D1609399

CASES AND MATERIALS ON
OIL AND GAS LAW

Sixth Edition

∎ ∎ ∎

By
John S. Lowe
George W. Hutchison Professor of Energy Law
Southern Methodist University

Owen L. Anderson
Eugene Kuntz Chair in Oil, Gas and Natural Resources
George Lynn Cross Research Professor
Director, John B. Turner LL.M. Program in Energy,
Natural Resources & Indigenous Peoples
The University of Oklahoma

Ernest E. Smith
Rex G. Baker Centennial Chair
in Natural Resources Law, The University of Texas

David E. Pierce
Professor of Law
Washburn University

Christopher S. Kulander
Assistant Professor of Law
Texas Tech School of Law
Of Counsel, Haynes and Boone, LLP

AMERICAN CASEBOOK SERIES®

WEST®
A Thomson Reuters business

Mat #41331968

American Casebook Series is a trademark registered in the U.S. Patent and Trademark Office.

COPYRIGHT © 1986, 1993 WEST PUBLISHING CO.
© West, a Thomson business, 1998, 2002
© 2013 Thomson Reuters

    610 Opperman Drive
    St. Paul, MN 55123
    1–800–313–9378

Printed in the United States of America

ISBN: 978–0–314–28516–4

Professors John Lowe, Owen Anderson, Ernest Smith, David Pierce, and Christopher Kulander dedicate this Sixth Edition to David P. Phillips, who for 42 years led the Rocky Mountain Mineral Law Foundation as its Executive Director, helping generations of lawyers and law professors advance the understanding and rationality of natural resources law.

PREFACE

Law is the long shadow of the people who serve it. Law has few absolute rules. Virtually every common-law principle has a rebuttal or a might-have-been. Ultimately, what becomes *the law* is shaped by the dedication, skill, and logic of the advocates, jurists, and commentators who participate in the legal process.

Eugene Kuntz, who led us in the preparation of the first two editions of this book, and whose influence remains strong in this sixth edition, casts a long shadow on oil and gas law. His work as a teacher, as a commentator, and—on occasion—as an advocate had a profound effect upon the development of oil and gas law in the second half of the Twentieth Century. Many of the concepts in this book, including the accommodation doctrine applied in surface use disputes, the meaning of "minerals," and the "marketable product" rule of royalty valuation, come from his work. Indeed, Gene Kuntz may have influenced the development of modern oil and gas law more than any other single individual. We miss Gene, but we were blessed by his friendship and counsel over the years, and we believe that he would have been pleased with this sixth edition of *Cases and Materials on Oil and Gas Law*.

But law is also heavily influenced by those who make possible the work of legal scholars. We dedicate this edition of our casebook to David Phillips, who has facilitated the work of generations of lawyers and law professors who research, write about, and teach resources law. David, who recently retired as the Executive Director of the Rocky Mountain Mineral Law Foundation after 42 years of service, "grew" the Foundation from a fledgling institute focused on resources law in the Rocky Mountain states to an educational institution that rivals many law schools and bar associations. The Foundation now has members throughout the United States and Canada, as well as 38 other countries, and conducts educational programs around the world. David also managed the editing and updating of numerous publications, including the *American Law of Mining*, the *Law of Federal Oil and Gas Leases*, and the Foundation's digital library, which contains approximately 250 volumes of scholarship produced over the 57 years of the Foundation's existence. In a very real sense, this casebook might not exist without David Phillips. He introduced John Lowe and Owen Anderson, saw to it that the Foundation financially supported the preparation of all six editions of this book, and administered a scholarship program that has provided hundreds of thousands of dollars of scholarships to our students over the years, including several students who have helped us with this book. Resources law—water law, mining law, public-land law, as well as oil and gas law—would not be nearly as well developed had it not been for David Phillips and the encouragement and support that his leadership of the Rocky Mountain Mineral Law Foundation has given legal scholars.

This casebook addresses the law of oil and gas by focusing first on ownership of the resource. Chapter 1 examines the common law of oil and gas ownership and the remedies that protect and restrict ownership rights. Chapter 2 focuses on the foundational business relationship used to develop oil and gas in the United States—the oil and gas "lease." Chapter 3 examines common problems encountered in oil and gas conveyancing. Chapter 4 explores legislative and regulatory responses to problems created by common-law ownership concepts, focusing on oil and gas conservation law. Chapter 5 examines the body of law designed to regulate environmental impacts by following the oil and gas development process chronologically, from land acquisition to abandonment. Chapter 6 considers transactions other than leasing and conveying that are frequently encountered in the industry, including assignments, farmouts, operating agreements, drilling contracts, and gas sales contracts. Finally, Chapter 7 examines the complex body of law that must be considered when oil and gas development is taking place on property owned by the federal, state, or tribal governments. Many instructors will build the basic oil and gas law course around Chapters 1 through 4 and save Chapters 5 through 7 for advanced courses.

We have adopted a number of conventions in the preparation of these materials. We have frequently omitted citations from cases and other quotations without inserting ellipses. Because oil and gas law is largely a matter of state law, we have modified the usual form for citation of federal cases that apply state law by including the state from which the case arose. The names of frequently cited treatises are abbreviated in accordance with the "Citation Abbreviations" page following this Preface. With the exception of cases, which each have their own internal set of consecutively-numbered footnotes, all footnotes are consecutively numbered within each chapter; however, we have endeavored to preserve the actual footnote numbers within the text of quoted materials.

The editors thank those who provided research and assistance in the preparation of the manuscript for the sixth edition. Thanks are also given to the Rocky Mountain Mineral Law Foundation for their financial assistance in the editing of this casebook. Professor Lowe appreciates the work of his research assistant, Eric Hoffman, as well as that of Underwood Law Library's Associate Director, Gregory Ivy, and IT Specialist Debbie Seiter. Professor Lowe also thanks John B. Attansio, Dean of the Dedman School of Law at Southern Methodist University, and William L. Hutchison, Esq. and the Hutchison Endowment, for their moral and financial support of his work on this project.

For support of his scholarship and research, Professor Anderson thanks Joe Harroz, Dean of the University of Oklahoma College of Law. He also appreciates the Dean's support of the College's energy curriculum, which is second to none, and of John B. Turner LL.M. Program in Energy, Natural Resources, and Indigenous Peoples. He thanks librarian Darin Fox and the entire staff of the Donald E. Pray Law Library for providing an outstanding petroleum law collection. Professor Anderson also thanks his former student, Christopher Kulander, for co-editing this sixth edition, his research assistant, Elizabeth Knox, Class of 2013, for her help in updating and reorganizing the casebook, and Kathie Anderson, for her editorial assistance.

Professors Lowe and Anderson express their appreciation to the faculty and staff of the University of Dundee's Centre for Energy, Petroleum & Mineral Law & Policy and to the University of Melbourne and University of Sydney's law faculties for the international perspectives that teaching at those institutions has given them.

Professor Smith expresses his deep gratitude to the late Rex G. Baker; his son, the late Rex G. Baker, Jr.; his grandson, Rex G. Baker III and his great-grandson, Rex G. Baker IV, for the support provided by the Rex G. Baker Centennial Chair in Natural Resources Law. He also thanks his many able student research assistants, and especially Amber Dobbs, who was quite adept at locating new and significant cases and updating existing citations.

Professor Pierce thanks Thomas J. Romig, Dean of Washburn University School of Law, for his support of this project.

Professor Kulander, who coordinated this sixth edition, thanks the other editors for welcoming him onto this project, and his parents Annie and Byron Kulander for their support of his academic career. In addition, he is appreciative of the editorial assistance of Byron Kulander and Kathie Anderson. Finally, he thanks student editors Blake Newton and Robert Shaw, Texas Tech School of Law Class of 2013, for their editorial work and assistance in preparing the manuscript for publication.

JOHN S. LOWE

OWEN L. ANDERSON

ERNEST E. SMITH

DAVID E. PIERCE

CHRISTOPHER S. KULANDER

September 5, 2012

CITATION ABBREVIATIONS

Throughout this casebook the following citation abbreviations have been used:

Brown: Earl A. Brown, The Law of Oil and Gas Leases (Update Editors: Earl A. Brown, Jr. & Lawrence T. Gillaspia) (Matthew Bender & Co. 2d ed. 2006).

Forms Manual: John S. Lowe, Owen A. Anderson, Ernest E. Smith, David E. Pierce, Forms Manual to Accompany Cases and Materials on Oil and Gas Law (Thomson/West 4th ed. 2004).

Hemingway: Owen L. Anderson, John S. Dzienkowski, John S. Lowe, Robert J. Peroni, David E. Pierce, and Ernest E. Smith, Hemingway Oil and Gas Law and Taxation (West 4th ed. 2004).

Kramer & Martin: Bruce M. Kramer & Patrick H. Martin, The Law of Pooling and Unitization (Matthew Bender & Co. 3d ed. 2006).

Kuntz: Eugene Kuntz, Oil and Gas Law (Update Editors: Owen L. Anderson, John S. Lowe, Ernest E. Smith, David E. Pierce) (Anderson 1987–2001 and Matthew Bender & Co. 2007).

Lowe: John S. Lowe, Oil and Gas Law in a Nutshell (West 4th ed. 2003).

Manual of Terms: Howard R. Williams and Charles J. Meyers, Williams & Meyers Manual of Oil and Gas Terms (Update Editors: Bruce M. Kramer & Patrick H. Martin) (Matthew Bender & Co. 13th ed. 2006).

Merrill: Maurice H. Merrill, The Law Relating to Covenants Implied in Oil and Gas Leases (Thomas Law Book Co. 2d ed. 1940).

O&GR: Oil and Gas Reporter (Bruce M. Kramer, Administrative Editor) (Matthew Bender 1952–2007) (specific Discussion Notes author identified by last name).

Pierce: Kansas Oil and Gas Handbook (Kansas Bar Association 1986).

Shade: Joseph Shade, Primer on the Texas Law of Oil and Gas (Matthew Bender 4th ed. 2008).

Smith:	Ernest E. Smith, John S. Dzienkowski, Owen L. Anderson, Garry B. Conine, John S. Lowe, and Bruce M. Kramer, International Petroleum Transactions (Rocky Mtn. Min. L. Found. 2 ed. 2000).
Smith & Weaver:	Ernest E. Smith and Jacqueline L. Weaver, Texas Oil and Gas Law (Matthew Bender & Co. 2d ed. 2006).
Sullivan:	Robert E. Sullivan, Handbook of Oil and Gas Law (Prentice Hall, Inc. 1955).
Summers:	W. L. Summers, The Law of Oil and Gas (Update Editor: John S. Lowe) (Vernon 1954 and Thomson 2007).
Williams & Meyers:	Howard R. Williams and Charles J. Meyers, Williams & Meyers Oil and Gas Law (Update Editors: Bruce M. Kramer & Patrick H. Martin) (Matthew Bender & Co. 2006).

SUMMARY OF CONTENTS

TABLE OF CONTENTS

—————

TABLE OF CASES

The principal cases are in bold type. Cases cited or discussed in the text
are in roman type. References are to pages. Cases cited in principal
cases and within other quoted materials are not included.

CASES AND MATERIALS ON
OIL AND GAS LAW

Sixth Edition

CHAPTER 1

HISTORY, ACCUMULATION AND OWNERSHIP

Table of Sections

A. HISTORICAL BACKGROUND

The oil and gas industry, and the body of law governing the industry, are largely products of the late 19th and early 20th Century. They are uniquely "American," as development of the resources, and development of the law in response to the resources, originated in places such as "Oil Creek," Pennsylvania. Although today's oil and gas industry is a huge

1

worldwide enterprise, the industry has recently returned to its Pennsylvania roots with the development of the Marcellus Shales and Utica Shales for natural gas.

"Colonel" Edwin Drake, wearing a top hat, is standing by his first oil well near Titusville, Pennsylvania, in 1859. Photograph courtesy of the Smithsonian Institution.

Apart from localized uses of oil from natural seeps and primitive hand-dug excavations, the story of oil really begins with whale oil—in particular oil from the sperm whale. Although oil could be recovered from the blubber of several whale species, spermaceti oil, obtained from the spermaceti organ in the head of the sperm whale and so-named because of its whitish, milky appearance, was the most valuable. In addition to other uses, spermaceti oil burned relatively smoke free in lamps. A large sperm whale could yield several tons of spermaceti oil. Commercial exploitation of sperm whales began in earnest in the 1740s.

By the early 1800s, however, tight supplies and strong demand led to increased prices. In response, the whaling industry built faster vessels, provisioned them for longer periods at sea, and ventured further away from home ports to harvest sperm whales. The whaling industry operated under the law of capture: a whale belonged to the whalers who could capture it and reduce it to possession.[1] Once a whale was captured, the whaling vessels processed the whale for its useful parts and stored the spermaceti oil in barrels. The whaling industry was centered in major seaports, especially ports in New England, such as Newport, Rhode Island.

As spermaceti oil increased in price, substitute products were developed. Kerosene distilled from coal was less expensive but smokier than spermaceti oil. In the 1850s, George Bissell, a New York lawyer, and James Townsend, a Connecticut banker, engaged the services of Professor Benjamin Silliman, Jr., a chemist at Yale, to develop a means of refining "rock oil" into suitable illuminating and lubricating oil. Silliman's research and experiments, for which he was grudgingly paid $528.08, proved that rock oil could be refined into excellent illuminating oil.

Proving that rock oil could serve as illuminating oil was only a first step. Bissell and Townsend then had to determine whether sufficient supplies of rock oil were available. Gathering small amounts of rock oil from seeps, springs, and shallow excavations would not result in a commercially successful enterprise, but their dream was to secure larger quantities of oil through drilling. Bissell learned that some rock oil was captured as a by-product of salt wells.

Townsend engaged Edwin L. Drake, a friend and sometimes railroad conductor, to travel to northwest Pennsylvania in 1857 to arrange the drilling of an exploratory rock-oil well. To add to Drake's credibility, he was introduced as Colonel Drake in 1857 to the locals in Titusville, Pennsylvania. The well was not drilled until 1859, owing to the need to arrange funding and engage drillers. "Uncle Billy" Smith and his two sons agreed to drill the well. As drilling operations continued slowly, only Townsend continued to furnish money and even his patience wore thin. In August, he wrote a letter instructing Drake to wind up operations. Before the letter arrived, the drillers found oil at a total depth of sixty-nine feet. Drake and Smith collected the flowing rock oil in every type of barrel[2] and other available containers; however, the stored oil was later consumed in a fire.

This discovery of rock oil, which may well have saved the sperm whale from being hunted to extinction, touched off an oil boom that would be

---

1. *See, e.g.,* Ghen v. Rich, 8 F. 159 (D. Mass 1881) (addressing wrongful conversion of a harvested whale) and Pierson v. Post, 3 Cai. R. 175, 2 Am. Dec. 264 (N.Y. Sup. Ct. 1805) (applying the law of capture to resolve a dispute between fox hunters).

2. Even today, oil is generally measured in "barrels," now standardized at 42 gallons.

"When oil first started flowing out of the wells in western Pennsylvania in the 1860s, desperate oil men ransacked farmhouses, barns, cellars, stores, and trash yards for any kind of barrel—molasses, beer, whiskey, cider, turpentine, salt, fish, and whatever else was handy. But as coopers began to make barrels specially for the oil trade, one standard size emerged, ... 42 gallons. The number was borrowed from England, where a statute in 1482 under King Edward IV established 42 gallons as the standard size barrel for herring in order to end skullduggery and 'divers deceits' in the packing of fish.... By 1866, seven years after Colonel Drake drilled his well, Pennsylvania producers confirmed the 42–gallon barrel as their standard, as opposed to, say, the 31 1/2–gallon wine barrel or the 32–gallon London ale barrel or the 36–gallon London beer barrel."

Daniel Yergin, The Prize (Simon & Schuster 1990).

repeated in other parts of the United States and in many other countries and continues to the present day. Within hours, the news of the discovery spread throughout the area and speculators began acquiring drilling rights. One Jonathan Watson, who had been observing the Drake well, upon hearing the word "oil," raced on his horse down the valley and began leasing as many farms as he could, later subleasing small well sites for drilling. Landowners reserved a portion of the oil as "royalty," ranging from 1/8 initially to as much as 5/8 within a year of the discovery. Many farmers were also able to negotiate firm drilling commitments in return for granting a lease. Many of the wells around Titusville produced oil for only a few weeks. Although the boom spread rapidly throughout the region, a bust soon followed.

This short summary of the Titusville oil boom has repeated itself numerous times since 1859. Oil exploration is a high-risk and high-cost enterprise, often requiring quick decisions and millions of dollars. Investors in oil must be risk takers who can move quickly in response to opportunity. Some investors, such as Bissell, are not able or willing to finance this risk. Others, such as Townsend, persevere and even convince others to share in the risk. Then, just about the time when they also lose heart, oil is found.

B. PHYSICAL BACKGROUND

Oil and gas law arose from issues and conflicts related to oil and gas production. Understanding how oil and gas are generated and deposited is necessary to comprehend how oil and gas law has evolved and how it might change in the future.

Early wildcatters[3] knew nothing of the science of petroleum geology.[4] They believed that oil and gas were constantly moving beneath the surface of the earth like a wild animal or a pinball. The key to success, therefore, was to drill a well at the right place and at the right time to capture these liquid and gaseous hydrocarbons before they migrated elsewhere. As will be seen in the next section, these notions also influenced the thinking of early courts and, hence, the law of oil and gas.

Oil and gas law has evolved—primarily from property law—in response to the unique physical realities associated with the exploration, development, and subsequent transport of oil and gas. This evolutionary process has been influenced by the knowledge—or lack of knowledge—regarding the nature of the occurrence of commercial oil and gas deposits as courts were called upon to resolve legal disputes. Some decisions, particularly those handed down in the early days of petroleum exploration and development, reflect broad and stark ignorance of the physical reali-

3. In the oil and gas context, the term *wildcatter* refers to a person who drills wildcat wells in search of petroleum. A *wildcat well* is an exploratory well drilled in an area and into a formation that is not known to contain petroleum.

4. Petroleum geology is largely the scientific search for traps that may contain oil and gas. The modern principles of petroleum geology began to gain acceptance in the 1930s.

ties of the location of oil and gas and the means of development. As late as 1921, a Texas Court noted that oil and gas "are supposed to percolate restlessly about under the surface of the earth, even as the birds fly from field to field and the beasts roam from forest to forest."[5] Legal disputes, however, do not wait on science and technology, and property regimes, once established, change slowly. Much of today's oil and gas law, and the cases and disputes that form and change the law, are products of the physical attributes of oil and gas and the decisions made through time that either respect, confuse, or ignore these physical realities.

The discovery of commercial quantities of "rock oil" in Drake's Well in 1859 signaled the beginning of our current understanding of how oil or gas is created, migrates, and comes to rest in geologic traps. Drake's Well also started the steady advancement of exploration, development, and deployment of technologies that make recovery of oil and gas commercially viable.

In times before drilling, oil had been recovered from surface seeps and pools. After drilling began, these surface quantities served largely to attract and focus the efforts of oil and gas producers to find the hidden underground reservoirs from which the seeps arose. Gas, often found with the oil, and called "associated gas," was at first considered a dangerous nuisance that was vented or flared at the drill site. In the early 1900s, a valuable liquid called natural gasoline could be separated from the gas and was marketed along with crude oil.

Natural gas production and marketing on a large scale came later, after the development of high-tensile steel, advanced welding, and pipe-rolling techniques in the 1920s. These developments allowed the gradual development of a nationwide natural gas delivery system. Further advances in natural gas processing led to the extraction and marketing of a host of natural gas liquids ("NGLs") from "wet" gas streams. The NGL content of natural gas varies, so some natural gas is largely "dry" when produced at the wellhead. Either wet or dry natural gas may be saturated with water, thus requiring dehydration. Natural gas may also be "sour," requiring the extraction of impurities, such as highly-toxic hydrogen sulfide (H_2S), to yield "sweet" gas. At the end of these processes, the remaining "residue" gas is pipeline quality methane.

1. ORIGIN OF OIL AND GAS

Deposition

The story of oil and gas formation begins with the deposit of organic material in shallow and tropical to subtropical water tens of millions of years ago. The fossil record strongly suggests that at certain points during the geologic past, the movement and collisions of continents as described by plate tectonics conspired to place parts of what is now North America near the equator and under warm and shallow marine and lacustrine (lake

5. Medina Oil Dev. Co. v. Murphy, 233 S.W. 333, 335 (Tex.Civ.App.1921, error dismissed).

and lagoonal) waters. This allowed great quantities of marine plant and animal life to thrive. When these organisms died, they joined other organic matter on the bottom, and the resultant accumulation began to undergo decomposition or degradation, or both. Meanwhile, great tropical rivers flowed from distant mountains to these tepid seas, carrying great volumes of mud, silt, and sand to be spread by currents and tides over the sea bottoms near the constantly changing shore lines. When the organic matter was deposited along with this inorganic sediment, the progressive burial and resultant overburden began to provide significant pressure and higher temperatures around the buried organic matter.

"Diagenesis", the process by which this organic material is first subjected to heightened temperatures and pressures is caused by burial under the first several hundred feet of overlying sediments. Through compaction and the passage of time, water is squeezed out of the organic material, and other chemical reactions leave a sticky residue called "kerogen" and a black tar-like substance called "bitumen." Critically, total decomposition is prevented by a lack of oxygen and by the presence of saltwater. The extent of the changes to the kerogen is reflected in its coloration, which characteristically changes from yellow to orange to brown to black with increasing depth and as the kerogen matures.

Generation

As temperatures and pressures increase with deeper burial, the process of "catagenesis" begins, being the thermal degradation of the kerogen to form hydrocarbons. As under diagenesis, the three ingredients necessary for catagenesis are time, heat, and pressure. Heat, which increases with depth, is provided by the earth's molten core and decay of radioactive isotopes. Pressure is provided by the thousands of feet of overlying sedimentary rock pressing down on the kerogen. The exact mix of time, heat, and pressure determines whether the kerogen will eventually turn into hydrocarbons and, if so, what type they will be. The oil forming "window" represents a range of time, heat, and pressure necessary to form oil, with each of the three variables being partially dependent on the others. If temperature and pressure higher than those found within the oil formation "window" are encountered, a more complete "cracking" of the kerogen occurs, resulting in the formation of natural gas. During catagenesis, the inorganic sediments around the kerogen are compressed, dewatered, and eventually lithified into sedimentary rock.

While the predominant theory explaining the generation of commercial oil and gas accumulations is that hydrocarbons are produced from biological material altered over millions of years by heat and pressure, another theory suggests that hydrocarbons, gas in particular, can be generated in the absence of biological organisms at depths of 100 to 300 kilometers. One view of this "inorganic" theory states that extraterrestrial hydrocarbon components were added to the igneous rocks of the earth's mantle during its formation. However, no considerable commercial quantities of inorganically-generated gas have been found in ancient crystalline rocks of continental shields, as would be expected if the inorganic gas was rising from great depths. The common opinion among petroleum geologists and petroleum engineers is that inorganic hydrocarbons exist only in small noncommercial quantities at reachable depths. Thus, these quantities could have only a negligible impact upon worldwide oil and gas estimates.

Migration and Trapping

Oil and gas are less dense than water. If the three are placed together within a closed system, water will be at the bottom overlain by the less dense oil, and gas on top. Therefore, once formed in its source beds, the oil and gas may percolate up through the overlying rock along a "migration path"—a pathway of rock or unconsolidated sediment with enough permeability to allow gas and oil to pass though it along a multitude of small interconnected pathways, commonly known as pore spaces. If the majority of the pores within a rock are interconnected, the rock is said to be permeable. Permeability, expressed in "millidarcies" ("md"), is defined as the capacity of a solid material to allow fluids to flow through it—the ability of a fluid to travel from pore space to pore space within the rock. The higher the millidarcies measured, the higher the permeability. Fewer than 1–15 millidarcies is poor to fair permeability; 15–50 is moderate; 50–250 is good; 250–1000 is excellent. Ten to one hundred millidarcies is adequate for a traditional oil reservoir; gas reservoirs require less.

Migration of hydrocarbons is also affected by the hydrocarbon's viscosity. Viscosity is the measure of a fluid's resistance to flow. "Heavy" oil, which has a low gravity (as described below) and a high viscosity, tends to resist flow through a rock having a low permeability, while a lighter crude, having higher gravity and a lower viscosity, will more readily flow through rock. Thus, heavy crudes do not readily infiltrate low permeability rock.

This upward and lateral migration of hydrocarbons along one or more migration paths will continue until either the surface is reached, with the gas venting into the atmosphere and the oil pooling on the surface, or an impermeable barrier of rock is encountered, which halts the migration and holds the hydrocarbons in place in the "trap." Thus, the oil and gas contained in the reservoir rock are held by a geologic trap comprised of rock that is impermeable to flow, such as shale or salt. Traps generally combine an impermeable rock layer with a geologic feature such as a dome, fold or fault. Even a "leaky" trap can provide an economic reservoir beneath it if the volume of migrating hydrocarbons entering is greater or equal to those passing through the trap toward the surface.

2. ACCUMULATION AND OCCURRENCE

The volume of rock in which the hydrocarbons stay after the trap stops their progress lies below or adjacent to the trap. Once the trap is encountered and the hydrocarbons have stopped their upward migration, the rock in which they are held is called the reservoir. A reservoir is a critical part of the petroleum system and occurs in conjunction with one or more traps. Many different shapes, sizes, and types of geologic structures and associated traps form hydrocarbon reservoirs.

Reservoir Geomorphology

A reservoir is a subsurface body of rock with sufficient void space ("porosity") to store hydrocarbons and connectivity between those void spaces ("permeability") to allow hydrocarbons to flow. Within a reservoir, hydrocarbons exist in the pore spaces between the matrix of rock grains that comprise the sedimentary rock. The ratio of the pore volume to the total rock volume is called porosity, and is usually expressed as a percentage. A good sandstone reservoir may have up to thirty percent (30%) porosity.[6] The geometry and volume of the rock comprising the trap define the reservoir from which producers will extract the oil and gas, likely by drilling a well.[7]

Reservoir rock is commonly sedimentary, being mostly comprised of grains of other rocks that have been eroded and transported by water and wind, and therefore has more porosity than most igneous and metamorphic rocks. In addition, metamorphic and igneous rocks form under temperature conditions at which hydrocarbons cannot be preserved. The most widespread rock in which hydrocarbons are found is sandstone that is made of sand grains usually mixed with particles of other materials. Porous and permeable limestone and dolomite are other types of sedimentary rocks in which oil and gas are found. Sandstones, limestone, and dolomite rocks comprise the majority of conventional reservoirs producing today.

Once the hydrocarbons are in place in the reservoir, the oil, gas, and any saltwater native to the reservoir separate according to their density, like oil, vinegar, and solids in a bottle of salad dressing and oil settles below. Saltwater, sometimes called "brine," settles below the oil-water contact "owc".

The picture can be further complicated, however, because significant quantities of saltwater can remain inside the pore spaces within the oil and gas zones of the reservoir. This remaining saltwater may entirely fill smaller pore spaces and lurk in the pore throats connecting the larger pore spaces, leaving the oil and gas to occupy the center of the largest pore spaces. The oil, or oil and gas, then occupy these water-jacketed pore spaces until production.[8] Often the pore spaces contain between about ten percent (10%) to over fifty percent (50%) saltwater in the midst of the oil

---

6. Usually ten to twenty percent (10% to 20%) porosity is adequate for an oil reservoir. Even less porosity is adequate for gas reservoirs.

7. NORMAN HYNE, DICTIONARY OF PETROLEUM EXPLORATION & PRODUCTION 372 (PennWell 1991).

8. The relative percentages of oil and water sharing the reservoir rock pores vary between 50% oil/50% water and 80% oil/20% water. Thus, many oil wells will produce both oil and salt water.

and gas accumulation. This presence of saltwater within the oil and gas accumulation causes wells to produce saltwater as well as oil and gas.

One way of classifying reservoirs is to group them according to their geologic source and geometry. Most reservoirs in which hydrocarbons are trapped can be placed into one of two broad categories—structural and stratigraphic. Structural traps, perhaps the easiest to conceptualize, are formed by stresses that cause deformation of the sedimentary rocks comprising the trap and reservoir. Such deformation, common during mountain building, can form folds and faults. Upward and lateral movement of salt can form salt domes that can produce traps in overlying and adjacent sedimentary formations that abut the salt. Stratigraphic reservoir/trap systems, a change within the formation itself, such as changes in permeability and porosity caused by increasing cementation of the rock grains or changes in grain sizes, provide the trap and reservoir. Stratigraphic reservoir/trap systems do not rely primarily on geologic structures, and thus may be more subtle and difficult for petroleum geologists to detect and image. Both oil and gas occur in all of the following general types of reservoir configurations.

Structural Reservoirs and Traps

Folds and Domes: Reservoirs formed by folding of the subsurface rock formations ("strata") usually have the shape of structural domes or upward-bent folds, or both, as shown in Figs. 1 and 2. An elongated upward fold in the rock (an "anticline") may not provide closure adequate to act as a trap. Nevertheless, where there is "four-way" closure along the long axis of the anticline, the resultant domal feature can provide the necessary trapping geometry to result in a potential trap below which the reservoir may occur. The porous and permeable rock below these traps is later filled by migration of oil or gas (or both).

Examples of reservoirs formed by domal structures are the Conroe Oil Field near Houston, Texas, and the historic Teapot Dome Field in Natrona County, Wyoming. Examples of reservoirs formed on anticlinal structures are gas fields in the Oriskany Sandstone in the Valley and Ridge Province of the central Appalachian Mountains, the Chevron Field in western Colorado near Rangely, and the enormous Yates Field in the Permian Basin of West Texas.

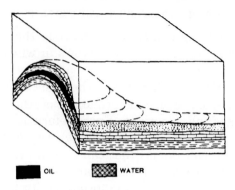

Figure 1. This sketch illustrates an oil accumulation in a dome-shaped structure. This done is circular in outline. Figure courtesy of the American Petroleum Institute.

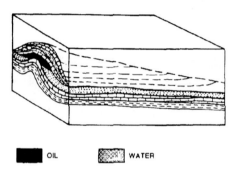

Figure 2. An anticlinal type of folder structure is shown here. An anticline differs from a dome in being long and narrow. Figure courtesy of the American Petroleum Institute.

<u>Faults</u>: A fault is a fracture or discontinuity in a volume of rock, across which there has been significant displacement relative to the other side. This displacement often results from earthquakes that can be felt on the surface. If the movement of rock juxtaposes an impervious layer of rock over a reservoir rock, this juxtaposition could act as a trap, as shown in Fig. 3. The fault plane or, if movement is not along a clearly defined boundary, a fault zone, must at least partially seal the reservoir if the movement of the rock juxtaposes a permeable layer opposite the potential reservoir.[9] Such a seal along the fault plane or zone can be provided by ground up rock debris, commonly clay or shale that is smeared along the fault plane or zone. Generally, however, a reservoir is positioned opposite an impermeable rock such as shale or salt. Examples of fields of this type are the Fahud Field in Oman, the faults around the Niger Basin, many

---

9. Faults without sealing capacity can actually act as conduits for flow, a fact necessary for hydraulic fracturing.

fields in the Gulf of Mexico, and the semi-radial faults that surround the Hibernian Field offshore the east coast of Canada.

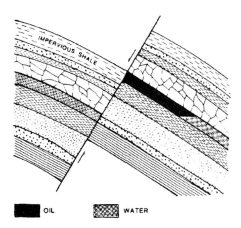

Figure 3. This is a trap resulting from faulting in which the block on the right has moved up with respect to the one on the left. Figure courtesy of the American Petroleum Institute.

Salt and Overpressured Shale: Salt and shale play an important role in the structural framework of many geologic basins, but their presence can lead to some of the most complex and challenging geology from which to find and recover hydrocarbons. Salt, like other sedimentary rocks, is deposited in large sheets, typically in shallow, hyper-saline seas in hot and dry environments that promote evaporation. Incoming fresh water is evaporated, leaving salt and other evaporate deposits. Modern analogies are the Great Salt Lake in Utah, the Dead Sea between Israel and Jordan, and the Garabogazköl Embayment just east of the Caspian Sea in Turkmenistan.

Salt and layers of highly-pressured shale are subject to "plastic flow" over short periods of geologic time, and thus flow and deform like butter left at room temperature. In addition, salt maintains a constant buoyant density as it is buried by overlying sediments, unlike other sedimentary rocks that increase in density with increasing burial depth. These two factors lead buried salt to eventually push up through overlying sediments and flow towards the surface to form a complex structure of domes and salt walls with salt withdrawal basins in between, as shown in Fig. 4. Overpressured shale, while not as subject to plastic flow as is salt, can also push through overlying sediment, leading to long linear ridges.

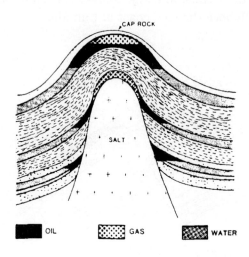

Figure 4. Salt domes often deform overlying rocks to form traps like the ones shown here. Figure courtesy of the American Petroleum Institute.

Salt and overpressured shale do not normally contain recoverable hydrocarbons, but oil and gas are commonly found in the sandstone formations abutting salt domes and overpressured shale, and such traps represent much of the oil and gas found in the Gulf of Mexico and in some other international regions. Onshore, some salt dome reservoirs include Avery Island and the Bay Marchand Fields in Louisiana and the historic Spindletop Field near Beaumont, Texas. Offshore, overpressured shale provides the trap mechanism along long ridges in the western Gulf of Mexico parallel to the coasts of Texas and Mexico.[10]

Stratigraphic Reservoirs and Traps

Channel Sandstones/Turbidites: The most common stratigraphic traps are sandstone and limestone, which are sealed along their upper surfaces bychanges in permeability or the interlayering of sandstone or limestone with impervious shale or mudstone. Hydrocarbons are thereby confined within porous and permeable parts of the rock ("sandstone") by the non-porous parts of the rock surrounding the porous and permeable reservoir rock (shale, clay, or "tight" sandstone with low porosity and permeability). Such sandstone found in ancient river channels and deltas, submarine canyons off of the continental shelf, and heaped at the bottom of continental slopes ("turbidites") have all been targets of successful exploration provided they are below impermeable seals of shale, clay or mudstone. For example, the Hugoton Field, a large, bowl-shaped structure that underlies most of southwest Kansas, is comprised of porous and permeable interbedded deposits of limestone and dolomite and shale deposited in a shallow

---

10. For further discussion of salt and over-pressured shale tectonics, *see* JOHN K. WARREN, EVAPORITES: SEDIMENTS, RESOURCES AND HYDROCARBONS (Springer 2006)

marine environment. Turbidite plays are common along the Gulf Coast of Louisiana and Texas.

Unconformities: Geological unconformities may contribute to hydrocarbon trap development. Such unconformities develop when a column of sedimentary rock layers are subjected to erosion and layers of younger sediments are deposited over the erosional surface. Such unconformities can be subtle, as when the older and much younger rock layers are parallel to the plane of the unconformity, like books stacked on top of one another. A more obvious unconformity develops when the older rock layers are first inclined to the place of the erosion surface and are overlying younger rocks. In this case, the older rocks were tilted and deformed before erosion.

The unconformity in Fig. 5 shows that the upward movement of oil has been halted by the impermeable younger rock deposited across the cut-off surfaces of the lower beds, possibly by water or wind erosion. Examples of reservoirs of this type are both the East Texas Field and the Oklahoma City Field. An unconformity is a significant part of the trapping mechanism for North America's largest field, Prudhoe Bay Field on the North Slope of Alaska, as well as other North Slope fields.

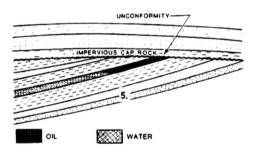

Figure 5. Oil is trapped under an unconformity in this illustration. Figure courtesy of the American Petroleum Institute.

Reefs: A reef or (more generally) a carbonate reservoir is an oil or gas deposit found in ancient reefs, clastic limestones,[11] chemical limestones,[12] or dolomite, as shown in Fig. 6. Prehistoric reefs that serve as reservoirs were created in warm seas by the calcium carbonate remains of shallow marine animals and plants that formed thick accumulations of limestones and dolomites. Many modern analogies exist today in tropical waters. Most prospective reef reservoirs are blessed with high porosity and permeability because they are made of large pieces and grains of carbonate and/or dolomite and because further dissolution of the carbonate and/or dolomite

---

11. Clastic limestones are comprised of pieces of carbonate rock transported from another source.

12. Chemical limestones are comprised of carbonate rock formed *in situ* by chemical processes such as precipitation or organic growth.

by fluids moving through the rock has opened even more pore space. The carbonates within the Delaware Basin in the western panhandle of Texas, the reef traps of the Chappel Limestone within the Bend Arch/Ft. Worth Basin in Texas, and the ancient reefs that sit upon the perimeter of the Michigan Basin are examples of reef reservoirs.

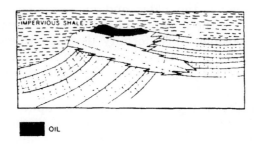

Figure 6. Reefs sometimes form reserviors similar to that shown here. Figure courtesy of the American Petroleum Institute.

Hybrid Trap: Components of two or more of the above described reservoir and trap systems are often incorporated into one reservoir. Typically, hybrid traps are a result of a series of events, perhaps related, which give rise to a complex mix of structural geometry and stratigraphic changes. For example, a reservoir could result from a combination of folding and faulting coupled with the introduction of magnesium and calcium carbonate into pore spaces and fractures within the strata. This combination changes the porosity by secondary cementation—a process whereby the rock grains are later bonded together by calcium carbonate, silica, or other cementing fluid long after deposition. This sequence of events may be followed by further faulting and folding instigated by tectonic stress from a second direction. The events need not even be sequential: for example, salt movement generally occurs synchronously with faulting. Unraveling the sequences of events to determine the best way to develop such reservoirs can be very challenging.

3. PETROLEUM MECHANICS AND RESERVOIR CHARACTERISTICS

While every reservoir is unique, and while there exist many broad categories of reservoir/trap combinations, all share several characteristics of concern to developers.

Porosity and Permeability

Once flow is halted by the trap, oil and gas reside in the pore spaces of the rock comprising the reservoir. Porosity and permeability, related but individual variables necessary for traditional recovery are affected by the types and shapes of the grains of rock, the presence of different grain sizes, and how the grains are packed. For example, the porosity and permeability of a rock containing rounded grains also partially depends on how these grains are packed. If packed such that the grains just touch one another at six points ninety degrees apart, as in a cubic packing scheme as shown in Fig. 7, porosity can theoretically increase to a maximum of over forty-six percent (46%). Alternatively, if the grains are packed in a tighter "rhombic" pattern, as shown in Fig. 8, maximum theoretical porosity is reduced to about twenty-six percent (26%). These maximums almost never

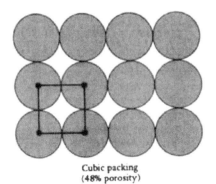

Cubic packing
(48% porosity)

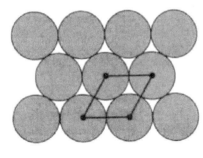

Rhombohedral packing
(26% porosity)

Figure 7 Cubic Packing. Figure 8 Rhombohedral Packing. Rock grain packing schemes with various resultant porosities. (Source: Luc Ikelle and Lasse Amundsen, Texas A&M University, *Introduction to Petroleum Seismology (Investigations in Geophysics No. 12)*)

occur in nature for a variety of reasons. If all the grains are nearly the same size, such as in eolian sandstone (sandstone deposited by wind), then porosity and permeability increase. Variance in the size of grains is a more common occurrence. In this case, the smaller grains take up space in the voids between the larger grains, lowering the overall porosity, and potentially clogging the pore throats (apertures between the pores), thus reducing overall permeability. Rounded grains may provide more pore space than angular grains, which may settle and be sorted in such a way to reduce overall porosity. Well-cemented rock, with the pore spaces between grains all or partially taken up by calcium carbonate or silica cement, can reduce both porosity and permeability, lowering both proportionately with heightening cementation.

Reservoir Pressure

During primary recovery operations, producers rely on the pressure caused by overlying strata and other natural forces in the reservoir to push hydrocarbons out of the reservoir and into a wellbore for development. Reservoir pressure increases with depth, and commonly falls between two values—"hydrostatic" pressure and "lithostatic" (or "overburden") pressure—as shown in Fig. 9. The hydrostatic pressure is the normal, predicted pressure for a column of freshwater from sea level to a given depth. Lithostatic pressure is the pressure of the weight of overburden, or overlying rock, on a formation. It is sometimes called "geostatic pressure" and is always higher than hydrostatic pressure because a column of rock weighs more than a column of water.

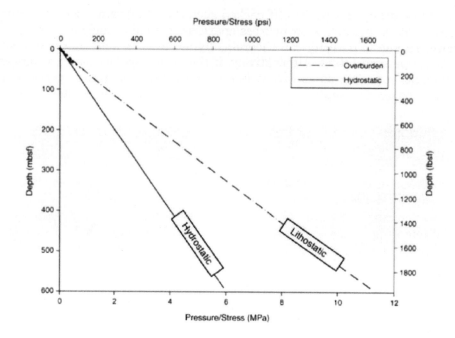

Figure 9. Pressure versus depth plot. A column of water (with a density of 1.0 g/cm³) shows increasing pressure with depth along the "Hydrostatic" track while a column of solid rock (with a density of 2.7 g/cm³) shows increasing pressure with depth along the "Lithostatic" track. (Source: modified after Luc Ikelle and Lasse Amundsen, Integrated Ocean Drilling Program, Texas A&M University)

The actual reservoir pressure will generally increase between these two boundaries, rising and falling at different rates depending on the conditions at depth. A zone of low pressure might occur in areas where oil or gas has already been drained. Abnormally high pressure might occur in areas where rocks containing natural gas have been buried quickly by overlying sediment and the resultant pressure caused by compressed gas has not been released. Such overpressured zones could cause an explosion or "blowout" on the surface when penetrated by a drill bit. Because reservoir pressure changes as fluids are produced from a reservoir, the pressure should be described as measured at a specific time, such as initial reservoir pressure (or "virgin" reservoir pressure), final reservoir pressure, etc.

Reservoir pressure, once lost, can generally only be replaced by slow natural processes or temporarily and locally through expensive secondary and tertiary recovery efforts, as the well will no longer flow without these potentially expensive recovery processes.

Reservoir Height

The reservoir height, sometimes called "net pay," is a measurement of the vertical thickness of a reservoir formation that contains prospective oil and gas and is open to flow. This value is used in calculations and mathematical models to assess reservoir performance or potential productivity. Highly heterogeneous reservoirs containing zones of unprospective rock interspersed within the prospective target may have higher "gross pay," which is reduced to "net pay" by removing the unprospective rock from the measurement equation. If the separate pay zones are not interconnected, however, the geologist will typically classify the smaller pay thicknesses separately and calculate the reserves individually.

Reservoir Heterogeneities

Although nearly all reservoirs can be placed into one of many categories, all have variations in rock properties, internal facies, faults, fractures, cementation, and other localized characteristics that make each reservoir unique. These variations can result in directional variations in porosity and permeability. Because there are so many types of reservoir heterogeneities, geologists and petroleum engineers must draw from their experience, surface mapping, core analysis, and well logs to determine if the reservoir is prospective and, if so, what recovery techniques should be deployed by production personnel.

4. NON-TRADITIONAL RESERVOIRS

While the four-step sequence described above—depositing, generating, migrating, trapping—is the process under which "traditional" oil and gas reservoirs were formed, some "non-traditional" reservoirs may form differently, or without the same four steps. For optimal development, some rock formations that serve as reservoirs require the use of specialized drilling techniques, such as horizontal drilling in a specific direction, or post-drilling processes, such as hydraulic fracturing, or both. These types of formations trap the hydrocarbons without being primarily dependent on the previously mentioned reservoir categories.

For example, the Austin Chalk in Texas is more prospective if horizontal drilling encounters the systemic fracture zones within the formation. These fractures, if not tightly closed, dramatically increase local permeability, allowing hydrocarbons to be more easily produced. Here, knowledge of the location and trend of these fracture zones derived by seismic reflection surveys and well cores is very important to maximize production from a single well.[13]

Shale Plays

Even more striking examples of "internally trapping" formations are layers of organic rich shale or "tight" sandstone that contain oil and gas that may have ample porosity but very low permeability, rendering traditional recovery methods unfeasible. "Shale gas" is natural gas found in shale formations. Unlike a traditional reservoir where the natural gas

---

13. For further discussion of well cores and fractured reservoirs *see* BYRON KULANDER, STUART DEAN & BILLY WARD, FRACTURE CORE ANALYSIS (AAPG Methods in Exploration Series, No. 8, 1990).

migrates from elsewhere, the shale acts as both the source *and* the reservoir for the natural gas—the gas stays where it was made. While older shale gas or oil wells were usually vertical, more recent shale gas and oil wells more commonly take advantage of advances in directional drilling technology to achieve a horizontal drainhole, discussed below, within the target shale or other formation, as shown in Fig. 10. Only shale formations with certain characteristics will produce gas or oil in commercial quantities—the shale needs organic material that has reached thermal maturity with a low permeability resulting in a large amount of gas in place. Commercial shale gas and oil deposits generally contain fewer hydrocarbons per volume of rock than traditional reservoirs but are far more continuous over large areas. This continuity increases the probability that a particular well will hit prospective rock.[14]

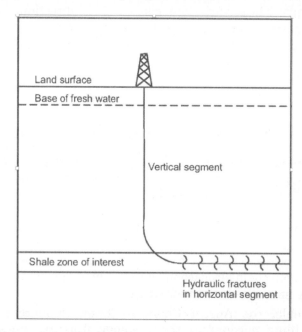

Figure 10. Schematic diagram of a horizontal well. (Source: Arizona Geology Magazine, Apr. 5, 2012)

Prospective shale formations have been identified in a multitude of states, most of which are shown in Fig. 11, and all perspective shale formations require some form of well stimulation such as modern hydraulic fracturing techniques that allow drillers to dramatically increase the permeability of the formation by forcing highly pressurized fluid into the rocks. The hydraulic fluid fractures the shale layers, opens existing fractures, and releases gas or oil that could not be recovered by traditional

14. For further discussion of shale plays in the United States and Canada *see* U.S. Department of Energy (DOE) Office of Fossil Energy, *Modern Shale Gas Development in the United States—A Primer*, (2008) and Tom Kurth, et al., *American Law and Jurisprudence on Fracing*, 47 *Rocky Mtn. Min. L. Found.* 2 (2010).

drilling techniques. Such fracing operations have helped make possible development of vast oil and natural gas reserves in the United States. To maximize recovery from these formations, wells are often drilled horizontally in the target formation and hydraulically fractured along the full length of the horizontal drainhole.

Figure 11. Location of major domestic shale oil and gas plays. (Source: ALL Consulting, www.all-llc.com)

Estimates suggest that the United States has almost 1,750 Tcf (trillion cubic feet) of technically recoverable natural gas, including over 200 Tcf of proved reserves (the discovered, economically recoverable fraction of the original gas in place). Technically recoverable unconventional gas—a category that includes gas derived from shale and "tight sandstone" formations as well as coalbed methane ("CBM")—accounts for approximately sixty percent (60%) of the onshore recoverable resource. At the production rates for 2007, about 19.3 Tcf, the current recoverable resource is sufficient to supply the United States for the next ninety (90) years. Separate estimates of the shale gas resource extend this supply to 116 years. Some shale gas reservoirs, like the Marcellus contain mostly "dry" natural gas—while others, such as the Utica, contain "wet" gas—gas saturated with natural gas liquids (NGLs).

The Bakken formation in North Dakota and the Eagle Ford formation in Texas are examples of shale oil formations, but they also contain substantial amounts of associated gas.

Coalbed Methane

Coalbed methane is methane found in coal seams. CBM is thought to be generated as either a result of microbial action or more typical thermogenic processes that arise from deep burial of the coal—thermogenesis similar to that seen in generation of "traditional" natural gas deposits. Methane is held in the coal by water pressure, and because CBM has very low solubility in water, it readily separates as pressure decreases. Extraction of CBM requires pumping both the water and the CBM from the coal seam. Water moving from the coal seam to the wellbore is beneficial, however, because it combines with reservoir pressure to encourage gas migration toward the well. Therefore, production of the CBM typically leads to co-production of large amounts of (often potable) water, particularly at the beginning of production until the methane "desorbs" (disconnects) from the coal due to depressurization caused by water production. According to the Wyoming Oil & Gas Commission, natural gas from coal beds accounts for approximately seven percent (7%) of the total natural gas production in the United States.

Oil Shale, Tar Sands and Gas Hydrates

If the source rock for oil and gas is itself near enough to the surface to be accessed by mining techniques, the immature hydrocarbons may be cooked out of the removed rock. "Cooking" requires that the ore be placed in a kiln-like apparatus to undergo pyrolysis, where the ore is distilled by temperatures ranging from 400–500° C. The process requires significant water and results in large volumes of slag comprised of coke and smectite, a type of clay, all laced with high concentrations of heavy metals such as vanadium and lead. Potential global oil shale reserves are estimated to roughly equal worldwide conventional oil reserves.[15]

Tar sands are loosely cemented sandstones into which oil has migrated at such a shallow depth and low temperature that the oil has been degraded by biological processes similar to those encountered by oil exposed to surface conditions, such as at oil seeps. The biological degradation by bacteria results in oil that is tar-like or asphaltic with such a high viscosity that it must be surface mined and then heated or heat treated *in situ* to allow it to flow to a well. The degradation can vary from merely low gravity oil to almost solid tar. In the case of extraction by wells, the heat necessary is usually provided by steam injected into the formation through a well in hopes of lowering the viscosity of the heavy oil and tar so it will flow to a nearby well. Currently, the largest known tar sands are in Alberta, Canada, and Venezuela. Like oil shale, production from tar sand requires significant volumes of water and, when surface mined, results in substantial surface destruction, requiring extensive reclamation.

Gas hydrates are slush-like solids comprised of methane and water frozen in various combinations. Generally found below the seafloor on

---

15. For further discussion on oil shales, tar sands and gas hydrates *see* KNUT BJORLYKKE, PETROLEUM GEOSCIENCE, § 21.2, 459–465 (Springer 2010).

continental slopes where the low temperatures necessary for their formation are found, one unit of volume of hydrate yields 160 volumes of gas. Although the potential of gas hydrates is great, techniques for economic development and subsequent marketing of hydrates remain elusive.

5. TYPES OF RESERVOIR DRIVES

Until a well is completed in the reservoir, the trap will prevent the hydrocarbons from escaping. Because oil, gas, and water are contained in the tiny pore spaces and fractures of the reservoir rock, hydrocarbons are not sucked or vacuumed from wells during primary recovery. Instead, oil and gas are pushed out of the reservoir and up the well by pore pressure provided from the very same oil, gas, and water under high pressure in the reservoir. Once the well is completed in the productive interval, the developer hopes that reservoir pressure originating in the reservoir itself will drive oil and gas to the surface.[16] Exactly how reservoir pressure is provided can be categorized as the reservoir's "drive" mechanism. When reservoir pressure is insufficient to drive oil to the surface, wells can be placed "on pump"; however, a pumpjack only lifts oil that is driven to the wellbore by reservoir pressure.

In addition to reservoir pressure provided by the weight of overlying rock, called "overburden" pressure, reservoir pressure can be provided by different reservoir-drive mechanisms, which include "gas drive" (where much of the reservoir pressure is provided by the presence of a gas cap or solution gas drive), "water drive" (where encroaching water from below or the edge of the reservoir provides the reservoir-drive mechanism), and a "combination drive," which has elements of the other reservoir-drive mechanisms. Reservoir-drive mechanisms are also called "natural drives," in contrast to drives provided by man-made processes.

"Gas Drive": Solution Gas Drive & Gas Cap Drive Reservoirs

Generally, oil in a reservoir is under such pressure that any gas present may be dissolved within the oil. If a reservoir has an internal pressure below the "bubble point"—that is, below the pressure at which gas can be contained in the oil solution without separating—the gas separates out of the liquid hydrocarbon and rises because of its lower density—analogous to a bottle of soda being first opened. The gas rises to form a gas-only "gas cap" from which this type of reservoir takes its name. [Fig. 12]. Typically, a reservoir featuring a gas cap drive is best produced by first drilling into the flanks of the reservoir to encounter the lower oil interval. Production of the oil causes a reduction in reservoir pressure, allowing the gas cap to expand and help push the remaining oil into the wells. Such a drive is called a "gas-cap drive" reservoir or, if no

---

16. Eventually, the reservoir energy may decline so that it can only push oil into the wellbore or perhaps only part of the way toward the surface. In this case, the well will be placed "on pump" to lift the oil that collects in the wellbore to the surface. Similarly, a compressor may be installed on a gas well to assist in lifting the gas and pushing it into a gathering line system at the surface.

separate gas cap exists and the gas is expanding in the oil itself, a "solution-gas drive" reservoir.

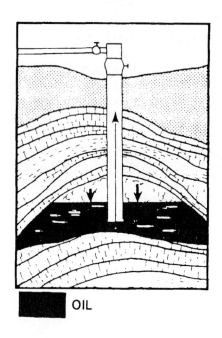
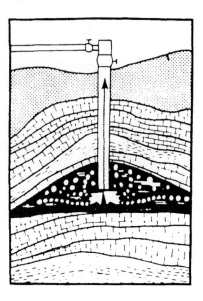

OIL

Figure 12. Gas-cap Drive. Figure courtesy of the American Petroleum Institute.

Figure 13. Solution-gas Drive. Figure courtesy of the American Petroleum Institute.

This solution gas drive mechanism, as shown in Fig. 13, is often the least effective type of reservoir drive because the gas will eventually cease to expand. The American Petroleum Institute ("API") has estimated that solution-gas drive reservoirs yield maximum recovery rates between ten and twenty-five percent (10–25%) of the oil originally found in the reservoir, increasing to twenty-five to fifty percent (25–50%) when augmented by a gas cap. Typically, solution-gas drive reservoirs are small, compartmentalized, or otherwise laterally discontinuous so that the reservoirs are essentially closed systems. If they were not, the gas might have left the oil solution before development.

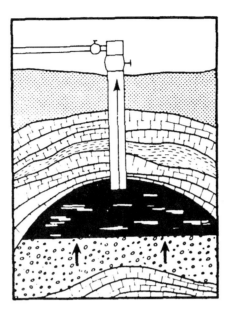

Figure 14. Water Drive. Figure courtesy of the American Petroleum Institute.

"Water Drive": Water–Drive Reservoirs

Water-drive reservoirs, as shown in Fig. 14, depend on release of reservoir pressure and the resultant expansion of the compressed water to provide the drive to force the hydrocarbons out of the reservoir and into the wellbore.

The "water-drive," which results from the decompression and expansion of the reservoir water after a wellbore releases the initial pressure through removal of oil and gas, is particularly effective in producing hydrocarbons from porous and permeable reservoirs that are continuous over a large area. As the water expands, it continues to push the oil and gas towards the wellbore. If extraction of the oil and gas is constrained by proper production practices, the water will gradually push the hydrocarbons toward a wellbore along a broad front. If extraction is uncontrolled and overproduction occurs, reservoir water will "channel" and begin to be produced alongside—or even exclusive of—the oil and gas. If correctly managed, water-drives are generally the most efficient type of drive for oil production and can often yield recoveries of thirty to fifty percent (30–50%) percent of the oil in place or higher.[17]

"Combination Drive"

In many cases, reservoirs have a combination of the above described characteristics, for example, both a gas cap and a solution gas drive. These "combination drives" can often be identified only through careful well

---

17. *Introduction to Oil and Gas Production*, American Petroleum Institute 6–7 (1983).

logging and analysis of bottom hole pressure tests as well as applied institutional knowledge of the target interval before production and the rates of hydrocarbon and water production after completion. Identifying the type of drive present is important for planning and implementing initial and secondary development of a maturing field, as the overall recovery of oil and gas in place depends on the development plan over the life of the field.

Retrograde Gas Reservoir

A "retrograde gas reservoir" (or "gas-condensate reservoir") contains only gas within the pressurized reservoir. Upon development, however, a portion of the gas converts to liquid as the gas approaches the surface. Additionally, the dramatic drop in pressure and temperature between the reservoir and the wellhead causes some of the gas produced at the surface to convert to liquid. This conversion is referred to as "flashing" from gas to condensate.[18] Thus, the hydrocarbons produced at the surface are a mixture of gas and condensate. Retrograde gas reservoirs tend to be deeper and have higher pressures and higher temperatures than conventional reservoirs, causing the fluids in the reservoir to behave differently than in conventional hydrocarbon reservoirs. The gaseous condensate initially remains a vapor, as in a conventional gas reservoir, but as the reservoir pressure decreases, the liquids drop out of the gas while still in the reservoir. When this occurs, condensate production declines dramatically. Condensate that drops out in the reservoir is much more difficult to produce and also inhibits flow through the reservoir rock.

6. TYPES OF OIL AND GAS

Oil and natural gas are composed of various hydrocarbon molecules, which in turn are primarily comprised of hydrogen ("H") and carbon ("C") atoms, hence "hydrocarbons." While natural gas can have a simple chemical composition (*i.e.* CH_4 for methane), naturally occurring oil ("crude" oil) can have a very complex composition. The most common hydrocarbons are known as "alkanes," sometimes called "paraffins," all of which have the same basic chemical formula of C_nH_{2n+2}. The number of carbon atoms in hydrocarbon molecules (C_n, with 'n' being the "carbon number") and how they are bonded to one another and the hydrogen atoms around them, determine in the aggregate the type of hydrocarbon(s) present, how much heat will be provided, and market value. Smaller molecules are typically gas, and "natural gas" consists of alkanes with familiar names such as "methane" (CH_4), "ethane" (C_2H_6), "propane" (C_3H_8) and "butane" (C_4H_{10}). Methane is the most abundant of the four, but propane and butane provide more heat than methane when burned. Paraffins with carbon numbers from five ("pentane"—C_5H_{12}) to fifteen ("pentadecane"—$C_{15}H_{32}$) are typically liquids at room temperature. The

---

18. Condensate (sometimes called distillate or retrograde gas) are liquid hydrocarbons that occur as gas under subsurface reservoir conditions. NORMAN HYNE, DICTIONARY OF PETROLEUM EXPLORATION & PRODUCTION 99 (PennWell 1991).

chemical characteristics and BTU[19] content of oil and gas vary substantially from one reservoir or field to another.

The density of crude oil is indicated by its °*API gravity*. A crude oil's "gravity" is expressed by a value inverse to its density, according to a standard density as defined by the American Petroleum Institute ("API"). This inverse density value is therefore, somewhat counter-intuitively, *higher* for lighter crudes and *lower* for heavier crudes. Very light crudes, such as those popularly associated with production in West Texas, might have API gravity values around 45 to 55 °API, while heavier crudes from Venezuela or California may have API gravities of 10 to 20 °API or lower. Light crude oils are typically rich in gasoline, which requires less refining, and are therefore more valuable.

Lighter crudes typically also have less sulfur than heavier crudes and often are referred to as "sweet" crudes, and generally are more valuable than "sour" crudes, which are defined as those crudes that contain more than one percent (1%) sulfur. Sulfur in hydrocarbons occurs as elemental sulfur, organic sulfur compounds or, in gas, as hydrogen sulfide (H_2S). Presence of the latter can be a concern, as H_2S gas is poisonous to both people and livestock and corrosive to oilfield equipment. The hydrogen sulfide gas must be extracted from the natural gas before it can be sold and transported in a pipeline, increasing processing costs. Similarly, natural gas without detectable hydrogen sulfide is "sweet gas," while gas with detectable amounts is "sour gas." Native sulfur produced from oil production accounts for most of the world's production of elemental sulfur. Petroleum geologists can often predict the gravity and sulfur content of oil before production even begins by considering the production history of other wells in the same field.

Oil and natural gas can be produced either together or separately. Gas is produced from an oil well is called "associated gas," "oil well gas" or "dissolved gas." "Casinghead gas" is gas which separates from the oil upon encountering the lower pressures and temperatures found at the surface. "Dry gas" or "gas well gas"—gas production that is not incidental to oil production—is natural gas which, at room temperature, does not produce a significant liquid phase. In contrast, "wet gas" contains significant amounts of heavy hydrocarbon molecules that separate from the gas at surface pressures and temperatures forming liquids which can then be sold separately from the natural gas. These "condensates," often called "drip gasoline" or "casinghead gasoline," can be almost pure gasoline and therefore the source of significant profit over the natural gas from which it was derived, particularly if the market price of natural gas is low compared to oil, as in the late 2000s.

The presence or absence of condensates can influence the decisions of production companies about whether to develop a field. If, during a period of high oil prices and low gas prices, one field produces significant

---

19. The British thermal unit (symbol BTU or Btu) is a unit of energy which represents the amount of heat required to raise the temperature of one pound of water (at or near 39.2 degrees Fahrenheit) by one degree Fahrenheit. One Btu is equal to about 252 small calories or 0.252 kilocalories, 778.17 foot pounds, or 1055.06 joules. A BTU represents approximately the amount of heat generated by one lighted match.

condensates while a second field does not, an oil company will favor production from the first over the second and will allocate its resources accordingly. For example, during a period of high oil prices and flat gas prices in 2012, producers preferred developing the Eagle Ford and Bakken plays in Texas and North Dakota, respectively, over development in the Fayetteville play in Arkansas because the former produce more condensates, which could be sold separately from the natural gas for significantly more profit over sales of just dry gas. Developers preferred the Utica in Ohio over the Marcellus in Pennsylvania for the same reason.

"Saturated crude" contains as much gas in solution as can be dissolved at the pressures and temperatures found in a typical reservoir while "unsaturated crude" has the capacity to hold more natural gas in solution at natural reservoir conditions. Unsaturated crudes are also typically "low shrinkage oils" as, after they are brought to surface conditions (low pressures and temperatures), they experience little volume reduction because little gas is present to bubble out of solution and deflate the oil. Conversely, saturated crudes are commonly also "high shrinkage oils" because at lower surface temperatures and pressures, they "shrink" when the dissolved natural gas separates and comes out of solution, significantly lowering the volume of remaining liquid crude.

C. TECHNICAL BACKGROUND

1. EXPLORATION TECHNIQUES AND EXPLORATION

The search for oil and gas typically begins when geologists conduct surface and subsurface geological studies in an effort to identify reservoirs suitable for the accumulation of oil and gas. Geologists mapping the surface on foot or with the assistance of aerial photography can identify outcropping rocks. Well logs and core samples taken from wells assist the geologist in identifying subsurface rocks, but neither can accurately describe the subsurface structural configuration. Therefore, the geophysicist employs devices and techniques that can sense remotely the subsurface geology and provide the geologist with useful subsurface information.

The biggest challenge to petroleum exploration is that the mineral wealth sought is located in rock layers often miles beneath the surface where no one can personally observe or locate for hydrocarbons. A geophysicist will typically never be able to visit personally the target formation.[20] Geophysicists involved in petroleum seismology use many techniques to sense remotely and image the shapes and patterns of various rocks far beneath the surface.

The devices used for geophysical exploration include the gravity meter, ground penetrating radar, the magnetometer, and the seismograph.

---

20. Geophysics is the study and measurement of the physical properties of the earth by either recording the earth's response to various stimuli (explosive compressive force or electricity) or merely measuring forces that already exist but which vary by location (gravity or magnetic forces) and using that data to detect remotely and to image buried features.

The density of subsurface rocks can be measured with a gravity meter, sometimes called a "gravimeter," which measures changes in the earth's gravitational pull caused by variations in density of objects in the earth's crust. This information helps the geologist determine whether the predominate local rock material is of a type commonly associated with oil and gas deposits. The "magnetometer" measures the intensity of the earth's magnetic field in a certain spot and can also be used to predict the type of rock being measured. Ground penetrating radar can provide a scan of geologic features several dozen feet below the surface.

Seismic imaging of the subsurface is the most widely used geophysical technique for analyzing the interior of the earth, and is used much more commonly by the petroleum industry than all the other techniques combined. Through World War I, the search for minerals and hydrocarbons was limited to those areas exhibiting surface expressions such as oil slicks or rock outcrops with "oil shows" (*i.e.* traces of oil). Seismic reflection data, originally used to locate artillery in World War I, but adapted for subsurface mapping, provided the crucial link that combined data taken from individual wells, well logs, and surface mapping so that the extent and thickness of various strata could be imaged and mapped over long distances. A modern geophysicist can model strata at depth without direct observation and can remotely sense the geometry of strata no one will ever personally encounter.

The petroleum industry has invested significant resources in improving the resolution of seismic reflection data. Although petroleum exploration and development focus on the upper portion of the earth's crust where most commercial oil and gas accumulations are developed—a zone of depths from approximately one to twenty thousand feet—seismic reflection technology has been applied to both greater and shallower depths. For example, surveys designed to image very shallow coalbed methane layers have been popular in the last twenty years.

Seismologists recognize a number of different types of seismic waves. "Body waves" travel through a body of rock and are typically faster than "surface waves" which travel along the earth's surface. Body waves include the two most important waves to petroleum seismologists, P-waves (also called "primary" or "compressive waves") and S-waves (also called "shear waves"). P-waves travel at higher velocities and are the waves usually recorded for seismic reflection data. They can be generated by explosions of dynamite or other charges placed in shallow holes, called "shot holes," in which the explosive is detonated. In addition, VibroSeis or "thumper" trucks can generate P-waves of a certain range of frequencies. Compressive airguns are commonly used offshore for marine geophysical surveys.

Once generated, P-waves travel through the rock until the energy encounters a reflector, whereupon a portion of the energy comprising the P-wave is reflected back to the surface, as shown in Fig. 15. Typical reflectors are caused by changes in density within a rock formation or by the boundary between one rock type and another. Returning P-waves are recorded by sensors called "geophones" onshore and "hydrophones" offshore placed at specified locations and intervals on land or dragged behind a boat in long arrays at sea.

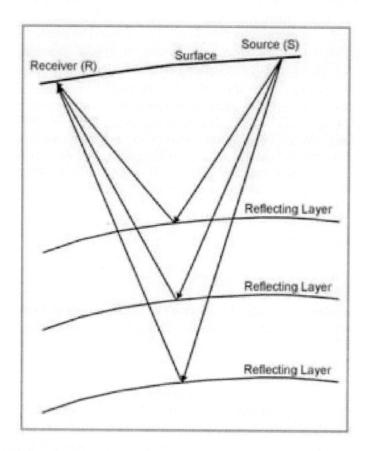

Figure 15. Primary or "P" waves being emitted from a source (S), traveling through multiple rock layers to various rock layer interfaces at which some of the energy is reflected back towards the surface and a receiver (R). (Source: Environmental Protection Agency)

Geophones consist of a mass hanging on a spring that is housed in a metal casing. When the reflected P-waves return to the surface, the ground and the geophone case moves ever so slightly while the hanging mass inside the geophone casing remains motionless. A strand of wire is wrapped around the mass, which is surrounded by a magnet. As the earth moves, the magnet moves up and down around the mass and wire. The magnetic field generated by the moving magnet produces an electrical voltage that can be amplified and recorded by an operator in a recording truck, sometimes called a "doghouse."

Once the data is recorded in the field, this raw seismic data is passed to the seismic processor. The processor uses advanced methods of computer-assisted signal processing and wave theory to render the raw data into a recognizable format so that interpretation and presentation can be made. Typically, the largest obstacle in seismic processing is "noise"— unwanted return multiples from indirect reflections or random events in the data that hide the true signal. In addition, objects seen on seismic records sometime need to be moved within the data so that they are represented as being in the same space in the data as in nature. The ultimate goal of seismic processing is to construct a data set that represents, as closely as possible, an accurate picture of subsurface rock structures.

Once seismic data has been processed so that it can be presented in a recognizable form, seismic interpretation can begin. The seismic reflection data section in Fig. 16 appears like a cross section of the earth, similar to a giant-scale roadcut of rock beside a highway, whereon various structures and strata are clearly evident. Because seismic reflection data consists of echoes, however, the vertical axis does not reflect *depth* but rather *time*— the time it takes for the seismic waves generated on the surface to travel through the rock, encounter a reflector, and return to the surface. If a portion of Fig. 16 was enlarged, we would see that the seismic section consists of many closely spaced "wiggle traces" which, when isolated, look like the traces on Fig. 17. Each wiggle trace is a series of echoes—a graphical representation of the P-waves echoing off reflecting horizons within the subsurface. The ultimate goal of seismic interpretation is to identify subsurface rocks, reservoirs, and the hydrocarbons themselves. This information will be used, along with other available geological data, to make drilling and development decisions.

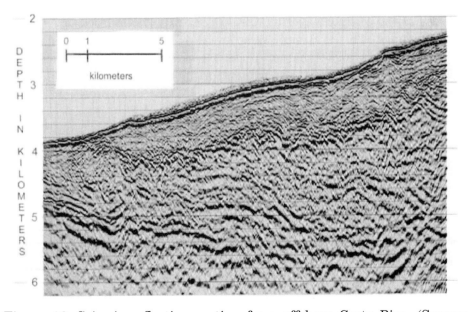

Figure 16. Seismic reflection section from offshore Costa Rica. (Source: Walter Kessinger)

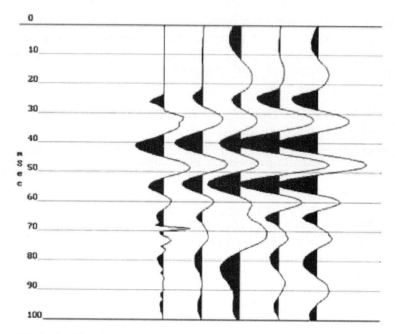

Figure 17. Individual seismic reflection traces that comprise a seismic reflection section. The vertical axis is measured in milliseconds while the horizontal axis represents distance between the traces. (Source: Kansas Geologic Survey).

Drilling costs increase dramatically as depth increases, so the time scale on the vertical axis must be converted to depth. To do this, the velocity of the seismic waves as they travel through the rock layers must be determined. This is usually done by taking well logs in the area and modeling the various types of rocks encountered. Accuracy can be a problem: even with good well control, a depth value estimated from a converted time scale may be five percent (5.0%) or more off the actual depth in the depth range of two to four (2–4) miles. Errors increase dramatically below those depths or where poor well control and/or deficient modeling take place. Seismic interpretation relies heavily on integration of other data and the geophysicist's experience.

Single seismic lines, representing a vertical plane-view of the earth, are called two-dimensional or "2D seismic" sections or lines. If a large number of parallel and perpendicular 2D seismic lines are acquired close enough to one another, typically 55, 110 feet, or 50 meters apart, then a three-dimensional cube of data can be interpreted on a computer. Three-dimensional or "3D seismic" can provide a much more accurate geometrical representation of the regional rock structure along with much better imaging of local faults and other smaller geologic structures.[21] This 3D seismic is expensive and requires many multiples of the seismic data acquired for a 2D seismic survey. The increased resolution and the computer's ability to produce custom 2D sections from any angle within a 3D seismic data cube, however, are generally considered to be worth the price once a production company makes the multi-million dollar decision to drill within a prospective area.

Recent advances in seismic exploration have revolutionized the petroleum industry. For example, hydrocarbon traps are often associated with complex structures comprised of immense sheets of salt. For many years, accurate seismic imaging of the traps under and adjacent to salt formations eluded petroleum seismologists because the complex structure of salt scattered the P-waves used to image geologic structure. While petroleum seismology associated with salt tectonics is still fraught with pitfalls creating doubt in many cases, advanced seismic data gathering and processing techniques have been combined with a better understanding of rock mechanics to allow for subsalt imaging in some cases. For example, discoveries over the last ten years in the Santos Basin offshore of Brazil were made possible partially by advanced seismic imaging techniques used on the salt layers that overlie the Tupi, Iara, and Iracema fields, which are thought to hold well over ten billion barrels of reserves, more than the entire reserve portfolio of Norway.[22]

Four dimensional seismic, typically called "4D" or "time-lapse" seismic, involves the analysis of two or more 3D seismic surveys repeated over the same target space over a period of time. 4D seismic has allowed geophysicists to monitor changes in reservoir properties over time.[23] Since gas and oil in place can sometimes be visible on seismic data, and since production removes a portion of gas and oil from a reservoir, 4D seismic can provide reservoir snapshots "before" and "after" production, allowing an interpreter to find pockets of remaining hydrocarbons for the operator to consider targeting.

Seismic surveys can involve significant number of workers, extensive surface use with small drill rigs and trucks, and potentially the use of small explosive charges. 3D seismic surveys require a field technician to place geophones along parallel lines only dozens of feet apart. Displeasure by surface owners at these intrusions and use represent a growing source of litigation and action by state legislatures.

---

21. For a comprehensive discussion of the recent state of 3D seismic, and its potential legal implications, see Anderson, Owen L. and John D. Pigott, *Seismic Technology and Law: Partners or Adversaries?*, 24 Energy & Min. L. Inst. Ch. 11 (2004).

22. *See* Carlos Caminada and Jeb Blount, *Petrobras' Tupi Oil Field May Hold Eight Billion Barrels*, BLOOMBERG, Nov. 8, 2007.

23. *See* Joel Watkins and Chris Kulander, *Finding Untested Compartments by Integrated Seismic and Production Analyses: A Case Study from Ship Shoal 274, Gulf of Mexico*, SOCIETY OF EXPLORATION GEOPHYSICISTS ANN. MTG. PROCEEDINGS (1999).

2. DRILLING A WELL

Introduction

Drilling a well is a costly gamble. Millions—or even tens of millions—of dollars can be at stake.[24] The long process and huge costs associated with making the decision about whether and where to drill, permitting, acquiring a rig and crew, drilling, testing and logging (and possibly completing) a well create a complex, expensive and time-consuming process. A brief summary of the steps that must be taken in drilling a well is helpful for understanding the risks inherent in the drilling business.

Oil companies generally hire drilling contractors to actually drill wells. The "operator"—the oil company in charge of drilling operations on behalf of group of co-developing companies will engage the services of the drilling contractor and other well-services providers. Drilling contractors employ a group of professionals to conduct the drilling. Each crewman typically has a specialty. The leader of the drilling contractor's team on the drillsite, the "toolpusher," is responsible for all rig floor activities and communicates with the operator's representative about drilling progress and about any problems encountered. The actual deck work is conducted by the drilling crew. Since drilling can continue around the clock, sometimes two or three drilling crews will work rotating schedules like factory shift workers. Each crew works under the direction of the "driller". In addition to directing the operation of the drilling and hoisting equipment, the driller is also responsible for the downhole condition of the well, operation of downhole tools, and maintaining well integrity. The deck crew will generally consist of a "derrickman" who works at the top of the derrick when drillpipe is being added or removed from the drillstem and who also tends the pumps while drilling, three "roughnecks" who work on the rig floor adding, removing, and connecting drillpipe and performing general rig maintenance, plus a support staff including mechanics, electricians, hoist operators, and various "roustabouts" who provide general labor.

The operator or occasionally the drilling contractor, will hire a myriad of other companies to provide wellsite services and provisions, such as electrical service, compressors, caterers, wireline and logging services, drillpipe, drilling mud and mudlogging services. The operator may contract for these services on a per-well basis or the basis of "master services agreements" (MSAs) that contemplate the drilling of multiple wells.[25]

Once the drilling contract and ancillary services contracts and MSAs have been executed, the drilling rig is transported to the drill site that has been selected by the operator's geologists. This task ranges from routine and inexpensive in flat, open land that is easily accessible by public roads

---

24. BP's 1982 Mukluk well, drilled from a man-made gravel island in the Beaufort Sea off Alaska's North Slope and costing in excess of $1 billion, has gained notoriety as the most expensive dry hole in history.

25. Drilling and services contracts will be further considered in Chapter 6, Section F. For an in-depth analysis of drilling contracts and operations, please see Owen L. Anderson, *The Anatomy of an Oil and Gas Drilling Contract*, 25 Tulsa L.J. 359–533 (1990).

to extremely difficult and very expensive in mountainous, forested, marshy, and offshore locations. In the latter situations, several service contractors may be involved in providing access and transporting the rig and other equipment to the drill site.

Rigs move from site to site on a tight schedule. During periods of high prices when rig availability is tight, if delays plague a certain project and the time window allocated for the rig visit to that project is missed, a long and costly delay may occur before another rig becomes available. Once the main drilling rig (usually a "rotary" rig) reaches the drill site, the "rigging up" process occurs. The rig is raised to a vertical position over the drill site and the various rig components are assembled to ready the rig for "making hole."

The Drilling Rig

Most rigs are rotary drilling rigs. This means that a "drillbit" is drilled into the earth by rotating the drillbit so that the bit rasps away the rock as it descends through the various formations. [Fig. 18]. "Cone" drillbits typically have three interlocking wheels held by a hollow metal casing. "Diamond" drillbits, as shown in Fig. 19, are studded with industrial-grade diamonds, the hardest substance available, on the end of a simple ring-shaped bit. Whatever the variety, the drillbit is attached to the "drill stem," which is comprised of a series of (generally) thirty-foot segments of pipe—"drill pipe". Drilling a modern oil and gas well involves placement of these tubes of steel drill pipe, fitted together, into a borehole. As the hole gets deeper, more drill pipe is added and hoisted into and out of the hole. Drill collars are heavier lengths of pipe connecting the lower end of the drill stem to the bit and providing weight on the bit, forcing it to drill or grind its way into the ground. Drilling mud is pumped down the drill string to provide additional weight and to lubricate the rotary bit.

The drill stem is hung in the wellbore by a hoist, a large block and tackle apparatus which raises and lowers the drill stem into and out of the hole. The hoist is hung on the derrick, which is the familiar structure that can rise high enough to allow the drill stem to be pulled out of the hole far enough so individual drill pipes may be removed from the drill stem.

The rotating components on the surface include the "swivel," "kelly," and "rotary table." The "swivel" attached to the bottom of the block is designed to rotate and to provide a high-pressure seal and passageway for drilling mud to enter the drill pipe. The "kelly" is a heavy four or six-sided pipe attached to the bottom of the swivel. Drilling mud passes through the kelly from the swivel and into the drill pipe. The kelly travels through bushings attached to the rotary table, and sometimes together they are called the "kelly bushing." The "rotary table" rotates the bushings, kelly, swivel, and drill stem. The rotary table also contains slips that hold the drill pipe in place when the kelly is removed.

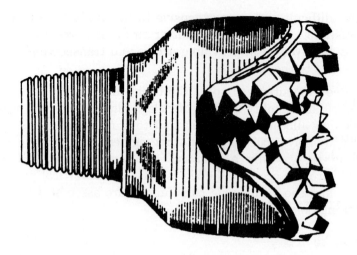

FIGURE 18. A conventional rock bit or cone bit. As the bit is rotated, the teeth on the cones turn and bite into the rock and chip off fragments. Drilling fluid passes through the bit to cool and to lubricate it and to carry the rock chips to the surface. Reprinted with permission of the North Dakota Geological Survey.

FIGURE 19. A diamond bit that is used for cutting a core out of the rock. It is used in conjuction with a core barrel. The surface of the bit is covered with industrial diamonds. The bit is hollow so that as it cuts into the rock, a core of rock is cut which passes through the bit and into the core barrel. Reprinted with permission of the North Dakota Geological Survey.

The circulation system facilitates the use of drilling mud. Drilling mud or drilling fluid consists of a mixture of water or oil (or both), clay, ballast (commonly barite), and various chemicals. Drilling mud is furnished by a service contractor commonly called a mud company. During drilling, the drilling mud is circulated continuously down the drill pipe, through the drillbit, and back out through the hole to the surface in the space between the rock and the drillstem. The flowing drilling mud removes the rock cuttings from the hole while cooling the hot drillbit.

The mud in the hole also provides weight so that the buried gas and/or liquids, which are under extreme overburden pressure, do not cause a "blowout" to the surface like the gusher wells of yore. In the event unexpected underground pressure is encountered, salt water, oil, or gas may enter the hole, causing mud suddenly to rise in the hole or to stop circulating. Detection of this so-called "kick" by bottom-hole detectors serves as the ominous first (and maybe only) warning of a possible blowout. A "kick" can lead to disaster if the gas or oil is allowed to push up the drill stem and reach the surface, where it may ignite in a lethal explosion.

If the kick cannot be controlled by adjusting the mud weight and circulation, one or more "blowout preventers" ("BOPs") will close. BOPs are a series of large valves at the top of the hole that may be closed if the drilling crew loses control of the mud and other formation fluids. By closing these valves (usually operated remotely via hydraulic actuators), the drilling crew tries to regain control of the reservoir, and procedures can then be initiated to increase the mud density until it is possible to open the BOP and retain pressure control of the formation. If the BOPs are closed, a choke manifold will allow limited and controlled circulation to occur, allowing heavier mud to be circulated into the hole to control the kick. BOPs come in a variety of styles, sizes, and pressure ratings. Some can effectively close over an open wellbore, some are designed to seal around tubular components in the well (drillpipe, casing or tubing), and others are fitted with hardened steel shearing surfaces that can actually cut through drillpipe. When the well is brought under control and mud circulation is restored, normal drilling operations may resume.

At the surface, the returning drilling mud is forced through a "shale shaker" vibrating screen that separates the rock cuttings from the mud and is then pumped into a pit where it is sampled, purified, allowed to settle so the solids fall out, and then used again. Geologists will analyze the cutting in the shale shaker or elsewhere to determine what formation the drillbit is currently penetrating.

The Drilling Process

At an onshore drill site, the drilling site or "pad" has to be surveyed, the rig must be erected on a reasonably level surface, a reserve pit has to be dug and lined, and a water supply has to be secured. Once the drilling rig is "rigged up" on the pad, the BOPs have been tested, and the necessary mud is on standby, the drilling crew is ready to commence "making hole." The crew will attach a drill bit to a drill collar and lower the bit and collar down the hole using the drawworks—the assembly of cables and hoists within the derrick necessary to raise and lower the drillstem. Additional drill collars and drill pipe sections will be added and lowered down the hole. When the bit nears the bottom of the hole, the crew will add the kelly to the top of the drill string. At this point, the circulating system and turntable will be activated, and the drawworks will lower the drilling string until the bit touches the bottom of the hole. At this point, the well is "making hole".

A main goal of any well is to ensure safe production of oil and gas in a way that protects groundwater and heightens production by keeping any hydrocarbons encountered inside the well and isolating the productive formations from aquifers and other formations. Sound well design and drilling ensure that no significant leakage will occur between any casing joints and that fluids introduced to the casing string at the surface or produced from the production zone must travel directly from the production zone to the surface inside the wellbore.[26]

A smaller "rathole," or water-well rig, may be used to set the initial conductor pipe in the drill hole. The deeper one goes in the well, the smaller the diameter of the drill stem—complete wells are similar to an extended sea captain's monocular. Steel tubes called "casing" are used to seal off the drilling and formation fluids from migrating into groundwater aquifers and to keep the wellbore from caving in.[27]

The first hole to be drilled is for the biggest tube of steel, the conductor pipe. The conductor pipe can also be pounded into place, like a structural caisson, by a cable-tool rig. This pipe is followed by (i) the surface casing, (ii) the intermediate casing (if necessary), and (iii) the production-zone casing. Each of these has a progressively smaller diameter.[28] (*See* Fig. 20, *Source: American Petroleum Institute*)

---

26. *Hydraulic Fracturing Operations—Well Construction and Integrity Guidelines 4*, AMERICAN PETROLEUM INSTITUTE (API Guidance Document HF1, First Edition), October, 2009, at 3.

27. *Manual of Oil and Gas Terms*, Casing 131, 132 (13th ed. 2006).

28. *Hydraulic Fracturing Operations—Well Construction and Integrity Guidelines 4, supra* note 26 at 2–4.

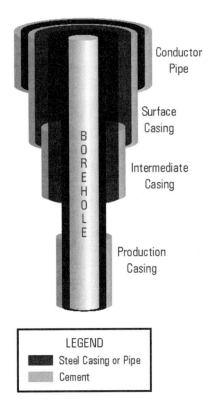

Figure 20. Typical Well Schematic (Source: Kirk Draut, used with permission)

The conductor pipe keeps out loose sediment at and near the surface and separates the groundwater zones from the drilling fluids. After the conductor pipe is installed and cemented into place, drilling continues and the surface casing is centered into the hole and cemented in place. Like the conductor pipe, the main purposes of the surface casing and cement are to provide stability for the subsequent deep drilling and completion operations and to provide a barrier to potable groundwater supplies. Casing is generally set and cemented into place by a special casing crew, and cementing is generally done by a cement-service contractor. The failure of surface casing can cause groundwater pollution, loss of a hole, and cratering, which can result in serious damage to the rig and other well equipment.

These first and second phases of drilling—constituting the "surface hole" portions of drilling—are sometimes completed with a smaller, cheaper drill rig and are commonly drilled using freshwater-based drilling fluids to prevent groundwater contamination. The surface hole is usually drilled to a predetermined depth established by the deepest occurrence of groundwater resources and can range from a couple hundred feet to more than a thousand feet deep. State regulations dictate the minimal setting depth of surface casing, with nearly all states requiring the surface casing to be set below the deepest freshwater aquifer. Generally, the surface casing is set at least one hundred feet below the deepest potable water encountered while drilling the well or the fresh/salt water boundary in the area, if known.

In addition to the protection of the groundwater provided by the steel casing, the API recommends that the surface casing be entirely cemented to completely isolate freshwater aquifers. The proper cementing of several layers of steel pipe in the hole isolates the groundwater zones near the surface from the borehole and the drilling/fracing fluid. After the casing has been inserted into the hole, it is cemented in place by pumping cement slurry into the well down through the casing and back up into place outside of the casing.

Subsequent to completion of the surface hole and casing, a larger drill rig is typically moved into position and drilling of the "intermediate hole" and the "production hole" is commenced. The intermediate hole is the broad zone of strata encountered between the surface groundwater zones and the area from which production or horizontal drilling will take place. As the hole becomes deeper, the crew will periodically stop the rotary table, shut off the mud pump, remove the kelly, and add another length of drill pipe. This is called making a connection and is repeated for each thirty feet—the length of one drill pipe.

Casing in the intermediate zone provides hole stability and prevents hole collapse from high-pressure zones encountered while drilling to the productive zones. Unlike the surface casing zone, complete cementing of the intermediate hole back to the surface is not usually necessary, but hydrocarbon-bearing zones are generally cemented. Once the intermediate zone is traversed by drilling, pressure testing is sometimes conducted to determine the maximum pressure that the casing string can withstand, to determine the integrity of previous cement jobs, and to determine the maximum mud weight that can be used for the next casing setting depth.[29]

If casing must be run, if the drill bit needs changing, or if equipment is lost down the hole, the crew must "trip out" (raise the drill string out of the hole). To accomplish this, the drill pipe and drill collars are detached as they are hoisted out of the ground, generally in three-length segments or as many as the height of the derrick will allow, and then stored vertically on the derrick. To resume making hole, the crew must "trip in" (reassemble the drill string and lower it down the hole). Once completed, the mud pump and turntable are engaged and the rig is again making hole.

Horizontal Drilling

The slowly developing drilling boom of 2000–2010 targeting hydrocarbons found in domestic shale and other "tight" formations has been made possible by horizontal drilling and the subsequent process of hydraulic

---

29. Apiwat Lorwongngam, The Validity of Leak–Off Test for In Situ Stress Estimation; the Effect of the Bottom of the Borehole (2008) (unpublished M.S. thesis, University of Oklahoma), on file with the University of Oklahoma Library *available at* http://mpge.ou.edu/research/documents/Lorwongngam.pdf (last visited March 28, 2010).

fracturing. "Horizontal" wells are wells that start as a typical vertical well but change direction at depth so that the drill stem and subsequent borehole are not vertical or straight but rather horizontal or curved. Horizontal wells remain in contact with the target formation much longer than a vertical well. Therefore, fewer wells are needed to develop a field. In addition, multiple wells can be drilled from the same pad, lessening the "surface footprint" left by the developer.

Horizontal drilling was first used successfully on a field scale in the Austin Chalk of Texas and the Bakken Shale in North Dakota, both in the 1980s. The Austin Chalk, a "tight" formation with little permeability, is productive only along certain naturally-occurring fracture trends. These fracture trends are large horizontal cracks in the formation wherein hydrocarbons can be commercially produced interspersed with intervals of low permeability chalk with no fractures, which stifled economic production. Production from the Austin Chalk by vertical wells was therefore hit or miss—miss a fracture zone and the well is dry. Traditional vertical wells were a poor risk to find the fractures as they ran parallel to the vertical fracture planes. The horizontal portion of a directional well, however, was far more likely to penetrate one or more fracture zones and result in a producing well because it would encounter the vertical fractures perpendicularly.

After the process of hydraulic fracturing—"fracing" (discussed below)—became commercially feasible on an industry-wide scale, the oil industry noticed that "tight" formations, which are oriented more or less laterally, could be fractured by man-made processes using a horizontal borehole. Specifically, wells were drilled into the Barnett Shale in Texas where the horizontal component remained within the Barnett over the entire lateral displacement of the well. Fracing allowed the gas in the shale to flow to the well all along the lateral extent of the borehole, and a new source of natural gas appeared.

Drilling a horizontal well is typically started in a way similar to a vertical well, with a rotary drill driving a string of drill pipe straight down from the rig. Drilling continues until the bottom of the hole is approximately five hundred feet above the target formation. At this "kick-off point"—the point where the well begins to turn from the vertical—a hydraulic motor is usually lowered into the hole directly above the drilling bit. Behind the motor on the drill string are one or more flexible points to allow the casing to turn from the vertical. The turn from vertical to the horizontal portion of the well—the "lateral"—can usually be accomplished over a lateral distance of less than a thousand feet. One or more co-axial portions of the stem then turn the bit in the direction sought while the downhole motor provides the continued impetus to drive the bit. The motor itself is connected to the surface string on a flexible mount, allowing it to also be pointed in the desired direction.

In the alternative, if the initial "bending" of the drill string is minor, the individual lengths of 30–foot drill pipe may be flexible enough to gradually turn the drill string without structural failure or buckling. The sub-horizontal portions of directional wells, however, are almost entirely drilled with downhole motors.

The location of the bit can be transmitted to the surface by a sensor/transmitter equipped with a global positioning system ("GPS") placed just behind the bit. As the borehole goes deeper and the sensor's progress is tracked and recorded over time, the eventual path of the borehole can be mapped at the surface. This allows for corrections to the direction of the casing string by the driller who is "steering" the hole from the rig floor. Steering allows the driller to maintain the designated borehole trajectory to encounter the most productive portions of the reservoir rock, and to eventually reach the desired endpoint without straying across the boundary of unleased tracts. Other sensors at various points in the drill string can provide more information, such as the temperature and pressure throughout the borehole and the weight of the overburden upon the non-vertical portion of the drill string. When the horizontal well is complete, many states require that the operator file with the state oil and gas agency a survey showing the borehole top, bottom, and trajectory in-between. The horizontal portion of a well can reach over 12,000 feet but is usually between 3,500 to 10,000 feet.

3. COMPLETING A WELL AND PRIMARY PRODUCTION

Finally, the possible production zone is reached. Once this depth is reached, an investigation must be conducted to discover if the hole is worth bringing in as a producing well or, if no hydrocarbons are found, to be plugged and abandoned. A mud logger, well-sitting geologist, or engineer gathers samples of well cuttings and examines the samples for petroleum. Another service contractor may provide logging services, which involves lowering various tools into the hole and taking measurements of the rock to indicate the presence of hydrocarbons. Since the produced fluid is allowed to flow through the drillstem or, as it is sometimes called, the drilling string, this test is termed a "drill-stem test" or "DST." A core-barreling device can also be lowered down the hole to cut actual core samples from a formation. After drilling, testing and plugging, or completion is accomplished, rigging down occurs. The drilling rig and related equipment are taken down and transported off the well site. Sometimes the drilling rig may be rigged down prior to completion so that completion operations may be conducted with a less-costly rig.

If investigations indicate nothing of value, the hole must be plugged and abandoned. This requires cement seals to be placed down hole and a cement cap to be installed beneath the surface, sealing the top of the hole. The reserve pit and well site are then reclaimed and restored.

If the gamble pays off and the well comes in as a producer, "production casing" is run and the producing formation is sealed off with expanding rings called "packers" and then cemented in place. Equipment that allows for the controlled flow of the hydrocarbons must be installed in the well. In most cases the first step in this operation is to place and cement production casing across the zone from which oil or gas will be withdrawn. A string of pipe, known as "production tubing," through which the hydrocarbons will flow, is then run inside the production casing so it may be pulled from the well if the string leaks or corrodes.

The production casing contains the downhole production equipment. In addition, like the casing in the intermediate zone, the production casing isolates the producing formations from other formations so that the only communication between the surface and the rock is through the perforated production casing. This isolation allows the drillers to recover the initial draw of oil and gas and, subsequently, to target the input of fracing fluids and other stimulation techniques directly into the producing formation without affecting any other formation or aquifer.

The result of this process, if followed with care and thoroughness, is a completed borehole where the freshwater aquifers are separated from communication with the fluids in the wellbore by two or three layers of steel tubing and one or two layers of impervious cement. The producing formations near the bottom of the hole are typically thousands of feet away from the uphole aquifers and separated by cement and packers.

When the packer is positioned just above the pay zone, its rubber seals are expanded to seal off the borehole between the production tubing and the production casing. To initiate production, the production casing is perforated by controlled explosive charges run down the tubing and positioned adjacent to the pay zone. Holes are then shot through the casing and cemented into the formation. The hydrocarbons flow into the wellbore and up the tubing to the surface. For gas wells, a complex set of valves and dials, known colloquially as a "Christmas tree" for its similarity in appearance to a metal abstract-art version of the real thing, is installed on the surface at the top of the wellhead. These Christmas trees are used to control the flow of gas once it reaches the surface. For oil wells, a pump is installed to raise the liquid hydrocarbons to the surface so the hydrocarbons can be placed in a tank battery. These pumps include the familiar "pumpjack" or "hammerhead" stripper wells found in mature oilfields across America.

At this point, as the tubing and spent perforating segments are removed, the rig is replaced by a contractor specializing in hydraulic fracturing. Development of oil and gas in "tight" formations such as shale, where the hydrocarbons will not flow naturally to a traditionally-drilled borehole, requires a well-completion process called hydraulic fracturing or "fracing." Critics of this process often incorrectly spell fracing "fracking" to give the word a pejorative connotation. The following material describes this process.

THOMAS KURTH, MICHAEL MAZZONE, MARY MENDOZA, CHRISTOPHER KULANDER, *AMERICAN LAW AND JURISPRUDENCE ON FRACING—2012*; **58 ROCKY MT. MIN. L. INST. § 4.05**

Hydraulic Fracturing—An Overview

Most people are familiar with the "gusher" well where reservoir pressure underground pushes oil up the wellbore. Oil and gas are harder to extract from "tight" rock formations, which do not allow passage of oil and gas through and up a well. Such formations, often shale or coal, may be filled with gas or oil, but allow those fluids to flow only along preexisting cracks or "fractures."

* * *

The usefulness and application of hydraulic fracturing only became apparent with the discovery that "tight" shale formations could be economically developed with hydraulic fracturing techniques—that is, by making *artificial* fractures. Now, instead of relying on natural fracture zones, developers made their own fractures.

Hydraulic fracturing—known colloquially as "frac'ing," "fracking," and, in this report, as "fracing"—is a process in which fluid is injected into a well at very high pressures in order to either widen and deepen existing cracks or create new fractures in the tight formation.[30] Generally, increased fracturing will allow more oil or gas to be produced from a well previously thought dry or in decline. Petroleum companies vary the type of fluid used for fracing depending on the rock type, depth, or other factors. The fluids used can include water, water mixed with solvents, or drilling mud. The fluid is mixed with the "proppant," which is typically sand, ceramic pellets or other small granular material that is carried into the fractures where it remains to prop the crack open thereby allowing oil or gas to flow.

* * *

Fracing Fluids and Operations

The process of hydraulic fracing requires a "fracing fluid" to be pumped into the well's production casing in the target formation at a very high pressure and rate. Therefore, the production casing string, the cement holding it in place, and the composite bridge plugs which separate the segments of the drainhole undergoing individual fracing salvos, must be capable of withstanding the pressure. If the integrity of the production casing is in doubt, a high pressure "frac string" may be used to direct the

---

30. The American Petroleum Institute *("API")* maintain a short video of current fracing techniques *available at* http://www.api.org/policy/exploration/hydraulicfracturing/hydraulic fracturing.cfm (last visited April 23, 2010).

fracing fluid to the prospective interval. The frac string is removed once operations are complete.[31]

The actual fracing takes place in three phases. The first phase, called the "pad," occurs when the hydraulic fluid is first pumped into the productive zone without any proppant. This is done to instigate the fractures in the rock and to prime the location so that any fluid leakage into immediately adjacent zones are accounted for. The second stage occurs when the proppant is added to the mix. Proppant can be sand of an optimum uniform grain size or man-made materials such as ceramic beads or sintered bauxite. The proppant holds the fractures open, allowing the gas to flow after the fracing fluid is pumped out. Without the proppant, the pressures at depth could largely reseal the the fractures, defeating the value of the operation. Finally, the last stage is the flushing of the reservoir to remove excess proppant from the borehole and to propel the proppant further into the formation. The flushing fluid can be either water or the same material used to start the process.[32]

The pressure in the hole is closely monitored throughout the process so that any significant leakage of the fracing fluid past the packers and away from the productive zone is immediately detected. If a leak is detected, the operation can be stopped. Leaks at or near the bottom of the casing string are separated by hundreds or thousands of feet of intervening strata from shallower freshwater aquifers.[33]

Nearly all oil and gas wells experience a gradual drop off in production over time; this is called a "decline curve" by petroleum engineers.[34] While the new "fraced" wells are initially prolific, their rates of production have been found to drop off quickly in the Barnett Shale and elsewhere. If this trend carries to shale gas plays, the productive lifespan of shale gas wells will be shorter than traditional gas wells. This means that to maintain high and steady gas production from a portfolio of assets, developers must continuously drill wells to replace wells to replace wells that quickly become uneconomic.[35]

* * *

The logistical and physical infrastructure demands of fracing operations involve a great deal of personnel and materials and traffic to and from the drillsite. Typically, fracing fluid is mixed offsite in the yard of the contractor conducting the fracing operations. Here, the water is mixed with any additives before being trucked onsite. Fracing operations often require one or two acres in addition to the original drilling pad where the

---

31. *Id.* at 18.

32. *Id.*

33. *Id.* at 21.

34. *Manual of Oil and Gas Terms, supra* note 8.

35. Arthur Berman, *Lessons from the Barnett Shale Suggest Caution in Other Shale Plays,* ASPO–USA, (August 10, 2009) *available at* http://www.aspousa.org/index.php/2009/08/lessons-from-the-barnett-shale-suggest-caution-in-other-shale-plays/ (last visited May 9, 2010).

multitude of tanker trucks and other vehicles and equipment can congregate.[36]

Oil companies typically hire specialized contractors to conduct fracing operations. These contractors are protective of the exact recipe of their fracing fluids, considering the ingredients and the ratio with which the ingredients are mixed with the water to make the fracing fluid to be trade secrets. The general constituents of fracing fluids are known, however, and in addition to 99.5% sand and water, made be 0.5% salt, acid, distillates, ethylene glycol, isopropanol and sodium or potassium carbonate.[37]

With today's technology, a typical fracing operation in the Marcellus Shale requires between one to five million gallons of fracing fluid, mostly water, per well.[38] About twenty to forty percent (20%–40%) of the fluid can be expected to return to the surface through the borehole after the proppant has been injected and the water is being drawn out. In general, there are three ways to deal with fracing fluid left over from operations: (i) inject it back via a disposal well, similar to those used to dispose excess brine from more traditional operations; (ii) treat the fluid through evaporation and/or settling at the surface; or (iii) gather the used fracing fluid, dilute it with freshwater, and truck or pipe it to another project and reuse it again.[39]

* * *

4. SECONDARY AND TERTIARY (ENHANCED) RECOVERY

Most oil that has been discovered remains in the ground, defying our efforts to produce it. Reservoir pressure eventually gives out, allowing the oil to sit "in situ" in the pore spaces between the rock grains comprising a reservoir and resulting in a typical pattern where a well experiences an initial burst of production and then a long decline until it no longer produces. Indeed, about 15% of total onshore domestic production comes from over 400,000 marginal or "stripper" wells that produce 10 or fewer barrels-of-oil-equivalent per day. You may be surprised to learn that about 3/4th of all the oil discovered still remains where it was found. Enhanced oil recovery provides a chance to increase production rates and even revive depleted fields and dormant wells.

---

36. Michele Rodgers, et al., *Marcellus Shale: What Local Governments Need to Know*, Penn State College of Agricultural Sciences (2008) p. 11, *available at* www.naturalgas.psu.edu (last visited May 9, 2010). The frequency of drilling activity in a locale, rural or urban, and its associated impact on the local populace can present a wide variety of challenges which require the formulation of solutions by the operators, service companies, and not uncommonly state and local regulatory Agencies. These challenges and their solutions will be addressed, *infra*.

37. Groundwater Protection Council, *Modern Gas Shale Development in the United States*, April 2009, p. 78, graphic representation *available at* http://www.energyindepth.org/frac-fluid.pdf (last visited May 1, 2010).

38. Michele Rodgers, et al., *supra* note 36, at 4.

39. Colter Cookson, *Technologies Enable Frac Water Reuse*, AMERICAN OIL & GAS REPORTER, March 2010, at 106.

Enhanced-recovery projects are expensive and may take a long time to show results. These operations typically target oil, as oil is more conducive to these efforts and is generally worth more than gas. If a fraction of the leftover oil is recovered, a significant increase in ultimate recovery results, improving the portfolio of oil reserves for the industry and providing, in the aggregate, security that comes from robust domestic oil reserves.

A typical oil well goes through three discrete stages during its lifetime. These are the primary recovery stage, the secondary recovery stage, and the tertiary recovery stage. After the reservoir pressure has diminished to the point that hydrocarbons are no longer forced to the surface (or into the wellbore) by reservoir pressure, the well leaves the primary recovery stage and enters the secondary and tertiary recovery stages provided the producer decides to continue developing the well.

To keep oil flowing, maintaining reservoir pressure is necessary. Secondary recovery entails subjecting the reservoir to gas or, more popularly, water injection, as a substitute for the lost reservoir pressure to move the oil to the surface. In some cases, secondary recovery can increase the ultimate production from a well up to a third or more of the total oil in place. Water injected into the producing formation to replace the volume of oil extracted provides not only a mechanism to force more oil toward a well, but also serves as a way to maintain reservoir pressure.[40]

But water flooding alone generally leaves more than half the original oil behind. Releasing that oil requires either chemicals, solvents, or heat. This is the role of "tertiary recovery." Tertiary recovery, also known as "enhanced oil recovery," injects certain liquids or gasses into the reservoir, lowering the viscosity of the oil remaining in the pore spaces which, in turn, allows that leftover oil to (hopefully) flow towards recovery wells. Tertiary recovery, usually (but not always) attempted after secondary recovery efforts have played out, can push the total oil recovered from a well from a third of the total oil in place to over half, depending on the reservoir stratigraphy and geology and the amount and ingenuity of the tertiary recovery methods that are attempted.

Several ways and methods may be used to conduct tertiary recovery. The first step, reservoir analysis determines what kind of process should be attempted. This usually involves using a core barrel to remove a cylindrical tube of rock from the reservoir upon which pressure experiments are conducted using a high-pressure pump and various samples of potential recovery-enhancing fluids or gasses. From these tests, the operator can determine the best methods of development.

Miscible Enhanced Recovery

Miscible enhanced recovery uses carbon dioxide (CO_2), nitrogen (N_2), or even hydrocarbons as miscible solvents to displace oil from a depleted oil reservoir containing low-viscosity light crude oil (typically oil with

---

40. Replacement of extracted oil with water has been attempted in places such as Long Beach, California, in an effort to diminish possible subsidence that may affect the land surface.

gravities greater than 20° API). Commercial deposits of CO_2 occur natural-ly in the earth. Currently, the largest domestic fields where CO_2 is widely used are in western Texas, where the proximity of semi-depleted fields to natural CO_2 deposits in New Mexico and Colorado and the necessary pipeline infrastructure to transport the CO_2 exist. CO_2 is a "greenhouse gas" and one by-product of combustion that can be recovered from power plant stacks or other industrial sources. Research and experiments con-cerning the capture of CO_2 from power and industrial plants for use in enhanced recovery efforts—while also gaining the possible benefit of sequestering this greenhouse gas underground—is underway. In deeper reservoirs where higher pressures are encountered, liquefied nitrogen has been used for miscible recovery. Approximately 78.1% of the earth's atmosphere is nitrogen, allowing for the construction of separation plants that can extract nitrogen for injection.

Miscible enhanced recovery relies on reducing the "interfacial ten-sion" between oil and water (or other injected fluid). "Interfacial tension" describes the molecular mechanics whereby liquids such as oil and water resist mixing. Injected miscible fluids such as CO_2 that encounter remnant light oils will mix such that the interfacial tension between the two materials will essentially disappear, allowing the CO_2 or other agent to dissolve into the oil, reducing its viscosity. Sometimes, CO_2 and water will be injected alternately, providing for better mixing with the remnant oil. Upon being drawn from the recovery well, the oil and carbon dioxide are separated. The oil is transported to a refinery and the CO_2 is recycled. Under the right conditions, CO_2 miscible flooding is popular because of its moderate cost and the fact that miscible displacement of oil by CO_2 or other recovery agents can result in the recovery of almost all of the oil from parts of the reservoir where the injected agents enter. The chief limitations particular to miscible enhanced recovery techniques are the availability and cost of CO_2 or other agents and poor control over the migration direction of injected fluids.

Thermal Enhanced Recovery

Thermal recovery, until recently, was the most widely-used enhanced recovery technique until recently, introduces heat to the reservoir to reduce the viscosity of the oil. Successive applications of steam are applied to the reservoir, heating the oil, lowering its viscosity, and enhancing its ability to flow. First attempted in Venezuela in the 1960s, thermal recovery now accounts for more than 50% of applied tertiary recovery in the United States, particularly in California.

Thermal tertiary recovery techniques are generally applied to relative-ly shallow reservoirs (less than 3,000 feet in depth) containing viscous heavy oils with gravities between 10°and 20°API. Heavy oil typically has such a high viscosity that it will not easily migrate through pore spaces unless diluted with a solvent or heated to raise the temperature of the reservoir oil to around 600 degrees Fahrenheit. As heat is absorbed in the reservoir, the thick, viscous oil in place becomes thinner so that it can move easily through tiny channels in the reservoir rock, and hopefully, towards a recovery well. Steam injection may continue for only a few days or for as long as a month. As temperatures near the well bore declines, and the oil cools and thickens once more, production rates decline. When production rates fall to the prestimulation level, the dilution or heating is repeated.

Thermal recovery can involve using injector wells through which the steam is introduced to the reservoir and recovery wells to produce the oil and cooled water. Alternatively, thermal recovery may use just one well for both roles through cyclic injection/production where the steam is injected and allowed to "soak." Then oil is produced out of the same well.[41] Depending on the topography of the reservoir, two well systems may utilize steam assisted gravity drainage; the steam is injected into one horizontal well and oils produced from a lower producing interval.

Steam Assisted Gravity Drainage ("SAGD") is a form of enhanced oil recovery used to help produce both heavy crude oil and bitumen. "SAGD" requires two parallel horizontal wells to be drilled into the target formation, usually about 15–25 feet apart, one above the other. The upper well continuously injects low pressure steam, possibly mixed with solvents, while the lower one collects the heated crude oil or bitumen drawn down due to lowered viscosity and gravity along with any water from the condensation of injected steam. The oil, bitumen, and water are then pumped out.

Another method of thermal recovery involves using a "flame front" or "fire flooding" in which a fire is started in one or more wells and (hopefully) spreads gradually through the reservoir and is then maintained by continuous injection of air or other gas mixtures with high oxygen contents. As the fire front burns, it moves in a wall toward production wells. The heat, in turn, reduces the viscosity of unburned oil near the recovery wells while also vaporizing reservoir water. The fire also breaks apart some heavier hydrocarbons into smaller molecules while vaporizing some of the lighter molecules to help further displace oil. This steam—which itself helps move nearby oil—and the lowered viscosity oil itself are then produced from the recovery wells.

Chemical Enhanced Recovery

Chemicals can also be introduced to the reservoir as a tertiary recovery method. Three popular chemical processes include polymer flooding, surfactant flooding, and alkaline-surfactant-polymer flooding ("ASP") flooding.

Surfactants are used in tertiary recovery to help mix water added to the reservoir with oil lying in situ (that is, left after primary and secondary recovery efforts) so that both water and oil can be produced. Surfactant, or "surface-active" agent, is a chemical that reduces interfa-

---

41. Such one-well thermal recovery schemes are colloquially known as "huff and puff" operations.

cial tension, such as soap reduces the interfacial tension between water and grease on a mechanic's hands. A surfactant may be mixed with water and injected into a producing formation to allow better mixing. There, the surfactant and water flood form an emulsion with the in situ oil. The emulsion moves through the formation toward a recovery well, sweeping much of the oil along with it. When the oil-water mix reaches a recovery well, it is produced and transported to a refinery. Generally, surfactant flooding is more effective than polymer flooding, and addition of surfactant to a water flood may, under some circumstances, actually reduce the oil-water interfacial tension to zero.

In polymer flooding, polymers are added to the injected water. While water floods are initially effective, injected water is prone to eventually begin "fingering" or "channeling," as the water favors certain paths in the reservoir and avoids other parts, leaving remnant oil behind. One way to prevent channeling is to add a polymer to the water injectant. The polymer thickens the injected water so that it tends to move through the formation as a wave, avoiding leaving pockets of oil behind. Generally, polymer floods are more common because they involve the least expensive chemicals.

ASP is a hybrid flooding process which involves using a low concentration of an alkaline chemical, such as sodium carbonate, which reacts with the oil to lower the interfacial tension between the trapped oil and either the injected fluid or formation water. This interaction makes them more "miscible" with one another—that is, capable of mixing with one another. When the alkaline solution injectant and the oil mix, they create "petroleum soap," a type of reservoir-born surfactant. A synthetic surfactant is injected simultaneously with the alkaline chemical to enhance the process. To increase the viscosity of the mixed injectant, a water-soluble polymer is also injected, both in a mixture with the alkaline chemical and surfactant and as an individual slug following the first mixed injectant. The surfactant mix is then moved through the reservoir by a displacing flood of water.

No single one of these processes within the definition of tertiary recovery works in all types of reservoirs or with all types of oils found therein. From reservoir data, petroleum engineers and geologists determine which method is best.

Secondary and tertiary oil recovery are crucial for domestic energy security. The majority of wells in the United States have, are now or will undergo some kind of secondary recovery process. Furthermore, the Department of Energy ("DOE") has estimated that CO_2 enhanced tertiary recovery in United States could generate an additional 240 billion barrels of recoverable oil resources. By comparison, the total undeveloped American domestic oil resources still in the ground total more than one trillion barrels, most of it remaining unrecoverable.

D. INTRODUCTORY NOTE ON LAND DESCRIPTIONS

References to land description are used throughout this casebook. To fully understand some of the cases, you must understand the land descriptions.

Most lands in the United States are described in accordance with a federal "rectangular" surveying system mandated by Congress in the Land Ordinance Act of 1785. Because the original surveys were performed by private contractors using crude equipment, surveys are not error free. Nevertheless, the rectangular survey system was a great improvement over the traditional "metes and bounds" description that relied upon historic boundaries and natural and artificial landmarks to describe tracts of land in deeds and other instruments. Over time, some landmarks might move (e.g., a stream) or disappear (e.g., a tree or post). Areas not subject to the federal rectangular system and thus still relying largely on metes and bounds descriptions include the original 13 states, Florida, Texas, and some portions of the Southwest settled under Spanish or Mexican rule.

Under the federal rectangular system, surveys were laid out from a principal (or prime) meridian longitudinal line and from a base latitudinal line. Various prime meridian lines and base lines have been established throughout the United States. For example, a major portion of the Louisiana Purchase was surveyed from the 5th Principal Meridian and from the Arkansas Base Line. These lines intersect in Eastern Arkansas. For a given survey area, other north-south lines, called range lines, are drawn at six-mile intervals east and west of the chosen principal meridian, and other east-west lines, called township lines, are drawn at six-mile intervals north and south of the chosen base line.

Range lines are described by counting east or west of the selected principal meridian. For example, Range 3 West would be three range lines west of (18 miles from) the chosen principal meridian. Range 5 East would be five range lines east of (30 miles from) the chosen principal meridian.

Likewise, township lines are described by counting north or south of the chosen base line. For example, Township 6 North would be six township lines north of (36 miles from) the chosen base line, and Township 1 South would be one township line south of (six miles from) the chosen base line.

Intersecting township and range lines create squares that are six miles on each side. These six-mile squares are townships. See Fig. 21. Each township is further subdivided into 36 numbered sections of one square mile each. Section 1 is always located in the northeast corner of a given township and the numbering progresses west in sequence to Section 6, located in the northwest corner of the township. Section 7 is then located immediately below Section 6, and the numbering continues in sequence back to the east to Section 12, which is located immediately below Section 1. This back-and-forth pattern continues until Section 36 is reached in the southeast corner of the township.[42] See Fig. 22. Each of these sections can be readily subdivided into various rectangular and square parcels. See Fig. 23. If you have difficulty visualizing the land descriptions mentioned throughout this book, refer back to Figures 21 through 23 for guidance.

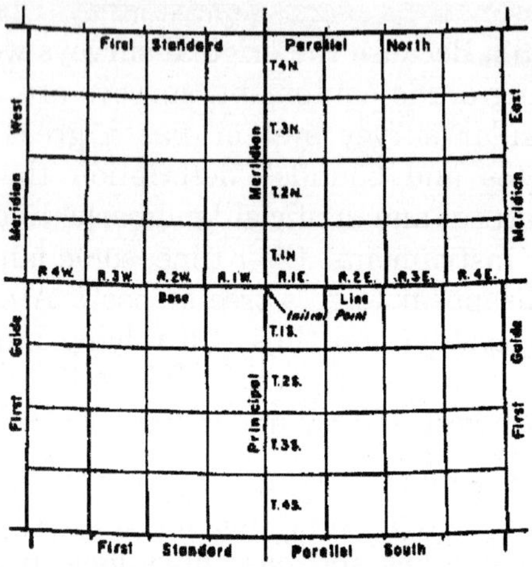

Figure 21.

Figure 23 also illustrates the acreage of various described tracts as well as the units of measurement. A "rod" is 16½ feet long and a "chain" is 66 feet or four rods long. A "standard" section (640 acres) is one mile by one mile. One mile equals 5280 feet, or 80 chains, or 320 rods in length. The units of measurement also described the instruments used to perform early surveys, such as "Gunter's chain." (For more information, see Andro Linklater, *Measuring America*, 16–18 (Walker & Company 2002)).

---

42. In his book, Measuring America, Andro Linklater describes this back-and-forth pattern as follows: "Within the township, the thirty-six sections were numbered in an idiosyncratic fashion established by the 1796 act, beginning with Section 1 in the northeast corner, and continuing first westward and then eastward, back and forth in 'boustrophedonic' fashion, that is, like an ox pulling a plow, until Section 36 was reached in the southeast corner." Andro Linklater, Measuring America 166 (Walker & Company 2002).

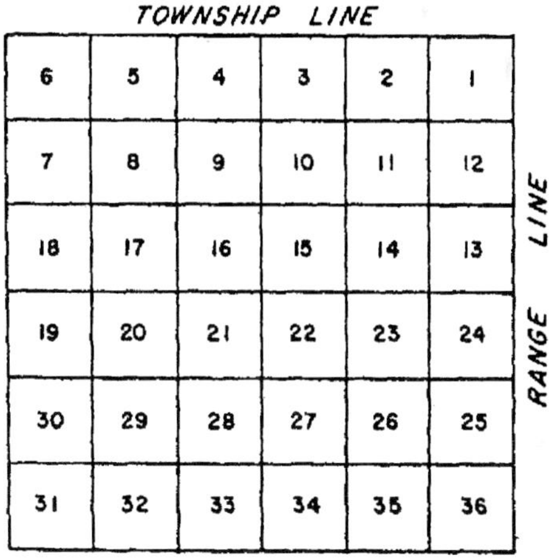

TOWNSHIP LINE

6	5	4	3	2	1
7	8	9	10	11	12
18	17	16	15	14	13
19	20	21	22	23	24
30	29	28	27	26	25
31	32	33	34	35	36

RANGE LINE

Figure 22

Unfortunately, "standard" sections are rarely encountered in the real world. Due to surveying errors and because the survey is corrected to treat all lands as being flat (e.g., a hilly standard 640–acre section of land would really contain more than 640 acres of land area), most sections vary in actual land area from the "standard" size. Moreover, although base lines and township lines are latitudinal and thus parallel, meridian lines converge at the North and South Poles. Thus, a township line intersects a range line at a point that is actually a bit shorter than six miles.

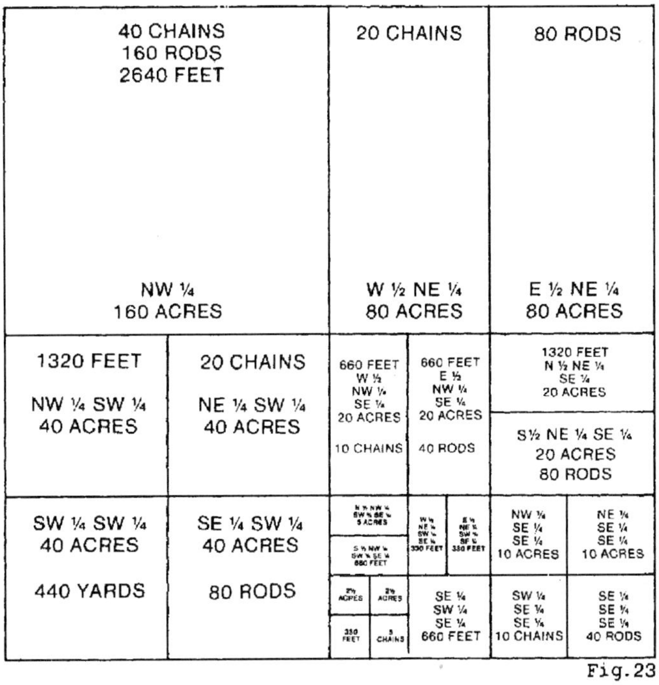

40 CHAINS
160 RODS
2640 FEET

20 CHAINS

80 RODS

NW ¼
160 ACRES

W ½ NE ¼
80 ACRES

E ½ NE ¼
80 ACRES

1320 FEET

NW ¼ SW ¼
40 ACRES

20 CHAINS

NE ¼ SW ¼
40 ACRES

660 FEET
W ½
NW ¼
SE ¼
20 ACRES
10 CHAINS

660 FEET
E ½
NW ¼
SE ¼
20 ACRES
40 RODS

1320 FEET
N ½ NE ¼
SE ¼
20 ACRES

S ½ NE ¼ SE ¼
20 ACRES
80 RODS

SW ¼ SW ¼
40 ACRES

440 YARDS

SE ¼ SW ¼
40 ACRES

80 RODS

N ½ N ½
SW ¼ SE ¼
5 ACRES

S ½ NW ¼
SW ¼ SE ¼
660 FEET

2½ ACRES | 2½ ACRES
330 FEET | CHAINS

NE ¼
SW ¼
SE ¼
330 FEET

E ½
SE ¼
SW ¼
SE ¼
330 FEET

SE ¼
SW ¼
SE ¼
660 FEET

NW ¼
SE ¼
SE ¼
10 ACRES

SW ¼
SE ¼
SE ¼
10 CHAINS

NE ¼
SE ¼
SE ¼
10 ACRES

SE ¼
SE ¼
SE ¼
40 RODS

Fig. 23

To correct for this gradual shortening, for the difficulty of laying squares out on the spherical surface of the earth, and for other surveying errors, periodic adjustments in the course of a survey are made. The main adjustment is that periodic full-width (six-mile) "correction" township lines are plotted at every fourth township line (24–mile intervals). Each correction township line creates a jog at its intersection with the range lines. That is, range lines will abruptly shift east or west every fourth township—something that is readily visible on a survey map covering a large area.

This scheme, as well as surveying errors, cause some sections to vary in acreage—either more or less than the standard 640 acres. For example, a survey plotted west of a prime meridian and north of a baseline will typically plot sections along the west and north lines of the township that contain significant variations in acreage, resulting in "lots" being surveyed within these sections to account for the acreage discrepancies.

Thus, rather than describing the NW¼ of the NW¼ of a particular Section 7 (which would theoretically be 40 acres), the correct description might be Lot 1 of Section 7, which might contain more or less than 40 acres. Immediately below that would be Lot 2 (in place of the SW ¼ of the NW ¼), then Lot 3 (in place of the NW ¼ of the SW ¼), and then Lot 4 (in place of the SW ¼ of the S/W ¼). In Section 6, which also borders a township line, Lot 1 would be in the Northeast corner of the section, Lot 2 would be immediately west of Lot 1, Lot 3 would be immediately west of Lot 2, and Lot 4 would be in the Northwest corner. Lot 5 would be immediately south of Lot 4, Lot 6 would be below Lot 5, and Lot 7 would be below Lot 6 in the southwest corner of Section 6.

To illustrate the above surveying discussion, the boyhood home of one of the co-authors of this casebook is a farm located in North Dakota. The land is located 148 Township lines north of the Arkansas baseline and 59 Range lines west of the 5th Principal Meridian. A portion of this land could be described as the W½ of Section 31, Township 148 North (of the Arkansas Base Line), Range 59 West (of the 5th Principal Meridian), Griggs County, North Dakota. However, because lots are surveyed in the western portion of this section, W½ (not technically the correct description) is actually comprised of 405.10 acres, not the "standard" 320–acre half section.

Further lots might be surveyed along streams and lakes. In theory, the beds of "navigable" waters were not surveyed, as they were reserved in trust for future states, under the Equal Footing Doctrine of the United States Constitution. See further discussion in Chapter 7. However, in theory, "nonnavigable" water bodies were surveyed. In reality, the decision to survey or not survey a water body was in the hands of the surveyor. Thus, whether a particular body of water is "navigable" or "nonnavigable" is not dependent upon whether it was surveyed. Where beds of waters were not surveyed, short, straight survey lines roughly paralleling the water lines were drawn along the bank or shore. These lines are called "meander" lines, and additional lots were surveyed from meander lines as a means of describing particular parcels of riparian or littoral lands.

The acreage variations in sections that result from lots and from survey errors are important to oil and gas title lawyers. As you will learn, lawyers prepare "division-order" title opinions that allocate oil and gas production based in part, upon acreage.

E. OWNERSHIP AND CAPTURE

1. *AD COELUM* DOCTRINE

From heaven to hell

PROBLEM

Assume that Sam discovers a valuable silver-bearing vein on his property, Blackacre. Sam extracts the ore by digging a shaft on Blackacre and mining the vein. Eventually, Sam mines the ore and extends the mine shaft to a point where he actually takes ore from beneath adjacent Whiteacre, a tract owned by Alice. Who is entitled to the ore that Sam extracts from beneath Whiteacre?

Property rights associated with land rely upon surface boundaries to define and identify the rights. Generally the property interests will be defined by a grant or reservation of a stated interest within a tract of land that is described by some form of surface description.

DEL MONTE MINING & MILLING CO. v. LAST CHANCE MINING & MILLING CO.

171 U.S. 55 (1898).

[The ultimate issue before the Court is whether the appellee has the right to follow a vein of silver and lead-bearing ore beyond the western boundary of its mining claim on federal public land and beneath the surface of the appellant's mining claim on federal public land. The Court's extensive discussion of federal statutory mining law has been deleted.]

MR. JUSTICE BREWER * * * delivered the opinion of the court.

* * * The general rule of the common law was that whoever had the fee of the soil owned all below the surface, and this common law is the general law of the states and territories of the United States, and, in the absence of specific statutory provisions or contracts, the simple inquiry as to the extent of mining rights would be, who owns the surface? Unquestionably, at common law the owner of the soil might convey his interest in mineral beneath the surface without relinquishing his title to the surface, but the possible fact of a separation between the ownership of the surface and the ownership of mines beneath that surface, growing out of contract, in no manner abridged the general proposition that the owner of the surface owned all beneath. [I]n certain parts of England and Wales so

called local customs were recognized which modified the general rule of the common law, but the existence of such exceptions founded upon such local customs only accentuates the general rule. The Spanish and Mexican mining law confined the owner of a mine to perpendicular lines on every side. * * * It is enough here to notice the fact that by the Mexican as by the common law the surface rights limited the rights below the surface. * * *

<h3 style="text-align:center">NOTES</h3>

1.   The principle expressed in this old hard rock mining case is based on the common law maxim, *Cujus est solum, ejus est usque ad coelum et ad inferos* (to whomsoever the soil belongs, he owns also to the sky and to the depths). Regarding mining lode claims on the federal public domain, this maxim is modified by the doctrine of extralateral rights. Under this doctrine, the owner of a lode claim may exclusively mine "all veins, lodes and ledges throughout their entire depth, the top or apex of which lies inside * * * [the vertical side-line boundaries of the claim] although such veins, lodes or ledges may so far depart from a perpendicular in their course downward as to extend outside the vertical side lines * * *." General Mining Law of 1872, 30 U.S.C. § 26. This doctrine of extralateral rights serves to extend the mining right beyond the staked boundaries of a lode claim.

2.   Common law governs the ownership of mineral rights in the United States, although Spanish and Mexican civil law has influenced mineral owner-ship rights in Texas, and French civil law has influenced mineral ownership rights in Louisiana.

3.   In most countries, including many common law countries, the govern-ment holds title to all valuable oil, gas, and mineral deposits, including deposits located beneath what may otherwise be privately-owned land. The United States is unique in having extensive private ownership of oil, gas, and other minerals. As will be seen, private ownership patterns tend to complicate mineral development. What reasons support recognizing private ownership of minerals? Public ownership?

Private Ownership

2. PETROLEUM OWNERSHIP THEORIES

As indicated in the prior historical segment at the beginning of this chapter and as is illustrated in the next case, the rule of capture governs entitlement to oil and gas production. A producer is entitled to all of the production from a well or wells drilled within the producer's land even if some of that production is drained from beneath the land of a neighboring landowner. As you might imagine, reconciling traditional concepts of land ownership with the rule of capture is difficult. For example, if, under the *ad coleum* doctrine, the owner of the surface "owns" the oil and gas beneath her land, how do we account for a rule that allows neighbors to acquire title to the oil and gas when it migrates into wells located on their lands?

Courts have responded by following one of two conceptual approaches. One approach addresses ownership and the rule of capture as two separate concepts, recognizing that, under appropriate facts, application of the rule of capture can result in a loss of ownership of oil and gas that migrate to other lands. The second approach combines the two concepts and accounts for the rule of capture as a limitation on the nature of the landowner's "ownership" in the oil and gas before it is produced. In his treatise, Professor Kuntz aptly describes the two approaches.

E. KUNTZ, A TREATISE ON THE LAW OF OIL AND GAS § 2.4 THEORIES OF OWNERSHIP OF OIL AND GAS (1987)

The peculiar characteristics of oil and gas which resulted in adoption of the law of capture also produced difficulties in the adoption of a theory of ownership. Because the rights in oil and gas were subject to being lost by drainage from operations on other land, it was difficult to describe, in conventional property terms, the nature of the rights to the oil and gas before capture. It is in the matter of description that theories differ. While courts and commentators have devoted considerable effort toward defining and justifying the various theories of ownership, the results of cases and the general course of the substantive law of oil and gas have been such that the distinction in theories is largely one of terminology. The acceptance of any one theory may result in subsequent difficulties for a court concerned with maintaining logical consistency; but, for the most part, logical consistency has not been exalted by the courts at the expense of sacrificing reasonable and realistic results. The adoption of a theory of ownership ultimately represents little more than the selection of an acceptable method of describing ownership in the light of the law of capture.

Although there have been various efforts to classify the theories of ownership into the categories of "ownership," "nonownership" and "qualified ownership," the theories may be reduced to two fundamental theories of "ownership in place" and "exclusive right to take." For purposes of convenience, such theories may also be referred to as the "ownership" as distinguished from the "nonownership" theory, although it must not be assumed that "nonownership" means the absence of property rights.

According to the ownership-in-place theory, the landowner owns all substances, including oil and gas, which underlie his land. Such ownership is qualified, however, in the case of oil and gas, by the operation of the law of capture. If the oil and gas depart from beneath the owned land, ownership in such substances is lost.

According to the exclusive-right-to-take theory, the landowner does not own the oil and gas which underlie his land. He merely has the exclusive right to capture such substances by operations on his land. Once reduced to dominion and control, such substances become the object of absolute ownership, but, until capture, the property right is described as an exclusive right to capture.

The difference between such theories is a matter of placing the emphasis in describing the rights of the owner and is about the same as the difference between describing a checkered pattern as consisting of black checks on a white background or as consisting of white checks on a black background. In the instance of the ownership-in-place theory, emphasis is placed upon the right of enjoyment, and the matter of possible drainage is treated as a qualification of ownership. In the instance of the exclusive-right-to-take-theory, emphasis is placed upon the possibility of drainage which is considered to be inconsistent with the concept of ownership, but advantages of ownership are recognized in the exclusiveness of the right to extract the substances by operations on the land.

3. RULE OF CAPTURE AND DOCTRINE OF CORRELATIVE RIGHTS

PROBLEM

Assume two adjoining tracts, Blackacre and Whiteacre, overlie a common reservoir of oil. Sam, the owner of Blackacre, extracts oil by drilling and completing a well within the boundaries of Blackacre; however, some of the extracted oil is drained from beneath Alice's Whiteacre. Who owns the extracted oil? Would your answer be different if gas were involved rather than oil?

KELLY v. OHIO OIL CO.

49 N.E. 399 (Ohio 1897).

Error to Circuit Court, Hancock County

* * * One John F. Hastings, of Findlay, in said county, is owner in fee, seised, and possessed of one hundred and sixty-five acres of valuable mineral oil land, in Findlay, Ohio * * *. [P]laintiff has a contract and agreement with said Hastings whereby plaintiff has the right to operate said lands for oil, and take the oil from said land, yielding to said Hastings a portion or royalty of the oil so produced, the balance to be retained by plaintiff as his own property; and in virtue of said contract plaintiff is now at work on said land, has two wells completed, and a rig up and ready to begin the drilling of a third well thereon. That said Hastings' land is joined on the east and west by lands now in the possession and control for oil purposes of the defendant, on which they now have producing oil wells; and the east eighty acres of said Hastings' farm is joined on the south by mineral oil lands owned in fee by the said defendant, and on which also the defendant has producing oil wells. That underlying the land of said Hastings, and the lands so adjoining the same on the south and west and east, as aforesaid, is a formation of porous sand or Trenton rock, so called, which is permeated with valuable mineral oil. That the nature of said mineral oil deposit is such that when, in the process of operating, an oil well is drilled from the surface down into and through said oil-bearing rock, and the usual pumping appliances attached to and employed on said

well to extract oil therein, the oil will be drawn to said opening from a long distance through said porous rock, and all the oil within a radius of from two hundred to two hundred and fifty feet surrounding such well will be drawn to and extracted by means of such well, so that in order to drain and exhaust all the oil in the land it is only necessary to drill the wells from four to five hundred feet apart. The defendants, well knowing the premises, and designing willfully and unlawfully to extract the mineral oil from, in, and under the said Hastings land, by means of surface operations on the land so owned and controlled by them, in fraud and violation of the plaintiff's right, and from motives of unmixed malice, have located a line of oil wells along the entire east line [and part of the west line] of said farm, and upon and along the said south line of the east eighty acres of said farm, which wells are so located just twenty-five feet from the line of Hastings' land * * *. That the defendants' holdings on the east consist of about one hundred and sixty acres in a body, and on the south a very large tract, to wit, several hundred acres, and there is in the defendants' operating said land for oil no sort of necessity or excuse for the defendants to locate their said wells so unusually near the Hastings line * * *. [T]hat the only motive of the defendant in so locating its said wells was to injure the plaintiff, and to get the oil which would be available to him in his operation of said farm. If the defendants are permitted to extract the plaintiff's oil in the manner as aforesaid, the plaintiff will suffer irreparable injury, and will have no adequate legal remedy, for the reason that it will be impossible to determine the exact proportion of the product belonging to the plaintiff. Wherefore the plaintiff prays that a temporary restraining order issue, enjoining the defendant from drilling and operating any oil well at any point within two hundred feet of the line of said Hastings farm, unless it should become necessary to approach nearer in order to protect the lines, and that on the final hearing that said injunction be made perpetual.

* * * That all of said wells are oil-producing wells of greater or less capacity, and that by means thereof the defendants are daily extracting large and valuable quantities of mineral oil, a large part of which mineral oil is so drawn and extracted from the deposits thereof in the land of said Hastings, and which oil the plaintiff has, by his contract with said Hastings, the right to take and use and enjoy. That said wells draw their supply so indiscriminately from the mines and lands of said Hastings and of the defendant that it is impossible to distinguish that of the defendant from that of the plaintiff, but all of said oil is so being taken by the said defendant and converted to its own use. Wherefore * * * the plaintiff prays [that defendant be enjoined from further operating the wells]; that the defendant be required to account to the plaintiff for the oil so taken; that the amount thereof be ascertained; and that the plaintiff may have a decree and judgment against the defendant therefor, and for all proper relief.

The circuit court was of opinion that the petition and supplemental petition failed to state a cause of action against the oil company, and therefore refused to hear any evidence, and found from the pleadings in favor of the defendant, to which plaintiff excepted.

BURKET, C.J.

* * *

The question is not as to the motive—fraud or malice—which may have induced the oil company to drill the wells sought to be enjoined. The only question of practical importance is, had the oil company the legal right to drill the wells? When a person has the legal right to do a certain act, the motive with which it is done is immaterial. The right to acquire, enjoy, and own property carries with it the right to use it as the owner pleases, so long as such use does not interfere with the legal rights of others. To drill an oil well near the line of one's land cannot interfere with the legal rights of the owner of the adjoining lands, so long as all operations are confined to the lands upon which the well is drilled. Whatever gets into the well belongs to the owner of the well, no matter where it came from. In such cases the well and its contents belong to the owner or lessee of the land, and no one can tell to a certainty from whence the oil, gas, or water which enters the well came, and no legal right as to the same can be established or enforced by an adjoining landowner. The right to drill and produce oil on one's own land is absolute, and cannot be supervised or controlled by a court or an adjoining landowner. So long as the operations are legal, their reasonableness cannot be drawn in question. * * * [I]t is intolerable that the owner of real property, before making improvements on his own lands, should be compelled to submit to what his neighbor or a court of equity might regard as a reasonable use of his property. Petroleum oil is a mineral, and while in the earth it is part of the realty, and, should it move from place to place by percolation or otherwise, it forms part of that tract of land in which it tarries for the time being, and, if it moves to the next adjoining tract, it becomes part and parcel of that tract; and it forms part of some tract until it reaches a well, and is raised to the surface, and then for the first time it becomes the subject of distinct ownership, separate from the realty, and becomes personal property,—the property of the person into whose well it came. And this is so whether the oil moves, percolates, or exists in pools or deposits. In either event, it is the property of, and belongs to, the person who reaches it by means of a well, and severs it from the realty, and converts it into personalty. While it is generally supposed that oil is drained into wells for a distance of several hundred feet, the matter is somewhat uncertain, and no right of sufficient weight can be founded upon such uncertain supposition to overcome the well-known right which every man has to use his property as he pleases, so long as he does not interfere with the legal rights of others. Protection of lines of adjoining lands by the drilling of wells on both sides of such lines affords an ample and sufficient remedy for the supposed grievances complained of in the petition and supplemental petition, without resort to either an injunction or an accounting. The * * * only complaint is that the oil company so used its own premises as to secure and appropriate to its own use that which came into its lands by percolation, or by flowing through unknown natural underground channels. This it had a right to do. While the drilled oil well is artificial, the pores and channels through which the oil reached the bottom of the well are natural. Judgment affirmed.

NOTES

1. Hall v. Reed, 54 Ky. 479 (1854), is thought to be the first case to address ownership of oil upon its capture. Hemingway § 1.3. In *Hall* the plaintiff completed a well on his land, and the defendants trespassed onto the plaintiff's land, operated the well, and removed three barrels of oil. Although defendant conceded that a suit for trespass onto the land would lie, the action in this case was in trover (conversion) to recover the oil, or its value. The facts indicate the value of a standard 42–gallon barrel of oil in 1854 was $52.50. When adjusted for inflation, this same oil would cost over $1250 today. The defendants argued the well tapped into a flowing stream of oil and had the defendant not produced these barrels of oil from the well, it would not have been produced but would have been forever lost as it flowed away from the well. The court rejected this argument, holding that once the oil was drawn out through the well, it became the property of the person who owned the well. Although nowhere does the court use the term "capture," the court did draw an analogy to produced groundwater, which among neighboring landowners was also governed by the law of capture at early common law. See Acton v. Blundell, 152 Eng. Rep. 1223 (1843) and Greenleaf v. Francis, 18 Pick. 117 (Mass. 1836).

For a comprehensive history of the rule of capture as applied to oil and gas, see TERENCE DAINTITH, FINDERS KEEPERS? HOW THE LAW OF CAPTURE SHAPED THE OIL AND GAS INDUSTRY (Earthscan 2010). Professor Daintith observes that capture was the accepted practice of oil drillers long before it became law. Id. 420. He concludes that the rule of capture is the least worst property rule that could have been applied to oil and gas. Id. 424. Professor Pierce is less enthused. He argues that the rule of capture should be replaced by a more modern property analysis. David E. Pierce, *Carol Rose Comes to the Oil Patch: Modern Property Analysis Applied to Modern Reservoir Problems*, 19 PENN. STATE ENVTL. L. REV. 241 (2011).

2. The "rule of capture," also referred to as the "law of capture," modifies the common law stated in *Del Monte* that "whoever had the fee of the soil owned all below the surface and * * * the surface rights limited the rights below the surface." Under the rule of capture, the landowner who extracts oil or gas from beneath his-or-her land acquires ownership of the extracted substances even though evidence discloses that a portion of the produced oil and gas was originally in place beneath the land of another. Edwards v. Lachman, 534 P.2d 670 (Okla.1974). See generally Kuntz §§ 4.1 and 4.2; Hemingway § 1.3; and Summers § 61. What reasons support the rule of capture? See Kuntz § 4.1.

3. As you learned in the introductory materials to this chapter, wells produce because the oil and gas in the reservoir are under tremendous

pressure. When a drill bit penetrates the reservoir, the reservoir pressure pushes the oil and gas toward and into the well bores. Accordingly, the manner in which an individual landowner develops his acreage for oil and gas production can affect reservoir pressure and production from neighboring lands. Yet, the rule of capture allows each owner to act independently to develop the resource and obtain title to oil and gas by capture.

Correlative rights

This right of capture is not unlimited. No individual landowner may negligently or intentionally damage the reservoir so as to impair the ability of other landowners to exercise their capture rights. Each landowner's right of capture is "correlative" with the rights of neighboring landowners whose land overlies a common reservoir. "Correlative rights" imply that every landowner has reciprocal "obligations" to act in a manner that does not unreasonably interfere with the rights of neighboring landowners. These reciprocal rights and duties also protect the public interest in assuring proper exploitation of oil and gas resources. Professor Pierce has conceptualized this relationship as follows:

> Society and the common law have historically placed limits upon a landowner's use of his or her property to prevent injury to neighbors and the general public. The rule of capture encouraged independent action to . . . exploit the oil and gas resource for maximum individual gain without regard for the best interests of the reservoir community. The landowner's rights under the rule of capture have been restrained to protect other proprietors overlying a common reservoir and to secure public interests in the oil and gas resource. Reciprocal rights and duties between landowners overlying a common reservoir are the essence of the correlative rights doctrine.

David E. Pierce, Coordinated Reservoir Development—An Alternative to the Rule of Capture for the Ownership and Development of Oil and Gas, 4 J. of Energy L. & Policy 1, 50 (1983).

In Elliff v. Texon Drilling Co., 210 S.W.2d 558 (Tex.1948), the court found that Texon negligently drilled a well, causing it to blow out, crater, and ignite, and resulting in a large amount of gas and distillate[43] being drained from beneath Elliff's adjacent property. The trial court awarded Elliff damages for the drained gas and distillate. The Civil Court of Appeals reversed, citing the rule of capture. The Texas Supreme Court reversed the Civil Court of Appeals, holding that the rule of capture was limited by the correlative rights doctrine, which protects owners from negligent or wasteful operations that injure or destroy the common source of supply. Because Texon wasted rather than capture and use or market the gas and distillate, the rule of capture did not protect Texon from liability for drainage.

4. The United States Supreme Court proclaimed the correlative rights doctrine in Ohio Oil Co. v. Indiana, 177 U.S. 190 (1900). An Indiana statute prohibited a well operator from allowing oil or gas to escape into the open air. Defendant drilled five producing oil and gas wells into a common reservoir but allowed the gas to escape into the air. Gas from this reservoir was exploited by nearby cities and manufacturing plants for fuel. Maintenance of "back pres-

---

43. The term *distillate* (also called *condensate* or *natural gasoline*) refers to liquid hydrocarbons produced with and recovered from *wet* gas. Oil and Gas Terms.

sure" upon the reservoir was necessary to prevent salt water encroachment, and the continued flow of gas from the defendant's wells greatly reduced this back pressure. Accordingly, the State of Indiana sued to enjoin the defendant from violating the statute. Defendant argued that enforcement of the statute would constitute a taking by depriving defendant of its right to produce oil, which defendant argued had a much greater value than the vented gas. In rejecting defendant's argument, Justice White noted:

> [A]s to gas and oil the surface proprietors within the gas field all have the right to reduce to possession the gas and oil beneath. They could not be absolutely deprived of this right which belongs to them without a taking of private property. But there is a co-equal right in them all to take from a common source of supply the two substances which in the nature of things are united, though separate. It follows from the essence of their right and from the situation of the things as to which it can be exerted, that the use by one of his power to seek to convert a part of the common fund to actual possession may result in an undue proportion being attributed to one of the possessors of the right to the detriment of the others, or by waste by one or more to the annihilation of the rights of the remainder. Hence it is that the legislative power, from the peculiar nature of the right and the objects upon which it is to be exerted, can be manifested for the purpose of protecting all the collective owners, by securing a just distribution, to arise from the enjoyment, by them, of their privilege to reduce to possession, and to reach the like end by preventing waste. * * * Viewed, then, as a statute to protect or to prevent the waste of the common property of the surface owners, the law * * *, in substance, is a statute protecting private property and preventing it from being taken by one of the common owners without regard to the enjoyment of the others.

177 U.S. at 209–210. See also, Manufacturers' Gas & Oil Co. v. Indiana Natural Gas & Oil Co., 57 N.E. 912 (Ind. 1900) (allowing a producer of natural gas to enjoin a production technique used by another producer where that technique injures or destroys the common source of supply).

5. As is apparent from *Kelly*, the rule of capture can lead to the drilling of too many wells. This results in (1) economic waste because more wells are drilled than are necessary for efficient and effective drainage, (2) surface waste due to the proliferation of production pipes, valves, fittings, and tanks that are prone to leakage, and (3) underground waste—leaving recoverable hydrocarbons in the ground—due to the inefficient dissipation of reservoir energy. This has led some courts to reject the rule of capture in circumstances when it might have been useful to resolve a dispute.

In *Borys v. Canadian Pacific Railway*,[44] the Judicial Committee of the Privy Council[45] held that the word "petroleum" under this reservation included liquid, but not gaseous, hydrocarbons in a reservoir, with

---

44. [1953] 2 D.L.R. 65 (P.C.), *aff'g* [1952] 3 D.L.R. 218 (Alta. C.A), *rev'g in part* [1951] 4 D.L.R. 427 (Alta. T.D.).

45. The Judicial Committee of the Privy Council, which sat in London, served as the highest appellate judicial body for cases arising within the British Empire and Commonwealth, including Canada, but outside of the United Kingdom. Today, the highest appellate judicial body for Canada is the Supreme Court of Canada.

ownership governed by the phase of the hydrocarbons in the ground.[46] The Privy Council reasoned that the term petroleum should be determined based upon its vernacular, not scientific,[47] usage at the time of the contract for sale of the land at issue; however, the Privy Council failed to clarify precisely "when" the physical nature of hydrocarbons, as liquid or as gas, was to be determined for the purpose of establishing ownership. This was the issue in *Anderson v. Amoco Canada Oil and Gas*.[48]

This rather narrow issue arises when there has been a "phase severance" such as what was decreed to have occurred with a reservation of "petroleum" in *Borys* and where a reservoir contains both oil and gas. At natural reservoir conditions, prior to human intervention, reservoirs are stable. Any gas in solution[49] with oil is in a liquid phase in the reservoir while any gas in the gas cap is in a gas phase. However, as a combined oil and gas reservoir is produced, reservoir pressures usually decrease, causing some of the gas that was originally in a liquid phase to come out of solution with the oil and to migrate as gas into the gas cap.[50] Thus, the volume of gas in the gas cap may increase as a reservoir is produced. Nevertheless, some of the gas in solution with oil is produced along with oil. Gas produced along with oil from an oil well and which may come out of solution at the wellhead is called "casinghead gas." Under *Borys*, because casinghead gas is in solution in the reservoir, it belongs to the petroleum owner.

At issue in *Anderson* is gas that comes out of solution and migrates into the gas cap. The *Anderson* courts called this gas "evolved gas."[51] The petroleum owners claimed ownership of this evolved gas on the ground that it was gas under original reservoir conditions prior to human intervention (i.e., gas in solution).[52] The gas owners claimed ownership of this evolved gas because, once it comes out of solution and migrates into the gas cap, it is indistinguishable from original gas-cap gas and because

---

46. 2 D.L.R. at 78. The Privy Council also ruled that the petroleum reservation included the implied right to use the surface to explore for and to produce petroleum. *Id.* at 74.

47. *Id.* at 70. Science regards oil and gas as similar hydrocarbons that exist in liquid or gaseous phase depending upon temperature and pressure. The liquid or gaseous phase of these hydrocarbons is measured from "Standard Temperature and Pressure" (STP) (15° Centegrade and 101.325 kPa, respectively). At higher pressure reservoir conditions, some hydrocarbons that would be gaseous at STP would be in liquid form or in solution.

48. [2004] 3 S.C.R. 3 (Can.), *aff'g* Anderson v. Amoco Canada Oil and Gas, [2002] 214 D.L.R. 272, *aff'g in part* Anderson v. Amoco Canada Oil and Gas, [1998] Alta. L.R. 669.

49. As explained [in a prior footnote not included in this excerpt], this gas refers to hydrocarbons that would become gaseous at lower temperature and pressure.

50. Gas may also be in solution with connate water. The Alberta Court of Appeal held that the petroleum owner did not own gas in solution with connate water. *Anderson*, [2002] D.L.R. ¶ 53. This issue was not appealed; however, the Supreme Court of Canada commented that it did not regard the court of appeal as having held that the gas owner owned this gas because, under Alberta law, the province of Alberta would own the ground water. Thus, ownership of gas in connate water was not finally determined. *Anderson*, [2004] S.C.R. ¶ 13.

51. *Anderson*, [2004] S.C.R. ¶ 9.

52. *Id.* ¶ 28.

it will be thereafter captured in the well bore as gas and not as gas in for the solution with oil.[53] The *Anderson* courts agreed with and held petroleum owners.[54]

* * * In essence, the Supreme Court of Canada held that *Borys* held that ownership of evolved gas was to be determined at natural reservoir conditions, prior to human intervention.[55] In other words, gas in solution at natural reservoir conditions belongs to the oil owner, including any gas that thereafter may come out of solution (*i.e.,* "evolved gas") and migrate into the gas cap.

The end result is that the ownership of liquid and gaseous hydrocarbons must be determined based upon estimates of the volumes of each phase in a reservoir prior to human intervention. Necessarily, these estimates must be based upon information gathered at and during the course of recovery and must be based upon expert determinations. The Court offers no specific guidance as to how these estimates are to be made, but does express confidence in the ability of experts to make this determination.[56]

* * *

The gas owners [unsuccessfully] attacked this reasoning by arguing that Canada did not adhere to the ownership-in-place (*in situ*) theory of ownership, but rather followed the non-ownership theory.[57] In other words, in Canada, an oil and gas owner does not own the oil and gas in place in a reservoir, but rather owns the right to explore for, produce, and reduce oil and gas to actual possession. In addition, the gas owners argued that Canada adhered to the rule of capture. Thus, the gas owners argued that ownership of hydrocarbons should be determined by their phase, whether liquid or gas, at the time of their capture in the well bore. Under this approach, the gas owners would be entitled to the evolved gas because it would be captured in the well bore as gas.

* * *

* * * The Court acknowledged that these [expert] estimates will "for the foreseeable future ... lack perfection"[58] and "will no doubt be the subject of some debate, [but] no system is flawless and a determination made at the time of recovery could be subject to manipulation by a dishonest producer."[59]

Regarding this last concern, although not cited in the opinion, the Court may have had in mind the infamous "white oil" debacle in the Texas Panhandle. Texas oil owners in a phase severance situation used wellhead refrigeration units so that gas in the reservoir was produced as a liquid at the wellhead, which they called "white oil."[60] [Although not

---

53. *Id.* ¶ 27.

54. *Id.* ¶ 44. In the interest of candor, Professor Anderson testified at trial at the request of the gas owners on phase severance case law in the United States.

55. *Id.* ¶ 34.

56. *Id.* ¶¶ 40–41.

57. *Id.* ¶¶ 35–39.

58. *Id.* ¶ 40.

59. *Id.* ¶ 40.

60. *See, e.g.,* Colo. Interstate Gas Co. v. HUFO Oils, 802 F.2d 133, 141 (Tex. 1986) (holding that "white oil" produced in gas well was "natural gas" rather than "crude petroleum oil" for

citing the rule of capture, the Texas Supreme Court held that since white oil was captured as gas in the wellbore, it must be regarded as gas for purposes of phase ownership. Amarillo Oil Co. v. Energy–Agri Prods., Inc., 794 S.W.2d 20, 27 (Tex. 1990). This was so even though the reservoir at issue was, like the one in *Anderson*, contained both gas in solution and a gas cap. Thus, the Texas court's decision was consistent with a rule-of-capture rationale.] * * *

* * *

Vernacularly speaking, which is how the Court construed the reservation of petroleum in *Borys*, the parties most probably would not have understood that the phase of hydrocarbons in a reservoir depended upon reservoir temperature and pressure. While they *might* have regarded "petroleum" as liquid oil, they may not have considered gas at all since gas had little value at that time without a nearby use or market,[61] and it was otherwise generally considered a nuisance by-product of oil production. Thus, our criticism of *Anderson* could have been answered by a holding in *Borys* that would have determined that the parties intended "petroleum" to be both oil and gas.[62]

There is also nothing certain about the Court's decision in *Anderson*. Indeed, although the issue was *when* the evolved gas entitlement is to be determined, the Court does not expressly state *when* the oil and gas reserve estimates are to be made. Implicitly, the Court's quote from the trial court mentions "modern estimation techniques."[63] This implies that estimates of the state of a reservoir prior to human intervention should not only be based on modern techniques but may therefore be revised from time to time as modern estimation techniques evolve. * * *

* * *

The court in *Anderson* accepted this scientific approach without seeming to realize the folly of estimating gas cap gas for every affected title for every reservoir, whether previously or hereafter discovered regarding all strata beneath each railroad tract subject to this type of phase severance. The intimation is that this issue can be revisited from time to time to more accurately determine ownership rights. This seem-

---

well classification purposes); Amarillo Oil Co. v. Energy–Agri Prods., Inc., 794 S.W.2d 20, 27 (Tex. 1990) (referring to precedential determinations that "white oil" does not count as oil for well classification purposes and citing *HUFO Oils v. R. R. Comm'n of Tex.*, 717 S.W.2d 405 (Tex. App. 1986)).

61. Regional and national markets for gas first developed in the late 1920s, following development of seamless pipe, which allowed gas to be transported long distances under high pressure. INSTITUTE OF GAS TECHNOLOGY, NATURAL GAS IN NONTECHNICAL LANGUAGE 11 (Rebecca L. Busby ed., 1999).

62. *See, e.g.*, Natural Gas and Oil Corp. v. Hamby, No. CA 80–27, 1981 WL 6185, at *4 (Ohio Ct. App. Mar. 20, 1981) (construing the term "petroleum" in a 1919 right-of-way instrument and concluding "[t]he term 'petroleum' shall be given a reasonable, nonrestrictive interpretation.... We conclude as a matter of law that natural gas is a natural derivative of petroleum and is included within the reasonable expectations of the parties to the 1919 right-of-way").

Apparently the parties to this 1919 Ohio right-of-way instrument had a significantly different vernacular intent than the parties had regarding the 1904–07 Alberta deeds!

63. *Anderson*, [2004] S.C.R. ¶ 40.

ing uncertainty is implicitly justified on the ground that determining ownership by application of the rule of capture would be unworkable and subject to manipulation. How so? Determining entitlements at the time of capture seems more workable and less subject to undiscoverable manipulation than do expert estimates of the state and volume of hydrocarbons in the ground prior to human intervention. Moreover, property law often determines ownership based upon events other than purely voluntary transfers. Consider the law of fixtures, commingling, accessions, abandonment, adverse possession, accretion, erosion, reliction, and increase. Also, consider avulsion under civil law. Using the law of capture to determine ownership in *Anderson* would be no less certain and no less unfair than these other property law doctrines—especially if that was what the parties, dealing in the vernacular, would likely have intended.

A case that is analogous to and yet stands in stark contrast with *Anderson* is *NCNB Texas National Bank v. West (NCNB)*[64]—a case not cited by the *Anderson* court. In this case, the Alabama Supreme Court held that ownership of coalbed methane gas was to be determined by the rule of capture. Cases dealing with the ownership of coalbed methane have most commonly arisen where coal has been severed from the surface and from the rest of the mineral interest by reservation or conveyance.[65] Although coal often contains methane reserves, this methane was historically regarded as a nuisance and safety hazard. Prior to actual coal mining, the methane embedded in the coal was often vented so that coal mining could safely proceed. Gradually, however, coalbed methane came to be considered a valuable by-product of coal mining and today is often the principle objective. Thus, since the 1970s, several courts have had to determine the ownership of coalbed methane gas. [See Chapter 3, Section E.]

* * *

The trial court in *NCNB* construed conveyances of "all coal and mining rights" that expressly reserved "all of the oil, gas, petroleum, and sulphur."[66] In ruling for the coal owners, the trial court held that the reservation of all gas did not include coalbed methane gas. In reversing, the Supreme Court of Alabama found, based upon the "plain language of the deed,"[67] that coalbed methane gas was included in the express reservation of "all" gas.[68] Nevertheless, the court determined that the

---

64. 631 So.2d 212 (Ala. 1993).

65. For other cases dealing with the issue of who owns the coalbed methane based on deeds that do not specifically mention that term, see *Amoco Production Co. v. Southern Ute Indian Tribe*, 526 U.S. 865 (1999); *United States Steel Corp. v. Hoge*, 468 A.2d 1380 (Pa. 1983); *Vines v. McKenzie Methane Corp.*, 619 So.2d 1305 (Ala. 1993); *Caballo Coal Co. v. Fidelity Exploration & Production Co.*, 84 P.3d 311 (Wyo. 2004); *Hickman v. Groves*, 71 P.3d 256 (Wyo. 2003); *McGee v. Caballo Coal Co.*, 69 P.3d 908 (Wyo. 2003); *Newman v. RAG Wyoming Land Co.*, 53 P.3d 540 (Wyo. 2002); *Rayburn v. USX Corp.*, No. 85–G–2261–W, 1987 U.S. Dist. LEXIS (N.D. Ala. July 28, 1987), *aff'd* 844 F.2d 796 (11th Cir. 1988); *Carbon County v. Union Reserve Coal Co.*, 898 P.2d 680 (Mont. 1995); *Harrison–Wyatt, LLC v. Ratliff*, 593 S.E.2d 234 (Va. 2004); and *Energy Development Corp. v. Moss*, 591 S.E.2d 135 (W. Va. 2003).

66. *NCNB*, 631 So.2d at 216.

67. *Id.* at 222.

68. *Id.* at 222–23.

ultimate ownership of coalbed methane gas should be determined on the basis of its location at the time of capture.[69] The court held that if coalbed methane gas is captured directly from the coal seam itself, the coal owner is entitled to the gas; however, if the coalbed methane gas migrates out of the coal and into the gob of a coal mine[70] or into non-coal strata, the gas owner is entitled to the gas.[71] In coalbed methane operations, methane may be captured directly from the coal seam by completing wells, including horizontal wells, into the coal seam, by wells drilled into the gob of a mine, and by wells drilled into strata overlying the coal seam or gob.[72] Out of concern that coalbed methane gas and natural gas may become commingled, gas entitlements under the court's decision depend upon the location from which gas is captured.

Although the court does not draw this analogy, the decision seems analogous to the following: *O*, the fee simple owner of Blackacre, conveys the west half to *X* in fee simple. *X* then drills a well on the west half, which produces oil and gas, some of which is drained from beneath the east half. Due to this vertical division of Blackacre into halves, the oil and gas produced from *X*'s west half is solely *X*'s personal property under the rule of capture. Based upon the court's decision in *NCNB*, the parties essentially horizontally divided Blackacre into coal strata and non-coal strata.

Recognizing the practical necessity of coal owners to be able to produce gas from their coal seams, the gas produced and captured directly from the coal seam could be claimed by the coal owner, just as casinghead gas could be claimed by the oil owners under *Borys*. However, once the coal strata disappeared through mining, no gas could be produced directly from the coal, and any gas that migrated out of the coal into other strata or into the gob could also no longer be produced and captured from the coal strata. Under *NCNB*, the gas owner would have the exclusive right to capture migrated gas, which may, in some cases, commingle with and become indistinguishable from natural gas. Thus, the rule of capture operates in the case of a horizontal division in much the same way as it operates in a vertical division. A similar decision could have been reached in *Anderson*, in which case any gas captured with the production of oil (i.e., casinghead gas) could be claimed by the oil owner; however, once the gas has migrated out of the oil into the gas cap (akin to the gob and overlying strata), the gas owners could claim that gas. In other words, entitlements to evolved gas would be determined at both the time and place of capture.

---

69. *Id.*

70. The gob of a coal mine is what is left of what was once a seam of coal after the coal has been extracted by a longwall mining process. A longwall mining process leaves no vacant "rooms" or "pillars" after mining. Rather the overlying strata is allowed to collapse into the void left by mining the coal. Gas not directly captured from the coal seam often migrates into the gob and into the overlying strata and into fractures created when the overlying strata collapses into the gob. *Id.* at 215.

71. *Id.* at 229.

72. *Id.* at 215–16.

● * * *

The trial court reduced the damages ... for drainage from $1 million to $543,776, in each instance the maximum amount supported by Salinas's evidence, and otherwise rendered judgment on the verdict.

The Court of Appeals * * * affirmed.

II

We begin with Salinas's contention that the incursion of hydraulic fracturing fluid and proppants into another's land two miles below the surface constitutes a trespass for which the minerals owner can recover damages equal to the value of the royalty on the gas thereby drained from the land. Coastal argues that Salinas has no standing to assert an action for trespass, and even if he did, hydraulic fracturing is not an actionable trespass. Because standing may be jurisdictional, we address it first.

A

As a mineral lessor, Salinas has only "a royalty interest and the possibility of reverter" should the leases terminate, but "no right to possess, explore for, or produce the minerals."[3] ... Since Salinas has no possessory right to the minerals in Share 13, Coastal argues he has no standing to sue for trespass.

* * * At common law, trespass included several actions directed to different kinds of wrongs.[4] Trespass *quare clausum fregit* was limited to physical invasions of plaintiff's possessory interest in land;[5] trespass on the case was not[6] and provided an action for injury to a non-possessory interest, such as reversion. Professors Prosser and Keeton explain:

> Thus a landlord cannot sue for a mere trespass to land in the occupation of his tenant. He is not without legal remedy, in the form of an action on the case for the injury to the reversion; but in order to maintain it, he must show more than the trespass— namely, actual permanent harm to the property of such sort as to affect the value of his interest.[7]

---

3. *Natural Gas Pipeline Co. of Am. v. Pool,* 124 S.W.3d 188, 194 (Tex.2003).

4. 1 Fowler V. Harper, Fleming James, Jr., & Oscar S. Gray, Harper, James and Gray on Torts § 1.3, at 7 (3d ed. 2006) (" 'Trespass' was really a 'family of writs' that summoned the defendant to show why ('ostensurus quare') he had done certain wrongs.").

5. *Id.* § 1.3, at 8; *Slye v. Guerdrum,* 29 App. D.C. 550 (1907) ("It is, of course, axiomatic that at common law the gist of the action of trespass *quare clausum fregit* is injury to the possession, and that, generally speaking, the plaintiff must show actual or constructive possession at the time of the trespass.").

6. Harper, *supra* note 4, § 1.3, at 9–10.

7. W. Page Keeton, Dan B. Dobbs, Robert E. Keeton & David G. Owen, Prosser and Keeton on the Law of Torts § 13, at 78 (5th ed.1984) (footnotes omitted); *see* Harper, *supra* note 4, § 1.2, at 5; *see also Gulf, Colo. & Santa Fe Ry. v. Settegast,* 79 Tex. 256, 15 S.W. 228, 230 (1891) ("The rule is well settled that the landlord may sue for and recover for damages to his reversionary interest; that is, he may bring an action for any permanent injury to the property."); *see generally* Restatement (First) of Property Y § 211 ("The owner of a future interest, in order to obtain any relief as against an act or omission to act of a third person, must establish that the conduct of such third person (a) is such conduct as would have been sufficient to entitle the owner of

Salinas's reversion interest in the minerals leased to Coastal is similar to a landlord's reversion interest in the surface estate. By his claim of trespass, Salinas seeks redress for a permanent injury to that interest—a loss of value because of wrongful drainage. His claim is not speculative; he has alleged actual, concrete harm whether his leases continue or not, either in reduced royalty revenues or in loss of value to the reversion. This gives him standing to sue for a form of trespass * * * Salinas's claim of trespass does not entitle him to nominal damages (which he has not sought). He must prove actual injury.

B

Had Coastal caused something like proppants to be deposited on the surface of Share 13, it would be liable for trespass,[8] and from the ancient common law maxim that land ownership extends to the sky above and the earth's center below, one might extrapolate that the same rule should apply two miles below the surface. But that maxim—*cujus est solum ejus est usque ad coelum et ad inferos*—"has no place in the modern world."[9] Wheeling an airplane across the surface of one's property without permission is a trespass; flying the plane through the airspace two miles above the property is not. Lord Coke, who pronounced the maxim, did not consider the possibility of airplanes.[10] But neither did he imagine oil wells. The law of trespass need no more be the same two miles below the surface than two miles above.

We have not previously decided whether subsurface fracing can give rise to an action for trespass. That issue, we held in *Gregg v. Delhi–Taylor Oil Corp.,* is one for the courts to decide, not the Railroad Commission [, the agency that regulates oil and gas operations].[11] In 1961, when we

complete property in the affected thing, to some relief; and (b) causes either harm or reasonable apprehension of harm to such owner of a future interest in view of the character of the act or omission to act and of the substantiality of his future interest."), and § 214 ("When conduct of a third person satisfies the requirements stated in § 211 and consists of acts or omissions to act affecting land, then (a) the owner of a future interest which consists of complete property in such land except for one or more prior estates for life is entitled to recover a judgment against the third person for the damages caused to the owner of the future interest by the conduct of such third person; and is entitled to the proceeds of such judgment * * *.").

8. *Glade v. Dietert,* 156 Tex. 382, 295 S.W.2d 642, 645 (1956) ("To constitute a trespass entry upon another's land need not be in person, but may be made by causing or permitting a thing to cross the boundary of the premises.") (internal quotes omitted).

9. *United States v. Causby,* 328 U.S. 256, 260–261 & n. 5, 66 S.Ct. 1062, 90 L.Ed. 1206 (1946) ("It is ancient doctrine that at common law ownership of the land extended to the periphery of the universe—*Cujus est solum ejus est usque ad coelum.*" (citing 1 Coke, Institutes (19th ed. 1832) ch. 1, § 1(4a); 2 Blackstone, Commentaries (Lewis ed.1902) p. 18; 3 Kent, Commentaries (Gould ed. 1896) p. 621)). The maxim continued *"et ad inferos"*—to the depths.

10. *See also* Harper, *supra* note 4, § 1.5, at 20 ("The maxim must be taken in the light of the actual decisions in which it found expression, and these all dealt with invasions of the airspace, close to the ground, that interfered with actual or potential use and occupation of the land (as by structures, trees, etc.).").

11. 162 Tex. 26, 344 S.W.2d 411, 415 (1961). Salinas points to language in our opinion that could be read to suggest that hydraulic fracturing below another's property constitutes an actionable trespass. For example, we offered that the allegations in that case were "sufficient to raise an issue" whether there was a trespass. *Id.* at 416. But we were not required to reach the issue.

decided _Gregg,_ the Commission had never addressed the subject, and we specifically indicated no view on whether Commission rules could authorize secondary recovery operations that crossed property lines. The next Term, in _Railroad Commission of Texas v. Manziel,_ we held that a salt water injection secondary recovery operation did not cause a trespass when the water migrated across property lines, but we relied heavily on the fact that the Commission had approved the operation.[12] Thirty years later, in _Geo Viking, Inc. v. Tex–Lee Operating Company_, we issued a per curiam opinion holding that fracing beneath another's land was a trespass,[13] but on rehearing we withdrew the opinion and expressly did not decide the issue.[14]

We need not decide the broader issue here. In this case, actionable trespass requires injury,[15] and Salinas's only claim of injury—that Coastal's fracing operation made it possible for gas to flow from beneath Share 13 to the Share 12 wells—is precluded by the rule of capture. That rule gives a mineral rights owner title to the oil and gas produced from a lawful well bottomed on the property, even if the oil and gas flowed to the well from beneath another owner's tract. The rule of capture is a cornerstone of the oil and gas industry and is fundamental both to property rights and to state regulation.[16] Salinas does not claim that the Coastal Fee No. 1 violates any statute or regulation. Thus, the gas he claims to

---

12. 361 S.W.2d 560, 568–569 (Tex.1962). We stated:

We conclude that if, in the valid exercise of its authority to prevent waste, protect correlative rights, or in the exercise of other powers within its jurisdiction, the Commission authorizes secondary recovery projects, a trespass does not occur when the injected, secondary recovery forces move across lease lines, and the operations are not subject to an injunction on that basis. The technical rules of trespass have no place in the consideration of the validity of the orders of the Commission. _Id._ We acknowledge that our opinions in _Gregg_ and _Manziel_ are in some tension and did not perfectly delineate the Commission's authority to regulate secondary recovery operations.

13. 839 S.W.2d 797 (Tex.1992) (No. D–1678) (per curiam op. withdrawn on reh'g) ("Although oil and gas are subject to legitimate drainage under the law of capture, the owner 'is accorded the usual remedies against trespassers who appropriate the minerals or destroy their market value.' _Elliff v. Texon Drilling Co.,_ 146 Tex. 575, 210 S.W.2d 558, 561 (1948). Fracing under the surface of another's land constitutes a subsurface trespass. _Gregg v. Delhi–Taylor Oil Corp.,_ 162 Tex. 26, 344 S.W.2d 411, 416 (1961); _Amarillo Oil v. Energy–Agri Products,_ 794 S.W.2d 20, 27 (Tex.1990). Therefore, the rule of capture would not permit [an operator] to recover for a loss of oil and gas that might have been produced as the result of fracing beyond the boundaries of its tract.").

14. 839 S.W.2d 797, 798 (Tex.1992) (per curiam) ("The per curiam opinion and judgment of this court issued April 22, 1992 are withdrawn. Further, the order of this court of April 22, 1992, granting the application for writ of error is withdrawn, as the application was improvidently granted. In denying petitioner's application for writ of error, we should not be understood as approving or disapproving the opinions of the court of appeals analyzing the rule of capture or trespass as they apply to hydraulic fracturing.").

15. _See Lyle v. Waddle,_ 144 Tex. 90, 188 S.W.2d 770, 773 (1945). As already noted, this case does not involve a trespass against a possessory interest, which does not require actual injury to be actionable and may result in an award of nominal damages. _See McDaniel Bros. v. Wilson,_ 70 S.W.2d 618, 621 (Tex.Civ.App.–Beaumont 1934, writ ref'd) ("[E]very unauthorized entry upon land of another is a trespass even if no damage is done or injury is slight, and gives a cause of action to the injured party."); _see also_ Restatement (Second) of Torts § 163 (1965) ("One who intentionally enters land in the possession of another is subject to liability to the possessor for a trespass, although his presence on the land causes no harm to the land [or] its possessor * * *.").

16. _See also_ 1 Ernest E. Smith & Jacqueline Lang Weaver, Texas Law of Oil and Gas § 1.1(A) (2d ed. 1998) ("The rule of capture may be the most important single doctrine of oil and gas law.").

have lost simply does not belong to him. He does not claim that the hydraulic fracturing operation damaged his wells or the Vicksburg T formation beneath his property. In sum, Salinas does not claim damages that are recoverable.

Salinas argues that the rule of capture does not apply because hydraulic fracturing is unnatural. The point of this argument is not clear. If by "unnatural" Salinas means due to human intervention, the simple answer is that such activity is the very basis for the rule, not a reason to suspend its application. Nothing is more unnatural in that sense than the drilling of wells, without which there would be no need for the rule at all. If by "unnatural" Salinas means unusual, the facts are that hydraulic fracturing has long been commonplace throughout the industry and is necessary for commercial production in the Vicksburg T and many other formations. And if by "unnatural" Salinas means unfair, the law affords him ample relief. He may use hydraulic fracturing to stimulate production from his own wells and drain the gas to his own property—which his operator, Coastal, has successfully done already. . . .[17]

Salinas argues that stimulating production through hydraulic fracturing that extends beyond one's property is no different from drilling a deviated or slant well—a well that departs from the vertical significantly—bottomed on another's property, which is unlawful. Both produce oil and gas situated beneath another's property. But the rule of capture determines title to gas that drains from property owned by one person onto property owned by another. It says nothing about the ownership of gas that has remained in place. The gas produced through a deviated well does not migrate to the wellbore from another's property; it is already on another's property. The rule of capture is justified because a landowner can protect himself from drainage by drilling his own well, thereby avoiding the uncertainties of determining how gas is migrating through a reservoir. It is a rule of expedience. One cannot protect against drainage from a deviated well by drilling his own well; the deviated well will continue to produce his gas. Nor is there any uncertainty that a deviated well is producing another owner's gas. The justifications for the rule of capture do not support applying the rule to a deviated well.

We are not persuaded by Salinas's arguments. Rather, we find four reasons not to change the rule of capture to allow one property owner to sue another for oil and gas drained by hydraulic fracturing that extends beyond lease lines.

---

17. In applying the rule of capture, the court of appeals drew a natural/unnatural distinction in *Peterson v. Grayce Oil Co.*, 37 S.W.2d 367, 370–374 (Tex.Civ.App.–Fort Worth 1931), *aff'd*, 128 Tex. 550, 98 S.W.2d 781 (1936), holding that drainage resulting from the use of vacuum pumps did not fall within the rule of capture because it did not "occur [ ] solely through the operation of natural agencies in a normal manner, as distinguished from artificial means applied to stimulate such a flow." But the distinction is either meaningless or circular because all extraction of oil and gas is by artificial means. In *Railroad Commission v. Manziel*, 361 S.W.2d 560, 568–569 (Tex.1962), we held that injecting water into a reservoir in a secondary recovery operation to increase production was not a trespass. The outcomes of these cases were different, not because water injection is less artificial than vacuum pumps, but because Railroad Commission rules allowed water injection and forbade vacuum pumps.

First, the law already affords the owner who claims drainage full recourse. This is the justification for the rule of capture, and it applies regardless of whether the drainage is due to fracing. If the drained owner has no well, he can drill one to offset drainage from his property. If the minerals are leased and the lessee has not drilled a well, the owner can sue the lessee for violation of the implied covenant in the lease to protect against drainage.... The Commission may also regulate production to prevent drainage. No one suggests that these various remedies provide inadequate protection against drainage.

Second, allowing recovery for the value of gas drained by hydraulic fracturing usurps to courts and juries the lawful and preferable authority of the Railroad Commission to regulate oil and gas production. Such recovery assumes that the gas belongs to the owner of the minerals in the drained property, contrary to the rule of capture. While a mineral rights owner has a real interest in oil and gas in place,[18] "this right does not extend to *specific* oil and gas beneath the property";[19] ownership must be "considered in connection with the law of capture, which is recognized as a property right"[20] as well. The minerals owner is entitled, not to the molecules actually residing below the surface, but to "a fair chance to recover the oil and gas in or under his land, *or* their equivalents in kind."[21] The rule of capture makes it possible for the Commission, through rules governing the spacing, density, and allowables of wells, to protect correlative rights of owners with interests in the same mineral deposits while securing "the state's goals of preventing waste and conserving natural resources".[22] But such rules do not allow confiscation; on the contrary, they operate to prevent confiscation.[23] Without the rule of capture, drainage would amount to a taking of a mineral owner's property—*the* oil and gas below the surface of the property—thereby limiting the Commission's power to regulate production to assure a fair recovery by each owner. * * *

Third, determining the value of oil and gas drained by hydraulic fracturing is the kind of issue the litigation process is least equipped to handle. One difficulty is that the material facts are hidden below miles of rock, making it difficult to ascertain what might have happened. Such difficulty in proof is one of the justifications for the rule of capture. But there is an even greater difficulty with litigating recovery for drainage resulting from fracing, and it is that trial judges and juries cannot take into account social policies, industry operations, and the greater good which are all tremendously important in deciding whether fracing should

---

18. *Brown v. Humble Oil & Ref. Co.,* 126 Tex. 296, 83 S.W.2d 935, 940 (1935).

19. *Seagull Energy E & P, Inc. v. R.R. Comm'n.,* 226 S.W.3d 383, 388–389 (Tex.2007) (emphasis added).

20. *Texaco, Inc. v. R.R. Comm'n,* 583 S.W.2d 307, 310 (Tex.1979); *see also Brown,* 83 S.W.2d at 940.

21. *Gulf Land Co. v. Atl. Ref. Co.,* 134 Tex. 59, 131 S.W.2d 73, 80 (1939) (emphasis added).

22. *Seagull Energy,* 226 S.W.3d at 389.

23. *Gulf Land,* 131 S.W.2d at 80.

or should not be against the law. While this Court may consider such matters in fashioning the common law, we should not alter the rule of capture on which an industry and its regulation have relied for decades to create new and uncertain possibilities for liability with no more evidence of necessity and appropriateness than this case presents. Indeed, the evidence in this case counsels strongly against such a course. The experts in this case agree on two important things. One is that hydraulic fracturing is not optional; it is essential to the recovery of oil and gas in many areas, including the Vicksburg T formation in this case. . . . The other is that hydraulic fracturing cannot be performed both to maximize reasonable commercial effectiveness and to avoid all drainage. Some drainage is virtually unavoidable. In this context, common law liability for a long-used practice essential to an industry is ill-advised and should not be extended absent a compelling need that the Legislature and Commission have ignored. No such need exists.

Fourth, the law of capture should not be changed to apply differently to hydraulic fracturing because no one in the industry appears to want or need the change. The Court has received amicus curiae briefs in this case from the Railroad Commission, the General Land Office, the American Royalty Council, the Texas Oil & Gas Association, the Texas Independent Producers & Royalty Owners Association, the Texas Alliance of Energy Producers, Harding Co., BJ Services Co., Halliburton Energy Services, Inc., Schlumberger Technology Corp., Chesapeake Energy Corp., Devon Energy Corp., Dominion Exploration & Production, Inc., EOG Resources, Inc., Oxy USA Inc., Questar Exploration and Production Co., XTO Energy, Inc., and Chief Oil & Gas LLC. These briefs from every corner of the industry—regulators, landowners, royalty owners, operators, and hydraulic fracturing service providers—all oppose liability for hydraulic fracturing, almost always warning of adverse consequences in the direst language.[24] Though hydraulic fracturing has been commonplace in the oil and gas industry for over sixty years, neither the Legislature nor the Commission has ever seen fit to regulate it, though every other aspect of production has been thoroughly regulated. Into so settled a regime the common law need not thrust itself.

Accordingly, we hold that damages for drainage by hydraulic fracturing are precluded by the rule of capture. It should go without saying that the rule of capture cannot be used to shield misconduct that is illegal, malicious, reckless, or intended to harm another without commercial justification, should such a case ever arise. But that certainly did not occur in this case, and no instance of it has been cited to us.

. . .

---

24. *E.g.* Brief of American Royalty Council as Amicus Supporting Petitioners at 2 ("[W]hile the prevailing parties in the case below are royalty owners, the long-term effect of the court of appeals' decision is disastrous for royalty owners throughout Texas. If operators are faced with the possibility of tort liability when engaging in hydraulic fracturing, they will likely fracture fewer and fewer wells, with the ultimate effect of royalty owners losing out on hundreds of millions of dollars in royalties and the economy of the entire state weakened.") * * *.

We reverse the court of appeals' judgment, render judgment that Salinas take nothing on his claims for trespass and breach of the implied covenant to protect against drainage, and remand the remainder of the case for a new trial.

JUSTICE WILLETT, concurring.

James Michener may well be right: "Water, not oil, is the lifeblood of Texas * * * "[25] But together, oil and gas are its muscle, which today fends off atrophy.

At a time of insatiable appetite for energy and harder-to-reach deposits—iron truths that contribute to $145 a barrel crude and $4 a gallon gasoline[26]—Texas common law should not give traction to an action rooted in abstraction. Our fast-growing State confronts fast-growing energy needs, and Texas can ill afford its finite resources, or its law, to remain stuck in the ground. The Court today averts an improvident decision that, in terms of its real-world impact, would have been a legal dry hole, jurisimprudence that turned booms into busts and torrents into trickles. Scarcity exists, but *above*-ground supply obstacles also exist, and this Court shouldn't be one of them.

Efficient energy production is profoundly important to Texas and to the nation: [Justice Willett's lengthy discussion of the strategic and economic importance of the Texas oil and gas industry is omitted.]

Bottom line: We are more and more over a barrel as "our reserves of fossil fuels are becoming harder and more expensive to find."[27] Given this supply-side slide, maximizing recovery via fracing is essential; enshrining trespass liability for fracing (a "tres-frac" claim) is not. I join today's no-liability result and suggest another reason for barring tres-frac suits: Open-ended liability threatens to inflict grave and unmitigable harm, ensuring that much of our State's undeveloped energy supplies would stay that way—undeveloped. Texas oil and gas law favors drilling wells, not drilling consumers. Amid soaring demand and sagging supply, Texas common law must accommodate cutting-edge technologies able to extract untold reserves from unconventional fields.

Two additional comments on the Court's decision:

First, it nixes trespass-by-frac suits for drainage (the only damages sought here) by invoking the rule of capture. I agree such suits would subvert this time-honored rule, but I would foreclose them a half-step sooner under the same "balancing of interests" approach we applied to

---

25.   James A. Michener, Texas v (1985).

26.   Energy Information Administration, Short–Term Energy Outlook, http://www.eia.doe.gov/steo (last visited Aug. 27, 2008). Fortunately, these all-time record highs from mid-July 2008 have fallen slightly. On August 27, 2008, the per-barrel price of light, sweet crude for October delivery settled at $118. New York Mercantile Exchange, Home, http://www.nymex.com/index.aspx (last visited Aug. 27, 2008). On the retail side, Texas motorists paid an average of $3.48 that day for a gallon of regular unleaded. American Automobile Association, Daily Fuel Gauge Report, http://www.fuelgaugereport.com/TXavg.asp (last visited Aug. 27, 2008).

27.   Bruce Wright, *The Texas Portfolio,* Fiscal Notes: Special Energy Issue, Apr. 2008, at 1, *available at* http://www.window.state.tx. us/comptro l/fnotes/fnEnergy08/fnEnergy08.pdf.

subsurface fluid injection nearly a half-century ago in *Railroad Commission of Texas v. Manziel.*[28] Such encroachment isn't just "no actionable trespass"; it's no trespass at all. As a practical matter, the distinction between "no actionable trespass" and "no trespass" may seem more rhetorical than real: recovery is denied either way. But orthodox trespass principles that govern surface invasions seem to me to have dwindling subterranean relevance, particularly as exploration techniques grow ever sophisticated. Given the pace of innovation, fueled by spiraling demand in a supply-constrained world, I would confront Lord Coke's maxim directly and decide whether land ownership indeed "extends to the sky above and the earth's center below,"[29] or alternatively, whether that ancient doctrine " 'has no place in the modern world.' "[30] The Court says there is no actionable trespass because there is no injury, and there is no injury because the rule of capture says so: "the gas he claims to have lost simply does not belong to him."[31] True, you cannot recover actual damages for trespass absent injury, but I would approach this case not as the Court does today but as the Court did in *Manziel,* focusing not on the injury caused by the alleged trespass but on whether the underlying act was wrongful to start with.[32] Injury is the *result* of trespass, not part of its definition, and this case should turn not on the absence of injury but on the absence of wrongfulness. Balancing the respective interests as we did in *Manziel,* this type of subsurface encroachment, like the waterflood in *Manziel,* simply isn't wrongful and thus isn't a trespass at all, not just a nonactionable trespass.

Second, the Court implicitly leaves trespass as a potentially viable theory in suits seeking "nondrainage" damages,[33] for example, when a reservoir or nearby drilling equipment is damaged. But plaintiffs alleging nondrainage injuries already have a ready theory: negligence. In such cases, where the rule of capture is inapposite, I would end definitively any lingering flirtation of Texas law with equating hydraulic fracturing with trespass. I would say categorically that a claim for "trespass-by-frac" is nonexistent in either drainage or nondrainage cases.

As for the dissent, it would take an indispensable innovation in an indispensable industry[34] and make it a tort. In doing so, it would usurp

---

28. 361 S.W.2d 560 (Tex.1962).

29. 268 S.W.3d at 11.

30. *Id.* at 11 (quoting *United States v. Causby,* 328 U.S. 256, 261, 66 S.Ct. 1062, 90 L.Ed. 1206 (1946)).

31. *Id.* at 13.

32. *Manziel,* 361 S.W.2d at 566–69; *see also Lyle v. Waddle,* 144 Tex. 90, 188 S.W.2d 770, 773 (1945) (distinguishing the wrongful act that constitutes trespass from the harm caused by the trespass). Black's Law Dictionary captures this view, defining "trespass" as an "unlawful act committed against the person or property of another; esp., wrongful entry on another's real property." Black's Law Dictionary 1541 (8th ed.2004).

33. 268 S.W.3d at 10–11.

34. The oil and gas industry is a mainstay of the Texas economy. Its share of gross state product was 15.7% in 2006, when it employed more than 312,000 Texans who earned almost $31 billion in total wages. *See* Texas Comptroller of Public Accounts, The Energy Report 2008, at 29–

the Railroad Commission's vast authority to oversee, through carefully balanced regulations, the production of oil and gas in this State, and replace that legislatively conferred discretion with wide-open tort liability for an essential recovery practice used in every producing region of Texas. It would take a meat-ax approach to a task that demands scalpel-like precision, all to address a problem that, even assuming it exists, surely has better solutions. The dissent's view would invite a nightmarish flood of litigation over unknowable facts. It would slow the spigot and make it far tougher to find that next barrel of crude, that next cubic foot of natural gas, particularly in less-desirable pockets. It would reward the free rider who would rather sue for trespass than drill his own well. And it would do all this at the worst possible time-one of falling production, surging demand, and near-record-high prices for both crude oil and gasoline. Under the dissent, the newest "enhanced-recovery technique" would be a wildcatting plaintiff who sues for multi-millions after his neighbor fracs a well. Why hire a drilling contractor and field geologist to drill an unsightly and unpredictable offset well when you can go for a gusher in the courtroom? Just hire a lawyer and retain a testifying expert who can summarize with mind-boggling precision the fluid dynamics and fracture geometry that transpired beneath millions of tons of earth.

I. A Comment on the Court's Decision

Another Reason for Barring Trespass-by-Frac Suits: Unbounded Tort Liability Would Impose Exorbitant Costs on Society

Although it disallows tres-frac damages under the rule of capture, the Court is unconvinced that tort exposure would necessarily crimp production and inflict broad-based economic harm. I am not nearly so sanguine. The dire alarms sounded in the amicus curiae briefs, including one from the State's oil and gas regulatory body, strike me as more factual than fanciful.

The amici depict a grim future for the Texas energy industry and economy if we permit trespass-by-frac lawsuits. These warnings—from public and private observers alike-counsel pause before we declare into existence a tort action they insist will undeniably imperil production. The Share 13 Plaintiffs label these concerns "a 'sky is falling' Chicken Little refrain," but if the warnings sound overwrought, it may be because, in this case, style is inextricable from substance: Allowing trespass-by-frac suits to impede what is perhaps the single most essential technique in modern oil and gas production would be a calamitous mistake.

i. Tres–Frac Liability Would Squeeze Much-Needed Production

The views of one amicus curiae merit particular attention: the Railroad Commission, legislatively commanded to superintend the Texas ener-

---

30 (2008) *available at* http://www.window.state.tx.us/specialrpt/energy [hereinafter Texas Energy Report].

gy industry and given jurisdiction over each and every one of our State's 200,000–plus producing oil and gas wells.

As to its irreplaceable role in modern energy exploration, fracing, says the Railroad Commission, is:

- "often necessary to maximize production and assure that the oil and gas reserves * * * are not left in the ground";

- "used widely and prolifically throughout Texas as a production technique";

- "a vital component of oil and gas production in Texas and, in those parts of the state where tight sands and shale formations are found, it is absolutely essential to the economic production of oil and gas"; and

- responsible for "the production of large quantities of oil and gas that otherwise would never have been recovered."

As to the devastating blow that tort liability would impose, such exposure, according to the Commission, would:

- "create a significant disincentive for oil and gas operators to continue to use and refine this longstanding and effective production technique";

- "result in many fewer wells being drilled and substantially decreased oil and gas production in Texas"; and

- "impede the exploration and development of, and lead to the 'waste' of, our state's oil and gas resources, a result that is completely contrary to the fundamental concept of oil and gas conservation and our agency's mission to support enhanced development and economic vitality for the benefit of Texans."

Fracing is not a luxury, but a must-have recovery tool that is vital today and will remain vital tomorrow (along with other promising recovery technologies). Easy-to-produce reserves are increasingly uncommon, and meeting spiking demand requires advanced techniques to make uneconomical fields economical.

.   .   .

Fracing is required but also imprecise. As the Court notes, we are talking about fissures of immeasurable length and uncontrollable direction. Whether a fracture's effective length actually crossed an adjacent lease line miles beneath the Earth's surface cannot be determined until after the fact.[35] As for controlling a fracture's precise direction, plaintiffs'

---

35. As described by plaintiffs' expert, who has written several books in this area, a fracture's *effective* length is shorter than its initial propped length. Even if the induced fracture crossed over the lease line momentarily, and even if experts had the wherewithal to confirm as much, who is to say the effective portion of the fracture—the part that actually captures oil and gas from the reservoir—did not remain completely within Coastal's Share 12 lease boundaries? Plaintiffs made no attempt to determine the fracture's effective length in this case. Because drainage occurs exclusively via this *effective* frac length, not the original frac penetration length, liability, if at all, must reasonably be limited to trespass that inflicts actual injury—drainage—not an encroach-

lead expert conceded there is no way to do so: "the fracture azimuth is preordained. There is very little that we can do to affect the fracture orientation." Creating a fracture is itself a geological and engineering marvel; controlling its length and direction (in three dimensions) is simply beyond present capabilities.

Risk-taking entrepreneurs contend daily with such uncertainties, but Texas law deserves greater predictability than permitting exemplary damages for invisible torts. Because operators of fraced wells lack absolute control, the specter of tort liability will convince many rational operators to forego fracing altogether and leave otherwise recoverable resources in the ground, to the detriment of the State as a whole. It defies belief that exposure to exemplary tort damages will do anything other than sharply curtail fracing and sharply curtail production (thus reducing supply, thus pushing up prices * * * for everything).[36]

We wisely took into account similar policy concerns in *Manziel,* where we rejected trespass liability for a waterflood that breached lease boundaries. We found it "obvious that secondary recovery programs could not and would not be conducted if any adjoining operator could stop the project on the ground of subsurface trespass."[37] The Railroad Commission urges the Court to accommodate real-world concerns here "as it has in the past," urging us to "give careful consideration to the policy implications of a decision recognizing a new cause of action." Like recovery by waterflood, recovery by fracturing is key to maximizing recovery.

ii. Less Fracing Means Less Tax and Royalty Revenue for Texas

Robust energy production enriches Texas' fiscal bottom line. In fiscal year 2007, severance taxes on oil and gas production produced more than $2.7 billion for the State, about 7% of all tax revenue, and preliminary figures for the current year suggest revenues may surpass $3 billion.[38] In

---

ment that produces no ill effect. This is particularly true where, as here, plaintiffs alleged felony theft in an attempt to avoid the statutory cap on punitive damages. *See* Tex. Civ. Prac. & Rem.Code § 41.008(b)(1), (c)(13). Only the fracture's *effective* length, not its hydraulic or propped lengths, speaks to whether the fracture is actually draining hydrocarbons. The cross-examination of Dr. Economides on this point was illustrative. Although he "estimated" that 25–35% of the fracture penetrated plaintiffs' property, plaintiffs' expert made no attempt to measure its *effective* length, the part that actually captures minerals and inflicts the complained-of injury: "I did not do any other elaborate calculation in terms of drainage and interference or whatever else."

36. Under the rules, a well may be as close as 467 feet from a lease line, but given that the center of a forty-acre square tract (the smallest permitted size) is only 660 feet from its edge, an operator realistically has no risk-free place to drill a fraced well without facing possible trespass liability. *See* 16 Tex. Admin.Code § 3.37 (spacing rules); *see* Laura H. Burney & Norman J. Hyne, *Hydraulic Fracturing: Stimulating Your Well or Trespassing?* 44 Rocky Mtn. Min. L. Inst. 19–1, at 19–14 (1998) (estimating the length of a fracture in tight sand reservoir at a few thousand feet); *see also* Ragsdale, *supra* note 15, at 338 n. 128 (noting that a typical fracture runs 2,500 to 4,500 feet from the wellbore).

37. *R.R. Comm'n of Tex. v. Manziel,* 361 S.W.2d 560, 568 (Tex.1962).

38. Terry D. Ragsdale, *Hydraulic Fracturing: The Stealthy Subsurface Trespass,* 28 Tulsa L.J. 311. Texas Comptroller of Public Accounts, Texas Net Revenue by Source–Fiscal 2007, http:// www.window.state. tx. us/taxbud/revenue.html (last visited Aug. 27, 2008); *see also* Texas Energy Report, *supra* note 34, at 30–31.

addition, drilling on State lands annually generates millions in oil and gas royalty revenue for the State's general fund.[39]

. . .

iii. Texas Statutory and Common Law Suggest the Court's Decision Should Be Informed by Concern for the Public Good

The interplay of common-law trespass and oil and gas law must be shaped by concern for the public good. In *Hastings,* we recognized a trespass cause of action to combat slant-hole drilling as "in line with the public policy of this state."[40] In *Manziel,* we stated that "[s]econdary recovery operations are carried on to increase the ultimate recovery of oil and gas," and that "[i]t cannot be disputed that such operations should be encouraged."[41] If anything, encouraging the use of leading-edge technology is a greater concern today than in 1962 when *Manziel* was decided. Hydraulic fracturing involves unique practical and policy considerations that Texas common law cannot ignore.

Our statutory law certainly doesn't. The Legislature, consistent with its focus on maximizing recoverable reserves, affirmatively champions fracturing by granting severance tax exemptions for production from dormant oil and gas wells brought back into production and from fields the Commission designates as tight sands areas, formations where fracing is the sole method capable of producing in commercial quantities.[42] Fracture stimulation is the "universal well completion technique in tight gas sands,"[43] and Texas law aims to facilitate economic production from areas with poor native porosity and permeability, like in South Texas. Coastal's expert testified that Hidalgo County, where this case arose, produces more than double the gas it produced a quarter-century ago, and the reason is undisputed: sophisticated fracing techniques. As of May 2008, the Railroad Commission had approved roughly 1,300 tight gas formations in the State,[44] and the Commission understands fully that "to be able to produce gas at volumes that are economical, reservoirs with low permeability must be treated."[45]

Given the omnipresence of fracing in modern industry practice, as recognized by Texas law, the Railroad Commission, and the Land Commis-

39. Texas Comptroller of Public Accounts, Biennial Revenue Estimate (2008–2009), http://www.window.state.tx.us/taxbud/bre 2008/html/sched_LGR.html (last visited Aug. 27, 2008).

40. *Hastings Oil Co. v. Tex. Co.,* 149 Tex. 416, 234 S.W.2d 389, 396 (1950).

41. *Manziel,* 361 S.W.2d at 568.

42. *See* Tex. Tax Code § 201.057; 16 Tex. Admin. Code § 3.101.

43. Burney & Hyne, *supra* note 36, at 19–17.

44. Railroad Commission of Texas, Oil & Gas–Statewide Rule 101—Approved Tight Gas Formation–Index Listing, http://www.rrc.state.tx. us/divisions/og/publications/hgindex.html (last visited Aug. 27, 2008).

45. [Study: Barnett Shale Boosting North Texas Economy, Dallas Bus. J., Mar. 28, 2008. As the Railroad Commission recently noted, "The Barnett Shale must be stimulated—treated to increase permeability—in order for the field to be economic." Railroad Commission of Texas, Water Use in the Barnett Shale, *available at* http://www.rrc.state.tx.us/divisions/og/wateruse_barnett shale.html (last visited Aug. 27, 2008).]

sion, it is unwise to expose operators to punitive sanctions and broader society to the manifold costs of reduced energy supply.

B. Fracing Is Not Merely Non–Actionable Trespass, But No Trespass at All

I agree with the Court as far as it goes. If the choice is (1) extend trespass liability to thwart a proven and widespread recovery technique or (2) extend the rule of capture—perhaps "the most important single doctrine of oil and gas law"[46]—I favor the latter.[47] To recognize a rule of capture yet at the same time prohibit fracing would create an asymmetry in Texas oil and gas law that leaves the rule of capture frozen in time (at the worst possible time), unable to adapt to essential new technologies.

My departure from the Court's reasoning is a narrow one. The Court says "no liability" because, while it presumes a trespass occurred, the rule of capture precludes injury: no injury, no lawsuit. I would instead tackle a more threshold issue, one we addressed in *Manziel* almost a half-century ago: whether formalistic trespass principles apply with equal force to the recovery of ever-dwindling supplies of natural resources miles below the surface.

To many people, a subsurface intrusion of fissures, fluid, and proppant invites a simple application of rudimentary trespass principles. Why not call a tort a tort? Well, *we* affix that common-law label, and not every technical intrusion, no matter how small, warrants damages, no matter how large. Trespass is a court-defined doctrine, and it falls squarely on this Court's shoulders to decide what is actionable. In doing so, we made clear in *Manziel* the common law must permit common-sense accommodations for technological breakthroughs that benefit society.

In *Manziel,* our watershed waterflood case, we flatly rejected an absolutist trespass standard, stressing that the definition of trespass must make room for industry innovations.[48] We unanimously rejected a theory of trespass based on an earlier-developed secondary recovery practice

---

46. 1 Ernest E. Smith & Jacqueline Lang Weaver, Texas Law of Oil & Gas § 1.1(A) (2d ed.2006). We have recognized for almost a century that drainage of oil or gas from beneath another's land is perfectly legal if the wellbore itself does not cross lease boundaries and the operator complies with Railroad Commission requirements. *See Bender v. Brooks,* 103 Tex. 329, 127 S.W. 168, 170 (1910); Smith & Weaver, *supra* § 1.1(E). Plaintiffs do not allege that Coastal's wellbore encroached into its property, and it is undisputed that Coastal complied with all pertinent Railroad Commission regulations.

47. The rule of capture has variously been explained as (1) a practical acknowledgment of the difficulties in determining the source of a well's production, (2) justified due to the availability of self-help, and (3) "a practical accommodation of the infant oil industry." Smith & Weaver, *supra* note 45, § 1.1(A). As to the last justification, "[a]n accounting for oil drained from other tracts would have placed the entire risk of a dry hole or unproductive well upon the driller while allowing neighboring landowners to benefit from a successful venture." *Id.* While the Texas energy industry is no longer in its infancy—indeed, it is quite mature (hence the imperative need for advanced recovery technologies)—these same concerns, including the free-rider problem, persist and are equally applicable to fracturing. The liability decision should not turn on whether proppant and frac fluid migrate across an imaginary vertical plane separating two properties miles underground (particularly when the fact of such migration is often unknowable). *See* Burney & Hyne, *supra* note 36, at 19–3 ("The extent of the fractures out from the wellbore can be determined only by *theoretical* calculations." (emphasis added)).

48. *R.R. Comm'n of Tex. v. Manziel,* 361 S.W.2d 560, 566–70 (Tex.1962).

(waterflooding) that was used to develop the giant East Texas field.[49] In a waterflood, usually conducted after primary production methods have ceased, water is injected under pressure into a reservoir to push residual oil toward certain output wells. The plaintiffs in *Manziel* complained the waterflood amounted to "trespass by injected water" that would drain oil from beneath their lease by pushing it to other properties and "result in the premature destruction of their producing * * * well."[50] We held that injected water that crosses lease lines did not constitute trespass * * * Basically, we held the law of trespass must not be applied in an unduly dogmatic manner to the oil and gas industry,[51] a statement I believe counsels against the *existence* of liability, not merely the *extent* of liability.[52]

Notably, we did not concede in *Manziel* that waterflood amounted to trespass but opt against liability because the good outweighed the bad. Indeed, if encroachment from waterflooding were deemed trespassory, then public policy considerations could not even be factored in.[53] Nor did we say the rule of capture precluded the plaintiffs whose oil was swept away from claiming a compensable injury. Rather, this Court, employing a balancing-of-interests analysis more common to nuisance cases, unanimously declared that injecting water beneath your neighbor's land was simply not a trespass because it was not wrongful:

* * *

C. Landowners Already Have Non–Trespass Remedies in Non–Drainage Cases

The Court reserves judgment on whether fracing might constitute trespass in non-drainage cases—for example, if Coastal's frac job had damaged the Share 13 plaintiff's wells or the Vicksburg T formation beneath their property. The plaintiffs claim no such injuries, but I would foreclose the possibility of trespass-based damages in non-drainage cases for a simple reason: settled Texas law already affords ample relief in such cases. Our precedent dating back 60 years makes clear that, notwithstanding the rule of capture, adjacent property owners may sue a driller who, through fracturing or otherwise, negligently damages a common reservoir,

---

49. *Id.* at 568–69 & n. 5.

50. *Id.* at 565.

51. *Id.*

52. As for the plaintiffs' contention that the rule of capture ceases to apply when a producer uses an "unnatural" recovery technique, I too, like the Court, am unpersuaded. Plaintiffs nowhere define "natural" production, but granting protection under the rule of capture only if the minerals flow totally unaided is assuredly un-natural and would deny protection to scores of everyday recovery techniques above and beyond fracturing—techniques that the Railroad Commission has long permitted. Indeed, all modern production technologies are artificial to some degree; oil and gas do not ordinarily seep out of the ground by themselves or when Jed Clampett's errant bullet sends up a geyser of "bubbling crude." This natural/artificial dichotomy has no support in Texas law and is rather hard to take seriously; the common law must be informed by common sense.

53. *Manziel,* 361 S.W.2d at 568–69.

thus reducing recoveries and causing waste.[54] Other settled precedent makes clear that Texas law affords no rule-of-capture immunity for waste or destruction stemming from a negligent well blowout.[55]

II. A Comment on the Dissent

A. Fracing Is Not Slant–Hole Drilling by Another Name

The dissent likens fracing to slant-hole drilling, intentionally bottoming a drill bit beneath the vertical boundaries of another's land. I see multiple and meaningful distinctions between fraced wells and deviated wells, as does the Railroad Commission.

First, a slant-hole driller exerts absolute control, knowing and directing with GPS-like precision *exactly* where the drillbit is and where it's going. Fracing, as plaintiffs' expert conceded, is highly unpredictable; under present-day petroleum engineering technology, a fracture's direction cannot be determined or controlled, except by Mother Nature, and a fracture's length cannot be precisely measured.[56] Second, a slant-hole well, encased in connecting pipe, remains open at its bottom-hole location, while only a portion of the initial fracture actually contributes to capturing minerals.[57] Third, nobody contends that bottoming a wellbore beneath your neighbor's property is indispensable to Texas oil and gas production; everybody-including plaintiffs' own expert-agrees that fracing is absolutely critical in low-permeability areas like South Texas.[58] Fourth, the Railroad Commission has never treated slant-hole drilling and frac drilling the same. In exercising its expertise, the Commission sees sharp distinctions between slant-hole wells and fraced wells, regulating the former heavily and the latter hardly at all * * * The Commission has always focused on the location of the wellbore itself, not any fractures or other subsurface features that might impact drainage.

B. We Should Defer to the Railroad Commission's Discretion, Not Usurp It

Oil and gas drilling is painstakingly regulated by the Railroad Commission, which possesses sweeping jurisdiction over all Texas oil and gas wells and all persons engaged in drilling or operating such wells.[59] The

---

54. *See Elliff v. Texon Drilling Co.,* 146 Tex. 575, 210 S.W.2d 558, 562–63 (1948) (recognizing negligence liability for harming the common reservoir); *see also HECI Exploration Co. v. Neel,* 982 S.W.2d 881, 886–88 (Tex.1998).

55. *See Comanche Duke Oil Co. v. Tex. Pac. Coal & Oil Co.,* 298 S.W. 554 (Tex. Comm'n App.1927, judgm't adopted) (jury finding that using 600 quarts of nitroglycerin to boost production ruined a nearby offset well).

56. *See* Ragsdale, *supra* note 36, at 338 n. 128.

57. Plaintiffs' expert testified that hydraulic fracturing produces four lengths: (1) fracture length, (2) hydraulic length, (3) propped length, and (4) effective length, stating "I not only agree [that those lengths exist], I'm the author of those definitions." No one disputes that only the effective length enhances mineral recovery.

58. As plaintiffs' expert testified, in such areas it is indispensable to viable production: "without hydraulic fracturing, there is no hope for economically attractive production in any * * * of the formations that I know of [in South Texas]." We have recognized that lessees have a duty to use successful modern production methods. *Amoco Prod. Co. v. Alexander,* 622 S.W.2d 563, 567 & n. 1 (Tex.1981). Hydraulic fracturing is a paradigm example of such a method. If the dissent's view controlled, an operator, particularly one operating on a smaller tract, would face a dilemma of fracing a well and thus risking a high-stakes trespass lawsuit from nearby landowners, or declining to frac and thus risking a high-stakes "failure to develop" lawsuit from its lessor.

59. Tex. Nat. Res.Code § 81.051.

Legislature has conferred open-ended authority to "adopt all necessary rules for governing and regulating persons and their operations" within the Commission's jurisdiction.[60] This jurisdiction includes "the use of techniques to enhance production and protect correlative rights."[61] More specifically, the Commission has the authority to make rules and issue orders that "require wells to be drilled and operated in a manner that will protect injury to adjoining property."[62]

In exercising that jurisdiction, the Railroad Commission has promulgated extensive regulations regarding oil and gas drilling generally but none that single out fracing specifically. If, in the course of advancing its legislative mandate to prevent waste and safeguard correlative rights, the Commission deems fracturing a practice potentially unfair to nearby landowners, it has wide discretion to weigh the competing interests and strike the proper regulatory balance. * * *

> * * *

I would defer to the Railroad Commission, whose competence in this matter far surpasses our own, to balance the competing interests and fine-tune the production of Texas hydrocarbons. If the Commission believes free-market practices have become too clamorous, it can flex its regulatory muscle over the offending production activities. But whether drainage results from honest mistake or dishonest misdeed, the Commission is best positioned to strike the smartest balance to protect landowners' rights and safeguard the viability of fracing amid shrinking reserves. We should leave the regulation of Texas' energy sector to the regulators as the Legislature intended.

C. Aggrieved Lessors Have Existing Remedies Short of Seeking Millions in Trespass Damages

The Share 13 Plaintiffs are not without alternative remedies. In this case, they pursued claims against their lessee, Coastal, for failure to protect against drainage and other claims. The clearest remedy is not a new-fangled tort action alleging trespass, but an old-fangled contract action alleging breach of the implied covenant to protect against uncompensated drainage, which the plaintiffs brought here.[63] * * *

Aside from litigation, a plaintiff [unleased landowner] can drill an offset well if he believes a fraced well on nearby property is causing drainage; self-help is the settled remedy under Texas law. As one venerable Texas oil and gas authority opined: "There is no reason for giving an injured party a cause of action for the violation of some legal right

---

60. *Id.* § 81.052.

61. *Amarillo Oil Co. v. Energy–Agri Prods., Inc.,* 794 S.W.2d 20, 26 (Tex.1990).

62. Tex. Nat. Res.Code § 85.202(a)(4); *see also Texaco, Inc. v. R.R. Comm'n,* 583 S.W.2d 307, 310 (Tex.1979) ("It is now well settled that the Railroad Commission is vested with power and charged with the duty of regulating the production of oil and gas for the prevention of waste as well as for the protection of correlative rights.").

63. *See Amoco Prod. Co. v. Alexander,* 622 S.W.2d 563, 567–68 (Tex.1981) (recognizing such liability where, as here, the lessee was the party doing the draining by producing from an adjacent tract).

resulting from a reasonable use of adjacent land if the aggrieved party's remedy of self-help is completely adequate for his proper protection."[64] Our law has long recognized that if a landowner desires the hydrocarbon riches beneath his property, he should drill a well. * * * The landowner should drill his own, not sue his neighbor for trespass; the rule of capture recognizes this simple concept, and I would preserve it. * * * Should the law be different when the neighbor uses an advanced recovery technique, without which drilling would be impractical?[65] The dissent thinks so, but in my view fails to reason so.

D. Allowing Tres–Frac Damages Would Portend Many Inconvenient Truths

Permitting trespass liability would be a grave blunder, auguring industry-wide tumult, the resulting tremors of which would be substantial and far-reaching. Both worldwide and in our energy-intensive State, energy is at once increasingly desired and increasingly scarce, and thus increasingly expensive. Courts shape the common law, but we cannot repeal the law of supply and demand any more than we can repeal the law of gravity. We occupy a petroleum-addicted world, and decades may pass before scalable fossil-fuel alternatives (wind, nuclear, solar, etc.) comprise a significantly larger piece of our diversified energy portfolio. Until then, letting neighbors file tresfrac suits against each other will only yield these stubborn realities: fewer wells will be drilled; fewer older (but still productive) wells will undergo remedial fracing to enhance recovery and will instead be plugged prematurely; huge swaths of Texas land will remain undeveloped, their resources utterly wasted.[66] The Texas economy would not grind to a halt, but it would feel the dampening effects of such a decision, and those effects would be real and acute.

* * *

Given Texas' unrivaled leadership in shaping the nation's dynamic energy sector, "[o]ther states frequently look to Texas decisions when confronted with a new or unsettled issue of oil and gas law."[74] While I would tackle the trespass issue slightly differently, the reasoning underlying the Court's no-liability outcome provides a valuable legal roadmap. I

---

64. A.W. Walker, Jr., *Property Rights in Oil and Gas and Their Effect Upon Police Regulation of Production,* 16 Tex. L.Rev. 370, 374 (1938).

65. In the pending case, expert testimony confirmed that drilling in this region would not be economically viable without fracturing. Certain "tight formations" produce gas in commercial quantities only through fracturing, and all the wells in the Vicksburg T field, including all of the wells drilled on Share 13, received fracture treatments. Coastal's expert testified that every well in South Texas has been subjected to at least one fracture treatment. The Share 13 Plaintiffs' expert testified that without fracturing "there is no hope for economically attractive production" in the Vicksburg T.

66. As the Texas Energy Planning Council reported on page 15 in its 2005 Texas Energy Plan: "Extending the useful and productive life of marginal wells encourages the domestic production of oil and gas. Once these wells are abandoned and plugged, Texas will lose access to this valuable natural resource." [Texas Energy Planning Council, Texas Energy Plan 2005 (Dec. 2004)].

74. Ernest E. Smith, *Implications of a Fiduciary Standard of Conduct for the Holder of the Executive Right,* 64 Tex. L.Rev. 371, 375 n.13 (1985).

agree that Texas law should not equate hydraulic fracturing across a lease boundary with actionable subsurface trespass. * * *

JUSTICE JOHNSON, joined by CHIEF JUSTICE JEFFERSON, and by JUSTICE MEDINA as to Part I, * * * dissenting in part.

I join the Court's opinion except for Part II–B. As to Part II–B, I would not address whether the rule of capture precludes damages when oil and gas are produced through hydraulic fractures that extend across lease lines until it is determined whether hydraulically fracturing across lease lines is a trespass. * * *

I. Rule of Capture

The rule of capture precludes liability for capturing oil or gas drained from a neighboring property "whenever such flow occurs solely through the operation of natural agencies in a normal manner, as distinguished from artificial means applied to stimulate such a flow." *Peterson v. Grayce Oil Co.*, 37 S.W.2d 367, 370–71 (Tex.Civ.App.–Fort Worth 1931), *aff'd,* 128 Tex. 550, 98 S.W.2d 781 (1936). The rationale for the rule of capture is the "fugitive nature" of hydrocarbons. *Halbouty v. R.R. Comm'n,* 163 Tex. 417, 357 S.W.2d 364 (1962). They flow to places of lesser pressure and do not respect property lines. The gas at issue here, however, did not migrate to Coastal's well because of naturally occurring pressure changes in the reservoir. If it had, then I probably would agree that the rule of capture insulates Coastal from liability. But the jury found that Coastal trespassed by means of the hydraulic fracturing process, and Coastal does not contest that finding here. Rather, Coastal contends that a subsurface trespass by hydraulic fracturing is not actionable. In the face of this record and an uncontested finding that Coastal trespassed on Share 13 by the manner in which it conducted operations on Share 12, I do not agree that the rule of capture applies. Coastal did not legally recover the gas it drained from Share 13 unless Coastal's hydraulic fracture into Share 13 was not illegal. Until the issue of trespass is addressed, Coastal's fracture into Share 13 must be considered an illegal trespass. I would not apply the rule to a situation such as this in which a party effectively enters another's lease without consent, drains minerals by means of an artificially created channel or device, and then "captures" the minerals on the trespasser's lease. *See id.* at 375 (limiting the rule of capture to oil and gas that is legally recovered); *see also SWEPI, L.P. v. Camden Res., Inc.,* 139 S.W.3d 332, 341 (Tex.App.–San Antonio 2004, pet. denied).

In considering the effects of the rule of capture, the underlying premise is that a landowner owns the minerals, including oil and gas, underneath his property. *Elliff v. Texon Drilling Co.,* 146 Tex. 575, 210 S.W.2d 558, 561 (1948). In *Halbouty,* this Court succinctly harmonized this property rule with the rule of capture:

> To infer that the rule of capture gives to the landowner the legally protected right to capture the oil and gas underlying his neighbor's tract is entirely inconsistent with the ownership theory. To harmonize

both rules, the rule of capture can mean little more than that due to their fugitive nature, the hydrocarbons when captured belong to the owner of the well to which they flowed, irrespective of where they may have been in place originally, without liability to his neighbor for drainage. That is to say that since the gas in a continuous reservoir will flow to a point of low pressure the landowner is not restricted to the particular gas that may underlie his property originally but *is the owner of all that which he may legally recover.*

357 S.W.2d at 375 (emphasis added). Coastal concedes that gas must be legally produced in order to come within the rule of capture. *See also Elliff,* 210 S.W.2d at 562–63 ("[E]ach owner of land in a common source of supply of oil and gas has legal privileges as against other owners of land therein to take oil or gas therefrom by *lawful* operations conducted on his own land.") (emphasis added) (citing 1 W.L. Summers, Oil and Gas § 63 (Perm. ed.)); *Comanche Duke Oil Co. v. Tex. Pac. Coal & Oil Co.,* 298 S.W. 554, 559 (Tex.1927) ("[O]ne owner could not properly erect his structures, surface or underground, in whole or part beyond the dividing line, and thereby take oil on or in the adjoining tract, or induce that oil to come onto or into his tract, so as to become liable to capture there or prevent the owner of the adjoining tract from enjoying the benefit of such oil as might be in his land or as might come there except for these structures."). The key word is "legally." Without it, the rule of capture becomes only a license to obtain minerals in any manner, including unauthorized deviated wells, and vacuum pumps and whatever other method oilfield operators can devise.

Today the Court says that because Salinas does not claim the Coastal Fee No. 1 well violates a statute or regulation, the gas that traveled through the artificially created and propped-open fractures from Share 13 to the well "simply does not belong to him." But that conclusion does not square with the underlying rationale for the rule of capture as we expressed it in *Halbouty,* and as seems only logical and just: an operator such as Coastal owns the oil and gas that is *legally* captured. *See Halbouty,* 357 S.W.2d at 375. And "legally" should not sanction all methods other than those specifically prohibited by statute or rule of the Railroad Commission. It simply cannot be a legal activity for one person to trespass on another's property. *See* Black's Law Dictionary 522 (7th ed.1999) (defining "legal duty" as a "duty arising by contract or by operation of law; an obligation the breach of which would be a legal wrong [such as] the legal duty of parents to support their children"); *Texas–Louisiana Power Co. v. Webster,* 127 Tex. 126, 91 S.W.2d 302, 306 (1936) (noting that a trespasser is one who enters upon the property of another without any right, lawful authority, or express or implied invitation). The question the Court does not answer, but which it logically must to decide this case, is whether it was legal for Coastal to hydraulically fracture into Share 13. The answer to the question requires us to address Coastal's primary issue: does hydraulic fracturing across lease lines constitute subsurface trespass.

We have held that a trespass occurs when a well begun on property where the operator has a right to drill is, without permission, deviated so the well crosses into another's lease. *See Hastings Oil Co. v. Tex. Co.*, 149 Tex. 416, 234 S.W.2d 389 (1950). Coastal argues that there are differences between taking minerals from another's lease through fracturing and taking them by means of a deviated well. Maybe there are, even though both involve a lease operator's intentional actions which result in inserting foreign materials without permission into a second lease, draining minerals by means of the foreign materials, and "capturing" the minerals on the first lease. The question certainly is not foreclosed. *See Gregg v. Delhi–Taylor Oil Corp.*, 162 Tex. 26, 344 S.W.2d 411, 414 (1961); Terry D. Ragsdale, *Hydraulic Fracturing: The Stealthy Subsurface Trespass*, 28 Tulsa L.J. 311, 339 (1993) (noting that "[f]rom both a functional and physical perspective, a hydraulic fracture is largely analogous to a directionally drilled well"). In *Gregg*, 344 S.W.2d at 414–15, we suggested that sand fracturing may constitute a trespass, and in *Railroad Commission of Texas v. Manziel*, 361 S.W.2d 560, 567 (Tex.1962), we implied that subsurface trespasses are not different from other trespasses.

To differentiate between a deviated well and a fractured well, the Court says that gas extracted from a neighboring lease through a deviated well is not subject to the rule of capture for two reasons: the neighbor cannot protect from such drainage by drilling a well, and there is no uncertainty that the deviated well is producing another owner's gas. I fail to follow the Court's logic. As to the first reason, the neighbor can protect from either a fracture extending into the neighbor's property or a deviated well. Both simply provide the means for gas to flow to an area of lower pressure and from there to the drilling operator's property where it is captured. The only difference is the degree of drainage that can be prevented by offset wells, and a fracture's exposure to the reservoir may be greater than that of the deviated well and thus drain more gas. As to the second reason, the purpose of both a deviated well and a hydraulic fracture is for gas to flow through them to be gathered at a distant surface. Coastal fractured its well so gas would flow through the fractures to the wellbore, and no one contends that gas did not do so. The evidence showed that the effective length of a fracture can be fairly closely determined after the fracture operation. Coastal's expert testified that the effective length of the fractures (that length through which gas will flow) did not extend into Share 13, while Salinas's expert opined that it did. As in most trials, the jury was called upon to resolve the conflicts in testimony. It resolved them in favor of Salinas. In sum, the jury decided that part of the gas produced from Coastal Fee No. 1 was a result of the channel created by Coastal's fracturing into Share 13. There was evidence to support the finding.

The Court gives four reasons "not to change the rule of capture" to allow a cause of action for drainage accomplished by hydraulic fracturing beyond lease lines. I disagree with some of the four reasons, but my fundamental disagreement is not with the reasons the Court gives. My fundamental disagreement is with the Court's premise that its decision is *not a change* of the rule of capture. I believe the Court is changing the rule, and I would not do so.

The Court says that mineral owners and lessors aggrieved by drainage because of hydraulic fracturing have numerous alternative remedies such as self-help, suits against their lessee, offers to pool, and forced pooling. That is true in many cases, as witnessed by the amici briefs. But not all property owners in Texas are knowledgeable enough or have the resources to benefit from those remedies. The rules of ownership and capture apply to them, also. Amici and the Court reference the importance of hydraulic fracturing to development of the Barnett shale field and other mineral interests in Texas. Who could quarrel with the facts? But those reports in many instances refer to mineral leasing and royalty payment benefits being received by small property owners, in many cases so small as to be single-family residence owners. Today's holding reduces incentives for operators to lease from small property owners because they can drill and hydraulically fracture to "capture" minerals from unleased and unpooled properties that would otherwise not be captured. Today's holding effectively allows a lessee to change and expand the boundary lines of its lease by unilateral decision and action—fracturing its wells * * *. Such a situation is exemplified by the facts facing this Court in *Gregg,* 162 Tex. 26, 344 S.W.2d 411. Gregg had a small lease surrounded by mineral interests owned by Delhi–Taylor. *Id.* at 412. Gregg planned to "expand" his lease by fracing a well and recovering minerals that he would not have been able to recover otherwise because of the tight gas formation. *Id.* The problem was that he was going to be recovering some of the minerals from Delhi–Taylor's part of the reservoir. *Id.* We did not have difficulty recognizing that Gregg's fracing into Delhi–Taylor's minerals, if it occurred, potentially was a trespass that the courts could enjoin. *Id.* at 416.

* * *

The Court, Coastal, and amici reference the importance of hydraulic fracturing to the development of mineral interests in Texas, and raise valid concerns about the effect on mineral production if hydraulic fracturing subjects the fracturing operator to exemplary damages. * * * Even if it were to be decided that hydraulic fracturing is subject to traditional trespass rules, equitable considerations are proper in determining the availability of damages for trespass related to the recovery of minerals, just as equitable considerations resulted in implied covenants protecting and promoting goals of mineral leases and lessors. * * *

In balancing the interests involved here, it seems that even if hydraulic fracturing is subject to trespass law, precluding recovery of *exemplary* damages for a trespass through a hydraulic fracture could be deemed reasonable. For example, the testimony in this case reveals that although the fracture length of an operation can be estimated before the job is done, the effective length—the length of the fracture through which gas will flow—cannot. Because there are clearly difficulties and technological limitations in these expensive but necessary operations, the law should be flexible in considering them. Preclusion of exemplary damages would be one way to minimize discouraging the use of advances in technology and recovery techniques, yet leave in place protection for rights of individual mineral owners to their property. A possible consideration for precluding exemplary damages if hydraulic fracturing were subject to trespass law could be the defense that, in light of industry standards at the time, a reasonably prudent lessee could have believed the fracturing operation was necessary to economically recover the minerals from the lessee's estate.

Whatever the result, I would decide the trespass issue.

* * *

NOTES

1.   As is obvious from the length and tone of the various opinions and by the number of amicus briefs, the outcome of this case was extraordinarily important to the Texas oil and gas industry. Given the overall tenor of the majority opinion, was the majority's careful distinction between trespass quaer clausum fregit and trespass on the case pivotal? In other words, would the case have been decided differently if the plaintiffs had been owners of unleased mineral interests? How would a court rule in a nonownership state such as Oklahoma on the right of owners of petroleum interests to sue for trespass?

A variety of common law actions are often grouped under the trespass heading. The particular actions pursued by a plaintiff will vary. Actions in trespass *quare clausum fregit* and trespass on the case typically allow recovery for the damage done to the land, measured by the diminution in value resulting from the trespass. An action in trespass de bonis asportatis allows recovery for the damage associated with taking something from the land. An action in trover may be maintained for the value of converted personal property wrongfully taken, e.g., oil and gas after it is severed from the real property. If circumstances allow, an action in replevin may be maintained to recover the personal property itself. Injunctive relief may also be available. In *Garza* what particular "trespass" remedy were the plaintiffs most likely seeking?

2.   What is most convincing about the majority opinion? Did the majority convincingly distinguish between a hydraulically fractured well and a slant well? What about the fact that some of the injected proppants likely remained in the reservoir rock beneath the plaintiffs' land?

3.   What is most convincing about Justice Willet's opinion? Is he correct that negligence should be the only appropriate remedy for a frac that does harm beyond just drainage?

4.   What is the most convincing part of the dissenting opinion? Should all subsurface intrusions be treated as a surface trespass, acknowledging that the remedy might be different for subsurface trespass?

5. In Browning Oil Co., Inc. v. Luecke, 38 S.W.3d 625 (Tex.App. 2000, writ denied), the court refused to apply the traditional rule of capture to a horizontal well bore,[75] that had been perforated to directly produce oil from several tracts. Instead the court held that the oil should be apportioned on the basis of the amount produced from each tract. The court offers no suggestions about how these amounts should be determined. Should an apportionment of production be based upon the acreage contained in the overlying tracts of land? Based upon the actual exposure of the well bore to the productive formation beneath each tract of land? Based upon the estimated volume of oil and gas beneath each tract? Should the landowner on whose surface the well is located be entitled to a share of production if the portion of the formation from which production is obtained does not lie beneath the well-site tract? Does the advent of horizontal drilling justify a departure from the rule of capture? The court in *Garza* did not discuss *Browning*; however, in light of Garza, would the Texas Supreme Court agree with the *Browning* court's refusal to apply the rule of capture to horizontal drilling?

6. In *Railroad Commission of Texas v. Manziel*, 361 S.W.2d 560 (Tex. 1962), the court was asked to set aside an order of the Texas Railroad Commission authorizing the injection of water into a reservoir to facilitate oil recovery. While acknowledging that it was not passing upon the tort aspects of the dispute, the court did discuss trespass law in considerable detail. The court reasoned that when the railroad commission properly authorizes secondary recovery projects, such as waterflooding of a reservoir, no trespass occurs if the injected water migrates beneath neighboring lands, even when such migration displaces oil from beneath those lands. In so reasoning, the court emphasized that the Railroad Commission had expressly authorized the waterflooding by issuing a permit. The majority in *Garza* certainly treated *Manziel* as a case about trespass law.

After *Garza*, the Texas Supreme Court reviewed a case involving the injection of fluid waste into the subsurface. FPL Farming Ltd. v. Environmental Processing Systems, L.C., 351 S.W.3d 306 (Tex. 2011). The injector had a permit from the Texas Commission on Environmental Quality. A neighboring landowner brought suit, alleging trespass. The court of appeals dismissed the action, citing *Garza* and *Manziel*. The Texas Supreme Court distinguished those cases and reversed and remanded:

> The court of appeals misinterpreted this Court's holding in *Manziel*. We stated there that we were "not confronted with the tort aspects" of subsurface injected water migration, nor did we decide "whether the [Railroad] Commission's authorization of such operations throws a protective cloak around the injecting operator who might otherwise be subjected to the risks of liability...." *Manziel, 361 S.W.2d at 566*. Instead, we held that Railroad Commission authorizations of secondary recovery projects are not subject to injunctive relief based on trespass claims. *Id. at 568*. Consistent with our suggestion in *Magnolia Petroleum* that the Railroad Commission has the authority and obligation to look to the parties' legal status in determining whether a permit should be

---

75. A horizontal well is initially drilled as a vertical well, but then re-directed so as to penetrate a producing reservoir horizontally.

issued, we noted that "[t]he technical rules of trespass have no place in the consideration of the validity of the orders of the [Railroad] Commission." *Id. at 569–70.* We made the point in *Manziel* that we were not deciding whether a permit holder is immunized from trespass liability by virtue of the permit. *Id. at 566.* The case is inapposite.

Our opinion in *Garza,* another opinion relied upon by the court of appeals, likewise did not hold that agency authorization or permission resulted in blanket immunity from trespass liability. *Coastal Oil & Gas Corp. v. Garza Energy Trust, 268 S.W.3d 1 (Tex.2008).* Although *Garza* dealt with a subsurface trespass issue, it also was a different case than the one before us. In *Garza,* the Salinases, mineral owners of one tract, sued Coastal Oil & Gas Corporation, the entity leasing their mineral interest and the mineral interest in an adjoining tract, for trespass based on the underground invasion of the Salinases' reservoir by injected proppant used by Coastal Oil in fracturing to recover minerals from the adjoining tract that it also leased. *Id. at 6–7.* Because the Salinases were mineral owners and had leased the minerals to Coastal Oil, they merely had a royalty interest and possibility of reverter but did not possess the minerals. *Id. at 9.* Although the Salinases had standing to sue for a form of trespass, we held that, because they were not in possession of the mineral rights, they were not entitled to sue for trespass based on nominal damages but had to prove actual injury. *Id. at 10–11.* We held that the rule of capture precluded damages for drainage by fracturing, and thus the Salinases could not recover. *Id. at 17.*

The issues in *Manziel* and *Garza* were factually similar. They dealt with injected substances per agency authorization that had possibly migrated underground across property lines. The case before us is distinguishable on several grounds. Both of those cases dealt with the extraction of minerals in the oil and gas industry, and thus the rule of capture. *Garza, 268 S.W.3d at 13, Manziel, 361 S.W.2d at 568.* The rule of capture, and administrative deference to agency interpretations, was critical to our holding in *Garza.* And although the Act contains provisions governing both Railroad Commission and TCEQ permits, injecting substances to aid in the extraction of minerals serves a different purpose than does injecting wastewater. Tex. Water Code § 27.011. We have recognized that "[i]t cannot be disputed that [secondary operations to recover oil and gas] should be encouraged" to "increase the ultimate recovery of oil and gas." *Manziel, 361 S.W.2d at 568.* Under the rule of capture, a "cornerstone of the oil and gas industry ... fundamental both to property rights and to state regulation," a mineral rights owner owns the oil and gas produced from his or her well even if the oil and gas migrated underground from a tract owned by someone else. *Garza, 268 S.W.3d at 13. Manziel* and *Garza* considered the justification for the rule of capture—greater oil and gas recovery—in their analyses. However, the rule of capture is not applicable to wastewater injection. *Id. at 17; see also Manziel, 361 S.W.2d at 568.* Mineral owners can protect their interests from drainage through means such as pooling or drilling their own wells. *Garza, 268 S.W.3d at 14.* That is not necessarily the case when a landowner is trying to protect his or her subsurface from migrating wastewater. *Manziel* and *Garza* did not decide the issues in this case, and because of the oil and gas interests at issue in *Manziel* and *Garza,* their reasoning does not dictate our analysis in this wastewater injection trespass case.

351 S.W.3d at 313–14.

In remanding the court said: "We do not decide today whether subsurface wastewater migration can constitute a trespass, or whether it did so in this case." Id. at 314–15. Didn't the *Garza* majority treat *Manziel* as a trespass case? Are the landowners in FPL entitled to at least nominal damages? If so, can they also enjoin the trespass?

The business of disposing of fluid wastes through injection wells into the subsurface is a major industry. Moreover, most oil wells also produce saltwater, which is commonly transported to disposal wells, which inject the saltwater into the subsurface. Saltwater disposal is an essential component of both conventional and unconventional oil production. Given the reasoning in Justice Willet's concurring opinion in *Garza*, why didn't he dissent in FPL?

The landmark decision on subsurface waste disposal is *Chance v. BP Chemicals, Inc.*, 670 N.E.2d 985 (Ohio 1996). BP Chemicals disposed of chemical waste underground under both federal and state regulatory permits. Neighboring landowners initiated a class-action suit, seeking damages and injunctive relief and asserting that the injected waste trespassed into their subsurface. The *Chance* court concluded that a landowner's subsurface right to exclude others encompasses only intrusions that "actually interfere with the [landowner's] reasonable and foreseeable use of the subsurface." Id. at 992. The court affirmed the trial court's excluding evidence that "environmental stigma associated with the deep wells had a negative effect on appellants' property values due to the public perception there may have been injectate under appellants' property and that the injectate may be dangerous." Id. at 993. The Ohio Supreme Court observed that plaintiff had offered no specific evidence of any actual damage but only opinion testimony that problems may arise in the future. Relying on *Willoughby Hills v. Corrigan*, 278 N.E.2d 658, 664 (1972) (addressing air space), the court observed that "ownership rights in today's world are not as clear-cut as they were before the advent of airplanes and injection wells." 670 N.E.2d at 992.

> "Just as a property owner must accept some limitations on the ownership rights extending above the surface of the property, we find that there are also limitations on property owners' subsurface rights. We therefore extend the reasoning of *Willoughby Hills,* that absolute ownership of air rights is a doctrine which 'has no place in the modern world,' to apply as well to ownership of subsurface rights." Id.

As in FPL, the *Chance* court indicated that the possession of permits does not shield the defendant from liability for actual harm. The class claims in *Chance* were deemed too speculative to merit recovery; however, the court did state that one class member might have a valid claim because the migrating waste may have caused him to abandon plans to drill for natural gas.

In *Chance*, notice of the action was sent to more than 20,000 landowners so they could opt out of the class. If the court had concluded that all class members were entitled to compensation merely because some hazardous waste had migrated into their pore space, then the underground fluid waste injection industry would most likely have ceased operations in Ohio.

In the future, deep subsurface strata may be used to store carbon dioxide captured from manmade sources to mitigate the effects of climate change, which is largely blamed on the burning of fossil fuels—coal, oil, and natural gas. Various studies indicate that CO_2 sequestered in the subsurface could migrate laterally from hundreds to thousands of square-miles.[76] Requiring project developers to obtain consent from all pore-space owners within the migratory path of the CO_2 plume could have the practical effect of prohibiting the development of many sequestration projects. Under *Chance*, developers of geologic carbon sequestration projects would not need to acquire pore-space rights prior to commencing operations, but they would have to compensate any landowner who suffered actual damages. See generally R. Lee Gresham and Owen L Anderson, Legal and Commercial Models for Pore–Space Access and Use for Geologic C Sequestration, 72 U. of Pitt. L. Rev. 701 (2011).

7. The Second Restatement of Torts addresses trespass as follows:

> Section 158. One is subject to liability to another for trespass, irrespective of whether he thereby causes harm to any legally protected interest of the other, if he intentionally
>
> > (a) enters land in the possession of the other, or causes a thing or a third person to do so, or
> >
> > (b) remains on the land, or
> >
> > (c) fails to remove from the land a thing which he is under a duty to remove.
>
> Section 159.
>
> (1) Except as stated in Subsection (2), a trespass may be committed on, beneath, or above the surface of the earth.
>
> (2) Flight by aircraft in the air space above the land of another is a trespass if, but only if,
>
> > (a) it enters into the immediate reaches of the air space next to the land, and
> >
> > (b) it interferes substantially with the other's use and enjoyment of his land.[77]

Comment m to Section 159 suggests that in cases of airspace intrusions that are not within the immediate reaches of the surface, liability should rest upon the basis of nuisance rather than trespass.

In light of *Garza* and the cases discussed in the preceding note, does the Restatement reflect current case law? Should the Restatement be changed?

---

76. *See* Pruess, K.; Xu, T.; Apps, J.; Garcia, J. *Numerical Modeling of Aquifer Disposal of CO₂. In SPE/EPA/DOE Exploration and Production Environment Conference, Society of Petroleum Engineers; San Antonio, TX (2001); Brennan, S.T.; Burruss, R.C.* Specific Storage Volumes: A Useful Tool for CO₂ Storage Capacity Assessment, *15 Nat. Resour. Res. 165, 182 (2006); R.L. Gresham, S.T. McCoy, J. Apt, and M.G. Morgan,* Implications of Compensating Property Owners for Geologic CO₂ Sequestration, *44 Environ. Sci. Technol. 2897, 2900 (2010).*

77. RESTATEMENT (SECOND) OF TORTS § 159 (1965).

See generally Owen L. Anderson, Lord Coke, The Restatement, and Modern Subsurface Trespass Law, 57th Ann. Inst. on Min. L. 22 (L.S.U. 2010), revised and reprinted 6 Tex. J. Oil Gas & Energy L. 203 (2011).

8. For somewhat contrasting views of *Garza*, compare David E. Pierce, Minimizing the Environmental Impact of Oil and Gas Development by Maximizing Production Conservation, 85 N. D. L. Rev. 759 (2009) and Owen L. Anderson, Subsurface Trespass After Coastal v. Garza, 60 Inst. On Oil & Gas L. 65 (2009).

PEOPLE'S GAS CO. v. TYNER

31 N.E. 59 (Ind. 1892).

Drilling the well is OK Shooting the well may not be "storing the glycerine" @ surface is private Nuisance

COFFEY, J. This was an action by the appellee against the appellants in the Hancock circuit court for the purpose of obtaining an injunction. The complaint alleges, substantially, that the appellee and his wife are the owners by entireties of the real estate therein described, which consists of four city lots in the city of Greenfield; that the lots are enclosed together by a fence, and that his dwelling house and residence, in which he and his family reside, is situated on the lots; that the lots are near the center of the city, and, with his residence thereon, are of the value of $4,000; that with full knowledge of all the facts the appellants, regardless of the rights of the appellee, and of the safety, peace, comfort, and lives of himself and family, have, without his consent and over his objections, within the last 40 days, dug and constructed a natural gas well to the depth of about 1,000 feet, and about 200 feet distant from the appellee's residence, with only a street 40 feet in width between the appellee's lots and the lot on which the well is sunk; that the appellants are about to "shoot" said well, and will do so unless restrained; that for the purpose of "shooting" the well[1] the appellants * * * unlawfully procured to be brought and unlawfully permitted a large quantity of nitroglycerin or other nitro explosive compound to be and remain upon Sycamore street, a public street in the city, and within less than 200 feet of appellee's residence, for about 3 hours, in the midst of and surrounded by a large number of people; that appellants, by their employees, threatened and attempted to "shoot" said gas well, and that they still threaten so to do, with their said nitroglycerin or other nitro explosive compound, and will do so unless restrained; that nitroglycerin is highly explosive, and very dangerous to property and life, and is liable to explode under any and all circumstances, and at any time or place, and that an explosion of 60 or 100 quarts of said explosive at any given place on the surface of the earth could and probably would destroy life and property for a distance of 500 yards in all directions from such explosion; that the handling or storing thereof in or about appellant's gas well will endanger the lives of his family, as well as the safety of his property, and that the shooting of said well with nitroglycerin will greatly injure and damage the appellee's said property, both above and under the

---

1. [Editors' Note] In "shooting" a well, the oil and gas bearing formation is fractured with explosives in an effort to improve permeability.

surface of the earth, and endanger his life and the lives of his family. This complaint was verified, and upon it and the affidavits filed in support of its allegations the court granted a temporary injunction, from which this appeal is prosecuted. The affidavits filed by the appellee tended to prove that the appellants' gas well is within the corporate limits of the city of Greenfield; that a short time prior to the filing of the complaint in this cause the appellants deposited in or near the derrick at the well described in the complaint about 117 quarts of nitroglycerin, weighing about 340 pounds, with the intention of exploding the same in the well. The affidavits further tend to show that nitroglycerin is very explosive, and that it is liable to explode at any time; that the explosion of that quantity of nitroglycerin upon the surface of the earth would be likely to destroy life or property at any point within 500 yards of such explosion.

It is contended by the appellants—*First,* that they had the right to use their own property as to them seemed best, and for that reason they could not be enjoined from exploding nitroglycerin in their well for the purpose of increasing the flow of natural gas, though such explosion might have the effect to draw the gas from the land of the appellee; *second,* that, as bringing nitroglycerin into the corporate limit of a town or city in a greater quantity than 100 pounds is made a crime by statute, it cannot be enjoined. On the other hand, it is contended by the appellee—*First,* that natural gas is property, and that the appellants have no legal right to do anything upon their own land which will draw such gas from his land, and appropriate it to their own use; *second,* that as he is liable to suffer an injury peculiar to himself, to which the public in general is not subject, by the unlawful act of the appellants in bringing nitroglycerin within the corporate limits of Greenfield, he is entitled for that reason to an injunction.

It has been settled in this state that natural gas, when brought to the surface of the earth and placed in pipes for transportation, is property, and may be the subject of interstate commerce. Water, petroleum, oil, and gas are generally classed by themselves as minerals possessing in some degree a kindred nature. As to whether the owner of the soil may dig down and divert a well-defined subterraneous stream of water, there is much diversity of opinion and conflict in the adjudicated cases; but the authorities agree that the owner of a particular tract of land may sink a well, and appropriate to his own use all the percolating water found therein, though it may entirely destroy the well on his neighbor's land. It is a familiar maxim that in contemplation of law, land always extends downward as well as upwards, so that whatever is in a direct line between the surface of any land and the center of the earth belongs to the owner of the surface. [It] would seem to follow from this maxim that whether what is subterranean be solid rock, mines, or porous soil, or salt springs, or part land and part water, the person who owns the surface may dig therein, and apply all that is there found to his own purposes *ad libitum.* Upon this principle, * * * if an adjoining land owner, in lawfully digging upon his own land, draws the water from the land of another, to his injury, such injury falls within the description of *damnum absque injuria,* which cannot become the ground of an action. * * * Mr. Gould, in his work on Waters, (2d Ed. § 291,) says: "Petroleum oil, like subterranean water, is included in the comprehensive idea which the law attaches to the word 'land,' and is a part of the soil in which it is found. Like water, it is not the subject of property, except while in actual occupancy, and a grant of either water or oil is not a grant of the soil, or of anything for which ejectment will lie." In recognition of the principles here announced in the case of Brown v. Vandergrift, 80 Pa.St. 142, it was said by the court that "the discovery of petroleum led to new forms of leasing lands. Its fugitive and wandering existence within the limits of a particular tract was uncertain, and assumed certainty only by actual development founded upon experiment." What is said of the fugitive character of percolating water and of petroleum oil applies with greater force to natural gas. In the case of Westmoreland & Cambria Nat. Gas Co. v. De Witt, Pa.St., 18 Atl.Rep. 724, it was said "Water and oil, and still more strongly gas, may be classed by themselves, if the analogy be not too strong, as mineral *ferae naturae.* In common with animals, and unlike other minerals, they have the power and the tendency to escape without the volition of the owner. Their fugitive and wandering existence within the limits of a particular tract is uncertain. * * * They belong to the owner of the land, and are part of it, so long as they are on or in it, and are subject to his control; but when they escape, and go into other land, or come under another's control, the title of the former owner is gone. Possession of the land, therefore, is not necessarily possession of the gas. If an adjoining or even a distant owner drills his own land and taps your gas, so that it comes into his well and under his control, it is no longer yours, but his." It is not denied by the appellee in this case that the appellants have the perfect legal right to sink a well into their own land, and draw therefrom all the gas that may naturally flow to it, but he contends that they have no right to explode nitroglycerin in the well to increase the natural flow. When it is once conceded that the owner of the surface has the right to sink a well and draw gas from the lands of an adjoining owner, no valid reason can be given why he may not enlarge his well by the explosion of nitroglycerin therein for the purpose of increasing the flow. The question is not as to the quantity of gas he may take, but it is a question of his right to take the gas at all. So far as this suit seeks to enjoin the appellants from exploding nitroglycerin in their gas well, upon the ground that it will increase the flow of the gas to the injury of the appellee, it cannot, in our opinion, be sustained. The rule that the owner has the right to do as he pleases with or upon his own property is subject to many limitations and restrictions, one of which is that he must have due regard for the rights of others. It is settled that the owner of a lot may not erect and maintain a nuisance thereon, whereby his neighbors are injured. If he does so, and the injury sustained by such neighbor cannot be adequately compensated in damages, he may be enjoined.

[handwritten: no explosion allowed]

If the appellants in this case have been guilty of the folly of sinking a gas well in the center of a thickly-populated city, where they cannot collect the necessary quantity of nitroglycerin to shoot it without endangering the property and lives of those who have no connection with their operations, they should be content with such flow of gas as can be obtained without such shooting. It certainly cannot be maintained that the destruction of human life is an injury which can be compensated in damages. No authority has been cited, and we know of none, supporting the position of the appellants that the appellee is not entitled to an injunction because the accumulation of nitroglycerin within the corporate limits of a town or city is a crime. It has long been settled that a private citizen may maintain an action for a public wrong if he suffers an injury peculiar to himself, and not sustained by the public in general. * * * In our opinion the court did not err in granting the temporary injunction in this case. Judgment affirmed.

Notes

1. *People's Gas* illustrates that a landowner's right to capture oil and gas, like all property rights, is not unlimited. The right is subject to a number of common law limitations, including nuisance, negligence, waste, and malice.

2. The right to capture can be further limited by the lawful exercise of the police power. For example, in Trail Enterprises, Inc. v. City of Houston, 957 S.W.2d 625 (Tex.App. 1997), the court upheld a city ordinance prohibiting the drilling of oil and gas wells within the city's watershed.

3. The following case illustrates how state police power in the form of oil and gas conservation statutes and regulations may limit the right to capture.

[handwritten: Violation of spacing pattern, overproduction where proration order controls amount field wide]

WRONSKI v. SUN OIL CO.
279 N.W.2d 564 (Mich.App.1979).

Holbrook, Judge.

[Plaintiffs own several tracts of land comprising 200 acres within the Columbus 3 oil pool or field. Defendant, Sun Oil has drilled several wells on nearby property within the field. The Supervisor of Wells, Michigan Department of Natural Resources,[1] issued an order,[2] under the authority of the Michigan oil and gas conservation act, establishing 20–acre well

---

1. Supervisor of Wells Act, M.C.L. § 319.1 et seq.; M.S.A. § 13.139(1) et seq.

2. The Supervisor of Wells Order of May 22, 1969, established:

"(B) DRILLING UNIT

The drilling unit for wells drilled for oil and gas in the pool defined in (A) above shall be a tract of approximately 20 acres, rectangular in shape, formed by dividing a governmental surveyed quarter-quarter section of land into an east half and a west half thereof.

"(C) WELL SPACING PATTERN

Permits shall be granted for the drilling of wells for oil and gas in the pool defined in (A) above provided the wells are located in the center of the northeast one-quarter (NE 1/4) or the center of the southwest one-quarter (SE 1/4) of a governmental surveyed quarter-quarter section of land."

drilling units for the field; this order limits the number of wells that may be drilled to one well for each designated 20–acre tract within the boundaries of the field. The Supervisor also issued an order[3] which limited production from each well within the field to a maximum of 75 barrels of oil per day.

Plaintiffs contend that Sun Oil illegally overproduced oil from three wells and that such oil was drained from beneath the plaintiffs' tracts. The court awarded compensatory and exemplary damages to the plaintiffs. Sun Oil appealed.]

* * *

* * * Review of the record discloses sufficient facts upon which the trial court could find that Sun Oil systematically, intentionally and illegally produced * * * 150,000 barrels over that allowed by the proration order. The record also supports the finding that one-third of this illegally produced oil was drained from the property of the plaintiffs. We are not convinced that had this Court been the trier of fact that we would have come to a different result, and do not reverse or modify these findings.

The trial court found that

* * * Sun Oil Company has violated the common law rights of Plaintiffs Wronski and Koziara by illegally, unlawfully and secretly draining valuable oil from beneath their properties.[4]

The nature of Sun Oil's violation, while not clearly stated by the trial court, was a claim for the conversion of oil.

* * *

Oil and gas, unlike other minerals, do not remain constantly in place in the ground, but may migrate across property lines. Because of this migratory tendency the rule of capture evolved. This rule provides:

The owner of a tract of land acquires title to the oil and gas which he produces from wells drilled thereon, though it may be proved that part of such oil or gas migrated from adjoining lands. Under this rule, *absent some state regulation of drilling practices,* a landowner * * * is not liable to adjacent landowners whose lands are drained as a result of such operations * * *. The remedy of the injured landowner under such circumstances has generally been said to be that of self-help— "go and do likewise". William and Meyers, *supra,* § 204.4, pp. 55–57 (Emphasis supplied.)

This rule of capture was a harsh rule that could work to deprive an owner of oil and gas underneath his land. To mitigate the harshness of this rule and to protect the landowners' property rights in the oil and gas beneath his land, the "fair share" principle emerged.

---

3. Supervisor of Wells Order of May 22, 1969.
4. Trial Court Opinion at 14.

As early as 1931, the Board of Directors of the American Petroleum Institute expressed this principle by declaring a policy:

> that it endorses, and believes the petroleum industry endorses the principle that each owner of the surface is entitled only to his equitable and ratable share of the recoverable oil and gas energy in the common pool in the proportion which the recoverable reserves underlying his land bears to the recoverable reserves in the pool. Graham, *Fair Share or Fair Game? Great Principle, Good Technology—But Pitfalls in Practice,* 8 Nat.Res.Law. 61, 64–65 (1975).

The API clarified the principle in 1942 by saying:

> Within reasonable limits, each operator should have an opportunity equal to that afforded other operators to recover the equivalent of the amount of recoverable oil [and gas] underlying his property. The aim should be to prevent reasonably avoidable drainage of oil and gas across property lines that is not offset by counter drainage. Id. at 65.

> This fair-share rule does not do away with the rule of capture, but rather acts to place limits on its proper application.

Texas has adopted both the ownership-in-place doctrine and the fair-share principle. Its courts have addressed the interrelationship between these two principles and the rule of capture.

> It must be conceded that under the law of capture there is no liability for reasonable and legitimate drainage from the common pool. The landowner is privileged to sink as many wells as he desires upon his tract of land and extract therefrom and appropriate all the oil and gas that he may produce, *so long as he operates within the spirit and purpose of conservation statutes and orders of the Railroad Commission.* These laws and regulations are designed to afford each owner a reasonable opportunity to produce his proportionate part of the oil and gas from the entire pool and to prevent operating practices injurious to the common reservoir. In this manner, if all operators exercise the same degree of skill and diligence, each owner will recover in most instances his fair share of the oil and gas. *This reasonable opportunity to produce his fair share of the oil and gas is the landowner's common law right * * *.* But * * * the right of each land holder is qualified, and is limited to legitimate operations. Elliff v. Texon Drilling Co., 210 S.W.2d 558, 562 (Tex.1948). (Emphasis supplied.)

The rule of capture is thus modified to exclude operations that are in violation of valid conservation orders.

Michigan recognizes the fair-share principle and its subsequent modifications of the rule of capture. When an adjacent landowner drilled an oil well too close to a property line the Supreme Court said that this:

> [D]eprived plaintiff of the opportunity of claiming and taking the oil that was rightfully hers; and defendants must respond in damages for such conversion. Ross v. Damm, 270 N.W. 722, 725 (Mich.1936).

The Supervisor of Wells Act also incorporated the fair share principle into Section 13. This section concerns proration orders and states in part that:

> The rules, regulations, or orders of the supervisor shall, so far as it is practicable to do so, afford the owner of each property in a pool *the opportunity to produce his just and equitable share of the oil and gas in the pool*, being an amount, so far as can be practically determined and obtained without waste, and without reducing the bottom hole pressure materially below the average for the pool, substantially in the proportion that the quantity of the recoverable oil and gas under such property bears to the total recoverable oil and gas in the pool, and for this purpose to use his just and equitable share of the reservoir energy. M.C.L. § 319.13; M.S.A. § 13.139(13). (Emphasis supplied.)

This right to have a reasonable opportunity to produce one's just and equitable share of oil in a pool is the common-law right that the trial court found Sun Oil violated. Under the authority of *Ross v. Damm, supra*, if it can be said that Sun Oil's overproduction deprived plaintiffs of the opportunity to claim and take the oil under their respective properties, then Sun Oil will be liable for a conversion.

Production in the Columbus 3 field was restricted to 75 barrels of oil per well per day. Compulsory pooling[5] was also in effect, limiting the number of oil wells to one per twenty acres, and specifying their location. The purpose behind proration is that the order itself, if obeyed, will protect landowners from drainage and allow each to produce their fair share. A violation of the proration order, especially a secret violation, allows the violator to take more than his fair share and leaves the other landowners unable to protect their rights unless they also violate the proration order. We therefore hold that any violation of a proration order constitutes conversion of oil from the pool, and subjects the violator to liability to all the owners of interests in the pool for conversion of the illegally-obtained oil. The trial court found that Sun Oil produced 150,000 barrels of oil from the Columbus 3 pool in contravention of the order of the Supervisor of Wells, and that 50,000 barrels of this oil had been drained from the lands of plaintiffs, which the trial court identified as a violation of the plaintiffs' common-law rights. The finding that Sun Oil is liable to plaintiffs for the conversion of 50,000 barrels of oil is affirmed.

The rule as to the amount of damages for a conversion of oil was established in Michigan in *Robinson v. Gordon Oil Co.*, 253 N.W. 218 (Mich.1934). The Court stated:

> "The general rule in the United States in actions for the conversion of oil, as in the case of conversion of minerals and other natural products of the soil is that, although a willful trespasser is liable for

---

5. [Editors' Note] The court should have said that well spacing and density regulations were in effect. Compulsory pooling refers to a regulatory order that combines small tracts into one well-spacing or well-drilling unit so that a well may be drilled on behalf of all owners within the unit.

the enhanced *value of the oil at the time of conversion* without deduction for expenses or for improvements by labor, an innocent trespasser is liable only for the value of the oil undisturbed; that is, he is entitled to set off the reasonable cost of production." (Citations omitted.) *Robinson, supra,* 253 N.W. at 219. (Emphasis supplied.)

This rule sets the liability of the convertor as the enhanced value of the oil at the time of conversion, but then subdivides this liability into two subrules depending upon the nature of the conversion. These two subrules are a "mild" rule which applies to innocent or nonwillful conversion and a "harsh" rule which applies to bad faith or willful conversions.

* * *

The trial court applied the "mild" rule with a royalty method of determining the value in situ and added exemplary damages. This method was improper since the court specifically found that Sun Oil was an intentional and willful convertor and that the oil was produced in violation of the leases. The "harsh" rule should have been applied in this instance, and plaintiffs awarded the value of the oil at the time of conversion. The addition of exemplary damages was also improper.

* * *

It is clear that the exemplary damages awarded were actually punitive damages. Application of the "harsh" rule of damages includes an amount for punitive damages and they may not be assessed twice.

* * *

Affirmed in part. Reversed in part. * * *

NOTES

1. Except for restraints imposed by the common law, by the correlative rights doctrine, and by the police power, a landowner exercising the right of capture may drill an unlimited number of wells and produce an unlimited amount of oil and gas without a duty to account to other landowners. See Kuntz § 4.2; Williams & Meyers § 204.4; and Summers §§ 61–65.

2. The next subsection explores ownership and rights to oil and gas after they have been produced.

4. OWNERSHIP AFTER EXTRACTION

CHAMPLIN EXPLORATION, INC. v. WESTERN BRIDGE & STEEL CO., INC.

597 P.2d 1215 (Okla.1979).

DOOLIN, JUSTICE:

We are called upon to decide, in this case, if a refiner loses title to refined hydrocarbons when they escape from him into the ground. To put it another way; are refined hydrocarbons subject to the law of capture when they escape into the ground?

We hold that an owner of refined hydrocarbons does not, ipso facto, lose title to escaped hydrocarbons unless it is shown by competent evidence that he has abandoned same.

Champlin Exploration, Inc.[1] (unit operator)[2] under a valid corporation commission order and operating agreement, brought suit against Champlin Petroleum Company (refiner) and other defendants who owned surface or mineral estates in the unit area; Western Bridge & Steel Company, Inc., Dosan Refining Company and Jim Peckham.

When the refiner discovered * * * leakage was occurring from its refinery, located within the unit area, it took immediate steps to recover what turned out to be refined hydrocarbons. Refiner caused trenches to be dug on its premises to recover and trap the escaped substances. Refiner pumped out the trenches and returned the hydrocarbons to its possession. The area of reclamation was subject to the operating agreement within the unit area.

Peckham, President of Western Bridge & Steel Company, Inc., as an individual and acting on his own, had for some time been collecting refined hydrocarbons in trenches or holes upon Western's premises which were adjacent to the refiner's premises. Western owned only the surface to these and adjoining premises, within the unit area. Peckham sold the hydrocarbons to Dosan Refining Company.

Unit operator brought suit seeking: (1) a declaratory judgment as to ownership of the escaped substances, and (2) an accounting against all defendants.

The evidence in this matter is not at variance. Both Peckham and the refiner took refined hydrocarbons from shallow holes or trenches from 6 feet deep to 18 or 20 feet deep. Natural forces such as gravity and water pressures caused the escaped hydrocarbons to collect in such areas where they were pumped into trucks or tanks. The substances had migrated a few hundred feet at most, from the leaking pipes or conduits installed by the refiner. The evidence disclosed the leaks have been repaired and for all intents and purposes the recovery by refiner and Peckham has ceased.

Trial court entered judgment for the defendant refiner and ordered case dismissed as to other defendants, holding the refiner was the owner of the escaped substances.

We affirm.

---

1. Despite the similarity in names the record indicates that Champlin Exploration, Inc. and Champlin Petroleum Co. are separate legal entities.

2. A unit operator is the entity having the legal right to drill and produce oil and gas. Where there are multiple owners of such a right, one entity is designated the "operator" by an oil and gas conservation agency, in this case, the Oklahoma Corporation Commission. The rights of other joint interest owners are protected by the terms of a Joint Operating Agreement (discussed in Chapter 5). A unit is the tract on which and from which the unit operator may conduct oil and gas drilling and production operations.

Unit operator relies primarily on our holding in Frost v. Ponca City, 541 P.2d 1321 (Okla.1975) to support its theory of error. Its contention basically is that once refined hydrocarbons escape into the ground, the escaped substance is again subject to the law of capture by virtue of having returned to the forces of nature under the surface of the earth.

In *Frost,* refined hydrocarbons had apparently seeped into and under property located within the city limits. The fumes from the seepage were creating a nuisance. The defendant city, pursuant to its police power, prohibited the plaintiff and any others, similarly situated, from drilling within the city by a city ordinance. The city then drilled wells, sold the recovered substances and kept the proceeds. Plaintiff, as owner of a mineral estate, brought a class action to recover the amount of hydrocarbons taken by the city, and this court found for plaintiff, allowing defendant credit for its expenses in producing, transporting and selling the hydrocarbons. In its brief, filed in the instant case, unit operator argues *Frost* holds that hydrocarbons which escape into the ground, even though previously refined and processed, were ipso facto, subject to the law of capture.

Refiner does not attack our holding in *Frost* but argues it has narrow or limited application. It points out that in the *Frost* case the escaped refined hydrocarbons had been abandoned for no one claimed previous title or ownership.

Ordinarily a landowner, lessee or unit operator who brings hydrocarbons to the surface and reduces them to actual possession acquires absolute ownership of the substances, subject to the operation agreement or lease, if any.

In Crosson v. Lion Oil & Refining Co., 275 S.W. 899 (Ark.1925) the Supreme Court of Arkansas turned the recovery of oil which had escaped from a pipe line of an owner upon the principles or theories of lost or abandoned properties. In *Crosson,* the owner who had reduced crude oil to his possession was allowed to recover the crude from a neighbor who had impounded it. In essence that court held title to lost property does not vest automatically in its finder or capturer for our purposes; there must have been an abandonment by its previous owner. Thus the law of capture in oil and as to chattels previously reduced to possession by an owner is conditioned on the well known and existing theory of abandonment of lost property. Professor Eugene Kuntz, in his definitive work on oil and gas, states the principle as follows: "If oil should escape from a well, tank, or pipeline, the owner may lose possession but he retains title unless the oil is abandoned." We can see no reason why his conclusions should not apply to refined hydrocarbons where problems of identity and other applications of the laws of evidence are comparatively simple and easy to apply.

The evidence in this case is clear and convincing; not only did the refiner capture his lost property, it was so pure and refined that it could be blended back into the marketable stock of the company with little or no treatment. We note also, refiner's operation to recover his lost property was confined to his premises; there was no abandonment under these circumstances.

It is uniformly held, once oil and gas is extracted from the earth, it becomes tangible, personal property and subject to absolute ownership.

We conclude that the refiner had not abandoned his refined hydrocarbons; there is no evidence of an intent to abandon by refiner.

Judgment affirmed.

NOTES

1. In the early days of wildcatting, productive wells often came in as "gushers." Until a gusher is brought under control and capped, it creates large pools of oil at the surface. Ruptured storage tanks and pipelines may create similar pools. If quantities are sufficient, salvage efforts will be undertaken. To resolve the ownership of salvaged oil, courts, as in the principal case, apply the law of finders.

2. Gushers, more commonly called "blow outs"[78] in contemporary jargon, rarely occur today; however, oil spills do occur from trucks, trains, tankers, and storage tanks. These occurrences are likely to trigger a number of common law and statutory claims by federal, state, and local governments, by neighboring property owners and businesses, and by various interest groups. Oil spills and other environmental issues are further considered in Chapter 5.

TEXAS AMERICAN ENERGY CORPORATION v. CITIZENS FIDELITY BANK & TRUST COMPANY

736 S.W.2d 25 (Ky.1987).

* * *

This court having granted discretionary review from an opinion of the Court of Appeals and being of the opinion that the Amended Opinion of the Hopkins Circuit Court by Honorable Thomas B. Spain, judge of said court, is correct, hereby adopts that opinion as the opinion of this court, as follows:

"This is a proceeding on a Joint Petition for a declaration of rights, pursuant to K.R.S. 418.020. [Movant], Texas American Energy Corporation (Texas American), is the successor by purchase to the assets and property of Western Kentucky Gas Company (Western), the principal business of which is the purchase of natural gas for resale to consumers.

"Effective June 29, 1983, Texas American entered into a $24,000,000 Revolving Loan Agreement with Respondent, Citizens Fidelity Bank &

---

78. The term *blow out* refers to the sudden and violent expulsion of oil, gas, drilling fluids, water, and other substances from a well resulting in an uncontrolled flow. "It occurs when high pressure gas is encountered in the hole and sufficient precautions * * * have not been taken." Manual of Oil and Gas Terms.

Trust Company, of Louisville, Kentucky, and Interfirst Bank Dallas, N.A.; The Northern Trust Company and Bank of the Southwest National Association, Houston (the Banks) to provide funds to Western for the periodic purchase of natural gas from its supplier. Such purchased gas is extracted from natural gas fields in Texas and Louisiana and piped to Western's pipeline distribution system in Kentucky. Western then stores surplus gas in its underground storage fields during the off-season and retrieves it during the peak demand mid-winter months for distribution to its customers.

"To secure the above-mentioned loan, Texas American, Citizens Fidelity and the Banks all agreed for a security interest to be conveyed in Texas American's gas in storage as discussed above. A dispute has arisen, however, as to whether such injected stored gas is personal property, susceptible of encumbrance merely by a security interest agreement as provided for in Article 9 of the Uniform Commercial Code (K.R.S. 355.9–102(1)(a)) as insisted by Texas American or whether such stored gas upon injection, once again becomes in the eyes of the law, an interest in real estate, the encumbrance of which could be accomplished only by a real estate mortgage, as argued by Citizens Fidelity and the Banks.

"Western has six storage fields, four of which are in Daviess County, Kentucky, and two of which are in Hopkins County, to wit: The St. Charles Storage Field and the Kirkwood Springs Storage Field. These storage fields are comprised of underground acreage leased from mineral owners containing various types of sandstone formations capable of accepting and containing natural gas because of being surrounded by strata that are impervious to the migratory characteristics of natural gas. These formations once contained indigenous or 'native' gas, but it has been long ago produced to depletion.

"It is not disputed that once foreign gas (sometimes called 'extraneous gas') is injected into these storage reservoirs, it is trapped, cannot escape, and remains exclusively within Western's control, because of Western's method of maintaining the integrity and viability of its storage fields through constant maintenance of 'cushion gas' therein. Furthermore, the Kentucky Department of Mines and Minerals has recently promulgated regulations requiring a 2,000 foot buffer zone around a gas storage field. Western has obtained permits for such buffer zones around its field, thus assuring their continued protection and integrity.

"With these facts in mind, we now move to the first question to be answered, namely whether natural gas, removed from its original 'home' and injected into a foreign location with confinement integrity, remains personal property as it is uniformly held to be upon its original production, or whether it reverts to an interest in real estate.

"The parties agree that until now the case law in Kentucky has considered such injected or extraneous gas not to be personal property when it is not confined. This is because of an opinion of the late revered Commissioner Osso Stanley of the former Court of Appeals in the now fifty-year-old case of *Hammonds v. Central Kentucky Natural Gas Co.,* Ky., 75 S.W.2d 204 (Ky.1934).

"In that case Della Hammonds owned 54 unleased acres located within the boundary of the gas company's 15,000 acre gas storage field. It was undisputed that the reservoir underlay her tract. She sued alleging trespass because the gas company's injected gas had 'invaded' the formation under her land without her consent. The trial Court found against her but Kentucky's highest Court * * * [affirmed], holding that once the foreign gas was injected back into the earth, (into an uncontrolled gas storage formation), it ceased being the property of the gas company, and would only become personal property again when and if it was produced or reduced to actual possession by extraction a second time.

"In reaching this conclusion, Commissioner Stanley traced the evolution of judicial thought with regard to oil and gas as distinguished from the 'solid minerals.' He adopted the then popular theory that because of their fugacious nature, oil and gas were 'wild and migratory in nature,' and hence similar to animals *ferae naturae* (i.e. wild by nature). This being so, he reasoned, the law as applied to wild animals ought to be applicable by analogy to oil and gas—minerals *ferae naturae*. Consequently, since a fox until his capture in the forest belonged to all mankind, and if trapped and released in another forest reverted to common property, shouldn't the same logic apply to 'captured' and injected natural gas? Commissioner Stanley also quoted from Thornton's Work on Oil and Gas, Sect. 1264, wherein Judge Willis equated injected gas in storage with timber. 'Standing in the woods, timber is a part of the land. When severed it becomes personal property. If made into lumber and used to construct a building it becomes again a part of the land to which it is attached. When gas is stored in the natural reservoir it is subject to all the properties that inhered in it originally. A neighbor could take it with impunity through adjacent wells, if he owned land within the radius of the reservoir. Hence it should be taxed only as part of the land in which it is placed, and in such circumstances could not be treated as personal property.'

"Texas American calls this Court's attention to the cases of *White v. New York State Natural Gas Corporation,* 190 F.Supp. 342 (W.D.Pa.1960) and *Lone Star Gas Company v. Murchison,* 353 S.W.2d 870 (Tex.1962). In both these cases *Hammonds* is referred to and rejected, along with the 'wild animal' analogy as applied to injected stored gas. The following portion of the opinion in *White* is particularly succinct:

'Generally stated, the law relating to ownership of wild animals is based on possessory concepts, with title being acquired only by reduction of the animal *ferae naturae* to possession and being divested by loss of possession through escape and return of the animal to its natural and ferocious state.' 2 Am.Jur., Animals § 8–13.

It becomes readily apparent, however, that a strict application of this analogy to the present facts is of no benefit to the plaintiff's cause. To begin with, the storage gas in question has not escaped from its owners. On the contrary, it is yet very much in the possession of the storage companies, being within a well-defined storage field, the Hebron–Ellisburg Field, and being subject to the control of the storage companies through the same wells by which the gas originally had been injected into the storage pool. Citing cases.

Moreover, there has been no return of storage gas to its 'natural habitat' since Southwest gas, differing materially in chemical and physical properties from native Oriskany gas, is not native to the Oriskany Sands underlying the Hebron–Ellisburg Field. Deferring to the analogy of animals *ferae naturae* under the circumstances of this case would no more divest a storage company of title to stored gas than a zookeeper in Pittsburgh to title to an escaped elephant. 2 Am.Jur., Animals § 13.

"In *Lone Star* the Court comments that our *Hammonds* case 'in its application of *ferae naturae* doctrine, has been the subject of violent adverse criticism by many authors and law review writers' (Citing Summers, 'Oil and Gas' permanent Ed. Vol. 1, p. 173; 21 U.Kan.City L.Rev. 217, 220 (1954), 35 Va.L.Rev. 947 (1950), 16 Tex.L.Rev. 370, and numerous others.) The Opinion then continues:

> * * * The analogy of wild animals upon which Hammonds is founded fails to undergird the ultimate decision of that case. Gas has no similarity to wild animals. Gas is an inanimate, diminishing non-reproductive substance lacking any will of its own, and instead of running wild and roaming at large as animals do, is subject to be moved solely by pressure or mechanical means. It cannot be logically regarded as personal property of the human race as are wild animals, instead of being turned loose in the woods as the fanciful fox or placed in the streams as the fictitious fish, gas, a privately owned commodity, has been stored for use, as required by the consuming public being, as alleged by appellant, subject to its control and withdrawal at any time. Logic and reason dictates the application of the White decision rather than Hammonds, to the end, that in Texas, the owner of gas does not lose title thereof by storing the same in a well-defined underground reservoir.

* * *

"Hammonds should be narrowly construed or limited as it applies to the instant case, for the reason that the fact situations in the two are distinguishable. In Hammonds there was a known 'leak' in the gas storage reservoir inasmuch as Mrs. Hammonds' land was, in fact, a part of the natural reservoir, though not controlled by the storage company. In the case at hand, however, it has been stipulated that the gas reservoir has total integrity, and the gas cannot escape nor can it be extracted by anyone except Western. Using the *ferae naturae* analogy, Western has captured the wild fox, hence reducing it to personal property. The fox has not been released in another forest, permitting it to revert to the common property of mankind; but rather, the fox has only been released in a private confinement zoo. The fox is no less under the control of Western than if it were on a leash.[1]

"Accordingly, the Court is of the opinion that *Hammonds* does not control in the instant case and that under the stipulated facts, the injected gas remains the personal property of Western.

"This being so, there is no more reason to require that it can only be hypothecated or encumbered by a real estate mortgage than there would be to require such of a recreational vehicle temporarily parked at a campground or of coal stockpiled at a tipple."

End of opinion of lower court.

It is therefore the opinion of this court that, in those instances when previously extracted oil or gas is subsequently stored in underground reservoirs capable of being defined with certainty and the integrity of said reservoirs is capable of being maintained, title to such oil or gas is not lost and said minerals do not become subject to the rights of the owners of the surface above the storage fields. Such previously extracted oil or gas, thus stored, is "goods" under the Uniform Commercial Code of Kentucky and the proper manner of encumbering an inventory of said minerals in storage is controlled thereby. Any language indicating the contrary in *Hammonds* * * * is specifically overruled.

NOTES

1. In *Hammonds v. Central Kentucky Natural Gas Co.*, 75 S.W.2d 204, 205–06 (Ky. Ct. App. 1934), the court took the analogy that oil and gas are like a wild animal a bit too far by reasoning that natural gas injected for storage was released back to nature and thus once again subject to capture. In essence the court concluded that the gas had been abandoned. While this reasoning cleverly avoided Hammonds' trespass claim, which was based upon the migration of the gas beneath her land, the court failed to recognize that the injector was storing the gas for later retrieval, not abandoning the gas. Thus, to protect the gas from being captured, the injector would have to secure the right to capture gas for every tract beneath which the gas migrated.

Hammonds has been widely criticized and rejected by several courts. See, e.g., Lone Star Gas Co. v. Murchison, 353 S.W.2d 870, 880 (Tex. Civ. App.– Dallas 1962); White v. New York State Natural Gas Corp., 190 F.Supp. 342 (E.D. Pa. 1960); Humble Oil & Ref. v. West, 508 S.W.2d 812, 817 (Tex. 1974); ANR Pipeline Co. v. 60 Acres of Land, 418 F. Supp.2d 933, 940 (W.D. Mich. 2006). Did the court in *Texas–American* overrule *Hammonds*?

---

1. [Editors' Note] William Jarrell Smith has noted:

If you are going to use the animal theory, then it seems to me that we are dealing with a domestic animal. If a horse strays over on a neighbor's land, the neighbor may be entitled to his damages, but he does not, by virtue of the trespass, acquire title to the horse.

William Jarrell Smith, Rights and Liabilities on Subsurface Operations, 8 Inst. on Oil & Gas L. & Tax'n 1, 26 (1957).

In *Lone Star*, the court held that natural gas injected for storage is not abandoned and subject to capture, but remains the personal property of the injector even if it migrates beneath neighboring tracts. *Lone Star* did not address the question of trespass directly. The court observed: "Appellees expend a great deal of space in their brief to the argument that appellant has trespassed upon their property. The status of this record is such, however, that we must, as Ulysses 'lash ourselves to the mast and resist Siren's songs' of trespass, or similar contention. This, for the simple reason that no action seeking redress or claimed trespass is here presented." 353 S.W.2d at 875.

In *ANR Pipeline Co. v. 60 Acres of Land*, 418 F.Supp.2d 933 (W.D. Mich. 2006), the court rejected the reasoning in *Hammonds* as follows: "Injected gas which has previously been produced, reduced to possession, and then reinjected into the ground is not subject to the rule of capture. Once severed from the realty, gas becomes personal property, and title to that property is not lost when it is injected into underground gas storage reservoirs. Accordingly, if injected [storage] gas moves across boundaries, then there may be a trespass." Id. at 939. The court further recognized that the presence of storage gas beneath private property may be grounds for an inverse condemnation action against an injector having condemnation authority; however, the "taking property for a public use must be accompanied by harm before it will be cognizable as a taking subject to an inverse condemnation claim." Id.

On the other hand, Kansas follows the *Hammonds* rule-of-capture view in the following circumstance: "[W]here a natural gas utility was not involved, where no certificate authorizing an underground natural gas storage facility had been issued by the Kansas Corporation Commission, and where a landowner had used the property of an adjoining landowner for gas storage without authorization or consent." Anderson v. Beech Aircraft, 699 P.2d 1023, 1032 (Kan. 1985). In Union Gas System, Inc. v. Carnahan, 774 P.2d 962 (Kan. 1989), the court applied the rule of capture to storage gas that had been produced by the neighboring landowners prior to the filing of a condemnation action, but refused to compensate the landowners for the pre-condemnation presence of storage gas beneath their property. The plaintiffs were allowed compensation for the value of the native gas beneath their property to the extent that it could be profitably produced from their land. The court rejected the injector's adverse-possession argument on the grounds that the pre-condemnation presence of the gas beneath plaintiff's property was not open and exclusive.

In 1993 the Kansas Legislature enacted Kan. Stat. Ann. § 55–1210, which provides, in part, as follows:

> (a) All natural gas which has previously been reduced to possession, and which is subsequently injected into underground storage fields, sands, reservoirs and facilities, whether such storage rights were acquired by eminent domain or otherwise, shall at all times be the property of the injector * * *.
>
> * * *
>
> (c) With regard to natural gas that has migrated to adjoining property or to a stratum, or portion thereof, which has not been condemned as allowed by law or otherwise purchased:

(1) The injector * * * shall not lose title to or possession of such gas if such injector * * * can prove by a preponderance of the evidence that such gas was originally injected into the underground storage.

(2) The injector * * * shall have the right to conduct such tests on any existing wells on adjoining property, at such injector's sole risk and expense including, but not limited to, the value of any lost production of other than the injector's gas, as may be reasonable to determine ownership of such gas.

(3) The owner of the stratum and the owner of the surface shall be entitled to such compensation, including compensation for use of or damage to the surface or substratum, as is provided by law, and shall be entitled to recovery of all costs and expenses, including reasonable attorney fees, if litigation is necessary to enforce any rights under this subsection (c) and the injector does not prevail.

(d) The injector * * * shall have the right to compel compliance with this section by injunction or other appropriate relief by application to a court of competent jurisdiction.

Kansas injectors have had difficulty meeting their statutory burden of proof, and landowners have successfully raised limitations to bar actions of conversion and unjust enrichment. Judge Brown has extensively reviewed some of these problems in the context of the Cunningham gas storage field in Kansas. See Northern Natural Gas Co. v. L.D. Drilling, Inc., 618 F. Supp.2d 1280 (D. Kan. 2009) and Northern Natural Gas Co. v. L.D. Drilling, Inc., 759 F. Supp.2d 1282 (D. Kan. 2010). While the above statute attempts to protect injectors from the rule of capture, the statute has also proved useful to landowners when seeking compensation for storage rights. The usual measure of damages is the fair rental value of the storage stratum. See Beck v. Northern Natural Gas Company, 170 F.3d 1018 (10th Cir. 1999).

Statutes in many states specifically authorize the use of eminent domain to acquire subsurface strata for gas storage. See, e.g., OKLA. STAT. ANN. Tit. 52, §§ 36.1–36.7. The Oklahoma statutes allow natural gas utilities to obtain storage rights by condemnation. Similarly to Kansas, the Oklahoma statutory regime provides that storage gas remains the property of the injector even though the gas migrates beneath neighboring lands; however, the injector bears to burden of proving migration and must compensate the neighboring landowner for the value of storage rights. Id. at § 36.6. For application, see Oklahoma Natural Gas Co. v. Mahan & Rowsey, Inc., 786 F.2d 1004 (10th Cir.Okla.1986).

2. Gas is most efficiently and safely stored in its natural underground reservoir until needed for consumption. The rule of capture, however, makes storing gas in place impractical. Also, gas is often extracted by necessity when it is produced as "casinghead" or "associated" gas in conjunction with the production of oil. Often gas is produced from its natural reservoir and moved to storage reservoirs located near the populated areas where it will be consumed. This allows gas suppliers to economically meet peak seasonal demands without constructing larger capacity pipelines or constructing and

maintaining man-made storage facilities that are more expensive and danger-ous than underground storage.

3.   To perfect a security interest in gas stored underground, is compli-ance with Article 9 of the Uniform Commercial Code sufficient, or should the lender also record a real estate mortgage covering the storage rights in the land? What if Texas American Energy Corporation had failed to record its storage lease in the real estate records of the county recorder? What if the mineral owners who leased storage rights to Texas American Energy Corpora-tion had previously executed an oil and gas lease to Wildcat Oil & Gas, Inc. that specifically included gas storage rights? What if the mineral owners had previously mortgaged their property to the First National Bank?

4.   If gas stored under high pressure migrates from the storage strata into a shallower oil-producing strata, making oil production more difficult and dangerous, is the owner of the gas liable to the oil producers? Would it matter that the oil lease was expressly "subject to" the natural gas storage agree-ment? See, e.g., Reese Exploration, Inc. v. Williams Natural Gas Co., 983 F.2d 1514 (10th Cir. 1993).

5.   Gas is often stored in underground reservoirs (formations) that contain native gas. Most often, any recoverable native gas will have been extracted. To maintain the integrity of the reservoir for storage, however, some native "cushion gas" may be left in the reservoir. This cushion helps prevent water encroachment and helps assure recovery of the stored gas. Should the owner of the native gas be entitled to both native and stored gas on a theory of commingling? See, e.g., Oklahoma Natural Gas Co. v. Mahan & Rowsey, Inc., 786 F.2d 1004 (10th Cir. Okla. 1986).

The royalty owner cannot require removal of all native gas, prior to injecting storage gas, because extracting all the native gas would cause water encroachment, which would ruin the reservoir for storage purposes. Moreover, an injector does not owe royalty on the native gas remaining in the reservoir when storage gas is injected into the reservoir; however, royalty will be owed on any native gas withdrawn with storage gas. The injector has the burden of proving the proportion of storage gas to native gas so that royalty owed on native gas can be determined at the time of withdrawal. Humble Oil & Refining Co. v. West, 508 S.W.2d 812 (Tex.1974).

6.   The Federal Energy Regulatory Commission is authorized to issue Certificates of Public Convenience and Necessity for gas storage in under-ground reservoirs. 15 U.S.C. § 717f. Once a certificate is issued, a pipeline company may acquire storage facilities by eminent domain. In Columbia Gas Transmission Corp. v. An Exclusive Natural Gas Storage Easement, 747 F.Supp. 401 (N.D. Ohio 1990), the court held that the Natural Gas Act, 15 U.S.C. §§ 717(b) preempts state trespass claims, leaving inverse condemna-tion as the only avenue for damages. The court concluded that the landowner bore the burden of proving damages and suggested that the operator of the storage reservoir need not condemn property into which its gas has migrated unless the integrity of the reservoir is threatened. See also, Mississippi River Transmission Corp. v. Tabor, 757 F.2d 662 (5th Cir. 1985). But see, Hum-phries v. Williams Natural Gas Company, 48 F. Supp. 2d 1276 (D. Kan. 1999).

7.   May storage rights be acquired pursuant to a general eminent domain statute? If so, what is the need for a special statute? What is the nature of the right acquired? How should the condemnation award be calculated where the storage reservoir contains some native gas? See, e.g., Union Gas System, Inc. v. Carnahan, 774 P.2d 962 (Kan.1989) and Pacific Gas & Electric Co. v. Zuckerman, 234 Cal.Rptr. 630 (Cal.App.1987).

8.   If one person owns the mineral estate and another person owns the surface estate, from whom should a gas storage right be obtained? Would it matter if the party seeking the storage right wanted to store gas in a depleted reservoir? See, e.g., Ellis v. Arkansas Louisiana Gas Co., 450 F.Supp. 412 (E.D.Okla.1978), affirmed 609 F.2d 436 (10th Cir. Okla.1979) and Mapco, Inc. v. Carter, 808 S.W.2d 262, 277 (Tex.App.1991), rev'd in part on other grounds, 817 S.W.2d 686 (Tex.1991). If the right is acquired by eminent domain, to whom should the award be paid and in what proportion? See, e.g., Mississippi River Transmission Corp. v. Tabor, 757 F.2d 662 (5th Cir.La.1985). See generally Kuntz § 2.6.

9.   Natural gas storage operations can be the source of surface damage. In January 2001, fires burned buildings and killed two people in Hutchinson, Kansas. The fires resulted from gas leaks from an underground gas storage reservoir located about 7 miles from the city. The gas reached the surface through abandoned but unplugged brine wells that had been drilled in the vicinity as early as the late 1800s. The integrity of the underground reservoir was apparently breached by over-pressurizing the reservoir to increase storage capacity. Consequently, some gas escaped into fractures in the rock adjacent to the reservoir and migrated to the unplugged brine wellbores, where the gas escaped at the surface within the city limits. See generally M. Lee Allison, *Natural Gas Explosions in Hutchinson, Kansas: Unraveling a Geologic Mystery (abs)*, Geological Society of America Abstracts with Programs, v33, #6, p132 (2001). *See also* Hayes Sight & Sound, Inc. v. ONEOK, Inc., 136 P.3d 428 (Kan. 2006) (upholding $1.7 million in actual damages to business properties caused by negligent over-pressuring and operation of gas storage facility; court also upheld $5.2 million in punitive damages).

This incident caused the State of Kansas to toughen its underground natural gas storage regulations. However, in Colorado Interstate Gas Company v. Wright, 707 F.Supp.2d 1169 (D. Kan. 2010), the court held that the Kansas regulations were preempted by the federal Natural Gas Act, 15 U.S.C. §§ 717 *et seq.* and by the federal Pipeline Safety Act, 49 U.S.C. §§ 60101 *et seq.*

F.   COMMON PATTERNS OF OIL AND GAS OWNERSHIP

This section summarizes frequently encountered business relationships that result in common patterns of oil and gas ownership. For example, landowners typically do not develop their oil and gas rights. Instead, landowners enter into a business relationship with a developer using a document titled "Oil and Gas Lease." Chapter 2 is devoted to the oil and gas lease. Conveyances by landowners and developers frequently follow a pattern that leads to specific types of disputes. Chapter 3 explores many of the commonly encountered conveyancing disputes. Relationships created beyond the oil and gas lease and conveyances of mineral interests are the focus of Chapter 6, which addresses these second-tier development agreements such as "farmout agreements," "operating agreements," "drilling contracts," and "gas purchase contracts." The goal of this introductory material is to list and describe the most commonly encountered interests so the materials that follow will be easier to understand. See Lowe, Chapter 3.B and Chapter 6.E.

In the oil and gas industry, the owner of a fee simple absolute is commonly identified as the owner of the *fee* (or *fee interest*). Traditionally, the term *fee* describes an estate in land that is capable of enduring forever. In other words, fee describes the duration of the estate. In oil and gas jargon, however, the fee or fee interest often refers to the totality of all private rights in the land. For example, Able, the *fee* owner of Blackacre, owns the surface, the airspace above the surface, and everything beneath the surface in fee simple absolute, an estate which is alienable, devisable, and inheritable. Various kinds of interests in oil, gas, and other minerals may be carved from the fee. In general, these interests may be created and conveyed or reserved as are other interests in real property.

The *mineral interest* (also called the *mineral estate* or the *mineral rights*) may be carved or "severed" from the fee interest in Blackacre. A "complete severance" occurs when Able, the fee owner of Blackacre, conveys Blackacre to Baker, reserving the mineral estate, or when Able conveys (by "mineral deed") all of the mineral interest in Blackacre to Baker. A "partial severance" occurs when Able either conveys Blackacre, reserving part of the mineral interest, or conveys part of the mineral interest in Blackacre. A partial severance may take many forms but would commonly be either a reservation or conveyance of (1) a fractional part of the minerals (e.g., Able conveys an undivided 1/2 of all minerals in Blackacre to Baker); (2) an interest in certain minerals (e.g., Able conveys Blackacre to Baker, reserving only oil, gas, and coal); or (3) a fractional part of certain minerals (e.g., Able conveys Blackacre to Baker, reserving an undivided 1/2 of the oil and gas).

A mineral interest consists of several "incidents," which courts identify and describe in a variety of ways. A common formulation divides the mineral interest into four incidents: (1) the right to use the surface; (2) the right to incur costs and to retain profits (the right to develop); (3) the right to alienate; and (4) the right to retain lease benefits. Each of these incidents may be carved separately from the mineral interest or from the fee.

(1) The right of access to and use of the surface. The owner of a mineral interest owns the mineral rights described in the conveyance or reservation, together with the right to use the surface and subsurface as reasonably necessary to explore for, develop, and produce the minerals. Even if this right of access and use (very similar to and often called an

easement) is not expressed in the severance instrument, it will be implied because access to and use of the surface and subsurface are generally necessary to exploit the minerals. Thus, implying such a right is consistent with what the parties to the instrument presumably intended. Indeed, most definitions of the mineral interest specifically refer to the right of access and use. For example, an oil and gas mineral interest is generally described as the right to enter and use the property described in the instrument as reasonably necessary to explore for, develop, and produce oil and gas. In states that follow the ownership in place theory (discussed in the preceding subsection), the mineral interest also includes a possessory right in the oil and gas in place beneath the property—subject, of course, to the law of capture. When this right of access and use is exercised, the surface owner may allege that the mineral owner's surface (or water) use is unreasonable. Terms such as *surface owner, owner of the surface interest,* or *surface estate* are often used to describe the interest of a landowner who owns the entire interest other than the mineral interest or owns a fractional mineral interest along with a possessory surface interest.

(2) The right to incur costs and to retain profits. A mineral owner who seeks to explore, develop, and produce minerals will incur the cost of these operations. When the extracted minerals are used or marketed, the owner may make a profit. Thus, the mineral interest is both a cost-bearing and profit-sharing interest. One who has the rights to use the surface, to incur costs, and to retain profits is generally identified as having a *working interest* (or *operating interest*) in the minerals. An owner who has only a right to share in any profits of an operation is commonly identified as having a *net profits interest.* If Doan, a co-owner of a tract, elects to develop minerals without co-owner Carr sharing in the cost of development, Carr would be commonly identified as the owner of a *carried interest* (or *nonparticipating working interest*), *i.e.*, a net profits interest. On the other hand, if Carr did participate with Doan in the costs of development, Carr would have a working interest.

(3) The right to alienate. A mineral interest is freely alienable. Accordingly, a mineral owner may transfer all or portions of the mineral interest to another party. A transfer may take the form of a "mineral deed," a "royalty deed," a "mineral (oil and gas) lease," or some other instrument. Examples of these instruments are found in the Oil and Gas Forms Manual. Whether the right to alienate may be owned separately from the other incidents of the mineral interest is uncertain—at least in some jurisdictions. The right to alienate, however, may be owned along with a smaller fractional interest in the minerals. For example, Able may own an undivided 1/4 mineral interest in Blackacre together with the right to alienate the full mineral interest. In this circumstance, as well as in other similar circumstances, Able's right to alienate is commonly called the *executive right.* The owner of the other 3/4 interest owns a *nonexecutive mineral interest.* The executive right may also be limited in scope. For example, Able's right to alienate may be limited to a right to lease the

minerals. In this situation, the nonexecutive mineral owners would retain the other alienation rights.

(4) The right to retain lease benefits. Fee owners and mineral owners commonly execute oil and gas leases. An oil and gas lease typically reserves certain lease benefits in the lessor. As consideration for executing and conveying the lease, the lessee pays the lessor an initial cash payment called a *bonus*. Most leases also provide for periodic *delay rental* payments to the lessor prior to development by the lessee. After development, the lessor may be entitled to *shut-in* royalty payments (typically where gas is discovered but not yet produced or where production of gas temporarily ceases). After production, the lessor is entitled to a *royalty,* a share of the production (or a share of the value of the production) free of production costs. Each of these lease benefits may be separately owned and quantified. For example, Able might convey the mineral interest in Blackacre to Baker, reserving all executive rights plus 1/2 of any lease bonus and 1/4 of any lease royalty.

The oil and gas *leasehold interest* is similar to a mineral interest in that the lessee receives all incidents of the mineral interest except those specifically reserved in the lessor. During the term of the lease, the lessee holds the rights to use the surface, to incur costs, and to retain profits (subject to the lessor's benefits, such as royalty). Accordingly, the lessee owns the *working interest* (or *operating interest*).

As discussed above, the lessor usually retains a right to a bonus, delay rental, shut-in royalty, and production royalty. In addition, the lessor retains what is often described as a *possibility of reverter;* that is, upon expiration of the oil and gas lease, all incidents of the mineral interest revert to the lessor. Because an oil and gas lease is generally issued for a specified term of years and "so long thereafter as oil or gas is produced in paying quantities," the lessee's interest is often described as being in the nature of a *fee simple determinable* or a *profit* of determinable duration. Accordingly, the lessor is often said to retain a *possibility of reverter,* although some courts may refer to this interest as a *reversion.* These matters will be further clarified in Chapter 2. For now, just be patient; however, if you surmise that the law of oil and gas leases bears little relationship to landlord-tenant law, you are correct!

The lessor's reserved royalty under an oil and gas lease has already been mentioned. A *royalty interest,* however, may be created in a number of circumstances. Each circumstance may be specifically identified. For example, Able, the fee owner (or mineral interest owner) of Blackacre, may convey a royalty interest (e.g. 1/16 royalty) to Baker. Or Able may convey Blackacre to Baker, reserving a 5 percent royalty interest. Royalties created by these two methods are often referred to as *nonparticipating royalties.* The lessor's reserved royalty under an oil and gas lease is often called the *landowner's royalty* or *lease royalty.* A royalty carved from the lessee's working interest is usually called an *overriding royalty.* For example, an oil and gas lessee may assign the lease, reserving an over-riding royalty, or simply convey an overriding royalty to a third party.

All of the above royalty interests have common characteristics. The owner of a royalty interest is entitled only to a share of production (or a share in the value or revenues of the production) as expressed in the instrument that creates the royalty interest. A royalty owner has no right to use the surface (except perhaps for the limited purpose of collecting the royalty), no right nor obligation to incur costs, and no right to share profits. Because a royalty owner is not obligated to incur costs of exploration, development, and production, a royalty interest is often called a "non-cost-bearing" interest. A person who owns only a royalty interest has no right to execute an oil and gas lease. Thus, by its nature, a royalty interest is a *nonexecutive* interest, although a royalty owner may convey the royalty interest itself.

The owner of a nonparticipating royalty interest does not share in the lessor's lease bonus and delay rental benefits; however, the royalty reserved in the lease may determine the nonparticipating royalty owner's share of production. For example, Able might convey Blackacre to Baker, reserving 1/2 of all royalties under any existing or future lease. Baker may lease Blackacre, reserving a 1/8 landowner's royalty. In this circumstance, Able's reserved nonparticipating royalty would be 1/16 (1/2 of 1/8).[79]

Some mineral interests, some royalty interests, and the typical oil and gas lease have determinable durations. These and other oil and gas interests having a duration less than a fee simple absolute are commonly called *term interests* (or more appropriately *terminable interests*). For example, Able may convey Blackacre to Baker, reserving "an undivided 1/2 interest in the oil and gas for a term of 10 years and so long thereafter as oil or gas is produced." This is a common example of a *term (terminable) mineral interest*. True *term mineral interests*, which are not common, have a flat duration (*e.g.*, 10 years).

Louisiana's civil law regime and Mineral Code do not recognize "common law" mineral and royalty interests. Instead, Louisiana law provides for a *mineral servitude* and a *mineral royalty*. These interests, along with the oil and gas lease, are the only severed interests that may be created respecting minerals, fugacious or otherwise. The holder of a mineral servitude has the exclusive right to explore for and to develop minerals. The holder of a mineral royalty has a right to share in gross production free from the costs of production. Both a mineral servitude and a mineral royalty automatically terminate and are prescriptively acquired by the landowner if the holder of the servitude fails to exercise the exploration and development rights for ten consecutive years. Accordingly, as a matter of law, the mineral servitude and mineral royalty are term interests.[80]

---

79. Due to the inherent differences between a mineral interest and a royalty interest, a drafter must be careful to prepare an instrument that creates the interest intended by the parties. Failure to do so often leads to litigation. These problems are discussed in Chapter 4.

80. Many other common law oil and gas interests may be carved from a mineral interest or fee. For example, Able may convey Blackacre to Baker, reserving 1/2 of all oil and gas produced

G. A FURTHER LOOK AT TRESPASS AND TRESPASS–RELATED CLAIMS

The physical and practical realities concerning the oil and gas resource often give rise to complex legal issues that would be fairly simple in other contexts. For example, as illustrated in *Garza*, above, subsurface trespass issues are more difficult to deal with than surface trespasses, but you have learned that drilling a slant hole beneath another's property without permission is a trespass. In *Wronski*, you learned that oil and gas can be converted. This section further considers trespass-related claims in other oil and gas contexts.

The complexity of oil and gas property interests, combined with their speculative and real values, creates doubt and dispute over "who" owns "what" in a particular property. When the existence or scope of a person's oil and gas property right is disputed, trespass will frequently be the underlying theory used to define the parties' rights. For example, the lessee may believe their oil and gas lease is still in effect; the landowner may think otherwise. The lessor purporting to grant lease rights may not have title to the underlying minerals. The parties to a lease may disagree concerning the scope of the rights granted. A lessee's activities on the premises may give rise to a trespass claim; the landowner's interference with the lessee's activities may give rise to a trespass claim. Either party may try to seek damages for slander of title when one denies the rights of the other. Once title is found lacking, the unauthorized production of oil and gas will generate conversion claims.

Third parties may raise claims when an exploration or development activity interferes with their property interests. For example, a lessee's geophysical activities may collect information concerning the mineral potential of surrounding lands. The drilling process may cause a well bore to penetrate adjacent lands; a frac job may create a fissure in the productive formation that extends into adjacent lands. Injected produced water may migrate to adjacent lands.

The threshold question in these cases is usually a determination of title to the interests in dispute. Once the title issue is resolved, the next problem is determining factually what has transpired regarding the property. If you can't "see" the property interest, it will be easier to interfere with it, either by accident or surreptitious design. What goes on at considerable depths below the surface of the earth is, by necessity, a matter of technical expertise and opinion. Once the facts are ascertained, the relative rights and obligations of the parties arising from their

---

until Able shall have received $50,000 worth of production. This interest is commonly called a *production payment,* an interest often used as a financing device. Like a royalty interest, it is non-cost bearing, but the interest terminates when the agreed sum has been paid. The oil and gas industry has devised a number of other agreements that create various contractual rights. These interests include letter agreements, farmout agreements, operating agreements, and pooling and unitization agreements. These agreements are defined and discussed in Chapters 2 and 5.

respective ownership interests must be defined and potential remedies identified.

1. GEOPHYSICAL AND EXPLORATION TRESPASS

When searching for oil and gas, geologists and geophysicists typically employ devices and techniques that can provide useful subsurface information. Among the devices used for geophysical exploration are the gravity meter, magnetometer, and seismograph. The density of subsurface rocks can be measured with a gravity meter, sometimes called a "gravimeter," which measures variations in the earth's gravitational pull. This information assists the geologist in determining whether particular rock material is of a type commonly associated with oil and gas deposits. The "magnetometer" measures the intensity of the earth's magnetic field and can also be used to predict the type of rock being measured. The seismograph has evolved as the primary device to predict subsurface geologic conditions.

The seismograph is used in seismic surveys of land which traditionally involve the drilling of shallow holes, called "shot holes," in which an explosive is detonated. Today, instead of using explosives to create the necessary shock waves, truck-mounted vibration devices are often used. The energy or shock waves generated by the explosions or vibrations are measured by "geophones" placed at specified locations and intervals on the surface. The shock waves travel at varying speeds through rock material and are reflected at different rates by the various types of subsurface rock. This data gathered by the geophones is transmitted to a seismograph. This data is enhanced by computer processing and then interpreted by a technician, typically a geophysicist. The ultimate goal is to construct an accurate "picture" of subsurface rock structures and to identify subsurface rock material. This information will be used, along with other available geological data, to make drilling and development decisions.

During the past three decades, significant advances have been made in seismic technology. Extensive geophysical research and improved computer technology have aided the progression of seismic technology from its original, and frequently unreliable, two-dimensional ("2D seismic") mode to three-dimensional ("3D seismic") status. 3D seismic can provide a much more accurate geometrical representation of the rock structure, rock material, and probable contents. For developed oil and gas fields, 3D seismic gathered through time can be used to map the actual movement of oil and gas within the reservoir. This time-lapse 3D seismic, sometimes called "4D seismic" can help maximize the recovery of hydrocarbons from a reservoir. For a comprehensive discussion of 3D seismic and its potential legal implications, see: Owen L. Anderson & John D. Pigott, 3D Seismic Technology: Its Uses, Limits, & Legal Ramifications, 42 Rocky Mtn. Min.L.Inst. 16–1 (1996).

PROBLEM

Geophysical Testing Services has hired you to assist in obtaining the right to conduct geophysical work on Blackacre, a 640–acre tract located in the county where you practice. The Blackacre property records reveal the following transactions:

2005—O, owner of fee simple absolute, conveys "all the oil, gas and other minerals in and under and that may be produced from" Blackacre to A.

2006—A Conveys 1/2 of "The Mineral Interest" to B.

2007—B Leases to X Company.

From whom must Geophysical Testing Services obtain permission to conduct seismic work on Blackacre? What are Geophysical Testing Services's potential liabilities if the required permission is not obtained? What should Geophysical Testing Services do if it cannot obtain the required permission?

ENRON OIL & GAS COMPANY v. WORTH

947 P.2d 610 (Okla.Civ.App.1997).

GOODMAN, PRESIDING JUDGE.

This is an appeal from an order denying the plaintiff's quest for an injunction to prevent surface owners from interfering with seismic exploration for minerals. The issue is whether the owner of an unleased, undivided mineral interest may authorize a third party to enter onto the surface of land owned by another to conduct seismic operations. Based upon our review of the record on appeal and applicable law, we reverse and remand with directions.

I

Defendant Virgil Worth and his mother, defendant Frieda M. Webb, own the surface of six quarter sections in Texas County, Oklahoma, used as farm land. The land owned by Worth and Webb is part of a multi-section prosect [sic] in which Enron Oil & Gas Company wanted to conduct seismic operations to test for oil and gas formations. In May 1996, an agent of Enron approached Worth and offered to pay $5 per surface acre, plus any incidental damage to crops, for permission to enter upon the land. Worth did not accept the offer and denied Enron access to his land.

On August 20, 1996, Enron filed a petition alleging the defendants "have interfered and prevented Enron, its agents and employees, from entering * * * to conduct seismic operations." Enron sought declaratory and injunctive relief. The trial court issued a temporary restraining order, and set a hearing for August 29 "at which time Defendants will be given an opportunity to show cause why the * * * restraining order should not be made a temporary injunction."

The defendants counter-claimed alleging seismic testing would cause "substantial damage" to their land, Enron had not agreed to compensate them for damages, and their actual damages would be compounded because portions of the proposed testing area were "designated for a 1996–97 wheat crop, which will need to be planted immediately * * * weather conditions permitting." The defendants sought actual and punitive damages.

After a hearing September 6, 1996, the trial court dissolved the temporary restraining order and granted Enron a temporary injunction covering the three quarter sections of the defendants' land for which Enron had obtained mineral leases or farmout agreements. With respect to the remaining three quarter sections, Enron argued it had "obtained its seismic permits from unleased mineral owners who clearly had the right to sever exploration rights (i.e. the right to conduct seismic testing) from the right to drill * * *." The court stated its belief that, although the mineral owners have the right to conduct geophysical exploration, they cannot sever that right from the right to drill and produce by granting permits to Enron. The court ordered the parties to submit briefs addressing the legal effect of the seismic permits.

On September 13, 1996, the court denied Enron's request for a temporary injunction covering the remaining three quarter sections. The court held that mineral owners "have an absolute right to go upon the property of the surface owner to the extent necessary to explore for or develop minerals located beneath the surface." However, because the "permits" did not grant Enron the right to drill and remove hydrocarbons, or require it to share the results of the seismic testing with the mineral owners, the court held that Enron did not have the right to go upon the land to conduct seismic testing, and that "Oklahoma law allows owners of surface interest only to allow geophysical exploration of minerals [which] would in no way damage or interfere with the right of the mineral owner." The court also held Enron had failed to prove irreparable harm, and the duration of seismic operations had been "totally unreasonable and * * * surface owners should not be subjected to having their farm land taken out of cultivation as a result of geophysical surveys for unreasonable durations of time." The court did not enter judgment on the defendants' counterclaims. * * * Enron appeals.

II

Enron contends the trial court erred in holding that, when the surface and mineral estates have been severed, an undivided mineral interest owner cannot separately convey the right of reasonable ingress and egress upon the surface for the limited purpose of conducting geophysical exploration, without conveying the other rights comprising the mineral estate, such as the right to develop and produce the minerals. We agree.

It is well settled that an owner of a mineral estate which has been severed from the surface has the exclusive right of reasonable ingress and egress upon the surface for purposes of exploration, development, and production of minerals. Even if a mineral owner has executed an oil and gas lease conveying his mineral rights to another, unless the terms of a lease expressly grant the lessee the exclusive right to conduct geophysical exploration, a lessor retains a corollary right to authorize a third party to conduct such operations. * * * And where, as here, the undivided mineral interest is not subject to a lease, all rights comprising the mineral estate are vested in the mineral owner.

In *Hinds v. Phillips Petroleum Company*, 591 P.2d 697 (Okla.1979), the lessee executed a contract conveying to a third party purchaser the right of "free entry" upon the surface to lay and maintain lines and equipment necessary for removal of hydrocarbons. The landowner sued to recover in trespass for unauthorized use of the premises by the third party. He argued the lessee's "attempt to sever and separately convey a portion of its surface rights in the oil and gas lease was legally a nullity [a]bsent assignment of [lessee's] entire 'dominant estate' in the oil and gas lease * * *." *Id.* at 698. The court disagreed, noting the distinction "recognized in our law between real estate and an estate in real property." *Id.* at 699. The lease-conferred easement to use the surface, said the court, is "clearly divisible if permissibly severed [and is] separately alienable under our law" without consent of the property owner. *Id.* The court concluded: "[L]easehold interests are freely alienable under our law, either in whole or in part. An exclusive right in the nature of a profit a-prendre, if granted in gross, may be transferred in gross, either in whole or in part. Divisibility is permissible so long as the servient owner's estate does not become burdened beyond the terms of the grant." *Id.*

We likewise find that a mineral owner may sever and assign the surface easement for the limited purpose of conducting geophysical exploration. The trial court erred in holding to the contrary, and in holding permission of the surface owner is required "to allow geophysical exploration of minerals * * * unless the grant of minerals excludes said right." We have examined the "seismograph permit[s]" executed by the mineral owners in favor of Enron, and "it is clear that alienation of separately severed lease-conferred interests was clearly within the parties' contemplation." *Id.* at 700. * * *

We hold the permits in question validly transfer to Enron the right of ingress and egress upon the surface of the defendants' land for the limited purpose of conducting geophysical exploration thereon.

III

The defendants argue that if such a conveyance is permissible, the "permission of all fractional minerals owners is necessary to conduct seismic exploration." We disagree.

When a mineral estate is divided among more than one owner without reservation, the undivided interest owners become tenants in common, and each "may enter upon the premises for the purpose of exploring for oil and gas and may drill and develop the premises [but not] to the exclusion of the other * * *." *Earp v. Mid–Continent Petroleum Corp.*, 167 Okla. 86, 89, 27 P.2d 855, 858 (1933). As we have seen, a mineral owner has the right to enter the servient estate for exploration purposes, and may sever that right and assign it to a third party. "While, as tenants in common, each has an undivided interest in the oil and gas under every part of the land, still each has a separate and distinct-right to enter and develop his portion when not to the exclusion of the other cotenants, and one has no more interest in the right of the other to develop than a stranger. It follows that when one assigns his right to develop the others have no interest in his efforts to cancel the assignment." *Knox v. Freeman*, 182 Okla. 528, 531, 78 P.2d 680, 682 (1938).

We hold that joinder of the other interest owners is not required to effectively transfer the rights of an individual owner of an undivided interest in a mineral estate. The defendants' argument is without merit.

IV

Finally, Enron contends the trial court erred in finding that Enron failed to prove its allegation it would suffer immediate and irreparable harm if an injunction is not granted, and that Enron's use of the surface since May 1996 had been unreasonable. We agree.

* * *

As discussed above, Enron had a legal right to enter the defendants' land to conduct geophysical exploration. In the unappealed portion of the proceedings below, the trial court correctly found Enron had a legal right to conduct geophysical exploration and, implicitly found Enron had sufficiently supported its petition for an injunction. We have carefully examined the evidence, and find and hold that same evidence demonstrates irreparable harm and necessity to support issuance of a temporary injunction for the land subject to this appeal. The appealed order is reversed, and the matter is remanded with directions to the trial court to grant Enron the relief requested.

REVERSED AND REMANDED WITH DIRECTIONS.

TAYLOR, V.C.J., and REIF, J., concur.

NOTES

1. In *Enron*, the court held that an owner of an undivided mineral interest can authorize geophysical exploration of the mineral interest. Thus, an owner of a tiny percentage of the mineral interest can authorize geophysical operations. Contrast the Oklahoma rule with the approach taken by the Louisiana Mineral Code, at La. Rev. Stat. Ann. § 31:166, which provides, in part:

> A co-owner of land may grant a valid mineral lease or a valid lease or permit for geological surveys, by means of a torsion balance, seismographic explosions, mechanical device, or any other method as to his undivided interest in the land but the lessee or permittee may not exercise his rights thereunder without consent of co-owners owning at least an

undivided eighty percent interest in the land, provided that he has made every effort to contact such co-owners and, if contacted, has offered to contract with them on substantially the same basis that he has contracted with another co-owner. * * *

Why does Louisiana have this statute?

2. Enron's petition alleged that the surface owners "have interfered and prevented Enron, its agents and employees, from entering * * * to conduct seismic operations." 947 P.2d at 612. What legal theory(ies) would Enron rely upon to support its claim against the surface owners?

3. Enron's agent offered to pay the surface owners $5 per surface acre plus compensation for damage to crops "for permission to enter upon the land." 947 P.2d at 612. Assuming the mineral deed severing the surface from the oil and gas rights was silent on the matter, would Enron owe the surface owners anything for the right to enter the surface? If not, why did it offer to pay the surface owners? Is there a danger in offering payment when none is due? See Ronald W. Polston, Surface Rights of Mineral Owners—What Happens When Judges Make Law and Nobody Listens? 63 N.D.L.Rev. 41, 62 (1987) ("If the mineral owner has no expectation that the use of the surface estate will be free of charge, then there is no problem with a statute that requires payment for surface damage.").

4. Would Enron owe the surface owners anything for damages to the surface arising out of the seismic operations? Would the Oklahoma surface damages act require surface damage payments? Okla.Stat.Ann. tit. 52, § 318.3 requires a party "preparing to drill for oil or gas" to negotiate surface damages with the surface owner "[b]efore entering upon a site for oil or gas drilling * * *." Anschutz Corp. v. Sanders, 734 P.2d 1290, 1291 (Okla.1987) (seismic exploration activity not encompassed by statute requiring negotiation of surface damages associated with "oil and gas drilling"). Many states have adopted surface damage acts that expressly include exploratory activities. E.g. N.D.Cent.Code § 38–11.1–03(2) (" 'Drilling operations' means the drilling of an oil and gas well and * * * oil and gas geophysical and seismograph exploration activities * * *."); S.D.Codified Laws Ann. § 45–5A–3(2) ("Mineral development" includes "the exploration for or drilling of an oil and gas well or mineral test hole which requires entry upon the surface estate"). In 1998 Oklahoma enacted the "Seismic Exploration Regulation Act," which requires persons conducting seismic work to register with the Oklahoma Corporation Commission and to obtain a permit for each seismic exploration operation. All applicants must post a bond and provide the surface owner with statutory notice regarding the proposed seismic operations. The Act prohibits conducting "seismic test hole blasting" within 200 feet of any "habitable dwelling, building or water well" unless written permission is obtained from the property owner. Okla. Stat. Ann. tit. 52, §§ 318.21 through .318.23.

5. Even though the surface owners have no agreement with Enron concerning surface damage compensation, suppose the oil and gas leases or exploration license agreements with the mineral owners stated: "Enron will compensate lessor/licensor for any damage done to the surface of the land during the conduct of seismic operations authorized by this agreement." Would such an agreement confer any rights on the surface owners? See

Cornwell v. Jespersen, 708 P.2d 515 (Kan. 1985) (lessor was third party beneficiary of surface reclamation covenants contained in drilling contract between lessee and drilling contractor); Hazelwood Farm, Inc. v. Liberty Oil and Gas Corp., 790 So.2d 93 (La.App.2001) (severed surface owner was third party beneficiary, beneficiary of a "stipulation *pour autrui,*" of lessee's promise to "be responsible for all damages caused by his operations" contained in oil and gas lease with mineral owner).

KENNEDY v. GENERAL GEOPHYSICAL CO.

213 S.W.2d 707 (Tex.Civ.App.1948, writ refused n.r.e.).

MONTEITH, CHIEF JUSTICE.

This action was brought by appellant, C.W. Kennedy, Jr., for the recovery of damages alleged to have been sustained by him by reason of the acts of appellees, General Geophysical Company and Skelly Oil Company in securing information as to the presence or absence of oil, gas or other minerals in and under a tract of 339 acres of land belonging to him in Houston County, Texas, and for an alleged trespass in the form of vibrations caused by explosions of dynamite in conducting geophysical operations in close proximity to appellant's land. He sought exemplary damages by reason of the alleged willful and malicious acts of appellees in conducting such operations and in the securing of such information.

In the trial before the Court, without a jury, judgment was rendered in favor of appellees and that appellant take nothing by his suit.

* * *

[The] appellant was the owner of 339 acres of land in the vicinity of these operations, and on or about August 1, 1947, an agent of appellee General Geophysical Company requested appellant's permission to conduct geophysical operations on his land, and that he was informed by appellant that he could neither "shoot" his land or the land along the road adjoining his land without paying for the right to do so;

The court found that neither appellees nor their agents or employees went upon or "shot" any part of appellant's land, and that the General Geophysical Company did not place any "shot-point," receiving set, or recording trucks on any part of said land, but that it did "shoot" land near plaintiff's land, one of such "shots" being within 10 or 15 feet of the boundaries thereof, but that on no occasion of such "shooting" did a straight line running from such "shot-point" to a "receiving set" or "jug" cross any part of plaintiff's land; that the shots and receiving sets were placed along or on a public road or highway adjoining the land at distances of 150 feet apart;

The court found that the vibrations received by these receiving instruments or "jugs" go down from the "shot-point" vertically and then back up to such receiving sets or "jugs," and that by the interpretation of these vibrations so received and recorded, information is gotten relative to the depth points under such receiving sets and that no interpretation or geophysical information as to plaintiff's land was given Skelly Oil Company by either the General Geophysical Company or its agents; and that no receiving sets were placed on said land; that the appellees got no reliable information as to the sub-surface structure under appellant's land by reason of the "shooting" and that any information that appellees may have gotten as to sub-surface structure under plaintiff's land would be based on assumption or supposition that the sub-surface structure under plaintiff's land, was the same as that along the road adjacent to the land on which the receiving sets were placed;

The court found that there was no evidence introduced upon the trial as to the extent and intensity of either the horizontal or vertical vibrations emanating from the explorations at the "shot-points" except that the vertical vibrations going straight down and back to the receiving sets were sometimes sufficient to be received by the "jugs" several hundred feet away from the points of "shooting"; and that it is a physical impossibility to control or govern the direction of the vibrations emanating from the explorations at the "shot-point"; that these vibrations extend horizontally and vertically from the points of explosion, and that the extent thereof is governed by the intensity of the explosion, and also by the character of the earth's structure through which the vibrations go;

He found that there was no evidence that appellant suffered any physical damage to his land by reason of the explorations at the point of shooting near his land; and

That neither the General Geophysical Company nor the Skelly Oil Company or their agents acted with malice or were prompted by malice in making the explorations complained of by appellant.

* * *

Only two witnesses testified on the trial of the case—appellant C.W. Kennedy and John Clements, an employee of General Geophysical Company, who was the party chief of the exploration truck which conducted the geophysical operation. Mr. Clements testified that by such geophysical explorations they obtained "depth-points" approximately directly beneath the "receiving sets" or "jugs." There is no evidence in the record as to whether any information was secured in reference to the sub-surface structure and/or the problematical presence of oil, gas or other minerals.

Under appropriate points of appeal appellant contends that the trial court erred in finding as a matter of fact that appellees gained no information as to plaintiff's land. He contends that the court should have taken judicial notice of the scientific fact, in the absence of evidence to the contrary, that the slope, dip or trend of a given subsurface formation continued with the same slope, dip or trend of the last point known, and that the court should have taken judicial notice of the scientific facts that appellees by the geophysical operations acquired information as to the sub-surface formation and the probable presence or absence of oil, gas, or other minerals in and under appellant's land and that such information was a valuable property right for the taking of which plaintiff should be entitled to damages.

There is no evidence in the record that, when a dip or slope of a sub-surface formation is determined in one locality, it will necessarily follow that the same dip or slope continues uniformly under adjoining land, and there is only one reference in the record to the value of information alleged to have been secured by appellees, for which appellant seeks damages, the testimony of appellant that he would not sell that information to his exclusion for $5000.

No testimony or evidence of any nature was introduced by appellant to dispute the statements by Mr. Clements that appellees gained no information in reference to appellant's land, nor was any evidence introduced tending to establish appellant's contention that the trial court should have taken judicial notice of the fact that the slope, or trend of a given sub-surface formation continues with the same slope, dip or trend past the last point definitely known.

* * *

* * * [T]he trial court could not, we think, have taken judicial notice of the scientific fact that the slope, dip or trend of a given sub-surface formation continued with the same slope past the last point definitely known. Further we think that appellant wholly failed to sustain his burden of proof that the appellees, by the use of seismograph operations, obtained information regarding the sub-surface structure or the presence or absence of oil, gas or other minerals in or under appellant's land, and, appellant having made the gaining of such information an indispensable element of his cause of action, his failure to make proof of his allegations with regard thereto renders the question irrelevant.

And the trial court, we think, correctly concluded that no trespass was committed upon appellant's land.

In discussing the question as to whether concussive waves transmitted into the lands of another constitutes a legal wrong and a trespass, it is said in 63 Corpus Juris, page 898, that:

> Trespass may also be committed by shooting onto or over the land, by explosions, by throwing inflammable substances, by blasting operations, by discharging soot and carbon, but not by mere vibrations.

* * *

In 4 Summers, Oil and Gas, § 661, at pages 68 and 69:

> It is submitted, therefore, that where one explodes a charge of dynamite to test his land for oil and gas purposes and thereby causes the earth to vibrate and as a proximate result of such vibration the personal property of a neighboring owner is injured, such injury should be compensated in damages. Taking into consideration the fact that the use of explosives is positively necessary for the discovery of mineral structure by this method (seismic exploration), that such

operations are not continuous, and that damage by vibration is of occasional occurrence, a court should not enjoin the use of the seismograph but leave the injured party to his remedy in damages.

It is unnecessary to place this liability for damage upon the ground that the explosives used in their nature or their use are inherently dangerous. Such a theory is only necessary to overcome the necessity of showing negligence in keeping explosives or establishing their use in certain localities as a nuisance per se. Nor does it seem advisable to attempt to base the liability upon the theory that the vibration amounts to an actual physical trespass. To constitute trespass there must be an entry upon the land. In many cases of injury by vibration the physical invasion might well be considered an entry upon the land, but certainly every vibration of a neighbor's land is not a trespass. Where is the line to be drawn? If at the point where the vibration causes appreciable physical injury, such a line coincides with the actor's liability for consequential injury.

* * *

In the case of *Universal Atlas Cement Company v. Oswald et ux.*, Tex.Civ.App., 135 S.W.2d 591, 593, affirmed 138 Tex. 159, 157 S.W.2d 636, it is said:

There is a conflict of authority as to whether one, who by blasting by powerful explosives produces severe concussions or vibrations in surrounding earth and air and so materially damages property belonging to others, is liable, irrespective of negligence on his part. All authorities hold that where there is an actual invasion of the premises of another by the throwing of dirt, stone or debris, proof of negligence is unnecessary to a recovery of damages. Others hold that in the absence of an actual physical invasion of the premises, no recovery can be had unless negligence is shown. 22 Amer.Jur. 180; 25 C.J. 192. There are some cases in Texas which seem to support this latter view. *Comanche Duke Oil Co. v. Texas Pacific Coal and Oil Co.*, Tex.Com. App., 298 S.W. 554; City of *Dallas v. Newberg*, Tex.Civ.App., 116 S.W.2d 476. This theory seems to have some reasonable foundation in those cases where the damage or annoyance is caused solely by noise or concussion of the air, for in those cases there is in fact no physical invasion of the premises; * * *.

* * *

In the instant case the trial court found on what we deem to be ample evidence that appellees were in no way negligent in their operations; that on no occasion did General Geophysical Company set up a receiving set so near appellant's land that a straight line drawn on the surface of the ground from the one shot-point from which waves were to be received by the receiving set crossed any part of plaintiff's land.

The trial court further found that neither the appellees nor their agents acted with malice or were prompted by malice. Appellant was, therefore, not entitled to exemplary damages, since exemplary or punitive damages may only be recovered in an action of trespass where actual damage has been sustained. * * *

It follows from these conclusions that the judgment of the trial court must be in all things affirmed. It is so ordered.

Judgment affirmed.

Notes

1. Geophysical operators have relied upon the principal case when they cannot obtain permission from the mineral owner of a given tract. Geophysical "lines" are "shot" as close as possible to the property to which access is denied, but information as to the geophysical structures under that property is not recorded. Does the reasoning of the principal case offer adequate protection for the geophysical explorer in such a situation?

2. By the reasoning of *Kennedy*, would damages for trespass have been awarded to the mineral owner if geophysical information from under his land had been recorded? See Ohio Oil Co. v. Sharp, 135 F.2d 303 (10th Cir.Okla. 1943). On what theory can damages be awarded where there is no physical trespass to the surface? Could you apply the theories of trespass, nuisance, invasion of privacy, theft of trade secrets, unjust enrichment, or interference with prospective advantage? See generally Sonya D. Jones, Comment, Time to Make Waves? A Discussion of the Outdated Application of Texas Law to Seismic Exploration, 38 Tex. Tech L. Rev. 429 (2006); Sean Laughlin, Comment, Why a Mineral Lessee Should Not Be Found Guilty of Geophysical Trespass: A Cogent Interpretation of Louisiana Revised Statute 30:217, 49 Loy. L. Rev. 975 (2003); Owen L. Anderson, Geophysical "Trespass" Revisited, 5 Tex. Wesleyan L. Rev. 137 (1999); Thomas M. Warner, Jr., Note, Oil and Gas: Recovery for Wrongful Geophysical Exploration—Catching Up with Technology, 23 Washburn L.J. 107, 118–126 (1983); Mark D. Christiansen, Note, Oil and Gas: Improper Geophysical Exploration—Filling the Remedial Gap, 32 Okla.L.Rev. 903 (1979); and Scott S. Slater, Note, The Surreptitious Geophysical Survey: An Interference With Prospective Advantage, 15 Pac.L.J. 381 (1984).

3. 3D seismic, due to its greater accuracy, can present even greater problems when it is acquired without the consent of all interest owners. Professor Anderson and Dr. Pigott offer the following thoughts on 3D seismic and geophysical trespass:

> A primary legal concern for a geophysical operator is to obtain permission from the owner of the exploration right to avoid what is often called "geophysical trespass." Proper permitting minimizes the possibility that a geophysical operator will be sued for trespass or other tort. This concern is greater for those engaged in 3D seismic operations because large areas may be involved, because detailed surveys require more intense surface use, and because the target of a 3D seismic survey may include the gathering of data from beneath tracts that are beyond the lands actually occupied during the course of geophysical operations. Moreover, because 3D seismic is often regarded as highly reliable, favor-

able information can be very valuable to those who have it, and unfavorable information can greatly lower the speculative value of "wildcat" acreage. Thus, actionable geophysical operations can have grave consequences for the culpable party.

Owen L. Anderson & John D. Pigott, 3D Seismic Technology: Its Uses, Limits, & Legal Ramifications, 42 Rocky Mtn.Min.L.Inst. 16–1, 16–67 to 16–69 (1996) (footnotes omitted) [hereinafter cited as Anderson & Pigott]. See also Harry L. Blomquist III, Geophysical Trespass? The Guessing Game Created by the Awkward Combination of Outmoded Laws and Soaring Technology, 48 Baylor L.Rev. 21 (1996).

    4. In some instances geophysical information may be obtained from overflights or from data relayed from space satellites.

> Where recovery is sought on the theory of assumpsit, tortious conduct is often involved but need not be present. Accordingly, recovery may be had in assumpsit for photographing and aerial reconnaissance whether or not a trespass is involved. For example, recovery in assumpsit has been allowed when the aerial reconnaissance did not involve a trespass. If the aerial reconnaissance includes landing on the land in question, the trespass so committed may be waived and recovery had in assumpsit if the value of the right of exploration is proved.
>
> If the value of the right exercised cannot be established and a trespass has not been committed, another avenue of recovery may be sought. It has been suggested that the law relating to improper means of obtaining trade secrets should be applied.

Kuntz § 12.7 at 349–50. As a practical matter, a mineral owner is not likely to know that geophysical information has been gathered from under his lands unless the acquiring party enters onto the surface.

    5. Following an exhaustive study of geophysical trespass, and 3D seismic technology, Professor Anderson and Dr. Pigott propose applying a "rule of capture" analysis to the acquisition of geophysical information:

> [W]e agree that the right to explore for minerals is a valuable property right and that a mineral owner should have the right to control geophysical oil and gas operations that involve direct entry onto or beneath such owner's parcel; however, we submit that the mineral owner of a target parcel should have no cause of action when seismic data are gathered from the target parcel solely through the use and occupancy of nearby parcels. In short, we reject the argument that the intentional gathering of seismic data from a target parcel solely by geophysical operations conducted on nearby parcels is wrongful, immoral, unethical, and unreasonable (and thereby constituting "geophysical trespass") if permission is not secured from a mineral owner of the target parcel. We reach these conclusions even though we concede that the use of 3D seismic techniques may often result in the gathering of information that geophysicists and their principals would regard as valuable, useful, and reliable. Nevertheless, we submit that this manner of gathering seismic data should fall within the venerable rule of capture.

* * * Accordingly, we submit that the gathering of seismic data by a mineral owner (or such owner's seismic permittee) by geophysical operations conducted on such owner's parcel and concerning the possible presence of oil or gas beneath a neighbor's parcel should be treated no more restrictively than the drilling of a producing well on such owner's parcel that drains oil or gas from a neighbor's parcel or than the drilling of a dry hole on such owner's parcel which results in the loss of speculative value to a neighbor's parcel.

Anderson & Pigott, at 16–111 to 16–113 (1996) (footnotes omitted). Would such an approach adequately protect the interest of the mineral owner? Could a court adopt this approach without "taking" existing property rights? See also Kendor P. Jones, Restrictions on Access and Surface/Subsurface Trespass Involving Exploration and Production Technologies, 40 Rocky Mtn.Min.L.Inst. 20–1, 20–33 to 20–34 (1994).

6.   In contrast to the facts of *Kennedy*, the land beneath public highways may be owned by the adjoining property owners, subject to an easement or right of way. Would the result in *Kennedy* have been different if the plaintiff had owned the fee beneath the adjacent road?

7.   Who owns geophysical information acquired by an oil and gas lessee in the process of exploring the leased land? See *Musser Davis Land Co. v. Union Pacific Resources*, 201 F.3d 561, 570 (5th Cir.La. 2000) (lessee "entitled to the ownership of the seismic data it develops pursuant to its prudent and reasonable geophysical operations incidental to its exercise of the exclusive right to explore and produce oil and gas under the lease."). What if the lessee was acting pursuant to an oil and gas lease from fewer than all of the mineral interest cotenants? Would it matter if the party acquiring the seismic information obtained permission from a cotenant through a seismic permit instead of an oil and gas lease? Why do you suppose Louisiana amended its Mineral Code to require the consent of 80% of the mineral co-owners to issue a "valid * * * permit for geological surveys, by means of a torsion balance, seismographic explorations, mechanical device, or any other method * * *."? La. Rev. Stat. Ann. § 31:166. Can a valid geophysical permit be obtained from a life tenant? What if the mineral estate has been severed by depth and the lessee owns only the deep rights in the property they wish to explore? See Owen L. Anderson, Geophysical "Trespass" Revisited, 5 Tex. Wesleyan L. Rev. 137, 150–59 (1999).

GRYNBERG v. CITY OF NORTHGLENN
739 P.2d 230 (Colo.1987).

LOHR, JUSTICE.

This case was brought by Jack J. Grynberg, the owner of a coal lease from the State of Colorado, claiming that his rights were violated when the City of Northglenn drilled a test hole within the lease boundaries without Grynberg's permission and disclosed the results of the test in a report filed in the public records of the state engineer. The test results showed an absence of commercially recoverable coal deposits. Northglenn had drilled the hole with the permission of the owner of the severed surface estate for the purpose of determining the suitability of the area as a site for a wastewater reservoir. The trial court granted summary judgment for defendant Northglenn and the other defendants, all of whom had participated in drilling the test hole, based on the finding and conclusion that they had no actual or constructive notice of Grynberg's lease, which had not been recorded in the county real estate records, and that the defendants were entitled to the protection of Colorado's recording statute, section 38–35–109(1), 16A C.R.S. (1982). The Colorado Court of Appeals affirmed in *Grynberg v. City of Northglenn*, 703 P.2d 601 (Colo. App.1985). We granted certiorari and now reverse the judgment of the court of appeals and remand the case for further proceedings.

I.

The relevant facts are established by documents in the record and are not in dispute. In late 1977, the City of Northglenn began a search for potential sites for a wastewater reservoir which would become part of a comprehensive wastewater treatment project. One of the sites selected was the West half of Section 36, Township 1 North, Range 68 West of the 6th P.M., in Weld County, Colorado (the site).

In order to assess the suitability of the site for construction of a reservoir, Northglenn made plans to drill test holes, including one deep hole to determine whether the site contained commercial deposits of coal. The exploration for coal deposits was to be accomplished to obtain information relevant to zoning and to securing the approval of the state engineer.

In order to ascertain the ownership of the site, Northglenn searched the Weld County records, including the records of the county clerk and recorder. This search revealed that the surface estate of the site was owned by a private corporation not a party to this lawsuit and that the severed mineral estate was owned by the State of Colorado. The search also disclosed that the State of Colorado had issued a coal lease to Clayton Coal Company (Clayton Coal), recorded June 6, 1975, that had a primary term of ten years and covered the site. Although the State of Colorado also had issued a coal lease to Jack J. Grynberg including the site together with the remainder of Section 36, Township 1 North, Range 68 West of the 6th P.M. (Section 36), dated July 13, 1977, for a primary term of ten years, that lease had not been recorded in the Weld County records. As a result, Northglenn's search did not disclose the existence of that lease. Northglenn had no actual knowledge of the existence of the Grynberg coal lease.

Prior to conducting any drilling, Northglenn contacted Clayton Coal and learned that it had assigned its coal lease to Adolph Coors Company (Coors). Northglenn then inquired of Coors and was informed that Coors had determined that any coal within the leasehold boundaries was not economically recoverable, and that Coors therefore had abandoned the coal lease.

In December 1977, Northglenn received a proposal for the sale of the surface estate from its owner. Following negotiations, Northglenn entered into an agreement to purchase the surface estate on March 3, 1978, and acquired that estate on June 1, 1978. In late February of 1978, during the course of the negotiations leading up to the sale, Northglenn obtained the permission of the surface owner and drilled test holes on the site. Northglenn never sought permission of the State of Colorado, the record owner of the mineral estate in the site, to accomplish the testing. * * *

The drilling conducted by Northglenn consisted of a number of shallow holes and one that was 600 feet deep. In performing this work defendant Sheaffer & Roland, Inc. acted as general contractor, defendant Chen and Associates, Inc. (Chen) was the soils engineering consultant and supervised the drilling, and defendant Arrow Drilling Company drilled the holes. None of these companies had actual knowledge of the existence of the Grynberg lease during the times relevant to this litigation.

Chen prepared a preliminary engineering geology and soils investigation report based in part on information obtained from the deep test hole drilled on the site. The report stated that the hole was drilled to evaluate the extent of coal deposits in the area and concluded that "it is our opinion that the coal in Section 36 * * * does not represent a potentially recoverable resource." Information in the report included the geologic and other data required by the state engineer in order to approve the proposed reservoir. On or about April 25, 1978, Chen filed the report in the state engineer's office where its contents became public information. The state engineer thereafter approved the plans and specifications for the proposed reservoir.

Northglenn first learned of the Grynberg lease when Grynberg contacted the city in mid-May of 1978 to express concern about the drilling activity on the property. Grynberg then brought suit against Northglenn, Sheaffer & Roland, Inc., Chen, and Arrow Drilling Company, based on theories of trespass, assumpsit, wrongful appropriation of geologic information, interference with prospective business advantage, and negligence. The asserted injury that provides the principal basis for all of these claims, directly or indirectly, is the loss of market value of Grynberg's coal lease as the result of the discovery and publication of information that the coal reserves on the property have no commercial value. The defendants filed answers and then moved for summary judgment. Plaintiff Grynberg filed a cross-motion for partial summary judgment on certain issues of liability. * * *

The defendants argued in support of their summary judgment motions that they had no actual notice of the Grynberg lease and were not on constructive notice of that lease because it had not been recorded with the Weld County Clerk and Recorder. Therefore, they argued, under Colorado's recording act, section 38–35–109(1), 16A C.R.S. (1982), the Grynberg lease was not valid as to them. * * * Although the district court acknowledged that Grynberg's lease was valid as to the State of Colorado, the court concluded that the lease was ineffective as to the defendants as a result of Grynberg's failure to record it in the county records. Consequently, the court ruled that Grynberg's claims, all of which were predicated on injury to his rights under the coal lease, must fail. Based on this analysis, the district court granted the defendants' motions for summary judgment and denied Grynberg's cross-motion for partial summary judgment.

Grynberg appealed, and the court of appeals affirmed the summary judgments. *Grynberg v. City of Northglenn,* 703 P.2d 601 (Colo.App.1985). That court held that the recording act by its own terms extends protection to "any class of persons with any kind of rights" and does not limit the persons protected to bona fide purchasers and encumbrancers. 703 P.2d at 602. The court also held that Northglenn obtained protected rights by securing permission to drill from the owner of the surface estate and ultimately purchasing the surface estate. *Id.* at 603. * * * Concluding that Northglenn was entitled to rely on the condition of title disclosed by the records of the county clerk and recorder, the court sustained the summary judgments. *Id.* Grynberg then petitioned for certiorari, and we granted that petition.

II.

It is well recognized that the surface and mineral estates in real property can be severed and separately owned. * * * Separate ownership of the surface and mineral estates creates obvious tensions in attempting to assure full use of each estate without injuring the other. The broad principle by which these tensions are to be resolved is that each owner must have due regard for the rights of the other in making use of the estate in question. The specific issue central to the resolution of the case now before us is whether the owner of a severed surface estate has the authority to grant permission to conduct drilling, a form of geologic testing, in order to explore for mineral deposits. This issue is critical because Northglenn relies entirely on permission from the surface owner to support the argument that its drilling activity was authorized.

A.

Courts in modern times have had occasions to consider the accommodation of the respective rights of mineral and surface owners in consenting to exploration for minerals. Generally, it can now be said that whoever has authority to execute a mineral lease on the land may grant a geophysical exploration permit.[1] Brown, *Geophysical Trespass,* 3 Rocky Mtn.

---

1. Geophysical exploration is described as "[t]he search for geologic structures favorable to the accumulation of petroleum by means of geophysical devices." H. Williams & C. Meyers, *Manual of Oil and Gas Terms* 318 (5th ed. 1981). Geophysical devices include gravity meters, magnetometers and seismographs. *Id.* Modern technology has further expanded the inventory of scientific devices used to accomplish geophysical exploration. Rice, *Wrongful Geophysical Exploration,* 44 Mont.L.Rev. 53 (1983). Although the geologic testing in the present case was conducted by core drilling and the object of the search was coal, not petroleum, the principles applicable to geologic testing are the same as those that apply to the broader category of testing procedures characterized as geophysical exploration. The essence of each type of exploration is the search for geologic information concerning the existence of a valuable natural resource. In the case of core

Min.L.Inst. 57, 59 (1957) (*"Brown"*). Where, as here, the surface estate has been severed from the mineral estate, "it is clear from the decided cases that the mineral owner, rather than the surface owner, is the one who has the right to conduct geological and geophysical operations." 1 E. Kuntz, *Law of Oil and Gas* § 12.7, at 280–81 (1962). * * * The recognition of the exclusivity of the right of the mineral owner to consent to such exploration is based upon the central importance of information concerning mineral deposits to the value of the mineral estate. * * * We conclude, therefore, that the permission obtained by Northglenn from the owner of the surface estate was insufficient to authorize Northglenn to drill in search of mineral deposits,[2] * * *.

* * *

III.

It is undisputed that Northglenn did explore the site for coal deposits, and that such exploration was without the consent of either Grynberg as the owner of the coal leasehold interest or the State of Colorado as the owner of the mineral estate.[3] Grynberg contends that Northglenn's actions, as pleaded, invaded his rights as lessee. We agree.

The issue of the right of the owner of a mineral estate or the lessee of such a mineral interest to complain of unauthorized geologic exploration has not yet been addressed by this court. However, several other jurisdictions have allowed recovery for damages incurred due to an unauthorized geophysical exploration, and a tort often characterized as geophysical trespass[4] appears to be well established.

---

drilling, the issue is somewhat simplified by the fact that this exploration method necessarily involves entry onto the land in question, whereas some types of geophysical exploration can be conducted from locations outside the boundaries of the property explored. *See, e.g., id.*

2. Northglenn did not seek permission from the State of Colorado, the record owner of the mineral estate as disclosed by the records in the clerk and recorder's office in Weld County. In oral argument before this court Northglenn confirmed that it does not assert that it derived any rights from Clayton Coal or from Coors, which had abandoned the coal lease that it had obtained by unrecorded assignment from Clayton Coal.

3. In the present case there remains a question whether the State of Colorado as owner of the mineral estate had joint authority with Grynberg to give permission for geologic testing of the property for coal or whether that authority was vested exclusively in Grynberg as lessee. The resolution of that issue is dependent upon the terms of the lease. *See Brown* at 61–62; R. Hemingway, *Law of Oil and Gas* § 4.1 (2d ed. 1983). It is undisputed that Northglenn did not obtain or seek permission to conduct geologic exploration from either the State of Colorado or Grynberg. Therefore, it is unnecessary to determine whether the state could have given permission for the testing.

4. In Rice, *Wrongful Geophysical Exploration,* 44 Mont.L.Rev. 53 (1983), it is argued that the tort should be recognized as a new one, wrongful appropriation of the right to explore, and that traditional legal theories such as trespass or conversion do not logically or historically fit this new tort. *Id.* at 53. One reason that the trespass theory is not always apt is that unauthorized geophysical exploration does not necessarily involve physical entry. Nevertheless, judges and commentators commonly use the term "geophysical trespass" as a rubric for this invasion of the right to explore for minerals. In the present case, the plaintiff asserts claims based on several different theories, including trespass. We consider it prudent to leave for the district court the determination of which, if any, of the plaintiff's theories of recovery are appropriate under the facts of this case.

[A] Geophysical trespasser [is] "one who conducts geophysical operations upon the lands of another without permission or consent. Such an explorer may also be deemed a trespasser where the consent or permission obtained is for any reason ineffectual, or where the operations conducted are in excess of the consent or permission granted."

Brown at 62–63 (quoting Hawkins, The Geophysical Trespasser and Negligent Geophysical Explorer, 29 Tex.L.Rev. 310, 314 (1951)). The reasons for recognizing unauthorized exploration of mineral rights as an invasion of the interest of the mineral owner are well explained in Layne Louisiana Co. v. Superior Oil Co., 209 La. 1014, 26 So.2d 20, 22 (1946), as follows:

It is a well-known and accepted fact in this, the third largest producing oil State, that the right to geophysically explore land for oil, gas or other minerals is a valuable right. Large sums of money are annually paid landowners for the mere right to go upon their land and make geophysical and seismograph tests. The information obtained as the result of such tests is highly valuable to the person or corporation by whom they are made. If the information thus obtained be favorable, it can be used and is used in dealing with the landowner for his valuable mineral rights. If the information be unfavorable, the fact quickly becomes publicly known and thus impairs the power of the landowner to deal advantageously with his valuable mineral rights. The average landowner is without means or funds to secure geophysical or seismograph information. Where that information, which is exclusively his by virtue of his ownership of the land, is unlawfully obtained by others, the landowner is clearly entitled to recover compensatory damages for the disregard of his property rights.

Although Northglenn did have the surface owner's permission to enter upon the land, it engaged in unauthorized geologic exploration contrary to the rights of the mineral interest holder and its lessee by drilling a test hole to determine the existence and extent of coal deposits. See 1 E. Kuntz, *Law of Oil and Gas* § 12.7 (1962).

IV.

Northglenn argues that even if its drilling activities would otherwise have contravened Grynberg's rights as lessee under the coal lease, Grynberg's claims are defeated by his failure to record that lease. We disagree. * * *

* * *

As discussed in part II of this opinion, rights to conduct geologic testing for minerals can be derived only from or through the owner of the mineral estate. Northglenn obtained no permission to conduct testing from the State of Colorado or Grynberg, the only possible sources of such permission. The ownership of the mineral estate by the State of Colorado clearly appeared from the county clerk and recorder's records. Northglenn sought and obtained permission only from the owner of the severed surface estate. That owner had no ability to give effective consent to geologic testing and nothing in the county records suggested to the contrary. Therefore, since Northglenn obtained no right from anyone who could authorize geologic testing or who appeared from the county clerk and recorder's records to possess such right, we conclude that Northglenn and the other defendants did not possess "any kind of rights" with respect to geologic testing that would entitle them to the protection of the recording act.

* * *

V.

We hold that the trial court erred in granting summary judgment for the defendants. * * *

The judgment of the court of appeals is reversed and the case is returned to that court for remand to the trial court with directions to conduct further proceedings consistent with the views set forth in this opinion.

NOTES

1.   Upon remand to the trial court, Grynberg abandoned its tort claims against the City of Northglenn and proceeded under an inverse condemnation theory to avoid the City's governmental immunity defense. The trial court awarded $862,155.05 in compensation, attorney fees, and prejudgment interest. The trial court's judgment was affirmed by the court of appeals. Grynberg v. City of Northglenn, 829 P.2d 473 (Colo.App.1991). However, on appeal, the Colorado Supreme Court ruled that no compensable "taking" had occurred and reversed the award. City of Northglenn v. Grynberg, 846 P.2d 175 (Colo.1993), cert. denied, 510 U.S. 815 (1993). Without purporting to determine whether geophysical information is a "trade secret," the court nevertheless employed a trade secret analysis to determine whether the City's wrongful acquisition and publication of the geophysical information constituted the taking of a property right. The court reasoned that since the same information was available from public sources, to recover, Grynberg, had to prove how the additional information obtained by the City's drilling and reporting had caused him damage. The United States Geological Survey ("USGS") and a prior coal lessee, Adolph Coors Co., had each previously drilled test holes in Section 36; their logs were available to the public and they were consistent with the Northglenn findings that no commercial deposit of coal was in the area. The court directed that the case be remanded to the trial court for dismissal of Grynberg's inverse condemnation action. Are you satisfied that nothing of value was taken from Grynberg? Assuming you represent Grynberg and the court remanded the case to the trial court for further proceedings, what evidence would you like to obtain to try to address the court's trade secret analysis? See generally James W. Griffin, Comment, Protectable Property Rights, Trade Secrets, and Geophysical Data After *City of Northglenn v. Grynberg*, 71 Denver U.L.Rev. 527 (1994).

2. Would a lessee having the exclusive right to explore for and produce "oil, gas, casinghead gas, other hydrocarbons (whether liquid or gaseous), carbon dioxide gas and sulfur" be entitled to information concerning coal core samples taken from the leased land by the lessor? Assuming the lessee's rights include methane gas, would the lessor be able to conduct desorption tests on the coal to determine its methane gas content? If the lessor's desorption tests indicated the coal contained potentially large quantities of methane gas, would the lessor have a duty to share this information with the lessee? See Mallon Oil Co. v. Bowen/Edwards Associates, Inc., 965 P.2d 105 (Colo.1998) (lessor of oil and gas rights, who was also owner of the coal rights, could conduct desorption tests to determine the methane content of the coal as part of the process of evaluating the value of their coal deposit; coal owner had no obligation to obtain permission from oil and gas lessee or to inform the lessee of the test results).

3. The oil and gas lease may not grant to the lessee the "exclusive" right to use the land for oil and gas purposes, and the lessor may have the right to permit others to conduct geophysical searches on the property. Justifying that result, the federal district court in Mustang Prod. Co. v. Texaco, Inc., 549 F.Supp. 424 (D.Kan.1982), aff'd, 754 F.2d 892 (10th Cir.Kan. 1982), noted that:

> These rights [to drill for, produce and market oil and gas] can hardly be granted to more than one person: oil can't be taken from the ground more than once, any more than a game animal can be hunted and eaten more than once. But there is no inherent inconsistency in granting different persons the right to conduct geophysical exploration, because they need not interfere with each other's activities, just as the game animal that can only be eaten once can be photographed innumerable times.

549 F.Supp. at 425.

Is this argument convincing? Is there a public policy rationale for the result reached in *Mustang Production Co.?* See Comment, Non–Exclusive Rights of Lessees to Conduct Geophysical Exploration—Federal and Wyoming State Oil and Gas Leases, 3 Land & Water L.Rev. 103, 106 (1968).

4. The City of Northglenn's exploratory activities revealed that the coal reserves beneath the land had no commercial value. Hasn't this action benefitted Grynberg since he will not have to spend his own money on fruitless exploration? Before attempting to answer this question, consider the case that follows.

2. DRY–HOLE TRESPASS

HUMBLE OIL & REFINING CO. v. KISHI

276 S.W. 190 (Tex.Com.App.1925).

BISHOP, J. In this case both the Humble Oil & Refining Company and K. Kishi have filed applications for writs of error, and there is here presented for review the holding of the Court of Civil Appeals on all questions discussed in its opinion. 261 S.W. 228. We agree with the conclusion reached by the Court of Civil Appeals on all questions except its holding that proof of the market value of the leasehold interest in the land involved did not in law furnish the measure of damages which should be awarded, and only such statement of the case is here made as is deemed necessary to a discussion of this holding.

K. Kishi, the owner of all the surface and three-fourths undivided interest in the oil and mineral rights, and Isaac Lang, the owner of the remaining one-fourth interest in the oil and mineral rights of 50 acres of land in Orange County, Tex., executed to the Humble Oil & Refining Company a lease granting to it the exclusive right to enter upon said land and drill oil wells and take therefrom the oil. This lease was of date December 23, 1919, but was not signed and acknowledged by Lang until January 29, 1920, and was thereafter delivered to said Humble Oil & Refining Company. By its provisions it was to remain in force for no longer period of time than three years from its date, unless within said three years drilling for oil was commenced. No drilling was begun within the time provided, and the lease expired. After the expiration of this lease, in January, 1923, oil was found on an adjoining tract of land in a well drilled near this 50 acres. On January 23, 1923, the Humble Oil & Refining Company entered upon this 50 acres of land, and began drilling an oil well thereon, claiming the exclusive right to the leasehold interest therein. It claimed that the lease had not expired, and that under its terms it did not expire until three years after it was signed and acknowledged by Lang and delivered. Kishi protested against this entry, and advised the Humble Oil & Refining Company that he would hold it responsible for any damages that might accrue to him. Lang, however, consented to the entry under the claim made.

The Humble Oil & Refining Company remained in possession under this entry until it completed the drilling of the well, which resulted in the failure to find oil, and it relinquished possession on May 10, 1923. As a result of the discovery of oil on the adjoining tract of land, the leasehold interest in the 50–acre tract was of the market value of $1,000 per acre. At the time the Humble Oil & Refining Company relinquished possession, and thereafter the leasehold interest had no value by reason of the failure to find oil on this tract.

In suit by Kishi against the Humble Oil & Refining Company for damages sustained by him, the district court awarded him nominal damages in the sum of $1 only, holding that the amount of damages sustained by him was uncertain and not susceptible of proof. On appeal from this judgment the Court of Civil Appeals held that he was under the facts entitled to recover the actual damages occasioned by reason of the wrongful entry and ouster which was the value to him of his three-fourths undivided leasehold interest, but that proof of the market value of the entire leasehold interest was not in law sufficient upon which to base the amount of his recovery.

Oil in place under the land is real estate. The exclusive right to enter upon the land, drill wells thereon, and remove therefrom the oil to exhaustion, paying therefor a portion of the oil when extracted or the equivalent of such portion, is a property right which the law protects. The Humble Oil & Refining Company, wrongfully claiming to own this right over the protest of Kishi, and excluding him therefrom, entered upon his 50 acres of land for the purpose of drilling the well. This was clearly a trespass and ouster. This right had a market value of $50,000, being $1,000 per acre. Had Lang not consented, and had he and Kishi joined in a suit to recover their damages for the wrongful entry, the measure of their damages would have been the market value of the leasehold interest which is here shown to be $1,000 per acre. Lang would have been entitled to one-fourth and Kishi to three-fourths of the amount recovered. We can conceive of no reason why Kishi should be permitted to recover either a larger or smaller amount, because it is shown that Lang consented to the entry.

The Humble Oil & Refining Company insists that it should not be required to pay as damages Kishi's proportionate share of the market value of this leasehold interest, because it entered upon the land in good faith, believing that its lease had not expired. Though it did so in good faith, without any intention to injure Kishi, it asserted a right it did not have. This right, at the time it was wrongfully asserted, had a market value. Had the oil company acquired this right by purchase before its entry, the presumption of law is that it would have been required to pay the market value therefor. Had it done so, Kishi would have been entitled to receive three-fourths of the market value of the leasehold interest. We think that in this case three-fourths of the market value of the leasehold interest was the measure of the damages which Kishi was in law entitled to recover, and that proof of the market value was in law sufficient upon which to determine the amount of judgment in his favor.

We therefore recommend that the judgment of the Court of Civil Appeals be reversed, and that the judgment of the district court be so reformed as to allow K. Kishi judgment against the Humble Oil & Refining Company for the sum of $37,500, with legal interest, and, as so reformed, that the judgment of the district court be here affirmed.

CURETON, C.J. Judgment of the Court of Civil Appeals reversed, and that of the district court reformed, and, as reformed, affirmed, as recommended by the Commission of Appeals.

NOTES

1. On the second motion for rehearing, the court in *Kishi* modified somewhat its stance on the issue of damages. The trial court had found that the land could be leased for $1,000 per acre. The Commission of Appeals recognized that a three-fourths undivided interest might not be worth $750 per acre, because the undivided nature of the interest might be taken into account by a lessee. The court thus remanded the case for a determination of

damages. Humble Oil & Refining Co. v. Kishi, 291 S.W. 538 (Tex.Com.App. 1927).

2. The nature of the wrong in *Kishi* has been obscure. In Byrom v. Pendley, 717 S.W.2d 602 (Tex.1986), the Texas Supreme Court undertook to clarify it.

> We disagree with Pendley's attempt to extend *Kishi* to cases involving entry by a cotenant while denying the validity of his cotenant's interest. Rather, we construe the *Kishi* decision as holding that a lessee of mineral interests who enters the land after termination of the lease and termination of the right to enter is liable to his nonconsenting lessor for injury resulting from such unlawful entry.

717 S.W.2d at 605.

3. Not all jurisdictions agree with the result of the *Kishi* case. See Martel v. Hall Oil Co., 253 P. 862, 866 (Wyo.1927) (court refused to grant damages for revealing the absence of mineral value noting "the defendants, by their trespass, made the truth known" thereby denying plaintiffs the ability to sell worthless mineral rights to an unsuspecting public).

4. In Phillips Petroleum Co. v. Cowden, 241 F.2d 586 (5th Cir. Tex. 1957), the court concluded that under Texas law the owner of a mineral estate that had been subjected to unauthorized seismic operations could waive the trespass and sue in assumpsit for the reasonable value of the use and occupation of the property. It rejected both the plaintiff's measure of damages, which was based on the value of the exploratory rights on the entire 2,682-acre ranch, and the defendant's argument that it was liable only for the value of the information pertaining to the perimeter around each seismic shot hole. The court reasoned that a recovery in assumpsit should be "based on an implied promise whose assumed terms should conform fairly closely to the sort of agreement that might actually have been reached by reasonable parties * * *." 241 F.2d at 593–94. Could the plaintiff in *Cowden* have recovered for the reduced market value of his mineral estate if the geophysical work had indicated the land was of minimal productive potential? See Angelloz v. Humble Oil & Refining Co., 199 So. 656 (La. 1940). Regarding loss of speculative value, see Kuntz § 12.10.

3. WET–HOLE TRESPASS

Where the wrongful interference results in production, the most common remedies are trespass and conversion, coupled with the equitable remedy of accounting. Normally the rightful owner will be able to recover the value of the trespasser's production. Disputes usually center on whether the wrongdoer will be able to recover any costs associated with its successful development activities. The ability of the wrongdoer to recover its development and operating costs will depend upon the wrongdoer's good faith, as well as the rightful owner's good faith and diligence in pursuing a remedy.

The refusal to reimburse development costs is a form of punitive damages designed to punish the wrongdoer for bad faith interference with another person's oil and gas interests. The court in Athens & Pomeroy Coal & Land Co. v. Tracy, 153 N.E. 240, 244 (Ohio App. 1925), characterized the rule as "nothing more or less than the application of a fixed rule for exemplary damages imposed as a matter of public policy." Some states employ a similar "fixed rule" regarding conversion. Recall in *Wronski*, above, Sun was held to have converted Wronski's oil by violating production limitations imposed by the State of Michigan. Although there was no trespass involved, the court applied the "harsh" rule of damages which valued the converted oil—the oil produced in excess of the production limits—at its value after extraction without allowing deduction of any costs associated with bringing the oil to the surface. The court noted that punitive damages could not be assessed when the "harsh" rule was applied because: "Application of the 'harsh' rule of damages includes an amount for punitive damages and may not be assessed twice." *Wronski*, 279 N.W.2d at 572. Cf., Leach v. Biscayne Oil & Gas Co., Inc., 289 S.E.2d 197 (W.Va. 1982) (trespassing operator who cleared an access road and installed equipment liable for punitive damages that were about five times greater than actual damages.)

Intentional trespass and conversion is rare. Disputes usually occur where the trespasser errs in claiming the right to develop and market minerals from the land in question. However, the trespasser's assertion of title must have been made in good faith for the trespasser to avoid the "harsh" measure of damages. See Alaska Placer Co. v. Lee, 553 P.2d 54 (Alaska 1976) (applying the rules developed in oil and gas cases to tin mining claims). Courts have generally defined good faith in broad terms. The definitions vary and are often unclear about whether good faith is to be measured by a subjective or an objective standard. See, e.g., Swiss Oil Corp. v. Hupp, 69 S.W.2d 1037, 1039, 1041 (Ky. 1934). For good faith, "the defendant must have an honest belief in the superiority of his right or title, and such belief must be a reasonable one in the light of the circumstances." Kuntz § 11.5.

Most courts treat good faith as a defense and place the burden of proof on the trespasser to prove that the trespass was in good faith; however, in Oklahoma, the plaintiff must prove the trespasser's bad faith to recover gross proceeds. See Sapulpa Petroleum Co. v. McCray, 277 P. 589 (Okla.1929).

Although good faith is usually a question of fact, some courts have ruled that a company acts in bad faith as a matter of law if it drills while litigation is pending over the validity of its claim to title. See Davis v. Cramer, 793 P.2d 605 (Colo.App.1990), judgment reversed on other grounds, 808 P.2d 358 (Colo.1991); Houston Prod. Co. v. Mecom Oil Co., 62 S.W.2d 75 (Tex.Com.App.1933); NRG Exploration, Inc. v. Rauch, 905 S.W.2d 405 (Tex.App.1995, writ denied). The Texas Supreme Court refused to apply this rule to an analogous situation involving cotenant lessees. In Byrom v. Pendley, 717 S.W.2d 602 (Tex.1986), a lessee filed suit seeking to have another party's lease of a fractional interest in the same land declared void. While the suit was pending, the plaintiff lessee entered and drilled a producing well. Although the plaintiff lessee was unsuccessful in having his cotenant's lease removed as a cloud on title, the court refused to treat him as a bad-faith trespasser. The court said there was no distinction between a cotenant who drills without another cotenant's consent and a cotenant who drills while asserting that his cotenant's lease is defective. Thus, the producing lessee had to account for the other cotenant's share of the net value of the oil and gas produced.

Most courts assume without discussion that an oil and gas lessee who remains in possession after the end of its lease is subject to a trespass action. For example, in Hunt v. HNG Oil Co., 791 S.W.2d 191 (Tex.App. 1990, writ denied), a lessee plugged back a deep dry hole to a shallower, producing formation after its lease had expired. The court held that the lessee had trespassed in good faith. But in Imperial Colliery Co. v. Oxy USA Inc., 912 F.2d 696 (4th Cir.W.Va.1990), a federal court, construing West Virginia law, held that an oil and gas lessee that continued in possession after its lease has ended should be treated as a holdover tenant. The court reasoned that the underlying wrong is a breach of contract, not a trespass; thus, the defendant's liability should be limited to the fair rental or royalty value of the leasehold plus any special damages. In Bryan v. Big Two Mile Gas Co., 577 S.E.2d 258 (W.Va.2001), the West Virginia Supreme Court rejected the holdover tenant/reasonable royalty analysis and applied an innocent(good faith)/willful (bad faith) trespass analysis to a lessee that remained in possession following a cessation of production that terminated the lease. Based on the facts, the court concluded that the lease terminated after cessation of production in 1979 but found that the lessee's failure to vacate the premises at that time was not willful; however, the court found the lessee's failure to leave the premises following a 1987 cessation was willful.

NOTES

1. When accounting to the true owner for produced oil and gas, a good-faith trespasser is entitled to deduct the reasonable costs of drilling, completing, equipping, and operating the well to the extent that such costs conferred benefits upon the true owner. Under what circumstances could the true owner successfully argue that he did not benefit from drilling and completion costs? See Edwards v. Lachman, 534 P.2d 670 (Okla.1974) and Carter Oil Co. v. McCasland, 207 F.2d 728 (10th Cir.Okla.1953). Would a true owner ever receive a benefit from a dry hole drilled by a trespasser? See Joyce v. Zachary, 434 S.W.2d 659 (Ky.1968) and Champlin Refining Co. v. Aladdin Petroleum Corp., 238 P.2d 827 (Okla.1951).

Other reasonable costs cannot be deducted if they were not incurred during the trespass. In Hunt v. HNG Oil Co., 791 S.W.2d 191 (Tex.App.1990, writ denied), a lessee recompleted a previously drilled dry hole as a producer after its lease had terminated. In determining the extent of its liability to the landowner, the lessee was not allowed to take into account its initial drilling costs, because at the time they were incurred it was operating under a valid lease and not as a trespasser.

2. May a good-faith trespasser remove any equipment, such as production tubing and casing? In computing costs, may a good-faith trespasser deduct interest or a charge for risk capital? Overhead? Bonus or royalties paid a third party? Income tax? Legal fees for the drilling title opinion? What about the costs of drilling an initial dry hole before the producing well was drilled? If the applicable statute of limitations bars the true owner from recovering damages for all of the produced oil, should the trespasser have to reduce this cost by the value of that oil? See discussion and cases cited at Kuntz § 11.6.

3. In some situations a state's "occupying claimants" statute may assist the good-faith trespasser. For example, Kan.Stat.Ann. § 60–1004 provides, in part:

> Where any person while peacefully occupying realty under color of title in good faith, including mineral leases, has in good faith made improvements thereon or paid obligations in connection therewith, such person shall not be dispossessed by a party, establishing a superior right, claim or title until he or she is fully compensated therefor.

4. The limitations periods for trespass and conversion actions vary from state to state. Usually both statutes of limitation will run from the time of the trespass or conversion. However, in the case of concealment, such as trespass by directional drilling, the statute of limitation may not commence running until the rightful owner acquires information that would cause a reasonable person to inquire.

In some jurisdictions, including North Dakota, the rules of the oil and gas conservation commission require that deviation tests be run when any well is drilled or deepened. N.D.Admin.Code § 43–02–03–25. In addition, the commission may order specific directional surveys when the location of the bottom of the well is in doubt. Any person furnishing well deviation ("whipstock") equipment or services must report the name of the operator and well to whom such equipment or services were furnished. Id.

5. In the case of a producing well, the trespass and conversion are continuing. Therefore, the rightful owner may recover damages for any period within the respective statutes of limitations for trespass and conversion so long as title to the underlying property has not been lost through adverse possession. See Pan American Petroleum Corp. v. Orr, 319 F.2d 612 (5th Cir.Tex.1963) and Alphonzo E. Bell Corp. v. Bell View Oil Syndicate, 76 P.2d 167 (Cal.App.1938).

6. Generally, oil companies and production purchasers are extremely careful about titles. In the course of drilling, development, and production, several title examinations may occur for the same property. Where lease bonuses are high, a lessee may secure a lease acquisition title opinion. Often, however, a lessee may rely on a landman's memorandum of title at the leasing stage, but before drilling, the lessee will obtain a drilling title opinion. Upon obtaining production, the lessee or the purchaser of production will obtain a division-order title opinion to determine the parties entitled to share in production and royalties, and their specific share, usually carried to several decimal points. In addition, in the event the lessee's property is mortgaged, sold, or placed into a larger production unit, further title opinions will be secured.

4. SLANDER OF TITLE

Slander of title claims often arise as an adjunct to litigation over the continuing validity of an oil and gas lease or ownership of an oil and gas interest. Courts and commentators usually list five elements that a plaintiff must prove to recover in such an action: (1) publication by the defendant; (2) falsity of the publication; (3) malice; (4) financial damage; and (5) an estate or interest in the property slandered. See, e.g., Kuntz § 12.1; Smith & J. Weaver § 7.1; Williams & Meyers § 232. Some Texas cases have listed loss of a specific sale as a sixth element, e.g., Williams v. Jennings, 755 S.W.2d 874 (Tex.App.1988, writ denied). However, proof of a lost sale would seem more properly to be a limitation on the type of financial damage that must be shown, rather than an entirely separate element.

If the parties have a legitimate dispute over ownership of the property interest at issue, it will be difficult to satisfy the "malice" element to establish slander of title. For example, the court in Voiles v. Santa Fe Minerals, Inc., 911 P.2d 1205 (Okla.1996), observed:

> To prove malice in its slander of title action Santa Fe must prove actual malice or want of good faith. * * * this malice is not ill will or hatred, but a lack of good faith and want of probable cause.

911 P.2d at 1209–10. Professor Kuntz offers the following explanation of why proof of malice is essential to the plaintiff's case:

> The element of malice is used as the basis for determining which of two important policies will control. One important policy is that a person should be free to assert his property rights without penalty in the form of damages if it should develop that his title is bad. The other policy of equal importance is that a property owner should be assured of enjoyment of his property and should be free from the assertions of false claims by others, when the asserted claims serve to impair the merchantability of his title and the value of his ownership. The balance between such policies turns upon the purpose and motive with which the assertion of the property right is made. if the assertion of the property right is made with malice, it is wrongful.

Kuntz § 12.1. Consider the policy role served by the malice requirement in the case that follows.

KIDD v. HOGGETT

331 S.W.2d 515 (Tex.Civ.App.1959, writ refused n.r.e.).

POPE, JUSTICE.

Pierce A. Hoggett and wife sued Barron Kidd, A.W. Cherry, and others, to remove the cloud of an unreleased but expired oil and gas lease, and for damages. There was no jury. Upon trial defendants disclaimed with respect to the oil and gas lease. The court rendered judgment removing the cloud but also awarded damages against defendants Kidd and Cherry in the amount of $8,400. Only Kidd and Cherry have appealed from the judgment. Kidd and Cherry urge that the judgment for damages was erroneous because (1) they were under no duty to release the oil and gas lease because it was still in force and effect when demand was made upon them, (2) this is an action for slander of title and the plaintiffs, prior to the motion for judgment, failed to prove malice, which is an essential element of such actions, (3) an implied finding of malice is against the great weight and preponderance of the evidence, and (4) the action for damages is barred by the two-year statute of limitations. We affirm the judgment.

On April 24, 1944, the then owners executed an oil and gas lease to 2,871 acres of land. Plaintiffs are the present owners of 2,831 acres of the land, and Howell Wright owns the other 40 acres. On January 25 and 26, 1954, by assignments, A.W. Cherry and Barron Kidd became the owners of the oil and gas lease. This was a short time before the primary term of the lease expired, so they commenced a well on the 40–acre Wright tract. Cherry and Kidd took the position that the well was a producing well but there was no market for the gas from February 23, 1954, the completion date. The lease contained a shut-in gas clause which provided:

> * * * where gas from a well producing gas only is not sold or used, Lessee may pay as royalty $50.00 per well per year, and upon such payment it will be considered that gas is being produced within the meaning of Paragraph 2 hereof; * * *

The well was shut in and lessees paid shut-in royalty for the year commencing in April, 1954, and again for the year commencing in April, 1955.

Plaintiffs became suspicious about the well, because the gas from the well was not sold at a time when the Junction Natural Gas Company needed gas. In November, 1955, after they had accepted the shut-in royalty, plaintiffs demanded a release of the oil and gas lease, but defendants refused upon assurances that the well was a producer. On January 9, 1956, plaintiffs entered into a specific lease with Ray Albaugh by which he agreed to pay $2 an acre bonus and $1 an acre for the first year's rental. This lease was subject to plaintiffs' obtaining a release from Kidd and Cherry of the oil and gas lease of record. When plaintiffs failed to obtain the release, Albaugh refused to enter into his lease and in January, 1957, released to plaintiffs. At the time of the trial, the tract had no value for oil and gas purposes. Plaintiffs, therefore, proved actual damages of at least $8,493.

* * * Kidd and Cherry do not complain of that part of the judgment which removes the cloud from the title. A greater portion of the briefs is devoted to the study of the nature of this action. Plaintiffs take the position that in a suit for removal of cloud and for damages, that malice is not a necessary element, but that in any event they both pleaded and proved malice. Defendants take the position that this is a suit for slander of title, that malice is a necessary element, and that it was not proved.

A lessee is under a duty in Texas to release of record an expired oil and gas lease. If the duty is imposed by the lease, an action rests on contract. Where, as here, there is no such contractual provision, there is nevertheless a duty. Speaking of a refusal to release an expired oil and gas lease, it was said in Witherspoon v. Green, Tex.Civ.App., 274 S.W. 170, 171: "The law charged appellee with the duty of removing this cloud from appellant's title by the execution of a release of his apparent, though not actual, interest in the land."

There may be some confusion as to nature of the action for damages for breach of the duty to release an oil and gas lease. Is malice necessary in such an action as this, and if so, what kind of malice? When there is an actual trespass upon property, an ouster of and a repudiation of the title of the true owner, allegations of malice are not required. Also, by way of analogy, in the case of a wrongful levy of an attachment, malice was not essential to the recovery of actual damages.

Malice is an essential element to the recovery of actual damages in a suit for slander of title. To recover damages against one who, to protect himself, buys an outstanding title there must be proof of a bad faith purchase of said title for the purpose of maliciously asserting a claim against and a repudiation of the lessor's title. Malice is an element in a suit for damages for the wrongful filing of an abstract of judgment.

One who sues to remove the cloud of an unreleased oil and gas lease and goes further and seeks actual damages occasioned by the loss of a specific sale of an oil and gas lease is, in our opinion, seeking recovery for the disparagement of his title, or, as it is termed, slander of title. The one clear case on the point is Wheelock v. Batte, Tex.Civ.App., 225 S.W.2d 591. In that case Mr. Justice Hughes reasons, and we agree, that a lessee should be permitted the right to assert his good faith claims to valuable properties without incurring great risk of damages just because he leaves disputed rights to the decision of courts. Hence, a plaintiff should prove malice on the part of the one refusing to give the release, and a defendant may defend against actual damages by proof of his good faith claim.

How malice is defined, however, is another matter. Malice as a basis for recovery of actual damages, as distinguished from punitive damages should mean that the act or refusal was deliberate conduct without reasonable cause. See, 8 Institute on Oil and Gas, 357. Malice as a basis for recovery of punitive damages should mean actual malice, that is, ill will, bad or evil motive, or such gross indifference to or reckless disregard of the rights of others as will amount to a willful or wanton act.

The decision in this case is not as difficult as the law on the subject may be indefinite, since whether malice, of whatever kind, is necessary or not, it was amply alleged and proved by the plaintiffs. The recovery was only for actual and not punitive damages. Since the case was tried without a jury, we presume all fact issues supported by the evidence were found in support of the judgment. In our opinion the evidence supports plaintiffs' contentions that the well was not a producing well when completed or afterwards. The evidence and the inferences from the evidence support a finding of malice and that finding is not against the great weight and preponderance of the evidence. * * *

The well has never actually produced anything. From February 23, 1954, the completion date, to the date of the disclaimer in 1959, defendants did not work on the well. A drilling contractor of thirty-eight years experience stated that he was at the well three days after its completion, and he thought it had enough gas to supply a farm house. * * * Jack Barker, a gas tester for U.J. Bremmer and Sons, stated that he tested the well just before the trial, that the well flowed on an absolute open flow, 9,185 cubic feet during a little more than twenty-three hours, but that it went down to 49.8 cubic feet on the sixth day. Thereafter there was not enough volume to record the gas. On this basis the gross income from the well would be less than twenty-five cents a day. * * *

Defendants reason that the shut-in royalty maintained the well in force. Also they reason that there were gas potentials under the lease. Shut-in royalty payments excuse production only if the well is actually capable of producing gas in paying quantities. The completion of a non-producing well in an area of known gas reserves does not excuse a well capable of actual production. Defendants' reasoning reduces itself to the contention, that if they had drilled a well properly or if they would now drill another one, because of the known gas reserves, it would be a producing well. That is not such proof of a producing well which will permit shut-in royalty in lieu of actual production.

Bearing further upon defendants' malice was proof that the Junction Natural Gas Company, as early as the summer of 1954, was in actual need of gas. * * * [T]he gas company informed Kidd's organization of a desperate need for gas, but none was available from the well. The gas company was within a half mile of the Wright well, but instead of obtaining gas from that well, the gas company went out and drilled two other wells at a different place. * * * This was evidence that there was a ready market for gas, but that defendants had nothing to sell from the Wright well. On March 6, 1956, plaintiffs' attorney asked for a release but Mr. Kidd assured plaintiffs he was then trying to market the gas from the well.

While Kidd and his organization were telling plaintiffs and their attorney that the well was a good producing well, that it was a commercial well, and that all that was needed was a market which would be obtained shortly, they were at that very time unable to provide gas to a purchaser who desperately needed it. Plaintiffs' attorney told Kidd and his organization that they were going to lose the lease with Albaugh unless they gave a release, but they still stood on the proposition that the well was a commercial well. This and other evidence amply supports all necessary findings, including the inference that defendants knew the well was not a commercial well, though they were leading the landowners to believe it was; that they could not furnish gas to an available market when they were representing to the landowner that they could not obtain a market. While defendants were willfully and deliberately deceiving plaintiffs, plaintiffs suffered damages. Plaintiffs proved malice, however defined.

There is no merit to defendants' contention that plaintiffs' action was barred by the two-year statute of limitations, Vernon's Ann.Civ.St. art. 5526. The sale to Albaugh was lost in January, 1957. This suit was brought on June 27, 1958. In a slander of title suit, one necessary element of a plaintiff's proof is that he suffered special damages. Unless he can allege and prove that fact he has no cause of action. If frustration of a specific sale is necessary to prove a cause of action, the cause of action did not mature until the frustration occurred. Any other rule would mean that limitation was running against a plaintiff before he had a cause of action. See 8 Institute on Oil and Gas 374.

The judgment is affirmed.

NOTES

1. Slander of title claims are often asserted by a lessee against a top lessee. In Voiles v. Santa Fe Minerals, Inc., 911 P.2d 1205 (Okla.1996), the court found:

> In 1989 Oklahoma Hugoton Corporation (Hugoton) approached the lessors of the Santa Fe leases, or their successors, and paid each for what is known as a top lease,[81] an oil and gas lease to take effect only if the pre-existing lease should expire or be terminated. In the process Hugoton obtained from each lessor his or her authority to take the necessary steps to bring suit, in the name of the lessor, but at the expense of Hugoton, to judicially terminate the earlier leases, called base leases.

> As a result ten cases were filed in the District Court of Texas County by the mineral owners/lessors to quiet title to their mineral interests—and to cancel the base leases owned by Santa Fe. The gravamen of each suit was that Santa Fe had, from time to time, withheld production for a period of more than sixty days, and each lease contained a "cessation of production" clause providing for cancellation if production ceased for more than sixty days without commencement of drilling operations.

> * * *

> In each of the ten cases Santa Fe filed a third-party claim against third-party defendant Hugoton. Santa Fe's claims were based upon allegations of tortious interference with contract, slander of title, and champerty and maintenance.

911 P.2d at 1207–08. The court held that Hugoton had not acted with malice because its cessation-of-production theory had been recognized in a trial court judgment against Santa Fe in a similar suit. Although the theory was

---

81. [Editors' Note] A *top lease* is an oil and gas lease that is taken on property that is already subject to an oil and gas lease. The party taking the top lease either believes the existing lease has terminated or they intend for the top lease to take effect when, and if, the existing lease terminates. Lessees may top lease themselves if they are concerned about the base lease expiring before they have an opportunity to secure production.

ultimately rejected by the Oklahoma Supreme Court in Pack v. Santa Fe Minerals, 869 P.2d 323 (Okla.1994), the court found Hugoton acted in good faith, believing the mineral owners had a "colorable" claim that the leases had terminated.

Courts differ on meaning of malice in the slander of title context. See Kuntz § 12.1. For discussions of the measure of damages and other remedies for slander of title, see Restatement (Second) of Torts § 633; Kuntz § 12.2; Smith & Weaver § 7.2(f); and Williams & Meyers § 232.

2.   In the *Voiles* case, Hugoton also argued that the act of obtaining top leases could not constitute slander of title because the leases were drafted to take effect only if Santa Fe's base leases expired or were terminated. Would the act of taking such a contingent interest constitute the "uttering and publishing of the slanderous words" to satisfy the "publication" element for slander of title? Is it possible to draft a top lease to avoid clouding the title of the base lease owner?

3.   The element of publication usually involves an affirmative act. In *Kidd*, however, the element was provided by a failure to act. In many states, a statutory duty exists to release a terminated or forfeited oil and gas lease upon demand by the lessor. Whenever the validity of a lease is being challenged, any statutory procedures for demanding a release should be carefully considered since the procedures often establish an independent basis for damages and recovery of attorney fees. For example, Kansas imposes a statutory duty on lessees to "surrender" in writing any "oil, gas or other mineral lease" within sixty days after it has become "forfeited". Kan.Stat. Ann. § 55–201. If the lessee fails to record a release of the challenged lease, Kan.Stat.Ann. § 55–202 provides, in part:

> Should the owner of such lease neglect or refuse to execute a release as provided by this act, then the owner of the leased premises may sue in any court of competent jurisdiction to obtain such release, and the owner may also recover in such action of the lessee, his or her successors or assigns, the sum of one hundred dollars as damages, and all costs, together with a reasonable attorney's fee for preparing and prosecuting the suit, and he or she may also recover any additional damages that the evidence in the case will warrant. * * *

See Pierce § 8.08.

4.   Sometimes developers will obtain "protection" leases if there appears to be a problem with their lessor's title. In Santa Fe Energy Oper. Partners v. Carrillo, 948 S.W.2d 780 (Tex.App.–San Antonio 1997), Santa Fe obtained an oil and gas lease from the Carrillos who claimed title to the leased land by adverse possession. After Santa Fe obtained protection leases and conveyances from the record title holders, the Carrillos sued Santa Fe for tortious interference with prospective contract and slander of title. The court held that since the Carrillo lease contained a proportionate reduction clause, and no clause specifically prohibiting Santa Fe from acquiring additional leases, "Santa Fe was justified, as a matter of law, in taking the leases from the record owners of the property claimed by the Carrillos." 948 S.W.2d at 785. This finding was relied upon by the court to reject the Carrillos' tortious interference and slander of title claims. "Malice" was lacking to support the slander of title

claim; the court noted: "Because we have held that Santa Fe was entitled to execute the disputed leases as a matter of law, we also hold, as a matter of law, that Santa Fe reasonably believed the record owners held title." Id.

5. Often the factual context for a slander of title claim might also support a "tortious interference" claim. See generally Voiles v. Santa Fe Minerals, Inc., 911 P.2d 1205, 1210 (Okla.1996) (unsuccessful tortious interference with contract claim) and Santa Fe Energy Oper. Partners v. Carrillo, 948 S.W.2d 780, 784 (Tex.App.–San Antonio 1997) (unsuccessful tortious interference with prospective business relations claim).

H. LOSS OF MINERAL OWNERSHIP

1. LOSS OF OWNERSHIP THROUGH NON–USE

Oil and gas rights, like other property rights, can be lost through application of various common law doctrines and statutory procedures. The common law doctrines of abandonment and adverse possession serve to extinguish title in a prior owner and establish title in a new owner. Abandonment is based upon the actions of the prior owner: did the owner have the requisite "intent" to abandon the property? Adverse possession is based upon the actions of the new owner and the statute of limitations: did they "adversely possess" the property for the period of time required by the applicable statute of limitations? To evaluate the possible impact of common law doctrines, first classify the property interest at issue. Although adverse possession concepts can be applied to real and personal property,[82] at common law abandonment could not be applied to possessory interests in real property. Therefore, if the interest is classified as personal property, or a nonpossessory (incorporeal) interest in real property, common law rules of abandonment can apply. If the interest is a possessory (corporeal) interest in real property, common law rules of adverse possession can apply. When evaluating a statutory procedure, the real/personal, possessory/nonpossessory classifications may have no relevance. Instead, the task is to define the interests encompassed by the statutory language.

(a) Adverse Possession

Adverse possession has two components: objective notice of the occupant's claim and a failure of the prior owner to respond in a timely manner to the occupant's possession. The "actual," "open," "notorious," and "continuous" elements of adverse possession are designed to provide evidence of the occupant's claim. The "hostile" and "exclusive" elements provide notice the interest being claimed is adverse to the current owner's rights, as opposed to being permissive. All of these elements are intended

---

82. Although we do not typically think in terms of adverse possession of personal property, the statute of limitations applicable to a cause of action for replevin or similar remedy will often have the same effect as adverse possession in the real property context. The major difference is that the statute of limitations for personal property will be much shorter, such as one to three years. Often the key issue in the personal property context is determining the date on which the statute of limitations will commence.

to give the current owner an opportunity to discover the occupant's possession, and its adversity, so the occupant can be ejected. Once the occupant is in adverse possession, the statute of limitations on the current owner's ejectment cause of action will commence. The limitations period varies from state-to-state but generally ranges from five to twenty-five years. Adverse possession, extending beyond the statute of limitations for bringing an ejectment action, will create new title to the property in the occupant and extinguish the rights of the prior owner.

(i) Entry Before Severance of Mineral Interest

If a mineral interest has not been severed from surface ownership, adverse possession of the surface will include limitation title to the minerals. If the owner of the land conveys a severed mineral interest after adverse possession of the surface has commenced, the severance will neither stop nor suspend the running of the limitation period as to the subsurface interests. As the Florida court pointed out in Ates v. Yellow Pine Land Co., 310 So.2d 772 (Fla.App.1975), once adverse possession has begun, only an actual ouster or a judicial ejectment will interrupt it. Similar reasoning has been used by other courts to reach the same result. See, e.g., Broughton v. Humble Oil & Refining Co., 105 S.W.2d 480 (Tex.Civ.App.1937, writ refused n.r.e.). Suppose the adverse claimant purports to convey the mineral estate before the running of the statute of limitations. Would a severance by the claimant stop the running of the statute as to the mineral estate? Contrast Houston Oil Co. v. Moss, 284 S.W.2d 131 (Tex. 1955) with Northcut v. Church, 188 S.W. 220 (Tenn. 1916). What if a severance took place prior to the adverse possessor's possession of the surface but the document severing the minerals had not been recorded at the time of the entry? What if the severing document remained unrecorded at the time the limitation period had run? See Taylor v. Scott, 685 S.W.2d 160 (Ark. 1985).

(ii) Entry After Severance of Mineral Interest

If a mineral interest is severed from surface ownership prior to the adverse possessor's entry, activities on the surface will not establish title to the severed mineral interest. An effective conveyance of all mineral rights will cause a severance. The execution of an oil and gas lease, in jurisdictions that view it as a transfer of a corporeal fee simple determinable in the minerals, will also cause a severance. See, e.g., Rogers v. Ricane Enterprises, Inc., 772 S.W.2d 76 (Tex.1989). In other jurisdictions the effect of an oil and gas lease is less certain. If it is a mere license to mine for minerals, it may not constitute a "severance" of the mineral interest for adverse possession purposes. If the owner of land severs a mineral interest, and subsequently reacquires the severed estate, a subsequent adverse possession of the surface will include title to the minerals only if there has been a merger of the two estates. Under traditional common law theory, however, two estates of equal dignity cannot merge and must remain separate. The few cases dealing with the issue have made the outcome hinge on intent, and have reached different results. See Ferguson v. Hilborn, 402 P.2d 914 (Okla.1965); Jones v. McFaddin, 382 S.W.2d 277 (Tex.Civ.App., writ dismissed); and Humphries v. Texas Gulf Sulphur Co., 393 F.2d 69 (5th Cir.Tex.1968). The common law theory is discussed in detail in Thomas K. McElroy, Adverse Possession of Mineral Estates, 11 Baylor L.Rev. 253, 258–65 (1959).

To acquire rights in the mineral interest, there must be adverse possession of the mineral for the statutory period. Therefore, adverse possession in the mineral context raises three basic issues: (1) What will cause a severance of a mineral interest from surface ownership? (2) When minerals have been severed prior to entry by the adverse claimant, what must the claimant do to provide notice to claim the mineral interest adversely? (3) When a claimant successfully possesses a mineral interest adversely for the statutory period, what is the scope and nature of the mineral interest acquired?

DIEDERICH v. WARE

288 S.W.2d 643 (Ky.App.1956).

MILLIKEN, CHIEF JUSTICE.

This case presents the question whether oil rights granted by an 1859 deed can be acquired through adverse possession by the owner of the surface of the land by the drilling and operation of two oil wells in a corner of a 56–acre tract.

The appellant, John T. Diederich, seeks a declaration of the rights of himself and others to royalties from two producing wells on a 56–acre tract, the surface rights to which are owned by the appellee, E. C. Ware, and the trial court adjudged that the appellee had acquired title to the oil by adverse possession through two wells which were sunk on the property by the surface owners in 1924 and which have been in open, notorious, and continuous operation ever since. The appellant bases his claim upon an 1859 recorded deed which severed the oil rights from the surface.

By recorded deed, dated April 2, 1859, an extremely early date for an oil deed, G. W. Webb and others conveyed to William P. Mellon and Algernon S. Gray the oil under their adjoining tracts of land in Johnson County, Kentucky. * * *

* * *

In 1923, B. H. Blanton, then owner of the particular tract involved in this suit and one of appellee Ware's predecessors in title, entered into a lease with Mid South Oil Company, giving that company a right to drill on this 56–acre tract. In 1924, Mid South drilled two wells which have been operated openly, notoriously and continuously on the property from 1924 until this suit was filed. Prior to the drilling of these wells other exploratory wells had been sunk on the property covered by the old mineral deed and appellant's predecessors knew of this exploration. The appellee claims as a remote vendee or assignee under the 1924 lease executed by his predecessor in title, Blanton, with Mid South, but since that lease gave merely exploration and producing rights, he claims more particularly as owner of the tract in question through the deed by which it was conveyed to him.

* * *

The old oil deed of 1859 appears valid, and as a result this question is presented: May the holder of a mineral deed granting to him the exclusive privilege of taking oil from a tract of land be divested of his rights under the deed through adverse possession if, subsequent to the severance of the mineral from the surface right, the surface owner or his successor in title permits others to sink oil wells on the property and to operate them under a lease for 32 years, paying royalties to the surface owner and his successors in title?

After severance of the mineral rights from the surface rights it is possible for the surface owner, or even a person having no interest in the surface, to acquire title to the minerals by adverse possession. Note, 35 A.L.R.2d 127. After such severance, title to the minerals cannot be gained through adverse possession without a penetration of the mineral estate. * * *

* * *

Here, the trial court found that the mineral owner's (appellant's) predecessors in title had actual and timely notice that oil was being taken from this tract under an adverse claim and made no effort within the 15–year statutory period to assert their rights. We accept this finding, for the truth of it appears to be conceded. CR 52.01.

The required factors to establish adverse possession of minerals are identical with those required for adverse possession of land. In other words, there must be exclusive, actual, peaceable, open and notorious, continuous and hostile possession of the minerals under a claim of right for the statutory period. * * * The trial court found that these requirements had been met and quieted title to the oil under the entire 56–acre tract in the appellee, E. C. Ware, without discussing the question of whether by operating two wells in a corner of this tract the appellee had acquired title by adverse possession to the oil under the entire 56 acres.

There are two general categories of cases where land is acquired by adverse possession—those where entry was made under color of title afforded by a written instrument, and those cases where the adverse possessor has staked off his claim by fencing and the like but has no paper title. In the first class color of title supplies the boundaries of the area claimed, while in the latter class the fences or physical markings define the area. When these categories and the law inherent in them are applied to severed mineral estates, they lead, as might be expected, to a lack of uniform results.

Where there has been a severance of title to minerals from the title to the surface of land, the authorities are not in harmony on the question of whether the working of a part of the mineral estate is sufficient to give title by adverse possession to the mineral underlying the whole of it. In a number of cases it has been held, or indicated, that such a working is not sufficient. * * * The holdings of these cases appear to be based on the conclusion that once one gets below the surface there are no clear boundaries for defining the limits of the mineral estate—that color of title boundaries underground are difficult to locate and that the fencing off of the subterranean area claimed can best be determined by confining it to the specific area actually mined. This reasoning ignores the fact that mineral estates are generally described by metes and bounds marked off on the surface. It is also said that an intruder on a mineral estate can have no "immediacy of use and occupation" of the whole of the minerals over which the law can by construction extend his actual possession. * * * This "immediacy of use" concept, applicable though it may be to solid minerals, is not particularly persuasive where a fugacious mineral is involved. Two geologists testified in the case at bar that the operation of two oil wells on this 56 acres since 1924 altered the entire subterranean structure underlying not only this particular tract but the entire 800 acres described in the old mineral deed as well, and caused movement of gases and other natural forces which ordinarily move oil to the mouth of a well. Thus, in a sense, the operators of the two oil wells exercised dominion over all of the oil under their tract when they withdrew it by means of their two wells. In the case of a solid mineral such as coal this is not necessarily true, for title to coal can be defeated only by acts which actually take the mineral. Piney Oil & Gas Co. v. Scott, above.

Several American cases are authority for the view that the rules of constructive possession applicable to surface estates are applicable to mineral estates, and that one working part of a well-defined, severed mineral estate may be deemed to be in constructive possession of the whole estate. * * * It is our opinion that this latter line of cases is more consistent with good reason, especially in view of the tendency of the courts to treat mineral estates and surface estates alike for most other purposes. * * *

Having concluded that the ordinary rules of constructive possession are applicable to mineral estates, in order to determine the extent of appellee's adverse possession under these rules, we must next determine whether appellee and his predecessors worked these two oil wells under "color of title." What is color of title is a question of law for the Court to decide. * * *

The question here is essentially this: Can a surface owner who works the minerals under his land relying on his general warranty deed, which does not except the prior severed minerals, be said to have color of title to those minerals? The Piney Oil case, Piney Oil & Gas Co. v. Scott, 258 Ky. 51, 79 S.W.2d 394, at page 400, suggests that in such a case the surface owner does not have color of title. Two American cases are authority for the view that such an intruding surface owner may have color of title to the prior severed minerals under his tract. Sanford v. Alabama Power Co., 256 Ala. 280, 54 So.2d 562; Vance v. Guy, 223 N.C. 409, 27 S.E2d 117, later appeal reported in 224 N.C. 607, 31 S.E.2d 766.

Considering the vagueness of the description employed in the 1859 mineral deed involved in this action and the difficulty of ascertaining just what land is embraced by that deed, and additionally considering the gap in the title between G. W. Webb, grantor of the minerals, and his son, C. W. Webb, to whom appellee traces his general warranty deed, and the many conveyances over a span of many years which ignored the mineral deed, we are of the opinion that appellee and his predecessors, in this instance, were working these two oil wells under color of title.

It is our conclusion that the operation of the two oil wells for the statutory period cut off the right of anyone else to drill for or extract oil on this 56–acre tract.

The judgment is affirmed.

SIMS, JUDGE (dissenting).

The majority opinion is so far from my conception of the law of adverse possession in minerals, and the question is of such importance in my judgment as to call for a short dissenting opinion.

I agree with the majority that the required factors to establish adverse possession of minerals are identical with those required to establish adverse possession of the surface of land. It is for this reason I sharply disagree with the majority. To my mind there can be no possession of fugacious minerals until they are brought to the surface.

After citing many authorities in referring to "color of title boundaries underground," the majority say these authorities ignore the fact that mineral estates are generally described by metes and bounds marked off on the surface. This may be true as to hard and stationary minerals, but certainly it has no applicability to fugacious minerals. It is impossible to give the boundaries of fugacious minerals underground. We have written that an owner of an oil or gas well is the owner of all oil or gas the well produces regardless of what boundary of land it drains. * * *

It is my opinion that adverse possession in oil or gas is limited to the oil or gas which is produced by the well or wells which has or have been drilled. This view is supported by Piney Oil & Gas Co. v. Scott, 258 Ky. 51, 79 S.W.2d 394, which the majority opinion overrules in part. Once established, this adverse possession lasts so long as the well or wells continue to produce.

For the reasons given I most respectfully dissent.

NOTES

1. The *Diederich* case discusses the geographic extent of the adverse claimant's oil and gas rights. Will the adverse claimant in *Diederich* obtain oil

and gas rights as to all depths beneath the property? Will the claimant obtain rights to other minerals such as coal and uranium within the property? Would the result in *Diederich* be different if the adverse claimant was not acting under "color of title?" Because of the paucity of cases in which a successful adverse possession claim has been established, most of these questions remain unanswered. What policy considerations should a court take into account in dealing with these issues? See Lowe, Chapter 5.D.3.

2. Efforts to establish adverse possession through pooling have not been successful. In Hunt Oil Co. v. Moore, 656 S.W.2d 634 (Tex.App.1983, writ ref'd n.r.e.), Hamilton, the owner of a one-tenth mineral interest in a 92–acre tract, executed an oil and gas lease which authorized pooling into units that could not exceed 40 acres in size. The lessee, Hunt Oil Co., purported to pool the interest into two separate units of approximately 160 acres each. The producing wells were located off the tract in which the lessor owned his interest, and under Texas law the unauthorized pooling did not maintain the lease. The lessee argued that it had acquired title by adverse possession to the leased interest by virtue of continuous production from the unit wells, which were draining the common reservoir underlying the lessor's tract. Rejecting Hunt Oil's argument, the court reasoned as follows:

> Upon execution of the Hamilton–Hunt lease on May 15, 1961, Hunt acquired constructive possession of the leasehold estate in Hamilton's one-tenth mineral interest. Such possession being in recognition of Hamilton's title, Hunt could not make it a hostile holding without a repudiation of Hamilton's title, evidenced by acts or declarations clearly manifesting such intention. There is no indication in the record that Hunt intended to repudiate their recognition of Hamilton's title until after this suit was filed.

> After termination of the Hamilton–Hunt lease on May 16, 1962, Hamilton, the record owner of the severed mineral interest, was in constructive possession thereof. Hunt's argument that they ousted Hamilton's possession of his unleased, severed mineral interest in the Hamilton tract by production of oil and gas from wells located on other land in the Hunt–Milner and Atlantic–Milner Units ignores the requirements of Art. 5509.[83] Hamilton's constructive possession could only be ousted by actual adverse possession of the land claimed—the unleased one-tenth mineral interest in place. The drilling of and production from wells not located on land covered by the Hamilton–Hunt lease was not an actual adverse appropriation of the land described therein and did not constitute a trespass of such mineral interest.

656 S.W.2d at 641. The court required a clear act by Hunt ousting Hamilton since Hunt's initial entry was permissive, pursuant to the Hamilton–Hunt oil and gas lease. The court also rejected Hunt's drainage argument noting drainage could have been caused by other wells in the area. Would the result have been different if Hunt was able to prove its wells were draining

---

83. Article 5509, which is now codified as Tex.Civ.Prac. & Rem.Code Ann. § 16.025, is a five-year statute of limitations requiring the adverse possessor to claim under a recorded deed and pay taxes on the property. See Sun Operating Ltd. Partnership v. Oatman, 911 S.W.2d 749 (Tex.App. 1995, writ denied).

Hamilton's 92–acre tract? See also Atlantic Richfield Co. v. Tomlinson, 859 P.2d 1088 (Okla.1993) (production from Commission-created 640–acre pooled unit would not constitute adverse possession of 40–acre tract included in unit when all drilling and production took place off of the 40–acre tract).

3. Would receipt of production proceeds over a 29–year period, and the payment of taxes on the production proceeds, establish adverse possession of the interest attributable to the production proceeds? Cornelius v. Moody Bible Institute of Chicago, 18 P.3d 1081 (Okla.Civ.App. 2000) (such acts insufficient as a matter of law; nothing to put the record title owner on notice of the adverse claim).

4. Although governmental entities can be adverse possessors, governmental property, absent statutory authorization, is not subject to adverse possession. See R. P. Davis, Annotation, Acquisition by Adverse Possession or Use of Public Property Held by Municipal Corporation or Other Governmental Unit Otherwise than for Streets, Alleys, Parks, or Common, 55 A.L.R.2d 554 (1957).

(b) Abandonment

Conceptually the common law does not permit the abandonment of a possessory interest in real property. At common law seisin could not be in limbo. Therefore, a freehold estate in real property[84] could not be abandoned. Conceptually a non-freehold estate, such as a tenancy for a term of years, could be abandoned since seisin was considered to remain with the landlord[85] and there was an identifiable estate in which it could be abandoned.[86] Through somewhat similar analysis the common law recognized the abandonment of an easement, which is classified as a nonpossessory interest in real property. Easement abandonment analysis is simpler because there is always a servient estate in which the abandoned easement can immediately merge upon abandonment.

As noted in previous sections, oil and gas mineral interests fall into two broad categories. For example, some states, such as Kansas and Texas, recognize a present possessory interest in oil and gas while in place. Therefore, in Kansas and Texas the mineral owner has a freehold estate in real property that cannot be abandoned. Other states, such as California and Oklahoma, do not recognize a possessory interest in oil and gas while in place. These states follow the "nonownership" or "exclusive-right-to-take" theory which dictates the mineral interest be classified as a nonpossessory interest in real property. Conceptually, in California and Oklahoma a mineral interest, and therefore any interest carved out of a

---

84. Fee simple, fee tail, or life estate.

85. Even though the tenant had "possession" of the leased land.

86. At common law the landlord had the option of refusing to accept the abandoned interest during the remaining term of the lease. This would permit the landlord to do nothing during the remaining lease term and then sue the defaulting tenant for recovery of the unpaid rent. Modern cases have generally taken away the landlord's option to refuse recognition of the tenant's abandonment of the leasehold. Instead, contract law mitigation of damages concepts have supplanted the landlord's property law option of refusing to acknowledge the reuniting of the tenant's abandoned leasehold with the landlord's freehold estate. See Sommer v. Kridel, 378 A.2d 767 (N.J.1977).

mineral interest, can be lost by abandonment. For example, in Gerhard v. Stephens, 69 Cal.Rptr. 612, 442 P.2d 692 (Cal. 1968), after noting a mineral interest in California creates a *profit a prendre*—an incorporeal hereditament—the court stated:

> If interests in real property can be and are abandoned, they do not become, as in the case of personal property, the property of the first appropriator * * * but instead return to the estate out of which they were carved. The abandonment of a profit a prendre, therefore, because the profit in essence is an easement, does not become subject to the void in ownership that the common law of land title sought to avoid. If a perpetual right of way or other easement is abandoned, the property interest reverts to the servient estate. * * * Similarly, a perpetual right to remove oil and gas * * * would ordinarily revert to the surface estate, thereby freeing that estate of its burden and permitting its owner more complete utilization and enjoyment of his property.

442 P.2d at 711. The court in *Gerhard* held that some of the mineral interests owned by shareholders of a defunct corporation had been abandoned, and some had not. Abandonment will occur only when there has been a lack of use of the interest coupled with the owner's intent to abandon the interest.

Abandonment analysis is a two-step process. First, the interest must be classified to determine whether abandonment is an available theory. If the interest passes the classification test, the second step is to determine whether the requisite intent to abandon exists. Since mineral interests are often held for long periods of time without development, nonuse alone will not support a finding of abandonment. As the court noted in *Gerhard*:

> In order to protect the owner of an unlimited profit a prendre or other incorporeal hereditament against "involuntary" abandonment under the circumstances in which conflicting inferences may be drawn from his nonuser we hold that the trial court must find either that the owner's future use of the right could result only from a palpably unsound business judgment or that the owner has given further indication of his intent to abandon.

442 P.2d at 716. In *Gerhard* the court found that some of the heirs who were entitled to a portion of the mineral interests disclaimed their interests in a prior probate proceeding where they rejected any interest in the defunct corporation as "being worthless and of no value." Coupled with fifty years of non-use, the court held this was sufficient evidence to support the trial court's finding of an intent to abandon the mineral interests.

Although a state may classify a mineral interest as a possessory interest in real property, interests carved from the mineral interest may be classified differently. For example, although in Texas an oil and gas lease is classified as a fee simple determinable in the minerals,[87] in Kansas the oil and gas lease creates a *profit a prendre*, a non-possessory interest in real property that is subject to abandonment. Oil and gas lease abandonment cases are rare because the habendum clause of the lease will typically terminate it long before abandonment becomes an issue. However, there can be instances where assignments of a segregated portion of a lease, either areal or by depth, create a situation where the activity of one lessee is maintaining the leasehold interest of an inactive lessee. The non-divisibility of the habendum clause permits such a situation to arise. Although courts recognize that any authorized activity described in the lease habendum clause will perpetuate the leased acreage, for abandonment analysis the court can focus on the actions of individual lessees to determine whether they have exhibited an intent to abandon their portion of the leased acreage.

In Rook v. James E. Russell Petroleum, Inc., 235 Kan. 6, 679 P.2d 158 (Kan. 1984), the lease habendum clause would perpetuate the lease either by production or by gas storage. The gas storage rights were assigned by the original lessee to Cities Service Gas Company. Cities maintained the lease through continuous gas storage operations. The oil and gas rights were subsequently assigned to Russell Petroleum in 1963 when there were sixteen producing oil wells on the leased land. By 1966 Russell Petroleum had ceased producing the wells and no production or exploration activity was conducted on the leased land from 1966 through 1980. The court found, based largely on fifteen years of nonuse, Russell Petroleum had abandoned its oil and gas lease rights. Russell Petroleum's explanation for not taking any action to regain production was simple: the lease was being maintained by Cities' gas storage activities so no immediate action was required on its part. Although the court found Russell Petroleum had breached the implied covenant of diligent and prudent operation by failing to restore production in a timely fashion,[88] the court relied on the following factors to hold the lease had been abandoned:

> [T]erminating production of all wells on these two leases with no further production activity on these leases for fifteen years, permitting equipment left on the property to rust or deteriorate, tearing down and removing the pump house after it was partially demolished in a storm, removing the power source equipment, and not physically going onto the premises in any manner after 1972.

---

87. Title to an oil and gas lease in Texas cannot be lost through abandonment. Rogers v. Ricane Enterprises, Inc., 772 S.W.2d 76, 80 (Tex.1989). However, in limited circumstances Texas courts have applied a concept referred to as "abandonment of purpose" where the underlying document contains specific language warranting such an analysis. Rogers v. Ricane Enterprises, Inc., 884 S.W.2d 763, 766–67 (Tex.1994) (discussing Texas Co. v. Davis, 254 S.W. 304 (Tex. 1923)).

88. Courts sometimes confuse the doctrines of abandonment and breach of implied covenants. See Phillip E. DeLaTorre, Recent Developments in Kansas Oil and Gas Law, 32 Kan.L.Rev. 595, 614 (1984) (discussing the intermediate appellate court's analysis in *Rook*); Phillip E. DeLaTorre, Recent Developments in Kansas Oil and Gas Law (1983–1988), 37 Kan.L.Rev. 907, 929–30 (1989) (discussing the supreme court's analysis in *Rook*).

679 P.2d at 167.[89]

NOTES

1. In a case such as *Rook v. James E. Russell Petroleum, Inc.*, why would a lessor prefer to rely upon an abandonment theory instead of an implied covenant theory? When might a lessee want to embrace an abandonment theory?

2. In the *Rook* case, the abandoned interest reverted to the owner of the mineral interest—the fee interest from which it was carved. Would this be the case in a state such as California where the mineral interest is a nonpossessory interest in land? The court in *Gerhard* made the following comments in a footnote:

> We state no absolute rule on this point because under certain circumstances not present here it may not apply. Thus, if the grantor carves out a perpetual profit to remove oil and gas and later conveys to another the fee ownership in an underground corporeal stratum, upon abandonment by the profit holder the ownership of the oil and gas removed from the stratum might well rest in the subsurface owner.
>
> We further recognize the possibility, not discussed by the parties, that when an incorporeal hereditament is held in cotenancy, the interest abandoned by one or more cotenants might revert to the remaining cotenants instead of to the servient estate. In view, however, of plaintiff's pleadings we decline to comment on this possibility at this time.

442 P.2d at 711.

3. What role can laches and estoppel play in causing a loss of title? In Perpetual Royalty Corp. v. Kipfer, 253 F.Supp. 571 (D.Kan.1965), affirmed, 361 F.2d 317 (10th Cir.Kan.1966), the plaintiffs brought suit to quiet title and for an accounting against the lessors, lessees, and purchaser of oil production from land in which the plaintiffs claimed various mineral interests. The court stated:

> It is generally considered that where, as in Kansas mineral interests create interests in realty, such mineral interests cannot be lost through mere abandonment. The equitable doctrine of laches, however, acting as a form of estoppel, can preclude a plaintiff from asserting in equity an alleged legal claim or interest * * *.
>
> * * *
>
> [T]he doctrine of laches is peculiarly appropriate to oil and gas and mineral interests which are subject to relatively rapid deviations in value. * * * In the case at bar plaintiffs and their predecessors made no attempt to develop the interest they presently claim from 1934 forward. And they remained utterly passive for some eight years while defendants were expending money, efforts and enterprise in developing the land for oil. * * * We feel that under such circumstances * * * it would be patently

---

89. But see Luman v. Davis, 196 P. 1078 (Kan. 1921) (removing machinery, casing, and property from the lease not sufficient, under the facts, to indicate an intent to abandon).

inequitable to entertain plaintiffs' claims after such prejudicial inaction on their part and on the part of their predecessors.

253 F.Supp. at 574–77. However, in Ford v. Willits, 688 P.2d 1230 (Kan.App. 1984), the court held that neither laches nor equitable estoppel would bar the quiet title action. In Rogers v. Ricane Enterprises, Inc., 772 S.W.2d 76, 80 (Tex.1989), the court held: "Laches is not a defense in a trespass to try title suit where the plaintiff's right is based on legal title." Is there a better way to "do equity" in cases where the occupying claimant is unable to perfect the title through abandonment or adverse possession?

4.   Most states have "unclaimed property" statutes designed to administer a broadly defined class of abandoned or forgotten personal property, including cash proceeds attributable to interests in minerals. The court in State v. Snell, 950 S.W.2d 108, 112 (Tex.App.1997), summarized the Texas unclaimed property regime as follows:

> The disposition of unclaimed property in the State of Texas is not left to the whim of the private citizens or the courts, and rightfully so. The Texas Legislature has imposed a specific and detailed procedure for identifying, reporting, and tendering, and has further provided for governmental custody and distribution of unclaimed property. * * *
>
> The Property Code prescribes a mandatory procedure whereby persons or entities holding property rightfully belonging to another, but which has been deemed abandoned property (due ordinarily to some form of inactivity on the part of the rightful owner), must turn that abandoned property over to the State of Texas for safe-keeping. * * * As required by statute, Appellants [State of Texas] have a duty to publish notice designed to apprise rightful owners that Appellants are holding abandoned property on behalf of the rightful owners. * * * Persons holding unclaimed property which has been deemed abandoned also have duties; they must report and deliver to Appellants all unclaimed property in their possession on an annual basis. * * * In order to enforce chapters 72 through 74 of the Property Code, the legislators have made available civil and criminal penalties in the event a person fails to pay or deliver property to the State of Texas within the time prescribed by the Property Code. * * * Once the money is delivered to the State, the rightful owners may claim their property without the fear of any statute of limitations barring their claim. * * *

In addition to the general unclaimed property laws found at Chapters 72, 73, 74 and 76 of the Texas Property Code, Chapter 75 addresses "Texas Minerals". Tex.Prop.Code Ann. §§ 75.001 to 75.102. The unclaimed property procedures apply to: "All mineral proceeds that are held or owing by the holder and that have remained unclaimed by the owner for longer than three years after they became payable or distributable and the owner's underlying right to receive those mineral proceeds are presumed abandoned." Tex.Prop. Code Ann. § 75.101(a). For a comprehensive discussion of unclaimed property issues see Paula Smith, Unclaimed Property Statutes and the Management of Production Proceeds, 44 Rocky Mtn. Min. L. Inst. 18–1 (1998).

(c) Liberative Prescription

In Louisiana a mineral servitude may be extinguished even in the absence of adverse possession. Under the doctrine of liberative prescription,[90] the servitude will terminate for nonuse at the end of ten years. The strength of the policy underlying this doctrine is illustrated by the following comments by a Louisiana court of appeals:

> If there is anything that seems to be well established in our jurisprudence, it is that any instrument which attempts to extend a mineral servitude beyond the prescriptive period set forth in our codal articles will be declared a nullity by our courts, if such fact is properly presented and established.

> * * *

> In the early period of judicial development of Louisiana's mineral laws, the efforts by the landowners to extend the life of the mineral servitude were by means of direct stipulations in the instrument. The first of these was an agreement between the landowner and the mineral owner that the minerals were reserved for a period in excess of ten years. Such provisions, being contrary to our public policy, were declared a nullity on the ground that prescription could not be renounced before it accrued. * * *

> Since it became increasingly clear that no direct contractual efforts to circumvent our public policy relating to prescription of mineral servitudes would be allowed, a resort was made to indirect attempts, carefully concealed in instruments which were valid on their face, but the underlying purpose being to defeat such public policy.

> It was maintained that the reservation of a royalty rather than a mineral interest would not fall within the legal category of "servitude" subject to the prescriptive period. The Supreme Court, however, held that the interest reserved prescribed in ten years, it being immaterial what term was used in characterizing the interest.

> Another effort was made by classifying the mineral owner as an agent, thus creating a mandate coupled with an interest, which effort was unsuccessful.

> A device was also used whereby undivided interests in outstanding minerals were conveyed to minors in the hope of suspending the running of the prescriptive period. The court again upheld the public policy of the state by holding that any conveyance to a minor for the purpose of suspending prescription would not be recognized. * * *

> * * *

---

90. Codal provisions dealing with the prescription of a mineral servitude are found in the Louisiana Mineral Code at La. Rev. Stat. Ann. §§ 31:28 to 31:79; those dealing with the royalty are §§ 31:80 to 31:104; those dealing with the mineral lease are §§ 31:114 to 31:148. Legislation extinguishing unused mineral interests in common law jurisdiction has taken the form of Dormant Mineral Acts discussed in the next section of this casebook.

Almost every device conceivable has been employed in an attempt to circumvent our law on this question. In every instance where the Supreme Court has found such an intent it has zealously protected the State's public policy. This vigilance of the Supreme Court has curtailed the attempts of those who seek to withhold mineral rights from commerce beyond the prescriptive period.

Chicago Mill & Lumber Co. v. Ayer Timber Co., 131 So.2d 635, 639–40 (La.App.1961).

What state or public interests are furthered by this strong position against private attempts to circumvent prescription of mineral rights?

The uses of the servitude that will interrupt the running of the 10–year period have been articulated through extensive case law and are now set out in detail in the Code. For example, good faith drilling is such a use:

§ 29.   How prescription of nonuse is interrupted

The prescription of nonuse running against a mineral servitude is interrupted by good faith operations for the discovery and production of minerals. By good faith is meant that the operations must be

> (1) commenced with reasonable expectation of discovering and producing minerals in paying quantities at a particular point or depth,

> (2) continued at the site chosen to that point or depth, and

> (3) conducted in such a manner that they constitute a single operation although actual drilling or mining is not conducted at all times.

La. Rev. Stat. Ann. § 31:29. The comment on this codal provision points out that it contains a mixture of subjective and objective standards. The operations that will interrupt the prescriptive period must be in "good faith," but for good faith to be established, a "reasonable expectation of production" must be shown. Drilling operations interrupt the prescriptive period at the time the well is actually spudded in, rather than at the time preparatory acts, such as erecting the drilling pad, are begun.[91] The period is interrupted by actual production even though the production is not in paying quantities.[92] A shut-in well also satisfies the production requirement, although in that situation the well must have been tested and shown capable of production in paying quantities.[93]

A mineral servitude may include several types of minerals, such as lignite, in addition to oil and gas. In Continental Group, Inc. v. Allison, 404 So.2d 428 (La.1981), the Louisiana Supreme Court, in applying pre-Mineral Code law, held that the production of oil and gas would not interrupt liberative prescription with respect to the right to strip-mine for lignite. The rule is different with respect to prescription after the January

---

91. La. Rev. Stat. Ann. § 31:30.

92. La. Rev. Stat. Ann. § 31:38.

93. La. Rev. Stat. Ann. § 31:34.

1, 1975, effective date of the Code. Under Article 40, acts that interrupt prescription as to one mineral included in a servitude will interrupt the prescriptive period as to all other minerals and all modes of use. La. Rev. Stat. Ann. § 31:40.

Even absent a qualifying use, liberative prescription may be interrupted by the landowner's acknowledgment of the rights of the mineral owner. Such acknowledgment, however, must be made with the intent of interrupting the prescriptive period. Thus a reference to a mineral servitude that is inserted in a deed to protect the grantor against a claim for breach of warranty should not have the effect of interrupting prescription of the servitude. La. Rev. Stat. Ann. §§ 31:54–56. For further discussions of the requirements for acknowledgment and the liberative prescription doctrine generally, see Kuntz § 10.7 and Williams & Meyers §§ 216.3–216.6. See also John M. McCollam, A Primer for the Practice of Mineral Law Under the New Louisiana Mineral Code, 50 Tulane L.Rev. 729 (1976).

(d) Dormant Mineral Interest Acts and Analogous Legislation

Commonly, as a result of speculative conveyancing, inheritance, or both, a large number of co-owners may hold title to a severed mineral interest. While in most states the lessee of one co-owner may lawfully develop the minerals, generally the lessee will be unwilling to assume the risk of development unless a lease is obtained from all co-owners because the developer must generally account to the other co-owners for their share of any net profits. Thus, the owner of a 1/32 fractional mineral interest is entitled to 1/32 of any net profits, but would assume all risk of a dry hole if the owner chose to drill.

Splintering of the mineral estate often makes it difficult and costly to locate the co-owners. This can impede development of the mineral interest. Since severed mineral interests typically include a right to make reasonable use of the surface to develop the minerals, they also impede development and marketability of the surface estate. Therefore, the developer must try to identify and locate mineral owners in order to negotiate oil and gas leases.

Many states have enacted various forms of statutes designed to reunite severed mineral interests with the surface estate. These statutes are typically called either "Dormant Mineral Interest Acts" or "Mineral Lapse Acts." Although the statutes vary in detail and effect, they can be placed in two general categories: (1) statutes designed primarily to terminate mineral interests and reunite them with the interest from which they were carved—typically the surface estate; and (2) statutes whose apparent but elusive aim is to identify and locate mineral owners. The Indiana Dormant Mineral Interests Act, Ind.Code Ann. §§ 32–23–10–1 through 32–23–10–8, is an example of the first category. The Kansas Mineral Lapse Act, Kan.Stat.Ann. §§ 55–1601 through 55–1607, is an example of the second category.

The United States Supreme Court, in a 5-4 decision, upheld the constitutionality of the Indiana act in Texaco, Inc. v. Short, 454 U.S. 516 (1982). The Indiana act provides for termination of a "mineral interest" if it has not been "used" for a period of 20 years—unless the mineral owner files a statement of claim in the county recorder's office within that period. In addition, from its effective date, the act established a two-year grace period in which existing mineral owners could take action to preserve their unused mineral interests by filing a statement of claim. Indiana's two-year grace period expired on September 2, 1973. In *Texaco, Inc. v. Short*, the mineral owners had not engaged in one of the statutorily-defined "uses" during the preceding twenty years or filed a statement of claim within the two-year grace period. Accordingly, their mineral interests were automatically extinguished and title passed to Short, the owner of the surface estate. The Act allows but does not require the surface owner to give notice of lapse to the mineral owners. When Short did so, the mineral owners responded by filing statements of claim; however, these were not timely.

The Court noted: "The statute does not require any specific notice be given to a mineral owner prior to a statutory lapse of a mineral estate." Id. at 454 U.S. at 520. Nevertheless, the Court upheld the Indiana act: "We have no doubt that, just as a State may create a property interest that is entitled to constitutional protection, the State has the power to condition permanent retention of that property right on the performance of reasonable conditions that indicate a present intention to retain the interest." Id. at 454 U.S. at 526. The Court rejected the mineral owners' due process argument, finding that the enactment of the law with the two-year grace period provided mineral owners with adequate notice and opportunity to preserve their interests by filing a statement of claim. Although the mineral owners in the *Texaco* case stipulated they had not used their mineral interests for over twenty years, the Court noted that had they contested their nonuse they would have been able to present their case in a subsequent quiet title action. The Court observed:

> [I]t is essential to recognize the difference between the self-executing feature of the statute and a subsequent judicial determination that a particular lapse did in fact occur. As noted by appellants, no specific notice need be given of an impending lapse. If there has been a statutory use of the interest during the preceding 20–year period, however, by definition there is no lapse—whether or not the surface owner, or any other party, is aware of that use. Thus, no mineral estate that has been protected by any of the means set forth in the statute may be lost through lack of notice. It is undisputed that, before judgment could be entered in a quiet title action that would determine conclusively that a mineral interest has reverted to the surface owner, the full procedural protections of the Due Process Clause—including notice reasonably calculated to reach all interested parties and a prior opportunity to be heard—must be provided.

Id. at 454 U.S. at 533–34.

Considerable variation exists in the statutory details among states that have adopted some form of Dormant Mineral Interest or Mineral Lapse Act. The statutes tend to differ concerning what constitutes a "mineral interest," the types of "use" that will preserve the mineral interest, the permissible period of nonuse, and as noted above, whether the statute is designed primarily to terminate unused mineral interests or to merely identify the owner of the interest. Unlike the Indiana act, the Kansas Mineral Lapse Act is designed primarily to identify and locate mineral owners.

SCULLY v. OVERALL

840 P.2d 1211 (Kan.App.1992).

E. NEWTON VICKERS, DISTRICT JUDGE RETIRED, assigned:

Plaintiffs Lewis Joseph Scully and Judith K. Scully appeal the trial court's granting of the motion of defendants Cleve Buford Overall, Judy A.C. Overall, and J.C.B. Resources, Inc., for judgment on the pleadings, holding that the Kansas mineral interest lapse statutes, K.S.A. 55–1601 et seq., entitle a mineral owner, who does not take any affirmative steps to maintain a mineral interest for over 20 years, to preserve the mineral interest by filing a statement of claim within 60 days after the surface owner files a notice of lapse. We affirm.

On April 26, 1961, plaintiffs Lewis and Judith Scully purchased real estate located in Anderson County, Kansas, from defendant Cleve Buford Overall. The contract excepted "the oil and gas in place which is reserved by the Vendor."

On August 1, 1991, the Scullys published a notice of lapse of mineral interest in The Anderson Countian, a local newspaper of general circulation in Anderson County.

On August 8, 1991, the Scullys filed a notice of lapse of mineral interest, claiming that no minerals from the property were used for 20 years and that the ownership of any mineral should revert to the Scullys, the current surface owners.

On August 12, 1991, the Overalls received a copy of the notice by registered mail from the Scullys regarding lapse of the mineral interest. On August 14, 1991, the Overalls filed a statement of claim to mineral interest in the office of the Register of Deeds of Anderson County.

On December 16, 1991, the Scullys filed a petition against the Overalls and J.C.B. to quiet title to real estate.

On January 9, 1992, the Overalls and J.C.B. answered, generally denying the allegations. The Overalls and J.C.B. jointly filed a motion for judgment on the pleadings on January 27, 1992.

The trial court granted the Overalls' and J.C.B.'s motion, holding as a matter of law that the Overalls' mineral interests were not extinguished or vested in the Scullys.

* * *

The primary issue before us is whether the Overalls' mineral interests lapsed and were extinguished and became vested in the surface owners, the Scullys, under the Kansas mineral interests lapse statutes, K.S.A. 55–1601 et seq. This is the first case to interpret these statutes since their enactment in 1983.

The pertinent statutes are set out in full.

K.S.A. 55–1601:

"As used in this act, 'mineral interest' means an interest created by an instrument transferring, by grant, assignment, reservation or otherwise, an interest of any kind in coal, oil, gas or other minerals."

K.S.A. 55–1602:

"An interest in coal, oil, gas or other minerals, if unused for a period of 20 years, shall lapse, unless a statement of claim is filed in accordance with K.S.A. 55–1604, and the ownership shall revert to the current surface owner."

K.S.A. 55–1603:

"(a) A mineral interest shall be considered to be used when:

(1) There are any minerals produced under the interest;

(2) operations are being conducted on the interest for injection, withdrawal, storage or disposal of water, gas or other fluid substances;

(3) rentals or royalties are being paid by the owner of the interest for the purpose of delaying or enjoying the use or exercise of the mineral rights;

(4) the use or exercise of the mineral rights is being carried out on a tract with which the mineral interest may be unitized or pooled for production purposes;

(5) in the case of coal or other solid minerals, there is production from a common vein or seam by the owners of the mineral interests; or

(6) taxes are paid on the mineral interest by its owner.

"(b) Any use pursuant to or authorized by the instrument creating the mineral interest shall be effective to continue in force all rights granted by the instrument."

K.S.A. 55–1604:

"(a) A statement of claim may be filed by the owner of a mineral interest prior to the end of the twenty-year period specified by K.S.A. 55–1602 or within three years after the effective date of this act, whichever is later. The statement shall contain the name and address of the owner of the mineral interest and a description of the land on or under which the mineral interest is located. The statement of claim shall be filed in the office of the register of deeds of the county in which the land is located. Upon the filing of the statement of claim within the time provided, it shall be considered that the mineral interest was being used on the date the statement of claim was filed.

"(b) Failure to file a statement of claim within the time prescribed by subsection (a) shall not cause a mineral interest to be extinguished if the owner of the mineral interest filed the statement of claim within 60 days after (1) publication of notice as prescribed by K.S.A. 55–1605, if such notice is published or (2) within 60 days after receiving actual knowledge that the mineral interest had lapsed, if such notice is not published."

The facts are undisputed in this case that the Overalls' mineral interest was unused for a period of 20 years as set forth in K.S.A. 55–1602 and 55–1603, and that no claim was filed by the Overalls prior to the 20–year period specified in K.S.A. 55–1602 or within three years after the effective date of the Act, whichever was later, as set forth in K.S.A. 55–1604.

The facts are further undisputed that the Scullys did publish in The Anderson Countian a "notice of lapse" pursuant to K.S.A. 55–1605 and that the Overalls filed a statement of claim within 60 days after publication of said notice pursuant to K.S.A. 55–1604(b)(1).

The Scullys' argument on appeal is that when a mineral owner files a statement of claim after publication of the lapse notice, this statement of claim "must be coupled with proof that the mineral interest was in fact 'used' during the 20–year period in order to preserve the mineral interest owner's rights."

The Scullys further argue that once the mineral interest has lapsed after the 20–year period of nonuse, the mineral owner has no ground to contest such lapse. The Scullys assert that the provision in K.S.A. 55–1604(b) is merely a notice requirement but does not provide any separate right to extend the mineral interest if the prior mineral owner cannot prove that the minerals were "used," as provided in K.S.A. 55–1603, or that the prior mineral owner did file with the register of deeds a statement of claim within 20 years of the last use of the minerals. The Scullys' interpretation of the statute is distorted.

According to the requirements in K.S.A. 55–1604(b), the mineral interest shall not be extinguished, even after the lapse of 20 years of nonuse, if the owner files a statement of claim. The statute does not require the mineral interest owner to provide proof of use at the time of the filing of the statement of claim. * * *

We agree with the analysis of the statute as stated by Associate Professor David E. Pierce, a professor of Oil and Gas law at Washburn University School of Law:

"Although the mineral interest will 'lapse' if unused for twenty years, and if a statement of claim is not filed on or before 1 July 1986, the interest will not be 'extinguished' until the surface owner gives notice of the lapse and the mineral interest owner fails to respond as required by K.S.A. 55–1605." Pierce, July 1 is Deadline for Filing Claims to Preserve "Unused Mineral Interests," 25 Circuit Rider 6 (Summer 1986).

The Scullys make reference to a United States Supreme Court case, Texaco, Inc. v. Short, 454 U.S. 516, 102 S.Ct. 781, 70 L.Ed.2d 738 (1982), but it is difficult to see what exactly Texaco offers to support their position. Texaco held the Indiana Dormant Mineral Interests Act constitutional. The Indiana act was used as a model for the Kansas statutes, K.S.A. 55–1601 et seq. However, there is a difference. The Indiana act does not require the surface owners to give notice to the mineral interest owners to allow them to avert the lapse of their interests. On the other hand, K.S.A. 55–1604(b) provides the chance to do exactly that.

The Scullys insist that only when there was some "use" of the mineral interest during the 20–year period should the mineral interest owner be allowed to dispute the lapsing of the mineral interest to the surface owner. They claim that this interpretation is the "most logical interpretation to achieve the intent of the legislature and to best serve the public policy behind the enactment of the Mineral Lapse Act." If the trial court's position is adopted, the Scullys argue, the whole purpose and intent of the statute is defeated. We are not convinced. Again, we agree with the analysis of Professor Pierce:

"The Kansas Mineral Lapse Act equitably balances the interests of the surface owner and mineral owner. The Kansas Act requires the surface owner to make reasonable efforts to identify and contact the owners of the lapsed interest. If the mineral interest owner responds, the interest is no longer forgotten, the name and address of the mineral interest owner is identified, the purposes of the Act are served. If the mineral interest owner fails to respond, the surface owner can perfect title to the interest in a subsequent quiet title action. The interest then becomes marketable because it is vested in a new, identified, owner." Pierce, 25 Circuit Rider at 9.

* * *

We hold that the mineral interest was not extinguished or vested in the surface owners after 20 years of nonuse, when the mineral interest owners filed a statement of claim within 60 days from the publication of notice under K.S.A. 55–1604(b)(1).

Affirmed.

NOTES

1. The Kansas act lacks the "self-executing" feature of the Indiana act. Non-use under the Kansas act merely permits the surface owner to serve notice on the mineral owner that a lapse has occurred. Non-use under the Indiana act still causes the mineral interest to "lapse" and become "extinguished," but only after the mineral owner is given notice of the lapse and fails to preserve their interest by filing a statement of claim within 60 days

following receipt of the lapse notice. The Kansas act addresses the major objection of the four dissenting justices in *Short*: "As applied to mineral interest owners who were without knowledge of their legal obligations, and who were not permitted to file a saving statement of claim within some period following the giving of statutory notice by the surface owner, the statute operates unconstitutionally." *Texaco*, 454 U.S. at 554, 102 S.Ct. at 805 (J. Brennan, dissenting).

Mailing notices to the last known addresses of mineral owners and publishing notices in official newspapers is expensive. To comply with the notice provisions, the surface owner ordinarily would have to secure a title opinion. What incentive does a surface owner have to do this under a Kansas-style act? What "due diligence" must be done by the surface owner to comply with the notice requirement? See Sorenson v. Alinder, 793 N.W.2d 797 (N.D. 2011).

2. Several state appellate courts, prior to *Texaco, Inc. v. Short*, found their dormant mineral acts, or portions of their acts, unconstitutional. Wilson v. Bishop, 412 N.E.2d 522 (Ill.1980); Van Slooten v. Larsen, 410 Mich. 21, 299 N.W.2d 704 (Mich.1980), appeal dismissed 455 U.S. 901 (1982); Wheelock v. Heath, 201 Neb. 835, 272 N.W.2d 768 (Neb.1978); Chicago & Northwestern Transportation Co. v. Pedersen, 259 N.W.2d 316 (Wis.1977). Even though an act passes scrutiny under the federal Constitution, it must also satisfy state constitutional requirements.

3. Indiana follows the nonownership-in-place theory of mineral ownership. Should the validity of dormant mineral acts depend upon the theory of ownership that a jurisdiction follows? See Ernest E. Smith, Evolution of Oil and Gas Rights in the Eastern United States, 10 Eastern Min.L.Inst. 16–1, 16–42 to 16–43 (1989).

4. Section 314 of the Federal Land Policy and Management Act of 1976 ("FLPMA") (codified as 43 U.S.C. § 1744) establishes a federal recording system designed to extinguish stale mining claims and to update data concerning the mining of public lands. For claims that were established before FLPMA's enactment, the claims had to be registered with the Bureau of Land Management ("BLM") within three years of FLPMA's enactment. In the year of initial recording, and "prior to December 31" of every year thereafter, the claimant must also file with state officials and with the BLM a notice of intention to retain the claim, an affidavit of assessment work performed on the claim, and a detailed reporting form. Failure to comply with any of these requirements "shall be deemed conclusively to constitute an abandonment of the mining claim * * *." Id. § 1744(c). In United States v. Locke, 471 U.S. 84 (1985), the appellees had purchased unpatented mining claims in 1960 and 1966 which were worth several million dollars and contained sand and gravel deposits that were being actively developed. The appellees met the initial registration requirement; however, at the end of 1980, they filed their annual notice of intention to retain their claims one day late—December 31 instead of December 30. The Court held the mining claims had been abandoned because FLPMA, and BLM regulations, required the filing to be made on or before December 30 of each year. The Court also held that Section 314 was constitutional, ruling that the statute was a valid exercise of Congressional

power, did not constitute a taking, and did not deny due process. Acquisition and maintenance of oil and gas leases on federal land are dealt with in Chapter 7.

5.   Can a title examiner safely rely upon dormant mineral act procedures as a basis for clearing title of mineral interests that have been of record for more than the statutory lapse period? Would it make a difference whether the statutes were similar to Indiana's "self-executing" approach as opposed to Kansas' "notice-and-failure-to-act" approach?

6.   In 1986, the National Conference of Commissioners on Uniform State laws promulgated a Uniform Dormant Mineral Interests Act, 7A U.L.A. 69–79.

7.   Dormant mineral acts have been the object of two major lines of criticism. First, critics contend they are merely designed to take valuable rights from mineral owners and give them to surface owners. Some would argue that the motivating force for "dormant" mineral interest legislation can be traced more directly to actively developed minerals instead of dormant minerals. Consider the plight of the surface owner who does not share in any of the wealth associated with mineral development but must suffer the surface disruptions associated with development. Although surface damage acts, enacted in several states, are designed to compensate the surface owner for surface disruption, many would view the dormant mineral acts as an attempt to give the surface owner a "piece of the action" in future mineral development. Second, critics note that dormant mineral procedures do not achieve an automatic clearing of title and often create new factual disputes such as whether a mineral interest has been "used" during the statutory period. Until these factual issues are resolved by court action or voluntary agreement, mineral developers are forced to expend additional time and money obtaining leases from all parties who may ultimately have a legitimate claim to the mineral interests at issue.

8.   In some states a marketable record title act may operate to extinguish a mineral interest. See, e.g., West's Fla.Stat.Ann. § 712.01 through 712.10 and § 704.05. Under a marketable record title act, one may determine the marketability of the record owner's title by relying on an examination of title spanning a specified time period, commonly ranging from twenty to forty years. These acts typically extinguish any interest appearing of record before the period specified in the act, unless the interest is preserved by possession or use or by recording a notice of claim within the statutory period. Exceptions may be made for certain types of interests, such as those evidenced by possession or owned by a governmental entity. However, many marketable title acts expressly exclude mineral rights from their operation, e.g. Utah Code Ann. § 57–9–6 ("This act may not be applied to * * * extinguish any right, title, estate, or interest in and to minerals, and any development, mining, production or other rights or easements related to the minerals or exercisable in connection with the minerals"); Kan.Stat.Ann. § 58–3408(d); Okla.St.Ann. tit. 16, § 76; and Wyo.Stat. § 34–10–108. Some acts also exclude easements, reversions, remainders, rights of entry, and possibility of reverters. E.g., Kan. Stat. Ann. § 58–3408(e), (g), & (h). Still others have been limited by court decision.

Similarly, the Marketable Record Title Act, Chapter 47–19.1, N.D.C.C., does not apply to protect Sickler's claim to the mineral estate. In order to come under the protection of this statute, one who claims an interest in real estate must have two qualifications. He must have an unbroken chain of title of record and he must be in possession of the interest which he claims. * * * As has been previously stated, the mineral interest in this case was severed from the surface estate by the reservation in 1941. By severance, separate estates are created and each is incapable of possession by the mere occupancy of the other. All that Reichert and his subsequent grantees obtained was title to the surface which did not in any way give them possession of the minerals. The presumption that one having possession of the surface has the possession of the subsoil does not exist where the surface and subsoil rights have been severed. * * * Because Sickler and her predecessors in interest have not been in possession of the mineral estate, they cannot claim any protection under the Marketable Record Title Act, Chapter 47–19.1, N.D.C.C.

See, e.g., Sickler v. Pope, 326 N.W.2d 86, 93–94 (N.D. 1982), citing Northern Pacific Railway Co. v. Advance Realty, 78 N.W.2d 705 (N.D. 1956)

9.   Property taxation can also be a means of extinguishing severed mineral interests. Over thirty states provide for the separate assessment and taxation of severed mineral interests either by specific statute, or as part of a general property taxation statute. To encourage the prompt listing of severed mineral interests for taxation, Kansas requires the severed mineral owner to record the conveyance creating the interest within 90 days after the deed is "executed." Unless the interest is recorded in a timely manner, or otherwise listed for taxation, the interest "shall become void." Kan.Stat.Ann. § 79–420. Compliance with the recording or listing requirements of the statute is a condition precedent to vesting title in the grantee. Becker v. Rolle, 508 P.2d 509, 513 (Kan. 1973) (mineral deed executed 22 April 1929 and recorded 5 April 1930 held void and subject to attack by grantor's successors 40 years later). See Pierce § 5.10.

Although many states have the statutory authority to tax mineral interests, actual practice may be similar to Kansas where minerals are assessed on a county-by-county basis. Unless the mineral has a recognized value at the time title is severed from the balance of the fee, the county treasurer may not bother to assess and tax the mineral as a separate property interest. Instead the owner of the balance of the fee will continue to pay taxes as before with the severed mineral owner never receiving a tax statement. This makes it possible for severed mineral interests to linger until they become valuable and hampers the ability of the property tax system to serve as a means to consolidate or eliminate forgotten mineral interests. For example, in North Dakota, property taxes are not assessed against severed minerals, although a production tax is levied on all oil and gas production.

Minnesota, historically a major iron mining state, but not an oil and gas producing state, taxes severed mineral rights at a flat rate and provides for their forfeiture to the state, rather than to the surface owner. See Minn. Stat. § 273.165 and §§ 93.52 through 93.58.

CHAPTER 2

THE OIL AND GAS LEASE

Table of Sections

A. PURPOSE OF THE LEASE AND NATURE OF THE RIGHTS CREATED

The oil and gas lease is the central document in oil and gas development. Lessors generally grant leases on printed forms provided by lessees, the terms of which vary substantially; there is no "standard" form.[1] Forms are the norm in the United States because, while millions of Americans own mineral rights, most mineral rights are in relatively small tracts of land, and the rights themselves have become fragmented with the passage of generations.[2]

While there are many different forms, form similarities are much more important than their differences. First, most courts treat oil and gas leases, whatever their precise language, as both conveyances and contracts. A lease is a conveyance because it is the instrument by which the mineral owner conveys a property right to an oil company to explore for and produce oil and gas, reserving a royalty interest in production. A lease is a contract because the oil company accepts the right to explore and produce, burdened by certain express and implied promises. Second, leases generally are executed like deeds, by lessors and not by lessees. The lessor's signature is acknowledged before a notary public, sometimes subscribed by witnesses, and recorded in the county real-property records. Third, although in many states consideration is not required to support the grant of a lease, lessors are generally paid a *bonus* for executing the lease, a payment that may range from a dollar to thousands of dollars per acre leased.

The parties often modify the printed lease form in the course of their negotiations. If alterations are minor, the lessor and the lessee make and

---

1. Many oil and gas lease forms are captioned "Producers 88," a term one court described as "incapable of definite application." Fagg v. Texas Co., 57 S.W.2d 87 (Tex.Com.App.1933). We include example forms in the Forms Manual. Leases are acquired and drilled after specialized title examinations, which are described in Joseph Shade, Petroleum Land Titles; Title Examinations and Title Opinions, 46 Baylor L. Rev. 1007 (1994).

2. In most other countries of the world, mineral rights belong to the Sovereign, which develops them either through a national oil company or by granting contract rights to domestic or international oil companies. Even in the United States, federal and state mineral ownership is significant, as we discuss in Chapter 7, below.

initial changes in the margins of the printed form. Extensive alterations are likely to be included in a lease addendum, executed with the same formalities as the lease, but usually signed by both the lessor and the lessee. Sometimes the parties modify the lease form by a supplemental agreement, which should be referred to in the lease.[3]

Oil and gas leases are often misunderstood by lessors and unappreciated by the courts. American courts subject lease language to close scrutiny and often construe it in favor of lessors, either because the lessee has drafted the lease or because the lease is an option agreement. In addition, U.S. courts have been quick to recognize *implied covenants* in oil and gas leases. Lease implied covenants arise from the ongoing relationship of the lessor and lessee created by the lease. The lease gives the lessee the exclusive cost-bearing right to explore and develop the leased property, potentially in perpetuity. The lessor has a cost-free interest in production or revenues or value, but no right to drill or produce. Because the typical oil and gas lease makes the lessor's royalty—the major compensation for grant of the lease—dependent upon the quantity and quality of the lessee's actions on the property, courts have concluded that the lessee has an obligation to perform certain unstated obligations, including testing the premises, protecting the lease against drainage, developing it after hydrocarbons are discovered, and marketing production.

1. PURPOSE OF THE LEASE

The key to understanding oil and gas lease provisions is to remember that the lease is a business transaction. A mineral owner, who generally lacks the capital or expertise to explore or develop, transfers those rights to an oil company, which generally has both capital and expertise. Both parties expect to make a profit from the transaction, and the lease form sets out their bargain.

Most oil and gas lease printed forms are drafted or chosen by the lessee.[4] As a result, printed lease forms generally used almost always reflect two fundamental goals of the lessee:

1. The lessee seeks the *right* to develop the leased land for an agreed term without any *obligation* to develop; and

2. If production is obtained, the lessee wants the right to maintain the lease for as long as it is profitable to do so.

Both of the lessee's goals arise from the economic realities of the oil and gas business. Because most mineral rights in the United States are privately owned in fragmented interests in small tracts, oil companies

---

3. For example, in Bay Petroleum Corp. v. May, 286 P.2d 269, 271 (Okla.1955), the court held the lessee liable under a supplemental letter agreement for a "cash bonus at the highest per acre rate paid to any other such owner during the term of [the] lease."

4. Lessees typically take the lead role in oil and gas leasing—choosing the form and approaching mineral owners—because mineral rights in the United States are usually small fractional interests in small tracts. Mineral owners generally lack both the skills and the incentives to develop or to market their mineral rights.

often acquire leases in a highly competitive environment before doing substantial evaluation of their prospects. Further, although application of modern geological and geophysical techniques increases the odds of finding and producing oil and gas profitably, there are no certainties until the lessee takes the risk of drilling. Whether taking that risk will make sense for a lessee depends upon a variety of economic factors that a lessee often cannot assess when it acquires a lease, including supply and demand for oil and gas, tax structure and incentives, and applicable regulatory policies. Therefore, the lessee's first goal in leasing is to obtain the right to drill without obligating itself to do so.

The lessee's second fundamental goal is to maximize profits from leases where the lessee has successfully taken the drilling risk. Because an oil company cannot predict how long a lease will produce profitably, the lessee does not want the lease to have a fixed term. Lessees generally attempt to satisfy this goal by including language in the oil and gas lease that maintains the lease for as long as there is "production in paying quantities," "capability of production in paying quantities," or "operations for oil and gas production."

In return for transferring the exclusive right to drill, from the surface to the center of the earth, unless that right is limited by the terms of the granting clause, the lessor usually receives an immediate cash payment, called a "bonus"; bonuses may run from a dollar to several thousands of dollars per acre leased. The lessor may also receive smaller payments, called "delay rentals," typically on an annual basis, pending production. If the lease proves to be productive, the lessor receives a royalty that is usually based upon the quantity of the production, its value, or the price the lessee receives when it is sold.

We will examine problems relating to delay rentals and royalties at length below. But the business transaction underlying lease formation is fraught with legal problems. Bonus payment is one. Rarely is the lessor's bonus mentioned in a lease; bonus is part of the "other good and valuable consideration" usually recited. Bonus is typically then specified on a simultaneously executed payment slip called a *bank draft*; we have included a sample bank draft in the Forms Manual. Though a bank draft often looks like a check, a draft is subject to conditions, while a check is an unconditional promise to pay. See Rodney D. Knutson and Sandra L. Magerfleisch, The Use and Misuse of Sight and Time Drafts in Oil and Gas Leasing Transactions, 29 Rocky Mtn. Min. L. Inst. 813 (1983). When a lessor deposits a draft, it is not cashed, but must be forwarded to another bank for collection.

Lessees frequently condition payment of lease-bonus drafts upon approval of the lessor's title within a stated period—perhaps 30 or 60 days. If the lessor's title is defective, the lessee can refuse to honor the draft, even if the lessee has recorded the lease, because title approval is a condition precedent to contract formation. Sun Exploration and Production Co. v. Benton, 728 S.W.2d 35 (Tex. 1987). But before the lessee has approved title, is the lessor free to revoke the lease if someone offers a better deal? Or can the lessee revoke before it approves title because a market downturn makes the bonus it had offered too high? See St. Romain v. Midas Exploration, Inc., 430 So.2d 1354 (Ct. App. La. 1983) (a lessee dishonored a draft claiming that its payment was conditioned upon his finding a buyer, which he failed to do. The only condition stated was approval of title, so the lessor was entitled to the full bonus payment.) And what if a lessee approves title and then fails to pay the promised bonus? See Clawson v. Berklund, 610 P.2d 1168 (Mont. 1980) (When the lessee has issued a draft and does not honor it, the lessor is entitled to choose either to cancel the lease or to recover the bonus.). But see Jones v. Bevier, 59 S.W.2d 945 (Tex.Civ.App. 1933) (when the $1 consideration stated in the lease was not paid, the lessor was without remedy, because an oil and gas lease conveys an interest in land and requires no consideration to be binding.)

Lease formation may also be troublesome. Lack of understanding of the oil and gas business and legal niceties by both unsophisticated lessors and unsophisticated oil company employees or agents may lead to claims of fraud or demands for rescission. See Kropa v. Cabot Oil & Gas Corp., 609 F.Supp.2d 372 (M.D. Pa. 2009) (defendant's motion to dismiss claim that lease had been granted by fraudulent inducement denied where the lessee's representative had stated that the lessee would never pay more for the lease than the lessee had offered, but subsequently paid others in the area more); Cascio v. Twin Cities Dev., LLC, 48 So.3d 341 (La. App. 2d Cir. 2010) (lessor not entitled to rescind an oil and gas lease on the theory that there was error regarding the object of the contract, even if the lessor did not know the land it was leasing was land with exceptional qualities— it overlaid the Haynesville Shale—and the lessee did not disclose the existence of the reservoir to the lessor. The court said that it should have been apparent to the lessor that the lessee sought the lease to explore for and produce from the land); Adams v. JPD Energy, Inc., 46 So.3d 751 (La. App. 2d Cir. 2010) (lease could be rescinded because there was no meeting of the minds, even though the lessor had read it before signing it, where the lessor contended that he had been promised a 1/4th royalty and a limit on the depth covered by the lease, but after signing the lease, he realized that it contained a 1/8th royalty provision and had no depth limitation, and the landman acknowledged that the 1/8th royalty provision was incorrect, stating that the lease actually should have contained a 1/5th royalty provision.) And there are frequent problems with the statute of frauds. See Sun–Key Oil Co. v. Whealy, 2006 WL 3114466 (Tex. App. 2006) ("150 acres of land out of the S/2 of the John Hibbins Survey, Abstract #225" does not permit the tract to be identified with sufficient certainty to satisfy the statute of frauds); Aurora Petroleum, Inc. v. Cholla Petroleum, Inc., 2011 WL 652843 (Tex.App.–Amarillo 2011) (an agreement providing that one company would assign its interest in leases to another company, which would drill a test well at a "mutually acceptable" location, was unenforceable).

2. NATURE OF THE LEASEHOLD INTEREST

Jurisdictions disagree about how to classify the rights that are created by an oil and gas lease. In general, however, the leasehold interest is more like the property right created by a real-estate deed than it is like an ordinary real-property lease. Some courts describe the lessee's interest as a fee simple determinable estate in the oil and gas in place, while other courts view the interest as a grant of an irrevocable license or *profit a prendre*. Typically, courts base their classification upon whether the state follows an ownership-in-place or exclusive-right-to-take theory of oil and gas rights.[5]

In states that follow the ownership-in-place theory, courts generally view the lessee's interest as a fee simple determinable estate in the oil and gas in place. The leasehold interest is a fee interest, because the lease contains a clause that allows the interest to continue indefinitely, "as long as there is production * * *," which merges with the term of years set in the primary term. The leasehold is determinable, because it may be terminated by one of the special limitations in the lease, such as the failure to pay delay rentals, the failure to commence operations or obtain production by the end of the primary term, or the cessation of production during the secondary term.

Most states that follow the ownership-in-place theory take the position that the terms of the lease granting clause are not significant in determining the nature of the interest created. Some states, however, have held that the granting clause language is controlling: if the granting clause purports to convey the oil and gas in place, it creates a fee simple interest, but if the granting clause merely grants the lessee the exclusive right to search, develop, and produce, it creates an irrevocable license or a *profit a prendre*.

In states that follow the nonownership or exclusive-right-to-take theory, the courts usually characterize the lessee's interest as an irrevocable license or a *profit a prendre* determinable. Since a conveyance of the oil and gas in place cannot be given literal effect in a nonownership state, the precise language of the granting clause is not significant. For a more complete discussion of the nature of the interest created by the granting clause of oil and gas leases, see Kuntz §§ 23.1–.29.

3. SIGNIFICANCE OF THE CLASSIFICATION OF LEASE INTERESTS

Classification of the lessee's interest as an irrevocable license, a *profit a prendre*, or a fee estate often determines the nature and extent of the lessee's rights. For example, a *profit a prendre* or a license is incorporeal and nonpossessory. Thus, if a state's courts classify the leasehold interest as a *profit a prendre*—as does Oklahoma, for example—or an irrevocable

---

5. See the discussion in Chapter 1.

license, the interest may be abandoned and is not subject to the possessory remedies of trespass and ejectment. The lessee's interest must be protected by nonpossessory actions, such as a quiet title suit. Conversely, if a state's courts classify the leasehold interest as a fee simple estate—as does Texas, for example—then the interest is corporeal and possessory in nature. Thus, the common law rules of abandonment should not apply, but the possessory remedies of trespass and ejectment will be available.

In addition to the corporeal and incorporeal distinction, how the courts classify the leasehold interest may also have substantial bearing upon the application of statutory provisions governing taxation, intestate succession, and judgment liens. The modern trend, however, is for the courts to regard oil and gas rights as *sui generis*. For further discussion, see Kuntz § 23.2.

Both the goals of lessees and the nature of oil and gas lease rights are often misunderstood by lessors and unappreciated by the courts. The courts subject lease language to close scrutiny and often construe it in favor of lessors, either because the lessee has drafted the lease or because the lease is an option agreement. In this chapter, we will survey lease clauses and examine the extent of the rights created by the modern lease. In the process, we will consider some of the interpretative problems that lawyers frequently encounter.

B. GRANTING CLAUSE: THE RIGHTS GRANTED BY A LEASE

The scope of the rights granted by an oil and gas lease is defined in the lease granting clause. A granting clause must address at least three factors that interact to determine the breadth of the rights granted: (1) what rights are given to use the land; (2) what substances are covered; and (3) what land and what interests are subject to the lease.

1. SURFACE USES GRANTED BY THE LEASE

The mineral owner who grants an oil and gas lease is likely to be focused upon the bonus offered and the prospect of royalties if the lessee obtains production. As a result, lessors often overlook the potential for conflict between the lessor and the lessee over use of the surface. The materials that follow illustrate the principles the courts apply to resolve surface use disputes.

HUNT OIL CO. v. KERBAUGH
283 N.W.2d 131 (N.D.1979).

SAND, JUSTICE.

Ivan and Shirley Kerbaugh appealed from an order of the district court enjoining them from interfering with geophysical explorations carried on over their property by the plaintiffs, Hunt Oil Co. and Williams Oil Co. The Kerbaughs asserted the oil companies do not have an unlimited right to conduct seismic exploration over their property and also that the record in this case was inadequate to grant the oil companies injunctive relief. We conditionally affirm.

This case involves geophysical exploration for oil and gas over approximately 1000 acres of land located in Williams County and owned by the Kerbaughs. * * *

The owners of the mineral estates in this case leased their oil and gas interests to Edward Mike Davis for a period of five years in 1974 and 1975, respectively.[1] Davis then conducted seismic exploration over the property in the early part of 1976. Ivan Kerbaugh testified that after the 1976 seismic activity, the flow from a spring which supplied water to his home and livestock, gradually decreased until it stopped in November 1976. Kerbaugh said he restored the flow of the spring, although at a reduced rate, at his own expense. Ivan also testified, that as a result of the 1976 exploration, open holes were left in his property, along with various types of debris.

In 1977, Davis assigned the oil and gas leases to Williams Exploration Co., who subsequently assigned a share of the same leases to Hunt Oil Co. The following summer the oil companies contracted with Pacific West Exploration Co. to conduct seismic exploration activities over certain lands in Williams County, including the Kerbaugh property. Pacific West Exploration contacted Ivan Kerbaugh for permission to conduct the exploration, offering to pay $50 per hole plus additional amounts for damages to growing crops. Kerbaugh rejected the offer and counteroffered with a request of $200 per hole, plus $1 per rod of tracks on the land, a commitment to cement shut any holes, and a guarantee of continued water supply. Although Kerbaugh later reduced his requests, they were rejected by Pacific.

When surveying for the exploration started, Kerbaugh requested the surveyors to leave until an agreement was reached as to compensation for damages to his surface rights. The oil companies then filed a summons and complaint seeking temporary and permanent injunctive relief restraining the Kerbaughs from interfering with the oil companies in the exercise of their rights under the oil and gas lease. Three affidavits were filed in support of the requested relief.

On 22 August 1978, the district court issued an order to show cause why Kerbaugh should not be restrained from interfering with the oil companies and issued an ex parte temporary injunction. Upon issuance of

---

1. The lease to Davis of the first tract of land was a form lease which provided:

"Lessee shall pay for damages caused by his operation to growing crops on said lands."

The leases covering the remaining lands were on what appear to be identical forms, although the above provision was altered to read:

"Lessee shall pay for damages caused by his operation on said lands & all surface & underground water."

the temporary injunction, Pacific West Exploration commenced the seismic activities. The Kerbaughs thereafter filed a motion to vacate the ex parte temporary injunction which was granted after a hearing held 28 August 1978. On 7 September 1978 the show cause hearing on the permanent injunction was held, after which the district court entered an order granting the restraint.

Kerbaughs appealed from the order contending the record was inadequate to grant injunctive relief, and that the oil companies did not have an unlimited right under the mineral leases to enter upon the Kerbaugh property for extensive exploration activities, particularly in light of prior harm to the Kerbaugh property from such activities.

* * *

The Kerbaughs argued the oil companies did not have an unlimited right to conduct seismic exploration over the Kerbaugh property. This court in Christman v. Emineth, 212 N.W.2d 543, 550, 70 A.L.R.3d 366 (N.D.1973), adopted the general rule set forth in 58 C.J.S. Mines and Minerals § 159b as to the implied rights of the mineral estate owner:

> * * * unless the language of the conveyance repels such a construction, as a general rule a grant of mines or minerals gives to the owner of the minerals the incidental right of entering, occupying, and making such use of the surface lands as is reasonably necessary in exploring, mining, removing, and marketing the minerals * * *. The incidental right of entering, occupying, and making such use of the surface lands as is reasonably necessary exists in the case of a reservation of mineral rights as well as a grant.

We have also considered the rights of the lessee under the usual oil and gas lease. In Feland v. Placid Oil Co., 171 N.W.2d 829, 834 (N.D. 1969), Chief Justice Teigen, speaking for the court, stated:

> Under a usual oil and gas lease, the lessee, in developing the leased premises, is entitled to use of the land reasonably necessary in producing the oil * * *.
>
> > Whether the express uses are set out or not, the mere granting of the lease creates and vests in the lessee the dominant estate in the surface of the land for the purposes of the lease; by implication it grants the lessee the use of the surface to the extent necessary to a full enjoyment of the grant. Without such use, the mineral estate obtained under the lease would be worthless. * * *
> > Texaco, Inc. v. Faris, 413 S.W.2d 147, 149 (Tex.Civ.App.1967).

The above cases recognize the well-settled rule that where the mineral estate is severed from the surface estate, the mineral estate is dominant. See Annot., 53 A.L.R.3d 16; 4 Summers, Oil and Gas, § 652; 58 C.J.S. Mines and Minerals § 159b. The mineral estate is dominant in that the law implies, where it is not granted, a legitimate area within which mineral ownership of necessity carries with it inherent surface rights to find and develop the minerals, which rights must and do involve the surface estate. Without such rights the mineral estate would be meaningless and worthless. Thus, the surface estate is servient in the sense it is charged with the servitude for those essential rights of the mineral estate.

In the absence of other rights expressly granted or reserved, the rights of the owner of the mineral estate are limited to so much of the surface and such use thereof as are *reasonably necessary* to explore, develop, and transport the minerals. In addition to, or underlying the question of what constitutes reasonable use of the surface in the development of oil and gas rights, is the concept that the owner of the mineral estate must have *due regard* for the rights of the surface owner and is required to exercise that degree of care and use which is a just consideration for the rights of the surface owner. Therefore, the mineral estate owner has no right to use more of, or do more to, the surface estate than is reasonably necessary to explore, develop, and transport the minerals. Nor does the mineral estate owner have the right to negligently or wantonly use the surface owner's estate.[2]

The requirement that due regard be given to the rights of the surface owner, defines, to a certain extent, a consideration in determining if the mineral owner's use of the surface is reasonably necessary. In Getty Oil Co. v. Jones, supra, the Texas Supreme Court set forth what has become known as the "accommodation doctrine":

> There may be only one manner of use of the surface whereby the minerals can be produced. The lessee has the right to pursue this use, regardless of surface damage. [Citations omitted.] And there may be necessitous temporary use governed by the same principle. But under the circumstances indicated here; i.e., where there is an existing use by the surface owner which would otherwise be precluded or impaired, and where under the established practices in the industry there are alternatives available to the lessee whereby the minerals can be recovered, the rules of reasonable usage of the surface may require the adoption of an alternative by the lessee. 470 S.W.2d at 622.

The Utah Supreme Court adopted the opinion of the Texas court in Flying Diamond Corporation v. Rust, 551 P.2d 509 (Utah 1976), where it said, at page 511:

---

2. This case does not present, nor does this opinion decide, the issue of whether or not the owner or lessee of the mineral estate is liable for damages arising from the reasonably necessary use of the surface incident to the exploration, development, and transportation of the minerals. The authorities which have considered the issue appear to be in agreement that such damages are *damnum absque injuria* and no recovery can be had against the mineral estate owner or lessee. This conclusion seems to rest on a principle that injury necessarily inflicted in the exercise of a lawful right does not create a liability, but rather, the injury must be the direct result of the commission of a wrong. We question, however, the social desirability of a rule which potentially allows the damage or destruction of a surface estate equal or greater in value than the value of the mineral being extracted.

Future mineral exploration and development can be expected to expand as our demands for energy sources grow. Equity requires a closer examination of whether or not the cost of surface damage and destruction arising from mineral development should be borne by the owner of a severed surface estate or by the developer and consumer of the minerals. Although we do not doubt the mineral estate owner's right to use the surface estate to explore, develop and transport the minerals, we specifically do not decide if the right of reasonable use also implies the right to damage and destroy without compensation. * * *

* * * wherever there exist separate ownerships of interests in the same land, each should have the right to the use and enjoyment of his interest in the property to the highest degree possible not inconsistent with the rights of the other. We do not mean to be understood as saying that such a lessee must use any possible alternative. But he is obliged to pursue one which is reasonable and practical under the circumstances.

We join with the Utah court in adopting the accommodation doctrine set forth in *Getty:*

The reasonableness of a surface use by the lessee is to be determined by a consideration of the circumstances of both and, as stated, the surface owner is under the burden of establishing the unreasonableness of the lessee's surface use in this light. The reasonableness of the method and manner of using the dominant mineral estate may be measured by what are usual, customary and reasonable practices in the industry under like circumstances of time, place and servient estate uses. What may be a reasonable use of the surface by the mineral lessee on a bald prairie used only for grazing by the servient surface owner could be unreasonable within an existing residential area of the City of Houston, or on the campus of the University of Texas, or in the middle of an irrigated farm. What we have said is that in determining the issue of whether a particular manner of use in the dominant estate is reasonable or unreasonable, we cannot ignore the condition of the surface itself and the uses then being made by the servient surface owner. * * * [I]f the manner of use selected by the dominant mineral lessee is the only reasonable, usual and customary method that is available for developing and producing the minerals on the particular land then the owner of the servient estate must yield. However, if there are other usual, customary and reasonable methods practiced in the industry on similar lands put to similar uses which would not interfere with the existing uses being made by the servient surface owner, it could be unreasonable for the lessee to employ an interfering method or manner of use. These [conditions] involve questions to be resolved by the trier of the facts. 470 S.W.2d at 627–628.

In this case the Kerbaughs sought to prevent the oil companies from conducting seismic exploration activities on their property. The oil companies, on the other hand, sought an injunction prohibiting the Kerbaughs from interfering with such exploration.

The Kerbaughs, in support of their argument for denial of injunctive relief, offered affidavits and testimony indicating the damages they had sustained as the result of prior seismic exploration; that the present seismic activity was causing damage to their grain crop, pasture, and other farmland; and that they fear additional damage to property from further seismic activity.

Whether or not the use of the surface estate by the mineral estate owner is reasonably necessary is a question of fact for the trier of facts. In addition, the burden of proof in such a determination is upon the servient estate owner. Getty Oil Co. v. Jones, supra.

The Kerbaughs presented evidence establishing the damage to their property that arose or was likely to arise as a result of seismic activity. They offered, however, no evidence of reasonable alternatives available to the oil companies to explore the properties. They offered no evidence that the same information could be obtained from the prior geophysical exploration; they offered no evidence that the same information could be obtained without traversing over cropland; and the record does not indicate that they offered evidence that the tests could be conducted in another manner which would cause less damage to the Kerbaughs. Although the Kerbaughs did offer evidence suggesting some damage could have been avoided by having the oil companies conduct the operations a few weeks later, the affidavits filed by the oil companies indicate this was not a reasonable alternative. On the basis of the evidence presented by the parties, the Kerbaughs failed to meet their burden of proof that the proposed activities of the oil companies were not reasonably necessary for the exploration of the leased mineral estate. Accordingly, the conclusion by the district court that the oil companies were entitled to injunctive relief was not in error.

It is important to note that the Texas Supreme Court in *Getty* concluded the accommodation doctrine is not a balancing type test weighing the harm or inconvenience to the owner of one type of interest against the benefit to the other. Rather the court said the test is the availability of alternative non-conflicting uses of the two types of owners. Inconvenience to the surface owner is not the controlling element where no reasonable alternatives are available to the mineral owner or lessee. The surface owner must show that under the circumstances, the use of the surface under attack is not reasonably necessary.

We agree a pure balancing test is not involved under the accommodation doctrine where no reasonable alternatives are available. Where alternatives do exist, however, the concepts of due regard and reasonable necessity do require a weighing of the different alternatives against the inconveniences to the surface owner. Therefore, once alternatives are shown to exist a balancing of the mineral and surface owner's interest does occur.

Kerbaugh argued and urged this court to adopt a rule of correlative rights and reasonableness, as discussed in Pennington v. Colonial Pipeline Company, 260 F.Supp. 643, 25 Oil and Gas Rptr. 514 (E.D.La.1966) affirmed 5 Cir., 387 F.2d 903. In that case the district court said the rights of the holder of a mineral lease, and the rights of the owner of the surface "are correlative rights, neither being superior to nor inferior to the other, and the rights of each party can only be exercised in such a manner as not to unreasonably interfere with the rights of the other. [Citations omitted.]'' Be that as it may, it does not change the basic rule that a servitude exists in favor of the oil and gas estate and thus it is the dominant estate and the surface estate is the servient estate. Although the rights implied in favor of the mineral estate can be exercised only by giving due regard to the rights of the surface owner, the mineral estate still remains dominant in the traditional real property sense. The district court in *Pennington,* although applying the right test of reasonableness, made an unfortunate use of the term "correlative rights" which is more appropriately used in referring to rights among various owners of mineral interests. See, Arnstad v. North Dakota State Industrial Commission, 122 N.W.2d 857 (N.D. 1963); 1 Kuntz, Oil and Gas § 43.

* * *

The Kerbaughs contended the oil companies failed to provide the proper statutory notice prior to engaging in the exploration drilling. The record indicates some irregularity in the manner in which the filing requirements of § 38–08.1–04, NDCC, were complied with. Chapter 38–08.1 provides, however, its own penalty for a person violating the provisions of the chapter. If the oil companies in this case failed to comply with Ch. 38–08.1, they may be subject to the penalty provided in § 38–08.1–07, NDCC. Such failure of compliance, however, does not affect the validity of the temporary injunction.

The Kerbaughs also asserted the oil companies failed to show the existence of an exigency as to support the issuance of an injunction.

The oil companies were not required to show their proposed activities were the most reasonable or even that other alternatives were unreasonable in the absence of the Kerbaughs' bringing the reasonableness of other alternatives into issue. The oil companies had the right to use the surface in exploring for their minerals. They also had the right to seek an injunction preventing the Kerbaughs from interfering with the right of exploration. It was the Kerbaughs' burden to show the proposed activities were unreasonable by reason of the existence of other alternatives.

In summary, the Kerbaughs, as the owner of the servient surface, failed to show the proposed exploration activities of the oil companies were not reasonably necessary as to prevent the issuance of a temporary injunction. What showing will or can be made on the merits of the case for a permanent injunction is not before us on this appeal.

* * *

The order of the district court is affirmed.

* * *

NOTES

1. As *Kerbaugh* indicates, courts generally hold that severing the minerals from the surface, whether by a mineral deed or an oil and gas lease,

impliedly creates in the mineral owner or lessee "inherent surface rights to find and develop the minerals." Among those implied rights are:

(a) *The right to use and occupy the surface of the land for purposes reasonably necessary to develop and operate the lease.* What is "reasonable" is determined by reference to the purpose of the easement. The implied right has been held to include the right to build storage tanks, power stations, and structures upon the leased land to produce, store, and take care of production, Gregg v. Caldwell–Guadalupe Pick–Up Stations, 286 S.W. 1083 (Tex.Com.App. 1926); to lay pipes on the land to gather production, Rostocil v. Phillips Petroleum Co., 502 P.2d 825 (Kan.1972); to build roads and residences for employees, Livingston v. Indian Territory Illuminating Oil Co., 91 F.2d 833 (10th Cir.Okla.1937); to construct salt water disposal pits, Feland v. Placid Oil Co., 171 N.W.2d 829 (N.D.1969); to conduct a waterflood program, Miller v. Crown Central Petroleum Corp., 309 S.W.2d 876 (Tex.Civ.App.1958); and to conduct seismographic tests, Yates v. Gulf Oil Corp., 182 F.2d 286 (5th Cir.Tex.1950).

A difficulty with the implied easement for surface use is that it is a "blanket" easement; its terms do not define its location or limits. Courts may construe such easements narrowly or broadly. Compare Southern Star Cent. Gas Pipeline, Inc. v. Cunning, 157 P.3d 1120 (Kan.App. 2007), holding that a garage located 41 inches from a natural gas pipeline did not materially interfere with the blanket easement, with Texas Eastern Transmission, LP v. Perano, 230 Fed.Appx. 134 (3rd Cir. Pa. 2007), holding that a pipeline was entitled to a right of way of 25 feet on either side, so that a homeowner was required to remove a mobile home that had been erected within 10 feet of the pipeline. Professor Pierce discusses the blanket-easement problem, and recommends lease language for landowners in Incorporating a Century of Oil and Gas Jurisprudence Into the "Modern" Oil and Gas Lease, 33 Washburn L. J. 786, 795 (1994).

(b) *The right to use and occupy the surface of the land at locations reasonably necessary to develop and operate the lease.* Again, "reasonable necessity" is judged by reference to the purpose of the easement and the courts may interpret it either narrowly or broadly. Compare Lierly v. Tidewater Petroleum Corporation, 2006 OK 47, 139 P.3d 897 (2006), where the court held the oil and gas operator was not entitled to an injunction to establish access at a new location on the lease when the operator already had access at another location and upheld a jury verdict finding the operator liable for malicious prosecution when it sued for injunctive relief, with Grimes v. Goodman Drilling Co., 216 S.W. 202, 203 (Tex.Civ.App.1919), where the court held a lessee entitled to locate a derrick, engine, boiler, and slush pit on a city lot in close proximity to a dwelling house, observing that:

> The slush pit connected with the well is near to and runs along the side of plaintiff's house, and slush spatters therefrom onto the sides of the house, the doors, and windows, and necessitates that side of the house being closed up. The running of the engine is very objectionable to the plaintiff's family and often prevents their sleeping at nights, and is so loud as to require them in ordinary conversation to speak in very loud tones. The evidence shows that conditions about this well, the noise, the slush, the

grease, etc., are similar to conditions prevailing around oil wells generally.
* * *

(c) *The right to use and consume the surface or its products in oil and gas operations*. A severed mineral owner or lessee may take potable groundwater belonging to the surface owner for secondary recovery operations (Sun Oil Co. v. Whitaker, 483 S.W.2d 808 (Tex.1972)), destroy growing crops without compensating the surface owner (Adkins v. United Fuel Gas Co., 61 S.E.2d 633 (W.Va.1950) and Robinson Drilling Co. v. Moses, 256 S.W.2d 650 (Tex. Civ.App.1953)); use clay dug on the leasehold to construct access roads (B.L. McFarland Drilling Contractor v. Connell, 344 S.W.2d 493 (Tex.Civ.App. 1961), judgment set aside on other grounds 347 S.W.2d 565 (Tex.1961)); and dispose of produced water from the lease into a previously drilled dry hole on the land (Leger v. Petroleum Engineers, Inc., 499 So.2d 953 (La.App.1986)).

A lessee generally may exercise these implied rights without the lessor's permission, with no obligation to compensate the lessor for surface damage and with no obligation to restore the premises. *Kerbaugh* outlines the underlying reasoning, though that court specifically declined to find that a lessee is not required to pay surface damages.

2.   The general principle that the mineral interest is dominant and the surface interest servient is limited by at least five countervailing principles, all of which interact to define the scope of the easement.

(a) *The mineral interest owner or lessee may make only such use of the surface as is reasonably necessary to produce oil and gas*. Consequently, as *Kerbaugh* notes, the scope of the implied easement is exceeded if the use is unreasonable. In Brown v. Lundell, 344 S.W.2d 863 (Tex.1961), the Supreme Court of Texas invoked the "reasonably necessary" limitation to find liability against a lessee for negligent pollution:

> The right of the lessee in exploring for and producing oil and gas embraces only the doing of those things expressly granted or necessarily implied in the lease as necessarily incidental thereto. All property rights not granted are reserved in the lessor. The rights of the lessor and lessee are reciprocal and distinct. If either party exceeds those rights he becomes a trespasser. Thus, if the lessee negligently and unnecessarily damages the lessor's land, either surface or subsurface, his liability to the lessor is no different from what it would be under the same circumstances to an adjoining landowner. The jury impliedly found that by taking reasonable precautions to dispose of the salt water that was accumulated as a necessary incident to the production of oil the operator could have avoided the pollution of the water. The operator did not obtain the right to permit the salt to drain and seep down into the subsoil and the resultant damage. The use of the lessor's land is limited. In other words the lessor has granted and leased to the lessee only so much of his land as will be reasonably necessary to effectuate the purpose of the lease, and to be used in a non-negligent manner.

344 S.W.2d at 866. In Tenneco Oil Co. v. Allen, 515 P.2d 1391 (Okla.1973), the Oklahoma Supreme Court applied the limitation of reasonableness to hold the lessee liable on a theory of nuisance for failure to fill and level abandoned wells and remove equipment and cement foundations, even though the

structures complained of had been placed on the land by previous oil opera-tors. The court said that "depriving the lessor of the use of portions of the leased land which were no longer reasonably necessary for the performance of the lessee's obligations under the oil and gas lease * * * constituted the use of that much of the surface which was not reasonably necessary." 515 P.2d at 1397.

Can a use of the surface that violates a conservation-agency statute or rule be reasonable? In Gerrity Oil & Gas Corporation v. Magness, 946 P.2d 913 (Colo. 1997), the Colorado Supreme Court held that violations of commis-sion rules were valid, but not conclusive, evidence that an oil and gas lessee had breached its duty of reasonable use.

Who decides whether a use is reasonable? What factors are relevant to determine reasonableness? Is it possible that abandoning a well without plugging and clean-up would have been considered reasonable at one time, but is no longer—that uses once deemed reasonable will become unreasonable as a result of legislative, societal, or technological changes? Is it possible that uses that were not contemplated by the parties will become reasonable as a result of legislative or societal change? See Pacific Gas Transmission Co. v. Richard-son's Recreational Ranch, Ltd., 773 F.Supp. 246 (D.Or.1991).

(b) *The use of the land must not violate the accommodation doctrine.* Discussed in *Kerbaugh*, the accommodation doctrine was first stated by the Texas Supreme Court in Getty Oil Co. v. Jones, 470 S.W.2d 618 (Tex.1971). In *Getty,* the surface owner sought to prevent an oil and gas lessee from installing pumping units that would have prevented the surface owner from continuing to use an automatic irrigation sprinkler system. For several years, Jones, the surface owner, had operated a "center-pivot" sprinkler system, a seven-foot high self-propelled device that rotated around a pivot point to distribute water. Getty, the mineral lessee, drilled oil wells and installed pumping units with upstrokes substantially greater than seven feet. As a result, Jones could not operate the irrigation system. Getty argued that its use of the land was reasonable because its pumping units were necessary to produce oil. The Texas Supreme Court disagreed, noting that Getty could have avoided the conflict by placing the pumping units in concrete cellars, and stating what has come to be called the accommodation doctrine:

> Where there is an existing use by the surface owner which will otherwise be precluded or impaired, and where under the established practices in the industry there are alternatives available to the lessee whereby the minerals can be recovered, the rules of reasonable usage of the surface may require the adoption of an alternative by the lessee.

470 S.W.2d at 622.

Under the *Getty* view, the surface owner must meet three requirements to invoke the accommodation principle: (1) there must be an existing use of the surface; (2) the mineral lessee's proposed use of the surface must preclude or impair the existing use of the surface; and (3) the mineral lessee must have a reasonable alternative available.

What constitutes an "existing" use is perhaps the most troublesome aspect of the accommodation doctrine. In Diamond Shamrock Corp. v. Phillips, 511 S.W.2d 160 (Ark. 1974), the Arkansas Supreme Court upheld a judgment of damages to a surface owner where a gas well was located on the site of a planned location for the surface owner's home. In Texas Genco, LP v. Valence Operating Company, 187 S.W.3d 118 (Tex. App. 2006), the court treated a dedication of land to waste storage as an existing use even though no waste had been stored. Should the protection of the accommodation doctrine be limited to situations where the surface owner is physically using the property? Why would the Texas Supreme Court so limit the doctrine in *Getty?*

The accommodation doctrine's requirement that a surface owner have an existing use of the surface to qualify for protection by the accommodation doctrine may be a big impediment to urban development. To address the tension, in 1983, the Texas legislature enacted a law permitting subdivision developers in heavily populated counties to require that oil and gas well sites and supporting locations be designated by the mineral owner or mineral lessee. See Tex. Nat.Res.Code Ann. §§ 92.001–92.007. The Texas statute is discussed at Smith & Weaver § 9.2. See also Jeffrey R. Fiske and Ann E. Lane, Urbanization of the Oil Patch: What Happens When They Pave Paradise and Put Up a Parking Lot, 49 Rocky Mtn. Min. L. Inst. 15–1 (2003).

In 1990, the Uniform Law Commissioners adopted a Model Surface Use and Mineral Development Accommodation Act that embraces and expands both the accommodation doctrine and the scheme of the Texas Statute. See Unif. Model Surface Use & Min. Dev. Accommodation Act (U.L.A.). In 2007, the Colorado legislature codified and broadened the accommodation doctrine, which the Colorado Supreme Court had adopted in Gerrity Oil & Gas Corporation v. Magness, 946 P.2d 913 (Colo. 1997).

Interference with surface use must be substantial to trigger the accommodation doctrine. The court in Davis v. Devon Energy Production Co., L.P., 136 S.W.3d 419 (Tex. App. 2004), relied on *Getty* to hold that "only when the conduct of the lessee destroys or substantially impairs the surface owner's use of the surface does the question arise whether that conduct is reasonably necessary." In this case, though there was some evidence that construction of permanent caliche roads might inconvenience the surface owner, the evidence did not support the surface owner's claim that the roads would destroy his ability to conduct a profitable farming operation.

The requirement that the lessee have a "reasonable alternative" also may be difficult for a surface owner claiming the protection of the accommodation doctrine to satisfy. Less than a year after the *Getty* decision, the Texas Supreme Court substantially limited the accommodation doctrine in Sun Oil Co. v. Whitaker, 483 S.W.2d 808 (Tex.1972). In *Whitaker,* the owner of severed surface rights who farmed by irrigation from the Ogallala aquifer (which supplies irrigation water for much of the irrigated lands of Colorado, Kansas, Oklahoma, and Texas) sued Sun to prevent the oil company from using potable water from the Ogallala formation in a secondary recovery water flood project. Evidence indicated that the amount of water to be taken from Sun's wells would adversely affect the amount of water flow available for irrigation and shorten the life of Whitaker's water supply by 15–20 percent. Evidence also showed that Sun could purchase and pipe in water for its purposes at economically feasible prices. The lower court found Sun's use of the ground water unreasonable, but the Texas Supreme Court reversed:

> To hold that Sun can be required to purchase water from other sources or owners of other tracts in the area, would be in derogation of the dominant estate.
>
> Our holding in Getty Oil Co. v. Jones, 470 S.W.2d 618 (Tex.1971), is not applicable under the facts of this case. It is limited to situations in which there are reasonable alternative methods that may be employed by the lessee *on the leased premises* to accomplish the purposes of this lease. (Emphasis in original).

483 S.W.2d at 812. Apparently, according to *Whitaker,* for the alternatives to be reasonable they must be available on the leased land. Does this distinction made by the Texas Supreme Court make sense to you? What is the impact of this distinction upon the accommodation doctrine in Texas? In determining the reasonableness of an alternative available to a lessee, of what relevance is the extra cost associated with that alternative? See *Getty,* 470 S.W.2d at 622.

For a critique of the accommodation doctrine as applied by Texas courts, see David E. Pierce, Developments in Nonregulatory Oil and Gas Law: Beyond Theories and Rules to the Motivating Jurisprudence, 58 Inst. on Oil & Gas L. & Tax'n 1–1 (2007) (§ 1.02[2] When Sticks Clash: The Accommodation Doctrine).

(c) *The surface use must be related exclusively to obtaining the minerals under the servient surface.* Thus, an oil and gas lessee may not use the surface of leased land to develop or to haul production from the lands of others. Mountain Fuel Supply Co. v. Smith, 471 F.2d 594 (10th Cir.Utah 1973). In Gill v. McCollum, 311 N.E.2d 741 (Ill.App.1974), the court held that a lessee could not put salt water from other leases in the area into a disposal well on its lease. In Robinson v. Robbins Petroleum Corp., 501 S.W.2d 865 (Tex.1973), the Texas Supreme Court applied the "exclusivity" principle to bar the taking of salt water from a well on the leased property to repressure an oil-bearing formation under a voluntary enhanced-recovery unit that included the leased property. On the other hand, in Dunn v. Southwest Ardmore Tulip Creek Sand Unit, 548 P.2d 685 (Okla.App.Div.1 1976), confronted with a similar problem in a compulsory enhanced-recovery unit, an Oklahoma Court of Appeals said that "[u]pon the creation of the unit the defendants had the right * * * to use the salt water well for the reasonable development of said unit." 548 P.2d at 688. In Delhi Gas Pipeline Corp. v. Dixon, 737 S.W.2d 96 (Tex.App.1987), the court followed similar reasoning in approving a gathering line across land included in a voluntary gas unit. In Kysar v. Amoco Production Co., 93 P.3d 1272 (N.M. 2004), the court held that a lessee could use the surface of leased land covered by a communitization agreement to gain access to a well on other lands within the unit, but could not use the surface of portions of leased acreage not within the pooled area, even though a portion of a lease was within the pooled area and shared in production. Is *Robinson, Dunn* and *Delhi,* or *Kysar* the more logically correct position? Or are they distinguishable? See generally W. C. Crais III, Annotation, Right of Owner of Title to or Interest in Minerals Under One Tract to Use Surface, or Underground Passages, in Connection with Mining Other Tract, 83 A.L.R.2d 665 (1962).

(d) *Application of the state's police power may limit the easement rights of the mineral owner or lessee through state statutes, city ordinances, and governmental regulations.* As the court notes in *Kerbaugh,* North Dakota law requires that notice be given to the surface owner before commencement of drilling. N.D.Cent.Code § 38–11.1–05. Many other states have similar provisions. See, e.g., Okla.Stat.Ann. tit. 52, § 318.3 and Colo. Rev. Stat. §§ 24–65.5–103.

Surface damage acts are a more controversial application of the police power of the state. Several states, including Colorado, New Mexico, North Dakota, Montana, Oklahoma, South Dakota, Tennessee, Washington, and West Virginia, have enacted statutes aimed at protecting surface uses from disruption by oil and gas operations. The statutes impose strict liability for surface damages caused by oil and gas operations, reversing the common law rule that the mineral owner has the right of reasonable surface use without any obligation to pay damages. Under the acts, oil companies are generally required to attempt to negotiate damage settlements before commencing operations. If the oil companies and surface owners cannot reach an agreement, the oil company has the right to proceed to develop, and damages will be resolved by litigation or arbitration. See, e.g., N.D.Cent.Code §§ 38–11.1–01 to 11.1–10, held constitutional in Murphy v. Amoco Production Co., 729 F.2d 552 (8th Cir.N.D.1984). There are many cases construing the Oklahoma Act. Two of the more important are Houck v. Hold Oil Corp., 867 P.2d 451 (Okla.1993) (holding inter alia that the appropriate measure of damages under the act is diminution in market value to the affected land, likening the act to a condemnation action) and Vastar Resources, Inc. v. Howard, 38 P.3d 236 (Okla.Civ.App. Div. 2 2001) (holding that the common law, not the Act, governs claims for willful or negligent conduct, such as claims relating to alleged groundwater and subsurface pollution). See also John S. Lowe, The Easement of the Mineral Estate for Surface Use: An Analysis of its Rationale, Status and Prospects, 39th Rocky Mtn. Min. L. Inst. Ch. 4.04[2] (1993), and Ronald W. Polston, Redefining the Relationship Between the Surface Owner and the Mineral Developer, 12 E.Min.L.Inst. 22–1 (1991).

(e) *Lease clauses, restrictive covenants, or other agreements may curtail the rights of use of the mineral owner or mineral lessee.* The parties to a lease may limit the implied rights by express language. As we have said in note 1 (c), above, the lessee's dominant easement generally includes the right to destroy growing crops without liability to the surface owner. But that right is often limited by an express lease clause. Consider the following example, which is somewhat different from the provision mentioned in *Kerbaugh:*

> When required by the Lessor, the Lessee shall bury its pipelines below plow depth and shall pay for damage caused by its operations to growing crops on said land. No well shall be drilled nearer than 200 feet to the house or barn on said premises as of the date of this Lease without written consent of the Lessor.

Is this clause sufficient to protect a surface user? How could it be improved? If you represented a potential lessee, would you recommend that the company accept such a clause?

Where the lease provides for payments to be made for "damages to growing crops," as in *Kerbaugh* and the language quoted above, are indigenous grasses and trees growing crops? If so, are damages to be measured by the value of the crops growing when operations begin or by the value of the crops that could be grown during the many years that operations may continue? Contrast Bell v. Cardinal Drilling Co., 85 N.W.2d 246 (N.D.1957), and Chambers v. Skaggs Cos., 732 P.2d 801 (Kan.App. 1987), with Okla.Stat. tit. 52, § 320. See generally V. Woerner, Annotation, Construction and Effect of Provision for Payment of Damages to "Crops" or "Growing Crops" in Mineral Deed or Lease, or in Conveyance of Pipeline or Other Underground Easement, 87 A.L.R.2d 235 (1963).

Landowners may also define reasonableness by imposing restrictive covenants. In The Mable Cleary Trust v. The Edward–Marlah Muzyl Trust, 686 N.W.2d 770 (Mich.App. 2004), the court held that a developer's 50% mineral interest in a subdivision was burdened by restrictive covenants the developer put in place before it severed its mineral interest from the surface estate, but that an oil and gas lease lessor's 50% interest in mineral rights, which it retained when it sold the land to the developer, was not burdened by them because its mineral rights were severed before the restrictive covenants were recorded. See also Devendorf v. Akbar Petroleum Corp., 577 N.E.2d 707 (Ohio App. 9 Dist.1989) (oil lessee who took lease subject to subdivision restrictive covenant barring "business of any type * * *" could not include land in a drilling unit), and Property Owners of Leisure Land, Inc. v. Woolf & Magee, Inc., 786 S.W.2d 757 (Tex.App.1990) (oil lessee who took lease before subdivision restrictions were imposed was not subject to the restrictions). Conservation easements are increasingly more important limitations upon surface use; conservation easements now encumber more than five million acres. Nancy A. McLaughlin, Conservation Easements: Why and How? 51 Rocky Mtn. Min. L. Inst. 22–1 (2005).

Also, landowners may be able to alter reasonable uses. The Restatement (Third) Of Property (Servitudes) § 4.8 cmnt. f (2000) provides that:

> Unless expressly denied by the terms of an easement, * * * the owner of the servient estate is entitled to make reasonable changes in the location or dimensions of an easement, at the servient owner's expense, to permit normal use or development of the servient estate, but only if the changes do not a) significantly lessen the utility of the easement, b) increase the burdens on the owner of the easement in its use and enjoyment, or c) frustrate the purpose for which the easement was created.

For discussion of the Restatement rule, see Roaring Fork Club, L.P. v. St. Jude's Co., 36 P.3d 1229 (Colo. 2001). Alternatively, some courts have applied equitable principles to permit landowners relief even when the lessee's use is "reasonable." See Mid–America Pipeline Co. v. Wietharn, 246 Kan. 238, 250–51, 787 P.2d 716 (1990) (refusing to order surface owner to remove encroaching buildings).

3. Many oil and gas leases contain express provisions authorizing the lessee to use water from the land.[6] Would a grant of "free use of water from said land, except water from lessor's wells, for all operations hereunder" give the lessee the right to use water from an artificial stock pond? Compare Arkansas Louisiana Gas Co. v. Wood, 403 S.W.2d 54 (Ark.1966) (lessee may not use the landowner's private ponds or tanks), with Wyckoff v. Brown, 11 P.2d 720 (Kan.1932), and Carroll v. Roger Lacy, Inc., 402 S.W.2d 307 (Tex.Civ.App.1966) (restriction limited to the lessor's wells). See also P. G. Guthrie, Annotation, Construction of Oil and Gas Lease Provision Giving Lessee Free Use of Water from Lessor's Land, 23 A.L.R.3d 1434 (1969). In a prior-appropriation jurisdiction, is a broad water-use provision an unauthorized grant that may put the lessor's water rights in jeopardy? See generally Comment, Changing Manner and Place of Use of Water Rights in Wyoming, 10 Land & Water L.Rev. 455 (1975).

4. If the grant of an oil and gas lease gives the lessee an implied right to use the surface of the land subject to the lease in ways and at locations as are reasonably necessary to enable the lessee to develop the oil and gas, why do most oil and gas leases contain a detailed statement of rights given to the lessee in the granting clause? Consider the following from a Louisiana form:

> Lessor, in consideration of the sum of _____ ($_____), hereby leases and lets unto Lessee, the exclusive right to enter upon and use the land hereinafter described for the exploration for, and production of oil, gas, sulphur and all other minerals, together with the use of the surface of the land for all purposes incident to the exploration for and production, ownership, possession, storage and transportation of said minerals (either from said land or acreage pooled therewith), and the right to dispose of salt water, with the right of ingress and egress to and from said lands at all times for such purposes, including the right to construct, maintain and use roads, pipelines and/or canals thereon for operations hereunder or in connection with similar operations on adjoining land, and including the right to remove from the land any property placed by Lessee thereon and to draw and remove casing from wells drilled by Lessee on said land; the land to which this lease applies and which is affected hereby being situated in _____ Parish, Louisiana, and described as follows, to-wit: [Legal description follows].

Does the language quoted give the lessee greater rights than it would have had without the clause? See East v. Pan Am. Petroleum Corp., 168 So.2d 426 (La.App.1964), for a discussion of the limits of this clause. See also Buffalo Mining Co. v. Martin, 267 S.E.2d 721 (W.Va.1980). In Caskey v. Kelly Oil Co., 737 So.2d 1257 (La.1999), the Louisiana Supreme Court held that a lease granting clause that gave the lessee the authority to construct roads in connection with mineral operations "on any adjacent lands" authorized the assignee of a non-operating fractional working interest in the lease to build an improved oilfield road across the lease to an adjacent tract on which the assignee had a lease but in which lessors owned no interest without having to prove that the lessors would receive some benefit. Could a severed mineral

---

6. See, for example, the Texas AAPL oil and gas lease in the Forms Manual.

owner validly grant a lessee the right to conduct operations on the lease in connection with operations on adjacent lands?

5. What remedies are available to a surface owner if a lessee abuses the easement for surface use? In Speedman Oil Co. v. Duval County Ranch Co., 504 S.W.2d 923 (Tex.Civ.App.–San Antonio 1973), the lessee argued that the surface owner should be limited to damages. The court rejected that argument:

> There is evidence of a long continued history of oil leaks and spillage resulting from the use of deteriorated equipment which has not been properly maintained. Where the trespass or injury to land is continuous, or frequently recurring, constantly adding to the damage, the legal remedy is inadequate because a jury cannot fix upon a time when the wrong may be said to be complete. Conduct that results in destruction or a serious change in the nature of property either physically or in the character in which it is being used does irreparable injury and justifies interlocutory injunctive relief.

504 S.W.2d at 929. In Thurner v. Kaufman, 699 P.2d 435, 439 (Kan. 1985), the court upheld lease cancellation as a remedy for "continuous unreasonable" breach of express surface use covenants. Ordinary property law permits suspension of an easement for abuse. See William B. Stoebuck & Dale A. Whitman, The Law of Property § 8.12 at 469 (3d ed. 2000).

Property owners may also sue for damages for use of their property beyond the reasonable use implied or specifically granted. As we discuss in Chapter 6, landowners may base surface damage claims on a variety of state and federal environmental statutes. In addition, however, property owners may—and usually do because of the possibility that they may recover punitive damages—rely on the common law theories of negligence, nuisance, or trespass to support claims for both compensatory and punitive damages. Marshall v. El Paso Natural Gas Co., 874 F.2d 1373 (10th Cir.Okla.1989), is a case in point. An oil company drilled an unsuccessful well on the Marshalls' land. When the company plugged the well, it allegedly failed to follow proper plugging procedures, though an Oklahoma Corporation Commission field inspector was at the site and approved of the operations. Marshall sued the oil company asserting that the plugging was a "time bomb" that would "explode" by polluting the groundwater beneath the property. The jury agreed with Marshall and awarded $350,050 for diminution in value of the property, $50,000 for nuisance damages, and $5,000,000 in punitive damages, which were upheld on appeal. In addition, it appears that the oil company was also required to clean up the site. The common law doctrines are alive and well even in an age of comprehensive environmental statutes.

The usual property-law rule limits a surface-owner's damages to the value of the property on the theory that it would be economically-inefficient to require payment of damages greater than the market value of the land. Corbello v. Iowa Production, 850 So.2d 686 (La. 2003), however, held that a lessee's liability for contamination of groundwater under an express agreement to "reasonably restore the premises as nearly as possible to their present condition" was not limited to the value of the property, which was 1/300th of the damage award, nor was the surface owner obliged to use the money to remediate the property, though by statute a lessee that pays a private restoration-damages award receives a credit against the costs of any cleanup later required by the Office of Conservation. The underlying rationale of the court's decision appeared to be the words of the contract, but the court also questioned the wisdom of the traditional rule in light of the possibility that the property owners might be liable in tort for the condition of their land. Subsequently, the Louisiana Legislature passed a law that requires that damages awarded for contamination or pollution affecting usable ground water must be used to evaluate and remediate the pollution. See 2003 La. Acts 1166. And in Terrebonne Parish School Board v. Castex Energy, Inc., 893 So.2d 789 (La. 2005), the Louisiana Supreme Court limited the application of *Corbello* by holding that lessees do not owe an implied duty to restore the surface to its pre-lease condition under Article 122 of the Mineral Code in the absence of an express lease provision or proof that the lessee unreasonably or excessively used the land surface.

One who purchases property that has been subjected to oil and gas exploration and development may not be able to sue for previous negligent use of the property unless the instruments of purchase expressly assign such causes of action. In Senn v. Texaco, Inc., 55 S.W.3d 222 (Tex. App.2001), the court recited the Texas rule that limits a cause of action for injury to real property to the owner of the property at the time it was damaged to support its conclusion that the Senns, who were subsequent landowners, lacked standing to sue for alleged damage to their property. The theory is that a damage claim is a chose in action, an item of personal property that accrues to the owner of the property when the damage occurs. The claim arises from the real property, but it is separate from it. When the owner transfers real property that has been damaged, the owner retains the personal property right unless it is assigned expressly.

May a lessee of the surface estate bar a subsequent oil and gas lessee from the premises? Compare Republic Natural Gas Co. v. Melson, 274 P.2d 543 (Okla.1954) (Yes), with Phillips Petroleum Co. v. Cargill, 340 S.W.2d 877 (Tex.Civ.App.1960) (No). See also John S. Lowe, How to Protect the Landowner in Oil and Gas Leasing Transactions, 31 Okla. L.R. 257, 262–263 (1978). May the severed mineral owner of Blackacre successfully challenge an operator who wishes to drill a directional well to Whiteacre from a surface location on Blackacre if the operator has permission of Blackacre's severed surface owner? Compare Chevron Oil Co. v. Howell, 407 S.W.2d 525 (Tex.Civ. App. 1966), with Humble Oil & Refining Co. v. L. & G. Oil Co., 259 S.W.2d 933 (Tex.Civ.App. 1953).

6. What are the remedies of a lessee who is wrongfully denied the right to use of the surface? Many cases hold that an interfering lessor or surface owner is liable for consequential damages to the lessee. See Ball v. Dillard, 602 S.W.2d 521 (Tex.1980); Short v. Wise, 718 P.2d 604 (Kan.1986); Reno Livestock Corp. v. Sun Oil Co., 638 P.2d 147 (Wyo.1981). State statutes may expose lessors and surface owners to penalties; for example, N.D.Cent.Code § 32–03–29 provides an aggrieved lessee treble damages. Second, the implied right of surface use may be enforced by an injunction, as well as damages. In Brown v. SEECO, Inc., 871 S.W.2d 580 (Ark.1994), for example, the court affirmed a preliminary injunction barring a landowner from interfering with a

lease operator, accepting the trial court's finding that the operator would suffer irreparable harm by having its drilling program interrupted and by drainage from off-setting wells, so that damages would be an insufficient remedy. And Montfort v. Trek Resources, 198 S.W.3d 344 (Tex. App. 2006), upheld a permanent injunction against a surface owner who had locked out the mineral owner's employees and made frivolous and false complaints to the state regulatory agency.

Finally, courts may apply the *obstruction doctrine*. The obstruction doctrine is predicated upon the implied covenant of quiet enjoyment. A lessor who obstructs the lessee either by denying access to the property or by attacking the lessee's title is precluded from denying the continued validity of the lease; implied covenants in oil and gas leases run *both* ways. Ordinarily, obstruction tolls the running of the lease primary term. If obstruction occurs close to the end of the primary term, however, the court may extend the lease for a period it deems reasonable. But what if the interference with the lessee is by a severed surface owner who is neither a lessor nor a mineral owner? Several cases apply the obstruction doctrine in that circumstance. See Burger v. Wood, 575 P.2d 977 (Okla.App. 1978); 21st Century Inv. Co. v. Pine, 734 P.2d 834 (Okla.App.1986); and Corley v. Craft, 501 So.2d 1049 (La.App.1987).

PROBLEM

O conveyed Blackacre to A, reserving all the minerals, without specifically mentioning surface access or use. Years later, O's successor leased to Industrious Oil Co. The lease granting clause specifically allowed Industrious Oil Co. to use Blackacre's surface for access to Industrious's operations on adjacent lands and to drill a salt-water disposal well on Blackacre to dispose of water produced from Blackacre and other lands in the area. What are the rights and liabilities of O's successor, A's successor, and Industrious?

2. SUBSTANCES GRANTED BY THE LEASE

When a lessor and lessee negotiate an oil and gas lease, their focus is usually on the prospect of producing oil and gas. Frequently, however, it turns out that the leased land contains other substances of value, so that the parties find themselves in disputes about what substances are covered by the lease granting clause.

Many oil and gas lease drafters attempt to deal with this problem by naming specifically the valuable substances that may be encountered. Thus, granting clauses frequently cover sulphur or carbon dioxide, as well as oil and gas, casinghead gas, and casinghead gasoline. Drafting is not a full solution, however, for a severed mineral owner who grants an oil and gas lease can give a lessee only the rights the lessor owns. As we will discuss infra in Chapter 2, there is an inherent ambiguity as to what substances belong to the owner of severed minerals.

A variation of the problem of substances covered by the lease occurs when the lease covers only oil or only gas. Who then owns casinghead gas (the gas that separates from oil shortly after production) or liquids extracted from the gas stream? Are such substances oil or gas or neither? In the Texas Panhandle in the early 1980s there was a raging dispute over the ownership of "white oil," a liquid produced when natural gas is chilled. Until the Texas Railroad Commission and FERC limited the practice, lessees of leases covering "oil and casinghead gas" produced natural gas as a liquid through refrigeration units—to the chagrin of the gas lessees. See Ralph A. Midkift, Note, Phase Severance of Gas Rights from Oil Rights, 63 Texas L.Rev. 133 (1984). See also Amarillo Oil Co. v. Energy–Agri Products, Inc., 794 S.W.2d 20 (Tex.1990).

A related issue is whether a lessor is entitled to royalty on a non-native substance, such as CO_2, that a lessee injects into a formation during enhanced recovery operations. Occidental Permian Ltd. v. The Helen Jones Foundation, 333 S.W.3d 392 (Tex. App. 2011), holds that the injected CO_2 remains the lessee's personal property.

3. LANDS AND INTERESTS GRANTED BY THE LEASE

The lease granting clause must identify the land and the interests covered by the lease. Land descriptions in areas in which governmental surveys have been conducted (for example, the "standard" or rectangular system established by congressional fiat), are generally in the survey form. Where property is not described by reference to a government survey, lease drafters use the *metes and bounds* system. A metes and bounds description locates property by establishing its exterior boundary lines by referring to natural or artificial "monuments" and directions and distances. Special applications of the metes and bounds description method include references to recorded plat maps and the "bounded by" method often used in Appalachia, which describes the property leased by referring to the ownership of surrounding properties at the time the lease was granted. All of these description methods are valid. All may create interpretative problems, which are more appropriate for a course in real-estate conveyancing than for this course.

The normal difficulties of property description are compounded in many parts of the country by the uncertainty of oil and gas titles. Title uncertainty arises largely from the unfamiliarity of many drafters and abstractors with oil and gas conveyancing, as we will discuss in Chapter 3. Oil and gas conveyances are frequently ambiguous and sometimes have been misinterpreted or totally ignored by abstractors.

Because land descriptions may be inaccurate and titles uncertain, oil and gas leases often include protective terms. These include (1) "in-gross" provisions, (2) "Mother Hubbard" provisions, and (3) "after-acquired title" provisions in the granting clause, and (4) warranty, (5) proportionate reduction, and (6) subrogation provisions, elsewhere.

In-gross provisions in a granting clause are similar to the following:

> For the purpose of determining the amount of any bonus, rental, and shut-in royalties hereunder, the number of gross acres above specified shall be deemed correct, whether actually more or less.

In other words, the payments provided for in the lease are for the gross acreage described, rather than being calculated on a per acre basis. An "in-gross" provision protects the lessee against lease failure if it turns out that the lease inaccurately describes the number of acres in the property.

Mother Hubbard provisions are included in oil and gas leases in areas where property descriptions are likely to inaccurately locate boundaries. This is particularly a problem where metes and bounds descriptions are used, because the "monuments" referred to may not be possible to locate. The "Mother Hubbard" clause, sometimes called the "cover-all" clause, generally provides that the lease is intended to cover all of the land owned by the lessor in the area:

> This lease also covers and includes any and all lands owned or claimed by the lessor adjacent or contiguous to the land described hereinabove whether the same be in such survey or surveys or in adjacent surveys, although not included within the boundary of the land described above.

We consider problems of application of the Mother Hubbard clause in Chapter 3.

Some oil and gas leases also contain *after-acquired title language.* The language may be included in the Mother Hubbard provisions:

> * * * it being the purpose and intent of lessor to lease, and lessee does hereby lease, all strips or parcels of land *now owned by lessor or hereafter acquired* which adjoin the land above described, and all interest in the land above described *now owned or hereafter acquired* by lessor. (Emphasis added).

Sometimes the after-acquired title language may be incorporated in a short phrase in the granting clause itself: "lessor * * * hereby grants, leases, and lets * * * the following described land, including any reversionary rights therein * * *." After-acquired title language is particularly important to a lessee if the lease warranty clause is struck or limited.

A lease *proportionate-reduction clause* (often called the lesser-interest clause) protects the lessee against being required to pay twice for the same lease interest. A common provision is that:

> [I]f Lessor owns an interest in the oil, gas, or other hydrocarbons in or under said land less than the entire fee simple estate, then the royalties and rentals to be paid Lessor shall be reduced proportionately.

The clause permits the lessee to reduce lease benefits to the extent that the lessor owns less than the full mineral interest described. This proportionate reduction clause also applies to reduce lease benefits to the lessor by the amount of outstanding nonparticipating royalty interests. For further discussion of the lease proportionate-reduction clause, see Kuntz § 52.4.

The lease *subrogation clause* empowers the lessee to protect its interest by paying taxes or mortgages encumbering the property and then stepping into the shoes of the former creditors. A typical provision is that:

> Lessor * * * agrees also that Lessee at its option may discharge any tax, mortgage or other liens upon said land either in whole or in part, and in the event Lessee does so it shall be subrogated to such lien with the right to enforce same and apply rentals and royalties accruing hereunder towards satisfying same.

This language may be overly broad, since it literally would give the lessee the power of subrogation even though liens on the property were not in default. How could it be limited? See Owen L. Anderson, David v. Goliath: Negotiating the "Lessor's 88" and Representing Lessors and Surface Owners in Oil and Gas Lease Plays, 27B Rocky Mtn.Min.L.Inst. 1029, 1051 (1981). For further discussion of the subrogation clause, see Kuntz § 52.3.

Most oil and gas leases contain a specific covenant of title from the lessor to the lessee. A typical lease *warranty clause* provides as follows: "Lessor hereby warrants and agrees to defend the title to said lands * * *." Note that the language is not a general warranty. It creates only a covenant of warranty, a promise to defend the lessee against future lawful claims and demands. There is no breach until the lessee is physically or constructively ousted from the property.

The lease warranty clause permits the lessee to recover damages from the lessor if there is a failure of title. In most states, the limit of the lessor's liability will be the lessee's actual damages up to the amount of compensation the lessor has received under the lease, plus interest. A warranty clause in a lease may also protect a lessee by making available the doctrine of after-acquired title. For further discussion of the lease warranty clause, see Kuntz § 52.2. Often, lessors will strike the warranty clause from leases. Is this important to lessors? Should lessees be willing to accept such a modification? How should the parties draft it?

The lease granting clause, the delay rental clause, the warranty clause, the proportionate reduction clause, and the subrogation clause are mutually supporting. Because mineral titles are so uncertain in many parts of the country, the lessee usually completes the granting clause property description without limiting the percentage of the interest granted, so that the lease literally purports to convey 100 percent of the mineral rights in the covered property.[7] The lessor is not liable if the lessor owns less than all the mineral rights or if there are easements and mortgages affecting the property, however, because the lease warranty does not include the present covenants for seisin, the right to convey, and against encumbrances. The lessee protects itself against the possibility that the

---

7.   This is an application of the "100 percent rule" of property law. See Lowe, Chapter 7.D.

size of the tract is greater than the parties believe by the in-gross provision or by providing for a flat amount as a rental payment rather than a per acre amount. If the lessor owns less than 100 percent of the mineral rights, the warranty clause permits the lessee to recover the proportionate bonus overpayment, the proportionate-reduction clause permits the lessee to reduce future payments of rentals and royalties, and the subrogation clause may permit the lessee to clear the cloud on title.

4. BASIC PRINCIPLES OF FEDERAL OIL AND GAS INCOME TAXATION

You should become familiar with several basic principles that distinguish oil and gas taxation from general federal income tax principles.

(a) Pool of Capital, Intangible Drilling Costs, and Percentage Depletion

As a result of historical accident, well-established practices, and congressional and treasury grace, the oil and gas industry obtains several federal income tax benefits that are not available to other industries and that profoundly affect both lessors and lessees. First, the *pool of capital doctrine* permits oil and gas investors to contribute capital to lease development in exchange for an interest in the minerals in place without triggering a tax. C.G.M. 22730, 1941–1 C.B. 214. This means that a lessee may exchange a working interest in an oil and gas lease for the drilling of a well or a production payment for geological and geophysical analysis on the lease without paying a tax on the transaction. The theory is that the parties are not exchanging goods or services but contributing to a pool of capital to establish an enterprise. Were it not for the pool of capital doctrine, each transfer of an interest would be a sale or exchange that would trigger gain or loss, and the party contributing services or equipment to the drill site would recognize the income from the contribution of services or equipment. The doctrine has been limited in recent years. See Hemingway § 12.1.

Second, an oil and gas investor may make a one-time *election to deduct all intangible drilling and development costs* when they are paid or incurred rather than capitalizing them as part of the leasehold property. I.R.C. § 263(c). Thus, a lessee can deduct in the current tax year the intangible costs necessary in drilling and developing a well site. For onshore wells, intangible drilling costs include payments for labor, vehicle rental, water, fuel, and repairs during the drilling and development stage and before the production stage. For offshore wells, such costs include the intangible costs for drilling developmental wells from a floating rig and the design, construction, transportation, and installation of a drilling platform. These costs can comprise 50 to 70 percent of the costs of drilling and completing a well. Without the deduction election, taxpayers would have to capitalize intangible costs and recover them over the life of the well. Congress has limited the deduction for integrated oil companies—

companies that produce, refine and market—to 70 percent of such costs. The remaining 30 percent must be capitalized and amortized ratably over 60 months. The intangible drilling and development costs election remains a powerful incentive for oil and gas investors, however.

Third, the oil and gas industry has obtained the option to use a cost recovery system called *percentage depletion,* which is not limited to the taxpayer's basis (its capital investment) in the minerals. Depletion—which is similar to depreciation—is the accounting method by in which a taxpayer recovers its capital investment in a mineral reservoir. Theoretically, depletion should be limited to a taxpayer's basis by *cost depletion*; if the taxpayer has capitalized $200,000 in a mineral reservoir, that taxpayer should be able to recover $200,000 over the time that taxpayer's share of minerals is produced. Congress in 1926, however, enacted a provision that gives a taxpayer who holds an economic interest in the minerals in place a right to deduct from gross income the greater of cost depletion or a flat percentage—currently 15%—of income. Treasury Regulation § 1.611–1(b) provides that the taxpayer holds an economic interest where the taxpayer acquires any interest in the minerals in place and secures, by any form of legal relationship, income from the extraction, to which he must look for return of his capital. Royalty interests, net profit interests, and carried interests are all generally recognized by the IRS as economic interests.

A taxpayer claiming cost depletion deducts its basis in the property from income as oil and gas are produced and sold. Cost depletion is calculated by a formula set forth in Treas.Reg. 1.611–2 that can be expressed as follows:

$$B \times \frac{S}{(U + S)}$$

B equals the adjusted basis of the property at the end of the period.

U equals units remaining at the end of the period.

S equals units sold during the period.

This formula relates the recovery of the taxpayer's investment to the proportion that current unit sales of oil and gas bear to the total anticipated sales of oil and gas from the property. Adjustments in estimates of units remaining are made prospectively and do not affect past tax years.

In contrast, a taxpayer using percentage depletion deducts a statutorily determined percentage of gross sales from the gross profits for the property. Because percentage depletion is unrelated to actual costs, it may greatly exceed cost depletion. Percentage depletion originally was calculated as 27½ percent of the gross income from the property, not to exceed 50 percent of the taxable income from the property. In 1975, however, the Congress reduced the percentage to an eventual 15 percent and significantly limited the availability of percentage depletion. Section 613A generally (1) limited percentage depletion to independent producers who do not engage in significant retailing or refining activities; (2) disqualified percentage depletion from proven properties transferred after 1974; (3) disqualified foreign properties from receiving percentage depletion; (4) placed annual quantity limitations on the number of barrels on which a taxpayer or related taxpayers can take percentage depletion; and (5) limited percentage depletion to 65 percent of the taxpayer's taxable income. In 1990, Congress modified the percentage depletion deduction to repeal the proven property transfer rule and to allow for a larger rate (16–25 percent) of depletion for marginal properties or "stripper" oil when the price of oil averaged below $20 for the prior year. Congress increased the rate of percentage depletion on marginal production by 1 percent for each $1 that the price of oil was below $20, up to a maximum increase in the rate of 10 percent. Congress also increased the taxable income limitation from 50 percent to 100 percent. The primary purpose underlying the 1990 changes was to encourage the continued production of marginal properties and to limit the effect of significant price drops in the oil markets.

Percentage depletion is particularly important to lessors, because they are not generally able to use cost depletion to shelter oil and gas income; cost depletion depends upon the taxpayer's basis in the minerals, and most lessors do not allocate any part of what they pay to minerals when they acquire land.

The oil and gas industry's special tax provisions have an important, positive impact upon oil and gas development. The pool of capital doctrine encourages venture formation. The immediate deduction of expenses permitted by the intangible drilling and development election encourages investment in oil and gas. The percentage depletion deduction allows taxpayers to recover their costs at a faster rate than cost depletion and to continue to deduct the depletion percentage even after they have recovered their costs. In a sense, the provisions are subsidies that make oil and gas investments more attractive than non-oil and gas investment opportunities.

Some scholars of tax policy argue that these special federal income tax provisions should be eliminated, because they violate the traditional principles of efficiency, simplicity, and horizontal equity. The pool of capital doctrine, the intangible drilling costs deduction, and percentage depletion are not efficient because (1) they make products that use oil and natural gas cheaper than they would be under the free market at the expense of the general treasury and (2) they cause distortions in oil and gas investments. These special provisions violate the principle of simplicity because they create a more complex tax system, which, in turn, discourages taxpayer compliance and increases the costs of government enforcement. The goal of horizontal equity is violated because a taxpayer in the oil and gas industry will pay less tax than a similarly situated taxpayer who has invested in a non-oil and gas industry. These scholars argue that if the energy industry should receive a subsidy, it should be accomplished through a federal subsidy program that directly offers benefits to parties who engage in the activities that are the target of the subsidy.

The Congress and industry, however, have prevailed in implementing much of this country's energy policy through our federal tax system for a number of reasons. First, the tax system requires the least interference with the capitalist marketplace. Participants who seek to obtain a tax benefit can anonymously obtain the benefit simply by engaging in the transaction. No large governmental agency must be created to hand out the subsidy with the high potential for corruption and favoritism. Second, the current tax system has a built-in enforcement agency—the Internal Revenue Service—with a system of penalties and criminal sanctions for noncompliance and fraud. Finally, the tax system offers a more permanent legal structure with no sunset provision or re-enactment requirements.

(b) Taxation of Lessor and Lessee

In the typical lease transaction, the lessor receives income from the lessee, and the money paid is an expense to the lessee. To determine federal income taxes from the lessor's perspective, one must generally examine two issues: Is the income ordinary or capital gain? And is the income subject to cost or percentage depletion?

From the lessee's perspective, one must examine three questions to determine tax treatment: Is the payment currently deductible, or must it be capitalized? If the payment is deductible, is it an ordinary deduction or a capital loss? And does the deduction qualify as a loss from an active activity, a passive activity, or a portfolio activity?

United States tax law views the grant of an oil and gas lease as a lease by the lessor and not as a sale or exchange of property. Thus, a *bonus payment* received by the lessor is ordinary income, rather than capital gain. Before the 1986 Tax Reform Act, a bonus was subject to percentage depletion. Present law permits percentage depletion only on payments related to actual production, however, so that a lessor may claim only cost depletion on bonus—which few lessors can do, as we have noted above. From the lessee's perspective, the bonus payment must be capitalized as part of the capital acquisition cost of the mineral reservoir, to be recovered through depletion, if the property is productive, or through an abandon-ment-loss deduction.

Royalty income is also ordinary income to lessors. The IRS views a royalty as a reservation of a mineral interest, and income generated from the royalty is ordinary income, subject to the greater of cost or percentage depletion. A lessee who pays the royalty does not include the portion of the production used to discharge the royalty in gross income.

Most leases contain provisions for *delay rental and shut-in royalty payments* to a lessor. These payments are treated as ordinary income to the lessor, not subject to any form of depletion; the theory is that delay rentals and shut-in royalties are similar to rental fees for extending the lease for a certain period and not for payments for production. From the lessee's perspective, delay rentals and shut-in royalties are viewed as expenses to extend the lease for a period, and thus they may be deducted as current expenses or capitalized under Section 266. Of course, most lessees elect to deduct them.

Because lessees can deduct delay rentals but must capitalize bonus payments, some lessees have attempted to couch bonuses as delay rentals by making them payable in installments. The courts have ruled that for a payment to qualify as a delay rental, it must be avoidable either by drilling, production, or abandonment of the lease. Otherwise, a payment is considered a bonus that must be capitalized. In 1986, Congress placed a new provision in the Code relating to the uniform capitalization of expenses relating to the production of assets. I.R.C. § 263A. The IRS has taken the position that delay rentals must be capitalized under this provision.

The final sets of payments under a typical oil and gas lease are payments for *property rights and damages to the surface*. A payment for a terminable right of way is rental income that is ordinary, non-depletable income to the landowner. A payment for a perpetual easement is a sale or exchange of a capital asset that will generate capital gain or loss to the landowner depending upon the basis allocated to the easement. Payments related to actual surface damage can be viewed as a return of capital that reduces the taxpayer's basis; the excess is capital gain. Of course, if damage payments are really bonuses in disguise, they must be treated as ordinary income. From the lessee's perspective, payments for rights of way must be capitalized as basis in the interest acquired and then either amortized over their life or as part of the life of the reservoir. Oil companies usually deduct damage payments as ordinary and necessary business expenses or intangible drilling costs.

5. STATE AND LOCAL TAXATION

State and local governments may also subject oil and gas facilities and production to taxation. Probably the most common tax is the *severance tax*. A severance tax, which may also be called a production tax, a license fee, or a conservation tax, may be defined as:

> a levy assessed at flat or graduated rates by government on the privilege, process, or act of commercially severing or extracting natural resources from the soil or water and measured by the amount of the gross or the net value of the natural resources produced or sold.[8]

Severance taxes come in two basic forms; unit and ad valorem. A unit severance tax is based upon the *amount* of resource produced; e.g., $.10 per barrel of oil. An ad valorem severance tax is based upon the *value* of the production; e.g., seven and one-half percent of the market value at the wellhead of natural gas produced and saved. Both are alike in that they

---

8. Allyn O. Lockner, The Effect of the Severance Tax on the Decisions of the Mining Firm, 4 Nat. Resources L.J. 468, 469 (1965).

are triggered by removal of the taxed resource from the ground. They are an excise tax upon the privilege of removing resources from the ground.

Two rationales are urged to justify severance taxes. One is that resource production imposes burdens upon the host community for which the community should be compensated; severance taxes repay the levying jurisdiction for damage to its infrastructure, environment, lifestyle, and heritage caused by extraction of natural resources. A second rationale supporting imposition of severance taxes is simply the need of the state for money to pay for public services, quite apart from those provided to the severing industry.

Severance taxes are particularly attractive as devices for fund raising because natural resources are immobile. Imposing a severance tax on oil and gas production is less likely to result in a movement of business activity from the state than would an increase in the corporate or individual income taxes. Indeed, to the extent that production is used outside of the state, a substantial proportion of the burden of severance taxes can be exported to the ultimate consumers. For discussion, see John S. Lowe, Severance Taxes as an Issue of Energy Sectionalism, 5 Energy L. J. 357 (1984).

C. HABENDUM CLAUSE: DURATION OF THE LEASE

The *habendum* or term clause of an oil and gas lease sets the lease's duration. Typically, modern term clauses provide for a primary term and a secondary term. The *primary term* of an oil and gas lease is a fixed term of years during which the lessee has the right, without any obligation, to explore for oil and gas or to drill for oil and gas on the premises. The *secondary term* is the extended period for which rights are granted to the lessee, if the lessee obtains production. A common formulation of an habendum clause is:

> This lease shall be for a term of ___ years from this date, called "primary term," and as long thereafter as oil or gas is produced * * *.

The lease habendum clause addresses the two fundamental goals sought by lessees in oil and gas leases. The primary term is the option period during which the lessee may explore the premises. The secondary term protects the lessee by allowing it to hold the leased premises indefinitely, so long as production continues.

1. THE LEASE PRIMARY TERM

The primary term of an oil and gas lease, which is the subject of this section, sets the maximum period for which the lessee can maintain the lease rights without drilling upon the property. The length of the primary term is determined by the bargaining leverage of the parties and the amount of the bonus that the lessee is willing to pay. Except in Louisiana and Tennessee, where it may not exceed ten years, the lease primary term may be as long or as short as the parties agree. Ten years was once a common primary term, and it is still frequently the primary term of leases in unproven or marginally producing areas. Primary terms of one to five years are more typical in states with established oil and gas production.

(a) Maintaining the Lease Primary Term by Paying Delay Rentals

Though the typical oil and gas lease does not expressly obligate the lessee to drill wells, there are several circumstances in which the lessee may have an implied duty to drill. Historically, one such duty commonly has been labeled the *implied covenant to test*. Early in the history of the oil and gas industry, the courts recognized an implied promise from the lessee to the lessor that the lessee would test the leased premises by drilling a well within a reasonable time after acquiring a lease. Their theory was that royalties were the primary consideration for the grant of the lease and that there would be no royalties unless the lessee tested the property. See generally Kuntz §§ 57.1–.5, and Hemingway, § 8.2.

Since a principal goal of the lessee is to have the option, without the obligation, to drill, the implied covenant to drill a test well was troublesome to lessees. To obviate the implied covenant, some oil and gas leases contain an express *delay rental clause* that specifically provides that the lessee may maintain the lease throughout the primary term, without drilling, by paying periodic (usually yearly) delay rentals. Except in Indiana, courts have generally held that the presence of a delay rental clause in an oil and gas lease obviates an implied obligation to drill a test well on the ground that there can be no such implied covenant where the lease explicitly provides a way for the lessee to maintain its rights without drilling. See, e.g., Warm Springs Dev. Co. v. McAulay, 576 P.2d 1120 (Nev.1978).

The lease delay rental clause allows the lessee to extend the lease from period to period (usually annually) during the primary term without drilling, by paying delay rentals that are usually nominal—often $1.00 per net mineral acre. But what happens if the lessee fails to pay the rentals properly? The answer depends upon the type of delay rental clause. The following case illustrates the result under the most common, "unless" form of delay rental clause.

Lease automatically terminates

SCHWARTZENBERGER v. HUNT TRUST ESTATE

244 N.W.2d 711 (N.D.1976).

ERICKSTAD, CHIEF JUSTICE.

Matt and Ruth Schwartzenberger, husband and wife, by complaint dated September 12, 1974, initiated a cause of action (claim for relief) against William Herbert Hunt Trust Estate. * * *

In the complaint, the Schwartzenbergers allege in essence that * * *

[1] on July 25, 1972, they executed in favor of the Trust Estate an oil and gas lease that provided for a primary term of ten years and which included a provision to the effect that if operations for drilling were not commenced on the premises or on lands pooled therewith, the oil and gas lease should be considered terminated *unless,* on or before one year from the date of the lease, the lessee should tender and pay to the lessors the rental of four hundred nineteen and 27/100 dollars ($419.27) which should cover the privilege of deferring commencement of drilling operations for a period of twelve months; [2] notwithstanding that drilling was not commenced, the Trust Estate failed to make payment of delay rentals in the sum due and owing of four hundred nineteen and 27/100 dollars ($419.27) on the anniversary date as provided in the lease and that accordingly the Trust Estate is now in default and in arrears in the payment of the delay rentals; [3] any and all deposits heretofore made as attempted payments of the said rentals by the Trust Estate to the Bank of Killdeer as the agent of the Schwartzenbergers, are rejected and refused as being insufficient to extend the time for drilling for oil and gas on the said premises; [4] on March 25, 1974, notice of termination and forfeiture of the oil and gas lease was given to the Trust Estate and that said Trust Estate has neglected, failed, and refused to file a release of the oil and gas lease; [5] the Schwartzenbergers have accordingly had to retain the services of legal counsel to commence an action for damages and for the termination of the oil and gas lease.

In their prayer for relief, the Schwartzenbergers ask that the oil and gas lease * * * be deemed in all things terminated, and that the Trust Estate be enjoined from exercising any control or authority over the premises, that it be determined and decreed that the Trust Estate has no interest in the said premises, and that the title to said oil and gas be quieted in the Schwartzenbergers.

The trustee for the Trust Estate responded by acknowledging the Schwartzenbergers' ownership of the lands and the provisions of the lease.

A pertinent part of the answer follows:

IV.

That on or about the 25th day of July, 1972, the Defendant herein did negotiate with the Plaintiffs herein for the purchase of an oil and gas lease. That the agent for the Defendant and the Plaintiffs herein did understand that there were 419.27 surface acres and that they did verily believe that the Plaintiffs did own 398.31 mineral acres lying in and under the property. That they did negotiate said oil and gas lease on the basis of a $3.00 per acre bonus for which they did tender to the Plaintiffs a draft on the 25th day of July, 1972, in the amount of One Thousand One Hundred Ninety-four and 93/100 Dollars ($1,194.93).

V.

That the draft was duly endorsed by the Plaintiffs herein and in due time was paid by the Defendant and that thereafter the Defendant did cause said oil and gas lease to be recorded in the Office of the Register of Deeds of McKenzie County, North Dakota, on the 28th day of July, 1972, at 10:50 A.M. in Book 165, Page 559.

VI.

That in accordance with the oil and gas lease, the Defendant was required, if it wished to sustain said lease, to pay delayed rental on or before the anniversary of said lease, being the 25th day of July, 1973, by tendering to the Bank of Killdeer delayed rental. That the Defendant did tender to said Bank the delayed rental on the 18th day of June, 1973, for the period of July 25, 1973 to July 25, 1974, the sum of Three Hundred Ninety-nine and 31/100 Dollars ($399.31),* which sum was deposited to the account of the Plaintiffs herein.

VII.

That on the 10th day of June, 1974, the Defendant did tender to the depository bank, the Bank of Killdeer, the sum of Three Hundred Ninety-nine and 31/100 Dollars ($399.31),* to cover the rental period of July 25, 1974 to July 25, 1975. That said monies were deposited into the account of the Plaintiffs herein.

VIII.

That the Defendant does hereby set forth that the actual net mineral acres underlying said property is 406.31 net mineral acres, whereas by mutual mistake Matt Schwartzenberger and Ruth Schwartzenberger and the William Herbert Hunt Trust Estate did understand and did verily believe that there were underlying said property a net mineral interest of 398.31 acres.

IX.

That the Defendant herewith does tender the difference of Three and no/100 Dollars ($3.00) per mineral acre as bonus consideration on eight (8) mineral acres, or the sum of Twenty-four and no/100 Dollars ($24.00) and does further tender the sum of Sixteen and no/100 Dollars ($16.00) for the delayed rental periods of July 25, 1973 to July 25, 1974; and July 25, 1974 to July 25, 1975.

X.

That the Plaintiffs having accepted said delayed rental payments are estopped from now claiming the insufficiency of those rental payments.

WHEREFORE, Subject to the tender hereinbefore set forth, the Defendant prays that the Complaint of the Plaintiffs be in all ways dismissed and that the title in and to the oil and gas lease on said property be quieted in favor of the William Herbert Hunt Trust Estate, John T. Livingston, Trustee.[1]

After a hearing at which testimony was taken and arguments made, the matter was taken under advisement and judgment in favor of the Hunt Trust Estate was subsequently entered. The findings of fact included a finding that Mr. Schwartzenberger, during the negotiations prior to the execution of the oil and gas lease, informed the agent for the Trust Estate that there was a five percent reduction in the mineral acreage due to a reservation by McKenzie County or the State of North Dakota and that, upon this information, the agent for the Trust Estate prepared an oil and gas lease covering 419.27 surface acres and 95% of the minerals, or 398.31 mineral acres, whereas in fact at the time of the execution of the oil and gas lease the Schwartzenbergers owned 100% of the minerals in the northeast quarter of section eighteen and 95% of the minerals in the remaining real property for a total mineral acreage of 406.24 mineral acres.

The trial court concluded that the oil and gas lease did not truly express the intentions of the parties because of a mutual mistake on the part of the parties and that therefore the lease should be reformed so as to express the true intention of the parties. The court found that the correct total surface acreage was 419.20 acres and that the oil and gas lease should be reformed to include, as delay rentals for the total surface acreage involved, the amount of $419.20, subject to the provision of the lesser interest clause found at paragraph 10 of the oil and gas lease which allows the Trust Estate to pay the delay rentals on the mineral interests which the court determined to be 406.24 acres, or a delay rental yearly of $406.24.

The court ordered the Trust Estate to pay the Schwartzenbergers the sum of $23.79 for the differences in the bonus payments actually made under the original lease and those required by the reformed lease and to pay to the Schwartzenbergers the sum of $15.79 for the difference between the delay rentals actually paid under the original lease and those required by the reformed lease.

On appeal the Schwartzenbergers seem to contend that the trial court was in error in its finding that Mr. Schwartzenberger, during the negotiations prior to the execution of the oil and gas lease, informed the agent for the Hunt Trust Estate that there was a 5% reduction in the mineral acreage due to a reservation by McKenzie County or the State of North Dakota.

* * *

Applying Rule 52(a) of the North Dakota Rules of Civil Procedure, which provides that unless findings of the trial court are clearly erroneous

---

1. [The actual amount deposited in each case was $398.31. The sum mentioned in the complaint includes an additional dollar for bank service charges.]

they shall not be set aside by the appellate court, we decline to set aside the trial court's finding relative to the circumstances surrounding the securement of the lease and the conclusion that a mutual mistake was made relative to the mineral acres. * * *

The next issue, however, is more difficult to determine. It relates to the trial court's conclusion that the lease should be reformed because of the existence of a mutual mistake and continued in effect as reformed after the payment of the deficiencies in the bonus payment and the deferred rentals.

* * *

The Schwartzenbergers contend that since this was an "unless" lease (as it is commonly denominated), then the lease terminated automatically when the Hunt Trust Estate failed to drill or to pay the correct amount of the deferred rentals. They rely on *Woodside v. Lee,* 81 N.W.2d 745 (N.D.1957).

In *Woodside* the court said:

> The generally accepted construction of the provisions for the termination of an "unless" lease is that the "unless" clause does not state a condition subsequent upon which the lease may be forfeited but states a common-law or special limitation upon which the interest of the lessee terminates immediately. [Citations omitted]

> Upon failure of the lessee to commence drilling operations within the limited time, such a lease terminates ipso facto without any notice or demand upon the part of the lessor unless delay rentals are paid as provided by the lease. [Citations omitted]

Id. at 746.

The Trust Estate contends that where a mutual mistake has occurred the lessor has a duty to notify the lessee of its mistake so that the lessee will have an opportunity to make a proper payment of the delay rentals. Hunt Trust Estate refers us to *Humble Oil & Refining Co. v. Harrison,* 146 Tex. 216, 205 S.W.2d 355, 361 (1947).

In *Humble* the Ottos owned a three-fourths interest in the minerals underlying a certain tract of land. They conveyed what the appellate court construed to be a one-half interest in those minerals to Harrison. Humble Oil, assuming the conveyance to be a one-half interest in the three-fourths interest, sent Harrison checks covering half of the three-fourths interest rather than half of the mineral interest. Harrison contended that the failure of Humble to pay him the correct amount of delay rentals terminated the lease.

The Supreme Court of Texas, in concluding that Harrison was estopped to assert that Humble's lease had been terminated because of its failure to make sufficient payments of delayed rentals to him, pointed out that there was no evidence that Humble did not act in good faith, no evidence that Humble acted negligently, and that there were provisions in the deed which made its meaning ambiguous and thus that the construction adopted by Humble's agent was not without reasonable foundation.

In finding Harrison estopped, the court said:

> * * * Where, as in this case, the lessee has in good faith made a mistaken construction of the lessors' partial conveyance of their interests and lessee has made a payment in accordance with such construction, of which the assignee has notice, the duty rests on the assignee to notify the lessee of its mistake so that the lessee will have an opportunity to make a proper payment of the delay rentals. Where the assignee, instead of giving the lessee such notice, remains silent, we hold that the assignee is estopped to assert that the lease has terminated as to his interest on the ground that the lessee has failed to pay him a sufficiently large share of the delay rentals.

Id., 205 S.W.2d at 361.

The Texas court pointed out that the leases in *Humble* executed by the Ottos contained the provision that "no change in the ownership of the land or part thereof, the minerals or interest therein, shall impose any additional burden on the Grantee." It concluded that it would be an imposition of an additional burden on the lessee to require that the lessee determine at its peril the proper construction of an ambiguous instrument thereafter executed by the lessors, conveying a part of their interest in the minerals and the royalty, bonuses and delayed rentals.

Humble is distinguishable from the instant case in that, in the instant case, there is evidence that the Trust Estate acted negligently in that its agent failed to discern when checking the records in the register of deeds' office, that the 5% reservation was not contained in the deed to the northeast quarter of section eighteen; further, there is nothing in the record before us and particularly in the abstracts of title that would constitute a reasonable foundation for the agent's mistake in checking the records at the office of the register of deeds; and further, in the instant case, the pertinent documents are not documents involving a change in the ownership of the lands or part thereof, the minerals or interest therein subsequent to the execution of the lease.

If we were to apply the rule laid down in *Humble* as a qualification to the rule in *Woodside,* we could not sustain the trial court's judgment in the instant case for the reason that we believe that adequate notice was given to the lessee in the instant case by the lessors prior to the commencement of the action in this case.

* * *

In other words, the record discloses that the Trust Estate, after written notice, first denied its obligation to pay a greater amount to retain its lease, and then ignored a repeated contention that it was in error until the Schwartzenbergers, some five months later in justified impatience, brought the present action. In *Humble* the company, while denying error, nevertheless tendered an amount more than sufficient to cover the disputed amount.

Whether we will in the future apply the rule that under circumstances of mutual mistake the lessee is entitled to receive notice of its mistake before the lease will be terminated, we need not decide today. It is sufficient to say that, under the circumstances of this case, the lessors are entitled to a termination of the lease under the principles enunciated in both *Woodside* and *Humble.*

For the reasons stated in this opinion, the judgment of the trial court is reversed and the case is remanded for the entry of a judgment consistent with this opinion.

* * *

NOTES

1. A typical lease habendum clause creates a potentially infinite, but determinable, interest. The lessee's term of years, set by the primary term of the lease, merges with the secondary term ("and so long thereafter") to form a fee-simple determinable, a *profit a prendre* determinable, or an irrevocable-license determinable in the minerals—depending upon how the jurisdiction's courts classify the leasehold interest. An "unless" delay rental clause creates one of the special limitations to which the lessee's interest is subject. The delay rental clause cuts the lease short automatically if the lessee fails to pay rentals or to commence drilling operations. The *Schwartzenberger* court paraphrased the unless delay rental clause before it. The unless delay rental clause from the Texas AAPL lease form in the Forms Manual provides:

> If operations for drilling are not commenced on said land, or on acreage pooled therewith as above provided for, on or before one year from the date hereof, the Lease shall terminate as to both parties, unless on or before such anniversary date Lessee shall pay or tender to Lessor, or to the credit of Lessor in the _____ Bank at _____, Texas, (which bank and its successors shall be Lessor's agent and shall continue as the depository for all rentals payable hereunder regardless of changes in ownership of said land or the rentals) the sum of ($__), herein called rentals, which shall cover the privilege of deferring commencement of drilling operations for a period of twelve months. In like manner and upon like payment or tender annually, the commencement of drilling operations may be further deferred for successive periods of twelve months each during the primary term hereof. * * *

To avoid lease termination or a declaration of forfeiture, a lessee who has not drilled within the period specified by an unless delay rental clause must pay the delay rentals provided for in the proper amount, on or before the due date, to the proper persons, and in the proper manner. Failure to comply strictly with any one of these elements will almost certainly result in loss of the lease:

(a) *In the proper amount.* In Young v. Jones, 222 S.W. 691, 694 (Tex.Civ. App.1920), a lessee tendered two checks totaling $73.29 under a lease that called for drilling delay rental payments totaling $76.25. In holding the lease terminated, the court stated:

> [T]he commencement of the well or payment of the rental were conditions precedent to an extension or continuation of the lessee's privileges and wholly optional with him; and, this being the nature of the contract equity will not relieve against the failure to exercise the option in strict accordance with its terms.

(b) *On or before the due date.* Tendering rental to the proper party, but at an improper address, results in termination of the lease if the rental payment does not reach the lessor before the due date. In Gillespie v. Bobo, 271 Fed. 641 (5th Cir.Tex.1921), the lessee's representative sent the payment to Box 43, Ft. Worth, Texas. The proper address was Box 43 A, Ft. Worth, Texas. As a result, the rental payment did not reach the lessor before the due date; the lessee did not learn of his mistake until after the due date had passed. The Fifth Circuit Court of Appeals held that the lease had terminated. Though the lease provided that rental payment rentals was effective upon mailing, as do most oil and gas leases,[9] the court held that use of an incorrect address invalidated the payment. See also Vaughan v. Doss, 245 S.W.2d 826 (Ark. 1952).

Even the most heart-wrenching excuses will not pardon a late rental payment. In Ford v. Cochran, 223 S.W. 1041 (Tex.Civ.App.1920), a lessee urged the court to protect his lease despite a late rental payment, because he was compelled to be with his sick family at the time the delay rental payment was due. The lessee's plea for mercy fell on deaf ears; the Texas court held that the lease had automatically terminated when delay rentals were not paid by the lessee on the due date.

(c) *To the proper persons.* In Empire Gas & Fuel Co. v. Saunders, 22 F.2d 733 (5th Cir.Tex.1927), a lessee mistakenly interpreted a conveyance of one-half of the mineral interest under one-half of the property subject to a lease as a conveyance of one-half of the mineral interest under all of the property. Accordingly, the lessee sent the lessor one-half of the delay rentals and sent the other one-half to the lessor's assignee. In holding the lease had terminated as to the lessee, the court stated: "The lessee is not obligated to do anything, but, if it fails either to drill wells or to make the payments of rent as and when due, its rights and privileges are at an end." 22 F.2d at 735. In Le Rosen v. North Central Texas Oil Co., 126 So. 442 (La. 1930), overruled on other grounds Jones v. Southern Natural Gas, 36 So.2d 34 (La.1948), a married man executed an "unless" oil and gas lease, and the lessee's assignee deposited rentals to the joint credit of the lessor and his wife. The Louisiana court held that the lease had terminated, because payment to the joint credit of the lessor and his wife did not comply with the terms of the lease.

(d) *In the proper manner.* Keeler v. Dunbar, 37 F.2d 868 (5th Cir.Tex. 1930), held that a lease terminated where, through no fault of the lessee, the delay rental payment reached the lessors on the day after the payment was due. Payment was due "on or before the 26th day of November, 1927." The lessee delivered the required amount to a telegraph company on October 19,

---

9. See paragraph 5 of the Texas AAPL lease in the Forms Manual for a typical provision.

1927, with proper instructions for delivery to the lessor. Without fault on the part of the lessee, the transfer was delayed and payment did not reach the lessor until November 27, 1927. The court stated:

> One using the telegraph, as plaintiffs allege they did in this case, must be held to have chosen their own agent for that purpose, and the failure to deliver or tender the money required to keep the lease alive within the time fixed by the contract, cannot be attributed to the [lessors].

37 F.2d at 869. The lease involved in *Keeler* required the lessee to "pay or tender" delay rentals before the due date. Would the result have been different had the lease provided that payment would be effective upon mailing? See Baker v. Potter, 65 So.2d 598 (La.1952).

2. A majority of jurisdictions follow the view expressed in *Schwartzenberger* that the "unless" delay rental clause creates a special limitation on the interest of the lessee so that failure to pay the delay rentals causes automatic termination as a matter of law. A few jurisdictions, however, view termination as an equitable forfeiture, which takes action by a court to enforce and which may be barred by equitable principles, such as estoppel or waiver. See, e.g., Ledford v. Atkins, 413 S.W.2d 68 (Ky.1967). Others vary in their treatment from case to case. Compare Morton v. Sutcliffe, 266 P.2d 734 (Kan. 1954), with Young v. Moncrief, 232 P. 871 (Kan.1925).

Louisiana reaches the same result as the majority, but for a different reason. Article 133 of the 1975 Mineral Code (La.Rev.Stat.Ann. § 31:133) provides that an oil and gas lease terminates at the end of the agreed term or "upon the occurrence of an express resolutory condition." Consequently, the failure either to commence drilling or to pay delay rentals properly under the terms of an "unless" drilling delay rental clause is an express resolutory condition that terminates the lease.

3. As *Schwartzenberger* recognizes, in a few circumstances, equity has been invoked even in majority rule states to preserve leases with "unless" clauses where there has been an improper payment or a failure to pay. These include:

(a) *Failure of an independent third party beyond the control of the lessee.* For example, in Oldfield v. Gypsy Oil Co., 253 P. 298 (Okla.1926), the Oklahoma Supreme Court held that timely mailing of a delay rental check in a properly addressed and stamped envelope was sufficient to preserve the lease even though the check was erroneously delivered by the post office to the wrong bank. But see Appling v. Morrison, 227 S.W. 708 (Tex.Civ.App. 1921). Most modern oil and gas leases avoid the issue by specifically making mailing the operative action for payment of delay rentals.

(b) *Lessor's acceptance of a late or inadequate tender of delay rental.* If a lessor accepts a late or inadequate payment, some courts may hold that estoppel or waiver prevents the lessor from asserting termination of the lease. See, e.g., Buchanan v. Sinclair Oil & Gas Co., 218 F.2d 436 (5th Cir.Tex.1955); Jones v. Southern Natural Gas Co., 36 So.2d 34 (La.1948), and Hove v. Atchison, 238 F.2d 819 (8th Cir.N.D.1956). Other cases hold that a lessor's acceptance of an inadequate delay rental payment continues the lease as to the number of acres for which payment was adequate; acceptance of a partial payment by the lessor gave the lessee a valid lease to a proportionate part of the acreage described. Kugel v. Young, 291 P.2d 695 (Colo.1955), and Borth v. Gulf Oil Exploration & Prod. Co., 313 N.W.2d 706 (N.D.1981).

(c) *Confusion or ambiguity caused by the lessor.* In Humble Oil & Refining Co. v. Harrison, 205 S.W.2d 355 (Tex.1947), discussed at length in *Schwartzenberger,* one of the factors noted by the court in refusing to find the lease terminated was that Humble Oil had reasonably misconstrued an ambiguous assignment of the lessor. See also Kouns v. Southwood Oil Co., 158 S.W.2d 37 (Ark.1942), and Cates v. Greene, 114 S.W.2d 592 (Tex.Civ.App. 1938).

(d) *Lessor's failure to notify lessee of mistake in payment.* Where a lessor knows that the lessee has made a mistake in paying delay rentals, some courts have held that the lease continues in effect unless the lessor notifies the lessee of his mistake. The classic case is Humble Oil & Refining Co. v. Harrison, supra. Is the North Dakota court's effort to distinguish *Humble* convincing?

Schwartzenberger suggests that the North Dakota Supreme Court might add to this list failure to pay properly because of mutual mistake. Can you see a basis for its addition? See generally William B. Browder, Estoppel, Waiver and Ratification Affecting Mineral and Leasehold Rights, 10 Rocky Mtn. Min.L.Inst. 139 (1965); Hemingway § 6.3(F); and 3 Kuntz § 36.4. For a later view of the North Dakota Supreme Court, see Norman Jessen & Associates, Inc. v. Amoco Prod. Co., 305 N.W.2d 648 (N.D.1981).

4.   Should equitable principles apply to save "unless" leases from termination for failure to pay delay rentals properly? The Hemingway Hornbook analyzes the problem this way:

> Whether or not a jurisdiction will relieve from an improper payment of delay rentals will depend, to a certain extent, upon the view of that jurisdiction as to the nature of the terminal provisions of the "unless" clause. A majority of jurisdictions appear to view the "unless" clause as creating a limitation upon the estate of the lessee, which will terminate automatically by its own terms in the event the lessee does not strictly comply with its provisions. On the other hand, a number of jurisdictions view the termination as a forfeiture in equity, and several jurisdictions appear to vary in their treatment of the effect of the clause.

* * *

> A jurisdiction that treats termination of the lease due to noncompliance with the delay rental clause as a forfeiture may apply equitable principles to prevent loss of the lease in situations in which the courts feel that it would be inequitable not to do so. On the other hand, a jurisdiction that views the termination as a limitation would technically be precluded from using equity principles to prevent loss of the lease.

Hemingway § 6.3(E) (citations omitted). The Oklahoma Supreme Court addressed the application of equity in the syllabus to Ellison v. Skelly Oil Co., 244 P.2d 832 (Okla.1951):

> The "unless" clause in an oil and gas lease is not a forfeiture provision, but rather a limitation on the period of the leasehold grant. When the

lessee fails to commence drilling operations or make payment of rental in lieu of said drilling on or before the date specified in the lease, the lease, ipso facto, as per its express terms, comes to an end, and the good faith intention and desire of the lessee to make timely payment of delay rentals will not relieve the lessee from the consequence of his failure to pay the delay rental on or before the time specified in the lease, when the lessor is not at fault and the fault is chargeable to the lessee.

244 P.2d at 833–34.

Professor Kuntz summarizes:

It is possible, however, to reconcile practicality with theory when the court takes equitable factors into account in determining whether or not an oil and gas lease has terminated for failure to comply with the terms of the drilling clause. In theory, the lease terminates automatically, and equity will not intervene to prevent such termination unless some traditional equitable doctrine which would bar the lessor can be invoked, such as estoppel or laches. The court may, however, construe the provisions of the drilling clause and determine that, if the lessee makes a bona fide effort to comply with the provisions of the drilling clause, the event which will result in a termination of the lease is not simply a failure to drill or to pay delay rentals in strict compliance with the lease, but is a failure to do so which may be attributed to the lessee's fault or dereliction and is not attributable to circumstances beyond the lessee's control.

Kuntz § 36.3.

5. Another legal theory that may preserve the rights of a lessee who makes a late or inadequate payment of rentals is *revivor*. An interest that has terminated may be "revived" if the parties to the lease act as if it were still valid. In Brannon v. Gulf States Energy Corp., 562 S.W.2d 219 (Tex.1977), the lessor complained to the lessee that her annual lease rental had not been paid. The lessee, who had assigned the lease, asked the assignee to pay the rentals. The Texas Supreme Court held that late payment and acceptance of a check endorsed "lease rental" had the effect of reviving the original lease. Because the premise of revivor is that the parties intended the interest to continue, however, should it not be a precondition to revivor that the lessor realize that the lease has terminated when the late rental is tendered?

6. Oil companies have developed elaborate administrative schemes to ensure that payments are made properly. The general industry practice is to mail a check for rentals and any bank handling fees to the bank by certified mail, return receipt requested, 30 to 60 days in advance of the rental payment date. The check is made payable to the bank and accompanied by written instructions to credit the accounts of the persons entitled to receive rental payments. The check is accompanied by a receipt for the rentals to be executed by an officer of the bank and returned to the lessee. Oil and gas leases almost always specifically permit delay rental payments to be made by check. Where a lease does not so provide, it is likely that a lessor could insist on payment in cash, but if the lessor does not refuse payment on that ground, the payment is good. 2 Summers Perm. Ed. § 345. If payment is made by check to a bank in accordance with the drilling delay rental clause, it is

immaterial that the bank does not collect payment for the check until after the rental payment is due. Gulf Refining Co. v. Bagby, 7 So.2d 903 (La.1942).

The court quotes typical transmittal letters and accompanying documents used in paying rentals to a depository bank in Gulf Prod. Co. v. Perry, 51 S.W.2d 1107 (Tex.Civ.App.–Texarkana 1932). The case holds that if a lease is made by several joint lessors providing for a payment of a stipulated rental, it will be considered as a joint rental. The lessee may tender the full amount of the rental to the lessors jointly at the depository bank without being required to deposit the specific part of the total rental to which each may be entitled. This principle is applied even in the situation where the lessee has actual knowledge that one of the persons signing as "lessor" is not entitled to any part of the rentals. York v. McBee, 308 S.W.2d 951 (Tex.Civ.App.1957). If there is any question as to the amount of the rentals due or to whom they are due, the lessee will seek a *rental division order*. A rental division order is a stipulation signed by those entitled to delay rentals stipulating their interests.[10] In addition, delay rentals are almost always paid well in advance of the due date either by certified mail with return receipt requested or by other methods that allow the lessee to assure itself that the payments have been properly made.

How far in advance may the lessee pay delay rentals? If the payments are made in advance, what happens if there is a change in the ownership of the underlying mineral interest between the time of payment and the due date? In Gulf Refining Co. v. Shatford, 159 F.2d 231 (5th Cir.La.1947), the lease in question contained a *change-of-ownership provision* that stated that no change in ownership of rentals or royalties would be binding on the lessee "until after the lessee has been furnished with a written transfer or assignment or a true copy thereof." Rental was due July 6. On May 3, Shatford advised Gulf that he had purchased an interest in the property from Gulf's lessor the previous November. Gulf replied immediately, referring to the lease clause and requesting photostatic or certified copies of Shatford's deeds. On June 25, Gulf mailed checks to the depository banks to pay the delay rentals due. No provision was made to pay Shatford. On June 26, Gulf received photostatic copies of Shatford's deeds. On June 28, Gulf notified Shatford that it had adjusted its records to show his interest, but it did not pay Shatford's share of the delay rentals to him. Shatford contended the lease had expired as to his interest. The court refused to find that the lease had terminated:

> Gulf did not direct the lessors' agent bank to deposit anything to the credit of Shatford because Gulf had not received a copy of any transfer or assignment in his favor. Had Shatford acted diligently and sent copies of his deeds prior to the time Gulf paid the rental money, he would have received a share in proportion to his holdings.

* * *

> To now permit Shatford to cancel the lease so far as it affects his one-eighth interest would be to reward him for his negligence and punish Gulf for living up to its contract.

---

10. We have included a rental division order example in the Forms Manual.

159 F.2d at 233. What if the payments were made three years in advance? See Gulf Prod. Co. v. Continental Oil Co., 164 S.W.2d 488 (Tex. 1942) and 3 Williams & Meyers § 606.4. How should the lessee have handled this situation to avoid a dispute?

Would the issues in *Gulf Refining Co. v. Shatford* and *Gulf Prod. Co. v. Continental Oil Co.* have been more easily resolved had the change-of-ownership provision read as follows?

> No change in the ownership of the land, or any interest herein, shall be binding on Lessee until thirty (30) days after Lessee shall have been furnished by registered U.S. Mail at Lessee's principal place of business with a certified copy of all recorded instruments, all court proceedings and all other necessary evidence of any transfer, inheritance or sale of said rights.

What if neither the lessor nor the lessor's assignee give notice to a lessee of a change of ownership, but the lessee learns of the change in the course of its business. Should the lessee pay rentals to the new owner or to the original lessor? Cf. Atlantic Refining Co. v. Shell Oil Co., 46 So.2d 907 (La. 1950).

7. Since dire results usually follow the improper payment of delay rentals under an "unless" delay rental clause, most leases contain language to minimize the risk of mistakes in rental payment. Practically all oil and gas leases stipulate that the lessee may pay delay rentals to a depository bank. The bank acts for the lessor in receiving rental payments, and mistakes or delays due to the fault of the depository bank are not chargeable to the lessee. A depository bank, however, has no agency power to bind a lessor by accepting a late or incorrect payment. The bank only has authority to receive payments made in accordance with the terms of the lease. Summers § 343.

Most leases also contain a *notice-of-assignment clause* to avoid disputes over the effect of an assignment by the lessee to a third party upon delay rental payments. A notice-of-assignment clause provides that the lessee may rely upon its records in making delay rental payments. Without such a clause, the lessee risks a finding that the lessee is obligated to review the public property records each year before the anniversary date and to interpret any conveyances found in the record to determine who should be paid delay rentals and in what proportions they should be paid. A typical notice-of-assignment clause follows:

> The rights of each party hereunder may be assigned in whole or in part, and the provisions hereof shall extend to their heirs, successors and assigns, but * * * no change or division in such ownership shall be binding on Lessee until thirty (30) days after Lessee shall have been furnished with a certified copy of recorded instrument or instruments evidencing such change of ownership.

Many leases also include a *separate-ownership clause*, sometimes called a "divisibility" clause, designed to protect the lessee after a partial assignment. Where a lessee assigns an interest covering a separate portion of the tract leased, the failure of either the assignee or the assignor to pay delay rentals on that portion of the lease will ordinarily cause termination of the entire lease; as *Schwartzenberger* illustrates, the lease is whole, and the whole rental is due on the date agreed. A typical separate-ownership provision intended to change that result follows:

> In the event of an assignment hereof in whole or in part, liability for breach of any obligation issued hereunder shall rest exclusively upon the owner of this Lease, or portion thereof, who commits such breach.

Could you devise better language? For further discussion of the separate-ownership clause, see Kuntz § 51.2(d).

A lease *surrender clause* permits a lessee to surrender the lease to the extent that it covers land thought to be unproductive. General real property law principles will not give him that right; the lease is a whole and cannot be severed at the lessee's whim. A surrender clause modifies the general rule by a specific provision:

> Lessee may at any time or times execute and deliver to lessor or to the depository above named, or place of record a release covering any portion or portions of the above described premises and thereby surrender this lease as to such portion or portions and be relieved of all obligations as to the acreage surrendered, and thereafter the rentals payable hereunder shall be reduced in the proportion that the acreage covered hereby is reduced by said release or releases.

For further discussion, see Kuntz § 53.2.

Another approach to avoiding loss of a lease because rentals are not properly paid is a savings clause designed to prevent automatic termination. Under the facts of *Schwartzenberger,* could the following provisions be relied upon to prevent automatic termination?

Clause 1

> In the event lessor considers that lessee has not complied with all its obligations hereunder, both expressed and implied, before production has been secured or after production has been secured, lessor shall notify lessee in writing, setting out specifically in what respects lessee has breached this contract. Lessee shall then have sixty (60) days after receipt of such notice within which to meet or commence to meet all or any of the breaches alleged by lessor.

Why? See Barbee v. Buckner, 265 S.W.2d 869 (Tex.Civ.App.1954).

Clause 2

> It is agreed that neglect or failure to pay rentals when due shall not operate to forfeit or cancel this lease, until Lessor gives Lessee notice by registered mail of said failure to pay rental; whereupon Lessee shall pay same within ten days of receipt of said registered letter, or this lease is void.

See Lewis v. Grininger, 179 P.2d 463 (Okla.1947); Clovis v. Carson Oil & Gas Co., 11 F.Supp. 797 (E.D.Mich.1935); and McDaniel v. Hager–Stevenson Oil Co., 243 P. 582 (Mont.1926).

Clause 3

> If Lessee shall, in good faith and with reasonable diligence, attempt to pay any rental but fails to pay or incorrectly pays part of the rental, this

lease shall not terminate unless Lessee fails to rectify the error or failure within thirty (30) days after written notice.

See Woolley v. Standard Oil Co., 230 F.2d 97 (5th Cir.Tex.1956).

How are these clauses different? What should be the standard for enforceability? See generally Hemingway § 6.3(F); Williams & Meyers § 681.2(3); and Kuntz § 30.3.

Would the argument that the lease in *Schwartzenberger* had not terminated for failure to pay rentals be stronger had the lease contained a delay rental savings clause like that in *Woolley,* plus a delay rental clause that provided:

> [T]his lease shall terminate * * * unless, on or before one year from the anniversary date Lessee shall pay or tender (or shall make a bona fide attempt to pay or tender) * * * delay rentals?

See Kincaid v. Gulf Oil Corp., 675 S.W.2d 250 (Tex.App.1984).

8. An increasingly popular way for lessees to avoid the problems inherent in payment of delay rentals is to use an oil and gas lease that does not require payment of delay rentals during the primary term—a "paid-up" lease. Generally, a lessee uses a lease with a specially drafted paid-up clause that recites that no rentals are due and disclaims the implied covenant to test:

> This is a PAID–UP LEASE. In consideration of the down payment, *Lessor agrees that Lessee shall not be obligated,* except as otherwise provided herein, *to commence or continue any operations during the primary term,* or to make any rental payments during the primary term.

Paid-up leases make good business sense in areas where lease bonuses are large and delay rental payments are relatively small. Occasionally, a lessee will either strike the delay rental clause from an "unless" form—risky because it may resurrect the implied covenant to test that the rental clause was designed to negate—or complete the clause, but in either situation make a notation that all rentals have been paid in advance. Are there circumstances in which it would be desirable or undesirable to use a paid-up lease? What is the best way to create a paid-up lease? See Kuntz §§ 28.6, 57.2. See also Lowe, Chapter 8.E.3.b(5).

9. An alternative widely used in the West Coast and Appalachian states is the "or" drilling-delay rental clause. In contrast to the "unless" clause, an "or" clause does not cause automatic lease termination upon a failure to commence drilling operations or to pay rentals in a timely fashion. The "or" clause merely imposes an affirmative duty upon the lessee to commence drilling *or* to pay rentals *or* to surrender the lease before the anniversary date. Because an "or" clause affirmatively obligates the lessee to do one of the alternatives, it is commonly referred to as an "or" clause. A typical "or" clause provides as follows:

> Commencing with the first day of the second year of the term hereof, if the lessee has not theretofore commenced drilling operations on said land or terminated this lease as herein provided [by surrender], the lessee shall pay or tender to lessor annually, in advance, as rental, the sum of one dollar per acre per year for so much of said land as may then be held

under this lease, until drilling operations are commenced or this lease terminated as herein provided.

For other examples of "or" forms, see the Forms Manual accompanying this casebook.

The effect of an "or" delay rental clause is the same as an "unless" lease in that the rental clause abrogates any implied covenant to test the premises by drilling an initial well. See generally Kuntz § 27.4. If a lessee fails to perform any of the alternatives, however, the "or" lease does not terminate, but the lessor is entitled to recover the rentals that the lessee should have paid; the courts will not require the lessee to drill because drilling would be more expensive and perhaps economically wasteful.

Note, however, that a lessor's rights may be altered by statute or by special lease terms. Kentucky Revised Statutes § 353.020 provides that where delay rentals are not paid or tendered, "the lessor or landowner may avoid the lease or contract unless before executing a new lease or contract he has accepted payment of the rental." The statute has been held to apply both to "unless" and "or" leases. Walter v. Ashland Oil & Refining Co., 187 S.W.2d 425 (Ky. 1945). West Virginia has a statute providing that a lease is void unless rentals due are paid within 60 days after the lessor's demand. W.Va. Code § 36–4–9a.

Many leases with "or" delay rental provisions also contain forfeiture clauses. For example:

> Upon the violation of any of the terms or conditions of this lease by the lessee and the failure to begin to remedy the same within 90 days after written notice from the lessor so to do, then, at the option of the lessor, this lease shall forthwith cease and terminate * * *.

Where the lease contains a forfeiture clause, what is the nature of the lessee's interest? Is it different from that under a lease with an "unless" delay rental clause?

Why do you suppose that leases with "or" delay rental clauses are not uniformly used? See McElroy, Unless vs. Or: An Appraisal, 6 Baylor L. Rev. 415 (1954). For further discussion of "or" delay rental clauses, see Kuntz § 27.4.

10. A final type of delay rental clause, in limited use and in great disfavor, is the "no term" clause. A "no term" drilling delay rental clause permits the lease to be extended indefinitely by payment of delay rentals; that is, the privilege is not limited by the primary term. Many courts have refused to enforce leases containing "no term" clauses on the ground that they create a mere estate at will, terminable at the will of either the lessor or the lessee. Other courts have upheld leases containing no term clauses, but with the stipulation that the lessee has an obligation to develop or release the lease within a reasonable time. For a discussion of the cases, see Kuntz § 28.3.

In Hite v. Falcon Partners, 13 A.3d 942 (Pa. Super. 2011), the lease stated:

> Lessee has the right to enter upon the Property to drill for oil and gas at any time within one [sic] (1) year from the date hereof and as long

thereafter as oil or gas or either of them is produced from the Property, or as operations continue for the production of oil or gas, or as Lessee shall continue to pay Lessors two ($2.00) dollars per acre as delayed rentals, or until all oil and gas has been removed from the Property, whichever shall last occur.

The court held that the provision did not permit the lessee to hold the lease beyond the initial year, reasoning that in Pennsylvania, until a lessee establishes production, a lease creates merely an inchoate interest that delay rentals cannot preserve indefinitely. But see Northup Properties, Inc. v. Chesapeake Appalachia, L.L.C., 567 F.3d 767 (6th Cir. Ky. 2009), where the court enforced a clause that allowed a lessee to maintain the lease in effect indefinitely without production by the payment of delay rentals, where rentals had been paid for nearly forty years, reasoning that Kentucky's public policy to encourage lease exploration and development was overridden by the plain terms of the lease. The court relied in part on Hemingway §§ 6.2, 6.4, and 2.3.

11. Lessors do not often reject leases with delay rental clauses. The clauses are customary in some parts of the country, and lessors have come to expect that the periodic payments will be made. But what should a lessor who wants drilling, rather than rental payments do?

(b) Maintaining the Lease Primary Term by Drilling

Most oil and gas leases provide that, as an alternative to payment of delay rentals, a lessee may maintain its rights during the primary term by commencing a well. The language quoted at note 1, following *Schwartzenberger,* above, states that rentals may be paid "if operations for drilling are not commenced * * *." What actions constitute "drilling operations" sufficient to maintain the lease present problems similar to those we have considered involving rental payments. Such problems also arise at the expiration of the lease primary term, when a lessee seeks to begin operations that it cannot complete before the end of the primary term, after an initial well has been completed as a dry hole, or after a well that initially produced has ceased to produce. See, e.g., the language of paragraph 6 of the Texas AAPL lease in the Forms Manual, which provide that "drilling or reworking operations" will maintain lease even though it is not actually producing; we will briefly revisit this matter below in connection with the discussion of the *dry-hole, operations, and cessation-of-production clauses.* Not surprisingly, however, lessors and lessees frequently disagree over what "operations" will preserve the lease in both contexts.

BREAUX v. APACHE OIL CORPORATION

240 So.2d 589 (La.App. 3d Cir.1970).

Before FRUGE, CULPEPPER and MILLER, JJ.

CULPEPPER, JUDGE.

The plaintiffs-lessors filed this suit to cancel an oil, gas and mineral lease on the grounds that the defendants-lessees did not "commence operations for the drilling of a well," nor pay delay rentals, within the time specified. The district judge granted defendants' motion for summary judgment dismissing plaintiffs' suit. Plaintiffs appealed.

The substantial issues on appeal are: (1) Is there a genuine issue of material fact as to whether defendants commenced operations for the drilling of a well on or before March 18, 1967? * * *.

For purposes of the motion for summary judgment, the pleadings and affidavits filed by the parties show the following: The lease in question is dated March 18, 1966 and covers 302.55 acres of land in Acadia Parish. It contains the following pertinent provisions:

"1. This lease shall terminate on March 18, 1967, unless on or before said date the Lessee either (1) commences operations for the drilling of a well on the land, or on acreage pooled therewith, in search of oil, gas or other minerals and thereafter continues such operations and drilling to completion or abandonment; or (2) pays to the Lessor a rental of One Hundred & No/100 Dollars ($100.00) per acre for all or that part of the land which Lessee elects to continue to hold hereunder, which payment shall maintain Lessee's right in effect as to such land without drilling operations for one year from the date last above mentioned * * *."

* * *

On March 16th or 17th, 1967, defendants commenced building a board road and turn-around to the well location. On March 18, 1967 the board road and turn-around were completed.

There is a dispute as to when the first rig equipment was moved to the well site. Affidavits submitted by defendant state that drilling equipment was moved to the location on March 18, 1967. Those introduced by plaintiffs state that no equipment was moved to the site until after March 18, 1967.

In any event, equipment was installed and actual drilling commenced on March 22, 1967 at the location approved in the amended order of the Commissioner of Conservation. These drilling operations were continued until the unit well was completed as a producer of gas and condensate.

In Hilliard v. Franzheim, 180 So.2d 746 (La.App. 3d Cir.1965) an overriding royalty sale was conditioned on the vendor drilling a well "to be started within 90 days." Within the 90-day period, plaintiff secured a drilling permit, staked the location, moved lumber onto it, leveled the site, installed a culvert and cattle guard and commenced construction of a board road to the well site. The rig was not on location and drilling was not begun until more than 90 days from the agreement. We held these activities satisfied the requirement that a well "be started." The law is stated as follows:

"For what applicability it may have to the interpretation of the present royalty contract, the general rule to be drawn from these decisions is that actual drilling is unnecessary to 'commence' a well within the meaning of the lease provisions; and that substantial surface preparations to drill are sufficient to be considered 'commencement' of drilling operations for the lease-clause purposes, such as making and clearing a location, delivering equipment to the well site, and the like, provided that such preliminary operations are continued in good faith and with due diligence until the well is actually spudded in." (citations omitted)

Plaintiffs first contend summary judgment is improper since there is a genuine issue as to material fact. Specifically, plaintiffs say cross-affidavits which they filed state that no equipment was moved to the well location until after March 18, 1967. This contradicts statements in affidavits submitted by defendant that drilling equipment was placed on the location on March 18, 1967.

Regardless of this contradiction in the affidavits, plaintiffs do not deny in their pleadings, affidavits or other documents that the board road and turn-around were completed to the well site on March 18, 1967. Under Hilliard v. Franzheim, supra, and the authorities cited therein, the completion of the board road and turn-around before the crucial date, followed by continuous operations until the well produced, is sufficient to satisfy the requirement that the lessee "commence operations for the drilling of a well." It is not necessary to determine whether drilling equipment was moved to the well site on or before March 18, 1967. Hence, there is no issue as to *material* fact. The case can be decided as a matter of law based on facts as to which there is no genuine issue.

* * *

For the reasons assigned, the judgment appealed is affirmed. All costs of this appeal are assessed against the plaintiffs/appellants.

Affirmed.

NOTES

1. In *Breaux,* the court ruled that "commencement" of drilling does not require actual drilling. That is the majority position. See, e.g., Whelan v. R. Lacy, Inc., 251 S.W.2d 175 (Tex.Civ.App.1952), Walton v. Zatkoff, 127 N.W.2d 365 (Mich.1964), Wilcox v. West, 114 P.2d 39 (Cal.App.1941), and Anderson v. Hess Corp., 649 F.3d 891 (8th Cir. N.D. 2011). The Arkansas Supreme Court expressed the rationale for the position vividly: "Does drilling commence with operations for a well or does it commence only with the piercing of the ground with the drill bit? Does 'baking a cake' begin with the preparations of the dough or only with the actual placing of the dough in the oven?" Vickers v. Peaker, 300 S.W.2d 29, 32 (Ark.1957). But see Solberg v. Sunburst Oil & Gas Co., 235 P. 761 (Mont.1925), where the Montana Supreme Court held that where a delay rental clause provided that the lessee's rights would terminate unless it "commence[d] drilling operations," the lessee was required to penetrate the ground with a drill bit. The court distinguished "commence

drilling operations" from "commence operations for the drilling of a well," holding that the latter requires the lessee only to perform preliminary work on the land. See also Hall v. JFW, Inc., 893 P.2d 837, 842 (Kan. App. 1995): "The lease provides that the lessee must 'commence to *drill* a well within the term of this lease.' (Emphasis added.) Under the plain terms of the lease, actual drilling was required prior to the termination date." Do such fine distinctions make sense?

2. If actual drilling is not necessary to "commence" drilling operations, what does it take? Professor Kuntz analyzed the issue as follows:

> The factors which have been considered in determining whether or not a well had been commenced include the factors of: (a) acts on the premises, (b) good faith of the lessee, and (c) diligence in continuing drilling operations.

* * *

> Recognizing that the described factors are all elements of the same ultimate fact finding, it is possible to state a general test for the determination of whether or not a well has been commenced. A lessee has commenced a well if operations have been conducted on the land in good faith preparation for the drilling of a well for oil or gas and has continued the operations in good faith and with due diligence.

Kuntz § 32.3. Is *Breaux* consistent with this analysis? In light of the general test, consider the following:

(a) What if the lessee staked the location of the well, delivered lumber to the premises and contracted for a drilling rig but was unable to get a rig to the leased premises until 10 days after the time prescribed for commencement of drilling operations? See Fast v. Whitney, 187 P. 192 (Wyo.1920). In *Whitney,* the Wyoming Supreme Court, ruling on an objection to the sufficiency of a pleading, held that the evidence did not establish as a matter of law that the lessee had failed to commence drilling operations. What if the lessee had not contracted for a drilling rig? See Herl v. Legleiter, 668 P.2d 200 (Kan.App.1983).

(b) What if the lessee entered onto the leased property at 10:00 p.m. on the last day of the primary term with a truck and a mounted searchlight to locate a previously abandoned borehole, and located it, but did not bring a drilling rig or crew to the property until the following day? See Moore Oil, Inc. v. Snakard, 150 F.Supp. 250 (W.D.Okla.1957). But see Veritas Energy, LLC v. Brayton Operating Corp., 2008 WL 384169 (Tex. App. 2008), where there was less than a day's work on the last day of the primary term by a "dirt-work" company hired by lessee, which used a backhoe to "back-drag" grass along a proposed new road to the well site.

(c) What if the lessee commenced actual drilling before the prescribed date using a water well rig? Would the lease be maintained? Compare Hughes v. Ford, 92 N.E.2d 747 (Ill.1950), Olinkraft, Inc. v. Gerard, 364 So.2d 639 (La.App.1978), and Wilds v. Universal Resources Corp., 662 P.2d 303 (Okla. 1983), with LeBar v. Haynie, 552 P.2d 1107 (Wyo.1976). Is the use of a water-well rig to commence an oil or gas well necessarily inconsistent with an intention to drill an oil or gas well?

(d) Before the end of the primary term of its lease, the lessee staked the well location, started road construction and began clearing the well site. The lessee did not obtain a drilling permit or enter into a drilling contract until after the end of the primary term, after another lessee had completed testing a nearby well. Lessor sued to have the lessee's lease declared terminated. What result? See Goble v. Goff, 42 N.W.2d 845 (Mich.1950), and Herl v. Legleiter, 668 P.2d 200 (Kan.App.1983). Compare D'Lo Royalties, Inc. v. Shell Oil Co., 389 F.Supp. 538 (S.D.Miss.1975).

(e) After obtaining three short extensions of the primary term of the lease, lessee commenced actual drilling. The drilling rig was not wired for electricity, so continuous operations were not possible. Delays occurred because the lessee did not pay workmen and suppliers timely. The lessor sued to terminate the lease on the theory that the lessee was stalling, awaiting the outcome of a well being drilled approximately a mile away. What result? See Louis Richardson Ranch, Inc. v. Gibson, 105 P.2d 143 (Cal.App.1940). Are continuous operations required to meet good faith and due diligence standards? Must the lessee have financing in hand? See Butler v. Nepple, 354 P.2d 239 (Cal.1960).

(f) A lessee sought to drill horizontally from one tract of land to a leased tract. After the lessee obtained permits from both the city and the state to drill a directional well, it prepared the drill site and began drilling prior to the end of the lease primary term; however, the drill bit did not penetrate the vertical plane of the leased tract by the end of the lease primary term. Was the lease maintained? See A & M Oil, Inc. v. Miller, 715 P.2d 1295 (Kan.App. 1986). See also Petroleum Energy, Inc. v. Mid–America Petroleum, Inc., 775 F.Supp. 1420 (D.C. Kan. 1991) and Manzano Oil Corporation v. Chesapeake Operating, Inc., 178 F.Supp.2d 1217 (D.C. N.M. 2001).

3. If, as in *Breaux*, a lease provides that it "shall terminate on March 18, 1967, unless on or before said date the Lessee * * * (1) commences operations for the drilling of a well* * *," when does the lease terminate—at the beginning of March 18 or at the end of the day? See Winn v. Nilsen, 670 P.2d 588 (Okla.1983).

4. Should commencement of operations on the last day of the primary term, or close to the last day, raise any inference as to the good faith of the lessee?

5. Would the result have been different in *Breaux* if the delay rental clause had stated that the lease would terminate on the anniversary date unless a well had been "completed" on the premises? See Baldwin v. Blue Stem Oil Co., 189 P. 920 (Kan.1920). See also Exxon Corporation v. Emerald Oil and Gas Co., L.C., 348 S.W.3d 194 (Tex. 2011), holding that "drilled and completed" within the meaning of lease continuous-development clauses required the lessee to drill, and if oil or gas in paying quantities was encountered, to perforate the casing or otherwise prepare the well to produce.

6. For further discussion of the meaning of "commencement," see generally Kuntz § 32.2; Summers Perm. Ed. § 349; Williams & Meyers § 606.1; Hemingway § 6.7; and Lowe, Chapter 8.

2. THE SECONDARY TERM: EXTENSION AND MAINTENANCE OF THE LEASE

The modern day oil and gas lease terminates at the end of its primary term unless the lease is maintained by "production." As we discussed in the introduction to this chapter, the purpose of the reference to "production" in the "secondary term" of the habendum clause is to give the lessee the right to hold a producing lease as long as it is economically viable to do so. Otherwise, if the lessee holds under a fixed term lease, say for fifty years, its rights will terminate at the end of that time, even if the property is still capable of prolific production. See Southland Royalty Co. v. Federal Power Comm'n, 543 F.2d 1134 (5th Cir.1976), reversed on other grounds 436 U.S. 519 (1978), for a fascinating (and horrific) story of leases with fixed terms. As the following materials illustrate, disputes frequently arise over the meaning of "production."

(a) Production "In Paying Quantities"

CLIFTON v. KOONTZ

325 S.W.2d 684 (Tex.1959).

SMITH, JUSTICE.

This suit brought by petitioners, Lillie M. Clifton, individually and as executrix of the estate of her husband, J.H. Clifton, deceased, et al., seeks the cancellation of an oil, gas, and mineral lease on the theory that after the expiration of its ten-year primary term, the lease terminated due to cessation of production.

* * *

The judgment of the trial court, entered after a trial before the court, without the aid of a jury, contains the court's findings of fact upon the basic questions. The court found that the existing gas well had at all material times continuously produced gas in paying quantities. Accordingly, the oil and gas lease was held to be in full force and effect, thus denying petitioners' prayer for judgment that the lease had terminated. * * *

Both petitioners and respondents appealed. The Court of Civil Appeals affirmed the trial court's judgment denying termination of the oil and gas lease and petitioners' claim for damages * * *. 305 S.W.2d 782.

We have concluded that the judgment of the Court of Civil Appeals must be sustained. We first consider the primary question, which is: Was there any evidence to sustain the finding of the trial court that production in paying quantities had not ceased?

One of the rules in determining this question is the well-settled rule that if there is any evidence reasonably tending to prove, either directly or by permissive inference, the essential facts, the judgment rendered thereon must be sustained.

* * *

Petitioners base their contention that the well had ceased to produce in paying quantities upon the showing that for the period of time from June, 1955 through September, 1956, the income from the lease was $3,250 and that the total expense of operations during the same period was $3,466.16—thus, a loss of $216.16 for the sixteen months' period selected by petitioners. During the period of time indicated, some months showed a gain and some a loss. For the months of July, August, and September 1956, the total net loss amounted to $372.37. These were the months immediately following June 1956, the date respondent, Koontz, acquired his 52 percent interest in the lease. Beginning July 1, 1956 he began making financial arrangements, securing the services of third parties, and commenced saving all oil produced from the lease to be used in reworking the well. The holding from the market of this oil accounts materially for the losses in the operations during the months of July, August, and September 1956. The record shows that for years, in view of the low allowable on gas, the oil production had made the difference between operating at a profit and at a loss. The respondent, Koontz, testified that from two to three months were required to accumulate a tank of oil and that after such accumulation a sale would be made. Respondents' evidence reflects that through 1955 and 1956 there was but little variation in gas production. For the same period of time there was a great variation in oil production, resulting in a showing of a profit in months when oil sales were made.

It is undisputed that reworking operations were commenced on September 12, 1956, and that such operations resulted in an 1800 percent increase of production. Reworking operations having thus been commenced on September 12, 1956, the evidence that there was a small operating loss for the period of time from July, 1956 through September, 1956 is not controlling in determining whether or not there had been a cessation of production in paying quantities through July 12, 1956, a date 60 days prior to the beginning of reworking operations. The question, therefore, is: Was there production in paying quantities from the existing well through July 12, 1956? Evidence, as contended for by the petitioners, as to profit or loss subsequent to July 12, 1956, is immaterial in determining whether or not there was production in paying quantities through that date. If there was production in paying quantities at all times through July 12, 1956, then the clause contained in the lease, which permits reworking within 60 days following cessation of production, if it ever came into operation, was complied with when reworking operations were begun on September 12, 1956, and later successfully completed. Thus, by considering only the evidence relative to production prior to July 12, 1956, we find that the lessee operated at a profit in the sum of $111.25, for the period of time beginning in June 1955 and continuing through July 12,

1956. The record shows a loss during the months of April and May, 1956. The record further shows that for the year 1954, a profit was earned each month, and that the aggregate profit was the sum of $1,575; that in 1955 the operations were profitable during nine months of the year, with a net profit of $894 for the year; and that for the first six months' period of 1956, the lease was operated at a profit of $145. These factual situations, when considered in the light most favorable to the findings of the trial court, support its finding and judgment that there was not a cessation of production in paying quantities through July 12, 1956.

Petitioners argue that it is settled under the Texas law that, after the primary term, the ordinary oil and gas lease absolutely terminates when its income no longer exceeds the cost of its operation, and that since the operations showed a loss for the months of April and May, 1956, the lease terminated. * * *

* * *

The lease instrument involved in this suit provides by its terms that it shall continue in effect after commencement of production, "as long thereafter as oil, gas, or other mineral is produced from said land." While the lease does not expressly use the term "paying quantities", it is well settled that the terms "produced" and "produced in paying quantities" mean substantially the same thing. Garcia v. King, 139 Tex. 578, 164 S.W.2d 509, 511.

The generally accepted definition of "production in paying quantities" is stated in the Garcia case, supra, to be as follows:

If a well pays a profit, even small, over operating expenses, it produces in paying quantities, though it may never repay its costs, and the enterprise as a whole may prove unprofitable.

In the case of a marginal well, such as we have here, the standard by which paying quantities is determined is whether or not under all the relevant circumstances a reasonably prudent operator would, for the purpose of making a profit and not merely for speculation, continue to operate a well in the manner in which the well in question was operated.

In determining paying quantities, in accordance with the above standard, the trial court necessarily must take into consideration all matters which would influence a reasonable and prudent operator. Some of the factors are: The depletion of the reservoir and the price for which the lessee is able to sell his produce, the relative profitableness of other wells in the area, the operating and marketing costs of the lease, his net profit, the lease provisions, a reasonable period of time under the circumstances, and whether or not the lessee is holding the lease merely for speculative purposes.

The term "paying quantities" involves not only the amount of production, but also the ability to market the product (gas) at a profit. Whether there is a reasonable basis for the expectation of profitable returns from the well is the test. If the quantity be sufficient to warrant the use of the gas in the market, and the income therefrom is in excess of the actual marketing cost, and operating costs, the production satisfies the term "in paying quantities". In the Hanks case, [Hanks v. Magnolia Petroleum Co., 24 S.W.2d 5 (Tex.Com.App.1930)] the trial court found that the well completed by Hanks did not produce in paying quantities within the contemplation of the terms of the lease, and this Court upheld such finding, holding that there was no evidence showing that there were any facilities for marketing the gas or any near-by localities or industries which might have furnished a profitable market therefor. The Court went further and pointed out the complete failure of the evidence to show what the gas could have been sold for at any probable market, and that there was no evidence "tending to show that the well was situated in such proximity to any prospective market which would justify the construction of a pipe line for marketing same."

In the present case we have a finding of the trial court that there was production in paying quantities, and that the lease had not terminated. The evidence supports the finding. Evidence of marketing facilities and that the gas was sold at a profit is present in the instant case, whereas the Hanks case, supra, was wholly devoid of such evidence.

Proration rules adopted by the Texas Railroad Commission are a factor in determining the productive capacity of a particular lease. The Railroad Commission may by its order, for example, permit the taking of a greater percentage of the daily volume from nonassociated gas wells to the end that adequate quantities of gas may be delivered during the winter months when the demand therefor is the greatest, and by its order reduce the percentage to be taken during the summer months when a much less quantity of gas is needed. Relative to individual leases or gas units, the Commission has taken the position that it may by its order allow an overproduction for a period of time to meet the market demand for that period, and, in order to balance such overproduction, it takes the position that it may order that the well be cut down to a minimum volume of production.

Petitioners contend that the trial court's finding that production in paying quantities had not ceased is erroneous because the profit and loss figures heretofore considered do not include charges for depreciation as an operating expense. We are of the opinion that the trial court correctly excluded depreciation as an operating expense in determining whether and when production in paying quantities ceases. The petitioners contend that depreciation of the original investment cost should be taken into consideration as a part of the expense in operating the well. With this contention we do not agree. We do not have before us the question of whether or not depreciation on producing equipment should be charged as an operating expense, and, therefore, do not decide the question.

As the Garcia case, supra, indicates, the term "paying quantities", when used in the extension clause of an oil lease habendum clause, means production in quantities sufficient to yield a return in excess of operating costs, and marketing costs, even though drilling and equipment costs may never be repaid and the undertaking considered as a whole may ultimately result in a loss. The underlying reason for this definition appears to be that when a lessee is making a profit over the actual cash he must expend to produce the lease, he is entitled to continue operating in order to recover the expense of drilling and equipping, although he may never make a profit on the over-all operation. Depreciation is nothing more than an accounting charge of money spent in purchasing tangible property, and if the investment itself is not to be considered, as is held by this Court, then neither is depreciation.

In Transport Oil Co. v. Exeter Oil Co. Ltd., 84 Cal.App.2d 616, 191 P.2d 129, it was held that operation of an oil and gas leasehold at an annual profit of about $4,300, without deduction of reserves for depletion and depreciation and after exclusion under terms of the lease and operating agreement of overriding royalties as an operating expense, was in "paying quantities" within the habendum clause of the lease. By not including depreciation as an operating expense, we more nearly accomplish a just result for lessors and lessees alike, for, if the rule were otherwise, many leases would be terminated and the lessees' incentive to drill decreased, regardless of the magnitude of the investment.

Petitioners present two cases to support their argument that depreciation should be treated as an expense item, but they are both distinguishable. In Persky v. First State Bank, Tex.Civ.App., 117 S.W.2d 861, 863, no writ history, the Court of Civil Appeals merely held:

> We *might* take judicial knowledge that all property of this kind has some depreciation from year to year, but we could not, in the absence of testimony to support it, take judicial knowledge of the percentage or amount of such depreciation. (Emphasis supplied.)

It is not held that depreciation is to be considered as operation expense, and, as such, is to be deducted from income. Also, we do not have pumping machinery involved in the case at bar, as was true in the Persky case.

The other case relied upon is United Central Oil Corporation v. Helm, 5 Cir., 11 F.2d 760, certiorari denied 271 U.S. 686. The Court in that case held that depreciation and overhead expenses are to be considered in determining paying quantities at the time of abandonment of a lease, in an action for damages against the lessee by the lessor. However, the lease was for a period of four years rather than "so long thereafter as oil and/or gas are produced." The holding in the Helm case does not conflict with our holding in the present case. The case merely demonstrates the variable meaning applied to the phrase "paying quantities".

Petitioners contend that the 8 percent overriding royalties outstanding, as shown by the record, should be excluded from the total income attributable to the working interest in determining whether or not production is being obtained in paying quantities. We do not agree. The entire income attributable to the contractual working interest created by the original lease is to be considered. Petitioners cite no Texas case, and we have found none, which supports their argument. While apparently there is no Texas decision in point on the particular question, we believe the case of Transport Oil Co. v. Exeter Oil Co., Ltd., supra, is authority supporting our view. In that case the basic oil and gas lease on a tract of land executed in 1921 required certain drilling operations and the payment of 16 2/3 percent royalty to the lessor based upon the gross income. After several assignments of the lease in which overriding royalties had been reserved, the plaintiff in the action became the owner of the lease subject to the overriding royalty. Thereafter, the plaintiff, Transport Oil Company, assigned this lease to the defendant, Exeter Oil Company, in which assignment the defendant obligated itself to pay out of the gross income from the lease, the basic landowner's royalty, the overriding royalty reserved in previous assignments, and the override to the plaintiff totaling almost 50 percent of the income per well. In 1942 the defendant plugged the well and abandoned the property, due to declining production. The abandonment terminated the plaintiff's interest as an overriding royalty owner, and it brought suit to recover damages. The court held that overriding royalty could not be excluded from the total income in determining whether there was production in paying quantities. See also, Vance v. Hurley, 1949, 215 La. 805, 41 So.2d 724.

* * *

The judgment of the Court of Civil Appeals is affirmed.

HAMILTON, J., not sitting.

NOTES

1.　The rule that production must be "in paying quantities" to the lessee, even where the lease habendum clause does not use the phrase, is virtually the unanimous position of the states. The rationale behind the rule is that the grant of the oil and gas lease is an economic transaction.

> The reasoning which has prompted many courts to give the term "produced" a meaning broader than its literal meaning, is that the basic purpose of the lease must be taken into account in construing the language of the lease. The view expressed is that the basic purpose of the lease is to secure development of the property for the mutual benefit of the lessor and lessee, and that the lessee should not be permitted to hold the lease for speculation.

Kuntz § 26.5.

> There are cases to the contrary, however. Professor Kuntz notes that:

> [T]here are cases in which it has either been held or assumed that the word "produced" means what it says and that production need not be in paying quantities to prevent a termination of the lease. * * * The reasoning behind the conclusion that the word "produced" does not mean that production must be in paying quantities is not uniform in the states where such conclusion has been reached. In West Virginia, the reasoning

is similar to the reasoning applied in the states where it is held that "production" means "production in paying quantities." The court seeks to construe the lease so as to give effect to the basic purposes of the parties. In West Virginia, however, the court does not consider that the basic purpose of the lease is simply to render the property productive for the benefit of both parties. According to such court, the fundamental purpose of the lease is to apply the skill and effort of the lessee to make the property productive. * * * The qualifying clause "as oil or gas is produced" really means "as long as the premises are diligently and efficiently operated, provided minerals shall have been discovered within the fixed term."

* * *

The other line of reasoning behind the conclusion that "production" does not require paying quantities is very simple and direct. Such reasoning proceeds upon the theory that the parties selected the language, that they intended for the word "produced" to have its literal meaning, and that if the parties contemplated that production should be in paying quantities, they could have so provided by the simple addition of the words "in paying quantities."

Id.

In United States v. 2,847.58 Acres of Land, 529 F.2d 682, 691 (6th Cir.1976), an example of the minority view, the court noted Kentucky law:

So long as a lessor is receiving royalties, "even though small," he may not cancel a lease which provides for continuance beyond its primary term for as long as oil or gas is produced without showing that such royalties are insufficient to compensate him for the occupancy and interference resulting from the operations of the lessee. * * * Statements in the various opinions requiring that such leases operate at a profit refer to the necessity that there be enough production to compensate the lessor [for the inconvenience of the lessee's occupancy and operations], not that the lessee show a profit. Many factors other than the size of production can determine the profitability of a particular operation.

Which of these approaches should be the rule of law? Why?

For an exhaustive discussion of production in paying quantities, see Douglas Hale Gross, Annotation, Meaning of "Paying Quantities" in Oil and Gas Lease, 43 A.L.R.3d 8 (1972).

2. Does "commercial quantities" mean the same as "in paying quantities"? In interpreting a statute requiring the plugging of wells that have ceased to produce in "commercial quantities" for a specified period, an Ohio court held in State v. Wallace, 369 N.E.2d 781 (Ohio App.1976), that "commercial quantities" is a sufficiently large amount to be sold by the owner to a buyer for transport elsewhere. But see the comment on the case at J. Richard Emens & John S. Lowe, Ohio Oil and Gas Conservation Law—The First Ten Years (1965–1975), 37 Ohio St. L.J. 31, 72–73 (1976). Contrast Pan Am. Petroleum Corp. v. Shell Oil Co., 455 P.2d 12 (Alaska 1969) with Texaco, Inc. v. Fox, 618 P.2d 844 (Kan.1980).

3. As *Clifton* illustrates, the "in paying quantities" standard is generally applied in a two-step process. First, the court will quantify the reasonable prudent operator standard by applying what might be called a "litmus test:"[11] looking to operating revenues and operating costs over a reasonable time to determine whether operations have been "profitable." If operations have resulted in a profit—however small—the inquiry is ended, and the lease is held to be producing "in paying quantities." If the test indicates that operating revenues have not exceeded costs over a reasonable time, however, the court usually applies the legal test articulated in *Clifton*: whether there is any reason that a reasonable prudent operator who expected to make a profit from the lease would continue to operate. Only if the answers to both steps of the analysis are negative, does the lease terminate. Oklahoma applies a two-step process, but couches the second step in the context of equity:

> Our law is firmly settled that the result in each case must depend upon the circumstances that surround cessation. Our view is no doubt influenced in part by the strong policy of our statutory law against forfeiture of estates. * * * In short, the lease continues in existence so long as the interruption of production in paying quantities does not extend for a period longer than reasonable or justifiable in light of the circumstances involved. But under *no* circumstances will cessation of production in paying quantities *ipso facto* deprive the lessee of his extended-term estate. A decree of lease cancellation may be rendered where the record shows that the well in suit was not producing in paying quantities and there are no compelling equitable considerations to justify continued production from the unprofitable well operations.

Stewart v. Amerada Hess Corp., 604 P.2d 854, 858 (Okla.1979) (Emphasis in original) (Citations omitted).[12] Other jurisdictions, however, use a one-step test. In Kansas, for example, "if the lessee's gross income from the lease exceeds lease operating costs, the paying quantities requirement is met. If gross income does not exceed operating costs, the lease terminates. * * * This objective approach is designed to keep the lessee from holding unprofitable leases for speculation." Pierce § 9.24, citing Reese Enterprises, Inc. v. Lawson, 553 P.2d 885 (Kan. 1976).

Some courts and commentators have described the two-step paying-quantities analysis as a "subjective test." See, e.g., T.W. Phillips Gas and Oil Co. v. Jedlicka, 42 A.3d 261 (Pa. 2012), and Hemingway § 6.4(A). But did the result in *Clifton v. Koontz* turn on the lessee's good faith judgment that production was still economically viable? Is a determination that a reasonable

---

11. It may be helpful to think of the quantification of operating revenues and operating costs over a reasonable time as a "litmus test," because, like its scientific counterpart, it is fallible. A lease may continue to produce "in paying quantities," even if it fails the litmus test; the test is determinative only when it shows that the lease *is* profitable.

12. In Smith v. Marshall Oil Corp., 85 P.3d 830 (Okla. 2004), the court held that fluctuating market prices "do not rise to the level of an equitable consideration." Id. at 836. And in Baytide Petroleum, Inc. v. Continental Resources, Inc., 231 P.3d 1144 (Okla. 2010), it addressed when an oil and gas lease terminates for failure to produce in paying quantities, stating:

> Our prior decisions make it clear that although a court order may be necessary to adjudicate the rights of the parties when allegations are that a lease has terminated for failure to produce in paying quantities, a lease terminates not because of the entrance of a court order but for failure to produce in paying quantities under the lease's habendum clause.

prudent operator would continue to produce with an expectation of profit or that "compelling equitable considerations" justify the producer's continued operations really "subjective"? Professor Kuntz said:

> The presence or absence of good faith must be proved by circumstantial evidence. In determining which circumstances are relevant, it is necessary to recognize some standard in order to determine when the lessee's judgment is reached by the exercise of good faith. By necessity, such standard requires the recognition of external circumstances and becomes external in nature.

Kuntz § 26.7(f).

4. Even if production "in paying quantities" is accepted as the standard and is defined as "operating revenues exceeding operating costs over a reasonable period," ascertaining what the term means in specific circumstances may be difficult. Consider the following:

(a) *Receipts taken into account.* As *Clifton* indicates, the share of production attributable to overriding royalty interests is taken into account in calculating operating income. All the income attributable to the working interest as it was originally created is counted; only income attributable to the landowner's royalty is excluded. See also Reese Enters., Inc. v. Lawson, 220 Kan. 300, 553 P.2d 885 (1976), and Article 124 of the Louisiana Mineral Code. But see Morgan v. Fox, 536 S.W.2d 644 (Tex.Civ.App.1976). Why should income, such as overriding royalties, that does not go to the lessee be considered as "production" to the lessee? Would the same rationale apply to production payments and other nonoperating interests? Should a payment from production to the lessor be taken into account if it is substantially greater than the usual royalty? See Vance v. Hurley, 41 So.2d 724 (La.1949).

(b) *Expenditures taken into account.* As *Clifton* states, it is well established that capital costs involved in the acquisition of the lease, as well as the initial costs of drilling and equipping the well, are *not* taken into account in determining whether or not the lease is producing in paying quantities. Such expenses are not relevant, because they have been incurred before the time that the lessee considers whether or not to continue production. In determining whether a lessee is acting as a reasonable prudent operator in continuing to operate the lease, "sunk" expenses are logically irrelevant. Even though such expenses will never be recovered, the prudent operator will continue to operate as long as operating revenues exceed operating costs, because operating will cut the ultimate loss on the venture.

Only actual and direct costs of continued production are considered in determining "paying quantities." An expenditure's classification as a capital or operating expense is generally determined by whether it is ordinary and recurring (in which case the expense is a lease operating expense), or extraordinary and largely non-recurring in nature (in which case the expense is a capital cost). Lege v. Lea Exploration Co., 631 So.2d 716 (La.App. 3 Cir. 1994). The value of the lessee's labor is not to be treated as an operating expense where no wages are actually accrued or paid. Blausey v. Stein, 400 N.E.2d 408 (Ohio 1980). A large expenditure to plug a leak in the well casing is analogous to the expense of initial drilling and, therefore, a capital expense rather than an operating expense. Pshigoda v. Texaco, Inc., 703 S.W.2d 416

(Tex.App.1986). Operating expenses generally include labor, trucking, transportation expense, replacement and repair of equipment, production taxes, license and permit fees, maintenance and repair of roads, and entrances and gates. Several classes of expenditures present substantial classification difficulties, however:

(1) Should overriding royalties paid out of production be deducted as expenses in determining "paying quantities"? In determining income for purposes of the "paying quantities" calculation, the *Clifton* court noted that receipts attributed to overriding royalty interests are generally credited to the lessee. In Hininger v. Kaiser, 738 P.2d 137 (Okla.1987), however, the Oklahoma Supreme Court held squarely that overriding royalties are not to be counted as lifting costs, because they are part of the lessee's initial capital investment: "if an overriding royalty is carved out of the lessee's estate, it is done in return for a benefit conferred." 738 P.2d at 140. Is that reasoning compelling?

(2) Should the cost of plugging wells, restoring the premises, and other statutorily or regulatorily imposed "clean up" expenses be included as operating costs? In Reese Enters., Inc. v. Lawson, 553 P.2d 885 (Kan.1976), the Kansas Supreme Court indicated that such costs should be included in operating costs. Professor Kuntz argues that cleanup costs should not be included, however, because the necessity for such expenditures arises when the well is first drilled and they are actually incurred after production has ceased. Therefore, they are not relevant to the issue of whether the reasonable prudent operator would continue production. Kuntz § 26.7(j). What is the better view?

(3) What about administrative and overhead expenses such as general supervision, office maintenance, bookkeeping and accounting, and the corporate jet? In Skelly Oil Co. v. Archer, 356 S.W.2d 774 (Tex.1961) and Sullivan & Garnett v. James, 308 S.W.2d 891 (Tex.Civ.App.1957), appellate courts included administrative and overhead costs in the calculation of paying quantities. In West v. Russell, 90 Cal.Rptr. 772 (Cal.App.1970), the court indicated that some administrative costs could be taken into account if established by the evidence. In Mason v. Ladd Petroleum Corp., 630 P.2d 1283 (Okla.1981), the court limited administrative and overhead costs to be considered to those related to the lease's producing operations. In Hininger v. Kaiser, 738 P.2d 137 (Okla.1987), the court ruled that administrative expenses paid under an operating agreement for supervision and accounting are not lifting costs. See also, Edwin M. Cage, Production in Paying Quantities: Technical Problems Involved, 10 Inst. on Oil & Gas L. & Tax'n 61 (1959). If such costs are to be considered, how should they be calculated and proved?

(4) Should depreciation of well equipment be considered in determining paying quantities? This issue has given the courts some difficulty, as the court's discussion in *Clifton* indicates. See also Texaco, Inc. v. Fox, 618 P.2d 844 (Kan.1980) and Ross Explorations, Inc. v. Freedom Energy, Inc., 8 S.W.3d 511 (Ark.2000). Another view of the law is found in the Oklahoma Supreme Court's statement in Stewart v. Amerada Hess Corp., 604 P.2d 854 (Okla. 1979):

Extant case law on the national scene has given little attention to depreciation as a mandatory lifting expense item. Some case law indicates, without actually so holding, that depreciation might be considered to be in this category. [Transport Oil Co. v. Exeter Oil Co., 191 P.2d 129 (Cal.App. 2 Dist. 1948); West v. Russell, 90 Cal.Rptr. 772, 43 A.L.R.3d 1 (Cal.App. 2 Dist. 1970).] Other out-of-state authority reasons that since the original investment in a well may not be considered in computing oil lifting expenses, neither should producing equipment depreciation. [Clifton v. Koontz, 325 S.W.2d 684 (Tex.1959).] The rationale for not including depreciation, given by one court, was that it would bring about termination of many leases and tend to diminish the incentive to drill. [Transport Oil Co. v. Exeter Oil Co., 191 P.2d 129 (Cal.App. 2 Dist. 1948).]

Depreciation of equipment used in lifting operations is regarded as production expense in some states. The rationale for this rule is that while depreciation of the original investment in the drilling of a well may not be *stricto sensu* an out-of-pocket lifting expense, production-related equipment does have value that is being reduced through its continued operation. We adopt this reasoning as sound and hold that depreciation should be mandatorily included as an item of lifting expense in determining whether there is production in "paying quantities." The base and the period of depreciation should be determined by reference to currently prevailing accounting standards.

604 P.2d at 857–58. Which approach makes more sense?

If depreciation of equipment is to be considered as an element of "in paying quantities," what items of equipment should be depreciated? For example, what about the casing in the well (the pipe that runs from the surface to the oil producing formation)? Casing could not be considered "lifting equipment," but it might be considered "production related equipment" in a producing well. And what method of depreciation should be used, that is, straight line, double declining balance, sum of the year's digits, or some other system? One writer has asserted that "[T]here are several methods of depreciation which would qualify as 'currently prevailing accounting standards' that could result in a broad range of depreciation expense charges for a particular lease." See Lawson, Depreciation of Equipment as an Element of Production in Paying Quantities: An Analysis of Stewart v. Amerada Hess Corp., 51 Okla.B.J. 2217, 2218 (1984). In Underwood v. Texaco Inc., 590 F.Supp. 289 (W.D.Okla.1981), the court held that tax depreciation was the appropriate basis.

(c) *Period taken into account.* As *Clifton,* 325 S.W.2d at 690, indicates, "there can be no limit as to time, whether it be days, weeks, or months, to be taken into consideration * * *." Professor Kuntz explains this standard as follows:

The volume of oil or gas which is produced will fluctuate from time to time. Normally, production will decline prior to final cessation, and in many instances may be periodically suspended completely. Moreover, the market price of oil and gas, as well as current operating costs are subject to considerable fluctuation. When these factors are taken into account, it

becomes apparent that it would be unreasonable to establish definite accounting periods during which the lease must be operated at a profit.
* * *

When the question of the period of time to be taken into account is considered along with the other factors which are taken into account in determining whether or not a lease is producing in paying quantities, it appears that such period of time should be sufficiently long to provide the information which a prudent operator would take into account in deciding whether to continue or to abandon the operation.

Kuntz § 26.7(u). As a rule of thumb, however, the courts have generally not considered a period less than a year.

5. Should the lessee or the lessor bear the burden of proof as to whether the lease is producing "in paying quantities"? The lessee (presumably) has a substantial investment at stake and if the lease is wrongfully terminated, the lessor receives a windfall in the form of a well capable of producing. But much of the information bearing on "in paying quantities" is solely under the control of the lessee, is it not? See Superior Oil Co. v. Devon Corp., 458 F.Supp. 1063, 1071 (D.Neb.1978), reversed on other grounds, 604 F.2d 1063 (8th Cir.Neb.1979), and Hydrocarbon Management, Inc. v. Tracker Exploration, Inc., 861 S.W.2d 427 (Tex.App.1993).

6. As a general rule, principles of equity do not apply to an interest subject to a special limitation, such as the lessee's interest under an oil and gas lease; a determinable interest terminates by its own terms rather than by an exercise of a right. In a few states, however, once a lessee's rights have vested by discovery of oil or gas, the lease continues "until there are no compelling equitable considerations to justify continued production from the unprofitable well operations." Stewart v. Amerada Hess Corp., 604 P.2d 854 (Okla.1979).

Should equitable defenses (for example, estoppel, waiver, or laches) be available to the lessee to maintain a lease in effect that is no longer producing "in paying quantities"? If a lessor continues to accept royalties, free gas, or other benefits tendered under the lease, can the lessee successfully assert that the lease continues? See the discussion at Williams & Meyers § 604.7; Kuntz § 26.14(c); and Lowe, Chapter 8.D.

7. In Louisiana, some cases indicate that the production must not only be "in 'paying quantities' to the lessee, but must also be sufficient to furnish an adequate consideration to the lessor. The adequacy of the consideration has been determined by comparing the royalties paid with the original bonus and rentals." See, e.g., Caldwell v. Alton Oil Co., 108 So. 314 (La.1926). The relevant section of the Louisiana Mineral Code, Article 125 (La. Rev. Stat. Ann. § 31:125), effective January 1, 1975, provides as follows:

[T]he amount of the royalties being paid may be considered only insofar as it may show the reasonableness of the lessee's expectation in continuing production. The amount need not be a serious or adequate equivalent for continuance of the lease as compared with the amount of the bonus, rentals, or other sums paid to the lessor.

The Reporter, Dean George Hardy, noted in the Comment to Article 125 that while the adequacy of consideration is not a legal requirement, Article 125 "maintains the relevance of the amount of royalties being paid as a factor for consideration in determining whether the lessee is acting as a reasonable, prudent operator in continuing to produce the property or is acting out of improper motives." In Edmundson Bros. Partnership v. Montex Drilling Co., 731 So.2d 1049 (La.App.1999), the court held that a lease that had produced an average of $139.00 per month profit over an eighteen-month period was not sufficient to justify the producer to continue production.

8.   What are a lessee's rights and obligations after lease termination? Most leases contain an *equipment-removal clause* permitting the lessee to remove equipment and fixtures. A common provision is that:

> Lessee shall have the right at any time during or after the expiration of this lease to remove all property and fixtures placed on the premises by Lessee, including the right to draw and remove all casing.

The purpose is to give the lessee the broadest possible discretion to determine when to plug and abandon wells and to protect the lessee against a finding that equipment left on a lease after termination has been abandoned or has become affixed to the land.

In fact, courts have generally permitted lessees to recover equipment after lease termination even without authorizing language. Moreover, provisions like the one quoted have been interpreted narrowly. They do not authorize the lessee to plug and abandon a well capable of commercial production, and despite the words "at any time," the lessee must recover his property from the premises within a reasonable time after lease termination. For further discussion, see Kuntz § 50.3.

9.   Lessors often insert in leases a *release-of-record provision*. A typical example follows:

> In the event that this lease expires for any reason as to all or any portion of the land described in this lease, lessee shall furnish lessor promptly, with a written, recordable release instrument covering all of the land as to which this lease has so expired.

The purpose of such a clause is to avoid clouds on title; an oil and gas lease extends as long as it is "produced," so a title examiner cannot tell by looking at the records in the county courthouse whether the lease has terminated. Most producing states have statutes requiring that lessees provide lessors with releases of record when leases terminate. Many laws provide for the lessor to recover nominal damages and reasonable attorney's fees if a lessee does not comply. See, e.g., Cal. Civ. Code § 883.140; Kan. Stat. Ann. §§ 55–201, 55–202, & 55–206. Regarding the Kansas procedure see Pierce § 8.08. For further discussion, see Kuntz § 12.4.

10.   In some states the oil and gas lease provides constructive notice of the lessee's rights only during the primary term unless the lessee files for record an affidavit indicating the production conditions of the lease have been met. For example, Kan. Stat. Ann. § 55–205 provides for the filing of what is known as an "affidavit of production" that describes the lease, the lease

owner, and states that the required contingency has occurred to extend the lease into the secondary term. See Pierce § 8.12.

(b) Actual Production or Capability of Production

While most courts agree that the economic meaning of "produced" is "in paying quantities," jurisdictions disagree about the physical nature of "produced." As the cases below illustrate, some states require actual production and marketing in paying quantities, while others require just a capability of production in paying quantities.

STANOLIND OIL & GAS CO. v. BARNHILL

107 S.W.2d 746 (Tex.Civ.App.1937).

STOKES, JUSTICE.

This appeal is from a judgment of the district court of Potter county in favor of the appellees, who were defendants in that court. The suit was filed by appellants, Stanolind Oil & Gas Company and J. A. Batson, each claiming to own a half interest in an oil and gas lease on 160 acres of land in Hutchinson county, the Stanolind Oil & Gas Company claiming to own the entire lease on the remaining portion of the tract involved of 960 acres. * * *

The lease was executed by appellees, J. R. Barnhill and wife and O. B. Carver, to J. A. Batson, and the interest claimed by Stanolind Oil & Gas Company duly assigned to it by the latter. It was dated February 4, 1930, and, by its terms, was to continue for a term of five years and as much longer as oil or gas or either of them should be produced from the land by the lessee. The sum of $10,000 was paid as cash consideration for the lease, and it contained further provisions for the payment of rentals in the sum of $1 per acre if no well were commenced on the land before February 4, 1931, and like payments annually in the absence of drilling operations.

Appellants commenced the drilling of a well on the land December 23, 1930, discovered gas and completed the drilling March 31, 1931, at a depth of 3,370 feet after plugging back from the total depth drilled of 3,498 feet. Tests showed a potential production of more than 7,000,000 feet of sour gas per day, and a pressure of 410 pounds. The well was gauged at intervals of about a month continuously from the date it was completed up to December 5, 1935, when the last test was made and the supply and pressure continued equally as good or better, with a slight increase toward the last portion of the period. No delay rentals were paid, and on May 11, 1932, appellees executed and filed in the office of the county clerk of Hutchinson county an affidavit setting forth this fact, and on May 26, 1932, appellants caused to be filed in the same office an affidavit in substance that the lease was in good standing. Appellants expended about $25,000 in drilling the well, in addition to the $10,000 paid to appellees for the lease.

There was no demand for sour gas, and no market for it, especially from small, isolated wells, such as the one involved here, until late in the year 1935, when House Bill No. 266, enacted by the Forty–Fourth Legislature, became effective, prohibiting the use of sweet dry gas in the manufacture of carbon black, and, though appellants made every reasonable effort to market the product of the well, they were unable to do so until about October, 1935. On the 9th of that month, appellant Stanolind Oil & Gas Company made a contract with Phillips Petroleum Company to begin the delivery of gas from the well on December 31, 1935, but, before the latter date, appellees notified the Phillips Petroleum Company and appellants that the lease had terminated and the Phillips Petroleum Company then declined to take the product of the well until the status of the lease was definitely determined. It was to determine that issue that this suit was filed.

The case was tried by the court, without a jury, and the trial judge filed findings of fact substantially in accordance with the foregoing statement. His conclusion of law was, in substance, that, regardless of what may have been the rights of appellees prior to February 4, 1935, as to forfeiture, there being no production of either oil or gas in paying quantities, as provided by the lease, it expired on that date, which was five years after its date, and judgment was entered denying appellants any relief, canceling the oil and gas lease and removing the cloud cast upon appellees' title to the land and vesting the title in them.

Appellants present the case in this court upon four propositions, the pertinent questions raised in all of which we think may be reduced to the contention that, under the oil and gas lease, appellants hold a determinable fee in the oil and gas conveyed by the same, which is not terminated by failure to sell the product on account of a non-existing market, there being no abandonment of the lease and, if the lessors have a remedy, it is one for damages and not for a cancellation of the lease.

It is not an open question in Texas as to the nature of the title or interest of the lessee in an oil and gas lease, such as the one involved here. It invests the lessee and his assigns with the title to oil and gas in place, which is a determinable fee * * *.

As we view the case, * * * it is a question of whether or not they have produced oil or gas in paying quantities as contemplated in the lease within the time provided by the lease itself. As we have stated, the estate held under the lease by appellants is what the law denominates a "determinable fee." It is a fee-simple title because it may continue, forever, and it is determinable because it may come to an end upon contingencies. The lease provides that it shall remain in force for a term of five years from its date, which was February 4, 1930, and as long thereafter as oil or gas, or either of them, is produced in paying quantities from the land by the lessee. If, within five years from the 4th of February, 1930, appellants have developed and produced oil or gas from said land in paying quantities, their interest in the estate continues. On the other hand, according to the terms of the lease, if oil or gas is not produced from the land within the period of five years, the lease comes to an end. It terminates, and no act on the part of the lessor is necessary in order to accomplish that result. The lease expires, and, after February 4, 1935, if no oil or gas was being produced, the lessee had no lease upon the land nor any interest whatever therein. The trial court seems to have taken this view of the controversy, and we think it is the proper one. * * *

* * *

The lease under which appellant holds provides that it shall remain in force for a term of five years from its date, and so long thereafter as oil or gas, or either of them, is produced in paying quantities. Under the above definition of the term employed by the parties in the contract, appellants, although they discovered gas to an extent and in quantity that would have complied with their obligation in the lease if a market had been available for the kind of gas discovered, did not, under the circumstances of this case, discover nor produce gas in such quantities as, under the law, would be "paying quantities," within the five years provided by the lease. Their estate, consisting of a determinable fee, determinable upon their failure to produce oil or gas in paying quantities within such term, came to an end on February 4, 1935, as found by the trial court, after which they did not possess any interest whatever in the land. The lease did not exist. The term had closed, and the interest they procured by the lease was gone. It is not a question of forfeiture for failure to continue to develop the land, nor does it rest upon any other contingency. Appellants did not contract for a term which would depend upon the possibility of procuring a market for the product at some date subsequent to its express date of expiration. The lease did not provide that it should remain in force and effect for five years, and as long thereafter as there may be prospects of a market for the product, and it is not the duty of the courts to make contracts for parties but only to construe such contracts as they make for themselves.

We have carefully considered all of the propositions and assignments of error made by appellants, and, finding no error committed in the trial of the case, the judgment is affirmed.

PACK v. SANTA FE MINERALS, A DIVISION OF SANTA FE INTERNATIONAL CORPORATION

869 P.2d 323 (Okla.1994).

SIMMS, JUSTICE:

Appellants, Santa Fe Minerals and other oil and gas companies, (lessees) appeal the judgments entered by the district court in the quiet title actions instituted by appellees * * *. The trial court entered judgment in favor of the mineral rights owners, canceling oil and gas leases and quieting title in the lessors.

The Court of Appeals affirmed, holding the leases terminated of their own terms under the provisions of the "cessation of production" clause.

Certiorari was granted to consider the first impression question of whether a lease, held by a gas well which is capable of producing in paying quantities but is shut-in for a period in excess of sixty (60) days but less than one year due to a marketing decision made by the producer, expires of its own terms under the "cessation of production" clause unless shut-in royalty payments are made. We find that under such circumstances, the lease does not expire of its own terms. * * *

* * *

The habendum clause provides for the primary term of the lease to be for ten (10) years and "as long thereafter as oil, gas, casinghead gas, casinghead gasoline or any of them is produced." The shut-in royalty clause provides for a fifty dollar ($50.00) royalty payment per year for each well from which gas is not sold. When the royalty payment is paid, the well is deemed a producing well for purposes of the habendum clause. The cessation of production clause provides for the lease to continue after the expiration of the primary term as long as production does not cease for more than sixty (60) days without the lessee resuming operations to drill a new well.

* * * Each of the wells continued to be capable of producing in paying quantities up until the time of trial, but lessees have chosen at times not to market gas from the wells for periods exceeding sixty (60) days. The lessees stipulated that they chose to overproduce the wells during the winter months when the demand for gas is higher and the price for gas increases. Because the Oklahoma Corporation Commission imposed annual allowable limitations as to how much gas may be produced from the wells, the lessees curtailed the marketing of gas from the wells during the summer months when prices were lower so as not to exceed the annual allowable limits. The intention and result of this practice was to obtain the highest price for the gas and still stay within the allowable production limits set by the Oklahoma Corporation Commission. Such a practice was common with most of the gas producers in the state.

Although some marketing of the gas continued during the warmer months, such sales were exceeded by the monthly expenses, so the wells were not profitable during that period. Additionally, the Pack well was shut-in for one month during this period in order to build up pressure in preparation for an annual well test to determine its annual allowable limit.

* * *

I.

The term "produced" as used in the lease clauses means "capable of producing in paying quantities" and does not include marketing of the product.

A.

The Habendum Clause

This Court has long held that the terms "produced" and "produced in paying quantities" have substantially the same meaning. State ex rel. Commissioners of the Land Office v. Carter Oil Co. of West Virginia, 336 P.2d 1086 (Okla.1958). Therein, we construed a typical habendum clause which extended the lease past its ten-year primary term as long thereafter as oil or gas is produced in paying quantities. We held that in order to extend the fixed term of ten years "and acquire a limited estate in the land covered thereby the lessee must have found oil or gas upon the premises in paying quantities by completing a well thereon prior to the expiration of such fixed term." 336 P.2d at 1094. The Court then rejected the lessors' argument that production in paying quantities required the lessees to not only complete a well capable of producing in paying quantities but also remove the product from the ground and market it. Thus, where a well was completed and capable of producing in paying quantities within the primary term, the lease continued, so far as the habendum clause was concerned, as long as the well remained capable of producing in paying quantities, regardless of any marketing of the product.

This rule of law has been consistently upheld. See, e.g., Gard v. Kaiser, 582 P.2d 1311 (Okla.1978) and McVicker v. Horn, Robinson and Nathan, 322 P.2d 410 (Okla.1958). Perhaps one of the best explanations for the rule was given in McVicker where we stated: "To say that *marketing* during the primary term of the lease is essential to its extension beyond said term, *unless the lease contains additional provisions indicating a contrary intent*, is to not only ignore the distinction between producing and marketing, which inheres in the nature of the oil and gas business, but it also ignores the difference between express and implied terms in lease contracts." 322 P.2d at 413 (Emphasis in original).

* * *

Finally, in State ex rel. Comm'rs of the Land Office v. Amoco Production Co., 645 P.2d 468 (Okla.1982), we held: "The provision about paying quantities adds little to the term production since it is settled that production must be in paying quantities even though a lease contains no such provision ... *It is the ability of the lease to produce that is the important factor rather than the actual production applied, as an example of ability to produce a shut-in gas well will hold a lease as long as the operator seeks a market with due diligence.*" 645 P.2d at 470 (Citations omitted) (Emphasis added).

Therefore, the lease in the case at bar cannot terminate under the terms of the habendum clause because the parties stipulated that the subject wells were at all times capable of producing in paying quantities. The habendum clause of these leases is satisfied. [Eds. note: the court also concluded that the lease cessation-of-production clauses did not apply because the leases were always capable of producing and the shut-in royalty clause did not apply because the leases had never ceased to produce for a full year.]

NOTES

1. Professor Kuntz summarizes the requirement of "production" to extend the oil and gas lease beyond the primary term as follows:

> [T]o the extent that generalization is possible, it may be said that three rules have been developed. According to one rule, the discovery of either oil or gas will satisfy the habendum clause. According to a second rule, gas and oil are distinguished because oil may be extracted and stored economically without marketing, whereas gas cannot be economically stored above ground. Under such rule, the discovery of gas is sufficient, but if oil is discovered, the oil must be actually extracted in order to satisfy the habendum clause. According to the third rule, mere discovery of oil or gas will not satisfy the habendum clause, but in both instances the product must be actually extracted. In the instance of gas, this necessarily involves marketing. As a matter of generality, each jurisdiction which has decided the point has adopted one of such rules.

Kuntz § 26.6.

Oklahoma and West Virginia are the main adherents of the first position Professor Kuntz described—that a capability of producing oil and gas in paying quantities before the end of the primary term is "produced" within the meaning of the term clause. Under this view, the main purpose of the lessor in granting a lease has been accomplished when oil and gas have been discovered. Cases in Montana, Wyoming, Kentucky, and Tennessee suggest that discovery of gas is sufficient to maintain the lease, but actual production of oil is required. The rationale for different rules for oil and gas is that oil can be produced and stored without actual marketing. The third rule, that "production" requires actual production and marketing, is the majority position. It has been adopted in Louisiana, Texas, New Mexico, Kansas, Illinois, Michigan, and Ohio.

Which approach is more appropriate to the purpose of the lease? Which approach do you think is closer to the intention of the parties—the view that requires actual production and marketing or the view that discovery is enough? Or, should one rule be applied to oil and another to gas? See generally Kuntz § 26.6. What is the practical effect in a state that holds that "produced" requires both production and marketing of using a lease like the Texas AAPL Form 675 in the Forms Manual?

2. Sometimes "capability of production" type language is found in leases used in "actual production" jurisdictions; for example, The American Association of Professional Landmen Form AAPL No. 690, approved for use in Kansas, provides:

> This lease shall remain in force for a primary term of ___ years and as long thereafter as oil, gas or other hydrocarbons *is or can be produced.* (Emphasis added.)

Should such language change the rule that applies? Anadarko Petroleum Corp. v. Thompson, 94 S.W.3d 550 (Tex.2002), holds that the "plain meaning" of the lease language controls. In Hunthauser Holdings, LLC v. Loesch, 2003 WL 21981961 (D. Kan. 2003), the court interprets similar language. Finding the reasoning of the Texas Supreme Court in *Anadarko Petroleum* persuasive, the court holds the lease can be extended either by actual production or a "capability to produce" from the leased land. What if the term clause provided that the lease would extend "as long as oil, gas or other hydrocarbons is *found*"? Compare Tate v. Stanolind Oil & Gas Co., 240 P.2d 465 (Kan.1952) and Bouldin v. Gulf Prod. Co., 5 S.W.2d 1019 (Tex.Civ.App.1928) (lease is extended if oil or gas is "discovered" or "found" in the primary term so long as the lessee exercised diligence in continuing operations to produce the discovered oil or gas) with Greenfield v. Thill, 521 N.W.2d 87 (N.D.1994); Reese Enters., Inc. v. Lawson, 553 P.2d 885 (Kan.1976); Cassell v. Crothers, 44 A. 446 (Pa.1899); and Tedrow v. Shaffer, 155 N.E. 510 (Ohio App.1926) ("found in paying quantities" requires "production in paying quantities").

(c) Savings Clauses as Substitutes for "Production"

As a practical matter, the definition of "production" adopted by the courts puts a heavy burden on the lessee of an oil and gas lease. As *Stanolind* and *Pack* illustrate, for a variety of reasons, a lessee who has acted in good faith and with sound planning may find it impossible to obtain and market production from the leased premises before the end of the primary term or to maintain profitable production in the secondary term.

Courts have developed a few doctrines that may protect lessees, including the temporary cessation-of-production doctrine and liberal applications of adverse possession. In addition, most modern oil and gas leases include savings clauses that address the circumstances that commonly prevent a lessee from obtaining or maintaining "production." Among the most important lease clauses are the shut-in royalty clause, the cessation-of-production clause, dry-hole and operations clauses, and the force-majeure clause. All of these savings clauses may be thought of as providing *substitutes for production* or *constructive production*, because they state that specified occurrences or actions will be considered to be production for purposes of the lease. The pooling clause also functions as a savings clause by expanding the area from which the required production can be obtained. The pooling clause, however, is addressed under a separate subheading because it has the potential to modify each of the major lease clause categories: Granting, Habendum, and Royalty.

We suggest an analytical approach that may help you understand complicated case facts and lease terms. In most jurisdictions, the grant of an oil and gas lease creates a determinable interest in real property. If there is no "production"—whether production is defined as production and marketing or as a capability of production—in paying quantities, the lease terminates after the end of the primary term unless some constructive production maintains it. Therefore, the focus of the courts in applying lease savings clauses is generally upon (1) whether the clauses provide for constructive production and (2) whether the definition of constructive production has been satisfied.

(i) Shut-in Royalty Clause

In states that equate "production" to actual production and marketing, a well that is shut in waiting for a pipeline connection to make marketing possible will not maintain the lease. Most modern oil and gas leases therefore contain a shut-in royalty clause providing that the lease will be maintained if a well capable of producing is shut in. A shut-in royalty clause provides for constructive production, typically in the form of periodic shut-in royalty payments.

FREEMAN v. MAGNOLIA PETROLEUM CO.

171 S.W.2d 339 (1943).

BREWSTER, COMMISSIONER.

This is a suit by petitioners to cancel an oil and gas lease of date April 7, 1930, covering 7,499 acres of land in Sherman and Hansford Counties, Texas. Respondents are the assignees of one Mager, original lessee. The provisions of the lease, relevant to the issues here, are as follows:

"2. Subject to the other provisions herein contained, which are not conditions, as is fully provided for in Article 8 hereafter, this lease shall remain in force for a term of ten years from this date (called 'primary term') and as long thereafter as oil, gas or other mineral is produced from said land.

"3. The royalties to be paid by lessee are: * * * a royalty of $50.00 per year on each gas well from which gas only is produced while gas therefrom is not sold or used off the premises, and while said royalty is so paid, said well shall be held to be a producing well under paragraph number 2 hereof; * * *.

* * *

"8. The covenants of lessee mentioned in this lease, as well as all implied covenants, are not to be understood as conditions, and the breach of one or all of same will not work a forfeiture, abandonment or termination of this lease * * *.

"After discovery of oil, gas or other minerals upon said premises, the title to all minerals in and upon and underlying the surface of the land described in this lease shall remain and be vested in lessee and shall not revert to lessor nor end until there is a complete, absolute and intentional abandonment by lessee of each and all of the purposes, either expressed or implied, of this lease and every part and parcel of the lands described herein. Such abandonment is the only manner by which lessee's title to said minerals can be ended and title to said minerals be reinvested in lessor."

After overruling petitioners' motion for an instructed verdict and their motion for judgment *non obstante veredicto*, the trial court rendered judgment for respondents on jury answers to special issues. That judgment was affirmed by the Court of Civil Appeals at Amarillo. 165 S.W.2d 111.

Although five points of error are assigned, our decision will turn on the third, which is that the court below "erred in holding that the provision for the payment of the $50 to declare a potential well a 'producing well' was an absolute and unconditional agreement on the part of the lessee, rather than an option, which had to be timely exercised, to-wit, before the expiration of the Primary Term, in order to keep the lease in force and effect."

We think the question is settled by the express terms of the lease. Paragraph 2 provides that the lease should remain in force for ten years from April 7, 1930, and as long thereafter as oil, gas or other mineral is produced from the leased land. It is not claimed that any oil or "other mineral" was being produced therefrom on April 7, 1940, when the primary term ended. In fact, it affirmatively appears that none was produced at any time during the primary term. Therefore, it only remains to determine whether gas was being produced from the land at the close of the primary term so as to continue the lease in force.

On December 22, 1939, respondents completed a well on the lease. It yielded gas in large quantities, but none of it was ever sold or used off the leased premises. No other well was thereafter drilled or attempted to be drilled on the land. Under these facts, was gas being "produced from said land" on April 7, 1940? The answer is found in the language of paragraph 3(b), as follows: "3. The royalties to be paid by lessee are: * * * (b) on gas, * * * a royalty of $50.00 per year on each gas well from which gas only is produced while gas therefrom is not sold or used off the premises, and *while said royalty is so paid, said well shall be held to be a producing well under paragraph 2 hereof.*" (Italics ours). Thus, in paragraph 2, the parties agree that the lease would end on April 7, 1940, unless gas was then being produced from the land. Then, in paragraph 3, they say that a well from which gas is not used or sold off the leased premises will be regarded as a producer by virtue of lessee paying fifty dollars per year; that is, in clear and unequivocal language, they say that *while it is so paid* the well shall be held to be a producer, *under paragraph 2.* It necessarily follows, conversely, that while the royalty is not so paid, the well will not be held to be a producer under that paragraph.

Respondents did not pay the fifty dollars royalty on or before April 7, 1940. They tendered it more than four months thereafter, contending that they could pay it at any time within the year. Petitioners declined the tender on the ground that the lease had terminated on April 7, 1940.

This court has recently held that upon cessation of production after termination of the primary term, the lease automatically terminates. Watson v. Rochmill, 137 Tex. 565, 155 S.W.2d 783, 137 A.L.R. 1032. Here the parties agreed that if no gas was being produced on April 7, 1940, the lease should terminate. They further agreed that a gas well from which gas was not being sold or used off the premises was a producing well provided a royalty of fifty dollars was paid. Clearly, then, if the fifty dollars was not paid on or before April 7, 1940, gas was not being produced from the premises on that date, and the lease terminated for nonproduction. That is precisely what the contracting parties said should follow, and they were privileged to define what they meant by the phrase "a producing well." If respondents had wanted to prevent lapsation of the lease for nonproduction, they could easily have done so by paying the fifty dollars on or before the last day of the primary term. They could thus have met the condition which they imposed upon themselves when they accepted assignment of the lease. For their failure to do so they have only themselves to blame. The lease lapsed as a matter of law when they so failed, and it could not be revived by their attempt to perform the condition more than four months after the contract said it should be performed.

Respondents stress the fact that paragraph 8, supra, provides that covenants of the lessee shall not be understood as conditions, breach of which would terminate the lease. It is sufficient to say that that paragraph does not even purport to make any condition a covenant. It merely says that no covenant shall be regarded as a condition. To give the language any other construction would be to ignore the distinction in the meaning of the two words; it would be to ignore the fact that express language of a lease may make an agreement for development a condition as well as a covenant. Gulf Production Co. v. Kishi, 129 Tex. 487, 103 S.W.2d 965. Moreover, despite the general provisions of that paragraph, it remained a question of law, to be determined under the express terms of the lease applicable thereto, as to which of the undertakings of the parties to the lease are covenants and which are conditions.

It is unnecessary to consider the other points of error or the many other propositions advanced by both parties. The jury findings are immaterial, since the trial court should have instructed a verdict for petitioners.

The judgments of the courts below are reversed, and judgment is here rendered for petitioners.

Opinion adopted by the Supreme Court.

NOTES

1. Professor Kuntz suggests that where a shut-in royalty payment is late, omitted altogether, made inaccurately to the wrong persons, or paid in the wrong amount, the result should turn on the language used in the clause. If payment of the shut-in royalty is made a condition for continuance of the lease or failure to pay is made a special limitation, improper payment terminates the lease. On the other hand, if the language creates a mere promise to pay, then the lease generally should not terminate if payment is

not made, but the lessor should be able to recover the payments. Kuntz § 46.3. As *Freeman* illustrates, the usual effect of a failure to pay shut-in royalties properly is lease termination. That is because most shut-in royalty clauses make failure to pay properly a special limitation or condition to the term of the lease. See also Williams & Meyers § 633.3; Summers Perm. Ed. § 299; and Hemingway §§ 6.5, 6.5(A).

If you have difficulty classifying shut-in royalty language in a lease as a condition, special limitation, or covenant, try analyzing the language by asking what it is that the clause defines as constructive production. If the constructive production defined by the clause is the existence of a well on the premises capable of production in paying quantities, then the lease should not terminate at the end of the primary term even if the lessee fails to pay the shut-in royalties properly. For example:

> If a well capable of producing gas in paying quantities is completed hereunder and is shut-in for a period of 90 consecutive days, this lease shall not terminate, but Lessee shall be obligated to pay or tender to Lessor as royalty for constructive production, an amount equal to one quarter of the rental specified in Paragraph 4 hereof for each 90–day period that such well is shut in during any calendar year. Such payment of tender shall be made promptly following the end of each such 90–day shut-in period.

See Risinger v. Arkansas–Louisiana Gas Co., 3 So.2d 289 (La.1941). If the language makes proper payment the constructive production, however, then if the lessee does not make the payment correctly the lease terminates because failure to have either actual or constructive production triggers the special limitation to the term of the lease. Thus under the language of the lease before the court in *Freeman,* failure to make proper payment of shut-in royalty terminated the lease; the lease was continued only "while said royalty is so paid * * *." See generally John S. Lowe, Shut–In Royalty Payments, 5 E.Min.L.Inst. 18–1, 18–8 (1984), and Robert E. Beck, Shutting–In: For What Reasons and For How Long?, 33 Washburn L.J. 749 (1994). See also Welsch v. Trivestco Energy Co., 221 P.3d 609 (Kan. Ct. App. 2009), where the court interprets "may pay" and "if such payments or tenders are made" language to create a condition to the term of the lease, so that when the lessee failed to pay, the lease automatically terminated.

2. Not all states follow the reasoning of *Freeman.* As we have seen, Oklahoma holds that a shut-in lease is still "producing" within the meaning of the habendum clause if it is capable of production in paying quantities. In effect, the line of cases illustrated by *Pack v. Santa Fe Minerals* holds that the shut-in royalty clause is not constructive production in Oklahoma. Geyer Brothers Equipment Co. v. Standard Resources, L.L.C., 140 P.3d 563, 566 (Okla.Civ.App.2006), stated the applicable rule "[W]here a well is capable of producing in paying quantities, a lessee's failure to market product from that well after expiration of the primary term does not automatically result in the termination of an oil and gas lease under the terms of the habendum clause," though it concluded that the lease had terminated because the lessee had taken no action secure a market for the gas over a 15–year period.

By different reasoning, a Louisiana court has also held that a lessee's failure to pay shut-in royalties does not result in automatic termination. In Acquisitions, Inc. v. Frontier Explorations, Inc., 432 So.2d 1095 (La.App. 1983), the court held that:

> Section 133 of the Louisiana Mineral Code provides: "A mineral lease terminates at the expiration of the agreed term or upon the occurrence of an express resolutory condition." When a mineral lease is violated an aggrieved party is entitled to any appropriate relief provided by law. La.M.C. § 135. A putting in default is required in those circumstances set forth in the Civil Code and is a prerequisite to a demand for damages arising from drainage of the property leased. La.M.C. §§ 135, 136. Also, written notice is a prerequisite to judicial demand for damages or dissolution of a lease occasioned by the lessee's failure to make timely or proper payment of royalties. La.M.C. § 137. "In a case where notice of failure to pay royalties is required, dissolution should be granted only if the conduct of the lessee, either in failing to pay originally or in failing to pay in response to the required notice, is such that the remedy of damages is inadequate to do justice." La.M.C. § 141.

> The requirement of notice as a prerequisite to judicial demand imposed by La.M.C. § 137, however, applies only to royalty payments. La.M.C. § 213(5) defines "Royalty" as follows:

> > Royalty, as used in connection with mineral leases, means any interest in production, or its value, from or attributable to land subject to a mineral lease, that is deliverable or payable to the lessor or others entitled to share therein. Such interests in production or its value are "royalty," whether created by the lease or by separate instrument, if they comprise a part of the negotiated agreement resulting in execution of the lease. "Royalty" also includes sums payable to the lessor that are classified by the lease as constructive production.

The comment following the original § 213 provides in pertinent part:

> *The term "royalty" also is defined to include payments classified as constructive production. This characterization would commonly in-clude shut-in royalty payments* and compensatory royalty payments that, *when paid under the terms of some leases are regarded as production under the habendum clause of the lease* or otherwise as the equivalent of production. (Emphasis in original.)

432 So.2d at 1100.

3. Lessees trying to make shut-in royalty payments on time may confront substantial interpretative difficulties. As *Freeman* illustrates, if the lease does not provide a grace period for payment, the courts have held that the payment must be made before shut in or before the end of the primary term, whichever is later. Gulf Oil Corp. v. Reid, 337 S.W.2d 267 (Tex.1960).

Most modern leases provide that the shut-in payment is to be made *after* a shut in and a grace period. For example:

> While there is a gas well on this Lease * * *, but gas is not being sold or used, Lessee shall pay or tender annually at the end of each yearly period

during which gas is not sold or used, as royalty an amount equal to the delay rental provided for * * *.

But is the "yearly period" measured by the calendar year, the lease anniversary date or the shut-in date? If the yearly period runs from the shut-in date (as your editors believe), note that the payment date may change from time to time. If the well is shut in on June 1, and then production is resumed from August 1 to September 15, the due date is changed to the following September 15; the shut-in royalty is due on the anniversary of shut in, rather than on the anniversary of the lease execution. It is easy for those making payments to become confused. Finally what if the grace period extends beyond the primary term? Must the payment be made before the end of the primary term, or will the grace period itself constitute constructive production? See Union Oil Co. v. Ogden, 278 S.W.2d 246 (Tex.Civ.App.1955), and Phillips Petroleum Co. v. Harnly, 348 S.W.2d 856 (Tex.Civ.App.1961).

4. Lessees may also find that they cannot rely on the shut-in royalty clause when they need it because of court-imposed limitations. First, the clause is available only when a well is capable of producing in paying quantities. Hydrocarbon Management, Inc. v. Tracker Exploration, Inc., 861 S.W.2d 427 (Tex.App.1993), illustrates this important implied condition of the clause. The *Tracker* case involved two pooled leases, both in their secondary term and held by the same gas well. In May 1989 the Railroad Commission ordered the operator to shut in the well for violating the production allowable. By the time that the operator received the Commission's letter the well had already ceased to produce as a result of mechanical difficulties. The well did not produce further until December 1989, after reworking operations were conducted. The trial court ruled that the leases terminated by their own terms. On appeal, the lessee contended that the lease was still within the one-year grace period of the shut-in royalty clause. The appeals court noted that the lessors had the burden of proof, but then went on to find that the shut-in royalty clause did not maintain the lease, because the well was not capable of producing gas in paying quantities:

> [F]or a well to be maintained by the payment of shut-in royalties, it must be capable of producing gas in paying quantities at the time it is shut-in. Kidd v. Hoggett, 331 S.W.2d 515, 519 (Tex.Civ.App.1959); Duke v. Sun Oil Company, 320 F.2d 853, 860 (5th Cir.1963); Hemingway, § 6.5. This is true even though the shut-in royalty clause makes no mention of capacity for paying production.

> * * *

> [T]he phrase "capable of production in paying quantities" means a well that will produce in paying quantities if the well is turned "on," and it begins flowing, without additional equipment or repair. Conversely, a well would not be capable of producing in paying quantities if the well switch were turned "on," and the well did not flow, because of mechanical problems or because the well needs rods, tubing, or pumping equipment.

861 S.W.2d at 433–434. See also Pray v. Premier Petroleum, Inc., 662 P.2d 255 (Kan.1983); Griffin Trustee v. Crutcher–Tufts Corp., 500 So.2d 1008 (Ala.1986); Bixler v. Lamar Expl. Co., 733 P.2d 410 (Okla.1987); and Taylor v.

Kimbell, 54 So.2d 1 (La.1951). But Levin v. Maw Oil & Gas, LLC, 234 P.3d 805 (Kan. 2010), rejected the argument that to be considered "capable" of producing a shut-in well must be able to flow gas when the valve is opened. Instead the court held that it is an issue of fact whether, under all relevant circumstances, a well is sufficiently completed to be considered "capable" of producing in paying quantities. The wells at issue in *Levin* were coalbed-methane wells on which dewatering operations (generally a necessary prerequisite to actual production of coalbed methane) had apparently not commenced. Blackmon v. XTO Energy, 276 S.W.3d 600 (Tex. App. 2008), held that the absence of downstream processing facilities required to improve the quality of gas to make it marketable did not render a well incapable of production in paying quantities. And in Wuenschel v. Northwood Energy Corp., 2008 Ohio 6879, 2008 WL 5389710 (Ohio App.2008), the court held wells not producing gas because leaking pipelines were being repaired were not "shut in" so that shut-in royalties were due, but continued to produce in paying quantities.

Of course the parties can address the issue specifically. In In re Reichmann Petroleum Corp., 399 B.R. 463 (Bkrtcy. S. D. Tex. 2009), the court applied a shut-in royalty clause to save a lease not capable of producing in paying quantities where the lease specifically provided that the provision applied if a well was "capable of producing oil or gas in paying quantities or log or testing results indicate that a well that has been drilled to its total depth will be capable of producing oil or gas in paying quantities upon final completion."

Second, the shut-in royalty clause may be limited by its history. Shut-in royalty clauses grew out of lessees' concern that there would be no market for gas. In the present deregulated gas markets, the issue is more likely to be whether the market is adequate. Can a lessee shut in a well and maintain a lease by making shut-in payments while waiting for a better market price? The Kansas Supreme Court, in Tucker v. Hugoton Energy Corp., 855 P.2d 929 (Kan.1993), appeared to conclude that the clause could not be invoked where a market, even a market at a low price, was available for the gas, relying upon Pray v. Premier Petroleum, Inc., 662 P.2d 255 (Kan.1983). Professor Anderson described *Tucker* as "perhaps the most alarming case of 1993, because it may force lessees to sell gas into unfavorable markets," which would be contrary to the interests of both lessees and lessors. Owen L. Anderson, Recent Developments in Nonregulatory Oil and Gas Law, 45 Inst. on Oil & Gas L. & Tax'n § 1.06 (1994). Subsequently, the Kansas Supreme Court, in Levin v. Maw Oil & Gas, LLC, 234 P.3d 805 (Kan. 2010), backed away from *Tucker*, noting that:

> Although *Tucker* asserts that the total absence of a market for natural gas is a prerequisite to classify a well as shut-in and thus bring into play a shut-in royalty clause, this assertion appears to arise out of an overinterpretation of *Pray* and insufficient attention to the subject leases' language. * * * In other words, *Pray* did not make the absence of a market a part of Kansas' definition of "shut-in."

Id. at 818.

Third, a shut-in royalty clause may be limited by its terms. Suppose that a shut-in royalty clause gives a lessee the right to hold the lease by payment of shut-in royalty "where there is a well producing gas *only* or capable of producing gas *only*." (Emphasis added). Subsequently the lessee drills and completes a well capable of producing both gas and oil. Because it cannot find a market for the gas production and conservation rules prohibit flaring of the gas, the lessee shuts in the well and tenders shut-in royalty payments. Is the lease still valid? See Vernon v. Union Oil Company of California, 270 F.2d 441 (5th Cir. Tex. 1959) and Duke v. Sun Oil Co., 320 F.2d 853 (5th Cir. Tex. 1963). Would it make a difference if the well were capable of producing both gas and distillate or condensate? See Shell Oil Co. v. Goodroe, 197 S.W.2d 395 (Tex.Civ.App. 1946). In all of these cases the courts said that the shut-in clause did not apply where substances other than gas could be produced. Can you think of a circumstance in which a shut-in royalty provision may be helpful to a lessee in conjunction with an oil well? See John S. Lowe, Shut–In Royalty Payments, 5 E.Min.L.Inst. 18–1, 18–13 (1984).

5. Because of the risks and difficulties inherent in shut-in royalty clauses, should the lessee include a savings clause addressing these issues in the oil and gas lease? See the discussion in note 7 following *Schwartzenberger v. Hunt Trust Estate*, above, about savings provisions in delay rental clauses. See also John S. Lowe, Shut–In Royalty Payments, 5 E.Min.L.Inst. 18–1, 18–34 (1984). If you were representing a lessor, would you want to limit the shut-in royalty clause? How?

(ii) Cessation-of-Production, Dry–Hole, and Operations Clauses

What if a well entirely ceases production for a time? Does the lease terminate automatically for lack of "production" if it is in the secondary term? This issue is particularly important in states that treat the lease-hold interest as a fee simple determinable estate, which logically terminates automatically and instantaneously when production stops during the secondary term. But the reality is that oil and gas wells, by their nature, do not produce constantly. Inevitably, there are cessations of production from time to time due to mechanical breakdowns, market conditions, reworking operations, or other problems.

Acting on the premise that the parties must have contemplated that production interruptions would occur from time to time, the courts generally recognize an implied lease term, the *temporary cessation-of-production doctrine*, where there is a complete cessation of production. There has been a *temporary* cessation of production, rather than a permanent cessation, when a lease, though not producing, is one that a reasonable prudent operator would continue to hold. Thus, the lessee seeking the doctrine's protection carries the burden of establishing that the cessation is "temporary," and temporary cessation is a question of fact in each case. The courts have considered the following factors:

(a) *The period over which the cessation extends:* The duration of the cessation is important but not controlling. In Saulsberry v. Siegel, 252

S.W.2d 834 (Ark.1952), a four-year production cessation was classified as temporary. In Logan v. Blaxton, 71 So.2d 675 (La.App.1954), a six-month cessation caused the lease to terminate. The difference in the cases is probably in their facts. In *Saulsberry,* the derrick over the well was destroyed by fire, and the lessor did not complain of the cessation of production until fifteen years after production was restored. In *Logan,* the lessee contended that seasonal rains prevented production and marketing, but the court noted that other wells in the area had produced during the same period. See also Red River Res., Inc. v. Wickford, Inc., 443 B.R. 74 (E.D. Tex. 2010), where in mid-January of 2009, the state issued an order prohibiting further production from the lease because of past production imbalances. The state agency lifted the order three months later, but the lessee did not resume production until August. The court held that the lessee had failed to resume production with reasonable diligence.

(b) *The cause of the termination:* A jurisdiction's view of the nature of the lease is a factor in determining what causes of production stoppage will trigger the temporary cessation-of-production doctrine. The Montana Supreme Court noted the issue in Somont Oil Company v. A & G Drilling, Inc., 49 P.3d 598, 605 (Mont. 2002):

> jurisdictions vary significantly on which causes contributing to the cessation may be considered in the temporary cessation of production analysis. Those jurisdictions which treat termination as a cancellation or forfeiture in equity generally hold that "the lease continues in force unless the period of cessation, *viewed in the light of all the circumstances,* is for an unreasonable time." See, e.g., Cotner v. Warren (Okla.1958), 330 P.2d 217, 219. Conversely, ownership-in-place jurisdictions generally limit temporary cessations to mechanical or production breakdowns. 49 P.3d at 605 (emphasis added by the court).

Relying in part on Watson v. Rochmill, 155 S.W.2d 783, 784 (Tex. 1941), which had stated that the doctrine applied where there is a cessation due to "sudden stoppage of the well or some mechanical breakdown of the equipment used in connection therewith, or the like," the Montana court adopted "Texas's narrow temporary cessation of production test." *Id. at* 605. Later, however, applying the temporary-cessation doctrine in Ridge Oil Co. v. Guinn Investments, Inc., 148 S.W.3d 143, 152 (Tex. 2004), a case in which production ceased because the operator released the lease, the Texas Supreme Court liberalized its version of the temporary cessation-of-production doctrine:

> although decisions at times have said that the temporary cessation of production doctrine applies when there is "sudden stoppage of the well or some mechanical breakdown of the equipment used in connection therewith, or the like," or that the doctrine applies when the cause of a cessation of production is "necessarily unforeseen and unavoidable," the circumstances in which this and other courts have

applied the doctrine have not been so limited. *Id. at* 605 (citations omitted.)

(c) *Lessee's efforts to restore production:* The lessee's diligence in working to regain production is clearly an important factor when courts determine whether cessation of production is temporary or permanent. Thus, if the lessee caps the well and does nothing, a court will likely rule that the lease has terminated. Locke v. Palmore, 215 S.W.2d 544 (Ky. 1948) and Tyson v. Surf Oil Co., 196 So. 336 (La.1940). But where the lessee proceeds expeditiously and in good faith to put the well back into production, the cessation is likely to be termed temporary. For discussion, see Summers Perm. Ed. § 305.

Still, there is little apparent consistency in the way courts classify particular situations as a "temporary" or "permanent" cessation of production. Consider the following:

(1) Would a lease terminate if production ceased because of the lack of funds of the lessee to maintain the well? Does a reasonable prudent operator ever encounter financial difficulties? Compare Fick v. Wilson, 349 S.W.2d 622 (Tex.Civ.App.1961); Lamb v. Vansyckle, 266 S.W. 253 (Ky. 1924); and Cotner v. Warren, 330 P.2d 217 (Okla.1958) (short delay in production because of lessee's financial difficulties is not unreasonable) with Gillespie v. Wagoner, 190 N.E.2d 765 (Ill.1963) (lessee's financial trouble shows a lack of reasonable diligence in producing the well).

(2) What if the reason the lease has stopped producing is that the formation has been depleted? Should the lease be held to have terminated? Or should the lessee have a reasonable period to explore for new production or to complete the well in another potential productive formation? See Blair v. Northwestern Ohio Natural Gas Co., 12 Ohio C.C. 78 (Ohio Cir. 1896); Reynolds v. McNeill, 236 S.W.2d 723 (Ark.1951); Frost v. Gulf Oil Corp., 119 So.2d 759 (Miss.1960); Western States Oil & Land Co. v. Helms, 288 P. 964 (Okla.1930); and Eastern Oil Co. v. Coulehan, 64 S.E. 836 (W.Va.1909) (production may cease without lease termination, if the lessee seeks to test and produce from a different formation). But see Sunray DX Oil Co. v. Texaco, Inc., 417 S.W.2d 424 (Tex.Civ.App.1967) (depletion of the formation no basis for temporary cessation-of-production doctrine).

Another possible protection for a lessee whose lease has ceased to produce is adverse possession. In Natural Gas Pipeline Co. v. Pool, 124 S.W.3d 188 (Tex. 2003), the court concluded that it did not have to determine if the leases at issue had been preserved by the temporary cessation-of-production doctrine because even if the leases had expired, the lessees had regained oil and gas leaseholds "on the same terms and conditions as the original leases" by adverse possession under the 10 year statute of limitations as a matter of law. The lessee had remained in possession and continued to produce and drill new wells for more than fourteen years after its lease had terminated. The court reasoned that actual repudiation, which is normally required of a tenant who remains in possession after a lease terminates, is not required in the case of an oil and gas lessee because repudiation can be inferred from the lessee's actions in depleting the estate by removing oil or natural gas. Other jurisdictions likely would reject that reasoning. See, e.g., Nelson v. Christianson, 343 N.W.2d 375 (N.D. 1984), holding that a plaintiff, who had once held land as a tenant in common with other tenants, who acquired interest of some cotenants by deed, and who relied only on constructive notice of his ouster of other cotenants, could not establish title to land by adverse possession. But BP Am. Prod. Co. v. Marshall, 342 S.W.3d 59 (Tex. 2011), rationalized the result in *Pool* on the grounds that a lessee's payment of the royalty percentage for more than 10 years, rather than the larger interest that would have been due had had the payments been made to unleased lessors, was "unmistakably hostile" and an "unequivocal assertion of title to leasehold interest" that put the lessors on notice that the lessee claimed the leasehold interest.

Because of the lack of predictability of the application of such doctrines, most oil and gas leases contain a *cessation-of-production clause*, often combined into a single lease paragraph with a *dry-hole clause* and an *operations clause*, as in the following case. Think of all of these clauses as substitutes for actual production and marketing in paying quantities. They are forms of *constructive production*.

ROGERS v. OSBORN

261 S.W.2d 311 (Tex.1953).

WILSON, JUSTICE.

This is a suit to terminate an oil and gas lease. The principal questions are: Whether work done upon a first well in an unsuccessful effort to make it produce at and after the expiration of the primary term kept alive the lease; and if so, whether the drilling of and production from a second well commenced after the expiration of the primary term will support the lease. Our answer to the first is "Yes" and to the second "No".

* * *

Before the primary term expired on September 21, 1947, Well No. 1 had been commenced on May 15. The derrick was torn down and drilling tools removed on July 30th. From then until November 12th the well was subjected to "periodic flowing". This was an effort to clean baroid and drilling mud out of the well by allowing it to build up a head of gas and then opening the flow valve into the pits. The head of gas was followed by a flow of oily mud. After the flow ceased it would be shut in to accumulate more pressure. At first this procedure was followed almost every day but it soon slowed down to once a week.

The uncontroverted evidence established that all cutting of new hole on Well No. 1 had been completed, all pipe cemented, and all flowing arrangements completed when the primary term expired on September 21st.

At that time there was no production from the lease. The word "production" means marketable oil or gas. Garcia v. King, 139 Tex. 578, 164 S.W.2d 509. There is positive testimony from lessees' witnesses that there was never any production from Well No. 1. The well was allowed to blow itself out a number of times in an effort to clean it, but neither party claims this as production. * * * We hold as a matter of law that there was no production from Well No. 1. Freeman v. Magnolia Petroleum Co., 141 Tex. 274, 171 S.W.2d 339.

The lease terminated on September 21, 1947 unless some provision other than the primary term kept it alive. To accomplish this, lessees rely (first) upon reworking operations upon Well No. 1 and (second) upon the drilling of and production from Well No. 2.

Paragraph No. 5 of the lease is as follows:

If prior to discovery of oil or gas on said land Lessee should drill a dry hole or holes thereon, or if after discovery of oil or gas the production thereof should cease from any cause, this lease shall not terminate if lessee commences additional drilling or reworking operations within sixty (60) days thereafter or (if it be within the primary term) commences or resumes the payment or tender of rentals on or before the rental paying date next ensuing after the expiration of three months from date of completion of dry hole, or cessation of production. If at the expiration of the primary term oil, gas or other mineral is not being produced on said land but lessee is then engaged in drilling or reworking operations thereon, this lease shall remain in force so long as operations are prosecuted with no cessation of more than thirty (30) consecutive days, and if they result in the production of oil, gas or other mineral so long thereafter as oil, gas or other mineral is produced from said land * * *.

We will first consider the first sentence of paragraph 5. If, prior to discovery of gas, lessees drilled a dry hole, they had 60 days in which to commence additional drilling or reworking operations. Lessees plead that oil and gas were discovered in the first well. They offered opinion evidence upon which the jury found that gas in paying quantities was discovered "prior to September 21, 1947." Since lessees sought and obtained a finding that Well No. 1 was not dry, the dry hole clause had no application. * * *

This presents a situation where gas was discovered in paying quantities in Well No. 1 but never produced. The second alternative in this first sentence of paragraph 5 is: "or if after the discovery of oil and gas the production should cease from any cause" the lessee had 60 days to commence additional drilling or reworking operations. If production never began, it could not "cease" and by ceasing give the lessee 60 days in which to commence additional drilling. Clearly the first sentence of paragraph 5 did not provide for discovering but not producing gas. Our construction is supported by the fact that the royalty provision * * * did provide for just this situation and required the payment of a specific shut-in royalty. And we have held that where the "year" of this shut-in gas royalty clause straddles the date for the expiration of the primary term, the "shut-in" payment must be made during the primary term, or the lease expires. Freeman v. Magnolia Petroleum Co., supra. Therefore the first sentence of paragraph 5 cannot be used to prolong the life of the lease.

We pass now to the second sentence.

The two conditions of the opening prepositional phrase are: (1) if "at the expiration of the primary term" gas was not being "produced on said lease," and (2) the lessee was "then engaged in drilling or reworking operations thereon". It is uncontroverted that no gas was being produced and the lessees were not "then engaged" in drilling hole. The second word "operations" ("so long as operations are prosecuted with no cessation of more than thirty (30) consecutive days"), undoubtedly means both "drilling" and "reworking operations". It is not necessary to determine whether this lessee's efforts to clean out the well be defined as "drilling" or "reworking" because without objection the trial court used almost the same definition for both drilling and reworking. It would include almost any type of work. Since it was not objected to it is part of the jury's finding. It was:

> You are instructed that the term "re-working operations," as used herein, means actual work or operations which have theretofore been done, being done over, and being done in good faith endeavor to cause a well to produce oil and gas or oil or gas in paying quantities as an ordinarily competent operator would do in the same or similar circumstances.

The jury found in response to Special Issues Nos. 1 and 2 that on the expiration date (September 21st) lessees were then engaged in both drilling and reworking operations. For convenience we will discuss lessees' efforts as "reworking". Is there evidence to support this?

There is conflicting testimony by experts on whether the lessees' attempts to complete Well No. 1 were a method by which an ordinarily competent operator would have completed Well No. 1. Under the charge used in this case, we cannot hold as a matter of law that periodic flowing or "bleeding" of a well for a limited period is not included within either the term "reworking operations" or the term "drilling" as defined in this charge. An actual reworking did occur during November 1947. We hold that there is some evidence supporting this finding but do not pass upon the trial court's definition of the words *drilling* and *reworking*.

* * *

Lessees offered opinion evidence that they still thought at the time of trial that Well No. 1 could be made into a producer. They testified that with the filing of this case on January 2, 1948 they ceased all efforts to make it produce. If the lessees had continued to work upon Well No. 1 it is possible that they might have made it into a producer, but there is no certainty that they would. And the record conclusively establishes that their total effort expended on Well No. 1 had not at the time of trial (January 17, 1951) resulted in production from it.

Lessees were upon notice when they drilled Well No. 2 that lessors then contended the lease had terminated. Under the facts of this case the lessees cannot tack the period of the drilling of and production from Well No. 2 to the period of reworking Well No. 1. In order to do that the lessees would have to borrow the words *commences additional drilling* from the first sentence of paragraph 5 and transpose them to the second sentence. The conditions contained in the two separate sentences should not be jumbled. See note in Oil and Gas Reporter, Vol. 1, No. 2, p. 1592. The second use of the word *operations* might be given the very broad construction used by the Court of Civil Appeals. This construction would allow a lessee to prolong a lease indefinitely and would take from the primary term much of its significance. The first two sentences apply to different factual situations. Since the first provides for "additional drilling" and the second does not, we hold that the second word *operates* as used in the second sentence does not include additional wells commenced after the expiration of the primary term. This sentence means that if production results from the continuous prosecution of the very operations being engaged in by the lessees upon the expiration of the primary term, the lease is good. This is not to be confused with the lessees' rights to drill additional wells under the "dry hole" and "if production ceases" sentence.

To sum up, this case reaches us with the lessees unable to avail themselves of the dry hole clause because Well No. 1 was not dry, with the lessees unable to avail themselves of the "if production ceases" clause because there was never any production, with the lessees keeping their lease alive through November 29, 1947 by the "reworking" clause, but with no finding on the date of termination and no definite evidence of reworking after November 29th, and with no production resulting from the reworking of Well No. 1.

Accordingly the judgments of the trial court and of the Court of Civil Appeals are reversed and judgment is here rendered for petitioners terminating the oil and gas lease on November 29, 1947 without prejudice to such salvage and other rights as lessees may have upon termination. Costs are taxed against respondents.

On Petition for Rehearing.

Rehearing denied.

* * *

CULVER, JUSTICE (dissenting).

I agree with both the analysis and conclusion reached by the Court of Civil Appeals in its opinion in this case, 250 S.W.2d 296, and would affirm that decision. It seems to me that it placed the proper construction upon the word "operations" as used in the latter part of paragraph 5 of the lease contract.[1] In the sense there used I think it should not be restricted to refer solely to the "drilling or reworking operations" in which the lessee was engaged at the expiration of the primary term, but should include additional drilling if prosecuted according to the terms of the contract with no cessation of more than thirty days. The desired result is the production of oil or gas. The lessor is interested only in the prosecution of the work with diligence and it is of little or no consequence to him whether the desired end is accomplished by reworking an old well or the drilling of a new one. I therefore dissent.

GARWOOD, J., joins in this dissent.

NOTES

1. *Rogers* illustrates the mechanical analysis that courts often apply to lease savings clauses. Which opinion do you think is the better interpretation of the language at issue in *Rogers?* In applying savings language in an oil and gas lease, should courts construe strictly the words of the lease or should they look to the purposes behind the inclusion of specific language?

2. Why did the dry-hole clause not preserve the lease in *Rogers?*

The dry-hole clause developed because of uncertainty over the effect of drilling a dry hole. One issue was whether a lessee that had drilled an unsuccessful well could maintain its lease for the remainder of the primary term without making delay rental payments. Another was whether the lessee had irrevocably elected the drilling option by commencing operations, so that it was subject to an implied obligation to continue to explore the premises. To the consternation of both lessors and lessees, there were cases that suggested an affirmative answer to both issues. As Professor Masterson commented:

> [T]heoretically a lessee would be better off without a dry hole clause, because under a literal construction of a lease on a usual ["unless" delay rental] form, omitting said clause, completion of a dry hole within the primary term would continue the lease in effect for the rest of the term without the necessity of further delay rentals or other activity. However, before the dry hole clause came into use, many courts held that once a lessee started drilling activity, he had to continue or lose his lease by abandonment. It was to avoid the possibility of abandonment that the dry hole clause came into use.

Masterson, Discussion Notes, 6 O & GR 360 (1956).

Dry-hole clauses have presented the courts with a variety of interpretative problems, including: (a) what is a "dry hole"; (b) when is a dry hole completed; and (c) when are rental payments due after a dry hole is drilled?

(a) *What is a "dry hole"?* It may be surprising, but most oil and gas leases do not define what is meant by a dry hole, leaving ambiguity as to

---

1. [Editors' Note] The court of civil appeals had reasoned that "No limitation is placed upon the word 'operations' the second time it is used in the clause, but it possesses the same broad connotation or meaning that it has when used the first time in the clause. There is no verbal basis for restricting 'operations' to those actually being prosecuted at the end of the primary term." Rogers v. Osborn, 250 S.W.2d 296, 298 (Tex.Civ.App.1952).

whether a "dry hole" must be a "duster" or merely a well not capable of producing in paying quantities. The cases are either inconclusive or not directly on point.

Professor Kuntz analyzed the problem as follows:

> Although there is no scientific or engineering definition of "dry hole," that term is widely used in the oil and gas industry to describe an unsuccessful drilling operation from which no benefit is derived other than the obtaining of additional geological data. It is the broad purpose of the dry hole clause to make provision for the rights of the parties in the event of an unsuccessful drilling operation. It is submitted that the generally accepted meaning that a dry hole is an unsuccessful drilling operation is the one intended by the parties. * * *. When such definition is applied, a dry hole is a well that is unsuccessful in that it does not satisfy the requirements of other provisions of the lease that require the drilling of a producing well.

* * *

> For example, if the question is raised during the primary term to determine whether or not the lessee must resume drilling or pay delay rentals in order to preserve the lease after having drilled a well, the other lease clause in question is the drilling clause, and the question is whether or not the well satisfies the requirements of that clause. If it does, it should not be regarded as a dry hole or an unsuccessful drilling operation.

Kuntz § 47.2(c).

(b) *When is a dry hole completed?* Most dry-hole clauses, like the one in the principal case, give the lessee a specified period after drilling a dry hole to commence additional operations or to pay delay rentals. Thus, *when* a well becomes a dry hole is important. Though "completion" of a well is not capable of precise definition, a well is not generally regarded as completed until the targeted formations are drilled to and tested. But what if the well is drilled in a "wildcat" area? Or what if it is drilled in an area in which there are two potential oil producing formations, one shallow and one deep, but only the shallow formation is tested? See A. W. Walker, Jr., Defects and Ambiguities in Oil and Gas Leases, 28 Tex.L.Rev. 895, 903 (1950). Could you draft a solution to avoid an ambiguity? See Williams & Meyers § 614.1.

(c) If a dry hole is completed early in the primary term, may the lessee preserve the lease by resuming rental payment, and if so, when are rental payments due after a dry hole is drilled? A well-drafted dry-hole clause will permit a lessee that has drilled a dry hole to maintain the lease for the remainder of the primary term by payment of rentals. Sometimes, however, the dry-hole clause may be unclear as to when payments are due. For example, in Superior Oil Co. v. Stanolind Oil and Gas Co., 230 S.W.2d 346 (Tex.Civ.App.1950), affirmed 240 S.W.2d 281 (Tex.1951), on March 3, 1944, Dodson executed an oil and gas lease to Richfield for a term of "10 years and so long thereafter as oil or gas is produced." The lease contained a delay rental clause providing that if no well were commenced on the land by March 3, 1945, the lease would terminate unless a rental was tendered. The lease provided that successive annual rentals could be paid to defer drilling throughout the primary term. The lease also contained the following dry-hole clause:

> Should the first well drilled on the above described land be a dry hole, then and in that event, if a second well is not commenced on said land within twelve months thereafter, this lease shall terminate as to both parties, unless the lessee on or before the expiration of said twelve months shall resume the payment of rentals in the same amount and in the same manner as hereinbefore provided. * * *

230 S.W.2d at 348.

Richfield commenced a well in January 1945 and completed it as a dry hole on February 3, 1945. In January of each of the following three years, 1946, 1947, and 1948, Richfield tendered delay rentals with a letter that stated that the check was "in payment of rentals for the period" February 3 of that year to February 3 of the following year. In December 1948, Richfield assigned the lease to Superior Oil Company and gave Superior copies of rental receipts that showed the periods for which rentals had been tendered. Superior tendered the next rental on February 5, 1949. Dodson refused the rentals, contending that the lease had terminated. Superior had assumed that rentals were due by March 3, 1949, the anniversary date of the lease. The court of appeals held that the lease terminated because the lease unambiguously required the lessee to tender rentals under these circumstance on or before the anniversary date of the dry hole, not the anniversary date of the lease. The Texas Supreme Court affirmed; the majority reasoned, however, that the lease was ambiguous about when the rental was due following the drilling of the dry hole. The majority concluded that the original parties' course of performance, which Superior had known, had fixed when the rental was due—i.e., on or before February 3 of each year. Two dissenting justices would have held that the lease was preserved. They argued that the dry-hole clause excused the lessee from paying "the annual rental on the succeeding March 3" and required the lessee to pay the first rental following the dry hole "by February 3, 1946, which it did * * *." 240 S.W.2d at 286. "When that was accomplished, the effect of the dry hole as well as the force of the dry-hole paragraph was spent." Id. Thereafter rentals were payable on or before the lease anniversary date pursuant to the delay rental clause. Which of these opinions is the better-reasoned? Applying the dissenters' analysis, when would the second rental have been due?

3. Why did the temporary cessation-of-production doctrine or the cessation-of-production clause not save the lease in *Rogers*?

Courts usually interpret the cessation-of-production clause as a derogation of the temporary cessation-of-production doctrine, so that the terms of the clause replace the doctrine. For example, in Samano v. Sun Oil Co., 621 S.W.2d 580 (Tex.1981), the Texas Supreme Court held that a lease upon which there had been no operations for 73 days after production ceased had terminated. The habendum clause provided that:

> [T]his lease * * * shall remain in force for a term of ten years from this date, called primary term * * * and as long thereafter as oil, gas or other mineral is produced * * * or as long thereafter as Lessee shall conduct

drilling or re-working operations * * * with no cessation of more than sixty consecutive days until production results * * *.

621 S.W.2d at 581. Applying the grammatical rule that modifiers are to be placed so that they will be connected immediately with the words they modify, the court reasoned that since the cessation of production language followed the secondary term language of the habendum clause, it modified both the primary and secondary terms. Thus, whether production ceased in the primary term or in the secondary term, "an inseparable part of this * * * was that there could be no cessation of drilling or reworking for more than sixty days—not seventy-three days." Id. See also Lone Star Producing Co. v. Walker, 257 So.2d 496 (Miss.1971). Is this logically correct? Welsch v. Trivestco Energy Co., 221 P.3d 609 (Kan. Ct. App. 2009), followed similar reasoning. (lessee cannot rely upon the temporary cessation doctrine because the parties' rights in the event of a cessation "from any cause" are addressed by the cessation-of-production clause).

If the cessation-of-production clause applies, what kind of actions by the lessee will maintain the lease? In Bachler v. Rosenthal, 798 S.W.2d 646, 650 n. 3 (Tex.App.1990), the court cautioned against an "overly rigid application" of the cessation-of-production clause, but suggested that the clause ought not be triggered unless the lessee could remedy the cessation of production by the kind of operations envisioned by the clause. Cox v. Stowers, 786 S.W.2d 102, 105 (Tex.App.1990), suggested a broad interpretation of the term "reworking," to include "any and all actual acts, work or operations in which an ordinarily competent operator, under the same or similar circumstances, would engage in a good faith effort to cause a well or wells to produce oil or gas in paying quantities." In French v. Tenneco Oil Co., 725 P.2d 275 (Okla.1986), however, the court held that where "operations for drilling" are required to maintain a lease that has ceased to produce, reworking or operations other than drilling will not suffice, and in Bargsley v. Pryor Pet. Corp., 196 S.W.3d 823 (Tex.App.–Eastland 2006), the court held that laying a pipeline, replacing a tank, providing electricity, and maintaining equipment did not establish that the lessee was "engaged in drilling for oil or gas." Which view of the cessation-of-production clause makes more sense? Which do you think that the trial court took in *Rogers*?

4. Suppose that a lessee begins drilling before the end of the primary term but does not complete drilling operations or does not complete the well by the end of the primary term. Will the lease terminate? Or does the right to "commence" drilling during the primary term imply that the lease extends until the lessee finishes what it has started?

One line of authority [followed in Kansas, Kentucky, Oklahoma, and Montana] takes the position that a conflict exists between the habendum clause, which requires a *completed* well (or at least discovery) before the end of the primary term, and the "unless" clause, which requires payment of rentals only if a well has not been *commenced* prior to the next rental payment date. The "unless" clause then customarily continues that the right to pay rentals and postpone development will continue for like periods with like payments. The clause usually neither refers specifically to the habendum clause nor limits the time for payments to the primary term of the lease. To "harmonize" the conflict, this line of cases permits a lessee a reasonable time to complete drilling a well begun during the primary term. The other line of authority finds no conflict between the lease habendum and "unless" clauses, or, if a conflict is found, holds the habendum clause is the dominant and controlling statement of intent.

* * *

The better reasoned view seems to be that the drilling provisions of the "unless" clause have no application after the end of the primary term. Because the provisions for payment of delay rentals are to permit delay of development during the primary term, drilling by the lessee that will discontinue the need for rental payments should be likewise limited. The apparent-majority view supports the conclusion that, unless the habendum clause is expressly and appropriately modified in the lease, the lessee may not finish a well drilling at the end of the primary term. (Emphasis in original).

Hemingway § 6.6. Do you think this view is compelling? May one argue with equal force that the right given by the typical lease to commence operations at any time within the primary term also gives the lessee the implied right to complete the well? Would it make sense to conclude that parties to a business transaction intended that one of them would have the right to commence operations at any time during the term of the lease up to and including the final day, but not the right to finish what was begun?

To avoid such arguments, most modern oil and gas leases contain language designed to make clear the lessee's right to complete what he has begun. The effect of the language is to make operations for drilling constructive production for purposes of the lease. For this reason, it is commonly called an *operations clause.*

Interpretative problems with operations clauses include (a) the meaning of "operations" and (b) the distinction between *well-completion* and *continuous-operations* clauses.

(a) *The meaning of "operations."* As *Rogers* illustrates, references to "operations" in an operations clause (or a dry-hole or cessation-of-production clause) generally are given the same liberal interpretation that is given to "operations" in the delay rental clause. Any substantial activity on the surface of the land that is directly related to securing production, begun in good faith, and diligently pursued is sufficient. Is this what the law should be? Can you develop an argument that "operations" within the meaning of the operations clause (or the dry-hole or cessation-of-production clause) should be more liberal (or more strict) than when "operations" is used in a delay rental clause?

(b) *The well-completion/continuous-operations distinction.* In *Rogers* the court held that the operations clause language gave the lessee the right to complete a well begun before the end of the primary term, but not to commence additional drilling operations. Such an operations clause is often called a *well-completion clause.* Consider whether the result in *Rogers* would have been different had the lease contained the following language?

If at the end of the primary term or at anytime thereafter this lease is not being kept in force by any other provision hereof, but is then engaged in drilling * * * or any other operations calculated to obtain * * * production on the leased premises, * * * this lease shall remain in force as long as the same *or any other* such operations are conducted without an interruption of more than 60 consecutive days, and, if such operations result in the production of oil or gas, * * * as long as production continues in paying quantities. (Emphasis added).

This kind of operations clause may be called a *continuous-operations clause.* It has been developed as a result of restrictive interpretations like *Rogers.*

Does the presence of an operations clause in an oil and gas lease affect the requirement in many states that the lessee have *actual production* from a lease to maintain it beyond the primary term? An operations clause permits the lessee to extend the lease beyond the primary term by operations. But what happens when those operations cease, and it is not possible to produce the well immediately? There is some authority to the effect that the presence of an operations clause in the lease shows the intention of the parties to give the lessee a reasonable time after drilling is completed to commence production. See, e.g., Sword v. Rains, 575 F.2d 810 (10th Cir.Kan.1978) (eight months between completion and marketing); Tate v. Stanolind Oil & Gas Co., 240 P.2d 465 (Kan.1952) (four months between completion and marketing); McClanahan Oil Co. v. Perkins, 6 N.W.2d 742 (Mich.1942) (nine months between completion and marketing); and Guleke v. Humble Oil & Refining Co., 126 S.W.2d 38 (Tex.Civ.App.1939) (three months delay between completion and marketing). But see Gulf Oil Corp. v. Reid, 337 S.W.2d 267 (Tex. 1960). Should an operations clause have such an effect? See generally Hemingway § 6.9.

5. The dry-hole clause, the operations clause and the cessation-of-production clause "are cumulative * * *." Hemingway § 6.9. Thus, the periods provided may be "tacked" to extend the lease. In Skelly Oil Co. v. Harris, 352 S.W.2d 950 (Tex.1962), commenting upon the interaction of the operations clause and the shut-in royalty clause, the Texas Supreme Court said:

[T]he habendum clause is required by its own terms to yield to any and all other provisions which affect the duration of the lease.

* * *

When the language of the 60–day clause is given its ordinary and commonly accepted meaning, it contemplates and permits either a temporary interruption or a final discontinuance of the operations in progress at the end of the primary term. If such operations result in production at a time when there has been no cessation of more than 60 consecutive days, the lease remains in force so long thereafter as production continues. The 60–day clause thus allows the lessee that period after completion of a well capable of producing within which to begin either actual or constructive production.

352 S.W.2d at 953. For example, a shut-in royalty payment tendered within the 60–day period provided in an operations clause would maintain the lease

even though it was not tendered until after the end of the primary term and the shut-in royalty clause did not allow for a "grace" period.

6. What makes a lease clause a "savings" clause or "constructive production"? Consider the following:

PROBLEM

Aggressive Oil Company took an oil and gas lease from Guerra. The lease had a three-year primary term and provided for one-eighth royalty. It also contained a cessation-of-production clause identical to the one in *Rogers v. Osborn*, supra, and a paragraph in an addendum that provided:

> Notwithstanding anything herein to the contrary, it is expressly agreed and understood that in the event that production of oil, gas and other minerals is obtained from the above-described land and the aggregate of the royalties paid to Lessor therefrom during any 12–month period of production amounts to less than five dollars per acre per annum for each acre subject to this lease during such 12–month period, then in that event the lessee, its successors and assigns, agrees to pay the Lessor (within sixty days after the expiration of such 12–month period by depositing same to Lessor's depository hereinabove named) the difference, if any, between the total amount of royalties paid to Lessor from this lease during such 12–month period and the aggregate of five dollars per acre for the acreage subject to this lease during such 12–month period.

Aggressive drilled, completed, and successfully produced oil from the leased property. In January of this year, however, Guerra filed suit to quiet title (to have the lease declared to be of no further effect), asserting that the lease had terminated because there had been no production of oil, gas, or other minerals from the lease premises for the previous 11 months (when oil prices took a nose dive) and because there had been no drilling or reworking operations on the lease within 60 days from the date of the cessation of production. Two days after the lawsuit was filed, Aggressive tendered to Guerra a check for the minimum royalties pursuant to the paragraph quoted above, which Guerra rejected. Aggressive then filed an answer asserting, among other affirmative defenses, that the payment of the minimum royalty preserved the lease. Both parties have moved for summary judgment. How should the court rule and why? See Morris Exploration, Inc. v. Guerra, 751 S.W.2d 710 (Tex.App.1988).

(iii) Force–Majeure Clause

A lessee often will try to protect itself against unforeseen interference with operations by including a *force-majeure clause* in its oil and gas lease. Literally, "force majeure" means superior or irresistible force. The term is generally applied to contract clauses designed to protect the parties against the possibility that the contract cannot be performed due to causes outside the control of the parties and that could not be avoided by due care. Black's Law Dictionary 674 (8th ed. 2004). See also Annot., 46 A.L.R. 4th 976 (1996), John S. Kirkham, Force Majeure—Does It Really Work?, 30 Rocky Mtn.Min.L.Inst. 6–1 (1984), and Christopher J. Costantini, Allocating Risk in Take-or-Pay Contracts: Are Force Majeure and Commercial Impracticability the Same Defense?, 42 S.W.L.J. 1047 (1989). In an oil and gas lease, the force-majeure clause often relates back to the habendum clause to provide a substitute for production.

As the following case illustrates, there are often disputes about applying force-majeure clause language.

PERLMAN v. PIONEER LIMITED PARTNERSHIP

918 F.2d 1244 (5th Cir.Tex.1990).

PER CURIAM:

William Perlman (Perlman) filed this diversity suit for a declaratory judgment against Pioneer Limited Partnership (Pioneer) and Kendrick Cattle Company (Kendrick) seeking to have an oil and gas lease and a surface lease declared unenforceable due to an alleged occurrence of a force majeure. He claimed that his performance of the contract had been hindered by state regulations in Wyoming and Montana. Pioneer and Kendrick counter-claimed for breach of contract seeking the amounts promised under the agreements, statutory penalties and attorney's fees. The district court found for Pioneer and Kendrick on all claims and ordered judgment against Perlman for $1,772,676.65. We affirm the district court's finding that Perlman breached his contract with Pioneer and Kendrick, but reverse the district court's award of attorney fees except for those awarded pursuant to Mont.Code Ann. § 82–1–202 in the amount of $2,500.

I.

Pioneer entered into an Oil and Gas Lease (the Lease) with Perlman to "explore, drill, prospect and operate" for oil and gas [on 131,120 acres] located in Montana and Wyoming. In return for these rights, Perlman agreed to (1) pay Pioneer $137,676.65 in initial rent, and (2) spend $1,500,000 in exploring and developing the acreage or, alternatively, to pay Pioneer the difference between $1,500,000 and the amount he spent. Perlman also obtained from Kendrick the right of access to and use of land in Wyoming and Montana overlying and adjoining Pioneer's acreage (the Surface Agreement) and in exchange, agreed to pay Kendrick $60,000. Incorporated into the Lease was a "force majeure" clause which states in pertinent part:

> 14. FORCE MAJEURE * * * This lease shall not be terminated * * * nor Lessee held liable in damages * * * if compliance [with covenants in lease] * * * is prevented or hindered by an act of God, of the public enemy, adverse field, weather or market conditions, labor disputes, inability to obtain materials in the open market or transportation thereof, inability to obtain governmental permits or approvals necessary or convenient to Lessee's operations * * * such circumstances of events being hereafter referred to as "force majeure" * * *. Lessee shall notify Lessor in writing * * * within fifteen (15) days of any force majeure which prevents or hinders any compliance, activity

or event hereunder * * *. Lessee shall use all reasonable efforts to remove such force majeure * * *.

Perlman obtained the right to produce oil and gas from all the depths and horizons subject to the lease. No one particular method to produce oil and gas was designated in the lease; however, Perlman anticipated using his patented "Perlman Process" to produce coal seam gas.[1] This process involves: (1) the injection of water into the ground during the drilling process (the fracturing phase), and (2) the production of water and gas resulting from the fracturing phase. This process usually produces substantial amounts of water. Apparently, other methods used in Wyoming to produce coal seam gas do not yield as much water.

After the Lease was signed, the Taylor 24 well in Wyoming was completed using the Perlman process.[2] Taylor 24 was not on the Pioneer/Kendrick tract and in fact was over 85 miles away from the subject acreage. Taylor 24 was drilled into a fault and, therefore, did not produce gas as expected, but produced only large volumes of water. Due to the substantial amounts of water produced by Taylor 24, the Wyoming Oil and Gas Conservation Commission (the Commission) ordered the owners either to permit the well as a water well or plug it. Pursuant to this order, the Wyoming officials requested a meeting (the October 26 meeting) with the parties having an interest in Taylor 24 to discuss the operations of that well.

The primary focus of this meeting between the Perlman representatives and the Wyoming officials was the problems associated with the Taylor 24 well; however, the proposed wells on the Pioneer/Kendrick acreage apparently were discussed as well. While the reports of what was actually discussed at the meeting conflict, it is clear that at the very least the State Engineer and the Commission required, *inter alia,* that studies be done for all of Perlman's proposed operations before the state could determine the impact of Perlman's operations and decide how the wells should be permitted. Primarily, the Wyoming officials requested more information in order to determine the effect of the Perlman process on Wyoming's water resources in the areas that Perlman planned to drill. Apparently this is a standard request of anyone using or who has the potential of using substantial amounts of water in Wyoming. Hydrology studies were the most pertinent studies needed and had to be done for the

---

1. [Editors' Note] Coalbed methane, or coal seam gas, as this court calls it, is natural gas found in and around coal beds. Created by the physical and chemical processes that create coal, coal seam gas exists in large quantities within the United States, which contains one of the world's largest deposits of coal. The U.S. Geological Survey estimates that there is 700 trillion cubic feet of coal seam gas in the United States, though less than 100 trillion cubic feet could be profitably developed. If that estimate is accurate, coal seam gas represents an energy source roughly equivalent to half the U.S. current proven reserves of natural gas. An excellent review of the legal issues presented by coal seam gas development is found in Phillip Wm. Lear & J Matthew Snow, Coal and Coalbed Methane Development Conflicts Revisited: The Oil and Gas Prospective, Rocky Mtn. Min. L. Spec. Inst. 10–1 (2003).

2. This well was not associated with Pioneer or Kendrick but it connected with the same aquifer as the Pioneer tract—the Fort Union Formation and its associated aquifer.

entire region affected by the drilling. Costs of these studies were estimated to be $50,000 to $200,000 per well.

After hearing the results of the meeting, Perlman concluded unilaterally that the actions of the Wyoming regulators hindered his performance under the contract. He also unilaterally concluded that because Montana regulated its water similarly or more stringently than Wyoming, he would also be hindered there. On the basis of such unilateral decisions, Perlman invoked the force majeure clause taking the position that he was no longer bound to perform under the Lease or the Surface Agreement. He notified Pioneer and Kendrick in December 1987 of the purported occurrence of the force majeure and filed this suit for declaratory judgment in April 1988.

At trial the district court rejected Perlman's force majeure argument on findings that Perlman made no effort whatsoever to drill on the lease even though he may not have encountered the same quantity of water as he did on the Taylor 24, and that Perlman failed to give timely notice of the force majeure. The court also found that, as a matter of law, the doctrine of force majeure did not excuse Perlman's failure to perform under the Lease because the circumstances alleged did not constitute force majeure and the event complained of was foreseeable to Perlman and within his control. * * * The district court therefore awarded Pioneer $137,676.65 plus interest pursuant to Section 2 of the Lease and $1,500,000 plus interest pursuant to Section 8 of the Lease. Pioneer was also awarded $100 for statutory penalties as a result of Perlman failing to file a required disclaimer. Kendrick was awarded $60,000 plus interest pursuant to the terms of the Surface Agreement. Finally, the district court awarded Pioneer and Kendrick a total of $75,000 for attorney's fees.

Perlman appeals claiming that the district court erred in finding that his performance was not excused by force majeure under the terms of the contract.

* * *

This action is governed by the law of the state of Wyoming as agreed upon in the contract. Unfortunately, there is a dearth of Wyoming caselaw dealing with the issues of this appeal. Therefore, we must look to the law of other common law jurisdictions, as would the state courts in Wyoming, to supply the rules of law.

III.

Force Majeure

At trial, the district court held that under the doctrine of force majeure Perlman's performance was not excused because the event complained of was within Perlman's control and was entirely foreseeable. The court also determined that Perlman could have performed because performance had not been rendered impossible or untenable. The district court rested its holding on the general principle that "a force majeure clause is to relieve [a] lessee from harsh termination due to circumstances beyond [his] control that would make performance untenable or impossible." *Edington v. Creek Oil Co.,* 690 P.2d 970 (Mont.1984). As Perlman aptly argues, however, the district court erred in using the "doctrine of force majeure" to interject terms into the contract that were not contemplated by the parties. Therefore, he urges, control and foreseeability are not at issue. The only issue in this instance, insists Perlman, is whether he was hindered by governmental regulations in his efforts to fulfill the contract.

Perlman is correct that this case is essentially one of contract interpretation. The language in the force majeure clause in the Lease is unambiguous and its terms were specifically bargained for by both parties. Therefore, the "doctrine" of force majeure should not supersede the specific terms bargained for in the contract. When the terms of a contract are unambiguous, the courts must give effect to the intentions of the parties expressed by the language they employ. Because the clause labeled "force majeure" in the Lease does not mandate that the force majeure event be unforeseeable or beyond the control of Perlman before performance is excused, the district court erred when it supplied those terms as a rule of law. But even under the terms of the Lease, Perlman's performance would not be excused unless he was hindered by the regulatory process in Wyoming or Montana.

Perlman argues that because the Wyoming officials refused to commit to permitting a gas well using Perlman's process once they received the hydrology and other expensive studies, and because the regulatory process itself might prevent his meeting the six-month drilling deadline, he was "hindered" by his "inability to obtain governmental permits or approvals necessary or convenient to [his] operations." Perlman's sole basis for this argument is his interpretation of the October 26 meeting between his representative and the officials from the Wyoming Gas and Water Commissions. Perlman's interpretation is that the Wyoming officials would refuse to permit any well that drew as much water as could a well using his process. But, as the district court found, the state officials never refused to permit Perlman's operations; they merely required advance studies of the use, quantity, drainage and quality of the water Perlman's process would affect. This requirement was apparently standard, or at least not unusual, for anyone likely to use substantial amounts of water in Wyoming. Furthermore, the amounts of water that would be produced on the Pioneer/Kendrick land using the Perlman process was not a certainty; neither was it known whether the wells might not show beneficial use under the Wyoming water regulations. And, significantly in this case, Perlman's obligation was not limited to use of his patented process.

From the evidence it is clear that no actual hindrance resulted from the regulations or the regulators in Wyoming because Perlman made no effort whatsoever to obtain the appropriate permits or to begin drilling the wells. Consequently, Perlman's self-serving conclusion that a force majeure condition existed was at best merely speculation as to what might have happened had he attempted to drill the wells as planned.

Perlman's reliance on supposition and speculation derived from his interpretation of the October 26 meeting is inadequate to support his argument that he was hindered by the regulatory process in Wyoming. We require more than the mere possibility or unsupported conclusion of the existence of hindrance by government regulations to relieve Perlman of his obligations under the contract—an actual, material hindrance must occur before performance is excused.

Furthermore, under the terms of the contract Perlman had a duty to make a reasonable effort to remove the force majeure condition should one occur. Perlman could have accomplished this either by beginning the permitting process or by using an alternative method of drilling for coal seam gas that would not produce as much water as his process and thus would not be subject to such strict regulation. That Perlman failed even to attempt to remove or overcome the purported force majeure defeats his claim under the contract. *See Phillips Puerto Rico Core, Inc. v. Tradax Petroleum, Ltd.,* 782 F.2d 314, 319 (2d Cir.1985); *see also Edington,* 690 P.2d at 974 ("the force majeure clause is not an escape way for those interruptions of production that could be prevented by the exercise of prudence, diligence, care, and the use of those appliances that the situation or party renders it reasonable that he should employ"). We therefore uphold the district court's conclusion that Perlman's obligation under the Lease and Surface Agreement was not excused by a force majeure, albeit for reasons other than those expressed by the district court.

The Lease's force majeure provision also included a fifteen day notice requirement. We need not address the adequacy of Perlman's notice, however, because we find that no event of force majeure in fact took place within the clear meaning of the contract.

* * *

For the foregoing reasons, the judgment of the district court is AFFIRMED in part and REVERSED in part. Costs of this appeal to be borne by Perlman.

NOTES

1. Mr. Perlman took an unusual oil and gas lease from Pioneer. The lease covered more than 131,000 acres, which is large for American transactions but typical of international concessions or production-sharing agreements, covering some of the land featured in *Butch Cassidy and the Sundance Kid.* He paid $1.00 per acre bonus and made a "work commitment" to spend $1,500,000 drilling wells, which is also unusual in U.S. leases but typical in international agreements.

2. United States' contract law does not recognize a force majeure doctrine, *per se.* The underlying premise of U.S. law is that if performance

was possible at the time a promise was made, a party should not be excused merely because performance becomes difficult or even impossible. Though jurisdictions generally do recognize narrow frustration of purpose[13] and commercial impracticability[14] doctrines as defenses to contract breach claims, oil and gas leases and other contracts generally include detailed force-majeure clauses that broaden protections for a non-performing party.

Professor Lowe summarizes the analysis of force-majeure clauses in oil and gas leases as follows:

> The operative factor in force-majeure clauses is the breadth of the exculpatory language. Analytically, a force-majeure clause will provide constructive production to maintain an oil and gas lease if (1) the event complained of is defined as a force-majeure event by the language of the clause, (2) production is excused by the event defined as force majeure, (3) there is a causal relationship between the event defined as force majeure and the failure of production, and (4) the lessee gives timely notice, if the clause requires it.

Lowe, Chapter 9.A.3. See also Kuntz § 53.5. Do you think that the court in *Perlman* applied a similar analysis?

3. Courts often construe force-majeure clauses narrowly, "glossing" them with the common-law limitations of frustration of purpose and commercial impracticability and requiring that (a) the event that the lessee claims triggers the clause be unknown and not expected by the parties, (b) that the lessee not control the condition or be at fault in creating the condition, and/or (c) that the lessee use due diligence to overcome the condition. See Joan Teshima, Annotation, Gas and Oil Lease Force Majeure Provisions: Construction and Effect, 46 A.L.R.4th 976 (1986).

Thus, in Logan v. Blaxton, 71 So.2d 675 (La.App.1954), a lessee contended that heavy rains had made the roads running into his lease impassable, making it impractical for him to produce and market. The clause defined force majeure as "lack of labor or means of transportation of labor or materials; Acts of God; insurrection; flood; strike." The court refused to apply the force-majeure clause to save the lease:

> We are not impressed, from the evidence, that the rains complained of constituted a flood or floods, or that they constituted such a Force Majeure or Act of God as would have prevented defendant from transporting, or causing to be transported, to market the oil from these leased premises * * * the rains were seasonal rains, and were such as to be expected. Even excessive seasonal rains to the extent as shown by the reports of the local Weather Bureau for the period involved, would not, in

---

13. The Restatement (Second) of Contracts § 265 (1981) provides:

Where, after a contract is made, a party's principal purpose is substantially frustrated without his fault by the occurrence of an event the non-occurrence of which was a basic assumption on which the contract was made, his remaining duties to render performance are discharged, unless the language or circumstances indicate the contrary.

14. Restatement (Second) of Contracts § 261 (1981) provides:

Where, after a contract is made, a party's performance is made impracticable without his fault by the occurrence of an event the non-occurrence of which was a basic assumption on which the contract was made, the duty to render that performance is discharged, unless the language or circumstances indicate the contrary.

our opinion, constitute Force Majeure so as to relieve the defendant of his obligation under the lease contract.

71 So.2d at 677.

Hydrocarbon Management, Inc. v. Tracker Exploration, Inc., 861 S.W.2d 427 (Tex.App.1993), is another example. In *Tracker*, the Railroad Commission ordered the operator to shut in a well for violating the production allowable. The order and other factors caused the lease to cease producing for more than six months. Considering the lessee's appeal from a trial court's finding that the lease had terminated, the court of appeals said:

> The purpose of a force majeure clause is to excuse the lessee from non-performance of lease obligations when the non-performance is caused by circumstances beyond the reasonable control of the lessee, * * * or when non-performance is caused by an event which is unforeseeable at the time the parties entered the contract. Inasmuch as force majeure as an excuse for non-performance is an affirmative defense, appellants bore the burden of proof to establish that defense.

> We note initially that the lease terms are controlling regarding force majeure, and common law rules merely fill in gaps left by the lease. See Texas City Refining v. Conoco, Inc., 767 S.W.2d 183, 186 (Tex.App.1989). Here, the leases specifically provide for the contingency that occurred. Under the terms of the leases, rules and regulations promulgated by a governmental body constitute an excuse for non-performance. The leases define an event of force majeure as an "occurrence or circumstance not within the reasonable control of lessee." Thus, to be able to claim the benefit of force majeure, appellants must show that the RRC's action in requiring the well to be shut-in, constituted an event beyond their reasonable control.

> * * *

> From the operator's statement that the well was "produced during December, 1988 at a rate close to the pipeline's nomination for this well for cash flow reasons," a reasonable trier of fact could have concluded that the operator intentionally overproduced, or at least was able to control the amount of production from the well. There was also testimony from individuals familiar with the oil and gas industry, that failure to follow the RRC guidelines, through overproduction of the well's allowable, will compel a shut-in order by the RRC.

> We conclude the evidence was sufficient to support the trial court's findings. * * * Appellants' failure to comply with the RRC's requirement, which resulted in the shut-in order from the RRC, was an event within the reasonable control of appellants. That being the case, the order would not be an event of force majeure, sufficient to maintain the leases.

861 S.W.2d at 436–437. See also Moore v. Jet Stream Inv., Ltd., 261 S.W.3d 412 (Tex.App.–Texarkana 2008), where the court held the force-majeure clause inapplicable where the Railroad Commission ordered a well shut in because the lessee had not provided a bond or letter of credit providing assurance that the well would be plugged upon abandonment.

And in Wiser v. Enervest Operating, L.L.C., 803 F.Supp.2d 109 (N.D.N.Y. 2011), the court held that even assuming that a state-imposed moratorium on hydrofracturing of shale structures constituted force majeure, the force-majeure provision did not keep a lease with an "unless" delay rental clause from terminating when lessees did not pay rentals. The court concluded that the "unless" special limitation was not affected by the force-majeure language.

> Assuming Governor Paterson's July 2008 memorandum triggered the force majeure clause, that event occurred during the primary term of the leases. If the force majeure clause was triggered at the time, by the terms of the leases "the delay or interruption shall not be counted against [the] Lessee[s]." As a result, both logic and the unambiguous terms of the leases dictate the conclusion that the primary terms of the leases were then extended indefinitely, which required that defendants continue making timely delay rental payments indefinitely in order to avoid termination.

PROBLEM

Because the courts tend to construe force-majeure language strictly, the precise terms of the clause may be crucial to the lessee's ability to maintain a lease under specific circumstances. Suppose that, at the end of the primary term, the lessee was prevented by heavy rains from gaining access to the leased premises to commence drilling. Would the following force-majeure clause preserve the lease?

> Whenever, as a result of any cause reasonably beyond Lessee's control, such as fire, flood, windstorm or other Act of God, decision, law, order, rule, or regulation of any local, State or Federal Government or Governmental Agency, or Court; or inability to secure men, material or transportation, and Lessee is thereby prevented from complying with any express or implied obligations of this Lease, and Lessee's obligations shall be suspended so long as such cause persists, and Lessee shall have ninety (90) days after the cessation of such cause in which to resume performance of this Lease.

See San Mateo Community College District v. Half Moon Bay Limited Partnership, 76 Cal.Rptr.2d 287 (Cal.App.1998). What if the language of the clause were as follows?

> Should lessee be prevented from complying with any express or implied covenant of this Lease, from conducting drilling, or reworking operations thereon or from producing oil or gas or other hydrocarbons therefrom by reason of scarcity of, or inability to obtain or to use equipment or material, or by operation of force majeure, or because of any federal or state law or any order, rule or regulation of a governmental authority, then while so prevented, Lessee's obligations to comply with such covenant shall be suspended, and Lessee shall not be liable in damages for failure to comply therewith; and this Lease shall be extended while and so long as Lessee is prevented by any such cause from conducting drilling or reworking operations on, or from producing oil or gas or other hydrocar-

bons from the leased premises; and the time while Lessee is so prevented shall not be counted against the Lessee, anything in this Lease to the contrary notwithstanding.

D. POOLING CLAUSE: MODIFYING THE GRANTING, HABENDUM, AND ROYALTY CLAUSES

Often lessees wish to conduct operations upon drilling unit configurations that do not fit neatly onto the surface acreage covered by the oil and gas leases they own. The lessees' desire may result from geological factors; the location of potential oil and gas producing formations underground obviously has nothing to do with who owns the land over those formations. Their wish may also result from the need to comply with orders of an oil and gas conservation agency; in many states, drilling units for oil and gas are set on the basis of section and quarter section lines and require minimum acreage commitments, which may not coincide with land ownership. Or lessees may seek to advance a plan to explore and develop systematically, and wish to maintain a block to leases to make that possible.

The *pooling clause* in an oil and gas lease gives a lessee the right to combine small tracts or fractional mineral interests for drilling and apportions production to each interest. An example of a pooling clause follows:

> Lessee may at any time or times pool any part or all of said land and lease or any stratum or strata, with other lands and leases, stratum or strata, in the same field so as to constitute a spacing unit to facilitate an orderly or uniform well spacing pattern or to comply with any order, rule or regulation of the state or federal regulatory or conservation agency having jurisdiction. Such pooling shall be accomplished or terminated by filing of record a declaration of pooling, or declaration of termination of pooling, and by mailing or tendering a copy to lessor, or to the depository bank. *Drilling or re-working operations upon or production from any part of such spacing unit shall be considered for all purposes of this lease as operations or productions from this lease. Lessee shall allocate to this lease the proportionate share of production which the acreage in this lease included in any such spacing unit bears to the total acreage in said spacing unit.*

Because the lessor grants this power to the lessee, and because the lessee must elect to exercise the power, pooling pursuant to a pooling clause is often described as "voluntary" pooling.[15]

A typical pooling clause changes the result that would otherwise occur under the lease in three ways, as the italicized language in the clause quoted illustrates. First, a pooling clause expands the lease grant by giving

---

15. Compulsory pooling is addressed in Chapter 3.

a lessee the power of attorney to pool the lessor's interests. Second, the pooling clause provides that operations anywhere on a pooled area will have the same effect in maintaining the lease as if they were conducted on the lease itself. This expands the habendum clause and allows the savings effect of actual production and constructive production to extend to all leases encompassed by the pooled area, if all contain pooling clauses.[16] Third, the pooling clause states that lessors agree to accept a royalty that reflects their proportionate acreage contribution to the pooled area. This expands, or contracts, the royalty clause depending upon the specific location of the well within the pooled area. If the well is located on the lessor's acreage, it will reduce their royalty by requiring them to share with other owners in the pooled area. The trade-off is that each lessor will enjoy expanded royalty rights to production from wells not on their leased lands but within the pooled area.

In jurisdictions that have broad compulsory pooling acts, lessors frequently bargain for and obtain the elimination or modification of the pooling clause. Absent a pooling clause, the lessee has no contractual authority to pool the lessor's interest, but the lessee may unilaterally seek and obtain a compulsory pooling order. See Nisbet v. Midwest Oil Corp., 451 P.2d 687 (Okla.1968). Another option, when the lease does not contain a pooling clause, or the pooling authority is inadequate to accomplish the lessee's development goals, is for the lessee to seek a separate pooling agreement from the lessors owning acreage within the proposed pooled area.

Disputes often arise about whether a lessee has properly exercised the pooling authority created by the lease pooling clause. Whether an exercise of the pooling power is valid involves two different issues: (1) is the exercise in accord with the terms of the pooling clause; and (2) if so, is it a "good faith" exercise.

If the lessee's purported exercise is not authorized by the pooling clause, it simply is not effective as to the lessor's interest. If the exercise is consistent with the terms of the clause but violates the lessee's implied duty of good faith, the lessor may have a choice of remedies available.

1. EXERCISE IN ACCORD WITH THE POOLING CLAUSE TERMS

Whether an exercise of the pooling power is within the authority granted by the pooling clause is discussed in Kuntz §§ 48.3(c), (d). The answer largely depends on what the pooling clause provides. A few of the more common issues are:

(1) Has the lessee complied strictly with the terms of the pooling clause? Many lease pooling clauses require the lessee to obtain the prior

---

16. Thus, if the owner of Blackacre grants a lease containing a pooling clause, and the Blackacre lessee pools a portion of Blackacre with Whiteacre, an adjoining property, production from or operations on any portion of Whiteacre will act as constructive production to preserve the Blackacre lease. See, e.g., Holland v. EOG Res., Inc., 2010 WL 1078480 (Tex.App.–Waco 2010).

approval of a conservation commission or to record a declaration of pooling. See, e.g., Sauder v. Frye, 613 S.W.2d 63 (Tex.Civ.App.1981). An example of a declaration-of-pooling form is included in the Forms Manual. A pooling clause may also require that unit production be allocated on an acreage basis among the various tracts within the unit; thus, allocation on any other basis would not be binding on the lessor. Some pooling clauses authorize the lessee to pool only to develop and produce gas and not oil.

Although courts have held that because the pooling clause is anticipatory in nature, it should be construed to grant very broad pooling authority in the lessee (see Phillips Petroleum Co. v. Peterson, 218 F.2d 926, 933 (10th Cir.Utah 1954)), they also tend to interpret pooling-clause language strictly. Jones v. Killingsworth, 403 S.W.2d 325 (Tex.1965), is an example. There the lease pooling clause provided that the lessee could pool the lease into units that were not larger than 40 acres for oil wells and 640 acres for gas wells. The clause also provided that "should governmental authority * * * *prescribe or permit*" larger units, units created under the lease pooling power "may conform substantially in size with those *prescribed* by governmental regulations." (Emphasis added). The Texas Railroad Commission set an 80–acre minimum unit size for oil wells, but encouraged operators to establish 160–acre units. Accordingly, the lessee designated a 160 acre drilling unit. The Texas Supreme Court held that the lease pooling clause meant what it said, that it could not be used to establish a drilling unit greater than 80 acres, since that was the area *prescribed* by Railroad Commission rules.

(2) Has the lessee exercised its pooling power when the lease is still effective? In Humble Oil & Refining Co. v. Kunkel, 366 S.W.2d 236 (Tex.Civ.App.1963), the lessee of Blackacre was drilling a well at the expiration of the primary term, but the lease was saved by a well-completion type operations clause. The well was completed as a dry hole. The lease contained both a dry-hole clause and a pooling clause. Within the 60–day grace period specified in the dry-hole clause, the lessee exercised the pooling power by pooling a small part of Blackacre with other land that was already productive. The court held that the lessee could not pool Blackacre after the primary term had expired. The only thing that could have saved the lease was compliance with the terms of the dry-hole clause, which required the lessee to begin additional "operations" within 60 days following the drilling of a dry hole. Cf. Harper v. Hudson Gas & Oil Corp., 299 F.2d 238 (5th Cir.La.1962), where the lease allowed pooling at any time while the lease was in force. See also Mobil Oil Exploration, Inc. v. Latham Exploration, Inc. 31 So.3d 1149 (La.App. 2 Cir. 2010), where a lease that provided that a pooling declaration must be executed in writing and filed for record terminated when the lessee executed a declaration of pooling (but failed to record it before the lease expiration date).

(3) May the lessee exercise the pooling power more than once? If the first drilling unit is dissolved, may the lessee create a new unit? See Texaco, Inc. v. Lettermann, 343 S.W.2d 726 (Tex.Civ.App.1961). If the

pooling power was exercised to pool a portion of the leasehold with other lands, may the lessee pool the remaining leasehold to create another unit? Kenoyer v. Magnolia Petroleum Co., 245 P.2d 176 (Kan.1952). May the lessee modify an existing unit through the exercise of the pooling power? See Grimes v. La Gloria Corp., 251 S.W.2d 755 (Tex.Civ.App. 1952) and Expando Prod. Co. v. Marshall, 407 S.W.2d 254 (Tex.Civ.App. 1966). Ordinarily, the answer to each of these questions is yes, but good drafting will avoid the issues.

(4) May the pooling power be exercised after production has been established? Some pooling clauses contemplate pooling only for purposes of securing development. Thus, exercise of the pooling power to include previously developed (producing) property may not be authorized. See Mallett v. Union Oil & Gas Corp., 94 So.2d 16 (La.1957). But see Odom v. Union Producing Co., 141 So.2d 649 (La.1961).

(5) May pooling be effective retroactively? In Tittizer v. Union Gas Corp., 171 S.W.3d 857 (Tex.2005), the lease pooling clause provided that the lessee could pool by recording a pooling declaration. The lessee filed a pooling declaration that purported to make the pooling effective retroactively to the date of first production. The Texas Supreme Court held that the declaration was an improper exercise of the pooling power and recognized the pooling declaration only as of the date it was recorded.

(6) May the pooling power be exercised to conduct field-wide unit operations? Many lease pooling clauses limit the size of units that may be formed, which usually effectively bars field-wide pooling.

(7) What is the lessor's remedy when the lessee exercises the pooling power improperly? Ordinarily, an improper pooling is simply ineffective to the extent that it exceeds the authority of the clause or the formalities of the clause have not been followed; see the discussions of *Jones v. Killingsworth* and *Tittizer v. Union Gas Corp.*, above. In Browning Oil Co., Inc. v. Luecke, 38 S.W.3d 625 (Tex.App. 2000), the court construed negotiated pooling clauses contained in three leases executed by the Lueckes as lessors. The pooling clauses expressly limited the lessee's pooling power through "anti-dilution" provisions that were designed to prevent the lessee from forming pooled units that contained small portions of the Lueckes' tracts. The lessee's assignee was found to have willfully breached these pooling provisions in forming units for the drilling of horizontal wells. One of the wells in question had been drilled on a Luecke tract. Rather than ignoring the pooling altogether and awarding all royalties to the Lueckes—which would have been an application of the rule of capture—or reforming the unit so it would comply with the clause, the court was persuaded by public-policy arguments regarding the importance of horizontal drilling in the prevention of waste (i.e., achieving the maximum recovery of oil in an efficient manner) to hold that the Lueckes should recover royalties based upon the production that can be "attributed to their tracts with reasonable probability." *Id.* at 647. How is a jury to make this determination? Given the negotiated pooling provisions, did the court

give the lessors the benefit of their lease bargain? Should the court have considered an alternate "public-policy" approach?

(8) May a lessee have a duty to exercise the lease pooling power? Lease pooling clauses are not usually drafted with language susceptible of interpretation as imposing a duty, and we find no case directly in point. But Professor Kuntz has said:

> It is possible for an affirmative duty to be found in a broader implied obligation on the part of the lessee. For example, drilling a well may be optional with the lessee according to the drilling clause, yet the lessee may be required to drill in order to comply with a broader obligation, such as the duty to protect against drainage. Similarly, a duty to pool may arise if pooling is required in order to comply with the broad requirements of prudent operation.

Kuntz § 48.3(h).

2. GOOD FAITH EXERCISE OF THE POOLING POWER

Pooling clauses rarely express any standard of conduct for the exercise of the pooling power. Yet, all jurisdictions that have addressed this matter have implied a standard of good faith. Cases dealing with the question of whether the pooling power has been exercised in good faith are similar, but—as you will see—not identical, to the cases concerning the reasonable prudent operator standard. Indeed, the good-faith pooling standard is an *implied covenant* that arises from the broad nature of the lessee's authority under the pooling clause coupled with the recognition that the pooling clause tends to favor the lessee's interests more than the lessor's. Do you understand why a pooling clause is more favorable to the lessee than to the lessor? Do you also understand why the pooling clause can be advantageous for the lessor?

AMOCO PRODUCTION CO. v. UNDERWOOD

558 S.W.2d 509 (Tex.Civ.App.1977).

McCLOUD, CHIEF JUSTICE.

This case involves the cancellation by lessors of a "gas unit" designated by lessee under the pooling provisions of eight oil, gas and mineral leases. . . .

Victory Petroleum Corporation entered into a "Farmout Contract" with Amoco Production Company whereby Victory agreed to drill a test well on Section 3, BS & F Survey, Wheeler County, Texas, and Amoco agreed to assign to Victory certain leases covering land located near Section 3. Amoco reserved an overriding royalty interest in the leases assigned. After the test well was completed as a gas well, Victory filed a gas unit declaration forming a 688.02 acre gas operating production unit designated as the Victory Petroleum Company et al., Circle Dot Ranch Gas

Unit No. 1. As designated, the unit perpetuated beyond the primary term eight different oil, gas and mineral leases containing 2,252.03 acres of land. The unit affected the eight leases as follows:

Lessor	Land Covered	Total Acres in Lease	Acres Included in Unit	Acres Excluded From Unit
Walser (Circle Dot)	Sec. 3	643.23	553.02	90.21
Walser (Circle Dot)	Sec. 81	647.90	45.00	602.90
Underwood	NW/4 & SE/4 of Sec. 2	320.90	10.00	310.90
Underwood	N/2 of Sec. 1	320.00	20.00	300.00
Wright	SE/4 of Sec. 1	160.00	10.00	150.00
American United Hefley	SW/4 SW/4 of Sec. 4	40.00	40.00	0
Johnson	N/2 SW/4 SE/4 SW/4 of Sec. 4	120.00	10.00	110.00
TOTALS		2,252.03	688.02	1,564.01

Plaintiffs, L.T. Underwood and wife, Ora Lee Underwood, and Circle Dot Ranch, Inc., sued defendants, * * * seeking, among other relief, cancellation of the Circle Dot Ranch Gas Unit No. 1. * * * [T]he jury found that the designation of the Circle Dot Ranch Gas Unit by Victory Petroleum Company, Westland Oil Development Corporation, L.C. Kung and Amoco Production Company "was not made in good faith".

Judgment was entered that the Unit Designation of the Victory Petroleum Company et al., Circle Dot Ranch Gas Unit No. 1 be canceled and held for naught; * * * that the oil, gas and mineral leases dated May 29, 1970, executed by the Underwoods and Walsers as lessors, covering the above described property have terminated for failure of production.

* * *

Appellants contend the court erred in overruling their motion for instructed verdict * * * because there is no evidence that appellants were not acting in good faith in designating the Circle Dot Ranch Gas Unit. Appellees argue the appellants "gerrymandered" the eight leases as set out in the unit designation to advance their own pecuniary interest without regard to the rights of appellees and the other mineral owners in and under the affected lands.

Appellees or their predecessors in title executed four oil, gas and mineral leases in favor of Amoco, dated May 29, 1970, with each containing a five-year primary term. The leases were assigned to Victory and each contained a pooling clause which, in part, provides as follows:

> Lessee, at its option, is hereby given the right and power to pool or combine the land covered by this lease, or any portion thereof, as to oil and gas, or either of them, with any other land, lease or leases when in Lessee's judgment it is necessary or advisable to do so in

order to properly develop and operate said premises, such pooling to be into a well unit or units not exceeding forty (40) acres, plus an acreage tolerance often percent (10%) of forty (40) acres, for oil, and not exceeding six hundred and forty (640) acres, plus an acreage tolerance of ten percent (10%) of six hundred and forty (640) acres, for gas, except that larger units may be created to conform to any spacing or well unit pattern that may be prescribed by governmental authorities.

The court in Elliott v. Davis, 553 S.W.2d 223 (Tex.Civ.App.–Amarillo 1977, writ filed) recently stated that the lessee must exercise "good faith" toward the lessor and royalty owners in making a pooling designation. As a general rule, the question of good faith is a fact question to be determined by the fact finder.

* * *

Westland Oil Development Corporation and Victory Petroleum Company are "associated companies" occupying joint offices. On May 20, 1975, A.B. Rothwell, Vice–President of Westland Oil Development Corporation and Victory Petroleum Company sent the following letter to Amoco:

We are still conducting completion operations on the Circle Dot Ranch No. 1 well in Wheeler County, Texas, although we have no doubt that we will be successful in making a Morrow Sand gas completion.

As you are aware, the majority of your leases included under your Farmout Contract (EA 56,278) will expire at the end of their primary term on May 29, 1975. It is imperative that we file a Gas Unit Declaration of record prior to this date.

We are forwarding herewith three (3) copies of Victory Petroleum Company et al's Circle Dot Ranch Gas Unit No. 1 Unit Declaration. *This unit has been designed to hold the majority of your leases which will expire on May 29, 1975,* and also takes into consideration our recent review of your seismic records. (Emphasis added)

The Victory Petroleum Circle Dot well was commenced on Section 3 in December 1974. It was completed in the Upper Morrow Formation on or about May 16, 1975, and the official potential test was conducted on May 21, 1975. The gas unit designation was signed on May 20, 1975, and filed on May 27, 1975, only two days before May 29, 1975, the termination date of the primary term of appellees' oil, gas and mineral leases.

At the time of trial, appellants had no plans to drill an additional well on any part of the 2,252 acres affected by their gas unit. Appellants excluded from the unit 90.21 acres in Section 3 where the well was located even though their records indicated the excluded acreage was probably productive, and included 45 acres in Section 81, which perpetuated beyond the primary term 602.90 acres, even though Section 81 was "lower structurally". One of appellants' witnesses testified that with the information at hand when the unit was designated, it would be "extremely stupid" to drill in Section 81, where the "seismic and subsurface" data indicated it was "lower". Their plan would be to move to a higher structural position. The Circle Dot well was drilled on a lease containing 643.23 acres. It was not necessary to bring in additional acreage in order to have a full spacing unit and receive full allowable under the Texas Railroad Commission's "spacing rules".

After May 29, 1975, the termination date of the primary term of the leases in question, appellees could have leased their land, other than Section 3 where the well was located, to other persons for a cash bonus of $75 per acre if it had not been "tied up" by the gas unit. * * *

The jury could have properly concluded from the evidence and inferences listed above that the configuration of the unit was not established in good faith, but designated as stated in Rothwell's letter to Amoco, "to hold the majority of the leases" which would otherwise expire on May 29, 1975.

* * * Judgment of the trial court is affirmed.

NOTES

1. A benchmark case establishing the lessee's duty to act in good faith on behalf of the lessor in the exercise of the pooling power is Imes v. Globe Oil & Refining Co., 84 P.2d 1106 (Okla.1938). In *Imes,* a group of landowners entered into a community oil and gas lease containing a broad pooling provision that provided as follows:

> It being understood and agreed that *any lot, lots* or parcels of land embraced within the outer boundary lines of the above described block or blocks, * * * may *at any time be included within the terms hereof and become a part of the leased premises covered hereby * * *.*

> * * * It is further agreed that lessee may *at any time* without the consent of lessors, *consolidate, jointly operate,* and develop this lease and the land covered hereby with any other lease or leases covering any lot, lots or parcels of land embraced within the outer boundary lines of the J.W. Craig's Sub. of Block 19, Fruitland Addition to Oklahoma City, Oklahoma * * *.

84 P.2d at 1107. [emphasis added]. Two successful wells were drilled on the leasehold within the primary term of the lease. Two and one-half years after the first well was completed, the lessee pooled the premises with six additional adjacent lots. The evidence showed that the lots were worthless for oil and gas production. The lessors of the community lease challenged the pooling, arguing that the phrase *at any time* contained in the pooling clause "meant within a reasonable time in view of the circumstances, and that the circumstances clearly support the finding of the trial court that a reasonable time had elapsed * * *." Id. The Oklahoma Supreme Court agreed. The court found: (1) that the lessee was *virtually the agent* of the lessors; and (2) that the evidence supported the lower court's finding that the adjacent lots were valueless. Given these factors, the court concluded that the phrase *at any time* did not mean that additional worthless tracts could be added to the producing unit after production was secured on the community lease. Id. The court held that the lessee owed the lessors a duty of good faith in the exercise of the

pooling power and that this duty prevented the inclusion in a unit of any interest antagonistic to the lessor.

2.   While cases concerning the good or bad faith exercise of the lessee's pooling power are similar to cases involving the reasonable-and-prudent-operator standard, they are not identical. Some courts describe the relationship established under the pooling clause as different from the relationship established in the balance of the lease. The court in *Imes* analogized the relationship of a lessor and lessee under the pooling clause with that of a principal and agent:[17] when the interests of the lessor and the lessee diverge, the lessee cannot, through an exercise of the pooling power, promote or acquire antagonistic interests to those of the lessor.

In general, an agent violates the fiduciary duty to the principal by having an adverse interest in any transactions conducted unless there is full disclosure to the principal who acquiesces to the transaction. Even if the agent's adverse interest is known to the principal, the agent owes a duty of full disclosure of all relevant facts prior to the transaction. W. Sell, Agency 120–21 (1975).

The requirement of full disclosure was applied to the exercise of the pooling power in Phillips Petroleum Co. v. Peterson, 218 F.2d 926 (10th Cir. Utah 1954). In *Peterson,* the court stated, "It is equally well settled that an agent may act with respect to matters involving interests adverse to his principal, where the principal possesses full knowledge of the facts and consents thereto." 218 F.2d at 934. The decision, however, does not explain the meaning of this principle in the context of an exercise of the pooling power, as the court avoided the question by finding that the lessor and lessee shared mutual interests. The court noted, however, that the lessee entered into the leases with the intent to exercise the power granted in the pooling clause and fully explained the effect of the clause to the lessors.

Regardless of the label given the relationship of the lessor and lessee under the pooling clause, the courts generally recognize that the lessee owes a duty to the lessor to exercise the pooling authority given by the clause in good faith to the lessor. Does the label of a principal and agent accurately describe the relationship between a lessor and lessee under the pooling clause? Should the lessee's duty to the lessor regarding the exercise of the pooling power be different from the lessee's duty under implied lease covenants or from the lessee's duty to pay royalty?

In Elliott v. Davis, 553 S.W.2d 223 (Tex.Civ.App.1977), the court refused to hold the lessee to a fiduciary standard when it exercised the pooling power.

> We conclude that the standard of good faith is correctly described in Kuntz, The Law of Oil & Gas, § 48.3, p. 224, as follows:
>
>> Although it has been said that the lessee has a fiduciary obligation in the exercise of the pooling power, it is submitted that the lessee is not a fiduciary and that standards applied to fiduciaries are entirely

---

17.   Other courts have not gone so far; see, e.g., Phillips Petroleum Co. v. Peterson, 218 F.2d 926 (10th Cir. Utah 1954); Expando Prod. Co. v. Marshall, 407 S.W.2d 254 (Tex.Civ.App.1966); Banks v. Mecom, 410 S.W.2d 300 (Tex.Civ.App.1966); and Tiller v. Fields, 301 S.W.2d 185 (Tex.Civ.App.1957).

too strict. This is so because the lessee has not undertaken to manage and develop the property for the sole benefit of the lessor. The lessee has substantial interests that must be taken into account, and he should not be required to subordinate the lessee's own interests entirely to the interests of the lessor. Since the lessee's interests frequently conflict with those of the lessor, however, the lessee must exercise the power in fairness and in good faith, taking into account the interests of both the lessor and lessee.

We have applied the foregoing standard of good faith to the summary judgment evidence, considering such evidence in the light most favorable to appellant defendants. We conclude that the summary judgment proof, including evidence of the configuration of the unit, the fact that expiration of the primary term of the leases was imminent at the time of the pool designation, and Elliott's testimony that he did not consider a geological basis in the formation of the unit, raises a fact issue for determination of the trier of fact. We do not find that the evidence so conclusively establishes bad faith that reasonable minds could not differ in considering that question.

The refusal by the Railroad Commission to approve the pooled acreage as a unit to be assigned to the well is not, in itself, determinative of the question of good faith. The Railroad Commission is a conservation body and does not have jurisdiction to effect a change of property rights. Likewise, the mere fact that the unit was declared and drilling begun shortly before the expiration date of some of the leases does not establish bad faith as a matter of law. In Boone v. Kerr–McGee Oil Industries, 217 F.2d 63 (10th Cir.Okla.1954), wherein the court found that the pooling designation was for the two-fold purpose of properly developing the premises and to extend the leases beyond their primary term, the court stated:

The mere fact that only a few months of the primary term remained * * * does not make arbitrary a decision which, based upon a consideration of relevant factors, was proper. Neither does the pooling arrangement, reached upon a consideration of relevant factors, become arbitrary merely because it relieves appellees from ruinous, wasteful drilling operations which would be necessary if it wanted to retain its leases, even if that was one of the factors it had in mind at the time it reached its decision.

Our holding that there is a jury issue on the question of the failure to exercise good faith in making the pooling designation is determinative of this appeal.

553 S.W.2d at 226–27. In Vela v. Pennzoil Producing Co., 723 S.W.2d 199, 206 (Tex.App.1986), the court noted that a lessee is not required to sacrifice its interests for those of the lessor, even though some cases suggest that the lessee owes a fiduciary duty to the lessor when it exercises the pooling power.

3. In Boone v. Kerr–McGee Oil Indus., 217 F.2d 63 (10th Cir.Okla.1954), the court addressed whether pooling of the leased premises just before the expiration of the primary term of the lease constituted bad faith. The court stated that the duty of good faith arose out of the contractual relationship.

Where discretion is lodged in one of two parties to a contract or a transaction, such discretion must, of course, be exercised in good faith. That simply means that what is done must be done honestly to effectuate the object and purpose the parties had in mind in providing for the exercise of such power.

217 F.2d at 65. The court said that the imminent expiration of the primary term of the lease was only one factor in determining whether the lessee had acted in good or bad faith. Other factors mentioned were:

(a) could the maximum amount of gas recovery be had through this one well, (b) would a fair distribution of the proceeds to all the interested parties be made, (c) was it economically feasible to drill additional wells under the other leases, (d) might the drilling of such additional wells detrimentally affect the ultimate amount of recovery of gas from such acreage, and (e) could such additional wells be drilled without probable damage to the recovery of oil from surrounding leases.

Id.

In *Boone,* good faith seemed to depend on an objective analysis of the above factors; a later case, however, Diggs v. Cities Serv. Oil Co., 241 F.2d 425 (10th Cir.Okla.1957), which also concerned pooling just before expiration of the primary term, suggests that a lessee's good faith must be measured in subjective terms.

The question of whether or not [lessees] were faithful to the duties and obligations imposed upon them by the terms of the lease so as to have acted in "good faith" in pooling gas rights is one of fact to be determined by a consideration of the circumstances and conditions existing at the time of the action. A careful review of the record and the mass of geological and other technical fact and opinion that explore [lessees'] good faith merely points to a conflict in most instances. * * * The trial court, in view of testimony that [lessees] pooled and drilled upon advice of their own experts and expended large sums of money in reliance thereon to bring in a well actually producing large quantities of gas, found no lack of good faith existed. This finding is of course justified for good faith may be probed by consideration of the subsequent actions of the person whose subjective intent is questioned.

241 F.2d at 427.

One writer advocating the objective standard states:

If the proper standard is whether the lessee complies with the prudent operator test when pooling is undertaken, it is submitted that the questions for determination will be whether the pooling would have been undertaken in nearly the same manner, at approximately the same time, by an ordinary prudent operator who, based upon information available at the time of exercise of the pooling power, is reasonably attempting to ensure that each lessor receives royalties reflecting the amount of oil and gas under his land by a pooling plan which is economically feasible to the lessee. A subjective test of the lessee's intention when exercising the pooling power would reward ignorance and protect unskilled operators.

John Ashworth, Selected Problems in Voluntary Pooling: A Suggested Rationale, 26 Ohio St.L.J. 420, 434 (1965).

Professor Kuntz submits that a determination of good faith involves both subjective and objective components:

> Because good faith is necessarily a subjective matter, the good faith standard is theoretically a subjective test, and there are judicial comments to support this conclusion. As it is applied, however, objective factors must be relied upon to make the determination of good faith. This is so, because in the absence of damaging admissions by the lessee, the presence or absence of good faith must be established by circumstantial evidence. The conclusion to be drawn from the circumstantial evidence is necessarily predicated on the premise that a lessee acts in good faith when doing what a prudent operator would do under the circumstances to obtain the greatest advantage from the operation for all parties interested in production and that the lessee acts in bad faith when he does otherwise.

Kuntz § 48.3 at 224–25. Professor Kuntz's analysis suggests that courts should deal with cases concerning the good faith exercise of the pooling power in the same manner as they deal with cases concerning the reasonable and prudent operator standard.[18]

4. Good faith is presumed. In other words, the lessor bears the burden of proof to show that the lessee did not act in good faith. There are a number of situations where pooling by the lessee raises the possibility that the lessee was chiefly motivated by self-interest. In these situations, a jury may be asked to decide whether the lessee exercised the pooling power in good faith. Some of the more common fact patterns, which may occur alone or together, are:

(a) Pooling After Production

PROBLEM

The lessee secures production on Blackacre. Thereafter, the lessee attempts to pool Blackacre with adjoining Whiteacre. The lessor of Blackacre objects because his share of production will be diminished.

Today many pooling clauses, like the following example, expressly provide that pooling may occur before or after production.

> Lessee may at its election exercise its pooling option before or after drilling operations have begun. The pooled unit may include land or leases upon which a well capable of producing oil or gas in paying quantities has been completed or upon which drilling operations have begun.

Nonetheless, the exercise of the pooling power (before or after production) must still be in good faith. Even in the absence of express authority, pooling after production does not, by itself, constitute bad faith.

---

18. For additional articles dealing with the subject of a good-faith exercise of the pooling power, see generally George C. Hardy, Pooling and Unitization in the Eastern United States: Part I, 2 E.Min.L.Inst. 16–1 (1981); Leo J. Hoffman, Pooling and Unitization: Current Status and Developments, 33 Inst. on Oil & Gas L. & Tax'n 245 (1982); and Allen L. Handlan & Kevin L. Sykes, Pooling and Unitization: Legal and Ethical Considerations, 19 Tulsa L.J. 309 (1984).

In *Imes,* above, the Oklahoma Supreme Court held that once production is had on a leasehold, the lessee cannot subsequently pool that leasehold with additional tracts that are valueless for oil and gas purposes. In Gillham v. Jenkins, 244 P.2d 291 (Okla.1952), a successful gas well was completed on an 80 acre tract. Because of federal wartime restrictions on steel, production was not allowed on units less than 160 acres. Here, the Supreme Court, in distinguishing *Imes,* upheld pooling after production:

> In the Imes case the principal factor for consideration was not the time of development but it was the good faith of the lessees in combining additional lots to the unit after production was had. * * * The joinder of these additional lots served no purpose and added nothing to value of the unit. It did serve to increase the interest of lessee in the oil and gas already being produced and to decrease the proportionate share of lessors. * * * The case is clearly distinguishable from the present case, where a real necessity and purpose existed at the time of the pooling, which was done in good faith to obtain the marketing of the gas from the well on plaintiff's land, and where the unitization was had, under compulsion, if the gas was to be marketed and benefit obtained by either party.

244 P.2d at 293.

(b) Pooling Just Before Expiration of the Primary Term

PROBLEM

The primary term of a lease covering Blackacre is about to expire. The lessee hastily pools Blackacre with Whiteacre where a well has been or is about to be drilled. The lessor of Blackacre objects, arguing that the lessor's motivation was to perpetuate the Blackacre lease beyond its primary term.

Although a lessee who acts in good faith should be allowed to pool any time during the primary term of the lease, pooling just before the expiration of the primary term raises doubts about the lessee's good faith. In *Boone,* above, the lessee (Kerr–McGee) pooled Whiteacre with Blackacre just before expiration of the primary term on Blackacre. The court noted that the evidence established that additional drilling would have been wasteful and "that such drilling would not have resulted in the ultimate recovery of additional quantities of gas and would have resulted in financial loss to the driller." 217 F.2d at 65. As to the timing of the pooling, the court held:

"The mere fact that only a few months of the primary term remained does not change the basic problem with which Kerr–McGee was faced and does not make arbitrary a decision which, based upon a consideration of relevant factors, was proper."

Id. *Boone* states the prevailing view that pooling just before expiration of the lease primary term does not by itself constitute bad faith. But see Wilcox v. Shell Oil Co., 76 So.2d 416 (La.1954).

(c) Gerrymandering

PROBLEM

The lessee of Blackacre, Redacre, Brownacre, Blueacre, and Greenacre pools a small portion of each of these leaseholds with Whiteacre to form a unit. The unit may be irregularly shaped, and Whiteacre may have been large enough to constitute a drilling unit by itself. The lessors of some or all of these tracts object, arguing that the lessee created a gerrymandered drilling unit to perpetuate as many leases as possible by drilling one well on the unit.

The general view, expressed in *Elliott* and *Underwood,* above, is that gerrymandering does not by itself constitute bad faith, but it may be a factor in determining bad faith. For example, in Southwest Gas Producing Co. v. Seale, 191 So.2d 115 (Miss.1966), the court sustained a challenge to a gerrymandered unit, but there was other evidence of bad faith. The lessee, Hayes, had already drilled a dry hole on a tract owned by Johnson. Thereafter, the Johnson lease expired. To obtain a new lease from Johnson, Hayes promised to form a unit by pooling some of Johnson's land with land under lease from Seale and further promised to drill a well on the pooled unit. The court's decision that the pooling power was not exercised in good faith was based on the following: (1) a considerable portion of Johnson's tract was not potentially productive; and (2) obtaining a new lease from Johnson in return for a promise to pool permitted Hayes to protect his lease block from competing fringe wells. The court then remanded the case to determine damages and to determine how much, if any, of the Johnson leasehold could have been pooled in good faith with the Seale tract.

(d) Pooling for Exploration and Orderly Development

PROBLEM

By exercising the power under a broadly worded pooling and unitization clause, the lessee of multiple leaseholds within a prospect area unitizes all leases to form a single large "exploratory" unit. The lessee drills a wildcat well and completes it as a producer. The lessors argue that the lessee formed the unit in bad faith, because one wildcat well holds all leases beyond their primary terms.

"Exploratory units" are most commonly created where some of the unit leasehold acreage consists of federal land. With the approval of the Bureau of Land Management, a lessee of federal acreage can form an exploratory unit to develop a wildcat area. Under applicable federal regulations, the pooling of federal acreage is called "communitization." 30 U.S.C. § 226(m). Exploratory units are generally formed where drilling and development costs are high. The exploratory unit allows the lessee time to develop fully what may be a very large area and to reap the full long-term benefit of its investment without the threat of competition. Without the unit, some of the leases might expire for lack of production. If some leases expire, competitors might acquire new leases in the area, or by offering higher bonuses, higher royalties, and more lessor-oriented lease terms competitors might increase the cost of acquiring and maintaining replacement leases.

Large exploratory units pose no threat to the interests of the federal government as lessor, because the Bureau of Land Management must consent to the inclusion of federal lands in a unit. Private mineral owners who have signed a lease that gives the lessee broad pooling and unitization powers, however, are often greatly distressed to learn that their lands have been included in a large unit. For example, in Amoco Prod. Co. v. Jacobs, 746 F.2d 1394 (10th Cir.N.M.1984), overruled in part, Amoco Prod. Co. v. Heimann, 904 F.2d 1405 (10th Cir.N.M.1990), private lessors unsuccessfully challenged the formation of a carbon-dioxide exploratory unit that included over one million acres of federal, state, and private lands. The pooling clause in *Jacobs* specifically allowed the lessee to "unitize, pool, or combine all or any part of the above described lands with other lands in the same general area * * *." 746 F.2d at 1406.

Courts have upheld the creation of exploratory units over the strong objection of private landowners. In Sotrana–Texas Corp. v. Mogen, 551 F.Supp. 433 (D.N.D.1982), the court, in sustaining the creation of an exploratory unit under a clause similar to the one construed in *Jacobs,* concluded that there was no need to consider the lessee's subjective intent as long as the formation of the unit was justified by geological data. In Froholm v. Cox, 934 F.2d 959 (8th Cir.N.D.1991), the Court of Appeals for the Eighth Circuit agreed with the reasoning of *Mogen.* In *Froholm,* the lessee formed an exploratory unit pursuant to a pooling clause that allowed the lessee "either before or after production * * * to pool or unitize * * * when in Lessee's judgment it is necessary and advisable to do so * * *." 934 F.2d at 962. The court upheld the formation of the unit even though the lessors had purposely divided their lands into several leaseholds to prevent the lessee from holding all of the lease acreage with one well. The *Mogen* court's failure to consider good faith was criticized in *Jacobs;* however, the *Jacobs* court (rather reluctantly and tentatively) found that the lessee had created the one million acre CO_2 unit in good faith. In Amoco Prod. Co. v. Heimann, 904 F.2d 1405 (10th Cir.N.M.1990), the Court of Appeals found that this same one million acre unit was properly formed and that a good faith inquiry was unnecessary where the New Mexico Oil Conservation Commission had approved of the unit operation.[19] And in *Froholm*, the court held that the proper forum for lessor's action was before the federal Interior Board of Land Appeals because the federal government had approved the establishment of an exploratory unit. For critical commentary see Professor Anderson's Discussion Note following *Froholm*, 117 O & GR 84. The lessors in these cases could have avoided this problem either by restricting the lessee's power or by deleting the pooling clause. Note that the clauses in question specifically used the word "unitize." Would the courts have upheld the units if the clauses had referred only to "pooling"?

Large exploratory units may generally not be formed by means of statutory compulsory pooling or compulsory unitization processes. Most pool-

---

19. The commission did not order compulsory pooling or unitization. It merely approved the unit plan of operations. In ruling that a good faith inquiry was unnecessary, *Heimann* overruled that portion of *Jacobs* that allowed a separate good faith inquiry by the court. 904 F.2d at 1414.

ing acts authorize pooling to form a drilling or proration unit, and most unitization acts authorize unitization for enhanced recovery, not for exploration. Nevertheless, a compelling argument can be made for the creation of compulsory exploratory unitization—especially for high-risk, high-cost prospects. See generally, Owen L. Anderson and Ernest E. Smith, The Use of Law to Promote Domestic Exploration and Production, 50 Inst. on Oil & Gas L. & Tax'n 2–86 to 2–94 (1999).

3. LEASE LIMITS ON THE POOLING AUTHORITY

Lessors often resist including pooling clauses in oil and gas leases. A mineral interest owner may view the pooling clause as giving the lessee a dangerous amount of discretion to preserve the lease and affect the amount of royalty. Lessors frequently simply strike the pooling clause from oil and gas leases. Deleting the pooling clause will likely substantially and adversely affect the value of the lease to the lessee, however, and the lessor may suffer a heavy trade-off in the form of lower bonus or royalty. There may be circumstances in which pooling is to the advantage of a lessor, particularly a small-tract owner.

Lessors may also negotiate to form lease provisions that limit the scope of the pooling clause. These provisions may include (1) **anti-dilution provisions**, (2) **Pugh clauses**, or (3) **retained acreage provisions**. All present drafting and interpretative problems.

NOTES

1. Where the lessee exceeds the grant of authority under the pooling clause or where the lessee does not act in good faith in the exercise of the pooling power, the lessor may by his conduct be prevented from contesting the lessee's actions. See Yelderman v. McCarthy, 474 S.W.2d 781 (Tex.Civ.App. 1971). Should a lessor who accepts royalty checks for production from a unit well be held to have ratified what may have been an invalid or improper exercise of the pooling power? Would the location of the well make any difference? Would it make any difference if the lessor had signed a division order that specified a unit share of production?

2. In the following situations, consider the proper remedy for an invalid or improper exercise of the pooling power:

(a) The producing unit well is located off the leasehold, and the primary term of the lease has expired.

(b) The unit well is located on the leasehold, and the primary term of the lease has expired.

(c) Reconsider the above situations, but assume the lease is being held by production from a well located on a portion of the leasehold not included in the unit.

(d) Reconsider the first two situations, but assume the lease is within the primary term.

See Kuntz § 48.3(i).

(a) Anti–Dilution Provisions

A lease anti-dilution clause seeks to protect the lessor by limiting the extent to which the lessor's royalty can be "diluted" by pooling. In HS Resources v. Wingate, 327 F.3d 432 (5th Cir. Tex. 2003), the anti-dilution clause provided that:

> Lessee shall not be granted the right to pool any of the leased premises for the drilling of or production from any well located on the leased premises which is anticipated to be classified, or ultimately classified, as a "gas" well by the governmental entity having jurisdiction over same *unless all of the leased premises is located either within the pooled unit for such well or within a unit for another gas well* producing in commercially paying quantities from the same formation. (Emphasis added).

The court applied Texas law to hold that the lessee, whose lease also limited the size of a pooled unit to 176 acres and required release of all property not included in a pooled unit, had satisfied the lease anti-dilution language where the lessee included both leased and unleased acreage in a 176 acre pooled unit and surrendered all of the rest of its leased acreage. Sabre Oil & Gas Corp. v. Gibson, 72 S.W.3d 812 (Tex.App.2002), rationalized a lease "anti-dilution" clause with a clause permitting partial assignments by holding that the anti-dilution clause applied only to the portion of the property assigned, so that an assignee complied with an anti-dilution clause that permitted pooling only if all the leased premises were included within the unit was satisfied where the assignee had pooled all of the acreage it owned.

(b) Pugh Clauses

A compromise often struck between lessors and lessees over the power to pool is what is commonly called a "Pugh" clause or, in Texas, a *Freestone rider*. A Pugh clause (named after the Louisiana lawyer who created it) limits the constructive-production effect of usual pooling language to provide that operations on or production from a pooled unit will not preserve the whole lease, but will sever the lease into pooled and unpooled portions. There are many variations. A simple formulation follows:

> Notwithstanding anything to the contrary herein contained, drilling operations on or production from a pooled unit or units established under the provisions of paragraph 4 [the pooling clause] hereof or otherwise embracing land covered hereby and other land shall maintain this lease in force only as to land included in such unit or units. The lease may be maintained in force as to the remainder of the land in any manner herein provided for, provided that if it be by rental payment, rentals shall be payable only on the number of acres not included in such unit or units.

A Pugh clause gives the lessee the flexibility to make pooling decisions, but limits the effect of decisions to that portion of the lease included in the pooled unit. The lessor's royalty is proportionate to the amount of his or her property included in the unit, but unit operations do not affect the remainder of his or her land. A Pugh clause takes away much of the incentive that lessees might otherwise have to try to hold large tracts of land by creation of small, multi-lease units.

A Pugh clause must be drafted to take into account the possibility of compulsory pooling. In Bibler Brothers Timber Corp. v. Tojac Minerals, Inc., 664 S.W.2d 472 (Ark.1984), the lease Pugh provision modified the pooling clause by providing that "In the event however that only a part of the lands embraced by this lease are included in a *unit created hereunder,* then the remaining portion of the lands embraced by this lease shall be subject to delay rental payments as provided in Paragraph 4." The court held that a statutorily-pooled unit was not subject to the language since it was not created under the lease. What should the Pugh language have said?

A Pugh clause may be either *vertical* or *horizontal*. The language quoted above severs the lease vertically, into a pooled tract from the surface to the center of the earth and an unpooled tract from the surface to the center of the earth. Pugh clauses can also expressly sever the leased premises horizontally between pooled formations and unproductive forma- tions. For example, in Sandefer Oil & Gas, Inc. v. Duhon, 961 F.2d 1207 (5th Cir.La.1992), a horizontal Pugh clause provided that following "expi- ration of the primary term, this lease shall terminate automatically as to all horizons situated 100 feet below the deepest depth drilled * * * from which a well * * * is producing in paying quantities." The well had been drilled to a depth of 17,609 feet but had been produced at a depth of 17,200 feet. The formation was between 17,100 feet and 17,250 feet deep. Below what depth should the lease terminate? Where a Pugh clause is not specifically limited to vertical severance, should the clause be construed as intending both vertical and horizontal severance? Compare Rogers v. Westhoma Oil Co., 291 F.2d 726 (10th Cir.Kan.1961) and Rist v. Westho- ma Oil Co., 385 P.2d 791 (Okla.1963), which construed the same clause and reached opposite conclusions.

Some compulsory pooling statutes also contain Pugh-like provisions. The Model Oil and Gas Conservation Act promulgated by the Interstate Oil and Gas Compact Commission in 2004 provides in § 10 that:

> (h) In case of a spacing unit of [one hundred sixty (160) acres] or more, no oil and gas leasehold interest outside the spacing unit involved may be held by production from the spacing unit more than [ninety (90) days] beyond the expiration of the primary term of the lease.

See also Miss.Code § 53–3–111, Okla.Stat.Ann. tit. 52, § 87.1(b); N.D.Cent.Code 38–08–09.8; Ark. Code Ann. § 15–73–201 (Mich.1987).

(c) Retained–Acreage Clauses

Pugh clauses operate only where there is a pooling. A retained- acreage clause, sometimes called a *continuous-development* clause, is broader. It divides a lease as drilling or proration units are formed, with the result that production from one unit propels the lease into the secondary term only as to land within the productive unit. A combination Pugh and retained-acreage provision follows:

> Notwithstanding any other provisions herein, upon the pooling of part of the leased premises or the completion of a producing well thereon this lease shall be severed and shall be considered as separate and distinct leases on (a) the pooled acreage or on the tract comprising the drilling unit for such well and (b) the rest of the leased premises; such severance shall result each time, and from time to time, whenever pooling occurs or any producing well is completed; and the term of each resulting lease caused by any such severance, and all the rights and obligations of Lessee under each such lease, shall apply separately to the acreage attributable to the particular lease under the foregoing severance, with every resulting lease being considered as separate and independent from every other lease.

This clause, which can also be drafted to divide the lease horizontally, operates independently of any pooling, and essentially is a modification of the secondary term of the habendum clause.

In Federal Land Bank of Spokane v. Texaco, Inc., 820 P.2d 1269 (Mont.1991), the Montana Supreme Court called the following provision a Pugh clause, but construed it as a retained-acreage clause:

> Should any of the lands hereunder be included in a unit or units, during the primary term, either by written consent of the lessor or as the result of action by any duly authorized authority having jurisdiction thereof, then operations or production from a well situated on lands embraced in such unit, shall serve to maintain this lease in force as to that portion of the leased premises embraced in such a unit, but shall not so maintain the lease on the remainder of the leased premises not embraced in such a unit and not otherwise maintained under the terms hereof * * *.

The clause was contained in its own numbered paragraph in a lease that covered 1,580 acres. Texaco, assignee of the original lessee, drilled a well on the premises and designated a 320 acre portion of the leased premises as the "spacing [drilling] unit" for the well, and the Montana Oil and Gas Conservation Board established 320 acre "drilling and spacing units" for the field. No pooling occurred because the drilling unit for Texaco's well consisted entirely of acreage embraced in the lease from the Federal Land Bank. The court held that the "Pugh clause * * * terminates the lease as to lands not embraced in a producing oil and gas [drilling and spacing] unit."

Pugh clauses and retained-acreage provisions are often inartfully drafted because they are commonly added to a printed lease form when a lease is negotiated. Consider the following clause:

Notwithstanding any provisions in this lease to the contrary, it is understood and agreed that this lease shall not (repeat not) extend beyond the primary term as to any part of the acreage described therein, excepting that part of the acreage which is then (at the end of the primary term) pooled or unitized for drilling, reworking operations, or production of oil and/or gas from such unit or units then (at the end of the primary term) formed by the LESSEE * * *.

In SMK Energy Corp. v. Westchester Gas Co., 705 S.W.2d 174 (Tex.App. 1985), the court construed this clause as a retained-acreage clause by holding implicitly that the lease would hold by production only the acreage that had been placed in some kind of unit, such as a drilling or proration unit. The lessee had argued that the clause was a Pugh clause that operated only in the event leased acreage was pooled or unitized with other lands.

E. ROYALTY PAYMENTS

1. GENERAL PRINCIPLES

Royalty is a major inducement for a wide variety of transactions in the oil and gas industry.[20] Mineral owners grant leases for a *landowner's royalty*, typically 1/8 to 1/3, and a cash bonus. Lessees assign leases to others for an *overriding royalty*, typically 1/32 to 1/16. Landowners often reserve a *nonparticipating royalty*, often 1/16, when they transfer land. In each situation the royalty owner hopes that oil and gas will be discovered and produced in the future so that the owner will receive royalty, measured as a percentage of production or its proceeds or value, free of costs of production.

---

20. Royalty comes to the oil and gas industry from the feudal system in England, where the term "royalty" was developed to distinguish the share of production reserved by the Crown from the production rights of those granted the right to work mines and quarries. "Royalty" was also used in feudal England in the context of landlord/tenant relations. Feudal lords received title to land directly from the Crown as a reward for services and on the condition that they would render future services. The lords in turn permitted their tenants to cultivate the land in return for a share of the products of the tenants' efforts. Feudal tenants held only a "working interest" in land, producing crops at their own labor and expense. The share of the products given to landlords by tenants was termed "royalty" since it was the portion accruing to the landowners as a result of the royal grant or favor. Taylor v. Peck, 116 N.E.2d 417, 418 (1953).

The civil law embodied a similar concept. Spanish law recognized the *dominio radical*, literally the "root ownership," the King's ownership of minerals contained in the soil of the lands of his subjects. The King's right derived from the Mining Ordinance of 1783, which listed royal minerals and set forth a procedure by which subjects could produce them. The ordinance authorized a miner's royalty to the King, the *derecho del quinto* ("the tax of the fifth part").

The form of a grant of the right to develop minerals, with a concomitant royalty to the mineral owner, evolved over the years for natural resources development generally. Modern U.S. oil and gas leases derived from forms used in the manufacture of salt from brine water, which in turn developed from solid minerals mining leases. For further discussion, see generally Leslie Moses, The Evolution and Development of the Oil and Gas Lease, 2 Inst. on Oil & Gas L. & Tax'n 1 (1951); John S. Lowe, Defining the Royalty Obligation, 49 SMU L.J. 223 (1996); and Owen L. Anderson, Royalty Valuation: Should Royalty Obligations Be Determined Intrinsically, Theoretically, Or Realistically? Part 1 (Why All The Fuss? What Does History Reveal?), 37 Nat.Res.L.J. 547 (1997). For a critique of one court's use of this historical information to resolve a royalty dispute see David E. Pierce, Defining the Role of Industry Custom and Usage in Oil & Gas Litigation, 57 SMU L. Rev. 387, 413–18 (2004).

A royalty is a hedge against the uncertainty of production. When parties can determine with certainty the quantity and value of things that they wish to buy or sell, they probably will fix a lump sum or a unit price. In the case of oil and gas, however, the existence of the substance—let alone the quantity, the quality, or its value—is uncertain. Common practice in the oil and gas industry, therefore, is that a part—perhaps the major part—of the compensation of those who contribute to the structure of exploration or development ventures is in the form of a *royalty*, a portion of production or its proceeds or value that is delivered or paid free of the costs of production. If production is prolific, the royalty owner benefits more than if production is slight.

The *landowner's royalty*, the most common kind of royalty, is provided by the oil and gas lease royalty clause. Typically, a lease royalty clause has separate provisions for oil and for gas. The provisions of the oil royalty clause usually assume that the oil royalty will be paid in kind by delivery to the lessor at the storage tanks.[21] On the other hand, the gas royalty clause is drafted so that the lessee disposes of production and then compensates the lessor, usually by check. The differences in the structure of the oil royalty clause and the gas royalty clause stem from the physical differences between oil and gas. Oil can be temporarily stored at or near the well and sold by the truckload. Natural gas, however, cannot be economically stored and must be delivered as it is sold into a pipeline.

Without royalty, a lessee would have to pay more for a lease. From a lessee's view, the money saved by offering royalty on potential future production is money that can be spent to buy more leases or to explore. From a lessor's perspective, the typical lessor prefers not to pass up the chance of profiting from production, which profits could be many times more than the money the lessee would be willing to pay for a lease without royalty. Note, however, that royalty puts the interests of lessors and lessees into conflict. As Judge Posner has observed:

> [A] conflict of interest is built into any royalty arrangement, or any other arrangement in which one party to a contract receives a percentage of gross revenues. The Finleys were entitled to one-sixth of all oil produced under the lease, and this was the equivalent of a 16.67 percent royalty on the gross revenues (minus selling costs) from the sale of all the oil. It was a matter of indifference to them, but intense interest to Marathon, how much the oil cost to produce. Suppose the oil had a value of 100, and cost 90 to produce. Production would then be profitable from the standpoint of the property as a whole and of course from the Finleys' standpoint. But Marathon would lose money because it would bear the entire cost and that cost (90) would exceed its share of the revenues (83.33). A similar conflict is created by royalty arrangements between publishers and authors and by contingent-fee contracts.

---

21. In fact, lessors rarely take actual possession of in-kind royalty. Rather, lessors sell their royalty using a "division order," which we will discuss below at Chapter 3.E.4.

Finley v. Marathon Oil Company, 75 F.3d 1225, 1230 (7th Cir.Ill.1996). Can you devise a compensation device that would avoid or mitigate the conflict of interest? In international transactions, the major compensation for host governments is often a net profits interest. Consider what are the advantages or disadvantages of net profits interests compared to royalties?

Because royalties are an important part of the lessor's compensation and a substantial cost to the lessee, they are the subject of many disputes. Royalty litigation has soared since federal price regulation was lifted in the 1980s.[22] The cases and notes that follow illustrate some common problems.

2. THE EXPRESS LEASE ROYALTY OBLIGATION

Lease royalty formulations are often similar to the following:

The royalties to be paid by Lessee are as follows: On oil, one-eighth of that produced and saved from said land, the same to be delivered at the wells or to the credit of Lessor into the pipe line to which the wells may be connected. Lessee shall have the option to purchase any royalty oil in its possession, paying the market price therefore prevailing for the field where produced on the date of purchase. On gas, including casinghead gas, condensate or other gaseous substances, produced from said land and sold or used off the premises or for the extraction of gasoline or other products therefrom, the market value at the well of one-eighth of the gas so sold or used, provided that on gas sold at the wells the royalty shall be one-eighth of the amount realized from such sale.

Not surprisingly, it is the "cash royalty" provisions that are usually the focus of disputes. While lessors and lessees may disagree about the measurement of "in kind" royalty, disputes are much more likely where royalty must be calculated based upon a hypothetical "market value" or by working back from the proceeds of a downstream sale price. The restructuring of the marketplace that occurred when oil and gas markets were deregulated in the 1980s exacerbated the situation, because it resulted in the development of market centers or "hubs" that may be many miles away from the lease.

One of the most widely litigated and expensive issues of the oil and gas industry during the 1970s and early 1980s was the meaning of "market value" in lease royalty clauses. Though falling gas prices and the end of federal gas price regulation in the mid–1980s quieted the disputes, the market value royalty issue remains a serious potential source of litigation under long-term contracts, and the law made in earlier litigation may have a bearing upon the resolution of apparently unrelated disputes. Professor Pierce discusses post-deregulation royalty issues in David E.

---

22. Some have suggested that the roots of the increase in royalty litigation rest in federal tax legislation in 1974 which lowered the percentage depletion allowance and tightened its limitations. Can you see a possible connection?

Pierce, Royalty Calculation in a Restructured Gas Market, 13 E. Min. L. Inst. 18–1 (1992), and David E. Pierce, The Royalty Value Theorem and the Legal Calculus of Post–Extraction Costs, 23 Energy & Min. L. Inst. 151 (2002).

The market value disputes arose from the language of lease royalty clauses that appear to distinguish between "market value" and "amount realized" as the basis for royalty calculation. For example, consider the language of the royalty clause quoted above:

> The royalties to be paid by Lessee are as follows: * * * *on gas* * * * produced and sold or used *off the premises* * * * the *market value at the well* of one-eighth of the gas so sold or used, provided that on gas sold *at the wells* the royalty shall be one-eighth of the *amount realized* from such sale.

(Emphasis added). The alternative bases for royalty calculation resulted in disputes, such as in the following case, over whether "market value" might exceed the "amount realized" from a sale when the lessee sold natural gas at a dedicated long-term contract price different from the current market price, a common occurrence during the 1970s and 1980s, when a combination of market forces and government regulation caused new gas contract prices to escalate faster than regulated long-term contract price adjustments.

PINEY WOODS COUNTRY LIFE SCHOOL v. SHELL OIL CO.

726 F.2d 225 (5th Cir.Miss.1984).

WISDOM, CIRCUIT JUDGE:

This case concerns the interpretation of royalty clauses in certain Mississippi oil and gas leases. The plaintiffs are the owners of mineral rights in the Thomasville, Piney Woods, and Southwest Piney Woods fields in Rankin County, Mississippi. They leased their rights to defendant Shell Oil Company through various conveyances beginning in the mid–1960s. The cause of this controversy, as in many similar suits across the country, was the unforeseen and unprecedented rise in natural gas prices brought on principally by the actions of the Organization of Petroleum Exporting Countries (OPEC) in the early 1970s. Unfortunately for both the plaintiff lessors and lessee Shell, Shell had already committed the gas for sale under long-term contracts at pre-OPEC prices. Unsurprisingly, the lessors brought this class action to recover royalties that they allege Shell owes and has not paid. The district court found for Shell, except on one relatively minor issue, and certified this appeal so that the questions of liability could be decided before the determination of damages. We affirm in part, reverse in part, and remand.

I. Facts

[Shell leased lands in Mississippi during the 1960s, using lease forms with royalty clauses similar to the clause quoted above and then drilled and completed gas wells.]

The gas from these fields is "sour"—it contains hydrogen sulfide. Before the gas can be put into the mainstream of commerce it must be processed. Rather than attempt to find someone to process the gas, Shell decided to do the processing itself. At its Thomasville plant, Shell treats the sour gas from the wells and recovers "sweet gas"—dry methane—and elemental sulfur.

Shell began efforts to market the gas from these fields in 1970. Shell sought buyers on the intrastate market because it wished to avoid restrictive federal regulations on interstate sales. See 15 U.S.C. §§ 717–717z (1982); 42 U.S.C. § 6399 (1976). After extensive negotiations with several potential buyers, Shell contracted with MisCoa, of Yazoo City, Mississippi, to sell up to 46,667 thousand cubic feet (Mcf) a day to MisCoa for 53 cents per Mcf, with an increase to 54.59 cents after 15 million Mcf were delivered, and price escalation of three percent a year thereafter. On May 23, 1972, Shell contracted to sell excess gas to Mississippi Power and Light (MP & L) for 45 cents per Mcf, with escalation of one percent a year. Both contracts appear to have been the best available at the time. Both contracts provide that title to the gas passes in the field, when the gas is still sour. But in fact the buyer does not take control of the gas until it is processed and "redelivered". In the MisCoa contract, the measurements of quality and quantity that determine how much MisCoa pays are not made until the gas is "redelivered", as sweet gas, in Yazoo City. The MP & L contract provides for "redelivery" near the Thomasville plant. Both contracts state that the sale price includes "substantial consideration" for Shell's agreement to gather and process the gas and, in MisCoa's case, to assume the risk of loss during transportation to Yazoo City. Apparently, the parties agreed that title would pass at the wells so that the parties could avoid state regulations on pipelines. But the passage of title at the wells is also relevant to the royalty clauses in Shell's leases. Because the gas is supposedly sold "at the wells", Shell has paid royalties based on the actual revenues received from its sales of sweet gas and sulfur, rather than on market value. Shell deducts from these royalties a substantial portion of the costs of processing the gas.

The lessors filed this class action on December 27, 1974, alleging that Shell computed royalty payments improperly. The case was tried without a jury in November and December 1979. On May 3, 1982, the court issued its findings of fact and conclusions of law. The court found that Shell properly deducted the costs of processing from the royalty payments and properly based royalties for gas sold on the actual revenues realized. * * *

Upon the plaintiffs' motion the court issued a final judgment on the claims decided, and certified the case for appeal under Federal Rule of Civil Procedure 54(b).

* * *

[The court first held that term "at the well" referred to gas in its natural state, before processing or transportation, rather than the point of sale, so that the gas Shell had sold was not "sold at the well" within the meaning of the lease royalty clauses. The "market value" portion of the royalty clause controlled.]

V. The Meaning of Market Value

* * *

The meaning of "market value" has been at the fore of lease litigation ever since the price of gas began to increase at a rate much faster than the price escalation clauses of existing gas contracts contemplated. As long as the price of gas increased at a rate substantially equivalent to the inflation rates provided in sale contracts, it made little difference whether current market value or actual proceeds formed the basis of royalty payments: the check to the lessor was the same. But when the price of gas began to rise much faster than anticipated, this distinction became of the utmost moment to lessors and lessees.

Until the 1970s the authority was clear that "market value" referred to market value at the time of production and delivery rather than when the applicable sale contract was made. *See, e.g., Wall v. United Gas Public Service Co.,* 1934, 178 La. 908, 913, 152 So. 561, 563; *Foster v. Atlantic Refining Co.,* 5 Cir.1964, 329 F.2d 485, 489–90 (Texas law); *Texas Oil & Gas Corp. v. Vela,* 1968, Tex., 429 S.W.2d 866. This rule has been upheld more recently in, *e.g., Lightcap v. Mobil Oil Co.,* 1977, 221 Kan. 448, 562 P.2d 1, 11; *Montana Power Co. v. Kravik,* 1978, 179 Mont. 87, 586 P.2d 298, 302; *Exxon Corp. v. Middleton,* 1981, Tex., 613 S.W.2d 240, 244–45. This line on cases, to which we refer as the *Vela* rule, was uncontradicted until very recently. A recent line of cases, however, holds that "market value" is equivalent to the price assigned in the sale contract, at least as long as that contract was made prudently and in good faith. The first case so to hold was *Tara Petroleum Corp. v. Hughey,* 1981, Okla., 630 P.2d 1269. *Tara* has been followed in *Hillard v. Stephens,* 1982, 276 Ark. 545, 637 S.W.2d 581, 583, and *Henry v. Ballard & Cordell Corp.,* 1982, La., 418 So.2d 1334.

The *Vela* rule is based principally on the doctrine that a gas sale contract is only executory until the gas is delivered, Martin v. Amis, 1926, Tex.Com.App., 288 S.W. 431, 433, and on the premise that the distinction made by the lease between market value and amount realized is meaningless under the *Tara* rule. *Tara,* on the other hand, found the *Vela* rule unfair because, when prices are rising, the *Vela* rule requires the lessee to pay the lessor an increasing percentage of the total revenues.

* * *

We fully agree with the district court's conclusions that a gas sale contract is executory and that the sale is executed only upon production and delivery. Under section 75–2–105 of the Mississippi Code the gas underground is future goods; no particular gas is sold until it is identified—i.e., brought to the surface. The sale contracts are not transfers of an interest in land; accordingly, under section 75–2–107(1) the contracts are contracts to sell and only become effective as sales when the gas is severed from the land. The logic of these provisions is clear. Under the leases, Shell has a *defeasible* interest in the gas underground. The most it could sell MisCoa or MP & L is that same defeasible interest: in effect, the right to possession of the gas if it is produced before Shell's lease terminates. The leases may terminate if Shell breaches implied or express covenants or if there is a cessation of production after the expiration of the primary term of the lease. If the leases terminate, Shell would no longer have the power to deliver title to the gas. MisCoa might be able to sue Shell for a breach of *contract to sell,* but it would have no claim to the gas itself or to specific performance of the contract, because all title to the gas would have reverted to the lessors. Shell could not "sell" the gas to MisCoa, because a "sale" consists in the passing of title, id. § 75–2–106.

We therefore conclude that the gas was not sold until it was produced. The sale contract itself provides that title passes when the gas is delivered. Accordingly, the basis of royalty should be "market value at the well" at the time of production and delivery, as the district court held.

We also find the district court's decision supported on other grounds. First, the explicit language of the leases distinguishes between gas sold at the well and gas sold off the lease, and between amount realized and market value. The *Tara* rule eliminates the differences: the lessor receives a royalty based on amount realized no matter where and in what form the gas is sold. * * *

Moreover, Shell and those from whom it received leases by assignment were or should have been aware that "market value" had been held to mean value at the time of production both in old cases like *Wall* and in new cases like *Foster* and *Vela*. * * * Though not binding on Mississippi lessees, these decisions were widely discussed in the industry and should have alerted the lessees to the potential legal effect of the royalty clause. Shell certainly had ample opportunity to change the language if in fact it intended a "proceeds" lease. It has long been doctrine that mineral leases are construed against the lessee and in favor of the lessor. But our decision that market value means value rather than proceeds is not simply an instance of interpretation against the lessee. It is rather a holding that, although the royalty clauses might have been less than lucid to laymen, they were quite readily understandable to those in the industry. Shell knew what a "market value" lease was and what a "proceeds" lease was. See *Lightcap v. Mobil Oil Corp.*, 1977, 221 Kan. 448, 457, 562 P.2d 1, 8; *Hillard v. Stephens*, 1982, Ark., 637 S.W.2d 581, 587 (Hickman, J., dissenting). Shell "cannot expect the court to rewrite the lease to [its] satisfaction". *Foster*, 329 F.2d at 490.[1]

---

1. For the same reason we reject the argument, accepted in Henry, 418 So.2d at 1338, that the "ultimate objective of the royalty provisions of a lease is to fix the division between the lessor and lessee of the economic benefits anticipated from the development of the minerals." If the purpose were to fix royalty at a permanent percentage of lessees' profits, the lessee could certainly devise language to say so. We hold to the contrary that the market value clause serves in part to protect the lessor from bad bargains by the lessee.

Shell asserts that "[r]oyalty payments based upon good faith contract prices have always been the custom in Mississippi". * * * The district court did not make a finding to this effect and we doubt its universal truth. * * *This allegation of "custom" is of course self-serving. The payment of royalties is controlled by lessees, and lessors have no ready means of ascertaining current market value other than to take lessees' word for it. See M. Merrill, *Covenants Implied in Oil and Gas Leases* 216 (2d ed. 1940). The formula for determining royalty and the statements issued to lessors may be, as in this case, complex; it is likely that many lessors have never known just what basis lessees were using. For a practice to be legally relevant custom, both parties to the contract must have actual or presumed knowledge of the practice. Those not engaged in an industry will not be presumed to know that words which have common meanings outside the industry have a different meaning inside it. Market value in these leases is most easily understood to mean current value: the lessors cannot be presumed to know that Shell and other producers made a practice of basing their royalty payments on a different criterion. We will not find "custom" binding on lessors from a practice within the control and understanding only of the lessees.

The most important rationale underlying the *Tara* rule is the concern that it is unfair to require the lessee to pay increasing royalties out of a constant stream of revenues. The reasoning is as follows: the lessee has a duty to market the gas; gas is customarily sold in long-term contracts; the lessee is thus forced by his duty to the lessor to enter into a long-term contract but then sees his profits whittled away as the market price of gas rises. *See Tara*, 630 P.2d at 1273. The *Tara* court reasoned further that its rule was not unfair to lessors, because they still receive royalties and are protected by the lessee's obligation to make a reasonable sale contract. *Id.* at 1274.

We appreciate that a lessee may find itself economically disadvantaged when its royalty obligations increase while its sale revenues remain constant. But this is no more than the risk assumed by every business venturer who undertakes the role of middleman. In this case it appears that Shell chose to market its gas to MisCoa at an initial price higher than any previously negotiated in the United States, but with a low annual escalation rate. Shell might instead have accepted a lower initial price but reserved the opportunity to redetermine the price at later intervals. Transcript at 1658–72. The district court held that Shell's decision was not a breach of the lease-created covenant to market, since the choice of the MisCoa contract was a prudent and reasonable one. But prudence does not relieve Shell of its obligations under the lease. To say that the gas contract was what a "prudent operator" would have negotiated under the circumstances begs the question. The question is whether the operator should be saved from loss of profits simply because it acted prudently and the world economy acted adversely. If Congress or the Mississippi legislature wishes, it may establish a relief fund or create tax credits to assist the unfortunate lessees. It is not the function of the courts, construing and enforcing contracts under state law, to intervene on behalf of producers experienced in the petroleum industry, and thereby deprive lessors of their legitimate contractual expectations. "Stripped of all its trimmings [the "fairness" argument] is simply: We cannot comply. This is no answer * * *. The fact that the ascertainment of future market price may be troublesome or that the royalty provisions are improvident and result in a financial loss to [the lessee] 'is not a web of the Court's weaving.' " *Foster*, 329 F.2d at 490 (footnote omitted).

We conclude that the *Tara* rule is unfair to lessors. A landowner may decide to accept a royalty based on a smaller fractional share of market value, rather than to hold out for a larger share of proceeds, because of an expectation that the market value will rise. If the courts then intervene and declare that "market value" is the same as "proceeds", this expectation is destroyed. Moreover, the lessor has no means with which to persuade the lessee to renegotiate the lease to reflect the changed legal rule. This is illustrated by the following hypothetical. A landowner is offered leases by two producers. The first offers a 1/8 market value royalty; the second offers a 1/6 proceeds royalty. The landowner decides to lease to the first operator, because he thinks the market value of gas will rise enough to compensate for the lower fractional share. This is a business risk: if the price does not rise enough, the lessor loses money. If, however, the price rises as the lessor thought, the lessor has won his bet, just as the lessee has lost his gamble that the price would not rise; and the lessor ought to profit. But if the *Tara* rule intervenes, it takes away the lessor's legitimate expectation of market value royalties without any compensation at all. The lessor would be frozen into 1/8 proceeds royalties on a long-term low-price sales contract made by his lessee.

By contrast, under the *Vela* rule, which we adopt, the lessor's royalties increase according to the provisions of the lease. At some point the lessee may find continued operation so unprofitable that it is more economical to cease production. At this point the lessor has a strong incentive to renegotiate the lease, because a cessation of production will mean the end of all royalties until another lessee can be found, and the present lessee has a comparative advantage over others in that it has the necessary facilities already in place. The lessee's buyers will have an incentive to renegotiate the sale contracts rather than seek new and more expensive sources of gas.

* * *

Accordingly, we affirm the district court's holding that market value means current market value at the time of production.

VI. Proof of Market Value

Max Powell, the plaintiffs' expert witness on the issue of market value, based his estimates of market value on the average of the top three prices for gas sold in seven counties that he had previously selected as a relevant market area. This technique is the same one that Powell used, and that the court approved without contest, in Butler v. Exxon Corp., 1977, Tex.Civ.App., 559 S.W.2d 410. It is similar to the method used in Exxon v. Middleton, 1981, Tex., 613 S.W.2d 240. The district court, however, found Powell's testimony unpersuasive. Shell challenged Powell's data on the ground that sales of sweet gas are not comparable with sales of sour gas. The district court rejected this argument, noting that the processing costs, which reflect the price of converting the sour gas to sweet gas, are deducted from royalty. But the court found Powell's data noncomparable because of "[t]he unprecedented volume, deliverability and reserves of production" in the Thomasville–Piney Woods fields. The court devised its own formula:

> "Once the relevant market area is defined and comparable sales are identified, the Court concludes that computation of market value should be made by the division of net sales receipts derived from sales of comparable gas (after necessary adjustments for variances in Btu content and compression changes) by the total volume sold."

The court made no findings on market value and directed the parties to consult the court for directions on further proof.

Although the district court did not certify this issue for appeal, the plaintiffs now ask us to order the district court to use Powell's method for determining market value on remand. This we decline to do. Market value is a question of fact, and it is up to the factfinder to determine the probative strength of relevant evidence. The plaintiffs contend that Powell's evidence was the only evidence on the issue, but the Shell–MisCoa contract, while not conclusive evidence of market value, was also plainly relevant to the issue. See E. Brown, The Law of Oil and Gas Leases § 6.09, at 6–66 to 6–67 (1983). The district court found that the sales used by Powell were made under conditions different enough to weaken their persuasiveness. The court was within its discretion to seek evidence of sales it considered more nearly "comparable".

A number of courts have struggled with the question of how to prove market value. See, e.g., Exxon v. Middleton, 1981, Tex., 613 S.W.2d 240; Montana Power Co. v. Kravik, 1978, 179 Mont. 87, 586 P.2d 298; Weymouth v. Colorado Interstate Gas Co., 5 Cir.1966, 367 F.2d 84. The only general rule that emerges from these cases is that the method of proof varies with the facts of each particular case. In determining market value at the well, the point is to determine the price a reasonable buyer would have paid for the gas at the well when produced. Comparable sales of gas at other wells may be used to do this. Another method is to use sales of processed gas and deduct processing costs. Yet another relevant measure is the one proposed by Shell, the actual sale price of the gas less costs. "This is the least desirable method of determining market price", Montana Power, 586 P.2d at 303–04, but its persuasiveness is a matter for the factfinder.

Completely comparable sales are not likely to be found.[2] Sales that have some different characteristics must be considered. "[O]bjections against uncomparable sales, irrelevancies and unreliable hearsay [go] to the weight which the [factfinder] ... should attach to the expert's opinion, and the protection to the other side as has always been true under our system [is] cross examination." Weymouth, 367 F.2d at 91. Especially when the court is factfinder, the court as well as counsel may question the expert opinions. But it should not dismiss fairly comparable sales out of hand because of certain incomparable qualities. The district court stated that there was a "lack of relevant evidence addressing comparability." The evidence produced by plaintiffs may, in the opinion of the court, have been insufficient, but it was plainly relevant. The plaintiffs produced evidence suggesting that, while some factors differentiate the Thomasville–Piney Woods wells from the wells upon which Powell based his data, those factors (abundance and availability) would increase, not decrease, the value of the plaintiffs' gas. It was, of course, for the court as factfinder to accord this testimony such weight as it saw fit, and to seek better information as well. We therefore reject the plaintiffs' request that on remand we mandate the use of the Powell formula as the exclusive measure of market value. But if, on remand, the search for better measures of market value at the well proves unsuccessful or inordinately burdensome, we think it the duty of the trier of fact to decide the question as best it can on the basis of the evidence that is presented. The plaintiffs must meet their burden of proof and produce sufficient relevant evidence to support their contentions. Having provided such evidence they should

---

2. Courts have identified a wide range of factors that may affect the price of natural gas. See, e.g., Hugoton Prod. Co. v. United States, 1963, 315 F.2d 868, 161 Ct.Cl. 274, listing the following relevant factors:

"(a) The volume available for sale. Generally the greater the volume or reserves, the greater the price the seller could command.

(b) The location of the leases or acreage involved, whether in a solid block or scattered, and their proximity to prospective buyers' pipelines.

(c) Quality of the gas as to freedom from hydrogen sulfide in excess of 1 grain per 100 cubic feet.

(d) Delivery point.

(e) Heating value of the gas.

(f) Deliverability of the wells. The larger the volume that could be delivered from a reserve, the greater the price the seller could command.

(g) Delivery or rock pressure. The higher the pressure, the less compression for transportation is required."

315 F.2d at 894–95. Exxon v. Middleton also contains a thorough discussion of the factors affecting market value, including the following: "Market value may be calculated by using comparable sales. Comparable sales of gas are those comparable in time, quality, quantity, and availability of marketing outlets. Sales comparable in time occur under contracts executed contemporaneously with the sale of the gas in question. Sales comparable in quality are those of similar physical properties such as sweet, sour, or casinghead gas. Quality also involves the legal characteristics of the gas; that is, whether it is sold in a regulated or unregulated market, or in one particular category of a regulated market. Sales comparable in quantity are those of similar volumes to the gas in question. To be comparable, the sales must be made from an area with marketing outlets similar to the gas in question. Gas from fields with outlets to interstate markets only, for instance, would not be comparable to gas from a field with outlets only to the intrastate market." 613 S.W.2d at 246–47.

not be faced with the impossible task of establishing market value with absolute certainty or perfection. It is Shell's responsibility to rebut the plaintiffs' evidence and provide evidence of its own to support its contentions. The decision is for the finder of fact, but the decision is made by balancing, not by erecting an insuperable barrier to relevant evidence.

* * *

NOTES

1.   As *Piney Woods* illustrates, one view (often called the *Vela* rule) is that "market value" is a "plain term" that must be given its usual meaning— the price a willing buyer and seller would agree upon at the time of production. Interpreting a royalty clause that called for royalty based upon the "market price at the wells," the court in Texas Oil & Gas Corp. v. Vela, 429 S.W.2d 866 (Tex.1968), made the classic statement of the analysis[23] in a five-to-four decision interpreting a lease that called for royalty to be based on "market price at the well:"

> [The parties to the lease] might have agreed that the royalty on gas produced from a gas well would be a fractional part of the amount realized by the lessee from its sale. Instead of doing so, however, they stipulated in *plain terms* that the lessee would pay one-eighth of the market price at the well of all gas sold or used off the premises. This clearly means the prevailing market price at the time of the sale or use.

Id. at 871 (emphasis added).

2.   The countervailing view is that "market value" is either ambiguous or is a term of art in the gas industry. Courts must therefore look beyond the four corners of the lease to the parties' intent, to implied covenants, or to fundamental fairness. Cases following this approach have concluded that the "market value" of gas is the long-term contract price set in a fair, arms-length contract, even though that price may be less than the current market price. As Judge Wisdom notes in *Piney Woods*, the leading statement of this line of reasoning is the Oklahoma Supreme Court's opinion in Tara Petroleum Corp. v. Hughey, 630 P.2d 1269 (Okla.1981), where the lease provided for royalties based upon "market price at the well":

> [c]onceding that competent parties should be held to their agreements even though improvident, the typical [royalty] clause ... seems to be freighted with inherent ambiguity when it is remembered that gas must be sold by long term contracts in which buyers have been able to obtain schedules of prices almost certain to get out of line with contemporary contracts * * *.

Id. at 1273. The Oklahoma Supreme Court relied upon the "well-known reality of the business" that the lessee has an implied covenant to market, the fundamental unfairness to producers of royalties based on a price higher than

---

23.   As the *Piney Woods* court notes, however, the first such decision came from the Fifth Circuit in Foster v. Atlantic Refining Co., 329 F.2d 485 (5th Cir.Tex.1964), where the lease provided that royalty was to be paid on "the market price therefor prevailing for the field where produced when run."

the contract price, and "the intent and understanding" of the parties to the lease. The court concluded that "'the ambiguity should be resolved in favor of the lessee as a matter of law, with inquiry restricted to whether the sale was a reasonable contract when made.'" 630 P.2d at 1274.

A Louisiana case, *Henry v. Ballard & Cordell Corp.*, 418 So.2d 1334 (La.1982), also treated "market value" as ambiguous because the parties to the lease had failed to state expressly whether "market value" means *current* "market value," Id. at 1337. Among the factors that the Louisiana court contended should be considered in resolving the ambiguity was the nature of the oil and gas lease as a "cooperative venture" between lessor and lessee in which "the lessor contributes the land and the lessee the capital and expertise necessary to develop the minerals for the mutual benefit of both parties," so that the parties "usually contemplate that the lessee will dispose of the gas (in a prudent manner) and pay the lessor the fractional part of the value which he is to enjoy from the enterprise." Id. at 1338 (citing Thomas A. Harrell, Developments in Non–Regulatory Oil & Gas Law, 30 Inst. on Oil & Gas L. & Tax'n 311, 334 (1979)).

The cooperative venture principle stated in *Henry* was an important, if unstated, premise of *Tara*, as well as *Hillard v. Stephens*, 637 S.W.2d 581 (Ark.1982). The view that "market value" cannot exceed the "amount realized" under the sales contract is based upon the implied covenant to market, which imposes upon the lessee the necessity of contracting at the market price available and, concomitantly, upon the lessor to accept royalty based upon that price. According to the Louisiana Supreme Court, it is the cooperative nature of the lease that gives rise to the implied covenant to market.

Professor Pierce offers his view of the "cooperative venture" concept as follows:

> When defining basic lease obligations, the parties are not concerned with "cooperation"; they are concerned with domination. The lessee wants to deduct the costs it incurs to move gas to a downstream marketing point; the lessor wants royalty calculated on the downstream value without any deduction of costs. "Cooperation" in this context means deciding that money must be taken from one party and given to the other. Who will be the first to "cooperate" in this situation? Which party should be forced to "cooperate" by the court? In the marketing context, cooperation would seem to function more as a justification for a "fairness" analysis than a viable interpretive tool. The concept of cooperation fails to acknowledge the basic conflicting interests of the lessor and lessee and that in most cases they will be competing to ensure the lease is interpreted to selfishly promote their individual economic interests.

David E. Pierce, Exploring the Jurisprudential Underpinnings of the Implied Covenant to Market, 48 Rocky Mtn. Min. L. Inst. 10–1, 10–29 to 10–30 (2002).

3. Which approach to the meaning of "market value" do you think is more appropriate—that market value is the value of the gas when produced and sold (the *Vela* or Texas rule), or that it is the proceeds of sale, if the sales contract is made prudently and in good faith (the *Tara* or Oklahoma rule)? If a lessor is entitled to a market value royalty when market value is higher than the proceeds of sale, is a lessor bound to accept a market value royalty

when market value is less than the price for which gas is sold? What if "market value" is less than the contract price? In Yzaguirre v. KCS Resources, Inc., 53 S.W.3d 368 (Tex.2001), the court rejected the royalty owners' argument that an implied covenant to market imposed an obligation on a lessee with an express "market value" royalty clause to pay royalties on a higher contract price.

What of changed circumstances? Is there a difference in the meaning of "market value" in states that follow *Vela* and in states that follow *Tara* when long-term gas sales contracts are no longer the norm, as became the case in the late 1980s? In Howell v. Texaco Exploration and Production, Inc., 112 P.3d 1154, 1160 (Okla. 2004), relying on *Tara* but without mentioning an implied covenant, the court concluded that "a royalty owner has a right to be paid on the best price available. * * * Whenever a producer is paying royalty based on one price but it is selling the gas for a higher price, the royalty owners are entitled to have their payments calculated based on the higher price."

4. What do you suppose the drafter of the lease at issue in *Piney Woods* had in mind when he or she used both the terms "market value at the well" and "amount realized" in the royalty clause? Professor Lowe commented as follows:

From the viewpoint of the oil and gas industry, the two terms usually meant the same thing. The market price or market value of gas from a particular well was the price that a willing buyer would pay a willing seller for that gas. Since economic regulation and the custom of the gas industry dictated that gas be sold under long-term gas contracts, the market value or market price at the well of gas from a particular well was the amount realized under the terms of a long-term gas contract entered into on the date of the first sale of gas at the wellhead. Where gas was sold off the premises, market value or market price at the well might well be less than the proceeds of the sale because the transportation or processing of the gas might substantially increase its value or add to its cost. Thus the market value or market price of gas at the wellhead might be the same or less than the proceeds or amount realized from sale but could never be greater than the proceeds or the amount realized.

John S. Lowe, Developments in Nonregulatory Oil & Gas Law, 32 Inst. on Oil & Gas L. & Tax'n 117, 146–47 (1981). By this view, the purpose of the contrasting use of "market value at the well" and "amount realized" in the royalty clause was to establish the right of the lessee to (1) keep all benefits of any increase in value of the gas resulting from a sale off the premises rather than at the well and (2) deduct from the lessor's royalty share costs such as transportation and cleaning, where gas was sold off the lease. The *Piney Woods* court rejected that analysis in a portion of the decision that we have omitted.

5. If current value at the well, or "market value," rather than amount realized at the well, is the appropriate royalty measure, how can a court establish what is market value from time to time?

Under the *Piney Woods* approach, "Market value is a question of fact * * *. [T]he point is to determine the price a reasonable buyer would have paid * * * at the well when produced." *Piney Woods*, 726 F.2d at 238–39. And the hierarchy of the methods to determine "market value" is intuitive. Market value is what a willing buyer and willing seller would agree upon under the circumstances. Where gas is actually sold at the wellhead as it is produced in a transaction negotiated at the time of sale, all elements of the definition and the transaction are in congruity unless the sale is not at arm's length or the parties act unreasonably; thus, an actual sale at the wellhead is the best evidence of value. Comparable sales illustrate an available market and are strong evidence of value where there are no actual sales. The circumstances of comparable sales, however, will never be completely the same as the circumstances at the wellhead. The work-back method is the hardest valuation method to use accurately because it begins furthest from the wellhead, so there are likely to be more variables to consider. But the work-back method "can be just as accurate as any other method * * *." Ashland Oil, Inc. v. Phillips Petroleum Co., 554 F.2d 381, 387 (10th Cir.1975).

Courts have had difficulty deciding what evidence is relevant to "value." One issue, during the time that gas prices at the wellhead were federally regulated, was whether a court could consider sales of gas of one regulatory classification in determining the market value of gas in another regulatory classification. Contrast First National Bank in Weatherford v. Exxon Corp., 622 S.W.2d 80 (Tex.1981) (whether quality is comparable requires consideration of the legal characteristics of gas) with Lightcap v. Mobil Oil Corp., 562 P.2d 1 (Kan.1977) ("market value" is independent of price regulation). Another issue has been whether a judge or jury can consider an existing long-term contract in determining current market value. When *Piney Woods* was retried, the district court held that the royalty owners had failed to establish that the market value of the gas in question was at any time greater than the amount that Shell received under its sales contract and determined value by working back from Shell's contract price. The court of appeals held that reliance on the contract price was "within its discretion." Piney Woods Country Life Sch. v. Shell Oil Co., 905 F.2d 840, 845 (5th Cir.Miss.1990). When the relevance of a long-term contract to current market value was challenged in Yzaguirre v. KCS Resources, Inc., 53 S.W.3d 368 (Tex.2001), however, the court said:

> According to the 1979 GPA, Tennessee was obligated to purchase KCS's gas at an ever-escalating price, regardless of its value on the open market. The gas was not free and available for sale, and its price was negotiated in 1979, not contemporaneously with the deliveries. Under these circumstances, the GPA price is not evidence of market value, and the trial judge properly excluded it.

53 S.W.3d at 374–375. Can both the Fifth Circuit and the Texas Supreme Court be right?

The work-back method of royalty payment has become increasingly common, because deregulation of the gas industry in the mid–1980s resulted in the development of downstream market centers or "hubs" at which "packages" of production can be marketed or transported. Today, producers can sell natural gas in the field, at market hubs, "at the burner tip," or anywhere in between. And most sales are on a short term—often a monthly—

basis. Some oil companies routinely pay royalty based upon the price for which they sell gas, adjusted for costs of transportation and marketing, whether they are administering "market value" or "amount realized" royalty clauses. Others determine "market value" by starting with a current "index" price or an average price at a market hub. Still others attempt to determine the price in the field where the production occurs or use a combination of devices. If sales are generally made under short-term contracts, is there any practical difference in the meaning of "market value" among the states?

In the almost-free-gas markets of the 21st Century what is appropriate evidence of market value? Is it current short-term or "spot" sales? Or should a trier-of-fact consider longer-term contracts too?

6. When royalty clauses are bifurcated, as they often are, it may be difficult to determine whether the "amount realized" or "market value" provisions apply. In *Piney Woods*, above, the Fifth Circuit Court of Appeals reasoned that "amount realized" applied only where the sale at the wells was of gas in its natural state, before processing or transportation. Where title to gas passed on the lease but the gas was then transported by a pipeline and redelivered to the producer for processing before final sale, the gas is "sold . . . off the premises" and market-value royalties are due. But the Texas Supreme Court in Exxon v. Middleton, 613 S.W.2d 240 (Tex.1981), took a more literal view. Exxon and Sun Oil Company gathered natural gas from leases in the Anahuac field near Houston, processed the natural gas at an Exxon-owned cleaning plant located on one of the leases in the field, and then sold the gas "at the tailgate" of the plant under a long-term low-priced contract. The royalty clause of the Middleton's lease was similar to the one quoted at the beginning of this section and at issue in *Piney Woods*. Reasoning that it must give effect to the plain language, the Texas Supreme Court upheld the lessors' contention that because the point of sale of the natural gas was off the leased premises they were entitled to royalties on the higher "market value" price. See also Occidental Permian Ltd. v. The Helen Jones Foundation, 333 S.W.3d 392 (Tex.App.2011), holding that lessors due royalty on the amount realized from sales "at the well" were entitled only to royalty on proceeds received from a percentage-of-proceeds contract with a processing plant that the lessee owned.

7. "Amount realized" royalty provisions became the subject of disputes analogous to the "market value" litigation ten years after the *Piney Woods* decision. The issue was whether gas contract take-or-pay benefits were part of the "amount realized" by producers for the sale of gas.[24] Courts generally

---

24. Royalty on take-or-pay disputes arose because the supply shortages that caused rapidly-rising prices for natural gas in the 1970s led some pipelines to compete for additional supply by offering to take or pay for high percentages of well delivery capacity; federal price regulation barred price competition, but not "take" competition. A take-or-pay clause might be very simply worded:

"Subject to all the other provisions of this Contract, Seller agrees to sell and deliver and Pipeline agrees to purchase and receive, or pay for if made available hereunder but not taken, a daily contract quantity of gas . . . equal to seventy-five percent (75%) of the maximum quantity of gas that Seller's wells can deliver to Pipeline."

Contract take-or-pay percentages increased from as low as twenty-five percent in the early 1970s to as much as ninety percent at the height of the gas boom of the late 1970s and early 1980s. When gas demand in the United States declined sharply, however, the gas boom became a

decided those disputes by applying the same analytical approaches that they had used in considering the meaning of "market value."[25]

The royalty on take-or-pay benefits litigation resulted in two lines of cases. One line held that "production" is the prerequisite for royalty, and that take-or-pay benefits were not generally subject to royalty because they were in lieu of production. The premise of those cases was that the lease royalty clause expresses the "plain meaning" of the parties and "production" or "sale"—the terms usually found in the royalty clause—should be given their usual meaning, just as was "market value"—so that royalty was not due on take-or-pay payments or settlements, except to the extent that they related to gas actually produced. The countervailing line of cases held that royalty was due on take-or-pay benefits because the lease royalty clause is but a statement of the general expectations of the parties. A lessor and a lessee are parties to a "cooperative venture," and if the lessee develops the minerals successfully, the lessor should share proportionately in all the benefits. Compare Diamond Shamrock Exploration Co. v. Hodel, 853 F.2d 1159 (5th Cir.1988) (dealing with federal oil and gas leases), State v. Pennzoil Co., 752 P.2d 975 (Wyo. 1988), TransAmerican Natural Gas Corp. v. Finkelstein, 933 S.W.2d 591 (Tex.App.1996); Roye Realty & Developing, Inc. v. Watson, 2 P.3d 320 (Okla.1996) and Harvey E. Yates Co. v. Powell, 98 F.3d 1222 (10th Cir.N.M. 1996), all holding that no royalty is due, with Frey v. Amoco Production Co., 603 So.2d 166 (La.1992) and Klein v. Jones, 980 F.2d 521 (8th Cir.Ark.1992), requiring that royalty be paid on take-or-pay benefits.

8. If a lease is a "cooperative venture," how far does the venture extend? Should a royalty owner share in the cash and overriding royalty that a lessee may receive for assigning the lease? What about payments indirectly associated with the sale of production? For example, gas sales contracts may provide for *producer demand charges*—monthly payments from purchasers to producers compensating the producers for committing to supply a stated amount of gas each month. Producers may receive a variety of marketing fees or "supply bonuses" from purchasers to induce them to make particular sales arrangements. Producers may receive money from a purchaser to buy or develop gas reserves, in return for a commitment to repay the amounts received when production occurs. And, producers routinely use investment devices such as hedges, trades and swaps of future production to minimize risks and generate current income. Are such receipts a part of the "amount realized" from the sale of production? See John S. Lowe, Defining the Royalty Obligation, 49 SMU L.Rev. 223, 264 (1996). Should such receipts be taken into account in determining "market value"?

9. Royalty formulations other than "market value" and "amount realized" are common, including "market price," "proceeds," "net proceeds," and "gross proceeds." Is "market price" different from "market value"? If so, how? Is "amount realized" different from "proceeds," "net proceeds," and "gross proceeds"? If so, how?

---

litigation boom. The total potential liability of interstate and intrastate pipelines was probably in the range of sixty to seventy billion dollars, and settlement costs were probably in the range of twelve to fifteen billion dollars.

25. The issue did not arise under a "market value" provision in a state like Mississippi or Texas. Can you see why?

3. IMPLIED LEASE COVENANTS THAT MAY AFFECT ROYALTY

Lessors' and lessees' interests coincide, because production benefits both. But their interests also conflict. The lease generally imposes upon the lessee all of the costs of exploring and producing, while the lessor's benefits are free and clear of such costs. Therefore, lessors and lessees often disagree about the need to spend money to explore or operate the lease. Because the typical oil and gas lease makes the lessor's royalty—the major compensation for grant of the lease—dependent upon the quantity and quality of the lessee's actions on the property, courts have been quick to conclude that the lessee has the obligation to perform certain unstated obligations, including production marketing, protection of the property against drainage, testing, reasonable development, and further exploration, even when the lease contains no specific provisions. See also Kuntz § 54.2, Hemingway § 8.1, Merrill § 1, and Lowe, Chapter 11.

One way of thinking about implied covenants is that American courts have "invented" a series of implied promises from lessees to protect lessors' interest in receiving royalty. The covenant to test assures that a lessee drills a well eventually so that royalty might result. The covenant to market ensures that royalty will be generated within a reasonable time and at an adequate price if the lessee finds oil or gas. The drainage covenant protects a lessor against loss of production that will generate royalty. The development covenant assures a full and timely royalty, if the lessee discovers oil or gas. Some courts recognize a covenant to explore further to assure that the lessee adequately tests a producing lease for additional production that might yield royalty. And some courts recognize a "catch-all" covenant that is intended to assure full and proper royalty by requiring the lessee to act diligently and prudently.

The theoretical underpinning for implied covenants is unclear. Commentators have engaged in lively debate about whether lease implied covenants such as the marketing covenant are implied in fact—i.e., predicated upon the intent of the parties—or implied at law—i.e., presumed from the relation of the parties and the object of the agreement. Consider the following statements:

> This implication [the duty to protect the lessor's interest] is based upon the thought that the prospective royalties constitute one of the primary inducements for the execution of the lease, and, since the lease makes the payment of this compensation to the lessor dependent upon the diligence and care with which operations are conducted by the lessee, the parties must have intended that these operations would be conducted with a reasonable regard for the interests of the lessor and not solely from the selfish standpoint of the lessee. If this is a correct interpretation of the theory of our cases the implication of these covenants is predicated upon the intention of the parties and is one of fact and not of law.

316   THE OIL AND GAS LEASE   **CH. 2**

A. W. Walker, "The Nature of the Property Interests Created by an Oil and Gas Lease in Texas," 11 Tex.L.Rev. 399, 404 (1933).

> The suggestion has been made * * * that the implied covenants are implied in fact rather than in law, that is, that the parties to the lease actually intend that these obligations shall attach to their relationship. While some judicial language may be cited in favor of the proposition, other language and the actual course of decision seem to be against this view. Thus in *Sauder v. Mid–Continent Petroleum Corporation,* the Supreme Court of the United States said that "a covenant on respondent's part to continue the work of exploration, development and production is to be implied *from the relation of the parties and the object of the lease * * *.*" The emphasized words stress the factors upon which the law seizes to impose the obligation. They say nothing about the intent of the parties, actual or apparent. They stress, instead, the relationship and the object of the lease.

Merrill § 220.

> Professor David Pierce has summed up the debate:

> [C]ourts imply covenants in oil and gas leases for two reasons: (1) to complete an incomplete contract; and (2) to make the 'unfair' contract 'fair,' or 'more fair.' These are the functional descriptions of the role of implied covenants. Typically courts and commentators refer to these two categories by their legal descriptions: 'implied in fact' and 'implied in law.' The implied-in-fact approach to implied covenants acknowledges their interpretive role: to complete an incomplete contract. The implied-in-law approach acknowledges their protective role: to protect the lessor's interests under the lease.

David E. Pierce, Exploring the Jurisprudential Underpinnings of the Implied Covenant to Market, 48 Rocky Mtn. Min. L. Inst. 10–1, 10–10 (2002). In the few instances where classification of implied covenants as implied in law or implied in fact has been directly material, the premise of the courts has generally been that they are implied in fact. Thus, covenants have been classified as implied in fact in concluding that the statute of limitations for actions on written contracts is applicable to implied covenants. Indian Territory Illuminating Oil Co. v. Rosamond, 120 P.2d 349, 138 A.L.R. 246 (1941) and Texas Pacific Coal & Oil Co. v. Stuard, 7 S.W.2d 878 (Tex.Civ.App.1928). See generally Kuntz § 54.3(b); R. Hemingway § 8.1; and Lowe, Chapter 11.A.

There are at least two more contemporary views of the theoretical basis of implied covenants. Professors Howard Williams and Charles Meyers have argued that implied covenants in oil and gas leases are an application of the contract law principle of cooperation, the rule that parties to a contract are required to cooperate to carry out the purposes of the contract. Williams & Meyers § 802.1. Their analysis is a synthesis of the implied-in-fact and implied-at-law debate; the principle of co-operation requires certain conduct by the parties, both as a matter of public policy (implied at law) and as conduct intended by the parties when they entered into the contract (implied in fact).

A second modern view of implied covenants is that they are a manifestation of the relational contract nature of an oil and gas lease. The theory is that classic contingent bargain-based analysis of contracts does not accurately describe the arrangement between the parties in contracts that are subject to complicated contingencies or unforeseen risks, particularly long term contracts. In such situations the parties seek to establish a relationship for mutual benefit, and the contract becomes a framework for negotiation and resolution, rather than a discrete and complete agreement. See Charles J. Goetz & Robert E. Scott, Principles of Relational Contracts, 67 Va. L. Rev. 1089, 1092 (1981). A relational contract is economically efficient, because it reduces the transactional costs of uncertain or complex agreements to acceptable levels—in a word, a relational contract makes it possible for the parties to make a deal under circumstances in which they probably could not make a deal if all details of the transaction had to be spelled out in the contract. Distributorships, franchises, and employment contracts are the classic examples of relational contracts, but oil and gas leases have been described as relational contracts, as well. See Charles J. Meyers & Steven M. Crafton, The Covenant of Further Exploration—Thirty Years Later, 32 Rocky Mtn. Min.L.Inst. § 1.04 at 1–17 to 1–25 (1986); Merrill § 220, and Kuntz § 54.3. Some compare a relational contract to a nineteenth-century marriage. In such a marriage, the parties had to consent to the union, but the rights and responsibilities of the spouses during the marriage were defined by the general law and custom. The parties' specific agreement triggered their obligations, but other forces determined what those obligations were. Wallace K. Lightsey, A Critique of the Promise Model of Contract, 26 Wm. & Mary L.Rev. 45, 68 (1984). Consider as you read the cases in this section whether that statement is an accurate description of the law of implied covenants.

What remedies should be available for breach of implied covenants? The Supreme Court of Alabama addressed that issue in Meaher v. Getty Oil Co., 450 So.2d 443 (Ala.1984):

> Three views exist throughout the oil and gas producing jurisdictions. A minority of jurisdictions hold that the exclusive remedy for breach of implied covenants is damages. In the majority of jurisdictions, cancellation may be sought as a remedy for breach of implied covenants only upon a showing that damages are wholly inadequate. Finally, a few jurisdictions allow cancellation as a remedy without first proving the inadequacy of damages.

> After reviewing the recognized authorities on the subject, we are of the opinion that the majority view is the most persuasive. Accordingly, we hold that an action for damages is the appropriate remedy for breach of the implied covenants to develop, produce, market, and prevent drainage. Only in the extraordinary circumstance where

damages are wholly inadequate as a remedy will our courts, exercising equity jurisdiction, subject the lease to cancellation.

This view is consistent with two principles of law pervasive in our jurisprudence. First, implied obligations are to be treated as covenants rather than conditions subsequent and as such cannot support forfeitures or cancellation unless remedies at law are wholly inadequate. Second, the law disfavors forfeitures and the cancellation of an oil, gas, and mineral lease is nothing less than a forfeiture of a recognized and protected property interest.

450 So.2d at 447. (citations omitted).

(a) The Implied Covenant to Market

The implied covenant to market has the most direct impact on royalty. The marketing covenant is the logical result of the reasonable prudent operator syllogism: the reasonable prudent operator, having taken the risks of drilling successfully, will seek to make a profit by marketing. The implied covenant to market requires a lessee to use the diligence of a reasonable and prudent business person in (a) finding a market and (b) negotiating a sale. Both steps often present difficulties in application.

(i) The Implied Covenant to Market Within a Reasonable Time

Until the lessee markets production, a lessor will receive no royalty. Therefore, courts will examine whether a lessee has acted prudently and diligently to market. How much time is reasonable for the lessee to take find a market will depend upon the facts and circumstances. But a "reasonable time" may be a long time. In Gazin v. Pan–American Petroleum Corporation, 367 P.2d 1010 (Okla. 1961), a gas well was shut in for three-and-a-half years while the lessee sought better contract terms. The court held that the lessee had not breached the covenant to market because the lessee had used due diligence in negotiating to obtain a satisfactory market. In Bristol v. Colorado Oil & Gas Corp., 225 F.2d 894 (10th Cir. Okla. 1955), the court held a delay of nearly eight years before marketing was reasonable because the gas was impure and there was no pipeline available.

The presence of a shut-in royalty clause in the lease may lengthen the time a court ultimately determines is reasonable to find a market; if the lease includes a shut-in royalty provision, logic suggests that the parties anticipate that marketing may not occur promptly. A shut-in royalty clause will not obviate the implied covenant to market, however, for the purpose of the shut-in royalty clause is to protect the lessee against loss of the lease for failure of production where marketing is not possible or advisable, not to relieve the lessee of the duty to market. Pray v. Premier Petroleum, Inc., 662 P.2d 255 (Kan.1983).

Determining whether marketing has occurred within a reasonable time requires an application of industry practice and common sense to specific circumstances. With all implied covenants, a lessee's prudence is judged as of the time the lessee made the decisions that give rise to the claim that the implied covenant has been breached. For example, in Robbins v. Chevron U.S.A., Inc., 785 P.2d 1010 (Kan.1990), the Kansas Supreme Court held that a lessee had not breached the implied covenant to market as a matter of law by shutting in wells capable of producing gas in paying quantities for two years during the pendency of a gas contract dispute. Prices under the contract were higher than market prices in the mid–1980s. Chevron refused to agree to the buyer's request that Chevron amend the contract to take lower prices and shut in the wells for two years when the purchaser refused to honor the contract. Robbins and other Chevron lessors argued that Chevron had acted imprudently, first in extending the contract in 1980 and then in shutting in the wells. The Kansas court reversed a summary judgment for the lessors, stating that: "Chevron's conduct must be judged upon what an experienced operator of reasonable prudence would have done under the facts existing at the time. The wisdom of hindsight cannot be utilized in making such determination. The individuals claiming imprudence have the burden of proving same." Id. at 1016. See also Tara Petroleum Corporation v. Hughey, 630 P.2d 1269, 1274 (Okla. 1981). One "operates" within given circumstances. Whether one operates "prudently" must be judged on the basis of the facts and circumstances at the time the operating decision is made.

When a lessor establishes a breach of the covenant to market within a reasonable time, many cases grant lease forfeiture or cancellation as a remedy. In Colorado, it appears that forfeiture is the preferred remedy. Davis v. Cramer, 837 P.2d 218, 225 (Colo.App.1992). In Oklahoma, a court has discretion to cancel a lease for breach of the implied covenant to market within a reasonable time; notice and an opportunity to correct the breach are ordinarily required, but demand for compliance may be excused when it would be useless. Crain v. Hill Resources, 972 P.2d 1179 (Okla. Civ.App. Div. 3 1998). In Kansas, forfeiture is available if damages are an inadequate remedy. Robbins v. Chevron U.S.A., Inc., 785 P.2d 1010, 1016 (Kan. 1990). In Texas, "in an extraordinary case, when damages would not furnish an adequate remedy, a court could conditionally order termination if a connection and actual production were not commenced within a reasonable time." Anadarko Petroleum Corp. v. Thompson, 94 S.W.3d 550, 560 (Tex.2002). Courts may also award damages equal to the amount of royalty the lessor would have received had production been marketed timely if evidence establishes with reasonable certainty the quantity of oil or gas that would have been produced. See Grass v. Big Creek Dev. Co., 84 S.E. 750 (W.Va. 1915). Would not the better damage measure be the interest that could have been earned on the royalty the lessor would have received had marketing occurred at a reasonable time. See Richard Maxwell, Appropriate Damages for Breach of Implied Covenants in Oil and Gas Leases, 42 Inst. on Oil & Gas L. & Tax'n § 7.07 (1991).

Historically, marketing covenant disputes have usually focused on gas, rather than oil. One reason is the difference between the physical characteristics of oil and gas. Oil is easily stored and is usually sold on a "spot" basis from storage tanks. Because gas must be produced into pipelines that have often been regulated as public utilities, gas has usually been sold under complicated long-term contracts. Delays of several years between well completion, contract negotiation, and pipeline hook-ups are common. Furthermore, as we have seen, most leases provide for payment of oil royalty in kind, allowing lessors to make independent arrangements for sale, while gas royalty is usually paid in cash.

Natural gas price controls were removed during the 1980s, however, and the Federal Energy Regulatory Commission restructured the gas pipeline industry to permit more competition. Price and pipeline deregulation caused two closely related phenomena: (1) spot markets now handle a substantial majority of natural gas supply and (2) price volatility. Today, it is likely that few lessees will be able to claim that they could not market gas sooner; in the 21st Century oil and gas industry in the United States, there is generally an available market either both oil or gas. The focus of disputes about a lessee's failure to market in a timely manner, therefor, is likely to be the reasonableness of the lessee's market-timing decisions. Consider the following:

PROBLEM

Aggressive Oil Company has drilled a prolific gas well on John and Jane Landowner's lease. Aggressive has decided that it will not market gas from the Landowner well at prices below $4.00 per MMBTU, because that is Aggressive's replacement cost—i.e., the cost of finding new gas—and because the price of a barrel of oil, which contains approximately six times the heating value of an MMBTU of gas, is hovering at $100.00; gas has an inherent worth far greater than $4.00. There is no drainage, but the Landowners are retired, and they want income now. How should a court decide the dispute? What if the reverse were true: Aggressive wanted to generate cash flow to service its debt, but the Landowners (successful lawyers, no doubt) wanted to wait for higher prices?

(ii) The Implied Covenant to Market at an Appropriate Price

The implied duty to market has pricing implications too. The "lessee under oil and gas leases * * * has an implied duty and obligation in the exercise of reasonable diligence, as a prudent operator, with due regard for the interest of both lessor and lessee, to obtain a market for the gas produced * * * at a prevailing market price * * *." Craig v. Champlin Petroleum Co., 300 F.Supp. 119, 125 (W.D.Okla.1969), rev'd on other grounds, 435 F.2d 933 (10th Cir.1971). The case that follows is a classic application of the *implied covenant to market* to a lessee's decisions about the terms of sale.

AMOCO PRODUCTION CO. v. FIRST BAPTIST CHURCH OF PYOTE

579 S.W.2d 280 (Tex.Civ.App.1979), writ refused n.r.e., 611 S.W.2d 610 (Tex.1980).

OSBORN, JUSTICE.

This case involves the issue of an implied covenant to market natural gas at fair market value under a lease which provides for a royalty based upon the amount realized from the sale of such gas. The trial Court awarded recovery for a sum based upon the price paid by other purchasers of gas from the same well. We affirm that part of the judgment, but reverse and render as to the part which requires that future royalties be based upon the price paid in the future by one specific purchaser of gas from the well in question.

Facts

The dispute between these parties concerns eighteen leases covering small tracts of land in the Townsite of Pyote, in Section 100, Block F, G & MMB & A Survey, Ward County, Texas. The Appellant owns oil and gas leases covering these tracts, each of which provides that on gas sold at the wells, the royalty shall be 1/8th of the amount realized from such sale. There is no dispute in this case concerning the fact that the gas is sold at the well.

The several owners of the oil and gas leasehold estates in tracts of land in Section 100 pooled the same to form the Caprito 100 Unit, containing 640 acres of land. The Appellant's leases, as pooled, cover 17.14240 percent of the unit. In 1973, the working interest owners drilled a well on this Section, and it was completed as a dual producer from both the Devonian and Ellenberger Formations. The working interest owners have been selling gas to one of four different purchasers, each of whom has its own gas pipeline connected to the well. Under the various gas purchase agreements with the different working interest owners, the total production from the well is sold approximately fifty-three percent to Lone Star Gas Company, twenty percent to Pioneer Natural Gas Company, fourteen percent to Delhi Gas Pipeline Corporation, and thirteen percent to Natural Gas Pipeline Company. All gas production attributable to the various interests of the Appellees has been sold to Pioneer Natural Gas Company and Odessa Natural Gasoline Company, who has acquired its rights under Pioneer.

Natural Gas Pipeline Company transports its gas interstate and the price paid under its contracts are subject to Federal Power Commission regulations, including price regulations. Both Lone Star and Delhi have contracts with their working interest owners which provide for an annual price redetermination provision to reflect current prices of gas each year. The prices they paid from initial production up to the time of trial were as follows:

Lone Star		Delhi	
Price		**Price**	
Per MCF		**Per MCF**	
.625	Dec. 73 to July 74	.80	Oct. 73 to Oct. 74
1.30	July 74 to July 75	1.30	Oct. 74 to Oct. 75
1.90	July 75 to July 76	1.90	Oct. 75 to Oct. 76
1.95	July 76 thru June 77	1.95	Oct. 76 thru June 77

By reason of production from other wells in neighboring sections, Amoco and Pioneer entered into a gas purchase contract in November, 1969 covering leases then owned by Amoco in nineteen sections of land in Ward County. This twenty-year gas purchase contract provided a price of 17per MCF through December 31, 1974, and basically a 1acceleration every five years of the contract. It also provided for the release of the dedication of acreage not assigned to a producing well as of December 31, 1974. There was no requirement for additional or subsequent dedication to the contract of other leases. In October, 1970, Amoco and Pioneer amended the 1969 gas contract and substituted a new list covering Defendant's leases in twelve sections of land, including six of the eighteen leases involved in this case. As of June 1, 1975, Amoco entered into a supplemental agreement with Pioneer and Odessa by which Amoco dedicated additional leases to the 1969 contract, including the other twelve leases involved in this litigation. In return for the dedication of these additional leases, Pioneer and Odessa agreed that the gas from the Caprito 100 Unit would be increased to 70per MCF retroactive to August 1, 1974, and that beginning on August 1, 1975 and each year thereafter, there would be a 1per MCF acceleration. Thus, by way of comparison, the Appellees were paid 17per MCF for gas produced prior to August, 1974, 70per MCF for the next twelve months, 71per MCF for the next twelve months, and 72per MCF for the remaining months through June, 1977.

Findings and Conclusions

The trial Court filed extensive findings of fact and conclusions of law, and determined that Amoco breached no duty with respect to the payment of royalty under the six leases where the gas was dedicated to the Pioneer contract under the 1970 amendment. There is no complaint about that part of the trial Court's decision. The trial Court further held that Amoco breached its legal duty with respect to the lessors under the twelve leases where gas was dedicated to the Pioneer contract by the 1975 supplement, and further that those parties were entitled to be paid the difference between the amounts which they were paid and the amounts which Lone Star was paying for gas purchased from this well during corresponding periods. In addition, the trial Court ordered that future payments shall be based upon the price paid by Lone Star Gas Company for gas produced from this particular well.

* * *

Marketing Duty

First and foremost is the question of whether Amoco breached any legal duty owed to these Appellees when, some twenty months after the

Caprito 100 Well began producing gas, it committed and dedicated such gas to a long-term contract on terms approximately one-half the amount at which gas was then being sold to other purchasers from the same well and with no right for future price redetermination based on market increases, and while doing so obtained for itself extra benefits in respect to other properties in which these Appellees had no interest.

In 1976, this Court in *Pritchett v. Forest Oil Corporation*, 535 S.W.2d 708 (writ ref'd n.r.e.), based upon the facts set forth in that opinion, concluded that a lessee was not in the position of a trustee with regard to a pooled royalty owner and did not have any fiduciary obligation to such royalty owner. But other cases have clearly recognized a duty, particularly with regard to implied covenants, for a lessee to act fairly and in good faith with regard to the interest of a lessor of a mineral interest.

In *McCarter v. Ransom*, 473 S.W.2d 235 (Tex.Civ.App.1971, no writ), the Court said:

> The doctrine of implied covenants applies with respect to oil, gas and mineral leases. Implied obligations are as much a part of the lease and are just as binding as though they were expressed. Implied covenants are justified on the ground of necessity and fair dealing.

* * *

In *Expando Production Company v. Marshall*, 407 S.W.2d 254 (Tex. Civ.App.1966, writ ref. n.r.e.), the Court said:

> There is no doubt but what there is a fiduciary obligation on the part of the lessee to exercise the utmost good faith toward the lessor in exercising the power granted under a pooling provision. * * *

> For other authorities holding that the lessee, in creating pooled units under a pooling provision in an oil, gas and mineral lease, is subject to the implied obligation that he act fairly, in good faith and with due regard for the interest of the lessor, see *Banks v. Mecom*, 410 S.W.2d 300 (Tex.Civ.App.1966, writ ref'd n.r.e.); *Tiller v. Fields*, 301 S.W.2d 185 (Tex.Civ.App.1957, n.w.h.).

In 1977, the Court in *Elliott v. Davis*, 553 S.W.2d 223 (Tex.Civ.App. writ ref'd n.r.e.), noted that there is an implied requirement that the lessee exercise good faith in making the determination to pool. That opinion relies upon the standard of good faith described in Kuntz, The Law of Oil and Gas, Vol. 4, Sec. 48.3 at 219 (1972), as follows:

> * * * Although it has been said that the lessee has a fiduciary obligation in the exercise of the pooling power, it is submitted that the lessee is not a fiduciary and that standards applied to fiduciaries are entirely too strict. This is so because the lessee has not undertaken to manage and develop the property for the sole benefit of the lessor. The lessee has substantial interests that must be taken into account, and he should not be required to subordinate his own interests entirely to the interests of the lessor. Since his interests frequently

conflict with those of his lessor, however, he must exercise the power in fairness and in good faith, taking into account the interests of both the lessor and lessee.

That decision was followed in *Amoco Production Company v. Underwood,* 558 S.W.2d 509 (Tex.Civ.App.1977, writ ref'd n.r.e.), where the Court affirmed a judgment based upon a jury finding that the designation of the pooled unit " 'was not made in good faith.' "

Those cases deal only with the pooling rights of the lessee and do not pass upon the marketing obligation of a lessee. Obviously, there is an obligation to market the product once it is discovered. Hemingway, The Law of Oil and Gas, Sec. 8.9(c) (1971). In this case, Amoco met that obligation by entering into a contract to sell the gas produced from the Caprito 100 Unit. But the most basic issue is whether there is a duty or implied covenant to market at any particular price, particularly when the lease provides for a royalty based on the "amount realized from such sale." We conclude there is an implied covenant to exercise good faith in the marketing of gas, and particularly so where the interests of the lessor and lessee are not identical. Professor Martin, in a recent article entitled "A Modern Look at Implied Covenants to Explore, Develop and Market Under Mineral Leases," says:

> * * * there is considerable authority that there is a duty owed by the lessee to obtain the best price possible for the gas, a duty which can arise either under a "market value" or a "proceeds" royalty clause.

Twenty–Seventh Annual Institute on Oil and Gas Law and Taxation (1976) 177 at 191.

In his text, Merrill, Covenants Implied in Oil and Gas Leases, 1940, the author on pages 212–214 says:

> * * * The concept of diligence in marketing should include the duty to realize the highest price obtainable by the exercise of reasonable effort. * * * [J]ustice toward the lessor would seem to require that he should receive the same return as those who had leased to other operators * * *. * * * [H]e is bound to get the best price he can.

The same pronouncement of this duty appears in Siefkin, "Rights of Lessor and Lessee with Respect to Sale of Gas and as to Gas Royalty Provisions," Fourth Annual Institute on Oil and Gas Law and Taxation (1953). In that article, the author on page 182 wrote:

> At all events, it is well settled that the lessee is impliedly obligated to "market"—to sell or otherwise utilize—the production obtainable from a commercial well. Probably this requires the lessee to secure the highest price reasonably obtainable therefor * * *.

Some of the historical development of implied covenants is set forth in Summers, The Law of Oil & Gas, Vol. 2, Sec. 416 at 641 (1959). He says:

> The development of standards of diligence for measuring the performance of the oil and gas lessee's express and implied covenants arising

from the policy of development, that is, covenants to test the land, to drill additional wells on discovery, to protect the land from drainage, and to market the product, has been an evolutionary process. These standards, their value for the purposes for which they were created, and their true meaning are perhaps best understood by tracing their origin and development through the decisions of the courts.

* * * Justice Van Devanter, in *Brewster v. Lanyon Zinc Company* said: "Whatever in the circumstances, would be reasonably expected of an operator of ordinary prudence, having regard to the interests of both the lessor and his lessee, is what is required." * * *

The marketing covenant is also discussed in Williams and Meyers, Oil and Gas Law, Vol. 5, Sec. 856.3 (1977). This text states:

> * * * The greatest possible leeway should be indulged the lessee in his decisions about marketing gas, assuming no conflict of interest between lessor and lessee. Ordinarily, the interests of the lessor and lessee will coincide; the lessee will have everything to gain and nothing to lose by selling the product. Where the interests of the two diverge and the lessee lacks incentive to market gas, closer supervision of his business judgment will be necessary.

As noted in footnote 7 on page 410.3 of that text, where the interests of the lessee and lessor do not coincide, the lessee must be held to a stricter standard.

In *Le Cuno Oil Company v. Smith,* 306 S.W.2d 190 (Tex.Civ.App.1957, writ ref'd n.r.e.), Chief Justice Chaddick considered the issue of marketing in a case where division orders provided for payment to the royalty owners based upon the price "received at the wells." In deciding this issue, he said:

> * * * It is in evidence that LeCuno took delivery of the royalty gas involved at the wellhead, ran it through its processing plant and delivered it to certain interstate gas transmission companies under contracts of sale which appellees had no part in making at a price agreed upon between LeCuno and the transmission companies. Such sales to the transmission pipe lines were bona fide arm's length transactions as between LeCuno and the transmission lines so far as this record reveals. Under the contractual relationship described above, LeCuno's division orders requiring it to account to the appellees for their royalty gas on the basis of *"the price received at the wells by LeCuno"* would require that LeCuno exercise the highest good faith in any contract it entered disposing of the royalty owners' gas.

Although the Court did not address the issue of the duty involved in marketing gas in *Livingston Oil Corporation v. Waggoner,* 273 S.W. 903 (Tex.Civ.App.1925, no writ), it did recognize the right of a lessor to receive a royalty on gas sold based upon the reasonable market value rather than the price at which the lessee had contracted to sell the gas. And in *Harding v. Cameron,* 220 F.Supp. 466 (W.D.Okla.1963), the Court recognized the existence of an implied duty or obligation imposed by law which requires a prudent operator, having due regard for the interest of both the lessor and lessee, "to obtain a market for gas at the best price obtainable." In *Greenshields v. Warren Petroleum Corporation,* 248 F.2d 61 (10th Cir.1957), the Court concluded that good faith must be explored by consideration of the circumstances then existing to see if more favorable terms could be obtained for the gas produced.

* * *

In this case, Amoco by dedicating additional leases, including those of the Appellees herein, in June, 1975, obtained an increased price for gas already dedicated under the prior contract from 17 to 70 per MCF. This was obviously a substantial benefit for Amoco and its royalty owners under the previously dedicated leases. But it also meant that as to twelve of the leases involved in this case, the royalty owners would receive a payment for gas which was approximately ½ of the amount soon to be paid by Lone Star and Delhi, and with a very limited provision for future acceleration. This was not a substantial benefit to them as compared to other royalty owners whose gas was soon to be purchased by Lone Star and Delhi for $1.30–$1.90 and $1.95 per MCF.

Having concluded that Amoco had an implied covenant or duty to act in good faith when selling the gas of its royalty owners, we overrule Appellant's points of error asserting it had no such obligation by reason of the lease provision providing for payment of royalty based upon the proceeds realized from the sale of gas.

Breach of Duty

We next turn to the issue of whether the evidence supports the trial Court's finding of a breach of the legal duty owed by Amoco to its royalty owners. Only one witness, Tom Johnson, testified in this case. The record does contain many exhibits relative to interest ownership, gas sales agreements, and a recapitulation of prices paid by each of the four purchasers of gas since the initial production in 1973. At no time did Mr. Johnson express an opinion as to the fair market value of gas in Ward County, or from a particular field, or even from this particular well. Nevertheless, his testimony and the exhibit with the recapitulation of prices paid for gas purchased show without dispute what was being paid at various times for gas from this particular well by one who purchased under federal regulations, one who purchased under a long-term contract, and those who purchased with annual redetermination clauses.

Market value of gas is to be determined by sales of gas comparable in time, quality and availability of marketing outlets. This is usually established by opinions from expert witnesses who have evaluated gas sales in a given field and arrived at a price which they consider to represent fair market value at a given time.

But that is not the exclusive manner of establishing market value. Professor Merrill, on page 213 of his book, notes that:

While the highest price paid by any purchaser in the area is not necessarily the highest obtainable by the exercise of reasonable effort on the part of the particular lessee, it certainly is pertinent evidence.

* * *

Future Payments

As set forth in finding No. 25, Amoco was ordered to pay royalty for gas produced after June, 1977 based upon the price at which Lone Star purchased gas from the well after that date. The judgment ordered future payments based on that standard. We conclude this was error.

First, these royalty payments are made monthly and the market can and does fluctuate at something other than annual periods. In addition, purchases by one individual buyer cannot be conclusive as to market price. Normally, market price is based upon a comparison of several sales of a given commodity at a given time and place. Generally, it is not tied exclusively to one particular sale. We recognize the question is a close one where there are several purchasers of gas from the same well with annual redetermination clauses. Nevertheless, we reverse that part of the judgment as to payments for gas sold after June, 1977, and order that those payments be made based upon market value at the time of sale. Obviously, the purchase price paid by Lone Star may be the best evidence of the market value, but it is not conclusive. We sustain Appellant's Point of Error No. 13.

The judgment of the trial Court is affirmed, except as to the provision for payments of gas after June, 1977, and that part of the judgment is reversed and rendered so as to provide for such payments based upon market value of the gas sold at the time and place of sale.

NOTES

1. Where did Amoco fail in *First Baptist Church?* Was Amoco's breach a failure to obtain the best available contract terms or that it obtained extra benefits for itself in properties in which the church had no interest? Would Amoco have breached an implied duty to its royalty owners with leases subject to low-priced contracts had it not renegotiated the 1969 contract with Pioneer?

2. There is debate over the standard that should be used to determine when there has been a breach of an implied covenant. Most courts have adopted the reasonable prudent operator standard discussed in *First Baptist Church* and classically articulated in Brewster v. Lanyon Zinc Co., 140 Fed. 801 (8th Cir.Kan.1905): "Whatever, in the circumstances, would be reasonably expected of operators of ordinary prudence, having regard to the interests of both lessor and lessee * * *." But some early courts adopted a mere good faith standard. See Colgan v. Forest Oil Co., 45 A. 119 (Pa.1899). And a few courts have embraced a "highest good faith" standard (see Le Cuno Oil Co. v. Smith, 306 S.W.2d 190 (Tex.Civ.App.1957), quoted in *First Baptist*

Church), or a "fiduciary obligation * * * to exercise the utmost good faith toward the lessor * * *." (Expando Prod. Co. v. Marshall, 407 S.W.2d 254 (Tex.Civ.App.–Fort Worth 1966)); but see HECI Expl. Company v. Neel, 982 S.W.2d 881, 888–889 (Tex.1998), observing that Texas law does not recognize a fiduciary relationship between a lessee and royalty owners. See also Finley v. Marathon Oil Company, 75 F.3d 1225 (7th Cir.Ill.1996), and Howell v. Texaco Inc., 112 P.3d 1154 (Okla.2004) (lease by itself does not create a fiduciary relationship). Is the reasonable prudent operator test an appropriate standard, or should the standard be higher or lower? See also, Gary B. Conine, Implied Covenants in Oil and Gas Leases—Past, Present & Future, 33 Washburn L.J. 670 (1994).

Some commentators, including Professor Lowe, have urged that implied covenants are best understood by a unified analysis, that there is only one implied covenant—the implied promise of the lessee to act as a reasonable prudent operator under the circumstances, which imposes the obligation to act (a) in good faith, (b) competently, and (c) with due regard to the lessor's interests. Lowe, Chapter 11.B. The Louisiana Mineral Code, La. Rev. Stat. Ann. § 31:122, provides:

> A mineral lessee is not under a fiduciary obligation to his lessor, but he is bound to perform the contract in good faith and to develop and operate the property leased as a reasonably prudent operator for the mutual benefit of himself and his lessor. Parties may stipulate what shall constitute reasonably prudent conduct on the part of the lessee.

The commentator, the late Dean George Hardy, noted that the Mineral Code's reasonable prudent operator standard is broad enough to cover the covenants usually implied in leases in common law jurisdictions, plus an obligation to restore the premises on completion of operations. A unified analysis is helpful because the reasonable prudent operator standard is the common denominator of all implied covenants in most states, but unified analysis does not fit the case method that fathered the covenants. Thus, implied covenants are usually identified more specifically, by reference to the actions demanded of the lessee by the lessor.

Professor Pierce rejects a unified analysis. David E. Pierce, Exploring the Jurisprudential Underpinnings of the Implied Covenant to Market, 48 Rocky Mtn. Min. L. Inst. 10–1, 10–12 (2002): "If the role of implied covenants is to assist in interpreting the oil and gas lease, there are an unlimited number of implied covenants because they will be fashioned as the express terms of the lease require."

3. What is the measure of the Lessee's duty under the implied covenant to market? To be "reasonable and prudent" should the lessee be obligated to sell at the highest possible price, or the best price currently available, or the prevailing market price, or merely at a price that is reasonable in light of other similar transactions? Would the index price at a market hub establish the lessee's obligation? Is price the only relevant issue in marketing? See the discussion of these issues in Smith v. Amoco Prod. Co., 31 P.3d 255, 268–269 (Kan.2001). If factors other than price are relevant, should the lessee's prudence in weighing those factors be judged on the basis of the subjective good faith business judgment of the lessee or on the basis of an objective

prudent operator standard? Compare the discussion in *First Baptist Church* with Jacqueline L. Weaver, Implied Covenants in Oil and Gas Law under Federal Energy Price Regulation, 34 Vand.L.Rev. 1473, 1515–19 (1981).

Apply your analysis to the following:

PROBLEM

Mineral Owner granted Aggressive Oil Company an oil and gas lease covering Greenacre, which provided for royalties of $\frac{3}{16}$ of the "amount realized" from the sale of gas. Aggressive drilled and completed a gas well upon Greenacre. Aggressive produced gas from Greenacre, put it into a pipeline with gas produced from Aggressive's other leases in the area, and sold the production under two gas contracts, one with Fertilizer Company at $3.00 per MMBTU and one with General Industries at $6.00 per MMBTU. Last month, equal amounts of gas were sold under the two contracts. Aggressive has paid royalties to Mineral Owner based upon the weighted average price received: $4.50 per MCF. Upon what amount is Mineral Owner's royalty due and why?

4. Should the implied covenant to market apply equally to both "market value" and "amount realized" royalty provisions? The court in *Craig v. Champlin Petroleum Co.*, quoted above in the introduction to this section, made no distinction. Neither did the Colorado Supreme Court in Davis v. Cramer, 808 P.2d 358, 361 (Colo.1991), nor the Arkansas Supreme Court in SEECO, Inc. v. Hales, 22 S.W.3d 157 (Ark.2000), nor the Kansas Supreme Court in Smith v. Amoco Prod. Co., 31 P.3d 255 (Kan.2001). But the Texas Supreme Court has held that the implied covenant to market does not apply to a "market value" royalty provision:

> * * *[T]he parties entered into a lease requiring a market-value royalty. Because the lease provides an objective basis for calculating royalties that is independent of the price the lessee actually obtains, the lessor does not need the protection of an implied covenant. Depending on future market behavior, this may be financially beneficial to the lessor, * * * or it may be less advantageous, as here. In either event, the parties have received the benefit of their bargain.

* * *

Essentially, the Royalty Owners wish to use an implied marketing covenant to negate the express royalty provisions in the leases and transform the "market value" royalty into a "higher of market value or proceeds" royalty. The Royalty Owners conceded as much at oral argument, stating that "the entire body of implied covenant law has been aimed at ... making sure the royalty owner gets the best deal." We disagree. The implied covenant to reasonably market oil and gas serves to protect a lessor from the lessee's self-dealing or negligence. *See Pyote,* 611 S.W.2d at 610. It does not override the express terms of the oil and gas lease whenever a lessee negotiates a sales contract that turns out to be especially lucrative. We will not now rewrite this lease's plain terms to give the Royalty Owners the benefit of a bargain they never made.

Yzaguirre v. KCS Resources, Inc., 53 S.W.3d 368, 374 (Tex.2001). Does the position taken by the courts in a particular jurisdiction on the meaning of "market value" affect the scope of the lessee's implied covenant to market? Or does a jurisdiction's view of implied covenants affect its interpretation of express lease provisions like "market value"?

5.   What about sales between related companies? Lessees often sell both oil and gas in the field where it is produced to related marketing companies, which then engage in a wide variety of marketing transactions. Lessors often suspect, and sometimes claim in law suits, that related companies have negotiated "sweetheart" terms of sale in the field or otherwise manipulated transactions to their benefit and the lessors' detriment. What should be the standard of a court's review of an affiliated sales transaction? Consider the following:

> Courts should take care not to allow lessors to be deprived or defrauded of their royalties by their lessees entering into illusory or collusive assignments or gas purchase contracts. Whenever a lessee or assignee is paying royalty on one price, but on resale a related entity is obtaining a higher price, the lessors are entitled to their royalty share of the higher price. The key is common control of the two entities.

Tara Petroleum Corp. v. Hughey, 630 P.2d 1269, 1275 (Okla.1981).

> A royalty owner has a right to be paid on the best price available. When the actual value is not obtainable because of a producer's self-dealing, the courts will carefully scrutinize the transactions on which the royalty payments are based. * * * We hold that an intra-company gas sale cannot be the basis for calculating royalty payments.

Howell v. Texaco Exploration and Production, Inc., 112 P.3d 1154, 1160 (Okla.2004).

> The mere fact that a subsidiary is wholly owned by the parent and there is an identity of management does not justify disregarding the corporate entity of the subsidiary, but where management and operations are assimilated to the extent that the subsidiary is simply a name or a conduit through which the parent conducts its business, the corporate fiction may be disregarded in order to prevent fraud and injustice.

Texas Oil & Gas Corp. v. Hagen, 683 S.W.2d 24, 28 (Tex.App.1984).[26] See also Ramming v. Natural Gas Pipeline Co. of America., 390 F.3d 366 (5th Cir. Tex.2004), and Occidental Permian Ltd. v. The Helen Jones Foundation, 333 S.W.3d 392 (Tex.App.2011). Is the Oklahoma or Texas view the better analysis? Why?

6.   What is the appropriate remedy for a breach of the covenant to market at an appropriate price? What should have been the remedy in *First Baptist Church?* By what reasoning did the majority uphold market value royalties in a proceeds lease?

---

26.   The *Hagen* case went to the Texas Supreme Court, which affirmed it in part and reversed it in part. Then the parties settled the case and judgment was set aside, 760 S.W.2d 960 (Tex.1988).

(iii) The Implied Covenant to Market and Post–Production Costs

By definition, royalty is free of the costs of production. The terms of the definition suggest, however, that royalty may be subject to other costs—costs *subsequent* to production. At issue is what costs associated with the production and marketing of oil and gas the producer must bear alone and what costs the producer can require royalty owners (or other nonoperating interest owners) to share proportionately to their interests in production. Another way to frame the issue is when is "production" complete for purposes of calculating royalty?

PINEY WOODS COUNTRY LIFE SCHOOL v. SHELL OIL CO.

726 F.2d 225 (5th Cir.Miss.1984).

WISDOM, CIRCUIT JUDGE:

VII. *Processing Costs*

The gas from these fields is extremely sour. It is an expensive proposition to convert the raw gas into marketable sweet gas and elemental sulfur and to transport the gas and sulfur to the buyers. Shell has passed on to the royalty owners a proportion of these costs, as determined by complex formulas that compensate Shell for expenses and capital investment. The plaintiffs argue that this is improper, since a royalty interest is "not chargeable with any of the costs of discovery and production", *Mounger v. Pittman*, 1959, 235 Miss. 85, 86–87, 108 So.2d 565, 566. They cite authority for the proposition that "production" includes the lessee's marketing efforts and that therefore any costs necessary to make gas marketable are to be borne exclusively by the lessee. *See West v. Alpar Resources, Inc.*, 1980, N.D., 298 N.W.2d 484; *Sterling v. Marathon Oil Co.*, 1978, 223 Kan. 686, 576 P.2d 635; *Schupbach v. Continental Oil Co.*, 1964, 193 Kan. 401, 394 P.2d 1; *Gilmore v. Superior Oil Co.*, 1964, 192 Kan. 388, 388 P.2d 602; *California Co. v. Udall*, D.C.Cir.1961, 296 F.2d 384; 3 E. Kuntz, *Law of Oil and Gas*, § 40.5 (1967); M. Merrill, *Covenants Implied in Oil and Gas Leases* 212–18 (2d ed. 1940). They argue that leases are construed against the lessee and that, in the absence of specific language authorizing deductions, no deductions may be permitted.

Shell responds, and the district court held, that production ends when the gas is extracted from the earth. Expenses incurred after production may be charged against royalty computed "at the well". 3 H. Williams, *Oil and Gas Law* § 645 (1981). Accordingly, the costs of processing and transportation may be deducted.

We agree with Shell that the specification in the leases that royalty is computed "at the well" controls. In Part III of this opinion, we discussed the purposes of distinctions between "amount realized" and "market value at the well". We concluded that "at the well" refers not only to the place of sale but also to the condition of the gas when sold. "At the well" means that the gas has not been increased in value by processing or transportation. It has this meaning in conjunction with "value" or "amount realized" as well as with "sold". The lessors under these leases are therefore entitled to royalty based on the value or price of unprocessed, untransported gas. *Freeland v. Sun Oil Co.,* 5 Cir.1960, 277 F.2d 154, 157. On royalties "at the well", therefore, the lessors may be charged with processing costs, by which we mean all expenses, subsequent to production, relating to the processing, transportation, and marketing of gas and sulfur.

We emphasize, however, that processing costs are chargeable only because, under these leases, the royalties are based on value or price at the well. Processing costs may be deducted only from valuations or proceeds that reflect the value added by processing. Thus, processing costs may not be deducted from royalties for gas "sold at the well", because the price of such gas is based on its value before processing.

The function of processing costs in determining royalties based on "market value at the well" is to adjust for imperfect comparisons. As we discussed in Part VI of this opinion, the best means of determining the market value at the well of the plaintiffs' gas would be to examine comparable sales of *sour gas* at other wells in the area. Apparently there were no such sales. The next-best method is to examine sales of sweet gas and sulfur, to determine the market value of the products resulting from processing at the Thomasville plant. Processing costs may then be deducted as an indirect means of determining what a buyer would have paid for the sour gas at the wellhead.

Under the Producers 88 (9/70) royalty provision, "amount realized by lessee, computed at the mouth of the well", is the basis of royalty for *all* gas sold, not merely that sold at the well (as in the other leases at issue here). Under this clause, processing expenses are deducted from the amount realized from the sales of sweet gas and sulfur to arrive at the royalty basis. *See Holbein v. Austral Oil Co.,* 5 Cir.1980, 609 F.2d 206 (per curiam); *Kretni Development Co. v. Consolidated Oil Corp.,* 10 Cir.1934, 74 F.2d 497.

The plaintiffs argue that Shell is entitled to deduct at most costs of sulfur production, but not to make deductions against residue gas. We see no basis for this distinction. The lessors are entitled to gas royalty at the well. This means royalty based on the value or price of the sour gas before it is separated into marketable constituents. The value or sale price of the residue sweet gas reflects Shell's processing costs just as surely as does the value or price of the sulfur.

We agree with the plaintiffs that the processing costs, under both the "market value" and "amount realized" provisions, must be reasonable. * * *

* * *

GARMAN v. CONOCO, INC.

886 P.2d 652 (Colo.1994).

ROVIRA, CHIEF JUSTICE

The following question of law was certified to this court by the United States District Court for the District of Colorado in accordance with C.A.R. 21.1: Under Colorado law, is the owner of an overriding royalty interest in gas production required to bear a proportionate share of post-production costs, such as processing, transportation, and compression, when the assignment creating the overriding royalty interest is silent as to how post-production costs are to be borne?

The district court provided three examples of post-production costs but left the term "post-production costs" undefined. We recognize that each of the activities posited in the certified question occurs throughout the gas production process. Gas may require processing to remove impurities for marketing, and once marketable may be further processed into additional component products. Transportation is required when gas is moved from the wellhead to a central location to prepare it for transmission and consumption, commonly referred to as gathering. See John C. Jacobs, Problems Incident to the Marketing of Gas, 5 Inst. on Oil & Gas L. & Tax'n 271, 273 (1954). If no market for the gas exists near the wellhead, transportation may be required to move the gas to a distant market. Compression may be required to create sufficient pressure for the gas to enter a purchaser's pipeline, or compression may occur to transform the gas into additional products. The parties understand the nature of the gas production, and agree that there exists a point in the production process when an overriding royalty owner may become obligated to bear a proportionate share of costs. They do not agree when proportionate allocation should occur. Because we cannot anticipate every conceivable type of post-production cost, and whether it occurs before or after a marketable product is obtained, we consider the certified question as if it were posed without the examples.

In addition, our consideration of the certified question is based on our understanding that "the assignment creating the overriding royalty interest" is indeed silent with respect to the allocation of post-production costs. The district court posed the certified question in general terms, and we answer to provide guidance when an assignment does not address the allocation of post-production costs. Had the district court wanted this court to consider the assignment from the Garmans to Lee A. Adams, who eventually assigned the leases to Conoco, we believe the question would have been framed to elicit a more specific response. However, the briefs submitted by the parties and amici curiae focused on the general principles of oil and gas law relating to the allocation of post-production costs. Other than a limited request by the Garmans to consider the language of the assignment in this case, they also assumed that the "response to the question should be a statement of the general principles of Colorado law applicable to the issue." While the Garmans asked us to "address the application of the legal principles announced to the undisputed facts of this case" we decline to do so. We believe we can respond appropriately to the district court on the law in Colorado without considering the specific assignment terms.

With this background in mind, limiting our response to those post-production costs undertaken to convert raw gas into a marketable product, and relying on the basic proposition that every oil and gas lease contains an implied covenant to market, we answer the certified question in the negative. We now turn to the facts which provide a foundation for the certified question and our answer.

I

During the years 1951 through 1953, M.B. and B.K. Garman acquired eight federal oil and gas leases covering approximately 10,742 acres situated in Rio Blanco County, Colorado (the leases). Through a series of assignments the leases were transferred to Conoco, Inc. (Conoco) subject to a reserved 4.00% overriding royalty interest now owned in equal shares by James P. Garman, Robert D. Garman and Mark Bruce Garman (collectively Garmans).

The leases are located in Dragon Trail Unit (Unit) and continue in full force and effect by the production of gas. Conoco operates both the Unit and the Dragon Trail Processing Plant (Plant). The Plant is located outside of both the Lease and the Unit boundaries. From the wellhead, gas enters a gathering line for transportation to the Plant. At the Plant, gas from the Unit is processed into three separate products: (1) residue gas; (2) propane; and (3) a combined stream of butane and natural gasoline (the "butane-gasoline stream"). The gross proceeds from the sale of the individual products are greater than the revenues which would have been obtained from the sale of the raw, unprocessed gas at the wellhead. Plant operations are typical of processing operations performed to enhance the value of gas. The parties have not stipulated as to the reasonableness of the processing costs.

Historically, Conoco has deducted the cost of certain post-production operations from the overriding royalty payments due to the Garmans. From January, 1987 until April, 1993, the Garmans' proportionate share of post-production costs was $459,511 on overriding royalty payments totaling approximately $2.2 million. In 1993, the Garmans filed an action in federal court requesting declaratory relief to determine the parties' rights under the original 1956 assignment creating the overriding royalty interest, and an accounting to determine whether post-production charges for the previous six years were properly assessed against their overriding royalty interest.

The Garmans argue post-production costs incurred to convert raw gas into a marketable product should not be charged against nonworking interest owners. Accordingly, they object to Conoco's deduction of the costs necessary to make gas from the Leases marketable. The Garmans concede that costs incurred after the gas is made marketable, which actually enhance the value of the gas, should be borne proportionately by all parties benefitted by the operations. They argue, however, that no evidence exists to show Conoco's operations increase the actual royalty amount paid to the Garmans. * * *

Conoco argues that all post-production costs incurred after gas is severed from the ground and reduced to possession should be borne proportionately by royalty, overriding royalty and working interest owners. Conoco asserts severance occurs at the wellhead and that all expenses incurred after severance improve or enhance the value of the gas from its natural, unprocessed state. Thus, it claims that royalty and overriding royalty interest owners who benefit from these operations ought to share in the cost of all post-production operations.

II

A

"The fundamental purpose of an oil and gas lease is to provide for the exploration, development, production and operation of the property for the mutual benefit of the lessor and lessee." Davis v. Cramer, 808 P.2d 358, 360 (Colo.1991). The lessor relinquishes its right to the mineral estate in exchange for a smaller non-risk and non-cost bearing royalty interest in any minerals discovered. Similar to a royalty, an overriding royalty is an interest in oil and gas produced at the surface, free of expense of production, generally assessed in addition to the usual mineral owner's royalty. While the lease agreement creates the royalty obligation, overriding royalty interests are typically reserved or created by separate agreement. Though their contractual origins may differ, both royalty and overriding royalty interests are non-risk and non-cost bearing interests. Naturally, the contracting parties are free to allocate the costs of compression, transportation and processing in their agreements. Often, however, these agreements fail to apportion expenses that may be incurred after the discovery of oil or gas.[1]

Though a lease is entered into for the mutual benefit of the parties, not all parties participate equally in lease development decisions. Royalty

---

1. While specific lease language is often determinative of cost allocation, see Martin v. Glass, 571 F.Supp. 1406, 1411 (N.D.Tex.1983) (" 'net proceeds' clearly suggests that certain costs are deductible ... defined as the sum remaining from gross proceeds of sale after payment of expenses;"), royalty clauses and overriding royalty reservations are often silent regarding allocation of these costs. Gas royalty clauses which provide for the payment of a royalty in money (rather than "in kind") typically require either payment of proceeds from the sale of the gas, or payment of the market value of the gas where it is produced. See 3 Eugene Kuntz, A Treatise on the Law of Oil and Gas, s 40.4 (1989 & 1994 Supp.) (hereinafter Kuntz); 3 Williams & Meyers § 643.2. This distinction does not answer the certified question, as Kuntz explains: Except in the case of a fixed gas royalty, the difficulty with respect to the additional costs of preparing the gas for market arises regardless of the type of royalty clause involved. If the royalty clause is the common type which provides for a payment of money to the lessor as a royalty on gas produced the question arises in determining the value of the gas. If the royalty clause is of the uncommon type which provides for the delivery of royalty gas in kind, then the question arises in determining what is required of the lessee in preparing the gas for delivery. 3 Kuntz § 40.5.

and overriding royalty interest owners (nonworking interest owners) defer to the risk-bearing parties (working interest owners) to decide where and when to drill, the formations to be tested and ultimately whether to complete a well and establish production. Here, Conoco objects to the Garmans' desire to get a "free-ride" on certain costs incurred after the gas is brought to the surface. We believe, however, that the relationship between the parties specifically provides for a "free-ride" on costs incurred to establish marketable production.

B

No consensus exists regarding the allocation of expenses incurred after the discovery of gas. See 3 Kuntz § 40.5.[2] Two lines of cases have developed in the oil producing states based upon differing views of when production is established and a royalty interest accrues. Texas and Louisiana have adopted the rule that nonoperating interests must bear their proportionate share of costs incurred after gas is severed at the wellhead. See, e.g., Danciger Oil & Refineries v. Hamill Drilling Co., 171 S.W.2d 321 (Tex.1943); Martin v. Glass, 571 F.Supp. 1406, 1415 (N.D.Tex.1983) ("Under the law of Texas, gas is 'produced' when it is severed from the land at the wellhead."), aff'd 736 F.2d 1524 (5th Cir.1984); see also Merritt v. Southwestern Elec. Power Co., 499 So.2d 210 (La.Ct.App.1986) (under Louisiana's reconstruction approach royalty payments are calculated by deducting costs incurred after gas reaches the wellhead). Conoco argues this interpretation best reflects the obligations of the parties.

In Kansas and Oklahoma a contrary rule has developed based on an operator's implied duty to market gas produced under an oil and gas lease. Wood v. TXO Production Corp., 854 P.2d 880, 882 (Okla.1992) ("[T]he implied duty to market means a duty to get the product to the place of sale in marketable form."); Gilmore v. Superior Oil Company, 192 Kan. 388, 388 P.2d 602, 606 (1964) ("Kansas has always recognized the duty of the lessee under an oil and gas lease not only to find if there is oil and gas but to use reasonable diligence in finding a market for the product."). Wyoming has codified the marketability approach.[3] The federal government also requires that a lessee "place gas in marketable condition at no cost to the federal government. . . ." 30 C.F.R. § 206.153(i) (1993).

---

2. Until relatively recently gas was often an unwanted by-product of oil production and was vented or flared without compensation to royalty or overriding royalty interest owners. See 3 Kuntz §§ 40.1—.4. After limited markets developed for gas, royalties on production were often calculated at a fixed rate for each producing gas well. Id. § 40.2. Kuntz explained the development of gas marketing: As the natural gas industry developed and natural gas pipelines were extended over the country creating and expanding the market for gas, the value of gas increased. It also became apparent that the ultimate value of gas and the value of the right to extract and sell gas could not be foreseen or determined at any given time of leasing. Accordingly, instead of merely increasing the amount of the fixed periodic payment to be made as the gas royalty, the parties to oil and gas leases changed their practices and began to provide for a royalty on gas which is measured either by volume or by the value of the gas produced. This evolution foreshadowed the type of dispute regarding calculation of gas royalties typified by the current case prompting the certified question now before this court.

3. Wyo.Stat. § 30–5–304(a)(vi).

Arkansas and North Dakota have reached similar conclusions when considering lease royalty clauses which are silent as to allocation of post-production costs. A lease which provides for the lessor to receive "proceeds at the well for all gas" means gross proceeds when the lease is silent as to how post-production costs must be borne. Hanna Oil & Gas Co. v. Taylor, 297 Ark. 80, 759 S.W.2d 563, 565 (1988); see also West v. Alpar Resources, Inc., 298 N.W.2d 484, 491 (N.D.1980) (when the lease does not state otherwise lessors are entitled to royalty payments based on percentage of total proceeds received by the lessee, without deduction for costs).

The Garmans and Amici Curiae advance three separate theories to support their claim that post-production costs are the sole responsibility of the lessee. The Garmans rely on the implied covenant to market which they assert imposes all costs associated with producing a marketable product on the lessee. The National Association of Royalty Owners urges us to consider the typical oil and gas lease habendum clause which generally requires production of oil or gas in paying quantities in order to extend the lessee's interest. Finally, a group of southwestern Colorado landowners argue production activities do not cease until the operator obtains a marketable product that can be delivered to a pipeline. While the parties have approached the question from slightly different angles, the common thread connecting these theories is the existence of an obligation upon the lessee, as the party charged with lease development, to complete all operations necessary to market the gas produced from the leasehold. This obligation is captured in what we have previously identified as the implied covenant to market.

* * *

Conoco argues that the implied covenant to market exists separately from the allocation of marketing costs. We disagree. Implied lease covenants related to operations typically impose a duty on the oil and gas lessee. See, e.g., 5 Kuntz §§ 57.1 to 62.5. Accordingly, the lessee bears the costs of ensuring compliance with these promises. Cf. Warfield Natural Gas Co. v. Allen, 261 Ky. 840, 88 S.W.2d 989, 991 (1935) (the lessee has the exclusive right to produce gas and find a market, and pays the expenses of doing both as consideration for its seven-eighths of production). The purpose of an oil and gas lease could hardly be effected if the implied covenant to drill obligated the lessor to pay for his proportionate share of drilling costs. In our view the implied covenant to market obligates the lessee to incur those post-production costs necessary to place gas in a condition acceptable for market. Overriding royalty interest owners are not obligated to share in these costs.

Allocating these costs to the lessee is also traceable to the basic difference between cost bearing interests and royalty and overriding royalty interest owners. Normally, paying parties have the right to discuss proposed procedures and expenditures and ultimately have the right to disagree with the course of conduct selected by the operator. Under the terms of a standard operating agreement nonoperating working interest owners have the right to go "non-consent" on an operation and be subject to an agreed upon penalty. See A.A.P.L. Form 610–1989 Model Form Operating Agreement Art. VI.b.ii. This right checks an operator's unbridled ability to incur costs without full consideration of their economic effect. No such right exists for nonworking interest owners.

We find Conoco's argument that industry practice allows proportionate allocation of post-production costs unpersuasive. Before one can be bound by industry custom "he must know of it or it must be so universal and well-established that he is presumed to have knowledge of its existence." Pittman v. Larson Distrib. Co., 724 P.2d 1379, 1384–85 (Colo.App. 1986). Further, the parties must have contracted with reference to the custom. Id. Custom and industry practice may be an appropriate consideration when Conoco deals with other oil exploration companies. Often, however, executing an oil and gas lease, or assigning a federal lease won under the previously existing federal lottery system is the extent of a party's contact with the oil industry. See Piney Woods Country Life Sch. v. Shell Oil Co., 726 F.2d 225, 240 (5th Cir.1984) ("[Shell's] allegation of 'custom' is self-serving. The payment of royalties is controlled by lessees, and lessors have no ready means of ascertaining current market value other than to take lessees' word for it."), aff'd in part on remand, 905 F.2d 840 (5th Cir.1990). Conoco cannot invoke industry custom to limit the rights of royalty and overriding royalty owners unsophisticated in the intricacies of mineral development. While we acknowledge that parties who reserve or create overriding royalty interests may be familiar with the oil and gas industry, no cogent argument exists to treat these nonworking interest owners differently from other royalty owners.[4]

* * *

C

Our answer is limited to those post-production costs required to transform raw gas into a marketable product.[5] As we explained at the outset, many different types of expenses may be involved in the conversion process. Upon obtaining a marketable product, any additional costs in-

4. Amicus Curiae Rocky Mountain Oil and Gas Association (RMOGA) urged us to distinguish royalty owners from overriding royalty interest owners. RMOGA argued overriding interest owners' familiarity with the industry justifies imposing upon them post-production costs. We cannot reconcile this argument with the decision by such knowledgeable parties to retain only an expense-free nonworking interest. If an overriding royalty owner familiar with the industry wanted to share in the risk and cost of exploration the retention of a working interest would achieve the desired result. Here, the reservation of an overriding royalty interest evidences the choice not to be burdened with costs of production and marketing.

5. Marketable means "fit to be offered for sale in a market; being such as may be justly and lawfully bought or sold ... wanted by purchasers." Webster's 3rd New International Dictionary at 1383 (1986). Williams and Meyers define marketable condition as gas "sufficiently free from impurities that it will be taken by a purchaser." 8 Williams & Meyers at 692. At oral argument counsel for the Garmans characterized marketing costs as those costs incurred to place the gas in a condition which meets pipeline standards. When the federal government has considered these processes it has distinguished between "operations that condition a product for market, for which a lessee is not entitled to an allowance, and those that transform it. If transformation is involved, a manufacturing allowance is appropriate." See Exxon Corp., 98 I.D. 110, 127, 118 I.B.L.A. 221 (1991).

curred to enhance the value of the marketable gas, such as those costs conceded by the Garmans, may be charged against nonworking interest owners. To the extent that certain processing costs enhance the value of an already marketable product the burden should be placed upon the lessee to show such costs are reasonable, and that actual royalty revenues increase in proportion with the costs assessed against the nonworking interest.[6] We are not, however, called upon today to consider the reasonableness of Conoco's expenses incurred to process, transport or compress already marketable gas.

For the above reasons our answer to the certified question is that, absent an assignment provision to the contrary, overriding royalty interest owners are not obligated to bear any share of post-production expenses, such as compressing, transporting and processing, undertaken to transform raw gas produced at the surface into a marketable product.

NOTES

1. As decisions in *Piney Woods* and *Garman* illustrate, a striking division of analysis has developed over the post-production cost issue. It is axiomatic that the working interest must bear all of the costs of producing oil or gas; royalty is free of "costs of production" because pre-production costs are required to create the production from which the royalty share comes. It is equally clear, however, that where royalty is valued after production is completed, by working back from downstream sales, the costs incurred by the working interest to move the product or to improve its quality—"costs subsequent to production"—must be deducted from the downstream sales price, whether the royalty clause calls for royalty based upon "market value" or "proceeds." The value of any commodity depends upon its proximity to market, and the value of oil or gas normally increases as it is moved closer to the burnertip.

The problem is to determine when "production" is complete. The "marketable-product" rule embraced by the Colorado Supreme Court in *Garman* says that "production" is complete when oil or gas is captured and made a marketable product. The approach of the Fifth Circuit in *Piney Woods*—what the *Garman* court describes as the "Texas and Louisiana" rule—treats

---

6. Some difficulty may arise in computing post-production marketing costs if the operations necessary to prepare the product for market, and operations to enhance the value of a marketable product, occur at the same facility. When the same company both extracts and processes the gas all operating costs must be closely scrutinized. See Amoco Production Co. v. First Baptist Church of Pyote, 579 S.W.2d 280 (Tex.Civ.App.1979): The greatest possible leeway should be indulged the lessee in his decisions about marketing gas, assuming no conflict of interest between lessor and lessee. Ordinarily the interests of the lessor and lessee will coincide; the lessee will have everything to gain and nothing to lose by selling the product. Where the interests of the two diverge and the lessee lacks incentive to market gas, closer supervision of his business judgment will be necessary. Id. at 286 (quoting Williams and Meyers § 856.3). Such a determination is a question of fact to be decided based on competent evidence in the record. See Davis v. Cramer, 837 P.2d 218, 222 (Colo.App.1992) (explaining the question whether the lessee was diligent in its marketing efforts is "based upon equitable considerations regarding the particular facts of the case."). The Federal Regulations are instructive on this point. 30 C.F.R. § 206.159(b) (1993) allows a processing deduction for "reasonable actual costs" incurred when a lessee has a "non-arm's-length processing contract or has no contract."

"production" as complete when oil or gas are severed, whether or not it is marketable. Professor Lowe has called this the "capture and hold" rule. Lowe, Chapter 10.F.

Which rule do you think is preferable and why? Commentators—including this book's authors—split about the rationality and wisdom of the marketable-product rule for determining the deductibility of expenses in calculating royalty.

Professor Anderson agrees with Professor Kuntz and generally with the *Garman* court. Anderson argues that royalty clauses should be, and historically have been, read with three principles in mind:

> (1) royalty should be payable on "production;" (2) production is not complete until a "first-marketable product" has been obtained; and (3) express provisions of the royalty clause should govern over the first two general principles, but royalty clauses, being both executory and anticipatory in nature, should be construed as a whole, in light of current market realities, and not narrowly construed by isolating certain words and phrases [e.g., "market value," "proceeds," "at the well," etc.] and ignoring general intent. [The] first two principles tie the royalty obligation to the point where the exploration and production segment of the oil and gas industry ends based upon factual marketplace realities.

Owen L. Anderson, Royalty Valuation: Should Royalty Obligations Be Determined Intrinsically, Theoretically, or Realistically? Part 1 Why All the Fuss? What Does History Reveal?, 37 Nat. R. J. 547, 549 (1997). His analysis was embraced virtually intact by Justice Opala's concurring and dissenting opinion in Mittelstaedt v. Santa Fe Minerals, Inc., 954 P.2d 1203 (Okla.1998), in which the majority opinion declared Oklahoma law on the issue to be consistent with *Garman,* which in turn is clearly based upon an implied covenant. Unlike some of the marketable-product cases, however, Professor Anderson—and Professors Kuntz and Merrill—would allow lessees to deduct costs incurred for "freight," including gathering and transportation-related compression. What is "marketable" may change over time; in the 1990s, for example, gas was often marketable at the lease if it was sweet and in a dehydrated state.

> Professors Pierce and Lowe have criticized the marketable-product rule:

> The court in *Garman* identified the implied covenant to market as the underlying basis for its marketable product rule. * * * But note that resort to the 'implied' in cases like *Garman* is not necessary to identify the assignee's royalty obligation. Instead, the 'express' terms of the assignment provide the formula for measuring the formula * * *—the market price for gas in the field. Since there is express language * * *, there is no need to resort to implied covenant concepts. When courts apply a marketable product analysis, they tend to push the royalty valuation point further downstream from the wellhead into separate business enterprises in which the lessor was never intended to participate. Often the result is that the lessor shares in the rewards of such separate businesses without exposure to any of the risks.

David E. Pierce, Developments in Nonregulatory Oil and Gas Law: The Continuing Search for Analytical Foundations, 47 Inst. on Oil & Gas L. & Tax'n § 1.07[b] (1996).

> One may challenge the very principle of the marketable-product rule. In the current almost-free markets, there is arguably no such thing as gas of unmarketable quality; if a producer does not choose to compress, transport and process gas to pipeline quality, someone else will. One may also argue that adopting a rule that the implied covenant to market requires the lessee to pay all expenses of developing a commercial product is bad policy. Adoption of such a rule is likely to mean that wells will be plugged and abandoned sooner than they would otherwise. Such a rule may also distort the efficient operation of markets by providing an artificial, non-economic incentive for sales at the well. Finally, the marketable-product rule will inevitably stick the courts in the factual quagmire of distinguishing between costs necessary to make a merchantable product and costs incurred to increase the value of an already-marketable product.

Summers Perm. Ed. § 589B (Lowe Supp.).

Professor Smith (the oldest and perhaps the wisest of us) has kept his own counsel.

2. The Colorado Supreme Court relies heavily on Professor Kuntz in embracing the "marketable-product" rule. The court's analysis is closer, however, to that of Professor Maurice Merrill, Professor Kuntz' colleague at the University of Oklahoma, who urged in 1940 that:

> If it is the lessee's obligation to market the product, it seems necessarily to follow that his is the task also to prepare it for market, if it is unmarketable in its natural form. No part of the costs of marketing or of preparation for sale is chargeable to the lessor.

Merrill 214–215.

The *Garman* court may have misread Professor Kuntz, who wrote:

> Although it is not difficult to reason from the presence of a general duty on the part of the lessee to market the produce to the conclusion that the lessee has authority to dispose of royalty gas on behalf of the lessor, it is considerably more difficult to reason from such general duty to a conclusion as to which party or parties must bear any added expense which might be incident to preparing the gas for market. * * * [T]he difficulty with respect to the additional costs of preparing the gas for market arises regardless of the type of royalty clause involved.

* * *

> Much of the difficulty can be avoided if it is recognized that there is a distinction between acts which constitute production and acts which constitute processing or refining of the substance extracted by production. * * * It is submitted that the acts which constitute production have not ceased until a marketable product has been obtained. After a marketable product has been obtained, then further costs in improving or transporting such product should be shared by the lessor and lessee.

Kuntz § 40.4. Is Professor Kuntz talking about the implied covenant to market or the meaning of "production" in the habendum clause? Are they different concepts? If so, how? Hemingway § 7.3(c) says:

> One reason for the uncertainty created by the marketable-product rule is that the rule stems from two distinct foundations. These foundations are best summarized by comparing the commentary of two leading oil and gas scholars: the late Eugene Kuntz and the late Maurice Merrill, both long-time professors at The University of Oklahoma. Professor Kuntz argued that, absent clarifying lease language, the default rule for royalty valuation should depend upon when oil and gas are deemed to be produced under the lease. He argued that "the acts which constitute production have not ceased until a marketable product has been obtained," and he reached this conclusion by considering the plain meaning of typical royalty clauses. While agreeing that the marketable-product rule was proper, Professor Merrill argued that the rule arose because of the lessee's "implied covenant to market" production. Although courts adopting the marketable-product rule have often cited Professor Kuntz, their opinions are often closer to, but in some cases go well beyond, the view of Professor Merrill. Courts following Professor Merrill's approach are more likely to ground the rule in the implied marketing covenant and to give less consideration to the language of the royalty clause. If courts followed Professor Kuntz's approach, they would start their analysis with the royalty clause itself and determine whether the language of the clause was consistent with the marketable-product rule.

3. What were the terms of the royalty provision before the court in *Garman*? How can a court determine a contractual royalty obligation without the contract terms?

The royalty provision at issue in *Garman* involved an overriding royalty carved from a lease. The Oklahoma Supreme Court, after adopting the *Garman* approach in a lease royalty dispute in Mittelstaedt v. Santa Fe Minerals, Inc., 954 P.2d 1203 (Okla.1998), subsequently rejected the *Garman* approach in the case of an overriding royalty payable "in kind." XAE Corp. v. SMR Property Management Co., 968 P.2d 1201 (Okla.1998). Why might the nature of the royalty interest—whether it is overriding or lease royalty or whether it is in-value or in-kind royalty—make a difference?

4. Does *Garman* tell us what it takes for gas or oil to become a "marketable product"? Must it be of "pipeline quality"—a quality that pipelines serving the area will accept? Or is it sufficient that the gas be saleable to an intermediary who will process it to a quality that will permit it to be transported through a pipeline? In Rogers v. Westerman Farm Company, 29 P.3d 887 (Colo.2001), the Colorado Supreme Court embraced the higher standard:

> Gas is marketable when it is in the physical condition such that it is acceptable to be bought and sold in a commercial marketplace, and in the location of a commercial marketplace, such that it is commercially saleable in the oil and gas marketplace. The determination of whether gas is marketable is a question of fact, to be resolved by a fact finder.

* * *

While we agree that a single purchaser, in a good faith purchase of gas, is evidence that there is a market for the gas, we do not agree that such a purchase conclusively establishes a market. The determination of whether a market exists is an issue of fact to be decided by a jury, based on the facts and circumstances, which may include factors other than a single purchase of gas. The jury instruction here erroneously implies that one sale to a purchaser in good faith establishes marketability. Instead, under our definition of marketability, the gas must be in such a physical condition and location that it is available for commercial exchange, in a viable market, i.e., a commercial marketplace.

29 P.3d at 906 and 910. Under this test, a producer's transportation costs of moving gas to the first available market are part of the costs of producing a marketable product. See also Tawney v. Columbia Natural Resources, LLC, 633 S.E.2d 22 (W.Va. 2006).

In contrast, the Kansas Supreme Court's analysis in Sternberger v. Marathon Oil Co., 894 P.2d 788, 806 (Kan.1995), adopted the rule that the lessee must bear all costs of making production marketable, but concluded that transportation costs to move gas to market were chargeable proportionately to the royalty interests:

This case turns on the fact that the royalty was to be paid based upon "market price at the well" and the gas was marketable at the well, but there was no market at the well. The parties in this case dispute Marathon's deduction of transportation expenses, but there has been no evidence or finding as to what the market price at the well was * * *.

The Oklahoma Supreme Court reached a similar result in Mittelstaedt v. Santa Fe Minerals, Inc., 954 P.2d 1203 (Okla.1998). See also Merrill 219.

5. The *Garman* court notes the generally accepted principle that the parties to the lease are free to agree how to apportion costs. But how explicit must they be? In the context of *Garman*, if the underlying oil and gas leases provided that royalty was "market value" or "amount realized" calculated "at the well," would the lessee possess sufficient authorization to deduct processing, transportation, and compression costs from the downstream sales price in calculating royalty due? The Colorado Supreme Court rejected the argument that "at the well" permitted deduction of downstream costs in Rogers v. Westerman Farm Company, 29 P.3d 887 (Colo.2001):

[I]n interpreting leases like those in this case, we are mindful of the generally accepted rule that oil and gas leases are strictly construed against the lessee in favor of the lessor. This rule is generally based on the recognition that the bargaining power between a lessor and lessee is similar to that historically found between an insurance company and its customers. * * * [T]he parties are in similar unequal positions. For example, lessors are not usually familiar with the law related to oil and gas leases, while lessees, through experience drafting and litigating leases, generally are.

Accordingly, based on our interpretation of the "at the well" and "at the mouth of the well" language common to the four lease types at issue, we conclude that the leases in this case are silent with respect to allocation of costs. We disagree with those jurisdictions that conclude that "at the well" is sufficient to allocate costs. Moreover, we disagree with the conclusion that "at the well" language addresses transportation costs, while not addressing other costs incurred in processing the gas. Instead, we conclude that because the leases are silent, we must look to the implied covenant to market, and our previous decision in *Garman v. Conoco,* to determine the proper allocation of costs.

29 P.3d 887, 901–902. And in Tawney v. Columbia Natural Resources, LLC, 633 S.E.2d 22 (W.Va. 2006), the West Virginia Supreme Court of Appeals held that language that indicates merely that royalty is to be calculated "at the well," "at the wellhead," or similar language, or that the royalty is "an amount equal to 1/8 of the price, net all costs beyond the wellhead," or "less all taxes, assessments, and adjustments" is "ambiguous" and not sufficient to permit a lessee to deduct any portion of the costs incurred between the wellhead and the point of sale. The court held that lease language intended to allocate between the lessor and lessee the costs of marketing the product and transporting it to the point of sale must expressly provide that the lessor shall bear some part of the costs incurred between the wellhead and the point of sale, identify with particularity the specific deductions the lessee intends to take from the lessor's royalty, and indicate the method of calculating the amount to be deducted from the royalty for such post-production costs. See David E. Pierce, Developments in Nonregulatory Oil and Gas Law: Beyond Theories and Rules to the Motivating Jurisprudence, 58 Inst. on Oil & Gas L. & Tax'n 1–1 (2007) (§ 1.04. Oil and Gas Lease Jurisprudence).

Would the following lease clause meet the standards set by the Colorado and West Virginia courts?:

> For gas (including casinghead gas) and all other substances covered hereby, the royalty shall be one-eighth of the proceeds realized by lessee from sale thereof, less a proportionate part of ad valorem taxes and production, severance, or other excise taxes and the costs incurred by lessee in delivering, processing or otherwise making such gas or other substances merchantable * * *.

Just how far the logic that "at the well" authorizes deduction of costs in calculating royalty might be taken is illustrated by Heritage Resources, Inc. v. NationsBank, 939 S.W.2d 118 (Tex.1996). *Heritage* involved a dispute over leases with royalty clauses that stated royalty as a percentage of "market value at the well," but which provided also in the same clause that "there shall be no deductions from the value of Lessor's royalty by reason of any required processing, cost of dehydration, compression, transportation, or any other matter to market such gas." Heritage sold gas off the premises and deducted the royalty owner's proportionate part of transportation costs in calculating the royalty due. NationsBank objected, but conceded that the charges were reasonable and that the sales price of the gas "reflected its market value at the point of sale." A fractionalized Texas Supreme Court held 7–2 in two opinions that the deductions were appropriate because of the literal language of the royalty formulation: where the royalty owner receives *"value at the well,"* downstream transportation costs are not a *"deduction from the value"* of the lessor's royalty.

6. As the *Garman* decision notes, some states have enacted statutes that attempt to define what deductions may be made in calculating royalty. Wyoming Statutes § 30–5–304(a)(i) and (vi) provide in part:

> The lessee pays all costs of production out of his interest, the lessor's interest being free and clear of all those costs;

> (vi) "Costs of production" means all costs incurred for exploration, development, primary or enhanced recovery and abandonment operations including, but not limited to lease acquisition, drilling and completion, pumping or lifting, recycling, gathering, compressing, pressurizing, heater treating, dehydrating, separating, storing or transporting the oil to the storage tanks or the gas into the market pipeline. "Costs of production" does not include the reasonable and actual direct costs associated with transporting the oil from the storage tanks to market or the gas from the point of entry into the market pipeline or the processing of gas in a processing plant.

Can such a law apply to royalty generated by production after its enactment under leases entered into before the statute was passed? If so, does this formulation solve the problem? For example, is "gathering" under the statute on-lease or in-field gathering, or does it include moving the gas to a pipeline that will deliver it to an end-user? And what is a "market pipeline"? Responding to a certified question, the Wyoming Supreme Court, in Cabot Oil & Gas Corp. v. Followill, 93 P.3d 238 (Wyo. 2004), concluded that "gathering" means "to collect gas and move it to a point where it can be processed or transported to the user." See also Nev. Stat. 522.115 and Mich. Comp. Laws § 324.61503(b).

7. Roughly equal numbers of jurisdictions have adopted or rejected the marketable-product rule. As note 5 points out, variations of the marketable-product rule have been recognized by Colorado, Kansas, Oklahoma, and West Virginia case law. As note 6 illustrates, Michigan, Nevada, and Wyoming have adopted the principle by statute. Federal lessees also have a duty to put production into a marketable condition at no cost to the government, including costs incurred by so-called marketing affiliates though the regulations permit some allowances for downstream transportation and processing. 30 C.F.R. §§ 206.106 (oil), 205.152(i) (unprocessed gas), 106.153(i) (processed gas), 206.52(i) (Indian oil), and 206. 174(h), (Indian gas). When production is moved downstream certain transportation deductions (allowances) are permitted. 30 C.F.R. §§ 206.156–206.157 (gas) and 206.109–206.111 (oil). 30 C.F.R. §§ 206.158–206.159.

On the other hand, as the *Garman* court notes, Texas and Louisiana have rejected the marketable-product rule. So have courts applying the law of California, Kentucky, Mississippi, Montana, New Mexico, North Dakota, Pennsylvania, and Utah. See Atlantic Richfield Co. v. State, 262 Cal.Rptr. 683, 688 (Cal.App. 2 Dist. 1989); Poplar Creek Development Co. v. Chesapeake Appalachia, L.L.C., 636 F.3d 235 (6th Cir. Ky. 2011); Elliott Indus. Ltd. P'ship v. BP America Prod. Co., 407 F.3d 1091 (10th Cir. N.M. 2005); Montana Power Co. v. Kravik, 586 P.2d 298, 303 (Mont. 1978); Bice v. Petro–Hunt LLC, 768 N.W.2d 496 (N.D. 2009); Piney Woods Country Life School v. Shell Oil Co., 726 F.2d 225 (5th Cir.Miss.1984); Kilmer v. Elexco Land Serv., Inc.,

990 A.2d 1147 (Pa. 2010); and Emery Resource Holdings LLC. v. Coastal Plains Energy, Inc., 2012 WL 1085718 (D.Utah 2012).

Generally, the cases permitting lessees to deduct compression, transportation, and processing costs in calculating royalty where production has been sold downstream from the lease have turned on the royalty clause language providing for royalty "at the well." " '*At the well*' language is clear and unambiguous. The parties intended for the royalty value to be determined based on the gas as it is produced from the wells and not at some point downstream." *Emory Resource Holdings, supra.* As the Fifth Circuit said in *Piney Woods*:

> "At the well" means that the gas has not been increased in value by processing or transportation.... The lessors under these leases are therefore entitled to royalty based on the value or price of unprocessed, untransported gas. On royalties "at the well," therefore, the lessors may be charged with processing costs, by which we mean all expenses, subsequent to production, relating to the processing, transportation, and marketing of gas and sulfur.

726 F.2d at 240.

But other cases rest on broader grounds. In the Pennsylvania case, *Kilmer v. Elexco*, the lease royalty clause called for royalty based on "sales proceeds actually received by Lessee from the sale of such production, less this same percentage share of all Post Production Costs," and expressly defined those costs. The lessors contended that the lease was invalid under Pennsylvania's Guaranteed Minimum Royalty Act, 58 Penn. Stat. § 33, which provides that:

> A lease or other such agreement conveying the right to remove or recover oil, natural gas or gas of any other designation from lessor to lessee shall not be valid if such lease does not guarantee the Lessor at least one-eighth royalty of all oil, natural gas or gas of other designations removed or recovered from the subject real property.

The lessors argued that a "standard dictionary definition" and the implied covenant to market required royalty at the point of sale, so that a net-back calculation starting with a downstream sales price and working back to proceeds at the well resulted in them receiving less than the statute required. The court reasoned, however, that the statute's reference to "royalty" must be considered in light of the conditions prevailing when the statute was enacted, in 1979, when virtually all sales of natural gas were at the wellhead. Further, the supreme court relied on the state's Statutory Construction Act, which requires that "technical words and phrases * * * as have acquired a peculiar and appropriate meaning * * * shall be construed according to such peculiar and appropriate meaning or definition." The court concluded that in the oil and gas industry, "royalty" is free of the expenses of production, which include the costs of drilling the well and bringing the production to the surface, but do not include the costs of getting the production to the point of sale. See also Wall v. United Gas Public Service Co., 152 So. 561 (La. 1934).

8.   The jurisdictions agree that, however post-production costs are defined, they must be reasonable. See, e.g., Garman v. Conoco, Inc., 886 P.2d

652, 661 (Colo.1994); Sternberger v. Marathon Oil Co., 894 P.2d 788, 800 (Kan.1995); Tawney v. Columbia Natural Resources, LLC, 633 S.E.2d 22, 23 (W.Va. 2006); Heritage Resources, Inc. v. NationsBank, 939 S.W.2d 118, 122 (Tex.1996); and Babin v. First Energy Corp., 693 So.2d 813, 815 (La.App. 1997). But they provide little guidance about what is reasonable, leaving the parties to squabble in the trial courts about whether lessees can charge royalty with costs such as depreciation, cost-of-money and overhead.[27] See the discussion at Atlantic Richfield v. Farm Credit Bank of Wichita, 226 F.3d 1138, 1150–1152 (10th Cir.Colo.2000). Huge sums of money may be involved. In Northern Natural Gas v. Grounds, No. KC–1969, slip op. (D. Kan. 1983), aff'd, Northern Natural Gas v. Hegler, 818 F.2d 730 (10th Cir.1987), the trial judge made "equity adjustments" in a suit over the value of helium between plant operators and producers. For each penny of adjustment in depreciation alone, the total valuation difference was $115,000.00. In Atlantic Richfield Co. v. State, 262 Cal.Rptr. 683 (Cal.App. 2 Dist. 1989), the court allowed the lessee to zero out royalty in some months through the deduction of post-wellhead costs. Is this reasonable? See Owen L. Anderson, Calculating "Freight" in a Marketable–Product Jurisdiction, 20 E. Min. L. Inst. 10–1 (1999). In Pursue Energy Corp. v. Abernathy, 77 So.3d 1094 (Miss. 2011), the court held that the assignee of a lease could not charge lessors for their proportional shares of the capital costs of the processing plant at issue in the *Piney Woods* case above, where the prior lessee had already charged and recovered the full capital costs through deductions from royalty payments.

(b) The Implied Covenant to Protect Against Drainage

The lessee's implied covenant to protect the lessor against drainage is the easiest of the implied covenants to understand. If operations on other land cause oil and gas under the leased property to drain away, the lessor loses royalty that the lessee would have paid had the oil or gas drained away been produced from the leased property. And the lease transfers to the lessee the lessor's right to search for, develop, and produce oil and gas from the property, so a lessor cannot protect himself. If drainage occurs, under what circumstances should the lessee have an obligation to protect the leased property, and what actions will satisfy the duty?

PROBLEM

Acme Oil Co. acquired an oil and gas lease on Section 1 from Xavier, the owner of that section. Acme also acquired an oil and gas lease on the adjoining Section 2 from Ysidro, the owner of that section. Geological and geophysical exploration indicated that a common formation underlay both sections. Acme drilled a well on Section 1 and discovered gas in paying quantities. A test of the well revealed, however, that there were not sufficient gas reserves to pay for the cost of drilling another well into the common source of supply. Ysidro has demanded that Acme drill an offset well to protect against drainage. How should Acme respond?

---

27. Note that the same legal and factual issues arise here as are presented in "paying quantities" disputes, but lessors and lessees generally take opposite positions.

AMOCO PRODUCTION CO. v. ALEXANDER

622 S.W.2d 563 (Tex.1981).

CAMPBELL, JUSTICE.

This is an action by royalty owners for damages because of fieldwide drainage. The trial court, after a jury verdict, rendered judgment for the Alexanders, lessors, for actual and exemplary damages against Amoco, lessee. The Court of Civil Appeals reformed the trial court's judgment and affirmed the judgment as reformed. 594 S.W.2d 467. We modify the judgment of the Court of Civil Appeals and affirm the judgment as modified.

The Hastings, West Field, in Brazoria County, is a water-drive field. Water and oil are in the same reservoir. Because water is heavier than oil, the water moves to the bottom of the reservoir driving the oil upward. As oil is removed, water moves up to fill the space.

As the oil is produced, the oil-water contact (a measure of the reservoir water level) gradually rises until the wells begin to produce water along with oil. As the wells are produced, the fluid from the wells contains increasingly higher percentages of water. When the wells produce almost all water, the wells are abandoned. The wells are then said to be "watered out" or "flooded out."

The Hastings, West Field, reservoir is not horizontal. It is highest (closer to the surface) in the southeast part. It is lowest in the northwest. Hence, the reservoir dips downward gradually from the southeast to the northwest. Leases on the higher part of the reservoir are called "updip leases" and on the lower, "downdip leases." The Alexanders' leases with Amoco are downdip. Amoco, with 80% of the field production, also has updip leases. Exxon, Amoco's chief competitor in the field, owns leases generally updip from the Alexanders and downdip from the remainder of the Amoco leases.

In water-drive fields, such as the Hastings, West Field, natural underground conditions and production of oil updip work to the disadvantage of downdip leases. As the oil is produced, the oil-water contact rises. The greater the production from updip leases, the sooner the wells on downdip leases will be "watered out" because of the water-drive pushing the oil to the highest part of the reservoir. The downdip leases, therefore, are the first to water out. Moreover, production anywhere in the field will cause the oil-water contact to rise and move from the downdip leases to the updip leases. This is field-wide drainage.

The Alexanders' theory of this lawsuit is that Amoco slowed its production on the Alexander–Amoco downdip leases and increased production on Amoco updip leases causing the Alexander–Amoco downdip leases to "water out" much sooner. Oil not produced from the Alexander leases will eventually be recovered by Amoco as the water pushes the oil to the Amoco updip leases. Their theory of liability is that Amoco owed the

Alexanders an obligation to obtain additional oil production from the Alexander leases by drilling additional wells and reworking existing wells to increase production. If Amoco had fulfilled that obligation, additional oil would have been produced from which the Alexanders would have been paid 1/6th royalty. The Amoco updip leases pay 1/8th royalty.

The Alexanders contend they pleaded two legal theories of recovery: (1) in contract, breach of Amoco by its implied obligation to take such steps as a reasonably prudent operator would have taken to protect the Alexander leases from drainage; and (2) in tort; for "intentional acts and omissions" undertaken by Amoco "for the purpose of increasing Amoco's production from its updip leases" and the deliberate waste of the Alexanders' royalty oil. The jury found:

> (1) Amoco failed to operate the Alexander leases as a reasonably prudent operator.

> (2) Amoco operated its leases under an intentional policy of maximizing its profits by producing less oil from the Alexander leases than would have been produced by a reasonably prudent operator, while increasing the drainage of oil from the Alexander leases by Amoco production on other leases.

The jury awarded actual and exemplary damages.

We must determine whether:

> (1) Amoco had a duty to protect from field-wide drainage, or a duty not to drain the Alexander downdip leases by its operations updip.

> (2) Amoco had a legal duty under the Alexander leases to apply to the Railroad Commission for permits to drill additional wells at irregular locations, to obtain the permits, and drill the wells.

* * *

> (4) The Alexanders are entitled to recover exemplary damages.

Field–Wide Drainage

Whether Amoco had a duty to protect the Alexander downdip leases from field-wide drainage, or a duty not to drain the leases by its updip operations has not been considered by the Texas courts. The Court of Civil Appeals held Amoco had a duty to protect the Alexanders from field-wide drainage.

An oil and gas lessee has an implied obligation to protect from local drainage. Local drainage is oil migration from under one lease to the well bore of a producing well on an adjacent lease. Local drainage depends upon production from wells in a specific area in a field. It will begin, increase, or decrease according to production. Local drainage may be in several directions in one field and can be prevented by drilling offset wells. Field-wide drainage in a water-drive field, however, is relatively independent of the location of particular wells. It depends on the water-drive and production from all wells in the field. Protecting from field-wide drainage, therefore, is more difficult than protecting from local drainage.

Amoco urges the Court of Civil Appeals correctly held the drainage in this case was field-wide but the court erred in holding the law imposes an obligation upon Amoco to prevent field-wide drainage, or an obligation not to drain the Alexander leases by its updip operations. Amoco recognizes the obligation to protect from local drainage, but states the Court of Civil Appeals was in error in extending that obligation to require a lessee to protect his lessor from field-wide drainage. Amoco argues this imposes a new implied obligation never previously held to exist.

Has the Court of Civil Appeals imposed a new obligation never previously held to exist? The terms "obligation," "duty," and "covenant" have been used interchangeably in oil and gas cases to describe the performance required of a lessee under an oil and gas lease. Traditionally, matters relating to the development of the lease and the protection of the lessor's interest are not expressly included in the written lease. Since the early history of oil and gas litigation, the courts have held that covenants are implied when an oil and gas lease fails to express the lessee's obligation to develop and to protect the lease. In recent years, implied covenants have been expanded to matters of management of the lease. The words "duty" or "obligation" are best used to express the requirements of a lessee in performance of the implied covenants.

Commentators differ on the classification of implied covenants in oil and gas leases. See Hemingway § 8.1; 5 E. Kuntz, a Treatise on the Law of Oil and Gas § 55.1 (1978); 5 H. Williams & C. Meyers, Oil and Gas Law § 804 (1980); Walker, *The Nature of the Property Interests Created by An Oil and Gas Lease in Texas,* 11 Texas L.Rev. 399 (1933). These covenants are usually grouped into categories according to the factual basis of the dispute between the lessor and lessee. 5 H. Williams & C. Meyers, Oil and Gas Law § 804 (1980). However, these categories are specific applications of three broad implied covenants to particular controversies. These broad implied covenants are: (1) to develop the premises, (2) to protect the leasehold, and (3) to manage and administer the lease.[1]

---

1. The Hemingway Hornbook summarizes the major implied covenants as follows:

(A) Implied covenants to develop the leases.

  (1) To drill an initial well.

  (2) To reasonably develop the lease after production has been acquired.

(B) Implied covenants of protection.

  (1) To protect against drainage.

  (2) Not to depreciate the lessor's interest.

(C) Implied covenants relating to management and administration of the lease.

  (1) To produce and market.

  (2) To operate with reasonable care.

  (3) To use successful modern methods of production and development.

  (4) To seek favorable administration action.

R. Hemingway, The Law of Oil and Gas § 8.1 (1971).

The standard of care in testing the performance of implied covenants by lessees is that of a reasonably prudent operator under the same or similar facts and circumstances. The reasonably prudent operator concept is an essential part of every implied covenant. Every claim of improper operation by a lessor against a lessee should be tested against the general duty of the lessee to conduct operations as a reasonably prudent operator in order to carry out the purposes of the oil and gas lease.

Amoco contends the Court of Civil Appeals' holding expands the offset drilling obligation beyond the point of fairness and workability by including within it the obligation to offset field-wide or regional drainage. Field-wide drainage affects all leases in the field; and if the duty exists, each lessee may be required to drill offset wells. The drilling of offset wells increases field-wide drainage and sets off a chain reaction the drilling of each additional well would trigger a field-wide obligation to drill more offsets and each drilling would further accelerate the field-wide drainage. Amoco argues, therefore the end result of carrying out the obligation would be self-defeating.

Amoco also says that updip leases enjoy a natural advantage over downdip leases. If the natural drainage is to be offset, the only valid way is through field-wide regulation by the Railroad Commission regulating rates of production to protect correlative rights in the field.

The implied covenant to protect against drainage is part of the broad implied covenant to protect the leasehold. The covenant to protect the leasehold extends to what a reasonably prudent operator would do under similar facts and circumstances. "As is true of the other implied duties, it is not easy to separate the duty from the standard of performance. The lessee is required generally to do what a prudent operator would do. Protection of the leased premises against drainage is but a specific application of that general duty." 5 E. Kuntz, a Treatise on the Law of Oil and Gas § 61.3 (1978). The covenant to protect from drainage is not limited to local drainage. It extends to field-wide drainage. Oil lost by field-wide drainage is just as lost as local drainage oil. The methods of safeguarding from the loss may be different and protecting from local drainage may be easier. However, it is no defense for a lessee to say there is no duty to act as a reasonably prudent operator to protect from field-wide drainage.

A lessor is entitled to recover damages from a lessee for field-wide drainage upon proof (1) of substantial drainage of the lessor's land, and (2) that a reasonably prudent operator would have acted to prevent substantial drainage from the lessor's land. * * * However, because of the complexity of the oil and gas industry and changes in technology, the courts cannot list each obligation of a reasonably prudent operator which may arise. The lessee must perform any act which a reasonably prudent operator would perform to protect from substantial drainage.

The duties of a reasonably prudent operator to protect from field-wide drainage may include (1) drilling replacement wells, (2) re-working existing wells, (3) drilling additional wells, (4) seeking field-wide regulatory action, (5) seeking Rule 37 exceptions from the Railroad Commission, (6) seeking voluntary unitization, and (7) seeking other available administrative relief. There is no duty unless such an amount of oil can be recovered to equal the cost of administrative expenses, drilling or re-working and equipping a protection well, producing and marketing the oil, and yield to the lessee a reasonable expectation of profit.

The Court of Civil Appeals has not imposed a new obligation upon Amoco. The jury, in finding that Amoco failed to operate the Alexander leases as a reasonably prudent operator, has determined that Amoco failed in its duties under the implied covenants to protect the leasehold.

Amoco argues the Court of Civil Appeals did not consider that Amoco has obligations to all of its lessors in the field. Anything it does to maintain or increase production from updip leases may accelerate the water drive and expose Amoco to liability to downdip lessors. If Amoco fails to maintain or increase updip production, it is exposed to liability from the updip lessors. Amoco argues the Court has placed it between contrary obligations from which there is no escape. The fulfilling of one obligation necessarily causes the breach of the other.

The conflicts of interest of Amoco, as a common lessee, cause us concern. The Alexander leases provided for 1/6th royalty while Amoco's updip leases provided for 1/8th royalty. There is no economic incentive for Amoco to increase production on the Alexander lease because it will eventually recover the Alexander's oil updip. Money invested in the Hastings, West Field, will have a longer productive life if invested updip. The greater the updip production the sooner Amoco's competitor Exxon will water out. Money spent updip will yield greater returns than money spent downdip because of higher daily production. With downdip operators out of production Amoco can produce its upper sands without competition and can begin production from its lower sands where it does not have significant production competition.

These conflicts would not occur if Amoco was not a common lessee (lessee common to downdip and updip lessors). If the Alexanders were the only Amoco lessor, their interests would more nearly coincide. Amoco's interest would be to capture the most oil possible from the Alexander leases before they watered out.

Amoco's responsibilities to other lessors in the same field do not control in this suit. This lawsuit is between the Alexanders and Amoco on the lease agreement between them and the implied covenants attaching to that lease agreement. The reasonably prudent operator standard is not to be reduced to the Alexanders because Amoco has other lessors in the same field. Amoco's status as a common lessee does not affect its liability to the Alexanders.

Duty to Apply for Administrative Relief

The Railroad Commission rules in the Hastings, West Field, prohibit the drilling of a well nearer than 660 feet to any other well and nearer than 330 feet to any property line or lease line. The rules allow the Railroad Commission to grant drilling permits as an exception to the spacing regulation. These exceptions are commonly referred to as Rule 37 permits. This rule provides:

> [T]he Commission in order to prevent waste or to prevent the confiscation of property will grant exceptions to permit drilling within shorter distance than above prescribed whenever the Commission shall determine that such exceptions are necessary to prevent waste or to prevent confiscation of property.

The Alexanders contend Amoco should have drilled replacement wells in the extreme updip corner of each lease. The wells would be within 50 feet of the lease line and 200 feet apart. The wells could not be drilled unless the Railroad Commission granted Rule 37 permits. Amoco did not apply for the permits.

The Court of Civil Appeals held that when Amoco determined the leases were watering out, prudent operation demanded drilling replacement wells unless it would be economically unfeasible. If Rule 37 permits were required, Amoco should have applied for them in furtherance of its duty to prudently operate the leases. Because Amoco failed to apply, the Court of Civil Appeals held, the Alexanders were entitled to show the exceptions most likely would have been granted and they suffered damages because of Amoco's failure.

Amoco states the holding of the Court of Civil Appeals amounts to the imposition of an implied covenant obligating a lessee to seek exceptions to regulations limiting the drilling and production of wells. Amoco argues there is no Texas authority for imposing an obligation to seek administrative relief and there is no duty to seek administrative relief.

We disagree with Amoco's argument that there is no duty to seek administrative relief. Amoco owed the Alexanders the duty to do whatever a reasonably prudent operator would do if the Alexanders were its only lessor in the field.

The duty to seek favorable administrative action may be classified under the implied covenants to protect the lease, or to manage and administer the lease. Regardless of the category, the standard of care in testing Amoco's performance is that of a reasonably prudent operator under similar facts and circumstances. *Shell Oil Co. v. Stansbury,* 410 S.W.2d 187, 188 (Tex.1966); 5 H. Williams & C. Meyers, Oil and Gas Law § 804 (1980).

We do not agree with the Court of Civil Appeals if its holding means that in every case of field-wide drainage the lessee must seek Rule 37 exceptions. There may be facts where the prudent operator would not seek administrative relief. The probability that the Railroad Commission will grant or deny the permit is a consideration to be made by the prudent operator. The jury, from evidence justifying granting or denying the permit, can determine if a reasonably prudent operator would have applied for the permit.

The jury found Amoco failed to operate the Alexander leases as a reasonably prudent operator. Does this finding, based in whole or in part on Amoco's failure to apply for Rule 37 permits, establish liability for failure to drill the replacement wells? If it does not, what remedies do the Alexanders have? They have no rights in the management or operation of the oil leases. Amoco, as operator, could quickly determine when the wells began watering out. Amoco, because of its conflicting interests, had no economic incentive to protect the Alexander leases. The downdip lessors, after their leases have watered out, have no opportunity to capture the oil updip.

It is the failure to act as a reasonably prudent operator that triggers the loss. If the Railroad Commission denies the Rule 37 permits, after a reasonably prudent application, the operator has no liability for not drilling the wells. We hold that an operator, who fails to act as a reasonably prudent operator by not seeking Rule 37 permits, is liable for loss caused by the failure to drill the wells.

* * *

Exemplary Damages

Amoco argues that exemplary damages are not recoverable because the Alexanders failed to plead and prove a tort allowing recovery of exemplary damages. We agree.

The Alexanders alleged "a breach by Amoco of both its express and implied covenants * * * under the lease contracts * * * to protect said leases from drainage and to operate said leases as a reasonable and prudent operator" and their "royalty interest under Leases A and B has been wasted and damaged * * *."

* * * Amoco argues that exemplary damages are not recoverable because a breach of the implied covenant to protect against drainage is an action sounding in contract and not in tort. The rights and duties of the lessor and lessee are determined by the lease and are contractual. The lease constitutes the contract. * * *

In *Texas Pac. Coal & Oil Co. v. Stuard,* 7 S.W.2d 878, 882 (Tex.Civ. App.1928, writ ref'd), the Court of Civil Appeals held that "the implication to develop after drilling the exploratory well is a part of the written contract and is governed by the four-year statute of limitation." In *Indian Territory Illuminating Oil Co. v. Rosamond,* 190 Okla. 46, 120 P.2d 349, 354 (1941), the Oklahoma Supreme Court held that "the implied covenant to protect against drainage is a part of the written lease as fully as if it had been expressly contained therein * * *" and applied the statute of limitations relating to actions on written contracts. We hold that the implied covenant to protect against drainage is a part of the lease and is contractual in nature.

Exemplary damages are not allowed for breach of contract. Even if the breach is malicious, intentional or capricious, exemplary damages may not be recovered unless a distinct tort is alleged and proved. We hold that a breach of the implied covenant to protect against drainage is an action sounding in contract and will not support recovery of exemplary damages absent proof of an independent tort.

* * *

Trial of Common Lessee Cases

The courts that have considered the common lessee problem have considered facts different from this case. In those cases the common lessee was causing the drainage by production on adjacent or adjoining land. The drainage was caused by production independent of water-drive and was local drainage. However, those decisions are analogous because of the common lessee. Professors Williams and Meyers have put these cases in three categories. See 5 H. Williams & C. Meyers, Oil and Gas Law § 824 (1980); Meyers & Williams, *Implied Covenants in Oil and Gas Leases: Drainage Caused by the Lessee,* 40 Texas L.Rev. 923 (1962). First, there are cases which state the lessee was causing the drainage but place no significance on that fact. Second, other cases state that the lessee caused the drainage but hold this fact does not alter the ordinary rules of liability for failure to protect from drainage. Third, there are cases holding the liability of the lessee is increased when the lessee is causing the drainage. * * *

This Court in *Shell Oil Co. v. Stansbury,* 410 S.W.2d 187, 188 (Tex.1966), * * * held that an express offset provision does not limit the lessee's obligation to protect from drainage when the lessee is the one causing the drainage. In drainage cases, Texas courts place upon the lessor the burden to prove that substantial drainage has occurred and that an offset well would produce oil or gas in paying quantities.

The judgment of the Court of Civil Appeals is modified to prohibit the recovery of exemplary damages and affirmed as modified.

NOTES

1. *Amoco v. Alexander*'s facts are unusual in that the lessor alleged that the lessee was permitting fieldwide drainage; the drainage the Alexanders complained about did not flow to an adjacent lease. Are the considerations for the courts different where fieldwide drainage is an issue? *Amoco v. Alexander* is also unusual in that it arose in Texas, which is one of the few oil-producing states without legislation for compulsory unitization.

2. As *Amoco v. Alexander* notes, the usual elements that a lessor must prove to maintain a claim upon the implied covenant to protect against drainage are (a) proof of substantial drainage and (b) proof that a reasonably prudent operator would have acted to prevent substantial drainage. Should the burden of proof be upon the lessor? What does a lessor have to prove to

satisfy these elements? See Breaux v. Pan Am. Petroleum Corp., 163 So.2d 406, 415 (La.App.1964). See also Lowe, Ch. 11.

    3. Is *Amoco v. Alexander* "good" law? Consider the following comment:

> The lessee of a single lease in a field could be expected to discharge these obligations in the lessee's self-interest, but * * * the common lessee operating competing leaseholds in the same pool may find irreconcilable conflict between the rule of capture and development obligations owed the various lessors with whom there are individual lease relationships * * *.

Summers Perm. Ed. § 401 (Lowe Supp.). Does it make economic sense to discourage the efficiencies of scale that accrue when a lessee operates several proximate leaseholds? See Amoco Prod. Co. v. Ware, 602 S.W.2d 620 (Ark. 1980). Does it make sense to require a lessee to seek administrative relief that is contrary to its business interests? Professor Jacqueline Weaver has urged that where the interests of the lessor and the lessee diverge, the lessee should be required only to give notice to the lessor so that the lessor can protect himself. Jacqueline L. Weaver, Implied Covenants in Oil and Gas Law Under Federal Energy Price Regulation, 34 Vand.L.Rev. 1473, 1541–47 (1981). See also Kuntz § 59.1. Amoco v. Alexander is also criticized in Stephen F. Williams, Implied Covenants' Threat to the Value of Oil and Gas Reserves, 36 Inst. on Oil & Gas L. & Tax'n § 3.06 (1985).

    4. Should it be significant in proving the elements of the implied covenant to protect against drainage that the lessee being sued is also the operator causing the drainage? What should be the law? Consider the merits of the following statements:

> The duty of an oil and gas lessee to operate the leased premises in a reasonable and prudent manner cannot prevent his operating the adjoining properties to the mutual advantage of the lessee and lessor there concerned.

Tide Water Associated Oil Co. v. Stott, 159 F.2d 174, 178 (5th Cir.Tex.1946).

> If plaintiffs' lessee (who also controls production from the adjacent draining well) should establish that it would be economically unfeasible for him to drill an offset well on plaintiffs' land, he nevertheless, under plaintiffs' interpretation of the law, would be compelled (1) to drill the offset well in spite of the cost, or (2) to surrender his lease, or (3) to discontinue producing from the adjacent well, or (4) to pay plaintiffs the value of a portion of the oil received from the adjacent well. We do not think the law would require the lessee under those circumstances to drill an offset well on plaintiffs' property when he could not hope to derive a profit from it, and in view of the established right of the adjoining landowner to capture and become the owner of the fugitive minerals which he may find under his land, we do not think plaintiffs have the right to compel their lessee to discontinue producing minerals from the neighboring tract or to pay to plaintiffs a portion of the oil produced from that tract.

Breaux v. Pan Am. Petroleum Corp., 163 So.2d 406, 417 (La.App.1964).

If the defendant had no interest in the adjoining leases on the north and south, it would seem that its defense [of lack of profitability of drilling] might be sound. But here the mind is haunted by the fact that the defendant is the beneficiary of the oil drained from plaintiffs' land by the wells on the north and south which belong to the defendant. It has not only been saved the cost of drilling, equipping and operating a protecting well but it gets all of the oil anyway without plaintiffs being paid for it.

Geary v. Adams Oil & Gas Co., 31 F.Supp. 830, 834 (E.D.Ill.1940).

The suit is based on the alleged fraudulent conduct of the lessee in draining gas from the Epling tract through wells owned and operated by it on adjoining leases. * * * What is fraud in such circumstances? Ordinarily it is considered to be fraud for a lessee of a given property, without protecting its boundaries by adequate offset wells, to take oil or gas from wells controlled by him on adjoining properties, which wells are so close to the boundaries of the given property as evidently to drain oil or gas from thereunder. * * * Though there may not be an actual dishonest intent on the part of the operator, the result is the same. And, even if such situation arise through the exercise of bona fide business judgment on the part of the lessee, if oil or gas from under the given tract is extracted through wells of the same lessee on adjoining tracts, equity considers it fraudulent conduct.

Dillard v. United Fuel Gas Co., 173 S.E. 573, 575 (W.Va.1934). See also Young v. Forest Oil Co., 45 A. 121 (Pa.1899).

We proceed next to a consideration whether there exists a duty in the lessee to protect the interests of his lessor against a depletion of the lessor's lands by the affirmative act of the lessee upon adjacent property.

* * *

The express provisions here involved absolved lessee from meeting his duty to the [lessor] by capturing lessors' oil in situ through wells drilled on lessors' lands. The equitable duty, existing as well under implication, to conserve the mineral resources of lessors or to refrain from depletory acts survives unimpaired.

Millette v. Phillips Petroleum Co., 48 So.2d 344, 346 (Miss.1950). See also Shell Oil Co. v. James, 257 So.2d 488 (Miss.1971).

The trial court also specifically concluded that a common lessee has a duty to prevent substantial drainage from the nonproducing lease land regardless of whether or not drilling of an offset well on the nonproducing land would be a prudent operation.

* * *

There are various reasons assigned for this exception to the reasonable prudent operator rule. It is sometimes emphasized that the common lessee is not a stranger to the situation and is operating on an arm's length situation; that he is subject to a duty to protect the lessee from the harm. Sometimes it is said that there is an unjust enrichment if the lessees are allowed to convert the gas with impunity. Some cases go so far as to characterize this as fraudulent drainage.

* * *

We conclude that the trial court was correct in its determination that the reasonable prudent operator limitation was not applicable to this case; that in view of the relationship of the parties there existed an implied covenant running to the plaintiff-appellee to refrain from any action which would deplete her property in the lease. There was a direct violation of this implied covenant. It is unnecessary then to consider whether it has undertones of inequitable conduct or unjust enrichment. The appellant companies have violated an implied covenant to refrain from activities that would injure her property interest.

Cook v. El Paso Natural Gas Co., 560 F.2d 978, 983–84 (10th Cir.N.M.1977).

In our view, the fact that it is the lessee's operations that cause drainage on lessor's land is an insufficient basis for eliminating the substantive requirement that an offset well be profitable. The most the law should seek to do is to require of the lessee the operations a reasonably prudent operator would undertake if he did not own the adjoining lease.

But because of the possibility of unfair dealing, the procedural law may properly be changed, although the substantive law should not be. The change we suggest would place the burden of going forward with evidence and the burden of persuasion of profitability on the lessee.

Thus, the plaintiff's case would consist of these elements:

(1) proof of substantial drainage;

(2) proof that the lessee's operations were the cause of the drainage;

(3) amount of the damages.

This evidence would be sufficient to withstand a motion to dismiss, and if defendant offered no evidence, plaintiff would get a directed verdict. Defendant can avoid liability, however, by proving that a protection well would not be profitable. Under this proposal, the only change in the law regarding the implied protection covenant is in the burden of proof on production in paying quantities. On this issue the lessee is ordinarily better informed anyway.

Williams & Meyers § 824.2. (used with permission)

5. What defenses should be available to a lessee if a lessor sues for breach of the implied covenant to protect against drainage?

(a) Suppose that the lessor has failed to give the lessee notice of the drainage. Should notice be a condition precedent to the lessee's implied obligation to protect the premises? The Supreme Court of Montana has observed that:

There is no sound reason to require a lessor to give a lessee notice of drainage in an action for damages, if the lessee already has such knowledge. Under the implied covenant to protect, a lessee is charged with the duty to act as a reasonable operator and to protect the leaseholder's interest. This duty requires the lessee to manage the leasehold in such a manner as to bring profit to both himself and the lessor. Obviously, if the lessee failed to drill an offset well, while knowing the leasehold was being drained, he would fail to meet this duty. In such a circumstance, he should not be excused for the sole reason that the lessee failed to comply with a requirement that is unnecessary.

* * *

[B]efore a lessee's duty to drill an offset well arises, he must have reasonable notice of the necessity to protect the leasehold. Such notice can either be express, from the lessor, or constructive, gained from the surrounding circumstances.

This rule is only applicable to those cases in which a lessor is seeking relief in the form of damages, however. If he is seeking other forms of relief, such as forfeiture of the lease, he must give written notice in order to give the lessor a chance to cure the breach. See Summers, Oil and Gas Volume 2 § 412 (1990).

The burden of proof is upon the lessor to establish the fact that the lessee knew of the drainage.

Sundheim v. Reef Oil Corp., 806 P.2d 503, 507–09 (Mont.1991).

(b) Should the lessee be able to defend against a lessor's claim of breach of the implied covenant to protect against drainage on the ground that the lessee has complied with existing spacing requirements? Why not? See U.V. Industries, Inc. v. Danielson, 602 P.2d 571 (Mont.1979). Had not the lessee complied with all existing conservation rules in *Amoco v. Alexander*?

(c) Should it be a defense that an offset well, while profitable, would not produce a reasonable rate of return on the lessee's investment? If so, what is a reasonable rate of return? See Forest Oil Corp., 141 IBLA 295 (1997).

(d) Can the lessor's implied rights be lost if the lessor accepts lease benefits? What if the lessor accepts delay rental payments covering the period during which the lessor alleges that the lessee has permitted drainage? Should the lessor be held to have waived the implied covenant to protect against drainage or to be estopped to assert it? Contrast Rogers v. Heston Oil Co., 735 P.2d 542 (Okla.1984) and Texas Co. v. Ramsower, 7 S.W.2d 872 (Tex.Com. App.1928) (no waiver or estoppel) with Clear Creek Oil & Gas Co. v. Bushmaier, 255 S.W. 37 (Ark.1923) (waiver or estoppel). If the lessor accepts royalty payments or executes a division order, should the lessor be barred from asserting the implied covenant to protect against drainage? See Elliott v. Pure Oil Co., 139 N.E.2d 295 (Ill.1956). See also Kuntz §§ 61.2, 61.4; and Lowe, Chapter 11.

(e) Should the rights of the lessor and lessee who are involved in a drainage dispute be different if the lease contains a clause that states:

> In the event a well or wells producing oil or gas in paying quantities should be brought in on adjacent land and within one hundred fifty (150) feet of and draining the leased premises, Lessee agrees to drill such offset wells as a reasonably prudent operator would drill under the same or similar circumstances.

See Williams v. Humble Oil & Refining Co., 432 F.2d 165, 174–76 (5th Cir.La.1970). See generally Kuntz § 61.2; Hemingway § 8.6; and Lowe, Chapter 11.C. What if the lease contains a statement that it is the complete agreement of the parties, and there are no other covenants or conditions, express or implied? Cf. Dallas Power & Light Co. v. Cleghorn, 623 S.W.2d 310 (Tex.1981).

6. What remedies should be available to a lessor who establishes that the lessee has breached the implied covenant to protect against drainage? See generally Daniel F. Sullivan, Annotation, Remedy for Breach of Implied Duty of Oil and Gas Lessee to Protect Against Drainage, 18 A.L.R.4th 147 (1982).

(a) If the lessor seeks damages, should the measure of damages be the royalty on the oil and gas drained away or the royalty that the protection well would have generated? Do you see the difference? Which measure would have been better for the lessors in Amoco v. Alexander and why? See Kuntz § 61.5(d).

(b) The Texas Supreme Court in Amoco v. Alexander denied exemplary (punitive) damages to the lessors. Why? Is the court's reasoning sound? See John S. Lowe, Developments in Non–Regulatory Oil and Gas Law: Are We Moving Toward a Kinder and Gentler Law of Contracts?, 42 Inst. on Oil & Gas L. & Tax'n § 1.02[c] (1991).

The Texas Supreme Court addressed the dividing line between tort and contract in Southwestern Bell Telephone Co. v. DeLanney, 809 S.W.2d 493 (Tex.1991), a non-oil and gas case. In *DeLanney,* the plaintiff sued for tort damages as a result of the telephone company's negligent failure to perform its contract to publish an advertisement in the Yellow Pages. A jury awarded DeLanney punitive damages for Bell's negligence, and a court of appeals affirmed, holding that Bell's failure was both a tort and a breach of contract. In reversing the award, the Texas Supreme Court discussed the distinction between tort and contract breaches:

> If the defendant's conduct—such as negligently burning down a house— would give rise to liability independent of the fact that a contract exists between the parties, the plaintiff's claim may also sound in tort. Conversely, if the defendant's conduct—such as failing to publish an advertisement—would give rise to liability only because it breaches the parties' agreement, the plaintiff's claim ordinarily sounds only in contract.

> In determining whether the plaintiff may recover on a tort theory, it is also instructive to examine the nature of the plaintiff's loss. When the only loss or damage is to the subject matter of the contract, the plaintiff's action is ordinarily on the contract.

809 S.W.2d at 494. (citations omitted). See also El Paso Marketing, L.P., v. Wolf Hollow I, L.P., 2012 WL 2161545 (Tex.).

In Zenith Drilling Corp. v. Internorth, Inc., 869 F.2d 560 (10th Cir.Okla. 1989), the Tenth Circuit Court of Appeals held that a drilling-rig lessor was not entitled to recover punitive damages for the lessees' material breach of contract in deliberately refusing to pay standby charges. Zenith had asserted that the lessees, by failing to pay the agreed charges, had committed an independent and willful tort to harm Zenith. The court rejected the claim, reasoning that Zenith had asserted an independent tort only to support its punitive damages claim and held that one may not recover punitive damages for breach of contract in Oklahoma unless one has also recovered actual damages for the tort. But in Okland Oil Co. v. Conoco Inc., 144 F.3d 1308 (10th Cir. Okla. 1998), the court permitted the operator of gas-producing wells to recover punitive damages from a gas purchaser where the purchaser had alleged and the jury had found breach of contract, fraud in the inducement, deceit by false representation, and deceit by nondisclosure or concealment with respect to the purchaser's failure to pay the operator under gas production contracts. And in Grynberg v. Citation Oil & Gas Corp., 573 N.W.2d 493 (S.D.1997), the South Dakota Supreme Court held that a lease operator who deliberately misallocated costs to a non-operating owner committed fraud that supported punitive damages because "Citation clearly invaded the property rights of the plaintiffs * * *." Id. at 501.

(c) Should a lessor be entitled to cancel the lease or have it declared forfeited for the lessee's breach of the implied covenant to protect against drainage? If so, what theory justifies cancellation? See Ramsey Petroleum Corp. v. Davis, 85 P.2d 427 (Okla.1938), and Elliott v. Pure Oil Co., 139 N.E.2d 295 (Ill.1956). Where courts permit cancellation, cancellation is likely to be conditional upon the lessee's failure to drill a protective well or to pay damages and is likely to affect only the area drained. See Kuntz § 61.5(e).

(d) Should a lessor whose property is being drained want the lease canceled?

7. What effect should the following lease clause, sometimes called a *notice-and-demand clause,* have upon the rights of the parties where a lessor complains that the lessee has failed to protect the property against drainage?:

> In the event lessor considers that lessee has not complied with all its obligations hereunder, both express and implied, lessor shall notify lessee in writing, setting out specifically in what respects lessee has breached this contract. Lessee shall then have sixty (60) days after receipt of said notice within which to meet or to commence to meet all or any part of the breaches alleged by lessor. The service of said notice shall be precedent to the bringing of any action by lessor on said lease for any cause, and no such action shall be brought until the lapse of sixty (60) days after service of such notice on lessee.

In Wiser v. EnerVest Operating, L. L. C., 803 F.Supp.2d 109 (N.D.N.Y. 2011), the court held that a notice-and-demand clause did not apply where the lessee had failed to pay delay rentals under an "unless" rental clause. Is a lessor's claim for breach of an implied covenant different from a claim that rentals have not been paid?

How is a notice-and-demand clause different from the following provision, sometimes called a *notice-before-forfeiture clause?*

> The breach by Lessee of any obligations arising hereunder shall not work a forfeiture or termination of this Lease nor cause a termination or reversion of the estate created hereby nor be grounds for cancellation hereby in whole or in part unless Lessor shall notify Lessee in writing of the facts relied upon in claiming a breach hereof, and Lessee, if in default,

shall have sixty (60) days after receipt of such notice in which to commence the compliance with the obligations imposed by virtue of this instrument * * *.

Some provisions, called *judicial-ascertainment clauses*, go even further to protect lessees. Typically judicial-ascertainment clauses provide that the lease may not be forfeited or declared terminated until the lessor has proved the breach complained of in court and then, after judgment, the lessee has been given a reasonable time to comply. Should the courts enforce such clauses? In Frick–Reid Supply Corp. v. Meers, 52 S.W.2d 115 (Tex.Civ.App.–Amarillo 1932), refusing to enforce a judicial ascertainment clause, the Texas court stated that "parties will not be permitted in the formation of their contracts to interfere with or retard the course of justice or to oust the court's jurisdiction * * * as prescribed by statute * * *." Id. at 118. Is that reasoning compelling? Is there any reason why a judicial-ascertainment clause should not be enforced? See Kuntz § 53.4. In Irish Oil & Gas, Inc. v. Riemer, 794 N.W.2d 715 (N.D. 2011), the court held that a judicial-ascertainment clause expressly applicable to an alleged breach of "implied covenants, conditions, or stipulations" did not apply to express provisions of the lease or to the lessee's failure to pay an agreed bonus.

(c) Implied Covenants to Drill

As *Amoco v. Alexander* illustrates, the essence of a lessor's claim for breach of the implied covenant to protect against drainage is that the lessee has failed to act as a reasonable prudent operator and has deprived the lessor of royalty by permitting oil or gas to be lost by drainage from the lease to another property. In contrast, when a lessor complains that a lessee has failed to test, to develop, or to explore, the lessor is complaining about the loss of the use of money that would have been paid as royalty had testing, developing, or exploring taken place—there is no loss of the oil and gas in place under the leased land. Consider as you ponder the following materials what difference this distinction should make, if any, in the burden of proof, the elements of proof, and the remedies for breach.

(i) The Implied Covenant to Test

As we have discussed above, early in the history of the oil and gas industry the courts held that a lessee was subject to an implied covenant to test leased premises by drilling within a reasonable time, on the theory that royalties were the primary consideration for the grant of the lease and that there would be no royalties unless the lessee tested the property. The implied covenant to test is relatively unimportant in modern practice because most leases contain a delay rental clause that specifically provides that the lessee may maintain the lease throughout the primary term, without drilling, by paying delay rentals. The implied covenant to test may be resurrected, however, where the lease contains no delay rental clause. Consider the following:

PROBLEM

Your client, the land manager of an oil company, has decided to pay delay rentals in advance for the entire primary term on a "package" of new leases she is negotiating, because the annual rental amounts are small in comparison to the administrative costs involved in paying them. Your client asks you whether she can safely delete the delay rental clause. What is your advice? See Kuntz §§ 28.6, 57.2. See also Lowe, Chapter 8.E.

(ii) The Implied Covenant to Develop

The implied covenant to develop is the corollary of the implied covenant to test. The implied covenant to test applies, if at all, during the primary term. The covenant to develop is not triggered until the lease is propelled into the secondary term by production or some substitute. Under a modern oil and gas lease, a lessee has no obligation to test the premises during the lease primary term. Once the lessee has drilled a well and the lease is held by "production" or some substitute, however, the lessee must continue to develop as would a reasonable prudent operator under the circumstances.

SUPERIOR OIL CO. v. DEVON CORP.

604 F.2d 1063 (8th Cir.Neb.1979).

BENSON, CHIEF JUDGE.

This is an appeal from an order and judgment of the district court cancelling an oil and gas lease for breach of an implied covenant to further develop the lease, * * *.

In 1949 Harlen C. and Velma R. Olsen executed an oil and gas lease in favor of plaintiff Superior Oil Company (Superior) covering 3,440 acres of land in Banner County, Nebraska. The lease was recorded in the office of the Register of Deeds of Banner County. The primary term of the lease was ten years and "as long thereafter as oil, gas, * * * or any of the products covered by this lease is or can be produced." Oil was discovered and produced on the leasehold within the primary term. In 1958, Superior assigned part of its interest in the lease to Lark Oil Company, which in turn made an assignment to plaintiff Petroleum, Inc. (Petroleum).

In 1961, that part of the Superior leasehold on which oil was being produced was unitized into the Willson Ranch Field "J" Sand Unit (Willson Ranch Unit).

After 1961, there was no further drilling by Superior or its assignees on the tracts covered by the Superior lease. In February 1976 the successors of the original lessors, hereinafter referred to as the Schuler–Olsens, executed oil and gas leases to Chris L. Christensen, Jr., on certain tracts that were subject to the prior Superior lease. An oil well was successfully completed in February 1977.

On June 30, 1977, Superior and Petroleum filed this action naming as defendants the Schuler–Olsens and the lessee and assignees under the

1976 top leases,[1] hereinafter referred to as the working interest defendants. Plaintiffs alleged that the Schuler–Olsens breached their contract with plaintiffs by executing the top leases and that the working interest defendants were trespassers and converters. * * *

In their amended answer and counterclaim, the Schuler–Olsens affirmatively alleged that plaintiffs had failed to perform the implied covenants of the lease and had abandoned the lease. They sought cancellation of the Superior lease for plaintiffs' breach of the implied covenant of further development.

* * *

The court * * * concluded that Superior had failed to meet the standards required of a prudent operator and that * * * it had breached the implied covenant to further develop. The court held that on the record in the case an adjudication of breach of the implied covenant to further develop was not barred by the failure of the lessor to demand further drilling, and ordered that portion of the Superior lease outside the Willson Ranch Unit cancelled unconditionally as of a time preceding the execution of the Christensen leases. * * *

We reverse the cancellation of the Superior lease and the dismissal of the working interest defendants, and do not reach plaintiffs' remaining specifications of error.

I. The Implied Covenant to Further Develop

In the field of oil and gas litigation a principle of law has arisen which incorporates in every oil and gas lease an implied covenant to further develop. The implied covenant becomes applicable only after production is obtained, and the life of the lease by its terms has been extended by reason of the production. Before production is obtained, the lease remains in effect for the primary term if delay rental payments are made as required. After production is obtained, the implied covenant of further development requires the lessee to act with reasonable diligence in developing the lease as would a reasonable and prudent operator under similar circumstances, having due regard for the mutual interests of both lessor and lessee. Concomitant with the duty on the part of the lessee to further develop the lease is a reasonable expectation of profit for the lessee. The reasonable expectation of profit for the lessor is not determinative of whether the lessee has complied with the implied covenant to further develop, for the lessor's royalty interest is not a costbearing interest. Any development will thus redound to the benefit of a lessor. The lessee bears the cost of development, and it is to his expectation of reasonable profit that the court must look in applying the reasonable and prudent operator standard.

* * *

---

1. [Editors' Note] A top lease is a lease that is granted to cover property already subject to an oil and gas lease. Generally, a top lease grants rights when the existing lease expires. Principles and problems of top leasing are considered in Chapter 4.

The rationale underlying the implied covenant to further develop has been stated by the Supreme Court as follows:

> The production of oil on a small portion of the leased tract cannot justify the lessee's holding the balance indefinitely and depriving the lessor, not only of the expected royalty from production pursuant to the lease, but of the privilege of making some other arrangement for availing himself of the mineral content of the land.

Sauder v. Mid–Continent Petroleum Corp., 292 U.S. 272, 281 (1934).

We further note that at this particular point in time the public interest in encouraging the prudent development of oil and gas leases is particularly important. The development of domestic sources of oil will reduce the amount of oil which has to be imported and will thereby redound to the national interest by helping to reduce the deficit trade balance and to render the nation less susceptible to economic dislocations arising from political disturbances in foreign oil producing nations. In this case the district court was justifiably concerned by the failure of Superior to develop. The district court was not persuaded that the reason for failure to develop was primarily economic, and as the court appropriately pointed out, had Superior availed itself of the opportunity to farm out, its interest would have been non-costbearing, as was the lessors' interest. The district court's error, however, was in ordering the cancellation of the Superior lease under the circumstances, where no notice or demand had been served on the lessee prior to lessors' execution of top leases to Christensen. The Schuler–Olsen defendants clearly misconstrued their remedies. They could have easily served their own interest, and in turn the national interest, by giving Superior notice, making demand for production, and subsequently bringing an action to cancel the lease if Superior failed to respond. They would have thereby accomplished their legitimate and reasonable objective without doing violence to well established principles of oil and gas law.

II.   The Requirements of Notice and Demand

An oil and gas lease is a recognized and protected property interest. A cancellation of an oil and gas lease effects a forfeiture of that interest. The law abhors a forfeiture. Therefore, an oil and gas lease will not be cancelled for breach of an implied covenant without the lessor having first given the lessee notice of the breach and demanding that the terms of the implied covenant be complied with within a reasonable time.

The rationale underlying the requirements of notice and demand is clear. A lessee, even though he may be in breach of the implied covenant, should be informed of that breach, and should be given an opportunity to redeem himself by commencing further development within a reasonable time. The lessee is in effect given a choice of development or forfeiture.
* * *

The concept that notice and demand are waived if there has been no development for an unreasonable period of time does not appear to be supported by the law. The only circumstance under which notice and demand are waived is when the lessee indicates to the lessor, by words or conduct, that he will not commence further development of the lease despite demand made by the lessor. Thus, where lessee states that he has no present intention of drilling at any time in the near or remote future, or claims the right to hold the property without development, or declares that he would not drill even if adequate demands were made, the requirements of notice and demand are waived. The mere passage of a period of time deemed to be unreasonable should not waive the notice and demand requirement, because a lessor retains the right to test the reasonableness of delay by giving notice and demanding development.

* * *

There appears to be no authority in the case law supporting the general equitable considerations upon which the court based its holding that notice and demand were not required in this case. Uncertainty in the established field of oil and gas law should not be introduced on the showing made by the Schuler–Olsens in this case.

* * *

IV.   Order

The orders of the District Court cancelling the Superior lease * * * are reversed, and the judgment entered on the orders is vacated. The case is remanded for disposition consistent with this opinion.

HEANEY, CIRCUIT JUDGE, dissenting.

I respectfully dissent. In my view, the District Court correctly terminated the portions of the Superior lease outside the Willson Ranch Unit because Superior breached its implied covenant to further develop.

I agree with the majority that this action is governed by Nebraska law and that the Nebraska courts would apply the implied covenant to further develop. I do not agree that the District Court erred in holding that notice was not required prior to the termination of the lease.

The requirement of notice is grounded in equitable principles and is designed to prevent unnecessary forfeitures by informing a lessee of a breach of an implied covenant and giving him an opportunity to repair the breach within a reasonable time. See generally 5 E. Kuntz, A Treatise on the Law of Oil and Gas § 58.4 (1978); 3 W. Summers, The Law of Oil and Gas § 469 (perm. ed. 1958). If, however, the lessee already knows that he has breached the implied covenant and within a reasonable time thereafter does not correct it, or indicates in some manner that he is not going to undertake further development, the notice requirement is dispensed with because its purposes have already been fulfilled. In such circumstances, requiring the lessor to give notice would be a useless act. Thus, notice is required only where it is equitable to do so in light of the policies behind the requirement.

In this case, Superior knew that it had breached the implied covenant to further develop and did not correct it within a reasonable time. Consequently, notice would serve no useful purpose.

The implied covenant to further develop requires the lessee to maintain an active interest in the lease after an exploratory well has been drilled. E. Kuntz, A Treatise on the Law of Oil and Gas § 58.1 (1978). Thus, after the lease is held by production, a lessee may not, consistent with its duty under the implied covenant, hold the remaining portions of the leasehold for speculative purposes. As noted by the court in *Doss Oil Royalty Co. v. Texas Co., supra,* 137 P.2d at 938:

> The implied covenants of a lease require the lessee to develop and operate the lease with due regard for the lessor's interest therein as well as his own. Neither the lessor nor the lessee is the arbiter of the extent to which, or the diligence with which, the lessee shall proceed, but such question is committed to the sound discretion of the courts to be determined from the facts and circumstances of each case. To permit the lessee to hold the lease for an unreasonable length of time for merely speculative purposes, is to allow him to protect his own interest and to disregard the interest of the lessor. If conditions do not indicate to him that further development will be profitable, it is but fair that, after a reasonable time has expired, he surrender the undeveloped portions of the lease and allow the lessor to procure development by others or assume the burden of showing why in equity and good conscience the undeveloped portion should not be cancelled so that the owner may, if possible, get it developed by others. (Citation omitted.)

Superior made a conscious decision not to develop the lease for speculative purposes and, in doing so, it intended to breach the implied covenant. Prior to 1960, Superior possessed geological evidence which indicated that further development of the lease was warranted. Superior did not act on this information. In addition, it refused to farm out any portion of its lease. Frank Baumgartner, for example, requested a farm out in March, 1960, on the same acreage where the Christensen well was successfully drilled seventeen years later. In rejecting the farm out, Superior noted in an inter-office memorandum:

> As the Olsen lease is held by production, I can see no reason at this time to grant an additional farmout [sic] to Frank Baumgartner. He still has the opportunity to earn additional acreage in Sec. 22. I feel we have moved too fast in this immediate area, as we have farmed out apparently good oil land to both British American and Baumgartner within the past year.

> As we are under no strain from a date standpoint, we can afford to await further drilling on acreage already farmed out.

It is difficult to see how Superior can claim that it is inequitable to terminate its lease without notice, or that it was surprised by the actions of the Schuler–Olsens. Once Superior made the decision to hold the lease for speculative purposes, it knowingly assumed the risk that the lessor would terminate the lease. Notice would serve no purpose in this case except to encourage such conduct in the future.

* * *

I would affirm the District Court.

NOTES

1. What is the rationale underlying the implied covenant to develop? In *Superior Oil,* the court observed that a failure to develop deprives the lessor of royalties and the opportunity to make other arrangements. Other courts have said that development was the main consideration for granting the lease (Stubbs v. Imperial Oil & Gas Products Co., 114 So. 595 (La.1927)); that development is required to further the original purpose of the lease (Smart v. Crow, 246 S.W.2d 432 (Ark.1952)); and that a failure to develop renders the leased premises susceptible to future drainage to other land if the field becomes fully developed (Vonfeldt v. Hanes, 414 P.2d 7 (Kan.1966)). One may also argue that additional drilling is needed to maintain proper reservoir pressure and to maximize ultimate recovery. A more realistic reason for an implied covenant for further development is given in Temple v. Continental Oil Co., 320 P.2d 1039 (Kan.1958):

> A lessor is entitled to the benefit of oil produced from the lease at the time it should be produced and not at some remote period of time in the future. The lessee is not the sole judge of what constitutes prudent development of the tract. The test is what would be expected of an operator of ordinary prudence, in the furtherance of the interests of both *the lessor* and the lessee. (Emphasis in original.)

320 P.2d at 1055. On rehearing, the court commented further on the "time element" as follows:

> [T]he *time* element must be reconciled with the established Prudent Operator Rule. It is well settled that where the existence of oil in paying quantities is made apparent, it is the duty of the lessee to continue the development of the property and to put down as many wells as may be reasonably necessary to deplete the oil and gas reserves underlying the premises for the common advantage of both the lessor and the lessee. Obviously, fulfillment of this obligation might require the drilling of several wells, despite the fact that one well alone *might ultimately* drain the entire reservoir *given unlimited time.* In other words, lessees cannot prove compliance with the Prudent Operator Rule by showing they have drilled enough wells to "adequately" drain the recoverable oil from the leased premises *"eventually".* (Emphasis in original)

Temple v. Continental Oil Co., 328 P.2d 358, 360 (Kan.1958).

2. What does a lessor have to prove to establish a breach of the implied covenant to develop? In Slaaten v. Amerada Hess Corp., 459 N.W.2d 765 (N.D.1990), the court identified several factors that should be considered in applying the reasonable prudent operator standard, including the quantity of oil and gas likely to be found, the market demand for oil and gas, the extent

and result of operations on adjacent lands, the character of the reservoir, usages of the industry, the costs of drilling and operation, the costs of transportation and storage, the prevailing price, the general market conditions as affected by supply and demand and regulation, the willingness of another operator to drill, the attitude of the present lessee toward further development, and the time that elapsed since drilling operations were last conducted. Professor Lowe has suggested that there are two elements of a breach of the implied covenant to develop: (1) proof that additional development will probably be profitable; and (2) proof that the lessee has acted imprudently in failing to develop. Lowe, Chapter 11.C. See also Kuntz § 58.3.

Would it be harder to prove breach of the covenant to develop than breach of the covenant to protect against drainage? Should the burden of proof be placed upon the lessor?

3. Does the statement that a "reasonable expectation of profit for the lessee" is a prerequisite to a finding of a breach of the implied covenant for further development mean the same thing as "production in paying quantities" under the habendum clause? See Kuntz § 58.3 and Lowe, Chapter 11.C.

4. Which opinion in *Superior Oil*—the majority or the dissent—do you think has the better argument as to whether the lessor should be required to give notice of the breach and demand for drilling to the lessee? Would the *Superior Oil* majority have been so insistent that notice be given if the lessors had sought damages, rather than lease cancellation? Generally, however, notice and an opportunity to correct the breach are prerequisites to a demand for forfeiture. For example, in James Energy Co. v. HCG Energy Corp., 847 P.2d 333 (Okla.1992), the Oklahoma Supreme Court refused to quiet title in lessors who failed to make a demand that a lessee produce and market gas before they sued for cancellation. The court reasoned that an action to cancel an oil and gas lease is an action in equity, so that the lessee must be given notice and a reasonable time to comply unless there are circumstances under which the giving of notice would be a "vain and useless thing."[28] Applying this standard in Crain v. Hill Resources, 972 P.2d 1179, 1181 (Okla.Civ.App. Div. 3 1998), an Oklahoma Court of Appeals held that evidence sustained a trial-court finding that "the sheer passage of time, i.e., 14 to 15 years, with no benefit to the Lessors * * * " indicated that "Lessees had exhibited no serious intention to market this gas."

5. Can the parties to a lease limit or define the implied covenant to further develop by express language? In *Superior Oil,* what would have been the effect of a lease provision that stated:

After the discovery of oil, gas, or other hydrocarbons in paying quantities on the lands covered by this lease, or pooled therewith Lessee shall reasonably develop the acreage retained hereunder, but in discharging this obligation Lessee shall not be required to drill more than one well per eighty (80) acres of area retained hereunder and capable of producing oil in paying quantities, and one well per six hundred forty (640) acres of the area retained hereunder and capable of producing gas or other

---

28. 847 P.2d at 338, *citing and quoting* Mitchell v. Amerada Hess Corp., 638 P.2d 441, 446 (Okla.1981).

hydrocarbons in paying quantities, plus a tolerance of ten percent in the case of either an oil well or a gas well.

Compare Gulf Prod. Co. v. Kishi, 103 S.W.2d 965 (Tex.Com.App.1937), with Sinclair Oil & Gas Co. v. Masterson, 271 F.2d 310 (5th Cir.Tex.1959). See also Kuntz § 58.2 and Lowe, Chapter 11.C. The lease in Exxon Corporation v. Emerald Oil and Gas Co., L.C., 348 S.W.3d 194 (Tex. 2011), contained a clause that required Exxon to "prosecute diligently a continuous drilling and development program until said tract is *fully developed* for oil and gas," and then stated that the lease "shall be deemed fully developed within the intent of the preceding paragraph of this Article" when at least one well had been "*drilled and completed*" in each horizon or stratum capable of producing oil or gas in paying quantities for each twenty acres of land for oil production and for each 160 acres of land for gas production. (Ital added.) The court held that "drilled and completed" required Exxon to drill, and if it encountered oil or gas in paying quantities, to perforate the casing or otherwise prepare the well to produce. It rejected, however, the lessors' argument that "fully developed" required Exxon to produce all of the oil from every stratum that could be produced in paying quantities; it concluded that "fully developed" was "primarily aspirational," and required merely that Exxon conform to industry best practices.

6.   What should be a lessor's remedy against a lessee for breach of the implied covenant to develop?

(a) If damages are the remedy, there is precedent for a variety of measures. The "lost royalty" rule awards the lessor the royalty that the lessor would have received had the lessee drilled development wells as a reasonable prudent operator. See, e.g., Howerton v. Kansas Natural Gas Co., 108 P. 813 (Kan.1910). The "lost interest" rule calculates the lessor's damages as the interest that the lessor would have received had the lessor been paid royalty on the wells that the lessee should have drilled. See, e.g., Grass v. Big Creek Dev. Co., 84 S.E. 750 (W.Va.1915). The "future credit" rule awards the lessor the lost royalty, but then permits the lessee to claim a dollar for dollar credit, without interest, when (and if) the lessee produces the oil or gas. See, e.g., Cotiga Dev. Co. v. United Fuel Gas Co., 128 S.E.2d 626 (W.Va.1962). What should be the measure of the lessor's recovery for breach of the implied covenant to develop and why? See Kuntz § 58.5(d).

(b) Because suits for breach of implied covenants are generally filed only after rancorous dealings between the lessor and lessee, lessors usually ask the courts for lease cancellation or forfeiture. If the implied covenants are implied contractual promises, cancellation or forfeiture should be available only where damages are an inadequate remedy, which would be highly unusual where the lessor's complaint was the lessee's failure to develop. Yet, lease cancellation or forfeiture for breach of the implied covenant to develop is commonplace, either on the theory that the lessee has shown an intent to abandon the lease by its inactivity or on general equitable principles. As the Oklahoma Supreme Court noted, "[w]e decline to become so involved in theories or distinctions as to render ourselves impotent to deal with the problem in the instant case." Doss Oil Royalty Co. v. Texas Co., 137 P.2d 934 (Okla.1943). On the other hand, because disputes over the obligation to develop further do not arise until there is a well producing on the lease or lands pooled with the lease, a cancellation decree is likely to be partial—to apply only to the lands that the court has found that the lessee should have developed—and conditional—to take effect only if the lessee fails to develop within a period set by the court. Total lease cancellation is likely only in extreme circumstances. For example, in ordering total cancellation in Waseco Chemical & Supply Co. v. Bayou State Oil Corp., 371 So.2d 305 (La.App.1979), a case in which the lessee had done nothing to develop the property for 24 years while other oil companies in the area had drilled hundreds of wells using advanced fire-flooding techniques, the trial court justified its action by noting that "frankly it appeared to the Court that Bayou State learned as much about fireflooding in the two weeks of our trial as it had in twenty years of operation." Id. at 307.

(iii) The Implied Covenant to Explore Further

Should a lessee who is producing oil or gas from a lease have an obligation to explore further? There has been considerable debate over whether the law should recognize an implied covenant to explore further separate from an implied covenant to develop. The concepts are clearly distinguishable in theory. A lessor who complains of a development-covenant breach alleges that the lessee has behaved imprudently in failing to develop known deposits of oil or gas that would have generated royalties. The lessor's complaint for breach of the exploration covenant is one step further removed—the lessor alleges that the lessee has acted imprudently in failing to explore undeveloped parts or formations of the land to determine whether there are deposits of oil or gas that might be profitably exploited to generate royalties.

The controversy concerns the lessor's burden in proving that a lessee failed to explore. If a lessor must prove the same degree of probability of profitability to establish a breach of the covenant to explore further as the courts require to establish a breach of the covenant to develop, a lessor will rarely be able to meet the burden. By definition, an exploratory well is riskier than a development well. The late Dean Charles Meyers started the formal debate. He argued that a lessee should not be allowed to hold an entire leasehold with production from only one area or one formation, but should be subject to a duty to explore unproductive areas, both laterally and vertically. To Meyers, prolonged delay without further exploration was the principal factor indicating breach, and conditional lease cancellation of the unexplored acreage or formations was the proper remedy. Citing cases such as Sauder v. Mid–Continent Petroleum Corp., 292 U.S. 272 (1934) and Doss Oil Royalty Co. v. Texas Co., 137 P.2d 934 (Okla. 1943), Professor Meyers concluded that courts had already given the exploration covenant de facto recognition, although none had fully spelled out all of its elements. The most controversial aspect of his proposed covenant was that the lessor should not be required to prove that exploration would be profitable. Meyers argued that what a reasonable prudent operator would do in developing or preventing drainage from proven formations had little bearing on what such an operator would do in exploring other areas or formations for new reserves. Charles J. Meyers, The Implied Covenant of Exploration, 34 Tex.L.Rev. 553 (1956).

Professor Meyers' proposal evoked a flood of commentary, including a vigorous complaint by Earl Brown that the creation of a duty to explore would impose an unfair, unreasonable, and unexpected burden upon oil companies. Brown argued that the profitability to the lessee was an essential element to the breach of any implied covenant and that the lessee's implied drilling obligations should not be extended beyond the implied covenants to protect against drainage and to drill additional development wells. Brown § 16.05.

Professor (later Judge) Stephen Williams criticized Professor Meyers's argument on economic grounds. Stephen F. Williams, Implied Covenants for Development and Exploration in Oil and Gas Leases—The Determination of Profitability, 27 Kan.L.Rev. 443 (1979). He suggested that what was primarily at issue was the rate of lease development and that a lessee's delay in exploratory drilling might be based upon a reasonable expectation that oil prices would increase or decrease drilling costs. Professor Williams was especially critical of the remedy of conditional lease cancellation, arguing that it might cause a lessee to engage in wasteful, unprofitable drilling to protect a leasehold that it was holding in anticipation of oil price increases. In other articles, he argued that a lessee's conduct should be deemed proper if the lessee was acting "as would a profit maximizing owner of [all] of the mineral under lease * * *." Stephen F. Williams, Implied Covenants in Oil and Gas Leases: Some General Principles, 29 Kan.L.Rev. 153, 171 (1981). See also Stephen F. Williams, Implied Covenants' Threat to the Value of Oil and Gas Reserves, 36 Inst. on Oil & Gas L. & Tax'n 3–1 (1985).

In response, Professor Meyers and lawyer-economist Steven Crafton chided Professor Williams for substituting the business judgment rule of corporate law for the traditional prudent operator rule standard and for failing to recognize that the oil and gas lease is a relational contract subject to opportunistic behavior by the lessee. Charles J. Meyers & Steven M. Crafton, The Covenant of Further Exploration—Thirty Years Later, 32 Rocky Mtn.Min.L.Inst. 1–1, 1–17 to 1–25 (1986).

Other commentators have been sympathetic to Professor Meyers's proposal. Professor Lowe states:

> Professor Meyers did not ignore profit potential. He identified a number of factors that bear on whether the operator acquitted itself properly in exploration, such as the feasibility of further exploratory drilling, which takes into account economic factors like the presence of geologic formations likely to contain oil or gas, the costs of drilling, the market for the product, and the size of the block necessary to drill a test well.

Lowe, Chapter 11.C.

Professor Mark Gergen uses an oil and gas lease to analyze generic problems in contracts where, in return for a royalty, the owner of an asset of uncertain value engages another party to develop the asset under a negligence-like performance standard (i.e. the reasonable and prudent operator standard). Mark P. Gergen, The Use of Open Terms in Contract, 92 Colum.L.Rev. 997 (1992). He demonstrates that without implied covenants an oil and gas lessee will perform below the level that maximizes the return on the lease. In particular, the article demonstrates that a lessee will not be diligent in developing new wells or exploring new areas, because the lessee bears the entire cost of development but reaps only part of the return. On the other hand, the lessee has an incentive to hold out areas that might be profitably developed or explored, because the lessee reaps most of the gain if the price of the mineral rises.

Professor Jacqueline Weaver has styled the debate over whether there is a separate implied covenant to explore further as:

> largely academic because regardless of whether the covenant is given a name that is distinct from the implied covenant to develop, the courts have recognized that the duty to act as a reasonably prudent operator may in some circumstances require the lessee to drill wells that the lessor has not been able to show would be profitable.

Jacqueline L. Weaver, Implied Covenants in Oil and Gas Law Under Federal Energy Price Regulation, 34 Vand.L.Rev. 1473, 1504 (1981).

The states have been as divided as the commentators. The Colorado Court of Appeals stated the case for a separate exploration implied covenant in the following manner:

> Colorado recognizes, in general, four implied covenants in oil and gas leases: to drill; to develop after discovery of oil and gas in paying quantities; to operate diligently and prudently. The basis for these covenants is founded on the concept that in the secondary term of an oil and gas lease:

> "[t]he work of exploration, development, and production should proceed with reasonable diligence for the common benefit of the parties, or the premises be surrendered to the lessor." *Brewster v. Lanyon Zinc Co.*, 140 Fed. 801 (8th Cir.1905).

> Reasonable diligence is, "whatever, in the circumstances, would be reasonably expected of all operators of ordinary prudence, having regard to the interests of both lessor and lessee." *Brewster, supra.*

> This obligation to explore, develop, and produce, once production is acquired, includes both an implied covenant of reasonable development and an implied covenant of further exploration. *H. Williams & C. Meyers, Oil & Gas Law* §§ 831–847 (1983). The implied covenant of reasonable development requires a determination that additional development will be profitable. This determination rests on proof that, more probably than not, production of oil or gas will be found in paying quantities. The implied covenant of further exploration does

not need such proof, but rather requires the lessor to show unreasonability by the lessee in not exploring further under the circumstances.

Among the circumstances relevant to determining whether there has been a breach of the promise of further exploration are: the period of time that has lapsed since the last well was drilled; the size of the tract and the number and location of existing wells; favorable geological inferences; the attitude of the lessee toward further testing of the land; and the feasibility of further exploratory drilling as well as the willingness of another operator to drill. *H. Williams & C. Meyers, supra.*

Gillette v. Pepper Tank Co., 694 P.2d 369, 372 (Colo.App.1984).

Kansas has codified a covenant to explore further. Kansas enacted in 1983 what has become known as the "Deep Horizons" Act (Kansas Stat. Ann. §§ 55–223 to 55–229), to promote exploration and development of leases lands held by production, as to formations that lie below "the base of the deepest producing formation as of the date of such action." K.S.A. § 55–227. The Act creates a presumption that "the lessee has breached and violated such [implied or expressed] covenant [of reasonable exploration or of reasonable development] insofar as it relates to such subsurface part or parts of land" when a lessor presents evidence that: (1) there is currently no mineral production from the deeper horizons; and (2) "initial oil, gas or other mineral production on the lease commenced at least 15 years prior to the commencement of such action. . . ." K.S.A. § 55–224. The Act is designed to place the burden of proof on the lessee to justify its failure to develop the deeper horizons once 15 years has passed since the last new production from the leased land. The statute was upheld against constitutional challenge in Amoco Prod. Co. v. Douglas Energy Co., 613 F.Supp. 730 (D.Kan.1985), and is discussed in Pierce § 10.06. In Lewis v. Kansas Production Co., 199 P.3d 180 (Kan. Ct. App. 2009), the court held that, for a lessor to be eligible for the remedy of outright cancellation under the Act, the lessor must first demand compliance with the covenant and provide the lessee with a reasonable opportunity to respond to the demand.

Louisiana also recognizes the implied covenant to further explore. The Comments to Article 122 of the Louisiana Mineral Code note that:

> [H]istorically in Louisiana the obligation of further exploration can be viewed as an evolutionary offshoot of the obligation of reasonable development. See Carter v. Arkansas Louisiana Gas Co., 213 La. 1028, 36 So.2d 26 (1948). Although the jurisprudence does not make a clear distinction between the obligation of further exploration and the obligation of reasonable development, the distinction nevertheless exists.

But both the Oklahoma Supreme Court and the Texas Supreme Court have rejected a free-standing implied covenant to explore further, however. In Mitchell v. Amerada Hess Corp., 638 P.2d 441 (Okla.1981), the Oklahoma Supreme Court observed that:

Failure to recognize the profit motive as an instrumental force in oil and gas leases on behalf of both lessee and lessor is to ignore the very essence of the contract. * * * To state otherwise is folly or worse. * * * Can the duties of the lessee be judged apart from the specter of profit where the activity is judged exploration rather than development? To do so is unwise and unnecessary. The machinery to adjudicate an "exploration" controversy exists presently in the form of the covenant to diligently develop.

638 P.2d at 447. See also Sun Exploration & Prod. Co. v. Jackson, 783 S.W.2d 202 (Tex.1989).

Which is the better approach? Would it not be reasonable and prudent for an operator to drill an exploratory well—a venture that does not meet the company's usual profitability standard for development wells—with one eye to profitability potential and the other on the need to locate additional development prospects?

If the courts recognize an implied covenant to explore further, separate from the implied covenant for further development, what should be the elements of its proof? Should they be different from elements of proof of the implied covenant to develop? What should be the victorious lessor's remedy? See Lowe, Ch. 11.C, and A. George Mason, The Yeas and Nays of Implying a Duty on a Producing Oil and Gas Lessee to Explore the Lease Further, 15 E.Min.L. Inst. 11–1 (1994).

Because the existence of an implied covenant to explore further is uncertain, many leases address the duty to explore directly. Lessors often break large tracts into several leases or include a *retained-acreage clause* like the following:

Notwithstanding any other provisions herein, upon the pooling of part of the leased premises or the completion of a producing well thereon this lease shall be severed and shall be considered as separate and distinct leases on (a) the pooled acreage or on the tract comprising the spacing unit for such well and (b) the rest of the premises; such severance shall result each time, and from time to time, whenever pooling occurs or any producing well is completed; and the term of each resulting lease caused by any such severance, and all the rights and obligations of Lessee under any such lease, shall apply separately to the acreage attributable to the particular lease under the foregoing severance, with every resulting lease being considered as separate and independent from every other lease.

See Nafco Oil & Gas, Inc. v. Tartan Resources Corp., 522 S.W.2d 703 (Tex.Civ.App.1975).

A lessor might also consider negotiating a liquidated-damages provision tied to a work program. In Presnal v. TLL Energy Corp., 788 S.W.2d 123 (Tex.App.1990), a lessor and lessee had agreed to a lease clause that provided for a $75,000 liquidated damages payment if the lessee failed to commence drilling as promised. The lessee failed to perform and challenged the liquidated damages clause as a penalty. The trial court granted the lessee summary judgment. The court of appeals reversed, applying *Stewart v. Basey*, 245 S.W.2d 484 (Tex.1952). In *Stewart*, the Texas Supreme Court held that a liquidated damages provision is enforceable only if (1) liquidated damages are a reasonable forecast of just compensation or (2) damages could not have been accurately estimated without difficulty. Both determinations must be made as of the date of contract formation. The *Presnal* court of appeals concluded, however, that the burden of proof is upon the party claiming that the liquidated damages provision is unreasonable. Since the lessee had presented no evidence, it had failed to meet its burden. By this view, a liquidated damages clause is presumptively valid.

Liquidated damages clauses remain, however, among the most difficult contract provisions to draft properly. First, the liquidated damages clause should contain the parties' stipulation that actual damages arising from a breach will be difficult to ascertain because of uncertainty or indefiniteness. Second, the liquidated damages amount should differ depending upon the extent of the performance before breach. While $75,000 in liquidated damages may be reasonable for a failure to commence drilling, $75,000 may be considered as a penalty for a failure to attempt to complete a well after the lessee has drilled to the total depth and has completed preliminary but disappointing tests.

(d) The Implied Covenant to Operate Diligently and Properly

The implied covenant of diligent and proper operation substantially overlaps the other implied covenants. For example, *Amoco Prod. Co. v. Alexander*, which you read when you considered the covenant to protect against drainage, may be viewed equally well as an example of the covenant of diligent and proper operation or as a specific implied covenant to seek administrative relief. See also Spaeth v. Union Oil Co., 710 F.2d 1455 (10th Cir.Okla.1983). But the covenant to operate diligently and properly may also be understood as a "catch-all" category; consider, for example, whether the requirement that a lessee exercise the lease pooling power in "good faith" or the implicit limitations on the right of a lessee to use the surface could not also be considered examples of the implied covenant to operate diligently and properly.

BALDWIN v. KUBETZ

307 P.2d 1005 (Cal.App.1957).

ASHBURN, JUSTICE.

* * *

The trustees of the Baldwin estate sued Kubetz, Kline and others for declaratory relief and declaration of forfeiture of their sublease. They alleged violation by Kubetz of (1) a covenant to operate in accordance with customary oil field practices, and (2) continuous drilling requirements of the sublease. The court found these charges to be true. Appellant Kubetz primarily claims insufficiency of the evidence to support the findings.

Concerning the manner of operation paragraph 3K of the Baldwin sublease provides: "Lessee agrees at all times to use diligence and observe customary oil field practices and modern methods, appliances and equipment to save all oil, gas or other products produced from said premises, which may be saved at a reasonable profit." The court found that Kubetz from time to time and "continuously on numerous occasions * * * violated the provisions of the Los Angeles County Fire Prevention Code, has created and maintained fire hazards, has failed to use and observe oil field practices customary in Los Angeles County, and has failed to use modern methods, appliances and equipment in accordance with standards customary in Los Angeles County. That such actions and course of conduct were willful and persistent despite repeated warnings and notices." The general nature of appellant's derelictions consisted of inadequacy of equipment to control the flow of oil, thus permitting it to overflow on various occasions; defective electric wiring; inflammable material permitted to collect near the well close to storage tanks and to the liquefied petroleum gas tank. These fire hazards existed before and after notice of default and down to the day of trial, and they resulted in conditions which were not in accordance with customary oil field practices and modern methods of operation. They constituted serious threats to the production and even the existence of the Kubetz well, also to two other producing wells in the immediate vicinity.

* * *

The obligation of continuous drilling is found in paragraph 4A of the sublease and requires (as the court found) the sublessee to "continuously drill additional wells, allowing not more than ninety (90) days between the completion of one well and the beginning of the next well, until an average of one well for each 10 acres of said lands shall be completed thereon, or a total of 44 wells." There is no dispute of the fact that Kubetz drilled but one well (known as Kubetz No. 1) and that his predecessor Kline had brought in two producers, nor is it denied that appellant did no drilling whatsoever after February, 1952. In this connection the court concluded: "That said sublease obligates defendant Sam Kubetz to continuously drill additional wells on said lands, to obtain zone exceptions as may be necessary to permit such drilling, to operate said Kubetz No. 1 well according to customary oil field practices and by the use of modern methods, appliances and equipment, and to keep said well in the most efficient productive state. * * * That defendant Sam Kubetz has not performed said obligations. * * * That none of said obligations has been suspended under the provisions of Paragraph 12 of said sublease, nor has the failure of defendant Sam Kubetz to perform said obligations been excused in any manner."

Appellant would overthrow this ruling by capitalizing paragraph 12 of the sublease which provides that the obligations of the lessee shall be suspended while lessee is prevented from performing by acts, rules or regulations of governmental agencies, or when prevented by other matters or conditions beyond control of the lessee, whether similar or dissimilar to matters or conditions specifically mentioned. The focal point of the argument is an alleged inability to procure a zoning exception which would permit further drilling. The property had been zoned for light agricultural use some three years before appellant acquired the sublease and a zone exception was necessary for oil drilling. Within ten days after he acquired the lease appellant applied for and obtained a permit to drill one well; that he did and placed it on production. About six months later he applied for another exception in order to do further drilling but that application was denied. "That at the time said application was made, heard and denied defendant Sam Kubetz was in violation of the conditions of his first permit, had violated various laws, regulations, or ordinances, and was operating said Kubetz No. 1 well in a manner materially detrimental to the public welfare and the property of other persons in the vicinity, and said application was denied for those reasons." (Finding X.) Appellant waited about a year, prepared a third application which was never filed and let the matter drop about the middle of 1953. Notice of default was served in October, 1954, and suit filed on March 9, 1955, but appellant did nothing further in an effort to drill or obtain permission to drill additional wells.

Appellant claims that there was no obligation to drill additional wells because the existence of the zoning brought the suspension[1] clause into operation and no duty rested on him to procure a zoning exception. First, he argues that the existing state of zoning—for uses exclusive of oil well drilling—precluded him from pursuing that activity, that he was thus prevented from performing his continuous drilling obligation by acts, rules or regulations of a governmental agency. There is no merit in this contention, for the applicable county zoning ordinance provided for the granting of an exception to permit the drilling of an oil well if "it appears probable that there is oil underneath the property under consideration or under adjacent property which oil cannot be otherwise extracted." It required as a condition to the granting of an exception the presentation of an application containing evidence that the applicant, if not the owner of the property, "has the permission of such owner to make such application." The zoning ordinance itself does not prevent drilling; it merely attaches a condition precedent which is easily fulfilled. * * * The court found, upon adequate evidence: "That at all times since June 14, 1951, and particularly since October 20, 1954, defendant Sam Kubetz could have applied for and obtained a zone exception to permit the drilling of additional wells on said lands."

Appellant next argues that no duty rested upon him to obtain the drilling permit: "Assuming appellants just did not wish to make application for zone variance, appellants submit that it would then be the

---

1. [Editors' Note] What the court calls the "suspension clause," we would call the force-majeure clause.

obligation of respondents to make such application and then either compel performance of the contract or sue for damages for the breach thereof." As appellant had the exclusive right to drill, this contention, which was also urged at the trial, ignores the basic requirement of fair dealing which is stated thus in Brawley v. Crosby Research Foundation, Inc., 73 Cal. App.2d 103, 112, 166 P.2d 392, 397: "In this, as in every contract, there is the implied covenant of good faith and fair dealing; that neither party will do anything that would result in injuring or destroying the right of the other to enjoy the fruits of the agreement. [Citations.] The law will therefore imply that under its agreement appellant was obligated in good faith and by its reasonable and best efforts to develop, exploit, produce and make sales of the rotary pump in question."

In consonance with this equitable principle it has become accepted law in this state that there is an implied covenant of diligent exploration and diligent operation of any producing wells. Immanent (sic) in this implied obligation is that of doing such incidental or subsidiary acts as may be reasonably necessary to accomplish the major purpose,—in this instance the procuring of the drilling permit through an easily obtained zoning exception.

Though the lease does not mention the point (having been made before the zoning for agricultural use) defendant acquired it with knowledge of the necessity of procuring an exception and by conduct placed a practical construction upon the lease to the effect that that was his obligation. Twice he prepared and presented such applications; also prepared a third which was abandoned without filing.

Appellant was subject to an implied obligation to obtain the necessary drilling permit through a zone variance. Of course, his failure to perform this obligation does not justify his falling back on the suspension clause.

* * *

We recognize in this state that equity's frown upon enforcement of forfeitures is not directed at cancellation of an oil lease for failure to perform its express or implied drilling obligations. Acme Oil and Mining Co. v. Williams, * * * 140 Cal. 681, 684, 74 P. 296, 297: "Covenants may be implied, as well as express; and in oil leases, and others of that particular character, where the consideration for the lease is solely the payment of royalties, there is an implied covenant not only that the wells will be sunk, but that if oil is produced in paying quantities, they will be diligently operated for the best advantage and benefit of the lessee and lessor." 140 Cal. at page 685, 74 P. at page 297: " * * * as the sole and only consideration to the lessor for the extension of this lease was the benefit and advantage in royalties which he might derive under it, and as this benefit could only accrue through diligent operation of the wells, the law raises an implied covenant for such diligent operations as of the very essence of the lease. As this covenant was implied from the nature of the lease, it stands upon the same footing as if it was expressly contained therein, and the lessor was warranted, if the condition was not performed, in re-entering and taking possession of the premises, and terminating the lease. While the general rule is that forfeitures are discountenanced in law, there are occasions when the only protection a landlord has is through the exercise of this reserved right, and the case at bar presents one of those occasions. If the right of forfeiture could not be exercised under such circumstances, a lessor would be at the mercy of his lessee. His land would be burdened by a lease which, while it could and should be made profitable through the diligence contemplated, would in fact be profitless through neglect. The lessor could not make other arrangements for the development of his property and his interest in the fee in the oil district might consist of a small holding, surrounding which numerous other operators would be successfully working, drawing off the oil to his irreparable injury. These are some of the peculiar circumstances surrounding leases of this character which favor the right of re-entry for condition broken." * * *

The foregoing authorities [citations to which were omitted] sustain the right of the court to declare terminated appellant's interest under the sublease with the possible exception of the existing producing well and ten acres surrounding it. They also render unimportant appellant's argument that he made unavailing attempts to induce the Pelisses, as owners, to join in the application for a zoning exception. In any event that defense could not prevail for defendant cannot excuse nonperformance of his obligation by a showing that he tried but was unable to perform, not unless the impossibility arises out of the nature of the act to be done rather than the inability of the obligor to do it.

With respect to the producing well, appellant relies upon paragraph 13A, which says: "If lessee shall fail to comply with any requirements or obligations in this lease contained, and such failure shall continue for a period of thirty (30) days after the receipt by lessee of written notice from lessor specifying the particulars in which the lease shall be in default * * * then, at the election of lessor this lease and all rights of lessee hereunder shall thereupon cease and terminate, except and only that lessee shall have the right to retain, subject to the terms of the within lease, any wells theretofore completed or on which work is then being done, in good faith at the time of such forfeiture, together with an area of *then* (10) acres of land surrounding each of said wells for the same period and upon the same terms as are set forth and provided in the within lease, hereinabove set out, in respect to wells completed during the term of this lease * * *. The forfeiture provided for in the within paragraph shall be the exclusive remedy of lessor against lessee in the event of failure of lessee to comply with any of the provisions of the within lease designated and relating to drilling requirements hereof." Respondents contend that 13A is not applicable and that the field is covered by paragraph 13B, thus precluding application of 13A. We are unable to agree with respondent in this respect, for 13B is general in its terms and must yield to the specific provisions of 13A to the effect that a general forfeiture does not terminate the lessee's rights with respect to a producing well and ten acres surrounding same.

* * *

The judgment is affirmed.

* * *

NOTES

1. Professors Williams and Meyers note that the most common complaints by lessors that are based upon the implied covenant to operate diligently and properly are: (a) that the lessee has damaged the property, (b) that the lessee has prematurely abandoned a well capable of producing profitably, (c) that the lessee has failed to use advanced production techniques, or (d) that the lessee has failed to protect the lessor by seeking favorable administrative action. Williams & Meyers § 861.

2. Because the implied covenant of diligent and proper operation is the broadest of the six covenants, the courts are likely to invoke it to respond to problems that do not fit neatly into one of the other categories. Environmental damage is an example. Where the lessee's operations have damaged the lessor's surface or water rights, the lessor may allege the excessive or unreasonable use of the property as a breach of the implied covenant of diligent and proper operation, rather than using one of the more traditional theories such as negligence or nuisance. Generally, however, lessors will prefer to emphasize their tort claims so that they can claim punitive damages. See, e.g., Briscoe v. Harper Oil Co., 702 P.2d 33 (Okla.1985).

3. When experts disagree, to what extent should a lessee be entitled to rely upon expert advice or to choose a course of action from among those recommended? In Sinclair Oil & Gas Co. v. Bishop, 441 P.2d 436 (Okla.1967), Woods obtained by assignment a lease from Bishop and drilled a well. After testing a deeper formation, Woods plugged back and completed and equipped the well. The well turned out to be a marginal producer, though nearby wells drilled to the same formation produced prolifically. Bishop sued Woods for breach of the implied covenant to operate diligently and prudently, claiming that Woods should have produced from the lowest possible portion of the zone. Bishop's expert witnesses testified that Woods had failed to complete the well in the proper interval and to use the proper equipment and completion methods. Woods presented an equal number of expert witnesses who testified that he had acted prudently. The trial court canceled the lease, but the Supreme Court of Oklahoma disagreed:

> The evidence on the part of lessors at most showed there might have been a better method of completion. The probative value of lessees' evidence does establish that Woods did complete the well according to the judgment of its experts.

* * *

We determine that in the completion of this well Woods was within its prerogatives by acting in reliance upon its own experts.

441 P.2d at 445. If Woods was an assignee of the original lessee, by what theory was the implied covenant enforceable against him?

4. DIVISION ORDERS

A troublesome issue is the extent to which the royalty obligation may be affected by a division order. In a division order, all parties who may have a claim to the proceeds of sale—working interest owners as well as royalty owners—agree how the proceeds are to be divided.[29] Lessees and purchasers of production use division orders to protect themselves against claims that they have improperly paid royalties. Typically, division orders identify the owners, their interests, and the producing property; certify the signatories' ownership of the production sold; transfer title of production to the purchaser; and provide for measurement of production, corrections, and the mode and time of payment. As the materials that follow illustrate, division orders give rise to frequent disputes.

GAVENDA v. STRATA ENERGY, INC.

705 S.W.2d 690 (Tex.1986).

SPEARS, JUSTICE.

This oil and gas case concerns the effect of division and transfer orders. The issue is whether division and transfer orders are binding until revoked when an operator who prepares erroneous orders underpays royalty owners, retaining part of the proceeds for itself. The trial court held the orders were binding until revoked and rendered summary judgment for the operators. The court of appeals affirmed. 683 S.W.2d 859. We reverse the judgment of the court of appeals in part and remand the cause to the trial court.

In 1967, the Gavenda family conveyed land in Burleson County to the Feinsteins. The Gavendas reserved a fifteen-year one-half non-participating royalty interest:

> PROVIDED, HOWEVER, the Grantors herein except from this conveyance and reserve unto themselves, their heirs and assigns, for a period of fifteen (15) years from the date of this conveyance, an undivided one-half (½) non-participating royalty of all of the oil and gas in, to and under that produced from the hereinabove described tract of land. Said interest hereby reserved is a non-participating royalty and shall not participate in the bonuses paid for any oil and/or gas lease covering said land, nor shall the Grantors participate in the rentals which may be paid under and pursuant to the terms of any lease with reference to said land.

The Feinsteins later sold the land, subject to the Gavendas' oil and gas reservation, to Billy Blaha. In 1976, Blaha executed an oil and gas lease for a 1/8th royalty.

---

29. The Forms Manual includes examples of division orders.

After various conveyances with overriding royalty interests taken, Strata Energy, Inc. and Northstar Resources, Inc. each acquired a working interest in the lease. They drilled one producing oil and gas well in July, 1979 and another in February, 1980. Strata and Northstar entered into a joint operating agreement naming Strata the lease operator and providing that Strata would disburse all royalties from production. The agreement also provided that Strata's actions were made on behalf of both Strata and Northstar.

Strata hired an attorney to perform a title examination, and he erroneously informed Strata that the Gavendas were collectively entitled to a 1/16th royalty, rather than the actual ½ royalty. Following the attorney's erroneous report, Strata prepared the division orders and disbursed the proceeds. When various Gavendas died and royalty ownership changed, Strata prepared and sent transfer orders to the new royalty owners reflecting the same collective 1/16th royalty. The Gavendas signed these division and transfer orders and received the disbursements. The Gavendas were underpaid by 7/16th royalty, 7/16th of gross production, and Strata and Northstar kept at least part of the underpayment.

On discovering this error, the Gavendas on September 29, 1982 revoked the division and transfer orders. Two days later, their royalty interest terminated under the express terms of their reservation. Later in 1982 the Gavendas filed suit to recoup more than 2.4 million dollars in underpaid royalties owed them under the deed reservation.

Both sides filed motions for summary judgment. The trial court and the court of appeals held for Strata and Northstar, maintaining the division orders were binding until revoked. The court of appeals, however, reversed summary judgment and remanded as to Victor Gavenda's estate. The court of appeals held that there were fact issues whether the division and transfer orders encompassed Victor Gavenda's estate.

Both parties have appealed to this court. The Gavendas bring three points of error, contending the rule that division orders are binding until revoked does not apply when there is unjust enrichment, and therefore they should be allowed to recover royalty deficiencies from Strata and Northstar.

Strata and Northstar contend the division and transfer orders were also binding on Victor Gavenda's estate. They, however, do not dispute: (1) the deed reserved a ½ royalty, or ½ of gross production; or (2) the amount of the royalty underpayment, $2,435,457.51 plus interest. The only issue then is whether under these facts division orders are binding until revoked.

Division orders provide a procedure for distributing the proceeds from the sale of oil and gas. They authorize and direct to whom and in what proportion to distribute funds from the sale of oil and gas. 4 H. Williams, Oil and Gas Law § 701 at 572 (1984). Transfer orders are later changes in the division order's distribution. *Id.*

In Texas, division and transfer orders do not convey royalty interests; they do not rewrite or supplant leases or deeds. The weight of authority clearly supports this rule.

The general rule in Texas, though, is that division and transfer orders bind underpaid royalty owners until revoked. One principle underlining this rule is detrimental reliance. 4 H. Williams, *supra,* § 707 at 614; 3 A. Summers, Oil and Gas § 590 at 139–140 (1958).

Detrimental reliance explains why purchasers and operators are usually protected by the rule that division orders are binding until revoked. In the typical case, purchasers and operators following division orders pay out the correct total of proceeds owed, but err in the distribution, overpaying some royalty owners and underpaying others. If underpaid royalty owners' suits against purchasers and operators were not estopped, purchasers and operators would pay the amount of the overpayment twice—once to the overpaid royalty owner under the division order and again to the underpaid royalty owner through his suit. They would have double liability for the amount of the overpayment. *Chicago Corp. v. Wall,* 293 S.W.2d 844 (Tex.1956). Exposing purchasers and operators to double liability is unfair, because they have relied upon the division order's representations and have not personally benefitted from the errors.

Generally, the underpaid royalty owners, however, have a remedy: they can recover from the overpaid royalty owners. The basis for recovery is unjust enrichment; the overpaid royalty owner is not entitled to the royalties. *See* 4 Williams, *supra,* § 707 at 613 (1984); 3A. Summers, *supra,* § 590 at 139–40 (1957).

In *Exxon v. Middleton,* 613 S.W.2d 240 (Tex.1981), we held the division orders were binding until revoked, even though there had been no detrimental reliance. To provide stability in the oil and gas industry, we held for the distributors of the proceeds because they had not profited from their error in preparing the division order—in short, because there was no unjust enrichment.

In *Middleton,* Sun and Exxon, the well operators, sold the gas off the premises to purchasers under long term contracts. They then prepared division orders and distributed to the royalty owners a 1/8th royalty based on the contract price. The leases, however, provided for gas sold off the premises for a 1/8th royalty based on market value at the well. The royalty owners sued for their royalty deficiencies—the difference between a 1/8th royalty based on market value at the well and a 1/8th royalty based on contract price.

Exxon and Sun could not have relied on the division orders' representations in making the long-term gas contracts, for they had executed these contracts before the royalty owners had signed the division orders. *Id.* at 249. More importantly, however, Exxon and Sun did not benefit from the discrepancy between the leases and the division orders. They paid out 1/8th of what they received from the purchaser—1/8th of the contract proceeds. Moreover, at the time of these transactions, long-term gas contracts were the best arrangement Exxon and Sun could obtain for the royalty owners.

When the operator, however, prepared erroneous orders and retained the benefits, we held that the division orders were not binding. *Stanolind Oil & Gas Co. v. Terrell,* 183 S.W.2d 743 (Tex.Civ.App.1944, writ ref'd). In *Terrell,* Stanolind Oil & Gas prepared the division orders and distributed the bonus and royalty accordingly. Stanolind Oil & Gas deducted the gross production tax from the bonus, although the lease provided that there would be no deductions. Despite the lease provision, Stanolind was shifting the gross production tax from itself to Terrell. It was profiting from its own error in drawing up the division order. There was unjust enrichment.

Applying the law to this case, we hold that the division and transfer orders do not bind any of the Gavendas. Strata both erroneously prepared the division and transfer orders and distributed the royalties. Because of its error, Strata underpaid the Gavenda family by 7/16th royalty, retaining part of the 7/16th royalty for itself. It profited, unlike the operators in *Exxon v. Middleton,* at the royalty owner's expense. It retained for itself, unlike in *Chicago Corp. v. Wall,* part of the proceeds owed to the royalty owners. Therefore, Strata is liable to the Gavendas for whatever portion of their royalties it retained, although it is not liable to the Gavendas for any of their royalties it paid out to various overriding or other royalty owners.

Strata also argues that it is not responsible for the loss because the attorney who prepared the title opinions was not Strata's agent but rather an independent contractor. We cannot agree. The attorney-client relationship is an agency relationship. The attorney's acts and omissions within the scope of his or her employment are regarded as the client's acts; the attorney's negligence is attributed to the client. We note that Strata and Northstar have filed a third party cross-action against the attorney.

* * *

We reverse the judgment of the court of appeals in part and remand the cause to the trial court to determine the amount of royalties owed by Strata and Northstar to the Gavendas * * *. Although the total amount of the royalty deficiency is undisputed, we cannot tell from the record what portion of the royalty deficiency was retained by Strata and Northstar.

NOTES

1. Can you understand how a title examiner might mistake a ½ nonparticipating royalty for a ¹⁄₁₆ royalty? There but for the Grace of God go you or we.

2. The *Gavenda* court distinguishes the facts before it from those in Exxon Corp. v. Middleton, 613 S.W.2d 240 (Tex.1981), on the ground that in *Middleton* there was no unjust enrichment of Exxon in enforcing the division order against the lessors. Is this a distinction without a difference? Professor Laura Burney has observed:

Arguably, the lessees in both Gavenda and Middleton were unjustly enriched. Just as the operator in Gavenda benefitted from the underpayment, caused by the use of the wrong fraction in calculating royalty, the lessees in Middleton and the other "market value royalty" cases benefitted by calculating royalties on a contract basis lower than the prevailing market value.

Despite this factual similarity in Gavenda and Middleton, the cases can be distinguished on the question of unjust enrichment. In Gavenda, the lessee retained money which had been received for the production, an unjust enrichment. In Middleton, however, the producers were not actually enriched, having never received payment for the gas based on the higher prevailing market value.

Laura H. Burney, The Interaction of the Division Order and the Lease Royalty Clause, 28 St. Mary's L.J. 353, 378–379 (1997); See also Smith & Weaver § 6.5. Why are you unjustly enriched if you keep money you are not entitled to receive, but not unjustly enriched if you fail to pay money that you are obligated to pay?

3. Why should a division order not be considered a contract amending the royalty clause of the oil and gas lease? The Kansas Supreme Court addressed that issue indirectly in Holmes v. Kewanee Oil Co., 664 P.2d 1335 (Kan.1983):

Appellant first argues the royalty owners signed division orders stipulating their royalty interest [which the lease stated was 1/8 of market value at the well] was 1/8 of the price under the gas purchase contracts, thereby altering the lease contracts. * * *

This issue was resolved in Maddox v. Gulf Oil Corp., 567 P.2d 1326 (Kan.1977). The court held:

A division order is an instrument required by the purchaser of oil or gas in order that it may have a record showing to whom and in what proportions the purchase price is to be paid. Its execution is procured primarily to protect the purchaser in the matter of payment for the oil and gas, and may be considered a contract between the sellers on the one hand and the purchaser on the other.

Where a division order prepared by the lessee of an oil and gas lease for the lessor's signature unilaterally attempts to amend the oil and gas lease to deprive the royalty owner of interest on royalties held in suspense, to which the royalty owner is otherwise entitled under the leasing contract, and the lessor signs the division order without consideration from the lessee, the provision waiving interest is null and void.

We hold the lessors' signatures on the division orders did not alter the leases.

664 P.2d at 1340–41.

Could you devise a division order that would meet the test established by the Holmes case? Do you think that it would satisfy the Gavenda court if it were applied to the facts of that case?

4. May a lessee refuse to pay royalty until a lease royalty owner has executed an appropriate division order? The Arkansas Supreme Court considered that issue with respect to gas royalties in TXO Prod. Corp. v. Page Farms, Inc., 698 S.W.2d 791 (Ark.1985):

> TXO also argues that the title was somehow rendered unmarketable by Page Farms's failure to sign the requested division order. To begin with, the oil and gas lease did not require the lessors to sign such an order. TXO submitted testimony that division orders are recognized by custom and usage as being required in the oil and gas industry, but there is no proof that Mr. and Mrs. Page were so familiar with the oil and gas business that their knowledge and acceptance of the particular usage must be presumed. Absent such proof, they were not bound by any such custom or usage. Additionally, the proposed division order contained provisions, unfavorable to the lessors, that were not authorized by the lease. Page Farms was not at fault in failing to sign the division order, nor is its title shown to be unmarketable.

698 S.W.2d at 792–93. See also Hull v. Sun Refining & Marketing Co., 789 P.2d 1272 (Okla.1989), holding that the terms of Okla.Stat. tit. 52 § 570.1, setting time periods and terms for payment of the proceeds of production, barred the lessee from insisting that the royalty owner sign a division order. Would the lessee's position be different in dealing with an oil royalty owner? What about a working interest owner?

5. Several states have enacted statutes that specifically address and limit the effect of oil and gas division orders. For example, § 91.402 of the Texas Natural Resources Code provides that a payor is entitled to a "signed division order" from any payee, sets what the division order may require, and provides that "such a division order does not amend any lease or operating agreement between the interest owner and the lessee or operator * * *." For other statutes that limit the effect of division orders, see La.Rev.Stat.Ann. § 31:138.1, Wyo.Stat. §§ 30–5–304,–305, N.D.Cent.Code § 47–16–39.3; and Okla.Stat. tit. 52, § 540B.

6. A division order is often used as a contract for sale of oil production. Under the common "in kind" oil royalty provision, a royalty owner owns the royalty share of oil production when it is produced. In practice, however, oil royalty owners rarely take their oil royalty in kind. Instead, they sell it, often to the lessee or an affiliated company, at a "posted field price" that the purchaser sets to purchase oil in the field. Where royalty oil is sold to a lessee or its affiliate, should there be an implied obligation upon the purchaser to set a posted price at least equal to a fair market price, regardless of the lease language? Cf. Taylor Oil & Gas Co. v. Pierce–Fordyce Oil Ass'n, 226 S.W. 467 (Tex.Civ.App.1920). Can the implied covenant to market impose such an obligation when the express royalty clause provisions state that royalty is due in kind? Cf. Yzaguirre v. KCS Resources, Inc., 53 S.W.3d 368 (Tex.2001). If no implied covenant applies, what standard governs the setting of the posted price? See U.C.C. § 2–305 and 1–201, and Shell Oil Co. v. HRN, Inc., 144 S.W.3d 429 (Tex.2004).

7. For further reading, see David E. Pierce, Resolving Division Order Disputes: A Conceptual Approach, 35 Rocky Mtn.Min.L.Inst. 16–1 (1989); and

Ernest E. Smith, Royalty Issues: Take–or–Pay Claims and Division Orders, 24 Tulsa L.J. 509 (1989).

5. REMEDIES FOR FAILURE TO PAY ROYALTIES

Royalty owners often suspect that royalty payments due to them are not being timely paid or paid in the correct amount. Delays or miscalculations of royalty may result from a variety of factors, ranging from clerical errors, to title problems, to outright fraud. Generally, improperly paid royalty owners want their leases cancelled. The following case discusses the royalty owners' rights.

CANNON v. CASSIDY

542 P.2d 514 (Okla.1975).

SIMMS, JUSTICE:

Can an oil and gas lease be cancelled for lessees' failure to pay accrued royalty when that failure is in violation of the express terms of the lease but such remedy is not expressly provided by the lease?

The trial court answered in the negative, granting judgment to lessees. The Court of Appeals reversed the trial court, cancelling the leases and quieting title thereto against lessees. We Grant Certiorari, Reverse the Court of Appeals, and Reinstate the District Court's judgment in favor of lessees.

The oil and gas leases in question provided for quarterly payments to lessors of one-eighth (1/8) royalty on gas sold. The leases do not provide for forfeiture in the event of lessees' failure to pay accrued royalties.

Lessees did not pay lessors royalties for gas produced and marketed for approximately eleven months. Lessors brought this action for cancellation of the oil and gas leases based upon the non-payment and they also sought to quiet their title to the real property. Lessors pled that the failure of lessees to pay accrued royalties breached both the express and implied covenants of the lease.

Trial was to the court on lessors' motion for judgment on stipulated facts. Briefs and exhibits were presented by the parties. The parties stipulated that: " * * * from August, 1971, until July, 1972, gas was produced from the subject tracts and sold to Cities Service Oil Company but lessees failed to account and remit to plaintiffs the proceeds attributable to their royalty interest derived from such sales in the amount of $1,693.62."

The trial court gave judgment for lessees based on the finding that cancellation of an oil and gas lease for lessees' failure to pay royalty as provided in the lease will not lie without an express provision in the lease which authorizes cancellation thereof for non-payment of royalties.

Lessees submit that the trial court's ruling is correct and in support thereof they cite the case of *Wagoner Oil & Gas Co. v. Marlow,* 137 Okla. 116, 278 P. 294 (1929), wherein the ninth syllabus by the Court states that:

> Failure to pay royalty or for injury to the land as provided by the lease will not give the lessors sufficient grounds to declare a forfeiture, unless by the express terms of the lease they are given that right and power.

Lessees further contend that cancellation of the lease would be harsh and inappropriate as lessors had a speedy and adequate remedy at law for money damages.

In their attempt to exempt this matter from the scope of the holding in *Wagoner, supra,* lessors present the novel argument that lessees' non-payment of royalties constituted more than a breach of the express terms of the lease. They submit that the non-payment was additionally a breach of the implied covenant to market.

However, lessors are unable to present any persuasive authority to the Court in support of this assertion. Primarily they rely on the suggestion by Earl A. Brown in his two volume work, Law of Oil and Gas Leases, 2d Ed., at § 6.02 that the implied covenant to market should be seen as a two-pronged obligation including both the sale of the products and payment to lessor of his share of the proceeds.

Cancellation, of course, is recognized as the proper equitable remedy for a breach of implied covenants where justice will be thus served.

From their premise that failure to pay royalties is a breach of the implied covenant to market, lessors' argument concludes with the claim that our decision in *Townsend v. Creekmore–Rooney Company,* Okla., 332 P.2d 35 (1958) is direct authority supporting cancellation of the leases involved herein. However, the facts in *Townsend, supra,* did not concern the payment of royalties. There we held only that the unexplained cessation of marketing of oil or gas from the leases for an extended period of several months was prima facie sufficient to justify cancellation as a breach of the implied covenant to market.

Neither Mr. Brown's opinion or lessors' arguments persuade us to adopt the notion that payment of royalties comes within the ambit of the implied covenant to market.

Consequently, we do not depart from the rule expressed in *Wagoner, supra,* that lessee's failure to pay royalty as provided by the lease will not give lessors sufficient grounds to declare a forfeiture unless by the express terms of that lease they are given that right and power.

We note in passing that the overwhelming majority of jurisdictions which have considered this issue are in accord.

* * *

Through stipulation of the parties lessors' damages were agreed to amount to $1,693.62. As lessees correctly contend, lessors had a plain, speedy and adequate remedy at law available to them which, if pursued, would have fully compensated them for this loss. This Court has repeatedly held that in such circumstances equity will not grant relief to a litigant who fails to pursue his remedy at law.

Therefore, the judgment of the Court of Appeals as modified and corrected by the Order of Amendment is Vacated and the Judgment of the Trial Court Granted in favor of lessees is Affirmed.

NOTES

1. Why should failure to pay royalties on production in a timely and correct manner be handled differently by the courts than failure to pay delay rentals or shut-in royalties? In Mitchell Energy Corp. v. Samson Resources Co., 80 F.3d 976 (5th Cir.Tex.1996), the Fifth Circuit Court of Appeals held under Texas law that even intentional non-payment of royalties does not terminate an oil and gas lease. The appeals court noted that Texas law treats an oil and gas lease as a conveyance of an estate in real property. As such, it could not be repudiated by the failure to pay royalties unless there was a specific clause in the lease to the contrary.

Royalty clause structural differences may also affect a lessor's rights if the lessee fails to pay royalty. As we have noted above, many oil royalty clauses provide for an in-kind oil royalty—a percentage of production, rather than the value or proceeds of production. Under an in-kind royalty clause a lessor owns the royalty share of production as it is produced. The lessee's disposition of it without the lessor's consent would be a conversion, and the lessor should be able to enforce a claim for payment against either the lessee or the production purchaser. If the lessor executed a division order to sell the royalty share, the terms of the division order should control. On the other hand, where the lessor merely has a right to a share of money received by the lessee from the sale of production, as is the case under most gas royalty clauses, the lessor's remedy is a contract action. So, for example, if the lessee sells gas production and the lessee's checking account is attached by creditors, the lessor probably has a contract claim against the lessee, but no right of action against the production purchaser.

2. Should lessors try to negotiate an express lease provision similar to the following?

> This lease shall be for a term of Three Years from this date (called "Primary Term") and as long thereafter as oil or gas, or either of them, is produced in paying quantities from said land or lands with which said land is pooled hereunder *and the royalties are paid as provided.*

> * * *

> (g) Within 120 days following the first sale of oil or gas produced * * * settlement shall be made by Lessee * * * for royalties due * * * and such royalties shall be paid monthly thereafter without the necessity of Lessor executing a division or transfer order. If said initial royalty payment is

not so made * * * this lease shall terminate as of 7 A.M. the first day of said 120–day period. After said initial royalty payment, with respect to oil and gas produced during any month, if royalty is not paid hereunder on or before the last day of the second succeeding month, this lease shall terminate at midnight of such last day.

Would such provisions be enforceable? See Hitzelberger v. Samedan Oil Corporation, 948 S.W.2d 497 (Tex.App.1997); Headley v. Hoopengarner, 55 S.E. 744 (W.Va. 1906). Would you advise a lessee client to accept a lease with such a clause?

3. The Louisiana rule alluded to in the principal case was modified in 1975 by the enactment of the Louisiana Mineral Code, which provides:

Art. 137. If a mineral lessor seeks relief for the failure of his lessee to make timely or proper payment of royalties, he must give his lessee written notice of such failure as a prerequisite to a judicial demand for damages or dissolution of the lease.

Art. 138. The lessee shall have thirty days after receipt of the required notice within which to pay the royalties due or to respond by stating in writing a reasonable cause for nonpayment. The payment or nonpayment of the royalties or stating or failing to state a reasonable cause for nonpayment within this period has the following effect on the remedies of dissolution and damages.

Art. 139. If the lessee pays the royalties due in response to the required notice, the remedy of dissolution shall be unavailable unless it be found that the original failure to pay was fraudulent. The court may award as damages double the amount of royalties due, interest on that sum from the date due, and a reasonable attorney's fee, provided the original failure to pay royalties was either fraudulent or willful and without reasonable grounds. In all other cases, such as mere oversight or neglect, damages shall be limited to interest on the royalties computed from the date due, and a reasonable attorney's fee if such interest is not paid within thirty days of written demand therefor.

Art. 140. If the lessee fails to pay royalties due or fails to inform the lessor of a reasonable cause for failure to pay in response to the required notice, the court may award as damages double the amount of royalties due, interest on that sum from the date due, and a reasonable attorney's fee regardless of the cause for the original failure to pay royalties. The court may also dissolve the lease in its discretion.

Art. 141. In a case where notice of failure to pay royalties is required, dissolution should be granted only if the conduct of the lessee, either in failing to pay originally or in failing to pay in response to the required notice, is such that the remedy of damages is inadequate to do justice. * * *

La. Rev. Stat. Ann. §§ 31:137 to 31:141. Should similar statutes be adopted in other states? See Joshua M. Morse III, Nonpayment of Production Royalties Under a Producers 88 Lease: A Legislative Prescription to Cure a New Disease, 9 Fla.St.L.Rev. 447 (1981).

4. Section 47–16–39.1 of the North Dakota Century Code provides as follows:

> The obligation arising under an oil and gas lease to pay oil or gas royalties to the mineral owner or his assignee, or to deliver oil or gas to a purchaser to the credit of such mineral owner or his assignee, or to pay the market value thereof is of the essence in the lease contract, and breach of such obligation may constitute grounds for the cancellation of such lease in such cases where it is determined by the court that the equities of the case require cancellation. * * * This section shall not apply when mineral owners or their assignees elect to take their proportionate share of production in kind, or in the event of a dispute of title existing which would affect distribution of royalty payments.

How are the rights given by this formulation different from those given by the Louisiana Mineral Code? In West v. Alpar Resources, Inc., 298 N.W.2d 484 (N.D.1980), the North Dakota Supreme Court upheld a trial court decision that royalty payments withheld were legitimately in dispute so that equity would not require lease cancellation. In Imperial Oil of North Dakota, Inc. v. Consolidated Crude Oil Co., 851 F.2d 206 (8th Cir.1988), however, the court upheld lease cancellation where a lessee had intentionally failed to pay royalties and disregarded requests for payment.

5. Some statutes and cases require interest on unpaid royalties. Vernon's Tex. Nat.Res.Code § 91.403 provides:

> (a) If payment has not been made for any reason in the time limits specified in Section 91.402 [120 days after the end of the month of the first purchase by a payor and thereafter 60 days after the end of the month in which oil production is sold and 90 days after the end of the month in which gas production is sold] of this code, the payor must pay interest to a payee beginning at the expiration of those time limits at two percentage points above the percentage rate charged on loans to depository institutions by the New York Federal Reserve Bank, unless a different rate of interest is specified in a written agreement between payor and payee.

Section 91.402 limits the obligation to pay interest:

> (b) payments may be withheld without interest beyond the time limits set out in Subsection (a) of this section where there is:
>
> > (1) a dispute concerning title that would affect distribution of payments;
> >
> > (2) a reasonable doubt that the payee:
> >
> > > (A) has sold or authorized the sale of its share of the oil or gas to the purchaser of such production; or
> > >
> > > (B) has clear title to the interest in the proceeds of production; or
> >
> > (3) a requirement in a title opinion that places in issue the title identity, or whereabouts of the payee and that has not been satisfied by the payee after a reasonable request for curative information has been made by the payor.

Similar statutes providing for interest on late payments of royalty have been adopted in a number of states including Alabama, Arkansas, California, Louisiana, Mississippi, Montana, Oklahoma, New Mexico, North Dakota, South Dakota, and Wyoming. Some provide for payment of reasonable attorney's fees and court costs in addition to the statutory interest. See, e.g., Okla.Stat. tit. 52, § 570.10. Do you think a provision for recovery of attorney's fees is necessary?

In California, a court has held that where the lease provides for a specific date for the payment of monthly delay rentals under an "or" lease, interest is due on each amount overdue because of the provisions of Cal.Civ.Code § 3302, which, in the absence of any contract provision, provides for interest to be awarded from the time money becomes due and payable. Howard Townsite Owners, Inc. v. Mills, 73 Cal.Rptr. 715 (Cal.App.1968). In Kansas, interest at the statutory rate has been awarded where royalty payments are "due and withheld by an unreasonable and vexatious delay of payment or settlement of accounts." Lippert v. Angle, 508 P.2d 920, 927 (Kan.1973). In Texas, interest was awarded even before § 91.403 was enacted, where a lessee held funds pending FPC approval of new rates. Phillips Petroleum Co. v. Stahl Petroleum Co., 569 S.W.2d 480 (Tex.1978). The principle is gaining acceptance that "where a party retains and makes use of money belonging to another, equitable principles require that it pay interest * * *." Lightcap v. Mobil Oil Corp., 562 P.2d 1, Syl. 12 (Kan.1977).

Do such statutory provisions or legal precedents provide adequate protection for royalty owners? Could you draft a lease provision that would afford better protection?

A legislative solution to the problem of nonpayment of royalties may be preferable to protective language in the lease, because the lessor under the typical lease will be an unsecured creditor of the lessee and the purchaser of production. Some states have enacted laws to create perfected security interests for unpaid owners of production. The Texas Legislature in 1983 enacted Texas U.C.C. § 9.343(b), a non-uniform amendment to Article 9 of the Uniform Commercial Code. Kansas enacted a virtually identical statute in 1991. Kansas U.C.C. § 84–9–339(a)–(b). In 1992, the Oklahoma Legislature enacted the Oklahoma Production Standards Act. 52 Okla. Stat. § 570–570.13. The applicable provision of the Production Standards Act, § 570.10, did not create a security interest for interest owners, but instead segregated the proceeds of production sales from other funds so that revenues and proceeds from the sale of production would never become subject to a U.C.C. security interest or a part of the estate of a bankrupt. In a series of related cases arising out of the huge SemCrude L.P bankruptcy in 2008, however, a bankruptcy court ruled that all three state statutes gave oil and gas interest owners rights that were junior to those of the perfected security interests of banks claiming priority. In Re SemCrude, L.P., 407 B.R. 82, 407 B. R. 112, 407 B.R. 140 (Bankr. D.Del. 2009).

6. What are the rights of an oil company that overpays royalty? Compare Matthews v. Sun Exploration and Production Co., 521 So.2d 1192 (La.App.1988) and Shanbour v. Phillips 66 Natural Gas Co., 864 P.2d 815 (Okla.1993) (reasonableness or equity permits recoupment), with Estate of

Hatch v. NYCO Minerals, Inc., 704 N.Y.S.2d 340 (N.Y.A.D. 3 Dept. 2000) (one who paid royalties it was not obligated to pay could not recover because it had voluntarily made a conscious decision to pay, and thus assumed the risk).

6. MISCELLANEOUS ROYALTY PROBLEMS

(a) Casinghead Gas and Processed Gas

Lessors and lessees often disagree over their rights and obligations when liquid products are extracted from casinghead gas or from "wet" gas.[30] One issue is whether the lessee is under any duty to extract liquid products from either casinghead gas or wet gas. A related question is whether the lessee incurs any royalty liability if casinghead gas is used for extraction of natural gasoline and the residue gas is vented or flared. Another issue is whether royalty is due upon liquids extracted.

The lessee generally has no duty to engage in extraction of liquid products. Likewise, the lessee has no special duty to preserve residue gas where casinghead gas is used for the extraction of natural gasoline. The only basis for an attack upon the conduct of the lessee in these instances is the lessor's assertion that there has been a violation of the implied covenant to operate the lease with due diligence for the mutual benefit of both parties or the implied covenant to market production as a reasonable prudent operator. In both instances, the prudent operator standard will be the measure of the propriety of the lessee's conduct, and unless a court finds imprudent conduct in failing to engage in extraction or in flaring or venting residue gas, the lessee is not liable.

Most modern leases specifically provide for royalties on casinghead gas and extracted liquids. In the absence of specific provisions, however, royalties must be paid on the basis of rather simple provisions providing for payment based on market value or amount realized at the well or in the field. Thus, in general, lessors are not due royalties for liquids extracted after gas has been sold.

(b) Production on Which Royalties Are Due

Many leases provide a free-use clause, stating that the lessee can use lease production for operations without paying royalty; see, for example, the last sentence of paragraph 3 of the Texas AAPL lease in the Forms Manual. Some, however, will limit free use to operations on the premises. Whether gas could be used without payment of royalty on production used for unit operations is certainly arguable in these circumstances. Other leases specifically provide that royalties are not due on production used for operations on the leased premises, on pooled or unitized acreage, or in a recycling project.

Many early leases did not contain express free-use clauses, probably because the right to free use was implicit in the lease grant. John S. Lowe,

---

30. Casinghead gas is natural gas that separates from oil at the top of the well bore, or casinghead. "Wet" gas is natural gas that contains liquids in solution.

The Lessee's Right to Free Use of Produced Substances: New Wine in Old Bottles, 37 Nat. Res. L. J. 729 (1997). See also Bice v. Petro–Hunt, L.L.C., 768 N.W.2d 496 (N.D. 2009), holding that residue gas processed and used off the leased premises at a treating/processing facility and then transported back to fuel the operation of heaters, treaters, and separators located at central tank batteries off the leases was in furtherance of lease operations and thus fell within the scope of the leases' free-use clauses, even though the clauses referred to "operations thereon" or "operations hereunder."

Anadarko Petroleum Corporation, IBLA 2010–228, 181 IBLA 388 (2012), held that the U.S. was due royalty on oil captured and sold from the water around BP's Macondo well blowout in 2010 because it was production "saved, removed, [and] sold from the leased area," even though the blowout occurred while BP was attempting to temporarily abandon the well, rather than secure "production" from it.

(c) Free–Gas Clauses

Some oil and gas leases contain clauses similar to the following that permit lessors to use gas produced free for domestic purposes:

> Lessor may lay a line to any gas well or wells on said lands and take gas produced from said well or wells for use for light, heat, and cooling in one dwelling house on said land and for use in lessor's farming and/or ranching operations, at lessor's own risk, subject to the use and the right of abandonment of the well by the lessee. The first 400,000 cubic feet of gas taken in each year shall be free of cost, but all gas in excess of 400,000 cubic feet taken in each year shall be paid for at the current market value at the well for the gas from said well, and the measurements and regulation shall be by meter and regulators set at lessor's cost at the tap on the line.

Generally, oil and gas lease provisions for the benefit of the lessor are covenants that run with the mineral title to the land. The free-gas clause, however, runs with the surface interest. See Hemingway § 7.12. If you represented a prospective lessee who was asked to include a free-gas clause in the lease, would you be concerned with potential liability? In Weiss v. Thomas & Thomas Development Co., 680 N.E.2d 1239 (Ohio 1997), the court held that a lessee owed a lessor the duty to use the same care in providing free-gas under a lease provision that a regulated public utility owed consumers. The court ignored exculpatory language in the lease that the lessor "covenants and agrees that his taking and use of gas shall be wholly at his own risk, and lessee shall not be held liable for any accident or damage caused thereby." The case and the issue is discussed at Nicholas J. Parrish, The Duties of a Well Owner to a Free Gas Consumer, 19 E.Min.L.Inst. Ch. 4 (1999). In Schell v. OXY USA, Inc., 822 F.Supp.2d 1125 (D. Kan. 2011), the court found that language in a free-gas clause that the gas would be used "for stoves and inside lights in the principal dwelling" required the lessee to put the gas in a form and condition that could be used for such purposes. The court suggested the lessee could perform its obligation by providing the lessor with an alternative source of gas. Would a surface owner be taxed on the value of free-gas taken? See Roundup Coal Mining Co. v. Commissioner, 20 T.C. 388 (1953).

(d) Fixed Gas Royalty

Fixed gas royalty is a problem of the gas-royalty clause peculiar to old leases, but many old leases exist. Until the 1930s, natural gas had little or no market value. Reflecting the economics of the time, many oil and gas leases drafted before World War II provided for a flat dollar amount as royalty for any well that produced natural gas; $50 to $200 per year per well that produced gas was common.

Rising gas prices beginning in the 1970s made fixed gas-royalty provisions unrealistic. Some oil companies voluntarily amended fixed gas-royalty clauses to give their lessors a fractional royalty. Others insisted upon recognition of the provisions of their leases and even continued to take such leases from unwary mineral owners. Some states took direct legislative action to deal with the problem. West Virginia Code, § 22–6–8 directed the administrator of the Office of Oil and Gas to refuse to issue drilling permits for leases with fixed gas-royalty provision, but the statute, now repealed, was held not to affect producing leases. Bruen v. Columbia Gas Transmission Corp., 426 S.E.2d 522, 526 (W.Va.1992). Pennsylvania's Guaranteed Minimum Royalty Act, 58 Penn. Stat. § 33, provides that:

> A lease or other such agreement conveying the right to remove or recover oil, natural gas or gas of any other designation from lessor to lessee shall not be valid if such lease does not guarantee the Lessor at least one-eighth royalty of all oil, natural gas or gas of other designations removed or recovered from the subject real property.

Are such statutes constitutional if they are applied to leases existing when the statutes are enacted? The Pennsylvania law addressed the issue by providing that existing leases "shall be subject to such an escalation when its original state is altered by new drilling, deeper drilling, redrilling, artificial well stimulation, hydraulic fracturing or any other procedure for increased production. A lease shall not be affected when the well is altered through routine maintenance or cleaning." If you were representing a lessor subject to a lease with a fixed gas-royalty clause in a state that did not have legislation, could you develop an argument to justify reformation to provide for a higher royalty? See John S. Lowe, Eastern Oil and Gas Operations: Do Recent Developments Suggest New Answers to Old Problems?, 4 E.Min.L.Inst. 20–1, 20–35 (1983), and McGinnis v. Cayton, 312 S.E.2d 765 (W.Va.1984).

CHAPTER 3

TITLES AND CONVEYANCES: INTERESTS IN OIL AND GAS

Table of Sections

———

Ownership of oil and gas and the type of ownership created by a transaction is one of the most complex issues encountered by an oil and gas attorney. The rule of capture, which has been a principal factor in the development of the various aspects of oil and gas law covered in the preceding chapters, has also played a role in the law relating to titles to oil and gas. Courts have been forced to wrestle with the question of what type of interest a grantee receives under a deed that conveys the oil and gas beneath a tract of land. Can the grantee be deemed to have received a fee interest in substances that can legally be drained and produced by a neighboring landowner? Or has he received merely a right to go on the land and produce oil and gas, which remain unowned until brought to the surface?

Regardless of which approach is taken, conveyances of oil and gas interests in most states must comply with the requirements that apply to conveyances of realty. Transfers must normally be by a writing that contains words of grant, identifies the parties to the transaction, adequately describes the property, and is properly executed. This chapter will not dwell on these formalities, since they are usually covered in courses in property or real estate transactions. Its focus will be on the special problems of construction and deed language encountered in mineral conveyances and the legal and practical uncertainties that result when a mineral estate is divided. Such a division can result in concurrent ownership among cotenants, successive ownership between a life tenant and remainderman, or the separation of the various incidents of mineral ownership among different persons. All such divisions pose unique problems.

The primary duty of a lawyer involved in such transactions is to make sure that the deed or other instrument clearly and accurately reflects the intent of the parties. The use of atypical language should always be avoided. For example, In re Estate of Slaughter, 305 S.W.3d 804 (Tex. App.–Texarkana 2010) a testator provided in his will that his three sons were always to share equally in "production royalty and unproduction royalty" from the land he had devised them. After the land was partitioned and an oil and gas lease executed on one of the tracts, a dispute arose over whether "unproduction royalty" referred to all lease benefits, including bonus and delay rentals, or only payments, such as shut-in royalty, paid in lieu of royalty on production. After extensive litigation the appellate court opted for the latter interpretation.

This chapter will provide some guidance in drafting appropriate language and will also present common instances where the parties (or their lawyers) failed to express their intent clearly. In this situation, a court may be required to determine the meaning of the language in question. Judicial construction of disputed language often entails a three-step process. Consider the following description of how a court traditionally goes about this process.

> First, the court will attempt to ascertain intent by examining the language in dispute * * *. When an instrument's substance is determined to be clear or unambiguous, the parties' intent must be

effectuated * * *. In cases in which an instrument is not so clear (e.g., different provisions of the instrument seem inconsistent or contradictory), the court will, if possible, harmonize the provisions in accord with the parties' apparent intent * * *. If examination solely of the language within the instrument's four corners does not yield a clear understanding of the parties' intent, the court will generally proceed to another tier in the three-tiered process. This entails discretionary implementation of applicable "canons" of contract construction * * *. Application of "canons" of construction may provide a court with an objective inference of the parties' intent. But if, at this step in the process, intent remains unascertainable (i.e., the instrument is still considered ambiguous), then the court may resort to a final tier in the three-tiered process of construction. This final tier entails consideration of extrinsic or parol evidence. * * *

Pursue Energy Corp. v. Perkins, 558 So.2d 349, 352–53 (Miss.1990).

Standard rules of construction that are commonly used in the "second tier" of the interpretative process include the doctrines that a deed should be construed to convey the largest estate possible, that the instrument should be construed against the party who drafted it (frequently the grantor, but with oil and gas leases normally the lessee), that handwritten or typed language prevails over inconsistent printed language, that the granting clause prevails if there is an irreconcilable conflict among clauses in a deed, and that a specific description prevails over a general description. There are many other such "canons," and as this brief listing suggests, they are frequently inconsistent. Thus the choice of the applicable "canon" to use during the second step of deed interpretation commonly determines the outcome. See Bruce M. Kramer, The Sisyphean Task of Interpreting Mineral Deeds and Leases: An Encyclopedia of Canons of Construction, 24 Tex.Tech.L.Rev. 1 (1992) for an excellent discussion of canons used in construing mineral deeds.

In reading the cases in this chapter, keep in mind the standard three-step process for construing instruments. Has the court followed this process in interpreting the instrument before it? If it reached the second step, why did it choose one canon of construction over another? Could it as easily have used a different constructional rule and thereby reached a different result? To what extent, if any, has the court chosen a construction that fosters title certainty and protects third party reliance in preference to a construction that more closely effectuates the parties' intent? See Mullinnix LLC v. HKB Royalty Trust, 126 P.3d 909 (Wyo. 2006) for an argument for construing mineral deeds in a way that promotes title certainty and the court's rejection of this approach as inconsistent with its "ultimate goal" of interpreting contracts and deeds in accordance with the intent of the parties.

A. DISTINCTION BETWEEN MINERAL INTERESTS AND ROYALTY INTERESTS

1. NATURE OF THE INTERESTS

BODCAW LUMBER CO. v. GOODE
254 S.W. 345 (Ark. 1923).

MCCULLOCH, C.J. This controversy involves the gas, oil, and other mineral rights in and under a certain tract of land, containing 40 acres, in Columbia county. Appellant, a corporation, formerly owned the land in fee simple, and in the year 1912 conveyed the land to appellee by warranty deed, but the granting clause contained a reservation (or exception) of the oil, gas, and other mineral rights, in the following language:

> Reserving to the grantor, its successors and assigns, all of the gas, oil and minerals and mineral rights in and under said land, with the right to prospect for and exploit the same, and use sufficient surface therefor, and the right to lay, maintain and operate pipe lines for oil and gas; and the right to erect, maintain and operate telephone and telegraph lines, with the right reserved to remove any building, machinery, pipe lines or other property erected or placed on said land in connection therewith; and reserving to said grantor, its successors and assigns, a right of way for railroad or tramroad not exceeding one hundred feet in width across said land, if same shall be necessary for, or desired by it, its successors or assigns—such pipe lines for oil and gas and such telephone and telegraph lines and such right of way, however, not to infringe upon or interfere with any improvements upon said land without payment of a reasonable amount for damages caused thereby.

Appellee instituted this action against appellant in the chancery court of Columbia county to cancel the reservation clause in said deed and to quiet his title. In the complaint he alleged that appellant had not explored this tract of land for oil, gas, or other minerals, nor any other land in that county, and that appellant had not paid any taxes on the mineral rights in the land. Appellee also pleaded the statute of limitations in bar of the right of appellant to assert any mineral rights in the land, and also pleaded in his complaint that appellant was barred by laches in not proceeding more expeditiously to explore the land for minerals.

* * * The court rendered a final decree in favor of appellee canceling the reservation clause in the deed and quieting appellee's title as against any claim of appellant to mineral rights.

* * *

The real question involved in the case is whether or not mineral rights in and under land can be severed from the fee to the surface and the title in perpetuity be retained by an exception, or whether such an exception, in whatever language it may be couched, amounts to no more than a mere servitude in the form of a license to use the surface for the purpose of enjoying the mineral rights.

The further question arises whether or not, if the exception operates as a retention of the title to the severed mineral rights, enjoyment of those rights can be barred by adverse occupancy of the surface of the land.

There has been a wealth of discussion on the subject whether or not there can be a severance of the surface and mineral rights in land so as to uphold a sale or reservation of the latter, and there is not entire harmony in the discussion; but it appears to us to be in accordance with the great weight of authority to say that there may be such separation and that mineral rights, even those including gas, a volatile substance and generally referred to as being of a vagrant character and liable to escape, may be the subject-matter of a separate sale or reservation so as to create or reserve a right in perpetuity. * * *

In two of our neighbor states (Texas and Oklahoma), where there are extensive gas and oil fields, it has been decided by the courts of last resort in accordance with the views now expressed. The Supreme Court of Texas, in the case of Texas Co. v. Daugherty, 107 Tex. 226, 176 S.W. 717, L.R.A.1917F, 989 (quoting from the syllabus), held:

> "The fact that oil and gas, from their fluid and fugitive character while in the ground, are capable of escaping from its owner or of being drawn off by an adjoining proprietor, while qualifying the title in them held by the owner of the soil, does not prevent them from being treated as minerals and a part of the realty, capable as such of transfer and separate ownership, the purchaser assuming the risk of reducing them to possession and absolute ownership."

* * *

The Supreme Court of Oklahoma has held in several cases that mineral rights may be severed so as to be the subject of a conveyance or an exception in a grant, that the title to that extent may be conveyed or retained, and that adverse occupancy of the surface for the statutory period of limitation does not bar the right to separate enjoyment of such mineral rights.

* * *

The Supreme Court of Louisiana has decided contrary to the views we now express and those expressed by the Oklahoma and Texas courts. * * *

* * *

Most of the cases which declare what we think is correct to term the minority rule make an exception as to gas and seem to be influenced by the character of that fluid and hold that it is of such a vagrant nature that it cannot be the subject of absolute ownership. * * *

According to many writers on this subject, the view most generally entertained by geologists at present is that gas and oil are not of a vagrant character and do not migrate but maintain their situs until they are drawn out or expel themselves by pressure through artificial openings in the surface, and the tendency of later decisions is to hold that oil and gas while in place and before being drawn out by artificial openings are as much a part of the realty as fixed minerals, such as coal or iron.

Our conclusion on this subject is that the majority rule is sound and that it works out a more definite result than the rule that mineral rights cannot be separated and that a conveyance thereof merely creates a servitude. It necessarily follows from the adoption of this view that the separate title to the minerals is retained in perpetuity and that the statute of limitations does not run against these rights unless there is an actual adverse holding which constitutes an invasion of these particular rights. Such is the unanimous view in all the authorities which hold that there is a right of separation and separate conveyance. * * * The rule of those authorities is that the title to minerals beneath the surface is not lost by nonuser nor by adverse occupancy of the owner of the surface under the same claim of title, and that the statute can only be set in motion by an adverse use of the mineral rights, persisted in and continued for the statutory period.

* * *

In the complaint it is alleged as grounds for the application of the doctrine of laches that appellant had not paid taxes on the land, but the answer is that appellant was not required to pay taxes on the land unless there was a separate assessment of the mineral rights, and the owner of the surface rights suffered no injury by the failure of the owner of the mineral rights to separately pay taxes.

Counsel for appellee also discuss the question of public policy involved in the separation of mineral rights from surface rights, but we perceive no question of public policy involved, in the absence of an express statute declaring such policy.

The decree of the chancery court, which is in direct conflict with the law as now declared, is reversed, and the cause is remanded, with directions to dismiss the complaint of appellee for want of equity.

Notes

1. The court in Humphreys–Mexia Co. v. Gammon, 254 S.W. 296, 302 (Tex. 1923), stated that "where the minerals in place were severed by the conveyance from the residue of the soil, * * * the original land [was] as effectively divided into two tracts as if the division had been made by superficial lines, or had been severed vertically by horizontal planes." Alternatively, the owner of the surface can sever the mineral estate below a specified depth and keep the shallower portion. What would be the reason for this type of severance?

2. As discussed in Chapter 2, the mineral estate is normally accorded the position of dominant estate. As a general proposition, the owner of the mineral estate has an implied right to use the surface and subsurface in any way that is reasonably necessary to accomplish the exploration, development, and drilling for the minerals. This right is, however, subject to limitations imposed by statute; state, county and municipal regulations; contractual agreement, or judicial doctrines such as the accommodation rule. Moreover, the mineral owner's right to use the surface estate may be affected by when the severance took place. For example, restrictive covenants imposed upon the land prior to severance are binding on the mineral owner and her oil and gas lessees; whereas the mineral estate is not subject to such covenants if they are imposed post-severance. See, e.g., The Mable Cleary Trust v. The Edward–Marlah Muzyl Trust, 686 N.W.2d 770 (Mich.App. 2004); Devendorf v. Akbar Petroleum Corp., 577 N.E.2d 707 (Ohio App.9 Dist. 1989), and Property Owners of Leisure Land, Inc. v. Woolf & Magee, Inc., 786 S.W.2d 757 (Tex.App. 1990).

3. A mineral estate can be severed horizontally into two or more horizontally separated estates. Although the owner in fee of the mineral estate can accomplish such a horizontal severance, it more commonly occurs through use of a horizontal Pugh clause in a lease, under which the lease extends downward only to a specified depth or formation. A horizontal severance of the mineral estate can also occur if a lessee that has received the entire mineral estate assigns a specified formation or depth to another lessee. In some instances the conveyance or assignment is to a depth of 100 feet below the deepest producing depth of the specified formation. A severance with a reference to depth may have unintended consequences, especially if shale formations are involved. In the case of some of the thicker shales, the severance may exclude a potentially productive part of the shale. Alternatively, the severance may include one productive formation and partially extend into another somewhat deeper productive formation. That would be true in areas where the Bakken formation is underlain by the Three Forks, which is another productive shale; or if the conveyance included the Austin Chalk, but was in an area where the "floor" of the Austin Chalk is the Eagle Ford shale. For a discussion of depth severances in the context of a Pugh clause, see John W. Broomes, "Spinning Straw into Gold: Refining and Redefining Lease Provisions for the Realities of Resource Play Operations," 57 Rocky Mt.Min. L.Inst. Ch. 26, § 26.04 (2011).

Suppose that the shallower conveyance is leased to Company A and includes both the Bakken but extends downward 100 feet through the Three Forks. The remaining depths are leased to Company B. Company A drills a horizontal well in the Bakken, hydraulically fractures it, and produces from the Bakken. Company B now decides to drill and develop the Three Forks. Does it have a right to do so, or must it obtain an assignment of rights in the Three Forks from Company A? Could Company A drill a horizontal well or frac a vertical well in the top portion of the Three Forks and Company B drill a horizontal well below that depth? Would compulsory pooling of the areas with the Three Forks leased to the two companies be possible?

4. A severance may be accomplished by an oil and gas lease as well as by a mineral conveyance. As the Texas Supreme Court pointed out in Cherokee Water Co. v. Forderhause, 641 S.W.2d 522 (Tex.1982),

> The term "lease," when used in an oil and gas context, is a misnomer. The estate created by the oil and gas lease is not the same as those interests created under a "lease" governed by the law of landlord and tenant. The common oil and gas lease creates a determinable fee. It vests the lessee with title to oil and gas in place. W.T. Waggoner Estate v. Sigler Oil Co., 118 Tex. 509, 19 S.W.2d 27 (1929) and authorities cited therein. It logically follows, and has long been held by this court, that an oil and gas lease is a sale of an interest in land.

Although some other states would agree that an oil and gas lease is in fact a deed that conveys a fee simple determinable, this view of the oil and gas lease is far from universal. The approach taken by a state's courts usually turns on whether oil and gas are viewed as susceptible of ownership in place and upon the language and duration of the lease. The relevance of lease language has been explained as follows:

> Although the nature of the interest created [by an oil and gas lease] may be determined by the granting clause, the duration of such interest is limited by the habendum clause. From the standpoint of duration of the lease, the parties may create any recognized estate. . . . Thus, the nature of the interest created may be an actual conveyance of oil and gas in place or may be a profit a prendre, but from the standpoint of duration, the estate created may be any of the various estates which may lawfully be created, such as an estate for years or a determinable fee.

Kuntz § 26.2.

5. Landowners in areas where wind farms are being built because of the strong, constant winds have executed deeds either conveying their land and reserving "wind rights" or conveying the wind rights and reserving the rest of the land. The deeds used are frequently modeled on deeds conveying or reserving rights in oil and gas. Can rights in wind be validly severed from the other incidents of land ownership? If so, what is the nature of the estate created in the wind? Can the "wind rights" equivalent of an NPRI be severed from the land? See Alan J. Alexander, "The Texas Wind Estate: Wind as a Natural Resource and a Severable Property Interest," U. of Mich. J. of Law Reform 429, 443–451 (Winter 2011); Michael J. Stephan, "Wind Severance," 40 Tex.J. Envt'l L. 73, 83–87 (2010); Ernest E. Smith & Becky H. Diffen, "Winds of Change: The Creation of Wind Law," 5 Tex. J. Oil, Gas & Energy L. 131 (2010); Ernest E. Smith, Steven DeWolf, Roderick E. Wetsel, Texas Wind Law § 4.02 (Lexis 2011).

McSWEYN v. MUSSELSHELL COUNTY, MONTANA

632 P.2d 1095 (Mont. 1981).

WEBER, JUSTICE.

This is an appeal by the defendants from a judgment of the District Court, Fourteenth Judicial District, Musselshell County, declaring certain oil and gas leases owned by the plaintiff, Donald McSweyn, to be valid. We reverse the judgment of the District Court.

* * *

This case comes to us on an agreed statement of facts. The County through tax proceedings had acquired the real property described in the oil and gas leases to McSweyn with which we are concerned. In 1933 the County entered into a contract with Shields for the sale to Shields of the real property. The contract contained the following reservation:

> * * * vendor [County] reserves to itself and its successors an undivided two and one-half percent of all oil, gas and other minerals lying in, under and beneath the premises hereinbefore described * * *.

All parties agree that the above language created a mineral reservation.

Before full payment had been made and deed delivered under the 1933 contract for deed, Shields filed a quiet title action against the County and other defendants which resulted in a 1943 decree. The decree in part stated:

> * * * A.D. Shields, is the owner, seized in fee and entitled to the possession of the following described real property * * * excepting and reserving to the said defendant Musselshell County, Montana, 2½% of all oil, gas or other minerals lying in, under and beneath [the said land] * * *.

Approximately one year later, in 1944, the County executed and delivered to Shields a deed covering the property in question which contained the following reservation:

> * * * and reserving unto * * * [the County] its successors and assigns, an undivided two and one-half percent royalty of all oil, gas, and other minerals lying in, and that may be produced from the premises hereinbefore described, delivered free of cost * * *.

The parties again agree that the foregoing deed language constitutes a royalty reservation as distinguished from the mineral reservation contained in the contract for deed.

After 1944 the lands described in the deed were transferred by Shields and his successors in interest to other parties. In 1974, 30 years after the deed, the successors in interest of Shields executed oil and gas leases to Exeter Company, which assigned its interest to Exeter Exploration Company, which in turn made partial assignments to True Oil Company. Oil wells were drilled on the lands in 1976 and four of the five wells drilled are presently producing oil.

In 1976, one day before drilling started on the first well, plaintiff, McSweyn, obtained from the County the first of his oil and gas leases covering the County's mineral interest in the lands. The second lease was obtained by McSweyn from the County 19 days later. The McSweyn leases, which are valid only if the County owned and retained a mineral interest rather than a royalty interest, contained the following disclaimer:

The execution of this instrument shall in no way prejudice the right of Musselshell County to claim its interest is a royalty interest rather than a mineral interest.

McSweyn brought this action in 1977 asking the District Court to declare and determine his rights and interests under his oil and gas leases from the County. * * *

The District Court held that the contract for deed contained a reservation of mineral interest and the issuance of the deed at a later date gave Shields more than he had bargained for. The court found that a mineral interest is more valuable than a royalty interest and that the deed by the County to Shields was an unconstitutional donation or gift by the County. * * * The District Court found the McSweyn leases to be valid.

* * *

Unconstitutional Gift

Although the issue had not been presented by either party, the District Court concluded that all things being equal, a mineral interest in real property is more valuable than a royalty interest. Reasoning from that position, the court concluded that the deed resulted in an unconstitutional gift or donation by the County to Shields.

Rist v. Toole County, (1945), 117 Mont. 426, 159 P.2d 340, points out that the holder of a *mineral* interest has an interest in the land and has the right to go on the property, to explore and drill for oil and gas and the obligation to pay for a proportionate share of development costs. A holder of a *royalty* interest does not have the right to go on the property to explore for undeveloped oil and gas, but the royalty holder is not obligated to pay the costs of development. The holder of the royalty interest simply shares in the profit from production. The District Court apparently concluded that because the *mineral* interest holder has greater rights with respect to real property itself than the *royalty* interest holder, such a mineral right has a greater value. There is nothing in the agreed statement of facts to show the comparative values of royalty and mineral interests in this particular land. The agreed statement of facts does show that the royalty interest which we find is owned by the County will have a much larger present share in production than would be true of a mineral interest. As a result, we conclude that the record does not show a 1944 gift, or the equivalent, by the County to Shields.

* * *

We find that Musselshell County owned a 2½ percent royalty interest in the lands involved in this case and not a mineral interest and conclude that the oil and gas leases from Musselshell County to McSweyn did not grant an effective lease upon a mineral interest. The judgment of the District Court is reversed, and the District Court is instructed to enter appropriate judgment in conformity with this opinion.

[The dissenting opinion of JUSTICE SHEEHY has been omitted.]

NOTES

1.   As Professor Emeritus Richard Maxwell has stated, a royalty "is less than a full mineral interest in conceptual terms since it encompasses only one attribute of such an interest; but it can be more than a mineral interest in economic terms when its share is stated as a share of gross production rather than as a percentage of [lease] royalty." Richard Maxwell, Mineral or Royalty—The French Percentage, 49 SMU L. Rev. 543, 544–45 (1996). What percentage of production is Musselshell County entitled to under the deed reservation as construed by the court? What percentage would the county probably have received under the construction urged by McSweyn?

2.   In most jurisdictions, a conveyance of the mineral estate is subject to the same formalities as are required for a conveyance of any other realty. E.g., Davis v. Griffin, 770 S.W.2d 137 (Ark. 1989) and Harlan v. Vetter, 732 S.W.2d 390 (Tex.App. 1987, writ refused n.r.e.). Would a conveyance of a nonparticipating royalty, as occurred in McSweyn have the same effect? Would the conveyance be subject to the same formalities? For a discussion of the applicability of such rules to oil and gas conveyances, see Lowe, Chapter 5.A.

3. As discussed in an earlier chapter, states differ on whether a severed mineral estate is a fee or a profit a prendre (or easement). In the latter jurisdictions, the mineral estate can, at least in theory, be lost be abandonment; whereas in jurisdictions where the mineral estate is viewed as a fee, abandonment is not possible. See Libby Placer Mining Co. v. Noranda Minerals Corp., 197 P.3d 924 (Mont. 2008). Louisiana oil and gas law, which has been greatly influenced by concepts originating in French civil law and continued in the Louisiana Civil Code, takes a somewhat different view of severed mineral rights than any other state. Two of its most significant aspects are the classification of an interest in minerals as a "servitude" and the doctrine of liberative prescription. Both are illustrated by Wemple v. Nabors Oil & Gas Co., 97 So. 666 (La. 1923), which involved rights in minerals that had been conveyed away more than ten years previously. The court stated that Louisiana law did not permit the creation of a separate corporeal estate in the minerals. The grantee in the deed had received a servitude that was subject to liberative prescription. Since no use had been made of the minerals for ten years, the servitude had automatically terminated, and rights in the minerals had returned to the successor in interest of the grantor.

4.   In Schlittler v. Smith, 101 S.W.2d 543 (Tex.Com.App. 1937), the grantor reserved in himself "an undivided one-half interest in and to the royalty rights on all of oil and gas and other minerals in, on and under or that may be produced from the land herein conveyed and described." While conceding that he had no right to join in an oil and gas lease, the grantor argued that he was entitled to receive one-half of all bonuses and delay rentals as well as one-half of all royalties provided for in a lease. The court disagreed with this contention.

The words "royalty," "bonus," and "rentals" have a well-understood meaning in the oil and gas business. Likewise, "minerals" and "mineral rights" have a well-recognized meaning. Broadly speaking, a reservation of minerals or mineral rights without limitation would include royalties, bonuses, and rentals. A conveyance of land without reservations would include all minerals and mineral rights. However, it is well settled that a grantor may reserve minerals or mineral rights and he may also reserve royalties, bonuses, and rentals, either one, more or all. Here we have a reservation of only "royalty rights." It is obvious, it seems to us, that this does not include a reservation of bonuses or rentals, but only of an interest in oil, gas or minerals paid, received, or realized as "royalty" under any lease existing on the land at the time of the reservation, or thereafter executed by the grantee, his heirs or assigns.

101 S.W.2d at 544.

5. The deed reservations litigated in the *Musselshell County* and *Schlittler* cases involved *nonparticipating royalty interests,* which, as indicated in an earlier chapter, is the term normally used to designate a royalty carved out of the mineral estate. In Lathrop v. Eyestone, 227 P.2d 136 (Kan. 1951), the Kansas Supreme Court held that a perpetual nonparticipating royalty violated the rule against perpetuities. The court stated:

[F]uture fee owners might never execute another lease. There is nothing in any of the instruments which imposes a duty on them to do so. * * * Moreover there is no limitation of time within which a future lease would be required to be executed, if one were actually executed. It is, therefore, wholly problematical when, if ever, such an interest under future leases would vest. Such a grant violates the rule against perpetuities, a rule against too remote vesting. In 41 Am.Jur., Perpetuities and Restraints on Alienation, § 24, it is said:

One of the essential elements of the rule against perpetuities is that at the time the future interest is created, it must appear that the condition precedent to vesting must necessarily happen, if it happens at all, within the period prescribed by the rule * * *. A possibility, or even a probability, that the interest or estate may vest within that time is not enough, for, it is said, the question of probabilities does not enter into the equation. If by any conceivable combination of circumstances it is possible that the event upon which the estate or interest is limited may not occur within the period of the rule, or if there is left any room for uncertainty or doubt on the point, the limitation is void.

The rule against perpetuities has played a significant role in determining the validity of perpetual nonparticipating royalties in Kansas. See, e.g., Cosgrove v. Young, 642 P.2d 75 (Kan. 1982); Drach v. Ely, 694 P.2d 1310 (Kan.App. 1985), rev'd on other grounds 703 P.2d 746 (Kan. 1985); and Fritschen v. Wanek, 924 P.2d 1288 (Kan.App. 1996). However, Kansas is apparently unique in taking this position, and the validity and scope of the application of the rule against perpetuities to NPRIs has been repeatedly questioned by the Kansas lower courts. For example, in Rucker v. DeLay, 235 P.3d 566 (Kan.App. 2010) the Kansas court of appeals, while stating that it was bound by precedent in ruling an NPRI invalid under the rule against perpetuities, encouraged the holders of the NPRI to seek review in the Kansas Supreme Court and urged that court to accept review, and if it determined that the rule against perpetuities was still applicable to royalty interests, determine whether production should continue to be deemed the vesting event.

Other states, e.g., Dauphin Island Property Owners Ass'n v. Callon Institutional Royalty Investors I, 519 So.2d 948 (Ala. 1988) and Conway Land, Inc. v. Terry, 542 So.2d 362 (Fla. 1989), have found the following reasoning, which was used by the Arkansas Supreme Court in Hanson v. Ware, 274 S.W.2d 359 (Ark. 1955), more persuasive:

> We are decidedly of the opinion that the rule against perpetuities was not violated by the conveyance to these appellees, for the reason that they acquired a present interest rather than a future interest in the land. To treat the appellees' royalty as a future interest involves a failure to distinguish between their estate in real property, which is an abstract legal conception, and the likelihood of their ultimately receiving a share in the production of oil and gas, which is purely a practical matter.

274 S.W.2d at 362.

Occasionally litigants in other jurisdictions argue that the language of a specific instrument compels the application of the Kansas rule. For example, the grantor in Luecke v. Wallace, 951 S.W.2d 267 (Tex.App. 1997) reserved "an undivided one-half (1/2) non-participating interest in any and all oil, gas and mineral royalties reserved by Grantee, his heirs and assigns at any time in the future and which may be payable to Grantee, his heirs and assigns under any future lease of the property." The grantee's successor argued that the grantor's retained interest violated the rule against perpetuities both because it was contingent upon a future reservation by the grantee or his successors and because it vested only if and when future leases were executed. How should the court have ruled on these arguments?

6. As preceding chapters have indicated, there are several kinds of rights to gross production in addition to the nonparticipating royalty. The *landowner's royalty,* which is reserved in an oil and gas lease, has been dealt with in Chapter 2. An *overriding royalty* is an interest carved out of the lessee's interest in the lease. Absent fraud or an express contractual provision to the contrary, an overriding royalty does not survive the termination of the lease from which it is created. See, e.g., Olson v. Continental Resources, Inc., 109 P.3d 351 (Okla. Civ. App.Div. 3 2005). A lessee that assigns all or part of its lease often retains such an interest. An overriding royalty may also be transferred.[1] The transfer or retention of an overriding royalty is subject to the same formal requirements as an oil and gas lease. In Texas, where an oil and gas lease is deemed to create a defeasible fee simple, Quigley v. Bennett, 227 S.W.3d 51 (Tex. 2007) presents a good example. A geologist, who had a sick friend who held several oil and gas leases that he wished to sell, orally agreed to analyze the leases and prepare a sales presentation in return for a 1% overriding royalty. The court ruled that the geologist was not entitled to the overriding royalty or its value. The court reasoned that an agreement to

---

1. In the first five or six decades of the Twentieth Century the term *overriding royalty* was occasionally used to designate a landowner's royalty to the extent that it exceeded one-eighth. This usage of the term is still occasionally encountered in instruments dating from that period, but is quite uncommon today.

transfer an overriding royalty must be in writing to be enforceable. Allowing a party to recover the value of such a royalty on the basis of fraud rather than a written agreement would circumvent the statute of frauds.

In addition to complying with the requirements for transferring real property interests, instruments creating an overriding royalty should be carefully drafted to make clear whether the fractional interest is payable out of the entire production of the well, for example, $\frac{1}{16}$ of $\frac{8}{8}$, or only out of the interest in production owned by the lessee, for example, $\frac{1}{16}$ of $\frac{4}{5}$.

7.   State courts typically rely upon their basic theory of oil and gas ownership in deciding how a royalty interest should be characterized. Consider, for example, the differing positions taken by the Texas and California courts when faced with the question whether the landowner's royalty could be subjected to a real property tax apart from the interest owned by the lessee. In Sheffield v. Hogg, 77 S.W.2d 1021 (Tex. 1934), rehearing denied 80 S.W.2d 741 (Tex. 1935), the Texas Supreme Court pointed out that a landowner owns the oil and gas in the ground and held that the lessor's royalty was a taxable interest in realty. Analogizing royalties to a right to unaccrued rents, the court stated that it made no difference whether the lessor was entitled to receive her fractional interest of the oil in kind, or whether the lessee was given a power to sell all of the oil and gas and required to account to the lessor for a fixed percentage in cash. California, which follows the nonownership theory, took the opposite approach. In Atlantic Oil Co. v. County of Los Angeles, 446 P.2d 1006 (Cal. 1968), the court upheld an assessment of oil and gas leases, which apparently included the value of the landowners' royalty in the assessed value of the lessees' interest. The court concluded that "the right to receive royalties is not classified as real property for purposes of taxation. * * * [I]n California the right to receive royalties is not a right appertaining to minerals 'in the land.' Rather, it is an interest in oil and gas when they are removed from the land and reduced to possession."

The specific language of the statute being applied is even more important than the local theory of ownership in determining whether an unaccrued royalty is subject to an ad valorem tax. For a discussion of such statutes, see Summers § 797.

PROBLEM

William Harris conveyed a 1,000 acre ranch to Clyde and Joan Smith. The deed contained a reservation clause in which Harris retained a right to "one-half ($\frac{1}{2}$) of all the oil royalty, gas royalty, casinghead gas and gasoline royalty, and royalty from other minerals or products, due and to be paid under the terms of any oil and gas lease" that might be executed on the land. Subsequently the Smiths negotiated an oil and gas lease which provided for a $500 an acre bonus and a $2.50 an acre delay rental. The lease also contained the following provisions:

¶ 3.

In the addition to the cash consideration above set out and as part of the consideration for the execution of this lease, and not as a part of the royalty hereinafter reserved, the lessors reserve unto themselves, their heirs and assigns, the following, to-wit: $\frac{1}{10}$ of $\frac{1}{5}$ of all oil, gas and other minerals, including casinghead gas or other gaseous substances which may be produced and saved, sold and used off from the lands above described under this lease, as, if and when produced and saved, free and clear of all costs of development or operation.

¶ 4.

The royalties reserved by lessors and which shall be paid by lessees are:

(a) On oil, one-fifth ($\frac{1}{5}$) of that produced and saved from said land, the same to be delivered at the wells or the credit of lessors in the pipe line to which the wells may be connected or at the option of the lessees, from time to time, the market price at the wells of such one-fifth ($\frac{1}{5}$) on the day it is run to the pipe line or storage tanks.

(b) On gas produced from said land and sold or used off the land or in the manufacture of gasoline, including casinghead gas, the market price at the well of one-fifth of the gas so sold or used, provided that if and when lessees shall sell gas at the wells, lessor's royalty thereon shall be one-fifth of the amount realized from such sale.

While there is a gas well on this lease or on acreage pooled therewith but gas is not being sold or used, Lessee may pay as royalty, on or before ninety (90) days after the date on which (1) said well is shut in, or (2) the land covered hereby or any portion thereof is included in a pooled unit on which a well is located, or (3) this lease ceases to be otherwise maintained, as provided herein, whichever is the later date, and thereafter at annual intervals, the sum of Two Thousand Five Hundred ($2,500) Dollars, and if such payment is made or tendered, this lease shall not terminate, and it will be considered that gas is being produced from this lease in paying quantities.

¶ 5.

In addition to all other reservations of royalties herein made and provided for the benefit of lessors, there is reserved to lessors, their heirs, and assigns, the title to an undivided one-tenth of four-fifths ($\frac{1}{10}$ of $\frac{4}{5}$) equal part of all oil, gas, and/or other minerals in, under, and that may be produced and saved from said land, as, if, and when so produced and saved, but not otherwise, until lessors shall have received free of cost of production, marketing, or handling, the sum of Sixty-four Thousand Dollars ($64,000), whereupon this reservation shall terminate and the title to said one-tenth of four-fifths ($\frac{1}{10}$ of $\frac{4}{5}$) undivided interest in said oil, gas, and/or other minerals shall thereupon vest in lessee, its heirs, successors, and assigns.

[handwritten margin note: production payment w/ end ~ bonus]

¶ 6.

During the primary term of this lease if the royalty paid under the provisions of Paragraph 4 hereof for any given year does not amount to as much as Two Thousand Five Hundred ($2,500) Dollars, then the difference between the amount so paid and the said sum of Two Thousand Five Hundred ($2,500) Dollars shall be paid to Lessors. After the expiration of the primary term of this lease if the royalties paid under the provisions of Paragraph 4 hereof for any given year, do not amount to as much as Two

[handwritten margin note: minimum royalty]

Thousand Five Hundred ($2,500) Dollars, then the difference between the amount so paid and the said sum of Two Thousand Five Hundred ($2,500) Dollars shall be paid to Lessors.

Which of the benefits provided for in the oil and gas lease is Harris entitled to share? Would either your answer or your calculation be different if Harris's reservation had entitled him to a "one-tenth ($\frac{1}{10}$) royalty in all oil, gas, casinghead gas, and other minerals"? In answering the question, you should consider the following material.

NOTES

1. In Lane v. Elkins, 441 S.W.2d 871 (Tex.Civ.App. 1969, writ refused n.r.e.), a Texas court made the following distinction:

> In the oil and gas industry a royalty interest is commonly understood to be the right to a proportionate share of the oil produced from a well during the life of an oil and gas lease. A "bonus" is the sum or amount paid for the execution of an oil and gas lease whether in cash or out of production.

> Because of the fact that a bonus payment is sometimes to be paid out of production it often becomes difficult to distinguish between the terms "royalty" and "bonus." However, there are certain characteristics of a royalty interest which are controlling when it is necessary to make the distinction. It is held that in determining whether the payment provided for in a lease is a royalty or bonus the provisions of the instrument must be construed for what they really are, regardless of the designation given by the parties.

> In Griffith v. Taylor, 291 S.W.2d 673 (Tex. 1956). Judge Calvert speaking for the court stated as follows:

>> it may be that the words "bonus" and "royalty" in their broadest concepts and meanings are conflicting and overlapping. On the other hand, when it is necessary that they be distinguished there is a narrower concept of the two terms as they are ordinarily and commonly used and understood in the oil and gas industry in which they do not conflict but are harmonious. In this narrower sense a reservation or a payment of a part or percentage of production under a lease which is to continue throughout the life of the lease is regarded as "royalty", and a sum certain to be paid in cash or out of production is regarded as "bonus".

441 S.W.2d at 874.

2. In Andretta v. West, 415 S.W.2d 638 (Tex. 1967), the plaintiffs, who had received a grant of one-fourth "of the oil royalty, gas royalty, and royalty in casinghead gas, gasoline, and royalty in other minerals in and under, and that may be produced and mined" from the land, were held entitled to share in a payment that the lessee had agreed to make to the defendants (lessors) in resolution of a dispute over whether it was obliged to drill an offset well to prevent drainage to an adjacent tract. The payment, which was to be made monthly, was to be the cash equivalent of one-eighth of the proceeds from the

sale of the oil produced from the nearby well. The Texas Supreme Court stated, "The monthly payments were based on production from the well on the adjoining property, which is characteristic of a 'lieu' or 'compensatory' royalty. * * * We recognize that calling the payments royalty is not conclusive as to their true nature, but words of art are given considerable weight in determining the intent of the parties. In this instance the basis and agreed effect of the payments are such that the same constitute royalty and not delay rentals, and the descriptive term used by the parties is entirely accurate." 415 S.W.2d at 640.

3. Paragraph 5 of the lease in the Problem provides for an interest commonly known as a *production payment*. Like a royalty, it is an expense free interest paid out of a specified fraction of production. The production payment terminates, however, when a specified sum has been received. It may be limited to a certain type of production, for example, oil, or casinghead gas, and may require the delivery of the substance rather than a payment in cash.

The interest set out in ¶ 6 of the Problem lease is a *minimum royalty*. It is typically inserted by the lessor of a large tract of land who wants assurance that royalties from production will at least equal the delay rental. A good example of the use of such a lease clause can be found in Morriss v. First National Bank, 249 S.W.2d 269 (Tex.Civ.App.–San Antonio 1952, writ refused n.r.e.). In rare instances, clauses providing for minimum royalty may require payment even though production terminates. See, e.g., the coal lease litigated in Bicknell Minerals, Inc. v. Tilly, 570 N.E.2d 1307 (Ind.App. 1991). Far more commonly, minimum royalties are payable only if some oil or gas is being produced. Thus, unlike shut-in royalties, payment of minimum royalty in lieu of production will not maintain a lease. Morris Exploration, Inc. v. Guerra, 751 S.W.2d 710 (Tex.App. 1988).

4. Another type of interest that has some similarity to a royalty is the *net profits interest*. As the term is normally used, it refers to a right to receive a share of profits without any exposure to personal liability for expenses or injuries. It is thus similar to a *carried interest,* although the carried interest is frequently restricted to specific operations, such as drilling as far as the casing point, whereas the net profits interest may be perpetual. A full discussion of the net profits interest and the various legal forms it can take is found in Kuntz, A Treatise on the Law of Oil and Gas § 63.5.

It is always well to keep in mind, however, that terms such as net profits interest do not necessarily have fixed legal definitions and may be used in atypical ways by persons in the industry. Moreover, the scope, nature and method of calculating a net profits interest depends upon the specific language of the instrument creating it. Ryan v. American Natural Energy Corp., 557 F.3d 1152 (10th Cir. 2009) provides a good example of the issues such an instrument may present. As part of a bankruptcy settlement, the parties agreed that the creditors would receive a 50% net profits interest in the oil and gas produced from existing wells; 15% net profits interest in production from new wells on existing leases; and a 6% net profits interest from new wells drilled in an area of mutual interest. The principal issue turned on whether in determining net profits interests the costs and proceeds should be calculated on a per-well basis; or whether net profits should be determined on a system-wide basis, under which the costs of all existing and new wells would be aggregated. Aggregate costs would then be deducted from the aggregate revenues of all wells, and the net profits interest would be payable occur only after all costs had been recouped. Determining the result required an extensive and detailed analysis of the language of a complex agreement and consideration of the distinctions that the agreement repeatedly made between new wells and existing wells and the record keeping requirements for each.

As the *Ryan* case illustrates, in most disputes over net profits or carried interests, the method of computation is more crucial than the nature of the interest, for the parties must be able to determine when "net profits" have been obtained or how far an interest is to be "carried." The costs that are to be taken into account and the method of amortizing or depreciating capital expenditures should be spelled out in detail in the instrument creating the interests. See Lowe, Chapter 3.B.

5. As the preceding notes have indicated, a variety of types of interests in production can be created. Is the same true of the mineral estate? One of the more interesting cases raising this question is Petro Pro, Ltd. v. Upland Resources, Inc., 279 S.W.3d 743 (Tex.App. 2007) where a lessee decided that a well on a 704 acre pooled gas unit was no longer sufficiently profitable and assigned to the plaintiff all of its "right, title and interest" in the pooled unit acreage "insofar and only insofar as said leases cover rights in the wellbore." The case and a discussion of the interests included in a wellbore assignment can be found in Chapter 6.

2. CREATION OF MINERAL AND ROYALTY INTERESTS

BARKER v. LEVY

507 S.W.2d 613 (Tex.Civ.App. 1974, writ refused n.r.e.).

Tunks, Chief Justice.

* * *

* * * Levy [who had represented Mrs. Sweet in several legal matters involving her real estate] proposed that he be given an interest in the minerals of the lands as a fee for his future representation of her interest. * * *

Mrs. Sweet approved the arrangement proposed by Levy. He thereupon prepared a deed dated July 21, 1930, from Mrs. Sweet to him * * *.

The deed, sometimes hereinafter called the Sweet deed, from Mrs. Sweet to Levy, which deed is the principal subject of this case, was in the following language:

THE STATE OF TEXAS   )
)
COUNTY OF GALVESTON   )

For and in consideration of One Dollar ($1.00) cash to me in hand paid by Adrian F. Levy of Galveston County, Texas, and other good and valuable considerations, the receipt of which is hereby acknowledged and confessed, I, Margaret Cade Sweet, a feme sole, of Queens County, State of New York, have granted, sold, conveyed, transferred and assigned, and by these presents do bargain, grant, sell, convey, transfer and assign unto the said Adrian F. Levy a One/one hundred and sixtieth ($\frac{1}{160}$th) part of all oil, gas, petroleum, sulphur and all other minerals that may be produced and saved from the following described lands, to wit:

[Description of Property Omitted]

TO HAVE AND TO HOLD the same unto the said Adrian F. Levy, his heirs, administrators, administrators [sic] and assigns forever.

I do hereby bind myself, my heirs, executors, and administrators to warrant and forever defend, all and singular, the interest hereby conveyed unto the said Adrian F. Levy, his heirs, assigns and legal representatives, against the lawful claim of every person lawfully claiming or to claim the same or any part thereof.

It is intended by this instrument to convey unto the said Adrian F. Levy a $\frac{1}{160}$th part of all the oil, gas, sulphur and other minerals that may be produced and saved from all lands in the State of Texas, the title to which is now owned in whole or in part by me, as well as such lands in the State of Texas which I have heretofore sold but in which I have retained an interest in the minerals.

Executed this the 21st day of July, A.D. 1930.

/s/ Margaret Cade Sweet

In 1933 Mrs. Sweet died intestate. * * * On January 15, 1971, Mrs. Barker, Mrs. Speer, and the trustee bank [the heirs and successors in interest of Mrs. Sweet] filed this suit. Adrian F. Levy and his two children, to whom he had transferred a part of his interest, were named as defendants. The case was tried to a jury. After the evidence was closed the trial judge withdrew the case from the jury and rendered judgment for the defendants. The plaintiffs appealed.

The plaintiffs in the trial court, appellants here, contend that the above quoted deed is unambiguous and conveyed to Levy a $\frac{1}{160}$ of the minerals in place. The defendants in the trial court, appellees here, contend that the deed is unambiguous and conveyed to Levy a royalty of $\frac{1}{160}$ of the oil produced from the lands described. Some of the Cade lands were, at the time of the deed, subject to an oil and gas lease to one Marrs McLean under which the lessors were entitled to $\frac{1}{8}$ royalty. In accordance with the contention of the plaintiffs-appellants Levy was, under that lease, entitled to $\frac{1}{160}$ or [of] $\frac{1}{8}$, or $\frac{1}{1280}$, of the oil produced, free and clear of the cost of production. According to the contention of the defendants-appellees, they were entitled to $\frac{1}{160}$ of all of the oil produced, free and clear of the cost of production. Alternatively, each side contends that if the deed is ambiguous it should, under the extrinsic evidence, be construed in that side's favor. * * *

* * *

Appellants contend that the Sweet deed is unambiguous and conveys to Levy ⅟₁₆₀ of the minerals in place. They state that the question is one of first impression as to any Supreme Court of Texas holding. They forthrightly admit that the language of two Texas courts of civil appeals' opinions, hereafter discussed, is contrary to their contention. They cite, as authority for their contention, three out-of-state judicial opinions and two texts.

The first case cited by appellants is Little v. Mountain View Dairies, 217 P.2d 416 (Cal. 1950). In that case the deed in question conveyed "Eight and one-third per cent (8⅓%) of all oil, gas and other hydrocarbon substances, and minerals, in, under and/or which may be hereafter produced and save [sic] from" the property. The Court held that the deed conveyed a ⅟₁₂ interest in the minerals in place. The Court said, at page 419:

> It is clear, therefore, that in California as in other jurisdictions, in the absence of extrinsic evidence or other controlling language in the deed, a grant of a fraction of all the oil in, under and that may be produced and saved from the land creates an expense-bearing mineral fee interest.

One of the texts cited by appellants is Richard Maxwell, A Primer of Mineral and Royalty Conveyancing, 3 U.C.L.A.L.Rev. 449 (1956). That article includes a discussion of the Mountain View Dairies case, supra. Appellants quoted the following language from page 457:

> There is ample basis in authority and practice in many jurisdictions, regardless of theories of ownership, to sustain the court's conclusion that more than the addition of the conveyancing formality "and which may be produced" is necessary for the creation of a royalty interest.

Other language from that same article at pages 456–458 is much more significant. The writer there said:

> One contention which the court considered in the *Mountain View Dairies* case was to the effect that the addition of the words, "and which may hereafter be produced and saved" to the grant of "eight and one-third percent of all oil, gas and other hydrocarbons," was indicative of an intent to grant an expense-free royalty interest. One reason for the rejection of this contention was the fact that California does not consider that oil and gas is owned "in place." The court opined that in view of the existence in California of the so-called non-ownership theory "the parties might well doubt the effectiveness of a conveyance limited to a fraction of all the oil and gas in and under the land and therefore add a reference to oil to be produced, without in any way intending to convey more than the stated fraction of all the oil rights appurtenant to the land." It is, however, common practice

to add the phrase "and which may be produced" to a document which purports to convey a specified portion of the oil and gas "in and under" the land without any other basis in the language for finding that the interest created is not an expense-bearing mineral interest.
* * *

The omission of the standard words of mineral ownership, "in and under," in a conveyance which speaks of oil and gas "produced," creates a context in which the latter language assumes greater significance. The reservation construed in Miller v. Speed is illustrative: "an undivided ¼₄ of all the oil, gas and other minerals produced, saved and made available for market." The court noted that "A ¼₄ of all the oil in and under and that may be produced from a tract of land is an interest in the minerals in place in the ground, but that is a different interest than a ¼₄ of all the oil that may be produced, saved and made available for market * * *." The opinion in the *Miller* case makes it clear that the absence of the words "in and under" was a critical factor in their interpretation of the reservation as a royalty reservation. In this the opinion is typical. That these words most often flag a mineral interest is supported by cases from many jurisdictions. That they have become a kind of shorthand for a statement that the interest described bears the expense of production and is therefore to be classified as a mineral interest is apparent from the judicial handling of them when they are used in the same conveyance with words such as "which may be produced" which tends toward an expense-free royalty interest. [Footnotes omitted]

That explanation of the holding in Mountain View Dairies renders it unpersuasive as to the appellants' claim relating to construction of the Sweet deed, which did not use the words "in and under."

The next case cited by appellants is Simson v. Langholf, 293 P.2d 302 (Colo. 1956). In that case the Court held that the grant of "forty-nine percent (49%) of all oil and/or gas that may be produced saved and marketed" granted a 49% interest in the minerals in place. In that case the successors to the grantee were contending that the instrument conveyed a 49% interest in the minerals in place—they claimed a right to participate in bonus and delay rental payments. The Court's opinion recited that there was no oil and gas lease covering the property in effect at the time the deed was executed and indicated that if there had been such a lease the Court would have held differently. At page 307 the Court said:

> [T]here being no oil or gas lease in existence at the time of the conveyance or reservation, the words of the grant or reservation "assigned and set over" are such as to convey a partial interest in the minerals in perpetuity, and an estate in fee simple is thus created.

At the time the Sweet deed was executed the Marrs McLean lease was in effect and still is. That fact distinguishes the Simson case. Furthermore, there is no requirement in Texas law that a lease be in effect before a royalty interest can be created.

The third out-of-state case cited by appellants is Mounger v. Pittman, 108 So.2d 565 (Miss. 1959). In that case the Court, in a five to three opinion, held that a reservation of "one-eighth of all the oil and gas which may be produced from said lands to be delivered in tanks and pipelines in the customary manner, and this shall be a covenant running with the land and all sales and other conveyances of said lands shall be subject to this reservation and agreement" reserved a ⅛ mineral interest instead of a ⅛ royalty interest in all oil and gas produced.

In that case, too, the land was not under lease at the time the reservation was made. In a later case, Gardner v. Pan–American Petroleum Corporation, 243 So.2d 399 (Miss. 1971), the same Court apparently considered that to be a distinguishing fact. In the Gardner case the Court held that a provision in a will devising to each of three persons ⅛ interest "in all Gas and Oil and other Minerals and Royalties that is or May be Proudeosed [sic]" created royalty interests in the devisees. The land involved was under lease at the time the will became effective. The Court distinguished the Mounger case saying, at page 402, "The land [in the Mounger case] was not under lease and there was no production." For the same reason the Mounger case is distinguished here because some of the Cade land was under lease at the time the Sweet deed was executed.

The other text authority cited by appellants is Emery, Conveyancing of Interests in Oil and Gas, 29 Okla.B.J. 1965 (1958). There the author says good draftsmanship requires that where a conveyance of a royalty is intended. "There should be added the proviso that 'it is the intention of the parties hereto to convey a royalty interest as distinguished from a mineral interest.'" It is quite probable that these appellees now heartily agree with this advice. However, it was written twenty-eight years too late to have been helpful to Mr. Levy and Mrs. Sweet. It is not authority for the proposition that the Sweet deed created a mineral interest.

* * *

Those are the principal authorities as to the construction of the Sweet deed presented by counsel for appellants. They are neither compelling nor very persuasive of the proposition that the Sweet deed was a conveyance of minerals in place. On the other hand, counsel for appellees have cited two Texas cases that are directly in point and sustain the conclusion that the Sweet deed conveyed a $\frac{1}{160}$ royalty. They are Miller v. Speed, 248 S.W.2d 250 (Tex.Civ.App.–Eastland 1952, no writ), and Pinchback v. Gulf Oil Corp., 242 S.W.2d 242 (Tex.Civ.App.–Beaumont 1951, writ ref'd n.r.e.).

The Miller case was discussed in the above quoted portion of the law review article of Professor Maxwell. It held that a deed reserving "an undivided $\frac{1}{24}$th of all the oil, gas and other minerals produced, saved and made available for market" reserved a $\frac{1}{24}$ royalty interest. In so holding the Court noted that the reservation clause used the word "all" and the words "produced, saved." The Court also noted the absence of the words "in and under." The Sweet deed has all three of those characteristics.

In the Pinchback case the deed in question reserved "⅛th of all minerals that may hereafter be produced and saved." The Court held that the grantor reserved a ⅛ royalty.

We, therefore, hold that the Sweet deed is unambiguous and that it conveyed to Levy a ¹⁄₁₆₀ royalty. Since the deed is clear and unambiguous the extrinsic evidence is immaterial on the issue of the intention of the parties in its execution. * * *

* * *

The judgment of the trial court is affirmed.

NOTES

1. Would the result in the principal case have been different if the grant had been "one/one hundred sixtieth (¹⁄₁₆₀) part of all oil, gas, petroleum, sulphur and all other minerals *in and under* and that may be produced and saved" from the land? See Little v. Mountain View Dairies, 35 Cal.2d 232, 217 P.2d 416 (1950) and Williams & Meyers § 304.5.

2. Whether language creates a royalty or a mineral fee interest is especially crucial in Kansas and has given rise to a large number of cases because as noted previously, a perpetual royalty is deemed invalid under the rule against perpetuities. In Rucker v. DeLay, 235 P.3d 566 (Kan.App. 2010) the successor of grantors who had reserved "60% of the land owner's one-eighth interest to the oil, gas or other minerals that may hereafter be developed under any oil and gas lease made by the grantee or by his subsequent grantees," unsuccessfully argued that their predecessors had reserved an interest in the mineral estate. They relied in part on Section 58–2202 of the Kansas Statutes Annotated, which provides that "every convey-ance of real estate shall pass all the estate of the grantor therein, unless the intent to pass a less estate shall expressly appear or be necessarily implied in the terms of the grant." Citing Professor David Pierce's Kansas Oil and Gas Handbook § 6.14, the court pointed out that a primary factor in determining the nature of an oil and gas interest is whether the instrument involved conveys a right to oil and gas "in and under" the land. The use of such language points toward the creation of a a mineral interest; whereas a mere reference to oil and gas "produced" from the land tends to indicate that a royalty interest was created. Equating the reference in the reservation to oil, gas or other minerals that may be "developed" as oil, gas or other minerals that may be "produced," the court concluded that the grantors had reserved a royalty.

3. The *Barker* and *Rucker* cases illustrate the prevailing view of the effect of "produced and saved" language. A similar construction is accorded the word "royalty." When used without additional language indicative of an interest in the mineral estate, a grant or reservation of a fractional royalty or a fraction *of* royalty normally creates an expense free interest in production. As in all such matters, however, there are exceptions. See, e.g., Laura H.

Burney, Interpreting Mineral and Royalty Deeds: The Legacy of the One–Eighth Royalty and Other Stories, 33 St. Mary's L. J. 1 (2001). Some of the most notable exceptions to the prevailing rules of interpretation are the following.

(a) A common law doctrine, which can be traced at least as far back as Lord Coke, holds that a grant of the profits from land constitutes a grant of the land itself. This doctrine was first applied to the construction of oil and gas instruments by the West Virginia Supreme Court of Appeals in Toothman v. Courtney, 58 S.E. 915 (W.Va. 1907). Its clearest expression by that court came ten years later in Paxton v. Benedum–Trees Oil Co., 94 S.E. 472 (W.Va. 1917), where the court was called upon to construe an instrument that included a grant of "the one-half of all the royalties, incomes and rentals that may hereafter arise therefrom or accrue upon the real estate hereinafter described by virtue of any oil and gas lease." Citing with approval the proposition that "there is no construction of words older and better settled than that a grant or devise of the profits of land passes the land itself," the West Virginia court held that the quoted language passed title to one-half of the mineral estate. West Virginia has not been entirely consistent in following the rule announced in its earlier cases. See, e.g., Davis v. Hardman, 133 S.E.2d 77 (W.Va. 1963) and Thomas Franklin McCoy, Note, Mineral Interests and the Executive Right in West Virginia, 66 W.Va.L.Rev. 221 (1964). The court did, however, follow Lord Coke's doctrine in Rastle v. Gamsjager, 153 S.E.2d 403 (W.Va. 1967), where it construed a devise of "my interest in the oil and gas that may be produced from the lands herein before devised" as including the mineral estate.

What language should a drafter in West Virginia use to create an expense free interest in the production of oil and gas? See generally L. Skeen, West Virginia Oil and Gas Law § 4.9 (1984).

The West Virginia view has been influential in a small number of states. The Colorado Supreme Court referred to the West Virginia cases and to Lord Coke's doctrine in Simson v. Langholf, 293 P.2d 302 (Colo. 1956), where it treated a grant of "49% of all oil and/or gas that may be produced saved and marketed" as creating an interest in the mineral estate. The Colorado court reaffirmed its position two years later in Corlett v. Cox, 333 P.2d 619 (Colo. 1958). In 1991, Colorado statutorily overruled *Simson* and *Corlett* with Colo.Rev.Stat. 38–30–107.5, which specifically permits the creation of nonparticipating royalty interests after July 1, 1991. A subsequent case held that the statute's primary purpose was to clarify confusing case law and that it had been possible to create perpetual nonparticipating royalties prior to the statutory date. Keller Cattle Co. v. Allison, 55 P.3d 257 (Colo.App. 2002). Alabama and Illinois have decisions which seem to approve the theory that a grant or reservation of royalty is a grant or reservation of an interest in the mineral fee. See, e.g., McCall v. Nettles, 37 So.2d 635 (Ala. 1948); Logue v. Marsh, 365 N.E.2d 1159 (Ill.App.4 Dist. 1977); and Vandenbark v. Busiek, 126 F.2d 893 (7th Cir. Ill. 1942).

(b) Oklahoma has also construed the word "royalty" in deeds as meaning an interest in the mineral estate. The Oklahoma courts have, however, advanced reasons in addition to Lord Coke's rule in support of their position.

The leading case is Melton v. Sneed, 109 P.2d 509 (Okla. 1940). In that case a grant of "one-third (⅓) of all royalties, from oil, gas or other minerals arising from or out of or produced upon the above described lands" was construed as transferring a one-third undivided interest in the mineral rights to the grantee, who was thereby entitled to join in any lease on the land and to receive one-third of the bonus, delay rentals, and royalty provided for by such a lease. The Oklahoma Supreme Court stated that

> [T]he word [royalty] was not used in its strict sense, but in the broader sense referred to in 3 Summers Oil and Gas, Perm.Ed., § 599, as denoting an interest in the minerals. That the word is frequently used in this State to denote an interest in the mineral rights is a matter of common knowledge. The conveyance in question here employed it in that sense. There is no reference therein to any lease, or to the royalty reserved thereunder, and the grant is expressly made perpetual. The term as used is ambiguous, and the trial court properly admitted evidence to denote the intent of the parties.

109 P.2d at 512–13.

What would be the result in Oklahoma if a deed grants a right to "one-half of royalties" on production under an existing lease and any future leases? See Meeks v. Harmon, 250 P.2d 203 (Okla. 1952). Would it make any difference if a grant of "one-half (½) of all royalties received from any oil and gas leases" is made at a time when no lease is outstanding? What if no lease is outstanding, but the deed specifies the fraction of gross production the grantee is entitled to, for example, "one-sixteenth (¹⁄₁₆) of all oil, gas or other minerals produced from said premises." See Wilson v. Hecht, 370 P.2d 28 (Okla. 1962); Federal Land Bank v. Nicholson, 251 P.2d 490 (Okla. 1952); Armstrong v. McCracken, 229 P.2d 590 (Okla. 1951); and Gardner v. Jones, 181 P.2d 838 (Okla. 1947). For a discussion of these and other Oklahoma cases, see Richard W. Hemingway, The Mineral–Royalty Distinction in Oklahoma, 52 Okla.B.J. 2791 (1981) and Hemingway, § 2.7(C).

The Oklahoma courts' treatment of the term "royalty" has been criticized as creating a high level of title uncertainty. It has been suggested that the average lawyer, who does not specialize in oil and gas law, has difficulty enough in understanding the difference between a royalty and a mineral interest. The added difficulty of determining which meaning "royalty" has inevitably resulted in title litigation. Hemingway § 2.7(C) at 77.

(c) Mississippi has reached a result similar to that of the West Virginia and Oklahoma courts, but on the basis of an entirely different rule of construction. In Mounger v. Pittman, 108 So.2d 565 (Miss. 1959), a reservation of "one-eighth of all the oil and gas which may be produced from said lands" was held to create an interest in the mineral estate, rather than a royalty because the clause "does not provide, either expressly or by implication, that the grantors' share of production is to be free of costs of discovery and production, an important provision in any instrument creating a nonparticipating royalty interest." Later cases have cast considerable doubt upon the state's continued adherence to this approach. See Castle v. Harkins & Co., 464 So.2d 513 (Miss. 1985); Gardner v. Pan–American Petroleum Corp., 243 So.2d 399 (Miss. 1971); and Lackey v. Corley, 295 So.2d 762 (Miss. 1974).

(d) Exceptionally large non-participating royalties have on occasion been construed as grants or reservations of an interest in the mineral estate. The rationale for such a construction was stated in Brooks v. Mull, 78 P.2d 879 (Kan. 1938), which involved a reservation of "an undivided one-half interest in and to all of the oil, gas, and, or, other minerals that may be produced from said land." In rejecting an argument that the grantor had retained a royalty, the court stated that "the construction of the reservation * * * for which defendants contend would utterly prevent any effective leasing of this 3,600 acre of land for oil and gas * * *, for certainly no sane man would lease and develop it if [grantor] is to receive an undivided one-half of all the oil and gas which the industry of the lessee may produce from the land." 78 P.2d at 880.

The reasoning that an NPRI of 1/8th or more would preclude leasing has lost some of its force in jurisdictions where the size of lease royalties have increased dramatically and seismic exploration, especially of oil or gas shales, has almost assured successful horizontal drilling. In some areas of the country one-fifth has become the standard lease royalty, and a one-fourth royalty is often successfully negotiated. Moreover, as Professor Smith has argued, large NPRIs do not necessarily prevent development. The practical effect of an exceptionally large nonparticipating royalty is that it enables the royalty owner to participate in the leasing process. "[I]n exchange for a bonus he can transfer a fraction of his royalty to the lessee for the term of the lease. The real danger, of course, is that the royalty interest will become dormant," that is, that it will be impossible to locate its owner. Ernest E. Smith, Methods of Facilitating the Development of Oil and Gas Lands Burdened with Outstanding Mineral Interests, 43 Tex.L.Rev. 129, 136 (1964). Does a large dormant royalty pose more serious problems for oil and gas development than a dormant fractional interest in the mineral estate?

(e) Regardless of the jurisdiction, "produced and saved" and "royalty" language will not necessarily create an expense-free interest if the instrument contains additional qualifying language that is more consistent with an interest in the mineral estate. Thus, an interest in the mineral estate may result if royalty language is coupled with grants of ingress and occupancy for the purposes of drilling, storing, and marketing oil and gas. Wynn v. Sklar & Phillips Oil Co., 493 S.W.2d 439 (Ark. 1973) and Williams v. J. & C. Royalty Co., 254 S.W.2d 178 (Tex.Civ.App. 1952, writ refused n.r.e.). A right to share in all lease benefits may be construed as having the same effect. See Loeffler v. King, 236 S.W.2d 772 (Tex. 1951). Should use of the word "all," for example "one fourth (¼) of all the oil, gas and other minerals produced and saved," also override a royalty construction? See Palmer v. Brandenburg, 651 P.2d 961 (Kan.App. 1982); Wilson v. Hecht, 370 P.2d 28 (Okla. 1962); and Sanders v. Bell, 350 P.2d 293 (Okla. 1960).

4. Often an instrument will use "in and under" or other language normally associated with ownership of a mineral fee interest, but then add qualifying language that cuts down the rights connected with that interest. The following case is an example of the constructional problems presented by such instruments.

FRENCH v. CHEVRON

896 S.W.2d 795 (Tex. 1995).

JUSTICE ENOCH delivered the opinion of the Court, in which all Justices join.

The controversy in this case is over the size of an interest conveyed by a mineral deed. Grantee's successor-in-interest claims to own a royalty interest equal to the value of 1/656.17 of all oil and gas produced from the entire tract of land involved. Grantor's successors-in-interest contend that the deed conveyed only a 1/656.17 portion of the royalty to be paid by the lessor. We agree with the grantor's successors-in-interest and consequently affirm the judgment of the court of appeals.

In 1943, George Calvert (Grantor), the owner of a 1/32 mineral interest in a 32,808.5 acre tract, deeded a fifty acre, 1/656.17 interest to Capton M. Paul (Grantee). The pertinent parts of the document, titled "Mineral Deed," read as follows:

[Paragraph I.]

That I, George Calvert, ... do grant, bargain, sell, convey, set over, assign and deliver unto Capton M. Paul, an undivided Fifty (50) acre interest, being an undivided 1/656.17th interest in and to all of the oil, gas and other minerals, in, under and that may be produced from the following described lands....

[Paragraph II.]

It is understood and agreed that this conveyance is a royalty interest only, and that neither the Grantee, nor his heirs or assigns shall ever have any interest in the delay or other rentals or any revenues or monies received or derived from the leasing of said lands present or future or any part thereof, or the renewal or extension of any lease or leases now on said lands or any part thereof. Neither the Grantee herein nor his heirs or assigns shall ever have any control over the leasing of said lands or any part thereof or the renewal or extending of any lease thereon or for the making of any lease contract to develop or prospect the same for oil, gas or other minerals, which is hereby specifically reserved in the Grantor.

(Emphasis added).

Petitioner Fuller Trust, the successor-in-interest to the grantee, brought suit against Grantor Calvert's successors to construe the deed as conveying a royalty interest. Fuller Trust maintains the deed conveyed a pure fixed royalty interest of 1/656.17 of all production. Respondent Chevron claims the deed conveyed a mineral interest with a reservation of all rights stated in paragraph II. If the deed conveyed a mineral interest reduced by reservations, the grantee would receive only a 1/656.17 fraction of any royalty payable under a lease.

Both parties sought summary judgment, asserting that the deed is unambiguous and that its construction is a question of law. If the language is unambiguous, the court's primary duty is to ascertain the intent of the parties from the language of the deed by using the "four corners" rule. Luckel v. White, 819 S.W.2d 459, 461 (Tex. 1991). The trial court denied Fuller Trust's summary judgment motion, finding only that the case constituted a proper declaratory judgment action, and granted Chevron's motion, holding that the deed conveyed a mineral interest with a reservation of certain rights.

* * *

The conflict in this case comes in reconciling language in paragraph one, which appears to convey a mineral estate, with the language in paragraph two, which explicitly states that only a royalty interest is being conveyed. A mineral estate consists of five interests: 1) the right to develop, 2) the right to lease, 3) the right to receive bonus payments, 4) the right to receive delay rentals, and 5) the right to receive royalty payments. Altman v. Blake, 712 S.W.2d 117, 118 (Tex. 1986). A conveyance of a mineral estate need not dispose of all interests; individual interests can be held back, or reserved, in the grantor. However, "[w]hen an undivided mineral interest is conveyed, reserved, or excepted, it is presumed that all attributes remain with the mineral interest unless a contrary intent is expressed." Day & Co. v. Texland Petroleum, 786 S.W.2d 667, 669 n. 1 (Tex. 1990).

While the first paragraph appears to grant a mineral estate, the second paragraph of the lease specifically states that the interest conveyed is a royalty interest only. The clause in the second paragraph, beginning "and that," sets forth the consequences of the royalty interest only declaration, by going further to specifically reserve in the grantor the four components of a mineral estate other than the royalty: the rights to lease, to receive bonus payments, to receive delay rentals and to develop or prospect.[1]

We interpret the transfer to have conveyed a 1/656.17 mineral interest with reservation of all developmental rights, leasing rights, bonuses, and delay rentals. The conveyance grants, in essence, only a royalty interest, as stated in the second paragraph. First, the granting clause must be read in light of the rest of the document. Paragraph one states that the grantor is conveying a fifty acre interest. A "fifty acre interest" is

---

1. The court of appeals held that the deed was silent as to the conveyance of the right to develop and therefore, that right was impliedly transferred to the grantee. This conclusion is incorrect for two reasons. First, the right to develop is a correlative right and passes with the executive rights. Day & Co. v. Texland Petroleum, 786 S.W.2d 667, 669 n. 1 (Tex. 1990). Second, we read the reservations clause in this conveyance as reserving the right to develop in the grantor. It states that the grantee has no control over "the making of any lease contract to develop or prospect." Consequently, we also conclude that the right to develop was reserved in the grantor.

For an exhaustive account of the various canons of construction used to interpret mineral deeds and leases, see Bruce M. Kramer, The Sisyphean Task of Interpreting Mineral Deeds and Leases: An Encyclopedia of Canons of Construction, 24 TEX.TECH.L.REV. 1 (1993).

1/656.17 of the 32,808.5 tract, and the deed then recites that it is conveying "an undivided 1/656.17th interest in and to all of the oil, gas, and other minerals in, under, and that may be produced from the described lands." Standing alone, this would convey a 1/656.17 interest in the minerals. Paragraph two indicates that the interest in the minerals conveyed in paragraph one is a royalty interest. The remainder of paragraph two is best interpreted as explaining the consequences of the "royalty only" description. It reserves in the grantor the right to receive delay or other rentals, or any revenues from the leasing or from any renewal or extension of any lease. This reservation would be redundant and would serve no purpose whatsoever if the interests in minerals being conveyed was a 1/656.17 royalty interest, that is, 1/656.17 of all production. A grant of a royalty interest, without any further grant, does not convey an interest to the grantee in delay or other rentals, or in bonus payments, nor would it convey executive rights. The meaning of this grant is to convey an interest in the nature of a royalty—a mineral interest stripped of appurtenant rights other than the right to receive royalties. From the four corners of the document, we conclude that the parties intended to convey a 1/656.17 mineral interest with the reservations described, thus conveying only the royalty portion of the mineral interest. This harmonizes and gives effect to all portions of the deed. Luckel, 819 S.W.2d at 461. In other words, when a deed conveys a royalty interest by the mechanism of granting a fractional mineral estate followed by reservations, what is conveyed is a fraction of royalty, not a fixed fraction of total production royalty. See, e.g., Brown v. Havard, 593 S.W.2d 939, 942, 946 (Tex. 1980) (distinguishing between conveyance of fraction of production as royalty and fraction of royalty).

The court of appeals correctly affirmed the trial court's summary judgment. We affirm the judgment of the court of appeals and render judgment by construing the Paul deed as conveying to Paul a 1/656.17 interest in the minerals and not 1/656.17 of production as royalty.

NOTES

1. Several Texas cases have construed deeds that begin with language indicative of a mineral fee but continue with clauses subtracting specific rights or benefits usually attached to mineral ownership. Altman v. Blake, 712 S.W.2d 117 (Tex. 1986) has been especially influential in determining the judicial approach to such deeds. The deed granted "an undivided one-sixteenth (1/16) interest in and to all of the oil, gas and other minerals in and under and that may be produced" from a described tract and provided that the grantee "does not participate in any rentals or leases. . . ." In rejecting the grantees' argument that they had received a 1/16 royalty, the court reasoned that the granting clause clearly conveyed an interest in the mineral estate; the proviso merely had the effect of stripping away two of the incidents normally associated with a mineral estate: the right to execute leases and the right to receive delay rentals. Thus the grantees were not entitled to 1/16 of gross production; their rights were limited to 1/16 of lease benefits other than

rentals, i.e., 1/16 of the royalty and 1/16 of the bonus paid under an oil and gas lease on the land.

In Mineral or Royalty—The French Percentage, 49 S.M.U. L.Rev. 543 (1996), Professor Emeritus Richard Maxwell has described this process by making an analogy to a "mineral bug."

> The mineral bug can be given a development head, a leasing power leg, a royalty leg, a rental leg, and a bonus leg, all attached to an expense-bearing body. The device works well in analyzing the common practice of first conveying a full mineral interest and then verbally stripping away some of the mineral attributes, to leave something less than full mineral interest in the grantee. For example, our mineral bug may have been divested of its development head and its leasing leg. Is a headless, three-legged mineral bug still a mineral bug? French v. Chevron U.S.A. illustrates and, to a degree, answers this and related questions. . . .

Id. at 548.

Some intermediate appellate courts have interpreted *Chevron* as requiring this method of analysis (absent the analogy) even where all incidents of the mineral estate except royalty are stripped away. For example, Bank One, Texas, Nat'l Ass'n v. Alexander, 910 S.W.2d 530 (Tex. App.–Austin 1995, writ denied) involved a reservation of "an undivided 1/16 interest in and to all minerals, . . . including oil and gas, in, upon and under said land," followed by language stipulating that the rights to control and manage, to execute oil and gas leases and to receive bonus and rentals were vested exclusively in the grantees. Citing *Chevron*, the court ruled that the grantors had reserved a 1/16 mineral fee stripped of all incidents except royalty. A clause providing that "an undivided 1/16 of any and all oil and gas . . . developed from said land shall be owned by grantors" did not enlarge the grantors' interest to a right to 1/16 of gross production.

2. In an earlier Texas Supreme Court case, Watkins v. Slaughter, 189 S.W.2d 699 (Tex. 1945), the grantor had retained "title to a 1/16 interest in and to all of the oil, gas and other minerals in and under and that may be produced from said land," without any right to participate in leasing or to share in delay rentals and bonus. The deed stipulated, however, that the grantor "shall receive the royalty retained herein only from actual production." After considering the deed as a whole, the Watkins court concluded that the grantor had retained a 1/16 royalty, rather than a 1/16 mineral fee stripped of all incidents except royalty. The court relied on the word "royalty," which "has a well understood meaning in the oil and gas industry," and the language indicating that the grantor would receive the royalty "from actual production."

Although *Chevron* might reasonably have been construed as impliedly overruling *Watkins*, the Texas Supreme Court treated the earlier case as controlling precedent in Temple–Inland Forest Products Corp. v. Henderson Family Partnership, Ltd., 958 S.W.2d 183 (Tex. 1997). There the deed granted an undivided 15/16 in the oil and gas in and under the land and provided that the 1/16 retained by the Grantor "is and shall always be a royalty interest, and shall not be charged with any of the costs which the grantee may incur in exploring, drilling, mining, developing and operating wells." Further language provided that the exclusive rights to lease and receive bonus and delay rentals were transferred to the grantee. Reversing the lower courts, the Texas Supreme Court held that that the grantor had reserved a full 1/16 royalty.

3. Occasionally, deeds are encountered that grant or reserve a royalty but contain additional language attaching rights or benefits normally associated with a mineral fee interest. An extreme example is the deed in Elick v. Champlin Petroleum Co., 697 S.W.2d 1 (Tex.App. 1985, writ refused n.r.e.), where the grantors reserved a one thirty-second royalty and then provided that they would also receive one-half of the bonus and delay rental and "shall join in the execution of any future oil, gas, or mineral lease." In construing such instruments, most courts have focused on whether the added rights indicate that the parties intended to create a mineral fee interest rather than a royalty. See, e.g., Acklin v. Fuqua, 193 S.W.2d 297 (Tex.Civ.App. 1946, writ refused n.r.e.).

Would a deed that grants rights of ingress and egress along with a royalty interest necessarily give rise to this type of issue? See Neel v. Alpar Resources, Inc., 797 S.W.2d 361 (Tex.App. 1990) and Smith & Weaver § 3.5(B)(2).

ANDERSON v. MAYBERRY

661 P.2d 535 (Okla.App.Div. 1 1983).

REYNOLDS, JUDGE:

Herbert S. Mayberry (Mayberry) contends that the trial court erred when quieting the title of Robert C. Anderson (Anderson) to two tracts of Logan County property.

Mayberry and three co-owners executed warranty deeds in 1966 which conveyed all the surface rights to the grantees, and which further provided:

> * * * excepting and reserving unto the grantors, [names omitted], and in the proportions now owned by them, and unto their respective heirs, devisees, successors and assigns, *an undivided one-half ($\frac{1}{2}$) interest in and to all of the oil, gas and other minerals in and under and that may be produced from said property,* for a term of twenty (20) years from the date hereof, and as long thereafter as oil or gas or other minerals are produced therefrom, *the said interest in the oil, gas and other minerals so reserved shall be nonparticipating in bonus and rental rights* on oil and gas leases, * * *. [Emphasis added.]

Anderson holds oil and gas leases from the grantees. He did not obtain a lease from Mayberry.

Mayberry asserts that he did not convey his right to execute oil and gas leases for his retained mineral interest. Anderson contends that by taking an interest which was " * * * * non-participating in bonus and rental rights on oil and gas leases * * * *" Mayberry has impliedly waived the right to execute leases. Mayberry demurred to Anderson's evidence and stood on his demurrer.

The case at bar is the inverse of McVey v. Hines, 385 P.2d 432 (Okla. 1963). The grantor in *McVey* reserved the right to collect bonuses and delay rentals, and conveyed a non-participating interest. The Supreme Court found that McVey intended to reserve all executive rights pertaining to oil and gas leases.

Mayberry has conveyed the right to collect bonuses and delay rentals, and has retained a non-participating mineral interest. The trial court found that Mayberry impliedly conveyed the right to execute leases since " * * * to hold otherwise would negate the whole idea of a non-participating interest * * *." We agree.

The leases executed by Mayberry's grantees reserve a ³⁄₁₆ of the oil and gas produced to the mineral owners. Mayberry owns a proportionate share of one-half the minerals. The trial court found that Mayberry was entitled to his proportionate share of ³⁄₃₂ of any production of oil or gas. This finding is without error.

* * *

Affirmed.

NOTES

1. In HNG Fossil Fuels Co. v. Roach, 656 P.2d 879 (N.M. 1982), the grantor executed two deeds, each of which conveyed to the Thomsons "25% of the minerals and mineral rights owned by the grantor relating to, within, upon, or underlying the real estate described on the exhibit attached here, * * * including, without limitation, oil, gas, and all other minerals of any types or character whatsoever, non-participating." The grantor's successors in interest agreed that the Thomsons were entitled to one-half of the royalty provided for in oil and gas leases on the property, but disputed their claim to share in bonus and delay rental. The New Mexico Supreme Court reasoned that the deed had conveyed an interest in the mineral estate, and then stripped away a portion of its normal incidents.

The issue disputed by the parties is the meaning of a "non-participating mineral interest."

A mineral interest includes the following incidents: the right to receive bonuses, delay rentals, and royalties; the right to execute oil, gas, and mineral leases; and the right of ingress and egress to explore for and produce oil and gas. A mineral interest may be created and, by appropriate language in the deed, be stripped of one or more of its normal incidents.

The question therefore is what incidents were removed from the Thomsons' mineral interest by the restriction that it be "non-participating." The term "non-participating royalty" has a well-understood meaning in oil and gas law, entitling its owner to a share of gross production but not to bonuses, delay rentals, the executive right, or the right of ingress and egress to explore for and produce oil and gas. Terminology that appears to create a "non-participating mineral interest" usually has been construed to create a royalty interest. * * * The court did not err in holding that the term "non-participating" as used in the deed in the instant case means that the owner of such interest is not entitled to participate in executing leases and does not participate or share in bonuses or delay rentals.

656 P.2d at 882.

2.   Compare the reasoning in *Anderson* and *HNG Fossil Fuels* with that used by the Nebraska Supreme Court in Antelope Prod. Co. v. Shriners Hosp. for Crippled Children, 464 N.W.2d 159 (Neb. 1991). The court concluded that a grantor who reserved an undivided one-half interest in the mineral fee but stipulated that the grantee would have the right to all bonuses and delay rentals had not impliedly relinquished the right to execute leases binding the reserved mineral interest. Pointing out that the executive right, like the right to receive bonuses, delay rentals, and royalties, is a distinct incident of ownership of a mineral estate, the court reasoned that this right, like any other incident of ownership, should be assumed to remain with the mineral estate unless expressly severed.

Do you agree with this reasoning? Should the court have reached a different result if the deed had stated that the grantor's interest "shall be nonparticipating in bonus and delay rentals"?

B. SHARED OWNERSHIP OF MINERAL ESTATE

Special problems may arise when the mineral estate is owned by two or more persons. Such ownership may be concurrent, as is the case of cotenants of a present estate, or successive, as occurs when there is a life estate followed by a remainder or reversion. This section focuses on the adjustment of rights in these shared ownership situations.

1. CONCURRENT OWNERSHIP

(a) Development and Leasing by Co-tenants

Co-owners of a mineral estate may be unable to agree upon how the minerals should be developed, or even *if* they should be developed. Moreover, identifying and locating all co-owners may be difficult or impossible because of the widespread fractionalization of mineral interests. The division of mineral estates into multiple small interests has occurred primarily because of generational transfers in which mineral owners devise their interests in equal shares to their children and the tendency of owners to retain a fractional interest in the minerals when conveying their land. By the first decade of the Twenty-first Century in Texas, Oklahoma and many other traditional oil and gas producing states the mineral estate beneath rural land was frequently owned by sixteen or more persons, with the number of owners increasing exponentially with each new generation. In instances where known owners cannot agree on development and other owners cannot be located, can one cotenant produce the oil and gas over the objection of the other owners? What legal devices are available for authorizing development in this situation? If production does occur, what are the producer's obligations to account? What difference should it make if the development is done by the lessee of one of the cotenants? These, and other questions, are dealt with in this section.

LAW v. HECK OIL CO.

145 S.E. 601 (W.Va. 1928).

MAXWELL, J. The plaintiff is the owner in fee of an undivided $\frac{1}{768}$ interest in the oil and gas underlying a tract of 131½ acres of land in Jackson county. The Heck Oil Company holds leases for development purposes on the remaining oil and gas interests in the said land, and, having failed to obtain a lease from the plaintiff, it undertook to drill a well without his consent, after it had given assurance to him that account would be made for his full proportionate share of the mineral production, if any, without deduction for expense of development or operation.

This is an appeal from a final order * * * permanently enjoining the oil company from drilling on said land for oil or gas without the consent of the plaintiff.

It appears that in the negotiations for a lease from plaintiff of his interest he offered to execute a lease in consideration of a bonus of $1,000. This amount was deemed grossly excessive, and the offer was not accepted. The company takes the position that the plaintiff's conduct is inequitable and unjust; that he does not come into equity with clean hands; and that the owner of such a small fractional interest, who is unable to obtain an exorbitant price which he has placed on his interest, ought not to be permitted to prevent development which is desired by all his co-owners, and which the lessee is willing and ready to undertake.

* * *

* * * Oil and gas in place is real estate. And an unqualified owner of real estate or an interest therein is entitled to have it remain in such condition as he sees fit subject of course, to the right of a cotenant to compel partition or sale as provided by statute, and to protect from dissipation, through drainage by operators on other land, estates in oil and gas. Where irreparable injury is involved, equity will enjoin waste, if the violation of a complainant's property rights be by a cotenant, and will enjoin the trespass, if the violation be by a stranger. Whether such complainant's undivided interest be large or small, the rules of property are the same.

To permit the defendant company to proceed with its proposed development of the oil and gas underlying the land in question without the plaintiff's consent, even though the company should faithfully turn over to the plaintiff his full proportionate share of such minerals, or account to him therefor, without cost of production, would be a compelling of the plaintiff to exchange his real estate for personal property. This the law will not require on a showing such as is here presented.

The action of the circuit court in perpetuating the injunction is approved, but the conditions which will relieve the restraint should * * * read "without the consent of the plaintiff, or until it shall affirmatively appear that development is necessary to protect the oil and gas under such land from drainage through wells on adjoining lands."

Modified in this particular, the decree is affirmed.

NOTES

1. In general, one cotenant may be liable to another cotenant for waste—especially affirmative waste; however, the rule expressed in *Law* is a minority view with regard to the extraction of oil and gas by a cotenant. This minority view, which stems from the Statute of Westminister II, has also been followed in Illinois, Louisiana, and Michigan, although these views have been modified by statute. See 765 ILCS 515/1–515/17; La. Rev. Stat. Ann. §§ 31:174–31:177; and Mich. Comp. Laws Ann. § 319.101. The Illinois and Michigan statutes allow the owners of a majority of the undivided mineral interests in land to obtain a court order authorizing drilling and producing for the benefit of all cotenants. In Louisiana, a co-owner may act to prevent waste, destruction, or extinction of the mineral servitude. Moreover, under La. Rev. Stat. Ann. § 31:166, the lessee of a co-owner can commence development if it obtains the consent of the co-owners of at least an undivided 80 percent interest in the land. For a discussion of law in these jurisdictions see Kuntz § 5.4.

Are there reasons for departing from the general view of waste where co-ownership of oil and gas rights are concerned? Even in West Virginia, when the issue arises after a well has been drilled, courts will adjust the rights of the parties through an accounting remedy as opposed to tort remedies. See, e.g., Eagle Gas Co. v. Doran & Associates, Inc., 387 S.E.2d 99, 103 (W. Va. 1989) ("It is conceptually impossible for tenants-in-common with a mutual right to possession of the whole, to trespass against one another. * * * But an action for an accounting will lie on such facts."). West Virginia courts will consider the "good faith" of the developing party in determining the non-consenting party's potential remedies. Thaxton v. Beard, 201 S.E.2d 298 (W. Va. 1973) (noting the developer had acted in good faith).

2. Most oil and gas development occurs pursuant to an oil and gas lease obtained from the mineral interest owner. Under the minority view, what rights, if any, are conferred in a lease from less than all of the cotenants? What if all cotenants agree to a lease, but the interest of one cotenant is subject to a restrictive covenant prohibiting oil and gas development? See The Mable Cleary Trust v. The Edward–Marlah Muzyl Trust, 686 N.W.2d 770 (Mich.App. 2004).

PRAIRIE OIL & GAS CO. v. ALLEN

2 F.2d 566 (8th Cir. Okla. 1924).

[In 1911, Good Land Company conveyed a 40 acre tract to J.C. Trout reserving "nine-tenths of all oil, gas and minerals in and under the surface * * * with the full and free right to enter upon said 40 acres and use so much of the surface thereof as may be reasonably necessary for operating, drilling and mining and marketing the production thereof." Trout conveyed this tract to Lizzie Allen. Thereafter, Good Land Company executed a lease of its rights in the tract to Kay–Wagoner Oil & Gas Company, which assigned three-fourths of its rights to Skelly Oil Company under an agreement giving Skelly control of operations.]

* * *

Phillips, District Judge. * * * On June 17, 1920, Skelly Company commenced the drilling of an oil well thereon and completed the same July 12, 1920, as a producing oil well. Thereafter it drilled two additional wells. It completed the last one February 9, 1921. From July 12, 1920, to the date of the trial it continuously produced oil from the premises in paying quantities. The reasonable and necessary expenditures of Skelly Company in the development and operation of the property up to and including February 1, 1922, amounted to $153,880.40. Skelly Company continued to operate the property from February 1, 1922, to the date of the trial (April 13, 1922), and incurred and paid the necessary expenses of such operation, but the items at the time of the trial had not been posted on Skelly Company's books.

On August 4, 1920, Skelly Company contracted with Prairie Company to sell the latter the oil produced from well No. 1, and from wells that might thereafter be drilled on the land. * * *

* * *

On February 25, 1921, Lizzie Allen procured W.W. Croom to write a letter to Skelly Company, in which he stated that Lizzie Allen owned one-tenth of the oil and gas rights in this land, that she had never received any payment for or statement concerning her share of the proceeds, and that he desired Skelly Company to advise him its interpretation of the rights of Lizzie Allen in the premises. On February 26, 1921, Skelly Company replied thereto by letter in which it stated that Lizzie Allen was being credited with one-tenth of the gross proceeds of oil sold from the premises and charged with one-tenth of the cost of drilling the wells and equipping and operating the property, and when the receipts exceeded the costs it would account to her for one-tenth of the net proceeds monthly, and that as soon as well No. 3 was completed it would furnish a statement to her of the cost of the wells and the amount received for oil sold.

On March 16, 1921, Skelly Company mailed to Lizzie Allen a statement setting forth the expenses of development and operation of the property and the amounts received for oil sold therefrom, and thereafter continued from time to time to mail her similar statements.

On May 7, 1921, Lizzie Allen, notified Skelly Company, in writing that she objected to its taking oil and gas from the land.

On May 12, 1921, Lizzie Allen made demand in writing upon the Prairie Company to surrender and deliver to her one-tenth of all the oil which had been produced from this land and received by it. The Prairie Company refused this demand.

It was expressly stipulated: "That * * * Lizzie Allen * * * is the owner of an undivided one-tenth interest in and to the oil, gas and mineral in and under said land. * * * "

* * *

Under the provisions of the deed to Trout, Good Land Company retained the ownership of nine-tenths of the oil, gas and mineral in and under the land, and reserved the right to enter upon the land and use so much of the surface thereof as might be reasonably necessary for operating, drilling, mining and marketing the same. Having reserved the right to use the surface, Good Land Company, being a tenant in common with Lizzie Allen, would have had the right to develop the land for oil, drill oil wells thereon, and produce oil therefrom, without her consent. Tenants in common are the owners of the substance of the estate. They may make such reasonable use of the common property as is necessary to enjoy the benefit and value of such ownership. Since an estate of a cotenant in a mine or oil well can only be enjoyed by removing the products thereof, the taking of mineral from a mine and the extraction of oil from an oil well are the use and not the destruction of the estate. This being true, a tenant in common, without the consent of his cotenant, has the right to develop and operate the common property for oil and gas and for that purpose may drill wells and erect necessary plants. He must not, however, exclude his cotenant from exercising the same rights and privileges.

* * *

In the case of Burnham v. Hardy Oil Co., [147 S.W. 330 (Tex.Civ.App. 1912)], the court said:

> It seems to us that the peculiar circumstances of a cotenancy in land upon which oil is discovered warrant one cotenant to proceed and utilize the oil, without the necessity of the other cotenants concurring. Oil is a fugitive substance and may be drained from the land by well on adjoining property. It must be promptly taken from the land for it to be secured to the owners. If a cotenant owning a small interest in the land had to give his consent before the others could move towards securing the oil, he could arbitrarily destroy the valuable quality of the land.

* * *

But counsel for Lizzie Allen say that since she did not join in the lease it was void as to her and that the Skelly Company, in going upon the land in question and developing and producing oil therefrom, was a trespasser. * * *

* * *

In the case of York et al. v. Warren Oil & Gas Co., 191 Ky. 157, 229 S.W. 114, the court after quoting extensively from the earlier case of New Domain Oil & Gas Co. v. McKinney, 188 Ky. 183, 221 S.W. 245, said:

> It will thus appear that this court is committed to the doctrine that one cotenant may lease his undivided interest in the joint real property for oil and other mineral and such lease contract is valid and binding on the cotenant making the same but not upon the other cotenants; however, the lessee becomes a cotenant in the mineral leased with the other joint owners and may, as could his grantor, enter upon the joint property and explore for, mine and market minerals, accounting to the other joint tenants for their proportion of the minerals recovered according to the rule adopted in the McKinney Case.

> In the case of Compton v. People's Gas Co., 75 Kan. 572, 89 P. 1039, 10 L.R.A.(N.S.) 787 the Kansas court held that where one tenant in common, owning one half of certain property, executed an oil and gas lease thereon to one party and the other tenants in common, owning the other half, executed another oil and gas lease thereon to another party, each lessee was entitled to the possession of the premises for the purpose of mining the same for oil and gas, but that neither was entitled to the exclusive possession.

> In the instant case the lease to the Kay–Wagoner Company, which was later assigned to Skelly Company, was not of the whole property but of the undivided interest therein belonging to Good Land Company and the rights of Lizzie Allen were fully recognized. We therefore conclude that Skelly Company was not a trespasser as against Lizzie Allen, but that the lease to it was valid, and that upon entry it became a tenant in common with Lizzie Allen during the continuation of the lease and occupied the same relation to Lizzie Allen and the property as the Good Land Company would have occupied, had it entered and developed and operated the property for oil and gas.

> The one question remaining then is: What is the proper basis of accounting between Skelly Company and Lizzie Allen? Under the general rule Skelly Company would be bound to account to Lizzie Allen for one-tenth of the net profits determined by deducting from one-tenth of the value of the gross production one-tenth of all reasonable and legitimate expenses for development and operating the property for oil and gas, but in the event of loss it could not compel her to reimburse it for any part of the loss.

In the case of New Domain Oil & Gas Co. v. McKinney, 188 Ky. 183, 221 S.W. 245, the Court of Appeals of Kentucky, after an exhaustive review of the authorities in passing upon the basis of accounting where one cotenant operated jointly owned oil property with the knowledge of his cotenant's interest, said:

> In cases of a willful trespasser the rule seems to be well settled * * * that the plaintiff is entitled to recover, in a suit for an accounting, the value of the mineral, without deducting any expenses incurred in mining it. But we do not understand that this stern rule should be applied in cases where a cotenant operates the mine with the knowledge of his cotenant's interest. Especially should this rule not be applied against a cotenant where the mineral involved is of a fugacious nature and liable to be exhausted by adjacent operators. In such case if one tenant is able and willing to develop the mine and extract the oil before it is entirely lost and his cotenant is not, he should be allowed to do so without incurring the penalty of accounting to his cotenant for the gross amount of oil produced; but since he may not convert, to any extent, his cotenant's interest, he must account to the latter for his proportion of the net value of the oil produced, which is its market value, less the cost of extracting and marketing. Any other rule, it seems to us, would be not only inequitable, but illogical; for, if the operating tenant could be made liable for the gross amount of the plaintiff's proportion of the oil produced, the rights of the former would be fixed according to the rules governing an operation by a willful trespasser who had no interest whatever in the mineral. We cannot believe that an exclusive operation by one joint tenant is so tainted with wrong as against his cotenant as to require the application of the same rules that should be applied to a willful trespasser. Moreover, it would be illogical to say that a cotenant could lawfully operate the joint property * * * and at the same time be compelled to divide the gross proceeds or profits with his joint tenant, thus circumscribing his rights according to the rule applicable to a willful and malicious trespasser without pretense of title or right. There is no rule of law known to us that would render the plaintiff cotenant immune from the observance of that healthy maxim, "He who seeks equity must do equity," and the equity which plaintiff in such cases is required to do is to pay his proportionate part of the actual expenses of operation and marketing, if they are not above that which is usual and customary in that locality.

* * *

We therefore conclude that Lizzie Allen is entitled to an accounting from Skelly Company for the market value of the oil produced less the reasonable and necessary expense of developing, extracting and marketing the same. The royalty paid by Skelly Company to the Good Land Company is not a part of the cost of production and should not be included in the same.

* * *

NOTES

1. The majority of jurisdictions agree with the *Allen* court's view that one cotenant should be allowed to extract oil and gas without the permission of other cotenants. Although the courts in several oil and gas producing states have not passed upon the issue, practitioners in those states have generally assumed that the courts would adopt the majority view.

A lessee from a co-owner in a majority jurisdiction acquires the same rights to explore and develop as were held by the lessor. Because the land agent who obtains the lease may be unable to perform an adequate title search, the lease may purport to cover 100% of the mineral estate, even though the lessor owns only a fractional interest. To avoid paying full lease benefits to a fractional owner, most lessees insist on the inclusion of a lease clause that reduces rentals and royalty in proportion to the interest actually owned by the lessor. This clause, which is variously referred to as a "proportionate reduction" clause and a "lesser interest" clause, is considered in a later section of this Chapter.

2. In most jurisdictions that have adopted the majority view, the developing co-owner, which is almost invariably a lessee, must account to other non-leasing cotenants for their proportionate share of the proceeds from production less the proportionate share of the reasonable and necessary costs of development and production. The developing party (whose interest is often called the "cost-bearing interest") may not collect costs directly from the other cotenants but may only deduct costs from the share of production attributable to the other cotenants (whose interest is often called a "noncost-bearing" or "carried interest"); thus, the developing party assumes all of the risk that the well will be dry.

3. Disputes often arise over what expenses can be deducted from the carried co-tenants share of production. If the developing co-tenant is using his own crew and equipment the costs may be challenged as excessive or unnecessary. See, e.g., White v. Smyth, 214 S.W.2d 967 (Tex. 1948). Overhead expenses, such as the cost of maintaining a field office or payments to supervisory personnel, may be challenged on the grounds either that they are not allocable to the well in question; or that an excessive amount is being allocated to the well. Most courts have refused to allow the operating co-tenant to deduct interest on the non-operator's share of cost. The Texas courts have reasoned that interest is non-deductible because the carried interest owner does not owe an enforceable obligation to the operating co-tenant and would not be liable to a personal judgment for reimbursement. See Cox v. Davison, 397 S.W.2d 200 (Tex. 1965). Courts in other states have reached the same result. See, e.g., Essley v. Mershon, 262 P.2d 417, 3 O & G Rep. (Okla. 1953).

4. Disputes over deductibility of expenses have also arisen in the situation where a cotenant's lease terminates while the other leases remain in effect. In Wagner & Brown, Ltd. v. Sheppard, 282 S.W.3d 419 (Tex. 2008) the plaintiff, who owned an undivided one-eighth mineral fee interest in a 63–acre tract, executed an oil and gas lease providing for lease termination if royalty was not paid within 120 days of the first sale of oil and gas. The lease contained a standard pooling clause, and the lessee, after drilling a gas well on the 63–acre tract, pooled it into a 122–acre unit. However the lessee failed to make a timely payment of royalty to the lessor, which resulted in termination of the plaintiff's lease. The lessee was held liable to account to plaintiff, who was now an unleased cotenant, for her share of net profits. However, as set out in Section H of this chapter, the court concluded that plaintiff's interest was still pooled and authorized the lessee to account to the plaintiff on the basis of non-leased co-ownership in the entire 122–acre pooled unit, rather than on the basis of one-eighth co-ownership of the 63–acre tract on which two producing wells had now been drilled. The court also held that the lessee could charge the plaintiff's share of production with her proportionate share of drilling and operating costs incurred prior to lease termination, and could deduct "leasehold, land/legal and overhead expenses" incurred in developing the entire pooled unit.

5. Even in majority jurisdictions multiple ownership makes mineral development difficult. See Marla E. Mansfield, A Tale of Two Owners: Real Property Co–Ownership and Mineral Development, 43 Rocky Mtn.Min.L.Inst. 20–1 (1997). Because of the risks inherent in drilling and development and the requirement of accounting to non-leasing co-owners, oil and gas companies will generally drill a well only if the interests of the carried cotenants are small. Obtaining the consent of the owners of all or almost all of the mineral estate has, however, become increasingly difficult because of the widespread fractionalization of mineral interests. As Professors Smith and Anderson have commented,

> The division of mineral fee interests and royalties into smaller and smaller fractional interests creates legal, practical and economic disincentives to mineral development. Fractionalization does this in at least three ways. Every increase in the number of owners who must sign a document makes it correspondingly more difficult to obtain unanimous or near-unanimous agreement. Moreover, as interests become fractionated, identifying, locating and dealing with owners becomes more time-consuming and more expensive. Indeed, because of dormancy, locating owners often becomes impossible. These problems are compounded by title uncertainties, for there is a frequent correlation between the number of owners and the number and difficulty of title problems.

Owen L. Anderson and Ernest E. Smith, The Use of Law to Promote Domestic Exploration and Production, 50 Inst. on Oil & Gas L. & Tax'n 2–1, 2–7 (1999).

As a later subsection indicates, partition is not always available for mineral estates and may in any event be an unsatisfactory remedy where there are dozens of owners. In some jurisdictions, however, there are alternatives to the remedy of partition. A few states have adopted specific statutes aimed at facilitating development of lands owned in cotenancy. The statutes of Illinois, Louisiana, and Michigan, minority view states, have already been noted. Several other states, including Arkansas, Ark.Stats. §§ 15–56–301 to–401, 15–73–406, Kansas, Kan. Stat. Ann. §§ 55–219 to 222, Kentucky, Ky.Rev. Stat. Ann. §§ 353.564–353.476, Mississippi, Miss.Code, §§ 11–17–33 to–34, North Dakota, N.D.Cent.Code § 38–13–01 to–04, and Texas, Tex.Civ.Prac. & Rem.Code Ann. § 64.091, have statutes authorizing co-owners to petition the court for the appointment of a trustee or receiver to execute a lease on behalf of unlocatable cotenants and hold funds for their benefit. Liberative prescription, dormant mineral interest acts and related doctrines that extinguish dormant mineral interests in specific situations are discussed in Chapter 1. All of these doctrines are quite limited in scope, however; and it is fair to say that with the possible exception of Louisiana, no state has a comprehensive method of dealing with extreme fractionalization. For discussions of state statutes, common law doctrines and possible solutions see Owen L. Anderson and Ernest E. Smith, The Use of Law to Promote Domestic Exploration and Production, 50 Inst. on Oil & Gas L. & Tax'n 2–1, 2–7 (1999); Victor A. Sachse III and Robert L. Atkinson, Reuniting Unused Mineral Interests with the Land, 44 Inst. on Oil & Gas L. & Tax'n 2–1 (1993) and Ernest E. Smith, Methods of Facilitating the Development of Oil and Gas Lands Burdened with Outstanding Mineral Interests, 43 Tex.L.Rev. 129, 136 (1964).

6.   There is limited authority for granting the carried cotenant a royalty on his share of production rather than a net profits interest. See Germer v. Donaldson, 18 F.2d 697 (3d Cir.Pa. 1927) and McIntosh v. Ropp, 82 A. 949 (Pa. 1912). In Kentucky, the developing cotenant who acts in the good faith belief that he owns the premises in fee simple absolute need only account for a royalty to the carried cotenant up to the time a suit is filed to determine the ownership of the property; after the filing of the suit, the carried cotenant is entitled to a net profits interest. Gillispie v. Blanton, 282 S.W. 1061 (Ky. 1926). A West Virginia case has awarded a royalty where the value of the gross production from the well was less than the costs of drilling and completion. South Penn Oil Co. v. Haught, 78 S.E. 759 (W.Va. 1913). West Virginia will consider the equities involved but generally allows the non-consenting cotenant an election of remedies between sharing as a royalty owner under an existing lease or sharing in their proportionate share of the net profits. Thaxton v. Beard, 201 S.E.2d 298, 303–04 (W. Va. 1973) ("The appellants have the option of either recognizing the lease and receiving their proportional share under the terms of the lease and unitization agreement [entered into under authority of the lease] or of rejecting the lease and receiving ⅛th of the oil produced less ⅛th of the cost of discovery and production."). To what extent, if any, do such doctrines mitigate the risk of drilling without the consent of all co-owners?

Even jurisdictions following the net profits view will award a royalty interest rather than a net profits interest if a lease purporting to cover the entire premises is executed by one cotenant and the other cotenant ratifies the lease. See, e.g., Texas & Pacific Coal & Oil Co. v. Kirtley, 288 S.W. 619 (Tex.Civ.App. 1926, writ refused n.r.e.). Ratification can be accomplished in several different ways, such as by executing an instrument for the express purpose of ratifying the lease, by accepting lease benefits, and in some instances by referring to the lease in an instrument of conveyance. See Ernest Smith & Jacqueline Weaver, Texas Oil & Gas Law §§ 2.3(A)(2) & 6.3(B). In what situations would a carried cotenant prefer a royalty to a net profits interest? Should a cotenant who has not joined in the lease have to ratify it within a reasonable time, or should he be able to wait to determine whether a well on the premises will pay out?

7. Assume that a cotenant drills two wells: a dry-hole and a producer. In a state requiring an accounting on the basis of net profits, should the developing cotenant be able to deduct the costs of both wells from the share of production attributable to the carried cotenants? A Texas court has answered this question in the negative, concluding that an operator must account to a non-leased co-owner on a well-by-well basis rather than a tract-wide basis. It refused to allow the operator to charge a pro rata share of the costs of an unsuccessful attempt to re-work a marginal well against the co-tenant's share of income from a second, profitable well. The court stated that the cost of drilling a dry hole and other, similar expenses that do not confer any benefit on a co-tenant cannot be deducted from that co-tenant's share of income from the tract. Wagner & Brown, Ltd. v. Sheppard, 198 S.W.3d 369 (Tex. App. 2006), *rev'd on other grounds*, 282 S.W.3d 419 (Tex. 2008). The court leaves open the issue of whether a lessee would be able to charge the cost of drilling an initial dry hole against a cotenant's share of production from a subsequent productive well if the initial drilling provided geological information that was useful in deciding where to drill the productive well.

There are many other contexts in which the carried interest owner may question whether certain types of expenses are reasonable and necessary. For example, should the operating cotenant be able to deduct a charge for overhead? Depreciation of equipment? Risk capital, that is, the cost of money? To the extent that any of these costs are deductible, how should they be computed and on what basis should they be allocated to the noncost-bearing interest? Which cotenant should have the burden of proof in the event of a dispute over the correctness of the operating cotenant's accounting? For cases dealing with these issues, see, e.g., Knight v. Mitchell, 240 N.E.2d 16 (Ill.App. 1968); Moody v. Wagner, 23 P.2d 633 (Okla. 1933); Cox v. Davison, 397 S.W.2d 200 (Tex. 1965); Wagner & Brown, Ltd. v. Sheppard, 198 S.W.3d 369 (Tex. App. 2006), *rev'd on other grounds*, 282 S.W.3d 419 (Tex. 2008); and Burnham v. Hardy Oil Co., 147 S.W. 330 (Tex.Civ.App. 1912), aff'd 195 S.W. 1139 (Tex. 1917).

A question may also arise about the amortization or depreciation of well costs. Can a carried cotenant argue that capital expenses should be allocated over the life of the well, and thus claim an accounting for profits within the first year of production, even though the developing cotenant has not yet recovered all drilling and completion costs? Is the tax treatment of tangible and intangible drilling costs relevant?

8. Most of the litigation involving rights of co-ownership has involved tenants in common. There are, however, other forms of concurrent ownership. Suppose that John and Sally Smith, husband and wife, own Blackacre in joint tenancy and that John leases his interest in Blackacre to Acme Oil Co. If John dies during the term of the lease, what are the rights of the surviving spouse

and the lessee? Assume that John and Sally both joined in executing the lease to Acme Oil Co. If John dies during the term of the lease, what are the rights of his heirs and devisees, Sally, and Acme Oil Co.? See Kuntz § 5.9. What if John and Sally owned Blackacre in a tenancy by the entirety? Id. § 5.10.

9.   A type of co-ownership between husband and wife also exists in the nine states that have adopted the community property system. These are the eight states—Texas, Louisiana, California, New Mexico, Idaho, Arizona, Nevada, and Washington—that derived their marital property systems from Spain, Mexico, or France, and Wisconsin, which more recently adopted a statutory form of community ownership. A person practicing in one of these states should be aware of the special requirements governing the rights of spouses in property acquired during marriage. In some instances, joinder of both spouses in a mineral deed or oil and gas lease may be required, even though title to the land is held in the name of only one spouse. The same requirement exists in several other states as the result of homestead laws. See generally Stephen J. Hull, Spousal Joinder Requirements in the Rocky Mountain States, 29 Rocky Mtn.Min.L.Inst. 545 (1983).

The most important factor that determines whether lease benefits are separate or community property is the classification of the underlying mineral estate. If the mineral estate is community property, all lease benefits, including bonus, delay rentals, and royalty, are community property also. If the mineral estate is separate, treatment of lease benefits depends upon a variety of legal doctrines that differ from state to state. In California all income from separate property is also separate. In Texas and Louisiana income from separate property is community, but proceeds from the sale of principal retain a separate-property classification. In those two states, treatment of lease benefits as separate or community turns upon the state's theory of oil and gas ownership. Texas is an ownership in place jurisdiction and treats money received as bonus and royalties as the sale price of the underlying separate estate. These proceeds are separate, whereas delay rentals are viewed as ordinary income and, hence, community. See, e.g., Commissioner v. Wilson, 76 F.2d 766 (5th Cir.Tex. 1935) and Lessing v. Russek, 234 S.W.2d 891 (Tex.Civ. App. 1950, writ ref'd n.r.e.). In Louisiana, which follows the non-ownership theory, all financial benefits from an oil and gas lease, including bonus and royalty as well as delay rentals, are apparently community. See Milling v. Collector of Revenue, 57 So.2d 679 (La. 1952).

Analogous problems of classifying lease benefits as principal or income are encountered in common law states when ownership of the mineral estate is divided between a life tenant and a remainderman. See Subsection B.2(a) of this chapter.

10.   Cotenants often execute oil and gas leases to different lessees. If one lessee drills and obtains production without entering into an agreement with the other, complex accounting issues arise. Earp v. Mid–Continent Petroleum Corp., 27 P.2d 855 (Okla. 1933) presents such a situation. Under the court's decision the producing lessee was required to pay the leasing cotenants' royalty proportionately reduced to their share of the mineral estate. It was also required to pay the non-producing lessee its proportionate share (which was 2/33) "of the market value of the oil and gas produced from the premises

after deducting the reasonable and necessary cost of developing, extracting, and marketing the same." This duty to account did not arise, however, until the producing company had recouped all of its costs and was making a net profit. Once the non-producing lessee began receiving payments, it was obligated to pay its own lessor a royalty retroactive to the date of first production. The non-producing lessee retained any sums that were left.

11. Not too surprisingly, when cotenants execute leases to different oil and gas companies, the lessees typically enter into a joint operating agreement, rather than going it alone.[2] An analogous situation arises when separately-owned tracts with different lessees are pooled. In that situation also one lessee is designated as the operator of the pooled unit under an agreement that provides for the sharing of the costs of the operation and typically entitles each lessee to market its proportionate share of production. A problem of accounting to the lessors arises when the lessees market production to different purchasers at different prices and in different ways. The problem is especially acute with respect to natural gas, where "split-stream" sales have long been common. (That is, the stream of production is split between two or more purchasers.) One lessee may market its share in a steady stream under a relatively long term contract; another may also sell its share in a steady stream, but under a contract with a different duration and a different price. A third lessee may sell intermittently on the spot market in an attempt to benefit from seasonal market peaks, and yet another lessee may forego marketing altogether for a year or longer.

States have dealt with this problem in different ways. A Texas case, Puckett v. First City Nat'l Bank of Midland, 702 S.W.2d 232 (Tex.App.– Eastland 1985) suggests that a lessor is entitled to royalty only on sales by his or her own lessee and has no right to benefit from the marketing decisions of any other lessees that have contributed working interests to the well. In a pooling context, this method of dealing with royalty claims is commonly referred to as the "tract allocation" approach. For an early Louisiana case adopting this method of accounting to lessors of pooled tracts, see Arkansas Louisiana Gas Co. v. Southwest Natural Production Co., 60 So.2d 9 (La. 1952).

The competing method of accounting is the "weighted average" approach, which originated with Shell Oil Co. v. Corporation Comm'n, 389 P.2d 951 (Okla. 1963), better known as the Blanchard case. Basing its decision largely on the language of the state pooling statute, the Oklahoma Supreme Court concluded that each royalty owner was entitled to share in 1/8 of all the sales of production from a unit well in the proportion that his or her acreage bore to the total acreage assigned to the well. Under this initial holding if a lessor's royalty exceeded 1/8, payment for the excess was based upon sales made by his or her own lessee. Subsequent legislative enactments extended the weighted average method of calculation to the entire royalty owed to a lessor (see Okla. Stat. Ann. tit. 52, § 87.1(e)) and shifted responsibility for royalty payments from the purchasers of a well's production to the marketing lessees, who are required to pay the royalty share of their gas proceeds to the operator

---

2. Joint operating agreements are dealt with in Chapter 6.

who, in turn, pays a weighted average royalty to the lessors and other royalty owners. Okla. Stat. Ann. tit. 52, § 570.4.

For discussions of the "tract allocation" and "weighted average" methods of accounting, see Bruce M. Kramer, Royalty Interests in the United States: Not Cut from the Same Cloth, 29 Tulsa L. J. 449, 477–79 (1994) and Kramer & Martin § 19.04(3). Operating agreements, gas marketing and the problem of "balancing," i.e., assuring that each owner ultimately receives credit for its proportionate share of natural gas produced, are addressed in Chapter 6.

12. Serious accounting question may also arise where a cotenant's fractional mineral interest is burdened by a nonparticipating royalty (NPRI). Suppose that all of the mineral interest owners except the cotenant with the burdened interest execute a lease. If the lessee obtains production, should the owner of the NPRI be paid immediately, or is she entitled to payment only after there are net profits to distribute to the carried, non-signing cotenant? Is the lessee or the cotenant primarily obligated to make the payments?

(b) The Community Lease

Subdivision of a single large tract and the resulting sale of portions of the subdivision often result in differing fractional co-ownership interests in the mineral estate beneath the various subdivided lots. A similar situation may result when a testator devises different parts of her land to her descendants in varying proportions. These co-owned lands may be adjacent to other land where the mineral estate is owned by a single person. To facilitate mineral development, all of the various owners of the mineral estates may join in a single lease, which is termed a "community lease." Such leases are no longer common, but are still occasionally encountered. If the lessee drills a productive well on one of the tracts covered by such a lease, is the royalty owed solely to the owners of the minerals beneath that tract or are the owners of the mineral estates beneath the other tracts also entitled to a share of the royalty? The court in French v. George, 159 S.W.2d 566 (Tex.Civ.App. 1942, writ ref'd n.r.e.) answered the question as follows:

> It seems to be established as a general rule of law that where several owners of adjoining tracts of land unite in a single lease to a third party for development of oil or gas as a single tract, and provision is made for delivery of the royalty to the lessors, in the absence of an agreement to the contrary, the royalties must be divided among the lessors in the proportion that the area of the tract owned by each bears to the total area covered by the lease, and the ownership of the tract upon which a well may be drilled and from which oil may be produced is a matter of no consequence. * * * We are, therefore, forced to the conclusion that it effected a pooling of the royalties between the lessors in proportion to their interests in the entire leased premises.

159 S.W.2d at 569.

In the earlier case of Parker v. Parker, 144 S.W.2d 303 (Tex.Civ.App.– Galveston 1940, writ ref'd n.r.e.), the court held that even though no waiver of offset obligations was included in the lease, a community lease resulted in pooling as a matter of law. In *French,* however, the court's holding is based on a rule of construction. Most jurisdictions that have addressed the matter have held that the intent of the parties determines whether a community lease results in a pooling of the tracts so leased. In Texas there is a strong presumption that the parties intended to pool. This presumption will apparently be overcome only where there is clear evidence to the contrary expressed in the lease itself. See Phillips Petroleum Co. v. McIlroy, 178 F.Supp. 107 (N.D.Tex. 1959). In Oklahoma, pooling is presumed, but the presumption can be rebutted by language in the lease, ancillary written or oral contracts, or by the conduct of the parties. See Peerless Oil & Gas Co. v. Tipken, 124 P.2d 418 (Okla. 1942) and Stroud v. D–X Sunray Oil Co., 376 P.2d 1015 (Okla. 1962). On the other hand, New Mexico courts do not presume an intention to pool or not pool by reason of a community lease. See Leonard v. Barnes, 404 P.2d 292 (N.M. 1965).

In Veal v. Thomason, 159 S.W.2d 472 (Tex. 1942), which involved a community lease executed by over 20 landowners and covering approximately 6,000 acres, the title to one of the lessors was challenged by a prior owner who had lost his land at a foreclosure sale and was claiming the foreclosure was invalid because of various irregularities in the proceedings. The plaintiff filed suit against the purchaser and the lessee. The court, however, held that all of the other lessors and royalty owners subject to the community lease were necessary parties to the litigation. It based its holding on what has come to be known as the "cross-conveyancing theory," i.e., by entering into the community lease, each lessor conveyed a fractional royalty interest to each of the other landowners signing the community lease. In other words, all the lessors became co-tenants of the royalty in each of the leases subject to the community lease, and a decision affecting the ownership of a tract covered by the lease would affect each signatory of the community lease. If the plaintiff prevailed in his lawsuit, he would eliminate the other twenty or so lessors' fractional share of royalty in the tract of land in question.

Citing a change in the statute requiring joinder of parties, a subsequent case reached a different result on the procedural issue that effectively defeated the plaintiff's claim in *Veal v. Thomason.* Sabre Oil & Gas Corp. v. Gibson, 72 S.W.3d 812 (Tex.App.–Eastland 2002, pet. denied) involved a community lease covering 38 separate tracts. Owners of three of the tracts brought suit, alleging that the lessee had violated the terms of the community lease by including land outside the leased acreage within a pooled gas unit. The court rejected the defendant's contention that *Veal v. Thomason* required the plaintiffs to join all 60 royalty owners in the newly formed pooled unit. It pointed out that *Veal* was decided before the 1971 amendments to the Texas Rules of Civil Procedure, which no longer distinguish between "necessary" and "indispensable" parties. The court reasoned that the joinder of the other royalty owners was not necessary in order for the court to determine if the defendant had breached the pooling clause of the community lease.

Most jurisdictions have rejected the "cross conveyancing" theory and view a community lease a contractual agreement to share royalties. Texas leases now often contain a specific provision stating the sharing of royalties is based upon a contractual agreement and that there is no cross conveying of royalties.

Suppose that Adams and Brown each own an undivided 50% interest in Tract One, which contains 100 acres. They join in a community lease with Castle, who owns Tract 2 containing 200 acres. The lease provides for a 1/5th royalty and contains a standard pooling clause. The lessee pools 20 acres from Tract 2 with 20 acres from an adjacent tract that is not subject to the community lease. A productive well is drilled on the 20 acres from the neighboring tract. How should the royalty be divided?

(c) Partition of Mineral Interests

Mineral interests can be partitioned by a voluntary agreement. The agreement is usually effectuated by cross-conveyances in which one cotenant conveys his interest in a specific portion of the land to the other cotenant, who conveys her interest in the remaining portion. See Smith & Weaver, § 2.3(A)(4). Such a partition does not have to include all mineral interests. In In re Estate of Slaughter, 305 S.W.3d 804 (Tex.App.–Texarkana 2010) three co-tenants partitioned the land owned in co-tenancy, with each owner acquiring sole ownership of all the incidents of mineral ownership in the tract received except for the royalty, which continued to be owned in equal shares in all three tracts. Often, however, in the absence of the rather unusual partition of the *Slaughter* case, one or more cotenants will be reluctant to accept the risk that the specific portion of land he receives may be less productive than the portions received by the other co-owners. Hence it is not uncommon for cotenants to partition the surface, where each parcel's value can be assessed fairly accurately, but retain undivided ownership of the mineral estate. In such situations, any owner who wishes to partition the minerals, must attempt to get a judicially ordered partition.

MOSELEY v. HEARRELL
171 S.W.2d 337 (Tex. 1943).

ALEXANDER, CHIEF JUSTICE.

This suit was brought by J.A.R. Moseley, Jr., against Mrs. Lola Hearrell and others for partition of the mineral interest in a one-acre tract of land. The trial court found that the mineral interest was incapable of partition in kind, and ordered it sold by a receiver and the proceeds divided. The judgment was reversed by the Court of Civil Appeals.

R.N. Wood originally owned the mineral interest in the tract of land in question. His interest was encumbered with a covenant that no more than one oil well would ever be drilled on the land. A firm of attorneys held an overriding royalty of $^{14}/_{128}$ interest in the minerals. Wood conveyed to Mrs. Lola Hearrell an undivided $^{49}/_{128}$ interest in the minerals. Afterwards a well was drilled and brought in as an oil producer. Wood and Mrs. Hearrell then entered into an oral understanding, by the terms of which Mrs. Hearrell was allowed to operate the well during the joint ownership of herself and Wood. Such understanding was not to extend beyond the period of such joint ownership. Thereafter Wood conveyed all of his remaining interest to the plaintiff J.A.R. Moseley, Jr. Moseley had knowledge of the previously existing oral operating agreement between Wood and Mrs. Hearrell at the time he purchased Wood's remaining interest in the property.

In this connection, it is proper to state that it was alleged by Mrs. Hearrell that Moseley, in seeking the partition of the property, was endeavoring to acquire her interest therein; that she would be financially unable to buy in the property at a receiver's sale; and that if her interest should be sold by the receiver it would not bring its full value, and in addition she would be compelled to pay a large federal income tax out of her receipts from the sale. These allegations were made for the purpose of showing that it would be inequitable to Mrs. Hearrell to compel partition of the property.

The Court of Civil Appeals was of the opinion that the joint ownership of the property and the parol operating agreement between Wood and Mrs. Hearrell created a mining partnership, and that when Moseley purchased Wood's interest he thereby became a partner in the venture. The court was further of the opinion that Moseley, as a member of the firm, was not entitled to dissolve the partnership and compel partition of the property without showing equitable grounds therefor. We are not in accord with this view.

In our opinion, it is not material whether the relationship between the parties created a mining partnership, nor whether the plaintiff showed equitable grounds for the partition. Our statutes relating to partition read as follows:

Art. 6082. Any joint owner or claimant of any real estate or of any interest therein or of any mineral, coal, petroleum, or gas lands, whether held in fee or by lease or otherwise, may compel a partition thereof between the other joint owners or claimants thereof in the manner provided in this chapter.

Art. 6096. Should the court be of the opinion that a fair and equitable division of the real estate, or any part thereof, cannot be made, it shall order a sale of so much as is incapable of partition, which sale shall be for cash, or upon such other terms as the court may direct, and shall be made as under execution, or by private sale through a receiver, if the court so order, and the proceeds thereof shall be returned into court and be partitioned among the persons entitled thereto, according to their respective interests.

The above statutes confer the right to compel partition in the broadest terms. There is no requirement for the showing of equitable grounds as a prerequisite to the exercise of the right, nor is there any provision that the right may be defeated by the showing of inequities. Article 6082 confers upon any joint owner or claimant of land the absolute right to demand segregation of his interest from that of his co-owner.

The above statute, Article 6082, was amended in 1917 by adding thereto the words "or of any mineral, coal, petroleum, or gas lands, whether held in fee or by lease or otherwise." This amendment enlarges the purpose of the statute so as to give the right of partition not only to joint owners of real estate, or of any interest therein, but as well to joint owners of any oil or gas lands, "whether held in fee or by lease or otherwise."

The rule which exists in some states to the effect that in order to dissolve a mining partnership by a decree in equity the bill must allege equitable grounds therefor (see Blackmarr v. Williamson, 57 W.Va. 249, 50 S.E. 254, 4 Ann.Cas. 265) cannot prevail in this State, in view of the positive and all-inclusive terms of our statute.

Respondents cite and rely on a line of cases in which it is held that a partition suit under our statute is governed by the rules of equity in all things not expressly provided for in the statute. See Thomas v. Southwestern Settlement & Development Co., 132 Tex. 413, 123 S.W.2d 290, 296. They also call attention to Revised Statutes, Art. 6106, which is a part of the title on partition, and provides as follows: "Art. 6106. No provision of this title shall affect the mode of proceeding prescribed by law for the partition of estates of decedents among the heirs and legatees, nor preclude partition in any other manner authorized by the rules of equity; which rules shall govern in proceedings under this title in all things not provided for in this title."

However, neither the above statute nor the cases relied on by respondents support their contention that equitable grounds must be shown as a prerequisite to the right to partition. Under the above statute and the authorities cited, equitable rules apply in determining *how* the property is to be partitioned, once partition is granted, but equitable principles are not material in determining whether or not the right of partition may be exercised.

It may sometimes be inequitable to one or more of the joint owners if another co-owner is permitted to enforce partition of the jointly owned property; but this is one of the consequences which one assumes when he becomes a co-tenant in land. If he does not provide against it by contract, he may expect his cotenant to exercise his statutory right of partition at will.

The judgment of the Court of Civil Appeals is reversed, and that of the trial court is affirmed.

NOTES

1. Although the right to compel a partition of a possessory interest in real property, including mineral interests, is frequently described as absolute and unconditional, in some jurisdictions fraud and oppression may be pleaded and proved as an affirmative defense to partition. See, e.g., Schnitt v. McKellar, 427 S.W.2d 202 (Ark. 1968); Strait v. Fuller, 334 P.2d 385 (Kan. 1959); Stern v. Great Southern Land Co., 114 So. 739 (Miss. 1927), and Cox v. Lasley, 639 P.2d 1219 (Okla. 1981). A suit for partition may also be defeated if the cotenants have agreed not to partition. Such an agreement must normally be express, although courts will imply an agreement not to partition if a partition is inconsistent with some other express agreement between the parties, such as an agreement to engage in joint operations in order to carry out a specific drilling program. See, e.g., Elrod v. Foster, 37 S.W.2d 339 (Tex.Civ.App. 1931, writ ref'd n.r.e.); Dimock v. Kadane, 100 S.W.3d 602 (Tex.App.–Eastland 2003, pet. denied); Dimock v. Kadane, 100 S.W.3d 608 (Tex.App.–Eastland 2003, pet. denied). In MCEN 1996 Partnership v. Glassell, 42 S.W.3d 262 (Tex.App. 2001) the court ruled that a lessee had waived its right to compel partition by entering into a pooling agreement which provided that the unit would continue as long as there was a well capable of production within the pooled unit.

2. Most jurisdictions favor partition in kind; however, where mineral interests are concerned, some jurisdictions hold that the only equitable method of partition is by sale, since it is not possible to determine whether valuable minerals are uniformly present throughout the property. The reasoning of the Michigan Supreme Court in Fortney v. Tope, 247 N.W. 751 (Mich. 1933), is illustrative. In responding to plaintiffs' objection that they lacked funds to protect their interest in the event of a partition by sale and that the other co-owners might thus procure the interest "at a mere pittance," the court stated that "[A] much greater injustice might be done if the parcel allotted the plaintiffs be found to have no oil thereon and the remainder be productive. This 40 acres lies in the oil and gas field of that part of the state, and it seems clear that on a sale buyers will be present and the plaintiffs be assured of a reasonable price for their interest in the property." 247 N.W. at 754.

The late Professor Eugene Kuntz has suggested the following analysis in determining whether the mineral estate should be partitioned in kind or by sale.

> First, if there is no evidence of oil and gas activity or other facts which would demonstrate that oil and gas are probably present, it must be assumed that any oil or gas is uniformly distributed under the surface, and partition in kind should be granted of severed mineral interests as well as of lands which might contain minerals. Second, if there is evidence that the land is producing oil or gas or that there is sufficient drilling activity in the immediate neighborhood to indicate the possible presence of oil or gas under the land, then it cannot be assumed that the oil and gas are evenly distributed, and partition in kind will be denied for fear of setting apart a barren portion for one co-tenant. Third, even though oil or

gas is being produced or even though there is sufficient drilling activity in the area to indicate the possible presence of oil or gas under the land, partition in kind may still be granted if it is proved that the subsurface structure is such that oil or gas would be uniformly distributed under the land if it were present.

Kuntz § 6.4.

3. Most jurisdictions have enacted statutes concerning partition. They do not, however, assure that all types of mineral interests can be partitioned. See Dorothy J. Glancy, Breaking Up Can Be Hard to Do: Partitioning Jointly Owned Oil and Gas and Other Mineral Interests in Texas, 33 Tulsa L.J. 705 (1998). There are four general elements of a statutory cause of action for partition: (a) Joint ownership (b) Possessory interest (c) Estates of equal dignity in the minerals (d) Throughout the land to be partitioned. Hemingway § 3.3(B).

(a) *Joint ownership:* Partition is uniformly available to tenants in common. Whether other types of concurrent estates are susceptible to partition varies from state to state, but the matter has generally been clarified by statute.

(b) *Possessory interest:* As a general matter, owners of non-possessory mineral interests, such as a landowner's royalty, NPRI, overriding royalty, production payment, and leases in non-ownership jurisdictions have no right to compel a partition. A nonpossessory interest, however, may be partitioned if incidental to the ownership of a possessory interest. For example, if Able and Baker own Blackacre as tenants in common and Able thereafter conveys a royalty interest to Carr, Baker may compel the partition of both Able's and Carr's interests. Can a working interest owner compel the partition of the overriding royalties as well as the other working interests? See Mulsow v. Gerber Energy Corp., 697 P.2d 1269 (Kan. 1985).

The modern trend, either as a result of case law or statute, recognizes the right to partition mineral interests and leasehold interests regardless of the ownership theory. Mineral interest owners whose interests are subject to a lease have been allowed to partition even though they did not have present possessory interests while the leases were in effect.

(c) *Estates of equal dignity:* In addition to a possessory interest, the plaintiff must have an estate of equal dignity to that of the defendant. For example, the owner of a lease to an undivided one-half interest in Blackacre may not force partition against a person who owns the other one-half interest in fee simple. Even though both may be possessory interests, the leasehold estate and the fee estate are not of equal dignity. On the other hand, the owner of an undivided one-fourth mineral interest may force partition against the owner of an undivided three-fourths interest. Although the estates are not of equal quantity, they are of equal quality (or dignity).

(d) *Throughout the land:* Where Able owns an undivided one-half mineral interest in the north one-half of Blackacre and Baker owns an undivided one-half mineral interest in all of Blackacre, Able may force Baker to partition of the north one-half of Blackacre because Able owns the mineral interest throughout the north one-half.

A logical corollary of the doctrine of severance is that a person who owns only an undivided interest in the surface cannot bring suit to partition both the surface and mineral rights. This doctrine is applied in Louisiana, even though the right in the minerals is classified as a servitude, rather than a separate estate. As the Louisiana Supreme Court has pointed out, "[T]he creation of a mineral servitude effectively fragments the title such that different elements of ownership are held by different owners (i.e., between the landowner and the mineral servitude owner), and there is not any 'thing held in common between them.'" Steele v. Denning, 456 So.2d 992, 998–99 (La. 1984). See also Sachse and Atkinson, Reuniting Unused Mineral Interests with the Land, 44 Inst. on Oil & Gas L. & Tax'n 2–1 (1993).

Does a person who owns only an undivided interest in the minerals have an equivalent possessory interest and an estate of equal dignity with a person who owns the remaining mineral interest and the surface? Some courts have answered this question in the affirmative, e.g., Henderson v. Chesley, 273 S.W. 299 (Tex.Civ.App. 1925), *aff'd* 292 S.W. 156 (Tex. 1927); but others would disagree. See, for example, Dunn v. Patton, 718 N.E.2d 264 (Ill.App.5 Dist. 1999), where the court reasoned that there was no unity of possession between common estates because the plaintiff, who sought a partition, had only the right to possess the mineral estate; whereas the defendant had the right to possess both the surface and the minerals.

2. SUCCESSIVE OWNERSHIP AND NONPOSSESSORY INTERESTS

(a) Life Estates and Remainders

WELBORN v. TIDEWATER ASSOCIATED OIL CO.

217 F.2d 509 (10th Cir.Okla.1954).

[Smith held a life estate in a certain parcel and she served as legal guardian to Garrett, a minor and the remainderman. In 1943, acting in her capacity as guardian, Smith issued a lease to Welborn of the remainder interest. In 1952, while the Welborn lease was still effective according to its stated terms, both Garrett (by now an adult) and Smith issued an oil and gas lease to McDaniel; this lease was subsequently assigned to Tidewater. Welborn sued Tidewater for slander of title. The trial court dismissed the action and Welborn appealed.]

PHILLIPS, CHIEF JUDGE.

* * *

It is well settled that a remainderman may not make an oil and gas lease to permit immediate exploration and production without the consent of the life tenant. Likewise, a life tenant cannot drill new oil or gas wells, or lease the land to others for that purpose. A life tenant and the remainderman may lease the land by a joint lease and they may agree as to the division of the rents and royalties. In the absence of such agreement, the life tenant is not entitled to any part of the royalties, but is entitled only to the income from such royalties.

The oil and gas lease to Welborn was wholly ineffective to permit Welborn to go upon the land during the existence of the life estate and explore for, develop, or produce oil and gas from the land.

The records in the probate court of Coal County clearly showed that Smith was the owner of the life estate and Garrett of the remainder interest. As such guardian, Smith could only give a lease on the remainder interest of Garrett. Smith as owner of the life estate did not individually, expressly consent to the developing of the land or the production of oil and gas therefrom under the Welborn lease. * * *

It follows that the most that Welborn acquired was a contingent right to go upon the land and develop it for oil and gas and produce oil therefrom after the death of the life tenant, in the event that death occurred prior to the expiration of the primary term of Welborn's lease. That primary term has now expired.

It follows that Welborn had no title which could be slandered by a lease executed jointly by the life tenant and remainderman.

While we doubt that it can be said that Smith is estopped to deny that she consented individually to the lease to Welborn, we refrain from passing on that question, because to so adjudicate would adversely affect the rights of Smith as life tenant, and she is not a party to the instant action. She would be an indispensable party to an action which would seek an adjudication that she is estopped to deny that she consented to the lease to Welborn and the immediate development of the land for oil and gas under such lease and during her life tenancy.

The judgment is affirmed.

NOTES

1. The principles stated in *Welborn* concerning the inability of either a life tenant or a remainderman, acting alone to develop minerals, are well established. Absent authority in the instrument creating the life estate, consent of the remainderman, or special circumstances a life tenant who produces oil and gas from the life estate commits waste. On the other hand, a remainderman who produces oil and gas without the consent of the life tenant commits a trespass. For a controversy in which a will devised the land to the testator's two children for life, remainder of each life tenant's share to his and her descendants per stirpes and authorized the life tenants to execute oil and gas leases, see Backhus v. Wisnoski, 2011 WL 4090394 (Tex.App.–Houston 2011).

Could a remainderman drill a directional well from property adjacent to the life estate property and produce the oil and gas without liability to the life tenant? Alternatively, could a life tenant avoid liability for waste by showing that drilling was necessary to prevent drainage to an adjacent tract?

2. As stated in *Welborn,* a life tenant and remainderman may execute a joint lease which will confer immediate development rights on the lessee. Immediate development rights may also be obtained where the lessee obtains a lease from the life tenant and has the lease ratified by the remainderman, or vice versa. See, e.g. VanAlstine v. Swanson, 417 N.W.2d 516 (Mich. App. 1987).

Separate leases may be obtained from the life tenant and the remainderman. By prevailing authority, such leases are valid and binding between the parties. If separate leases having substantially equivalent terms are held by a common lessee, the leases merge and confer immediate development rights on the lessee. Where, however, the leases contain different terms and cover different time periods no merger will result. Cf. Rowe v. Bird, 304 S.W.2d 775 (Ky. 1957); Orndoff v. Consumers' Fuel Co., 162 A. 431 (Pa. 1932); McIntosh v. Ropp, 82 A. 949 (Pa. 1912); Weekley v. Weekley, 27 S.E.2d 591 (W.Va. 1943); and Albert A. Haller, Note, Oil and Gas—Leases—Validity When Executed by Life Tenant and Remainderman at Different Times, 56 Mich. L.Rev. 654 (1958). Where both the life tenant and remainderman have executed leases with different terms to the same lessee, can either complain about the lessee's entry?

3. If oil and gas land is held in trust, the authority of the trustee to lease and develop the property for oil and gas must be found in the trust instrument or in general trust law. At common law a trustee was liable for waste if minerals were developed without express authorization in the trust instrument. Statutes have modified this view in many jurisdictions, and most trust instruments expressly authorize the trustee to lease or develop minerals. The powers of a trustee, however, are often subject to specific statutory conditions that may vary from state to state. The trust instrument may also limit the trustee's general statutory authority. As a result, leases and other interests granted by trustees are often the source of title problems.

In the absence of a trust, land that is subject to future interests in minors or unborn or unascertained persons can usually be protected against drainage by a court of equity, which can order the property sold or leased. Generally, all ascertainable living persons must consent, and the sale or lease must be mutually advantageous to the holders of both the present and future interests. See Robinson v. Barrett, 45 P.2d 587 (Kan. 1935) and Pierce § 4.25. See generally Darrel Hester, Note, Remainders—Doctrine of Representation—Binding the Interest of Unborn Contingent Remaindermen, 26 Tex.L.Rev. 349, 349–51 (1948). Several states have enacted statutes expressly authorizing courts to appoint receivers or trustees to execute leases covering contingent future interests. See, e.g., Colo.Rev.Stat. § 38–43–101; Neb.Rev.Stat. § 57–222 et seq.; N.D.Cent.Code § 38–10–12 et seq.; Okla.Stat.Ann.tit. 60, § 71–73; and Tex.Civ.Prac. & Rem.Code Ann. § 64.092. Some of these statutes also address the distribution of lease proceeds. These statutes were usually enacted to facilitate oil and gas development, while preserving the rights of contingent remainderman.

4. Occasionally courts are called upon to reconcile doctrines relating to life estates with those developed in connection with co-ownership. Suppose, for example, that Smith holds an undivided one-half life estate interest in

Blackacre, that Garcia holds the remainder, and that Nguyen owns the other undivided one-half interest in fee simple. May Nguyen lease the property for oil and gas development and may the lessee drill and produce the property? See Davis v. Atlantic Oil Producing Co., 87 F.2d 75 (5th Cir.Tex.1936) and H.M.W., Note, Oil and Gas—Rights of Statutory Life Tenant in Share of a Tenant in Common Where Remainderman and Tenants in Common Lease Whole Tract, 16 Tex.L.Rev. 420 (1938).

HYNSON v. JEFFRIES

697 So.2d 792 (Miss.App. 1997).

Before THOMAS, P.J., and DIAZ and SOUTHWICK, JJ.

SOUTHWICK, JUDGE, for the Court:

The only issue in this case is whether the owner of a life estate in a trust that contains producing oil and gas properties will receive the entire royalties from those minerals, or whether the royalty must be invested and the life tenant receive only the interest on that investment. The chancellor found that under the common law doctrine of waste the life tenant would receive only the interest on the royalties, while the royalty itself would be added to corpus and later be received by the remaindermen. We hold that the chancellor erred in finding that the Mississippi Uniform Principal and Income Law was inapplicable. We reverse and remand for further proceedings.

FACTS

Robert C. Hynson was the owner of substantial oil and gas properties. At his death, he left a detailed last will and testament, prepared by a highly competent and experienced attorney. The provisions that are relevant for this dispute are found in Item VII. In summary, the will gave to trustees of the Robert C. Hynson Marital Deduction Trust all interests in oil and gas of any kind. During the lifetime of Mr. Hynson's widow, all income after the payment of certain expenses would be disbursed to her....

The following are the specific provisions:

ITEM VII.

I give, devise and bequeath unto the Trustees hereinafter named in trust and on the terms and conditions as are herein set forth, all of the interests I own in oil, gas and other similar minerals including all mineral rights, working interests, royalty interests and any and all other interests in oil, gas and other similar minerals, excluding, however, all oil, gas and other similar mineral interests in, on and under lands where I also own the surface thereof.

A. NAME

This trust shall be known as the "ROBERT C. HYNSON MARITAL DEDUCTION TRUST," or "TRUST A."

B. TRUSTEES

The Trustees shall be JOHN L. JEFFRIES, Laurel, Mississippi, and MALCOLM COOPER, Austin, Texas. . . .

C. BENEFICIARY

The primary beneficiary of this trust shall be my wife, CAROLYN HARRIS HYNSON.

F. PAYMENT OF EXPENSES AND DISTRIBUTION OF INCOME

The gross income of the trust property and estate shall be used first for the payment of all necessary expenses, taxes, and repairs or other charges against the trust property or incurred in connection with the use or management of the said trust property and in the administration of this trust including reasonable Trustees' fees. The balance of the income from the trust property and estate remaining after the payment of all such items of expense shall be regarded as net income. However, capital gains on the sale or exchange of trust property shall not be regarded as net income, but shall become a part of the corpus or principal of the trust.

All of the income of the trust shall be paid to my said wife during her lifetime in periodic installments, the frequency of such payments to be determined by the Trustees, except that in no event shall such payments be made less frequently than annually.

I direct that if the trust at any time contains any unproductive property, my wife may require the Trustees to make such property productive or convert such property to productive property within a reasonable time.

     * * *

G. TERMINATION AND DISTRIBUTION

Upon the death of my said wife, any undistributed income shall be paid over to my wife's estate.

(1) From the corpus of the trust, there shall be paid any and all estate taxes which shall become due as a result of the corpus of the trust being includible in my said wife's estate for estate tax purposes.

(2) The entire remaining corpus shall be divided into three equal parts. One part shall be distributed per stirpes to the descendants of my daughter, JULIE HYNSON JEFFRIES.

One part shall be distributed per stirpes to the descendants of CAROLYN HARRIS HYNSON.

One part shall be distributed per stirpes to the descendants of my son, ROBERT GARDINER HYNSON.

This trust shall thereby be terminated. . . .

Some of the remaindermen are minors. Guardians ad litem were appointed for them. In the lower court, the widow Mrs. Carolyn Harris

Hynson argued that she was entitled to the entire royalty, and not just interest on royalty. One of the co-trustees of the trust and the two guardians ad litem took the position that Mrs. Hynson was only entitled to the interest on invested royalty. The second co-trustee took no position. After summary judgment motions by Mrs. Hynson and by the co-trustees, the court ruled that Mrs. Hynson was not entitled to the entirety of the royalty, but only the interest. She appealed.

DISCUSSION

Life estate and remainder interests in oil and gas have frequently led to litigation. Rarely is it an academic discussion of meaningless legal concepts. Substantial sums of money have usually been at stake and presumably such is the case here. Mrs. Hynson raises several different reasons for reversal. These include that the language of the will clearly required that Mrs. Hynson receive all the income, that the open mines doctrine should apply, that the Uniform Principal and Income Law is controlling, and that the provisions of the will requiring that the trust terms be altered if necessary to permit the marital deduction to be received, all require that the trial court be reversed. Though we need not address all these questions because of our resolution of one of them, we will proceed by stages to explain our analysis.

* * *

1. Language of Will

A testator or other creator of successive interests in real property may override all the doctrines that the parties discuss in their briefs merely by adopting sufficiently clear language in the relevant instruments. Not surprisingly, both parties believe that was done here. We have already quoted the relevant sections of the will.

Mrs. Hynson, hoping to acquire the right to receive all the royalty during her lifetime, makes the following argument. The will first refers to "gross income of the trust property and estate," and provides that this income "shall be used first for the payment of all necessary expenses," etc. All of the "balance of the income from the trust property and estate remaining after the payment of all such items of expense shall be regarded as net income." Mrs. Hynson therefore argues that there are only two forms of income recognized in the will, "gross" and "net." The former is all income. The latter is all income except that which is necessary for the payment of expenses. Mrs. Hynson according to the will is to receive "[a]ll of the income of the trust . . . ." Her argument is this: gross income is all income of the trust; net income is gross income less expenses; Mrs. Hynson is to receive "all income," which means net income. We agree that "income," un-modified by the words "gross" or "net," is not some third category of income. We further accept that "all income" must mean "all net income." The problem is not in defining the modifiers, but in defining the word modified. "Income" is not a defined word in the will. Had the will stated that income of the trust included royalty on oil and gas, then Mrs. Hynson's position would be persuasive. Instead, a review of the will from Mrs. Hynson's perspective leaves us where we started: does the conversion of the minerals to a royalty create income, or only principal that must be deposited in the corpus?

* * *

The result of this review is that if—but only if—royalty is "income" of the trust, the will provides that it is to be paid to Mrs. Hynson. The will left the term undefined, and therefore we must determine the default definition. We turn next to the common law, together with exceptions and statutory additions, for the definition of "income."

2.   Law of Waste: General Principles

The starting point for examining the common law issues is Martin v. Eslick, 229 Miss. 234, 90 So.2d 635 (1956). In that case, Mississippi joined most other states that had considered the question and determined that to permit a life tenant to receive all the payments of royalty would constitute waste:

> It is manifest to us that oil in place is part of the real estate and cannot be withdrawn without injury to the inheritance, and that, therefore, portions of the oil produced and paid as royalties represent principal or corpus and only the interest thereon derived from any investment of such funds should be paid to the life tenant.

Martin, 229 Miss. at 253, 90 So.2d at 641. This rule has been followed in numerous subsequent decisions. See, e.g., Whittington, 608 So.2d at 1280.

The application of a more fundamental rule has led to occasional deviations from the hard and fast rule of interest on royalty to the life tenant, the royalty itself to corpus. Martin v. Eslick and similar cases are applying the common law doctrine of waste to interests in real property that are not described in great detail in the document that creates them. If a grantor or testator specifically states a division of income that is different from the Martin v. Eslick rule, the specific language will control.

* * *

Mrs. Hynson argues that two reasons exist to reach a different result from the Martin v. Eslick interpretation. One is a common law corollary to the doctrine of waste, and the other is a statute that did not exist when the Martin decision was handed down. We will examine each.

* * *

A decision that predates Martin v. Eslick states the following:

> It is settled beyond controversy with reference to coal mines that a life tenant has no interest in or right to open and work new mines not in operation at the time he becomes vested with the estate. To do so

amounts to the commission of waste, as a lasting injury to the inheritance, and equity will enjoin him from its commission.

Pace v. State ex rel. Rice, 191 Miss. 780, 800–801, 4 So.2d 270, 275 (1941). From this early date the supreme court recognized a distinction between what a life tenant could do with an "open mine," and with minerals that were not yet being "wasted" prior to the creation of the life estate. The "open mines doctrine" is a well-established common law principle. It is explained by one of the common treatises on oil and gas law:

> The most important exception to the general rules limiting the power of a life tenant to sever and remove minerals without the concurrence of the owner of a future interest arises from the operation of the "open mine" doctrine. If a mine has been opened before the creation of the life estate and a future interest in land, the life tenant may be entitled to continue and operate the opened mine and retain the proceeds of such operation. . . . The basis of the open mine doctrine appears to be that a life tenant given the beneficial enjoyment of land is entitled to enjoy the land in the same manner as it was enjoyed before the creation of the life estate.

2 HOWARD R. WILLIAMS & CHARLES J. MEYERS, OIL AND GAS LAW, § 513 at 654–655 (1989) (emphasis added).

Factually this doctrine has never had to be applied by the Mississippi Supreme Court beyond such statements as in Pace. The appellees as well as the trial court point to this fact and say "Mississippi has never adopted the open mines doctrine." Though that appears true, the references to the doctrine have hardly been couched in terms of revulsion: "[i]t is settled beyond controversy," the court noted, that the open mine doctrine applied to life tenants of coal. Pace, 191 Miss. at 800, 4 So.2d 270. As recently as 1992 the supreme court referred to the doctrine this way:

> The general rule [of impeachment for waste] is, however, subject to exceptions. One such exception is the so-called open mine doctrine which provides that the life tenant is entitled to the entire royalty, and not impeachable for waste, where a well had either been opened or authorized prior to the creation of the life estate. [citations of 2 Texas cases and a treatise omitted]; Martin v. Eslick, 229 Miss. at 253, 90 So.2d at 641 (life tenant may not open new mines). This exception is not applicable here because no lease authorizing the drilling of a well had been executed prior to the creation of the life estate.

Whittington, 608 So.2d at 1280–81. The only fair reading of that language is that the open mine doctrine is part of the common law principles of waste recognized by the supreme court. The Whittington court cited Martin v. Eslick as standing for the proposition that a "life tenant may not open new mines." Whittington, 608 So.2d at 1281. The supreme court for decades has applied "the general rule" of impeachment for waste, and has never indicated a reluctance to invoke the open mine exception.

It would be difficult not to find that the open mine doctrine is part of the general rules to be applied to interpreting the common law principles of waste in Mississippi oil and gas law. Under the concept of open mines, Mrs. Hynson would be entitled to all the royalty for her lifetime from wells that were "opened or authorized prior to the creation of the life estate." Whittington, 608 So.2d at 1280. However, before actually holding such to be the law, we need to conclude whether that is relevant to the resolution of this case, or if it would only be dicta. The mere fact that the open mines doctrine is not some questionable principle that has been kept at arm's length by the supreme court, does not mean that it applies here. To complete our analysis we must examine one final point.

4. *Uniform Principal and Income Law*

In 1966 the legislature adopted the "Uniform Principal and Income Law." Miss.Code Ann. §§ 91–17–1 et seq. Two sections are relevant to this case:

§ 91–17–5 Duty of trustee as to receipts and expenditures

A trust shall be administered with due regard to the respective interests of income beneficiaries and remaindermen. A trust is so administered with respect to the allocation for receipts and expenditures if a receipt is credited or an expenditure is charged to income or principal or partly to each:

> (a) In accordance with the terms of the trust instrument, notwithstanding contrary provisions of this chapter.

> (b) In the absence of any contrary terms of the trust instrument, in accordance with the provisions of this chapter.

* * *

§ 91–17–19. Disposition of receipts from taking natural resources from land.

(1) If any part of the principal consists of a right to receive royalties, overriding or limited royalties, working interests, production payments, net profit interests, or other interests in minerals or other natural resources in, on, or under land, the receipts from taking the natural resources from the land shall be allocated as follows:

* * *

> (c) If received as a royalty, overriding or limited royalty, or bonus, or from a working, net profit, or any other interest in minerals or other natural resources, receipts not provided for in the preceding paragraphs of this section shall be apportioned on a yearly basis in accordance with this paragraph, whether or not any natural resource was being taken from the land at the time the trust was established. Twenty-seven and one-half per cent

(27½%) of the gross receipts (but not to exceed fifty per cent (50%) of the net receipts remaining after payment of all expenses, direct and indirect, computed without allowance for depletion) shall be added to principal as an allowance for depletion. The balance of the gross receipts, after payment therefrom of all expenses, direct and indirect, is income.

This statute has rarely been the subject of interpretation or application by the supreme court. It may well be a forgotten or never-known part of our statutory law, but it is no less conclusive despite its lack of notoriety. The statute applies "[i]n the absence of any contrary terms in the trust instrument...." Miss.Code Ann. § 91–17–5(b). The chancellor refused to apply the statute, as he found Mr. Hynson's intent on division of the royalty to be clear from the will. In the first section of our discussion we addressed that conclusion, and found that the terms that are controlling on the division of royalty have to be defined from outside of the trust instrument. What made the terms clear to the chancellor and contrary to the statute were the common law definitions of those terms, not language in the will itself. We agree with the chancellor that the terms are not used ambiguously. The statute controls over the common law, however, when seeking definitions of the terms.

Having found the statute applicable, this necessarily means that the common law definitions of waste, open mines, and assorted other principles are inapplicable. The legislature is entitled to amend or abolish common law doctrines, which they have under this statute. Thus the royalty division does not depend on whether a well had been producing or authorized prior to Mr. Hynson's death, and all royalty is treated the same. This statute does not affect other legal doctrines that limit a life tenant's power to grant the right to explore for minerals, Hathorn v. Amoco Prod. Co., 472 So.2d 403, 408 (Miss. 1985), but only divides the payment of royalty from validly executed and producing leases.

Section 91–17–19 of the Uniform Principal and Income Law specifically deals with a trust that contains a right to receive royalty on mineral interests. Twenty-seven and one-half percent of the gross receipts is to be considered an allowance for depletion. That amount will be added to principal, and the remainder to income for the life tenant. We hold that this section is applicable to the trust in question.

We remand the case for further proceedings to compute the division of past proceeds and any subsequent royalty or other income. Mrs. Hynson raises other issues regarding the perceived error in the trial court's decision, but we need not address them as our decision on the applicability of the Uniform Principal and Interest Law renders the remaining issues moot.

NOTES

1. The question of how to allocate lease proceeds is likely to arise whenever ownership of leased land is divided between a life tenant and

trates, one common issue is whether the language of the controlling instrument actually provides for a different distribution than would otherwise be applicable. In the absence of such an instrument, a life tenant and remainderman who join in a lease can disregard the common law method of allocation and specify how the proceeds will be divided between them.

6.   Statutes authorizing the appointment of a trustee to execute an oil and gas lease on behalf of contingent future interest owners may address the issue of distribution, although this is not invariably the case. The North Dakota law, for example, contains fairly detailed provisions; whereas the Texas statute is entirely silent on the matter, leaving the courts free to apply common law principles to their distribution. See Kemp v. Hughes, 557 S.W.2d 139 (Tex.Civ. App. 1977). In Rush v. In re the Application for Appointment of a Trustee, 897 P.2d 1150 (Okla.App.Div. 4 1995) an Oklahoma court treated the state's act as part of a general statutory scheme that included the Oklahoma version of the Uniform Principal and Income Act, Okla.Stat.Ann. tit. 60 § 175.33, and held that the life tenant was entitled to the bonus, delay rentals, 80% of the royalty, and interest on the remaining royalty, leaving only 20% of royalty in trust for the contingent remaindermen.

The statutory allocation of proceeds applied in *Rush* has been criticized on two grounds. First, if the property is primarily valuable for its speculative mineral content, several dry holes or extensive 3D seismic testing that reveals no favorable geologic structures may effectively destroy the property's value; yet the contingent remaindermen will have received none of the lease bonus that was paid for the right to conduct these operations. Second, when coupled with the treatment of other lease benefits, the division of royalty between income and corpus inequitably favors the life tenant and does not accomplish the goal of facilitating mineral development while protecting the rights of unascertained and possibly unborn contingent remainderman. See Anderson, Discussion Notes, 156 O & GR 284 (1997). Is there any reason why the allocation of proceeds from a lease executed by a court-appointed trustee should differ from the allocation of proceeds generally made in all other situations?

(b) Tenants for Years and Holders of Defeasible Fees

Most controversies involving tenants for years are between surface lessees and mineral owners and center on the latter's right of surface access. The surface tenant often has an agricultural lease and fears that entry for exploratory, drilling or related purposes will disrupt his operations. If mineral rights have been severed or an oil and gas lease has been granted before the agricultural lease is executed, there is little question that the mineral owner or lessee has superior rights of access. The more difficult issue arises when the agricultural or other surface lease is prior in time and the tenant seeks to prohibit a subsequent oil and gas lessee from entering and drilling on the land. In Republic Natural Gas Co. v. Melson, 274 P.2d 543 (Okla. 1954) the court treated an oil and gas lease as granted "subject to" the pre-existing agricultural lease and held the oil and gas lessee liable for all damage done to crops. Conversely, in Ball v. Dillard, 602 S.W.2d 521 (Tex. 1980) a prior agricultural tenant was held liable in damages to an oil and gas lessee that he prevented from entering the property. Are these decisions necessarily inconsistent?

A somewhat different issue was raised in Mobile Pipe Line Co. v. Smith, 860 S.W.2d 157 (Tex. App.–El Paso 1993, writ disms'd w.o.j.), where the landowner, whose property had been farmed by the same tenant for 10 years, granted a pipeline easement, rather than an oil and gas lease. When the tenant denied the pipeline company access to the property, the company sought a temporary injunction. The court relied on cases such as Ball v. Dillard that suggest the agricultural tenant is in a legal position analogous to that of the owner of a severed surface estate and therefore takes his interest subject to an implied right of access to the minerals. This reasoning has been questioned in Kuntz § 9.2. The lessor's implied right of access is an incident of the mineral estate which the lessor implicitly retains when she executes the agricultural lease; whereas a pipeline easement given to a party without an oil and gas lease creates a new and technically different type of servitude burdening the surface. Can the result in *Mobile* be justified on the ground that it facilitates the efficient acquisition of easements while still permitting the agricultural tenant to recover for injury to his crops?

[Conflicting claims of rights to surface use are especially likely to arise in areas where wind farms—often consisting of 100s of wind turbines—either already have been built or are being constructed on land where mineral rights have been severed from the surface ownership. In Windows of Change: The Creation of Wind Law, 5 Tex. J. of Oil, Gas & Energy L. 166, 181–186 (2009–2010) Prof. Ernest Smith and Becky Diffen have argued that "the wind lessee is in logically the same legal position as an agricultural lessee." An opposing theory has been advanced in K. K. DuVivier & Roderick E. Westel, Jousting at Windmills: When Wind Power Development Collides with Oil, Gas and Mineral Development, 55 Rocky Mtn. Min. L. Inst. 9–1 (2009), where the authors argue that since wind is a natural resource, it should be treated as minerals are treated when rights in different minerals, e.g. coal, uranium, oil and gas, have been severed and transferred to different persons or entities. Although there is a variety of judicial positions in this situation, the most common approach is "first in time; first in right." If applied to wind farms, a wind lessee would prevail over a later oil and gas lessee in disputes over the location of drilling rigs, wind turbines, roads, etc. At the time this book was going to press, the issue of the relative rights of a wind lessee versus the holder of the mineral estate was being litigated in The Osage Nation v. Wind Capital Investment Management Group, 2011 WL 5864368 (N.D. Okla.).]

The holders of defeasible fees, whether subject to a condition subsequent, possibility of reverter, or executory limitation, may usually develop or lease the property for oil and gas without the consent of the future interest owner. Moreover, the owner of the present interest is generally permitted to retain all of the proceeds of development. See Davis v. Skipper, 83 S.W.2d 318 (Tex.Com.App. 1935). Of course, except in highly unusual situations, an owner cannot transfer an interest that will outlast his own interest. Hence, if the defeasible fee terminates, the lease also terminates unless the owner of the reversionary interest has joined in the lease or ratifies it. The Arkansas Supreme Court, however, has suggested that the owner of a defeasible fee commits waste by developing oil and gas where it is certain that the defeasible interest will terminate. See Dickson v. Renfro, 634 S.W.2d 104 (Ark. 1982). This ruling is consistent with the doctrine of equitable waste as applied in such circumstances. Kuntz § 7.1.

(c) Creditors

In many jurisdictions a secured creditor, such as a mortgagee or the beneficiary under a deed of trust, is deemed to have legal title to the land that has been put up as security for a loan. Because the creditor's interest is limited to protecting its security, however, the right to create rights in oil and gas is held by the debtor. This does not mean that the debtor will have complete freedom in transferring oil and gas interests. The terms of the instrument creating the security may require the consent of the creditor. Moreover, unless the owner of the security has waived its priority or executed a subordination agreement, the debtor's grantee or lessee receives the interest subject to the security. In the event of a foreclosure, the lease or other interest will be extinguished.

In many mortgages and deeds of trust there are other types of clauses that must also be taken into account by the parties to an oil and gas transaction. As Professor Lowe has pointed out:

> Many mortgages and deeds of trust contain "due on sale clauses;" e.g., "if the ownership of any portion of the premises shall be changed * * * then, at the mortgagee's discretion, the entire indebtedness secured hereby shall become immediately due and payable." Others contain assignments of proceeds; e.g., "there are specifically assigned to the mortgagee all rents, revenues, damages and payments * * * on account of any and all oil, gas, mining and mineral leases, rights or privileges of any kind now existing or that may hereafter come into existence."

Lowe, Chapter 6.C.

Another form of security device that is frequently used is the land contract. The vendor typically retains legal title until the entire purchase price has been paid; upon default by the purchaser, the vendor's traditional remedy has been to declare the vendee's equitable title forfeited and to repossess the premises. Although many states have modified the vendor's rights somewhat, he will still normally reacquire full legal title in the event of a continuing default by the purchaser. Hence, a lessee should seek either a subordination of the vendor's rights or else a ratification of the lease by the vendor along with a present grant of after-acquired rights.

(d) Owners of Easements, Covenants, and Servitudes

The owner of an easement, covenant or servitude has no right to lease or develop the minerals. He can, however, prevent his grantor and his grantor's successors in interest from interfering with the enjoyment of his interest. In the case of rights of way, an oil and gas developer need only avoid conducting operations within the boundaries of the right-of-way corridor. In the case of restrictive covenants or servitudes that limit the use of property to a specific purpose (for example, single family dwellings) development of minerals, including oil and gas, may be barred unless all parties benefiting from the interest consent to development. See, e.g., Devendorf v. Akbar Petroleum Corp., 577 N.E.2d 707 (Ohio App.9 Dist. 1989) (covenant prohibiting use for "business of any type, whether commercial, retail, manufacturing or otherwise" barred oil and gas development.)

Of course such doctrines presuppose that the easements, covenants or servitudes were created prior to the transfer of mineral rights in a third party. Except for interstate gas pipeline easements, where, as in Panhandle Eastern Pipe Line Co. v. Tishner, 699 N.E.2d 731 (Ind. App. 1998), federal statutes and regulations dealing with pipeline operations and safety preempt state law, a prior mineral owner's right to use the surface estate usually has priority over subsequently created easements, covenants or servitudes. See, e.g., The Mable Cleary Trust v. The Edward–Marlah Muzyl Trust, 686 N.W.2d 770 (Mich.App. 2004); Property Owners of Leisure Land, Inc. v. Woolf & Magee, Inc., 786 S.W.2d 757 (Tex.App. 1990).

The owner of a *profit a prendre* has the right to enter and take whatever substance is subject to the profit; this may include timber, minerals, or gravel. A pure profit rarely includes an interest in oil and gas. As was indicated earlier in this chapter, however, many jurisdictions characterize an oil and gas lease as a *profit a prendre*.

C. TERMINABLE INTERESTS

Terminable mineral and royalty interests are encountered with some frequency in states with a long history of oil and gas production. (Courts sometimes erroneously refer to such interests as "term" interests.) A typical conveyance is "for a period of ten (10) years from the date of this instrument, and as long thereafter as oil, gas or other minerals are produced or mined from the lands herein described in paying quantities."[4] The interest received by the grantee under such a deed terminates at the end of the specified period if there is no production; if there is production extending beyond the stated period, the interest terminates when the production terminates. Occasionally, the intended duration of the royalty may be in issue. Whether the royalty will terminate when the existing lease expires, or whether it will continue in perpetuity may not be clear. In Browning v. Grigsby, 657 S.W.2d 821 (Tex.App. 1983) there was a reservation of one-half of the mineral estate with a proviso that "this

---

4. An example of a terminable royalty deed using this language is set out in its entirety in the Forms Manual.

mineral exception and reservation shall expire on October 25, 1958, unless at that time the above named minerals or either of them, is being produced from said premises in paying quantities." The court held that production on the date stipulated maintained the grantor's interest in perpetuity; it did not terminate when production later ceased. See also Bellport v. Harrison, 255 P. 52 (Kan. 1927) and Hasty v. McKnight, 460 S.W.2d 949 (Tex.Civ.App. 1970, writ ref'd n.r.e.).

One of the most common questions that arises under a terminable-interest deed is what constitutes "production" that will maintain the interest past the primary term. The following case illustrates the usual judicial approach to this issue.

ARCHER COUNTY v. WEBB

338 S.W.2d 435 (Tex. 1960).

HICKMAN, CHIEF JUSTICE.

* * * Archer County, Fred Turner, Jr., and Juliette Turner, as trustees for Dorothy Scarbauer, and Fay Durham, hereinafter called petitioners, sued respondents, C.R. Webb and others, trustees of the Shannon West Texas Memorial Hospital and of the Margaret A. Shannon Estate, in trespass to try title and for a declaratory judgment establishing the continued existence of a term royalty interest in League 3, Crockett County, Texas. Phillips Petroleum Company, hereinafter called Phillips, and Fred Turner, Jr., sued the same defendants in trespass to try title and for a declaratory judgment establishing the continued existence of an oil and gas lease covering 202 acres of land in League 3, Crockett County, Texas. The trial court held that the royalty interest of petitioners subsisted to the extent that it pertained to the 202–acre tract under lease to Phillips and Turner. It further held that the lease owned by Phillips and Turner remained in effect. The Court of Civil Appeals affirmed the judgment of the trial court insofar as it held that the oil and gas lease remained in effect, but reversed and rendered that part of the judgment maintaining in effect the royalty interest in the 202 acres, holding that all rights under the royalty deed under which petitioners claimed had reverted to the respondents. 326 S.W.2d 250.

The somewhat complicated facts are recited in detail in the opinion of the Court of Civil Appeals. We think a brief statement of the facts is sufficient to disclose how the law questions presented here arose. On May 7, 1929, Margaret A. Shannon, owner in fee simple of a league of a land in Crockett County, known as Survey 3, executed a deed to James E. Ferguson, conveying

> * * * an undivided one-half interest in and to all oil and gas royalty that may be produced under oil and gas leases outstanding or to be hereinafter outstanding on the aforesaid lands, or any part thereof, for the full term of fifteen (15) years from this date, or so long as oil

or gas shall be produced from said premises, or any part thereof in commercially paying quantities * * *

* * *

If no commercially paying oil or gas be produced from aforesaid lands within fifteen years, this conveyance to become null and void.

By mesne conveyances all the interests acquired by Mr. Ferguson under that deed passed to the petitioners herein.

Margaret A. Shannon died testate on December 13, 1931. By her will all of her interest in League 3[1] passed to respondents as trustees of her estate and of the Shannon West Texas Memorial Hospital. On April 24, 1940, respondents, as lessors executed to R.G. Carr an oil and gas lease covering 202 acres of League 3. The lease was for a primary term of ten years "and as long thereafter as oil, gas or other mineral is produced from said land hereunder." The lease provided for payment of shut-in gas well royalty of $50 per well per year where gas from a well producing gas only was not sold or used. Carr assigned his interest under the lease to Phillips, which in turn assigned an interest in 40 acres thereof to Fred Turner, Jr. Delay rentals were paid to respondents sufficient to keep the lease in force until April 24, 1944. Phillips and Turner, however, completed a well on the 40 acres as a potential producer on September 24, 1943. Subsequently, during a period from September 15, 1948, to January 5, 1949, gas from this well was produced and sold, but except during that period no gas has been produced from the well. Since the completion of the well, Phillips and Turner have annually tendered payment of the shut-in gas well royalty provided for in the lease to the respondents, all of which tenders, except one made by Turner in 1943, were refused.

* * *

The first question presented is whether the terms of the royalty deed, which provide for the continuation of the grantees' interest after the original 15–year term as long "as oil or gas shall be produced from said premises, or any part thereof in commercially paying quantities," have been met. The deed does not define "production in commercially paying quantities"; in the absence of such definition, and considering the language alone, that expression must be construed as requiring actual production in commercially paying quantities and not merely the completion of a well capable of producing. * * *

We consider next whether the terms of the royalty deed were modified by the execution of the oil and gas lease above mentioned. The primary term of the lease was for ten years "and as long thereafter as oil, gas or other mineral is produced from said land hereunder." But the lease provided that "where gas from a well producing gas only is not sold or used, Lessee may pay as royalty $50.00 per well per year, and upon such payment it will be considered that gas is being produced within the

1. [Editors' Note] A League contains about 4,428 acres.

meaning of paragraph 2 hereof.'' Petitioners contend that respondents, by executing this lease, effected a modification of the royalty deed so that payment of the shut-in gas well royalty would not only keep the lease in force, but it would also maintain the royalty interest in force.

To our minds, the language of the lease does not either expressly or by implication extend the term of the royalty deed. Under the express provision of the lease, payment of the shut-in gas well royalty is considered "production" "within the meaning of paragraph 2 hereof." Paragraph 2 of the lease prescribes its own duration, and the effect of the provision quoted is merely to extend the term of the lease and not the term of the royalty deed. There is no provision in the royalty deed which would extend its term by the payment of shut-in gas well royalty, and as held in Union Producing Co. v. Scott, D.C., 173 F.Supp. 361, affirmed in 5 Cir., 267 F.2d 469, 470, "It is the mineral deed, not the lease, which should have contained the provision securing to the term mineral owners the benefits of the shut-in gas well provision."

* * *

Petitioners also contend that respondents are estopped to assert that their royalty interest expired by its own terms. They base that contention, as we understand it, upon the proposition that respondents' claim of benefits under the lease to the exclusion of petitioners for whom they acted in a fiduciary capacity in executing the lease is unfair. We can discover no unfairness to the term royalty owners in the execution of the oil and gas lease by respondents. No injustice resulted to them. In fact, the execution of the lease could well have resulted in great benefit to the petitioners. Had the well actually produced oil or gas in commercial quantities, the effect would have been to extend their royalty deed. But petitioners argue that to uphold the execution by the respondents of the type of lease here involved would be to open the door to all kinds of fraud and collusion between lessors and lessees, for the purpose of terminating the interests of term royalty owners. In our view, the holding that the execution of the lease in this case was not a breach of any duty owing to petitioners does not condone any fraudulent act or open the door to fraud.

* * *

In summary, we hold that the term royalty deed expired at the termination of the fifteen-year period provided therein, * * *. The result is that the judgment of the Court of Civil Appeals is affirmed.

WALKER, J., not sitting.

* * *

ON MOTION FOR REHEARING.

HAMILTON, JUSTICE.

* * *

I respectfully dissent from the majority opinion in so far as it holds that payment of shut-in gas well royalty did not serve to extend the term royalty beyond its fixed term.

In arriving at an answer to the above question, it is necessary to construe the royalty deed and the oil and gas lease together, because the interest conveyed by the royalty deed is contained in the oil and gas lease. We must go to the oil and gas lease to find out what the royalty is. The royalty deed does not define "production", nor does it define "royalty". The lease sets out specifically of what the royalty payable under the lease consists, and in defining royalty it also defines production as it applies to a producing gas well from which gas is not being sold or used. The deed recites an agreement to convey

> an undivided 1/2 interest in and *to all oil or gas royalty* that may be paid under oil and gas leases or development work * * *.

and that the interest is to be

> subject to oil and gas leases now outstanding or that may be *hereinafter outstanding* on the aforesaid land or any part thereof; said conveyance limited to 15 years, *plus production period.* (Our emphasis.)

The lease recites:

> The royalties to be paid Lessor are: * * * where gas from a well producing gas only is not sold or used, Lessee may pay as royalty $50.00 per well per year, and upon such payment it will be considered that gas is being produced within the meaning of paragraph 2 hereof; * * *

Paragraph 2 referred to provides:

> Subject to the other provisions herein contained, this lease shall be for a term of ten years from this date (called "primary term") and as long thereafter as oil or gas or other mineral is produced from said land hereunder.

The majority opinion construes the reference in the royalty provision to paragraph 2 as having the effect of restricting the definition of production to the lease itself to the exclusion of any outstanding term royalty interest. I do not think that such construction necessarily follows. All the royalty interest owned by petitioner is contained within this lease and of whatever royalty is provided therein the petitioners own an undivided one-half for a period of fifteen years *"plus production period".* The royalty provision itself defines the production period in so far as gas not being sold or used from a producing well is concerned. The reference to paragraph 2 is merely to emphasize what the parties meant by this substitute production. They made it clear that it was such a production as would extend the lease beyond its primary term and that the two provisions would not be in conflict. Petitioners bought an interest in the royalty under this lease for fifteen years *"plus the production period",* Petitioners received and were without question entitled to their part of the royalty paid prior to the end of the fifteen-year term. Morriss v. First National Bank of Mission, Tex.Civ.App., San Antonio, 249 S.W.2d 269 (n.r.e. 1952), wherein it was held that a shut-in gas well payment is a *royalty on production* and that the holder of a nonparticipating royalty interest is entitled to his fractional part thereof. Generally a royalty deed or a royalty reservation does not specify what kind of lease the one holding the leasing rights is to make. All that a royalty owner has is the right to participate in whatever royalty is provided for in any lease.

* * *

With the single exception of the pooling cases, reversioners, under the majority opinion, can execute leases which define any set of circumstances as production and the effect of such lease provisions will be to extend the oil and gas lease but not to extend term interests. To so hold is to express a judicial policy against term interests for it requires the draftsman of the royalty deed to anticipate and seek to cover all of the various contractual provisions for substitute production which the lessee and lessor may, at some time in the future, agree upon. Term interests will necessarily be prejudiced thereby because the lessee, by reason of lease definitions of production, is freed of the most effective incentive to accomplish actual production and certainly may be tempted to operate in such a fashion that the lease will continue but the term interests will expire. Purely from a policy standpoint, as well as a legal one, we submit that the majority opinion reaches an incorrect result.

* * *

I would hold, then, that the payment of the shut-in royalty by lessee is such production as would prevent the termination of the term royalty of petitioners, and would affirm the judgment of the trial court.

NOTES

1. The holding in the principal case has been followed in a series of decisions by the Texas courts of appeals which have repeatedly rejected arguments attempting to distinguish it on its facts.[5] What should be the result if the lessors in *Archer County* had reached an agreement with their lessee that the lessee could satisfy its obligation to drill an offset well by paying an "in lieu" royalty based upon production from an adjacent well which it had drilled? Compare Andretta v. West, 415 S.W.2d 638 (Tex.1967).

2. Oklahoma has long taken the position that a lease will be maintained past the primary term by the completion of a well capable of producing gas in

5. See Campbell v. Dreier, 382 S.W.2d 179, 21 O & GR 165 (Tex.Civ.App.–San Antonio 1964, writ ref'd n.r.e.); Midwest Oil Corp. v. Lude, 376 S.W.2d 18, 20 O & GR 224 (Tex.Civ.App.–Corpus Christi 1964, writ ref'd n.r.e.); Ramage v. Potter, 373 S.W.2d 399, 19 O & GR 711 (Tex.Civ.App.–Texarkana 1963, writ ref'd n.r.e.); Midwest Oil Corp. v. Mengers, 372 S.W.2d 247, 19 O & GR 600 (Tex.Civ.App.–Waco 1963, writ ref'd n.r.e.); Investors Royalty Co. v. Childrens Hospital Medical Center, 364 S.W.2d 779, 18 O & GR 349 (Tex.Civ.App.–San Antonio 1963, writ ref'd n.r.e.); and Holland v. Vela De Pena, 343 S.W.2d 750, 14 O & GR 264 (Tex.Civ.App.–San Antonio 1961, writ ref'd n.r.e.).

paying quantities, even though the well is shut in at the end of the primary term. See, e.g., McVicker v. Horn, Robinson & Nathan, 322 P.2d 410 (Okla. 1958). Its courts have, however, refused to extend that doctrine to terminable interests. The courts in Fransen v. Eckhardt, 711 P.2d 926 (Okla. 1985) and McEvoy v. First National Bank & Trust Co., 624 P.2d 559 (Okla.App.Div. 1 1980) both cited with approval the distinction made by Professor Kuntz:

> The view taken by the Oklahoma court is supported by the reasoning that it should be recognized that the situation involving leasing is not the same as the situation present in the granting or reserving of terminable interests in the minerals. In the case of the lease, development by the lessee is contemplated, and it is assumed that the lessee will have it within his power to attempt to extend the lease by production. In the case of the terminable interest, however, the parties do not contemplate activity by the grantee to make the minerals productive for the mutual benefit of the grantee and the reversioner. The owner of a terminable royalty interest has no right of ingress and egress, and although the owner of a terminable mineral interest enjoys such right to the extent that it is not impaired by an outstanding oil and gas lease, such right is for his own benefit. The duration of the fixed term of the terminable interest may be fixed by caprice, by the anticipated duration of a current wave of speculation, or by references to purposes other than that of stimulating operations. While the lessor contemplates operations by the lessee for the mutual benefit of the lessor and lessee, the grantor of a terminable interest contemplates no such thing. The parties have picked an event which is not related to their mutual interests except that it defines when one interest terminates and the other vests in present enjoyment.

Kuntz § 15.8.

3. In Texaco, Inc. v. Fox, 618 P.2d 844 (Kan. 1980), the grantors reserved a royalty for twenty years and "as long as oil/or gas is produced in commercial quantities." An oil and gas lease that was subsequently executed provided that the lease would continue beyond the primary term "as long thereafter as oil, gas, casinghead gas, casinghead gasoline, or any of them is produced." In determining whether the reserved interest or the lease or both had terminated, the Kansas Supreme Court first pointed out that the habendum clause of an oil and gas lease is dependent upon continued production of oil or gas in paying quantities. It then stated that "the 'thereafter' clause has the same meaning when used to create a separate estate or interest in oil and gas as when it is used in the habendum clause of an oil and gas lease. Having determined the habendum clause of an oil and gas lease and of a mineral reservation have the same meaning, we must determine whether the term 'commercial quantity' is synonymous with the term 'paying quantity.' * * * We hold the terms are synonymous." 618 P.2d at 847.

Is the position of the Kansas court consistent with the distinction made by Professor Kuntz? Can an argument be made in support of construing language in terminable mineral deeds the same way identical language is construed in oil and gas leases?

4. In Dewell v. Federal Land Bank of Wichita, 380 P.2d 379 (Kan. 1963), the grantor had reserved an interest in the mineral estate for twenty years and "so long thereafter as oil, gas and/or other minerals or any of them are produced therefrom, or the premises are being developed or operated." He later executed an oil and gas lease containing a shut-in royalty clause. The Kansas Supreme Court, citing *Archer County,* held that the payment of shut-in royalty under the lease did not maintain the terminable interest past the twenty year period. "Mineral reservations are to be construed in accordance with the intent and purpose of the parties as gathered from an examination of the entire instrument. * * * The shut-in royalty clause contained in the leases was for the sole benefit of the lessee. It is a privilege granted the lessee in lieu of production. It does not purport to convey any estate or rights to anyone else. Neither does it purport to extend the interest of the holders of the mineral rights. * * * The payment of shut-in royalty is not the equivalent of 'production' or 'being developed or operated.' As the land was not being produced, developed or operated, the mineral interest was not perpetuated or extended beyond the primary term." 380 P.2d at 381–83.

Has the Kansas court used a consistent method of construing terminable interests in the *Dewell* and *Fox* cases? What result would you expect from the Kansas court if it were faced with the question raised in Note 1—that is, the effect of an "in lieu" royalty upon a terminable interest?

5. There seems to be little question about the validity of a terminable interest that is transferred to a grantee. Like an oil and gas lease, the grantee's interest can be viewed as analogous to a fee simple determinable. The possibility of reverter reserved by the grantor is a presently vested right that does not violate the rule against perpetuities.

A more difficult issue is presented if the grantor *retains* a terminable mineral or royalty interest. In that event the interest of the grantee in the mineral interest may be viewed as an executory interest that violates the rule against perpetuities because it may not vest for an indefinite period in the future. See Victory Oil Co. v. Hancock Oil Co., 270 P.2d 604 (Cal.App. 1954). This argument has been rejected in several cases, although the courts have used different lines of reasoning. A later California case, Rousselot v. Spanier, 131 Cal.Rptr. 438 (Cal.App. 1976), distinguished *Victory Oil Co.* on its facts and took the position that a grant of land with a retained terminable interest should be analyzed as a conveyance of a present possessory interest subject to an incorporeal hereditament in the nature of a *profit a prendre* in the grantor; when the grantor's interest ceases, it simply frees the land of the burden and no new estate is vested in the grantee. The same reasoning was used by a Michigan court in Stevens Mineral Co. v. State, 418 N.W.2d 130 (Mich.App. 1987). Texas appellate courts have adopted the fiction that a grant and re-grant have taken place. They have pointed out that the parties could have created incontestably valid interests if they had used two instruments, with the grantor first conveying all rights in the land to the grantee and the grantee immediately reconveying a defeasible royalty interest to the original grantor. The courts have stated that the law will imply that such an exchange has taken place, even though the parties have used only a single instrument. See Bagby v. Bredthauer, 627 S.W.2d 190 (Tex. App. 1981) and Walker v. Foss, 930 S.W.2d 701 (Tex. App. 1996). A somewhat similar rationale was adopted by the Alabama Supreme Court in Earle v. International Paper Co., 429 So.2d 989 (Ala. 1983). The court reasoned that a retained terminable mineral interest was a reservation rather than an exception and that under the common law concept of a reservation the grantee had "recreated the one-half [terminable] mineral interest in" the grantor. The Wyoming Supreme Court, on the other hand, classified the grantee's interest following a retained terminable mineral interest as a vested remainder. It stated that if it had not come to that conclusion, the court "would not be able to give effect to what all justices acknowledge was the intent of the parties. * * * [T]he interest remaining after the determinable fee would, if it were designated an executory interest, be in violation of the rule against perpetuities and therefore void. This would leave fee title absolute in the [grantor]—a result which would defeat the intent of all parties." Williams v. Watt, 668 P.2d 620, 633 (Wyo. 1983). Judge Thomas, specially concurring in the *Williams* case, argued that the grantee's mineral interest was clearly an executory interest; relying upon the argument advanced in 2 Williams & Meyers § 335, he would not have applied the rule against perpetuities to the grantee's interest on the ground that such interests tend to remove title complications and, therefore, promote one of the purposes served by the rule.

Which, if any, of these arguments do you find persuasive?

D. EXECUTIVE RIGHT IN MINERAL INTERESTS

Of all the rights contained within the mineral estate fee, the executive right to lease is possibly the right whose exact extent, purpose and limitations are the least clearly defined by case law. Definitions of the executive right can be read very broadly. The most sweeping definition of executive right would be "the right to take or authorize all actions which affect the exploration and development of the mineral estate * * * [including] the right to engage in or authorize geophysical exploration, drilling or mining, and producing oil, gas and other minerals." Smith & Weaver § 2.6. However courts rarely use the term in this broad sense. More commonly, they equate the executive right with the right to execute oil and gas leases. See, e.g., Altman v. Blake, 712 S.W.2d 117 (Tex. 1986). See also Patrick A. Martin, Unbundling the Executive Right: A Guide to Interpretation of the Power to Lease and Develop, 37 Nat.Res.J. 311 (1997) and Williams & Meyers § 339.1.

The executive right must be analyzed as a separate interest in land, because it is frequently severed from other incidents of mineral ownership. We have already encountered such a severance in our consideration of royalties. The owner of a royalty normally has no right to participate in the leasing process, and hence is dependent upon the action of the mineral estate owner in realizing any income from his interest. The executive right may also be severed from an interest in the mineral estate itself. The owner of Blackacre may convey away an undivided one-half interest in the minerals, retaining the other one-half interest plus the exclusive executive right. The grantee in such a transaction has received an interest commonly referred to as a *nonparticipating mineral fee*. This type of interest differs from a royalty in that its owner is entitled to one-half of all benefits allocable to the mineral estate under an oil and gas lease, including the bonus and delay rentals. The right to execute the lease itself, however, is held entirely by the grantor. See generally Charles J. Meyers & Pamela Ray, Perpetual Royalty and Other Non-executive Interests in Minerals, 29 Rocky Mtn.Min.L.Inst. 651 (1983).

Little evidence is found explaining why the executive right exists as a separate property interest. It seems likely that the executive right was derived in response to the fractionalization of mineral fee interests to ease the leasing of oil and gas interests. This seems to be the informal consensus of oil and gas practitioners and commentators as to why the executive right was recognized. Persons acquiring interests in cotenancy may recognize that each division of ownership makes oil and gas development more difficult, not only because of the potential for disagreement among the cotenants, but also because of the likelihood that some of the interests may become owned by minors or other persons under a legal disability. Hence, leasing will be greatly facilitated if one of the cotenants has the exclusive authority to execute leases. Similarly, co-owners—especially family members—may decide it is in their best interests to rely upon the special skill, contacts or expertise that one of them has acquired through previous experience or work in the oil industry. Among practitioners, the purpose of the power is to facilitate leasing—mineral cotenants and potential lessors can put the leasing negotiations in the hands of the most sophisticated party among them. This provides potential lessees the benefit of only having to negotiate one lease instead of many.

On the other hand, it is also possible that the severance of the executive right has nothing to do with a desire to facilitate mineral development. A purchaser who is primarily interested in surface use may insist upon acquiring the exclusive executive right to protect his surface investment. Since he has the exclusive right to execute oil and gas leases, he can impose limitations upon surface use in any lease that he may subsequently execute. This could lead to problems for both the executive rights owner and the owner of the nonparticipating mineral fee, particularly if their interests in mineral development diverges. Consider the following problem:

PROBLEM

Hobbs Houses, Inc. owns one hundred percent (100%) of the surface and an undivided twenty percent (20%) portion of the minerals under Brownacre, a three thousand acre tract in the heart of the Barnett Shale region fifty miles from Ft. Worth, Texas. Hobbs Houses, Inc. also owns 100% of the executive rights to lease all the minerals under Brownacre. Anna Mary Sullivan is the nonparticipating mineral fee owner of the other seventy-five percent (75%) of the minerals. Hobbs Houses, Inc., a company from outside Texas with no interest in developing the minerals, decides it wants to divide up the surface of Brownacre into three to seven-acre "ranchettes". Further, in order to entice buyers seeking undisturbed surface use, it prints sales brochures which advertise the facts that no drilling will ever take place on Brownacre and that anti-drilling covenants will be included in the homeowner association rules under which all prospective buyers will have to take title in Brownacre.

Seeing natural gas prices rise, Ms. Sullivan demands that Hobbs Houses, Inc. seek a lessee to lease the land for drilling. Hobbs Houses, Inc. refuses and goes forward with its surface development plans. Ms. Sullivan asks you, her lawyer, if she has a legal basis for complaint.

Would your answer change if Hobbs Houses, Inc. agreed to lease just the interest of Ms. Sullivan but not its own? How about if Hobbs Houses, Inc. was first approached by a lessee? What if Hobbs Houses, Inc. agreed to lease all the minerals but included in the leases a provision that the lessee had no right to access the surface? Before answering these questions, you should consider the following material.

IN RE LEE M. BASS

113 S.W.3d 735 (Tex. 2003).

SCHNEIDER, JUSTICE

Here, non-participating royalty interest owners are attempting discovery of the mineral estate owner's geological seismic data to prove that the mineral estate owner breached an implied duty to develop its land. The mineral estate owner claims that the data are trade secrets. The trial court found that the royalty owners met their burden of establishing necessity and ordered the mineral estate owner to produce the data under a protective order. The court of appeals denied the mineral estate owner's requested mandamus relief. The mineral estate owner now seeks mandamus relief from this Court to prevent discovery of the claimed trade secrets.

* * *

I. BACKGROUND

Real parties in interest, the non-participating royalty interest owners (the McGills), sued Relator, the mineral estate owner (Bass), for multiple claims in the trial court. The relevant claim for the purpose of this mandamus is the McGills' assertion that Bass breached an implied duty to the McGills to develop his land.

Bass owns the surface and mineral estate of La Paloma Ranch—a large tract of land in Kenedy and Kleberg counties, Texas. The Ranch is made up of multiple tracts of land, which Bass purchased from the McGills and their predecessors in interest. The disputed land tract here is the former Erck property—approximately 22,000 acres within the La Paloma Ranch. The Erck property was originally part of the McGill family ranch. The McGill family ranch was partitioned between three brothers, J.C. McGill, H.F. McGill, and Scott McGill in 1954. Although both surface and minerals were partitioned, each of the brothers retained a 1/3rd of 1/8th non-participating royalty interest in the other two brothers' partitioned land.

As sole daughter and heir of J.C. McGill, Anne McGill Erck inherited her father's land. Bass purchased the Erck property in 1990. The Erck property general warranty deed to Bass clearly recognizes the encumbrance of the royalty interests that the other McGill brothers own. Here, Relators are the heirs of Scott McGill, and their non-participating royalty interest in the Erck property is less than 2.0%.

In the mid-nineties, Bass contracted with Exxon to run a geological survey of seismic activity on the entire La Paloma Ranch. Bass has never opted to lease the land for development. The McGills claim that by refusing to lease and thus develop the land, Bass has breached an implied duty to the royalty interest holders. To prove that Bass breached this duty, the McGills claim access to Bass' seismic data is necessary because the data will reveal whether development would be profitable. The trial court ordered production of the data subject to a protective order.

The trial court order did not expressly find that the seismic activity data are trade secrets. Bass contends the data are trade secrets, and thus, Bass sought mandamus relief from the court of appeals, which denied relief in a *per curiam* order. Bass now seeks relief from this Court, arguing that the data are trade secrets and that the McGills have not shown entitlement to the seismic information.

* * *

It is undisputed that the oil and gas industry typically treats seismic data and other methods for obtaining subsurface geological information as trade secrets. Other jurisdictions have recognized this industry wide practice of treating seismic data as trade secrets. See *Musser Davis Land Co. v. Union Pac. Res.*, 201 F.3d 561, 569 (5th Cir. 2000); *Tidelands Royalty "B" Corp. v. Gulf Oil Corp.*, 804 F.2d 1344, 1351 (5th Cir. 1986); *Phillips Petroleum Co. v. Stryker*, 723 So. 2d 585, 587 (Ala. 1998); *Amoco Prod. Co. v. Laird*, 622 N.E.2d 912, 918 (Ind. 1993).

* * *

We therefore hold that the seismic data and its interpretations are trade secrets protected by Texas Rule of Evidence 507.

* * *

[T]he McGills claim that the trade secret data are necessary to show that Bass breached a fiduciary duty to the McGills to develop Bass' land. The duty to develop, according to the McGills, arises from the existing relationship between the mineral estate owner—Bass—and the royalty interest holders—the McGills. However, a duty to develop a mineral estate arises not from a fiduciary relationship, but from the implied covenant doctrine of contracts law in which courts read a duty to develop into an oil and gas lease when necessary to effectuate the parties' intent. *Danciger*

Oil & Ref. Co. v. Powell, 137 Tex. 484, 154 S.W.2d 632, 635 (Tex. 1941). Conversely, a fiduciary duty arises out of agency law based upon a special relationship between two parties. *Johnson v. Brewer & Pritchard, P.C.*, 73 S.W.3d 193, 200, 45 Tex. Sup. Ct. J. 470 (Tex. 2002). The McGills' argument confuses a fiduciary duty with a duty to develop; yet these two duties are distinct and have developed under different legal theories. Thus, we will first address whether Bass owes the McGills a duty to develop Bass' land under the implied covenant doctrine. And, we will then address whether Bass owes the McGills a fiduciary duty based upon the two parties' existing relationship under the Erck property deed.

a) Implied Covenant to Develop Land

We have consistently stated that implied covenants are not favored by law and will not be read into contracts except as legally necessary to effectuate the plain, clear, unmistakable intent of the parties. *Powell*, 154 S.W.2d at 635; *Freeport Sulphur Co. v. Am. Sulphur Royalty Co.*, 117 Tex. 439, 6 S.W.2d 1039, 1042 (Tex. 1928). "It is not enough to say that an implied covenant is necessary in order to make the contract fair ... It must arise from the presumed intention of the parties as gathered from the instrument as a whole." *Powell*, 154 S.W.2d at 635. From these propositions, oil and gas jurisprudence recognizes an implied covenant to develop land in oil and gas leases after oil and gas are discovered in paying quantities. *Powell*, 154 S.W.2d at 635. "The evident intent of the parties in the execution of [the mineral lease] being the production of such minerals, possible only through operation and development, the obligation to operate with reasonable diligence and to reasonably develop the land, will be implied in order to effectuate this intent." *Grubb v. McAfee*, 109 Tex. 527, 212 S.W. 464, 465 (Tex. 1919).

No oil and gas lease exists here. Bass owns the Erck property, surface and mineral estate, in fee simple absolute. The McGills hold less than a 2% non-participating royalty interest in the Erck mineral estate. Bass acquired the general warranty deed to the Erck estate in Ann McGill's bankruptcy sale in 1990. There is nothing in the record to indicate this general warranty deed is anything other than a typical real estate transaction involving the conveyance of a fee simple estate. *Powell*, 154 S.W.2d at 635–636. An implied covenant to develop a mineral estate has never been read into general warranty deeds in Texas because the parties' intent in transferring a fee simple absolute estate could rarely, if ever, be said to place the grantor in a position to develop the land for the grantee. Id. at 635. We see no reason today to imply such a covenant as doing so would potentially place many Texas landowners in a position of owing a duty to remote royalty interest holders that would burden fee simple estates in a manner contrary to traditional property law. Accordingly, we refuse to imply a covenant into the Erck property deed. Bass, as the Erck property owner, therefore owes no implied duty to develop his land to the McGills, as remote royalty interest holders, under the doctrine of implied covenants.

b) Fiduciary Duty

The McGills rely on our holdings in *Manges v. Guerra*, 673 S.W.2d 180, 183, 27 Tex. Sup. Ct. J. 421 (Tex. 1984), and *Schlittler v. Smith*, 128 Tex. 628, 101 S.W.2d 543, 545 (Tex. 1937), for the proposition that a mineral estate owner owes non-participating royalty interest owners a fiduciary duty, or in the alternative, a duty of good-faith and fair-dealing to develop the mineral estate.

Smith involved a dispute over the meaning of the word "royalty" in a general warranty deed. Id at 543. The grantor claimed that the reservation of a "royalty" interest included bonuses and rental payments. Id. at 544. Nonetheless, we held that the word "royalty" has a specific meaning in oil and gas law that does not include bonuses and rental payments. Id. And, although the deed did not explicitly state the royalty interest amount the grantor would receive if the land were developed, we stated that "self-interest on the part of the grantee may be trusted to protect the grantor as to the amount of royalty reserved. Of course, there should be the utmost fair dealing on the part of the grantee in this regard." Id. at 545.

Hence, *Smith* involved a very narrow duty in which a grantee, after executing a mineral lease, owes a duty of the utmost fair dealing to protect the amount of the grantor's royalty. Id. The Smith duty, therefore, arises in conjunction with the execution of a lease. Here, Bass has not executed an oil and gas lease. Accordingly, as grantee, Bass' duty to protect the amount of the McGill's royalty reservation does not arise until Bass executes a lease. Id. at 544–45. Hence, the McGill's reliance on *Smith* is misplaced. Furthermore, even if an oil and gas lease existed in this case, the McGills' royalty reservation amount is explicitly stated in the general warranty deed. Under the execution of a lease, Bass would be aware of exactly how much to pay the McGills if oil and gas were ever discovered on the Erck property. In *Smith*, the deed did not explicitly state the amount of the royalty reservation Id. at 544. Therefore, the McGills' reliance on *Smith* is misplaced as Smith does not give rise to a duty in Bass because no lease has been executed and no royalty payment exists.

The McGills also rely on our holding in *Manges* to support their breach of fiduciary duty claim against Bass. 673 S.W.2d at 180. *Manges* involved a dispute between mineral estate co-tenants. Manges purchased one-half of the mineral estate and executive leasing rights from the Guerra family with the Guerras retaining the other 50% ownership interest in the mineral estate. The Guerras sued Manges for self-dealing in leasing a portion of the estate to himself at unfair terms. Id. We stated that "[a] fiduciary duty arises from the relationship of the parties ... that duty requires the holder of the executive right, Manges in this case, to acquire for the non-executive every benefit that he exacts for himself." Id. at 183–84. Accordingly, we held that Manges breached his fiduciary duty to the Guerras by making a lease to himself under numerous unfair terms. Id. at 184.

Manges extends the *Smith* duty by creating a fiduciary duty between executive and non-executive interest holders in mineral deeds. Id. at 180. Here, the McGills hold a non-participating royalty interest in Bass' mineral estate. By definition, all non-participating royalty interests are non-executive interests. Thus, like *Manges*, the relationship between Bass and the McGills is one of executive and non-executive. Because *Manges* held that the executive owes the non-executive a fiduciary duty, the McGills correctly state that Bass owes them a duty to acquire every benefit for the McGills that Bass would acquire for himself. Id. at 184.

What differentiates this case from *Manges*, however, is that no evidence of self-dealing exists here. Bass has not leased his land to himself or anyone else. Bass has yet to exercise his rights as the executive. Because Bass has not acquired any benefits for himself, through executing a lease, no duty has been breached. Thus, the present facts are distinguishable from *Manges*.

Traditionally, a duty to develop land arises under an oil and gas lease either through an explicit provision in the lease or through an implied covenant to develop. No lease exists in this case. Furthermore, without exercising his power as an executive, Bass has not breached a fiduciary duty to the McGills as non-executives. Because the record both fails to demonstrate the existence of an oil and gas lease that would create an implied duty to develop and fails to show that Bass has breached his duty as the executive, we hold the trial court abused its discretion in compelling trade secret production. *In re Continental*, 979 S.W.2d at 615; *Walker*, 827 S.W.2d at 839.

B. ADEQUATE REMEDY BY APPEAL

When an abuse of discretion exists, we must next determine whether the party resisting trade secret discovery has an adequate appellate remedy. We have held that no adequate appellate remedy exists if a trial court orders a party to produce privileged trade secrets absent a showing of necessity. *In re Continental*, 979 S.W.2d at 615. We have determined that the data are trade secrets and that the record is bare of any viable claim against Bass that would necessitate the production of the 3–D seismic trade secret data in this case. Thus, because the district court abused its discretion in compelling Bass to produce the data, there is no adequate appellate remedy, and therefore, we hold the McGills are not entitled to trade secret production.

IV. CONCLUSION

Bass met his burden to show geological seismic data are trade secrets. Furthermore, because the record fails to establish the existence of a duty to develop or that Bass has breached a fiduciary duty, the McGills have not made the requisite showing of necessity under *In re Continental*. Hence, the trial court abused its discretion compelling Bass to produce the trade secrets, and no adequate appellate remedy exists. Therefore, we conditionally grant mandamus relief and order the trial court to vacate its order compelling the production of Bass' seismic data. The writ will issue only if the trial court fails to act in accordance with this opinion.

NOTES

1. The problem included before the case above reflects the facts of Veteran's Land Bd. v. Lesley, 281 S.W.3d 602 (Tex. App.–Eastland 2009, pet. granted). In *Lesley*, the 11th Court of Appeals overruled the district court, holding that since the developer in *Lesley* had not leased the land, the fiduciary duty had not been activated and suggested the rule, "The court's analysis in *Bass* establishes that no breach of fiduciary duty can occur until the executive exercises the executive rights." Id. at 605.

After the Texas Supreme Court accepted certiorari (352 S.W.3d 479), the executives and the nonexecutives tried to align the situation in *Lesley* with the two main cases they each saw as favorable to their cause. The executives cited *Bass*, echoing the 11th Court of Appeals notion that the executive's duty does not arise until leasing. In contrast, the nonexecutives invoked *Manges* and the self-dealing involved in that case, arguing that the executive's reading of *Bass* which allows no leasing could not be reconciled with both *Manges* and the executive self-dealing they claim in *Lesley*.

Instead of establishing a specific rule regarding the fiduciary duty of executive in relationship to a refusal to lease, the Texas Supreme Court instead reasoned that "an executive's refusal to lease must be examined more carefully. If the refusal is arbitrary or motivated by self-interest to the non-executive's detriment, the executive may have breached his duty." (Id. at 491) and remanded the issue for the trial court to decide whether the executive breached its duty by not entering into leases. Instead of expanding on the issue, the court briefly explained that it would not give a "general rule" because of the varying circumstances from which an executive could be liable for breaching his fiduciary duty, stating, "We need not decide here whether as a general rule an executive is liable to a non-executive for refusing to lease minerals, if indeed a general rule can be stated, given the widely differing circumstances in which the issue arises." Id.

The Texas Supreme Court held that the executive right owner violated its fiduciary duty by placing the restrictive covenants on the individual lots. Although the court recognized that the executive wanted to protect the homeowners from disruptive activity related to drilling, the court stated that protection could be achieved through the accommodation doctrine. Id. at 492.

Do you think *Lesley* can be distinguished from *Bass* on the basis of the existence of self-dealing contrary to the fiduciary duty owed by the executive to the non-executive interests?

Contrast also the result in *Bass* with the suggestion in Hlavinka v. Hancock, 116 S.W.3d 412 (Tex. App. 2003) that a landowner whose mineral estate is burdened with an NPRI and who is offered several opportunities to lease at the going rates in the area, but arbitrarily refuses to lease under any circumstances may have breached the duty owed to the nonexecutives.

2. Can an owner of a non-executive mineral fee interest compel the executive rights holder to lease the non-executive fee minerals? Even if a non-executive mineral owner can compel an executive to lease its own interest, can it compel the executive mineral right owner to lease the minerals of the executive? Consider the situation where the Party A owns seventy-five percent (75%) of the minerals but none of the executive rights of Blackacre and Party B owns twenty-five percent (25%) of the minerals and all of the executive rights of Blackacre. Even if Party B leases Party A's interest, if it does not lease its own 25% interest, the prospect will likely not be economic to develop at all. This is because, in the event a producing well is drilled, the unleased interest requires the lessee/developer pay 25% of all proceeds to Party B without first multiplying that amount by the royalty fraction in the lease.

3. The concept of executive rights can also encompass the duty that the holder of executive rights has towards non-participating royalty interest (NPRI) holders and other such non-participating interests. In Mims v. Beall 810 S.W.2d 876 (Tex. App. 1991, no writ) the court considered a case where the holder of executive rights leased to a family member for a 1/8 royalty. The holders of NPRIs covering the same tract sued, claiming that the lessor had breached its fiduciary duty to the NPRI holders because the 1/8 royalty was unreasonably low when compared to similar leases in the region. Echoing *Manges*, the trial court instructed the jury to hold the executive rights to the "utmost good faith and fair dealing" standard and the jury found that the lessor had breached their duty to the NPRI holders. The court of appeals opined the trial court had properly charged the jury with "utmost good faith and fair dealing" being defined as,

> "[T]he use of the same degree of diligence and discretion in exercising the rights and powers held by an executive owner as would be utilized by the average landowner seeking to obtain all the benefits that could be reasonably obtained for himself and for his non-participating royalty owner from a disinterested third party in an arms-length transaction."

Id. at 879.

This charge is almost identical in content to that found in *Manges* and *Hlavinka*, and like those cases, the result in *Mims* centered upon the breach of duty that the executive rights holder had to the non-executive right interests. In addition, in finding for the NPRI holders, the court seized upon the similarity of the self-dealing in *Manges* and its similarity to the lessors' 1/8 royalty lease to their son in the case before them.

4. In Luecke v. Wallace, 951 S.W.2d 267 (Tex. App. 1997) Union Pacific Resources Company offered to lease land from the defendant, who owned the mineral estate subject to the plaintiff's right to a 1/2 nonparticipating interest of all royalties and 1/2 of all bonus exceeding $50 per acre. Union Pacific initially offered a 1/5 royalty and a $150 per acre bonus. At the defendant's request, the transaction was restructured. The defendant first leased the land to his solely owned oil company for a 1/8 royalty and a bonus of less than $50 an acre. The defendant's company then transferred the lease to Union Pacific for a $150 per acre bonus and a 1/5 royalty. Plaintiff sued for actual and punitive damages, alleging the defendant had breached his duty of utmost

good faith and fair dealing. The trial court granted plaintiff a summary judgment.

On appeal, defendant argued that plaintiff should not have prevailed on her summary judgment motion because she had failed to establish that she could have made a better deal than the 1/8 royalty and low bonus that the defendant's company had paid for the lease. How should the appellate court have ruled on this argument?

Evidence in *Luecke* indicated that Union Pacific had discovered the plaintiff's interest in the royalties and bonus while performing a title search and had sent the defendant a letter notifying him that he must provide the lessee with "evidence of payment of 1/2 of excess bonus money above $50.00 per acre and a Ratification and Rental Division Order setting for the interest division." Defendant asked Union Pacific to restructure the transaction two days after defendant received the letter, and Union Pacific agreed.

Could Union Pacific have been held liable for breach of any obligation it owed the plaintiff? See Kimsey v. Fore, 593 S.W.2d 107 (Tex.Civ.App. 1979, writ ref'd n.r.e.) and Ernest E. Smith, The Standard of Conduct Owed by Executive Right Holders and Operators to the Owners of Nonparticipating and Nonoperating Interests, 32 Inst. on OIL & GAS L. & TAX'N 241, 253–55 (1981).

5.   Non-executive mineral interest owners have no power to lease their minerals. Rather, that power resides in the hands of the owner of the executive right. The power of the executive right owner, and the level of consideration that he or she must give the non-executives is still being litigated.

Current case law in Texas also does not allow a non-executive mineral rights owner to self-develop. Lesley at 492. In *French v. Chevron*, the Texas Supreme Court held that a non-executive cannot self-develop his own minerals, saying, "The right to develop is a correlative right and passes with the executive right." French at 797.

Consider a scenario wherein one party owns only the executive right, and a second party owns one hundred percent (100%) of the rest of the mineral estate. From a public policy standpoint, which favors oil and gas development, do you think that in such a situation that the second party should not be allowed to self-develop? While the above may be an extreme case, a more realistic scenario might involve one or more non-executives with a strong majority of the mineral interest, high oil and gas prices, and an executive right holder with an associated minority or even trivial mineral interest that may not have a motivation to lease. If the non-executive(s) are willing and able to self-develop, even if it may mean carrying the executive right holder's smaller interest, should the executive rights holder still be able to prevent production? One commentator posits that it should not be so: "The public policy of Texas that favors regulated mineral development and basic tenants of real property law both argue that the executive right does not prevent the non-executive mineral co-tenants from conducting self-development efforts. The right of development is one of five 'sticks' that comprise the total package of mineral ownership, a separate and equal right to that of the executive right. By claiming that the owner of the executive right can also prevent the non-executive mineral co-tenants from self-development, the two sticks of self-development and executive rights have been impliedly combined, leaving the non-executive with only the rights to the money from leasing and possible production—the rights to collect bonus, delay rentals and royalty." Christopher Kulander, Big Money vs. Grand Designs: Revisiting the Executive Right to Lease Oil & Gas Interests, 42 TEX. TECH. L. REV. 1 (2009).

6. Utmost fair dealing has long been urged as the appropriate standard of conduct that the holder of the executive right should owe to the owner of a royalty or other nonparticipating interest. The author of an early and influential article, Lee Jones, Jr., Non-participating Royalty, 26 TEX. L. REV. 569 (1948), argues that the imposition of a fiduciary duty is not consistent with the probable intent of the parties, especially where an arm's length transaction is involved, whereas the ordinary good faith required of parties to the typical contract does not adequately protect the owner of the nonparticipating interest. Utmost fair dealing is characterized as an intermediate standard that requires the holder of the executive right to act with a reasonable regard for the interests of the other party. "The courts should require the same degree of diligence and discretion on the part of the holder of the exclusive-leasing privilege as would be expected of the average landowner who, because of self-interest, is normally willing to take affirmative steps to co-operate with a prospective lessee and make a *bona fide* effort to agree upon the bonus payable for, and the delay rentals and royalties to accrue under, an oil, gas and mineral lease." Id. at 581. Does this statement mean that the holder of the exclusive leasing power must execute a lease with the same terms as he would have executed in the absence of any outstanding interest in a third party?

The "utmost fair dealing" standard is not without its critics. In "New Remedies for Executive Duty Breaches: The Courts Should Throw J.R. Ewing Out of the Oil Patch," 40 Ala.L.Rev. 187, 217 (1988), Professor Joshua Morse and Ms. Jaimie Ross argue that the utmost fair dealing standard:

> [G]ives with one hand while it takes with the other. The proponents of this standard say that where parties' interests diverge, the executive will not be "bound to a standard of selfless conduct" but may protect his self-interest as though no outstanding nonexecutive interest existed; then they restrict this freedom by forbidding the executive to act "for the purpose of benefiting himself at the expense of nonexecutives." Thus, this definition declares that executives can act for self-interest, but cannot act to benefit themselves at the nonexecutives' expense. * * * No directions tell the courts how to resolve this conflict. Executives and nonexecutives compete for lease benefits, so if one gains the other loses. How can executives act for their self-interest, but not at nonexecutives' expense? The standard contains internal contradictions that render it unusable.

The authors go on to argue that a fiduciary standard is not only appropriate for the relationship between the executive and nonexecutive but also provides the courts with needed flexibility in devising proper remedies for breach.

Most jurisdictions have adopted the utmost fair dealing standard. See, e.g., Welles v. Berry, 434 So.2d 982 (Fla.App.1983); Schroeder v. Schroeder, 479 N.E.2d 391 (Ill.App.5 Dist. 1985); Murdock v. Pure–Lively Energy 1981–A

Ltd., 775 P.2d 1292 (N.M. 1989); and J.M. Huber Corp. v. Square Enterprises, Inc., 645 S.W.2d 410 (Tenn.App. 1982). Others have applied standards ranging from mere absence of fraud to the highest fiduciary obligation. See Hemingway § 2.2(D). One Texas appellate court has suggested that the duty of utmost good faith requires the executive to obtain "the highest royalty possible," although later language in the opinion indicates that a lease providing "for at least the fair market royalty prevalent in the surrounding area" will satisfy the requirement. Dearing, Inc. v. Spiller, 824 S.W.2d 728, 733 (Tex.App.–Fort Worth 1992).

7. Although most litigation involving the executive right has dealt with the duty owed by the executive, questions have also arisen concerning its duration, assignability and divisibility. Most courts that have addressed the issue have concluded than an exclusive executive right is not personal to the original holder and survives her death. E.g. Stone v. Texoma Prod. Co., 336 P.2d 1099 (Okla. 1959) and Mull Drilling Co., Inc. v. Medallion Petroleum, Inc., 809 P.2d 1124 (Colo.App. 1991). The Texas Supreme Court in Day & Co., Inc. v. Texland Petroleum, Inc., 786 S.W.2d 667 (Tex. 1990) characterized the executive right as "an interest in property, an incident and part of the mineral estate like the other attributes such as [the rights to receive] bonus, royalty and delay rentals." The case involved the right to lease an undivided 1/2 non-executive interest in the mineral estate. Keaton and Young had reserved the non-executive interest in a deed that conveyed the other undivided half interest in the mineral estate plus the exclusive executive right to Day & Co. Subsequently Day & Co. executed a deed that conveyed an undivided 1/4 interest in the mineral estate, reserved the remaining undivided 1/4 in Day & Co. but made no mention of the right to lease the Keaton and Young 1/2 non-executive interest. Both Day & Co and its grantees later claimed the exclusive right to execute a lease binding the non-executive interest. Overruling an earlier case that had treated the executive right as analogous to a power of appointment, the court held that the transfer of the executive right was governed by principles of property law. Since Day & Co. did not expressly reserve the right to lease the Keaton and Young non-executive interest, that right passed under the deed to Day & Co.'s grantee.

8. Is the multiplicity of ownership that often results from the assignment or inheritance of an exclusive executive right consistent with the probable purpose for creating such a right? Dividing the executive right among several owners can create serious problems. For example, suppose that Morales conveys an undivided one-half interest in the mineral estate and the exclusive right to execute leases to Vasquez. Upon Vasquez's death all of her interests in the land are inherited by her four children. Each now owns an undivided 1/8 interest in the mineral estate. What rules govern their ability to lease the nonparticipating mineral interests retained by Morales? If only one of the holders of the executive right executes a lease can he bind any part of the nonparticipating interests? Alternatively, what if a majority wish to lease the land, but one of the four refuses to sign the lease? Should all of the current holders of the executive right have to join in the lease to bind Morales's interest? For a suggested solution to these types of problems, see W. Randolph Elliott, The Executive Right, 42 Tex.L.Rev. 865, 884–85 (1964).

How could a lawyer avoid the problem of multiple ownership when drafting a deed that creates an executive right?

9. There is some authority for the proposition that an exclusive executive right divorced from any ownership interest in the mineral estate is subject to the rule against perpetuities. In Dallapi v. Campbell, 114 P.2d 646 (Cal.App. 1941) the California Supreme Court treated such a right as a special power of appointment and held that it was void because it could be exercised beyond the period permitted by the rule. Would the result be different in a jurisdiction that follows the *Day & Co.* view that the executive right is a severable interest in property?

E. MEANING OF "MINERALS" AND NAMED SUBSTANCES

Lawyers frequently see mineral deeds containing grants or reservations of "oil, gas, and other minerals" or "coal and other minerals" or even "all minerals." Although somewhat less common, single-substance grants and reservations, such as those referring only to "oil," or "gas" or "coal," may also be encountered. Whether expansive ("all minerals"), narrow ("all the coal") or inclusive of several named substances ("coal, oil and gas"), these formulations can raise difficult problems of interpretation.

1. GRANTS AND RESERVATIONS OF "OTHER MINERALS"

Historically, one of the most contentious issues has been the meaning of the term "other minerals" in a conveyance or reservation of "oil, gas and other minerals." The origin of general references to "other minerals" following specific references to "oil and gas" is historically obscure. One possibility is that it grew out of the concern that casinghead gas or distillate produced with oil and gas would not be covered by a deed or lease references to "oil and gas." There is Oklahoma precedent to that effect. Mullendore v. Minnehoma Oil Co., 246 P. 837 (Okla. 1926). Alternatively, the reference may have begun as a hedge against the discovery of unrelated valuable substances. Where one valuable substance is found, there are likely to be other different but valuable substances as well; oil and gas and coal, for example, are frequently found in sedimentary strata in the same geographic areas. Finally, there may well have been a purely speculative motive behind use of the term. It would not be surprising if the general reference to "other minerals" is frequently used simply in the hope that the extra language will give the grantee (who usually prepares the deed) rights that he would not otherwise have. Professor Horner has suggested that the term is used "hoping that it would catch anything that may be valuable in the future." Edwin P. Horner, Lignite—Surface or Mineral, 31 Ark.L.Rev. 75, 97 (1977).

Whatever the historical reason for the use of "other minerals," its interpretation is of substantial economic importance. Natural resources are finite, and many substances that may be found while searching for oil and gas or that may be produced with oil and gas are dwindling in supply. Furthermore, there have been rapid technological and economic advances that have radically changed the value of substances once viewed as valueless or even dangerous by-products. Coalbed methane gas, which is the subject of the next subsection, and natural gas in shale deposits are an excellent examples, but they are far from the only ones. Sulphur, which was once regarded as a troublesome impurity in natural gas and oil, is now often a profitable byproduct. What may be especially significant is the impact of some methods of extraction—especially strip mining—upon the surface estate. Where open pit mining is involved, courts have frequently defined—and redefined—the term "minerals" in an attempt to make an equitable adjustment of the rights of the surface and mineral owners.

MOSER v. UNITED STATES STEEL CORP.

676 S.W.2d 99 (Tex.1984).

On Motion for Rehearing

Campbell, Justice.

This is a suit to quiet title to an interest in uranium ore. We must determine whether uranium is included in a reservation or conveyance of "oil, gas and other minerals." The trial court awarded title to the defendant mineral owners, and the court of appeals affirmed the trial court judgment. We affirm the judgments of the courts below, and hold that uranium is a part of the mineral estate.

The Mosers, plaintiffs, and the Gefferts, defendants, own neighboring tracts of land in Live Oak County. Prior to 1949, the boundary between the Mosers' land and that of the Gefferts was a winding road. In 1949, the road was straightened and, as a result, no longer represented the true boundary between the two ranches. The new road separated a 6.77 acre tract of the Geffert ranch on the Moser's side of the road and a 6.42 acre tract of the Moser ranch on the Geffert's side of the road. To avoid crossing the highway to reach their tracts, the Mosers' predecessor in title and the Gefferts executed similar deeds conveying the surface estates of the isolated tracts to the other party. The 1949 deeds contain identical language reserving:

> [A]ll of the oil, gas, and other minerals of every kind and character, in, on, under and that may be produced from said tract of land, together with all necessary and convenient easements for the purpose of exploring for, mining, drilling, producing and transporting oil, gas or any of said minerals.

Substantial quantities of uranium were discovered on the 6.77 acre tract. The Mosers, as surface owners of the 6.77 acre tract, sued the Gefferts to establish ownership of the uranium. The Gefferts, as owners of the mineral estate under the 6.77 acre tract, counterclaimed to establish that uranium is one of the "other minerals" reserved from the conveyance of the surface.

At trial, the parties offered conflicting evidence on the depth of the uranium deposits and the effect its removal would have on the surface. Special issues were submitted based on the test set out by this Court in Reed v. Wylie, 554 S.W.2d 169 (Tex. 1977) (*Reed* I): if substantial quantities of the mineral lie so near the surface that extraction, as of the date of the severance of the surface and mineral estates, would necessarily have destroyed the surface, the surface owner has title to the mineral. The jury found there would have been no substantial surface destruction at the time the deed was executed. The trial court accordingly held the uranium was a part of the mineral estate retained by the Gefferts in the 1949 deed.

After the Mosers' appeal to the court of civil appeals, but prior to final disposition by that court, we rendered our decision in Reed v. Wylie, 597 S.W.2d 743 (Tex. 1980) (*Reed* II). The court of civil appeals held that *Reed* II should govern the appeal. In *Reed* II, we modified the rule of *Reed* I by holding that a substance "near the surface" is a part of the surface estate if it is shown that any reasonable method of production, at the time of conveyance or thereafter, would consume, deplete, or destroy the surface. 597 S.W.2d at 747. A deposit within 200 feet of the surface was held to be "near the surface" as a matter of law. In addition, we held if a surface owner establishes ownership of a substance at or near the surface, the surface owner owns the substance beneath the tract at whatever depth it may be found. Id. at 748. The *Moser* court of civil appeals found, as a matter of law, that at the time of trial the only reasonable method of mining uranium from the tract was by in-situ leaching or solution mining, a process which it found did not result in substantial destruction of the surface. 601 S.W.2d at 734.[1] Accordingly, the court of civil appeals affirmed.

We have previously attempted to create a rule to effect the intent of the parties to convey valuable minerals to the mineral estate owner, while protecting the surface estate owner from destruction of the surface estate by the mineral owner's extraction of minerals. In so doing, we decided that determinations of title should be based on whether a reasonable use of the surface by the mineral owner would substantially harm the surface. Application of this rule has required the determination of several fact issues to establish whether the owner of the surface or the mineral estate owns a substance not specifically referred to in a grant, reservation or exception. As a result, it could not be determined from the grant or reservation alone who owned title to an unnamed substance. Determining the ownership of minerals in this manner has resulted in title uncertainty. We now abandon, in the case of uranium, the *Acker* and *Reed* approach to

---

1. We note that under *Reed* II, however, the correct time frame for determining the existence of a surface destructive method of mineral extraction was not solely at the time of trial (the time used by the court of civil appeals), or solely at the time of conveyance, but the time of conveyance or *thereafter*. See Reed v. Wylie, 597 S.W.2d 743, 747 (Tex. 1980).

determining ownership of "other minerals" and hold that title to uranium is held by the owner of the mineral estate as a matter of law.

In Texas, the mineral estate may be severed from the surface estate by a grant of the minerals in a deed or lease, or by reservation in a conveyance. This severance is often accomplished by a grant or reservation of "oil, gas and other minerals." Consequently, Texas courts have had many occasions to construe the scope of the term "other minerals." We have determined that some unnamed substances have been impliedly conveyed or reserved in mineral conveyances by cataloging each, on a substance-by-substance basis, as part of the surface or mineral estate as a matter of law. See, e.g., Sun Oil Co. v. Whitaker, 483 S.W.2d 808 (Tex. 1972) (fresh water not included in mineral estate reservation of "oil, gas, and other minerals"); Heinatz v. Allen, 217 S.W.2d 994 (Tex. 1949) (devise of "mineral rights" held not to include limestone and building stone); Atwood v. Rodman, 355 S.W.2d 206 (Tex.Civ.App.–El Paso 1962, writ ref'd n.r.e.) ("oil, gas, and other minerals" did not include limestone, caliche, and surface shale); Union Sulphur Co. v. Texas Gulf Sulphur Co., 42 S.W.2d 182 (Tex.Civ.App.–Austin 1931, writ ref'd) (solid sulphur deposits conveyed by ordinary oil and gas lease); Praeletorian Diamond Oil Ass'n v. Garvey, 15 S.W.2d 698 (Tex.Civ.App.–Beaumont 1929, writ ref'd) (gravel and sand not intended to be included in lease for "oil and other minerals"); Reed v. Wylie, 597 S.W.2d 743 (Tex. 1980) (near surface lignite, iron and coal is part of the surface estate as a matter of law).

In making these determinations of ownership, our courts have considered a number of construction aids. We have refused to employ the *ejusdem generis* rule of construction to limit the term "oil, gas and other minerals" to hydrocarbons. Likewise, we have acknowledged that the scientific or technical definition of a disputed substance is not determinative of whether it is a mineral, because the term "other minerals" would then "embrace not only metallic minerals, oil, gas, stone, sand, gravel, and many other substances but even the soil itself." Heinatz v. Allen, 217 S.W.2d 994, 997 (Tex. 1949). Such a construction would eliminate any distinction between the surface and the mineral estates. We have, however, approved of considering whether the substance is thought to be a mineral within the ordinary and natural meaning of the term. The knowledge of the parties of the value, or even the existence of the substance at the time the conveyance was executed has been found to be irrelevant to its inclusion or exclusion from a grant of minerals. * * * In Acker v. Guinn, 464 S.W.2d 348 (Tex. 1971), we quoted with approval Professor Eugene Kuntz' theory that the proper focus when construing an implied grant of minerals is the general, rather than the specific, intent of the parties. We adopted the view that the general intent of parties executing a mineral deed or lease is presumed to be an intent to sever the mineral and surface estates, convey all valuable substances to the mineral owner regardless of whether their presence or value was known at the time of conveyance, and to preserve the uses incident to each estate. Id. at

352; Kuntz, *The Law Relating to Oil and Gas in Wyoming,* 3 Wyo.L.J. 107, 112 (1949).

Professor Kuntz suggested the apparently irreconcilable conflict between the rights of the surface fee and the right of a mineral owner who takes a mineral under an implied grant to extract his mineral could be compromised as follows:

> The rights of the surface owner to subjacent support and his right to the use of the top-soil in its place would have to be respected, and at the same time, the owner of the mineral fee should have a right of extraction. Since the right of extraction could only be exercised by destruction of the surface owner's enjoyment, it could only be accomplished with compensation for the damages to the surface estate * * *. Specific mention of the substance, however, together with the usual provisions for extraction, would demonstrate a specific intention to make the surface right subject to the rights of access for purposes of extraction and would not make the mineral owner accountable for necessary damage flowing therefrom.

Kuntz, "The Law Relating to Oil and Gas in Wyoming," 3 Wyo.L.J. 107, 115 (1949).

We now hold a severance of minerals in an oil, gas and other minerals clause includes all substances within the ordinary and natural meaning of that word, whether their presence or value is known at the time of severance. We also hold uranium is a mineral within the ordinary and natural meaning of the word and was retained in the Gefferts' conveyance of the 6.77 acre tract to the Mosers. We continue to adhere, however, to our previous decisions which held certain substances to belong to the surface estate as a matter of law. See, e.g., Heinatz v. Allen, 217 S.W.2d 994 (Tex. 1949) (building stone and limestone); Atwood v. Rodman, 355 S.W.2d 206 (Tex.Civ.App.–El Paso 1962, writ ref'd n.r.e.) (limestone, caliche, and surface shale); Fleming Foundation v. Texaco, 337 S.W.2d 846 (Tex.Civ.App.–Amarillo 1960, writ ref'd n.r.e.) (water); Psencik v. Wessels, 205 S.W.2d 658 (Tex.Civ.App.–Austin 1947, writ ref'd) (sand and gravel); Reed v. Wylie, 597 S.W.2d 743 (Tex. 1980) (near surface lignite, iron and coal).

Having established that the mineral owner has title to uranium, we now must determine the issue of reasonable use of the surface estate by the uranium owner. The mineral owner, as owner of the dominant estate, has the right to make any use of the surface which is necessarily and reasonably incident to the removal of the minerals. This is an imperative rule of mineral law; a mineral owner's estate would be worthless without the right to reach the minerals. A corollary of the mineral owner's right to use the surface to extract his minerals is the rule that the mineral owner is held liable to the surface owner only for negligently inflicted damage to the surface estate.

Restricting the mineral owner's liability to negligently inflicted damage to, or excessive use of, the surface estate is justified where a mineral is specifically conveyed. It is reasonable to assume a grantor who expressly conveys a mineral which may or must be removed by destroying a portion of the surface estate anticipates his surface estate will be diminished when the mineral is removed. It is also probable the grantor has calculated the value of the diminution of his surface in the compensation received for the conveyance. This reasoning is not compelling when a grantor conveys a mineral which may destroy the surface in a conveyance of "other minerals."

We hold the limitation of the dominant mineral owner's liability to negligently inflicted damages does not control in a case such as this, in a general conveyance of "other minerals." When dealing with the rights of a mineral owner who has taken title by a grant or reservation of an unnamed substance such as this, liability of the mineral owner must include compensation to the surface owner for surface destruction.[2]

This holding does not affect the right of the mineral owner to enter the surface estate and use so much of the surface as is reasonably necessary to remove the minerals. As in the case of the mineral owner who takes under a specific grant, the mineral owner under a grant of "other minerals" is restricted in his use of the surface estate by the dictates of the "due regard" or "accommodation doctrine." This rule is applied when the surface owner and mineral owner are attempting to use the surface estate for two conflicting and incompatible uses. We held, in Getty Oil Co. v. Jones, 470 S.W.2d 618 (Tex. 1971), that even though the mineral owner held the dominant estate, he must exercise his rights of surface use with due regard for the rights of the surface owner.

Because of the extent of public reliance on our holdings in Acker v. Guinn, 464 S.W.2d 348 (Tex. 1971), and Reed v. Wylie, 597 S.W.2d 743 (Tex. 1980), and because of an inability to foresee a coming change in the law, the rules announced in this case are to be applied only prospectively from the date of our original opinion, June 8, 1983.

We affirm the judgments of the courts below. We hold as a matter of law the Gefferts are the owners of the uranium in the 6.77 acre tract.

RAY, JUSTICE, dissenting. [deleted]

NOTES

1. Not all courts would agree with the statement that a mineral owner's right to use the surface in any way that is "necessarily and reasonably

---

2. This holding does not affect the statutory duty of the mineral owner, or his lessee, to reclaim the surface after surface mining. See Texas Uranium Surface Mining and Reclamation Act, NAT.RES.CODE ANN. §§ 131.001 to–.270. See also Surface Mining Control and Reclamation Act of 1977, 30 U.S.C. § 1201 et seq. The Texas Act requires an operator who is surface mining uranium to submit and effect a reclamation plan or lose his performance bond and face civil and criminal penalties. TEX.NAT.RES.CODE ANN. § 131.101 to–.270. The Code provides the surface owner with an opportunity to have the land classified as unsuitable for surface mining if he believes the land cannot be reclaimed to the Code's strict standards. Id. §§ 131.038.,–.039,–.047. The Code also demands all reclamation efforts to proceed as contemporaneously as practicable with the surface mining operation. Id. § 131.102(b)(14).

incident to the removal of the minerals" is "an imperative rule of mineral law." Contrast the position of a Pennsylvania court, which held that the owner of the mineral estate has no right to engage in strip mining unless the grant or reservation contains specific language authorizing such a method of extraction. The court ruled that deed language authorizing the mineral owner to "perform all acts incident or appertaining to the mining, drilling and carrying away of coal" was insufficient. In re Condemnation by County of Allegheny, 719 A.2d 1 (Pa.Commnwlth. 1998). See also Fiore v. County of Allegheny, 16 A.3d 1179 (Pa. Commnwlth. 2011) (placing the burden on the owner of the coal estate to show that the parties to the original deed intended to allow strip mining).

2.   In *Moser*, the Texas Supreme Court said that it was abandoning the surface destruction test that it had adopted in Acker v. Guinn and developed in the two Reed v. Wylie cases, because those decisions had resulted in title uncertainty. Texas is not unique in having changed the test that is applied in construing grants of "other minerals." In North Dakota, for example, there was uncertainty over whether the courts would apply the surface destruction test. See Robert E. Beck, "And Other Minerals" as Interpreted by the North Dakota Supreme Court, 52 N.D.L.Rev. 633 (1976). This uncertainty of deed construction was compounded by a series of legislative definitions of "minerals," which vacillated between a narrow and a broad construction of the term. Compare 1955 N.D.Sess.Laws ch. 235, § 1 and 1975 N.D.Sess.Laws ch. 422, § 1 with N.D.Cent.Code § 47–10–24,–25. See also George E. Reeves, The Meaning of the Word "Minerals," 54 N.D.L.Rev. 419 (1978).

3.   The *Moser* court excludes from the scope of its ruling substances such as sand and gravel, building stone, limestone and surface shale, caliche, water, and near surface lignite, iron ore and coal, because those substances had previously been held "to belong to the surface estate as a matter of law." Is the clarity of the new rule enhanced by the court's reaffirmation of its holding in *Acker* that near surface iron ore is not a mineral? Equally important, is the listing exclusive? If not, how does one tell whether a court's ruling that a substance is or is not a mineral is based upon the intention of the parties or is a holding as a matter of law?

4.   The significance of the *Moser* decision to Texas mineral titles is limited by its application only to instruments executed after June 8, 1983. Thousands of deeds severing mineral and surface ownership had been executed before that date. In spite of the court's stated goal of providing a more definite standard than the surface destruction test, the Texas Supreme Court reaffirmed the prospective-only nature of the ordinary and natural meaning test in Friedman v. Texaco, Inc., 691 S.W.2d 586 (Tex. 1985), and applied the surface destruction test in construing a reservation of "other minerals" in a deed executed in 1959. In Plainsman Trading Co. v. Crews, 898 S.W.2d 786 (Tex. 1995) the court resolved a conflict in appellate court decisions by holding that the surface destruction test also applies to non-participating royalties created before June 8, 1983. Although royalty owners have no right to authorize mining of any kind and so cannot endanger the surface estate, the court reasoned that a royalty interest is carved from the mineral estate and so cannot include a substance that is not a part of the mineral estate. Is this a convincing rationale in a case like *Plainsman*, where the non-participat-

ing royalty was created before the mineral and surface estates had been severed? Is there some other rationale that would support applying the surface destruction test to pre-*Moser* royalties?

5. The *Moser* approach to the meaning of "other minerals" is expansive. Consider the merits of the more restrictive definition used in the following case.

OKLAHOMA EX REL. COMMISSIONERS OF LAND OFFICE v. BUTLER

753 P.2d 1334 (Okla. 1987).

SIMMS, JUSTICE.

* * *

Claude Butler, the appellee, brought action to quiet title in the rights to the coal on land he owned in fee simple. His predecessors in interest acquired the property by three separate patents from the Commissioners of the Land Office by public sale of state-owned lands with notice as provided by law. One patent reserved to the state "an undivided fifty per centum of all oil, gas, and other mineral rights" and the other two patents contained reservations of "an undivided fifty per centum of all oil, gas and other minerals and mineral rights". The notice of sale stated that the land would be sold subject to the state's reservation of fifty percent of "all the oil, gas and other mineral rights". The Commissioners counterclaimed to quiet the state's claimed interest in the coal based on the reservations.

Mr. Butler sought summary judgment arguing that the phrase "oil, gas and other minerals" has an established meaning in Oklahoma; that it includes only oil and gas and other minerals produced as a component or constituent thereof. The Commissioners disagreed, urged the Court to hold that the phrase was ambiguous and to allow extrinsic evidence of the intent of the original parties at the time of the conveyances to be introduced.

The trial court found no significant distinction between the language of the patents, held that the reservations were unambiguous and disallowed any extrinsic evidence of intent. Based on our decision in *Panhandle Cooperative Royalty Co. v. Cunningham*, Okla., 495 P.2d 108 (1972), the trial court held that the state had reserved only fifty percent of the oil, gas and minerals produced as constituents and components thereof, whether hydrocarbon or non-hydrocarbon, and that no other mineral, including coal, was reserved by the state. The trial court granted summary judgment in favor of Mr. Butler and quieted title to all the coal in him.

The Commissioners bring this appeal contending primarily that the trial court erred by disallowing extrinsic evidence to show intent of the original parties. They argue that the phrase "oil, gas and other minerals" is ambiguous and that extrinsic evidence should therefore be allowed to show the intent of the original conveying parties. The same arguments have been presented and rejected repeatedly by this Court.

The phrase "oil, gas and other minerals" is, of course, common in the oil and gas industry. It, and its close variants, are standard terms which appear in very early oil and gas leases, and have commonly been used in fee conveyances and reservations, such as those before us today. The meaning of "oil, gas and other minerals" has been the subject of frequent and spirited litigation nationwide as well as in Oklahoma. Questions as to which unspecified minerals are included within the phrase have been answered with differing results under different rationales. See, for instance the annotation Grant, Lease, Exception, or Reservation of "Oil, Gas, and Other Minerals", or the Like, as Including Coal or Metallic Ores, 59 A.L.R.3rd 116 (1974).

We have a consistent line of cases which offer no possible result except that a reservation of "oil, gas and other minerals", standing alone, does not include coal. See, e.g., *Barker v. Campbell–Ratcliff Land Co.*, 167 P. 468 (Okla. 1917)—reservation of "mineral rights" includes oil and gas; *Beck v. Harvey*, 164 P.2d 399 (Okla. 1945)—reservation of "mineral royalty" does not include gravel; *State, ex rel., Comm'rs of Land Office v. Hendrix*, 167 P.2d 43 (Okla. 1946)—conveyance of an interest in and to all the oil, petroleum gas, coal, asphalt and all other minerals of every kind and character does not include gravel; *Cronkhite v. Falkenstein*, Okla., 352 P.2d 396 (1960)—mineral deed for "oil, gas and other minerals" does not include gypsum rock; and *Holland v. Dolese Co.*, Okla., 540 P.2d 549 (1975)—reservation of an interest in "the mineral rights" did not include quarried limestone.

In Oklahoma we have relied primarily on the rule of ejusdem generis to determine the scope of such mineral conveyances. Ejusdem generis is simply a rule of interpretation. It gives guidance to the ordinary insight that when specific words are followed by general words those specific words restrict the meaning of the general. Thus, where the phrase "other minerals" follows the enumeration of particular classes of minerals such as oil and gas, the general words will be construed as applicable only to minerals of the same kind or class as those specifically named. *Wolf v. Blackwell Oil & Gas Co.*, 186 P. 484 (Okla. 1920).

* * *

There is no longer room for question in Oklahoma. The rule of law has evolved in this state that "oil, gas and other minerals" is not ambiguous. "Oil, gas and other minerals" is not a description of the entire mineral estate. The phrase has a certain and definite meaning: it includes only oil and gas and those minerals produced as constituents and components thereof.

In *Panhandle* supra, the Court upheld the trial court's determination that a mineral deed granting interest in "oil, gas and other minerals" was not ambiguous and that extrinsic evidence of the parties' intent as to the inclusion of metallic minerals such as gold, silver and copper was inadmissible. There the defendants had also argued that the phrase was ambiguous and included "all minerals", and that extrinsic evidence should be allowed to show the parties' intention to include metallic minerals. The Court there did not rely on ejusdem generis, although it recognized it as a rule of construction which is a useful part of our law, but the Court did cite and rely on *Cronkhite v. Falkenstein,* Okla., 352 P.2d 396 (1960), which was an ejusdem generis case.

In *Panhandle* the Court conducted a historical review of litigation on the issue which left no doubt that the phrase "other minerals" resulted from early litigation over rights to other distinct substances produced at the well head—particularly casinghead gas—under mineral deeds and conveyances of interest in "oil and/or gas" and "oil and gas". The phrase "other minerals" has a special purpose in extending the connotation of "oil and gas".

Applying the statutory rules of interpretation, 15 O.S.1961, § 151, et seq., the Court held that the deed in question granted interest in oil and gas and other minerals produced as oil or gas or produced as a component or constituent thereof whether hydrocarbon or non-hydrocarbon, but did not grant any other mineral or the right to produce any other mineral, including copper, silver, gold, or any other types of metallic ores or metallic minerals. *Panhandle,* supra at 113.

Following *Panhandle* the Court decided Allen v. Farmers Union Cooperative Royalty Co., Okla., 538 P.2d 204 (1975), where metallic minerals were once again the subject of a quiet title action brought to determine whether they were included in a reservation of "all oil, gas and mineral rights". The same arguments which were presented and rejected in *Panhandle* and are now presented in the instant case, were before the Court in *Allen,* and were summarily rejected.

The appellants there criticized the decision in *Panhandle,* and contended that the reservation is unambiguous and clearly meant "all minerals" of every kind. Relying on the rule of ejusdem generis the Court determined that a reservation of "all oil, gas and mineral rights" has essentially the same meaning as "all oil, gas and other minerals" as set forth in *Panhandle* * * * i.e., oil, gas and other minerals produced as a component or constituent thereof, whether hydrocarbon or non-hydrocarbon, and does not convey any other mineral or the right to produce any other mineral including copper, silver, gold or any other types of metallic ores or metallic minerals. The Court reaffirmed its holding in *Panhandle* that a deed granting oil, gas and other minerals is not ambiguous and consequently no extrinsic evidence of an interpretative nature could be introduced to ascertain the intention of the parties.

* * *

The rule of law is clearly well settled in Oklahoma. "Oil, gas and other minerals" or similar phrases are not, standing alone, ambiguous and do not allow the introduction of parol evidence. The meaning of the words must be derived from common understanding which means that "other minerals" shall be limited to minerals similar in kind and class to "oil and gas''. Coal is not similar in kind and class to oil and gas. Appellant urges us to find that since all three belong to the class hydrocarbons, they are similar and belong together. It is not, however, the chemical composition which is important, but rather those traits which a man of common understanding would find to be similar or dissimilar. While coal has some chemical similarities to oil and gas, dissimilarities dominate. Coal is a solid substance extracted from the land in ways fundamentally different from those used to obtain oil, gas or a "component or constituent thereof", *Panhandle*, 495 P.2d, at 113. We therefore reaffirm our consistent position that "oil, gas and other minerals" and similar phrases are not ambiguous. They do not include coal or other unspecified minerals.

Appellants also suggest that slight differences in the wording between the minutes of resolution of the Commissioners to sell the property, the notice of sale, and the patent support their argument that extrinsic evidence should be allowed as to intent of the original parties.

It is fundamental that a patent is solemn evidence of title; it is a written public grant of the highest character, and high evidence of its own validity. Where government officers have issued a patent in due form which on its face is sufficient to convey title to land described, it is to be treated as valid in actions of law. The recitals of the patent are conclusive as to the estate conveyed, and no evidence can be received for construction thereof. A patent is deemed to have been issued regularly and the presumption exists that all usual necessary steps were taken before the title was perfected by patent.

* * *

Appellants' final argument is that a sacred trust of the school lands existed for the benefit of the beneficiaries and that as part of that trust, Commissioners were forbidden by the Constitution to diminish the corpus. They contend that by conveying coal rights without specific remuneration therefor, a diminution of the corpus was effected which was beyond the Commissioners authority. In support of this argument, appellants rely on *Lassen v. Arizona*, 385 U.S. 458 (1967), which held that when trust lands are obtained by anyone, including the state, the trust must be compensated in money for the full appraised value. *Lassen* is inapplicable here for, inter alia, this land sold for more than its appraised value. Appellants' argument would mean that every time a new mineral was discovered on subject lands, appellants could argue in retrospect that at the time of sale it did not receive full compensation. We reject the argument and find the notion contrary to the language and spirit of the Enabling Act, the Oklahoma Constitution, and common sense.

The trial court correctly granted the motion for summary judgment and we affirm.

JUDGMENT AFFIRMED.

DOOLIN, C.J., and HODGES, KAUGER and SUMMERS, JJ., concur.

HARGRAVE, V.C.J., and LAVENDER, OPALA and WILSON, JJ., dissent. [The dissenting opinion has been omitted.]

NOTES

1. Other courts have been more receptive to the argument that "oil, gas and other minerals" is ambiguous and that extrinsic evidence should be admitted to determine its meaning. A somewhat different approach was taken in Christensen v. Chromalloy Am. Corp., 656 P.2d 844 (Nev. 1983). The Nevada Supreme Court spoke favorably of the surface destruction test that had once been espoused by the Texas courts as a method for determining the meaning of "other minerals," but then remanded the case for admission of extrinsic evidence as to whether the parties intended to allow strip mining.

2. As the two preceding principal cases illustrate, courts have usually rejected claims that grants or reservations of "minerals" include sand, gravel, caliche, limestone and similar substances. They have, however, used different rules of construction in reaching this result. Several have adopted a test similar to that used in *Moser* and concluded that in the absence of clear deed language to the contrary, sand, gravel, clay and other road building materials are not regarded as minerals under the ordinary meaning of the term. See, e.g., Florman v. Mebco Ltd. Partnership, 207 S.W.3d 593 (Ky.App. 2006); Farley v. Booth Bros. Land & Livestock Co., 890 P.2d 377 (Mont. 1995), and Miller Land & Mineral Co. v. Wyoming State Highway Commission, 757 P.2d 1001 (Wyo. 1988). An Illinois court used the "ejusdem generis" rule to reach the same result with respect to limestone. In construing a reservation of "coal and other minerals" it pointed out that limestone is unlike coal in that it cannot be burned or mined without destroying the surface, as is generally the case with coal. Save Our Little Vermillion Environment, Inc. v. Illinois Cement Co., 725 N.E.2d 386 (Ill.App.3 Dist. 2000). See also Keith v. Kinney, 140 P.3d 141, 150 (Colo.App. 2005) ("oil, gas and other minerals").

3. Throughout much of the west and southwest subsurface fresh water is a highly valuable commodity. Many of the states in this region have adopted the prior appropriation doctrine. See, e.g. Yeo v. Tweedy, 286 P. 970 (N.M. 1929) (discussing the rejection of the traditional English common law of water rights in favor of the prior appropriation doctrine in the western states). Other states, however, adhere to the doctrine that the overlying landowner has a right to the water beneath his land. To the extent permitted by state and local regulation, such landowners often drill wells and sell the water. In Texas, a deed severing the right to water beneath the surface owner's land was upheld in City of Del Rio v. Clayton Sam Colt Hamilton Trust, 269 S.W.3d 613 (Tex. App.–San Antonio 2008, pet. denied). To date, rather limited authority holds that fresh water is not included in a grant or reservation of "oil, gas and other minerals." See Vogel v. Cobb, 141 P.2d 276 (Okla. 1943), Fleming Foundation v. Texaco, Inc., 337 S.W.2d 846 (Tex.Civ.App. 1960, writ ref'd n.r.e.); Dyegard Land Partnership v. Hoover, 39 S.W.3d 300 (Tex. App. 2001); Kuntz § 50.2. Should the result be different with respect to subsurface salt water, which usually has value only for use in connection with water flooding or other oil and gas related operations? See Robinson v. Robbins Petroleum Corp., 501 S.W.2d 865 (Tex. 1973); Kuntz § 50.2.

4. By majority view, oil and gas are "other minerals." McCormick v. Union Pacific Resources Co., 14 P.3d 346 (Colo. 2000), which adopts the majority position, contains a good discussion of the position taken by most courts on this issue. The minority view, under which oil and gas are not deemed included within a grant or reservation of "minerals," is followed in Pennsylvania, and perhaps Ohio, Arkansas, and Indiana. See Kuntz § 13.3.

5. Few issues have produced as many and as diverse judicial approaches as the meaning of "other minerals." In this regard note the comment of Professor Anderson:

> [O]nly two polar views are defensible on policy grounds. Either "minerals" should include all substances enjoyed by the process of extraction/depletion, with the exception of common variety substances encountered at the surface (e.g., sand and gravel), or the term should include only those substances that are specifically mentioned in the reservation or grant of minerals. These polar views are preferable because they promote efficiency and certainty of title, they allow title examiners to counsel clients on ownership in a consistent and clear manner, and they recognize the futility of a case-by-case approach that searches for the parties' subjective intent by considering extrinsic evidence.

Anderson, Discussion Note, 146 O & GR 246, 248 (2001).

As Professors Anderson, Kuntz and Lowe have all noted, the flaw in any process that seeks to determine the parties' intent is that the parties almost certainly never considered the issue. If the parties had been aware of the presence or value of the disputed substance or of the manner of its removal, they would have included express language in their deed. As an alternative to a fruitless search for the parties' intent, Professor Lowe and the late Professor Kuntz have urged adoption of the "manner of enjoyment" test under which a grant or reservation of "other minerals" would include "all substances presently valuable in themselves, apart from the soil, whether their presence is known or not, and all substances which become valuable * * *." Lowe Chapter 7.B.3 and Eugene O. Kuntz, The Law Relating to Oil and Gas in Wyoming, 3 Wyo.L.J. 107, 112–13 (1947), reprinted in 34 Okla.L.Rev. 28, 33–34 (1981). Is Professor Anderson's exception for "common variety substances encountered at the surface" consistent with this test?

Would the "manner of enjoyment" test mean that the mineral owner has the right to destroy the surface if that is necessary to extract a newly discovered substance, such as potash, that would have value "apart from the soil"? See Spurlock v. Santa Fe Pacific R. Co., 694 P.2d 299 (Ariz.App. 1984) and John Lowe, Developments in Nonregulatory Oil and Gas Law, 39 Inst. on Oil & Gas L. & Tax'n 1–1, 1–9 to 1–12 (1988).

6. Patents and deeds from the federal government frequently contain reservations of "minerals" or specific substances and "other minerals." In interpreting these terms federal courts have looked to legislative intent in the statute authorizing the reservation and have often interpreted that intent broadly in favor of the retention of substances in the government. Thus, in United States v. Union Oil Co., 549 F.2d 1271 (9th Cir.Cal. 1977), a reservation of "coal and other minerals" in a patent issued under the Stock–Raising Homestead Act of 1916, 43 U.S.C. §§ 291 to 301, was held to include

geothermal rights. In Millsap v. Andrus, 717 F.2d 1326 (10th Cir.Okla. 1983), a reservation of "oil, coal, gas or other minerals" included in a deed given under the Osage Allotment Act was held to include limestone-dolomite, and in Watt v. Western Nuclear, Inc., 462 U.S. 36 (1983), gravel was held to be a mineral reserved to the United States under the Stock–Raising Homestead Act of 1916. Contrast the result reached in BedRoc Ltd. L.L.C. v. United States, 541 U.S. 176 (2004) where the court refused to extend the holding in *Western Nuclear* to a reservation of "coal and other valuable minerals" in a patent granted under the Pittman Underground Water Act of 1919. The court reasoned that the term "valuable" indicated a Congressional intent not to include substances such as sand and gravel. A still different approach was taken in United States v. Hess, 194 F.3d 1164 (10th Cir. 1999), which involved a reservation of "all oil and gas, coal and other minerals" in a patent given by the United States pursuant to an exchange of Indian-trust land[6] for private land. The court vacated the district court's ruling that gravel had been reserved as a matter of law and remanded the case for a determination of the parties' intent. The court pointed out that, unlike the statutes under which other federal patents had been awarded, the statute authorizing the land exchange did not require any minerals to be reserved; rather, it merely required that exchanged lands be of equal value and gave the Secretary of the Interior discretion to issue exchange patents with or without mineral reservations.

State courts have also often taken a broad approach in construing mineral reservations in a state. In Schwarz v. Texas, 703 S.W.2d 187 (Tex. 1986), the Texas Supreme Court, distinguishing earlier cases involving conveyances between private parties, concluded that the state's reservation of minerals in land sold for agricultural purposes under the Land Sales Act of 1895 included coal and lignite, even though they were extracted by strip mining. *Schwarz* was followed in Texas v. Cemex Construction Materials, 350 S.W.3d 396 (Tex.App.–El Paso 2011), which involved a reservation of minerals in a grant of state school lands. The court held that, as a matter of law, the state had retained ownership of all deposits of granite, limestone, gravel, sand, and any other mineral substances of economic or commercial value. A vigorous dissent in *Butler* criticized the majority for failing to take a similar approach based upon a careful scrutiny of statutory language authorizing the sale of Oklahoma's state-owned lands. 753 P.2d at 1341–1342. In New Mexico, where there appears to be some support for the surface destruction test in conveyances between private landowners, the courts have held that whether a reservation of minerals by the state includes surface substances, such as quarry rock, is determined by the intent of the parties at the time the patent was issued. See Prather v. Lyons, 267 P.3d 78 (N.M.Ct.App. 2011) (holding that "based on the sale transaction documentation, including the patent, and also based on all of the surrounding circumstances, the intent of the conveyance transaction was that the rock was included in the reservation of 'all minerals of whatsoever kind' in the patent.")

7. Difficult issues arise if different substances in the mineral estate are conveyed to different owners. As the following section illustrates, this situa-

---

6. Tribal lands and issues involved in leasing them are covered in Chapter 7.

tion has often occurred when one person owns rights to gas and another owns the rights to coal and lignite in which natural gas has been adsorbed. Conflicts are likely to arise in a variety of situations, but are almost certain to occur if the only feasible method of mining one of the substances precludes or makes the extraction of the other far more expensive. In some situations development by one party may not only conflict with development by the other party, but may even preclude it. American Energy Corp. v. Datkuliak, 882 N.E.2d 463 (Ohio App. 7 Dist. 2007) provides a good example. The defendants had conveyed: "all the coal," but reserved the right oil and gas along with the right to drill through the coal. Although the case was ultimately dismissed as moot, the court held that the grantee, by receiving "all the coal," had the right to extract all the coal and in doing so could require any well drilled through the coal to be plugged.

As discussed earlier, analogous conflicts are likely to arise where land is subject to both a wind lease and an oil and gas lease. See, e.g., Ernest E. Smith, Steven K. DeWolf & Roderick E. Wetsel, Texas Wind Law § 3.02 (LexisNexis 2011). What property-law and common-law principles could be applied? Is the "first-in-time" doctrine an appropriate way to resolve such disputes? For a brief discussion of possible approaches, see K.K. Duvivier & Roderick E. Wetsel, "Jousting at Windmills: When Wind Power Development Collides with Oil, Gas and Mineral Development," 55 Rocky Mt. Min. L. Inst. § 9.01 at § 9.06 (2009).

2. OWNERSHIP OF COALBED METHANE GAS; CONSTRUING "COAL," "OIL," "GAS," "OIL AND GAS," AND OTHER NAMED SUBSTANCES

Problems similar to those encountered in construing "minerals" also arise with respect to a named substance or substances, such as "coal" or "oil and gas." The issue has gained increased importance with the development of coalbed methane gas and gas shales.

At this point in time most of the reported cases involve claims of ownership to coalbed methane gas. The usual controversy is whether a grant of "coal" or, conversely, a grant of "oil and gas" includes ownership of coalbed methane gas. Coalbed gas is formed as a by-product of the process by which peat turns into coal, and is primarily a lower quality mixture of the same hydrocarbons found in natural gas. The coal acts as a reservoir of the gas, which is found in and around coal seams and is absorbed in the micropores of coal. When coal is mined, the gas is released. It can also be commercially exploited separately from the coal.

NCNB Texas National Bank, N.A. v. West, 631 So.2d 212 (Ala. 1993) contains a brief description of the three basic methods of producing coalbed methane gas:

A gob well is one drilled from the surface of the earth down to a stratum where Coalbed Gas released from a coal mine 'gob' can be extracted. The gob is produced by the longwall mining method, in which a huge machine grinds progressively into a face, or 'wall,' in the coal seam to tear away the coal, which is then conveyed to the surface. As the mining machine grinds further and further into the wall, it leaves behind it a void into which the ceiling of the mine collapses [creating a 'gob' of rubble] and into which great quantities of Coalbed Gas collect.... Some degree of subsidence extends all the way to the surface, and the fractures in the overlying strata extend from the gob area upward toward the surface. Thus, Coalbed Gas from the gob may travel upward into non-coal strata, where it may be collected and extracted through the gob well. Of all three methods of Coalbed Gas production, this one is the most prolific.

A horizontal borehole is, as the name implies, a hole bored horizontally into the coal seam from a point within the coal mine itself. The seam releases some of its adsorbed or trapped Coalbed Gas into the borehole from which the gas may then be produced.

Finally, a vertical degasification well is one drilled more or less vertically from the surface and directly into an unmined coal seam to extract such Coalbed Gas as may be trapped or collected. The release of the Coalbed Gas from the coal seam into the vertical degasification well may be increased by various methods of fracturing the coal seam in the vicinity of the bottom of the well. The fracturing methods generally involve forcing water, other substances, or a combination thereof down the well and into the coal seam. An emerging method is to blast water out the bottom end of the well so violently that it rips out an area of coal. This method may evolve into a way of producing not only Coalbed Gas but also coal itself.

631 So.2d at 215.

The issue of ownership of coalbed methane gas arises in situations where rights in coal and rights to oil and gas are held by different parties and necessarily involves a consideration of the various methods of producing the gas. If a court concludes that the owner of the coal also owns coalbed methane gas, does the owner have the right to drill "gob wells" to produce the gas from overlying strata where it has migrated? Conversely, if the coalbed methane gas is deemed to belong to the owner of "gas," can the owner use either the "horizontal borehole" or "vertical degasification" methods of production?

CENTRAL NATURAL RESOURCES, INC.
v. DAVIS OPERATING CO.,

201 P.3d 680 (Kan. 2009).

The opinion of the court was delivered by JOHNSON, J.:

Central Natural Resources, Inc. (Central) appeals the district court's order denying its motion for partial summary judgment and granting the defendants' summary judgment motions in a quiet title action to determine ownership of methane gas in the coal formations of 16 tracts of Labette County land. Agreeing with the district court's determination that the warranty deeds conveying the coal to Central's predecessor in title did not convey the methane gas contained within the coal, we affirm.

FACTUAL OVERVIEW

During a period from 1924 through 1926, Central's predecessors in interest paid money to the owners of 16 separate tracts of land in Labette County, Kansas, in return for coal warranty deeds. All of the deeds recited that the landowners were conveying "all coal without reference to quality or quantity, ... together with the right to mine and remove same."....

Neither Central nor any of its predecessors in title have ever exercised the right to mine and remove coal from any of the tracts .....

Three-quarters of a century after the coal transfers, the defendant oil and gas companies obtained oil and gas leases on some of the tracts. Pursuant to those leases, certain defendant companies drilled for and obtained production of CBM. Thereafter, Central filed a quiet title action, claiming ownership of the CBM in all 16 tracts through the 1924–26 coal deeds, and seeking damages for trespass and conversion for the drilling and production activities.

* * *

Subsequently, the district court issued a memorandum decision and order, granting summary judgment to the defendants on the issue of CBM ownership, i.e., finding that the deeds conveying "all coal" to Central's predecessors in title did not transfer ownership of the CBM. However, the court clarified that its order was not intended to address the plaintiff's claim for trespass or for damages to the coalbed inflicted by defendants in the process of extracting CBM.

* * *

COALBED METHANE GAS

Central's arguments rely in part on the physical properties of CBM. It stresses that CBM is created during the natural process by which coal is formed. In Amoco Production Co. v. Southern Ute Indian Tribe, 526 U.S. 865, 872–73, 119 S.Ct. 1719, 144 L.Ed.2d 22 (1999), the United States Supreme Court explained that process as follows:

"We begin our discussion as the parties did, with a brief overview of the chemistry and composition of coal. Coal is a heterogeneous, noncrystalline sedimentary rock composed primarily of carbonaceous materials. See, e.g., Gorbaty & Larsen, Coal Structure and Reactivity, in 3 Encyclopedia of Physical Science and Technology 437 (R. Meyers ed.2d ed.1992). It is formed over millions of years from decaying plant material that settles on the bottom of swamps and is converted by microbiological processes into peat. D. Van Krevelen, Coal 90 (3d ed.1993). Over time, the resulting peat beds are buried by sedimentary deposits. As the beds sink deeper and deeper into the earth's crust, the peat is transformed by chemical reactions which increase the carbon content of the fossilized plant material. The process in which peat transforms into coal is referred to as coalification.

"The coalification process generates methane and other gases. R. Rogers, Coalbed Methane: Principles and Practice 148 (1994). Because coal is porous, some of that gas is retained in the coal. CBM gas exists in the coal in three basic states: as free gas; as gas dissolved in the water in coal; and as gas 'adsorbed' on the solid surface of the coal, that is, held to the surface by weak forces called van der Waals forces. These are the same three states or conditions in which gas is stored in other rock formations. Because of the large surface area of coal pores, however, a much higher proportion of the gas is adsorbed on the surface of coal than is adsorbed in other rock. When pressure on the coalbed is decreased, the gas in the coal formation escapes. As a result, CBM gas is released from coal as the coal is mined and brought to the surface."

Central further urges us to consider the historical context in which the coal deeds were executed. At that time, the parties would have been well aware that coal contained a gas, sometimes referred to as "marsh gas" or "fire damp," which posed a significant danger of explosion as the coal was being mined. Cf. Amoco, 526 U.S. at 875–76, 119 S.Ct. 1719 (in 1909–10, CBM considered a dangerous waste product of coal mining which frequently sparked explosions). Statutes and regulations of the time placed a duty upon the owner/operator of a coal mine to provide for the safety of miners, including the proper control or ventilation of the CBM. Cf. Amoco, 526 U.S. at 876, 119 S.Ct. 1719 (federal coal mine safety law of 1891 prescribed specific ventilation standards for coal mines of a certain depth to dilute and render harmless the noxious or poisonous gases).

Therefore, the context within which the coal deeds were executed was that CBM was a dangerous substance which had no economic value, but which, to the contrary, placed an additional burden and expense on the coal mine owner/operator to insure their miners' safety. Moreover, as Central conceded at oral argument, the parties could not have been privy to the current scientific knowledge as to the manner in which CBM is adsorbed within the coal and, accordingly, would have considered the CBM to be a gas that was separate and distinct from the solid coal.

* * *

PROPOSED LEGAL THEORY

Central's first tack is to propose that we adopt a "first severance/container theory" rule of law. Under that "rule," if a coal deed is the first conveyance which severs any mineral interest from the fee simple absolute estate, the grantee acquires ownership of everything that is contained within the coal formation, unless the deed contains a specific reservation of other minerals . . . . .

Central relies on case law from Alabama, Illinois, and Pennsylvania, contending that those states have adopted the "container theory." See

Vines v. McKenzie Methane Corp., 619 So.2d 1305 (Ala.1993); Continental Resources v. Illinois Methane, 364 Ill.App.3d 691, 301 Ill.Dec. 887, 847 N.E.2d 897 (2006); United States Steel Corp. v. Hoge, 503 Pa. 140, 468 A.2d 1380 (1983). However, other jurisdictions have held that the ownership of coal does not include the ownership of CBM. See Michael F. Geiger, LLC v. United States, 456 F.Supp.2d 885, 886 (W.D.Ky. 2006); Carbon County v. Union Reserve Coal Co., 271 Mont. 459, 898 P.2d 680 (1995); Harrison–Wyatt, LLC v. Ratliff, 267 Va. 549, 593 S.E.2d 234 (2004). Decisions in Wyoming have gone both ways, focusing on the facts and circumstances of each particular deed. See Mullinnix LLC v. HKB Royalty Trust, 126 P.3d 909 (Wyo. 2006); Caballo Coal v. Fidelity Exploration, 84 P.3d 311 (Wyo. 2004); Hickman v. Groves, 71 P.3d 256 (Wyo. 2003); McGee v. Caballo Coal Co., 69 P.3d 908 (Wyo. 2003); Newman v. RAG Wyoming Land Co., 53 P.3d 540 (Wyo. 2002). Given the unique facts of each case, together with differing state laws, the cases from other states are not easily synthesized or particularly persuasive.

In this state, all minerals belong to the landowner and are considered part of the realty so long as they reside on, in, or under the land. However, "[w]hen they escape and go into other lands, or come under another's control, the title of the former owner is gone." Lanyon Zinc Co. v. Freeman, 68 Kan. 691, 696, 75 Pac. 995 (1904). A severance of the surface and mineral rights is accomplished by either a conveyance of the land with an express reservation of the minerals, or by a conveyance of the mineral or mining rights. After the severance, two separate estates exist, each being a distinct freehold estate of inheritance....

Central's argument recognizes that the mineral interest in land can be further divided by severing a particular mineral. In other words, only one mineral, such as coal, can be conveyed, resulting in different entities owning different minerals. Indeed, at oral argument, Central acknowledged that the coal deeds did not give it ownership of the gas which had escaped from the coalbed, i.e., it does not claim to own all of the gas under the subject real estate. Thus, Central's theory would effect a split ownership of all the remaining minerals, with the landowner still owning all noncoal minerals except those that may be located within a seam of coal, even though the deeds did not explicitly convey any mineral other than coal.

Pointedly, the coal deeds did not purport to convey any particular stratum or horizon, e.g., the Pittsburg–Weir formation. They conveyed all the coal, wherever situated, presumably because there might be several seams of coal underlying the property. Nevertheless, Central claims that the coal deeds must, by necessity, convey the entire stratum because the mining of the coal consumes all of the structure and destroys all of the minerals within the stratum. Granted, each deed specifically grants the right to mine and remove the coal, which would permit the removal of the entire stratum, plus such of the surrounding strata as may be necessary to effect the coal removal. However, that right does not convey ownership of the entire stratum, any more than it conveys ownership of the dirt and rock outside the coalbed which might be removed to allow for a safe mining operation.

Moreover, Central offers nothing persuasive to recommend the adoption of its proffered temporal rule, which gives the grantee of the first mineral interest to be severed superior rights in and to the other minerals conveyed to another grantee (or still held by the landowner) simply based on the timing of the deed. While a "first-in-time, first-in-right" rule is a logical manner in which to deal with competing claims to the same property, it makes scant sense as a rule to enlarge or expand the property conveyed beyond that which was described in the deed.

In short, we decline to adopt an artificial rule of law mandating that a conveyance of all coal, with the right to remove and mine the same, always effects a transfer of everything that may be contained within the strata where coal may be found. Rather, if a coal deed is to include the CBM, that inclusion must emanate from the parties' intent.

RULES OF DEED INTERPRETATION

As an alternative to its proposed first severance/container theory rule of law, Central argues that the deeds should be interpreted as manifesting an intent to convey the CBM. The district court found that the parties to the deeds did not contemplate the transfer of CBM, because at that time, it was simply a dangerous by-product of coal mining. Central asks us to revamp the way in which we interpret deeds in order to divine such an intent.

We have well-established rules that are applied to the interpretation of both deeds and contracts. The primary consideration, when construing the meaning of a deed, is the intention of the grantor as gathered from an examination of the instrument as a whole.

We ordinarily recite that the first step is to determine whether the instrument is ambiguous. In doing so, we apply the plain, general, and common meaning of the terms used in the instrument. We refrain from adding words into the instrument which would impart an intent that was wholly unexpressed when it was executed . . . . .

An instrument is ambiguous when the application of pertinent rules of interpretation to the whole "fails to make certain which one of two or more meanings is conveyed by the words employed by the parties. If we find ambiguity, then

> "facts and circumstances existing prior to and contemporaneously with its execution are competent to clarify the intent and purpose of the contract in that regard, but not for the purpose of varying and nullifying its clear and positive provisions."

* * *

Central challenges the efficacy of our long-standing rules of interpretation, declaring that "[t]he most fickle of the analytical tools used to 'interpret' documents is the declaration that a document is either 'ambiguous' or 'unambiguous.' " It argues that extrinsic evidence is always necessary to establish a context for ascribing a meaning to the words the parties employed . . . . .

However, we do agree that whenever one endeavors to ascertain the meaning of written words, it is necessary to consider them within the context that they are used. Hence, we examine the whole document when determining its meaning. Moreover, certain terms may have a commonly understood meaning within a trade or industry, so that a commercial contract between parties that are regularly engaged in that trade or industry would be construed in the context of that common usage. However, that does not mean that the words employed are, inherently, always ambiguous, i.e., subject to two or more meanings. The ambiguity analysis endeavors to simply give effect to what the parties actually said they meant at the time of contracting. We are not prepared to abandon that analytical tool.

Likewise, we decline Central's invitation to divine from selected statements in prior cases a reasonably intelligent business person interpretive model. Our focus is to discern the actual agreement between these particular people, rather than what was the most intelligent agreement which could have been reached . . . . .

* * *

APPLICATION OF R.S.1923, 67–202

Central also contends that the provisions of R.S.1923, 67–202, the predecessor to K.S.A. 58–2202, control the extent of the property transferred by the coal deeds, notwithstanding any problem ascertaining the parties' intent. As noted above, that statute provided, in relevant part, that "every conveyance of real estate shall pass all the estate of the grantor therein, unless the intent to pass a less estate shall expressly appear or be necessarily implied in the terms of the grant." R.S.1923, 67–202. . . .

* * *

Central argues that the statute provides a presumption that the transfer of the "coal estate," together with the right to mine and remove the coal, transfers all of the grantors' interest in that estate, in the absence of an express reservation. Then, to make the argument work, Central declares that CBM is a part of the "coal estate" because it is a byproduct of the coalification process, it exists as part of the coal seam, and it is released as part of the coal mining process. We find the argument unavailing on more than one level.

The purpose of the statutory provision at issue is to clarify that a real estate conveyance passes all of the grantor's interest in the land, unless an intent to pass a lesser interest is manifested in the terms of the grant. For instance, in the cases relied upon by Central, the provision was applied to clarify that the grantors conveyed all the interest they owned in the subject real estate, because the deeds did not express an intent to retain any interest.

In this case, the grantors owned the entire fee simple absolute in the subject real estate. Obviously, the coal deeds did not pass all of that interest to Central's predecessors. By the express terms of the coal deeds, each grantor stated an intent to pass a lesser estate, i.e., only the coal. Given that the deeds expressly tell us that not all of the grantors' estates passed to the grantees, we need not resort to the statutory presumption.

Even if the statute could be construed as meaning that a conveyance of a lesser estate passes all of the grantor's interest in that lesser estate, it would not help in this instance. No one disputes that the deeds conveyed all of the grantors' interests in the coal. The disconnect in Central's argument is its declaration that CBM is part of the "coal estate."

Central does not dispute that coal, CBM, and oil are separate minerals which have different chemical compositions and which exist in different states, i.e., solid, gas, and liquid. However, it points out that CBM is produced by the coalification process, implying that the common origin makes the gas part of the coal estate. At oral argument, Central acknowledged that the gas which has escaped from the coalbed is not part of the "coal estate," but rather it is part of a "gas estate" which defendants have a right to produce. Of course, the escaped gas was formed in exactly the same manner as the gas which is currently held captive by the pressure on the coalbed. Thus, the genesis of CBM is not determinative.

* * *

Further, the fact that CBM escapes during the traditional coal mining operation does not persuade us that gas is coal. Today, it is apparently possible to drill from the surface and relieve the pressure, allowing the CBM to "desorb" and be collected, while leaving the coal rock in place. While Central complains that such a process invades and damages the coalbed, the issue of whether the gas producer must compensate the coal owner for damages resulting from the process of liberating the gas is not before us. The point is that CBM is a gas that can be produced without mining the coal rock, contradicting the assertion that the CBM is part and parcel of the "coal estate."

In short, we reject the notion that "all coal" should be read as meaning a "coal estate" that includes such of the natural gas which may be currently held captive within the coal formation. Therefore, CBM is not statutorily presumed to be conveyed by a grant of "all coal."

THE PARTIES' INTENT

* * *

As Central painstakingly sets forth in its brief, at the time of the subject deeds, the parties would have been aware that a gas, commonly referred to as "fire damp" or "marsh gas," was released during the process of digging coal out of the ground and that the gas was a source of great danger to life in coal mines. See Amoco, 526 U.S. at 874, 119 S.Ct. 1719. They would not have been privy to our current scientific knowledge about the manner in which a portion of the CBM remains captive within the coal, i.e., adsorbed to the surface of the rock. Rather, the common understanding at that time was that the term "coal" did not encompass CBM, "both because it is a gas rather than a solid mineral and because it was understood as a distinct substance that escaped from coal as the coal was mined, rather than as a part of the coal itself." Amoco, 526 U.S. at 874–75, 119 S.Ct. 1719. Therefore, the facts and circumstances existing in 1924–26 would suggest that a grantor's use of the term, "coal," was intended to refer only to the solid mineral. Accordingly, a grantor would have no reason to include a reservation of gas in a coal deed.

Moreover, the primary energy source of that era was coal. See Amoco, 526 U.S. at 875, 119 S.Ct. 1719 ("In contrast to natural gas, which was not yet an important source of fuel at the turn of the century, coal was the primary energy for the Industrial Revolution."). In historical context, the obvious purpose of the coal deeds was to effect the sale of the commodity which was valuable at the time, i.e., coal. In reality, the parties to the coal deeds probably had no specific intent regarding other unspecified minerals, such as coalbed methane. Pierce, Evaluating the Jurisprudential Bases for Ascertaining or Defining Coalbed Methane Ownership, 4 Wyo. L.Rev. 607 (2004).

* * *

Central wants us to consider that CBM was dangerous and life threatening for the miners and that the mine operator had a legal duty to ventilate and control the gas during the mining process. It then argues that a landowner surely would not have intended to reserve ownership of such a deadly substance. But, of course, on the flip side, one would not expect a grantee to voluntarily seek full ownership of the CBM, knowing it to be a worthless and hazardous material. To the contrary, one would suspect that a mine operator in those days would have been ecstatic if the landowner had removed the CBM prior to the commencement of mining operations, thus relieving the operator of the cost of meeting its legal responsibility to dispose of the gas.

* * *

In short, at the time the coal deeds were executed, the purpose of each grantor was to consummate the sale of the solid mineral coal. CBM was simply a hazardous by-product of the coal mining process. The parties did not intend, either expressly or impliedly, for the coal deeds to pass ownership of the CBM. The district court's granting of summary judgment on the issue of ownership is affirmed.

Affirmed.

NOTES

1. In Amoco Production Co. v. Southern Ute Indian Tribe, 526 U.S. 865 (1999), which is extensively cited in the principal case, the U.S. Supreme Court was faced with a claim that coalbed methane gas was included in patents issued under the Coal Lands Acts of 1909 and 1910. These patents conveyed all rights in the land except for coal, which was reserved by the United States.[7] In determining whether the grantees or the government owned the coalbed methane gas beneath these lands, the U.S. Supreme Court emphasized the hazardous nature of coalbed gas and the coal companies' need to control and vent the gas to prevent explosions. The Court reasoned that because coalbed methane gas was generally viewed as a dangerous waste product that posed a serious threat to mine safety, Congress would not have considered it as part of the solid rock fuel that the government was retaining, but as a hazardous by-product. The court also relied on the common understanding of coal in 1909 and 1910 as a solid mineral that was entirely distinct from the gas that escaped from the coal as it was mined.

2. Disputes involving deeds granting coal rights, but reserving rights to oil and gas in the grantor have also presented difficult problems of construction. United States Steel Corp. v. Hoge, 468 A.2d 1380 (Pa. 1983) was the earliest case fully to consider this issue. It involved a 1920 deed granting rights to "all the coal" and "all the rights and privileges necessary and useful in the mining and removing of said coal, including * * * the right of ventilation," while reserving in the grantor "the right to drill and operate through said coal for oil and gas without being held liable for any damages." In holding that the grantor had not retained ownership of coalbed methane gas, the Pennsylvania Supreme Court used reasoning similar to that of the U.S. Supreme Court in *Southern Ute*. The court stated that it was construing the deed language in accordance with its "plain meaning, in the common understanding, of the provisions * * * in light of conditions existing at the time of its execution." It then pointed out that

> [A]t the time this coal severance deed was entered into, although commercial exploitation of coalbed gas was known such operations were very limited and sporadic. Indeed for the most part coalbed gas was a dangerous waste product which had to be vented from the coal seam to allow for safe mining of the coal * * *

> Although the unrestricted term "gas" was used in the reservation clause, in light of the conditions existing at the time of its execution we find it inconceivable that the parties intended a reservation of all types of gas. * * * We find implicit in the reservation of the right to drill through the severed coal seam for 'oil and gas' a recognition of the parties that the gas was that which was commercially exploitable. It strains credulity to think that the grantor intended to reserve the right to a valueless waste product. * * * We find more logical and reasonable the interpretation

---

7. The lands patented to homesteaders under the 1909 and 1910 acts had previously been part of the Southern Ute Indian Tribe's reservation. In 1938 the U.S. granted the Tribe equitable title to the coal the U.S. had reserved in lands, but continued to hold legal title to the coal in trust for the benefit of the Tribe.

* * * that the reservation intended only a right to drill through the seam to reach the unconveyed oil and natural gas generally found in strata deeper than the coal.

468 A.2d at 1384–85.

Using somewhat similar reasoning the West Virginia court rejected an argument that a standard oil and gas lease gave the lessee the right to produce coalbed methane gas. The court expressed a concern that drilling into coal seams could make subsequent production of coal more hazardous and pointed out that in any event the lease in question was executed before the widespread commercial production of coalbed methane gas in the state. Energy Development Corporation v. Moss, 591 S.E.2d 135 (W.Va. 2003).

3. Several courts, including the Pennsylvania court in the preceding note, have invoked the "plain meaning" doctrine in attempting to resolve controversies over ownership of coalbed methane gas. However the plain meaning rule has led to different results in different jurisdictions. See, e.g., NCNB Texas National Bank, N.A. v. West, 631 So.2d 212 (Ala. 1993), where the Alabama Supreme Court applied the "plain meaning rule" in concluding that a grantor's reservation of "all" gas included the right to coalbed methane gas that migrated from the source coal beds into other strata, including "gob gas" that had migrated into the rubble resulting from longwall mining; but that the reservation did not include coalbed gas still contained within its source coal seam, which belonged to the owner of the coal and which could be produced by that owner.

4. The Wyoming court has rejected the argument that it should adopt a "plain meaning" approach and, instead, considers surrounding circumstances in determining ownership of coalbed methane gas under unambiguous deeds that sever the coal estate from rights in oil and gas. The court did not disagree that a "plain meaning" approach would result in greater predictability of ownership, facilitate title examination, and protect third-party reliance, but concluded that it would be inconsistent with the court's ultimate goal of construing a document in accordance with the intent of the parties. Mullinnix LLC v. HKB Royalty Trust, 126 P.3d 909 (Wyo. 2006). In other cases the Wyoming court has carefully parsed the language of each deed to determine ownership of coalbed methane gas. In McGee v. Caballo Coal Co., 69 P.3d 908 (Wyo. 2003) the court construed a 1973 deed conveying "all coal and all other minerals * * * contained in or associated with coal and which may be mined and produced with coal" and reserving "oil, gas and other minerals" in the grantor. In holding that coalbed methane gas was not included in the grant, the court reasoned that the word "with" refers to minerals that can be mined together with the coal and at the same time as the coal. It pointed out that neither today nor at any time in the past has coalbed methane gas been mined and produced *with* coal. The court reached the opposite result in Caballo Coal Co. v. Fidelity Exploration & Production Co., 84 P.3d 311 (Wyo. 2004), which involved a determination of rights to coalbed methane gas under deeds conveying "all of grantor's undivided interest in and to the coal upon and within and underlying the following described lands * * * together with * * * all other minerals, metallic or nonmetallic, contained in or associated with the deposits of coal conveyed hereby or which may be mined and produced with

said coal." Unlike the deed in *McGee*, the deeds at issue in *Caballo Coal Co.* did not require that minerals other than coal be mined *with* coal, but broadly granted *all* other minerals, both metallic and nonmetallic, *contained* in coal deposits. In view of an earlier ruling that coalbed methane gas is a mineral, the court held that the gas was clearly included within the granting clause. The Wyoming cases are discussed in David E. Pierce, Evaluating the Jurisprudential Bases for Ascertaining or Defining Coalbed Methane Ownership, 4 Wyoming L. Rev. 607 (2004).

5. As the principal case and notes indicate, state courts are sharply divided over whether coalbed methane gas should be deemed part of a coal seam or included within an oil and gas lease. Cimmaron Oil Corp. v. Howard Energy Corp., 909 N.E.2d 1115 (Ind.App. 2009), involves a controversy in which the landowners treated coalbed methane gas in still a third way: As a form of gas distinct from the "ordinary" natural gas included in an oil and gas lease. The landowners executed an oil and gas lease to defendants's predecessor, and several years later executed a coalbed gas lease to plaintiff. In a dispute over whether plaintiff or defendants had the right to drill for and produce coalbed methane gas the Indiana Court of Appeals ruled for the plaintiff. The court's conclusion was based primarily on the original parties' intent. It reasoned what when the oil and gas lease was executed the parties could not have contemplated that production of coalbed methane gas would be profitable and the lessors could not have intended to grant the oil and gas lessee the right to invade the underlying coal seam by fracturing it in order to release the gas it contained.

6. A similar dispute, based on reasoning similar to that used in *Cimmaron Oil*, has arisen in Pennsylvania with respect to the gas in the Marcellus shale formation. As noted previously, Pennsylvania has ruled that a grant or reservation of "minerals" does not include oil and gas. See Dunham v. Kirkpatrick, 101 Pa. 36 (Pa. 1882); Highland v. Commonwealth, 161 A.2d 390 (Pa.1960), *cert. denied*, 364 U.S. 901, (1960), and has also ruled that coalbed methane gas is a component of coal, which is clearly a mineral under Pennsylvania law; hence coalbed methane gas belongs to the owner of the coal, rather than to the owner of oil and gas rights. See United States Steel Corp. v. Hoge, 468 A.2d 1380 (Pa.1983). In Butler v. Charles Powers Estate, 29 A.3d 35 (Pa. Super. 2011) the defendant who had reserved an undivided half interest in the minerals, asserted a claim to one-half of the gas in the Marcellus shale beneath the land. His argument was based in significant part on the difference between "free flowing" gas in conventional reservoirs and gas contained in shale, which is extracted by hydrofracing. As such, it is similar to coalbed methane gas, which is contained in coal pores and is also often extracted by hydrofracing. Hence the ownership of both types of gas should be treated identically. The court remanded the case for a determination of whether Marcellus Shale is a "mineral" and therefore included within the defendant's reservation and, if so, is more similar to coal than to conventional oil and gas reservoirs. Until the issue is resolved, development of the Marcellus Shale in Pennsylvania may come to a near halt as a result of the concern of oil and gas companies that they have obtained leases from the wrong person.

7.   In EnerVest Producing, LLC v. Sebastian Mining, LLC, 2012 WL 1448549 (C.A. 8 Ark.) the 8th Circuit Court of Appeals considered two deeds that split the coal and all other minerals into two estates. An oil and gas company held the first deed that conveyed to it all the oil, gas, and other mineral rights, with the exception of coal rights, while a coal company held the coal and surface rights. The oil and gas company argued that it should not have to pay royalty on any natural gas to the coal company, including gas traceable to the coal. The coal company argued that coal bed methane gas was not considered valuable at the time the oil, gas, and mineral rights were conveyed and thus the original grantor had no intention for the mineral rights to include natural gas rights. The federal court of appeals held that a deed transferring surface and mineral rights included vapors and liquids and any other substance that is "embraced within the meaning of the word 'mineral.'"

8.   Controversies over the meaning and ownership of "gas" have arisen in other contexts. In some areas, such as the Texas Panhandle, gas and oil have been leased separately. A precise chemical or scientific definition of each is virtually impossible, because variations in pressure and temperature, both within the reservoir and at the point of extraction, determine whether hydrocarbons exist in a liquid or gaseous state. The issue is further complicated, because the owners of oil may also own casinghead gas. See, e.g., Amarillo Oil Co. v. Energy–Agri Products, Inc., 794 S.W.2d 20 (Tex. 1990), where the court concluded that in the absence of some clearly expressed intent to the contrary, an instrument severing rights in oil and casinghead gas from rights in natural gas would be construed as having incorporated the statutory definitions of the crucial terms. Thus "casinghead gas" was "any gas or vapor indigenous to an oil stratum and produced from the stratum with oil." Tex.Nat.Res.Code Ann. § 86.002(10). For a discussion of the regulatory aspects of the Panhandle Field controversy, see Smith & Weaver § 10.2(B).

Controversies over the meaning of "gas" can also arise in the context of an oil and gas lease. Since lease forms almost always provide for a higher royalty on "gas" than on "other minerals" or specifically named substances (other than oil), it is to a lessor's advantage to argue that any marketable substance that is in a gaseous form when produced is a "gas." Several cases have dealt with the issue of how the royalty on sulphur extracted from sour gas should be calculated. See First Nat'l Bank of Jackson v. Pursue Energy Corp., 799 F.2d 149 (5th Cir. Miss. 1986); Schwartz v. Prairie Producing Co., Inc., 727 S.W.2d 289 (Tex. App. 1987, writ ref'd n.r.e.) and Schwartz v. Prairie Producing Co., Inc., 833 S.W.2d 629 (Tex. App. 1992). The granting clause may also present a constructional issue. For example, the court in Northern Natural Gas Co. v. Grounds, 441 F.2d 704 (10th Cir. Kan. 1971) was asked to determine if leases covering "oil and gas" conveyed to the lessees the right to produce helium.

9.   Even though a grant or reservation does not include a particular substance, the mineral owner may still have a right to use or dispose of the substance. For example, the general rule that the mineral estate is dominant to the surface estate means that the mineral owner or mineral lessee can use substances owned by the surface estate to develop the minerals on or under the premises. Thus, in Sun Oil Co. v. Whitaker, 483 S.W.2d 808 (Tex. 1972),

the mineral owner's lessee was permitted to use groundwater belonging to the surface estate for waterflood operations beneath the premises. In Carbon County v. Union Reserve Coal Co., Inc., 898 P.2d 680 (Mont. 1995) the Montana Supreme Court indicated that even though coalbed methane gas was not a part of the coal owner's estate, the coal owner had an incidental right to "extract and capture coal seam methane gas for safety purposes during the mining process."

F. CONVEYANCES AND RESERVATIONS OF MINERAL AND ROYALTY INTERESTS

1. SIZE OF GEOGRAPHIC AREA: "CATCH–ALL" CLAUSES, HORIZONTAL SEVERANCES, AND RELATED ISSUES

Boundary issues are common throughout all types of land transactions. There are, however, certain issues that are encountered more often in mineral conveyances than in other types of transactions or are unique to mineral conveyances. As noted in Section A, one such issue is depth boundaries. A mineral owner may convey rights either above or below a certain depth or downward to include a specified formation. In some instances the conveyance is to a depth of 100 feet below the base of the specified formation. Such conveyances may include one productive reservoir and partially extend into another somewhat deeper reservoir, raising the issue of the grantee's right to drill and produce from the deeper reservoir. A more traditional and hence more common issue results from the use of "catch-all" clauses, in which a grantor or lessor states that the conveyance covers not only the mineral or royalty interest in the area specifically described in the granting clause but also includes all other mineral or royalty interests that she owns in a general area, such as a named county. The following case illustrates some of the constructional problems that may arise from the use of such a clause.

J. HIRAM MOORE, LTD. v. GREER[1]
172 S.W.3d 609 (Tex. 2005).

CHIEF JUSTICE JEFFERSON delivered the opinion of the Court . . .

Mary Greer, her three sisters, and their widowed mother partitioned an 80–acre tract into four 20–acre tracts, designated 1 through 4. The land is all in the I. & G.N. R.R. Survey No. 6, A–232 ("the Railroad Survey"), in Wharton County. Each sister received title to the surface and minerals in one tract and one-fourth of a non-participating royalty interest in each of the other three tracts. Greer received Tract 3.

In 1988, the two sisters who owned Tracts 1 and 2 leased their minerals to Larry K. Childers. The SixS Frels #1 Well was completed on

---

1. Some of the footnotes in the various opinions in this case have been omitted and most citations have been moved into the text.

an adjacent 106–acre tract in the Wm. Barnard Survey No. 14, A–801 ("the Barnard Survey"), and in 1991 that tract was pooled with Tracts 1 and 2 and four other tracts, at a specified horizon, to form the 350–acre SixS Frels Gas Unit. * * *

After 1991, Greer was thus entitled to receive 1/4 of the royalty for each of Tracts 1 and 2 from the SixS Frels #1 Well. There was no production—hence no royalty due Greer—with respect to Tracts 3 and 4.

In May 1997, Greer and her sister leased the minerals in Tracts 3 and 4, respectively, to J. Charles Holliman, Inc. The following September, Greer executed a royalty deed to Steger Energy Corp. At the time, there was still no production with respect to Tracts 3 and 4, and despite her lease to Holliman four months earlier, Greer was unaware of any drilling activity planned for the future. Greer's royalty deed to Steger consisted of nine numbered paragraphs in small print on a single page. The first paragraph conveyed all mineral royalties—

> that may be produced from the following described lands situated in the County of Wharton, State of Texas, to wit:

> All of that tract of land out of the AB 801 SEC 14/W M BARNARD #14 SURVEY, Wharton County, Texas known as the MEDALLION OIL–SIXS FRELS UNIT. Grantor agrees to execute any supplemental instrument requested by Grantee for a more complete or accurate description of said land. Reference is made to this unit(s) for descriptive purposes only and shall not limit this conveyance to any particular depths or wellbores. In addition to the above described lands, it is the intent of this instrument to convey, and this conveyance does so include, all of grantors [sic] royalty and overriding royalty interest in all oil, gas and other minerals in the above named county or counties, whether actually or properly described herein or not, and all of said lands are covered and included herein as fully, in all respects, as if the same had been actually and properly described herein.

The first quoted sentence, a specific grant, describes land "known as the ... SIXS FRELS UNIT" in the Barnard Survey. As already noted, the SixS Frels unit comprised tracts in both the Barnard Survey and the adjacent Railroad Survey, but Greer owned no interests in the Barnard Survey.[2] Greer's only royalty interests in the SixS Frels unit were in Tracts 1 and 2, both of which were in the Railroad Survey. But the fourth sentence, a general grant, refers to all Greer's interests in Wharton County, thus including not only her royalty interests in Tracts 1 and 2 in the SixS Frels Unit, but her interests in Tracts 3 and 4 as well.

During September and October, Steger acquired other royalty interests in Wharton County, and in December it sold twenty-five such interests, including the one acquired from Greer, to J. Hiram Moore, Ltd. for

---

2. We do not address whether, via pooling, Greer may have owned some interest in the Barnard Survey, as Moore stipulated below that "Greer owns no interest in the W.M. Barnard No. 14 Survey."

$360,000, which was market value. At that time, there was no production from Greer's Tract 3, nor was it pooled with any producing property.

Two years later, in December 1998, Kaiser–Francis Oil Co., successor to the working interest in Tract 3 that Greer conveyed to Holliman, pooled about 313 acres, including Tracts 1–4, at a different horizon than the SixS Frels Gas Unit, for production from the Greer #1 Well which had been completed in Tract 3. Moore claimed all royalties with respect to the interests partitioned to Greer in Tracts 1–4, and when Greer disputed the claim, Kaiser–Francis suspended payments for those tracts.

Moore sued Greer to determine their respective rights, and Greer counterclaimed for declaratory relief as well as rescission and reformation based on mutual mistake and fraud. Moore moved for summary judgment, contending that it had acquired all of Greer's royalty interests in Wharton County by purchasing her royalty deed to Steger. Greer responded that she had intended to convey to Steger only her interests in the SixS Frels Unit in the Barnard Survey. In her supporting affidavit, she stated: "I did not intend to convey any other property. I specifically did not intend to convey any of my interest in the I & GNRR Co. Survey No. 6, Abstract 232 Wharton County, Texas." The trial court granted Moore's motion for summary judgment and severed Greer's claims for rescission and reformation. Those claims remain pending.

The court of appeals reversed the summary judgment with this explanation:

> Here the question is not whether the property [claimed by Moore] was described specifically enough [in Greer's royalty deed to Steger], but whether the "catch-all" language is sufficient to effect a conveyance of a significant property interest that Greer contends she had no intention of conveying by this deed. Jones v. Colle[, 727 S.W.2d 262 (Tex. 1987)] sets forth the longstanding rule in Texas that a clause, like the one at issue here, can only convey small interests that are clearly contemplated within the more particularly described conveyance, and they are not effective to convey a significant property interest not adequately described in the deed or clearly contemplated by the language of the conveyance. Because the interest in Tract 3 was a substantial one, we hold that the rule disallowing such "cover-all" clauses to effectively convey a substantial property interest is the controlling law in this case. 72 S.W.3d 436, 441.

We granted the petition for review to determine the extent of the interest conveyed in the deed. 46 Tex. Sup.Ct. J. 793 (June 19, 2003).

We may construe the deed as a matter of law only if it is unambiguous. See Westwind Exploration, Inc. v. Homestate Sav. Ass'n, 696 S.W.2d 378, 381 (Tex. 1985). Citing Holloway's Unknown Heirs v. Whatley, 133 Tex. 608, 131 S.W.2d 89, 92 (Com.App. 1939), Moore argues that the deed is unambiguous and that the general description establishes that the parties intended the deed to convey all of Greer's royalty interests in the county. Pointing to a line of cases in which our courts have recognized the validity of geographic grants, Moore contends that the general description falls into that category of conveyances and thus enlarges the specific grant. See, e.g., Holloway's Unknown Heirs, 131 S.W.2d at 90.

Greer, on the other hand, contends that she intended a specific conveyance only. She argues that the second grant does not enlarge the first. Citing Jones v. Colle, 727 S.W.2d 262 (Tex.1987), and Smith v. Allison, 157 Tex. 220, 301 S.W.2d 608 (1957), she argues, and the court of appeals agreed, that the language following the specific grant was intended to convey only small unleased strips of land adjacent to the described property. 72 S.W.3d at 441.

In Smith v. Allison, 157 Tex. 220, 301 S.W.2d 608, 611 (1956), we held that a deed was ambiguous when its general description conveyed a significantly greater interest (surface and minerals in land included within the specific description) than the specific grant (minerals only) and when the amount paid for that conveyance appeared to relate only to the mineral interest specifically described. Accordingly, we noted that "the deed under question contain[ed] material inconsistent provisions that render[ed] it uncertain as to the property conveyed." Smith, 301 S.W.2d at 612. * * *

Because the deed was ambiguous, it was correctly submitted to the jury, and we affirmed the judgment on that verdict. Id. at 615.

We face a similar problem here. The specific description in Greer's deed points to a survey in which Greer apparently owns no interest. The deed purports to convey "[a]ll of that tract of land out of the AB 801 SEC 14/W M BARNARD #14 SURVEY, . . . known as the MEDALLION OIL–SIXS FRELS UNIT." As previously noted, Greer owns a 1/4 nonparticipating royalty interest in Tracts 1 and 2, which were pooled in the SixS Frels Unit; however, neither tract is in the W M Barnard Survey. Therefore, the specific description either does not describe any royalty interests owned by Greer, or it incorrectly describes her royalty interests in Tracts 1 and 2 that are part of the SixS Frels Unit by stating that they are in the W M Barnard Survey instead of the I. & G.N. R.R. Survey. The general description conveys "all of grantors [sic] royalty and overriding royalty interest in all oil, gas and other minerals in the above named county or counties, whether actually or properly described herein or not, and all of said lands are covered and included herein as fully, in all respects, as if the same had been actually and properly described herein." The deed in effect states that Greer conveys nothing, and that she conveys everything. We cannot construe this deed as a matter of law.

Given the deed's ambiguity, the trial court erred in granting summary judgment. A jury should therefore hear evidence and determine the parties' intent. See Columbia Gas Transmission Corp. v. New Ulm Gas, 940 S.W.2d 587, 589 (Tex. 1996). Accordingly, we affirm the court of appeals' judgment[3] and remand to the trial court for further proceedings consistent with this opinion.

---

3. In doing so, we express no opinion on the court of appeals' holding that "a clause, like the one at issue here, can only convey small interests that are clearly contemplated within the more

JUSTICE HECHT, concurring.

The dissent discerns no principle in the Court's decision, but there is one, and a very venerable one at that: hard cases make bad law.[4] * * *

Moore argues that general grants must always be read literally, or land titles will become uncertain, and chaos will descend. Greer argues that general grants can never include more than small strips adjacent specifically described property, or unsophisticated, perhaps careless, grantors will be duped out of property they never intended to convey. We have squarely rejected Greer's argument in two cases,[5] and the argument is at least inconsistent with three others.[6] But we stopped short of endorsing Moore's argument in Smith v. Allison, 157 Tex. 220, 301 S.W.2d 608 (1956). There the grantor specifically conveyed a mineral interest in two adjoining quarter-sections–320–acres then-added, with this general language:

> any and all other land and interest in land owned or claimed by the Grantor in said survey or surveys in which the above described land is situated or in [sic] adjoining the above described land. Id. at 610.

As it happened, the grantor owned the surface and minerals in 1,440 acres adjoining the two specifically described quarter-sections. Id. at 611. We held that the general grant did not unambiguously convey all of the grantor's interest in the 1,440 acres and affirmed a judgment on a jury verdict finding that it was not her intent to do so. Id. at 613–615.

* * *

Situations in which general grants cannot be given effect have not arisen frequently. * * * But while it only rarely happens that general grants cannot be given literal effect, I am not prepared in the unusual circumstances of this case to adopt a rigid rule that always construes general grants literally. The dissent poses five situations in which, I agree, a general grant should be construed according to its terms, but it is just as easy to pose other circumstances in which it will seem highly unlikely that the parties fully intended what they actually said, and unjust to hold one of them to it. We should not use this case to make bad law. As long as a rule that gives effect to general grants with a few exceptions seems to manage the cases that arise, I would not change it simply because it could,

particularly described conveyance, and they are not effective to convey a significant property interest not adequately described in the deed or clearly contemplated by the language of the conveyance." 72 S.W.3d at 441 (citing Jones v. Colle, 727 S.W.2d 262 (Tex.1987)).

4. Northern Sec.Co. v. United States, 193 U.S. 197, 400, 24 S.Ct. 436, 48 L.Ed. 679 (1903) (Holmes, J., dissenting) ("Great cases, like hard cases, make bad law."); Robinson v. Central Tex. MHMR Ctr., 780 S.W.2d 169, 172 n. 1 (Tex.1989) (Hecht, J., dissenting).

5. Holloway's Unknown Heirs v. Whatley, 133 Tex. 608, 131 S.W.2d 89, 90–92 (1939); Sun Oil Co. v. Burns, 125 Tex. 549, 84 S.W.2d 442, 445, 446–447 (1935) (quoting Lauchheimer v. Saunders, 27 Tex.Civ.App. 484, 65 S.W. 500, 501 (1901, no writ)).

6. Sun Oil Co. v. Bennett, 125 Tex. 540, 84 S.W.2d 447 (1935); Gulf Prod. Co. v. Spear, 125 Tex. 530, 84 S.W.2d 452 (1935); Strong v. Garrett, 148 Tex. 265, 224 S.W.2d 471 (1949); see also Texas Consol. Oils v. Bartels, 270 S.W.2d 708, 712 (Tex.Civ.App.–Eastland 1954, writ ref'd); Smith v. Westall, 76 Tex. 509, 13 S.W. 540 (1890); Witt v. Harlan, 66 Tex. 660, 2 S.W. 41 (1886).

possibly, prove unworkable. Smith did not destabilize land titles. Neither will this case.

With these few additional thoughts, I join in the Court's opinion.

JUSTICE OWEN, joined by JUSTICE MEDINA dissenting.

* * *

This grant is unambiguous. It purports to grant Greer's interest in a specific section of a specific survey, and it also purports to grant all of Greer's royalty interests in Wharton County, whether described in the deed or not. As it turns out, Greer does not own what she purported to convey in the specific grant. But she does own royalty interests in Wharton County, and she unequivocally conveyed all those royalty interests in the general granting section of this deed. I would give effect to this grant unless and until the deed is reformed or rescinded.

* * *

If the Court were to faithfully apply our precedent which is considerable,[7] it would give effect to what the written words unmistakably say in this royalty deed. This Court's decision in Smith v. Allison, 157 Tex. 220, 301 S.W.2d 608 (1957) does not support the result reached today. The general clause in Smith v. Allison purported to convey fee simple title to all land adjoining the parcels specifically described, while the specific descriptions as well as the habendum clause and warranty clause limited the conveyance to minerals only. Id. at 610. The general grant was therefore in conflict with and repugnant to the specific grant, and we have long held that when that occurs, the specific grant "will ordinarily control."[8]

I have several questions for the Court: Would the Court hold that the deed in this case, including the general grant of all royalty interests in Wharton County, is ambiguous if:

(1) a metes and bounds description of the land in which royalty interests were conveyed had been used as the specific description, but the description did not close;

(2) there were three tracts of land specifically described in which royalty interests were granted, and all were effective, but there was one other royalty interest in Wharton County, not specifically described, that Greer owned;

(3) there were three tracts of land specifically described in which royalty interests were granted, but one failed because Greer owned no interest in that one tract;

---

7. Smith v. Westall, 76 Tex. 509, 13 S.W. 540 (1890); Witt v. Harlan, 66 Tex. 660, 2 S.W. 41 (1886); Holloway's Unknown Heirs v. Whatley, 133 Tex. 608, 131 S.W.2d 89 (1939); Sun Oil Co. v. Burns, 125 Tex. 549, 84 S.W.2d 442 (1935); Tex. Consol. Oils v. Bartels, 270 S.W.2d 708 (Tex.Civ.App.–Eastland 1954, writ ref'd).

8. Burns, 84 S.W.2d at 446.

(4) there were 100 tracts of land specifically described in which royalty interests were granted, but one failed because Greer owned no interest in that one tract; or

(5) there were 100 tracts of land specifically described in which royalty interests were granted, and all were effective, but there were three other royalty interests in Wharton County, not specifically described, that Greer owned?

What principle of law does the Court announce today that will give stability and predictability in construing deeds, wills, oil and gas leases, liens, and deeds of trust? I can discern none. We are told only that when there is at least one specific grant and it fails, an unambiguous general grant is rendered ambiguous. Accordingly, there will be trials, sometimes years after the grantors and grantees have passed on, to determine what a conveyance meant.

We have received a number of amicus briefs in this case. [These briefs] tell us that the failure to give effect to the plain meaning of the deed before us will lead to severe adverse consequences including the failure of previously certain titles and security interests and a proliferation of litigation that can only be resolved by a trial to determine the meaning of "ambiguous" instruments. I fear that these amici are correct in their assessment of the damage today's decision will inflict on the stability and predictability of titles. Geographic grants are commonly used in large acquisitions as well as small, personal transactions in which individuals cannot afford to have deed records scoured and legal descriptions prepared and reviewed by lawyers. But all lay people know what they mean when they say, "I intend to convey all the royalty interests I own in Wharton County."

* * *

Because the Court does not give effect to a direct, unambiguous grant, I dissent.

NOTES

1. The majority opinion in the principal case takes the traditional view set out in the introductory comments to this chapter that a court's primary duty is to determine the intent of the parties. If their intent cannot be discerned from the language of the instrument and appropriate canons of construction, extrinsic evidence should be admitted to aid in determining that intent. The dissenting judges reject this approach in preference to one that will assure the stability of land titles. Judge Hecht in his concurrence points out that every rule has exceptions, and the decision creates a minor exception to the rule that general grants are given effect as written. Which position is preferable? Which position would a title attorney prefer?

2. The dissent describes two situations in which general or "catch-all" grants are commonly made: Large acquisitions of all of a company's mineral interests in an area and the sale of small fractional interests whose value

doesn't justify the cost of a detailed title examination. "Catch-all" language is also commonly used in the granting clause of oil and gas leases. When used in this context the clause is often referred to as a "Mother Hubbard" or "cover-all clause," and follows a detailed description of the land subject to the lease. This description is typically taken from a prior deed in the lessor's chain of title, and an oil and gas lessee wants assurance that the lease will also cover any additional land owned by the lessor that is not described in the deed. Such additions may result from errors in the original deed's description, subsequent acquisition of limitation title to fenced-in-strips, a prior grantor's ignorance of the strip-and-gore doctrine (discussed below in Note 6), inaccuracies in surveys, or other factors. There is considerable variation in the wording of such clauses. An example of one form of Mother Hubbard clause is the one involved in Law v. Stanolind Oil & Gas Co., 209 S.W.2d 381 (Tex.Civ.App.–Galveston 1948, writ refused n.r.e.):

> It is the intention that this shall also include all land owned or claimed by Lessor adjacent or contiguous to the land particularly described above, whether the same be in said survey or surveys or in adjacent surveys.

When used in a lease, should this type of clause have the same all-inclusive effect given a catch-all clause in the two situations described by the dissenting judges? In Jones v. Colle, 727 S.W.2d 262 (Tex. 1987), the Texas Supreme Court held that a Mother Hubbard clause in an oil and gas lease was effective to include only small adjoining pieces of land and did not bring large adjacent tracts within the coverage of the lease. In omitted portions of their opinions both the dissenting and concurring judges in the principal case stated that the *Jones* court had misread precedent, and in a footnote the majority stated that it was expressing no opinion on the court of appeals' holding, which was explicitly based upon *Jones*.

Suppose that a lessor owns 1,200 acres that are adjacent to an 80 acres tract that is specifically described in an oil and gas lease containing a Mother Hubbard clause like the one set out earlier in this note. What advice should you give to another oil company that would like to obtain a lease on the 1,200 acres?

3. In Bergeron v. Amoco Prod. Co., 789 F.2d 344 (5th Cir.La. 1986) a cover-all clause that was contained in each of three leases covering a total of 330 acres was held to bind the lessors' 2367/2880 interest in a contiguous 40–acre tract. At the time the leases were executed, the lessors believed that their mother, who had executed an oil and gas lease to the same lessee, owned full title to the 40–acre tract. The court stated that the parties had clearly intended to lease the entirety of the family interests in the 40 acres as well as the 330 acres.

4. The Kansas Legislature has addressed "Mother Hubbard" or "cover-all" clauses by statute. Kan. Stat. Ann. § 58–2273. Although the wording is convoluted, the intent is to negate such clauses by requiring the beneficiary of the clause to record a reformed document limited to the specifically stated property boundaries. Failure to record the reformed document following a demand can result in a penalty equal to the greater of "up to $10,000 per title affected" or the "fair market value of the mineral or royalty interests" affected by the general language. The statute provides for attorney fees,

"additional damages," and expedited judicial proceedings in the event the reformed document is not filed for record.

The impact of the statute is narrowed by the definition of "Mother Hubbard clause" which is limited to a conveyance of "all of the grantor's property in a certain county." § 58–2273(e)(1). "General conveyance provision" is defined as "a provision in a deed or other instrument describing an interest in real estate which, in addition to referring to the real estate specifically described in such deed or other instrument, describes unspecified other mineral or royalty rights or interests of the grantor in an entire township, county or state * * *." § (e)(2). However, the most limiting aspect of the statute is the triggering event:

> When a recorded deed or conveyance covering mineral or royalty rights purports to cover mineral or royalty rights not owned by the grantor, or such deed or conveyance includes a general conveyance provision, including, but not limited to, a 'mother hubbard' clause or other cover-all clause, for other property conveyed by grantor *and such general conveyance provision should not have been included in such deed or conveyance*, then any party with an interest in the real estate covered by such deed or conveyance may make written demand upon the grantee or grantor, as applicable, by certified mail, return receipt requested, to rescind or reform the general conveyance provision.

Kan. Stat. Ann. § 58–2273(a). This appears to limit the statute to situations where the clause was included in a conveyance by mistake or fraud. The likely defense in these cases will be: the parties intended the clause to be included in the conveyance.

5. Problems in addition to determining the scope of the grant may arise from using Mother Hubbard and other catch-all clauses. There may be an issue of notice to a third party purchaser who has acquired land that has been made subject to a recorded deed or oil and gas lease by such a clause. In a situation analogous to the *Bergeron* case, a grantee may claim that the clause transfers the entire interest of a grantor who owns three-fourths of the mineral fee but purports to grant only one-half. If a deed contains a catch-all clause and excepts a specified area from the grant, does the clause have the effect of transferring the excluded area to the grantee? For a discussion of these and other problems, see Hemingway § 7.7.

6. A deed or oil and gas lease may be held to include minerals beneath land not specifically described in the instrument even though there is no Mother Hubbard or similar clause. This may occur through application of the common law strip-and-gore doctrine. Suppose, for example, that a county or other governmental body acquires a roadway easement across two adjacent tracts of land, with each tract contributing land to the center of the road. If one of the landowners or his successor subsequently sells or executes an oil and gas lease, the land may be described as bounded on one side by the highway. Unless there is a clear expression to the contrary, the strip-and-gore doctrine applies and the grant is presumed to include fee title to the center of the roadway. See, e.g., Escondido Services, LLC v. VKM Holdings LP., 321 S.W.3d 102 (Tex. App.–Eastland 2010). Should the same presumption apply if a road crosses through the middle of a tract, and the landowner later conveys

the land north of the highway by a deed describing the land granted as bounded by "the north line" of the highway? Courts of appeals in Texas have reached different conclusions. Compare Reagan v. Marathon Oil Co., 50 S.W.3d 70 (Tex. App. 2001) with Krenek v. Texstar North America, Inc., 787 S.W.2d 566 (Tex. App. 1990, writ denied).

Although the strip-and-gore doctrine is most commonly applied to deeds and oil and gas leases that describe the land as bounded by a public road or railway, it has not been restricted to these situations. In Moore v. Energy States, Inc., 71 S.W.3d 796 (Tex. App. 2002) grantors conveyed land described as "South of the T & P Ry. Co. right of way and South of the Public road which lies immediately south of said T & P Ry. Co. right of way." The court ruled that the strip-and-gore doctrine and estoppel by deed precluded the grantors' successors from claiming title to a narrow strip of land between the railway easement and the public road.

Other courts have taken a more limited view of the doctrine. In Town of Moorcroft v. Lang, 779 P.2d 1180 (Wyo. 1989) the Wyoming Supreme Court refused to apply the strip-and-gore doctrine to a severed mineral estate beneath the streets of a residential subdivision. The court distinguished between a common law dedication of subdivision streets and a statutory dedication. In the first situation the municipality acquires only an easement, and the court agreed that the developer's subsequent conveyances of each subdivided lot included the fee to the middle of the streets. The court reasoned that such a result was necessary because an easement requires a servient estate into which the easement can merge if it terminates. Under a statutory dedication, however, the municipality receives a fee simple determinable in the surface estate, thus effectuating a severance of the underlying mineral estate. The court indicated that in this situation the developer's subsequent conveyances of subdivision lots to abutting lot owners included the possibility of reverter in the surface of the streets, but did not include any part of the mineral estate underlying the streets, which the developer retained. The court reasoned that since a statutory dedication created a fee simple determinable in the surface which, upon being vacated, would vest a fee simple absolute in the adjacent lot owners, there was no adequate rationale for passing any portion of the title to the mineral estate to the abutting lot owners as they received conveyances from the developer. The court felt that applying the strip-and-gore doctrine in this situation would be inconsistent with the concept that a severance creates two separate freehold estate of equal dignity, separate and independent of each other.

7. The doctrine of accretion may change the size and location of a mineral estate. For example, in Nilsen v. Tenneco Oil Co., 614 P.2d 36 (Okla. 1980) the boundary between two properties was described as the center line of the South Canadian River. As the river slowly migrated northward, new land was accumulated on the south bank. Under the common law doctrine of accretion[8] a riparian landowner may lose or gain land as a result of the movement of a bounding body of water. As the court explained the doctrine:

> [W]hen nature causes a gradual shift in the line which separates riparian land from the abutting water due either to rescission of the water or the

---

8.   Oklahoma has codified the common law doctrine in Okla.St.Ann. tit. 60, § 335.

deposit of soil against the margin of the land, there occurs a change in the boundary between the land and the waterbed so that the owner of the original waterbed has lost title to that part of it which is now land and the owner of the original body of land has acquired title to the new land thus formed.

614 P.2d at 41. Prior to the center line shift of the river bed, mineral interests had been severed from the surface on several tracts on both sides of the South Canadian River. The trial court reasoned that if title to a severed mineral estate could not be acquired by adverse possession of the surface, then title could not be lost by accretion or erosion on the surface; the change in location of the river could affect only surface ownership. The Oklahoma Supreme Court rejected the trial court's reasoning and held the severed mineral interests were also subject to adjustment under the doctrine of accretion. See also Ely v. Briley, 959 S.W.2d 723 (Tex.App. 1998), holding that a severed one-half mineral interest was subject to the accretion doctrine.

Issues over title to streambeds, navigable waters and coastal lands are dealt with in Chapter 7.

2. SIZE OF FRACTIONAL INTERESTS

One of the most persistently fertile sources of title problems has been the conveyance or reservation of fractional mineral and royalty interests. The problem in its classic form involves double fractions: A grantor who owns a fractional interest executes a warranty deed that conveys or reserves a fractional interest. As the following case and the notes following it illustrate, very slight variations in deed language may determine whether the interest set out in the grantor's deed is a fraction of the entire estate or only of the estate actually owned by the grantor.

AVERYT v. GRANDE, INC.

717 S.W.2d 891 (Tex.1986).

SPEARS, JUSTICE.

The issue in this declaratory judgment action is whether a mineral reservation in a general warranty deed reserves a fraction of the entire mineral estate or only a fraction of the undivided one-half mineral interest owned and conveyed by the grantor. The trial court held that the reservation reserved a fraction of the entire mineral estate. The court of appeals affirmed. 686 S.W.2d 632. We affirm.

On September 30, 1977, Respondent Grande, Inc. conveyed the real property in question to the Fogelmans. The Fogelmans then conveyed the property to Petitioner James R. Averyt, trustee for R.M. Hopkins, Jr. Averyt, individually and as Hopkin's trustee, sued to determine what portion of the mineral interest Grande conveyed to the Fogelmans.

The Grande to Fogelman deed contains the following pertinent provisions:

[T]hat Grande, Inc. * * * have GRANTED, SOLD and CONVEYED, * * * unto the said Gordon V. Fogelman and wife, Clarice E. Fogelman, * * * the following described real estate:

FIRST TRACT:

All that certain tract or parcel of land, situated in Fayette County, Texas, * * *.

* * *

[C]ontaining 86.82 acres of land.

SECOND TRACT:

An undivided ½ interest in and to all that certain tract or parcel of land, situated in Fayette County, Texas, * * *.

* * *

[C]ontaining 0.03 acres of land.

LESS, HOWEVER, AND SUBJECT TO *an undivided ½ interest in the oil, gas, sulphur, and all other minerals,* described in that deed from Rubie Keilers and Annie Keilers, to Texas Osage Cooperative Royalty Pool, et al, dated May 2, 1930, and recorded in Volume 152, Pages 75–76, Deed Records of Fayette County, Texas.

* * *

There is hereby excepted from this conveyance and reserved to Grantor, its successors and assigns, an undivided ¼th of the royalty covering all of the oil, gas and other minerals, including but not limited to uranium, coal, lignite, iron, gold, silver, and all other minerals, whether or not now known to be valuable and whether by drilling, strip mining, or any other method, *in, to and under or that may be produced from the lands above described * * *.*

* * *

TO HAVE AND TO HOLD the above described premises, together with all and singular, the rights and appurtenances thereto in any wise belonging unto the said Gordon V. Fogelman and wife, Clarice E. Fogelman, their heirs and assigns, forever. And Grande, Inc., does hereby bind itself and its successors, to warrant and forever defend, all and singular, the said premises unto the said Gordon V. Fogelman and wife, Clarice E. Fogelman, their heirs and assigns, against every person whomsoever lawfully claiming, or to claim the same or any part thereof. (emphasis added)

The question presented is whether Grande reserved one-fourth of the royalty from the entire 86.82 and 0.003 acres or one-fourth of the royalty from the undivided one-half mineral interest Grande owned at the time of the conveyance. Grande argues that the deed reserves one-fourth of the royalty of the entire mineral estate. Averyt argues that the deed reserves one-fourth of the royalty only from the undivided one-half mineral interest Grande owned at the time of the conveyance to the Fogelmans.

* * *

Specific rules of construction apply to cases in which a grantor owns an undivided mineral interest and reserves a fraction of the minerals under the land in the deed. If the deed reserves a fraction of the minerals under the land *conveyed,* then the deed reserves a fraction of the part of the mineral estate actually owned by the grantor and conveyed in the deed. *Hooks v. Neill,* 21 S.W.2d 532 (Tex.Civ.App.–Galveston 1929, writ ref'd). In *Hooks,* the grantor conveyed all of his undivided one-half interest in a tract of land. He then reserved "a one-thirty second part of all oil on and under the said land and premises herein described and conveyed." The *Hooks* court focused on the word "conveyed" to hold that the reservation clause applied "only to the interest which [grantors] have in the land and ore which they conveyed." *Hooks,* 21 S.W.2d at 538.

If, on the other hand, the deed reserves a fraction of the minerals under the land *described,* the deed reserves a fraction of the minerals under the entire physical tract, regardless of the part of the mineral estate actually conveyed. *King v. First National Bank of Wichita Falls,* 144 Tex. 583, 192 S.W.2d 260 (1946). In *King,* the grantor conveyed all of his undivided one-half interest in the described land. The deed later reserved "an undivided one eighth of the usual and customary one eighth royalty . . . in oil and gas and other minerals that may be produced from the hereinabove described land." This court focused on the word "described" to hold that the grantor reserved an undivided one eighth of the royalty from the minerals under the entire described tract, not just the grantor's undivided one-half. *King,* 192 S.W.2d at 262. We distinguished *Hooks* on the basis that the deed in that case limited the reservation to part of the estate conveyed while the *King* deed contained no such restricting language. *Id. See* Masterson, *Double Fraction Problems In Instruments Involving Mineral Interests,* 11 Southwestern L.J. 281, 281 (1957) (disapproves distinction but states that *King* better effects intent of parties).

* * *

The Grande to Fogelman deed reserves one-fourth of the royalty from minerals "that may be produced from the lands above described." This places the reservation within the *King* rule. Averyt argues, however, that the exception of one-half of the minerals in the "subject to" clause is part of the description of the land. Averyt asserts that the "lands above described," therefore, are the two tracts minus the one-half mineral interest excepted from the grant in the "subject to" clause. * * *

* * *

We hold that a "subject to" clause which excepts fractional mineral interests from lands and minerals conveyed does not form part of the description of the land. The "subject to" clause does limit the estate granted and warranted. There is a difference, however, between the estate granted and the land described. "Land" is the physical earth in its natural state, while an estate in land is a legal unit of ownership in the physical land. 1 Thompson, *Thompson on Real Property* § 51 (1939). To define the estate granted is to set out the portion of the physical land conveyed. In contrast, "[T]o describe land is to outline its boundaries so that it may be located on the ground, *and not to define the estate conveyed therein.*" *Sharp v. Fowler*, 151 Tex. 490, 252 S.W.2d 153, 154 (1952).

Because "land" includes the surface of the earth and everything over and under it, including minerals in place, Thompson at § 51, a description of land includes the land and all the minerals naturally existing underneath. In other words, minerals under "the lands described" refers to all the minerals under the entire land because minerals "would necessarily be produced from the whole land, irrespective of the ownership of undivided shares thereof." *King,* 192 S.W.2d at 263. The "subject to" clause affects "the ownership of the undivided shares" of the minerals, not the description of the land containing them. *Id.* Thus, when the Grande to Foglellman deed reserved a fraction of the minerals in the "lands above described," it meant the minerals under the entire physical tracts described in the deed by metes and bounds. *Id.* at 262. The dissent correctly notes that here the interest conveyed is the same as the interest described. However, Grande reserved one-fourth of the royalty from the *lands* described, not from the interest described.

The deed further evidences an intent to reserve one-fourth of the royalty from the minerals under the entire land when it reserved "¼th of the royalty covering *all* of the oil, gas and other minerals * * * in and under and that may be produced from the lands above described" (emphasis added). We therefore hold that the Grande to Foglellman deed reserved to Grande an undivided one-fourth of the royalty from the minerals produced from the whole of the tracts described in the deed.

* * *

We overrule all of Averyt's points of error. Accordingly, we affirm the judgment of the court of appeals and that of the trial court.

KILGARLIN, JUSTICE, dissenting.

I respectfully dissent. How can Grande, Inc. reserve to itself a one-fourth royalty interest in the half of the mineral estate in which it had no interest? The Grande to Fogelman deed clearly evidences that Texas Osage already owned the other one-half mineral interest.

* * *

RAY and WALLACE, JJ., join in this dissent.

NOTES

1.   The rule applicable to deeds such as that involved in *Averyt* continues to have significant vitality and is often applied. See, e.g., Winegar v. Martin,

304 S.W.3d 661 (Tex. App. 2010). It has been summarized in Will G. Barber, Duhig to Date: Problems in the Conveyancing of Fractional Mineral Interests, 13 Sw.L.J. 320 (1959), as follows: "Where a fraction designated in a deed is stated to be a mineral interest in land *described* in the deed, the fraction is to be calculated upon the entire mineral interest. * * * Where a fraction designated in a reservation clause is stated to be a mineral interest in land conveyed by the deed, the fraction is to be calculated upon the grantor's *fractional* mineral interest except where the granting clause *purports* to convey the *entire* mineral interest." Id. at 322–23.

Occasionally, however, the language of a reservation in a deed does not fall squarely within either type of language presupposed by this rule. In Phillipello v. The Nelson Family Farming Trust, 349 S.W.3d 692 (Tex.App.–Houston 2011) the grantor owned less than 100% of the mineral estate, but the size of its fractional interest was in dispute and was being litigated in another case. In the case at issue the grantor conveyed its entire interest by a deed that reserved "for a period of ten (10) years from the date of this conveyance, one-eighth (1/8) of the royalty in oil, gas and other minerals in and under and that may be produced with the oil and gas." The reservation clause made no reference to either the land described in the deed or the fractional interest being conveyed by the deed. The court concluded that since the deed did not stipulate what fractional interest was being conveyed and since the reference to the oil and gas produced was not specifically limited to the grantor's fractional interest, the deed reserved a terminable one-eighth fractional interest in the entire mineral estate.

Do you agree with the court's statement that the reservation was unambiguous and therefore the court should not apply the canon of construction under which any doubt about a deed's meaning is construed against the grantor?

2. A double-fraction problem analogous to that presented in *Averyt* arises if a grantor who owns a fractional interest conveys or reserves a fraction either "of" her interest or "out of" her interest. As the late W. D. Masterson, Jr. has pointed out, in a conveyance the word "of" has the same meaning as "times" in a multiplication formula. See Note, 6 O & GR 1372 (1956). Thus a deed that grants "$\frac{1}{16}$ of the usual $\frac{1}{8}$ royalty" transfers a $\frac{1}{128}$ royalty. Conversely, a deed that grants a fraction "out of" the grantor's fractional interest merely specifies the source from which the grant is taken and does not affect the size of the interest transferred. See, e.g., Minchen v. Hirsch, 295 S.W.2d 529 (Tex. Civ. App. 1956, writ ref'd n.r.e.). Following this rule of construction, the court in Black v. Shell Oil Co., 397 S.W.2d 877 (Tex.Civ.App. 1965) concluded that grantors who owned an undivided half interest in the mineral estate had conveyed their entire interest when they executed a deed which stated that their intent was "to convey one-half of the minerals out of the interest owned by them."

3. Rules of grammar may be invoked in litigation over the size of an interest conveyed or reserved. For example, in Stewman Ranch, Inc. v. Double M. Ranch, Ltd., 192 S.W.3d 808 (Tex. App. 2006) the grantors had executed a deed providing that the conveyance was subject to various outstanding mineral and royalty interests and reserving "an undivided one-half ($\frac{1}{2}$) of the

royalties to be paid on the production of oil, gas and other hydrocarbons from the described lands which are presently owned by Grantors * * *." In a subsequent dispute over whether the grantors had reserved one-half of all royalties payable on production from the land or only one-half of the royalties owned by the grantors at the time of the conveyance, the grantors attempted to invoke the grammatical rule that a restricting clause that is not set off by commas modifies the word or phrase immediately preceding it. They argued that the phrase "which are presently owned by Grantors" referred to "the described lands" rather than to "royalties." While acknowledging the existence of the rule of the grammar, the court nonetheless rejected it on the ground that its application would make the restricting clause superfluous. The court held that "which are presently owned by Grantors" referred to "royalties" and that the grantors had thus reserved only half of the royalties that they owned at the time of the conveyance. Contrast the result reached in *Stewman* with James v. Beckwith, 805 P.2d 117, 111 O & GR 294 (Okla.App. Div. 1 1990) where the court applied the rule of grammar to a granting clause that excepted "oil, gas and other minerals, reservations and conveyances and oil and gas leases and easements of record." The court held that the phrase "of record" did not modify "oil, gas and other minerals," and that the conveyance did not include any interest in the mineral estate.

4. Deeds executed in the middle decades of the Twentieth Century, when the parties often assumed that one-eighth would forever remain the standard lease royalty, have given rise to a significant amount of litigation now that lease royalties often exceed one-eighth. These deeds usually granted or reserved a stated fraction "of royalty," e.g. "one-half of royalty," and then contained other language indicating that the fraction was of a 1/8 royalty, e.g., a right to 1/16th of production from future leases. The legal issues arising from these types of deeds are discussed in Section G.1, dealing with conveyances "subject to" an existing lease.

3. OVERCONVEYANCES: *DUHIG* AND ITS PROGENY

One of the most difficult problems encountered by title examiners and drafters arises in a situation like *Averyt* if the deed makes no mention of the third person's outstanding interest. Since the deed on its face grants full title to everything but the interest retained by the grantor, it appears to govern a larger interest in the land than the grantor has the power to deal with. The leading case dealing with this situation is set out below.

DUHIG v. PEAVY–MOORE LUMBER CO.
144 S.W.2d 878 (Tex. 1940).

SMEDLEY, COMMISSIONER.

Through conveyance from the executor of the estate of Alexander Gilmer, deceased, W.J. Duhig became the owner of the Josiah Jordan survey in Orange County, subject however, to reservation by the grantor of an undivided one-half interest in the minerals. Thereafter Duhig conveyed the survey to Miller–Link Lumber Company, and in the deed it was agreed and stipulated that the grantor retained an undivided one-half interest in all of the mineral rights or minerals in and on the land. Peavy–Moore Lumber Company became the owner of whatever title and estate Miller–Link Lumber Company acquired by the deed from Duhig in 574⅜ acres of the said survey.

The suit is by defendant in error, Peavy–Moore Lumber Company, against plaintiffs in error, Mrs. W.J. Duhig and others, who claim under W.J. Duhig, for the title and possession of the 574⅜ acres in the Jordan survey. The trial court's judgment was that the plaintiff, Peavy–Moore Lumber Company, recover the title and possession of the land, except all minerals and mineral rights therein, and that as to the minerals and mineral rights, it take nothing against the defendants. On appeal by Peavy–Moore Lumber Company, the Court of Civil Appeals reversed the judgment of the trial court and rendered judgment in favor of that company. 119 S.W.2d 688.

The ownership by Gilmer's estate, and its assignees of an undivided one-half interest in the minerals in the land through the reservation in the first deed, which was duly recorded, is admitted by the parties. Plaintiffs in error, Mrs. Duhig and others, make no claim of title to the surface estate, but their contention, sustained by the trial court and denied by the Court of Civil Appeals, is that W.J. Duhig, their predecessor, reserved for himself in his conveyance of the land to Miller–Link Lumber Company the remaining undivided one-half interest in the minerals. Defendant in error, Peavy–Moore Lumber Company, takes the position that the deed last referred to did not reserve to or for the grantor such remaining one-half interest that had theretofore been reserved by Gilmer's estate and invested the grantee with title to the surface estate and an undivided one-half interest in the minerals.

The deed from W.J. Duhig to Miller–Link Lumber Company is a general warranty deed, describing the property conveyed as that certain tract or parcel of land in Orange County, Texas, known as the Josiah Jordan Survey, further identifying the land by survey and certificate number and giving a description by metes and bounds. After the metes and bounds the following matter of description is added: " * * * and being the same tract of land formerly owned by the Talbot–Duhig Lumber Company, and after the dissolution of said company, conveyed to W.J. Duhig by B.M. Talbot". After the habendum and the clause of general warranty and constituting the last paragraph in the deed, appears the following: "But it is expressly agreed and stipulated that the grantor herein retains an undivided one-half interest in and to all mineral rights or minerals of whatever description in the land."

We cannot agree with plaintiffs in error's contention that the granting paragraph of the deed purports to convey only the surface estate and an undivided one-half interest in the minerals. It is our opinion that the statement in the deed, that the land described is the same tract as that formerly owned by Talbot–Duhig Lumber Company and conveyed to Duhig by Talbot, is not intended to define or qualify the estate or interest conveyed but that it is inserted to further identify the tract or area described by metes and bounds. The deed, of course, does not actually convey what the grantor does not own. Richardson v. Levi, 67 Tex. 359, 365, 3 S.W. 444. But the granting clause in this deed describes what is conveyed as the tract or parcel of land known as the Jordan survey. This description includes the minerals, as well as the surface, and thus the granting clause purports to convey both the surface estate and all of the mineral estate. Likewise the clause of general warranty has reference to "the said premises", meaning the land described in the granting clause, and, but for the last paragraph of the deed retaining an undivided interest in the minerals, would warrant the title to the land including the surface estate and all of the minerals.

The writer believes that the judgment of the Court of Civil Appeals should be affirmed for substantially the same reasons as those set out in the opinion of that court, that is, that the language of the deed as a whole does not clearly and plainly disclose the intention of the parties that there be reserved to the grantor Duhig an undivided one-half interest in the minerals in addition to that previously reserved to Gilmer's estate, and that when resort is had to establish rules of construction and facts taken into consideration which may properly be considered, it becomes apparent that the intention of the parties to the deed was to invest the grantee with title to the surface and a one-half interest in the minerals excepting or withholding from the operation of the conveyance only the one-half interest theretofore reserved in the deed from Gilmer's estate to Duhig. It is the court's opinion, however, that the judgment of the Court of Civil Appeals should be affirmed by the application of a well settled principle of estoppel.

The granting clause of the deed, as has been said, purports to convey to the grantee the land described, that is, the surface estate and all of the mineral estate. The covenant warrants the title to "the said premises". The last paragraph of the deed retains an undivided one-half interest in the minerals. Thus the deed is so written that the general warranty extends to the full fee simple title to the land except an undivided one-half interest in the minerals.

The language used in the last paragraph of the deed is that "grantor retains an undivided one-half interest in * * * the minerals". The word "retain" ordinarily means to hold or keep what one already owns. If controlling effect is given to the use of the word "retains", it follows that the deed reserved to Duhig an undivided one-half interest in the minerals and that the grantee, Miller–Link Lumber Company, acquired by and through the deed only the surface estate. We assume that the deed should be given this meaning. When the deed is so interpreted the warranty is breached at the very time of the execution and delivery of the deed, for the deed warrants the title to the surface estate and also to an undivided one-half interest in the minerals. The result is that the grantor has breached his warranty, but that he has and holds in virtue of the deed containing the warranty the very interest, one-half of the minerals, required to remedy the breach. Such state of facts at once suggests the rule as to after-acquired title, which is thus stated in American Jurisprudence: "It is a general rule, supported by many authorities, that a deed purporting to convey a fee simple or a lesser definite estate in land and containing covenants of general warranty of title or of ownership will operate to estop the grantor from asserting an after-acquired title or interest in the land, or the estate which the deed purports to convey, as against the grantee and those claiming under him." Vol. 19, p. 614, § 16.

* * *

In the instant case Duhig did not acquire title to the one-half interest in the minerals after he executed the deed containing the general warranty, but he retained or reserved it in that deed. Plaintiffs in error, who claim under him, insist that they should be permitted to set up and maintain that title against the suit of defendant in error and to require it to seek redress in a suit for breach of the warranty. What the rule above quoted prohibits is the *assertion* of title in contradiction or breach of the warranty. If such enforcement of the warranty is a fair and effectual remedy in case of after-acquired title, it is, we believe, equally fair and effectual and also appropriate here.

We recognize the rule that the covenant of general warranty does not enlarge the title conveyed and does not determine the character of the title. The decision here made assumes, as has been stated, that Duhig by the deed reserved for himself a one-half interest in the minerals. The covenant is not construed as affecting or impairing the title so reserved. It operates as an estoppel denying to the grantor and those claiming under him the right to set up such title against the grantee and those who claim under it.

For the foregoing reasons, the judgment of the Court of Civil Appeals is affirmed.

Opinion adopted by the Supreme Court.

NOTES

1. Would the result in the principal case have been different if the deed from Duhig to the Miller–Link Lumber Co. had not contained a general warranty clause? Several courts have reasoned that the key factor is what the deed purports to convey, rather than the presence or absence of a general warranty. Hence, special warranty deeds, Miller v. Kloeckner, 600 N.W.2d 881 (N.D. 1999) and even no-warranty deeds, Blanton v. Bruce, 688 S.W.2d 908 (Tex.App. 1985), have been construed as precluding a grantor from asserting a reservation that would reduce the interest purportedly conveyed to the grantee. Several courts have refused to give this effect to a quitclaim deed. See Hill v. Gilliam, 682 S.W.2d 737 (Ark. 1985), Rosenbaum v. McCaskey, 386 So.2d 387 (Miss. 1980) and Young v. Vermillion, 992 P.2d 917 (Okla.Civ.App.

No Warranty - No Duhig

Div. 1 1999). However if the focus of *Duhig* is on whether the parties intended to convey certain land and interests in land and effectuating that intent would result in an overconveyance, the Duhig rule might well be applied even under a quitclaim deed.

Consider the point made by Professor Anderson:

> Under most quitclaim deeds, the operative language quitclaims "my [or *his*, *her* or *their*] right, title and interest," meaning whatever interest that is, which may be no interest. Occasionally, one may encounter a quitclaim deed that quitclaims "*all* right title and interest," or "*all that* right, title and interest." These forms of quitclaim deeds arguably purport to convey all the interest in the subject property, but do not contain a warranty. In these instances, a court might choose to apply the *Duhig* doctrine.

Anderson, Discussion Notes, 145 O & GR 381, 382 (2001)

2.   In Gawryluk v. Poynter, 654 N.W.2d 400 (N.D. 2002) the North Dakota supreme court rejected the argument that an overconveyance of the grantor's mineral interest creates an ambiguity that should be resolved by the introduction of extrinsic evidence of the parties' intent. The court stated that in this situation the *Duhig* rule of construction determined the interests received by the grantee and reserved by the grantor.

3.   Combs v. Sherman, 267 P.3d 150 (Okla.Civ.App.2011) involved an attempt to apply *Duhig* to conveyances by two sisters who owned land as common law joint tenants. Each sister executed a warranty deed to a neighboring landowner that contained a reservation of "an undivided 3/4ths interest in and to the oil, gas and other minerals lying in and under the property * * * it being the intent of Grantor herein to convey to Grantee herein, an undivided 1/4th mineral interest." There was a subsequent dispute over whether the grantee received an undivided one-half of the mineral estate (one-fourth from each sister) or only a total of one-fourth. As the court pointed out, the sisters, as joint tenants, held the entire property in a single ownership, but each also held a specific share which was all she could alienate. In the deeds in question each sister conveyed one quarter of her share, which amounted to one-eighth of the mineral estate. Among other arguments, the grantee's successor cited Duhig for the proposition that a grantor cannot assert title in contradiction of her warranty. The court distinguished *Duhig* and the Oklahoma cases following it on the ground that the 3/4ths interest reserved by each sister had not been previously reserved by another grantor and that the deeds in question specifically stated that only one-fourth was being conveyed.

4.   Although *Duhig* has been widely followed, the estoppel doctrine upon which it is based has not met with universal approval. Some courts and commentators have preferred the position supported by Commissioner Smedley, the opinion's author, who states near the middle of the opinion that he prefers the rationale of the court of appeals, which was that the language of the deed did not clearly indicate that the parties intended for the grantor to reserve an undivided one-half interest in the minerals in addition to the interest previously reserved in the Gilmer estate. See, e.g., Anderson, Discussion Notes, 145 O & GR 381 (2001); Willis H. Ellis, Rethinking the *Duhig*

Doctrine, 28 Rocky Mtn.Min.L.Inst. 947 (1982). See also O'Brien v. Village Land Co., 794 P.2d 246 (Colo. 1990), where the court pointed out that the terms "reservation" and "exception" are often used interchangeably and refused to construe the deed's reservation of an undivided one-half interest in the minerals as an attempt by the grantor to retain one-half of the minerals. The court construed the reservation as a reference to the one-half interest in the minerals owned by a third party.

A few courts have rejected the *Duhig* result in its entirety. In Hartman v. Potter, 596 P.2d 653 (Utah 1979), the Utah Supreme Court was called upon to construe a deed which reserved "three-fourths (¾) of all the oil, gas, and mineral rights to the above land." It rejected a traditional estoppel analysis and treated the grantor as having retained three-fourths of the one-half interest in the minerals which he actually owned at the time of the conveyance. See Willis H. Ellis, Rethinking the *Duhig* Doctrine, 28 Rocky Mtn. Min.L.Inst. 947 (1982).

Even in the state of its origin there are several exceptions to the Duhig rule. For a discussion of these, see Terry E. Hogwood, "Ding Dong Duhig Is Dead," 43 Oil, Gas and Energy Law (Tex. Oil, Gas & Energy Law Section, Sept. 2010). Perhaps the most impost important of these is its limited application to oil and gas leases. In McMahon v. Christmann, 303 S.W.2d 341 (Tex. 1957), the Texas Supreme Court reasoned that there are many instances in which the lessor executes a lease purporting to cover the entire mineral fee even though he owns only an undivided interest in the leased premises: application of the *Duhig* rule in this situation would estop the lessor to assert his reserved royalty and thus permit a lessee to take the lessor's entire mineral estate without an obligation to make any payment from production to the landowner. Since the lessee, rather than the lessor, traditionally drafts the oil and gas lease, the court felt that such a result would be grossly unfair. The lessee can avoid overpaying the lessor in this situation by making sure the lease contains a proportionate reduction clause. This type of clause is discussed in the following section.

For additional arguments in favor of distinguishing between grantors and lessors in the application of the *Duhig* doctrine, see Richard C. Maxwell, Some Comments on North Dakota Oil and Gas Law—Three Cases from the Eighties, 58 N.D.L.Rev. 431 (1982).

5. In Benge v. Scharbauer, 259 S.W.2d 166 (Tex. 1953), an undivided one-fourth mineral interest was outstanding in a third party when the grantors conveyed away several sections of land, purporting to reserve in themselves an undivided three-eighths interest in the oil and gas. The deed gave the grantees the sole power to execute oil and gas leases, but provided that "said leases shall provide for the payment of three-eighths (⅜ths) of all the bonuses, rentals and royalties to the grantors." A dispute later arose between the parties over the correct division of delay rentals under an oil and gas lease that had been executed by the grantees. The court reasoned that under the *Duhig* doctrine the deed warranty was breached because of the existence of the outstanding one-fourth mineral interest; hence, to remedy the breach a one-fourth mineral interest was taken from what the grantors had tried to reserve, leaving them with only a one-eighth interest in the minerals.

The grantees won a Pyrrhic victory, however, for the remainder of the court's reasoning was as follows:

> The fractional part of the bonuses, rentals and royalties that one is to receive under a mineral lease usually or normally is the same as his fractional mineral interest, but we cannot say that it must always be the same. The parties owning the mineral interests may make it different if they intend to do so, and plainly and in a formal way express that intention. Here that intention is expressed by clear language in the deed that leases executed by the grantee under the power given shall provide for the payment of ⅜ths of all bonuses, rentals and royalties to the grantors. The provision is not an agreement that the parties to the deed shall participate in the bonuses, rentals and royalties in proportion to their ownership of mineral interests. It is rather a contractual provision that the grantors shall receive a specified part of the bonuses, rentals and royalties; namely, ⅜ths. * * * The rule of the Duhig case, in order to remedy the breach of warranty, takes from the grantors part of what the deed purported to reserve to them, but that rule should not be extended to change the express agreement as to what interests the grantors shall receive in bonuses, rentals and royalties under leases to be executed by the grantee.

259 S.W.2d at 169.

6. Quite commonly, a drafter, wanting to avoid a claim for breach of warranty, specifically excepts from a deed an interest reserved by a remote grantor; the *Duhig* doctrine, however, estops the remote grantor from claiming the interest. What effect should be given such a deed recital that overstates the size or misstates the ownership of an outstanding mineral interest? Many jurisdictions still adhere to the common law doctrine that an interest cannot be reserved in a third party who is a stranger to the deed. See, e.g., Lighthorse v. Clinefelter, 521 N.E.2d 1146 (Ohio App.9 Dist. 1987); In re Condemnation by County of Allegheny, 719 A.2d 1 (Pa.Commnwlth. 1997), and Little v. Linder, 651 S.W.2d 895 (Tex.App. 1983, writ refused n.r.e.). In such states an exception or reservation clause cannot transfer an interest to the remote grantor. Canter v. Lindsey, 575 S.W.2d 331 (Tex.Civ.App. 1978, writ refused n.r.e.) Other jurisdictions, however, have rejected the common law doctrine in its entirety. See, e.g., Willard v. First Church of Christ, Scientist, Pacifica, 498 P.2d 987 (Cal. 1972); Malloy v. Boettcher, 334 N.W.2d 8 (N.D.1983); and Simpson v. Kistler Inv. Co., 713 P.2d 751 (Wyo.1986). In this latter type of jurisdiction, what would be the effect of a deed recital that erroneously attributes a mineral interest to a prior owner?

PROBLEM

In 1950 Owens conveyed Blackacre to Able and reserved an undivided one-half interest in the minerals in himself. Five years later, Able gave Brown a warranty deed that made no reference to the prior reservation in Owens, but that purported to reserve in Able an undivided one-fourth interest in the minerals beneath Blackacre. Brown subsequently conveyed the tract to Crane. This deed did not reserve any interest in Brown, but specifically excepted an undivided one-half of the minerals in Owens and an undivided one-fourth of the minerals in Able. What interest does Crane own in the minerals? What other parties own an interest in the minerals? In what fractions? Compare Canter v. Lindsey, 575 S.W.2d 331 (Tex.Civ.App. 1978, writ refused n.r.e.) with Jackson v. McKenney, 602 S.W.2d 124 (Tex.Civ.App. 1980, writ refused n.r.e.).

Crane has now contracted to sell Blackacre to Daniels. How should you draft the reservation and exception clauses if Crane wants to retain a one sixty-fourth royalty? An undivided one-eighth interest in the mineral fee?

ACOMA OIL CORP. v. WILSON

471 N.W.2d 476 (N.D.1991).

In 1915 H.O. Moen obtained fee simple title to the 160–acre tract of land in McKenzie County described as:

Township 153 North, Range 95 West

Section 20: NW¼

In 1937 Moen made three separate royalty conveyances, cumulatively transferring a 6.5% royalty of all oil and gas produced from the 160 acres, to third parties. The primary dispute in this case is whether the burden of that 6.5% royalty is proportionately shared by the current mineral interest owners.

Moen and his wife conveyed the 160 acres to Clayton D. Wilson, Sr., by warranty deed dated December 18, 1944, and recorded February 7, 1945. Moens' warranty deed did not reserve any mineral interests or mention the prior royalty assignments. Clayton, Sr., then conveyed the 160 acres to himself and his wife, Alma E. Wilson, as joint tenants. The parties to this lawsuit all obtained their interest in the 160 acres through conveyances originating from Clayton, Sr., and Alma Wilson.

By separate mineral deeds, both dated June 17, 1952, and recorded on June 26, 1952, Clayton, Sr., and Alma conveyed an "undivided $^{35}/_{320}$th" and "an undivided $^{5}/_{320}$th interest in and to all the oil, gas, casinghead gas, casinghead gasoline and other minerals in and under" the N ½ of Section 20 to Thomas W. Leach. The two mineral deeds identified a specific intent to convey 35 and 5 "mineral acres," respectively, in the N ½ of Section 20. Neither mineral deed indicated that the conveyed interest was burdened by the outstanding 6.5% royalty. * * *

* * *

Leach obtained a title opinion, dated June 21, 1952, which noted the outstanding 6.5% royalty in the NW ¼ of Section 20.

[Leach subsequently executed mineral deeds conveying various fractions of the mineral estate to United Properties and Clarke Bassett. United reconveyed to Acoma Oil Corp. None of these deeds referred to the outstanding 6.5% royalty.]

* * *

When Clayton, Sr., died on February 8, 1978, his interest in the NW ¼ of Section 20 passed to his wife, Alma, as joint tenant. Alma died on March 11, 1984, and by probate of her estate and a personal representative's deed of distribution from her estate, dated November 25, 1986, and recorded December 16, 1986, her interest in the NW ¼ of Section 20 passed to her sons, Clayton D. Wilson, Jr. and Allan LeRoy Wilson (the Wilson children), with each getting an undivided ½ interest.

Universal Resources Corporation (Universal) has operated a producing oil and gas well on the NW ¼ of Section 20 since 1983. A dispute arose as to whether the burden of the 6.5% royalty should be shared proportionately by Acoma, Bassett,[1] and the Wilson interests, or entirely by the Wilsons. Acoma commenced this action against the Wilson children for breach of warranty and to quiet title. Acoma sought a determination that its mineral interests in the 160–acre tract of land were not burdened by the 6.5% royalty and that the Wilson interests were burdened by that royalty. * * * Bassett intervened as a plaintiff, essentially raising the same claims and seeking the same relief as Acoma.

The parties submitted stipulated facts to the trial court. The court concluded that the rationale of *Duhig et al. v. Peavy–Moore Lumber Co.,* 135 Tex. 503, 144 S.W.2d 878 (1940), was not applicable to this fact situation. The court observed that equitable estoppel[2] applied to fact situations which did not conform to the classic *Duhig* scenario. The trial court applied equitable estoppel and determined that Leach was aware of the outstanding 6.5% royalty because of a contemporaneous title opinion and that he was not "destitute of all knowledge of the true state of the title [and] of the means of acquiring such knowledge." The court concluded that "[e]quity dictates that the royalty burden of six and a half percent created in 1937 by the former owner, Moen, be proportioned among the present mineral owners." * * *

We initially consider the trial court's determination that the 6.5% royalty should be proportionately shared by the present mineral owners. Acoma and Bassett contend that the trial court erred in determining that

---

1. The decimal equivalent of Acoma's interest in proceeds from the well with a proportionate reduction for the royalty is .0104062 and without a proportionate reduction for the royalty is .0140625. The decimal equivalent of Bassett's interest in proceeds from the well with a proportionate reduction for the royalty is .0022969 and without a proportionate reduction for the royalty is .00351563.

2. The trial court quoted the following "equitable estoppel" test to determine whether or not a grantor should be estopped from asserting title:

"1. The party making the admission by his declaration or conduct was appraised of the true state of his own title;

"2. That he made the admission with the express intention to deceive or with such careless and culpable negligence as to amount to constructive fraud;

"3. The other party was not only destitute of all knowledge of the true state of the title, but of the means of acquiring such knowledge;

"4. That he relied directly upon such admission and will be injured by allowing its truth to be disproved;"

See Wehner v. Schroeder, 354 N.W.2d 674 (N.D.1984); *Gilbertson v. Charlson,* 301 N.W.2d 144 (N.D.1981).

Duhig, supra, was not applicable and in determining that equitable estoppel dictated a proportionate sharing of the 6.5% royalty by the present mineral owners. Relying on *Duhig,* they argue that the Wilson interests should bear the entire burden of the 6.5% royalty, because Clayton, Sr., and Alma had sufficient remaining mineral interests to satisfy the outstanding 6.5% royalty when they made their conveyances to Leach.

The defendants respond that *Duhig* is not applicable to this case because there was no mineral reservation clause in the mineral deeds from Clayton, Sr., and Alma to Leach. They argue that the trial court correctly determined that the 6.5% royalty should be shared proportionately under equitable estoppel because Leach had actual or constructive knowledge of the outstanding royalty.

Under *Duhig* " 'a grantor who, by warranty deed, purports to convey a fractional mineral interest is estopped from asserting title to a reserved fractional mineral interest in contradiction to the interest purportedly conveyed.' " *Mau v. Schwan,* 460 N.W.2d 131, 133 (N.D.1990), *citing Sibert v. Kubas,* 357 N.W.2d 495, 496 n. 1 (N.D.1984). *See generally* 1 Williams & Meyers, Oil & Gas Law § 311 et seq. (1990).

* * *

Duhig resolves a conflict between grant and reservation clauses under principles of estoppel by warranty, a subset of estoppel by deed, which precludes a warrantor of title from disputing the title warranted. *Mau, supra.* The effect of *Duhig* is that a grantor cannot grant and reserve the same mineral interest, and if a grantor does not own a large enough mineral interest to satisfy both the grant and the reservation, the grant must be satisfied first because the obligation incurred by the grant is superior to the reservation. * * *

In *Mau, supra,* we observed that several North Dakota statutes reinforced the result in *Duhig.*

* * *

In this case the plaintiffs obtained their mineral interests by conveyances originating from the Wilson parents' transfer to Leach. We thus look to that conveyance to determine the applicability of *Duhig* and those statutes to this case because estoppel by deed precludes a party to a deed and privies from asserting against another party and privies any right or title in derogation of the deed, or from denying the truth of any material facts asserted in the deed. That analysis is supported by the language of Section 47–10–08, N.D.C.C., that "[e]very grant of an estate in real property is conclusive against the grantor and everyone subsequently claiming under him."

The parties to this action are successors in interest to the Wilson parents. The Wilson parents conveyed an "undivided" fractional "interest in and to all the oil, gas, casinghead gas, casinghead gasoline and other minerals in and under" the NW ¼ of Section 20 to Leach. Those mineral deeds included language stating a specific intent to convey 35 and 5 "mineral acres," respectively, in the N ½ of Section 20. Neither deed indicated that the mineral acres were burdened by the outstanding 6.5% royalty and each deed included language granting a warranty of title.

A mineral acre is the full mineral interest in one acre of land. 8 Williams & Meyers, Manual of Terms, p. 561 (1987). * * * A royalty interest is a smaller interest in a mineral estate which is a share of the product or proceeds reserved to the owner for permitting another to develop or use the property. * * * Although royalty interests are part of the full spectrum of a mineral estate, the interest in minerals in place and the interest in royalty based on the production of those minerals are separate and distinct estates. *Selman v. Bristow,* 402 S.W.2d 520 (Tex.Civ. App.1966).

Instruments conveying "mineral acres" generally have been construed to convey the full spectrum of oil and gas rights recognized in the law and instruments granting interests in oil, gas and other minerals "in and under" described land have also been construed to convey full mineral interests. In this case, the mineral deeds from the Wilson parents to Leach warranted conveyances of "mineral acres" and interests in oil, gas, and other minerals "in and under" the 160 acres. The Wilson parents thus warranted conveyances of an undivided fraction of the full bundle of mineral rights in the 160–acre tract of land to Leach. After the conveyances to Leach, the Wilson parents owned enough royalty interest in that tract of land to satisfy the previous 6.5% royalty assignments made by Moen without a reduction of any royalty from the "mineral acres" conveyed to Leach.

Under those circumstances, we believe that Sections 47–09–13, 47–09–16 and 47–10–08, N.D.C.C., and the *Duhig* rationale are applicable to the Wilson parents' conveyances of mineral acres to Leach. Like *Duhig,* in cases where a grantor conveys some mineral interests while keeping some mineral interests in the same tract of land without an explicit reservation, the focus is on whether or not the grantor has enough mineral interests in that tract of land to satisfy the conveyance. We believe that result follows under our law even though the Wilson parents' mineral deeds did not contain a specific reservation clause because "a grant [without a reservation] shall be interpreted in favor of the grantee" [Section 47–09–13, N.D.C.C.] and "a conveyance of land, without any exception or reservation of the minerals constitutes a conveyance of 100 percent of the minerals as well as the surface." *Sibert supra,* 357 N.W.2d at 496, citing *Schulz v. Hauck,* 312 N.W.2d 360 (N.D.1981).

We are not persuaded that equitable estoppel and Leach's actual or constructive knowledge of the outstanding 6.5% royalty is applicable to this case because the Wilson parents owned enough mineral interests in the 160–acre tract of land to fulfill their grant to Leach. *See Sibert, supra* [grantee's actual or constructive notice of a third party's outstanding mineral interest does not jeopardize a grantee's rights against a grantor who has made a conveyance by warranty deed].

Wehner v. Schroeder, 354 N.W.2d 674 (N.D.1984),[3] is distinguishable. In that case there was a discrepancy between two instruments executed by the original grantor and grantee which should have given a successor in interest sufficient notice of a potential problem to prompt further investigation. Here, the record title shows that there was an outstanding 6.5% royalty in the 160 acres, but the Wilson parents' mineral deeds do not indicate that the mineral acres conveyed by them were burdened by that royalty and they owned enough remaining mineral interests in that land to fulfill their grant of mineral acres to Leach. Leach's actual or constructive knowledge of the outstanding 6.5% royalty does not diminish the Wilson parents' warranty because the risk of title loss is on the grantor. We conclude that *Duhig* and our previously cited statutory provisions govern this case.

Other courts have used the *Duhig* rationale to conclude that conveyances of undivided fractional mineral interests in a tract of land were not proportionately burdened by prior royalty conveyances. *Atlantic Refining Co. v. Beach,* 78 N.M. 634, 436 P.2d 107 (1968); *Selman v. Bristow,* 402 S.W.2d 520 (Tex.Civ.App. 1966).

* * *

The rationale of *Selman* and *Atlantic Refining* is consistent with our statutory provisions and *Duhig.* * * * Because the Wilson parents owned enough mineral interests in the 160–acre tract of land to fully satisfy their conveyances to Leach, we conclude that the interests of Leach's successors in interest, Acoma and the Bassett Trust, are not burdened by the 6.5% royalty. * * * We therefore conclude that the trial court erred in determining that the 6.5% royalty should be proportionately shared by Acoma and Bassett.

* * *

The district court judgment is reversed, and we remand for further proceedings consistent with this opinion.

VANDE WALLE, JUSTICE, concurring specially.

Because, as the majority opinion recognizes, mineral and royalty interests are separate property interests with different characteristics, it would not be unreasonable to conclude, as did the district court, that the

---

3. We are aware of the analysis of our "equitable estoppel" decisions in *Wehner* and *Gilbertson. See* Richard C. Maxwell, "Some Comments on North Dakota Oil and Gas Law—Three Cases From the Eighties," 58 N.D.L.Rev. 431 (1982); Willis A. Ellis, "Rethinking the Duhig Doctrine," 28 Rocky Mtn. Min. Law Institute 947 (1983); Lisa B. Plumly, "Conveyances of Fractional Interests: North Dakota Supreme Court Repudiates the Duhig Rule, Gilbertson v. Charlson," 17 Tulsa Law Journal 117 (1981); Owen L. Anderson and Charles T. Edin, "The Growing Uncertainty of Real Estate Titles," 65 N.D.L.Rev. 1 (1989).

The elements of estoppel by deed and equitable estoppel are different [compare 28 Am.Jur.2d, Estoppel and Waiver, §§ 5 and 35], and it has been stated that it is a mistake to equate an estoppel by deed to an estoppel in pais. 28 Am.Jur.2d, Estoppel and Waiver § 4, citing *McAdams v. Bailey,* 169 Ind. 518, 82 N.E. 1057 (1907).

burden of the 6.5% royalty assignment was to be shared by all the owners of mineral acres in the 160 acres. * * *

* * *

Under a different set of facts, for example where the original grantor, after conveying a royalty interest conveys all the grantor's remaining mineral acres or conveys mineral acres to the extent that the grantor no longer retains sufficient interest to satisfy the previously conveyed royalty interest, the result would be different. I write separately to note that the majority opinion does not, nor does it purport to resolve those factual situations. In such instances, depending upon the facts, the burden of the previously conveyed royalty interest might well be shared proportionately by the present mineral owners.

NOTES

1. Does the *Duhig* doctrine permit a grantee to claim an interest reserved by the grantor if that interest is not identical to the one that the grantee fails to receive? What, for example, is the effect of a deed that reserves a one-sixteenth royalty in the grantor, but fails to except an undivided one-half interest in the minerals owned by a third party? How would the court in *Acoma* construe the deed? The concurring judge?

2. In Gilstrap v. June Eisele Warren Trust, 106 P.3d 858 (Wyo. 2005) the grantee (Ray) owned the surface and an undivided half interest in the mineral estate. His brother (William) owned the remaining half interest in the minerals, and his sister (Daisy) owned no interest whatsoever in the land. Nonetheless, William and Daisy joined as grantors in a warranty deed that purported to convey the entire property, both surface and minerals, to Ray and to reserve an undivided one-third interest in the minerals to each of the grantors. In subsequent litigation over ownership of the minerals, Ray's heirs contended, among other arguments, that since Daisy had owned no interest in the land, the deed purported to convey an undivided two-thirds interest in the mineral estate to the grantee. Under *Duhig*, which had been followed in Wyoming, William was thereby estopped to assert any interest in the undivided half of the minerals that he had owned. In ruling against this argument the Wyoming Supreme Court reasoned that since the grantee was already the owner of an outstanding half interest, that interest should be subtracted from the interest purportedly warranted by the grantors. Hence, all that William warranted title to was the undivided half interest that he actually owned. Moreover, even though Daisy owned no interest in the land, the deed on its face purported to convey only an undivided one-third interest in the minerals. Applying *Duhig*, the court concluded that this was the size of the mineral estate that passed to the grantee, and it could be deducted from the half-interest owned by William, who was thereby left with an undivided one-sixth interest in the mineral estate.

3. Virtually any application of the *Duhig* rule presents the possibility that the grantee is receiving more than he bargained for. Thus the courts have frequently refused to apply the rule where the grantee has actual notice

that the grantor's land is subject to an outstanding interest. Actual notice may result from the language in the deed itself. This was true of the deed in the *Averyt* case, which specifically described the third party's interest. Should a grantee also be deemed on notice of the outstanding interest if his deed, while not mentioning the outstanding interest, nonetheless specifically refers "for all purposes" to the earlier deed in which the outstanding interest was created? See Harris v. Windsor, 294 S.W.2d 798 (Tex. 1956).

Is there justification for distinguishing between a grantee's actual notice and the constructive notice that a grantee is deemed to have of all recorded documents in his chain of title?

4. Although the doctrine of estoppel by deed is usually applied against a grantor, it is also occasionally invoked against a grantee. Sauceda v. Kerlin, 164 S.W.3d 892 (Tex. App. 2005) involved warranty deeds to land on Padre Island that were executed in 1937 by the heirs of Padre Juan Jose Balli, who had received the original grant of the island from Mexico in the preceding century. Each deed contained a reservation clause providing that the grantors therein reserved "a one-sixty-fourth ($\frac{1}{64}$th) of the royalty of one-eighth ($\frac{1}{8}$th) of any and all oil and/or gas or other minerals in and under * * * the above described premises." The grantees under these deeds later filed suit against other persons who had claims to Padre Island based on 1902 and 1923 court judgments. In order to reach a settlement with these claimants, the grantees abandoned their claims based on the Balli deeds and accepted conveyances of approximately 7,500 acres from the judgment claimants. They later sold the surface of the 7,500 acres and executed oil and gas leases on the underlying mineral estate. The descendants of the Balli grantors filed suit for a share of royalties on production from the leases. The court ruled for the plaintiffs, holding that the doctrine of estoppel by deed prevented defendant-grantees from disavowing the reservations in the 1937 deeds.

4. PROPORTIONATE REDUCTION CLAUSE

Even though both parties to an oil and gas lease are aware that the lessor owns only a fractional interest in the fee, the lessee normally prefers that the lease purports to convey the entire mineral fee. This practice assures that no outstanding interest will be inadvertently left in the lessor. It also gives the lessee the benefit of the after-acquired title doctrine if the lessor later acquires a greater interest in the land. The lessee protects itself against having to pay royalties upon a larger fee interest than the lessor actually owns by including a proportionate reduction clause in the lease. There are many variants of such provisions, which are sometimes referred to as "lesser interest" clauses, but they all typically provide for the reduction of payments to the lessor if his interest is less than that which he purports to lease. An example of such a clause is as follows:

> Without impairment of Lessee's rights under the warranty in event of failure of title, it is agreed that if Lessor owns an interest in said land less than the entire fee simple estate, then the royalties and rentals to be paid Lessor shall be reduced proportionately.

Although such provisions are usually adequate to adjust the amount of royalty owed to the lessor of a fractional fee interest, they must be carefully drawn if, like the above clause, they are intended to apply to other leasehold benefits as well. The following case should serve to illustrate the problem.

TEXAS CO. v. PARKS

247 S.W.2d 179 (Tex.Civ.App.1952, writ refused n.r.e.).

RENFRO, JUSTICE.

Suit was brought by appellees, L.D. Parks and wife, as owners and lessors, to terminate a lease and assignment thereunder and remove same as a cloud upon their title. From a judgment terminating the lease, because of failure of appellant, The Texas Company, to pay the rental provided in the lease, this appeal resulted.

The facts are undisputed. On February 4, 1950, L.D. Parks and wife executed an oil and gas lease to W.L. Simmons covering their undivided one-half interest in the E/2 of Sec. 208, Block D of the John H. Gibson Survey in Yoakum County, Texas. On February 10, 1950, Simmons assigned the lease to The Texas Company.

The lease was for a period of ten years from February 4, 1950, and for as long thereafter as oil and gas or other minerals were produced. The lease provided for the payment of $160 per year delay rental.

On January 18, 1951, appellant tendered to the First National Bank of Fort Worth the sum of $80 to be deposited to the credit of L.D. Parks et ux. to cover the annual rental for the privilege of deferring commencement of drilling operations for a period of twelve months from February 4, 1951. L.D. Parks refused to accept the $80, contending the proper amount of annual rental was the sum of $160. Operations for drilling on the E/2 of Sec. 208, Block D, John H. Gibson Survey, were not commenced on or before February 4, 1951.

Appellant did not pay or tender to L.D. Parks and wife, or to the First National Bank of Fort Worth, the sum of $160 to constitute the delay or annual rental on said lease. The contention of The Texas Company has been at all times since receiving the assignment from Simmons that "$80 is the correct amount."

At the time of the execution of the oil and gas lease on February 4, 1950, L.D. Parks and wife, Una W., were the owners of an undivided one-half interest in the property therein described. There has been no failure of title as to the leasehold interest in such undivided one-half interest.

* * *

The three points raised by appellant may be summarized in one question, namely, whether, in the situation presented by the undisputed facts, appellant was entitled under the proportionate reduction clause to reduce proportionately the amount of rental stated in the rental clause.

In determining whether appellant was entitled to reduce proportionately the amount of the rental, we must ascertain, if possible, from the lease instrument the true intention of the parties. The intent of the parties, if it can be ascertained from the instrument, will prevail.

Appellant cites King v. First National Bank of Wichita Falls, 144 Tex. 583, 192 S.W.2d 260, 263, 163 A.L.R. 1128, as authority for its contentions. In that case the granting clause of a warranty deed conveyed an undivided one-half interest in certain property which was then described as a whole. Certain royalty interest was reserved. The Supreme Court said, " * * * looking forward from the granting clause and backward from the reservation clause it seems evident that the terms 'following described land', 'hereinabove described land', 'said land', and 'premises', refer not to the one-half interest actually conveyed, * * * but relate to the intervening paragraphs of the deed wherein the '1st Tract' and the '2nd Tract' are particularly described as a whole in units of 160 acres and 80 acres, respectively."

Different from the description in King v. First National Bank, supra, the lease before us conveys the whole leasehold interest of grantors in and to an undivided one-half interest in the E/2 of Sec. 208, Block D, John H. Gibson Survey. The only question before the court in the King case was the amount of royalty interest reserved by the grantor in a warranty deed. The question of rental was not involved. In the instant case the amount of annual delay rental agreed upon in an oil and gas lease is the only question to be determined.

Par. 4 of the lease provides that if drilling operations are not commenced within one year on said land, the lease shall terminate as to both parties unless the lessee deposit in the First National Bank of Fort Worth to the credit of lessors the sum of $160 rental.

In Par. 9, lessor agrees to warrant title to said land, and the same paragraph provides that if lessor owns an interest in said land less than the entire fee simple estate, then the rentals shall be reduced proportionately.

Looking forward from the granting clause and backward from the rental clause, we reach the conclusion that as to the rental, the lease referred to the undivided one-half interest of lessors, and when lessee agreed to pay $160 rental on said land, said land referred to the interest therein conveyed by lessor, namely, lessors' undivided one-half interest.

The agreement to pay $160 rental on said land referred to the undivided one-half interest in the whole tract and not to the 320 acres in its entirety.

The property referred to as the land is the same as that actually owned and conveyed by the lessors.

The delay rental clause is for the benefit of the lessee. The provision for payment of delay rentals is designed to enable a lessee who finds it undesirable to begin drilling on the agreed date to avert a forfeiture, and retain his rights by paying periodical rentals for the privilege of deferring operations. 31A Tex.Jur., pp. 247–8, Sec. 145.

The lease does not specify any particular rental rate per acre. On the contrary, it provides a lump sum payment to lessor of $160. If the parties had intended the rental to appellees to be any other sum, the lease could have so provided. The parties could agree upon any amount of rental they desired. In our opinion, it is inescapable that by the terms of the lease before us, it was the intention of the parties, and they agreed, that lessors would receive an annual rental of $160 for their interest conveyed. There is nothing in the lease to indicate that the parties were fixing the rental on a percentage or fractional basis, or in proportion to lessors' interest in the entire tract. It was an agreement to pay the lessors in the particular lease the lump sum of $160 per year rental. The language employed does not support the contention that lessee agreed to pay a total of only $160 to all the owners of the 320 acre tract.

* * *

Having determined that the lessee agreed to pay lessor $160 annual delay rental for the interest conveyed, it necessarily follows that appellant could not rely upon the reduction clause to reduce the payment from $160 to $80. The appellees' title has not failed. They owned the entire fee simple in what they conveyed, to-wit, their undivided one-half interest.

The court did not err in holding that appellees were entitled to cancellation of the lease.

* * *

The judgment of the trial court canceling the lease and removing said lease and assignment as a cloud on appellees' title is affirmed.

Affirmed.

ON MOTION FOR REHEARING

HALL, CHIEF JUSTICE.

Hazarding the probability of repeating findings expressed in our original opinion, we shall undertake to explain in more detail the reason for our holding, and, at the same time, answer some of the vigorous contentions advanced in appellant's motion for rehearing.

The scrivener used an oil and gas lease form known as "Producers 88—Revised 8–42, Texas Standard Lease Form," which in our opinion was prepared for the purpose of leasing from a lessor his entire interest in a tract of land, regardless of whether he owned the whole tract or only a proportionate part thereof. The provisions of each paragraph are so synchronized, one with the other, in order for the scrivener to describe the tracts of land involved as a whole; then after the parties have agreed upon the amount of annual delay rental to be paid upon the whole tract to insert such amount in the rental clause, so that under the provisions under the last sentence in the proportionate reduction clause the lessee will pay rental in proportion to the amount of interest lessor has in the land. Evidently, for convenience, this or a similar form is consistently used by the oil industry and its niceties are well recognized by this court. This form of preparing an oil and gas lease, however, is not necessarily suitable where the lessor owns a lesser interest than the whole tract but does not intend to grant a lease on all of his interest. Neither should it become effective where the lessor owns the entire tract but is only leasing a portion thereof.

Be that as it may, let us review the provisions of the lease as written, and undertake to distinguish them from the above formula as outlined. We find the scrivener using a more orthodox method of describing the real estate, in that he only describes the interest lessor is to convey, which description is referred to in the instrument as "said lands" or "lands above described." Then we find in paragraph 4 the parties agreeing that $160.00 is the amount of annual rental to be paid on *said land*. At this point, no complication has arisen. However, under the last sentence in said paragraph 4, 320 acres more or less are referred to as the total amount of land considered for the purpose of executing releases and assignments, etc., by lessee. As to this particular phase of the written instrument, the scrivener was following the first formula, supra, which, among other things, requires that the tract be described as a whole. Thus, we have our first real diversity as the 320 acres last mentioned conflict with the description of the land conveyed in the granting clause. No doubt, the scrivener should have continued to follow his orthodox rule by describing *said land* as being *a one-half undivided interest in 320 acres more or less*.

Having the main issue in mind, the substance of appellant's argument is that we should consider the description in the granting clause as though it did cover the entire east half of the section in question. While appellant, in substance, is asking us to double the amount of acreage called for in the granting clause, yet it is not willing for us to raise the amount of rentals called for in the rental clause in the same proportion. If we were to change the number of acres in the granting clause without changing the amount of rental due under the rental clause, then we would be writing a new lease for the parties, which, under the law, the court is prohibited from doing. In other words, by applying such construction, we would reduce by fifty per cent the amount of rentals which the instrument calls for to be paid upon said proportionate interest in the whole tract of land.

The saving clause, or what is here termed the proportionate reduction clause, is designed to protect the lessee in the event the lessor owns a lesser interest in the land which he undertakes to convey.

While seeking to ascertain, from the four corners of the instrument, the true intention of the original parties pertaining to their agreement relative to the amount of delay rentals which might become due lessor, we would not be applying the "common-sense rule" by finding that both parties agreed to rely upon said proportionate reduction clause to determine such amount.

* * *

We do not agree with appellant's contention "that where a lease covers a fractional or undivided interest, lessee may under the proportionate reduction clause reduce the rental stated in the lease," as being the law applicable in a case where no greater interest in a tract of land is described than the portion being leased. Neither do we agree with appellant's argument that the effect of our opinion "is to place in jeopardy the right of the lessee to reduce royalty under every producing oil and gas lease in this State in which an undivided or fractional interest was described, rather than the entire fee simple interest, in the granting clause." Looking to the description of the land leased, we believe the lessee, or his assigns, would have no difficulty in determining the amount of royalty interest which appellees should receive if and as oil is produced from said land. We need not state here that a formula used or the reason given for determining amount of rental due under a lease should necessarily be the same formula used to ascertain proportionate royalty interests in the oil if and when produced. * * *.

* * *

Neither appellees nor appellant offered any extraneous evidence to aid the court in determining the facts of this case. It is not shown who drew the instrument or furnished the printed form in order that the court might construe same most strongly against such person. The following general rule that is used in construing written instruments pertaining to real estate, to the effect that the instrument must be construed most strongly against the lessor, does not necessarily apply as to oil and gas leases. As stated in 31A Tex.Jur., p. 178, sec. 108: "In many instances a contrary rule has been followed and the lease construed most strongly against the lessee." Obviously this rule does not apply where the lease is free from ambiguity.

Most other established rules governing the courts while construing description of lands in conveyances do generally apply to oil and gas leases. Therefore it is not amiss for an oil and gas lease to contain as near as possible a proper and accurate description of the land to be leased. The lease should also definitely define the lessee's duties and obligations in respect to continuing the life thereof, that is, in the instant case, to either commence a well or pay the "agreed delay rentals." 31A Tex.Jur., p. 218, sec. 134.

All emphases are ours.

Appellant's motion for rehearing is overruled.

NOTES

1. How should a lease be drafted to avoid the problem in the principal case?

2. If Cohen, who owns an undivided 3/4 interest in the mineral estate, executes a lease purporting to cover the entire mineral fee, the proportionate reduction clause would reduce her royalty to 3/4 of the royalty amount stated in the lease, e.g., from 1/8 to 3/32. See Baker v. Vanderpool, 178 S.W.2d 189 (Ky. 1944). What should be the result if Cohen owned 100% of the mineral estate, but the estate is burdened by an outstanding 1/16 non-participating royalty (NPRI)? By the weight of authority, the *Duhig* doctrine, rather than the proportionate reduction clause applies in this latter situation. If the lease royalty is 1/8, the holder of the NPRI would receive 1/16 and Cohen would receive the remaining lease royalty, in this situation the remaining 1/16. See, e.g., Klein v. Humble Oil & Refining Co., 86 S.W.2d 1077 (Tex. 1935).

E.H. Lester Leasing Co. v. Griffith, 779 S.W.2d 226 (Ky. App. 1989) illustrates the effect of applying the proportionate reduction clause, rather than the *Duhig* doctrine where the lessor's interest is burdened by a non-participating royalty. In that case the lessor, who owned land subject to a one-eighth nonparticipating royalty in third parties, executed an oil and gas lease providing for a one-eighth landowner's royalty and containing a proportionate reduction clause virtually identical to the one set out in the preceding note. The lessee, apparently relying on the *Duhig* doctrine, argued that the lessor was not entitled to any share of production, because the entire lease royalty was used in satisfying the outstanding nonparticipating royalty interests. Ruling against the lessee, the court concluded that the dispute was governed by the lesser interest clause.

> Here we find a situation in which the lessor's right to lease the mineral estate is encumbered by a 1/8 perpetual royalty interest. The bargain he struck pursuant to the lesser interest clause requires that his [royalty] interest be reduced to 1/8 x 7/8 or 7/64's because that is the extent of his interest. Were it otherwise, we believe the lease should be cancelled due to failure of consideration—it would be an absurd inequity to require the lessor to give up his interest in the minerals below his land, put up with the inconvenience attendant to production and receive nothing in return * * *.

Id. at 228.

The court's rationale for applying the proportionate reduction clause rather than *Duhig* is to avoid a result that seems unduly harsh to the lessor. What is the impact of *Lester Leasing* on the lessee? For a critique of the case, see Anderson, Discussion Notes, 107 O & GR 254 (1991).

3. Suppose that Jones and Morales each owns an undivided half interest in the mineral estate in Blackacre, but that Jones' interest is burdened by a 1/16 nonparticipating royalty held by Nguyen. Jones and Morales each execute separate, but identical oil and gas leases. Each lease provides for a 1/8 royalty, contains a proportionate reduction clause, and purports to cover 100% of the mineral estate. The lessee drills and obtains production. How much

royalty must the lessee pay? To whom is it paid? See Hooks v. Rocket Oil Co., 130 P.2d 846 (Okla. 1942).

4. In Horizon Resources, Inc. v. Putnam, 976 S.W.2d 268 (Tex. App. 1998) the lessor, who owned less than a full 100% interest in the minerals, executed a lease that provided for a 1/7th royalty. An addendum to the lease provided

> As additional bonus for the making of this lease, LESSOR shall receive an overriding two/thirty-fifths (2/35) royalty in all oil, gas, liquid hydrocarbon and sulfur associated with their production, produced from these lease premises.

The lease also contained a standard proportionate reduction clause. It stipulated that

> If this lease covers a less interest ... than the entire undivided fee simple estate ... the royalties, delay rental and other monies accruing from any part ... shall be paid only in the proportion which the interest therein ... bears to the whole and undivided fee simple estate therein.

In holding that the additional payment in the addendum as well as the basic royalty was subject to proportionate reduction, the court relied on the absence of language in the addendum stating that the payment was "net" or "without reduction." Neither the placement of the provision in an addendum nor use of the terms "bonus" and "overriding" indicated an intent to exclude the payment from the proportionate reduction clause, which by its express terms applied to "other monies" paid under the lease.

Should the result have been different if the addendum had provided for an oil payment? See Probst v. Ingram, 373 P.2d 58 (Okla.1962),where a typewritten rider to a lease provided that

> In addition to the royalty on oil provided for above, lessee agrees to deliver to lessor one-sixteenth (1/16th) of eight-eighths (8/8) of all oil which may be produced and saved by lessee from oil wells located on the leased premises, until the cumulative total value of the oil so delivered shall equal $82,500 ($1200 per acre for interest herein covered), at which time the obligation of this provision shall terminate.

For a similar case dealing with an overriding royalty, see Downen Enters. v. Gem Oil & Gas Co., 476 N.E.2d 42 (Ill.App.5 Dist. 1985).

G. CONVEYANCES OF INTERESTS IN LEASED LAND

Conveyances of interests in land subject to an oil and gas lease occasionally give rise to misunderstandings between the lessee and the parties to the conveyances. For example, if a lessor subdivides her property, the owners of the resulting tracts may assume that the lessee must now treat each tract as a separate unit. Some owners may argue that the lessee is obligated to protect them against drainage to the other tracts, or that the lessee should undertake development on a per-tract rather than a lease-wide basis. If the lessor transfers a fractional interest in her lease royalty, the transferee may contend that the lessee must provide separate measuring devices and receiving tanks for each royalty owners' share of oil production.

Many oil and gas leases contain provisions making clear that transfers by the lessor will not increase the lessee's duties. Such provisions are commonly referred to as "no-increase-of-burden clauses" and contain language like the following:

> No change or division in the ownership of the land, rentals or royalties, however accomplished, shall operate to enlarge the obligations, or diminish the rights of the Lessee * * *

Issues arising from conveyance of interests in leased land are not limited to those between the lessee and the lessor's successors. Indeed, as the following material illustrates, far more difficult problems arise in drafting and construing the conveyance itself.

1. CONVEYANCES "SUBJECT TO" AN EXISTING LEASE

If an oil and gas lease is outstanding of her land, a grantor contemplating a conveyance by warranty deed may be concerned that the lease will breach her deed warranty. To protect the grantor against such a claim by her grantee, the conveyance is normally made "subject to" the outstanding lease; to assure the grantee of receiving his share of lease benefits, the clause may then go on to state that the deed "covers and includes" lease rentals and royalties. As the following material indicates, the drafter should exercise extreme care to make sure that the interests referred to in the granting clause and in these subsequent clauses are consistent with each other.

HOFFMAN v. MAGNOLIA PETROLEUM CO.
273 S.W. 828 (Tex.Com.App.1925).

STAYTON, J. Peter L. Hoffman, as plaintiff, brought this suit for the recovery of the proceeds of royalties that accrued under an oil lease on a half section of land, basing his right of action upon a deed from lessors to himself. The district court sustained general demurrers to his petition, and the parties who demurred aver as the basis of the decision, and as correct law, the point that the deed only conveyed the royalty earned by wells drilled upon a tract of 90 acres out of the larger leased tract, whereas the petition did not allege that any wells had been brought in upon this particular 90 acres. The Court of Civil Appeals was of the same opinion, 260 S.W. 950. The defendants give assurance that this was and is the only question in the case; and for that reason, without a critical examination of the petition in other respects, the disposition of the cause will be governed accordingly. The specific inquiry is whether the deed gave plaintiff a right to participate in any royalties under the lease, unless production were had from a well upon the 90 acres.

As is shown by the allegations of the petition, the lease was in ordinary form to one R.O. Harvey as lessee; covered and conveyed the oil and gas under 320 acres out of a section of land in Comanche county; provided for a one-eighth royalty on oil, money royalty on gas, and rentals of $330 every six months, as consideration for deferring the commencement of a well, up to five years; made the rights under it perpetual during production; and negated all obligation upon lessee to drill upon any particular part of the premises.

The deed to plaintiff is averred to have passed from lessors, Duke and wife, before the completion of any well on the half section, in consideration of $10,000 paid by him. It was delivered nine months after the date of the lease, and granted:

> The following, to wit: One-half (1/2) interest in and to all of the oil, gas and other minerals in and under and that may be produced from the following described lands situated in Comanche county, Texas, to wit: A certain 90 acres (giving metes and bounds and describing the tract as out of the section already mentioned) together with the rights of ingress and egress at all times for the purpose of mining, drilling and exploring said lands for oil, gas, and other minerals and removing the same therefrom.

The instrument continued:

> Said above-described lands being now under an oil and gas lease originally executed in favor of R.O. Harvey and now held by ___. It is understood and agreed that this sale is made subject to said lease but covers and includes one-half of all the oil royalty and gas rental or royalty due to be paid under the terms of said lease. It is agreed and understood that one-half of the money rental which may be paid to extend the term within which a well may be begun under the terms of said lease is to be paid to the said Peter L. Hoffman and in the event that the said above-described lease for any reason becomes cancelled or forfeited then and in that event the lease interest and all further rentals on said land for gas and mineral privilege shall be owned jointly by Jas. N. Duke and wife, and ___ Hoffman, each owning one-half interest in all oil, gas and other minerals in and upon said land, together with one-half interest in all future rents. * * * To have and to hold the above-described property, together with all and singular the rights and appurtenances thereto in anywise belonging unto the said Peter L. Hoffman heirs and assigns, forever.

The plaintiff contends that the conveyance to him of "one-half of all of the oil royalty * * * due to be paid under the terms of said lease" is not confined to wells upon the smaller tract. The defendants reply that, since the smaller tract is the subject-matter of the deed, the quoted language should be construed as having reference to it alone, and that any other interpretation would be unreasonable.

Before deciding the question, the court would call to mind that, if the deed is capable of the meaning contended for by plaintiff, there would be nothing unreasonable in holding under the circumstances alleged that, for so substantial a cash consideration, the lessors, having previously conveyed to lessee all of the oil, gas, and minerals under the whole half section, and retained the surface for their own consistent uses, consented to part, not only with their possibility of a reverter in the oil, etc., of the 90 acres, but also with a full one-half of their right to royalties under the lease as an entirety, especially in view of the fact that the reverter was uncertain and the control over the placing of wells impossible. * * *

* * *

The deed, in the first part, conveys an undivided one-half interest in the possibility of a reverter of the oil in place under the 90 acres. For, "subject" to the lease, the one-half interest in the oil under that particular tract is conveyed to Hoffman. In the last part of the instrument it is provided that, if the lease shall be forfeited or canceled, the grantor and grantee shall share equally in all mineral interests and rights in "said land"; that is, the 90 acres. Gas and other minerals take the same course, but are not here involved.

Those passages have regard to minerals, the title to which has passed to the lessee, but which may revert to lessor and his assigns if the lease should terminate. But they are not the sole subject-matter of the conveyance. There follow other words regarding not the reverter but rents and royalties prior to the time the lease terminates, and while it is still in force, both before any well at all is drilled and after the drilling of a productive well.

The deed, after conveying the interest in oil, gas, and minerals, and referring, as the description and the allegations show, to the particular "lease" now under consideration, reads:

> It is understood and agreed that this sale is made subject to said lease, but covers and includes one-half of all the oil royalty and gas rental or royalty due to be paid under the terms of said lease. It is agreed and understood that one-half of the money rentals which may be paid to extend the term within which a well may be begun under the terms of said lease is to be paid to said Peter L. Hoffman. * * *

This is plainly a statement that the deed conveys a one-half interest in the royalty to accrue under the terms of the lease as an entirety; that is, the lease upon the whole half section.

Instead of restricting these royalties to wells on the 90 acres, the conveyance covers one-half of "all" the oil royalty under the terms of the lease. That this passage refers to an interest in the whole instead of a part of the royalty, irrespective of where the wells shall be located, is corroborated by the provisions for one-half of the delay rentals payable under the lease. These, by the provisions of the latter instrument, are to accrue before any well at all is begun, and the conveyance of them can only refer to the lease as a whole, and hence not to a particular 90 acres of it; thus showing that in this connection a segregated 90–acre tract is not intended to be the measure of the rights granted.

The Court of Civil Appeals correctly decided that, under this lease, a subdivision of the land would not affect the rights and obligations of the lessee—that the purchaser occupies no better position than his vendor does. As to the lessee the lease remained an entirety, as did his duty to pay rents and royalties. The deed said the 90 acres was subject to the lease. It was. But a conveyance of a part of the land did not subdivide the lease and turn it into two leases, one upon the 90 and the other upon the remaining 320. There was therefore no lease covering solely 90 acres, and, when the deed refers to the "lease," it can only refer to the lease on the whole 320 acres.

The words of the two instruments show this meaning, and it is one that may reasonably be viewed as the real intention of the parties.

* * *

It is suggested that there was a mistake with regard to the provisions of the deeds. If so, it may be remedied upon another trial.

* * *

We recommend that the judgment of the Court of Civil Appeals be reversed, and that the cause be remanded for new trial.

NOTES

1. In Caruthers v. Leonard, 254 S.W. 779 (Tex.Com.App. 1923), the Texas Commission of Appeals held that the grantee of a fractional interest in a mineral estate that was subject to a pre-existing oil and gas lease did not receive a right to proportionate benefits under the lease. Language stating that the conveyance "covers and includes" lease rentals and royalties was thereafter routinely inserted into deeds to avoid this result. The *Caruthers* case was overruled twenty years later by Harris v. Currie, 142 Tex. 93, 176 S.W.2d 302 (1943). See Thomas H. Lee, Ambiguity and the "Subject To" Clause in Texas Mineral Conveyancing, 5 So.Tex.L.J. 313 (1961) and Howard R. Williams, Hoffman v. Magnolia Petroleum Co.: The "Subject–To" Clause in Mineral and Royalty Deeds, 30 Tex.L.Rev. 395 (1952). For a discussion of these issues and the importance of historical context when interpreting documents, see David E. Pierce, Interpreting Oil and Gas Instruments, 1 Texas J. of Oil, Gas, and Energy L. 1, 23–29 (2006).

Is there any longer a reason to include "covers and includes" language in the deed? How else might the drafter deal with the problem posed by *Hoffman?*

2. The doctrine employed in the *Hoffman* case is commonly referred to as the "two-grant" theory. Its most controversial application has been to deeds where the fractions used in the granting clause and in the "covers and includes" clause, or its equivalent, are not consistent with each other. If, for example, the land is subject to an oil and gas lease providing for a one-eighth

royalty, the granting clause may purport to convey one thirty-second of the oil and gas beneath the tract, while the "subject to" clause states that the deed covers and includes one-fourth of all rents and royalties under the outstanding lease and under all future leases. The following case illustrates the problems involved in construing this type of deed.

CONCORD OIL CO. v. PENNZOIL EXPLORATION AND PRODUCTION CO.

966 S.W.2d 451 (Tex. 1998).

OWEN, JUSTICE, announced the judgment of the Court in an opinion in which PHILLIPS, CHIEF JUSTICE, HECHT and ABBOTT, JUSTICES, join.

The motions for rehearing were granted, and the opinion of the Court dated October 18, 1996 is withdrawn.

This case presents an issue with which this Court, other courts, and practitioners have struggled for many years: What interest has been conveyed in an oil and gas property when two differing fractions appear within the conveying instrument? The granting clause of the mineral deed in controversy describes the interest conveyed as a 1/96 interest in minerals, but a subsequent clause states that the conveyance covers and includes 1/12 of all rentals and royalty of every kind and character. We hold that the conveyance at issue, when considered in its entirety, constituted a grant of a 1/12 interest in any rights or benefits under the lease in existence at the time of the grant and the possibility of reverter of a 1/12 interest in the mineral estate. Accordingly, we reverse the judgment of the court of appeals and render judgment in favor of Concord and Crenshaw.

I

The mineral deed at issue, which we refer to as the Concord deed, was executed in 1937 by A.B. Crosby as the grantor. * * * The grantee was Southland Lease and Royalty Corporation.... Crenshaw acquired Southland's interest and subsequently executed two oil and gas leases under which Concord is the lessee. * * * The Concord deed provides in relevant part:

> That I, A.B. Crosby ... Grant, Sell and Convey unto Southland ... an undivided one-ninety sixth (1/96) interest in and to all of the oil, gas and other minerals in and under, and that may be produced from Survey Sixty-four ... together with the right ... of ingress and egress at all times for the purpose of prospecting, drilling, mining and exploring said lands for oil, gas and other minerals ... together with all rights of every kind and character necessary and convenient to the full use and enjoyment of such estate herein conveyed....

> While the estate hereby conveyed does not depend upon the validity thereof, neither shall it be affected by the termination thereof, this conveyance is made subject to the terms of any valid subsisting oil, gas and/or mineral lease or mineral lease or leases on above described land or any part thereof, but covers and includes one-twelfth (1/12) of

all rentals and royalty of every kind and character that may be payable by the terms of such lease or leases insofar as the same pertain to the above described land, or any part thereof.

This deed was executed on August 5. The day before, the grantor Crosby had acquired an undivided 1/12 interest in the minerals under a deed identical to the Concord deed in all respects but one: the fraction in the granting clause. The granting clause in the deed to Crosby contained the fraction "one-twelfth (1/12)" rather than 1/96.

The parties have stipulated that at the time each of these deeds was executed, an oil and gas lease that provided for a 1/8 royalty was outstanding. That lease expired before any of the parties to this case entered into leases covering Survey Sixty-four.

[Long after the original lease expired Robinson, who was the grantor's successor in interest, executed an oil and gas lease to Pennzoil Producing Co.]

* * *

Pennzoil completed producing wells on the property, and this dispute ensued. Concord sought a determination of its interest and sued for damages equal to the value of past production by Pennzoil. Pennzoil counterclaimed seeking a determination of its rights. * * * Concord's primary contention was that the deed at issue unambiguously conveyed a 1/12 interest in the minerals. * * *

Pennzoil contended that the Concord deed conveyed only a 1/96 interest in the minerals. Pennzoil acknowledged that the deed had also conveyed 1/12 of rentals and royalty, but took the position that the 1/12 interest was limited to the lease that existed at the time the deed was executed. Under Pennzoil's view of the case, the 1/12 interest terminated upon the expiration of that lease, which occurred well before the Crosby conveyance to Robinson, Pennzoil's lessor.

The trial court found in favor of Pennzoil and entered a take-nothing judgment against Concord. The court of appeals affirmed. 878 S.W.2d 191. The basis of the court of appeals' holding was that the Concord deed did not convey any interest in future leases. The court concluded that the grant of 1/12 of rentals and royalty was limited to the lease in existence at the time of the conveyance, and that upon expiration of that lease, Concord was left with only a 1/96 interest in the minerals. The court relied on what has been termed the "two-grant" or "multiple-grant" theory in concluding that the deed did not convey a single estate, but instead conveyed a 1/96 interest in the minerals in addition to a 1/12 interest in the lease existing at the time of the grant. Id. at 196. For the reasons discussed below, we disagree with this construction of the deed.

II

This case is not the first one in which we have considered deeds or other conveyances of mineral interests that contain two or more differing fractions. The proper construction of such instruments has been a recurring issue. * * *

In Luckel [v. White, 819 S.W.2d 459 (Tex.1991)], we held that the primary objective in construing mineral and other grants is to determine the intent of the parties from all the language in the instrument. We recognized that the intent of the parties must be determined from what they expressed in the instrument, read as a whole, and that the actual, subjective intent of the parties will not always be given effect even if we were able to discern that subjective intent. We declined to rely on labels given to clauses, such as "granting," "warranty," "habendum," and "future lease." We expressly overruled our decision in Alford v. Krum, 671 S.W.2d 870 (Tex.1984), which had elevated the granting clause over another provision in the conveying instrument and had given it controlling weight.

Commentators have written fairly extensively about our decisions in this area of oil and gas law, often debating what theories were or were not applied.[1] However, with the exception of Alford, our decisions contain a unifying principle: the entire document must be examined to glean the parties' intent. Apparent inconsistencies in the conveying instrument must be harmonized, if possible, by looking at the document as a whole. 46 Baylor L.Rev. 1007 (1994).

A

One of the first decisions that confronted a conveyance with more than one fraction was Tipps v. Bodine, 101 S.W.2d 1076 (Tex.Civ.App.–Texarkana 1937, writ ref'd). The granting clause was couched in terms that typically would indicate that a 1/16 interest in the minerals had been conveyed. Standing alone, this language would indicate that the grantee would receive only 1/16 of royalties payable under any lease, 1/16 of delay rentals, and 1/16 of bonuses paid upon execution of future leases. But the mineral deed in Tipps contained three other clauses under which the grantor effectively conveyed a larger fraction of each of the incidents of the mineral estate. The grantor conveyed: a 1/2 interest in benefits under the existing lease, a 1/2 interest in the possibility of reverter and executive rights (the "lease interest"), a 1/2 interest in all benefits under future leases (which would have been the result of a grant of 1/2 of the possibility of reverter in any event), and, for good measure, a 1/2 interest in "all

---

1. A sampling of treatises and articles addressing so-called multiple-grant conveyances and decisions of this Court includes: RICHARD W. HEMINGWAY, THE LAW OF OIL AND GAS §§ 9.1–.2 (3d ed.1991); Laura H. Burney, The Regrettable Rebirth of the Two–Grant Doctrine in Texas Deed Construction, 34 S. TEX. L.J. 73 (1993); Tevis Herd, Deed Construction and the "Repugnant to the Grant" Doctrine, 21 TEX. TECH L.REV. 635 (1990); Stuart C. Hollimon & Robert E. Vinson, Jr., Oil, Gas, and Mineral Law, Annual Survey of Texas Law, 45 SW. L.J. 1965 (1992); Bruce M. Kramer, The Sisyphean Task of Interpreting Mineral Deeds and Leases: An Encyclopedia of Canons of Construction, 24 TEX. TECH L.REV. 1 (1993); Phillip E. Norvell, Pitfalls in Developing Lands Burdened by Non–Participating Royalty: Calculating the Royalty Share and Coexisting with the Duty Owed to the Non–Participating Royalty Owner by the Executive Interest, 48 ARK. L.REV. 933 (1995); Joseph Shade, Petroleum Land Titles: Title Examination & Title Opinions, 46 BAYLOR L.REV. 1007 (1994).

future events." The Tipps court held that these provisions accomplished the conveyance of a 1/2 interest in the minerals even though the granting clause contained the fraction "1/16." The intent of the parties was evident from the four corners of the instrument.

The facts in Garrett v. Dils Co., 157 Tex. 92, 299 S.W.2d 904 (1957), were similar to those in Tipps. The granting clause purported to convey a 1/64 interest in the minerals. However, a subsequent clause identified an existing lease and provided that "this sale . . . covers and includes one-eighth of all . . . rental or royalty due." The deed in Garrett also had a clause addressing future events that stated that the grantee was to own "an undivided one-eighth of the lease interest and all future rentals . . . and other mineral privileges . . . [the grantee] owning one-eighth of one-eighth of all oil, gas, and other minerals . . . together with one-eighth interest in all future rents." We held that because the grantee had the right to receive 1/8 of the royalty together with 1/8 of the lease interest (the executive rights) and future rentals, he was "in reality . . . the owner of one-eighth of the minerals in the land." Id. at 907. Once again, the instrument spelled out what the grantee was to receive, which amounted to 1/8 of all the attributes of mineral ownership.

The conflict in the royalty deed at issue in Luckel was not as readily apparent as those in Tipps and Garrett. In Luckel, as long as the royalty payable under any given lease was a 1/8 royalty, the granting clause seemed consistent with other parts of the deed. The granting and warranty clauses of the royalty deed at issue spoke of a 1/32 royalty. 819 S.W.2d at 461. A clause addressing an existing lease and another clause dealing with subsequent leases stated, respectively, that the grantee "shall receive one-fourth" and "shall be entitled to one-fourth" of all royalties, which would equal a 1/32 royalty under a 1/8 royalty lease. Problems in construing the deed arose when leases providing for a 1/6 royalty were subsequently obtained. We held that 1/4 of royalty, rather than a fixed 1/32 royalty interest, was conveyed. Id. at 464. The grant of a 1/32 royalty, however, was held to be a floor for the royalty interest. Id. at 464–65. The 1/4 of royalty otherwise payable under any given lease could not result in less than a 1/32 royalty.

On the same day that we decided Luckel, we also decided Jupiter Oil Co. v. Snow, 819 S.W.2d 466 (Tex. 1991). The granting clause of the mineral deed in Jupiter Oil described a 1/16 interest in the minerals. Although not set out fully in this Court's opinion, another paragraph in the deed dealt with an existing lease and stated that the parties intended that the grantee "receive 1/16 part of the oil, gas or other mineral" produced under the lease then in effect and that the grantors intended to convey "one-half of the interest they now have in such production under said lease." Snow v. Jupiter Oil Co., 802 S.W.2d 354, 356 (Tex.App.–Eastland 1990), rev'd, 819 S.W.2d 466 (Tex. 1991). That lease provided for a 1/8 royalty. Jupiter Oil, 819 S.W.2d at 467. Another provision in the mineral deed dealt with termination of the then-existing lease and recited that upon that event, the grantee was to "have and hold" 1/2 of all minerals. We held that this deed conveyed a 1/2 interest in the possibility of reverter and that the grantee owned a 1/2 interest in the minerals upon termination of the lease that was outstanding at the time of the conveyance. The result in Jupiter Oil was fully consistent with Luckel, Garrett, and Tipps.

* * *

C

In each of the cases in which the fraction in the granting clause was smaller than those in subsequent parts of the conveyance, the conveyance contained explicit, unambiguous provisions that directed what interest the grantee was to receive under various circumstances. In each of these cases, the fraction was consistent in all clauses except the granting clause. And, in each of these cases, when all the rights of the grantee under the specific provisions following the granting clause were considered and aggregated, the grantee had in fact received an estate larger than that otherwise indicated by the granting clause.* * *

This does not mean that no deed or grant should be construed to convey mineral and royalty interests of different magnitudes. The owner of a mineral interest may convey one or more, or fractions of one or more, of any attribute of the mineral estate, including but certainly not limited to a fraction of the mineral interest, a fraction of royalties, the right to receive delay rentals, and the executive rights. But when differing fractions appear in a conveyance, we must discern the intent of the parties from the four corners of the document. * * *

III

The Concord deed does not give as much guidance as the conveyances considered by this Court in other cases. One of the primary points of dispute is whether the provision that refers to "one-twelfth (1/12) of all rentals and royalty" applies only to leases in existence at the time the grant was made or whether it applies to all leases. The court of appeals framed the issue as whether the Concord deed contained a "future lease" clause and concluded that it did not.

Whether a deed such as the one under consideration contains a "future lease" clause is not necessarily dispositive of what interest was conveyed. The substance of what has been conveyed must be determined taking into account all provisions of the conveyance. The parties' intent must be determined from the document as a whole, not by the presence or absence of a certain provision.

A

One of the first questions that must be answered is whether it is evident within the four corners of the conveyance that two differing interests were to be conveyed. Although the Concord deed gives only sparse direction, we conclude that it does not evidence an intent to convey two separate interests. The opening paragraph of the deed describes a 1/96 interest in the "estate" conveyed. The second paragraph recites that "the estate hereby conveyed . . . covers and includes one-twelfth (1/12) of all rentals and royalty of every kind and character." This language indicates that only a single "estate" is being conveyed, not two separate interests. Moreover, if the estate were only a 1/96 interest in the minerals, it would cover and include only 1/96 of the rents and royalty. A 1/96 mineral interest could not "cover [ ] and include[ ] one-twelfth (1/12) of all rentals and royalties."

Another indication that a single estate rather than two estates with differing durations was conveyed is the recitation in the deed that the estate being conveyed "does not depend upon the validity . . . [nor] shall it be affected by the termination" of leases. If the estate conveyed was a 1/12 mineral interest only for the life of the lease that was in effect at the time the deed was executed and became a 1/96 mineral interest upon expiration of that lease, "the estate hereby conveyed" is unquestionably "affected by the termination" of that lease. The construction placed on the deed by the court of appeals and by the dissent ignores the express direction of the deed. The dissent and the court of appeals concede, as they must, that the grantee was entitled to 1/12 of rents and royalties as long as the lease in existence at the time of the conveyance continued in effect. They cannot explain how, upon termination of that lease, "the estate hereby conveyed," which included 1/12 of rents and royalties under the existing lease, became 1/96 of rents and royalties under all future leases and yet was not "depend[ent] upon" or "affected by" the termination of the existing lease.

The construction adopted by the court of appeals also does violence to the express provisions of the conveyance in concluding that two separate estates were conveyed, a 1/96 mineral interest and "in addition," a "1/12 interest in the existing lease which expired when the lease terminated." No language in the conveyance indicates that the 1/12 interest in rents and royalties was meant to be in addition to or separate from the estate granted in the opening clause. Such a construction also raises a knotty problem. The court of appeals concluded that the grant of a 1/96 mineral interest and the grant of 1/12 interest in the existing lease took effect at the same time, specifically, that the grant of a 1/96 mineral interest "remained the same throughout." If that were the case, the deed would have granted 1/96 of the minerals pursuant to which the grantee would receive 1/96 of the rents and royalties under the then-existing lease plus a 1/12 interest pursuant to which the grantee would receive another 1/12 (8/96) of rents and royalties. The sum of these two grants would be 9/96 of rents and royalties under an existing lease, which is more than 1/12. See David E. Pierce, Developments in Nonregulatory Oil and Gas Law: The Continuing Search for Analytical Foundations, in 47 INSTITUTE ON OIL & GAS LAW & TAXATION § 1.05 (1996) (criticizing the decision of the court of appeals in this regard). * * *

* * *

Our decision in this case does not depend on the presence or absence of a "future lease" clause, which the court of appeals found dispositive. As we have seen, the intent to convey a single estate that includes 1/12 of rents and royalties, rather than two estates of differing magnitudes and duration, is evident from the conveyance. We do note, however, that the deed should be construed to include future leases, not just the lease in existence at the time this deed was executed. The conveyance provides in this regard that it is subject to "the terms of any valid subsisting oil, gas and/or mineral lease or mineral lease or leases" and "covers and includes one-twelfth (1/12) of all rentals and royalty of every kind and character that may be payable by the terms of such lease or leases." The court of appeals found the word "subsisting" to mean only leases in existence at the time of the conveyance and held that the provision did not extend to future leases. If the deed had simply said "any valid subsisting oil, gas and/or mineral lease," we might be inclined to agree. But it says "any valid subsisting oil, gas and/or mineral lease or mineral lease or leases." (emphasis added). The deed covers and includes 1/12 of the rentals and royalty on any "mineral lease or lease" as well as those leases subsisting at the time of the grant. Any other construction ignores the phrase "or mineral lease or leases."

* * *

Concord and some commentators suggest that conflicting fractions appear in so many deeds because of a common misconception of what an owner of a mineral interest retains after the execution of a lease. See, e.g., 2 HOWARD R. WILLIAMS & CHARLES J. MEYERS, OIL AND GAS LAW § 327.2, at 94.1 (1980); Frank W. Elliott, Jr., The Fractional Mineral Deed "Subject To" a Lease, 36 TEX. L.REV. 620, 622 (1958). Commentators have also observed that most grantors do not intend to convey interests of different magnitudes. See, e.g., 2 WILLIAMS & MEYERS, supra, § 340.2 (1995); Ernest E. Smith, The "Subject To" Clause, 30 ROCKY MTN. MIN. L. INST. § 15.02[1] (1985). Under a typical lease providing for a 1/8 royalty, the lessor may think that the interest retained is 1/8 of the minerals including 1/8 of the royalties. This misconception is evidenced in a few decisions. See, e.g., Tipps, 101 S.W.2d at 1078 (lessor of mineral interest "retained one-eighth of all the minerals in place, subject to the lease"); Jupiter Oil, 819 S.W.2d at 468–69 (citing and following Tipps on this point). In actuality, a lease conveys a fee simple determinable with the possibility of reverter. When the lessor owns all the mineral estate (8/8) and executes an oil and gas lease, the lessor has conveyed all the mineral estate (8/8) but has retained a possibility of reverter in the entire mineral estate (8/8). See generally Luckel, 819 S.W.2d at 464. The lessor also receives, of course, all rights that are bargained for in connection with the lease, which usually include the payment of royalties, delay rentals, and bonuses.

The decision in Tipps, which helped to foster this so-called "estate misconception," went so far as to say that the use of differing fractions was the proper method of conveyance when a mineral lease was outstanding at the time of the grant. 101 S.W.2d at 1079. In referring to the conflicting fractions, the court said, "No language has been suggested, and we know of none, that would more clearly and accurately express the intention of the parties or that would have the legal effect intended by them than that used." Id. The Tipps court thus blessed the use of "1/16" in the granting clause and "1/2" in subsequent clauses when the grantor owned the possibility of reverter in the entire mineral estate and wished to convey 1/2 of that interest at a time when the property was subject to a mineral lease providing for a 1/8 royalty. Tipps was decided in 1936, and the Concord deed was executed in 1937. Under the rationale of Tipps, it would have been appropriate for Crosby to have inserted "1/96" in the granting clause and "1/12" in other provisions of the Concord deed if he intended to convey a 1/12 interest in the minerals.

We are thus mindful of extant circumstances at the time the Concord and other deeds were executed. But we do not base our decision in this case on the theory of an "estate misconception." An understanding of the misconceptions under which some operated is helpful and instructive, but not dispositive. We cannot say categorically that no conveyance with differing fractions effectuated a grant of one fractional interest in the mineral estate and a different fractional interest in royalties under either existing or future leases.

Concord and amici urge this Court to adopt "firm" or "bright-line" rules for construing mineral and royalty conveyances that contain differing fractions. Bright-line tests that focus only on the predominance of one clause over another or that strictly construe each provision in a conveyance as a separate, independent grant, or that choose the larger of conflicting fractions are arbitrary. They will not always give effect to what the conveyance provides as a whole. The principles *461 set out in Luckel and the approach taken in Garrett are designed to give effect to the intent of the parties as actually expressed within the four corners of the conveyance and to harmonize provisions that appear to conflict.

* * *

For the foregoing reasons, we reverse the judgment of the court of appeals and render judgment in favor of Concord.

ENOCH, JUSTICE, concurring.

The original opinion from this Court was seriously flawed in two respects. First, the Court presupposed that the typical grantor does not intend to make two grants in one deed. Concord Oil Co. v. Pennzoil Exploration, 40 Tex. Sup.Ct. J. 33, 35, 1996 WL 596657 (Tex. 1996). Second, the Court anchored the opinion on a conclusion that the Crosby deed's "subject to" clause included future leases. 40 Tex. Sup.Ct. J. 33, 38. * * *

Pennzoil rightly contends that whether "most grantors" intend to make two grants in one deed is an irrelevant inquiry unless the Court determines that the document, standing alone, contains internal inconsistencies. * * * Further, we were wrong to conclude that the "subject to" clause of the Crosby deed includes future leases. It does not—at least not clearly. * * *

Today, the plurality undermines its reasoning by continuing to rely on both the improper presupposition about a typical grantor's intent and the improper reading of the Crosby deed's "subject to" clause. * * * But, there is one other, dispositive reason that dictates the actual judgment in this case. * * *

* * *

A proper review of the Crosby deed begins with the four-corners rule, under which we attempt to ascertain the intent of the parties from the language of the deed. See Luckel, 819 S.W.2d at 461. * * * At the time of Crosby's deed to his grantee, Southland, a mineral lease covered the property. The lessee held title to the mineral estate subject to the possibility that title would revert to Crosby and the other lessors in the future. Crosby, therefore, owned the possibility of a 1/12 mineral interest. Crosby's reverter interest included the right to royalties under the then-current lease, as do all reverter interests in the absence of language to the contrary. Therefore, the Crosby deed's granting clause transferred to Southland 1/96 of Crosby's reverter interest, carrying with it a corresponding 1/96 share of the royalties due under the then-current lease. If the "subject to" clause were a separate conveyance, it would transfer to Southland an additional 8/96 interest in the royalties due under the then-current lease. Under the dissent's construction, the granting clause and the "subject to" clause would convey 1/96 plus 8/96 for a total of 9/96 interest in the royalties, a larger interest than Crosby owned. This construction is not reasonable.

As Professor David Pierce has noted in looking at the court of appeals' opinion in this case, the dissent's two-grant conclusion makes sense only if one assumes that only one grant operates at a time. See David E. Pierce, Developments in Nonregulatory Oil and Gas Law: The Continuing Search for Analytical Foundations, in 47 OIL & GAS LAW & TAXATION § 1.05, at 1–24 (1996). That assumption, however, is contrary to the clear language of both the granting and "subject to" clauses.

I do not disagree with the content of the plurality's dissertation on policy and historical justifications, but the dissertation requires the practitioner to dig to find the nugget that resolves this case. Giving the Crosby deed a reasonable construction, I must conclude that the deed conveyed all of Crosby's 1/12 mineral interest. Therefore, I concur.

GONZALEZ, JUSTICE, joined by SPECTOR, BAKER and HANKINSON, JUSTICES, dissenting on motion for rehearing.

We agree with both the trial court and the court of appeals that the deed in question unambiguously conveyed two estates of different sizes and duration: a 1/96 perpetual interest in the minerals, and a 1/12 interest in rentals and royalties which ended with the existing lease. Accordingly, we would affirm the judgment of the court of appeals.

* * *

Guided by Luckel, we conclude that the A.B. Crosby deed to Southland Leasing Co. (which the Court refers to as the "Concord deed") unambiguously makes two grants: (1) the granting clause conveyed a 1/96 perpetual mineral interest and the corresponding royalty; and (2) the subject-to clause conveyed a separate and additional 1/12 royalty estate from subsisting leases. The Court errs because it begins with a presumption that different fractions in different provisions necessarily conflict. If we can give the differing fractions meaning according to the plain language of the deed, then we must do so.

Understanding the deed as two separate grants, we need not apply rules of construction to rewrite one of the fractions, as the Court has done. Under well-settled case law, a grantor may convey a different interest in the leased minerals and in the existing royalty income by the same instrument. Thus, the fact that the deed purports to grant two different fractional estates does not create a conflict.

* * *

For this reason, the cases the Court cites involving conveyances with irreconcilable provisions do not apply here. * * * The deed at issue in this case is more like the one in Pan American Petroleum Corp. v. Texas Pacific Coal & Oil Co., 340 S.W.2d 548 (Tex.Civ.App.–El Paso 1960, writ ref'd n.r.e.). There, the granting clause conveyed an undivided 1/32 mineral interest, and the subject-to clause "cover[ed] and include[d] one fourth 1/4 of all of the oil royalty and gas royalty" in existing leases. Like the Crosby–Southland deed, the Pan American deed contained no future-lease clause. The court held that the deed at issue conveyed two independent interests: (1) the granting clause conveyed 1/32 of all the minerals and the corresponding royalty interest; and (2) the subject-to clause conveyed a separate and additional royalty estate of 1/4 of the royalties allocated in existing leases.

The subject-to clause states that the conveyance was subject to "any valid subsisting oil, gas and/or mineral lease or mineral lease or leases." The deed plainly limits the subject-to clause to existing leases, but the Court avoids this construction by interpreting the conclusion of the phrase "or mineral lease or leases" to mean future leases. It is unlikely that after carefully limiting the subject-to clause to existing leases, Crosby meant "or mineral lease or leases" to include an entirely different interest— future leases. * * *

* * * Thus, Crosby retained a possibility of reverter in future lease benefits that vested when the existing lease expired. The Court's construction ignores the word "subsisting," which unlike "or mineral lease or leases" has substantive meaning.

The Court and Justice Enoch contend that the lease may not be enforced as written because the granting clause includes within the "bundle of sticks" a royalty interest which must be added to the interest in existing leases conveyed in the subject-to clause. * * * The deed says "subject to," not "added to." ... Crosby intended to convey to Southland a 1/96 interest in all of his rights, except for the rentals and royalties in subsisting leases, of which he conveyed a 1/12 interest. The net effect is that Crosby conveyed to Southland all of his royalty interest from existing leases, being 1/12, and a 1/96 interest in the possibility of reverter; Crosby retained the other 7/96 interest in the possibility of reverter. The right to royalty from subsisting leases and the possibility of reverter are two different interests which should not be added together. Under this interpretation, Crosby conveyed all of his right to royalty in subsisting leases and less than his interest in the possibility of reverter; it does not require us to assume that Crosby meant to convey 1/12 when he wrote 1/96.

* * * The Court's opinion promotes ad-hoc analysis of every mineral deed and wreaks havoc on title stability. For these reasons, we would affirm the court of appeals' judgment.

NOTES

1. All three opinions in the principal case rely upon the earlier Texas Supreme Court case of Luckel v. White, 819 S.W.2d 459 (Tex. 1991), which was also decided by a badly split court (4–1–4). *Luckel* expressly disapproved the repugnant-to-the-grant rule of construction that had been adopted in Alford v. Krum, 671 S.W.2d 870 (Tex. 1984) in construing a deed with multiple fractions. The court in *Alford* had concluded that there was an "irreconcilable conflict" between the clauses of a deed that conveyed a 1/16 interest in the minerals and in current lease royalty, but a 1/2 interest in future lease benefits. The court held that the fraction in the granting clause prevailed in instances where other deed clauses used fractions that were inconsistent with the fraction used in the granting clause.

2. Conveyances or reservations of fractional royalty interests in land subject to an oil and gas lease and containing references to rights in future leases continue to be fertile sources of litigation. An example is Hausser v. Cuellar, 2010 WL 2844046 (Tex. App.–San Antonio 2010). In 1936, defendants' predecessors, whose land was subject to an oil and gas lease providing for a 1/8 royalty, executed a deed granting "an undivided (1/2) interest in and to all of the oil royalty, gas royalty, * * *" and providing that if a future lease was executed after the termination of the existing lease, "the Grantees shall receive under such future lease or leases one sixteenth (1/16) part of all oil, gas and other minerals * * *" In 2006, long after the original lease had terminated, the grantor's successors executed a new lease providing for a 1/4 royalty. Plaintiffs, who were the successors of the grantees in the 1936 deed, brought suit for a declaratory judgment that they were entitled to one half of the 1/4 royalty, i.e., 1/8 of production, rather than only 1/16th of production, as contended by the defendant. In ruling for the plaintiffs, the court pointed to the absence of any language in the 1936 deed suggesting that two different

estates were being conveyed, i.e., a present right to one-half of royalty and a future right to a 1/16th royalty; rather the deed conveyed a single, fixed estate of one-half of royalty. Contrast the court's decision with its earlier construction of a similar deed in Neel v. Killam Oil Co. Ltd., 88 S.W.3d 334 (Tex. App.–San Antonio 2002, pet. denied) in which it had reached the opposite result. The court distinguished the two cases on the ground that the *Neel* decision did not rely entirely upon the language of the deed at issue, but was based, in part, upon an earlier deed in which the grantor of the deed in *Neel* had received only a one-sixteenth royalty and hence could convey only as much as he owned.

Coghill v. Griffith, 358 S.W.3d 834 (Tex.App. 2012) provides another good example of the issue. In 1961 Wood, Coghill's predecessor who had executed an oil and gas lease providing for a 1/8 royalty, conveyed the leased land to Welch, the Griffiths' predecessor. In the deed the grantor reserved "an undivided one-eighth (1/8) interest in and to all of the oil royalty [and] gas royalty" under the existing lease "as well as an undivided one-eighth (1/8) of the usual one-eighth (1/8) royalties provided for in any future oil, gas and/or mineral lease * * *" A further provision stipulated that the grantee would never execute a new oil and gas lease unless the lease provided "for at least a royalty on oil of the usual one-eighth (1/8)" and if the grantee or a successor developed the minerals, the grantor was entitled to receive "as a free royalty hereunder an undivided one-sixty-fourth * * *" After the original lease terminated, Welch, the original grantee, executed two new oil and gas leases providing for a 3/16ths royalty, and subsequently signed a division order showing that both he and Coghill, who had inherited the grantor's interest, were each entitled to 1/8th of the 3/16th royalty.[9] Subsequently the Griffiths purchased Welch's interest in the property, and disputed Coghill's claim to one-eighth of the lease royalty. They argued that the original deed had reserved only a right to 1/64th of production. The court held that the 1961 deed specifically reserved a right to 1/8th of royalty in the existing lease and in future leases. The references to the usual 1/8th royalty do not compel a conclusion that the parties to the deed intended to limit the reservation to a fixed 1/64th royalty. Similarly, the requirement that future leases provide for "at least" a 1/8th royalty and that the grantor would receive 1/64th of production if the grantee or his successors developed the land were included to guarantee that the reserved royalty would never be less than 1/64th of production. Setting a floor on the royalty did not indicate an intent to limit the royalty to the amount guaranteed by the floor.

3. Modern lawyers are often puzzled as to why drafters of early mineral deeds inserted different fractions in the granting, subject-to, and future leases clauses. Consider the explanation provided by the Kansas Supreme Court in Heyen v. Hartnett, 679 P.2d 1152 (Kan. 1984). The case involved a 1925 deed that granted "an undivided 1/16 interest in and to all of the oil, gas and other minerals" and provided that if the land was subject to an oil and gas lease, the grantees "shall have an undivided 1/2 interest in the Royalties, Rentals, and Proceeds therefrom * * *." The court stated that:

---

9. The case does not state this, but the various fractions of lease royalty claimed by the parties suggest that Wood, the original grantor, owned only 1/4th of the mineral estate along with the executive right.

the use of the fraction "1/16" in the initial clause of this mineral deed was simply an error commonly made in the early days of oil and gas conveyancing. The confusion is not uncommon today. In Shepard, Executrix v. John Hancock Mutual Life Ins. Co., 368 P.2d 19 (Kan. 1962), there is an excellent discussion of this early day misconception and misuse of the fraction "1/16th" when "1/2" was really intended:

* * *

As the most common leasing arrangement provides for a one-eighth royalty reserved to the lessor, the confusion of fractional interests stems primarily from the mistaken premise that all the lessor-landowner owns is a one-eighth royalty. In conveying minerals subject to an existing lease and also assigning a corresponding fractional interest in the royalties received, mistake is often made in the fraction of the minerals conveyed by multiplying the intended fraction by one-eighth. Thus, if a conveyance of an undivided one-half of the minerals is intended, the parties will multiply one-half by one-eighth and the instrument will erroneously specify a conveyance of one-sixteenth of the minerals upon the assumption that one-sixteenth is one-half of what the grantor owns. An ambiguity is created because the instrument will also show that the conveyance of one-sixteenth of the minerals is meant to entitle the grantor to one-half of the royalty. Of course, an undivided one-half of the minerals is needed to carry one-half of any royalties reserved. (l.c. 576.)

And so here. In computing the fractional interest reserved the parties were aware of the existence of the Jennings leases providing for 1/8 th royalty to the landowner, and it is obvious the scrivener multiplied 1/4 th by 1/8 th and the instrument erroneously specified a reservation of 1/32 nd as the interest reserved, apparently upon the assumption that 1/32 nd interest in and to all oil, gas or other minerals, would constitute ownership of 1/4 th of the landowners' 1/8 th royalty, when the intention of the reservation as disclosed by its other terms indicate that the fraction 1/4 th should have been used instead of the fraction 1/32 nd. When this is done, the intent of the grantor is clear and no ambiguity exists. Hence, contrary to plaintiffs' contention, no occasion exists for the application of any rule of construction to aid in the interpretation of the reservation.

On the basis of the reasoning set forth above, we hold that the ambiguous mineral deed of 1925 should be construed to convey to the grantees an undivided 1/2 interest in the oil and gas and other minerals in and under the land in question, so as to carry out the intention of the parties to give the grantees and their successors in title an undivided 1/2 interest in the royalties produced under the Iannitti lease.

679 P.2d at 1158–59.

4. An ingenious but unsuccessful argument based on the prevalence of the one-eighth landowner's royalty throughout most of the Twentieth Century was advanced in Hudspeth v. Berry, 2010 WL 2813408 (Tex. App. 2010). The case involved a 1943 conveyance in which two brothers granted their two

one-third interests in a mineral estate to their third brother and reserved an "undivided 1/40th royalty interest (being 1/5th of 1/8th)" in each of the two grantors. Over 60 years later the successor of the grantee executed an oil and gas lease providing for a 1/5 royalty. The successors of the grantors argued that because 1/8 was the standard lease royalty for several decades in the early and middle part of the 20th century, the term "1/8th" was synonymous with "landowner's royalty," and they were therefore each entitled to 1/5th of the 1/5th royalty that the plaintiff had reserved in the oil and gas lease. The court rejected the argument, pointing out that the 1943 deed did not contain conflicting fractions, but plainly reserved two fixed 1/40th royalty interests.

See Laura H. Burney, Interpreting Mineral and Royalty Deeds: The Legacy of the One–Eighth Royalty and Other Stories, 33 St. Mary's L.J. 1 (2001) for a discussion of the influence the traditional one-eighth royalty has had upon drafting and judicial construction. See also David E. Pierce, Interpreting Oil and Gas Instruments, 1 Texas J. of Oil, Gas and Energy L. 1 (2006); Noelle C. Letteri, Recent Developments: Resolving the Multi–Fractional Deed Dilemma—Concord Oil Co. v. Pennzoil Exploration & Production Co., 30 St. Mary's L.J. 615 (1999).

5. The traditional function of the "subject to" clause has been to protect the grantor from breach of warranty by making clear that the grantee receives the land subject to existing rights in third parties. For this reason, the clause is frequently inserted in a deed even though there is some uncertainty about the existence or validity of such outstanding interests. Not surprisingly, its use in this context frequently creates problems. For example, a grantor may make her conveyance subject to mineral reservations made by prior grantors, even though no valid reservations exist. Claims by the grantor or her successors to own the minerals have generally been rejected on the ground that the "subject to" clause merely operates to protect the grantor's warranty of title and is not sufficient to reserve mineral rights. See, e.g., Walker v. Foss, 930 S.W.2d 701 (Tex. App. 1996). Some courts, however, have made a distinction between a global "subject to" clause that simply refers to all outstanding mineral interests and a more restrictive clause that refers to a specific grant of a specific interest. In the latter case, if the referenced interest doesn't exist, the "subject to" clause is treated as a limitation on the grant and the grantor retains title to the referenced interest. Compare, e.g., Miller v. Lowery, 468 So.2d 865 (Miss. 1985) with Knight v. Minter, 749 So.2d 128 (Miss. 1999). What is the rationale for the difference in result?

Should a "less and except" clause be given a different interpretation than a "subject to" clause? The grantors in Boswell Energy Corp. v. Arrowhead Homes, Inc., 976 P.2d 1113 (Okla.Civ.App.Div. 3 1999) conveyed land by a deed that the included the phrase "less and except all mineral interests" immediately after the warranty clause. Both the grantors and the grantee executed oil and gas leases. In a dispute between the two lessees over which had a valid lease, the Oklahoma Court of Appeals concluded that the deed was ambiguous and remanded the case to the trial court for a determination of the parties' intent with respect to ownership of the minerals.

6. Conveyances are normally made subject to outstanding oil and gas leases. The provisions of the lease will, of course, have a significant bearing on

the interest received by the grantee. An unusual example is Schwarm v. Mexia Holdings, L.P., 720 N.E.2d 330 (Ill.App. 1999) involving a terminable mineral interest that was conveyed subject to a lease that covered two additional tracts. The terminable interest was maintained by production from the other leased tracts for several decades after production on the terminable-interest tract had ceased.

If a grant is made subject to an inoperative lease, the lessee may assert that the grantee, by accepting the deed, has ratified or revived the lease. In McVey v. Hill, 691 S.W.2d 67 (Tex.App. 1985, writ refused n.r.e.), defendant received an assignment of a contract to purchase a tract of land. The assignment was made "subject to the terms, conditions and stipulations embodied in said contract of Sale and Purchase." The contract, in turn, was made "subject to any reservations or exceptions set out in the Deed" to the contract vendor. The deed made reference to an oil and gas lease, which apparently had expired at the time of the assignment. In rejecting the lessee's argument that the acceptance of the assignment ratified the lease, the court stated that "the subsequent execution of a formal document must expressly recognize in clear language the validity of an expired instrument to create a ratification," and held that the language of the assignment was insufficient to constitute such a recognition of the lease.

7. Although the terms *ratification* and *revivor* are frequently used interchangeably, they refer to different situations. As Professor Smith has pointed out,

> [R]atification can occur only with respect to a lease which, although intended to be binding, contains some defect in drafting or execution; whereas the lease which has already terminated can not be ratified, but only revived. Failure to make this distinction can introduce unnecessary confusion into an already overly-confused body of law; for the requirements for reviving an instrument which has ceased to have any legal effect have traditionally been somewhat different than those for validating an instrument which was never legally binding. Revival has typically required the execution of an instrument which incorporates the language of the terminated instrument, either expressly or by reference, and which itself takes effect as a conveyance. Ratification, on the other hand, usually occurs through the execution of a document which simply recognizes the validity of the previously ineffective instrument.

Ernest E. Smith, The "Subject to" Clause, 30 Rocky Mtn.Min.L.Inst. 15–1, 15–12 (1984).

For other discussions of ratification and revivor, see William B. Browder, Jr., Estoppel, Waiver, and Ratification Affecting Mineral and Leasehold Rights, 10 Rocky Mtn.Min.L.Inst. 139 (1965); Note, Revival and Ratification of Leases—Synonyms or Antonyms? 26 Baylor L.Rev. 455 (1974), and Smith & Weaver § 6.3.

2. NONAPPORTIONMENT DOCTRINE

If land subject to an oil and gas lease is divided in severalty, rather than by the sale of an undivided fractional interest, there is less likelihood of a dispute over the size of the interests actually created. As the following case indicates, however, there may still be a serious dispute over the right to benefits under the lease.

JAPHET v. McRAE

276 S.W. 669 (Tex.Com.App.1925).

POWELL, P.J. In December, 1915, Wilbur Fisher and wife executed an oil, gas and mineral lease to the Producers' Oil Company on a certain 15–acre tract of land out of the William Bloodgood augmentation survey in a portion of what is now called Barbers' Hill oil field, in Chambers county, Tex. Subsequently, Fisher, the original lessor, conveyed to Walter Keeble, one of the defendants in error here, the north 5 acres of said 15 acres. Keeble then conveyed to Charles C. McRae, the other defendant in error here, an undivided 3 acres out of his north 5 acres. Some 18 months after he sold 5 acres of the land to Keeble, Fisher, the original lessor as aforesaid, sold to the same Walter Keeble the remaining south 10 acres of the 15–acre tract. On the same day Keeble conveyed that very same 10–acre tract, for a very large profit, to Dan A. Japhet, one of the plaintiffs in error here.

The various deeds conveying these lands were in the usual form of general warranty deeds, and all referred to the lease to the Producers' Oil Company, which was itself in the usual or commercial form of oil leases. There is nothing whatever in any of the deeds providing for an apportionment of the one-eighth royalty retained by the owner of the fee among the various subdivisions of the 15–acre tract. The deeds contained no language from which it could be said that any apportionment of royalty was in the mind of the parties at the time they were executed. Keeble, undoubtedly, could have written his deed to Japhet in such a way as to provide that the latter should take the 10 acres of land by metes and bounds, but should have only ten-fifteenths of the one-eighth of any oil produced from any part of the 15 acres. But no such provision is in the deed. On the contrary, the deed expressly provided that Japhet should have all the rights which the original lessor had in the 10 acres. This is a case where it is contended that the law itself, in the absence of contract to the contrary, requires an apportionment of the one-eighth royalty. In this respect, it is unlike the case of Hoffman v. Magnolia Petroleum Co., 273 S.W. 828, very recently decided by this section of the Commission of Appeals and the Supreme Court. We will discuss this law point more fully later.

After Japhet bought the 10 acres of land, he succeeded in having the oil company, as the lessee, develop his 10 acres. Under the lease, of which all parties had notice when these various deeds were written, the lessee could develop any part of the 15 acres just as it saw fit to do. Much oil was discovered on the 10 acres. McRae and Keeble filed this suit for five-fifteenths of the one-eighth royalty from this oil, although their 5 acres had never been developed. The trial court, upon an agreed statement of facts, denied the recovery sought, and awarded all the money to Japhet.

The money itself, under agreement of the parties, is being deposited in a Houston bank to await the termination of this suit.

The Court of Civil Appeals at Galveston reversed the judgment of the trial court and rendered judgment in favor of McRae and Keeble for one-third of the royalty. * * *

Counsel for Japhet contend that:

Where the lessor of land for oil and gas, subsequently to the execution of the lease, but prior to the development of the land and the production of oil or gas under the lease, sells a portion or portions of the land to others, and oil and gas are thereafter produced under the lease from some portion of the leased premises, the royalties therefrom belong to the owner of the particular tract upon which the well is located, and the owner or owners of other portions of the leased premises have no interest therein.

If this rule is correct, then the trial court's judgment should be affirmed. On the other hand, if the converse of the rule just stated is correct, as Keeble and McRae contend, the judgment of the Court of Civil Appeals should be affirmed. Which is the correct rule in this connection presents an interesting question. * * * We have concluded that the rule contended for by plaintiffs in error is the better one, and that the judgment of the trial court was correct. In this conclusion, we follow the great weight of authority. For instance, we are in line with the following states:

Arkansas: Osborn et al. v. Arkansas Territorial Oil & Gas Co., 103 Ark. 175, 146 S.W. 122.

Indiana: Fairbanks v. Warrum, 56 Ind.App. 337, 104 N.E. 983, 1141.

Ohio: Northwestern Ohio Natural Gas Co. v. Ullery, 68 Ohio St. 259, 67 N.E. 494.

Oklahoma: Kimbley v. Luckey, 72 Okla. 217, 179 P. 928; Pierce Oil Corporation v. Schacht et al., 75 Okla. 101, 181 P. 731; Galt v. Metscher, 103 Okla. 271, 229 P. 522; Gypsy Oil Co. v. Schonwald, 107 Okla. 253, 231 P. 864.

West Virginia: Pittsburgh & West Virginia Gas Co. v. Ankrom, 83 W.Va. 81, 97 S.E. 593, 5 A.L.R. 1157; Musgrave v. Musgrave, 86 W.Va. 119, 103 S.E. 302, 16 A.L.R. 564.

The only opinions contrary to our views, so far as counsel cite or we can find, are the Pennsylvania case of Wettengel v. Gormley, 160 Pa. 559, 28 A. 934, 40 Am.St.Rep. 733, and 184 Pa. 354, 39 A. 57, and the Texas case of Gillette v. Mitchell, 214 S.W. 619. The latter case was by the Court of Civil Appeals at Galveston, and that court has again held the same way in the case at bar. It has continued to follow the Wettengel Case in Pennsylvania. * * *

* * * We think the reasoning by the majority of the courts is sound. They answer every contention of any possible merit on the contrary side.

If the rule we approve is just in all the states where it is followed, it is also just in Texas. We are not unlike the other states in any matter of substance which affects this matter. Our Supreme Court has held that oil is a part of the realty until brought to the surface, and that it can be sold in place. Japhet unquestionably bought the realty in the 10 acres. He bought one-eighth of the oil in or under that land. The lessee had the right to take full charge of the land so far as necessary to get the oil from under it. He had the title to the oil for that purpose. But, when it was brought to the surface, Japhet had the right to his one-eighth thereof. He had an equitable title to his interest in that oil, and if the lessee had made any effort to take it away from him, Japhet would have been entitled to sue him as for conversion of his property. It seems to us that the only possible justification for permitting McRae and Keeble to participate in these royalties coming out of the Japhet wells would be on the presumption, as a matter of law, that a part of the oil from the wells on the 10 acres was being drained from their 5 acres. Should there be any such legal presumption? We think not. It is well known that oil wells and dusters are found side by side within a very few feet of each other. If the Japhet wells were draining oil from the lands of anyone else, it would be impossible in the absence of proof, to say whether such drainage was north, south, east or west of the Japhet tract. But, before the drainage could possibly affect defendants in error, it must come from the north. It is entirely possible that if McRae and Keeble should be allowed one-third of this money, they would be receiving it when there was not a drop of oil on their land. It is, in any event, unjust to take away the property apparently belonging to one party and give it to another until it is shown that the latter party has been deprived of it.

If the oil on the 15 acres in this suit should be apportioned, because the entire tract of land was under one lease, then where will we stop? Will the courts say they will apportion royalties provided the lease does not cover more than 1,000 acres, or more than 10,000, or more than some other acreage arbitrarily fixed? Or will they say that apportionment will apply, unless the contrary is expressly provided for, in all lands under the same original lease? If this rule should be enforced, we would have a situation of this kind. Upon the submission of this case, it was stated, and not questioned, that the Humble Oil & Refining Company has one lease covering 1,000,000 acres of land from the same owner. One corner of that land is 75 miles from one of its other corners. The land is in several counties. Suppose the owner of the land should sell 75 acres in one corner to a party interested in oil, and who thinks he knows oil land when he sees it. He counts confidently on the one-eighth royalty attaching to that 75–acre tract. He induces the original lessee to develop his land, and a gusher is forthcoming. Under the rule urged by defendants in error, the man discovering this 75–acre tract as the most valuable of the entire million acres for oil purposes would be entitled to only seventy-five one-millionths of the one-eighth royalty of the oil coming out of the gusher on the 75–acre tract. Can we say such a rule is just? A party owning another 75 acres, 75 miles distant, would get as much from the oil as the man whose 75 acres has the producing gusher. And yet this man without the gusher might not have a single drop of oil under his land, which is 75 miles distant from the gusher. Such a rule would, in our opinion, be entirely impracticable. Many oil leases cover thousands of acres of land. As our Supreme Court has held, oil is fugitive in its nature, and ordinarily should belong to him who captures it and brings it to the surface. The quest for it involves tremendous expense and a vast element of chance. In spite of the scientific knowledge of the geologists, the industry still partakes largely of a gamble. It seems to us that the only safe rule, and the only one free from much confusion, is one which gives the oil to the man who owns the land upon which the well is located. Clearly, it would not be right to award the oil to those who, like Keeble and McRae, offered no proof that any of it was drained from under their 5–acre tract.

Our conclusion is not unjust, as we see it, even if there were a possibility that the 5 acres were being drained by the Japhet wells. Keeble knew that the lessee had the right to drill anywhere at its pleasure. He knew that part of the 15 acres might never be developed. Still, he allowed Japhet to select 10 definite acres. He traded with his eyes wide open to the rights of the various parties. He expressly sold to Japhet the one-eighth royalty retained by the original lessor so far as the 10 acres were concerned. He must be held to have known that the 10 acres might be first developed, and, if so, that the oil thereunder would belong to Japhet and the lessee. Keeble was not required to sell any of the 15 acres. If he wanted the oil which might be found under any part of the 15 acres, he should have retained it all or expressly sold off only an undivided interest in the royalty under the entire 15 acres. That course seems fairer than to wait for others to develop a certain portion of the tract and then ask for a division of the developed tract.

While the majority rule does not seem to perpetrate any injustice on defendants in error, the contrary rule would work a grave injustice to Japhet. He paid $10,000 cash for this 10–acre tract, practically worthless except as an oil prospect. Keeble made a profit of $2,000 on the deal, and he turned it in one day. His money was not invested long. Japhet could have bought the 10 acres and accepted a deed to an undivided ten-fifteenths of the royalties in the 15 acres. But he did not do so. If he had known that Keeble wanted one-third of the oil coming from wells on the 10 acres he was buying, he doubtless would have vigorously objected to it. He bought no partnership interest in oil. It is an injustice to him to make him divide his oil after he had exercised his own best judgment and selected the 10 acres where he thought the oil was. The description of the 10 acres by metes and bounds was utterly useless under the minority rule. Under that doctrine, Japhet would get only ten-fifteenths of the oil royalty whether he bought a certain 10 acres or merely an undivided 10 acres. It is wrong to force him to do something he did not contract to do.

The various states are beginning by statute and supervision to make certain rules governing the duties of lessees. Particularly is this true with reference to the duty on the part of the lessees to drill offset wells on adjoining leases. As this great industry develops, other laws will doubtless be passed regulatory of operation by lessees. But such laws will not take away the rights of parties which have already become vested. The courts should not make contracts for people overturning those they have voluntarily and fairly made for themselves.

In the Gormley Case, the Pennsylvania court said there would be no apportionment of coal or other solid minerals. But, the court said, oil and gas were different. The court seemed to think that each of the 600 acres would probably produce an equal amount of oil. This case was written 30 years ago, and the courts did not know as much about the mysteries of oil as they do now. Actual experience shows that the Pennsylvania court is very much in error in assuming that oil is anything like equally distributed on 600 acres of land, or any other number of acres.

For the reasons stated by the great majority of all the courts which have passed upon this question, as well as those stated by ourselves, we think the judgment of the Court of Civil Appeals should be reversed and that of the district court affirmed. We so recommend.

CURETON, C.J. The judgment recommended in the report of the Commission of Appeals is adopted, and will be entered as the judgment of the Supreme Court.

NOTES

1. An opinion recommending the opposite result in the *Japhet* case was considered and rejected by the Texas Supreme Court. The text of the rejected opinion, along with introductory comments, was later published as a law review article by the judge who had proposed it. Robt. W. Stayton, Apportionment and the Ghost of a Rejected View, 32 Tex.L.Rev. 682 (1954).

2. The nonapportionment doctrine is still the majority rule, although its fairness has frequently been questioned, and the courts and legislatures have been strongly urged to adopt in its stead a rule dividing royalties among the owners of the subdivided tract. See, e.g., William O. Huie, Apportionment of Oil and Gas Royalties, 78 Harv.L.Rev. 1113, 1534 (1965). Professor Lowe, on the other hand, argues that, depending upon the facts involved, either rule may be onerous in its application; hence, which rule is adopted is not of crucial importance. What is important is the stability and certainty of land titles. Thus, whichever rule is adopted, it should be clearly defined and clearly applicable to all situations. Lowe, Chapter 7.E.2. Which argument is more persuasive?

3. Compare the prevailing nonapportionment rule with the Texas rule on community leases, where owners of different tracts sign a single lease covering all the tracts and each lessor receives a share of royalty that is proportionate to his interest in the entire area covered by the lease. Can these rules be reconciled?

4. The nonapportionment doctrine has been applied in Texas even though the spacing and density rules of the Railroad Commission prohibit

drilling on one of the tracts resulting from the subdivision and treat such tract as being drained by the producing well. See Mueller v. Sutherland, 179 S.W.2d 801 (Tex.Civ.App. 1943, writ ref'd w.o.m.) and Ryan Consol. Petroleum Corp. v. Pickens, 285 S.W.2d 201 (Tex. 1955).

In some situations compulsory pooling or the application of the doctrine of judicial pooling provide relief from the nonapportionment doctrine, see Chapter 2; see also William O. Huie, Apportionment of Oil and Gas Royalties, 78 Harv.L.Rev. 1113, 1142–45 (1965). State statutes may also modify the rule. Legislation in Oklahoma provides that owners of mineral interests within a spacing unit must receive their royalty on all production from the unit. Arkansas has similar legislation requiring apportionment of the first 1/8 royalty. As Professor Lowe has pointed out, it is unclear how royalty in excess of 1/8 is to be allocated, and suggests that the non-apportionment rule would probably apply. Lowe, Chapter 7.E.2.

5.   The problem of apportioning royalty is not limited to the traditional "vertical" subdivision of the surface. It may also arise if there is a horizontal division of the mineral estate. Suppose that a lessor conveys title to all minerals that lie below the depth of 5,000 feet and that the lessee subsequently obtains production from a well drilled to a depth of 3,000 feet.

How should royalty be paid under the apportionment doctrine? How should royalty be paid under the nonapportionment rule?

6.   The parties to a lease or other instrument can provide by contract for the apportionment of royalties among different owners of a subdivided tract. Such a provision is commonly called an entirety clause. Because the clause is usually drafted in contemplation of vertical transfers, its applicability to a horizontal severance of the mineral estate, such as that described earlier, may be unclear. For a suggested approach to the problem, see Kuntz § 48.2(d)(4).

7.   The entirety clause is not used as frequently today as it once was. The following case illustrates one reason why lessees may now be disinclined to include such a provision.

**THOMAS GILCREASE FOUNDATION
v. STANOLIND OIL & GAS CO.**

266 S.W.2d 850 (Tex. 1954).

CULVER, JUSTICE.

Suit was brought by petitioner, Gilcrease Foundation, against the respondent, Stanolind Oil and Gas Company in the district court for declaratory judgment to sustain its right to receive as royalty under an oil and gas lease ½ of the ⅛th royalty produced from all of the land covered by such lease in the proportion that its interest bore to the entire tract and the corresponding right to the satisfaction of an oil payment or overriding royalty provided for in the lease. The trial court entered summary judgment in favor of the petitioner on its motion, which decision was reversed and remanded by the Court of Civil Appeals. 262 S.W.2d 756. A somewhat extended statement of the factual background will be necessary.

To begin with, First National Bank of Fort Worth owned all of the mineral estate in the N.E. quarter and an undivided ½ interest in the N.W.

quarter of Section 32, Block 44, of a survey in Ector County. By separate instruments, in 1929 the Bank conveyed to Gilcrease Oil Company an undivided ¾ths interest in the N.E. quarter and an undivided ¼th interest in the N.W. quarter. On the 19th day of February 1946 the Bank executed an oil and gas lease to Stanolind covering the north ½ of Section 32 containing a lesser estate clause which provided "that if lessor owns an interest in said land less than the entire fee simple estate then the royalties and rentals to be paid lessor shall be reduced proportionately." The Bank therefore owned and conveyed only a lease, on an undivided ¼th interest in the N.E. quarter and an undivided ¼th interest in the N.W. quarter. In the following month Gilcrease Company executed an oil and gas lease to Stanolind similar to the one executed by the bank except, (1) Gilcrease reserved an oil payment for $160,000, being figured at $500 per acre upon the 320 acres described, having the legal status of an overriding royalty, but reduced proportionately to accord with lessor's actual ownership; and (2) the inclusion of a so-called "entirety clause" reading as follows:

> If the leased premises *are now or shall hereafter be owned in severalty or in separate tracts,* the premises, nevertheless, shall be developed and operated as one lease, and all royalties accruing hereunder shall be treated as an entirety and shall be divided among and paid to such separate owners in the proportion that the acreage owned by each such separate owner bears to the entire leased acreage.

Thereafter Gilcrease Company conveyed all of its interest in the leased property to petitioner Foundation.

Upon the development of the property the N.W. quarter proved to be much more productive of oil than the N.E. quarter. * * * Petitioner owns an undivided ¾ths of the mineral interest in the N.E. quarter and only an undivided ¼th in the N.W. quarter. * * *

Petitioner's contention is that it is entitled to receive as royalty ½ of the ⅛th royalty produced from the entire half section and likewise should have applied to its oil payment an undivided ¹⁄₁₆th of ⅞ths of all of the production from the half section by reason of the provisions of the "entirety clause." On the other hand respondent asserts that the "entirety clause" does not bring about that result, but that petitioner is limited to receive ¾ths of the ⅛th royalty produced on the N.E. quarter and ¼th of the royalty on the N.W. quarter, according to its actual ownership of the minerals in the two quarter sections respectively, and that the oil payment is to be retired on the same basis. The point has not been heretofore squarely passed upon by the courts of this state.

In the situation where the lessor of an oil and gas lease has granted a part of his estate to another, there is considerable conflict of authority as to whether the grantee would participate pro rata in the royalties accruing from the entire leased tract or would be confined to the royalty from oil produced from his portion only of the premises. Some states, notably Pennsylvania, early adopted the apportionment theory, holding that the grantee would participate in the royalty paid from the production on the entire tract according to the ratio that his interest bore to the premises leased. This rule does not obtain in Texas. Nor is it the majority rule. * * *

The obvious difficulties and hardships encountered under the Texas and the majority rule have brought into common use what is known as the "entirety clause." This provision has been upheld in many jurisdictions and its validity is not here under attack, merely its application. Thus it is conceded that, were we concerned with the subsequent assignment of a tract of a certain specified acreage out of the whole amount leased, the provisions of the clause would be applicable. The difficulty here arises by reason of the undivided ownership of the petitioner in the two quarter sections, which interests are not the same and which were owned at the time of the execution of the lease just as they are now, the only change in ownership being that Gilcrease Company has conveyed all of its interest in both quarter sections to the Foundation. The key to the problem at least partially turns on the meaning and interpretation of the phrase "owned in severalty or in separate tracts."

* * *

The word "severalty" as used in the expression "tenants in severalty" means for the sole, separate and exclusive dominion of the tenants.

* * *

A state of separation. An estate in severalty is one that is held by a person in his own right only, without any other person being joined or connected with him, in point of interest, during his estate therein. Black's Law Dictionary, 2d Ed. p. 1080.

But, however the term "in severalty" may be applied in this connection, we think that in purview of the "entirety clause" under the facts here before us the ownership of petitioner is in "separate tracts," and the words "are now" must be given the effect of making the clause applicable at the time of the execution of the lease. We have been cited no authority to the effect that ownership in different undivided interests in segregated portions of the leased premises does not qualify as an ownership "in separate tracts." In fact Stanolind is here seeking to treat the ownership as being "in separate tracts" in contending that royalty must be paid not in proportion that the ownership by the Foundation bears to the entire leased premises, but only from oil separately produced on each of the two quarter sections.

Respondent cites the following provision of the lease:

The rights of either party hereunder may be assigned, in whole or in part, and the provisions hereof shall extend to the heirs, successors and assigns of the parties hereto, but no change or division in ownership of the land, rentals, or royalties, however accomplished shall operate to enlarge the obligations or diminish the rights of lessee.

It asserts that this provision would be completely disregarded if petitioner's contention is sustained, citing Shell Petroleum Corporation v. Calcasieu Real Estate & Oil Co., 185 La. 751, 170 So. 785.

In the Calcasieu case the lease was held to be a joint lease and the "entirety clause" was applied. However, we think the quoted provision means exactly what it says, that is: whatever obligations are imposed by the terms of the lease the same cannot be increased, altered or modified by any subsequent change or ownership. The extent of the obligations imposed by the lease upon the lessee is the very question here to be determined and the quoted provision sheds no light on that problem, nor indeed does it have any bearing.

* * *

Respondent maintains that the "entirety clause" is always included for the benefit of the lessee and is intended to relieve the lessee of additional burdens that might be occasioned by virtue of there being a separate ownership and separate tracts so as to allow the lessee to develop the premises as one entire lease and was never intended to impose any additional burden by increasing the royalty over and above that contained in the royalty provision. Generally speaking we agree. It is to be borne in mind, however, that the lease from Gilcrease to Stanolind was executed prior to the development of the properties and apparently at a time when it was not known which quarter section, if either, would be more productive. If the N.E. quarter had produced more oil the situation would have been reversed, and petitioner would have received less royalty under the provisions of the "entirety clause." In fact the right to operate the property as one lease is granted by the clause. So far as petitioner is concerned there is no reason why the two quarter sections could not be operated under one lease and the ownership by Tidewater and Sunray of undivided interests in the N.W. quarter, which entails upon Stanolind the duty of operating the two quarter sections independently, can hardly be said to affect the rights of petitioner. The fact that Stanolind did not obtain leases from Tidewater and Sunray who together owned an undivided one-half interest in the N.E. quarter, but rather executed operating agreements with these companies, cannot be held to vary the terms of the leases executed by Gilcrease nor does it have any bearing on the meaning and construction of the "entirety clause."

The affidavits filed in the trial court reveal that Gilcrease desired to make separate leases on the two quarter sections, possibly to eliminate the question of interior drainage, but at the insistence of Stanolind agreed to one lease and to the inclusion of the "entirety clause" in the lease. It is possibly of some significance that the lease from the Bank to Stanolind did not contain the "entirety clause" inasmuch as the Bank owning the same interest in each quarter section (an undivided ¼th) would receive the same royalty whether the "entirety clause" had been inserted or not.

We hold, therefore, that at the time the lease was made to Stanolind, Gilcrease did own the premises "in severalty or in separate tracts" notwithstanding that the interest in each quarter section was an undivided interest and that the terms of the "entirety clause" apply. The petitioner is entitled to share the royalty in proportion that the interest owned by it bears to the entire leased premises and naturally the same ruling will obtain so far as the satisfaction of the overriding royalty or oil payment is concerned. The judgment of the Court of Civil Appeals is reversed and that of the trial court is affirmed.

NOTES

1. A lessee may find that an entireties clause imposes a heavy administrative burden if the land subject to lease is subdivided into many small tracts, as may happen with a residential subdivision.

What contractual remedy, other than the deletion of the entirety clause, can be used to deal with this problem?

2. As discussed earlier in this chapter, in some jurisdictions, an apportionment of royalties among owners of separate tracts results from the execution of a community lease. A community lease results if the owners of two or more tracts of land join in executing the same lease or execute separate but identical leases that purport to cover the entire acreage owned by the various lessors.

In Verble v. Coffman, 680 S.W.2d 69 (Tex.App. 1984) a lease covering 149 acres contained the following clause:

> If this lease now or hereafter covers separate tracts, no pooling or unitization of royalty interest as between any such separate tracts is intended or shall be implied or result merely from the inclusion of such separate tracts within this lease. * * * [T]he words "separate tract" mean any tract with royalty ownership differing, now or hereafter, either as to parties or amounts, from that as to any other part of the leased premises.

A producing well was located on the northern half of the leased premises. Ratification of the lease by the owner of royalty in the southern one-half of the tract was held to result in a communitization of royalty in spite of the quoted language. The court stated that the request for lease ratification by the lessor constituted an offer to pool in accordance with the pooling clause within the lease.

Why should ratification be effective as to the pooling clause of the lease, but not as to the anti-communitization clause? For one possible explanation, see London v. Merriman, 756 S.W.2d 736 (Tex. App. 1988, writ denied).

3. TOP LEASING

A landowner, while his property is still subject to an oil and gas lease, may execute a second lease that gives the new lessee possessory rights in the property upon the expiration of the existing lease. This practice, known as top leasing, has existed for some time and may become relatively widespread whenever a sharp increase in oil and gas prices results in heightened competition for oil and gas leases.

Top leasing frequently occurs near the end of the primary term of an existing lease whose owner has made no apparent plans to drill or pool. The landowner commonly receives a small bonus at the time he enters into the top lease and a right to an additional payment when the existing, or "bottom," lease expires. He thus foregoes the bargaining advantage he will have if the existing lease terminates while there is still a seller's market for oil and gas leases. In exchange, he protects himself against a collapse in the market for leases and assures himself of another bonus, albeit small, even though the existing lease is maintained past the primary term.

The reasons why an oil company may take a top lease vary. The holder of the existing lease may use this device to gain an extension of time for drilling. A third-party lessee may be willing to run the risk that the bottom lease will not expire to obtain the property for a smaller bonus than would otherwise have to be paid.

The risks and judgments involved in top leasing are not solely economic. Several legal issues must be considered by all parties affected by a top lease. As the following case illustrates, not the least of these is the rule against perpetuities.

HAMMAN v. BRIGHT & CO.

924 S.W.2d 168 (Tex.App.1996).

DODSON, JUSTICE.

This is an appeal from a summary judgment. Appellants, the Hammans, request that we reverse the trial court's determination that certain oil and gas top leases violate the Texas constitutional rule against perpetuities (the Rule).

* * *

BACKGROUND

The record shows in 1917, George and John Hamman acquired the Hamman ranch located in Hidalgo County. In April of 1951, the Hammans leased 20,715.83 acres to Shell Oil Company (the Shell lease). Shell later released a portion of this land, and on November 4, 1952, the Hammans leased 1,853.48 acres to Superior Oil Company (the Superior lease). The leases to Shell and Superior became "bottom leases" nine days later, when the Hammans executed two top leases[1] and a third lease in favor of John Hamman, Jr. The top leases corresponded to the property descriptions in the bottom leases, and the third lease (the other lease) covered all acreage

---

1. A top lease is one granted by a landowner, during the existence of a recorded lease, which is to become effective if and when the existing lease expires or is terminated. Williams and Meyers, 8 Oil and Gas Law 1147 (Matthew Bender & Co., Inc. 1995).

not subject to the bottom leases. Except for the property descriptions and references to the underlying bottom leases, the two top leases are identical.

On December 27, 1952, George and John executed a deed to Rio Grande (the Deed) conveying certain mineral interests in the property under lease. The Deed provided that such conveyance was subject to the bottom leases, the top leases, the other lease, a reservation of one-half of the royalties accruing under the existing leases, and a perpetual one-sixteenth royalty interest in the grantors. After several transactions spanning approximately ten years, Atlantic succeeded to the mineral interest originally conveyed by the Deed.

In December 1987, the Hammans sued Bright, a sublessee/assignee under the top leases, to recover on the top leases for underpaid royalties, excessive fees, fraud, and conversion. They later sued Bright for wrongful pooling, and Atlantic was joined as a party. Bright denied liability and joined Shell as a third-party defendant. Atlantic responded by denying liability and further pleaded that the Rule voided . . . the top leases . . . ab initio. Bright, Shell and Atlantic then counterclaimed against the Hammans based upon the voidness of the instruments, and sought to recover previously paid royalties.

* * *

APPLICABLE PRINCIPLES

* * *

The Texas Constitution provides that "[p]erpetuities . . . are contrary to the genius of free government, and shall never be allowed." Tex. Const. art. I, § 26. Courts have enforced this provision by applying the rule against perpetuities. Under the Rule, no interest is valid unless it must vest, if at all, within twenty-one years after the death of some life or lives in being at the time of the creation of the interest.

The Rule relates only to the vesting of estates or interests, not vesting of possession, and is not applicable to present interests, or future interests which vest at their creation. We must therefore, examine the challenged conveyances as of the date the instruments were executed, and the conveyances are void if, by any possible contingency, the interests could vest outside the perpetuities period.

Upon creation of an oil and gas lease, the grantee receives a fee simple determinable estate in the minerals, and the grantor is left with a possibility of reverter. Jupiter Oil Co. v. Snow, 819 S.W.2d at 468. This possibility of reverter is the right to the mineral estate upon termination of the lease, and is a freely assignable vested right. Id. In that regard, Texas courts have long recognized that the owner of a mineral estate can bargain, sell, convey, assign, retain, reserve, or except all or a portion of the possibility of reverter.

Moreover, being a presently vested interest, the possibility of reverter is not subject to the Rule. Consequently, a conveyance or reservation of a present interest in all or a portion of the possibility of reverter does not violate the Rule. Bagby v. Bredthauer, 627 S.W.2d 190, 197 (Tex.App.–Austin 1981, no writ). Alternatively, if the conveyance is of an executory interest which cannot vest until a condition precedent occurs, the interest is subject to, and indeed may be void under the Rule. Peveto v. Starkey, 645 S.W.2d at 772.

Since all parties assert the instruments are unambiguous, the court's primary duty is to ascertain the intent of the parties as expressed in the agreement. Under the *172 applicable rule of construction, we must confine our inquiry to the four corners of the instrument and cannot consider extrinsic evidence. Luckel v. White, 819 S.W.2d 459, 461 (Tex. 1991); Sun Oil Co. (Delaware) v. Madeley, 626 S.W.2d 726, 728 (Tex.1981).

. . . In the top leases, the lessors specifically retained unto themselves all vested interests fixed by the underlying leases, and thereby expressed an intent not to convey any presently vested interests to the lessee. . . .

THE TOP LEASES

By three points of error, the Hammans contend the trial court erred in determining that the Rule invalidates the top leases as a matter of law. They assert the top leases conveyed vested possibilities of reverter to John Hamman, Jr., and therefore, are not subject to the Rule. After carefully analyzing the words used in the top lease conveyances, we disagree.

In Peveto v. Starkey [645 S.W.2d 770 (Tex.1982)], the Supreme Court relied specifically upon the words used in a grant in finding the grant to be void under the Rule. The Court stated:

> The printed portion of the granting clause conveyed a presently vested three-fourths royalty interest. However, following the property description, the parties inserted: 'this grant shall become effective only upon the expiration of [Peveto's] . . . Deed. . . .' This additional clause causes the Jones–Starkey deed to violate the rule.
>
> * * *
>
> [t]he words used here postpone the vesting of Starkey's interest until some uncertain future date. A grant "effective only upon" the termination of a determinable fee cannot vest until the prior interest has terminated. . . . The words "effective only upon" created a springing executory interest in Starkey which may not vest within the period of the Rule; therefore, the deed is void.

Peveto v. Starkey, 645 S.W.2d at 772. (emphasis added).

Turning to the language used in these top leases, we point out the following provisions inserted by the parties below the property description:

... this lease shall be for a term and period (now called "primary term") covering and embracing, and including also, ten (10) years after and subsequent to the forfeiture, or to the expiration, of said lease [to Shell/Superior]....

It being particularly agreed and understood that during the existence and continuance of said prior lease that the rights, interests, estate, privileges and royalties, as fixed thereby, of said Lessors shall remain vested in and held and possessed by said Lessors, free of all claims and demands whatsoever by said John Hamman, Jr ..... (emphasis added).

Under these lease provisions, George and John expressed an intent to preclude a present conveyance of any interest whatsoever to the lessee, by stating that any interest or estate owned by them under the bottom leases was to remain vested in them throughout the existence of the bottom leases, and free of all claims and demands by John Hamman, Jr. These top leases were made subject to, and specifically designated to commence after and subsequent to the expiration of, the bottom leases. Furthermore, the parties marked through the printed provision in each lease stating that the lease would be for a primary term "from date hereof," indicating the lease term was not to begin on the date of the document's execution.

Thus, although George and John owned possibilities of reverter at the time of the conveyances, under the express language of these top leases, they did not make present conveyances of their interests. Instead, the top leases conveyed interests that would vest in the grantee only upon termination of the bottom leases, and it is undisputed that the bottom leases could continue for an indeterminate amount of time. Consequently, the interests conveyed by the top leases had the potential for vesting outside the period provided by the Rule, and are void as a matter of law.[2]

* * *

The Hammans assert that a series of events, occurring after the execution of the top leases, removed any invalidity which may have existed with respect to those leases. They point to ratification agreements signed by John Hamman and George Hamman's successor in interest, division orders acted upon by various defendants, multiple assignments made "subject to" the top leases, subleases obtained by Bright from lessees of the top leases, and ratification agreements executed by Atlantic at Bright's request. The Hammans argue that because these actions occurred after the bottom leases had in fact expired, the perpetuity issue no longer existed, and the later ratifications were valid. We disagree.

All parties cite cases in support of their respective positions concerning ratification, and we recognize the emergence of competing lines of

---

2. In reaching our conclusion, we need not decide whether all top leases violate the rule against perpetuities, as the inserted language in these leases prevented any present vesting. For suggested "Ways To Avoid The Peveto Snare," see Nelson Roach, The Rule Against Perpetuities: The Validity Of Oil And Gas Top Leases And Top Deeds In Texas After Peveto v. Starkey, 35 Baylor L.Rev. 399, 410 (1983).

authority with respect to ratification of void instruments. However, we have not been cited to, nor have we found, any case which specifically determines or even addresses whether a conveyance, found to be void ab initio as violative of the rule against perpetuities, subsequently can be ratified after the potential perpetuity has, in fact, expired. Consequently, we must follow the unequivocal mandate of our constitution with respect to perpetuities.

An agreement made in violation of the constitution or a statute is illegal and absolutely void, and is not subject to ratification. In that regard, the constitutional mandate that perpetuities shall never be allowed must be relentlessly enforced. Brooker v. Brooker, 106 S.W.2d at 254. Having determined that the top leases were void ab initio under the Rule, and if enforced would violate the constitutional provision against perpetuities, we conclude that they could not be ratified.

* * *

NOTES

1.   The parties in the principal case entered into a settlement agreement after the appellate court handed down its decision and asked the Texas Supreme Court to vacate the judgments of lower courts. The supreme court did so "without reference to the merits" and remanded the case to the trial court for entry of judgment in accordance with the parties' settlement. See Bright & Co. v. Hamman, 938 S.W.2d 718 (Tex. 1997).

Although this subsequent history casts some doubt on the precedential value of the principal case, the court's reasoning on the perpetuities issue is squarely in accord with Peveto v. Starkey, 645 S.W.2d 770 (Tex. 1982), which the court heavily relied on. *Peveto* involved a "top deed," which is far less common than a top lease. The grantors had conveyed a terminable royalty "for a period of fifteen years" and "as long thereafter as oil, gas or other minerals, or either of them is produced * * * in paying commercial quantities." Thirteen years later the grantors executed a second royalty deed which, according to its express terms, would "become effective only upon the expiration" of the initial terminable royalty. The supreme court held that the second royalty was invalid. "The words 'effective only upon' created a springing executory interest in [the grantee] which may not vest within the period of the Rule [against Perpetuities]; therefore, the deed is void."

2.   The Hammans attempted to avoid the Rule against Perpetuities by arguing that the top lease had been carved out of the possibility of reverter remaining in the lessors after the bottom lease had been granted. Since the possibility of reverter is a presently vested interest, neither it nor any interests carved from it can violate the Rule. The court rejected this argument because it was not consistent with the actual language used in the top lease.

Suppose that the top lease had included a clause stipulating that the lease "is granted on lessor's reversionary interest and is hereby vested in interest, but is subject to an existing oil and gas lease and will become possessory only upon the termination of that lease." Would the result in Hamman have been different? Are there less legally abstruse ways to draft a top lease that does not violate the Rule against Perpetuities?

For specific examples of top leases that have been drafted to avoid the *Peveto/Hamman* problem, see the Forms Manual. See also Eugene O. Kuntz, The Rule Against Perpetuities and Mineral Interest, 8 Okla. L.Rev. 183, 186 (1955); Nelson Roach, Note, The Rule Against Perpetuities: The Validity of Oil and Gas Top Leases and Top Deeds in Texas After Peveto v. Starkey, 35 Baylor L. Rev. 399 (1983) and J. Suzanne Hill, Comment, Top Leases and the Rule Against Perpetuities, 10 Pepperdine L. Rev. 773 (1983).

3. In states that have modified the common law Rule Against Perpetuities, a top lease that commences once the bottom lease expires may be deemed valid even though it has no perpetuities savings clause. In Nantt v. Puckett Energy Co., 382 N.W.2d 655 (N.D. 1986) the North Dakota Supreme Court applied the "wait and see" doctrine and concluded that the top lease was valid because the bottom lease had not been extended by production beyond its primary term. In Stoltz, Wagner & Brown v. Duncan, 417 F.Supp. 552 (W.D.Okla. 1976) the court applied an Oklahoma statute authorizing reformation of interests that violate the Rule if reformation will effectuate the general intent of the grantor. The court reformed the top lease by eliminating the proviso under which the top lease would begin "from and after the expiration of the existing oil and gas lease" and sustained its validity under an alternative clause that provided that the top lease would begin on a specified date if the bottom lease had expired by that time.

4. The *Hamman* court ruled that a top lease that violates the Rule against Perpetuities cannot be ratified, even if the actions constituting ratification take place after the bottom lease has terminated. Several courts have allowed a grantee to ratify an originally void instrument once the reason for invalidity is no longer present. For example, the court in TCA Building Co. v. Northwestern Resources Co., 922 S.W.2d 629 (Tex. App. 1996) recognized the validity of a long-term coal and lignite lease and option that had been ratified after a statute prohibiting such leases on Veteran Land Board Tracts had been amended. In Humble Oil & Refining Co. v. Clark, 126 Tex. 262, 87 S.W.2d 471 (1935) the court indicated that a lease executed on behalf of a minor by a person who had no authority to act could be ratified by the minor once she reached her majority. Is there a convincing rationale for distinguishing between these situations and the top lease? What state constitutional policy is served by disallowing ratification of a top lease after the bottom lease terminates?

5. The Rule Against Perpetuities is not the only legal issue raised by top leasing. A lessor risks a suit for breach of warranty if she top leases when there is still a possibility that operations will extend the life of the bottom lease. In Siniard v. Davis, 678 P.2d 1197 (Okla.App.1984), the lessor executed a top lease on a standard form which contained a covenant of general warranty. When the bottom lease was unexpectedly maintained by production, the top lessees brought suit for breach of warranty and forced a return of the bonus and prepaid delay rentals. The court refused to imply any modification of the warranty because of the plaintiffs' knowledge of the existing lease. It

pointed out that the lessor could have protected herself by striking the warranty or inserting language making it subject to the prior lease.

In Pilkinton v. Ashley Ann Energy, L.L.C., 77 So.3d 465 (La.App.2 Cir. 2011) the lessor did essentially these things. In early August the defendant oil and gas company contracted for a top lease on plaintiffs' land that would commence the day after the termination of the existing lease's primary term, which would end on December 1. The prospective top lessee gave plaintiffs a draft, payable in 20 days, for one-fourth of the bonus and agreed to pay the remaining three-fourths when the top lease became effective. Although the agreement contained an express disclaimer of warranty of title by the land-owners, the draft for the initial payment was conditioned "upon approval of title." About two weeks after the draft was issued, the existing lessee received a drilling permit for the pooled unit which included the plaintiff landowners' tract. The defendant refused to authorize payment of the draft on the ground that the drilling permit constituted a title defect, in that drilling by the current lessee would extend the lease past the primary term. In holding that the landowners were entitled to the initial payment, the court pointed out that the parties had expressly agreed that the land was subject to an existing lease and that the plaintiff had included a disclaimer of warranty in the agreement. Even assuming that the landowners agreed to the condition contained in the draft, a permit to drill did not, by itself, extend the bottom lease beyond its primary term and did not constitute a flaw in the landowner's title,

Something of the reverse situation was presented in Petroleum Energy, Inc. v. Mid–America Petroleum, Inc., 775 F.Supp. 1420 (D.Kan. 1991), where the bottom lessee sued the lessor for breach of warranty of title and the covenant of quiet enjoyment, because the lessor had executed a new lease to a third party after the primary term had expired but while the plaintiff was in the process of preparing the drill site. Although the court agreed that the bottom lessee had maintained its lease by drilling operations, it rejected the claims for breach of covenant, pointing out that the covenants:

> [W]ould only protect a lessee from an eviction under a paramount title which existed at the time the lease was signed. [Plaintiff] was not evicted as a result of an assertion of a paramount title which allegedly existed at the time the 1979 lease was signed. [Plaintiff] was evicted under the terms of a 1984 lease entered into between [lessor] and [his new lessee] when the two latter parties believed that the 1979 lease had expired.

Id. at 1428.

6. A top lease that purports to vest while the bottom lease is still in effect can give rise to a variety of tort claims against the lessor and the top lessee, including tortious interference with a contract and tortious interference with a prospective business advantage. One of the most common claims is slander of title, which was discussed in Chapter One. For the bottom lessee to prevail under this theory, it must establish several elements, including malice. Courts have been generally reluctant to find that the lessor and top lessee acted with malice if the continued validity of the bottom lease depends upon the resolution of a genuine fact question or a legal question of first impression. See, e.g., Petroleum Energy, Inc. v. Mid–America Petroleum, Inc.,

775 F.Supp. 1420 (D.Kan. 1991) and Voiles v. Santa Fe Minerals, Inc., 911 P.2d 1205 (Okla. 1996). See also Marichiel Lewis, Note, Oil and Gas: Top Leasing after Voiles v. Santa Fe Minerals—Unethical Claim Jumping or Prudent Business Practice? 52 Okla.L.Rev. 127 (1997).

7. Top leasing by the existing lessee has occasionally given rise to a claim that the new lease supercedes or is now substituted for the original lease, even though the original lease has not yet expired according to its terms. This theory, which has received some support in Louisiana cases, such as Placid Oil Co. v. Taylor, 325 So.2d 313 (La.App. 1975), is criticized in Michael L. Brown, Effect of Top Leases: Obstruction of Title and Related Considerations, 30 Baylor L.Rev. 213, 231–37 (1978).

Which party is more likely to negotiate for a novation: the lessor or the original lessee who is seeking to gain additional time in which to drill?

H. EFFECT OF POOLING ON PROPERTY INTERESTS

The pooling clause in an oil and gas lease typically authorizes the lessee to join all or part of the land subject to the lease with adjacent leased land to form a unit that does not exceed a specified size. It then provides that production from a well on any part of a pooled unit is deemed to come from all portions of the unit and will be allocated on a surface acreage basis to all tracts within the unit. Legal issues connected with the exercise of the pooling clause are discussed in Chapter Two. This section deals with a different set of issues: What is the effect of pooling on property interests, such as the lessor's reversionary interest and NPRIs, within the pooled unit?

1. EFFECT ON LESSOR'S INTERESTS

WAGNER & BROWN, LTD. v. SHEPPARD

282 S.W.3d 419 (Tex. 2008).

JUSTICE BRISTER delivered the opinion of the Court.

* * *

I. BACKGROUND

Jane Sheppard, a CPA and retired family lawyer, owns 1/8th of the minerals underlying a 62.72–acre tract in Upshur County, Texas. C.W. Resources, Inc. leased her 1/8th interest, and along with Wagner & Brown, Ltd. leased the other 7/8ths of the minerals from other owners. Sheppard's lease had a special addendum providing that if royalties were not paid within 120 days after first gas sales, her lease would terminate the following month.[1]

---

1. Within 120 days following the first sale of oil or gas produced from the lease premises, or lands pooled therewith, settlement shall be made by Lessee, or by Lessee's agent, for royalties due

Sheppard's lease also authorized pooling with adjacent tracts. On September 1, 1996, C.W. Resources, Wagner & Brown, and mineral lessees on adjacent tracts signed a unit agreement pooling the Sheppard tract and eight others to form the W.M. Landers Gas Unit.[2] One month later, a gas well was successfully completed and began producing, and a second well was completed in September 1997. Both wells were physically located on the Sheppard tract, but pursuant to the unit agreement proceeds and costs were split among all the tracts in proportion to acreage.

The original unit agreement designated C.W. Resources as operator of the unit. In September 2000, Wagner & Brown took over that position, and discovered that Sheppard had not been paid royalties within 120 days of the first gas sales. Wagner & Brown offered Sheppard a new lease, but with two producing wells already on her property, she declined. The parties agree that Sheppard's lease terminated on March 1, 1997, and since then she has been an unleased co-tenant, entitled to her share of proceeds from minerals sold less her share of the costs of production and marketing.

The dispute here concerns both the proceeds and the costs. Regarding the proceeds, the question is whether the termination of Sheppard's lease also terminated her participation in the unit (in which case she is entitled to 1/8th of 100 percent of production, as both wells are on her tract), or did not do so (in which case she is entitled to 1/8th of only 51.3 percent of production—the proportion her tract bears to total acreage in the unit).[3] Regarding the costs, the question is whether Sheppard should bear any costs incurred before her lease terminated, or any costs incurred after the lease terminated that relate to the unit but not her lease.

The trial court granted summary judgment for Sheppard, finding that termination of the lease also terminated her participation in the unit, that she was not liable for any costs incurred before termination, and that she was liable for costs incurred after termination only if they pertained solely to her lease; the court of appeals affirmed.[4] For the reasons stated below, we disagree.

II. DOES TERMINATION OF THE LEASE ALSO TERMINATE THE UNIT?

Sheppard's 1994 lease contained a standard industry pooling clause that provided:

> Lessee shall have the right but not the obligation to pool all or any part of the leased premises or interest therein with any other lands or interests.... Production, drilling or reworking operations anywhere

---

hereunder with respect to such oil or gas, and such royalties shall be paid monthly thereafter without the necessity of Lessor executing a division or transfer order. If said initial royalty payment is not so made under the terms hereof, this lease shall terminate as of 7:00 A.M. the first day of the month following the expiration of said 120 day period.

2. The other parties joining in the unit agreement were defendants Thompson Interests, Inc., Carl A. Westerman, Westerman Royalty Company, Bernie Wolford, and H.G. Westerman.

3. Sheppard's 62.72 acre tract compared to a total of 122.15954 acres in the unit.

4. 198 S.W.3d 369.

on a unit which includes all or any part of the leased premises shall be treated as if it were production, drilling or reworking operations on the leased premises, except that the production on which Lessor's royalty is calculated shall be that proportion of the total unit production which the net acreage covered by this lease and included in the unit bears to the total gross acreage in the unit.... In the absence of production in paying quantities from a unit, or upon permanent cessation thereof, Lessee may terminate the unit by filing of record a written declaration describing the unit and stating the date of termination. Pooling hereunder shall not constitute a cross-conveyance of interests.

The Designation of Unit signed by the lessees of the various "leases and lands" included in the pool provided that they "hereby pool and combine said leases and the lands ... into a single pooled unit or unitized area for the development of and production of gas and associated hydrocarbons...."

* * *

[A] proper interpretation of these documents indicates the termination of Sheppard's lease did not terminate her participation in the unit. A lease is not necessarily required for pooling; mineral owners can join a pool even if no lease exists. Here, both Sheppard's lease and the unit agreement pooled certain "premises" and "lands," not just their leased interests. Although Sheppard's lease expired, the lands themselves obviously did not. Thus, while termination of Sheppard's lease changed who owned the mineral interests in the unit, it did not cause the unit to terminate because it was a pooling of lands, not just leases.

On precisely this basis, the Second Court of Appeals held in Ladd Petroleum Corp. v. Eagle Oil & Gas Co. that termination of a lease does not terminate a unit.[5] The lease in Ladd allowed pooling with "other lands" as well as other leases, so the unit survived the termination of one lease because "the continuing validity of any such pooling was not dependent upon a subsisting leasehold estate in the adjacent land."[6] In this case as in Ladd, lands as well as leases were pooled, so the tracts dedicated to the unit survived even if the related leases did not.

The court of appeals here distinguished Ladd on the ground that it involved termination of an entire pool, while Sheppard seeks only termination of her participation in it.[7] But there cannot be one rule of contract interpretation for small mineral interests and a different rule for large ones. If Sheppard's original mineral interest had been 8/8ths rather than 1/8th, the ruling she seeks would have cut off all production for the other members in the pool just as occurred in Ladd. And if her original interest

5.   695 S.W.2d 99, 106 (Tex.App.–Fort Worth 1985, writ ref'd n.r.e.).

6.   Id.

7.   198 S.W.3d at 375.

had been 5/8ths or more, her share would have curtailed their share, even though they had nothing to do with letting her lease terminate.[8]

The court of appeals relied on Texaco, Inc. v. Lettermann, in which the Seventh Court of Appeals held that the termination of two out of the three leases in a unit resulted in termination of the pool.[9] But the lease in Lettermann only authorized pooling "with the gas leasehold estate" of adjacent lands.[10] Thus, when those leasehold estates terminated, so did the pool. But that does not mean a unit formed by pooling lands must terminate on the same basis as one formed by pooling only leases.

The court of appeals also reasoned from the premise that the pooling agreement transferred only the operator's interest, leaving Sheppard's possibility of reverter unimpinged. But her lease allowed pooling of "all or any part of the leased premises or interest therein," and Sheppard's reverter was certainly an interest in the leased premises. "When a unit is properly pooled, the owners of the minerals or reversionary interests in a separate tract within the unit surrender their right to receive their interest in all production from wells located on their own tract...."[11] Just as pooling impinges on a mineral owner's royalty interest,[12] it also may impinge on an owner's possibility of reverter.

The parties invite us to decide the question here based on general principles rather than the terms of the particular documents involved. Wagner & Brown urges that termination of a lease should never terminate a pool, pointing out that pooling benefits mineral owners, operators, the state, and the environment by reducing the number of wells needed to maintain efficient production while protecting correlative rights.[13] Sheppard urges adoption of a treatise's view that "pooling can extend no longer than the lease itself" because a lessor grants only "a power to pool the leasehold rights."[14]

---

8. A co-tenant owning 5/8ths of the minerals would be entitled to 62.5 percent of production, whereas the other pool members here were entitled to 49.7 percent of production based on their proportional acreage in the pool.

9. 343 S.W.2d 726, 730 (Tex.Civ.App.–Amarillo 1961, writ ref'd n.r.e.).

10. Id. at 727 (emphasis added).

11. Mengden v. Peninsula Prod. Co., 544 S.W.2d 643, 648 (Tex.1976) (emphasis added); Southland Royalty Co. v. Humble Oil & Ref. Co., 151 Tex. 324, 249 S.W.2d 914, 916 (1952).

12. See Southland Royalty, 249 S.W.2d at 916; Brown v. Smith, 141 Tex. 425, 174 S.W.2d 43, 46 (1943).

13. See Mengden, 544 S.W.2d at 647; Howard R. Williams, Conservation of Oil and Gas, 65 Harv. L.Rev. 1155, 1164 (1952) (recommending compulsory pooling as a conservation measure because "dense spacing dissipates reservoir energy, occasions some wastage of oil or gas while the wells are being cleaned out, increases the hazards of fire or other accidents which cause loss of minerals or damage to the producing structure, and results in uneconomic use of materials and labor in the drilling of unnecessary wells").

14. 1 Bruce M. Kramer & Patrick H. Martin, The Law of Pooling & Unitization § 15.04 (3d. ed.2006). The authors acknowledge that the question here is "difficult," that "another way of viewing the pooling clause" is that it continues under the normal rules of principal and agent, and that "[i]t is necessary to look at all the circumstances of the pooling in order to determine whether there is a continuation of the pooling once a lease that has been pooled may be said to have terminated." Id. The authors also serve as editors of another treatise stating that "[e]xpiration or other extinguishment of a unitized interest will cause termination of the unit as to such interest." 6 Howard R. Williams & Charles J. Meyers, Oil & Gas Law § 931.2 (Patrick H. Martin & Bruce M. Kramer eds., 2007). Both entries rely almost entirely on Texaco, Inc. v. Lettermann, in which (as we have noted) the polling clause unitized leases rather than lands.

But oil and gas leases in general, and pooling clauses in particular, are a matter of contract.[15] Just as owners and operators generally must agree to create a pool,[16] they should also be able to agree when one terminates. If the parties want pooling to expire (or not) upon termination of one lease, they should be free to say so.[17] The lease here allowed the Sheppard tract (rather than just the lease) to be pooled for purposes of production, and that is what the unit designation did. As termination of the lease changed none of the lands committed to the unit, we hold that it did not terminate the unit. Thus, while Sheppard is entitled as a co-tenant to 1/8th of the proceeds due to the mineral owners of her tract, that does not entitle her to 1/8th of the proceeds that must be shared with mineral owners of other tracts by the terms of the unit agreement.

* * *

NOTES

1. The issue of whether Sheppard's carried interest was liable for expenses attributable to the entire pooled unit and what those expenses included was dealt with in Section B of this chapter.

2. The pooling clause in Sheppard's lease has been widely used for many years, and the ruling in the principal case has raised a variety of questions that are extremely troublesome to title examiners. For example, if Sheppard's interest remains pooled after the expiration of the lease on her interest, do *all* of the leased interests remain pooled after production ceases and all of the leases have terminated? If in 1932 portions of three different tracts were pooled under clauses like that in Sheppard's lease and the well maintaining the leases on the pooled unit ceased producing in 1970, do the portions of the tracts in the pooled unit remain pooled? Does a prospective lessee of one of the tracts also need to obtain leases on the portions of the other two tracts that were within the original pooled unit?

Do the decisions in Ladd Petroleum Corp. v. Eagle Oil & Gas Co. and Texaco, Inc. v. Lettermann, which were cited by the court and also involved claims of termination of a pooled unit, provide any help in resolving the issue?

3. In Holland v. EOG Resources, Inc., 2010 WL 1078480 (Tex. App.– Waco 2010), the lessors entered into an agreement providing that the lessee "will spud a well on the [plaintiff's] tract no later than December 31, 2007, and if it fails to do so, shall make a one-time payment in the total amount of $25,000 * * *" The lease contained a pooling clause, and the lessee drilled a well on land pooled with plaintiff's land within the time limit specified in the agreement and extended a horizontal line beneath the plaintiffs' tract. The court rejected the plaintiffs' claim to $25,000 on the ground that operations anywhere within a pooled unit are deemed to have taken place on each tract within that unit. It reasoned that spudding a well on land pooled with plaintiffs' tract was the legal equivalent of spudding a well on the plaintiffs' tract. There was no breach of the agreement.

---

15. Tittizer v. Union Gas Corp., 171 S.W.3d 857, 860 (Tex.2005).

16. Id.

17. See Southland Royalty, 249 S.W.2d at 917 (holding that nothing prevented mineral owner "from protecting their estates by express stipulation").

4. As noted earlier in the section on community leases, Veal v. Thomason, 159 S.W.2d 472 (Tex. 1942), which involved a community lease, adopted the theory that by entering into the community lease, each lessor conveyed a fractional royalty interest to each of the other landowners signing the community lease. In other words, all the lessors became co-tenants of the royalty in each of the leases subject to the community lease. There is some authority that the same theory applies to pooling.

5. Section 956 of the Summers treatise offers this commentary regarding the Texas cross-conveyancing theory. It states,

> There is authority pro[10] and con[11] whether this cross-conveyance theory applies to consolidations effected by other than the community lease device. If the cross-conveyance theory is to be a jurisdiction's property law for any pooling and unitization situations, no reason is apparent why the line should be drawn short of including all voluntary methods resulting in true poolings and unitizations.

The treatise goes on to state that a majority of jurisdictions follow the "contract theory" under which property rights remain unchanged and there is an implied agreement that production from the pooled or unitized area will be shared.

One effect of the cross-conveyancing theory is that lessees within a pooled unit are now deemed co-tenants of the working interests. Although a cotenant can normally compel a partition, the various clauses within the lessees' pooling agreement may be deemed to constitute a waiver of the right to partition. See MCEN 1996 Partnership v. Glassell, 42 S.W.3d 262 (Tex. App. 2001).

Because of the problems posed by the cross-conveyancing theory, many lease pooling clauses and unitization agreements expressly disclaim cross-conveyancing and provide that the sharing of production is based on a contractual agreement among the parties.

6. How do the cross-conveyance and contract theories determine the application of the rule against perpetuities to a pooling agreement? In analyzing this question, consider the fact that most pooling clauses specifically allow the lessee to pool "at any time." See Kuntz § 17.2 and Williams & Meyers § 936.

2. EFFECT ON ROYALTY AND RELATED INTERESTS

LONDON v. MERRIMAN

756 S.W.2d 736 (Tex.App. 1988, writ denied).

OPINION

NYE, CHIEF JUSTICE.

Appellant, Dorothy London, asks this Court to determine her rights as lessor under an oil and gas lease, as well as the rights of the non-

---

10. Tex.—Miles v. Amerada Petroleum Corp., 241 S.W.2d 822 (Tex.Civ.App.–El Paso 1950, error refused n.r.e.).

11. Tex.—Sohio Petroleum Co. v. Jurek, 248 S.W.2d 294 (Tex.Civ.App.–Fort Worth 1952, writ ref'd n.r.e.).

participatory royalty interest owners (the Merrimans). London appeals from a judgment awarding the Merrimans gas royalties. We affirm.

London owns two adjoining tracts of land and holds the executive right (the right to lease) to all the minerals. She owns a 3/16 royalty interest in the eastern tract and a 1/8 royalty interest in the western tract. The Merrimans own a 1/16 non-participating (no right to lease) royalty interest in the western tract, created by reservation when Mr. Merriman conveyed the land to London.

In 1980, London executed a single oil and gas lease which included both tracts. The lessee later assigned its interest to the McCord Exploration Company. In 1982, McCord brought in successful gas wells on the eastern tract, in which London owns all the royalty interest. No wells have been drilled on the western tract.

In 1983, the Merrimans sued McCord and London, claiming that McCord breached a duty to protect the tract in which they owned a royalty interest against drainage by the other tract. In 1984, they successfully sought statutory forced pooling of their royalty interest with London's by the Railroad Commission, enabling them to share in the royalties paid on the wells since the effective date of the Commission's order, March 7, 1984. The Merrimans pursued their suit for a common law recovery of royalties allegedly lost by drainage until the effective date of the order. In 1986, they filed a supplemental petition, alleging an alternative theory— that they had ratified the lease between McCord and London and so had accepted London's alleged offer in the lease to pool their royalty interest with hers.

The case proceeded to trial on both pled theories. The ratification theory was tried to the court, while the breach of duty theory was tried to the jury. The Merrimans were successful on both. They elected to have judgment on the ratification theory, and the trial court awarded them $390,051.35 for royalty payments due them * * *. In its judgment, the court found that the Merrimans ratified the lease by filing suit on July 14, 1983, entitling them to their share of royalties from that date until the effective date of the Railroad Commission's forced pooling order, March 7, 1984. London asserts that the oil and gas lease by its terms precluded ratification and the consequent pooling of the royalty interests.

The oil and gas lease executed by London is a standard "Producer's 88" lease. It contains a provision which authorizes the lessee, at its option, "to pool or combine the acreage covered by this lease, or any portion thereof, as to oil and gas, or either of them, with any other land * * *".

Absent consent, the executive does not have the legal right to authorize the lessee to pool the royalty rights of the non-participating royalty interest owner with other royalty interest owners. Montgomery v. Rittersbacher, 424 S.W.2d 210, 215 (Tex. 1968); Brown v. Getty Reserve Oil, Inc., 626 S.W.2d 810, 814 (Tex.App.–Amarillo 1981, writ dism'd.). A lease which purports to do so is essentially an offer by the lessor to the other royalty interest owners to create a community lease by ratifying the lease; if they do ratify it, the lease effects a cross-conveyance of interests and a pooling or combining of royalty interests. See Ruiz v. Martin, 559 S.W.2d 839, 842–44 (Tex.Civ.App.–San Antonio 1977, writ ref'd n.r.e.) and cases cited therein.

* * *

The instant case is nearly indistinguishable from *Ruiz,* where the court there also interpreted a Producer's 88 lease. The lease included several royalty interest owners and covered separate tracts, and a gas well was brought in on one of the tracts. The owner of a non-producing tract claimed a part of the royalties from the well under the pooling clause. The court, interpreting *Montgomery,* held that the non-participating royalty owner was able to ratify the lease and so claim a percentage of the royalty. See also Standard Oil Co. v. Donald, 321 S.W.2d at 606. We have carefully analyzed *Ruiz* and agree that it was correctly decided.

London argues, however, that a clause in the lease here distinguishes *Ruiz.* At the end of the same paragraph which grants the power to pool to the lessee, the lease contains a clause which London characterizes as a "non-unitization" or "anti-communitization" clause:

> If this lease now or hereafter covers separate tracts, no pooling or unitization of royalty interest as between any such separate tracts is intended or shall be implied or result merely from the inclusion of such separate tracts within this lease but Lessee shall nevertheless have the right to pool as provided above with consequent allocation of production as above provided. As used in this paragraph 4, the words "separate tract" mean any tract with royalty ownership differing, now or hereafter, either as to parties or amounts, from that as to any other part of the leased premises.

No such clause appears in the *Ruiz* opinion.

London contends that this clause negated any intent to pool or unitize the royalties and keeps the royalties separate, so that the Merrimans are entitled to recover only for production from the western tract. The Merrimans counter that the clause is ineffective and they are entitled to a proportionate share of royalty from production anywhere on the leasehold, under *Ruiz* and *Montgomery.*

We agree with the Merrimans. The purported non-unitization clause simply provides that no pooling or unitization of royalties is intended "merely from" the inclusion of the two tracts in one lease. We agree that no such pooling results *merely* because the lease included two tracts.

Rather, it results from the previous lease provisions which authorize the unitization or pooling of the royalties should the lessee pool the tracts of land in any fashion. The purported non-unitization clause expressly does not detract from this authorization.

Pooling of the royalties resulted from London's attempted authorization for the lessee to pool the Merrimans' interest without their consent, enabling the Merrimans to ratify the unauthorized act. *Montgomery,* 424 S.W.2d at 215,[1] *Ruiz,* 559 S.W.2d at 842–44.

* * *

London's lease with McCord attempted to authorize an unauthorized act, thereby offering the Merrimans an opportunity to ratify the lease. The Merrimans accepted the offer by ratifying the lease, which the trial court found occurred when suit was filed in 1983. Bringing suit constitutes an implied ratification of an unauthorized act. *Montgomery,* 424 S.W.2d at 214. By ratifying the lease, the Merrimans became a party to it, and the rule that the execution of an oil and gas lease by more than one mineral interest owner effects a pooling of their interests applied.

* * *

The judgment of the trial court is AFFIRMED.

NOTES

1.   In Brown v. Getty Reserve Oil, Inc., 626 S.W.2d 810 (Tex.App. 1981, writ dism'd), the executive leased Sections 27 and 29 in a single lease. Section 27 was subject to a royalty interest owned by X, and Section 29 was subject to a royalty interest owned by Y. Neither X nor Y ratified the lease. The lessee brought in a gas well on Section 29 and attempted, by use of a division order, to pool the entire lease acreage. X executed the division order, but Y refused. The court held that Sections 27 and 29 were not pooled and therefore Y was entitled to royalty on all production from the well on Section 29. X was not entitled to any royalty from the well on Section 29. The court concluded that Y could claim full royalty without having to ratify pooling because the well was located on Section 29 (the land subject to Y's royalty interest) and that the executive had clear authority to subject Y's interest to a lease but no

1. The Supreme Court in *Montgomery* suggested that if the executive wishes to prevent this result, he should take "affirmative steps" to exclude the interest from the operation of the entirety clause or pooling clause. See Montgomery, 424 S.W.2d at 213. The Court did not provide guidance on what those steps might be; however, the Court of Civil Appeals in Standard Oil Co. v. Donald, 321 S.W.2d 602, 606 (Tex.Civ.App.–Fort Worth 1959, writ ref'd n.r.e.), suggested the exclusion of the mineral estate of the other interest owners from the lease or the execution of separate leases. Id. at 844, cited in Ruiz, 559 S.W.2d at 844. It may also be possible for a lease covering more than one tract and including more than one royalty interest to expressly negate any unauthorized pooling of the non-executive interest, but because of its pooling clause, the standard form Producer's 88 lease involved here does not do so. It is ill-equipped to handle the complexities inherent in multi-tract and multi-royalty situations.

Dean Ernest Smith advances the theory that the lessor of a non-producing tract cannot exclude the non-executive's interest from a pooled unit without the non-executive's consent. Smith, Implications of a Fiduciary Standard of Conduct for the Holder of the Executive Right, 64 Texas L.Rev. 371, 391–95 (1985).

authority to pool Y's interest. Why was X's execution of a division order insufficient to give X a royalty share of the Section 29 well even though Y had not executed a division order? If Y had ratified the pooling by executing the division order, could Y later revoke this ratification? Cf. Exxon Corp. v. Middleton, 613 S.W.2d 240 (Tex.1981).

In MCZ, Inc. v. Triolo, 708 S.W.2d 49 (Tex.App.–Houston 1986, writ ref'd n.r.e.), the executive issued a lease covering Blackacre. Blackacre was subject to a royalty interest owned by X. The lease contained a pooling clause. The lessee later pooled a portion of Blackacre with Whiteacre. X specifically ratified the pooling; however, the ratification provided that it did "not apply to all or any portion of" Blackacre not included within the pooled unit. A producing well was completed on Whiteacre, and X accepted royalty payments in accordance with the pooling. Later, the lessee pooled the balance of Blackacre with Redacre and drilled a producing well on Blackacre. X refused to consent to this pooling and claimed royalty on the entire production. The court held that because X's ratification of the pooling was limited to the Whiteacre unit, X was entitled to royalty on the entire production from the Blackacre well. The court reached this decision even though the holding resulted in a reduction of the executive's royalty in the Blackacre well. Why would the executive's royalty in the Blackacre well be reduced?

Does the holder of the executive right or the lessee have a duty to notify owners of nonoperating interests of their right to ratify community leases or pooling agreements? See De Benavides v. Warren, 674 S.W.2d 353 (Tex.App. 1984, writ ref'd n.r.e.). See generally Smith The Standard of Conduct Owed by Executive Right Holders and Operators to the Owners of Nonparticipating and Nonoperating Interests, 32 Inst. on Oil & Gas L. & Tax'n, 241, 252–55 (1981). For a thorough discussion of the Texas cases dealing with rights of nonoperating interests regarding pooling, see Smith & Weaver § 4.7(B).

2. In Montgomery v. Rittersbacher, 424 S.W.2d 210 (Tex. 1968), Montgomery was the owner of a royalty interest in 80 acres of land, designated in the record as the "First Tract." The respondents held the executive rights to the First Tract and also owned executive rights in adjacent land, designated in the record as the "Second Tract." Respondents leased both the First Tract and the Second Tract under a single lease. The lease contained a pooling clause and an entireties clause. The entireties clause provided as follows:

> If the leased premises are now or shall hereafter be owned in severalty or in separate tracts, the premises, nevertheless, shall be developed and operated as one lease, and all royalties accruing hereunder shall be treated as an entirety and shall be divided among and paid to such separate owners in the proportion that the acreage owned by each such separate owner bears to the entire leased acreage.

424 S.W.2d at 212.

Sun Oil Co., the lessee, formed several units out of the original leased acreage. A portion of the Second Tract was pooled with other land, designated in the record as the Crutchfield tract. Sun completed a producing well on the Crutchfield tract but drilled a dry hole in the unit that included the First Tract. Montgomery brought suit claiming to have ratified the lease and claiming a share of the royalties by virtue of the entireties clause from the production on the Crutchfield Tract. The court of appeals ruled in favor of respondents, and Montgomery appealed. The supreme court reversed in favor of Montgomery:

> We can see no distinction between the pooling clause, insofar as it has the effect of changing the aggregate ownership of the non-participating royalty owner, and the entirety clause, which, in effect, would allow the holder of the executive rights to either diminish or enlarge the ownership of that of the royalty owner. In either case, the consent of the owner must be obtained.

> * * * The lease executed by Respondents and the original lessee explicitly described the entire tract in which Montgomery had a non-participating interest as being covered by the lease. The unambiguous entirety clause clearly indicates that it was to apply to all the interests covered by the lease. The clause points out that even if the premises are owned in severalty *at the time of the execution of the lease,* as the premises were in this case, "the [leased] premises, nevertheless shall be developed and operated *as one lease,* and *all royalties* accruing hereunder shall be treated as an entirety and shall be divided among and *paid to such separate owners in the proportion that the acreage owned by each bears to the entire leased acreage.*" (Emphasis added.) This Court has held that an "are now" entirety clause as was contained in the present lease applies to minerals held in severalty at the time of the execution of the lease. Thomas Gilcrease Foundation v. Stanolind Oil & Gas Co., 19 266 S.W.2d 850, 853 (Tex. 1954).

* * *

This Court has never been called upon to decide the question of whether a holder of non-participating royalty has an option to make an entirety clause operative on his interest. We think that the non-participating royalty owner, so far as the existence of an option is concerned, occupies a comparable position to that of a cotenant under a lease made by his cotenant or a non-participating royalty owner under a pooling agreement made by the holder of the executive rights. As to the cotenant, it has been held that he has the right to ratify or repudiate a lease made by his cotenant which covers his interest. Likewise, in the pooling area, if a non-participating royalty owner ratifies a pooling agreement, either by joining in the execution of the agreement or by accepting royalties from the pool, his interest is bound by the pooling agreement. Therefore, we hold that the non-participating royalty owner has the option to ratify or repudiate a lease containing provisions which as to his interest the holder of the executive rights had no authority to insert in the lease.

Montgomery, in bringing this suit, seeks two things under the lease—royalties that have already accrued and royalties that are to accrue in the future. We have held that Montgomery has ratified the lease in question by filing suit; consequently, he is only entitled to receive royalties accruing from and after May 12, 1964, the date this suit was filed. In this connection, we point out that Montgomery, having thus ratified the lease, is as much bound thereby as if he had joined in the original execution thereof. As long as the lease is in force, he is not free to claim his full 1/2 non-participating interest under "First Tract."

Id. at 213–15.

The well located on the Crutchfield Tract was completed in October 1956, shut-in, and put on production in May 1958. The dry hole drilled on land pooled with the First Tract was plugged in 1961. By the court's ruling, Montgomery ratified the lease on May 12, 1964.

Could respondents have successfully argued that Montgomery should have exercised his ratification within a reasonable time? See the dissenting opinion of Chief Justice Calvert. Id. at 215. What did Montgomery gain by waiting so long to ratify? What did he lose?

Could Montgomery have ratified the lease insofar as the entireties clause is concerned but have disavowed the pooling? Under what circumstances would Montgomery want to do this? Conversely, could Montgomery have ratified the pooling clause but have disavowed the entireties clause? Under what circumstances would Montgomery want to do this?

3.   Louisiana courts have held that the owner of a mineral servitude has the power to pool on behalf of the owner of a mineral royalty. Le Blanc v. Haynesville Mercantile Co., 88 So.2d 377 (La.1956). Is this a better view? Is the holder of an executive right restricted in other ways when he negotiates an oil and gas lease on behalf of himself and nonoperating interests?

4.   Does an assignee of the oil and gas lease working interest have the right to pool an overriding royalty if the instrument of assignment is silent on the matter? In Rice Bros. Mineral Corp. v. Talbott, 717 S.W.2d 515 (Ky.App. 1986), the Bakers executed a lease to Rice Brothers. The pooling clause was deleted. Rice assigned the lease to Talbott, reserving an overriding royalty. Talbott negotiated a pooling agreement with the Bakers, but Rice refused to pool voluntarily. Talbott, who did not seek compulsory pooling, treated Rice's interest as if it had been pooled, completed a producing well on the Baker lease, and reduced Rice's overriding royalty in accordance with the pooling. Rice sued for additional royalty, and the trial court granted Talbott's motion for summary judgment. The Kentucky Court of Appeals affirmed. In holding that Talbott could pool on behalf of Rice, the court relied on language in the compulsory pooling act that gave "the owners of all oil and gas interests" the right to pool voluntarily. The court concluded by noting that under the Kentucky nonownership theory, Rice was not an "owner" of the "an oil and gas interest" within the meaning of the statute. Is this sound reasoning? In Union Pacific Resources Co. v. Hutchison, 990 S.W.2d 368 (Tex. App. 1999) the court considered the terms of the underlying oil and gas lease to determine the intent of the parties. Since the pooling clause of the lease authorized pooling without the consent of the lessors, the court thought it unlikely that the parties to the assignment intended that the assignee should have to obtain the prior consent of the assignor in order to pool the retained overriding royalty.

5.   When a nonexecutive interest is created, the parties could specifically authorize the executive to pool the property on the nonexecutive's behalf, to execute a lease that contains an entireties clause, or both.

3. EFFECT ON TERMINABLE INTERESTS

EDMONSTON v. HOME STAKE OIL & GAS CORPORATION

762 P.2d 176 (Kan.1988).

HOLMES, JUSTICE:

This case is before the Kansas Supreme Court on a certified question from the United States Court of Appeals for the Tenth Circuit pursuant to the Uniform Certification of Questions of Law Act, K.S.A. 60–3201 et seq. The question as presented by the certifying court is:

"When a term mineral interest in several tracts has been conveyed by a single instrument and one of those tracts has been unitized under the Kansas Compulsory Unitization Act, Kan.Stat.Ann. 55–1301 et seq., is the entire mineral interest extended by the unitized production or only the interest in the tract included within the unit?"

As pointed out by the Court of Appeals, the facts are stated in the United States District Court opinion. Edmonston v. Home Stake Oil & Gas Corp., 629 F.Supp. 620 (D.Kan.1986). For convenience, a plat or map of the area involved is attached as an appendix to this opinion. The Hon. Patrick F. Kelly, speaking for the United States District Court for the District of Kansas, stated the facts which are pertinent to the question before this court as follows:

"This is a quiet title action concerning three-quarters of a section of land, the North Half (N/2) and Southeast Quarter (SE/4) of Section 31, [Township 29 South, Range 18 West] in Kiowa County, Kansas. Defendants own a defeasible term mineral interest, an undivided 1/4 interest in and to all oil, gas and other minerals in the entire three-quarters tract. Plaintiff Edmonston purchased title to the tract in 1979, succeeding to the original grantors' reversionary rights against the defendants. The dispositive issue is whether defendants' defeasible term mineral interests in the entire tract were extended by a Kansas Corporation Commission compulsory unitization order, which included only a portion of the tract, followed by off-tract production on the unitized acreage * * *.

* * *

"In 1962, within the 10–year primary term of defendants' interest, the Lewis 'C' Well was drilled and completed on the SE/4. The well produced oil and/or gas in paying quantities until plugged and abandoned on April 7, 1973. The parties agree the development, production and operation of the Lewis 'C' extended beyond the primary term defendants' term mineral interest in the entire tract, the SE/4 and the N/2 of Section 31. Baker v. Hugoton Production Co., 182 Kan. 210, Syl. ¶ 1, 320 P.2d 772 (1958).

"Pursuant to the Kansas Compulsory Unitization Act, K.S.A. 55–1301 et seq., on May 24, 1968 the Kansas Corporation Commission (KCC) ordered unitization of the Nichols Pool in Kiowa County. The unitized area included the SE/4, but not the N/2, of Section 31. The KCC order incorporated by express reference the plan of unitization agreed upon by the necessary 75% of the royalty, term and working interest owners of the Nichols Pool. (R. 10, Ex. C, p. 3.) Paragraph 3.4 of that plan provided operations or production anywhere on the unit shall be considered as operations or production in each tract within the unit, the effect being to 'continue in effect each lease, term royalty, or other agreement as to all lands covered thereby just as if such operations had been conducted and a well had been drilled on and was producing from each tract.' * * * The KCC terminated the Nichols Unit effective November 20, 1984.

"After the Lewis 'C' Well on the SE/4 was plugged in 1973, no producing oil well or gas well was physically located on the N/2 of Section 31 * * *.

"At no time after the Lewis 'C' Well was plugged on April 7, 1973, has any producing oil well or gas well ever been physically located or drilled upon the SE/4 of Section 31." 629 F.Supp. at 621–22.

The district court held that the statutory unitization of the Nichols Pool extended the defendants' defeasible term mineral interests only as to the SE/4 which was included in the unit. We agree.

* * *

In Wilson v. Holm, [164 Kan. 229, 188 P.2d 899 (1948)] a quiet title action brought by a reversioner, this court set out certain rules pertaining to defeasible term mineral interests of the type at issue here. The court stated that "the ultimate test as to whether an estate created by a deed has terminated depends entirely upon its own provisions," and that the "deed must be construed in accord with the intent and purpose of the parties after it has been examined in its entirety." 164 Kan. at 239, 188 P.2d 899.

This court has consistently followed the rule, asserted in Wilson v. Holm, that the instrument which creates a defeasible term mineral interest is controlling on the question of whether the interest has terminated. While the foregoing cases cover a multitude of factual situations and establish numerous principles of law, one common thread that permeates the opinions is that the extent and duration of a term mineral interest is ordinarily controlled by the provisions of the document creating the interest. The cases also reflect that to perpetuate a term mineral interest beyond the primary term contained in the original document, there must be production from or operations on a portion of the property contained in the original grant. It is also the rule in Kansas that where defeasible term mineral interests are voluntarily unitized with other property, production from the other property within the unit will operate to continue the term mineral interests only as to property actually included within the unit. Classen v. Federal Land Bank of Wichita, 228 Kan. 426, 617 P.2d 1255. There is nothing in the original deed in this case which would extend the term mineral interest in the N/2 of the section by off-tract production from the Nichols Unit. Insofar as the deeds in this case are concerned, the term mineral interest in the N/2 terminated when the actual production from the SE/4 terminated.

Does the fact that the Nichols Unit was created pursuant to the Kansas compulsory unitization law, K.S.A. 55–1301 et seq., rather than by voluntary agreement alter the foregoing general principles under the facts of this case? We think not.

The plaintiffs rely heavily upon Classen v. Federal Land Bank of Wichita, 228 Kan. 426, 617 P.2d 1255, and the applicable unitization statutes. In considering *Classen*, it is necessary to also consider the companion case of Friesen v. Federal Land Bank of Wichita, 227 Kan. 522, 608 P.2d 915. *Friesen* was a quiet title action against the holder of a reserved undivided 1/4 interest in minerals under a quarter section of land. The Federal Land Bank by deed conveyed three quarter sections, referred to in the opinion as Tracts 1, 2, and 3, subject to a reservation of an undivided one-fourth interest in the oil, gas, and other minerals for a period of 20 years "and so long thereafter as oil, gas and/or other minerals or any of them are produced therefrom, or the premises are being developed or operated." 227 Kan. at 522–23, 608 P.2d 915. The Friesens subsequently became the owners of Tract 2 by a deed from the original grantees of the bank. At the end of the primary term, no actual drilling had occurred on any of the three tracts, but Tract 1 had been pooled by its owners with other property to form a production unit, and production had commenced from the other property within the unit. Evidence was presented that the unit well was physically draining gas from under Tract 1, and the defendant bank contended that this was production from the tract sufficient to extend the term of the mineral interest as to all three of the tracts within the meaning of the mineral reservation clause. The court reviewed several of our earlier cases and held that the mineral reservation as to Tract 2 had expired at the end of the primary term.

In Classen v. Federal Land Bank of Wichita, 228 Kan. 426, 617 P.2d 1255 (1980), the Classens, the original grantees in the conveyance from the bank, brought suit to quiet title to their claimed reversionary interest as to Tracts 1 and 3 of the same property as described in *Friesen*. The defendant bank claimed its mineral interest by virtue of the same mineral reservation described in *Friesen*, arguing again that unit production outside Tract 1 but allegedly draining gas from under Tract 1 extended its mineral interest not only as to Tract 1 but also as to Tract 3. The Classens argued that, to extend the mineral interest beyond the primary term, production must actually come from a well located on one of the three tracts or operation or development must physically occur upon one of the tracts. As Tract 1 had been voluntarily placed in the unit by the parties, the court held that production from the unit continued the Federal Land

Bank mineral interest in that tract. However, as in *Friesen,* we held that production from the unit did not perpetuate the mineral interest in Tract 3 which was not included in the unit. One authority has succinctly summarized our holdings in *Friesen* and *Classen* as follows:

> 'A defeasible term mineral interest cannot be extended unless there is a well physically located on the land which is subject to the grant. However, if a portion of the land is effectively pooled or unitized, the duration of the grant will be extended as to acreage which actually participates in production from the pooled or unitized operation. Acreage included in the grant, but not participating in unit production, will not be held by pooled or unitized operations. [citing *Classen*].' Pierce, Kansas Oil and Gas Handbook § 9.21 p. 9–20 (1986).

We are of the opinion our prior decisions, including *Classen,* are controlling unless the Kansas compulsory unitization law requires a different conclusion.

K.S.A. 55–1303 sets forth the requisites for statutory unitization by the Kansas Corporation Commission. The statute requires, *inter alia,* that the applicant submit a proposed plan of unitization along with a copy of a proposed operating plan. There is no contention in this case that there was not a valid unitization order issued by the Kansas Corporation Commission. The order which was issued approved the proposed plan of unitization and the proposed operating plan. The plan of unitization provided in part:

> "3.4 *Continuation of Leases and Term Royalties.* Operations, including drilling operations, conducted with respect to the Unitized Formation on any part of the Unit Area, or production from any part of the Unitized Formation, shall be considered as operations upon or production from each Tract, and such operations or production shall constitute a compliance with and continue in effect each lease, term royalty, or other agreement as to all lands covered thereby just as if such operations had been conducted and a well had been drilled on and was producing from each Tract."

The term "Tract" is defined by ¶ 1.8 of the plan as follows:

> "1.8 *Tract* means each parcel of land described as such and given a Tract number in Exhibit A."

The SE/4 of Section 31 is listed as Tract #20 in Exhibit A attached to the plan.

K.S.A. 55–1306 and–1308 are also relevant to our decision in this case. K.S.A. 55–1308 provides in part:

> "*Property rights,* leases, contracts and other rights or obligations *shall be regarded as amended and modified only to the extent necessary to conform to the provisions and requirements of this act* and to any valid order of the commission providing for the unit operation of a pool or a part thereof, but otherwise shall remain in full force and effect." (Emphasis added.)

K.S.A. 55–1306 provides in pertinent part:

> "All operations, including, but not limited to, the commencement, drilling, or operation of a well upon any part of the unit area shall be deemed for all purposes the conduct of such operations upon each separately owned tract in the unit area by the several owners thereof. The portion of the unit production allocated to a separately owned tract in a unit area shall, when produced, be deemed, for all purposes, to have been actually produced from such tract by a well drilled thereon. Operations conducted pursuant to an order of the commission providing for unit operations shall constitute a fulfillment of all the express or implied obligations of each lease or contract covering lands in the unit area to the extent that compliance with such obligations cannot be had because of the order of the commission.

> * * *

> "Except to the extent that the parties affected so agree no order providing for unit operations shall be construed to result in a transfer of all or any part of the title of any person to the oil and gas rights in any tract in the unit area."

We think it is clear that compelled unitization pursuant to the statutes must be limited in its scope to the accomplishment of the objectives of the unit formed. Statutory unitization or compulsory unitization is done pursuant to the police power of the state and the power of the Kansas Corporation Commission to prevent waste, conserve oil and gas, and protect the correlative rights of persons entitled to share in the production of oil and gas. K.S.A. 55–1301. Under such circumstances the statutes should be strictly construed and limited so as to minimize disruption of interests in property not included in the unit. As specifically provided in K.S.A. 55–1308, property rights can only be amended and modified to the extent necessary to meet statutory requirements and the order providing for the operation of the unit. If, as we held in *Classen,* a voluntary pooling or unitization will not operate to extend a term mineral interest as to any property not included in the unit, a compelled statutory unitization certainly will not do so. Here the N/2 of the section was not a part of the unit, was not affected by the off-tract production from the unit, and did not benefit from such production. Defendants were free to pursue development and production from the N/2 regardless of what took place on the Nichols Unit, but apparently elected not to do so.

* * *

We conclude the decision of the federal district court is correct. * * *.

* * *

We hold that under the facts submitted only the interest in the tract included within the unit is extended by the unitized production when there is no actual production from a well upon the tract within the unit.

HERD, JUSTICE, dissenting:

* * *

The majority is affirming the mistake we made in Classen v. Federal Land Bank of Wichita, 228 Kan. 426, 617 P.2d 1255 (1980). By these opinions, we allow property to be taken from owners without just compensation.

* * *

APPENDIX

R 18 W

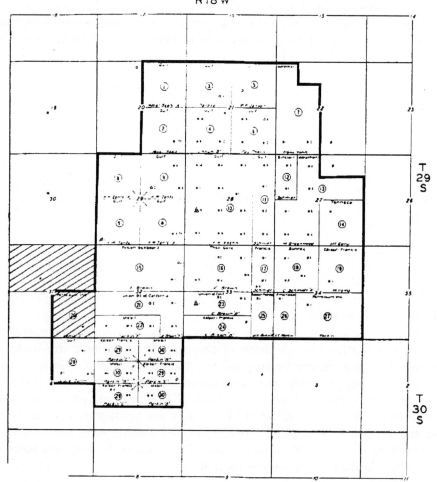

Edmonston Tract

NICHOLS UNIT
KIOWA COUNTY, KANSAS
EXHIBIT "B"

Nichols Unit Boundary

NOTES

1. *Edmonston* provides an introduction into the murky subject of pooling and its effect on defeasible term (terminable) interests. In general, if pooling is not involved, when several tracts are subject to a common defeasible term mineral interest, production on any tract perpetuates the terminable interest beyond its primary term as to all tracts unless a contrary intent is expressed in the instrument. See Baker v. Hugoton Prod. Co., 320 P.2d 772 (Kan. 1958) and Turner v. McBroom, 565 P.2d 44 (Okla. 1977). Where all or part of the premises subject to a defeasible term mineral interest (Blackacre) are voluntarily pooled (by both the term and reversionary interest owners) with other lands (Whiteacre) and production is obtained from a well located on Whiteacre, Texas courts have held that such production holds the terminable interest as to all of Blackacre. See Williamson v. Federal Land Bank, 326 S.W.2d 560 (Tex.Civ.App.–Texarkana 1959, writ ref'd n.r.e.); Southland Royalty Co. v. Humble Oil & Refining Co., 249 S.W.2d 914 (Tex. 1952); and Spradley v. Finley, 302 S.W.2d 409 (Tex. 1957). The Texas courts base these decisions on the intent of the parties to modify the terminable mineral interest so that production anywhere within the unit perpetuates the interest into the secondary term.

A similar result was reached in Panhandle Eastern Pipe Line Co. v. Isaacson, 255 F.2d 669 (10th Cir.Okla. 1958), a federal diversity case interpreting Oklahoma law. See also Fox v. Feltz, 697 P.2d 543 (Okla.App. Div. 2 1984). In *Isaacson*, part of the premises subject to the defeasible term interest (Blackacre) was included in a drilling unit established by the Corporation Commission. This unit also included Whiteacre, where a gas well had already been completed and shut in. The court held that the Whiteacre well was sufficient to extend the entire terminable interest into its secondary term. Recall that in Oklahoma, the formation of a drilling unit effectively pools unit production and that discovery of gas is sufficient to extend an oil and gas lease into its secondary term (see Chapter Two)[12] Because only one well could be drilled on a drilling unit, the court reasoned that a contrary holding would eliminate the possibility of extending the terminable interest by operations on the portion of Blackacre that was included within the unit. The court also concluded that the establishment of a drilling unit does not divide a mineral interest; hence, the entire terminable interest was extended by the unit well. Of the possible rules, which is preferable? Should the rule be the same for oil and gas leases? See Kuntz § 15.8 and Williams & Meyers § 961.4.

In Smith v. Home Royalty Ass'n, Inc., 498 P.2d 98 (Kan. 1972), the Kansas Supreme Court held that a defeasible term interest could be perpetuated by production only if the well was physically located on land that was subject to the terminable interest. *Smith* was partially overruled by Classen v. Federal Land Bank, 617 P.2d 1255 (Kan. 1980). In *Classen*, the court held that a unit well located off the terminable interest tract was sufficient to perpetuate the term interest beyond its primary term as to the portion of the

---

12. In Fransen v. Eckhardt, 711 P.2d 926 (Okla. 1985), the Supreme Court of Oklahoma, rejecting a portion of *Isaacson*, held that "discovery" of gas was insufficient to extend a defeasible mineral interest into its secondary term.

tract included in the unit. In Kneller v. Federal Land Bank, 799 P.2d 485 (Kan. 1990), the court refused to make *Classen* retroactive. Justice Herd, who dissented in *Edmonston,* filed this concurring opinion in *Kneller:*

> This is a difficult decision for me because I feel so strongly about the wrongness of our decision in *Smith* * * *.
>
> Since it is impossible to ascertain what has happened to the myriad of interests which have expired or how many innocent purchasers for value have changed positions because of *Smith,* it appears the most stable way to handle the issue is to treat *Classen* as prospective. To make *Classen* retrospective would constitute an improper taking of property without just compensation just as had occurred with *Smith.* Our dilemma brings to mind an old baseball metaphor where the umpire mistakenly called a strike against a batter. That constituted one mistake. Feeling guilty, and wanting to be fair, the umpire then purposely miscalled the next pitch in the batter's favor, to even the score. The umpire had now made two mistakes. Similarly, *Smith* was our mistake number one, and I do not think that we should compound it by making *Classen* retrospective.

799 P.2d at 490–91.

2. The preceding discussion and the principal cases have assumed that both the owner of the terminable interest and the owner of the reversionary interest have either expressly or implicitly consented to pooling or that pooling has occurred by an order of the conservation agency. Implied consent may result from executing a lease containing a pooling clause, ratifying such a lease, or executing a community lease.

Where the owner of the terminable interest has neither expressly nor implicitly consented to pooling by the owner of the reversionary right, a different analysis is necessary. Generally, the owner of the reversionary right cannot bind the owner of a terminable mineral interest to a pooling arrangement, and, under the Texas view, the owner of a terminable royalty or terminable nonexecutive mineral interest also could not be bound. Could the owner of the terminable interest ratify a pooling? If so, under what circumstances would the owner of the terminable interest want to ratify? What should constitute ratification? Do the answers to these questions affect the lessee's obligations under the implied covenants? Reconsider the effect of the following clause in light of a nonexecutive defeasible term interest:

> Lessee shall not be obligated to drill any offset wells on the leased premises to wells drilled upon any unitized area that includes any part of the leased premises.

Would the defeasible term interest be extended where the owner of the terminable interest consented to pooling, but the owner of the reversionary right did not? Would the answer depend on the location of the well? Compare Williams & Meyers § 961.3 and Summers § 962 with Kramer & Martin § 20.02(3)(b). Would the answer depend on the nature of the term interest— for example, a terminable royalty interest? See Kuntz § 15.8 and Williams & Meyers § 961.4.

In Shelton v. Andres, 478 N.E.2d 311 (Ill.1985), S.D. Broyles owned the surface and an undivided seven-twelfths mineral interest in an 80 acre tract.

In 1962, Broyles conveyed the tract to plaintiffs by warranty deed reserving "all of his undivided interest in and to all of the oil, gas and other minerals * * * as long as there is production on said described real estate." At the time of this conveyance there was one producing well on the 80 acre tract. In 1964, Broyles entered into a unit agreement with other interest owners in the field to conduct secondary recovery by waterflooding. Under the terms of the unit agreement, each tract within the unit was allocated a share of unit production. The plaintiffs did not execute the unit agreement. In 1973, the well on the 80 acre tract ceased production. Plaintiffs sued Broyles's successor in interest (defendant) to quiet title to the seven-twelfths mineral interest. The trial court ruled for plaintiffs. The appellate court reversed relying on a provision of the Illinois conservation act which provided that where the owners of separate tracts of land agree to form a unit "production from any tract in such established unit shall be regarded as production from all presently owned tracts * * *." Ill.Rev.Stat.1961, ch. 104, § 84b(a). The Supreme Court of Illinois affirmed the appellate court on other grounds.

> A fair and reasonable reading of the deed here indicates that "production on said described real estate" was intended to include production from a unit which encompassed the 80–acre tract. Although the deed in question was phrased in terms of "production," it is reasonable to assume that the parties here intended the reservation to continue as long as the grantor, his heirs or assigns, reaped a financial benefit from oil and gas production from the property. As Professor Kuntz noted in his treatise on oil and gas law:

> Although the duration of terminable interest may be expressed in terms of production from the premises, the parties were most likely thinking in terms of enjoyment of benefits. It is most likely intended in such instances that if the interest proves to be productive within the fixed term the interest is to endure as long as it yields tangible benefits in the form of royalty payments or payments in lieu of royalty, regardless of how the payments are computed. 1 E. Kuntz, Oil and Gas sec. 15.8, at 356–57 (1962).

> Plaintiffs contend that the phrase contained in the deed requiring production "on said described real estate" means that production must come from a well located on the 80–acre tract. We disagree. As the appellate court noted, oil and gas are always produced from under the land, not on it. The source of the oil, at all relevant times, remained the same. * * * Thus, in the absence of any contrary language in the deed, or subsequent actions of the parties amounting to a modification of the deed, we hold that production from another parcel in the Unit constitutes "production on said described real estate" so as to extend defendant's interest in the minerals underlying the 80–acre parcel.

478 N.E.2d at 315.

Would the pooling of a terminable interest pursuant to a compulsory pooling statute require a different analysis?

3. In Louisiana, whether established by compulsory or voluntary pooling or unitization, drilling operations, or production from any location within a unit interrupts prescription *liberandi causa* as to all of the property burdened

by the mineral servitude located within the unit. But to interrupt prescription as to burdened lands outside the unit, the well must be located on the portion that is within the unit. See La. Rev. Stat. Ann. §§ 31:33, 31:37. The landowner and the owner of the mineral servitude, however, may specifically agree in writing that any unit operation or production interrupts prescription as to all lands burdened by the servitude. Id. § 31:75.

As discussed in the previous subsection, in Louisiana the owner of executive rights has the power to pool an outstanding royalty interest. Whether established by compulsory or voluntary pooling or unitization, production from any location within a unit that includes all or part of a tract burdened by a mineral royalty interrupts prescription of the royalty. But if the unit well is not located on the burdened land, the interruption extends only to that portion of the burdened land that has been included in the unit. Id. § 31:89.

I.   TITLE EXAMINATION

As the preceding material should have made clear, "Who owns the minerals?" might sound like a simple question but it is often one of the most difficult challenges encountered during the acquisition, assignment and development of oil and gas. Mineral rights, once granted by the sovereign to a private patentee, can be sold, subdivided and devised many times over, leaving a mineral interest owned by dozens or hundreds of co-tenants, each with an undivided portion. Certain other rights, such as royalties and select minerals, may have been retained by grantors whose successors and assigns have no idea of their current rights.

Mineral title examination is the process by which a lawyer provides his client with information on the ownership of the mineral estate of a particular tract of land. Like title examination on the surface, it is done to put the client, who may be a landowner, oil and gas company, or financing institution, on notice of the status of the "subject tract"—the land about which the client is interested. The examination is often conducted when the client is considering either developing the minerals underlying a subject tract or when the client is assigning the leasehold covering the subject tract. Sometimes the client may be a lender interested in confirming title for collateralization purposes as lenders generally require some form of assurance that the borrower owns what it claims to own, and mineral title examination is often required to "prove up" title to the collateral so that it can be mortgaged and a security interest placed upon the production therefrom.

Unlike title examination for surface development, mineral title examination is not done for the purpose of issuing title insurance. No title insurance is typically available for mineral ownership. Therefore, millions of dollars can be dependent on the examination and subsequent calculations, analysis and declarations of title. In addition, perfect title is almost non-existent, and the title attorney will generally have to advise his client on which flaws are more hazardous than others. Finally, oil and gas developers are usually on a tight schedule and want title answers more quickly than a title attorney can accurately provide them, creating tension between the attorney and his client.

The most thorough method of mineral title examination is to examine instruments compiled in an abstract. An abstract is a chronological assemblage of all the documents of record in the chain of title which is compiled and certified to by the local abstract company. If certified abstracts are not available or if time constraints prevent their acquisition, a title attorney may be required to go to the courthouse of the county wherein the subject tract lies in order to conduct a "stand up" examination—the personal inspection of the public property and district court records and tax assessor's office. Such an examination is often completed using a "run sheet"—a list of all the instruments and their recording information pertinent to the subject tract—prepared and certified to by an abstractor.

States are split as to how public property records are indexed. Texas, California and other states maintain grantor-grantee indexes. A grantor-grantee index consists of two lists of real property transfers maintained in alphabetical order of the last name of the entity of the individual or entity transferring, or accepting the transfer, of the property. One list is the *grantor index*, an alphabetized list of sellers—the grantors. The other list is the *grantee index*, an alphabetized list of buyers—the grantees. In each entry is listed the location of the affected tract and the book and page number where the full text of the deed or other recorded instrument describing the transfer may be found. Granter-grantee indexes make title examination more difficult because instruments that affect the tract are more easily missed as no separate compendium of instruments is available in the courthouse. A further examination of the records of the local abstractor may be necessary.

Title examiners have an easier time in New Mexico, Oklahoma, Utah, Wyoming and other states which require tract indexing and provide a title examiner with just such a compendium. The information is organized by section in the township-range system. In each quarter-section area, all transfers are listed in chronological order. Each entry generally includes several cross-reference details, such as the names of the grantor and grantee, the book and page of recording, the date, and other identifying characteristics of the transfer, such as the name of the instrument.

As discussed in Section F.1 of this chapter, some instruments can affect ownership of real property but not specifically describe a tract or interest. For example, in addition to instruments which affect the ownership rights within a specifically described and identifiable tract of land, Texas and many other states allow a grantor of minerals or an assignor of leasehold to convey all of their property within a particular county or even the entire state. Such blanket—or "catch-all"—conveyances do not provide the legal description of the real property conveyed, but rather grant all or a fraction of the owner's interest within that county or state. Such blanket conveyances are common, for example, when large estates are probated and conveyed to devisees or when title is affected by bankruptcy or litigation. These instruments are among those filed in the "general index" of abstractor's offices and can make the jobs of abstractors constructing certified abstracts, landman compiling a run sheet or attorneys doing a stand up very difficult. In addition, despite examining all the relevant documents of record, a title examiner will find the chain of title to also be affected by matters entirely outside of the record such as adverse possession, signatures by unauthorized corporate officers, missing exhibits, misfiled instruments, or faulty plats and surveys.

Ultimately, all present private title must originally have resulted from a valid award or patent from a sovereign, whether by the federal or state government. In addition, courts in some states recognize the patents of other sovereigns. For example, the records of the General Land Office of Texas contain records of the distribution of all Texas lands and Texas courts have recognized patents from the King of Spain, the Emperor of Mexico, and the Republic of Texas.

The format and information contained in an opinion depends on the purpose and intention of the client. Different levels of thoroughness are required at different stages of mineral development. Oil and gas producers will first seek to lease acreage wherein they believe prospects may exist. For this first phase of development where tens of thousands of acres may be leased in a short period of time, full title opinions may be too focused, expensive and time consuming. Instead, teams of landmen will descend on the county courthouses and abstract offices of the counties where the minerals of potential interest lie to research, copy and photograph public records to determine mineral ownership. Later, this information is compiled by landmen (and, sometimes, law students) in the offices of oil and gas companies or lease brokerages. Actual leasing is then conducted based upon this information. In some cases, actual title attorneys may draw up a "leasehold acquisition opinion" which seeks only to ascertain the mineral or leasehold owners.

Once an oil and gas producer has consulted with its geoscience, financial and engineering staff and decided on the location of its drilling prospects within the leased acreage, closer scrutiny of those tracts is required, often in the form of a formal "drilling title opinion". In a drilling title opinion, an attorney provides the period of time over which the opinion covers, a legally-sufficient description of the subject tract(s) and the materials examined. These materials may include prior certified abstracts that cover all or a portion of the subject tract, prior title opinions covering the same subject (provided the attorney is satisfied as to the accuracy and coverage of the prior opinion), information from the local tax and district court, and any other information or instruments affecting ownership of the subject tract(s). Like the ownership report or leasehold acquisition opinion, the client is generally still not yet interested in the allocation of leasehold or overriding royalty, but is focused on who owns the minerals, whether the minerals have been leased, the terms of the lease(s), and whether the minerals can be accessed for exploration and development.

While examining the instruments in the chain of title, a title examiner sometimes must decide whether an interest being conveyed is a mineral or royalty interest, a problem described in Section A of this chapter, and closely follow reservations and term grants. Sometimes the intention of the parties cannot be discerned from the language of the instrument. Title attorneys must also be careful to keep track of sometimes hundreds of tiny fractional interests whose owners may be unaware, dead or missing. Examiners must be aware of pooled units and how the rights of leases covered by the pool or unit are affected, or whether the lease in question allows for pooling at all and on what terms.

After examination of all the title materials available and connection of all the links in the chain of title from the sovereign down to the current owners, the title attorney will ascertain and describe the ownership of record of the surface and mineral estate and, in some cases, leases that may cover either estate. In addition and where possible, if ownership of the subject tract is subject to the terms of contracts such as farmout agreements or drill-to-earn contracts, the title attorney will generally list the "beneficial ownership"—the record ownership that may exist in the future if assignments are recorded based on the terms of the private contracts examined. In cases where numerous mineral or royalty deeds and leasehold assignments are a part of the record and result in a diversity of ownership, the title attorney will often construct a chart describing the chain of title in order to help accurately set forth the ownership of the mineral estate. Such a chart will identify which groups of interests are subject to prior reservations of royalty or other nonparticipating interests or which groups of owners may be subject to a particular title defect that may not affect the other parties in the chain of title.

If no production has yet been achieved, it generally is enough at this stage to simply describe the oil and gas leasehold coverage of the tract upon which the well may be drilled. Hopefully, the company ordering the drilling title opinion will either be the same entity listed as the lessee of record or at least be aware of the identity of all or most of the current lessees and lessors, whether one or more.

While knowledge of the exact identity, location and quantum of ownership of all the lessors and lessees may not be necessary prior to drilling, accurately describing whether or not the producer will have trouble accessing the prospective drillsite is a critical portion of any title opinion. Therefore, title opinions will generally describe what could impede access and development of the subject tract, such as the presence of surface use agreements, pipeline and surface easements, or prior leases covering the surface or other minerals. Some opinions may even describe access issues off of the subject tract if the scope of examination is broadened to include descriptions of access across intervening tract between the subject tract and one or more particular roads or facilities.

Issues encountered during title examination can include almost all aspects of civil law. No chain of title is perfect and many contain so many problems, qualifiers and risks that a developer may decide that the chance of title failure is not worth the cost of exploration and development. Title examiners must be careful to identify any significant legal problem discovered in the chain of title and describe these problems as "title requirements" to which the ownership data described in the beginning of the opinion are subject. Along with the requirement, the examiner should also describe the curative work which may be necessary prior to leasing or development in order to clear the chain of title of that problem. Some title opinions have dozens of requirements.

In the happy circumstance that a well is brought in and production is achieved in paying quantities, the producer will be required to pay its fellow working interest owners as well as the owners of non-participating interests such as royalty. This requires a type of opinion called a "division order title opinion" or "DOTO" because it is the opinion upon which the division order which describes all the parties and their associated quantum of ownership to which payments of royalty and production payments are due. Since a DOTO typically follows a basic title opinion and covers the same subject tract, it does not usually provide the same extensive coverage of surface access, easements, and other obstacles to exploration and development.

Title opinions are sometimes required by lenders seeking to confirm ownership of minerals or leaseholds so that a mortgage or deed of trust can placed on the assets and to assure the lender that their lien will be first in priority. Title is also examined in connection with purchase and sale agreements or "PSAs". Such agreements will generally express that the grantor is providing some level of warranty, whether general, special or quitclaim, and will allow for a period of title due diligence.

CHAPTER 4

OIL AND GAS CONSERVATION LAW AND REGULATION

Table of Sections

A. THE RULE OF CAPTURE REVISITED

PROBLEM

Acme Oil Co., Baxter Oil Co., and Carter Oil Co. each hold leases to contiguous tracts. Each has drilled a prolifically producing oil well. Acme has decided to drill another well on its tract and to locate the well close to the boundaries of Baxter's and Carter's tracts. What are the likely legal and practical consequences of Acme's decision?

W. RUNDELL, JR., EARLY TEXAS OIL: A PHOTOGRAPHIC HISTORY, 1866–1936, AT 35–38 (1977)[1]

Since 1892 Pattillo Higgins had promoted the possibilities of oil around the salt dome known as Sour Spring Mound, Big Hill, and later Spindletop. Drillers, such as Walter B. Sharp, had put down test wells but with disappointing results. Higgins and the Gladys City Oil, Gas and Manufacturing Company did not despair but kept searching for a driller who could find the oil trapped by the salt dome. Higgins' advertisement in a trade journal attracted the attention of Captain Anthony F. Lucas, a mining engineer who had experience with Louisiana salt domes. After corresponding with Higgins, Lucas journeyed to Beaumont to look at the land. On June 20, 1899, the company sold its leases to Lucas for $33,150. Recognizing Higgins' assistance, Lucas awarded him a 10 percent interest in the lease.

Lucas' first well went to 575 feet and produced only a small amount of oil before his money ran out. Local financiers scoffed at his efforts and offered no assistance. [Lucas was able to secure financing for an additional well from James McClurg Guffey, a Pittsburgh oil speculator, and his partner, John H. Galey.]

The backing of Galey and Guffey laid the foundation for Lucas' success at Spindletop. Galey arranged with the Hamill brothers—Curt, Jim, and Al—* * * to go to Beaumont as drillers for Lucas, with Galey and Guffey guaranteeing payment and supplying all the pipe. The Hamills would get $2 per foot for a 1,200–foot well. They spudded in, or began, the well on October 27, 1900, with a rotary rig * * *. There they had used water to soften the ground, cool the bit, and flush out the cuttings, but at Spindletop water could not accomplish the last objective. Curt Hamill improvised an ingenious experiment. He drove some cattle into a shallow pond nearby, hoping their milling around would produce mud that would be sufficiently viscous when pumped down the drill stem to bring up the cuttings. The experiment worked, and from that time forward drilling mud became a mainstay in rotary operations.[2]

* * *

The Hamills encountered numerous difficulties with their well. For their boiler they could get only water-soaked logs, so the fireman had difficulty keeping enough fire going to produce steam. The quicksand

---

1. Reprinted by permission of Texas A & M University Press.

2. As with many technological innovations, mud possessed some highly desirable attributes other than that originally intended. It came to have four main functions. Most important, it counteracted pressures exerted by gas, oil, or water, preventing dangerous and costly blowouts. It served as a lubricant, cooling the whirling bit and keeping it from burning out from the intense friction. It flushed out cuttings from around the bit, eliminating frequent stops to clean away fragments of sand, clay, and rock. And it plastered and exerted pressure on the sides of the hole, thereby lessening the danger of cave-ins and helping prevent water or gas from entering through the side walls. When the industry became more advanced and technology more sophisticated, artificial muds were devised to meet exacting specifications.

through which they had to drill slowed the operation to a few feet per day. One of the four members of the crew, Henry McLeod, left because the work was too strenuous. The remaining members * * * had to go to eighteen-hour shifts or tours (pronounced towers) so that drilling could continue. By Christmas Eve, Galey, who had come from Pittsburgh to observe the test well, realized that the crew was exhausted and recommended that they shut down for a Christmas holiday, the well having reached 880 feet.

The Hamills returned to Corsicana to spend the vacation, arriving back at Spindletop on New Year's Day. In a week they had drilled to 1,020 feet, where the bit got deflected by a crevice. Needing a different kind of bit, Al wired Jim in Corsicana to send a fishtail bit, which arrived on the train on January 10. Al inserted the new bit to a depth of 700 feet, when the well started regurgitating mud high up the derrick. Al noticed that it was 10:30 A.M. Immediately after the mud, the four-inch drill pipe shot up through the derrick, knocking down the crown block. As the pipe ascended, several joints broke off at a time. Then the well became quiescent. The disheartened drillers surveyed their spoiled well and started shoveling the muck off the derrick floor. Suddenly, the well disgorged vast quantities of mud with an explosive roar. The frightful noise continued as gas propelled upward. Then oil shot above the derrick too—the black plume doubling the derrick height, more oil gushing than any Texan had seen. More than anyone had ever seen, for the Lucas discovery well at Spindletop broke the world's record. In its first nine days, the well produced 800,000 barrels of oil. But what to do with that oil flowing freely over the rice fields? Lucas hastily commandeered forty four-horse teams to throw up levees to contain the oil. They also plowed under the oil-soaked grass to lessen chances of fire. On the third day, however, a careless smoker set the grass afire, but the fire was smothered before it got to the well.

On January 10, 1901, Captain Anthony F. Lucas brought in the world's greatest gusher at Spindletop.   The well flowed between 75,000 and 100,000 barrels a day. Photograph courtesy of the American Petroleum Institute and Standard Oil Co. of Ohio.

Lucas' ultimate concern, of course, was how to regulate the well. As he put it to the drillers, "Now that we have got her, boys, how are we going to close her up?" Since the gusher spewed up large rocks periodically, the crew hesitated to cap the well too soon for fear that a rock would knock off the valve. On January 16 the Hamills imposed their fittings over the geyser of oil: an eight-inch T that had an eight-inch gate valve and an eight-inch nipple screwed into it. The side opening in the T connected with a six-inch pipe that had a gate valve through which the oil flowed. The Hamills bolted this apparatus over the casing until Al could prepare the drill pipe to receive the T. By the tenth day it appeared safe to try this daring feat. With Galey and J.S. Cullinan offering advice, Al undertook the job of sawing through the iron pipe to remove a "protector" that could not be unscrewed and then dressing the threads so that the T could be screwed on. As he worked in a deluge of oil, Hamill knew that one spark from his hacksaw would blow him—and the Lucas well—into kingdom come. He worked steadily for several hours, finally screwing the T onto the casing, and his brother Curt closed the valve. "Just like that, it was over," Al commented.

Only the gushing of the Lucas well was over, for the boom had just begun for Beaumont. Within three months the sedate city of 9,000 had swelled to 50,000 as speculators, oil-field workers, adventurers, and spectators swamped the town.

As could be imagined, speculation was rife throughout Beaumont and the surrounding countryside. Pig wallows sold for $35,000 and cow pastures for $100,000. Land 150 miles from Beaumont sold for $1,000 per acre, and land within the proven Spindletop field sold for $900,000 an acre. Because of the sharp and shady practices of many lease dealers, the area got the nickname of Swindletop. The development of the field was likewise frenzied, with wells being drilled as close together as physically possible. In fact, the desire to exploit the field quickly ran so high that on occasion four wells were drilled beneath one derrick floor.

* * *

Spindletop's Boiler Avenue, 1903. In the first year, over 400 wells were drilled. This unfettered development left much oil unrecovered because the gas pressure in the reservoir, which forced the oil to the surface, was quickly and inefficiently dissipated. Photograph courtesy of the American Petroleum Institute (Fred A. Schell).

B. CONSERVATION LAW AND PRACTICE

1. INTRODUCTION AND OTHER REGULATION

AMERICAN INSTITUTE OF MINING AND METALLURGICAL ENGINEERS, PETROLEUM CONSERVATION

248–251 (S.E. Buckley Ed.1951).3

Control of production rate, preservation of gas caps, injection of gas and water, pressure maintenance, cycling, and the many auxiliary controls now employed to recover oil and gas efficiently have not always been in use. Oil and gas were produced for many years before such techniques were even thought of. They were simply produced by the direct process of drilling wells and producing them wide open. The objective of each producer was to drill his wells as fast as possible and to produce as much oil as possible before the pool could become exhausted. It was always a race against time and against the other fellow.

Surface waste was evident enough in the enormous volumes of gas that were blown to the air and in the oil that sprayed over the countryside from the top of a derrick. Under the conditions then existing, oil could not be retained in the ground but had to be produced. Over-production periodically flooded the market, drastically depressed prices, and brought about conditions of near chaos in the industry. The rapid production and resultant waste raised fears that our oil resources were in grave danger of being completely dissipated by wasteful practices.

* * *

The root of the difficulty lay in the inevitable result of the combination of two seemingly innocuous factors. One of these was a rule of law popularly known as the rule of capture. * * * It was adopted at a time when little was known of the underground character and behavior of petroleum, when it was utterly impossible to determine the ultimate source of the oil and gas produced by a well. Even today, specific identification of the original underground abode of each barrel of oil or cubic foot of gas produced by a well would be impractical.

The other part of the combination was the migratory or fugacious nature of petroleum. Even though little was known of their quantitative behavior, and although fluid mechanics as now applied was yet to be heard of, it was very well known that oil and gas were fluid substances that could and did flow from one underground location to another when a well was produced.

When the known fluid nature of petroleum was combined with the rule of capture there could be but one result. Once a reservoir had been

---

3. Reprinted by permission of the Society of Petroleum Engineers, American Institute of Mining, Metallurgical and Petroleum Engineers.

discovered and oil was produced, the owner of the discovery well would own all of the oil he could produce and recover regardless of whether it came from beneath his own property or drained from beneath the land of his neighbors. An adjacent landowner had no recourse. If oil and gas underlay his property they would escape to his neighbor unless he reduced them to possession beforehand by drilling wells on his own property. Self-protection forced each owner of a tract of ground overlaying an oil pool to drill quickly as many wells as he could and to produce each well at its utmost capacity. If he could not market his oil as quickly as it was produced, he was forced to provide surface storage, in a dammed creek or earthen pit if necessary, for only after his oil was at the surface could he call it his own and be assured of its possession. The gas produced with the oil was often flared or blown to the air.

The inevitable result is obvious. There was a tendency to deplete each pool as fast as it was physically possible for the wells to produce the oil. Drilling was continued until the declining production of old wells indicated that a new well would not recover its cost. This resulted in very close spacing of wells in rich pools and wider spacing in pools of lower yield. The density of drilling bore no relation to the number of wells actually required to recover the oil, and tremendous waste in the form of unnecessary development costs resulted.

It was obvious to many that this situation was not in the public interest, was of no advantage to the oil industry, and provided a poor and risky basis on which to depend for oil for a growing industrial economy, let alone possible national emergencies, should such ever arise. It was equally obvious that individual landowners and lessees were powerless to correct the situation, for if they refrained from drilling, or restricted the output of their wells the only result would be loss of some of their recoverable oil through subsurface drainage to others. It seemed highly questionable that concerted action to restrict production could be obtained through voluntary agreement by all the producers in a pool, or that if such action were taken it would be legal.

* * *

In spite of the many difficulties, control of production was initiated by the producers in several pools, primarily to prevent surface waste. It soon became evident that the waste that had been occurring underground often exceeded that visible at the surface. The results of research and of technical studies in these controlled pools as well as in uncontrolled pools demonstrated that proper control of production could substantially improve recoveries. Such conclusions were corroborated by the increase in production being obtained through secondary-recovery operations in some semi-depleted pools.

More and more producers began to recognize that it was to their interest to adopt conservation practices, and that cooperative action was needed in order to exploit effectively the rapidly developing technical knowledge. It was apparent, however, that such action was difficult to achieve without some kind of conservation legislation. Furthermore, there were "rugged individualists" who vigorously protested and actively opposed every restrictive proposal. These difficulties led finally to a recognition that the adoption of efficient recovery practices would be greatly facilitated by the enactment of state conservation laws.

* * *

NOTES

1. The term "correlative rights" concerns the fair treatment of owners when their development rights are curtailed by regulation. This relationship between the landowners' development rights and state conservation regulation is described by Professor Pierce as follows:

> If the Rule of Capture determines an owner's basic property right in oil and gas, any attempt to restrain an owner's capture rights must be administered in an equitable manner. Any action limiting the Rule of Capture will impact all owners in the reservoir—their rights are correlative. If the conservation laws permit A to produce while restraining B, there must be a sound basis for the action or B's correlative rights will be violated. Since spacing, prorationing, and most other techniques designed to prevent waste limit capture rights, the conservation authorities must ensure that all persons possessing rights in the reservoir are treated fairly. For example, A cannot be given a spacing rule exception without considering the effect it might have on adjacent property owners. Perhaps the permissible production rate of A's well will need to be reduced to account for the off-pattern spacing of A's well. In this manner, the rights of other owners in the reservoir are protected.

David E. Pierce, Reconciling State Oil and Gas Conservation Regulation with the Natural Gas Act: New Statutory Revelations, 1989 BYU L. Rev. 9, 16–17 (1989).

2. The economies of major producing states became heavily dependent on a healthy oil and gas industry. Accordingly, these states enacted comprehensive oil and gas conservation laws, creating administrative agencies charged with a duty to conserve oil and gas. In the oil and gas context, "conservation" means the effective and efficient recovery and marketing of oil and gas resources.

3. In challenging the constitutionality of conservation legislation, the following objections have been raised: (1) taking of property without due process and without just compensation; (2) denial of equal protection; (3) impairment of contract; (4) interference with interstate commerce; and (5) unlawful delegation of legislative authority to an administrative agency. Generally, however, conservation statutes have been upheld as a proper exercise of the police power to prevent waste of an irreplaceable natural resource and to protect the correlative rights of diverse owners of a common source of supply. Sullivan § 143. See e.g. Robert–Gay Energy Enters., Inc. v. State Corp. Comm'n, 685 P.2d 299 (Kan.1984).

4. The Interstate Oil & Gas Compact Commission (formerly the Interstate Oil Compact Commission), an association of state oil and gas regulatory officials and industry advisors, promulgated a Model Conservation Act in 1941. Although not adopted verbatim in any state, the Model Act is similar to conservation statutes encountered in many states. Notable exceptions are the unique conservation acts of Oklahoma and Texas. The most recent revision of the Model Act defines the protection of correlative rights as an action or regulation by an oil and gas conservation agency that affords "a reasonable opportunity to each Operator to recover or receive without causing waste his Just and Equitable Share of the Production." A Form For an Oil and Gas Conservation Statute § 1.1.15 (I.O.C.C.1981) [hereinafter cited as I.O.C.C.]. The phrase "Just and Equitable Share of the Production" is defined as "that part of the authorized production from a reservoir that the amount of recoverable Oil and Gas under the Developed Area of the separately owned tract or tracts bears to the recoverable Oil or Gas in the total of the Developed Areas in the Reservoir." Id. § 1.1.8.

5. Besides oil and gas conservation agencies, *operators*[4] must deal with other administrative agencies, particularly agencies that carry out and enforce laws that address environmental protection, public health, and safety in the workplace.[5] If fresh water is used in a water flooding operation or used in drilling a well, an operator may have to obtain a water permit from the state water conservation agency.[6] Consider the following example from Colorado.

VANCE v. WOLFE

205 P.3d 1165 (Colo. 2009).

JUSTICE EID delivered the Opinion of the Court.

This is an appeal from a declaratory judgment action brought in District Court, Water Division 7 by William S. Vance, Jr., Elizabeth S. Vance, James G. Fitzgerald, and Mary Theresa Fitzgerald (collectively, the "Ranchers"). The Ranchers asked the water court to determine the legal obligations of the State Engineer and Division Engineer for Water Division 7 (collectively the "Engineers") regarding well permits and augmentation plans[1] when ground water is diverted for the purpose of coalbed methane ("CBM") production. Specifically, the Ranchers sought a declara-

---

4. The term "operator" is commonly used to describe a party having the right to drill for and produce oil and gas, usually an oil and gas lessee. Thus, an operator owns a *working interest* in property, although it may only be a fractional interest. As used in oil and gas conservation law, the operator is the party who is authorized by the conservation agency through the issuance of drilling permit to drill a well at a particular location.

5. See, e.g., Petroleum Equipment Tool Co. v. State Board of Health, 567 So.2d 328 (Ala. Civ. App. 1990) (approving a preliminary injunction by the Board of Health to enforce its order to clean up radiation contamination at a well site).

6. In State ex rel. Corporation Comm'n v. Texas County Irrigation & Water Resources Ass'n, Inc., 818 P.2d 449 (Okla.1991), the court noted that, while the corporation (conservation) commission could authorize a water-flooding operation, the state water permitting agency would also have to issue a water permit authorizing the use of potable water.

1. [Editors' Note] Augmentation is a term used in Colorado to refer to the means by which a junior appropriator may take water out of priority by taking steps to assure that more senior users are not deprived of the water needed to satisfy their priority. This is often accomplished by supplying the senior users with substitute water.

tion that withdrawal of ground water during the CBM process constitutes a "beneficial use" giving rise to appropriative water rights subject to administration and permitting by the Engineers under the Water Right Determination and Administration Act of 1969, §§ 37–92–101 through– 602, C.R.S. (2008) ("1969 Act"), and the Colorado Ground Water Management Act, §§ 37–90–101 through–143, C.R.S. (2008) ("Ground Water Act").

The Engineers and BP America Production Company ("BP"), an intervenor in the action, opposed the Ranchers' request for a declaratory judgment, arguing that the use of water during CBM production is not a "beneficial use." The water court held for the Ranchers, finding that CBM production constitutes an appropriation for a "beneficial use," and that consequently, the Engineers cannot allow out-of-priority diversions for CBM production without a well permit and, where necessary, a decree adjudicating an augmentation plan. Dist. Ct. Water Div. 7 Order: Motions for Summary Judgment, July 2, 2007. This direct appeal followed.

We now affirm the water court. The 1969 Act defines "beneficial use" as "the use of that amount of water that is reasonable and appropriate under reasonably efficient practices to accomplish without waste the purpose for which the appropriation is lawfully made." § 37–92–103(4), C.R.S. (2008). Under the language of the 1969 Act, the CBM process "uses" water—by extracting it from the ground and storing it in tanks— to "accomplish" a particular "purpose"—the release of methane gas. The extraction of water to facilitate CBM production is therefore a "beneficial use" as defined in the 1969 Act. We reject the Engineers' and BP's argument that water used in CBM production is merely a nuisance rather than a "beneficial use." On the contrary, the use of water in CBM production is an integral part of the CBM process itself. The presence and subsequent controlled extraction of the water makes the capture of methane gas possible. As our precedent in the gravel cases makes clear, the fact that the water used during the CBM process may become a nuisance *after* it has been extracted from the ground and stored in above-ground tanks (that is, after it has been beneficially used) does not prevent a finding that the water is put to a beneficial use. * * * Accordingly, we affirm the order of the District Court for Water Division 7 and remand for further proceedings consistent with this opinion.

I.

Coalbed methane natural gas is produced from more than 4,000 existing wells drilled into deep coalbed formations in the San Juan Basin in southwestern Colorado. CBM wells are drilled between 2,000 and 3,000 feet below the surface and exist to facilitate the extraction of methane gas. The gas is naturally absorbed on the internal surface of the coal and held in place by hydrostatic pressure from ground water that fills the cleats of the coal. When pressure is reduced by removing water from the cleats and bringing it to the surface, methane gas desorbs from the coal and flows through the cleat system to a collection well. The removed water, which has been brought to the surface, is held in storage tanks. At this point, a small quantity of the water is lost to evaporation. At a later time, the water is typically reinjected via underground injection control wells into designated geologic formations that lie deeper than the aquifer from which the methane is produced. The reinjection control wells are regulated by the Colorado Oil and Gas Conservation Commission ("COGCC"). Except under limited circumstances, the Engineers have not, thus far, issued permits for the CBM wells because they believe they are under no obligation to do so.

The Ranchers possess water rights located in Water Division 7 that lie in sources tributary to the Piedra River and the Pine River. The Ranchers use their water rights for irrigation, stock watering, domestic uses, farming, and piscatorial uses. In their declaratory judgment action before the water court, the Ranchers argued that the water used in CBM production constitutes out of priority depletions that are injurious to their vested senior water rights.[2] They contended that the use of water in the CBM process is a "beneficial use" and that the Engineers are statutorily obligated to require well permits for CBM wells pursuant to the Ground Water Act. The Engineers asserted that the CBM wells are not "wells," as defined by the Ground Water Act, because they do not put water to a "beneficial use." Instead, they claimed that the extracted water is merely "produced water," which is exempt from the prior appropriation doctrine and instead regulated exclusively by the COGCC.

In granting summary judgment in the Ranchers' favor, the water court began with the assumption, unchallenged here, that this case involves tributary water.[3] *See Safranek v. Limon,* 123 Colo. 330, 334, 228 P.2d 975, 977 (1951) (holding that under Colorado law, all ground water is presumed to be tributary until proven otherwise). The water court found that the extraction of water during the CBM process was a beneficial use constituting both a "well" under the Ground Water Act and an "appropriation" under the 1969 Act, because "the removal of water ... is not incidental" but rather "occurs as the result of the active and intentional pumping of water to accomplish the intended purpose." The water court therefore concluded that CBM production requires a water well permit and, where necessary, a decree adjudicating an augmentation plan. The water court noted that "[t]he conclusion is bolstered by the overall intent of the water law scheme. By passing the 1969 Act, the General Assembly intended to integrate the appropriation, use, and administration of underground water ... [because under Colorado law] adjudication and adminis-

---

2. The Ranchers relied on a study by the U.S. Forest Service and the Bureau of Land Management entitled, "A Draft Environmental Impact Statement for the Northern San Juan Basin Coal Bed Methane Project Volume I," that concluded, "[b]efore CBM development in the northern San Juan Basin, discharge from the Fruitland aquifer to the Animas, Florida, *Pine* and *Piedra* Rivers totaled approximately 195 acre-feet per year, [and] [m]odeling by Cox et al. (2001) has demonstrated that CBM development has and will continue to intercept groundwater that would normally discharge to these rivers." (emphasis added).

3. [Editors' Note] The presumption that the water at issue is tributary is important because tributary groundwater is subject to the prior appropriation doctrine and is considered part of the stream system for purposes of determining priorities of use.

tration are essential to protection of water rights." (internal citations and quotations omitted). In finding beneficial use, the water court declined to defer to the Engineers' interpretation of the term and found that the regulation of CBM production by the COGCC was not exclusive.

The Engineers and BP appealed to this court * * *.

We now affirm * * *.

II.

Through the enactment of the Ground Water Act and the 1969 Act, the General Assembly delegated responsibility for the administration, distribution, and regulation of the waters of the state to the state and division engineers. *Danielson v. Jones*, 698 P.2d 240, 247 (Colo.1985). The issue presented by this appeal is whether the Engineers are required to permit CBM wells under the provisions of the Ground Water Act—that is, whether CBM production puts water to a beneficial use such that CBM wells are "wells" as defined in that Act.

Under the Ground Water Act, "no new wells shall be constructed outside the boundaries of a designated ground water basin[4] ... unless the user makes an application in writing to the state engineer for a permit to construct a well." § 37–90–137(1), C.R.S. (2008). The act defines "well" as "any structure or device used for the purpose or with the effect of obtaining ground water for a *beneficial use* from an aquifer." § 37–90–103(21)(a), C.R.S. (2008) (emphasis added). Thus, the primary question is whether CBM production obtains water for a "beneficial use," such that it requires a well permit under the Ground Water Act in connection with an "appropriation" under the 1969 Act.

As we have noted in the past, "beneficial use" is the essential premise of Colorado water law. * * * In Colorado, "the right to divert the unappropriated waters of any natural stream to *beneficial use* shall never be denied," and the water of every natural stream is "the property of the public," Colo. Const., art. XVI §§ 5, 6 (emphasis added), subject to appropriation and actual beneficial use. * * *.

An "appropriation" is "the application of a specified portion of the waters of the state to a *beneficial use*." § 37–92–103(3)(a), C.R.S. (2008) (emphasis added). Once an appropriation occurs, it gives rise to a vested water right subject to permitting and adjudication. * * *. Prior appropriated rights have priority over subsequent junior rights. * * *.

Consequently, we begin with the central question presented by this case—whether CBM production is a "beneficial use" giving rise to an appropriative water right subject to water well permitting, water court adjudication, and administration by the Engineers. We find that it is. We then turn to the Engineers' and BP's assertion that we must defer to the Engineers' interpretation of the term "beneficial use" and conclude that

---

4. " 'Designated Ground Water Basin' means that area established by the ground water commission in accordance with section 37–90–106." § 37–90–103(7), C.R.S. (2008).

we need not defer. Finally, we consider, and ultimately disagree with, the argument that the regulation of CBM production is exclusively within the province of the COGCC.

A.

While the term "beneficial use" is undefined in the Colorado Constitution, the 1969 Act defines it broadly as "the use of that amount of water that is reasonable and appropriate under reasonably efficient practices to accomplish without waste the purpose for which the appropriation is lawfully made." § 37–92–103(4), C.R.S. (2008). Under the language of the 1969 Act, the CBM process "uses" water—by extracting it from the ground and storing it in tanks—to "accomplish" a particular "purpose"— the release of methane gas. The extraction of water to facilitate CBM production is therefore a "beneficial use" as defined in the 1969 Act.

Arguing against this interpretation, the Engineers and BP assert that the use of the water during the CBM process cannot be a "beneficial" one because the water is merely a nuisance. They stress that the goal of the CBM process is to capture the gas, not the water. The water, they continue, is simply an unwanted byproduct of the process. In sum, they question how the use of the water in this case can be termed "beneficial" when they consider it to be a hindrance. First, based on the gravel cases, we disagree. *See Three Bells Ranch Assocs. v. Cache La Poudre Water Users Ass'n,* 758 P.2d 164 (Colo.1988), and *Zigan Sand & Gravel, Inc. v. Cache La Poudre Water Users Ass'n,* 758 P.2d 175 (Colo.1988). In *Three Bells* and *Zigan,* gravel mining operators dug pits in the ground that were deeper than the water table in order to excavate the gravel. *Three Bells,* 758 P.2d at 166; *Zigan,* 758 P.2d at 177. The gravel pits then filled up with water, some of which was lost to evaporation. *Zigan,* 758 P.2d at 177. The gravel pits were eventually reclaimed and turned into ponds that could support recreation and wildlife. *Id.* at 182. In both cases, the operators argued that the water involved in the mining process was merely a nuisance to their operations and, therefore, could not effectuate an appropriation of the water. *See Three Bells,* 758 P.2d at 170; *Zigan,* 758 P.2d at 182. We rejected this argument, holding that the pits constituted "wells" for the purpose of obtaining water by appropriation for the "beneficial use" of wildlife habitats and recreation. *See Three Bells,* 758 P.2d at 175; *Zigan,* 758 P.2d at 181–82; *see also State v. Sw. Colo. Water Conservation Dist.,* 671 P.2d 1294, 1322 (Colo.1983) (holding that land reclamation and dust suppression are beneficial uses of water).

In *Three Bells,* we noted that "[a]lthough [the operator] is not digging the pits for the purpose of capturing ground water, and the water that accumulates hinders mining operations, the interception of ground water is the *inevitable result* of excavating pits to a depth below the water table." 758 P.2d at 174 (emphasis added); *see also Zigan,* 758 P.2d at 181. The same is true with the CBM process. While the purpose of the mining operation is to obtain gas, not water, the withdrawal of water and its accumulation in the storage tanks is the "inevitable result" of the CBM process.

In fact, the presence of water and its subsequent extraction during CBM production is far more than an "inevitable result." Indeed, the presence and extraction of water are integral components to the entire CBM process. CBM producers rely on the presence of the water to hold the gas in place until the water can be removed and the gas captured. Without the presence and subsequent extraction of the water, CBM cannot be produced. As both *Three Bells* and *Zigan* make clear, the fact that the water used during the CBM process may become "a nuisance" *after* it has been extracted from the ground and stored in above ground tanks (that is, after it has been "beneficially used") does not prevent a finding that the water is put to a beneficial use. While the Engineers and BP are correct that no Colorado case has *specifically* held that water used during CBM production is a beneficial use, this fact does not prevent us from finding such a beneficial use where our case law and the language of the 1969 Act so dictate. *See Sw. Colo. Water Conservation Dist.*, 671 P.2d at 1321–22.

That the water used in CBM production is integral to the process itself distinguishes this case from a host of other instances in which nuisance water is merely removed but not beneficially used. The Engineers and BP argue that the use of water in CBM production is akin to snow removal, removal of flood water from a subsurface mine, and storm water control at construction sites—all of which constitute mere removal of nuisance water rather than beneficial uses.[5] We find the analogy attempted by the Engineers and BP to be a faulty one. In their examples, the water is exclusively a nuisance and not integral to the task at hand. In contrast, CBM production cannot occur without the presence and controlled removal of the water.

The Engineers and BP point out that the beneficial use of the water in the gravel cases—the creation of ponds for recreation and wildlife—came *after* the extraction of the water. They argue that the gravel cases therefore create a requirement that the beneficial use be "subsequent" or "collateral" to the withdrawal of the water. The use of water in CBM production cannot be deemed such a beneficial use, they conclude, because the withdrawal and benefit, if any, occur simultaneously.

Again, we find that our case law forecloses this argument. While it is true, as the Engineers and BP point out, that the gravel cases describe the beneficial use as the subsequent wildlife and recreational use, *see, e.g., Zigan,* 758 P.2d *passim,* those cases do not set a *requirement* that the beneficial use always be subsequent or collateral to the withdrawal and collection of water. Indeed, we have previously recognized beneficial uses that actually coincide with the withdrawal and storage of water. For example, in *Pueblo West Metropolitan District v. Southeastern Colorado Water Conservancy District,* 689 P.2d 594, 603 (Colo.1984), we held that

---

5. For purposes of this appeal, we assume without deciding that the examples cited by the Engineers and BP are not beneficial uses.

the capture and storage of flood water is a beneficial use of the water. There, as here, the capture and storage of the water coincided with the beneficial use—the prevention of floods. Furthermore, we note that the statutory definition of "beneficial use" contains no such temporal element. *See* § 37–92–103(4), C.R.S. (2008).

Finally, the Engineers and BP argue that to find a beneficial use in this case would be inconsistent with section 37–90–137(7), C.R.S. (2008) of the Ground Water Act, which provides: "In the case of dewatering of geologic formations by removing *nontributary*[6] ground water to facilitate or permit mining of minerals: (a) No well permit shall be required unless the *nontributary* ground water being removed will be beneficially used." (emphasis added). The Engineers and BP contend that this statutory provision demonstrates a difference between dewatering a mine to facilitate mining and doing so for a beneficial use. They also assert that, if we find a beneficial use in this case, the phrase "unless the nontributary ground water being removed will be beneficially used" would be rendered meaningless.

Contrary to the argument of the Engineers and BP, we find that section 37–90–137(7)(a) actually supports a finding of beneficial use in this case. Section 37–90–137(7)(a) recognizes that permitting is required where, as here, the removed water is beneficially used.

Furthermore, we observe that the provision does not control our inquiry because the water at issue here is presumed to be tributary. *See Safranek v. Limon,* 123 Colo. 330, 334, 228 P.2d 975, 977 (1951). To the extent that the Engineers and BP assert that the water is nontributary, they must overcome the presumption of tributariness in an evidentiary hearing in the water court below. *See American Water Dev., Inc. v. Alamosa,* 874 P.2d 352, 389 (Colo.1994). Because nontributary groundwater is not subject to the constitutional right of prior appropriation, the General Assembly has plenary authority and can wholly exempt it from regulation. *See In re the Application for Water Rights of Park County Sportsmen's Ranch LLP,* 986 P.2d 262, 269 (Colo.1999). In sum, we find that section 37–90–137(7)(a) does not change our conclusion that the extraction of water during CBM production is a beneficial use in the tributary water context, which we presume in this case.

As the water court noted, the Ranchers' central concern is the protection of their vested senior water rights. We agree with the district court that our prior appropriation system exists to protect water rights holders. Here, the extraction, storage, and reinjection of water during CBM make the water inaccessible to other water rights holders such as the Ranchers. When the water is stored in surface tanks, a small quantity is lost to evaporation. At a later time, the water is typically reinjected, via underground injection control wells, into designated geologic formations

---

6. Nontributary ground water is defined as "ground water, located outside the boundaries of any designated ground water basins in existence on January 1, 1985, the withdrawal of which will not, within one hundred years, deplete the flow of a natural stream ... at an annual rate greater than one-tenth of one percent of the annual rate of withdrawal." § 37–90–103(10.5), C.R.S. (2008).

that lie deeper than the aquifer from which the methane is produced.[7] Consequently, "beneficial use" also means use of water for a designated purpose—the result of which is to make the water inaccessible to other water rights holders. *See, e.g., Three Bells,* 758 P.2d at 171 (noting, "we believe that when mining operations *affect water rights* it is necessary for the operator to achieve compliance with the Ground Water Management Act and the 1969 Act." (emphasis added)).

In response to the Ranchers' concern about injury to their vested senior water rights, the Engineers, joined by BP, argue that their duty under the 1969 Act to curtail material injury[8] is sufficient to protect the Ranchers' interests. In other words, the Engineers and BP argue that it is not necessary to deem the extraction of water during the CBM process a "beneficial use" of water. But the fact that the Engineers concede that they are required to protect against material injury pursuant to the 1969 Act does not eliminate the Ranchers' concerns about protecting their vested senior water rights. The 1969 Act provision, requiring the Engineers to curtail material injury, does not afford the same protection as permitting and permanent augmentation plans. Permitting is a comprehensive process that provides notice to potentially injured parties and involves the determination of whether there is unappropriated water available for appropriation and whether an appropriation can be made without injury. *See Buffalo Park Dev. Co. v. Mountain Mut. Reservoir Co.,* 195 P.3d 674, 683–86 (Colo.2008). The statutory design places the determination of the presence or absence of a water right with the water court, not the Engineers. *See Santa Fe Trail Ranches Prop. Owners Ass'n v. Simpson,* 990 P.2d 46, 58 (Colo.1999) ("Our state legislature and courts ... have never accepted the proposition that water officials may determine the water rights of citizens; this is a judicial function under the adjudication statutes."). Finally, we note that the Engineers took no action with regard to diversions in this case.

We emphasize that determining the boundaries of "beneficial use" requires careful case-by-case factual analysis, *Zigan,* 758 P.2d at 182, and our holding today addresses the unique circumstances involved in CBM production. The definition of "beneficial use," however, is a "broad" one, *see id.,* and we agree with the Ranchers that it is broad enough to cover the extraction of water to facilitate CBM production. In rendering our decision, we observe that the General Assembly may choose to make modifications to the statutes in light of our opinion.[9] *See Sw. Colo. Water Conservation Dist.,* 671 P.2d at 1323–24.

---

7. [Editors' Note] This finding means that the water withdrawn from the coal seam is fully consumed. The consumptive use of water that is not replaced through augmentation presumably would adversely affect senior users.

8. Pursuant to section 37–92–502(2)(a), C.R.S. (2008) of the 1969 Act, [The Engineer] shall also order the total or partial discontinuance of any diversion in his division to the extent that the water being diverted is required by persons entitled to use water under water rights having senior priorities, but no such discontinuance shall be ordered unless the diversion is causing or will cause material injury to such water rights having senior priorities.

9. Although the Colorado Constitution subjects tributary water to constitutional constraints, it does not define the term "beneficial use." The General Assembly thus has authority to define the term within those constraints, as it has done in the 1969 Act.

B.

The Engineers and BP argue that because "beneficial use" is an ambiguous term, we should defer to the Engineers' interpretation and hold that the extraction of water to facilitate CBM production is not a beneficial use of water. While we may take into account agency interpretations, we are not bound by them. *See Colo. Mining Ass'n v. Bd. of County Comm'rs,* 199 P.3d 718, 731–32 (Colo.2009). Here, the Engineers' interpretation of the term "beneficial use" is contrary to the 1969 Act's definition of that term. Their interpretation also conflicts with our case law interpreting the term. We therefore decline to defer to the Engineers' interpretation.

C.

In their final argument, the Engineers assert that the legislature intended that CBM wells be regulated not by them but rather exclusively by the Colorado Oil and Gas Conservation Commission. They contend that, rather than subjecting oil and gas wells to possibly overlapping, inconsistent, or conflicting regulatory requirements, the General Assembly recognized and sought to protect the regulatory authority of the COGCC. We disagree with the Engineers' argument and hold that COGCC does not have exclusive regulatory authority over the extraction of water in CBM production.

In support of their argument, the Engineers point to the fact that the COGCC has been given extensive authority to regulate the production of oil and gas. *See* Oil and Gas Conservation Act, §§ 34–60–101 through–129, C.R.S. (2008). Yet, as the Engineers acknowledge in their brief, simply because "the General Assembly granted the COGCC primary authority over oil and gas operations does not exempt oil and gas wells from complying with applicable Colorado water law." *See also Three Bells,* 758 P.2d at 171 ("'[W]hen mining operations affect water rights, it is necessary for the operator to achieve compliance with the [Ground Water Act and the 1969 Act].'"). The Engineers fail to point to a specific provision in the Oil and Gas Conservation Act that exempts oil and gas production from the 1969 Act or the Ground Water Act, and we decline to create such an exemption here.

The Engineers also point to section 37–91–102(16)(b)(I), C.R.S. (2008) of the Water Well Construction and Pump Installation Contractors Act, which exempts from regulation "those wells subject to the jurisdiction of the [COGCC], as provided in article 60 of 34, C.R.S." The Engineers' reliance on this provision misses the mark as well. While section 37–91–102(16)(b)(I) might exempt oil and gas wells from the provisions governing water well construction, *see generally* § 37–91–101, C.R.S. (2008) (noting, among other things, the importance of the "proper location, construction, repair, and abandonment of wells"), it does not exempt them from the requirements of the 1969 Act and the Ground Water Act.

In sum, while the production of oil and gas is subject to extensive regulation by COGCC, it is also subject to the 1969 Act and the Ground Water Act. * * *

III.

Accordingly, we affirm the order of the District Court Water Division 7 and remand for further proceedings consistent with this opinion.

* * *

JUSTICE COATS, concurring in part and dissenting in part.

Although I agree that the extraction of groundwater in the coalbed methane ("CBM") production process falls within the administrative responsibilities of the state and division engineers, I do not agree that this process, in itself, amounts to a "beneficial use" of the water extracted, for either constitutional or statutory purposes. Furthermore, since the engineers have an obligation to regulate the removal of the waters of the state from their natural course or location, whether they are diverted for beneficial use or not, I do not consider it either necessary or appropriate to resolve the question of beneficial use as a declaratory judgment for the protection of senior appropriators. I therefore respectfully dissent from all but the conclusion of part II. C. of the majority's opinion.

The division engineer has a statutory obligation to order the discontinuance of any diversion not necessary for application to a beneficial use, *as well as* any diversion of water required to satisfy senior rights. § 37–92–502(2)(a), C.R.S. (2008). * * *

The CBM process therefore does not escape administration by the engineers, whether it amounts to a beneficial use of the extracted water or not. * * *

While I would therefore not address the question of beneficial use at all, I believe that in resolving the matter as it has, the majority erroneously (and unnecessarily) ties the hands of the legislature by suggesting that CBM producers have a constitutional right to appropriations for this purpose. Of even greater concern, it appears to me that the majority interprets "beneficial use" so broadly as to encompass virtually any diversion of the waters of the state that is not an inefficient way of accomplishing its purpose, whatever that purpose may be. By no longer requiring that these waters even be put to some use, but rather that it simply be advantageous to someone to relocate them from their natural course or location, I believe the majority has effectively eliminated the requirement altogether, making an efficient act of diverting sufficient for an appropriation.

* * *

Whether the General Assembly chooses to authorize the displacement of waters of the state for the production of methane gas, and if so, in what manner it chooses to best regulate that process, I consider to be matters entirely within its purview. I do not believe, however, it has yet done so.

By so loosening the requirement of beneficial use for valid appropriations, and by tying its expanded definition of "beneficial use" to constitutional protections against curtailing the right to appropriate unappropriated waters, I fear the majority not only authorizes appropriation under the existing statutory scheme for virtually any reason but also inadvertently implies a constitutional limitation on the power of the legislature to limit this protection in the future.

Except to the extent that I believe the extraction of groundwater in the coalbed methane production process necessarily falls within the administrative responsibilities of the state and division engineers, regardless of its beneficial use, I therefore respectfully dissent.

Justice MARTINEZ does not participate.

NOTES

1. In some prior-appropriation states, the legislature has defined categories of beneficial use. These statutory categories will generally include oil and gas exploration and development either expressly, as a part of "mining," or within "industrial" use. *See* Mathers v. Texaco, Inc., 421 P.2d 771 (N.M. 1966) ("the order of the State Engineer granting Texaco the right to use 350 acre feet of water per year for the stated purpose of recovery of oil by flooding 1,360 acres, should have been affirmed"). In North Dakota, industrial use is defined as "use of water for the furtherance of a commercial enterprise wherever located, including but not limited to manufacturing, mining, or processing." N.D. Cent. Code § 61–04–01.1(6).

2. Of the three primary uses of water—preparation of drilling mud; water flooding for secondary recovery, and hydraulic fracturing, fracing has been the most controversial, and state legislatures have been begun to legislate that fracing is an acceptable development method, thus clearing the way for treating it as a beneficial use of water. *See, e.g.,* N.D. Cent. Code § 38–08–25. Due the large volumes of water used in fracing and concerns about disposal, additives, and natural pollutants that may be mixed in with fracing fluids when withdrawn from the target formation, the oil and gas industry has increased efforts to recycle and reuse fracing waters. In addition, some states may require the use of nonpotable freshwater wherever suitable supplies are available. See, e.g., Northern Great Plains Water Consortium Bakken Water Opportunity Assessment Water Resource Opportunities Meeting (Dec. 10, 2009).

3. Eastern states generally follow riparian-rights doctrine for lakes and streams, generally limiting the use of surface waters to adjacent riparian lands and some limited non-riparian uses. Western states follow the prior-appropriation doctrine for lakes and streams but a few western states—e.g., California and Oklahoma—also recognize limited riparian rights.

Groundwater law is more variable. The absolute-ownership doctrine or English Rule is followed in Texas and perhaps a few other states.

The regulated-ownership/reasonable-use or American Rule is followed in most states. Many courts have defined this as the Arizona Supreme Court did in Town of Chino Valley v. State Land Dep't, 580 P.2d 704, 709 (Ariz. 1978), "Under the doctrine of reasonable use property owners have the right to capture and use the underground water beneath their land for a beneficial purpose on that land, but no landowner can transport water off the land from which it came if the transfer injured the water supply of neighboring property owners." Regulatory regimes have tended to do away with the limitation that the groundwater be used only on land above the water.

The correlative-rights/reasonable-share rule is followed in California. The balancing rule, RESTATEMENT OF (SECOND) OF TORTS § 858, is followed in Nebraska and perhaps in Indiana, Michigan, and Ohio. The prior-appropriation doctrine is applied to at least some groundwater in Alaska, Colorado, Kansas, Montana, Nevada, New Mexico, North Dakota, South Dakota, Utah, Wyoming and some others states.

Special groundwater rules may apply to certain "critical areas" or to 'designated groundwater basins,' e.g., Arizona, California, Colorado, Kansas, Nebraska, Montana, Nevada, New Mexico, Oklahoma, Texas, and Wyoming."

Where landowners have ownership rights in groundwater, they may be able to transfer the right to use the water to an oil and gas lessee. *See* Oklahoma Water Resources Bd. v. Texas County Irrigation and Water Resources Ass'n, Inc., 711 P.2d 38, 43 (Okla. 1984), where the majority stated: "[P]rior to the approval of Mobil's application for allocation of fresh ground water, it was incumbent upon Mobil to present evidence that the intended use was reasonable by establishing: (1) *it owns or leases lands overlying the Ogallala formation*; (2) that its intended use is a beneficial use; and, (3) that waste will not occur. Mobil's intended use . . . in secondary or tertiary oil recovery falls within the enumerated beneficial uses provided . . . agricultural, domestic, municipal, industrial and other beneficial uses." *Id.* at 44.

4. For a discussion of water law as it relates to upstream oil and gas operations, see generally, Robert E. Beck, Water and Oil and Gas, A Survey of North Dakota Water Law, 87 N. Dak. L. Rev. 4 (2012); Robert E. Beck, *Current Water Issues in Oil and Gas Development and Production: Will Water Control What Energy We Have?*, 49 WASHBURN L.J. 423 (2010); and Eva N. Neufeld, The Kansas Water Appropriation Statutes and Their Effect Upon the Oil and Gas Industry in Kansas, 50 J. Kan. B. Ass'n 43 (1981). Further discussion of state water-use law is beyond the scope of this book. See generally, DAVID H. GETCHES, WATER LAW IN A NUTSHELL (4th ed. 2009).

Basic Introduction to Administrative Law

While coverage of administrative law is beyond the scope of this text, a brief introduction to basic principles of administrative law will facilitate your understanding of the materials that follow.

When a state legislature enacts a comprehensive oil and gas conservation law, it creates a conservation agency and confers onto the agency executive, legislative, and judicial powers. The legislature authorizes the agency to execute, administer, and enforce the conservation act. However, because the statutory law lacks detail, the legislature delegates legislative power to the agency, authorizing the agency to enact rules and regulations in furtherance of the broad policies set forth in the conservation act. The most basic policies are preventing waste and protecting correlative rights. The legislature also empowers the agency to hold hearings and to adjudicate certain disputes among operators and other working interest owners concerning oil and gas operations.

While the authority of the legislature to delegate legislative powers to an administrative agency is well recognized, an agency may not act *ultra vires*—beyond the scope of its delegated authority or inconsistent with its nondiscretionary regulations. For example, a conservation agency generally has no delegated authority to adjudicate private disputes concerning property or contract rights; however, an agency is empowered to regulate private rights to the extent authorized by statute.[7]

An agency has *primary jurisdiction* over matters that are within the scope of its delegated authority. Thus, a party seeking to engage in conduct or seeking to resolve a dispute regarding an activity within an agency's authority must petition the agency and must exhaust all administrative remedies before pursuing an appeal in the courts. Moreover, after the agency issues its final order regarding a matter and after the time for appeal has expired, the order is not subject to a *collateral attack* in an ancillary action; however, an administrative agency usually has continuing jurisdiction to review and modify or rescind a prior final order if conditions change or if new material evidence becomes available.

In addition to specific regulatory acts, many states have an administrative procedures act (APA) that sets forth general procedures that all nonexempt agencies must follow when exercising their legislative and judicial functions. Because the APA is a general act, the provisions of specific regulatory acts prevail in the event of a conflict.

Regarding an agency's legislative function, the APA commonly provides that administrative agencies must give advance notice of proposed regulations and must provide an opportunity for public comment, often at a hearing. Regarding an agency's judicial function, the APA commonly provides for an adjudication hearing, requires notice to all interested parties, and requires the agency to issue an order.

A substantive judicial order must contain conclusions of law supported by findings of fact. Common issues include: whether a party is interested[8] and

---

7. The Oklahoma Supreme Court has struggled to find a "bright line" distinguishing private disputes, which are beyond the jurisdiction of the Corporation Commission, from public or regulatory disputes, which are within Commission jurisdiction. See, e.g., Samson Resources Co. v. Corporation Comm'n, 702 P.2d 19 (Okla.1985). See generally, Patrick H. Martin and Bruce M. Kramer, Jurisdiction of Commission and Court: The Public Right/Private Right Distinction in Oklahoma Law, 25 Tulsa L.J. 535 (1990).

8. In an adjudicatory proceeding, an *interested* party is one having a sufficient stake in the proceeding to participate fully and to appeal an adverse order. Conservation agencies often allow parties to participate in a hearing even though they have no standing to appeal. In the conservation arena, disputes may arise as to whether a mineral lessor or royalty owner has standing to participate in proceedings that concern drilling, development, and production. Do you understand why such a dispute might arise? See, e.g., Grace Petroleum Corp. v. Corporation Comm'n, 841 P.2d 1172 (Okla.App. Div. 3 1992) (holding that the owner of a working interest who elected to take an overriding royalty in lieu of participating in drilling did not have standing to apply for an increase in well density) and Turley v. Flag–Redfern Oil Co., 782 P.2d 130 (Okla. 1989) (holding that a surface owner has no standing to appeal an order increasing drilling density even though additional drilling would adversely affect surface use).

has standing; whether necessary parties have received proper notice and an opportunity to be heard; whether the agency has acted within the scope of its authority; whether the agency has issued an order that contains sufficient fact findings to permit a meaningful review, and whether the agency has made conclusions of law that are supported by the evidence and by agency's findings of fact.

The APA also sets forth the procedure to appeal an adverse order and commonly establishes a standard of review for the courts. If an agency's rulemaking is challenged in court, the court will affirm the agency's regulations if they are not *ultra vires* and if they are not arbitrary and capricious. In most states, a court will affirm an agency's findings of fact in an adjudicatory proceeding if the findings are supported by any *substantial and credible evidence*; however, in a few jurisdictions, courts must grant a *trial de novo* when hearing an appeal of an agency's adjudication. Regardless of the applicable standard of review, courts commonly defer to the agency's rulemaking or adjudication, including the agency's interpretation of its own rules or orders, because the agency has special expertise in a highly technical area— *e.g.*, oil and gas operations. Accordingly, a court is usually reluctant to substitute its judgment for that of a conservation agency that employs petroleum geologists and petroleum engineers. The following passage from Railroad Comm'n v. Rowan and Nichols Oil Co., 310 U.S. 573, 580 (1940), exemplifies this very well.

> A controversy like this always calls for fresh reminder that courts must not substitute their notions of expediency and fairness for those which have guided the agencies to whom the formulation and execution of policy have been entrusted. * * * Certainly in a domain of knowledge still shifting and growing and in a field where judgment is therefore necessarily beset by the necessity of inferences bordering on conjecture even for those learned in the art, it would be presumptuous for courts, on the basis of conflicting expert testimony, to deem the view of the administrative tribunal, acting under legislative authority, offensive to the Fourteenth Amendment. * * * It is not for the federal courts to supplant the Commission's judgment even in the face of convincing proof that a different result would have been better.

> As long as geological and engineering theories are applied uniformly, a conservation agency's discretionary orders will generally be upheld.

On the other hand, if the agency does not set forth relevant fact findings and its legal rationale for its conclusions of law, the reviewing court will reverse and remand.

> The Commission's findings of fact must be sufficient to enable this Court to understand the basis for its decision. * * * Even in subject areas that entail administrative expertise, 'that expertise must be directed toward the statutory standards set forth by the legislature so that reviewing courts may have the benefit of that expertise.' * * *. If the reasons given do not enable us to understand the basis for the decision, the Commission's decision cannot be sustained."

Gadeco, LLC v. Industrial Commission, 812 N.W.2d 405 (N.D. 2012), citing *Hystad v. Industrial Comm'n,* 389 N.W.2d 590, 598 (N.D.1986).

If the issue on appeal concerns a question of law, such as the agency's scope of delegated authority, or constitutional rights, the agency's decision is more fully reviewable. Nevertheless, courts often defer to an agency's interpretation of its authority and mandate, as well as the agency's view of what is proper public policy concerning matters within its area of expertise. As stated in Railroad Comm'n v. Humble Oil & Refining Co., 193 S.W.2d 824, 833 (Tex.Civ.App.–Austin 1946, writ ref'd n.r.e.) (quoting Corzelius v. Harrell, 186 S.W.2d 961, 967 (Tex.1945)):

> The conservation orders of the Commission are presumptively valid, and before they can be set aside by the courts, their invalidity must clearly be shown.

> "The Railroad Commission is not required in administering the oil and gas statutes to be absolutely accurate in its rules and orders. This would be impossible. It is the duty of the Commission to treat all interested parties justly and impartially, and the actions and rulings of the Commission in attempting to accomplish such results will not be disturbed by the courts unless such rules or orders are clearly illegal, unreasonable, or arbitrary. The power to make rules rests exclusively with the Railroad Commission."

5. The following case illustrates the conflict that may arise between a state regulatory agency and a political subdivision.

RANGE RESOURCES—APPALACHIA, LLC v. SALEM TOWNSHIP

964 A.2d 869 (Pa. 2009).

JUSTICE SAYLOR.

The primary question raised in this appeal by allowance pertains to the preemptive scope of Pennsylvania's Oil and Gas Act. As such, this decision is issued in conjunction with our disposition in *Huntley & Huntley, Inc. v. Borough Council of the Borough of Oakmont*, 600 Pa. 207, 964 A.2d 855, 2009 WL 413723 (2009), which also addresses the same issue within the context of a somewhat different set of facts.

In 2005, Appellant Salem Township, Westmoreland County (the "Township") enacted a general ordinance directed at regulating surface and land development associated with oil and gas drilling operations. Shortly thereafter, Appellees, oil and gas producers, commenced an action in the common pleas court, seeking declarations that: the ordinance was invalid due to non-compliance with the Municipalities Planning Code ("MPC") (Count I); the ordinance's regulations were preempted by Pennsylvania's Oil and Gas Act (the "Act") (Count II);[1] the regulations were

---

1. Act of December 19, 1984, P.L. 1140 (as amended, 58 P.S. §§ 601.101–601.605). Preemption is governed by Section 602, which provides:

> Except with respect to ordinances adopted pursuant to the ... Municipalities Planning Code, and the ... Flood Plain Management Act, all local ordinances and enactments purporting to regulate oil and gas well operations regulated by this act are hereby superseded. No ordinances or enactments adopted pursuant to the aforementioned acts shall contain provisions which impose conditions, requirements or limitations on the same features of oil and

also preempted by other state and federal enactments (Counts III and IV); the regulations violated due process (Count V); and they effected a regulatory taking (Count VI). Only Count II, relating to Oil and Gas Act preemption, is relevant to this appeal.

After pleadings closed, the parties filed cross-motions for summary judgment. In July 2006, while these motions were pending, the Township enacted, for the first time, comprehensive subdivision and land development legislation, thereby supplanting the earlier ordinance. This new legislation was adopted pursuant to the MPC, and included two appendices. Appendix B (hereinafter, the "Ordinance") comprised a wholesale re-enactment of the oil and gas regulations found in the prior legislation. In addition to its substantive restrictions on oil and gas drilling activities, the Ordinance established a fee for permit applications and provided for criminal penalties upon failure to comply with its terms. The parties stipulated that any decision on the pending motions for summary judgment would affect the validity of the replacement oil and gas regulations contained in the Ordinance, and Appellees withdrew Count I of the complaint.

Acting on the pending motions, the trial court granted partial summary judgment in favor of Appellees on the basis that the Act preempted the Township's oil and gas regulations. The court additionally granted the Township's application for a determination of finality under Rule of Appellate Procedure 341(c). See Pa.R.A.P. 341(c). The Township then appealed to the Commonwealth Court.

The trial court issued an opinion setting forth the rationale for its conclusion that each of the oil and gas regulations challenged in the complaint was preempted by state law. In particular, the court found that the Ordinance requires a permit for all drilling-related activities; regulates the location, design, and construction of access roads, gas transmission lines, water treatment facilities, and well heads; establishes a procedure for residents to file complaints regarding surface and ground water; allows the Township to declare drilling a public nuisance and to revoke or suspend a permit; establishes requirements for site access and restoration; and provides that any violation of the Ordinance is a summary offense that can trigger fines and/or imprisonment. The court then summarized some relevant aspects of the Act's "comprehensive regulatory scheme with regard to the development of oil and gas and coal," including those pertaining to such things as casing requirements, protection of water supplies, safety devices, and the plugging of wells. * * *

The trial court also enumerated the purposes of the Act as stated by the General Assembly, including: to allow the optimal development of oil and gas resources consistent with the protection of citizens' health, safety,

---

gas well operations regulated by this act or that accomplish the same purposes as set forth in this act. The Commonwealth, by this enactment, hereby preempts and supersedes the regulation of oil and gas wells as herein defined.

58 P.S. § 601.602 (emphasis added to highlight language supplied by a 1992 legislative amendment).

environment, and property; to protect the safety of personnel and facilities employed in gas and oil exploration, development, and storage; to protect the safety and property rights of persons residing in areas where such activities occur; and to protect natural resources. See id. at 6–7 (quoting 58 P.S. § 601.102). In light of all of the above, the court found that the Ordinance "places conditions, requirements, or limitations on some of the same features of oil and gas well operations regulated by the Oil and Gas Act," id. at 7, and indeed, is even more stringent than the Act with regard to the manner in which many activities are regulated.[2] The court suggested that the Township was attempting, through the Ordinance, to impose requirements with regard to the location of activities necessarily incident to the development of wells, and that these types of restrictions fall within the purview of the Act and the oversight of the Department of Environmental Protection (the "Department"). See id. at 7–8. The trial court ultimately concluded as follows:

> Although the township expresses laudable goals in its concern for the health, safety and property of its citizens, the hazardous nature of oil and gas well drilling operations, and the potential for an adverse impact on environmental resources, those purposes have been addressed by the legislature in its passage of the act. While the township may have traditionally been able to pursue such purposes, once the state has acted pursuant to those purposes, the township is foreclosed from exercising that police power. I would add that the comprehensive nature of the statutory scheme regulating oil and gas well operations reflects a need for uniformity so that the purposes of the legislature can be accomplished.

* * *

The Commonwealth Court affirmed. * * * The court noted that the Township's primary contention on appeal was that the trial court had erred in concluding that, because some of the Ordinance provisions conflicted with the Act, the entire ordinance was invalid. Specifically, the Township maintained that the court should have examined the Ordinance on a provision-by-provision basis to ascertain whether any provisions were severable. The Commonwealth Court did not directly address this claim, but instead, affirmed based on the analysis set forth in the trial court's opinion.

In seeking permission to appeal to this Court, the Township questioned whether the Act's preemptive scope is as broad as the trial court indicated—and particularly, whether the items regulated by the Ordinance, including oil and gas well access roads, gas transmission lines, road maintenance agreements, and the location of water cleaning facilities associated with coal bed methane operations, fall under the rubric of

---

2. The Township indicates that the court's use of the word "some" implies that other ordinance provisions must be valid. * * * This contention is in error as the court was speaking of the state enactment, not the local one.

"features of oil and gas well operations" for purposes of Section 602 of the Act. This Court allowed appeal here, as in *Huntley*, to address the topic of Oil and Gas Act preemption. We additionally invited the Department to file an amicus brief articulating its view of whether the Act and its associated administrative regulations preempt the local regulations at issue. * * *

In *Huntley*, we concluded that the Act's preemptive scope is not total in the sense that it does not prohibit municipalities from enacting traditional zoning regulations that identify which uses are permitted in different areas of the locality, even if such regulations preclude oil and gas drilling in certain zones. In reaching this determination, we agreed with the Department's position that the statutory term, "features of oil and gas well operations," refers to the "technical aspects of well functioning and matters ancillary thereto (such as registration, bonding, and well site restoration), rather than the well's location," *Huntley*, 600 Pa. at 223, 964 A.2d at 864, and that the traditional purposes of zoning are distinct from the purposes set forth in the Act, see *id.* at 224, 964 A.2d at 865. We clarified, however, that our holding should not be understood to suggest that any and all zoning regulation of oil and gas development would be allowable under Section 602 of the Act simply because the ordinance in question was enacted pursuant to the MPC. See id. at 226 n. 11, 964 A.2d at 866 n. 11 ("We do not, for instance, suggest that the municipality could permit drilling in a particular district but then make that permission subject to conditions addressed to features of well operations regulated by the Act.").

Presently, the Township forwards arguments that overlap to some degree with those of the municipality in the *Huntley* case. It maintains, for example, that local land-use regulations adopted pursuant to the MPC are only preempted to the degree they address the technical, operational aspects of oil and gas drilling, but that they are permissible otherwise so long as their provisions are consistent with ordinary zoning principles. To the extent these assertions subsume the "how-versus-where" distinction articulated in *Huntley*, they are plainly supported by that case's reasoning. In advancing the validity of the Ordinance's comprehensive regulatory scheme, however, the Township suggests that this Court adopt two additional prongs as part of the preemption analysis. Thus, the Township proffers that local regulation of a particular surface activity ancillary to oil and gas drilling should only be deemed preempted if the activity: (a) relates to the technical operations of the oil and gas industry, (b) flows directly from the operation an oil or gas well, and (c) is unique to the oil and gas industry. See Brief for Appellant at 9, 31. Under this proposed standard, the Township maintains the Ordinance's regulations pertaining to the submission of site plans, storm water management plans, erosion and sediment control plans, grading of access roads, road bonding requirements, and other related surface disturbance activities or surface elements (such as the placement and subsequent removal of water treatment facilities), are all permissible inasmuch as they comprise traditional local controls over land use.[3]

The Township also avers that it is affirmatively required or permitted to enact some of these regulations under the provisions of other state enactments such as the Storm Water Management Act,[4] and the Dam Safety and Encroachments Act.[5] As a separate matter, the Township renews its contention that the trial court erred in invalidating the Ordinance wholesale, rather than undertaking a section-by-section analysis of the ordinance against the Act's regulatory provisions in view of the Ordinance's severance clause. * * * The Township then offers its own such analysis and, as to each section of the Ordinance, concludes that all of its provisions are valid * * *. The Township's amici add that the Act should be read in a manner consistent with constitutional guarantees relating to the preservation of natural resources, see Pa. Const. art. I, § 27 (guaranteeing the "right to clean air, pure water, and the preservation of the natural, scenic, historic and esthetic values of the environment"), giving due weight to the shared state and local responsibilities to protect the environment.

Appellees counter that the Act preempts all local oil and gas regulations that either seek to accomplish the Act's purposes or overlap the Act's regulatory features. * * * They maintain that the arguments of the Township and its amici address only the latter test and ignore the former. This is relevant, they argue, because the Ordinance is directed exclusively at regulating oil and gas development in the municipality, thereby seeking to accomplish the purposes of the Act. They aver, in this regard, that general local regulations pertaining to the bonding of municipal roads and bridges and the use of municipal facilities by all industries might pass the Act's test for preemption because these potential features of operations are not addressed in the Act; but, they argue, an ordinance, such as the one under review, that specifically targets the oil and gas industry, incorporates by reference the provisions of the Act, and "overlap[s] the Act at nearly every turn," is clearly preempted as it amounts to local legislation seeking to accomplish the purposes set forth in the Act. * * *

As regards severance of specific portions of the ordinance, Appellees assert that the Township waived the issue as it did not raise this concern

---

3. The Township submits the following list as a sample of the items that the Ordinance requires or regulates: (1) the location and grading of access roads from public roads to well sites; (2) the creation of tire cleaning areas along access roads where they intersect with public roads; (3) the slope of access roads for storm water management purposes; (4) the construction of cross pipes under access roads for storm water management purposes; (5) the entry of excess maintenance agreements requiring operators to repair public roads damaged by heavy equipment; (6) the location and grading of gas transmission lines running from the well heads to ensure and maximize surface development; (7) a minimum depth at which transmission lines should be located to ensure they do not interfere with farming or other surface development; (8) the installation of marking ribbons on transmission lines for easy identification to ensure they are not subject to damage or disruption by other excavation in the area; (9) mandatory testing of potable water supplies; and (10) the location of water cleaning facilities associated with coal bed methane operations which are not provided for under the Act. * * *

4. Act of Oct. 4, 1978, P.L. 864, No. 167 (as amended, 32 P.S. §§ 680.1–680.17).

5. Act of Nov. 26, 1978, P.L. 1375, No. 325 (as amended, 32 P.S. §§ 693.1–693.27).

before the trial court in defending against Appellees' motion for summary judgment, and that, in all events the remainder of the ordinance would be unintelligible after severance of the offending provisions.

Finally, Appellees proffer a public and legislative policy rationale for invalidating the ordinance. They assert that the statewide economic benefits of developing Pennsylvania's vast oil and natural gas reserves can best be realized if producers are required to comply with a uniform regulatory scheme administered by the Department. In this respect, they emphasize their view that fashioning and maintaining such a uniform regulatory scheme without substantial interference from local non-expert governing bodies is a primary legislative objective underlying the Act. Thus, Appellees contend that any ruling by this Court which permits the Commonwealth's thousands of local governmental units to establish their own substantive oil and gas regulations (as the Township has done) would undermine the Act and its broad policy goals by effectively removing the regulation of the oil and gas industry from the expert statewide regulators charged with its oversight. * * *

The Department agrees with Appellees' position regarding the need for statewide uniformity in the regulation of the oil and gas industry. It highlights that the Act and its associated administrative regulations already provide a comprehensive framework for permitting, bonding, registering, operating, and plugging oil and gas wells, and develops that any municipal ordinance contradictory to, or inconsistent with, the state statutory and regulatory scheme cannot be sustained under general rules of preemption. While the Department qualifies its advocacy by recommending—as in *Huntley*—an interpretation of the Act that leaves room for municipal regulations bearing only a tangential relationship to oil and gas drilling and extraction, it avers that the common pleas court and the Commonwealth Court reached the correct result in this case because "the purposes of the Ordinance are duplicative of the purposes of the Act," Brief for Department as Amicus Curiae at 12, and are thus preempted.

Upon review, we find that the Ordinance reflects an attempt by the Township to enact a comprehensive regulatory scheme relative to oil and gas development within the municipality. Accord Brief for the Department as Amicus Curiae at 11 ("[T]he ordinance covers the full panoply of issues related to oil and gas drilling."). Indeed, there are numerous aspects of the Ordinance's regulations pertaining to features of well operations that substantively overlap with similar regulations set forth in the Act, falling under the express preemptive language of Section 602.[6] For example, the

---

6. We agree with Appellees that the Township's proposed three-prong test for statutory preemption is "divorced from the language of the Act and unreasonably narrow." Brief for Appellees at 33. The Act does not indicate that preemption is only accomplished if the regulated activity is unique to the oil and gas industry and flows directly from the operation of a well. Rather, it states more generally that no feature of oil and gas well operations may be subject to any further conditions, requirements, or limitations by MPC-enabled local legislation. See 58 P.S. § 601.602. Here, the concept of a "feature of" oil and gas well operations is statutorily limited only by the qualifier, "regulated by this Act." 58 P.S. § 601.602. On its face, therefore, it is

Ordinance purports to: establish permitting procedures specifically for oil and gas wells, see Ordinance, Article I, § II; RR. 537b; impose bonding requirements before drilling can begin, see id., § III(A)(6); RR. 540b; regulate well heads, including the capping of the same once they are no longer in use, see id., § III(D)(2); RR. 543b; and regulate site restoration after drilling operations cease, see id., § III(A)(5); RR. 543b. The Ordinance's permitting and bonding procedures constitute a regulatory apparatus parallel to the one established by the Act and implemented by the Department. See 58 P.S. § 601.215 (relating to well bonding); id., §§ 201–202 (relating to drilling permits and objections thereto); id., § 203 (relating to well registration); id., § 204 (relating to wells attaining inactive status). Likewise, the topic of site restoration is addressed by the Act, see id., § 206, as is the subject of well casing and plugging upon cessation of use, see id., §§ 207, 210.

As developed by the trial court, moreover, in many instances the Ordinance's requirements are even more stringent than the corresponding provisions of the Act.[7] Further, some of the ordinance's provisions appear to impose excess costs on entities engaged in oil and gas drilling, such as the requirement of restoring nearby streets to their pre-drilling conditions regardless of whether the wear and tear on such roadways was caused by vehicles associated with drilling activities. See Brief for Appellant at 42 (quoting Ordinance, Article I, § III(A)(9); RR. 541b).

Notably, as well, the Ordinance does not guarantee issuance of a permit even if the applicant complies with all requirements, stating expressly that it reflects only the "minimum terms acceptable" and that, upon compliance, a conditional permit "may" be issued by the Township, "subject to final approval by the Board of Supervisors at a public meeting." Ordinance, Article I, § 2(C); RR. 538b. While the Township may be correct in arguing that there are some aspects of the Ordinance that are not expressly covered directly by the Act, even these are bound up with the overall regulatory scheme which includes strict permitting and penalty provisions, and phrased in such general terms—e.g., "the most direct and feasible means," "shall not unreasonably restrict access," etc.—as to provide the Township with virtually unbridled discretion to deny permission to drill. This is in stark contrast to, and in conflict with, the Act's more permissive approach. See, e.g., 58 P.S. 601.201(f) (providing that "the well operator may proceed with the drilling of the well" upon

potentially broad enough to include items that flow both directly and indirectly from the operation of an oil or gas well, as well as features that are shared by other industries.

7. One example highlighted by Appellees pertains to the protection of water supplies in the vicinity of drilling operations. The Act and its associated administrative regulations specify that any well operator who affects a water supply through pollution or diminution of the amount of available water must restore or replace the affected supply with an alternate source of water. See 58 P.S. § 601.208(a); 25 Pa.Code § 78.52. Well operators may, however, conduct pre-drilling water testing to establish a defense to future charges of water pollution, see id., § 601.208(d), or they may elect not to conduct such testing and risk future liability. Under the Ordinance, pre-operation water testing is mandatory relative to all water sources within 1,000 feet of a well site. See Ordinance Section II (relating to required approvals); RR. 537b. Because the Ordinance thus forbids an operator from foregoing pre-drilling water testing and risking liability, while the Act allows such a course of action, the Ordinance is in direct conflict with the Act. * * *.

issuance of the departmental permit and the giving of 24 hours' notice to various interested parties (emphasis added)). Hence, we find that the Ordinance is qualitatively different from the zoning enactment at issue in *Huntley* that sought only to control the location of wells consistent with established zoning principles.[8]

We also agree with Appellees that the Township's advocacy is deficient in that it fails to account for the independent statutory basis for preemption relative to local ordinances that seek to accomplish the same objectives as are set forth in the Act. * * * As developed in *Huntley* and by the trial court, the Act's purposes, broadly speaking, pertain to optimizing oil and gas development, ensuring the safety of the personnel and facilities used in such development, protecting the property rights of neighboring landowners, and preserving the natural environment. * * * Similarly, the Ordinance focuses, not on zoning or the regulation of commercial or industrial development generally, but solely on regulating oil and gas development, with specific objectives that include "enabling continuing oil and gas drilling operations . . . while ensuring the orderly development of property through the location of access ways, transportation lines and treatment facilities necessarily associated with the same." Ordinance, Preamble; RR. 535b. The goals of the Ordinance also subsume protecting the development of neighboring properties, see *id.*, and protecting natural resources. As the common pleas court expressed, these may all be laudable ends, but they are addressed by the Act.

Finally, the Township urges this Court to uphold the Ordinance to the degree it controls ancillary features of oil and gas operations. See Brief for Appellants at 39–49 (arguing that the Ordinance is valid to the extent it restricts water treatment facilities, oil and gas transmission lines, and the location, grading and construction of access roads). Even to the extent these provisions pertain to items that are not specifically addressed in the Act, within the framework of an ordinance specifically directed to oil and gas well operations, they plainly constitute an impermissible form of regulation, as the last sentence of Section 602 prohibits even such restrictions as these. See 58 P.S. § 601.602 ("The Commonwealth, by this enactment, hereby preempts and supersedes the regulation of oil and gas wells as herein defined."); see also supra note 6.

In sum, not only does the Ordinance purport to police many of the same aspects of oil and gas extraction activities that are addressed by the Act, but the comprehensive and restrictive nature of its regulatory scheme

---

8. This also answers the Township's argument predicated upon its obligations under other statutes such as the Storm Water Management Act. While such enactments may encourage local management of certain environmental problems, Appellants have not shown that they authorize implementation of administrative controls specifically targeted at the oil and gas industry. Thus, because the Oil and Gas Act is industry-specific, its express preemptive language remains unaffected by provisions in other statutes generally imposing duties upon localities that are not phrased with particular reference to oil and gas development. Cf. 1 Pa.C.S. § 1933 (where two statutes conflict, special provisions prevail over general ones). Consistent with our treatment of the zoning controls at issue in *Huntley*, however, our holding here should not be construed to preclude local regulations duly enacted pursuant to other state laws that incidentally affect oil and gas development.

represents an obstacle to the legislative purposes underlying the Act, thus implicating principles of conflict preemption. * * * Furthermore, its stated purposes overlap substantially with the goals as set forth in the Oil and Gas Act, thus implicating the second statutory basis for express preemption of MPC-enabled local ordinances. In view of the Ordinance's focus solely on regulating oil and gas drilling operations, together with the broad preemptive scope of Section 602 of the Act with regard to such directed local regulations, we agree with the common pleas court's conclusion that each of the oil and gas regulations challenged in Appellees' complaint is preempted by the Oil and Gas Act and its associated administrative regulations.

For the reasons stated, the order of the Commonwealth Court is affirmed.

CHIEF JUSTICE CASTILLE, and JUSTICES EAKIN, BAER, TODD, McCAFFERY and JUSTICE GREENSPAN join the opinion.

NOTES

1. In *Huntley*, an oil company proposed drilling a well on residential property. The city council denied a conditional use application to allow the drilling. Although the court held that the zoning ordinance was not preempted by the oil and gas conservation act, the court found that the ordinance permitted drilling as a conditional use. The city unsuccessfully argued that the ordinance, which permitted the extraction of "minerals" as a conditional use of property, did not permit the drilling of a natural gas well as a conditional use.

> The Statutory Construction Act of 1972 commands that words and phrases should ordinarily be understood according to their common and approved usage. See 1 Pa.C.S. § 1903(a). * * * "Feature" means a "prominent or conspicuous characteristic," RANDOM HOUSE WEBSTER'S COLLEGE DICTIONARY 481 (2d ed. 2000), and "operation" refers to a process and manner of functioning, see id. at 929. Although one could reasonably argue that a well's placement at a certain location is one of its features in a general sense, it is not a feature of the well's operation because it is not a characteristic of the manner or process by which the well is created, functions, is maintained, ceases to function, or is ultimately destroyed or capped. Therefore, we find the resolution of this issue as advanced by Appellants and the Department to be persuasive and, accordingly, conclude that, absent further legislative guidance, Section 602's reference to "features of oil and gas well operations regulated by this act" pertains to technical aspects of well functioning and matters ancillary thereto (such as registration, bonding, and well site restoration), rather than the well's location. * * *

> This leads to the second inquiry: whether the challenged zoning restrictions accomplish the same purposes as set forth in the Act. The "as set forth" qualifier signifies that this Court should not attempt to glean the Act's objectives from its substantive provisions, but instead should consult the list of purposes enumerated in the Act itself, namely, to:

(1) Permit the optimal development of the oil and gas resources of Pennsylvania consistent with the protection of the health, safety, environment and property of the citizens of the Commonwealth. (2) Protect the safety of personnel and facilities employed in the exploration, development, storage and production of natural gas or oil or the mining of coal. (3) Protect the safety and property rights of persons residing in areas where such exploration, development, storage or production occurs. (4) Protect the natural resources, environmental rights and values secured by the Pennsylvania Constitution.

58 P.S. § 601.102.

By way of comparison, the purposes of zoning controls are both broader and narrower in scope. They are narrower because they ordinarily do not relate to matters of statewide concern, but pertain only to the specific attributes and developmental objectives of the locality in question. However, they are broader in terms of subject matter, as they deal with all potential land uses and generally incorporate an overall statement of community development objectives that is not limited solely to energy development. * * * More to the point, the intent underlying the Borough's ordinance in the present case includes serving police power objectives relating to the safety and welfare of its citizens, encouraging the most appropriate use of land throughout the borough, conserving the value of property, minimizing overcrowding and traffic congestion, and providing adequate open spaces. * * *

There is some overlap between these goals and the purposes set forth in the Oil and Gas Act, most particularly in the area of protecting public health and safety. As we read the ordinance, however, the most salient objectives underlying restrictions on oil and gas drilling in residential districts appear to be those pertaining to preserving the character of residential neighborhoods, see Ordinance § 205–3(A)(7), and encouraging "beneficial and compatible land uses." Id., § 305–3(A)(10). In this regard, the highest appellate court of one of our sister states has observed as follows:

> While the governmental interests involved in oil and gas development and in land-use control at times may overlap, the core interests in these legitimate governmental functions are quite distinct. The state's interest in oil and gas development is centered primarily on the efficient production and utilization of the natural resources in the state. A county's interest in land-use control, in contrast, is one of orderly development and use of land in a manner consistent with local demographic and environmental concerns. Given the rather distinct nature of these interests, we reasonably may expect that any legislative intent to prohibit a county from exercising its land-use authority over those areas of the county in which oil development or operations are taking place or are contemplated would be clearly and unequivocally stated. We, however, find no such clear and unequivocal statement of legislative intent in the Oil and Gas Conservation Act.

Board of County Comm'rs of La Plata County v. Bowen/Edwards Assocs., Inc., 830 P.2d 1045, 1057 (Colo.1992). We find the Colorado court's emphasis on a political subdivision's land-use authority appropriate here because, as discussed, the express preemptive language of Section 602 pertains to features of well operations and the Act's stated purposes. This limitation on preemption regarding MPC-enabled legislation appears to reflect the General Assembly's recognition, as Appellants contend, that, while effective oil and gas regulation in service of the Act's goals may require the knowledge and expertise of the appropriate state agency, the MPC's [Municipal Planning Code's] authorization of local zoning laws is provided in recognition of the unique expertise of municipal governing bodies to designate where different uses should be permitted in a manner that accounts for the community's development objectives, its character, and the "suitabilities and special nature of particular parts of the community." 53 P.S. § 10603(a) * * * Accordingly, and again, absent further legislative guidance, we conclude that the Ordinance serves different purposes from those enumerated in the Oil and Gas Act, and hence, that its overall restriction on oil and gas wells in R–1 districts is not preempted by that enactment. * * *

Having determined that the challenged portion of the zoning ordinance was not preempted by the Oil and Gas Act, we must now resolve whether the ordinance permits such drilling as a conditional use in an R–1 district. When Huntley applied for a conditional use permit, the Ordinance allowed the extraction of minerals as a conditional use in such a district, and defined that activity as "any use consisting of the mining and extraction of coal or other minerals." See Ordinance § 205–10 (relating to definitions). As may be expected, the parties are in sharp disagreement over the propriety of the Commonwealth Court's determination that Council should not have excluded natural gas drilling from the scope of such activities.

Appellants argue that the Commonwealth Court mistakenly superimposed the MPC's definition of mineral upon the relevant portion of the zoning code. They observe that the MPC's definitions generally attach to terms as they are "used in this act [the MPC]," 53 P.S. 10107(a), and reference *Boyd* [476 A.2d 499 (Pa. Commw. 1984)] for the position that local ordinances need not utilize the same definition of such words. Appellants also aver that the Ordinance makes reasonable provision for natural gas development, as required by the MPC, see 53 P.S. § 10603(i), because drilling is permitted as a special exception in other areas of the municipality besides R–1 residential districts. Additionally, Appellants point out that the Ordinance's definition of "extraction of minerals" includes the term mining and, on this basis, the Borough's construction of the activity to exclude drilling was reasonable.

Huntley responds by observing that, when it first applied for conditional-use approval, it did so upon the Borough's directive in which the Borough stated explicitly that it had considered the matter and determined that the drilling of a gas well fell within the zoning ordinance's definition of "extraction of minerals." Huntley states that the Commonwealth Court properly concluded that the Borough's post-hoc effort to redefine "mineral" to exclude natural gas was impermissible, particularly as it was entirely inconsistent with the MPC's definition of the same term. Further, Huntley maintains that *Boyd* is inapposite for the reason articulated by the Commonwealth Court, namely, that the ordinance in *Boyd* defined "structure" in a way that was consistent with the MPC's definition, and that the Commonwealth Court appropriately looked to the MPC in the present dispute to supply a default definition of "mineral" in the absence of one provided by the Ordinance. Finally, Huntley states that this Court has previously acknowledged that natural gas is a mineral.

As discussed, the Commonwealth Court developed that the Ordinance does not define "mineral," and determined that it should employ the definition of that term contained in the enabling statute. We find this approach to have been appropriate: while Appellants are correct in stating that the MPC's definitions are limited in application to their use in that statute, they overlook that the code's utilization of defined terms is always in relation to the requirements of local comprehensive plans and ordinances. See 53 P.S. §§ 10301, 10603. Thus, contrary to Appellants' portrayal, the MPC contemplates application of its definitions in the manner adopted by the Commonwealth Court. * * * Therefore, the Commonwealth Court properly utilized the MPC's definition of the term "mineral" to include natural gas, a usage that accords with this Court's understanding of the term. See, e.g., United States Steel Corp. v. Hoge, 503 Pa. 140, 146, 468 A.2d 1380, 1383 (1983) ("Gas is a mineral, though not commonly spoken of as such [.]"); Kelly v. Keys, 213 Pa. 295, 299, 62 A. 911, 913 (1906) (recognizing a distinction between minerals that are fugacious in nature, such as oil and gas, and those that have a fixed situs). This advances the MPC's policy directive that, where doubt exists as to the extent of a land-use restriction, local ordinances should be interpreted in favor of the property owner. See 53 P.S. § 10603.1.

The Borough maintains, however, that it is in the best position to determine what types of mining activities are best suited to each type of district, see Brief for Appellants at 37–38, and invokes the deference that courts ordinarily give to municipalities in interpreting their ordinances. See Broussard v. Zoning Bd. of Adjustment of City of Pittsburgh, 589 Pa. 71, 81, 907 A.2d 494, 500 (2006). As to the first of these points, the Borough's argument is not persuasive because it does not explain why drilling for fugacious minerals is less compatible with the common use of land in an R–1 district than is mining for coal or other solid substances, an arguably counterintuitive notion that would appear to require some justification.

Relative to the second point, we find the application of deference problematic in the present context for several reasons. For one, the principles that underlie the rule of deference are undermined where, as here, the municipality arrives at one interpretation of its ordinance—which it then conveys to the interested party as the basis for its command to apply for a conditional use permit—before adopting an alternate interpretation following the filing of the application and a hearing at which community members express their opposition to the project in question. In this regard, in the correspondence sent to Huntley in the pre-hearing timeframe, the Borough Solicitor specifically indicated that the pertinent Borough officials had considered the matter and determined that natural gas drilling was permitted as a conditional use. * * *

Furthermore, we believe it would be unwise to defer automatically to a local governing body concerning the proper interpretation of a term that is expressly defined by the MPC and used in a zoning ordinance adopted pursuant to that statute, where the ordinance does not supply an alternate definition. Such an approach would invite litigation by fostering uncertainty as to the meaning of zoning terms, while opening the door for local agencies to adopt positions arbitrarily and/or based on interests unrelated to the legislative intent underlying the ordinance's enactment. * * *

Accordingly, we hold that the Commonwealth Court's resolution of the issue was reasonable, and that Council improperly denied conditional use approval predicated on its after-the-fact, restrictive interpretation of the phrase, "extraction of minerals."

Huntley & Huntley, Inc. v. Council of Oakmont, 964 A.2d 855, 864–868 (Pa. 2009). In 2012, the Pennsylvania General Assembly enacted Act 13, which, in part, restricted the authority of local governments to regulate oil and gas operations. Further, local governments must allow "reasonable development of oil and gas." 2012 Pa. Laws Act No. 13. When this casebook edition went to press, portions of this law were being challenged on the ground that they violate the Pennsylvania Constitution.

2.   Could a municipality, through a land-use ordinance, prohibit the extraction of minerals within city limits? Cf, Marblehead Land Co. v. City of Los Angeles, 47 F.2d 528 (9th Cir. Cal. 1931) (upholding a ban on new wells); Beverly Oil Co. v. City of Los Angeles, 254 P.2d 865 (Cal. 1953) (upholding a ban on redrilling and deepening of wells); Blancett v. Montgomery, 398 S.W.2d 877 (Ky. Ct. App. 1966) (upholding a ban); and Tri–Power Resources, Inc. v. City of Carlyle, 967 N.E.2d 811 (Ill. App. Ct. 2012) (upholding a ban) with Voss v. Lundvall Bros., Inc., 830 P.2d 1061 (Colo. 1992) (overturning a ban). In Zimmerman v. Board of County Comm'rs, 218 P.3d 400 (Kan. 2009), the court upheld a county-wide ban on commercial wind farms. In a related case, the court held such denial was not a taking because a property owner has no property right to a conditional use permit. Zimmerman v. Hudson, 264 P.3d 989 (Kan. 2011).

Would a ban on drilling within areas zoned for residential use be permissible? Cf., Newbury Twp. Bd. of Trustees v. Lomak Petroleum, Inc., 583 N.E.2d 302 (Ohio 1992) (zoning ordinance cannot validly bar drilling for oil and gas contrary to an express state policy that encourages drilling and cannot ban drilling in a residentially zoned subdivision that also contains farmland suitable for drilling) and Excalibur Exploration, Inc. v. Board of Trustees of Springfield Twp., 549 N.E.2d 224 (Ohio App. 9 Dist. 1989) (upholding ordinance that barred drilling in all but commercial-industrial zones).

In Van Meter v. H.F. Wilcox Oil & Gas Co., 41 P.2d 904 (Okla. 1935), the court held that the zoning authority cannot, under the guise of exceptions and variances, modify, amend, repeal, or nullify the zoning ordinance by establishing new zoning lines and creating new areas for the drilling of oil and gas wells and thereby essentially change and substantially derogate the fundamental character, intent, and true purpose of the zoning law. Its power to review in granting variations and exceptions is limited to adjusting practical difficulties and unusual emergencies which may arise in a particular case when the strict enforcement of the provisions of the ordinance would constitute an unnecessary hardship.

For a case affirming the grant of drilling variance on the ground of unnecessary hardship, see Beveridge v. Westgate Oil Co., 44 P.2d 26 (Okla. 1935) and Indian Territory Illuminating Oil Co. v. Larkins, 31 P.2d 608 (Okla. 1934).

In Shelby Operating Co. v. City of Waskom, 964 S.W.2d 75 (Tex. App.–Texarkana 1997), the court held that a statute requiring that permit applications be considered under ordinances in effect at time of filing did not preclude applying an amended version that denied drilling near buildings where the amended version was enacted after denial of the initial drilling-permit application but before the second application. The court further held that the applicant had no vested right in the granting of a drilling permit. Walton v. City of Midland, 287 S.W.3d 97 (Tex. App.–Eastland 2009).

3. Historically, local governments were the first to regulate oil and gas activity. For example, by the mid–1910s, Oklahoma City ordinances limited the density of drilling within city limits. Nevertheless, because exploration and development largely occurred in sparsely populated rural areas,[9] local land-use regulations did not greatly affect oil and gas operations. This changed dramatically in the 1980s, particularly along the Colorado Front Range and more recently in the Barnett Shale play near Forth Worth, Texas, where expanding oil and gas operations met expanding urbanization.

Regarding the effect of local land-use regulation on oil and gas operations, the fundamental legal issue is the extent to which the state conservation act and regulations preempt local regulation. Because the answer varies from state to state, the Model Oil and Gas Conservation Act provides optional bracketed language of a general nature. "The [commission] shall have exclusive authority [,subject only to any applicable local zoning and land-use regulations] * * *." Model Oil and Gas Conservation Act Alt. § 4 (Interstate Oil & Gas Compact Comm'n 2004).[10]

Preemption analysis usually differs for statutory local government and "home-rule" cities.[11] For a statutory entity, such as a township, county, local

---

9. An important exception is the Oklahoma City Field, discovered in 1928. As this field was developed, oil wells were even drilled on the grounds of the state capitol.

10. Likewise, the Model Act recognizes that other state agencies may regulate particular oil and gas activities. "Without limiting the general authority of the [commission], the [commission] has the additional exclusive authority to regulate the following [, subject only to the authority of ___ to regulate air pollution, water pollution, and water-use permits]...." Model Oil and Gas Conservation Act Alt. § 4 (Interstate Oil & Gas Compact Comm'n 2004).

11. Home-rule cities have adopted a home-rule charter for local self governance. Residents of a home-rule city may choose their own form and manner of municipal government. Home-rule cities are not subject to the Dillon doctrine, which limits a political subdivision's powers to those

district, or nonhome-rule city, the first issue is whether state has given the statutory entity authority to enact regulations. Generally, the answer is yes.

The second issue is whether the local regulations impermissibly conflict with state law. If state law fully and expressly preempts local regulation, then there is preemption—sometimes called "field preemption." However, state law is seldom as clear. Where state law is unclear, the issue becomes whether, in enacting a comprehensive regulatory law, the legislature intended to preempt local law. If not, then the question is whether the operation of particular local regulation impermissibly conflicts with the operation of state regulatory law, in which case there may be either full or only partial preemption. Some local ordinances may run afoul of so-called "conflict preemption," i.e., where a regulated party is unable to comply with both the local regulation and the related state regulation. Michael J. Wozniak, Home Court Advantage? Local Government Jurisdiction Over Oil and Gas Operations, 48 Rocky Mtn. Min. L. Inst. 12–1, 12–27 (2002)[hereafter Wozniak].

Home-rule cities have either implicit or explicit regulatory authority to protect public health, safety, and welfare. Nevertheless, most state legislatures may be partially or fully preempt that authority. Thus, if a conflict between a home-rule city ordinance and state law is at issue, then the above analysis generally begins with the second issue.

In a few states, including California and Colorado, however, the state legislature may not preempt home-rule cities from regulating matters that are purely local. See, e.g., Colo. Const. art. IX, § 9. Accordingly, in these states, preemption depends on whether the regulatory matter is purely a local concern, purely a state concern, or a mixed concern. If purely local, then the local regulation will control over state regulation. If purely state, then preemption occurs. If mixed, then the preemption issue depends upon several factors: whether statewide uniformity is necessary; whether the local regulation has extra-territorial consequence; whether state or local law has traditionally regulated the area; and whether the state constitution expressly allocates regulatory authority over the matter. Wozniak at 12–27 and 12–28. Although oil and gas regulation is certainly not a purely local concern, no state has completely preempted local regulation of oil and gas operations.

In the context of oil and gas operations, Colorado courts have frequently dealt with the issue of preemption of local land-use regulations. See, e.g, Board of County Comm'rs v. Bowen/Edwards Assoc., 830 P.2d 1045 (Colo. 1992) (finding that the issue of operational conflicts between state and local regulations is a case-by-case inquiry); Board of County Comm'rs v. Colorado Oil and Gas Conservation Commission, 81 P.3d 1119 (Col. Ct. App. 2003) (invalidating a state conservation regulation that would have preempted all local regulation of drilling); Oborne v. Board of County Comm'rs, 764 P.2d 397 (Colo.App. 1988) (preempting county regulations that operationally conflicted with state regulations governing well drilling); Town of Frederick v. North American Resources Co., 60 P.3d 758 (Colo. Ct. App. 2002) (upholding some local regulations of oil and gas drilling operations but finding partial preemption of others due to operational conflict); Voss v. Lundvall Bros., Inc.,

---

expressly granted by the state. See Clinton v. Cedar Rapids & Missouri River R.R., 24 Iowa 455 (1868).

830 P.2d 1061 (Colo. 1992) (finding that, in light of state interest, a home-rule city may not completely bar oil and gas operations).

Because homeowners may view oil and gas operations as undesirable in their neighborhoods, city and other local-government officials may be politically pressured to enact zoning ordinances intended to discourage, if not thwart, oil and gas development. Many cases illustrate that zoning ordinances relating to public health, safety, and welfare may lawfully restrict oil and gas operations. See, e.g., Wood v. City Planning Comm'n, 130 Cal.App.2d 356, 279 P.2d 95 (1955) and Beveridge v. Harper & Turner Oil Trust, 168 Okla. 609, 35 P.2d 435 (Okla. 1934), overruled on other grounds, Oklahoma City v. Harris, 191 Okla. 125, 126 P.2d 988 (1941). However, courts may take a dimmer view of ordinances that purport to prohibit drilling completely. See, e.g., Clouser v. City of Norman, 393 P.2d 827 (Okla. 1964) and Indian Territory Illuminating Oil Co. v. Larkins, 31 P.2d 608 (Okla. 1934). Unfortunately, the outcome of particular disputes is not easy to predict, and depends upon whether the particular jurists choose to take a "hard look" or a "soft glance" at the regulation. Bruce M. Kramer, Local Regulation of Oil and Gas Operations: Don't All Homeowners Want a Pumpjack in Their Backyard, Eugene Kuntz Conference on Oil and Gas Law and Policy 7–8 (2004).

Particular cases may turn on related issues—e.g., whether the operator had a "vested right" to drill before a restrictive ordinance was enacted or whether the operator had already drilled a well that became a legally protected "nonconforming use" after a restrictive ordinance was enacted. Kramer at 8–10. Regarding these issues, the dispute may arise or be revisited when the operator seeks a "variance" so that an existing operation may be expanded or modified.

For further discussion, in addition to the previously cited authority, see generally, Bruce M. Kramer, Drilling in the Cities and Towns: Rights and Obligations of Lessees, Royalty Owners, and Surface Owners in an Urban Environment, Part I, 23 Pet. Acct'g & Fin'l Mgt. J 58 (Spring 2004) and Part II, 23 Pet. Acct'g & Fin'l Mgt. J. 39 (Summer 2004); Jeffrey R. Fiske & Ann E. Lane, Urbanization of the Oil Patch: What Happens When They Pave Paradise and Put in a Parking Lot?, 49 Rocky Mtn. Min. L. Inst. 15–1 (2003); and Bruce M. Kramer, The Pit and the Pendulum: Local Government Regulation of Oil and Gas Activities Returns From the Grave, 50 Inst. on Oil & Gas L. & Tax'n 4–1 (1999).

4. Just as the state may act to preempt local law, the federal government may act to preempt state law. Federal law may preempt the field or preempt state law to the extent state law conflicts with federal law. Federal preemption of state oil and gas conservation law regarding federal and Indian lands is discussed in Chapter 6, Section A.1(e). Preemption of state environmental law related to oil and gas operations is discussed in Chapter 7. Preemption of state authority to regulate underground gas storage was discussed in Chapter 1. Preemption of state authority to regulate the marketing of natural gas is addressed briefly in this chapter.

5. If government regulation, whether federal, state, or local, effectively deprives a property interest of all of its economic value or utility, then there will be a taking, requiring compensation. Lucas v. South Carolina Coastal

Council, 505 U.S. 1003 (1992). Most regulations do not constitute a total taking, in which case compensation is due only if the owner's investment and reasonable intended use is outweighed by the government's interest in protecting public health, safety, and welfare. Penn Central Transportation Co. v. City of New York, 438 U.S. 104 (1978). See generally, Bruce M. Kramer, Local Regulation of Oil and Gas Operations: Don't All Homeowners Want a Pumpjack in Their Backyard, Eugene Kuntz Conference on Oil and Gas Law and Policy 17–32 (2004). Generally, when the dispute falls into this latter category and the regulation seems reasonable, courts tend to balance the scale in favor of the regulation and thus no taking.

Because mineral rights are often severed from surface rights, a government may elect to exercise its power of eminent domain to acquire only the surface for a public use but not the mineral rights. In these circumstances, the public-use activity on the surface could interfere with the mineral owner's practical ability to exploit the minerals in the future, causing the mineral owner to file an inverse-condemnation action. Absent proof that the enjoyment of known minerals is impossible, courts have not required the government to acquire the mineral interest. See, e.g., City of Abilene v. Burk Royalty, 470 S.W.2d 643 (Tex. 1971) and Tarrant County Water Control and Improvement District v. Haupt, Inc., 854 S.W.2d 909 (Tex. 1993). See generally, Kramer at 32–34.

6.   Comprehensive oil and gas conservation acts address exploration, drilling, well completion, well plugging, production, marketing, unit operations, some end uses, and environmental protection. This chapter discusses all of these topics, but environmental regulation is addressed in greater detail in Chapter 5.

2. REGULATING EXPLORATION, DRILLING, WELL COMPLETION & PLUGGING

(a) Exploration and Well Permitting

Historically, exploration activities, including geophysical (seismic) exploration, were not regulated. Today, however, either the state conservation agency or local governments or both may require a permit to engage in geophysical exploration. This regulation has largely arisen from concerns about geophysical trespass from complaints by surface owners about sloppy geophysical contractors who may leave debris behind or fail to reclaim shot holes. Thus, the regulations, which may be either state or local, typically address the need to notify affected surface owners, the cleanup of work sites, and the reclamation of shot holes. Although concerns have been raised about possible environmental harm resulting from geophysical operations, these concerns are largely unproved, and seismic operations seem preferable, both from environmental and economic standpoints, to the random drilling of wildcat wells.

Under the rule of capture, a landowner could drill oil or gas wells at will. Today, the conservation acts of most states prohibit the drilling of an oil or gas well without a permit.[12] A drilling permit specifies the location of the well, the maximum depth of the well, and the targeted geological formations. In many states, the operator must post a bond to assure the proper *plugging and abandonment* of the well.[13]

A holder of a permit must drill the well in strict compliance with regulations aimed at preventing waste. To avoid groundwater pollution and to prevent the hole from caving in, the operator must install steel pipe called *surface casing* from the surface to below the deepest known fresh or potable water supply.[14] The operator may be required to install additional strings of casing to prevent the escape of oil and gas from one stratum to another or to prevent undesirable fluids or gases from polluting an oil and gas reservoir or potable groundwater. Regulations commonly require the operator to install high-pressure valves and fittings to prevent a blow out of the well.[15]

During drilling, the operator must keep the well site clear of debris to prevent fires and must contain all drill cuttings, drilling mud, and drilling wastes from polluting the surface and subsurface.[16] During completion as a well in being completed, completing a producing well, the operator must install and test *flow string*[17] (*tubing* or *production casing*) to facilitate production and to control reservoir pressures.

Upon *completion* or upon *plugging and abandoning* a well, the operator must file a report with the conservation agency, indicating that the well is a producer of oil or gas, or both, or a dry-hole. The operator may have to include test data on the reservoir, a core sample from the targeted formation, and indicate whether the well is flowing or on pump.

An operator may complete a well to produce from more than one formation. The conservation agency must specifically approve a *dual-* or *multiple-completion*. Ordinarily, the operator must install additional tubing to prevent the commingling of the oil and gas from the different strata and must separately meter the production from each stratum.[18]

Conservation regulations generally require vertical drilling. Due to well-location rules and trespass concerns, the operator must obtain special permission to deviate from vertical—*i.e.*, to drill a *directional* or *horizontal well*.[19] A conservation agency most commonly issues a directional-well permit for topographical or environmental reasons and a horizontal-well

---

12. A sample drilling permit form is included in the forms manual accompanying this casebook.

13. See, e.g., N.D.Admin.Code § 43–02–03–15.

14. See e.g., Tex.R.R.Comm'n, 16 Tex.Admin.Code § 3.13.

15. See, e.g., N.D.Admin.Code § 43–02–03–23.

16. See,e.g., Lone Star Salt Water Disposal Co. v. Railroad Comm'n, 800 S.W.2d 924 (Tex. App., no writ).

17. *Flow string* is the casing or tubing that is perforated in the producing zone and through which the oil flows to the surface. Norman J. Hyne, Dictionary of Petroleum Exploration, Drilling & Production (PennWell 1991).

18. See, e.g., Okla.Admin.Code § 52–3–220 and Tex.R.R.Comm'n, 16 Tex.Admin.Code § 3.6.

19. See, e.g., N.D.Admin.Code § 43–02–03–25.

permit to increase the ultimate recovery of oil. Horizontal drilling has increased both the rate and volume of recoveries in certain vertically fractured reservoirs, because the well bore laterally penetrates the reservoir, thereby intersecting the vertical fractures, horizontal drilling has also increased recoveries from tight formations by facilitating more effective use of hydraulic fracturing to increase permeability.[20] Deviation surveys or *measurement while drilling* (MWD) equipment can measure the direction and distance of a directional or horizontal well bore.

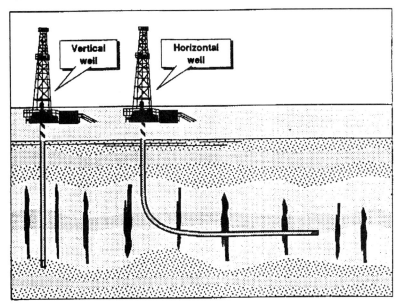

In a vertically fractured reservoir, a vertical well may result in a dry hole or may recover only a small amount of oil. On the other hand, a horizontal well is capable of intersecting several vertical fractures, thereby increasing oil recovery. The cost of drilling a horizontal well, however, greatly exceeds the cost of drilling a vertical well. Diagram by Don Cook, courtesy of the Fort Worth Star Telegram.

Historically, conservation agencies protected only correlative rights and prevented waste, primarily the waste of oil or money. Today, conservation agencies also protect the environment.[21] Thus, a host of regulations govern both drilling and production operations to prevent pollution, waste, and other avoidable harm to the environment.

---

20. An operator initially commences a directional or horizontal well by using special directional drilling equipment to drill vertically and deviating the well downhole.

21. For example, in Colorado, the conservation agency "may regulate ... [o]il and gas operations so as to prevent and mitigate significant adverse environmental impacts on any air, water, soil, or biological resource...." Colo. Rev. Stat. Ann. § 34–60–106(2)(d). In Michigan, the conservation agency must balance the environmental harm that may occur if a drilling permit is issued against the underground waste of oil if the permit is denied. See Michigan Oil Co. v. Natural Resources Comm'n, 276 N.W.2d 141 (Mich.1979) (drilling permit denied due to impact on wildlife). See also Gulf Oil Corp. v. Wyoming Oil & Gas Conservation Comm'n, 693 P.2d 227 (Wyo.1985) (affirming commission order conditioning approval of drilling permit on relocation of access road to lessen surface impacts.) See generally Michael J. Wozniak, Expanding Authority of Oil and Gas Conservation Commissions, 51 Rocky Mtn. Min. L. Inst. 15–1 (2006).

For example, upon completion of a well as a dry hole or after a well has produced hydrocarbons for its economic life, the operator must properly *plug and abandon* the well and reclaim the well site. If a well is improperly plugged, then oil and brine may rise in the well bore, corrode the surface casing, invade fresh-water supplies, and pollute soils and subsoils. Thus, an operator must plug a well bore—commonly with cement—in accordance with conservation rules.[22]

Civil penalties, bonds, and special funds provide revenue for plugging wells if an operator or other working interest owners are financially unable to pay plugging costs. Environmental regulation of oil and gas drilling and production is further addressed in Chapter 7.

(b) Well Spacing and Density

The most significant limitations on drilling are regulations that govern *well distance and density*. These regulations greatly modify the rule of capture by limiting the number and location of wells that may be drilled into a reservoir.[23] Spacing rules mandate minimum distances between wells and minimum distances between wells and spacing-unit boundary lines.[24] While a statewide spacing rule provides for default minimum distances, special field-wide spacing orders may govern known oil or gas reservoirs. In addition to regulating distances, most conservation agencies regulate well density through the establishment of *spacing units* (or *drilling units*). The Model Conservation Act authorizes the conservation agency to regulate "the spacing and location of wells, including the authority to establish spacing units." Model Oil and Gas Conservation Act § 7 (Interstate Oil & Gas Compact Comm'n 2004).

MODEL OIL AND GAS CONSERVATION ACT (INTERSTATE OIL & GAS COMPACT COMM'N 2004)

Section 10. WELL SPACING.

(a) * * * [After] discovery of oil or gas, the [commission], to prevent waste and to protect correlative rights, shall issue an order establishing a field and reservoir, providing for allowable production, and providing for uniform well spacing units, which may be established in accordance with applicable statewide spacing rules. Except as otherwise provided in subsection (b), and in light of the information

22. See, e.g., Tex.R.R.Comm'n, 16 Tex.Admin.Code § 3.14.

23. The rule of capture continues to govern to the extent that it has not been limited by conservation law. See INB Land & Cattle Co. v. Kerr–McGee Rocky Mountain Corporation, 190 P.3d 806 (Col. App. 2008).

24. For example, in Texas a well must ordinarily be located at least 467 feet from the property line and 1200 feet from any well completed in, or drilled to, the same reservoir on the same tract. Tex.R.R.Comm'n, 16 Tex.Admin.Code § 3.37. In many states, the minimum distance between wells is not limited to wells on the same tract. Minimum distances for statewide spacing regulations vary from state to state and may vary with the depth of the well.

available to the [commission] at the time of an order establishing spacing units for a reservoir, a spacing unit must consist of the maximum area of a reservoir that may be efficiently and economically drained by one well, and an order establishing spacing units for a reservoir must cover lands determined or reasonably believed to be underlain by that reservoir.

(b) If reasonably necessary to prevent waste or to protect correlative rights, the [commission] may establish a spacing unit that is larger or smaller than the uniform spacing units for a reservoir, but that larger or smaller spacing unit must produce in proportion to the size of the uniform units established for that reservoir.

(c) * * *

(d) * * *

(e) An order establishing spacing rules may be modified by the [commission] from time to time to prevent waste or to protect correlative rights, including the addition of lands determined to be underlain by the reservoir or to the exclusion of lands determined not to be underlain by the reservoir. The [commission], if reasonably necessary to prevent waste or to protect correlative rights, may change the size or shape of one or more spacing units or permit the drilling of additional wells on a reasonably uniform spacing pattern.

(f) Unless specifically authorized by the [commission], upon completion of a producing well not subject to applicable spacing rules, additional wells may not be commenced for production from that reservoir until an order establishing spacing rules is adopted. The [commission] shall provide for the retroactivity of an initial order establishing spacing rules for a reservoir to the date that notice of a hearing to establish spacing units for the reservoir was issued, but may provide for retroactivity to the date of first production for the discovery well for that reservoir.

(g) The [commission] may establish horizontal well spacing units for horizontal drilling and development of a common source of supply. A horizontal well is an oil or gas well drilled, completed or recompleted in a manner in which the horizontal component of the completion interval in the geological formation exceeds the vertical component in the geological formation and which horizontal component extends a minimum of [one hundred fifty (150) feet] into the formation. A horizontal well spacing unit may be established for a common source of supply for which there are already established non-horizontal well spacing units. A horizontal well spacing unit may include within the boundaries thereof more than one existing non-horizontal well spacing unit for the common source of supply. A horizontal well spacing unit may exist concurrently with producing non-horizontal well spacing units; however, where there are no producing non-horizontal well spacing units, a horizontal well spacing unit shall supersede existing non-developed non-horizontal well spacing units for the duration of the horizontal well spacing unit.

* * *

NOTES

1.   A spacing unit initially means that only a single well may be drilled in the unit to produce from a *common reservoir* or (*common source of supply*). In a minority of states, the conservation agency sets production limits (*allowables*)[25] for spacing units, which removes the incentive to drill more than one well if that well is capable of producing the full allowable. In either case, however, as production matures, the agency may authorize the drilling of additional *infill* (or *increased density*) wells if evidence indicates that additional drilling is economical and will result in greater hydrocarbon recovery.

2.   The purpose of spacing is to prevent surface, underground, and economic waste[26] and to protect correlative rights. Spacing prevents *surface waste* because fewer wells will occupy the surface, thereby reducing surface impacts as well as reducing the number of valves, fittings, pipes, storage tanks, and other leakage-prone components. Spacing prevents *underground waste* because fewer wells more efficiently use and conserve the natural reservoir energy, thereby more effectively draining hydrocarbons from the reservoir. Spacing prevents *economic waste* by reducing the number of wells, thereby saving the costs associated with drilling wells not needed to drain the reservoir.[27] Spacing *protects correlative rights* by giving working interest owners the opportunity to recover their fair share by drilling wells in accordance with a uniform drilling pattern and density and by requiring minimum distances between wells and property lines.[28]

----

25.   An allowable is the maximum amount of oil or gas that a well, parcel, field, or all fields within a state are allowed to produce over a given period, e.g., daily or monthly. For example, a well allowable might be set as 400 barrels a day for a period of 25 days in each calendar month. Norman J. Hyne, Dictionary of Petroleum Exploration, Drilling, and Production (PennWell 1991).

26.   The Model Conservation Act defines waste as:

(A) the inefficient, excessive, or improper use of reservoir energy or unnecessary dissipation of reservoir energy;

(B) the inefficient storing of oil or gas;

(C) the locating, drilling, equipping, operating, or producing of an oil or gas well in a manner that causes or tends to cause a reduction in the quantity of oil or gas ultimately recoverable from a reservoir under prudent and proper operations, the drilling of unnecessary wells, or the loss or destruction of oil or gas either at the surface or below the surface;

(D) the production of oil or gas in excess of pipeline, marketing, or storage capacities, in excess of reasonable market demand, in excess of the amount reasonably required for properly drilling, completing, testing, or operating a well or other facilities for recovering, processing, or transporting oil, gas, or by-products, or in excess of the amount otherwise utilized on the acreage from which the oil or gas is produced; or

(E) other dissipation, production, or use of oil or gas underground or above ground, or in storage, that is careless, needless, or without valuable result.

Model Oil and Gas Conservation Act § 1 (24)(Interstate Oil & Gas Compact Comm'n 2004).

27.   One goal of spacing is to prevent the drilling of *unnecessary wells*: wells that are not needed to drain the reservoir effectively and efficiently. Under the rule of capture, many wells were drilled solely for the purpose of quickly capturing oil to prevent drainage to neighboring tracts.

28.   For further discussion, see generally Kramer & Martin § 5.02 and Kuntz §§ 77.2, 77.3.

LARSEN v. OIL & GAS CONSERVATION COMMISSION

569 P.2d 87 (Wyo.1977).

ROSE, JUSTICE.

This is an appeal from a judgment of the district court affirming an order entered by the Wyoming Oil and Gas Conservation Commission which established eighty-acre drilling units in the North Rainbow Ranch Field, Campbell County, Wyoming. These units were to run horizontally or east-west, except for those located in the SW 1/4 of Section 24, which were to run vertically or north-south. At the conclusion of this opinion is a plat, marked Appendix "A," indicating the area with which we are concerned, with the wells located thereon. Appellants are owners of royalty and overriding royalty interests under leases covering the W 1/2 SE 1/4, the SE 1/4 SE 1/4, the SW 1/4 NE 1/4 and the SW 1/4 of Section 24. Appellee, Apache Exploration Corporation, is the owner of working interests in, and operator of, all wells drilled in the Minnelusa formation within the spaced area. The remaining appellees are owners of working interests under United States oil and gas leases covering the NE 1/4 SE 1/4 and other portions of Section 24.

On December 21, 1972, Apache filed an application with the Commission seeking to establish eighty-acre drilling units for the production of hydrocarbons from the Minnelusa formation. The application was based on the discovery of oil and associated hydrocarbons in the NW 1/4 NE 1/4 of Section 24. Without notice to the appellants, a hearing on the application was conducted before the Commission on January 9, 1973. On January 18, 1973, the Commission entered an order which established eighty-acre drilling units and provided that wells would be permitted only in the center of the SE 1/4 and the center of the NW 1/4 of each quarter section. This order was made temporary for a period of ninety days because the Commission found that the need for eighty-acre spacing was not yet conclusive. Although not approved by the United States Geological Survey until May 7, 1973, the appellees entered into communitization[1] agreements covering the NE 1/4 and the N 1/2 SE 1/4 of Section 24, which were effective February 1, 1973. During February, 1973, producing wells were completed in the S 1/2 NE 1/4 and the S 1/2 NW 1/4 of Section 24, and a dry hole was encountered in the W 1/2 SW 1/4. On April 1, 1973, a producing well was completed in the NW 1/4 SE 1/4. It is this well which is at the center of the present controversy. On its own motion, the Commission called a hearing to review its original order, which was conducted on April 10, 1973. Again, appellants were not personally notified of the hearing, but they did appear to object to a continuation of the prior order, especially as it related to the horizontal drilling units in the SE 1/4 of Section 24. Appellants' objection to the spacing-unit direction was premised on a belief that the two forty-acre tracts comprising the N

---

1. [Editors' Note] *Communitization* is similar to *pooling*; the term is most commonly used to describe the pooling of federal tracts or of federal and private tracts.

1/2 SE 1/4 of Section 24 did not contribute equally to the well located in the NW 1/4 SE 1/4. On April 23, 1973, the Commission affirmed its previous order. Pursuant to an application made by Apache, the Commission force pooled all interests in the N 1/2 SE 1/4 of Section 24.

The appellants' petition for review of the April 23 order culminated in a judgment, entered by the district court on January 16, 1974, which declared the Commission's orders of January 18 and April 23, 1973, to be void and of no further force or effect, and remanded the matter to the Commission for rehearing, with the direction that all evidence in existence at the time of the new hearing should be considered. Subsequently, appellees Aquarius and Double U filed their application for a reestablishment and continuation of the drilling units referred to previously. On the basis of this application and its own motion, the Commission held another hearing on July 16 and 19, 1974, at which time all interested parties presented evidence and argument. Some of the evidence presented at this hearing will be discussed in the course of this opinion. On August 13, 1974, the Commission entered findings of fact and conclusions of law, which in effect continued the previously-established drilling and spacing units. Appellants again filed a petition for review of the Commission's decision. On June 23, 1975, the district court entered its order summarily affirming the decision. The matter is now before this court for disposition.

On appeal, appellants raise essentially four issues, which are stated as follows:

I.

The Commission acted without [sic] and in excess of its powers when it ordered a drilling and spacing unit established in the N 1/2 of the SE 1/4 of Section 24 as such order does not protect the correlative rights of all the property owners and does not prevent or assist in the prevention of waste.

[The other three issues are omitted]

* * *

With respect to the first issue, appellants contend that the Commission's Conclusion of Law No. 8 is not supported by findings of underlying or basic facts. Conclusion of Law No. 8 states:

Eighty (80) acre drilling and spacing units will protect correlative rights of each owner (as that term is defined by Sec. 30–216(e), [sic] [should be § 30–216(i)] Wyoming Statutes 1957) in the field and will prevent or assist in preventing the various types of waste defined in the Oil and Gas Conservation Act.

We agree with appellants' observation and, therefore, will remand the case for further findings of fact; and inasmuch as the case is not yet ripe for review, we will not reach the remaining issues.

The authority of the Commission to establish drilling and spacing units is set forth in § 30–221(a), W.S.1957, (1967, 1975 Cum.Supp.), which states:

When required, to protect correlative rights or, to prevent or to assist in preventing any of the various types of *waste* of oil or gas prohibited by this act [§§ 30–216 to 30–231], or by any statute of this state, the commission, upon its own motion or on a proper application of an interested party, but after notice and hearing as herein provided shall have the power to establish drilling units of specified and approximately uniform size covering any pool. [Emphasis supplied]

The statutory language mandates that before a drilling unit can be established, the Commission must first find that such a unit is necessary to protect correlative rights or to prevent waste. After this initial determination is reached, the Commission must also determine the acreage to be embraced within each unit and the shape thereof—based on evidence adduced at the hearing—but each unit "shall not be smaller than the maximum area that can be efficiently drained by one well." § 30–221(b), W.S.1957, (1967).

* * *

Throughout these proceedings, appellants have been concerned about the direction of the drilling units established in the SE 1/4 of Section 24. They contended below, and contend here, that the horizontal spacing direction established by the Commission deprives them of their correlative rights in oil and associated hydrocarbons purported to exist in the SW 1/4 SE 1/4 of Section 24. Their contention is premised, as previously mentioned, on a belief that substantial amounts of oil are being drained from the SW 1/4 SE 1/4 by the well located in the NW 1/4 SE 1/4, and that little or no oil is contributed by the government forty-acre tract in the NE 1/4 SE 1/4. Appellants' argument is one which is rooted in the theory of protecting correlative rights, but we find that the Commission's findings of fact make absolutely no mention of appellants' correlative rights. More specifically, such findings make no reference to the amount of recoverable oil under any of the tracts in the SE 1/4, or any other portion of Section 24. Additionally, the findings do not indicate the amount of oil that can be recovered *without waste,* as that phrase is defined by the statutes. The only finding which even approaches a consideration of these factors is Finding of Fact No. 19, which states:

19. The Minnelusa "A" sand in said field has produced 324,298 barrels of oil up to May 31, 1974: 229,599 barrels from the Sherard 1–24 well in the N–SE 1/4 [sic] [should be N 1/2 SE 1/4] of Sec. 24; 58,586 barrels from the Carter 1–A in the S 1/2 NW 1/2 of Section 24; 9400 barrels from the Peterson 1–24 well in the S 1/2 NE 1/4 of Section 24; and 26,713 barrels from the Wolff 1–24 well in the N 1/2 NE 1/4 of Section 24. Primary production to the economic limit of all Minnelusa "A" sand wells in the field will be approximately 1.1

million barrels of oil representing ten (10) to fourteen (14) percent of the "A" sand oil in place in the pool.

From this finding we know the approximate amount of oil that can be economically recovered from the pool, and can surmise that the greatest production comes from the well located in the NW 1/4 SE 1/4 of Section 24. In addition, the Commission has found (1) that all of Section 24 is underlain by a reservoir containing a common accumulation of oil or gas, or both; (2) that there is no oil-water contact in any of the wells drilled in the Minnelusa formation "A" zone; and (3) that when the NW 1/4 SE 1/4 well was tested the reservoir pressure declined, indicating communication between wells. Taking into account these determinations, it is, nevertheless, clear to this court that the Commission has wholly failed to make the requisite findings of fact required by law which would support its conclusion that the correlative rights of all interested parties will be protected by establishing eighty-acre spacing units along an East–West direction in the SE 1/4 of Section 24.

At a minimum, in order to determine the extent of the correlative rights in question, the Commission must establish: (1) the amount of recoverable oil in the pool; (2) the amount of recoverable oil under the various tracts; (3) the proportion that #1 bears to #2; and (4) the amount of oil that can be recovered without waste. See Continental Oil Co. v. Oil Conservation Commission, 70 N.M. 310, 373 P.2d 809. These findings were not made in this case. Without such findings, a reviewing court has no way to determine whether the owner of each property has been afforded the opportunity to produce without waste, so far as it is reasonably practicable, his *just and equitable share* of the oil in the pool (§ 30–216(i)). In other words, it cannot determine whether correlative rights are being protected. As the court said in the *Continental Oil* case:

> * * * That the extent of the correlative rights must be determined before the commission can act to protect them is manifest.

We will, therefore, require that the Commission make such findings, insofar as it is reasonably practicable to do so. Given the facts available, including the extent of drilling and production in Section 24 at the time of the hearing, we are unable to understand the administrative agency's failure to discharge these fact-finding obligations in this case.

Although we are unable to reach the merits of this case for reasons set out above, we, nevertheless, consider it advisable, in light of the fact that the matter must be remanded for further decision-making, to comment concerning legal standards which are apparently being misinterpreted or misapplied by the Commission. The findings of fact and conclusions of law relative to the eighty-acre spacing resolution carry with them strong overtones of a misunderstanding or misapplication on the part of the Commission of an important facet of the term "waste" as employed by the statute. The Commission's Conclusion of Law No. 8 provides that eighty-acre drilling units "will prevent or assist in preventing the various types of waste defined in the Oil and Gas Conservation Act." Concerning the word "waste," we call attention to Conclusion of Law No. 9, which says:

> The area herein spaced is fully developed and further wells are unnecessary to recover the oil in the Minnelusa 'A' sand pool. The drilling of additional wells in said pool would constitute *economic* and physical *waste*. [Emphasis supplied]

It would appear, then, that the Commission considers "economic waste" to be contemplated by the statutory definition of "waste" under § 30–216(a), supra. If this is indeed the Commission's position, and its decisions are being made with an economic-waste factor ground into its ultimate conclusions, we find it to be erroneous in light of the legislative history which stands behind this provision of the statute. As originally introduced on January 25, 1951, this Section 15 of H.B. No. 130 provided:

> (a) The term "waste" in addition to its ordinary meaning, shall include: * * * (5) *the drilling of wells not reasonably necessary to effect an economic maximum ultimate recovery of oil or gas from a pool:* * * * *the drilling of unnecessary wells creates waste,* such as wells create fire and other hazards conducive to waste, *and unnecessarily increase production costs and thus also unnecessarily increase the costs of products to the consumer.* [Emphasis supplied]

This language was rejected by the legislature and is not contained in the present § 30–216(a), supra. The rejection stands for the proposition that the legislature did not want economic matters considered. See 2A Sutherland, Statutory Construction, § 48.04 (4th ed.1975). We could find no other reference to economic matters in the Oil and Gas Conservation Act. As a result, when the Commission makes an ultimate finding concerning waste, in this and similar considerations, it should do so only on the basis of the various types of waste enumerated in § 30–216(a), supra.[2]

* * *

For the reasons stated, the judgment of the district court is reversed with instructions to enter a judgment vacating the order of the Commission and remanding the proceeding to the Commission for further consideration consistent with this opinion.

Reversed with instructions.

See "Appendix A" on next page.

---

2. When utilizing the term "economic waste," we do so in the same context used in the Memorandum Opinion of Special Assistant Attorney General Sutton at page 403, where he says in a footnote on that page:

> "In this opinion, when referring to 'economics' the reference relates to the economic position of oil and gas producers and their internal financial ability or inability to drill all of the well locations required by any given spacing order. Or stated differently, whether well spacing must be determined by the financial ability of producers to drill wells or by principles of conservation as defined by the conservation act."

APPENDIX "A"

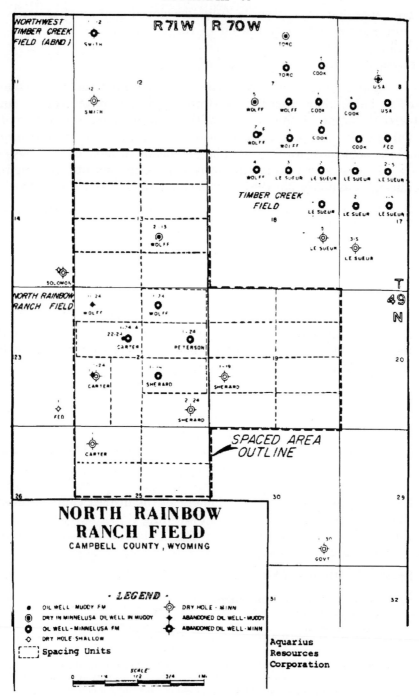

NORTH RAINBOW RANCH FIELD

CAMPBELL COUNTY, WYOMING

- LEGEND -

Spacing Units

Aquarius
Resources
Corporation

NOTES

1. *Larsen* is useful as a summary of the evidence ideally needed to establish special field-wide spacing rules for an established field. The Wyoming Supreme Court distinguished *Larsen* in Anschutz Corporation v. Wyoming Oil and Gas Conservation Commission, 923 P.2d 751 (Wyo.1996). In *Anschutz*, the court held that a temporary spacing order issued to govern the initial development of wildcat acreage was lawful even though the agency knew little about the geology of the area and based its order on information concerning oil fields six to ten miles away that the agency found to be geologically analogous. Noting the "reasonably practicable" phrase in *Larsen*, the court in *Anschutz* stated: "We are ill-equipped to determine whether the Commission correctly analyzed and weighed the evidence presented to it. However, we are equipped to examine the record and recognize that the experts * * * testified that the only way to obtain accurate information * * * is to drill a well." Id. at 757.

2. Many conservation acts, including the model act, expressly allow the conservation agency to consider economic waste before issuing orders. For example, Oklahoma has consistently recognized the importance of preventing economic waste. Thus, testimony about drilling economics is relevant in determining the appropriate size of a spacing unit, but preventing economic waste must also be balanced against other factors, including the correlative rights of affected interest owners. In Brooks v. LPCX Corp., 587 P.2d 1358 (Okla.1978), LPCX applied for an order establishing 160–acre spacing units in two sections of land for the production of gas and gas condensate from the Red Fork formation. The Corporation Commission granted the application over the protest of Brooks, who also had production from the Red Fork formation from lands that were subject to 640–acre spacing and located about two miles from the acreage of LPCX. On appeal, Brooks cited expert testimony that one well would adequately drain gas from the Red Fork formation for about a 1/2–mile radius around the well.[29] Brooks argued that, if 160–acre spacing were permitted on the LPCX acreage, interest owners in surrounding property subject to 640–acre spacing would have to seek permission to drill additional wells "to recover their fair share of the gas in the same common source of supply as fast as the owners in the 160–acre spacing units." 587 P.2d at 1359. The court rejected this argument and affirmed the commission's order:

> This argument might be more persuasive if only the economic interests of the working interest owners were involved; however, the economic interests of the royalty owners must also be considered. Sec. 86.1 defines "Common Source of Supply" as " * * * that area which *is underlaid* or

---

29. Absent evidence to the contrary, engineers will presume that drainage will be radial to a well. In other words, drainage will occur from within the radius of an estimated circle, the center of which is the well bore. Because the true nature of a reservoir is rarely homogeneous, the concept of radial drainage is largely an engineering fiction; however, the concept is a useful tool in determining appropriate spacing patterns for a field.

which, from geological or other scientific data, or from drilling operations, or other evidence *appears to be underlaid,* by a common accumulation of oil or gas or both * * * "(emphasis added). Under Sec. 87.1(a), the Commission is authorized to establish spacing units " * * * of approximately uniform size and shape covering any common source of supply, or prospective common source of supply * * * ". For these reasons, it was necessary for the Commission to consider the question of which portions of the area concerned (Sec. 4 and the East Half of Sec. 33, immediately adjoining it on the north) were underlaid by the Red Fork Formation.

On this question we find testimony by an expert witness, the gist of which is summarized on a map prepared by him as an exhibit, to the effect that, as it runs through this portion of Kingfisher County, the Red Fork Formation is " * * * nothing but a river channel delineated by the lines on the exhibit that look about a quarter of a mile wide; the productive limits are probably somewhat less, maybe a thousand feet". The exhibit shows that the formation runs generally from the northeast to the southwest through this portion of Kingfisher County, in a slightly meandering way.

* * *

The exact delineation of an underground channel such as the Red Fork Formation is admittedly difficult and a proper subject for expert testimony. In the first paragraph of Sec. 87.1(b)(1), the factors to be considered by the Commission in establishing a spacing unit are listed. The first one is "The lands embraced in the actual or prospective common source of supply" (meaning as we have seen, the lands *underlaid* by the producing formation). All factors listed are subject to the requirement in the same paragraph, that " * * * due and relative allowance for the correlative rights and obligations of the producers *and royalty owners* interested therein" (emphasis supplied) be made. The expert witness for the applicant-appellee was of the view that the southeast quarter of Section 4 is not underlaid by the Red Fork Formation, merely touching the edge of it at the northwest corner. If this is correct, a 640–acre spacing unit for Sec. 4 would have been unfair to the royalty owners in the other three quarter sections, because they would have had to share the royalty payments with owners of royalty in the southeast quarter section. On the other hand, under the 160–acre spacing units established by the Commission, if a producing well is drilled on the southeast quarter, the payments will be made to the royalty owners properly entitled thereto.

* * *

Id. at 1359–60.

3.   In Calvert Drilling Co. v. Corporation Comm'n, 589 P.2d 1064 (Okla. 1979), the Corporation Commission established two 320–acre spacing units on the edge of an existing field. Some evidence indicated that only about 75 percent of the new unit areas would produce oil and gas. No hard evidence supported the potential productivity of the remaining unit area. The Oklahoma Supreme Court addressed whether a spacing unit could only overlie those portions of a formation producing of oil and gas:

The appellant advances Panhandle Eastern Pipe Line Co. v. Corporation Comm'n, 285 P.2d 847 (Okla.1955) for our consideration as authority for reversing Order No. 129314 here, stating this Court said therein that the Commission has no power to include land not overlying the common source of supply in a drilling and spacing unit. * * *

* * * In *Panhandle,* supra, we note the following discussion pertaining to acreage subject to a spacing order which is material to the issues before us:

* * * "Only so much of a common source of supply as has been defined and determined to be productive of oil and gas by actual drilling operations may be so included within the unit area." [Okla.Stat.Ann. tit. 52, § 287.4 (West 1951).] No provision requiring a common source of supply to be exactly defined by drilling operations before a well-spacing or pooling order may be entered with reference to it, has yet been enacted by our Legislature. Perhaps, until some means other than drilling is devised to conclusively ascertain productivity, such a statutory provision would be desirable *as more certainly precluding the owner whose interest may not be underlain* by the spacing area's common source of supply, *or the productive part of the producing sand* or structure, *from participating in its production.* But this might, in many instances, defeat the purposes of well-spacing and pooling. Our Legislature has apparently thus far been persuaded that chancing the possibility of some owners receiving benefits, to which subsequent explorations indicate they have not been entitled, is preferable to such a result. As the matter now stands, the lesser hazard is tolerated in preference to the greater hazard to the greater number of owners, and to the State in the dissipation of its natural resources by excessive drilling. [Emphasis added]

* * *

In order to secure a reversal of the spacing order on the grounds the Commission had no authority to space land not overlying the common source, the appellant must preclude the existence of a present or prospective common source.

Here the experts agreed that only further drilling on the east half of the section would determine the configuration of the prospective common source and the record confirms the presence of the established common source over 75% of the requested spacing unit. Those facts are substantial evidence supporting the extension of the spacing units to the newly discovered common source, and areas constituting the prospective common source spaced in this order.

The Commission's Order No. 129314 is affirmed.

589 P.2d at 1067–69. As a practical matter, will further drilling occur that more accurately defines the limits of the reservoir?

4. At what stage in the development of a reservoir should a conservation agency consider the need for special field-wide spacing? Some development is necessary to arrive at the proper spacing for an oil and gas pool. A period of unregulated development under the rule of capture or regulated development under a statewide-spacing rule may defeat the purpose of spacing. Several states, including New Mexico, North Dakota, and Utah, address this dilemma

by following a three-step process. First, a statewide-spacing rule governs the drilling of wildcat wells (wells drilled in previously unproven and unproductive areas or pools). Second, upon a wildcat discovery, the conservation agency will hold a hearing and issue a temporary spacing order that establishes an initial spacing and density pattern for development of the area surrounding the discovery well. This temporarily spaced area will encompass all acreage that the agency believes may prove productive from the same reservoir. Third, after initial development proceeds for a specified period, or until more information about the reservoir is available, the conservation agency will hold another hearing and issue a proper spacing order.

In Oklahoma, in contrast, spacing is ordinarily established on a well-by-well basis, although a single proceeding may establish spacing for several units. In Florida, Montana, and several other states, conservation agencies have promulgated general statewide spacing regulations that provide for initial spacing by depth. Under these rules, the minimum spacing distances and spacing-unit size increase with the depth of the well. The Oklahoma spacing statute contains the following provision:

> [T]he Commission shall not establish well spacing units of more than forty (40) acres in size covering common sources of supply of oil, the top of which lies less than four thousand (4,000) feet below the surface as determined by the original or discovery well in said common source of supply, and the Commission shall not establish well spacing units of more than eighty (80) acres in size covering common sources of supply of oil, the top of which lies less than nine thousand nine hundred ninety (9,990) feet and more than four thousand (4,000) feet below the surface as determined by the original or discovery well in said common source of supply.

Okla.Stat.Ann. tit. 52, § 87.1(d). What is the rationale for spacing by well depth?

5. When may a conservation agency modify a spacing order? In general, a conservation agency has continuing jurisdiction to modify any existing order, not just a spacing order, when necessary to prevent waste or to protect correlative rights. A Texas case states that this well-established principle requires no citation of authority. Railroad Comm'n v. Humble Oil & Refining Co., 193 S.W.2d 824, 828 (Tex.Civ.App.–Austin 1946, writ refused n.r.e.). See generally R. M. Williams, "Nature and Effect of Conservation Orders: Their Finality, Modification, Restriction on Production and Consequences of Violation—Duty of Lessees," 8 Rocky Mtn.Min.L.Inst. 433 (1963).

A series of Oklahoma cases, beginning with Wood Oil Co. v. Corporation Comm'n, 239 P.2d 1021 (Okla.1950), suggests that agency authority exists only where there has been a substantial change of condition that warrants the modification.[30] Otherwise, an application to modify an order is an impermissible collateral attack on the commission's prior order. The required change of condition includes one or more of the following: a change in the behavior of a reservoir resulting from development and production, French v. Champlin Exploration, Inc., 534 P.2d 1302 (Okla.1975); a realization that the reservoir was incorrectly interpreted in the first place, Application of Peppers Refining

---

30. New Mexico has similar case law. See, e.g., Uhden v. New Mexico Oil Conservation Comm'n, 817 P.2d 721 (N.M. 1991).

Co., 272 P.2d 416 (Okla.1954); as well as the development of new technological advances in reservoir interpretation, development, or production, or a change in statutory or regulatory provisions. See generally Howard H. Harris, Modification of Corporation Commission Orders Pertaining to a Common Source of Supply, 11 Okla.L.Rev. 125 (1958). An analysis of the Oklahoma cases suggests that the change-of-condition requirement is merely another way of stating that the Corporation Commission's decision to modify a prior order must be supported by substantial and credible evidence that is different in some material respect from the evidence submitted in the prior proceeding. See, e.g., Harding & Shelton, Inc. v. Sundown Energy, Inc., 130 P.3d 776 (Okla.Civ.App. Div. 1 2006) and Mustang Prod. Co. v. Corporation Comm'n, 771 P.2d 201 (Okla.1989).

In general, courts tend to construe liberal conservation-agency authority to accomplish the fundamental objectives of preventing waste and protecting correlative rights. For example, in Amoco Prod. Co. v. North Dakota Indus. Comm'n, 307 N.W.2d 839 (N.D.1981), the court affirmed a spacing order that changed existing 320–acre spacing units from the South 1/2–North 1/2 of a section (customarily called *lay-down* or *prone* units) to the West 1/2–East 1/2 of the section (customarily called *stand-up* units). The spacing statute authorized the agency to increase or decrease the size of spacing units but did not specifically authorize this type of change. Nevertheless, the court affirmed the agency's order because the change better protected correlative rights by more fairly allocating production to particular tracts based upon the geology of the reservoir in that section.

6.   When a conservation agency increases drilling density, it may order a reduction in the size of spacing units or simply authorize the drilling of additional wells in each existing unit. These approaches are not equally suitable and each presents problems. Do you understand why? See Kuntz § 77.3(g), (h), and (j)(1991).

7.   The procedure adopted by a commission to establish special field-wide spacing units varies from state to state; however, the following excerpt provides a basic summary of common practice and procedure:[31]

> The statutes of the subject states empower their respective Commissions, after notice and hearing,[32] to establish drilling units covering any pool. Accordingly, discovery of a pool is obviously a prerequisite to such action.

> * * *

> [The Commission or any] party having an interest in the discovered pool is authorized to file an application to establish drilling units.

> * * *

---

31. William M. Balkovatz, Practice and Procedure Before Oil and Gas Commissions—Some Nuts and Bolts, 25 Rocky Mtn.Min.L.Inst. 14–1, 14–9 to–18 (1979). Copyright 1980 by Matthew Bender & Co., Inc. and reprinted with permission from Rocky Mountain Mineral Law Foundation.

32. [Editors' Note] For spacing hearings, agency rules may provide for notice by publication rather than by personal notice. Proponents of notice by publication argue that such notice is sufficient because well spacing is a legislative or "rulemaking" function, not a judicial function. Proponents of personal notice argue that field-specific well spacing is a judicial or "adjudicatory" function involving the rights of specific property owners having interests in the field. The New Mexico Supreme Court, while noting that the adoption of statewide spacing rules is rulemaking, held that field-specific spacing hearings are adjudications requiring personal notice to interested parties whose identity and location are ascertainable. Uhden v. New Mexico Oil Conservation

Three knowledgeable witnesses should be utilized at the spacing hearing—a landman, a petroleum geologist, and a petroleum engineer. The testimony of both a geologist and engineer is necessary because if either witness attempts to testify as to facts within the area of expertise of the other,[33] an objection could be made and sustained, resulting in the record being devoid of critical testimony which is essential for entry of the requested order.

* * *

A landman should be utilized in spacing hearings because he is qualified to answer any and all questions that may be raised concerning the percentage ownership of working, royalty, and perhaps unleased interests, within the entire area sought to be spaced and within each proposed drilling unit therein. Further, if the applicant notified other interested parties, he will explain how, when, and upon whom such notice was served.

* * *

Subsurface geologic testimony is critical because all of the statutes of the subject states, in essence, require that the order establishing drilling units cover all lands determined or believed to be underlain by the pool. When the Commission acts to space a pool, its areal extent is usually unknown; thus, the words "believed to be underlain by the pool" come into play because "It is universally recognized that geology is not an exact science."[34]

* * * The geologist's testimony will include such matters as the name of the formation and pool, the tops of each, correlation markers used, formation lithology, and gross and net pay thickness of the producing zone.

* * *

Engineering testimony is also critical because the Commission must find that the acreage (based on surface acres) within each drilling unit is not smaller nor greater than the area that can be efficiently and economically drained by one well.[35]

* * *

Comm'n, 817 P.2d 721 (N.M.1991). Accord Cravens v. Corporation Comm'n, 613 P.2d 442 (Okla.1980).

33. [Editors' Note] A landman is a man or woman who secures oil and gas leases and other instruments on behalf of an oil company. In addition, a landman may do title curative work and perform cursory title examinations. A petroleum geologist is principally concerned with finding oil and gas. A petroleum engineer is principally concerned with developing and producing oil and gas fields.

34. Stamper v. Jones, 364 P.2d 972 (Kan.1961). "Because most geological facts are not directly observable, much of the lore of geology must rest on reasonable conclusions drawn from facts indirectly observed and sometimes imperfectly known." Texas Oil & Gas Corp. v. Railroad Comm'n, 575 S.W.2d 348, 351 (Tex.Civ.App., no writ).

35. [Editors' Note] A static bottom-hole pressure test is one way to establish the drainage area of a well. Generally, all wells in a field are shut in for a period (e.g., 72 hours) to allow the

8. Modern horizontal drilling has led to somewhat different spacing patterns than what is illustrated by the map in *Larsen*. Wells are commonly located at the far end of rectangular units, in some cases even beyond the boundaries of the unit, so that the wellbore can penetrate more of the targeted reservoir beneath the unit. Regulations establish a minimum distance from the ends of the unit lines for the perforation of the wellbore's production tubing and cement liner to allow for hydrocarbons to enter the wellbore. In addition, the wellbore must maintain certain minimum distances from the unit side lines. As an example, a drilling unit may be a half section (320 acres) or stacked half sections to allow the horizontal section of a wellbore to extend nearly two miles. The drainage pattern of a horizontal wellbore is then presumed to drain a cylinder with two half spheres at either end of the unit.

As horizontal drilling became increasingly common, the Texas Railroad Commission issued Statewide Rule 86 in 1990. At this time horizontal drilling was almost invariably used to produce from natural vertical fractures, such as those found in the Austin Chalk formation. The wells were not cased or cemented, but were entirely open hole in order to produce oil or gas from any fracture in the path of the well that contained such substances. Rule 86, which was enacted to deal with such wells, permitted horizontal drilling, but imposed the same 467 foot/1,200 foot spacing that was applicable to vertical wells. This rule is entirely inappropriate for horizontal wells in shale fields, such as the Barnett Shale and Eagle Ford Shale, where the wells are cased and cemented and perforated and hydraulically fractured only at various points along their length.

As a result, several special field rules have been adopted for many of the shale fields. One such rule, which recognizes the extremely low permeability of shale formations, reduces the required distance from the property line from 467 feet, which is the statewide rule, to 330 feet.

An exceptionally important special field rule is the "Take Point Rule." It defines a "take point" as any point along a horizontal well where oil or gas can be produced. In wells that are cased and cemented, a "take point" is where the well has been perforated (and presumably hydraulically fractured). The take-point rule precludes the need for a Rule 37 exception where any part of a horizontal well is closer to a property line than the spacing rule allows so long as no perforation is closer to a property line than authorized by the spacing rule. Such a rule is especially significant—indeed almost essential due to the absence of an effective compulsory pooling act in Texas (discussed later)—in a field such as the Barnett Shale that partially underlies urban and suburban areas where there are hundreds—perhaps thousands—of very small lots, many of which are unleased and lie within a few feet of the horizontal line of the well.

Another special field rule is the Off–Lease Penetration Point Rule. Rule 86(a)(4) requires that drilling and proration units for a horizontal well include

---

reservoir pressure to stabilize. Then one or more wells are placed on production. Communication between wells will be shown by a decrease in pressure at the remaining shut-in wells. Some communication demonstrates that the reservoir is being effectively drained, but too much communication, shown by a large decrease in pressure, may indicate that reservoir energy is being wasted because the wells are too closely spaced.

the entire area from the point where it first penetrates the reservoir (referred to as the "correlative interval") to its terminus, *i.e.*, where it ends. Given the nature of horizontal drilling, the slanted or curved portion of the well enters a shale formation before the horizontal extension begins and the well can be perforated. If the well can be drilled from an off-lease site, the first perforation can be as close to the lease line as authorized by Rule 37 or by the special field rule applicable to the field in question. The Off–Lease Penetration Point Rule, which now applies as a special field rule in more than 60 Texas fields, allows an operator to drill a well with an off-lease penetration point. Of course this rule does not preclude the necessity of obtaining drilling rights on the off-lease tract. From whom would an operator need permission to drill from an off-lease tract? The surface owner(s), the mineral owner(s), or both?

Some fields also have what is referred to as the "Box Rule," which was adopted in recognition of the fact that horizontal wells often deviate, sometime intentionally, from the precise path that the application indicated it would follow. The rule provides that a well is not in violation of its permit as long as it extends no more than a specified number of feet from each side of the specified path, i.e., so long as it stays within an imaginary box or elongated cube within the target formation.

(c) Spacing & Density Exceptions ("Exception Locations")

PROBLEM

Acme Oil Company wishes to drill a well on its tract, but, believing that the legal location will result in a dry hole, wants to drill a well at a location that is too close to the property line to comply with the applicable distance requirements. Under these circumstances, should Acme be permitted to drill a well at its desired location?

MODEL OIL AND GAS CONSERVATION ACT (INTERSTATE OIL & GAS COMPACT COMM'N 2004)

Section 10. WELL SPACING.

* * *

(c) The [commission] may grant exceptions to applicable spacing rules when the [commission] determines that one or more of the following conditions exist:

    (1) A topographic condition makes drilling in compliance with spacing rules unduly burdensome.

    (2) An environmental consideration makes drilling in compliance with spacing rules unduly harmful or potentially harmful to the environment.

    (3) A spacing unit is partly outside the reservoir.

(4) A well drilled in compliance with spacing rules is or will be noncommercial.

(5) Oil and gas confiscation will be prevented.

(6) The exception will otherwise prevent waste or protect correlative rights.

(7) The owners adversely affected by an exception to applicable spacing rules consent to that exception.

(d) If an exception to applicable spacing rules is granted, the [commission] shall take whatever action may be reasonably necessary to protect correlative rights, including adjustment of the well's rate of production.

PATTIE v. OIL & GAS CONSERVATION COMMISSION

402 P.2d 596 (Mont. 1965).

JAMES T. HARRISON, CHIEF JUSTICE.

This action arose out of plaintiffs' dissatisfaction with an order made by defendant, Oil and Gas Conservation Commission, hereinafter called Commission, denying a request to drill a gas well at a place other than that prescribed by the spacing requirements.

The plaintiff-respondents, Pattie and others, are oil and gas lessees of the W 1/2 of Section 14, T. 37 N., R. 3 E., Toole County, Montana. The Sumatra Oil Corporation also has leases in this vicinity including the NE 1/4 of Section 15, which is immediately to the west of respondents' lease.

Sumatra filed a notice of intention to drill an oil well in the SE 1/4 NE 1/4 Section 15 at a point 330 feet west of the section boundary separating the Sumatra lease from the Pattie lease. Rule 203(b) of the General Rules and Regulations of the Oil and Gas Conservation Commission provides that when drilling for oil the well location shall be no closer than 330 feet from any legal subdivision line and no closer than 1,320 feet from any other well producing from the same reservoir. The Commission rules further provide that gas wells are to be more sparsely located over the reservoir—at least 1,320 feet from a lease or property line and not less than 3,700 feet from a neighboring gas well on the same reservoir. Rule 203(c). These rules apply in the absence of special field rules. Special field rules are promulgated after a field is developed and usually are tailor-made to fit the requirements of the specific reservoir. The above rules are merely the general spacing rules that have been arrived at by statistical studies of many oil and natural gas fields, reservoirs, and pools.

Instead of hitting oil as planned Sumatra struck natural gas in commercial quantities. Since this was a newly discovered gas field no special field rules were in effect, so the provisions of Rule 203(c) were applicable. As a gas well the Sumatra well was clearly in violation of the general spacing rules. Sumatra applied to the Commission to have either special field rules or the rule of 203(c) established as the spacing rules for the newly discovered gas field. Included in that application was a request that their gas well be declared an exception to the rules so that time and money would not be lost in having to drill anew.

Respondents, Pattie and others, applied for an exception also, and requested permission to drill an off-set to the Sumatra well in Section 15. This would place the requested well 330 feet from the Section 14–15 boundary line and 660 feet from Sumatra's well.

On September 13, 1962, the Commission held the hearing and declared the field to be called the Whitlash West Field. Spacing of gas wells was prescribed to be on the basis of one well per 160–acre unit (quarter section) located within a 660 foot square in the center of each such 160–acre unit.

The testimony, based upon known geological factors established by known producing oil wells and dry holes, was that the likely eastern edge of the gas reservoir follows a line from the center of Section 11 southwest to the center of Section 22. The field may be roughly sketched as a slender oval extending from the center of Section 21 to the center of Section 11; the western line passes through the northwest corner mark of Section 15 and just to the east of the center of the dividing line between Sections 14 and 15. The Sumatra well, in the SE 1/4 NE 1/4 Section 15, lies inside the eastern edge of the reservoir. If plaintiffs are granted their off-set, their well will be in the SW 1/4 NW 1/4 of Section 14, or just inside the eastern edge of the new field. If, however, plaintiffs' request is denied they will have to drill at the center of the NW 1/4 of Section 14 (within a 660–foot square, allowed for tolerance). This position lies just outside the projected eastern edge. The Commission granted Sumatra the requested exception for the well already drilled but plaintiffs were denied permission to drill the off-set.

Plaintiffs * * * filed a complaint directly in the district court of Toole County for a trial de novo as provided for in section 60–135, R.C.M.1947.

The complaint alleged that the order of the Commission was unreasonable and inequitable in that it causes plaintiffs injury by gas being drained from under their land without their being able to protect themselves with a well. It was asserted that to allow them to drill the off-set would not be damaging to the conservation protection sought by the spacing units.

Testimony was received and the matter was finally submitted to the court on motions for summary judgment filed by both sides on February 26, 1964. In April 1964, District Judge R.V. Bottomly denied the Commission's motion, granted plaintiffs' motion, and ordered the Commission to reconsider plaintiffs' request. * * *

The Commission brings this appeal and urges * * * that the Commission lacks jurisdiction to determine correlative rights or private rights because there is no authorization to do so provided by the legislature. * * *

* * *

* * * Montana is the only state we can find that produces substantial quantities of oil and gas, has a modernized Conservation Act, and belongs to the Interstate Oil Compact Commission, but has no specific reference to correlative or private rights in the legislation. This case is truly unique. No similar cases have been found and no oil and gas law treatise or other writing has been found disclosing to us a guide for the solution. Unless the Montana Act is flexible enough to permit the Commission to make orders with an eye to the interests of adjacent landowners in sharing in the common supply the legislation would have to be held unconstitutional as a deprivation of property without due process of law. * * *

* * *

In the instant case, the Commission did not consider the correlative rights but we hold that it should have. The transcript shows that plaintiffs attempted to convince the Commission that if they were confined to drilling in the center of the NW 1/4 of Section 14 (with tolerance) the result would be either no gas or less gas than Sumatra would produce. A considerable portion of the plaintiffs' lease, however, overlies the projected boundary of the gas reservoir. Plaintiffs desired * * * a well over the reservoir * * *.

Section 60–129, subd. C, provides:

Subject to the provisions of this act, the order establishing spacing units shall direct that no more than one (1) well shall be drilled and produced from the common source of supply on any spacing unit, and that the well shall be drilled at a location authorized by the order, with such exception as may be reasonably necessary where it is shown, upon application, notice, and hearing, and the commission finds, that the spacing unit is located on the edge of a pool or field and adjacent to a producing unit, or, for some other reason, the requirement to drill the well at the authorized location on the spacing unit would be inequitable or unreasonable.

Where, as here, the landowners lie on the projected edge of a petroleum reservoir the section above clearly indicates that an exception may be granted where "the requirement to drill the well at the authorized location on the spacing units would be inequitable or unreasonable." Certainly, the Commission would not say that in determining where the authorized location is "inequitable" or "unreasonable" it is confined to a scientific waste prevention study alone. The correlative rights of the parties as a general principle of conservation of natural resources must also be considered in studying the equities of the well-spacing regulations with respect to fringe owners. It is the very essence of "conservation" that the private rights be respected. Counsel for the Commission make frequent reference in the brief to the fact that plaintiffs only presented a case showing that the "equities" are on their side. But this is what the section quoted above demands.

* * *

It would be "inequitable" and "unjust" not to allow one to have an exception to the drilling pattern in order to allow that driller to get his share of petroleum—provided, of course, that the exception does not cause waste.

* * *

The order of the district court is affirmed.

NOTES

1. In Denver Producing & Refining Co. v. State, 184 P.2d 961, 964 (Okla.1947), the Oklahoma Supreme Court stated: "In striking a balance between conservation of natural resources and protection of correlative rights, the latter is secondary and must yield to a reasonable exercise of the former." But in Application of Peppers Refining Co., 272 P.2d 416, 424 (Okla.1954), the court stated:

> In our opinion it is more important to secure to each lessor, lessee, and owner of mineral rights in a field, his ratable share of the production therefrom and to prevent underground waste, than it is to secure to some, the maximum profits from drilling and producing operations. In view of the evidence in this case, we think the Commission gave undue consideration to what it apparently termed "economic waste," to the detriment of other more important considerations, including the correlative rights of the various owners of interests in the common reservoir.

How are these two statements to be reconciled? In light of the constitutional basis for the doctrine of correlative rights, how can protecting correlative rights be secondary to the prevention of waste?

2. Unlike Montana, most courts do not conduct a trial de novo when considering an appeal from the order of a regulatory agency. Moreover, except in Oklahoma, in reviewing a conservation order, courts may not modify or amend an order. Rather, they are confined to either affirming or setting aside the order. See, e.g., Atlantic Refining Co. v. Railroad Comm'n, 346 S.W.2d 801 (Tex.1961).

3. Exception locations to protect correlative rights are generally of two types. The first type is illustrated in *Pattie*, where an exception location serves to prevent drainage to a neighboring well or to locate the well above the reservoir. The second type is an exception location permitted on a tract of land too small to comprise a spacing unit or too small to meet minimum distance requirements from boundary lines or neighboring wells. Cases concerning this type are common in Texas and are discussed in Section C.5., below.

4. Occasionally, an exception location may be granted to avoid particular topographical problems. This may serve the purpose of protecting the environment, avoiding a hazardous or costly well location, or moving the location

away from particular surface improvements, such as a dwelling. In some states, the need for these exceptions is lessened through so-called "island" or "window" spacing orders that allow operators more flexibility to locate wells. Traditionally, to assure a uniform pattern of wells, spacing orders prescribed a precise well location based upon specific distances from the unit boundary.

EXXON CORP. v. RAILROAD COMMISSION

571 S.W.2d 497 (Tex.1978).

GREENHILL, CHIEF JUSTICE.

This is a direct appeal involving a Railroad Commission order which grants appellee BTA Oil Producers a permit to drill at a requested location under the Commission's Statewide Spacing Rule 37. The central issue in the case is whether BTA Oil Producers was entitled to a permit under the Rule 37 waste exception, taking into consideration economic factors arising from the presence of an existing well bore at the requested location. On appeal of the Commission's order, the district court held that BTA Oil Producers was so entitled, and we agree. * * *

BTA Oil Producers [hereinafter BTA] is the owner of a lease on a 673–acre tract in the Beall (Devonian) Field, Ward County, Texas. The Devonian Field has been classified by the Railroad Commission as an oil field with an associated gas cap. The field contains an upper gas producing zone and a lower oil producing zone. * * *

Under the applicable field rules, spacing for the Devonian Field is governed by the Railroad Commission's Statewide Spacing Rule 37. That rule provides as follows:

> (A)(1) No well for oil or gas shall hereafter be drilled nearer than twelve hundred (1200) feet to any well completed in or drilling to the same horizon on the same tract * * * provided that the Commission, in order to prevent waste or to prevent the confiscation of property, may grant exceptions to permit drilling within shorter distances * * *.

The present suit arises from an application filed by BTA to obtain an exception under this rule. Exxon contested the application as an offset operator.

At the time of the proceedings in question, the Devonian Field contained four wells classified as oil wells and two wells classified as gas wells. The gas wells are the Exxon Herd Gas Unit No. 1 and the BTA Wedge Gas Unit No. 1. On the same tract as its Wedge Gas Unit No. 1, BTA has a well known as the Wedge No. 2. This well was originally drilled as a test well to the Ellenberger Formation, which lies considerably deeper than the Devonian Field.[1] Upon discovering the Ellenberger to be non-productive, BTA completed the Wedge No. 2 in the Montoya Reservoir,

---

1. The Ellenberger Formation lies approximately 15,500 feet below the surface, whereas the Devonian Field begins approximately 12,000 feet from the surface. An intermediate reservoir, the Montoya, lies approximately 13,000 feet below the surface.

which is between the Ellenberger and the Devonian. The Wedge No. 2 was a commercial producer of gas in the Montoya Reservoir; but, according to the testimony in the present case, the Montoya reserves are nearing depletion. BTA therefore applied to the Commission for a permit to plug back and recomplete the Wedge No. 2 in the Devonian Field. Such recompletion required a Rule 37 exception because, at Devonian depth, BTA's Wedge No. 2 and BTA's Wedge No. 1 are only 265 feet apart, rather than the 1,200 feet required by the Rule for a "regular" location.

* * *

At the hearing before the Railroad Commission, BTA produced evidence designed to show that recompletion of the Wedge No. 2 well in the Devonian Field was necessary to prevent waste of oil from the field. BTA's evidence indicated that, at least in the Wedge No. 2 well bore, the lower oil productive strata (Lower Devonian) was completely separate from the upper gas productive strata. Because BTA's tests showed the Lower Devonian pressure to approximate the original reservoir pressure in the area, BTA concluded that none of the four oil wells presently existing in the Devonian Field were able to recover oil in the vicinity of the Wedge No. 2 well bore; BTA's expert witness testified that, although the oil could be recovered by drilling a completely new well at a regular location, BTA could not economically justify such drilling. Thus, BTA's position was that the Rule 37 exception was economically necessary to prevent waste of the Lower Devonian oil. BTA's witness testified that, because the economics would not justify the drilling of a new well, the oil reserves were only recoverable through use of the existing Wedge No. 2 well bore.

The Railroad Commission, in adopting the Findings of Fact and Conclusion of Law found in the Hearing Examiner's Proposal for Decision, agreed with BTA's position.

* * *

Based on these findings and conclusions, the Commission entered its order in Rule 37 Case No. 75,332, granting BTA a permit to plug back and recomplete the Wedge No. 2 in the Devonian Field. Exxon, alleging interest as an offset operator, brought suit in the District Court of Travis County to set aside the Commission's order and to enjoin BTA from producing from the Devonian Field through its Wedge No. 2 well. The district court upheld the Commission's order and denied Exxon's prayer for injunctive relief. Exxon then perfected this direct appeal to this court * * *.

As noted at the outset, the central issue in this case is whether BTA was entitled to a Rule 37 exception on the basis of economic conditions arising from the presence of an existing well bore. Both parties agree that the exception may only be granted where necessary to prevent waste or confiscation. Exxon argues that, in addition, a Rule 37 exception may only be granted upon a showing of unusual reservoir conditions. * * *

* * *

* * * Exxon argues that it is a longstanding rule of law in Texas that unusual reservoir conditions must be shown before a Rule 37 permit may be granted to prevent waste. Because the Commission expressly found that BTA's Wedge No. 2 well bore would encounter approximately the same thickness of Devonian formation as would a well at a regular location, Exxon urges that BTA has failed to show such unusual conditions as would support the granting of the permit.

* * *

In the present case, the requirements * * * for a showing of unusual conditions has been met. The most obvious condition which differentiates the permit location from regular locations on BTA's tract is the presence of an existing well bore. While it is agreed that the Wedge No. 2 well bore will encounter the Devonian Field at approximately the same thickness that a regular location would, there is also evidence that it is not economically feasible to drill at a regular location. In addition, there is a finding, supported by evidence, that the oil that would be produced from the Wedge No. 2 well cannot be produced by any other existing well. * * *

In its briefs to this court, Exxon argues that there is a great potential for abuse in allowing the Railroad Commission to consider the presence of an existing well bore as a relevant factor in granting a Rule 37 exception. Exxon urges that the existence of well bores is entirely within the oil and gas operators' control, and that operators will be encouraged to drill to deeper formations in such a way as to be able to later disregard spacing rules in intervening formations. Because of this threat, Exxon urges that this court must devise a test limiting the circumstances in which an existing well bore is a proper consideration in a Rule 37 case. We conclude that an appropriate test is whether the existing well was drilled and completed in the original formation legitimately and in good faith, and not as a subterfuge to bolster a later Rule 37 exception. In the present case, there is not even a suggestion that BTA did not meet such a test. The Wedge No. 2 was drilled first to the deeper Ellenberger, and was then completed as a producing gas well in the Montoya Reservoir; and, as the Commission expressly found, the Montoya reserves were nearing depletion at the time BTA sought this permit to plug back the well. Should a case arise in which there is a suggestion that a well has been drilled as a subterfuge to bolster a later Rule 37 application, the Commission, upon finding such a subterfuge, may properly refuse to consider the existing well bore as a factor in granting the Rule 37 exception.

Consideration of reasonable economic factors upon which operators must act is one of the underlying bases for Rule 37 itself. * * *

In the present case, common sense dictates that the economic waste that would result from BTA's drilling a completely new well, simply so as not to crowd its existing well, is a most relevant consideration. BTA's economic argument becomes even more cogent in light of the fact that completion of the Wedge No. 2 well in the Devonian Field can do Exxon no greater harm than would the completion of a well at a regular location.

Exxon's own position is that geological conditions are the same * * *. Thus, the only advantage Exxon would gain in having BTA drill at a regular location instead of at the exception location lies in the delay factor that would be involved in drilling a completely new well. * * *

* * *

In the context of the present case, economic factors were relevant to BTA's application and were properly considered by the Commission in determining whether a Rule 37 exception was necessary to prevent the waste of oil.

The judgment of the district court is affirmed.

NOTES

1. Did the court sustain the Railroad Commission's order because it was necessary to prevent the physical waste of oil or the economic waste of BTA's assets? Cf. Schlachter v. Railroad Comm'n, 825 S.W.2d 737 (Tex.App.–Austin 1992, writ den.) (denying an exception location to re-enter an existing well bore where evidence showed that other existing wells could recover the remaining oil reserves and showed that applicant could profitably drill and produce a well at a regular location). Did the order in *Exxon* also protect correlative rights? Why did Exxon object when recompletion of the existing well as an exception location could do no greater harm to Exxon than a well drilled at a regular location?

2. Exception locations may be granted to prevent underground, surface, or economic waste. The geology of a reservoir may require exception locations to maximize recovery from a field. For example, an otherwise productive formation may contain an area of poor porosity and permeability. To prevent underground waste, the commission may grant an exception location that will avoid a nonproductive area and yet secure production from an area that is not being effectively drained by existing wells. Economic waste is also prevented by avoiding the drilling of a nonproductive well. See Application of Gulf Oil Corp., 313 P.2d 1101 (Okla.1957).

3. REGULATING PRODUCTION OPERATIONS, PRODUCTION, AND MARKETING

Production may be regulated to protect correlative rights, to prevent waste, or to correct market failures. Additionally, an agency may order the curtailment or outright cessation of production operations for noncompliance with its regulations. See, e.g., Hawley v. Board of Oil and Gas Conservation, 993 P.2d 677 (Mont.2000). Depending upon the jurisdiction and upon the underlying objective, production from completed wells may be largely unregulated or may be strictly regulated on a per-well, field-wide, or statewide basis.

In some states, each well may be assigned an allowable to protect correlative rights. Recall that, in *Wronski v. Sun Oil Co.,* see Chapter 1,

Section D, Sun Oil unlawfully produced wells in excess of assigned allowables established to protect correlative rights. Not all states would establish field-wide allowables for that purpose. In many states, operators are allowed to produce wells at their "potential" or at their "maximum efficient rate." Thus, the rule of capture still applies to the extent that it has not been limited or modified by conservation laws and regulations. See generally Bruce M. Kramer and Owen L. Anderson, The Rule of Capture— An Oil and Gas Perspective, 35 Envt'l L. 899 (symposium 2005), reprinted, 43 Rocky Mtn. Min. L. Found. J. 321 (2006).

Well allowables are most commonly assigned on an acreage basis. Thus, in setting an allowable for an individual well, acreage must be assigned to the well. The acreage assigned is commonly called a "proration unit." In theory, the amount of acreage assigned to a spacing unit is usually the acreage that one well may effectively and efficiently drain; however, a proration unit may or may not correspond to the applicable spacing unit, and the shape of the proration unit may not conform to the actual or assumed drainage pattern.[36]

Under an acreage-based allowable, a well in a standard proration unit for a field (e.g. 160 acres) would receive a standard field-wide allowable (e.g. 400 barrels a day); however, a smaller unit (e.g. 120 acres) would receive a proportionately reduced allowable (e.g. 300 barrels a day), while a larger proration unit (e.g. 320 acres) would receive a proportionately enlarged allowable (e.g., 800 barrels a day). In addition to acreage, however, allowables may be partially determined by the depth of the well, the net-acre feet of reservoir beneath the proration unit, the open flow capability of the well, and other factors.[37]

To prevent unfair drainage from adjacent tracts, conservation agencies may restrict production from wells drilled as exception locations. This practice is illustrated in Chevron Oil Co. v. Oil & Gas Conservation Commission, below. Historically, the Texas Railroad Commission gave owners of small tracts disproportionately larger allowables than it gave owners of large tracts so that the small-tract owners could profitably drill and produce wells. This unique Texas practice is further explored in Section C.5.(d)(ii), below.

To prevent underground waste, allowables may be assigned to increase ultimate recovery:

---

36. Conservation agencies usually presume that oil and gas reservoirs are homogeneous. Accordingly, in the case of vertical wells drilled into a common reservoir, drainage is presumed to be radial and equal both in volume and in area from well to well. The acreage assigned to a drilling or proration unit, however, need not conform to this radial drainage pattern because all wells (and thus their owners) are capable of recovering a fair share of the oil and gas in a homogeneous reservoir. In other words, because all wells will drain in a similar fashion, oil drained from Unit A by wells on another unit will be made up by drainage to the Unit A well from other units and so on from well-to-well across the field. This is often called the doctrine of "compensatory drainage."

37. For example, Texas has a statewide rule establishing a schedule of so-called yardstick allowables for wells based upon the time the field was discovered, the depth of the well, and the acreage assigned to the well. Tex.R.R.Comm'n, 16 Tex.Admin.Code § 3.45. For a detailed explanation of how this system works, see Smith & Weaver § 10–3(C).

The maintenance of reservoir pressure increases the ultimate primary recovery of oil and gas from a reservoir. The natural pressure in a reservoir is sometimes sufficient to push oil to the surface without the assistance of any artificial lift. When pressures decline to a point where oil is no longer naturally pushed to the surface, wells are placed on pump. A beam-type pump, sometimes referred to as a horsehead pump, is then installed at the surface to lift the oil to the surface. Wells that flow either naturally or on the pump are in a *primary recovery* stage.

To assure the maximum recovery of oil, well production may be restricted to a *maximum efficient rate of recovery "MER."* MER is the designation for the maximum efficient rate or the most efficient rate at which a well can produce without impairing the efficiency of reservoir drive with consequent physical, underground waste. MER is the upper limit of production beyond which any increase will mean a decrease in the amount of oil ultimately recoverable.

Sullivan § 165.

In a water-drive reservoir, oil production may be restricted on a yearly basis to keep the rate of oil production consistent with the rate of water encroachment. If production is not restricted, water tends to "finger" through some formations, leaving lenses of oil trapped in the reservoir rock.

Restricting production also prevents swift pressure declines that, in turn, cause gas to come out of solution and cause oil viscosity to increase. In a solution-gas reservoir, oil is pushed toward well bores by the expansion of gas dissolved in the oil. If wells are produced too rapidly, this expanding gas reaches the bubble point: the point of declining pressure at which gas escapes from solution. As pressure declines, gas production increases and ultimate oil recovery decreases. MER allowables may be established to maintain reservoir pressures above the bubble point for as long as possible, thereby increasing ultimate recovery.

To prevent the inefficient dissipation of gas, some wells in a field may be assigned smaller than normal allowables. For example, in some gas-drive reservoirs, specific wells—often a cluster of wells in the heart of a field—may produce a large quantity of gas relative to the amount of oil. To conserve the reservoir energy, and thereby prevent underground waste, these wells may be assigned a lower allowable than other wells in a field. This practice of regulating gas-oil ratios is illustrated in *Denver Producing & Refining Co.*, below.[38]

To prevent surface waste, a conservation agency will commonly have a rule that prohibits or at least greatly curtails the flaring of gas.

---

38. Similar underground waste may occur from wells located lower on the structure of a water-drive reservoir. To conserve the water drive, wells that produce a large quantity of water relative to oil may be given a lower allowable than other wells in the field, although regulating water-oil ratios is not as common as regulating gas-oil ratios.

When the proceeds of production attributable to working-interest owners are sufficient to cover drilling and completion costs, the well is said to have reached payout. To allow for more rapid recovery of well drilling and completion costs, new wells may be assigned higher allowables until these costs are recovered.[39] Assigning higher allowables prior to payout prevents economic waste because the cost of money is reduced.

Historically, the rule of capture encouraged the rapid production of oil, which was often in excess of transportation and refining capacities. Production that could not be immediately transported or refined was stored in tanks and open pits at the surface. As a result of this storage, large quantities of oil were lost through seepage, leakage, or fire. As more fields were discovered and produced (culminating with the discovery of the huge East Texas Field in 1930), excessive oil supplies reduced prices to a point where wells could no longer be profitably drilled or produced. Many existing wells were prematurely abandoned. This surplus of oil, caused by the discovery of new fields and rapid rule-of-capture production devastated the economies of producing states. Ultimately, to address this market failure, many conservation agencies were authorized to restrict production to reasonable market demand.

The regulation of production and marketing is briefly explored in the materials that follow. When you read these materials, try to determine the primary, and any secondary objectives, of the particular regulation or order. If you conclude that one objective is to prevent waste, try to determine the kind of waste addressed by the regulation or order. Consider whether the objective is being achieved or is being achieved at the expense of another objective. Finally, consider whether there is a better means of achieving the objective.

PROBLEM

In *Pattie*, above, suppose that Sumatra's well had been initially located at a legal location for gas (near the center of the NE 1/4 of Section 15). Then Pattie's claim for its proposed exception location would have been based solely upon evidence that a well drilled at a legal location would be a dry hole. Suppose Sumatra contended, that if Pattie's exception well is permitted, the well's production should be curtailed on the grounds that the off-pattern location will drain Section 15 and that the reservoir extends only partially beneath Pattie's tract. Should production from the Pattie well be curtailed?

In Chevron Oil Co. v. Oil & Gas Conservation Commission, 435 P.2d 781 (Mont.1967), Chief Justice Harrison, speaking for the court, said the following about a similar situation.

> * * * We said in *Pattie* that * * * the Commission had the authority and duty to consider correlative rights in granting exceptions to field spacing

---

39. For example, in addition to its schedule of statewide yardstick allowables, the Texas Railroad Commission has adopted a separate schedule of discovery allowables for new wells. These allowables are based upon the depth of the well and the location of the well (onshore or offshore). Because drilling costs generally increase with the depth of the well, the deeper the well, the higher the allowable. Likewise, offshore wells, which are more expensive to drill, are given higher allowables than onshore wells. Tex. R.R.Comm'n, 16 Tex.Admin.Code § 3.42.

rules. * * * [Now the applicants for an exception location to protect correlative rights] contend that the consideration of correlative rights must be limited to only the rights of the applicant for the exception location. We cannot agree. Correlative rights are not a one-way street. The authority of the Commission to limit production to protect the correlative rights of adjoining owners when an exception location well is granted is a natural facet of the authority to consider correlative rights when granting the exception location. * * *

The Commission has the authority to restrict the production of the exception well, on a proper showing, so that it does not result in a taking of production from an adjacent owner's property. This authority is only an incident of the authority to grant exceptions to established spacing rules. Such order must naturally be consistent with the purpose of the Conservation Act and not result in waste.

Just as the Act protects the rights of the owner to capture his share of the oil and gas when the pool is only under part of his land, it must protect the adjoining landowners from having their share of the oil and gas appropriated by the exception location well. * * *

Although no exact or precise determination can be made as to the amount of oil or gas under each tract, it can be made within reasonable limits and subject to redetermination as more knowledge is acquired about the particular field. All factors involved in the production from the exception location well should be taken into account.

Notes

1. In the case of Application of Gulf Oil Corp., 313 P.2d 1101 (Okla. 1957), an adjacent owner appealed a commission order, which permitted Gulf Oil to drill a directional well as an exception location but limited production to 75% of the allowable production for standard wells in the field.

The unit here involved was the west half of the southwest quarter of a specified section. The applicant had drilled a well in the center of the north 40 acres thereof to a depth of more than 13,000 feet in accord with those previous general orders. The hole penetrated the said Simpson Sand Series but it was found that a fault existed in the sand to the extent that the porosity and permeability had been destroyed making it impossible to produce from the formation.

Thereupon, applicant filed its application for permission to set a whipstock at about the 10,000 foot level and directionally drill said well in a southerly direction to the extent that the bottom of the hole would be some 1,320 feet south of the surface hole or approximately in the center of the south 40 acres of the drilling unit. The protestant was the owner of an undivided one half royalty interest in the drilling unit lying immediately west of the one here involved. A well had been drilled and was producing from protestant's unit at the regular pattern location in the center of the south 40 acres thereof. Thus the bottom of the hole proposed to be drilled directionally by applicant would be some 1,320 feet east of protestant's well and about the same distance south off the regular pattern in the area.

* * *

The correlative rights of mineral estate owners of applicant's drilling unit would have to be disregarded by the Commission if the permission to directionally drill out of the fault were to be denied. * * * Protestant's unit, lying immediately west, was productive merely because, although crossed by the same fault, the drilling pattern placed the location of its well south of the fault. The chance location of the well site should not let one owner develop and produce oil which his neighbor was prohibited from developing and producing, all because of requiring strict compliance with an arbitrarily fixed drilling pattern. * * *

* * * The 75% allowable from the 80 acres was, in effect, a finding that the unit contained 60 acres of productive formation. Protestant's contention is based upon the fact that the witnesses testified that the productive area thereof approximated between 40 and 55 acres. However, those estimates did not include the acreage which might lie north of the fault. Also * * * protestant's unit, which was producing the full allowable, was traversed by the same fault and its productive acreage was proportionately decreased. Therefore, percentage-wise, applicant's productive acreage was approximately the same as the protestants' productive acreage. Furthermore, there was no conclusive evidence that the off pattern well of applicant would reduce, to any marked extent, the ultimate recovery from protestant's well.

* * *

The order and judgment appealed from is sustained and affirmed.

313 P.2d at 1102–04. Since the fault also crossed protestant's tract, making the productive acreage of each unit approximately the same, should Gulf's allowable have been curtailed at all? On the other hand, should the protestant's allowable have been curtailed? Might your answer depend on the productive areas beneath other nearby wells?

In the matter of Application of Anderson, 214 P.2d 896 (Okla.1950), the applicant requested an increase in the allowable of a proposed well that had been previously authorized as an exception location.

After hearing the evidence the Commission * * * made an order increasing the allowable production of such well to that allowed other wells in the pool until such time as the cost of the well had been repaid, with the provision that after the cost of the well had been repaid the Commission would set the matter for further hearing, and at such time reduce the allowable of such well below one half the usual allowable in order to make up the over production.

* * *

The applicant, Frank Anderson, was the only witness who testified at the hearing. He testified that he had theretofore drilled a well [in accordance with the general spacing order] * * * which proved dry; that his lease was being drained by three wells on the west which had been producing for more than a year; that there were wells one half mile south of the proposed location, and that his associates in the drilling venture, who apparently were interested in the well with him, refused to consider the drilling of the well so long as the allowable was placed at one half of the allowable permitted to the wells in the field. This testimony was not in any manner controverted.

* * *

From the testimony of the applicant Anderson it plainly appears that the [exception] well which he had theretofore been authorized to drill * * * was located on the edge of the pool. Whether the well would produce any oil or gas when completed was questionable. But it was to the interest of the state and the land owner, as well as to the interest of the lessee, that the well be drilled if there was a possibility of production. Otherwise the only oil recovered from this area would be that drained by offset wells. * * *

* * * There is no showing in the record that such well would drain any appreciable quantity of oil from the adjoining lands, and apparently the Commission was of opinion that it would not. However, under the order of the Commission, if the proposed well was a producing well, the production therefrom would be limited after the well had been paid for to offset the probability of the well having drained oil from the adjoining tracts.

* * *

Order affirmed.

214 P.2d at 897–98. In such cases, which party should bear the burden of proof regarding the necessity for an exception location? For the curtailing of the allowable? For the later increase of the allowable? For the later decrease of the allowable? Does a conservation agency have an affirmative duty to protect correlative rights in these situations, or need the agency be concerned only in the event of a protest?

2.   In Masonite Corp. v. State Oil & Gas Bd., 240 So.2d 446 (Miss.1970), the Mississippi Supreme Court upheld a conservation statute prohibiting the conservation agency from reducing the allowables of an exception well on the ground that the unit did not fully overlie the reservoir. Noting that the rule of capture was still in effect, except as specifically abrogated by the conservation act, the court concluded that "[t]he nature of oil and gas is such that conservation measures cannot be designed so as to grant as a matter of law to each owner the exact amount of oil under his tract." However, in Stack v. Harris, 242 So.2d 857 (Miss.1970), the Mississippi Supreme Court upheld an order restricting production from an exception well where the operator, after receiving permission for the location, intentionally drilled the well directionally (without agency permission) to a point where the well bore nearly intersected the junction of four spacing units. The agency later approved the directional well but reduced its allowable because it crowded a nearby well belonging to Harris. On appeal, the circuit court reversed, holding that reducing allowables

for exception wells was prohibited by statute. The Supreme Court reversed the circuit court, holding that, under the particular circumstances, the agency could lower allowables because the well had not been drilled in accordance with the permit. Should the conservation agency have ordered the operator to plug the well?

3. Suppose an operator in a field where the spacing units were 80 acres desired to drill only one well on a 160–acre tract. Could the operator obtain a "double" allowable for the well? Why might an operator wish to do this? See, e.g., Dodds v. Ward, 418 P.2d 629 (Okla.1966).

PICKENS v. RAILROAD COMMISSION

387 S.W.2d 35 (Tex.1965).

GREENHILL, JUSTICE.

The main question here is the validity of the order of the Texas Railroad Commission prorating the production allowable of oil from the Fairway (James Lime) Field in Anderson and Henderson Counties, Texas. The order fixed the rate at which the various owners of the oil could produce. The district court found the order to be reasonably supported by substantial evidence and upheld it. W.L. Pickens and others have brought the case to us by direct appeal. The main law question before us is the same as that before the district court: Is the Commission's proration order reasonably supported by substantial evidence?

The formula under attack has two basic elements: (1) the number of surface acres in the production unit on which there is a well, usually 160 acres; and (2) the number of acre-feet of productive sand or rock which are within, or below, the 160 surface acres. The acre-foot is a measure of volume. Some surface acres of the field have, vertically, a thicker section of productive sand below them. An acre-foot, as used here, refers to a horizontal square acre with a thickness of one foot of productive sand. An acre-foot contains 43,560 cubic feet of oil or gas-bearing formation.

In addition to pleading that the order was unreasonable because it did not protect their correlative rights and would permit uncompensated drainage, Pickens et al. pleaded that any formula which was not "based solely on net-acre-feet of pay underlying each unit tract" would be unreasonable, would fail to protect their correlative rights, and would deprive them of their property without due process of law. Their witness's testimony was that the formula should have been based 100 percent on acre-feet of productive sand.

The proration order was arrived at in the following manner: the Commission each month determines the amount of oil to be produced from all fields in Texas. It divides this amount among the various fields. The total amount this particular field may produce is determined from time to time and is not fixed in the proration allowable formula here attacked. What the proration order does is to allocate to the wells in the field the part of the total field allowable which each well may produce. There are some exceptions because some wells have but limited capacity, others have a high gas-oil ratio, and so forth. Those wells are given particular allowables and are not here involved. The remaining volume of oil, whatever it is, is divided in half: one half of the oil is allocated to the wells in that proportion which their assigned surface acreage in the oil field (usually 160 acres) bears to the total acreage in the field (about 21,000 acres); and the other half is distributed among the same wells in that proportion which their assigned acre-feet, their net acre-feet, bears to the total acre-feet in the field. Thus it is said that the formula allows 50 percent for acreage (up to 160 surface acres), and 50 percent for acre-feet.

* * *

* * * This "50 percent acreage, 50 percent acre-feet" formula will be hereafter referred to as the "50–50 formula." * * * The witness Latimer testified that when the field was prorated on a 100 percent acreage basis, Appellant Pickens' three wells on 480 of the field's 21,000 acres had an allowable of 333 barrels per day each. The effect of the 50–50 formula was to raise his allowable to between 362 and 378 barrels per well per day. The allowables on other wells having fewer acre-feet were lowered. * * *

Pickens and others filed suit in Travis County on April 8, 1963, to attack this order of March 6, 1963. They contend, among other things, that it was unreasonable and was not supported by substantial evidence, mainly, in that it discriminates against people who have the most oil in place under their surface acres, i.e., the most acre-feet; and it allows, they say, an undue advantage to those having the same surface acreage over the oil but fewer acre feet of oil in place. They also contend that it will bring about undue uncompensated draining which will ultimately result in their great financial loss. * * *

The Commission's order is presumed to be valid. The question is not whether the Commission came to a proper factual conclusion on the basis of conflicting evidence, but whether it acted arbitrarily and without regard to the facts. Railroad Commission v. Manziel, 361 S.W.2d 560 (Tex.1962). Our duty is to look to the record as a whole to see whether the order of the Commission is reasonably supported by substantial evidence. While we look to the record as a whole, our duty is to determine whether there is in the record competent evidence which reasonably supports the order. The evidence is voluminous; of necessity it must be greatly condensed.

The oil-bearing strata in question is several miles across, and is elevated about 130 feet toward its center. The thickest of the oil-saturated sand or rock (some 115 feet vertically) is in the central part of the strata or field. It is not located over subsurface water. If the field could be sliced and looked at vertically, the oil-bearing portion or strata could roughly be compared to an elongated, very gradually sloping crescent, the entire center of which is elevated toward the surface. It may be described as a symmetric recumbent anticline. The "thick" area of the field, which has the most acre-feet of oil-bearing rock, is updip (at a higher elevation in the structure) from the thinner sections which are toward the ends of the crescent. The thinnest producing rock or sand is some 15 feet thick. The average thickness is about 77 feet. The argument of Pickens is that since there is an average of 77 acre-feet of producing sand below each average surface acre, the 50–50 formula is weighted overwhelmingly in favor of surface acres as contrasted to acre-feet of producing sand. There is not, they say, one acre-foot for each surface acre (which they say would make a 50–50 allocation more equitable), but an average of 77 acre-feet for each surface acre. Hence the areas of thickest sands are not being allowed to produce in proportion to the reserves in place.

Pickens and others relied upon the testimony of H.J. Gruy, a consulting petroleum engineer and geologist. He projected the 77–to–1 figures mentioned above to show that Pickens et al. will ultimately recover amounts substantially less under the 50–50 formula than they would if the formula used were based 100 percent on the number of acre-feet under each tract. His testimony was that oil wells would drain in excess of 160 surface acres, and that Pickens et al. would be the victims of net uncompensated drainage.

Gruy disputed the assertion that there was any water drive or water encroachment in the field. He testified that any water in the wells toward the edge of the field was due to poor cementing of the wells. * * *

The Appellees called five expert witnesses, who were petroleum or production engineers, a petroleum reserve engineer, and a petroleum consultant. These experts agreed that the field was virtually surrounded by water which was in contact with the oil in the field, and that a substantial portion of the field was located over water which was also in contact with the oil. Their testimony was that there was a marked difference in the bottom-hole pressures in the various wells in the field. The wells toward the center of the field and the thick section of the oil-bearing strata had a lower pressure than the wells toward the edge of the field, particularly to the southeast.

The discovery wells were in the southeast part of the field, and that portion of the field had produced almost a year longer than the center section. Yet the pressure in that southeast area has not declined as much, proportionately, as the pressure in the center or thicker section of the field where Appellants Pickens et al. (as well as many of the Appellees, including the Appellee Hunt Oil Company) had their wells. The explanation was that as the oil was withdrawn from the field, water moved into the field around its edges to replace the oil, thus keeping up the pressure. There was evidence that edge wells were making water and that the amount of water in the wells was increasing.

* * *

The witness J.R. Latimer, Jr., testified * * * that substantial quantities of water are in fact moving into the field, and its movement will continue. * * *

The water, he said, encroaching from the edges of the field, would push the oil updip toward the thicker sections of the strata where

Appellant Pickens' wells are located. The thinner sections would be watered out first. In his opinion, a 100 percent acre-foot proration formula would cause an acceleration of the influx of water, and the allowables from the watered-out wells on the thinner tracts would then be transferred to the wells on the thick tracts toward the center of the field.

The witness Latimer further testified to pressure differentials in the field. Oil, he said, will drain toward low pressure. It cannot drain against pressure. The area in the center of the field, around the wells of Pickens et al., has lower pressure than the pressure around the thin or edge tracts.

So his testimony was that net drainage was not *away* from the wells of Appellants Pickens et al. but *toward* them because of (1) the difference in pressure and (2) the force of the water pushing the oil updip. He concluded that the 50–50 formula more nearly gave all the owners an equal opportunity to produce their in-place reserves. He doubted that even under that formula the edge wells would come even close to producing what was considered to be originally in place because the oil is being pushed past them, updip.

* * * There was an abundance of testimony that under the Commission's formula, each operator would have the opportunity to recover his in-place oil reserves. This Court held in the Quitman Field case[1] that in a Rule 37 case (involving a permit to drill a well on a small tract), the landowner is entitled to a fair chance to recover the oil and gas in and under his land or its equivalent in kind to prevent confiscation of his property. * * *

While the Appellants' witness Gruy testified that Appellants would suffer uncompensated drainage under the Commission's formula, there was an abundance of competent testimony that the net drainage was *toward* the Appellants' portion of the field, not only because of water encroachment but because of the difference in pressure. * * * There is competent testimony here that there would be little if any drainage toward the edge wells which did not have a thick section of oil-bearing sand or rock; i.e., those wells which did not have as many acre-feet as those wells in the center.

This Court has taken note before that oil moves to areas of low pressure and that drainage is from areas of high pressure to areas of low pressure. * * *

Moreover, there is an acceptable reason for allowing the thinner tracts with fewer acre-feet to produce at a higher rate. As set out above, there is evidence that as the oil is withdrawn from the entire field (not just the edge tracts), water rises or comes into the thin or outside areas. This does two things: it cuts down on the recoverable oil in those tracts, and it pushes oil updip toward the thick tracts. If this oil is not recovered before that happens, it is lost to the owners of that tract. Their correlative rights are not protected.

---

1. Railroad Commission v. Shell Oil Co., 380 S.W.2d 556 (Tex.1964). See also Railroad Commission v. Williams, 356 S.W.2d 131 at 136 (Tex.1961) as to Rule 37 cases.

This Court has taken the position that it is not the function of the Court to substitute itself for the Commission in determining the wisdom or advisability of a particular order. The power to regulate the production of oil and gas has been delegated by the Legislature to the Commission. The Court will not usurp that authority. It will not invalidate an order of the Commission because some other order might be thought by the Court to be better or more equitable. Railroad Commission v. Shell Oil Co., 139 Tex. 66, 161 S.W.2d 1022 at 1029 (1942). The Commission's order will be sustained if it is reasonably supported by substantial evidence. Railroad Commission v. Mackhank Pet. Co., 144 Tex. 393, 190 S.W.2d 802 (1945). Our holding is that this order of the Commission is reasonably supported by substantial evidence.

* * *

The judgment of the trial court is affirmed.

NOTES

1. In many states, the conservation agency does not set general pro-ration unit allowables to protect correlative rights. Except in the case of an exception well, production continues to be governed by the rule of capture. When allowables are set, a straight surface-acreage allocation is the most common unless field-wide unitization for enhanced recovery is involved, in which case the formulas may be very complicated. Why is a surface-acreage allocation the most common? How should production be allocated from a horizontal well?

2. In *Pickens,* the stated reason for using the allowable formula at issue was to provide each person with a fair opportunity to produce the oil and gas in place beneath his tract. Is that what the doctrine of correlative rights requires? Would the requirements of the doctrine depend upon the theory of ownership followed in a given jurisdiction?

3. If a well operator overproduces the allowable for a given period, civil penalties may either be assessed or the "overage" may be charged against future allowables. Depending on individual circumstances and the policy of the conservation agency, "underage" may or may not be recouped from future production.

4. Allowables may be transferred to other wells when transfer would help to conserve reservoir energy or to protect correlative rights.

MODEL OIL AND GAS CONSERVATION ACT (INTERSTATE OIL & GAS COMPACT COMM'N 2004)

Section 5. SPECIFIC AUTHORITY OF THE COMMISSION.

Without limiting the general authority of the [commission], the [commission] has the exclusive authority to require the following:

* * *

(h) the operation of wells at efficient gas-oil or water-oil ratios and the limiting of production from wells with inefficient gas-oil or water-oil ratios;

* * *

DENVER PRODUCING & REFINING CO. v. STATE

184 P.2d 961 (Okla.1947).

BAYLESS, JUSTICE.

On June 26, 1945, the Corporation Commission promulgated Order No. 17920, Cause CD 979, establishing a limited permissible producing gas-oil ratio of 2,000 cubic feet per barrel of oil in the West Edmond Hunton pool. Application was filed by plaintiff in error, Denver Producing & Refining Company, hereafter referred to as applicant, before the Corporation Commission on September 7, 1945, to amend said order by fixing a gas-oil ratio of 5,000 cubic feet per barrel of oil. After a hearing in which considerable evidence was taken for and against the application, the Commission entered an order denying the application, from which order applicant has appealed to this court. For a period of three years prior to the filing of the application herein the Commission had fixed flat allowables for the West Edmond Hunton pool, and at the time of the hearing the daily per well allowable was 150 barrels.

The effect of the two separate orders, i.e. the flat allowable order and the gas-oil ratio order, was that each well was limited to a maximum daily production of 300,000 cubic feet of gas or 150 barrels of oil, whichever was produced first. If the order had been amended as requested by applicant, the maximum allowable per well would have been 750,000 cubic feet of gas or 150 barrels of oil, whichever was produced first. There were 571 oil producing wells in this pool. Of this number, eight wells produced with a gas-oil ratio in excess of 5,000–to–1; 13 wells in excess of 4000–to–1; 48 wells in excess of 3000–to–1; and 128 wells in excess of 2000–to–1. The average of gas-oil ratio for the entire pool at the time of the hearing was 1895 cubic feet per barrel of oil. Thirty-five per cent of the oil wells in the pool were penalized by the order complained of. Applicant had 27 or 28 producing wells, 13 of which were high gas-oil ratio wells. The penalty to applicant for not being able to produce the full amount authorized by the flat allowable order amounted to $30,000 per month. Applicant's wells were high on the structure and therefore had a high gas-oil ratio since gas migrates up structure. Approximately 142,000,000 cubic feet of gas was produced daily from the field, one-half of which was being vented into the air. If the application had been granted an additional 34,000,000 cubic feet of gas would have been vented into the air, also only one and one-half per cent of the wells in the entire pool would have been restricted in the production of gas.

Applicant did not challenge the validity of the flat allowable order nor did it seek to have it set aside or amended. It complains that the fixing of a flat allowable and further restricting said flat allowable by an arbitrary gas-oil ratio of 2000-to-1 is such a departure from ratable taking as fixed by the statute, and does such violence to the correlative rights as to amount to a confiscation of property without due process of law.

Three petroleum engineers testified that no conservation would be practiced so far as reservoir energy was concerned if the ratio were raised to 5000-to-1, that a greater ultimate recovery of oil could be had if the gas-oil ratio remained at 2000-to-1. Applicant's expert witness testified that reservoir energy dissipated in one place will dissipate the energy for the entire field. * * *

* * *

Title 52 O.S.1941 § 86, as amended, Laws 1945, p. 156, section 3, 52 O.S.Supp. § 86, provides that the Commission shall have authority and is charged with the duty of preventing the inefficient or wasteful utilization of gas in the operation of oil wells producing from a common source of supply, of preventing the production of gas in such quantities or in such manner as unreasonably to reduce reservoir pressure or unreasonably to diminish the quantity of oil or gas that might be recovered from a common source of supply, and of preventing the escape of gas from oil wells into the air in excess of the amount necessary in the efficient drilling, completion or operation thereof.

* * *

* * * [T]he application of conservation measures necessarily results in curtailment of production of oil, gas or both in order to prevent waste and to obtain the greatest ultimate recovery from the pool. Experience has taught us that the heedless dissipation of gas reservoir energy of oil pools has resulted in the loss of many millions of barrels of oil. We take judicial knowledge of this fact. In most instances it is impossible to use a formula which will apply equally to all persons producing from a common source. In striking a balance between conservation of natural resources and protection of correlative rights, the latter is secondary and must yield to a reasonable exercise of the former. If the 5000-to-1 ratio had been established, the efficacy of the order from a conservation standpoint would have been negligible. The Commission has the power and is charged with the duty of conserving gas and oil resources. The Commission may, subject to the rule of reasonableness, promulgate an order directed against allowing natural gas not conveniently necessary for other purposes to come to the surface without its lifting power having been utilized to produce the greatest quantity of oil. The Commission did not use an arbitrary figure in establishing the 2000-to-1 ratio. This was based upon the average gas-oil ratio for the entire pool. Perhaps the Commission could have applied a formula which would have resulted in greater equality and less inequity but the court must not substitute its notion of expediency and fairness for that which guided the Commission to whom the formulation and execution of policy have been entrusted. The continuing supervising power of

the Commission makes it possible to keep such inequities to a minimum. The order was not arbitrary and it does not unreasonably discriminate against the applicant.

The order is affirmed.

NOTES

1. The need for a conservation agency to order the curtailment of production from wells with high gas-oil ratios has been explained as follows:

> Gas is usually present in a deposit of oil, either in solution or as a gas cap. If the gas is not utilized when oil is produced, waste of gas occurs at the surface, and the practice is subject to regulation as a wasteful practice. Whether or not the gas is utilized, waste may occur in the ground. The gas provides reservoir pressure which serves to lift the oil, and dissipation of that reservoir energy at a too rapid rate results in loss of oil underground. Gas-oil ratio regulation is designed to prevent such waste.

Kuntz § 76.2 at 387.

2. The following excerpt from Bandini Petroleum Co. v. Superior Court, 284 U.S. 8, 16 (1931) (quoting People ex rel. Stevenot v. Associated Oil Co., 294 P. 717, 724 (Cal.1930)), explains the importance of efficiently using gas to achieve the maximum primary recovery of oil.

> For present purposes it need only be noted that oil in this state is found under layers of rock in a sand or sandstone formation termed a lentille or "lentil," under pressure caused by the presence of natural gas within the formation. The layers of rock thus form a gas-tight dome or cover for the oil reserve. The oil adheres in the interstices between the sand particles. The natural gas may be in a free state at the top of the dome, but is also in solution with the oil, thus increasing the fluidity of the oil and the ease with which the oil is lifted with the gas in solution when the pressure on the gas is released by drilling into the oil "sand." It is estimated that only from ten to twenty-five per cent of the total amount of oil deposited in a reservoir is ultimately recovered, depending on the natural characteristics of the reservoir and the methods employed in utilizing the lifting power of the gas. The importance of gas in the oil-producing industry has, therefore, become a question, of great concern to the industry itself and to government, to the end that its function may be fully utilized without waste. It fairly appears on this application that, depending on its location in the oil reservoir, the extent of the oil "sand," the degree of pressure within the formation, the amount of oil in the "sand," the amount of gas in solution with the oil, the porosity of the "sand" and other considerations, each oil and gas well has a best mean gas and oil ratio in the utilization of the lifting power of the gas and the production of the greatest quantity of oil in proportion to the amount of gas so utilized, and which may be computed as to each individual well to a reasonable degree of certainty and be regulated accordingly.

In some water-drive reservoirs, the same reasoning applies regarding wells having high water-oil ratios.

3. Prorationing may serve the dual purposes of preventing waste and protecting correlative rights. When those purposes are in conflict, the prevention of waste is primary. Texaco, Inc. v. Railroad Comm'n, 583 S.W.2d 307 (Tex.1979). In the principal case, are these purposes in conflict?

In Big Piney Oil & Gas Co. v. Wyoming Oil and Gas Conservation Comm'n, 715 P.2d 557 (Wyo.1986), Belco, the operator of a secondary-recovery unit, filed an application with the Wyoming Oil and Gas Conservation Commission alleging that Big Piney, a party who had refused to participate in the unit operations, was depleting the gas cap in the reservoir, causing underground waste of oil and violating correlative rights. The evidence showed that Big Piney had already produced more gas than was originally in place under its lease and that as much as 800,000 barrels of oil would be lost to underground waste if Big Piney's production from the gas cap was not curtailed. The commission issued an order curtailing Big Piney's wells, and Big Piney appealed, contending, *inter alia,* that the commission could not protect correlative rights unless it restricted all wells in the field on a ratable basis. In rejecting this argument, the court stated:

> Testimony at the hearing demonstrated that the waste in question was caused by the production of gas cap gas. Testimony indicated further that while Belco was producing casinghead gas, it was not producing gas cap gas; thus, there was no production by Belco to restrict in order to prevent waste. Should Belco begin production of gas cap gas in the future, appellant would clearly be entitled, under the above statutes, to an allocation of production so that each operator would have the opportunity to produce its equitable share.

> Furthermore, the record reflects that, due to migration of gas into the gas cap, appellant has already produced more gas from the common pool than was estimated to be under its lease. For this reason, it would be inequitable to restrict production of gas cap gas by Belco until such production has reached the level already produced by appellant.

> Finally, we note that the rights granted by the statutory provisions cited above are limited. That is, although the owner of each property in a pool has the right to produce its equitable share of the oil and gas in the pool, that right is always subject to the need to prevent waste. For these reasons, we find that the Commission had the authority to restrict appellant's production without similarly restricting Belco's production.

Id. at 563.

MODEL OIL AND GAS CONSERVATION ACT (INTERSTATE OIL & GAS COMPACT COMM'N 2004)

Section 1. DEFINITIONS

(17) "Reasonable market demand" means:

    (A) the amount of oil reasonably needed for current consumption, use, storage, and working stocks, within and without this state; or

(B) the amount of gas reasonably needed for current consumption, use, and storage, within and without this state.

Section 9. RATABLE PRODUCTION OF OIL AND GAS

(a) To prevent unreasonable discrimination in favor of one pool against another, and on written complaint and proof of discrimination, the [commission] may allocate or apportion the allowable production of oil on a fair and reasonable basis among the various pools in this state. In fixing the allowable production of oil based on reasonable market demand, the [commission] is not required to determine the reasonable market demand applicable to a single field or reservoir, except in relation to other fields and reservoirs and in relation to the reasonable market demand applicable to this state. In allocating the allowable production of oil to fields and reservoirs, the [commission] may consider, but is not bound by, nominations of purchasers to purchase from particular fields or reservoirs. In allocating or ascertaining the reasonable market demand for the entire state, the reasonable market demand of one pool shall not be discriminated against in favor of another pool. The [commission] shall determine the reasonable market demand of the respective pool as the basis for determining the allotments to be assigned to the respective pool so that discrimination may be prevented.

(b) If full production from wells producing gas, including a gas by-product, from a common source of supply of gas in this state is in excess of the reasonable market demand, the [commission] shall inquire into the production and reasonable market demand for the gas and shall determine the allowable production from the common source of supply. The allowable production from a common source of supply is that portion of the reasonable market demand that can be produced without waste. The [commission] shall allocate, distribute, or apportion the allowable production from the common source of supply among the various owners on a reasonable basis and shall limit the production of each owner to the amount allocated or apportioned to the owner. The [commission] may give priority to the production of gas from oil wells when allocating the allowable production of gas under this section.

Dad, Doc, Boy and the Black Giant[40]

Although you could not tell by their looks, "Dad" and "Doc" were ladies' men. Dad walked hunched over, and Doc was corpulent. Yet, each had an uncanny talent for separating widows from their money and often

---

40. For more information, see, BRYAN BURROUGH, THE BIG RICH: THE RISE AND FALL OF THE GREATES TEXAS OIL FORTUNES, ch. 4 (Penguin 2009); DIANA DAVIS OLIEN & ROGER M. OLIEN, OIL IN TEXAS, THE GUSHER AGE, 1895–1945, ch. 7 (Univ. of Tex. 2002) (hereafter OIL IN TEXAS); DANIEL YERGIN, THE PRIZE 244–259 (Simon & Schuster 1990); Harry Hurt III, "How to Become a Billionaire," TEXAS MONTHLY 94 (August 1980).

from their virtue. Dad, whose real name was Columbus Marion Joiner, was a "poor-boy wildcatter." Doc Lloyd, born Joseph Idelbert Durham, used many aliases throughout his life, apparently to hide from several wives, lovers, and children. Doc was a patent-medicine salesman who falsely claimed to also be a physician, geologist, engineer, or other convenient expert when the need arose. Neither Dad nor Doc was successful in the oil business until Doc convinced Dad that oil could be found on the Daisy Bradford farm in East Texas—an idea that was laughable to real geologists at that time. Nevertheless, using Doc's "trendologist's" report,[41] Dad was able to raise drilling capital by selling interests in the well—totaling more than 100% as it turns out—and by occasionally paying the drilling crew and purchasing supplies with promises of production shares.

The Daisy Bradford No. 1 and No. 2 wells failed when drill pipe became stuck in the holes, but the Daisy Bradford No. 3 blew in October 3, 1930, gushing oil from the Woodbine Sand formation. Daisy Bradford No. 3 was the discovery well for the East Texas Field, commonly called the "Black Giant." This field would prove to be the biggest oilfield in the continental United States: over 40 miles long and up to 10 miles wide.

Soon after the discovery, Dad's overly zealous promotion came back to haunt him. He had promised more in production shares than he could deliver. He was rescued—some might say conned—by H. L. Hunt, a former gambling hall operator, who had become a moderately successful oil man in Arkansas. Dad called Hunt "Boy." In some ways, Boy was like Dad and Doc. Boy had a knack for spending other peoples' money, and he was maintaining two wives and families.

Boy had tried to secure an interest in the discovery well before it was even completed, but Dad did not need additional funds at that moment. After the well blew in, Boy and Dad negotiated at Boy's room in the Baker Hotel in Dallas, cater-cornered from the Adolphus Hotel, where Dad maintained his office. During the course of their 36–hour marathon negotiation, Hunt was secretly fed information about the Deep Rock well, which would help confirm the size of the field. Shortly after Hunt received news that the Deep Rock was a producer, he struck a final deal with Dad at near midnight on the evening of November 26, 1930. The terms were $30,000 cash and $1.3 million in production payments. Because Boy had his own investors, Boy had bought out Dad's well and leases in East Texas without using a penny of his own funds.

Boy would become the wealthiest man in the world. Doc died in poverty in a Chicago a flophouse hotel in 1941. Dad drilled dry holes in search of another giant oilfield and died in 1947 owning little more than a house and a car.

---

41. "Lloyd's 'reports' told investors that it was possible to locate these riches by studying the color of surface rock, soil, and vegetation, as well as by drawing lines on a map that connected oil-producing areas, and then by drilling where the lines intersected." OIL IN TEXAS at 169.

Dad Joiner shakes hands with the corpulent Doc Lloyd after discovering the huge East Texas oil field on October 3, 1930. H.L. Hunt (smoking a cigar) rescued Joiner from financial difficulties and in the process acquired his immensely valuable leases.

The Immediate Aftermath of The Big Giant

Within eight months of the Daisy Bradford No. 3 discovery, the field was producing 500,000 barrels per day. Production would greatly increase as additional wells were drilled. This additional oil could not have come onto the market at worse time. The country was in the grip of the Great Depression and had no need for additional oil supplies. Soon oil prices plummeted across the country from over a dollar per barrel to below a nickel in East Texas—well below the cost of production. To try to stem the tide of oil, the governor of Oklahoma declared martial law, directing the state militia to take control of large fields. The Texas governor sent the Texas Rangers to East Texas to deal with "insurrection."

The Oklahoma Corporation Commission exercised its authority to regulate production to a level of reasonable market demand. The Texas Railroad Commission had no such authority but did so anyway. The Texas orders were invalidated by the courts. Legislation was passed in Texas in a special legislative session and new market-demand-prorationing orders were issued. These new orders were not restrictive enough, and many producers ignored the restrictions. Production that exceeded the allowable quota came to be called "hot oil."

Following the inauguration of Franklin D. Roosevelt in March of 1933, Harold L. Ickes, the newly appointed Secretary of the Interior, was given broad powers to deal with hot oil by executive order and by the National Industrial Recovery Act (NIRA).[42] Under this Act, Ickes could establish production quotas for each state. This federal system worked reasonably well until the United States Supreme Court held in January of 1935 that a key provision of the NIRA was unconstitutional.[43] Then in May of that year, the Court declared much of the rest of the Act unconstitutional.[44] These decisions stripped Ickes of his authority to establish state production quotas.

In the interim, Congress passed the Connally Hot Oil Act,[45] which reestablished federal authority to stem the tide of hot oil. The federal Bureau of Mines still published recommended quotas for states. For the most part, these recommendations were followed. Using these guidelines, the petroleum regulatory agency in each state established quotas for each field and then for each well in each field. This practice was formalized in the Interstate Oil Compact,[46] initially proposed in 1931 and finally approved by Congress on August 27, 1935.[47] In the 1970s, the Organization of Petroleum Exporting Countries (OPEC) began establishing production quotas for its member countries in a manner somewhat similar to the Interstate Oil Compact.

NOTES

1. A conservation agency typically uses the following three-step process to limit production to reasonable market demand:

> (1) a determination of the maximum allowable production figure for the state as a whole; (2) a determination of the share of this top allowable that shall be allocated to each producing field in the state; and (3) a formula for the ratable distribution of this field allowable among the operators therein.

Sullivan § 163. Separate determinations for different types of crude oil may be made due to variations in market demand and refining capabilities for particular crude oils. For example, not all refineries can refine sour crude oils and heavy crude oils. To assist the conservation agency in determining the statewide production allowables, purchasers and refiners of crude oil made periodic nominations of the amount of oil they could handle. From these projections, the conservation agency then determined statewide, field-wide, and per well[48] allowables for the period in question.

---

42. Pub. L. 73–90, 48 Stat. 195 (June 16, 1933); Exec. Order 6199 (July 11, 1933); and Exec. Order 6204 (July 14, 1933).

43. Panama Refining Co. v. Ryan, 293 U.S. 388 (1935)

44. A.L.A. Schechter Poultry Corp. v. United States, 295 U.S. 495 (1935).

45. 49 Stat. 33, 15 U.S.C. § 715 et seq.

46. The authority for states to enter into compacts is found in the United States Constitution, art. I, § 10, cl. 3.

47. H.R. Res. 407, 74th Cong. (1935) (enacted).

48. A marginal or "stripper" well (often defined as a well that produces fewer than 10 barrels of oil a day) is typically exempt from market demand or other prorationing to prevent the underground and economic waste that may result if the well were abandoned. For similar

Although a few states still observe the formalities of this process, "market-demand prorationing" is largely of historical interest. Occasionally, this process is useful to address temporary reductions in refining capacity, such as reductions caused by refinery explosions or natural catastrophes.

2.   Not all producing states have statutes expressly authorizing market-demand prorationing, but that authority has been implied and upheld under the general authority to prevent waste. See Lion Oil Refining Co. v. Bailey, 139 S.W.2d 683 (Ark.1940). On the other hand, because market-demand prorationing has been controversial, several states have provisions in their conservation acts that expressly or impliedly prohibit market-demand prorationing. Among these states are California, Colorado, Illinois, Kentucky, Mississippi, Montana, Ohio, Utah, and Wyoming.

3.   The constitutionality of market-demand prorationing of oil was upheld in Champlin Refining Co. v. Corporation Comm'n, 286 U.S. 210 (1932).

4.   While oil market-demand prorationing is largely of historical interest, nondiscriminatory gas marketing has been and remains a controversial matter. Most natural gas is transported in pipelines from the area where the gas is produced (e.g., the Southwest) to the area where the gas is consumed (e.g., the Northeast).

Like a railroad, a pipeline tends to serve particular markets and is subject to regulation as a common carrier. Historically, however, unlike railroads, pipeline companies purchased gas in the field and then transported and resold the gas to consumers—commonly local distribution companies, such as a public utility. Thus, pipeline companies exercised both monopsony and monopoly powers. To curb abuse of these powers, Congress enacted the Natural Gas Act of 1938, 52 Stat. 821. [T]o further curb abuse of monopsony power and to protect correlative rights, state conservation acts required pipeline companies to purchase gas ratably from producers without price discrimination.[49]

State ratable-take regulation, however, was not viewed favorably by the federal courts. Just five years after sustaining oil market-demand prorationing, the Supreme Court struck down a ratable-take order for the Panhandle Field in Texas, where the pipeline,[50] although having monopsony power, could satisfy its demand from its own wells. Thompson v. Consolidated Gas Utilities Corp., 300 U.S. 55 (1937).[51] In 1963, the Court held that general statewide and field-wide ratable-take orders were preempted by the Natural Gas Act.

reasons, marginal wells may be subject to lower production taxes. See, e.g., Gofor Oil, Inc. v. State, 427 N.W.2d 104 (N.D.1988). Marginal wells are important contributors to domestic oil supplies. Taken as a whole, they account for 17 percent of all domestic onshore oil production and 9 percent of all domestic onshore gas production. Interstate Oil & Gas Compact Commission, Marginal Wells: Fuel for Economic Growth (2007).

49.   In contrast, oil market-demand prorationing requires producers to curb production for the primary purpose of preventing waste

50.   In the natural gas industry, the term "pipeline(s)" is often used to refer to a pipeline company, rather than an actual gas pipeline.

51.   In 1950, the Court held that gas prorationing orders issued to prevent waste were enforceable even though the orders effectively fixed the wellhead price of gas and required ratable taking. Cities Service Gas Co. v. Peerless Oil & Gas Co., 340 U.S. 179 (1950). The state's power to fix wellhead gas prices was later overturned in Natural Gas Pipeline Co. v. Corporation Commission of Oklahoma, 349 U.S. 44 (1955), a case that built upon Phillips Petroleum Co. v.

Northern Natural Gas Co. v. State Corp. Comm'n, 372 U.S. 84 (1963). The Court did suggest, however, that an order that required ratable production would be permissible.

In 1978, with passage of the Natural Gas Policy Act (NGPA), Pub.L.No. 95–621 (1978), Congress mandated the gradual deregulation of gas and the conversion of pipeline operators from being regulated merchants of gas to being regulated transporters of gas. Thereafter, the Mississippi Supreme Court upheld a state ratable-take order on the grounds that the NGPA demonstrated Congressional intent to retreat from federal regulation of gas and to allow states to again regulate sales of wellhead gas. Transcontinental Gas Pipeline Corp. v. State Oil & Gas Bd., 457 So.2d 1298 (Miss.1984). This holding was reversed by the United States Supreme Court in a 5–4 decision. Transcontinental Gas Pipe Line Corp. v. State Oil & Gas Bd. (Transco), 474 U.S. 409 (1986). While *Transco* reaffirmed the position that states cannot mandate ratable taking, in 1989 the Supreme Court implicitly upheld a state's right to set gas allowables, or in other words, to require ratable production. Northwest Central Pipeline Corp. v. State Corp. Comm'n, 489 U.S. 493 (1989).

Allowables for gas wells are generally set by establishing an allowable for each reservoir based upon the estimated market demand for gas from that reservoir. The reservoir allowable is then divided among the wells according to an allocation formula that may consider acreage, deliverability,[52] reservoir pressures, net-acre-feet of reservoir beneath each proration unit, and the number of wells in the field.

To further protect gas producers from discriminatory marketing practices, Oklahoma's Natural Gas Market Sharing Act, Okla. Stat. tit. 52, § 581.1 et seq., protects gas producers from discriminatory purchasing practices by allowing them to elect to share in the nonexempt gas markets of other producers.

5. Gas that is produced from an oil well is called *casinghead* or *associated gas*. To prevent waste, associated or casinghead gas is usually given a higher marketing priority than gas produced from gas wells.[53] Associated gas may be unmarketable because the well may be too far from a pipeline connection, because the gas may be *sour*,[54] or because there may be no

---

Wisconsin, 347 U.S. 672 (1954), wherein the Court held that the Federal Power Commission had authority to control the wellhead price of gas.

52. Deliverability is a measure of a well's production capability; an estimate of a well's flow rate against a working wellhead back pressure. Norman J. Hyne, Dictionary of Petroleum Exploration, Drilling, and Production (PennWell 1991).

53. Wells are classified, for purposes of conservation regulation, as either gas or oil wells in accordance with a regulatory definition. A common classification would define an oil well as any well that produces one or more barrels of oil for each 100,000 cubic feet of gas. A gas well is any well that produces only gas or more than 100,000 cubic feet of gas for each barrel of oil. See, e.g., V.T.C.A., Nat.Res.Code § 86.002. A regulatory classification, however, does not resolve disputed ownership rights to the production where the oil rights and the gas rights are owned by separate parties (commonly called a "phase severance"). See, e.g., Colorado Interstate Gas Co. v. HUFO Oils, 626 F.Supp. 38 (W.D.Tex.1985), affirmed 802 F.2d 133 (5th Cir. 1986), rehearing en banc denied 806 F.2d 261 (5th Cir.1986); and Amarillo Oil Co. v. Energy–Agri Prod., Inc., 794 S.W.2d 20 (Tex.1990).

54. Sour gas is gas that contains hydrogen sulfide in concentrations that exceed pipeline or sales specifications. Norman J. Hyne, Dictionary of Petroleum Exploration, Drilling, and Production (PennWell 1991).

market demand for the gas. Historically, operators flared or vented unmarketable associated gas. Today, however, conservation agencies either prohibit or greatly limit the flaring of gas.

4. REGULATING END USE

Some uses of oil and gas, such as for the manufacture of carbon black, a historically common use for gas that could not otherwise be marketed, are prohibited under the provisions of some conservation acts on waste-prevention grounds. As a result of the energy "crisis" in the 1970s, some public utility commissions prohibited the sale of natural gas for outdoor decorative lighting.

In the 1970s and 1980s, state public utility commissions and the federal government took steps to discourage the construction or expansion of electrical-generation facilities that convert oil or gas to electricity. For example, the Powerplant and Industrial Fuel Use Act of 1978, Pub.L.No. 95–620, 92 Stat. 3289 (1978), codified at 42 U.S.C. §§ 8301 *et seq., inter alia,* prohibited utilities and large industrial users from building new plants designed to burn oil or gas. This act was part of an over-all effort to encourage conversion to coal or other forms of energy. Various sections of the act were repealed or amended by the act of May 21, 1987, Pub.L.No. 100–42, 101 Stat. 310 (1987). Because gas is a relatively clean-burning fuel, the electric-power industry has constructed many new gas-fired power plants.

5. THE PROBLEM OF SMALL TRACTS & COMPULSORY POOLING

Assume that Tracts A, B, and C comprise one spacing or proration unit and that one well has been drilled somewhere within the unit. Assume further that the respective owners of these tracts have equitably shared the costs of drilling and completing the well and are equitably sharing production and production costs. Combining of these tracts for the purpose of sharing production and expenses is called "pooling." While most commonly done to comply with spacing and density requirements, pooling can be done for other reasons and can encompass larger acreages.

Pooling can occur voluntarily, such as by the execution of a *community lease*[55] in some jurisdictions (discussed in Chapter 4, Section B.1.(b)); by the lessee's exercise of the pooling power under a lease *pooling clause*[56]

---

55. A community oil and gas lease is a single lease covering two or more separately-owned mineral tracts. A community lease typically is a single lease signed by the multiple owners of separate mineral tracts but could also result from the execution of separate but identical leases by the owners of separate mineral tracts where each lease provides that it covers the entire acreage encompassed by all the tracts. Royalties are typically apportioned in proportion to the size of the individual interests owned in the entire leased acreage.

56. While a lessee may pool its lease working interest with other acreage, the lease pooling clause authorizes the lessee to act on the lessor's behalf to pool the lessor's retained royalty interest with other acreage. The lessee must exercise this authority in good faith and in

(discussed in Chapter 3, Section C.2.(c)(iii)); or by agreement. Pooling has occasionally occurred as a matter of law through so-called judicial or equitable pooling in Mississippi and commonly occurs in many states through a regulatory process called *forced pooling* or *compulsory pooling*.

(a) Introduction

The most difficult problem in spacing is the small tract. Suppose Able is the owner of Blackacre, a 10–acre tract in an oil field that must be developed on a 40–acre spacing unit pattern. Assume Baker is the owner of Whiteacre, a 30–acre tract in the same field adjacent to Blackacre. Historically in Texas, Able and Baker would each be entitled to drill one well on their respective tracts is as an exception to the normal spacing pattern. This approach protected the correlative rights of owners of tracts that were too small to qualify for a routine well permit under applicable spacing regulations.

In most producing states, however, Able and Baker would have to *pool* their interests and drill one well in accordance with the 40–acre drilling pattern. If they fail to pool their interests by voluntary agreement, the conservation agency would, upon the application of either party, *force pool* their interests under authority of a compulsory pooling statute. Once pooled, Able and Baker would proportionately share in the production from the one well to be drilled on the spacing unit.

Disagreements among various interest owners often prevent the successful negotiation of a pooling agreement. Disagreements can occur over the desirability of drilling, the timing of drilling, the allocation of production and drilling costs, the location of the well, the designation of the operator, and the particular acreage to be included in the unit. The most common solution to the inability to pool voluntarily is for the party or parties desirous of pooling to apply to the conservation agency for an order force pooling the interests in a spacing or proration unit.

Statutes authorizing compulsory pooling have been enacted in all major producing states except Kansas. The statutory details vary from state to state but generally provide that in order to meet the minimum requirements for a drilling permit any person seeking a drilling permit may force the inclusion of the necessary adjacent tracts, as well as force pool undivided interests within the proposed unit.[57]

(b) Judicial and Equitable Pooling

The terms *judicial pooling* and *equitable pooling* describe a doctrine set forth in several Mississippi cases. According to this doctrine, when a

---

accordance with the terms of the applicable pooling clauses. If the lessee exercises this power to pool leases that only it holds, the lessee "declares" a pooling. If two or more lessees exercise their respective pooling powers to pool leases, they do so through a voluntary pooling agreement.

57. Similar problems exist in *unitization*, discussed in Section 6 of this chapter. Although pooling and unitization are quite different, these terms of art are often improperly used interchangeably. In pooling, small tracts and interests are joined within a single drilling or proration unit. By contrast, in unitization, the tracts and interests in all or in a significant portion of a field are joined to facilitate the use of enhanced-recovery techniques to increase production.

well is drilled on an established spacing unit, the land within the unit is automatically pooled as a matter of law. See Superior Oil Co. v. Foote, 857, 59 So.2d 85 (Miss.1952) and Green v. Superior Oil Co., 59 So.2d 100 (Miss.1952). Although the decisions in *Foote* and *Green* were handed down following the enactment of a compulsory pooling act, both cases concerned wells that were drilled before the passage of the act.

Equitable pooling has not been adopted in any other jurisdiction, although there may be some support for the doctrine in Louisiana.[58] Texas, Kansas, and other jurisdictions have specifically rejected the concept.[59] Since all major oil and gas producing states except Kansas have compulsory pooling statutes, the concept of equitable pooling is largely of historical interest.

(c) Kansas: Allowable Adjustments and Acreage Attribution

Although Kansas does not have a compulsory pooling statute, it has adopted the following statute dealing with oil and gas development within cities:

> Whenever the governing body of any city authorizes the development of minerals within the corporate limits of the city, it may adopt an ordinance dividing the city into drilling units for the production of those minerals. The ordinance shall require any persons having the right to produce minerals in a drilling unit to pool their rights for the production of such minerals.

Kan. Stat. Ann. §§ 55–1611. If a city fails to provide for pooling within its jurisdictional boundaries, or if the property lies outside of municipal boundaries, then pooling is possible only by voluntary agreement.

Kansas spaces wells using property line set-backs and minimum blocks of acreage to form a "drilling unit." Kan. Admin. Reg. § 82–3–108 (set-back), § 82–3–207 (oil drilling unit), § 82–3–312 (gas drilling unit). For example, the standard drilling unit for gas wells is 10 acres. The "standard" drilling unit can be adjusted by requesting special field rules. Well allowables are used to ensure compliance with the set-back and drilling unit requirements. For example, Kan. Admin. Reg. § 82–3–312 establishes a "standard daily allowable" for gas wells limited to 50 percent of the well's actual open-flow potential. However, "[i]f any gas well is located nearer than 330 feet to any lease or unit boundary line, the standard daily allowable or minimum allowable shall be reduced in the same proportion that the acreage attribution to the well bears to 10 acres."

If the mineral interests at issue are within an area governed by special field rules, the field rules will define the set-backs and drilling unit

---

58. Placid Oil Co. v. North Central Texas Oil Co., 19 So.2d 616 (La.1944).

59. See Ryan Consol. Petroleum Corp. v. Pickens, 266 S.W.2d 526 (Tex.Civ.App. 1954), affirmed 155 Tex. 221, 285 S.W.2d 201 (Tex.1955), cert. denied 351 U.S. 933 (1956) [included at Subsection A.1(a) of this Chapter], and Republic Natural Gas Co. v. Baker, 197 F.2d 647 (10th Cir.Kan.1952).

acreage. Under the "Basic Integrated Proration Order for the Hugoton Gas Field and the Panoma Council Grove Gas Field," the standard drilling unit is set at 480 acres and operators have the option to drill up to three wells on the drilling unit and dual-complete them in both the Hugoton (Chase) and the Panoma Council Grove formations. Although the Order requires that the standard drilling unit must be comprised of "contiguous and adjoining" acreage, an exception can be requested to attribute "non-contiguous acreage" to the unit when certain conditions are met, including: "That a reasonable attempt has been made to form a unit made up of wholly contiguous acreage and there is no acreage in closer proximity to the well site available on approximately the same economic basis for attribution thereto; * * *" Basic Integrated Proration Order, p. 8, § H.2.(a)(2) (available through the Kansas Corporation Commission's website at www.kcc.state.ks.us). This provides the developer some leverage to encourage acreage owners within the standard unit to voluntarily pool their interests.

In Mobil Oil Corp. v. State Corp. Comm'n, 608 P.2d 1325 (Kan.1980), Mobil had obtained the consent to pool from the mineral owners in three quarter sections, and the owner of a 4/7ths interest in the remaining quarter section, to create a 571–acre (160 + 160 + 160 + 91) pooled area for assignment of its allowable. The conservation agency refused to attribute the 91 (4/7 x 160) acres associated with the 4/7ths interest because the owner of the remaining 3/7ths mineral interest had refused to pool. The Kansas Supreme Court reversed the conservation agency's conclusion that it lacked jurisdiction to attribute the 91 acres to the prorated unit:

> The rather dog-in-the-manger position of the owners of the 3/7 interest is that if Mobil won't pay them a premium for joining the unit then it is unfair to let the owners of the 4/7 interest into the unit. The Commission, by its order, permits the 3/7 to use the 4/7 as a tool to improve their bargaining position. The Commission is acting upon what might be referred to as equitable considerations when it is cloaked with no equitable jurisdiction.

608 P.2d at 1337. The practical result was that the 3/7ths interest owner is forced to accept Mobil's pooling offer. Does this practice protect the correlative rights of the 3/7ths interest owner? The 4/7ths interest owner? See generally Mobil Exploration v. State Corp. Comm'n, 908 P.2d 1276, 1303 (Kan.1995) (equating correlative rights to an "opportunity" to produce).

Although the acreage-attribution mechanism provides an incentive to pool voluntarily, very few fields in Kansas are subject to field rules that allow the attribution of noncontiguous acreage to fill out a drilling unit. Therefore, in the vast majority of situations, this outside force will not be available to promote voluntary pooling.

The absence of compulsory pooling has, in the past, not created a serious problem for Kansas oil and gas operators. Compared to states such as Oklahoma or Texas, Kansas oil and gas ownership patterns are relatively simple and spacing patterns are relatively small. Most developers have adapted to the situation by including broad pooling authority in their oil and gas leases whenever possible;[60] however, sophisticated Kansas lessors delete these provisions whenever possible. Kansas landowners enjoy greater leverage when negotiating an oil and gas lease because the developer will lack the coercive option of compulsory pooling. However, with the advent of a major horizontal drilling play in Kansas, the topic of compulsory pooling was again before the Kansas Legislature when this edition went to press. Kansas landowners are executory oil and gas leases containing pooling clauses allowing 1280–acre pooled areas in return for the payment of large bonuses that had not been seen in Kansas prior to the current horizontal drilling activity.

(d) Texas Regulations: Rule 37 Exceptions

Because Texas did not have a compulsory pooling act until 1965, the means by which Texas has addressed the problem of the small tract is unique.[61] In 1919, the legislature enacted a law giving the Texas Railroad Commission ("RRC") broad enforcement powers to prevent waste in the production of oil and gas. Pursuant to this authority, the Commission promulgated a series of regulations governing drilling, production, and marketing. Rule 37[62] is the best known rule and the one that has prompted the most litigation. Like all Railroad Commission rules, it was promulgated when virtually all legal drilling was by vertical wells. As a result it and almost all other RRC rules have posed special problems when applied to horizontal wells.

Rule 37 is a statewide spacing rule, which now provides that a vertical well has to be located at least 467 feet from any property line and at least 1,200 feet from other wells on the same tract and producing from the same source of supply. This statewide rule is sometimes altered by the adoption of special field-wide rules on spacing. For shale fields where horizontal drilling is typically used, the minimum distance from lease or pooled unit lines is often 330 feet, although here, also, other special field-wide rules may be promulgated for different fields, but the provisions of Rule 37 still govern the granting of exception locations.

Under Rule 37, spacing exceptions may be granted to prevent waste or to prevent "confiscation" of property. This portion of the rule has become especially significant in fields with horizontal drilling, for the extended well bore may pass within 330 feet of an unleased tract, especially in urban and suburban areas where there are many small lots with unleased mineral rights. In some fields special field rules have been

---

60. A lease pooling clause authorizes the lessee to pool the lease with other lands, including the power to pool the lessor's interest. Lease pooling clauses are discussed in Chapter 3, Section C.2.(c)(iii).

61. The discussion on the history of Rule 37 is largely a synopsis of Hafley, Rule 37 Exceptions: Well Spacing and Density Requirements, Paper H (State Bar of Tex.Inst.1982). See also Robert E. Hardwicke, Oil–Well Spacing Regulations and Protection of Property Rights in Texas, 31 Tex.L.Rev. 99 (1952).

62. R.R. Comm'n, Tex.Admin.Code § 3.37.

adopted under which an exception is not necessary if a horizontal well has been cased and cemented and only a cased and cemented portion of the well is closer than 330 feet to an adjoining unleased property. In these fields the exception would have to be sought only if a perforation or "take point" is within 330 feet of adjacent property. As of the time this edition was being prepared, the Railroad Commission was under considerable pressure to amend Rule 37 to eliminate the need for exceptions in all situations where a cased and cemented portion of a horizontal line was closer than 330 feet (or other spacing rule applicable to the field) to unleased property.

The Commission's Rule 38[63] governs drilling density. This rule, adopted in the late 1930s, provides the minimum acreage required for a well based on the size of the spacing units[64] established for a field. If field-wide proration units have not been established, the minimum acreage is 40 acres. The commission may also grant exceptions to Rule 38 to prevent waste or to prevent confiscation of property.

(i) Exceptions to Prevent Confiscation

The spacing or density exception to prevent waste has already been discussed in this chapter. The peculiarity that distinguishes Texas conservation law from that of other major oil and gas producing states is the exception to prevent confiscation. This exception is predicated upon the proposition that every mineral interest owner is entitled, as a matter of law, to drill at least one well to produce the oil and gas beneath the tract no matter how small or irregular in shape the tract may be.[65]

If several vertically separated reservoirs underlie a tract, the right to one well applies to each reservoir. In Benz–Stoddard v. Aluminum Co. of America., 368 S.W.2d 94 (Tex.1963), the applicant for a Rule 37 permit owned approximately one-tenth of an acre overlying ten vertically separated gas reservoirs. The Railroad Commission granted her petition to drill a single well that would have multiple completions in six of the reservoirs.[66] On appeal the opponent argued that the Rule 37 permit should have been limited to a single completion. The opponent contended that production from a single reservoir would result in enough drainage from surrounding property to permit petitioner to recover more than her fair share of the oil

---

63. Id. § 3.38.

64. In Texas, a proration unit is the acreage assigned to a specific well for the purpose of calculating and allocating a well allowable.

65. The term confiscation was defined by the Texas Supreme Court in Gulf Land Co. v. Atlantic Refining Co., 131 S.W.2d 73, 80 (1939), as follows:

As used in Rule 37 * * * the term "confiscation" evidently has reference to depriving the owner or lessee of a fair chance to recover the oil and gas in or under his land, or their equivalents in kind. It is evident that the word refers principally to drainage. * * * It is the law that every owner or lessee of land is entitled to a fair chance to recover the oil and gas in or under his land, or their equivalents in kind. Any denial of such fair chance would be "confiscation" within the meaning of Rule 37 * * *

Most oil and gas conservation acts charge the agency with the duty to protect correlative rights rather than the duty to prevent the confiscation of property.

66. The permit was apparently limited to six completions, because it was not technically feasible to make completions in all ten reservoirs from a single well bore.

and gas in place in all ten reservoirs.[67] In upholding the Railroad Commission's action, the Texas Supreme Court held that petitioner who had mineral rights in all ten reservoirs was entitled to protect each reservoir from confiscation.

The right of an owner of a tract, however small the tract, to drill a well suggests a problem with its application. As stated by a Texas court of appeals,

> If the owner of a tract of land which is capable of development as a whole in such manner as to extract therefrom all the oil he is entitled to under the conservation laws of the state, be permitted, under the guise of vested rights, either to lease same in small tracts, or to lease a portion thereof and reserve unto himself a small strip * * * and thus secure one or more wells on each small tract, it is obvious that the conservation laws would be rendered nugatory.

Sun Oil Co. v. Railroad Comm'n, 68 S.W.2d 609, 611 (Tex. Civ.App.1933), affirmed 84 S.W.2d 693 (Tex.1935). To avoid this result, the Railroad Commission and the courts developed a major limitation upon rights of owners of small tracts—the voluntary subdivision rule, which is set forth in Statewide Spacing Rule R.R. Comm'n, Tex.Admin. Code § 3.37(g) (West Apr. 1, 1991)

As interpreted by the Texas courts, a voluntary subdivision occurs when a tract entitled to at least one well is subdivided and one or more of the subdivided tracts is smaller than 40 acres. An obvious example is a 40 acre tract that is subdivided into a 20-acre tract and two 10-acre tracts. None of the tracts is entitled to a well as a matter of right. This rule applies, however, only if the decision was made in contemplation of oil and gas development (such as by executing separate leases on each of the 20-acre tracts) or if the subdivision occurred after the field underlying the 40-acre tract had been discovered. The fact that the field extended laterally beneath the tract was not known as of the date of the subdivision is irrelevant. (The Administrative Code does contain a provision authorizing the Railroad Commission to provide exceptions to protect the rights of innocent parties.)

The voluntary subdivision rule raises an obvious question: Is it ever possible to drill on small tracts resulting from a voluntary subdivision? The answer is yes. In fact three options are usually available: The Century doctrine, voluntary pooling, and forced pooling under the Mineral Interest Pooling Act.

The Century doctrine[68] was summarized in Humble Oil & Refining Co. v. Lasseter, 120 S.W.2d 541, 542 (Tex.Civ.App.1938, writ dismissed) as follows:

---

67. Alcoa alleged that as of the date of the case, Claire Benz–Stoddard had completed her well in three reservoirs and had already recovered seven times the gas in place beneath all ten reservoirs. Alcoa calculated that 84 percent of the gas produced by the petitioner had been drained from Alcoa's property.

68. The Century Doctrine, which was set forth in Railroad Comm'n v. Magnolia Petroleum Co., 109 S.W.2d 967 (Tex.1937), got its name from the Century Refining Company, the party that sought the Rule 37 exception.

> Where, independently of the voluntary segregation, the larger
> tract, including the segregated tract, is entitled to an additional
> well in order to protect the vested rights of the owners of such
> larger tract to recover their fair share of the oil thereunder in
> place, the permit to drill on the segregated tract will be upheld.
> And this, although the application be made to drill only upon the
> voluntarily segregated tract and only by the owners of that tract,
> and be contested by the owners of the remaining portion of the
> larger tract.

In other words, the Century doctrine provides that a well permit should be granted or denied on the basis of whether the requested well would prevent confiscation of oil and gas under the original, pre-subdivided tract. If so, the well permit should be granted even though only the owner of a small subdivided tract that was once part of a larger tract applies for the permit and uses the acreage of some or all the subdivided tracts to reach the 40 acres required, and even in the face of opposition by the owners of the remaining portions of the larger tract.[69]

Assume the original hypothetical in which a 40-acre tract was subdivided into a 20-acre and two 10-acre tracts after the field underlying the acreage had been discovered. The owners of the three tracts execute leases to different oil and gas companies and each lessee applies for the single Century Doctrine drilling permit to be issued for the "reconstructed" 40-acre tract. How does the Railroad Commission determine which applicant should receive the permit? What are the rights of the parties whose applications are denied? Over a vigorous dissent, the Texas Supreme Court in Ryan Consolidated Petroleum Corp. v. Pickens, 285 S.W.2d 201 (Tex.1955), came to the rather surprising conclusion that under the rule of capture, the applicant who received the permit was entitled to all of the production from the well, and did not have to share it with owners and lessees of other tracts, even though those tracts had been included in the application for a well on the "reconstructed" tract.

The Century doctrine is not often invoked today, in part because of the reasoning and result of *Ryan*. If there are several applicants, no one applicant can be sure to receive the drilling permit. The applicants that do not receive the permit will not be entitled to any of the production of the well. The case thus created an incentive for the owners or lessees of tracts resulting from a voluntary subdivision to enter into a voluntary pooling agreement.

If the parties cannot reach a voluntary agreement, a third alternative became available in 1965 with the passage of Texas' Mineral Interest Pooling Act (MIPA), which authorized forced pooling. The MIPA will be discussed later in this section.

---

69. The editors gratefully acknowledge the assistance of Professor Jacqueline Weaver of the University of Houston Law School in preparing this explanation of the Century Doctrine.

(ii) Well Allowables

The complexity of the Rule 37 exception to prevent confiscation is some indication of the large number and variety of situations in which it has been invoked. Since voluntary pooling is usually available as an alternative method for procuring the benefit of the underlying oil and gas, you may wonder why so many small-tract owners asserted their right to drill. The reason lies in the fact that for many decades the Railroad Commission, with the blessings of the courts, assigned Rule 37 exception wells a so-called "living allowable." For example, in Railroad Commission v. Humble Oil & Refining, 193 S.W.2d 824 (Tex.Civ.App.–Austin 1946, writ ref'd n.r.e.), called the *Hawkins Field* case, the court affirmed the use of a "50–50 allowable," wherein half of the field-wide allowable was allocated on a per-well basis and half was allocated on a per-acre basis. This resulted in small tracts receiving a proportionately much larger allowable at the expense of larger tracts. The standard density rule for the Hawkins Field was 20 acres. A townsite, consisting of about 137 acres of town lots had 91 Rule 37 exception wells, 87 of which were located on lots comprising less than 74 acres total. The 50–50 allowable formula effectively gave the exception wells the right to drain a quantity of oil that far exceeded a fair share.

The *Hawkins Field* case is but one example of the basic principle governing well allowables in the early days of Railroad Commission regulation: Except for limitations imposed by doctrines such as the voluntary subdivision rule, an owner had the right to drill at least one well and the right to an allowable sufficient to operate the well at a reasonable profit. The Commission would protect these rights by issuing special well permits and by establishing sufficiently large allowables to assure profitable production.

> The result of this choice favoring the small-tract owner was a widespread disruption of the spacing pattern in any field containing a large number of small tracts. A desirable conservation method was frustrated at least in part, and fire and other safety hazards in the small-tract area were greatly increased. Equally as important to the oil industry was the economic waste involved. Several wells were drilled to produce the same amount of oil which one well could have produced. Not only was the ultimate cost of petroleum products raised, but money which could have been used for exploration or research was spent for unnecessary wells.

> Although these disadvantages flowing from the small-tract policy of the Commission and courts could have been largely remedied by voluntary pooling agreements, there was little or no incentive to enter such agreements. Indeed, the incentive was *not* to pool, for under the proration formulas usually adopted the owner of a one-acre tract frequently would receive far more profit by drilling a well on his own

tract than by pooling his land with his neighbors and sharing the expenses of drilling on a forty-acre unit.[70]

From the standpoint of owners and lessees of large tracts, the increased well allowables were unjust because the owners of small tracts received a disproportionately large part of the field allowable set forth in the proration orders.

In 1961, the Texas Supreme Court finally abandoned the principle that a small-tract owner was entitled to a "living allowable." In Atlantic Refining Co. v. Railroad Commission, 346 S.W.2d 801 (Tex.1961) (commonly called the *Normanna* decision), the Court struck down a 1/3 wells and 2/3 acreage proration formula that the Commission had established for the Normanna gas field. Special field rules had established a proper well density as 320 acres. Under the formula, the owner of three-tenths of an acre would recover $2,500,000 over the life of the well even though the value of the gas beneath the tract was worth approximately $7,000. In other words, the owner of a well on three-tenths of an acre would recover over 200 times as much gas per acre as the owner of a well drilled on 320 acres. The Supreme Court of Texas addressed a similar situation in Halbouty v. Railroad Commission, 357 S.W.2d 364 (Tex.1962), in which it expanded upon its reasoning in the *Normanna* case. The *Normanna* case had been widely viewed as a holding limited to the particular facts before the court, where the production allowed the tract in question was arbitrary and unreasonable and not sustained by substantial evidence. In Halbouty, which is frequently referred to as the *Port Acres* case, the court specifically rejected the argument advanced by the small tract owners that a formula allowing them to produce significantly more than the oil or gas beneath their tracts was supported by the rule of capture. The court reasoned that a proration formula that does not afford all parties a reasonable opportunity to produce their fair share of the minerals beneath their tracts is inconsistent with the ownership-in-place theory. The result was essentially a holding that the Railroad Commission was in error in promulgating field formulas that allowed small tract owners to drill and produce an amount that would reasonably assure them a profit at the expense of surrounding large tract owners.

The 1/3–2/3 formula, which was successfully challenged in the *Normanna* and *Port Acres* (as *Halbouty* is commonly called) cases, was applied to gas reservoirs overlain by small tracts. The 50–50 formula, which was the subject of litigation in the earlier *Hawkins Field* case, was invalidated in Railroad Commission v. Shell Oil Co., 380 S.W.2d 556 (Tex.1964) (the *Quitman Field* case).

70.　Ernest E. Smith, The Texas Compulsory Pooling Act (pt. 1), 43 Tex.L.Rev. 1003, 1004–5 (1965). As early as the mid–1930s, two pre-eminent oil and gas lawyers and scholars, Robert E. Hardwicke and A.W. Walker, were urging the adoption of compulsory pooling as a method of solving the small-tract problem in Texas. See Robert E. Hardwicke, The Rule of Capture and Its Implications as Applied to Oil and Gas, 13 Tex.L.Rev. 391 (1935); A. W. Walker, The Problem of the Small Tract Under Spacing Regulations, 57 Tex.Bar Ass'n Proceedings 157, 167–69 (1938); and A. W. Walker, Property Rights in Oil and Gas and Their Effect Upon Police Regulation of Production, 16 Tex.L.Rev. 370, 380–81 (1938).

Both the 1/3–2/3 and 50–50 formulas allocated a disproportionate amount of a field's production on a per-well basis, rather than an acreage or acre-foot basis. In other words, the mere existence of a well on a small tract allowed production of oil or gas disproportionately large compared to the oil or gas actually underlying the tract.

In Railroad Commission v. Aluminum Co. of Am., 380 S.W.2d 599 (Tex.1964) (the *Appling Field* case), the Texas Supreme Court stated that its opinions striking down proration formulas with large per-well factors were to be applied only prospective. The court reiterated its statement in the *Normanna* case that "where producers have acquiesced in and have failed to complain of the Commission's proration orders for a long period, during which time other operators have expended vast sums in exploration and drilling operations, such producers should not be heard to complain." 346 S.W.2d at 811. Pointing out that thousands of wells had been drilled on small tracts under Rule 37 exceptions, the court concluded that stable proration formulas were essential to the prosperity of the oil and gas industry and that the expectations and reliance of the operators, investors, lenders, and taxing authorities might be substantially disrupted if proration formulas in several hundred fields were set aside. In V–F Petroleum, Inc. v. A. K. Guthrie Operating Co., 792 S.W.2d 508 (Tex. App.–Austin 1990, no writ), the court upheld the Railroad Commission's refusal to change the 50–50 allocation formula to a 100% acreage-based formula in an old field.

In Texas an oil well's allowable is determined by application of what is generally referred to as the "yardstick."[71] The allowable is based on a combination of the depth of the well and the size of the field's proration unit. For example, in an established field discovered after 1965 with a 40-acre proration unit, a well drilled one mile deep would have a maximum daily allowable of 102 barrels of oil. If the proration unit was 80 acres, the allowable would be 171 barrels a day; whereas if the proration unit was 80 acres and the well was drilled a mile and a half deep, the well's allowable would be 198 barrels a day. Wells drilled in fields with larger proration units receive a greater allowable under the theory that the well is draining a larger area. The increased allowable for deeper wells is presumably based on an attempt to encourage deeper drilling, which is usually more expensive than more shallow drilling. A larger allowable (assuming the well can actually produce the maximum amount specified) permits the company to recoup its drilling costs more rapidly. As with other RRC rules, some fields have a special allowable that deviates from the ones set out in the yardstick. This is especially the case in fields with small tracts, for the yardstick allowable is based on the proration unit established for the field, rather than the amount of acreage assigned to a well.

Horizontal wells have different allowables than allowables for vertical wells. The allowable is based on the amount of acreage required for a

---

71. There are, in fact, seven yardsticks, and the one used depends upon when the well was drilled; whether the well was drilled offshore, in a wildcat area, etc.; but the one most widely used is the 1965 yardstick, and the examples given above.

vertical well in the field plus the additional acreage allowed by Rule 86(d). The additional acreage is based on the wells "horizontal drainhole displacement," i.e., the length of the well from the initial point where it penetrates the producing stratum to its termination point. For example, in a field with a density rule of 40 acres for a vertical well, a horizontal well extending 2,500 feet in the producing stratum is assigned 40 acres plus an additional 100 acres. The well's maximum allowable is determined by multiplying the maximum allowable of a vertical well in the field by the ratio assigned to the horizontal well. In the example given, the vertical well's maximum allowable is 102 barrels a day. 102 would be multiplied by 140/40, resulting in a maximum allowable of 357 barrels a day. A well with a longer horizontal leg would have a correspondingly larger maximum allowable. See Smith & Weaver § 9.9 for a full discussion of horizontal drilling and allowables.

(iii) The Mineral Interest Pooling Act

In direct response to the decisions that invalidated allocation formulas favoring small tracts, the Texas Legislature enacted the Texas Mineral Interest Pooling Act,[72] a limited compulsory pooling act, in 1965. Many of the act's unusual provisions are directly traceable to its origin.

Unlike the compulsory pooling acts of most other states, the Texas act is limited in scope. The act is only applicable to fields discovered after the *Normanna* decision, March 8, 1961. Further, unless an applicant for a pooling order has exhausted efforts to reach an agreement to pool with other interest owners within the proposed proration unit,[73] the applicant is not entitled to a pooling order. Moreover, if the applicant's offers for voluntary pooling were not "fair and reasonable," the Railroad Commission lacks jurisdiction to compel pooling. Accordingly, and as the following case illustrates, the MIPA has been described as "an Act to encourage voluntary pooling—rather than an Act to provide compulsory state action." Ernest E. Smith, The Texas Compulsory Pooling Act, 43 Tex.L.Rev. 1003, 1009 (1965).

CARSON v. RAILROAD COMMISSION

669 S.W.2d 315 (Tex.1984).

WALLACE, JUSTICE.

This is an appeal from a judgment of the trial court upholding an order of the Texas Railroad Commission favorable to BTA Oil Producers

---

72. Texas Mineral Interest Pooling Act, Tex.Nat.Res. Code Ann. §§ 102.001–.112. For a thorough discussion of the Texas Mineral Interest Pooling Act, see Smith & Weaver, Texas Law of Oil and Gas § 12 (1990). See also, Ernest E. Smith, The Texas Compulsory Pooling Act (pts. 1 & 2), 43Tex.L.Rev. 1003 (1965), 44 Tex.L.Rev.387 (1966).

73. In Texas, separate tracts or undivided interests within a "proration unit" (not a "drilling unit") may be pooled under the Mineral Interest Pooling Act. Recall that a drilling unit refers to the acreage assigned to a well in compliance with well-density restrictions. A proration unit refers to the acreage assigned to a well to determine an allowable. In Texas and a few other states, the proration and drilling units for a given reservoir need not be identical in size or shape.

(BTA). The court of appeals in an unpublished opinion affirmed the judgment of the trial court. We reverse the judgments of the court of appeals and the trial court and remand the cause to the Railroad Commission with instructions to dismiss BTA's application for want of jurisdiction.

Petitioners John Lee Carson, Donald R. Broadland, David C. Carson, Jeanne L. Carson, Betty Jo Rife and Stanford G. Rife (Carson) are owners of 13/64 of a 1/8 royalty interest in several contiguous tracts subject to a number of oil and gas leases. Two of these tracts are subject to a forced pooling order of the Railroad Commission. Of the 97 interest owners in the pooled unit, petitioners are the only ones who refused to ratify a voluntary pooling agreement proposed by BTA, the working interest owner, and a respondent herein.

Carson's lease, covering tracts 5 and 7 of the pooled unit, was executed in 1926 and retained a 1/8 royalty. This lease gave the lessee no authority to pool. Some of the leases on the other tracts, executed at a later date, retained a 1/6 royalty and gave the lessee pooling authority. BTA commenced drilling a well on Tract 7 on January 13, 1980, and completed it as a producer on July 3, 1980. Prior to this time the Commission had approved a proration unit of 642.39 acres. Sales commenced from the well in September of 1980. The well is located on one of the tracts in which Carson owns a royalty interest.

In November of 1980, some four months after the producing well was completed, and some two months after sales from the well commenced, BTA made a written proposal to all royalty interest owners in the 642.39 proration unit to share in production from the well on an acreage basis. This offer would have reduced Carson's interest in the gross production from the subject well by approximately two-thirds, while allowing owners of royalty interests who would not otherwise participate in production from the well (owners of royalty interests in non-drillsite tracts) to share in these proceeds. Carson was the only royalty owner who refused to ratify the voluntary pooling unit.

The issue in this case is whether the offer made by BTA to Carson was fair and reasonable. If so, the Railroad Commission was correct in ordering the unit to be force-pooled. If not, the Railroad Commission did not have jurisdiction of BTA's application for forced pooling and should have dismissed the application. * * * BTA contends that § 102.013(c) of MIPA controls in this case and that it made an offer in compliance with that section, which states:

> An offer by an owner of a royalty or any other interest in oil or gas within an existing proration unit to share on the same yardstick basis as the other owners within the existing proration unit are then sharing shall be considered a fair and reasonable offer.

* * *

BTA contends * * * that the only criteria for a fair and reasonable offer was that it offer each owner an opportunity to share on the same yardstick basis as other participants in the unit. We disagree.

* * *

Considering that the Legislature added subsection (c) in response to Coleman, wherein the Supreme Court had interpreted the MIPA to limit the availability of involuntary pooling orders to applicants who had drilled or proposed to drill; and considering further that Coleman was a "muscle in" situation, we find that the intent of the Legislature in adding subsection (c) was to permit small acreage owners to "muscle in" to a larger established proration unit, and to provide that the only offer required from the small acreage owner in order to "muscle in" is to offer to share in the royalties on an acreage basis.

Having determined that an offer, made by an operator who has drilled or proposes to drill, to a royalty interest owner is not necessarily fair and reasonable just because it would allow the royalty owner to share on an acreage basis, we must turn to the offer by BTA to determine if it was fair and reasonable.

The offer was made in November of 1980 after BTA had completed a producing well on the tract in which Carson owns a royalty interest. The letter to Carson containing the offer stated that Carson was required to sign the ratification agreement in order to share in the proceeds of the well and that "we cannot issue a division order to you until we have received your executed ratification." BTA placed this condition on the offer even though there was no question concerning Carson's title to the royalty interest and no impediment to the issuance of division orders.

BTA acknowledged in this letter that Carson's lease did not contain authorization for the lessee to pool as did other leases in the unit, but it noted that it expected the Railroad Commission to grant it such authority. Carson responded to BTA's letter by suggesting that BTA compensate him for reducing his interest in the well proceeds by increasing the 1/8 royalty interest under the lease to reflect prevailing royalties under modern leases, but BTA refused to negotiate, stating that it did not feel obligated to do so.

In this particular case, the time at which the offer was made is a factor to be considered in determining if it was fair and reasonable. BTA had complete discretion as to when it would make the offer. Had an offer to share on an acreage basis been made before it was determined where the well was to be drilled, there would have been some incentive for Carson to join the voluntary pooling unit: it would have assured him that he would have the right to receive royalties from the well wherever it was drilled. After the producing well was completed on Carson's tract, he was entitled to his proportionate share of 1/8 royalty from the entire production of the well, unless he either agreed to join the voluntary pooling unit or, after refusing to accept a fair and reasonable offer, he was properly force-pooled by order of the Railroad Commission.

It would not be logical, or even rational to interpret MIPA § 102.013(c) to allow an operator in BTA's position to drill and complete a producing well, and then to obtain a forced pooling order which would substantially reduce its royalty obligation to interest owners, based only on an initial demand that the royalty owners join in a proposed "voluntary" unit and a subsequent refusal to negotiate. As noted by Ernest Smith in a leading article on the MIPA, "The Texas Compulsory Pooling Act," 44 Tex.L.Rev. 387 (1966):

> [i]n the absence of a finding of reasonable offers a dismissal rather than a compulsory pooling may be more in keeping with the spirit of the act. As has been pointed [out] in the previous installment of this article, the Texas statute differs from similar statutes of other states by its emphasis on voluntary pooling * * *. *If a bona fide attempt to reach a contractual agreement is not considered a condition precedent to invoking the compulsory process, much of the deliberately unique language in the Texas statute is rendered meaningless.* Id. at 393 (emphasis added).

We do not attempt to define a fair and reasonable offer, or to determine the various elements thereof. We do agree that the offer must be one which takes into consideration those relevant facts, existing at the time of the offer, which would be considered important by a reasonable person in entering into a voluntary agreement concerning oil and gas properties.

We hold as a matter of law that the proposal made by BTA to Carson in November of 1980 was not a "fair and reasonable offer."

The judgments of the court of appeals and the trial court are reversed and we remand the cause to the Railroad Commission with instructions to dismiss BTA's application for want of jurisdiction.

NOTES

1. Under most compulsory pooling acts, the conservation agency may pool only the acreage necessary to form a standard-sized drilling or proration unit. However, under the Texas Mineral Interest Pooling Act (MIPA), the owner of a small tract that "reasonably appears to lie within the productive limits of a reservoir", Tex.Nat.Res.Code § 102.018, who was not given "a reasonable opportunity to pool voluntarily, id. § 102.014(2), can muscle into an existing proration unit by offering to share on the same yardstick basis as the other owners in the existing proration unit are then sharing." Id. § 102.013(c). If this occurs, the Railroad Commission "may authorize a larger allowable for the unit if it exceeds the size of the standard proration unit for the reservoir." Id. § 102.014(b). The "muscle in" provisions underscore a major objective of MIPA—to protect the owners of small tracts in post-*Normanna* fields. The ability of small-tract owners to muscle into units that

they were not fairly and reasonably invited to join further illustrates the point that MIPA is an act to encourage voluntary pooling.

2. An operator seeking to form and develop a standard-sized unit may offer the lessee of an adjacent small tract the same opportunity for participating in the proposed well as a party may have to participate in subsequent operations under a typical joint operating agreement (JOA). Under the typical JOA, a party may consent to the operation and pay its share of the expenses as they accrue or may elect to "go nonconsent" and be carried. If the JOA participant elects to be carried, it will not be entitled to share in any production resulting from the subsequent operation until the consenting parties have recouped some additional percentage (*e.g.*, 200%, 300%, or more) of the non-consenter's share of the cost from the non-consenter's share of production.[74] Is such an offer "fair and reasonable"? The Mineral Interest Pooling Act contains the following provision:

> As to an owner who elects not to pay his proportionate share of the drilling and completion costs in advance, the commission shall make provision in the pooling order for reimbursement solely out of production, to the parties advancing the costs, of all actual and reasonable drilling, completion, and operating costs plus a charge for risk not to exceed 100 percent of the drilling and completion costs.

Tex.Nat.Res.Code Ann. § 102.052(a).

Can an offer be "fair and reasonable" if it is less favorable to the offeree than the pooling order would be? Should it make any difference that the offer is in accordance with widespread industry custom?

Whether a pooling offer is fair and reasonable has often been litigated, especially where the applicant is trying to "muscle in" to an existing proration unit. See, e.g., American Operating Co. v. Railroad Comm'n, 744 S.W.2d 149 (Tex.App.–Hous. 1987, writ den.) ("muscle in" pooling upheld where, applicant's offer included unproductive acreage and failed to include a risk penalty) and Railroad Comm'n v. Broussard, 755 S.W.2d 951 (Tex.App.–Austin 1988, writ den.) ("muscle in" pooling denied because well was not draining applicant's tract).

In Buttes Resources Co. v. Railroad Comm'n, 732 S.W.2d 675 (Tex.App.–Hous. (14 Dist.) 1987, writ ref'd n.r.e.), Buttes drilled a wildcat well, discovered a small gas field, and created a 179–acre proration unit. When Buttes allowed its leases (comprising 55 acres) adjoining the unit to expire, Schneider leased the acreage and made Buttes a pooling offer either to pay his share of actual drilling and completion costs or to be carried for a 100 percent risk penalty. When Buttes rejected the offer, Schneider sought to "muscle in" under MIPA. The Railroad Commission issued an order pooling 22 of Schneider's acres with Buttes's unit. On appeal, the court upheld the Railroad Commission's finding that Schneider's offer was fair and reasonable. Buttes had argued that Schneider should pay the risk penalty up front. The court rejected this because Schneider did not own an interest in the acreage when the well was drilled and thus had not taken a risk-free ride on the well. Even

---

74. The options given a nonconsenting interest owner under the typical joint operating agreement are discussed in Chapter 6, Section E.

though a portion of the 55 acres offered by Schneider had already been drained by Buttes's well,[75] the court also held that the offer was fair on the ground that Schneider was merely trying to protect the correlative rights of his lessors—lessors that Buttes had failed to protect from its own drainage when it had the 55 acres under lease.

MIPA gives little guidance as to what constitutes a fair and reasonable offer; however, offers that contain any of the following terms are unfair and unreasonable:

(1) preferential right of the operator to purchase mineral interests in the unit;

(2) a call on or option to purchase production from the unit;

(3) operating charges that include any part of district or central office expense other than reasonable overhead charges; or

(4) prohibition against nonoperators questioning the operation of the unit.

Tex.Nat.Res.Code Ann. § 102.015. The fair and reasonable offer requirement of MIPA is extensively reviewed in Smith & Weaver, § 12.3(B). Professors Smith and Weaver offer the following summary of the case law:

1. The courts will judge fairness from the standpoint of the party being force-pooled at the time of the offer.

2. Applicants must negotiate seriously with the parties with whom they are trying to pool. * * *

3. Opponents of the pooling must also negotiate seriously with the parties proposing the pooling. * * *

4. Provisions in MIPA that limit the authority of the Railroad Commission to issue compulsory pooling orders do not necessarily define what is fair and reasonable in the voluntary offers required as conditions precedent.

5. MIPA will be construed to favor small-tract owners or lessees who are either being pooled against their will or who are seeking to muscle-in to a larger unit.

Id. § 12.3.B.1.d.

3. If compulsory pooling is granted, production is allocated among the pooled tracts on a surface-acreage basis. There is, however, an exception.

[I]f the commission finds that allocation on a surface-acreage basis does not allocate to each tract its fair share, the commission shall allocate the production so that each tract will receive its fair share, which for any nonconsenting owner shall be no less than he would receive under a surface-acreage allocation.

---

75. Buttes had argued that an offer to pool nonproductive acreage was unfair, because MIPA provides that the Railroad Commission may "pool only the acreage which at the time of its order reasonably appears to lie within the productive reservoir." Tex. Nat. Res. Code Ann. § 102.018. The court held that this provision was not relevant to the issue of whether an offer was fair and reasonable.

Id. § 102.051(b). Is this provision consistent with the holdings of the *Norman-na* and *Port Acres* cases? See Ernest E. Smith, The Texas Compulsory Pooling Act (pt. 2), 44 Tex.L.Rev. 387, 409–13 (1966).

4. Section 102.013 of MIPA provides:

(a) The applicant shall set forth in detail the nature of voluntary pooling offers made to the owners of the other interests in the pooled unit.

(b) The commission shall dismiss the application if it finds that a fair and reasonable offer to pool voluntarily has not been made by the applicant.

(c) An offer by an owner of a royalty or any other interest in oil or gas within an existing proration unit to share on the same yardstick basis as the other owners within the existing proration unit are then sharing shall be considered a fair and reasonable offer.

Tex.Nat.Res.Code Ann. § 102.013. Throughout *Carson,* the court treats the requirement of a fair and reasonable offer as a prerequisite to commission jurisdiction. Although the issue of whether a pooling offer was fair and reasonable is necessarily a question of fact, Texas courts, in response to *Carson,* reviewed this issue as a question of law under a jurisdictional standard rather than as a question of fact to be supported by substantial and credible evidence. In Railroad Comm'n v. Pend Oreille Oil & Gas Co., Inc., 817 S.W.2d 36 (Tex.1991), the Texas Supreme Court clarified its use of a jurisdictional standard in *Carson:*

In *Carson,* the threshold issue was the meaning of section 102.013(c) of the MIPA. Subsection (c) gives some meaning to the phrase "fair and reasonable offer to pool voluntarily" contained in section 102.013(b). The *Carson* court of appeals' construction of subsection (c) would simply have required that an offer by an interest owner to share on the same yardstick basis as other interest owners in the proposed unit is all that is required under section 102.013. This, we said, is not the only criterion. * * *.

Because of the *Carson* court of appeals' misinterpretation of subsection (c), its application of the established facts to the statutory phrase "fair and reasonable offer to pool voluntarily" in subsection (b) was incorrect as a matter of law. We, therefore, were not constrained by the substantial evidence rule in reviewing its construction, because there was no need to examine the administrative record for substantial evidence supporting the court of appeals' construction. We nevertheless held that courts are required to review commission *findings about and conclusions of* fair and reasonable offers to pool by examining those relevant facts which existed at the time of the offer. To do so, courts must apply the substantial evidence rule * * *.

"Jurisdictional review" was limited to the narrow issue presented in *Carson.* It is not some talismanic incantation that permits courts to freely substitute their judgment for that of the administrative agency.

817 S.W.2d at 41–42 (emphasis in original).

5. Because of MIPA's legislative history, the Texas Railroad Commission has generally construed its jurisdiction to order pooling under MIPA rather

narrowly. With the increasingly widespread use of horizontal drilling and hydraulic fracturing in shale reservoirs, arguments have been strongly advanced for a less restrictive reading of the act. See, e.g., Ronnie Blackwell,, Forced Pooling with the Barnett Shale: "How should the Texas Mineral Interest Pooling Act Apply to Units with Horizontal Wells?" 17 Tex. Wesleyan L. Rev. 1 (2010). The language of the act itself, however, often precludes its use where horizontal drilling is involved. Under MIPA, units cannot exceed 160 acres for oil wells or 640 acres for gas wells, plus a 10 percent tolerance; but under Rule 86, where the size of a unit depends in large part upon the length of the horizontal portion of a horizontal well, units often substantially exceed these size limitations. The result precludes the use of the MIPA by an operator who wishes to incorporate a small tract into the unit or by the owner of a small tract who would like to "muscle into" a horizontal unit. The latter situation is especially likely to occur when a horizontal well is hydraulically fractured, and the fractures extend beneath an adjacent small tract. Damages for drainage are precluded by the Texas Supreme Court's holding in Coastal Oil & Gas Corp. v. Garza Energy Trust, 268 S.W.3d 1 (Tex. 2008) and the size of the unit may preclude the use of the "muscle-in" pooling clause, leaving the owner of the tract being drained without any effective remedy.

6. Horizontal drilling in urban and suburban areas has presented other problems under the MIPA. Some of the areas where horizontal drilling is taking place underlie urban and suburban developments with hundreds of small lots. Operators are thus occasionally confronted with a situation where one or more owners of small lots that lie directly in the path of a proposed horizontal well refuse to execute a lease or authorize pooling. Because MIPA had been so effective at promoting voluntary agreements and permitting small tract owners to "muscle into" existing units, this was the first time the Railroad Commission was confronted with applications to force pool unwilling parties. The issue came to a head in an application by a company that proposed to form a 96+ acre pooled unit beneath a subdivision of over 300 lots. Owners of 26 lots, covering close to 6 acres, refused to lease. The company made three alternative offers to these lot owners: a lease with a $2,100 acre bonus and a 20% royalty; participation as a working interest owner who would pay a pro rata share of well costs based on a surface acreage allocation, and a farm out in which the owner would convey an 80% net revenue interest to the operator and retain a proportionately allocated 20% overriding royalty convertible to a 25% proportionally allocated working interest when the well paid out. When the lot owners rejected these offers, the operator sought compulsory pooling. The Railroad Commission examiners recommended denial on the grounds that the history of MIPA indicated that it was enacted to help small tract owners either to form a pooled unit or to force their way into an existing unit, and that MIPA did not permit an operator to force-pool unwilling lot owners. The Railroad Commission ultimately overruled the examiners and issued an order allocating production on a surface-acreage basis. The force-pooled lot owners were not assessed a risk penalty and received a 20% royalty and an 80% working interest, based on each owner's proportionate contribution to the entire unit.

Not surprisingly, the order has raised a variety of issues, such as whether an offer to lease is the equivalent of an offer to pool (which is required before an applicant can seek pooling under MIPA) and whether the Railroad Commission's order was so generous to the force-pooled lot owners that it will encourage other lot owners to refuse to lease or pool in anticipation of receiving similar favorable rulings from the RRC. When this edition was being prepared, the RRC was considering whether to adopt formal rules implementing the various provisions of MIPA.[76]

7.   The "fair and reasonable offer" requirement distinguishes MIPA from the compulsory pooling acts of many other states. Smith & Weaver, § 12.3(B)(1)(a). For example, in North Dakota, the Industrial Commission may issue a pooling order "[i]n the absence of voluntary pooling." N.D.Cent. Code § 38–08–08(1). In other words, the commission need not inquire about whether an effort has been made to pool voluntarily, although a risk penalty may be assessed "only if the paying owner has made an unsuccessful, good-faith attempt to have the unleased nonparticipating owner execute a lease or to have the leased nonparticipating owner join in and participate in the risk and cost of drilling the well." Id. In any event, in those states that do require an effort to pool voluntarily, the burden is not as exacting as it is in Texas. See, e.g., Okla. Admin. Code 165:5–7–7.

The Colorado compulsory pooling act was amended in 1988 to allow a nonconsenting, unleased mineral owner to protest the issuance of a pooling order. If a protest is filed, the pooling applicant must show that the protesting party was "tendered a reasonable offer to lease upon terms no less favorable than those currently prevailing in the area at the time application for such order is made * * *." Colo.Rev.Stat. § 34–60–116.

The Alabama compulsory pooling act contains a requirement similar to MIPA where the applicant seeks a risk penalty. Before a penalty may be assessed, the applicant must meet several requirements. One requirement is that the applicant must have "made a good faith effort to * * * offer each nonconsenting owner the opportunity to lease or farm out on reasonable terms or to participate in the cost and risk of * * * the unit well involved on reasonable terms." Ala.Code § 9–17–13.

8.   Generally, compulsory pooling acts apply to state-owned lands in the same manner as private lands. MIPA, however, does not apply "to land owned by the State of Texas nor to land in which the State of Texas has an interest directly or indirectly." Tex.Nat.Res.Code § 102.004.

(e) Compulsory Pooling

In 1935, Oklahoma and New Mexico became the first states to enact statewide compulsory pooling acts.[77] Under such an act, at the request of an interested party, a conservation agency *may*, or under many acts *must*, issue an order pooling tracts and interests within a spacing unit.[78] The

---

76. This discussion is based on H. Philip Whitworth, "Regulatory Update: Recent Developments at the Railroad Commission and General Land Office," paper 1, 38th Annual Ernest E. Smith Oil, Gas and Mineral Law Conference (Houston, Mar. 30, 2012.)

77. Cities in Texas, Kansas and other states, however, had previously enacted pooling ordinances to control oil development within city limits. See Marrs v. City of Oxford, 32 F.2d 134 (8th Cir.Kan.1929) and Tysco Oil Co. v. Railroad Comm'n, 12 F.Supp. 202 (S.D.Tex.1935).

78. The following states have enacted compulsory pooling statutes: Alabama, Alaska, Arizona, Arkansas, California (limited), Colorado, Florida, Georgia, Idaho, Illinois, Indiana, Iowa, Ken-

pooling order may be issued even though some interest owners are opposed to pooling. A pooling order allows a routine well permit to be issued in accordance with applicable spacing laws, regulations, or orders; however, pooling orders may be issued after a well has been drilled.[79] A compulsory pooling act eliminates the need for small-tract exceptions, avoids the drilling of unnecessary wells, and, in turn, helps prevent the inefficient dissipation of reservoir energy.[80]

These acts protect the correlative rights of owners of oil and gas interests within the pooled unit by giving each owner a fair share of the production from the well. Each working interest owner also pays, either directly or out of its share of production, for a fair share of the drilling and operating costs of any productive well.

NOTES

1. Without the specific approval of the Secretary of the Interior, a state pooling order does not apply to federally owned land. See Kirkpatrick Oil & Gas Co. v. United States, 675 F.2d 1122 (10th Cir.Okla.1982) and the Mineral Lands Leasing Act of 1920, as amended, 30 U.S.C. § 226(j) (Supp.1991). However, the Secretary, generally by delegating authority to lesser officials in the Department of the Interior, will often ratify state pooling orders. See generally Owen L. Anderson, State Conservation Regulation—Single Well Spacing and Pooling—Vis–À–Vis Federal and Indian Lands, Special Institute on Federal Onshore Oil and Gas Pooling and Unitization (Rocky Mtn. Min. L. Foundation 2006).

2. Similarly, a state pooling order does not pool Indian tribal and trust lands without federal consent. See Assiniboine & Sioux Tribes v. Calvert Exploration Co., 223 F.Supp. 909 (D.Mont.1963), reversed on other grounds Yoder v. Assiniboine & Sioux Tribes, 339 F.2d 360 (9th Cir.Mont.1964). Whether state conservation orders are effective as to non-Indian fee lands within reservations is uncertain. Many states, however, have asserted conservation jurisdiction over these lands. But see, Montana v. United States, 450 U.S. 544 (1981), wherein the United States Supreme Court noted that a tribe has inherent power to exercise jurisdiction over "non-Indians on fee lands within its reservation when that conduct threatens or has some direct effect

tucky, Louisiana, Maine, Michigan, Mississippi, Missouri, Montana, Nebraska, Nevada, New Mexico, New York, North Carolina (limited), North Dakota, Ohio, Oklahoma, Oregon, Pennsylvania, South Dakota, Tennessee, Texas (limited), Utah, Washington, West Virginia, and Wyoming. In addition, the Canadian provinces of Alberta, British Columbia, Manitoba, and Saskatchewan have compulsory pooling laws. The limited Texas Act was discussed in the prior subsection.

Under the California Act, a tract comprising less than one acre may be pooled with surrounding lands if the drilling of a well on the tract would constitute a public nuisance. West's Ann.Cal.Pub. Res. Code § 3608 (1984). In addition, in certain specified circumstances, the oil and gas conservation supervisor may adopt a spacing plan requiring pooling for pools discovered after 1973. Id. § 3609.

79. See Superior Oil Co. v. Foote, 59 So.2d 85 (Miss.1952).

80. The constitutionality of compulsory pooling acts has been upheld as a proper exercise of the police power of a state. See Patterson v. Stanolind Oil & Gas Co., 77 P.2d 83 (Okla.1938), appeal dismissed 305 U.S. 376 (1939).

on the political integrity, the economic security, or the health or welfare of the tribe." 450 U.S. at 566.

MODEL OIL AND GAS CONSERVATION ACT (INTERSTATE OIL & GAS COMPACT COMM'N 2004)

Section 11. POOLING

(a) When two or more separately owned tracts or interests are within an existing or proposed spacing unit, the persons owning the tracts or interests may voluntarily pool their tracts or interests.

(b) In absence of voluntary pooling and upon application by an owner within a unit, the [commission] may, either before or after drilling, enter an order pooling all tracts and interests within the spacing unit. All operations, including the commencement, drilling, operation, or production of a well, upon a portion of a pooled spacing unit shall be deemed the commencement, drilling, operation, or production of a well upon each separately owned tract or interest in the unit. That portion of the production allocated to a separately owned tract or interest included in a unit shall be deemed produced from that tract or interest. To protect correlative rights, the [commission] may provide for the retroactivity of a pooling order to the date that notice of a hearing to establish spacing units for the reservoir was issued and may provide for retroactivity to the date of first production for the discovery well for that reservoir.

(c) In a pooling order, the [commission] shall designate an owner to serve as operator of the unit to manage and supervise the drilling, completion, operation, and plugging and abandonment of the well or wells on a pooled unit. All owners shall share in reasonable costs of drilling, completing, operating, and plugging and abandonment of the well or wells on a pooled unit. Production and costs associated with a pooled unit must be allocated among the owners in that unit in the same proportion each owner's acreage in the unit bears to the total acreage in the unit or must be allocated according to a method approved by the [commission]. The [commission] may reallocate production and costs to prevent waste or to protect correlative rights and may equitably reallocate costs.

(d) An owner whose tract or interest has been involuntarily pooled may elect not to participate in a proposed operation in which case the operator may recover on behalf of all participating owners that owner's share of the costs of the operation out of any resulting production, plus a risk and interest penalty not to exceed [three hundred (300)] percent of the owner's share of these costs.

BENNION v. ANR PRODUCTION CO.

819 P.2d 343 (Utah 1991).

DURHAM, JUSTICE:

This is a case of first impression on the rights of a nonconsenting mineral owner under the forced pooling provisions of the Utah Oil and Gas Conservation Act. The case raises questions regarding the drilling of increased density wells in a drilling unit already subject to a forced pooling order. The operative facts span nearly two decades, from 1971 to 1990. During that period, the Oil and Gas Conservation Act underwent several amendments and a complete repeal and reenactment. We discuss the effect of those changes on the parties' rights and liabilities, and we examine constitutional and statutory challenges to certain changes in the act.

In 1971 and 1972, in the exercise of its statutory powers, the Utah State Board of Oil, Gas and Mining (the Board) established oil and gas drilling units for large areas of the state. *See Bennion v. Utah State Bd. of Oil, Gas & Mining*, 675 P.2d 1135, 1137 (Utah 1983). The Board made each 640–acre geographical section a drilling unit and authorized the drilling of only one well on each unit. *Id.* Sam H. Bennion is the owner of an unleased mineral interest in certain property located in Section 1, Township 2 South, Range 5 West in Duchesne County. The property was included in one of the drilling units established in 1971. By issuing the 1971 order, the Board fixed the location of the unit well and precluded Bennion from drilling his own wells.

Under a communitization agreement dated June 12, 1973, all of the owners of working interests in the drilling unit except Bennion voluntarily pooled their interests pursuant to Utah Code Ann. § 40–6–6(5) (then codified at § 40–6–6(f)). The Tew 1–1–5 well (the first well) was designated as the unit well. It was completed as a producing well on July 7, 1974. In 1975, Bennion filed a petition requesting that the Board order the interests in the unit pooled pursuant to its statutory power under section 40–6–6(5) (then codified at § 40–6–6(f)).[1] A statutory pooling order was entered by the Board on April 30, 1981, retroactively effective July 26, 1979.[2] The terms of the 1981 order were the result of negotiations

---

1. This is termed "forced" or "compulsory" pooling, as opposed to voluntary pooling. "In order to reap maximum benefits from his position as the owner of a mineral interest in a producing well, Bennion had to enter a pooling arrangement and pay his share of the producing costs along with the owners of the other working interests." Bennion v. Utah State Bd. of Oil, Gas & Mining, 675 P.2d at 1138. Because Bennion did not join the voluntary pooling agreement, the only way for him to achieve this end was to be "force pooled" with the other mineral owners by the Board under its statutory powers.

2. A drilling unit order, such as the one entered in this case in 1971, "establishes spacing (drilling) units of a certain size over what appears to be a common source of supply and fixes the well location within the unit." Ward v. Corporation Comm'n, 501 P.2d 503, 507 (Okla.1972). A forced pooling order is issued subsequent to a drilling unit order and determines the interest of each owner in a drilling unit and, in the absence of a voluntary agreement, the relative income,

between the Board, Bennion, and the unit operator. The order accounted for and applied only to the first well, providing that once the well reached payout,[3] Bennion was to receive a share of production upon payment of a share of the monthly operating costs. The order made no finding concerning the sharing of costs between consenting and nonconsenting owners.

In April 1985, the Board issued an increased density well order permitting an additional well on the subject drilling unit.[4] In 1986, ANR Production Company (ANR) became the operator of the first well. On February 6, 1990, ANR commenced drilling the Miles 2–1–5 well (the second well) within the boundaries of the drilling unit. Bennion was given the opportunity to participate in the drilling of the second well, but he refused.

In a petition dated April 10, 1990, ANR requested that the Board either enter a new order or modify the 1981 order to lay out the costs Bennion would be required to pay and the revenues he would be entitled to receive as a result of the second well. On September 20, 1990, the Board entered an order modifying the 1981 order. The modified order incorporates the second well, allowing Bennion to receive a royalty from the time of first production. Before he can receive a working interest share of production, however, the new order requires Bennion to pay his share of 100 percent of the costs of surface equipment beyond the wellhead, 100 percent of the operating costs, and 175 percent of the costs of drilling, completing, and equipping the well.

In this appeal, Bennion requests that this court review the Board's 1990 action modifying the 1981 order. He raises four issues: (1) whether the imposition of a statutory nonconsent penalty is inconsistent with the declaration of public interest contained in the Utah Oil and Gas Conservation Act; (2) whether the penalty is unconstitutional, either on its face or as applied, as a taking or a violation of due process; (3) whether the Board lacks statutory authority to modify a forced pooling order; and (4) whether the 1985 order requires the operator to make a showing of economic feasibility to the Board prior to the drilling of a second well. We treat these issues in order.

I. Conflict With the Declaration of Public Interest

Bennion argues that the imposition of a nonconsent penalty in this case is inconsistent with the statutory declaration of public interest contained in the Oil and Gas Conservation Act. This is a question of law to

---

investment, and costs to be allocated to different parties in the drilling unit. See Bennion v. Utah State Bd. of Oil, Gas & Mining, 675 P.2d at 1140–41.

3. At "payout," the cumulative value of production from a well exceeds the initial costs of drilling, equipping, and completing the well.

4. Increased density wells are drilled for simultaneous production when it is determined that one well per drilling unit is not draining a pool. This type of well is to be distinguished from an alternative production well, which is drilled as a substitute for the original well. See Bennion v. Gulf Oil Corp., 716 P.2d 267, 268 (Utah 1985). Increased density wells were not permitted under the Utah statute until after the 1983 repeal and reenactment of the Oil and Gas Conservation Act. Prior to that date, only one producing well was allowed per unit. Id. at 269.

be reviewed under a correction-of-error standard. * * * In pertinent part, the declaration of public interest contained in the Oil and Gas Conservation Act provides:

> It is declared to be in the public interest to foster, encourage, and promote the development, production, and utilization of natural resources of oil and gas in the state of Utah in such a manner as will prevent waste; to authorize and to provide for the operation and development of oil and gas properties in such a manner that a greater ultimate recovery of oil and gas may be obtained and that the correlative rights of all owners may be fully protected * * *.

Utah Code Ann. § 40–6–1. Bennion argues that the modification of the 1981 order requiring him to pay nonconsent penalties for the second well does not protect his correlative rights pursuant to the statutory directive.

"Correlative rights" are defined under section 40–6–2 of the Utah Code as "the opportunity of each owner in a pool to produce his just and equitable share of the oil and gas in the pool without waste." The statute requires the protection of all owners' correlative rights, of course, not just Bennion's. A nonconsent penalty clearly protects the *participating* parties by compensating them for the risk they assume in drilling the well.[5] In addition, such an allocation of risk and benefits protects *nonconsenting* parties' rights by allowing them to receive revenues (in addition to a royalty) from a well for whose drilling costs they are not liable. The imposition of a penalty on nonconsenting working interest owners is a reasonable way to allocate risks and balance the diverse interests involved in the pooling of oil and gas interests. See Application of Kohlman, 263 N.W.2d 674, 678–79 (S.D.1978). Taken as a whole, forced pooling in general "prevents waste," provides for "a greater ultimate recovery of oil and gas," and protects "the correlative rights of all owners" pursuant to the purposes of the Oil and Gas Conservation Act. Accord Palmer Oil Corp. v. Phillips Petroleum Co., 231 P.2d 997, 1005 (Okla.1951), appeal dismissed for lack of substantial federal question, 343 U.S. 390 (1952). As part of the statutory scheme, the nonconsent penalty is entirely consistent with those objectives.

---

5. Bennion does not dispute his liability for 100 percent of his share of the costs of preparing, drilling, completing, equipping, and operating the second well. What he objects to is the assessment of the additional 75 percent nonconsent penalty for some of those costs. The Oil and Gas Conservation Act requires a 100 percent assessment of the costs of well operation and of the costs of equipment beyond the wellhead, Utah Code Ann. § 40–6–6(6)(a), and requires a 150 percent to 200 percent assessment "of the costs and expenses of staking the location, wellsite preparation, rights of way, rigging up, drilling, reworking, deepening or plugging back, testing and completing, and the cost of equipment in the well," Utah Code Ann. § 40–6–6(6)(b). A 100 percent assessment on some costs allows the consenting parties to recover 100 percent of a nonconsenting party's share of those costs out of that party's share of production. A 175 percent assessment on other costs (often termed a 175 percent penalty) allows the consenting parties to recover 100 percent of the nonconsenting party's share plus an additional 75 percent as a risk penalty. If a well never produces (i.e., it is a dry hole), the nonconsenting party is not liable for any of the drilling costs. If the well is not productive enough to allow the consenting parties to recover their costs and the amount of the penalty (i.e., it is an unprofitable well), the nonconsenting party will not have to pay any portion of the remaining costs or penalty. In this way, a nonconsenting working interest owner avoids the financial risks of a dry hole or an unprofitable well.

II. The Constitutionality Question

* * *

In 1955, the Utah legislature first enacted the legislation now known as the Utah Oil and Gas Conservation Act.1955 Utah Laws ch. 65. The statute created the Oil and Gas Conservation Commission (now known as the Board of Oil, Gas and Mining), id. at § 3, and gave that agency the power to establish drilling units, id. at § 6(a), and to enter orders pooling "all interests in [a] drilling unit for the development and operation thereof," id. at § 6(f). The original statute provided that pooling orders should allow for the reimbursement of nonconsenting working interest owners' shares of costs out of production from the unit, id. at § 6(g) (codified at § 40–6–6 (Supp.1959)); it contained no nonconsent penalty for failure to participate in a well. In 1977, the Oil and Gas Conservation Act was amended to add such a penalty; the amount of the penalty was 120 percent for a well in a proven field and 150 percent for a well drilled "to a different common source of supply or in an area not proven for production." 1977 Utah Laws ch. 161, § 1. In 1983, the Utah Code was amended to its current form, which provides for a statutory nonconsent penalty ranging between 150 percent and 200 percent.[6] 1983 Utah Laws ch. 205, § 1 (codified at § 40–6–6(6)(b)). In this case, the allocation of costs and revenues established by the Board in its 1990 order conforms to the 1983 version of the statute.

Bennion argues that the statute mandating a nonconsent penalty is unconstitutional on its face and as applied because it is a taking of a property right without just compensation. This argument is without merit. Bennion confuses the concept of a vested property right with an obligation to pay a share of drilling costs. The modification of the 1981 order and the imposition of a nonconsent penalty did not divest Bennion of any property right. He still owns a mineral interest and has a right to a royalty. See Bennion v. Utah State Bd. of Oil, Gas & Mining, 675 P.2d at 1142. Any right he has to a statutory share of production as a nonconsenting working interest owner is, however, subject to the payment of a share of costs and expenses, including a share of risk compensation which results from his election not to contribute to the drilling costs.

Bennion had the right to participate—or not participate—in the second well on condition that certain requirements were met. That he had the option of participating in the costs of drilling or being subject to a penalty was a grant to him (at the expense of the participating working

---

6. The statutory nonconsent penalty established in the Oil and Gas Conservation Act applies only to forced pooling orders entered by the Board. The interest owners in any given drilling unit are at liberty to voluntarily pool their interests under their own terms. See Utah Code Ann. § 40–6–6(5). In that event, the voluntarily pooled owners can agree to be subject to any reasonable penalty for nonconsent to the drilling of a well. See In re SAM Oil, 817 P.2d 299, 302–303, 304 n. 6 (Utah 1991). This occurred in the instant case, where all of the owners except Bennion voluntarily pooled their interests in an agreement providing for a 300 percent nonconsent penalty. In addition, nonconsenting parties under the voluntary agreement did not receive a royalty until payout, whereas under the 1990 order Bennion receives a royalty share from the time of first production.

interest owners) because of the statute's recognition of correlative rights.[7]
See Anderson v. Corporation Comm'n, 327 P.2d 699, 703 (Okla.1957),
appeal dismissed for lack of substantial federal question, 358 U.S. 642
(1959). The parties were forced to cooperate for their mutual benefit and
for the protection of the public generally. Id. A nonconsent penalty is
"designed to ensure that nonparticipating owners do not benefit from the
successful outcome of risks they do not take." In re SAM Oil, 817 P.2d at
302.

Clearly, a drilling unit order cannot constitutionally prohibit a mineral owner from drilling a well on his property unless it also gives the owner
the opportunity to participate in production from the unit well. See
Bennion v. Utah State Bd. of Oil, Gas & Mining, 675 P.2d at 1142; Ward
v. Corporation Comm'n, 501 P.2d at 507. But where, as in this case, the
nonconsenting party is not only given a royalty from production but is also
given the opportunity to elect to participate in the drilling, the subsequent
imposition of a nonconsent penalty constitutes a valid exercise of the
police power. See Summers § 977 at 136 ("[U]nlike the judgments of
courts dealing with claims fixed by past events which are res judicata,
[orders of oil and gas regulatory agencies] are prospective, subject to
change, and fundamentally designed to prevent waste and protect correlative rights, with effects upon private property when they occur only
incidental to these two police power purposes."). The penalty is not an
unconstitutional taking of property.

Bennion also argues that under federal due process principles, the
Utah statutory nonconsent penalty is invalid on its face because it does
not have a rational relation to a permissible state interest. We disagree.

According to the United States Supreme Court, "a state has constitutional power to regulate production of oil and gas so as to prevent waste
and to secure equitable apportionment among landholders of the migratory gas and oil underlying their land, *fairly distributing among them the
costs of production and of the apportionment*." Hunter Co. v. McHugh, 320
U.S. 222, 227 (1943) (emphasis added). As discussed earlier, the purpose of
a nonconsent penalty is to balance the costs, benefits, and risks of drilling
a well among the diverse parties. The nonconsenting parties avoid any
risk; the participating parties assume it. The statutory nonconsent penalty
is an integral part of the compulsory pooling process which protects the
correlative rights of all of the mineral owners. See supra section I.
Further, the penalty provides an incentive for parties to participate in
drilling, resulting in increased production consistent with the public policy
of this state. There is, therefore, a rational relation between the Utah
statutory nonconsent penalty and a permissible state interest.

Bennion also argues that his right to due process was violated because
the Board arbitrarily and capriciously imposed the nonconsent penalty on

---

7. In this way, the nonconsent penalty avoids, among other things, "the serious constitutional
problem which would arise if the state simply compelled participation in a speculative venture."
Summers § 975 at 128.

him without taking into account the risks involved in his particular case. He argues that he is being assessed a very high penalty when in fact the risks of drilling a dry well in the area were "virtually zero." This argument is likewise without merit.

Inherent in the drilling of *any* well is a risk of mechanical problems, price fluctuations, or insufficient production to cover costs. For this reason, the legislature has decided that a minimum nonconsent penalty of 150 percent is justified in all cases. Because not all wells carry the same risks, however, the legislature has provided for a higher risk penalty when warranted. It is left to the Board to decide in each case whether the risks of a particular well warrant the minimum statutory penalty of 150 percent, the maximum of 200 percent, or an amount in between.

Although in the case of the second well the risk of a dry hole was minimal, the drilling process itself was not risk-free. In this particular case, the Board found that there was enough risk to warrant the imposition of a 175 percent nonconsent penalty. Under the Utah Administrative Procedures Act, Bennion can obtain relief only if we find that the amount of the nonconsent penalty imposed on him "is based upon a determination of fact, made or implied by the agency, that is not supported by substantial evidence when viewed in light of the whole record before the court," Utah Code Ann. § 63–46b–16(4)(g), or if the Board's action was "otherwise arbitrary or capricious," Utah Code Ann. § 63–46b–16(4)(h)(iv). With regard to the 175 percent penalty, in light of the record before us, we hold that the Board's finding is supported by substantial evidence and was neither arbitrary nor capricious. By means of the 175 percent penalty, the consenting parties will recoup a fair and reasonable amount from Bennion's share of production.

III. Modification of the 1981 Order

Bennion contends that the Board lacks statutory authority to modify the 1981 pooling order. Under the Utah Administrative Procedures Act, this court shall grant Bennion relief if an agency has acted beyond the jurisdiction conferred on it by any statute. Utah Code Ann. § 63–46b–16(4)(b). This is a question of law and, more particularly in this case, a question of statutory construction. The particular statutory terms do not expressly grant the Board discretion; therefore, this court is in as good a position as the Board to interpret the statutory language. See Savage Indus., 811 P.2d at 668. Thus, our review is governed by a correction-of-error standard, with no deference to the Board's conclusion that it has the authority to modify a pooling order.[8]

---

8. Specifically, in the 1990 order, the Board concluded:

The Board has the necessary and inherent authority, pursuant to [the Oil and Gas Conservation Act] to amend, modify or supplement its previous pooling orders where there has been a substantial change in circumstances or an omission in a prior order and where failure to modify the order would result in the continued enforcement of terms which are not just and reasonable or which would fail to protect correlative rights.

Bennion argues that the Utah Code gives the Board the authority to modify an order establishing a *drilling unit* but that the Board does not have a corresponding power to modify an order pooling the unit. We look first at the language of the statute.

When a drilling unit is initially established, the Oil and Gas Conservation Act contemplates that only one well will be drilled per unit. See Utah Code Ann. § 40–6–6(1)(a) * * * (an order establishing a drilling unit shall include "the acreage to be embraced within each drilling unit and the shape of each drilling unit as determined by the board but the unit shall not be smaller than the maximum area that can be efficiently and economically drained by one well"); Utah Code Ann. § 40–6–6(1)(b) * * * (an order establishing a drilling unit shall direct "that no more than one well shall be drilled for production from the common source of supply on any drilling unit"). Yet, even in 1981, when the drilling unit at issue in this case was force pooled by the Board, the statute contemplated that additional wells *could* be permitted under the right circumstances. The statute provided: "When found necessary for the prevention of waste * * * or to protect correlative rights, an order establishing drilling units in a pool may be modified by the board * * * to permit the drilling of additional wells on a reasonably uniform plan in the pool, or any zone thereof." Utah Code Ann. § 40–6–6(d) (Supp.1977). Under the 1983 amendments to the Oil and Gas Conservation Act, the Board, without qualification, can "permit additional wells to be drilled within the established units." 1983 Utah Laws ch. 205, § 1 (codified at § 40–6–6(4)). Based on the language of the statute, therefore, it is perfectly logical that the Board's 1981 order force-pooling the subject drilling unit did not apply to or anticipate the drilling of additional wells in the unit or the consequences if a party elected not to participate in a future well. It is just as logical, however, that the legislature intended to permit the Board to amend its pooling orders to accommodate the drilling of additional wells.

This court has held that in addition to those powers expressly conferred upon an administrative agency, the agency has such implied powers as are reasonably necessary to effectuate its express powers or duties. Williams v. Public Serv. Comm'n, 754 P.2d 41, 50 (Utah 1988); Basin Flying Serv. v. Public Serv. Comm'n, 531 P.2d 1303, 1305 (Utah 1975) * * *. Consistent with that principle is a recognition of the authority of the administrative agency charged with the regulation of the oil and gas industry to change or modify its orders. Although we have never before ruled on this issue, several courts of other oil and gas producing states have recognized such an inherent power. See, e.g., Application of Bennett, 353 P.2d 114, 118–19 (Okla.1960) ("We are * * * of the opinion that the Legislature intended and contemplated that orders * * * could and should be modified when it is shown that modification is necessary in order to conserve oil or gas or bring about a fair and equitable production of the oil or gas."); Railroad Comm'n v. Aluminum Co. of America, 380 S.W.2d 599, 602 (Tex.1964) ("[T]he Commission's power to regulate oil and gas production in the interest of conservation and protection of

correlative rights is a continuing one and its orders are subject to change
or modification where conditions have changed materially, new and unforeseen problems arise or mistakes are discovered."); see also Application
of Kohlman, 263 N.W.2d at 678; Summers § 977 at 138 ("with regard to
those matters fairly within the areas of prevention of waste and protection
of correlative rights there is broad continuing jurisdiction to alter, amend,
and modify and interpret previous orders" within the oil and gas regulatory agencies). A pooling order, while based on facts existing at the time of
its entry, addresses future conduct and relationships. In this case, the
anticipated drilling of an additional well in the unit caused the 1981 order
to become inadequate to define the relationships among the owners in the
unit. Because the modification of the pooling order promoted the stated
policies and goals of the Oil and Gas Conservation Act without compromis-
ing Bennion's correlative rights, it follows that amendment of the order
was proper.

Moreover, upon close examination, it is evident that the legislature
intended that the statutory nonconsent penalty be determined on a well-
by-well basis. The language of section 40–6–6(6)(b) stipulates that the
Board is to determine an amount "not less than 150% nor to exceed 200%
of that portion of the costs and expenses * * * in the well." The nonconsent penalty is therefore to be determined by the risks associated with
each particular well.[9] That can only be done if the Board has the power to
amend the original pooling order to accommodate the particular risks of
an additional well.[10]

In conclusion, although the Utah Oil and Gas Conservation Act does
not explicitly authorize the Board to modify a pooling order to accommodate the drilling of additional wells in a drilling unit, such an authoriza-

9. When additional wells are drilled, for example, there will be improved knowledge of the
geologic and economic factors involved. That change and any others in connection with additional
wells should be taken into account in allocating the costs and benefits among the parties.

Bennion cites Oklahoma case law for the proposition that pooling under a forced pooling statute
is on the basis of the area of the drilling unit rather than only on an individual wellbore. See, e.g.,
Inexco Oil Co. v. Oklahoma Corp. Comm'n, 767 P.2d 404, 405 (Okla.1988); Amoco Prod. Co. v.
Corporation Comm'n, 752 P.2d 835, 837 (Okla.Ct.App.1987); Amoco Prod. Co. v. Corporation
Comm'n, 751 P.2d 203, 206 (Okla.Ct.App.1986) (adopted by the Oklahoma Supreme Court Dec.
16, 1987). Those Oklahoma cases are distinguishable. Pursuant to Oklahoma law, nonconsenting
interest owners are often given the option of participating in unit-wide drilling or accepting a cash
bonus and/or an overriding or excess royalty interest. Where these options are present, the
election is exercisable only once, prior to the drilling of the initial well. Under those circumstances, the "initial risk capital investors" have a vested right in their interest in the unit rather
than in any given well. See, e.g., id. at 207. Under the statutory scheme established by the Utah
statute, however, a nonconsent penalty is determined on a well-by-well basis. An election to
participate is made anew each time an additional well is drilled, and the policy considerations are
therefore different.

10. In his reply brief, Bennion argues that in electing not to participate in the second well, he
assumed that his costs would be allocated according to the 1981 order. Yet the 1981 order is silent
as to the rights of consenting and nonconsenting interest owners to reimbursement for costs out
of production and share of production. In his original brief, Bennion admitted that he refused to
participate in the second well despite the fact that ANR informed him that such failure would
subject him to the nonconsent penalties mandated by statute. Moreover, the letter dated March
20, 1990, in which ANR offered Bennion the opportunity to participate in the second well clearly
states that nonconsenting parties will be subject to the statutory penalty of 150 percent to 200
percent. For these reasons, we find Bennion's reliance argument unpersuasive.

tion is implied in the statute's grant of authority to the Board to modify *drilling orders* to that effect. When a modification of a drilling order results in the drilling of wells not specifically addressed in the previous pooling order, in the absence of a voluntary agreement as to the treatment of additional wells within the pool, the Board has the implied authority to modify the pooling order under terms consistent with the Oil and Gas Conservation Act. In this case, the conditions that existed at the time the original pooling order was entered have changed appreciably. It was necessary that the pooling order be modified to the extent necessary to fix the amount of drilling and operational costs for the second well. As has been demonstrated, the Board has done so in a manner consistent with the express language of and the policies behind the Oil and Gas Conservation Act.

IV. Showing of Economic Feasibility

As a final argument, Bennion asserts that the 1985 order allowing the drilling of additional wells in the unit requires an operator to make a showing to the Board of economic feasibility prior to drilling a second well. He further asserts that ANR made no such showing in the case of the second well. The 1985 order states, "Additional wells may be drilled at the option of the operator of the unit, based upon geologic and engineering data for that unit which will justify the drilling of an additional well in order to recover additional oil, provided the additional well appears to be economically feasible." Bennion raised this issue in his response to petitioners' request for agency action, but the Board made no express finding in this regard in its 1990 order. Although the Oil and Gas Conservation Act does not require the Board to give prior approval for the drilling of additional wells on existing units, the language of the 1985 order could be interpreted to require such approval. That language requires clarification from the Board.

V. Conclusion

We uphold the Board's 1990 action modifying the 1981 order. The imposition of a statutory nonconsent penalty is not inconsistent with the declaration of public interest contained in the Utah Oil and Gas Conservation Act. The statutory nonconsent penalty is not unconstitutional as a taking or a violation of due process. Under appropriate circumstances, the Board has statutory authority to modify a forced pooling order. Finally, we remand this case for the Board to make a finding on the question whether the 1985 order requires an operator to make a showing of economic feasibility to the Board prior to the drilling of a second well and, if so, whether such a showing was made in this case.

NOTES

1. In Application of Kohlman, 263 N.W.2d 674 (S.D.1978), the South Dakota Supreme Court upheld the imposition of a risk penalty in a pooling order even though the pooling statute did not specifically authorize a penalty.

2. A *nonparticipating working interest owner,* sometimes called a *carried interest owner* in conservation statutes or regulations, is a party who does not participate in the drilling of a well. For example, if an operator drills a well without reaching an agreement with other working-interest owners to participate in the drilling venture and without securing a forced pooling order that includes a risk penalty, the carried interest owners will usually get a risk-free "ride" on the well. In other words, although the carried interest owners assume none of the risk that the well may be a dry hole, they may still be able to claim a working interest in a productive well either as a cotenant or, after the well is completed, by seeking compulsory pooling. In contrast, the operator and participating working interest owners assume the full risk of a dry hole, even though they may ultimately have to share some of the production with carried owners who have assumed no risk. Drilling risk is significant, especially when drilling wildcat wells.

To obtain a risk penalty, in some states, the operator must seek compulsory pooling prior to drilling. See, e.g., Traverse Oil Co. v. Chairman, Natural Resources Comm'n, 396 N.W.2d 498 (Mich.App.1986). But see the principal case and Matter of SAM Oil, Inc., 817 P.2d 299 (Utah 1991) (distinguishing *Traverse* and upholding the assessment of a risk penalty where a nonparticipating working interest owner delayed seeking compulsory pooling until after the well had been completed as a producer).

In Superior Oil Co. v. Humble Oil & Refining Co., 165 So.2d 905 (La.App.1964), writ ref'd 167 So.2d 668 (La.1964), Humble, the lessee of Whiteacre, sought an order pooling Whiteacre with Blackacre after Superior, the lessee of Blackacre, had completed a producing well. Humble argued that it was entitled to treatment as a carried interest owner; hence, its proportionate share of costs was to be payable out of production from the well. The court held that Humble could be required to advance its share of the costs in cash. The court was influenced by the fact that Humble, the nonparticipating party, was engaged in the oil and gas business and had sought the pooling order after Superior had drilled a producing well.

In Davis Oil Co. v. Steamboat Petroleum Corp., 583 So.2d 1139 (La.1991), the operator sought compulsory pooling, secured a pooling order, and drilled two dry holes. In a suit by the operator to recover costs, the Louisiana Supreme Court held that the nonparticipating party's share of costs could be recouped only from production. The court commented favorably on *Superior,* noting that Humble had essentially agreed to participate when it had elected to seek the pooling order; however, the court distinguished *Superior* on the grounds that the nonparticipating party in *Davis* had refused to participate in the drilling of the well and was not the party who had sought the pooling order. As a practical matter, when should an operator seek compulsory pooling? When should a nonparticipating working interest owner seek compulsory pooling? Does it matter whether the well is a wildcat or development well?

Without an inducement, such as a risk penalty, the nonoperating working-interest owners are not likely to participate in a drilling venture if they believe that the operator will drill a well anyway. For example, Procrastinator Oil Co., the lessee of a tract contained within a larger drilling or proration unit, may be anxious to drill a well to save a lease that is nearing the end of its primary term. The working interest owners of other tracts within the unit will likely know of Procrastinator's predicament and decide to take a risk-free ride if they believe Procrastinator will drill without their participation. In such a circumstance, the owner of a present working interest in the unit who also holds a top lease[81] to Procrastinator's tract is even more likely to take a risk-free ride. Do you understand why?

A working-interest owner may also refuse to participate when its interest is small compared to the total size of the spacing unit. For example, the owner of a 5–acre tract within a 640–acre spacing unit may refuse to participate in drilling, because the owner may conclude that the operator and other working-interest owners will elect to drill and "carry" such a small interest rather than expend the time and cost of seeking a pooling order.

What other circumstances might prompt a working-interest owner not to participate in the drilling of a well? Are there instances where the assessment of a risk penalty would be unfair?

3. A carried party will not receive any share of production until the operator has recouped all reasonable and necessary drilling and completion costs, including any risk-penalty charges assessed against the carried party's interest. Once the well has reached "payout" and any risk penalty has been recouped, the carried party is entitled to its share of production, less its share of reasonable and necessary operating costs. Occasionally, disputes may arise over whether costs incurred are "reasonable and necessary." These disputes may arise between the operator and either a participating party or a carried party. Conservation agencies are authorized to adjudicate disputes that arise from compulsory pooling.[82]

4. In most jurisdictions, including Michigan, New Mexico, North Dakota, and Texas, the pooling order allocates both production and costs among working-interest owners who own separate tracts within the pooled unit. In some jurisdictions, including Louisiana, Mississippi, and Oklahoma, production is apportioned by the spacing order among all owners within a spacing unit. In these latter jurisdictions, the purpose of the pooling order is not to divide production. Rather, its purpose is to provide a coercive administrative remedy for the operator who wishes to drill but who cannot reach an agreement with other working-interest owners about the allocation of costs and risks. In states such as Oklahoma, where spacing and pooling orders are issued simultaneously and generally cover only one unit, this distinction often has little practical importance.

As illustrated in *Bennion*, the practice in most jurisdictions is to require each working-interest owner to make an election, within the time and manner specified in the order, to participate in drilling the well or to be carried with a risk penalty. Under typical Oklahoma practice, however, the nonoperating working-interest owners must elect to participate in the drilling operation or to transfer their interests in the well to the operator and other participating working-interest owners who elect to acquire a proportionate interest in the

---

81. A top lease is a lease that is subject to an existing prior lease.

82. If a dispute arises from voluntary pooling or from the execution of a joint operating agreement, the dispute is a contractual one to be settled in court.

nonparticipating party's share. Under either practice, owners who do not make a timely election are bound by the "nonconsent" default option specified in the order—to be carried with a risk penalty in most states or to transfer their interest in return for compensation.

Owners who elect to participate must either pay their share of the estimated costs to the operator or post a bond to secure payment. An election to participate is often made by executing an "authorization for expenditure" (AFE). While the AFE may contain a cost estimate, execution of the AFE obligates the signing party to pay a full share of all reasonable and necessary costs incurred in drilling, completing, and operating the well even though the estimate may have been too low. See, e.g., W.L. Kirkman, Inc. v. Oklahoma Corporation Comm'n, 676 P.2d 283 (Okla.App. Div. 2 1983) (noting that cost figures set forth in the pooling order are merely estimates).

In Oklahoma, lessees who elect to transfer their interests to the operator must do so as provided in the order. This transfer is generally made in return for cash or cash and an overriding royalty ("ORRI" or "ORR"). The conservation agency determines the amount of the case payment based upon evidence concerning the value of the transferred interest.[83]

When an election is made to transfer an interest in return for cash, or a royalty, or both, the nature of the interest transferred may be determined by the pooling statute, the order, or a court. Where the pooled owner is a lessee, the operator acquires the lessee's working-interest in the pooled formation in the unit, as if there was an assignment of the exploration rights in the pooled formation in a unit, even if the pooling order specifically pooled "the well." Inexco Oil Co. v. Oklahoma Corp. Comm'n, 767 P.2d 404 (Okla.1988) and Ranola Oil Co. v. Corporation Comm'n, 752 P.2d 1116 (Okla.1988) (prohibiting the pooled owner from electing to participate in additional "increased density" wells within a unit). Where the pooled party is an unleased owner, the election to accept a bonus has been characterized as the "sale" of a lease. Anderson v. Corporation Comm'n, 327 P.2d 699 (Okla.1957). Where the order specified that the cash payment was in lieu of the right to participate in the proposed well, the operator's acquired interest terminated when the well was completed as a dry hole. Southern Union Prod. Co. v. Eason Oil Co., 540 P.2d 603 (Okla.App. Div. 1 1975). Although the Corporation Commission can interpret a pooling order's continued efficacy in light of a dry hole, it does not have the power to declare the rights of parties affected by an interpretation. Southern Union Prod. Co. v. Corporation Comm'n., 465 P.2d 454 (Okla. 1970). Later case authority demonstrates that the effect of a forced pooling order upon the mineral interest in a spacing unit is subject to the Corporation Commission's jurisdiction to interpret, clarify, amend, repeal, modify, or supplement the order under Okla. Stat. Ann., tit. 52 § 112, Harding & Shelton Inc. v. Sundown Energy, Inc., 130 P.3d 776 (Okla.Civ.App. Div. 1 2006) and Nilsen v. Ports of Call Oil Co., 711 P.2d 98 (Okla. 1985). It is now well settled that an order force pools the working interest on a spacing-unit basis. Thus, if production occurs from a pooled common source of supply, the order will pool the unit until there is a further Commission order affecting the

---

83. Once a pooling order is issued and the election is made, the operator is obligated to make the cash payment even if the well is not drilled. Buttram Energies, Inc. v. Corporation Comm'n, 629 P.2d 1252 (Okla.1981).

initial order. See Amoco Prod. Co. v. Corporation Comm'n., 751 P.2d 203 (Okla.App. Div. 1 1986, adopted by Okla. Sup. Ct. February 9, 1988), (the Commission's order force pools the spacing unit as a unit and, absent express provision in an order, a pooling order does not automatically terminate).

On very rare occasions, an Oklahoma pooling order may provide for a risk-penalty option. For example, a risk-penalty option has been included in a pooling order at the request of a working interest owner who is not actively engaged in the oil business. See Texas Oil & Gas Corp. v. Rein, 534 P.2d 1280 (Okla.1974) and Wakefield v. State, 306 P.2d 305 (Okla.1957). A risk penalty of 250 percent has been found to be reasonable where the evidence suggested that a smaller penalty would make drilling uneconomical. Holmes v. Corporation Comm'n, 466 P.2d 630 (Okla.1970).

What are the pros and cons of the various methods of allocating risk? In the case of risk penalties, what is a fair percentage? What factors should be considered in determining a fair percentage? Should the percentage be the same for all pooling orders? Should the risk penalty percentage in pooling orders be based on negotiated risk penalty percentages found in operating agreements? These percentages may range from 300 percent to 500 percent or more.

Where the operator pays cash in return for an assignment of the nonparticipating party's working interest, should the assigning party be entitled to a payment based on present and future values? Should the matter be treated as a condemnation? See Home–Stake Royalty Corp. v. Corporation Comm'n, 594 P.2d 1207 (Okla.1979) and Coogan v. Arkla Exploration Co., 589 P.2d 1061 (Okla.1979).

5. Where an unleased mineral interest owner is not force pooled until after the well is drilled, there is some authority for giving the owner a 1/8 royalty plus a 7/8 working interest. This assures the unleased owner of royalty income from a well that may never pay out. Absent a risk penalty assessed against the 7/8 working interest, the owner receives a risk-free ride on the well. See Barton v. Cleary Petroleum Corp., 566 P.2d 462 (Okla.App. Div. 1 1977). In *Barton*, the spacing and pooling orders were issued *after* the well had been drilled. The order was based on a statute specifying that an unleased owner was to be a lessee to the extent of seven-eighths of the production and a lessor to the extent of the remaining one-eighth. See Okla.Stat.Ann. tit. 52, § 87.1(d). The ordinary practice is to secure a pooling order *before* drilling, in which case the unleased interest would receive a royalty but then be subject to elections similar to those discussed in the prior note regarding the balance of the unleased interest in Oklahoma or perhaps to a risk penalty in some other states.

A North Dakota case also gave an unleased owner a royalty plus a carried working interest without a risk penalty under a pooling statute that provided that each owner was entitled to receive a "just and equitable share." See Slawson v. North Dakota Industrial Commission, 339 N.W.2d 772 (N.D.1983). Since *Slawson*, the North Dakota Statute has been amended to provide that:

> any unleased mineral interest pooled by virtue of this section is entitled to a cost-free royalty interest equal to the acreage weighted average royalty interest of the leased tracts within the spacing unit, but in no

event may the royalty interest of an unleased tract be less than a one-eighth interest. The remainder of the unleased interest must be treated as a * * * cost bearing interest.

N.D.Cent.Code § 38–08–08(1). The statute then provides for the assessment of a risk penalty as follows:

If the nonparticipating owner's interest in the spacing unit is not subject to a lease or other contract for development, the risk penalty is fifty percent of the nonparticipating owner's share of the reasonable actual costs of drilling and completing the well and may be recovered out of production from the pooled spacing unit * * * exclusive of any royalty provided for in subsection 1.

Id. § 38–08–08(3)(b). In contrast, the owner of a lease who elects to be carried may be subject to a 200% risk penalty. Id. § 38–08–08(3)(a). Why this distinction?

In Bennion v. Utah State Board of Oil, Gas & Mining, 675 P.2d 1135 (Utah 1983), based upon an interpretation of the pooling statute, a nonconsenting unleased mineral owner was awarded a 1/8th royalty from date of production on a pre-existing spacing unit to date of payout and a prorata share of production proceeds, less a prorata share of costs, from date of payout to date of pooling. Following pooling, the unleased owner was given the right to take its prorata share of production in kind. In Bennion v. Graham Resources, Inc., 849 P.2d 569 (Utah 1993), the court recognized that a nonconsenting party has vested, correlative rights to share in production within an established spacing unit, but that these rights must be enforced through voluntary or forced pooling. In Bennion v. Utex Oil Co., 905 F.2d 324 (10th Cir.Utah 1990), the court characterized the failure of an operator to account to a nonconsenting unleased mineral owner as akin to a breach of contract rather than a wrongful taking of property in tort. Accordingly, the court denied the nonconsenting owner punitive damages on the ground that Utah law does not allow the recovery of punitive damages in a contract action.[84]

6.   Under the provisions of most compulsory pooling acts, undivided (concurrent) interests in the same tract may be pooled. Compare the allocation of costs and production among undivided interests under case law. See Texaco, Inc. v. Industrial Comm'n, 448 N.W.2d 621 (N.D.1989); Earp v. Mid-Continent Petroleum Corp., 27 P.2d 855 (Okla.1933); and Chapter 4, Section B.1.

7.   Compulsory pooling can also affect the nonapportionment rule (discussed in Chapter 4, Section G.2.). For example, assume that Jefferson, the owner of Blackacre, issues an oil and gas lease to Liberty Oil Company and, during the term of the lease, conveys the East Half of Blackacre to Madison. Under the nonapportionment rule, which is the prevailing rule of construction in most states, if Liberty completes a producing well in the East Half, Madison would be entitled to all lease royalty—even though Liberty, under

---

84. Note, however, that Utah and many other states authorize the conservation agency to impose penalties for noncompliance with conservation law; however, whether such penalties are payable to an aggrieved party or to the state varies. Cf., Utah Code Ann. § 40–6–9(7) and N.D. Cent. Code 38–08–16.

the lease habendum clause, would continue to hold the entire Blackacre lease by production. However, if all or a portion of the West Half of Blackacre were to be included in a spacing unit for the well, Jefferson could obtain a share of production through compulsory pooling. In states such as Oklahoma, where spacing pools production, spacing can affect the nonapportionment rule in the same way.

8.   The establishment of a spacing unit does not give the owner of one tract within the unit the right to drill the well on another tract. Subject to acquisition of a drilling permit, each owner is entitled to drill on land in which the owner owns a working interest. However, after a pooling order is issued, the operator may use any land within the unit for access, drilling, production, and transportation, including, in most states, land that is not subject to an oil and gas lease. See, e.g., Kysar v. Amoco Prod. Co., 93 P.3d 1272 (N.M. 2004); Delhi Gas Pipeline Corp. v. Dixon, 737 S.W.2d 96 (Tex.App. 1987, writ denied); and Texas Oil & Gas Corp. v. Rein, 534 P.2d 1277 (Okla. 1974). See generally Kuntz § 77.4(l). In Continental Resources, Inc. v. Farrar Oil Co., 559 N.W.2d 841 (N.D.1997), the conservation agency pooled acreage owned by Farrar to form a 640-acre unit on which a horizontal well was authorized. The well would be drilled to a vertical depth of 9,200 feet at a surface location in the northwest quarter and then travel horizontally for 4,385 feet through the Red River "B" formation and end at a point 660' from the south section line of the southwest quarter. Farrar contended that any penetration of its leasehold by the horizontal well bore would be an illegal subsurface trespass. The court rejected Farrar's argument and held:

> The police powers exercised by the Commission here effectively superseded Farrar's right to use its oil and gas properties as Farrar pleases.

> Since force-pooled oil and gas operations are "deemed, for all purposes," to be the proper "conduct of such operations upon each separately owned tract in the drilling unit by the several owners thereof" under NDCC 38–08–08(1) of the Resources Act, the property law of trespass does not affect those authorized operations and, to that extent, property law is necessarily superseded.

559 N.W.2d at 846.

9.   Where the conservation agency increased drilling density as it did in *Bennion,* should the prior large drilling and pooled unit be maintained, or should new smaller units be formed? See, e.g., Hystad v. Industrial Comm'n, 389 N.W.2d 590 (N.D.1986). Assuming statutory authority to do either, which option is more protective of correlative rights?

10.   The drilling of a deep well that will pass through several potentially productive formations may result in a *multiple completion* (a well completed to produce from more than one reservoir). Pooling of such a well presents special problems because separate spacing units of potentially different sizes and shapes are generally created for each formation or reservoir. Thus, one tract may contain several overlapping spacing units. In addition, ownership may vary, based on depth or strata, and a given pooling order may apply to any one or more of these units. Is a pooled owner entitled to an election for each spacing unit and strata?

In Oklahoma, a pooling order may allow a working interest owner to make separate elections regarding each vertical-well spacing unit, although the order may provide that an election to participate in one unit constitutes an election to participate in all units established for any more shallow formation. In the event a working-interest owner elects to participate in fewer than all units, costs are commonly allocated by assigning the actual costs attributable to specific formations, such as the cost of testing a formation for the presence of oil or gas. These actual costs are then deducted from total costs. The remaining unassigned costs are divided among the units based on guidelines derived from industry custom and practice, especially the Council of Petroleum Accountants Societies (COPAS) Bulletin #2/Accounting Guideline AG–1. This guideline entails use of formulas based on the ratios of days-of-penetration or the footage of penetration. For example, with regard to a days-of-penetration ratio, if drilling took 90 days but the more shallow formation was reached in 30 days, the parties participating to the more shallow formation would be responsible for one-third of the unassigned costs. C.F. Braun & Co. v. Corporation Comm'n, 739 P.2d 510 (Okla.1987). A pooling order for a deep formation may allocate costs on the basis of the ownership rights in that particular unit, even though the proposed well passes through and is also a unit well in other productive formations in which the poolee has no interest. Marathon Oil Co. v. Corporation Comm'n, 651 P.2d 1051 (Okla.1982). In Viking Petroleum, Inc. v. Oil Conservation Comm'n, 672 P.2d 280 (N.M.1983), the New Mexico Supreme Court upheld a pooling order that failed to allow a pooled party to elect to participate in the costs associated with fewer than all zones. See Kuntz § 77.4(j).

Assume Hapless Oil Company, owner of the oil rights in Blackacre, obtains a permit to drill an oil well but instead discovers gas. Could Lucky Oil Company, the owner of the gas rights in Blackacre, acquire the well through compulsory pooling or some other method, rather than negotiating to buy the well from Hapless?

MODEL OIL AND GAS CONSERVATION ACT (INTERSTATE OIL & GAS COMPACT COMM'N 2004)

Section 11. POOLING (OKLAHOMA–STYLE ALTERNATIVE)

(a) When there are separately owned tracts, or when there are separately owned undivided interests, or when there are both separately owned tracts and separately owned undivided interests embraced within a well spacing unit, the owners thereof may validly pool their interests and develop their lands as a unit. Where, however, the owners within a well spacing unit have not agreed to pool their tracts and interests for joint operations and development and where one or more owners have drilled or propose to drill a well on a well spacing unit to the common source of supply, the [commission], to prevent waste or to protect correlative rights, shall require all owners to pool and develop their interests and lands in the well spacing unit.

(b) The pooling applicant shall give all owners whose addresses are known or could be known through the exercise of due diligence proper notice of the application and hearing as required by law.

[(b) [Alternative] The pooling applicant shall give all owners whose addresses are known or could be known through the exercise of due diligence at least [thirty (30)] days' notice by mail, return receipt requested. The applicant shall also give notice by one publication, at least [thirty (30)] days before the hearing, in [the official newspaper] [newspaper of general circulation published] in the county or counties where the affected tracts or interests are located. The applicant shall file proof of publication and an affidavit of mailing with the [commission].]

(c) An order requiring pooling shall be made after notice and hearing, and upon terms and conditions that are just and reasonable and will afford to the owner of a tract or interest in the unit the opportunity to recover or receive without unnecessary expense his just and fair share of the oil and gas.

(d) The portion of the production allocated to the owner of each tract or interest included in a well spacing unit formed by a pooling order shall, when produced, be considered as if produced by the owner from the separately owned tract or interest by a well drilled thereon.

(e) The pooling order of the [commission] shall designate an operator and make definite provisions for the payment of costs of the development and operation, which shall be limited to the actual expenditures required for that purpose not in excess of what are reasonable, including a reasonable charge for supervision. In the event of a disputed cost, the [commission] shall determine proper costs after due notice to interested parties and a hearing.

(f) The operator of a pooled unit, in addition to other rights provided by the pooling order of the [commission], shall have liens on the oil or gas estates or rights of the other owners therein and upon their shares of the production from the unit to the extent that costs incurred in the development and operation upon the unit are a charge against the estates or interests by order of the [commission] or by operation of law. These liens shall be separable as to each separate owner within the unit, and shall remain liens until the operator has been paid the amount due under the terms of the pooling order.

(g) The [commission] is authorized to provide that the owner or owners paying for the drilling or operation of a well shall be entitled, subject to the payment of royalty, if any, to that production from the well that would be received by the nonpaying owner or owners for whose benefit the well was drilled or operated until the paying owners have been paid the amount due under the terms of the pooling order or order settling the dispute. No part of the production or proceeds accruing to an owner of a separate tract or interest in a well spacing unit shall be applied toward payment of costs properly chargeable to another tract or interest in the well spacing unit.

(h) For the purpose of this section, the owner or owners of oil or gas estates or rights in an unleased tract of land shall be regarded as a lessee to the extent of not more than a [seven-eighths (7/8)] interest in and to the rights and a lessor to the remaining interest therein.

(i) In the event a producing well or wells are completed upon a well spacing unit where there are, or may thereafter be, two or more separately owned tracts or interests, each royalty interest owner shall share in all production from the well or wells drilled within the unit, or in a shut-in royalty as to which the royalty interest owner may be entitled under a lease or other instrument and covering a separately owned tract or interest in the unit, to the extent of the royalty interest owner's interest in the unit. Each royalty interest owner's share in the unit shall be the percentage of royalty owned in each separate tract or interest by the royalty interest owner, multiplied by the proportion that the acreage in each separately owned tract or interest bears to the entire acreage of the unit.

ANDERSON v. CORPORATION COMMISSION

327 P.2d 699 (Okla. 1957).

DAVISON, JUSTICE.

This is a proceeding * * * instituted by W. E. Anderson, as plaintiff, against the Corporation Commission of Oklahoma and Kenneth A. Ellison, as defendants, on appeal from an order * * * authorizing the drilling of an oil well on an eighty-acre tract of land * * * and directing the terms of participation in the production therefrom.

Anderson was the owner of 36.96% of the fee in a forty-acre tract of land. Ellison was the owner of 25.2% of the leasehold estate in the adjoining forty acres. The two tracts had been, by prior order of the Commission, designated as a single drilling or spacing unit in which the parties' respective percentage interests were one-half that in the individual forties as above set out. On * * * application of Ellison, the Commission made an order finding the percentage ownership of said unit and that all other owners except Anderson had agreed with Ellison on a plan of development of the unit. Ellison was authorized to drill a well, the cost of completing the same being near $300,000. Anderson was authorized to participate in the working or lessee interest by paying to Ellison his proportionate share of the drilling and completion costs of the well. The Commission further found that $800 per acre was the reasonable bonus value of the leasehold and ordered that Anderson have the option of electing to participate in the working-interest in the well or to accept from Ellison $800 per acre bonus for a lease on his undivided interest. It was further ordered that, if Anderson had not made an election within thirty days thereafter, he would be presumed to have "elected to take the said

$800 per acre bonus for the acreage owned by him underlying said tract." It is from that order that this appeal has been perfected.

Anderson's attack upon the order is founded upon the assertion that, by reason of the pooling * * * order, a co-tenancy relationship was created between himself and Ellison; that the order appealed from was in violation of the rights of co-tenants and outside the authority conferred by the statute—52 O.S.1951 § 87.1; that, if said statute authorized the order, it violates the provisions of the State and Federal Constitutions in that it amounted to a taking of private property for private use and without due process of law; that, if said statute authorized that order, it is further unconstitutional in that it compels citizens to contract against their wills and it also impairs vested contractual rights; and lastly, that the Corporation Commission could not exercise such judicial powers except by a due process of law wherein a litigant is entitled to a trial by jury.

Petroleum and petroleum products have, in less than two generations, become most vital in life and industry over the entire world. They have, by reason thereof, become probably the most important of natural resources. It was only natural that, with the increase in importance and use, the necessity for conservation was recognized. To curtail over-production and waste for the benefit and protection of the general public, restraints had to be placed around the individual's rights to develop and produce beyond the demand or need. The only logical method of restraint, other than limitation of production per well, was the curtailment of drilling by exercise of the police power. There evolved the well spacing laws. But, with well spacing alone, the object of curtailment was met, although often at the expense of serious inequalities and inequities between the various mineral owners and lessees. Under such primary restraints, when Ellison drilled a well on the forty acres in which he owned an interest, Anderson would have no rights whatever therein, his ownership being of an interest in an adjoining forty acres. Thus, consideration of the correlative rights of such owners and lessees became a necessary part of the legislation. The results were the acts authorizing * * * pooling in each common source of supply in order that the exercise of the police power in the conservation of natural resources would not effect too serious an unbalancing of correlative rights. The act under consideration, 52 O.S.1951 § 87.1, authorized the order complained of as a necessary and integral part of securing those various rights. In that connection, we are here dealing with rights of the owners of what is commonly called the 'working-interest.' No issue is presented as to the other one eighth or 'royalty interest.'

By the order, Ellison, who had made agreements with all other owners of interests in the minerals underlying the eighty-acre drilling unit for development of the same, was granted a permit to drill a well on the forty acres in which he owned an interest but in which Anderson owned none. By the same order, Anderson was granted the privilege of participating in the production from that well if he met the requirements. He could pay his proportionate part of the drilling and completion costs of the well and receive his portion of the seven eights working-interest of the production or he could accept $800 per acre as a bonus therefor and share only in the [1/8] royalty interest.

We need not consider the reasonableness of the order since Anderson's contention goes solely to the authority of the Commission to make it. His argument is that, because the former order made him and Ellison co-tenants in the eighty acres, the only method by which Ellison could recover * * * Anderson's proportionate part of the cost was by deducting it from the production, if the well proved to be good. However, with so many interdependent rights and burdens to be established it is not a simple proposition of determining the existence of co-tenancy. In the case of Amis v. Bryan Pet. Corp., 185 Okla. 206, 90 P.2d 936, 939, an almost identical relationship existed by reason of municipal zoning ordinances controlling drilling. It was there said that,

> 'Here the city created the relationship as it now exists between the parties. Had it not been for the zoning ordinance none of the lot owners would have held an interest in the oil and gas rights beneath the lots of the others. The relationship in the nature of a tenancy in common resulted merely as an incident to the application of the city's police powers. The tenancy * * * is entirely subject thereto. The parties cannot successfully assert their common law rights as tenants in common, for such a tenancy actually does not exist.'

* * *

The limitation of co-tenancy rights and privileges of some of the mineral owners is no greater burden on them than is the limitation of the rights and privileges of capture of the operating mineral owners. In the case at bar, Anderson, had no more justification for complaint of being required to elect whether to pay his portion of the costs or accept the fixed bonus for a lease, than Ellison had to complain of being required to share with him the object of his capture—the production from the well. Both were prerequisites to other rights and privileges granted by the same order under authority of the same statute.

This court has, on several occasions, held that * * * pooling statutes were constitutional, where the question was raised by the producer. * * *

* * *

* * * The order complained of did not constitute a taking of property of Anderson in any manner. It granted him the right to participate in the production from a well on Ellison's property, but on condition that certain requirements were met. The limitation of one well to eighty acres was a proper exercise of the police power in furtherance of conservation of natural resources. That he was allowed to share in the production or to receive a bonus instead of that participation was a grant to him at the expense of Ellison merely because of the recognition of correlative rights. On the other hand, Ellison was not deprived of anything because he was granted the right to drill the only well which would be permitted on the eighty-acre drilling unit upon condition that Anderson (and other owners

of leasehold interests) could participate in the production upon payment of his part of the cost. Both were forced to co-operate for the benefit of both and for the protection of the public generally.

The Supreme Court of the United States, in the case of Hunter Co. v. McHugh, 320 U.S. 222, 64 S.Ct. 19, 21, 88 L.Ed. 5, made the following statement, supporting it with citation of numerous earlier cases,

> 'A state has constitutional power to regulate production of oil and gas so as to prevent waste and to secure equitable apportionment among landholders of the migratory gas and oil underlying their land, fairly distributing among them the costs of production and of the apportionment.'

* * *

* * * [T]he order of the Commission did not deprive Anderson of any property rights. He was granted the right to participate in oil produced from another's well upon compliance with fixed requirements. Therefore he was not entitled to have a jury trial. This situation was in addition to the proposition that the order was regulatory and in the exercise of the police power. By such exercise, the State may do away with a cause of action and, the right to jury trial being incidental thereto, is thereafter no longer involved. Adams v. Iten Biscuit Co., 63 Okla. 52, 162 P. 938. * * *

* * *

For the reasons stated, the order of the Corporation Commission appealed from is affirmed.

HALLEY, JOHNSON and JACKSON, JJ., concur.

WILLIAMS, J., concurs by reason of stare decisis.

WELCH, C. J., and BLACKBIRD and CARLILE, JJ., dissent.

NOTES

1. *Anderson* illustrates a classic Oklahoma compulsory-pooling matter and answers the fundamental constitutional concerns.

The Arkansas Oil & Gas Commission follows a pooling practice that is similar to Oklahoma's. In Walls v. Arkansas Oil & Gas Commission, 2012 Ark. App. 110 (2012), the applicant for a pooling order proposed that unleased mineral interest owners who were unwilling to participate in drilling the well should be compensated at the rate $800 per mineral acre and a 1/6 royalty or, alternatively, $225 per mineral acre and a 3/16 royalty. The mineral owners argued that this sum was too low because evidence showed that the Arkansas Game and Fish Commission had received over $1600 per mineral acre and 1/5 royalty for an oil and gas lease. In a prior hearing, a landman for the applicant testified that more acres scattered over a wider area were more valuable to an operator than one small tract in a proposed pooled unit. The landman also testified that public agencies are often paid a premium for their leases—exceeding market value—to foster public relations and goodwill. Another landman for the applicant testified that the state agency could not be force pooled and thus had to be induced to lease voluntarily. The Commission's pooling order provided for $800 per mineral acre and a 1/6th royalty. The pooling statute provides that the pooled party must receive "reasonable consideration and on a reasonable basis." Ark.Code Ann. § 15–72–304(b)(4).

On appeal, the mineral owners argued that the statute required the applicant to pay fair market value based on the highest price that would be paid in a transaction between informed parties as in an eminent domain action. The court affirmed the order of the Commission on the ground that the legislature had not required either fair market value or the highest price but had opted for a standard based upon reasonable price. The court declined to rule on the argument by the mineral owners that they should be been granted a rehearing to provide evidence of higher values in pooling orders in nearby tracts. In Oklahoma, the Corporation Commission considers lease values paid for lands within the unit and for lands adjoining the unit to be pooled but not leases sold at auctions, such as leases for state-owned lands. Thus, in the case of a pooled section of land, the Corporation Commission considers evidence of lease values within the section to be pooled and in the surrounding eight sections.

2. A case that further illustrates the effect of an Oklahoma pooling order is Youngblood v. Seewald, 299 F.2d 680 (10th Cir.Okla.1961). In this case, Seewald owned the oil and gas leases covering a section of land except for 64.22 acres leased to McLain and a smaller tract not relevant to the dispute. McLain's leases were originally acquired by Youngblood. The leases provided for a 3/16 royalty interest to the lessors. Youngblood assigned the leases to McLain, reserving an overriding royalty of 1/8 of 7/8. When Seewald was unable to reach an agreement with McLain for the development of the section, he sought a pooling order. A pooling order named Seewald the operator, and determined McLain's interest to be worth $50 per acre or an overriding royalty of 1/8 of 8/8 if McLain elected not to participate in the drilling of the well. McLain elected to take the overriding royalty in lieu of participating in the well. The pooling order was issued under 52 Okla.St.Ann. § 87.1(d), which provided, in part, as follows:

> provided, where a lease covering any such separately owned tract or interest included within a spacing unit stipulates a royalty in excess of one-eighth (1/8) of the production, or said lease shall be subject to an overriding royalty, to production payment or other obligation, then the lessee of said lease out of his share of the working-interests from the well drilled on said unit, shall sustain and pay said excess royalty, overriding royalty, or production payment, and therefrom meet any other obligation due in respect to the separately owned tract or interest held by him.

Seewald contended that, by virtue of the statute and the pooling order, he acquired the full working-interest in the leases formerly owned by Youngblood, subject only to the statutory 1/8th royalty and the 1/8th of 8/8ths overriding royalty created when McLain elected to take an overriding royalty. The trial court agreed with Seewald and reasoned that, under the pooling statute, all of the burdens against the lease over and above the statutory 1/8th royalty should be the obligations of the owner of the working-interest just prior to the time the order was entered. On appeal, the Court of Appeals for the Tenth Circuit reversed, stating:

> The statute contemplates that the owner of the working-interest shall satisfy the burdens, but it does not specify whether the owner should be determined before or after the pooling order. It seems clear that the Commission determined the cost of drilling the well and the value of the working-interest for the purpose of giving to McLain the option of participating in the well, by paying his proportionate share of the cost, or accepting the value of his working-interest and transferring the same to Seewald. The value of McLain's working-interest could not be determined without considering the burdens on the lease. It could well be that without any overriding burdens the value would have been far in excess of the $50.00 per acre or 1/8th of 8/8ths royalty stipulated by the Commission order. When McLain elected to accept the 1/8th of 8/8ths royalty option, in exchange for his working-interest, his right to drill on the leases was surrendered, and the working-interest became the property of Seewald by operation of law. There is no language in the order which indicates that the Commission intended that the Youngblood royalty and the 1/16th excess royalty of the lessors should be paid out of the 1/8th overriding royalty accepted by McLain. The result of the trial court's interpretation is that McLain would receive nothing, and he would be unable, out of the 1/8th he accepted, to pay the lessors' excess royalty and Youngblood's override in full.

* * *

> McLain, as owner of the working-interest in the unit, could have retained this interest by paying his proportionate share of the cost of the well. In that event he would have received 7/8ths of the production allotted to his land, and would have been required to pay therefrom the excess royalty and other burdens on the lease. If he did not elect to participate in the well, he had the option of accepting the $50.00 per acre bonus or 1/8 of 8/8ths overriding royalty for his interest. Upon the acceptance of either of these options his working-interest became the property of Seewald. The Commission did not attempt to disturb the royalty burden on the leases over and above the statutory 1/8th, and the Oklahoma statute does not require it. But, the construction given the Commission's order by the trial court would exclude McLain from participating in the production, and still, the share he elected to receive would be insufficient to satisfy the remaining overriding burdens. We need not consider whether the Commission has the power to restrict overriding burdens when all the parties are before the Commission. We hold, however, that the Commission did not undertake to disturb the excess royalty of the lessors or the overriding royalty of Youngblood, and these burdens, in addition to the 1/8th of 8/8ths which McLain elected to take for his working interest, must be satisfied by the owner of the working-interest, Seewald, who is now the "lessee" referred to in the statutory provision in question.

Note that the total royalty burdening the 64–acre tract exceeds 42 percent; however, that burden is limited to approximately 10% of the 640–acre unit.

In light of *Youngblood*, should conservation agencies have authority to reduce or eliminate excessive nonoperating interests to avoid the *de facto* nullification of a compulsory pooling act? On what basis might this authority be grounded?

This question was addressed in O'Neill v. American Quasar Petroleum Co., 617 P.2d 181 (Okla.1980). In *O'Neill*, several parties had overriding royalties totaling over 9 percent on one tract under lease to O'Neill. These overriding royalties were in addition to the 12.5 percent royalty reserved to the lessor and were convertible to working-interests upon "payout" of the well. American Quasar, the lessee of another tract in the same spacing unit, wanted to drill a well and sought a pooling order. The Corporation Commission's pooling order gave the owners of the overriding royalty interests the option of participating in the drilling of the well as working-interest owners or of taking a reduced overriding royalty interest. The Supreme Court of Oklahoma held that the Commission did not have the authority to "completely rearrange contractual rights and duties of the owners of all overriding royalty interests * * * by converting their non-participating investment into a working-interest * * *." 617 P.2d at 184. The court stated:

> The Commission's authority * * * to require owners to pool their interests and contribute to the costs of development and operation, does not authorize the Commission to require owners of an override to contribute as they are * * * not owners [of a right to drill under the pooling statute.] This conclusion is confirmed by the fact that no order pooling the royalty interests in a unit is necessary or contemplated by the statute because the creation of a unit, by operation of law, pools royalty interests.

Id.[85] The court also held that where the original lessee elects not to participate in the cost of drilling the well, overriding royalty interests must be paid by the drilling operator—the party who succeeds to the pooled party's working-interest.

Four dissenting justices argued that excessive "overriding royalty interests, production payments, etc., may be amended and modified to the extent necessary to conform to the requirements of forced pooling" and that "the pooler may not be required to pay a bonus or satisfy a burden in excess of the fair and reasonable value of the 7/8ths working-interest." Id. at 186–87.

The majority in *O'Neill* acknowledged that under its holding "a lessee acting in bad faith might burden a lease to the point it becomes useless." Id. at 186. Given the holding, can anything be done to discourage this?

Today in Oklahoma, most if not all, pooling orders take into account excessive burdens by more severely restricting the electing party's options if the interest is burdened by excessive royalty. However, so long as a royalty burden is established by an arm's length transaction, the royalty burden cannot be directly reduced or converted to a working-interest.

---

85. The Oklahoma compulsory pooling statute, like most pooling acts, refers to pooling "owners." Okla.Stat.Ann. tit. 52, § 87.1(e) (1991). The Oklahoma conservation act defines "owner" as the "person who has the right to drill * * *." Id. § 86.1 (1991). The owner of a royalty interest has no right to drill a well.

The Alabama compulsory pooling act places a cap on the obligation of the operator to pay excess royalties attributable to carried interest owners and to provide a minimum royalty to unleased carried interest owners. Under the Act,

> 13/16ths (or if said tract or interest is leased, the working-interest fraction or percent if it is greater) of the oil and gas production allocated to such [carried] * * * interest may be appropriated by the operator * * * for the payment of [the carried party's share of costs] * * *, but that a 3/16ths part (or the actual landowner royalty if it is less) of the unit production allocated to each [carried] * * * interest shall in all events be regarded as royalty and shall * * * be distributed to * * * the person or persons owning royalty or unleased mineral interests (as the case may be) in such [carried] tract * * * free and clear of the development and operating costs and of any risk compensation fee * * *.

Ala. Code § 9–17–13. A party who owns a royalty interest "in excess of 3/16 of production * * * is subrogated to all the rights of the operator with respect to the [carried party] * * *." Id. Apparently, after payout, a royalty owner could satisfy its excess royalty interest by claiming production proceeds allocated to the carried party. Would a carried lessee be personally liable to its lessor for excess royalties that were not paid by the operator to the lessor? Assume that Clements is the assignee of a lease covering Blackacre, and that Blackacre is burdened by royalty totaling 25 percent: a 5 percent royalty interest owned by Jackson; a 15 percent landowner's royalty (in addition to Jackson's 5 percent royalty interest) reserved in the oil and gas lease by Rose, the lessor; and a 5 percent of eight-eighths overriding royalty that was carved out of the lease by Ryan, the initial lessee who assigned the lease to Clements. If Blackacre is pooled and carried under the Alabama Act, how should the operator divide the statutory three-sixteenths (18.75 percent) royalty? What if any of these royalty owners had the right to take royalty in "kind"?

The Kansas Supreme Court has suggested that a solution to the problem of excessive overriding royalty interests that frustrate pooling or development may be found in partition out of "equitable necessity." See Mulsow v. Gerber Energy Corp., 697 P.2d 1269 (Kan.1985).

For a comment on the authority of the Texas Railroad Commission to limit excessive nonoperating interests, see Ernest E. Smith, The Texas Compulsory Pooling Act, (pt. 2), 44 Tex.L.Rev. 387 (1966).

3. In pooling orders, production and costs are generally allocated on an acreage basis. Assume Blackacre comprises a total of 640 acres described as the East 1/2 of Section 9 and the West 1/2 of Section 10. Whiteacre comprises 160 acres described as the Southeast Quarter of Section 10. Greenacre comprises 160 acres described as the Northeast Quarter of Section 10. Assume that Section 10 constitutes a 640-acre spacing unit and has a productive well. Assume further that the owners of each of the tracts participated in the drilling of the well. If all three tracts are separately owned, unleased tracts, the division of costs and production on an acreage basis would be as follows:

$$\frac{320 \text{ Blackacre acres (w/i unit)}}{640 \text{ Unit Acres}} = \frac{1}{2} \text{ of production and costs}$$

$$\frac{160 \text{ Whiteacre acres}}{640 \text{ Unit acres}} = \frac{1}{4} \text{ of production and costs}$$

$$\frac{160 \text{ Greenacre acres}}{640 \text{ Unit acres}} = \frac{1}{4} \text{ of production and costs}$$

Note that although Blackacre comprises a total of 640 acres, only 320 acres have been included in the spacing unit. When production and costs are allocated, only the acreage contained in the spacing unit is considered.

When some or all of the tracts are under lease, or subject to royalty interests, the allocation is more complex. Assume in the above situation that Able, the owner of Blackacre, has leased it to Xavier Oil Co., reserving a one-eighth royalty. Baker, the owner of Whiteacre, has leased the property to Yucca Oil Co., reserving a one-eighth royalty, and Carr, the owner of Green-acre, has leased to Zebra Oil Co., reserving a one-sixth royalty. Assume further that Yucca Oil Co., intending to drill a well on the spacing unit, obtains a pooling order that gives Xavier and Zebra the option of participating as full working-interest owners according to their respective interests. If Xavier and Zebra choose to participate, the costs would be divided among Xavier, Yucca, and Zebra as shown above, but production would be allocated as follows:

Nonworking (Nonoperating) Interests

Able: $\frac{1}{8}$ royalty   x $\dfrac{320 \text{ Blackacre acres}}{640 \text{ Unit acres}}$ $= \frac{1}{16}$ of production

Baker: $\frac{1}{8}$ royalty   x $\dfrac{160 \text{ Whiteacre acres}}{640 \text{ Unit acres}}$ $= \frac{1}{32}$ of production

Carr: $\frac{1}{6}$ royalty   x $\dfrac{160 \text{ Greenacre acres}}{640 \text{ Unit acres}}$ $= \frac{1}{24}$ of production

Working (Operating) Interests

X: $\frac{7}{8}$ w.i.   x $\dfrac{320 \text{ Blackacre acres}}{640 \text{ Unit acres}}$ $= \frac{7}{16}$ of production

Y: $\frac{7}{8}$ w. i.   x $\dfrac{160 \text{ Whiteacre acres}}{640 \text{ Unit acres}}$ $= \frac{7}{32}$ of production

Z: $\frac{5}{6}$ w. i.   x $\dfrac{160 \text{ Greenacre acres}}{640 \text{ Unit acres}}$ $= \frac{5}{24}$ of production

By converting each fraction to decimals, you can see that all production has been allocated:

Able	.06250
Baker	.03125
Carr	.04167
X	.43750
Y	.21875
Z	.20833
	1.00000 = All interests within the drilling unit

This is a very simple example. The existence of overriding royalties, production payments, and undivided (fractional) interests in each tract within the spacing unit can result in very complex production allocations.

4. Are allocations based on an acreage basis protective of correlative rights? Consider the following statement by Professor Kuntz:

> When production from a unit is apportioned among owners in the unit, it is first apportioned among the tracts in the unit on the basis of surface acreage. That is, production is allocated to each tract included in the unit and to the mineral owners thereof in the proportion that the surface acres of such tract bears to the total surface acres in the unit. This is different from the allocation that is made in the event of field-wide unitization wherein various factors as to the quality of the producing formation are taken into account. The difference is justified, and an allocation on the basis of surface areas is fair and reasonable in most instances, because drilling units are ordinarily not large in area and the variations in quality of the formation do not produce significant variations in the production that could be realized from each tract if all owners were permitted to exercise their rights under the law of capture. It has been said that such formula has the "merit of simplicity and certainty."

> As technology improves, as discoveries are made at greater depths, and as costs of drilling increase, there is a tendency to create larger drilling units. It is submitted that the surface acreage formula may or may not be fair and reasonable and may or may not protect correlative rights when applied to very large units because of the increased possibility of variations in the underground formations underlying a large area that can result in considerable variations in the share of production that would be realized by each owner under the law of capture.

Kuntz § 77.3(c) at 487–88. How should a pooling order allocate production from a horizontal well that traverses two or more tracts? By acreage, by length of wellbore within the formation, by perforations in the flow string, or on some other basis?

5. Assume Alexander owns Blackacre, an eighty-acre tract, and Baxter owns Whiteacre, an eighty-acre tract. Assume Alexander has leased Blackacre to Xavier Oil Co. and Baxter has leased Whiteacre to Yucca Oil Co. Yucca has drilled and completed a producing wildcat well on Whiteacre, and Xavier has refused to participate in the venture. Subsequently, the conservation agency dockets a spacing hearing and later issues a spacing order establishing 160-acre spacing units for the field, with Blackacre and Whiteacre comprising one spacing unit. Yucca applies for a pooling order, requesting that the Commission determine the interests of Alexander, Baxter, Xavier, and Yucca. Should the pooling order allocate production and costs retroactively? If so, to what point in time?

To protect correlative rights where pooling occurs after production, the conservation agency may issue pooling orders that are retroactive, either to the date of spacing or to the date of first production (generally whichever is later). See, e.g., Desormeaux v. Inexco Oil Co., 298 So.2d 897 (La.App.1974), writ denied 302 So.2d 37 (La.1974); Farmers Irrigation Dist. v. Schumacher,

194 N.W.2d 788 (Neb.1972); Texaco Inc. v. Industrial Comm'n, 448 N.W.2d 621 (N.D.1989); Barton v. Cleary Petroleum Corp., 566 P.2d 462 (Okla.App. Div. 1 1977); and Cowling v. Board of Oil, Gas & Mining, 830 P.2d 220 (Utah 1991). Occasionally, a conservation agency may refuse retroactive relief where sophisticated parties fail to seek pooling in a timely manner. See, e.g., Hegarty v. Board of Oil, Gas and Mining, 57 P.3d 1042 (Utah 2002). See generally Owen L. Anderson, Compulsory Pooling in North Dakota: Should Production Income and Expenses Be Divided From Date of Pooling, Spacing, or 'First Runs'?, 58 N.D.L.Rev. 537 (1982). What is the better policy?

6. Spacing, density, and pooling orders, as well as other conservation orders, may conflict with various voluntary agreements. See, e.g., General Gas Corp. v. Continental Oil Co., 230 So.2d 906 (La.App.1970) (operating agreement and a pooling order); Texaco, Inc. v. Vermilion Parish School Bd., 145 So.2d 383 (La.App.1962), reversed in part 152 So.2d 541 (La.1963) (unit agreement and a spacing order); Sylvania Corp. v. Kilborne, 271 N.E.2d 524 (N.Y.1971) (farmout agreement and a spacing order); Tenneco Oil Co. v. El Paso Natural Gas Co., 687 P.2d 1049 (Okla.1984) (operating agreement and a pooling order); and Hladik v. Lee, 541 P.2d 196 (Okla. 1975)(spacing order and pooling agreement). In general, resolution of this conflict is based upon the following general principles:

> First, spacing unit orders and pooling orders are an exercise of the police power of the state to conserve oil and gas resources and to protect the correlative rights of the owners involved. Where conflict exists, private contractual rights must yield to the valid exercise of the police power. To the extent a private voluntary agreement is not necessarily superseded by the overlapping governmental order, however, the intention of the parties will govern.

Morris G. Gray & Hugh V. Schaefer, Conflict Between Voluntary Pooling Agreements and State Spacing and Pooling Orders, 27 Rocky Mtn.Min.L.Inst. 1517, 1552 (1982). See also Kramer & Martin § 13.08.

7. The typical working-interest owner holds an oil and gas lease from a lessor who is relying on the lessee's expertise regarding decisions relating to petroleum operations. As discussed in Chapter 3, Section D.3., the lessee must act in good faith as a reasonable and prudent operator for the parties' mutual benefit. Thus, a lessee may have a duty to pool acreage so that drilling may occur, the duty to seek exception locations, or a duty to pursue other administrative relief for the benefit the parties. Concerning the duty to *pool,* Professor Kuntz states:

> It is possible for an affirmative duty to be found in a broader implied obligation on the part of the lessee. For example, drilling a well may be optional with the lessee according to the drilling clause, yet the lessee may be required to drill in order to comply with a broader obligation, such as the duty to protect against drainage. Similarly, a duty to pool may arise if pooling is required in order to comply with the broad requirements of prudent operation.

Kuntz § 48.3(h).

8. In Hebble v. Shell Western E & P, Inc., 238 P.3d 939 (Okla.Civ.App. Div. 3 2009), the Oklahoma Court of Civil Appeals held that an operator under a compulsory pooling order owes a fiduciary duty to the pooled parties. Given what you have learned so far about the nature of the lessee-lessor relationship, the executive-nonexecutive relationship, and the exercise of the pooling power under the pooling clause, is a fiduciary duty appropriate for the operator of compulsorily pooled unit?

6. UNITIZATION

The preceding materials illustrate legal problems related to pooling, but that discussion also applies to unitization. The following materials discuss unitization and problems that, although relevant to pooling, are either more commonly encountered or more serious in unitization.

(a) Shortcomings of Traditional Conservation Policy

OWEN L. ANDERSON AND ERNEST E. SMITH, THE USE OF LAW TO PROMOTE DOMESTIC EXPLORATION AND PRODUCTION, 50 INST. ON OIL & GAS L. & TAX'N 2–1, 2–64 to 2–76 (1999)

*Mandatory unitization * * * would have a number of important advantages over the present state and federal systems of conservation regulation. First, and most importantly, it would result in conservation in a meaningful sense. * * * Second, by holding out to explorers the prospect of being able to develop and produce new discoveries on the most economical terms, it would encourage exploration and contribute to * * * equating supplies of oil and gas with growing demand in the years ahead. Third, it would result in true protection of correlative rights. And fourth, it would allow us to dispense with all of the elaborate and expensive machinery of present detailed regulation except that necessary to restrain drilling and production in the preunitization period of information-gathering and to protect the environment * * *.*[86]

Unitization has been long recognized as the ultimate conservation tool.[87] * * * It addresses fractionalization and subdivision [of mineral rights] by consolidating multiple tracts and interests into a single unified block to allow for orderly development and efficient operations to prevent surface, underground and economic waste. If properly implemented, unitization also serves to protect fully correlative rights. * * *

---

86. McDonald, Unit Operation of Oil Reservoirs as an Instrument of Conservation, 49 Notre Dame L. Rev. 305, 311 (1973).

87. *See generally* JACQUELINE L. WEAVER, UNITIZATION OF OIL AND GAS FIELDS IN TEXAS (Johns Hopkins Press 1986); WALLACE F. LOVEJOY & PAUL T. HOMAN, ECONOMIC ASPECTS OF OIL CONSERVATION REGULATION (Johns Hopkins Press 1967) [hereinafter LOVEJOY & HOMAN]; and McDonald, above.

* * *

Prior to spacing and pooling legislation and regulation, the rule of capture governed the development of oil and gas reservoirs. Under the rule, if one operator drilled a producing well, neighboring operators had no judicial remedy for any resulting drainage.[88] Thus, their only remedy was self-help. That is, they had to drill offsetting wells if they wanted to prevent drainage of oil and gas from beneath their acreage. Theoretically, the rule of capture protected correlative rights. Diligent landowners above a common reservoir could protect their interests by matching the drilling patterns of other wells. Unfortunately, development under the rule of capture caused waste. More wells were drilled to offset drainage than were necessary to efficiently drain the reservoir, thereby causing economic waste. The proliferation of wells led to the proliferation of related surface storage tanks, pipes, and valves, all of which were prone to leakage and to catching fire, thereby causing surface waste. The flush production that resulted from too many wells inefficiently dissipated the reservoir energy that pushed the oil and gas through the reservoir, thereby causing underground waste (the failure to recover hydrocarbons in the reservoir). In addition, the high production rates caused oil prices to drop to the point where wells could not be drilled and produced at a profit. Because there were typically many interest owners overlying a common reservoir, high transaction costs and strategic behavior prevented the successful negotiation of a voluntary agreement to curtail this frenzied, costly and wasteful development.

The standard legislative responses to the problems that result from rule-of-capture development have been spacing and density regulations, compulsory pooling, and in some states, market-demand prorationing. As typically practiced, spacing and density regulations require the conservation agency to determine theoretically the area that can be efficiently and effectively drained by one well for a given reservoir. Well spacing and density regulations are then established for that reservoir. Each drilling unit is entitled to one well.

If a given unit contains multiple tracts or interests, the conservation agency may consolidate these tracts and interests through the issuance of a pooling order, thereby providing that the single unit well will serve all tracts and interests within that drilling unit. Compulsory pooling is used to protect the correlative rights of the owners of tracts that are too small to comprise a drilling unit. * * *

[I]n theory, spacing and density regulations limit the numbers of wells to those that are necessary to drain the reservoir efficiently and effectively. Unfortunately, as will be developed below, the actual application of these regulations does not ordinarily achieve this theoretical objective.

In some states, spacing and pooling regulations are further supplemented by limiting production. Under one form, all wells are limited to

---

88. *See, e.g.*, Kelly v. Ohio Oil Co., 49 N.E. 399 (Ohio 1897).

protect correlative rights.[89] In theory, this form of production limit is designed to allow each interest owner a fair opportunity to recover the oil and gas beneath their individual tracts. Of course, for this to work in practice, other owners would have to promptly drill a well. Thus, there is no guarantee that correlative rights will be protected.

* * *

Yet another form of production limit curtails production of oil wells that produce high ratios of gas in the case of a gas-cap reservoir, or high ratios of water in the case of a water-drive reservoir.[90] This is done to preserve natural reservoir energy so as to prevent underground waste. This form of curtailment may serve as a prelude to field-wide unitization.

Unfortunately, these traditional regulations addressing well numbers, well locations, and production are fraught with problems. For example, the agency may prescribe drilling units that are too small or too large. If too small, more wells are drilled than necessary, resulting in economic waste and perhaps underground waste. If too large, some hydrocarbons may not be recovered. The latter is usually less of a problem, because the conservation agency can allow the drilling of an additional well or wells within a drilling unit. These additional wells are commonly called "in-fill" wells. The drilling of in-fill wells raises the correlative-rights issue of whether the drilling units should be preserved in their original size or "de-spaced" into smaller units.[91]

"Exception-location" wells are another problem. Exception-location wells are wells that are drilled or produced not in compliance with the normal well-spacing pattern. Oftentimes, exception-location wells can only be drilled after a separate regulatory proceeding. There are many reasons for exception-location wells. Due to surface topography or reservoir geology, one location may be far preferable over another.[92] An existing well may have been initially completed in another reservoir that was developed on a different well spacing pattern. To save money, the operator of the well may wish to re-complete the well in the subject reservoir as an exception-location well.[93] Or a well may have been legally located in contemplation of finding oil, but completed as a gas well.[94] In short, exception-location wells are permitted to prevent waste, protect correlative rights, or both. If an exception-location is permitted by the conservation agency, neighboring landowners may present expert testimony on the need to limit the production of the exception-location well to protect their property from unfair drainage. The exception-location applicant will most

89. *See, e.g.,* Wronski v. Sun Oil Co., 279 N.W.2d 564 (Mich.Ct.App.1979) (illustrating this form of regulation in the context of a conversion case).

90. *See, e.g.,* Denver Producing & Ref. Co. v. State, 184 P.2d 961 (Okla.1947) (illustrating this form of production limit).

91. *See, e.g.,* Hystad v. Industrial Comm'n, 389 N.W.2d 590 (N.D.1986).

92. *See, e.g.,* In re Gulf Oil Corp., 313 P.2d 1101 (Okla.1957).

93. *See, e.g.,* Exxon Corp. v. Railroad Comm'n, 571 S.W.2d 497 (Tex.1978).

94. The drilling unit for a gas well is ordinarily larger than the drilling unit for an oil well, because a gas well will commonly efficiently drain a larger area than an oil well. * * *

likely present expert testimony in rebuttal.[95] These disputes further complicate the regulatory process and increase regulatory costs.

Another problem with a well-by-well regulatory approach is that the true nature of the typical oil and gas reservoir is largely ignored. Well spacing and density rules are based upon three related assumptions. First, that oil and reservoirs are homogeneous; that is, they have the same characteristics throughout. Second, that all wells completed in such a reservoir will drain in a radial pattern. And third, that, although drilling units are usually square or rectangular, the drainage pattern of one well will be fairly offset by the drainage pattern of neighboring wells so that each unit well will recover a fair share of hydrocarbons.[96] One problem is that the initial assumption, that reservoirs are homogeneous, is usually false. As a result, the next two assumptions are also typically false. Moreover, the third assumption is often further nullified by off-pattern exception-location wells.

Reservoirs are typically heterogeneous. The typical reservoir has varying porosity and permeability throughout, varying thickness, and varying quantities and types of hydrocarbons. Nevertheless, relying upon the above three assumptions, the conservation agency, in administering a typical spacing and pooling regulatory regime, will usually treat all tracts the same. Thus, tracts having structural advantage (*e.g.*, tracts located above the apex of an anticline and above the thickest part of the reservoir) are treated the same as tracts having poor structural advantage (*e.g.*, tracts located on the edge of an anticline and above a thinner portion of the reservoir).[97] The end result is often too many wells drilled at less than ideal locations that fail to adequately protect correlative rights.

Other problems with a well-by-well regulatory approach arise from compulsory pooling practices. Although compulsory pooling is often effective in protecting the correlative rights of the owners of tracts that are too small to comprise a drilling unit and may be used to consolidate fractional interests in drilling units, it is far from a perfect way to achieve even these limited objectives. * * * [C]ompulsory pooling continues to presuppose a well-by-well regulatory approach in which compulsory pooling practices often fail to protect fully correlative rights. This occurs when some working interest owners, who are unwilling to assume the risk of drilling, simply speculate at the expense of those who have assumed the risk. * * *

[Illustration of risk-penalty style of compulsory pooling is omitted.] * * * Although the details differ, this style of pooling is common throughout much of the mid-continent and Rocky Mountain Region * * *, but such penalties [typically ranging from 50%—250%] do not approach those typically found in joint operating agreements.[98]

---

95. *See, e.g.,* Chevron Oil Co. v. Oil & Gas Conservation Comm'n, 435 P.2d 781 (Mont.1967).

96. This latter assumption is often called the "compensatory drainage doctrine." R. B. Giles, The Technological Underpinnings of Conservation Law, Paper 2, 2–13, Oil and Gas Conservation Law and Practice (Rocky Mtn. Min. L. Found.1985).

97. *See, e.g.,* Pickens v. Railroad Comm'n, 387 S.W.2d 35 (Tex.1965). * * *

98. Penalties in joint operating agreements typically start at 300% and commonly are as high as 800%. We have seen agreements that contain penalties as high as 1800%.

The problem with the risk penalty approach, particularly a relatively low one * * *, is that the penalty bears no real relation to the risk assumed by the drilling party. * * *

Oklahoma compulsory pooling better addresses the speculation problem, at least with respect to initial wells, but the pooling process itself is more involved and time-consuming, leading to high regulatory costs that are usually incurred on a drilling unit basis. Commonly, Oklahoma regulatory practice enlarges a newly discovered field on a drilling unit basis by combining spacing and pooling into one proceeding. Due to land ownership patterns, this often can require a separate proceeding for almost every well in a field. * * * Under Oklahoma compulsory pooling, working-interest owners who elect not to participate in drilling are commonly forced to relinquish their working interest in the proposed well in return for money, an overriding royalty, or both. * * * Ordinarily unleased interest owners may elect to participate and receive a royalty or to relinquish their interest in return for money and a royalty. * * *

[A problem encountered in all jurisdictions is that the successful development of wildcat acreage invites competition from speculative operators. These operators will have leased or top-leased nearby acreage for speculative purposes. In areas where tracts have been subdivided and the mineral rights have been fractionalized, it is highly unlikely that any one operator will be able to acquire lease rights to all of the acreage in the area. Accordingly, when the wildcat operator assumes the high risk of drilling a wildcat well that turns out to be a prolific well, the speculators, who have taken minimal risk in acquiring their acreage position in the area, stand to profit handsomely from the wildcatter's efforts. Indeed, such profits often come at the expense of the wildcatter who suffers offsetting wells on adjacent drilling units. In the end, the wildcatter shares the benefits of the new discovery with other operators who took comparatively little risk.]

The preceding discussion has endeavored to illustrate some of the problems with a well-by-well regulatory approach. A reader unfamiliar with conservation practices is cautioned not to assume that this discussion offers a summary of "normal" conservation regulatory practice. Indeed, another problem with traditional oil and gas conservation regulatory practices is a lack of uniformity from state-to-state. Conservation law practice tends to be highly specialized. Knowing how to practice conservation law in one state does not suffice for all. Thus, this lack of uniformity serves to increase regulatory costs for the many operators that drill wells and produce oil and gas in more than one state.

For several decades, leading oil and gas economists have recognized the shortcomings of a well-by-well regulatory approach.[99] Professor Stephen McDonald, while acknowledging that traditional spacing, pooling and prorationing regulations have been helpful, has pointed out that these regulations have two serious defects:

---

99. *See generally* Lovejoy & Homan above and McDonald, above.

First, they do not adequately protect correlative rights.... In the ordinary situation where some wells in a reservoir have structural advantage or disadvantage depending on whether oil is driven toward or away from them by expanding gas or water, producers' rights to the oil originally in place beneath their surface leases are not protected by allowing each well draining a tract of given size to produce at the same rate as every other in the reservoir as long as it can.... Second, by aiming at physical efficiency—or the prevention of physical waste in the language of the typical conservation statute—existing regulatory measures do not necessarily benefit the industry or society in every instance and certainly do not maximize the benefit we derive from our oil resources over an extended period of time.[100]

Professors Wallace Lovejoy and Paul Homan conclude that a well-by-well regulatory approach reduces but does not eliminate the drilling of unnecessary wells. * * * They further conclude that development of reservoirs by numerous working-interest owners, acting on their own, increases costs and decreases ultimate recovery. They strongly support field-wide unit operations, arguing that, because self-interest would be unitized, the unit operator would determine the proper rates of production and investment without the need for extensive conservation agency oversight on a well-by-well basis.[101]

Early unitization would decrease drilling and operational costs because fewer wells would be drilled and greatly reduce overall regulatory costs for both interest owners and for states. Unit operators would be free to efficiently use the surface of the entire unitized acreage. * * * The result would be less surface use overall and far fewer conflicts with surface owners * * * and fewer land-use * * * and environmental concerns * * * because there would be fewer well bores, and even fewer well locations, * * * access roads, tank batteries, and gathering systems. Moreover, the unit operator would be allowed to use a variety of modern tools, including 3–D seismic surveying * * * and hydraulic fracturing, * * * without risking liability for trespass. Field-wide unitization would greatly reduce the liability to third parties because there would be no owners of non-unitized tracts to file suit for damages allegedly resulting from unit operations. * * * Although the regulatory costs of achieving unitization may be quite high, overall regulatory costs should be much lower because there should be far less regulatory oversight and fewer regulatory requirements and proceedings. * * *

(b) What Is Enhanced Recovery?

Traditionally, unitization has been used as a tool to combine the various oil and gas interests in all or a portion of an existing oil or gas field so that secondary or enhanced-recovery operations may be conduct-

---

100. McDonald *above* at 308.

101. Lovejoy & Homan, above at 31.

ed.[102] Methods of enhanced recovery are divided into two broad categories: secondary and tertiary (enhanced) recovery. Secondary recovery refers to more conventional methods: water flooding and gas injection. Tertiary or enhanced recovery refers to more complex and relatively new techniques, such as surfactant flooding, carbon dioxide flooding, steam injection, and fire flooding. See the more detailed description in Chapter 1, Section C.4.

(c) Achieving Unitization

OWEN L. ANDERSON, MUTINY: THE REVOLT AGAINST UNSUCCESSFUL UNIT OPERATIONS, 30 ROCKY MTN.MIN.L.INST. 13–1, 13–3 TO 13–8 (1984)[103]

[Unitization combines the individual holdings of all or a significant portion of a common reservoir for the purpose of conducting joint operations, usually involving pressure maintenance, water flooding, gas injection, or other means of enhanced recovery.][104] This * * * discussion focuses primarily on units created under the provisions of compulsory unitization acts.

* * *

Unitization for enhanced recovery is perhaps the ultimate conservation tool. Ideally, unitization should occur at an early stage so that the natural energy of the reservoir can be conserved and even enhanced to achieve a greater ultimate recovery of oil and gas.

Under voluntary unitization, all of the various working-interests and nonworking-interest owners in a field, or a portion thereof, agree to joint operations to enhance recovery. For a variety of reasons, however, the unanimous consent of all interest owners is difficult to achieve.[105] Thus, compulsory unitization laws are often relied upon to implement an enhanced-recovery plan.

Under compulsory unitization acts,[106] a conservation agency can issue an order compelling unitization. While in some jurisdictions a conserva-

---

102. Unitization can occur in wildcat areas for purposes of exploration, but exploratory units are common only to federal lands. Federal exploratory units are briefly discussed in Chapter 7, Section A.6.

103. Copyright © 1985 by Matthew Bender & Co., Inc., and reprinted with permission from Rocky Mountain Mineral Law Institute © 1985, 30th Annual Institute.

104. Norman J. Hyne, Dictionary of Petroleum Exploration, Drilling, and Production (PennWell 1991).

105. Production from a unit must be fairly and equitably allocated among the various interest owners, but there may be great disagreement over what is fair and equitable. Many interest owners, especially those with highly productive wells in the heart of a field, may believe that their interests are best served by refusing to share any production with outlying properties. Some interest owners are simply suspicious of unitization plans and characterize them as a ploy by lessees to hold on to leased acreage without having to fully develop the fields.

106. [Updated by editors] The following states have enacted compulsory unitization acts: Alabama; Alaska; Arizona; Arkansas; California; Colorado; Florida; Georgia; Illinois; Kansas; Kentucky; Louisiana; Michigan; Mississippi; Missouri; Montana; Nebraska; Nevada; New Mexico; New York; North Dakota; Ohio; Oklahoma; Oregon; South Carolina; South Dakota; Tennessee; Utah; Vermont; Washington; West Virginia; Wyoming. Texas, a major oil and gas producing state, does not have a compulsory unitization act. For commentary on the need for a unitization statute in Texas see, Murray & Cross, Case for a Texas Compulsory Unitization Statute, 23 St. Mary's L.J. 1099 (1992).

tion agency may issue a unitization order on its own motion, such an order is usually issued upon the application of working-interest owners.

Achieving unitization is usually a lengthy and involved process. The process may begin when the working-interest owners form a field-wide operating committee. This committee, or a specially formed unit committee, investigates the feasibility of enhanced recovery from both engineering and economic standpoints and determines which enhanced-recovery method will obtain the maximum recovery of hydrocarbons from the field. Because implementing an enhanced-recovery plan may be very expensive, the amount of expected increased recovery must be sufficient to recoup all costs and produce a reasonable profit.

If the committee decides that unitization is warranted, tract participation formulas must be calculated for the allocation of production from the unit and for the allocation of unit costs.[107] In contrast to pooling, where production and costs are customarily allocated on a surface-acreage basis, unitwide allocations are usually based on a combination of factors, such as the acreage of each tract, the net-acre feet of pay and the volume of oil in place beneath each tract, the differences in porosity within the field, current production, cumulative production, the projected primary recovery from each well, and other factors. Reaching an agreement on a fair allocation formula is difficult, especially when some tracts may have no past or existing production.[108]

[The committee must also allocate costs among the working-interest owners. As existing wells and equipment will be used for unit operations, the committee must consider development expenses already incurred by each owner. Usually a portion of these costs are attributed to primary recovery; the well owner remains solely responsible for these costs. The balance is attributed to future secondary recovery and charged against all working-interest owners in the unit on a fair share basis, as are costs of enhanced recovery.]

---

107. [Editors' Note] To illustrate the need for a participation formula, assume that an existing oil field consists of the separately owned and leased tracts of Blackacre, Whiteacre, Redacre, and Greenacre with the outlines of the reservoir and location of wells as indicated on the following map.

If the unitization plan is implemented, assume that two wells on Blackacre, one well on Whiteacre, and two wells on Greenacre will be converted into water injection wells. Production will come from the remaining wells. When water flooding begins, oil will be pushed toward the production wells and some of this oil will be pushed across property lines.

Without equitably allocating production on a unit-wide basis, the lessee of Redacre, who loses no production wells, may recover more than a fair share of production from the reservoir. Conversely, the owners of Blackacre, Whiteacre, and Greenacre, who lose production wells, may recover less than their fair share. To protect correlative rights, production must be allocated on a unit-wide basis.

108. Unproductive tracts are commonly included in a unit. These tracts are often on the fringes of the field and, in some cases, may not contain sufficient hydrocarbons to justify economically the drilling of a well. But drilling and seismic data collected from nearby properties may substantiate that the reservoir targeted for unitization may lie under these tracts. Since the enhanced-recovery technique may sweep the entire reservoir, these tracts are often included in the unit plan and are entitled to receive a just and equitable share of production.

To secure the payment of each working-interest owner's share of unit costs, the unit operator and each working-interest owner are given a lien on each other's share of unit production. To encourage an owner to advance his share of costs, unit agreements give an owner the option of advancing his share of costs, having his share of costs taken out of his share of production, or, in some cases, selling his interest in return for a bonus or overriding royalty or both.

Once the unit committee has reached accord on the basics of the unit plan and allocation formulas, it will draft a unit agreement and unit operating agreement.[109] The unit agreement is the basic document which identifies and combines the various tracts and interests forming the unit. The agreement outlines the basic plan for unitization and the formulas for allocating costs and production. In addition, the agreement will designate the unit operator, usually the owner of the largest share of unit production.

The unit operating agreement governs the day-to-day operation of the unit. This agreement sets forth the specific responsibilities and duties of the unit operator and working-interest owners, voting procedures for working-interest owners, insurance, valuation of equipment contributions, accounting procedures, winding up provisions, and other matters.

Once the plan, unit agreement, and unit operating agreement have been formulated, the proposal is submitted to the conservation agency for approval.[110] After notice to all interested parties, the plan and agreements are outlined at a hearing. Following the hearing, if the commission finds that the proposed unit is economically feasible and will prevent waste and protect correlative rights, it may enter an order approving the plan and agreements. In issuing its order, the commission may require modifications to the plan or amendments to the agreements, which may be proposed by interested parties or may originate with the commission itself. Often, however, the plan and agreements are approved as submitted.

Once commission approval has been obtained, the designated unit operator and other proponents of unitization will begin the task of obtaining the required ratification of working and nonworking-interest owners in the proposed unit. Nearly all compulsory unitization acts require the ratification of working interest owners who collectively will be required to pay a specified percentage of the costs of unitization under the terms of the unitization agreement. In addition, the acts require the ratification of nonworking interest owners who collectively will be entitled to a specified percentage of the production or proceeds of production under

109. These agreements are made on standardized forms that are usually not materially changed. * * * [For examples of a unit agreement and unit operating agreement, see the Forms Manual accompanying this casebook.]

110. If the unitization is to be entirely voluntary, the unit committee will seek the necessary ratifications from all interest owners. The oil and gas conservation commission may be asked to approve the unitization, but its approval is typically sought to avoid any possible antitrust problems. Some statutes, however, provide that approval by the conservation commission is a prerequisite to engaging in any unit operations. See N.D.Cent.Code 38–08–09.

the terms of the unitization agreement.[111] Among the major oil and gas producing states, the required percentage specified in the acts varies from 63% to 85% of each of the working and nonworking-interests. In a few states, nonworking-interests carved from the lessee's interest are excluded for purposes of meeting the minimum percentage of nonworking-interests. In Kansas, the percentage is lower (63%) for both working and nonworking-interests if unitization is needed to prevent the imminent abandonment of wells. Otherwise, the percentage is 63% for working-interests and 75% for nonworking-interests. In both situations, nonworking-interests carved from the lessee's interest are excluded.[112]

Once the necessary ratifications have been obtained, and in some jurisdictions certified by order of the conservation agency following a second hearing, the unit is established and enhanced-recovery operations may begin. The unit remains in effect for its economic life. * * *

A common variation of the above procedure is to have only one unitization hearing following preparation of the unit plan and the ratification process. Under this approach, the unit plan (having already been ratified) is put to the conservation agency on essentially a "take it or leave it" basis. This approach is more prone to accusations that the allocations of costs and production are unfair to those parties who refused to ratify the unit. Nevertheless, because conservation agencies are generally more concerned about preventing waste than protecting correlative rights, the agency is likely to approve the unitization.

MODEL OIL AND GAS CONSERVATION ACT (INTERSTATE OIL & GAS COMPACT COMM'N 2004)

Section 13. COMPULSORY UNIT OPERATION—CREATION.

The [commission], upon its own motion or upon application of an owner, shall conduct a hearing to consider the need for unit operation of an entire reservoir or portion thereof, to increase ultimate recovery of oil or gas from that reservoir or portion thereof. The [commission] shall issue an order requiring unit operation if it finds that unit operation of the reservoir or portion thereof is reasonably necessary to prevent waste or to protect correlative rights; that unit operation of the reservoir or portion thereof is reasonably necessary for maintaining or restoring reservoir pressure, or to implement cycling, water flooding, enhanced recovery, horizontal drilling, de-watering, or a combination of these operations or other operations or objectives to be cooperatively pursued with the goal of increasing the ultimate recovery of oil or gas; and that the estimated cost to conduct the unit operation will not exceed the value of the estimated recovery of additional oil or gas resulting from unit operation.

---

111. The Alaska Compulsory Unitization Act requires no voluntary ratifications. See Alaska Stat. § 31.05.110 (1985).

112. Kan. Stat. Annot. §§ 55–1304 and 55–1305.

Section 14. COMPULSORY UNIT OPERATION—APPLICATION.

(a) An application for compulsory unitization shall contain, at a minimum, a description of the proposed unit and the vertical limits to be included therein with a map or plat thereof attached; a statement that the reservoir or portion thereof involved in the application area has been reasonably defined by development; a statement of the type of operations contemplated for the unit area; the proposed plan of unitization; a proposed operating plan that addresses the manner in which the unit will be supervised and managed and costs allocated and paid.

(b) The [commission] may, by regulation, impose additional requirements for an application for compulsory pooling.

Section 6. COMPULSORY UNIT OPERATION—ORDER FOR UNIT OPERATION.

(a) An order for a unit operation must be upon just and reasonable terms and conditions and shall include all of the following:

    (1) a precise definition of the vertical and horizontal limits of the unit area;

    (2) a statement of the nature of the operation contemplated;

    (3) a provision designating one of the owners as operator of the unit and providing a means to remove the operator and designating a successor operator;

    (4) a provision for recording in the [county] land records documents sufficient to give constructive notice of the establishment of the unit operation respecting all lands included in the unit area;

    (5) a provision to protect correlative rights, allocating to each separately owned tract in the unit area a just and equitable share of the production that is produced and saved from the unit area, other than production used or unavoidably lost in the conduct of the unit operation;

    (6) a provision for credits and charges to adjust among owners in the unit area for their interest in wells, tanks, pumps, machinery, materials, and equipment that contribute to the unit operation;

    (7) a provision that describes:

        (A) how the costs of unit operation, including capital investments and costs of terminating the unit operation, are to be determined and charged to each owner or the interest of each owner;

        (B) how, when, and by whom the share of unit production allocated to an owner who does not pay the share of those costs charged to that owner or to the interest of that owner may be sold and the proceeds applied to the payment of that owner's share of those costs; and

(C) how accounts will be settled upon termination of the unit.

(8) a provision, if reasonable, for carrying or otherwise financing an owner who elects to be carried or otherwise financed, which allows a reasonable charge for the cost and risk of that service payable out of that owner's share of the production;

(9) a provision for the supervision and conduct of the unit operation, in respect to which each owner is entitled to a vote whose value corresponds to the percentage of the costs of the unit operation chargeable to that owner or to the interest of that owner;

(10) a time when the unit operation is to commence and the manner in which, and the circumstances under which, the unit operation is to terminate and the unit is to be dissolved; and

(11) additional provisions found to be appropriate to carry on the unit operation, to prevent waste, and to protect correlative rights.

(b) An order for a unit operation may provide for a unit operation of less than the whole of a reservoir so long as the unit area is of size and shape reasonably required for that purpose and the conduct thereof will have no significant adverse effect upon other portions of the reservoir.

* * *

Section 17. UNIT AGREEMENT—EFFECTIVE DATE OF COMPULSORY UNIT. An order requiring a unit operation shall not become effective until a unit agreement, approved by the [commission], has been signed and approved in writing by the owners of at least [sixty (60)] percent as costs are shared under terms of the allocation of costs under [Section 15(a)] and the royalty interest owners of at least [sixty (60)] percent, excluding owners of overriding royalties, production payments, and other interests carved from a working-interest, in the unit area as revenues are distributed under the terms of the allocation under [Section 15(a)]. The unit agreement is subordinate to the terms of an order requiring a unit operation and to an order amending an order requiring a unit operation.

* * *

Section 19. EFFECT OF COMPULSORY UNITIZATION.

(a) Operations, including the commencement, drilling, or operation of a well upon a portion of a unit area, are deemed conducted on each separately owned tract in the unit area by the owner or owners thereof. That portion of a unit's production allocated to a separately owned tract in a unit area, when produced, is deemed produced from a well drilled on that tract. Operations conducted under an order of the [commission] providing for a unit operation shall constitute fulfillment of expressed or implied obligations of a lease or contract covering lands within the unit area to the extent that compliance with those obligations is not possible without a further order of the [commission].

(b) That portion of unit production allocated to a tract and the proceeds of sale for that portion are deemed the property and income of the several persons to whom or to whose credit that portion is allocated or payable under the order providing for unit operation.

(c) A division order or other contract relating to a sale or purchase of production from a separately owned tract or combination of tracts remains in force and applies to oil and gas allocated to the tract until terminated in accordance with provisions of the order providing for unit operation.

(d) Except to the extent that all affected parties agree, an order providing for unit operation does not result in a transfer of all or part of a person's title to the oil and gas rights in a tract in the unit area.

(e) All property, whether real or personal, that may be acquired in the conduct of a unit operation hereunder is deemed acquired for the account of the owners within the unit area and is deemed the property of the owners in the proportion that the expenses of the unit operation are charged.

(f) The creation of a unit operation shall not constitute approval or permitting of underground injection operations for a well or wells. Injection operations, whether for storage, disposal, or enhanced recovery, must be separately approved and permitted.

———

Unitization hearings tend to be complex and divisive. Moreover, the stakes can be high for interested parties. The following case illustrates these characteristics and teaches much about conservation practices and fundamentals of administrative law.

THE TREES OIL COMPANY v. STATE CORPORATION COMMISSION

105 P.3d 1269 (Kan. 2005).

* * *

This is an administrative appeal pursuant to K.S.A. 77–601 *et seq.* from the decision of the district court of Haskell County, Kansas, affirming the order of the State Corporation Commission of Kansas (KCC or Commission) granting the application of Chesapeake Operating Inc. (Chesapeake) to allow the compulsory unitization and unit operation of the South Eubank Waterflood Unit (Unit) pursuant to the Kansas Unitization Act, K.S.A. 55–1301 *et seq.*, over the continuing objection of The Trees Oil Company (Trees).

The first issue was one of first impression involving the statutory definition of an oil and gas "pool" as defined in K.S.A. 55–1302, when considered by the KCC and district court. This issue becomes one of last impression as the result of 2004 amendments to K.S.A. 55–1302, which now clearly grant the rights Trees contests, as will be fully discussed in our opinion. See L.2004, ch. 115, sec. 1.

Trees' second, third, and fourth issues involve the application of administrative law to the KCC orders and relate to the involuntary inclusion of Trees' property within the Unit, whether there was substantial competent evidence to uphold the KCC findings and rulings, and if the KCC acted arbitrarily and capriciously in refusing to allow Trees to present additional geological evidence at a second hearing the Commission ordered to consider only the fairness of the terms of the Unit Operating Agreement.

      *   *   *

Procedural History and Factual Background

Several oil and gas operators, Chesapeake, OXY–USA, Inc. (OXY), and Anadarko Petroleum Corporation (Anadarko), own 16 oil and gas wells that produce oil out of a 3.7 miles long and 500–to 1,500–foot wide incised Chester and Morrow formation channel and desired to inject water into the Chester formation to produce substantial additional oil production beyond that possible with conventional pumping methods.

Trees owns and operates one oil and gas well on 80 acres within the southern boundary of the proposed water flood project and, after attending two planning meetings in mid–2000, informed the other operators it did not wish to voluntarily participate in the project.

Planning on the project continued and, on June 27, 2001, Chesapeake filed an application with the Commission that sought unitization and unit operations of the area above described. OXY and Anadarko were allowed to intervene.

      *   *   *

The hearing took place on September 20, 2001, with the Commission taking testimony from five technical witnesses and admitting exhibits. Posthearing briefs were filed, the record was closed, and the Commission took the matter under advisement.

On March 12, 2002, the KCC issued an Interim Order Requiring Additional Evidence, in which it stated: "The Commission has before it ample record and is ready to rule on the conditions in K.S.A. 55–1302(a) and (b)," but reopened the record for the specific purpose of receiving additional testimony as to whether specific terms of the Unit Operating Agreement were fair and equitable to all parties.

On April 3, 2002, the Commission heard additional evidence concerning the fairness of the specific terms of the Unit Operating Agreement. The Commission refused to reopen the record to allow Trees to present additional geological testimony.

On April 18, 2002, the KCC issued a detailed 26–page order of findings and conclusions granting Chesapeake's application for unitization and unit operations of the South Eubank Waterflood Unit. Trees' petition for reconsideration was denied, and it then filed a petition for judicial review before the Haskell County District Court.

* * * District Judge Tom R. Smith issued a comprehensive 18–page decision in which the rulings and orders of the Commission were affirmed. Trees appealed.

* * *

[At the Commission proceedings], Rodney J. Vaeth, a Chesapeake expert landman, presented copies of the Unit Agreement and the Unit Operating Agreement, which he testified incorporated the statutory requirements of the Kansas Unitization Act and met the required statutory percentages of both royalty and working interest owners who had approved both agreements. He testified 93.39152 percent of the working-interest owners had approved Phase I of the agreements and 94.47862 percent had approved Phase II of the agreements. He further testified 69.396548 percent of the royalty owners on a surface-acre basis had approved the agreements, that 64.00343 percent of the royalty owners had approved Phase I and 67.35903 percent of the royalty owners had approved Phase II of the agreements.

Jimmy W. Gowens, a petroleum geologist, testified for Chesapeake and described the reservoir and unit areas as portions of the Morrow and Chester sand formations in an incised channel 3.7 miles long and between 500–to 1,500–foot wide and described how the boundaries were established by the technical committee by seismic data and other factors. He noted that, within the field, Chesapeake operated 12 wells, Anadarko 4 wells, and Trees operates 1 well. He described the Chester sand as continuous from the north boundary of the Unit to the south boundary.

Gowens had personally been involved in drilling all of the Chesapeake wells. He testified seven of the wells within the proposed unit area have commingled production from both the Chester and Morrow formations and, as the result of such dual completions, both of the formations are in pressure communication.

Gowens testified he had prepared the hydrocarbon pore volume (HPV) maps * * * used in determining the participation formulas. On cross-examination, he said the HPV values are a very reliable measure of oil in place.

In rebuttal testimony, Gowens said he doubted the ability of Trees to use the Lou Ethel well (a well south of Trees' Josephine well which was included in the Unit) as an injection well for a mini waterflood. He questioned whether there was communication between the two wells because of the possibility of a separating fault.

Chesapeake then presented the testimony of Dan Scott, a petroleum engineer with 22 years of experience. He testified the unit area is underlain by productive Chester sand, which is in good pressure communication throughout the Unit making it an excellent waterflood candidate.

Scott testified the project was economic and would result in incremental secondary recovery of at least 690,000 barrels of oil, a figure he believed to be conservative. He said the increased recovery would not be achievable through primary operations and would therefore prevent waste. The project, based on an oil price of $20 per barrel, was expected to achieve a gross profit of $6.2 million.

Scott then testified in detail regarding the determination of the unit participation percentages and formula. The parameters used included remaining primary reserves, current production, Chester well bores, Chester HPV, and Chester ultimate recovery. He opined that the use of these parameters and resulting unit formula was fair and equitable and that 94 percent of the working-interest owners had approved the two-phase participation formula.

The two-phase formula was described as Phase I with 50 percent remaining primary reserves and 50 percent current production and Phase II being 5 percent Chester well bores, 47.5 percent Chester HPV, and 47.5 percent Chester estimated ultimate recovery. Scott said he had been working on the waterflood since the summer of 1999 and had devoted over 1,000 hours to the study of the project.

Scott also testified in rebuttal to Trees' witnesses. He opined that the Trees' Josephine well was in pressure communication with the other Chester wells in the proposed unit. He said the reservoir pressure at that time was approximately 400 psi but that, through injection under pressure, they intended to bring reservoir pressure back to 1,500 psi. He testified the Trees' Josephine well, if allowed to remain a producer, would become much more productive as the result of the proposed waterflood with much of the production coming from the unit area as the result of migration of oil across the lease line in violation of correlative rights.

Scott strongly disagreed with Trees' witness Hupp that efficient operation of the Leather's Land 2–10 well (located directly north of the Josephine well) could prevent migration of oil. He noted that the initial production rate of the Leather's Land 2–10 well was only 87 barrels of oil a day and that injection rates would be as high as 1,100 barrels per day causing oil to bypass the Leather's Land 2–10 well and be pushed to the Josephine well in violation of correlative rights. Scott disagreed with Hupp, who had suggested the narrowness of the channel would prevent migration, pointing out a well bore is only 7 or 8 inches wide and the reservoir at the Leather's Land 2–10 well is over 1,000 feet wide, approximately the length of over 3 football fields. Scott estimated the amount of oil that could be lost by migrating of oil off the Unit onto the Trees' well could be as much as 18,000 barrels if Trees were omitted from the Unit.

Scott testified the natural state of the formations had been altered by commingling the Morrow and Chester formations in seven of the well bores, and the two zones are in pressure communication, which means, from a pressure standpoint, they are one and the same. He further said it was intended to leave both sets of perforations open in the commingled wells that would become injection wells, which could lead to additional recovery and production from the Morrow formation.

Scott opined the value of the Josephine lease without water flooding would be approximately $130,000 but by implementation of the project the value could increase to $390,000 and that the increase in present net worth at a 10 percent discount rate was approximately $250,000.

Finally, Scott testified the wells in the proposed unit are in imminent danger of being abandoned due to economics and low levels of primary production.

Trees presented the testimony of Thomas G. Pronold, a geologist, and Kenton Hupp, a petroleum engineer.

Pronold testified the Chester formation in this area has different pressure compartments, which could minimize the effectiveness of the proposed waterflood. He did not present any pressure studies to support this statement. Pronold acknowledged he could not determine whether interest owners were receiving credit for Morrow pay that was not actually producing. He did not present any seismic data on behalf of Trees, although it was available, in support of the possibility that the Morrow formation might be productive in the area of the Josephine well and acknowledged he would not recommend Trees to drill a well there for Morrow production.

Pronold acknowledged that seven of the wells in the area had been commingled between the Chester and Morrow formations as had been permitted by Commission orders.

Hupp testified that the technical committee undervalued the remaining reserves under the Josephine 1–15 well because it did not honor late term amounts of Trees' production. He did acknowledge that September 2000 through February 2001 production amounts would have been below the decline curve and that he did not account for those points in developing his exhibit.

Hupp said that geologic mapping was prepared without input from Trees but did acknowledge that he knew Trees had representatives at two technical committee meetings and a geophysicist present at the meeting on July 10, 2000. Hupp admitted that he believed the project was valid from an engineering standpoint and that the Chester formation is floodable.

Hupp expressed concern that Trees would not get credit for Morrow reserves but did acknowledge that he was not aware of any other operation in the Unit that was to receive credit for Morrow production that was not actually being produced. He acknowledged Trees would be getting a share of Morrow production from the Unit even though there would be no Morrow production from the Trees' tract itself.

Hupp criticized the use of HPV or oil in place as a parameter in the participation formula as being unreliable and speculative, although he acknowledged he had previously advocated use of oil in place before the

Commission and that the Commission had used HPV on unit orders before.

Chesapeake and Trees presented additional testimony on April 3, 2001, in response to the Commission's interim orders limited to the fairness of the terms of the Unit Operating Agreement.

Professor David E. Pierce of the Washburn University School of Law, who teaches in the oil and gas law area, qualified as an expert witness and testified on behalf of Chesapeake. He was familiar with the agreements and said they were patterned after the model forms of the American Petroleum Institute. They are standardized provisions generally used in the oil and gas industry and satisfied the statutory requirements of the Kansas Unitization Act, K.S.A. 55–1301 *et seq.*

Professor Pierce opined the agreements were fair in that all owners were treated the same. Decisions were required to be made in good faith and provided adequate protection for the interests of an unwilling participant. Pierce specifically testified the "recovery of costs" provision of the Unit Operating Agreement was authorized by statute and was fair in that if a nonoperating working-interest owner elected not to assume additional risk, it compensated the operator for the additional risk it assumed when it financed the operation.

Gayle Gentry Bishop testified on behalf of Trees. She is its president, principal shareholder, and has had operating responsibility for the past 17 years. Bishop said she felt the agreement was unfair to Trees because, as an unwilling participant, it was being forced to take risks it did not wish to take. It had no practical way to protect itself from majority decisions that Trees believed to be adverse to its interests. She objected to lost cash flow and being required to contribute to unit expenses.

Bishop said Trees had not known it could be forced to participate in the project and had not perceived a need to be involved in Unit planning.

There were three provisions of the agreement which Bishop believed to be unfair. Article 4.3 was objected to because it allowed decisions by a majority vote and, consequently, the other participants would effectively control unit operations. She further objected to Chesapeake and OXY determining the values of personal property delivered to the Unit and expressed concern about the future use of a tank battery that was also used for Trees' Lou Ethel No. 15 well.

Chesapeake presented Scott on rebuttal. He testified the cash flow impact on Trees was proportionate to all participants. As to the equipment valuation objection, he testified that all equipment owned by Trees in connection with the Josephine well, except for the casing, would be pulled and returned to Trees so no valuation would be needed. As to the tank battery in question, it would not be disturbed by unit operation and would remain fully available for use in connection with Trees' Lou Ethel well which was not a part of the Unit.

Rulings and Orders of the Kansas Corporation Commission

The Commission order first recited the evidence presented as has been summarized above. It was then noted that Trees raised a threshold legal issue that the proposed unitization could not go forward because it violated the statutory requirements for unit operation of a "pool," defined in K.S.A. 55–1302 as

> an underground accumulation of oil and gas in a single and separate natural reservoir characterized by a single pressure system so that production from one part of the pool affects the reservoir pressure throughout its extent.

Trees' argument was said to center on the wording "single and separate natural reservoir" as precluding unitization of two reservoirs connected by well bores completed so that the formations become commingled.

The Commission declined to apply what it characterized as a narrow and restricted reading of the statute because it deemed that doing so would result in substantial waste including loss of 690,000 barrels of oil production and economic loss of approximately $6.2 million of gross profits after expenses.

It was noted this was a matter of first impression in Kansas, although two Oklahoma cases had determined a pool such as exists here would be acceptable under the Oklahoma statute. The word "natural" is not used in the Oklahoma statute, so the Commission determined it must address that feature of the Kansas statute to determine if it should result in denial of the Chesapeake application.

The Commission pointed out that the Kansas Unitization statute is founded on the public policy of prevention of waste, conservation of oil and gas, and protection of correlative rights. Parkin v. Kansas Corporation Commission, 234 Kan. 994, 1006, 677 P.2d 991 (1984). There is no indication the legislature intended to prevent oil bearing reservoirs from unit operation because of commingled production of what was originally separate reservoirs. The fact deemed the most significant was that waste could be prevented by allowing unit operation of the Chester formation.

The Commission's order then looked to the rule of statutory construction set forth in *Todd v. Kelly*, 251 Kan. 512, 516, 837 P.2d 381 (1992), that

> 'courts are not permitted to consider only a certain isolated part or parts of the act, but are required to consider and construe together all parts *in pari materia. When the interpretation of some one section of an act according to the exact and literal impact of its words would contravene the manifest purpose of the legislature, the entire act should be construed according to its spirit and reason, disregarding so far as may be necessary the strict letter of the law.*' [Citation omitted.]

The order pointed out the legislature had previously amended the act to make unitization easier to accomplish by lowering the 75 percent sign up requirement in the original act to 63 percent. The clear intent of the statute would not be advanced by giving "natural" the significance Trees urged. It was noted the word "natural" may have been used for unrelated reasons and there was no reason within the statutory scheme for such a narrow interpretation.

The Commission noted this specific question, while not the subject of any Kansas cases, had been addressed by Professor Ernest E. Smith in an article on the Kansas Unitization Act, Smith, *The Kansas Unitization Statute: Part II*, 17 Kan. L.Rev. 133, 137 (1968), which the Commission quoted as follows in its order:

> '[The Kansas statute] requires "a single and separate natural reservoir characterized by a single pressure system so that production from one part of the pool affects the reservoir pressure throughout its extent." If "natural" is read as defining "reservoir" and not "single pressure system"—as, indeed seems the most obvious construction— then a series of vertically separated reservoirs which have been brought into pressure communication through multiple-completion drilling and production techniques would qualify as a "pool" under the statute and could be developed as a single unit under the act. Such a construction would be entirely consistent with the definition, in that production from one such reservoir would affect the pressure throughout all the reservoirs. It would also be consistent with the purposes of the act insofar as these include the avoidance of economic waste and uneconomical methods of production.'

The Commission stated it agreed with this reasoning. It also noted the Chester and Morrow formations had previously been authorized to be commingled by a Commission order[1] and there was not expected to be any significant recovery from the Morrow formation, with the primary production coming from the secondary recovery of the Chester formation.

The Commission noted it would not be prudent to separate the formations at this time as it would be costly, without benefit, and any possible Morrow production would be lost. The Commission's order concluded that the interpretation called for by Trees is not required and it "will not interpret the statute to require foregoing over $6 million in additional production because the reservoir to be unitized for secondary recovery is incidentally connected to a reservoir, such as the Morrow formation, with no secondary-recovery potential of its own."

The Commission order then looked at the additional issues Trees raised as to the fairness of the allocations and the Unit Operating Agreement itself as it impacts a minority working-interest owner. The Commission said that it had taken a closer look at the agreement but was satisfied that the proposed unit is fair and equitable to all participants.

---

1. [Editors' Note] Conservation agencies often prohibit commingling of production from separate formations. In this particular circumstance, the KCC expressly authorized commingling, perhaps because, without commingling, production from the Morrow formation would not be economic. That is, the oil in the Morrow would be wasted—left in the reservoir—if producers were forced to incur the extra expense of having to segregate production. Absent commingling, the statutory interpretation question would not have arisen.

As to the allocation formula, it was found to use well recognized measures and was reasonable. The cut-off point was reasonable, and the fact Trees gave fracture treatment to its Josephine well to temporarily increase production in April 2001, after the January to May 2000 period used, did not improperly affect the allocations of interests. The allocation of the Morrow production to Phase I of the allocation was found to be reasonable because of the existence of some Morrow production.

While a short-term revenue loss to Trees would result from conversion of the Josephine well from a producing well to an input well, there was substantial credible evidence that the value of Trees' lease with unit operation is higher than without. All participants lose short-term cash flow but will recover its allocated share of unit production.

The Commission order then moved to the three Trees' claims of unfairness in the Unit Operating Agreement addressed by the April 3, 2000, hearing and found: (1) There was nothing inherently unfair about majority rule where the majority was obligated to use good faith and equally treated all participants, (2) valuations of personal property must be treated fairly and, based on the Scott testimony, there would be no valuation questions, and (3) the Trees' tank battery remained usable in conjunction with another well.

The Commission order noted Trees' protest had not been helpful in improving the agreement and that "[Trees] only wants out." Trees' request to be omitted from the Unit would violate the public interest as well as correlative rights. Under the statute, waste or harm to correlative rights would occur without Trees being included in the Unit. Convincing evidence of this is that omission of the Trees' tracts and Josephine well would allow as much as 18,000 barrels of oil to migrate from the Unit onto the Trees tracts. The remaining well on that end of the Unit would not adequately prevent this migration. The Commission concluded this discussion by stating: "Prevention of harm to correlative rights is one of the principal goals of the Unitization statute and supports keeping the Trees tract in the Unit."

The Commission's order held that the Chester and Morrow formations had been commingled and now constituted one common source of supply, approved the described unit area for a waterflood operation, found without unit operations substantial waste would occur, found participation percentages were fair to Trees and other participants, approved the Unit Operating Agreement as fair and equitable, held exclusion of Trees from the Unit would violate correlative rights by allowing 18,000 barrels of oil to migrate from the Unit to Trees' tracts, and found all applicable statutory requirements had been satisfied.

It is from these findings and orders that Trees appealed * * *.

District Court Decision

* * *

[The district court found that there was substantial evidence to uphold the KCC's findings and that, as trier of fact, it determines the credibility of the witnesses and the weight to give their testimony. The court found substantial evidence in the record that correlative rights would be violated if the KCC granted Trees' request to be excluded from the Unit, because Trees would gain substantial additional oil from the water flooding operations. The court found that the KCC did not act unreasonably, arbitrarily, or capriciously in refusing to allow Trees to offer additional evidence on whether the waterflood and unitization plan was sound. The court noted that Trees attended two meetings to discuss the Unit in mid–2000 and could have submitted the additional evidence that it offered at the April 3, 2002, at the prior September 2001 hearing. The court found substantial and credible evidence to support the KCC's findings that the participation factors or percentages assigned to Trees were fair and equitable. The court further found that Trees did not meet its burden of proof regarding its equal-protection claim.]

[Regarding the statutory-construction claim] * * * relating to the definition of "pool" in K.S.A. 55–1302 * * * [the district court] noted that, by virtue of the two formations being commingled with seven wells, they were in pressure communication and, therefore, no longer separate pools. * * *

* * *

The court found "that the Kansas definition of 'pool' is most influenced by a single pressure system. Indeed, to prevent waste, or to most effectively produce oil or gas, reservoir pressure is the single most important issue."

The court noted the KCC's reliance on the Smith article in the Kansas Law Review and that Smith relied on two Oklahoma cases, *Jones Oil Company v. Corporation Commission*, 382 P.2d 751 (Okla.) * * * and *Jones v. Continental Oil Co.*, 420 P.2d 905 (Okla.1966).

In the first *Jones* case, 275 wells were unitized with 61 of the wells producing from two or three separate sands. The Oklahoma Corporation Commission's finding that, because of the three producing strata, there was one common source of supply and that the pressure in the three strata were substantially the same was affirmed by the Oklahoma Supreme Court.

The facts were even more striking in the second *Jones* case as there were 204 wells in the field having 21 different producing sand formations. Some wells produced from as many as 14 or 15 well bores although no one well was opened in all 21 zones. The court found that openings in common well bores were now a common source of supply having direct or indirect pressure communication.

The district court restated Professor Smith's analysis, which we have previously set forth and Smith's observations that Kansas should reach the same result despite the difference in statutory language.

* * *

The court then noted the broad authority of the Commission to regulate production of oil, to prevent waste, and to prevent inequitable or unfair taking from a common source of supply. * * * It pointed to the long-time holding that the interpretation of a statute by an administrative agency charged with the responsibility of enforcing a statute is entitled to judicial deference, called the doctrine of operative construction, and deference to an agency's interpretation is particularly appropriate when the agency is one of special competence and experience. * * *

The court stated that legislative intent must be determined from consideration of the entire Unitization Act and every part thereof, that the KCC is an agency of special competence and experience in oil and gas matters with prevention of waste being of primary importance, and held "to this end the decision by the State Corporation Commission to find that two separate oil reservoirs that have been penetrated by common well bores and that are in pressure communication [with each other] are in [e]ffect a single pool and unit operations may be ordered." With this finding, the orders of the KCC were affirmed, and Trees' appeal was denied.

Scope of Review of Agency Actions to the Kansas Supreme Court

This appeal by Trees is from the orders and findings of the KCC as allowed by the KJRA and brings into application the following scope of review sections of K.S.A. 77–621:

(a) Except to the extent that this act or another statute provides otherwise:

(1) The burden of proving the invalidity of agency action is on the party asserting invalidity; and

(2) the validity of agency action shall be determined in accordance with standards of judicial review provided in this section, as applied to the agency action at the time it was taken.

. . . .

(c) The court shall grant relief only if it determines any one or more of the following:

(1) The agency action, or the statute or rule and regulation on which the agency action is based, is unconstitutional on its face or as applied;

. . . .

(4) The agency has erroneously interpreted or applied the law;

. . . .

(7) The agency action is based on a determination of fact, made or implied by the agency, that is not supported by evidence that is substantial when viewed in light of the record as a whole * * *; or

(8) the agency action is otherwise unreasonable, arbitrary or capricious.

As we are instructed by Reed v. Kansas Racing Comm'n, 253 Kan. 602, 609–10, 860 P.2d 684 (1993):

We exercise the same review of the agency's action as does the district court. * * * We must accept as true the evidence and all inferences to be drawn therefrom which support or tend to support the findings of the trial court. We are to disregard any conflicting evidence or other inferences which might be drawn therefrom. * * * 'A rebuttable presumption of validity attaches to all actions of an administrative agency and the burden of proving arbitrary and capricious conduct lies with the party challenging the agency's action.' * * *

Because one of the principal issues here involves the interpretation of a statute, we are obligated to apply the doctrine of operative construction * * *:

The interpretation of a statute by an administrative agency charged with the responsibility of enforcing that statute is entitled to judicial deference.... Further, if there is a rational basis for the agency's interpretation, it should be upheld on judicial review. If, however, the reviewing court finds that the administrative body's interpretation is erroneous as a matter of law, the court should take corrective steps. The determination of an administrative body as to questions of law is not conclusive and, while persuasive, is not binding on the court. * * *

However, * * * "when a statute is ambiguous, the interpretation placed upon it by an administrative agency whose duties are to carry the legislative policy into effect should be given great weight and may be entitled to controlling significance when the scope and limitations of the powers of the agency must be determined in judicial proceedings. * * *"

* * *

I. Interpretation of the term "pool" in K.S.A. 55–1302 of the Kansas Unitization Act, K.S.A. 55–1301 et seq.

The history of unitization of oil and gas operations is well described in Smith, *The Kansas Unitization Statute: Part I,* 16 Kan. L.Rev. 567 (1968), where it is observed: "Unfortunately, the very factors which make field-wide unitization desirable frequently prevent its being achieved through voluntary agreement."

The factors which must be found for the Commission to order unitization and unit operations are set forth in K.S.A.2003 Supp. 55–1304 as the following:

(a) (1) The primary production from a pool or a part thereof sought to be unitized has reached a low economic level and, without introduction of artificial energy, abandonment of oil or gas wells is imminent; or (2) the unitized management, operation and further development of the pool or the part thereof sought to be unitized is economically feasible and reasonably necessary to prevent waste within the reservoir and thereby increase substantially the ultimate recovery of oil or gas;

(b) that the value of the estimated additional recovery of oil or gas substantially exceeds the estimated additional cost incident to conducting such operations; and

(c) that the proposed operation is fair and equitable to all interest owners.

The Unitization statutes make many other references to operations of a "pool," which is defined in K.S.A. 55–1302 as follows:

The term 'pool' as herein used shall mean an underground accumulation of oil and gas in a single and separate natural reservoir characterized by a single pressure system so that production from one part of the pool affects the reservoir pressure throughout its extent.

In its protest to Chesapeake's Application for Unitization and Unit Operations to the KCC, to the district court, and to our court, Trees argues that the commingled Morrow and Chester formations do not constitute "a single and separate natural reservoir" and that the Commission erred in its interpretation of the statute and must be reversed.

The Commission and the district court refused to apply what each deemed to be Trees' "narrow" interpretation in the face of establishing a unit that would allow recovery of substantial additional production, prevent unnecessary waste, and protect correlative rights of the parties. We have previously set forth the findings of the Commission and district court which in effect hold that the "pool" definition more properly encompasses a single pressure system where production from one part of the pool affects the reservoir pressure throughout the pool.

This issue brings into focus numerous rules of statutory construction whose applications could give rise to different results. The Commission most strongly relies on the statement from *Todd v. Kelly,* 251 Kan. 512, 516, 837 P.2d 381 (1992):

In order to ascertain the legislative intent, courts are not permitted to consider only a certain isolated part or parts of the act, but are required to consider and construe together all parts *in pari materia. When the interpretation of some one section of an act according to the exact and literal import of its words would contravene the manifest purpose of the legislature, the entire act should be construed according to its spirit and reason, disregarding so far as may be necessary the strict letter of the law.* * * *

Trees argues that "natural" has a limited meaning that does not justify the expanded definition as found by the Commission because "ordinary words are to be given their ordinary meaning and a statute should not be so read to add that which is not readily found therein as to read out what as a matter of ordinary English is in it. * * * " *GT, Kansas, L.L.C.,* 271 Kan. at 316, 22 P.3d 600.

As was said in *Williamson v. City of Hays,* 275 Kan. 300, 305, 64 P.3d 364 (2003): "The fundamental rule of statutory construction to which all other rules are subordinate is that the intent of the legislature governs if that intent can be ascertained. The legislature is presumed to have expressed its intent through the language of the statutory scheme it enacted." In *State ex rel. Morrison v. Oshman Sporting Goods Co. Kansas,* 275 Kan. 763, Syl. ¶ 2, 69 P.3d 1087 (2003), after stating that statutes must be construed to give effect, if possible, to the entire act, it was said:

> To this end it is the duty of the court, as far as practicable, to reconcile the different provisions so as to make them consistent, harmonious, and sensible. The court must give effect to the legislature's intent even though words, phrases, or clauses at some place in the statute must be omitted or inserted.

Because there has been an amendment by the 2004 Kansas Legislature to K.S.A 55–1302, specifically to the "pool" definition, see L.2004, ch. 115, sec. 1, we must also look to and consider conflicting maxims which state:

> When the legislature revises an existing law, it is generally presumed that the legislature intended to change the law. * * * This presumption, however, may be weak according to the circumstances and may be wanting altogether. * * * When a statute is ambiguous, an amendment may indicate a legislative purpose to clarify the ambiguities in the statute rather than to change the law. * * *

It is clear that the Kansas Legislature has intended for the Unitization Act to be construed so that unit operations can be fostered and enhanced. This is shown by the 2000 amendment to reduce the approval requirement from 75 percent to 63 percent (L.2000, ch. 15, sec.2), and the 2004 amendment clarifying the pool definition and not requiring Commission approval if all mineral and royalty owners and not less than 90 percent of working interest owners approve in writing the contract for unit operation. (L.2004, ch. 115, secs. 1 and 3.)

Trees places an unrealistic emphasis on the single word "natural" in the pool definition as defining "reservoir," when consideration of all of the wording of K.S.A. 55–1302 much more logically shows that a pool is to be "characterized by a single pressure system so that production from one part of the pool affects the *reservoir pressure* throughout its extent." [Emphasis added.]

"Natural" is defined in Black's Law Dictionary 1054 (8th ed.2004) as being "[i]n accord with the regular course of things in the universe and without accidental or purposeful interference." There can be no question but that oil and gas drilling and producing operations have the effect of changing producing formations from their natural state. This, along with our obligation to look to the legislative intent of the Unitization Act and the legislative intent, requires us to look beyond the restrictive interpretation Trees requests.

With the absence of prior Kansas cases on this issue, the most on-point discussion does come from Professor Smith's Kansas Law Review article previously set forth in our summary of both the Commission's order and the district court's decision. A reading of the entire pool definition as well as the adjoining sections of the Kansas Unitization Act clearly support Professor Smith's statement that a "series of vertically separated reservoirs which have been brought into pressure communication through multiple-completion drilling and production techniques would qualify as a 'pool' under the statute and could be developed as a single unit under the Act." 17 Kan. L.Rev. at 137. Smith also correctly notes that such a construction is consistent with the purposes of the Act, which are to avoid economic waste and uneconomical methods of production. 17 Kan. L.Rev. at 137. We, like the Commission and the district court, agree with and adopt this construction of the "pool" definition.

Trees correctly argues that the Oklahoma cases cited in the Smith article and district court ruling relate to an Oklahoma statute which defines an area to be unitized as covering a "common source of supply." Okla. Stat. Annot. 52 Oil and Gas § 287.4 (2004) and as defined by Okla. Stat. Annot. 52 Oil and Gas § 86.1(c) (2000). Because of this difference in language, we must discount the precedential value of the two Oklahoma *Jones* cases. However, in doing so, we do point out that K.S.A. 55–1307, which relates to enlargement of unit areas and creation of new units, does state that unit areas may be enlarged to "include adjoining portions of the *same common source of supply*." [Emphasis added.]

* * *

We do agree with all of the observations of both the Commission's order and the district court decision as to the purpose of the Unitization Act, the necessity of reading the entire Act together and not one phrase in isolation, the legislative intent, and the overriding obligation of the Commission to prevent waste, foster economic development, and protect correlative rights. * * *

This then leads us to the final factor that we must consider. After the district court decision in late 2003 was pending on appeal, the 2004 Kansas Legislature enacted House Bill 2652, which amended K.S.A. 55–1302 in the following manner applicable to our case:

"Section 1. K.S.A. 55–1302 is hereby amended to read as follows: 55–1302. *As used in this act:*

. . . .

(b) 'Pool' means *an underground accumulation of oil and gas in one or more natural reservoirs in communication so as to constitute* a single pressure system so that production from one part of the pool affects the pressure throughout its extent. . . .

. . . .

(d) 'Waste,' in addition to its meaning as used in articles 6 and 7 of chapter 55 of the Kansas Statutes Annotated *and amendments there-*

to, includes both economic and physical waste resulting from the development and operation separately of tracts that can best be operated as a unit. . . .

. . . .

New Sec. 2. The amendment by this act of the definition of 'pool' shall not be considered a statement of legislative intent for the purpose of interpretation of the definition of 'pool' prior to its amendments by this act." L.2004, ch. 115, secs. 1 and 2.

* * * Trees contends the 2004 Legislature intended to change the meaning and intent of the definition of "pool" and points to the testimony of Dr. M. Lee Allison, state geologist, who stated, "The existing law allows only single and separate reservoirs to be unitized." See Minutes, Sen. Comm. on Utilities, March 10, 2004. Trees argues [that,] because of the language of new Section 2, a legislative change was prospectively effected.

The Commission, Chesapeake, and OXY equally persuasively point to the testimony of Edward Cross, executive vice president of Kansas Independent Oil & Gas Association, and E.R. Brewster for BP America, which show the amendment was simply a clarification of legislative intent so there would be no doubt in the future. See Minutes, Sen. Comm. on Utilities, March 10, 2004. They further argue Section 2 was added because the legislature was aware of this case and did not want to adjudicate its outcome.

Anadarko's argument differs and suggests any reference in this case to H.B. 2652 and the amendment to the pool definition "is inappropriate and that such reference, as well as the statute and testimony of conferees . . . should be totally disregarded . . ." There is considerable logic in this argument as new Section 2 states the amendment "shall not be considered a statement of legislative intent."

The sharp conflict this case presents leads to the clear conclusion that we are being asked to resolve language [that] * * * is clearly ambiguous, at least in the minds of the appellees herein. Trees argues against this conclusion. But, different interpretations of the pool definition lead to different results. This is "an uncertainty of meaning or intention, as in a contractual term or statutory provision," which is how Black's Law Dictionary, 88 (8th ed.2004) defines ambiguity.

It is more logical to hold that the amendment does nothing more than "clarify the ambiguities in the statute rather than to change the law." * * *

We are also taught that statutes are to be construed to avoid unreasonable results. * * * If we follow Trees' arguments and deny unitization here because of the "pool" definition, the legal effect of our decision is immediately ineffective. Chesapeake has only to file a new application with the Commission and, assuming the facts remain as previously presented, a unitization order would be expected.

We hold that the 2004 amendment to the "pool" definition contained in H.B. 2652 should either not be considered or, if it is considered, should represent nothing more than a clarification. In either event, it does not change this court's affirmance of the decisions of the Commission and district court insofar as they relate to allowing unit operation of the commingled Chester and Morrow formations as a single pressure system falling within the K.S.A. 55–1302 definition of a "pool."

* * *

II. The Commission followed all requirements of the Kansas Unitization Act in including the Trees' acreage in the Unit for which it will be fairly compensated.

Trees argues that the unit participation factors or percentages assigned to it do not fairly and equitably value Trees' acreage. It further contends its minority interests were not adequately protected. As the result of these alleged injustices, the KCC unitization order amounts to an unconstitutional taking of Trees' property. It further contends it is being compelled to take business risks it cannot control and does not want to take.

What this actually boils down to is whether the KCC's finding that the Unit Operating Agreement was fair and equitable was supported by substantial competent evidence. * * *

The Commission's orders are not in any way a "taking" as Trees argues. K.S.A.2003 Supp. 55–1304 and K.S.A.2003 Supp. 55–1305 set out in detail the findings that must be made and the provisions required in the unitization and unit operation order. There is clearly legislative authority for the Commission's actions, and all of the statutory requirements were followed.

Trees' argument that the technical committee used outdated production data is based on its late April 2001 fracture treatment of the Josephine well which resulted in higher recent production. The Unit Operating Agreement divides participation into two phases. Phase I weighs current production during December 1999 through May 2000, along with remaining recoverable primary reserves. Trees argues that had late term production been used, it would have received a higher level of unit production.

The KCC order found that the data had to be cut off at some point and computations could not deal with a "constantly moving target." The order pointed out the fracture treatment did not take place until after notice of the intended unit was known and the formulas for the proposed unit had been discussed. The Commission recognized that fracture treatment resulted in a temporary increase in production but noted that a well then returns to its original decline. It was held to have been extremely difficult and possibly improper to use the enhanced production in the computations.

There was substantial competent evidence to support the Commission's order approving the use of the prior data. The formula was fair and equitable, and the Commission's order in approving it was not arbitrary or capricious.

There was clearly sufficient evidence to sustain the use of Morrow formation production in the Unit even though Trees' acreage was currently unproductive in the Morrow. There was expert testimony of the commingling of the Morrow and Chester formations and that additional Morrow production could be anticipated in which Trees would share. While significant amounts of Morrow production would not be expected from the waterflood, it was prudent to leave the formations open and unnecessary cost and waste would result from closing the Morrow. A review of the record shows substantial competent evidence supports the KCC's findings relating to the Morrow formation.

Trees' arguments concerning the usage of the estimated Chester hydrocarbon pore volume (HPV) factor are not persuasive. Gowens' testimony explained this usage, and it was not refuted. Even Hupp acknowledged he had previously advocated the use of HPV before the Commission. The geology may not be constant and the formula may not be perfect, but it was fairly and logically developed, supported by substantial competent evidence, and its adoption by the KCC was clearly justified.

Trees' argument that its minority interest was not adequately protected is without merit. The Commission ordered a second hearing to satisfy itself precisely on this point. The testimony of Professor Pierce of the Washburn Law School was unchallenged. He said the agreements satisfied all statutory requirements, were fair and equitable in following industry standards, and adequately protected interests of unwilling minority participants. Trees offered no changes or improvement. The small issue of property valuation became a nonissue with control remaining in Trees, and the tank battery usage it questioned remained under its control and usage. There was clearly substantial competent evidence that the Unit Operating Agreement was fair and equitable.

Testimony showed that including Trees' acreage in the Unit increases its value from approximately $130,000 to $390,000 based on testimony before the KCC. The present net worth of the acreage increases approximately $250,000. Trees will share in the expected $6.2 million profit from the Unit. Trees might lose absolute control of its property, which is statutorily allowed, but it will benefit economically from being in the Unit.

We have examined all of Trees' arguments, whether responded to in detail or not, and none satisfy its burden of showing improper or unlawful agency action. There was substantial competent evidence for all of the Commission's findings and orders, and none were arbitrarily or capriciously made.

III. Inclusion of the Trees' tracts in the South Eubank Unit was clearly supported by substantial competent evidence.

* * *

Trees' main contention is that Chesapeake failed to provide "tangible evidence" of pressure communication between Trees' acreage and the other portions of the proposed unit. Trees claims drill stem tests should have been submitted to support Chesapeake's contention of pressure communication of the Chester sand throughout the Unit. This contention is not persuasive based on the evidence submitted to the KCC through various studies and expert testimony.

Gowens and Scott both opined that the whole Unit, including the Trees' tracts, were in the same reservoir and were pressure connected. Gowens testified as to how the Unit boundaries were established by the technical committee. Gowens specifically stated the southern boundary of the reservoir was an oil-water contact at the subsea datum of 2515 identified at the Trees' Josephine well.

Scott testified the unit area including the Trees' acreage was an excellent waterflood candidate because it is in good pressure communication. Even Trees' witness Hupp conceded there was pressure communication between the Trees' Josephine 1–15 well and the balance of the Unit.

Scott further testified that exclusion of the Trees' tracts and Josephine well from the Unit would violate correlative rights. Correlative rights, as defined in K.A.R. 82–3–101(a)(21) means

"the privilege of each owner or producer in a common source of supply to produce from that supply only in a manner or amount that will not have any of the following effects:

(A) Injure the reservoir to the detriment of others; or

(B) take an undue proportion of the obtainable oil and gas; or

(C) cause undue drainage between developed leases."

* * * Scott opined that if the Josephine well were allowed to remain a producer outside the Unit, there would be a migration of oil from the Unit of as much as 18,000 barrels which would violate the correlative rights of the other owners within the Unit. Scott described this increase in Josephine production as a "certainty."

Trees' expert Pronold testified there was a significant degree of lateral compartmentalization within the Eubank Unit which resulted in pressure communication making a flood risky. Gowen testified the article Pronold relied on described only sections at the north boundaries of the Unit and that no such compartmentalization existed in the rest of the Unit.

Trees' disagreement with Gowens' and Scott's testimony is not sufficient to establish substantial competent evidence does not exist. This is in fact the very evidence the Commission relied on as is previously stated herein in summarizing its order.

There was substantial competent evidence to support the Commission's findings that the Eubank Unit should include the Trees' tracts because there was pressure communication with the rest of the Unit.

There was further evidence that the Commission properly protected correlative rights by requiring the Trees' tracts to be included in the Unit. The Commission is obligated to resolve conflicts of the experts' opinions. * * *

* * *

> *IV.   The KCC did not err in denying Trees' motion*
> *to present supplemental technical testimony at*
> *the April 2, 2002, hearing.*

* * *

The Commission, in an abundance of caution, was concerned about the fairness to Trees of the Unit Operating Agreement. The Interim Order, which was issued on March 12, 2002, specifically stated: "The Commission has before it ample record and is ready to rule on the conditions in K.S.A. 55–1304(a) and (b)."

The Commission's order specifically stated: "[T]he record should be reopened for the specific purpose of receiving explanation or argument as to whether the specific terms of the Unit Operating Agreement are fair and equitable to all parties and to take additional evidence on that issue."

Despite this clear statement, Trees, on March 25, 20032, filed a motion seeking to introduce supplemental geological and engineering evidence at the April 2, 2002, hearing. The Commission correctly refused to allow this additional technical evidence.

Trees' argument that it was somehow denied due process by the Commission's Interim Order is not persuasive. Trees points to the limited time to prepare for the September 2001 hearing. However, it had early knowledge of the studies of the proposed unit through its representatives' attendance of early technical meetings. It had knowledge of the proposed unit with its inclusion by May 16, 2001.

The initial filing before the Commission on June 27, 2001, was 85 days before the hearing was held.

Virtually, all the data relied on in the supplemental testimony was available before the September 20, 2001, hearing. The data to prepare the 2–D seismic study was done in July 1997 and was available long before Trees finally studied it in March 2002. The Trees' experts, Hupp and Pronold, were hired 6 weeks before the initial hearing.

Allowance of supplemental technical evidence would in effect allow Trees a second chance to retry the case. It would have forced the applicants to prepare rebuttal testimony. The Commission found that Trees' belief that it could not be included in the Unit was an erroneous conclusion of Trees' own making.

The Commission, as the trier of fact, must be given wide latitude and discretion in establishing time limits and admitting evidence. Trees was given several extensions of the initial hearing date, and the denial of Trees' request is not unreasonable, arbitrary, or capricious.

Affirmed.

LUCKERT, J., dissenting:

I dissent from the majority's interpretation of K.S.A. 55–1302 which, in effect, deletes the word "natural" from the definition as written by the legislature. The legislature clearly and unambiguously restricted the definition to single and separate natural reservoirs stating: "The term 'pool' as herein used shall mean an underground accumulation of oil and gas in a single and separate *natural* reservoir characterized by a single pressure system so that production from one part of the pool affects the reservoir pressure throughout its extent." (Emphasis added.) K.S.A. 55–1302.

In essence, the majority concludes that the legislature did not mean to use the phrase "single and separate *natural* reservoir," at least as the phrase would ordinarily be understood, because restricting application of the unitization statutes to only single and separate natural reservoirs eliminates coverage from the unitization statutes for those reservoirs, such as the ones at issue, where pressure communication resulted from multiple drilling and production operations. Therefore, the majority concludes that what the legislature meant to say is that a pool is to be characterized by a single pressure system and it does not matter whether this single pressure system is a naturally occurring single and separate reservoir or is the result of multiple-completion drilling and production techniques. The majority rationalizes that its reading is consistent with legislative intent and the Kansas Corporation Commission's (KCC) obligation to prevent waste, foster economic development, and protect correlative rights.

However, the majority's interpretation ignores one of the most basic rules of statutory construction:

The legislature is presumed to have expressed its intent through the language of the statutory scheme it enacted. When a statute is plain and unambiguous, the court must give effect to the intention of the legislature *as expressed* rather than determine what the law should or should not be. * * *(Emphasis added.) * * *

* * * As written, K.S.A. 55–1302 need not be reconciled with other statutory provisions; it simply gives other provisions a narrower application. Furthermore, as written, K.S.A. 55–1302 advances the legislative goals, albeit in a manner limited to natural reservoirs. The majority's interpretation gives a wider application and may maximize the opportunities to apply the unitization statutes. However, the court's role is not to rewrite the statute to a version [that] * * * the court perceives as maximizing the legislative goals; the court's role is to apply an unambiguous statute as written. To do otherwise interferes with the policy decision made by the legislature, which in this case was clearly to limit the coverage of unitization provisions to oil and gas accumulations in a single and separate natural reservoir.

In essence, the majority's holding reaches the same result as the 2004 amendments which, as stated in the Supplemental Note on H.B. 2652 (2004), "change" and "expand the definition" of the term "pool." Similarly, the majority's interpretation of K.S.A. 55–1302 is a change and expansion of the unambiguous definition provided by the legislature. As such it is inaccurate to cast the majority's interpretation as a clarification or reconciliation, terms which the majority uses to justify its position.

As further justification for its analysis, the majority cites Professor Ernest E. Smith's article, Smith, *The Kansas Unitization Statute: Part II*, 17 Kan. L.Rev. 133 (1968). Professor Smith reaches his conclusion based upon case law which interprets the Oklahoma statute to apply to any accumulations of oil and gas separated by a strata of earth but connected by common well bores * * * 17 Kan. L.Rev. at 137. The majority recognizes that because of the differences in the Oklahoma and Kansas statutes, the Oklahoma authorities have little precedential value. However, the majority seemingly accepts Professor Smith's argument that a *natural* result of drilling may be to place two separate formations in pressure communication and such a result must have been what the legislature meant to address.

While this may be what Professor Smith, the appellees, the KCC, and the majority wish the statute said, it is clearly not what the statute provides. "Ordinary words are to be given their ordinary meaning, and a statute should not be so read as to add that which is not readily found therein or to read out what as a matter of ordinary English language is in it." * * * The majority, citing Black's Law Dictionary 1054 (8th ed.2004) recognizes the ordinary definition of "natural": "In accord with the regular course of things in the universe and without accidental or purposeful interference." However, the majority does not apply this ordinary meaning to the facts of this case. Well-bore drilling is an act of purposeful interference. The unitization provisions do not apply to separate reservoirs commingled by purposeful interference. K.S.A. 55–1302 limits the definition of "pool" to natural reservoirs.

K.S.A. 55–1302 is plain and unambiguous; therefore, this court should give effect to the intention of the legislature as expressed rather than determine what the law should or should not be. Under the clear and unambiguous language of the statute, Trees' property should not be included in the unit and the remaining issues should be treated as moot.

ALLEGRUCCI and BEIER, JJ., join the foregoing dissenting opinion.

NOTES

1. Compulsory unitization can be difficult to achieve. Other than in Alaska, where the federal government, state government, and native corporations hold most mineral rights, the voluntary agreement of a high percentage of both working-interest and royalty interest owners is necessary before a conservation agency may force unitization. Among major producing states, the

required percentage ranges from 63 to 80 percent. Voting self-interest and variances in the parties' respective ownership shares influence unitization plans. Thus, owners opposed to a particular unitization plan may view the participation formula as being unfair—even confiscatory.

In Gilmore v. Oil & Gas Conservation Comm'n, 642 P.2d 773 (Wyo.1982), the working-interest owners held several meetings following the issuance of a conservation order curtailing production pending unitization. In an attempt to agree on a formula for allocating production, the 81 working-interest owners considered 71 formulas and voted on about 60 formulas. None of the formulas received sufficient votes to seek compulsory unitization. The owners then used computers to analyze the voting records and developed a compromise formula that divided production based upon eleven factors. This formula received 75.89 percent approval. The conservation agency then exercised its statutory authority to reduce, in certain circumstances, the required ratification from 80 percent to 75 percent, and the commission authorized compulsory unit operations. On appeal, the Wyoming Supreme Court upheld the commission.

> We * * * hold that substantial waste cannot be countenanced by a slavish devotion to correlative rights. We are faced with a delicate balancing problem between prevention of waste and correlative rights, but prevention of waste is of primary importance. * * *

> > Here the Commission strived mightily to strike an equitable balance between correlative rights and prevention of waste. We agree with the Commission's acting Chairman, "And when that public interest conflicts with the private interest, the public interest has to come first." * * *

> There is no indication that a more equitable formula could be devised. * * * Appellant did not suggest a better formula to the Commission, the district court, or to us. It would appear, therefore, that there is little chance that anyone involved could devise a better formula, nor is it likely that a different formula could receive the necessary approval. * * *

> > The owners and technical committees worked for three years, trying to develop a formula that would get the necessary approval. As appellant says, 'All operators worked long and hard, in good faith, to attempt to get a satisfactory unit agreement.' * * * The group effort at compromise should not be discarded because of appellant's general disagreement with the plan. Appellant seems to expect perfection. Justice was accomplished here, as much as could be under the circumstances. This litigation should end.

642 P.2d at 779–81. As illustrated in *Gilmore,* obtaining the requisite voluntary agreement to a unitization participation formula can be extremely difficult and time consuming. Given a court's reluctance to second-guess the conservation agency and given the agency's primary concern for preventing waste, could a large majority of interest owners engage in strategic voting to secure a participation formula that is especially favorable to them? Cf. Williams v. Arkansas Oil & Gas Comm'n, 817 S.W.2d 863 (Ark.1991) (holding that working-interest owners could not be forced to pay a greater percentage share of expenses than their percentage share of production).

What factors should the parties use to arrive at an allocation formula? Possibilities include the type of natural reservoir energy, the prior operations of each working-interest owner, prior tract production, existing well productivity, well density, production allowables, and recoverable reserves under each tract. Often a split formula is used. Initially, the formula allocates production to each tract based on the hydrocarbons that existing wells would have produced under continued primary-recovery operations. After reaching that level of production, remaining production is then attributable to enhanced recovery and allocated among all tracts in the unit—including tracts within the reservoir that may not have been in production when the unit became effective.

2. To "encourage" unitization, a conservation agency may issue an order curtailing production on waste-prevention grounds, pending unitization. For example, an order might curtail production from wells having high gas-oil ratios, limit or prohibit the flaring of gas where gas injection is desirable, or lower production allowables for nonunitized wells. These efforts to encourage unitization ordinarily meet with court approval. See e.g. Santa Fe Exploration Co. v. Oil Conservation Commission, 835 P.2d 819 (N.M.1992); Mobil Oil Corp. v. State Corp. Comm'n, 608 P.2d 1325 (Kan.1980); California Co. v. Britt, 154 So.2d 144 (Miss.1963); Corley v. Mississippi State Oil & Gas Board, 105 So.2d 633 (Miss.1958); Railroad Comm'n v. Sterling Oil & Refining Co., 218 S.W.2d 415 (Tex.1949); and Big Piney Oil & Gas Co. v. Wyoming Oil & Gas Conservation Comm'n, 715 P.2d 557 (Wyo.1986). But see Union Pac. R. Co. v. Oil & Gas Conservation Comm'n, 284 P.2d 242 (Colo.1955).

In Majority of working-interest Owners in Buck Draw Field Area v. Wyoming Oil and Gas Conservation Comm'n, 721 P.2d 1070 (Wyo.1986), the Conservation Commission ordered an entire field shut in until the operators in the field could agree on an enhanced-recovery program. Expert witnesses who testified on behalf of the minority of working-interest owners convinced the commission that either gas miscible flooding or water flooding was economically feasible and that either method would recover substantial quantities of oil and gas that would otherwise be lost. The witnesses further testified that these methods would succeed only if flooding commenced before the field pressure fell below the bubble point—the point at which gas comes out of solution in a reservoir, which can reduce ultimate recovery. Although expert witnesses who testified on behalf of the majority of working-interest owners disputed this testimony, the commission, finding that field pressure would soon fall below the bubble point, ordered the entire field shut in, pending unitization for enhanced recovery. On appeal, the Wyoming Supreme Court upheld the commission's order. In response to the argument that the commission was forcing the majority of owners to unitize against their will,[113] the Court stated:

> In reality, none of the interest owners have been forced into a unit. The commission's order gives the owners a choice of voluntarily forming a unit or ceasing their wasteful production. If the commission could not

---

113. Under the Wyoming Compulsory Unitization Act, the conservation commission may not issue a compulsory unitization order until, *inter alia*, the working-interest owners who are responsible for at least 80 percent of the unitization costs voluntarily agree to unit operations.

force this choice on the appellants, then it would be prevented from exercising its primary function, the prevention of waste. * * *

When the legislature passed the waste prevention statutes, it apparently understood that producers would sometimes use wasteful methods out of ignorance or self-interest. That is why the commission was given the power to order a halt to such practices. If, under the facts of a given case, the commission must choose between a producer's economic well-being and the prevention of waste, it must choose the latter. * * * Under extreme circumstances, the commission's decision might drive a producer out of business.

In the case at bar, the commission's duty to prevent waste has forced it to issue an order that is unpalatable to the majority of the interest owners. They must either shut-in their wells, which might drive some of them out of business, or they can unitize for secondary operations. It may be unpalatable, but it is a legitimate choice. If, as a practical matter, the commission's order causes the parties to unitize, then that result can be attributed to the commission's overriding duty to prevent waste rather than an improper decision to force these parties to unitize.

721 P.2d at 1080. Could this order cause some producers, especially those in need of revenues, to agree to an unfair allocation formula for the sharing of unit production and unit costs?

3. The State of Texas does not have a compulsory unitization act. Nevertheless, owing to Railroad Commission orders designed to "encourage" unitization, a substantial number of "voluntarily" unitized fields exist in Texas. For a detailed history and analysis, see J. Weaver, Unitization of Oil and Gas Fields in Texas: A Study of Legislative, Administrative and Judicial Policies (1986).

4. As was discussed in Chapter 2, Section D.2., oil and gas leases may contain a pooling clause authorizing the lessee to pool the lease on the lessor's behalf. Some leases also authorize the lessee to unitize a lease on the lessor's behalf. See, e.g., Amoco Prod. Co. v. Jacobs, 746 F.2d 1394 (10th Cir.N.M. 1984), overruled in part, Amoco Prod. Co. v. Heimann, 904 F.2d 1405 (10th Cir.N.M.1990) (confirming the power of the lessee to unitize, on behalf of the lessor, a voluntary carbon-dioxide unit encompassing over 1,000,000 acres). Does the lessee's ratification of a plan on behalf of the lessor, pursuant to a lease unitization clause, count toward the necessary percentage needed for a conservation agency to exercise its compulsory unitization authority?

5. Professor Pierce comments on *Trees*:

> Although not addressed in the justices' opinions, one of the more interesting discussions during the hearing before the Commission was the essence of Trees' working-interest "ownership" in a pressure-connected reservoir. During the hearing I noted that the concept of "correlative rights" consists of two elements: "rights" that are "correlative." This is best demonstrated by Trees' major objection: they have a well producing on their leased land that is generating a positive cash flow for the company. How can they be forced to give up this cash flow for potential income in the future? The answer

concerns the "connected" nature of their lease. Because they are part of a reservoir, and actions on their land can impact the rights of the owners of 16 other wells in the proposed unit (and those well owners can, in turn, impact the Trees well), the correlative nature of their interest is a *limitation* on their rights. The correlative nature of their interest also gives them rights in the reservoir as a whole—these are the reciprocal rights being exercised by the other owners to make Trees go along with decisions that have been reviewed and approved by the Commission. The Commission is concerned with protecting the correlative rights of *all owners in the reservoir* while also seeking to conserve the oil and gas resource through the prevention of "waste."

The major focus of the justices' opinions concerned the definition of a "pool." This decision reveals the result-oriented nature of statutory interpretation. As the majority notes: "This issue brings into focus numerous rules of statutory construction *whose applications could give rise to different results.*"

Discussion Notes, Oil and Gas Reporter, 162 OGR 498, 499–500:

6. In addition to the correlative-rights and statutory-construction issues, *Trees* provides a short course in administrative law. First, the case illustrates one reason why legislative bodies establish administrative agencies: to resolve factually complex technical disputes—in this case, reservoir engineering—beyond the expertise of most trial judges. Such disputes often play out as a battle of expert witnesses. The party that loses at the agency level faces an up-hill battle on appeal because courts are unlikely to reject the conservation agency's findings of fact.

Note the different standards of review employed by the court, depending upon the issue. But note also that the court is very deferential to the views of the agency, including the agency's construction of the statute. The court also defers to the agency's view of the evidence and to the agency's timetable for the consideration of evidence. When working-interest owners discuss the need for unitization and negotiate allocation formulas, they customarily agree to deadlines for the submission of data to avoid what might otherwise become a never-ending study.

(d) Unitization Liabilities & Obligations

Although conservation agencies prefer to unitize an entire field, as in *Trees*, above, an agency may approve voluntary or compulsory unitization of a portion of a field. For example, partial unitization may result when some interest owners refuse to participate in the formation of a field-wide unit.[114] In such a circumstance, the owners of nonunitized interests may claim to suffer injury from the unit operations. For example, in the case of water flooding, some of the injected water may enter nonunitized property, displacing hydrocarbons.

---

114. For example, in compulsory unitization, if the unit proponents cannot secure the necessary threshold of ratifications to unitize the entire field, they may settle for a partial unitization by securing the required ratifications for a particular portion of the field.

PROBLEM

Assume that three tracts—Blackacre, Whiteacre, and Redacre—are of equal size and overlie a common reservoir of oil. Chance owns Blackacre, Tinker owns Whiteacre, which lies west and adjacent to Blackacre, and Evers owns Redacre, which lies east and adjacent to Blackacre. All three are producing oil from their respective tracts, but production has started to decline. Because they are producing from a water drive reservoir, Tinker and Evers would like to conduct water flooding, but they have been unable to induce Chance to participate. What potential exposure to liability do Tinker and Evers face if they conduct the water flooding operation without Chance's participation?

BAUMGARTNER v. GULF OIL CORP.

168 N.W.2d 510 (Neb.1969).

SPENCER, JUSTICE.

This is an action at law for willful trespass and conversion. Plaintiff sued for the value of oil claimed to have been displaced and swept from land under lease to him by defendant into its waterflood unit recovery wells.

Plaintiff was the holder of an oil and gas lease granted by the State of Nebraska, the owner of the minerals underlying Section 16, Township 18 North, Range 53 West of the 6th P.M., Banner County, Nebraska. Plaintiff acquired the lease June 13, 1960, and allowed it to lapse June 13, 1965.

Defendant is the owner of the Kenmac "J" Sand Unit, Banner County, Nebraska, hereinafter referred to as Kenmac, which was formed to increase the ultimate recovery of oil and to prevent waste. In consequence of the depletion of the field the lessees thereon had, before plaintiff obtained his lease, commenced studies as to the feasibility of unitizing the field. This involved the merger of all of the interests in the oil pool and the designation of an operator for the unit. Defendant was so designated for Kenmac. Except for Kenmac there would have been no recovery of secondary oil. The Nebraska Oil and Gas Conservation Commission, hereinafter called the commission, entered an order April 24, 1961, approving the unit agreement, which provided for the secondary recovery of the oil by water flooding. It was signed by all of the working interest owners in the field except the plaintiff, and by the owners of more than 80 percent of the royalty interests, including the plaintiff's lessor, the Nebraska Board of Educational Lands and Funds. When the plaintiff refused to join the unit, Section 16 was excluded from it and plaintiff's lessor withdrew its consent.

Kenmac offsets plaintiff's lease on the east and the north. Exhibit 2, which is reproduced herewith, shows the boundaries of Kenmac as well as the outline of the oil-bearing stratum involved herein:

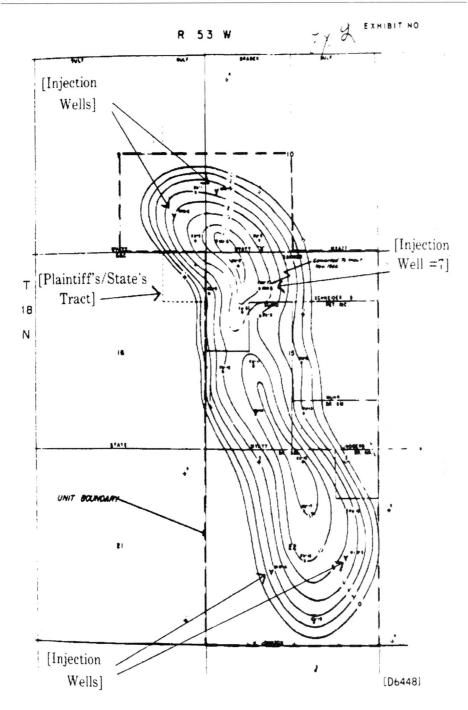

[The editors apologize for the poor quality of the stratigraphic map. You need only focus on the locations of the specially labeled Injection Wells and the Plaintiff's/State's Tract.]

Water flooding is the controlled introduction of water into an oil-producing stratum or oil reservoir for the purpose of recovering oil which cannot be produced by normal primary methods. Water is injected into selected wells to create pressure to force the oil toward producing wells. In this instance water was injected on the north into wells 1 and 2, and on the south into wells 3 and 4. These wells forced the oil toward wells 10, 11, and 12, the final point of recovery. In November 1964, it was necessary to convert well 7 to an injection well. The introduction of water into an oil reservoir causes oil and water to migrate across lease lines and it is impossible to restrict the advance of the water to lease lines. Because of this encroachment it is necessary to unitize a field to protect the correlative rights of all those holding interests in the field.

A prior lessee of Section 16 had drilled a dry hole in the northeast quarter of the section. This dry hole and other wells on the adjoining sections had established that the oil-bearing sands under plaintiff's lease were in the northeast quarter of the northeast quarter of the northeast quarter, hereinafter referred to as NENENE, with a thin and narrow strip along the east edge of the section.

Plaintiff's engineer testified that prior to the formation of the unit, oil had been drained from Section 16 by the off-setting wells to the north and the east. The 23 producing wells shown on the plat had so depleted the field that the nearest well off-setting plaintiff's lease had been temporarily abandoned because of insufficient production. The parties stipulated that as of June 6, 1961, there were only 2,254.2 barrels of recoverable primary oil, worth $6,063, under the plaintiff's lease. The amount of oil underlying Section 16 for recovery by secondary methods was stipulated to be 36,624.1 barrels, while the recovery from the entire reservoir was 1,658,-955 barrels. It is undisputed that the cost of drilling a well to recover the primary oil on Section 16 was far in excess of $6,063.

Plaintiff's engineer also testified that in the absence of Kenmac there would not have been any secondary oil recovered on Section 16. Plaintiff refused to join the unit, and after it was approved he applied for a permit to drill a well in the NENENE. This permit was refused by the commission because plaintiff was able to include his section in Kenmac, but its order was subsequently reversed by the district court. No well was drilled because the recoverable oil by this time had been swept from the section. Plaintiff's engineer conceded that if plaintiff had been permitted to drill a well on the NENENE it would have resulted in the drainage of oil from Kenmac. The testimony clearly would indicate that plaintiff could not have profitably developed his lease. In the absence of Kenmac no secondary oil could have been recovered from Section 16 so the independent development of Section 16 would have resulted in an economic loss except for the water flooding by Kenmac.

Plaintiff's manager of operations, who was his principal witness, actually had been instrumental in setting up the unit agreement and the operator's agreement for Kenmac. This was before he entered plaintiff's employment in June 1962. He admitted that Kenmac was properly formed; that a common assessment formula was used for all undeveloped acreages; and that the assessment formula and the amount allocated to plaintiff's tract were fair and equitable. Plaintiff refused to join the unit unless this assessment was waived as to his section. This the other parties to the agreement would not do, and plaintiff's section was excluded from the unit.

If the plaintiff had joined Kenmac and borne his share of the development and operating costs, his profit would have been $27,455, and the State of Nebraska would have received $7,377 for royalties. The evidence would indicate that if plaintiff had drilled his own well, the highest estimate of his profit would be $12,224.

The trial court applied the common law doctrine of willful trespass, and entered judgment against the defendant in the amount of $89,933 for the value of the oil drained from Section 16, without the deduction of any development or operating costs necessary to produce that oil. Defendant perfected an appeal to this court.

This is a case of first impression in this state. However, in view of the objectives of the Nebraska Oil and Gas Conservation Act, hereinafter referred to as act, and the apparent public policy inherent therein, as well as the nature of oil and gas, we cannot accept the premise on which judgment was rendered by the trial court.

Section 57–901, R.R.S.1943, provides as follows: "It is hereby declared to be in the public interest to foster, to encourage and to promote the development, production and utilization of natural resources of oil and gas in the state in such a manner as will prevent waste; to authorize and to provide for the operation and development of oil and gas properties in such a manner that the greatest ultimate recovery of oil and gas be had; and that the correlative rights of all owners be fully protected; and to encourage and to authorize cycling, recycling, pressure maintenance and secondary recovery operations in order that the greatest possible economic recovery of oil and gas be obtained within the state to the end that the landowners, the royalty owners, the producers and the general public realize and enjoy the greatest possible good from these vital irreplaceable natural resources."

* * *

To appreciate the importance of the legislative policy, one needs only to understand the importance of secondary oil recovery in Nebraska. We quote herewith from reports made by the director of the commission to the Interstate Oil Compact Commission: "As in previous years, the recovery of secondary oil formed a prominent part of Nebraska's producing picture. To January 1, 1966, Nebraska reservoirs had contributed over 36 million barrels of secondary oil. This volume was recovered as a direct result of the application of secondary energy for production. The quantity represents 15 percent of all oil produced in the state since the original oil

discovery in 1939." (The Interstate Oil Compact Bulletin, June 1966)
* * *

" 'At this time, 76 secondary-recovery or pressure-maintenance projects are underway in Nebraska—72 involve water injection, two involve miscible slugs while one project consists of gas recycling and one involves both gas recycling and water injection. Approximately 40 percent of Nebraska's current oil production comes as a direct result of the introduction of extraneous fluids into the State's reservoirs.' (The Interstate Oil Compact Bulletin, December, 1966)"

* * *

There is no claim for the oil which naturally migrated from Section 16 by reason of the offsetting wells to the north and east, because this is governed by the law of capture. Under the law of capture, an owner of land acquires title to oil or gas which he produces from wells on his land although part of the oil or gas may have migrated from adjoining wells. He may thus appropriate the oil and gas that have flowed from adjacent lands without the consent of the owner of those lands and without incurring liability to him for drainage.

The rule of capture is applied to oil which migrates without the introduction of extraneous substances into the oil-producing stratum to induce migration. Here an extraneous substance, water, was injected into wells on adjoining sections which induced migration. It is this inducement which plaintiff alleges constitutes a willful trespass as to his property.

We cannot ignore the fact that the operation of Kenmac was specifically authorized and approved by commission, effective April 18, 1961, and that the project was at all times conducted in conformity with the order of the commission. Plaintiff concedes this fact, but maintains that the order of commission was applicable to only the lands in the unit, and that Section 16 was not a part of it. Although Section 16 was excluded from the project, everyone involved, including the plaintiff, would understand that there was no way to seal off the oil under Section 16 from the pool, and that from its very nature water injected into wells 1 and 2 would eventually reach the narrow portion of the reservoir in Section 16 and sweep oil from it. It is this very fact which required that plaintiff be afforded an opportunity to join the project. Plaintiff was offered this opportunity on a fair and equitable basis. As an oil operator, he was fully cognizant of the fact that unless the other operators in the field were willing to abandon the project and thus waste more than a million and a half barrels of recoverable oil, they would either be forced to meet his demand for an unreasonable return at their expense, or go ahead with the project without him and incur possible liability for sweeping oil from under his leased land in the process. They did the latter. Did they incur liability for willful trespass? We hold they did not. Plaintiff contends no issue of waste is presented in this case. We do not agree. Defendant's every action was premised on the prevention of waste.

We have reached the conclusion that where the primary recoverable oil has been exhausted, all interested parties in the field must be offered an opportunity to join in any unitization project to recover secondary oil on a fair and equitable basis, and if any interested party refuses to join he should not be permitted to capitalize on that refusal. To hold otherwise would discourage unitization and encourage rather than avoid waste. Consequently, we hold where a secondary-recovery project has been authorized by the commission the operator is not liable for willful trespass to owners who refused to join the project when the injected recovery substance moves across lease lines.

While the fact situation is not analogous, some of the language in Railroad Commission of Texas v. Manziel, Tex., 361 S.W.2d 560, 93 A.L.R.2d 432, is pertinent herein. That case was a water-flooding operation on a lease rather than a unit basis. The regular location for a lease input well was 660 feet from the property line, but the commission authorized the appellant to place an input well 206 feet from the Manziels' property line. The evidence indicated Manziels were producing far in excess of the original oil in place on their land and, without the specific limitations of the water input well, would continue to obtain more than their fair share. The following language is of interest herein: "To constitute trespass there must be some physical entry upon the land by some 'thing,' Gregg v. Delhi—Taylor Oil Corp., 162 Tex. 26, 344 S.W.2d 411 (1961); but is injected water that crosses lease lines from an authorized secondary project the type of 'thing' that may be said to render the adjoining operator guilty of trespass? * * * "

"A problem analogous to the situation that confronts this court is found in instances where gas is produced, the gasoline content removed therefrom, and the dry gas reinjected into the original reservoir from whence it was produced to preserve bottomhole pressure; the process thus displacing the more valuable wet gas under adjoining leases with the dry reinjected gas. * * * "

"In considering the legal consequences of the injection of secondary-recovery forces into the subsurface structures, one authority, Williams and Meyers [§ 204.5] has stated:

" 'What may be called a 'negative rule of capture' appears to be developing. Just as under the rule of capture a land owner may capture such oil or gas as will migrate from adjoining premises to a well bottomed on his own land, so also may he inject into a formation substances which may migrate through the structure to the land of others, even if it thus results in the displacement under such land of more valuable with less valuable substances (e.g., the displacement of wet gas by dry gas).' "

"Secondary-recovery operations are carried on to increase the ultimate recovery of oil and gas, and it is established that pressure maintenance projects will result in more recovery than was obtained by primary methods. It cannot be disputed that such operations should be encouraged, for as the pressure behind the primary production dissipates, the greater is the public necessity for applying secondary-recovery forces. It is obvious that secondary-recovery programs could not and would not be conducted if any adjoining operator could stop the project on the ground of subsurface trespass. * * *

"The orthodox rules and principles applied by the courts as regards surface invasions of land may not be appropriately applied to subsurface invasions as arise out of the secondary recovery of natural resources. If the intrusions of salt water are to be regarded as trespassory in character, then under common notions of surface invasions, the justifying public policy considerations behind secondary-recovery operations could not be reached in considering the validity and reasonableness of such operations. Certainly, it is relevant to consider and weigh the interests of society and the oil and gas industry as a whole against the interests of the individual operator who is damaged; and if the authorized activities in an adjoining secondary-recovery unit are found to be based on some substantial, justifying occasion, then this court should sustain their validity.

"We conclude that if, in the valid exercise of its authority to prevent waste, protect correlative rights, or in the exercise of other powers within its jurisdiction, the Commission authorizes secondary-recovery projects, a trespass does not occur when the injected, secondary-recovery forces move across lease lines, and the operations are not subject to an injunction on that basis. The technical rules of trespass have no place in the consideration of the validity of the orders of the Commission."

* * *

Plaintiff throughout his brief asserts that he was precluded from drilling his unorthodox well by the objections of the defendant, and that this action indicates the willfulness of defendant's trespass. There is no merit to this suggestion. Without passing on plaintiff's right to drill a well, we find the evidence is conclusive that it could not have been profitable except for Kenmac, and even plaintiff's witness admits it would have resulted in plaintiff recovering secondary oil from Kenmac. Suffice it to say that we consider it to be a basic and fundamental principle of all conservation legislation that the correlative and constitutional right of a landowner or leaseholder is not the right to drill but the right to recover his just and equitable share of the oil and gas underlying his property. * * *

Plaintiff was given every opportunity to secure his just and equitable share of the oil in the pool by being offered fair, reasonable, and equal participation with the other interested parties in Kenmac. He refused to participate as he had every right to do. As an oil operator we must assume that he was fully aware of the consequences of his refusal. While we agree he had a perfect right to refuse to join the project, he should not be rewarded because he did. Neither should he be permitted to recover what he would have received if he had assumed the risks of that project. To hold either way would serve to defeat the purpose of our conservation act and would promote waste by effectively discouraging the formation of second-ary-recovery units which are so essential to the oil industry in this state.

The statute provides and plaintiff insists his correlative rights in the oil underlying his lease must be protected. That oil, however, was oil which could not be profitably produced by primary methods. The evidence is also conclusive that plaintiff could not have recovered secondary oil except for Kenmac. Under the facts herein the most that plaintiff should have a right to recover is what he can prove by a preponderance of the evidence he could have obtained through his own efforts if he had drilled, developed, and operated his property outside the unitization project; that is, as if no unitization had occurred. There is evidence that any operation by plaintiff would have resulted in an economic loss. If the testimony of his manager of operations is accepted, then the profit he could have realized from his own operations for both primary and secondary recovery would have been $12,224. This would be the limit of plaintiff's just and equitable share for oil displaced from Section 16 by Kenmac in the absence of other evidence.

* * *

Reversed and remanded.

NEWTON, JUSTICE (dissenting).

Notwithstanding that I heartily concur in the facts and the proposi-tions of law set forth in the majority opinion, I find that I must respectful-ly dissent from the result reached. * * *

* * *

* * * Quite conclusively, plaintiff would have lost money had he made an attempt to recover his share of the primary oil and he could not have shown a profit without the efforts of Kenmac in producing secondary oil, a project in which he refused to join. If, therefore, he is permitted to recover, he is then being permitted to capitalize on his refusal to cooperate and to join in Kenmac.

In my opinion, the judgment should be reversed and the cause dismissed.

NOTES

1. In Syverson v. North Dakota State Industrial Comm'n, 111 N.W.2d 128 (N.D.1961) and in Railroad Comm'n v. Manziel, 361 S.W.2d 560 (Tex. 1962), nonunit owners attempted to set aside a conservation order authorizing voluntary unit operations. In both cases, the courts held that the order authorizing a voluntary unit was in the public interest and that an interest owner who refused a fair opportunity to participate could not enjoin the unit operations on a theory of trespass. See also California Co. v. Britt, 154 So.2d 144 (Miss.1963) (denying liability for drainage where plaintiff rejected a fair offer to participate in a unit) and Tide Water Associated Oil Co. v. Stott, 159 F.2d 174 (5th Cir.Tex.1946) (denying liability of lessees engaged in gas

recycling operations on nearby lands that displaced lessor plaintiffs' wet gas with dry gas where plaintiffs refused a fair opportunity to participate in the recycling operations).

Professors Williams and Meyers have referred to the rule of nonliability for displacement of hydrocarbons by water-flooding or gas injection as the "negative rule of capture." They suggest that this rule should be limited to situations where the injection of substances is "pursued as part of a reasonable program of development and without injury to producing or potentially producing formations." Williams & Meyers § 204.5.

Is the court's decision in *Baumgartner* proper? What constitutes a fair opportunity to participate? What standard should courts use in determining whether an opportunity to participate in secondary-recovery operations is fair? If an owner is not offered any opportunity to participate or is offered an unfair opportunity to participate, what remedy is appropriate?

2. Several cases have sustained the recovery of damages even though the conservation agency approved of unit operations. See Hartman v. Texaco Inc., 937 P.2d 979 (N.M.App.1997); Greyhound Leasing & Fin. Corp. v. Joiner City Unit, 444 F.2d 439 (10th Cir.Okla.1971); Boyce v. Dundee Healdton Sand Unit, 560 P.2d 234 (Okla.App. Div. 1 1975); and Mowrer v. Ashland Oil & Refining Co., 518 F.2d 659 (7th Cir.Ind.1975). These cases suggest that a cause of action may lie in trespass, nuisance, strict liability, or confiscation.

In Tidewater Oil Co. v. Jackson, 320 F.2d 157 (10th Cir. Kan.1963), the court sustained a verdict awarding actual damages for injury caused by water flooding conducted pursuant to a voluntary unitization that had been approved by the conservation agency but reversed the award of punitive damages. Although the defendants argued that plaintiff had received a fair offer to unitize, the court did not regard this fact as germane. The court also reasoned that conservation-agency approval of the unit operations was also not germane because the agency lacked authority to resolve private tort claims. The court, however, limited its decision to voluntary unitization. Should the court treat compulsory unitization differently?

In Jameson v. Ethyl Corp., 609 S.W.2d 346 (Ark.1980), Ethyl held mining rights covering about 15,000 acres to extract bromide from formations containing salt water. Following the extraction of bromide, Ethyl reinjected the mined salt water into the producing formation. Ethyl sought a declaratory judgment to establish the validity of this enhanced-recovery process. Jameson, the owner of a 95–acre tract surrounded by Ethyl's interests, counterclaimed for damages on grounds of trespass and private nuisance. Jameson argued that the recycling operation increased drainage from her tract and replaced valuable bromide-bearing salt water with noncommercial salt water. Specifically, Jameson asserted that the injected salt water invaded her tract and "pushed" or "swept" the bromide-bearing water from beneath her property. Ethyl argued that its process merely assisted in "pulling" salt water from beneath the land of Jameson and, therefore, was lawful under the rule of capture. Ethyl had offered to lease the Jameson property by making a rental offer in lieu of royalty. This offer was substantially the same as offers accepted by other landowners. In ruling for Jameson, the Arkansas Supreme Court stated:

Viewed from a judicial perspective it seems clear that the law as developed with respect to the rule of capture, trespass and nuisance fails to adequately provide a resolution of the issue with respect to bromine-enriched brine where secondary-recovery methods are utilized, the results of which materially alter the natural drainage consequences of extracting from encircled properties lying within a common pool. It seems equally clear that the law should not turn upon the issue of whether the activities are characterized as "pushing" or "pulling", or whether a differential pressure is created by injection or the addition of larger quantities of brine. Similarly, the obviously necessary steps of secondary recovery (which by definition create alterations to the norm) from a common pool area (be it oil, gas, brine or other fluid minerals) should not be subject to the arbitrary control of a limited number of landowners. Nor should the law permit those persons who are in an economically advantaged posture to be able to gain negotiating clout by being allowed to undertake, with impunity, processes that go beyond extracting transient minerals or gasses which have drained or flowed by natural process to their drilling sites.

* * *

In Budd v. Ethyl Corporation, 474 S.W.2d 411 (Ark.1971) this Court had occasion to address the issue of whether Ethyl's operations in the Field which forcibly injected brine into input (injection) wells were entitled to the benefit of the rule of capture. As to a 240–acre tract lying next to but outside of Ethyl's 15,000 area block, this Court held that the rule of capture applied and that Ethyl was not obligated to account for any minerals which may have flowed as a result thereof into its wells from the 240–acre tract. However, as to a 40–acre tract lying within Ethyl's peripheral area of input (injection) wells, this Court concluded that a separate analysis was necessary. Because of the limited nature of the lessee's interest in the 40–acre tract within Ethyl's peripheral area of input wells and certain equities noted, this Court also rejected Budd's claim against Ethyl concerning the 40–acre tract. Obviously, this Court would not have treated the encircled 40–acre tract differently if this Court had reached the decision in the *Budd* case that it was immaterial whether the lands were inside or outside of Ethyl's peripheral area of input wells. Because of this the 8th Circuit Court of Appeals in the diversity case of Young v. Ethyl Corporation [521 F.2d 771 (8th Cir.Ark. 1975) and 581 F.2d 715 (8th Cir.Ark.1978)] attempted to construe the Arkansas law in a comparable situation and concluded that the rule of law should not be expanded to permit the so-called "sweeping" process without liability for damages.

While Arkansas' [oil and gas] unitization laws are not * * * involved in this case, we do believe that the underlying rationale for the adoption of such laws, i.e., to avoid waste and provide for maximizing recovery of mineral resources, may be interpreted as expressing a public policy of this State which is pertinent to the rule of law of this case. Inherent in such laws is the realization that transient minerals such as oil, gas and brine will be wasted if a single landowner is able to thwart secondary-recovery processes, while conversely acknowledging a need to protect each land-owner's rights to some equitable portion of pools of such minerals. A determination that a trespass or nuisance occurs through secondary-recovery processes within a recovery area would tend to promote waste of such natural resources and extend unwarranted bargaining power to minority landowners. On the other hand, a determination that the rule of capture should be expanded to cover the present situation could unnecessarily extend the license of mineral extraction companies to appropriate minerals which might be induced to be moved from other properties through such processes and, in any event, further extend the bargaining power of such entities to reduce royalty payments to landowners who are financially unable to "go and do likewise" as suggested by Ethyl.

* * * By adopting an interpretation that the rule of capture should not be extended insofar as operations relate to lands lying within the peripheral area affected, we, however, are holding that reasonable and necessary secondary-recovery processes of pools of transient materials should be permitted, when such operations are carried out in good faith for the purpose of maximizing recovery from a common pool. The permitting of this good faith recovery process is conditioned, however, by imposing an obligation on the extracting party to compensate the owner of the depleted lands for the minerals extracted in excess of natural depletion, if any, at the time of taking and for any special damages which may have been caused to the depleted property. By this holding we believe that the interests of the owners and the public are properly protected and served.

609 S.W.2d at 349–51.

Notwithstanding the court's discussion, didn't the *Jameson* Court essentially decide that "pulling" bromide from outside the unit periphery was protected by the rule of capture but that "pushing" bromide from within the periphery was not? What is the justification for differentiating between lands inside and outside the enhanced-recovery area, assuming drainage occurs from both? What "formula of damages" should the court devise? Does the remedy in *Jameson* differ from the remedy in *Baumgartner*?

3.   May a unit operator use any part of the surface within a unit to carry out the unit plan without permission from surface owners, whether or not they hold an interest in the minerals? See generally Nelson v. Texaco, Inc., 525 P.2d 1263 (Okla.App. Div. 1 1974).

4.   Compare *Baumgartner* to Snyder Ranches, Inc. v. Oil Conservation Comm'n, 798 P.2d 587 (N.M.1990), wherein the court states that a permit to inject salt water into a disposal well does not authorize an actual trespass or other tort. Is the disposal of salt water legally distinguishable from water flooding, or are *Snyder* and *Baumgartner* irreconcilable?

5.   Injection or disposal of salt water (or brine) poses a threat to fresh-water zones. To assure that injected brine enters the targeted formation, operators use pumps to pressurize and force the brine through tubing into the desired formation. Operators seal off the targeted formation in the well bore with *packers*. They seal off fresh-water zones by installing and cementing pipe, called *surface casing*, from the surface through known fresh-water zones. Thus, the tubing, packers, and surface casing serve as barriers against

fresh-water pollution. Pressure gauges in the *annulus* of the well (the space between the surface casing, cement, and tubing) detect leaks in the tubing. The federal Safe Drinking Water Act[115] provides for underground injection control (UIC) programs[116] to protect fresh groundwater supplies. For further discussion, see Chapter 5, Section B.1.

6. Because the typical working-interest owner holds an oil and gas lease from a lessor who is relying on the expertise and ability of the lessee, the lessee has an implied duty to act in good faith and to conduct reasonable and prudent operations for the parties' mutual benefit. This may include an implied obligation to unitize for enhanced recovery. See, e.g., Waseco Chemical & Supply Co. v. Bayou State Oil Corp., 371 So.2d 305 (La.App.1979) (addressing the failure to implement modern enhanced-recovery operations); Amoco Prod. Co. v. Alexander, 622 S.W.2d 563, 568 (Tex.1981) (addressing the lessee's failure to pursue unitization and other means to prevent field-wide drainage). See generally Maurice Merrill, Implied Covenants and Secondary Recovery, 4 Okla.L.Rev. 177, 181 (1951). Implied covenants are discussed in more detail in Chapter 2, Section E.3.

Upon unitization, the unit operator must conduct enhanced-recovery operations reasonably and prudently. An operator may be liable to both unit participants and nonparticipants for negligence, including the use of experimental methods that harm the reservoir or for violating the terms of the conservation agency's unitization order. See, e.g., Empire Oil & Ref. Co. v. Hoyt, 112 F.2d 356 (6th Cir. Mich. 1940) (negligent acidization). See generally Kuntz §§ 59.1–.5 and Hemingway § 8.5. In *Baumgartner*, does the State of Nebraska, owner of the minerals in Section 16, have a cause of action against the plaintiff for failing to join in the unit operations?

Unit operators may be accountable for failing to implement an approved unitization plan in good faith, and the conservation agency may terminate the unit for such failure or if it otherwise fails to achieve its objectives. See Parkin v. State Corp. Comm'n, 677 P.2d 991 (Kan.1984). See generally Owen L. Anderson, Mutiny: The Revolt Against *Unsuccessful* Unit Operations, 30 Rocky Mtn.Min.L.Inst. 13–1 (1984).

Regarding the termination of unsuccessful unitizations, the Model Oil and Gas Conservation Act provides:

Section 16. COMPULSORY UNIT OPERATION—TERMINATION.

The [commission], upon its own motion or upon the application of an owner, may for good cause terminate a unit operation and dissolve the unit on just and equitable terms. If not terminated earlier, the unit operation shall terminate upon final cessation of production from the reservoir or unitized portion thereof and the plugging and abandonment of unit wells and facilities. At the time of dissolution of the unit operation, the operator shall file with the [commission] and record in the [county] land records of the [county] or [counties] documents sufficient to give constructive notice of the dissolution of the unit operation respecting the lands that were included in the unit area.

---

115.   42 U.S.C. §§ 300f to 300j–26.

116.   Id. §§ 300h(a), (b).

Model Oil and Gas Conservation Act (Interstate Oil & Gas Compact Comm'n 2004).

Many unitization acts, orders, plans, and agreements do not address the involuntary dissolution of enhanced-recovery units because of unsuccessful or imprudent unit operations. Typical unitization agreements provide for dissolution of the unit by agreement of the working-interest owners, for cessation of production, or both. See, e.g., Christmas v. Raley, 539 S.W.2d 405 (Ark. 1976) (terminating unit upon cessation of production). If a unit is terminated prior to ultimate recovery, are there any correlative-rights concerns?

CHAPTER 5

ENVIRONMENTAL REGULATION OF THE OIL & GAS INDUSTRY

Table of Sections

Oil and gas development impacts the environment. This chapter introduces students to the major federal environmental laws that regulate the upstream oil and gas activities of exploration, development, and production. "Environmental law" in the United States is the product of piecemeal legislative responses to an array of environmental issues. Environmental protection is achieved by applying many self-contained federal and state statutes which address a particular problem, such as air pollution or water pollution. This makes the practice of environmental law challenging because the lawyer must work with a complex maze of statutes and common law concepts to effectively represent their clients. This chapter examines the major federal environmental laws that can potentially apply to oil and gas exploration, development, and production activities. However, state and local law should always be consulted since the federal statutes routinely permit more stringent regulation and, in many cases, delegate administration of federal statutory programs to state authorities.

The environmental laws can be placed into three general categories for analysis. First, are laws that impose land-use restrictions, usually to achieve a preservationist goal, such as protecting a particular specie of plant or animal, or a resource, such as wetlands. Second, are laws that impose precise performance standards on a regulated activity, usually to achieve a numerical standard which is representative of either a legislative goal for environmental quality or the best the industry can do given the available, or soon-to-be available, technology. Third, are laws that impose liability on defined classes of persons to address environmental problems. Under this third category, the goals are to clean up existing environmental problems and deter creation of new problems. A single law can employ all three regulatory techniques. For example, the Clean Water Act imposes land-use restrictions on wetlands,[1] numerical effluent limitations on industry discharges,[2] and cleanup liability for oil and hazardous substance spills.[3] Oil and gas development activities are impacted by all three types of environmental laws. To appreciate how the environmental laws can apply to the oil and gas industry, this chapter reviews the oil and gas exploration, development, and production processes chronologically from lease acquisition to production of the oil and gas.

Often the oil and gas developer's most difficult task is to merely identify the environmental laws they must consider before undertaking an activity. When development takes place on private lands, there will typically be no single coordinating agency charged with identifying environmental impacts. Therefore, the attorney representing the developer, landowner, regulatory agency, or environmental interest group, must anticipate the possible environmental impacts and be able to extract from the mass of environmental laws those that may apply to the various components of the proposed development activity. This chapter focuses on oil and gas development of private lands; Chapter 7 addresses development on federal, state, and Indian lands.

A. OBTAINING THE OIL & GAS LEASE

Analysis of environmental issues must take place even before acquisition of the oil and gas lease. The two major areas of concern include: (1) Can the proposed activity take place on the leased land? and (2) What sort of environmental cleanup liability might be associated with obtaining, or giving, an oil and gas lease covering the land?

---

1.   33 U.S.C. § 1344.

2.   Id. at § 1311.

3.   Id. at § 1321.

1. LAND USE CONSIDERATIONS

Land use considerations include any potential restriction that is unique to the land where the activity will take place. The most common examples are local zoning regulations that limit certain types of development to specified "zones" within a geographic area. See generally David E. Pierce, Municipal Development of Oil and Gas, 19 Tulsa L.J. 337 (1984), reprinted at, 22 Pub.Land & Resources L.Dig. 66 (1985). Instead of focusing on these traditional forms of state and local government land use regulation, this section examines federal environmental laws that may limit or prohibit the use of private land for oil and gas development. The two environmental laws the oil and gas developer is most likely to currently encounter in a land use context are the wetlands provision of the Clean Water Act ("CWA")[4] and the "take" provision of the Endangered Species Act ("ESA").[5] The CWA and ESA provide an interesting dichotomy of land use restrictions. The CWA regulates activities on a particular type of land because of its "wetlands" classification. Under the ESA the classification of the land is secondary; the primary focus is upon the specie of plant or animal that is dependent upon the land.

(a) Wetlands Protection

Under section 404[6] of the Clean Water Act the U.S. Army Corps of Engineers (the "Corps") is authorized to issue permits "for the discharge of dredged or fill material into the navigable waters * * *."[7] "Dredged material" generally includes anything that is excavated from a regulated area[8] while "fill material" includes anything that is used to fill or build up a regulated area.[9] For example, construction of a drill site and associated facilities, such as an access road, typically require excavation and filling of the drill site area. If these activities impact "navigable waters" a § 404 permit may be required.

The CWA defines "navigable waters" to mean "waters of the United States * * *."[10] By regulation, the Corps has defined "waters of the United States" very broadly to include any source of surface water that could affect interstate commerce, tributaries connected to such water sources, and wetlands adjacent to such water sources or their tributaries.[11] "Wetlands" are defined to include "those areas that are inundated

---

4. 33 U.S.C. § 1344.

5. 16 U.S.C. § 1538.

6. It is common to refer to many of the federal environmental laws by their section designation in the original session laws instead of their section designation in the United States Code. Therefore, if you refer to section "404" of the Clean Water Act most environmental practitioners will know you are talking about the "dredged or fill" permits provision of the Act codified at 33 U.S.C. § 1344.

7. CWA § 404(a), 33 U.S.C. § 1344(a). However, the Environmental Protection Agency ("EPA") is given the authority to review the permit decisions of the Corps and to limit or prohibit issuance of a permit. CWA § 404(c), 33 U.S.C. § 1344(c).

8. 33 C.F.R. § 323.2(c).

9. Id. at §§ (e) & (f).

10. CWA § 502(7), 33 U.S.C. § 1362(7).

11. 33 C.F.R. § 328.3(a). The EPA has adopted a similar definition of "waters of the United States." See 40 C.F.R. § 230.3(s). Portions of this regulation have been invalidated by the courts. The status of the Corps' regulation is explored in Rapanos v. United States, 547 U.S. 715 (2006).

or saturated by surface or ground water at a frequency and duration sufficient to support, and that under normal circumstances do support, the prevalence of vegetation typically adapted for life in saturated soil conditions."[12] One of the most important issues, under the CWA and the Oil Pollution Act ("OPA"),[13] is the regulatory reach of "waters of the United States." To what extent can the Corps and the EPA broadly define the phrase "waters of the United States" to extend to non-navigable water bodies or to tributaries or lands that are not directly connected to navigable water bodies?

RAPANOS v. UNITED STATES

547 U.S. 715 (2006).

JUSTICE SCALIA announced the judgment of the Court, and delivered and opinion, in which THE CHIEF JUSTICE, JUSTICE THOMAS, and JUSTICE ALITO join.

In April 1989, petitioner John A. Rapanos backfilled wetlands on a parcel of land in Michigan that he owned and sought to develop. This parcel included 54 acres of land with sometimes-saturated soil conditions. The nearest body of navigable water was 11 to 20 miles away. * * *. Regulators had informed Mr. Rapanos that his saturated fields were "waters of the United States," 33 U.S.C. § 1362(7), that could not be filled without a permit. Twelve years of criminal and civil litigation ensued.

The burden of federal regulation on those who would deposit fill material in locations denominated "waters of the United States" is not trivial. In deciding whether to grant or deny a permit, the U.S. Army Corps of Engineers (Corps) exercises the discretion of an enlightened despot, relying on such factors as "economics," "aesthetics," "recreation," and "in general, the needs and welfare of the people," 33 CFR § 320.4(a) (2004). The average applicant for an individual permit spends 788 days and $271,596 in completing the process, and the average applicant for a nationwide permit spends 313 days and $28,915—not counting costs of mitigation or design changes. * * *

The enforcement proceedings against Mr. Rapanos are a small part of the immense expansion of federal regulation of land use that has occurred under the Clean Water Act-without any change in the governing statute— during the past five Presidential administrations. In the last three decades, the Corps and the Environmental Protection Agency (EPA) have interpreted their jurisdiction over "the waters of the United States" to cover 270–to–300 million acres of swampy lands in the United States— including half of Alaska and an area the size of California in the lower 48 States. And that was just the beginning. The Corps has also asserted jurisdiction over virtually any parcel of land containing a channel or

---

12. 33 C.F.R. § 328.3(b); 40 C.F.R. § 230.2(t).

13. OPA § 1001(21), 33 U.S.C. § 2701(21) (defining "navigable waters" as "waters of the United States" for purposes of the OPA).

conduit—whether man-made or natural, broad or narrow, permanent or ephemeral—through which rainwater or drainage may occasionally or intermittently flow. On this view, the federally regulated "waters of the United States" include storm drains, roadside ditches, ripples of sand in the desert that may contain water once a year, and lands that are covered by floodwaters once every 100 years. Because they include the land containing storm sewers and desert washes, the statutory "waters of the United States" engulf entire cities and immense arid wastelands. In fact, the entire land area of the United States lies in some drainage basin, and an endless network of visible channels furrows the entire surface, containing water ephemerally wherever the rain falls. Any plot of land containing such a channel may potentially be regulated as a "water of the United States."

I

Congress passed the Clean Water Act (CWA or Act) in 1972. The Act's stated objective is "to restore and maintain the chemical, physical, and biological integrity of the Nation's waters." 86 Stat. 816, 33 U.S.C. § 1251(a). The Act also states that "[i]t is the policy of Congress to recognize, preserve, and protect the primary responsibilities and rights of States to prevent, reduce, and eliminate pollution, to plan the development and use (including restoration, preservation, and enhancement) of land and water resources, and to consult with the Administrator in the exercise of his authority under this chapter." § 1251(b).

One of the statute's principal provisions is 33 U.S.C. § 1311(a), which provides that "the discharge of any pollutant by any person shall be unlawful." "The discharge of a pollutant" is defined broadly to include "any addition of any pollutant to navigable waters from any point source," § 1362(12), and "pollutant" is defined broadly to include not only traditional contaminants but also solids such as "dredged spoil, . . . rock, sand, [and] cellar dirt," § 1362(6). And, most relevant here, the CWA defines "navigable waters" as "the waters of the United States, including the territorial seas." § 1362(7).

The Act also provides certain exceptions to its prohibition of "the discharge of any pollutant by any person." § 1311(a). Section 1342(a) authorizes the Administrator of the EPA to "issue a permit for the discharge of any pollutant, . . . notwithstanding section 1311(a) of this title." Section 1344 authorizes the Secretary of the Army, acting through the Corps, to "issue permits . . . for the discharge of dredged or fill material into the navigable waters at specified disposal sites." § 1344(a), (d). It is the discharge of "dredged or fill material"—which, unlike traditional water pollutants, are solids that do not readily wash downstream—that we consider today.

For a century prior to the CWA, we had interpreted the phrase "navigable waters of the United States" in the Act's predecessor statutes to refer to interstate waters that are "navigable in fact" or readily susceptible of being rendered so. *The Daniel Ball,* 10 Wall. 557, 563, 19

L.Ed. 999 (1871) * * * After passage of the CWA, the Corps initially adopted this traditional judicial definition for the Act's term "navigable waters." * * * After a District Court enjoined these regulations as too narrow, *Natural Resources Defense Council, Inc. v. Callaway,* 392 F.Supp. 685, 686 (DC 1975), the Corps adopted a far broader definition. See 40 Fed.Reg. 31324–31325 (1975); 42 Fed.Reg. 37144 (1977). The Corps' new regulations deliberately sought to extend the definition of "the waters of the United States" to the outer limits of Congress's commerce power. * * *

The Corps' current regulations interpret "the waters of the United States" to include, in addition to traditional interstate navigable waters, 33 CFR § 328.3(a)(1) (2004), "[a]ll interstate waters including interstate wetlands," § 328.3(a)(2); "[a]ll other waters such as intrastate lakes, rivers, streams (including intermittent streams), mudflats, sandflats, wetlands, sloughs, prairie potholes, wet meadows, playa lakes, or natural ponds, the use, degradation or destruction of which could affect interstate or foreign commerce," § 328.3(a)(3); "[t]ributaries of [such] waters," § 328.3(a)(5); and "[w]etlands adjacent to [such] waters [and tributaries] (other than waters that are themselves wetlands)," § 328.3(a)(7). The regulation defines "adjacent" wetlands as those "bordering, contiguous [to], or neighboring" waters of the United States. § 328.3(c). It specifically provides that "[w]etlands separated from other waters of the United States by man-made dikes or barriers, natural river berms, beach dunes and the like are 'adjacent wetlands.'" *Ibid.*

We first addressed the proper interpretation of 33 U.S.C. § 1362(7)'s phrase "the waters of the United States" in *United States v. Riverside Bayview Homes, Inc.,* 474 U.S. 121, 106 S.Ct. 455, 88 L.Ed.2d 419 (1985). That case concerned a wetland that "was adjacent to a body of navigable water," because "the area characterized by saturated soil conditions and wetland vegetation extended beyond the boundary of respondent's property to ... a navigable waterway." * * * Noting that "the transition from water to solid ground is not necessarily or even typically an abrupt one," and that "the Corps must necessarily choose some point at which water ends and land begins," * * * we upheld the Corps' interpretation of "the waters of the United States" to include wetlands that "actually abut[ted] on" traditional navigable waters. * * *

Following our decision in *Riverside Bayview,* the Corps adopted increasingly broad interpretations of its own regulations under the Act. For example, in 1986, to "clarify" the reach of its jurisdiction, the Corps announced the so-called "Migratory Bird Rule," which purported to extend its jurisdiction to any intrastate waters "[w]hich are or would be used as habitat" by migratory birds. 51 Fed.Reg. 41217; * * * In addition, the Corps interpreted its own regulations to include "ephemeral streams" and "drainage ditches" as "tributaries" that are part of the "waters of the United States," see 33 CFR § 328.3(a)(5), provided that they have a perceptible "ordinary high water mark" as defined in § 328.3(e). 65 Fed.Reg. 12823 (2000). This interpretation extended "the waters of the

United States" to virtually any land feature over which rainwater or drainage passes and leaves a visible mark-even if only "the presence of litter and debris." 33 CFR § 328.3(e). * * * Prior to our decision in [Solid Waste Agency of Northern Cook County v. Army Corps of Engineers, 531 U.S. 159 (2001)] *SWANCC,* lower courts upheld the application of this expansive definition of "tributaries" to such entities as storm sewers that contained flow to covered waters during heavy rainfall, *United States v. Eidson,* 108 F.3d 1336, 1340–1342 (C.A.11 1997), and dry arroyos connected to remote waters through the flow of groundwater over "centuries," *Quivira Mining Co. v. EPA,* 765 F.2d 126, 129 (C.A.10 1985).

In *SWANCC,* we considered the application of the Corps' "Migratory Bird Rule" to "an abandoned sand and gravel pit in northern Illinois." * * * Observing that "[i]t was the *significant nexus* between the wetlands and 'navigable waters' that informed our reading of the CWA in *Riverside Bayview,*" * * * we held that *Riverside Bayview* did not establish "that the jurisdiction of the Corps extends to ponds that are not adjacent to open water." * * * On the contrary, we held that "nonnavigable, isolated, intrastate waters," * * *—which, unlike the wetlands at issue in *Riverside Bayview,* did not "actually abu[t] on a navigable waterway," * * *— were not included as "waters of the United States."

Following our decision in *SWANCC,* the Corps did not significantly revise its theory of federal jurisdiction under § 1344(a). The Corps provided notice of a proposed rulemaking in light of *SWANCC,* 68 Fed.Reg.1991 (2003), but ultimately did not amend its published regulations. Because *SWANCC* did not directly address tributaries, the Corps notified its field staff that they "should continue to assert jurisdiction over traditional navigable waters ... and, generally speaking, their tributary systems (and adjacent wetlands)." 68 Fed.Reg.1998. In addition, because *SWANCC* did not overrule *Riverside Bayview,* the Corps continues to assert jurisdiction over waters " 'neighboring' " traditional navigable waters and their tributaries. 68 Fed.Reg.1997 (quoting 33 CFR § 328.3(c) (2003)).

Even after *SWANCC,* the lower courts have continued to uphold the Corps' sweeping assertions of jurisdiction over ephemeral channels and drains as "tributaries." For example, courts have held that jurisdictional "tributaries" include the "intermittent flow of surface water through approximately 2.4 miles of natural streams and manmade ditches (paralleling and crossing under I–64)," *Treacy v. Newdunn Assoc.,* 344 F.3d 407, 410 (C.A.4 2003); a "roadside ditch" whose water took "a winding, thirty-two-mile path to the Chesapeake Bay," *United States v. Deaton,* 332 F.3d 698, 702 (C.A.4 2003); irrigation ditches and drains that intermittently connect to covered waters, *Community Assn. for Restoration of Environment v. Henry Bosma Dairy,* 305 F.3d 943, 954–955 (C.A.9 2002); *Headwaters, Inc. v. Talent Irrigation Dist.,* 243 F.3d 526, 534 (C.A.9 2001); and (most implausibly of all) the "washes and arroyos" of an "arid development site," located in the middle of the desert, through which "water courses ... during periods of heavy rain," *Save Our Sonoran, Inc. v. Flowers,* 408 F.3d 1113, 1118 (C.A.9 2005).

These judicial constructions of "tributaries" are not outliers. Rather, they reflect the breadth of the Corps' determinations in the field. The Corps' enforcement practices vary somewhat from district to district because "the definitions used to make jurisdictional determinations" are deliberately left "vague." * * * But district offices of the Corps have treated, as "waters of the United States," such typically dry land features as "arroyos, coulees, and washes," as well as other "channels that might have little water flow in a given year." * * * They have also applied that definition to such manmade, intermittently flowing features as "drain tiles, storm drains systems, and culverts." * * *

In addition to "tributaries," the Corps and the lower courts have also continued to define "adjacent" wetlands broadly after *SWANCC*. For example, some of the Corps' district offices have concluded that wetlands are "adjacent" to covered waters if they are hydrologically connected "through directional sheet flow during storm events," * * * or if they lie within the "100–year floodplain" of a body of water—that is, they are connected to the navigable water by flooding, on average, once every 100 years, * * *. Others have concluded that presence within 200 feet of a tributary automatically renders a wetland "adjacent" and jurisdictional. * * * And the Corps has successfully defended such theories of "adjacency" in the courts, even after *SWANCC's* excision of "isolated" waters and wetlands from the Act's coverage. One court has held since *SWANCC* that wetlands separated from flood control channels by 70–foot–wide berms, atop which ran maintenance roads, had a "significant nexus" to covered waters because, *inter alia,* they lay "within the 100 year floodplain of tidal waters." *Baccarat Fremont Developers, LLC v. Army Corps of Engineers,* 425 F.3d 1150, 1152, 1157 (C.A.9 2005). In one of the cases before us today, the Sixth Circuit held, in agreement with "[t]he majority of courts," that "while a hydrological connection between the non-navigable and navigable waters is required, there is no 'direct abutment' requirement" under *SWANCC* for " 'adjacency.' " 376 F.3d 629, 639 (2004) *(Rapanos II).* And even the most insubstantial hydrologic connection may be held to constitute a "significant nexus." One court distinguished *SWANCC* on the ground that "a molecule of water residing in one of these pits or ponds [in *SWANCC*] could not mix with molecules from other bodies of water"—whereas, in the case before it, "water molecules currently present in the wetlands will inevitably flow towards and mix with water from connecting bodies," and "[a] drop of rainwater landing in the Site is certain to intermingle with water from the [nearby river]." *United States v. Rueth Development Co.,* 189 F.Supp.2d 874, 877–878 (N.D.Ind. 2002).

II

In these consolidated cases, we consider whether four Michigan wetlands, which lie near ditches or man-made drains that eventually empty into traditional navigable waters, constitute "waters of the United States" within the meaning of the Act. Petitioners in No. 04–1034, the Rapanos and their affiliated businesses, deposited fill material without a permit into wetlands on three sites near Midland, Michigan: the "Salzburg site," the "Hines Road site," and the "Pine River site." The wetlands at the Salzburg site are connected to a man-made drain, which drains into Hoppler Creek, which flows into the Kawkawlin River, which empties into Saginaw Bay and Lake Huron. * * * The wetlands at the Hines Road site are connected to something called the "Rose Drain," which has a surface connection to the Tittabawassee River. * * * And the wetlands at the Pine River site have a surface connection to the Pine River, which flows into Lake Huron. * * * It is not clear whether the connections between these wetlands and the nearby drains and ditches are continuous or intermittent, or whether the nearby drains and ditches contain continuous or merely occasional flows of water.

The United States brought civil enforcement proceedings against the Rapanos petitioners. The District Court found that the three described wetlands were "within federal jurisdiction" because they were "adjacent to other waters of the United States," and held petitioners liable for violations of the CWA at those sites. * * * On appeal, the United States Court of Appeals for the Sixth Circuit affirmed, holding that there was federal jurisdiction over the wetlands at all three sites because "there were hydrological connections between all three sites and corresponding adjacent tributaries of navigable waters." 376 F.3d, at 643.

Petitioners in No. 04–1384, the Carabells, were denied a permit to deposit fill material in a wetland located on a triangular parcel of land about one mile from Lake St. Clair. A man-made drainage ditch runs along one side of the wetland, separated from it by a 4–foot–wide man-made berm. The berm is largely or entirely impermeable to water and blocks drainage from the wetland, though it may permit occasional overflow to the ditch. The ditch empties into another ditch or a drain, which connects to Auvase Creek, which empties into Lake St. Clair. * * *

After exhausting administrative appeals, the Carabell petitioners filed suit in the District Court, challenging the exercise of federal regulatory jurisdiction over their site. The District Court ruled that there was federal jurisdiction because the wetland "is adjacent to neighboring tributaries of navigable waters and has a significant nexus to 'waters of the United States.'" * * * Again the Sixth Circuit affirmed, holding that the Carabell wetland was "adjacent" to navigable waters. 391 F.3d 704, 708 (2004) *(Carabell)*.

We granted certiorari and consolidated the cases * * * to decide whether these wetlands constitute "waters of the United States" under the Act, and if so, whether the Act is constitutional.

III

The Rapanos petitioners contend that the terms "navigable waters" and "waters of the United States" in the Act must be limited to the traditional definition of *The Daniel Ball,* which required that the "waters" be navigable in fact, or susceptible of being rendered so. * * * But this definition cannot be applied wholesale to the CWA. The Act uses the phrase "navigable waters" as a *defined* term, and the definition is simply "the waters of the United States." 33 U.S.C. § 1362(7). Moreover, the Act provides, in certain circumstances, for the substitution of state for federal jurisdiction over "navigable waters ... *other than* those waters which are presently used, or are susceptible to use in their natural condition or by reasonable improvement as a means to transport interstate or foreign commerce ... including wetlands adjacent thereto." § 1344(g)(1) (emphasis added). This provision shows that the Act's term "navigable waters" includes something more than traditional navigable waters. We have twice stated that the meaning of "navigable waters" in the Act is broader than the traditional understanding of that term, * * *. We have also emphasized, however, that the qualifier "navigable" is not devoid of significance, * * *.

We need not decide the precise extent to which the qualifiers "navigable" and "of the United States" restrict the coverage of the Act. Whatever the scope of these qualifiers, the CWA authorizes federal jurisdiction only over "waters." 33 U.S.C. § 1362(7). The only natural definition of the term "waters," our prior and subsequent judicial constructions of it, clear evidence from other provisions of the statute, and this Court's canons of construction all confirm that "the waters of the United States" in § 1362(7) cannot bear the expansive meaning that the Corps would give it.

The Corps' expansive approach might be arguable if the CWA defined "navigable waters" as "water of the United States." But "the waters of the United States" is something else. The use of the definite article ("the") and the plural number ("waters") show plainly that § 1362(7) does not refer to water in general. In this form, "the waters" refers more narrowly to water "[a]s found in streams and bodies forming geographical features such as oceans, rivers, [and] lakes," or "the flowing or moving masses, as of waves or floods, making up such streams or bodies." Webster's New International Dictionary 2882 (2d ed.1954) (hereinafter Webster's Second). On this definition, "the waters of the United States" include only relatively permanent, standing or flowing bodies of water.[1] The definition refers to water as found in "streams," "oceans," "rivers,"

---

1. By describing "waters" as "relatively permanent," we do not necessarily exclude streams, rivers, or lakes that might dry up in extraordinary circumstances, such as drought. We also do not necessarily exclude *seasonal* rivers, which contain continuous flow during some months of the year but no flow during dry months—such as the 290–day, continuously flowing stream postulated by Justice STEVENS' dissent (hereinafter the dissent), *post,* at 2259–2260. Common sense and common usage distinguish between a wash and seasonal river.

Though scientifically precise distinctions between "perennial" and "intermittent" flows are no doubt available * * * we have no occasion in this litigation to decide exactly when the drying-up of a stream bed is continuous and frequent enough to disqualify the channel as a "wate[r] of the United States." It suffices for present purposes that channels containing permanent flow are plainly within the definition, and that the dissent's "intermittent" and "ephemeral" streams, *post,* at 2260 (opinion of STEVENS, J.)—that is, streams whose flow is "[c]oming and going at intervals ... [b]roken, fitful," Webster's Second 1296, or "existing only, or no longer than, a day; diurnal ... short-lived," *id.,* at 857—are not.

"lakes," and "bodies" of water "forming geographical features." *Ibid.* All of these terms connote continuously present, fixed bodies of water, as opposed to ordinarily dry channels through which water occasionally or intermittently flows. Even the least substantial of the definition's terms, namely "streams," connotes a continuous flow of water in a permanent channel—especially when used in company with other terms such as "rivers," "lakes," and "oceans."[2] None of these terms encompasses transitory puddles or ephemeral flows of water.

The restriction of "the waters of the United States" to exclude channels containing merely intermittent or ephemeral flow also accords with the commonsense understanding of the term. In applying the definition to "ephemeral streams," "wet meadows," storm sewers and culverts, "directional sheet flow during storm events," drain tiles, man-made drainage ditches, and dry arroyos in the middle of the desert, the Corps has stretched the term "waters of the United States" beyond parody. The plain language of the statute simply does not authorize this "Land Is Waters" approach to federal jurisdiction.

In addition, the Act's use of the traditional phrase "navigable waters" (the defined term) further confirms that it confers jurisdiction only over relatively *permanent* bodies of water. The Act adopted that traditional term from its predecessor statutes. * * * On the traditional understanding, "navigable waters" included only discrete *bodies* of water. For example, in *The Daniel Ball,* we used the terms "waters" and "rivers" interchangeably. * * * Plainly, because such "waters" had to be navigable in fact or susceptible of being rendered so, the term did not include ephemeral flows. As we noted in *SWANCC,* the traditional term "navigable waters"—even though defined as "the waters of the United States"—carries *some* of its original substance: "[I]t is one thing to give a word limited effect and quite another to give it no effect whatever." * * * That limited effect includes, at bare minimum, the ordinary presence of water.

Our subsequent interpretation of the phrase "the waters of the United States" in the CWA likewise confirms this limitation of its scope. In *Riverside Bayview,* we stated that the phrase in the Act referred primarily to "rivers, streams, and other *hydrographic features more con-*

---

2. The principal definition of "stream" likewise includes reference to such permanent, geographically fixed bodies of water: "[a] current or course of water or other fluid, flowing on the earth, as a *river, brook, etc.*" *Id.,* at 2493 (emphasis added). The other definitions of "stream" repeatedly emphasize the requirement of *continuous* flow: "[a] *steady flow,* as of water, air, gas, or the like"; "[a]nything issuing or moving with *continued succession* of parts"; "[a] *continued current* or course; current; drift." *Ibid.* (emphases added). The definition of the verb form of "stream" contains a similar emphasis on continuity: "[t]o issue or flow in a stream; to issue freely or move in a *continuous flow or course.*" *Ibid.* (emphasis added). On these definitions, therefore, the Corps' phrases "intermittent streams," 33 CFR § 328.3(a)(3) (2004), and "ephemeral streams," 65 Fed.Reg. 12823 (2000), are-like Senator Bentsen's " 'flowing gullies,' " *post,* at 2260, n. 11 (opinion of STEVENS, J.)—useful oxymora. Properly speaking, such entities constitute extant "streams" only while they are "continuous[ly] flow[ing]"; and the usually dry channels that contain them are never "streams." Justice KENNEDY apparently concedes that "an intermittent flow can constitute a stream" only "*while it is flowing,*" *post,* at 2243 (emphasis added)—which would mean that the channel is a "*water*" covered by the Act only during those times when water flow actually occurs. But no one contends that federal jurisdiction appears and evaporates along with the water in such regularly dry channels.

ventionally identifiable as 'waters' " than the wetlands adjacent to such features. * * * We thus echoed the dictionary definition of "waters" as referring to "streams and bodies *forming geographical features* such as oceans, rivers, [and] lakes." Webster's Second 2882 (emphasis added). Though we upheld in that case the inclusion of wetlands abutting such a "hydrographic featur[e]"—principally due to the difficulty of drawing any clear boundary between the two, * * *—nowhere did we suggest that "the waters of the United States" should be expanded to include, in their own right, entities other than "hydrographic features more conventionally identifiable as 'waters.' " Likewise, in both *Riverside Bayview* and *SWANCC*, we repeatedly described the "navigable waters" covered by the Act as "open water" and "open waters." * * * Under no rational interpretation are typically dry channels described as *"open* waters."

Most significant of all, the CWA itself categorizes the channels and conduits that typically carry intermittent flows of water separately from "navigable waters," by including them in the definition of " 'point source.' " The Act defines " 'point source' " as "any discernible, confined and discrete conveyance, including but not limited to any pipe, ditch, channel, tunnel, conduit, well, discrete fissure, container, rolling stock, concentrated animal feeding operation, or vessel or other floating craft, from which pollutants are or may be discharged." 33 U.S.C. § 1362(14). It also defines " 'discharge of a pollutant' " as "any addition of any pollutant *to* navigable waters *from* any point source." § 1362(12)(A) (emphases added). The definitions thus conceive of "point sources" and "navigable waters" as separate and distinct categories. The definition of "discharge" would make little sense if the two categories were significantly overlapping. The separate classification of "ditch[es], channel[s], and conduit[s]"—which are terms ordinarily used to describe the watercourses through which *intermittent* waters typically flow-shows that these are, by and large, *not* "waters of the United States."

Moreover, only the foregoing definition of "waters" is consistent with the CWA's stated "policy of Congress to recognize, preserve, and protect the primary responsibilities and rights of the States to prevent, reduce, and eliminate pollution, [and] to plan the development and use (including restoration, preservation, and enhancement) of land and water resources. . . ." § 1251(b). This statement of policy was included in the Act as enacted in 1972 * * * prior to the addition of the optional state administration program in the 1977 amendments * * *. Thus the policy plainly referred to something beyond the subsequently added state administration program of 33 U.S.C. § 1344(g)–(*l*). But the expansive theory advanced by the Corps, rather than "preserv[ing] the primary rights and responsibilities of the States," would have brought virtually all "plan[ning of] the development and use . . . of land and water resources" by the States under federal control. It is therefore an unlikely reading of the phrase "the waters of the United States."

Even if the phrase "the waters of the United States" were ambiguous as applied to intermittent flows, our own canons of construction would establish that the Corps' interpretation of the statute is impermissible. As we noted in *SWANCC*, the Government's expansive interpretation would "result in a significant impingement of the States' traditional and primary power over land and water use." * * * Regulation of land use, as through the issuance of the development permits sought by petitioners in both of these cases, is a quintessential state and local power. * * * The extensive federal jurisdiction urged by the Government would authorize the Corps to function as a *de facto* regulator of immense stretches of intrastate land—an authority the agency has shown its willingness to exercise with the scope of discretion that would befit a local zoning board. * * * We ordinarily expect a "clear and manifest" statement from Congress to authorize an unprecedented intrusion into traditional state authority. * * * The phrase "the waters of the United States" hardly qualifies.

Likewise, just as we noted in *SWANCC*, the Corps' interpretation stretches the outer limits of Congress's commerce power and raises difficult questions about the ultimate scope of that power. * * * Even if the term "the waters of the United States" were ambiguous as applied to channels that sometimes host ephemeral flows of water (which it is not), we would expect a clearer statement from Congress to authorize an agency theory of jurisdiction that presses the envelope of constitutional validity. * * *

In sum, on its only plausible interpretation, the phrase "the waters of the United States" includes only those relatively permanent, standing or continuously flowing bodies of water "forming geographic features" that are described in ordinary parlance as "streams[,] ... oceans, rivers, [and] lakes." See Webster's Second 2882. The phrase does not include channels through which water flows intermittently or ephemerally, or channels that periodically provide drainage for rainfall. The Corps' expansive interpretation of the "the waters of the United States" is thus not "based on a permissible construction of the statute." *Chevron U.S.A. Inc. v. Natural Resources Defense Council, Inc.,* 467 U.S. 837, 843, 104 S.Ct. 2778, 81 L.Ed.2d 694 (1984).

IV

In *Carabell,* the Sixth Circuit held that the nearby ditch constituted a "tributary" and thus a "water of the United States" under 33 CFR § 328.3(a)(5) (2004). * * * Likewise in *Rapanos,* the Sixth Circuit held that the nearby ditches were "tributaries" under § 328(a)(5). * * * But *Rapanos II* also stated that, even if the ditches were not "waters of the United States," the wetlands were "adjacent" to *remote* traditional navigable waters in virtue of the wetlands' "hydrological connection" to them. * * * This statement reflects the practice of the Corps' district offices, which may "assert jurisdiction over a wetland without regulating the ditch connecting it to a water of the United States." * * * We therefore address in this Part whether a wetland may be considered "adjacent to" remote "waters of the United States," because of a mere hydrologic connection to them.

In *Riverside Bayview,* we noted the textual difficulty in including "wetlands" as a subset of "waters": "On a purely linguistic level, it may appear unreasonable to classify 'lands,' wet or otherwise, as 'waters.' " * * * We acknowledged, however, that there was an inherent ambiguity in drawing the boundaries of any "waters":

> "[T]he Corps must necessarily choose some point at which water ends and land begins. Our common experience tells us that this is often no easy task: the transition from water to solid ground is not necessarily or even typically an abrupt one. Rather, between open waters and dry land may lie shallows, marshes, mudflats, swamps, bogs—in short, a huge array of areas that are not wholly aquatic but nevertheless fall far short of being dry land. Where on this continuum to find the limit of 'waters' is far from obvious." *Ibid.*

Because of this inherent ambiguity, we deferred to the agency's inclusion of wetlands "actually abut[ting]" traditional navigable waters: "Faced with such a problem of defining the bounds of its regulatory authority," we held, the agency could reasonably conclude that a wetland that "adjoin[ed]" waters of the United States is itself a part of those waters. * * * The difficulty of delineating the boundary between water and land was central to our reasoning in the case: "In view of the breadth of federal regulatory authority contemplated by the Act itself and *the inherent difficulties of defining precise bounds to regulable waters,* the Corps' ecological judgment about the relationship between waters and their adjacent wetlands provides an adequate basis for a legal judgment that adjacent wetlands may be defined as waters under the Act." * * *[3]

When we characterized the holding of *Riverside Bayview* in *SWANCC,* we referred to the close connection between waters and the wetlands that they gradually blend into: "It was the *significant nexus* between the wetlands and 'navigable waters' that informed our reading of the CWA in *Riverside Bayview Homes.*" * * * In particular, *SWANCC* rejected the notion that the ecological considerations upon which the Corps relied in *Riverside Bayview*—and upon which the dissent repeatedly relies today * * * provided an *independent* basis for including entities like "wetlands" (or "ephemeral streams") within the phrase "the waters of the United

---

3. Since the wetlands at issue in *Riverside Bayview* actually abutted waters of the United States, the case could not possibly have held that merely "neighboring" wetlands came within the Corps' jurisdiction. *Obiter* approval of that proposition might be inferred, however, from the opinion's quotation without comment of a statement by the Corps describing covered "adjacent" wetlands as those " 'that form the border of *or are in reasonable proximity to* other waters of the United States.' " * * * The opinion immediately reiterated, however, that adjacent wetlands could be regarded as "the waters of the United States" in view of "the inherent difficulties of defining precise bounds to regulable waters," * * *—a rationale that would have no application to physically separated "neighboring" wetlands. Given that the wetlands at issue in *Riverside Bayview* themselves "actually abut[ted] on a navigable waterway," * * * given that our opinion recognized that unconnected wetlands could not naturally be characterized as " 'waters' " at all, * * * and given the repeated reference to the difficulty of determining where waters end and wetlands begin; the most natural reading of the opinion is that a wetlands' mere "reasonable proximity" to waters of the United States is not enough to confer Corps jurisdiction. In any event, as discussed in our immediately following text, any possible ambiguity has been eliminated by *SWANCC* * * *.

States." *SWANCC* found such ecological considerations irrelevant to the question whether physically isolated waters come within the Corps' jurisdiction. It thus confirmed that *Riverside Bayview* rested upon the inherent ambiguity in defining where water ends and abutting ("adjacent") wetlands begin, permitting the Corps' reliance on ecological considerations *only to resolve that ambiguity* in favor of treating all abutting wetlands as waters. Isolated ponds were not "waters of the United States" in their own right * * * and presented no boundary-drawing problem that would have justified the invocation of ecological factors to treat them as such.

Therefore, *only* those wetlands with a continuous surface connection to bodies that are "waters of the United States" in their own right, so that there is no clear demarcation between "waters" and wetlands, are "adjacent to" such waters and covered by the Act. Wetlands with only an intermittent, physically remote hydrologic connection to "waters of the United States" do not implicate the boundary-drawing problem of *Riverside Bayview,* and thus lack the necessary connection to covered waters that we described as a "significant nexus" in *SWANCC.* * * * Thus, establishing that wetlands such as those at the Rapanos and Carabell sites are covered by the Act requires two findings: First, that the adjacent channel contains a "wate[r] of the United States," (*i.e.,* a relatively permanent body of water connected to traditional interstate navigable waters); and second, that the wetland has a continuous surface connection with that water, making it difficult to determine where the "water" ends and the "wetland" begins.

* * *

VIII

Because the Sixth Circuit applied the wrong standard to determine if these wetlands are covered "waters of the United States," and because of the paucity of the record in both of these cases, the lower courts should determine, in the first instance, whether the ditches or drains near each wetland are "waters" in the ordinary sense of containing a relatively permanent flow; and (if they are) whether the wetlands in question are "adjacent" to these "waters" in the sense of possessing a continuous surface connection that creates the boundary-drawing problem we addressed in *Riverside Bayview.*

* * *

We vacate the judgments of the Sixth Circuit in both No. 04–1034 and No. 04–1384, and remand both cases for further proceedings.

It is so ordered.

CHIEF JUSTICE ROBERTS, concurring.

* * *

It is unfortunate that no opinion commands a majority of the Court on precisely how to read Congress' limits on the reach of the Clean Water

Act. Lower courts and regulated entities will now have to feel their way on a case-by-case basis. * * *

JUSTICE KENNEDY, concurring in the judgment.

These consolidated cases require the Court to decide whether the term "navigable waters" in the Clean Water Act extends to wetlands that do not contain and are not adjacent to waters that are navigable in fact. In * * * [SWANCC] the Court held, under the circumstances presented there, that to constitute " 'navigable waters' " under the Act, a water or wetland must possess a "significant nexus" to waters that are or were navigable in fact or that could reasonably be so made. * * * In the instant cases neither the plurality opinion nor the dissent by Justice STEVENS chooses to apply this test; and though the Court of Appeals recognized the test's applicability, it did not consider all the factors necessary to determine whether the lands in question had, or did not have, the requisite nexus. In my view the cases ought to be remanded to the Court of Appeals for proper consideration of the nexus requirement.

* * *

II

Twice before the Court has construed the term "navigable waters" in the Clean Water Act. In * * * *Riverside Bayview Homes* * * * the Court upheld the Corps' jurisdiction over wetlands adjacent to navigable-in-fact waterways. * * * The property in *Riverside Bayview,* like the wetlands in the *Carabell* case now before the Court, was located roughly one mile from Lake St. Clair, though in that case, unlike *Carabell,* the lands at issue formed part of a wetland that directly abutted a navigable-in-fact creek, * * *. In regulatory provisions that remain in effect, the Corps had concluded that wetlands perform important functions such as filtering and purifying water draining into adjacent water bodies, * * * slowing the flow of runoff into lakes, rivers, and streams so as to prevent flooding and erosion, * * * and providing critical habitat for aquatic animal species, * * *. Recognizing that "[a]n agency's construction of a statute it is charged with enforcing is entitled to deference if it is reasonable and not in conflict with the expressed intent of Congress," * * * the Court held that "the Corps' ecological judgment about the relationship between waters and their adjacent wetlands provides an adequate basis for a legal judgment that adjacent wetlands may be defined as waters under the Act," * * *. The Court reserved, however, the question of the Corps' authority to regulate wetlands other than those adjacent to open waters. * * *

In *SWANCC*, the Court considered the validity of the Corps' jurisdiction over ponds and mudflats that were isolated in the sense of being unconnected to other waters covered by the Act. * * * The property at issue was an abandoned sand and gravel pit mining operation where "remnant excavation trenches" had "evolv[ed] into a scattering of permanent and seasonal ponds." * * * Asserting jurisdiction pursuant to a regulation called the "Migratory Bird Rule," the Corps argued that these isolated ponds were "waters of the United States" (and thus "navigable waters" under the Act) because they were used as habitat by migratory birds. * * * The Court rejected this theory. "It was the significant nexus between wetlands and 'navigable waters,'" the Court held, "that informed our reading of the [Act] in *Riverside Bayview Homes*." * * * Because such a nexus was lacking with respect to isolated ponds, the Court held that the plain text of the statute did not permit the Corps' action. * * *

Riverside Bayview and *SWANCC* establish the framework for the inquiry in the cases now before the Court: Do the Corps' regulations, as applied to the wetlands in *Carabell* and the three wetlands parcels in *Rapanos,* constitute a reasonable interpretation of "navigable waters" as in *Riverside Bayview* or an invalid construction as in *SWANCC?* Taken together these cases establish that in some instances, as exemplified by *Riverside Bayview,* the connection between a nonnavigable water or wetland and a navigable water may be so close, or potentially so close, that the Corps may deem the water or wetland a "navigable water" under the Act. In other instances, as exemplified by *SWANCC,* there may be little or no connection. Absent a significant nexus, jurisdiction under the Act is lacking. Because neither the plurality nor the dissent addresses the nexus requirement, this separate opinion, in my respectful view, is necessary.

A

* * *

[T]he plurality proceeds to impose two limitations on the Act; but these limitations, it is here submitted, are without support in the language and purposes of the Act or in our cases interpreting it. First, because the dictionary defines "waters" to mean "water '[a]s found in streams and bodies forming geographical features such as oceans, rivers, [and] lakes,' or 'the flowing or moving masses, as of waves or floods, making up such streams or bodies,'" * * * the plurality would conclude that the phrase "navigable waters" permits Corps and EPA jurisdiction only over "relatively permanent, standing or flowing bodies of water," * * * a category that in the plurality's view includes "seasonal" rivers, that is, rivers that carry water continuously except during "dry months," but not intermittent or ephemeral streams * * *. Second, the plurality asserts that wetlands fall within the Act only if they bear "a continuous surface connection to bodies that are "waters of the United States' in their own right"— waters, that is, that satisfy the plurality's requirement of permanent standing water or continuous flow. * * *

The plurality's first requirement—permanent standing water or continuous flow, at least for a period of "some months," * * * makes little practical sense in a statute concerned with downstream water quality. The merest trickle, if continuous, would count as a "water" subject to federal regulation, while torrents thundering at irregular intervals through otherwise dry channels would not. Though the plurality seems to presume that such irregular flows are too insignificant to be of concern in a statute focused on "waters," that may not always be true. Areas in the western parts of the Nation provide some examples. The Los Angeles River, for instance, ordinarily carries only a trickle of water and often looks more like a dry roadway than a river. * * * Yet it periodically releases water-volumes so powerful and destructive that it has been encased in concrete and steel over a length of some 50 miles. * * * Though this particular waterway might satisfy the plurality's test, it is illustrative of what often-dry watercourses can become when rain waters flow. * * *

To be sure, Congress could draw a line to exclude irregular water-ways, but nothing in the statute suggests it has done so. * * *

The plurality's second limitation-exclusion of wetlands lacking a continuous surface connection to other jurisdictional waters—is also unpersuasive. To begin with, the plurality is wrong to suggest that wetlands are *"indistinguishable"* from waters to which they bear a surface connection. * * * Even if the precise boundary may be imprecise, a bog or swamp is different from a river. The question is what circumstances permit a bog, swamp, or other nonnavigable wetland to constitute a "navigable water" under the Act—as § 1344(g)(1), if nothing else, indicates is sometimes possible * * *. *Riverside Bayview* addressed that question and its answer is inconsistent with the plurality's theory. There, in upholding the Corps' authority to regulate "wetlands adjacent to other bodies of water over which the Corps has jurisdiction," the Court deemed it irrelevant whether "the moisture creating the wetlands ... find[s] its source in the adjacent bodies of water." * * * The Court further observed that adjacency could serve as a valid basis for regulation even as to "wetlands that are not significantly intertwined with the ecosystem of adjacent waterways." * * * "If it is reasonable," the Court explained, "for the Corps to conclude that in the majority of cases, adjacent wetlands have significant effects on water quality and the aquatic ecosystem, its definition can stand." * * *

The Court in *Riverside Bayview* did note, it is true, the difficulty of defining where "water ends and land begins," * * * and the Court cited that problem as one reason for deferring to the Corps' view that adjacent wetlands could constitute waters. Given, however, the further recognition in *Riverside Bayview* that an overinclusive definition is permissible even when it reaches wetlands holding moisture disconnected from adjacent water-bodies, * * *. *Riverside Bayview's* observations about the difficulty of defining the water's edge cannot be taken to establish that when a clear boundary is evident, wetlands beyond the boundary fall outside the Corps' jurisdiction.

For the same reason *Riverside Bayview* also cannot be read as rejecting only the proposition, accepted by the Court of Appeals in that case, that wetlands covered by the Act must contain moisture originating in neighboring waterways. * * * Since the Court of Appeals had accepted that theory, the Court naturally addressed it. Yet to view the decision's reasoning as limited to that issue—an interpretation the plurality urges here, * * * would again overlook the opinion's broader focus on wetlands' "significant effects on water quality and the aquatic ecosystem," * * *. In any event, even were this reading of *Riverside Bayview* correct, it would offer no support for the plurality's proposed requirement of a "continuous surface connection," * * *. The Court in *Riverside Bayview* rejected the proposition that origination in flooding was necessary for jurisdiction over wetlands. It did not suggest that a flood—based origin would not support jurisdiction; indeed, it presumed the opposite. * * * Needless to say, a continuous connection is not necessary for moisture in wetlands to result from flooding—the connection might well exist only during floods.

SWANCC, likewise, does not support the plurality's surface-connection requirement. *SWANCC*'s holding that "nonnavigable, isolated, intrastate waters," * * * are not "navigable waters" is not an explicit or implicit overruling of *Riverside Bayview's* approval of adjacency as a factor in determining the Corps' jurisdiction. In rejecting the Corps' claimed authority over the isolated ponds in *SWANCC,* the Court distinguished adjacent nonnavigable waters such as the wetlands addressed in *Riverside Bayview.* * * *

As *Riverside Bayview* recognizes, the Corps' adjacency standard is reasonable in some of its applications. Indeed, the Corps' view draws support from the structure of the Act, while the plurality's surface-water-connection requirement does not.

* * *

B

While the plurality reads nonexistent requirements into the Act, the dissent reads a central requirement out—namely, the requirement that the word "navigable" in "navigable waters" be given some importance. Although the Court has held that the statute's language invokes Congress' traditional authority over waters navigable in fact or susceptible of being made so, * * * the dissent would permit federal regulation whenever wetlands lie alongside a ditch or drain, however remote and insubstantial, that eventually may flow into traditional navigable waters. The deference owed to the Corps' interpretation of the statute does not extend so far.

Congress' choice of words creates difficulties, for the Act contemplates regulation of certain "navigable waters" that are not in fact navigable. * * * Nevertheless, the word "navigable" in the Act must be given some effect. * * * Thus, in *SWANCC* the Court rejected the Corps' assertion of jurisdiction over isolated ponds and mudflats bearing no evident connection to navigable-in-fact waters. And in *Riverside Bayview,* while the Court indicated that "the term 'navigable' as used in the Act is of limited import," * * * it relied, in upholding jurisdiction, on the Corps' judgment that "wetlands adjacent to lakes, rivers, streams, and other bodies of water may function as integral parts of the aquatic environment even when the moisture creating the wetlands does not find its source in the adjacent bodies of water," * * *. The implication, of course, was that wetlands' status as "integral parts of the aquatic environment"—that is, their significant nexus with navigable waters—was what established the Corps' jurisdiction over them as waters of the United States.

Consistent with *SWANCC* and *Riverside Bayview* and with the need to give the term "navigable" some meaning, the Corps' jurisdiction over wetlands depends upon the existence of a significant nexus between the wetlands in question and navigable waters in the traditional sense. The required nexus must be assessed in terms of the statute's goals and purposes. Congress enacted the law to "restore and maintain the chemical, physical, and biological integrity of the Nation's waters," 33 U.S.C. § 1251(a), and it pursued that objective by restricting dumping and filling in "navigable waters," §§ 1311(a), 1362(12). With respect to wetlands, the rationale for Clean Water Act regulation is, as the Corps has recognized, that wetlands can perform critical functions related to the integrity of other waters—functions such as pollutant trapping, flood control, and runoff storage. 33 CFR § 320.4(b)(2). Accordingly, wetlands possess the requisite nexus, and thus come within the statutory phrase "navigable waters," if the wetlands, either alone or in combination with similarly situated lands in the region, significantly affect the chemical, physical, and biological integrity of other covered waters more readily understood as "navigable." When, in contrast, wetlands' effects on water quality are speculative or insubstantial, they fall outside the zone fairly encompassed by the statutory term "navigable waters."

Although the dissent acknowledges that wetlands' ecological functions vis-á-vis other covered waters are the basis for the Corps' regulation of them, * * * it concludes that the ambiguity in the phrase "navigable waters" allows the Corps to construe the statute as reaching all "non-isolated wetlands," just as it construed the Act to reach the wetlands adjacent to navigable-in-fact waters in *Riverside Bayview* * * *. This, though, seems incorrect. The Corps' theory of jurisdiction in these consolidated cases—adjacency to tributaries, however remote and insubstantial—raises concerns that go beyond the holding of *Riverside Bayview;* and so the Corps' assertion of jurisdiction cannot rest on that case.

As applied to wetlands adjacent to navigable-in-fact waters, the Corps' conclusive standard for jurisdiction rests upon a reasonable inference of ecologic interconnection, and the assertion of jurisdiction for those wetlands is sustainable under the Act by showing adjacency alone. That is the holding of *Riverside Bayview.* Furthermore, although the *Riverside Bayview* Court reserved the question of the Corps' authority over "wetlands that are not adjacent to bodies of open water," * * * and in any event addressed no factual situation other than wetlands adjacent to navigable-in-fact waters, it may well be the case that *Riverside Bayview's* reasoning—supporting jurisdiction without any inquiry beyond adjacency—could apply equally to wetlands adjacent to certain major tributaries. Through regulations or adjudication, the Corps may choose to identify categories of tributaries that, due to their volume of flow (either annually or on average), their proximity to navigable waters, or other relevant considerations, are significant enough that wetlands adjacent to them are likely, in the majority of cases, to perform important functions for an aquatic system incorporating navigable waters.

The Corps' existing standard for tributaries, however, provides no such assurance. As noted earlier, the Corps deems a water a tributary if it feeds into a traditional navigable water (or a tributary thereof) and possesses an ordinary high-water mark, defined as a "line on the shore established by the fluctuations of water and indicated by [certain] physical characteristics," § 328.3(e). * * * This standard presumably provides a rough measure of the volume and regularity of flow. Assuming it is subject to reasonably consistent application, * * * it may well provide a reasonable measure of whether specific minor tributaries bear a sufficient nexus with other regulated waters to constitute "navigable waters" under the Act. Yet the breadth of this standard—which seems to leave wide room for regulation of drains, ditches, and streams remote from any navigable-in-fact water and carrying only minor water-volumes towards it-precludes its adoption as the determinative measure of whether adjacent wetlands are likely to play an important role in the integrity of an aquatic system comprising navigable waters as traditionally understood. Indeed, in many cases wetlands adjacent to tributaries covered by this standard might appear little more related to navigable-in-fact waters than were the isolated ponds held to fall beyond the Act's scope in *SWANCC*. * * *

When the Corps seeks to regulate wetlands adjacent to navigable-in-fact waters, it may rely on adjacency to establish its jurisdiction. Absent more specific regulations, however, the Corps must establish a significant nexus on a case-by-case basis when it seeks to regulate wetlands based on adjacency to nonnavigable tributaries. Given the potential overbreadth of the Corps' regulations, this showing is necessary to avoid unreasonable applications of the statute. * * *

III

In both the consolidated cases before the Court the record contains evidence suggesting the possible existence of a significant nexus according to the principles outlined above. Thus the end result in these cases and many others to be considered by the Corps may be the same as that suggested by the dissent, namely, that the Corps' assertion of jurisdiction is valid. Given, however, that neither the agency nor the reviewing courts properly considered the issue, a remand is appropriate, in my view, for application of the controlling legal standard.

* * *

In these consolidated cases I would vacate the judgments of the Court of Appeals and remand for consideration whether the specific wetlands at issue possess a significant nexus with navigable waters.

JUSTICE STEVENS, with whom JUSTICE SOUTER, JUSTICE GINSBURG, and JUSTICE BREYER join, dissenting.

* * *

The narrow question presented in No. 04–1034 is whether wetlands adjacent to tributaries of traditionally navigable waters are "waters of the United States" subject to the jurisdiction of the Army Corps; the question in No. 04–1384 is whether a manmade berm separating a wetland from the adjacent tributary makes a difference. The broader question is whether regulations that have protected the quality of our waters for decades, that were implicitly approved by Congress, and that have been repeatedly enforced in case after case, must now be revised in light of the creative criticisms voiced by the plurality and Justice KENNEDY today. Rejecting more than 30 years of practice by the Army Corps, the plurality disregards the nature of the congressional delegation to the agency and the technical and complex character of the issues at stake. Justice KENNEDY similarly fails to defer sufficiently to the Corps, though his approach is far more faithful to our precedents and to principles of statutory interpretation than is the plurality's.

In my view, the proper analysis is straightforward. The Army Corps has determined that wetlands adjacent to tributaries of traditionally navigable waters preserve the quality of our Nation's waters by, among other things, providing habitat for aquatic animals, keeping excessive sediment and toxic pollutants out of adjacent waters, and reducing downstream flooding by absorbing water at times of high flow. The Corps' resulting decision to treat these wetlands as encompassed within the term "waters of the United States" is a quintessential example of the Executive's reasonable interpretation of a statutory provision. * * *

* * *

IV

While I generally agree with Parts I and II–A of Justice KENNEDY's opinion, I do not share his view that we should replace regulatory standards that have been in place for over 30 years with a judicially crafted rule distilled from the term "significant nexus" as used in *SWANCC*. To the extent that our passing use of this term has become a statutory requirement, it is categorically satisfied as to wetlands adjacent to navigable waters or their tributaries. *Riverside Bayview* and *SWANCC* together make this clear. *SWANCC's* only use of the term comes in the sentence: "It was the significant nexus between the wetlands and 'navigable waters' that informed our reading of the [Clean Water Act] in *Riverside Bayview*." * * * Because *Riverside Bayview* was written to encompass "wetlands adjacent to navigable waters and their tributaries," * * * and reserved only the question of isolated waters, * * * its determination of the Corps' jurisdiction applies to the wetlands at issue in these cases.

Even setting aside the apparent applicability of *Riverside Bayview*. I think it clear that wetlands adjacent to tributaries of navigable waters generally have a "significant nexus" with the traditionally navigable waters downstream. Unlike the "nonnavigable, isolated, intrastate waters" in *SWANCC,* * * * these wetlands can obviously have a cumulative effect on downstream water flow by releasing waters at times of low flow or by keeping waters back at times of high flow. This logical connection alone gives the wetlands the "limited" connection to traditionally navigable waters that is all the statute requires, * * * and disproves Justice KENNEDY's claim that my approach gives no meaning to the word " 'navigable,' " * * *.

V

* * * While Justice KENNEDY's approach has far fewer faults, nonetheless it also fails to give proper deference to the agencies entrusted by Congress to implement the Clean Water Act.

I would affirm the judgments in both cases, and respectfully dissent from the decision of five Members of this Court to vacate and remand. I close, however, by noting an unusual feature of the Court's judgments in these cases. It has been our practice in a case coming to us from a lower federal court to enter a judgment commanding that court to conduct any further proceedings pursuant to a specific mandate. That prior practice has, on occasion, made it necessary for Justices to join a judgment that did not conform to their own views. In these cases, however, while both the plurality and Justice KENNEDY agree that there must be a remand for further proceedings, their respective opinions define different tests to be applied on remand. Given that all four Justices who have joined this opinion would uphold the Corps' jurisdiction in both of these cases-and in all other cases in which either the plurality's or Justice KENNEDY's test is satisfied-on remand each of the judgments should be reinstated if *either* of those tests is met.

JUSTICE BREYER, dissenting.

In my view, the authority of the Army Corps of Engineers under the Clean Water Act extends to the limits of congressional power to regulate interstate commerce. * * * I therefore have no difficulty finding that the wetlands at issue in these cases are within the Corps' jurisdiction, and I join Justice STEVENS' dissenting opinion.

* * *

NOTES

1. In *Riverside Bayview Homes* the Court noted: "We are not called upon to address the question of the authority of the Corps to regulate discharges of fill material into wetlands that are not adjacent to bodies of open water * * * and we do not express any opinion on that question." 474 U.S. at 131, n.8. The Court had the opportunity to address this issue in Solid

Waste Agency of Northern Cook County v. U.S. Army Corps of Engineers, 531 U.S. 159 (2001) ("SWANCC"), but chose to limit its holding to the propriety of the Corps' migratory bird rule. See note 2 below. However, the Court offered the following comments regarding the scope of the Corps' § 404 jurisdiction:

> We thus decline * * * [the Corps'] invitation to take what they see as the next ineluctable step after *Riverside Bayview Homes*: holding that isolated ponds, some only seasonal, wholly located within two Illinois counties, fall under § 404(a)'s definition of 'navigable waters' because they serve as habitat for migratory birds * * * We cannot agree that Congress' separate definitional use of the phrase 'waters of the United States' constitutes a basis for reading the term 'navigable waters' out of the statute * * * The term 'navigable' has at least the import of showing us what Congress had in mind as its authority for enacting the CWA: its traditional jurisdiction over waters that were or had been navigable in fact or which could reasonably be so made.

SWANCC, 531 U.S. at 171–72.

2.   In *SWANCC* the Corps asserted § 404 jurisdiction over an abandoned gravel mining site which was used as a habitat for migratory birds. The Corps relied upon a 1986 "clarification" of its regulations defining the scope of § 404(a) to include intrastate waters: "Which are or would be used as habitat by birds protected by Migratory Bird Treaties" or "Which are or would be used as habitat by other migratory birds which cross state lines * * *." This is known as the Corps' "Migratory Bird Rule." The Court invalidated the Migratory Bird Rule holding that the mere presence of migratory birds on a body of water does not make it "waters of the United States." There still must be some nexus between the body of water and "navigable waters." See John W. Broomes, Note, Navigating in Isolated Waters: Section 404 of the Clean Water Act Revisited, 41 Washburn L. J. 209 (2001) (observing the Court arrived at the right conclusion but failed to use "the richest sources of support for the holding" consisting of "strong legislative history" applying what key legislators referred to as the "highway test" to define navigable waters under the CWA).

3.   Most United States Courts of Appeals, when seeking to identify "waters of the United States" and adjacent wetlands, have applied the *Marks* rule, also known as the "narrowest-grounds-rule", which has been explained as follows: "When a majority of the Supreme Court agrees only on the outcome of a case and not on the grounds for that outcome, 'the holding of the Court may be viewed as that position taken by those Members who concurred in the judgments on the narrowest grounds.' " United States v. Bailey, 571 F.3d 791, 798 (8th Cir.Minn. 2009). The *Bailey* case reviews the approaches taken by the Courts of Appeals as of 2008 noting: "Because there is little overlap between the plurality's and Justice Kennedy's opinions, it is difficult to determine which holding is the narrowest." *Id.* The 7th, 9th, and 11th Circuits have concluded Justice Kennedy's opinion is the "narrowest" because it is least limiting on federal authority to assert jurisdiction over wetlands. "Thus if a wetland meets the substantial nexus test, the federal authority has jurisdiction to regulate the wetland under the Act." *Id.* However, the 7th and

9th Circuits did not foreclose the possibility that the plurality's test might apply in some cases. The 1st Circuit decided the Marks rule was unworkable in light of the differing tests and therefore it will find jurisdiction to act "if either the plurality's test or Justice Kennedy's test is met." *Id.* at 799.

4. Section 404(f) excludes certain land uses, such as existing "normal farming, silviculture, and ranching activities," from the § 404 permitting process. 33 U.S.C. § 1344(f). However, absent an exclusion, whenever an activity is proposed on jurisdictional "wetlands" an individual § 404 permit, or coverage by a "nationwide" permit, will be required. If an individual § 404 permit is required, the issuance of a permit may be considered a major federal action significantly impacting the environment which will trigger the environmental assessment/environmental impact statement process under the National Environmental Policy Act ("NEPA"). 42 U.S.C. § 4332(C).[14] Regulations governing the Corps' administration of its NEPA obligations can assist in predicting whether an environmental assessment or impact statement will be required.[15] Pursuant to § 404(e) of the CWA the Corps has created a number of nationwide permits designed to streamline, to varying degrees, compliance with § 404. The current version of the Corps' nationwide permit program is contained in: "Reissuance of Nationwide Permits; Final Notice," 77 Fed.Reg. 10184 (Feb. 21, 2012). This regulation authorizes 48 categories of Nationwide Permits, including, for example, Nationwide Permit No. 8 "Oil and Gas Structures on the Outer Continental Shelf." 77 Fed. Reg. at 10271. See generally David E. Pierce, Assessing Thirty Years of Federal Environmental Regulation of Upstream Oil and Gas Activities, 50 Inst. Oil and Gas L. & Tax'n 5–1, 5–5 to 5–11 (1999). For a comprehensive treatment of this topic see: Special Institute Manual on Water Quality & Wetlands: Regulation and Management in the Development of Natural Resources, Rocky Mountain Mineral Law Foundation (Jan. 2002) (available through rmmlf.org).

5. Often the first time an owner discovers they may be filling a "wetland" is when they receive a notice of violation and an order directing that the affected land be restored to its previous condition. The violation gives rise to a potential daily fine of $37,500 and a failure to comply with the restoration order adds an additional daily fine of $37,500, for a total fine of $75,000 for each day the owner fails to act. The EPA has taken the position, supported by several federal courts, that a compliance order is not subject to judicial review. The United States Supreme Court, in *Sackett v. Environmental Protection Agency*, 132 S.Ct. 1367 (2012), held the party receiving a compliance order is able to seek judicial review under the Administrative Procedure Act to determine whether the lands are "wetlands" subject to the EPA's jurisdiction. The Court leaves for another day whether it will allow pre-enforcement review of the terms and conditions of a compliance order. Most of

14. NEPA is also discussed in Chapter 7. For a thorough discussion of the NEPA process as it applies to oil and gas operations see: Ezekiel J. Williams & Kathy Schaeffer, What Every Land Professional Should Know About NEPA, 53 Rocky Mtn. Min. L. Inst. 4–1 (2007).

15. 33 C.F.R. §§ 230.1 to 230.26. For example, § 230.7 identifies activities that normally require an environmental assessment but not necessarily an environmental impact statement. Section 230.9 contains a list of the Corps' "categorical exclusions" for activities which, under normal circumstances, should not require an assessment or impact statement. For example, § 230.9(i)(4) excludes rights-of-way for "[o]il and gas seismic and gravity meter survey for exploration purposes."

the environmental statutes discussed in this chapter provide for some form of compliance order procedure coupled with fines of up to $37,500 per day. Although the jurisdictional issue may not be as nebulous as the Clean Water Act's "waters of the United States," the *Sackett* decision will be used to seek judicial review of compliance orders under other environmental statutes.

6. What happens if an oil and gas lessee discovers their drill site is located in a wetland area and there is insufficient time remaining in the primary term to obtain the necessary § 404 permit to begin operations? See Erickson v. Dart Oil & Gas Corp., 474 N.W.2d 150 (Mich.App.1991) (lessee needed wetlands permit to construct road to access drill site; lease was not extended by force majeure clause and terminated at the end of the primary term).

7. What if an activity on a "wetland" adversely impacts an endangered species?

(b) Species Protection

The presence of an endangered species can have significant land use implications. Often the major cause of species extinction is alteration of its habitat.[16] Therefore, once a species is found to be endangered its protection will depend, in part, upon controlling development activities taking place in areas necessary for its life cycle. These essential feeding, breeding, and sheltering areas frequently encompass private lands.

PROBLEM

Suppose an oil and gas developer obtains oil and gas leases covering land outside Austin, Texas. The developer is unaware that the black-capped vireo, a small bird, is known to inhabit the area. The black-capped vireo is a listed endangered species[17] known to exist in the Austin area.[18] What impact does the potential presence of the black-capped vireo have on the ability to develop the oil and gas leases?

BABBITT v. SWEET HOME CH. OF COMMUN. FOR GREAT OR.
515 U.S. 687 (1995).

JUSTICE STEVENS delivered the opinion of the Court.

The Endangered Species Act of 1973, 87 Stat. 884, 16 U.S.C. § 1531 (1988 ed. and Supp. V) (ESA or Act), contains a variety of protections

---

16. The first Congressional finding under the Endangered Species Act is that "various species of fish, wildlife, and plants in the United States have been rendered extinct as a consequence of economic growth and development * * *." 16 U.S.C. § 1531(a)(1). The process for determining whether a species is endangered, or threatened, considers, among other factors, "the present or threatened destruction, modification, or curtailment of its habitat or range * * *." Id. at § 1533(a)(1)(A).

17. 50 C.F.R. § 17.11(h).

18. "Endangered and Threatened Wildlife and Plants; Determination of the Black-capped Vireo to be an Endangered Species," 52 Fed.Reg. 37420, 37421 (Oct. 6, 1987) (the Austin area contains the largest known concentration of black-capped vireos).

designed to save from extinction species that the Secretary of the Interior designates as endangered or threatened. Section 9 of the Act makes it unlawful for any person to "take" any endangered or threatened species. The Secretary has promulgated a regulation that defines the statute's prohibition on takings to include "significant habitat modification or degradation where it actually kills or injures wildlife." This case presents the question whether the Secretary exceeded his authority under the Act by promulgating that regulation.

I

Section 9(a)(1) of the Endangered Species Act provides the following protection for endangered species:[1]

> "Except as provided in sections 1535(g)(2) and 1539 of this title, with respect to any endangered species of fish or wildlife listed pursuant to section 1533 of this title it is unlawful for any person subject to the jurisdiction of the United States to—

> * * *

> "(B) take any such species within the United States or the territorial sea of the United States[.]" 16 U.S.C. § 1538(a)(1).

Section 3(19) of the Act defines the statutory term "take":

> "The term 'take' means to harass, harm, pursue, hunt, shoot, wound, kill, trap, capture, or collect, or to attempt to engage in any such conduct." 16 U.S.C. § 1532(19).

The Act does not further define the terms it uses to define "take." The Interior Department regulations that implement the statute, however, define the statutory term "harm":

> "*Harm* in the definition of 'take' in the Act means an act which actually kills or injures wildlife. Such act may include significant habitat modification or degradation where it actually kills or injures wildlife by significantly impairing essential behavioral patterns, including breeding, feeding, or sheltering." 50 CFR § 17.3 (1994).

This regulation has been in place since 1975.[2]

A limitation on the § 9 "take" prohibition appears in § 10(a)(1)(B) of the Act, which Congress added by amendment in 1982. That section authorizes the Secretary to grant a permit for any taking otherwise prohibited by § 9(a)(1)(B) "if such taking is incidental to, and not the purpose of, the carrying out of an otherwise lawful activity." 16 U.S.C. § 1539(a)(1)(B).

---

1. The Act defines the term "endangered species" to mean "any species which is in danger of extinction throughout all or a significant portion of its range other than a species of the Class Insecta determined by the Secretary to constitute a pest whose protection under the provisions of this chapter would present an overwhelming and overriding risk to man." 16 U.S.C. § 1532(6).

2. The Secretary, through the Director of the Fish and Wildlife Service, originally promulgated the regulation in 1975 and amended it in 1981 to emphasize that actual death or injury of a protected animal is necessary for a violation. See 40 Fed.Reg. 44412, 44416 (1975); 46 Fed.Reg. 54748, 54750 (1981).

In addition to the prohibition on takings, the Act provides several other protections for endangered species. Section 4, 16 U.S.C. § 1533, commands the Secretary to identify species of fish or wildlife that are in danger of extinction and to publish from time to time lists of all species he determines to be endangered or threatened. Section 5, 16 U.S.C. § 1534, authorizes the Secretary, in cooperation with the States, see 16 U.S.C. § 1535, to acquire land to aid in preserving such species. Section 7 requires federal agencies to ensure that none of their activities, including the granting of licenses and permits, will jeopardize the continued existence of endangered species "or result in the destruction or adverse modification of habitat of such species which is determined by the Secretary ... to be critical." 16 U.S.C. § 1536(a)(2).

Respondents in this action are small landowners, logging companies, and families dependent on the forest products industries in the Pacific Northwest and in the Southeast, and organizations that represent their interests. They brought this declaratory judgment action against petitioners, the Secretary of the Interior and the Director of the Fish and Wildlife Service, in the United States District Court for the District of Columbia to challenge the statutory validity of the Secretary's regulation defining "harm," particularly the inclusion of habitat modification and degradation in the definition. * * * Respondents challenged the regulation on its face. Their complaint alleged that application of the "harm" regulation to the red-cockaded woodpecker, an endangered species,[3] and the northern spotted owl, a threatened species,[4] had injured them economically. App. 17–23.

Respondents advanced three arguments to support their submission that Congress did not intend the word "take" in § 9 to include habitat modification, as the Secretary's "harm" regulation provides. First, they correctly noted that language in the Senate's original version of the ESA would have defined "take" to include "destruction, modification, or curtailment of [the] habitat or range" of fish or wildlife, * * * but the Senate deleted that language from the bill before enacting it. Second, respondents argued that Congress intended the Act's express authorization for the Federal Government to buy private land in order to prevent habitat degradation in § 5 to be the exclusive check against habitat modification on private property. Third, because the Senate added the term "harm" to the definition of "take" in a floor amendment without debate, respondents argued that the court should not interpret the term so expansively as to include habitat modification.

---

3. The woodpecker was listed as an endangered species in 1970 pursuant to the statutory predecessor of the ESA. See 50 CFR § 17.11(h) (1994), issued pursuant to the Endangered Species Conservation Act of 1969, 83 Stat. 275.

4. See 55 Fed.Reg. 26114 (1990). Another regulation promulgated by the Secretary extends to threatened species, defined in the ESA as "any species which is likely to become an endangered species within the foreseeable future throughout all or a significant portion of its range," 16 U.S.C. § 1532(20), some but not all of the protections endangered species enjoy. See 50 CFR 17.31(a) (1994). In the District Court respondents unsuccessfully challenged that regulation's extension of § 9 to threatened species, but they do not press the challenge here.

The District Court considered and rejected each of respondents' arguments, finding "that Congress intended an expansive interpretation of the word 'take,' an interpretation that encompasses habitat modification." 806 F.Supp. 279, 285 (1992). * * *

A divided panel of the Court of Appeals initially affirmed the judgment of the District Court. 1 F.3d 1 (C.A.D.C.1993). After granting a petition for rehearing, however, the panel reversed. 17 F.3d 1463 (C.A.D.C.1994). Although acknowledging that "[t]he potential breadth of the word 'harm' is indisputable," *id.*, at 1464, the majority concluded that the immediate statutory context in which "harm" appeared counseled against a broad reading; like the other words in the definition of "take," the word "harm" should be read as applying only to "the perpetrator's direct application of force against the animal taken. . . . * * *"

* * *

The Court of Appeals' decision created a square conflict with a 1988 decision of the Ninth Circuit that had upheld the Secretary's definition of "harm." See *Palila v. Hawaii Dept. of Land and Natural Resources*, 852 F.2d 1106 (1988) (*Palila II*). The Court of Appeals neither cited nor distinguished *Palila II*, despite the stark contrast between the Ninth Circuit's holding and its own. We granted certiorari to resolve the conflict. 513 U.S. 1072, 115 S.Ct. 714, 130 L.Ed.2d 621 (1995). Our consideration of the text and structure of the Act, its legislative history, and the significance of the 1982 amendment persuades us that the Court of Appeals' judgment should be reversed.

II

Because this case was decided on motions for summary judgment, we may appropriately make certain factual assumptions in order to frame the legal issue. First, we assume respondents have no desire to harm either the red-cockaded woodpecker or the spotted owl; they merely wish to continue logging activities that would be entirely proper if not prohibited by the ESA. On the other hand, we must assume *arguendo* that those activities will have the effect, even though unintended, of detrimentally changing the natural habitat of both listed species and that, as a consequence, members of those species will be killed or injured. Under respondents' view of the law, the Secretary's only means of forestalling that grave result—even when the actor knows it is certain to occur * * *—is to use his § 5 authority to purchase the lands on which the survival of the species depends. The Secretary, on the other hand, submits that the § 9 prohibition on takings, which Congress defined to include "harm," places on respondents a duty to avoid harm that habitat alteration will cause the birds unless respondents first obtain a permit pursuant to § 10.

The text of the Act provides three reasons for concluding that the Secretary's interpretation is reasonable. First, an ordinary understanding of the word "harm" supports it. The dictionary definition of the verb form of "harm" is "to cause hurt or damage to: injure." Webster's Third New

International Dictionary 1034 (1966). In the context of the ESA, that definition naturally encompasses habitat modification that results in actual injury or death to members of an endangered or threatened species.

Respondents argue that the Secretary should have limited the purview of "harm" to direct applications of force against protected species, but the dictionary definition does not include the word "directly" or suggest in any way that only direct or willful action that leads to injury constitutes "harm." * * * Moreover, unless the statutory term "harm" encompasses indirect as well as direct injuries, the word has no meaning that does not duplicate the meaning of other words that § 3 uses to define "take." A reluctance to treat statutory terms as surplusage supports the reasonableness of the Secretary's interpretation. * * *

Second, the broad purpose of the ESA supports the Secretary's decision to extend protection against activities that cause the precise harms Congress enacted the statute to avoid. In *TVA v. Hill*, 437 U.S. 153, 98 S.Ct. 2279, 57 L.Ed.2d 117 (1978), we described the Act as "the most comprehensive legislation for the preservation of endangered species ever enacted by any nation." *Id.*, at 180, 98 S.Ct., at 2294. Whereas predecessor statutes enacted in 1966 and 1969 had not contained any sweeping prohibition against the taking of endangered species except on federal lands, see *id.*, at 175, 98 S.Ct., at 2292, the 1973 Act applied to all land in the United States and to the Nation's territorial seas. As stated in § 2 of the Act, among its central purposes is "to provide a means whereby the ecosystems upon which endangered species and threatened species depend may be conserved. . . ." §§ 16 U.S.C. § 1531(b).

In *Hill*, we construed § 7 as precluding the completion of the Tellico Dam because of its predicted impact on the survival of the snail darter. See 437 U.S., at 193, 98 S.Ct., at 2301. Both our holding and the language in our opinion stressed the importance of the statutory policy. "The plain intent of Congress in enacting this statute," we recognized, "was to halt and reverse the trend toward species extinction, whatever the cost. This is reflected not only in the stated policies of the Act, but in literally every section of the statute." *Id.*, at 184, 98 S.Ct., at 2297. Although the § 9 "take" prohibition was not at issue in Hill, we took note of that prohibition, placing particular emphasis on the Secretary's inclusion of habitat modification in his definition of "harm."[5] In light of that provision for habitat protection, we could "not understand how TVA intends to operate Tellico Dam without 'harming' the snail darter." *Id.*, at 184, n. 30, 98 S.Ct., at 2297. Congress' intent to provide comprehensive protection for endangered and threatened species supports the permissibility of the Secretary's "harm" regulation.

---

5. We stated: "The Secretary of the Interior has defined the term 'harm' to mean 'an act or omission which actually injures or kills wildlife', including acts which annoy it to such an extent as to significantly disrupt essential behavioral patterns, which include, but are not limited to, breeding, feeding or sheltering; *significant environmental modification or degradation* which has such effects is included within the meaning of 'harm.' " *TVA v. Hill*, 437 U.S. 153, 184–185, n. 30, 98 S.Ct. 2279, 2297, n. 30, 57 L.Ed.2d 117 (1978) (citations omitted; emphasis in original).

* * * Given Congress' clear expression of the ESA's broad purpose to protect endangered and threatened wildlife, the Secretary's definition of "harm" is reasonable. * * *

Third, the fact that Congress in 1982 authorized the Secretary to issue permits for takings that § 9(a)(1)(B) would otherwise prohibit, "if such taking is incidental to, and not the purpose of, the carrying out of an otherwise lawful activity," 16 U.S.C. § 1539(a)(1)(B), strongly suggests that Congress understood § 9(a)(1)(B) to prohibit indirect as well as deliberate takings. * * * The permit process requires the applicant to prepare a "conservation plan" that specifies how he intends to "minimize and mitigate" the "impact" of his activity on endangered and threatened species, 16 U.S.C. § 1539(a)(2)(A), making clear that Congress had in mind foreseeable rather than merely accidental effects on listed species. * * * No one could seriously request an "incidental" take permit to avert § 9 liability for direct, deliberate action against a member of an endangered or threatened species, but respondents would read "harm" so narrowly that the permit procedure would have little more than that absurd purpose. * * * Congress' addition of the § 10 permit provision supports the Secretary's conclusion that activities not intended to harm an endangered species, such as habitat modification, may constitute unlawful takings under the ESA unless the Secretary permits them.

* * *

Nor does the Act's inclusion of the § 5 land acquisition authority and the § 7 directive to federal agencies to avoid destruction or adverse modification of critical habitat alter our conclusion. Respondents' argument that the Government lacks any incentive to purchase land under § 5 when it can simply prohibit takings under § 9 ignores the practical considerations that attend enforcement of the ESA. Purchasing habitat lands may well cost the Government less in many circumstances than pursuing civil or criminal penalties. In addition, the § 5 procedure allows for protection of habitat before the seller's activity has harmed any endangered animal, whereas the Government cannot enforce the § 9 prohibition until an animal has actually been killed or injured. The Secretary may also find the § 5 authority useful for preventing modification of land that is not yet but may in the future become habitat for an endangered or threatened species. The § 7 directive applies only to the Federal Government, whereas the § 9 prohibition applies to "any person." Section 7 imposes a broad, affirmative duty to avoid adverse habitat modifications that § 9 does not replicate, and § 7 does not limit its admonition to habitat modification that "actually kills or injures wildlife." Conversely, § 7 contains limitations that § 9 does not, applying only to actions "likely to jeopardize the continued existence of any endangered species or threatened species," 16 U.S.C. § 1536(a)(2), and to modifications of habitat that has been designated "critical" pursuant to § 4, 16 U.S.C. § 1533(b)(2). * * * Any overlap that § 5 or § 7 may have with § 9 in particular cases is unexceptional, * * * and simply reflects the broad purpose of the Act set out in § 2 and acknowledged in *TVA v. Hill.*

* * *

III

Our conclusion that the Secretary's definition of "harm" rests on a permissible construction of the ESA gains further support from the legislative history of the statute. * * *

* * *

The history of the 1982 amendment that gave the Secretary authority to grant permits for "incidental" takings provides further support for his reading of the Act. The House Report expressly states that "[b]y use of the word 'incidental' the Committee intends to cover situations in which it is known that a taking will occur if the other activity is engaged in but such taking is incidental to, and not the purpose of, the activity." * * * This reference to the foreseeability of incidental takings undermines respondents' argument that the 1982 amendment covered only accidental killings of endangered and threatened animals that might occur in the course of hunting or trapping other animals. Indeed, Congress had habitat modification directly in mind: both the Senate Report and the House Conference Report identified as the model for the permit process a cooperative state-federal response to a case in California where a development project threatened incidental harm to a species of endangered butterfly by modification of its habitat. * * * Thus, Congress in 1982 focused squarely on the aspect of the "harm" regulation at issue in this litigation. Congress' implementation of a permit program is consistent with the Secretary's interpretation of the term "harm."

IV

When it enacted the ESA, Congress delegated broad administrative and interpretive power to the Secretary. See 16 U.S.C. §§ 1533, 1540(f). The task of defining and listing endangered and threatened species requires an expertise and attention to detail that exceeds the normal province of Congress. Fashioning appropriate standards for issuing permits under § 10 for takings that would otherwise violate § 9 necessarily requires the exercise of broad discretion. The proper interpretation of a term such as "harm" involves a complex policy choice. When Congress has entrusted the Secretary with broad discretion, we are especially reluctant to substitute our views of wise policy for his. * * * In this case, that reluctance accords with our conclusion, based on the text, structure, and legislative history of the ESA, that the Secretary reasonably construed the intent of Congress when he defined "harm" to include "significant habitat modification or degradation that actually kills or injures wildlife."

In the elaboration and enforcement of the ESA, the Secretary and all persons who must comply with the law will confront difficult questions of proximity and degree; for, as all recognize, the Act encompasses a vast range of economic and social enterprises and endeavors. These questions must be addressed in the usual course of the law, through case-by-case resolution and adjudication.

The judgment of the Court of Appeals is reversed.

It is so ordered.

NOTES

1.   Building on the Problem, would the construction of a lease road and drill site constitute a "take" of the black-capped vireo that is prohibited by § 9 of the ESA? Must the activity result in actual injury to the black-capped vireo or will the mere potential for injury be sufficient?

2.   In addition to listing the endangered species, § 4(a)(3) directs the Secretary, "to the maximum extent prudent and determinable", to concurrently "designate any habitat of such species which is then considered to be critical habitat * * *." 16 U.S.C. § 1533(a)(3)(A). The ESA defines "critical habitat" to include the areas actually occupied by the species at the time it is listed plus areas necessary for its conservation. Id. at § 1532(5)(A). Noting the important role of the critical habitat designation, Professor Rodgers observes in his treatise:

> The designation of critical habitat is a pivotal issue for the biological reason that habitat is *the* crucial parameter for species survival, for the legal reason that critical habitat is protected from impairment or modification under Section 7, and for the political reason that the geography staked out as "critical" suddenly is burdened by servitudes for the benefit of the protected species.

William H. Rodgers, Jr., Environmental Law § 9.9, 1007. Despite the importance of critical habitat designation, it appears most endangered species are listed without ever having a critical habitat designated.[19] For example, the black-capped vireo was listed in 1987 and no critical habitat was designated at that time or since. When listed, the Fish and Wildlife Service determined:

> [T]here is no demonstrable benefit to the vireo in designating critical habitat and therefore such an action is not prudent. The habitat of the black-capped vireo occurs in scattered, small patches; occupied habitat would be difficult to delineate and may vary over time due to succession. Service recovery actions will continuously update and address the vireo's habitat management needs. In addition, * * * the black-capped vireo is popular among bird-watchers. Possible increased harassment could occur due to the publication of critical habitat maps.[20]

Although the designation of critical habitat could assist developers in defining areas known to be impacted by the presence of an endangered species, designation is not necessary for protection offered by § 9 of the ESA. The

---

19.   See Oliver Houck, The Endangered Species Act and Its Implementation by the U.S. Departments of Interior and Commerce, 64 Colo.L.Rev. 277, 302 (1993) (16% of listed species have critical habitat designations).

20.   52 Fed.Reg. at 37422.

actual presence of the endangered species will trigger § 9 whether it is within a critical habitat area or somewhere else.

3.   Building on the question posed in note 1, if the oil and gas developer is aware that their activities are likely to "harass, harm, * * * wound, [or] kill" the black-capped vireo, they will need to consider applying for an "incidental take" permit under § 10 of the ESA which provides, in part: "The Secretary may permit, under such terms and conditions as he shall pre-scribe—* * * (B) any taking otherwise prohibited by section 1538(a)(1)(B) of this title [§ 9] if such taking is incidental to, and not the purpose of, the carrying out of an otherwise lawful activity." 16 U.S.C. § 1539(a)(B). The permit process requires a detailed application which the Secretary will use to make specific findings concerning the request. Id. at § 1539(a)(2). See also 50 C.F.R. § 17.22(b) (incidental take permit requirements). Large-impact propos-als may require preparation of an environmental impact statement.[21] Permit issuance may be conditioned upon an agreement by the developer to "miti-gate" known impacts by creating and maintaining an approved conservation area. For example, as a condition to issuance of an incidental take permit for a 1,746–acre lakefront development in Austin, Texas, the developer proposed to compensate for its disruption of golden-cheeked warbler habitat "by preserv-ing and maintaining a 827–acre conservation area * * * in perpetuity."[22] Operations in certain geographic areas may trigger the need to consider other laws, such as the Marine Mammal Protection Act, 16 U.S.C. §§ 1361–1407 ("MMPA"). The MMPA prohibits the "taking" of marine mammals but, like the ESA, provides for issuance of "incidental take" permits.[23]

4.   How should an oil and gas developer determine whether they are in an area that is habitat for one or more endangered species? When should they consider applying for an "incidental take" permit? What if the permit is denied or the conditions attached to its issuance unacceptable to the develop-er? See generally GDF Realty Investments, Ltd. v. Norton, 326 F.3d 622 (5th Cir.Tex. 2003), cert. denied, 545 U.S. 1114 (2005) (incidental take permit denied to develop surface of land that would interfere with caves where six endangered species of subterranean invertebrates are found).

---

21.   For example, the U.S. Fish and Wildlife Service prepared an Environmental Assessment covering a 210–acre residential development that would impact the black-capped vireo. The Service determined that an Environmental Impact Statement was not required since issuance of the permit, under the circumstances, would not be a major federal action significantly affecting the environment. "Finding of No Significant Impact for an Incidental Take Permit for the Construction and Operation of the Davenport Ranch Subdivision in Austin, Travis County, Texas," 60 Fed.Reg. 13169 (March 10, 1995). However, a regional incidental take permit sought by the City of Austin and Travis County, covering a series of projected development activities impacting between 30,000 and 60,000 acres, required an Environmental Impact Statement. "Availability of Final Environmental Impact Statement for Proposed Issuance of a Permit to Allow Incidental Take of Golden-cheeked Warbler, Black-capped Vireo, and Six Karst Inverte-brates in Travis County, Texas," 61 Fed.Reg. 11859 (March 22, 1996).

22.   "Notice of Availability of an Environmental Assessment/Habitat Conservation Plan (EA/HCP) and Receipt of Application for Incidental Take Permit for Construction and Operation of the Reed Estate Property by the Volente Group, Inc. in Austin, Travis County, Texas," 61 Fed.Reg. 37760 (July 19, 1996).

23.   16 U.S.C. § 1371(a)(5). See 50 C.F.R. §§ 18.121 to 18.129 (Taking of Marine Mammals Incidental to Oil and Gas Exploration, Development, and Production Activities in the Beaufort Sea and Adjacent Northern Coast of Alaska) (covering incidental take of polar bear and walrus).

5. Section 7 of the ESA requires all federal agencies to "insure that any action authorized, funded, or carried out by such agency * * * is not likely to jeopardize the continued existence of any endangered or threatened species or result in the destruction or adverse modification of habitat of such species which is determined by the Secretary * * * to be critical * * *." 16 U.S.C. § 1536(2). This section weaves the ESA into the other federal laws and requires the agency, in pursuing its basic administrative function or mission, to ensure it does not do something that is "likely to jeopardize the continued existence of any endangered or threatened species * * *." For example, under the Army Corps of Engineers' § 404 nationwide permit program one of the "General Conditions" to qualify for a permit is:

> 18. Endangered Species: (a) No activity is authorized under any NWP which is likely to directly or indirectly jeopardize the continued existence of a threatened or endangered species or a species proposed for such designation, as identified under the Federal Endangered Species Act (ESA), or which will directly or indirectly destroy or adversely modify the critical habitat of such species * * *[24]

Note that the burden of species and critical habitat identification is placed on the permit applicant.

6. Section 7 of the ESA requires other federal agencies to engage in "consultation" with the Secretary whenever their action is likely to "jeopardize" an endangered or threatened species or its habitat. Following consultation, the Secretary will issue a written opinion, known as a "Biological Opinion", identifying the impact the proposed agency action is likely to have on a species and its habitat.[25] If the species or habitat is found to be in "jeopardy" the Secretary will identify in the Biological Opinion "those reasonable and prudent alternatives" the agency can follow to avoid jeopardizing the species or its habitat.[26] Suppose the Corps consults with the Secretary regarding a § 404 permit application submitted by an oil and gas developer. If the Secretary concludes that no oil and gas operations should be allowed within the area, and the Corps thereby rejects the permit application, would the developer have any recourse under the ESA?

7. The ESA contains a broad citizen suit provision which provides, in part: "[A]ny person may commence a civil suit on his own behalf—* * * (C) against the Secretary where there is alleged a failure of the Secretary to perform any act or duty under section 1533 of this title which is not discretionary with the Secretary." 16 U.S.C. § 1540(g)(1). Suppose in our example the developer argues that the practical effect of the Secretary's Biological Opinion was to designate the proposed drilling area as a "critical habitat" for the endangered species without following the procedural requirements of § 1533, particularly § 1533(b)(2) which states:

> The Secretary shall designate critical habitat * * * on the basis of the best scientific data available and after taking into consideration the

---

24. "Reissuance of Nationwide Permits; Final Notice," 77 Fed.Reg. 10184, 10283 (Feb. 21, 2012).

25. 16 U.S.C. § 1536(b)(3)(A); 50 C.F.R. §§ 402.14(g)(4) and 402.15.

26. 16 U.S.C. § 1536(b)(3)(A).

economic impact, and any other relevant impact, of specifying any particular area as critical habitat.

Does an oil and gas developer have standing to bring a citizen suit that is not motivated by a desire to preserve or protect an endangered species? See Bennett v. Spear, 520 U.S. 154 (1997) (yes).

2. LIABILITY CONSIDERATIONS

In addition to land use considerations, the prospective oil and gas lessee (and their lessors) must also be concerned with environmental statutes that impose cleanup liability on persons having an ownership or other defined interest in contaminated property.[27] The statute posing the greatest risk is the Comprehensive Environmental Response, Compensation and Liability Act ("CERCLA"), 42 U.S.C. §§ 9601 to 9675, popularly known as the "Superfund" law. Under CERCLA the Environmental Protection Agency ("EPA") can order defined parties to clean up areas where "hazardous substances" are found that may present "an imminent and substantial endangerment to the public health or welfare or the environment * * *." CERCLA § 106(a), 42 U.S.C. § 9606(a). CERCLA also gives private parties, as well as federal, state, and Indian governmental entities, the authority to sue liable third parties for costs associated with the cleanup of a hazardous substance. CERCLA § 107(a), 42 U.S.C. § 9607(a).

The liable parties under CERCLA, commonly known as "potentially responsible parties" ("PRPs"), are identified by their statutory status either with the property where the hazardous substance is found, or with a hazardous substance found on the property. The CERCLA status liability categories include the following:

- Current owners of the contaminated property.
- Current operators of the contaminated property.
- Owners of the property at any time disposal of a hazardous substance occurred.
- Operators of the property at any time disposal of a hazardous substance occurred.
- Parties that created the hazardous substance and arranged for its transport, disposal, or treatment.
- Parties who arranged for the transport, disposal, or treatment of a hazardous substance created by another.
- Parties who transported the hazardous substance and selected the site where it was taken.

---

27. CERCLA uses "liability-forcing" as a regulatory device whereas the major environmental laws of the 1970s relied primarily upon "technology-forcing" to achieve environmental goals. David E. Pierce, The Emerging Role of "Liability–Forcing" in Environmental Protection, 30 Washburn L.J. 381, 382 (1991) ("Liability-forcing refers to regulatory programs that require designated 'responsible parties' to *fix* the environmental problem which they have, in part, created.").

CERCLA § 107(a)(4), 42 U.S.C. § 9607(a)(4). Section 101(35)(C) of CERC-LA creates an eighth category of liable party which can include owners that are not current owners or operators, and were not owners or operators at the time of disposal. Although these intermediate owners would normally have no owner liability under CERCLA § 107(a)(4), they can lose their non-liable status if they: "obtained actual knowledge of the release or threatened release of a hazardous substance at such facility when the defendant owned the real property and then subsequently transferred ownership without disclosing such knowledge * * *." CERC-LA § 101(35)(C), 42 U.S.C. § 9601(35)(C).

(a) Developer Concerns

The developer's primary concern is to avoid acquiring an oil and gas lease or other interest in property that may have lingering environmental liabilities. Although under state law the developer is typically concerned with unplugged wells[28] or tort claims,[29] a much greater potential liability may lurk under federal law. As the case that follows demonstrates, merely taking an ownership interest in a contaminated site can give rise to substantial environmental liabilities.

AMOCO OIL CO. v. BORDEN, INC.

889 F.2d 664 (5th Cir.1989).

Before BROWN, REAVLEY and HIGGINBOTHAM, CIRCUIT JUDGES.

REAVLEY, CIRCUIT JUDGE:

In a private action brought under the Comprehensive Environmental Response, Compensation, and Liability Act of 1980 ("CERCLA"), 42 U.S.C.A. §§ 9601–9675 (1983 & Supp.1989), * * * Amoco Oil Co. ("Amoco") sought a declaratory judgment for liability and response cost damages from Borden, Inc. ("Borden"), from which Amoco had purchased contaminated industrial property. Finding that Amoco had failed to establish CERCLA liability, the district court entered judgment for Borden. Holding that Amoco has met the liability requirements, we reverse and remand for determination of damages.

---

28. See Smith & J. Weaver § 14.2.D.; Scott Lansdown, A Checklist for the Abandonment of Properties (or, "Turn Out the Lights, the Party's Over"), 47 Inst. Oil & Gas L. & Tax'n 2–1, 2–3 to 2–10 (1996); Susan G. Zachos, Liabilities Arising from Ownership or Operation of Dead and Dying Oil Fields, 42 Rocky Mtn.Min.L.Inst. 17–1, 17–34 to 17–38 (1996).

29. E.g., Marshall v. El Paso Natural Gas Co., 874 F.2d 1373 (10th Cir.Okla.1989) (landowner sued lessee for improper drilling and plugging of oil and gas well; court affirmed jury verdict awarding $350,050 for diminution in property value, $50,000 in nuisance damages, and $5,000,000 in punitive damages). See Robert N. Barnes, Patranell Britten Lewis, Roy B. Short, Tort Liability for Past Mineral Development, 44 Rocky Mtn. Min. L. Inst. 17–1 (1998). But see Terrebonne Parish School Board v. Castex Energy, Inc., 893 So.2d 789 (La. 2005) (absent a contractual obligation to restore, and absent proof of unreasonable or excessive use of the surface, lessee has no implied obligation to restore surface to the condition it was in prior to lease operations). In Texas many of these landowner claims have been avoided by holding the cause of action for the pre-existing condition was not expressly assigned when the land was conveyed to the current landowner. Cook v. Exxon Corp., 145 S.W.3d 776 (Tex. App. 2004); Exxon Corp. v. Tyra, 127 S.W.3d 12 (Tex. App. 2003); Senn v. Texaco, Inc., 55 S.W.3d 222 (Tex. App. 2001).

I. Background

The property at issue is a 114–acre tract of land in Texas City, Texas. For many years, Borden operated a phosphate fertilizer plant on the site. As a by-product of the fertilizer manufacturing process, large quantities of phosphogypsum were produced. The site now contains a large inactive pile of phosphogypsum covering approximately 35 acres.

Phosphogypsum alone contains low levels of radioactivity. More highly radioactive sludges and scales from processing equipment, however, were dumped into the phosphogypsum pile, creating "hot" areas within the pile. Additionally, during processing, radioactive materials became concentrated in manufacturing equipment, pipe, and filter cloths used in production. These materials constitute "off-pile" wastes and were left primarily near a junkyard on the property and near the abandoned manufacturing buildings. Some of the off-pile sites contain over 500 times the background level of radiation.[1]

In 1977, Amoco became interested in purchasing the property. The parties discussed two prices: $1.8 million for the site "as is," or $2.2 million if Borden would remove the phosphogypsum. Allegedly unaware of the site's radioactivity, Amoco accepted the "as is" option.

Amoco claims it had no knowledge of the radioactive nature of phosphogypsum until it was so informed by the Texas Department of Water Resources in 1978. Amoco then hired several consultants to measure the radioactivity, to determine geology and hydrology, and to characterize the data. The consultant's reports revealed the various elevated radiation levels throughout the site. The site is currently unused and is secured with fences and guards to prevent access. Amoco claims that permanent remedial action will cost between $11 million and $17 million.

In 1982, Amoco brought this action in diversity, alleging various state law claims, including fraud and breach of contract. It later added the CERCLA claim to recover response costs incurred as a result of the radioactive contamination. The state law claims were tried to a jury. The jury found that Borden did not fraudulently misrepresent the condition of the property, but did find that Borden did not deliver the building, equipment, and machinery in a "clean and healthful" condition, as it had expressly warranted. Yet, because the jury also found that Amoco should have known about the radioactivity prior to April 16, 1978, that claim was barred by the statute of limitations.

Amoco continued to pursue its CERCLA cost recovery claim, which the district court bifurcated into liability and remedial phases. Borden's primary defenses against liability were: (1) that it had sold the property on an "as is" basis, and that this fact and the doctrine of caveat emptor should preclude a finding of liability; and (2) that the levels of radiation emanating from the site are not high enough to be considered a release of a hazardous substance within the meaning of CERCLA.

---

1. Background levels indicate natural soil radiation in the area. The background levels for the property were determined from samples obtained at a neighboring city, La Marque, Texas.

On February 2, 1987, the district court issued a Memorandum and Order denying Amoco's motion for entry of judgment on the CERCLA claim. In that order, the court rejected Borden's caveat emptor argument, holding that common-law defenses do not apply to CERCLA claims and that there can be no implied transfer of CERCLA liability. The court further held, however, that Amoco must prove that some threshold level of radioactivity exists at the site in order to establish CERCLA liability and selected the standards for remedial actions at inactive uranium processing sites, see 40 C.F.R. Part 192 (1988) ("Inactive Tailings Standards"), promulgated by the Environmental Protection Agency ("EPA") under the Uranium Mill Tailings Radiation Control Act, 42 U.S.C.A. §§ 7901–7942 (1983 & Supp.1989), to determine hazardous radionuclide levels.

After hearing evidence at a later trial, the court used data that averaged radiation levels throughout the phosphogypsum pile and concluded that the property's radiation levels did not exceed the Inactive Tailings Standards. It then entered judgment for Borden. Amoco appeals the court's holding that a threshold level of radionuclides must be shown to exist at the site to establish CERCLA liability, the appropriateness of the Inactive Tailings Standards for defining that threshold, and the court's application of that standard.

II. Discussion

A. CERCLA

Congress enacted CERCLA in response to well-publicized toxic waste problems. * * * Yet, because the final version was enacted as a "last-minute compromise" between three competing bills, it has "acquired a well-deserved notoriety for vaguely-drafted provisions and an indefinite, if not contradictory, legislative history." * * *

CERCLA substantially changed the legal machinery used to enforce environmental cleanup efforts and was enacted to fill gaps left in an earlier statute, the Resource Conservation and Recovery Act of 1976 ("RCRA"), 42 U.S.C.A. §§ 6901–6987 (1983 & Supp.1989), as amended by Solid Waste Disposal Act Amendments of 1980, Pub.L. No. 96–482, 94 Stat. 2334. * * * The RCRA left inactive sites largely unmonitored by the EPA unless they posed an imminent hazard. * * * CERCLA addressed this problem "by establishing a means of controlling and financing both governmental and private responses to hazardous releases at abandoned and inactive waste disposal sites." * * * Section 9607(a), one of CERC-LA's key provisions for furthering this objective, permits both government and private plaintiffs to recover from responsible parties the costs incurred in cleaning up and responding to hazardous substances at those sites.

* * *

B. Liability

To establish a prima facie case of liability in a CERCLA cost recovery action, a plaintiff must prove: (1) that the site in question is a "facility" as defined in § 9601(9); (2) that the defendant is a responsible person under § 9607(a); (3) that a release or a threatened release of a hazardous substance has occurred; and (4) that the release or threatened release has caused the plaintiff to incur response costs. * * * If the plaintiff establishes each of these elements and the defendant is unable to establish the applicability of one of the defenses listed in § 9607(b),[2] the plaintiff is entitled to summary judgment on the liability issue. * * *

A plaintiff may recover those response costs that are necessary and consistent with the National Contingency Plan ("NCP"). § 9607(a)(4)(B); see 40 C.F.R. Part 300 (1988). Thus, once liability is established, the court must determine the appropriate remedy and which costs are recoverable. The court then must ascertain, under CERCLA's contribution provision, each responsible party's equitable share of the cleanup costs. § 9613(f).

It is undisputed that Amoco's property falls within the statutory definition of a "facility";[3] that Borden is a responsible party within the meaning of CERCLA;[4] and that the statutory defenses to liability are inapplicable. The question of liability centers around the determination of whether a release of a hazardous substance has occurred. Amoco and the EPA, as amicus curiae, specifically claim that the district court erred in requiring Amoco to show that the property's radioactive emissions violated a quantitative threshold to establish the release of a hazardous substance within the meaning of § 9607(a)(4). That section provides in relevant part:

> [A]ny person who accepts or accepted any hazardous substances for transport to disposal or treatment facilities, incineration vessels or sites selected by such person, from which there is a release, or a threatened release which causes the incurrence of response costs, of a hazardous substance, shall be liable for—
>
> . . . .
>
> (B) any other necessary costs of response incurred by any other person consistent with the national contingency plan;
>
> . . . .

1. Hazardous Substance

Radium–226, the primary radioactive waste on the property, decays to form a gas, radon–222, and solid "daughter products."[5] Radon and its

---

2. To establish a defense to liability, a defendant must prove by a preponderance of the evidence that the release or threat of a release of a hazardous substance and the resulting damages "were caused solely by—(1) an act of God; (2) an act of war; [or] (3) an act or omission of a third party. . . ." § 9607(b).

3. CERCLA defines "facility" as "(A) any building, structure, installation, equipment, pipe or pipeline . . ., well, pit, pond, lagoon, impoundment, ditch, landfill, storage container, motor vehicle, rolling stock, or aircraft, or (B) any site or area where a hazardous substance has been deposited, stored, disposed of, or placed, or otherwise come to be located. . . ." § 9601(9).

4. Under § 9607(a) liability is imposed on "any person who at the time of disposal of any hazardous substance owned or operated any facility at which such hazardous substances were disposed of." The definition of "person" includes "an individual, firm, corporation, association, partnership, consortium, joint venture, [or] commercial entity. . . ." § 9601(21).

daughter products are considered radionuclides, which are defined as "any nuclide that emits radiation." 40 C.F.R. § 61.91(c) (1988). The term hazardous substance includes "any element, compound, mixture, solution, or substance designated pursuant to section 9602 of [CERCLA], . . . [and] any hazardous air pollutant listed under section 112 of the Clean Air Act. . . ." § 9601(14). The EPA has designated radionuclides as hazardous substances under § 9602(a) of CERCLA. See 40 C.F.R. § 302.4 (1988). Additionally, the regulations promulgated by the EPA under § 112 of the Clean Air Act, 42 U.S.C. § 7412, list radionuclides as a hazardous air pollutant. See 40 C.F.R. § 61.01(a) (1988).

The plain statutory language fails to impose any quantitative requirement on the term hazardous substance and we decline to imply that any is necessary. Radionuclides meet the listing requirements and therefore the radioactive materials on Amoco's property are hazardous substances within the meaning of CERCLA.

* * *

2. Release

The term "release" is defined to mean: "any spilling, leaking, pumping, pouring, emitting, emptying, discharging, injecting, escaping, leaching, dumping, or disposing into the environment (including the abandonment or discarding of barrels, containers, and other closed receptacles containing any hazardous substance or pollutant or contaminant). . . ." § 9601(22). As with "hazardous substance," the plain statutory language fails to impose any quantitative requirement on the term "release." We believe that the definition of "release" should be construed broadly, * * *

Borden's actions met the release requirement in two ways. First, it did so by disposing of the phosphogypsum and highly radioactive wastes on the property. See § 9601(22). Second, the gas emanating from the radionuclides constitutes a release within the meaning of the statute. See 54 Fed.Reg. 22524, 22526 (1989).

3. Response Costs

The statutory provision suggesting a threshold for liability is the requirement that a release or threatened release have "caus[ed] the incurrence of response costs." § 9607(a)(4). Response costs are generally and specifically defined to include a variety of actions designed to protect the public health or the environment.[6] To justifiably incur response costs,

---

5. The new element resulting from the atomic disintegration of a radioactive element is called the daughter of the original element.

6. In § 9601(25) "response" is defined to mean "remove, removal, remedy, and remedial action. . . ." In turn, these terms are further defined in the statute.

Section 9601(23) defines "remove" or "removal" to include[:]

> the cleanup or removal of released hazardous substances from the environment, such actions as may be necessary taken in the event of the threat of release of hazardous substances into the environment, such actions as may be necessary to monitor, assess, and evaluate the

one necessarily must have acted to contain a release threatening the public health or the environment.

In our interpretation of the requirement that a release "cause[ ] the incurrence of response costs," we are notably entering unexplored territory. As with many of CERCLA's provisions, the legislative history is bereft of discussion about the causal nexus between releases and response costs. Additionally, courts have not been faced with a scenario suggesting that a plaintiff's action was not justified by the hazard posed. * * *

Borden has pointed out that all matter is radioactive to some degree. While harmless at low concentrations, at some point on a continuum it poses an unacceptable risk to human life and the environment. Given CERCLA's broad liability provisions and the pervasive nature of radionuclides, Borden argues that without a quantitative limit CERCLA liability could attach to the release of any substance and theoretically could reach "everything in the United States."[7] The district court was apparently persuaded by Borden's argument. In finding a standard essential, it noted that "[m]ost of the radionuclides in the atmosphere come from natural sources [and that] radionuclides are used or produced in thousands of locations throughout the United States."

Yet, concerns about the most extreme reach of liability—extending to naturally occurring hazardous substances—are misplaced. Remedial actions taken in response to hazardous substances as they occur naturally are specifically excluded from the NCP and are therefore not recoverable. § 9604(a)(3)(A). The only concern that should support the use of a quantitative measure at the liability phase is potential abuse of the broad provisions, which may subject some defendants to harassing litigation.

Amoco and the EPA argue that CERCLA liability attaches upon the release of any quantity of a hazardous substance and that the extent of a release should be considered only at the remedial phase. However, we must reject this approach because adherence to that view would permit CERCLA's reach to exceed its statutory purposes by holding parties liable who have not posed any threat to the public or the environment. * * * Accordingly, we find use of a standard of justification acceptable for determining whether a release or threatened release of a hazardous substance has caused the incurrence of response costs. In the absence of any specific direction from Congress, we believe that the question of

---

release or threat of release of hazardous substances, the disposal of removed material, or the taking of such other actions as may be necessary to prevent, minimize, or mitigate damage to the public health or welfare or to the environment, which may otherwise result from a release or threat of release.

Section 9601(24) defines "remedy" or "remedial action" to include, among others, "those actions consistent with permanent remedy taken instead of or in addition to removal actions in the event of a release or threatened release of a hazardous substance into the environment, to prevent or minimize the release of hazardous substances so that they do not migrate to cause substantial danger to present or future public health or welfare or the environment."

7. We note also that this is not unique to radionuclides. The EPA has listed several other substances, such as zinc, sodium, and selenium, that are present in most soil. See 40 C.F.R. § 302.4 (1988). Harmless and, indeed, essential to humans at low levels, they are also toxic in higher concentrations.

whether a release has caused the incurrence of response costs should rest upon a factual inquiry into the circumstances of a case and the relevant factual inquiry should focus on whether the particular hazard justified any response actions. CERCLA's provisions provide guidance for making this determination.

Section 9621(d) governs the extent of cleanup, which is required "at a minimum [to] assure[ ] protection of human health and the environment." § 9621(d)(1). To attain that goal, the scope of remedial action may be established by any "legally applicable or relevant and appropriate ... requirement" ("ARAR"). § 9621(d)(2)(A). ARARs include "any standard, requirement, criteria, or limitation under any Federal environmental law" or any more stringent "State environmental or facility siting law." *Id.* As these standards define the limits of appropriate response costs, and therefore recoverable expenses, they are also useful for establishing the limits of liability. While not the exclusive means of justifying response costs, we hold that a plaintiff who has incurred response costs meets the liability requirement as a matter of law if it is shown that any release violates, or any threatened release is likely to violate, any applicable state or federal standard, including the most stringent.

Amoco has clearly met this requirement by showing that the radioactive emissions exceeded the limits set in Subpart B of the Inactive Tailings Standards,[8] which provides that:

> (a) The concentration of radium–226 in land averaged over an area of 100 square meters shall not exceed the background level by more than—
>
> > (1) 5 pCi/g,[9] averaged over the first 15 cm of soil below the surface, and
> >
> > (2) 15 pCi/g, averaged over 15 cm thick layers of soil more than 15 cm below the surface.

40 C.F.R. 192.12 (1988).

Amoco presented evidence that the background level of radium–226 was 0.5 pCi/g. The phosphogypsum pile contains an average radium concentration of 40 pCi/g. Samples from the buildings and the junkyard contained radium levels ranging from 661 pCi/g to 816 pCi/g. Some materials found in the junkyard had concentrations up to 24,000 pCi/g and residue in a pipe between the junkyard and a surge pond contained a concentration of over 60,000 pCi/g. As these measurements clearly exceed an applicable standard, Amoco was justified in incurring response costs as a matter of law. Moreover, the excessive radiation in the hot spots, which

---

8. While these standards were not devised to regulate phosphogypsum piles, all parties agree that these standards are applicable because the inactive uranium mill tailings piles, which they regulate, emit the same radioactive materials and present similar environmental problems.

9. Radioactivity is measured in picocuries. A picocurie is a unit of radioactivity equal to one-trillionth of a curie and represents 2.22 radioactive disintegrations per minute. Radium–226, one of the radioactive substances on the property, is measured by weight in pCi/g, or picocuries per gram of the substance measured.

exceeds any possible standard protective of public health, justified response actions regardless of any overall measure of the site's radiation.

The district court determined that there was an insufficient release of a hazardous substance based on its application of Subpart A, a less stringent standard. In applying this standard, the district court used an average measure of radiation from the site. Samples from which this average was derived were taken primarily from the pile. While the average included a few measurements from off-pile sites, these samples were apparently not taken from the most highly radioactive areas. * * * Since that figure did not exceed the Subpart A standard, the district court held that Amoco failed to establish CERCLA liability.

The district court erred initially by using a less stringent standard. The error, however, was compounded by using a measurement of site radioactivity that excluded the most contaminated materials. That reading portrayed the property as containing only the most minimal contamination.

Amoco's security measures and site investigation are acceptable response costs within the meaning of CERCLA. * * * As there has been a release of a hazardous substance that justified the incurrence of response costs and the other elements of a prima facie case have been met, Amoco is entitled to summary judgment on the liability issue.

C. Damages

Under CERCLA, a private plaintiff may recover only those response costs that are necessary and consistent with the NCP. § 9607(a)(4)(B). The NCP has been promulgated by the EPA, 40 C.F.R. Part 300 (1988), and "establish[es] procedures and standards for responding to releases of hazardous substances. . . ." § 9605(a). Under the NCP, cleanup efforts are designed to meet CERCLA's goals for cost-effective remedial action that adequately protects public health and the environment. See § 9621(a)–(b). ARARs define the limits of remedial efforts and must be selected from applicable federal standards or more stringent state standards. § 9621(d). Once the applicable ARARs are established, a district court must determine which of the standards will provide remedial action most consistent with the NCP.

While the strictest standard may be used for the purposes of establishing liability, it will not govern remedial actions unless consistent with the NCP. See 40 C.F.R. § 300.68(i) (1988) * * * The justification standard provides a broad net for establishing liability, consistent with CERCLA's liability provisions, leaving remedial and responsibility determinations for a later stage.

In this case, the district court considered only one possible ARAR, the Inactive Tailings Standards. The court, however, will have to revisit its application of the standard and determine whether other ARARs are more appropriate. See 40 C.F.R. § 300.68(i) (1988). Some other standards to consider include the EPA's new regulations for radionuclide emissions from phosphogypsum piles, which should be finalized soon, see 54 Fed. Reg. 9612, 9612 (1989); the EPA's maximum contaminant levels for Radium–226, adopted under the authority of the Safe Drinking Water Act, 42 U.S.C. § 300g–1, see 40 C.F.R. 141.15 (1988); any appropriate regulations for groundwater contamination; and any Texas standards concerning radiation contamination of soil, vegetation, or groundwater.

The hazard on the property constitutes an indivisible harm. * * * As an owner of a facility that continues to release a hazardous substance, Amoco shares joint and several liability for remedial actions with Borden. * * * When one liable party sues another to recover its equitable share of the response costs, the action is one for contribution, which is specifically recognized under CERCLA. See § 9613(f).

Under that provision a court has considerable latitude in determining each party's equitable share. After deciding the appropriate remedial action, the court will have to determine each party's share of the costs. Possible relevant factors include: "the amount of hazardous substances involved; the degree of toxicity or hazard of the materials involved; the degree of involvement by parties in the generation, transportation, treatment, storage, or disposal of the substances; the degree of care exercised by the parties with respect to the substances involved; and the degree of cooperation of the parties with government officials to prevent any harm to public health or the environment." * * * Additionally, the circumstances and conditions involved in the property's conveyance, including the price paid and discounts granted, should be weighed in allocating response costs. * * *

Borden does not challenge the *caveat emptor* holding, but does claim that the equities in this case require Amoco to bear the full cost of cleanup. However, because both parties are liable under CERCLA, this is a question more properly decided by the district court, after it has determined the proper scope of the cleanup efforts. Accordingly, we REVERSE the judgment and REMAND the case for proceedings not inconsistent with this opinion.

REVERSED AND REMANDED.

NOTES

1. The *Amoco* case illustrates the importance of carefully evaluating the potential environmental liability associated with becoming an owner or operator of property. In this case Amoco purchased property for a total capital outlay of 1.8 million dollars and ended up acquiring a potential 11 to 17 million-dollar cleanup liability. It would have been impossible, however, for Amoco to anticipate its CERCLA liability since it acquired the property three years before CERCLA was enacted. Nevertheless, courts have held that CERCLA can be applied retroactively to address sites created prior to its December 11, 1980 enactment date. E.g., United States v. Olin Corp., 107 F.3d 1506, 1515 (11th Cir.Ala.1997) ("[W]e find clear congressional intent

favoring retroactive application of CERCLA's cleanup liability provisions."); United States v. Alcan Aluminum Corp., 315 F.3d 179, 188–89 (2d Cir.N.Y. 2003), cert. denied, 540 U.S. 1103 (2004) (collecting cases on the issue).

2. Which CERCLA status liability categories would apply to Borden? Which would apply to Amoco?

3. Applying the court's analysis in *Amoco*, how much of a CERCLA "hazardous substance" must be found at a facility to be deemed a CERCLA hazardous substance? Once a hazardous substance is found to exist, how much must be present to support a cleanup action? Must some state or federal standard be violated to trigger a cleanup action?

4. The Fifth Circuit addressed the issue again in Licciardi v. Murphy Oil U.S.A., Inc., 111 F.3d 396 (5th Cir.1997), where it reviewed a district court ruling that ' "the presence of any hazardous substances [above background levels] on plaintiffs' property is sufficient to justify their incurring response costs.' " *Licciardi*, 111 F.3d at 398. The Court of Appeals rejected this conclusion on two grounds: First, evidence that the hazardous substance concentration exceeds background levels, without more, will not satisfy the *Amoco* requirement of a factual inquiry that reveals some threat to the public or the environment. Second, in this case even the evidence of background levels may have been irrelevant since it was based upon measurements 30 to 50 miles away from the site at issue.

5. Not all courts follow the *Amoco/Licciardi* minimum quantity approach to determine when an actionable CERCLA release has occurred. For example, in Johnson v. James Langley Operating Co., Inc., 226 F.3d 957 (8th Cir. 2000), a landowner filed a CERCLA action against prior oil and gas lessees alleging: "the defendants' oil and gas production activities caused the properties at issue to become contaminated with radioactive scales, salt water, oil and grease, heavy metals and other hazardous substances." 226 F.3d at 959. The trial court relied upon the *Amoco* decision to dismiss the action because the plaintiffs failed to establish the hazardous substances at issue exceeded any applicable, appropriate, or relevant state or federal standard. The Court of Appeals for the Eighth Circuit rejected the Fifth Circuit's *Amoco/Licciardi* analysis stating:

> We disagree with *Amoco* and *Licciardi* to the extent they saddle a landowner with the costs of testing and sampling in response to a release or threat of a release of hazardous substances. CERCLA plainly contemplates liability for site assessment. The statute defines "response" to include removal actions * * * Removal, in turn, includes 'such actions as may be necessary to *monitor, assess, and evaluate the release or threat of release* of hazardous substances.' * * * Moreover, CERCLA's plain language does not incorporate any quantitative threshold into its definition of hazardous substances. See United States v. Alcan Aluminum Corp., 964 F.2d 252, 260–61 (3d Cir.1992) (collecting cases)

* * *

> To fashion a quantitative minimum threshold for CERCLA liability under the guise of a non-statutory 'justification' theory is to undo the policy decision Congress has already made: that the threat posed by hazardous

substances does not depend upon a minimum concentration or quantity. [citing cases from the First, Eighth, and Ninth Circuits that reject the Fifth Circuit's approach]

* * *

CERCLA allocates to the generator of hazardous substances the cost of ascertaining the danger posed by an actual or threatened release of hazardous substances, even if such testing determines that levels do not warrant cleanup action

* * *

[R]esponse costs must be caused by an actual release or threatened release * * * We have previously speculated in dicta that the degree of connection required 'may be slight indeed.' * * * Our rejection of *Amoco* confirms that speculation inasmuch as the causation requirement does not include an unstated quantitative threshold. Rather, it requires that plaintiffs prove either that there was a release of hazardous substances, or that such a release was threatened.

Johnson, 226 F.3d at 962–63.

6. As oil, gas, and associated saltwater are produced from the reservoir, radium can become deposited on the inside of pipes, tanks, and other well facilities in the form of a scale known as "naturally occurring radioactive materials" ("NORM"). As described by the EPA:

NORM is formed by co-precipitation of soluble radium from the formation water (produced water) along with barium sulfate, calcium carbonate, and other scale-producing constituents. These precipitates (as scale) collect in the separator tanks bottoms (solids) along with the produced sand.[30]

Although the radioactive concentration of scale may be minimal when it is deposited, higher radiation levels can be created when scale and similar contaminated wastes are removed and centralized through cleaning, salvage, or disposal operations. Many states now regulate the management and disposal of NORM oilfield wastes. E.g., Tex.Admin.Code tit. 16, §§ 4.601 to 4.632. The Texas rules governing NORM are discussed in Smith & Weaver at § 14.6. NORM guidelines have also been addressed by the Interstate Oil & Gas Compact Commission ("IOGCC") through its Council on Regulatory Needs. See Interstate Oil & Gas Compact Commission, IOGCC Environmental Guidelines for State Oil & Gas Regulatory Programs § 7 (1994). Is NORM a CERCLA hazardous substance? See Johnson v. James Langley Operating Co., Inc., 226 F.3d 957, 959 (8th Cir.2000) (CERCLA action by landowner against oil and gas lessees for produced water contamination causing "mineral scales that contain measurable quantities of natural radioactivity"). How can the move by states to adopt regulatory guidelines for NORM impact its status as a CERCLA hazardous substance?

7. Suppose that instead of purchasing the fertilizer plant Amoco merely entered into an oil and gas lease with Borden covering the 114–acre tract where the plant was located. The EPA issues Amoco an order to clean up the

---

30. "Oil and Gas Extraction Point Source Category; Offshore Subcategory Effluent Guidelines and New Source Performance Standards," 58 Fed.Reg. 12454, 12467 (March 4, 1993).

site and Amoco wants to know if it is required, by CERCLA, to comply with the order. CERCLA § 106(b)(1) provides:

> Any person who, without sufficient cause, willfully violates, or fails or refuses to comply with, any order of the President [EPA] under subsection (a) of this section may * * * be fined not more than $25,000 for each day in which such violation occurs or such failure to comply continues.

42 U.S.C. § 9606(b)(1). The fine amount is now $37,500 per day. "Civil Monetary Penalty Inflation Adjustment Rule," 74 Fed.Reg. 626, 628 (Jan. 7, 2009). This penalty provision is further bolstered by CERCLA § 107(c)(3) which provides, in part:

> If any person who is liable for a release or threat of release of a hazardous substance fails without sufficient cause to properly provide removal or remedial action upon order of the President [EPA] pursuant to section * * * 9606 * * * such person may be liable to the United States for punitive damages in an amount at least equal to, and not more than three times, the amount of any costs incurred by the [Super]Fund as a result of such failure to take proper action.

42 U.S.C. § 9607(c)(3). How will you go about analyzing the situation for Amoco? Would your answer be different if instead of entering into an oil and gas lease Amoco purchased all or part of the mineral interest in the 114–acre tract from Borden? See David E. Pierce, Structuring Routine Oil and Gas Transactions to Minimize Environmental Liability, 33 Washburn L.J. 76, 88–95 (1993), reprinted at 31 Pub.Land & Resources L.Dig. 176 (1994) (analyzing CERCLA owner, operator, arranger, and transporter liability in the oil and gas context). Consider also the possibility of judicial review of a 106 remedial action order applying the principles set out in Sackett v. Environmental Protection Agency, 132 S.Ct. 1367 (2012).

8. Suppose an oil and gas lessee obtains a lease on a pristine 160–acre homestead owned by Fred Farmer. In the process of drilling wells on the leased land the oil company disposes of hazardous substances in drilling pits on the property. Several years later, the EPA issues Fred a CERCLA § 106 order instructing him to clean up the drilling pits. Is Fred a liable party under CERCLA? See David E. Pierce, The Impact of Landowner/Lessor Environmental Risk on Oil and Gas Lessee Rights and Obligations, 31 Tulsa L.J. 731, 731–37 (1996), reprinted at 34 Pub.Land & Resources L.Dig. 127 (1997) (analyzing landowner's CERCLA liability associated with their oil and gas lessee's activities).

(b) Landowner Concerns

When a landowner enters into an oil and gas lease, or conveys a mineral interest, they give third parties access to their property to engage in oil and gas development activities which can result in surface and subsurface contamination. In addition to the damage such activities may cause to the fair market value of their land, landowners must also consider the potential cleanup liability they may be creating for themselves.

QUAKER STATE CORP. v. U.S. COAST GUARD

681 F.Supp. 280 (W.D.Pa.1988).

GERALD J. WEBER, DISTRICT JUDGE.

On July, 2 1985, the Coast Guard and Environmental Protection Agency (EPA) observed a sheen on the surface of the water on Pine Run in McKean County, PA. Nearby they discovered an abandoned and refilled waste water containment pit with evidence of petroleum residues. Over the following year the Government executed a cleanup operation which entailed the excavation and removal of 115 truckloads of material. The cost of the operation totaled $430,000.00 and the Coast Guard demanded payment of those costs, plus interest and penalties, from Quaker State.

Quaker State filed this declaratory judgment action seeking to determine the single discrete issue of whether it was an "owner or operator" of the site within the meaning of the Clean Water Act, 33 U.S.C. § 1321(f), as charged by the Government. The Coast Guard asserted a counterclaim, seeking to establish strict liability under § 1321(f). Subsequently, the Government sought leave to amend its counterclaim to assert an alternative basis for liability under § 1321(g).

We scheduled trial solely for a determination of whether Quaker State was an "owner or operator" within the meaning of the Act. Quaker State then filed a motion for summary judgment arguing that the Act by its terms defined "owner or operator" as of the time of discovery of the spill. Because Quaker State's lease expired in 1975 and operations ceased in 1978, Quaker State contends it could not be an "owner or operator" in 1985 when the spill was discovered.

On the other hand, the Government contends that "owner or operator" is defined as of the date of initial discharge. It argues that the date of discovery, even if years after the discharge, is irrelevant. In this case the government contends that the initial discharge occurred in 1977 or 1978 while Quaker State was still engaged in operations on the site.

Therefore, for the Government to prevail on the strict liability claim under § 1321(f) we must accept the Government's interpretation of "owner or operator", and we must conclude that the initial discharge occurred while Quaker State was still on site. If we reject either premise, then Quaker State is not strictly liable under § 1321(f), though it may ultimately be liable on another provision of the Act or otherwise.

We reserved ruling on the statutory interpretation issue concerning the timing element in the definition of "owner or operator" and proceeded to trial on the factual question of when the discharge first occurred. We also considered a tardily advanced argument that Quaker State had paid taxes on the subject site through 1985, thereby evidencing some ownership interest at the time of discovery of the spill. Our findings of fact and conclusions of law are contained below:

Facts

On July 2, 1985, Commander Patrick of the U.S. Coast Guard took a break from his worries and waded up Pine Creek in the Allegheny National Forest, absorbing the subtle pleasures of a summer day in the woods. As he waded upstream he noticed a silvery sheen on the surface of the water. Closer inspection revealed black deposits on stones in the stream which, when disturbed, generated a rainbow sheen on the water, characteristic of oil contamination.

Oil in streams in Northwestern Pennsylvania is not uncommon, and not always unnatural. Natural seepage from subterranean oil deposits has leaked into these streams for hundreds of years. Indians skimmed oil from the surface of streams for religious and medicinal purposes. The sheen of oil on the water first attracted the embryonic oil industry in the 19th Century and the natural contamination of streams still occurs today.

However, the last century has added manmade sources of stream contamination. Neglected or abandoned wells, pipelines, drilling sites, and waste containment pits have created myriad opportunities for the discharge of oil into Pennsylvania's streams. The occurrence of such discharges in the Allegheny National Forest prompted increased Governmental activity in the area in 1985 and culminated in the creation of an interagency task force in August of that year.

As administrator of the Government's cleanup fund, Commander Patrick came to the Allegheny National Forest on July 2, 1985. After inspecting several cleanup operations already underway in the area, Commander Patrick began his leisurely walk up Pine Run. Now he followed the silver sheen upstream about 50 yards. There he found an encrusted stripe of semi-solidified oil on the bank of the stream. Clambering up the steep bank he stepped into a clearing.

The Commander stood in a flat, oval meadow. Vegetation grew in clumps and the ground was spongy underfoot. A short distance from the crest of the stream bank he found an area where an oily substance lay on the surface of the ground. Within an hour the EPA and a private contractor, in the area on other cleanups, were on site.

The meadow was in fact the site of a covered, abandoned containment pit. In the production of oil in this region, water is commonly pumped into the underground oil field, forcing the oil and water out of the well heads. The oil and water mixture pumped from the ground is then placed in separation tanks where the oil floats to the surface. The waste water at the bottom of the tank is then drained into a containment pit. A certain amount of oil and sludge drains with the water into the pit. This residue generally is absorbed into the underlying soil and strata.

Some containment pits date back to the 19th Century. The age of the pit involved here is unknown. We do know that the pit existed prior to 1968, and that Quaker State did not use the pit in its operations after that date. Indeed there is no evidence here that Quaker State ever used this pit.

But the pit was located on Lot 128 of Warrant 2244, a site under lease to Quaker State. When the company chose not to renew the lease in 1975, it began abandonment operations, capping and abandoning well sites and removing equipment. At some time in 1977, at the direction and under the supervision of the U.S. Forest Service, the owner of the surface rights, Quaker State covered the pit by bulldozing earth over it, compacting and seeding it. Quaker State completed its abandonment operations early in 1978.

Discussion

We begin with the Government's assertion, first raised in its cross motion for summary judgment filed two weeks before trial, that local tax records establish Quaker State's ownership interest in the site as late as 1985. Because the discharge was first discovered in 1985, the Government contends that Quaker State is strictly liable as an "owner" under § 1321(f), even under Quaker State's interpretation of the Act.

* * *

The burden of proof on ownership is on the Government. * * * We cannot tell from these records whether Quaker State was paying taxes on Lot 128 or only on other lots it held within the Warrant. A Quaker State official denied that any taxes were paid on Lot 128 after the expiration of the lease. While this ambiguity may be the fault of the records and not the United States, the evidence being equivocal the Government fails to satisfy its burden.

Thus we come to the question of the date of initial discharge. While counsel have raised many issues, directly and obliquely, we will confine ourselves to determining whether the initial discharge occurred in 1977 or early 1978 when Quaker State was arguably still in operation on the site, and wells were capped and the pit was filled.

Although Commander Patrick discovered a discharge on July 2, 1985, the Government contends that the spill had in fact begun by April 1978, at the latest. * * *

* * *

The simplest and most obvious rejoinder to the Government is the absence of any complaints of oil on Pine Run in the eight years between the covering of the pit and the discovery of a discharge. * * *

* * *

For the reasons stated above, we conclude that 1.) the Government failed to establish that Quaker State was an "owner" of Lot 128 in 1985, the tax records being equivocal at best, and 2.) that the initial discharge from the site did not occur in 1977 or 1978 when Quaker State was still in occupation on the site. As a result, Quaker State is not an "owner or operator" under either proffered construction of that term, and cannot be liable under 33 U.S.C. § 1321(f).

We have also considered the statutory construction issue raised by Quaker State's Motion for Summary Judgment. As described above, Quaker State contends that "owner or operator" is defined as of the date of discovery of a spill, while the Government argues that the date of initial discharge, even if years in the past, is the pertinent time element.

Although there are no reported decisions on this issue, perhaps because discharge and discovery are usually contemporaneous, our review of the Act and its purpose compel the conclusion that Congress intended to hold strictly liable the "owner or operator" at the time a discharge is discovered.

First of all, the Act defines owner or operator in the present tense with the single exception of abandoned offshore facilities. 33 U.S.C. § 1321(a)(6). In that situation, because there may not be a present owner or operator, the Act holds strictly liable the last owner or operator prior to abandonment. An abandoned onshore facility does not present the same problem—there is always a readily identifiable property owner who may be held strictly liable.

The definition is stated in the present tense because Congress sought to encourage the immediate cleanup of spills. When a spill is discovered, response must be swift. If the Government must bear the cost of cleanup, there must be a ready pocket for reimbursement. It is the owner or operator at the time the spill is first discovered who has control of the site and the source of discharge. He is readily identifiable. He is most likely to be in position to halt the discharge, to effect an immediate cleanup, or to prevent a discharge in the first place. If the onus of cleanup falls on the Government, he is the clearest and most expeditious source for reimbursement.

On the other hand, if the Government must search in the past for the date of initial discharge and the identity of some past owner or operator, the purpose of the Act is thwarted. Determining the date of initial discharge may require extensive investigation and expert opinion. It will almost certainly be the subject of litigation. Identifying the past owner or operator may also require considerable effort and be fraught with uncertainty. In any event that owner or operator may no longer be in control of the site, or may not longer exist. Congress' desire for immediate cleanup or in the alternative for a ready source for reimbursement would certainly be frustrated by the definition advanced by the Government.

We conclude therefore that "owner or operator" is to be defined as of the date of discovery of a spill and not at some date in the past. We recognize that in the present case there was no "operator" in 1985 and the "owner" at the time of discovery of the spill was the U.S. Forest Service. Therefore, the Government itself would be the strictly liable party under § 1321(f). Though the fact setting in the present case yields a bad result for the Government on the strict liability provisions, we will not torture the Act to achieve a result not intended by Congress.

* * *

Conclusion

For the reasons stated above, we will dismiss Count I of the Government's counterclaim and grant Quaker State declaratory judgment on the owner or operator issue. Also, we will grant the Government leave to amend its counterclaim to assert a direct cause of action under 33 U.S.C. § 1321(g). An appropriate order will be entered.

NOTES

1. When a financially solvent landowner exists, the government would not normally be as persistent at pursuing a past oil and gas lessee with such nebulous association to the contamination problem. Instead, they would merely look to the current owner of the property where the problem exists. However, in *Quaker State* the surface owner of the property was the National Forest Service. Following the court's ruling that Quaker State was not an "owner or operator" under § 311(f) of the CWA, the government pursued Quaker State under § 311(g) which imposes third party liability when the owner or operator can demonstrate the discharge was caused by the third party. Quaker State Corp. v. U.S. Coast Guard, 716 F.Supp. 201 (W.D.Pa. 1989) (*Quaker State II*). The government ultimately failed in its efforts to shift cleanup liability from the surface owner to Quaker State. Quaker State Corp. v. U.S. Coast Guard, 1990 WL 272708 (W.D.Pa.1990) (*Quaker State III*).

2. Would a severed mineral interest owner be an "owner or operator" for purposes of § 311? Kendall Refining Company owned the oil and gas mineral interest in the land where the containment pit was located. Judge Mincer, in *Quaker State III*, entered the following conclusions of law regarding Kendall's status:

> 20. Kendall Refining Company not only was Quaker State's lessor, but was the owner of the oil and gas rights to Lot 128, at least from 1965 through the time of the discharge. Ownership of the oil and gas carries with it the right to use the surface of the land for oil and gas purposes.

> 21. Quaker State as a matter of law could not be the sole cause of the discharge, due to Kendall's status and involvement with the site, including its request for Quaker State to perform abandonment activities thereon to Kendall's benefit, and due to others' prior use of the site and pit.

Quaker State III, 1990 WL 272708 at *8. Would a nonparticipating mineral interest owner be subject to "owner or operator" liability? What about a nonparticipating royalty interest owner? See Thomas F. Cope, Environmental Liabilities of Non–Operating Parties, 37 Rocky Mtn.Min.L.Inst. 1–1, 1–30 to 1–31 (1991); David E. Pierce, Structuring Routine Oil and Gas Transactions to Minimize Environmental Liability, 33 Washburn L.J. 76, 151–53, 164–65 (1993).

3.   The landowner's exposure to CERCLA liability has been summarized by Professor Pierce as follows:

> Liability is based upon the "status" of the party, not their "fault." Therefore, if a third party, such as an oil and gas lessee, contaminates land in the course of its operations, the "owner" of the land can be liable for the cleanup. The landowner's liability arises not from their culpability or causation, but rather their status as the owner of an interest in the contaminated property. This creates an entirely new category of concerns for property owners who convey mineral interests in their property while retaining the surface interest. These concerns are equally compelling for a landowner who enters into an oil and gas lease.

David E. Pierce, The Impact of Landowner/Lessor Environmental Risk on Oil and Gas Lessee Rights and Obligations, 31 Tulsa L.J. 731, 732–33 (1996) (footnotes omitted).

4.   Similar "status" liability problems exist for surface owners, mineral owners, lessors, and lessees under state law. E.g., Wells Fargo Bank v. Goldzband, 61 Cal.Rptr.2d 826 (Cal.App. 1997) (mineral owner ordered to plug and abandon nine oil wells and clean up well sites); White v. Regan, 575 N.Y.S.2d 375 (N.Y.App.Div.1991) (current owner of land liable for petroleum discharge under New York statute and government need not seek out other parties who caused or contributed to the discharge.).

5.   If permissible under state and federal law, can a lessee dispose of naturally occurring radioactive material ("NORM"), generated by lease operations, on the leased land? If the lessee has previously disposed of NORM on the leased land, can they remove it and take it to a commercial hazardous waste facility without the landowner's consent? See Gray v. Murphy Oil USA, Inc., 874 F.Supp. 748, 750 (S.D.Miss.1994) (noting plaintiff landowners had legitimate concern about their liability under CERCLA if their oil and gas lessee removed NORM from their land to another site for disposal).

6.   How might a grantor of a mineral interest, who is reserving the surface estate, address these environmental risks? How about a landowner entering into an oil and gas lease? See David E. Pierce, Incorporating a Century of Oil and Gas Jurisprudence Into the "Modern" Oil and Gas Lease, 33 Washburn L.J. 786, 796–800 (1994) (suggesting ways a landowner might try and leverage environmental risk when entering into an oil and gas lease); David E. Pierce, Structuring Routine Oil and Gas Transactions to Minimize Environmental Liability, 33 Washburn L.J. 76, 154–62 (1993) (same); David E. Pierce, Assessing Thirty Years of Federal Environmental Regulation of Upstream Oil and Gas Activities, 50 Inst. Oil and Gas L. & Tax'n 5–1, 5–20 (1999) (same).

B. DRILLING AND COMPLETION OPERATIONS

The oil and gas drilling process generates several wastes that may be subject to federal environmental regulation. Drilling operations create large volumes of solid waste and the potential for water discharges. The solid wastes must be evaluated under the Solid Waste Disposal Act, 42 U.S.C. §§ 6901 to 6992k, while the water discharges will be evaluated under the Clean Water Act.

1. MANAGING DRILLING WASTES

The Solid Waste Disposal Act ("SWDA") consists of several solid waste management programs.[31] The most extensive SWDA program was added in 1976 as the Resource Conservation and Recovery Act ("RCRA"), 42 U.S.C. §§ 6921 to 6939e, to regulate hazardous wastes.[32] RCRA establishes a detailed command-and-control regulatory program for materials classified as "hazardous waste" under the EPA's regulations.[33] Congress directed the EPA, in RCRA § 3001, 42 U.S.C. § 6921, to promulgate characteristics and lists to identify wastes that must be regulated as "hazardous waste" to effectively protect human health or the environment. However, with regard to "drilling fluids, produced waters, and other wastes associated with the exploration, development, or production of crude oil or natural gas," a 1980 amendment to RCRA[34] instructed the EPA to conduct a special study of such wastes before it considered listing any of them as hazardous under Subtitle C.

EPA completed its study in 1987[35] and in 1988 issued its decision to exempt from Subtitle C regulation certain wastes generated during the exploration, development, and production of oil, gas, and geothermal resources.[36] The exemption is established by the following regulation:

> The following solid wastes are not hazardous wastes:
>
> * * *
>
> (5) Drilling fluids, produced waters, and other wastes associated with the exploration, development, or production of crude oil, natural gas or geothermal energy.[37]

The EPA's regulatory determination contains a list of wastes it believes are examples of the types of wastes encompassed by the exemption.[38]

---

31. For example: Subtitle C (Hazardous Waste Management); Subtitle D (State or Regional Solid Waste Plans); Subtitle I (Regulation of Underground Storage Tanks). Certain subtitles apply generally to the Act: Subtitle A (General Provisions/Definitions); Subtitle G (Miscellaneous Provisions/Enforcement and Judicial Review).

32. The RCRA portion of the SWDA comprises "Subtitle C" of the SWDA (designated "Subchapter III" in the codified version of the SWDA).

33. 40 C.F.R. Part 261.

34. Codified at 42 U.S.C. § 6921(b)(2)(A) and 42 U.S.C. § 6982(m).

35. U.S. Environmental Protection Agency Report to Congress, Management of Wastes from the Exploration, Development, and Production of Crude Oil, Natural Gas, and Geothermal Energy, (Dec. 28, 1987) (NTIS #PB88–146212).

36. "Regulatory Determination for Oil and Gas and Geothermal Exploration, Development and Production Wastes," 53 Fed.Reg. 25446 (July 6, 1988).

37. 40 C.F.R. § 261.4(b)(5).

38. However, the EPA has cautioned that:

The Regulatory Determination included a list of example wastes that generally are exempt and a list of example wastes that generally are not exempt. Neither of these lists was intended to be

Among the numerous wastes on the EPA's list are the following: produced water, drilling fluids, drill cuttings, rigwash, and well completion, treatment, and stimulation fluids.[39] Among examples of wastes expressly excluded from the list of exempt wastes are "unused fracturing fluids or acids" and "oil and gas service company wastes."[40] In 1993 the EPA sought to clarify the scope of the exemption by addressing specific activities and by offering the following general guidance:

> [F]or a waste to be exempt from regulation as hazardous waste under RCRA Subtitle C, it must be associated with operations to locate or remove oil or gas from the ground or to remove impurities from such substances and it must be intrinsic to and uniquely associated with oil and gas exploration, development or production operations (commonly referred to simply as exploration and production or E & P); the waste must not be generated by transportation or manufacturing operations.

> * * *

> A simple rule of thumb for determining the scope of the exemption is whether the waste in question has come from down-hole (i.e., brought to the surface during oil and gas E & P operations) or has otherwise been generated by contact with the oil and gas production stream during the removal of produced water or other contaminants from the product (e.g., waste demulsifiers, spent iron sponge). If the answer to either question is yes, the waste is most likely considered exempt.

Clarification of the Regulatory Determination for Wastes from the Exploration, Development and Production of Crude Oil, Natural Gas and Geothermal Energy, 58 Fed.Reg. 15284, 15284–85 (Mar. 22, 1993).

If a waste is not exempt, the oil and gas developer generating the waste must test it to determine whether it is "hazardous" under the RCRA regulatory regime.[41] If the waste is found to be hazardous, the party creating the waste, the "generator," must comply with detailed recordkeeping, labeling, manifest, reporting, training, and management requirements.[42] Transporters of hazardous waste must comply with equally detailed requirements.[43] The waste can only be taken to licensed hazardous waste treatment, storage, and disposal facilities.[44] As a hazardous waste it would also be subject to the "land ban" which prohibits the

---

a complete itemization of all possible exempt or non-exempt wastes. Also, because definitions of the terms used in these lists vary, the criteria identified in the Report to Congress ["Management of Wastes from the Exploration, Development, and Production of Crude Oil, Natural Gas, and Geothermal Energy"] remain the authoritative source for determining the scope of the exemption.

58 Fed.Reg. at 15285.

39. 53 Fed.Reg. at 25453.

40. 53 Fed.Reg. at 25454.

41. 40 C.F.R. § 262.11.

42. RCRA § 3002, 42 U.S.C. § 6922; 40 C.F.R. Part 262.

43. RCRA § 3003, 42 U.S.C. § 6923; 40 C.F.R. Part 263.

44. RCRA § 3004, 42 U.S.C. § 6924; 40 C.F.R. Part 264.

disposal on land of most hazardous wastes unless they are treated to "substantially diminish the toxicity of the waste or substantially reduce the likelihood of migration of hazardous constituents from the waste * * *."[45] In contrast, if the waste is encompassed by the exemption, and is not discharged into surface waters[46] or placed in an underground injection well,[47] it will typically be governed only by state regulatory programs. Also, the exempt wastes are still "solid waste" subject to the EPA's authority under Subtitle D of the SWDA.

In addition to the EPA's authority under Subtitle D, it also possesses broad authority under the "imminent hazard" provisions of the SWDA. Section 7003 provides, in part:

> Notwithstanding any other provision of this chapter, upon receipt of evidence that the past or present handling, storage, treatment, transportation or disposal of any solid waste or hazardous waste may present an imminent and substantial endangerment to health or the environment, the Administrator may bring suit on behalf of the United States in the appropriate district court against any person (including any past or present generator, past or present transporter, or past or present owner or operator of a treatment, storage, or disposal facility) who has contributed or who is contributing to such handling, storage, treatment, transportation or disposal to restrain such person from such handling, storage, treatment, transportation, or disposal, or to order such person to take such other action as may be necessary, or both.

SWDA § 7003, 42 U.S.C. § 6973. This provision applies to non-hazardous "solid waste" as well as "hazardous waste."

The definitions of "solid waste" and "hazardous waste" used in § 7003 are broader than those used for purposes of Subtitle C of RCRA. Section 7003 relies upon the *statutory* definitions of solid waste and hazardous waste instead of the EPA's *regulatory* definitions found at 40 C.F.R. Part 261. See Connecticut Coastal Fishermen's Association v. Remington Arms, 989 F.2d 1305, 1314–16 (2d Cir.1993) (noting broader "solid waste" definition used for "imminent hazard" citizen suit provisions than used for Subtitle C program). The statutory definition of hazardous waste employs a qualitative approach to identifying potential hazards instead of the quantitative conclusions used by the EPA for Subtitle C regulation. Section 1004(5) of the SWDA defines "hazardous waste" as:

> [A] solid waste, or combination of solid wastes, which because of its quantity, concentration, or physical, chemical, or infectious characteristics may—

---

45. RCRA § 3004(m), 42 U.S.C. § 6924(m).

46. In which case the Clean Water Act may be implicated. See infra § B.2. of this Chapter.

47. In which case the Safe Drinking Water Act would be implicated. See infra § C.1.(c) of this Chapter.

(A) cause, or significantly contribute to an increase in mortality or an increase in serious irreversible, or incapacitating reversible, illness; or

(B) pose a substantial present or potential hazard to human health or the environment when improperly treated, stored, transported, or disposed of, or otherwise managed.

42 U.S.C. § 6903(5). The SWDA also has a citizen suit provision that includes a provision almost identical to the EPA's imminent hazard authority. See SWDA § 7002(a)(1)(B), 42 U.S.C. § 6972(a)(1)(B). This provision is discussed in further detail infra at § C.2.(a) of this Chapter.

The critical requirement under § 7003, and its citizen suit counterpart at § 7002, is that the solid waste "may present an imminent and substantial endangerment to health or the environment." If it does, the persons who generated, transported, or otherwise contributed to the problem can be ordered to take action to abate the imminent hazard. Among parties who can be ordered to take action are those who own or operate a treatment, storage, or disposal facility.

NOTES

1. Suppose an oil and gas developer decides to dispose, on the leased land, drilling fluids, drill cuttings, and other exempt E & P wastes associated with drilling a well. The developer carefully follows all existing state laws concerning the land disposal of such wastes, which permit them to be buried at the well site. Although the wastes are exempt from RCRA's hazardous waste program, they contain concentrations of chemicals, such as benzene and lead, that would make them "hazardous" under the RCRA program—but for the E & P waste exemption. Under common forms of oil and gas leases, would the oil and gas developer have the authority to dispose of these wastes on the leased premises without the lessor's consent? How would the analysis vary if there had been a severance of the minerals from the surface prior to the oil and gas lease? Could the severed surface owner object? The severed mineral owner? David E. Pierce, The Impact of Landowner/Lessor Environmental Risk on Oil and Gas Lessee Rights and Obligations, 31 Tulsa L.J. 731, 739–40 (1996).

2. Although the exempt E & P wastes are not RCRA Subtitle C "hazardous *wastes*," could they ever become CERCLA "hazardous *substances*?" See Jastram v. Phillips Petroleum Co., 844 F.Supp. 1139, 1142 (E.D.La.1994) ("pit or production sludges" associated with oil and gas exploration and production are subject to CERCLA) and Nixon–Egli Equipment Co. v. John A. Alexander Co., 949 F.Supp. 1435, 1443, n. 7 (C.D.Cal.1996) (drilling wastes are not encompassed by petroleum exclusion). Compare Landowner/Lessor Environmental Risk, supra, at 739–40 ("waste exempt under RCRA can be considered hazardous substances under CERCLA.") with Michael M. Gibson & David P. Young, "Oil and Gas Exemptions Under RCRA and CERCLA: Are They Still 'Safe Harbors' Eleven Years Later?" 32 S.Tex.L.Rev. 361, 365–83 (1991) (arguing that exempt RCRA wastes should also be exempt under CERCLA). Could E & P wastes ever trigger an imminent hazard action under SWDA

§ 7002 or § 7003? The EPA, as part of its Regulatory Determination concerning E & P wastes, noted:

> EPA is concerned over the lack of Federal authority under Subtitle D of RCRA [SWDA] to address treatment and transportation of oil and gas wastes. The Administrator therefor will work with Congress to develop any additional legislative authorities that may be needed to address these issues. In the interim, EPA will use section 7003 of RCRA and sections 104 and 106 of CERCLA to seek relief in those cases where wastes from oil and gas sites pose substantial threats or imminent hazards to human health and the environment. Oil and gas waste problems can also be addressed under RCRA section 7002 * * *.

53 Fed.Reg. at 25458.

3. Should exploration and production wastes exempt under RCRA be exempt from CERCLA?

2. MANAGING WATER DISCHARGES

Regulated discharges can occur at several stages of the oil and gas development process. The Clean Water Act ("CWA") prohibits the "discharge of a pollutant" unless the source of the discharge obtains and complies with a "permit" that incorporates specific "effluent limitations" for the discharge. As with other environmental statutes, the regulatory program is revealed only after an interlocking maze of terms are defined. "Discharge of a pollutant" is defined as the addition of a "pollutant" to "navigable waters" from a "point source."[48] The term "navigable waters" is defined as "waters of the United States"[49] and subject to the same interpretive problems noted in § A.1.(a) of this Chapter regarding wetlands regulation.[50] "Point source" is another defined term of art which includes "any discernible, confined and discrete conveyance * * * from which pollutants are or may be discharged."[51] In United States v. Earth Sciences, Inc., 599 F.2d 368 (10th Cir.1979), the court noted the need for a broad interpretation of the term "point source" stating:

> The touchstone of the [CWA's] regulatory scheme is that those needing to use the waters for waste distribution must seek and obtain a permit to discharge that waste, with the quantity and quality of the discharge regulated. The concept of a point source was designed to further this scheme by embracing the broadest possible definition of any identifiable conveyance from which pollutants might enter the waters of the United States.

* * *

---

48. CWA § 502(12), 33 U.S.C. § 1362(12).

49. CWA § 502(7), 33 U.S.C. § 1362(7).

50. The jurisdictional scope of the CWA, as applied to point sources, is examined in detail infra at § C.1.

51. CWA § 502(14), 33 U.S.C. § 1362(14).

We believe it contravenes the intent of FWPCA [CWA] and the structure of the statute to exempt from regulation any activity that emits pollution from an identifiable point.

599 F.2d at 373. The term "pollutant" includes a wide range of waste material but also includes such things as "heat."[52] At the drilling stage of operations the most common "pollutant" discharges that may require a permit consist of drilling fluids, drill cuttings, well treatment, workover, completion, and frac fluids, produced sand, deck drainage, and storm water discharges.

The permit is called a "National Pollutant Discharge Elimination System" ("NPDES") permit.[53] Section 402 of the CWA specifies the requirements for issuance of the NPDES permit, including the applicant's agreement to comply with specific "effluent limitations"[54] established for its category of industrial activity. The EPA has placed upstream oil and gas development activities into the "Oil and Gas Extraction Point Source Category." 40 C.F.R. Part 435. To account for different environmental and operational settings, the EPA has divided the Oil and Gas Extraction Point Source Category into five Subcategories: Offshore, Onshore, Coastal, Agricultural and Wildlife Water Use, and Stripper. It is important to accurately classify an operation into the proper Subcategory since the effluent limitations can vary. For example, any operation within the Onshore Subcategory must meet the following effluent limitation: "there shall be no discharge of waste water pollutants into navigable waters from any source associated with production, field exploration, drilling, well completion, or well treatment (i.e., produced water, drilling muds, drill cuttings, and produced sand)."[55] However, within specified parameters, deck drainage, drilling fluid, drill cuttings, well treatment, workover, and completion fluids may be discharged during operations within the Offshore Subcategory.[56]

The Environmental Protection Agency has scheduled rulemakings to develop effluent guidelines for two additional Oil and Gas Extraction Point Source subcategories: a Coalbed Methane Extraction Subcategory and a Shale Gas Extraction Subcategory. Notice of Final 2010 Effluent Guidelines Program Plan, 76 Fed.Reg. 66286 (Oct. 26, 2011). As part of this rulemaking process the EPA also plans to issue a pretreatment standard for produced water that is discharged into publicly-owned treatment works.

Before any discharge can take place, the operator of the discharging facility must have a permit. There are two ways a permit can be obtained.

---

52. CWA § 502(6), 33 U.S.C. § 1362(6).

53. CWA § 402, 33 U.S.C. § 1342.

54. "Effluent limitation" is defined to mean "any restriction established by a State or the [EPA] Administrator on quantities, rates, and concentrations of chemical, physical, biological, and other constituents which are discharged from point sources * * *." CWA § 502(11), 33 U.S.C. § 1362(11).

55. 40 C.F.R. § 435.32.

56. 40 C.F.R. §§ 435.12, 435.13, 435.14, 435.15.

First, an application can be made for an individual permit that covers a single discharging facility.[57] Second, the activity may be covered by a "general permit" which specifies a procedure for a class of applicants to become subject to the general permit.[58] Many general permits have been issued for activities covered by the Oil and Gas Extraction Point Source Category. E.g., Final Reissuance of the NPDES General Permit for Facilities Related to Oil and Gas Extraction in the Territorial Seas of Texas, 77 Fed. Reg. 8854 (Feb. 12, 2012).

Drilling activities can also trigger the need for a storm water discharge permit. Section 402(p) of the CWA establishes a permit program to control the discharge of "storm water,"[59] which is defined as "storm water runoff, snow melt runoff, and surface runoff and drainage."[60] Oil and gas operations may become subject to the program in one of two ways. First, the regulations require a permit for "industrial activity" which is defined to include:

> [O]il and gas exploration, production, processing, or treatment operations, or transmission facilities that discharge storm water contaminated by contact with, any overburden, raw material, intermediate products, finished products, byproducts or waste products located on the site of such operations; * * *[61]

When the CWA was amended in 1987 to add the storm water permit program, the following exemption was included for the oil, gas, and mining industries:

> The Administrator shall not require a permit under this section, nor shall the Administrator directly or indirectly require any State to require a permit, for discharges of stormwater runoff from mining operations or oil and gas exploration, production, processing, or treatment operations or transmission facilities, composed entirely of flows which are from conveyances or systems of conveyances (including but not limited to pipes, conduits, ditches, and channels) used for collecting and conveying precipitation runoff and which are not contaminated by contact with, or do not come into contact with, any overburden, raw material, intermediate products, finished product, byproduct, or waste products located on the site of such operations.[62]

The exemption was designed to encourage oil, gas, and other mineral developers to channel storm water around their facilities so it would not come into contact with contaminants.[63] However, if the operator has

---

57. 40 C.F.R. § 122.21.

58. 40 C.F.R. § 122.28. Subsection (c) of § 122.28 authorizes Regional EPA Administrators to establish general permits covering discharges from offshore oil and gas exploration and production facilities within the Region's jurisdiction.

59. CWA § 402(p)(3), 33 U.S.C. § 1342(p)(3).

60. 40 C.F.R. § 122.26(b)(13).

61. 40 C.F.R. § 122.26(b)(14)(iii) (including facilities in Standard Industrial Classifications 10 through 14; SIC 13 is "Oil and Gas Extraction").

62. CWA § 402(l)(2), 33 U.S.C. § 1342(l)(2). See also 40 C.F.R. § 122.26(a)(2).

63. National Pollutant Discharge Elimination System Permit Application Regulations for Storm Water Discharges, 55 Fed.Reg. 47990, 48029 (Nov. 16, 1990). It was perceived that

experienced a discharge which has been contaminated through contact with an operations site, a storm water discharge permit will be required.[64]

The EPA viewed the § 402(*l*)(2) exemption as being limited to existing oil and gas facilities and asserted the installation of new facilities could trigger a second basis for regulation as a "construction activity." This meant that construction of a drill site or other related facility may require a permit. The EPA's regulations require a permit for storm water discharges associated with "construction activity" which includes the following:

> Construction activity including clearing, grading and excavation, except operations that result in the disturbance of less than five acres of total land area. Construction activity also includes the disturbance of less than five acres of total land area that is a part of a larger common plan of development or sale if the larger common plan will ultimately disturb five acres or more.[65]
>
> . . . .
>
> [Small] Construction activities including clearing, grading, and excavating that result in land disturbance of equal to or greater than one acre and less than five acres. Small construction activity also includes the disturbance of less than one acre of total land area that is part of a larger common plan of development or sale if the larger common plan will ultimately disturb equal to or greater than one and less than five acres.[66]

The construction of a lease road and drill site will in many situations exceed the one-acre threshold. In response to this second basis for regulation, the oil and gas industry was successful in obtaining an amendment to the Clean Water Act as part of the Energy Policy Act of 2005.[67] The amendment added the following definition designed to expand the scope of the CWA § 402(*l*)(2) exemption:

> (24) OIL AND GAS EXPLORATION AND PRODUCTION.—The term "oil and gas exploration, production, processing, or treatment operations or transmission facilities" means all field activities or operations associated with exploration, production, processing, or treatment operations, or transmission facilities, *including activities necessary to prepare a site for drilling and for the movement and placement of drilling equipment, whether or not such field activities or operations may be considered to be construction activities.*[68]

---

requiring operators to obtain a permit would discourage the practice of collecting storm water runoff to avoid contact with mining facilities.

64. 40 C.F.R. § 122.26(c)(1)(iii).

65. 40 C.F.R. § 122.26(b)(14)(x).

66. 40 C.F.R. § 122.26(b)(15)(i).

67. Energy Policy Act of 2005, Pub. L. No. 109–58, § 323, 119 Stat. 594 (2005).

68. CWA § 502(24), 33 U.S.C. § 1362(24) (emphasis added).

The EPA responded to this legislative change by revising 40 C.F.R. § 122.26(a)(2)(ii) to make it clear that construction activities will not trigger a permit obligation unless they result in a discharge of a regulated contaminant other than "sediment."[69] This interpretation of the amendment was rejected by the court in Natural Resources Defense Council v. U.S. Environmental Protection Agency, 526 F.3d 591 (9th Cir. 2008) (sediment is a contaminant that can trigger a permit under the § 402(l)(2) of the Act). Therefore, because "sediment" is created by construction activities, and most drilling activities will exceed the one-acre threshold, a storm water discharge permit will be required if the sediment is likely to be washed into "waters of the United States" by storm events.

NOTES

1.   Discharges of industrial wastes into ocean waters that are beyond the CWA's jurisdictional reach are generally prohibited by the Marine Protection, Research and Sanctuaries Act, 33 U.S.C. §§ 1401 to 1445, which is better known as the "Ocean Dumping Act." Professor Conine has described the operation of the Act as follows:

> The Act precludes, among other actions, the removal of virtually any material or waste from the United States for the purpose of dumping it in ocean waters without first obtaining a permit. Disposal of waste pursuant to provisions of the Act is not considered "dumping" under the Act. Consequently, disposal under an NPDES permit will not require additional permitting under the Ocean Dumping Act.

> Ocean dumping permits are to be issued by the EPA upon consideration of a number of factors, including need, environmental effects and alternatives, and determination that the disposal will not "unreasonably degrade or endanger human health, welfare or amenities, or the marine environment, ecological system, or economic potentialities." Industrial wastes, including wastes from processing plants, are not entitled to a permit after December 31, 1991, except in emergencies.

Gary Conine, "Environmental Issues in Offshore Exploration and Production Activities," 42 Inst.Oil & Gas L.and Tax'n 8–1, 8–19 (1991) (footnotes omitted). *See also* CLAUDIA COPELAND, OCEAN DUMPING ACT: A SUMMARY OF THE LAW, CONGRESSIONAL RESEARCH SERVICE (Dec. 15, 2010), *available at* http://www.gc.noaa.gov/documents/gcil_crs_oda.pdf.

2.   When considering the need for a NPDES permit, particularly a storm water discharge permit, it must be remembered that only discharges into "waters of the United States" require permits under the CWA.

3.   HYDRAULIC FRACTURING ISSUES

The following article excerpts discuss the potential environmental issues associated with hydraulic fracturing.

---

69. Amendments to the National Pollutant Discharge Elimination System (NPDES) Regulations for Storm Water Discharges Associated With Oil and Gas Exploration, Production, Processing, or Treatment Operations or Transmission Facilities, 71 Fed. Reg. 33628, 33639 (June 12, 2006).

THOMAS E. KURTH, MICHAEL MAZZONE, MARY MENDOZA, CHRISTOPHER KULANDER, *"AMERICAN LAW AND JURISPRUDENCE ON FRACING—2012"*

58 Rocky Mt. Min. L. Inst. **70**

Fracing Fluids and Operations

* * *

Fracing operations are noisy. All natural gas production results in temporary noise from drilling and subsequent fracing that can last from two weeks to over a month. Noise curtailment is usually a function of local law and is measured and controlled in multiple ways. The simplest type of local noise ordinance sets a direct limit on noise caused by drilling and fracing operations. Such regulations typically prohibit noise greater than 70–90 decibels as measured from 200–400 feet from the edge of a site. To cut down on fracing noise, companies have put "sound blankets" resembling large, heavy quilts around the equipment. In other municipalities, an averaging method is used. For example, Ft. Worth, Texas requires that drilling and fracing be no more than five decibels higher during the day than the ambient (background) noise and no more than three decibels higher at night. In such cases, wellsites are usually situated as close to a road as possible to minimize access costs and to take advantage of a higher ambient (*i.e.* masking) noise level caused by the road traffic.[71]

* * *

[A] typical fracing operation in the Marcellus Shale requires between one to five million gallons of fracing fluid, mostly water, per well.[72] About twenty to forty percent (20%–40%) of the fluid can be expected to return to the surface through the borehole after the proppant has been injected and the water is being drawn out. In general, there are three ways to deal with fracing fluid left over from operations: (i) inject it back via a disposal well, similar to those used to dispose excess brine from more traditional operations; (ii) treat the fluid through evaporation and/or settling at the surface; or (iii) gather the used fracing fluid, dilute it with freshwater, and truck or pipe it to another project and reuse it again.[73]

The third method is the least expensive and is favored for its seemingly sound environmental underpinnings. However, the used fracing fluid typically must be treated upon its return to the surface. Used fracing fluid

---

70. © 2012 Haynes and Boone, LLP, and reprinted with permission from the authors, Haynes and Boone, LLP, and the Rocky Mountain Mineral Law Foundation.

71. Ft. Worth Municipal Code, Chapter 15, Article II, §§ 15–30 *et seq.* (2006).

72. Michele Rodgers, et al. *Marcellus Shale: What Local Governments Need to Know*, Penn State College of Agricultural Sciences (2008) p. 11, *available at* www.naturalgas.psu.edu (last visited Sep. 30, 2012). The frequency of drilling activity in a locale, rural or urban, and its associated impact on the local populace can present a wide variety of challenges which require the formulation of solutions by the operators, service companies, and not uncommonly state and local regulatory agencies.

73. Colter Cookson, *Technologies Enable Frac Water Reuse*, AMERICAN OIL & GAS REPORTER, March 2010, at 106.

must have solids removed for optimum results upon re-injection and to prevent the hydrogen sulfide (H_2S) or iron sulfide (FeS) from returning with the "flowback" on the fracing fluid as it returns to the surface through the borehole. Disposal of the fracing fluid is another option, with costs dependent on the number and proximity of disposal wells near the fracing operations.[74] This method is more difficult in areas such as the Appalachians as less disposal wells are currently available than in regions where prior development has occurred. Solids in the used fracing fluid are again a concern as they could block up disposal wells or contain naturally occurring radioactive materials (*"NORM"*). * * * Treatment at the surface is potentially the most expensive, as pits for settling and transportation of the fluid to a crystallization/evaporation treatment plant—if either is available—is potentially expensive. However, such costly treatment may be necessary if environmental regulations require a complete reduction of additives and no reuse or injection outlets are allowed or available.[75]

Moreover, the rapid growth of hydraulic fracturing technologies has witnessed a parallel growth of companies developing sophisticated technologies for treatment of the residual water.[76] [These developments are] most welcome at a time when water is increasingly regarded by individual states, localities and commentators as a vital natural resource whose conservation and management is paramount.[77] The scarcity of water is likely to witness significant further development in technologies which will require lesser volumes of water to accomplish the same objectives.

* * *

74. *Id.*

75. *Id.* at 108.

76. Melissa McEver, *Companies Developing Tech to Recycle Fracking Water*, HOUSTON BUSINESS JOURNAL, August 19, 2011, *available at* http://www.bizjournals.com/houston/print-edition/2011/08/19/companies-developing-tech-to-recycle.html; Erica Gies, *Shale Gas Boom Creates Market Opportunity to Clean Fracking Water*, FORBES (Aug. 23, 2011, 12:06 PM), http://www.forbes.com/sites/ericagies/2011/08/23/game-changing-vacuum-creates-market-opportunity-to-clean-fracking-water/; Kevin Robinson–Avila, *Shale-gas water provides new business for Altela*, NEW MEXICO BUSINESS WEEKLY (Oct. 7, 2011, 4:00 AM), http://www.bizjournals.com/albuquerque/print-edition/2011/10/07/shale-gas-water-provides-new-business.html; Jeff McMahon, *Names You Need To Know: Osorb*, FORBES (May 2, 2011, 8:12 AM), http://www.forbes.com/sites/jeffmcmahon/2011/05/02/fracking-pollution-may-be-solved-doe-says/.

77. Matthew Bieniek, *Bill would ban wastewater created by hydraulic fracturing process*, CUMBERLAND TIMES-NEWS (Jan. 30, 2012), http://times-news.com/local/x431317452/Bill-would-ban-wastewater-created-by-hydraulic-fracturing-process; Joe Carroll, *Worst Drought In More Than A Century Strikes Texas Oil Boom*, BLOOMBERG (Jun. 13, 2011, 3:29 PM), http://www.bloomberg.com/news/2011-06-13/worst-drought-in-more-than-a-century-threatens-texas-oil-natural-gas-boom.html; *Hydraulic Fracturing Using Too Much Water?*, CBS7 (Jan. 21, 2011), http://www.cbs7kosa.com/news/details.asp?ID=27486; Mike Lee, *Parched Texans Impose Water–Use Limits for Fracking Gas Wells*, BLOOMBERG BUSINESSWEEK (Oct. 6, 2011, 10:35 AM), http://www.businessweek.com/news/2011-10-06/parched-texans-impose-water-use-limits-for-fracking-gas-wells.html; Nick Snow, *Deloitte report sees crucial energy role for water management*, OIL & GAS JOURNAL (May 28, 2012), http://online.qmags.com/OGJ052812?sessionID=A5611671BEE3148CD05EE88D2&cid=2181944&eid=17285#pg27&mode2.

Contamination

Surface owners often allege that fracing has contaminated the property's air, water, and soil. Landowners seek retribution for the alleged contamination by asserting a variety of causes of action, including, but not limited to, negligence, gross negligence, trespass, and nuisance.[78] In regard to water, surface owners claim that nearby drilling has turned their water either an orange or yellow color, or that it contains gray sediment.[79] They claim that the water tastes and smells bad, and in some cases has become flammable.[80] Filed complaints contain a long list of chemicals alleged to have been found in their water wells: benzene, arsenic, lead, iron, potassium, zinc, ethyl benzene, toluene, barium, and even methane gas.[81]

With regard to the methane gas, according to the petitions, fracing releases underground methane gas, the gas migrates to groundwater aquifers, and gets into the landowners' water wells.[82] The methane escapes the wells via home faucets, creating a fire hazard.[83] Landowners contend that other chemicals, like benzene, are entering the water supply via above-ground contamination, e.g., from spills and improper disposal techniques.[84] Landowners claim that careless treatment of fracing fluids— the mixture of water, sand, and various chemicals that facilitates the breaking of the rock layer (shale) in which minerals are located—causes chemicals to enter groundwater aquifers and water wells.[85] Soil contami-

---

78. See generally, e.g., Complaint, Harris v. Devon Energy Production, 4:10–CV–00708–ALM (N.D. Tex. April 8, 2011); Complaint, Scoma v. Chesapeake, No. 3:10–cv–01385–N, (N.D. Tex. Aug. 11, 2010); Complaint, Fiorentino, et. al. v Cabot Oil and Gas Corp, No. 3:09–cv–02284–JEJ, (M.D. Pa. May 17, 2010); Petition, Lipsky v. Range Resources, et. al., Case No. CV11–0798 (Parker County, District Court, June 10, 2011); Complaint, Becka v. Antero Resources, Cause No. 2:11–CV–01040–MRH (W.D. Penn. July 15, 2011); Complaint, Dillon v. Antero Resources, Cause No. 2:11–CV–01038–MRH (W.D. Penn. July 12, 2011); Complaint, Boggs v. Landmark 4, LLC, No. 1:12–CV–00614–LW (N.D. Ohio, March 12, 2012).

79. See, Scoma Complaint, note 78; Harris Complaint, note 78.

80. See Scoma Complaint, note 78; Fiorentino Complaint, note 78.

81. Id.; see also Casey Junkins, Firm Denies Methane Liability, HERALD STAR (April 17, 2012), available at http://www.heraldstaronline.com/page/content.detail/id/572600/Firm-denies-methane-liability.html?nav=5010.

82. See Fiorentino Complaint, note 78; see also Bryan Walsh, Another Fracking Mess for the Shale–Gas Industry, TIME (May 9, 2011), available at http://www.time.com/time/health/article/0, 8599,2070533,00.html (reporting lawsuit filed in April 2012 against Chesapeake alleging that hydraulic fracturing caused water well to be contaminated with methane).

83. The Internet is littered with home movies of people setting their water on fire to demonstrate the combustibility of tap water. http://www.youtube.com/watch?v=VEQMA0zwMM4; http://www.youtube.com/watch?v=U01EK76Sy4Al; http://www.youtube.com/watch?v=TEtgvwllNpg.

Notably, the veracity of these videos has been called into question by oil and gas companies, sometimes resulting in counterclaims for defamation. See Order of Feb. 16, 2012 Denying Plaintiffs' Anti–Slapp Motion to Dismiss Range's Counterclaims, in Lipsky v. Range Resources, et. al., Case No. CV11–0798 (Parker County, District Court, June 10, 2011) (denying Plaintiffs' motion to dismiss counterclaims by Range alleging that a water-on-fire video released by Plaintiffs' to the news media constituted a conspiracy to defame Range).

84. Scoma Complaint, note 78; Complaint, Berish, et al v. Southwestern Energy Production Company, 3:2010cv01981, (M.D. Pa. Sept. 22, 2010); Complaint, Mitchell v. EnCana Oil & Gas; Chesapeake, 3:10–cv–02555–L (N.D. Tex. April 25, 2011).

85. Id.

nation claims are similar: when the companies spill fracing fluid, produced water and/or oil, the soil becomes contaminated.[86]

In cases alleging air pollution, landowners contend that fumes from the diesel-powered engines are causing them to inhale large quantities of chemicals, like nitrogen oxides and carbon monoxide, on a daily basis.[87] Additionally, landowners claim that fracing creates particulate matter, like smog and dust. Landowners have asserted claims for assault, battery, and intentional infliction of emotional distress, because the "severe air pollution" they allege caused physical distress and injuries like tremors, confusion, irregular heartbeat, headaches, and rashes.[88] * * *

Noise, Odors, and Light

In addition to contamination allegations, plaintiffs often bring nuisance claims. Surface owners aver that unpleasant odors, the operation of the drilling equipment, and the constantly shining lights interfere with the use and enjoyment of their property.[89] They allege that the production activities are abnormal, out of place in their current locations, and create harmful living conditions.[90] As drilling activities occur more often in populous areas, the frequency of nuisance claims may also increase.

* * *

Air Quality Permitting and Controls

The fracing process can result in the emissions of air pollutants from engines associated with mobile, construction and pumping equipment on the surface, from the materials pumped into the well and from the resulting produced gases and liquids. Emissions may include products of combustion from engines or other combustion sources, particulate matter from construction and vehicle movement, and methane, volatile organic compounds and hydrogen sulfide from the well and the recovered liquids.

---

86. Complaint, *Rine v. Chesapeake Appalachia, LLC,* Case No. 5:11–cv–00004–FPS, N.D. W.Va.(April 10, 2011); Petition, *Ruggiero v. Aruba Petroleum, Inc.,* Cause No. CV–10–10–801 (Wise County, District Court, Oct. 18, 2010).

87. Petition, Parr v. Aruba Petroleum, Inc.; Ash Grove Resources, LLC; EnCana Oil & Gas (USA), Inc.; Halliburton Company; Republic Energy Inc.; Ryder Scott Oil Company; Tejas Production Services, Inc.; Tejas Western Corp., No. 2011–01650–E, (Dallas County Court at Law, no. 5, March 16, 2011); Boggs Petition, supra note 78; see also, John Colson, Class Action Suit Filed Against Antero Resources, GLENWOOD SPRING POST INDEPENDENT (July 21, 2011) available at http://www.postindependent.com/article/20110721/VALLEYNEWS/110729994 (describing a class action filed in Colorado state court alleging health consequences suffered as a result of nearby drilling). A similar lawsuit was filed against Antero in March 2011. Ryan Wyrick, Company Dumping in Eagle County Slapped with Lawsuit, VAIL DAILY (Aug. 21, 2011) available at http://www.vaildaily.com/article/20110818/NEWS/110819834.

88. *Id.*

89. Ruggiero Petition, *supra* note 86; Petition, Dow, et. al. v. Atmos Energy Corp; Crosstex North Texas Gathering, L.P.; Enbridge Gather (North Texas) L.P.; Energy Transfer Fuel, L.P.; and Texas Midstream Gas Services, LLC; and Enterprise Texas Pipeline, LLC, No. 2011–30097–211 (Denton County, Tex. Feb. 28, 2011); Petition, Sciscoe v. Atmos Energy Corp; Crosstex North Texas Gathering, L.P.; Enbridge Gather (North Texas) L.P.; Energy Transfer Fuel, L.P.; and Texas Midstream Gas Services, LLC; and Enterprise Texas Pipeline, LLC, No. 2011–70084–431 (Denton County, Tex. Feb. 28, 2011).

90. *Id.*

Potential concerns under the federal and state clean air acts include permitting of stationary sources of emissions and the impact of the emissions.

NOTES

1. Highly publicized claims that hydraulic fracturing causes groundwater contamination have prompted a focus on whether fracing is being adequately regulated. The regulation issue was heightened by a provision of the Energy Policy Act of 2005 which expressly excluded hydraulic fracturing from regulation as "underground injection" under the Safe Drinking Water Act. This in turn focused attention on state regulation of hydraulic fracturing. It was discovered that the states did not have specific regulations addressing "hydraulic fracturing," but instead regulated the practice incidentally as part of each state's long-standing regulation to ensure well integrity and management of surface operations.

2. To date allegations that hydraulic fracturing is causing groundwater contamination have been proven unfounded. For example, landowners in Parker County, Texas alleged their water wells had been contaminated with natural gas due to hydraulic fracturing operations conducted by Range Resources Corporation. These allegations resulted in the EPA issuing an "Imminent and Substantial Endangerment Administrative Order," under the Safe Drinking Water Act, against Range Production Company and Range Resources Company. The Texas Railroad Commission investigated the matter and found no basis for the allegations. Final Order, Commission Called Hearing to Consider Whether Operation of the Range Production Company Butler Unite Well No. 1H (RRC ID 253732) and Teal Unit Well No. 1H (RRC ID 253729) in the Newark, East (Barnett Shale) Field, Hood County, Texas are Causing or Contributing to Contamination of Certain Domestic Water Wells in Parker County, Texas, Oil & Gas Docket No. 7B–0268629 (March 22, 2011). Apparently, the EPA was also persuaded by the evidence and dismissed its enforcement proceedings against the Range entities. United States v. Range Prod. Co., 2012 WL 1108785 (2012) (Joint Stipulation of Dismissal Without Prejudice Pursuant to Fed. R. Civ. P. 41(a)(1)(A)(ii) and (a)(1)(B)).

3. Consistent with other studies on hydraulic fracturing, the Energy Institute at the University of Texas, in February 2012, issued its report refuting the media-created perceptions that fracture fluids are migrating into aquifers and contaminating water wells. CHARLES G. GROAT & THOMAS W. GRIMSHAW, FACT-BASED REGULATION FOR ENVIRONMENTAL PROTECTION IN SHARE GAS DEVELOPMENT, SUMMARY OF FINDINGS 22–23, (Energy Institute, University of Texas at Austin, Feb. 2012), available at http://www.energy.utexas.edu/images/ei_shale_gas_reg_summary1203.pdf.

C. PRODUCTION ACTIVITIES

After the well is drilled, the production process will include several periodic and continuous activities that impact the environment. For example, when oil is produced it must be moved from the wellhead to storage tanks, often water must be separated from the oil, sometimes the oil must be treated to remove impurities. Disposal of produced water will often require the drilling of an underground injection well. When gas is produced it may require treatment to remove condensed liquid hydrocarbons or impurities, such as water and hydrogen sulfide. Pipelines will need to be constructed to move production from the wellhead. Gas may require varying stages of compression as it moves from the wellhead to a major pipeline system. The gas may be taken to centralized "gas plants" to convert its heavier hydrocarbon components into gas liquids such as propane. Throughout the life of a well it will be necessary to perform various maintenance or reworking operations to ensure its continued production. Once all production economically recoverable has been obtained at the primary stage of operations, the lessee may decide to pursue enhanced recovery opportunities which may require additional production facilities.

Several federal environmental laws apply to production operations. As with the drilling phase of operations, the Clean Water Act ("CWA"), Solid Waste Disposal Act ("SWDA"),[91] and the Comprehensive Environmental Response Compensation and Liability Act ("CERCLA"), will each be implicated. Production is typically the stage of development where several other federal environmental statutes will apply, to include the: Clean Air Act ("CAA"), Safe Drinking Water Act ("SDWA"), Oil Pollution Act ("OPA"), Migratory Bird Treaty Act ("MBTA"), and the Emergency Planning and Community Right-to-Know Act ("EPCRA"). First we revisit the role the CWA plays in oil and gas operations by examining the disposal of produced water.

1. MANAGING PRODUCED WATER

By volume, produced water is often the major waste associated with oil and gas production. As noted by one court:

> Oil production brings to the surface water which was originally trapped with oil or natural gas in a geological formation, as well as water and other fluids that have been mixed with oil or gas during the production process. These fluids are known as produced water.

Natural Resources Defense Council v. U.S. E.P.A., 863 F.2d 1420, 1425 (9th Cir.1988). See generally Marion Yoder & Thomas H. Owen, Jr., Disposal of Produced Water, 37 Rocky Mtn.Min.L.Inst. 21–1 (1991). In the past, produced water has been discharged into evaporation or percolation pits, or into surface waters. Today most produced water associated with onshore operations is disposed of through underground injection wells. This shift in disposal practices is due primarily to the Clean Water Act prohibition of the discharge of pollutants into "waters of the United States."

---

91. To include the portion of the SWDA known as the Resource Conservation and Recovery Act ("RCRA").

(a) "Waters of the United States" Revisited

As noted with the identification of "wetlands" in § A.1., and the regulation of drill site discharges and storm water in § B.2., the jurisdictional reach of the Clean Water Act ("CWA") is limited, and defined, by the concept of "waters of the United States." The definition of "waters of the United States" is a particularly important issue for the oil and gas industry. Not only does it define the activities that require a permit under the CWA, it also defines the scope of the oil spill prevention, cleanup, and liability programs under § 311 of the Act.[92] Equally significant is the use of identical language to define the jurisdictional reach of the Oil Pollution Act. See OPA § 1001(21), 33 U.S.C. § 2701(21) (" 'navigable waters' means the waters of the United States * * *.").

QUIVIRA MIN. CO. v. UNITED STATES E.P.A.

765 F.2d 126 (10th Cir.1985), cert. denied, 474 U.S. 1055 (1986).

Before HOLLOWAY, CHIEF JUDGE, DOYLE, CIRCUIT JUDGE, and SAFFELS, DISTRICT JUDGE.[1]

SAFFELS, DISTRICT JUDGE.

Petitioners in these consolidated cases challenge the authority of the Environmental Protection Agency [hereinafter EPA] under the Clean Water Act, as amended, 33 U.S.C. § 1251, *et seq.*, to regulate the discharge of pollutants from uranium mining and milling facilities into gullies or "arroyos."

* * *

The companies contend that Arroyo del Puerto and San Mateo Creek are not "waters of the United States," and therefore the EPA has no jurisdiction under the Clean Water Act to require permits authorizing discharges into these waters.

* * *

Viewed in the light of the substantial evidence test, the court finds that both the Arroyo del Puerto and the San Mateo Creek flow for short distances from the discharge points. Although neither the Arroyo del Puerto nor the San Mateo Creek is navigable-in-fact, surface flow occasionally occurs, at times of heavy rainfall, providing a surface connection with navigable waters independent of the underground flow. Additionally, the waters of the Arroyo del Puerto and the San Mateo Creek soak into the earth's surface, become part of the underground aquifers, and after a lengthy period, perhaps centuries, the underground water moves toward eventual discharge at Horace Springs or the Rio San Jose.

---

92. These programs are discussed in § C.2. of this Chapter.

1. Honorable Dale E. Saffels, United States District Judge, District of Kansas, Sitting by Designation.

It is the national goal of the Clean Water Act to eliminate the discharge of pollutants into navigable waters. 33 U.S.C. § 1251(a)(1). The term "navigable waters" means "the waters of the United States, including the territorial seas." In *United States v. Earth Sciences, Inc.*, 599 F.2d 368 (10th Cir.1979), this court noted that the Clean Water Act is designed to regulate to the fullest extent possible * * * sources emitting pollution into rivers, streams and lakes. *Id.* at 373. "The touchstone of the regulatory scheme is that those needing to use the waters for waste distribution must seek and obtain a permit to discharge that waste, with the quantity and quality of the discharge regulated." *Id.* It is the intent of the Clean Water Act to cover, as much as possible, all waters of the United States instead of just some. *Deltona Corp. v. United States*, 657 F.2d 1184, 1186, 228 Ct.Cl. 476 (1981).

The extent of the Clean Water Act's coverage of discharges of pollution is illustrated by a review of some of the cases which have been before the United States Court of Appeals for the Tenth Circuit. In *Ward v. Coleman*, 598 F.2d 1187 (10th Cir.1979), *reversed on other grounds* 448 U.S. 242, 100 S.Ct. 2636, 65 L.Ed.2d 742 (1980), the court found that Boggie Creek, a tributary of the Arkansas River, is a navigable water of the United States for purposes of the Clean Water Act because the Arkansas River is navigable in fact. *Id.*, 598 F.2d at 1188, n. 1. In *United States v. Earth Sciences, Inc., supra,* the court found the Rito Seco to be a "water of the United States," although it is not navigable in fact nor does it transport any goods or materials, and although it is located entirely in Costilla County, Colorado. Although the Rito Seco did not provide a very significant link in the chain of interstate commerce, the court found that the stipulation of facts indicated at least some interstate impact from the stream and that was all that was necessary under the act. There, the facts were that the stream supported trout and some beaver, the water collected in the reservoirs was used for agricultural irrigation, and the resulting products were sold into interstate commerce. The court stated, "It seems clear Congress intended to regulate discharges made into every creek, stream, river or body of water that in any way may affect interstate commerce. Every court to discuss the issue has used a commerce power approach and agreed upon that interpretation." *Id.* at 375. In *United States v. Texas Pipe Line Co.*, 611 F.2d 345 (10th Cir.1979), the court found that the Clean Water Act covered oil spilled into an unnamed tributary of Caney Creek, which discharges into Clear Boggie Creek, itself a tributary of the Red River. The record reflected that there was a small flow of water in the unnamed tributary at the time of the spill, but there was no evidence that the other streams were or were not flowing. The court stated, "Congress did not in this Act use the term 'navigable waters' in the traditional sense; Congress intended to extend the coverage of the act as far as permissible under the commerce clause." *Id.* at 347. Even though nothing in the record supported an interstate commerce effect of this unnamed tributary, the court found that it was "without question" within the intended coverage of the Clean Water Act. The result was based substantially on the fact that the tributary was flowing a small amount of water at the time of the spill. "It makes no difference that a stream was or was not at the time of the spill discharging water continuously into a river navigable in the traditional sense." *Id.*

This court's findings in *Earth Sciences* and *Texas Pipe Line* compel a finding herein affirming the decision of the EPA. Substantial evidence here supports the Administrator's findings that both the Arroyo del Puerto and San Mateo Creek are waters of the United States. Substantial evidence before the Administrator supports his finding that during times of intense rainfall, there can be a surface connection between the Arroyo del Puerto, San Mateo Creek and navigable-in-fact streams. Further, the record supports the finding that both the Arroyo del Puerto and San Mateo Creek flow for a period after the time of discharge of pollutants into the waters. Further, the flow continues regularly through underground aquifers fed by the surface flow of the San Mateo Creek and Arroyo del Puerto into navigable-in-fact streams. The court finds that the impact on interstate commerce is sufficient enough to satisfy the commerce clause. And, as noted above, it was the clear intent of Congress to regulate waters of the United States to the fullest extent possible under the commerce clause.

The decision of the Administrator is AFFIRMED.

NOTES

1.   Judge Saffels concludes his opinion in *Quivira* stating: "[I]t was the clear intent of Congress to regulate waters of the United States to the fullest extent possible under the commerce clause." Was the holding in *Quivira* correct even though some of the court's statements may be questionable after Rapanos v. United States, 547 U.S. 715 (2006) and Solid Waste Agency of Northern Cook County v. U.S. Army Corps of Engineers, 531 U.S. 159 (2001) ("SWANCC")? After *Rapanos* and *SWANCC* what is the proper analysis of the issues presented in *Quivira*?

Regarding broad commerce clause statements made by courts prior to *Rapanos* and *SWANCC*, consider the following commentary:

Congress never intended to divest the term navigable of all its traditional meaning. The legislative history of the FWPCA of 1972 shows that Congress simply intended to broaden the definition of 'navigable waters' to encompass waterways that had the potential to become part of the system of 'highways' over which interstate or foreign commerce is conducted. The statements made about 'broadest possible constitutional interpretation' simply indicate that, in 1972, Congress felt the 'highway test' *was* as far as it could go under the Commerce Clause. Thus we must avoid the temptation to quote the general limits ('broadest possible constitutional interpretation') while ignoring the specific limits ('highway test') presented in the debates.

The stated goal of Congress in enacting the CWA was 'to restore and maintain the chemical, physical, and biological integrity of the Nation's waters.' With that purpose in mind, the logic of Congress in trying to reach waterways that were 'potentially navigable' makes sense. It seems irrational to prohibit pollution of a navigable river, while permitting pollution of non-navigable creeks, streams and other tributaries that feed into the river. Pollution injected into these tributaries will inevitably reach the river, frustrating Congress' purpose for enacting the CWA. The lack of any discernible hydrologic connection between small, isolated, intrastate waters and more traditionally navigable waterways casts considerable doubt on congressional intent to regulate isolated waters, like the SWANCC [Cook County] ponds, with the 1972 Act.

John W. Broomes, Navigating in Isolated Waters: Section 404 of the Clean Water Act Revisited, 41 Washburn L. J. 209, 224–25 (2001).

2. If the discharge in *Quivira* was into a large pit or land depression from which the discharged material evaporated and percolated into the soil, would a NPDES permit be required? Must there be a hydrological connection between the discharge pit and surface waters? Will a hydrological connection solely with groundwater be sufficient? Will an "ecological" connection between the pit and interstate commerce be sufficient?

3. Should the "waters of the United States" analysis be the same for the § 402 NPDES permit program as it is for the § 404 dredged or fill permit program?

(b) NPDES Permit Requirements

Once the required nexus with "waters of the United States" is established, the next step is to determine whether a "pollutant" is being discharged. Expressly excluded from the CWA definition of "pollutant" are the following:

[W]ater, gas, or other material which is injected into a well to facilitate production of oil or gas, or water derived in association with oil or gas production and disposed of in a well, if the well used either to facilitate production or for disposal purposes is approved by authority of the State in which the well is located, and if such State determines that such injection or disposal will not result in the degradation of ground or surface water resources.[93]

This exclusion removes produced water from regulation under the CWA if it is being disposed of in an injection well under a state-approved injection permit. It also exempts water, gas, and other injected substances intended to enhance recovery of oil and gas. Injection well permits are issued pursuant to the federal Safe Drinking Water Act ("SDWA") underground injection control ("UIC") program. 42 U.S.C. §§ 300h to 300h–7.[94] The SDWA and underground injection are discussed in § C.1.(c) infra. However, if the produced water is not injected, or the injection is done without state authority, it may constitute a discharge of a pollutant under the CWA.

93. CWA § 502(6)(B), 33 U.S.C. § 1362(6)(B).

94. In most producing states, the state oil and gas conservation commission administers the federal UIC program. For a discussion of the Texas program see Smith & Weaver § 14.4.

As noted in § B.2. of this Chapter, the EPA has placed upstream oil and gas operations into the "Oil and Gas Extraction Point Source Category" for CWA regulation. 40 C.F.R. Part 435. This Category is then divided into five subcategories for the creation of effluent limitations that must be incorporated into NPDES permits. Three of the subcategories are based primarily upon geographical distinctions and separates the industry into "onshore," "coastal," and "offshore" operations. The "stripper" subcategory is intended to account for the unique resource choices associated with the economics of marginal oil production. The stripper subcategory applies to an oil well that produces 10 barrels or less each day.[95] Since the EPA has not adopted specific effluent limitations for the stripper subcategory, such discharges must comply with state water quality standards and standards that reflect the permit writer's best professional judgment concerning the required level of control.[96] The "agricultural and wildlife water use" subcategory has both geographic and qualitative components. To come within this category the onshore operation must be located west of the 98th meridian and the produced water must be of a quality that it can be used for agricultural purposes and which is actually used for wildlife or livestock watering or other agricultural activities.[97]

With regard to coalbed methane wells, the EPA initially elected to address discharges on a case-by-case basis instead of applying the national effluent limitations. EPA Region 8 describes the rationale for treating coalbed methane wells differently stating:

> There are two approaches for developing technology-based limits for industrial facilities: (1) National effluent limitations guidelines ("ELGs") and (2) in the absence of ELGs, limitations developed on a case-by-case basis using best professional judgment. Because CBM activities were not significant and widespread when EPA developed ELGs for the Oil and Gas Point Source Category (40 CFR 435), EPA did not consider CBM in developing these guidelines and has not applied them to CBM. Therefore, according to 40 CFR 125.3(c)(2), technology-based limits for the CBM permits need to be developed using a BPJ case-by-case analysis.[98]

The EPA has announced its plan to address coalbed methane wells and shale gas wells by adopting two new effluent limitation industry subcategories: the Coalbed Methane ("CBM") Extraction subcategory and the Shale Gas Extraction ("SGE") subcategory. Notice of Final 2010 Effluent Guidelines Program Plan, 76 Fed.Reg. 66286 (Oct. 26, 2011).

"Onshore" operations encompass everything landward from the ordinary low water mark of the coastlines.[99] "Offshore" operations extend

---

95. 40 C.F.R. § 435.60.

96. CWA § 402(a)(1), 33 U.S.C. § 1341(a)(1) and 40 C.F.R. § 125.3(a)(2).

97. 40 C.F.R. §§ 435.50 to 435.52.

98. EPA Region 8 "Best Professional Judgment" (BPJ) Determination of Effluent Limitations That Represent Best Available Technology Economically Achievable (BAT) for Coalbed Methane (CBM) Activities; Announcement of Meeting, 66 Fed. Reg. 46455 (Sept. 5, 2001).

99. 40 C.F.R. § 435.30. If the activity falls within the agricultural, stripper, or coastal subcategory, it will not be governed by the onshore subcategory.

from the low water mark seaward.[100] "Coastal" operations encompass any onshore operation which takes place in or on "waters of the United States" or in areas specified as coastal by regulation.[101] Varying effluent limitations exist for each subcategory so the first task is to identify the appropriate subcategory that corresponds to an operation. If an "onshore" operation is involved, the applicable effluent limitation on produced water is "no discharge" into waters of the United States.[102] Contrast this with an operation that qualifies under the "agricultural and wildlife water use" subcategory where the produced water can be discharged so long as the daily "oil and grease" limitation of 35 mg/l is not exceeded.[103] Discharges of produced water are permissible under the offshore and coastal subcategories but the specific effluent limitation will vary—from "no discharge" to discharges meeting numeric "oil and grease" limits—depending upon the precise geographic location of the discharging facility and the level of technology that must be applied.[104] Once the appropriate effluent limitations are identified, they will be incorporated into any individual or general NPDES permit covering the operation. See supra § B.2. of this Chapter for a discussion of the NPDES permitting process. For discharges into publicly-owned treatment works from shale gas operations, the EPA is proposing pretreatment standards. Notice of Final 2010 Effluent Guidelines Program Plan, 76 Fed.Reg. 66286 (Oct. 26, 2011).

(c) Underground Injection

The Safe Drinking Water Act ("SDWA"), 42 U.S.C. §§ 300f through 300j–26, establishes national drinking water standards by defining "maximum contaminant levels" ("MCLs")[105] for water delivered to any user of a "public water system."[106] One of the major components of the SDWA is the protection of ground water resources through the regulation of underground injection. "Underground injection" is defined as "the subsurface emplacement of fluids by well injection" but excludes:

> (i) the underground injection of natural gas for purposes of storage; and

> (ii) the underground injection of fluids or propping agents (other than diesel fuels) pursuant to hydraulic fracturing operations related to oil, gas, or geothermal production activities.[107]

---

100. 40 C.F.R. § 435.10.

101. 40 C.F.R. § 435.40.

102. 40 C.F.R. § 435.32.

103. 40 C.F.R. § 435.52(b).

104. Compare 40 C.F.R. § 435.13 (produced water discharge allowed with application of "best available technology" in offshore subcategory) with 40 C.F.R. § 435.43 (no discharge of produced water allowed with application of "best available technology" in coastal subcategory—except for discharges into Cook Inlet).

105. 42 U.S.C. § 300f(1).

106. A "public water system" means: "a system for the provision to the public of water for human consumption through pipes or other constructed conveyances, if such system has at least fifteen service connections or regularly serves at least twenty-five individuals." 42 U.S.C. § 300f(4).

The term "well" is defined broadly to include: "[a] bored, drilled, or driven shaft whose depth is greater than the largest surface dimension; or, a dug hole whose depth is greater than the largest surface dimension; or, an improved sinkhole; or, a subsurface fluid distribution system."[108]

Section 300h instructs the EPA to establish minimum requirements for state underground injection control ("UIC") programs, including the prohibition of underground injection which "endangers drinking water sources."[109] Drinking water sources are endangered if the injection:

> [M]ay result in the presence in underground water which supplies or can reasonably be expected to supply any public water system of any contaminant,[110] and if the presence of such contaminant may result in such system's not complying with any national primary drinking water regulation or may otherwise adversely affect the health of persons.

42 U.S.C. § 300h(d)(2). The SDWA contemplates that each state will take the lead in developing and administering UIC programs in accordance with the minimum requirements established by the SDWA.

Underground injection is prohibited unless a permit is obtained and it is found that the proposed injection will not endanger drinking water sources;[111] the operator of the injection well must also comply with inspection, monitoring, record-keeping, and reporting requirements.[112] For regulatory purposes injection wells have been placed into five classes.[113] Most injection operations associated with oil and gas development will fall under Class II which includes wells that inject fluids:

> (1) Which are brought to the surface in connection with natural gas storage operations, or conventional oil or natural gas production and may be commingled with waste waters from gas plants which are an integral part of production operations, unless those waters are classified as a hazardous waste at the time of injection.

> (2) For enhanced recovery of oil or natural gas; and

> (3) For storage of hydrocarbons which are liquid at standard temperature and pressure.

40 C.F.R. § 144.6(b). For a discussion of how the State of Texas administers its UIC program see Smith & Weaver § 14.4.

---

107. 42 U.S.C. § 300h(d)(1).

108. 40 C.F.R. § 144.3.

109. 42 U.S.C. § 300h(b)(1).

110. "Contaminant" includes "any physical, chemical, biological, or radiological substance or matter in water." 42 U.S.C. § 300f(6).

111. Id. at 300h(b)(1)(A) & (B).

112. Id. at § 300h(b)(1)(C).

113. 40 C.F.R. § 144.6.

NOTES

1. If the wastes are produced in conjunction with the operation of a carbon dioxide well can they be injected into a Class II well? See Arco Oil And Gas Co. v. E.P.A., 14 F.3d 1431 (10th Cir.1993) (no).

2. In 1997 a citizen's group successfully challenged the adequacy of Alabama's UIC program because it failed to require UIC permits to regulate hydraulic fracturing associated with methane gas production. LEAF v. EPA, 118 F.3d 1467 (11th Cir.1997). See also Legal Environmental Assistance Fdn., Inc. v. U.S. Environmental Protection Agency, 276 F.3d 1253 (11th Cir. 2001) (when considering adequacy of Alabama UIC program EPA must properly classify wells used for the injection of hydraulic fracturing fluids as Class II wells; not as a "Class II-like underground injection activity"). Congress responded to these cases in the Energy Policy Act of 2005 by amending the Safe Drinking Water Act to exclude hydraulic fracturing, employing fluids other than diesel fuels, from the definition of "underground injection." Energy Policy Act of 2005, Pub. L. No. 109–58, § 322, 119 Stat. 594 (2005). Hydraulic fracturing is addressed at § B.3. of this Chapter.

3. Some of the most interesting provisions of the SDWA concern the establishment of "critical aquifer protection areas" and "wellhead protection areas." A critical aquifer is "an aquifer which is the sole or principal drinking water source for the area and which, if contaminated, would create a significant hazard to public health * * * " 42 U.S.C. § 300h–3(e). A wellhead protection area consists of "the surface and subsurface area surrounding a water well or wellfield, supplying a public water system, through which contaminants are reasonably likely to move toward and reach such water well or wellfield." 42 U.S.C. § 300h–7(e). The goal is to have states develop programs that regulate, through land use restrictions and other techniques, activities on the surface of land that could impact subsurface water supplies. For example, the location of an injection well in a designated area may be prohibited to ensure it does not impact water supplies.

2. THE SPECIAL ENVIRONMENTAL STATUS OF OIL

Many of the environmental impacts associated with oil and gas development can be traced to the extracted resource. In addition to the wastes created to find, extract, produce, transport, refine, and distribute oil and gas, the oil itself can become a major pollutant when released into the environment. Section 311 of the Clean Water Act ("CWA") establishes a self-contained regulatory program designed to prevent oil spills, report them when they occur, clean them up, and punish those responsible for the spill.[114] In 1990 the Oil Pollution Act ("OPA") was enacted to add to the EPA's oil spill prevention authorities and to expand the liability of a facility owner or operator in the event of a spill.[115] Although primarily designed to address refined petroleum releases, in 1984 a new Subchapter IX was added to the Solid Waste Disposal Act ("SWDA") to address the

---

114. CWA § 311, 33 U.S.C. § 1321.

115. OPA §§ 1001 to 7001, 33 U.S.C.A. §§ 2701 to 2761.

storage of petroleum in "underground storage tanks."[116] Above ground storage is addressed under CWA § 311.[117]

(a) CERCLA's "Petroleum Exclusion"

As noted in § A.2. of this Chapter, wastes generated as part of the oil and gas exploration, development, and production process can give rise to liability under the Comprehensive Environmental Response, Compensation and Liability Act ("CERCLA"). The first step in analyzing a potential CERCLA problem is to determine whether a "hazardous substance" is involved. CERCLA § 101(14) defines hazardous substance broadly to include substances listed under § 102 of CERCLA and substances identified as toxic or hazardous under the Clean Water Act, Clean Air Act, Resource Conservation and Recovery Act, and the Toxic Substances Control Act. However, of particular importance to the oil and gas industry, the definition contains the following provision, commonly known as the "petroleum exclusion:"

> The term [hazardous substance] does not include petroleum, including crude oil or any fraction thereof which is not otherwise specifically listed or designated as a hazardous substance under subparagraphs (A) through (F) of this paragraph, and the term does not include natural gas, natural gas liquids, liquefied natural gas, or synthetic gas usable for fuel (or mixtures of natural gas and such synthetic gas).

CERCLA § 101(14), 42 U.S.C. § 9601(14). Therefore, if the waste itself is "petroleum"—as opposed to a waste generated in the process of producing the "petroleum"—it will most likely fall within CERCLA's "petroleum exclusion."

PROBLEM

An oil and gas developer used a large earthen pit to store oil back in the 1920s. When use of the pit for oil storage ceased, the developer removed all the oil they could and abandoned the remaining contents of the pit in place.

---

116. 42 U.S.C. §§ 6991 to 6992k. "Underground storage tank" is defined as:

[A]ny one or combination of tanks (including underground pipes connected thereto) which is used to contain an accumulation of regulated substances, and the volume of which (including the volume of the underground pipes connected thereto) is 10 per centum or more beneath the surface of the ground. Such term does not include any—

* * *

(D) pipeline facility (including gathering lines) * * *

(E) surface impoundment, pit, pond, or lagoon, * * *

* * *

(H) liquid trap or associated gathering lines directly related to oil or gas production and gathering operations * * *.

§ 6991(1). "Regulated substance" includes listed "hazardous substances" that are not regulated as a RCRA "hazardous waste" plus "petroleum" which is defined as "petroleum, including crude oil or any fraction thereof which is liquid at standard conditions of temperature and pressure (60 degrees Fahrenheit and 14.7 pounds per square inch absolute)." § 6991(2) & (8).

117. CWA § 311(j)(5), 33 U.S.C. § 1321(j)(5).

Several decades later the surface owner of the property had the pit filled with dirt, the area leveled, and grass planted. Your client purchased the property and began constructing houses as part of a new subdivision. While excavating a foundation a tar-like substance was discovered, about six feet beneath the surface of the land, which contained several hazardous substances typically found in crude oil. The areal distribution of the tar-like material corresponds with the bottom area of the earthen oil storage pit. Does your client have a potential CERCLA claim against the oil and gas developer that created and used the pit? Against the person who sold them the property?

COSE v. GETTY OIL CO.

4 F.3d 700 (9th Cir.1993).

PREGERSON, CIRCUIT JUDGE:

Don A. Cose and Darlene A. Cose ("the Coses") appeal the district court's grant of summary judgment dismissing their Comprehensive Environmental Response, Compensation and Liability Act ("CERCLA"), 42 U.S.C. § 9601 et seq., action against the Getty Oil Company ("Getty Oil"), *et al.* The CERCLA action sought recovery for response costs needed to clean subsurface crude oil tank bottom waste discovered on property purchased from Getty Oil. The tank bottom waste contains substances deemed hazardous under CERCLA. The district court based its dismissal on its conclusion that crude oil tank bottoms fall within CERCLA's petroleum exclusion. We disagree and therefore reverse.

Background

Getty Oil produced crude oil from wells in the Tafts–Fellow area of Kern County, California. The oil was transported by Getty to its Avon refinery in Martinez, California via a pipeline route and pumping stations located at twelve-mile intervals. The crude oil was stored at the pumping stations in tanks and heated to reduce its viscosity. The oil was then pumped farther along the pipeline.

When crude oil is stored in tanks, suspended sedimentary solids in the crude oil settle to the bottom. Because water is heavier than oil, it separates from the oil and also collects at the bottom of the tank. The bottom layer of the tank is known as basic sediment and water, or "crude oil tank bottoms." Crude oil tank bottoms are typically drained from crude oil storage facilities and disposed of in nearby sumps.

One pumping station used by Getty Oil was located in Tracy, California. The sump facility for the Tracy pumping station was situated on nearby property called the "Gravel Pit." About once a week, the crude oil tank bottoms from the Tracy pumping station storage tanks were drained and dumped in the Gravel Pit. Getty Oil closed the Tracy pumping station by 1968, when a new pipeline system on a different route rendered the Tracy station obsolete.

In May 1974, Don A. Cose purchased the Gravel Pit, a 40–acre parcel of undeveloped land, from Getty Oil * * * for $50,000. The complaint alleges that when Cose purchased the property, a layer of topsoil concealed the crude oil tank bottom materials dumped on the property and hence, a reasonable inspection of the premises did not disclose the dumped materials. The Coses contend that they discovered the presence of a "subsurface asphalt or tar-like material" on the property in November 1987 when they undertook to develop the property for housing. They then commissioned Kleinfelder, Inc., a soils and environmental engineering firm, to investigate the property further. The investigation included a preliminary assessment of the chemical composition of the oily waste found on the property. Of particular concern, the investigation revealed a "high concentration" (10.5 ppm) of Chrysene, a known carcinogen. Kleinfelder Report, at 4. The concentration level of Chrysene in crude oil in the region was determined to be 28.0 ppm. The Kleinfelder report recommended that "the waste, which contains concentrations of [petroleum hydrocarbons] that are considered hazardous by many regulatory agencies, be removed or stabilized prior to development of the site." Kleinfelder Report, at 1.

Based on the results of the Kleinfelder investigation, the Coses filed suit in federal district court under CERCLA to recover "response costs" needed to clean up the Gravel Pit property.[1] 42 U.S.C. § 9607(a)(3).

In response, Getty Oil moved for summary judgment. In its summary judgment motion, Getty Oil contended that the Coses could not prove that Getty Oil had disposed of a "hazardous substance" on the Gravel Pit property because CERCLA excludes from its "hazardous substances" definition crude oil tank bottoms.

The district court agreed and granted summary judgment in favor of Getty Oil. This appeal followed.

Analysis

* * *

On appeal, the Coses do not allege that summary judgment was improper due to a genuine issue of material fact. Rather, this appeal rests solely on a claim that the district court incorrectly applied the relevant substantive law. Hence, we must review the relevant substantive law underlying CERCLA claims in this context.

Congress enacted CERCLA in 1980 "to facilitate the cleanup of leaking hazardous waste disposal sites." * * * To further this purpose, Congress created a private cause of action for certain "response costs" against various types of persons who contributed to hazardous waste dumping at a specific site. * * *

To state a prima facie case under CERCLA, 42 U.S.C. § 9607(a), a plaintiff must allege that: (1) the waste disposal site is a "facility" within the meaning of 42 U.S.C. § 9601(9); (2) a "release" or "threatened release" of a "hazardous substance" from the facility has occurred, *id.*

---

1. The Coses also brought pendent state claims seeking damages for public and private nuisance, negligence, strict liability based on a defective product, statutory tort, and fraud.

§ 9607(a)(4); (3) such release or "threatened release" will require the expenditure of response costs that are "consistent with the national contingency plan," *id.* §§ 9607(a)(4) and (a)(4)(B); and, (4) the defendant falls within one of four classes of persons subject to CERCLA's liability provisions. *Id.* at §§ 9607(a)(1)–(4) * * *

Here, the district court granted summary judgment in favor of the defendants because it concluded as a matter of law that crude oil tank bottoms are not "hazardous substances" under CERCLA. Hence, the court held that the Coses could not establish a prima facie case under CERCLA because they could not show that Getty Oil had released a "hazardous substance."

CERCLA defines "hazardous substance" by reference to substances listed under various other federal statutes. * * * See 40 C.F.R. § 302.4 (comprehensive listing of CERCLA hazardous substances). But § 9601(14) of CERCLA expressly excludes from its "hazardous substance" definition "petroleum, including crude oil or any fraction thereof which is not otherwise specifically listed or designated as a hazardous substance under subparagraphs (A) through (F) of [§ 9601(14)]...."

Both the EPA and our court interpret the petroleum exclusion to apply to petroleum products, even if a specifically listed hazardous substance, such as Chrysene, is indigenous to such products. *See* EPA Memorandum, July 31, 1987; *Wilshire Westwood Assoc.*, 881 F.2d 801 (leaded gasoline falls within the petroleum exclusion despite hazardous indigenous components and additives). In Wilshire, we analyzed the plain meaning of CERCLA, its post-enactment legislative history, and the EPA's interpretation of the statute to reach the following conclusion:

> [T]he petroleum exclusion in CERCLA does apply to unrefined and refined gasoline *even though certain of its indigenous components and certain additives during the refining process have themselves been designated as hazardous substances within the meaning of CERCLA.*

881 F.2d at 810 (emphasis added).

The EPA has followed this interpretation through its rules and memoranda. As the EPA explained in a Final Rule published April 4, 1985,

> EPA interprets the petroleum exclusion to apply to materials such as crude oil, petroleum feedstocks, and refined petroleum products, *even if a specifically listed or designated hazardous substance is present* in such products. However, EPA does not consider materials such as *waste oil to which listed CERCLA substances have been added* to be within the petroleum exclusion.

50 Fed.Reg. 13,460 (April 4, 1985) (emphasis added). *See also Mid Valley Bank v. North Valley Bank*, 764 F.Supp. 1377, 1384 (E.D.Cal.1991) (waste oil containing CERCLA hazardous substances does not fall under CERCLA's petroleum exclusion); *United States v. Western Processing Co.*, 761 F.Supp. 713, 722 (W.D.Wash.1991) (tank bottom sludge *does not* fall

within the petroleum exclusion in part because the sludge at issue contained contaminants that were not indigenous to the crude oil itself).

If a specifically listed hazardous substance is indigenous to petroleum and is present as a result of the release of petroleum, such substance will fall within the petroleum exclusion *unless* it is present at a concentration level that exceeds the concentration level that naturally occurs in the petroleum product. *See, e.g., State of Washington v. Time Oil Co.*, 687 F.Supp. 529, 532 (W.D.Wash.1988) (contaminants in excess of amounts that would have occurred during the oil refining process and substances that would not have occurred due to the refining process do not fall under the petroleum exclusion).

Our court has not yet addressed the question whether the separated sediment and water that constitute crude oil tank bottoms fall within CERCLA's petroleum exclusion. This is the issue that we must decide.

The Coses contend that crude oil tank bottoms are discarded waste products and not fractions of the crude oil. Hence, the Chrysene, which is part of the tank bottom material dumped at the Gravel Pit, does not fall within the petroleum exclusion. In contrast, Getty Oil contends that crude oil tank bottoms are *components* of the crude oil. Hence, because the concentration level of the Chrysene found in the Gravel Pit does not exceed the concentration level found in regional crude oil, the tank bottoms fall within the petroleum exclusion. We address each argument in turn.

A. Argument that Crude Oil Tank Bottoms Are Not "Petroleum, Including Crude Oil or a Fraction Thereof" Under CERCLA, 42 U.S.C. § 9601(14)

1. Definition of "Fraction" and "Petroleum"

As a starting point, we will examine the definitions of the words "fraction" and "petroleum." Our court took judicial notice of these definitions in *Wilshire Westwood Assoc. v. Atlantic Richfield*, 881 F.2d at 803. In Wilshire, we defined "fraction" to mean "one of several portions (as of a distillate or precipitate) separable by fractionation and consisting either of mixtures or pure chemical compounds." *Id.* (citing *Webster's Third New International Dictionary Unabridged* (1981)).

Likewise, in *Wilshire* we defined "petroleum" as:

[A]n oily flammable bituminous liquid . . . that is essentially a compound mixture of hydrocarbons of different types with small amounts of other substances (as oxygen compounds, sulfur compounds, nitrogen compounds, resinous and asphaltic components, and metallic compounds) . . . and *that is subjected to various refining processes* (a fractional distillation, cracking, catalytic reforming, hydroforming, alkylation, polymerization) *for producing useful products* (as gasoline, naphtha, kerosene, fuel oils, lubricants, waxes, asphalt, coke, and chemicals. . . .)

Id. (emphasis added). Crude oil tank bottoms do not fall within the plain meaning of the definition of "fraction" or "petroleum."

Crude oil tank bottoms are comprised of water and sedimentary solids that settle out of the crude oil and create a layer of waste at the bottom of the crude oil storage tanks. Such tank bottoms accumulate naturally before the crude oil even reaches the refinery. Crude oil tank bottoms are not "one of several portions separable by fractionation" of crude oil, as required by our definition of "fraction."

Likewise, crude oil tank bottoms are never "subjected to various refining processes" as required by our "petroleum" definition.[2] Moreover, such tank bottoms are not used "for producing useful products." Rather, as evidenced at the Gravel Pit property, the substance is simply discarded waste.

Accordingly, the definitions of "fraction" and "petroleum" as adopted by our court urge a conclusion that crude oil tank bottoms *do not* fall within CERCLA's exclusion of "petroleum, including crude oil or a fraction thereof."

2. United States v. Western Processing Co.

The only federal court to address whether tank bottom material is "petroleum" applied reasoning similar to the reasoning reflected in the definition of petroleum. In *United States v. Western Processing Co.*, 761 F.Supp. at 721, the district court concluded that "tank bottom sludge is a contaminated waste product, and *not a petroleum fraction, as that term is used in [CERCLA]*." *Id.* (emphasis added).[3] In so ruling, the court focused in part on the tank bottom's status as "waste" in contrast to a useful petroleum product, which would be considered a petroleum fraction under CERCLA.

The decision in *Western Processing* relied heavily on EPA interpretations of CERCLA's petroleum exclusion. In so doing, the district court noted that, as the agency with the relevant CERCLA expertise, EPA's interpretations of the petroleum exclusion are entitled to "considerable deference." *Id.* The court further observed that "the [EPA's] interpretations harmonize the petroleum exclusion with the goal of CERCLA in order that the fullest remedial nature of the statute may be realized." *Id.*

The district court noted a "theme" running through two EPA documents: that *wastes are distinguishable from recyclables.* Id. The court cited an EPA Final Rule published April 4, 1985 in which the EPA states in

---

2. The separation of the tank bottoms from the crude oil does not occur as part of the "fractional distillation" process. Rather, fractional distillation is an industrial (refinery) process whereby the crude oil is partially vaporized and the vapor and residue recovered separately. *Encyclopedia of Chemistry*, "Distillation," at 326 (4th ed. 1984).

3. It is important to note that *Western Processing* is factually distinguishable from the case at hand because that case involved tank bottom material to which sand and rust contaminants from the sides of the storage tanks had been added. Here, the Coses do not contend that the tank bottoms that were disposed of in the Gravel Pit property were contaminated with any substances other than those that separated from the stored crude oil. Nonetheless, much of the *Western Processing* analysis is relevant to the case at hand.

Section 1, Hazardous Substances Subject to This Rule, a. ICRE Substances:

> If a nondesignated ICR substance is spilled and immediately cleaned up for repackaging, reprocessing, recycling, or reuse, it is not a waste and the spill need not be reported.
>
> ... However, if the substance is not cleaned up for eventual disposal, it is then a waste (and thus a hazardous substance) which has been released to the environment and must be reported if it exceeds the RQ.
>
> ... [T]oday's final rule has been clarified to show the distinction between substances that are wastes prior to their initial release and substances that become wastes after their initial release.

Id.

Similarly, the court in *Western Processing* cited a December 13, 1990 EPA Memorandum, which stated that "[t]he wastes from the interior of the tank [that] include *unrecovered* product, water, sludge, scale, etc. *are presumed to be hazardous. . . .* The only method to remove the presumption is to test the waste for characteristics of a hazardous waste." *Id.* (citation omitted) (emphasis added).

Applying the EPA's approach, the court in *Western Processing* held:

> [The] tank bottom material was certainly "waste" as it was being hauled away for disposal, not for reuse. For whatever reason Congress may have elected to treat "petroleum" releases differently under CERCLA, *conceptually there is a difference between releases of petroleum, products from tanker spills or from leaking storage tanks and the delivery of petroleum related waste material to a disposal or treatment facility.* The former releases have unique characteristics, while in the latter case, the wastes are just one more waste product delivered to a facility where other such wastes accumulated from deliveries by others.

Id. at 721 (emphasis added).

Here, the crude oil tank bottoms are clearly "waste materials." Getty Oil disposed of the tank bottom materials with no intention of recycling such materials.[4] Hence, the "waste vs. recyclable" distinction further supports a conclusion that crude oil tank bottoms are *not* a fraction of crude oil and that the tank bottoms therefore do not fall within CERCLA's petroleum exclusion.[5]

---

4. Getty Oil's argument that the discarded tank bottoms may indeed be "recyclable" at this time is irrelevant because Getty disposed of the substances with no intention to recycle or reuse such materials, as evidenced by the fact that the company sold the Gravel Pit to the Coses without attempting any reuse options.

5. As further support for the contention that Congress intended the petroleum exclusion to protect "useful" products only, the Coses also note additional CERCLA language that excludes "natural gas, natural gas liquids, liquefied natural gas, or synthetic gas *usable for fuel. . . .*" from the definition of "hazardous substance." 42 U.S.C. § 9601(14).

3. Legislative History

CERCLA's legislative history regarding the scope of the petroleum exclusion lends further support for the conclusion that tank bottom substances disposed of in dump sites do not fall within CERCLA's petroleum exclusion. An EPA Memorandum dated July 31, 1987, which specifically addresses the petroleum exclusion, characterizes these remarks of Congresswoman Mikulski as reflecting Congressional intent:

> I realize that it is disappointing to see no oil-related provision in the bill, but we must also realize that this is our only chance to get hazardous waste dump site cleanup legislation enacted.
>
> Moreover, there is already a mechanism in place that is designed to deal with spills in navigable waterways. There is not, however, any provision currently in our law that addresses the potentially ruinous situation of abandoned toxic waste sites.

EPA Memorandum, July 31, 1987 (citing 126 Cong.Rec. H11796) (daily ed. December 3, 1980). Congresswoman Mikulski's remarks indicate that CERCLA's focus is on cleanup of hazardous waste dump sites. We should interpret the petroleum exclusion in light of CERCLA's overall purpose. This purpose further compels us to conclude that crude oil tank bottoms, which include hazardous components such as Chrysene, that are dumped at waste sites should not find protection under CERCLA's petroleum exclusion.

B. The District Court's Grant of Summary Judgment

The district court based its decision to grant summary judgment in favor of Getty Oil on: (1) a 1981 EPA Memorandum that states that petroleum waste or waste oil[6] not specifically listed under the Resource Conservation and Recovery Act ("RCRA") is excluded from the definition of "hazardous substance" under CERCLA;[7] and (2) a 1982 opinion by the EPA General Counsel that states that the petroleum exclusion encompasses hazardous substances inherent in petroleum, but not those added to or mixed with petroleum or those found at concentrations exceeding those normally found in petroleum. A closer review of these considerations indicate that the district court erred in its conclusion of law.

The 1981 and 1982 memoranda do not bear upon whether crude oil tank bottoms are "petroleum" within the meaning of CERCLA. As discussed above, crude oil tank bottoms are not "petroleum waste" or "waste oil" because such tank bottoms are not "petroleum" to begin with. Crude oil tank bottoms are merely comprised of water and suspended solids that settle out of crude oil and collect at the bottom of the crude oil storage tanks en route to the refineries. The 1981 and 1982 memoranda on which the district court relied in granting summary judgment address the application of the petroleum exclusion to a *petroleum* product, either one

---

6. The EPA subsequently interpreted "waste oil" to include only *unadulterated* waste oil. EPA Memorandum, July 31, 1987, n. 2.

7. Crude oil tank bottoms are not specifically listed under RCRA.

that is a "waste" petroleum product or one that contains indigenous hazardous products. Because crude oil tank bottoms are not "petroleum products," the memoranda do not apply.

The district court further based its decision to grant summary judgment on the fact that *leaded* tank bottoms in the refining industry are specifically listed as "hazardous substances" under CERCLA. Getty Oil argued that such listing demonstrates that the EPA considered tank bottoms *in general* in establishing the "hazardous substances" list. Accordingly, Getty Oil contends that the EPA implicitly decided *not* to list *crude oil* tank bottoms as a hazardous substance. Getty Oil concludes then that we should deem crude oil tank bottoms to fall within CERCLA's petroleum exclusion. As support, Getty Oil cites an EPA advisory letter dated May 21, 1981 from the Chief of EPA's Discovery and Investigation Branch to Mobil Oil. The letter concluded that, despite the specific listing of leaded tank bottoms in the oil *refining* industry as "hazardous substances" under CERCLA, leaded tank bottoms in the petroleum *marketing* industry fall *within* the petroleum exclusion.

Getty Oil's argument, however, incorrectly assumes that *all* types of tank bottoms are considered "petroleum, including crude oil or a fraction thereof" under CERCLA. In this way, Getty argues that, unless a particular type of tank bottoms is *specifically* listed as a hazardous substance and thereby removed from the petroleum exclusion, we must assume that such tank bottoms fall within CERCLA's petroleum exclusion.

In interpreting CERCLA's petroleum exclusion, however, we can identify critical distinctions between *leaded* tank bottoms and *crude oil* tank bottoms. *Leaded* tank bottoms consist of waste generated from cleaning leaded gasoline storage tanks. Patricia Broussard–Welther, *Thermal Desorption Meets BDAT Standards at Louisiana Refinery*, Oil & Gas Journal, Nov. 2, 1992, at 58. As such, such substances have been "subjected to various refining processes" in the production of leaded gasoline. Leaded gasoline in turn is considered a "useful product" within the definition of petroleum, as judicially noticed by our court. See *Wilshire*, 881 F.2d at 803.

Accordingly, leaded tank bottoms constitute "petroleum or a fraction thereof" under CERCLA. As the EPA has observed, leaded tank bottoms will fall within the petroleum exclusion, *unless otherwise excluded as a "hazardous substance" under CERCLA. See* 40 C.F.R. § 302.4.

In contrast, as discussed in detail above, *crude oil* tank bottoms are *not* "petroleum, including crude oil or a fraction thereof" under CERCLA and therefore do not fall within CERCLA's petroleum exclusion in the first instance. *See* discussion *supra*. Hence, unlike *leaded* tank bottoms, crude oil tank bottoms do not have to be specifically exempt from the petroleum exclusion as a "hazardous substance" to invoke CERCLA. Accordingly, the fact that crude oil tank bottoms are not listed as a "hazardous substance" under CERCLA does not preclude CERCLA's application.

Getty Oil also cites as support a statement made by Senator Simpson during Senate debate on related legislation, the Superfund Amendments and Reauthorization Act of 1986 ("SARA"), Pub.L. 99–499, 100 Stat. 1613.[8] Senator Simpson stated:

This bill will not diminish the scope of the present petroleum exclusion. That provision, found in section 101(14) of the Act excludes from the definition of "hazardous substances" all types of petroleum, including crude oil, *crude oil tank bottoms*, refined fractions of crude oil, and tank bottoms of such which are not specifically listed or designated as a hazardous substance under the other subparagraphs of that provision.

132 Cong.Rec. S14931–32 (daily ed. Oct. 3, 1986) (emphasis added).

Post-enactment legislative history merits less weight than contemporaneous legislative history. *See Wilshire*, 881 F.2d at 806. Senator Simpson's stray comment was made *six years* after the enactment of CERCLA's petroleum exclusion, which remains unaltered to this date. Hence, we confer little, if any, weight to the comment.

C. Application of Non–Petroleum Classification

Because we conclude that the crude oil tank bottoms here at issue are not "petroleum" and therefore not subject to CERCLA's exclusion, the Chrysene found within the Gravel Pit's environmental samples is properly viewed as an independent "hazardous substance," rather than as a component of petroleum. Liability is imposed under CERCLA *regardless of* the concentration of the hazardous substances present in a defendant's waste, *as long as* the contaminants are listed "hazardous substances" pursuant to 40 C.F.R. § 302.4(a). *See Louisiana–Pacific Corp. v. ASARCO, Inc.*, 735 F.Supp. 358, 361 (W.D.Wa.1990), *aff'd* 909 F.2d 1260 (9th Cir.1990). Hence, the Coses need only show *the presence* of Chrysene to recover cleanup costs from Getty Oil under Sections 107(a)(3) of CERCLA, 42 U.S.C. § 9607(a)(3). Because the presence of Chrysene in the Gravel Pit is undisputed, we reverse the district court's grant of summary judgment and remand this matter to the district court for further proceedings consistent with this opinion.

REVERSED and REMANDED.

Notes

1. The court in *Cose* felt compelled to try and distinguish tank bottoms associated with refined petroleum from those associated with the handling of crude oil prior to being refined. The court was confounded by the EPA's

---

8. In 1986, Congress enacted Section 205 of SARA, which amended subtitle I of the Solid Waste Disposal Act by adding Section 9003(h), 42 U.S.C. § 6991b(h). Section 9003(h) established a separate response program for petroleum leaking from underground storage tanks. SARA did not alter the meaning of the petroleum exclusion initially set forth under CERCLA but did amend CERCLA by adding a definition of the term "pollutant or contaminant" to CERCLA in Section 101(33), 42 U.S.C. § 9601(33). *See Wilshire*, 881 F.2d at 807. This definition contains a petroleum exclusion identical to the exclusion in Section 9601(14).

specific listing of refinery "leaded tank bottoms" as a hazardous substance. Did the EPA intend that these would be the only tank bottoms subject to CERCLA regulation? Was the EPA's listing done to bring them within the "exception" to the "exclusion" that makes "crude oil or any fraction thereof" subject to CERCLA only when they are "specifically listed or designated as a hazardous substance?" See CERCLA § 101(14), 42 U.S.C. § 9601(14). When the EPA listed leaded tank bottoms its focus was not on CERCLA but rather on RCRA. The EPA determined that certain solid wastes generated during petroleum refining should be managed as RCRA hazardous wastes and therefore designated "tank bottoms (leaded) from the petroleum refining industry" as "EPA hazardous waste No. K052." 40 C.F.R. § 261.32 (list of hazardous wastes from specific sources). Under CERCLA § 101(14) the K052 RCRA "hazardous waste" *automatically* became a CERCLA "hazardous substance." The decision to regulate leaded tank bottoms associated with refinery operations had nothing to do with whether the material was, or should be, encompassed by the petroleum exclusion. The court's "product vs. wastes generated to produce or refine the product" analysis could just as easily be applied to tank bottoms generated from storage of refined products. The only relevance of an express listing under RCRA is the tank bottoms would then be deemed covered by CERCLA so a product/waste analysis would not be necessary.

2. Referring to the Problem, who should have the burden of proof to establish that the tar-like material is, or is not, "crude oil" vs. "tank bottoms?" Compare Ekotek Site PRP Committee v. Self, 932 F.Supp. 1319, 1322–23 (D.Utah 1996) (petroleum exclusion is a "statutory exception" so defendant has burden of proof to establish that its waste comes within the exclusion) and Nixon Egli Equipment Co. v. John A. Alexander Co., 949 F.Supp. 1435, 1443 (C.D.Cal.1996) (adopting *Ekotek* analysis) with United States v. Poly–Carb, Inc., 951 F.Supp. 1518, 1526, n. 6 (D.Nev.1996) ("Since the petroleum exclusion does not appear as one of the § 9607(b) affirmative defenses, and since there is no other language in § 9601(14) supporting a contrary interpretation, we hold that Plaintiff bears the burden of persuading us that the petroleum exclusion does not apply.").

In Tosco Corp. v. Koch Industries, Inc., 216 F.3d 886 (10th Cir.2000) the court held the party seeking to rely upon the petroleum exclusion has the burden of proof. Without citing the *Ekotek* case, the court stated:

> In any CERCLA case, once the plaintiff alleges a release or threatened release of hazardous substances, which Tosco has alleged and supported with evidence here, the party asserting the benefit of the petroleum exclusion bears the burden of proof on that issue. *See Organic Chem. Site PRP Group v. Total Petroleum Inc.*, 58 F.Supp.2d 755, 763 (W.D.Mich. 1999) (because petroleum exclusion is an exception to a statutory prohibition, the defendant bears the burden of showing the exclusion applies.).

Tosco, 216 F.3d at 894, n.5. The court summarized the *Cose* holding as follows: "crude oil tank bottoms are not 'petroleum' and therefore not subject to CERCLA's exclusion. * * *" *Tosco*, 216 F.3d at 893. The Eighth Circuit followed the Tenth Circuit's approach in Johnson v. James Langley Operating Co., Inc., 226 F.3d 957, 663 n.4 (8th Cir.Ark. 2000) ("We agree with the Tenth

Circuit's conclusion that once plaintiffs have presented evidence to support their allegation of a release or threatened release, defendants bear the burden of showing the petroleum exclusion applies."). The court in Cariddi v. Consolidated Aluminum Corp., 478 F. Supp.2d 150 (D. Mass. 2007), follows the *Johnson* analysis, characterizing it as the "majority approach." Id. at 154.

3. CERCLA's petroleum exclusion imposes a major limitation on recovery of cleanup costs when the contaminating material is some form of oil. In most cases the complaining party will be relegated to state tort or statutory law for a possible remedy. In 1990 the Oil Pollution Act ("OPA") was passed in part to fill the liability void created by CERCLA's petroleum exclusion. The OPA applies to the discharge of "oil," which is defined as:

> [O]il of any kind or in any form, including, but not limited to, petroleum, fuel oil, sludge, oil refuse, and oil mixed with wastes other than dredged spoil, *but does not include petroleum, including crude oil or any fraction thereof, which is specifically listed or designated as a hazardous substance under * * * [CERCLA § 101(14)]*

OPA § 1001(23), 33 U.S.C. § 2701(23) (emphasis added). Are CERCLA and the OPA mutually exclusive? Could the tank bottoms in *Cose* be considered "sludge, oil refuse, and [or] oil mixed with wastes?"

4. Although the OPA was designed to fill some of the void created by CERCLA's petroleum exclusion, the OPA has two limiting jurisdictional requirements that are not found in CERCLA. First, the OPA only applies to "an incident occurring after the date of the enactment of * * * [the OPA]" which was August 18, 1990. OPA, Pub.L.No.101–380, 104 Stat.484, 506 (1990) (OPA § 1020); see also OPA § 1017(e), 33 U.S.C. § 2718(e) ("Nothing in this title shall apply to any cause of action or right of recovery arising from any incident which occurred prior to August 18, 1990."). Second, the OPA only applies to discharges or threatened discharges "into or upon the navigable waters" which is defined as—you guessed it—"waters of the United States." OPA § 1002, 33 U.S.C. § 2702 (elements of liability); OPA § 1001(21), 33 U.S.C. § 2701(21) ("navigable waters").

5. Returning to the oil storage pit Problem, could your client use the OPA to address the problem? Should a court be willing to read "waters of the United States" more broadly under the OPA than the CWA? Should the scope of CERCLA have a greater impact on the scope of the OPA than CWA interpretations of "waters of the United States?" Compare Avitts v. Amoco Production Co., 840 F.Supp. 1116, 1122 (S.D.Tex.1994), rev'd on procedural grounds, 53 F.3d 690 (5th Cir.1995) (broad interpretation of "navigable waters" under the OPA) with Sun Pipe Line Co. v. Conewago Contractors, Inc., 1994 WL 539326, at *12 (M.D.Pa.1994) (narrow interpretation of "navigable waters" under the OPA). In Rice v. Harken Exploration Co., 250 F.3d 264 (5th Cir.2001), the court held Congress intended the scope of the OPA to be the same as the scope of the Clean Water Act. Relying upon the Supreme Court's actions in Solid Waste Agency of Northern Cook County v. U.S. Army Corps of Engineers, 531 U.S. 159 (2001), the court in *Rice* held the jurisdictional reach of the OPA did not extend to groundwater nor to oil spills on dry ground that did not reach "waters of the United States." The court went one step further and held that spills on dry land, that enter groundwater, and

which may then later reach navigable waters, are not actionable under the OPA. The oil spills at issue in the *Rice* case were described by the oil and gas lessee as "discharges * * * of the sort that inevitably accompany any oil production operation * * *" *Rice*, 250 F.3d at 265. How might the analysis in Rapanos v. United States, 547 U.S. 715 (2006) affect the court's holding in *Rice*? See generally United States of America v. Chevron Pipe Line Co., 437 F. Supp.2d 605 (N.D. Tex. 2006) (post-*Rapanos* analysis in light of Fifth Circuit precedent).

6. If hazardous constituents are still migrating from the pit area into underlying ground water, would this constitute a post-August 18, 1990 "incident?" The OPA defines "incident" as "any occurrence or series of occurrences having the same origin, involving one or more vessels, facilities, or any combination thereof, resulting in the discharge or substantial threat of discharge of oil; * * *." OPA § 1001(14), 33 U.S.C. § 2701(14). "Discharge" is defined as "any emission (other than natural seepage), intentional or unintentional, and includes, but is not limited to, spilling, leaking, pumping, pouring, emitting, emptying, or dumping; * * *." OPA § 1001(7), 33 U.S.C. § 2701(7). See In re Energy Cooperative, Inc., 1995 WL 330876, at *6 (N.D.Ill.1995), where the court observed:

> The fact that ARCO ceased to own the Facility in 1976 may or may not affect ECI's contribution rights under OPA. The entire gist of ECI's Counterclaim is that ARCO is solely responsible for the environmental damage caused at the Facility—including incidents occurring after 1990—based on ARCO's action while ARCO owned and operated the facility through 1976.

7. The OPA provides for broader categories of damages than are available under CERCLA. For example, a litigant under CERCLA can recover clean-up costs. However, under the OPA the litigant can recover clean-up costs plus:

> Damages for injury to, or economic losses resulting from destruction of, real or personal property, which shall be recoverable by a claimant who owns or leases that property.
>
> * * *
>
> Damages equal to the loss of profits or impairment of earning capacity due to the injury, destruction, or loss of real property, personal property, or natural resources * * *.

OPA § 1002(b), 33 U.S.C. § 2702(b). See generally Liability–Forcing, supra, at 407–416.

8. In § B.1. of this Chapter we were introduced to RCRA's "imminent hazard" provisions. If a waste material falls within CERCLA's "petroleum exclusion," could a private litigant nevertheless use RCRA § 7002 to obtain a cleanup of the material as a "solid or hazardous waste which may present an imminent and substantial endangerment to health or the environment?"

MEGHRIG v. KFC WESTERN, INC.

516 U.S. 479 (1996).

JUSTICE O'CONNOR delivered the opinion of the Court.

We consider whether § 7002 of the Resource Conservation and Recovery Act of 1976 (RCRA), 42 U.S.C. § 6972 (1988 ed.), authorizes a private cause of action to recover the prior cost of cleaning up toxic waste that does not, at the time of suit, continue to pose an endangerment to health or the environment. We conclude that it does not.

I

Respondent KFC Western, Inc. (KFC), owns and operates a "Kentucky Fried Chicken" restaurant on a parcel of property in Los Angeles. In 1988, KFC discovered during the course of a construction project that the property was contaminated with petroleum. The County of Los Angeles Department of Health Services ordered KFC to attend to the problem, and KFC spent $211,000 removing and disposing of the oil-tainted soil.

Three years later, KFC brought this suit under the citizen suit provision of RCRA, 90 Stat. 2825, as amended, 42 U.S.C. § 6972(a) (1988 ed.),[1] seeking to recover these cleanup costs from petitioners Alan and Margaret Meghrig.

KFC claimed that the contaminated soil was a "solid waste" covered by RCRA, see 42 U.S.C. § 6903(27) (1988 ed.), that it had previously posed an "imminent and substantial endangerment to health or the environment," see § 6972(a)(1)(B), and that the Meghrigs were responsible for "equitable restitution" of KFC's cleanup costs under § 6972(a) because, as prior owners of the property, they had contributed to the waste's "past or present handling, storage, treatment, transportation, or disposal." See App. 12–19 (first amended complaint).

The District Court held that § 6972(a) does not permit recovery of past cleanup costs and that § 6972(a)(1)(B) does not authorize a cause of action for the remediation of toxic waste that does not pose an "imminent and substantial endangerment to health or the environment" at the time

---

1. Section 6972(a) provides, in relevant part:

"Except as provided in subsection (b) or (c) of this section, any person may commence a civil action on his own behalf—

* * *

"(1)(B) against any person, including ... any past or present generator, past or present transporter, or past or present owner or operator of a treatment, storage, or disposal facility, who has contributed or who is contributing to the past or present handling, storage, treatment, transportation, or disposal of any solid or hazardous waste which may present an imminent and substantial endangerment to health or the environment....

* * *

"... The district court shall have jurisdiction ... to restrain any person who has contributed or who is contributing to the past or present handling, storage, treatment, transportation, or disposal of any solid or hazardous waste referred to in paragraph (1)(B), to order such person to take such other action as may be necessary, or both...."

suit is filed, and dismissed KFC's complaint. App. to Pet. for Cert. A21–A23. The Court of Appeals for the Ninth Circuit reversed, over a dissent, 49 F.3d 518, 524–528 (1995) (Brunetti, J.), finding that a district court had authority under § 6972(a) to award restitution of past cleanup costs, *id.*, at 521–523, and that a private party can proceed with a suit under § 6972(a)(1)(B) upon an allegation that the waste at issue presented an "imminent and substantial endangerment" at the time it was cleaned up, *id.*, at 520–521.

The Ninth Circuit's conclusion regarding the remedies available under RCRA conflicts with the decision of the Court of Appeals for the Eighth Circuit in *Furrer v. Brown*, 62 F.3d 1092, 1100–1101 (1995), and its interpretation of the "imminent endangerment" requirement represents a novel application of federal statutory law. We granted certiorari to address the conflict between the Circuits and to consider the correctness of the Ninth Circuit's interpretation of RCRA, 515 U.S. 1192, 116 S.Ct. 41, 132 L.Ed.2d 922 (1995), and now reverse.

II

RCRA is a comprehensive environmental statute that governs the treatment, storage, and disposal of solid and hazardous waste. See *Chicago v. Environmental Defense Fund*, 511 U.S. 328, 114 S.Ct. 1588, 1590–1591, 128 L.Ed.2d 302 (1994). Unlike the Comprehensive Environmental Response, Compensation and Liability Act of 1980 (CERCLA), 94 Stat. 2767, as amended, 42 U.S.C. § 9601 *et seq.* (1988 ed. and Supp. V), RCRA is not principally designed to effectuate the cleanup of toxic waste sites or to compensate those who have attended to the remediation of environmental hazards. Cf. *General Electric Co. v. Litton Industrial Automation Systems, Inc.*, 920 F.2d 1415, 1422 (C.A.8 1990) (the "two ... main purposes of CERCLA" are "prompt cleanup of hazardous waste sites and imposition of all cleanup costs on the responsible party"). RCRA's primary purpose, rather, is to reduce the generation of hazardous waste and to ensure the proper treatment, storage, and disposal of that waste which is nonetheless generated, "so as to minimize the present and future threat to human health and the environment." 42 U.S.C. § 6902(b) (1988 ed.).

Chief responsibility for the implementation and enforcement of RCRA rests with the Administrator of the Environmental Protection Agency (EPA), see §§ 6928, 6973, but like other environmental laws, RCRA contains a citizen suit provision, § 6972, which permits private citizens to enforce its provisions in some circumstances.

Two requirements of § 6972(a) defeat KFC's suit against the Meghrigs. The first concerns the necessary timing of a citizen suit brought under § 6972(a)(1)(B): That section permits a private party to bring suit against certain responsible persons, including former owners, "who ha[ve] contributed or who [are] contributing to the past or present handling, storage, treatment, transportation, or disposal of any solid or hazardous waste which *may present* an *imminent* and substantial endangerment to health or the environment." (Emphasis added.) The second defines the remedies a district court can award in a suit brought under § 6972(a)(1)(B): Section 6972(a) authorizes district courts "to restrain any person who has contributed or who is contributing to the past or present handling, storage, treatment, transportation, or disposal of any solid or hazardous waste ..., *to order such person to take such other action as may be necessary*, or both." (Emphasis added.)

It is apparent from the two remedies described in § 6972(a) that RCRA's citizen suit provision is not directed at providing compensation for past cleanup efforts. Under a plain reading of this remedial scheme, a private citizen suing under § 6972(a)(1)(B) could seek a mandatory injunction, *i.e.*, one that orders a responsible party to "take action" by attending to the cleanup and proper disposal of toxic waste, or a prohibitory injunction, *i.e.*, one that "restrains" a responsible party from further violating RCRA. Neither remedy, however, is susceptible of the interpretation adopted by the Ninth Circuit, as neither contemplates the award of past cleanup costs, whether these are denominated "damages" or "equitable restitution."

In this regard, a comparison between the relief available under RCRA's citizen suit provision and that which Congress has provided in the analogous, but not parallel, provisions of CERCLA is telling. CERCLA was passed several years after RCRA went into effect, and it is designed to address many of the same toxic waste problems that inspired the passage of RCRA. Compare 42 U.S.C. § 6903(5) (1988 ed.) (RCRA definition of "hazardous waste") and § 6903(27) (RCRA definition of "solid waste") with § 9601(14) (CERCLA provision incorporating certain "hazardous substance[s]," but not the hazardous and solid wastes defined in RCRA, and specifically not petroleum). CERCLA differs markedly from RCRA, however, in the remedies it provides. CERCLA's citizen suit provision mimics § 6972(a) in providing district courts with the authority "to order such action as may be necessary to correct the violation" of any CERCLA standard or regulation. 42 U.S.C. § 9659(c) (1988 ed.). But CERCLA expressly permits the Government to recover "all costs of removal or remedial action," § 9607(a)(4)(A), and it expressly permits the recovery of any "necessary costs of response, incurred by any ... person consistent with the national contingency plan," § 9607(a)(4)(B). CERCLA also provides that "[a]ny person may seek contribution from any other person who is liable or potentially liable" for these response costs. See § 9613(f)(1). Congress thus demonstrated in CERCLA that it knew how to provide for the recovery of cleanup costs, and that the language used to define the remedies under RCRA does not provide that remedy.

That RCRA's citizen suit provision was not intended to provide a remedy for past cleanup costs is further apparent from the harm at which it is directed. Section 6972(a)(1)(B) permits a private party to bring suit only upon a showing that the solid or hazardous waste at issue "may present an imminent and substantial endangerment to health or the environment." The meaning of this timing restriction is plain: An endangerment can only be "imminent" if it "threaten[s] to occur immediately,"

Webster's New International Dictionary of English Language 1245 (2d ed.1934), and the reference to waste which "may present" imminent harm quite clearly excludes waste that no longer presents such a danger. As the Ninth Circuit itself intimated in *Price v. United States Navy*, 39 F.3d 1011, 1019 (1994), this language "implies that there must be a threat which is present *now*, although the impact of the threat may not be felt until later." It follows that § 6972(a) was designed to provide a remedy that ameliorates present or obviates the risk of future "imminent" harms, not a remedy that compensates for past cleanup efforts. Cf. § 6902(b) (national policy behind RCRA is "to minimize the present and future threat to human health and the environment").

Other aspects of RCRA's enforcement scheme strongly support this conclusion. Unlike CERCLA, RCRA contains no statute of limitations, compare § 9613(g)(2) (limitations period in suits under CERCLA § 9607), and it does not require a showing that the response costs being sought are reasonable, compare §§ 9607(a)(4)(A) and (B) (costs recovered under CERCLA must be "consistent with the national contingency plan"). If Congress had intended § 6972(a) to function as a cost-recovery mechanism, the absence of these provisions would be striking. Moreover, with one limited exception, see *Hallstrom v. Tillamook County*, 493 U.S. 20, 26–27, 110 S.Ct. 304, 309, 107 L.Ed.2d 237 (1989) (noting exception to notice requirement "when there is a danger that hazardous waste will be discharged"), a private party may not bring suit under § 6972(a)(1)(B) without first giving 90 days' notice to the Administrator of the EPA, to "the State in which the alleged endangerment may occur," and to potential defendants, see §§ 6972(b)(2)(A)(i)–(iii). And no citizen suit can proceed if either the EPA or the State has commenced, and is diligently prosecuting, a separate enforcement action, see §§ 6972(b)(2)(B) and (C). Therefore, if RCRA were designed to compensate private parties for their past cleanup efforts, it would be a wholly irrational mechanism for doing so. Those parties with insubstantial problems, problems that neither the State nor the Federal Government feel compelled to address, could recover their response costs, whereas those parties whose waste problems were sufficiently severe as to attract the attention of Government officials would be left without a recovery.

Though it agrees that KFC's complaint is defective for failing properly to allege an "imminent and substantial endangerment," the Government (as *amicus*) nonetheless joins KFC in arguing that § 6972(a) does not in all circumstances preclude an award of past cleanup costs. See Brief for United States as *Amicus Curiae* 22–28. The Government posits a situation in which suit is properly brought while the waste at issue continues to pose an imminent endangerment, and suggests that the plaintiff in such a case could seek equitable restitution of money previously spent on cleanup efforts. Echoing a similar argument made by KFC, see Brief for Respondent 11–19, the Government does not rely on the remedies expressly provided in § 6972(a), but rather cites a line of cases holding that district courts retain inherent authority to award any equitable remedy that is not expressly taken away from them by Congress. * * *

RCRA does not prevent a private party from recovering its cleanup costs under other federal or state laws, see § 6972(f) (preserving remedies under statutory and common law), but the limited remedies described in § 6972(a), along with the stark differences between the language of that section and the cost recovery provisions of CERCLA, amply demonstrate that Congress did not intend for a private citizen to be able to undertake a cleanup and then proceed to recover its costs under RCRA. As we explained in *Middlesex County Sewerage Authority v. National Sea Clammers Assn.*, 453 U.S. 1, 14, 101 S.Ct. 2615, 2623, 69 L.Ed.2d 435 (1981), where Congress has provided "elaborate enforcement provisions" for remedying the violation of a federal statute, as Congress has done with RCRA and CERCLA, "it cannot be assumed that Congress intended to authorize by implication additional judicial remedies for private citizens suing under" the statute. " '[I]t is an elemental canon of statutory construction that where a statute expressly provides a particular remedy or remedies, a court must be chary of reading others into it.' " Id., at 14–15, 101 S.Ct., at 2623 (quoting *Transamerica Mortgage Advisors, Inc. v. Lewis*, 444 U.S. 11, 19, 100 S.Ct. 242, 247, 62 L.Ed.2d 146 (1979)).

Without considering whether a private party could seek to obtain an injunction requiring another party to pay cleanup costs which arise after a RCRA citizen suit has been properly commenced, cf. *United States v. Price*, 688 F.2d 204, 211–213 (C.A.3 1982) (requiring funding of a diagnostic study is an appropriate form of relief in a suit brought by the Administrator under § 6973), or otherwise recover cleanup costs paid out after the invocation of RCRA's statutory process, we agree with the Meghrigs that a private party cannot recover the cost of a *past* cleanup effort under RCRA, and that KFC's complaint is defective for the reasons stated by the District Court. Section 6972(a) does not contemplate the award of past cleanup costs, and § 6972(a)(1)(B) permits a private party to bring suit only upon an allegation that the contaminated site presently poses an "imminent and substantial endangerment to health or the environment," and not upon an allegation that it posed such an endangerment at some time in the past. The judgment of the Ninth Circuit is reversed.

It is so ordered.

NOTES

1. If the "imminent and substantial endangerment" threshold can be met, RCRA § 7002 can be used to address a vast range of environmental problems, including those associated with petroleum. However, as the *Meghrig* opinion illustrates, timing is critical. If the RCRA "citizen" responds to an imminent hazard by spending their own money to eliminate the problem, they will not have a remedy under RCRA. If they are able to delay action at the site, and instead seek a mandatory injunction against those who contrib-

uted to the problem, they may be able to force a cleanup without spending their own money. The issue left unresolved by the Court in *Meghrig* is whether the RCRA "citizen" can begin cleanup work at the site and simultaneously seek injunctive relief and reimbursement from parties contributing to the problem. The result may turn on whether the hazard is still "imminent and substantial" at the time injunctive relief is sought.

2. Suppose an oil and gas developer has unreclaimed well sites located on a producing lease that include inactive, unplugged wells. The surface owner has brought suit under RCRA § 7002 asserting the unreclaimed well sites contain "solid waste" which, in conjunction with unplugged wells that provide a pathway to underground sources of drinking water, "may present an imminent and substantial endangerment to health or the environment." What might the oil and gas developer do to try and avoid the surface owner's RCRA § 7002 claim? Would plugging the wells—eliminating the "pathway"—be sufficient to avoid the surface owner's § 7002 claim? Even though the contaminants remain on site? See Leister v. Black & Decker (U.S.) Inc., 117 F.3d 1414 (4th Cir.1997) (unpublished opinion) (filtration system that removes contaminants from groundwater eliminated immediate threat of serious harm even though contaminants remained in untreated groundwater); Davies v. National Co–op. Refinery Ass'n, 1996 WL 529208, at *3 (D.Kan. 1996) (*Davies I*) (court stated: "Although there is a 'pathway' to the contaminated water in this case—namely, the wells on plaintiffs' property—it would seem that any imminent risk to the plaintiffs' health has been diminished by plaintiffs' awareness that their water should not be consumed and by the availability of an alternative water supply."). In Trinity American Corp. v. U.S. Environmental Protection Agency, 150 F.3d 389 (4th Cir.1998), the court found that supplying well owners with bottled water would not eliminate "an imminent and substantial endangerment" under the Safe Drinking Water Act. The court limited its prior holding in *Leister* to a situation where the defendant "had installed a sophisticated filtration system that remedied previous groundwater contamination * * *" 150 F.3d at 400.

3. If a state agency is addressing the problem, would the doctrine of primary jurisdiction be available to a defendant seeking to have the federal court abstain from considering RCRA citizen suit claims? See Davies v. National Co–op. Refinery Ass'n, 963 F.Supp. 990 (D.Kan.1997) (*Davies II*) (court abstains from pursuing plaintiffs' § 7002 claim while the state environmental agency completed its site investigation and developed a remedial plan). In *Davies II* Judge Brown followed-up on his statement in *Davies I* noting:

> Here, plaintiffs have been warned of the danger and are able to occupy the property without serious risk to their health by using an alternative water supply. In making this observation, the court does not mean to suggest that an endangerment to health cannot be considered imminent whenever the plaintiff has a means of avoiding the hazard. The threat of exposure can always be avoided by evacuating property where hazardous waste is found or by taking other extraordinary measures. See e.g., *Morris v. Primetime Stores of Kansas, Inc.*, 1996 WL 563845 (D.Kan. 1996) (plaintiffs moved out of their house because of the presence of explosive vapors). In contrast to the situation in Morris, the plaintiffs here are able to occupy the property and can operate the radio station

without a threat to their health. The fact that they must use bottled water instead of groundwater is undoubtedly an inconvenience and an economic burden, but it is the type of injury for which an action at law provides an adequate remedy.

963 F.Supp. at 999. In applying the doctrine of primary jurisdiction, and deciding to abstain from pursuing the plaintiffs' § 7002 claim, the court noted: "[T]here is no evidence that an imminent danger to the health of any person will arise if the court abstains to permit KDHE [Kansas Department of Health & Environment] to pursue the investigation and remediation of the site." Id. In *Davies* the defendants had entered into consent orders with the KDHE in which the defendants agreed: "to cooperate with KDHE in investigating and remediating the potential threat to health and the environment from the contamination at the site." 963 F.Supp. at 998. Although the court observed that the KDHE had been involved at the site since 1984 "and still has no definitive plan for remediation," it found "the KDHE investigation has been more diligently conducted since 1995 and appears now to be on the verge of addressing remediation." Id.

4. Regardless of the action taken by state officials, if there is an "imminent and substantial endangerment" must the court act under RCRA? Is abstention ever appropriate? Was the court in *Davies II* really holding there was no imminent hazard in part because the state and the responsible parties were finally focusing on the problem? See Charlotte Gibson, Note, Citizen Suits Under the Resource Conservation and Recovery Act: Plotting Abstention on a Map of Federalism, 98 Mich. L. Rev. 269 (1999).

5. As with the other "citizen suit" provisions of the environmental laws, RCRA § 7002 contains a rather elaborate pre-suit notification requirement. RCRA § 7002(b)(2), 42 U.S.C. § 6972(b)(2). Compliance with the pre-suit notification provisions "are mandatory conditions precedent to commencing suit under the RCRA citizen suit provision; a district court may not disregard these requirements at its discretion." Hallstrom v. Tillamook County, 493 U.S. 20, 31 (1989), rehearing denied, 493 U.S. 1037 (1990). Under RCRA § 7002(b)(2)(C) the RCRA citizen is prohibited from bringing a citizen suit when the state "has commenced and is diligently prosecuting" its own RCRA § 7002 action, "is actually engaging in a removal action" under CERCLA, or "has incurred costs to initiate a Remedial Investigation and Feasibility Study" under CERCLA. 42 U.S.C. § 6972(b)(2)(C). Is it proper for a district court judge to create additional exceptions to the availability of RCRA's imminent hazard authority through abstention?

6. Under CERCLA the cleanup trigger for a private cost recovery action will be whether the situation justifies the incurrence of response costs. As noted at § A.2. of this Chapter, the violation of any applicable or relevant state or federal standard can be sufficient to justify the incurrence of response costs under CERCLA. Amoco Oil Co. v. Borden, Inc., 889 F.2d 664, 671 (5th Cir.1989). Is the CERCLA cleanup trigger less demanding than the RCRA imminent hazard requirement?

7. If the substance at issue is clearly a CERCLA hazardous substance, would there be any reason to pursue a RCRA § 7002 action in addition to the CERCLA action? As noted at the beginning of this Chapter, Congress has not

attempted to coordinate the various environmental laws. Instead, each act must be analyzed as a separate regulatory program to ascertain the unique obligations they create—and to ascertain the unique remedies each act has to offer. For example, in dicta the Court in *Meghrig* noted: "Unlike CERCLA, RCRA contains no statute of limitations * * *." *Meghrig*, 116 S.Ct. at 1255. The Supreme Court has also created its own important distinction between RCRA and CERCLA concerning the recovery of attorney fees and litigation costs. Section 7002(e) of RCRA provides, in part:

> The court, in issuing any final order in any action brought pursuant to this section * * * may award costs of litigation (including reasonable attorney and expert witness fees) to the prevailing or substantially prevailing party, whenever the court determines such an award is appropriate.

42 U.S.C. § 6872(e). In Key Tronic Corp. v. United States, 511 U.S. 809 (1994), the Court held that under CERCLA attorney fees can be recovered from a liable party only to the extent they are necessary for the actual cleanup of the CERCLA site. This excludes fees for work performed to try and recover costs from third parties.

(b) Oil Spills

At the federal level, oil spills are regulated by the Clean Water Act ("CWA") and the Oil Pollution Act ("OPA"); in addition, many states have enacted their own elaborate programs to address oil spills. E.g., Alaska Stat. §§ 46.03.740 to 46.03.790. Oil spill regulation consists of four basic components: reporting, liability, cleanup, and prevention. The CWA oil spill prohibition provides, in part:

> The discharge of oil or hazardous substances (i) into or upon the navigable waters of the United States, adjoining shorelines, or into or upon the waters of the contiguous zone, or (ii) in connection with activities under the Outer Continental Shelf Lands Act * * * or the Deepwater Port Act * * * or which may affect natural resources belonging to, appertaining to, or under the exclusive management authority of the United States * * * in such quantities as may be harmful as determined by the President under paragraph (4) of this subsection, is prohibited, except * * * [certain discharges specifically authorized by the CWA].

CWA § 311(b)(3), 33 U.S.C. § 1321(b)(3). Paragraph (4) of § 311(b) authorizes the EPA to designate, by regulation, "those quantities of oil and any hazardous substances the discharge of which may be harmful to the public health or welfare or the environment of the United States * * * " § 1321(b)(4). The EPA has determined that a "harmful" quantity of oil for purposes of § 311 means discharges of oil that either violate an applicable water quality standard or that:

> Cause a film or sheen upon or discoloration of the surface of the water or adjoining shorelines or cause a sludge or emulsion to be deposited beneath the surface of the water or upon the adjoining shorelines.

40 C.F.R. § 110.3(b). This is known as the "sheen test".[118]

The CWA prohibits discharges that "may be harmful;" it is not necessary to prove the discharge in fact caused harm. Chevron, U.S.A., Inc. v. Yost, 919 F.2d 27, 30 (5th Cir.1990). Therefore, a discharge of oil creating a sheen on "navigable waters" will give rise to liability. The phrase "navigable waters" under the § 311 oil spill program is defined by the EPA,[119] and the courts,[120] as broadly as it is under the § 402 NPDES and § 404 dredged and fill permit programs. See supra § A.1.(a) and § C.1.(a) of this Chapter. Although the Supreme Court's analysis in Rapanos v. United States, 547 U.S. 715 (2006) concerned CWA authority under § 404, its limiting scope would similarly apply to § 311 and other CWA programs.

The oil spill reporting obligation is imposed by CWA § 311(b)(5) which provides, in part:

> Any person in charge of a vessel or of an onshore facility or an offshore facility shall, as soon as he has knowledge of any discharge of oil or a hazardous substance from such vessel or facility in violation of paragraph (3) of this subsection [for oil this is the "sheen test"], immediately notify the appropriate agency of the United States Government of such discharge.

33 U.S.C. § 1321(b)(5). By regulation, the EPA requires that all oil spill reports be made to the National Response Center ("NRC") by calling 800–424–8802. 40 C.F.R. § 110.6. Because prompt self-reporting is essential to the timely cleanup of oil spills, and the identification of responsible parties, failure to report is made a crime punishable by fine and imprisonment for up to 5 years. CWA § 311(b)(5), 33 U.S.C. § 1321(b)(5).[121]

---

118. "Sheen" is defined as "an iridescent appearance on the surface of water." 40 C.F.R. § 110.1.

119. Id. ("navigable waters" mean "waters of the United States" which is then extensively defined to include a wide range of water sources, tributaries to a water source, and their adjacent wetlands).

120. E.g., United States v. Texas Pipe Line Co., 611 F.2d 345, 346–47 (10th Cir.1979) ("navigable waters" included spill into "an unnamed tributary of Caney Creek, which discharges into Clear Boggy Creek, itself a tributary of the Red River."). Compare the approach taken in the post-*Rapanos* decision of United States of America v. Chevron Pipe Line Co., 437 F. Supp.2d 605 (N.D. Tex. 2006).

121. CERCLA has a somewhat similar reporting requirement for release of a "reportable quantity" of a "hazardous substance:"

> Any person in charge of a vessel or an offshore or an onshore facility shall, as soon as he has knowledge of any release * * * of a hazardous substance from such vessel or facility in quantities equal to or greater than those determined pursuant to section 9602 [CERCLA § 102] of this title, immediately notify the National Response Center established under the Clean Water Act [33 U.S.C. § 1251 et seq.] of such release. * * *

CERCLA § 103(a), 42 U.S.C. § 9603(a). The list of hazardous substances and their corresponding reportable quantities is found at Appendix A to 40 C.F.R. Part 302.4. The list contains CERCLA "hazardous substances" and "hazardous substances" designated under § 311(b)(2)(A) of the CWA. 40 C.F.R. § 302.1. As noted previously, the corresponding "reportable quantity" for oil is defined by the "sheen test." 40 C.F.R. § 110.3. Like oil spills, a hazardous substance release must be reported to the National Response Center by calling (800) 424–8802. 40 C.F.R. § 302.6(a).

Subject to very limited statutory defenses,[122] an oil spill can result in several forms of liability under the CWA: fines under § 311(b)(6) and (7), cleanup obligations under § 311(c) and (e), and government cleanup cost reimbursement obligations under § 311(f). Liability under the OPA includes reimbursement of cleanup costs incurred by private parties,[123] and damages associated with injury to: natural resources, real and personal property, subsistence use of natural resources, and profits and earning capacity.[124] Governmental entities can also recover damages associated with increased expenses to provide public services and reductions in tax, royalty, rental, and fee collections resulting from the spill.[125]

Although CWA § 311 and the OPA intersect in many ways, § 311 contains the statutory command to the "owner or operator" of a vessel or facility to report and respond to an oil spill. The OPA provides the mechanism for injured parties to make claims against the "owner or operator" for damages and reimbursement of cleanup costs associated with a spill. Unlike CERCLA, the OPA has a statutory claims procedure that must be followed when third parties are seeking damages or reimbursement from the "responsible party." Subject to certain exceptions, "all claims for removal costs or damages shall be presented first to the responsible party * * *." OPA § 1013(a), 33 U.S.C. § 2713(a).[126] When a spill occurs, the appropriate agency will identify the source of the spill and designate the "responsible party." OPA § 1014(a), 33 U.S.C. § 2714(a).

Section 1002 of the OPA creates the basic private right of action for oil spill damages by providing:

> [E]ach responsible party for a vessel or a facility from which oil is discharged, or which poses the substantial threat of a discharge of oil,

---

122. E.g., CWA § 311(f)(2) provides, in part:

Except where an owner or operator of an onshore facility can prove that a discharge was caused solely by (A) an act of God, (B) an act of war, (C) negligence on the part of the United States Government, or (D) an act or omission of a third party without regard to whether any such act or omission was or was not negligent, or any combination of the foregoing clauses, such owner or operator of any such facility from which oil or a hazardous substance is discharged in violation of subsection (b)(3) of this section [the sheen test] shall be liable * * *

33 U.S.C. § 1321(f)(2). The OPA and CERCLA each have somewhat similar statutory defenses except there is no "negligence on the part of the United States Government" defense and the "third party" defense is limited as follows:

[A]n act or omission of a third party, other than an employee or agent of the responsible party or a third party whose act or omission occurs in connection with any contractual relationship with the responsible party * * *.

OPA § 1003(a)(3), 33 U.S.C. § 2703(a)(3) (1994). See also CERCLA § 107(b)(3), 42 U.S.C. § 9607(b)(3).

123. OPA § 1002(b)(1), 33 U.S.C. § 2702(b)(1).

124. Id. at § (2)(A), (B), (C), and (E).

125. Id. at § (D) & (F).

126. Compare Boca Ciega Hotel v. Bouchard Transp. Co., 51 F.3d 235, 240 (11th Cir.Fla. 1995) (OPA § 1013 claims presentation procedure is a mandatory condition precedent to the filing of private lawsuits against responsible party) with Marathon Pipe Line Co. v. LaRoche Industries Inc., 944 F.Supp. 476, 477–78, 480 (E.D.La.1996) (OPA § 1013 claims presentation procedure does not apply to suit by responsible party seeking to establish liability of third party nor does it apply to one third party seeking recovery from another third party).

into or upon the navigable waters or adjoining shorelines or the exclusive economic zone[127] is liable for the removal costs and damages specified in subsection (b) that result from such incident.

§ 1002(a), 33 U.S.C. § 2702(a). Like CERCLA, the OPA addresses a "threat" of a discharge.[128] The CWA analog is found at § 311(e)(1) which authorizes relief when "the President determines there may be an imminent and substantial threat to the public health or welfare of the United States * * * because of an actual or threatened discharge of oil or a hazardous substance * * *." 33 U.S.C. § 1321(e)(1).

The OPA, like § 311 of the CWA,[129] initially places all liability on the "owner" or "operator" of the vessel or facility.[130] It then becomes incumbent upon the "innocent" owner or operator to either establish a statutory defense[131] or comply with the cleanup order and then seek reimbursement either from a liable third party[132] or from the Oil Spill Liability Trust Fund.[133] The OPA, like the CWA and CERCLA, contains limits on liability depending upon the size of the vessel or the location of the facility. For example, the limit of liability under the OPA for any onshore facility is $350,000,000.[134] The EPA, by regulation, can reduce the liability limit for onshore facilities to not less than $8,000,000 considering the actual risk posed by the "size, storage capacity, oil throughput, proximity to sensitive areas, type of oil handled, history of discharges, and other factors relevant to risks posed by the class or category of facility."[135] However, any statutory limit can be lost when the spill is caused by a responsible party's "gross negligence or willful misconduct," "violation of an applicable Federal safety, construction, or operating regulation," or failure to report the spill and cooperate with authorities.[136] CERCLA and the CWA have similar provisions providing for a loss of limited liability.[137]

---

127. "Exclusive economic zone," as defined by the OPA, "comprises the coastal waters surrounding the United States, extending seaward for a distance of two hundred miles from the United States coastline." Sun Pipe Line Co. v. Conewago Contractors, Inc., 1994 WL 539326, at *2 (M.D.Pa.1994).

128. CERCLA § 107(a)(4), 42 U.S.C. 9607(a)(4) authorizes action whenever there is "a release, or a threatened release" of a hazardous substance which causes the incurrence of response costs.

129. See Quaker State Corp. v. U.S. Coast Guard, 681 F.Supp. 280 (W.D.Pa.1988), reproduced supra at § A.2.(b) of this Chapter.

130. OPA § 1001(32), 33 U.S.C. § 2701(32) (defining "responsible party"); CWA § 311(a)(6), 33 U.S.C. § 1321(a)(6) (defining "owner or operator").

131. See supra note 129.

132. OPA § 1009, 33 U.S.C. § 2709 (contribution action).

133. OPA § 1013(b)(1)(B), 33 U.S.C. § 2713(b)(1)(B).

134. OPA § 1004(a)(4), 33 U.S.C. § 2704(a)(4). See also CWA § 311(f)(2), 33 U.S.C. § 1321(f)(2) ($50,000,000 limit) and CERCLA § 107(c)(1)(D), 42 U.S.C. § 9607(c)(1)(D) ("the total costs of response plus $50,000,000 for any damages").

135. OPA § 1004(d), 33 U.S.C. § 2704(d). The parallel provision in the CWA is found at CWA § 311(q), 33 U.S.C. § 1321(q).

136. OPA § 1004(c)(1), 33 U.S.C. § 2704(c)(1).

137. CERCLA § 107(c)(2), 42 U.S.C. § 9607(c)(2) ("willful misconduct or willful negligence within the privity or knowledge of such person," "violation * * * of applicable safety, construction, or operating standards or regulations," or failure to cooperate with officials); CERCLA

To ensure funds are available in the event of a spill, the OPA imposes enforceable "financial responsibility" requirements on vessel and facility owners and operators. OPA § 1016, 33 U.S.C. § 2716 and § 1016a, 33 U.S.C. § 2716a. Financial responsibility can be achieved through such means as insurance, surety bond, and letter of credit.[138] Claims can be made directly against the "guarantor" providing the financial responsibility and the act limits defenses a guarantor can raise against a claimant.[139]

Although there are limitations of liability that may apply at the federal level, state laws may impose broader liability. Section 1018(a) of the OPA provides, in part:

> Nothing in this chapter or the Act of March 3, 1851 [Limitation of Liability Act of 1851, 46 U.S.C. §§ 183–189 (1994)] shall—
>
> > (1) affect, or be construed or interpreted as preempting, the authority of any State or political subdivision thereof from imposing any additional liability or requirements with respect to—
> >
> > > (A) the discharge of oil or other pollution by oil within such State; or
> > >
> > > (B) any removal activities in connection with such a discharge; * * *.

33 U.S.C. § 2718(a).

The CWA and OPA both rely upon the National Contingency Plan ("NCP") as the guide for conducting cleanup activities.[140] To ensure that cleanup expenses are eligible for reimbursement, parties incurring the expense must comply with the NCP. In addition, anyone seeking to establish rights under the federal environmental laws should be aware that most acts have their own self-contained procedural codes. For example, in addition to the OPA's special claims procedure, the act also contains various statutes of limitation,[141] and provisions governing jurisdiction, venue, and judicial review.[142]

Another major goal of the CWA and OPA is to prevent oil spills from occurring. A substantial portion of the OPA is dedicated to improving vessel design and operation, personnel training, and emergency prepared-

---

§ 103(c), 42 U.S.C. § 9603(c) (failure to report); CWA § 311(f), 33 U.S.C. § 1321(f) ("willful negligence or willful misconduct within the privity and knowledge of the owner").

138. OPA § 1016(e), 33 U.S.C.A. § 2716(e).

139. Id. at § (f).

140. The NCP is found at 40 C.F.R. Part 300. 40 C.F.R. § 300.1 describes the NCP as follows:

The purpose of the National Oil and Hazardous Substances Pollution Contingency Plan (NCP) is to provide the organizational structure and procedures for preparing and responding to discharges of oil and releases of hazardous substances, pollutants, and contaminants.

The NCP also governs cleanup actions under CERCLA. CERCLA § 107(a)(4)(A) & (B), 42 U.S.C. § 9607(a)(4)(A) & (B); 40 C.F.R. § 300.3.

141. OPA § 1012(h), 33 U.S.C. § 2712(h) (period of limitations for claims against Oil Spill Liability Trust Fund); OPA § 1017(f), 33 U.S.C. § 2717(f) (limitations periods for damages, removal costs, contribution, subrogation, and for minors and incapacitated persons).

142. OPA § 1017(a) & (b), 33 U.S.C. § 2717(a) & (b).

ness.[143] Section 311 of the CWA requires the adoption of regulations "establishing procedures, methods, and equipment and other requirements for equipment to prevent discharges of oil and hazardous substances from vessels and from onshore facilities and offshore facilities, and to contain such discharges * * *." CWA § 311(j)(1)(C), 33 U.S.C. § 1321(j)(1)(C). In response to this directive the EPA has adopted Spill Prevention Control and Countermeasure ("SPCC") Plan regulations. 40 C.F.R. Part 112.[144] As described by the EPA: "The SPCC Plan shall be a carefully thought-out plan, prepared in accordance with good engineering practices, and which has the full approval of management at a level with authority to commit the necessary resources." 40 C.F.R. § 112.7. The goal is to plan for spills and then incorporate measures and practices to prevent them from occurring.

The SPCC Plan is required under Part 112 if the following criteria are met:

1. The total capacity of all above-ground storage tanks at the onshore or offshore facility is in excess of 1,320 gallons, or the total capacity of all underground storage tanks at the facility is in excess of 42,000 gallons;

2. The facility is a "non-transportation-related" facility;[145]

3. "[E]ngaged in drilling, producing, gathering, storing, processing, refining, transferring, distributing, using, or consuming oil and oil products"; and

4. The facility is located in an area from which it could "reasonably be expected to discharge oil in quantities that may be harmful," applying the sheen test, into waters of the United States, or "that may affect natural resources belonging to, appertaining to, or under the exclusive management authority of the United States * * *"

40 C.F.R. § 112.1. To evaluate the location element of the test, the regulations state:

This determination shall be based solely upon consideration of the geographical and location aspects of the facility (such as proximity to navigable waters or adjoining shorelines, land contour, drainage, etc.) and must exclude consideration of manmade features such as dikes, equipment or other structures, which may serve to restrain, hinder, contain, or otherwise prevent a discharge * * *.

---

143. See generally J.B. Ruhl & Michael J. Jewell, Oil Pollution Act of 1990: Opening A New Era in Federal and Texas Regulation of Oil Spill Prevention, Containment and Cleanup, and Liability, 32 S.Tex.L.J. 475, 507–17 (1991).

144. Although the first SPCC regulations were effective in 1973, the EPA, since 1991, has been in the process of amending its SPCC regulations. The amended regulations took effect for offshore facilities in 2010 with a November 10, 2011 compliance date for onshore facilities. Oil Pollution Prevention; Spill Prevention, Control, and Countermeasure (SPCC) Rule—Compliance Date Amendment, 75 Fed.Reg. 63093 (Oct. 14, 2010).

145. This would exclude transportation pipelines beyond the lease area and related breakout storage tanks needed for operation of the pipeline. See generally Appendix A to Part 112— Memorandum of Understanding Between the Secretary of Transportation and the Administrator of the Environmental Protection Agency, 40 C.F.R. Part 112.

§ 112.1(d)(1)(I).

The OPA amended § 311 of the CWA to require the preparation of a "Response Plan" for spills from facilities that could cause a "substantial harm" to the environment. CWA § 311(j)(5), 33 U.S.C. § 1321(j)(5). The "substantial harm" category includes "tank vessels," offshore facilities, and certain onshore facilities that have a total oil storage capacity of 1 million gallons or more, or have a capacity of 42,000 gallons or more and transfer oil over water to or from vessels. 40 C.F.R. § 112.20(f)(1). The Response Plan must "plan for responding, to the maximum extent practicable, to a worst case discharge, and to a substantial threat of a discharge, of oil or a hazardous substance." § 311(j)(5)(A). See Appendix F to Part 112—Facility Specific Response Plan, 40 C.F.R. Part 112.

NOTES

1. Would the EPA exceed its authority by requiring a SPCC plan for a discharge that "may affect natural resources belonging to * * * the United States"—even when those resources are not associated with "waters of the United States"? For example, could the EPA require SPCC plans to protect grazing lands belonging to the United States? Does the § 311 goal of protecting waters of the United States suggest a broader regulatory scope than would apply under CWA §§ 402 and 404?

2. Does the "owner" of the oil that is spilled have any liability under the CWA or OPA? "Owner or operator" under the OPA is defined as:

> (i) in the case of a vessel, any person owning, operating, or chartering by demise, the vessel, and (ii) in the case of an onshore or offshore facility, any person owning or operating such facility, (iii) in the case of any abandoned offshore facility, the person who owned or operated such facility immediately prior to such abandonment * * *.

OPA § 1001(26)(A), 33 U.S.C. § 2701(26)(A). The CWA definition is substantially the same. CWA § 311(a)(6), 33 U.S.C. § 1321(a)(6). If you were an oil producer would you prefer not to own, operate, or lease the vessel carrying your oil? See Antonio J. Rodriguez & Paul A.C. Jaffe, The Oil Pollution Act of 1990, 15 Tul.Mar.L.J. 1, 27–28 (1990). Under CERCLA the party that generated the polluting "hazardous substance" is liable as well as the owner or operator of the facility where the polluting material is found. CERCLA § 107(a)(3), 42 U.S.C. § 9607(a)(3). Does it matter that oil is a useful product immediately prior to its discharge?

3. Suppose an oil and gas developer is maintaining a number of inactive wells on a lease as "temporarily abandoned" under state law. The lessor/landowner wants the wells plugged but the developer refuses. Even though the unplugged wells are not currently discharging oil, does the OPA offer the landowner a potential remedy? What if the lease had terminated several years ago and the developer failed to plug the wells? Would the landowner be the "owner" of the wells and the abandoned *onshore* facilities? Will the landowner become the "responsible party" under the OPA? With regard to abandoned facilities, the OPA defines "responsible party" as "the persons who would

have been responsible parties immediately prior to the abandonment of the vessel or facility." § 1001(32)(F), 33 U.S.C. § 2701(32)(F). "Facility" includes "any structure, group of structures, equipment, or device (other than a vessel) which is used for one or more of the following purposes: exploring for, drilling for, producing, storing, handling, transferring, processing, or transporting oil." § 1001(9), 33 U.S.C. § 2701(9). Would the landowner fare as well under § 311 of the CWA?

4. The blowout of British Petroleum's Macondo well in the Gulf of Mexico provided an opportunity to evaluate the OPA's regulatory programs. For a discussion of the OPA post-Macondo, see: John Wyeth Griggs, *BP Gulf of Mexico Oil Spill*, 32 ENERGY L. J. 57 (2011).

3. WILDLIFE PROTECTION

Birds are attracted to water—and stuff that looks like water. During the oil and gas production process, pits and open tanks may be used which contain mixtures of produced water and oil that can be lethal to wildlife, particularly birds. The technological fix for the problem is fairly simple: either avoid using pits and open tanks or ensure those in use are fitted with protective netting to screen out wildlife. The incentive for the oil and gas developer to screen their pits and open tanks is provided by the Migratory Bird Treaty Act ("MBTA"), 16 U.S.C. §§ 703 to 712, which provides, in part:

> [I]t shall be unlawful at any time, by any means or in any manner, to pursue, hunt, take, capture, kill, attempt to take, capture, or kill * * * any migratory bird * * *.

16 U.S.C. § 703. "Migratory bird" includes hundreds of bird species and many will be found virtually everywhere there is a producing oil and gas well.[146] For example, the list of migratory birds includes thirty-three different species of sparrow, seven blackbird species, seven species of dove, and three species of robin. 50 C.F.R. § 10.13 (list of migratory birds). Violation of the MBTA is a crime punishable as a misdemeanor unless the party violating the Act does so "knowingly," in which case it is a felony. 16 U.S.C. § 707.

If a migratory bird gains access to a pit or open tank, and is killed, the U.S. Fish and Wildlife Service will view it as an unlawful "take, capture, [and/or] kill" by the owner or operator of the oil and gas facility. For example, in United States v. Corbin Farm Service, 444 F.Supp. 510 (E.D.Cal.1978), aff'd, 578 F.2d 259 (9th Cir.1978), an alfalfa field was treated with a pesticide which poisoned migratory birds feeding in the field. The court noted that the MBTA made it illegal "at any time, by any

---

146. In Mahler v. U.S. Forest Service, 927 F.Supp. 1559, 1576 (S.D.Ind.1996), Judge Hamilton observed:

The list of birds now protected as "migratory birds" under the MBTA is a long one, including many of the most numerous and least endangered species one can imagine. Although the MBTA initially protected only a small number of birds, in 1971, the Secretary of the Interior expanded its coverage to apply to nearly all birds indigenous to the North America, including the wren, robin, crow, chickadee, oriole, sparrow, warbler, blackbird, bluebird, and many others.

means or in any manner, to * * * kill * * * any migratory bird * * *."
444 F.Supp. at 532. The court concluded the MBTA was not intended to
regulate merely those who hunt or capture migratory birds but included
those who "kill" migratory birds. Id. The court also held it was unnecessary for the killing to be intentional. Id. at 536. Therefore, the court
refused to dismiss the MBTA charges against the farmer who owned the
alfalfa field, the pesticide dealer who provided pesticide advice to the
farmer, and the pilot who applied the pesticide.

In discussing the strict liability aspect of the MBTA, the court in
Corbin Farm referred to a case, United States v. Union Texas Petroleum,
73–CR–127 (D.Colo., July 11, 1973), where Union was prosecuted for
maintaining "open oil sludge pits in which migratory birds landed, became
coated with oil and died". 444 F.Supp. at 533. The court also referred to
United States v. Equity Corp., Cr. 75–51 (D.Utah, Dec. 8, 1975), which
concerned ducks killed in "oil sump pits." Id. at 527, n.7. In United States
v. FMC Corp., 428 F.Supp. 615 (W.D.N.Y.1977), aff'd, 572 F.2d 902 (2d
Cir.1978), FMC was held strictly liable for the deaths of birds that were
poisoned when they landed in a wastewater storage pond. The wastewater
in the pond had become contaminated with a pesticide FMC was manufacturing. 572 F.2d at 904–05. The court on appeal affirmed FMC's convic-
tion reasoning that FMC was strictly liable for creating a condition on its
property that was dangerous to birds. 572 F.2d at 907.

The *Corbin Farm* and *FMC Corp.* cases suggest the MBTA should be
given a broad reading to encompass industrial activities where migratory
birds are unintentionally killed. However, a series of more recent cases
have caused courts to reexamine the underlying purpose, and the corresponding scope, of the MBTA. Several environmental organizations have
attempted to use the MBTA to prevent timber sales by the National
Forest Service, asserting the resulting logging activities will "kill" migratory birds. The first line of argument attempted to equate the destruction
of migratory bird "habitat" with a "taking or killing" of the migratory
bird.[147] This argument, to date, has been rejected by the courts. E.g.,
Seattle Audubon Society v. Evans, 952 F.2d 297, 302–03 (9th Cir.1991)
(noting fundamental differences between Endangered Species Act and
MBTA). The second line of argument is that allowing logging during the
nesting season will result in a direct take or killing of a migratory bird.
One court rejected this argument by holding the MBTA did not apply to
the federal government. Sierra Club v. Martin, 110 F.3d 1551, 1555 (11th
Cir.1997). Such an approach merely defers the issue until the successful
private bidder attempts to exercise their logging rights.[148] Other courts
have addressed the issue directly by limiting the scope of the MBTA.

147. Essentially attempting to extend to the MBTA the reasoning applied to the Endangered Species Act in Babbitt v. Sweet Home Ch. of Commun. for Great Or. See supra § A.1.(b) of this Chapter.

148. The district judge in the *Martin* case noted: "In this case, however, a killing of young migratory birds occurs because Defendants are allowing tree cutting and logging during nesting season." Sierra Club v. Martin, 933 F.Supp. 1559, 1564 (N.D.Ga.1996), rev'd, 110 F.3d 1551 (11th Cir.1997).

When presented with the nesting season argument, the court in Newton County Wildlife Ass'n v. U.S. Forest Service, 113 F.3d 110, 115 (8th Cir.1997), cert. denied, 522 U.S. 1108 (1998), rejected the argument and offered the following reasoning:

> [I]t would stretch this 1918 statute far beyond the bounds of reason to construe it as an absolute criminal prohibition on conduct, such as timber harvesting, that indirectly results in the death of migratory birds. Thus, we agree with the Ninth Circuit that the ambiguous terms "take" and "kill" in 16 U.S.C. § 703 mean "physical conduct of the sort engaged in by hunters and poachers, conduct which was undoubtedly a concern at the time of the statute's enactment in 1918."

Judge Hamilton, in Mahler v. U.S. Forest Service, 927 F.Supp. 1559, 1579 (S.D.Ind.1996), addressed the issue in depth and concluded:

> Properly interpreted, the MBTA applies to activities that are intended to harm birds or to exploit harm to birds, such as hunting and trapping, and trafficking in birds and bird parts. The MBTA does not apply to other activities that result in unintended deaths of migratory birds.

This view of the MBTA was rejected by Judge Babcock in United States v. Moon Lake Electric Ass'n, Inc., 45 F.Supp.2d 1070 (D.Colo.1999), where an electric cooperative was held strictly liable under the MBTA for killing protected birds that were electrocuted when landing on its power poles. The cooperative's power poles served an oil field near Rangely, Colorado and provided perching and roosting places in this relatively treeless area of Colorado.

These varying interpretations of the MBTA are illustrated, in the oil and gas context, by the court's approach in United States v. Apollo Energies, Inc., 611 F.3d 679 (10th Cir. 2010), contrasted with the court's approach in United States v. Brigham Oil and Gas, L.P., 840 F.Supp.2d 1202 (D.N.D. 2012). In *Apollo* the oil and gas operator was held liable for migratory birds that died when they became trapped within heater-treater equipment at a well site. 611 F.3d at 686 ("The question here is whether unprotected oil field equipment can take or kill migratory birds. It is obvious the oil equipment can."). The court in *Brigham Oil* held:

> This Court expressly finds that the use of reserve pits in commercial oil development is legal, commercially-useful activity that stands outside the reach of the federal Migratory Bird Treaty Act. Like timber harvesting, oil development and production activities are not the sort of physical conduct engaged in by hunters and poachers, and such activities do not fall under the prohibitions of the Migratory Bird Treaty Act. The Eighth Circuit Court of Appeals' decision in *Newton County* is controlling precedent which this Court is obligated to follow.

840 F.Supp.2d 1202 at *1211,

NOTES

1. If the reasoning in the *Newton County* and *Mahler* cases is followed, can an oil and gas developer be held liable under the MBTA for the death of migratory birds that land in the developer's pits and open tanks? Considering the *Moon Lake* decision, what if the developer was aware that migratory birds, on prior occasions, had been killed when they landed in the pits and open tanks? What if the migratory bird was a blacked-capped vireo?

2. If the reasoning of the *Corbin Farm* and *FMC Corp.* cases is followed, could a landowner be held liable under the MBTA for the death of migratory birds that land in abandoned oil pits left on their land by a prior oil and gas lessee?

3. Violating the MBTA can be expensive. Although 16 U.S.C. § 707(a) makes it a misdemeanor to violate the act, punishable by a fine of "not more than $500" and imprisonment for "not more than six months," under the Alternative Fines Act an "individual" violating the MBTA could be fined up to $5,000 and an "organization" up to $10,000.[149] Anyone who "knowingly" violates the MBTA "shall be guilty of a felony and shall be fined not more than $2,000 or imprisoned not more than two years, or both." 16 U.S.C. § 707(b). Under the Alternative Fines Act the fine could be up to $250,000 for an individual and $500,000 for an organization. 18 U.S.C. § 3571(b)(3) & (c)(3).

4. If ten dead birds are found in a pit is the maximum fine ten times the applicable amount? In the *Corbin Farm Service* case the court found that a single application of pesticide had caused the death of ten migratory birds. The government took the position that each bird death constituted a separate violation of the statute. The trial court dismissed nine of the ten counts noting that "when all the deaths are caused by a single act" there is only one offense. *Corbin Farm Service*, 444 F.Supp. at 521. This was the issue that prompted the appeal to the Ninth Circuit where the court affirmed noting that "multiple bird deaths resulting from a single transaction cannot be separately charged under the MBTA." 578 F.2d at 260. If a migratory bird was killed by flying into an open pit each day for ten days, would each day the pit remained open to migratory birds constitute a new "transaction" or "act"—or failure to act? See United States v. FMC Corp., 572 F.2d 902, 903 (2d Cir.1978). Who has to prove when the bird flew into the pit? Who has to prove the bird carcass is that of a listed migratory bird?

5. "Marine mammals" are protected under the Marine Mammal Protection Act ("MMPA"), 16 U.S.C.A. §§ 1361 to 1407. Mammals "morphologically adapted to the marine environment" or which "primarily inhabits the marine environment," are included. 16 U.S.C.A. § 1362(6) (defining "marine mammal"). In language reminiscent of the Endangered Species Act, the MMPA makes in unlawful to "take" a marine mammal without a permit. § 1371. "Take" is defined broadly to mean "harass, hunt, capture, or kill, or attempt to harass, hunt, capture, or kill any marine mammal." § 1362(13). "Harass-

---

149. Under 18 U.S.C. § 3559(a)(7) such a violation is classified as a Class B misdemeanor which, under 18 U.S.C. § 3571(b)(6) & (c)(6), authorizes the enhanced $5,000/$10,000 fines.

ment" is also defined as "any act of pursuit, torment, or annoyance which * * * has the potential to injure a marine mammal * * * or has the potential to disturb a marine mammal * * * by causing disruption of behavioral patterns, including, but not limited to, migration, breathing, nursing, breeding, feeding, or sheltering." § 1362(18). See "Taking and Importing of Marine Mammals; Offshore Seismic Activities in the Beaufort Sea," 62 Fed.Reg. 38263 (July 17, 1997) (issuance of Incidental Harassment Authorization to "take" small numbers of bowhead whales and other marine mammals by harassment incidental to conducting seismic surveys in the Western Beaufort Sea).

4. MANAGING AIR EMISSIONS

Oil and gas exploration and production activities create air emissions which may be regulated under the Clean Air Act ("CAA"), 42 U.S.C. §§ 7401 to 7671q. Internal combustion engines used to drill, produce, and market oil and gas are a source of emissions. Lease equipment, such as heater-treaters and glycol dehydrators, create emissions. The oil and gas product itself is a source of emissions, particularly volatile organic compounds ("VOCs"). VOCs are unburned hydrocarbons that interact with nitrogen oxides in the presence of sunlight to form ozone which is the major component of photochemical smog. The underlying goal of the CAA is "to protect and enhance the quality of the Nation's air resources so as to promote the public health and welfare and the productive capacity of its population." CAA § 101(b)(1), 42 U.S.C. § 7401(b)(1). The regulatory strategy for attaining the goal is to establish uniform air quality standards at the federal level which the states can supplement and implement with federal assistance and oversight. The states implement the CAA by adopting state implementation plans ("SIPs") designed to meet and maintain federal air quality standards by prohibiting and regulating air emissions through various permit programs.[150]

Not all air emissions are regulated under the CAA. The oil and gas developer's task will be to determine whether their emissions require a permit under federal law; even when covered by federal standards, the operations may also be covered by more stringent or special state requirements, such as the obligation to inventory emissions and pay an emissions fee.[151] Determining a facility's regulatory status under the CAA generally involves two inquiries: First, how much of each regulated pollutant is the

---

150. Offshore facilities are generally governed by the SIP of the state bordering the operation. CAA § 328(a)(1), 42 U.S.C. 7627(a)(1) provides, in part:

> For such sources located within 25 miles of the seaward boundary of such States, such requirements shall be the same as would be applicable if the source were located in the corresponding onshore area [generally the onshore attainment or nonattainment area closest to the source], and shall include, but not be limited to, State and local requirements for emission controls, emission limitations, offsets, permitting, monitoring, testing, and reporting.

See 40 C.F.R. § 55.15 (specific designation of corresponding onshore areas). See generally Offshore Environmental Issues, supra, at 8–24 to 8–28.

151. E.g., Tex.Admin.Code tit. 30, § 101.10 (requiring emissions inventories from certain non-major sources of air pollution) and Tex.Admin.Code tit. 30, § 101.27 (requiring payment of emissions fees by certain air pollution sources).

facility capable of emitting during a year of operation? Second, where is the facility located and what is the geographic impact of the facility's emissions? The CAA regulates "major sources" of air pollution so the first task is to evaluate an emitting source to determine if it is "major." However, the definition of "major" can vary depending upon where the polluting source is located. For example, a source emitting less than 100 tons per year ("tpy") of VOCs in a geographic area classified as "attainment" for ozone is not a major source.[152] However, if the same source were located in an area classified as "extreme" nonattainment for ozone, VOC emissions as low as 10 tpy would make it a major source.[153]

Major source classification varies with the pollutant involved. The CAA employs two distinct regulatory approaches to achieve air pollution goals. First, an ambient air quality approach is used to regulate six "criteria" air pollutants.[154] The ambient air is monitored at selected locations to determine if primary and secondary ambient air quality standards are being met. Areas failing the national ambient standards are designated "nonattainment" and states, through their SIPs, are required to adopt a mix of controls designed to achieve and maintain the ambient standards. The second regulatory approach relies upon specific source reductions of pollutants instead of an ambient measure of progress. This is the approach used for hazardous air pollutants.[155] Hazardous air pollutants closely associated with the oil and gas industry include: benzene, toluene, ethyl benzene, xylenes, methanol, mercury compounds, formaldehyde, hexane, and asbestos.

The definition of "major source" for hazardous air pollutants focuses on the annual volume of the pollutant emitted. If the air pollutant source emits[156] 10 tpy or more of any single hazardous air pollutant, or 25 tpy or more of any combination of hazardous air pollutants, it will be deemed a "major source."[157] Although the source may escape regulation as a "major" source, any non-major source of a hazardous air pollutant can be regulated as an "area source" when additional regulation is necessary to

---

152. CAA § 302(j), 42 U.S.C. § 7602(j).

153. Id. at § 182(d), 42 U.S.C. § 7511a(e).

154. Sulfur oxides, particulate matter, carbon monoxide, ozone, nitrogen dioxide, and lead. See 40 C.F.R. Part 50.

155. CAA § 112(d), 42 U.S.C. § 7412(d).

156. CAA § 112(a)(1) provides, in part:

The term "major source" means any stationary source or group of stationary sources located within a contiguous area and under common control that emits or has the potential to emit considering controls, in the aggregate, 10 tons per year or more of any hazardous air pollutant or 25 tons per year or more of any combination of hazardous air pollutants.

42 U.S.C. § 7412(a)(1). See National Min. Ass'n v. U.S. E.P.A., 59 F.3d 1351, 1364–65 (D.C.Cir. 1995) (addressing the "considering controls" portion of § 112(a)(1)).

157. However, pursuant to CAA § 112(a)(1), the definition of "major source" can be reduced:

The Administrator may establish a lesser quantity, or in the case of radionuclides different criteria, for a major source than [the 10/25 ton per year levels] * * * on the basis of the potency of the air pollutant, persistence, potential for bioaccumulation, * * * or other relevant factors.

42 U.S.C. § 7412(a)(1).

protect human health or the environment.[158] Hazardous emissions from oil and gas wells, and pipeline facilities, receive special treatment through CAA § 112(n)(4) which provides, in part:

> (A) Notwithstanding * * * [the definitions of major source and area source], emissions from any oil or gas exploration or production well (with its associated equipment) and emissions from any pipeline compressor or pump station shall not be aggregated with emissions from other similar units, whether or not such units are in a contiguous area or under common control, to determine whether such units or stations are major sources, and in the case of any oil or gas exploration or production well (and its associated equipment), such emissions shall not be aggregated for any purpose under this section.
>
> (B) the Administrator shall not list oil and gas production wells (with its associated equipment) as an area source category under subsection (c), except that the Administrator may establish an area source category for oil and gas production wells located in any metropolitan statistical area with a population in excess of 1 million,[159] if the Administrator determines that emissions of hazardous air pollutants from such wells present more than a negligible risk of adverse effects to public health.

42 U.S.C. § 7412(n)(4). This no-aggregation provision means the EPA is unable to combine emissions from several individual well sites to determine whether the 10/25 tpy major source threshold is met.

Major source classification for the criteria air pollutants begins with the uniform requirement that any source that emits 100 tpy or more of any criteria air pollutant is a major source. Depending upon the pollutant, and the severity of the nonattainment status of the area impacted by the source, the major source annual emissions trigger can range from 10, 25, 50, or 70 tpy. For example, the VOC emission limits for defining major sources of ozone are: 50 tpy ("serious" nonattainment area), 25 tpy ("severe" nonattainment area), and 10 tpy ("extreme" nonattainment area).[160] The practical effect of the CAA's ambient regulatory approach is to divide the United States into air quality zones based upon the level of nonattainment for each criteria pollutant.

Section 819 of the Clean Air Act Amendments of 1990 created a limited exemption for "stripper" wells located in an area designated nonattainment.[161] However, the exemption does not apply to areas classified as "severe" or "extreme;" nor will the exemption apply in an area classified as "serious" with a population of 350,000 or more. The stripper well exemption includes oil wells that produce an average of 10 barrels or

---

158. CAA § 112(c)(3), 42 U.S.C. § 7412(c)(3).

159. This is one instance where the "location" of the operation can impact its status under the CAA's hazardous air pollutant provisions.

160. CAA § 182(c)–(e), 42 U.S.C. § 7511a(c)–(e).

161. Clean Air Act Amendments of 1990, Pub.L.No. 101–549, § 819, 104 Stat. 2423, 2698–99 (1990).

less each day and gas wells that produce an average of 60 Mcf or less each day.[162]

A notable exception to the 100 tpy threshold is the regulation of asbestos. When a client plans to remove, renovate, or demolish anything possibly containing asbestos, the CAA's pre-work notice and work practice requirements must be carefully reviewed. See 40 C.F.R. § 61.145. This is probably the CAA regulation that is most often innocently overlooked by the public but nevertheless consistently, and unforgivingly, enforced by the EPA. See, e.g., United States v. Trident Seafoods Corp., 60 F.3d 556, 558 (9th Cir.Wash. 1995) (failure to give advance notice of asbestos removal resulted in EPA demand for a $346,000 fine).

In addition to the nonattainment program, the CAA also has a program designed to protect air that is cleaner than the national standards. This is known as the "prevention of significant deterioration" or "PSD" program. CAA § 160, 42 U.S.C. § 7470. To be subject to the PSD permitting process the source must either emit 250 tpy of any criteria pollutant, or be one of a listed group of sources and emit 100 tpy or more. Among listed facilities are petroleum refineries and large petroleum storage and transfer facilities. CAA § 169(1), 42 U.S.C. § 7479(1). The CAA also has a visibility protection program for listed facilities that emit 250 tpy of any criteria pollutant that can impact certain parks and wilderness areas classified as "mandatory class I Federal areas." CAA §§ 169A & 169B, 42 U.S.C. §§ 7491 & 7492.

As with the other environmental laws, the CAA has the usual menu of administrative fines, civil penalties, and criminal sanctions to encourage compliance. CAA § 113(b)–(d), 42 U.S.C. § 7413(h)–(d). The CAA also provides for citizen enforcement. CAA § 304, 42 U.S.C. § 7604.

The first comprehensive regulation of air pollutants associated with the exploration, production, and marketing of oil and gas, including VOC emissions associated with hydraulic fracturing, occurred on April 17, 2012 when the Environmental Protection Agency adopted New Source Performance Standards and National Emission Standards for Hazardous Air Pollutants for the Oil and Natural Gas Sector. The following excerpts are from the EPA's executive summary of its new regulations:

> **New Source Performance Standards ("NSPS").** The newly established NSPS for the Crude Oil and Natural Gas Production source category regulate Volatile Organic Compound ("VOC") emissions from gas wells, centrifugal compressors, reciprocating compressors, pneumatic controllers, storage vessels and leaking components of onshore natural gas processing plants, as well as sulfur dioxide (SO2) emissions from onshore natural gas processing plants * * *.

> **Gas wells.** The rule covers any gas well that is "an onshore well drilled principally for production of natural gas." Oil wells (wells drilled principally for the production of crude oil) are not subject to

---

162. Id.

this rule. For fractured and refractured gas wells, the rule generally requires owners/operators to use reduced emissions completions, also known as "RECs" or "green completions," to reduce VOC emissions from well completions. To achieve these VOC reductions, owners and/or operators may use RECs or completion combustion devices, such as flaring, until January 1, 2015; as of January 1, 2015, owners and/or operators must use RECs and a completion combustion device * * *

Storage Vessels. Individual storage vessels in the oil and natural gas production segment and the natural gas processing, transmission and storage segments with emissions equal to or greater than 6 tons per year ("tpy") must achieve at least 95.0 percent reduction in VOC emissions * * *

Certain controllers. The rule sets a natural gas bleed rate limit of six TcfM/hour for individual, continuous bleed, natural gas-driven pneumatic controllers located between the wellhead and the point at which the gas enters the transmission and storage segment * * *.

Certain compressors. The rule requires a 95.0 percent reduction of VOC emissions from wet seal centrifugal compressors located between the wellhead and the point at which the gas enters the transmission and storage segment. The rule also requires measures intended to reduce VOC emissions from reciprocating compressors * * *.

For onshore natural gas processing plants, this final action revises the existing NSPS requirements for Leak Detection And Repair ("LDAR") to reflect the procedures and leak thresholds established in the NSPS for Equipment Leaks and VOCs in the Synthetic Organic Chemicals Manufacturing Industry * * *

National Emissions Standards for Hazardous Air Pollutants (NESHAP). This section also revised the NESHAP for glycol dehydration unit process vents and LDAR requirements. In the final rule for major sources at oil and natural gas production facilities, we have lowered the leak definition for valves at natural gas processing plants to 500 parts per million ("ppm") and thus require the application of LDAR procedures at this level. In this final rule, we also have established MACT standards for "small" glycol dehydration units, which were unregulated under the initial NESHAP. Covered glycol dehydrators are those with an actual annual average natural gas flow rate less than 85,000 standard cubic meters per day ("scmd") or actual average benzene emissions less than 1 ton tpy, and they must meet unit-specific limits for Benzene, Ethylbenzene, Toluene and Xylene ("BTEX").

In the final rule for major sources at natural gas transmission and storage facilities, we have established MACT standards for "small" glycol dehydrators also not regulated under the initial NESHAP * * *.

Final Rule, Oil and Natural Gas Sector: New Source Performance Standards and National Emission Standards for Hazardous Air Pollutants Reviews (April 17, 2012), http://www.epa.gov/airquality/oilandgas/pdfs/2012041finalrule.pdf.

NOTES

1. What are the statutory bases for the EPA's New Source Performance Standards and emission standards for Hazardous Air Pollutants for the Oil and Natural Gas Sector?

2. To avoid CAA problems, the oil and gas developer must be aware of the volume and chemical composition of all air emissions created by their operations. Once these are known, the operations can be evaluated to determine whether major sources, or regulated area sources, exist. Any major source analysis will have to account for the location of the facilities involved and the attainment status, and nonattainment categories, for the area. The final step in the analysis will consider any special or additional requirements imposed by the state where operations are conducted.

3. Many oil and gas exploration and production operations, because of their emission volumes, will not be subject to any regulation—state or federal. Is there any business reason why an operator might nevertheless want to keep track of their emissions and consider ways they might be reduced?

5. EMERGENCY PLANNING OBLIGATIONS

The Emergency Planning and Community Right–To–Know Act ("EPCRA"), 42 U.S.C. §§ 11001 to 11050, requires persons that have hazardous material on site to provide information to the local fire department, local emergency planning agency, and state emergency planning agency, regarding the existence, location, and nature of the hazardous material. The goal is to assist all parties in responding effectively to a release of hazardous material. The program is administered at the state and local levels but the regulatory obligations are imposed by EPCRA and its state counterparts.[163] EPCRA also represents one of the first direct links between workplace employee-protection legislation and general environmental legislation. In defining the "hazardous chemical" central to EPCRA's reporting requirements, EPCRA incorporates the hazard communication program under the Occupational Safety and Health Act ("OSHA").[164] The primary OSHA hazardous chemicals which will be at oil and gas production sites, above threshold levels, are the produced hydrocarbons—typically the crude oil stored on the leased premises awaiting sale. The presence of any OSHA hazardous chemical at a facility, in excess of 10,000 pounds, will trigger an initial reporting obligation under § 311 of EPCRA and annual reports under § 312. 42 U.S.C. §§ 11021 & 11022.

---

163. See generally 40 C.F.R. Part 355.

164. 29 C.F.R. Part 1910.

In addition to reporting hazardous chemicals, EPCRA imposes emergency planning obligations whenever a listed "extremely hazardous substance" is on site in a "threshold planning quantity." EPCRA § 302, 42 U.S.C. § 11002. The list of extremely hazardous substances, and their threshold planning quantities, are found at 40 C.F.R. Part 355, Appendix A. Section 304 of EPCRA requires reporting of any release of a listed "extremely hazardous substance," or a CERCLA "hazardous substance," when the release exceeds a regulatory "reportable quantity" and results in exposure to persons beyond the site on which the facility is located. 42 U.S.C. § 11004. To be subject to the § 304 reporting requirement the facility must produce, use, or store a "hazardous chemical." As noted above, the presence of crude oil at a site can satisfy the hazardous chemical requirement. Although petroleum is not an extremely hazardous substance, nor is it a CERCLA hazardous substance, the operator must determine whether the oil contains any hazardous substances, such as benzene, in such concentration and volume as to independently trigger a § 304 report. The § 304 reporting obligation is more extensive than those under the CWA and CERCLA. In addition to reporting the release to the National Response Center, the facility owner or operator must also report to all impacted local emergency planning committees and state emergency response commissions. EPCRA § 304(b), 42 U.S.C. § 11004(b); 40 C.F.R. § 355.40(b).

EPCRA also requires that certain manufacturing operations prepare and file an annual toxic chemical release report which itemizes all toxic releases from the facility during the preceding calendar year. EPCRA § 313, 42 U.S.C. § 11023. Although exploration and production activities will typically not meet the toxic release reporting thresholds, some large treatment or processing facilities may and the general trend has been to expand this program to encompass more facilities and substances.

NOTES

1. What "emissions," "discharges," or "releases" are prohibited by EPCRA? You will note that EPCRA is solely an information statute; persons who possess hazardous chemicals must provide information to federal, state, and local officials. Civil penalties can be assessed for a failure to comply with EPCRA's information requirements. Willful violations can result in criminal prosecution. EPCRA § 325, 42 U.S.C. § 11045. A citizen can bring suit to enforce compliance with the Act, to have civil penalties assessed against the violator, and to have the violator pay the citizen's attorney and expert witness fees. EPCRA § 326, 42 U.S.C. § 11046.

2. EPCRA is a good law to end this Chapter with; it reminds us of the importance of knowing the characteristics of, and consequences associated with, the instrumentalities used to find, develop, and produce oil and gas. To avoid environmental problems, both ecological and legal, the oil and gas developer must have a clear understanding of the activity they are undertaking, the materials and methods to be used, the wastes that will be created, and the resources that will be affected.

CHAPTER 6

CONTRACTS AND TRANSFERS
BY THE LESSEE

Table of Sections

————

Transfers by an oil and gas lessee of all or part of its interest take a wide variety of forms. They often include all or portions of one or several leases. Contracts executed by lessees range from standard form contracts for materials and services to complicated agreements with other companies for exploration and joint development of thousands of acres. This chapter will cover the most common types of transfers and several of the basic contracts that lessees commonly enter into.

A. LEASE ASSIGNMENTS

A lease may be assigned in whole or in part; or several leases may be assigned simultaneously. The recipient may be an oil and gas company or several companies. Partial assignments can take a variety of forms. Geologic stratum above or below a designated depth may be assigned. The right to extract one or more specific substances covered by the lease, such as coal or natural gas, can be severed by a partial assignment. A single well may be assigned, entirely apart from the leased acreage. More commonly, a partial assignment transfers either an undivided interest in the lease or a specific geographic area covered by the lease. Other types of interests, such as overriding royalties, production payments, and carried interests may be assigned or reserved.

The reasons for such assignments are as varied as the types available. For example, a company planning to engage in horizontal drilling may wish to obtain leases that are in the path of the planned horizontal extension of its well and that are held by other companies. Alternatively, lease brokers who have neither the intention nor the ability to undertake exploration, drilling, and development may lease land through a corporation that they control with the expectation of selling the leases. Thus a person, hearing rumors that wildcat exploration or horizontal drilling will take place in an area, may lease one or two tracts in the general vicinity with the idea that the leases will increase substantially in value if the exploration or horizontal drilling takes place and is successful. Alternatively, several persons with extensive knowledge of geology and the petroleum industry may lease a large block of land that they will attempt to market to an oil company as an attractive drilling prospect. In these and similar situations, if the original lessee assigns the lease in full it will typically retain an overriding royalty and may provide that the retained interest can be converted into a working interest at a later time.

Something of the reverse of the situations just described occurs when the lessee plans to explore and develop the land itself but must obtain money, equipment, or services to carry out such operations. The lessee may sell undivided interests in the leasehold or specific portions of the leasehold to investors or to other companies; or it may carve overriding royalties, production payments, or other nonoperating interests out of the working interest and transfer them to persons who will perform specified services for the endeavor. Thus an independent geologist may agree to assess a prospect's potential in exchange for a two percent overriding royalty in the prospect area.

Full or partial lease assignments quite commonly occur in the context of a farmout agreement. Such agreements are covered in detail later in the chapter. Under the traditional farmout an oil company that has a lease covering a large area may transfer its interest in specified acreage to an operator who agrees to drill a well to a specified depth and at a specified location on the acreage transferred. Such drilling will probably enable the transferor to maintain its lease on the rest of the acreage without incurring any out-of-pocket drilling costs and also provide it with information concerning the desirability of drilling on the retained acreage. With the advent of widespread horizontal drilling, farmouts typically include multiple leases, may involve several companies, and be limited to a specific formation, especially if the purpose of the farmout is the development of a shale formation.

Partial assignments are often used as a risk-spreading device. A lessee wishing to drill on a new or risky prospect can sell interests in the leasehold to other companies or investors. An investor concerned about the risk of unsuccessful drilling can acquire partial interests in a wide variety of prospects instead of only one or two. Additionally, a partial assignment may serve as a vehicle for obtaining equity or debt financing. For a fuller discussion of these and other reasons for assigning interests in an oil and gas lease, see Peter K. Reilly & Christopher S. Heroux, When Should Interests in Oil and Gas Be Considered Securities?: A Case for the Industry Deal, 34 So. Tex. L.Rev. 37, 38–41 (1993); D.C. Pohland, Partial Assignments of Oil and Gas Interests, 10 Eastern Min.L.Inst. 14–1 (1989). See also Lawrence P. Terrell, Limited Assignments—Who Gets What?, 35 Rocky Mt.Min.L.Inst. 17–1 (1989).

1. LEGAL REQUIREMENTS AND DRAFTING CONSIDERATIONS

Like most sales or assignment of interests in real estate, an assignment of all or part of a lease (or several leases) is preceded by a contractual agreement between the parties. The following case illustrates some of the issues that may arise when one of the parties attempts to enforce the contract.

PRESTON EXPLORATION COMPANY, L.P. v. GSF, L.L.C. AND CHESAPEAKE ENERGY CORP.

669 F.3d 518 (C.A.5 [Tex.] 2012).

MICAELA ALVAREZ, DISTRICT JUDGE[1]:

I. BACKGROUND

Plaintiffs/Appellants Preston Exploration Company, L.P.; PEC Partnership; T.S.C. Oil & Gas, Inc.; and Frank Willis, III (collectively

---

1. District Judge of the Southern District of Texas, sitting by designation.

"Preston") appeal the district court's entry of judgment in favor of Defendants/Appellees GSF, L.L.C. and Chesapeake Energy Corporation (collectively "Chesapeake") on Chesapeake's statute of frauds defense to Preston's lawsuit demanding specific performance of three Purchase and Sale Agreements ("PSAs") entered between the parties for the sale/purchase of certain oil and gas leases. Following a bench trial, the trial court granted judgment on the statute of frauds issue in favor of Chesapeake, determining that the PSAs did not comply with the statute of frauds as neither the PSAs, nor the exhibits attached to the PSAs, furnished the means or data by which to identify the leases to be conveyed with reasonable certainty. Preston appeals the judgment granted in Chesapeake's favor. For the reasons set forth below, we VACATE the judgment of the trial court and REMAND to the district court.

A. FACTUAL BACKGROUND

In June 2008, Preston and Chesapeake began discussions regarding the sale/purchase of certain oil and gas leases owned by Preston. In time, the parties agreed to pursue a transaction and entered into a letter of intent with a closing date of August 20, 2008. This closing date was later pushed back by a month to September 19th, then to September 26th and again to October 7th. By early October, for various reasons, the parties were not yet ready to proceed to closing. In an effort to move forward with the transaction, the parties agreed to enter into purchase and sale agreements.

The dispute herein arises in connection with the documents attached to the PSAs. The PSAs were executed on October 7 and 8, 2008.[2] Prior to signing the PSAs, the parties exchanged drafts of the PSAs along with drafts of the exhibits attached to the PSAs. The exhibits were specifically referenced in the PSAs, including a reference to one of the exhibits as the document describing the oil and gas leases to be conveyed and a reference to a different exhibit as the document setting out the form of the assignments to be delivered at closing.

The drafts of the PSAs, including the attached exhibits, were exchanged by e-mail between Preston and Chesapeake in the days immediately preceding the actual execution of the documents. During this time, Chesapeake specifically requested to review the final schedules and exhibits. After some back and forth, Preston executed the PSAs on October 7th. On the following day, Chesapeake executed the PSAs without any complaints regarding the attached exhibits. The PSAs now provided for a November 7th closing date. The PSAs also provided for payment of a non-refundable deposit of 10% of the unadjusted purchase price. The deposit amounted to $11,000,000.00.

---

2. Ultimately, three PSAs were executed between the parties. The PSAs are substantially identical except that each pertains to a distinct Preston entity.

Following execution of the PSAs, the parties moved towards closing. Chesapeake continued performing its due diligence examination of the title to the leases to be conveyed. However, on November 6, 2008, upon inquiry by Preston, Chesapeake confirmed that it would not close. This suit followed.

B. Procedural Background

Soon after answering Preston's complaint, Chesapeake filed its motion for summary judgment asserting that enforcement of the PSAs was barred by the statute of frauds. Preston thereafter filed its own motion for summary judgment on its claim for specific performance and on Chesapeake's counterclaim to recover its down payment.

* * *

Following the bench trial, the trial court issued findings of fact and conclusions of law. Of significance to the issues presented in this appeal, the trial court determined that the exhibits referenced as Exhibit A and attached to the PSAs did not contain sufficient information to be statute of frauds compliant. The trial court also determined, as a factual matter, that the exhibits referenced as the Assignment Exhibits were not finalized at the time the PSAs were executed; thus, the trial court determined that those exhibits could not be incorporated into the PSAs. Based upon these findings, the trial court determined that the PSAs did not comply with the statute of frauds and were not enforceable as neither the PSAs, nor the attached exhibits, furnished the means or data by which to identify the leases to be conveyed with reasonable certainty. The trial court also held that Chesapeake was not entitled to return of the $11,000,000.00 paid to Preston as a down payment on the transaction. Chesapeake did not cross-appeal this issue.

* * *

C. PSA Relevant Terms

The terms of the PSAs as a whole are not in dispute. Thus, only those terms pertinent to the statute of frauds issue are referenced herein.

Section 1(a)(i) of each of the PSAs describes the properties to be conveyed as "[a]ll of Seller's right, title and interest in and to all oil and gas leases ... [as] defined in Exhibit 'A' attached and made a part hereof...." Exhibit A to the PSAs is a listing of the leases to be conveyed. That exhibit includes a county reference in the overall heading and ten columns with the following headings: lease Id, Lease Name, Lessee, eff. date, gross acres, net acres, royalty, ORRI, NRI to be conveyed, and value of net.

Section 2 of the PSA sets out the purchase price with a provision for a 10% nonrefundable deposit.

Section 3, entitled Effective Date and Closing provides that the conveyance of the properties shall be effective as of September 26, 2008 and "title thereto shall be delivered at the Closing which shall take place on November 7, 2008...."

Section 8(b)(i) provides that at closing Seller shall deliver an "Assignment executed and acknowledged by Seller ... the form of which is attached hereto as Exhibit 'C' (the Assignment form)."

Section 12(b) provides that "[t]his agreement together with the Exhibits attached hereto and the Assignment and other documents to be delivered pursuant to the terms hereof, shall constitute the complete agreement between the parties...." Section 12(q)(vii) provides that "[t]he Schedules and Exhibits listed in the List of Schedules and Exhibits are attached hereto. Each such Schedule and/or Exhibit is incorporated herein by reference for all purposes, and reference to this Agreement shall also include such Schedule and/or Exhibit unless the context in which used shall otherwise require."

Also included was a provision for post-closing adjustment of the purchase (Section 10); a provision for curing any title defects pertaining to any particular lease (Section 6); and a provision obligating Seller to make available to Buyer all of its "title files" (Section 6(b)).

II. DISCUSSION

A. STANDARD OF REVIEW AND APPLICABLE LAW

"The standard of review for a bench trial is well established: findings of fact are reviewed for clear error and legal issues are reviewed de novo." Kona Tech. Corp. v. S. Pac. Transp. Co., 225 F.3d 595, 601 (5th Cir.2000). As the case was brought to the district court on diversity jurisdiction, the substantive law of Texas applies. See Erie R.R. v. Tompkins, 304 U.S. 64, 78–79, 58S.Ct. 817, 82 L.Ed. 1188 (1938).

B. TEXAS STATUTE OF FRAUDS

The Texas Statute of Frauds provides that a contract for the sale of real estate is not enforceable unless it is in writing signed by the person to be charged. TEX. BUS. & COM. CODE ANN. § 26.01 (West 2009). The statute of frauds applies to any transfer of an interest in land, including oil and gas leases. Minchen v. Fields, 162 Tex. 73, 345 S.W.2d 282, 287–88 (1961). Further, to be valid, the writing must contain a sufficient description of the property to be conveyed. Pick v. Bartel, 659 S.W.2d 636, 637 (Tex.1983). A property description is sufficient if the writing furnishes within itself, or by reference to some other existing writing, the means or data by which the particular land to be conveyed may be identified with reasonable certainty. Wilson v. Fisher, 144 Tex. 53, 188 S.W.2d 150, 152 (1945). * * * "The written memorandum, however, need not be contained in one document." Padilla v. LaFrance, 907 S.W.2d 454, 460 (Tex.1995) (citing Adams v. Abbott, 151 Tex. 601, 254 S.W.2d 78, 80 (1952)).

C. THE CONTRACT

The contracts between the parties are the three PSAs entered into on October 7th and 8th. In determining that the conveyance at issue here did not comply with the statute of frauds, the trial court found that the PSAs standing alone (i.e. considered without the related incorporated documents) did not contain a description of the property to be conveyed. This issue is not disputed. However, the PSAs do contain some indication of what is to be conveyed. The PSAs specifically provide that Preston is to convey "[a]ll of Seller's right, title and interest in and to all oil and gas leases" as defined in Exhibit A.

D.   The Exhibits

As noted above, the PSAs specifically referenced and incorporated various exhibits. Because it is undisputed that certain of those exhibits do provide specific reference to the recording information for each lease, Chesapeake argued that these documents should not be incorporated into the PSAs because the documents were not finalized. The trial court agreed with Chesapeake.

Exhibit C is the assignment form to convey the leases at closing. Exhibit C is specifically referenced in the PSAs and is incorporated into the PSAs by the language of Section 12(q)(vii). Section (a) of Exhibit C provides language that is almost identical to the conveyance language contained in the PSAs. Specifically, Section (a) of Exhibit C provides that the assignment is of "[a]ll of Assignor's right, title and interest ... [in the] oil and gas leases ... defined in Exhibit 'A'...." Exhibit C has an Assignment Exhibit attached to it as Exhibit A and it is undisputed that this Assignment Exhibit includes recording information for the leases to be conveyed. The dispute arises from Chesapeake's contention that it did not consider this document to be part of the PSAs because it was not yet final. However, the assignment documents could not be final at the signing of the PSAs because it was clearly intended by the parties that title work remained to be completed. The PSAs specifically include provisions for curing title defects and for adjusting the contract price for any title defects which could not be cured. It is undisputed that title work continued to be done by Chesapeake even after the execution of the contract as the PSAs also included a title work completion date of October 14th in Section 6(c). Therefore, the trial court's factual finding that the assignment documents were not yet final is not disturbed.

However, the PSAs clearly reflect the intention of the parties and a recognition that there was still some title work to be done before a final determination could be made as to the leases which would ultimately be conveyed. Thus, the trial court misconstrued this lack of finality as to the assignment documents as evidence that there was no meeting of the minds as to the subject of the contract. As a result, the trial court determined that the exhibits could not be construed as part of the contract. Such analysis reflects the conflating of two distinct principles—whether parties come to a meeting of the minds as to the subject matter of a contract with whether a writing's legal description is sufficient to meet the statute of frauds. The trial court relied on certain discrepancies between the exhibits attached to the PSAs to determine that there was no meeting of the minds as to the properties to be conveyed. While discrepancies certainly exist between the exhibits, the PSAs themselves clearly reflect the essential terms of the contract—to convey certain leases for a particular price by a certain date. If in fact there was no meeting of the minds, there would be no contract whatsoever and the statute of frauds issue would be moot.

The Texas Supreme Court has repeatedly held that multiple writings pertaining to the same transaction will be construed as one contract. [Citations omitted.] Furthermore, "[i]t is uniformly held that an unsigned paper may be incorporated by reference in the paper signed by the person sought to be charged." Owen v. Hendricks, 433 S.W.2d 164, 166 (Tex. 1968). Additionally, "[o]ne writing may be connected with another either expressly or by necessary inference because of internal evidence of the subject matter and occasion, that is, that they relate to the same transaction." Oliver v. Corzelius, 215 S.W.2d 231, 237 (Tex.Civ.App.El Paso1948), rev'd on other grounds, 148 Tex. 76, 220 S.W.2d 632 (1949).

Here, it is clear that the intention of the parties was to convey leases that complied with the specifications set forth in the PSAs. The PSAs define the type of leases [to] be conveyed—those oil and gas leases that had marketable title and that would continue for at least a one year period after the effective date (Section 6). Prior to execution of the PSAs, the parties exchanged the documents pertaining to the transaction, including the attached exhibits, certain of which provide the recording information for the leases. The attached exhibits are specifically referenced in, and incorporated into, the PSAs. By the very terms of the PSAs, the parties intended that title work would continue and that certain leases might ultimately be excluded from the contract. Clearly, the PSAs and the attached exhibits were all part of the same transaction and should be construed together. [Citation omitted.]

It was clearly the intent of the parties that the assignments would not be finalized until such time as the title work was complete. Thus, the trial court erred in its holding that the lack of finality prevented consideration of the exhibits attached to the PSAs as a part of the contract to convey the property. The exhibits were specifically incorporated into the contract. The exhibits contain a sufficient legal description to meet the statute of frauds. Thus, the PSAs are enforceable by specific performance.

To the extent that certain leases are listed on Exhibit A of the PSAs but contain no corresponding recording information on the Assignment Exhibit A that is part of Exhibit C, enforcement is limited to those leases identified by recording information. * * * Therefore, this Court holds that Preston may obtain specific performance of those leases listed in Assignment Exhibit A of Exhibit C which include recording information.

III. CONCLUSION

Accordingly, the district court's judgment in favor of Chesapeake is VACATED and the case is REMANDED for proceedings consistent with this opinion.

NOTES

1. As the principal case indicates, in jurisdictions where an oil and gas lease is deemed to create an interest in realty an assignment and contracts for an assignment are subject to the rules governing conveyances of real property. See, for example, Masgas v. Anderson, 310 S.W.3d 567 (Tex. App. 2010) where the court refused to recognize an interest in a party because of a written agreement with a lease owner that made reference to the properties that the party owned an interest in, but neither the agreement nor the attached JOA and division orders contained language indicating an intent to grant the interests in dispute to the claimant. The court pointed out that an instrument could not be effective as a grant unless it contained words of conveyance. In John O. Schofield, Inc. v. Nikkel, 731 N.E.2d 915 (Ill.App. 5 Dist. 2000), the court refused to enforce an oral agreement between an oil company and a petroleum geologist for an assignment of an interest in leases in exchange for geological assessments. Similarly, in Fontaine Trust v. P & J Resources, 2010 WL 1529399 at *9 (E.D.Ky. 2010) the court held that oral modification of letter agreements for the assignments of working interests were unenforceable.

More commonly, as in the principal case, there is a written contract or deed that clearly evinces an intent to assign all or part of a lease or leases and one party challenges whether the interests to be assigned are described with sufficient certainty to satisfy the statute of frauds. In Carpenter v. Phelps, 2011 WL 1233312 (Tex. App. 2011) the defendant, in an effort to raise money to further develop a lease containing 48 wells, began to correspond by email and letter with the plaintiffs as potential investors. In the correspondence the defendant represented that, as investors, each plaintiff would receive a stated percentage in the "M.T. Cole 'A' lease in Gregg County," which was also described as the Railroad Commission "Oil Lse/Gas ID no. 08294." Plaintiffs, who invested various sums with defendant, subsequently brought suit to enforce the agreement. The court ruled that the correspondence failed to furnish, either within itself or by reference to some other existing writing, a means by which the land in question could be identified with reasonable certainty. Plaintiff's landman was unable to provide a legal description of the M.T. Cole "A" lease either through an internet search using the lease number or by reference to any Gregg County documents containing a legal description. Further, the court held that there was no authority for the proposition that a reference to a Railroad Commission lease number could serve as a basis for an adequate legal description. Somewhat similarly, in The Long Trusts v. Griffin, 222 S.W.3d 412 (Tex. 2006) an agreement to assign leases that were described as located "in the Northeast portion of Rusk County, Texas, and consist[ing] of 50+ leases covering approximately 2100+ net mineral acres in the Dirgin and Oak Hill Fields area" as "described in the attached Exhibit 'A'" was deemed unenforceable under the statute of frauds, even though the attached exhibit provided the lessor's name, the survey name, the term, and the net acreage for each lease at issue. What additional information would have been necessary to make the agreement enforceable?

2. In Kansas an oil and gas lease is classified as a form of personal property (a profit a prendre), but is nonetheless subject to the state's

recording statute. See Kan. Stat. Ann. § 58–2221. Depending upon the circumstances, compliance with homestead laws and requirements for the transfer of community property may also be necessary. If tangible personal property is being assigned along with the leasehold, the transaction will be subject to the U.C.C.

3. Attorneys involved in facilitating assignments are likely to be advertent to the need to determine state law requirements, but they may be unaware that an assignor of leasehold interests may also be subject to certain requirements of federal and state law. The key federal legislation that may affect a company engaged in these transfers includes the Securities Act of 1933 (codified as amended at 15 U.S.C. § 77a–77bbb) and the Securities Exchange Act of 1934 (codified as amended at 15 U.S.C. § 78a–78lll). The Securities Act of 1933 primarily regulates the original distribution of securities by an issuer to the public. Consequently, an oil and gas company can be exposed to regulation if it is involved in any of the three basic categories of oil and gas securities that are required to be registered under the Act. These categories include:

1) any stock, certificate of interest, or certificate of participation in any profit-sharing agreement;

2) investment contracts, which include any arrangement where the purchaser looks to the efforts of others to make their investment profitable, and;

3) fractional undivided interest in oil, gas, or other mineral rights that are created for the intent of public sale. See 15 U.S.C. § 77b(1).

In Securities & Exchange Commission v. C. M. Joiner Leasing Corp., 320 U.S. 344 (1943) the 1933 Act was invoked to enjoin "Dad" Joiner, who discovered the giant East Texas Field, from soliciting investments in a 3,002 acre, undrilled lease located hundreds of miles from the known limits of the field. Joiner had mailed sales promotion literature to over 1,000 people in at least eighteen states promising "a good chance for splendid returns on the investment * * * [in] a new oil field," but insisted that the solicitations were exempt because he was seeking buyers for specific blocks of acreage (ranging from 2 1/2 to 20 acres in size). The Court dealt with that argument as follows:

It is urged that because the definition mentions "fractional undivided interest in oil, gas or other mineral rights," it excludes sales of leasehold subdivisions by parcels. Oil and gas rights posed a difficult problem to the legislative draftsman. Such rights were notorious subjects of speculation and fraud, but leases and assignments were also indispensable instruments of legitimate oil exploration and production. To include leases and assignments by name might easily burden the oil industry by controls that were designed only for the traffic in securities. This was avoided by including specifically only that form of splitting up of mineral interests which had been most utilized for speculative purposes. We do not think the draftsmen thereby immunized other forms of contracts and offerings which are proved as matter of fact to answer to such descriptive terms as "investment contracts" and "securities."

320 U.S. at 352.

The Securities Act of 1933 does expressly provide for some exempted transactions, including for example, private offerings. See id. § 77d(2). In addition to these express exemptions, as a general rule an oil and gas company can transfer an entire leasehold interest without risking subjugation to securities regulation. The courts have also held that the transfer of a lease subject to a retained royalty or other payment from production is not the transfer of a security. See Graham v. Clark, 332 F.2d 155 (6th Cir. 1964). Several courts have, however, held that the transfer of any fractional undivided mineral interest is a securities transaction for purposes of the anti-fraud provisions of federal law. See Penturelli v. Spector, 779 F.2d 160 (3d Cir.Pa. 1985); Adena Exploration, Inc. v. Sylvan, 860 F.2d 1242 (5th Cir.1988). Moreover, a securities transaction will be found even if the buyer of the fractional undivided mineral interest is an active participant in the mineral operations. See Adena at 1248–49. There is, however, limited authority to the contrary, See, e.g., Ballard & Cordell Corp. v. Zoller & Danneberg Exploration, Ltd., 544 F.2d 1059, 1063–64 (10th Cir. 1976), holding than an offering of fractional undivided interest in oil and gas leases is not a security where the transaction is among friends and acquaintances and involves purchasers with sophisticated discernment about oil and gas business, and the transaction is entered into after on-the-ground inspection and negotiation. When circumstances indicate that a purchaser of an entire leasehold interest is buying in expectation of profiting from the continued activities of the seller instead of operating the lease himself, the interest will be classified as a security. See Mansfield v. United States, 155 F.2d 952 (5th Cir.1946).

The Securities Act of 1934 also affects a variety of transactions, but the most important provision of this Act affecting oil and gas securities is Rule 10b–5. See 15 U.S.C. § 78j(b) (codified version of Securities Exchange Act of 1934 § 10(b)). This provision grants investors a private right of action for misrepresentation, omission of a material fact, or fraud in connection with the purchase or sale of a security. Due to the time and expense associated with securities regulation, oil and gas companies often carefully structure their transactions to fit within the statutory exemptions. Even so, oil and gas securities must still be sold in compliance with "blue sky" security laws of the states because civil or criminal sanctions may be enforced when the state requirements are not met. For further discussion, see Alan R. Bromberg & Lewis D. Lowenfels, Securities Fraud & Commodities Fraud (1997); see also David H. Barber, Applicability of United States Federal and Securities Acts to Sales of Oil and Gas Interests, 1 Canadian–American L.J. 43 (1982), and J. Richard Emens, Securities Laws Applicable to Financing Oil, Gas, and Hard Mineral Exploration, 1 E.Min.L.Inst. 11–1 (1980). See also John Burritt McArthur, Coming of Age: Initiating the Oilfield into Performance Disclosure, 50 SMU L.Rev. 663 (1997) detailing a wide variety of ways in which investors can be misled by lack of full disclosure by oilfield operators and arguing that current common law and statutory remedies, including securities law, are inadequate.

Although the states' "blue sky" laws impose civil or criminal sanctions when state requirements for the sale of securities are not met, since 1996 federal law has partially preempted state laws governing securities in order to create a more unified system of regulation. For example, states may no longer require the registration and qualification of many types of securities. In response to federal preemptive legislation, many states have tailored their securities rules to make them consistent with federal regulations. See, e.g., Paull v. Capital Resource Management, Inc., 987 S.W.2d 214 (Tex. App. 1999) (showing the similarity of state exemptions from registration with Regulation D of the 1933 Securities Act) and Denise Voight Crawford, Exemptions Update Under Texas Law, 35 Tex. J. Bus. L. 1 (Winter 1999). While the states' powers to register and qualify securities have been significantly curtailed, states still retain considerable authority in regulating securities fraud. There are many articles discussing state blue sky laws. These include Nelson S. Ebaugh, Remedies for Defrauded Purchasers of Oil and Gas Interests Under the Securities Laws, 1 Tex. J. Oil Gas & Energy L 51 (2006) (pointing out that the Texas Blue Sky Law has a broad definition of "security" that includes more oil and gas transactions than the federal securities acts); George Lee Flint, Jr., Securities Regulation, 57 SMU L. Rev. 1207 (2004); Rick A. Fleming, 100 Years of Securities Law: Examining A Foundation Laid in the Kansas Blue Sky, 50 Washburn L.J. 583 (2011); Jay H. Knight, Esq. & Garrett P. Baker, Kentucky Blue Sky Law: A Practitioner's Guide to Kentucky's Registrations and Exemptions, 34 N. Ky. L. Rev. 485 (2007); Keith A. Rowley, The Sky Is Still Blue in Texas: State Law: Alternatives to Federal Securities Remedies, 50 Baylor L. Rev. 99 (1998); Keith A. Rowley, Muddy Waters, Blue Skies: Civil Liability Under the Mississippi Securities Act, 70 Miss.L.J. 683 (2000); Keith A. Rowley, They Toil Not, Neither Do They Spin: Civil Liability Under the Oregon Securities Law, 37 Willamette L.Rev. 335 (2001), and Joseph Shade, Financing Exploration: Requirements of Federal and State Securities Laws, 37 Nat.Res.L.J. 749 (1997).

4.   The attorney drafting an assignment must not only comply with the requirements of state and federal law, she must also take into account the terms of the parties' deal and attempt to anticipate the variety of legal and relational issues that may arise after the instrument has been executed; otherwise there is a significantly increased possibility of litigation. This approach is especially important if the assignment is of a type that is relatively new and there is little case law to provide guidance. The following "wellbore assignment" case provides a good example.

PETROPRO, LTD. v. UPLAND RESOURCES, INC.

279 S.W.3d 743 (Tex.App. 2007).

OPINION

PATRICK A. PIRTLE, JUSTICE.

This appeal concerns a dispute between assignors, assignees, and intervening royalty owners regarding the construction of two oil and gas wellbore assignments, wherein the assignments expressly limited the assigned interest to "rights in the wellbore" of a given well. . . .

BACKGROUND FACTS

Original Oil and Gas Leases

The two assignments in question pertain to rights in the wellbore of the King "F" No. 2 gas well, located on a 704–acre pooled gas unit in

Roberts County. The material facts surrounding the well are not disputed. In September 1992 and 1993, Upland Resources, Inc. (hereinafter individually referred to as "Upland Resources") entered into five oil, gas, and mineral leases involving separate tracts of land in Roberts County. In 1993, Medallion Production Company ("Medallion") acquired the leasehold and spud the King "F" No. 2 well on one of the leased tracts consisting of 500 acres. The tract covered multiple gas-producing formations, including the Brown Dolomite formation, located at depths of approximately 3,400 to 3,600 feet, and the Cleveland formation, located approximately 6,500 to 6,600 feet beneath the surface. The King "F" No. 2 well was completed as a gas well in the Cleveland formation and produced gas in paying quantities. Several months after the well was completed, Medallion pooled the 500–acre tract with 204 acres from an adjacent tract to create an irregular shaped, 704–acre gas unit. The leasehold interest in the 704–acre unit was subsequently acquired by KCS Medallion Resources ("KCS") and MB Operating Co., Inc. ("MB"). Eventually, the leasehold area situated horizontally outside the 704–acre unit and vertically below 6,800 feet was released.

"Wellbore Only" Assignments

In 1998, for reasons undisclosed in the record, KCS and MB decided that the King "F" No. 2 well was no longer economically viable. Consequently, in November of that year, KCS and MB sold their interests in the well at an auction of oil and gas properties. The winning bidder, L & R Energy ("L & R"), received the interests from KCS and MB via the two assignments in controversy. The assignments were identical in that they both conveyed the following:

> All of Seller's right, title and interest in and to the oil and gas leases described in Exhibit "A" attached hereto and made a part hereof ("Subject Leases") *insofar and only insofar as said leases cover rights in the wellbore* of the King "F" No. 2 Well.

(Emphasis added). Pursuant to the express terms of the assignments, L & R's leasehold interest became effective on December 1, 1998.

New Development Activity

Several years after the assignments, operators in the area began drilling and completing gas wells in the shallower Brown Dolomite formation. In May 2003, pursuant to a farmout agreement with KCS, Upland Resources entered the pooled gas unit and completed a horizontal gas well in the Brown Dolomite formation. The well, dubbed the Skeeterbee No. 1, traversed within 600 feet of the King "F" No. 2 well. By June 2004, Upland Resources had completed two more gas wells within the 704–acre pooled gas unit, the horizontal Skeeterbee No. 2 and the vertical Skeeterbee No. 3. Both those wells were completed in the Brown Dolomite formation. Meanwhile, in April 2004, L & R assigned its interest in the King "F" No. 2 well to Petro Pro Ltd. (hereinafter individually referred to as "Petro Pro"). Concerned with Upland Resource's drilling activities,

Petro Pro sent a letter to Upland Resources and KCS requesting that both parties clarify their respective interests in the pooled gas unit. Both parties promptly responded with letters stating their belief that Petro Pro did not acquire any leasehold interest outside the confines of the King "F" No. 2 wellbore. Petro Pro replied with a letter stating claims for trespass and conversion and demanding that Appellees vacate the leasehold and cease production from the Skeeterbee wells.

Suit Filed

Finally, in September 2004, citing Upland Resources and KCS's refusal to resolve the dispute, Petro Pro and L & R (hereinafter collectively referred to as "Petro") filed the underlying suit against Upland, KCS, and other interested parties, . . . for trespass, bad faith trespass, conversion, and money had and received. Petro claimed they owned the exclusive right to produce gas from the entire 704–acre pooled gas unit, from the surface to a depth of 6,800 feet. Petro also sought a declaratory judgment declaring the property rights and ownership interests acquired by the respective parties by virtue of the assignments and an accounting of all proceeds from the sale of gas produced from the Skeeterbee wells. Petro also filed a motion requesting that any production revenue from the Skeeterbee wells be placed into the court's registry until the dispute was resolved. Upland initially responded to the allegations by filing a general denial. Upon learning of the pending dispute between Petro and Upland, the royalty interest owners in the 704–acre pooled gas unit, Nancy Wilson Briscoe, Judith Brock Seitz, and Carolyn Rogers (hereinafter collectively referred to as "Intervenors") filed a plea of intervention seeking damages for the alleged breach of implied covenants and for tortious interference with existing contracts. Intervenors contended that Petro's lawsuit and wrongful claims of ownership prevented Upland from fully developing the lease and protecting the lease from drainage from adjacent wells.

Competing Motions for Summary Judgment

On February 1, 2005, Upland filed a motion for summary judgment contending that Petro's rights were limited to the right to produce gas from the Cleveland formation only and the right to "enhance" that production. Upland further contended that Petro's rights were restricted to the physical confines of the King "F" No. 2 well only, without the right to deepen the well to other zones or horizons, or the right to perforate the wellbore casing for the purpose of producing any other zone or horizon lying between the surface and the presently producing section of the Cleveland formation. Subsequently, Intervenors filed a motion for partial summary judgment contending Petro had the right to produce from any formation subject to governmental regulations, which limited the horizontal extent of Petro's rights to forty acres surrounding the King "F" No. 2 wellbore. Finally, Petro filed their own motion for summary judgment restating their position that they were the exclusive owners of any portion of leasehold estate that could "reasonably be reached and produced" through the King "F" No. 2 wellbore.

The Trial Court's Judgment

Following hearings on the parties' competing motions for summary judgment, the trial court ruled that the King "F" No. 2 wellbore assignments were unambiguous and granted Upland Resources' motion for summary judgment.... The court denied Petro and Intervenors' motions for summary judgment and Petro's motion to have funds from production tendered into the court's registry. The trial court also severed and abated Intervenors' damage claims against Petro.

As drafted, the trial court's judgment does not set forth a declaration of the interest and rights conveyed by the assignments.[1] ...

* * *

The questions presented in this case are, what interest is conveyed by the assignments, and what are the rights of the parties? Therefore, this Court will construe the assignments in question and declare the interests conveyed and rights of the parties as to those matters upon which the parties have joined issue.

* * *

[W]e begin by determining the applicability of some established canons of contract construction.

Applicability of Canons of Contract Construction

The goal when construing an unambiguous agreement is to determine and give effect to the parties' intent as expressed within the "four corners" of the instrument. See Gulf Ins. Co. v. Burns Motors, Inc., 22 S.W.3d 417, 423 (Tex.2000); Luckel v. White, 819 S.W.2d 459, 461–63 (Tex.1991). Such intent is garnered from the language used in the writing when read as a whole. Cross Timbers Oil Co. v. Exxon Corp., 22 S.W.3d 24, 26 (Tex.App.–Amarillo 2000, no pet.). Stated differently, we must analyze the entire instrument to understand and harmonize all parts of the instrument so as to give effect to all of its provisions. [Citations omitted.]. Construction of an unambiguous instrument is a question of law to be resolved by the court. Luckel, 819 S.W.2d at 461....

By their brief, Petro contends that the absence of express limiting language means that Upland intended to assign their leasehold interest in the entire 704–acre pooled gas unit, including the right to extend one or more horizontal drainholes from the King "F" No. 2 wellbore into other productive areas of the lease. Similarly, Petro insists that the conveyance of "[a]ll of Seller's right, title and interest" in the leases gives them title to all the oil, gas, and minerals beneath the leasehold regardless of where

---

1. The judgment merely recites that the assignments in question are "unambiguous" and "grant[s] Defendant's motion for summary judgment and den[ies] Plaintiff's motion for summary judgment and Intervenors' motion for summary judgment...."

it is located. Petro contends that this interpretation is consistent with the various canons of construction that pertain to conveyances of real property, namely the canon to "construe in favor of the grantee" and the canon of "conveyance of the greatest estate," which they claim is embodied in § 5.001(a) of the Property Code.[2] Furthermore, Petro urges us to consider Upland's actions with respect to other assignments, which are unrelated to the present case but contain similar language.

At the opposite extreme, Upland contends that the assignments should be construed in light of the facts as they existed at the time of conveyance, thereby restricting Petro's rights to the production of gas from the existing wellbore and the Cleveland formation only. While Intervenors agree that operations should be confined to the existing wellbore, they claim that Petro's rights should be construed in such a way that they are limited, in accordance with Railroad Commission well density rules, to an undetermined forty surface acres surrounding the wellbore. Intervenors further contend that the assignments should be construed so as to allow Petro the right to plug back the wellbore and recomplete the well in the Brown Dolomite formation.

* * *

Here, none of the parties allege that the assignments are ambiguous, and we agree that they are not. Therefore, we restrict our analysis to the plain language of the assignments to determine the nature and scope of the assigned interest. See Yzaguirre v. KCS Resources, Inc., 53 S.W.3d 368, 372–73 (Tex.2001).

Nature and Scope of the Assigned Interest

As recited above, the assignment language describes the assigned interest as "[a]ll of Seller's right, title and interest in and to the oil and gas leases ... insofar and only insofar as said leases cover rights in the wellbore of the King 'F' No. 2 Well." While the parties agree that this language unambiguously assigns leasehold rights in the King "F" No. 2 wellbore, their interpretations regarding the nature and extent of the estate conveyed differ greatly.

An oil and gas lease conveys an interest in real property, as does the assignment of all or a portion thereof. Cherokee Water Co. v. Forderhause, 641 S.W.2d 522, 525 (Tex.1982); ExxonMobil Corp. v. Valence Operating Co., 174 S.W.3d 303 (Tex.App.–Houston [1st Dist.] 2005, pet. denied). A lessee under an oil and gas lease owns a determinable fee in the oil and gas in place. Cherokee Water Co., 641 S.W.2d at 525. In this case, the

---

2. The canon of conveyance of the greatest estate provides that the instrument should be construed to confer to the grantee the largest estate that the terms of the instrument will permit. *See generally* Bruce M. Kramer, *The Sisyphean Task of Interpreting Mineral Deeds and Leases: An Encyclopedia of Canons of Construction,* 24 Tex. Tech L.Rev. 1, 117–24. Section 5.001(a) states that "[a]n estate in land ... is a fee simple unless the estate is limited by express words or unless a lesser estate is conveyed or devised by construction or operation of law." Tex. Prop.Code Ann. § 5.001(a) (Vernon 2004). *See also Ladd v. DuBose,* 344 S.W.2d 476, 480 (Tex.Civ.App.–Amarillo 1961, no writ), *citing Waters v. Ellis,* 158 Tex. 342, 312 S.W.2d 231, 234 (1958).

estate conveyed was part of the leasehold estate created by the underlying oil and gas leases. Therefore, the assignments assigned to Petro a determinable fee interest in the oil and gas in place.

Like the phrase "subject to," the phrase "insofar and only insofar" constitutes a limitation of the grant. See, e.g., Walker v. Foss, 930 S.W.2d 701, 707 (Tex.App.–San Antonio 1996, no writ) (stating that the principal function of such a limitation is protecting the grantor against a claimed breach of warranty). It neither conveys an interest to the assignee, nor does it reserve or retain an interest in favor of the assignor. It merely limits the extent of the interest granted. Id. at 706–07. Consequently, it does not serve to limit the "rights" conveyed to Petro, nor does it reserve to Upland any exclusive rights. Therefore, the assignee, in this case Petro, received all of the rights appurtenant to the estate conveyed. So, what was the estate conveyed and what are the rights appurtenant thereto?

Estate Conveyed

To settle this dispute and define the estate conveyed, we must first determine the depth (vertical rights) and area (horizontal rights) covered by the assignments. [Citations omitted.] This information, in turn, will allow us to define the extent of assignees' leasehold rights in the King "F" No. 2 wellbore.

Vertical Limit of Assignment

Regarding this issue, Upland contends that the "plain, grammatical meaning" of the words used in the assignments limits the assigned interest to the horizon that was open in the wellbore on the date of the assignments. In other words, Upland claims Petro's rights are strictly limited to the Cleveland formation. But adopting this stance would be inserting language into the assignments that does not exist. Furthermore, it would require a determination of the facts, outside the four corners of the assignment, to ascertain the extent of the interest transferred. Contrary to Upland's contention, the assignments are completely devoid of language limiting Petro's leasehold interest to the Cleveland formation. Without such limiting language, we find no support for Upland's contention and agree with Petro and Intervenors' contention that the assignment language does not limit wellbore operations to a specific depth or formation. Therefore, we hold that the vertical limit of the assignments is defined by the depth of the wellbore as assigned.

Horizontal Limit of Assignment

Similarly, there is a lack of support for Petro's claim that it acquired horizontal rights coextensive with the 704–acre pooled gas unit and Intervenors' claim that Petro acquired leasehold rights in forty surface acres surrounding the King "F" No. 2 wellbore. Just as the assignment language does not restrict Petro's operations to a specific vertical producing interval, it also does not expressly or impliedly convey leasehold rights in any horizontal surface acreage. Cf. David E. Pierce, An Analytical

Approach to Drafting Assignments, 44 Sw. L.J. 943, 955 (1990) (explaining that, presumably, the assignee is entitled to the production allocated to the [lease] well even though he owns none of the required leasehold acreage).

On the issue of the horizontal extent of the estate conveyed, Intervenors cite the language in the assignments stating that the assigned interests are "subject to . . . governmental regulations." Relying on this "governmental regulations clause," Intervenors contend that, pursuant to Railroad Commission Rule 38, when Petro acquired rights in the King "F" No. 2 wellbore, it also acquired rights in the minimum amount of surface acreage needed to obtain a plug back permit for recompletion in the Brown Dolomite formation. See 16 Tex. Admin. Code §§ 3.5, 3.38 (2007) (Tex. R.R. Comm'n, Application To Drill, Deepen, Reenter, or Plug Back; Well Densities). We disagree.

As Intervenors acknowledge, the Railroad Commission is a regulatory agency and lacks the authority to determine ownership of land or property rights. See, e.g., Amarillo Oil Co. v. Energy–Agri Products, Inc., 794 S.W.2d 20, 26 (Tex.1990). The government regulations clause does not provide for additional leasehold rights contingent upon the assignee seeking to commence certain wellbore operations. Simply put, there is nothing in the assignments that suggests that, because the assigned interest is subject to governmental regulation, the nature and scope of the interest assigned may vary. For this reason, we find Intervenors position to be inconsistent with the plain language of the assignments.

Because the assignments are limited to "rights in the wellbore" we must determine what the parties intended by that term. The assignments do not describe the King "F" No. 2 wellbore or even define the term "wellbore," therefore, we must turn to its generally accepted meaning. A wellbore, sometimes called a borehole, is the hole in the ground created by the process of drilling or boring a well. 8 Patrick H. Martin & Bruce M. Kramer, Williams & Meyers Oil and Gas Law, Manual of Terms, 107, 1207 (9th ed.1998). A well, meanwhile, is defined as the "orifice in the ground made by drilling, boring or any other manner, from which any petroleum or gas is obtained or obtainable. . . ." Id. at 1205. When read in context with the assignment language, these definitions indicate that Petro's leasehold rights extend horizontally only to the area of the hole identified as the King "F" No. 2 well and, by implication, such surface area adjacent thereto as is reasonably necessary to operate the well.

Rights Appurtenant

Consistent with the horizontal and vertical limitations of Petro's interest, the assignments also conveyed all rights appurtenant to the underlying oil and gas leases. One of those rights was the right to develop the leased premises for the purpose of "exploring, drilling, mining, operating for and producing oil, gas and other minerals." To that extent, Petro's interest was not limited to production of gas from the Cleveland formation. Therefore, subject to governmental regulations, the assignments in question granted Petro the right to rework the King "F" No. 2 well so as to produce from any formation that might possibly be reached from the existing wellbore. This right to develop, however, does not extend beyond the present confines of the wellbore. In other words, Petro does not have the right to extend the present well beyond its current depth, nor does it have the right to drill horizontally beyond the confines of the existing wellbore.

Another one of the rights assigned was the right to produce. Subject to the duties imposed by the lease (e.g., the duty to pay the original lessor a royalty for oil or gas taken, the duty to pay for damages occasioned by its operations, and the duty to restore the surface upon abandonment of the well), Petro has the exclusive right to produce oil and gas from the King "F" No. 2 well. Conversely, because the assignments in question did not transfer Upland's determinable fee interest in the oil and gas in place outside of the wellbore, Petro does not own an interest in the oil and gas in place outside the confines of the King "F" No. 2 well. For these reasons, completion of the Skeeterbee wells did not constitute a trespass onto property which Petro owned. For these same reasons, the production of gas from the Skeeterbee wells did not constitute conversion of property belonging to Petro. Because Petro does not have an ownership interest in the gas produced from the Skeeterbee wells, Petro is not entitled to a portion of the proceeds or to an accounting.

* * *

To the extent that the leases embodied other rights not exclusive to the possession and use of the wellbore in question (e.g., the right to extend the lease by the payment of shut-in royalties), the assignment created a co-tenancy with the other lessees, with each party sharing those incorporeal appurtenant rights.

The practical effect of this construction is that Petro owns the exclusive right to produce any oil, gas, or other minerals that may be produced from the King "F" No. 2 wellbore, consistent with the terms and conditions of the original leases. Subject to governmental regulations, Petro also owns the right to develop the wellbore and conduct any operations within the wellbore that would facilitate or enhance that development and production, including the right to produce from other formations. Upland retained the exclusive right, subject to the terms and conditions of the original leases and any applicable governmental regulations, to produce any oil, gas, or other minerals that may be extracted from the leased premises, other than through the King "F" No. 2 wellbore. Although this construction describes a relatively restrictive leasehold interest, it is consistent with the fact that, from an area standpoint, a wellbore assignment is the narrowest form of oil and gas assignment. Lawrence P. Terrell, Limited Assignments—Who Gets What?, 35 Rocky Mtn. Min. L. Inst. 17, § 17.02 (1989).

Our learned colleague's dissenting opinion states, "Rather than concluding the parties intended to grant Petro the right to recomplete the well to produce gas it does not own, we would construe the assignments' language in a manner consistent with our state's ownership-in-place theory." ... While the concept of producing oil and gas that one does not own may seem unfair, it is hardly inconsistent with the ownership-in-place theory of mineral ownership. To the contrary, it is entirely consistent with over a hundred years of precedent pertaining to the corollary doctrine of the "rule of capture." ... Even though the legal effect of this Court's interpretation is to allow Petro the right to produce gas that it does not own until it captures it, and merely because that result may seem to be inconsistent with what reasonable people would consider fair, that interpretation does give effect to the intent expressed within the "four corners" of the instrument. It has long been recognized that, absent exigent circumstances, even though the intent of the parties may seem illogical, the law will not protect you from an improvident bargain.

CONCLUSION

In summary, we find that the trial court erred in rendering its declaration of the rights of the parties. To that extent, Intervenors' sole issue and Petro's issues one through three are subsumed within the disposition of Petro's fourth issue, which is sustained in part (as to the granting of summary judgment in favor of Upland's construction of the assignments) and overruled in part (as to the denying of Petro's Motion for Partial Summary Judgment and Intervenor's First Amended Motion for Partial Summary Judgment in favor of their respective construction of the assignments). Because we also find that Petro did not have title to the oil and gas in place outside of the King "F" No. 2 wellbore, we conclude that they would not be entitled to an accounting of future production from the Skeeterbee wells....

We reverse the judgment of the trial court and render judgment declaring that the wellbore assignments in question transfer to the assignee an estate that extends to the physical limits of the wellbore, together with all of the appurtenant rights incident to the underlying lease. Accordingly, the plain language of the assignments conveys to Petro the oil, gas and other minerals in place within the confines of the King "F" No. 2 wellbore, together with those rights appurtenant to the original leases as may be necessary to the production of those minerals and to the full use and enjoyment of that wellbore, including, but not limited to the right to produce from any formation traversed by the wellbore. As a result, Petro did not acquire title to the gas in place outside of the King "F" No. 2 wellbore or the right to extend the existing wellbore into other areas of the lease. We further hold that Upland retains their respective interest in the remainder of the leasehold estate, and the rights appurtenant thereto. Petro's claims of trespass, bad faith trespass, conversion, and money had and received are dismissed and its request that monies from current production from the Skeeterbee wells be placed into the registry of the court is denied.

JAMES T. CAMPBELL, JUSTICE, concurring and dissenting.

There is much in the Court's opinion with which I agree.

* * *

My difference with the Court involves its conclusion that the language used by the parties in the wellbore assignments reflects their intention that the assignee was conveyed the right to recomplete the King "F" No. 2 well in the Brown Dolomite formation. From the language used in these assignments, I would not find the parties intended both the assignor and assignee to have the right to produce gas from the same formation.

* * *

Rather than concluding the parties intended to grant Petro the right to recomplete the well to produce gas it does not own, I would construe the assignments' language in a manner consistent with our state's ownership-in-place theory.

My conclusion is that the trial court was correct to adopt the position asserted by Upland.[3] With respect to the leasehold rights that were at issue before the trial court, I would enter judgment declaring that the assignments in question did not convey the right to recomplete the King "F" No. 2 well for production of gas from the Brown Dolomite formation.[4] To the degree the Court's judgment is otherwise, I respectfully dissent.

* * *

NOTES

1.   Under what circumstances would parties enter into a "wellbore-only" assignment? If the operator had determined that the well was "no longer economically viable," why would the assignee have any interest in acquiring the well? Is the parties' failure to define the relative rights of the assignors and assignee relevant to the answer of this question?

2.   Ideally, potential issues that may arise as a result of an assignment, whether it be a wellbore-only assignment or an assignment of the assignor's entire interest in a lease, should be anticipated and addressed at the drafting stage rather than after they have arisen. A comprehensive discussion of the substantive law and negotiating points that should be considered can be found in David E. Pierce, An Analytical Approach to Drafting Assignments, 44 Sw. L.J. 943 (1990).

---

3. The court expresses the concern that adoption of Upland's position requires us to imply language the assignments do not contain. I do not agree. By the assignments, the assignee received all the assignor's right, title and interest in and to the leases, "insofar and only insofar as said leases cover rights in the wellbore of the King 'F' No. 2 well." It seems to me we do not read language into the assignments merely by acknowledging the undisputed, and indisputable, fact that the well referred to in the assignments as the King "F" No. 2 (but not further identified or described in the assignments) is a well producing only from the Lips, West (Cleveland) Field. *See, e.g., Texas Pac. Coal & Oil Co. v. Masterson,* 160 Tex. 548, 334 S.W.2d 436 (Tex.1960) (court's construction of unambiguous deed included references to stipulated facts).

4. Although title to gas in the Cleveland formation is not at issue, Upland's brief acknowledges that the assignments conveyed the "Cleveland Zone which was then open to production in the wellbore...."

Professor Pierce concludes his article with a hypothetical situation in which Big Oil Company has agreed to assign an undivided half interest in an oil and gas lease that it obtained by a prior assignment from a landman. The lease is thus already subject to the lessors' 1/8 royalty and a 1/16 of 7/8 overriding royalty reserved by the landman when he transferred the lease in full to Big Oil Co. Professor Pierce suggests that the following assignment document could be used for this situation:

ASSIGNMENT

Big Oil Company ("Big"), for valuable consideration, conveys to XYZ Petroleum Corporation ("XYZ"), subject to the terms of this ASSIGNMENT, an UNDIVIDED 50% INTEREST in the following property:

a. Oil and Gas Lease between John Doe and Mary Doe as lessor and Larry Landman as lessee, dated September 15, 2002, recorded in Book 105, Page 152, of the Miscellaneous Records of Eureka County, Texas, covering the North Half of Section 30, Township 36 South, Range 10 East, in Eureka County, Texas ("Lease").

b. All personal property, to include fixtures, currently located on the Lease and used or useable in connection with oil and gas exploration and production activities ("Personal Property") [could itemize in assignment or incorporate an itemized list from a Bill of Sale].

The Lease and Personal Property are collectively referred to as the "Assigned Property."

ASSIGNMENT terms:

1. NO WARRANTY. Big makes this ASSIGNMENT without any warranty, express, implied, or statutory. XYZ accepts the Personal Property AS IS, WITH ALL FAULTS.

2. ADMINISTRATION OF DELAY RENTAL. Big will pay 100% of the delay rental necessary to keep the Lease in effect. If Big fails to properly pay delay rental, thereby resulting in Lease termination, Big will pay to XYZ an amount equal to the greater of: (1) the price paid by XYZ as consideration for this ASSIGNMENT, or (2) the fair market value of XYZ's interest in the Lease as of the date immediately prior to termination.

3. INDEMNITY. Big agrees to indemnify XYZ against any liability, claim, demand, damage, or cost arising out of a failure, prior to the date of this ASSIGNMENT, to fulfill the express or implied covenants created by the Lease. XYZ's indemnity rights include reasonable attorney fees and litigation costs necessary to defend any matter covered by Big's indemnity or to enforce Big's obligation to indemnify.

4. ALLOCATING EXISTING BURDENS. In addition to lessor's royalty rights created by the Lease, production from the Lease is subject to an overriding royalty retained by Larry Landman in an assignment by Larry Landman to Big dated September 20, 1988 and filed for record in Book 106, Page 24, of the Miscellaneous Records of Eureka County, Texas ("Landman Override"). To the extent the Landman Override continues in effect, and relates to production from the Lease, XYZ agrees to share in satisfying the Landman Override up to, but not exceeding, an amount equal to 50% of

1/16th of 7/8ths of 8/8ths of production from the Lease. To the extent this is not sufficient to meet the requirements of the Landman Override, Big will pay or deliver the balance.

5. BINDING EFFECT. This ASSIGNMENT, and all related terms and conditions, are binding upon the successors and assigns of Big and XYZ.

[Provisions for signatures, acknowledgment and seal have been omitted.]

NOTES

1. The assignment set out above includes a specific disclaimer of warranty. Why might the assignor be unwilling to give a warranty? Why is the disclaimer necessary?

2. In Geodyne Energy Income Production Partnership v. The Newton Corp., 161 S.W.3d 482 (Tex. 2005) the defendant, which owned a 10% working interest in a lease held by a single well that had stopped producing, listed it for sale along with other properties at a lease auction. The properties were listed for sale "as is * * * without warranty of merchantability and without warranty of title." Transfer was to be by quitclaim deed. Upon discovering that the lease had terminated, and that it was liable for 10% of plugging costs, the purchaser at the auction brought suit, alleging that the defendant had misrepresented the validity of the lease and thus had violated the Texas Securities Act. The Texas Supreme Court reversed a judgment for plaintiff. It reasoned that a quitclaim deed of an oil and gas lease puts a buyer on notice that the seller's title may be doubtful, and that the plaintiff was precluded from claiming that the seller misrepresented or omitted a material fact even though the underlying lease had in fact terminated.

Would a buyer who received an expired leased under the assignment set out above also be barred from an action against the seller?

3. Oil and gas leases frequently contain language providing that if a specific geographic portion of the lease is assigned, delay rentals are thereafter apportioned on a surface acreage basis among the parties to the assignment and that default by one party will terminate the lease only as to that party's portion of the lease. Does this lease provision eliminate the need for parties to an assignment to contract between themselves as to obligations for delay rental payments?

What recourse is available against a party who contractually assumes the obligation to make payments of delay rentals but fails to do so? In Isler v. Texas Oil & Gas Corp., 749 F.2d 22 (10th Cir. N.M. 1984), the assignor had agreed to use its best efforts to pay the delay rentals, but inadvertently failed to make the payments and did not give the assignee timely notice of the default. After the lease expired, the assignee completed two wells on the premises. In rejecting the assignee's action in tort for damages caused by the assignor's negligence, the Tenth Circuit held that the assignee was limited to damages for breach of contract. Is this the same remedy as that provided for in the assignment by Big Oil Co.?

If an assignee agrees to pay delay rentals or give the assignor timely notice that it chooses not to do so, can it relieve itself of both the obligation and liability for breach by reassigning the lease? Shore Exploration & Prod. Corp. v. Exxon Corp., 976 F.Supp. 514 (N.D.Tex. 1997) presents a textbook case of the issues involved and variety of possible results. The plaintiff assigned three leases by an instrument providing that both the initial assignee and that party's "successors and assigns" were obligated to give plaintiff notice of non-payment of delay rentals. One lease was assigned directly to Texaco, which subsequently re-assigned it to another company. Texaco was a remote assignee of the other two leases, which it also later re-assigned. Plaintiff lost its retained overriding royalties in the three leases when the company to which Texaco had reassigned them failed to pay delay rentals and did not give notice. The court held that Texaco remained liable for breach of the notice provision in the lease that it had received directly from the plaintiff because it had expressly agreed to continuing liability. However since Texaco was a remote assignee of the second and third leases, it could not be held liable under the contractual provision binding the initial assignee; and since it had reassigned them, it would normally be exempt from liability for breach because it no longer owned the estate burdened by the notice obligation. The court concluded that that was the correct result with respect to only one of the leases. Texaco was held liable with respect to the remaining lease because the company contractually assumed all obligations agreed upon between the plaintiff and the original assignee.

The decision in *Shore* was based on the law of Virginia, where the oil and gas leases were located. Professor Smith has argued that different results under the three leases would probably be reached in jurisdictions that do not view oil and gas leases as traditional leases.

> Since landlord/tenant law is not strictly applicable, the liability of an initial assignee and the parties to which it reassigns in a jurisdiction such as Texas [which views an oil and gas lease as conveying a fee simple determinable in the mineral estate] should be determined by the rules governing covenants attached to fees simple. (These are commonly referred to as covenants running with the land.) Under this body of law there is considerable question whether an initial covenanting party can still be held liable on the covenant after the land is transferred to another party.

Ernest E. Smith, Recent Developments in Nonregulatory Oil and Gas Law, 49 Inst. on Oil & Gas L. & Tax'n 1–1 1–30 (1998).

He cautions, however, that regardless of jurisdiction a company would be well advised to clearly state in the agreement with its original assignor that it will not be liable for breach of covenants in the assignment if it reassigns the lease to another company. See also John S. Lowe, Recent Significant Cases Affecting Farmout Agreements, 50 Inst. on Oil & Gas L. & Tax'n 3–1, 3–30 to 3–32 (1999).

4. The duration of an assignee's interest is dependent upon the language of the assignment. In Rogers v. Ricane Enterprises, Inc. (Ricane I), 772 S.W.2d 76 (Tex.1989), the assignor sought to terminate the defendant's interest after twenty years had elapsed without either production or additional drilling on the assigned acreage. In overturning a summary judgment for the plaintiff, the court pointed out that the assignment had been made on the

condition that the assignee's rights "will cease and terminate * * * unless within thirty (30) days * * * [the assignee] shall commence the actual drilling of a well for oil and gas" upon the assigned acreage and that the assignee had complied with this condition by drilling an initial well. In a subsequent appeal of the same case, Rogers v. Ricane Enterprises, Inc. (Ricane II), 884 S.W.2d 763 (Tex. 1994) the court refused to uphold the lower courts' conclusion that the assignment was impliedly terminable upon the assignee's failure to comply with an unstated purpose of continuing production or drilling activity.

On the other hand in Riley v. Meriwether, 780 S.W.2d 919 (Tex.App.1989, writ denied), the assignee's interest was held to have terminated even though the assignee had drilled and shut in gas wells that maintained the leases into the secondary term. The court construed the assignment as requiring the assignee to obtain actual production to continue its interest.

2. RIGHTS AND OBLIGATIONS OF THE ASSIGNOR AND ASSIGNEE

If a specific geographic area or depth is assigned, the assignor usually retains an interest, such as an overriding royalty, in the acreage or strata transferred. What types of problems should the drafter of an overriding royalty clause provide for? What language should be drafted to handle such problems? The following cases may help you in answering these questions.

REYNOLDS–REXWINKLE OIL, INC. v. PETEX, INC.

1 P.3d 909 (Kan. 2000).

LARSON, J.:

The difficult legal question in this appeal is whether an overriding royalty interest held by Reynolds–Rexwinkle Oil, Inc., (Reynolds) in an oil and gas lease terminated upon expiration of the lease or whether it extended to a subsequent oil and gas top lease on the same acreage negotiated by the assignee of the initial lease, Petex, Inc., (Petex) and the landowners.

* * *

The trial court granted summary judgment on what are essentially uncontroverted facts, with the following being material to the issues we consider.

On February 5, 1992, Herman and Loretta Schippers granted Hess, Inc., an oil and gas lease covering the northeast quarter (NE/4) of section 8, Township 11 South, Range 32 West in Logan County, Kansas. The lease was for a 1–year term; consideration was $1,000; the lease reserved a 1/8th royalty interest and an additional overriding royalty of 1/32nd of 7/8ths; and an attached option allowed the lease to be extended for an additional term of 1–year by paying a delay rental of $6.25 multiplied by the number of net mineral acres owned by the lessors. On February 5,

1992, Hess, Inc., assigned all of its right, title, and interest in and to the above-described oil and gas lease to Reynolds. Reynolds paid the Schippers the $1,000 required by the option to extend and thereby extended the term of the lease to February 5, 1994.

Daniel M. Reynolds, an officer and principal of Reynolds knew Larry Childress, an officer and principal of Petex, from a casual introduction in previous years. Mr. Reynolds called Mr. Childress and offered to sell Petex the Schippers oil and gas lease described above for $1,000 and a reserved 1.5% of 8/8ths overriding royalty interest. [Mr. Childress accepted the offer the same day.]

Pursuant to the agreement, Reynolds, on May 14, 1993, assigned all of its right, title, and interest in and to the original Schippers oil and gas lease to Petex with the assignment containing the following provision:

"The Assignor herein hereby expressly excepts, reserves, and retains title to an undivided 1.5% of 8/8ths of all oil, gas, and casinghead gas produced, saved, and marketed from the described land under the provisions of the aforesaid lease, *or any extension or renewal thereof,* as an overriding royalty, free and clear of any cost and expense of the development and operation thereof, excepting taxes applicable to said interest and the production therefrom." (Emphasis added.)

On August 30, 1993, prior to the expiration of the extended term of the existing oil and gas lease, the Schippers and Petex entered into a new oil and gas lease covering the same acreage with the second lease to take effect February 6, 1994, the day after the expiration of the extended term of the original lease. The terms of the second lease were substantially similar to the initial Schippers lease. A 1/8th royalty interest and 1/32nd of 7/8ths overriding royalty interest was reserved by the Schippers, the second lease provided for an additional years' term upon payment of a $800 delay rental, and the sum of $800 was paid as consideration for the lease. The second lease contained no mention of the overriding royalty interest reserved by Reynolds in the earlier lease.

During the primary and extended term of the original Schippers lease, no oil or gas development or exploration activities were carried out by any of the parties. Petex began seismic and geological work on the acreage in October 1994, and around November 18, 1994, commenced drilling of an oil test well which was completed as a producing oil well on or about January 6, 1995.

In December 1994, Reynolds filed an affidavit claiming an overriding royalty interest in production from the Schippers property. In March 1995, Reynolds demanded payment of the overriding royalty, which was denied by Petex.

The parties filed cross-motions for summary judgment. In its motion, Reynolds acknowledged that an overriding royalty interest normally expires with the expiration of the oil and gas lease out of which it is carved, but claimed there are exceptions to this rule (a) where the lease assignment contained an extension/renewal clause, and (b) where the lessee or assignee acted in bad faith or breached a duty of fair dealing owed to the holder of the overriding royalty interest. Reynolds argued that when Petex took the second lease, it was with the intention of destroying or washing out Reynolds' overriding royalty interest and that either through the construction of the assignment or the facts regarding the taking of the second lease, the overriding royalty properly existed. Reynolds denied that any confidential or fiduciary relationship was needed in order for it to recover under either exception.

Petex argued that in the absence of a confidential relationship, which it claimed did not exist in this instance, or evidence of collusion, fraud, or bad faith, that an overriding royalty interest always ends with the expiration of the oil and gas lease which it burdens. . . .

[The trial court ruled for Reynolds, and Petex appealed. In reversing, the Court of Appeals held that

> "absent a contract provision that an overriding royalty interest in an oil and gas lease survives a subsequent top lease, a top lease extinguishes the overriding royalty interest, unless the holder of the overriding royalty interest proves a breach of duty of fair dealing by showing that the lessor committed fraud, collusion, or bad faith in granting the top lease. The district court erred in granting summary judgment when it failed to require Reynolds–Rexwinkle to prove that Petex's actions were fraudulent, collusive, or in bad faith." 25 Kan. App.2d at 715–16, 969 P.2d 906.

We accepted Reynolds' petition for review. . . .]

* * *

ALLEGATIONS OF PETEX

Petex contends the facts show no confidential relationship between the parties and that it owed no fiduciary duty to Reynolds. Reynolds has not alleged any fraudulent conduct by Petex nor is there a claim of collusion on the part of Petex and the landowners. Consequently, Petex's basic claim is that we must recognize and apply the rule that the duration of an overriding royalty is limited by the oil and gas lease under which it is created. Campbell v. Nako Corp., 195 Kan. 66, Syl. p 2, 402 P.2d 771.

Petex primarily relies on Drilling, Inc. v. Warren, 185 Kan. 29, 340 P.2d 919 (1959), where the court found a duty of good faith existed in a situation where an operator acquired a second lease after having earlier held a lease burdened by an overriding royalty interest. It was not contended that the second lease was an extension or renewal of the first lease, and despite wording in the assignment that the overriding royalty shall be deemed a covenant running with the land and binding upon successors and assigns of the parties, we held that "[w]e cannot therefore construe 'covenant running with the land' to mean that the overriding royalty applied to production under any unrelated new lease subsequently acquired, in good faith, on the same property." 185 Kan. at 35, 340 P.2d 919.

Petex argues that the only other exceptions to the well-settled rule that an overriding royalty has no duration beyond the life of the underlying lease it burdens were stated in Howell v. Cooperative Refinery Ass'n, 176 Kan. 572, 271 P.2d 271 (1954), where the parties' agreements created a confidential relationship in the nature of joint interests and joint ownership, and in Campbell, 195 Kan. 66, 402 P.2d 771, where there was an allegation of bad faith, fraud, and collusion between the assignee and the lessor, Petex claims that neither circumstance exists here.

The other case relied on by Petex is Lillibridge v. Mesa Petroleum Co., 907 F.2d 1031, where an overriding royalty was held not to extend to "new" leases because there were several, rather than one, lease; a larger landowner royalty; a 3–year rather than a 10–year term; and new consideration of $130,200 for the new leases. Petex argues the top lease it took from the Schippers was similar to the situation in Lillibridge.

ALLEGATIONS OF REYNOLDS

Reynolds first argues that a duty of fair dealing exists between an assignee and an overriding royalty holder. Reynolds relies on a statement in Campbell that in controversies between the lessee and the overriding royalty holder "there seems [to be] clearly emerging a duty of fair dealing required on the part of the lessee (see 2 Williams and Meyers, Oil and Gas Law, s 420.2 [1999]) to which doctrine this court has definitely [been] inclined [to follow] (Howell v. Cooperative Refinery Ass'n, 176 Kan. 572, 271 P.2d 271)." 195 Kan. at 73, 402 P.2d 771.

Reynolds further contends that while Campbell established the rule that fraud or collusion would prohibit a washout, there does not have to be fraud or collusion in order for a duty of fair dealing to exist between the parties. Reynolds contends that the early Kansas case of Matthews v. Ramsey–Lloyd Oil Co., 121 Kan. 75, 245 P. 1064 (1926), protected a nonoperating interest in spite of the assignment of the lease back to the lessor by holding that "[e]quity would not countenance a merger of interests by Ramsey to the prejudice of plaintiff." Campbell, 195 Kan. at 73, 402 P.2d 771 (citing Matthews, 121 Kan. at 82, 245 P. 1064).

* * *

Reynolds, citing Howell, Otter Oil Co. v. Exxon Co., U.S.A., 834 F.2d 531, 533 (5th Cir.1987), and Avatar Exploration, Inc. v. Chevron, U.S.A., Inc., 933 F.2d 314, 319 (5th Cir.1991), claims that case law and scholarly opinion agree that "washout" actions are a violation of fair dealing and that the overriding royalty owner must be protected through strongly enforced extension and renewal clauses.

Finally, Reynolds notes Lillibridge is not binding on state courts and criticizes its reasoning and the result which relied on the Texas decision of Sunac Petroleum Corp. v. Parkes, 416 S.W.2d 798 (Tex.1967). Reynolds also attempts to minimize Lillibridge's authority through the following statement from Note, Protecting Overriding Royalty Interests in Oil and Gas Leases: Are the Courts Moving to Washout Extension or Renewal Clauses? 31 Washburn L.J. 544, 563 (1992):

> "Thus, Lillibridge opens the door for those operators who can get their case into federal court to evade the obligations of an extension or renewal clause included in a lease assignment. The only requirement is that the operator must obtain a second lease on terms substantially different from those of the original lease."

Reynolds also asserts Lillibridge is factually distinguishable because there was no extra bonus paid here or increased royalty as there was in Lillibridge. In addition, the terms of the second leases in Lillibridge were for 3 years, not 10 as in the first; and the number of leases in Lillibridge was 5 rather than the one first lease. In our case, the first and second Schippers' lease are substantially similar.

ANALYSIS

The relationship between operating and nonoperating interests in oil and gas exploration and development is fraught with potential disputes because they arise out of a leasehold estate. While some agreements do set out with specificity the respective rights of the parties, in many instances (like the one we face here), courts are left with the difficult task of determining the scope and extent of protections to afford nonoperators (overriding royalty holders) against the acts of operators that either intentionally or inadvertently extinguish the nonoperating interests.

Rather than first attempting to either distinguish or harmonize the Kansas cases with cases from other jurisdictions that have dealt with this precise issue, we first turn to the general statements of the treatise writers who have summarized the issue we face.

[The court's lengthy quotations from Kuntz § 63.2; Williams & Meyers § 420.2 and Summers § 554 have been deleted.]

Perhaps the most helpful of the discussions of the issue is that of Professor David E. Pierce in 1 Pierce, Kansas Oil and Gas Handbook s 7.15 (1991), where he instructs that, in Kansas, two attacks have been advanced by nonoperating interest holders against "washout" conduct: (1) express provisions in the document creating the nonoperating interest to protect against such conduct; and (2) assertion of fiduciary duties between the lessee and the nonoperating interest owner.

* * *

The Kansas case most discussed by Professor Pierce is Howell, 176 Kan. 572, 271 P.2d 271, where the assignment creating the overriding royalty contained or "extension or renewal" clause. Pierce notes the opinion defined a confidential relationship and adopted the general rule relating to the assignor/assignee relationship from 24 Am.Jur., Gas and Oil s 82.

" 'Thus when an assignment expressly provides that any extension or renewal of the lease shall be subject to the overriding royalty therein agreed upon, the courts will regard a new lease procured by the assignee as an extension or renewal of the old one and charge it with the royalty so reserved, even though it was not granted until production under the former lease had come to an end.' " Howell, 176 Kan. at 576, 271 P.2d 271.

Pierce then notes that despite this statement, the ultimate holding in Howell was based on the entire transaction between Howell and Cooperative Refinery Association, which was held to have become a joint interest in development and a confidential relationship between the parties in turn, resulting in the overriding royalty attaching to the later lease even though there was a 1–year lapse between the termination of the original lease and the acquisition of the new lease. Professor Pierce concludes:

"The court's statements in Robinson v. Eagle–Picher Lead Co and Howell v. Cooperative Refinery Ass'n suggests the importance of the 'extension and renewal' clause in assignments and subleases. Not only will it provide some express contractual guidance on the duration of the nonoperating interest, it will also, under appropriate factual circumstances, give rise to fiduciary obligations between the assignor/assignee or sublessor/sublessee. A sample extension and renewal clause follows:

"The obligation to pay the overriding royalty required by this assignment shall exist for the life of the oil and gas lease plus any extensions or renewals of the lease. For purposes of this Section, any leasehold interest acquired by assignee within ____ years following the termination, cancellation, or surrender of the oil and gas lease shall be deemed an 'extension or renewal.'

"See K & E Drilling Inc. v. Warren, 185 Kan. 29, 340 P.2d 919 (1959)." Pierce, Kansas Oil and Gas Handbook s 7.15 p. 7–20 (1991)."

The precise issue we face has been the subject of a recent law journal article, Ney, Note, Protecting Overriding Royalty Interests in Oil and Gas Leases: Are the Courts Moving to Washout Extension or Renewal Clauses? 31 Washburn L.J. 544 (1992). It emphasizes the holding in Lillibridge v. Mesa Petroleum Corporation, 907 F.2d 1031 (10th Cir.1990), and after suggesting that the Lillibridge opinion relies on the reasoning of the case of Sunac Petroleum Corporation v. Parkes, 416 S.W.2d 798 (Tex.1967), rather than the Oklahoma case of Probst, 143 Okla. 11, 286 P. 875, or the Kansas case of Howell, 176 Kan. 572, 271 P.2d 271, the note suggests:

"Lillibridge greatly narrows the scope of protection provided by an express extension or renewal clause, at least in the Tenth Circuit. Unless the terms and conditions of the second lease are essentially the same as those of the original lease, the Tenth Circuit Court of Appeals will not give effect to an extension or renewal clause." 31 Washburn L.J. at 563.

The note recognizes that the expressed concern of Lillibridge appears to be that protecting overriding royalty interests would prevent operators from acquiring new leases on property covered by an existing lease with an attaching overriding royalty interest in extensions and renewals because the circuit court states "we will not create such an irrational impediment to the business of oil exploration and development." 907 F.2d at 1036. In its conclusion, however, the note suggests:

"Courts should recognize that the purpose and intent behind the inclusion of an extension or renewal clause is two-fold. First, the clause as a contract term represents the direct express intent of the parties to prevent washouts. Secondly, courts should also recognize and give effect to the underlying intent to impose heightened or fiduciary obligations on the relationship." 31 Washburn L.J. at 571.

* * *

We have previously discussed the Kansas cases Howell, Drilling, Inc., and Campbell and also the Tenth Circuit case Lillibridge that the parties to this appeal rely on or distinguish. While each is helpful, each is somewhat different factually from our case.

We view Howell as most helpful to the result we reach. While the ultimate decision there was based on the confidential relationship in the form of a joint enterprise between the holder of the overriding royalty and the operator obtaining the second lease, we consider the following language from that opinion extremely important:

"The cases have been examined, and in our opinion the proper conclusion to be drawn from them is. . . .

'when an assignment expressly provides that any extension or renewal of the lease shall be subject to the overriding royalty therein agreed upon, the courts will regard a new lease procured by the assignee as an extension or renewal of the old one and charge it with the royalty so reserved. . . .' 176 Kan. at 576, 271 P.2d 271.

This is strong language and clearly precedent to require that the overriding royalty of Reynolds attached to the second lease that was obtained by Petex during the time the first lease was in full force and effect.

Even though Drilling, Inc., reaches a result that is favorable to Petex's arguments, we discount its specific authority for two reasons. First, the extension and renewal clause was not precisely in issue as the "covenant running with the land" argument was the basis for the overriding royalty holder's attempt to perpetuate its rights in the property. 185 Kan. at 35, 340 P.2d 919. Second, and most important, the subsequent lease was not a top lease acquired while the first lease was still in effect.

We do not believe the holding in Campbell is helpful to either party to this appeal since the opinion more precisely involved the right to set aside and defend a default judgment. Campbell holds that where there is fraud, bad faith, or collusion in canceling an oil and gas lease to extinguish an overriding royalty interest, a court of equity will grant relief to allow the holder of the overriding royalty interest to defend against such a forfeiture or surrender. There is no bad faith, fraud, or collusion here, and Campbell is not helpful except for the statement relied on by Reynolds that "there seems clearly emerging a duty of fair dealing required on the part of the lessee ... to which doctrine this court has definitely inclined." 195 Kan. at 73, 402 P.2d 771.

Finally, with regards to Lillibridge we note that in KPERS v. Reimer & Koger Assocs., Inc. 262 Kan. 635, 669–70, 941 P.2d 1321 (1997), we stated that federal decisions on issues of state law are not binding on and have limited precedential effect in state courts. Nevertheless, Lillibridge is an important decision and deserves our consideration.

Essentially, the facts that drove the result in Lillibridge were that there was no fraud, collusion, bad faith, or breach of fiduciary duty, and the second leases were deemed to be "new" leases rather than extensions or renewals because (1) there were several leases (five rather than one); (2) a larger landowner royalty was required in the later leases (3/16ths rather than 1/8th); (3) the later leases had a 3–year term rather than a 10–year term; and (4) there was new consideration of $130,200 paid for the later lease. 907 F.2d at 1033.

We find Lillibridge factually different and not authority to require the result that either party to this appeal champions.

CONCLUSION

We hold the Court of Appeals erroneously reversed and remanded to require Reynolds to prove either fraud, collusion, or bad faith. The undisputed facts do not show that Petex was guilty of fraud, collusion, or bad faith. Nevertheless, the fact Petex took the second lease while the original lease it held was still in full force and effect requires a ruling that the overriding royalty of Reynolds attaches to the later lease. But, this is because of the extension and renewal language in the assignment and not due to any finding of bad faith on Petex's part.

Although Petex points to small differences in the language, the fact is the second lease is substantially identical to the first lease it replaced. The royalty was the same, the overriding royalty the landowners reserved was the same, the term was not substantially different, and the lease is, as a matter of law, considered and held to be an extension and renewal of the initial lease Reynolds assigned to Petex.

We look to the language quoted earlier from Kunz, Williams & Meyers, Summers, and Pierce. The general language from each treatise would require, under the facts we face here, the protection of the overriding royalty reserved in the Reynolds-to-Petex assignment. The terms of the lease specifically state that the overriding royalty applies to extensions and renewals, and we hold the second Schippers' lease was such an extension and renewal as a matter of law.

We agree with and follow our statement in Campbell that a duty of fair dealing exists under the facts of this case. This duty, coupled with the "extension or renewal" wording of the assignment, and the taking of the subsequent lease while the first one was in full force and effect compels a ruling, as a matter of law, that the overriding royalty interest of 1.5% of 8/8ths applies to and burdens the second oil and gas lease upon which production was obtained. . . .

This case is remanded to the trial court to enter a money judgment in favor of Reynolds and against Petex for such amount as is determined to be due and owing.

NOTES

1.   The court distinguishes the earlier Tenth Circuit case of Lillibridge v. Mesa Petroleum Co., 907 F.2d 1031 (10th Cir.Kan. 1990) on the ground that the top lease in the principal case was substantially identical to the original bottom lease, whereas in *Lillibridge* the lessee took five new leases rather than one, increased the royalty from 1/8th to 3/16ths, reduced the primary term from 10 years to 3 years, and paid a new, substantial bonus. Should the similarity of terms between the bottom lease and the top lease be determinative of whether the new lease is or is not a renewal and extension of the bottom lease? Consider the following comments by Professor Pierce:

> The issue is not similarity but rather whether the documents or documents constitute an effective extension or renewal of the preexisting lease. In this contest, even the *Lillibridge* leases were extensions or renewals. Most well informed, or well represented, lessors try to negotiate better terms when their lessee seeks to avoid letting their acreage return to the open leasing market. The new lease will reflect the current leasing market [which would almost certainly include a shorter primary term than 10 years, a royalty larger than the traditional 1/8th, new consideration and possibly leases based on regulatory spacing units rather than a landowner's entire acreage.] Pierce, Discussion Notes, 146 O & GR 111, 112 (2001).

Professor Pierce goes on to suggest that the timing of the top lease was the principal factor that triggered the extension or renewal clause. "By taking the top lease while the bottom lease was still in effect, Petex denied Reynolds–Rexwinkle the ability to compete for a lease on the premises." 136 O & GR at 113.

2.   In Sunac Petroleum Corp. v. Parkes, 416 S.W.2d 798 (Tex. 1967) the Texas Supreme Court relied on both the different provisions of the new lease and the fact that the old lease had expired when the new lease was executed in holding that the extension or renewal clause was inapplicable. It reasoned that the new lease was not an extension of the old lease because "[a]n extension * * * generally means the prolongation or continuation of the term of the existing lease." Similarly, the new lease could not be viewed as a

renewal because it was executed over a year after the old lease had expired and "when an oil and gas lease has expired, the lessor is free to deal with the property as he sees fit." 416 S.W.2d at 802.

3. In the absence of an extension or renewal clause, courts have generally rejected arguments that a top lease is subject to an overriding royalty reserved by an assignor of the original bottom lease. See, for example, Brannan v. Sohio Petroleum Co., 260 F.2d 621 (10th Cir.Okla.1958) where the plaintiff unsuccessfully argued that the assignment created a fiduciary relationship between the parties and that the court should impose a constructive trust upon the new lease for the amount of the overriding royalty reserved in the assignment of the original lease. Is the "duty of fair dealing" articulated in the principal case limited to situations where the assignor includes an extension or renewal clause in the assignment or does it apply to all assignments in which the assignor reserves an overriding royalty or similar interest?

See Hemingway § 9.11 for a discussion of the assignor/assignee relationship.

COOK v. EL PASO NATURAL GAS CO.

560 F.2d 978 (10th Cir.N.M.1977).

WILLIAM E. DOYLE, CIRCUIT JUDGE.

In this action the question is whether the plaintiff, who owns a five percent overriding royalty interest in an oil and gas lease, is entitled to recover a compensatory royalty on the basis that the defendants who own a gas well which is located on an adjoining lease have drained gas from a lease under which plaintiff has the five percent overriding royalty interest.

The case was first filed in the State District Court for New Mexico, Eddy County. The defendants, El Paso Natural Gas Company and Phillips Petroleum Company, petitioned for removal to the United States District Court for the District of New Mexico, where the case was tried to the court on December 15, 1975. Judgment was entered for plaintiff-appellee on February 25, 1976.

Mrs. Cook was the owner of a United States Oil and Gas Lease in which the legal description is the W 1/2 of Section 29, Township 23 South, Range 31 East, N.M.P.M., Eddy County, New Mexico. She assigned this lease to Phillips Petroleum Company on June 26, 1964, reserving a five percent overriding royalty. In the lease there was a so-called potash stipulation which provided that no wells would be drilled for oil or gas at a location which, in the opinion of the Oil and Gas Supervisor of the Geological Survey, would result in undue waste of potash deposits or would constitute a hazard to or an undue interference with mining operations being conducted for the extraction of potash deposits.

On November 1, 1971, Phillips assigned to El Paso an interest in the lease covering the description mentioned. On February 12, 1973, El Paso completed a well in the E 1/2 of Section 29. This was called the Mobil Federal Well No. 1.

* * *

On May 8, 1974, the United States Geological Survey determined that oil and gas drilling operations to a depth sufficient to test the so-called Morrow formation underlying the W 1/2 of Section 29 would result in undue waste of potash and would constitute a hazard to future potash mining. It entered an order prohibiting the drilling of an oil or gas well on the W 1/2 of Section 29.

At the conclusion of the trial both sides submitted proposed findings of fact and conclusions of law. The trial court ruling for plaintiff-appellee made findings of fact and conclusions of law in which it determined that: the Mobil Federal No. 1 Well was some 660 feet from the East line of the lease which plaintiff had owned covering the W 1/2 of Section 29; thereafter, production was commenced on the Mobil Federal Well on March 22, 1973, and on May 8, 1974, the United States Geological Survey (USGS) issued its prohibition against the drilling of a well on the W 1/2 of Section 29. The court also found that the Morrow gas pay zone reservoir for the Mobil Federal No. 1 Well extended into the W 1/2 of Section 29, whereby this underground area was contributing approximately 26% of the gas contained in the Morrow gas pay zone reservoir for the Mobil Federal No. 1 Well.

The court further found that the Mobil Federal No. 1 Well was draining gas in substantial quantities from the underground area beneath the W 1/2 of Section 29.

The court concluded that since the law implies a duty on an oil and gas lessee to protect the leased premises from offsetting adjoining land drainage of oil and gas, and since this is a covenant which runs with the land and the owner of an overriding royalty interest has standing to invoke the implied covenant to protect against drainage, and where a common lessee exists for two abutting oil and gas leases, the common lessee is obligated to protect its lessor from oil and gas drainage from a well located in the other lease. This is not controlled or limited by the test as to whether a reasonable prudent operator would in the circumstances drill an offset well.

The court further concluded that the common lessee is under a duty to prevent drainage regardless of whether or not the drilling of an offset well on nonproducing land would satisfy the standards of the prudent operator rule.

A further conclusion of the trial court was that the defendants-appellants as common lessees under separate leases covering the E 1/2 and W 1/2 of Section 29 were under a duty to the plaintiff to protect her interest in the oil and gas under the W 1/2 of Section 29 against drainage from the defendants' Mobil Federal No. 1 Well, located in the E 1/2 of Section 29.

The court's next conclusion was that the plaintiff had not waived her rights to protection from drainage as a result of the existence of a potash stipulation nor by reason of the USGS prohibition against a well being drilled.

Nor did she waive or disclaim her rights by assigning her lease to Phillips Petroleum Company.

The terms of the lease do not circumscribe plaintiff's right to be protected from drainage.

The payment of compensatory overriding royalty as an alternative to the drilling of an offset well where the interest owner is suffering losses as a result of drainage is appropriate.

The court finally concluded that as a result of the governmental prohibition, an offset well cannot be drilled upon the W 1/2 of Section 29. However, the alternative compensatory remedy is available to her and for that reason she is entitled to judgment.

The contentions of the defendants-appellants are:

First, that any right which plaintiff may have had to a compensatory royalty was nullified by the government prohibition issued by the Geological Survey.

* * *

Fifth, plaintiff is precluded, as an overriding royalty interest owner, from invoking the implied covenant to protect against drainage.

I.

The thrust of the first argument of the appellant companies is that the government prohibition against drilling in the W 1/2 of Section 29, the purpose of which was to protect potash deposits under that section, had the effect of excusing performance of any contractual duty including the implied covenant to protect appellee from drainage of the defendants-appellants, and that it was not limited to excusing the drilling of an offset well in the W 1/2 of Section 29. They maintain that compensatory royalties need only be paid when there is an obligation, either express or implied, to drill an offset well and since the government prohibited the drilling of a well in the W 1/2, the argument goes, there can be no further obligation to perform the covenant to drill an offset well nor can there be an obligation to respond to an implied covenant to protect the plaintiff-appellee from drainage. To accept this argument is to determine that all performance by defendants-appellants is excused.

Contractual performance can indeed be excused where the intervention of a government regulation or law makes performance impossible. In recognizing also that spacing regulations can render a covenant to drill a second well inoperative, it does not follow that this vitiates all other alternative remedies. The result of acceptance of this argument is to give appellant companies a license to drain the gas from the area under the plaintiff-appellee's assigned lease without paying a royalty—all because the government has prevented the drilling of a well. It would be grossly inequitable to confer such windfalls. It is difficult to see how a prohibition against drilling (governmental intervention) can excuse the party draining gas under another's land from compensating that person for the gas being so taken.

The case of Pan American Petroleum Corporation v. Udall, 192 F.Supp. 626 (D.D.C.1961), furnishes clarification as to the nature of the compensatory royalty. It was there explained that:

> In the oil industry compensatory royalties are royalties paid to a landowner whose land lies adjacent to a producing well, but on whose land no well has been drilled. They are intended to compensate the landowner for losses suffered due to subterranean drainage of oil from his land resulting from the adjacent producing well. They are an alternative to the drilling of a so-called "offset well" to recover the oil before it drains away.

192 F.Supp. at 628. The court went on to rule that the compensatory royalties which had been assessed by the Department of the Interior in that case were arbitrary. The court did acknowledge that some compensatory royalties in a reasonable amount were due. The cause was remanded for redetermination of the amount of royalty.

Appellants rely on this court's decision in Ashland Oil & Refining Co. v. Cities Service Gas Co., 462 F.2d 204 (10th Cir.1972). But in *Ashland* we held that where there is impossibility of performance with respect to one of two alternatives, the result is not to relieve the promisor of all obligation in the premises. He does not escape performance of an alternative remedy if one exists. * * * [W]e concluded that "failure of the withdrawal promise could not frustrate performance of either the entire contract or the optional alternative of performance."

In summary, the appellants' position that the government regulations broadly apply so as to excuse them from all legal obligations which might arise from the lease and the facts is not tenable. Contrary to the appellants' arguments, the purpose of the government regulation is not that of relieving the companies from all their legal obligations.

The purpose of the prohibition against drilling was to protect the potash deposits. It cannot be held to include the release of Phillips and El Paso from their duty to protect the plaintiff-appellee, their assignor, from unlawful drainage of gas.

* * *

IV.

Does the plaintiff as an overriding royalty interest owner have standing to bring an action claiming violation of the implied covenant to protect against drainage?

It is argued without citing any persuasive authority that the plaintiff as the owner of an overriding royalty does not have standing in court to enforce the obligation of the lease and therefore of the implied covenant to protect against drainage. We disagree.

This problem is fully considered by Williams and Meyers in their treatise on oil and gas law. See 5 Oil and Gas Law (1975). It is true that there is very little case law on this subject. The authors, however, have collected the authorities and have set forth the general rule as being that a successor in interest to the original lessor may enforce the covenants implied in the lease. This is said to be a matter of traditional land law. The elements which must be satisfied are that the covenant be in writing; the parties intend that the covenant run to the successor; the covenant touches and concerns the land; and the parties are in privity of estate.

The requirement of writing is satisfied because the covenants are implied in a written instrument. The intent requirement is satisfied in the typical lease which provides for assignment by either party and for the covenants to be binding on heirs, executors, administrators, successors, or assigns. The authors also explain that the privity of estate as well as the touch and concern requirements are both fulfilled in this kind of lease.

The underlying rationale for the right of the royalty interest owner to enforce the implied covenant is that the covenants run with the land. Hence, even a transferee of a nonparticipating royalty interest or nonexecutive mineral interest is said to have the same right. In our case, of course, the plaintiff is the successor to the original lessor who upon transfer retained an overriding royalty interest.[1]

The authors also call attention to the cases of Warren v. Amerada Petroleum Corp., 211 S.W.2d 314 (Tex.Civ.App.1948), and Compton v. Fisher–McCall, 298 Mich. 648, 299 N.W. 750 (1941). These are not directly in point, but they lend some support to the conclusion that the plaintiff here has standing. In *Warren,* the court stated that the plaintiff, a holder of a nonparticipating royalty interest, had the same right as the lessor to enforce implied covenants in a lease pertaining to mineral rights. In *Compton,* the court held that the lessor-plaintiff had not failed to join a proper party by failing to join a postlease transferee of a nonparticipating royalty interest. In stating that the implied covenants of the lease were divisible, the court implied that the royalty interest holder could bring its own action.

There is somewhat of a dearth of case authority on denying the right of a royalty interest owner to bring such an action.

Also to be noted is that in the case at bar the plaintiff is in a very difficult position due to the fact that the lessor has no incentive to bring an enforcement action because the United States, the lessor, is collecting its royalty both from the E 1/2 of Section 29 and from the W 1/2 as well. Since the United States is not being deprived of anything, the only thing remaining is for the plaintiff to bring the action herself. It is impossible to say that she lacks standing or interest to bring the action since she is the only one who has a pecuniary interest which is affected.

The judgment of the district court is affirmed.

---

1. [Editors' Note] This statement is somewhat misleading. Cook was the initial lessee from the United States, which retained a landowner's royalty.

NOTES

1.   Courts have taken different positions on the circumstances, if any, in which covenants should be implied in assignments of oil and gas leases. In XAE Corp. v. SMR Property Management Co., 968 P.2d 1201 (Okla. 1998), the Oklahoma Supreme Court rejected a claim by an assignor who had reserved an overriding royalty that the assignee was subject to an implied marketing covenant. The court stated that the assignor's rights were determined by the terms of the instrument creating the overriding royalty and that no covenants would be implied unless they were necessary to achieve the fundamental purpose of the transaction. Since the assignor had reserved an in-kind royalty and the well-head is the point of delivery of an in-kind interest, the assignee had no implied duty to make the product marketable. See also McNeill v. Peaker, 488 S.W.2d 706 (Ark. 1973), which also refused to imply a covenant in favor of an assignor who had retained an overriding royalty.

The Fifth Circuit took a different approach in In Tidelands Royalty B Corp. v. Gulf Oil Corp., 804 F.2d 1344 (5th Cir.Tex.1986). The plaintiff had received an overriding royalty in one of the defendant's offshore leases in exchange for confidential geophysical data. In evaluating the plaintiff's argument that the defendant had breached an implied covenant to protect against drainage from wells defendant had drilled on adjacent leases, the court rejected the analogy to a lessor-lessee relationship, pointing out that the plaintiff had never had a right to explore and produce from the area in question and had no reversionary interest in the tract being drained. The court concluded that the plaintiff's interest was more like a nonparticipating royalty that had been conveyed by a landowner who had the exclusive right to lease and develop. The court then remanded for a determination of whether the defendant had breached the implied obligation that an executive owes a nonexecutive.

Would the *Tidelands* court have found the lessor-lessee analogy more convincing under the facts of Cook v. El Paso? Is there a reason to distinguish between an assignor who retains an overriding royalty and a person who receives an overriding royalty in exchange for goods or services?

2.   Commentators also disagree over whether covenants should be implied in assignments. Contrast the following positions.

> The argument that implied terms are necessary to evoke relative equality of bargaining power between the lessor and lessee loses impetus once it is applied to the parties of an assignment agreement. Assignors and assignees of oil and gas leases are presumed to have acquired a degree of sophistication alien to the traditional surface owner's aptitude. * * * It is submitted, therefore, that the assignor of an oil and gas lease should be allowed to enforce an implied covenant only where the lessor has joined as a plaintiff in an action against the breaching assignee or where the lessor has assigned his cause of action to the assignor.

Michael D. Salim, Comment, Implied Covenants Between Assignors and Assignees of Oil and Gas Leases: Policy and Precedent, 31 Sw.L.J. 905, 923–25 (1977).

Non-operating interest holders should be protected by implied covenants just as are lessors. * * * Extension of the protection of implied covenants to a lessee that transfers its operating rights in exchange for a non-operating interest will not materially affect the obligations of the holder of the lease. The lessee's transferee will have no obligation to test the premises, unless the assignment imposes a specific drilling obligation. The transferee will ordinarily have no liability to the original lessee for letting the lease terminate by failing to pay delay rentals. The transferee will merely have an obligation to the lessee, as well as to the lessor, to protect the premises against drainage, to reasonably develop and explore once production is obtained, and to perform as would a reasonable prudent operator under the circumstances.

Lowe, Chapter 12.C.1.

3. Does an assignee have the right to pool an overriding royalty if the instrument of assignment is silent on the matter? The court in Union Pacific Resources Co. v. Hutchison, 990 S.W.2d 368 (Tex. App. 1999) looked to the terms of the underlying lease to help determine the probable intent of the parties. Since the lease authorized pooling without the consent of the lessors the court thought it unlikely that the parties to the assignment intended that the assignee should have to obtain the prior consent of the assignor in order to pool her retained overriding royalty.

3. LESSOR RIGHTS AGAINST ASSIGNEE

Free alienability of the oil and gas lease may pose problems for the lessor. In some instances, the landowner has relied upon the reputation and expertise of the original lessee and would have been unwilling to entrust the exploration and drilling of her land to a different, less experienced company. She may have foregone attempts to negotiate extensive lease provisions dealing with surface damages because she had had prior dealings with the original lessee and was confident that it would be careful in its use of the surface or would fully compensate her for any injury to the surface. Even in the absence of such considerations, the lessor will wish to know the identity of the ultimate transferee of the lease. Without such information, she may be unable to determine the rightfulness of an entry by a drilling company or a geophysical survey crew claiming authorization from the new owner of the lease. She may be unable to give immediate notice if there is an emergency or some disagreement over drilling or rights of surface use.

Attempts by lessors to restrict assignability of leases have met with limited success, for some courts have been reluctant to enforce such restrictions in the lease. For example, in Shields v. Moffitt, 683 P.2d 530 (Okla.1984), the Oklahoma Supreme Court held that a clause that prohibited assignment without the consent of the lessor but that failed to provide a remedy for breach, was void as an impermissible restraint on alienation. See Hemingway, Discussion Notes, 81 O & GR 159 (1984). Is there a way to redraft such a clause to meet the court's objections? See generally, Robert E. Nowack, Restrictions Against Alienation in Agreements Relating to Oil and Gas Interests, 23 Alberta L.Rev. 62 (1985). The lessor used a more successful device in Trafalgar House Oil & Gas Inc. v. De Hinojosa, 773 S.W.2d 797 (Tex.App.1989), where the court upheld a lease clause requiring the lessee, its successors, and assigns to notify the lessor of the name and address of an assignee within thirty days of an assignment or pay $1,000 in liquidated damages for each failure to give notice. The court concluded that the clause provided a reasonable estimate of the harm that might be caused a lessor who needed to locate the party responsible for lease operations on her property and might be forced to hire a lawyer or landman to examine courthouse records to determine who had received a lease assignment.

Under traditional landlord-tenant law if a lessee assigns his or her interest, the assignee is primarily liable for performing the lease covenants that run with the estate, but the original lessee remains secondarily liable under the concept of privity of contract. Most printed form oil and gas leases attempt to negate this continuing liability by including a clause like the following: "In case Lessee assigns this lease, in whole or in part, Lessee shall be relieved of all obligations with respect to the assigned portion or portions arising subsequent to the date of the assignment." This type of provision is commonly referred to as the "separate owner-ship" clause.

If a lease is assigned in its entirety, the assignee will normally be subject to the same duties as required of the original lessee. See Lowe, Chapter 12.B.1. This is not the case, however, if the assignment is terminable and the assignor retains a reversionary interest. In Tawes v. Barnes, 340 S.W.3d 419 (Tex. 2011), a lessee that was subject to a joint operating agreement (JOA) refused to consent to additional operations and, under the terms of the JOA relinquished its interest to the consent-ing parties until they had recovered 200% of the non-consenting party's share of costs. The court rejected the claim by the lessor of the non-consenting lessee that there was privity of estate between the lessor and the consenting parties. The court pointed out that the period during which consenting parties own a non-consenting party's interest is limited until a certain level of the non-consenting party's share of expenses has been recovered. Because the consenting parties did not receive a permanent interest in the plaintiff's lease, there was no privity of estate between the lessor and the other lessees subject to the JOA.

The issue of an assignee's liability arises much more frequently when the lease is divided geographically among several assignees. The following cases raise the issue of the lessor's rights in such a situation.

OAG v. DESERT GAS EXPLORATION CO.

659 N.Y.S.2d 654 (App. Div. 1997).

Before GREEN, J.P., and PINE, LAWTON, DOERR and FALLON, JJ.

MEMORANDUM

Plaintiffs commenced this action seeking compensatory damages for breach of an oil and gas lease covering their property in Chautauqua County, rescission of the lease and a declaration that the lease is null and void. On June 21, 1990, defendant was assigned an interest in a portion of an oil and gas lease on plaintiffs' property known as "Oag units #3A and #6". Those units were originally part of a larger lease granting exclusive rights to drill for, produce, and market oil and gas upon the land.

Supreme Court properly granted summary judgment in favor of defendant declaring, inter alia, that the subject oil and gas lease is in full force and effect. The court properly applied the general rule prevailing in all oil and gas producing States except Louisiana that, in an oil and gas lease, "the habendum clause, and modifying clauses of the habendum clause such as the well completion, continuous drilling, shut-in royalty, and dry hole clauses, are treated as being indivisible" (Hemingway, Law of Oil and Gas § 9.10, at 642 [3d ed. 1991]). Where, as here, there is no provision to the contrary, "if the assignor obtains production on the part retained, such production will not only satisfy the habendum clause of the lease as to [the] part retained but also as to the part or parts assigned" (2 Kuntz, Law of Oil and Gas § 26.12, at 404; see, Hemingway, Law of Oil and Gas, op. cit., § 9:10[A], at 643). Thus, because it is uncontroverted that at least eight wells are producing on the original leased premises and plaintiffs have received royalties thereon, defendants were not contractually obligated to tender further shut-in royalties for Oag units #3A and #6.

We have considered the remaining contentions raised on appeal and conclude that they are without merit.

Judgment unanimously affirmed without costs.

NOTES

1.   The principal case illustrates the prevailing view that the habendum clause and those provisions that modify it, such as the well completion and the shut-in royalty clauses, are indivisible. Even though a lease has been divided into separate geographic parts held by different assignees, if production, drilling operations or other action sufficient to maintain the lease takes place anywhere on the original lease premises, the lease is maintained as to all segregated portions.

2.   The indivisibility doctrine can be changed by express language to the contrary. As noted in the preceding section, leases frequently contain such language with respect to delay rentals. If the lease is segregated, delay rentals are apportioned on an acreage basis, and failure by an assignee to pay delay rentals allocable to its portion does not affect the right of parties holding other segregated portions of the lease. See Hemingway, § 9.10. A similar change may result from a continuous drilling or retained acreage clause, which terminates all acreage except a specified amount surrounding each well

unless drilling is done at specified time intervals. See Nafco Oil & Gas, Inc. v. Tartan Resources Corp., 522 S.W.2d 703 (Tex.Civ.App.1975, writ refused n.r.e.).

3. The *Oag* court states that production from eight wells located on other portions of the lease not only maintains the lease as to the defendant's portion but also relieves the defendant from the obligation to pay shut in royalty on its wells. Suppose the shut in royalty clause provides as follows:

> While there is a gas well on this Lease, or on acreage pooled therewith, but gas is not being sold or used Lessee shall pay or tender annually at the end of each yearly period during which such gas is not sold or used, as royalty, an amount equal to the delay rental provided for in Paragraph 5 herein, and while said royalty is so paid or tendered this Lease shall be held as a producing Lease under Paragraph 2 [the habendum clause].

What argument might the lessor make based on this clause? What would be the lessee's counterargument? Which party should prevail?

KOTHE v. JEFFERSON

455 N.E.2d 73 (Ill. 1983).

THOMAS J. MORAN, JUSTICE:

The plaintiff, Vera Shaw, filed suit in the circuit court of Clark County against numerous individuals seeking to cancel portions of an oil and gas lease due to an alleged breach of the implied covenant to reasonably develop the property. She sought cancellation of the lease as it applied to 318.5 acres of the 438.5–acre leasehold which she owned. A number of the original defendants defaulted and, pursuant to plaintiff's motion, the circuit court cancelled the lease as to those individuals. Plaintiff also moved for, and was granted, summary judgment against the remaining defendants, Mary Jefferson and her heirs and John Ryan (defendants), with respect to 120 acres (hereinafter referred to as the subject tract), of the 318.5 acres, in which they claimed an interest. A divided appellate court reversed, holding that the implied covenant to develop is indivisible and therefore development of some tracts of the leasehold property served as compliance with the covenant on all other tracts. We granted plaintiff leave to appeal.

Three issues are raised for review: (1) Did defendants waive the right to challenge the sufficiency of the complaint? (2) Do defendants have standing to contest plaintiff's motion for a summary judgment? (3) Should the implied covenant to develop be construed as indivisible or divisible?

On February 19, 1959, Shaw leased 11 parcels of real estate, consisting of 438.5 acres, to John Jefferson for the production of oil and gas. The lease agreement provided that the lease would remain in effect for a primary term of three years, and as long thereafter as oil or gas is produced "from said leased premises" or operations for drilling are continued. In consideration for the lease, Shaw received one dollar and a 1/8 royalty interest in any gas or oil produced.

In 1964, Jefferson and his wife assigned their interest in 120 of the acres, located in the northeast quarter of section 4, township 11 north, range 14 west, Clark County (the subject tract), to J.L. Cowan. They reserved an overriding royalty interest in the property. Prior to his death in 1967, Cowan made numerous assignments of his working interest in the subject tract.

In January of 1980, plaintiff filed a complaint against all individuals who "have or may claim a record interest in" 318.5 acres of the leasehold (including the subject tract), seeking to cancel the lease as it applied to that property. Plaintiff alleged in the complaint that these individuals "have wholly failed" to develop and produce the leasehold property, and that there has been no activity directed toward production during the preceding 10 years. The remaining 120 acres of the leasehold (40 of which are located in section 4), upon which oil and gas were being produced, were not affected by the complaint.

On March 20, 1980, the heirs of John Jefferson, now deceased, purportedly assigned a working interest in the subject tract to John Ryan, and reserved an overriding royalty interest in the property. The Jefferson heirs claimed that the working interest in the property reverted to them when Cowan ceased to develop the subject tract. Pursuant to plaintiff's motion, Ryan was subsequently joined as a defendant.

With the exception of the Jefferson heirs and Ryan, none of the individuals named in the complaint appeared or filed an answer. Default judgments were entered against them, including the Cowan heirs and assigns. Shubrick T. Kothe (who, as executor of Vera Shaw's estate, was substituted as plaintiff following Shaw's death in February of 1980) subsequently filed a motion requesting cancellation of the lease as to all individuals who claim to have working interests in the subject tract. He also moved for summary judgment against the nondefaulting defendants. He alleged in the motion that the only individuals who owned a working interest in the subject tract (the Cowan heirs and assigns) had been defaulted. The nondefaulting defendants owned only overriding royalty interests, which cannot exist apart from the working interests.

Defendants filed objections to the motion for summary judgment, alleging that oil and gas leases are indivisible, and that plaintiff therefore cannot seek cancellation of the lease as to certain property if there is production on other tracts in the leasehold. Defendants submitted affidavits indicating there has been continuous development on portions of the leased premises. In defendants' brief opposing the motion for summary judgment, they argued that plaintiff's complaint was insufficient to state a cause of action. The trial court determined that defendants waived the right to raise this issue because they answered the complaint instead of challenging it by motion. The court therefore granted plaintiff's motion for summary judgment and cancelled the lease as to the 120 acres. In reversing, the appellate court determined that defendants adequately raised the issue of indivisibility, which, it stated, could be construed as an affirmative defense.

[The court's discussion of the issue of waiver has been omitted].

We next consider whether the covenant to reasonably develop the premises, implied in oil and gas leases, should be construed as indivisible or divisible. Where the covenant is deemed indivisible, compliance therewith on one tract of the leased premises serves to perpetuate the lease as to all tracts. If the covenant is divisible, failure to reasonably develop one tract will not affect other tracts subject to the lease. (R. Hemingway, Oil and Gas sec. 9.10 (1971).) Plaintiff relies on Baker v. Collins (1963), 29 Ill.2d 410, 194 N.E.2d 353, and Elliott v. Pure Oil Co. (1956), 10 Ill.2d 146, 139 N.E.2d 295, for the proposition that the covenant is divisible, and that he may therefore seek partial cancellation of the lease. We find these cases distinguishable.

In *Baker,* the lessors sought cancellation of an oil and mineral lease as it applied to the undeveloped portions of the leasehold premises. It was alleged that the lessees unreasonably delayed drilling efforts for a period of 11 years, between 1950 and 1961. Subsequent to 1961, however, the lessees explored and developed the premises "without objection from, and apparently at the insistence of, the [lessors]." (29 Ill.2d 410, 414, 194 N.E.2d 353.) This court determined that it would be inequitable to permit cancellation of the lease on the basis of the 11–year drilling delay, since the lessors acquiesced in subsequent exploratory drilling.

Similarly, *Elliott* did not specifically address the issue of whether the implied covenant to develop is indivisible or divisible. In that case, the lessor sought cancellation of an oil lease on the grounds that the lessee failed to develop the property and failed to protect the tract from drainage. The trial court ruled that, unless a well was drilled within 60 days, the lease would be cancelled as it applied to 10 acres of a 20–acre tract. In affirming, this court noted that the 10 acres in question were threatened by drainage from nearby wells, a situation which the lessee was required to prevent. (See R. Hemingway, Oil and Gas sec. 9.10 (1971).) Further, the lessee did not raise indivisibility as a defense.

Dickerson v. Ray (1960), 20 Ill.2d 107, 169 N.E.2d 341, cited by defendants, is more closely analogous to the instant case. In *Dickerson,* the separate owners of two tracts of land executed a mineral deed in which they conveyed to the grantee an undivided one-half interest in any oil and gas discovered on the properties. The habendum clause provided that the deed would remain in effect for a certain primary term and for as long thereafter as oil or gas was produced. Production on one of the tracts eventually ceased, and the owners claimed that the deed thereby expired as to that tract. In rejecting their contention, this court stated:

> Arising first in decisions relating to oil-and-gas leases, it is the rule of the vast majority that where a number of land owners demise their lands in a single lease, whether contiguous or not, and provide that after a designated period the interest covered by the said instrument

will continue for as long as there is production upon said land, production which is sufficient to continue the interest as to any of the land described is sufficient to continue the interest as to all of the land described. (20 Ill.2d 107, 113–14, 169 N.E.2d 341.)

Although, in the instant case, there are numerous lessees and only a single lessor, we agree with the appellate court that "the divisibility or indivisibility of covenants does not depend on where diversity of [interest] lies." (109 Ill.App.3d 247, 251, 64 Ill.Dec. 863, 440 N.E.2d 415.) Nor is it significant that Dickerson involved a deed rather than a lease, since the court based its decision on the rules pertaining to oil and gas leases.

Further, while there is authority to the contrary, it is generally held that the implied covenant to develop should be construed as indivisible unless the lease expressly provides otherwise. (See R. Hemingway, Oil and Gas sec. 9.10 (1971); 3 W. Summers, Oil and Gas secs. 513, 516 (1958) (and cases cited therein); cf. Annot., 9 A.L.R. 4th 1121 (1981) (covenants to develop, implied in mineral deeds, are generally deemed indivisible); 38 Am.Jur.2d 526, *Gas and Oil* sec. 51 (1968) (pursuant to the rule applied in oil and gas lease cases, the implied covenant to develop, in conveyances transferring term interests, is construed as indivisible).) Based upon our interpretation of *Dickerson,* and the above-related authorities, we hold that the implied covenant to reasonably develop the premises is indivisible. Since plaintiff's complaint sought to affect only certain tracts of the leased premises, thus treating the covenant as divisible, the appellate court did not err in holding the complaint failed to state a cause of action.

We recognize that the principle of indivisibility could operate to the disadvantage of the lessor. As long as there is reasonable development of the property, as a whole, the lease is perpetuated even as to substantial tracts of land which may remain undeveloped. However, this seemingly harsh result is one which the lessor could easily avoid. The principle of indivisibility only applies where the parties to the lease agreement fail to manifest a contrary intent. (See 3 W. Summers, Oil and Gas sec. 516 (1958).) If the lessor wishes to preclude assignments of interest, or otherwise seeks to treat the covenant to develop as divisible, he need only include a provision to that effect in the lease agreement.

* * *

As previously stated, the appellate court reversed on the ground that the implied covenant to develop is indivisible. The court concluded that, since defendants showed there was continuous production on portions of the leasehold, the trial court should not have granted plaintiff's motion for summary judgment. However, the principle of indivisibility requires more than mere production; it requires that the production and development be reasonable. (See Baker v. Collins (1963), 29 Ill.2d 410, 194 N.E.2d 353; R. Hemingway, Oil and Gas sec. 9.10 (1971).) The appellate court made no express findings as to whether the premises were reasonably developed. Although plaintiff failed to specifically allege that development of the leasehold was unreasonable, defendants did not address this pleading deficiency in the trial court. Indeed, our review of the record indicates that the parties were not particularly specific in their pleadings. Consequently, we believe that plaintiff should be afforded an opportunity to prove that the premises, as a whole, were unreasonably developed. We note that counsel for defendants, during oral argument, conceded that a remand might be appropriate under the circumstances of this case.

For the above-stated reasons, the judgment of the appellate court reversing the entry of summary judgment is affirmed, and the cause is remanded to the circuit court of Clark County for further proceedings consistent with this opinion.

Affirmed and remanded.

NOTES

1. As the opinion in the principal case indicates, jurisdictions disagree as to whether an oil and gas lease is divisible with respect to implied covenants. The leading case supporting divisibility is Cosden Oil Co. v. Scarborough, 55 F.2d 634 (5th Cir.Tex.1932). The court there made the following analysis:

> Of oil and gas leases generally it may be said that ordinarily they are regarded as indivisible as to the express conditions which fix the vesting of the determinable fee, such as the drilling of a certain number of wells, when that is required, or the obtaining of production in the absence of specific requirement, and that assignees under an original lease hold their titles to their several tracts without the necessity of further rental payments, or of further compliance with these express drilling conditions when they have been complied with on any part of the lease. On the other hand, as to the implied covenant, which running with the land is imposed on each taker of any part of the lease as a consideration for his holding it, we think it is quite generally held that the contract is severable, imposing upon the holder of each segregated part the obligation to develop that part without reference to the others.

* * *

> This construction gives meaning and effect to the instrument of lease. Without enlarging the rights of either lessor or lessee, it not only gives effect to the implied covenant to develop, the prime purpose of the leasing, but it prevents complicating the performance of that covenant with considerations such as are sought to be raised in this case. In short, while the lease is entire as to the vesting not only in the original lessee, but in all of his assigns, of a determinable fee in each as to the part of the land he owns, that determinable fee as to each owner stands or falls, is abandoned or ceases, according to his own acts, subjecting him to the obligation for damages not at all for what is being done or not done upon the tract in general, but only for what he does. Any other construction would lead to interminable confusion.

> If the idea of indivisibility or entirety is persisted in after production obtained, then the lessor is unable to protect himself as to the particular part leased, though the lessee abandons it, ceases to operate it, or fails in

his covenant of diligence, without having to take into account all other assignees and their supposed collateral rights in the acreage and operations thereon.

There is ample authority for the view we take, that the lease is indivisible as to the fixing of the term; divisible as to the implied covenant to develop. It accords with reason and common sense. * * *

55 F.2d at 637–38

2. Several commentators have been critical of the position taken by the *Cosden* court. Brown has argued that there is no satisfactory rationale for treating a lease as indivisible with respect to some covenants but divisible with respect to others. The original developmental obligation relates to the lease in its entirety, and that obligation should not be increased or rendered more burdensome merely because the lease is divided into different areas geographically. See Earl A. Brown, Assignments of Interests in Oil and Gas Leases, 5 Inst. on Oil & Gas L. & Tax'n 25, 43–44 (1954). A similar argument is advanced in Hemingway § 9.10.

Williams and Meyers have concluded that the dispute over the divisibility of a lease is almost entirely academic. They point out that if part of the lease has been adequately developed and the remainder neglected, most courts will conditionally cancel the lease as to the undeveloped portion, regardless of whether the undeveloped part has been assigned or whether the lease is still owned in its entirety by the original lessee. Williams & Meyers § 409.4.

From the lessor's standpoint, is there any practical advantage to treating the developmental covenant as a separate obligation as to each segregated portion of the lease?

3. In Hartman Ranch Co. v. Associated Oil Co., 73 P.2d 1163 (Cal. 1937), the lessor sought to enforce the implied covenant to prevent drainage against a transferee of the original lease. The defendant argued that under the law of California it had received a sublease, rather than an assignment, because the original lessee had retained a right of re-entry for breach of condition.[1] Further, as a sublessee it could not be held liable for breach of covenants in the original lease, because they were real covenants binding only persons who have acquired the exact estate owned by the original covenantor. While not disputing these traditional common law doctrines, the court held the defendant liable for breach of the drainage covenant on the ground that in accepting the sublease it had expressly agreed to perform all of the covenants provided for in the parent lease. The court reasoned that the lessor was the "creditor beneficiary" of this promise and entitled to enforce it against the defendant.

The distinction between an assignment and a sublease is firmly rooted in Louisiana oil and gas jurisprudence—see, e.g., Willis v. International Oil & Gas Corp., 541 So.2d 332 (La.App.1989)—but has doubtful validity in most

---

1. The traditional common law rule treated a transfer of the entire remaining term of a lease as an assignment. A subleasing occurred if the lessee transferred less than the remaining term. The rule applied in California and several other states, under which retention of a right of re-entry creates a sublease, is usually referred to as the "Massachusetts rule." A good discussion of these rules and the distinction between an assignment and a sublease can be found in Jaber v. Miller, 219 Ark. 59, 239 S.W.2d 760 (1951). See also, Kuntz, § 64.2.

other states. In Holman v. North Dakota, 438 N.W.2d 534, 540 (N.D.1989), the North Dakota Supreme Court refused to hold "that the mere retention of an overriding royalty without anything else should cause the transfer of a lease to be classified as a sublease rather than as an assignment," and cited authorities questioning whether a distinction that developed in connection with traditional landlord-tenant law should ever be applied in the context of an oil and gas lease. In jurisdictions such as Texas, which view the oil and gas lease as a fee simple determinable, a court is unlikely to apply the distinction because the underlying document is not a "lease" in the traditional common law sense. See Brown § 11.04.

B. SUPPORT AGREEMENTS

A classic problem in economics arises when oil and gas leases are held by two or more companies in an unexplored prospect. The first company to drill incurs a significant risk, but confers a benefit on the other companies. Without any expenditure or risk of loss non-drilling companies will learn whether the prospect is productive or not. In practice, they are likely to learn far more; for the drilling company will be required to file a variety of reports with the state regulatory agency, including total depth drilled, the result of initial well tests and monthly production records if the well is productive. The non-drilling companies can now plan their course of action accordingly.

Support agreements (which are also sometimes referred to as letter agreements) provide a mechanism for spreading the risks and benefits of drilling among two or more lessees in the field. For example, one lessee may agree to pay a specified sum to a second lessee in exchange for drilling logs and well completion reports if the second lessee drills a well to a specified depth. This type of understanding is often referred to as a bottom hole contribution agreement. A variant is the dry hole agreement, under which the first party makes the cash payment only if the drilling lessee gets a dry hole. Typically these agreements do not impose any drilling obligation; an enforceable obligation arises—either to pay a set sum or supply information—only if the second party actually drills a well. Support agreements may also incorporate a provision for a lease assignment. Paine v. Moore, 464 S.W.2d 477 (Tex.Civ.App. 1971), contains a good example of a bottom hole purchase letter. If the lessee drilled a well to a specified depth, the other party agreed to make a cash payment in exchange for an assignment of an undivided 1/8 interest in the drilling party's 400 acre lease.

Although standardized forms for support agreements and other forms of letter agreements are available, the documents relied on are often a series of written exchanges that attempt to memorialize the parties' oral negotiations. Enforceability is a common problem. The written correspondence may fail to set out all essential elements of the agreement or specifically contemplate a later, formal contract. See, e.g., Lynx Exploration & Production Co., Inc. v. 4–Sight Operating Co., Inc., 891 S.W.2d 785

(Tex.App. 1995, writ denied) and EP Operating Co. v. MJC Energy Co., 883 S.W.2d 263 (Tex.App. 1994), involving attempts to enforce lease acquisition agreements. Paine illustrates one of the most common problems: failure to describe the interest to be transferred with sufficient certainty to satisfy the statute of frauds. The contributing party under the bottom hole purchase letter successfully resisted payment after a dry hole was drilled by arguing that the agreement did not contain an adequate description of either the 400 acres or the lease. For a discussion of the real property description and information necessary to satisfy the statute of frauds see Hemingway § 9.7.

Even if the letter agreement is enforceable, it may lack detailed provisions that are necessary to avoid disputes or misunderstandings. For example, the parties may not spell out the precise information that the drilling party must furnish, or they may fail to define critical terminology. Is the driller entitled to payment under a dry hole letter if some production is possible, but not production in paying quantities? If the well will produce in paying quantities, but will never pay out?

Many words and phrases commonly used in an oil and gas lease have been defined by the courts. See, e.g., Clifton v. Koontz, 325 S.W.2d 684 (Tex. 1959) (production in paying quantities) and Humphrys v. Skelly Oil Co., 83 F.2d 989 (5th Cir.Tex. 1936) (commencement of drilling operations). Do the same definitions apply to such terms when they are used in a letter agreement? For example, are the operations that the driller must commence on or before a certain date to earn the payment under a dry hole letter identical with the drilling operations that will maintain a lease in effect past the primary term? See Vickers v. Peaker, 300 S.W.2d 29 (Ark.1957) and Davis v. Zapata Petroleum Corp., 351 S.W.2d 916 (Tex.Civ. App.1961, writ refused n.r.e.).

Similarly, to what extent should concepts developed in connection with the oil and gas lease control the rights of parties under a letter agreement? For example, is the driller entitled to payment for a dry hole if the well produces in paying quantities but will never pay out? If a well will not produce in paying quantities, is it a dry hole even though some production is possible?

C. FARMOUT AGREEMENTS

A farmout is basically an agreement under which one who owns an oil and gas lease (the farmor) assigns an interest in it to another person (the farmee) in exchange for testing and drilling operations. There are many reasons why the parties may enter into such an arrangement. The farmor may use the agreement to maintain the lease by securing production before the expiration of the primary term or to comply with offset drilling or development covenants; it may wish to acquire geological information that will enable it to assess the productive potential of retained acreage or simply to obtain an interest in production without costs. The farmee may view the farmout as a way to acquire leased acreage not otherwise available or at lower cost than would otherwise be possible. The farmout may be used as a mechanism for sharing the risk of drilling an expensive or high-risk well. For a discussion of the various factors that may motivate parties to enter into a farmout, see John S. Lowe, Analyzing Oil and Gas Farmout Agreements, 41 Sw.L.J. 763, 778–892 (1987). This article is widely viewed as the definitive work on traditional farmout agreements. Other excellent discussions of farmouts include Blair Klein & Noel Burke, The Farmout Agreement: Its Form and Substance, 24 Rocky Mt.Min. L.Inst. 479 (1978); John R. Scott, How to Prepare an Oil and Gas Farmout Agreement, 33 Baylor L.Rev. 63 (1981); Hugh V. Schaefer & James E. O'Byrne, The Ins and Outs of Farmouts: A Practical Guide for the Landman and the Lawyer, 32 Rocky Mtn.Min.L.Inst. 18–1 (1986); and Kender P. Jones, "Something Old, Something New: The Evolving Farmout Agreement," 49 Washburn L.J. 477 (2010).

Whether the drilling provision in the farmout agreement is a condition precedent or a firm obligation, the farmee who complies with its terms is entitled to the assignment specified in the agreement. This assignment may be of the entire leasehold estate owned by the farmor or some portion of it. A partial assignment may be limited to an undivided interest in the lease, a specific amount of the land covered by the lease, a specific depth or formation, or even a type of production, such as natural gas. The assignment may or may not be combined with the reservation of a noncost-bearing interest in the farmor. In spite of these possibilities, the most common assignment resulting from a farmout involving a vertical well has traditionally been the entire working interest in the drilling site, subject to an overriding royalty in the farmor, which is convertible into a 50 percent working interest upon payout and a 50 percent interest in the working interest in the remainder of the land subject to the farmout.

1. STRUCTURE AND TAX IMPLICATIONS

In the oil industry even the simplest and most informal agreement may have significant tax ramifications, and farmouts are certainly no exception. The following revenue ruling describes a common farmout arrangement and the tax consequences that flow from it.

REVENUE RULING 77–174
1977–1 Cum.Bull. 77 (May 9, 1977).

Advice has been requested regarding the Federal income tax consequences of the transaction described below.

Corporation *X* uses the cash receipts and disbursements method of accounting and files its Federal income tax returns on the calendar year basis. *X* has properly exercised the option provided by section 1.612–4 of the Income Tax Regulations, implementing section 263(c) of the Internal Revenue Code of 1954, to treat drilling and development costs as expenses.

X entered into a written agreement with corporation *Y*, the owner of an oil and gas lease on a single undeveloped 16*x* acre tract of land. Pursuant to the terms of the agreement, *X* assumed the obligation for the drilling of a well to a specified depth at a designated location on the leased acreage, for the completing and equipping of the well if commercially productive, or for the plugging and abandoning thereof if dry. In consideration of the undertaking by *X*, the agreement provided that upon the abandonment or completion of the well pursuant to the agreed terms, *Y* would assign to *X* the following: (1) the entire working or operating interest in the 3*x*–acre drill site (the spacing unit assigned to the well by the state regulatory body), subject, however, to the reservation by *Y* of an overriding royalty interest of an undivided 1/16 of all oil, gas, and other hydrocarbons produced, saved, and sold from such drill site; and (2) an undivided one-half of the working or operating interests in the portion of the tract exclusive of the drill site. The agreement provided further that after recovery by *X* of all costs of drilling, equipping, and operating the well out of the proceeds from the working interest share of all oil, gas, and other hydrocarbons, produced, saved, and sold from the drill site, *Y* will have the right to convert the overriding royalty interest to an undivided one-half of the working interest in the drill site.

X successfully drilled and completed the well as a commercial producer of oil and gas. In accordance with the agreement, *Y* thereupon promptly assigned to *X* the entire working interest in the drill site, subject to the reservation by *Y* of an overriding royalty interest of an undivided 1/16 of all oil, gas, and other hydrocarbons produced, saved, and sold from such drill site, and an undivided one-half of the working interest in the balance of the tract of land.

Section 61(a) of the Code provides, in part, that gross income means all income from whatever source derived, including, insofar as is pertinent here, compensation for services.

Section 1001(a) of the Code provides, in part, that the gain from the sale or other disposition of property is the excess of the amount realized therefrom over the adjusted basis for determining gain, and the loss is the excess of the adjusted basis over the amount realized.

Section 1001(b) of the Code defines the amount realized from the sale or other disposition of property as the sum of money received plus the fair market value of the property (other than money) received.

Section 1.61–2(d)(1) of the regulations provides, in part, that if services are paid for other than in money, the fair market value of the property or services taken in payment is includible in income.

Section 1.451–1(a) of the regulations provides that under the cash receipts and disbursements method of accounting income is includible in gross income when actually or constructively received.

In the case of the compensatory receipt of property other than cash, the fair market value of such property, determined as of the date of transfer or receipt, actual or constructive, is includible in the gross income of the taxpayer in the taxable year such property is actually or constructively received.

When property other than cash is transferred as compensation for services that are not readily subject to independent valuation or in satisfaction of an unliquidated claim, the courts have held that the transfer is treated as the sale for the equivalent of the fair market value on the date of transfer of the property with the transferor realizing gain if the transferor's basis in the property is less than the fair market value and loss if such basis is greater.

G.C.M. 22730, 1941–1 C.B. 214, provides, in part, that when drillers or equipment suppliers and investors contribute materials and services in connection with the development of a mineral property in exchange for an economic interest in such property, the receipt of the economic interest does not result in realization of income. The contributors are viewed as not performing services for compensation, but as acquiring capital interests through an undertaking to make a contribution to the pool of capital. To come within the holding of G.C.M. 22730, the economic interest acquired must be in the same property to the development of which the materials and services are contributed. With respect to the transferor of the economic interest, G.C.M. 22730 states that such transferor has parted with no capital interest but has merely given the transferee (driller, equipment supplier, or investor) a right to share in production in consideration of an investment made.

Section 263(c) of the Code, as a specific exception to the basis provision of section 263(a), directs the Secretary of the Treasury or the Secretary's delegate to prescribe regulations corresponding to the regulations that granted the option to deduct as expenses intangible drilling and development costs in the case of oil and gas wells and that were recognized and approved by Congress in House Concurrent Resolution 50, Seventy-ninth Congress.

Section 1.612–4(a) of the regulations provides, in part, as follows:

In accordance with the provisions of section 263(c), intangible drilling and development costs incurred by an operator (one who holds a working or operating interest in any tract or parcel of land either as a fee owner or under a lease or any other form of contract granting working or operating rights) in the development of oil and gas properties may at his option be chargeable to capital or to expense * * *. Included in this option are all costs of drilling and development undertaken (directly or through a contract) by an operator of an oil and gas property whether incurred by him prior or subsequent to the formal grant or assignment to him of operating rights (a leasehold interest, or other form of operating rights, or a working interest); except that in any case where any drilling or development project is undertaken for the grant or assignment of a fraction of the operating rights, only that part of the costs thereof which is attributable to such fractional interest is within this option. In the excepted cases, costs of the project undertaken, including depreciable equipment furnished, to the extent allocable to fractions of the operating rights held by others, must be capitalized as the depletable capital cost of the fractional interest thus acquired.

Section 1.614–1(a)(1) of the regulations provides, in part, that for purposes of subtitle A of the Code, in the case of mines, wells, and other natural deposits, the term "property" means each separate interest owned by the taxpayer in each mineral deposit in each separate tract or parcel of land.

Rev.Rul. 69–332, 1969–1 C.B. 87, deals with a situation in which a taxpayer, in consideration of drilling a test well on a specified lease, received an undivided 5/8 interest in the lease, and was to receive a sum of money equal to its total costs from all of the proceeds of all production from the well for the complete payout period. Rev.Rul. 69–332 holds that, because the taxpayer was the owner of the entire working or operating interest in the well under the agreement that provided for complete recoupment of all costs, the taxpayer was entitled to deduct 100 percent of the intangible drilling and development costs incurred in the drilling of the well.

Rev.Rul. 71–207, 1971–1 C.B. 160, deals with a situation in which the assignee, in consideration of the receipt, of an undivided one-half operating interest in an undeveloped oil and gas lease, agreed to drill, complete, equip, and operate a well on the lease. The assignee would completely recoup all costs of drilling, completing, equipping, and operating the well before the assignor and the assignee became co-owners of the lease, sharing equally in the costs and income from the well. Since the assignee owned the entire operating interest in the oil and gas lease during the period of complete payout, the assignee was entitled to deduct as expense all the intangible drilling and development costs of drilling the well.

Before the assignment of the working interests to X in the instant case, the oil and gas lease was, within the meaning of section 614(a) of the Code and section 1.614–1(a) of the regulations, one property in the hands of Y. Upon assignment, X received two separate economic interests in the tract or parcel of land, each such interest being a separate section 614 property. The entire working interest in the drill site to which X made a contribution in the form of drilling was one property, and the undivided one-half of the working interest in the portion of the tract exclusive of the drill site was a second property. Likewise, Y retained two separate properties in the tract or parcel of land. The overriding royalty interest reserved in the drill site was one property, and the undivided one-half of the working interest retained by Y in the balance of the tract exclusive of the drill site was a second property.

Having received the entire working interest in the drill site for the period of complete payout, X is regarded under the holdings of Rev.Rul. 69–332 and Rev.Rul. 71–207 as having received the grant of the entire working or operating interest in the drill site, the separate oil and gas property on which the well was drilled.

Inasmuch as X received all of the operating rights in the drill site, X is entitled, under section 1.612–4(a) of the regulations, to deduct all of the intangible drilling and development costs that were actually paid or incurred in the drilling and completion of the well, regardless of the fact that in consideration of such drilling X also received property in addition to the working interest in the drill site.

Neither X nor Y realized income as a result of the transfer of the entire working interest in the drill site from Y to X. This working interest is in the same property to which X made its contribution in the form of drilling. The receipt by X of the working interest in the drill site does not represent payment in the property for services rendered or supplies furnished, but is, instead, a capital interest acquired through the under-taking of X to make a contribution to the pool of capital. Y does not realize income upon the transfer of the working interest in the drill site to X, because Y is not regarded as having parted with a capital interest but has only lessened the required investment and the risks and burdens attend-ing development of the drill site.

Because the acreage exclusive of the drill site is a property separate from that to which the development contribution was made, drilling by X on the drill site did not represent a capital investment in the development of the acreage exclusive of the drill site, and the Federal income tax consequences of the transfer from Y to X of the undivided one-half of the working interest in such acreage is not determined under the pool of capital concept.

With respect to X, the undivided one-half of the working interest in the acreage exclusive of the drill site is compensation in the form of property received by X for undertaking the development project on the drill site. Because the rights of X to receive the assignment of such working interest were conditioned upon the abandonment or completion of the well pursuant to the terms of the agreement, the fair market value of such working interest, determined as of the date of transfer to X, is includible in the gross income of X in the year the well was completed or when the working interest was received by X, whichever is the earlier.

With respect to Y, the tax consequences of the assignment to X of the undivided one-half of the working interest in the acreage exclusive of the drill site are determined by regarding Y as having sold such interest for its fair market value on the date of transfer, and having paid the cash proceeds to X as additional compensation for the undertaking by X of the development project on the drill site. Depending upon whether the fair market value on the date of transfer is more or less than the adjusted basis of Y in such undivided one-half of the working interest, Y will realize gain or loss in the year of transfer. The nature of such gain or loss, whether ordinary or resulting from the sale or disposition of property used in the trade or business for purposes of section 1231(b) of the Code, will depend upon the period that *Y* held such property on the date of transfer, and whether the oil and gas lease was held by *Y* primarily for sale to customers in the ordinary course of its trade or business.

The adjusted basis of *Y* in the overriding royalty interest reserved in the drill site is increased by the fair market value of the undivided one-half of the working interest in the acreage exclusive of the drill site on the date of transfer of such working interest to *X*.

If under alternative facts the transfer of the property for Federal income tax purposes occurred at an earlier date, then the fair market value of the property would be determined as of such earlier date.

Pursuant to the authority contained in section 7805(b) of the Code, the conclusions of this Revenue Ruling will not be applied to transfers made before April 27, 1977, or to transfers made pursuant to binding contracts entered into before such date.

NOTES

1. Before the issuance of Revenue Ruling 77–176, the quite common type of farmout arrangement described therein was treated by most people in the oil and gas industry as not giving rise to any taxable income. This treatment was based upon the "pool of capital" concept, which originated in Palmer v. Bender, 287 U.S. 551 (1933), and which seemed to be applicable to the farmout situation under the reasoning of a tax memorandum, G.C.M. 22730, 1941–1 C.B. 214. Under this concept, the farmee, who had drilled a well in exchange for an economic interest in the leasehold, was not viewed as having received compensation for services performed but rather as having acquired a capital interest in the entire property assigned by having made a contribution to the "pool of capital" necessary for the development of the property. The farmor was deemed to have given the farmee a right to share in the income from the property in exchange for the drilling, which the farmee had undertaken. This arrangement was not viewed, however, as constituting a transfer by the farmor of an economic interest in the property. Thus, under this interpretation of G.C.M. 22730, no taxable income would result to either the assignor or assignee until the sale of the actual production.

Revenue Ruling 77–176 does not change this tax treatment with respect to the drill site. Neither the farmor nor farmee realizes any income as a result of its transfer. The transfer of the remaining acreage, however, which the revenue ruling treats as a separate property, does result in substantial adverse tax consequences to both parties. See Emily A. Parker, Contribution of Services to the Pool of Capital: General Counsel Memorandum 22730 to Revenue Ruling 83–40, 35 Inst. on Oil & Gas L. & Tax'n 313 (1984); Juan E. Arrache, Is Revenue Ruling 83–46 a 'Duster' for Service Contributors Seeking 'Tax Free' Pool of Capital Treatment? 24 Santa Clara L.Rev. 857 (1984); and Ron Morgan, Comment, 22 Houston L. Rev. 813 (1985). See also Hemingway § 12.1, arguing that treating drill site and the lands surrounding it as separate properties is inconsistent with § 614 of the Internal Revenue Code.

2. Since the issuance of Revenue Ruling 77–176, the Internal Revenue Service has sought to restrict the applicability of the pool of capital concept. In a subsequent ruling, Revenue Ruling 83–46, 1983–1 C.B. 16, the Service identified three circumstances that would seem to fall within the pool of capital doctrine; however, each of the cases was interpreted to involve a taxable event. In the first situation, a corporation received an overriding royalty from a partnership in exchange for locating oil and gas properties for the partnership. In the second situation, a lawyer received an overriding royalty interest in exchange for title and lease drafting work. In the third situation, an employee of a closely held corporation arranged financing for oil and gas properties and received an overriding royalty interest. The ruling does not mention the pool of capital doctrine and simply identifies each of the situations as creating a taxable event for the recipient of the overriding royalty interest.

The pool of capital concept itself has been called into question by a Seventh Circuit decision. In Zuhone v. Commissioner, 883 F.2d 1317 (7th Cir.1989), an individual taxpayer was the president and sole shareholder of a corporation involved in the sale of fractional interests in oil and gas. The taxpayer received overriding royalties in several properties in exchange for promotional work in acquiring and selling the properties. Some of the transfers occurred before and others occurred after the properties were developed. The taxpayer sought to exclude the value of the overriding royalties from income under the pool of capital doctrine. The Service challenged the taxpayer's exclusions of these royalty interests from gross income, and the taxpayer took the case to tax court. In 1988 the Tax Court in a memorandum decision held that the receipt of these overriding royalty interests did not qualify for pool of capital treatment and that the taxpayer must include the fair market value of such overriding interest in gross income in the year of receipt. The Seventh Circuit not only affirmed the Tax Court's decision but also took this opportunity to place into question the viability of the doctrine. After reviewing the "murky" history underlying the doctrine, the *Zuhone* court cast "doubt as to the wisdom of judicially endorsing this exception to Sections 61 and 83 of the Code for the oil and gas industry in the absence of legislative intent." See John S. Dzienkowski & Robert J. Peroni, A Critical View of *Zuhone*'s Pool of Capital Dicta, Nat.Res.Tax Rev. 93 (May–June 1991); Hemingway § 12.1.

3. One method that has been suggested for reducing the adverse tax consequences of the revenue ruling is the assignment of the entire farmout acreage before the drilling of the well. Why might the timing of the assignment affect the parties' tax? See Blair Klein & Noel Burke, The Farmout Agreement: Its Form and Substance, 24 Rocky Mtn.Min.L.Inst. 479, 489–91 (1978) and Arnold C. Wegher, Taxation of Earned Interest—The Impact of Revenue Ruling 77–176, 24 Rocky Mtn.Min.L.Inst. 521 (1978).

An obvious goal of a farmor who makes such an up-front assignment is to include provisions that protect the farmor in the event of default by the assignee but do not result in a loss of the tax benefit. In this connection note the farmout litigated in Rogers v. Ricane Enterprises, Inc. (Ricane I), 772 S.W.2d 76 (Tex. 1989) on subsequent appeal Rogers v. Ricane Enterprises, Inc. (Ricane II), 884 S.W.2d 763 (Tex. 1994). It provided that "[a]ll of the right, title, interest and privileges herein conveyed to * * * Western [the farmee] will cease and terminate and shall revert to and revest in Superior [the farmor], unless within thirty (30) days after the date hereof, Western shall commence the actual drilling for oil and gas * * *'' Professor Lowe has characterized the *Ricane* farmout as

> a classic illustration of a *drill-to-earn, divided interest, single-well condi-tional-assignment* farmout agreement. It was a *drill-to-earn, divided interest* and *single-well* farmout because Western obtained its rights in a separate part of a larger lease by drilling a well, not by completing a well capable of producing in paying quantities. And Western obtained a *conditional assignment* of its interest before it performed, rather than an assignment after it had drilled the earning well.

John S. Lowe, Recent Significant Cases Affecting Farmout Agreements, 50 Inst. on Oil & Gas L. & Tax'n 3–1, 3–16 (1999).

Conditional assignments have become increasingly common. Which party holds equitable title under such an arrangement? Should it make any differ-ence if the reassignment provision is phrased as a contractual obligation to reconvey or an automatic reversion in the event the terms of the farmout are not fulfilled? Will either form of conditional assignment provide the tax benefits derived from the traditional farmout?

4. The alternative usually suggested for avoiding the adverse tax conse-quences of the Ruling is to create the "tax partnership."

> The general rule is that no gain or loss is recognized either by the partners or the partnership as a result of the formation of the partner-ship and the contribution to it of property.

> The contributing partner obtains as his basis for his interest in the partnership his adjusted basis for the property contributed plus the amount of any money that he contributes to the partnership capital. The partnership obtains as its basis for the property contributed, the adjusted basis that that property had in the hands of the contributing partner. * * * One partner may contribute property and another services deter-mined to be of equal value. Nevertheless, the share of each partner in the income, deductions, credits, gains or losses may be different from the 50 percent value of his initial contribution.

* * *

> The basic partnership rule is that each partner's share of each item of income and expense is to be determined in accordance with the partner-ship agreement if that agreement covers the matter. If the agreement contains no provision as to one or more of the items, the partners' distributive shares of those items are determined in accordance with their shares of the taxable income or loss. The partnership agreement may make special allocations of income gains, loss deductions or credit among the partners in a manner that is disproportionate to their capital contri-butions. A special allocation of an item will be denied if its principal purpose is to avoid or evade the tax. Likewise, the business purpose and economic effect of the allocation is important.

Arnold C. Wegher, Taxation of Earned Interests—The Impact of Revenue Ruling 77–176, 24 Rocky Mtn.Min.L.Inst. 521, 540–42 (1978).[2]

Pʀᴏʙʟᴇᴍ

Assume that the parties wish to enter into the type of farmout agreement discussed in Revenue Ruling 77–176: The farmee will receive a full working interest in the well site, plus a 50 percent working interest in additional contiguous acreage. The farmor will retain a convertible one-sixteenth override in the well site, which at his option may be changed to a 50 percent working interest at pay out. He will also retain 50 percent of the working interest in the additional acreage.

The farmor's cost allocable to the well site is $3,000, and his cost allocable to a 50 percent interest in the additional acreage is $6,000. At the time of the farmout 50 percent of the working interest in such additional acreage is worth $10,000; upon completion of the well it is worth $100,000.

What would be the tax consequences to both the farmor and the farmee under the three alternative methods for accomplishing this transaction that have been previously discussed: assignment of the acreage upon completion of the well, assignment of the acreage at the time of the farmout agreement, and setting up a tax partnership agreement? What other alternatives are available? See John S. Lowe, Analyzing Oil and Gas Farmout Agreements, 41 Sw.L.J. 759, 771–77 (1987).

2. DRILLING OBLIGATIONS

Occasionally farmout agreements are entered into that are predicated upon one party undertaking some sort of seismic testing. Far more commonly, the agreement requires drilling a test well or wells. Such a requirement is rarely free of ambiguity or other uncertainties. For example, a provision that the farmee will drill a test well at a location that is "mutually acceptable" to both parties is unenforceable because the parties have merely agreed to agree to a material term at some time in the future. See, e.g., Aurora Petroleum, Inc. v. Cholla Petroleum, Inc., 2011 WL 652843 (Tex. App. 2011). More commonly, the lawyer for the farmor who is drafting or reviewing such an agreement may be unfamiliar with the geological terms the parties have used or the assumptions which they are making. Thus if the farmor's primary interest is in testing a specific formation, a provision that the well called for in the agreement must be completed to a stated depth may be inadequate if it turns out that the desired formation is below the specified depth at that particular location. See Blair Klein & Noel Burke, The Farmout Agreement: Its Form and Substance, 24 Rocky Mtn.Min.L.Inst. 479 (1978) and John R. Scott, How to Prepare an Oil and Gas Farmout Agreement, 33 Baylor L.Rev. 63 (1981). The requirement that the well be "completed" may also be subject to differing interpretations. See Barrett v. Ferrell, 550 S.W.2d 138 (Tex. Civ.App.1977, writ refused n.r.e.) and Seale v. Major Oil Co., 428 S.W.2d 867 (Tex.Civ.App.1968). The agreement also must make clear exactly what is required for the farmee to earn an interest. The more common agreement for vertical wells contains a produce-to-earn provision under which the farmee is entitled to an assignment only by completing a well capable of producing in paying quantities. Under a drill-to-earn agreement, the farmee earns its interest merely by drilling to the required depth.

The description of the requirements for earning acreage by drilling a horizontal well is more complex. The horizontal extension of the well may cross beneath several leases, causing typically more than one party to be involved. Because of the high cost of drilling and fracing a horizontal well, each party to the farmout may agree to contribute a specified percentage of the costs. The agreement may then further stipulate that each party earns an undivided interest in the acreage covered. The interest earned by the farmee may thereby be limited to a specified percentage of each lease contributed to the farmout. In some instances, the parties may need to negotiate for the assignment of a lease whose lessee is unable or unwilling to participate in the agreement.

The farmee's lawyer must be alert to the risks and uncertainties of the drilling operations. Not only must the depth or stratigraphic formation be specified, but the agreement must indicate the length of the well's horizontal extension. Predicting the length that it will be possible to drill may be difficult; for there is a risk of encountering impenetrable rock or fault zones that make continued extension impossible. The farmee's attorney may argue for the inclusion of a clause providing that the farmee has complied with the drilling requirements if the company has drilled horizontally in the specified formation a distance that is a percentage, e.g., 50%, of the length called for in the farmout agreement; but can drill no farther because of unanticipated geological formations. Special clauses must be included providing for the possibility that not all leases will be reached by the well and what affect this will have upon the rights of those lessees. Because of these and other complexities, further discussion of a horizontal farmout is best left to an advanced course in oil and gas.

The traditional farmout frequently contains a requirement that the farmee complete the well "within _____ days after commencement." Under such a clause, a farmee that has spent large sums of money in drilling a well may nonetheless lose its right to an assignment of the acreage if it encounters impenetrable substances or unforeseeable delays in drilling. (This possibility is especially likely in the case of a horizontal well.) As has been pointed out in John R. Scott, How to Prepare an Oil and Gas Farmout Agreement, 33 Baylor L.Rev. 63, 69 (1981), "[f]armouts containing such limitations rarely contain definitions of 'commencement' or adequate force majeure clauses. * * * Unless there is some compelling reason to fix a deadline for completing the well, it is better merely to require 'diligent and continuous' drilling operations."

What would be an example of a compelling reason for fixing a deadline for a well's completion? If an agreement states a definite time either for the commencement or completion of a well, should a court automatically conclude that time was of the essence of the drilling obligation? See Argos Resources, Inc. v. May Petroleum, 693 S.W.2d 663 (Tex.App.–Dallas 1985, writ ref'd n.r.e.).

If the drilling provision is stated in terms of a condition precedent, failure to comply with its terms merely disqualifies the farmee from receiving the stipulated assignment of acreage. A more difficult legal problem is presented if the drilling clause is stated in terms of a covenant or contractual obligation. What is the liability, for example, of a farmee who enters into a firm drilling agreement and then fails to drill in the time or manner specified?

MARTIN v. DARCY

357 S.W.2d 457 (Tex.Civ.App.1962, writ refused n.r.e.).

POPE, JUSTICE.

Plaintiff, Harris P. Darcy, sued Glen A. Martin for breach of a farm-out agreement, and recovered $3,500 damages under the express terms of the contract, and an additional $3,000 for loss of profits. Martin, by this appeal, insists that the trial court erred (1) in submitting the first special issue which called upon the jury to construe the legal instrument, (2) in submitting the second issue and rendering judgment upon it, when there was no evidence in support of the issue, and (3) in making its own findings upon the amount of lost profits, when there was no evidence of the elements of lost profits. In our opinion, Martin is correct in his contentions about the first and third points, and wrong about the second.

In early July of 1959, Darcy owned the minerals under 671 acres of McMullen County land by force of an assignment from Sun Oil Company. Sun's assignment obligated Darcy to "begin by August 10, 1959, the actual drilling of a well" on the tract. Darcy also held three dry hole contribution letters by which Ohio Oil Company agreed to contribute $6,500, Western Natural Gas Company, $3,150, and El Paso Natural Gas Company, $3,150 toward the drilling of a well. Sun's assignment to Darcy and each of the dry-hole letters to Darcy, prohibited his assignment without prior written consent.

Darcy and Martin began negotiations by which Darcy would assign his rights and obligations to Martin. On July 29, 1959, Martin accepted the terms of a letter which Darcy had written him. By that agreement, Darcy assigned his rights and obligations to Martin. The letter described each of the four documents which Darcy had from the four oil companies. Martin assumed the obligation to drill the well. The contract provided that Darcy would receive $1,500 in the event Martin completed the well as a producer, or $3,500 in the event it was a dry hole. Darcy also retained one-eighth of the oil and other minerals in the property.

Martin's letter of transmittal, from San Antonio to Darcy in Houston, called on Darcy to send him the consents to the assignment from the four oil companies. On July 31, upon receipt of Martin's acceptance, Darcy wrote each oil company based in Texas, and asked for its consent. On August 4, Martin wrote Darcy, "since I do not have letters giving permission for you to assign cannot take the deal as outlined in our letter of agreement." On August 6, Darcy went to Martin's office with consents from Ohio and Western. Martin refused to examine or consider them. On August 7, Darcy returned to Martin's office with the Sun consent and a telegram from El Paso, which stated that its consent was already mailed. It was received on August 8. During Darcy's visit on August 7, he delivered a letter to Martin with attached consents from all but El Paso Oil Company, whose telegram was attached. Darcy by his letter called on Martin to comply with his drilling obligation. Martin did not drill the well. It was later drilled by other persons and was completed as a dry hole. The parties treat the well as a dry hole. Darcy claimed that he was entitled to the contract amount of $3,500 because the well was a dry hole. Martin claimed that Darcy breached the contract by failing to furnish the consents.

* * *

Defendant Martin's next point is that there is no evidence which supports the jury's finding to the second issue. The jury found that Darcy obtained the required written consents in sufficient time for Martin, in the exercise of reasonable diligence, to have commenced the actual drilling of the well by August 10, 1959. Martin's sole attack upon that finding is that there is no evidence to support it. Our search of the record shows that there is much direct evidence and many inferences which support the finding. When Martin accepted the contract and mailed his letter on July 29 from San Antonio to Houston, he knew that he had only thirteen days before the crucial date. In a sense, both parties knew from the beginning that time was limited. Both parties knew that the consents were necessary. Sun's consent to move on the premises was available on August 7. All consents were in hand on August 8. Martin still had August 8 and all of August 9 and 10, to begin actual drilling. The question is not whether this Court disagrees with the finding, but to decide if there is more than a scintilla of evidence upon which the jury could have made such a finding. Martin details the steps incident to actual drilling. One must reach an agreement with a driller; a drilling permit must be obtained; the site must be surveyed, staked and cleared; pits must be dug; water must be obtained; the rig must be moved, set up, and the bit actually turned. However, the evidence in the record shows that these steps usually are taken simultaneously. While one thing is being done, others are also being executed. There is proof that many steps, short of entering upon the premises, as normal procedure, would be taken even before Sun gave its consent. The proof shows that Martin had in fact already engaged a driller for the well, but let him go on August 4. The driller's rig was in Live Oak County, which adjoins McMullen County, and was available. Martin could have taken steps to obtain a drilling permit. The proof from several witnesses is that even after August 8 he could have obtained a permit as a routine matter. The Railroad Commission has an office in San Antonio. There was evidence that applications may be made by telegraph and are often granted on the same day. One witness testified at length and offered several of his former telegraphic applications and permits in evidence. One permit was obtained in three hours. Witnesses testified that staking, clearing and digging the pits would take about half a day, and such work is usually and often done while the rig is moving along the highway to the premises. * * * The most compelling evidence, however, is supplied by Martin himself. When Darcy went to Martin's office on August 6, after receiving Martin's letter that he was withdrawing from the deal, according to Darcy, Martin told him, "I don't need an extension. I can drill it tomorrow if I want to." Certainly there was evidence, and the court properly submitted the dispute to the jury. On the basis of that jury finding, Martin had time to commence actual drilling, and in failing to do so breached the contract.

The trial court granted Darcy an additional $3,000 for lost profits. This was error. There were no jury issues submitted, but the court found as facts that Darcy proved that his retained one-eighth mineral interest had a market value of $6,000, and that he would have sold one-half of it for $3,000 prior to completion of the well. Martin urges that there is no evidence in the record which supports such findings. The point is good. For breach of a contract to drill one may recover the loss of value of royalty and mineral interest during drilling but prior to completion as a dry hole. Such a recovery gives the wronged party the benefit of performance of the contract.

It is not the rule of law, but the failure to prove the elements of such damages which defeats Darcy's recovery of profits. Whiteside v. Trentman, [141 Tex. 46, 170 S.W.2d 195 (1943)], permits such recovery upon proof (1) that the profits may reasonably be supposed to have been in the contemplation of the parties when the contract was made, and (2) that Darcy would have sold his interest prior to completion as a dry hole. Darcy's proof failed to meet either of these tests.

The critical time at which profits must have been in the contemplation of the parties, according to Whiteside v. Trentman is "when the contract was made." The only proof as of that time is that it is well known in the oil industry that some persons do make sales of their royalty and mineral interest during drilling operations. But it is equally well known that other persons hold their interest in the hope of a producing well. The proof, therefore, was that some sell and others do not. This record does not show that Martin, or even Darcy, at that time, had any reason to believe that the mineral interest would or would not be sold. The proof shows that nobody knew what would be done.

The general rule about lost profits is stated in Whiteside v. Trentman, and it is apparent that the rule is taken verbatim from Hadley v.

Baxendale, 9 Exch. 341, 26 Eng.L. & E. 398. The balance of the Baxendale rule, with respect to notice of contemplated profits, is applicable to this case for the reasons that are well expressed by that opinion:

> We think the proper rule in such a case as the present is this: Where two parties have made a contract which one of them has broken, the damages which the other party ought to receive in respect of such breach of contract should be either such as may fairly and substantially be considered as arising naturally, i.e., according to the usual course of things, from such breach of contract itself, or such as may reasonably be supposed to have been in the contemplation of both parties at the time they made the contract, as the probable result of the breach of it. Now, if the special circumstances under which the contract was actually made were communicated by the plaintiff to the defendant, and thus known to both parties, the damages resulting from the breach of such a contract which they would reasonably contemplate, would be the amount of injury which would ordinarily follow from a breach of contract under these special circumstances so known and communicated. But, on the other hand, if those special circumstances were wholly unknown to the party breaking the contract, he, at the most, could only be supposed to have had in his contemplation the amount of injury which would arise generally, and in the great multitude of cases, not affected by any special circumstances, for such a breach of contract. For had the special circumstances been known, the parties might have expressly provided for the breach of contract by special terms as to the damage in that case, and of this advantage it would be very unjust to deprive them. The above principles are those by which we think the jury ought to be guided in estimating the damages arising out of any breach of contract.

Darcy did not prove by more than a scintilla of evidence the other element—that he would have sold his retained interest. There is scarcely anything in the record about the matter. Darcy stated that he could have sold one-half of his retained interest. He said he had a verbal trade. The person with whom he said he had such a trade, described it as a "tentative" deal which was never consummated. There was no evidence, as that term is used in Joske v. Irvine, 91 Tex. 574, 44 S.W. 1059, that Darcy had a $3,000 loss of profits.

The judgment is affirmed insofar as it awarded damages of $3,500 provided in the contract. It is reversed and rendered by denying the additional recovery of $3,000 for lost profits. Since the appeal was prosecuted with effect, costs are adjudged against appellee, Darcy.

NOTES

1. What measure of damages would a Texas court use if the assignor did not retain an interest in the portion of its lease block that it had assigned? See Whiteside v. Trentman, 141 Tex. 46, 170 S.W.2d 195 (Tex.Com.App. 1943).

2.   A party in Darcy's position occasionally attempts to establish damages based on the share of production he would have received if the well had been drilled as promised. The court in County Management, Inc. v. Butler, 650 S.W.2d 888, 890 (Tex. App. 1983), suggested that a plaintiff in this situation:

> [C]an satisfy this burden through the introduction of evidence showing the initial and continued production of wells drilled on the lands in controversy (if available) and on other lands in the area. A qualified expert witness should then be produced who, after examining the logs and other relevant information from the surrounding wells, gives an opinion as to the probability of obtaining production and the extent of such production on the land in question. "Such matters as production costs, geological trends, proration, kind and quality of the oil and countless other items," where applicable, should also be referred to by the expert in making his opinion.

3.   Under Oklahoma law, a farmee who breaches a contract to drill a well is liable for the reasonable cost of drilling the well to the specified depth. See, e.g., Eysenback v. Cardinal Petroleum Co., 110 Okla. 12, 236 P. 10 (1925) and Mid–Continent Petroleum Corp. v. Russell, 173 F.2d 620 (10th Cir.Okla.1949). Could the problems that the principal case posed for the assignor have been avoided by specifically providing in the farmout agreement for the Oklahoma measure of damages?

4.   Questions concerning the proper measure of damages for breach of a contract to drill also arise where a farmee or other operator has entered into a drilling contract with a third party driller. See Section F, infra, of this chapter. See also Own L. Anderson, The Anatomy of an Oil and Gas Drilling Contract, 25 Tulsa L.J. 359, 404–08 (1990) and Richard C. Maxwell, Damages for Breach of Express and Implied Drilling Covenants, 5 Rocky Mtn. Min.L.Inst. 435 (1960).

3.   RETAINED INTERESTS

The interest retained by the assignor in a farmout varies greatly from agreement to agreement, although an overriding royalty, such as the one retained by Darcy in his assignment to Martin, is fairly common in farmouts involving vertical wells. A second common type of reservation is an overriding royalty that equals the difference between a stated percent of production and any other royalties, overriding royalties, or production payments outstanding at the time of the farmout. Suppose, for example, that the stated percentage is 25%. If the lease when assigned is subject to a one-eighth royalty in the lessor and a production payment of $25,000 payable out of one-sixteenth of production, which is owed to a third party, the assignor would be entitled to one-sixteenth of production until termination of the production payment, at which time he would be entitled to one-eighth of production. The effect of such a reservation is to give the assignee a "net revenue interest" of 75 percent of production.

In addition to these fairly simple provisions for an overriding royalty, many farmout agreements also contain a "back-in" provision. Under such a clause the farmor has the option of converting his overriding royalty into a share of the working interest once payout has occurred. Like the overriding royalty, the size of the share of the working interest that the assignor is entitled to will vary. As Professor Lowe has pointed out, the attorney drafting an acceptable conversion provision must deal with a variety of formidable problems, such as determining when and if the well has paid out. See John S. Lowe, Analyzing Oil and Gas Farmout Agreements, 41 Sw.L.J. 759, 832–36 (1987). Especially difficult problems are presented if the back-in interest is conditioned upon payout on a leasehold or "package" basis, as it was in Howell Petroleum Corp. v. Leben Oil Corp., 976 F.2d 614 (10th Cir. Okla. 1992). As the late Dean Eugene Kuntz has pointed out, without careful drafting the farmor will find it difficult to keep informed as to when payout occurs, and in any event "an enterprising farmee may be able to defer payout interminably by drilling or causing to be drilled additional wells." Kuntz, Discussion Notes, 121 O. & G.R. 264 (1994).

Courts have occasionally come to the aid of farmors who have failed to include salient provisions in the farmout agreement. In Energen Resources MAQ, Inc. v. Dalbosco, 23 S.W.3d 551 (Tex. App. 2000) plaintiff farmor, who had converted his overriding royalty to a 25 percent working interest after the well drilled by farmee paid out, successfully sued the farmee for damages for failing to give him an opportunity to take over operation of the well before it was plugged and abandoned. Although the farmout agreement was silent on any obligation to notify the farmor that the farmee planned to plug the well, the court held such a duty was supported by evidence of custom and usage. Notice of intent to plug and abandon was typically given either in order to collect a working interest owner's proportionate cost of the plugging operations or to give the working interest owner an opportunity to buy out other working interest owners and take over operations.

4. EARNED INTERESTS

Under the usual farmout agreement involving a vertical well, a farmee who complies with the drilling obligation receives the working interest in the drill site acreage. He may also be entitled to an interest in additional acreage. As discussed previously, this may include an undivided interest in acreage outside the drill site as soon as the initial well has been completed as specified. Another type of arrangement frequently encountered is referred to as "drill to earn." Under this type of agreement, the farmee receives a working interest only in the drill site when he completes the well; he is, however, then entitled to earn an interest in additional sites as he drills on them. Typically such drilling must be done at specified time intervals for the farmee to earn the additional acreage.

PROBLEM

A farmout contains the following clause: "This Agreement is subject to all existing lease burdens, overrides and payments out of production relating to the area covered by this Agreement, which obligations you agree to assume."

Suppose that the landowner, in leasing the area covered by the agreement, had reserved a three-sixteenths royalty. The original lessee, Reata Oil Co., assigned the lease in its entirety to Sabine Exploration Co. but reserved a one-sixteenth overriding royalty in itself. The farmout agreement is between Sabine and the Uvalde Drilling Co. Sabine has reserved an overriding royalty of one-sixteenth of production until payout, at which time it will be entitled to a 50 percent share of the working interest.

What proportion of the production is Uvalde entitled to before payout? What proportions of production are Sabine and Uvalde each entitled to after payout? See Hemingway § 9.8.

———

The farmout agreement is rarely recorded. Indeed, the agreement may not qualify for recordation under the state's recording statute, because it does not have the prescribed form of acknowledgment or notarization.[3] If the document contains a present assignment of acreage, a clause may prohibit recordation until the well has been drilled and accepted by the farmor. There is thus some risk to the farmee that his interest, when finally earned, will have been burdened by claims of the farmor's subsequent creditors.

A more substantial problem may result if the farmout agreement has been transferred through a succession of farmees. To what extent will the ultimate farmee take subject to unrecorded interests retained by prior farmees? The following case may provide some insights into this issue.

WESTLAND OIL DEVELOPMENT CORP. v. GULF OIL CORP.

637 S.W.2d 903 (Tex.1982).

McGee, Justice.

This case involves the adjudication of the parties' interests in certain oil and gas leases located on six sections of land in Pecos County, Texas. We must determine the effect that a letter agreement, dated November 15, 1966 (hereinafter referred to as "the November 15, 1966, letter agreement"), had upon the respective interests in those leases. The trial court granted summary judgment in favor of Westland Oil Development Corporation and L.C. Kung (hereinafter referred to as "Westland"), petitioners herein and plaintiffs in the trial court, holding that Gulf Oil Corporation and the Superior Oil Company (hereinafter referred to as

---

3. E.g., Cal.Gov't. Code § 27287 (West 1988); S.D. Codified Laws Ann. 43–28–8 (1983); and Tex.Prop.Code Ann. § 12.001 (1991).

"Gulf and Superior"), respondents herein and defendants in the trial court, were on notice as a matter of law of the November 15, 1966, letter agreement, and that said agreement was enforceable as to all six sections. The court of appeals reversed the judgment of the trial court and remanded the cause for a determination of the notice issue. We reverse the judgment of the court of appeals and render judgment that Gulf and Superior were on notice of the November 15, 1966, letter agreement as a matter of law, and that the statute of frauds does not prohibit enforcement of said agreement as to three of the six sections under dispute.

Prior to August 4, 1966, Mobil Oil Corporation (hereinafter referred to as "Mobil") owned oil and gas leases covering twenty-nine sections in the Rojo Caballos Field in Pecos County, Texas. The six sections comprising the subject matter of this suit were a part of those twenty-nine sections, and are identified as sections 23, 24, 25 and 26, Block 49, and sections 19 and 30, Block 48. From this point forward, we will refer to the sections by number only and eliminate any corresponding reference to the block number.

On August 4, 1966, Mobil and Westland entered into a farmout agreement (hereinafter referred to as the Mobil/Westland farmout agreement). The leases which were the subject matter of the farmout agreement covered, among others, sections 19, 23 and 24. The agreement provided that at such time as Westland complied with its drilling obligations and completed a producing well, it would be entitled to receive an assignment of one-half of Mobil's interest in those sections. The Mobil farmout obligated Westland to commence a wildcat well by September 1, 1966. Westland sought more time, and Mobil granted an extension of time to December 1, 1966, in a letter dated August 29, 1966.

A Midland partnership, Chambers & Kennedy (hereinafter referred to as "C & K"), became interested in taking over Westland's obligations under the Mobil/Westland farmout agreement. The agreement made to accomplish this was the November 15, 1966, letter agreement. This agreement contains a provision which is the center of the controversy in this case. Under the terms of this agreement, C & K assumed all of the obligations imposed by the Mobil/Westland farmout agreement, agreed to pay Westland $50,000.00 in cash, and assigned to Westland a 1/16 of 8/8 overriding royalty interest on any acreage earned from Mobil, 1/32 of the working interest obtained from Mobil under the farmout agreement, and a production payment of $150,000.00 payable out of the production from the test well.

The November 15, 1966, letter agreement also contained what shall be referred to as an area of mutual interest agreement. This is the controversial provision referred to above. In an area of mutual interest agreement, the parties attempt to describe a geographic area within which they agree to share certain additional leases acquired by any of them in the future. This necessarily contemplates that oil and gas leasehold interests will be conveyed. Therefore, the agreement is in the nature of a contract to convey interests in oil and gas leases.

The area of mutual interest agreement was contained in paragraph 5 of the November 15, 1966, letter agreement and reads as follows:

> 5. If any of the parties hereto, their representatives or *assigns,* acquire any additional leasehold interests affecting any of the lands covered by said farmout agreement, or any additional interest from Mobil Oil Corporation under lands in the area of the farmout acreage, such shall be subject to the terms and provisions of this agreement; provided, however that in no event shall the owners of the working interest under any portion of such acreage be entitled to less than 75% working interest leases.

(emphasis added). It is this covenant or obligation which Westland seeks to enforce against Gulf and Superior.

* * * The farmout well was spudded on December 1, 1966, and completed on January 23, 1968. The well was marginal but earned the acreage. By assignment dated March 7, 1968, Mobil conveyed to C & K, Union Texas as operator, and the other investors in the well, one-half of its leasehold interests in the farmout block, which included the leases covering sections 19, 23 and 24. This assignment provided that as to all the lands and depths assigned, with one exception, the assignment would be subject to all the provisions of a certain operating agreement dated March 1, 1968. The precise language of that assignment was as follows:

> This Assignment is made without warranty of title, either express or implied. In addition, as to all the lands and depths herein assigned (except as to said Section 18), *this Assignment shall be subject to all the provisions of that certain Operating Agreement dated March 1, 1968,* by and between Assignor and Assignee.

> The provisions hereof shall be binding upon, and shall inure to the benefit of, the parties hereto and their respective heirs, devisees, legal representatives successors and assigns.

(emphasis added). The March 7, 1968, assignment is the only instrument mentioned thus far which was recorded. It was filed for record May 16, 1968, in the lease records of Pecos County, Texas.

The March 1, 1968, operating agreement was executed by Mobil, C & K, Union Texas, and the other owners of the interests in the six sections of land described in the Mobil/Westland farmout agreement. This operating agreement is critical to an understanding of the case because of the provisions contained within paragraph 31, the last clause of the agreement. Captioned above paragraph 31 was the heading, "OTHER CONDITIONS, IF ANY, ARE:."

Subparagraphs B and C referred to the Mobil/Westland farmout agreement and the November 15, 1966, letter agreement as follows:

B. This Agreement shall supersede and replace that certain Operating Agreement attached as Exhibit "A" to the said Farmout Letter Agreement dated August 4, 1966 between Mobil Oil Corporation and Westland Oil Development Corporation. *In the event of any conflict between this Contract and the Farmout Letter Agreement dated August 4, 1966, between Mobil Oil Corporation and Westland Oil Development Corporation as amended by letter dated August 29, 1966, and November 11, 1966, and a Letter Agreement between Chambers and Kennedy and Westland Oil Development Corporation and L.C. Kung dated November 15, 1966, then such prior agreements shall prevail over this Agreement.*

(emphasis added).

The court of appeals quoted the last sentence of paragraph 31.B. but did not quote the next paragraph:

C. Exhibit "A" lists all of the parties, and their respective percentage or fractional interests under this Agreement. *Such interests are specifically subject to all terms, conditions and reservations set forth in that Farmout Agreement Letter dated August 4, 1966 between Mobil Oil Corporation and Westland Development Corporation, as amended, and that certain Assignment dated March 7, 1968 from Mobil Oil Corporation to C. Fred Chambers and W.D. Kennedy and Union Texas Petroleum.*

(emphasis added).

Gulf and Superior obtained their interests in the leases covering sections 19, 23 and 24 through dealings with one Bernard Hanson. By letter dated April 18, 1972, Mobil entered into a farmout agreement with Hanson wherein Mobil agreed that if Hanson commenced a test well on Section 25, Block 49, to a depth sufficient to test the Ellenberger formation and completed it as a producer, Mobil would assign all of its leasehold rights below a depth of 15,000 feet in section 25, and an undivided 60% of its leasehold rights in sections 19 and 30, Block 48, and Sections 23, 24 and 26, Block 49. Sections 19, 23 and 24 were the three southernmost sections involved in the Mobil/Westland farmout agreement. Sections 25, 26 and 30 abut those three sections to the south. The farmout agreement with Hanson stated that the lands and leases covering sections 19, 23 and 24 were covered by the March 1, 1968, operating agreement between Mobil, C & K and Union Texas, and that any interest earned by Hanson from Mobil would be subject to that agreement. Hanson then assigned this farmout agreement to Gulf and Superior.

Hanson also approached C & K, Union Texas and their other partners, and obtained from them farmouts similar to the one received from Mobil. These farmouts covered part of their interests in leases covering sections 19, 23 and 24 which were earned pursuant to the Mobil/Westland farmout agreement and the November 15, 1966, letter agreement. Most of these farmout agreements refer to the March 1, 1968, operating agreement. Hanson also assigned these farmout agreements to Gulf and Superior.

In 1972, Gulf and Superior drilled the test well as required by the Hanson farmout agreements. This well was completed in March 1973, as a large gas producer. Gulf and Superior thereby earned the acreage under these farmout agreements, and the earned leasehold estates were assigned directly to Gulf and Superior. The assignment from Mobil was dated May 22, 1973, and was expressly made subject to the March 1, 1968, operating agreement.

Upon learning of the last assignments from Mobil, Westland filed suit and sought a declaratory judgment that the November 15, 1966, letter agreement was valid and applied to the interests acquired by Gulf and Superior from Mobil, and would cover any acreage so acquired in the Rojo Caballos Field. Westland moved for summary judgment, their motion being based on the November 15, 1966, letter agreement, various instruments, letters between the parties which included those instruments previously referred to and several depositions. Westland contended that all of these supported their claim that Gulf and Superior were on notice of the November 15, 1966, letter agreement, and that, by references made therein to other existing instruments, their interests acquired under the letter agreement covered the interest acquired by Gulf and Superior from Mobil. The trial court granted Westland's motion for summary judgment and declared the November 15, 1966, letter agreement enforceable as to the interests and acreage acquired by Gulf and Superior from Mobil. The decree vested title in Westland in the manner set forth in the November 15, 1966, letter agreement.

* * *

There are two questions before us in this case. The first concerns the issue of whether Gulf and Superior were on notice of Westland's prior equitable title. The second issue deals with whether the description of the leases covered by the area of mutual interest agreement contained in paragraph 5 of the November 15, 1966, letter agreement is legally insufficient, thereby rendering the agreement unenforceable under the statute of frauds. We will first address the issue of notice.

The court of appeals held that a question of fact existed as to whether Gulf and Superior, as reasonable purchasers, would have been placed on the duty to conduct complete inquiry of the operating agreement by the reference to it in their assignment from Mobil. The court believed that the normal function of an operating agreement was to define and control the development operations of a certain tract of land, and not to affect title to property. Thus, a question of fact existed as to what a reasonable purchaser would have done under the circumstances.

This, however, is not the rule with regard to references made in documents appearing in one's chain of title. It is well settled that "a purchaser is bound by every recital, reference and reservation contained in or fairly disclosed by any instrument which forms an essential link in the chain of title under which he claims." (emphasis added). Wessels v. Rio Bravo Oil Co., 250 S.W.2d 668 (Tex.Civ.App.–Eastland 1952, writ ref'd). * * *

Since it was the duty of Gulf and Superior to make investigation of the operating agreement, they are also charged with notice of the contents of the operating agreement. Subparagraph 31.B. makes a clear reference to the November 15, 1966, letter agreement and therefore Gulf and Superior were charged with the duty of inspecting that document. We also believe that subparagraph 31.C., when read in conjunction with 31.B., is capable of a construction which would supply a reference to the November 15, 1966, letter agreement. However, it is unnecessary for us to decide this question in light of the unambiguous reference made in subparagraph 31.B.

It is not unusual for an operating agreement, as was the case here, to not be placed of record. An entirely different result might obtain on the issue of notice if, upon diligent inquiry and search, Gulf and Superior were simply unable to obtain a copy of the operating agreement. However, Gulf and Superior have never contended such was the case, and there is evidence to the effect that Gulf and Superior had a copy of the operating agreement in their files. Therefore, we hold that the reference to the March 1, 1968, operating agreement contained in the May 22, 1973, assignment from Mobil to Gulf and Superior, as a matter of law, charged Gulf and Superior with the duty of inspecting said agreement. As a result, Gulf and Superior were charged with notice of the November 15, 1966, letter agreement and the equitable claim of Westland, and cannot enjoy the status of innocent purchasers.

We next address the issue of whether paragraph 5 of the November 15, 1966, letter agreement supplies a legally sufficient description of the property covered thereby. It is an agreement to assign an interest in an oil and gas leasehold estate, and therefore is subject to the requirements of the statute of frauds as set out in section 26.01 of the Texas Business and Commerce Code. Tex.Bus. and Com.Code Ann. § 26.01 (Supp.1980–1981); The paragraph actually contains two different descriptions which are separated by the word "or." To illustrate this, we will insert each description separately into the body of paragraph 5. Employing this method, the first description would read as follows:

If any of the parties hereto, their representatives or assigns, acquire *any additional leasehold interests affecting any of the lands covered by said farmout agreement,* * * *, such shall be subject to the terms and provisions of this agreement,

(emphasis added). Westland contends this constitutes a sufficient description of sections 19, 23 and 24, thereby rendering the area of mutual interest agreement enforceable as to those sections.

The second description would provide: If any of the parties hereto, their representatives or assigns, acquire * * * any additional interest from Mobil Oil Corporation *under lands in the area of the farmout acreage,* such shall be subject to the terms and provisions of this agreement; * * *

(emphasis added). Westland contends this second description applies to sections 25, 26 and 30, and is legally sufficient to permit enforcement of the area of mutual interest agreement as to those three sections.

We believe the first description is legally sufficient to satisfy the statute of frauds. The operative words are "leasehold interests affecting any of the lands covered by said farmout." In the introductory paragraph to the November 15, 1966, letter agreement, the parties expressly agreed that the Mobil/Westland farmout would be referred to as "said farmout." Copies of that instrument were attached to the November 15, 1966, letter agreement. The caption to the Mobil/Westland farmout agreement reads as follows:

> PROPOSED FARMOUT OF MOBIL'S LEASEHOLD INTEREST IN THE DRILLSITE SECTION AND AN UNDIVIDED ONE–HALF OF OUR LEASEHOLD INTEREST IN SECTIONS 7, 18 and 19, BLOCK 48, TWP. 8, T. & P., AND SECTIONS 13, 23 and 24, BLOCK 49, TWP. 8, T. & P. LESS THE DRILLSITE SECTION FOR THE DRILLING OF A PROJECTED ELLENBURGER TEST TO BE LO- CATED IN THE SE 1/4 SECTION 13, BLOCK 49, TWP. 8, T. & P. RY. CO. SURVEY, PECOS COUNTY, TEXAS (MOC T–29063, T– 29165, T–30931–C, T–31229–C, D, AND T–31230–D, E, G–O).

In Wilson v. Fisher, 144 Tex. 53, 188 S.W.2d 150 (1945) this court stated:

> In so far as the description of the property is concerned the writing must furnish within itself, *or by reference to some other existing writing,* the means or data by which the particular land to be conveyed may be identified with reasonable certainty.

* * *

We believe that the words "said farmout" sufficiently provide that nucleus of description. The introductory paragraph defines "said farmout" and one is expressly directed to an instrument which contains an adequate legal description. Therefore, the area of mutual interest agreement pro- vides a description of sections 19, 23 and 24 which is legally sufficient.

We reach a different conclusion with respect to the second description. The phrase "lands in the area of the farmout acreage" does not meet the test set out above. Westland contends that one should substitute "Rojo Caballos Area" for the word "area" contained in the phrase recited above. Westland then argues that parol evidence could be introduced to supply a legal description for "Rojo Caballos Area."

Westland's argument asks us to indulge in an impermissible infer- ence. The description necessary to meet the requirements of the statute of frauds cannot be arrived at from tenuous inferences and presumptions of doubtful validity. When resort to extrinsic evidence is proper, it should be used only for the purpose of identifying the land with reasonable certainty from the data in the memorandum, and not for the purpose of supplying its location or description. There is nothing contained within the November 15, 1966, letter agreement which necessarily leads to the conclusion that "area" means "Rojo Caballos Area." We believe that "lands in the area of the farmout acreage" simply means lands in close proximity to the farmout acreage. Such a description, under the established authority, is not legally sufficient. We hold the second description contained within paragraph 5 of the November 15, 1966, letter agreement is within the statute of frauds and unenforceable. Accordingly, the area of mutual interest agreement cannot be enforced with respect to sections 25, 26 and 30.

* * *

Gulf and Superior also contend that the area of mutual interest agreement is a personal covenant between Westland and C & K, and therefore not binding upon them as assignees of C & K. They argue that privity of estate does not exist, and the covenant does not "touch and concern" the land. We disagree. The agreement contained within paragraph 5 of the November 15, 1966, letter agreement is a contract to convey interests in oil and gas leases. Such an agreement, at least with respect to sections 19, 23 and 24, involved covenants running with the land.

In order for the covenant to run with the land there must be privity of estate between the parties to the agreement. This means there must be a mutual or successive relationship to the same rights of property. Privity of estate exists in this case by virtue of the assignment of sections 19, 23 and 24 to Gulf and Superior.

We further believe that the agreement touches and concerns the land. The tests involved in making this determination are far from absolute. The courts have consistently relied upon rather general statements in their analyses of the touch and concern requirement. As stated in Reno, *Covenants, Rents and Public Rights,* 2 Amer.L. of Prop. § 9.4 (1952):

> One of the two often cited statements of the requirement is that a covenant will run "if it affected the nature, quality or value of the thing demised, independently of collateral circumstances, or if it affected the mode of enjoying it" * * *.

It has also been said,

> If the promisor's legal relations in respect to the land in question are lessened—his legal interest as owner rendered less valuable by the promise—the burden of the covenant touches or concerns that land; if the promisee's legal relations in respect to that land are increased—his legal interest as owner rendered more value by the promise—the benefit of the covenant touches or concerns the land.

Bigelow, The Content of Covenants in Leases, 12 Mich.L.Rev. 639 (1914); Williams, Restrictions on the Use of Land: Covenants Running with the Land at Law, 27 Tex.L.Rev. 419 (1949).

We believe that the promise to convey the prescribed interests in the leases covering sections 19, 23 and 24 clearly affected the nature and value of the estate conveyed to C & K. It burdened the promisor's estate and could be considered to have rendered it less valuable. Accordingly, we are of the opinion that the covenant affecting Gulf and Superior's interest in sections 19, 23 and 24 was one which runs with the land.

The judgment of the court of appeals is reversed. We render judgment that Gulf and Superior were on notice of the equitable claim of Westland, and that the November 15, 1966, letter agreement is enforceable as to Section 19, Block 48, and Sections 23 and 24, Block 49, and unenforceable as to Sections 25 and 26, Block 49, and Section 30, Block 48.

* * *

WALLACE, JUSTICE, dissenting.

I respectfully dissent. While I agree with the Court's holding that the description contained in Paragraph 5 of the November 15 Letter Agreement is sufficient to satisfy the Statute of Frauds as to sections 19, 23, and 24, I do not agree with the holding that Gulf and Superior were on notice, as a matter of law, of the equitable claim of Westland.

* * *

It is helpful to begin with the assignment through which Gulf and Superior gained title and work backward to see exactly what Gulf and Superior knew or should have known. To begin with, Gulf and Superior received an assignment dated May 22, 1973, from Mobil Oil of 60% of its interest in sections 19, 23, 24, 26 & 31, and 100% of its interest in section 25. This assignment was expressly made subject to the March 1, 1968 operating agreement. Gulf and Superior received this assignment by drilling a well on section 25 and earning the acreage pursuant to farmout agreements from Mobil, Chambers/Kennedy (C & K), and others. The operating agreement contains two possible references to the November 15 Letter Agreement. Paragraph 31B states:

> * * * (i)n the event of any conflict between this contract and the Farmout Letter Agreement dated August 4, 1966, between Mobil Oil Corporation and Westland Oil Development, as amended by Letter dated August 29, 1966 and November 11, 1966 and a Letter Agreement between Chambers & Kennedy and Westland Oil Development Corporation and L.C. Kung dated November 15, 1966, then such prior agreements shall prevail over this Agreement.

Paragraph 31C states the following:

Exhibit A lists all of the parties, and their * * * interests * * *. Such interests are specifically subject to all terms, conditions, and reservations set forth in that Farmout Agreement Letter dated August 4, 1966 between

Mobil Oil Corporation and Westland Development Corporation as amended and that certain assignment dated March 7, 1968 from Mobil to C. Fred Chambers and W.D. Kennedy and Union Texas Petroleum.

It is the letter agreement dated November 15, 1966 between Westland/Kung and Chambers/Kennedy which contains the area of mutual interest clause which Westland contends Gulf and Superior are on notice of and therefore bound by.

* * * [T]he duty of inquiry extends only to matters which are fairly suggested by the facts really known. * * * An operating agreement and a "conflict between an operating agreement and a letter agreement" do not necessarily suggest a title matter. As pointed out by the Court of Appeals, the function of an operating agreement is to explain in detail the operation between the various interests in the development of a tract for economical production of the minerals, not to establish interests of any kind. Therefore, a reference to any conflict with an operating agreement might well have alerted a reasonably diligent purchaser to check the letter agreement if he was concerned with the operations, not for title reasons. Nor does paragraph 31B in any way suggest that the letter agreement between C & K and Westland involves title. The reference in 31C does not even refer to the November 15, Letter Agreement between Westland and C & K, unless one assumes the words "as amended," refers to it. However, "as amended," just as logically refers only to the actual amendments to the farmout between Mobil and Westland of August 29, 1966, and November 11, 1966. The letter agreement between Westland and C & K is not an amendment to the agreement between Mobil and Westland, but a new agreement between different parties.

* * * Ordinarily, summary judgment will not be awarded where the issue is inherently one for a jury, such as the exercise of judgment. Actual notice is normally a question of fact, it will only become a question of law when there is no room for ordinary minds to differ as to the proper conclusion to be drawn from the evidence.

I am not willing to hold that as a matter of law, Gulf and Superior were on notice of an equitable right expressed in an unrecorded farmout agreement between Westland/Kung and Chambers/Kennedy, ambiguously referred to in an operating agreement between Chambers/Kennedy and Union Texas Petroleum, which was expressly referred to in the assignment from Mobil to Gulf and Superior. That is a question of fact, raised by the summary judgment proof and properly reserved for the trier of fact.

* * *

* * * I would hold that a question of fact remains for the trier of fact to decide and, therefore, would remand the cause to the trial court on the issue of notice.

NOTES

1. How far does the notice requirement extend? If the November 15 letter had not itself contained the area of mutual interest provision but rather had made reference to yet another document that contained the provision, would the defendants still have been on notice of the clause as a matter of law?

2. An area of mutual interest clause usually provides that both parties to a farmout will share in any future leases that either acquires in a defined geographical area. In the principal case, Gulf and Superior were not parties to the agreement containing the clause, but the court nonetheless held that it could be enforced against them as a covenant running with the land. It should be noted that the clause dealt with land other than that assigned to the defendants. Should such a clause have been deemed to "touch and concern" the land actually assigned? For a criticism of both the notice and covenant aspects of the case, see Angus Earl McSwain, Note, Westland Oil Development Corp. v. Gulf Oil: New Uncertainties as to Scope of Title Search, 35 Baylor L.Rev. 629 (1983).

In Grimes v. Walsh & Watts, Inc., 649 S.W.2d 724 (Tex.App.1983, writ refused n.r.e.), an area of mutual interest clause was ruled unenforceable as a covenant running with the land because privity of estate was lacking. The court held that such a clause was enforceable as a covenant only so long as the lease, which was the subject of the parties' agreement, was in existence. Once the original lease terminated, the clause could be enforced, if at all, only as a personal obligation.

3. In First National Bank & Trust v. Sidwell Corp., 678 P.2d 118 (Kan. 1984), an area of mutual interest agreement was entered into between a geologist, who was engaged in a joint venture with two other persons, and a petroleum landman. The agreement stated that the parties contemplated the acquisition of additional acreage and provided that if the landman acquired any oil and gas leases on the acreage, he would assign an undivided one-fourth interest in the leases to the geologist, free of cost; if the geologist acquired leases on the acreage, the landman could receive an assignment of an undivided three-fourths interest upon payment of the bonus and broker's commission. The landman, in appealing the imposition of a constructive trust against him for the benefit of the two deceased joint venturers, argued that the area of mutual interest clause violated the rule against perpetuities. The Kansas Supreme Court rejected that argument on the ground that the agreement imposed purely contractual obligations and did not involve the vesting of future interests in realty.

The same reasoning was used to uphold a similar area of mutual interest clause in Courseview, Inc. v. Phillips Petroleum Co., 258 S.W.2d 391 (Tex.Civ. App.–Galveston 1953), on appeal after remand 298 S.W.2d 890 (Tex.Civ.App.– Galveston 1957), aff'd 312 S.W.2d 197 (Tex. 1957).

4. There are other doctrines, such as the statute of frauds and the common law rule against restraints on alienation, that may serve as the basis for attacking an area of mutual interest clause. For an analysis of these

doctrines and suggestions for drafting, see Dante L. Zarlengo, Area of Mutual Interest Clauses Regarding Oil and Gas Properties: Analysis, Drafting and Procedure, 28 Rocky Mtn.Min.L.Inst. 837 (1982).

D. FINANCING OIL AND GAS TRANSACTIONS[4]

Numerous methods are used in the oil and gas industry to finance the acquisition of acreage for development, as well as the development of acreage into producing oil and gas properties. While various exotic financing techniques exist, such as the sale of net profits interests and volumetric production payments, the establishment of royalty trusts, or structuring credit agreements with equity conversion rights or other equity kickers, the most common structure used by oil and gas exploration and production companies (outside of equity financing by the operating company itself) is the senior secured reserve based credit agreement (Credit Agreement) from a lender or syndicate of lenders.

While the Credit Agreement may sound fairly simple, there is a great deal of negotiation related to the document itself and the Credit Agreement is only one of many documents that are prepared in connection with a standard secured credit facility. In addition, before a lender is willing to advance any funds to a borrower, the lender and its counsel must complete the due diligence process, which may drive a number of changes to both the Credit Agreement and the other loan documents.

1. DILIGENCE DOCUMENTS

Other than a lender's discussions with a potential borrower and a cursory review of the information a potential borrower provides, formal due diligence typically begins contemporaneously with or immediately after a term sheet and commitment letter have been signed by the lender and the borrower. Conducting diligence for oil and gas transactions includes many of the standard document reviews that would be conducted in virtually any loan transaction, including a review of the borrower's organizational structure, formation and governance documents, qualifications to do business, lien searches, etc. However, the following are some of the key oil and gas specific diligence reviews that should be completed prior to closing and funding under the Credit Agreement.

(a) Title Review

The preferred method to determine the current ownership of the leases and related mineral interests that will be pledged to secure the obligations incurred by a borrower under a Credit Agreement is a mineral interest title opinion (Title Opinion) prepared by counsel licensed in the jurisdiction in which the underlying minerals are located. Depending on

---

4. The authors thank Michael D. Cuda, Senior Counsel in the Dallas, Texas office of Patton Boggs LLP, for preparing this section.

the jurisdiction, the Title Opinion will either track the mineral interests back to the original land grant from the state, territory or country (the "sovereignty of the soil") or to a statutorily determined time period prior to which a claims limitation period applies.

Title Opinions in form and substance acceptable to the lenders (or the agent for the lenders in a syndicated transaction) with respect to a certain percentage of the properties included in the Credit Agreement borrowing base are expected in large syndicated credit facilities. Generally, these Title Opinions must cover between 60% and 100% of the value of borrowing base credited properties. Lender's counsel must review each Title Opinion to determine whether there are any material exceptions or qualifications to the mineral interests owned by the borrower. Title Opinions are expensive and time consuming to prepare. If a borrower does not have Title Opinions available for closing, the lender must decide whether Title Opinions will be required (which can be driven by internal lender policies) or whether there are alternative forms of title evidence that are acceptable to the lenders for closing.

Assuming that Title Opinions are not available for the borrower's properties, a lender and its counsel may look to other third party documentation for evidence that a borrower owns a particular mineral interest. If the borrower is not the operator and the properties are producing oil or gas, lenders generally will rely on division orders from the operator to the borrower that set out the working interest and net revenue interest owned by the borrower. If the borrower does not have the division order and can not obtain a copy from the operator on a timely basis, the lender may be willing to accept copies of check stubs from distributions that have been made to the borrower, provided that the check stubs contain working interest and net revenue interest information regarding the borrower's ownership of the minerals.

While other third party evidence of title may be available, such as evidence of joint interest billing reimbursements, if all else fails, the lender may be willing to accept a truncated form of title review that tracks the mineral interests transferred to the borrower back through a 20 to 30 year limitations period (depending on the state), provided that the transfers come from parties unrelated to the borrower. Note that title to oil and gas properties may be acquired in a manner that does not provide a Title Opinion, such as a mineral interest auction. In those cases, it is up to the lender and its counsel to determine whether there is adequate third party evidence of ownership to provide financing to the borrower.

(b) Oil and Gas Leases

The terms of individual oil and gas leases (Lease(s)) will have a significant effect on the value of the underlying mineral interests. If a Title Opinion has been issued, the key terms (and any defects) of the Lease(s) are generally summarized in the Title Opinion. Additionally, to the extent that there is production on a leased property, the Lease (or a portion of the Lease) may be held by production. Nevertheless, the lender also must know if any portion of the Lease will expire if the lessor fails to drill within a certain period of time.

The primary and secondary terms of the Lease become even more critical if a significant amount of the property is in early stages of development. In this case, it is crucial that the lender structure the Credit Agreement to allow the borrower access to funds for continued development, but also to make sure that the loan matures (or an event of default is triggered) early enough to allow the lender time to foreclose on the property and sell it to an operator that can develop the property before the Leases expire.

(c) Joint Operating Agreements

Any joint operating agreements ("JOA") should be reviewed to determine the penalties to which a non-operator is subject for failure to reimburse a joint interest billing (JIB) invoice in a timely manner. The lender should be aware that generally, the failure to reimburse a JIB under the JOA allows the operator to place a lien on the non-operator's interest, and this lien will prime a lender's perfected security interest under the collateral documents. Additionally, the JOA will generally provide that the operator is entitled to foreclose on the lien and sell the non-operator's interest to repay the unpaid obligations under the JOA.

(d) Farm-in—Farm-out Agreements

Farm-in and Farm-out Agreements (sometimes spelled "farmin" and "farmout," respectively) should be reviewed to determine whether a borrower will acquire additional lease interests as a result of testing and drilling operations on behalf of the lessee (a Farm-in Agreement) or whether the borrower may give up a portion of the lender's collateral as the result of a third party performing testing and drilling operations on a lease owned by the borrower (a Farm-out Agreement). If the borrower is the farmee under a Farm-in Agreement, the lender may want to limit the amount the borrower can invest in testing and drilling under the Farm-in Agreement unless the borrower is obligated to pledge any earned interest to the lender as a part of the collateral pool. In the case of a Farm-out Agreement, the lender must understand that it may be required to release certain pledged collateral if a non-borrower farmee earns an interest in pledged leases under the terms of the Farm-out Agreement.

(e) Hedging Agreements

If a borrower holds interests in oil or gas producing properties, the borrower may have already entered into hedging agreements ("Hedges") with a commodity hedge party. A Hedge is designed to allow an oil or gas producer (or a borrower/producer for its own benefit and the benefit of its lender) to lock in a price today for the delivery of oil or gas at some predetermined time in the future. Hedges are extremely common for exploration and production companies and in many cases, are required as a condition to the lender advancing funds under a Credit Agreement.

Hedges are designed to mitigate losses as the result of a significant drop in the price of oil or gas. By locking in a delivery price today, a borrower knows that as long as they have the production to deliver the oil or gas on the specified future date, the borrower will have a steady revenue source. However, once the Hedge is executed, the borrower is no longer eligible to participate in any continued increase in the price of oil or gas through the delivery date (although some more exotic hedges can allow for this type of upside participation).

When reviewing Hedges, the lender and its counsel should determine whether the contracts are assignable to the lender or any other party and the hedge counter-party's rights to terminate the hedge. Additionally, the lender will want to know the volume of the oil or gas that has been hedged, the Hedge price per barrel or mcf, and the delivery date. Finally, the lender will want to know what impact the Hedge can have on the lender if the lender forecloses on the Hedge or takes the Hedge by assignment from the borrower.

Typically, a Hedge provider will require a borrower to provide collateral to secure any losses that the borrower may incur under the Hedge, such as an inability to deliver the oil or gas on the date delivery is due under the terms of the Hedge. In order to avoid the requirement that the borrower pledge security to a third party, the lender will frequently allow the Hedge provider to share in the collateral pledged to secure the Credit Agreement. If the Hedge provider is allowed to share in the collateral, the borrower, the lender and the Hedge party will generally enter into an intercreditor agreement that spells out the respective rights of each party to receive payments from collateral proceeds in the event that the collateral must be liquidated.

(f) Lien Searches

Lien searches allow a lender to assure itself that it is receiving the priority it expects with respect to the collateral pledged to support the obligations under a Credit Agreement. A secondary benefit of lien searches is that the search may identify financial problems that the borrower is encountering with its suppliers, service providers or taxing authorities.

Lien searches will need to be run in several locations. In connection with UCC filings, searches should be run where the borrower is located. In general, corporations, LLCs and limited partnerships are deemed located in the jurisdiction in which those entities are organized. With respect to individuals or other entities, counsel should consult their local UCC rules for both filing and search provisions. At a minimum, UCC lien searches should be run with the secretary of state of the state in which an entity is organized.

In connection with a borrower's ownership of leases or other mineral interests, because those interests are generally deemed to be real property interests, the county (or parish in Louisiana) records must be searched in the county or parish in which the leases or mineral interests are located.

Special rules apply to offshore leases in federal waters, however ownership transfers (but not security interest perfection) can be checked with the Bureau of Ocean Energy Management (formerly the Bureau of Ocean Energy Management, Regulation and Enforcement, which was previously the Mineral Management Service). Lender's counsel will likely require real property lien searches in multiple counties (and possibly multiple states depending on the location of the lease) to confirm that no other liens have been granted on leases in federal waters.

(g) Environmental

Environmental diligence has become increasingly important over the last several decades due to the expanding scope and detail of regulation. A single unresolved environmental problem can doom the loan transaction due to the uncertain remediation costs. Lender's counsel should request disclosure of any environmental issues known to the borrower, and will need to review all Phase One Environmental Assessments performed on the proposed collateral. To the extent that a Phase One Environmental Assessment has identified environmental issues, a Phase Two Environmental Assessment may be necessary, and environmental specialists should be consulted. Lenders may also have specific internal environmental policies that must be considered during the diligence phase.

2. CREDIT AGREEMENTS

Generally, as the due diligence is being conducted, the Credit Agreement is being drafted in accordance with the terms and conditions set forth in the term sheet that was delivered along with the executed commitment letter. The Credit Agreement is the primary document used to determine the deliveries the borrower must make to close the transaction (conditions precedent); the preliminary and certain ongoing standards the borrower must meet (current and ongoing representations and warranties); the loan amount available to the borrower; the methods by which a loan can be advanced; the ongoing performance obligations of the borrower (affirmative and negative covenants); events of default; and remedies of the lender after an event of default. As additional information about the borrower, the borrower's operations or the borrower's assets is uncovered while conducting due diligence, the provisions of the Credit Agreement may be modified from the terms outlined in the term sheet to reflect the borrower's actual operations and assets.

Exploration and production Credit Agreements are asset based loans and are secured by a pledge of the borrower's assets including, but not limited to owned leases and other mineral interests. Other assets such as pipelines on the properties, drilling or storage equipment, and Hedges and other contract rights may also be pledged as collateral; however, the value of the leases and other mineral interests form the basis of the borrowing base. Additionally, a typical Credit Agreement covenant will require the borrower to enter into Hedges to support the collateral values against which the lender is advancing funds.

One of the closing conditions of the Credit Agreement will require the borrower to deliver a current reserve report ("Reserve Report") to the lender setting out the value of the mineral interests owned by the borrower. The Reserve Report must be prepared by an independent third party oil and gas reservoir engineer and it will be prepared with the assumptions that the lender requires. The Reserve Report will always value the Proved, Developed, and Producing ("PDP") reserves, generally over a ten year horizon, and will then discount those cash flows to a present value based on the then current interest rate environment. In a very low interest rate environment, a 9% to 10% discount rate will be applied. The Reserve Report will also generally provide a discounted cash flow value for the Proved, Developed and Non–Producing ("PDNP") reserves as well as the Proved, Undeveloped ("PUD") reserves. The Reserve Report is generally required to be updated and delivered to the lender every six months, and the borrowing base is adjusted according to the new Reserve Report calculations.

Once the lender receives the Reserve Report, the lender's in-house engineer or energy staff then reviews and evaluates the report. At a small financial institution, this review may be conducted by a knowledgeable loan officer. A multiple lender Credit Agreement with an administrative agent may have a group of "technical banks" with expertise in the industry and engineering staffs that review the Reserve Report and related documents. In either case, a typical borrowing base advance rate will fall between 50% and 60% of the discounted present value set out in the Reserve Report, assuming that the lender has a lien on all the assets included in the Reserve Report.

The Credit Agreement will also set forth additional conditions to the effectiveness of the document and the obligation of the lender to make advances under the document. While each of the conditions precedent to the effectiveness of the Credit Agreement are important, the execution and delivery of the collateral documents in proper form are generally considered to be the most important.

3. COLLATERAL DOCUMENTS AND PERFECTION OF LIENS

(a) Notes

Depending on the nature of the Credit Agreement, a note may or may not be required. Typically, the Credit Agreement is the best evidence of the terms and conditions of the loan repayment terms, however some lenders prefer that a separate note be prepared. Most large syndicated credit transactions are "noteless" and a note is only executed by the borrower for lenders that specifically request a note for internal documentation purposes.

(b) Mortgages and Deeds of Trust

Mortgages and deeds of trust (together, Mortgages) are prepared to grant a security interest in real property interests, such as leases (and in most states, net profits interests). Whether a mortgage or deed of trust is the appropriate document to perfect a security interest in an oil and gas interest is a matter of state law, although some states allow either document to be used. In order to perfect a security interest in oil and gas interests, a properly drafted Mortgage must be filed in the county (or parish) and state in which the underlying oil and gas interest is located. Because these documents are governed by local state law, local counsel should always be consulted in order to conform a negotiated Mortgage to the requirements of local law. Generally, local counsel is requested to comment only on those provisions in the document that would affect the perfection or enforceability of the Mortgage and to issue a legal opinion that the form of the document is enforceable, and upon proper filing, would grant the lender a perfected security interest in the collateral.

Several provisions of any Mortgage deserve special attention, because a minor error can cause significant issues for the lender (and by extension, its counsel). While it sounds simple, always review the granting clause to make sure that the borrower is actually *granting* a security interest in the collateral the lender expects to receive. Mortgages in oil and gas transactions generally also serve as security agreements. In this case, there are generally two separate grants of a security interest, one for the interests in real property and one for the standard UCC personal property interests. If the document is also serving as a security agreement, make sure that Hedges are specifically included as a part of the contract rights pledged by the borrower.

Lender's counsel should confirm that the debt that the collateral is being pledged to secure properly tracks to all the obligations being incurred by the borrower under the Credit Agreement. In particular, make sure that any Hedge obligations are covered by the Mortgage.

Finally, if at all possible, include both the specific lease descriptions and oil and gas well descriptions as the mortgaged property being pledged to secure the obligations under the Credit Agreement. If only the producing well descriptions are included as security, new wells that are drilled and producing will not secure the indebtedness under the Credit Agreement. Additionally, as wells produce, they also deplete their reserves. Hence, if the lender does not adequately tie the loan amortization schedule to well depletion (or if the Reserve Report does not accurately estimate well depletion), the lender may find itself undersecured. Therefore, the best practice is to include both well and lease descriptions on the exhibits to the Mortgage.

(c) Pledge Agreement and Equity Securities

A pledge agreement is a collateral document under which a borrower or other securities owner pledges a security interest in equity securities (i.e. stock, LLC member interests, partnership interests, etc.). Generally, a borrower will not be executing a pledge agreement unless it owns subsidiaries. However, the parent entity of the borrower, or individual equity owners, if the borrower is owned by individuals, will execute a pledge agreement in favor of the lender pledging all their respective equity interests in the borrower. The pledge agreement is helpful to a lender in a foreclosure scenario because it makes it easier for the lender to liquidate the borrower and its subsidiaries. If stock certificates have been issued, the lender will need to take physical possession of the certificates to be perfected. Additionally, the lender will require each of the equity owners to execute a "stock power" in blank in favor of the lender. The stock power is a document executed by an equity owner that directs an equity issuer (the borrower, for example) to transfer the equity securities evidencing ownership of the borrower into the name of the lender, and issue new stock certificates naming the lender as the securities owner. "Stop transfer letters" executed by the securities owner and directing the securities issuer not to transfer ownership of the securities on the books and records of the securities issuer may also be required by the lender, particularly if the equity interests are "uncertificated". As discussed above, Lender's counsel should carefully review the debt description that the collateral pledged under the pledge agreement secures

(d) Guaranties

A guaranty may be required by a lender for additional borrower financial support. Guarantees in large syndicated credit facilities may be required of a subsidiary of the borrower, but generally would not be required of the borrower's parent corporation. However, is not unusual for a lender to require a family owned corporate borrower to have its debt guaranteed by some or all of the family members. Additionally, a lender may require a guaranty of the owners of relatively new exploration and production company. A guaranty may be "unlimited" (pay all obligations under all circumstances) or "limited" (the limitations, such as a set dollar amount, will be set forth in the guaranty). Guarantees may take many forms with many limitations which can be negotiated between the lender and the proposed guarantors.

(e) Deposit Account Control Agreements

A deposit account control agreement ("DACA") may be necessary if the borrower has bank accounts at a financial institution other than the lender. The DACA is a three party agreement executed by the borrower, the depository bank and the lender pursuant to which the borrower grants the lender the ability to direct and control the deposit account after the occurrence of certain events, most commonly, an event of default under the Credit Agreement. Prior to an event of default, the depository bank is exercising "control" over the funds in the account on behalf of the lender so that the lender's security interest in the account is perfected under the UCC (possession required for perfection of cash). Under the terms of the

DACA, after the occurrence of an event of default, the lender is authorized to notify the depository bank of the event of default and to direct the depository bank with respect to the disposition of the funds in the account.

(f) Letters in Lieu of Transfer

Letters in lieu of transfer (Letters in Lieu) are designed to allow a lender to act quickly and without the additional consultation of the borrower to direct production payments into the account of the lender's choosing. Letters in Lieu are executed in blank by the borrower at closing and specifically grant the lender the authority to direct a well operator to make all future production payments to any party or into any account set out in the Letter in Lieu delivered to the operator. Letters in Lieu are generally used only after an event of default has occurred under the Credit Agreement and the lender has been unable to negotiate an acceptable resolution to the default.

(g) UCC–1 Financing Statements

A financing statement is generally filed in the offices of the secretary of state (or equivalent) of the jurisdiction in which the borrower is organized. The financing statement should include the non-real estate collateral in which the borrower has granted a security interest to the lender under the Mortgage (or security agreement if used separately) as well as the pledge agreement. The financing statement should track the language from the collateral description in the mortgage/security agreement and pledge agreement, and should specifically include the "proceeds" therefrom. Ultimately, if (i) the borrower has rights in the collateral, (ii) the lender has given the borrower value for the collateral pledge, and (iii) a proper grant of an interest in the collateral is contained in the Mortgage/security agreement and/or pledge agreement, upon filing the financing statement in the proper filing office, the lender will have a "perfected" security interest in the pledged collateral.

NOTES

1. What effect is an increasing interest rate environment likely to have on a borrower's borrowing base under a reserve based Credit Agreement? Will a 1% increase in interest rates have only a 1% impact on the borrowing base?

2. Why would a lender be interested in a borrower using loan proceeds in connection with a Farm-in Agreement. What types of notices should a borrower be required to give a lender with respect to a Farm-in Agreement? Commencement of drilling? Completion of a well? Production from the well? The time of transfer of the interest to the farmee? What actions should a lender take when the farmee actually earns its interest in the minerals?

3. If a borrower successfully completes its obligations under a Farm-in Agreement, what adjustments might be necessary to the borrowing base? Will any adjustments to the borrowing base be necessary if a farmee successfully completes its obligations under a Farm-out Agreement?

4. Why would a lender require a borrower to enter into a Hedge for the benefit of the lenders? If a Hedge is such a good idea, why do lenders generally place a cap on the maximum amount of production that a borrower may hedge against? Are there times that hedging more than current production may be a good idea?

5. The ownership and transfer of lease interests in federal waters is filed with the Bureau of Ocean Energy Management. The perfection of a security interests in the same lease interests as collateral is governed by state law filing rules. However, the county (or parish) and sometimes the state in which the filing is required may not be entirely clear, requiring lenders to file Mortgages in multiple states and counties. See generally, Oil, Gas and Energy Resources Law Section Report, State Bar of Texas, Vol. 27, No. 2, December 2002.

E.   OPERATING AGREEMENTS AND RELATED DOCUMENTS

Joint ownership of development rights may come about in a variety of ways. Cotenants of a mineral estate may lease their interests to different companies, or companies leasing adjacent acreage may be required to pool their leases to form a standard sized spacing unit. More commonly, joint ownership is the result of a deliberate decision to spread the cost and risk of drilling and development. The nature of the current petroleum industry makes such decisions increasingly necessary. Because the lower continental United States has been thoroughly explored, most major exploratory efforts are offshore or in harsh Arctic environments where the initial capital investment is quite high or else in emerging countries where there are considerable political risks. Even where oil or gas is known to exist in large quantities in the United States, such as in shale formations, the hydrocarbons can frequently be recovered only by the use of highly expensive technology, such as that involved horizontal drilling coupled with fracing operation or through the use of tertiary recovery operations.

Few companies are willing to assume the entire risk or entire cost of such undertakings. Hence a lessee with a promising "prospect" may farm out part of its acreage, or it may do the drilling itself, but only after selling interests in the leasehold to investors or to other companies. Alternatively, several companies that already have leases in the area may agree to combine their efforts for exploratory and developmental purposes.

Whenever joint operations are contemplated, either as the result of multiple ownership of a single lease or of combining two or more leases for drilling and development purposes, an agreement has to be reached on a variety of matters including initial drilling, payment of expenses, operation of the well, division of production, and further development of the property. The operating agreement serves this function. It describes the geographic area that it covers[5] and specifies the fractional interests owned

---

5. The agreement designates this as the Contract Area. In some older agreements, it is called the Unit Area or some similar term.

in this area by the various contracting parties. Typically one of these parties is designated the operator, and the authority to incur expenses and make operational decisions is delegated to it. Occasionally, however, a party, such as the holder of leases who has assigned all of its interest in the leases to investors, is named as operator. Such a party has standing to enforce the operating agreement or bring suit on behalf of the participants, even though it lacks any interest in the area covered by the JOA. See Basic Energy Service, Inc. v. D–S–B Properties, Inc., 367 S.W.3d 254 (Tex.App.–Tyler 2011); Long v. Rim Operating, Inc., 345 S.W.3d 79 (Tex.App.–Eastland 2011). The other contracting parties are referred to as nonoperators. Each nonoperator's share of both costs and production is usually based on his fractional interest in the contract area.

Several forms for operating agreements are available, and some companies have developed agreements that are designed for their particular needs. The most widely used form for on-shore operations is the Model Form Operating Agreement developed by the American Association of Petroleum Landmen. Originally developed in 1956, it was revised in 1977, 1982, and again in 1989. Like any standardized form, it obviously does not contain provisions that fit every situation or that are necessarily acceptable to all the parties to an operating agreement. This is especially the case if the parties plan on drilling a horizontal well; for the model forms were drafted entirely in the context of traditional vertical wells, and their provisions and definitions are not adapted to horizontal drilling. Nonetheless, many attorney use an existing model form as a basis for a JOA for horizontal drilling, even though extensive modifications are necessary.

1. OPERATOR AUTHORITY AND RESPONSIBILITY

A Joint Operating Agreement is often entered into after some period of discussion and negotiation among the participants. Whether they are co-lessees of pooled mineral interests, investors who are participating in a promoted prospect for the first time, or experienced companies that have decided to undertake a high risk or high cost project jointly, before executing a formal agreement the participants will make some initial decisions, such as the geographic scope of the agreement, and the location and depth of the first well. Horizontal wells often present special problems because it may be difficult to determine in advance the exact length of the lateral extension of the well, especially if the formation is very deep, and whether lateral extensions will be possible, even if the initial drilling proves highly successful. Because unexpected faulting or other unanticipated geological problems may be encountered, one commentator has suggested that, as in the case of farmouts, the operator may want to insert a clause providing that the operator has complied with the initial-well provision if the distance drilled equals a specified percentage, such as 50% of the length decided upon by the parties to the JOA. Lamont C. Larsen, "Horizontal Drafting: Why Your Form JOA May Not Be Adequate for

Your Company's Horizontal Drilling Program," 48 RMMLF J. 51, 63 (2011).

Such an addition broadens still further the broad authority that the typical JOA gives the operator in carrying out the initial exploration and drilling decisions and acting as manager of all operations within the specified area. The language of article V.A. of the 1989 Model Form, which is fairly representative, provides that the operator "shall conduct and direct and have full control of all operations on the Contract Area * * *" The operator's discretionary authority is not totally unlimited, however. For example, the operator has no power to pool unleased mineral interests or royalties contributed to the Contract Area by non-operators unless it is given express power to do so. See PYR Energy Corp. v. Samson Resources Co., 456 F.Supp.2d 786 (E.D.Tex. 2006), on motion for reconsideration, 470 F.Supp.2d 709 (E.D.Tex. 2007). The operator is required to maintain specified types of insurance at a certain level, and some decisions require input or approval of the nonoperators. The operator cannot incur costs in excess of a stated maximum unless all parties consent, and cannot deepen or plug and abandon a well without consent of the nonoperators. JOAs used in offshore and international operations, where costs and risks are frequently quite high, usually go much further in requiring nonoperator approval or consent to decisions. They usually provide for a management committee composed of representatives of the parties to the agreement and grant it some supervisory power over the operator. The same is true of some JOA's governing horizontal drilling in shale formations.

Most operating agreements give the nonoperators the right to remove the operator, but restrict this right to removal for specified reasons, such as refusal to carry out duties or bankruptcy. The 1989 Model Form authorizes removal "for good cause," which it defines as gross negligence, willful misconduct, material breach of operating standards, or material failure or inability to perform obligations. See generally Brian R. Bjella, Removing the Operator Under the Joint Operating Agreement: Breaking Up Is Hard to Do, 45 Rocky Mtn.Min.L.Inst. 7–1 (1999) and Robert C. Bledsoe, The Operating Agreement: Matters Not Covered or Inadequately Covered, 47 Rocky Mtn.Min.L.Inst. 15–1, 15–19 to 15–22 (2001). A majority vote of at least two nonoperators who together own a majority interest in the Contract Area, exclusive of the operator's interest, is normally required to remove the operator and to select a successor operator. Can the operator avoid removal by assigning a significant part of its working interest to a wholly owned subsidiary who will vote against operator removal? See Pennmark Resources Co. v. Oklahoma Corporation Comm'n, 6 P.3d 1076 (Okla.Civ.App. Div. 3 2000).

Even if an operator can be removed, there are many situations in which a nonoperator may conclude that he has been damaged by operator misconduct or failure to abide by the terms of the JOA. The following case illustrates such a situation.

SHELL ROCKY MOUNTAIN PROD., LLC
v. ULTRA RESOURCES, INC.

415 F.3d 1158 (10th Cir. Wyo. 2005).

SEYMOUR, CIRCUIT JUDGE.

Ultra Resources, Inc. (Ultra) and Shell Rocky Mountain Production, LLC (Shell) operate oil and gas wells on jointly leased properties in Sublette County, Wyoming. Shell filed suit in federal district court requesting a declaration that it is the operator of certain wells on the jointly leased properties pursuant to a previous settlement agreement binding the parties.

* * *

In July 2002, Ultra filed a complaint in Wyoming state court seeking damages for Shell's alleged breach of the Settlement and an order requiring compliance with the Settlement. It also sought reformation of the JOAs to bring them into compliance with the terms of the Settlement. Shell filed a timely notice of removal, prompting the district court to order removal and consolidate the cases.

Ultra's answer to Shell's federal complaint included three counterclaims. The first two were identical to Ultra's state court claims as detailed above. The third alleged that Shell breached the JOAs by imposing excessive drilling and operations costs. Both parties moved for summary judgment. The district court granted Shell's motion, holding that (1) the Settlement granted Shell the right to operate the wells that were located on surface lands in which it held a majority interest, irrespective of the depth to which those wells are drilled; (2) the Settlement provision addressing directional drilling wells created an exception to the Settlement's general rule for designating well operators; and (3) the exculpatory clauses in the JOAs barred Ultra's excessive costs claim against Shell.

* * *

THE EXCESSIVE COSTS ISSUE

Ultra's final contention is that the district court erred in barring its counterclaim against Shell for breach of the JOAs by invoking the exculpatory clause of Article V, section A of each JOA. Article V of each JOA includes two relevant provisions to the breach of contract dispute: section A includes a general conduct requirement with an exculpatory clause, while section D includes a specific duty provision. The exculpatory clause of section A provides that the operator "shall conduct all such operations in a good and workmanlike manner, but it shall have no liability as Operator to the other parties for losses sustained or liabilities incurred, except such as may result from gross negligence or willful misconduct." *Id.* The specific duty provision of section D requires that the operator (1) incur costs that are commensurate with those incurred by other operators in the contract area to drill and complete wells and (2) drill and complete wells at the generally prevailing rates:

> All wells drilled on the Contract Area shall be drilled on a competitive contract basis at the usual rates prevailing in the area. If it so desires, Operator may employ its own tools and equipment in the drilling of wells, but its charges therefor shall not exceed the prevailing rates in the area and the rate of such charges shall be agreed upon by the parties in writing before drilling operations are commenced, and such work shall be performed by Operator under the same terms and conditions as are customary and usual in the area in contracts of independent contractors who are doing work of a similar nature.

Id.

Ultra alleges that Shell, acting as operator, breached the competitive rate provision of section D by charging drilling costs to the nonoperating working interest owners in excess of the prevailing rates in the area. Shell's defense is that section A absolves it of all liability under the JOA unless its actions amount to gross negligence or willful misconduct.[1] Relying exclusively on this court's decision in Palace Exploration Co. v. Petroleum Dev. Co., 316 F.3d 1110 (10th Cir.2003), the district court held that the exculpatory clause of section A bars Ultra's breach of contract claim against Shell. Shell Rocky Mountain Prod., 266 F.Supp.2d at 1337 ("[t]he *Palace* decision applies directly to the issue the Court is deciding here. As the Tenth Circuit held, this exculpatory clause bars suit against an operator for breach of contract, or for anything else other than willful acts or gross negligence"). According to the district court,

> [*Palace*] held that the plaintiff "did not articulate any theory of recovery whereby it could recover legal damages based on breach of contract, for the above-referenced exculpatory clause limited [the defendant's] potential liability to willful acts or acts that resulted from gross negligence."

Id. (citing *Palace*, 316 F.3d at 1114).

The district court's decision to bar Ultra's excessive costs claim on the basis of the exculpatory clause in section A of the JOAs constitutes reversible error for two reasons. First, Ultra is correct to assert that the district court misconstrued the *Palace* decision. The language quoted by the district court is found in the "Background" or facts section of *Palace* and thus does not represent a holding of this court. Indeed, the "facts"

---

1. * * * Shell also contends that Ultra has no standing to complain about well costs because it chose not to participate in the wells once it was made aware of Shell's cost estimate. We disagree. A party that refuses to consent does not forever relinquish its interest in the well to the consenting parties. Relinquishment lasts only until "payout," the point at which the consenting parties have recovered a percentage—here 300%—of the well's cost. This percentage is commonly referred to as the "nonconsent penalty" and is found in Article VI, section B(2) of the JOAs. Once payout is reached, nonconsenting parties are entitled to begin receiving production revenue commensurate with their ownership interest. *Id.* It therefore follows that if Shell is incurring excessive costs, as alleged by Ultra, both the amount of revenue and the date at which Ultra will receive any revenue are directly affected. Thus, Ultra has standing to sue for breach of the competitive rate provision of the JOAs.

quoted from *Palace,* which were recited by this court to explain why the plaintiff selected only certain claims in its complaint, were not relevant to the legal analyses in that case. *Palace* also did not address the scope of the JOA exculpatory clause.[2]

Second, the district court did not discuss relevant circuit case law regarding the scope of JOA exculpatory clauses. In *Amoco Rocmount,* we construed an exculpatory clause—nearly identical to one at issue in the instant case[3]—and its application to breach of *express terms* in JOAs. We rejected the plaintiff's contention that the exculpatory clause applied to "nonperformance of duties imposed by the contract," such as the duties at issue here:

> We would have no trouble upholding the application of [the exculpatory clause] if this case involved tortious acts related to the performance of the contract, such as an error in dealing with a third party that caused loss to the whole operation. But the issues in the instant counterclaim, and in the two other counterclaims to which Amoco seeks to apply the clause, relate to actions taken deliberately and, as the district court found, in breach of the contract involving shifting costs between the contracting [entities]. Applying strict construction we do not believe the exculpatory language applies to these counterclaims. *The breaches at issue here are nonperformance of duties imposed by the contract, and do not hinge on whether the breaching party's failure to perform was negligent, grossly negligent, or willful.*

Id. at 923. Thus, the exculpatory clause has no application to claims that an operator has failed to abide by specific and express contractual duties assigned in the JOA. Rather, it applies to tortious actions and, as the section A clause plainly states, implied duties that come with the covenant of good and workmanlike performance.

---

2. This court's more recent decision in Palace Exploration Co. v. Petroleum Dev. Co., 374 F.3d 951 (10th Cir.2004) (*Palace II*), supports our analysis and clarifies the holding of Palace Exploration Co. v. Petroleum Dev. Co., 316 F.3d 1110 (10th Cir.2003) (*Palace*). In *Palace II,* the court stated:

> Appellant admits that "neither party disputed [at the district court level] that the exculpatory clause of the joint operating agreement set the standard for determining PDC's liability as operator for breach of duties *not affirmatively set forth in the agreements.*"

Id. at 954 n. 2 (emphasis added).

In the instant case, the exculpatory clause does not set the standard for determining Shell's liability for excessive drilling costs because there is *an express contractual provision* directly on point in Article V, section D of the JOAs. *Palace* is inapposite as it involved implied contractual duties rather than express provisions.

3. The clause at issue in Amoco Rocmount Co. v. Anschutz Corp., 7 F.3d 909 (10th Cir.1993), stated in relevant part:

> The Unit Operator shall conduct all operations hereunder in a good and workmanlike manner and in accordance with prudent operating practices but the Unit Operator shall not be liable to the Parties for any losses, costs or expenses resulting from any act or omission on the part of the Unit Operator, its agents or employees, save and except such losses, costs or expenses which shall result from the gross negligence or willful misconduct of the Unit Operator, its agents or employees.

Id. at 922.

Both parties cite law professor and noted oil and gas commentator Gary Conine's article, *The Prudent Operator Standard: Applications Beyond the Oil and Gas Lease*, 41 Nat. Resources J. 23 (2001), as support for their respective interpretations of the scope of the JOAs' exculpatory clause. In addressing exculpatory clauses exactly like the one at issue here, Mr. Conine is concerned with the construction of the requirement that the operator "shall conduct ... operations in a good and workmanlike manner." Conine, *supra*, at 67. According to the professor, the exculpatory language limiting liability to "gross negligence and willful misconduct" implies that a standard more similar to "the business judgment rule" than the "prudent operator" standard should apply to claims that an operator performed in less than a "good and workmanlike manner." *See id.*

A thorough perusal of Mr. Conine's article makes it clear that all of Shell's quotations derived from that source come from the professor's discussion of an operator's liability for performing in less than a "good and workmanlike manner," *i.e.,* the discussion of an operator's liability for breaching the *implied duties* that go hand in hand with the good and workmanlike manner covenant. Indeed, none of Mr. Conine's language cited by Shell is directed at *express contractual provisions*. Moreover, Shell argues that Mr. Conine's article supports its contention that the evolution of standard JOA language included the deletion of an exception for "breach of contract" in the exculpatory clause specifically to preclude a non-operator from suing an operator for breach of contract. Mr. Conine maintains in his article, however, that the deletion of that language occurred as a result of concern that courts would imply standard contract terms, such as the prudent operator standard, into modern JOAs. *See* Conine, *supra,* at 67 & n. 163.

Mr. Conine also addresses this court's *Amoco Rocmount* decision and favorably contrasts it with the more expansive interpretation of the standard exculpatory clause by the Fifth Circuit in *Stine v. Marathon Oil Co.*, 976 F.2d 254 (5th Cir.1992). The *Stine* court held, much like the district court in this case, that the exculpatory clause bars suits for breach of express contractual terms. As Mr. Conine explained:

> [t]he restrictive interpretation of the exculpatory clause in the [*Amoco Rocmount*] decision applies to express provisions in the operating agreement where the parties have clearly negotiated an allocation of risks and costs. Consequently, the one area in which [*Stine*] and [*Amoco Rocmount*] are in agreement is the application of the exculpatory clause to those "operations" that are the subject of the paragraph containing the exculpatory clause. This would include implied duties arising from the covenant to perform those "operations" in a good and workmanlike manner. Restricting [*Stine*] in this fashion allows a more sensible application of the exculpatory clause. It is difficult to perceive why the parties would include explicit and detailed directions on administrative matters that are supplemental to "operations" if they did not intend the operator to be liable for breach

of those matters. This is particularly true because the performance of those administrative duties does not generally involve extraordinary risks against which the operator should be protected. Performance of "operations" and implied duties connected with those operations are another matter. The operating agreement does not function well if the risks associated with these activities are borne by the operator alone.

Conine, *supra,* at 68 n. 168. Incurring costs at a rate commensurate with those of other operators in the area is clearly one of those "administrative duties" that does not "involve extraordinary risks" to Shell. Moreover, it would make little sense for the parties to include detailed directives concerning what the operator can and cannot do in incurring costs if the parties did not intend to be legally bound by them. While a higher standard for breach might apply to drilling, extraction, and other risky "operations" because most operators have the same incentive as non-operators to do well in physical operations, it is nonsensical to apply such a standard to administrative and accounting duties where the operator can profit by cheating, or simply overcharging, its working interest owners. We hold that the exculpatory clause does not bar Ultra's counterclaim for breach of the JOAs.

We AFFIRM the district court's grant of summary judgment to Shell on the operatorship issue, but we REVERSE it on the excessive costs issue and REMAND that claim to the district court for further proceedings consistent with this opinion. We also DENY Shell's motion to supplement its appendix.

NOTES

1.   Stine v. Marathon Oil Co., 976 F.2d 254 (5th Cir. Tex. 1992), which is briefly discussed in the principal case, might be characterized as the highpoint of operator non-liability. The court held that the protection granted an operator by the JOA's exculpatory clause "extends to [the operator's] various administrative and accounting duties, including the recovery of costs under the authority of the JOA. It is clear to us that the protection of the exculpatory clause extends not only to 'acts unique to the operator,' as the district court expressed it, but also to any acts done under the authority of the JOA 'as Operator.' This protection clearly extends to breaches of the JOA." 976 F.2d at 261.

Stine was a diversity case in which the court stated it was applying Texas law. Subsequent to that decision, three Texas courts of appeals have agreed with the position taken in the principal case that a showing of gross negligence or willful misconduct is required only if the complaint is based on the operator's physical activity, and is not necessary for causes of action based on breach of contract or accounting issues. Abraxas Petroleum Corp. v. Hornburg, 20 S.W.3d 741 (Tex. App. 2000); Cone v. Fagadau Energy Corp., 68 S.W.3d 147 (Tex.App.2001) and IP Petroleum Co., Inc. v. Wevanco Energy L.L.C., 116 S.W.3d 888 (Tex.App.2003). See PYR Energy Corp. v. Samson Resources Co., 470 F.Supp.2d 709 (E.D.Tex. 2007) for an excellent discussion of whether in a diversity case a federal district court applying Texas law should follow *Stine* or *Abraxas* in ruling on the scope of the JOA's exculpatory clause.

2. Whether the operator's physical operations constitute gross negligence is a question of fact and requires a finding of extreme misconduct rather than a series of missteps and misdeeds. In IP Petroleum Co., Inc. v. Wevanco Energy L.L.C., 116 S.W.3d 888, 160 Oil & Gas Rep. 1125 (Tex.App.–Hous. 2003), the court held that the operator's failure to prepare a written drilling plan for the well; failure to use drilling mud and getting stuck during the drilling operation as a result; spending over $100,000 trying to get unstuck; failure to run a drill stem test on the well; failure to tell the non-operators and investors that setting pipe would mean the well could not be deepened if it were not productive, and allowing the farmout under which it was operating to expire while it was still operating, were "legally sufficient evidence of negligence," but did "not rise to the level of gross negligence."

3. In *Wendell Reeder v. Wood Country Energy, LLC et al.*, Opinion No. 10–0887, the Texas Supreme Court considered the case of an operator who faced claims by non-operators that he had failed to maintain production in paying quantities, causing oil and gas leases potentially worth millions of dollars to expire and the Texas Railroad Commission to break apart a unit and suspend operations therein. The operations were conducted pursuant to the 1989 form JOA and at trial, a jury found the operator had breached his duty to the non-operators by failing to maintain production in paying quantities. The court of appeals held that the exculpatory clause in the JOA at issue should not have applied to shield the operator from the claims of the non-operators because the clause did not apply to breach of contract claims like the ones before the court, and therefore it was not necessary that the operator first be found to have behaved with either gross negligence or willful misconduct.

The Supreme Court of Texas first noted that, unlike the earlier versions of the form JOA that stated that "[Operator] shall conduct *all such operations* in a good and workmanlike manner, but it shall have no liability as Operator to the other parties for losses sustained or liabilities incurred, except such as may result from gross negligence or willful misconduct," the 1989 form JOA provided that "[Operator] shall conduct *its activities under this agreement* as a reasonable prudent operator, in a good and workmanlike manner, with due diligence and in accordance with good oilfield practice, but in no event shall it have any liability as Operator to the other parties for losses sustained or liabilities incurred except such as may result from gross negligence or willful misconduct." (emphasis added)

Drawing upon the difference between the exculpatory language of "its activities under this agreement" versus "all such operations," and noting that commentators such as Robert Bledsoe (*The Operating Agreement: Matters Not Covered or Inadequately Covered*, 47 ROCKY MTN. MIN. L. INST. § 15.03[1] (2001)) and Wilson Woods (Comment, *The Effect of Exculpatory Clauses in Joint Operating Agreements*, 38 TEX. TECH. L. REV. 211, 214–15 (2005)) have concluded the 1989 form JOA provided for a more expansive exoneration of the Operator, the Supreme Court held the 1989 form JOA exculpatory language broadened the range of operator activities covered by the exculpatory clause.

Specifically, this expended coverage of the 1989 Form JOA exculpatory clause covered not only basic oilfield operations but also all activities covered under the form JOA. The Court opined "The [1989 Form JOA exculpatory clause] implicates a broader scope of conduct following the language of the contract. The agreed standard exempts the operator from liability for its activities unless its liability-causing conduct is due to gross negligence or willful misconduct." After subsequently finding that the operator had not acted with gross negligence or willful misconduct, the Supreme Court reversed and ruled in favor of the operator.

4. Several cases have rejected attempts by non-operators to impose liability upon an operator that moved the drill site some distance from the site initially proposed without obtaining the non-operators' consent to the changed location. Matrix Production Co. v. Ricks Exploration, Inc., 102 P.3d 1285 (N.M.App. 2004) held that the plaintiffs had not met their burden of showing gross negligence or willful misconduct. See also IP Petroleum Co., Inc. v. Wevanco Energy L.L.C., 116 S.W.3d 888 (Tex.App.–Hous. 2003) (involving operator's alleged failure to drill to the depth agreed upon). The Tenth Circuit relied on industry custom and expert testimony that the first proposed location is usually tentative and the drill site is commonly moved without notice and fine-tuned in light of new information. Palace Exploration Co. v. Petroleum Development Co., 316 F.3d 1110 (10th Cir. Okla. 2003).

5. Both parties and the court in the principal case relied heavily upon an article by Professor Gary Conine. In his article Professor Conine argues that the "good and workmanlike" standard imposed by Article V.A. of the JOA should not be equated with the prudent operator standard.

> While both the good and workmanlike standard and the prudent operator standard require reasonable conduct by the performing party, they do not necessarily impose the same specific duties in every contract * * *. It is one thing to say that all oil and gas leases that follow a standard format contain certain implied obligations that must be performed by all lessees. It is quite another to say that any party in the petroleum industry agreeing to perform its responsibilities in a reasonable manner must assume all additional duties that will promote the interests of both parties.

Gary Conine, The Prudent Operator Standard: Applications beyond the Oil and Gas Lease, 41 Nat. Resources J. 23, 46 (2001).

6. Claims by non-operators that the operator owes them a fiduciary duty have had mixed success. For example, in Texas Oil & Gas Corp. v. Hawkins Oil & Gas, Inc., 668 S.W.2d 16 (Ark. 1984) the nonoperator used a theory of fiduciary relationship to obtain the benefit of leases that the operator had acquired within the Contract Area. The nonoperator had originally contributed leases on the same acreage to the venture. When the operator discovered that the leases had been executed by the wrong person, it proceeded to lease the land itself without notifying the nonoperator. In holding that the nonoperator was entitled to share in the new leases, the court stated that the execution of the JOA had given rise to a relationship of trust and confidence

and that the operator had breached the duty of fair dealing owed to the nonoperator. On somewhat analogous facts the court in Schmude Oil Co. v. Omar Operating Co., 458 N.W.2d 659 (Mich.App.1990) based the operator's fiduciary duty on a joint venture that had arisen out of the parties' negotiations prior to entering into the JOA.

Contrast the result reached in Dime Box Petroleum Corp. v. Louisiana Land and Exploration Co., 938 F.2d 1144 (10th Cir.Colo.1991), which denied recovery to a nonoperator who alleged that the operator had overcharged lease acquisition costs, failed to comply with an agreement to buy part of the nonoperator's interest, and refused to refund an overpayment. The court stated that the JOA created a joint venture between the parties and would have imposed a fiduciary standard of conduct upon the operator had the parties not modified this obligation by agreeing to the exculpatory clause. The court reasoned that the exculpatory clause relieved the operator of all liability except that arising from the operator's gross negligence or willful misconduct.

7.   Although a finding of a joint venture has been the most common basis for imposing fiduciary duties upon the operator, other rationales have also been used. Various courts have viewed the operator as an agent operating the project for the benefit of the participants; a trustee; or a cotenant bound to act as a fiduciary with respect to commonly owned property. For a discussion of the strengths and weaknesses of these various positions, see Ernest E. Smith, Duties and Obligations Owed by an Operator to Non–Operators, Investors, and Other Interest Owners, 32 Rocky Mtn.Min.L.Inst. 12–1, 12–7 to 12–13 (1986).

Professor Smith has suggested a somewhat different position. Agreeing that the parties would almost certainly be viewed as joint venturers with mutual fiduciary duties if they had no operating agreement, he argues that the appropriate question is whether that relationship continues after the operating agreement has been entered into. Assessment of the parties' relationship depends upon an analysis of a variety of factors, including the specific terms of the operating agreement, which may modify any general fiduciary duties otherwise imposed upon the operator; the type of activity in question; and the location of the activity. Ernest E. Smith, Joint Operating Agreement Jurisprudence, 33 Washburn L.J. 834 (1994) and Ernest E. Smith, Duties and Obligations Owed by an Operator to Non–Operators, Investors, and Other Interest Owners, 32 Rocky Mtn.Min.L.Inst. 12–1 (1986). See also John R. Reeves & J. Matthew Thompson, Significant Cases Governing the Onshore Operating Agreement, 49 Inst. on Oil & Gas L. & Tax'n 2–1, 2–6 to 2–26 (1998); Smith & Weaver § 17.4(A). Edward Evans, The Oil and Gas Operator as Fiduciary, 10 J.Energy & Nat.Res.L. 172 (1992), describes a somewhat analogous approach taken by Canadian courts with respect to the duties owed by oil and gas operators. For the argument that the typical joint operating agreement contains all elements of a joint venture, see Howard L. Boigon, Liabilities and Relationships of Co–Owners under Agreements for Joint Development of Oil and Gas Properties, 37 Inst. on Oil & Gas L. & Tax'n 8–1 (1986); Howard L. Boigon & Christine L. Murphy, Liability of Non–Operating Mineral Interest Owners, 51 U.Colo.L.Rev. 153 (1980); and Frank Erisman & Elizabeth Jennings Dalton, Multi–Party Ownership of Minerals—Real Property Consequences of Joint Mineral Development, 25 Rocky Mtn.Min.L.Inst. 7–1 (1979).

2. NONOPERATOR LIABILITY FOR COSTS

(a) Initial Drilling

Decisions to drill an initial well or conduct additional operations are usually based upon a document known as the Authority for Expenditure ("AFE"), which has been prepared and circulated by the operator. In the case of an initial well the parties examine and agree to this document, which specifies the well's location, its depth, and the time when it must be commenced, before they execute the operating agreement. If the well is to be a horizontal well, the AFE should clearly specify this and include a description of the completion operations. Of course the provisions of a traditional JOA must also be modified if the parties are planning to drill a horizontal well rather than a vertical well. For example, "drillsite," which in the vertical well context refers to the oil and gas lease where the well is to be located, should include a reference not just to the location of the vertical portion of the well but also refer to every tract that will be penetrated by the well's horizontal extension. Similarly, "sidetrack," which is defined in the 1989 JOA as "deviation of a well from vertical," should be re-defined as meaning a deviation of the lateral extension from the direction originally proposed. See Mark D. Christiansen & Wendy S. Brooks, "A Different 'Slant' on JOAs: New Developments in Shale Plays and Recent Court Rulings," 57 Rocky Mt. Min. L. Inst., Ch. 25 (2011). Of course the proposed length of the lateral extension as well as the depth of the well must be included, although the operator may wish to include a provision giving it some flexibility if geological conditions make it impossible to drill to the specified length. See Lamont C. Larsen, "Horizontal Drafting: Why Your Form JOA May Not Be Adequate for Your Company's Horizontal Drilling Program," 48 Rocky Mt.Min.L.Fdn.J. 51, 62 (2011).

One important aspect of the AFE is that it contains an estimate of the cost of drilling the well. Regardless of whether the well is vertical or horizontal, this estimate leads to one of the most common risks facing the parties to the operating agreement: the possibility of substantial cost overruns. A drilling operation that was projected to cost $1,000,000 may encounter drilling difficulties that result in an actual cost of twice that amount.

The following case illustrates the basic resolution of this problem.

M & T, INC. v. FUEL RESOURCES DEVELOPMENT CO.
518 F.Supp. 285 (D.Colo.1981).

* * *

KANE, DISTRICT JUDGE.

Jurisdiction of this diversity case is admitted by the parties. It is a contract case concerning development and operation of oil and gas leases in the Johnny Moore Area in Jackson County, Colorado and concerns the pivotal question of when a party may, as they say in the trade, "go non-consent." M & T and McBride have sued to recover the unpaid balance of Fuelco's share of the costs, amounting to $150,927, incurred in the drilling of an oil well known as No. 1–25 Unit Well. The theory of recovery is based upon express and implied agreements among the parties, or their predecessors in interest, as well as upon the doctrine of estoppel. Plaintiffs also ask for attorney fees, pre-judgment interest and costs.

* * *

The instant dispute arises from the 1–25 Unit Well. The parties agreed to share drilling costs 56.25% M & T, 25% Fuelco and 18.75% McBride. This was in accord with the 1973 Operating Agreement and the course of dealing that the parties or their predecessors had followed from the 42–26 State Well forward. However, in the middle of drilling, when the pre-drilling costs estimates contained in the Authority for Expenditure, or AFE, were reached, Fuelco announced that it would cease to pay its share of the drilling costs. M & T and McBride were thereafter left to continue the drilling alone or to throw away their entire investment in the well to that point. They continued drilling until the Dakota–Lakota formations were tested, and at that point, in light of the test results and the burden of Fuelco's absence, they agreed to terminate drilling.

An AFE is a form which is widely used in the oil and gas industry when wells are drilled by multiple parties. The AFE sets forth the location of the well, its objective geological formation, an estimated depth at which that formation will be encountered, the estimated costs of drilling and completion, and miscellaneous other information. It is prepared by the "operator" of the well, and execution of the AFE by the non-operating owners of working interests in the underlying leaseholds is a written manifestation of their consent to participate in the well. It is axiomatic that drilling costs cannot be estimated with certainty and that an AFE is at best a good-faith estimate. AFE's are usually exceeded, often by very substantial amounts. This is particularly true in the North Park Basin, which includes the Johnny Moore Prospect. In drilling the 25–1 State Well, the 42–26 State Well, and the 1–10 Unit Well, the AFE estimates were all exceeded by substantial amounts.

In the oil and gas industry, it is understood and accepted that when one signs an AFE, he is committed to his proportionate share of the necessary costs in drilling to the objective specified in the AFE, unless the parties mutually agree to terminate drilling earlier or to attempt a completion at a shallower formation. The industry norms are consistent with the contracts and the parties' course of dealing with each other in the Johnny Moore Prospect.

In the instant case, the AFE reflected M & T's intention, as "opera-tor," to drill and complete a test of the Entrada formation. The AFE further indicated M & T's belief that the objective formation would be encountered at a depth of 9,070 feet and that the "dry-hole" cost of the well would be $739,400.

Between the date of Fuelco's withdrawal and the date that drilling operations were concluded, M & T and McBride incurred expenditures in the amount of $603,708, in connection with the drilling operations on the 1–25 Unit Well, i.e., the AFE was exceeded by that amount. Of that amount, three-fourths was paid by M & T and one-fourth was paid by McBride. M & T and McBride contend that Fuelco is liable for 25% of this amount, or $150,927 plus interest.

Fuelco contends that it did not agree to pay more than its share of the AFE cost estimate, but I find that it agreed to pay its share of the costs of drilling the well to its objective or to casing point. Fuelco contends that it could withdraw its consent (go "non-consent") at the AFE estimate. I find that it could not and that such constituted a breach of the contracts, the AFE, the parties' prior dealings, and industry custom and practice. Further, Fuelco contends that the drilling costs were exorbitant. I find that the costs were necessary and reasonable in light of the difficult drilling conditions. Further, Fuelco was informed of the problems as they were incurred and participated in finding solutions to them.

I find that plaintiffs relied on Fuelco's participation when they undertook the drilling of the 1–25 Unit Well and that Fuelco is estopped to deny its full participation in the drilling of the well and in its responsibility for paying its full proportionate share of the costs.

Fuelco's obligation to pay 25% of the costs is established in the 1973 Operating Agreement which is incorporated into the 1973 Agreement. The Operating Agreement provides in Article 3 that the costs of drilling the initial test well shall be borne by the parties "in accordance with separate agreement among themselves." I find that the "separate agreement" is the 1973 Operating Agreement. * * *

The method of allocation for the Johnny Moore wells is set forth in the 1973 Operating Agreement, paragraph 4 of which states:

> Unless changed by other provisions of the [1973] Agreement, all costs and liabilities incurred in operations under this contract shall be borne and paid * * * by the parties as their interests are given in Exhibit A.

Those interests are: 25% Fuelco; 18.75% McBride; 56.25% other parties [since 1976, M & T]. Paragraph 11(a) provides that when a party consents to the drilling of a well, he consents to bear his proportionate share of all necessary drilling costs to the casing point.

I find that Fuelco consented to the drilling of the 1–25 Unit Well and is thus liable for its proportionate share of all necessary drilling costs to the casing point. In March 1978, Fuelco agreed to the location of the well. In April, Fuelco signed the AFE for the well. Further, Fuelco participated fully in the unitization procedures including the drilling of the requisite test well. When the 1–10 Unit Well did not qualify as a test well, the 1–25 Unit Well was drilled and Fuelco issued its AFE.

Fuelco's contention that the AFE set a ceiling upon the expenditures to which it consented is without merit. It is novel and somewhat imaginative, but nevertheless meritless. The overwhelming weight of the evidence establishes that an AFE is nothing more than an estimate. In the drilling of the three previous Johnny Moore wells the cost estimates were exceeded yet Fuelco paid its proportionate share of the overruns. The Tenth Circuit has already ruled in Cleverock Energy Corp. v. Trepel, 609 F.2d 1358 (1979) that AFE's do not limit or otherwise qualify the consent given to participate in a particular drilling operation. The rule is bedded not only in law and logic, but even more so in practicality. Given the uncertainties and risks implicit in drilling ventures, the oil and gas drilling industry could not function if forced to march to the exact measure of a budget which is considered to be at best an educated guess.

We next consider Fuelco's equally meritless assertion that it had the right to go non-consent at the time the AFE estimate was surpassed. Consent to drilling has certain limitations; it does not extend to completion attempts, deepening or plugging back. Typically non-consent elections can be made at those times or, usually, at the casing point. None of these events is related to the AFE estimate. Fuelco's attempt to go non-consent in the instant case was harnessed to the AFE and unrelated to any triggering event such as the casing point. The attempt to go non-consent here was in mid-phase of drilling and, as such, must be impermissible.

As previously indicated the testimony discloses that the drilling costs were reasonable and necessary. The drilling event was seriously affected by specific geologic and mechanical problems. Fuelco received daily reports of these problems and actively participated in formulating solutions to the problems. None of the parties to the enterprise was incompetent. In fact all were highly skilled and knowledgeable. There is no doubt that the conditions found in the North Park Basin make drilling particularly difficult. Anticipation of consequent high costs and overruns of substantial amounts are the rule rather than the exception. Suffice it to say that drilling in the North Park Basin is not an appropriate activity for timid souls. Given these conditions and the acknowledged skill and expertise of the parties, I find that the costs incurred were reasonable and necessary.

The final defense of Fuelco to avoid meeting its responsibility is that the plaintiffs did not drill to the Entrada formation which was the objective of the project. Fuelco cannot be heard to complain since it dropped out when the well had reached 5,700 feet and the decision to terminate was not made by the survivors of the agreement until drilling reached 9,401 feet. Had Fuelco stayed in, a different result might be reached, but Fuelco's dropping out was itself a significant factor to be considered by the survivors when they mutually agreed to stop.

In sum, I hold that the AFE was only an estimate; that approval of an AFE is a commitment to pay one's proportionate share of all reasonable and necessary costs incurred until the objective formation or casing point[1] is reached or until the parties mutually agree to terminate. Further I hold that an AFE gives no right to go non-consent and that the point at which a party can go non-consent, in the absence of express written agreement, is determined by industry custom and practice.

IT IS THEREFORE ORDERED that plaintiffs shall have judgment against defendant in the amount of $150,927 plus prejudgment interest * * *.

NOTES

1. In "Coming of Age: Initiating the Oilfield into Performance Disclosure," 50 S.M.U. L.Rev. 663, 745–750 (1997) John McArthur points to the inability of nonoperators to hold operators' to their cost estimates as one of several examples of the JOA's failure to provide adequate protection for investors. He faults the limited pool of drafters and the industry orientation of the American Association of Professional Landmen (AAPL), which has promulgated the standard form JOA, and suggests that the AAPL lacks any incentive to side with investors in drafting provisions in which the investors' interests conflict with those of the operators.

Contrast the following comment made by Professor Ernest E. Smith in Joint Operating Agreement Jurisprudence, 33 Washburn L.J. 834, 840 (1994):

> With the possible exception of some "promoted" prospects, such as those in the late seventies and early eighties, the parties to an operating agreement are either oil or gas companies or experienced investors. Nonoperators normally have access to geological data relating to the Contract Area prior to signing the operating agreement * * *. Agreement to the AFE, which can be evaluated by the parties' in-house geologists, engineers and accountants or outside consultants, precedes agreement to the joint operating agreement. Nonoperators should be able to bargain from an information and economic base that is not widely dissimilar from that of the operator. Such factors would suggest that in the absence of special circumstances, nonoperators can include special self-protective clauses in the operating agreement and only need an implied standard that protects them from outright fraud.

What contractual devices would you suggest including in the JOA to protect nonoperators against the risk of unlimited cost overruns? See Smith & Weaver § 17.3(C)(1) for a discussion of various types of protective clauses.

2. In the absence of contract modification, nonoperators can challenge the costs assessed them by the operator only if the costs were incurred in bad faith or are excessive, unreasonable, or unauthorized by the AFE. For a successful challenge on the latter ground, see Haas v. Gulf Coast Natural Gas Co., 484 S.W.2d 127 (Tex.Civ.App.1972). In True Oil Co. v. Sinclair Oil Corp.,

---

1. [Editors' note] Under the typical JOA for a vertical well each participant can elect whether to participate in completing the well once it has reached the agreed-upon depth (the "casing point election"). With horizontal wells, however, once the lateral extension is begun, drilling is both a drilling and completion operation so there is no clearly identifiable point at which to make a casing point election.

771 P.2d 781 (Wyo.1989), the court rejected an argument that the operator was required to drill the well "at cost" and that the operator's affiliated companies were not entitled to profits for the services and equipment they had furnished. The court pointed out that the operator could have contracted out drilling and other services to nonaffiliated companies and in at least one instance had done so. "[C]ompetitive rates were what was mutually contemplated [under the parties' agreement] * * *. Under these circumstances * * * the fiduciary duty to be met by True Oil [the operator] was to obtain drilling and related services at a reasonable cost as reflected by competitive rates." 771 P.2d at 793.

3. In addition to the costs of initial drilling, non-operators are liable for ordinary operating costs associated with the initial well and the plugging and other expenses incurred at the end of the well's productive life. In Seagull Energy E & P, Inc. v. Eland Energy, Inc., 207 S.W.3d 342 (Tex. 2006) the defendant non-operator sold its interest in two oil and gas leases on the Outer Continental Shelf shortly before the wells ceased producing. The buyer, which had received an assignment of all of the defendant's rights and obligations under the JOAs along with the leasehold interests, defaulted on its obligation to reimburse the operator for its proportionate share of operating costs, plugging costs and the expenses incurred in dismantling the offshore facility. The operator then brought suit against the assignor. The Texas Supreme Court rejected the defendant assignor's argument that it was not liable for any costs incurred after the assignment, ruling that in the absence of a clear agreement to the contrary, the general rule of contract law applied, under which a party remains liable for its contractual obligations after an assignment.

Operations covered by a JOA often last for decades. Suppose an original participant in an off-shore well assigns its interest shortly after the well is completed and that the interest is re-assigned several times. A final re-assignment is made to an insolvent company shortly before extensive plugging, reclamation and dismantling costs are incurred. Can the operator sue the initial owner of the interest without first attempting to recover from the ultimate assignee and the intermediate assignees?

4. The JOA gives the operator several remedies against a defaulting participant. The operator can assert a lien against the nonoperator's working interest, share of production and share of equipment; the operator also has the right to collect the proceeds from the sale of the nonoperator's share of production.

The exercise of these remedies is a common source of dispute. Other creditors of the nonoperator may challenge the priority of the operator's lien. See, e.g., MBank Abilene, N.A. v. Westwood Energy, Inc., 723 S.W.2d 246 (Tex.App. 1986) and Enduro Oil Co. v. Parish & Ellison, 834 S.W.2d 547 (Tex.App. 1992). In Andrau v. Michigan Wisconsin Pipe Line Co., 712 P.2d 372 (Wyo. 1986) defaulting nonoperators argued that the operator was subject to a fiduciary duty that precluded him from foreclosing a lien against their working interests. They contended that the operator was obligated to use the least onerous remedy available, and that remedy was to sell their share of gas under his own sales contract that provided for a price three times above current market price. In rejecting this argument, the Wyoming Supreme Court concluded that any fiduciary duty owed by the operator had been limited by the express JOA provision giving the operator the right to foreclose against the nonoperators' working interests.

Because of the value of the information obtained through horizontal drilling, it has been suggested that a JOA for a horizontal well should provide not only that the operator can withhold the delinquent non-operator's share of costs from its share of production, but that the operator can also withhold information about the well until the non-operator pays its bills. See Mark D. Christiansen & Wendy S. Brooks, "A Different 'Slant' on JOAs: New Developments in Shale Plays and Recent Court Rulings," 57 Rocky Mt. Min. L. Inst., Ch. 25 (2011).

(b) Additional Development

As the preceding section indicates, non-operators are liable for all costs connected with the operations agreed upon when entering into the JOA. However both offshore and on-shore JOAs limit the operator's authority to commit non-operators to the costs of drilling additional wells or other major operations, such as deepening or re-working an existing well. In the case of a horizontal well, the term "deepen" should be defined to mean drilling a greater distance than the distance initially agreed to. The JOA should also make clear that, with respect to a horizontal well, additional operations may include drilling lateral wells.

Most agreements include a "nonconsent" provision that any party can invoke with respect to all operations other than those connected with the initial well.[6] Many commonly used JOAs provide that participants have a specified number of days (typically either 30 or 60, depending which AAPL form is being used) in which to respond to the proposal for additional operations, and that a party that does not respond within the specified period is deemed to have opted to go "non-consent." The JOAs further provide that the party making the proposal will commence work on the proposed operations within a specified period after the expiration of the notice period. Should the "deemed non-consent" provision apply if the party proposing the additional work begins operations during the notice period? See Valence Operating Co. v. Dorsett, 164 S.W.3d 656 (Tex. 2005). What if a new well is drilled *before* notice has been given?

In Bonn Operating Co. v. Devon Energy Production Co., 613 F.3d 532 (5th Cir. [Texas] 2010) the operator sent the nonoperator notice *after* it had drilled and completed a new well. The non-operator responded that it elected to go non-consent, and then objected when the operator charged the nonoperator's share of production with the non-consent penalty as well as its proportionate share of the total costs of the new well. In subsequent litigation the nonoperator contended that the operator could

---

6. In some instances involving vertical wells the operating agreement may provide a nonconsent option at the casing point of the initial well, thus permitting a party to refuse to spend funds for completing a well that it does not believe will be commercially productive.

not charge the non-consent penalty because the operator had failed to give notice prior to drilling the well, as required by the JOA.

The court rejected this argument, pointing out, as the Texas Supreme Court did in Valence v. Dorsett, that the JOA does not place any limitation on when the operator can commence work on a project. Moreover, because the operator's drilling and related operations were essentially completed before notice was sent to the nonoperator, the nonoperator had the highly unusual advantage of being able to determine all costs associated with drilling and any risk associated with the well before deciding whether to consent or not.

If, after receiving notice of a proposal to drill a new well, a party makes an election, can it change its election if the change is made before the end of the period? A divided court ruled to the contrary in XTO Energy, Inc. v. Smith Production, Inc., 282 S.W.3d 672 (Tex.App.–Houston 2009). The plaintiff non-operator initially notified the operator of its decision to go non-consent as to the subsequent operations. All of the other nonoperators elected to participate and advised the operator that they would carry the non-consenting party's share of expenses. Before the notification period elapsed, plaintiff notified operator that it was revoking its prior non-consent and had elected to participate in the new wells. The operator responded that the plaintiff could not change its election and it would be deemed to have relinquished its interest in the new wells to the consenting parties, who would recover plaintiff's share of expenses from its share of production in the new wells plus a 300% penalty, as provided for in the JOA. Plaintiff filed suit against the operator, arguing that it had the right to change its decision within 30 days after receiving notification of the proposal for subsequent operations and that the operator and other parties were not entitled to withhold the non-consent penalty.

In ruling against the plaintiff, the court relied on Section VI. B of the JOA which states that when the party proposing the new operations receives all notifications, the proposing party must "immediately * * * advise the Consenting Parties of the total interest of the parties approving" the proposal, and if it recommends that the proposal operations proceed, the Consenting Parties have 48 hours in which to notify the proposing party whether they wish to carry a proportionate part of the Non–Consenting Parties' share. The court reasoned that although the JOA does not deal expressly with changes of election within the notice day period, a construction that precludes changes is more consistent with the "immediate" notification requirement. It also accords with the time-sensitive nature of the proposing party's obligations so that it can make the necessary arrangements to begin drilling within the 90 days specified under the parties' JOA.

The parties who agree to undertake additional operations must bear the entire cost of the operation. Depending upon the terms of the agreement, the party who refuses his consent to such operations may lose all interest in the new or deeper portion of the well. This is, indeed, quite often the case with horizontal wells that are lengthened or when laterals are drilled. With vertical wells, it is more common, as is indicated in the previous paragraphs, to provide that the nonconsenting party acquires a carried interest[7] in the operation, but is not entitled to any share of the production from the well until the operator and other consenting parties have recouped the nonconsenting party's share of the costs several times over from the non-consenting party's share of the production. These costs include "all production, severance, excise, gathering and other taxes, and all royalties, overriding royalties and other burdens applicable to the non-consenting party's share of production." The court in Tawes v. Barnes, 340 S.W.3d 419 (Tex. 2011) ruled that the lessor of a non-consenting lessee is not a third-party beneficiary of this JOA provision and cannot sue the consenting lessees for the royalty that would otherwise be owed by her lessee. It reasoned that the JOA lists the expenses owed by consenting participants in order to provide clarity to the operator, which must keep an accurate record of accounting, and does not contain any statement or indication of an intent to make the lessor of a participant that goes non-consent a third-party beneficiary of the consenting parties' obligation to pay royalty.

The JOA clause that entitles consenting parties to recover the non-consenting parties' share of costs several times over has been attacked as an unenforceable penalty clause and defended as a provision for liquidated damages. See, e.g., Hamilton v. Texas Oil & Gas Corp., 648 S.W.2d 316, 321 (Tex.App.1982). The Texas Supreme Court has disagreed with both characterizations. It has pointed out that the non-consenting party is not being punished or made liable in damages for breaching a contract; for that party had the express option not to consent to additional operations. The clause is thus a contractual mechanism for compensating the consenting parties for the risk they incur in going forward with additional operations without the participation of the non-consenting parties. Valence Operating Co. v. Dorsett, 164 S.W.3d 656 (Tex. 2005). A special JOA clause providing that a non-consenting party would forever relinquish its interest has been upheld on similar grounds. See Long v. RIM Operating, Inc., 345 S.W.3d 79 (Tex. App. 2011).

Although a party that exercises its non-consent option has a carried interest that does not entitled it to any current income or other rights in the well, it may still be subject to regulatory control and to penalties for actions of the operator. In Railroad Commission v. Olin Corp., 690 S.W.2d 628 (Tex.App.–Austin 1985, writ ref'd n.r.e.), a well plugging statute, Vernon's Texas Code Ann., Nat.Res.Code § 89.042(b), was held applicable

---

7. The term "carried interest" has no fixed meaning, but varies in accordance with the terms of the agreement involved. In the case of a party "who goes nonconsent," the term means that the nonconsenting party "will receive none of the proceeds of the production until the parties who put up the money to 'carry' his interest receive some multiple of the costs they have expended with respect to the carried interest." Lowe, Chapter 3.H. If a party is carried "to the casing point," it is free of the costs of drilling and testing, but is liable for its share of the costs of completing, equipping, and producing. A party who is carried "to the tanks or pipeline" will be free of the equipment and completion costs, and liable only for the costs of operation. Id.

to nonoperators who had gone nonconsent as to a gas well that was being reworked. The operator abandoned the well, which subsequently blew out. Upon a showing that the operator lacked the assets to pay for properly plugging the well, the nonconsenting parties were held jointly and severally liable for controlling and plugging the well.

As noted in the preceding section, the Texas Supreme Court has ruled that a non-operator that assigned its interest remained bound by its contractual its obligations under the JOA and was thus liable for plugging and abandonment costs incurred after the assignment. Seagull Energy E & P, Inc. v. Eland Energy, Inc., 207 S.W.3d 342 (Tex. 2006). Suppose that a non-operator assigns its interest to a party that agrees to costly but unsuccessful additional drilling. If the assignee defaults on its share of the costs, can the operator hold the assignor liable?

(c) Liability to JOA Creditors

The operator has the exclusive right and duty to contract for material and services for the Contract Area and is clearly liable for payment. If the operator fails to pay or become insolvent, the creditors may attempt to hold nonoperators liable. The following case deals with this issue.

BLOCKER EXPLORATION CO. v. FRONTIER EXPLORATION, INC.

740 P.2d 983 (Colo. 1987).

VOLLACK, JUSTICE.

* * *

I.

This dispute arises from a series of agreements concerning the exploration and development of oil and gas leases in the State of Michigan. In January 1981, Lewis entered into an agreement with Great Lakes Niagaran [hereinafter GLN] whereby GLN assigned its rights in certain Michigan oil and gas leases to Lewis. The GLN–Lewis agreement designated Lewis as the operator for exploration and development of the leases, and provided that Lewis and GLN would enter into an operating agreement before any drilling began. An unexecuted operating agreement was appended to the GLN–Lewis agreement....

In February 1981, Lewis entered into an agreement with Frontier. Frontier was to conduct seismic work on the Michigan leases, in exchange for fees and expenses as set out in the agreement.

In March 1981, Lewis assigned a portion of its interest in the Michigan leases to Blocker. The Lewis–Blocker agreement ... provided that unless otherwise indicated, the parties' rights would be governed by the GLN–Lewis contract.

Frontier performed the reconnaissance seismic work for Lewis, from March through September of 1981. In February 1982, Lewis filed bankruptcy. At that time, Frontier had only been paid a portion of the fees it was owed for the seismic work it had performed under the Lewis–Frontier agreement. Unable to satisfy the outstanding debt through Lewis' bankruptcy proceeding, Frontier filed suit against Blocker, claiming that Blocker was liable for Lewis' debts because a mining partnership existed between Lewis and Blocker.

Frontier and Blocker both filed motions for summary judgment, with Frontier alleging that a mining partnership existed by operation of law, and Blocker contending that such a partnership did not exist.

Based on the agreements presented by the parties (which were not disputed), the trial court granted Blocker's motion for summary judgment. The trial court held that because one of the required elements of a mining partnership—namely, joint operation—was absent, no mining partnership existed. * * *

II.

A.

ELEMENTS OF MINING PARTNERSHIP

"Mining Partnerships developed as a special type of partnership peculiarly adapted to serve the mining industry (including the oil and gas field)." ... Mining partnerships have been recognized for the purpose of "impos [ing] joint and several liability on nonoperating interest owners in favor of third parties transacting business with or injured by a mineral venture." Boigon & Murphy, Liabilities of Nonoperating Mineral Interest Owners, 51 U.Colo.L.Rev. 153, 154 (1980). Oil and gas partnerships are treated as a type of mining partnership for purposes of analysis.

The three essential elements of a mining partnership are: (1) joint ownership; (2) joint operation; and (3) an express or implied agreement to share profits and losses. This mining partnership test has been adopted in the jurisdictions which have addressed this issue. See Fiske, Mining Partnership, 26 Inst. on Oil & Gas L. & Tax'n 187, 193 (1975).

If a mining partnership exists, the partners are characterized as operators and have a limited power (less than the power of a general partner) to bind other members of the partnership. Frontier asks us to find that Lewis and Blocker were partners, and that Lewis had the power to bind Blocker, leaving Blocker liable on the Lewis–Frontier contract.

The parties conceded the existence of joint ownership. The record shows, and the parties do not dispute, that Lewis and Blocker agreed to share profits and losses. The element of joint operations is the critical issue presented by these facts.

B.

JOINT OPERATIONS

As pointed out by the court of appeals, other jurisdictions have formulated various standards for determining what constitutes joint operation. Co-ownership alone does not give rise to a mining partnership. All investors are not mining partners by virtue of holding a working interest in an oil or gas lease. The court of appeals correctly held that "the determining factor is related to the degree of active participation in control or management of the venture that is exercised by a co-tenant or co-owner."

The issue then becomes: what rights and actions of co-owners rise to the level of active participation in control or management, rendering them mining partners and not mere co-owners or investors?

Texas has held that the right of a co-owner to give counsel to the company does not make the co-owner a partner. Nor does the right to approve certain expenditures, the right to take in kind, or the right of access to the site. In Berchelmann v. Western Co., 363 S.W.2d 875 (Tex.Civ.App.1962), the appellants were held not liable as partners because "the very operating agreements themselves, wherein appellants were designated as the 'non-operators' and Texita as the 'operator' do not contain the basic elements of sharing of liability, control, risk and profits, along with the elements of agency, necessary to constitute a partnership or mining partnership." Id. at 876–77. Other factors in Berchelmann included the non-operators' contribution of a portion of the operator's expenses (while the operator controlled drilling and production), the operator's exclusive management and control of operations, and the fact that the operator's purchase of labor and materials was charged to accounts in the operator's name only. Id. at 877. The Texas Court of Appeals has held that joint operation was not established by proof that the non-operator counseled the operator, was present at the well and interested in the drilling results, and knew there was a contract which failed to authorize the operator to create liability to third parties binding on the non-operator. U.S. Truck Lines v. Texaco, Inc., 337 S.W.2d 497, 500 (Tex.Civ.App.1960).

Oklahoma has held that the assignee of an interest in an oil and gas lease was not liable to a third party creditor as a mining partner because his actions did not amount to "actively joining in the promotion, conduct or management of the joint venture." Edwards v. Hardwick, 350 P.2d 495, 502 (Okla.1960). The non-operator had contributed use of equipment, which he had authorized to be ordered while he was present at the well. Compare Oklahoma Co. v. O'Neil, which involved a dispute between co-owners in a venture. The same court there found that a partnership existed, even though "[t]he only cooperation by the defendants reflected by the record in this case [was] the visit to and the examination of the leases by the defendants ... shortly prior to the purchase of the leases. Subsequent cooperation by the defendants appears to have been minimal." 440 P.2d 978, 985 (Okla.1968). This evidence was held sufficient to uphold the trial court's holding that a mining partnership existed, even though "the defendants left the management and operation of the leases to the plaintiff." Id.

Illinois has held that co-owners "never exercised any control in the management or operation," when the non-operator did not give orders, hire personnel, or buy equipment, and was only on the premises a few times. *Bovaird Supply Co. v. McClement*, 32 Ill.App.2d 224, 234, 177 N.E.2d 430, 434 (1961). In *Dunbar v. Olson*, Illinois declined to find a mining partnership where the non-operators "knew nothing about the operations other than" what the operator told them, were not "oil men," and did not have skill or knowledge in oil exploration. 349 Ill.App. at 310, 110 N.E.2d at 665.

In a dispute between co-owners, the Tenth Circuit Court of Appeals applied Oklahoma law and found existence of a mining partnership where the non-operator furnished funds and materials, made many trips to the field, personally wrote letters asking the operator to keep expenses down, and the general plan was for the operator and non-operator "both to counsel together." *Dana v. Searight*, 47 F.2d 38, 41 (10th Cir. 1931).

Kansas found existence of a mining partnership, and permitted a third party creditor to recover from all five co-owners of a well in *Mountain Iron & Supply Co. v. Branson*, 134 Kan. 818, 8 P.2d 407 (1932). The five co-owners shared regularly in production, used materials bought from the plaintiff-third party creditor for two years without payment, and paid wages to their hired employee individually on a pro rata basis.

A review of these cases makes it clear that the "joint operations" question requires application of the mining partnership test on a case-by-case basis.

C.

JOINT OPERATIONS TEST

The test to determine whether the joint operations element is met requires a court to look at the express agreement between the parties and, in some cases, the actions and conduct of the co-owners. If a co-owner takes an active role in the conduct of operations of a mining venture, and the other two elements of the mining partnership test are met, then a mining partnership does exist.

If there has not been actual control or participation by the co-owners, then it must be determined whether there was an express agreement between the parties and, if so, whether the agreement gave the co-owners a right of participation in the management or control of the operation. If no agreement exists, or the agreement does not give a co-owner the right to actual control or participation, then no mining partnership exists. However, if the agreement gives a co-owner a right of actual control or participation there may be joint operations, even if the rights described in the agreement have not been exercised by the co-owner.

Here, the parties did not allege that there was any conduct by the co-owners outside the rights set forth in the agreement. To determine whether the joint operations element was met, we must look at the rights and responsibilities as set out by the two agreements, and decide whether they constitute actual participation in control or management.

* * *

The GLN–Lewis agreement expressly designated Lewis as "the operator." Lewis agreed to provide information to GLN regarding the drilling permits, drilling reports and progress, and evidence from "the operator" regarding the testing and showings of oil and gas. The GLN–Lewis agreement also gave GLN the right to require "the operator" to carry insurance. Lewis was responsible for the reconnaissance seismic program, and entered into a contract with Frontier to have that work done. Lewis agreed to undertake a detailed seismic investigation to establish drilling prospects and to undertake and manage the drilling program.

Blocker agreed to contribute certain sums to overhead and seismic program costs, and to a detailed seismic survey, if Blocker elected to participate at that stage. Blocker had the right to receive "all data and all interpretations" and the right to be consulted before detailed seismic investigations, if any, were established. By incorporation of the GLN–Lewis agreement, Blocker also had access to regulatory reports, daily drilling reports, logs, core samples, and the right to be present at the site.

We agree with the court of appeals' holding that these facts do not support Frontier's argument that Blocker's rights rose to the level of active participation in control or management. Rather, Blocker invested funds, and enjoyed the right to receive data and to elect whether to continue participation in particular phases of the exploration or development. "[A] non-operating working-interest [member] should not be considered, without more, a mining partner if his only rights are to take in kind, receive reports, inspect books, make an election of whether to join in a particular phase of exploration/development (commonly known as a 'go-no-go' decision), or has the right of approval of specified expenditures." Frontier Exploration, Inc., 709 P.2d at 42–43.

Blocker's role was that of an investor, not a partner; the rights to receive certain data, to have access to the site, and to be consulted do not convince us that Blocker actively controlled the exploration. Blocker had no power to veto Lewis' decisions, did not enter into any contracts on behalf of the alleged partnership, and only enjoyed the right to make a "go-no-go" election at a certain stage of the exploration. We agree no mining partnership existed here.

* * *

QUINN, C.J., dissents.

[The dissenting opinion has been omitted.]

NOTES

1. Creditors are normally subrogated to the operator's claims against nonoperators who have failed to pay their proportionate share of drilling,

operating and related costs. A nonoperator faces far more serious problems if, as in the principal case, one or more creditors attempt to hold him liable for all of the operator's unpaid debts. As the principal case illustrates, participation in a mining partnership is the typical theory of nonoperator liability advanced by third party tort and contract claimants.

According to Howard L. Boigon & Christine L. Murphy, Liabilities of Nonoperating Interest Owners, 51 U. Colo. L.Rev. 153 (1980), delegation of operational control to one person may not be an entirely effective mechanism for shielding the nonoperating co-owners from liability. A few jurisdictions may be inclined to find the crucial element of control in the provisions of the JOA giving certain limited decision-making rights to the nonoperators, such as the clause that requires consent of all nonoperators before the operator can plug and abandon the initial well. In Lavy v. Pitts, 29 S.W.3d 353 (Tex.App. 2000) a workman who was injured when natural gas that was leaking from a well exploded sought-albeit unsuccessfully—to find the requisite element of nonoperator control in the JOA provision authorizing removal of the operator if it failed to conduct operations in a good and workmanlike manner.

Even in jurisdictions whose courts view the JOA's provisions as negating a mining partnership or joint venture, a nonoperator who disregards the terms of the agreement and takes an active role in the conduct of operations will probably be held liable for the operator's debts or tort liabilities. Moreover, if the JOA is expressly made subject to some other contract, such as a farmout, that grants partial managerial rights to a nonoperator, the nonoperator may be deemed to have sufficient control over the operations, even though he has never exercised his rights.

2.   As noted in an earlier section, nonoperators often urge a joint venture theory when attempting to impose liability on the operator. Could a jurisdiction that has adopted the joint venture theory in litigation between nonoperators and the operator reject it in suits brought by third party creditors against nonoperators? Texas has rejected the theory that a joint operating agreement creates a joint venture in both types of litigation. See, e.g., Hamilton v. Texas Oil & Gas Corp., 648 S.W.2d 316 (Tex.App. 1982, writ ref'd n.r.e.), rejecting nonoperator's claim that operator owed him a fiduciary duty based on a joint venture, and Berchelmann v. Western Co., 363 S.W.2d 875 (Tex.Civ.App. 1962, writ ref'd n.r.e.), rejecting creditor's argument that the nonoperators had entered into a mining partnership with the operator.

3.   OWNERSHIP AND MARKETING OF PRODUCTION

Except in limited situations, such as where a party goes non-consent as to additional drilling or to lengthening a horizontal well, each participant in the JOA owns a share of production in accordance with its proportionate interests in the Contract Area and "shall take in kind or separately dispose of its proportionate share." Most controversies over marketing have arisen where a party has failed to dispose of its share of natural gas or, more rarely, oil. JOAs typically make provision for this contingency by authorizing the operator to purchase the nonoperator's share or to sell it for the account of the nonmarketing party "at the best price obtainable in the area." If gas is involved, the operator may also have the right to treat all undisposed production as belonging to it, in which event the operator will need to and make adjustments (or "balance") at a later date.

What sorts of obligations, if any, do these provisions impose on an operator when a nonoperator fails to market? The following case addresses this issue.

ATLANTIC RICHFIELD CO. v. THE LONG TRUSTS

860 S.W.2d 439 (Tex.App. 1993).

OPINION

GRANT, JUSTICE.

* * *

BACKGROUND

Henderson Clay Products (HCP)—ARCO's predecessor—and The Long Trusts drilled gas wells during the early 1980s. The wells became producers, and HCP created B & A Pipe Line Company as its wholly owned subsidiary to build and maintain the pipe line and facilities transporting the gas to purchasers. On May 10, 1982, HCP and B & A entered into a contract whereby HCP dedicated its gas to B & A at the "applicable maximum lawful price per MMBTU [One Million British Thermal Units] as provided by the Federal Energy Regulatory Commission." On May 11, 1982, B & A entered into a ten-year contract with Lone Star Gas in which B & A dedicated its gas to Lone Star, to be purchased at the price that B & A had agreed to pay HCP. Lone Star also agreed to pay B & A an operations fee on all volumes of gas delivered by B & A at the point of delivery, in addition to the gas cost. ARCO purchased HCP and stands in its position for all purposes.

ARCO (as successor of HCP) was operating under joint operating agreements with The Long Trusts and other investors. Section VI.C of each agreement stated that:

> In the event any party shall fail to make the arrangements necessary to take in kind or separately dispose of its proportionate share of the oil and gas produced from the Contract Area, Operator shall have the right, subject to the revocation at will by the party owning it, but not the obligation, to purchase such oil and gas or sell it to others at any time and from time to time, for the account of the non-taking party at the best price obtainable in the area for such production. Any such purchase or sale by Operator shall be subject always to the right of the owner of the production to exercise at any time its right to take in kind, or separately dispose of, its share of all oil and gas not previously delivered to a purchaser.

The Long Trusts contend that they were defrauded by ARCO because the phrase "best price obtainable in the area for such production" mandated that B & A keep in effect the right to receive the "maximum lawful price" for the gas delivered under the terms of the May 10, 1982, contract between HCP and B & A. They argue that subsequent amendments to the initial contract between ARCO and B & A and between B & A and Lone Star Gas defrauded them by lowering the gas price.

Those amendments were made as part of the settlement of a take-and-pay lawsuit between B & A and Lone Star Gas. The original contract between B & A and Lone Star was negotiated and signed at a time when natural gas prices were at their zenith. Very shortly thereafter, the prices began to drop drastically, and Lone Star Gas failed to take the quantities of gas to which they had agreed under the contract or pay at the high price specified by the contract. B & A filed suit on the contract. The settlement of the suit provided that Lone Star Gas would agree to take substantially higher quantities of gas at a new, lower price. Even with the reduction in the purchase price, the price remained substantially above the going price for gas on the spot market.

The Long Trusts' Appeal

The primary issue: By modifying its long-term contract with Lone Star so that Lone Star paid less for the gas purchased, did ARCO—through its wholly-owned subsidiary B & A—violate the portion of its joint operating agreements with The Long Trusts stating that if ARCO sold The Long Trusts' gas, it would do so "at the best price obtainable in the area for such production?" We find that it did not.

Determination

The Long Trusts focus on the portion of the previously quoted Article VI.C of the joint operating agreements stating that the operator could sell their gas but only for the "best price obtainable in the area for such production." To prevail, their argument must necessarily be that the best price available was the "maximum lawful price" that was contained in the original contract between B & A and Lone Star. They must also be able to show that they had some right to obtain that price under the agreements. Although The Long Trusts had benefited incidentally from the terms of that contract, they were not third-party beneficiaries of the contract, i.e., there was no showing that these contracts were entered into for the purpose of directly benefiting The Long Trusts. ARCO and B & A had committed its production to Lone Star over a ten-year period in order to obtain that premium price. On the other hand, The Long Trusts had a right to terminate ARCO's selling of its gas at any time. Neither B & A nor ARCO had any future obligations to The Long Trusts because, by the terms of the contract, these transactions could be terminated at any time by either party.

The phrase "best price obtainable in the area for such production" necessarily requires that the gas prices available be compared only to similarly uncommitted production and not to gas committed to a long-term sales contract. If The Long Trusts had wished to obtain a higher price over a longer period of time, it had the option of negotiating separately with any gas purchaser. The joint operating agreements did not require that ARCO sell gas on behalf of The Long Trusts or that The Long Trusts must allow ARCO to sell their gas. Rather, the agreements provided that ARCO or The Long Trusts could terminate the selling of the gas at any time. This agreement cannot be rewritten by judicial fiat to say that ARCO's option had abruptly become ARCO's duty. So long as ARCO continued to sell for The Long Trusts, The Long Trusts enjoyed the same benefits that ARCO had obtained for itself.

The Long Trusts could not prevent ARCO from renegotiating its contracts to sell its own gas and had no vested interest in these contracts. In claiming such an interest, The Long Trusts seek to enjoy all the benefits of contracts to which they were not parties and at the same time bear none of the obligations of the terms of the contracts. The Long Trusts could have entered into their own long-term contract at the best price they could obtain, and B & A would have been required to transport their gas at a reasonable transportation fee. The term "for such production" in the joint operating agreements meant the undedicated gas of The Long Trusts. The term applied to what could be obtained for such undedicated gas or what actually was obtained. The Long Trusts were not entitled to any damages as a result of B & A's amendments to its contracts with Lone Star or with ARCO.

The trial court did not err in refusing to award The Long Trusts damages of $6,327,693.

* * *

FAILING TO ACCOUNT

We first examine the determination that ARCO failed to account to The Long Trusts at the best prices obtainable in the area for such production by not accounting to them for their share of the production at the price set forth in the B & A amendment[1] for gas marketed from June 1, 1985, to January 31, 1991. . . .

Nothing in the joint operating agreements prohibited ARCO or B & A from becoming the purchaser of the gas, if The Long Trusts were willing to sell the gas to ARCO or B & A. The operating agreements, however, did not contemplate that ARCO could become both the seller and the purchaser or that ARCO could make a profit directly or indirectly from selling the gas of The Long Trusts.

By the terms of the operating agreements, The Long Trusts expressly authorized ARCO to sell its gas at a controlled price, being the "best price

---

1. The B & A amendment was defined in the jury charge as the "agreement between B & A Pipeline Company and Lone Star Gas dated effective February 1, 1986."

obtainable in the area for such production." This creates a special agency limited to the sale of The Long Trusts' gas from the wells involved.

We recognize that the Texas Supreme Court has determined that, unless a lease document itself creates a trust, the relationship between the operator and the royalty owners is based upon an implied covenant and that the operator owes the royalty owners a duty of good faith. Amoco Production Co. v. Alexander, 622 S.W.2d 563 (Tex.1981); Amoco Production Co. v. First Baptist Church of Pyote, 611 S.W.2d 610 (Tex.1980). A lessee, however, is not an agent with respect to the sale of the lessor's gas because the lessor has no gas to sell. An oil and gas lease conveys to the lessee title to the gas in place, subject only to the contractual obligation to pay royalty on gas that is produced. Hurd Enterprises, Ltd. v. Bruni, 828 S.W.2d 101, 109 (Tex.App.–San Antonio 1992, writ denied).

The present case does not concern royalty owners, and an agency relationship does arise when an operator is selling gas belonging to a nonoperator. See Johnston v. American Cometra, Inc., 837 S.W.2d 711 (Tex.App.–Austin 1992, writ denied). The act of selling on behalf of the nonoperator, unlike a direct purchase of the nonoperator's share of production, implies a principal-agent relationship. See Ernest E. Smith, Gas Marketing by Co–Owners: Disproportionate Sales, Gas Imbalances and Lessors' Claims to Royalty, 39 Baylor L.Rev. 365, 373 (Spring 1987).

ARCO correctly contends that it was not receiving any remuneration from The Long Trusts for selling its gas; however, a gratuitous agent is subject to the same duty to account as a paid agent. Whether the relationship can be described as one of agency or trust, there is a duty owed to The Long Trusts to account for the monies received for selling its gas, to avoid conflicts of interests, and not to act as an adverse party in its capacity as the seller of its gas.

The jury, having found that ARCO was the alter ego of B & A, and B & A being the wholly owned subsidiary of ARCO, then The Long Trusts were entitled to damages for any profit from the sale of the gas by B & A. Whether ARCO was selling the gas as an accommodation to The Long Trusts or was selling it to recoup the drilling costs owed by The Long Trusts, the gas was sold under the authority of the operating agreements. Because B & A was found to be the alter ego of ARCO, B & A's selling of gas to Lone Star for profit was tantamount to ARCO selling it to Lone Star for profit and not properly accounting to The Long Trusts for that profit. There was expert testimony that B & A received $2.90 per MMBTU for gas belonging to The Long Trusts that had been sold by ARCO to B & A for prices of $1.60 and $1.40 per MMBTU. An expert established that The Long Trusts lost more than one million dollars because ARCO did not account to it for the price at which the gas was sold by B & A.

We find that the operating agreements provide a basis for recovery for The Long Trusts on the facts proven in this case, that the trial court did not err in failing to disregard the jury answers and in failing to direct a verdict because there was some evidence on the essential jury findings that supported the judgment. These points of error are overruled.

* * *

NOTES

1. As the court in the principal case points out, an operator that markets a non-operator's share of production as authorized by the JOA is acting as agent for the non-operator. The agency relationship imposes a fiduciary duty on the operator with respect to its actions in marketing the non-operator's gas; but it does not preclude the operator from exercising its contractual right under the JOA to stop marketing the non-operator's share of production at any time. See The Long Trusts v. Griffin, 144 S.W.3d 99 (Tex.App. 2004).

2. In Oklahoma, where royalty owners are entitled to payment based on the weighted average of gas sales from a well, serious accounting problems are posed when participants in a JOA sell gas under different contracts for different prices or do not sell their shares of production at all for an extended period. An initial legislative attempt to require each "first purchaser" to account to every royalty owner within the Contract Area apparently met with widespread industry resistance and was replaced with the Production Revenue Sharing Act, Okla. Stat. tit. 52, § 570.1. The act places the responsibility for accounting to royalty owners on the unit operator, rather than on the purchasers of production. The statute requires each working interest owner who is marketing natural gas to pay the royalty share of proceeds to the operator every month. The operator, who is deemed to be acting in a ministerial capacity, distributes the royalty proceeds and is protected against liability if it properly distributes all proceeds paid to it by the various working interest owners. Alternatively, a working interest owner who is concerned that the operator might not properly distribute royalty payments has the option to pay all royalty owners within the Contract Area directly.

3. As part of Senate Bill 168 the Oklahoma legislature also passed the Natural Gas Market Sharing Act ("NGMSA"), Okla. Stat. tit. 52, § 581.1, which supplemented earlier legislation designed to deal with situations in which some of the working interest participants in a unit well are unable to find markets for their shares of gas. Under the NGMSA working interest owners are entitled to share proportionately in the proceeds received by a "designated marketer," less marketing and post-production costs. Unless the participants choose a substitute, the operator is deemed to be the designated marketer with the obligation either to obtain a contract with a nonaffiliated purchaser or to account to the other working interest owners who elect to share in the proceeds from the operator's existing contract. The NGMSA also contains provisions exempting some sales from its coverage and barring working interest owners from participating under specified circumstances.

4. As Professor Lowe has noted, there may well be a question as to when an operator should be deemed to be selling gas on behalf of a nonoperator and hence subject to the JOA requirement that it sell for the best price obtainable in the area. "The fact that an operator opens a valve that causes a

jointly owned stream of gas (or oil) to flow form a well to a purchaser does not mean that the operator has elected to sell for the nonoperator." Lowe, Discussion Notes, 334 O & GR 335 (1999). The presence of gas balancing provisions in the JOA or an attachment to the JOA recognize that a single party may at various times be selling the entire stream of gas solely on that party's behalf.

Indeed, there are many reasons other than inability to obtain a market why a participant in a JOA may not market its share of gas. For example, one company may seek to take advantage of seasonal peaks in price and sell its share only during winter months, while another may have contract commitments that require it to delay sales until proper pipeline transportation arrangements can be made. In all such situations the working interest owners who do not market their shares of production are said to be "underproduced," whereas the marketing owners are "overproduced." There are two accepted methods of bringing the parties into balance. The method traditionally preferred by the industry is balancing in kind, whereby the underproduced party makes up the underage by taking its share plus a percentage of the overproduced parties' share. Under the alternative method the overproduced party accounts to the underproduced party in cash, either periodically or upon reservoir depletion. See generally Ernest E. Smith, Gas Marketing by Co–Owners: Disproportionate Sales, Gas Imbalances and Lessors' Claims to Royalties, 39 Baylor L.Rev. 365 (1987); Claude E. Upchurch, Split Stream Gas Sales and the Gas Storage and Balancing Agreement, 24 Rocky Mtn. Min. L. Inst. 665 (1978); Cannady, Duties of Operator in Marketing Nonoperator's Production, Buying and Selling Gas: A Practical Guide for Operators, Nonoperators and Royalty Owners 21—50 (P. Strohl ed. 1990), and Smith & Weaver § 17.6.

Because the model form operating agreements do not clearly address the most crucial issues that arise in imbalance situations, parties to an operating agreement frequently enter into a separate gas balancing agreement that is added as an attachment to the JOA. Some courts have viewed the gas balancing agreement as the exclusive determinant of the parties' rights, and in several instances where the parties have provided for balancing in kind have refused to grant cash balancing, even though the reservoir became depleted before the underproduced party could exercise its make-up rights. See, e.g., Amoco Production Co. v. Fina Oil & Chemical Co., 670 So.2d 502 (La.App. 1996) and Chevron U.S.A., Inc. v. Belco Petroleum Corp., 755 F.2d 1151 (5th Cir. La. 1985).

4. MISCELLANEOUS PROVISIONS, ATTACHMENTS AND EXHIBITS

Like most complex contractual arrangements, the JOA contains provisions dealing with a wide variety of specific subjects. Many provisions deal with the property interests of the participants and govern such matters as maintenance of title, liens and encumbrances, and the acquisition or transfers of interests. For a detailed description of these clauses and their purpose, see Gary Conine, Property Provisions of the Operating Agreement—Interpretation, Validity, and Enforceability, 19 Texas Tech L.Rev. 1263 (1988).

The property provision that has generated the most litigation is the right of purchase. This clause gives the JOA participants a preferential right to purchase the interest of any party who has offered it for sale to a third person. Professor Conine has suggested that this clause is intended to accomplish two principal purposes: First, it rewards risk by giving the JOA participants the opportunity to enlarge their interests within the Contract Area in preference to a third person who did not share in the initial risks. Second, it enables the parties to exclude new and possibly undesirable participants who may be financially weak or have management styles or philosophies that conflict with those of the original participants. See Gary Conine, 19 Texas Tech L. Rev. at 1317. These rationales support the conclusion reached in Fina Oil and Chemical Co. v. Amoco Production Co., 673 So.2d 668 (La. App. 1996) that the clause was not triggered when a participant transferred its interest in the Contract Area to its subsidiary. Do they support the court's further conclusion that the clause did not apply when the subsidiary's stock was subsequently sold to an unrelated company?

Although not involving a JOA, the following case considers that issue.

TENNECO INC. v. ENTERPRISE PRODUCTS CO.
925 S.W.2d 640 (Tex. 1996).

Abbott

This case poses a question of first impression concerning the effect of a stock sale on a right of first refusal. The dispute involves ownership rights in a natural gas fractionation plant. Respondents filed this lawsuit, contending that three transactions among several Tenneco and Enron entities violated the fractionation plant's operating agreement. The trial court granted summary judgment for Petitioners. The court of appeals reversed. We reverse the judgment of the court of appeals and render judgment for Petitioners.

I

Enterprise Products Company, Texaco Exploration and Production, Inc., El Paso Hydrocarbons Company, Champlin Petroleum Company and Tenneco Oil Company shared ownership in a natural gas liquids fractionation plant. Meridian Oil Hydrocarbons, Inc. and Union Pacific Fuels, Inc. later succeeded to the El Paso and Champlin interests. Plant operations were governed by a contract called the Restated Operating Agreement. This agreement provided the plant owners with a preferential right to purchase ownership interest in the plant. Under this preferential right, or "right of first refusal," a plant owner had to make its share available to the other owners before selling to a non-owner. Additionally, the agreement obligated each owner, under certain circumstances, to deliver raw natural gas liquids, or "raw make," to the plant for processing.

Enterprise, Texaco, Meridian and Union Pacific (collectively called "the Enterprise Parties") claim that three transactions, or "transfers," involving Tenneco Oil's ownership share of the plant breached the Restated Operating Agreement. In the First Transfer, Tenneco Oil conveyed its share to Tenneco Natural Gas Liquids Corporation. At the time of the First Transfer, the stock of Tenneco Natural Gas Liquids was wholly owned by Tenneco Oil. In the Second Transfer, Tenneco Oil sold all of Tenneco Natural Gas Liquids' stock to Enron Gas Processing Company, and Tenneco Natural Gas Liquids' name was changed to Enron Natural Gas Liquids Corporation. In the Third Transfer, Enron Gas Processing sold Enron Natural Gas Liquids' stock to Enron Liquids Pipeline Operating Limited Partnership. . . .

The Enterprise Parties sued Tenneco Oil and its parent corporation, Tenneco Inc. (the Tenneco Defendants), Enron Gas Processing and its parent, Enron Corp., as well as several other Enron affiliates (the Enron Defendants) for injunctive relief and damages for breach of contract, breach of fiduciary duty, and tortious interference with contract. The Enterprise Parties alleged that Tenneco Natural Gas Liquids did not comply with the raw-make delivery obligations that arose under the Restated Operating Agreement as a result of the First Transfer. The Enterprise Parties also claimed that the Second and Third Transfers violated the plant owners' right of first refusal.

II

In the First Transfer, Tenneco Oil conveyed its interest in the plant to its wholly owned subsidiary, Tenneco Natural Gas Liquids. The Enterprise Parties do not claim that this transfer triggered a right of first refusal because the Restated Operating Agreement allows transfers to wholly owned subsidiaries. Instead, the Enterprise Parties assert that this transaction invoked Section 12.2 of the Restated Operating Agreement. That Section provides:

> No sale, transfer, or assignment of Ownership Interest authorized by Section 12.1 shall be effective hereunder until. the assignee enters into an agreement with Operator to put through the Facilities a volume of raw make per day at least equal to the volume set forth opposite the name of the Selling Owner on Schedule C hereto.

. . . . The volume attributed to Tenneco Oil by Exhibit A was 31,000 barrels. To comply with Section 12.2, ... Tenneco Natural Gas Liquids (the assignee) should have agreed to deliver at least 31,000 barrels per day. At no point, however, did Tenneco Natural Gas Liquids either agree to provide, or actually deliver, the capacity attributed to it. The Enterprise Parties argue that Tenneco Natural Gas Liquids' failure to commit to the 31,000–barrel requirement is a breach of the Restated Operating Agreement.

The trial court granted the Tenneco Defendants' motion for summary judgment regarding the First Transfer without specifying the grounds.[1] The court of appeals reversed, holding that none of the bases upon which the Tenneco Defendants presented their motion supported the summary judgment ... To reverse the court of appeals and reinstate the trial court's judgment, we need to sustain only one of the Tenneco Defendants' summary judgment grounds. Rogers v. Ricane Enterprises, 772 S.W.2d 76, 79 (Tex.1989).

One theory upon which the Tenneco Defendants sought summary judgment was the Enterprise Parties' waiver of any complaint about the First Transfer. The affirmative defense of waiver can be asserted against a party who intentionally relinquishes a known right or engages in intentional conduct inconsistent with claiming that right. Sun Exploration & Prod. Co. v. Benton, 728 S.W.2d 35, 37 (Tex.1987). A waivable right may spring from law or, as in this case, from a contract. Ford v. Culbertson, 158 Tex. 124, 308 S.W.2d 855, 865 (1958); see also Alford, Meroney & Co. v. Rowe, 619 S.W.2d 210, 213 (Tex.Civ.App.–Amarillo 1981, writ ref'd n.r.e.). A party's express renunciation of a known right can establish waiver. Rowe, 619 S.W.2d at 213. Silence or inaction, for so long a period as to show an intention to yield the known right, is also enough to prove waiver. Id.

The Tenneco Defendants included in their summary judgment evidence deposition excerpts from the plant owners' designated representatives. Those excerpts demonstrate the following: (1) various owners knew that Tenneco Oil had transferred its ownership interest to Tenneco Natural Gas Liquids; (2) Tenneco Natural Gas Liquids had not executed an agreement in satisfaction of Section 12.2; and (3) Tenneco Natural Gas Liquids was delivering substantially less than 31,000 barrels per day.

Other summary judgment evidence shows that the plant owners accepted Tenneco Natural Gas Liquids as a full-fledged fellow owner and that they had elected not to enforce any rights arising under Section 12.2.

* * *

In this case, the Tenneco Defendants have shown that until this lawsuit was filed, the plant's owners accepted Tenneco Natural Gas Liquids as a fellow owner without enforcing Section 12.2. The Tenneco Defendants' proof of waiver, which includes testimonial admissions by the plant owners' designated representatives, establishes the affirmative defense of waiver as a matter of law. Accordingly, we reverse the judgment of the court of appeals regarding the First Transfer.

* * *

III

The Enterprise Parties claim that the Second and Third Transfers invoked the right of first refusal provisions of the Restated Operating

---

1. The Enron Defendants did not request summary judgment on this issue because they were not involved in the First Transfer.

Agreement. A right of first refusal, also known as a preemptive or preferential right, empowers its holder with a preferential right to purchase the subject property on the same terms offered by or to a bona fide purchaser. See Palmer v. Liles, 677 S.W.2d 661, 665 (Tex.App.–Houston [1st Dist.] 1984, writ ref'd n.r.e.). The right of first refusal upon which the Enterprise Parties base their claims arises from Section 12.5 of the Restated Operating Agreement:

> Preferential Right to Purchase. Except as provided in Section 12.6 hereof, if any Owner should desire to sell, transfer or assign all or any part of its Ownership Interest, the other Owners shall have the prior and preferential right and option to purchase proportionately the interest to be sold by such Owner upon the same terms and conditions as the bona fide prospective purchaser or purchasers (collectively "Offeror") are offered by such Owner. . . .

Section 12.6 allows transfers to wholly owned subsidiaries such as occurred in the First Transfer. The Second and Third Transfers do not fall within the exception provided in Section 12.6.

A

The Tenneco and Enron Defendants each filed substantially identical motions for summary judgment contending that the Second Transfer did not invoke the right of first refusal provision. In those motions, the Tenneco and Enron Defendants contend that: (1) the Second Transfer consisted only of a sale of Tenneco Natural Gas Liquids' stock from Tenneco Oil to Enron Gas Processing; (2) a stock sale is merely a transfer of ownership in an entity, not a sale of assets or ownership interest in a plant; (3) Tenneco Natural Gas Liquids' stock, rather than Tenneco Natural Gas Liquids' ownership interest in the plant, was transferred to Enron Gas Processing; and (4) as such, the transfer could not trigger any preferential rights.

* * *

In response, the Enterprise Parties offered three distinct pieces of summary judgment evidence: (1) proof that Tenneco Inc. had offered Tenneco Natural Gas Liquids' assets for sale before it finally settled upon the stock-sale transaction; (2) press releases in which Tenneco Inc. and Enron Corp. announced the completion of the Second Transfer; and (3) testimony from Tenneco Inc. and Tenneco Oil representatives indicating that, for tax purposes, the Tenneco Defendants and Enron Corp. had treated the Second Transfer as an asset sale rather than a stock sale.

B

The court of appeals held that the absence of the Second Transfer's written agreement from the summary judgment evidence raised a fact issue concerning whether at transfer was a stock sale or an asset sale. We disagree. The Tenneco and Enron Defendants proved that the transfer was a stock sale without including a copy of the relevant agreement in the summary judgment evidence. In the absence of controverting proof, Potempa's affidavit testimony is enough to establish the character of the transaction. See First Gibraltar Bank, FSB v. Farley, 895 S.W.2d 425, 428 (Tex.App.–San Antonio 1995, writ denied); Christian v. University Fed. Sav. Ass'n, 792 S.W.2d 533, 534 (Tex.App.–Houston [1st Dist.] 1990, no writ). Moreover, there were no objections to the affidavit.

Furthermore, the Enterprise Parties' summary judgment evidence does not undermine Potempa's affidavit. First, regardless of whether the parties originally proposed to transfer Tenneco Oil's ownership interest to Enron Gas Processing in an asset sale, the only relevant transaction was the completed stock sale. Preliminary negotiations between offerors and potential purchasers do not trigger preemptive rights. See Holland v. Fleming, 728 S.W.2d 820, 822–23 (Tex.App.–Houston [1st Dist.] 1987, writ ref'd n.r.e.); see also K.C.S., Ltd. v. East Main Street Land Development Corp., 40 Md.App. 196, 388 A.2d 181, 183 (1978).

* * *

Finally, the Enterprise Parties incorrectly argue that the election to treat the Second Transfer as an asset sale for tax purposes shows that it may not have been a stock sale. State law, not the Internal Revenue Code, controls the transaction's characterization. How the parties portray their transaction for federal tax purposes is immaterial. Questa Energy Corp. v. Vantage Point Energy, Inc., 887 S.W.2d 217, 221 (Tex.App.–Amarillo 1994, writ denied).

We hold that the summary judgment evidence establishes as a matter of law that the Second Transfer embodied a stock sale and not a transfer of assets. "[T]he purchaser of stock in a corporation does not purchase any portion of the corporation's assets, nor is a sale of all the stock of a corporation a sale of the physical properties of the corporation." McClory v. Schneider, 51 S.W.2d 738, 741 (Tex.Civ.App.–Amarillo 1932, writ dism'd); accord Engel v. Teleprompter Corp., 703 F.2d 127, 131 (5th Cir.1983). The transaction was not, therefore, a transfer of Tenneco Natural Gas Liquids' ownership interest in the fractionation plant.

C

Because the Second Transfer was not a conveyance of Tenneco Natural Gas Liquids' ownership interest in the plant, the Tenneco and Enron Defendants further argue that the transaction did not trigger the Enterprise Parties' preferential right to purchase. Conversely, the Enterprise Parties maintain that no matter how the parties structured the transaction, it was, in substance, a transfer of an ownership interest which invoked the right of first refusal.

The Enterprise Parties argue that we should look to the parties' intent to determine the nature of the transaction. The Enterprise Parties expressly rely upon Galveston Terminals, Inc. v. Tenneco Oil Co., 904 S.W.2d 787 (Tex.App.–Houston [1st Dist.] 1995), set aside without reference to the merits, 922 S.W.2d 549 (Tex.1996). In Galveston Terminals,

Tenneco Oil transferred its interest in a tract of land to a wholly owned subsidiary and then sold all of the subsidiary's stock to a third party. Id. 904 S.W.2d at 788–89. The party that originally conveyed the land to Tenneco Oil claimed that the sale of the subsidiary's stock triggered its preferential right to purchase the land. Id. at 789. The court of appeals held that "the character of a legal transaction depends upon the intent and purpose of the parties." Id. at 791. To determine the parties' intent, the court explained, Tenneco Oil's transfer of the property to the subsidiary and its subsequent sale of the subsidiary's stock should be viewed as a single transaction. Id. Considering the facts in that light, the court held that Tenneco Oil failed to prove as a matter of law that its stock sale did not actually amount to an asset sale. Id. at 792.

We expressly disapprove of the court's reasoning in Galveston Terminals. Sound corporate jurisprudence requires that courts narrowly construe rights of first refusal and other provisions that effectively restrict the free transfer of stock. See Consolidated Bearing & Supply Co. v. First Nat'l Bank, 720 S.W.2d 647, 650 (Tex.App.–Amarillo 1986, no writ); Gulf States Abrasive Mfg. v. Oertel, 489 S.W.2d 184, 187 (Tex.Civ.App.–Houston [1st Dist.] 1972, writ ref'd n.r.e.); see also Frandsen v. Jensen–Sundquist Agency, Inc., 802 F.2d 941, 946 (7th Cir.1986) (Posner, J.); Engel, 703 F.2d at 134. Viewing several separate transactions as a single transaction to invoke the right of first refusal compromises the law's unfavorable estimation of such restrictive provisions. See Consolidated Bearing, 720 S.W.2d at 650; Gulf States, 489 S.W.2d at 187.

Moreover, the plain language of the Restated Operating Agreement provides that only a transfer of an ownership interest triggers the preferential right to purchase; it says nothing about a change in stockholders. The Enterprise Parties could have included a change-of-control provision in the agreements that would trigger the preferential right to purchase. None of the agreements among the parties contained such a provision. We have long held that courts will not rewrite agreements to insert provisions parties could have included or to imply restraints for which they have not bargained. See Dorroh–Kelly Mercantile Co. v. Orient Ins. Co., 104 Tex. 199, 135 S.W. 1165, 1167 (1911); see also Great Am. Ins. Co. v. Langdeau, 379 S.W.2d 62, 65 (Tex.1964).

D

In holding that the sale of a corporation's stock does not trigger rights of first refusal, we join courts from other jurisdictions that have considered this issue. See, e.g., LaRose Mkt. v. Sylvan Ctr., 209 Mich.App. 201, 530 N.W.2d 505, 508 (1995); K.C.S., Ltd. v. East Main Street Land Development Corp., 40 Md.App. 196, 388 A.2d 181, 183 (1978); Cruising World, Inc. v. Westermeyer, 351 So.2d 371, 373 (Fla.Dist.Ct.App.1977), cert. denied, 361 So.2d 836 (Fla.1978); Torrey Delivery, Inc. v. Chautauqua Truck Sales & Serv., 47 A.D.2d 279, 366 N.Y.S.2d 506, 510 (N.Y.App. Div.1975). We also recognize the insight of commentators who have long maintained that stock sales do not invoke preemptive rights. See, e.g.,

Conine, Property Provisions of the Operating Agreement—Interpretation, Validity and Enforceability, 19 Tex. Tech L. Rev. 1263, 1320 & 1320 n. 231 (1988); Reasoner, Preferential Purchase Rights in Oil and Gas Instruments, 46 Tex. L. Rev. 57, 72 (1967); Abright, Comment, Preferential Right Provisions and Their Applicability to Oil and Gas Instruments, 32 Sw. L.J. 803, 811–12 (1978). A contrary conclusion is an unwarranted impingement on the free transfer of stock.

* * *

V

We hold that the sales of Tenneco Natural Gas Liquids' and Enron Natural Gas Liquids' stock did not invoke any right of first refusal and that the Enterprise Parties waived any complaint concerning Tenneco Natural Gas Liquids' delivery obligations. Accordingly, we reverse the judgment of the court of appeals and render judgment for the Petitioners.

OWEN, J., did not participate in the decision.

NOTES

1.   The procedure litigated in the principal case is sometimes referred to as "the Texas two-step." Not all courts would agree with the reasoning or result reached in the principal case. See, e.g., Williams Gas Processing–Wamsutter Co. v. Union Pacific Resources Co., 25 P.3d 1064, 163 O & G Rep. 926 (Wyo. 2001), where two companies that jointly owned a gas processing plant had an agreement containing a preferential right to purchase clause that applied if an owner proposed to all or part of its interest to a non-affiliate. One of the parties transferred its entire interest in the plant to a subsidiary, and then created a holding company to which all of the stock of the subsidiary was transferred. The holding company then merged with a third, unrelated company. The Wyoming Supreme Court rejected the argument that the latter transaction was a "merger" rather than a sale and held that it triggered the plant's other owner's preferential right of purchase.

2.   The court in Questa Energy Corp. v. Vantage Point Energy, Inc., 887 S.W.2d 217 (Tex. App. 1994) held that the right of first refusal was not triggered by a participant's agreement to trade its interest for shares of stock in another company. Should it make a difference whether the trade gives the seller control over the purchasing company? Should the preferential right apply to a non-participating, non-cost-bearing interest, such as an overriding royalty, that a JOA participant owns in the Contract Area? See Coral Production Corp. v. Central Resources, Inc., 730 N.W.2d 357 (Neb. 2007); El Paso Production Co. v. Geomet, Inc., 228 S.W.3d 178 (Tex. App. 2007).

3.   Although the preferential right to purchase typically contains no time limit on its exercise, at least two courts have ruled that it does not violate the rule against perpetuities. In Murphy Exploration & Production Co. v. Sun Operating Ltd. Partnership, 747 So.2d 260 (Miss. 1999). the Mississippi Supreme Court reasoned that the purpose of the rule against perpetuities is to avoid fettering real property with future interests and the preferential right

to purchase "amounts to no more than a continuing and preferred right to buy at the market whenever [a JOA participant] desires to sell." The Oklahoma Supreme Court reached the same result in Producers Oil Co. v. Gore, 610 P.2d 772 (Okla. 1980). Even if the preferential right to purchase does not violate the rule against perpetuities, might it be challenged as an invalid restraint on alienation? See Terry I. Cross, The Ties that Bind: Preemptive Rights and Restraints on Alienation that Commonly Burden Oil and Gas Properties, 5 Tex.Wesleyan L.Rev. 193 (1999).

4.   In addition to the variety of clauses contained in the body of the JOA, the instrument contemplates the attachment of several exhibits. At least three of these are expressly referred to in various clauses of the operating agreement and are essential to its validity and coherence. Exhibit A identifies the Contract Area and sets out the parties' fractional ownership interests. The contents of this exhibit must, of course, be separately drafted for each operating agreement. Exhibit C establishes the procedure for billings, payments and charges to the parties' joint account. Like the JOA itself, Exhibit C is usually a form instrument. The one most commonly used was promulgated by the Council of Petroleum Accountants Societies and is referred to as "the COPAS." One commentator has pointed to the value of having a widely accepted form that has "standar[ized] practices that would be far too costly for parties to negotiate in every new investment," while criticizing the form's bias in favor of the operator. John Burritt McArthur, A Twelve–Step Program for COPAS to Strengthen Oil and Gas Accounting Protections, 49 SMU L. Rev. 1447 (1996). Exhibit D lists both the types and amounts of insurance the operator is required to carry. See Michael E. Smith & Robert D. McCutcheon, Joint Operating Agreement Exhibits: A Survey, 47 Rocky Mtn.Min.L.Inst. 14–1 (2001) and Smith & Weaver § 17.5 for a description of the types of exhibits typically attached to a JOA.

Other documents or exhibits, such as the gas balancing agreement described earlier in this chapter, a statement of nondiscrimination, or a tax partnership agreement, may or may not be attached to the JOA, depending upon the particular circumstances of the transaction and the intent of the parties. One frequent attachment is an Area of Mutual Interest Clause. To avoid unequal and unfair distribution of benefits generated by joint operations, most operating agreements provide that any cash or acreage received under a bottom hole, acreage contribution, or other support agreement must be distributed proportionately for the benefit of all parties. Such clauses do not apply, however, to properties acquired inside or outside the contract area for consideration that is unrelated to drilling or other joint operations. As noted in Conine, 19 Tex.Tech L.Rev. at 1345–48 (1988), this situation leaves the parties free to engage in competitive lease acquisitions based on information obtained from joint operations. Because such conduct may be both unfair and detrimental to the smooth functioning of the operating agreement, area of mutual interest clauses are often added to the agreement, so that any party acquiring an oil and gas interest within the area governed by the operating agreement or within a specified distance from its perimeter must give all other parties an option to participate on a proportional basis.

If the acquisition was made possible by information obtained through joint operations, should the party acquiring the interest be compelled to share it with the other parties even in the absence of an express area of mutual interest clause? See Kaye v. Smitherman, 225 F.2d 583 (10th Cir.Kan.1955); Foley v. Phillips, 508 P.2d 975 (Kan. 1973); and Smith v. Bolin, 271 S.W.2d 93 (Tex. 1954).

F. DRILLING AND SERVICE CONTRACTS

The operator responsible for lease operations, whether it is the original lessee, a farmee, or the party named as the operator under a joint operating agreement, often has no seismic, drilling, or well-service equipment of its own. Accordingly, the operator typically enters into multiple contracts with service companies, including a seismic surveyor, a well-site surveyor, a road and well-pad builder, a utility company, a drilling contractor, a drilling-mud company, a well-logging company, a service company that specializes in directing and measuring horizontal well bores, and perhaps a company that may hydraulically fracture a well. Producing wells are often monitored, maintained, and occasionally "reworked" by service contractors. Although service contracts are customarily performed on either a daywork or turnkey basis, depending on the type of service provided, the operator may wish to consider other alternatives. For example, a drilling contractor may be engaged on a turnkey, footage, or daywork (day rate) basis.

> On a "turnkey" basis, the parties agree on a fixed sum of money that will be paid to the drilling contractor in return for his furnishing a drilling crew, drilling equipment and certain specified materials and services, to be due and payable only after the hole is drilled to contract depth; all other services, materials and equipment are furnished at the cost of the well owner. On a "footage basis," the drilling contractor furnishes the drilling crew, drilling equipment and certain specified services, materials and supplies; he is paid an agreed sum of money for each foot actually drilled, irrespective of whether the proposed depth is reached or not; all other materials, supplies and equipment are furnished by the well owner. On a "day rate" basis, the drilling contractor furnishes the drilling crew and drilling equipment; he is paid an agreed sum of money for each day spent in drilling regardless of the number of days involved; all materials, services and supplies that are not agreed to be furnished by the contractor are furnished by the well owner.

Haas v. Gulf Coast Natural Gas Co., 484 S.W.2d 127, 131 (Tex.Civ.App. 1972) Joint operating agreements frequently require that wells be drilled "on a competitive contract basis." If the drilling contract allows bids, is it possible to compare bids made on the basis of different types of contract? Can an operator justify entering into a daywork or turnkey contract if the AFE sent to nonoperators said that the drilling contract would be bid on a footage basis? See Haas v. Gulf Coast Natural Gas Co., 484 S.W.2d 127 (Tex.Civ.App.1972).

In most situations, the operator's preferred type of drilling contract turns upon an evaluation of cost and control versus risk. In a turnkey contract, the operator does not control how the well is drilled and thus assumes significantly less down-hole risk; however, the cost will be greater, when compared to a hypothetical daywork well completed on schedule, because the drilling contractor assumes more of the down-hole risk and will want to be compensated accordingly. In the more common daywork drilling contract, the operator directs the overall drilling operation and thus assumes greater down-hole risk; thus, if the well is completed on schedule with no unexpected additional costs, the operator will pay the drilling contractor less than if the well were drilled on a turnkey basis. The footage contract represents a middle ground and is the preferred choice in certain markets, such as Kansas, but is less common than the daywork contract.

In some situations, the choice of type of drilling contract may depend on which party is in the superior bargaining position; the operator may prefer one type of contract (usually turnkey or perhaps footage), whereas the contractor prefers another type (usually daywork). In boom times when rigs are in short supply, drilling contractors tend to have the upper hand; the reverse is true when drilling activity drops precipitously. And large operators probably have more bargaining power than small operators. The type of contract used will also be influenced by site location, projected well depth, drilling conditions, general availability of the kind of rig and equipment required, and the operator's experience. Contracts for drilling in deep offshore waters and in arctic areas are usually of the daywork type. The same is true of "international" contracts—wells drilled outside the United States and Canada.

Nothing precludes the parties from using their own, specially crafted contract that does not follow any of the traditional types. For example, in Boger & Boger v. Continental Fire & Casualty Ins. Corp., 234 S.W.2d 133 (Tex.Civ.App.1950, writ ref'd n.r.e.), the drilling company contracted to furnish the rig, equipment, and drilling services in exchange for a conveyance of an undivided interest in the oil and gas lease and an agreement by the operator to pay "all out-of-pocket expense" connected with the drilling. Under the terms of what is often referred to as a risk-service contract, a drilling or service contractor is compensated based upon the contractor's success in completing assigned tasks ahead of schedule, under budget, or to a specified threshold level of success.

As is true of the operating agreement and the oil and gas lease, parties negotiating a drilling contract often begin with a printed form, such as one of the forms promulgated by the International Association of Drilling Contractors ("IADC") or a pre-prepared form furnished by one of the parties. Not surprisingly, the IADC forms are contractor oriented. Nevertheless, many operators, especially companies with little bargaining power, often execute IADC forms with little or no changes because they may not fully appreciate the potential risks involved or may have little choice if they want a well drilled in time to save a lease. Larger operators have their own drilling contract forms that are more operator oriented, and they also have their own service contract forms.

If a well-service contractor is engaged to perform services on a number of wells and leaseholds over an extended period of time, the parties may enter into a "Master Service Agreement," which is then implemented for each service provided through separate "work orders." Some service contractors will attempt to use a one-operation "work order" or "rig ticket" as the form of service contract. Not surprisingly, a contractor-furnished work order will typically allocate most of the risk to the operator. Such an arrangement is therefore unpopular with operators and leaves both parties uncertain regarding a number of important legal issues that may arise during and after the period during which the contractor provides services.

A Master Service Agreement ("MSA") is similar to any other contract in that it states the responsibilities and obligations of one party towards another. An MSA differs from a typical service contract in that it defines rates, services, responsibilities, and other obligations of both parties as applied to a series of similar activities to be repeated at many locations over an extended or even indefinite period of time. And MSA alleviates the need to negotiate a completely new service contract every time a contractor performs an operation under a work order or rig ticket by providing terms that the contractor and operator want to cover all services or material furnished by the contractor for the operator.

MSAs generally stipulate the level and measure of care and conduct under which the individual services will be provided, the choice of state law to govern the MSA terms and any legal action that may occur over the provision of services under future work orders, and a choice of forum, perhaps arbitration, for the settlement of disputes. MSAs also typically describe force majeure conditions, termination, and contact information of parties that may be used in emergency situations.

Generally, the most important and complex provisions in an MSA are the cross indemnities (often called "knock-for-knock" indemnities) between the parties wherein each party typically agrees to indemnify the other party against liability for harm to indemnitor's property or employees. These indemnities may also expressly cover harm to the indemnitor's subcontractors (or other contractors) and the indemnity protection may expressly extend to the other party's other contractors (or subcontractors). These contractual indemnities are often given regardless of cause, including negligence of the indemnified party or parties.

Indemnities and the allocation of risk is illustrated by the two principal cases in this section. Depending on the state wherein the services and materials are to be provided, drafters of MSAs and other service contracts must contend with particular state statutory law or case law addressing the enforceability of indemnities against negligence For example, Texas courts require that an indemnity against negligence, as well as a release from negligence liability, must be "conspicuous." See Dresser

Industries, Inc. v. Page Petroleum, Inc., 853 S.W.2d 505 (Tex.1993). Thus, Texas contracts customarily boldface, capitalize, or otherwise highlight indemnity clauses.

MSAs are not a substitute for certain types of service contracts. Drilling and construction contracts, for example, cover very complex and expensive single operations and are therefore better covered with a single contract tailored to that one unique event or operation. Other types of contracts, such as equipment rental contracts, rolling purchase orders, or service contracts that provide for operations at many different locations may contain specially tailored indemnity provisions.

Indemnity provisions are subject to revocation or curtailment by specific oilfield anti-indemnity statutes found in a handful of states with a long history of petroleum production and may be vulnerable to general anti-indemnity laws in states where indemnities covering tortious conduct are unenforceable on public-policy grounds.

MSAs and other service contracts commonly include insurance provisions, which, in part, are required to support indemnities. These provisions describe the types of insurance that each party must carry and the minimum amount of coverage required for each type of insurance. In many service contracts, only the contractor is required to secure insurance since it is the party providing the services and materials, but some contracts may require both parties to carry insurance, although major oil and gas companies generally self-insure.

A matter of special concern in choosing the type of drilling contract and negotiating its specific provisions is allocation of risks. Generally speaking, an operator assumes the most risk under a daywork contract. Under this arrangement, the operator generally makes decisions concerning the day-to-day drilling and is responsible for paying the specified day rate—generally regardless of progress. The contractor assumes the most risk under a turnkey contract, because the contractor promises to drill the well for a fixed price, regardless of problems encountered in the course of drilling. The drilling contractor's risk is somewhat mitigated by a provision, common in both turnkey and footage contracts, that converts the contract to a daywork basis, both in terms of compensation and risk allocation, if specified problems are encountered or if the operator elects to continue drilling below the initial contract depth. Drilling contracts, and most service contracts, contain detailed provisions allocating the risk of loss. The precise language may be partially driven by the terms of underlying insurance policies.

Both parties must be careful that the contract provisions regarding risk allocation, indemnities, and insurance are internally consistent and especially careful that insurance coverages dovetail with contract terms. In addition, the operator will be concerned that its contracts with other contractors at the work site achieve a consistent risk allocation. The contractor will have the same concern with its subcontractors, if any. All types of drilling and service contracts customarily contain detailed provisions addressing potential liability for personal injury or property damage resulting from hazards inherent in almost all drilling and service operations, and drilling contracts, as well as some service contracts, allocate risks of unexpected costs and delays and potential liability for violating safety and environmental regulations.

Rather than allocating risk "at law," the parties will typically allocate risk by contract—usually without regard to the negligence of either party. Why would parties choose to do this? The rationale is generally explained as an attempt to promote certainty and an effort to allocate certain risks to the party most able to control, insure, or accept such risks. Of course, neither party can avoid potential tort liability to third parties, but they can contractually allocate the risks of tort and other liability between each other through indemnity provisions. Thus, as between the parties, responsibility for certain losses arising from a particular accident or event can be determined by reading the contract. The following case illustrates how risks are typically allocated between an operator and drilling contractor in the event of a well blowout.

CAZA DRILLING (CALIFORNIA), INC. v. TEG OIL & GAS U.S.A., INC.

142 Cal.App.4th 453 (2006).

Epstein, P.J.

Appellants TEG Oil & Gas U.S.A., Inc. (TEG) and its parent company Sefton Resources, Inc. (Sefton) appeal the grant of summary judgment on their cross-complaint against respondent CAZA Drilling (California), Inc. (CAZA). TEG hired CAZA pursuant to a written agreement to drill a well on an oil field leased by TEG and Sefton and operated by TEG. CAZA argued, and the trial court agreed, that exculpatory and limitation of liability provisions in the parties' agreement precluded the recovery of the types of damages sought in the cross-complaint: compensation for economic loss and physical harm to equipment and facilities. The court entered judgment on the cross-complaint, despite appellants' contention that CAZA was both negligent and in violation of various regulations governing oil drilling operations.

On appeal, appellants take the position that the exculpatory and limitation of liability provisions in the parties' agreement are invalid under Civil Code section 1668 (section 1668), which prohibits enforcement of contracts that have for their object the exemption of parties from responsibility for fraud, willful injury, or violations of law. We conclude that the contractual provisions represented a valid limitation on liability rather than a complete exemption from responsibility, and that, in any event, appellants have failed in their repeated efforts to identify a specific law or regulation potentially violated by CAZA. We shall affirm the trial court judgment.

FACTUAL AND PROCEDURAL BACKGROUND

Certain background facts are not disputed. In 2002, CAZA was hired by TEG to drill a well at the Tapia oil field, located in Castaic, California. The well was referred to as "Yule 6." The work was performed under a standardized contract entitled "Daywork Drilling Contract—U.S."[1] A few days after drilling began, there was a blowout, resulting in the death of a CAZA employee, injury to others, and complete destruction of Yule 6.

It is appellants' position the blowout was the result of the negligence of CAZA's crew in pulling the drillstring out of the wellhole too quickly (referred to as "swabbing in"), which caused a fire to ignite. Under appellants' theory, the crew committed further negligence by failing to close the blowout preventer after the fire began. Nonetheless, TEG felt constrained to engage CAZA to do additional work to help repair the damage. In 2003, the parties signed a second Daywork Drilling Contract and a "Payment Schedule" to deal with outstanding invoices due under the 2002 agreement.

Complaint

In November 2003, CAZA sued TEG for breach of contract, open book account, account stated, quantum meruit, and foreclosure of oil and gas liens. Initially, the complaint was based on the Payment Schedule. CAZA claimed to be owed $33,219.94, plus interest.

Subsequently, CAZA amended the complaint to include claims for breach of the two Daywork Drilling Contracts. The claim for unpaid work was increased to $117,824.73, based on work performed under the 2003 agreement.

Cross–Complaint

TEG and Sefton cross-claimed against CAZA for breach of contract, negligence, and negligence per se based on violations of various safety provisions contained in state and federal regulations. The cross-complaint alleged that as a result of CAZA's actions appellants suffered "damage to the Well and the hole, as well as unexpected and otherwise unnecessary cleanup and remediation damage, and losses to [appellants'] business operations." Although there is a reference to the related lawsuit by the survivors of the deceased worker (*Currington et al., v. TEG Oil & Gas U.S.A. et al.* (Super. Ct. Los Angeles County, 2003, No. PC033424 (*Currington*)), the cross-complaint does not seek indemnification for damages paid to the plaintiffs in that lawsuit.

Daywork Drilling Contract

The 2002 Daywork Drilling Contract consists of a standardized form agreement with a number of blanks for the name of the operator, the contractor, the location of the well, the commencement date of drilling operations, the rates to be charged for various tasks, and other items.

---

1. The same document also contained the "Drilling Bid Proposal" from CAZA.

TEG was designated the "Operator" and CAZA was described as the "Contractor." The contract begins with a statement that "Operator [TEG] engages Contractor [CAZA] as an Independent Contractor to drill the hereinafter designated well or wells in search of oil or gas on a daywork basis" and that "Contractor shall furnish equipment, labor, and perform services as herein provided, for a specified sum per day under the direction, supervision and control of Operator." "Daywork basis" is defined to mean that "Contractor shall furnish equipment, labor, and perform services as herein provided, for a specified sum per day under the direction, supervision and control of Operator (inclusive of any employee, agent, consultant or subcontractor engaged by Operator to direct drilling operations)." The contract also provides that: "When operating on a daywork basis, Contractor shall be fully paid at the applicable rates of payment and assumes only the obligations and liabilities stated herein. Except for such obligations and liabilities specifically assumed by Contractor, Operator shall be solely responsible and assumes liability for all consequences of operations by both parties while on a daywork basis, including results and all other risks or liabilities incurred in or incident to such operations."

Paragraph 8, entitled "DRILLING METHODS AND PRACTICES" includes the following pertinent subparagraphs:

> 8.1 Contractor [CAZA] shall maintain well control equipment in good condition at all times and shall use all reasonable means to prevent and control fires and blowouts and to protect the hole.
>
> . . .
>
> 8.3 Each party hereto agrees to comply with all laws, rules, and regulations of any federal, state or local governmental authority which are now or may become applicable to that party's operations covered by or arising out of the performance of this Contract.

Paragraph 14 governs "RESPONSIBILITY FOR LOSS OR DAMAGE, INDEMNITY, RELEASE OF LIABILITY AND ALLOCATION OF RISK." Under subparagraph 14.1, the contractor (CAZA) "assume[s] liability" for "damage to or destruction of Contractor's surface equipment," unless the damage fell under paragraph 10, which requires the operator (TEG) to prepare a "sound location" to support the drilling rig, or subparagraph 14.3, which requires the operator to assume liability for damage to or destruction of the contractor's equipment "caused by exposure to highly corrosive or otherwise destructive elements, including those introduced into the drilling fluid." Subparagraph 14.2 requires the operator to assume liability for "damage to or destruction of Contractor's in-hole equipment."

Subparagraph 14.4 requires the operator (TEG) to assume liability "for damage to or destruction of Operator's equipment . . . regardless of when or how such damage or destruction occurs," and to "release Contractor of any liability for any such loss or damage." Similarly, under subparagraph 14.5, the operator is to "be solely responsible for . . .

damage to or loss of the hole, including the casing therein" and the operator is to "release Contractor [CAZA] of any liability for damage to or loss of the hole" and in addition "protect, defend and indemnify Contractor from and against any and all claims, liability, and expense relating to such damage to or loss of the hole."

In subparagraph 14.6, the operator releases the contractor from liability for, and agrees to indemnify the contractor from and against claims "on account of injury to, destruction of, or loss or impairment of any property right in or to oil, gas, or other mineral substance or water" unless "reduced to physical possession above the surface of the earth," and for "any loss or damage to any formation, strata, or reservoir beneath the surface of the earth."

Subparagraphs 14.8 and 14.9 require the parties to indemnify each other for claims based on injuries to their own employees "without regard to the cause or causes thereof or the negligence of any party or parties."

Subparagraph 14.10 states that the operator is liable "for the cost of regaining control of any wild well, as well as for cost of removal of any debris."

The parties focus particular attention on subparagraph 14.11. Entitled "Pollution and Contamination," it provides:

"Notwithstanding anything to the contrary contained herein, except the provisions of Paragraphs 10 and 12,[2] it is understood and agreed by and between Contractor and Operator that the responsibility for pollution and contamination shall be as follows: [¶] (a) Unless otherwise provided herein, Contractor [CAZA] shall assume all responsibility for, including control and removal of, and shall protect, defend and indemnity Operator from and against all claims, demands and causes of action of every kind and character arising from pollution or contamination, which originates above the surface of the land or water from spills of fuels, lubricants, motor oils, pipe dope, paints, solvents, ballast, bilge and garbage, except unavoidable pollution from reserve pits, wholly in Contractor's possession and control and directly associated with Contractor's equipment and facilities.

"(b) Operator [TEG] shall assume all responsibility for, including control and removal of, and shall protect, defend and indemnify Contractor from and against all claims, demands, and causes of action of every kind and character arising directly or indirectly from all other pollution or contamination which may occur during the conduct of operations hereunder, including, but not limited to, that which may result from fire, blowout, cratering, seepage of any other uncontrolled flow of oil, gas, water or other substance, as well as the use or disposition of all drilling fluids, including, but not limited to, oil emulsion, oil base or chemically treated drilling fluids, contaminated

---

2. As we have seen, paragraph 10 obligates the operator to prepare a sound location. Paragraph 12 provides for termination of the contractor's liability after restoration of the location.

cuttings or cavings, lost circulation and fish recovery materials and fluids. Operator shall release Contractor of any liability for the foregoing."

Subparagraph 14.12 provides that neither party is liable to the other for "special, indirect or consequential damages resulting from or arising out of this Contract, including, without limitation, loss of profit or business interruptions including loss or delay of production, however same may be caused."

Finally, subparagraph 14.13 entitled "Indemnity Obligation" provides: "Except as otherwise expressly limited herein, it is the intent of parties hereto that all releases, indemnity obligations and/or liabilities assumed by such parties under terms of this Contract, including, without limitation, Subparagraphs 14.1 through 14.12 hereof, be without limit and without regard to the cause or causes thereof (including preexisting conditions), strict liability, regulatory or statutory liability, breach of warranty (express or implied), any theory of tort, breach of contract or the negligence of any party or parties, whether such negligence be sole, joint or concurrent, active or passive."

There are two nonstandardized provisions. A handwritten term provides for a $10 million umbrella policy, in addition to the statutory workers' compensation insurance and the comprehensive general and automobile liability insurance policies. The other change is the deletion by interlineation of a provision requiring TEG to pay motel expenses for CAZA employees.

CAZA's Motion for Summary Judgment

CAZA moved for summary judgment on the cross-complaint on the ground that the 2002 Daywork Drilling Contract allocates liability for all damages claimed by appellants in the cross-complaint to TEG. * * *

In its memorandum of points and authorities, CAZA relied primarily on the 2002 Daywork Drilling Contract provision that "Operator shall be solely responsible and assumes liability for all consequences of operations by both parties while on a Daywork basis, including results and all other risks or liabilities incurred in or incident to such operations" to establish that it could not be liable to appellants on the cross-complaint. The memorandum also references subparagraph 14.11 governing liability for environmental pollution, subparagraph 14.5 governing liability for damage to the hole, and subparagraph 14.12 prohibiting the recovery of consequential damages.

Appellants' Opposition

* * * With respect to their losses, appellants stated that "Cross–Complainant claims that it is owed money for damages to its well and other costs and expenses resulting from CAZA's breach of the contract and from CAZA's gross negligence and violation of law." They further stated that "[t]he blowout and fire at the Yule 6 well caused injury and death

and completely destroyed the well, forcing [appellants] to expend funds for remediation and clean-up, and for other costs and expenses, leaving TEG without income and resulting in Sefton having to sell its stock at a depressed price to raise capital."

Appellants disputed that any of their employees was expert in drilling. They asserted that CAZA "had the only drilling rig available for work which would allow TEG to begin drilling work during the latter part of 2002" and that "[f]or financial reasons and because of duties to stockholders, [appellants] could not wait for other companies to have a rig available at a later time."

The remainder of appellants' SOF describes in detail the actions or omissions of CAZA's crew that appellants believe caused the blowout and fire. These assertions were supported by the declaration of expert witness, Gregg S. Perkin. Perkin expressed the opinion that "the CAZA crew swabbed in TEG's well as the drill stem was being pulled from the well"; that "the swabbing of the Yule 6 wellbore by the actions of the CAZA crew, and not an earlier reduction in the drilling mud's weight, caused the well to kick" resulting in "the well's blowing out and catching fire"; and that "[m]ore likely than not . . . the drill stem was being pulled out of the hole [in a] negligent manner." He based this opinion on his review of the report of the Department of Gas and Geothermal Resources, the "Data-Hub EDR Log," and CAZA's "Master Driller Reference Guide." Perkin stated that in undertaking these actions, CAZA violated "Part 30 of the Code of Federal Regulations, Part 250.410(b), which stated that: [¶] '4) Drill pipe and downhole tool running and pulling speeds shall be at controlled rates so as not to induce an influx of formation fluids from the effects of swabbing nor cause a loss of drilling fluid and corresponding hydrostatic pressure decrease from the effects of surging. [¶] 5) When there is an indication of swabbing or influx of formation fluids, the safety devices and measures necessary to control the well shall be employed. The mud shall be circulated and conditioned, on or near the bottom, unless well or mud conditions prevent running the drill pipe back to the bottom.' " (Emphasis omitted.)

Trial Court Order

The trial court granted the motion for summary judgment on the cross-complaint, stating in its order: "[CAZA] asserts that the cross-complaint is barred by the provisions of the contract between the parties assigning liability 'for all consequences of operations by both parties' to [TEG]. Therefore, the issue is one of contract interpretation and is a matter of law for the court to decide. [¶][TEG] points to clauses in the contract requiring [CAZA] to maintain and control well equipment and follow the law. These provisions, however, do not negate the provisions assigning liability to [TEG] 'for all consequences of operation.' [TEG] argues further that the exculpatory provisions of the contract are void as against public policy under Civil Code Section 1668. The court disagrees for the reasons set forth in the moving papers."

Judgment was entered on the cross-complaint, and both Sefton and TEG purported to appeal, although TEG was a party to the still pending complaint.

DISCUSSION

I

* * *

II

We now turn to the merits. According to the 2002 Daywork Drilling Contract, "[e]xcept for such obligations and liabilities specifically assumed by [CAZA], [TEG] shall be solely responsible and assume liability for all consequences of operations by both parties." This was the provision chiefly relied upon by CAZA in seeking summary judgment. Preliminarily, appellants contend this general language cannot control over more specific provisions of subparagraphs 8.1, requiring CAZA to use "all reasonable means" to prevent fires and blowouts, and 8.3, requiring that both parties comply with all federal, state, and local laws, rules, and regulations.

Appellants are correct that when general and specific provisions are inconsistent, the latter control. (Code Civ. Proc., § 1859; 1 Witkin, Summary of Cal. Law (10th ed. 2005) Contracts, § 754, p. 845.) However, as we have seen, the general provision just quoted is not the only provision in the agreement relating to allocation and limitation of liability. Paragraph 14 describes in detail the parties' respective "RESPONSIBILITY FOR LOSS OR DAMAGE, INDEMNITY, RELEASE OF LIABILITY AND AL-LOCATION OF RISK." Under its terms, each party was to be liable for damage to its own equipment, with certain limited exceptions, and for injury to its own employees. Responsibility for damage to the hole and the underground minerals and for regaining control of a "wild well" was fixed on the operator. Liability for "Pollution and Contamination" was allocated between the parties depending on the cause. Neither party was to be liable for the other's consequential damages. These provisions are more specific with respect to allocation and limitation of liability than the language cited by appellants.

Beyond that, we do not believe that the allocation and limitation of liability provisions are contradicted by subparagraphs 8.1 and 8.3. The latter describes CAZA's duties under the contract. To the extent TEG can establish that CAZA failed to perform these duties, it is entitled to raise that breach as a defense to CAZA's claim for payment under the 2002 Daywork Drilling Contract. The provisions of paragraph 14 are intended to limit contract damages by excluding consequential damages and allocating liability for tort damages for injuries to persons or property in the case of negligence. There is nothing inherently inconsistent in a party to a contract agreeing to do "X," but stating that if it does not, the other party may not recover consequential damages or stating that if negligence occurs during the performance of "X," liability will be limited.

The authorities upon which appellants rely [citations omitted] were decided before the Supreme Court's seminal decision in Tunkl v. Regents of University of California (1963) 60 Cal.2d 92, 32 Cal.Rptr. 33, 383 P.2d 441 (Tunkl), which we discuss more fully below. Their conclusion that a party cannot limit its liability for a duty it has undertaken to perform by contract when that duty is negligently performed does not represent the current state of the law in this area.

Appellants also contend that the provisions of the various subparagraphs of paragraph 14 cannot be read as excluding liability for negligence because negligence was not specifically mentioned in every subparagraph. It is true that "[f]or an agreement to be construed as precluding liability for 'active' or 'affirmative' negligence, there must be express and unequivocal language in the agreement which precludes such liability" and that "[a]n agreement which seeks to limit liability generally without specifically mentioning negligence is construed to shield a party only for passive negligence, not for active negligence." [citations omitted] But it is equally true that "[w]hether an exculpatory clause 'covers a given case turns primarily on contractual interpretation, and it is the intent of the parties as expressed in the agreement that should control. When the parties knowingly bargain for the protection at issue, the protection should be afforded. This requires an inquiry into the circumstances of the damage or injury and the language of the contract; of necessity, each case will turn on its own facts.'" [Citations omitted]

Subparagraph 14.13 specifically states that the allocations of liability set forth in subparagraphs 14.1 through 14.12 are "without limit" and "without regard to the cause or causes thereof," including "regulatory or statutory liability," "breach of contract or the negligence of any party or parties, whether such negligence be sole, joint or concurrent, active or passive." Read as a whole, the provisions of paragraph 14 make clear the parties' intent—to limit "the Operator's" ability to recover for injury resulting from accidents, even those caused by the negligence of "the Contractor." As a matter of contractual interpretation, there is nothing to hinder a "voluntary transactions in which one party, for a consideration, agrees to shoulder a risk which the law would otherwise have placed upon the other party." (Tunkl, supra, 60 Cal.Rptr. 33, 383 P.2d 441.) Such an agreement may, however, run afoul of section 1668, to which we now turn.

III

Section 1668 provides that "[a]ll contracts which have for their object, directly or indirectly, to exempt any one from responsibility for his own fraud, or willful injury to the person or property of another, or violation of law, whether willful or negligent, are against the policy of the law." As explained in Tunkl, early interpretations of this provision expressed the view that section 1668 absolutely prohibited a party from limiting its liability for its own negligence. (Tunkl, supra, 60 Cal.2d at p. 95, 32 Cal.Rptr. 33, 383 P.2d 441, citing England v. Lyon Fireproof Storage Co.

(1928) 94 Cal.App. 562, 271 P. 532.) In Mills v. Ruppert (1959) 167 Cal.App.2d 58, 333 P.2d 818, however, the court pointed out that "the only use of the word negligent in said section is in a restrictive sense and only in connection with violations of law." (Id. at p. 62, 333 P.2d 818.) It necessarily followed that " 'contracts seeking to relieve individuals from the results of their own negligence are not invalid as against the policy of the law as therein provided, and hence are neither contrary to public policy nor expressed provision of the law....' " (Id. at p. 63, 333 P.2d 818; accord, Werner v. Knoll (1948) 89 Cal.App.2d 474, 475–476, 201 P.2d 45.)

In Tunkl, the Supreme Court limited the holding in Mills v. Ruppert. The court concluded that exculpatory clauses relieving a party from the consequences of its own negligence cannot be enforced where the public interest was involved, even if the conduct did not involve a violation of law. The court described factors or characteristics which identify a transaction implicating the public interest: (1) the transaction "concerns a business of a type generally thought suitable for public regulation"; (2) "[t]he party seeking exculpation is engaged in performing a service of great importance to the public, which is often a matter of practical necessity for some members of the public"; (3) "[t]he party holds himself out as willing to perform this service for any member of the public who seeks it, or at least for any member coming within certain established standards"; (4) "[a]s a result of the essential nature of the service, in the economic setting of the transaction, the party invoking exculpation possesses a decisive advantage of bargaining strength against any member of the public who seeks his services"; (5) "[i]n exercising a superior bargaining power the party confronts the public with a standardized adhesion contract of exculpation, and makes no provision whereby a purchaser may pay additional reasonable fees and obtain protection against negligence"; and (6) "[a]s a result of the transaction, the person or property of the purchaser is placed under the control of the seller, subject to the risk of carelessness by the seller or his agents." (Tunkl, supra, 60 Cal.2d at pp. 98–101, 32 Cal.Rptr. 33, 383 P.2d 441, fns. omitted.)

Appellants contend these factors are present here. We disagree. Although the Supreme Court did not specifically exclude contracts between relatively equal business entities from its definition of contracts in the public interest, it is difficult to imagine a situation where a contract of that type would meet more than one or two of the requirements discussed in Tunkl. With respect to the second and third factors, for example, CAZA did not hold itself out as performing services for the public, but only for the small number of entities that happened to be oil field operators. While the production of oil is of great importance to the public, the drilling of a particular oil well is generally only important to the party who will profit from it. With respect to the fourth and fifth factors, appellants' argument that it was forced into an adhesion contract boils down to this: "Although two provisions in the agreement were altered during negotiations, we did not know we could alter any provisions during negotiations." The fact that TEG found itself backed into a corner in late 2002 as a result of failure to plan ahead and had no choice but to deal with the only company that had a suitable drill rig available at that specific point in time, is not the sort of unequal bargaining power to which the court in Tunkl referred.

* * * CAZA's services may have been essential to TEG, but the agreement between the parties did not implicate the public interest in the way required to abrogate exculpatory provisions limiting liability for negligence under Tunkl.

IV

If Tunkl were the only basis raised by appellants for the applicability of section 1668, we could end our analysis. However, in their cross-complaint and their opposition to the motion for summary judgment, appellants contend that CAZA violated various statutes and regulations in performing drilling activities. They argue that section 1668 invalidates any exculpatory language that would relieve CAZA of liability for performing drilling operations in violation of law "without regard to whether any public interest [was] involved." They cite for support this court's recent decision in Capri v. L.A. Fitness International, LLC (2006) 136 Cal. App.4th 1078, 39 Cal.Rptr.3d 425 (Capri).

* * *

Capri is significantly different from the present case because it involved personal injury to a consumer. Here, the contract was between two business entities and the damages claimed are entirely economic. In only one recent case has a court applied section 1668 to invalidate provisions in a contract between business entities: Health Net of California, Inc. v. Department of Health Services (2003) 113 Cal.App.4th 224, 6 Cal.Rptr.3d 235 (Health Net). * * *

The holding in Health Net does not apply to this case because, as the court explained, the exculpatory clause at issue in that case "prohibit[ed] ... the recovery of any damages at all for DHS's statutory for regulatory violations" and "exempt[ed] DHS completely from responsibility for completed wrongs." (113 Cal.App.4th at pp. 240–241, 6 Cal.Rptr.3d 235, italics added.) The court believed that even in a commercial case, "an exculpation of any liability for any damages for any statutory violation surely rises to the level of an 'exempt[ion] from responsibility' within the meaning of the plain language of section 1668." (Id. at p. 239, 6 Cal. Rptr.3d 235.) The provisions at issue here do not exempt CAZA from all liability, but merely limit its responsibility with respect to economic damages. * * * * * * In the majority of commercial situations, courts have upheld contractual limitations on liability, even against claims that the breaching party violated a law or regulation. [Discussion of various such cases omitted.]* * *

* * *

Based on these authorities, we conclude that the challenged provisions in the 2002 Daywork Drilling Contract represent a valid limitation on liability rather than an improper attempt to exempt a contracting party from responsibility for violation of law within the meaning of section 1668. CAZA did not seek or obtain complete exemption from culpability on account of its potential negligence or violation of any applicable regulations. It merely sought to limit its liability for economic harm suffered by TEG. The parties foresaw the possibility that a blowout could occur and agreed between themselves concerning where the losses would fall. Significantly, the agreement required CAZA to accept responsibility for damage to its equipment, injury to its employees, and certain pollution and contamination removal and control activities. Thus, the limitation of liability provisions did not adversely affect the public or the workers employed by CAZA. As appellants concede, CAZA accepted liability for the bodily injury that occurred as the result of the blowout, and has defended and indemnified appellants, through its carrier, in the Currington litigation. Under these facts, * * * where the only question is which of two equal bargainers should bear the risk of economic loss in the event of a particular mishap, there is no reason for the courts to intervene and remake the parties' agreement.

V

Finally, appellants made no serious effort to identify a specific law or regulation potentially violated by CAZA so as to trigger application of section 1668. In their cross-complaint, appellants contended that CAZA violated Public Resources Code section 3219, as well as California Code of Regulations, title 14, sections 1722, subdivisions (a) and (c), 1722.2, 1722.5, 1722.6, and 1744, and title 8, sections 3202, 6507, and 6573, subdivision (a). Appellants did not mention any of these provisions in opposing the summary judgment motion. * * *

* * *

At first glance, the statutory and regulatory provisions cited in the cross-complaint seem more relevant. Public Resources Code section 3219 appears in chapter 1 of division 3, which covers "oil and gas" wells. (Pub. Resources Code, § 3008.) Section 3219 provides: "Any person engaged in operating any oil or gas well wherein high pressure gas is known to exist, and any person drilling for oil or gas in any district where the pressure of oil or gas is unknown shall equip the well with casing of sufficient strength, and with such other safety devices as may be necessary, in accordance with methods approved by the supervisor, and shall use every effort and endeavor effectually to prevent blowouts, explosions, and fires." But, on examination, the flaw in appellants' attempt to hold CAZA accountable for ensuring compliance with this chapter of the Public Resources Code and the safety regulations promulgated under it becomes apparent.

Section 3219 of the Public Resources Code refers to persons engaged in "operating" oil or gas wells. Section 3009 defines "[o]perator" as "any person who, by virtue of ownership, or under the authority of a lease or any other agreement, has the right to drill, operate, maintain, or control a well." It would be stretching the definition of "operator" to include a company performing drilling work by the day. This is confirmed by other statutory provisions found in this chapter of the Public Resources Code, which imposes duties on "the operator" that a drilling company such as CAZA could not reasonably be expected to fulfill. (See Pub. Resources Code, § 3203 [operator must file a written notice of intent to commence drilling]; § 3204 [operator must post an indemnity bond prior to engaging in drilling; §§ 3210–3211 [owner or operator required to keep a log of the history of the drilling of the well showing, among other things, the formations encountered or passed through]; § 3227 [owner required to file monthly production reports]; Wells Fargo Bank v. Goldzband (1997) 53 Cal.App.4th 596, 605–606, 61 Cal.Rptr.2d 826 ["It would be illogical to impose upon someone who has no authority or responsibility for a well the duty to: file a notice of intent to drill (§ 3203); post an indemnity bond prior to engaging in drilling (§ 3204); maintain a log of drilling operations (§ 3211); employ specific safety devices on wells and drilling techniques (§§ 3219, 3220); file monthly production reports (§ 3227); or abandon a well in accordance with the instructions of the Division (§§ 3228, 3229, 3230, and 3232)"].)

Review of the governing regulations further illustrates the point that "operator" means something more than a daywork contractor. Section 1722.1.1 of title 14 of the California Code of Regulations requires that there be posted at each well location a sign "with the name of the operator." Section 1722, subdivision (b) of title 14 requires "the operator" to "develop an oil spill contingency plan." Section 1722, subdivision (c) of title 14 requires "the operator" to submit "a blowout prevention and control plan, including provisions for the duties, training, supervision, and schedules for testing equipment and performing personnel drills." Other regulations, while not specifically referencing owners or operators, similarly impose duties that a drilling company hired on a daywork basis could not reasonably be expected to undertake. Section 1722.2 of title 14 requires wells to have casings "designed to provide anchorage for blowout prevention equipment" and "to withstand anticipated collapse, burst, and tension forces." Sections 1722.3 and 1722.4 of title 14 require cement casings of a certain depth and strength.

Appellants draw our attention to California Code of Regulations, title 14, sections 1722.5 and 1722.6, which are specifically designed to prevent blowouts and "uncontrolled flow of fluids from any well." While neither provision expressly imposes responsibility for compliance on well owners and operators, there is no reason to interpret them as imposing legal responsibility on a contractor like CAZA, when all the other statutes and regulations in this area are clearly directed at the owner or operator.

In short, * * * appellants have failed to set forth a specific statute or regulation purportedly violated. Accordingly, no basis has been presented that justifies invalidating the exculpatory provisions of the 2002 Daywork Drilling Contract.

DISPOSITION

The judgment is affirmed.

NOTES

1. Given the court's holding, what should TEG have done in addition to negotiating to be named an "additional insured" under CAZA's comprehensive liability policies? In hindsight, was the special provision requiring CAZA to pay the motel expenses of the drilling crew a significant matter?

2. Drilling contracts contain numerous so-called "carve outs" that expressly allocate particular risks—mostly to the operator. Several of these provisions are mentioned in *Caza*. What is the rationale for allocating to the operator the risk of loss of the drilling contractor's "in-hole" equipment? Assuming this provision is generally acceptable to the operator, would you change this provision in any way if you were the operator's counsel? What are the reasons behind the provision making the operator responsible for damage to or destruction of the contractor's equipment "caused by exposure to highly corrosive or otherwise destructive elements"?

3. The following case illustrates the importance of carefully drafting the basic indemnity provisions.

FOREMAN v. EXXON CORP.

770 F.2d 490 (5th Cir. 1985).

ROBERT MADDEN HILL, CIRCUIT JUDGE:

The issue presented on this appeal is whether Exxon Corporation (Exxon) is entitled to receive indemnification from Offshore Casing Crews, Inc. (Offshore), pursuant to their contract, not only for amounts Exxon paid to plaintiff directly as a result of its share of fault in causing plaintiff's injury but also for amounts Exxon paid to Diamond M Company (Diamond M) as a result of Exxon's contractual agreement with Diamond M to indemnify Diamond M for its share of fault in causing plaintiff's injury. The district court determined that Offshore is required to indemnify Exxon for the amounts for which Exxon is directly liable to the plaintiff; the court also determined, however, that Offshore is not required to indemnify Exxon for the amounts which Exxon owes in contractual indemnity to Diamond M. We agree * * *.

I. *Procedural History*

Plaintiff, Randy Foreman, an employee of Offshore, brought this action against Exxon and Diamond M for personal injuries he sustained while working on a fixed platform located in the Gulf of Mexico off the coast of Louisiana. The platform was owned by Exxon and the drilling rig that was located atop the platform was owned by Diamond M.

Prior to the date of the incident giving rise to Foreman's injuries, Exxon had contracted with both Diamond M and Offshore to perform services aboard its platform. The contract with Diamond M for performance of drilling services was executed on July 15, 1975. The contract with Offshore for installation of well casing pipe was executed thereafter on January 12, 1976.

Subsequent to Foreman's initial action against Exxon and Diamond M (the principal claim) and pursuant to the terms of the Exxon–Diamond M contract, Diamond M filed a cross-claim against Exxon for indemnity and/or contribution relative to any sums for which Diamond M might be liable to Foreman;[1] Exxon also filed a similar cross-claim against Diamond M (the cross-claims). In addition, pursuant to the Exxon–Offshore contract,[2] Exxon filed a third-party complaint against Offshore seeking indemnity for (a) any sums for which Exxon might be liable directly to Foreman for its negligence and (b) any sums for which it was required to indemnify Diamond M (the third-party complaint). Further, Northwestern Insurance Company (Northwestern) filed a complaint in intervention to recover benefits paid to Foreman pursuant to the Longshoremen's and Harbor Workers' Compensation Act. The parties went to trial on these three issues: the principal claim, the cross-claims and the third-party complaint.

After trial on the issue of liability, the jury found that Exxon, Diamond M, and Offshore were negligent and that each contributed to the accident which caused Foreman's injuries. The district court then submitted to the jury a special interrogatory asking the jury to apportion the negligence as between Exxon, Diamond M and Offshore.[3] The jury found Exxon, Diamond M and Offshore to be negligent with respect to Foreman in the following proportionate degrees: Exxon–10%; Diamond M–55%; and Offshore–35%.

After trial on the issue of damages and prior to the conclusion of the jury's deliberations, the parties reached a settlement agreement with respect to the quantum of damages recoverable by Foreman. Specifically, the parties agreed that Foreman would receive $323,000 in a settlement fund and that Northwestern would be paid $23,000 from this fund. They further agreed that the district court would decide the contractual indemnity issues that were the basis of the cross-claims and of the third-party complaint. In addition, all parties reserved their right to appeal to this Court.[4]

---

1. *See infra* note 8.

2. *See infra* note 7.

3. Offshore objected to its inclusion in the jury interrogatory because it was not a defendant in the principal claim and because it was immune as Foreman's employer. *See infra* Part II. Overruling the objection, the district court stated that the apportionment of the various degrees of negligence "is not going to determine how the money is going to be paid. But in view of the contracts, I have to find the percentage of fault." Explaining its position more concisely, the court later indicated that "a determination by the Court on the contractual indemnity issues necessitated a finding by the jury, as trier-of-fact, relative to Offshore's fault or negligence."

4. The settlement agreement also provided that should the district court's determination of each party's proportionate contribution to the settlement fund be reversed and/or reapportioned on appeal, then the party who had underpaid the settlement would reimburse the party who had overpaid the settlement to the extent of the overpayment and legal interest from the date the settlement was funded.

The district court then issued its reasons for judgment setting forth its decision on the contractual issues. The court noted that the jury had found the parties at fault in the proportionate degrees above set out and proceeded to review various indemnity provisions of the Exxon–Diamond M contract and the Exxon–Offshore contract. The court then concluded that Offshore was obligated to contribute 45% of the settlement fund: this contribution represents 35% attributable to Offshore's fault and 10% attributable to Exxon's fault for which Offshore contractually agreed to indemnify Exxon. In addition, the court concluded that Exxon was obligated to contribute the remaining 55% of the settlement fund: this contribution represents the percentage of fault attributable to Diamond M for which Exxon contractually agreed to indemnify Diamond M. The court did not allow Exxon indemnity from Offshore for this 55% contribution that Exxon was assessed; it found that Offshore had agreed only to indemnify Exxon for Exxon's direct liability and that Offshore had not agreed to assume Exxon's contractual liability to Diamond M pursuant to the Exxon–Diamond M contract.

Offshore then timely perfected its appeal from the district court's judgment arguing that the 35% of fault assigned to it should have been apportioned between Exxon and Diamond M and that it should not have been required to indemnify Exxon for Exxon's direct liability to Foreman under the contractual indemnity terms of the Exxon–Offshore contract. Exxon filed a cross-appeal arguing that Offshore should have been required to indemnify it for amounts it owes Diamond M under the contractual indemnity terms of the Exxon–Diamond M contract.

II. *Apportionment of Fault*

Offshore contends that the district court erred in submitting a special interrogatory to the jury that requested an apportionment of fault between not only Exxon and Diamond M, defendants, but also Offshore, third-party defendant. Because it was not a tort defendant, Offshore argues, the jury should have been required to apportion fault between Exxon and Diamond M only. In response to Offshore's objection to submission of the special interrogatory, however, the district court stated, "this [the special interrogatory] is not going to determine how the money is going to be paid. But in view of the contracts, I have to find the percentage of fault." Submission of the special interrogatory was not error, as the district court observed, because disposition of the contractual indemnity claims necessitated a jury finding on Offshore's percentage of fault.

Nevertheless, despite the district court's correct reasoning for submitting the special interrogatory and despite Exxon's acknowledgement that "the District Judge, and all of the parties to this suit, clearly recognized that Offshore is immune from tort liability by virtue of its status as the employer of Plaintiff, and its payment to him of compensation benefits," the court erroneously determined that Offshore should bear the burden for 35% of the settlement fund in accordance with the 35% of fault assigned it by the jury. To support its determination, the court stated that "although Offshore could not have been held directly liable to the plaintiff, absent its agreement to compromise, its potential exposure under the indemnity agreements was significant." We find that neither "potential exposure under the indemnity agreements" nor the settlement agreement permitted the district court to impose upon Offshore the obligation to pay any portion of the settlement fund as a result of its fault in causing Foreman's injury.

* * * [N]otwithstanding the district court's assertion that a determination by the jury of Offshore's percentage of fault would not "determine how the money was going to be paid," the court did require Offshore to contribute to the settlement fund the same percentage of the fund as the percentage of Offshore's fault. The court did so after ruling on the contractual issues. [W]e conclude that the district court should have first determined the proper apportionment of negligence as between defendants Exxon and Diamond M before apportioning the settlement fund.

Notwithstanding the district court's implication that the 35% share of the settlement fund imposed upon Offshore represents some undefined contractual exposure, the court, without further explanation, held Offshore was liable to pay, as tort damages, the exact percentage of the settlement fund as its percentage of fault as found by the jury. It is well established, however, that because of Offshore's status as employer of Foreman and because Foreman is subject to the Longshoremen's and Harbor Workers' Compensation Act (the Act), 33 U.S.C. §§ 901–950, employees' compensation represents the exclusive liability of Offshore to Foreman. 33 U.S.C. § 905(a). * * * Consequently, Offshore should not have been required to pay, as tort damages, 35% of the settlement fund.

* * * [W]e decline to remand this action for a redetermination of the respective percent of the settlement fund to be paid by Exxon and Diamond M.[5] Exxon and Diamond M must bear proportionately the 35% fault that the jury attributed to Offshore. Accordingly, because Exxon was found 10% liable and Diamond M 55% liable, Exxon will now bear approximately 15.4% of the total damages and Diamond M will bear the other approximately 84.6%.

III. *Offshore's Indemnity Obligation for Exxon's Direct Liability to Foreman*

Offshore argues that the first paragraph of the indemnity provision of the Exxon–Offshore contract does not require that Offshore indemnify Exxon for amounts for which Exxon is directly liable to Foreman since the cause of action arose in favor of an Offshore employee who is expressly excluded from the operation of that paragraph.[6] Offshore fails, however, to

---

5. Also, we note that at oral argument the parties indicated they would prefer a reapportionment by this Court of Offshore's 35% fault between Exxon and Diamond M rather than a retrial to determine the percentages of fault attributable to Exxon and Diamond M.

6. The first paragraph of the indemnity provision is set out in note 7, *infra.*

read the indemnity provision in its entirety. The second paragraph of the indemnity provision provides that:

> Contractor [Offshore] further agrees to protect, indemnify and hold harmless Exxon, its agents, servants and employees from and against any and all claims, demands and causes of action of every kind which may be brought against them *by an employee of Contractor,* including any person judicially determined to be an employee of Contractor, on account of personal injury, illness, death or loss of services or damage to or loss of property where:
>
>> (a) The personal injury, illness, death or loss of services or damages to or loss of property in any way results from the willful or negligent acts or omissions of Contractor, Contractor's agents, employees representatives, or subcontractors, *whether or not such personal injury, illness, death or loss of or damage to property arose out of the joint and/or concurrent negligence of Exxon,* its agents, employees or representatives and/or the unseaworthiness of any vessel....

(emphasis added).

* * * This additional indemnity provision unambiguously requires Offshore to indemnify Exxon for liability which Exxon incurs on claims by Offshore's employees for personal injury resulting from Offshore's negligence.

Based upon the jury's finding that Offshore was negligent, and despite the joint and/or concurrent negligence of Exxon, Exxon is entitled to indemnity for the amount for which it is directly liable to the plaintiff. Accordingly, Offshore must contribute to the settlement fund that percentage which Exxon would otherwise be required to contribute on account of its direct liability to Foreman, approximately 15.4%. *See supra* Part II.

IV.   *Offshore's Indemnity Obligation for Exxon's Contractual Liability to Diamond M*

The district court determined that Offshore was not required to indemnify Exxon for amounts Exxon owed pursuant to Exxon's contract of indemnity with Diamond M. On cross-appeal, Exxon argues that the first paragraph of the indemnity provision of the contract between Exxon and Offshore unambiguously provides for such indemnity and in the alternative that the parties intended to provide for such indemnity.[7] * * *

---

7. The first paragraph of the indemnity provision provides that:

Contractor further agrees to protect, indemnify, and hold harmless Exxon, its agents, servants and employees, from and against all claims, demands and causes of action of every kind and character arising in favor of Exxon's employees or third parties (third parties being defined for purposes of this provision as any party other than employee of Exxon or an employee of Contractor) for injury to or death or illness of persons or loss of or damage to property in any way resulting from the willful or negligent acts or omissions of Contractor, Contractor's agents, employees, representatives, or subcontractors, whether or not such personal injury, illness,

[W]e affirm the district court's determination that Exxon is not entitled to indemnity for amounts for which it is liable to Diamond M pursuant to their indemnity agreement.[8] * * *

* * * [T]he agreement between Exxon and Offshore provides for indemnity "against all claims, demands and causes of action ... *for injury to or death or illness of persons* ... in any way resulting from the willful or negligent acts or omissions of Contractor...." (emphasis added) Exxon's argument that the language of the indemnity provision unambiguously provides that Offshore must reimburse Exxon for Exxon's contractual liability to Diamond M ignores the limiting language "for injury to or death or illness of persons." * * *

Further, Exxon argues that Offshore's agreement to indemnify it against *"all claims,* demands, and causes of action of every kind and character arising in favor of ... third parties" includes Diamond M's "third party" contractual claim against Exxon. (emphasis added) [We decline to read the phrase "all claims" to include contractual claims when that phrase was limited by language requiring some claim based "on account of personal injury." * * * Exxon's liability to Diamond M is not "for injury to ... persons;" rather, it is for, or the result of, its agreement to indemnify Diamond M. * * *

* * * [W]e find no indication in the Exxon–Offshore contract that Offshore has accepted this unusual extension of its normal obligations.

* * *

We believe that the district court properly interpreted the intent of the parties to this contract, and that it properly concluded that the parties failed to clearly and expressly provide that Offshore indemnify Exxon for Exxon's contractual liability to Diamond M.

> Generally, Louisiana law requires the Court to give legal effects to agreements, according to the true intent of the parties. The true intent of the parties is to be determined by the clear and explicit terms of the agreements.

Leenerts Farms, Inc. v. Rogers, 421 So.2d 216, 218 (La.1982); La.Civ.Code Ann. art. 1945 (West 1977). Because * * * we agree that the parties to this contract * * * did not intend to shift to Offshore the contractual indemnity exposure of Exxon to Diamond M, we reject Exxon's cross-appeal. Exxon will be required to contribute approximately 84.6% of the proceeds comprising the settlement fund.[9]

---

death or loss of or damage to property arose out of the joint and/or concurrent negligence of Exxon, its agents, employees, or representatives and/or the unseaworthiness of any vessel.

8. There is no dispute that the Exxon–Diamond M contract requires Exxon to indemnify Diamond M. Pursuant to our reapportionment, *see supra* Part II, as indicated this amount represents approximately 84.6% of the settlement fund.

9. *See supra* Part II. The reapportionment of the parties' share of the settlement fund should be effected pursuant to the terms of the settlement agreement, *see supra* note 4.

The judgment of the district court is AFFIRMED in all respects except as to the apportionment of fault between Exxon, Diamond M and Offshore, as to which it is REVERSED. Accordingly, the cause is RE-MANDED to the district court with directions to reform its judgment reapportioning the percentage of Offshore's fault between Exxon and Diamond M pursuant to this opinion.

AFFIRMED in part; REVERSED in part and REMANDED.

NOTES

1. How could Exxon have changed the wording of the indemnity provisions in its contracts so that it would have prevailed?

2. Statutes in several states proscribe clauses that purport to indemnify a party to a drilling or well-service contract against liability for its own negligence, but they differ in significant details. For example, Wyoming (Wyo.Stat.Ann. § 30–1–131 to 39–1–133) and New Mexico (N.M.Stat.Ann. § 56–7–2) proscribe clauses that indemnify against negligence causing death, personal injury, or property damage. Louisiana law (La.Rev.Stat.Ann. § 9:2780) proscribes clauses that indemnify against negligence causing death or personal injury, but does not proscribe indemnities relating to property damage. The Louisiana Act also permits clauses indemnifying against negligence for injury from a wide range of specified causes, including radioactivity and the performance of services to bring a wild well under control. Louisiana case law permits insurers to waive subrogation in some circumstances, Fontenot v. Chevron U.S.A. Inc., 676 So.2d 557 (La. 1996), and enforces additional insured provisions when the additional insured party directly pays the additional premium for that coverage to the insurer or insurer's agent, Marcel v. Placid Oil Co., 11 F.3d 563 (5th Cir.1994). The New Mexico Act does not allow indemnities even if backed by insurance or enforce promises to procure insurance to cover indemnity liability. Amoco Prod. Co. v. Action Well Service, 755 P.2d 52 (N.M. 1988). What is the rationale for anti-indemnification statutes? For specific statutory exemptions?

In Bolack v. Chevron U.S.A., Inc., 963 P.2d 237 (Wy.1998), an operator sought to compel nonoperators to share settlement costs and attorney fees associated with a suit brought by well-service employees injured when a well caught fire during a reworking operation. The court held that the unit operating agreement purported to indemnify the operator for its negligence and thus was unenforceable under Wyoming oil field anti-indemnity statute where operator was clearly attempting to compel non-negligent nonoperators to contribute proportionately to settlement of claims caused by operator's negligence. What are the ramifications of this ruling? See, Section D.2., above. The Texas Act excludes joint operating agreements from its scope, and the Louisiana Act excludes both joint operating agreements and farmout agreements.

Texas has one of the most complex anti-indemnity statutes. Tex.Civ.Prac. & Rem.Code Ann. §§ 127.001–127.007. It voids agreements pertaining to oil, gas, or water wells or to mines that purport to indemnify a party against loss or liability resulting from personal injury, death, or property damage that is caused by the party's own negligence. Like the Louisiana act, the Texas statute contains exceptions for indemnities relating to specific matters, such as radioactivity. It also specifically exempts indemnification agreements "if the parties agree in writing that the indemnity obligation will be supported by liability insurance coverage to be furnished by the indemnitor." Initially, a "mutual indemnity obligation" was valid to the limits of insurance or qualified self-insurance each party agreed to provide in equal amounts, whereas a "unilateral indemnity obligation" is limited to $500,000. In Ken Petroleum Corp. v. Questor Drilling Corp., 24 S.W.3d 344 (Tex.2000), the Texas Supreme Court upheld a mutual indemnity where the parties had procured different amounts of liability insurance coverage. The court held that a mutual indemnity would be enforced up to the policy limits of the policy with the lowest dollar coverage. The court reasoned that requiring the parties to contract for and acquire insurance in exactly equal amounts was inconsistent with practical reality; for operators and drilling contractors are likely to have taken out and maintained insurance policies for years before any particular drilling contract is entered into. Moreover, such an interpretation of the Texas statute would lead to the peculiar result that a party could avoid its indemnity obligation if the other party had taken out a larger insurance policy. While *Ken Petroleum* case was still pending, the Texas statute was amended to delete the specific reference to "equal amounts" instead providing that the indemnity was enforceable to the "extent of the coverage and dollar limits of insurance or qualified self-insurance each party as indemnitor has agreed to obtain for the benefit of the other party as indemnitee." Tex.Civ.Prac. & Rem.Code § 127.005(b). What policy supports the Texas approach to indemnity agreements supported by insurance? Is the New Mexico position, as stated in the principal case, preferable?

In addition to these oilfield indemnity acts, many states have general statutes that limit or proscribe indemnities against negligence in certain "construction" contracts. See, e.g., Ill.Comp.Stat.Ann. ch. 740 ¶¶ 35/0.01–35/3; Ind. Code § 26-2-5-1; Kan. Stat. Ann. § 16-121; Miss.Code Ann. § 31-5-41; Ohio Rev.Code § 2305.31; and W.Va.Code § 55-8-14. The extent to which such statutes may apply to oilfield drilling and service contracts is uncertain and would turn on whether the drilling of an oil and gas well was deemed to be "construction." Some of these statutes contain quite specific definitions of what constitutes a construction contract. See, e.g., Kan. Stat. Ann. § 16-121.

3. Courts may impose special requirements upon indemnity agreements even apart from a statute. For example Kansas, which has no anti-indemnity statute, requires that such contracts be "clear and unequivocal." Bartlett v. Davis Corp., 219 Kan. 148, 547 P.2d 800 (Kan. 1976). In Texas an indemnity against negligence must be sufficiently explicit to satisfy an "express negligence" requirement. The Texas Supreme Court explained the rationale for this stringent test as follows:

> [T]he scriveners of indemnity agreements have devised novel ways of writing provisions which fail to expressly state the true intent of those provisions. The intent of the scriveners is to indemnify the indemnitee for its negligence, yet to be just ambiguous enough to conceal that intent from the indemnitor * * *. The express negligence doctrine provides that

parties seeking to indemnify the indemnitee from the consequences of its
own negligence must express that intent in specific terms.

Ethyl Corp. v. Daniel Construction Co., 725 S.W.2d 705, 707–08 (Tex.1987).
Texas law does not, however, impose this same requirement on provisions
requiring a party to obtain liability insurance naming the other party as an
additional insured. Getty Oil Co. v. Insurance Co. of North America, 845
S.W.2d 794 (Tex.1992).

The 10th Circuit Court of Appeals has held that limitation of liability
provisions can be invalid due to unequal bargaining positions even among oil
and gas entities. In Arnold Oil Properties LLC v. Schlumberger Technology
Corporation, 672 F.3d 1202 (2012), the plaintiff (Arnold) hired defendant
(Schlumberger) to conduct completion operations on its natural gas well. The
service contract contained indemnity and limitation-of-liability provisions.
After a slipshod completion job on the well and resultant additional expenses,
Arnold sued Schlumberger.

Schlumberger argued the service contract precluded recovery based on
what it called the "exculpatory" provision. Alternatively, Schlumberger also
argued the service contract limited recovery by Arnold to the cost of work
performed by Schlumberger and not the additional costs incurred by Arnold.
The federal district court ruled the "exculpatory" clause was actually an
indemnification clause, allowing Arnold to seek recovery. The district court
also held that fact issues existed as to the parties relative bargaining positions, and thus denied Schlumberger's summary judgment motion to enforce
the limitation-of-liability provision.

On appeal, the 10th Circuit Court focused on the relative bargaining
position of the parties. Applying Oklahoma law that allows courts to not
enforce contractual provisions limiting a party's liability for ordinary negligence if the parties are found to not have equal bargaining power, the court of
appeals found the "exculpatory" clause to be unenforceable.

4. Since the operator and contractor may be domiciled and contract in a
different state than the one where drilling or service takes place, litigation
over the provisions of the agreement may give rise to a choice-of-law issue.
The parties can usually avoid this problem by specifying that the law of a
particular state is to govern their contract. Subject to additional restrictions
for offshore wells, this contractual decision is likely to be questioned only if
the state chosen has "no substantial relationship to the parties or the
transaction" or if the governing law is "contrary to a fundamental policy of a
state which has a materially greater interest than the chosen state in the
determination of the particular issue and which * * * would [otherwise] be
the state of the applicable law." Restatement (Second) of Conflict of Laws
§ 187.

Would a comprehensive anti-indemnification statute constitute a statement of "fundamental policy" overriding a clause choosing the law of a state
that enforced indemnity agreements? Cf., Maxus Exploration Co. v. Moran
Bros., Inc., 817 S.W.2d 50, 57 (Tex.1991) (applying Kansas law to a drilling
contract negotiated in Texas where the parties did not make an express choice
of law for the drilling of a well in Kansas). See generally Russell Weintraub,
Commentary on the Conflict of Laws § 3.6 (4th ed. 2001). In Reagan v.

McGee Drilling Corp., 933 P.2d 867 (N.M.App.1997), the New Mexico Court of Appeals upheld the parties' choice of Texas law as the governing law of a drilling contract for the drilling of a well by two Texas companies in New Mexico on the ground that the Texas Oilfield Anti–Indemnification Act, although substantially different in detail, reflected the same public policy goals as the New Mexico Act, the promotion of safety. Because the primary difference between the statutes was the insurance exceptions, which was not considered to be contrary to New Mexico public policy, the choice-of-law provision was upheld. A subsequent amendment to the New Mexico Act, 1999 N. M. Laws ch. 205, § 1, appears to have nullified this ruling by specifically stating that an insurance provision is also against public policy. This was confirmed by the New Mexico Court of Appeals in Piña v. Gruy Petroleum Management Company, 136 P.3d 1029 (N.M. Ct. App. 2006), which invalidated a Texas choice of law provision in a Master Service Agreement covering drilling operations in various states, including New Mexico. The court of appeals examined the amendments to the New Mexico Act and concluded the Legislature was responding to the *Reagan* decision.

While other jurisdictions apply the same general choice-of-law principles, application has not been uniform. In Roberts v. Energy Development Corp., 235 F.3d 935 (5th Cir. 2000), an accident occurred in Louisiana state waters, but the parties chose Texas as the governing law of their contract. The court concluded that the choice-of-law provision was invalid as against Louisiana public policy, at least to the extent one party to the contract was a Louisiana contractor. *Id.* at 943. On the other hand, in a case involving a drilling operation in Louisiana, the Texas court of appeals, in Chesapeake Operating, Inc. v. Nabors Drilling USA, Inc., 94 S.W.3d 163 (Tex.App. 2002), held the trial court properly applied Texas law. In doing so, the court, sitting en banc, reversed the earlier panel opinion which had held that the trial court should have applied Louisiana law, because, despite the parties' express choice of Texas law, the contract should be subject to the provisions of the Louisiana Oilfield Anti–Indemnity Act, which rendered the applicable indemnity provisions of the contract void and unenforceable. Relying on the Texas Supreme Court's decision in *Maxus* and applying Restatement (Second) Conflict of Laws § 187, the Houston Court of Appeals for the 14th District held that Texas law should apply because the contracting parties had a substantial relationship to Texas, the suit had been filed in Texas, and the parties had contractually selected Texas law. However, the court expressly stated that it was not suggesting that "choice-of-law agreements in indemnity contracts are *per se* enforceable." Chesapeake, 94 S.W.3d at 179 n. 35. In the subsequent decision in Sonat Exploration Company v. Cudd Pressure Control, Inc., 271 S.W.3d 228 (Tex. 2008), the Court held under similar facts—accident in Louisiana, but significant Texas contacts and suit in Texas—that Louisiana law should apply, thus leading to a different result, because the parties did not expressly choose Texas law. *Id.* at 908–909.

5. Some drilling contract forms requires the contractor "to perform all work * * * with due diligence and care, in a good workmanlike manner, and in accordance with good drilling practices." In construing a contract containing almost identical language, the court in W.E. Myers Drilling Corp. v. Elliott, 695 S.W.2d 809 (Tex.App.1985, writ ref'd n.r.e.), upheld a jury verdict

that a contractor under a daywork agreement was not entitled to payment for the full 12 1/2 days spent in drilling the well. Although the well had concededly been drilled in a "good and workmanlike manner," the operator was also entitled to performance "with due diligence."

What recourse, if any, would an operator have for a contractor's unreasonable delays in drilling under a footage or turnkey contract? The IADC form contracts for daywork and footage drilling contain no statement of drilling standards. Should a court imply the same standard as is set out in more operator-oriented forms?

6. The contractor's breach of a drilling contract presents the same difficult problems of determining damages as breach of a firm drilling obligation in a farmout agreement. Surprisingly, although use of a standardized drilling contract form (promulgated by the IADC) is far more common than use of a standardized farmout agreement, the most commonly used printed drilling-contract form contains relatively few provisions dealing with remedies and damages in the event of the contractor's default. The most obvious remedy—liquidated damages—is typically limited to an early termination of the drilling contract by the operator. Both drilling and service contracts commonly contain provisions whereby both parties waive the right to recover consequential damages, such as lost profits. If the contract fails to define "consequential damages," its application is then left to the courts. See, e.g., Wil–Roye Invest. Co. II v. Alleder, Inc., 2001 WL 903179 (Tex. App. 2001) (unreported) (holding that reservoir damage, increased production costs, and decreased production are direct damages).

7. For more information on drilling contracts, see Owen L. Anderson, Drilling for Black Gold: Understanding the Fine Print in Model Form Drilling Contracts, 15 E. Min. L. Inst. 293 (1995); Owen L. Anderson, The Anatomy of an Oil and Gas Drilling Contract, 25 Tulsa L.J. 359, 464–521 (1990); and H. Harold Calkins, The Drilling Contract—Legal and Practical Considerations, 21 Rocky Mtn.Min.L.Inst. 285 (1975).

G. GAS PURCHASE CONTRACTS

Probably more than any other instrument considered in the casebook, natural gas purchase contracts owe their form and content to the long history of federal regulation and current deregulation of the gas industry. Until well into the 1980's pipelines served as both natural gas transporters and marketers, buying natural gas in the field and transporting it to a point, often hundreds or thousands of miles away, where the pipelines resold it to industrial users or to local distribution companies and public utilities for ultimate distribution to consumers. Federal regulatory orders in the 1980's and early 1990's that required pipelines to "unbundle" their services resulted in a radical restructuring of this system. Producers and customers could now choose to use only specific types of pipeline services, such as gathering or transportation, and could deal directly with each other rather than solely with natural gas pipelines. When coupled with price deregulation, this change moved the locus of gas sales from the gas pipeline connections in the field to distant processing plants, electric generating companies, end-user facilities, and other downstream locations. It also generated an extraordinarily complex gas market.

The excerpts from following article present a brief overview of the regulatory history of the natural gas industry.

MARTIN, "SUMMARY OF SIGNIFICANT GAS MARKET AND TRANSPORTATION CHANGES AFFECTING PRODUCERS IN THE 1990's"

37 Rocky Mtn.Min.L.Inst. 16–1, 16–7 to 16–10 and 16–45 to 16–54 (1991).[8]

* * *

STATUTORY FRAMEWORK FOR FEDERAL REGULATION OF NATURAL GAS

* * *

The Natural Gas Act of 1938 (NGA), was enacted to eliminate a perceived gap in the regulation of the interstate transportation and sale of natural gas resulting from court holdings that certain areas were beyond the power of the states to regulate. The resulting statute, the NGA, was designed to plug the gaps, not supplant the power of the states. Accordingly, the NGA only granted to the Federal Power Commission (now the Federal Energy Regulatory Commission; both referred to herein as FERC) authority over "transportation of natural gas in interstate commerce," "sales in interstate commerce of natural gas for resale," and the companies engaged in such transportation or sale. Although the NGA specifically excludes production or gathering of natural gas from its jurisdictional ambit, the United States Supreme Court's 1954 decision, *Phillips Petroleum Co. v. Wisconsin,* found the exclusion did not exempt sales in interstate commerce for resale by gas producers from the FERC's NGA jurisdiction. However, because of its limited scope, the NGA did not regulate the intrastate transportation and sale of gas.

* * *

* * * Producer price regulation under the NGA has been largely superseded by the Natural Gas Policy Act of 1978 (NGPA) and NGWDA.

The NGPA was enacted to eliminate the inherent bifurcation of the natural gas market into an unregulated intrastate market and a regulated interstate market. Regulated prices for producer sales of gas had trailed market prices, with the result that shortages had developed in the interstate market as producers sold gas into the unregulated intrastate market. Congress in the NGPA responded by regulating all sales of domestically produced natural gas. For pricing purposes, a series of different prices, or vintages, were established with qualifying criteria. A schedule of partial deregulation was put in place, with the first category of gas deregulating

---

8. © 1991 by Matthew Bender & Co., Inc., and reprinted with permission from the author and Rocky Mountain Mineral Law Institute © 1991, 37th Annual Institute.

one year after enactment, and additional categories deregulating in 1985 and 1987. So long as gas was regulated, the price for the gas was subject to maximum lawful prices (MLPs), all of which had inflation-based adjustments. Additionally, FERC was granted authority under the NGPA which permitted it to relax interstate transportation requirements and to allow intrastate pipelines to engage in interstate transactions without becoming subject to the NGA.

13.   15 U.S.C. § 3301 *et seq.* (1988).

* * *

The wellhead price controls of the NGPA initially applied to all "first sales" of natural gas; as previously stated, there was also a schedule for the full deregulation of certain categories of natural gas. The term "first sale" was so defined that it included *any* producer sale of gas. In addition, it included any other sale of natural gas to a pipeline, end-user, or local gas distributor except a sale by a pipeline or local distribution company.

President Bush signed the Natural Gas Wellhead Decontrol Act of 1989 (NGWDA) into law on July 26, 1989. The NGWDA provides for permanent elimination of all wellhead price controls on first sales of natural gas, including all wellhead sales, on January 1, 1993, at which time Title I of the NGPA will be repealed. Prior to the total removal of price controls in 1993, the NGWDA deregulates gas sold under three categories of contracts and from one category of wells.

* * *

NOTES

1.   Take-or-pay clauses, which were commonly included in the long-term gas contracts entered into before the early 1980s, were a significant factor in causing the crisis in the gas pipeline industry in the early 1980's. As the name suggests, the take-or-pay clause required a pipeline purchaser to pay for a specified quantity of gas, whether it was taken or not. Such clauses were almost always coupled with a make-up provision that gave the pipeline a specified number of years in which to take the gas it had already paid for. Excessive commitments under such clauses caused a crisis in the gas pipeline industry in the 1980s. Purchaser attempts to avoid take-or-pay obligations through the use of traditional contract doctrines, such as force majeure and commercial impracticability, were generally unsuccessful. See, e.g., Golsen v. ONG Western, Inc., 756 P.2d 1209 (Okla.1988). However in determining damages for breach at least one court refused to grant the producer the full amount of the pay obligation and instead applied the Uniform Commercial Code provision that awards the difference between the market price and the unpaid contract price for the unproduced gas. See Roye Realty & Developing, Inc. v. Arkla, Inc., 863 P.2d 1150 (Okla. 1993). See also Owen L. Anderson, Recent Developments in Nonregulatory Oil and Gas Law, 45 Inst. on Oil & Gas L. & Tax'n 1–1, 1–89 to 1–92 (1994).

Most disputes between producers and pipeline purchasers over take or pay contracts were ultimately settled, often for millions of dollars.

2. The federal regulatory orders requiring pipelines to "unbundle" their services resulted in interstate pipelines abandoning sales function and offering a variety of services, including transportation and storage. As a result, producers could sell directly to purchasers or to merchants who bought and re-sold. Today natural gas has become a widely sold and traded commodity. There are dozens of gas market centers where natural gas is sold and traded and prices reported almost contemporaneously with the sales or trades. However the three basic types of contracts used to sell natural gas at the time the article excerpted above was written: spot purchase contracts, multi-month contracts, and long-term firm or warranty contracts, are still widely used. One significant change in these contracts has been in the vastly shortened length of long-term contracts and the increased use of short-term contracts. Prior to the repeal of federal regulation, the typical long-term contract was for 20 years and some were even for the life of a well or, indeed, a field. Today, the term "long-term" is used to describe any contract longer than one year. See Jeffrey M. Petrash, "Long–Term Natural Gas Contracts: Dead, Dying or Merely Resting," 27 Energy L.J. 545 (2006). The decline in the length and number of long-term contracts has been accompanied by an increase in the use of short-term contracts, which can range from one day purchases in the "spot market" through the use of marketers or the producer's marketing staff to contracts for several months. Both long-term and short term contracts can be "interruptible," i.e., the buyer agrees that if the seller has over-committed the gas available to it for any specific period, supply to the buyer will be "interrupted" without penalty.

The sharply increased use of short term contracts is attributable to a variety of factors in addition to the end of federal regulation. One of the most important has been the steadily increasing use of gas for electric generation. The need for electricity varies enormously with the weather. Additionally, in several states electric utilities no longer have a monopoly in a specific area; rather, customers can choose among retail providers. Utilities may deal with these uncertainties by entering into contracts under which a utility's purchase obligations range between a minimum and maximum volume. See Petrash, *supra*.

3. In addition to the differences in length of term (10 to 20 years as compared to 2 to 5 years) the long-term contracts entered into before the 1980s and the longer term contracts currently negotiated typically differ in the identity of the purchaser. The earlier contracts were almost invariably between producers and pipelines, which bought gas for resale to local distribution companies. These companies, in turn, sold to residential customers, businesses, industries, and companies generating electricity. Largely because of the FERC's efforts to force pipelines to act as third-party transporters as well as marketers, producers now sell directly to other parties, including local distributing companies and end-users, as well as to pipeline

4. Matters of crucial importance in long-term contracts are whether a contract for the sale of gas has actually been consummated and, if so, the measure of damages if the selling party refuses to perform. The following case addresses both of those issues.

MANCHESTER PIPELINE CORP. v.
PEOPLES NATURAL GAS CO.

862 F.2d 1439 (10th Cir. [Okla.] 1988).

STEPHEN H. ANDERSON, CIRCUIT JUDGE.

This diversity case arises out of an alleged gas purchase contract between the seller, Manchester Pipeline Company ("Manchester"), a corporation formed to sell natural gas produced from a reservoir in Oklahoma, and the buyer, Peoples Natural Gas Company ("PNG"), a natural gas distribution company. Manchester brought suit in district court in Oklahoma, claiming that PNG had breached the gas purchase contract and seeking damages. A jury returned a verdict for Manchester and awarded Manchester damages in the amount of $1,450,000. The district court denied PNG's post-trial motions for judgment n.o.v., for a new trial and for a remittitur.

* * *

Manchester thereafter filed a motion to tax costs and attorney's fees. The district court awarded Manchester its costs and referred the question of attorney's fees to a magistrate, who, after conducting an evidentiary hearing, assessed $175,000 in attorney's fees against PNG. The district court affirmed that award. PNG's appeal from the award of attorney's fees has been consolidated with its appeal from the jury verdict and award of damages to Manchester. For the reasons set forth below, we AFFIRM the jury verdict finding that PNG breached the contract with Manchester, but REVERSE and REMAND for a recalculation of damages. Because we partially remand, we do not address at this time the propriety of the award of attorney's fees to Manchester.

BACKGROUND

William H. Davis and others discovered and developed a natural gas reservoir known as the Manchester Field (the "Field"), located in Grant County, Oklahoma. By the end of 1983, there were four completed wells in the Field. Ultimately, eleven wells were completed in the Field. In late 1983, Davis began contacting several natural gas purchasers, including PNG, to explore possibilities for selling the gas.

Actual negotiations between Manchester and PNG commenced in November, 1983. There were several meetings between Manchester representatives and PNG representatives. PNG's representatives on several occasions provided Davis with sample gas purchase contracts for his review. In April, 1984 Davis met with Rod Donovan, PNG's gas contracts representative. Donovan testified that he often, but not always, told prospective sellers that any offer he made was subject to PNG management approval. Donovan further testified that his superior, Bill Eliason, never told Donovan that any of the offers or letters he [Donovan] sent in connection with the negotiations with Manchester were "improper or inappropriate." Eliason testified that he approved the terms Donovan was negotiating with Manchester at each stage of those negotiations and communicated those terms to other members of PNG's management. Eliason's superior in PNG management, Richard Coil, testified that he was generally aware of the terms being negotiated with Manchester and that he never disapproved of any such terms. . . .

Donovan sent Davis a letter dated May 14, 1984 "offering" to purchase natural gas from Manchester, at the price of $2.65 per Million British Thermal Units ("MBTUs"), for a 20 year period.

The parties continued to negotiate over the following months. On three or four occasions during those months, Donovan sent to Davis a single copy of a sample gas purchase contract. On those copies, "draft copy" was stamped in red ink. On September 12, 1984, Donovan sent to Davis three copies of a document titled "Gas Purchase Contract" (the "Document"), covering six wells in the Field. These did not have "draft copy" stamped in red on the front page. The Document provided for a term of ten years and contained detailed provisions concerning price, minimum "take" obligations, determination of reserves, and the right of PNG to reduce the price paid for gas taken in order to remain competitive in the gas market.[1] The copies were accompanied by a letter, which stated in pertinent part:

> "Enclosed for your review and approval, please find three copies of our Gas Purchase Contract covering acreage referenced above.

> "If you find this Contract acceptable, please fully execute all three copies, (including notary pages) and return to this office. Following [PNG's] execution, one completed Contract will be forwarded to you."

. . . . On September 18, 1984, the Vice President of Manchester, Richard Massengale, executed the three copies and returned them to Donovan. PNG never executed the copies and denies that a contract for the purchase of gas has ever been formed between the parties. PNG's explanation for its failure to sign the contract is that it lost its largest industrial gas customer and there was a general "softening" of the gas market, the combined effect of which rendered it unable to enter into a contract.[2] Coil testified that he began to be concerned about PNG's loss of market even before the Document was sent to Manchester for signature, but that he "did let them go ahead and send out the contract with the understanding that it may not get approved. . . ."

---

1. This latter is the so-called "market-down" or "market-out" provision, which is frequently included in long term purchase contracts and which the parties argue here impacts upon any damages Manchester suffered from PNG's alleged breach of contract. See 37 Institute on Oil and Gas Law and Taxation, § 6.06[2] (1986).

2. PNG raises but does not stress the argument that, assuming the existence of a contract between the parties, performance could be excused under the force majeure clause of the contract on the theory that a failure of the gas market constitutes a force majeure. A recent Oklahoma case forecloses the availability of that and related arguments. See Golsen v. ONG Western, Inc., 756 P.2d 1209 (Okla.1988).

The parties presented conflicting evidence as to the custom in the oil and gas industry regarding entering into gas purchase contracts. Both Donovan and Davis testified that gas purchasers always drafted the contracts. Donovan testified that, after a gas contract representative such as himself had drafted the contract, he would forward it to the producer for execution. He testified that after the gas contract representative had received the executed copy from the producer, he would "forward it to . . . management for their review and finally their execution." Coil testified similarly as to the custom in the industry. He stated that "we do not feel we have a contract with the producer until it is signed by both parties." PNG presented an expert witness who testified that this practice was followed without exception. Davis testified that, in practice, while the buyer always expected the producer to sign and execute the contract first, the buyer always returned an executed contract once the producer had executed the document. Manchester's expert, William Dutcher, testified that it was the custom in the oil and gas industry to only formally exchange executed documents after the producer and buyer had agreed, at least verbally, on all the terms. . . .

During the negotiations between PNG and Manchester, the parties had agreed that Manchester would acquire any necessary rights of way and construct a pipeline from the Field to PNG's pipeline system. This obligation was embodied in the Document. Davis testified that in July and August, he instructed Massengale, who was an engineer, to commence the engineering studies necessary for Manchester to build the pipeline. He further testified that, at PNG's request, Manchester used larger pipe in building the pipeline (six-inch instead of four-inch) "to match up with the system they [PNG] already had in place." Donovan testified that he had a number of conversations with Massengale concerning the pipeline, and that he told Massengale "that it would be more prudent to wait until after the contract had been approved and executed by my management before he would go ahead with [the pipeline]."

After Manchester returned the executed copies of the Document, Davis met with Donovan and Eliason in September, 1984 to discuss the pipeline. There was conflicting evidence as to what happened at that meeting. Manchester presented testimony that Davis was assured that, despite PNG's failure to return the executed copy of the Document, PNG wanted to purchase Manchester's gas but was experiencing some internal gas allocation problems, and that Davis should continue in his efforts to construct the pipeline. Donovan and Eliason testified that Eliason explained to Davis PNG's hesitancy to sign the Document, and urged Davis to discontinue construction on the pipeline until PNG's management had signed it. Eliason testified that, at that meeting, PNG was only "considering" whether to purchase Manchester's gas. Donovan further testified that Davis said he would continue with the pipeline and sell to another buyer if PNG refused to sign the Document.

* * *

Donovan sent a letter to Davis dated October 29, 1984 in which he said there would be no binding contract until PNG's management signed and executed the Document, and advising Manchester not to proceed with installation of the pipeline until PNG's management had done so.

* * *

On December 27, 1984, PNG informed Manchester that it would not sign the Document. In an effort to mitigate its damages, Manchester contracted with Scissortail Natural Gas Company and extended the pipeline to connect with this buyer's facilities. The contract with Scissortail ("Scissortail Contract"), dated December 1, 1984, was a one year "spot market" contract, with a renewal option.[3] Under that contract, Manchester sold gas from the Field at a lower price, $2.58 per MBTU, than that stipulated under the contract with PNG.

Manchester sued PNG, claiming breach of contract. PNG's response was that there was never a contract between itself and Manchester and, even if there was, it denied that Manchester suffered any damages from PNG's breach.

With regard to the existence of a contract, PNG argues that its motion for judgment n.o.v. should have been granted because there was insufficient evidence that the parties had entered into a binding contract to sell gas. It argues that the evidence produced at trial shows that "the parties intended that the reduction to writing and execution of the contract was a condition precedent to its existence." Relying on Sections 26 and 27 of the Restatement (Second) of Contracts, PNG argues that Manchester had "reason to know" that PNG did not intend to become bound by the agreement until it signed and executed the copies.[4]

---

3. Davis testified that a "spot market" contract is based on "month to month marketing," rather than a "long term firm agreement." R.Vol. II at 91. Manchester's expert, Dutcher, described the "spot market" as referring to "direct sales from a producer to an end user, such as a large industry or an electric utility, or a local distribution company directly, as opposed to the producers selling the gas ... to a pipeline, who would ... resell it to these end users." R.Vol. III at 47. Typically, a spot market contract has a term of from one month to one year, has no "take or pay" provision, no "minimum take" provision, and provides the producer with a lower price than it would get under a long term contract.

4. Section 26 of the Restatement provides as follows:

"A manifestation of willingness to enter into a bargain is not an offer if the person to whom it is addressed knows or has reason to know that the person making it does not intend to conclude a bargain until he has made a further manifestation of assent."

Restatement (Second) of Contracts § 26 (1979). Comment a to Section 26 states as follows:

" 'Reason to know' depends not only on the words or other conduct, but also on the circumstances, including previous communications of the parties and the usages of their community or line of business."

Id. at § 26 comment a.

Section 27 provides as follows:

"Manifestations of assent that are in themselves sufficient to conclude a contract will not be prevented from so operating by the fact that the parties also manifest an intention to prepare and adopt a written memorial thereof; but the circumstances may show that the agreements are preliminary negotiations."

Restatement (Second) of Contracts § 27 (1979). Comment b to section 27 states as follows:

Manchester responds that the conflicting evidence as to the custom in the oil and gas industry concerning formalization of gas purchase contracts at least created a jury question as to whether Manchester had "reason to know" that PNG did not intend to be bound until it had signed the Document, and the jury resolved that question in Manchester's favor. Manchester further argues that, under Okla.Stat. tit. 12A, § 2–206, PNG's letter was an offer "inviting acceptance in any manner and by any medium reasonable in the circumstances" and that Manchester reasonably accepted by returning the executed copies to PNG.[5]

With regard to the damages awarded Manchester, PNG argues that the district court erred in instructing the jury on the method for computing Manchester's damages and on incidental damages and argues that the jury's award of damages was not supported by credible evidence.

DISCUSSION

"In this circuit, the sufficiency of the evidence to go to the jury is a matter of federal law even in diversity cases." Fed. Deposit Ins. Corp. v. Palermo, 815 F.2d 1329, 1335 (10th Cir.1987); see also Suggs v. State Farm Fire and Casualty Co., 833 F.2d 883, 887 n. 5 (10th Cir.1987), cert. denied, 486 U.S. 1007, 108 S.Ct. 1732, 100 L.Ed.2d 196 (1988); Brown v. McGraw–Edison Co., 736 F.2d 609, 612 (10th Cir.1984). We should only grant judgment n.o.v. "when all the inferences to be drawn from the evidence are so in favor of the moving party that reasonable persons could not differ in their conclusions." Palermo, 815 F.2d at 1335. We "may not weigh the evidence, pass on the credibility of witnesses, or substitute [our] judgment for that of the jury." Brown, 736 F.2d at 613. And, while federal standards govern the sufficiency of the evidence, Oklahoma provides the substantive law applicable to the underlying causes of action. Id.

Similarly, the denial of a motion for a new trial in a diversity case is governed by federal law. See Suggs, 833 F.2d at 887 n. 5; Whiteley v. OKC Corp., 719 F.2d 1051, 1058 (10th Cir.1983). PNG argued before the district court that a new trial was required because the verdict was against the weight of the evidence.

* * *

"[I]f either party knows or has reason to know that the other party regards the agreement as incomplete and intends that no obligation shall exist until other terms are assented to or until the whole has been reduced to another written form, the preliminary negotiations and agreements do not constitute a contract."

Id. at § 27 comment b.

5. Alternatively, Manchester argues that the Oklahoma Supreme Court has recognized that the doctrine of equitable estoppel can estop a party from denying the existence of an agreement. The jury was instructed on both the contract and estoppel theories. Since the jury only returned a general verdict for Manchester, we cannot tell whether the jury found that there was a contract between Manchester and PNG or whether it found for Manchester based on an equitable estoppel theory. As we discussed more fully in the text of this opinion, there was sufficient evidence in this case from which the jury could find that a contract existed between the parties. Additionally, there was sufficient evidence to support a jury verdict for Manchester on equitable estoppel grounds.

Here, the jury was instructed that, in order to find for Manchester, it had to find by a preponderance of the evidence that a contract existed between Manchester and PNG. Alternatively, the jury was instructed that, if it found no contract existed between Manchester and PNG, it should consider whether PNG is equitably estopped from denying that it was reasonable for Manchester to rely on PNG's promise to buy Manchester's gas.

As the district court instructed the jury, in order for there to be a contract between two parties, there must be a meeting of the minds on all material elements of the contract. See Watkins v. Grady County Soil and Water Conservation District, 438 P.2d 491, 494 (Okla.1968) ("there must be a meeting of the minds of the parties on all material parts of the agreement in order to settle a valid contract."). Furthermore, since the alleged contract related to the sale of natural gas reserves to be severed from the earth by the seller, Oklahoma's codification of the Uniform Commercial Code applies. See Golsen v. ONG Western, Inc., 756 P.2d 1209, 1220 (Okla.1988) (Kauger, J., concurring); Okla.Stat. tit. 12A, § 2–107.7 Under Okla.Stat. tit. 12A, § 2–206:

> "(1) Unless otherwise unambiguously indicated by the language or circumstances
>
>> "(a) an offer to make a contract shall be construed as inviting acceptance in any manner and by any medium reasonable in the circumstances."

Manchester argues that the September 12 transmittal of the letter and three copies of the Document was an "offer" and that Manchester's prompt return of the executed copies was "acceptance in any manner and by any medium reasonable in the circumstances." PNG argues that, following the Restatement (Second) of Contracts, there could be no "offer" as long as Manchester had "reason to know" that PNG did not intend to become bound until PNG had itself executed the Document.

In Oklahoma, as under the law of most states, the question of the existence of a contract is a question of fact for the jury to resolve. [Citations omitted] The questions of PNG's intent not to be bound by the Document until it had executed copies of it and of whether Manchester had "reason to know" that PNG did not intend to conclude a bargain until further indication from PNG, are factual questions. As we have indicated, comment a to section 26 of the Restatement explains that:

> " 'Reason to know' depends not only on the words or other conduct, but also the circumstances, including previous communications of the parties and the usages of their community or line of business."

Restatement (Second) of Contracts § 26 comment a (1979).

The jury in this case heard conflicting testimony as to the substance of numerous conversations and communications between PNG representatives and Manchester representatives concerning PNG's purchase of Manchester's gas and concerning the Document.... After carefully reviewing the record, we conclude that there was sufficient evidence from which the jury could conclude that PNG's transmittal of the three copies of the Document, with the September 12 letter, constituted an "offer" which Manchester accepted in a reasonable manner by returning the copies, signed and executed, thereby forming a contract on the terms contained in the Document as modified, if at all, by any later mutual agreement.[6]

We remand, however, for a redetermination of the damages payable by PNG for breach of the contract. PNG argues that the court misinstructed the jury on the computation of damages for years two through ten of the contract. The district court's instruction was as follows:

> "In order to determine the amount of damages: (1) for the first year, you may consider the evidence presented with regard to the difference between the agreed to price, if any, for the gas and the price obtained at resale of the gas to Scissortail Natural Gas Company, but that price is not conclusive, except to the extent that it reflects a standardized market price at the time and place defendant [PNG] would have had to take the amount of gas agreed, if there was an agreement, to be taken for the first year; plus (2) for the years two through ten, you may consider the evidence presented with regard to the difference, if any, between the market price for the gas at the time and place in the future when defendant [PNG] would have had to take that portion of plaintiff's [Manchester's] reserves as agreed, if agreed, and the agreed price, if any."

PNG argues that this instruction conflicts with Oklahoma's statutory provisions for calculating damages for non-acceptance or repudiation of a contract. We agree.

Under Okla.Stat. tit. 12A, § 1–106, "[t]he remedies provided by this Act shall be liberally administered to the end that the aggrieved party may be put in as good a position as if the other party had fully performed...." PNG argues that Okla.Stat. tit. 12A, §§ 2–708 and 2–723 govern the measure of a seller's damages for non-acceptance or repudiation of a contract. Section 2–708 provides in pertinent part:

> "Subject to subsection (2) and to the provisions of this Article with respect to proof of market price (Section 2–723), the measure of damages for non-acceptance or repudiation by the buyer is the differ-

---

6. The parties both address the question of Donovan's authority to enter into a contract on PNG's behalf. PNG argues "Davis admitted that he was aware that ... Donovan lacked authority to enter into a contract on behalf of [PNG]." Brief of Appellant at 16. Thus, PNG suggests Donovan lacked authority to bind PNG. In the face of conflicting evidence, the question of whether Donovan was PNG's agent with respect to any contract is a question of fact. See Agee v. Gant, 412 P.2d 155, 160 (Okla.1966); cf. Mitchell v. Ford Motor Credit Co., 688 P.2d 42, 46–47 (Okla.1984) (where facts concerning agency are undisputed and no conflicting inferences can be drawn therefrom, question of agency is one of law for court to decide). Here, there was conflicting evidence as to what representations were made to Manchester concerning Donovan's authority, and, while there was evidence that Donovan was not authorized to execute contracts binding PNG, there was evidence that all of Donovan's actions, including the transmittal of the Document with the September 12 letter, were approved by Donovan's superiors at PNG. In such a situation, we do not disturb the jury's implicit finding that Donovan was PNG's agent for the purposes of the contract between Manchester and PNG.

ence between the market price at the time and place for tender and the unpaid contract price together with any incidental damages provided in this Article (Section 2–710), but less expenses saved in consequence of the buyer's breach."

Okla.Stat. tit. 12A, § 2–708(1). Section 2–723 provides in pertinent part:

"If an action based on anticipatory repudiation comes to trial before the time for performance with respect to some or all of the goods, any damages based on market price (Section 2–708 or Section 2–713) shall be determined according to the price of such goods prevailing at the time when the aggrieved party learned of the repudiation."

Id. at § 2–723(1). Accordingly, PNG argues Manchester's damages should be determined in accordance with the price of gas "prevailing at the time when the aggrieved party learned of the repudiation."

* * *

In its order denying PNG's motions for judgment n.o.v. or for a new trial, the court stated:

"The Court acknowledges that in most circumstances the measure of damages for repudiation is determined according to the price of the goods prevailing at the time when the aggrieved party learned of the repudiation. Okla.Stat. tit. 12A. § 2–723(a) (1981). Nevertheless, the unique circumstances of a gas purchase agreement with a take or pay obligation requires that the jury consider the extreme unpredictability of the future market. Giving the jury such discretion, provides the opportunity to find plaintiff is or is not entitled to recover damages for any alleged loss in the future. Because the nature of the gas market is uniquely nonstandard and the terms of gas purchase agreements are not easily analogized to commercial contracts in general, this Court finds the circumstances of this case, as presented at trial, fell within the scope of the commentary to Section 2–723, that states other reasonable methods of determining market price or measuring damages are not excluded from use where necessary."

* * *

In determining the proper measure of damages for breach of a long term contract such as the one between Manchester and PNG, we must bear in mind the fundamental objective of the remedies provisions of the Uniform Commercial Code—to place "the aggrieved party ... in as good a position as if the other party had fully performed." Okla.Stat. tit. 12A, § 1–106. As indicated, section 2–723 provides that, in an anticipatory repudiation action which is brought before the time for performance, damages are calculated on the basis of the market price at the time the aggrieved party learned of the repudiation. That section has, as the Oklahoma Code Comment indicates, the virtue of certainty. The jury need not "speculate by attempting to predict what the future market value will be." Id. at § 2–723, Oklahoma Code Comment. Because Manchester's action was brought long before the time for full performance under the ten year contract had passed, section 2–723 appears to apply. Nonetheless, we are aware of the peculiar difficulties presented by attempting, at the end of the first year of a ten year contract, to calculate damages for the entire contract period.[7] The fact that damages are difficult to ascertain does not, however, mean they are unascertainable.... We therefore see no reason to depart from section 2–723's mandate to calculate market price at the time Manchester learned of the repudiation, and we therefore remand for a redetermination of damages. Because we believe that the focus of the parties' damages evidence was misplaced, however, we offer the following additional guidance to the trial court on retrial.

In our view, the central problem with the evidence and arguments presented regarding Manchester's damages was that they primarily focused on the difference between the long term contract price between Manchester and PNG and the spot market price under a spot market contract such as the Scissortail Contract. While Manchester's expert, Dutcher, expressed an opinion as to the average price of gas under long term contracts containing market down provisions in November, 1985, the bulk of his testimony, as well as both Manchester's and PNG's exhibits, was on the difference between the spot market price and the Manchester–PNG contract price. Insufficient evidence was presented on the average price of gas under long term contracts in November or December, 1984, the time at which Manchester learned of the repudiation. As the evidence presented clearly indicated, however, the spot market is very volatile and uncertain. That contrasts with the predictability of a long term contract with a minimum take provision and a take or pay provision.[8] Spot market contracts differ significantly from long term contracts. In our view, Manchester's damages should be calculated by reference to the difference between the Manchester–PNG contract price and the market price of gas under a similar long term contract at the time Manchester learned of PNG's repudiation.[9]

---

7. In support of its argument that section 2–723 provides the proper measure of damages, PNG refers us to a recent Second Circuit case involving breach of a long term aluminum supply contract. See Trans World Metals, Inc. v. Southwire Co., 769 F.2d 902 (2d Cir.1985). The court in Trans World Metals applied the damages remedy of section 2–708. In dicta, the court stated "[w]e would accept Southwire's argument that the date Trans World learned of the repudiation would be the correct date on which to calculate the market price had this action been tried before the time for full performance under the contract." Id. at 909 (emphasis original).

8. PNG argues strenuously that the market down provision contained in the contract with Manchester would have resulted in a decreasing price each year. Nonetheless, Manchester's expert testified that it was as reasonable to estimate that, despite the market down provision, the price would average out to $2.75 per MBTU throughout the ten year term. In any event, evidence as to the market price of gas under long term contracts containing market-down provisions will take into account the existence of such provisions and their likely effect on the price of gas.

9. We note that at least one commentator views section 2–723 differently. See Jackson, " 'Anticipatory Repudiation' and the Temporal Element of Contract Law: An Economic Inquiry into Contract Damages in Cases of Prospective Nonperformance," 31 Stan.L.Rev. 69, 104 (1978) ("While silent on the issue, section 2–723 appears to envision 'the price of such goods prevailing at the time the aggrieved party learned of the repudiation,' the spot price prevailing on that date.") (emphasis original). The commentator goes on, however, to make a persuasive case that

PNG also challenges the district court's jury instruction regarding incidental damages. The challenged instruction stated:

> "You may also consider, in order to determine the amount of damages, incidental damage the plaintiff may have suffered. Incidental damages include any commercially reasonable charges, expenses or commissions, incurred in stopping delivery of the gas, in the transportation, care and custody of the gas after defendant failed to comply with its agreement, in connection with return or resale of the gas or otherwise resulting from defendant's failure to comply with its agreement, if any. Plaintiff claims its incidental damages include the cost of building the pipeline and then extending the pipeline. Defendant denies such costs are incidental damages and claims plaintiff would have had to incur them anyway.

* * *

> [Defendant argues that] "Under the terms and conditions of the disputed contract, Manchester was solely responsible for the cost of constructing the pipeline to the point of delivery. Thus, even if a contract exists and [PNG is] liable to Manchester for damages, it cannot be held liable for the cost of constructing the pipeline to point of delivery specified in the contract. Only that portion of its pipeline costs which are directly attributable to [PNG's] alleged breach may be considered. However, even this portion of pipeline expense may not be laid entirely at [PNG's] feet. The cost of extending the pipeline should have been apportioned between the parties. Manchester used the pipeline to sell the gas from five wells not included in the disputed contract. It enjoyed gas sales of $5,246,621.44 during an eight month period ending September, 1985. [PNG] would have been obliged to purchase only $346,130.00 worth of gas during this period. However, Manchester did not deduct that portion of its pipeline expenses attributable to the enormous sales which it enjoyed from these five wells. The Trial Court's failure to properly instruct the jury in this regard is error."

We find no error in the instruction. The instruction correctly defined "incidental damages." See Okla.Stat. tit. 12A, § 2–710. It then simply stated that Manchester claimed the pipeline costs as incidental damages but that PNG argued that they were not incidental damages and that Manchester would have incurred them anyway. It further cautioned the jury to deduct any amounts Manchester saved from PNG's repudiation. That instruction is correct.

* * *

We have considered all of PNG's arguments on appeal, and for the foregoing reasons the district court opinion is AFFIRMED in part, REVERSED and REMANDED in part.

"hypothetical market-based-damages ... should ... be based on the forward market price as of the date of the repudiation." Id. at 72.

NOTES

1. One way to incentivize the parties to a long-term contract to carry out their obligations for the full period covered by the contract is to include a provision for damages in the event of non-performance, coupled with an option for the performing party to terminate the agreement. Would such provisions have benefitted the purchaser in the principal case?

2. At least two "Base Contracts for the Sale and Purchase of Natural Gas" have been developed, one by the Gas Industry Standard Board, which is intended for use for short-term agreements of one month or less, and the other by the North American Energy Standards Board, which is designed for use in either short-term or long-term agreements. There are, of course, significant differences between short-term and long-term agreements.

In a short-term spot transaction, the parties are focused on a one-time acquisition or sale of natural gas at a given price. In addition, typically the period of time between reaching an agreement on the terms of a spot transaction and the actual execution of the transaction is very close at hand, usually within hours or days. As a result, parties involved in spot contracts are more interested in being able to execute a transaction swiftly than in protecting interests and addressing issues that could arise over a more extended period of time * * *.

> Parties to a long-term contract, however, generally have entered into such an arrangement in order to secure a long-term supply of, or market for, natural gas at a certain price. Simply liquidating a transaction and being reimbursed for any expenses incurred with respect to failure to perform will likely not be entirely satisfactory to the performing party as it is likely to have long term obligations on which it depends on timely deliveries or sales of natural gas and will need to find some type of comparable replacement arrangement. In addition, the likelihood that circumstances will change or some event take place that could adversely affect a party's ability to perform, or implement the provisions of the contract, over time is much greater the longer the term of the contract.

Karen Goepfert, "For the Long Haul: The Suitability of the Base Contract for the Sale and Purchase of Natural gas for Long–Term Transactions," 27 Energy L.J. 583, 585–86 (2006).

CHAPTER 7

FEDERAL, STATE, AND INDIAN LANDS

Table of Sections

———

Some of the largest remaining domestic oil and gas reserves in the United States are located on public lands, particularly in and offshore of Alaska and on the Continental Shelf of the Atlantic Ocean and Gulf of Mexico, and on land owned either communally or individually by American Indians. Development of these often remote areas is expensive, occasionally dangerous, and sometimes controversial. Environmental interest groups have generally opposed development of certain public lands out of concern for fish, fauna, flora, and aesthetics. After the 2009 Deepwater Horizon disaster in the Gulf of Mexico off Louisiana, various citizens groups also fear further offshore oil spills. Thus, the federal government has continued to bar leasing and development of many potentially oil-rich offshore areas in the Atlantic and Pacific and off the western coast of Florida.

This chapter, a brief introduction to the leasing and development of public lands, is divided by ownership and type of land: federal onshore lands; federal offshore areas; American Indian lands; state onshore lands; and state aquatic and offshore areas. Many of the same issues addressed in prior chapters may arise with respect to these lands and are often resolved in a similar manner. Accordingly, this chapter concentrates on matters unique to federal, Indian, and state lands. For example, concerns about the conservation of oil and gas on governmental lands are the same as for private lands, but a state conservation agency does not have general jurisdiction over federal lands absent federal consent or over Indian lands absent tribal and, in most cases, federal consent. Federal and state oil and gas lease forms are similar to leases used for private lands, although some modern state lease forms are more lessor-oriented. The law of implied covenants applies to federal, Indian, and state leases in much the same manner as the law applies to private leases, although modern governmental lease forms, underlying statutes, or regulations often contain express covenants to protect against drainage, to develop proven properties and to market production prudently. Disputes over a government's title to land are uncommon;[1] nevertheless, private parties frequently litigate development rights on federal land.

A. DEVELOPMENT OF FEDERAL AND INDIAN LANDS[2]

In Fiscal Year 2011, the federal government generated over $11.2 billion in bonuses, rents, royalties, and other revenues from mineral leasing activities on federal (onshore and offshore) and Indian lands. Nearly $6.5 billion of these revenues were generated by offshore oil and gas leasing activities. Just over $4.1 billion came from onshore mineral leasing, and the balance, not including bonuses collected by the Bureau of Indian Affairs, came from mineral leasing of Indian lands.[3] Federal royalties are the third largest source of revenue for the United States Treasury.

Professor George Coggins has noted that, although the federal oil and gas leasing regime is patterned after private leasing transactions,

> [t]he government as mineral lessor is still the government, with all of the procedural trappings and substantive subtleties that inevitably accompany activities of the sovereign. Prospective lessees are not free to negotiate lease terms and covenants because most requirements are set by law. Unlike private lessors, the United States sometimes tries harder to keep leases in force than to terminate them. Federal lessees by statute acquire interests and procedural remedies unknown to the common law. But, unlike private leases, federal oil and gas leases do not necessarily convey a "dominant estate" with all appurtenant rights and easements. Other areas of difference between federal

---

1. One major exception is the title to the beds of lakes and streams. Generally, the state owns the beds of navigable lakes and streams, while the riparian owner owns the bed of a non-navigable lake or stream. There has been substantial litigation over whether a particular lake or stream is navigable and over the precise boundary and location of state ownership along a navigable stream. In the context of oil and gas development, see, e.g., North Dakota ex rel. Board of University and School Lands v. United States, 770 F.Supp. 506 (D.N.D.1991) (*but cf.* Defenders of Wildlife v. Hull, 18 P.3d 722 (Ariz. Ct. App. 2001)) (statute disclaiming state's interest in watercourse bedlands held invalid.); Kim–Go, H.K. Minerals, Inc. v. J.P. Furlong Enterprises, Inc., 484 N.W.2d 118 (N.D.1992); Kim–Go, H.K. Minerals, Inc. v. J.P. Furlong Enterprises, Inc., 460 N.W.2d 694 (N.D.1990); and J.P. Furlong Enterprises, Inc. v. Sun Exploration & Production Co., 423 N.W.2d 130 (N.D.1988).

2. The Editors wish to acknowledge the assistance of Peter J. Schaumberg in the preparation of this chapter. Mr. Schaumberg is Of Counsel in the Washington, D.C. office of Beveridge & Diamond, P.C. He is the former Deputy Associate Solicitor for the Division of Mineral Resources, U.S. Department of the Interior, where his responsibilities included providing legal advice to the minerals programs of the Bureau of Land Management and the former Minerals Management Service for almost 25 years. For prior editions, the editors also acknowledge the assistance of Geoffrey R. Heath. Mr. Heath was the Assistant Solicitor for Federal and Indian Royalty in the Division of Mineral Resources. Mr. Heath was assisted by Milo Mason, an attorney in the Branch of Petroleum Resources, Office of the Solicitor. Any views expressed herein are the personal views of the authors and are not necessarily the official position of the Department of the Interior.

3. Department of the Interior, Office of Natural Resources Revenue *available at* http://www.onrr.gov/ (last visited Aug. 27, 2012). Onshore figures include revenues generated from many different minerals, but most of these revenues were derived from oil, gas, and coal leasing activities.

and private leases include acreage limitations, diligence requirements that affect other leaseholds, and minimum bonus systems. On the other hand, federal leases may be integrated with private leases in spacing, pooling, and unitization agreements if the federal agency agrees. All in all, practitioners will seldom be able to transpose their expertise in private oil and gas law bodily into federal oil and gas leasing.

2 George C. Coggins, Public Natural Resources Law § 23.01[1] (1992).

1. PUBLIC LANDS

Federal Public lands comprise almost 655 million acres or about 29 percent of the total land area of the fifty states.[4] Most of this acreage is classified as "public domain:" lands that have never left federal ownership and lands that were acquired in exchange for public domain lands or timber on those lands. The balance is generally classified as "acquired lands:" lands obtained by the federal government by purchase, condemnation, gift, or exchange. In addition, the United States has reserved 700 million acres of federal minerals, including reserved oil and gas rights to over 37 million acres of patented lands.[5]

While the surface acreage of federal lands may be managed by a variety of agencies, the oil and gas assets of nearly all federal lands are currently managed by the Department of the Interior through the Bureau of Land Management ("BLM") and the Bureau of Ocean Energy Management ("BOEM"). Nonetheless, other federal agencies, including the National Park Service ("NPS"), the Fish and Wildlife Service, and the Forest Service, manage the surface of federal lands assigned to their respective jurisdictions. In general, each of these agencies has the right to decide whether the lands that it manages may be leased for oil and gas exploration and development, and to decide the extent to which the lessee has access to and use of the surface for exploration and development. The President, through the use of an executive order, or the Congress may declare certain public lands unavailable for oil and gas exploration and development.

(a) History

Federal law governing oil and gas operations on public lands has tended to evolve in response to specific controversies respecting federal lands. Under the Oil Placer Act of 1897,[6] oil and gas were classified as "locatable" minerals and thereby subject to placer claims under the General Mining Law of 1872.[7] Under this law, a person could enter upon the public domain, explore for ("locate") oil and gas, and, without pay-

---

4. Department of the Interior, Public Land Statistics, *available at* http://www.blm.gov/public_land_statistics/pls10/pls10_combined.pdf (last visited Aug. 27, 2012).

5. Id. at 7.

6. Act of Feb. 11, 1897, 29 Stat. 526.

7. Act of May 10, 1872, ch. 152, 17 Stat. 91 (codified as amended at 30 U.S.C. §§ 22–47).

ment to the federal government, acquire a valid right to produce oil and gas and the right to secure a patent to the land.[8] In the early 1900s, however, oil became strategically important to the United States Navy, which converted its ships from coal-fired to oil-fired power at about the same time that miners were filing placer claims on federal oil reserves. In 1909, in the interest of national security, President William H. Taft withdrew certain federal oil reserves from the "location" rules of the Mining Law of 1872.[9]

In 1920, the Congress passed the Mineral Leasing Act ("MLA").[10] As amended, the MLA classifies "coal, phosphate, sodium, potassium, oil, oil shale, [tar sands,] gilsonite (including all vein-type solid hydrocarbons) or gas" as "leasable minerals and, therefore, these minerals are withdrawn from location under the Mining Law."[11] "Oil" includes "all nongaseous hydrocarbon substances other than those substances leasable as coal, oil shale, or gilsonite (including all vein-type solid hydrocarbons)."[12] The Department of the Interior treats coalbed methane gas, carbon dioxide, helium, nonflammable gas, and other gases as "gas," except that the MLA specifically reserves ownership of all helium to the United States.[13] Under the MLA, when the federal government issues an oil and gas lease, it reserves a royalty of not less than 12 1/2 percent of the amount or value of oil and gas production.[14]

As the MLA evolved, six categories of lands were required to be leased by competitive bidding, including lands that contained a "Known Geological Structure" ("KGS"), Alaskan lands within a "favorable petroleum geological province," and lands subject to drainage.[15] Nevertheless, most lands were leased noncompetitively to the first qualified applicant who properly filed a lease application with the BLM.[16] This seemingly simple "over-the-counter" leasing system proved unworkable. Upon the expiration of the primary term of a lease that included acreage having a high speculative value, a crowd of applicants would often rush to the BLM

8. There are still some existing unpatented pre–1920 oil and gas and oil shale placer claims.

9. Congress ratified this action with passage of the Pickett Act of 1910, ch. 421, 36 Stat. 847 (1910). The United States Supreme Court upheld President Taft's executive withdrawal in United States v. Midwest Oil Co., 236 U.S. 459 (1915).

10. Act of Feb. 25, 1920, ch. 85, § 1, 41 Stat. 437.

11. 30 U.S.C. § 181.

12. *Id.*

13. 30 U.S.C. § 181. The United States reserved helium because in the early twentieth century helium was a strategic mineral used for military and other purposes.

14. Numerous "hardrock" minerals are still classified as locatable. The federal government has not reserved a royalty on locatable minerals; however, various proposals to amend or repeal the General Mining Law of 1872 are still being debated. Why did the Congress authorize the private exploitation of federal minerals without reserving a royalty or obtaining some type of compensation for these resources?

15. 43 C.F.R. § 3120.1. For current amended version see 43 C.F.R. § 3120.1.

16. 43 C.F.R. §§ 3112.0 to 3112.7 (no longer in current regulations). An over-the-counter lease could also be issued for a previously leased non-KGS tract if there were no applications to lease the tract after it had been re-offered under the simultaneous filing system.

office in an effort to be the first person to file for a new over-the-counter lease.

To address the problem of multiple applicants,[17] the system was revised in 1960.[18] Although previously unleased acreage could be leased "over the counter," previously leased acreage was leased through a "simultaneous filing" program. Under this program, applicants were given a "window of time" to apply for a lease to lands that had been previously leased. All applications filed within this time (together with a nonrefundable application fee) were treated as having been simultaneously filed. The lessee was then selected by a random drawing. The "simultaneous filing" program was in reality a national oil and gas lease lottery with winners receiving leaseholds having a wide range of values. Although applicants were technically limited to a single application per tract, this limit was easily circumvented through various "ballot box stuffing" schemes. Additionally, various lottery filing "services" took advantage of unsophisticated parties by charging a fee for questionable advice and for processing applications that could easily have been filed directly with the BLM.

In 1987, in response to certain abuses of the existing over-the-counter leasing system, Congress passed the Federal Onshore Oil and Gas Leasing Reform Act ("FOOGLRA"), amending several MLA leasing provisions. This Act created a new leasing system, which eliminated the KGS classification and replaced the old three-tiered over-the-counter, simultaneous filings, and competitive systems. Under the MLA, as amended by FOOGLRA, all federal onshore lands, with few exceptions, must be offered for lease under the competitive leasing system. 30 U.S.C. § 226(b).

On May 17, 2010, the Department of Interior announced another round of oil and gas leasing reforms for BLM managed sub-surface lands, meaning the new rules apply to leasing of federal minerals under land surfaces managed by the BLM, state surface lands, and private surface owners. Generally, in addition to "Master Development Plans" ("MDPs"), which govern individual post-lease development decisions, the new rules require "Master Leasing Plans" ("MLPs"), which include a more detailed environmental review before leasing and development.

Currently, Resource Management Plans ("RMPs") complied by the BLM govern the leasing decisions for fluid minerals. BLM field offices are required to periodically examine resource management decisions to determine whether the RMPs currently on file adequately protect important resource values regarding new data and regulations and changing circumstances. But while RMPs primarily deal with just oil and gas planning and leasing decisions, the Department of the Interior through the BLM believes that MLPs will provide necessary *additional* planning and analysis over a broader scope of factors.

---

17. See Arkla Exploration Co. v. Texas Oil and Gas Corp., 734 F.2d 347 (8th Cir. 1984).

18. 43 C.F.R. §§ 3112.0–5 to 3112.7 (no longer in current regulations).

Generally, the MLP analyzes the type and extent of disruption that the proposed development might cause regarding a variety of features on the lands under consideration for leasing. The interdisciplinary teams that conduct the MLPs consider the impact that oil and gas development may have on air quality, recreation, flora and fauna, cultural properties of American Indian communities or paleontological resources, watersheds and aquifers, erosion and soils, and health and safety.

The preparation of an MLP is required when a "substantial" portion of the area to be developed is not currently leased but is majority-owned by the federal government and when the oil and gas industry has expressed a specific interest in leasing due to the moderate to high potential for a commercial discovery. If these circumstances are met, an MLP will be compiled if additional analysis/information is necessary to "address likely resource or cumulative impacts if oil and gas development were to occur where there are: multiple-use or natural/cultural resource conflicts; impacts to air quality; impacts on the resources or values of any unit of the National Park System, national wildlife refuge, or National Forest wilderness area...; or impacts on other specially designated areas."[19]

After the MLP is completed, typically in the form of an Environmental Assessment or Environmental Impact Statement, the BLM Field Manager or District Manager will forward the results and a recommendation to the BLM State Director. The field office recommendation may vary from offering a lease parcel under standard conditions to withholding the parcel and closing the area to further leasing.

NOTES

1. In 1947, in response to a request from the Department of the Interior, which had chosen to narrowly construe its authority under the MLA, Congress enacted the Mineral Leasing Act for Acquired Lands ("MLAAL") Act of Aug. 7, 1947, ch. 513, 61 Stat. 913 (codified as amended at 30 U.S.C. §§ 351–359). This Act provides that acquired lands (including millions of acres acquired by the federal government during the depression of the 1930s) could be leased, subject to certain limitations, under the general provisions of the MLA. These limitations include a provision requiring "the consent of the head of the executive department * * * having jurisdiction over the lands * * * and subject to such conditions as that official may prescribe to insure the adequate utilization of the lands for the primary purposes for which they have been acquired or are being administered." 30 U.S.C. § 352.

2. For MLA leases, the state where the lease is located receives 50 percent (90 percent in Alaska) of the bonus, rental, and royalty revenues received for that lease. 30 U.S.C. § 191. Leases on acquired lands are subject to various revenue distribution requirements established in the laws under which the lands were acquired.

---

19. Instruction Memorandum No. 2010–117 from Robert Abbey, BLM Director, to all Field Officials, May 17, 2010, p. 15.

3. Throughout the history of the United States, and especially in the 1800s, the cash-starved but land-rich federal government made large land grants for the construction of public improvements, particularly to railroad companies to entice them to build tracks through the American West to transport settlers and goods.[20] Various railroad companies received grants totaling about 94 million acres, and certain states received an additional 37 million acres to aid in the construction of railroads.[21] Although initially more limited, many of these grants conveyed fee title to the railroad, including all mineral rights. The lands granted were usually sections of land granted in a checker-board pattern (e.g., odd-numbered sections within twenty miles on either side of the track). If any of these lands were already privately owned, then the railroad was ordinarily allowed to select "in lien" lands (substitute). Railroads forfeited their grant lands if the railroad was not completed.

Commonly, the railroad resold most of these lands to investors and settlers, often reserving coal and iron, which were important, respectively, to powering locomotives and laying track. When selling lands in the 1900s, many railroads began reserving oil, gas, and other minerals as well. Thus, railroads such as the Central Pacific, Northern Pacific, and Union Pacific, held vast acreages of mineral rights in the Western United States. For the most part, these mineral rights are now held largely by other entities. For example, the grant lands and reserved mineral rights of the Union Pacific are now held by Anadarko Petroleum Corporation, one the largest independent oil and gas operators in the United States.

4. Railroads were also granted rights-of-way for the construction of tracks. Railroad rights-of-way vary from a range of 100 feet wide to 400 feet wide, depending on the Act, and may include additional rights to harvest timber, secure water supplies, gravel, and other necessary resources beyond the right-of-way corridor. These rights-of-way were not granted by instrument. Rather, the railroad filed maps with the federal government indicating the location of the track and hence the rights-of-way, which were perfected when the railroad was constructed. Northern Pacific R. Co. v. Townsend, 190 U.S. 267, 270 (1903). Other entities were granted rights-of-way or easements for various purposes, including pipelines, telephone and telegraph lines, electric lines, water reservoirs, and roads. BLM records, local county land records, or a physical inspection of land may reveal the existence of a valid right-of-way. For example, as late as the 1970s, the holder of a public-lands grazing right could establish a valid water reservoir right-of-way on federal land without governmental approval. When developing public land, oil and gas lessees must respect the prior rights of rights-of-way and easements holders.

The issue of mineral title beneath rights-of-way through federal land is complicated. See, e.g., United States v. Union Pacific R.R. Co., 353 U.S. 112

---

20. The earliest such grants were only for rights-of-way, but later included grants of millions of acres of land that the railroads could pledge or sell for financing railroad construction. See. e.g., Act of July 1, 1862, ch. 120, 12 Stat. 489, 493–94, amended by Act of July 2, 1864, ch. 216, 13 Stat. 356 (Union Pacific Railroad and Central Pacific Railroad grants); Act of July 2, 1864, ch. 217, 13 Stat. 365, amended by Act of May 31, 1870, 16 Stat. 378, 378–79 (Northern Pacific Railroad grant); Act of July 27, 1866, ch. 278, 14 Stat. 292 (commonly called the Southern Pacific Railroad grant); Act of Mar. 3, 1871, ch. 122, 16 Stat. 573, 578 (Texas Pacific Railroad grant).

21. Frank Wilner, Railroad Land Grants: Paid in Full, U.S. Office of Information and Public Affairs 8, 24–25 (1984).

(1957) (construing Acts of July 1, 1862, 12 Stat. 489). Because certain rights-of-way across federal lands have been viewed as granting "limited fee" title, generally only lasting as long as use of the right of way continued, with the federal government retaining a reverter right in the right-of-way acreage, the Secretary of the Interior did not assume authority to lease these rights-of-way under the Mineral Leasing Act of 1920, but the Secretary did assume a right to bar the right-of-way holder from leasing. In response, Congress enacted the Right-of-Way Leasing Act of 1930.[22]

Where applicable, the Act of 1930 authorizes the Secretary to lease acreage beneath rights-of-way, "whether the same be a base fee or mere easement."[23] 30 U.S.C. § 301. Nevertheless, because of the assumed reversionary nature of the government's title, the lease must also be offered to the owner of the right-of-way or the owner's assignee (§ 301), subject to a minimum royalty of one-eighth (§ 305). Prior to the issuance of the lease, however, the Secretary must give the adjacent landowner or oil and gas lessee the opportunity to offer "compensatory royalty" for the privilege of draining the right-of-way from wells on the adjacent land. The Secretary must also allow the owner of the right-of-way or its assignee an opportunity to make a competing offer. If competing offers are made, then the Secretary awards the development right to the bidder whose offer, in the Secretary's opinion, is the "most advantageous to the United States." 30 U.S.C. § 303.

Because the holder of only a right-of-way lease could not ordinarily locate a well on the surface of the right-of-way, the matter boils down to how much the holder of the adjacent rights is willing to pay to acquire the rights to drain the right-of-way. Railroads regard the Right-of-Way Leasing Act of 1930 as giving them, or their assigns, the right to apply to the Secretary for an oil and gas lease to the right-of-way acreage. Commonly, a railroad will assign its right to apply for particular right-of-way acreage to a third party in return for a bonus. If the assignee succeeds in obtaining a lease, then the assignee may be obliged to pay an additional bonus and overriding royalty to the railroad. For a thorough discussion of the Right of Way Leasing Act, see 1 Rocky Mtn.Min.L. Found., Law of Federal Oil and Gas Leases, Chapter 8 (1997).

Regarding rights-of-way established over federal lands prior to 1871, a railroad right-of-way grant often expressly included coal and iron rights beneath the right-of-way.[24] In Wyoming v. Udall, 379 F.2d 635 (10th Cir. 1967), the court held that State of Wyoming did not receive title to the land

22. Act of May 21, 1930, ch. 307, 46 Stat. 373 (codified as amended at 30 U.S.C. §§ 301–306).

23. Current regulations, however, purport to limit the application of the Right-of-Way Leasing Act to railroad rights-of-way and easements issued pursuant to the Act of March 3, 1875, 43 U.S.C. §§ 934–939 and earlier railroad rights-of-way statutes, and to irrigation and drainage ditch rights-of-way and easements issued pursuant to the Act of March 3, 1891, 43 U.S.C. §§ 946–949. 43 C.F.R. § 3109.1–1. Other rights-of-way and easements are deemed to be governed by the Mineral Leasing Act of 1920. These regulations are intended to limit the application of the Right-of-Way Leasing Act as much as possible and still comply with case law. See, e.g., Champlin Petroleum Co., 68 IBLA 142 (1982). Nevertheless, in view of the express language of § 301 of the Right-of-Way Leasing Act, the validity of these regulations is questionable. See discussion, 1 Rocky Mtn.Min.L. Found., Law of Federal Oil and Gas Leases § 8.04(1) (1997).

24. One of the more significant acts was the Right of Way Act of 1852, ch. 80, 10 Stat. 28. Earlier acts included Resolution of June 25, 1834, ch. 3, 4 Stat. 744; Act of Jan. 31, 1837, ch. 9, 5 Stat. 144; Act of June 28, 1838, ch. 150, 5 Stat. 253; Act of Sept. 20, 1850, ch. 61, 9 Stat. 466.

beneath a pre–1871 railroad right-of-way granted to the Union Pacific[25] when the federal government subsequently granted certain land along the railroad to the state. Accordingly, the federal government retained title to the minerals beneath the right-of-way, other than coal and iron. Thus, the federal government could lease the oil and gas rights within the right-of-way under the provisions of the Right-of-Way Leasing Act of 1930.

After 1871, right-of-way grants over federal lands did not include an express grant to any minerals and came to be issued under the General Railroad Right-of-Way Act of 1875, which granted a 200–foot wide right-of-way.[26] In Amerada Hess Corporation, 24 IBLA 360 (1976), the Interior Board of Land Appeals held that the subsequent patentee of federal land along an 1875 Act right-of-way received title (including any minerals not expressly reserved in the patent) to the lands beneath the right-of-way. Accord, Samuel C. Johnson 1988 Trust v. Bayfield County, 649 F.3d 799 (7th Cir. 2011).

Beginning in the 1970s, the rail industry began abandoning many of its spur services to small communities, particularly in the Great Plains. These abandonments spawned litigation over title to abandoned right-of-way acreage.[27] Where the railroad received its right-of-way by virtue of federal law to cross public lands, the effect of abandonment turns on the relevant federal act.

---

25. Act of July 1, 1862, 12 Stat. 489, as amended by the Act of July 2, 1864, 13 Stat. 356.

26. 18 Stat. 482. The 1871 date is significant, as the federal government made no new land grants to railroads after 1871 but did provide for railroad rights-of-way in the General Railroad Right of Way Act of 1875.

27. The Congress passed a statute regarding abandoned tracts as early as 1922, but this law did little to resolve to clear title to railroad rights-of-way. It provides:

Whenever public lands of the United States have been or may be granted to any railroad company for use as a right of way for its railroad or as sites for railroad structures of any kind, and use and occupancy of said lands for such purposes has ceased or shall hereafter cease, whether by forfeiture or by abandonment by said railroad company declared or decreed by a court of competent jurisdiction or by Act of Congress, then and thereupon all right, title, interest, and estate of the United States in said lands shall, except such part thereof as may be embraced in a public highway legally established within one year after the date of said decree or forfeiture or abandonment be transferred to and vested in any person, firm, or corporation, assigns, or successors in title and interest to whom or to which title of the United States may have been or may be granted, conveying or purporting to convey the whole of the legal subdivision or subdivisions traversed or occupied by such railroad or railroad structures of any kind as aforesaid, except lands within a municipality the title to which, upon forfeiture or abandonment, as herein provided, shall vest in such municipality, and this by virtue of the patent thereto and without the necessity of any other or further conveyance or assurance of any kind or nature whatsoever: Provided, That this section shall not affect conveyances made by any railroad company of portions of its right of way if such conveyance be among those which have been or may after March 8, 1922, and before such forfeiture or abandonment be validated and confirmed by any Act of Congress; nor shall this section affect any public highway on said right of way on March 8, 1922: Provided further, That the transfer of such lands shall be subject to and contain reservations in favor of the United States of all oil, gas, and other minerals in the land so transferred and conveyed, with the right to prospect for, mine, and remove same.

43 U.S.C. § 912. The Court of Appeals for the Seventh Circuit has ruled that a court of competent jurisdiction included the Interstate Commerce Commission (now the STA). Samuel C. Johnson 1988 Trust v. Bayfield County, 649 F.3d 799 (7th Cir. 2011). In Phillips Co. v. Denver & Rio Grande Western R.R. Co, 97 F.3d 1375 (10th Cir. 1996), the court held that abandonment could not occur without prior authorization by Interstate Commerce Commission (ICC). In contrast to this statute, the National Trails Systems Act, 16 U.S.C. § 1248, preserves the United States' interest, if any, in rights-of-way for the purpose of establishing recreational trails unless the right-of-way was abandoned prior to October 4, 1988.

Courts have variously classified the property interest in railroad rights-of-way.[28] Courts have construed several acts as conveying title to the right-of-way in fee simple absolute.[29] Courts have construed other acts as conveying limited title, which terminates when the right-of-way is abandoned.[30] Rights-of-way under General Railroad Right-of-Way Act of 1875 grant only easements across federal lands.[31] Numerous acts were passed concerning railroad rights-of-way across American Indian lands, most of which granted only easements.[32]

In Hash v. United States, 403 F.3d 1308 (Fed. Cir. 2005), the court held that the United States retained no interest in rights-of-way granted under the 1875 Act where the land along the right-of-way was subsequently patented into private ownership. Accordingly, the patentees and their successors in interest took fee title subject to the pre-existing railroad right-of-way. Upon abandonment, their fee title was no longer encumbered by that easement.

5.   As an aside, similar problems are encountered regarding railroad rights-of-way across state and private lands. The following is but a sampling of the case law: Use of the term "right-of-way" may be enough to cause a court to rule that a mere easement was conveyed. See, e.g., Consolidated Rail Corp., Inc. v. Lewellen, 682 N.E.2d 779 (Ind. 1997) (finding easement) and Swan v. O'Leary, 225 P.2d 199 (Wash. 1950) (finding easement). But see, Roeder Co. v. K & E Moving & Storage Co., Inc., 4 P.3d 839 (Wash. App. 2000) (finding fee simple). In Hash v. United States, 454 F. Supp.2d 1066 (D. Idaho 2006), in construing an instrument to land in Idaho, the court held that a conveyance of a right-of-way "forever" conveyed title in fee simple distinguishing Neider v. Shaw, 65 P.3d 525 (Idaho 2003) (finding that a hand written "right of way" clause added to a printed deed form was substantive and thus limited the conveyance to an easement). But see, Blendu v. United States, 79 Fed. Cl. 500 (Fed. Cl. 2007) (holding that the railroad was given an

---

28.   One commentator has argued that the various classifications cannot be explained by differences in the Acts but rather reflect a change in political and judicial attitudes about the railroads. Danaya C. Wright, The Shifting Sands of Property Rights, Federal Railroad Grants, and Economic History: *Hash v. United States* and the Threat to Rail–Trail Conversion, 38 Envtl, Law 711 (2008).

29.   *Missouri, K & T Ry. Co. v. Oklahoma*, 271 U.S. 303, 304, 308 (1926) (discussing Act of July 26, 1866, ch. 270 § 4, 14 Stat. 289); Winston v. U.S. Trust, 172 U.S. 303, 304, 309 (1898) (discussing Act of July 27, 1866, ch. 278, 14 Stat. 292); *Missouri, K & T Ry. Co. v. Roberts*, 152 U.S. 114 (1894) (Same); (discussing Act of July 23, 1866, c. 212, 14 Stat. 210); Union Pacific R. Co. v. City of Atoka, 6 Fed. Appx. 725 (10th Cir. Okla. 2001) (discussing Act of July 25, 1866, ch. 241 §§ 1–8, 14 Stat. 236–38); and Missouri–Kansas–Texas R.R. Co. v. Early, 641 F.2d 856 (10th Cir. 1981) (discussing July 25 and July 26 Acts).

30.   United States v. Union Pac. R.R. Co., 353 U.S. 112, 113, 118–19 (1957) (discussing Act of July 1, 1862); Great Northern Ry. Co. v. United States, 315 U.S. 262, 271, 273 n. 6, 277–78 n. 18 (Act of March 3, 1875); Union Pac. R.R. Co. v. Laramie Stock Yards Co., 231 U.S. 190 (1913) (discussing Act of July 1, 1862); Northern Pac. Ry. Co. v. Townsend, 190 U.S. 267, 267–68, 271 (1903) (discussing Act of July 2, 1864); Territory of New Mexico v. United States Trust Co., 172 U.S. 171 (1898) (discussing Act of July 27, 1866); Railroad Co. v. Baldwin, 103 U.S. 426, 429–30 (discussing Act of 1866); Wyoming v. Andrus, 602 F.2d 1379, 1380 n. 2 (10th Cir.1979) (discussing Act of July 1, 1862, ch. 120, 12 Stat. 489, as amended by Act of July 2, 1864, ch. 216, 13 Stat. 356); and Wyoming v. Udall, 379 F.2d 635, 637 (10th Cir.) (same).

31.   Great Northern Ry. Co. v. United States, 315 U.S. 262, 271 (1942) (implicitly overruling Rio Grande Western Ry. Co. v. Stringham, 239 U.S. 44 (1915), which had regarded rights-of-way under the 1875 Act as limited fees).

32.   See, e.g., Act of Feb. 28, 1902, ch. 134, 32 Stat. 43, 44.

easement under Idaho law even though the deed's habendum clause conveyed "a perpetual right of Way for said second party's Rail Way Line unto the said party of the second part and its successors and assigns forever"). Cf., Kershaw Sunnyside Ranches, Inc. v. Yakima Interurban Lines Assoc., 126 P.3d 16 (Wash. 2006) (holding that conveyance of a "right of way for a railway forever" conveyed only an easement). If the deed expressly conveys "fee simple title," then the railroad most likely takes title in fee simple absolute. See Brown v. State, 924 P.2d 908 (Wash. 1996). Cf., State v. Hess, 684 N.W.2d 414 (Minn. 2004) (holding that a conveyance "for so long as the said strips of land shall be used for Right of Way and for Railway purposes, but to cease and terminate if the Railway is removed" conveyed a fee simple determinable but further held that Marketable Record Title Act terminated the possibility of reverter). Cf., State ex. rel. Commissioners of the Land Office v. Bruce, 25 P.3d 953 (Okla.Civ.App. 2001) (holding that the state did not retain any rights to a railroad right-of-way easement that was abandoned after the state conveyed its interest in adjacent acreage to a third party).

6. A series of acts and regulations specifically govern federal lands in Alaska. Under the Alaska Statehood Act, Alaska was granted over 100 million acres of federal land. Act of July 7, 1958, Pub.L.No. 85–508, 72 Stat. 339. federal patents issued to the state include all mineral rights, but the patents are subject to valid existing rights, including oil and gas leases.

To achieve a final allocation of federal lands in Alaska, Congress enacted the Alaska National Interest Lands Conservation Act of 1980 ("ANILCA"). Act of December 2, 1980, Pub.L. No. 96–487, 94 Stat. 2371. Except for specified areas, most federal lands were withdrawn from oil and gas leasing. Under the Act, the Arctic National Wildlife Refuge ("ANWR") was designated as "Wilderness" and the "production of oil and gas from [ANWR] is prohibited and no leasing or other development leading to production of oil and gas from the [Refuge] shall be undertaken until authorized by an act of Congress." This effectively proscribed oil and gas development in ANWR except within an approximately 1.5 million acre-strip on the ANWR coastal plain adjacent to the Beaufort Sea known as "Area 1002" (due to the numerical designation of the portion of ANILCA describing the tract, Section 1002). Congress deferred a decision regarding future management of Area 1002 in recognition of the area's potentially enormous oil and gas resources and its importance as wildlife habitat. In 1987 DOI submitted to Congress a report on the resources (including petroleum) of Area 1002. This DOI report was followed by a report from the United States Geological Survey ("USGS")[33] which deemed Area 1002 as potentially prospective for oil and gas development after analysis of 1,400 miles of 2–D seismic reflection lines in Area 1002 and other studies including surface rock sampling, mapping, and geochemical testing. This work was undertaken by a private exploration firm and funded by a consortium of oil companies.

Lands authorized for leasing under ANILCA are leased pursuant to the MLA. Prior to exploration and leasing, however, the Secretary must gather and study environmental and other data and seek the views of many federal

---

33. The U.S. Geological Survey (USGS) is often asked to provide the federal government with timely scientific information about decisions regarding land management, environmental quality, and economic and strategic policy.

and state officials, Alaskan Natives, the oil and gas industry, conservation groups, and the public. Once issued, leases may be canceled for environmental reasons, and all surface and subsurface activities must be conducted in accordance with an approved plan of development. Leases of lands within the Petroleum Reserve are offered in the same manner as offshore leases. Thus, in many respects, the Alaska leasing process is similar to the offshore leasing process discussed in Section B.2 below.

With declining production in the Prudhoe Bay field and possible future competition with the proposed Keystone XL pipeline extension which will carry Canadian crude from northern Alberta to refineries and markets in Texas and Oklahoma, the Alaska Pipeline will have excess capacity. Accordingly, the State of Alaska, which depends heavily on oil and gas revenues for its economy and state treasury, is desirous of opening up more of the North Slope to oil and gas exploration. The state and federal government have leased certain of their respective offshore lands, and the BLM is actively leasing in the National Petroleum Reserve–Alaska, west of Prudhoe Bay, pursuant to the Naval Petroleum Reserves Production Act, 42 U.S.C. § 4208; however, drilling is still barred in ANWR, east of Prudhoe Bay. Access to ANWR is strictly regulated by the Fish and Wildlife Service. 50 C.F.R. pt. 37.

For more information about leasing federal lands in Alaska, see 2 Rocky Mtn.Min.L. Found., Law of Federal Oil and Gas Leases, Chapter 27 (1997).

(b) Lands Available for Leasing

The BLM manages the public lands under the Federal Land Policy and Management Act ("FLPMA"), 43 U.S.C. §§ 1701–1785, using a multistep planning and decision process that precedes any leasing decisions. Before the BLM can decide which lands to lease for oil and gas development, it must first prepare a Resource Management Plan ("RMP") that sets long-term goals for management of mineral, timber, grazing, recreational, and other resources on BLM-administered lands. 43 U.S.C. § 1712(a). The RMP identifies the public land available for each use, often calling for multiple use management. For mineral development activities such as oil and gas leasing, the RMP also sets the conditions under which development of each resource should occur within a particular resource planning area. 43 C.F.R. § 1601.0–5(k). BLM regulations require that RMPs be prepared on a district-wide or area-wide basis, unless the BLM State Director authorizes a more appropriate scope. 43 C.F.R. § 1601(b). The BLM prepares an Environmental Impact Statement pursuant to the National Environmental Policy Act, 42 U.S.C. 4332(2)(C), to support the resource allocation decisions included in the RMP. A RMP is amended or revised as necessary, based on monitoring and evaluation, new data, or revised policies that affect the entire plan or significant portions of the plan. 43 C.F.R. § 1610.5–6. Generally, a RMP does not constitute a decision to undertake a particular site-specific action. 43 C.F.R. § 1601.0–5(k). Rather, the BLM implements the RMP through project-specific decisions, such as oil and gas lease sales, which must conform to the RMP. See 43 U.S.C. § 1712(e); 43 C.F.R. § 1610.5–3. See also Headwaters, Inc. v. Bureau of Land Management, 914 F.2d 1174, 1178 (9th Cir. Or. 1990).

Under the MLA, the Department of the Interior ("DOI") may lease available lands that are "known or believed to contain oil or gas deposits."[34] Rather than identifying and classifying lands available for leasing, the MLA, other federal statutes, and regulations classify lands that cannot be leased. Lands that may not be leased include lands within national parks, national monuments, recreational areas, wildlife refuges, lands acquired under the Appalachian Forest Act,[35] lands within incorporated cities, towns, and villages, lands within strategic petroleum and oil-shale reserves, and lands within Indian reservations.[36] Pursuant to the Wilderness Act,[37] federal lands within wilderness study areas, lands recommended for wilderness allocation, and lands within wilderness areas may not be leased.[38] Corridors adjacent to federally designated "wild and scenic rivers" are also unavailable for leasing.[39] The DOI, through the BLM, may lease most National Forest System lands[40] but only by consent of the Secretary of Agriculture.[41] Finally, the Secretary of the Interior generally has unfettered discretion to withhold lands from the leasing process.[42]

(c) Eligibility and Continuing Requirements for Leasing and Lease Ownership

(i) Citizenship and Corporate Control

Under the laws and regulations in the United States, various restrictions or controls exist on foreign nationals and foreign companies for holding a mineral right or to be a shareholder of a holder of a mineral right. To own, hold, or control an interest in a federal lease, a person must meet citizenship[43] and other requirements.[44] Subject to certain exceptions, "[n]o person or entity shall take, hold, own or control more than 246,080 acres[45] of federal oil and gas leases in any one State [except Alaska] at any

---

34. 30 U.S.C. § 226(a). For further information, see Lewis C. Cox, Jr., The Road Map to Administering Federal Onshore Oil and Gas Leases, 38 Rocky Mtn.Min.L.Inst. 20–1 (1992).

35. Act of March 1, 1911, ch. 186, 36 Stat. 961.

36. 30 U.S.C. § 181. See also 43 C.F.R. § 3100.0–3(a)(2)(ii)–(iv). The Secretary of the Interior claims implied authority to lease lands that are subject to drainage even if they are not otherwise open to leasing. Id. § 3100.0–3(d). Five national recreational areas are specifically subject to oil and gas leasing. Id. §§ 3100.0–3(g)(4)(i)–(iv), 3109.2(c)(1)–(4). Leasing of Indian lands is discussed in Subsection 3, below.

37. 16 U.S.C. §§ 1131–1136.

38. 30 U.S.C. § 226–3.

39. The Wild and Scenic Rivers Act, 16 U.S.C. § 1280(a)(iii).

40. 30 U.S.C. § 181.

41. Id. § 226(h). The Secretary of Agriculture is the cabinet member in charge of the United States Forest Service, the agency having primary jurisdiction over the National Forest System.

42. Udall v. Tallman, 380 U.S. 1 (1965); Marathon Oil Co. v. Babbitt, 966 F.Supp. 1024 (D.C.Colo.1997), aff'd without opinion, 166 F.3d 1221 (10th Cir.1999). The Secretary of Agriculture may bar the leasing of National Forest System Lands, including National Grasslands.

43. A person qualifies if he is a citizen of the United States or an alien stockholder in a corporation organized under state or federal law.

44. 43 C.F.R. § 3102.5–1.

45. Section 352 of the Energy Policy Act of 2005, Pub. L. No. 109–58, amended section 27(d)(1) of the MLA, 30 U.S.C. 184(d)(1), by excluding from the acreage limitation all acreage

one time."[46]

Mineral rights in oil and gas under public domain lands and lands returned to the public domain are subject to lease under the Mineral Leasing Act of 1920 ("MLA")[47] and its amendments, and may be acquired and held by an alien only through stock ownership, holding, or control, and only if the laws, customs, or regulations of the alien's home country do not deny similar or like privileges to citizens or corporations of the United States. Offshore federal mineral rights are also covered under this umbrella. An alien corporation may not acquire or hold any direct or indirect interest in mineral prospecting permits or mineral rights, except that it may own or control stock in corporations holding a permit or mineral rights if the laws of its country do not deny similar or like privileges to citizens of the United States.[48]

No joint venture is expressly required in the case where an alien or alien company is a shareholder or owner of domestic mineral rights, but since alien companies cannot directly own federally-issued oil and gas leases or other mineral rights issued by the federal government, an American subsidiary is typically formed to own or control stock in corporations holding such permits, leases, or mineral rights. Alien companies can own other non-federal minerals and leases in the United States, such as those bought or issued from private owners or even states.

Generally, if the alien corporation is based in a country hostile to the United States, ownership of mineral rights is disallowed or seriously curtailed. Similarly, if ownership is sought by an alien corporation from a country that, in turn, does not allow entities from the United States to own mineral rights in the foreign country, then ownership of American mineral rights is likewise curtailed. If any appreciable percentage of stock of a corporation is held by aliens who are citizens of a country denying similar privileges to United States citizens, then that corporation's application or bid for an oil and gas mineral right will be rejected and that corporation's mineral right is subject to cancellation.[49]

(ii) Survey Act of 1976

Ownership or effective control of ten (10) percent or more of a corporation's voting securities activates the International Investment Survey Act of 1976 (the Survey Act).[50] This information is collected by the Bureau of Economic Analysis (the "BEA").

---

committed to a federally approved unit or communitization agreement or for which royalty was paid in the preceding calendar year.

46. Id. § 3101.2–1(a). Alaska is divided into two leasing districts. A person or entity is limited to 300,000 acres of federal leases in each district. Id. §§ 3102.5–1(b) and 3101.2–1(b).

47. 30 U.S.C.A. §§ 181–196,

48. 43 C.F.R. §§ 3472.1–2(d), 3502.13. Qualification Stipulations for alien ownership of mineral rights are described in 43 C.F.R. § 3502.10.

49. 43 C.F.R. § 3472.1–2(d).

50. See generally 21 U.S.C. §§ 3101–3108 (1988), amended by the Trade and Tariff Act of 1984, Pub. L. No. 98–573, § 306(b)(1), 98 Stat. 2948, 3009 (1984); Pub.L. 101–533, § 6(A), Nov. 7,

While the Survey Act does not impose restrictions on domestic investment by alien entities, it does generally require an alien investor to submit periodic reports of its business activity if: (a) its direct investment exceeds five million dollars; (b) if it has more than five million dollars net income from its direct investment; (c) owns more than 200 acres of land in the United States.[51]

More specifically, these reports require information about direct investment, financial and operating data of U.S. affiliates, and entity establishment and acquisition data. The reports also must contain the following disclosures: abbreviated income statements and balance sheets, employment and employee compensation, a separation of sales data into components (including bills of sale, sales of services, and sales to U.S. citizens or to foreign persons), structure and source of external financing, capital expenditures, changes in property, plant, and equipment, research and development expenditures, taxes paid, trade in goods, and numerous other data.[52]

In addition, every five years the U.S. Department of Commerce issues a mandatory survey requesting information on the amount and type of foreign direct investment in U.S. business enterprises. This survey is known as the Form BE–12 Benchmark Survey. All alien corporations, organizations, associations, branches, or ventures investing in U.S. real property must complete the report. The data obtained remains confidential and is used by the Bureau of Economic Analysis for evaluating the effect of foreign investment on the U.S. economy.

(iii)　Foreign Investment and National Security Act

Acquisition by an alien entity of control over strategically important domestic assets such as oil and gas may also trigger the Foreign Investment and National Security Act of 2007 ("FINSA").[53]

The "Exon–Florio provision," first implemented in 1988, gives the President the power to "suspend or prohibit any acquisition, merger, or takeover, of a person engaged in interstate commerce" by an alien entity, provided the President determines that the acquisition will threaten the national security of the United States. FINSA codified the regulations and guidelines created by the Committee on Foreign Investment in the United States ("CFIUS"). CFIUS was created by Presidential order and is a federal inter-agency group of twelve members chaired by the Secretary of

1990, 104 Stat. 2348, overview of Surface Act *available at* http://ww.bea.gov/papers.pdf/Mar04 OverviewPaper3.pdf (last visited Sep. 11, 2011).

51.　*Id.* (Note, however, that several exemptions mentioned in the statute may exempt certain foreign entities from being required to file the reports).

52.　*Id.*; *see also* Kozlow, Ralph H., Foreign Direct Investment in the United States—Bureau of Economic Analysis, Directorate for Economic Co-operation and Development (OECD) Workshop on International Investment Statistics, Paris, France, March 22–24, 2004.

53.　50 App. U.S.C.A. § 2170; 31 U.S.C. § 301; 5 U.S.C. 5315

the Treasury. The law requires a mandatory investigation of any transaction involving an "entity controlled or acting on behalf of a foreign government."[54]

FINSA requires an alien entity to address several concerns when seeking approval of an acquisition or merger. First and most importantly, the foreign entity must address the extent to which the transaction will affect the U.S.'s "critical infrastructure" in national security. Based on the extent to which the transaction will impact this critical infrastructure, government regulators may impose a "mediation agreement" on the parties seeking CFIUS approval for the transaction.

Under FINSA, the CFIUS review process has been codified and made more rigorous. Although there is no requirement that an alien entity seek CFIUS approval for a proposed transaction before it occurs, the federal government may suspend or unwind any transaction after closing if it determines that the transaction represents a threat to the critical infrastructure described above. Before bringing in CFIUS, two threshold questions should be considered:

1) Does the transaction give an alien entity control over a U.S. firm?

2) Does the acquisition implicate interests that could be characterized as important for national defense?

When considering the first question, the regulations promulgated under Exon–Florio define "control" as the power to direct key matters affecting that firm, such as the power to sell the corporation's assets, dissolve the firm, close its facilities, and terminate its contracts.

Prior actions by CFIUS show that mineral rights purchases in general are considered to implicate interests that could be characterized as important for national defense and that oil and gas interests are considered strategic, as are the companies that own them. Nevertheless, the only recent acquisitions of mineral rights by foreign entities that have given rise to CFIUS concerns have been proposed acquisitions of large corporations with extensive U.S. domestic and foreign operations by foreign entities that are citizens of countries that represent a potential strategic challenge to the United States. In addition, CFIUS review generally is not required for asset acquisitions; therefore, the acquisition of a passive investment (for example, a royalty interest or overriding royalty interest) probably does not require CFIUS review.

Generally, in the case where an alien or alien company holds a mineral right or is a shareholder of a holder of a mineral right, the company is not required to supply the minerals produced by operations based on the mineral right to the domestic market.

---

54. 31 C.F.R. 800, *et al.*

(d) Competitive Leasing Under the MLA and MLAAL

(i) Competitive Lease Sale

The MLA[55] permits and describes the leasing of public lands for developing all liquid and gaseous hydrocarbons as well as deposits of coal, phosphates, sodium, potassium, and oil shale. All federally-owned onshore lands available for leasing may be offered only through a competitive bidding process.[56] A notice of sale, listing the sale acreage and specifying the time, date, and place of sale, must be posted at least forty-five days prior to the sale in the appropriate BLM office in the state where the lands are located and in the offices of any surface management agencies having jurisdiction over the lands.[57] Competitive onshore lease sales are held quarterly at every BLM state office, and bids must be made orally.[58] A lease is conditioned upon the payment of a royalty at a rate of not less than twelve-and-a-half percent (12.5%) in amount or value of the production removed or sold from the lease.[59] The leases are sold to the highest qualified bidder, so long as the bid equals or exceeds the "national minimum acceptable bid."[60]

Following a lease sale, the highest qualified bidder must submit to the BLM by the close of that business day: (1) the national minimum acceptable bid; (2) the total amount of the first year's delay rental;[61] and (3) a nominal administrative fee.[62] The winning bidder has up to ten days after the last auction day to submit the balance of the bonus bid.[63] If a bid is rejected, the lands must be re-offered competitively.[64]

(ii) Competitive Lease Requirements

Tracts offered for lease must be "as nearly compact as possible" and may not exceed 2,560 acres (5,760 acres in Alaska).[65] The primary term of a competitive lease is ten years.[66] If drilling operations are commenced

55. 30 U.S.C. §§ 181–196.

56. Id. § 3120.4–1. This basic rule applies to lands that are otherwise not available for leasing, but that are subject to drainage. If federal lands are being drained, the BLM may either enter into compensatory royalty arrangements with offsetting lessees or lease the tract being drained using the competitive bid process.

57. Id. § 3120.4–2.

58. Id. § 3120.1–2(a)–(c).

59. 30 U.S.C. § 226(b)(1)(A).

60. 30 U.S.C. § 226(b)(1)(B). When this edition went to press in 2012, the national minimum acceptable bid was $2.00 per acre, but the Secretary of the Interior has the discretion to increase this amount. 43 C.F.R. § 3120.1–2(c).

61. Note that annual rentals are assessed for each year of the primary term, including the first year.

62. 43 C.F.R. §§ 3120.5–2; 3120.1–2(c); and 3000.12.

63. Id. § 3120.5–2(c).

64. Id. § 3120.5–3(c).

65. 30 U.S.C. § 226(b)(1)(A). Tar sand leasehold tracts may be as large as 5,760 acres. Id. § 226(b)(2).

66. 30 U.S.C. § 226(e). The primary term for competitive oil and gas leases for designated tar sands areas is 10 years. 30 U.S.C. § 226(e).

prior to the expiration of the primary term and are being diligently prosecuted at the end of the primary term, the lease is extended for two years subject to continued payment of rentals.[67] The secondary term is for so long as "oil or gas is produced in paying quantities."[68]

Annual rentals are $1.50 per acre for the first five years of a lease and $2.00 per acre thereafter.[69] Upon discovery of oil or gas, the lessee must pay a minimum royalty of not less than what the rental would be for that year.[70] If annual rentals are not timely or properly paid, the lease automatically terminates by operation of law;[71] however, the lease can be reinstated if the lessee meets the reinstatement criteria.[72] The BLM regulations authorize royalty rate reductions for leases on a case-by-case basis to encourage the greatest ultimate recovery of oil or gas, and to serve the interest of conservation.[73]

Except for Alaska, one-half of all bonuses, rentals, royalties, and interest on royalties received for leases on public domain lands leased under the MLA are paid to the state where the leased acreage is located.[74] Alaska receives 90 percent of such income.[75] For leases issued pursuant to the Mineral Leasing Act for Acquired Lands ("MLAAL"),[76] the statute

---

67. 43 C.F.R. § 3107.1.

68. 43 C.F.R. § 3107.2–1. A copy of the competitive lease form in use at the time this edition went to press is included the Forms Manual that accompanies this casebook.

69. 30 U.S.C. § 226(d). See also 43 C.F.R. § 3103.2–2(a).

70. Id.

71. 43 C.F.R. § 3103.2–2.

72. 30 U.S.C. § 188(d) and 43 C.F.R. §§ 3108.2–2, 3108.2–3. Reinstatement of oil placer mining claims validly located prior to February 24, 1920 is also possible. 30 U.S.C. § 188(f) and 43 C.F.R. § 3108.2–4. How does the typical private oil and gas lease address the reinstatement of a lease for failure to pay rentals in a timely or proper manner?

73. Id. § 3103.3–1(a). Previously, the federal government sometimes used sliding scale royalties for some leases. Under this scheme, the royalty rate increased with the rate of production from the lease.

Section 39 of the Mineral Leasing Act authorizes the Secretary of the Interior to waive, suspend, or reduce the rental, or minimum royalty, or reduce the royalty on an entire leasehold, or on any tract or portion thereof segregated for royalty purposes, for the purpose of encouraging the greatest ultimate recovery of oil, gas, and other minerals, and in the interest of conservation of natural resources (1) whenever, in his judgment, it is necessary to do so in order to promote development; or (2) whenever, in his judgment, the leases cannot be successfully operated under the terms provided therein (30 U.S.C. 209).

BLM regulations previously authorized rate reductions for certain categories of wells. Categorical royalty relief pursuant to the existing codified regulations is no longer available for current production, since the BLM has terminated the regulatory programs that established royalty relief and Congress has enacted a superseding relief program for marginal wells. The current regulations provide for royalty relief on a case-by-case basis. (30 C.F.R. § 3103.4–1).

While royalty relief is no longer available for current production, prior production continues to be subject to audits and, when appropriate, corrective actions. The BLM may still terminate relief retroactively, however, if such relief was initially granted based on manipulation of normal production or adulteration of oil sold or if the BLM determines that the total of overriding royalty currently encumbering the tract in question should be lowered before granting relief.

74. 30 U.S.C. § 191.

75. Id.

76. The MLAAL provides that lands acquired by the United States "may be leased by the Secretary under the same conditions as contained in the leasing provisions of the mineral leasing laws...." 43 U.S.C. § 352. Therefore, because the same leasing standards apply to public domain

under which the lands are acquired specifies how the Secretary must distribute revenues.[77]

(e) Noncompetitive Leasing Under the MLA and MLAAL

(i) Noncompetitive Sale

Generally, lands must first be offered through the competitive bidding process. If a tract of land offered competitively does not receive a bid, it then becomes available for noncompetitive leasing for a two-year period beginning on the first business day following the auction.[78] If any such lands are not leased within that period, those lands revert to the competitive leasing process.[79]

The procedure for obtaining a lease noncompetitively is a hybrid of the former "over-the-counter" and simultaneous filing methods. Noncompetitive leases are awarded to the first qualified applicant.[80] All offers received during the first business day following a competitive sale, however, are deemed simultaneously filed.[81]

Certain lands are subject to a pre-sale noncompetitive application process.[82] Under this process, an applicant may apply for a noncompetitive lease prior to the competitive bid and sale process, gaining priority over all subsequent noncompetitive applicants. The property must still be offered competitively with a notice that a pre-sale offer has been made. If the land is not leased competitively, the first pre-sale applicant, if any, may secure an "over-the-counter" lease.[83] Pre-sale offers may not be made for lands that were subject to a lease within the preceding year or for lands that have already been listed in the Notice of Competitive Lease Sale or the List of Lands Available for Competitive Nominations.[84] What are the ramifications of pre-sale noncompetitive offers?

and acquired lands, the BLM oil and gas leasing regulations in 43 C.F.R. part 3120 apply to both categories of lands. The "AUTHORITY" section cites to both the MLA and the MLAAL as authority for the regulations. Thus, while we refer only to the MLA, the statutory and regulatory provisions apply equally to oil and gas leasing on acquired lands.

77.   For example, see Act of May 24, 1939, Pub. L. No. 76–85, 53 Stat. 753. The Act relates to the disposition of funds derived from the Coos Bay Wagon Road grant lands and designates 75 percent of the revenues generated to the local counties in which the federal lease is located.; See also 33 U.S.C. § 701c–3 which stipulates that 75 percent of all money received and deposited in the Treasury of the United States during any fiscal year on account of the leasing of lands acquired by the United States Corps of Engineers for flood control, navigation, and allied purposes, be paid to the State in which such property is situated.

78.   30 U.S.C. § 226(b)(1)(A) and 43 C.F.R. § 3110.1(b).

79.   30 U.S.C. § 226(c)(2)(A).

80.   43 C.F.R. § 3110.2(a).

81.   Id.

82.   Id. § 3110.1(a).

83.   An "over-the-counter" lease is a federal oil and gas lease that is issued without a bidding process first being conducted.

84.   Id. § 3110.1(a)(i)–(ii).

(ii) Noncompetitive Lease Requirements

Noncompetitive lease terms are the same as competitive lease terms. The income from these leases is shared with the states in the same manner as income is shared from competitive leases.

(f) Environmental and Land Use Considerations

(i) Pre-leasing NEPA

Although the MLA has few environmental provisions, the National Environmental Policy Act ("NEPA") is an important vector of environmental regulation on federal onshore leasing.[85] Any action taken by a federal agency, including decisions to lease federal lands and the approvals of drilling plans, are subject to NEPA. Under NEPA, federal agencies must prepare a "detailed statement" for inclusion in every recommendation or report on proposals for any major federal action that significantly affects the quality of the human environment.[86] A "detailed statement" can refer to a major study called an Environmental Impact Statement ("EIS") or it can mean a less detailed Environmental Assessment ("EA"). The agency proposing federal action must first prepare an EA to determine whether the proposed action is "significant" enough to require an EIS. An EA sets forth the need for the proposed action, the reasonable alternatives to the action, and the impacts of those alternatives. If an agency concludes (based on its EA) that the proposed action will not significantly affect the environment, it will issue a Finding of No Significant Impact ("FONSI"). If an agency finds (based on its EA) that the proposed action could significantly affect the environment, it must then prepare an EIS.

As part of the process for issuing the Resource Management Plan (RMP), which covers the proposed acreage to be leased, the BLM prepares an EIS to assess the environmental impacts of oil and gas leasing. A RMP is a report compiled by the BLM to communicate to the public the BLM plan for resource development and management within a designated area and to chart the future biological, physical, and social condition of the area in question once all the development, management, and reclamation actions in the RMP have been implemented. At the time the BLM decides to proceed with a lease sale within the area covered by the RMP, the BLM must decide whether the EIS performed on the RMP is adequate to support its leasing decision, or whether it must prepare a new EIS or EA to examine the impacts of leasing in a particular area. A new NEPA review is more likely where the lease sale decision raises new environmental impacts not previously considered by the RMP. To assess the adequacy of previous NEPA documents, the BLM generally prepares a "Documentation of Land Use Plan Conformance and NEPA Adequacy" or "DNA." The DNA, unlike an EA or a FONSI, is not a document recognized in NEPA or its implementing regulations. DOI's Board of Land Appeals

---

85. 42 U.S.C. §§ 4321–4370.

86. Id. § 4332(2)(c).

("IBLA") has stated that "DNAs cannot properly be used to supplement previous EAs or EISs or to address site-specific environmental effects not previously considered in them."[87] Rather, the DNA merely assesses whether the existing EISs or EAs that address oil and gas leasing for an area are adequate for the next lease sale decision.

The adequacy of a RMP EIS to support a lease sale may become an issue as the RMP and the corresponding EIS age. Many years may pass before the BLM amends or revises a RMP. The issue of adequacy is especially relevant when there is new information or impacts that were not previously considered by the original EIS. This question was presented in a number of cases that examined whether the impacts of coalbed methane ("CBM") development were adequately considered in EISs that examined only conventional oil and gas development. Because in certain regions CBM production involves increased potential for surface discharge of large amounts of water, environmental plaintiffs argued the EIS for conventional oil and gas development was inadequate to cover CBM development.

PENNACO ENERGY, INC. v. U.S. DEPT. OF INTERIOR

377 F.3d 1147 (10th Cir. 2004).

BRISCOE, CIRCUIT JUDGE.

Plaintiff Pennaco Energy, Inc. (Pennaco), brought this suit in the District of Wyoming, pursuant to the Administrative Procedure Act, 5 U.S.C. §§ 701–06 (APA), against the United States Department of the Interior (DOI) to challenge a decision of the Interior Board of Land Appeals (IBLA). The challenged IBLA decision reversed a decision of the Bureau of Land Management (BLM) to auction three oil and gas leases (successfully bid upon by Pennaco). The IBLA concluded the requirements of the National Environmental Policy Act (NEPA) had not been satisfied prior to issuing the leases and remanded the matter to the BLM for additional appropriate action. * * *

I.

The factual and procedural background of this case is best understood in the context of the relevant statutes and regulations.

National Environmental Policy Act

The NEPA, 42 U.S.C. §§ 4321–70, "prescribes the necessary process" by which federal agencies must "take a hard look" at the environmental consequences of the proposed courses of action. "The statute does not impose substantive limits on agency conduct." Rather, once environmental concerns are "adequately identified and evaluated by the agency, NEPA places no further constraint on agency actions." (internal citations omitted).

---

87. Southern Utah Wilderness Alliance, 166 IBLA 270, 283 (2005).

For proposed "Major federal actions significantly affecting the quality of the human environment," agencies must prepare an environmental impact statement (EIS) in which they consider the environmental impact of the proposed action and compare this impact with that of "alternatives to the proposed action."

See 42 U.S.C. § 4332(2)(C). * * *

"Agencies 'need not prepare a full EIS,' however, if they initially prepare the less detailed environmental assessment (EA) and, based on the EA, issue a finding of no significant impact (FONSI), concluding that the proposed action will not significantly affect the environment." (citations omitted). Further, an agency need not prepare a new EIS to address a proposed action as long as it already has taken a "hard look" at the action's potential environmental consequences.

* * *

Oil and gas leasing decisions

The DOI manages the use of federal oil and gas resources through a three-phase decision-making process. At the earliest and broadest level of decision-making, the DOI develops land use plans-often referred to as resource management plans (RMPs).

* * *

Once a RMP has been issued, "subsequent more detailed or specific planning, shall conform to the [RMP]." 43 C.F.R. § 1610.5–3(a). In the context of oil and gas development, the BLM is initially charged with determining whether the issuance of a particular oil and gas lease is consistent with the RMP. The lessee must obtain BLM approval of an Application for Permit to Drill (APD) before commencing any "drilling operations" or "surface disturbance preliminary thereto." 43 C.F.R. § 3162.3–1(c).

II.

BLM's decision to auction leases

At issue in this case is whether the BLM satisfied the NEPA prior to auctioning three oil and gas leases on February 1, 2000, for the development of tracts of land in the Powder River Basin in Wyoming. In August 1999, interested parties nominated 49 parcels of land for inclusion in the next available oil and gas lease sale. It is undisputed that the planned use of the leases was the extraction of coal bed methane (CBM). It is also undisputed that a CBM exploration and development boom is occurring in the Powder River Basin. The hotly contested issue underlying this case is whether the environmental impacts of CBM development are significantly different than the environmental impacts of non-CBM oil and gas development.

On September 28, 1999, Richard Zander, the acting field manager of the BLM Buffalo Field Office, prepared separate but identical Interim

Documentation of Land Use Conformance and NEPA Adequacy work-sheets (DNAs) for each of the 49 nominated parcels. DNAs are forms designed to allow BLM employees to determine whether they properly can rely on existing NEPA documents. In this case, Zander concluded that two existing NEPA analyses (the Buffalo Resource Management Plan EIS (Buffalo RMP EIS) and the Wyodak Coal Bed Methane Project Draft EIS (Wyodak DEIS)) satisfied the NEPA requirements with regard to issuance of the leases.

The first document relied upon by Zander, the Buffalo RMP EIS, was published in October 1985 in conjunction with the development of the Buffalo RMP. In the Buffalo RMP EIS, the BLM discussed the potential environmental impacts of oil and gas development within the Buffalo Resource Area, an area encompassing the three parcels at issue in this case. However, the Buffalo RMP EIS did not specifically address CBM extraction.

The second document relied upon by Zander, the Wyodak DEIS, was published in May 1999. Unlike the Buffalo RMP EIS, the Wyodak DEIS addressed the potential environmental impacts of CBM mining. However, as the Wyodak DEIS was a post-leasing project level study, the BLM did not consider whether leases should have been issued in the first place. Further, the geographic scope of the Wyodak DEIS did not encompass two of the three parcels at issue in this case.

Having concluded the NEPA requirements were satisfied in regard to the proposed leases, Zander further concluded that issuance of the leases conformed to the Buffalo RMP. Thus, the BLM auctioned the leases at a competitive sale on February 1, 2000, and Pennaco was the successful bidder.

On January 27, 2000, the Wyoming Outdoor Council (WOC) and the Powder River Basin Resource Council (PRBRC) filed a formal protest with the BLM, alleging the "environmental impacts of CBM development and extraction are not comparable to the impacts of other oil and gas develop-ment." Aplt. App. VI, Doc. 22 at 3. Given the alleged differences between CBM extraction and conventional oil and gas extraction, WOC and PRBRC argued that the BLM was required by NEPA to prepare a new EIS before issuing the leases. More generally, WOC and PRBRC argued the BLM had failed to take a "hard look" at the potential environmental impacts of issuing the leases. On April 7, 2000, the BLMs acting deputy state director dismissed the protest as "unfounded." Aplt. App. VI, Doc. 23 at 3. * * *

IBLA decision

WOC and PRBRC timely appealed the decision of the BLM to the IBLA.

* * *

The primary issue addressed by the IBLA was whether the BLM correctly determined that existing NEPA documentation "adequately ana-lyzed the environmental effects of the proposed inclusion of the affected parcels in the February 2000 competitive lease sale or whether the agency violated NEPA by failing to undertake additional site-specific environmental reviews before deciding to offer the parcels for oil and gas leasing." Id. at 357. The BLM and Pennaco, as an intervenor, contended the NEPA was satisfied by existing NEPA documents, namely the Buffalo RMP EIS and the Wyodak DEIS.

The IBLA concluded the Buffalo RMP EIS was inadequate because it "did not specifically discuss CBM extraction and development, which were not contemplated uses in 1985, although they are the planned uses for the leases issued for the disputed parcels." Id. at 358. The IBLA rejected the BLM's position "that the techniques and impacts associated with CBM extraction and production are not significantly different from those analyzed in the Buffalo RMP/EIS." Id. Further, the IBLA stated:

> We find ... that not only does the record amply demonstrate that the magnitude of water production from CBM extraction in the Powder River Basin creates unique problems and that CBM development and transportation present critical air quality issues not adequately addressed in the RMP/EIS, but [the] BLM itself has also acknowledged the inadequacy of the RMP/EIS as far as the analysis of CBM issues is concerned.... Because the Buffalo RMP/EIS failed to take the requisite hard look at the impacts associated with CBM extraction and development, which clearly are relevant matters of environmental concern in this case, [the] BLM could not rely on that document to satisfy its NEPA obligations for the proposed leasing decisions at issue here.

> In apparent recognition of the deficiencies in the Buffalo RMP/EIS, [the] BLM also relies on the October 1999 Wyodak Final EIS.... The Wyodak EIS is a project-level EIS designed to analyze the impacts of developing federal CBM properties by drilling, completing, operating, and reclaiming approximately 5,000 new productive CBM wells and related production facilities in the eastern Powder River Basin [...]. Since leases authorizing surface occupancy had already been issued for the lands involved in the proposed action, the Department lacked the authority to deny all federal drilling activity based on environmental concerns unrelated to threatened or endangered species.... Given that the leasing decisions had already been made and the leases issued, the EIS did not consider reasonable alternatives available in a leasing decision, including whether specific parcels should be leased, appropriate lease stipulations, and NSO [no surface occupancy] and non-NSO areas. Thus, despite the Wyodak EIS's detailed analysis of the impacts of CBM development, which we note parenthetically undercuts [the] BLM's claim that the impacts of CBM extraction are the same as those of other methane production, that documents failure to consider reasonable alternatives relevant to a pre-leasing environmental analysis fatally impairs its ability to serve as the requisite pre-leasing NEPA document for these parcels.

Since the existing NEPA documents relied upon by [the] BLM, whether viewed separately or taken together, do not constitute the requisite hard look at the environmental consequences of the proposed action, [the] BLM was required to conduct further NEPA analysis before deciding whether to approve the sale of the parcels at issue. The [DNAs], dependent as they were on the Buffalo EIS/RMP and the Wyodak EIS, fail to even identify, much less independently address, any of the relevant areas of environmental concern or reasonable alternatives to the proposed action and thus do not satisfy [the] BLM's NEPA obligations in this case.

Id. at 358–59.

* * *

District court decision

Pennaco appealed the IBLA's decision to the District Court of Wyoming. The district court reversed the IBLA's decision and reinstated the decision of the BLM. The district court concluded the Wyodak EIS and the Buffalo RMP EIS, taken together, were sufficient to satisfy NEPA. Further, the district court concluded "the IBLA's opinion arbitrarily and capriciously elevates form over substance by separating the two documents and refusing to consider them together." Pennaco Energy, Inc. v. U.S. Dept of Interior, 266 F. Supp. 2d 1323, 1330 (D. Wyo. 2003).

III.

* * *

"We afford no particular deference to the district court's review of an agency action; our review of the administrative record pertaining to the challenged action is independent." Colo. Envtl. Coalition v. Dombeck, 185 F.3d 1162, 1167, n.5 (10th Cir. 1999). Instead, we defer "to the decisions of the IBLA, and we will set aside an IBLA decision only if it is arbitrary, capricious, otherwise not in accordance with law, or not supported by substantial evidence." IMC Kalium Carlsbad, Inc. v. Bd. of Land Appeals, 206 F.3d 1003, 1009 (10th Cir. 2000) (internal quotation omitted).

* * *

Application of arbitrary and capricious standard

We conclude the IBLA gave due consideration to the relevant factors and that the IBLA's conclusion was supported by substantial evidence in the administrative record. To determine whether additional NEPA documents were needed, the IBLA was required to consider whether existing NEPA documents were sufficient to allow the agency to take a "hard look" at the environmental impacts of CBM development on the three parcels at issue. Appropriately, the IBLA's decision turned on its answer to that precise question. Further, the administrative record contains substantial evidence to support the IBLA's conclusion that the proposed action raised significant new environmental concerns that had not been addressed by existing NEPA documents.

* * *

We begin our review of the record with an affidavit which the IBLA did not rely upon but which Pennaco contends is very significant. In support of its position that the Buffalo RMP EIS, by itself, satisfies NEPA, Pennaco relies primarily on a December 2000 affidavit by Zander. In his affidavit, Zander states that "CBM well requirements and impacts fall within the range of those for other oil and gas wells." Aplt. App. V, Doc. 20 at 5. Further, Zander avers that "CBM wells produce substantial water, but much less than that asserted by Appellants in this proceeding." Id. at 6. According to Zander, some CBM wells produce less water than some conventional oil and gas wells. In support of its argument that the IBLA acted arbitrarily and capriciously, Pennaco contends the IBLA ignored Zander's purportedly uncontroverted affidavit.

The IBLA specifically referred to the Zander affidavit, noting Pennaco's contention that "CBM activities are not unique but fall within the range of those for other oil and gas wells." Wyoming Outdoor Council, 156 IBLA at 354. Further, Zander's affidavit is not uncontroverted. Zander's own 1990 internal BLM memorandum, which the IBLA did rely upon, described CBM development as a "non-traditional type of oil and gas activity" that "was not considered" in the Buffalo RMP EIS. Aplt. App. I, Doc. 4 at 162. Further, in its 2002 budget request (another piece of evidence relied upon by the IBLA), the BLM asserted that existing NEPA documents were not adequate to address the environmental impacts of CBM development.

There is additional evidence in the record, not cited by the IBLA, that the BLM previously had concluded existing NEPA analyses were not adequate to address the impacts of CBM development. In a September 6, 2001, statement to Congress, the BLM assistant secretary Tom Fulton stated:

> While [CBM] development on the public lands occurs in several western states, a dramatic increase in new [CBM] exploration and development is occurring in the Powder River Basin in Wyoming. Currently in Wyoming, there are more than 5,500 CBM-producing wells under an EIS completed in 1999 and a supplemental drainage environmental assessment completed in 2001. At the time of the original EIS, no one anticipated or planned for the rapid development of this resource. Consequently, there is a need for a new EIS which is currently scheduled for completion in May 2002, with a Record of Decision expected in July 2002. This EIS will analyze the effects of the drilling of 50,000 CBM wells, and 3,000 conventional oil and gas wells, expected to be drilled in the next 10 years.

Id., Vol. V, Doc. 21 at 1264–65.

Water Quantity

The administrative record also contains evidence to support the IBLA's conclusion that water production associated with CBM extraction is significantly greater than water production associated with non-CBM oil and gas development.

* * *

After reviewing the entire record, we conclude it contains substantial evidence to support the IBLA's conclusion that CBM development poses unique environmental concerns related to water discharge that were not addressed by the Buffalo RMP EIS. The fact that the administrative record contains some evidence arguably contrary to the IBLA's findings (such as the Zander affidavit) does not render the IBLA's decision arbitrary and capricious.

* * *

Air Quality

We further conclude the record contains substantial evidence to support the IBLA's conclusion that CBM development poses unique environmental concerns related to air quality that were not addressed in the Buffalo RMP EIS. * * *

The Wyodak EIS

Pennaco's alternative position is that the Wyodak EIS cured any deficiencies in the Buffalo RMP EIS. In some circumstances, agencies may satisfy the NEPA by looking at multiple documents. See Nat'l Indian Youth Council v. Watt, 664 F.2d 220, 228 (10th Cir. 1981) (holding various NEPA documents, taken together, "adequately informed the Secretary [of the Interior] of the [mining] project's potential effect on the human environment" and, therefore, there was no "substantial procedural" reason to set aside the Secretary's decision); see also 40 C.F.R. § 1502.21 ("Agencies shall incorporate material into an environmental impact statement by reference when the effect will be to cut down on bulk without impeding agency and public review of the action.").

In this case, the IBLA concluded the Wyodak EIS had one significant shortcoming. The Wyodak EIS was a post-leasing analysis and, therefore, the BLM did not consider pre-leasing options, such as not issuing leases at all. In the Wyodak EIS, the BLM acknowledged its limited discretion in regard to the Wyodak project. The Wyodak EIS provides:

> None of the stipulations imposed (on the leases within the project area) would empower the Secretary of the Interior to deny all drilling activity because of environmental concerns where leases have been issued with surface occupancy rights.

* * *

Aplt. App. IV, Doc. 8 at 750. This language reflects that lessees already had acquired certain rights, subject only to stipulations contained in their leases.

* * *

Therefore, in light of the Wyodak EIS' failure to consider the pre-leasing options, we conclude the IBLA did not act arbitrarily and capriciously in deciding that the Wyodak EIS did not adequately supplement the Buffalo RMP EIS.

Park County

Finally, we note that Pennaco relies heavily on Park County, 817 F.2d 609. In Park County, the plaintiffs (environmental interest groups) claimed the BLM "unlawfully issued an oil and gas lease, and thereafter unlawfully approved an [APD] filed by the Marathon Oil Company, in contravention of . . . NEPA." Id. at 612. In recounting the facts, we noted that prior to issuing the lease in question the BLM had prepared an "extensive" EA which addressed the "issuance of federal oil and gas leases" in the Shoshone National Forest where the tract at issue was located. Id. The EA exceeded 100 pages and addressed various leasing alternatives, including "issuance of no leases." Id. The EA concluded that merely issuing the leases would create no environmental impacts, and a FONSI was issued with respect to the lease issuance. Approximately three years after issuance of the FONSI and the sale of the lease, Marathon submitted an APD. In response, the BLM and the Forest Service prepared a comprehensive EIS with respect to the drilling application.

The Park County plaintiffs challenged both the adequacy of the pre-drilling EIS and issuance of the oil and gas lease prior to preparation of an EIS. We concluded plaintiffs' challenge to the adequacy of the pre-drilling EIS had been rendered moot by the lessee's development and subsequent abandonment of the site in question. On the other hand, we concluded the challenge to issuance of the lease was not moot because the lease remained operative. We employed a reasonableness standard to review the BLM's issuance of a FONSI and concluded:

> In light of the substantial EA, of the mitigating lease restrictions requiring further environmental appraisal before any surface disturbing activities commence, of the nebulousness of future drilling activity at the time of leasing, and of the continuing supervision of the federal agencies involved over future activities, the agency's decision in this case that the lease issuance itself was not a major federal action significantly affecting the quality of the human environment was not unreasonable.

Id. at 624 (emphasis added).

Park County has been overruled to the extent it held that a reasonableness standard of review should be used when reviewing an agency's decision to not prepare an EIS. In Marsh, 490 U.S. at 385, the Court held that an agency's decision to not prepare an EIS or to not supplement an existing EIS should only be reversed when it is arbitrary and capricious. See also Village of Los Ranchos de Albuquerque v. Marsh, 956 F.2d 970, 972–73 (10th Cir. 1992) (recognizing Park County was overruled, in part, by Marsh). Nevertheless, according to Pennaco, Park County is controlling. Pennaco argues "the analyses on which the BLM relied here far exceed that which passed muster in Park County." Aplee. Br. at 28.

This case differs significantly from Park County. First, in Park County, plaintiffs challenged an agency decision to issue an oil and gas lease prior to preparation of a comprehensive EIS. We concluded that the BLM's decision to not prepare an EIS at the leasing stage was "not unreasonable." In comparison, the question before us is not, as Pennaco suggests, whether the documents relied upon by the BLM pass muster. The central issue is whether the IBLA's determination that the documents did not "pass muster" was arbitrary and capricious. In Park County, this court did not conclude the agency would have abused its discretion if it decided that an EIS was necessary at the pre-leasing stage.

Moreover, in Park County, we relied in part on the fact that the BLM issued a FONSI after having prepared an "extensive" EA that addressed the potential environmental impacts of issuing the leases and considered the option of not issuing leases. In comparison, in this case, the BLM did not prepare such an EA, did not issue a FONSI, and did not prepare any environmental analysis that considered not issuing the leases in question. Instead, the BLM determined, after filling out DNA worksheets, that previously issued NEPA documents were sufficient to satisfy the "hard look" standard. DNAs, unlike EAs and FONSIs, are not mentioned in the NEPA or in the regulations implementing the NEPA. See 40 C.F.R. § 1508.10 (defining the term "environmental document" as including environmental assessments, environmental impact statements, findings of no significant impact, and notices of intent). As stated, agencies may use non-NEPA procedures to determine whether new NEPA documentation is required. For reasons discussed above, however, we conclude the IBLA's determination that more analysis was required in this case was not arbitrary and capricious.

IV.

We REVERSE and REMAND to the district court with instructions to reinstate the IBLA's decision.

(ii) NEPA at the Development Stage

NEPA also is involved at the development stage of an oil and gas lease. FOOGLRA amended the MLA to add a new provision in 30 U.S.C. § 226(g) prescribing that "No permit to drill on an oil and gas lease issued under this chapter may be granted without the analysis and approval by the Secretary concerned of a plan of operations covering proposed surface disturbing activities within the lease area." Therefore, before a lessee may begin drilling operations on its lease, the BLM must approve an Application for Permit to Drill (APD). 43 C.F.R. § 3162.3–1(c).[88] The BLM's decision whether to approve the APD must be supported by adequate NEPA analysis. Unless the proposed drilling operations present new impacts not previously considered, or are proposed in an area that is particularly environmentally sensitive, the BLM generally is able to support its decision of approving an APD with an EA. However, in response to concerns raised by the oil and gas industry that APD approvals were taking too long and delaying oil and gas production, Congress enacted section 390 of the Energy Policy Act of 2005, Pub. L. No. 109–58, entitled "NEPA REVIEW." Under this new provision, action by the Secretary of the Interior respecting certain enumerated MLA oil and gas activities on public lands is subject to a "rebuttable presumption" that the use of a categorical exclusion under NEPA applies to that activity. These activities include:

(1) Individual surface disturbances of less than 5 acres so long as the total surface disturbance on the lease is not greater than 150 acres and site-specific analysis in a document prepared pursuant to NEPA has been previously completed.

(2) Drilling an oil or gas well at a location or well pad site at which drilling has occurred previously within 5 years prior to the date of spudding the well.

(3) Drilling an oil or gas well within a developed field for which an approved land-use plan or any environmental document prepared pursuant to NEPA analyzed such drilling as a reasonably foreseeable activity, so long as such plan or document was approved within 5 years prior to the date of spudding the well.

(4) Placement of a pipeline in an approved right-of-way corridor, so long as the corridor was approved within 5 years prior to the date of placement of the pipeline.

(5) Maintenance of a minor activity, other than any construction or major renovation of a building or facility.

Energy Policy Act of 2005 Pub. L. No. 109–58, § 390 (2005).

The BLM determined that these statutorily-prescribed categorical exclusions are different from the standard categorical exclusions authorized under NEPA and its implementing regulations.[89] The BLM has used the new categorical exclusions to streamline its processing of APDs. Are these categorical exclusions really different? Why didn't Congress just provide an exemption from NEPA for APDs that met certain criteria?

---

88. In addition to its onshore oil and gas operations regulations at 43 C.F.R. part 3160, the BLM has established requirements for oil and gas operations on federal leases through Onshore Orders. The BLM recently issued a revised Onshore Order Number 1 which, among other things, established requirements for application, review and approval of APDs. 72 Fed.Reg. 10308 (March 7, 2007). The revised Onshore Order Number 1 also includes the new timeframes for processing APDs prescribed in section 366 of the Energy Policy Act of 2005, Pub. L. No. 109–58. These timeframes are intended to expedite APD processing for federal leases.

89. See the BLM policy guidelines implementing the categorical exclusions in section 390. IM No. 2005–247, Sept. 30, 2005.

Notes[90]

1.   As only a small percentage of federal lands are actually leased for oil and gas and only a small percentage of the lands leased are ever actually developed, the question becomes: When should an EIS be prepared?

Apparently, the IBLA has decided that the law is settled—BLM must assess the specific impacts of CBM development in RMPs prior to leasing only when CBM development would cause significantly greater and previously unconsidered environmental impacts. See Biodiversity Conservation Alliance, 171 IBLA 313, 322 (2007) ("It is simply not enough to continue to pull at the threads of the [Pennaco decision] in an effort to unravel subsequent Board and federal court precedent affirming that the question of whether additional environmental analysis is required in any case depends on whether it can be shown that existing NEPA documents failed to analyze the likely effects of the action at hand.")

The Ninth Circuit Court of Appeals in Conner v. Burford, 848 F.2d 1441 (9th Cir.1988), held that the preparation of an EIS was not required when a lease to National Forest Service lands was issued if the lease contained stipulations of "no surface occupancy" ("NSO"), but an EIS would be required if a lease were issued without an NSO stipulation.[91] In Sierra Club v. Peterson, 717 F.2d 1409 (D.C.Cir.1983), the D.C. Circuit reviewed a Forest Service FONSI that was issued as part of a recommendation to lease 247,000 acres of remote land in Idaho and Wyoming. Some of the leases issued contained NSO stipulations, and others allowed surface occupancy subject to certain environmental restrictions. The D.C. Circuit Court of Appeals held that a site-specific EIS must be prepared prior to issuing any leases that do not contain NSO provisions. Thus, the D.C. Circuit and the Ninth Circuit agree that an EIS must precede the issuance of an oil and gas lease unless the lease contains NSO provisions. In contrast, in Park County Resource Council, Inc. v. United States Department of Agriculture, 817 F.2d 609 (10th Cir. 1987), the Tenth Circuit Court of Appeals upheld a Forest Service FONSI concerning a lease issued without an NSO stipulation but with specific surface use conditions. The court concluded that the requirement of an EIS may be deferred until the prospects for drilling (e.g., APD stage) are more certain. What rights does the holder of an NSO lease actually have?

Two recent opinions from the district court of New Mexico suggest the unsettled nature of the law regarding whether new EISs must be prepared before issuance of site-specific leases. In New Mexico v. BLM, 459 F.Supp.2d 1102 (D.N.M. 2006), plaintiffs challenged the BLM's decision to amend a RMP and approve a lease covering a portion of the area included in the amended

90.   For further information, see Charles L. Kaiser & Scott W. Hardt, Surface Use Regulation of Federal Oil and Gas Leases: Exploring the Limits of Administrative Discretion, 38 Rocky Mtn.Min.L.Inst. 19–1 (1992).

91.   NSO stipulations in a lease prohibit any surface disturbing operations without environmental review. After review, the NSO stipulation may or may not be removed. Thus, the Ninth Circuit concluded that no irreversible commitment of resources had been made at the leasing stage that would have required an EIS. *Conner* further held that when rendering a biological opinion, the U.S. Fish and Wildlife Service was required to consider the effects of all stages of oil and gas activity in connection with the issuance of leases.

RMP. Following Pennaco, the court found that the amended RMP did not address all issues affecting the use of the land and ruled that the BLM must conduct site-specific environmental review before issuing leases. Less than one year later, in June, 2007, the district court of New Mexico rejected the plaintiff's reliance on Pennaco and Conner v. Burford and agreed with the reasoning of Park County to hold that BLM was not arbitrary and capricious in deciding not to perform site-specific analyses on lands offered for lease pursuant to an older RMP EIS. Chihuahuan Grasslands Alliance v. Norton, 507 F.Supp.2d 1216 (D.N.M. 2007).

In practice, NEPA review regarding oil and gas development occurs in stages with new environmental analysis supplementing the prior analysis. For example, the NEPA process may be triggered when a leasing feasibility study is done, when an application for a permit to drill is filed, when the anticipated level of development of new reserves is reasonably known, and when a major revision in development is foreseen, such as the anticipation of a major enhanced recovery project. In preparing an EA or an EIS in contemplation of oil and gas leasing, what level of development should be anticipated? For example, should an initial EA or EIS address only the immediate prospects of site-specific exploration activity, or should the EA or EIS consider long-term development possibilities? For commentary and analysis, see generally John Shepherd, Key NEPA Issues Affecting Oil and Gas Development on Federal Lands, 37 Rocky Mtn.Min.L.Inst. 15–1 (1997); Jan Laitos, Paralysis by Analysis in the Forest Service Oil and Gas Leasing Program, 26 Land & Water L.Rev. 105 (1991); and Marla Mansfield, Through the Forest of the Onshore Oil and Gas Leasing Controversy Toward a Paradigm of Meaningful NEPA Compliance, 24 Land & Water L.Rev. 105 (1989).

Courts are often asked to review federal agency usage of prior information and data, particularly if new developments have transpired. For example, on June 22, 2012, the 11th Circuit Court of Appeals denied a petition filed by several environmental organizations that challenged the issuance of approvals by the Bureau of Ocean Energy Management of the exploration plan for ten exploratory wells to be drilled by Royal Dutch Shell off the shore of Alabama and Mississippi in the Gulf of Mexico. By determining that the Bureau had met all of the requirements of NEPA, the court rejected the environmentalists' argument that the Bureau had not conducted a site-specific analysis of potential devastating spills and had thus underestimated the risk of such oil spills. In addition, the court rejected the environmentalists' second argument that the Bureau's reliance on certain "biological opinions" issued before the 2007 BP oil spill violated the Endangered Species Act. These opinions concluded that Shell's exploration plan would not jeopardize any endangered or threatened species or destroy habitat associated with such species, but the opinions necessarily did not account for any effects stemming from the subsequent 2007 spill. Despite this, the court found the Bureau's ruling that the opinions remained operative until issuance of new or revised opinions to be reasonable and not arbitrary and capricious.

2.   BLM may not issue an oil and gas lease on national forest system lands if the Secretary of Agriculture objects to lease issuance. 30 U.S.C. § 226(g). The MLA also vests the Secretary of Agriculture with the authority to regulate all surface-disturbing activities conducted pursuant to a BLM-

issued MLA lease on national forest lands. In addition, the Secretary of Agriculture must approve APDs for leases on these lands. 30 U.S.C. 226(g).

In 2005, the Forest Service relied on language from two U.S. Supreme Court decisions, Ohio Forestry Ass'n v. Sierra Club, 523 U.S. 726 (1998) and Norton v. Southern Utah Wilderness Alliance, 542 U.S. 55 (2004), to categorically exempt Land and Resource Management Plans ("LRMPs") from the NEPA EIS/EA requirement. 36 C.F.R. § 219.4. The regulations characterize LRMPs as strategic documents providing guidance rather than binding the agency to actions identified by the plan. 36 C.F.R. §§ 219.2, 219.3 Under the regulations, environmental impact analysis is still required when APDs are processed and when considering project-specific decisions, such as whether to make specific forest service lands available for leasing, 36 C.F.R. § 228.102(c). Nevertheless, environmental plaintiffs successfully challenged the regulations. Citizens for Better Forestry v. USDA, 481 F.Supp.2d 1059 (N.D. Cal. 2007) (enjoining the Forest Service from implementing and relying on the regulation). Specifically, the district court held the regulation procedurally defective for failing to comply with the NEPA, APA, and ESA.

3.   The Alaska National Interest Lands Conservation Act requires special land-use planning and regulations to protect subsistence hunting, fishing, and gathering activities by native Alaskans. 16 U.S.C. § 3120. Although subsistence activities are not given primacy, the Act sets forth a costly and time-consuming procedure for considering the impacts of any activity that would significantly restrict subsistence uses. The activity may be undertaken only if "necessary and if the adverse effects are minimized." Amoco Prod. Co. v. Village of Gambell, 480 U.S. 531, 544 (1987).

4.   Under the Endangered Species Act, 16 U.S.C. §§ 1531–1544, federal agencies must protect endangered and threatened species and insure that federal agency activity will not jeopardize the continued existence of any such species or result in the destruction of such species' critical habitat. Id. § 1536(a)(1), (2). Agencies must consult with the United States Fish and Wildlife Service ("USFWS") to determine whether agency activity is likely to jeopardize a species on the endangered or threatened lists. In preparation for this consultation, the BLM (or Forest Service) must prepare a biological assessment. The USFWS must respond with a biological opinion. 50 C.F.R. § 402. If the opinion concludes that the activity is likely to jeopardize an endangered species, the USFWS must suggest reasonable and prudent alternatives to the action, which may include a refusal to lease or to allow lease development. Id. § 402.14(g)(3).

(g) Compliance With the National Historic Preservation Act

Several BLM oil and gas lease sales have been challenged on grounds that the BLM failed to comply with the requirements of the National Historic Preservation Act, 16 U.S.C. § 470 et seq. ("NHPA"). Similar to NEPA, the NHPA is basically a procedural statute designed to ensure that federal agencies identify and consider effects on significant historic and cultural resources in their decision-making processes. Section 106 of NHPA requires that the head of any federal agency having authority to license any undertaking take into account the effect of the undertaking on any property eligible for inclusion on the National Register of Historic Places maintained by the Secretary of the Interior. 16 U.S.C. § 470f. The Advisory Council for Historic Preservation issued regulations at 36 C.F.R. part 800 implementing section 106 of the NHPA. If an undertaking has no potential to affect historic properties, the agency is not required to take any further action. If an undertaking does have a potential to affect cultural or historic properties, then the agency must undertake a consultation process with the State Historic Preservation Officer, and possibly other interested parties, before it approves the license.

A BLM oil and gas lease sale is an undertaking under the NHPA. Montana Wilderness Ass'n v. Fry, 310 F.Supp.2d 1127 (D. Mont. 2004). Therefore, as part of the lease sale process, BLM must determine whether there will be any potential effects on cultural and historic properties, including historic properties of religious and cultural significance to Indian tribes. BLM sometimes undertakes its NHPA responsibilities in phases, with a more general review at the time the Resource Management Plan for an area is adopted or amended, and a progressively more focused review at the lease sale and the subsequent APD approval stages. DOI's Board of Land Appeals has held that the BLM's phased approach to NHPA complies with the statute's requirements.[92]

(h) Preemption of State and Local Law

When the MLA was enacted in 1920, the West was sparsely populated. In fact, until recent years, oil and gas development on federal lands rarely conflicted with other uses of the public lands. However, with the rapidly increasing population and evolving demographics of the West, interest in recreation and other non-development uses has intensified. Concerns about the effects of mineral development on health and other environmental factors increase the potential for controversy as well. Nevertheless, the high demand for energy and the search for significant new sources of oil and gas continue to drive exploration and development activities into areas that are now highly populated.

As people move into areas that only a decade or two ago were isolated and where oil and gas operations on federal land previously caused no concerns, states and local governments are under increasing pressure to curtail, or even to halt, mineral development. Because the Supremacy Clause of the constitution, U.S. Const. art. VI, cl.2, prevents states and local jurisdictions from "regulating" the federal government, any non-federal restrictions on development of federal oil and gas leases raise issues of preemption and inter-governmental immunity.

The leading case about preemption and inter-governmental government immunity is California Coastal Comm'n v. Granite Rock Co., 480 U.S. 572 (1987). The case involved a challenge to a California statute requiring Granite Rock to obtain a state permit to continue its mining operations on federal mining claims that Granite Rock located under the

---

92. The Mandan, Hidatsa and Arikara Nation, 164 IBLA 343 (2005).

Mining Law of 1872. The issue was whether the California law constituted land use planning, which would be preempted, or reasonable environmental regulation, which might be permissible. In a narrowly focused opinion, the Supreme Court held that the requirement that Granite Rock apply for a state environmental permit was not facially preempted. A more recent decision, South Dakota Mining Ass'n v. Lawrence County, 155 F.3d 1005 (8th Cir. S.D. 1998), also arose under the Mining Law of 1872. Here, the regulation at issue was a county ordinance prohibiting issuance of any new or amended permits for surface metal mining in a particular area. Under the facts presented, the ordinance acted as a *de facto* ban on mining the plaintiffs' federal mining claims. The court of appeals struck down the county ordinance as a clear obstacle to Congress' encouragement of exploration and mining under the Mining Law.

An important distinction exists between preemption issues that arise under the Mining Law and those that might arise where a state or local jurisdiction seeks to impermissibly impede oil and gas development under a MLA lease. The Mining Law is essentially a public land grant statute which grants property interests on a self-initiated basis and authorizes citizens to enter upon public lands to explore for and develop minerals that they locate. No proceeds from sale or revenues from development accrue to the federal government. In contrast, when the BLM holds a lease sale under the MLA, the government has made an affirmative decision to lease and expects revenues in the form of bonuses, rentals, and royalties for the oil and gas resources it has leased.

One court had the opportunity to address the preemption and intergovernmental immunity issues that may arise in situations where a state or local government attempts to severely limit development of a MLA oil and gas lease. Ventura County v. Gulf Oil Corp., 601 F.2d 1080 (9th Cir. 1979), aff'd mem, 445 U.S. 947 (1980) (barring county from enforcing a zoning ordinance on federal land that would have prohibited the federal lessee from drilling unless it received a special use permit from the county government). How much regulation of oil and gas development on federal leases may a state or local jurisdiction undertake to protect the health and welfare of its citizens? At what point do environmental restrictions become so onerous as to constitute a de facto ban on operations? Do you think states and local jurisdictions should have less ability to regulate activities on federal oil and gas leases than on federal mining claims?

Preemption also is relevant to issues regarding applicability of state conservation laws and regulations to federal oil and gas leases within the state. Congress certainly could partially or completely preempt oil and gas conservation regulation under the Supremacy Clause or Commerce Clause of the Constitution, or preempt state regulation of federal and Indian lands under the Property Clause of the Constitution.

The Congress shall have Power to dispose of and make all needful Rules and Regulations respecting the Territory or other Property belonging to the United States; and nothing in this Constitution shall be so construed as to Prejudice any Claims of the United States, or of any particular State.[93]

As construed, this clause bars the states from regulating federal lands in a manner inconsistent with federal legislation.[94] Thus, the key to preemption is whether federal legislation has preempted or partially preempted state regulation. Regarding state oil and gas conservation regulation, the answer is somewhat uncertain. Thus, the Model Oil and Gas Conservation Act includes the following alternative jurisdiction provision, which acknowledges partial preemption, for use by states with large tracts of federal or Indian lands:

> This [Act] shall apply to all lands within this state, except as follows:
>
> (a) As to lands of the United States or lands which are subject to its supervision, this [Act] shall apply only to the extent necessary to permit the [commission] to protect the correlative rights, health, safety, and the environment. The other provisions of this [Act] shall also apply if the officer of the United States having jurisdiction over the lands approves an order, permit, rule, or regulation of the [commission] purporting to affect the lands.
>
> (b) This article shall not apply to lands committed to federal exploratory unit or federal communitized unit except to the extent approved by the Department of Interior and except as to affected privately owned or state lands.

Model Oil and Gas Conservation Act Alt. § 3 (Interstate Oil & Gas Compact Comm'n 2004).

Generally, the BLM cooperates with states regarding certain conservation issues, such as communitization of leases (or pooling of tracts to form a drilling unit). Ordinarily, communitization is accomplished when the Secretary "consents" to the communitization of federal lands by agreeing to the terms of a communitization agreement;[95] however, the Secretary may also coerce federal lessees to communitize.[96] In either case, when communitization is consistent with state spacing and pooling orders, which is often the case, the Secretary has acceded to state regulatory authority for that particular communitization. Thus, the Secretary may and often does accede to state spacing, density, and pooling regulatory authority because the Secretary decides that doing so is in the public interest. On the other hand, the Secretary may occasionally decline to accede to a state spacing, density, or pooling order because the Secretary

---

93. U. S. Const. art. IV, § 3, cl. 2.

94. Kleppe v. New Mexico, 426 U.S. 529, 543 (1976) (barring states from regulating wild burros in a manner that is inconsistent with federal legislative policy).

95. For communitization regulations, see 43 C.F.R. § 3105.2. This regulation applies to both public domain, 43 C.F.R. § 3100.0–3(a), and to acquired lands, 43 C.F.R. § 3100.0–3(b).

96. The federal oil and gas lease form specifies that "Lessor reserves the right . . . to require lessee to subscribe to a cooperative or unit plan, within 30 days of notice, if deemed necessary for proper development and operation of the area, field, or pool embracing these leased lands." United States Dep't of the Interior, Bureau of Land Management, Offer to Lease and Lease for Oil and Gas, Form 3100–11 (January 2006).

concludes that doing so is not in the public interest. In any case, as explained earlier, state and local regulations barring oil and gas development by a lessee of federal lands,[97] as well as a state regulation that is inconsistent with mandatory provisions of the MLA or underlying federal regulations, are not enforceable.[98]

For a review of the case law exploring the uncertainty surrounding federal preemption of state conservation law and discussing the longstanding practice of federal-state cooperation regarding the conservation of oil and gas, see Owen L. Anderson, State Conservation Regulation—Single Well Spacing and Pooling—Vis–À–Vis Federal and Indian Lands, Special Institute on Federal Onshore Oil and Gas Pooling and Unitization (Rocky Mtn. Min. L. Foundation 2006).

(i) Lease Termination, Suspension, and Cancellation

IN RE GREAT PLAINS PETROLEUM, INC.
117 IBLA 130 (1990).

Appeal from a decision of the Montana State Office, Bureau of Land Management, declaring oil and gas lease NDM 25321 terminated by cessation of production. * * * Affirmed.

Opinion by ADMINISTRATIVE JUDGE HUGHES

Great Plains Petroleum, Inc. (Great Plains), appeals from a decision of the Montana State Office, Bureau of Land Management (BLM), dated August 3, 1988, declaring oil and gas lease NDM 25321 terminated effective October 31, 1987, by cessation of production. Lease NDM 25321 was issued effective July 1, 1973, for a period of 10 years and so long thereafter as oil or gas was produced in paying quantities. On April 11, 1988, the Dickinson, North Dakota, District Office, BLM, notified Great Plains, which had been the designated operator, that BLM records showed no production from the lease since October 1987. BLM reminded Great Plains that the lease was issued for a primary term of 10 years and so long thereafter as hydrocarbons were produced from the leasehold. BLM advised that, unless the lease contained a well capable of producing hydrocarbons in paying quantities, the lease would be considered to have terminated effective October 31, 1987. BLM informed Great Plains that, if it considered the lease capable of producing hydrocarbons in paying quantities, it had to furnish adequate test data showing the well's current potential production within 60 days of receipt of the notice and continue to produce the lease. Otherwise, BLM stated, the lease would terminate.

A conversation record in the case file indicates that on July 20, 1988, a BLM employee from the District Office spoke with a representative of

---

97. Ventura County v. Gulf Oil Corp., 601 F.2d 1080 (9th Cir. 1979), *aff'd mem*, 445 U.S. 947 (1980).

98. *See, e.g.*, Kirby Exploration Co. of Texas, 149 IBLA 205 (1999), *aff'g in part, rev'g in part*, 143 IBLA 133 (1998) (finding that the Oklahoma "weighted average" approach to the payment of royalty on pooled acreage was inconsistent with the "gross proceeds" approach to the payment of royalty mandated by the MLA).

Great Plains concerning the status of the Signalness 24–2 well, which was the last producing well on the lease. The representative stated that the well was shut-in and that Great Plains had filed for bankruptcy. The BLM employee reported that although the representative had added that the well was capable of producing, Great Plains had not submitted any data.

On July 27, 1988, the Acting District Manager advised the Montana State Director, BLM, that Great Plains had not responded to BLM's 60-day notice letter of April 11, 1988, and that it therefore appeared that the Signalness 24–2 well was not capable of producing hydrocarbons in paying quantities. The District Manager recommended that the lease be declared terminated effective October 31, 1987, the last day of the month in which production ceased.

In its decision dated August 3, 1988, BLM, referring to the report of the District Office, stated that the last producible well on the leasehold ceased production October 31, 1987. BLM concluded that, since there was no production to continue the lease, the lease term was exhausted and declared terminated by cessation of production effective October 31, 1987. Great Plains appealed.

In its statement of reasons, Great Plains explains that it was the operator of the Signalness 24–2 well until April 1986, when it agreed to be placed into bankruptcy, with a court-appointed trustee running operations at Great Plains from April 1986 through July 1987, during which time several wells, including the Signalness 24–2 well, were allowed to be shut-in; that no attempt was made by the trustee to place wells back on production; that upon the trustee's resignation in July 1987, the court appointed another company as operator of Great Plains' wells with the exception of five wells, including the Signalness 24–2, which were given back to Great Plains to operate; that the Signalness 24–2 well was not operating at that time and, due to insufficient income, Great Plains was unable to get the Signalness 24–2 "up and running"; and that eventually all of Great Plains' wells were shut down.

Great Plains asserts that it has continued to search for a solution to renew operations of all wells, noting that in May 1988 the court approved its Plan for Reorganization. According to Great Plains, it was in the process of "getting wells back up and running." Great Plains stated that it planned to have work completed on the Signalness 24–2 during the month of September 1988, and sought more time to get the well back into production. Great Plains filed no further information concerning its activities on the lease.

Under section 17(f) of the Mineral Leasing Act, as amended, 30 U.S.C. § 226(f), an oil and gas lease in its extended term terminates by operation of law when paying production ceases on the lease, subject to three statutory exceptions. C & K Petroleum, Inc., 70 IBLA 354 (1983); Michael P. Grace, 50 IBLA 150 (1980); John S. Pehar, 41 IBLA 191 (1979). The exceptions provide that no lease shall terminate for cessation of production if: (1) Reworking or drilling operations are begun within 60 days after cessation and are continued with reasonable diligence until production resumes; (2) the Department has ordered or consented to suspension of operations or production; or (3) for lands on which there is a well capable of production, the lessee places the well in production within 60 days after receipt of notice to do so. See 43 C.F.R. § 3107.2–2, 3103.4–2, 3107.2–3.

In this case, there is no evidence that any reworking or drilling operations were under way within 60 days after cessation of production, and the Department did not order or consent to a suspension of operations or production on the lease. In its letter of April 11, 1988, BLM properly notified Great Plains that it had 60 days from receipt of the letter to submit to BLM adequate test data showing the wells then current potential production and to continue to produce the lease. See Michael P. Grace, supra at 151; Cf. C & K Petroleum, Inc., supra. Great Plains did not respond to this notice.

Upon a determination that production has ceased on an oil and gas lease in its extended term by reason of production because the well on the lease is no longer capable of production in paying quantities, the affected parties, including the lease operator and the lessees of record, are entitled to notice and an opportunity to request a hearing on the issue of the productive capacity of the well where they have presented evidence raising an issue of fact regarding the status of the well. Daynon D. Gililland, 108 IBLA 144 (1989); C & K Petroleum, Inc., supra; John Swanson, 51 IBLA 239 (1980). In this case, Great Plains has not contested BLM's finding that the Signalness 24–2 well, the last producible well on the leasehold, ceased production October 31, 1987. Nor has Great Plains submitted any evidence regarding the productive capacity of the well. There is no allegation of facts which, if proven, would show compliance with the statute and prevent the lease from terminating. See John S. Pehar, supra at 193; C & K Petroleum, Inc., supra. Therefore, BLM properly declared the lease terminated.

Therefore, pursuant to the authority delegated to the Board of Land Appeals by the Secretary of the Interior, 43 C.F.R. § 4.1, the decision appealed from is affirmed.

NOTES

1. Under the typical private oil and gas lease and under the circumstances outlined in Great Plains Petroleum, Inc., would a private landowner have to give sixty days' notice?

2. Any person adversely affected by a Bureau of Land Management lands decision has the right to appeal that decision to the Interior Board of Land Appeals ("IBLA") in the Office of Hearings and Appeals. 43 C.F.R. part 4, subpart E. In most cases IBLA appeals are decided on a written record filed by the appellant, the BLM, and any other party to the appeal. However, in case of a factual dispute, the IBLA may refer the matter to the Hearings Division of the Office of Hearings and Appeals ("OHA") for a hearing before

an administrative law judge (43 C.F.R. § 4.415). The IBLA's review is de novo. Because the IBLA is delegated by the Secretary of the Interior's authority to decide matters finally for the Department (43 C.F.R. § 4.1), decisions issued by the IBLA are final decisions of the Department subject to judicial review under the Administrative Procedure Act (APA), 5 U.S.C. §§ 701–706 (43 C.F.R. § 4.21(c)).

Assistant Secretaries in the Department of the Interior also are delegated all the Secretary's authority over the various matters under their jurisdiction. Therefore, if an Assistant Secretary issues or concurs in a decision, the IBLA will not review such a decision. (Blue Star, Inc., 41 IBLA 333 (1979); Marathon Oil Co., 108 IBLA 177 (1989)). An Assistant Secretary's decision is final for the Department and is subject to judicial review under the APA. In addition, the Secretary of the Interior may take jurisdiction at any time of any matter pending before any person and issue a final decision for the Department. (43 C.F.R. § 4.5(a)).

3. The BLM may direct or permit the suspension of operations or production "in the interest of conservation of natural resources" or upon request of the lessee for reasons of force majeure. 43 C.F.R. § 3103.4–4(a). When the BLM suspends operations or production, the lease is extended by the period that production or operations are suspended; thus, a lease will not expire during that period. Id. § 3103.4–4(b).

4. Cancellation of a lease by the Secretary may occur only after the lessee is given notice of noncompliance and an opportunity to cure. If the leasehold contains a well capable of production in paying quantities and the lessee has failed to comply with a law, regulation, or lease provision, the lease may be canceled but only by a judicial proceeding. Improperly issued leases are also subject to cancellation, either by a judicial proceeding or by the Secretary, depending on whether the leasehold contains a well capable of production in paying quantities. Id. § 3108.3(a). In addition, for noncompliance with regulations or directives, the BLM may assess civil penalties, may order remedial work, and may even order the immediate shut down of operations. Id. Subpart 3163.

2. OFFSHORE LANDS

In addition to its onshore lands, the United States government also claims, subject to state title claims to certain territorial waters, the exclusive right to control the exploitation of oil and gas resources to most of the Outer Continental Shelf ("OCS") and other submerged lands bordering the United States seaward 200 nautical miles. The federal OCS includes all submerged lands that lie seaward of state-owned submerged lands ceded to the states by the Submerged Lands Act of 1953[99] and that are subject to the jurisdiction and control of the United States.[100] Under

---

99. 43 U.S.C. §§ 1301–1315.

100. 30 C.F.R. § 251.3–1(ff). Under Presidential Proclamation No. 5030, the United States claims the sovereign rights to the Exclusive Economic Zone (EEZ), an area extending seaward for a distance of 200 miles from the coast of the United States and its territories and possessions. 48 Fed.Reg. 10,605 (1983). The 1982 U.N. Convention on the Law of the Sea, 21 I.L.M. 1261 (1982),

the Submerged Lands Act, all coastal states except Texas and Florida hold title to the inlets and offshore lands within three miles of their respective shore lines.[101] Florida, on its Gulf coast, and Texas hold title to offshore lands within three marine leagues of their shore lines.[102]

The first documented offshore wells were drilled in the 1890s from piers off the coast of California. The first freestanding offshore well was drilled in 1938 in 14 feet of water off the coast of Louisiana. Modern offshore wells in the Gulf of Mexico have achieved production through almost 10,000 feet of water.[103] Approximately one-fifth of domestic oil and one-third of domestic gas production occur in the Gulf of Mexico.

Modern 3–D seismic technology has lowered the risk of drilling dry holes in high-cost deep water areas. The Outer Continental Shelf Deep Water Royalty Relief Act, Pub. L. 104–58, Title III, §§ 301 *et seq.*, 109 Stat. 563–566 (November 28, 1995), improved the economics of drilling in deep water by enacting certain provisions for suspending the royalty ordinarily owed the federal government for certain volumes of production from wells drilled in deep water.

The Outer Continental Shelf Lands Act of 1953 ("OCSLA"), as amended most significantly in 1978, governs the leasing of federal offshore lands.[104] From 1982 to 2010, the offshore leasing program was adminis-tered by the Mineral Management Service ("MMS"). After the Deepwater Horizon disaster, the MMS was replaced by the Bureau of Ocean Energy Management, Regulation and Enforcement ("BOEMRE"). On October 1, 2011, as part of a major reorganization, BOEMRE was in turn replaced by the Bureau of Ocean Energy Management ("BOEM"), the Bureau of Safety and Environmental Enforcement ("BSEE"), and the Office of Natural Resource Revenue. BOEM is responsible for managing offshore leasing, resource evaluation, review and administration of oil and gas exploration and development plans, renewable energy development, and the National Environmental Policy Act ("NEPA") analysis and environ-mental studies. BSEE is responsible for safety and environmental over-

---

addresses a sovereign nation's right to develop natural resources from the seabed. Although the United States has not ratified it, the EEZ claimed by the United States is consistent with arts. 55–75 of the Convention. In 1945, President Truman issued what has become known as the Truman Proclamation, Proclamation No. 2667, 10 Fed. Reg. 12303 (1945) wherein the United States laid claim to the continental shelf. When other countries followed suit, these claims were given legal recognition in the U.N. 1958 Geneva Convention on the Continental Shelf, 52 Am.J.Int'l L. 858 (1958); however, after only about 50 countries became parties to this Conven-tion, the Law of the Sea Convention was negotiated.

101.   43 U.S.C. § 1312.

102.   Under the Act, coastal states were given the right to prove greater historical boundaries. Only Texas and Florida have succeeded. For background, see United States v. Louisiana, et al., 364 U.S. 502 (1960). A marine league is equal to three geographical or nautical miles. A geographical or nautical mile is about 6,075 feet, whereas a statute mile is 5,280 feet.

103.   Xiong Tong, *Shell Produces Oil from World's Deepest Subsea Well in Gulf of Mexico*, ENGLISHNEWS.CN, Nov. 18, 2011.

104.   43 U.S.C. §§ 1331–1356. A host of other federal laws also apply to certain offshore oil and gas operations, including the Jones Act, 46 U.S.C. § 688; the Longshore and Harbor Workers' Compensation Act, 33 U.S.C. §§ 901–950; the Coastal Zone Management Act, 16 U.S.C. §§ 1451–1464; and the Rivers and Harbors Act, 33 U.S.C. § 403.

sight of offshore oil and gas operations, including permitting and inspections. The Office of Natural Resource Revenue collects revenues from leasing and production of federal offshore lands.

A major focus of the 1953 Act was to establish a leasing and development program for offshore lands. The primary focus of the 1978 amendments addressed environmental concerns, which provided for state involvement in the formulation of leasing plans and in the conduct of offshore operations that affect the states' coastal zones.[105] Under the 1978 amendments, the Secretary of the Interior may suspend lease operations and cancel leases when the potential harm outweighs benefits and where operators are not in compliance with environmental requirements.[106]

The amended OCSLA has four steps for the development of an offshore oil well on federal offshore lands: (1) development of a five-year leasing plan; (2) offering, sale, and issuance of leases (solicitation of bids and issuance of offshore leases); (3) exploration operations; and (4) drilling, development, and production operations. Each of these steps has environmental analysis components.

(a) Five–Year Leasing Plan

Under OCSLA, the DOI must first prepare a five-year leasing plan for offshore leases.[107] This plan, which is a schedule of the proposed lease sales, must indicate the size, timing, and location of the leasing activity that the Secretary of the Interior determines will best meet the nation's energy needs for the following five years.[108] In making this determination, the Secretary must consider the economic, social, and environmental impact of the plan, including an equitable sharing of developmental benefits and environmental risks among the various regions.[109] The Secretary must also solicit comments from all interested federal agencies and from the governors of states that might be affected by the proposed operations.[110] The Secretary must submit the proposed final program and any comments to the President and the Congress[111] and must give final approval to the plan. This process can take as long as two years. Many federal waters remain off-limits for drilling. Currently, despite strong evidence that commercial oil and gas deposits can be found off both the Atlantic and Pacific coasts and off the southern and western coast of the Florida peninsula, federal leases for oil and gas development have been

---

105. In general, offshore activities must be consistent with an affected state's coastal zone management plan as promulgated pursuant to the Coastal Zone Management Act of 1972, as amended. 16 U.S.C. §§ 1451–1464.

106. 43 U.S.C. § 1334(a)(1).

107. Id. § 1344(a).

108. Id.

109. Id.

110. Id. § 1344(c)(1). Under the Coastal Zone Management Act of 1972, any federal offshore leasing activities "directly affecting the coastal zone" must be consistent with each coastal state's approved coastal zone management plan.

111. Id. § 1344(d)(2).

issued only off certain Alaskan waters and off the coasts of Texas, Louisiana, Mississippi, Alabama, and the western portion of Florida.

(b) Bid Solicitation and Lease Issuance

After the final five-year leasing plan has been approved, the next step in the offshore development process is the solicitation of bids and the issuance of offshore leases. Under OCSLA, the Secretary of the Interior must set the timing of leases and the location of leased tracts to strike a proper balance among the potential for environmental damage, the potential for the discovery of oil and gas, and the potential for any adverse impact on the coastal zone.[112] Since the 1990 amendments to the Coastal Zone Management Act ("CZMA"), lease sales are subject to CZMA section 307(c)(1)'s so-called "consistency provisions" for federal agency activities. 16 U.S.C. § 1456(c)(1).

The following table enumerates the steps involved in issuing an offshore lease and the anticipated time schedule for each step:

Steps	Lower 48	Alaska
Identify Areas of Hydrocarbon Potential, Call for Information and Nomination, and Publish Notice of Intent to Prepare an EIS	Month 1	Month 1
Area Identification	Month 4	Month 4
Draft EIS	Month 12	Month 15
Public Comment Period	Month 14	Month 17
Final EIS	Month 18	Month 21
Proposed Notice of Sale	Month 19	Month 22
Governors' Comments	Month 21	Month 24
Final Notice of Sale	Month 22	Month 25
Sale	Month 23	Month 26
Bid Review	Month 24	Month 27
Lease Issued	Month 25	Month 28

Following the call for information and nomination, BOEM identifies areas of potential hydrocarbon resources.[113] The oil and gas industry is invited to comment on these areas and to nominate areas for leasing. The governors of affected states may also make comments regarding environmental concerns[114] and consult with the Secretary to determine whether leases in close proximity to the coast may contain oil or gas reservoirs underlying state lands.[115]

---

112. Id. § 1344(a)(3).

113. 30 C.F.R. § 256.23.

114. Id. § 256.25.

115. Id. § 256.25(b). Since coastal states hold title to offshore lands within 3 miles (Texas and Florida (on the Gulf coast) hold title to 3 marine leagues) of their respective shorelines, a 3-mile "buffer zone" of federal offshore land lies seaward of each state's offshore limits. This area is commonly referred to as the "8(g) Zone," because Section 8(g) of OCSLA (43 U.S.C. § 1337(g)) governs federal leasing of submerged lands within 3 nautical miles of a coastal state's seaward boundary. In other words, two separate zones apply to federal offshore lands: (1) the 8(g) Zone, the innermost 3–mile strip of federal offshore land lying immediately seaward of state owned

Next, a draft environmental impact statement ("EIS") is usually prepared (unless a multi-sale EIS has been issued for an area with recurring sales). The EIS identifies the planning area, possible environmental impacts, potential coastal zone management conflicts, and alternatives to the proposed leasing program. The release of the draft EIS is followed by a public comment period. Comments on the proposal and on the draft EIS are evaluated in the final EIS. In the case of a subsequent lease sale in an area with recurring sales, BOEM does an environmental assessment ("EA") to determine whether a supplemental EIS needs to be prepared or whether BOEM can make a Finding of No New Significant Impact ("FONNSI"—similar to an original Finding Of No Significant Impact ("FONSI") but a subsequent issuance after a follow-up EA or EIS is conducted).

After the final EIS is released, a proposed notice of sale is published in the Federal Register. This announcement contains the proposed terms and conditions of sale, the bidding systems, the lease blocks, special lease stipulations, and any required mitigation measures. The notice of sale is also sent to governors of affected states. These governors are invited to comment upon the size, timing, and location of the proposed lease sale. The Secretary must respond in writing to their comments. In the final notice of sale, which is an invitation to submit bids, the Secretary may include any comments that are deemed "valid." The final notice is published in the Federal Register at least thirty days before the actual date of bidding and sale.

Leasing of federally controlled offshore land is by competitive sealed bid.[116] The BOEM, with approval of the Secretary, may use alternative bidding systems to increase income to the government or to give smaller oil and gas companies a better opportunity to acquire offshore leases.[117] To achieve these somewhat inconsistent goals, the Secretary is authorized to use any of the following bidding systems:[118] a cash bonus with a royalty of twelve-and-a-half percent (12.5%) or more; a variable royalty bid with either a fixed work commitment or a fixed cash bonus; a cash bonus bid or a work commitment bid and a diminishing sliding scale royalty beginning at twelve-and-a-half percent (12.5%); a cash bonus with a fixed net profits share of not less than thirty percent (30%); a net profits share bid with a fixed cash bonus; a cash bonus bid with a royalty of at least twelve-and-a-half percent (12.5%) and a fixed net profits share of at least thirty percent (30%); a work commitment bid with a fixed cash bonus and a fixed royalty; or any other bidding system with variables, terms, and conditions that the Secretary determines to be useful to accomplish the purposes and policies of the Act. The overwhelming number of offshore leases were issued under the variable cash bonus and fixed rate royalty system. What

offshore lands; and (2) all federal offshore land lying seaward of the 8(g) Zone. Texas v. Secretary of Interior, 580 F.Supp. 1197, 1198 (E.D.Tex.1984).

116. 43 U.S.C. § 1337(a)(1).

117. 30 C.F.R. § 256.32(e).

118. 43 U.S.C. § 1337(a)(1)(A)–(H).

might be some of the reasons for this? Do other available bidding systems involve particular potential problems or offer any advantages?

The Secretary may accept or reject any bid within ninety days of the sale.[119] Tied highest bids are rejected, unless the tied bidders (within fifteen days after notification of the tie) file an agreement with the BOEM to accept the lease jointly.[120] Before any bids are accepted, the Attorney General and the Federal Trade Commission review the highest bid for each lease to determine whether any bids violate antitrust laws and to assure that fair market value has been realized.[121] Before a lease is issued, the successful bidder must post a bond of at least $50,000 with the BOEM; the BOEM may require additional bonds when offshore operations are commenced.[122]

Because the costs and risks of offshore oil and gas development are high, several operators may submit joint bids to acquire joint interests in offshore leases.[123] Joint bidders enter into agreements that name the parties, identify targeted lease blocks, address allocation of interests in the lease, require disclosure of certain information and provide for confidentiality of that information, set procedures for determining a bid, provide for termination of the agreement regarding certain parcels for which there is no mutual interest, provide for execution of a joint operating agreement, and provide that the agreement shall not be construed as a partnership or joint venture.[124] A key provision addresses antitrust aspects of a joint bidding agreement: parties to the agreement are allowed to submit their own bids or to participate in other joint bids; however, parties are generally given a participation option to acquire interests in any lease obtained by any other party to the agreement. Although no case law addresses antitrust aspects of joint bidding for oil and gas leases, parties are advised not to submit a bid lower than the highest suggested bid proposed by a member of the joint bidding group.[125] Pursuant to a federal regulation, the Department of the Interior periodically publishes a list of

---

119. 30 C.F.R. § 256.47(e)(2). See also Kerr–McGee Corp. v. Morton, 527 F.2d 838 (D.C.Cir. 1975) (holding that the Secretary may reject the highest bid if the Secretary believes that the bid is too low).

120. 30 C.F.R. § 256.47(c).

121. 43 U.S.C. § 1337(c).

122. Id. § 256.58(a).

123. See generally, A. Hoppe, Offshore Agreements, Paper 3, 18 Annual Oil, Gas & Min. L.Inst., (The University of Texas School of Law 1992) and Terry E. Hogwood, Bidding Agreements: Tailoring the Right One for Your Company, Monograph Series No. 3, 1986 ABA Sec. on Nat. Res., Energy, and Envt'l L.

124. Joint operating agreements covering offshore wells are lengthy and detailed documents, but they contain many of the same provisions commonly found in onshore agreements. One major difference, however, is that offshore agreements commonly contain lengthy and onerous nonconsent penalties for a party's refusal to participate in the drilling of an offshore well. Due to the high cost of offshore operations, offshore operating agreements often contain detailed provisions concerning the construction, ownership, and operation of platforms and other offshore facilities, including detailed provisions on preferential purchase rights in the event any party wishes to sell its interest.

125. Terry E. Hogwood, Bidding Agreements: Tailoring the Right One for Your Company, Monograph Series No. 3, 1986 ABA Sec. on Nat.Res., Energy, and Environmental L.

parties prohibited from entering into joint bidding arrangements with other listed parties.[126] This list includes companies whose daily production exceeded 1.6 million barrels of oil or natural gas or liquefied petroleum equivalent in the preceding six months.[127]

Offshore tracts are awarded to the "highest responsible qualified bidder."[128] To be deemed "responsible," a bidder must be financially capable of fulfilling the lease conditions and have fully complied with the conditions of any prior leases.[129] To be deemed "qualified," a bidder must meet the same requirements detailed in Section A.1.(c) above, including the requirements to be a United States citizen, an alien lawfully admitted for permanent residence, a private, public, or municipal corporation organized under United States law, or associations thereof.[130] All leases become effective on the first day of the month following the date of execution by the Secretary.

Generally, federal offshore leases include the following terms and provisions: a leasehold consisting of a compact area not exceeding 5,760 acres;[131] a lease primary term of five years (up to ten years for certain deep water leases) and a secondary term for so long as oil or gas is produced in paying quantities or approved drilling or well reworking operations are being conducted;[132] payment of the amount or value specified by the bidding system;[133] the right to explore, develop, and produce oil and gas conditioned upon due diligence requirements and upon approval of a plan of development;[134] suspension or cancellation of the lease;[135] annual rentals;[136] payment of royalties;[137] and offers of production to small or independent refiners under the Emergency Petroleum Allocation Act of 1973.[138] A copy of a federal offshore lease in use at the time this edition went to press is included in the Forms Manual that accompanies this casebook.

Unlike the leasing of federal onshore lands where the affected state shares in the revenues produced under the lease, coastal states have generally not shared in revenues produced under federal offshore leases. An exception is where leaseholds are located within the "buffer" or

---

126. See, e.g., 56 Fed.Reg. 55,928.

127. 30 C.F.R. § 256.41.

128. 43 U.S.C. § 1337(a)(1).

129. 43 U.S.C. § 1337(d).

130. 30 C.F.R. § 256.35(b).

131. 43 U.S.C. § 1337(b)(1). Larger leaseholds are allowed if the leasing of a larger tract is necessary to secure a reasonable economic production unit. Id.

132. Id. § 1337(b)(2). To encourage development in deep water or under adverse conditions, the lease may provide for a primary term of up to ten years.

133. Id. § 1337(b)(3).

134. Id. § 1337(b)(4).

135. Id. § 1337(b)(5).

136. Id. § 1337(b)(6).

137. The royalty rate is commonly one-sixth; however, pursuant to alternate bidding systems, the rate could be higher, lower, or not reserved.

138. Id. § 1337(b)(7).

"Section 8(g) Zone." Section 1337(g) of OCSLA provides that where a federal lease lies wholly within three nautical miles of a coastal state's seaward boundary, the federal government must remit to the state twenty-seven percent (27%) of the revenues generated by the lease.[139] Where a federal lease lies only partially within the Section 8(g) Zone, the amount remitted to the coastal state must equal the percentage of the lease lying within the Section 8(g) Zone multiplied by twenty-seven percent (27%) of the revenues generated by the lease.[140]

In 2006, Congress passed the Gulf of Mexico Energy Security Act ("GOMESA"), which was signed into law by President George W. Bush on December 20, 2006.[141] GOMESA requires that fifty percent (50%) of "qualified OCS revenues" be disbursed (1) to Gulf producing states and their coastal political subdivisions (seventy-five percent (75%) of the fifty percent (50%)), and (2) as financial assistance to states under Section 6 of the Land and Water Conservation Fund Act of 1965 (16 U.S.C. § 4601–8) (twenty-five percent (25%) of the fifty percent (50%)). However, the revenues to which that requirement applies are limited to those derived from leases issued after the date of GOMESA's enactment in two relatively small areas made available for leasing under the Act for fiscal years 2007 through 2016. For FY 2017 and thereafter, the disbursement requirements will apply to leases issued after the date of GOMESA's enactment in the entire federal area subject to leasing in the Gulf of Mexico except for areas under leasing moratorium and leases in the Section 8(g) Zone.[142] GOMESA also contains laws establishing areas within the Gulf of Mexico that are prohibited for oil and gas leasing, including areas off Florida.

(c) Exploration

Before exploration, an operator must file an exploration plan with the Department of the Interior.[143] This plan is subject to an environmental analysis that could lead to an EIS. The plan must be consistent with any affected state's approved coastal zone management plan and must set a

---

139. Id. § 1337(g)(2). In Louisiana ex rel. Guste v. United States, 832 F.2d 935 (5th Cir.La.1987), the Court of Appeals for the Fifth Circuit ruled that the State of Louisiana was not entitled to relief against drainage by federal wells or to unitization since the share the state received from 8(g) Zone leases was intended to settle such problems between sovereigns permanently. (Thus, this case could be viewed as upholding the "rule of capture" on the Federal OCS.)

140. 43 U.S.C. § 1337(g)(2).

141. Pub.L.No. 109–432, 120 Stat.2922.

142. The seventy-five percent (75%) of the fifty percent (50%) paid to Gulf-producing states is allocated among those states under a formula that the Secretary must establish by rule, under which the allocated amounts are inversely proportional to the distances between the closest point on the state's coastline and the geographic center of each leased tract (with no state receiving less than 10 percent of the total) for FY 2007–2016. A similar formula is prescribed for FY 2017 and thereafter. The Secretary must pay 20 percent of the amount allocated to each Gulf-producing state to the coastal political subdivisions, according to the complicated inverse distance allocation prescribed for the Coastal Impact Assistance Program enacted by section 384 of the Energy Policy Act of 2005, 43 U.S.C. § 1356a. In addition, the total amount of revenues to be disbursed may not exceed $500 million for each of FY 2016—FY 2055.

143. Id. § 1340(c)(1).

schedule of anticipated exploration activity, a description of the equipment to be used, the general location of each well to be drilled, and other pertinent information.[144] The DOI must approve or reject the plan within thirty days.[145] Plans that are rejected may be revised. If revision is necessary, the Secretary may suspend the running of the lease term and any lease activity until the plan is approved.[146] If the plan cannot be altered to avoid harm to the environment,[147] the lease may be canceled if the lessee commences exploration without having filed an approved exploration plan or fails to comply with an approved plan.[148]

(d) Development and Production

Before beginning this phase of operations, the lessee must file a development and production plan with the Department of the Interior.[149] The plan must be consistent with any affected state's coastal zone management plan and must set forth all facilities and operations proposed by the lessee, including the location of the operations, all environmental and safety standards to be implemented, and other pertinent information.[150] Within ten days of receipt of this plan from the lessee, the Secretary must forward the plan to the governor of any affected state.[151] An environmental analysis must also be done and, if approval of the plan is a "major federal action," the Secretary must prepare an EIS.[152] The governor has sixty days from receipt of the plan to submit comments and recommendations that might influence the Secretary's approval of the plan.[153] Affected states can veto any plan that is inconsistent with its state coastal zone management plan, but the Secretary of Commerce may override a state veto.[154] If the plan is not approved by the Secretary and cannot be altered to avoid harm to the environment, the lease may be canceled.[155]

(e) Lease Suspension and Cancellation

(i) Suspension of Operations or Production

The Regional Supervisor may suspend production (including the requirement to produce) or any other operations on an offshore leasehold either on his own initiative or at the lessee's request for reasons that include the following:

---

144. Id. § 1340(c)(3).

145. Id. § 1340(c)(1).

146. Id. § 1340(e)–(f).

147. Id. §§ 1340(c), 1334(c)–(d).

148. Id. § 1351(j).

149. Id. § 1351(a)(1).

150. Id. § 1351(a)(2).

151. Id. § 1351(a)(3).

152. Id. § 1351(f).

153. Id. § 1351(g).

154. Id. § 1351(d), 16 U.S.C. § 1456(c)(3)(B).

155. 43 U.S.C. § 1351(h).

(1) to facilitate proper development;

(2) to allow for construction or negotiation for use of transportation or production facilities;

(3) to allow time to enter into gas or oil sales contracts;

(4) to avoid operations that would result in premature abandonment of a producing well;

(5) to allow a reasonable time to commence drilling;

(6) to comply with the law or lease terms;

(7) to prevent harm to the environment;

(8) in the interest of national security;

(9) to comply with NEPA;

(10) to install equipment for safety or environmental reasons;

(11) when lessees are subject to inordinate governmental delays in obtaining permits; or

(12) to comply with judicial orders prohibiting production or other operations.[156]

A suspension may not exceed five years. If a lease is suspended, the term of the lease is extended for the period of the suspension, unless the suspension is the result of the lessee's gross negligence or willful violation of a permit, lease, or regulation.[157]

(ii) Cancellation of Lease

If a lessee fails to comply with a law, regulation, or lease provision, the lease is subject to cancellation. If the owner of a *nonproducing* lease fails to comply with the law or with the lease terms, the Secretary of the Interior may cancel the lease, subject to judicial review.[158] If the owner of a *producing* lease fails to comply with the law or with the lease terms, only a federal district court may cancel the lease.[159] Nevertheless, if the Secretary determines, after a hearing, that continued activity on the lease would probably harm the environment, that the threat of harm will not decrease, and that the advantages of cancellation outweigh the advantages of continuing the lease, the Secretary may cancel the lease whether or not the lease is productive.[160] The lease may also be canceled if the lessee fails to submit an exploration plan or fails to comply with an approved plan. If an exploration plan or development and production plan is rejected and cannot be altered to avoid harm to the environment, the lease may be canceled before exploration or development begins.

---

156. 30 C.F.R. §§ 250.172–250.175.

157. 30 C.F.R. §§ 250.170(a), 250.169.

158. 43 U.S.C. § 1334(c).

159. Id. § 1334(d).

160. Id. § 1334(a).

As the following case illustrates, if the federal government causes the delay in development, the federal offshore lessee is not without a remedy if a court should find that the federal government has breached its obligations.

MOBIL OIL EXPLORATION & PRODUCING SOUTHEAST, INC. v. UNITED STATES

530 U.S. 604 (2000).

JUSTICE BREYER delivered the opinion of the Court.

Two oil companies, petitioners here, seek restitution of $156 million they paid the Government in return for lease contracts giving them rights to explore for and develop oil off the North Carolina coast. The rights were not absolute, but were conditioned on the companies' obtaining a set of further governmental permissions. The companies claim that the Government repudiated the contracts when it denied them certain elements of the permission-seeking opportunities that the contracts had promised. We agree that the Government broke its promise; it repudiated the contracts; and it must give the companies their money back.

I.

A.

A description at the outset of the few basic contract law principles applicable to this case will help the reader understand the significance of the complex factual circumstances that follow. "When the United States enters into contract relations, its rights and duties therein are governed generally by the law applicable to contracts between private individuals." United States v. Winstar Corp., 518 U.S. 839, 895 (1996) (plurality opinion) (internal quotation marks omitted). The Restatement of Contracts reflects many of the principles of contract law that are applicable to this case. As set forth in the Restatement of Contracts, the relevant principles specify that, when one party to a contract repudiates that contract, the other party "is entitled to restitution for any benefit that he has conferred on" the repudiating party "by way of part performance or reliance." Restatement (Second) of Contracts § 373 (1979) (hereinafter Restatement). The Restatement explains that "repudiation" is a "statement by the obligor to the obligee indicating that the obligor will commit a breach that would of itself give the obligee a claim for damages for total breach." Id., § 250. And "total breach" is a breach that "so substantially impairs the value of the contract to the injured party at the time of the breach that it is just in the circumstances to allow him to recover damages based on all his remaining rights to performance." Id., § 243.

As applied to this case, these principles amount to the following: If the Government said it would break, or did break, an important contractual promise, thereby "substantially impair[ing] the value of the contract[s]" to the companies, Id., then (unless the companies waived their rights to restitution) the Government must give the companies their money back. And it must do so whether the contracts would, or would not, ultimately have proved financially beneficial to the companies. The Restatement illustrates this point as follows:

> "A contracts to sell a tract of land to B for $100,000. After B has made a part payment of $20,000, A wrongfully refuses to transfer title. B can recover the $20,000 in restitution. The result is the same even if the market price of the land is only $70,000, so that performance would have been disadvantageous to B." Id., § 373, Comment a, Illustration 1.

B.

In 1981, in return for up-front "bonus" payments to the United States of about $158 million (plus annual rental payments), the companies received 10–year renewable lease contracts with the United States. In these contracts, the United States promised the companies, among other things, that they could explore for oil off the North Carolina coast and develop any oil that they found (subject to further royalty payments) provided that the companies received exploration and development permissions in accordance with various statutes and regulations to which the lease contracts were made "subject." App. to Pet. for Cert. in No. 99–253, pp. 174a–185a.

The statutes and regulations, the terms of which in effect were incorporated into the contracts, made clear that obtaining the necessary permissions might not be an easy matter. In particular, the Outer Continental Shelf Lands Act (OCSLA), 67 Stat. 462, as amended, 43 U.S.C. § 1331 et seq. (1994 ed. and Supp. III), and the Coastal Zone Management Act of 1972 (CZMA), 16 U.S.C. § 1451 et seq., specify that leaseholding companies wishing to explore and drill must successfully complete the following four procedures.

First, a company must prepare and obtain Department of the Interior approval for a Plan of Exploration. 43 U.S.C. § 1340(c). Interior must approve a submitted Exploration Plan unless it finds, after "consider[ing] available relevant environmental information," § 1346(d), that the proposed exploration

> "would probably cause serious harm or damage to life (including fish and other aquatic life), to property, to any mineral . . ., to the national security or defense, or to the marine, coastal, or human environment." § 1334(a)(2)(A)(i).

Where approval is warranted, Interior must act quickly—within "thirty days" of the company's submission of a proposed Plan. § 1340(c)(1).

Second, the company must obtain an exploratory well drilling permit. To do so, it must certify (under CZMA) that its Exploration Plan is consistent with the coastal zone management program of each affected State. 16 U.S.C. § 1456(c)(3). If a State objects, the certification fails, unless the Secretary of Commerce overrides the State's objection. If

Commerce rules against the State, then Interior may grant the permit. § 1456(c)(3)(A).

Third, where waste discharge into ocean waters is at issue, the company must obtain a National Pollutant Discharge Elimination System permit from the Environmental Protection Agency. 33 U.S.C. §§ 1311(a), 1342(a). It can obtain this permit only if affected States agree that its Exploration Plan is consistent with the state coastal zone management programs or (as just explained) the Secretary of Commerce overrides the state objections. 16 U.S.C. § 1456.

Fourth, if exploration is successful, the company must prepare, and obtain Interior approval for, a Development and Production Plan—a Plan that describes the proposed drilling and related environmental safeguards. 43 U.S.C. § 1351. Again, Interior's approval is conditioned upon certification that the Plan is consistent with state coastal zone management plans—a certification to which States can object, subject to Commerce Department override. § 1351(a)(3).

C.

The events at issue here concern the first two steps of the process just described—Interior's consideration of a submitted Exploration Plan and the companies' submission of the CZMA "consistency certification" necessary to obtain an exploratory well drilling permit. The relevant circumstances are the following:

1. In 1981, the companies and the Government entered into the lease contracts. The companies paid the Government $158 million in upfront cash "bonus" payments.

2. In 1989, the companies, Interior, and North Carolina entered into a memorandum of understanding. In that memorandum, the companies promised that they would submit an initial draft Exploration Plan to North Carolina before they submitted their final Exploration Plan to Interior. Interior promised that it would prepare an environmental report on the initial draft. It also agreed to suspend the companies' annual lease payments (about $250,000 per year) while the companies prepared the initial draft and while any state objections to the companies' CZMA consistency certifications were being worked out, with the life of each lease being extended accordingly.

3. In September 1989, the companies submitted their initial draft Exploration Plan to North Carolina. Ten months later, Interior issued the promised ("informal" pre-submission) environmental report, after a review which all parties concede was "extensive and intensive." App. 179 (deposition of David Courtland O'Neal, former Assistant Secretary of the Interior) (agreeing that the review was "the most extensive and intensive" ever "afforded an exploration well in the outer continental shelf (OCS) program"). Interior concluded that the proposed exploration would not "significantly affect" the marine environment or "the quality of the human environment." Id., at 138–140 (U.S. Dept. of Interior Minerals

Management Service, Environmental Assessment of Exploration Plan for Manteo Area Block 467 (Sept.1990)).

4. On August 20, 1990, the companies submitted both their final Exploration Plan and their CZMA "consistency certification" to Interior.

5. Just two days earlier, on August 18, 1990, a new law, the Outer Banks Protection Act (OBPA), § 6003, 104 Stat. 555, had come into effect. That law prohibited the Secretary of the Interior from approving any Exploration Plan or Development and Production Plan or to award any drilling permit until (a) a new OBPA-created Environmental Sciences Review Panel had reported to the Secretary, (b) the Secretary had certified to Congress that he had sufficient information to make these OCSLA-required approval decisions, and (c) Congress had been in session an additional 45 days, but (d) in no event could he issue an approval or permit for the next 13 months (until October 1991). § 6003(c)(3). OBPA also required the Secretary, in his certification, to explain and justify in detail any differences between his own certified conclusions and the new Panel's recommendations. § 6003(c)(3)(A)(ii)(II).

6. About five weeks later, and in light of the new statute, Interior wrote a letter to the Governor of North Carolina with a copy to petitioner Mobil. It said that the final submitted Exploration Plan "is deemed to be approvable in all respects." It added:

> "[W]e are required to approve an Exploration plan unless it is inconsistent with applicable law or because it would result in serious harm to the environment. Because we have found that Mobil's Plan fully complies with the law and will have only negligible effect on the environment, we are not authorized to disapprove the Plan or require its modification." App. to Pet. for Cert. in No. 99–253, at 194a (letter from Regional Director Bruce Weetman to the Honorable James G. Martin, Governor of North Carolina, dated Sept. 28, 1990).

But, it noted, the new law, the "Outer Banks Protection Act (OBPA) of 1990 . . . prohibits the approval of any Exploration Plan at this time." It concluded, "because we are currently prohibited from approving it, the Plan will remain on file until the requirements of the OBPA are met." In the meantime a "suspension has been granted to all leases offshore the State of North Carolina." Id. See also App. 129–131 (letter from Lawrence H. Ake, Minerals Management Service, to William C. Whittemore, Mobil Exploration & Producing U.S. Inc., dated Sept. 21, 1990 (notice of suspension of leases, citing 30 CFR § 250.10(b)(7) (1990) as the basis for the suspensions)).

About 18 months later, the Secretary of the Interior, after receiving the new Panel's report, certified to Congress that he had enough information to consider the companies' Exploration Plan. He added, however, that he would not consider the Plan until he received certain further studies that the new Panel had recommended.

7. In November 1990, North Carolina objected to the companies' CZMA consistency certification on the ground that Mobil had not provided sufficient information about possible environmental impact. A month later, the companies asked the Secretary of Commerce to override North Carolina's objection.

8. In 1994, the Secretary of Commerce rejected the companies' override request, relying in large part on the fact that the new Panel had found a lack of adequate information in respect to certain environmental issues.

9. In 1996, Congress repealed OBPA. § 109, 110 Stat. 1321–177.

D.

In October 1992, after all but the two last-mentioned events had taken place, petitioners joined a breach-of-contract lawsuit brought in the Court of Federal Claims. On motions for summary judgment, the court found that the United States had broken its contractual promise to follow OCSLA's provisions, in particular the provision requiring Interior to approve an Exploration Plan that satisfied OCSLA's requirements within 30 days of its submission to Interior. The United States thereby repudiated the contracts. And that repudiation entitled the companies to restitution of the up-front cash "bonus" payments it had made. Conoco Inc. v. United States, 35 Fed.Cl. 309 (1996).

A panel of the Court of Appeals for the Federal Circuit reversed, one judge dissenting. The panel held that the Government's refusal to consider the companies' final Exploration Plan was not the "operative cause" of any failure to carry out the contracts' terms because the State's objection to the companies' CZMA "consistency statement" would have prevented the companies from exploring regardless. 177 F.3d 1331 (C.A.Fed.1999).

We granted certiorari to review the Federal Circuit's decision.

II.

The record makes clear (1) that OCSLA required Interior to approve "within thirty days" a submitted Exploration Plan that satisfies OCSLA's requirements, (2) that Interior told Mobil the companies' submitted Plan met those requirements, (3) that Interior told Mobil it would not approve the companies' submitted Plan for at least 13 months, and likely longer, and (4) that Interior did not approve (or disapprove) the Plan, ever. The Government does not deny that the contracts, made "pursuant to" and "subject to" OCSLA, incorporated OCSLA provisions as promises. The Government further concedes, as it must, that relevant contract law entitles a contracting party to restitution if the other party "substantially" breached a contract or communicated its intent to do so. [citations omitted] Yet the Government denies that it must refund the companies' money.

This is because, in the Government's view, it did not breach the contracts or communicate its intent to do so; any breach was not "substantial"; and the companies waived their rights to restitution regardless. We shall consider each of these arguments in turn.

A.

The Government's "no breach" arguments depend upon the contract provisions that "subject" the contracts to various statutes and regulations. Those provisions state that the contracts are "subject to" (1) OCSLA, (2) "Sections 302 and 303 of the Department of Energy Organization Act," (3) "all regulations issued pursuant to such statutes and in existence upon the effective date of" the contracts, (4) "all regulations issued pursuant to such statutes in the future which provide for the prevention of waste and the conservation" of Outer Continental Shelf resources, and (5) "all other applicable statutes and regulations." App. to Pet. for Cert. in No. 99–253, at 175a. The Government says that these provisions incorporate into the contracts, not only the OCSLA provisions we have mentioned, but also certain other statutory provisions and regulations that, in the Government's view, granted Interior the legal authority to refuse to approve the submitted Exploration Plan, while suspending the leases instead.

First, the Government refers to 43 U.S.C. § 1334(a)(1)(A), an OCSLA provision that authorizes the Secretary to promulgate regulations providing for "the suspension . . . of any operation or activity . . . *at the request of a lessee,* in the national interest, to facilitate proper development of a lease." (Emphasis added.) This provision, as the emphasized terms show, requires "the request of a lessee," i.e., the companies. The Government does not explain how this requirement was satisfied here. Hence, the Government cannot rely upon the provision.

Second, the Government refers to 30 CFR § 250.110(b)(4) (1999), formerly codified at 30 CFR § 250.10(b)(4) (1997), a regulation stating that "[t]he Regional Supervisor may . . . direct . . . a suspension of any operation or activity . . . [when the] suspension is necessary for the implementation of the requirements of the National Environmental Policy Act or to conduct an environmental analysis." The Government says that this regulation permitted the Secretary of the Interior to suspend the companies' leases because that suspension was "necessary . . . to conduct an environmental analysis," namely, the analysis demanded by the new statute, OBPA.

The "environmental analysis" referred to, however, is an analysis the need for which was created by OBPA, a later enacted statute. The lease contracts say that they are subject to then-existing regulations and to certain future regulations, those issued pursuant to OCSLA and §§ 302 and 303 of the Department of Energy Organization Act. This explicit reference to future regulations makes it clear that the catchall provision that references "all other applicable . . . regulations," * * * must include only statutes and regulations already existing at the time of the contract, * * * a conclusion not questioned here by the Government. Hence, these provisions mean that the contracts are not subject to future regulations promulgated under other statutes, such as new statutes like OBPA. Without some such contractual provision limiting the Government's power to impose new and different requirements, the companies would have spent $158 million to buy next to nothing. In any event, the Court of Claims so interpreted the lease; the Federal Circuit did not disagree with that interpretation; nor does the Government here dispute it.

Instead, the Government points out that the regulation in question—the regulation authorizing a governmental suspension in order to conduct "an environmental analysis"—was not itself a *future* regulation. Rather, a similar regulation existed at the time the parties signed the contracts, 30 CFR § 250.12(a)(iv) (1981), and, in any event, it was promulgated under OCSLA, a statute exempted from the contracts' temporal restriction. But that fact, while true, is not sufficient to produce the incorporation of future statutory requirements, which is what the Government needs to prevail. If the pre-existing regulation's words, "an environmental analysis," were to apply to analyses mandated by *future* statutes, then they would make the companies subject to the same unknown future requirements that the contracts' specific temporal restrictions were intended to avoid. Consequently, whatever the regulation's words might mean in other contexts, we believe the contracts before us must be interpreted as excluding the words "environmental analysis" *insofar as* those words would incorporate the requirements of future statutes and future regulations excluded by the contracts' provisions. Hence, they would not incorporate into the contracts requirements imposed by a new statute such as OBPA.

Third, the Government refers to OCSLA, 43 U.S.C. § 1334(a)(1), which, after granting Interior rulemaking authority, says that Interior's

> "regulations ... shall include ... provisions ... for the suspension ... of any operation ... pursuant to any lease ... *if there is a threat of serious*, irreparable, or immediate *harm* or damage to life ..., to property, to any mineral deposits ..., or to the marine, coastal, or *human environment*." (Emphasis added.)

The Government points to the OBPA Conference Report, which says that any OBPA-caused delay is "related to ... environmental protection" and to the need "for the collection and analysis of crucial oceanographic, ecological, and socioeconomic data," to "prevent a public harm." H.R. Conf. Rep. No. 101–653, p. 163 (1990) [U.S. Code Cong. & Admin. News 1990, pp. 722, 842]; see also Brief for United States 32. At oral argument, the Government noted that the OBPA mentions "tourism" in North Carolina as a "major industry ... which is subject to potentially significant disruption by offshore oil or gas development." § 6003(b)(3). From this, the Government infers that the pre-existing OCSLA provision authorized the suspension in light of a "threat of ... serious harm" to a "human environment."

The fatal flaw in this argument, however, arises out of the Interior Department's own statement—a statement made when citing OBPA to explain its approval delay. Interior then said that the Exploration Plan "fully complies" with current legal requirements. And the OCSLA statutory provision quoted above was the most pertinent of those current requirements. * * * The Government did not deny the accuracy of Interior's statement, either in its brief filed here or its brief filed in the Court of Appeals. Insofar as the Government means to suggest that the new statute, OBPA, *changed* the relevant OCSLA standard (or that OBPA language and history somehow constitute findings Interior must incorporate by reference), it must mean that OBPA in effect created a *new* requirement. For the reasons set out * * *[in the above quoted OCSLA provision], however, any such new requirement would not be incorporated into the contracts.

Finally, we note that Interior itself, when imposing the lengthy approval delay, did not rely upon any of the regulations to which the Government now refers. Rather, it relied upon, and cited, a different regulation, 30 CFR § 250.110(b)(7) (1999), which gives Interior the power to suspend leases when "necessary to comply with judicial decrees prohibiting production or any other operation or activity." The Government concedes that no judicial decree was involved in this case and does not rely upon this regulation here.

We conclude, for these reasons, that the Government violated the contracts. Indeed, as Interior pointed out in its letter to North Carolina, the new statute, OBPA, *required* Interior to impose the contract-violating delay. See App. 129 ("The [OBPA] contains provisions that specifically prohibit the Minerals Management Service from approving any Exploration Plan, approving any Application for Permit to Drill, or permitting any drilling offshore the State of North Carolina until at least October 1, 1991"). It therefore made clear to Interior and to the companies that the United States had to violate the contracts' terms and would continue to do so.

Moreover, OBPA changed pre-existing contract-incorporated requirements in several ways. It delayed approval, not only of an Exploration Plan but also of Development and Production Plans; and it delayed the issuance of drilling permits as well. It created a new type of Interior Department environmental review that had not previously existed, conducted by the newly created Environmental Sciences Review Panel; and, by insisting that the Secretary explain in detail any differences between the Secretary's findings and those of the Panel, it created a kind of presumption in favor of the new Panel's findings.

The dissent argues that only the statements contained in the letter from Interior to the companies may constitute a repudiation because "the enactment of legislation is not typically conceived of as a 'statement' of anything to any one party in particular," and a repudiation requires a "statement by the obligor to the obligee indicating that the obligor will commit a breach." * * * (quoting Restatement § 250). But if legislation passed by Congress and signed by the President is not a "statement by the obligor," it is difficult to imagine what would constitute such a statement. In this case, it was the United States who was the "obligor" to the contract. See App. to Pet. for Cert. in No. 99–253, at 174a (lease, identifying "the United States of America" as the "Lessor"). Although the dissent points out that legislation is "addressed to the public at large," * * * that "public" includes those to whom the United States had contractual obligations. If the dissent means to invoke a special exception such as the "sovereign acts" doctrine, which treats certain laws as if they simply created conditions of impossibility, see Winstar, 518 U.S., at 891–899 (principal opinion of SOUTER, J.), 923–924 (SCALIA, J., concurring in judgment), it cannot do so here. The Court of Federal Claims rejected the application of that doctrine to this case, see 35 Fed.Cl., at 334–336, and the Government has not contested that determination here. Hence, under these circumstances, the fact that Interior's repudiation rested upon the enactment of a new statute makes no significant difference.

We do not say that the changes made by the statute were unjustified. We say only that they were changes of a kind that the contracts did not foresee. They were changes in those approval procedures and standards that the contracts had incorporated through cross-reference. The Government has not convinced us that Interior's actions were authorized by any other contractually cross-referenced provision. Hence, in communicating to the companies its intent to follow OBPA, the United States was communicating its intent to violate the contracts.

B.

The Government next argues that any violation of the contracts' terms was not significant; hence there was no "substantial" or "material" breach that could have amounted to a "repudiation." In particular, it says that OCSLA's 30–day approval period "does not function as the 'essence' of these agreements." Brief for United States 37. The Court of Claims concluded, however, that timely and fair consideration of a submitted Exploration Plan was a "necessary reciprocal obligation," indeed, that any "contrary interpretation would render the bargain illusory." 35 Fed.Cl., at 327. We agree.

We recognize that the lease contracts gave the companies more than rights to obtain approvals. They also gave the companies rights to explore for, and to develop, oil. But the need to obtain Government approvals so qualified the likely future enjoyment of the exploration and development rights that the contract, in practice, amounted primarily to an *opportunity* to try to obtain exploration and development rights in accordance with the procedures and under the standards specified in the cross-referenced statutes and regulations. Under these circumstances, if the companies did not at least buy a promise that the Government would not deviate significantly from those procedures and standards, then what did they buy? Cf. Id., at 324 (the companies bought exclusive rights to explore and develop oil *"if they met"* OCSLA requirements (emphasis added)).

The Government's modification of the contract-incorporated processes was not technical or insubstantial. It did not announce an (OBPA-required) approval delay of a few days or weeks, but of 13 months minimum, and likely much longer. The delay turned out to be at least four years. And lengthy delays matter, particularly where several successive agency approvals are at stake. Whether an applicant approaches Commerce with an Interior Department approval already in hand can make a difference (as can failure to have obtained that earlier approval). Moreover, as we have pointed out, OBPA changed the contract-referenced procedures in several other ways as well. * * *

The upshot is that, under the contracts, the incorporated procedures and standards amounted to a gateway to the companies' enjoyment of all other rights. To significantly narrow that gateway violated material conditions in the contracts. The breach was "substantia[l]," depriving the companies of the benefit of their bargain. Restatement § 243. And the Government's communication of its intent to commit that breach amounted to a repudiation of the contracts.

C.

The Government argues that the companies waived their rights to restitution. It does not deny that the United States repudiated the contracts *if* (as we have found) OBPA's changes amounted to a substantial breach. The Government does not claim that the United States retracted its repudiation. Cf. Id., § 256 (retraction will nullify the effects of repudiation if done before the other party either changes position in reliance on the retraction or communicates that it considers the repudiation to be final). It cannot claim that the companies waived their rights simply by urging performance. Id., § 257 (the injured party "does not change the effect of a repudiation by urging the repudiator to perform in spite of his repudiation"); see also 11 Williston § 1334, at 177–178. Nor has the Government convinced us that the companies' continued actions under the contracts amount to anything more than this urging of performance. [citations omitted] Consequently the Government's waiver claim must come down to a claim that the companies *received* at least partial performance. Indeed, acceptance of performance under a once-repudiated contract can constitute a waiver of the right to restitution that repudiation would otherwise create. Restatement § 373, Comment *a;* cf. Restatement of Restitution § 68, Comment b (1936).

The United States points to three events that, in its view, amount to continued performance of the contracts. But it does not persuade us. First, the oil companies submitted their Exploration Plan to Interior two days *after* OBPA became law. * * * The performance question, however, is not just about what the oil companies did or requested, but also about what they actually received from the Government. And, in respect to the Exploration Plan, the companies received nothing.

Second, the companies subsequently asked the Secretary of Commerce to overturn North Carolina's objection to the companies' CZMA consistency certification. And, although the Secretary's eventual response was negative, the companies did at least receive that reply. * * * The Secretary did not base his reply, however, upon application of the contracts' standards, but instead relied in large part on the findings of the new, OBPA-created, Environmental Sciences Review Panel. See App. 224, 227, n. 35, 232–233, 239, 244 (citing the Panel's report). Consequently, we cannot say that the companies received from Commerce the kind of consideration for which their contracts called.

Third, the oil companies received suspensions of their leases (suspending annual rents and extending lease terms) pending the OBPA-mandated approval delays. * * * However, a separate contract—the 1989 memorandum of understanding—entitled the companies to receive these suspensions. See App. to Brief for United States 2a (letter from Toni D. Hennike, Counsel, Mobil Exploration & Producing U.S. Inc., to Ralph Melancon, Regional Supervisor, U.S. Dept. of Interior Minerals Management Service, dated Feb. 21, 1995 (quoting the memorandum as a basis for the requested suspensions)). And the Government has provided no convincing reason why we should consider the suspensions to amount to significant performance of the lease contracts in question.

We conclude that the companies did not receive significant post-repudiation performance. We consequently find that they did not waive their right to restitution.

D.

Finally, the Government argues that repudiation could not have hurt the companies. Since the companies could not have met the CZMA consistency requirements, they could not have explored (or ultimately drilled) for oil in any event. Hence, OBPA caused them no damage. As the Government puts it, the companies have already received "such damages as were actually caused by the [Exploration Plan approval] delay," namely, none. Brief for United States 43–44; see also 177 F.3d, at 1340. This argument, however, misses the basic legal point. The oil companies do not seek damages for breach of contract. They seek restitution of their initial payments. Because the Government repudiated the lease contracts, the law entitles the companies to that restitution whether the contracts would, or would not, ultimately have produced a financial gain or led them to obtain a definite right to explore. * * * If a lottery operator fails to deliver a purchased ticket, the purchaser can get his money back— whether or not he eventually would have won the lottery. And if one party to a contract, whether oil company or ordinary citizen, advances the other party money, principles of restitution normally require the latter, upon repudiation, to refund that money. Restatement § 373.

III.

Contract law expresses no view about the wisdom of OBPA. We have examined only that statute's consistency with the promises that the earlier contracts contained. We find that the oil companies gave the

United States $158 million in return for a contractual promise to follow the terms of pre-existing statutes and regulations. The new statute prevented the Government from keeping that promise. The breach "substantially impair[ed] the value of the contract[s]." Id., § 243. And therefore the Government must give the companies their money back.

For these reasons, the judgment of the Federal Circuit is reversed. We remand the cases for further proceedings consistent with this opinion.

It is so ordered.

JUSTICE STEVENS, dissenting.

Since the 1953 passage of the Outer Continental Shelf Lands Act (OCSLA), 43 U.S.C. § 1331 *et seq.,* the United States Government has conducted more than a hundred lease sales of the type at stake today, and bidders have paid the United States more than $55 billion for the opportunity to develop the mineral resources made available under those leases. * * * The United States, as lessor, and petitioners, as lessees, clearly had a mutual interest in the successful exploration, development, and production of oil in the Manteo Unit pursuant to the leases executed in 1981. If production were achieved, the United States would benefit both from the substantial royalties it would receive and from the significant addition to the Nation's energy supply. Self-interest, as well as its duties under the leases, thus led the Government to expend substantial resources over the course of 19 years in the hope of seeing this project realized.

From the outset, however, it was apparent that the Outer Banks project might not succeed for a variety of reasons. Among those was the risk that the State of North Carolina would exercise its right to object to the completion of the project. That was a risk that the parties knowingly assumed. They did not, however, assume the risk that Congress would enact additional legislation that would delay the completion of what would obviously be a lengthy project in any event. I therefore agree with the Court that the Government did breach its contract with petitioners in failing to approve, within 30 days of its receipt, the plan of exploration petitioners submitted. As the Court describes, * * * the leases incorporate the provisions of the OCSLA into their terms, and the OCSLA, correspondingly, sets down this 30–day requirement in plain language. 43 U.S.C. § 1340(c).

I do not, however, believe that the appropriate remedy for the Government's breach is for petitioners to recover their full initial investment. When the entire relationship between the parties is considered, with particular reference to the impact of North Carolina's foreseeable exercise of its right to object to the project, it is clear that the remedy ordered by the Court is excessive. I would hold that petitioners are entitled at best to damages resulting from the delay caused by the Government's failure to approve the plan within the requisite time.

I.

To understand the nature of the breach, and the appropriate remedy for it, it is necessary to supplement the Court's chronological account.

From the time petitioners began discussing their interest in drilling an exploratory well 45 miles off the coast from Cape Hatteras in the fall of 1988, until (and even after) the enactment of the Outer Banks Protection Act (OBPA), § 6003, on August 18, 1990, their exploration proposal was fraught with problems. It was clear to petitioners as early as October 6, 1988 (and almost certainly before), that the State of North Carolina, whose approval petitioners knew they had to have under their lease terms in order to obtain the requisite permits from the Department of the Interior (DOI), was not going to go along readily. App. 61–63 (letter from North Carolina Governor James G. Martin to Ralph Ainger, Acting Regional Manager, Minerals Management Service (MMS) (a [former] division of the DOI)). As the Court explains, * * * without the State's approval pursuant to the Coastal Zone Management Act (CZMA), 16 U.S.C. § 1451 et seq., incorporated into the OCSLA by multiple references, no DOI licensing, permitting, or lessee exploration of any kind could ensue, 43 U.S.C. § 1340(c).

That is why petitioners pursued multiparty negotiations with the Federal Government and the State to help facilitate the eventual approval of their proposal. As part of these negotiations, petitioners entered into a memorandum of understanding with North Carolina and the Federal Government, and, according to the terms of that agreement, submitted a draft plan of exploration (POE) to DOI and to the State. App. 79–85. The Government also agreed to prepare draft and final environmental impact reports on petitioners' draft POE and to participate in public meetings and hearings regarding the draft POE and the Government's findings about its environmental impact. Id., at 81–82. Among other things, this agreement resulted in the Government's preparation in 1990 of a three-volume, 2,000–page special environmental report on the proposed project, released on June 1 of that year.

Although the State thereafter continued to express its dissatisfaction with the prospect of exploration and development, voicing its displeasure with the Government's draft environmental findings, Id., at 86–95, and rejecting petitioners' application for a separate required permit, Id., at 96–97, * * * petitioners nonetheless submitted a final POE to DOI on August 20, 1990, pursuant to the lease contract terms. This final plan, it must be noted, was submitted by petitioners two days *after* the enactment of the OBPA—the event petitioners claim amounted to (either) an anticipatory repudiation of the lease contracts, or a total breach, Brief for Petitioner in No. 99–244, p. 19 ("[I]n enacting the OBPA, the Government anticipatorily repudiated its obligations under the leases . . ."); Brief for Petitioner in No. 99–253, p. 21 ("The enactment of the OBPA placed the United States in total breach of the petitioners' leases").

Following petitioners' submission of the final POE, DOI then had a duty, under the terms of the OCSLA as incorporated into the lease contract, to approve that plan "within thirty days of its submission." 43 U.S.C. § 1340(c)(1). In other words, DOI had until September 19, 1990, to consider the submitted plan and, provided that the plan was complete and otherwise satisfied the OCSLA criteria, to issue its statement of approval. (Issuing its "approval," of course, is different from granting petitioners any "license or permit for any activity described in detail in an exploration plan and affecting any land use or water use" in a State's coastal zone, § 1340(c) (2); actual permission to proceed had to wait for the State's CZMA certification.) Despite this hard deadline, September 19 came and went without DOI's issuance of approval.

DOI's explanation came two days later, on September 21, 1990, in a letter to Mobil Oil from the MMS's Acting Regional Supervisor for Field Operations, Lawrence Ake. Without commenting on DOI's substantive assessment of the POE, the Ake letter stated that the OBPA "specifically prohibit[s]" the MMS from approving any POE "until at least October 1, 1991." App. 129. "Consequently," Mr. Ake explained, the MMS was suspending operation on the Manteo Unit leases "in accordance with 30 CFR § 250.10(b)(7)," Id., a regulation issued pursuant to the OCSLA and, of course, incorporated thereby into the parties' lease agreement. One week after that, on September 28, 1990, the MMS's Regional Director, Bruce Weetman, sent a letter to Governor Martin of North Carolina, elaborating on MMS's actions upon receipt of the August 20 POE. App. to Pet. for Cert. in No. 99–253, pp. 193a–195a. According to Weetman, the POE "was deemed complete on August 30, and transmitted to other Federal Agencies and the State of North Carolina on that date. Timely comments were received from the State of North Carolina and the U.S. Coast Guard. An analysis of the potential environmental effects associated with the Plan was conducted, an Environmental Assessment (EA) was prepared, and a Finding of No Significant Impact (FONSI) was made." Id., at 193a. Based on these steps taken by the MMS, it concluded that the POE was "approvable" but that the MMS was "currently prohibited from approving it." Thus, the letter concluded, the POE would "remain on file" pending the resolution of the OBPA requirements, and the lease suspensions would continue in force in the interim. Id., at 194a.

II.

In my judgment, the Government's failure to meet the required 30–day deadline on September 19, 1990, despite the fact that the POE was in a form that merited approval, was a breach of its contractual obligation to the contrary. * * * After this, its statement in the September 21 Ake letter that the OBPA prohibited approval until at least October 1991 must also be seen as a signal of its intent to remain in breach of the 30–day deadline requirement for the coming year. The question with which the Court is faced, however, is not whether the United States was in breach, but whether, in light of the Government's actions, petitioners are entitled to restitution rather than damages, the usual remedy for a breach of contract.

As the Court explains, * * * an injured party may seek restitution as an alternative remedy only "on a breach by non-performance that gives rise to a claim for damages for total breach or on a repudiation."

Restatement (Second) of Contracts § 373 (1979). Whether one describes the suspect action as "repudiation" (which itself is defined in terms of total breach, * * * or simply "total breach," the injured party may obtain restitution only if the action "so substantially impairs the value of the contract to the injured party ... that it is just in the circumstances to allow him to recover damages based on all his remaining rights to performance.") Restatement (Second) § 243. * * * In short, there is only repudiation if there is an action that would amount to a total breach, and there is only such a breach if the suspect action destroys the essential object of the contract. It is thus necessary to assess the significance or "materiality" of the Government's breach.

Beyond this, it is important to underscore as well that restitution is appropriate only when it is "just in the circumstances." Restatement (Second) § 243. This requires us to look not only to the circumstances of the breach itself, but to the equities of the situation as a whole. Finally, even if a defendant's actions do not satisfy the foregoing requirements, an injured party presumably still has available the standard contract remedy for breach—the *damages* petitioners suffered as a result.

III.

Given these requirements, I am not persuaded that the actions by the Government amounted either to a repudiation of the contracts altogether, or to a total breach by way of its neglect of an "essential" contractual provision.

I would, at the outset, reject the suggestion that there was a repudiation here, anticipatory or otherwise, for two reasons. First, and most basic, the Government continued to perform under the contractual terms as best it could even after the OBPA's passage. * * * Second, the breach-by-delay forecast in the Ake letter was not "of sufficient gravity that, if the breach actually occurred, it would of itself give the obligee a claim for damages for total breach." Restatement (Second) § 250, and Comment d * * *.

While acknowledging the OBPA's temporary moratorium on plan approvals, the Ake letter to petitioner Mobil states that the Government is imposing a lease *suspension*—rather than a cancellation or rescission—and even references an existing, OCSLA regulatory obligation pursuant to which it is attempting to act. The Weetman letter explains in detail the actions the MMS took in carefully considering petitioners' POE submission; it evaluated the plan for its compliance with the OCSLA's provisions, transmitted it to other agencies and the State for their consideration, took the comments of those entities into account, conducted the requisite analyses, and prepared the requisite findings—all subsequent to the OBPA's enactment. It cannot be doubted that the Government intended to continue performing the contract to the extent it thought legally permissible post-OBPA.

Indeed, petitioners' own conduct is inconsistent with the contention that the Government had, as of August 18, 1990, or indeed as of September 19, 1990, fully repudiated its obligations under the parties' contracts. As I have mentioned, it was *after* the enactment of the OBPA that petitioners submitted their final plan to the DOI—just as if they understood there still to be an existing set of contractual conditions to be fulfilled and expected to fulfill them. Petitioners, moreover, accepted the Government's proffered lease suspensions, and indeed, themselves subsequently requested that the suspensions remain in effect * * * under 30 CFR § 250.10(b)(6) (1990) * * *.

After the State of North Carolina filed its formal CZMA objections on November 19, 1990 (indicating that the State believed a contract still existed), petitioners promptly sought in December 1990—again under statutory terms incorporated into the contracts—to have the Secretary of Commerce override the objections, 43 U.S.C. § 1340(c)(1), to make it possible for the exploration permits to issue. In a response explainable solely on the basis that the Government still believed itself to be performing contractually obligatory terms, the Secretary of Commerce undertook to evaluate petitioners' request that the Secretary override the State's CZMA objections. This administrative review process has, I do not doubt, required a substantial expenditure of the time and resources of the Departments of Commerce and Interior, along with the 12 other administrative agencies whose comments the Secretary of Commerce solicited in evaluating the request to override and in issuing, on September 2, 1994, a lengthy "Decision and Findings" in which he declined to do so.

And petitioners were not finished with the leases yet. After petitioners received this adverse judgment from Commerce, they sought the additional lease suspensions described, see App. to Brief for United States 1a (letter from Toni Hennike, Counsel, Mobil Oil, to Ralph Melancon, Regional Supervisor, MMS, Feb. 21, 1995), insisting that "the time period to seek judicial review of the Secretary's decisions had not expired when the MMS terminated the [pre-existing] suspensions," and that "[s]ince the Secretary's decision is being challenged, it is not a final decision and will not be until it is upheld by a final nonappealable judgment issued from a court with competent jurisdiction," Id., at 2a. Indeed, petitioners have pending in the United States District Court for the District of Columbia at this very moment their appeal from the Secretary of Commerce's denial of petitioners' override request of North Carolina's CZMA objections. Mobil Oil Exploration & Producing Southeast, Inc. v. Daley, No. 95–93 SSH (filed Mar. 8, 2000).

Absent, then, any repudiation, we are left with the possibility that the nature of the Government's breach was so "essential" or "total" in the scope of the parties' contractual relationship as to justify the remedy of restitution. As above, I would reject the suggestion that the OBPA somehow acted *ex proprio vigore* to render a total breach of the parties' contracts. * * *. The OBPA was not passed as an amendment to statutes that the leases by their terms incorporated, nor did the OBPA state that its terms were to be considered incorporated into then existing leases; it was, rather, an action external to the contract, capable of affecting the parties' actions but not of itself changing the contract terms. The OBPA did, of course, impose a legal duty upon the Secretary of the Interior to take actions (and to refrain from taking actions) inconsistent with the Government's existing legal obligations to the lessees. Had the Secretary chosen, despite the OBPA, to issue the required approval, he presumably could have been hauled into court and compelled to rescind the approval in compliance with the OBPA requirement. * * * But that this possibility remained after the passage of the OBPA reinforces the conclusion that it was not until the Secretary actually took action inconsistent with his contractual obligations that the Government came into breach.

In rejecting the Government's argument that the breach was insufficiently material, the Court's reliance on the danger of rendering the parties' bargain illusory,* * * is simply misplaced. I do not contest that the Government was contractually obliged to give petitioners' POE prompt consideration and to approve the POE if, after that consideration, it satisfied existing OCSLA demands; nor would I suggest that petitioners did not receive as part of their bargain a promise that the Government would comply with the procedural mechanisms established at the time of contracting. But that is all quite beside the point; the question is not whether this approval requirement was part of the bargain but whether it was so "essential" to the bargain in the scope of this continuing contract as to constitute a total breach.

Whether the breach was sufficiently "substantial" or material to justify restitution depends on what impact, if any, the breach had at the time the breach occurred on the successful completion of the project. * * * In this action the answer must be close to none. Sixty days after the Government entered into breach—from September 19, 1990, to November 19, 1990—the State of North Carolina filed its formal objection to CZMA certification with the United States. App. 141–148. As the OCSLA makes clear, "The Secretary *shall not grant any license or permit for any activity described* in detail in an exploration plan and affecting any land use or water use in the coastal zone of a State with a coastal zone management program ... unless the State concurs or is conclusively presumed to concur with the consistency certification accompanying such plan ..., or the Secretary of Commerce makes the finding [overriding the State's objection]." 43 U.S.C. § 1340(c)(2) (emphasis added); see also § 1351(d). While this objection remained in effect, the project could not go forward unless the objection was set aside by the Secretary of Commerce. Thus, the Government's breach effectively delayed matters during the period between September 19, 1990, and November 19, 1990. Thereafter, implementation was contractually precluded by North Carolina.

This fact does not, of course, relieve the Government of liability for breach. It does, however, make it inappropriate to conclude that the Government's pre-November 19 actions in breach were sufficiently "material" to the successful completion of the parties' project to justify giving petitioners all of their money back. At the time of the Government's breach, petitioners had no reasonable expectation under the lease contract terms that the venture would come to fruition in the near future. Petitioners had known since 1988 that the State of North Carolina had substantial concerns about petitioners' proposed exploration; North Carolina had already officially objected to petitioners' NPDES submission—a required step itself dependent on the State's CZMA approval. App. 106–111. At the same time, the Federal Government's own substantial investments of time and resources, as well as its extensive good-faith efforts both before and after the OBPA was passed to preserve the arrangement, gave petitioners the reasonable expectation that the Government would continue trying to make the contract work. And indeed, both parties continued to behave consistently with that expectation.

While apparently recognizing that the substantiality of the Government's breach is a relevant question, * * * the Court spends almost no time at all concluding that the breach was substantial enough to award petitioners a $156 million refund * * *. In a single brief paragraph of explanation, the Court first posits that the Government "did not announce an ... approval delay of a few days or weeks, but of 13 months minimum and likely much longer." * * * The Court here is presumably referring to the Ake letter to Mobil written a few days after the expiration of the 30–day deadline. But the Government's "statement" to this effect could matter only in the context of evaluating an intended *repudiation;* because, as I have explained, that "announcement" cannot be seen as a repudiation of the contract, I do not see how the statement itself exacerbates the effect of the Government's breach. What matters in evaluating a breach, of course, is not what the Government said, but what the Government did. And what the Government did was, as I have explained, continue to perform in every other way possible—evaluating the August 20 POE; suspending the leases, including suspensions in response to petitioners' express requests (suspensions that continue in effect to this day); and responding over years to petitioners' appeal from the State's CZMA objection. * * *

The Court also asserts, without support, that "[w]hether an applicant approaches Commerce with an Interior Department approval already in hand can make a difference (as can failure to have obtained that earlier approval)." Id. Although the Court thereby implies that the Secretary of Commerce's handling of petitioners' CZMA override request was somehow tied to the DOI's failure to issue the required approval, there is record evidence that petitioners' CZMA appeals were not "suspended, impeded, or otherwise delayed by the enactment or implementation of the ... OBPA...." App. 187 (declaration of Margo E. Jackson, Conoco Inc. v. United States, No. 92–331–C (Fed.Cl., Apr. 6, 1994) (Commerce Department supervisor in charge of handling Mobil's appeals)). Whether or not the Secretary's decision was influenced by OBPA-required findings is, of course, a question of fact that, despite the Court's assertion, * * * none of the lower courts in this action decided. Regardless, there is certainly no *contractual* basis for the proposition that DOI's approval is a condition precedent or in any respect material to overcoming a state-filed CZMA objection. That objection, petitioners most certainly knew, was coming whether or not DOI approved the submitted POE.

In the end, the Court's central reason for finding the breach "not technical or insubstantial" is that "lengthy delays matter." * * * I certainly agree with that statement as a general principle. But in this action, that principle does not justify petitioners' request for restitution. On its face, petitioners' contention that time was "of the essence" in this bargain is difficult to accept; petitioners themselves waited seven years into the renewable 10–year lease term before even floating the Outer Banks proposal, and waited another two years after the OBPA was passed before filing this lawsuit. After then accepting a full 10 years of the Government's above-and-beyond-the-call performance, time is now suddenly of the essence? As with any venture of this magnitude, this undertaking was rife with possibilities for "lengthy delays," indeed "inordinate delays encountered by the lessee in obtaining required permits or consents, including administrative or judicial challenges or appeals," 30 CFR § 250.10(b)(6) (1990). The OBPA was not, to be sure, a cause for delay that petitioners may have anticipated in signing onto the lease. But the State's CZMA and NPDES objections, and the subsequent "inordinate delays" for appeals, certainly were. The Secretary's approval was indeed "a gateway to the companies' enjoyment of all other rights," but the critical word here is "a"; approval was only one gateway of many that the petitioners knew they had to get through in order to reap the benefit of the OCSLA leases, and even that gate was not closed completely, but only "narrow[ed]," * * *. Any long-term venture of this complexity and significance is bound to be a gamble. The fact that North Carolina was holding all the aces should not give petitioners the right now to play with an entirely new deck of cards.

IV.

The risk that North Carolina would frustrate performance of the leases executed in 1981 was foreseeable from the date the leases were signed. It seems clear to me that the State's objections, rather than the enactment of OBPA, is the primary explanation for petitioners' decision to take steps to avoid suffering the consequences of the bargain they made. As a result of the Court's action today, petitioners will enjoy a windfall reprieve that Congress foolishly provided them in its decision to pass legislation that, while validly responding to a political constituency that opposed the development of the Outer Banks, caused the Government to breach its own contract. Viewed in the context of the entire transaction, petitioners may well be entitled to a modest damages recovery for the *two months* of delay attributable to the Government's breach. But restitution is not a default remedy; it is available only when a court deems it, in all of the circumstances, just. A breach that itself caused at most a delay of two months in a protracted enterprise of this magnitude does not justify the $156 million draconian remedy that the Court delivers.

Accordingly, I respectfully dissent.

NOTE

Any person adversely affected by a decision of the DOI's Offshore Minerals Management Program (this does not include royalty decisions—see section 4 below) may appeal the decision to the IBLA, 30 C.F.R. part 290 subpart A. The DOI regulations further provide that IBLA will consider the appeal under procedures applicable to BLM land appeals in 43 C.F.R. part 4, subpart E (30 C.F.R. 290.2). See the discussion above at the end of Subsection A.2., which describes the Department's administrative review process.

(f) Application of Maritime Law[161]

Whenever oil and gas exploration or development occurs on navigable waters, including inland and offshore waters, the applicability of maritime (admiralty) law must be considered. Indeed, the general maritime law of the United States, if applicable, will preempt state law. The full body of maritime law consists of regulations, statutes, case law, and even international law. Although much of the body of maritime law has some impact on oil and gas activities on the offshore and inland navigable waters, a few maritime statutes and cases are especially important. While maritime law is also relevant to operations on inland navigable waters and on state coastal waters, the interplay of maritime law and OCSLA is not relevant to these waters. For further discussion of maritime law in the context of offshore oil and gas operations, see W. M. Daniel Wellons, Maritime Law Impacts on Offshore Development, 52 Inst. on Oil & Gas L. & Tax'n 8–1 (2001). The following discussion relates to offshore oil and gas operations specifically.

Federal courts are given express maritime jurisdiction under Article III, Section 2 of the United States Constitution. Under federal statutory law, 28 U.S.C. § 1333, federal district courts have original jurisdiction over maritime matters; however, maritime claimants may also pursue certain *in personam* actions in state courts under the so-called "Savings to Suitors" Clause. Id. For maritime law to apply, there must be some nexus between the dispute and maritime commerce, which, under 46 U.S.C. § 30101, includes claims for damage and loss that occur on land resulting from wrongful conduct on navigable water. In addition, certain maritime statutes can trigger federal-question jurisdiction under 28 U.S.C. § 1331, and diversity of citizenship can provide an additional basis for federal jurisdiction over maritime claims. In general, if maritime law does not apply through its own force or by the parties' express choice of law, then state law applies, either through its own force or as surrogate federal law under OCSLA.

The general test for maritime jurisdiction is whether the matter involves or relates to the use and operation of a "vessel" in navigation. See Stewart v. Dutra Const. Co., 543 U.S. 481, 487 (2005) (defining a

---

161. The editors wish to acknowledge the assistance of William W. Pugh and John G Almy, Attorneys, Liskow & Lewis, Houston, Texas, for reviewing this section.

"vessel"). Generally, a vessel is any floating structure having a significant transportation use. In the oil and gas context, marine seismic ships, drilling barges, jack-up drilling rigs,[162] and semi-submersible rigs[163] are vessels; however, fixed platforms[164] and other more permanent production facilities (such as tension-leg platforms[165] and spars[166]) are not. For a list of various factors used to determine whether a facility is a "vessel," see Burchett v. Cargill, Inc., 48 F.3d 173 (5th Cir.1995). See generally F. Maraist, Admiralty in a Nutshell 14–25 (3d ed. 1996) [hereinafter Maraist]. Thus, if a drilling contractor agrees to furnish a drilling barge, jack-up rig, or semi-submersible rig, the drilling contract will be considered a maritime contract, subject to maritime law; however, if the use of a vessel is merely incidental to the work performed, the contract will be considered non-maritime and will ordinarily be governed directly by state law (or by state law adopted as surrogate federal law under OCSLA). Whether the use of a vessel is "merely incidental" to the work performed is a difficult question. Cf., Thurmond v. Delta Well Surveyors, 836 F.2d 952 (5th Cir.1988) (holding that a work order relating to work on a fixed platform pursuant to a contract to furnish a vessel, crew, and wireline services was primarily non-maritime in nature and thus governed by state law) and Texaco Exploration and Production, Inc. v. AmClyde Engineered Products Co., Inc., 448 F.3d 760 (5th Cir. 2006) (holding that, where claims arose

162. Offshore Co. v. Robison, 266 F.2d 769 (5th Cir.1959). A jack-up rig is a mobile floating drilling rig with adjustable legs that can be placed on the ocean floor to hold the rig in place, and allow the rig to be jacked up out of the water, during drilling operations.

163. A semi-submersible rig is a mobile offshore drilling rig that has large underwater compartments in the hull(s) that can be flooded with ballast to stabilize the rig for drilling operations.

164. A fixed platform is a drilling and production structure built on the seabed and extending above the surface. Because fixed platforms are not mobile, they are classified as artificial islands, not vessels. Moreover, a contract to build a fixed platform offshore is governed by state law, even though performance of the contract contemplates the hiring of vessels and seamen. Laredo Offshore Constructors, Inc. v. Hunt Oil Co., 754 F.2d 1223, 1230–31 (5th Cir.1985).

165. Overstreet v. Transocean Offshore, Inc., 1998 WL 709809 (E.D.La.1998). A tension leg platform or tension leg well platform is a floating platform used in deep waters that is held in place by steel tendons attached to the platform and to a foundation on the seabed. The tendons are under tension to pull the hull down into the water to minimize motion. Norman Hyne, Dictionary of Petroleum Exploration & Drilling Production, p. 519 (PennWell 1991). See also McKay v. Offshore Specialty Fabricators, Inc., 1997 WL 289365 (E.D.La.1997). In a tax context, a tension leg platform has also been held to be a fixed platform. Gulf Oil Corporation v. Commissioner, 87 T.C. 324 (1986). But see Jordan v. Shell Offshore, Inc., 2007 WL 128313 (S.D.Tex. 2007) (slip copy) (stating, contrary to existing precedent, that a tension leg platform is a vessel).

166. Fields v. Pool Offshore, Inc., 182 F.3d 353 (5th Cir.1999) (holding that a spar designed and used primarily as a stationary work platform is not a vessel). A spar is a floating structure that is tensioned by and attached to the seabed by cables so that it remains relatively stationary, much like a buoy. Like the tension leg platform, a spar does not have a significant transportation function once it has been placed in position offshore. When this edition went to press, no court had considered whether a floating production, storage, and off-loading (FPSO) facility is a "vessel." Many FPSOs are converted oil tankers and many are flagged as vessels; however, they are used much as a spar is used. The difference is they can generally navigate from place-to-place under their own power, and they can also remain in fixed locations under their own power, often through the use of computer-controlled propellers at each corner of the facility (vessel). At least theoretically, FPSOs can be used in multiple locations, although their actual use is generally limited to one location for the productive life of a reservoir. FPSOs are also attached to the seabed by cable and production lines.

from an offshore crane barge dropping a platform section into the water during installation, any connection to maritime law was eclipsed by the work's connection to the development of the Outer Continental Shelf). In general, if the objective of the contract is to perform services on the vessel that contribute to the mission of the vessel, then the contract is maritime in nature. But see Hoda v. Rowan Companies, Inc., 419 F.3d 379, 381 (5th Cir. 2005) (stating that "[t]he maritime or non-maritime status of the contract ultimately depends on its 'nature and character,' *not* on its place of execution or performance"). The following case illustrates both the importance and difficulty of determining the maritime or non-maritime nature of a contract and contract work.

DAVIS & SONS, INC. v. GULF OIL CORPORATION

919 F.2d 313 (5th Cir.La.1990).

ALVIN B. RUBIN, CIRCUIT JUDGE:

Whether a contract is or is not maritime in nature is a quotidian issue whose resolution is governed by no broad rubric discernible from the numerous decided cases. Once again, therefore, we examine a contract for services associated with offshore oil and gas production to determine whether its validity and interpretation are governed by maritime or state law. The parties had entered into what they called a "blanket" contract, the terms of which were to be incorporated into agreements for actual services they contemplated. These later agreements were periodic work orders calling for the performance of specific services. The district court held that since the principal obligation of the blanket contract was non-maritime in nature, an indemnity provision contained in it was subject to state law, which rendered the provision invalid. Because we find that the blanket contract was inchoate, was amended and supplemented by the subsequent work orders, and the work order in question required the performance of a maritime obligation, we hold that maritime law applies. We, therefore, reverse and remand.

I.

In 1981, Davis & Sons, Inc. entered into Master Service Agreement No. 05–114 with Gulf Corporation to provide "labor and general contracting services for the Eastern offshore area onshore and offshore facilities." The document did not further specify any work to be performed by Davis for Gulf. This blanket contract included an indemnity clause requiring Davis to "protect, indemnify and save Gulf harmless from and against all claims, demands and causes of actions, suits or other litigation * * * " that might arise out of the contractual relationship.

Pursuant to the terms of this document, and as contemplated by the parties, Gulf from time to time issued work orders directing Davis to provide labor to perform maintenance work in Black Bay Field, an area in Plaquemines Parish, Louisiana, leased by Gulf, in which Gulf operated approximately 150 wells producing natural gas and crude oil. The Black

Bay Field is located primarily beneath open water, consisting of lakes, bays, and canals with a limited amount of marshland and virtually no firm ground. After a well has been completed, the wellhead is surrounded by a work platform or grating approximately seven feet in diameter. Maintenance of the wellheads, flow lines, storage tank batteries, and related production equipment is performed primarily through the use of self-propelled work barges each of which is equipped with spuds to anchor the barge in a given work location.

Pursuant to work orders issued weekly, Davis supplied labor for two barge crews and two individual pumpers to work in Black Bay Field during 1981 and 1982. The tasks performed by the contract labor included acting as crew for the vessels. Mark P. Brenaman, a Davis employee, was assigned to work as a "pusher" aboard Barge No. 11171 in Black Bay Field, beginning in January 1981. The crew of Barge 11171 were land-based; the barge had neither sleeping quarters nor bathroom facilities. The barge had spuds but no jack-up facilities, so any work on the barge was done either while it was afloat or spudded down adjacent to a platform.

Brenaman's primary duty was to supervise the Davis employees. Barge 11171 went on daily routine maintenance runs wherever the services of the Davis employees were needed within Black Bay Field to make repairs, lay pipe, and work on flow lines; it also transported chemicals and supplies. Most of the service work was performed on the barge itself since the wellheads did not provide adequate work space. The Davis employees were also responsible for maintenance of the barge, which included: painting the quarters, crane and other equipment; inspecting and repairing the engines and cranes; and operating and navigating the barge. Although Brenaman had no captain's license, he supervised all of these functions.

On July 2, 1982, while assigned to work on Barge 11171, Brenaman drowned. The precise circumstances of his death are unknown. At the time of his death, Davis's employees were assigned to Barge 11171 pursuant to service order 728113, covering the period from June 28–July 4, 1982. The order provided only: "Vendor: Davis; Service Description: Labor Gang 11171."

On the day of the accident, Barge 11171 was spudded down adjacent to a fixed platform. The crew were all on the barge, building a walkway to be placed on a tank battery, filling a pollution tank with water, and checking the tank for leaks. Brenaman was both supervising their work and fitting paneling for an office being built on the barge. He left this area and several hours later was discovered to have drowned in nearby waters.

Brenaman's representatives sued Davis and Gulf. After that suit had been settled, Davis filed suit for a declaratory judgment that Louisiana law governs the interpretation of the contractual indemnity provision in the blanket contract and that the Louisiana Oilfield Indemnity Act[1] voids that provision. Gulf counterclaimed that maritime law applies to the interpretation of the indemnity clause and that it is therefore valid. Gulf and Davis brought cross-motions for summary judgment. The district court granted Davis's motion and denied Gulf's motion, holding that this court's analysis in Thurmond v. Delta Well Surveyors[2] required a finding that the blanket contract was non-maritime in nature.

II.

The attempt to determine whether a contract, particularly one linked to offshore gas and oil production, is governed by state or maritime law has led to much confusion. For those looking for a bright line delineating the boundary between maritime and non-maritime contracts, our previous cases offer little assistance; some assert that "oil and gas drilling on navigable waters aboard a vessel is recognized to be maritime commerce,"[3] or hold that a turnkey contract to drill an offshore well[4] or a contract to furnish a casing crew to a submersible drilling barge[5] are maritime in nature, while others state that there is nothing inherently maritime about the activities involved in offshore oil production.[6] These apparent inconsistencies, however, can be traced to the highly fact-specific nature of the inquiry necessary to determine whether a contract is governed by maritime law. While we can discern no single method of analysis in the many cases addressing this subject, they do appear to be based on a fairly consistent underlying approach, which we now articulate.

* * *

A contract may either contain both maritime and non-maritime obligations or, as in the Gulf–Davis blanket agreement, contemplate future detailed contracts having different characteristics. If separable maritime obligations are imposed by the supplementary contracts, or work orders, these are "maritime obligations [that] can be separately enforced [in admiralty] without prejudice to the rest,"[7] hence subject to maritime law.[8] If, therefore, an injury occurs in the performance of a separable maritime obligation even though it is provided for by an initial blanket

1. La.Rev.Stat.Ann. § 9:2780 (West 1990).

2. 836 F.2d 952 (5th Cir.1988).

3. Theriot v. Bay Drilling Corp., 783 F.2d 527, 538–39 (5th Cir.1986).

4. Lewis v. Glendel Drilling Co., 898 F.2d 1083 (5th Cir.1990).

5. Corbitt v. Diamond M. Drilling Co., 654 F.2d 329 (5th Cir.1981); see Transcontinental Gas Pipe Line Corp. v. Mobile Drilling Barge, 424 F.2d 684 (5th Cir.1970); Halliburton Co. v. Norton Drilling Co., 302 F.2d 431 (5th Cir.1962).

6. Houston Oil & Minerals Corp. v. American Int'l Tool Co., 827 F.2d 1049 (5th Cir.1987); Sohyde Drilling & Marine Co. v. Coastal States Gas Producing Co., 644 F.2d 1132 (5th Cir.1981); see Herb's Welding, Inc. v. Gray, 470 U.S. 414 (1985).

7. Compagnie Francaise De Navigation A Vapeur v. Bonnasse, 19 F.2d 777, 779 (2d Cir.1927), quoted in Hale v. Co–Mar Offshore Corp., 588 F.Supp. 1212, 1217 (W.D.La.1984).

8. Hale, 588 F.Supp. at 1215; Home Ins. Co. v. Garber Industries, Inc., 588 F.Supp. 1218 (W.D.La.1984); Heath v. Superior Oil Co., 617 F.Supp. 33 (W.D.La.1985).

contract that is principally non-maritime, the complete contract is nevertheless subject to maritime law.[9]

Whether the blanket agreement and work orders, read together, do or do not constitute a maritime contract depends, as does the characterization of any other contract, on the "nature and character of the contract,"[10] rather than on its place of execution or performance. "A contract relating to a ship in its use as such, or to commerce or navigation on navigable waters, or to transportation by sea or to maritime employment is subject to maritime law."[11] What constitutes maritime character is not determinable by rubric. The Supreme Court has resorted to the observation that a contract is maritime if it has a "genuinely salty flavor."[12] As Gilmore and Black interpret the jurisprudence, "[t]he resultant conception of our admiralty jurisdiction has been one of fairly complete coverage of the primary operational and service concerns of the shipping industry, with a few anomalous exceptions."[13]

Determination of the nature of a contract depends in part on historical treatment in the jurisprudence and in part on a fact-specific inquiry. We consider six factors in characterizing the contract: 1) what does the specific work order in effect at the time of injury provide? 2) what work did the crew assigned under the work order actually do? 3) was the crew assigned to work aboard a vessel in navigable waters; 4) to what extent did the work being done relate to the mission of that vessel? 5) what was the principal work of the injured worker? and 6) what work was the injured worker actually doing at the time of injury?

III.

By its own terms, the blanket agreement between Gulf and Davis provides for services for "onshore and offshore facilities." Davis asserts that approximately 70% of the labor provided under this contract was land-based, the contract's principal obligation was demonstrably non-maritime, and the holding of *Thurmond v. Delta Well Surveyors*[14] therefore mandates the application of state law. Gulf contests both the evidentiary and legal basis of this assertion. Even if we assume Davis's factual assessment to be correct, however, this does not foreclose the application of maritime law to the work orders applicable to some or all of the 30% vessel-based services as maritime obligations rendered pursuant to the final contract for these services. The choice of state law in *Thurmond* did not rest solely on the non-maritime nature of the principal obligation of the preliminary blanket agreement to provide wireline services for off-

---

9. Lefler v. Atlantic Richfield Co., 785 F.2d 1341 (5th Cir.1986); Hale, 588 F.Supp. at 1215.

10. North Pacific S.S. Co. v. Hall Bros. Marine Ry. & Shipbuilding Co., 249 U.S. 119, 125 (1919); Kossick v. United Fruit Co., 365 U.S. 731 (1961).

11. E. Jhirad, A. Sann, B. Chase, & M. Chynsky, Benedict on Admiralty, § 182 (1988).

12. Kossick, 365 U.S. at 742.

13. G. Gilmore & C. Black, The Law of Admiralty 22 (2d ed. 1975).

14. 836 F.2d 952 (5th Cir.1988).

shore wells, but also on the fact that the suit arose out of the performance of that non-maritime obligation.[15]

On the day of his death, Brenaman and his crew were working pursuant to weekly service order 728113, which specifically assigned them to Barge 11171. This service order contained no further details of their assigned work. The workers' time sheets from June 28—July 4, however, indicate that during that week Brenaman's crew actually repaired leaks on wells and tanks, repaired and replaced flowlines, transported materials, and built a walkway. To fulfill these tasks, the crew of Barge 11171 travelled aboard the barge from one job site to another within Black Bay Field and performed their work predominantly aboard the barge. The particular nature of the terrain and production equipment involved required a special purpose vessel like Barge 11171 that could function as a mobile work platform. Its transportation function was more than "merely incidental" to its primary purpose of serving as a work platform.[16] The mission of this vessel, therefore, was to serve as a mobile maintenance unit in Black Bay Field, and "in the light of the function or mission of the special structure to which they were attached, [its crew] served in a capacity that contributed to the accomplishment of its mission in the same way that a surgeon serves as a member of the crew of a floating hospital."[17] The work done by the crew of Barge 11171 was inextricably intertwined with maritime activities since it required the use of a vessel and its crew.

Brenaman's principal work was to supervise Davis's employees in the accomplishment of the vessel's mission. He had been assigned to Barge 11171 for more than eighteen months and performed a substantial part of his work on the barge itself. He was, in effect, a Jones Act seaman with regard to Barge 11171.[18] At the time of his death, he was engaged in his principal activity of overseeing Davis's employees who in effect constituted the crew of the vessel, as well as temporarily helping to build an office on board.

We hold, therefore, that the entire agreement between Davis and Gulf to provide labor for Barge 11171 for the period June 28 to July 4, 1982, constitutes a maritime contract and that the validity of the indemnity provision of the blanket contract between Davis and Gulf must be assessed according to maritime law. We REVERSE the district court's grant of summary judgment to Davis and its denial of summary judgment to Gulf, and REMAND for further action consistent with this opinion.

NOTES

1. As the court's discussion in *Davis* illustrates, offshore oil and gas contracts that have a "genuine salty flavor" are governed by maritime

15. Id. at 955.

16. Sharp v. Johnson Bros. Corp., 917 F.2d 885 (5th Cir.1990); Brunet v. Boh Bros. Construction, 715 F.2d 196, 198 (5th Cir.1983).

17. Offshore Co. v. Robison, 266 F.2d 769, 776 (5th Cir.1959).

18. Id. Barrett v. Chevron, U.S.A., Inc., 781 F.2d 1067 (5th Cir.1986).

(admiralty) law. Unfortunately, the large number of cases addressing this salty-flavor issue indicates that salt is not as easily detected in law as in water. See, e.g., Campbell v. Sonat Offshore Drilling, Inc., 27 F.3d 185 (5th Cir.1994) and Demette v. Falcon Drilling Company, 280 F.3d 492 (5th Cir.2002). The frustration of judges is evident in the following opening sentence of an opinion written by Judge John R. Brown for the Fifth Circuit Court of Appeals: "Once more we embark on a voyage through the familiar marshland area of the law set aside for classifying the oil and gas exploration services as wet or dry." Domingue v. Ocean Drilling & Exploration Co., 923 F.2d 393 (5th Cir.1991) (dubiously holding that a contract to perform wireline services on a jack-up drilling rig located 30 miles off the coast of Louisiana was non-maritime and thus governed by Louisiana law, even though a jack-up drilling rig is a "vessel" governed by maritime law). In Smith v. Penrod Drilling Corp., 960 F.2d 456, 460 (5th Cir.1992), the court commented: "Application of [the Davis] * * * factors to the instant case is unenlightening, as each factor simply turns on the question of whether workover operations are maritime." The Court noted:

> The following summary of caselaw demonstrates the lack of a consistent approach for dealing with these cases. A drilling contract is maritime. Lewis, 898 F.2d at 1086; Theriot v. Bay Drilling Corp., 783 F.2d 527 (5th Cir.1986). A contract for the construction of drilling platforms is non-maritime. Laredo Offshore, 754 F.2d at 1232. A contract for the construction of gathering lines is non-maritime. Union Texas Petroleum, 895 F.2d at 1050. A contract for providing wireline services to drilling platforms is non-maritime. Domingue, 923 F.2d at 398; Thurmond, 836 F.2d at 955. A contract for maintenance of oil wells using a non-jackup barge is maritime. Davis, 919 F.2d at 317. A drilling and workover contract is maritime. Corbitt, 654 F.2d at 332.

960 F.2d at 461, n. 3. Nevertheless, this classification issue is critical in many contract and tort cases dealing with offshore oil and gas operations, because the ultimate outcome often turns on whether the case is governed by state or maritime law. Detailed discussion of this issue is a principal focus of admiralty law courses and is, therefore, beyond the scope of a basic oil and gas law text. Thus, we offer only a few general observations. For a more thorough discussion, see Maraist, 14–44, 136–151, 171–393, 304–323 (3d ed. 1996).

2. In addition to classifying the contract as maritime or non-maritime, courts must determine the governing law in light of the situs of the events giving rise to the dispute, whether in tort or contract. Generally, if the contract is not maritime, state law governs of its own force within a state's territorial waters. Moreover, the law of the adjacent state[167] may govern beyond its territorial waters as surrogate federal law under OCSLA: (1) if the controversy arises on a situs covered by OCSLA, such as the subsoil, seabed or artificial structures attached thereto (e.g., fixed platforms), 43 U.S.C. § 1333(a)(1) and (2)(A); (2) if federal law does not apply of its own force; and (3) if state law is not inconsistent with federal law. Id. § 1333(a)(2)(A). Union

---

167. Determining the "adjacent state" is itself an important and potentially thorny issue. See, e.g., Snyder Oil Corp. v. Samedan Oil Corp., 208 F.3d 521 (5th Cir.2000), and Reeves v. B & S Welding, Inc., 897 F.2d 178 (5th Cir.1990). Although OCSLA gives the President authority to make this determination, 43 U.S.C. § 1333(2)(A), this determination has never been made.

Texas Petroleum Corp. v. PLT Engineering, Inc., 895 F.2d 1043, 1047 (5th Cir.1990). Generally, if federal (e.g., maritime) law applies on its own, state law will not apply except in some contracts cases where the parties have made an express choice of state law having a substantial relationship to the parties. Stoot v. Fluor Drilling Services, Inc., 851 F.2d 1514 (5th Cir.1988). If adjacent state law applies as surrogate law under OCSLA, that state's law will govern even if the parties have attempted to contract out of OCSLA or that state's law. Matte v. Zapata Offshore Co., 784 F.2d 628 (5th Cir.1986). A host of maritime doctrines and statutes govern maritime matters. The following notes highlight those doctrines and statutes that are most relevant to offshore oil and gas operations, and discuss also the potential application of state law.

3. When a worker is injured in connection with an offshore oil operation, the worker's remedies will depend in part on whether the injured worker is classified as a seaman, maritime worker, or regular (non-seaman, non-maritime) worker. If the employee is a regular worker, the employer would ordinarily be immune from suit under applicable state workers' compensation acts, but the injured employee will generally be able to sue third parties for negligence or other wrongdoing. While these third parties may have the benefit of contractual indemnities from the employee's employer, they might not be able to enforce their contractual indemnity rights against the employer due to state oilfield anti-indemnity statutes. See discussion in Chapter 6, § E.

On the other hand, if the employee is a "seaman," the Jones Act allows the employee to sue his employer for injuries resulting from negligence. 46 U.S.C. app. § 688. Together with the additional rights to sue for maintenance and cure[168] and for unseaworthiness[169] under general maritime law, injured seamen have far greater recovery rights than employees who are limited to workers compensation benefits. Whether the injured employee is a seaman is of critical importance, but this issue can be difficult to answer. See, e.g., Theriot v. Bay Drilling Corp., 783 F.2d 527, 538–39 (5th Cir.1986). In general, to be classified as a seaman, one must be more or less permanently assigned to a vessel or group of identifiable vessels under common control and perform a job that contributes to the mission and function of the vessel. Harbor Tug and Barge Co. v. Papai, 520 U.S. 548 (1997) and Offshore Co. v. Robison, 266 F.2d 769, 776 (5th Cir.1959). Thus, a member of the crew of a jack-up or semi-submersible drilling rig is a seaman, even though an employee performing somewhat similar work on a fixed platform is not.

If the injured employee is not a seaman, he may nevertheless be a maritime worker (longshoreman or harbor worker). A maritime worker's rights vis-à-vis his employer are governed by the Longshore and Harbor Workers' Compensation Act, 33 U.S.C. §§ 901–950 ("LHWCA"), a form of federal workers' compensation coverage that is automatically extended to offshore platform employees by OSCLA. The LHWCA permits a maritime worker to sue his employer for negligence if the employer is the owner or charterer of a vessel and the injury is caused by vessel-based negligence. 33

---

168. Maintenance and cure refers to the duty of a vessel and vessel owner to care for a seaman who is injured or falls ill while in service to the vessel.

169. A vessel and its owner are strictly liable for unseaworthiness. Unseaworthiness includes a vessel that fails to withstand the perils of an ordinary voyage, a vessel that could not reasonably be expected to make a voyage, and a vessel manned with an incompetent crew.

U.S.C. § 905(b). Vessel-based negligence generally refers to negligence of the vessel owner or charterer and the captain and crew as opposed to an unseaworthy condition of the vessel that was not created by or known by the vessel crew. The LHWCA also preserves the injured maritime worker's rights against third parties.

The Outer Continental Shelf Lands Act ("OCSLA") provides longshoremen with worker's compensation coverage under the LHWCA. 43 U.S.C. 1333(b). Until recently, the Fifth Circuit held that, to be eligible for benefits under § 1333(b), the injury must occur on the OCS. *See, Mills v. Director, Office of Workers' Compensation Programs,* 877 F.2d 356 (5th Cir. 1989). In January, 2012, the Supreme Court addressed the split between the 3rd, 5th, and 9th Circuits when it decided *Pacific Operators Offshore, LLP v. Valladolid,* ___ U.S. ___, 132 S.Ct. 680 (2012). In *Valladolid,* the Court determined that the 5th Circuit's situs test was too restrictive and not supported by the text of the statute and that the 3rd Circuit's "but for" operations on the OCS was too broad. The court adopted the test of the 9th Circuit, which requires the claimant to show a "substantial nexus" between the injury and the employer's extractive operations on the OCS.

In case of death caused by tort on the high seas beyond a marine league from shore, a wrongful death claim arises against those responsible under the Death on the High Seas Act (DOHSA), 46 U.S.C. §§ 761–768. Professor Maraist notes that a DOHSA action may arise even though the accident does not have a maritime flavor. Maraist, 37.

Catastrophic losses can occur when cargo on board a vessel is lost or where a vessel collides with another vessel, offshore structure, or harbor facility. Where the potential claims exceed the value of the vessel and the cargo, the vessel owner (or demise charterer) may limit its liability to the value of the vessel and cargo after the casualty. Limitation of Vessel Owner's Liability Act, 46 U.S.C. App. § 181–195. Depending on the language of the insurance policy, this limitation of liability may also extend to the vessel owner's insurers. Crown Zellerbach Corp. v. Ingram Indus., Inc., 783 F.2d 1296 (5th Cir. La. 1986). Limitation of liability, however, is not available unless the casualty results from a cause that is not within the privity or knowledge of the vessel owner or demise charterer. This limitation of liability is generally intended to apply to transient conditions or operational errors as opposed to problems of which the vessel owner was or should have been aware. Proving the value of both the culpable vessel and the damaged property, particularly unique and aging offshore oil installations, and then determining the appropriate measure of damages, can also be difficult tasks.

Yet another limitation of liability in maritime law is court made. In Robins Dry Dock & Repair Co. v. Flint, 275 U.S. 303 (1927), Justice Holmes held that a plaintiff may not recover for economic loss resulting from damage to property in which plaintiff had no proprietary interest. Thus, an offshore operator who transported production from its platform through a third-party pipeline was barred from recovering damages for lost profits from a vessel that disabled the pipeline with its anchor. Texas E. Transmission Corp. v. McMoran Offshore Exploration, 877 F.2d 1214 (5th Cir. La. 1989).

4. Despite the aforementioned limitations, however, the oil and gas industry is strictly liable for the consequences of oil spills. Major focuses of the Federal Oil Pollution Act of 1990 ("OPA") are the prevention of and reaction to oil spills resulting from offshore oil operations and the shipping of oil. Pub. L. No. 101–380, 104 Stat. 486 (1990). The OPA, which is further discussed in Chapter 5, overrides a vessel owner's limited liability under the Limitation of Vessel Owners Liability Act and the limitations of *Robins Dry Dock*. The OPA limits monetary damages to $75 million for losses to private parties, such as property damage or lost profits from businesses affected by the spill, but the culpable parties are still liable for all cleanup costs. In addition, the OPA liability limits do not apply if the responsible party is grossly negligent, and the Act does not preempt actions filed under state law. Following the 2010 Deepwater Horizon oil spill in the Gulf of Mexico, several bills were introduced which would substantially raise the $75 million cap.

5. A host of offshore oil and gas workers qualify as maritime workers[170] or seamen; however, oil and gas workers employed on a fixed platform in state territorial waters have often been classified as regular workers protected only by state workers' compensation laws;[171] however, the *Valladolid* decision may affect future cases. Regardless of status, an employee who is injured on the job may generally sue any third party responsible for the injury. In anticipation of such tort claims, the parties to offshore oil and gas contracts commonly agree to indemnify each other against negligence and other claims made by their respective employees. Clearly expressed indemnity obligations are generally valid under maritime law[172] but may be invalid under the laws of certain states.[173] Hence, whether maritime law governs the contract and events giving rise to the dispute, or if not, which state's law governs, is often critical to the enforceability of the indemnity provisions.

In *Hollier v. Union Texas Petroleum Corp.*, 765 F.Supp. 330 (W.D.La. 1991), reversed 972 F.2d 662 (5th Cir.1992), an employee of a service contractor attempted to transfer from a vessel to a fixed platform located on the outer continental shelf off the coast of Louisiana. The employee slipped between the vessel and the platform, was crushed, and drowned. The service contract required the contractor to perform certain tests on a well that had been drilled from a fixed platform; however, the contractor's employees lived, ate, and slept on a vessel that had been chartered by the operator of the

---

170. OCSLA provides that the provisions of the Longshore and Harbor Workers' Compensation Act apply to all oil and gas workers on the OCS who are not classified as seamen or public employees. 43 U.S.C. § 1333(b) (1994). Nevertheless, some oil and gas workers (e.g., an employee working on a fixed platform in state waters) remain protected only by state workers' compensation law. In light of *Valladolid*, *supra*, however, this may no longer be the case.

171. For detailed discussion of the classification of offshore employees and remedies for injury, see Maraist, 171–293.

172. Id. 298–303. Nevertheless, the Longshore and Harbor Workers' Compensation Act restricts indemnity by the employer of a longshoreman in favor of a "vessel" (including the owner and a time charterer, such as the operator of a jack-up drilling rig), unless the indemnity is reciprocal. 33 U.S.C. §§ 905(b) and (c). However, insurance coverage is not prohibited even if the indemnity is invalid. Price v. Zim Israel Navigation Co., Ltd., 616 F.2d 422 (9th Cir. 1980); Voisin v. O.D.E.C.O. Drilling Co., 744 F.2d 1174, 1177–78 (5th Cir. 1984). In addition, a tower cannot get indemnity for its own negligence from its tow, Bisso v. Inland Waterways Corporation, 349 U.S. 85 (1955). Nevertheless, similar protection can often be obtained through an additional-insured provision or a waiver of subrogation.

173. See discussion of state oilfield anti-indemnity acts in Chapter 6.

platform. The operator settled a claim made by the employee's survivors under the Death on the High Seas Act, maritime law, OCSLA, and Louisiana law, and then sued the service contractor for indemnification pursuant to the indemnity provisions of the service contract. Under Texas law, the parties' express choice of law, and under maritime law, the indemnity was valid, but under the Louisiana Oilfield Indemnity Act, the indemnity was void. The district court held that the work was not maritime in nature and thus was governed by state law and further upheld the parties' choice of Texas law, the home office of the operator. The Texas Oilfield Anti–Indemnity Act authorizes a mutual indemnity that is supported by insurance. Hence, the operator prevailed in federal district court. On appeal, however, the Court of Appeals for the Fifth Circuit reversed on the ground that, under OCSLA, Louisiana law governed the incident, notwithstanding the parties express choice of Texas law. The court noted that in *Matte v. Zapata Offshore Co.*, 784 F.2d 628, 631 (5th Cir. 1986), "[w]e held that the choice-of-law provision violated both Louisiana law and federal public policy as expressed in OCSLA, 'which seeks to apply the substantive law of adjacent states to problems arising on the Shelf.' "

On the other hand, in *Smith v. Penrod Drilling Corp.*, 960 F.2d 456 (5th Cir.1992), Chevron, the operator of a fixed platform, sued Penrod, a contractor who had furnished a jack-up drilling barge and crew to perform workover services on the platform. Chevron sought indemnity from Penrod's insurer for damages Chevron had paid in settlement of a suit by a Penrod employee, who had been injured when he was standing on the safety fencing on the platform while reaching for some equipment on the drilling barge. Although the court found that the accident occurred on the platform, an OCSLA situs, the court concluded that the contract was maritime in nature and thus governed by maritime law. Had state law applied as surrogate federal law under OCSLA, Chevron's action would have been barred by the Louisiana Oilfield Indemnity Act. The facts of this case prompted the Fifth Circuit to criticize its own precedent as in possible conflict with OCSLA and with itself.[174] 960 F.2d at 460–61. The Fifth Circuit noted that it had narrowed its application of maritime *law* in response to Congressional intent, as expressed in OCSLA, that state law should apply to matters having an OCSLA situs, and that the United States Supreme Court had criticized the Circuit's expansive view of maritime *employment* in *Herb's Welding v. Gray*, 470 U.S. 414, 422–23 (1985). Nevertheless, the Fifth Circuit also observed that it had not narrowed its expansive view of maritime *contracts*. 960 F.2d at 460.

In *Hodgen v. Forest Oil Corp.*, 87 F.3d 1512 (5th Cir.1996), a worker employed by a service contractor sued the platform operator, as well as the owner of the vessel, for injuries suffered during a swing-rope transfer from a fixed platform to a vessel in high seas. The vessel had been time chartered (non-demise) by the operator. In a non-demise charter, the owner of the vessel controls the vessel and furnishes the crew and captain. Against the advice of the captain and the workers, the operator's employee ordered that the workers be transported by the vessel to a platform to take certain meter

---

174. See also Lewis v. Glendel Drilling Co., 898 F.2d 1083, 1084 (5th Cir.1990), wherein the court lamented that "because of an apparent contradictory line of cases in our circuit and the uncertain policy underpinning our result, the appellant would justly ask 'Why'?".

readings. Because weather conditions were bad, that the timing for this task was not critical, and a helicopter could have been used later in the day to transport the workers, the district court found that the operator was eighty-five percent (85%) negligent and that the vessel owner was only fifteen (15%) negligent even though, at the time of the accident, the operator's employee was at a different platform and the captain of the vessel had the final authority to abort the transfer. *Hodgen* illustrates that liability for offshore accidents can potentially rest with a number of parties and their insurers due to comparative fault. The district court also held that the contract with the service contractor was not maritime in nature, that the situs of the accident was governed by OCSLA, that Louisiana law applied as surrogate federal law, and that the indemnity provisions in the master services contract were thus unenforceable. In affirming, the Fifth Circuit panel again reviewed its prior case law and reaffirmed the six-part contract test of *Davis* and the three-part governing-law test of *Union Texas*.

The platform operator in *Hodgen* also argued that, because it was exonerated in that capacity (and culpable only in its capacity as time charterer), it should be allowed to enforce the indemnity regarding those costs incurred in defending itself as a nonculpable platform operator. In Louisiana, under Meloy v. Conoco, Inc., 504 So.2d 833, 839 (La.1987), an oilfield-related indemnity is enforceable to the extent that the indemnitee seeks recovery of its defense costs when found not at fault. The Fifth Circuit panel certified the question of attributing culpability, along with questions relating to the respective liability of various insurers, to the Louisiana Supreme Court. The Louisiana Supreme Court, however, declined to accept certification. Hodgen v. Forest Oil Corp., 681 So.2d 354 (La.1996). In response, the Fifth Circuit panel held that Louisiana law barred any indemnity under the circumstances. Hodgen v. Forest Oil Corp., 115 F.3d 358 (5th Cir.La.1997).

In *Grand Isle Shipyard, Inc. v. Seacor Marine*, LLC, 589 F.3d 778 (5th Cir. 2009) (en banc), the Fifth Circuit seized the opportunity to clarify the otherwise confusing precedent about which law applied to an indemnity claim. This case involved a Grand Isle employee who was injured aboard a Seacor vessel while it was traveling in open water between the rig platform and the residential platform. Grand Isle contracted with BP to perform repair and maintenance operations on BP platforms, and Seacor contracted with BP to provide vessel services. The injured Grand Isle employee filed suit against Seacor, and Seacor claimed defense and indemnity from Grand Isle based on an indemnity provision in the contract between Grand Isle and BP. The Fifth Circuit made clear that, despite previous holdings that indicated otherwise, a "focus-of-the-contract" test should be used to determine the situs of the controversy in contract cases under OCSLA. The "situs of the tort" analysis was intended only for tort claims. Under the "focus of the contract" test, the situs is where the majority of the contracted work is to be performed, not where the tort occurred. If the majority of the contracted work is to be performed on a site recognized by the OCSLA (in this case on fixed platforms), the OCSLA then applies the substantive law of the adjacent state as surrogate federal law. Hence, in this case, the indemnity provisions were deemed unenforceable under Louisiana law. To complete the analysis, the Fifth Circuit explicitly overruled several cases including *Hollier*, and *Hodgen* to the extent the cases held that a contract claim was governed by the law of the situs of the tort.

6. Federal maritime law (but not OCSLA) also governs maritime activities on inland navigable waters and state territorial waters. As a curious example, Volume 1, page 1, of the reports of the Supreme Court of Dakota Territory, one of the most land-locked areas of the United States, is a maritime law case. United States v. The Cora, 1. Dak. Rep. 1, 46 N.W. 503 (1867) (involving seizure of a steamboat for introducing "spirituous and intoxicating liquors" into Indian country).

3. INDIAN LANDS

(a) Ownership and Development of Minerals in Indian Country and the Trust Doctrine

(i) Sources and Characteristics of Indian Mineral Ownership

American Indian tribes have either acquired mineral ownership themselves or had their real property interests recognized through several outlets. Such outlets include their original occupancy rights (including federal recognition of rights granted by prior governments such as Great Britain), recognition through treaty or through executive order and acts of Congress, or through purchase.

Following cases such as *Johnston v. M'Intosh*, wherein the Supreme Court first provided for the right of Indian tribes to occupy lands subsequently discovered and settled by Europeans, the "discovery doctrine" recognizing eventual federal appropriation of Indian title took hold.[175] This doctrine vested title in the colonizing power which 'discovered' the land, exclusive of all other competing European powers, but—at least initially—allowed Indian tribes to continue to occupy their native lands even after title to such real property had become vested in the discovering sovereign. In *Johnson*, Chief Justice Marshall explains that this discovery and vesting power descended from Great Britain to the United States at independence.

The position of the Indian tribes (hereafter, "Indians" or "Tribes"), as occupiers without fee title in their lands, is subject to termination by the federal government.[176] Indians, however, may invoke their aboriginal occupancy rights in a way similar to adverse possession, by proving that the real property being claimed is currently occupied and in the possession of the tribe and that the tribes' use of the land was open, notorious, continuous, and exclusive.[177]

---

175. Johnson v. M'Intosh, 21 U.S. (8 Wheat.) 543 (1823); Confederated Tribes of Chehalis Indian Reservation v. State of Washington, 96 F.3d 334 (9th Cir.1996).

176. Oneida Indian Nation v. County of Oneida, 414 U.S. 661 (1974).

177. United States v. Santa Fe Pac. R.R. Co., 314 U.S. 339 (1941); Narragansett Indian Tribe of Rhode Island v. Narragansett Elec. Co., 89 F.3d 908 (1st Cir.1996); Menominee Indian Tribe of Wisconsin v. Thompson, 922 F.Supp. 184 (W.D.Wisc. 1996).

Tribes have been described as "domestic, dependent nations"[178] in recognition that, while they do not all possess the same powers as independent states, such as the power to raise armies or print currency, they do possess some powers which run parallel to federal and state power, such as the right to tax as well as powers to provide for health and safety regulations if the tribe or its members are affected. Thus, the tribes still possess powers not surrendered to, or taken over by, the federal government via case law, treaty, law, or regulation. As the U.S. Supreme Court noted in *South Dakota v. Bourland*,[179] Indian nations retain "attributes of sovereignty over both their members and their territory." This sovereignty can apply as well to some control of activities by non-Indians that take place inside Indian Country.

Before American independence and for roughly the first half of the existence of the United States, land dealings with tribes were dealt with through treaties in a way similar to treaty making with other independent nations. Treaties covering land trades usually followed a pattern of the tribes ceding their claims to certain lands while the United States officially recognized the tribe's claims to other lands. As with treaties with other independent powers, only the federal government—not the individual states—had the right to enter into treaties with the tribes.

Treaties involving land settlements were sometimes one-sided in favor of the federal government and often signed in the aftermath of bloodshed or fraud, or both, between the government and a tribe, sometimes by Indian parties whose authority to represent a particular tribe was questionable. With the advent of the westward growth of the United States across the continent and the corresponding decrease in the numbers and power of the tribes, the tribal nations gradually ceased to be recognized as entirely independent entities with which treaties should be negotiated. Congress eventually stopped entering into treaties with Indian nations in 1871 and thereafter dealt with Indian tribes as a plenary power.[180]

From 1871 until 1938, the ownership of minerals under reservation land acquired from treaties was in doubt. Then, the Supreme Court in United States v. Shoshone Tribe[181] held that the grant and recognition of the land for a reservation in that case also included the minerals under the reservation surface.[182] This case established the rule that minerals passed with the granting of reservation lands provided that the treaty did not reserve the minerals for the federal government. Of course, treaties may have expressly reserved minerals in the federal government, so title examination of Indian minerals should include analysis of any pertinent treaty.

---

178. Cherokee Nation v. Georgia, 30 U.S. (5 Pet.) 1, 17 (1831).

179. 508 U.S. 679 (1993).

180. Appropriations Act of March 3, 1871, ch. 120, § 1, 16 Stat. 544, 566 (1871) (codified in part at 25 US.C. § 71).

181. 304 U.S. 111 (1938).

182. Id.

After 1871, the federal government has instead relied upon congressional action and, for a period from 1871 to 1919, Presidential executive orders[183] to conduct most land dealings with Indian nations. These acts and orders generally provided for either setting aside federal lands for reservation use or allowed for the purchase of additional acreage for the tribe named. No blanket policy exists to determine the passage of mineral rights in these laws or executive orders, so each must be analyzed individually to determine whether or not the minerals passed to the tribe. Such oil and gas rights that pass to tribes by recognition and conveyance may be leased and developed by the tribe under the laws and regulations described below.

Of course, Indian tribes have also purchased land to add to their communal holdings. Although this proactive approach has been approved by Congress, the purchased land is then subject to the same restraints on sale and other restrictions as was the previously-owned tribal land.[184] Congress also has allowed the government, through the Department of the Interior, to purchase new communal tribal lands and to approve exchanges of land. This procedure permits better amalgamation of tribal lands into a more contiguous mass where non-Indian land holdings within the general boundaries of tribal lands have led to a "checkerboard" pattern of Indian/non-Indian ownership.[185]

Finally, in keeping with the general federal policy of recognizing land grants from prior governments to private individuals and other non-government entities, the rights to lands established in, or conveyed or patented to Indian nations by prior governments have been recognized by both Congress and the courts.[186]

Various attempts have been made to curtail or even eliminate communal ownership of Indian land. To varying degrees, these attempts have, led to unfortunate results ranging from outright theft and fraud to loss of Indian title to non-Indian purchasers in return for below-market consideration. The broadest of these laws was the General Allotment Act of 1887—known popularly as the "Dawes Act"—that authorized the allotment of communally-held reservation land to individual Indians.[187]

With the Dawes Act, the federal government acted on the seemingly good intention that the best way to integrate Indians into the culture and economic system of the broader United States was by conveying parcels of land to individual Indians, thereby gradually eliminating the communal system of ownership.[188] As provided in the Dawes Act, each Indian was to receive a tract of varying size, commonly between 80 to 160 acres of land,

---

183. The use of executive orders to create reservations or change reservation boundaries was ended by congressional action by the Act of June 30, 1919, ch. 4, 41 Stat. 34 (1919) (codified at 43 U.S.C. § 150 (1982)).

184. Law of Federal Oil and Gas Leases, Rocky Mtn. Min. L. Found., 2 § 26.01[2][e].

185. Id., citing 25 U.S.C. §§ 464, 465.

186. Id. at 2 § 26.01[2][f].

187. Ch. 119, 24 Stat. 388 (1887) (codified in part as 25 U.S.C. §§ 331–381).

188. Montana v. United States, 450 U.S. 544 (1981).

with the size of each tract dependent on the type of land and its potential use, as well the characteristics of the individual Indian, such as gender, family size, and age. After allotment, the tracts were held in trust by the federal government for twenty-five years. This period of trust supervision was deemed sufficient so that the Indian would be sufficiently assimilated and knowledgeable to accept fee title. Until that time, he had little control over alienation and other property rights of the fee title, such as leasing or mortgaging of mineral rights—all of which had to be approved by the Secretary of the Interior—and generally could not sell the minerals outright.

Although the original intent of the Dawes Act and other allotment acts was to eventually give over full control of all the allotted acreage to the individual Indians, the trust period for much allotted land has been continually extended by executive orders, as authorized by statute.[189] As a consequence of this restriction on alienation, the typical allotment tract is now held in trust for numerous descendants of the original allottee. This fractionalization of the beneficial title has created, in some cases, difficulties in ascertaining all the Indian owners. Federal trust control can be modified or partially or wholly terminated by approved fee patent releases after a determination of "competency" in the allottee(s), the death of all allotted owners and subsequent inheritance by non-Indians, foreclosure of an approved mortgage or deed of trust, pipeline or other condemnation, and Secretary-approved leasing.[190]

Allotment continued until 1934 when the Indian Reorganization Act[191] ended the policy of distribution of communal tribal land. This Act both disallowed continued allotment of tribal land as well as continued federal retention of any lands then held in trust. By 1934, almost twenty-seven million acres of communal tribal land had been allotted, and many lands were still had in trust, creating two new categories of Indian-owned land—fee lands owned by individual Indians and lands held in trust by the government for individual Indians.[192]

(ii) Status of Indian Lands and the Trust Doctrine

Lands owned all or in part by Indian tribes represent some of the largest unexplored regions in the lower forty-eight states. If the present boom in domestic drilling continues, interest in developing Indian lands will remain high.

In general, the parallels are numerous between tribal lands—managed to various degrees by federal agencies—and federal lands. Tribal

189. 25 U.S.C. § 391 (1988).

190. *See supra* [note 182] at § 26.01[3] (citing that the statutory authority for such termination may be found in the following, among others: 25 U.S.C. § 349 (patents in fee to allottees)); Id. at § 372 (patents in fee to heirs); Id. at § 372 (sales by the Secretary of the Interior); Id. at § 483a (mortgages); Id. at § 357 (condemnation); Id. at §§ 393, 393a, 394, 395, 396a–396g, 397, 398, 398a–398e (leasing).

191. Act of June 18, 1934, ch. 576, 48 Stat. 984 (codified at 25 U.S.C. §§ 461–495).

192. JUDITH V. ROYSTER and MICHAEL C. BLUMM, NATIVE AMERICAN NATURAL RESOURCES LAW, Chapter 3(E), p. 167 (Carolina Academic Press 2002).

lands introduce complexities, however, not found elsewhere. "Indian Country" consists of a patchwork of land owned and controlled by a variety of authorities.[193] Tribal lands are communally held and individual tribal members have no inheritable interest in tribal land.[194] These facts raise the interesting notion of intra-tribal friction between those members that want the minerals developed and those whose surface use is disrupted. In addition to the actual communally-owned reservation lands, some plots are owned by individual Indians both in trust with the federal government and by themselves in fee. "Indian Country" can include non-Indians who own land within the reservation boundaries. Tribal lands also contain sacred religious/cultural sites whose nature, number, and location may bewilder those not familiar with the particular tribe.

Tribal land is exceptional because the equitable title is held by the whole tribe for the benefit of all the individuals in the tribe.[195] Individual members have no inheritable title in tribal land.[196] Most lands held by tribes is by aboriginal title arising from governmental recognition of the Indians' right to quiet enjoyment of the lands even after the fee of such land becomes vested in the federal government.[197] A majority of the lands protected under aboriginal title were recognized by treaty.[198]

Treaties typically involve federal recognition of aboriginal title.[199] In 1871, in United States v. Shoshone Tribe, the Supreme Court noted that the overall goal of the federal government in treaties was to deal equitably with tribes and to seek no reward for itself.[200] Thus, a treaty could be found to include the mineral rights under the land turned over to the tribe, even though the treaty made no mention of the mineral rights.[201] Such an inquiry is usually conducted on a case-by-case basis and requires examination of the treaty.[202] After the treaty period, the government has relied on statutes to carry out its land dealings with Indian tribes.[203]

---

193. 18 U.S.C. § 1151. Although this statute is part of the federal criminal code, it has also been cited in civil cases. The statute defines the term "Indian Country" as:

"(a) all land within the limits of any Indian reservation under the jurisdiction of the United States Government, notwithstanding the issuance of any patent, and, including rights-of-way running through the reservation, (b) all dependent Indian communities within the border of the United States whether within the original or subsequently acquired territory thereof, and whether within the original or subsequently acquired territory thereof, and whether within or without the limits of a state, and (c) all Indian allotments, the Indian titles to which have not been extinguished, including rights-of-way running through the same."

Alaska v. Native Village of Venetie Tribal Government, 522 U.S. 520 (1998) and *Mustang Production Co. v. Harrison*, 94 F.3d 1382 (10th Cir. 1996) *cert. denied*, 520 U.S. 1139 (1997).

194. F. Cohen, Handbook of Federal Indian Law 606 (1982 Ed.).

195. Rocky Mt. Min. L. Found., Law of Federal Oil and Gas Leases, § 26.01[2], (Tribal Lands) (2001).

196. *Id.*

197. *Id.* at § 26.01[2][a].

198. *Id.*

199. *Id.* at § 26.01[2][b].

200. United States v. Shoshone Tribe, 304 U.S. 111 (1938).

201. LAW OF FEDERAL OIL AND GAS LEASES, *supra* note 195 at § 26.01[2][b].

202. *Id.*

203. *Id.* at § 26.01[2][c].

Tribes are considered "domestic, dependent sovereigns," a status rooted in the ancient nature of the tribes, which long predate both the sovereignty of the United States and the previous period of European colonization.[204] As a result of this status, the federal government recognizes a fiduciary relationship between the United States and Indian tribes and their individual members.[205] Because of this relationship, the federal government is the guardian of tribes and members, and must assure that all government actions affecting tribes, individual Indians, or their property are in the Indians' "best interest."[206] The federal government, through the Secretary of the Interior, must therefore meet the strictest fiduciary principles.[207]

This duty, often called the "Trust Doctrine," places the government in the position of the guardian of the tribes[208] and individual members.[209] The Trust Doctrine affects a tribe's dealings with private parties such as mineral developers through questions of statutory interpretation[210] and has even been used as a reason to "unravel" (*i.e.* declare invalid) development agreements between producers and tribes.

(iii) Tribes as Mineral Lessors

Beginning in 1790, Congress passed a series of acts, commonly known as the Indian Non-intercourse Acts, to govern and regulate the sale of tribal lands.[211] These acts commonly stipulated that no sale of land by a tribe or individual Indian was valid unless concluded in accordance with a treaty between the federal government and the appropriate tribe.[212] These acts still exist today and are important to mineral lessees because all leases and mineral agreements entered into by a tribe or individual Indian must be examined and approved by the Secretary.[213] In addition, any lease farmout agreements and modifications of a previously approved lease or agreement must also be approved by the Secretary.[214]

The Indian Mineral Leasing Act ("IMLA") of 1938 arose from a need to consolidate and simplify lease provisions and practices.[215] The 1938 Act had three express aims.[216] First, the Act attempted to establish one single

---

204. *Id.* at § 26.02[a].

205. *Id.* at § 26.02[b].

206. *Id.* quoting Assiniboine & Sioux Tribes of the Fort Peck Indian Reservation v. Board of Oil and Gas Conservation of the State of Montana, 792 F.2d 782, 794 (9th Cir. Mont. 1986).

207. *Id.*

208. Jicarilla Apache Tribe v. Supron Energy Corp., 782 F.2d 855 (10th Cir.1986).

209. Pawnee v. United States, 830 F.2d 187 (Fed.Cir.1987).

210. *See* Citation Oilfield Supply and Leasing, Ltd. and Murphy Oil U.S.A. Inc. v. Acting Billings Area Director, 27 IBIA 210 (1995).

211. LAW OF FEDERAL OIL AND GAS LEASES, *supra* note 195 at § 26.02[c].

212. *Id.*

213. *Id.*

214. *Id.*

215. Judith V. Royster, *Mineral Development in Indian Country: The Evolution of Tribal Control over Mineral Resources,* 29 Tulsa L.J. 541, 558 (1994).

216. *Id.*

set of leasing procedures.[217] Second, the IMLA was passed to help achieve the goal of tribal revitalization—the primary goal of the Indian Reorganization Act of 1934.[218] Third, the Act was to encourage economic development and to insure tribes "the greatest return for their property."[219]

Specifically, the Act established requirements for surety bonds, bonuses, rents, and royalties for mineral leases.[220] Unfortunately, the IMLA leasing system was fraught with implementation problems which led to corruption.[221] The Act also gave the tribes a limited right to sue for breach of trust.[222] During the duration of a lease, the Secretary is required to watch over the lessee's performance to guard the Indian's mineral assets and economic potential, which includes overseeing actions mandated by both federal regulations and the terms of the lease.[223]

Although flawed, particularly in its "one size fits all tribes" approach to development, the IMLA represented a major advance for mineral-owning tribes.[224] In *Jicarilla Apache Tribe v. Supron Energy*, after listing the extensive responsibilities of the government in representing tribes in leasing negotiations, the court noted, "the evident purpose of the statute is to ensure that Indian tribes receive the maximum benefit from mineral deposits on their lands through leasing."[225]

Current federal policy promoting tribal self-government also affects producers in Indian country. This policy encourages tribes to seek greater control over tribal lands and resources while also recognizing that some tribes are currently more capable than others in negotiating and managing their own mineral development without significant inefficiency and corruption. As described below, the Indian Mineral Development Act of 1982[226] recognized this desire by allowing qualifying tribes to attract, negotiate and manage their own mineral development, subject only to final approval by the BIA. This policy of self-determination has also been relied upon by courts to support exercises of tribal authority directed against developers.

The IMLA makes all oil and gas lease activities on Indian lands subject to the regulations of the Secretary.[227] In addition, a 1909 Act authorizing the leasing of allotted lands also authorizes the Secretary to "make such rules and regulations as may be necessary...."[228] Section 8

---

217. *Id.*

218. *Id.*

219. *Id.*

220. *Id.* at 565.

221. *Id.* at 567.

222. *Id.* at 569.

223. *Id.* at 570.

224. *Id.* at 560.

225. Jicarilla Apache Tribe v. Supron, 728 F.2d 1555, 1570 (10th Cir. N.M. 1984).

226. 25 U.S.C. §§ 2101–2108.

227. LAW OF FEDERAL OIL AND GAS LEASES, *supra* note 195 at § 26.01[2][b].

228. 25 U.S.C. § 396.

of the IMLA mandates that the Secretary will execute regulations to assist achievement of the Act's purpose.[229] The chief purpose of the operating regulations for leases is to help assure that exploitation activities are performed so as to achieve the greatest recovery with minimum waste.[230]

Royalty accounting and payments for Indian leases are generally governed by the lease provisions, related regulations, and by the notices of oil and gas lease sales. Royalties are set by the Secretary. The MMS regulations, controlling the value of royalties for oil and gas from Indian lands, are very similar to the regulations addressing valuation for federal oil and gas leases.[231] The regulations are generally the same for leases on both reservation lands and allotted lands, and broadly provide that, with the exception of advance payments to the superintendent of the reservation after the first year of the lease, payments of rentals and royalties are controlled by statute.[232]

Interpretations of these regulations and statutes by federal agencies are watched closely by tribes and developers alike. When the issue is how to interpret a regulation or statute and when the outcome affects the amount of royalty due a tribe, litigation is almost certain to follow, often times questioning whether the government has met its duty as an agent for the tribe under the Trust Doctrine.

THE SHOSHONE INDIAN TRIBE OF THE WIND RIVER RESERVATION, WYO. v. THE UNITED STATES

56 Fed. Cl. 639 (2003).

HEWITT, JUSTICE:

I. Background

This case was filed in 1979 and has been divided into four phases for adjudication. * * * The current phase involves plaintiffs' claims of breach of fiduciary duty by the Minerals Management Service ("MMS") and its predecessors in the management and payment of royalties. This opinion addresses the statutory and regulatory framework pursuant to which the Tribes receive royalties for the oil and gas extracted from their land and the interpretation of a 1989 settlement agreement between several oil companies regarding oil and gas extraction.

The statutory framework at issue here includes the Act of August 21, 1916 (1916 Act), which authorized the Secretary of the Interior (Secretary) to lease for oil and gas production certain lands ceded from the Wind River Reservation under such terms and conditions as shall be by him prescribed. The Indian Mineral Leasing Act of 1938, 25 U.S.C. §§ 396a–396g (IMLA) was later passed to further govern the leasing of land on

---

229. LAW OF FEDERAL OIL AND GAS LEASES, *supra* note 195 at § 26.01[2][b].

230. *Id.*

231. *Id.*

232. 30 C.F.R. Sec. 218.51

Indian reservations for oil and gas [leasing, exploration, and production]. In 1982, the Federal Oil and Gas Royalty Management Act, 30 U.S.C. §§ 1701–1757 (FOGRMA) was passed to provide greater legislative guidance on the valuation of the oil and gas as to which royalties were owed the Tribes.

Based on this statutory framework, regulations were promulgated by * * * the Bureau of Indian Affairs ("BIA"). * * * The text of these rules remained substantially consistent until 1988, when the MMS rewrote its royalty valuation rules, and 1996 when the BIA rules were amended to reference the MMS rules for the establishment of the valuation of oil and gas for royalty purposes.

The "Arco settlement" was an agreement reached between Atlantic Richfield Company, Arco Oil and Gas Company, and Arco Natural Gas Marketing, Inc. (collectively, Arco), as lessee/producer, and MDU Resources Group, Inc. and Williston Basin Interstate Pipeline Company (collectively, MDU), as purchaser, on October 17, 1989 in settlement of a case [then] pending in the 95th District Court of Dallas County, Texas, captioned *Atl. Richfield Co. v. MDU Res. Group.* Under the terms of the Arco settlement, MDU paid Arco $39 million. Arco paid royalties to plaintiffs on 53% of this amount. Plaintiffs claim that Arco attributed 47% of the settlement amount to "Take-or-Pay at Sec. 107 Pricing." Arco did not pay royalties on this portion of the settlement on the grounds that royalties were not due under [the royalty valuation rules of the BIA from 1996].

The "Take-or-Pay" portion referred to a provision in most long-term gas sales contracts. This provision "obligated the purchaser to take a specified minimum volume of gas during an identified period or to pay for that quantity even if not taken in full." The dispute here, as was the case in other litigation in the 1980s, is whether the settlement amount allocated for gas not actually produced, but due under the terms of the contract, was royalty-bearing or not.

* * *

As to plaintiffs' claim [that the federal government failed in their fiduciary duty owed to the tribe by not maximizing the royalty profits of the tribe], the defendant relies primarily on the decision of the Supreme Court in *Navajo Nation* and, particularly, the Court's holding that there was no general fiduciary duty to "maximize" the profits of Indian Tribes absent statutory, regulatory, or contractual obligations. Defendant argues that there is an absence here of any statute or regulation which requires the government to "maximize" plaintiffs' royalty income. Defendant further argues that because plaintiffs have not identified any duty that has been breached by the government's alleged failure to "maximize" profits from the Tribes' oil and gas leases, the court is without jurisdiction to hear this case.

Plaintiffs contend that the regulations and statutory authority governing defendant's management of the Tribes' oil and gas establish a fiduciary duty of the government. Plaintiffs further argue that defendant has breached its duty established by the IMLA and subsequent regulations in failing to ensure that the Tribes' received full value for their oil and gas. Plaintiffs argue that the specific statutory and regulatory language here makes this case distinguishable from *Navajo Nation,* and therefore no precedent precludes the Tribes' recovery.

As to plaintiffs' Take-or-Pay claim, defendant argues that under the applicable law and precedents, the Take-or-Pay portions of the Arco settlement at issue are not royalty producing. While defendant acknowledges an obligation under various leases to pay royalties at certain percentage rates, it argues that the leases do not define what oil and gas shall be subject to the obligation to pay royalties. That subject, according to defendant, is governed by the regulations which are in effect when the royalties are due.

Plaintiffs counter that defendant seeks to apply retroactively current regulations but that the regulations that were in effect when the lease was entered into should govern. Plaintiffs argue that the agency's interpretation at the time the leases were entered into was what was relied upon by the parties, and that to allow the agency to change the rules now would punish the Tribes by binding them into long-term leases that can be altered at any time at the whim of defendant.

II. Discussion

A. Motion to Dismiss on Duty to "Maximize" Profits

Defendant relies primarily on two cases in support of its argument that the government has no duty to "maximize" the Tribes' oil and gas revenue, *Pawnee v. United States,* 830 F.2d 187 (Fed.Cir.1987), *cert. denied* 486 U.S. 1032, 108 S.Ct. 2014, 100 L.Ed.2d 602 (1988), and *Navajo Nation.* In *Pawnee,* Indian tribes brought suit under the Indian Long–Term Leasing Act, 25 U.S.C. § 396, claiming that the government "breached a fiduciary obligation to provide that plaintiffs received royalty based on 'the highest price paid or offered for like quality gas.'" Defendant argues that, while the court in *Pawnee* found that the United States has a general fiduciary obligation as to the management of oil and gas leases, the existence of a "general fiduciary relationship does *not* mean that any and every claim by the Indian lessor necessarily states a proper claim for breach of trust." Defendant urges close attention to the particular standards and responsibilities imposed by the statutory and regulatory scheme. Defendant relies on the following language from *Pawnee:*

> "[T]he fiduciary relationship springs from the statutes and regulations which "define the contours of the United States' fiduciary responsibilities." *United States v. Mitchell,* (463 U.S. at 224). Where, as in this case, the regulations and the leases deal directly with the problem and are not challenged, the Indians cannot demand that the

United States ignore those provisions or act contrary to them. The scope and extent of the fiduciary relationship, with respect to this particular matter, is established by the regulation and leases. Appellants cannot create a viable fiduciary claim purely by insisting that this court (or the Claims Court) establish different or higher standards." *Pawnee*, 830 F.2d at 192.

Defendant argues that plaintiffs' maximization claims are effectively the same as the *Pawnee* plaintiffs' claims for "the highest price paid or offered for like quantity gas." Because the "valuation regulations applicable to production from tribal leases are identical to the regulations applicable to allotted leases that were involved in *Pawnee*," that case is controlling and plaintiffs' claim must be dismissed.

Defendant also relies on *Navajo Nation* to support its position that the applicable statutes and regulations do not create a duty to "maximize" plaintiffs' profits. Defendant relies on the Supreme Court's statement in *Navajo Nation* that:

"[N]either the IMLA nor any of its regulations establishes anything more than a bare minimum royalty. Hence, there is no textual basis for concluding that the Secretary's approval function includes a duty, enforceable in an action for money damages, to ensure a higher rate of return for the Tribe concerned. Similarly, no pertinent statutory or regulatory provisions requires the Secretary, on pain of damages, to conduct an independent 'economic analysis' of the reasonableness of the royalty to which a Tribe and third party have agreed." (123 S.Ct. at 1094)

To defendant, *Navajo Nation* sets the bar that plaintiffs must reach to show a duty on defendant's part to "maximize" their revenues: they must identify specific statutory and regulatory provisions which establish such duties.

When the maximization issue was posed at oral argument after supplementary briefing on the impact of *Navajo Nation,* plaintiffs conceded that they could not maintain a claim for "maximization." Plaintiffs now focus their argument on the existence of a money-mandating statutory and regulatory framework. Specifically, plaintiffs point to the detailed statutory and regulatory framework applicable to oil and gas leasing, a framework not present in the coal leasing regime considered in *Navajo Nation.*

Because of the specific language of the oil and gas leasing regime, plaintiffs argue that this case is more akin to *United States v. Mitchell,* (Mitchell II), where the Court found a money-mandating fiduciary obligation, than to *Navajo Nation.* Under both the timber regulations considered in *Mitchell II* and the oil and gas regulations applicable here, the government has control over advertising and bidding of sales and leases of the Tribes' resources. Both sets of regulations require the Secretary to establish guidelines for sales and to approve all contracts and leases. The

Secretary must also closely supervise the lease during contract performance under both sets of regulations.

Plaintiffs also point to the fact that in *Navajo Nation,* " 'no pertinent statutory or regulatory provision requires the Secretary, on pain of damages, to conduct an independent "economic analysis" of the reasonableness of the royalty to which a Tribe and third party have agreed,' " while the oil and gas regulations here require the Secretary to conduct an economic analysis. * * *

Defendant counters that the regulatory language merely vests the Secretary with the "discretion" to conduct an economic analysis in this case. Plaintiffs argue, however, that "the existence of 'discretion' in carrying out statutory or regulatory duties does not make the Government immune from suit." Accordingly, "[t]he Government's failure to consider any factor contemplated by a specific statutory or regulatory provision can give rise to a breach of trust claim." Further, the Secretary's exercise of that discretion is limited by the regulations and defendant's fiduciary responsibilities. Therefore, plaintiffs argue that defendant " 'cannot escape [its] ... role as trustee by donning the mantle of administrator' to claim that courts must defer to [its] ... expertise and delegated authority." (quoting *Cobell v. Norton*, 240 F.3d 1081, 1099 (D.C.Cir.2001) (quoting *Jicarilla Apache Tribe v. Supron Energy Corp.*, 728 F.2d 1555, 1567 (10th Cir.1984)).

In *Navajo Nation,* the Supreme Court clearly outlined what was needed for a Tribe to state a claim cognizable under the Indian Tucker Act [which allows Tribes to bring suit against the government for breach of fiduciary duty]:

> "[A] Tribe must identify a substantive source of law that establishes specific fiduciary or other duties, and allege that the Government has failed faithfully to perform those duties. *See* [Mitchell II,]. If that threshold is passed, the court must then determine whether the relevant source of substantive law 'can fairly be interpreted as mandating compensation for damages sustained as a result of a breach of the duties [the governing law] imposes.' *Id.,* at 219. Although 'the undisputed existence of a general trust relationship between the United States and the Indian people' can 'reinforce' the conclusion that the relevant statute or regulation imposes fiduciary duties, *Id.,* at 219, that relationship alone is insufficient to support jurisdiction under the Indian Tucker Act. Instead, the analysis must train on specific rights-creating or duty-imposing statutory or regulatory prescriptions. Those prescriptions need not, however, expressly provide for money damages; the availability of such damages may be inferred. * * * " *Navajo Nation,* 123 S.Ct. at 1092.

In *Navajo Nation,* the Court considered a situation where, in the course of setting a royalty rate for coal extracted from Tribal land, the Secretary engaged in ex parte communications to the detriment of the Tribe. While the IMLA, one of the statutes applicable in this case, was the statute governing the setting of royalties for coal extracted from Tribal lands, the Court explicitly stated that it was ruling only on the Government's role in the coal leasing process under IMLA.... [B]oth the IMLA and its implementing regulations address oil and gas leases in considerably more detail than coal leases. Whether the Secretary has fiduciary or other obligations, enforceable in an action for money damages, with respect to oil and gas leases is not before us.

Based on the statutory and regulatory language that applied to coal royalties, the Court found that the facts of the case before it were distinguishable from those before the Court in *Mitchell II:*

> Unlike the "elaborate" provisions before the Court in Mitchell II, at 225, the IMLA and its regulations do not "give the Federal Government full responsibility to manage Indian resources ... for the benefit of the Indians," The Secretary is neither assigned a comprehensive managerial role nor, at the time relevant here, expressly invested with responsibility to secure "the needs and best interests of the Indian owner and his heirs." *Navajo Nation*, 123 S.Ct. at 1092 (quoting Mitchell II, at 224).

In light of the analysis of the Supreme Court in *Navajo Nation,* the court finds that the facts of this case are closer to *Mitchell II* than *[Navajo Nation]*. Initially, the court notes that this case involves oil and gas leases, so there is a much more elaborate statutory and regulatory framework than the coal leasing regime involved in *Navajo Nation*. Also, the dispute here involves the setting of "value" upon which the rate of royalty was to be paid, and therefore is more closely involved with the statutory and regulatory framework than the *ex parte* communications complained of in *Navajo Nation*.

Valuation in this case is the subject of two statutory frameworks; the IMLA, 25 U.S.C. §§ 396a–396g, and FOGRMA, 30 U.S.C. §§ 1701–1757. The regulations applicable to this case, promulgated under the IMLA and FOGRMA, specifically addressed valuation in much greater detail than the regulations at issue in *Navajo Nation,* which merely set a minimum royalty rate. Here, the regulations state:

> "The value of production, for the purpose of computing royalty, *shall* be the estimated reasonable value of the product as determined by the Associate Director, *due consideration* being given to the highest price paid for a part or a majority of production of like quality in the same field, to the price received by the lessee, to posted prices, and to other relevant matters." (emphasis added).

The lease terms, though "technically" negotiated by the Tribes, reserve for the Secretary the task of valuing the Tribes' oil and gas upon which royalties are paid.

Plaintiffs argue that even more detailed "benchmarks" were established for determining the value of oil and gas beginning in 1988. The parties agree that the 1988 regulations stated:

"For any Indian leases which provide that the Secretary may consider the highest price paid or offered for a major portion of production in determining value for royalty purposes. If data are available to compute a major portion, MMS [Mineral Management Service] will, where practicable, compare the value determined in accordance with this section with the major portion. The value to be used in determining the value of production, for royalty purposes, shall be the higher of those two values."

* * *

The court agrees with plaintiffs that this comprehensive valuation framework creates fiduciary responsibilities on the part of the government. This, however, is not the end of the argument; defendant contends that even if this is the case, the Federal Circuit's decision in *Pawnee*, and the discretion built into the regulatory framework, require that this case be dismissed. The court turns to *Pawnee* first.

In *Pawnee,* the Federal Circuit interpreted a regulatory framework that was virtually identical to the framework in this case. There, the court stated:

"Because the statutes and regulations at issue in this case clearly establish fiduciary obligations of the Government in the management and operation of Indian land's and resources, they can fairly be interpreted as mandating compensation by the Federal Government for damages sustained. Given the existence of a trust relationship, it naturally follows that the Government should be liable in damages for the breach of its fiduciary duties." *Pawnee,* 830 F.2d at 190.

However, the court went on to state "[t]hat there is such a general fiduciary relationship does *not* mean that any and every claim by the Indian lessor necessarily states a proper claim for breach of the trust—a claim which must be fully tried in the Claims Court." *Id.* at 191.

* * *

Because appellants in *Pawnee* wanted the Secretary "to go contrary to and beyond the regulations and the leases in order to fulfill its alleged fiduciary obligation to appellants," the court found that appellants had not stated a proper claim for breach of trust based on the statutes and regulations that "define the contours of the United States' fiduciary responsibilities." Here, to the extent their claims can be read as a claim for "maximization" barred by *Pawnee,* the Tribes have conceded the point.

However, the Tribes also claim that "[t]he Government failed to collect royalties based on the proper value of oil and gas." This proper value can be determined by application of the regulations above. Unlike the plaintiffs in *Pawnee,* in this statement of their claim the Tribes are not asking the Secretary to go "contrary to and beyond the regulations and the leases in order to fulfill its alleged fiduciary obligation to appellants," *Pawnee*, 830 F.2d at 191; rather, plaintiffs are merely asking that the Secretary comply with her own regulations. This is a cognizable claim, and therefore *Pawnee* does not bar the Tribes' claim.

Defendant, relying on *Navajo Nation,* also argues that the discretion afforded the Secretary under the regulations bars the Tribes' claim. Defendant argues that because "[p]laintiffs have not shown a statute or regulation which makes [economic] analysis mandatory," any alleged failure to perform that analysis cannot form a basis for damages. The court, however, agrees with plaintiffs that the discretion afforded the Secretary here is not so wide as to protect defendant from liability.

* * *

The pre–1988 regulatory framework mandated that the supervisor give "due consideration" to enumerated factors and directed that the resulting valuation be an "estimated reasonable value:"

> "The value of production, for the purpose of computing royalty, *shall be the estimated reasonable value* of the product as determined by the Associate Director, *due consideration* being given to the highest price paid for a part or a majority of production of like quality in the same field, to the price received by the lessee, to posted prices, and to other relevant matters." (emphasis added).

This regulation provides the Secretary with guidelines within which to exercise her discretion, and provides the court with guidelines within which to evaluate the Secretary's action. The court does not agree with the government that the fact that the value is "as determined by the Associate Director" is, in the context of the regulation, an indication that the supervisor's action is entirely discretionary. Such an interpretation would render the balance of the regulation (e.g., the words "shall be the estimated reasonable value") meaningless, a result to be avoided in statutory interpretation. The court finds that the discretion afforded the Secretary under the regulations is not so broad as to require the dismissal of this claim. Defendant's Motion to Dismiss Plaintiffs' Claim of Breach by Defendant's Failure to "Maximize" the Tribes' Oil and Gas Revenues is DENIED IN PART as to defendant's failure to collect royalties based on the proper value of oil and gas and GRANTED IN PART as to defendant's failure to "maximize" the Tribes' oil and gas revenues.

B. Motion for Summary Judgment on Take-or-Pay Claims

The Take-or-Pay dispute requires the court to decide whether the portion of the Arco settlement attributable to Take-or-Pay claims is royalty-bearing. Plaintiffs argue that the terms of their leases, properly interpreted, make the Take-or-Pay portion of the settlement royalty-bearing, so that the government's failure to obtain royalties on that portion of the settlement is a breach of its money-mandating trust obligations.

After many years of interpreting the leases to include take-or-pay amounts in the calculation of royalties, the government issued a regulation to that effect in January 1988. The agency's interpretation to include take-or-pay payments in gross proceeds was overturned. In late 1988, the government issued a regulation excluding take-or-pay payments from the calculation of royalties. The regulation that excluded take-or pay amounts from the calculation of royalties was in effect when the settlement was executed.

* * *

Plaintiffs acknowledge that "the leases ... are silent as to whether the value of what was 'produced and saved' includes take-or-pay amounts received in relation to those products," and is therefore royalty-bearing. But plaintiffs contend that "the Government had a well-established policy in effect which made it clear that take-or-pay amounts were to be included in calculating royalties." Plaintiffs rely on the agency's longstanding interpretation, in effect before 1988, that "gross proceeds" included take-or-pay amounts, and argue that the application of 1988 regulations excluding take-or-pay amounts from "gross proceeds" was improperly retroactive.

Plaintiffs further argue that "it is firmly established that a regulation cannot be retroactively applied absent 'express authorization' from Congress to do so." The Tribes argue that retroactivity is especially important here, where the regulations governing Indian leases specifically state that "[n]o regulation that becomes effective after the date of approval of any lease or permit shall operate to affect the duration of the lease or permit, rate of royalty, rental, or acreage unless agreed to by all parties to the lease or permit. It is not the law that the Tribes are indefinitely locked into the royalty rate set in those leases while the Government is free to alter to the Tribe's detriment the definition of the proceeds upon which the royalty is to be paid."

Even if the 1988 regulation in effect at the time of the settlement could be viewed as detrimental to the Tribes, however, the court finds that the government was entitled to rely on it. Notwithstanding plaintiffs' general statements of the law of property rights, the "retroactive" application of regulations is clearly addressed in the leases. The leases at issue state that the parties will "abide by and conform to any and all regulations of the Secretary of the Interior now or hereafter in force relative to such leases." The only exception to the agreement that regulations "hereinafter in force" will govern the lease is that "no regulation hereafter shall effect a change in rate of royalty or annual rental herein specified without the written consent of the parties to this lease." In the court's view the "rate of royalty" is the numerical percentage of value to which plaintiffs are entitled. This view is confirmed by the text of the leases in which the rate of royalty is separately stated as a percentage. Because the November 1988 regulation was the proper regulation to apply to the settlement under the terms of the lease, the agency was entitled to rely on it when the agency collected royalties on the Arco settlement.

Therefore, Defendant's Motion for Summary Judgment on Plaintiffs' Claims of Breach of Trust on Plaintiffs' Take-or-Pay Claims is GRANTED IN PART.

III. Conclusion

For the foregoing reasons, defendant's Motion to Dismiss Plaintiffs' Claim of Breach by Defendant's Failure to "Maximize" the Tribes' Oil and Gas Revenues is DENIED IN PART as to defendant's failure to collect royalties based on the proper value of oil and gas and GRANTED IN PART as to defendant's failure to "maximize" the Tribes' oil and gas revenues. Defendant's Motion for Summary Judgment on Plaintiffs' Claims of Breach of Trust on Plaintiffs' Take-or-Pay Claims is GRANTED IN PART as to the applicability of the November 1988 regulations to the Arco settlement.

IT IS SO ORDERED.

NOTES

1. A goal of the IMLA was to insure tribes "the greatest return for their property." This broad goal, however, yields to specific particulars when considering the actual terms of the lease and the government's fiduciary duty. The court in *Pawnee* ruled that the tribe wanted the Secretary to go beyond the regulation, but that, despite the general duty to bring in the greatest return, the specific duty called for in *Pawnee* stipulated that the royalty was only a component of the income from the lease and therefore did not need to be maximized if, overall, the lease was negotiated by the government with due regard for their fiduciary duty to the tribe. Therefore, the court in *Pawnee* ruled the tribe hadn't proved that the Secretary had breached this duty and had asked the federal government to go beyond what was required in the lease. The court in *Shoshone* ruled the same argument applied here and dismissed the claims of the tribes.

Did you think that same argument applies? One editor of this casebook has argued that, when the choice is simply between maintaining the long-standing policy of royalty collection on take-or-pay payments or using the 1988 regulation to stop collecting money on *pre-existing* leases until actual production, the payments should be included since the take-or-pay gas contract settlement will not be royalty bearing otherwise.[233]

2. Practically speaking and absent a specific regulation to maximize a particular aspect of a lease, it is easy to understand why a court would hesitate to allow a breach of trust claim for every possible instance where value was not maximized. As we have amply seen, oil and gas leases can be very complex and they also can last years or even decades. Leases commonly involve a great deal of risk and speculation. Often times, only when the lease

---

233. Christopher Kulander, *Take-or-Pay Royalties, the Trust Doctrine, and the* Shoshone *Case,* 29 AM. INDIAN L. REV. 101, 118–119 (2005).

has expired and production is long done can hindsight effectively image what would have been the optimal position the government should have taken to fulfill its fiduciary duty to a tribe. If a breach of trust action arose from every possible lack of maximization claim not rooted in a specific statute or regulation, but rather in the general fiduciary duty of the government to the tribe, the potential for litigation would multiply.

For example, in *Pawnee*, as in many royalty calculation disputes, the correct values may be difficult to determine. Should the court use the "amount received" or the "market value" approach to determine royalty? Are the post-production sales really being conducted at arm's length? Should the "work back" method for royalty calculation be employed? These can be difficult questions even with regulations and statutes to guide the government. In the *Shoshone* case, in contrast, the question over valuation is clear. The tribe either received the royalty on the 47% of $39 million or they did not. Can you understand the difference?

3. Oil and gas development on tribal and allotted lands in Oklahoma has an infamous and tragic history. Unlike other tribes, the Osage tribe retained the mineral rights to all lands allotted to individual tribal members. Through an act of Congress in 1906, the Osage National Council was allowed to negotiate and issue oil and gas leases with the consent of the Secretary of the Interior,[234] ch. 3572, § 3, 34 Stat. 539, 543–44 (1906). Most royalties from production were paid in the form of "headrights" to individual members of the tribe. These payments have totaled hundreds of millions of dollars. When probate and guardianship jurisdictions were transferred to the state in 1912, guardianship fraud schemes developed, whereby many members were systematically robbed of their headright payments. Non–Indian guardians were appointed for Osages who were minors or for adults who were routinely deemed incompetent. Other non-Indians acquired control of headrights through marriage. Some adult Osages were even murdered so that guardians could be appointed to "manage" the assets of minor heirs. These abuses occurred until at least 1925, when the Congress gave the Osage Agency and county courts joint supervision of guardianships. For a detailed discussion of what has been called the Osage Reign of Terror, see K. Franks, The Osage Oil Boom, Chapter 8 (Western Heritage Books 1989).

Members of the Five Civilized Tribes of Oklahoma were given allotments, which included mineral rights. Several major oil fields, including the Glenn, Cushing, Healdton, and Seminole Pools, were discovered in the first quarter of the twentieth century on allotted lands. During these booms, some Indian families became very wealthy, while others remained poor. Guardianship and other scams emerged similar to those that occurred during the Osage boom.

> Forgery, embezzlement, criminal conspiracy, misuse of notary's seals, and other crimes against Indian property continued with monotonous regularity, but these grosser and slightly more dangerous forms of swindling were not as common as the more respectable methods of investing Indian money in worthless real estate, padding guardians' accounts, and allowing excessive fees to guardians and attorneys. * * *

---

234. The Osage oil boom actually began in earnest in 1896 when the Osage National Council granted a lease covering the entire Osage Nation to Henry Foster.

[During the height of the boom, the courts became] hopelessly congested. In Creek County, where guardianship frauds were especially notorious and were rarely corrected, a newspaper [Sapulpa Herald] reported in 1916 that there were 219 civil cases on the district court docket, involving oil property worth fifteen to twenty million dollars. Some of these cases had been pending ever since the discovery of oil in the county, but for the preceding two years they had been piling up enormously because of the uncertainty over Indian titles and the sudden value of Creek County land since the discovery of the Cushing Pool. There was no prospect that one out of twenty of these cases would be disposed of during the few days that the court would be in session—it was estimated that continuous sessions for two years would not clear the docket—and about the only recourse open to litigants was settlement out of court. As to criminal prosecutions, the same newspaper stated, "The dismissal of these cases makes a record for the attorney general's office in Creek County that is perfect so far as acquittals are concerned."

Angie Debo, And Still the Waters Run: The Betrayal of the Five Civilized Tribes 312–13 (1940).

4. Fraud against Indians, especially regarding oil and gas rights, is not just an historical event. In 1989, a special committee of the United States Senate reported:

[D]espite the federal government's long-standing obligation to protect Indian natural resources, they have been left unprotected, subject to, at best, benign neglect and, at worst, outright theft by unscrupulous private companies.

* * * [S]ophisticated and premeditated theft by mismeasuring and fraudulently reporting the amount of oil purchased has been the practice for many years of the largest purchaser of Indian oil * * *. The Department of the Interior and its relevant agencies, charged with stewardship of federal and Indian land, have knowingly allowed this widespread oil theft to go undetected for decades, at the direct expense of Indian owners.

Senate Special Committee on Investigations of Select Committee on Indian Affairs, 101st Cong., 1st Sess., S.Rep.No. 216 (1989).

5. Problems associated with communitization and unitization of Indian Lands are discussed in [Subsection 6], below.

6. For a more detailed discussion of general Indian Law, see Felix Cohen, Handbook of Federal Indian Law (1982 ed.). For a more detailed discussion of Indian natural resources law, see Peter Maxfield, Mary Dieterich & Frank Trelease, Natural Resources Law on American Indian Lands (1977), and Judith Royster, Equivocal Obligations: The Federal–Tribal Trust Relationship and Conflicts of Interest in the Development of Mineral Resources, 71 N.D. L. Rev. 327 (1995). For a thorough analysis of the landmark case of *Johnson v. M'Intosh*, see Lindsay G. Robertson, Conquest by Law: How the Discovery of America Dispossessed Indigenous Peoples of Their Lands (2005).

(b) General Regulatory Control in Indian Country

Non–Indian landowners—and who can govern them—provide a source of consternation among the state, tribal, and federal governments. Generally, tribes may assert regulatory control over non-natives on reservation lands whether the specific land in question is considered tribal or is held in fee by non-Indians. State regulation, particularly if a strong state interest is not implicated, is pre-empted by tribal and federal authority. This is especially the case if state regulatory control would disrupt a tribal regulatory scheme. Likewise, as described in *Montana v. United States*, 450 U.S. 544 (1981), the general rule is that a tribe's inherent government authority does not allow the regulation of non-native activity on non-native land within "Indian country." This rule is subject to two major exceptions. The first is that non-natives can enter into consensual dealings with tribes, thus subjecting themselves to tribal regulation and liability. The second is that tribes can regulate non-native behavior in Indian country where the non-native behavior significantly affects the health and welfare of a tribe.

Development of the mineral estate sometimes entails both exceptions. The first is often seen in modern oil and gas development agreements executed by tribes operating under the auspices of the 1982 Indian Mineral Development Act ("IMDA"), which allows tribes to negotiate more directly with developers than the IMLA of 1938—subject, of course, to the approval of the Secretary of the Interior. Tribes have often insisted on clauses within these agreements that subject the non-Indian developer to the jurisdiction of tribal court. The second exception would be entailed, at least in theory, when development activities lead to surface damage or groundwater contamination that adversely affects a tribe.[235]

Federal environmental regulations did not provide any role for tribes until the Safe Drinking Water Act ("SDWA")[236] was expanded by the federal courts in *Phillips Petroleum Co. v. U.S. Environmental Protection Agency*, 803 F.2d 545, 562 (10th Cir. 1986) in 1986 to cover Indian country, giving the Environmental Protection Agency ("EPA") power to apply the SDWA to tribal lands. Five years later, with the blessing of President George H.W. Bush, the EPA established a "government-to-government" relationship with tribes, recognizing that tribes are sovereign entities.

The SDWA and the Clean Water Act ("CWA")[237] are two of the overarching controlling statutes relevant to tribes when considering possible oil and gas development. The SDWA controls injection of contaminated water into aquifers. Like the SDWA, the CWA was amended to give tribes the same standing as states, allowing tribes to assume responsibility for water quality control in Indian country. The scope of tribal control reflects the complex landholding situation on many reservations, allowing the tribe to regulate reservation, trust lands, allotted lands, and fee lands of both Indians and non-Indians. A tribe may gain the ability to invoke and enforce environmental regulations through the tribes-as-states ("TAS") provisions in the SDWA and CWA.

---

235. This second Montana exception has proved an elusive protection for tribes to invoke.

236. 42 U.S.C. §§ 300f–300j

237. 33 U.S.C. § 1251 *et seq.*

The authority for the bonding of oil and gas wells on Indian land currently lies with the Bureau of Indian Affairs ("BIA").[238] Unlike other categories of federal land, tribal lands require bond coverage at the time an oil and gas lease is issued, and a bond is typically secured by the lessee.

(c) Laws and Concepts Affecting Exploration and Development in Indian Country

Indian lands are an important source of energy from oil, gas, and coal. Although both tribes and individual Indian families directly share in energy development revenues, development of Indian lands is both controversial and complex. The following materials provide a summary of the general principles of Indian land law especially relevant to exploration and drilling on Indian lands. Important concepts to remember when negotiating and contracting for exploration and development in Indian country are also covered.

2 ROCKY MTN. MIN. L. FOUND., LAW OF FEDERAL OIL AND GAS LEASES CH. 26 (2001)[239]

§ 26.03 Identification of Lands Subject to Lease–Title Examination of Indian Lands

Knowing the status of title to any tract of land is essential before that tract can be developed.[240] While consideration of the nuances of examining title to a tract of Indian land is beyond the scope of this paper,[241] any complete title examination will include a review of records maintained by the Bureau of Land Management (BLM), Bureau of Indian Affairs (BIA), the applicable Indian tribe, and the county wherein such tract is located. These basic repositories are:

1. BLM State Land Office—this office has primary responsibility for retaining federal historical records, and any title matters requiring BLM approval;[242]

2. BIA Land Titles and Records Office—this is the office of record for land records and title documents pertaining to Indian lands while

---

238. BIA Well Bonding Regulations, 25 C.F.R. §§ 211–213.

239. Reprinted with permission of the Rocky Mountain Mineral Law Foundation and Matthew Bender & Company, Inc.

240. Ownership determinations for Indian lands are perhaps of even greater importance since many state law concepts often relied upon to cure title problems (i.e. adverse possession) have no application to Indian lands. In addition, as federal law provides that in any trial concerning the right of property in which an Indian is a party on one side and a white person on the other, the burden of proof rests on the white person once the Indian party has established prior ownership in the property. 25 U.S.C. § 194 (1988).

241. The examination of title to Indian lands has been extensively covered in the following: 3 Am.L. of Mining § 96 (2d Ed. 1984); M. Webster Examination of Title to Indian Lands, Mineral Title Examination III, Paper No. 5 (Rocky Mtn. Min. L. Fdn. 1992).

242. The state offices of the BLM, and their jurisdictional areas, are identified in 43 C.F.R. § 1821.2–1(d). In addition, the BLM maintains district and area offices, a listing of which can be obtained at any BLM state office or at the BLM's Washington, D. C. office.

such lands remain in trust status;[243]

3. BIA [Regional]* * * Office—this is the office which exercises jurisdiction over Indian Agency offices within its jurisdiction;[244]

4. BIA Agency and Sub—Agency offices—these officers possess primary responsibility for approving and retaining documents affecting title to lands within each particular Agency's jurisdiction;[245]

5. County records—the records maintained by the county wherein the land is located will disclose documents not requiring BIA approval, documents which are subject to state recording laws,[246] and matters affecting title to Indian land previously owned in fee status;

6. General tribal records—records maintained by the tribe involved will include tribal court records, records of tribal tax commissions, tribal mineral department records and any other records which involve title to the lands under review.

§ 26.04   Exploration of Indian Lands

The permitting of geological and geophysical operations on Indian lands is generally controlled by regulations for both tribal[247] and allotted[248] lands. These regulations generally permit, subject to Secretarial approval, exploration activities for oil and gas so long as such activities do not conflict with an existing mineral lease covering such lands and so long as the appropriate mineral owner has consented to the exploration activities.

The regulations provide, for both tribal and allotted lands, that the exploration permit describe the area to be explored, the time period for completion of the exploration, and the consideration to be paid to the Indian mineral owner. Unless the permit provides to the contrary, there is no grant of any option or any preference right to lease associated with the issuance of the permit. Similarly, unless the permit otherwise provides, the permittee may not produce or remove oil, gas or other minerals during exploration except for samples required for assay or experimental purposes.

A party exploring Indian lands must provide copies of all data collected in the process of exploring such lands to the Secretary. In addition, such data is also to be given to the tribe where tribal lands are involved and made available to individual Indians if allotted lands are involved. The regulations provide that this dissemination of information by the permit-

243. 25 C.F.R. § 150.4 (2001) identifies the location and service areas for five such offices. The BIA also maintains an office in Sacramento, California for all California tribes.

244. 25 C.F.R. § 150.5 vests certain [Regional] * * * offices with additional record keeping functions and responsibilities.

245. Agreements creating overriding royalties or payments out of production, and agreements designating operators, are to be filed with the Superintendent. 25 C.F.R. (§ 211.539d); 25 C.F.R. § 212.53.

246. See, e.g. 25 C.F.R. § 103.28 (2001) (financing documents).

247. 25 C.F.R. § 211.56.

248. 25 C.F.R. § 212.56.

tee may be modified by the terms of the permit. The regulations further provide that the Secretary shall treat data received by the Secretary as being proprietary and privileged for so long as is set forth in the permit, or, in the absence of any time period, for six years. Thereafter, the Secretary may release such data with the consent of the Indian mineral owner.

For allotted lands, a permit for exploration activities may be granted where less than all trust mineral owners consent in certain identified circumstances. Consent to a permit may be granted where the mineral interest to be explored is owned by more than one party and the owners of a majority interest in the minerals consent to the permit. The permit may also be granted where the whereabouts of one owner is unknown and all of the remaining owners consent to the permit. A permit may also be issued where the owner of the land or an interest therein is deceased and the owner's probate has not been completed; provided, however, the Secretary finds that the activity can take place without substantial injury to the land or any owner thereof. Finally, a permit for exploration purposes may also be granted where the Secretary determines not only that there are so many owners of a tract of land that it would be impractical to obtain their consent, but also that the desired activity can occur without substantial injury to the land or any owner thereof.

The allotted land regulations, but not the tribal land regulations, provide that no permit for geological or geophysical activities is required where the exploring party holds a current mineral lease covering the property to be explored and the lessor is also the surface owner. Where the allotted lands mineral lessor is not the surface owner, the regulation requires that the lessee intending to conduct exploration activities obtain "any additional necessary permits or rights of ingress or egress from the surface occupant."[249]

§ 26.05   Statutory Authority for Development of Indian Lands

Development of Indian mineral resources can only occur where some legal authority sanctions the development. Primary authority for developing tribal minerals is found in the Omnibus Indian Mineral Leasing Act of 1938[250] and in the Indian Mineral Development Act of 1982.[251] Primary authority for developing mineral resources owned by individual Indians is found in the Allotted Lands Leasing Act of 1909.[252]

[1]   Tribal Lands

[a]   Early Legislation

The first statute which authorized tribal leasing of oil and gas was the Act of February 28, 1891.[253] This Act applied only to lands "bought and

---

249.   25 C.F.R. § 212.56(c).

250.   Codified at 25 U.S.C. §§ 396a–396g.

251.   Codified at 25 U.S.C. § 2101–2108.

252.   Codified at 25 U.S.C. § 396.

253.   Ch. 383, 26 Stat. 795 (1891) (codified at 25 U.S.C. § 397 (1988)).

paid for" by Indians and, further, limited such leases to a term of 10 years. The 1891 statute was broadened first by the Act of May 29, 1924,[254] which provided for the leasing of all unallotted lands on Indian reservations (other than lands of the Five civilized Tribes and the Osage Reservation, which Congress had previously provided for by separate legislation) for periods up to 10 years and as long thereafter as oil or gas is found in paying quantities. The 1924 legislation established a public auction requirement and provided for state taxation of production from leased lands, including the tribe's royalty share, in a manner identical to taxation of production from non-Indian lands.[255]

Reservations lands reserved for agency or school purposes were made subject to lease by the Secretary at public auction through the Act of April 17, 1926.[256] Similar legislation relating solely to the Fort Peck and Blackfeet reservations in Montana had previously been enacted,[257] as had legislation pertaining solely to the Kaw reservation in Oklahoma.[258]

After enactment of the 1924 Act, the applicability of that Act and other leasing legislation to executive order reservations was uncertain. To clarify this, Congress passed the Act of March 3, 1927, which specifically made the leasing provisions of the 1924 Act[259] applicable to executive order reservations.[260] The 1927 Act also authorized the Secretary of the Interior to recognize and confirm the validity of prospecting permits filed for Indian lands under the Mineral Leasing Act of 1920[261] provided the applications for such permits had been filed before May 27, 1924. Upon establishing full compliance with the terms of the permit, including discovery of oil and gas, the permittee was entitled to a lease on a portion of the permitted lands and a preference right to a lease on the balance.[262]

[b]   Omnibus Indian Mineral Leasing Act of 1938[263]

---

254.   Ch. 210, 43 Stat. 244 (1924) (codified at 25 U.S.C. § 398).

255.   The United States Supreme Court has held that the provisions authorizing state taxation of Indian royalty interests on oil and gas produced within reservations have no application to lands leased pursuant to the 1938 Indian Mineral Leasing Act. Montana v. Blackfeet Tribe of Indians, 471 U.S. 759 (1985).

256.   Ch. 156, 44 Stat. 300 (1926) (codified at 25 U.S.C. § 400a (1982)).

257.   Act of September 20, 1922, ch. 347, 42 Stat. 857 (codified at 25 U.S.C. § 400); *see* British–American Oil Producing Co. v. Board of Equalization of State of Montana, 299 U.S. 159 (1936) (construing Act of 1922).

258.   Act of April 28, 1924, ch. 135, 43 Stat. 111 (codified at 25 U.S.C. § 401). The legislation applied to the Kaw reservation lands, which had been reserved from allotment to be used as a cemetery when such land was unneeded for that purpose.

259.   Ch. 210, 43 Stat. 244 (1924) (codified at 25 U.S.C. § 398).

260.   Ch. 299, 44 Stat. 1347 (1927) (codified at 25 U.S.C. §§ 398a–398e); *see* United States v. Truckee–Carson Irrigation Dist., 649 F.2d 1286 (9th Cir.1981) (executive order reservations merit the same protection as reservations created by treaty or statute).

261.   30 U.S.C. §§ 181–263.

262.   25 U.S.C. § 398e.

263.   The Act does not apply to the Osage Reservation in Oklahoma, and to the ceded lands of the Shoshone Reservation in Wyoming. The Act originally had no application to various other tribes, but various Public Laws have made the Act applicable to most reservations.

The Omnibus Indian Mineral Leasing Act of 1938 (1938 Act) was, for nearly 45 years, the main mechanism for developing tribal mineral resources. This Act authorizes leasing lands "owned by any tribe, group or band of Indians under Federal jurisdiction," subject to approval of the Secretary.[264] Leases under the 1938 Act are limited by statute to "terms not to exceed ten years and as long thereafter as minerals are produced in paying quantities."[265] The Act requires that oil and gas leases be offered at a public sale following notice and advertisement. No similar statutory requirement exists for other minerals.[266] To hold a lease, the Act requires lessees to furnish a bond or other acceptable collateral, in an amount deemed satisfactory to guarantee compliance with the lease terms.[267] The Act authorizes the Secretary to promulgate rules and regulations governing operations under the 1938 Act Lease; such regulations are found at 25 C.F.R. Part 211.

Leasing of tribal land for oil and gas under the 1938 Act is generally initiated through a resolution by the tribal council, or by a designated tribal committee. The resolution typically stems from nominations or requests from parties who are interested in prospective acreage. On occasion, tribes will offer lands for leasing solely in an effort to generate exploration interest and income. Following tribal authorization, the superintendent of the reservation, through the Bureau of Indian Affairs Agency Realty Section, will obtain title status reports covering all lease tracts, and seek recommendations of Bureau of Indian Affairs and Bureau of Land Management minerals specialists.

Oil and gas leases to be issued under authority of the 1938 Act must be offered at public sale for at least 30 days.[268] * * * [Rental and royalty rates are established in the sales notice and are not subject to negotiation.][269] Each notice must acknowledge the Secretary's right to reject bids and that acceptance of the lease bid by the tribe is required prior to approval of the lease.[270] Strict compliance with these sale requirements is required.[271]

---

264. 25 U.S.C. § 396a (1988). The Secretary may delegate this authority to others. 25 U.S.C. § 396c. The Secretary has a duty to approve or reject a lease within a reasonable time.

265. 25 U.S.C. § 396a.

266. 25 U.S.C. § 396b. Under this section, the Secretary reserves the right to reject any and all bids. Where the Secretary rejects a bid, the tribe may be allowed to conduct private negotiations. This section specifically provides that it shall not restrict those tribes organized under the Indian Reorganization Act from leasing their lands in accordance with any applicable tribal constitution or charter.

267. 25 U.S.C. § 396d.

268. 25 C.F.R. § 211.2(b)(1).

269. Id.

270. 25 C.F.R. § 211.20(b)(2).

271. Jicarilla Apache Tribe v. Andrus, 687 F.2d 1324 (10th Cir.1982). Many lease sales conducted prior to 1982 failed to strictly comply with these advertising requirements. The Secretary recognized the need for a method of curing defects resulting from deficient sale notices; and, as a result, the Secretary approved a procedure whereby lease amendments called "waivers" or "ratifications" acknowledging technical deficiencies in the notice of sale, and waiving the same, are executed by lessors and lessees following renegotiation of bonuses. Authority to approve the waiver and ratification documents was delegated to area directors and superintendents (except for

[Sales may be conducted through a sealed bid process or an oral auction. Payment of bonus, advertising costs, filing fees, bonds, and rentals and the filing of an executed lease with the Secretary are governed by detailed regulations. The failure of a successful bidder to fully comply with these regulations can lead to loss of the lease and the forfeiture of bonus deposits.][272] If the Secretary rejects the highest bid, or no bid is received, or if the successful bidder fails to complete all requirements necessary for lease approval, the Secretary may re-advertise the tract or authorize the tribe to enter into private negotiations for a lease.[273]

Tribal leases should be executed by those tribal officials who are duly authorized to act for and on behalf of the tribe. In most instances, the persons authorized to execute tribal oil and gas leases are executive officers of the tribe, but on occasion the authorized party may be the chairman or some other member of a committee designated by tribal ordinance, charter, or constitution to manage oil and gas resources and execute lease documents. In some cases, the tribal resolution which authorizes the leasing or the acceptance of bids will contain authorization for lease execution. In other instances, separate resolutions dealing with execution of the lease will be utilized.

* * * The regulations for 1938 Act leases require corporate lessees to supply various financial and corporate information.[274] In addition, all lessees must file adequate bonds to hold any lease issued pursuant to the Act. * * *[275] Leased lands are to be in a reasonably compact body, covering no more than one governmental survey section of land, not to exceed 640 acres.[276]

The regulations provide that leases shall be for a primary term not to exceed 10 years, and, unless otherwise provided, for so long thereafter as minerals covered by the lease are produced in paying quantities. Unless otherwise provided, the effective date of the lease runs from the date of approval of the lease by the Secretary.[277] Tribal leases may contain "commencement of drilling clauses" which may extend the term of tribal leases over the end of the primary term, but only if the lessee has commenced actual drilling by midnight of the last day of the primary term utilizing a drilling rig designed to reach the proposed depth, with actual drilling operations being diligently prosecuted. The regulations provide that such a clause will not act to continue the term of the lease for more than 120 days beyond the primary term without actual production being obtained. The regulations recognize, however, that the "commencement of

---

superintendents under the Navajo office) pursuant to a February 24, 1983, memorandum from the Deputy Assistant Secretary for Indian Affairs.

272. 25 C.F.R. § 211.20(b)(5).

273. 25 C.F.R. § 211.20(b)(6).

274. 25 C.F.R. § 211.23.

275. 25 C.F.R. § 211.24.

276. 25 C.F.R. § 211.25.

277. 25 C.F.R. § 211.27(a).

drilling" clause will not extend a lease past the 10 year maximum primary term provided by statute.[278]

Operations may not begin until Secretarial approval of the lease[279] and BLM approval of the proposed operations.[280] Lessees must conduct operations in a manner insuring diligent development while also preventing waste of the lessor's minerals.[281] The Secretary may restrict operations to protect the lessor's interests.

[c]   Indian Mineral Development Act of 1982[282]

In 1982, Congress enacted the Indian Mineral Development Act (IMDA). The IMDA authorizes tribes, with Secretarial approval (and subject to any limitation contained in the tribe's constitution or charter), to enter into private negotiations for joint ventures, operating or production sharing agreements, service or managerial contracts, leases, or any other type of agreement providing for the exploration, extraction, processing or development of tribal energy resources.[283] Any negotiated agreement must be submitted to the Secretary for approval in order to become valid and effective. * * *[284] In reaching a decision on whether to approve or disapprove a mineral agreement, the Secretary must determine if the agreement is in the tribe's best interest, taking into account, inter alia: the potential economic benefit to the tribe; the possible environmental, social and cultural impacts on the tribe; and the means for dispute resolution built into the agreement.[285] The Secretary must provide the tribe with written findings forming the basis of the Secretary's decision to approve or disapprove the agreement at least 30 days before final Secretarial action.[286] These findings are considered proprietary information.[287] Only the Secretary or the Assistant Secretary for Indian Affairs may disapprove an IMDA agreement, and disapproval constitutes final agency action reviewable de novo by a federal district court.[288] A tribe may withdraw its consent to an agreement at any time prior to final Secretarial approval of an IMDA agreement.[289] Terms of IMDA agreements have no statutory limitation, nor does the Act contain any standards which must be satisfied for continuation of agreements. The Act also contains no acreage limitations.

---

278.   25 C.F.R. § 211.27(b).

279.   25 C.F.R. § 211.48(a).

280.   25 C.F.R. § 211.48(b); 25 C.F.R. § 211.4.

281.   25 C.F.R. § 211.45.

282.   25 U.S.C. §§ 2101–2108.

283.   25 U.S.C. § 2102(a).

284.   25 U.S.C. § 2103(a).

285.   25 U.S.C. § 2103(b).

286.   25 U.S.C. § 2103(c) (1988).

287.   Id.

288.   25 U.S.C. § 2103(d).

289.   Quantum Exploration, Inc. v. Clark, 780 F.2d 1457 (9th Cir.1986).

* * * Regulations implementing the IMDA were finally promulgated in final form effective as of March 30, 1994.[290] The regulations governing IMDA agreements are located at 25 C.F.R. Part 225. These regulations state that they are intended to permit Indian mineral owners (both tribes and individual Indians) to enter into mineral agreements which are structured to allow development in a manner desired by the Indian mineral owner.[291]

The regulations partially clarify the roles which the Bureau of Land Management[292] and the Minerals Management Service[293] are to play in conjunction with the Bureau of Indian Affairs in the administration of any IMDA agreement. The regulations also set forth a de facto checklist of matters which should be considered and/or incorporated into any IMDA agreement.[294]

* * * When a mineral developer negotiates for an IMDA agreement with a tribe, several matters must be considered during the negotiation process.[295] The following are of particular importance to developers, given the sovereign status of Indian tribes: every agreement should contain a waiver of the tribe's sovereign immunity,[296] since the sovereign status of tribes[297] otherwise makes them immune from suit;[298] agreements should ideally contain dispute resolution provisions since any dispute will generally be resolved in tribal court, applying tribal laws, in the absence of any contractual provision to the contrary;[299] an agreement should also address taxation by the tribes of the developers property[300] and production;[301] and tribal employment issues should be addressed.[302]

[2]   Allotted Lands

[a]   Act of March 3, 1909

The primary authority for leasing allotted Indian lands is the Act of March 3, 1909 (1909 Act).[303] This Act[304] permits individual Indians[305] to

---

290.   59 Fed.Reg. 14971 (March 30, 1994).

291.   25 C.F.R. § 225.1.

292.   25 C.F.R. § 225.4.

293.   25 C.F.R. § 225.6.

294.   25 C.F.R. § 225.21.

295.   A number of provisions have been identified by regulation. 25 C.F.R. § 225.21.

296.   McClendon v. United States, 885 F.2d 627, 630 (9th Cir.1989).

297.   Worcester v. Georgia, 31 U.S. 515 (1832).

298.   Santa Clara Pueblo v. Martinez, 436 U.S. 49 (1978).

299.   Iowa Mutual Ins. Co. v. LaPlante, 480 U.S. 9 (1987); National Farmers Union Ins. Cos. v. Crow Tribe, 471 U.S. 845 (1985).

300.   [Editors' note] Big Horn County Elec. Co-op, Inc. v. Adams, 219 F.3d 944 (9th Cir. Mont. 2000).

301.   Merrion v. Jicarilla Apache Tribe, 455 U.S. 130 (1982).

302.   Arizona Public Service Co. v. Aspaas, 77 F.3d 1128 (9th Cir.1995).

303.   Act of March 3, 1909, ch. 263, 35 Stat. 783 (now codified at 25 U.S.C. § 396 (1988)).

304.   The Act does not apply to allotments made to members of the Five Civilized Tribes and to the Osage Indians in Oklahoma.

305.   See, Poafpybitty v. Skelly Oil Co., 390 U.S. 365 (1968).

lease their lands for mining purposes "for any term of years as may be deemed advisable by the Secretary of the Interior." As amended in 1955, this Act authorizes the Secretary to lease allotted lands where the allottee is deceased and the heirs or devisees of any interest in the lands are not yet determined, or if determined, some or all cannot be located.[306] In such a situation, the lands must be offered for lease at public auction or on sealed bids, after notice and advertisement.[307] The Secretary may reject bids if rejection is in the Indian owner's best interest.[308]

Regulations promulgated under the 1909 Act at 25 C.F.R. Part 212 largely mirror the regulations for 1938 Act tribal leases found at 25 C.F.R. Part 211.

* * *

The 1909 Act regulations [in general are the same as the 1938 Act regulations]. * * *

Several 1909 Act regulations are unique to allotted lands. One such regulation purportedly empowers the Superintendent to execute leases on behalf of minors and persons judged incompetent by reason of mental incapacity, provided there is no parent, guardian, conservator or other person otherwise lawfully entitled to execute a lease on such party's behalf.[309] * * *

* * * [Until the Congress took steps to rectify the problem in 2000, every fractional interest owner of an allotment tract had to consent to the issuance of an oil or gas lease for such allotment. Under the 2000 legislation, codified at 25 U.S.C. § 2218, the number of owners of interests in allotments that must consent to an oil and gas lease depends upon the total number of owners of the allotment as reflected in the records of the Secretary. Once the requisite number of owners of interests in allotments have consented to the lease, the Secretary can approve the lease agreement on behalf of the remaining allottees, if the Secretary determines that such approval is in the best interests of such owners.]

* * *

[b]   Indian Mineral Development Act of 1982

The primary focus of the IMDA is on developing tribal resources. Although the IMDA permits the inclusion of allotted lands "in a tribal minerals agreement subject to the concurrence of the parties and a finding by the Secretary that such participation is in the best interest of the Indian,"[310] allotted lands have only occasionally been included within an IMDA agreement.

---

306. Act of August 9, 1955, ch. 615 § 3, 69 Stat. 540, 25 U.S.C. § 396.

307. 25 U.S.C. § 396.

308. The Secretary owes a general fiduciary duty to individual Indians with respect to the development of their mineral resources. *See,* Pawnee v. United States, 830 F.2d 187 (Fed.Cir. 1987).

309. 25 C.F.R. § 212.21(b). No statutory authority directly supports this power.

310. 25 U.S.C. § 2102(b).

§ 26.06   Commencing and Conducting Operations on Indian Lands

[1]   Bonding

Parties operating or conducting operations on Indian lands must furnish to the Secretary a surety bond or personal bond in an amount sufficient to insure compliance with the terms and conditions of any lease[311] or mineral agreement.[312] * * *

* * *

[2]   Drilling Permits

No action to drill a well for oil and gas on Indian lands may be taken until the BLM has issued to the lessee or operator a drilling permit for such well.[313] The procedures for obtaining a drilling permit are primarily found in 43 C.F.R. Part 3160 and in Onshore Oil & Gas Order No. 1.[314]

The prospective operator should have a map of the proposed project available for review by the appropriate surface managing agency for determination of whether or not a cultural or biological inventory or other information may be required.[315] Generally, a lessee or operator will employ an independent archaeologist to conduct an archaeological inspection of the surface of any lands to be disturbed by development activities. In most instances, permits for this inspection must be obtained from both the BIA and the tribe. * * *

BLM approval in advance of any surveying or staking of either the well location or any necessary access road is unnecessary.[316] However, an operator must contact the BIA prior to engaging in such activity. It is the responsibility of the operator to make all arrangements with the surface owner necessary to obtain access. If the property is held in trust for a tribe or individual Indians, the BIA must approve any access agreements.

Consideration of issuance of a drilling permit is initiated by the lessee or operator filing with the BLM an [Application for a Permit to Drill, Deepen or Plug–Back] APD (BLM Form 3160–3),[317] or by the filing of a [Notice of Staking] NOS, followed by the filing of an APD.[318] A technically and administratively complete APD is required for each well drilled on Indian lands. * * *

* * *

---

311.   25 C.F.R. § 211.24 (tribal); 25 C.F.R. § 212.24 (allotted).

312.   25 C.F.R. § 225.30.

313.   See, William Perlman, 93 I.D. 159 (1986); 43 C.F.R. § 3162.3–1(c); see 43 C.F.R. Subpart 3164, which authorizes both Onshore Oil and Gas Orders and Notices to Lessees (NTL's).

314.   48 Fed. Reg. 48916 (October 21, 1983), as corrected in 48 Fed. Reg. 56226 (Dec. 20, 1983).

315.   Onshore Oil & Gas Order No. 1, Section III.B.

316.   Onshore Oil & Gas Order No. 1, Section III.B–C.

317.   Onshore Oil & Gas Order No. 1, Section III.D; 43 C.F.R. § 3162.3–1.

318.   Id.

[3]   Operating the Lease

Section 4 of the Omnibus Leasing Act[319] makes all operations under an Indian lands oil and gas lease subject to rules and regulations promulgated by the Secretary of the Interior. Similarly, the 1909 Act authorizing the leasing of allotted lands also authorizes the Secretary to "make such rules and regulations as may be necessary. . . ."[320] Finally, Section 8 of the Indian Mineral Development Act required the Secretary to implement rules and regulations to facilitate implementation of the Act.[321] The majority of regulations addressed to oil and gas operations are contained in 43 C.F.R. Part 3160, which provides general operating instructions for both federal and Indian oil and gas leases. The regulations found in Part 3160 are intended to control the exploration, development, and production of oil and gas deposits from Indian lands. Such regulations are primarily administered under the direction of the Bureau of Land Management. * * *

* * *

The regulations governing operations on Indian lands provide in essence that the lessee or developer shall exercise diligence in drilling and operating and shall do all things required to insure that Indian resources are developed in a manner that maximizes economic benefits while minimizing environmental and cultural impacts.[322]

[4]   Rents and Royalties

Rental and royalty accounting and remittances on Indian reservations are generally governed by regulations[323] as well as by the lease forms and by the notices of oil and gas lease sales. The regulations are substantially the same for both tribal and allotted leases, and provide generally that, except advance payments for the first year (which are usually paid directly to the superintendent of the reservation when the leases are first filed), payments of rentals and royalties are controlled by the provisions of 30 C.F.R. § 218.51.

* * * On newer lease forms and in accordance with current regulations, rental payments are not credited against royalties; * * * full rentals must be paid throughout the life of the lease, even if production is obtained in quantities where the royalty generated would exceed the rental payments required.[324]

As is implied from the above, rentals must be paid regardless of production. Also, delay rentals on Indian leases are contractual obligations and if not paid, the lessor may have recourse against the lessee's bond. At present, an Indian lease does not terminate automatically upon improper

---

319. 25 U.S.C. § 396d.

320. 25 U.S.C. § 396.

321. 25 U.S.C. § 2107.

322. 25 C.F.R. § 211.1(a) (tribal); 25 C.F.R. § 212.1(a) (allotted); 25 C.F.R. § 225.1(a) (mineral agreements).

323. 25 C.F.R. §§ 211.40, 211.41 (tribal); 25 C.F.R. §§ 212.40, 212.41 (allotted); 35 C.F.R. ch. II, subchs. A and C.

324. 25 C.F.R. § 211.41(a) (tribal); 25 C.F.R. § 212.41(a) (allotted).

or untimely rental payments. Nevertheless, care should be taken to pay rentals on time, since the failure to timely make a rental payment may allow the lessor to seek cancellation, and it is unclear whether acceptance of late rental payments would constitute a waiver of the right to claim a forfeiture.[325]

Rental and royalty rates are set by the Secretary or his representative, and vary from reservation to reservation. * * * [Subject to some "grandfathered" leases,] [c]urrent regulations require the payment of at least $2.00 per acre per year annual rental,[326] and the current minimum royalty is now set at 16–2/3%.[327]

[The Minerals Management Service regulations addressing the value for royalty purposes of oil and gas production from Indian leases are similar in most respects to the regulations addressing valuation for federal oil and gas leases. See section 4 below. In addition, standard form Indian leases have certain unique provisions.]

In 1982, Congress passed the Federal Oil & Gas Royalty Management Act of 1982 (FOGRMA),[328] to require the Secretary to "aggressively" carry out his trust responsibilities relative to Indian oil and gas interests[329] in order to fulfill the trust responsibilities of the United States in the administration of Indian oil and gas resources.[330] FOGRMA directed the Secretary to establish comprehensive inspection, collection, and auditing schemes to insure that all oil and gas royalties, interest, fines and any other monies due as a result of production of oil and gas were properly and timely paid.[331] * * *

The primary duty for enforcing the requirements of FOGRMA rests on the MMS.[332] By regulation, the MMS is charged with responsibility for collecting royalties, reviewing sales and production reports, determining royalty liability, auditing royalty payments, and for all other similar functions relating to the royalty management of Indian oil and gas leases.[333] In fulfilling its obligations, the MMS has implemented extensive systems for the reporting of and accounting for royalties attributable to Indian lands. Regulations set forth valuation standards for production,[334] identify forms and reports that must be completed relative to production,[335] and provide directives on the payment of rentals and royalties.[336]

* * *

---

325. United States v. Forness, 125 F.2d 928 (2d Cir.1942).

326. 25 C.F.R. § 211.41(a) (tribal); 25 C.F.R. § 212.41(a) (allotted).

327. 25 C.F.R. § 211.41(b) (tribal); 25 C.F.R. § 212.41(b) (allotted).

328. Public Law 97–451, 96 Stat. 2448, codified at 30 U.S.C. §§ 1701–1757.

329. 30 U.S.C. § 1701(a)(4).

330. 30 U.S.C. § 1701(b)(4).

331. 30 U.S.C. § 1711(a).

332. See 25 C.F.R. § 211.6 (tribal leases); 25 C.F.R. § 212.6 (allotted leases); 25 C.F.R. § 225.6 (mineral agreements).

333. 30 C.F.R. § 201.100.

334. 30 C.F.R. Part 206.

335. 30 C.F.R. Part 210 and Part 216.

336. 30 C.F.R. Part 218.

§ 26.08   Other Concerns

[1]   Secretarial Approval

All leases, mineral agreements, lease assignments, lease modifications, communitization agreements and other similar agreements are void until and unless validly approved by the Secretary. This requirement presents several potential concerns for developers of Indian lands. Included within these concerns are:

[a]   Exposure for Environmental Review Costs

Mineral agreements entered into under authority of the IMDA are of no force or effect until approved by the Secretary.[337] Under the IMDA, significant time delays exist before the Secretary approves or disapproves an agreement, particularly where any significant environmental review is required.[338] The developer may be financially liable for costs associated with any extensive environmental review. Because an Indian tribe may withdraw its consent to an IMDA agreement at any time before final Secretarial approval, a developer may find that it has expended significant sums of money on environmental studies only to have the Tribe, at the last minute, withdraw its consent to the mineral agreement.

There is no statutory mechanism available to restrict a tribe's ability to withdraw its consent to an IMDA agreement. It may be possible, however, to negotiate a shifting of the financial burden of such an event from the developer to a surety of the tribe or to the tribe itself. Thus, a developer may attempt to negotiate a separate agreement with a tribe, approved by the Secretary, whereby the tribe would guarantee, through a non-Indian surety company, the reimbursement of a developer's environmental review costs required by the Secretary should the tribe unilaterally withdraw its consent to the agreement prior to final Secretarial approval or disapproval.[339]

[b]   "Best Interests" Standard for Approval

Secretarial approval of any agreement affecting Indian lands is only to occur where approval is in the "best interests" of the Indian, unless the Secretary's actions are carried out pursuant to a clear directive of Congress.[340] This "best interests" [fiduciary] standard injects uncertainty into any Secretarial action, and court actions have been successfully advanced by tribes based upon allegations that the Secretary has failed to satisfy this standard. * * *

[c]   Failure to Obtain Secretarial Approval

The failure to obtain Secretarial approval of any lease, mineral agreement, assignment, or other similar agreement means that such

---

337.   Quantum Exploration Inc. v. Clark, 780 F.2d 1457 (9th Cir.1986).

338.   25 U.S.C. § 2103(a); 25 C.F.R. § 225.24.

339.   See, White Mountain Apache Tribe v. Smith Plumbing Co., 856 F.2d 1301 (9th Cir.1988) relative to utilizing a non-Indian surety company.

340.   Yellowfish v. City of Stillwater, 691 F.2d 926 (10th Cir.1982).

agreement is, under the law, void.[341] While the effect of this is clear as to leases or development agreements—there simply is no agreement and the developer has no rights—the ramifications flowing from lack of Secretarial approval of other agreements are just as important, albeit less obvious.

Most tribal and allotted lands leases provide that they may be canceled if the lessee breaches any of the terms of the lease or any of the applicable regulations. These same forms, almost without exception, require that any assignment be approved by the Secretary. This requirement is also found in the regulations.[342] Nevertheless, county records often disclose multiple lease assignments for trust oil and gas leases which have never been approved by the BIA. While no case is known where this failure to obtain approval of an assignment has resulted in lease cancellation, the possibility of such an attack on a lease or agreement cannot be ruled out.

The failure to obtain BIA approval of an assignment can also have economic implications for the party remaining the record title owner of the lease, since that owner remains liable for plugging and abandoning until that process is satisfactorily completed.[343] Additionally, the record title owner will remain liable for other damages, including environmental harm, occasioned by the operations on the lease. Finally, the record title owner remains liable for any unpaid royalties or production taxes.[344]

[2]   Sovereign Immunity

[a]   Tribal Sovereign Immunity

Indian tribes, as "domestic, dependent nations,"[345] possess those attributes of sovereignty which have not been lost through voluntary surrender by the tribe, through actions of Congress, or by necessary implication as a result of a tribe's dependent status.[346] One of these attributes of sovereignty is that of immunity from suit. Thus, in the absence of an effective waiver of immunity, a tribe may assert its immunity from suit as an absolute defense against a mineral developer which finds itself engaged in a dispute with a tribe, even where the dispute originates off the reservation.[347]

Courts have indicated that tribes may waive their immunity from suit by contract.[348] Where the waiver is part of a lease or mineral agreement, the agreement must be approved by the Secretary before the waiver of

---

341.   Craig McGriff Exploration, Inc. v. Acting Anadarko Area Director, Bureau of Indian Affairs, 22 IBIA 265, 269 (1992).

342.   See, e.g. 25 C.F.R. § 211.53(a) (tribal leases); 25 C.F.R. § 212.53 (allotted lands leases); 25 C.F.R. § 225.33 (mineral agreements).

343.   American Surety Co. of New York v. United States, 112 F.2d 903 (10th Cir. 1940).

344.   Mesa Operating Ltd. Partnership, 125 IBLA 28 (1992) GFS (O & G) 2 (1993).

345.   Cherokee Nation v. Georgia, 30 U.S. (5 Pet.) 1, 17 (1831).

346.   Oliphant v. Suquamish Indian Tribe, 435 U.S. 191 (1978); State of Alaska v. Native Village of Venetie, 856 F.2d 1384, 1387 (9th Cir.1988).

347.   In Re Greene, 980 F.2d 590 (9th Cir.1992).

348.   McClendon v. United States, 885 F.2d 627, 630 (9th Cir.1989).

immunity clause is effective.[349] Additionally, the waiver must be unequivocally expressed.[350] Contractual provisions which merely provide for remedies for breach of contract will likely be found to be unenforceable in the absence of an effective waiver.[351] Similarly, [although] the presence of an arbitration clause in an agreement may * * * constitute an effective waiver of a tribe's immunity, [it is certainly good practice to expressly provide for a waiver * * *].[352]

An effective immunity waiver should be included in every IMDA agreement. * * * Any negotiated waiver should ideally be broad enough to permit the developer not only to enforce the terms of the mineral agreement, but also to prosecute suits of a declaratory nature to resolve uncertainties relating to the rights and obligations of the developer under both the agreement and under any present or future tribal law or ordinance.

While a developer may negotiate for a waiver of tribal immunity under the IMDA, standard 1938 Act leases contain no waivers of immunity. Although it is possible to obtain a modification of 1938 Act leases to include a waiver, Secretarial approval of the modification would be required.[353] Approval would be appropriate only if the waiver were in the tribe's best interest, a standard unlikely to be satisfied by such a modification. Nevertheless, it may be argued that tribal immunity should not shield a tribe from compliance with the 1938 Act and the terms of the tribe's lease, since a tribe should not reap the benefits of the 1938 Act and lease while at the same time refusing to comply with their provisions.[354] In addition, a developer under a 1938 Act lease may be able, in certain circumstances, to bring suit against tribal officials or the Secretary.[355]

[b]   Immunity of Tribal Officials

Governing bodies of Indian tribes, like the tribe itself, enjoy common law immunity from suit.[356] This immunity shields tribal officials from suit when the officials are acting in their official, representative capacity, and within the scope of their authority.[357] Such immunity does not extend to individual tribal members,[358] nor will a tribe's immunity from suit extend to shield tribal officials acting pursuant to an allegedly unconstitutional

---

349. A. K. Management Co. v. San Manuel Band of Mission Indians, 789 F.2d 785 (9th Cir.1986).

350. Pit River Home and Agr. Coop. Ass'n. v. United States, 30 F.3d 1088 (9th Cir.1994).

351. American Indian Agricultural Credit Consortium, Inc. v. Standing Rock Sioux Tribe, 780 F.2d 1374 (8th Cir.1985).

352. * * * C & L Enterprises, Inc. v. Citizen Band of Potawatomi Indian Tribe of Oklahoma, 532 U.S. 411 (2001). Cf., First American Casino Corp. v. Eastern Pequot Nation, 2001 WL 950243 (Conn.Super.2001).

353. 25 C.F.R. § 211.53(c).

354. See, e.g. Ross v. Flandreau Santee Sioux Tribe, 809 F.Supp. 738, 744 (D.S.D.1992).

355. United Nuclear Corporation v. United States, 912 F.2d 1432, 1438 (Fed.Cir.1990).

356. Stock West Corporation v. Lujan, 982 F.2d 1389, 1398 (9th Cir.1993).

357. Imperial Granite Co. v. Pala Band of Mission Indians, 940 F.2d 1269 (9th Cir.1991).

358. United States v. James, 980 F.2d 1314, 1319 (9th Cir.1992).

statute.[359] Because an official's immunity is predicated on the official acting within the scope of their authority, immunity will not exist where the official involved is acting outside that authority, or implicitly where the authority given by the tribe exceeds the level of authority possessed by the tribe.[360] Thus, a developer faced with actions by a tribe which appear to be beyond the tribe's sovereign authority may be able to challenge such actions, even in the absence of a tribal waiver of immunity, by prosecuting an action against the appropriate tribal officials.

[c]   Immunity of Other Tribal Entities

As tribes have become more sophisticated regarding on-reservation economic development, more and more tribes have formed separate tribally-owned and operated businesses to conduct commercial activities for and on behalf of the tribe.[361] Tribal construction companies, mineral development companies, marketing entities and other similar businesses all may be involved in a developer's on-reservation operations, and the unique status of these companies must be understood and addressed by the developer.

While generalities in Indian law are dangerous, particularly in areas implicating tribal sovereignty and the extent or limits thereof, a developer would be prudent to assume that every tribally-owned and operated business or other entity with which the developer does business enjoys the same immunity from suit otherwise enjoyed by the tribe.[362] Thus, in dealing with a tribal business entity, a developer should seek to obtain from the tribe a written waiver of the tribal entity's immunity,[363] or the developer should verify that the corporate charter of the tribal entity contains a waiver of immunity, most commonly in the nature of a "sue and be sued" provision.[364]

[3]   Dual Taxation

One attribute of tribal sovereignty which has been recognized by the courts is the ability of tribes to tax non-Indian mineral developers on production obtained from Indian lands.[365] In addition, states may also tax production from Indian lands so long as the state's taxes are found to be reasonable and not otherwise preempted by federal law.[366] The preemption test employed by the courts provides no bright line test for determining where preemption will be found,[367] other than to suggest that a state

---

359. Burlington Northern Railroad v. Blackfeet Tribe, 924 F.2d 899 (9th Cir.1991).

360. Tenneco Oil Company v. Sac & Fox Tribe of Indians of Oklahoma, 725 F.2d 572, 574 (10th Cir.1984).

361. See, e.g., In Re Greene, 980 F.2d 590 (9th Cir.1992).

362. See, e.g., Weeks Construction Inc. v. Oglala Sioux Housing Authority, 797 F.2d 668 (8th Cir.1986).

363. Altheimer & Gray v. Sioux Manufacturing Corp., 983 F.2d 803 (7th Cir.1993).

364. Rosebud Sioux Tribe v. A & P Steel, Inc., 874 F.2d 550 (8th Cir.1989).

365. Merrion v. Jicarilla Apache Tribe, 455 U.S. 130 (1982); Kerr–McGee Corp. v. Navajo Tribe, 471 U.S. 195 (1985).

366. Cotton Petroleum Corp. v. New Mexico, 490 U.S. 163 (1989).

367. Gila River Indian Community v. Waddell, 967 F.2d 1404 (9th Cir.1992).

severance tax of 30% will be too high,[368] while a state severance tax of 8% may be valid.[369] A state may not tax a tribe's royalty interest under 1938 Act leases.[370] It also seems clear that the same rationale prohibiting taxation of the tribe's share of production under 1938 Act leases would also apply to any tribal share of production and/or income resulting from development under an IMDA agreement.

The exposure to dual taxation clearly has a negative economic impact on mineral development of Indian lands. To offset this negative impact, some tribes have agreed to tax holidays or to tax credits equal to the amount of state taxes paid on production from Indian lands which a developer may then utilize to offset tribal taxes. This is often done to enhance arguments that state taxes are preempted since the economic consequences of the state tax in such circumstances falls directly on the tribe. Other tribes have agreed to ceilings on the total tax and royalty burdens applicable to a lease in order to provide some level of certainty on the uppermost economic burden which must be borne by the developer. Developers and tribes have also looked to alternative business structures under the IMDA to take advantage of the tribal immunity from state taxes.

[4]   Tribal Employment Laws

Many tribes have enacted employment laws requiring that employers give preference in employment to Indians residing on or near the reservation.[371] Some tribal employment laws create quotas for Indian employees or set specific limitations on the total number of non-Indians that may be employed by a developer. Some tribes have drafted their employment laws to apply to both trust and fee lands located within the reservation, and at least one court has upheld a tribe's employment laws as applied to the on-reservation operations of a non-Indian employer doing business on fee lands.[372] Many tribal employment ordinances require the employer to give preference specifically to members of the tribe enacting the ordinance. * * *

Many tribal employment ordinances also require employers to pay fees to the tribe to assist the tribe in its compliance efforts or to help fund job training programs. These fees may be relatively small or quite significant.[373] In addition to this direct cost, tribal employment laws often require that Indian contractors be awarded bids for projects if the Indian contractor's bid is within some fixed percentage of the lowest non-Indian

---

368. Crow Tribe of Indians v. State of Montana, 819 F.2d 895 (9th Cir.1987), *summarily aff'd.* 484 U.S. 997 (1988).

369. Cotton Petroleum Corp. v. New Mexico, 490 U.S. 163 (1989).

370. Montana v. Blackfeet Tribe of Indians, 471 U.S. 759 (1985).

371. See, e.g., Comprehensive Code of Justice of the Assiniboine and Sioux Tribes–Fort Peck Indian Reservation, Title XVI (1989).

372. FMC v. Shoshone–Bannock Tribes, 905 F.2d 1311 (9th Cir.1990).

373. See, e.g., Employment Ordinances of Crow Tribe, which sets a fee percentage on all contracts entered into on the reservation.

contractor's bid. These types of requirements can have a significant impact on the economic viability of a project.

While developers may have little ability to negotiate concerning tribal employment laws where the developer is acting pursuant to a 1938 or 1909 Act lease, a developer negotiating an IMDA agreement may attempt to negotiate for specific contractual provisions on employment. Agreements may include provisions which excuse a developer's non-compliance with tribal employment laws where compliance would result in the developer's violation of other laws applicable to it. Agreements may also include limitations or waivers of fees otherwise required under such ordinances to be paid by the developer to the tribe. Additionally, developers may negotiate provisions requiring that Indian contractors meet the lowest bids received for projects without additional allowances. Any contractual modifications of tribal employment ordinances touch upon the sovereignty of the tribe and should be confirmed by an appropriate resolution from the tribal governing body.[374]

[5]   Tribal Zoning, Health and Environmental Laws

Indian tribes possess the sovereign authority to implement zoning laws, health and safety laws, and other similar laws controlling activities and development taking place on Indian lands.[375] In certain limited circumstances, tribes may also validly extend these laws to non-Indian parties resident or doing business on non-Indian owned fee land within reservations.[376] Additionally, Congress has also authorized tribes to enforce several federal environmental laws.[377]

Developers must be mindful of a tribe's ability to enact laws which can impact, directly or indirectly, an on-reservation development project.[378] Developers contemplating activities on a reservation for the first time should obtain from the tribe copies of all existing laws, ordinances, rules or regulations directed at controlling development activities within the reservation. A developer should pay particular attention to any tribal environmental programs or laws which might impact the developer's activities in order to ascertain any compliance problems which might arise in the course of planned activities. Finally, developers should, where possible, negotiate for a waiver of a tribe's immunity from suit in terms

374. [Cf., Arizona Public Service Co. v. Aspaas, 77 F.3d 1128 (9th Cir. Ariz. 1995) (enforcing a contractual waiver of the Tribe's authority to regulate a utility's employment decisions beyond those expressed in the contract) and Dawavendewa v. Salt River Project Agr. Imp. and Power Dist., 276 F.3d 1150 (9th Cir. Ariz. 2002) (dismissing suit by non-Indian who was denied job due to Indian employment preference provision in contract with employer on ground that Tribe was indispensable party to suit and that Tribe enjoyed sovereign immunity).]

375. Brendale v. Confederated Tribes & Bands of Yakima Indian Nation, 492 U.S. 408 (1989).

376. Cardin v. De La Cruz, 671 F.2d 363 (9th Cir.1982); Knight v. Shoshone & Arapahoe Indian Tribes, 670 F.2d 900 (10th Cir.1982).

377. See, e.g., Clean Air Act, Clean Water Act, Safe Drinking Water Act; *see also*, November 8, 1984 EPA Policy for the Administration of Environmental Programs on Indian lands.

378. Governing Council of Pinoleville Indian Community v. Mendocino County, 684 F.Supp. 1042 (N.D.Cal.1988) (upholding tribal ordinance imposing moratorium on new businesses within reservation).

broad enough to permit the developer to challenge current or future tribal zoning, health or environmental laws or ordinances.

[6]   Production Requirements

Most standard oil and gas leases covering Indian lands expire at the end of their primary term unless actual production has been obtained by that time, although current regulations do recognize that "commencement" of operations clauses may permit the drilling and completion of a well over the end of the primary term of a lease in those instances set forth in the regulation.[379] Thus, drilling operations commenced prior to the expiration of the primary term of the lease will not act to extend an Indian lands oil and gas lease unless the lease itself so provides, and then only if such operations are diligently conducted as provided for in the regulations.[380] Additionally, by the terms of the 1938 Act, tribal leases entered into under the authority of the 1938 Act are for a maximum 10 year primary term, with production in paying quantities at the end of such term being essential for continuation of the lease.[381]

* * *

[7]   Dispute Resolution

[a]   Utilization and Exhaustion of Tribal Courts

Most tribes now have established their own judicial systems for resolving civil disputes arising within their reservation and involving trust lands, the tribe, or its members. Similarly, most tribes have also enacted their own tribal law codes to provide the statutory framework for controlling legal relationships within reservation boundaries. The existence of these court systems, and issues associated with their utilization by non-Indians, are significant to those engaged in the development of Indian lands.

The United States Supreme Court has indicated that considerations of comity direct that tribal remedies be exhausted before the issue of the tribal court's jurisdiction is reviewed by a federal court.[382] The Court has reasoned that exhaustion of tribal court remedies will promote tribal self-government, while also providing a reviewing federal court with the benefit of the tribal court's analysis and expertise.[383] The Supreme Court noted, however, that under certain circumstances, exhaustion would not be required.[384]

---

379.   25 C.F.R. § 211.27(b) (tribal); 25 C.F.R. § 212.27 (allotted).

380.   Id.

381.   25 U.S.C. § 396a; 25 C.F.R. § 211.27(b).

382.   National Farmers Union Insurance Companies v. Crow Tribe of Indians, 471 U.S. 845 (1985); Iowa Mutual Insurance Company v. LaPlante, 480 U.S. 9 (1987).

383.   National Farmers Union Insurance Companies, 471 U.S. at 856, 857; Iowa Mutual Insurance Company, 480 U.S. at 15,16.

384.   National Farmers Union Insurance Companies, 471 U.S. at 856, n.21. The Court indicated that exhaustion would not be required where tribal jurisdiction was motivated by a desire to harass or in bad faith, where the action is patently violative of express jurisdictional prohibitions, or where exhaustion would be futile due to a lack of any adequate opportunity to challenge the tribal court's jurisdiction. See also Strate v. A-1 Contractors, 520 U.S. 438 (1997)

Courts have interpreted the exhaustion doctrine as requiring exhaustion even where no on-going dispute exists in a tribal court,[385] and even where the complaint in another court was filed by the sole Indian party to the dispute.[386] Additionally exhaustion has been required even though the suggestion of a need to exhaust tribal remedies was presented to a non-tribal court only after significant proceedings had occurred in that court.[387]

* * *

There is no way to assure a developer doing business within a reservation that it can avoid becoming involved in a tribal court proceeding. While it may be possible to include a mandatory arbitration provision in a mineral lease or agreement, such provision is only binding on the parties to the contract. Tribal members or others who are not signatories to the agreement would remain as potential plaintiffs free to pursue claims against a developer in tribal court. * * *

[b] Arbitration

The common-held desire to avoid long and protracted legal disputes has led many developers to look to mandatory arbitration provisions in their development agreements. While arbitration provisions are rarely found in standard 1909 Act or 1938 Act leases, arbitration clauses are increasingly included within negotiated leases, and the current regulations for IMDA agreements recognize that dispute resolution issues should be considered and addressed by the parties as they negotiate such an agreement.[388] Regarding these regulations, it should be noted that the use of arbitration clauses has been upheld as valid and proper in leases of trust property.[389] To be enforced, however, arbitration clauses must be mandatory, rather than permissive.[390] The arbitration provision must be part of the lease or agreement at the time it is approved, or separate Secretarial approval of such a provision must be obtained.[391] * * *

[c] Choice of Law and Venue Provisions

Because many non-Indian parties are uncomfortable utilizing tribal forums and because many developers are reluctant to have their legal interests and relationships determined by laws with which the developer has little, if any, familiarity, developers may attempt to address these

---

wherein the court stated "... when tribal court jurisdiction over an action such as this one [automobile accident on state highway] is challenged in federal court, the otherwise applicable exhaustion requirements ... must give way, for it would serve no purpose other than delay."

385.   Burlington Northern Railroad v. Crow Tribal Council, 940 F.2d 1239, 1245 (9th Cir. 1991).

386.   Wellman v. Chevron U.S.A. Inc., 815 F.2d 577 (9th Cir.1987).

387.   Crawford v. Genuine Parts Co. Inc., 947 F.2d 1405 (9th Cir.1991).

388.   25 C.F.R. § 225.21(b)(13); 25 C.F.R. § 225.25.

389.   Pittsburg & Midway Coal Mining Co. v. Acting Navajo Area Director, 21 IBIA 45 (1991).

390.   American Indian Land Development Corp. v. Sacramento Area Director, Bureau of Indian Affairs, 23 IBIA 208 (1993).

391.   See, Mr. & Mrs. W. A. Merrill v. Portland Area Director, Bureau of Indian Affairs, 19 IBIA 81 (1990).

concerns by including venue provisions and choice of law provisions in negotiated leases and agreements entered into with tribes. Most often, these provisions will work together to provide that disputes between the parties will be resolved in a designated court, other than the tribal court, utilizing some agreed upon set of laws.

In Altheimer & Gray,[392] the Seventh Circuit held that these types of contractual provisions could be properly adopted by a tribe, based upon the self-governing powers of a tribe. * * *

[8]   Rights-of-Way and Access Issues

[a]   General

Any mineral developer of Indian lands must pay particular attention to the existence and validity of its rights-of-way and surface use rights in order to insure that it will have the ability to get to the lands it intends to develop, and that it will have the ability to move any resources it may locate and produce to market.[393] Where access is required across Indian lands, the acquisition of rights-of-way will be controlled by federal law.[394] State law concepts, such as easements by prescription, do not apply to Indian lands and thus cannot be looked to by one attempting to gain access rights across a tract of Indian land.[395] Generally, rights-of-way across tribal lands will be obtained through voluntary tribal consent to the grant of an easement by the Secretary in accordance with one of the federal acts which authorize such rights-of-way.[396] Rights-of-way across allotted lands can be obtained either by grant from the Secretary (generally following consent from the individual Indian owner) in accordance with an applicable federal statute, or by condemnation.

[b]   Voluntary Grants of Rights-of-Way

Primary authority for rights-of-way for all purposes is provided by the Act of February 5, 1948.[397] Under this Act, consent of all tribes organized under the Indian Reorganization Act (IRA) is required prior to Secretarial grant of any right-of-way.[398] By regulation this requirement of tribal consent has also been extended to those tribes which chose not to organize

---

392.   Altheimer & Gray v. Sioux Manufacturing Corp., 983 F.2d 803, 815 (7th Cir.1993).

393.   See, e.g., 43 C.F.R. § 3164.3(a), which provides that a lessee/operator shall have the right to use the surface of a leased tract only to the extent specifically granted by the lease, and any other use must be authorized by written agreement executed by surface owner and approved by Superintendent.

394.   For a more in-depth consideration of rights-of-way across Indian lands, See Michael E. Webster, Native American Jurisdiction and Permitting Oil and Natural Gas Pipelines–Wellhead to End User, 13–1 (Rocky Mountain Mineral Law Foundation, 1995).

395.   Imperial Granite Co. v. Pala Band of Mission Indians, 940 F.2d 1269, 1272 (9th Cir.1991).

396.   Plains Electric Generation & Transmission Cooperative v. Pueblo of Laguna, 542 F.2d 1375 (10th Cir.1976).

397.   Act of February 5, 1948, 62 Stat. 17, 25 U.S.C. § 323–328. In addition to the 1948 Act, special rights-of-way acts do exist; See, e.g., 25 U.S.C. § 321 (rights-of-way for pipe lines); 25 U.S.C. § 312 (rights-of-way for railways, telegraphs, telephone lines).

398.   25 U.S.C. § 324.

under the IRA.[399] Consent of individual Indian owners prior to Secretarial grant of a right-of-way is also required, although the 1948 Act does provide that rights-of-way across allotted lands can be granted by the Secretary in certain limited circumstances.[400]

Under the 1948 Act, rights-of-way may be granted for a perpetual term, or for any other term of years agreed to by the parties.[401] The 1948 Act requires that compensation for rights-of-way be paid to the trust owner,[402] and the regulations provide detailed procedures for calculating the value of any right-of-way.[403] The regulations also set forth detailed procedural steps which must be followed by any party attempting to obtain a grant of a right-of-way for Indian lands.[404]

In obtaining a right-of-way from a tribe, a developer should be concerned with, and attempt to address in the right-of-way grant matters not considered in typical easement negotiations. A developer should attempt to obtain in any right-of-way grant from a tribe a waiver of the tribe's immunity from suit, particularly if the developer's only contractual relationship with the tribe is through such easement.[405] In addition, a developer may wish to address regulation of the right-of-way at the time the right-of-way is obtained. Finally, the developer may wish to try to obtain, in the right-of-way agreement, some limitation on the tribe's power to tax either the right-of-way or the value of property or products crossing over or through the right-of-way.

NOTE

Some of Alaska's early grant-land selections conflicted with the rights of Alaska Natives. Ultimately, these conflicts were addressed in the Alaska Native Claims Settlement Act of 1971. Act of Dec. 18, 1971, Pub.L. No. 92–293, 85 Stat. 688 (codified as amended at 43 U.S.C.A. §§ 1601–1629f). Under this Act, all of the native claims were extinguished, and previous entries that were made in reliance on federal or state authority were recognized. Alaska Natives, through Village and Regional Corporations established by the Act, were allowed to select 60 million acres of land. In addition, the Village Corporations also acquired the surface rights to about 22 million acres within and adjacent to certain Alaska Native villages, and the Regional Corporations were given title to the subsurface of those lands. Also, the Secretary of the Interior was given broad authority to withdraw lands from entry, leasing, or disposal. Millions of acres were withdrawn by the Secretary, subject to valid existing rights, such as an oil and gas lease.[406]

---

399. 25 C.F.R. § 169.3.

400. 25 U.S.C. § 324 (1988); 25 C.F.R. § 169.3.

401. 25 U.S.C. § 323 (1988); 25 C.F.R. § 169.18.

402. 25 U.S.C. § 325.

403. 25 C.F.R. § 169.12–169.14.

404. 25 C.F.R. § 169.3–169.11.

405. See, Imperial Granite Co. v. Pala Band of Mission Indians, 940 F.2d 1269 (9th Cir.1991).

406. For further information, see James D. Linxwiler, The Alaska Native Claims Settlement Act: The First 20 Years, 38 Rocky Mtn.Min.L.Inst. 2–1 (1992) and James D. Linxwiler, The

4. ROYALTY VALUATION AND PAYMENT[407]

Each of the mineral leasing statutes previously discussed grants the Secretary of the Interior general rulemaking authority to implement its provisions. E.g., 30 U.S.C. § 189 (Mineral Leasing Act); 30 U.S.C. § 359 (Mineral Leasing Act for Acquired Lands); 43 U.S.C. § 1334(a) (Outer Continental Shelf Lands Act (OCSLA)); 25 U.S.C. § 396d (Indian tribal leases); and 25 U.S.C. § 396 (Indian allotted leases). That authority takes on particular importance in the context of establishing the value of minerals produced for purposes of computing royalty.

Federal and Indian oil and gas lease instruments are on standard forms that the Secretary revises from time to time. The lease terms include many statutorily-required terms. For example, the Mineral Leasing Act prescribes a minimum royalty rate of not less than 12.5 percent (one eighth) of the amount or value of the production removed or sold from the lease. 30 U.S.C. § 226. The Outer Continental Shelf Lands Act contains a similar royalty rate provision of not less than 12.5 percent of the amount or value of the production saved, removed, or sold, 43 U.S.C. § 1337(a)(1), although many newer offshore leases have a royalty rate as high as 18.75 percent. This royalty rate is applied to the volume and value of the oil and gas the lessee produces to determine the amount of royalty owed (*i.e.*, volume x royalty value x royalty rate = amount owed). Lessees generally must pay royalties monthly, with payment due by the end of the month following the production month. 30 C.F.R. § 1210.53(a).

All of the federal and Indian leases contain two important terms. One is that the lessee agrees to be subject to all reasonable rules and regulations in force when the lease is entered into or that thereafter may be promulgated. The other lease term of particular importance to this discussion is the term in virtually all federal and Indian leases that expressly reserves to the Secretary the authority to establish the reasonable value of production for royalty purposes. Regulations promulgated under the authority of the several leasing statutes that prescribe the methods of determining royalty value in various circumstances (*see* 30 C.F.R. part 1206) likewise reflect this principle.

Most private mineral lease arrangements do not contain this kind of reservation of authority to the lessor. While it may be an unusual characteristic of federal and Indian leases, the courts have uniformly upheld the Secretary's broad authority and discretion to establish the reasonable value of production for royalty purposes under the statutes, lease terms, and regulations.[408] However, the Secretary's final determinations are subject to judicial review under the Administrative Procedure Act, 5 U.S.C. §§ 701–706. The Secretary's discretion therefore is not

---

Alaska Native Claims Settlement Act at 35: Delivering on the Promise, 53 Rocky Mtn. Min. L. Inst. 12–1 (2007).

407. The Editors again wish to acknowledge the assistance of Peter J. Schaumberg, Beveridge & Diamond, P.C., Washington, D.C.

408. See, e.g., Independent Petroleum Association of America v. DeWitt, 279 F.3d 1036 (D.C. Cir. 2002); Marathon Oil Co. v. United States, 604 F.Supp. 1375 (D.Alaska 1985), aff'd, 807 F.2d

unfettered. The Secretary's authority has been delegated to the Director of the Office of Natural Resources Revenue ("ONRR"). ONRR is the successor to the Minerals Management Service ("MMS"). Although most of the regulations were issued by MMS and the administrative and federal court decisions likewise involved that agency, we refer to the agency by its new name.

ONRR regulations prescribing how lessees are to calculate the royalty value of production are found in 30 C.F.R. part 1206. They are divided according to Indian crude oil (§§ 1206.50–1206.62), federal crude oil (§§ 1206.100–1206.120), federal gas (§§ 1206.150–1206.160), and Indian gas (§§ 1206.170–1206.181).[409]

The method for determining royalty value prescribed under the rules depends on several factors. The single most important threshold factor in applying the valuation rules is the relationship of parties to a sales transaction (particularly arm's-length versus non-arm's-length). If the transaction is at arm's length, one set of valuation principles applies based on the lessee's "gross proceeds." If the transaction is not at arm's length, another set of valuation criteria applies using market-based indicia of value external to the specific transaction.

If lessees enhance the value of oil or gas production by transporting the production closer to market before selling or processing the gas into more valuable constituent products, the regulations allow the lessee to deduct a transportation allowance or processing allowance. 30 C.F.R. §§ 1206.156–1206.157 (transportation); §§ 1206.158–1206.159 (gas processing).

In natural gas and crude oil valuation under federal leases, fundamental valuation concepts and principles have been the subject of considerable litigation and development over time. The basic concepts and principles are reflected in various provisions of both past and current ONRR regulations. Valuation issues are also broadly disputed between the ONRR and the producing oil and gas industry. The following subsections highlight several of the most important principles and issues.

(a) Gross Proceeds

(i) Basic Concept—Total Consideration Paid for Production

For federal onshore and Indian leases, since the 1930s and since offshore leasing began in 1954, the regulations have provided that under

---

759 (9th Cir.1986); United States v. Ohio Oil Co., 163 F.2d 633 (10th Cir. Wyo. 1947); Shoshone Indian Tribe v. Hodel, 903 F.2d 784 (10th Cir.1990); Continental Oil Co. v. United States, 184 F.2d 802 (9th Cir.1950); California Co. v. Udall, 296 F.2d 384 (D.C.Cir.1961).

409. Valuation for royalty purposes of oil and gas produced from Indian leases is in many respects similar to valuation of production from federal leases and gives rise to issues that are the same as or similar to those discussed below. However, there are some differences in valuation rules. Indian leases also present unique issues by virtue of certain lease terms and regulations that are not discussed in this section. The discussion that follows will address royalty valuation under federal oil and gas leases, and mention only some regulatory and statutory enforcement differences between federal and Indian leases.

no circumstances may the value of production be less than the "gross proceeds" accruing to the lessee for the disposition of the production.[410] The lessee's gross proceeds are the total consideration paid (in whatever form) for sale or disposition of the production.[411] Under the valuation regulations, with limited exceptions, if the lessee sells its production under an arm's-length contract, the royalty value is the gross proceeds accruing to the lessee under that contract.

Controversies arise as to whether various forms of payments between the lessee and its purchaser constitute part of gross proceeds. For example, gross proceeds include any reimbursements paid by purchasers to lessees for state severance taxes paid on the share of the production equal to the working interest, because the tax reimbursements are part of the consideration paid under the sales contract for all of the production.[412]

The consideration paid to the lessee when production is sold constitutes the lessee's gross proceeds even if the production is not sold in the local area. The following case is an example of how the gross proceeds rule operates.

MARATHON OIL COMPANY v. UNITED STATES

604 F.Supp. 1375 (D.Alaska 1985), *affirmed*, 807 F.2d 759 (9th Cir. 1986).

JAMES M. FITZGERALD, CHIEF JUDGE.

* * * [Editors' note: The following statement of facts is taken from the Ninth Circuit's Opinion affirming Judge Fitzgerald]

[Marathon owns a 50% working interest in certain federal oil and gas leases in the Kenai Field Unit in Alaska. The leases require Marathon to pay 12 1/2% royalty on the reasonable value of production from the leased lands "computed in accordance with the Oil and Gas Operating Regulations (30 C.F.R. Pt. 221) [now codified in relevant part at 30 C.F.R. § 206.103 (1985)]." The statutory authorization for promulgating the Oil and Gas Operating Regulations is found at 30 U.S.C. § 226(c). The government, the State of Alaska, and Cook Inlet Region, Inc. (Cook Inlet) are each entitled to receive a percentage of the royalties. Marathon transports about 16% of its share of the gas produced in the Kenai Field Unit to a liquefied natural gas plant owned by Marathon and Phillips Petroleum Company. After the gas is reduced to a liquid state, Marathon

---

410. Current codifications of the rule are found at 30 C.F.R. §§ 1206.152(h) and 1206.153(h) (federal unprocessed and processed gas); 1206.52(h) (Indian crude oil); and 1206.174(g) (Indian gas where an index-based method cannot be used). The gross proceeds rule applied uniformly to crude oil produced from federal leases before June 1, 2000 (former 30 C.F.R. § 206.102(h) (1999)), but new rules adopted on that date provide for index-based values for oil not sold under an arm's-length contract, and a limited option for a lessee to choose index-based valuation even when it sells its oil at arm's length. See 30 C.F.R. §§ 1206.102(a) and (d) and 1206.103. Otherwise, the lessee's gross proceeds are the value of production sold at arm's length.

411. See, e.g., 30 C.F.R. § 1206.151 definitions (federal gas); Hoover & Bracken Energies, Inc. v. U.S. Dep't of the Interior, 723 F.2d 1488 (10th Cir. Okla. 1983).

412. Hoover & Bracken Energies, Inc. v. U.S. Dep't. of the Interior, supra; Enron Oil & Gas Co. v. Lujan, 978 F.2d 212 (5th Cir. Tex. 1992).

transports the liquefied natural gas in tankers to Japan where it is sold. Marathon computed royalties on the liquefied natural gas sold in Japan based on the price paid for Kenai Field Unit gas under a long-term contract it had to sell unliquefied gas to the Alaska Pipeline Company.

* * *

In 1983, the Mineral Management Service (the Service), which succeeded USGS as the government agency responsible for managing the involved leases, notified Marathon that it intended to redetermine the reasonable value of production of the Kenai gas delivered to the liquefied natural gas plant. * * *

Although it was not required to do so by statute, the Service held a public hearing at which Marathon appeared and was permitted to make comments, to state opinions, and to provide statements of facts concerning the new royalty valuation formula. * * * [Thereafter,] the Service issued an order directing Marathon to pay royalties based on the revised royalty valuation formula. Marathon appealed the order to the Director of the Service * * *. In addition, Marathon ceased paying royalties based on the agreed-to Phillips formula [the prior method used to value the gas] and began computing royalties based on the long-term contract price paid to the Alaska Pipeline Company.

The Service issued a second order directing Marathon to compute royalties according to the Phillips formula from the date Marathon began computing royalties based on the terms of the long-term contract to the effective date of the order requiring compliance with the revised royalty valuation formula. Marathon did not comply with this second order either. The Department of the Interior (the Department) then issued a third order, at the direction of the Secretary of the Interior (the Secretary), directing Marathon to comply with the previous two orders.]

* * *

Scope of Review

Since the federal defendants have moved for summary judgment in this case, the test is whether, with respect to any dispositive issue, there is any genuine issue as to any material fact. If not, I must decide whether, construing the evidence in the light most favorable to the plaintiff Marathon, the defendants are entitled to judgment as a matter of law.

Section 706 of the Administrative Procedure Act (APA) establishes the appropriate standard of judicial review of agency decision. Under that provision, the agency's determination must be set aside if found to be arbitrary or capricious, or in violation of constitutional, statutory, or procedural requirements.

Given my earlier rejection of Marathon's constitutional claims, I must now make a three-part determination. First, did the agency act within the scope of its statutory authority? In making this inquiry, I need only determine whether the agency was in substantial compliance with the applicable statute(s). Second, was the agency decision "arbitrary, capricious, an abuse of discretion, or otherwise not in accordance with law"? As the Supreme Court has observed:

> To make this finding the court must consider whether the decision was based on a consideration of the relevant factors and whether there has been a clear error of judgment. Although this inquiry into the facts is to be searching and careful, the ultimate standard of review is a narrow one. The court is not empowered to substitute its judgment for that of the agency.

Citizens to Preserve Overton Park v. Volpe, 401 U.S. 402, 416. Third, did the agency comply with all procedural requirements? [Footnote omitted]

In reviewing an agency decision, the agency's own interpretation of the applicable statutes is entitled to substantial deference. Deference is even more clearly in order where an administrative regulation, rather than a statute, is involved. According to the Supreme Court, "the ultimate criterion is the administrative interpretation, which becomes of controlling weight unless it is plainly erroneous or inconsistent with the regulation." Bowles v. Seminole Rock & Sand Co., 325 U.S. 410, 414 (1945).

To uphold the MMS orders, I need not find that the MMS's interpretation of the statutes and regulations is the only reasonable interpretation, nor that it is the interpretation a court would reach if initially faced with the question. I need only find that it is a reasonable interpretation. I must ascertain whether MMS "articulate[d] a rational connection between the facts found and the choice made." Bowman Transportation, Inc. v. Arkansas–Best Freight System, Inc., 419 U.S. 281, 285 (1974).

Discussion

* * *

Under the Minerals Lands Leasing Act, "[t]he Secretary of the Interior is authorized to prescribe necessary and proper rules and regulations and to do any and all things necessary to carry out and accomplish the purposes of [the Act]." 30 U.S.C. § 189. These regulations have the force and effect of statutes when not in conflict with such statutes. The leases at issue in this case, in addition to being subject to the terms of the Mineral Lands Leasing Act, are also "subject . . . to all reasonable regulations of the Secretary of the Interior now or hereafter in force" unless inconsistent with the leases themselves.

Administrative regulations governing MMS are found in 30 C.F.R. ch. II (1984). The particular regulation at issue in this case is 30 C.F.R. § 206.103 [1985], which provides:

§ 206.103   Value basis for computing royalties.

> The value of production, for the purpose of computing royalty, shall be the estimated reasonable value of the product as determined by the Associate Director due consideration being given to the highest price

paid for a part or for a majority of production of like quality in the same field, to the price received by the lessee, to posted prices, and to other relevant matters. Under no circumstances shall the value of production of any of said substances for the purposes of computing royalty be deemed to be less than the gross proceeds accruing to the lessee from the sale thereof or less than the value computed on such reasonable unit value as shall have been determined by the Secretary. In the absence of good reason to the contrary, value computed on the basis of the highest price per barrel, thousand cubic feet, or gallon paid or offered at the time of production in a fair and open market for the major portion of like-quality oil, gas, or other products produced and sold from the field or area where the leased lands are situated will be considered to be a reasonable value.[1]

Under this regulation, royalties are to be based on "the estimated reasonable value of the product as determined by the Associate Director [for Royalty Management]" with the proviso that "[u]nder no circumstances shall the value of production of any of said substances for the purposes of computing royalty be deemed to be less than the gross proceeds accruing to the lessee from the sale thereof."

* * *

The federal gas leases at issue in this case are by their own terms "subject to the terms and provisions of [the Mineral Lands Leasing Act] and to all reasonable regulations of the Secretary of the Interior now or hereafter in force, when not inconsistent with any express and specific provisions herein." The leases also provide that the lessee shall pay the lessor "12 1/2 percent royalty on the production removed or sold from the leased lands computed in accordance with the Oil and Gas Operating Regulations." The leases further state:

> It is expressly agreed that the Secretary of the Interior may establish reasonable minimum values for purposes of computing royalty on any or all oil, gas, natural gasoline, and other products obtained from gas, due consideration being given to the highest price paid for a part or for a majority of production of like quality in the same field, to the price received by the lessee, to posted prices, and to other relevant matters and, whenever appropriate, after notice and opportunity to be heard.

Both the regulations and the leases, as discussed above, vest in the administrative agency the authority to establish the basis for computing royalties. The regulations require that the basis for royalty purposes "shall be the estimated reasonable value of the product as determined by the Associate Director." The leases expressly provide that "the Secretary

---

1. [Editors' note: The regulations cited and quoted in this opinion have been substantially revised and are more complex; however, in general, they remain consistent with the result in this opinion. For current regulations, see 30 C.F.R. §§ 1206.150–160 (federal gas).]

of the Interior may establish reasonable minimum values for purposes of computing royalty."

* * *

The regulation requires that the value of production for royalty purposes be not less than "the gross proceeds accruing to the lessee from the sale thereof." 30 C.F.R. § 206.103. * * * By its own language, the provision aims to ensure that the gross proceeds accruing to the lessee is the absolute minimum value for computation of royalties.

* * *

The gas Marathon delivers to the LNG plant is neither sold at the wellhead, nor at the LNG plant. Thus there is no simple way for MMS to value this production. The first arm's-length transaction involving this gas is the sale of the LNG in Japan. Recent changes in economic conditions suggested to MMS that neither the contract price for gas sold to Alaska Pipeline Co., nor the Phillips formula set out in the 1981 settlement agreement, represented a "reasonable value" for royalty computation purposes. MMS gave "due consideration" to the various factors and information before it in arriving at its decision. [Footnote omitted.] To capture the true value of the LNG being sold in Japan, MMS determined it was necessary to look at the landed price in Japan and work back to arrive at a reasonable wellhead value. To do this, MMS proposed to make allowances for costs of liquefaction and transportation, and for a reasonable rate of return on the LNG plant. Deducting these allowances from the sales price in Japan would thus yield an estimated wellhead value for the gas.

Is there "good reason" supporting MMS's decision to look to the sales price in Japan, rather than to open market contracts for the sale of other gas from the Kenai field? Again, I conclude yes. The regulation provides:

> In the absence of good reason to the contrary, value computed on the basis of the highest price per ... thousand cubic feet ... paid or offered at the time of production in a fair and open market for the major portion of like-quality ... gas ... produced and sold from the field or area where the leased lands are situated will be considered to be a reasonable value.

Marathon contends that this provision should be followed to arrive at a reasonable value of gas delivered to the LNG plant for royalty purposes. I conclude, however, that there exists "good reason to the contrary" warranting use of another method.

By its terms, the provision refers to "the price ... paid or offered at the time of production in a fair and open market for the major portion of like quality ... gas ... produced and sold from the field or area." This assumes that reasonable value can be ascertained based on arm's-length transactions negotiated by unrelated parties each acting in their own self-interest in competition with others.

It is obvious that market value of gas in any field will vary depending upon a wide variety of factors. So far as the Kenai field is concerned, 42% of the gas produced in 1982 was delivered to the ammonia and urea plant at Nikiski owned by Collier Chemical, a subsidiary of Union Oil. An additional 16% of production was delivered to the LNG plant owned by Marathon and Phillips. Alaska Pipeline Company bought 31% of production for distribution in the Anchorage market and 9% of production was rented to the Swanson River Field Unit for pressure maintenance. The gas delivered to the LNG plant presents a special, unique situation. At the plant the gas is cooled until it becomes liquid, then transported to Japan, and there sold. To capture the true value of this gas, it is reasonable for MMS to look to the proceeds accruing to Marathon in Japan.

The regulation requires that "Under no circumstances shall the value of production ... for the purposes of computing royalty be deemed to be less than the gross proceeds accruing to the lessee from the sale ... or less than the value computed on such reasonable unit value as shall have been determined by the Secretary." Did MMS satisfy the explicit requirement that the value for royalty purposes be not less than the "gross proceeds" accruing to Marathon from the sale of the gas? I conclude the answer is yes. In fact, MMS determined that the net back method was necessary to satisfy the gross proceeds requirement. I agree with this determination.

Obviously the February 1981 settlement agreement demonstrates that the price paid for gas by Alaska Pipeline on its long-term contract failed to provide reasonable value for purposes of computing royalty on that portion of the gas delivered to the LNG plant for sale in Japan. Even under the so called Phillips formula of 36% of the price received in Japan, the additional royalties from January 1, 1980 through February 1981 were computed to be $1,834,160.00. Thus Marathon's argument that "the 'gross proceeds' received by the lessee from the sale of [the LNG] with its enhanced values in a distant market are not indicative of the value of the raw material feedstock gas produced at the lease" has a hollow ring. [Footnote omitted.] Since January 1, 1980, the effective date of the settlement agreement, Marathon paid royalties based on a "value" derived from the sales price in Japan. Marathon expressly agreed to this method in the February 1981 settlement agreement. Marathon cannot now credibly argue that landed sales price in Japan is irrelevant to the reasonable value for purposes of computing royalties.

Is MMS's net back method consistent with the regulatory language directing the agency to determine the "value of production" for royalty purposes? Marathon argues that this language requires that royalties be based on the value of production at the lease. I agree with this basic premise. However, nothing in the regulation precludes MMS from looking at the sales price in Japan as a means to determine the reasonable value of production at the lease. MMS has done just this by taking the landed sales price, making allowances for liquefaction and transportation costs, and thereby deriving a reasonable value at the lease. The regulation does not preclude such computations, but rather requires them to ensure that the value chosen is not less than the gross proceeds accruing to the lessee. Thus I conclude that in deriving a value for royalty purposes from the sales price in Japan, MMS complied with the regulatory requirement that royalties be based on the "value of production."

MMS is charged with managing these national resources and ensuring that full royalties are levied and collected. Deriving an estimated wellhead value from the sales price of the LNG in Japan is, I conclude, a reasonable method of establishing a basis for computing royalties.

* * *

For these reasons, I conclude that the MMS orders directing Marathon to use the net back method fall within the agency's authority under the statutes and regulations. I also conclude that the orders neither violated nor were inconsistent with provisions of the leases. The leases by their express terms provide for a royalty to be paid "on the production removed or sold from the leased lands computed in accordance with the Oil and Gas Operating Regulations." Marathon argues that like the regulatory language, this lease language requires royalties to be computed on value of production at the lease. However, I have concluded that the net back method is a valid means of estimating the value of production for royalty purposes. Moreover, the leases themselves provide that the Secretary of the Interior has the authority to establish reasonable values for computation of royalties. I conclude that the MMS orders did not violate the terms of the leases.

* * *

Conclusion

* * * I GRANT the federal defendants' Motion for Summary Judgment and Partial Dismissal. Marathon's claims against the federal defendants are accordingly DISMISSED. I further find that the federal defendants are entitled to an injunction. Marathon is accordingly ORDERED to comply with the terms of the three MMS royalty orders.

* * *

NOTES

1. During the course of this litigation, Marathon did not request a stay of the ONRR and Departmental orders to pay royalty and did not pay the disputed amounts pending appeal. Accordingly, the ONRR proposed a civil penalty assessment under section 109(c) of the Federal Oil and Gas Royalty Management Act, 30 U.S.C. § 1719(c), in the amount of $70,000 per day for knowingly or willfully failing to pay royalty as required by the orders. An administrative law judge upheld the assessment of a penalty for the period from July 13, 1984, through April 30, 1985, in the cumulative amount of $20,440,000. On appeal to the Interior Board of Land Appeals, the grounds for the penalty were upheld, but the penalty was reduced to $10,220,000. Marathon Oil Co. v. Minerals Management Service, 106 IBLA 104 (1988).

2.   When production is sold at a point remote from the producing lease or unit, ONRR rules and case precedents have allowed the lessee to deduct the reasonable actual costs of transporting the production to the point away from the lease to arrive at the value of the production at or near the lease or unit.[413] The *Marathon* case reflects this principle. Value at the lease was determined by the landed sales price in Japan less the costs of liquefaction and tankering—*i.e.*, the transportation costs.

3.   Federal leases effectively are a hybrid between the two principal types of leases found in oil and gas leases between private parties. Many private leases are "value" leases—i.e., royalty is determined based on market value independent of what the lessee may actually receive for the disposition of the production. Many other leases are so-called "proceeds" leases—i.e., royalty is a specified percentage of the proceeds the lessee derives from selling the oil or gas, regardless of whether it is worth more on the market. By statute and lease terms, federal leases are "value" leases, but with the gross proceeds rule, they are "value" leases with a "proceeds" minimum.

(ii) What Payments Are Payments for Production?

The way that sales transactions may be structured, particularly in light of regulatory requirements, has led to disputes between lessee-producers and the government about whether certain payments are payments for "production" so as to be part of the lessee's gross proceeds. The most prominent disputes have arisen in the context of the former natural gas price regulations and the restructuring of the gas industry that occurred in roughly the same time as price deregulation.

Until the mid–1980s, most natural gas produced in the United States was sold under long-term contracts at or near regulated ceiling prices established by the Federal Energy Regulatory Commission ("FERC"). In most cases, the purchaser was a pipeline who then resold the gas to public utilities, industrial consumers, and others. Under these long-term regulated contracts, gas reserves were committed by contract to the purchaser at fixed or increasing prices. The producer (the federal or Indian lessee) was not free to sell gas to someone else without a certificate of abandonment from FERC.

Most of these contracts contained "take-or-pay" provisions, which obligated the purchaser to take a specified minimum volume of gas during an identified period or to pay for that quantity even if not taken in full. The purpose of a take-or-pay clause was to ensure a dependable revenue flow to the producer to cover operations, maintenance, and investment costs during periods of slack demand due to seasonal changes, etc., because the producer's reserves were dedicated to that contract.

---

413.   30 C.F.R. §§ 1206.109–1206.112 (federal crude oil); 1206.156–1206.157 (federal gas); 1206.56–1206.57 (Indian crude oil); and 1206.177–1206.178 (Indian gas). Before the 1988 regulations, transportation costs were allowed under judicial and administrative cases. See, e.g., United States v. General Petroleum Corp., 73 F.Supp. 225 (S.D.Cal.1946), aff'd, Continental Oil Co. v. United States, 184 F.2d 802 (9th Cir.1950); Arco Oil and Gas Co., 109 IBLA 34 (1989); Shell Oil Co., 52 IBLA 15 (1981); Shell Oil Co., 70 I.D. 393, 396 (1963).

If a purchaser took less than the required minimum quantity during the period but paid for the minimum quantity under the take-or-pay clause, the payment for the difference between the minimum take volume and the lesser volume taken was called a "take-or-pay" payment. The contract provision usually allowed the purchaser a period of time in which to recoup, or "make up," a take-or-pay payment by taking gas in excess of the required minimum quantity. Amounts previously paid as take-or-pay payments would be credited against the purchase price of the volume taken in excess of the contractual minimum take requirement (so-called "make-up gas"). (The purchaser would have to pay additional money if the market price had increased at the time of actual production.) Under most contracts, if the purchaser never took make-up gas, the lessee kept the take-or-pay payment.[414]

ONRR assessed royalty on take-or-pay payments when received, which led to several lawsuits that resulted in conflicting district court rulings. Diamond Shamrock Exploration Co. v. Hodel, 1987 WL 5986 and consolidated cases (E.D. La. 1987) (upholding royalty assessment), and Mesa Petroleum Co. v. U.S. Dep't. of the Interior, 647 F.Supp. 1350 (W.D. La. 1986) (overturning royalty assessment). The losing parties' appeals were consolidated before the Fifth Circuit.

In Diamond Shamrock Exploration Co. v. Hodel, 853 F.2d 1159 (5th Cir. 1988), the ONRR had argued that the take-or-pay obligation (and, therefore, a payment made under that obligation) was part of the consideration paid for all gas under the contract, not just "make-up" gas. In rejecting the government's argument, the Fifth Circuit held that "royalties are not owed unless and until production, the severance of mineral from the formation, occurs." Id. at 1165. The "production" to which the court referred was "make-up" gas. In other words, the court held that royalties were not due on a take-or-pay payment when received, but would become due later (as part of the lessee's gross proceeds) as and to the extent that the purchaser took "make-up" gas. To the extent that the purchaser did not take make-up gas, the lessee kept the take-or-pay payment royalty-free.

NOTES

1. Under what circumstances should a payment under an oil or gas sales contract not be regarded as a payment for the oil or gas purchased under that contract? Are there principled distinctions that can be made that will avoid abuses?

2. In your view, which was more in accord with the economic reality of the transaction—the court's decision or the government's theory? What was the contractual take-or-pay obligation a payment for?

---

414. Gas sales contracts currently in use in the United States do not often include take-or-pay clauses. However, the issue illustrates the potential complexity of the gross proceeds determination.

The take-or-pay controversy was followed a few years later by questions about whether and to what extent payments made to reform or terminate existing contracts are part of a lessee's gross proceeds. In the 1980s, due to both market and regulatory changes, the price of gas began to decline. Pipeline purchasers who could not resell the high-priced gas they were obligated to take under their long-term contracts began to violate the contract terms and sought to escape their price provisions. Because the pipelines could not resell the volumes their long-term contracts required them to take, they could not take those volumes from the producers and as a result also began to accrue large take-or-pay liabilities.

During the same period, FERC promulgated a series of regulatory changes with the objective of opening the industry to competition and changing the role of interstate pipelines from acting as purchasers to acting primarily as transporters.[415] The consequence of these developments was that producers and purchasers entered into agreements to revise or terminate their long-term higher-priced contracts. These agreements often were referred to as gas contract settlements and generally included a lump-sum payment to the producer.

In Independent Petroleum Association of America v. Babbitt, 92 F.3d 1248 (D.C. Cir. 1996), the D.C. Circuit held that a lump-sum payment made to compromise past accrued take-or-pay liabilities and to terminate a contractual relationship completely (often called a "buyout") was not part of the consideration the lessee received for gas sold after the settlement to third parties at reduced prices and was not royalty-bearing. The court emphasized that the compromise payment for the take-or-pay liability and the buyout payment were "non-recoupable" and therefore were not like make-up gas to which part of a take-or-pay payment is allocated.

The particular contract settlement at issue in the IPAA v. Babbitt case involved a settlement in which the producer and the purchaser terminated their relationship entirely. The purchaser did not continue to take production after the settlement. An entirely new and unrelated purchaser entered into a new contract with the producer.[416]

In contrast, United States v. Century Offshore Management Corp., 111 F.3d 443 (6th Cir. Ky. 1997), involved a situation in which the purchaser made a lump-sum payment to replace the contract with a new contract with changed prices, and the same purchaser continued to take production after the settlement. In that case, the court held that the continued sale of production to the same purchaser at changed prices under the replacement contract provided a sufficient nexus between the payment and the production such that the lump-sum payment constituted

---

415. See, respective FERC Order series numbered 380, 436, 500, 528, and 636.

416. The *IPAA* decision was a 2–1 decision with an extensive dissent (by Judge Rogers). She found that it was reasonable for the Department to attribute the "buyout" payment to gas that was subject to the contract between the lessee and the original purchaser and sold by the lessee to a different purchaser after the settlement but during the term of the original contract. She found that doing so was consistent with *Diamond Shamrock* because royalty was not assessed until after the gas to which the payment was attributed was produced.

part of the payment for production sold, even though the payment was not in form "recoupable." The court distinguished the D.C. Circuit's decision in the *IPAA* case.

NOTES

1. Should express attribution of a payment to particular production (or "recoupability") be a precondition for regarding a payment under (or in settlement of) a gas sales contract as part of the consideration for production sold under that contract? What issues arise for both affirmative and negative answers?

2. Would the D.C. Circuit reach the same result as in IPAA v. Babbitt if it were confronted with a fact situation similar to that in United States v. Century Offshore Management Corp., in which the original purchaser continued to take production after the contract settlement?

(iii) What Is Production Subject to Royalty?

In Diamond Shamrock v. Hodel, supra, the Fifth Circuit held that royalties are not owed unless and until production occurs. Following the explosion and sinking of the Deepwater Horizon rig in the Gulf of Mexico, some of the oil volumes discharged from the damaged Macondo well were recovered and sold by lease operator BP. The ONNR issued an order to Anadarko Petroleum Corporation, 25 percent owner of the Macondo lease, requiring it to pay royalties on its share of the discharged and recovered oil volumes. Anadarko appealed the order to the Interior Board of Land Appeals asserting that these volumes were not "production" within the meaning of OCSLA.

ANADARKO PETROLEUM CORPORATION

IBLA 2010–228   Decided January 20, 2012

* * *

OPINION BY ADMINISTRATIVE JUDGE ROBERTS

Anadarko Petroleum Corporation (Anadarko) has appealed from the August 24, 2010, order to pay (demand letter) of the Director, Bureau of Ocean Energy Management, Regulation, and Enforcement (BOEMRE or BOEM) * * * holding that, as "owner of 25 percent of the legal record title in Lease OCS–G 32306," Anadarko is liable for 25 percent of the royalty payments due on the Lease, and requiring Anadarko to "report and pay royalties immediately for 25 percent of all oil and gas captured from the Macondo well" subsequent to the BP Deepwater Horizon Oil Spill. * * * For general background information pertaining to the BP oil spill, we have relied, to some extent, on both the Chief Counsel's Report and the National Commission on the BP Deepwater Horizon Oil Spill and Offshore Drilling, Report to the President, entitled *Deepwater: The Gulf Oil Disaster and the Future of Offshore Drilling*. We refer to these reports in this opinion as the Chief Counsel's Report and the National Commission Report. Decision at 1.

Anadarko raises two basic arguments on appeal. First, it claims that the captured oil is not "production" as that term is defined by section 2 of the Outer Continental Shelf Lands Act (OCSLA), 43 U.S.C. § 1331(m) (2006) (hereinafter occasionally referred to as § 1331(m)), and, consequently, that no royalty is owed on spilled oil captured and sold following the catastrophe. Second, it argues that the August 24, 2010, decision should be vacated because it is "facially inadequate and unsupported by the administrative record." Statement of Reasons (SOR) at 28. In this opinion, we reject Anadarko's reasoning and hold that the definitions in section 2 of OCSLA and section 3 of the Federal Oil and Gas Royalty Management Act (FOGRMA), 30 U.S.C. § 1702 (2006), are inclusive of the oil captured and sold by BP Exploration Production, Inc. (BP), from the Macondo Well, and that Anadarko is obligated to pay 25 percent of royalty due on that production in accordance with the terms of Lease OCS–G 32306. Further, as explained below, we summarily reject as without merit Anadarko's contention that the decision and record involved herein are inadequate.

I.   LEGAL AND FACTUAL BACKGROUND

An understanding of the imperatives at work in this appeal is not possible without a general understanding of the governing statutes; the Lease and assignment agreements between MMS and BP and between BP and the Anadarko companies; and relevant operational details that led to the blowout and that impact our analysis here.

A.   The Statutes

The relevant statutory criteria governing this appeal are found in OCSLA, which governs the exploration for and development of oil and gas originating in the OCS, and FOGRMA, which governs the federal royalty interest that attaches to oil and gas produced from all federal lands. We begin with OCSLA.

OCSLA was passed in 1953 to establish federal ownership and control over the mineral wealth of the OCS and to provide for the development of those natural resources. Gulf Offshore Co. v. Mobil Oil Corp., 453 U.S. 473, 480 n.7 (1981). The OCSLA thus vests the federal government with a proprietary interest in the OCS and establishes a regulatory scheme governing leasing and operations there. EP Operating Limited Partnership v. Placid Oil Co., 26 F.3d 563, 566 (5th Cir. 1994); Laredo Offshore Constructors, Inc. v. Hunt Oil Co., 754 F.2d 1223, 1227 (5th Cir. 1985).

Congress amended OCSLA significantly in 1978. We are indebted here to the Court's opinion in *Ensco Offshore Co. v. Salazar* (*Ensco v. Salazar*), 786 F. Supp. 2d 1151, 1156–58 (E.D.La. 2011), for its synopsis of the law pertaining to the Outer Continental Shelf. See Pub. L. No. 95–372, 92 Stat. 629 (Sept. 18, 1978). As amended, OCSLA establishes a national policy to make the OCS "available for expeditious and orderly development, subject to environmental safeguards, in a manner which is consistent with the maintenance of competition and other national needs." 43 U.S.C. § 1332(3). Before 1978, OCSLA did not define the terms "exploration," "development," or "production." Secretary of the Interior v. California, 464 U.S. 312, 336 (1984). Since 1978, "four distinct statutory stages to developing an offshore oil well" have been recognized: "(1) formulation of a five year leasing plan by the Department of the Interior; (2) lease sales; (3) exploration by the lessees; (4) development and production." Id. at 337. As conceptualized by Congress, "[e]ach stage involves separate regulatory review that may, but need not, conclude in the transfer to lessees of rights to conduct additional activities on the OCS." Id.

As in Ensco v. Salazar, 786 F. Supp. 2d at 1156–58, the third stage—exploration—and the fourth stage—development and production—are relevant to our inquiry here. Accordingly, we quote provisions of OCSLA that govern these phases. Under OCSLA, "exploration" is

> the process of searching for minerals, including (1) geophysical surveys where magnetic, gravity, seismic, or other systems are used to detect or imply the presence of such minerals, and (2) any drilling, whether on or off known geological structures, including the drilling of a well in which a discovery of oil or natural gas in paying quantities is made and the drilling of any additional delineation well after such discovery which is needed to delineate any reservoir and to enable the lessee to determine whether to proceed with development and production.

43 U.S.C. § 1331(k). "Development" is defined as "those activities which take place following discovery of minerals in paying quantities, including geophysical activity, drilling, platform construction, and operation of all onshore support facilities, and which are for the purpose of ultimately producing the minerals discovered." Id. § 1331(*l*). "Production" comprises "those activities which take place after the successful completion of any means for the removal of minerals, including such removal, field operations, transfer of minerals to shore, operation monitoring, maintenance, and workover drilling." Id. § 1331(m); Ensco v. Salazar, 786 F. Supp. 2d at 1156–57.

Two sections of FOGRMA are relevant to our later analysis. The first, section 102(a) of FOGRMA, was relied upon by BOEMRE in its August 24, 2010, letter to Anadarko demanding royalties. Section 102(a) addresses, among other things, who shall be liable for royalty payments:

> The person owning operating rights in a lease shall be primarily liable for its pro rata share of payment obligations under the lease. If the person owning the legal record title in a lease is other than the operating rights owner, the person owning the legal record title shall be secondarily liable for its pro rata share of such payment obligations under the lease.

30 U.S.C. § 1712(a).

The second, section 308 of FOGRMA, has been either distinguished or analogized by the parties to the facts here. Section 308 provides that lessees are

> liable for royalty payments on oil or gas lost or wasted from a lease site when such loss or waste is due to negligence on the part of the operator of the lease, or due to the failure to comply with any rule or regulation, order or citation issued under this chapter or any mineral leasing law.

30 U.S.C. § 1756.

B.   The Lease and the Assignment Agreements

Lease OCS–G 32306, Mississippi Canyon Block 252 (MC 252), was issued to BP pursuant to section 8 of OCSLA, 43 U.S.C. § 1337, effective June 1, 2008. * * * The Lease is located about 50 miles off the coast of Louisiana and about 5,000 feet below the surface of the water.

Lease OCS–G 32306 was issued with a royalty rate of 18 3/4 per cent. Section 6(a) of the Lease provides that "[t]he Lessee shall pay a fixed royalty as shown on the face hereof in amount or value of production saved, removed, or sold from the leased area"; that "gas (except helium) and oil of all kinds are subject to royalty"; and that "[a]ny Lessee is liable for royalty payments on oil or gas lost or wasted from a lease site when such loss or waste is due to negligence on the part of the operator of the lease, or due to the failure to comply with any rule or regulation, order, or citation issued" under FOGRMA or OCSLA. Section 6 of the attached "Sale 206 Lease Addendum" provides that, under certain conditions, the lessee may be eligible for royalty relief, including a royalty suspension of 12 million barrels of oil equivalent (royalty suspension volume (RSV)), under section 345 of the Energy Policy Act of 2005, which provides for royalty relief for production from deep water wells. Paragraph 2(f) of that section provides that "[f]ull royalties are owed on all production from a lease after the RSV is exhausted * * *." The Aug. 24, 2010, demand letter does not address the impact, if any, of this addendum. (Emphasis added.) Additionally, standard terms of the Lease provide that it is subject to all regulations issued pursuant to OCSLA "in the future which provide for the prevention of waste and conservation of the natural resources of the Outer Continental Shelf and the protection of correlative rights therein; and all other applicable statutes and regulations." Lease, § 1.

Anadarko became a co-lessee on Lease OCS–G 32306 effective October 1, 2009, by acquiring a 2.5 percent share of the Lease. That same day, Anadarko's subsidiary, Anadarko Exploration and Production Company, L.P. (Anadarko Exploration), acquired a 22.5 percent share of Lease OCS–G 32306, and BP acquired a fourth partner, MOEX Offshore 2007 LLC (MOEX), who acquired and currently holds a 10 percent share of the Lease. These assignments were executed on MMS Form MMS–150, which contains standard language making clear that by executing the contract, an assignee agrees to accept all applicable terms, conditions, stipulations, and restrictions pertaining to Lease OCS–G 32306, as well as the provisions of OCSLA and implementing regulations. By December 17, 2009, all assignees had designated BP as operator of the Lease. * * * Effective April 1, 2010, Anadarko acquired all of Anadarko Exploration's interest in the Lease, thus achieving a 25 percent share of Lease OCS–G 32306.

C.   The Macondo Well: Relevant Operational Details

* * *

For BP, the goal of temporary abandonment of the Macondo was to secure the well and remove its blowout preventer and riser so the well could be brought into production when the collection and production rig arrived. National Commission Report at 103.

The procedures undertaken by BP to temporarily abandon the Macondo well are well-documented and unnecessary for us to narrate here, except for two observations. First, it is important to note that all the temporary abandonment procedures undertaken with respect to the Macondo well were performed with the foreknowledge that this well had tapped an economically viable reservoir that was in fact being prepared for subsequent production. Id. at 94. Second, at least one job normally reserved for the completion and production crew—setting the lockdown sleeve in place—was performed by the drilling crew. Id. at 104. * * *

On April 20, 2010, subsequent to attempts to cement the casing in place and plug the well, a catastrophic blowout occurred, resulting in the deaths of 11 oil rig workers, the burning and sinking of the Deepwater Horizon, and the discharge of large amounts of federally-owned oil and gas into the atmosphere and waters of the Gulf of Mexico. National Commission Report at 87. The National Commission Report, at 87, estimates that nearly 5 million barrels of oil escaped from the Macondo well before it was capped on July 15, 2010. The discharge occurred through two leaks in the riser pipe, which was severed from the rig during the explosion, but remained connected to the well head. Id. at 132.

From April 21 through September 19, 2010, BP engineers and outside experts from government, industry, and academia worked to "kill" the flow spewing from the well and, in the interim, to contain and/or capture it, and finally, to permanently seal the reservoir. See National Commission Report at 131, 145–150, 155–160, 167, 169. While early attempts failed, on June 3, 2010, a successful collection device was installed over the wellhead. Id. at 159. Production that BP captured and removed by this device, or "top hat," as it was called, was conveyed by a new riser pipe extending from the device to a collection vessel, the Discoverer Enterprise, stationed above the Macondo well. Id. By June 8, the Discoverer Enterprise was collecting nearly 15,000 barrels of oil per day. Id. A second ship, the Q4000, became operational on June 16, amassing up to 10,000 additional barrels of oil per day. * * *

The oil captured from the Macondo well by these collection vessels was conveyed to off-lease facilities, where it was metered, processed, and sold. BOEMRE Answer at 5. According to ONRR, BP reported that approximately 679,000 barrels of oil from the Macondo well were produced, removed, and sold, generating approximately $47.3 million in proceeds for the lessees, and 35% of those proceeds, or approximately $11.8 million, are attributable to Anadarko and MOEX. See BOEMRE Answer at 5, ¶¶ 17, 18 n.4, referring to the attached Exs. 2 and 3, Affidavits of Robert Prael, dated May 27, 2011. ONRR asserts that "[t]he $47.3 million in total proceeds generated approximately $8.2 million in total royalties due and owing to the United States"; and that "[t]he amount of royalty owed by Appellant to the United States from its $11.8 million share of these proceeds is approximately $2 million." The Board makes no findings here as to the volumes of oil BP ultimately measured, processed, or sold, or the value of those volumes. The sole question before us here is one of law: *i.e.*, whether, as assignee of 25% of the record title interest in Lease OCS–G 32306, Anadarko is legally responsible for paying royalty on the portion of proceeds from oil recovered and sold from the Macondo spill attributable to its ownership interest. Answer at 5–6, ¶¶ 19 to 22.

D.   The Demand Letter

On July 15, 2010, BOEMRE issued an order requiring BP to immediately report and pay royalties on all oil captured from the Macondo well. Answer at 6, 23. According to Anadarko, on or about July 30, 2010, BP sent Anadarko a letter seeking 25 percent payment by Anadarko and enclosing a check that, according to BP, reflected 25 percent of BP's realized proceeds from its measurement and sale of oil captured from the Lease during June 2010. SOR at 5. Anadarko returned BP's check, explaining that Anadarko was not entitled to any of those volumes or the proceeds from their disposition because they were not "production" from the Lease. Id. On August 2, Anadarko informed BP that it believed that BP was responsible for payment due, but BP did not agree; also on August 2, BP informed BOEMRE that it would pay royalties for its 65 percent share of the total proceeds. SOR at 5; Answer at 6.

After failing to receive the full amount due from BP under the July 15 order, ONRR issued Anadarko the August 24 demand letter, or order to pay, that is the subject of this appeal. ONRR also issued a nearly identical letter to MOEX the same day, corresponding to its 10 percent record title interest in the Lease. Citing section 8 of OCSLA, 43 U.S.C. § 1337 (2006), and section 102 of FOGRMA, 30 U.S.C. § 1712(a) (2006), the one-page demand letter to Anadarko states that, as a 25 percent record title owner, "Anadarko is liable for 25 percent of the royalty payments due on the Lease"; and, "[u]ntil notified otherwise, Anadarko is required to report and pay royalties immediately for 25 percent of all oil and gas captured from the Macondo well using Form MMS 2014." The demand letter warns Anadarko that failure to comply may trigger civil penalties under 30

U.S.C. § 1719 (2006). Thereafter, Anadarko and MOEX began making royalty payments under protest. Answer at 6. On August 31, 2010, Anadarko and MOEX appealed.

II. ARGUMENTS OF THE PARTIES

Anadarko's central argument is that the discharged volumes captured and sold from the Lease do not constitute "production" as that term is defined by OCSLA, 43 U.S.C. § 1331(m), and that, therefore, they do not meet the "specific conditions under which a 'royalty' obligation is owed to the United States as lessor." SOR at 2. Anadarko maintains that "BOEM exceeded its authority by ordering Anadarko to pay a royalty where none is due." Id.

Anadarko challenges BOEMRE's reliance upon section 8 of OCSLA, 43 U.S.C. § 1337(a), in demanding royalty payments from Anadarko. Anadarko emphasizes that under section 8 of OCSLA, royalty is owed "at not less than 121/2 per centum . . . in amount or value of the production saved, removed, or sold." 43 U.S.C. § 1337(a)(1)(A) (emphasis added). Similarly, states Anadarko, OCSLA's implementing regulations BOEMRE explains that the Department recently promulgated a direct final rule recodifying its royalty regulations within the newly created ONRR. *See* 75 Fed. Reg. 61051 (Oct. 4, 2010). The regulatory provisions cited by BOEMRE previously existed at 30 C.F.R. §§ 202.100 and 202.150, and were otherwise left unchanged by the 2010 final rule. provide that "[r]oyalties [are] due on oil production from leases subject to the requirements of [Part 1200]" (30 C.F.R. § 1201.100(a)); that "[a]ll oil [subject to certain exceptions] produced from a federal or Indian lease to which this part applies is subject to royalty" (30 C.F.R. § 1202.100(b)); and that gas produced from a federal or Indian lease is subject to royalty (30 C.F.R. § 1202.150). SOR at 9. Anadarko also refers to Section 6(a) of BP's Lease document as requiring the payment of "a fixed royalty . . . in amount or value of production saved, removed, or sold from the leased area," and to an Addendum to the Lease providing that "[f]ull royalties are owed on all production from a lease after the RSV [royalty suspension volume] is exhausted." Id. (quoting Ex. 2 to SOR).

Anadarko posits that OCSLA, the regulations, and the Lease "set forth two principal prerequisites for the imposition of royalty on oil and gas volumes derived from the OCS." Id. "First," states Anadarko, "the oil and gas must constitute 'production,'" and "[s]econd, that production must be 'saved, removed, or sold' from the Lease." Id. Anadarko asserts that "[t]his appeal concerns only the first criterion." Id. (emphasis added). In Anadarko's view, "[b]ecause the captured volumes do not constitute 'production' in the first instance, the method of their disposition is irrelevant for royalty determination purposes." Id. at 9–10.

Anadarko quotes the definition of "production" in OCSLA, 43 U.S.C. § 1331(m), i.e., "those activities which take place after the successful completion of any means for the removal of minerals" (emphasis added by Anadarko), for the proposition that, "[f]or deepwater oil and gas on the OCS, production is accomplished via a successfully completed well." SOR at 10. Anadarko states that "successful completion" is not separately defined in OCSLA, OCSLA's legislative history, or relevant case law, but that "BOEM's regulations supply a consistent definition of 'completion,' recognizing that well completion must precede production." Id. (citing, inter alia, 30 C.F.R. §§ 250.105, 250.501; 75 Fed. Reg. 63376 (Oct. 14, 2010) (amending 30 C.F.R. § 250.1500 to separately define "well completion/well workover" to mean "those operations following the drilling of a well that are intended to establish or restore production")).

Anadarko argues that "by defining 'production,' Congress has expressly established the prerequisite conditions under which royalty may be assessed." SOR at 11. Anadarko states those conditions in unequivocal terms: "In short, only oil and gas volumes derived from a successfully completed well constitute production, and in royalty. Conversely, if oil and gas volumes do not meet this legal definition of production, the statutory, regulatory, and lease royalty obligations are not triggered." Id. Anadarko's argument in this regard is set forth below:

> The captured oil volumes at issue clearly do not meet the statutory definition of production. First, the discharge and capture of hydrocarbons resulting from the Deepwater Horizon incident did not follow the "completion" of a well. The well was in fact never completed. Although drilling operations were finished at the time of the incident, several remaining steps necessary to complete the well for production had not been planned or performed. Indeed, as of April 20, operations were underway to cement and temporarily abandon the well. Necessary well-completion steps to interface between the reservoir and the surface to enable production had not been taken, including but not limited to pressure-testing, installation of the "Christmas tree," and perforation of the well.... Moreover, ... the BOEM plans and approvals required to transition from exploration to development and production were neither sought nor granted.
>
> Second, the Macondo well plainly was not "successfully" completed. As illustrated by the April 20 blowout and premature discharge of oil volumes until July, and the eventual "bottom kill," the exploration well obviously was the essence of unsuccessful.

Id. at 12.

Anadarko reasons that "[a]t the time of the Deepwater Horizon incident, the Lease was indisputably only in its initial exploration phase," and that "[b]ecause exploration activities had not yet concluded, and the necessary regulatory approvals to commence production had not yet been sought or granted, production could not take place at MC 252 and no royalty was due." Id. at 13. According to Anadarko, OCSLA "divides OCS leases into three different sequential phases: exploration, development, and production." Id. Thus, Anadarko states:

OCSLA defines "exploration" as "the process of searching for minerals," including drilling "to enable the lessee to determine whether to proceed with development and production." 43 U.S.C. § 1331(k). In turn, "development" consists of activities, "following discovery of minerals in paying quantities," conducted "for the purpose of ultimately producing the minerals discovered." Id. § 1331(*l*). Finally, as detailed above, "production" may begin "after the successful completion" of a well. Id. § 1331(m).

Id. Applying these definitions of exploration, development, and production, Anadarko claims that "[t]he activities underway at MC 252 as of April 20, 2010, only constituted exploration," and that "[n]o development, let alone production, had begun." Id. (citing Congressional Research Service, Deepwater Horizon Oil Spill: Selected Issues for Congress, at 32 n.164 (July 30, 2010) ("At the time of the incident, the oil and gas formation was still being explored, and was not yet in the production phase of the project. . . . [I]t would have taken some years to develop the project into a producing facility.")). In addition, Anadarko asserts that BOEMRE's regulatory program parallels OCSLA in defining exploration, development, and production. See 30 C.F.R. § 250.105.

Anadarko states that section 11 of OCSLA and BOEMRE's regulations require submission and approval of an Exploration Plan (EP) before exploration. See 43 U.S.C. § 1340(c)(1) (2006); 30 C.F.R. § 250.201. Anadarko states that at the time of the explosion and blowout, exploration of MC 252 was proceeding pursuant to BP's Initial EP, approved by MMS early 2009, before Anadarko acquired its interest in the Lease. On the accompanying OCS Plan Information Form (Form MMS–137, Ex. 3), BP's proposed activities included only "exploration drilling," and later activities, including "development drilling," "well completion," and "commence production," were not selected on Form MMS–137. SOR at 16. Such later "activities were not permitted, and production could not occur," under the Initial EP. Id. In its Application for Permit to Drill (APD), BP designated the Macondo well as "exploration," and BP's drilling plan summary indicated that "[t]he well will either be P & A'ed [plugged and abandoned] or temporarily abandoned for future completion." Id. (quoting Ex. 4). Anadarko states that "BP never requested approval to complete the Macondo well," and that none of the revised and additional APDs or Applications for Permit to Modify (APMs) to adapt its activities to circumstances on MC 252, "including but not limited to the need to substitute the Transocean Deepwater Horizon rig for the Transocean Marianas rig and to conduct bypass operations[,] . . . altered the Macondo well's status as an uncompleted exploration well." Id. at 17.

"[B]efore the operator may 'conduct any development and production activities on a lease or unit in the Western GOM [Gulf of Mexico],' including MC 252," Anadarko argues that BOEMRE requires submission and approval of a Development Operations Coordination Document (DOCD). Id. (citing 30 C.F.R. § 250.201, 250.241 to 250.273; Mobil Oil Exploration & Producing Southeast v. United States, 530 U.S. 604, 610

(2000) (noting that if exploration is successful, the company must prepare and obtain Interior approval for a Development and Production Plan—a Plan that describes the proposed drilling and related environmental safeguards)). Further, states Anadarko, a deepwater lease like MC 252, i.e., water depths greater than 1,314 feet, requires the filing of a Conservation Information Document (CID) with the DOCD. See 30 C.F.R. § 250.201. "The CID must be submitted and approved before the operator may 'commence production.'" SOR at 18 (citing 30 C.F.R. §§ 250.201, 250.299). Moreover, water depths at MC 252 necessitate submission and approval of a Deepwater Operations Plan (DWOP) in advance of production. 30 C.F.R. §§ 250.201, 250.286. The DWOP process consists of two components—a "Conceptual Plan" and the DWOP, id. §§ 250.296 to 250.295, both of which must be approved prior to production. Id. § 250.290.

Thus, Anadarko argues, based upon the OCSLA's statutory definitions and scheme, as implemented in BOEMRE's regulatory program, that the "several prerequisites to 'production' . . . were not satisfied at MC 252." SOR at 20. Anadarko asserts that "[t]he blowout on the Lease occurred before exploration work was finished under the approved EP"; that "BOEM authorized BP to drill and temporarily abandon the exploration well, and nothing more, at MC 252"; and that "[n]one of the other prerequisite approvals for completion, development, and production was sought, let alone secured." Id. Anadarko concludes, therefore, that "the uncontrolled flow of hydrocarbons from the blowout of the sole Macondo Exploration well drilled could not, and did not, constitute production, and BOEM may not assess royalty on those oil volumes if they are captured and then disposed of." Id.

Anadarko further disputes BOEMRE's reliance upon section 102 of FOGRMA, 30 U.S.C. § 1712(a), in ordering Anadarko to pay royalty on the captured oil. Section 102 of FOGRMA, as amended by the Royalty Simplification and Fairness Act of 1996 (RFSA), Pub. L. No. 104–285, requires lessees to pay royalty in proportion to their share of ownership in a lease. Anadarko argues that section 102 of FOGRMA triggers "[p]roportionate royalty payments . . . only where royalty is due in the first instance." SOR at 21. According to Anadarko, since "[t]he volumes uncontrollably discharged from the Lease and later captured and sold by BP are not subject to 'royalty' under OCSLA because they do not meet the definition of 'production.' . . . [N]o royalty is owed, [and] Anadarko's 25 percent ownership interest in the Lease is irrelevant for royalty purposes." Id. Anadarko speculates that the federal government might, in a subsequent action, "assert entitlement to a different form of compensation for the discharged and captured volumes from the Lease." SOR at 21. However, unlike the requirement to pay royalty under OCSLA, "potential liability or other compensation is not statutorily proportionate among co-lessees." Id. at 21–22. Anadarko would hold BP solely responsible for non-performance of Lease obligations and resulting damages. We offer no opinion on the merits of this theory.

Anadarko next argues that the only other existing legal vehicle for BOEMRE to assess the equivalent of a royalty is the "[e]xpanded royalty obligations" in section 308 of FOGRMA, 30 U.S.C. § 1756. As noted, section 308 provides that "[a]ny lessee is liable for royalty payments on oil or gas lost or wasted from a lease site when such loss or waste is due to negligence on the part of the operator of the lease, or due to the failure to comply with any rule or regulation, order or citation issued under this Act or any mineral leasing law." 30 U.S.C. § 1756. Thus, Anadarko states, "[s]ection 308 requires payment equivalent to a royalty for oil or gas negligently (i.e., 'avoidably') lost or wasted, even if production has not occurred." SOR at 23.

According to Anadarko's reasoning, the expanded royalty obligations of section 308 do not apply since oil discharges from Lease MC 252 were not "lost or wasted." Id.; see also Reply at 4. Anadarko states that the term "lost or wasted" is not defined by statute, but that "[t]he ordinary meaning of [the term] applies to volumes that are gone and cannot be recovered, i.e., the opposite of the ordinary meaning of 'capture,' the term employed by BOEM's Order." Id. (footnote omitted). According to Anadarko, "BOEM recognizes this difference." Id. (citing 30 C.F.R. §§ 250.1160(e), 250.1162(b), under which the term "lost or wasted" includes oil that is burned or gas that is flared or vented). Anadarko argues that "while FOGRMA may expand royalty obligations to cover volumes of oil or gas that are lost or wasted, it does not impose royalty on volumes that are instead captured and sold." Id. at 24.

Anadarko engages in what ONRR refers to as "an amorphous discourse about circumstances in which discharged oil may not constitute 'production.'" Id. at 24–26. Anadarko reviews the regulatory history on the subject of lost or wasted volumes and states that "[t]he end result is a legal scheme that provides separately for compensation on avoidably lost or wasted volumes as opposed to royalty on production, despite both being styled as a 'royalty.'" Id. at 24–25. In addition, Anadarko claims that "no case has squarely addressed the government's remedy for uncontrollably discharged and later captured volumes from a lease during exploration activities due to operator misconduct." SOR at 26. According to Anadarko, "the case law ... does not support imposition of a royalty here." Id. Anadarko reviews Chevron U.S.A. Inc., 110 IBLA 216 (1989), and Diamond Shamrock Exploration Co. v. Hodel (Diamond Shamrock), 853 F.2d 1159 (5th Cir. La. 1988), and argues that neither of those opinions supports BOEMRE's attempt to assess royalty on "the uncontrollable discharge and later recovery of volumes as a result of a blowout while drilling an uncompleted exploration well." Id. at 28. Anadarko concludes that "the volumes that prematurely escaped from MC 252 and were later captured by BP are not production and thus are not subject to a corresponding royalty on production." Id.

ONRR answers that "[t]his case is about a company which is attempting to avoid paying royalties for oil produced, removed and sold from a federal lease ... despite the facts that approximately 679,000 barrels of oil were produced, removed and sold from its lease, and that sale of this oil generated $47.3 million in proceeds from the three leases." Answer at 1. In ONRR's view, "[t]his attempt to avoid a clear legal obligation is especially egregious in light of the circumstances." Id. ONRR devotes much of its Answer to addressing Anadarko's "core argument," i.e., that "oil captured, removed and sold from the Macondo well on Lease OCS–G 32306 does not meet the definition of 'production'" under OCSLA, and "[t]herefore, . . . that no royalty is owed on that oil." Id. at 2.

ONRR contends that the oil captured from the Macondo well was "[o]il produced, removed, and sold" from Lease OCS–32306, and in fact meets the definition of "production" in § 1331(m) of OCSLA. Answer at 9–13. Relying upon Diamond Shamrock, 853 F.2d at 1165–66, ONRR argues that the "plain language reading" of § 1331(m) is not intended to exclude accepted industry meanings for the term, "including the actual products of an oil and gas well." Id. at 11. ONRR argues that Anadarko's "attempts to distinguish Diamond Shamrock" are not supportable because "the Fifth Circuit's interpretation of the term 'production' was not contingent upon or linked to the facts of that case," and "[t]here is no indication" that the Court intended to ignore the phrase "by any means" set forth in § 1331(m). Answer at 11–13 (citing Murphy Exploration, 148 IBLA 266, 273 n.2 (1999)). Moreover, ONRR argues that the appellant and its partners "would realize a multi-million dollar windfall if not required to pay royalty on the oil captured and sold from the Macondo well," and that the Board has traditionally declined to interpret the law in a manner that creates windfalls, citing Steve Crooks, 167 IBLA 39, 46 (2005), and Mesa Petroleum Co., 111 IBLA 201, 203–04 (1989). Answer at 16.

Anadarko replies that Diamond Shamrock is distinguishable because it addressed the meaning of the value of production within the context "of whether contractual 'take-or-pay' clauses required royalty payments to be made prior to the actual severance of the minerals from the lease." Reply at 5–6. In distinguishing Diamond Shamrock, Anadarko states: "In reality, Diamond Shamrock held only that if there was no severance of minerals, then there was no production. This holding does not mean that whenever there is severance of minerals, there is production." Id. at 5. Anadarko argues that the Board's decision in Chevron U.S.A. Inc., 110 IBLA 216 (1989), also is not on point, even though it involved a blowout situation, because at issue was a large quantity of gas that was lost during drilling through "venting and flaring," and because the Board held that the statutory basis for collecting royalty on the lost gas in that case was not 43 U.S.C. § 1331(m), but rather "the expanded royalty in FOGRMA section 308 [30 U.S.C. § 1756 (2006)]." Id. at 26–27. With the Deepwater Horizon disaster, Anadarko argues, the captured oil was not "lost" and therefore was not subject to section 308 of FOGRMA. Id.; Reply at 4.

The Government's loss is a tort issue rather than a royalty issue, Anadarko maintains (SOR at 26), as, under § 1331(m), "production" is properly limited to that product which is removed and sold from a well after the well's successful completion, and does not extend to the capture and sale of oil emanating from a blowout during exploratory drilling. SOR at 26; Reply at 8. Anadarko argues that this limited approach to defining production is consistent with Congress's recognition that not all discharged oil volumes constitute "production subject to royalty," referring to volumes (1) unavoidably lost or wasted, (2) used for the benefit of the Lease, or (3) lost due to drainage. SOR at 24–26. Anadarko asserts that ONRR is mistaken in its assertion that Anadarko will receive a windfall if royalty is not paid. In Anadarko's view, there is no windfall because no royalty inures to the lessor since there was no production. Anadarko argues that the proper remedy for the government's loss is a damages claim against BP, the operator. Reply to Answer (Reply) at 6–8.

In a Sur–Reply to Anadarko's Reply, ONRR argues that Anadarko's arguments ignore the plain language of OCSLA and its implementing regulation, 30 C.F.R. § 250.105, defining "production." Sur–Reply at 3. ONRR maintains that, "[b]y its plain language, the definition of 'production' is not limited solely to completion of a well, but rather to "the successful completion of any means for the removal of minerals." Id. (emphasis by ONRR). ONRR argues that in its Answer it has demonstrated (1) "that there was 'successful completion' of at least one 'means for the removal of minerals' "; and (2) "that the oil removed and sold from Lease OCS–G 32306 meets multiple meanings applicable to the term 'production.' " Id. at 2–5. Further, ONRR asserts, its interpretation of the statutory definition of "production" "conforms to the plain language of the statute and precedent," and prevents all record title lessees from obtaining "a windfall of royalty-free oil." Sur–Reply at 5–9.

III. ANALYSIS

[1, 2] We reject Anadarko's central premise, i.e., that the oil captured, removed, and sold from the Macondo well is not "production" under OCSLA, 43 U.S.C. § 1331(m). As discussed below, we find no support for Anadarko's limited definition of "production."

We agree with ONRR that the phrase "successful completion" in § 1331(m) must be read with the phrase "of any means"; that "[l]imiting the ability to realize royalties from a lease based on the way in which those minerals were taken would not effectuate Congress's goal of reimbursing the United States for those minerals"; and that "[s]uch a limitation would particularly run afoul of Congress's goal in the present case, given that 679,000 barrels of oil were removed from the Macondo well using non-typical means, then sold on the lessees' behalf for $47.3 million in proceeds." Id. To accept Anadarko's argument that the captured oil is not royalty-bearing would undermine OCSLA's primary objective, i.e., "the efficient exploitation of the minerals of the OCS, owned exclusively by the United States." Amoco Production Co. v. Sea Robin Pipeline Co., 844 F.2d 1202, 1210 (5th Cir. 1988) (emphasis added; quoted in EP Operating Limited Partnership v. Placid Oil Co., 26 F.3d at 570 ("The government's interest in the minerals of the OCS is proprietary.... It leases out the minerals and receives a royalty on the amount produced.

Thus, the government is concerned with the total recovery of the federally-owned minerals from the reservoirs underlying the OCS.'')).

Anadarko's efforts to distinguish Diamond Shamrock are not persuasive. That case involved take-or-pay payments pursuant to a take-or-pay clause in a gas sales contract, and the Fifth Circuit denied the demand for royalty on the basis that the production had not yet been physically severed from the ground. The Fifth Circuit looked to the lease itself, to the contract between the producer and the pipeline-purchaser, and a common-sense definition of the term "production" to reach its conclusion "[f]or purposes of royalty calculation and payment, production does not occur until the minerals are physically severed from the earth." 853 F.2d at 1168. The Fifth Circuit stated that "[t]he word 'production' is a horse of many colors." 853 F.2d at 1165. In observing that the term "production" has a variety of meanings in the oil and gas industry, the Fifth Circuit stated:

> The term "production" is used in the oil and gas industry in several different but related senses. The term can be used to refer to an abstract noun: (i) the act or process of producing. It can also refer to either of two concrete nouns: (ii) the products of an oil and gas well, or (iii) the well itself.

853 F.2d at 1166. ONRR rightly states that "the oil which emanated from the Macondo well clearly fits the second definition posited by the Fifth Circuit": this oil is obviously "the product of an oil and gas well." Answer at 10. ONRR also correctly observes that "[t]he first definition is also appropriate: BP engaged in 'the act or process of producing' oil by using various devices to capture it as it emanated from a well which BP had drilled (and, for some of the oil, after it had reached the surface of the water)." Id.

The Court's explicit rejection of a limited interpretation of the term "production," as used in § 1331(m), undermines Anadarko's argument:

> Even accepting the proposition that "production" in these leases is used in the abstract noun sense, as in (i) above, this court cannot accept "the conclusion that § 1331(m) was intended to define production to exclude all other accepted meanings in the industry, including (ii) above, the actual products of an oil and gas well.

Id. at 1166 (emphasis added; footnote omitted). The Court stated that "[i]n the interests of consistency, logic and economics," it was "adopt[ing] as the legal definition of the word 'production,' as used in the context of calculating royalty payments, the actual physical severance of minerals from the formation." Id. at 1168 (citing, e.g., Christian v. A.A. Oil Corp., 506 P.2d 1369, 1373 (Mont. 1973)) (production is mineral withdrawn from land and reduced to possession). The Fifth Circuit emphatically rejected the Department's argument that the definition of production in § 1331(m) "relates to only one possible interpretation," and stated: "With all due deference to the Secretary, juxtaposing the definition of § 1331(m) onto these oil and gas leases makes little sense, either economically, logically or geologically." 853 F.2d at 1166. The same can be said about Anadarko's definition of "production" in the present case.

In Diamond Shamrock, as with Lease OCS–G 32306, the royalty provision provided that royalty will be paid on "the amount or value of the production saved, removed, or sold from the leased area." 853 F.2d at 1166 (emphasis added). This is a very broadly phrased provision. The Fifth Circuit stated that in 30 C.F.R. § 206.150 the Department has defined "value of production" as "fair market value." Id. The Fifth Circuit then stated: "At a minimum, fair market value is at least 'the gross proceeds accruing to the lessee from the disposition of the produced substances.'" Id. (quoting 30 C.F.R. § 206.150). Accepting Anadarko's argument means that the gross proceeds accruing to Anadarko and its co-lessees are not from the disposition of produced substances. According to Anadarko's theory, the substances were not "produced." Such a rendering is contrary to the specific holding in Diamond Shamrock that "[f]or purposes of royalty calculation and payment, production does not occur until the minerals are physically severed from the earth." Id. at 1168. The Fifth Circuit made this point again, stating: "Royalty payments are due only on the value of minerals actually produced, i.e., physically severed from the ground." 853 F.2d at 1168. In the face of the Fifth Circuit's analysis in Diamond Shamrock, Anadarko's protestations that the oil from the Macondo well is royalty-free because the minerals were not produced are unconvincing.

The oil emanating from the Macondo well was "physically severed," even if the manner in which it was severed involved a series of unfortunate events that were unplanned and unpermitted. In characterizing the captured oil, Anadarko carefully avoids any wording that would suggest that the oil was "produced" or constitutes "production" within the limited meaning that Anadarko projects onto § 1331(m). Anadarko uses such terms, inter alia, as "uncontrollable discharge" (SOR at 1); "discharged volumes" (id.); "captured oil volumes" (id. at 12); "uncontrolled flow of hydrocarbons" (id. at 20); the "subject volumes" (id.); "volumes uncontrollably discharged" (id. at 21); "volumes that prematurely escaped" (id. at 28); "captured hydrocarbons" (id. at 29); "discharged and captured volumes" (id.); and "recovered oil volumes" (id. at 30). We conclude that production by any other name is still production.

Anadarko would have us construe and apply § 1331(m) only in those circumstances when the sequence of stages and events (i.e., exploration, development, and production) takes place as contemplated in OCSLA and the regulations. As ONRR states, the regulatory scheme embodied in § 1331(m) and the implementing regulations "envisions an orderly progression, in which a lessee obtains the necessary authorizations, drills and completes a well, then extracts oil through the well by conventional means." Answer at 12. We are in complete agreement with the following summation, offered by ONRR:

The flaw in Appellant's narrow reading of the term "production" is perfectly illustrated by the present case. Here, large quantities of oil were severed from the formation by the drilling of the Macondo well. This oil then emanated from the Macondo well. A significant amount of this oil, 679,000 barrels, was captured by various devices. This oil was then removed from the lease, metered, processed, and sold, just like oil produced through more conventional means. Arguing that this oil is not royalty bearing because there was not the standard orderly progression ignores reality.

Id. at 13. The logical end to application of Anadarko's narrow definition of "production" would be to allow an operator to avoid paying royalty on oil severed and sold by deliberately not securing the permits required prior to development and completion of a well, since under Anadarko's theory there is no production because the mineral has not been extracted as planned and in accordance with the phases Anadarko would impose onto § 1331(m). In the world imagined by Anadarko, the lessees would be entitled to keep the proceeds from the sale of the recovered oil and the federal government's recourse would be a tort action for damages. We find no support for such an approach. Imposing Anadarko's "interpretation of § 1331(m) onto these oil and gas leases makes little sense, either economically, logically or geologically." 853 F.2d at 1166.

In Chevron U.S.A., which Anadarko also deems inapplicable, the Board considered the assessment of royalty in a blowout scenario in which an uncompleted OCS well suffered a blowout during drilling, resulting in a large quantify of gas being lost through venting and flaring. 110 IBLA at 217. The MMS sought to impose a royalty on the lost gas. On appeal, Chevron U.S.A. argued that by its definition of "production" in § 1331(m), "Congress intended that royalty would accrue [only] on that oil or gas severed after successful completion of a well, but no royalty would accrue on that gas which escaped into the atmosphere during exploration and development, regardless of the reason for its loss." Id. at 218. The Board noted that "[t]he fact that Well No. 1 had not been successfully completed at the time of the blowout [was] not in dispute." Id. The Board did not resolve the issue as to whether § 1331(m) applied because it concluded that the expanded royalty obligation in section 308 of FOGRMA, 30 U.S.C. § 1756 (2006), "fills this gap" and requires payment of royalty on avoidably lost gas volumes. Id. at 221. Anadarko argues that the "recovered oil volumes" at the Macondo well "were not lost," and so "FOGRMA does not apply or preclude a Board determination that the subject volumes are not royalty-bearing 'production' within the meaning of OCSLA, the regulations, and the Lease." SOR at 27. Indeed, Anadarko argues that FOGRMA's provisions do not include volumes discharged as a result of a blowout and subsequently captured. The end result of Anadarko's logic is that, had BP not captured the oil it in fact captured, but that all of the oil was lost and none captured, royalty would be payable on all oil as lost under section 308 of FOGRMA. According to Anadarko, the Secretary is entitled to collect royalty on the lost oil, but not oil reduced to

BP's possession and sold on the market. See id. at 21. Such an argument is not sustainable. We note that by Anadarko's own reasoning BOEMRE would be well within its authority under section 308 of FOGRMA to demand payment of royalty on the oil and gas that was in fact *lost* as a result of the Deepwater Horizon blowout. That issue is not before us, however.

The very nature of the Deepwater Horizon catastrophe is inconsistent with Anadarko's position that a successful completion for royalty purposes takes place only when a well is completed and oil and gas are extracted on schedule and in accordance with the required permits. In enacting OCS-LA, Congress was aware that the phases of exploration, development, and production on the OCS are not always distinctly separated. According to the testimony of the Chairman of the Council on Environmental Quality reported in the legislative history of the 1978 amendments to OCSLA, the statute would, of course, provide "[a]uthority for a distinct pause between exploration and development to reevaluate how and whether to proceed." H.R. 95–590, 95th Cong. (1977) reprinted in 1978 U.S.C.C.A.N. 1450, 1520. And the House Report stated that section 25 of the Act, "Oil and Gas Development and Production," codified at 43 U.S.C. § 1351, "provides a means to separate the federal decision to allow private industry to explore for oil and gas from the federal decision to allow development and production to proceed if the lessee finds oil and gas." Id. While this testimony shows an understanding that exploration, development, and production in connection with an OCS lease may take place in discrete stages, those phases are defined largely for regulatory convenience. The Committee demonstrated a sophisticated working knowledge of the realities of oil and gas development, where, as the National Commission Report on the BP spill vividly demonstrates, decisions are made under the pressure of the moment:

> The committee recognize[s], that in many cases, there is no real separation between exploration and production. Exploration activities, including delineation drilling, can continue in a lease area even after production has commenced. However, the committee also recognize[s] that there is a point in time when the lessee has to make a decision whether or not he is going to order a platform, seek related, onshore support facilities, and commence substantial development and production in a lease area. This decision is perhaps, with the exception of the purchase of a lease, the key decision, with the most significant effects, relating to OCS activities. This section utilizes the natural pause that occurs when a lessee determines he is to commence major development as the basis to supply needed information to affected states and other interested persons, and to provide a mechanism for decisions as to continued activity on a lease.

H.R. 95–590, 1978 U.S.C.C.A.N. at 1570–71 (emphasis added).

What the Deepwater Horizon catastrophe demonstrates in stark and tragic terms is that there was very little that was "natural" about the blowout and the series of efforts taken to stymie the uncontrolled flow of oil from the well. The Chief Counsel's and National Commission Reports make clear that, as the disaster unfolded, there was in reality no "natural pause" between "exploration" and "production." The plan for orderly development of MC 252 was destroyed with the blowout. The capture of the oil was prudent from the viewpoint of minimizing, to the extent possible, the environmental harm that would result if the oil were not captured. The capture was also prudent from the perspective of preventing the waste of federally-owned minerals. However, there was no "natural pause" between development and production. Any suggestion that BP and Anadarko should be excused from paying royalty because the project failed to materialize according to plan is meaningless. The Deepwater Horizon plan, even though thwarted by the blowout, was aimed at the production of oil and gas. See Tennessee Gas Pipeline v. Houston Casualty Ins. Co., 87 F.3d 150, 154 (5th Cir. 1996) ("[T]he operation involves 'exploration, development, or production' of minerals on the OCS. These terms denote respectively the processes involved in searching for minerals on the OCS; preparing to extract them by, inter alia, drilling wells and constructing platforms; and removing the minerals and transferring them to shore.").

Anadarko argues that, under the terms of OCSLA, there was no "successful completion" of the well and that, therefore, there was no production upon which to base a royalty demand. ONRR argues, on the other hand, that the operative language is the phrase "by any means," such that there is a successful completion for the purpose of collecting royalty even if the production phase contemplated by the statute was never reached, and that royalty is properly demanded under the rationale set forth in Diamond Shamrock. Thus, we are asked to interpret a statutory definition containing two phrases that may be seen as inconsistent under the opposing arguments presented.

In construing the seemingly ambiguous language in dispute, we will interpret the provision "with common sense in order to accomplish a reasonable result." 3 Singer, Sutherland Statutory Construction § 57:3 at 16 (6th ed. 2001) (citation omitted); see also United States v. Ryan, 284 U.S. 167, 175 (1931) ("All laws are to be given a sensible construction. A literal application of a statute which would lead to absurd consequences is to be avoided whenever a reasonable application can be given which is consistent with the legislative purpose.") (citations omitted); see Jerry Grover d.b.a. Kingston Rust Development (Grover III), 160 IBLA 234, 255 (2003).

OCSLA has very little to say regarding the effective collection of royalty for oil and gas inuring to the United States from federal oil and gas leases. The 1978 amendments to OCSLA predated FOGRMA by over 4 years; FOGRMA became law in January 1983. Congress stated that the purpose to be accomplished by FOGRMA is "to clarify, reaffirm, expand, and define the authorities and responsibilities of the Secretary of the Interior to implement and maintain a royalty management system for oil and gas leases on federal lands, Indian lands, and the Outer Continental

Shelf." 30 U.S.C. § 1701(b)(2) (emphasis added). Under section 3 of FOGRMA, "production" is defined as "those activities which take place for the removal of oil or gas, including such removal, field operations, transfer of oil or gas off the lease site, operation monitoring, maintenance, and workover drilling"; and "royalty" means "any payment based on the value or volume of production which is due to the United States ... on production of oil or gas from the Outer Continental Shelf ... under any provision of a lease." 30 U.S.C. § 1702(13) and (14).

There can be no doubt that, for purposes of determining royalty on the value of production saved, removed, or sold from the leased area, the "successful completion" of a well under § 1331 of OCSLA is not a limiting factor, at least in the sense that Anadarko would define "successful completion." Moreover, a reasonable construction of the definition of "production" for royalty-bearing purposes is that, to the extent the two statutory definitions may be viewed as inconsistent, the definition of production in section 3 of FOGRMA, embracing "activities which take place for the removal of oil or gas," without regard to the sequence of those activities, amended and clarified the definition of "production" set forth in § 1331(m) of OCSLA. This reasonable construction, which is consistent with both OCSLA and FOGRMA, avoids many potential "absurd consequences" of Anadarko's literal application of § 1331(m). U.S. v. Ryan, 284 U.S. at 175.

However, we do not find the two definitions inconsistent. The legislative history quoted supra indicates that Congress was indeed aware of the realities of oil and gas exploration and development. Thus, a reasonable interpretation of the clause "by any means" in § 1331(m) is that it operates as a limitation on the phrase "successful completion," and thereby acknowledges, and is consistent with, the comment in the House Report accompanying OCSLA that "in many cases, there is no real separation between exploration and production," quoted supra. This interpretation renders the definition of "production" in § 1331(m) consistent with the definition of "production" set forth in FOGRMA. There is no question that the Macondo well was drilled, and there is no question that the subject oil emanated from the well as the result of the operator's drilling activities. Thus, we hold that the capture and sale of oil severed from the ground as the result of the BP oil spill is properly deemed a "successful completion" for purposes of determining whether royalty must be paid to the United States, pursuant to the definitions of "production" under both OCSLA and FOGRMA.

We have no doubt that section 102(a) of FOGRMA, 30 U.S.C. § 1712(a) (2006), as well as the agreements between Anadarko and BP as assignee and assignor, respectively, and MMS' successor, BOEMRE, as the lessor, clearly define Anadarko's legal obligation to the United States as required by BOEMRE's August 24, 2010, Order. Accordingly, we conclude that the oil collected from the Macondo well was production "saved, removed, [and] sold from the leased area," and, therefore, was royalty-bearing under section 6(a) of the Lease and under section 3 of FOGRMA,

30 U.S.C. § 1702(13). Under BP's assignments to Anadarko of 25 percent of the record title interest, a pro rata amount of the royalty to be collected was properly chargeable to Anadarko pursuant to section 102(a) of FOGRMA, 30 U.S.C. § 1712(a) (2006).

To conclude otherwise would mean that "the lessees would realize a $47.3 million windfall in royalty-free oil." Answer at 16. Of this $47.3 million amount, approximately $11.8 million is attributable and owed to Anadarko in accordance with its 25 percent interest in the Lease. The royalties due on Anadarko's proportionate share of the proceeds amounts to $2 million. Anadarko's premise would have us ignore the fact that "the minerals of the OCS [are] owned exclusively by the United States." Amoco Production Co. v. Sea Robin Pipeline Co., 844 F.2d at 1210. The lessees severed, captured, removed, metered, processed, and sold the Government's oil. In construing OCSLA, FOGRMA, and the Lease to mean that such oil may be sold free of royalty, Anadarko positions itself to realize a windfall of $2 million. Anadarko's argument that the captured and sold oil is royalty-free runs contrary to the Government's interest in the "total recovery of the federally-owned minerals from the reservoirs underlying the OCS." EP Operating Limited Partnership v. Placid Oil Co., 26 F.3d at 570.

* * *

NOTES

1. Did the IBLA correctly analyze the law? Was its decision driven more by its concerns about a possible windfall?

2. If ONRR issues orders to the lessees to pay royalties on the oil and gas volumes lost (i.e., not recovered) from the Macondo well, does the IBLA decision control?

(b) Duty to Put Production Into Marketable Condition at No Cost to the Lessor

The gross proceeds rule often may operate in tandem with other requirements. For example, longstanding Interior Department rules for both onshore and offshore leases have required lessees to put production into marketable condition and to pay royalty on the value of the gas in marketable condition without deduction for the costs of treatment.[417] In the onshore lease context, the District of Columbia Circuit held that the Secretary had discretion under the Mineral Leasing Act and the regulations to define the term "production removed or sold" as production in marketable condition and upheld the rule that treatment costs were not deductible from royalty value.[418]

---

417. Current rules are found at 30 C.F.R. §§ 1206.106 (federal crude oil); 1206.152(i) and 1206.153(i) (federal unprocessed and processed gas); 1206.52(i) (Indian crude oil); and 1206.174(h) (Indian gas).

418. California Co. v. Udall, 296 F.2d 384 (D.C.Cir.1961).

Treating crude oil for marketable condition typically involves removal of basic sediment and water. Treating gas for marketable condition usually involves gathering (joining gas from multiple wells for compression and marketing), compression, dehydration, and desulphurization (or "sweetening"). Under the definition in the regulations, "marketable condition" means production sufficiently free from impurities and otherwise in a condition that a purchaser will accept under a sales contract typical for the field or area. See, 30 C.F.R. §§ 1206.101 (crude oil) and 1206.151 (gas). What condition is typical for the field or area may vary. See, Branch Oil & Gas Co., 144 IBLA 304 (1998).

This "marketable condition" principle led to a consequence under the gross proceeds rule in the context of FERC price controls formerly applicable to natural gas. Under section 110 of the Natural Gas Policy Act of 1978 ("NGPA"), 15 U.S.C. § 3320, FERC was authorized to allow, by rule or order, gas producers to charge, within the allowed "first sale price," more than the otherwise applicable ceiling price to recover certain costs, including the costs of compression, gathering, and treatment—in other words, the costs of putting production into marketable condition. FERC implemented section 110 by issuing Order No. 94 and its progeny (codified to 18 C.F.R. Part 271 Subpart K).[419] The FERC Order 94 series allowed sellers to charge purchasers and receive reimbursements for production-related costs, which included the same costs incurred to put gas into marketable condition, in addition to the otherwise permitted maximum lawful price as part of the allowed first sale price of the gas.

The question then arose whether cost reimbursements paid under the FERC Order 94 series were part of the lessee's gross proceeds. (Although FERC price controls have ended, the case is instructive because the gross proceeds principles that the case applies have continued applicability.) The Fifth Circuit held that they were and upheld the marketable condition rule.

* * *

MESA OPERATING LIMITED PARTNERSHIP
v. UNITED STATES

931 F.2d 318 (5th Cir.1991).

* * *

III.   The Merits

A.   *The Marketable Condition Rule*

The DOI relies heavily on the Marketable Condition Rule to reach its conclusion that § 110 payments are subject to royalty valuation. In short,

---

419. See FERC Order Nos. 94, 45 Fed. Reg. 53099 (Aug. 11, 1980); 94–A, 48 Fed. Reg. 5152 (Feb. 3, 1983); and 94—, 48 Fed. Reg. 5190 (Feb. 3, 1983), as amended by Order 334, 48 Fed. Reg. 44495 (Sept. 29, 1983); 48 Fed. Reg. 52031 (Nov. 16, 1983); and Order No. 408, 49 Fed. Reg. 49625 (Dec. 21, 1984).

the DOI interprets the regulations to provide that: royalties are due on the gross proceeds accruing to the lessee; the term "gross proceeds" includes payments for the costs of treatment including measuring, gathering, compressing, sweetening, and dehydrating "where such services are necessary to place gas in marketable condition," whether the costs are absorbed in the price the purchaser pays pursuant to the set NGPA ceiling or are ultimately borne by the purchaser under § 110; accordingly, where the purchaser reimburses the lessee for treatment costs in accordance with § 110 and the Order 94 regulations, these payments become part of the value of production (gross proceeds) subject to royalty. Mesa argues that the DOI order is unacceptable and the district court should be reversed because the regulations do not support such a construction. While Mesa's reading of the regulations may be plausible, we may reject the DOI's Order (and, consequently, the district court's judgment) only if the agency's interpretation is impermissible or unreasonable. [Footnote omitted.] Granting this deference, we conclude that the DOI's construction certainly does not rise to this level.

* * * Mesa acknowledges that the Marketable Condition Rule, which prohibits lessees from deducting treatment costs incurred in complying with the Rule when figuring royalty due, has some relevance to the calculation of royalties. However, Mesa contends that the Rule prohibits producers from deducting costs of treatment from the calculated royalty amount itself rather than the royalty base against which the royalty rate is applied (that is, the total proceeds from sale on which royalty is due).

In addition, Mesa maintains that this prohibition does not translate into an affirmative obligation to pay royalties on § 110 reimbursements for treatment costs. Such a requirement, Mesa argues, would have the anomalous result of entitling the DOI to inverse recovery of greater royalties roughly proportionate to the poor quality of the gas and the difficulty of treatment.

* * *

Mesa's contention that the Marketable Condition Rule applies to the royalty amount itself rather than the royalty base evidences a fatal misreading of the Rule and its accepted construction, undermining much of Mesa's argument on appeal. Its reading is indeed contrary to the interpretation the DOI has given the Marketable Condition Rule for decades, that is, that marketing costs cannot be deducted from the gross proceeds, equal to the value of production, before royalty is calculated. [Citing, inter alia, California Co. v. Udall, 296 F.2d 384 (D.C.Cir.1961).] As the Interior Board of Land Appeals recently stated in ARCO Oil & Gas Co. [115 IBLA 393 (1990)], only such marketing allowances "as have been expressly recognized may properly be deducted from value [of production] for royalty purposes." [Id. at 396; footnote omitted.] As did the D.C. Circuit in *California Co.*, in the context of this case we define "production" in the phrase "amount or value of the production" as meaning "gas conditioned for market." [296 F.2d at 388.]

* * *

Second, any anomaly which results from allowing higher royalty on lower quality gas by assessing royalty on § 110 payments is a consequence of the NGPA/FERC price regulation system and not of the scheme setting out the royalty owner's rights. Indeed, this is a uniform result. The DOI-lessor simply obtains a flat percentage of all "gross proceeds" whether they be within the ceiling price or exceed it under § 110, obtaining more royalty where the lessee obtains a greater price, including costs reimbursements, from the pipeline purchaser. [Footnote omitted.]

* * *

Moreover, because the motives behind special relief measures such as were put forth by the FPC [Federal Power Commission], and by FERC pursuant to § 110, did not change, we are unconvinced that including § 110 reimbursements in the royalty-bearing "gross proceeds" from the sale of gas necessarily thwarts Congress' intention to provide incentives for exploration and production of low quality gas by allowing for producers to be reimbursed for certain actual costs. Knowing that the FPC had allowed royalties on special relief prices in the past, it was for Congress, if it had intended the incentive to be greater than under the NGA [Natural Gas Act], to provide that NGPA § 110 payments not be subject to royalty.

* * *

Therefore, we conclude that the DOI's construction of the impact of the Marketable Condition Rule on the royalty-bearing nature of NGPA § 110 reimbursement payments is entirely reasonable and permissible.

B. The Effect of Diamond Shamrock

Mesa relies heavily on our 1988 decision in *Diamond Shamrock* [853 F.2d 1159], arguing that it uncategorically prohibits assessment of royalties on costs for treatment of gas after the gas is physically severed from the earth. The DOI counters, and the district court found, that Diamond Shamrock involved a different question than the case before us and does not provide support for Mesa's position. We agree.

In *Diamond Shamrock* we were asked to determine whether the DOI could obtain royalties on take-or-pay monies received by the producing lessee for gas not taken. We held that producers leasing offshore lands from the DOI were not required to pay royalties on monies received from pipeline purchasers as take-or-pay payments under the purchase contract. [Id. at 1168.]

* * *

Conclusion

For the foregoing reasons, we conclude that the district court properly determined that the DOI correctly interpreted the regulations as they apply to royalty owing on § 110 reimbursements.

AFFIRMED.

NOTE

The *Mesa* holding and rationale were applied and reaffirmed in Amerada Hess Corp. v. Department of the Interior, 170 F.3d 1032 (10th Cir. 1999), in which the court upheld the Department's assessment of royalties on reimbursements for gas gathering costs under the gross proceeds rule and the marketable condition rule. The D.C. Circuit also considered the application of the marketable condition rule to natural gas produced from coal seams in Amoco Production Co. v. Watson, 410 F.3d 722 (D.C. Cir. 2005), cert. denied in relevant part sub nom., BP America Production Co. v. Burton, 547 U.S. 1068 (2006). Coal seam gas has higher levels of carbon dioxide (CO_2), an acid gas impurity. In *Amoco*, the court held that the costs of removing carbon dioxide to the level of pipeline tolerances and the costs of transporting to the treatment plant the CO_2 in excess of the pipeline tolerances were not deductible in calculating royalty value.

The Interior Board of Land Appeals has held that a lessee may not avoid the requirements of the marketable condition rule by transferring the treatment or conditioning function to the purchaser in return for a lower price. See, Branch Oil & Gas Co., 144 IBLA 304 (1998); Bailey D. Gothard, 144 IBLA 17 (1998), affirmed, Bailey D. Gothard v. United States, No. CV 98–103 (D. Mont. 1999).

Whether certain gas treatment costs are costs of placing production in marketable condition, which the lessee may not deduct in determining its royalty value, or whether they are allowable deductions for transportation or gas processing, has been the subject of disputes between ONRR and industry. See 30 C.F.R. §§ 1206.156–1206.157 (transportation); 30 C.F.R. §§ 1206.158–1206.159 (gas processing). (Transportation and processing allowance are discussed later in this section). The D.C. Circuit addressed this question in a decision that had significant consequences for gas producers on federal leases.

DEVON ENERGY CORPORATION v. KEMPTHORNE
551 F.3d 1030 (D.C. Cir. 2008).

EDWARDS, SENIOR CIRCUIT JUDGE.

* * * This case arises from a final order issued by the United States Department of the Interior ("DOI" or "Interior") requiring Devon retroactively to recalculate royalties owed to the Government pursuant to its lease to extract coalbed methane from federal land in Wyoming.

At issue is the agency's interpretation of its "marketable condition rule." The rule was included as a part of DOI's 1988 Revision of Gas Royalty Valuation Regulations, which establish the framework for calculating the royalty value of coalbed methane gas production. In its disputed order, DOI held that the marketable condition rule precluded Devon from deducting certain costs associated with compression and dehydration when calculating the "gross proceeds" upon which royalties are owed. DOI determined that gas cannot enter a pipeline and move to a purchaser unless it meets the requirements of the pipeline, which typically requires compression to raise its pressure and dehydration to reduce its water content. Thus, DOI concluded that if gas is not sufficiently compressed and dehydrated to be deliverable to the point of purchase through the pipeline, it is not in marketable condition. Devon filed suit in the District Court to challenge Interior's order. The District Court denied Devon's motion for summary judgment and granted the Secretary's cross-motion. On appeal, Devon argues that DOI's order is inconsistent with the plain language of the marketable condition rule, and also inconsistent with DOI's own prior interpretation of the rule.

We affirm the judgment of the District Court. First, we find that Interior's interpretation of the marketable condition rule reflects a perfectly reasonable construction of the rule. It is clear that the agency's order is not at odds with the plain language of the rule, nor does it effectively "amend," rather than reasonably construe, the rule. Second, we reject Devon's claim that DOI's order conflicts with a prior interpretation of the marketable condition rule. Devon argues that its position finds support in guidance documents distributed by agency personnel after DOI's promulgation of the 1988 regulations. However, as Devon concedes, these contested guidance documents were distributed by agency individuals who had no authority either to amend the marketable condition rule or to issue authoritative guidelines on behalf of the agency.

I. Background

A. Statutory and Regulatory Framework

* * *

The Mineral Leasing Act gives DOI the authority "to prescribe necessary and proper rules and regulations and to do any and all things necessary to carry out and accomplish the purposes of" the Act. 30 U.S.C. § 189. Pursuant to this directive, DOI has issued a number of regulations governing the royalty valuation process. In 1988, DOI conducted a major rulemaking that modified the then-existing gas royalty valuation regulations. See Revision of Gas Royalty Valuation Regulations and Related Topics, 53 Fed.Reg. 1230, 1272 (Jan. 15, 1988); 30 C.F.R. § 206.152 (1988). The 1988 regulations establish the framework for calculating the royalty value of the coalbed methane gas production at issue here. Under this regulatory framework, royalties are calculated on the basis of the total value a lessee receives for its production. The regulations specify that the "value of production" should be no less "than the gross proceeds accruing to the lessee for lease production," minus certain allowable deductions. 30 C.F.R. § 206.152(h); see also Amoco Prod. Co. v. Watson, 410 F.3d 722, 725 (D.C.Cir.2005), aff'd sub nom., BP Am. Prod. Co. v. Burton, 549 U.S. 84, 127 S.Ct. 638, 166 L.Ed.2d 494 (2006).

When calculating "gross proceeds," DOI regulations have long interpreted the Mineral Leasing Act to require lessees to put the gas into marketable condition at no cost to the United States-the so-called "marketable condition rule." The 1988 regulations confirmed this requirement. See 30 C.F.R. § 206.152(i) (governing unprocessed gas); 30 C.F.R. § 206.153(i) (governing processed gas); see also California Co., 296 F.2d at 387–88 (affirming marketable condition requirement). Marketable condition is defined in the DOI regulations as "lease products which are sufficiently free from impurities and otherwise in a condition that they will be accepted by a purchaser under a sales contract typical for the field or area." 30 C.F.R. § 206.151. If a lessee sells "unmarketable" gas at a lower price, the gross proceeds are "increased to the extent that the gross proceeds have been reduced because the purchaser, or any other person, is providing certain services" to place the gas in marketable condition. 30 C.F.R. § 206.152(i); Amoco, 410 F.3d at 725–26.

The 1988 regulations also provide that the lessee may deduct its actual costs of transporting the gas from the wellhead to the point of sale when gas produced from the lease is sold at a market remote from the lease. 30 C.F.R. § 206.157(a)–(b). This "transportation allowance" includes "only those costs which are directly related to the transportation of lease production." 53 Fed.Reg. at 1261. A transportation allowance is defined as "an allowance for the reasonable, actual costs of moving [gas] to a point of sale or delivery off the lease ? or away from a processing plant." 30 C.F.R. § 206.151.

B.   Facts and Proceedings Below

Devon leases land from the United States in Wyoming's Powder River Basin, which contains the natural gas known as coalbed methane. These leases cover three fields-Kitty, Spotted Horse, and Rough Draw-each of which contains a large number of individual gas-producing wells. The gas produced from the wells is gathered at central delivery points ("CDPs") that have been approved by the Bureau of Land Management as the points of measure for the royalty due on the gas. After the gas leaves a CDP, it goes through a complex series of compression and dehydration processes as it travels "downstream" to the Buckshot processing plant in preparation for eventual sale. See Valuation Determination for Coalbed Methane Production from the Kitty, Spotted Horse, and Rough Draw Fields, reprinted in Joint Appendix ("J.A.") 57 ("Valuation Determination"); see also Chart, J.A. 460.

The production process varies slightly in the three fields, but the differences are not material. Essentially, each CDP is connected to a small diameter pipeline. Gas travels from the CDP through the pipeline to one of several "screw compressors," which compress the gas to raise its pressure. The gas then travels through the pipeline to a "field booster," a reciprocating compressor that further raises the pressure of the gas. The gas then enters a dehydrator, which removes water. Valuation Determination, J.A. 61. At this point, the gas enters a 24–inch high-pressure gas pipeline, which begins at what is known as the Landeck Station and runs 126 miles to the Buckshot Gas Plant. Approximately 30 miles from the Landeck Station, the gas enters a large compressor called the "MTG Booster," which compresses the gas to raise the pressure from 450–500 pounds per square inch ("psi") to approximately 1,200 psi. The gas travels the remaining 96 miles to the Buckshot Gas Plant, losing approximately one-third of its pressure on the way. Id. at 66.

When the gas arrives at the Buckshot Gas Plant, excess carbon dioxide is removed, the gas is dehydrated, and the gas is compressed from approximately 800 psi to 1,100 psi. At that pressure, Devon delivers the treated gas into one of two lateral pipelines. The gas is transported to various purchasers through these pipelines. Id.

On November 2, 1995, DOI and MMS personnel serving on a group called the Royalty Policy Board met to discuss how the royalty calculation regulations should be applied to coalbed methane production. See Royalty Policy Board Meeting Minutes, Nov. 2, 1995, reprinted in J.A. 102. Subsequently, on December 7, 1995, and December 8, 1995, the then-Deputy Director of MMS issued two documents captioned "Coalbed Methane Valuation and Reporting Guidelines" and "Compression Guidance," respectively. See Coalbed Methane Valuation and Reporting Guidelines, Dec. 7, 1995, reprinted in J.A. 157; Compression Guidance, Dec. 8, 1995, reprinted in J.A. 160 [hereinafter, along with the "Dear Operator" letter, infra, "guidance documents"]. These documents were memoranda from the Deputy Director to the Associate Director for Royalty Management and the Associate Director for Policy and Management Improvement. J.A. 83. Although they were not promulgated pursuant to the notice-and-comment procedures of the Administrative Procedure Act ("APA"), 5 U.S.C. § 553 (2000), the guidance documents nonetheless suggested that certain costs of compression and dehydration after the gas leaves the CDP were deductible as transportation costs.

Subsequently, on April 22, 1996, MMS's Associate Director for Royalty Management distributed a "Dear Operator" letter detailing how to calculate royalties on coalbed methane production. The letter stated:

> If you sell your coalbed methane at the tailgate of a carbon dioxide removal or other treating facility, ... [y]ou can include costs of dehydration occurring after metering at the royalty measurement point in your transportation allowance but you cannot deduct costs of dehydration occurring at the wellhead. You can include costs for compression occurring downstream of the royalty measurement point, to the extent the compression is necessary for transportation. This

> includes compression at the CDP and in the transportation system to the [carbon dioxide] removal facility.

MMS Dear Operator Letter, Apr. 22, 1996, reprinted in J.A. 162, 164 [hereinafter, along with the "Coalbed Methane Valuation and Reporting Guidelines" and the "Compression Guidance," supra, "guidance documents"].

From 1995 to 2002, Devon deducted the following costs as transportation allowances: the cost of compressing the gas at the screw compressors, the field boosters, the MTG Booster, and the Buckshot Gas Plant, as well as the cost of dehydrating the gas. Devon apparently assumed that these expenses were deductible transportation costs under the guidance documents. On January 11, 2002, however, Devon sought guidance from MMS to confirm that it was properly deducting (as part of its transportation allowance) dehydration and compression costs incurred after the gas leaves the CDPs. Request for Valuation Determination, Jan. 11, 2003, reprinted in J.A. 166. On October 9, 2003, the Acting Assistant Secretary issued a decision rejecting Devon's reliance on the guidance documents. See Valuation Determination, J.A. 57.

In its Valuation Determination, the agency found that statements in the guidance documents were either ambiguous, J.A. 84–85, or reflected an incorrect application of the marketable condition rule, J.A. 84, or were simply "inconsistent" with the rule, J.A. 85. The DOI Valuation Determination held that Devon's deductions of the costs of dehydration and of compression performed at the screw compressors, the reciprocating compressors, and the Buckshot Plant were inconsistent with the marketable condition rule, because the compression and dehydration functions were necessary to put the production into marketable condition.

> Devon could not meet the requirements of any of its sales contracts without compressing the gas to the pressure necessary to get it into those [pipe]lines. That is the pressure that would enable the gas to be "accepted by a purchaser under a sales contract typical for the field or area," in the words of the definition [of the marketable condition rule] at 30 C.F.R. § 206.151. In other words, to meet the requirements of the "sales contract[s] typical for the field or area," Devon had to compress the gas to pipeline pressure.

Id. at 88.

> Both before and after the 1988 regulations, the lessee's obligation is to dehydrate gas to the water content required for delivery to the pipeline (as necessary for sale under contracts that are typical for the disposition of gas produced from the field or area).

> Devon has not shown that the dehydration performed after the reciprocating compressors and at the Buckshot Plant is for anything other than what is required to put the production into marketable condition and what is necessary for it to meet pipeline and purchaser requirements.

Id. at 91.

Devon's request for reconsideration of the DOI Valuation Determination was denied in March 2004. Final Order to Perform Restructured Accounting and Pay Additional Royalties ("Final Order"), Mar. 19, 2004, reprinted in J.A. 46. The DOI Final Order largely reaffirmed the reasoning and conclusions reached in the DOI Valuation Determination. Devon was instructed to "perform a restructured accounting and pay additional royalties on the coalbed methane produced from the federal leases" that were the subject of the DOI Valuation Determination. J.A. 55. Devon was also instructed that, in the future, it was to "report and pay royalties under the regulations and guidelines discussed" in the DOI Final Order. Id.

Devon filed suit in the District Court seeking to overturn the Final Order. The District Court denied Devon's motion for summary judgment and granted Interior's cross-motion for summary judgment. Devon Energy Corp. v. Norton, No 04–Civ0821, 2007 WL 2422005 (D.D.C. Aug. 23, 2007). This appeal followed.

II. Analysis

A. Standard of Review

"In a case like the instant one, in which the District Court reviewed an agency action under the APA [5 U.S.C. § 706], we review the administrative action directly, according no particular deference to the judgment of the District Court." Holland v. Nat'l Mining Ass'n, 309 F.3d 808, 814 (D.C.Cir.2002); see also Troy Corp. v. Browner, 120 F.3d 277, 281 (D.C.Cir.1997); Gas Appliance Mfrs. Ass'n, Inc. v. Dep't of Energy, 998 F.2d 1041, 1045 (D.C.Cir.1993). We will uphold the contested agency action unless we find it to be "arbitrary, capricious, an abuse of discretion, or otherwise not in accordance with law." 5 U.S.C. § 706(2)(A).

An agency's interpretation of its own regulation is entitled to "substantial deference," unless "plainly erroneous or inconsistent with the regulation." Thomas Jefferson Univ. v. Shalala, 512 U.S. 504, 512, 114 S.Ct. 2381, 129 L.Ed.2d 405 (1994) (internal quotation marks omitted). However, an agency may not "evade [the] notice and comment requirements [of § 553 of the APA, 5 U.S.C. § 553(b)(A),] by amending a rule under the guise of reinterpreting it." Envtl. Integrity Project v. EPA, 425 F.3d 992, 995 (D.C.Cir.2005) (quoting Molycorp, Inc. v. EPA, 197 F.3d 543, 546 (D.C.Cir.1999)); see also Am. Hosp. Ass'n v. Bowen, 834 F.2d 1037, 1044–48, 1052–57 (D.C.Cir.1987). In determining whether an agency action effectively "amends" a rule without adhering to the requirements of the APA, we must consider, inter alia, whether the agency officials involved in the disputed actions had the authority to issue binding regulations or otherwise act with the force of law on behalf of the agency. See generally Harry T. Edwards & Linda A. Elliott, Federal Standards of Review—Review of District Court Decisions and Agency Actions 130–35 (2007).

B. Plain Language

Under the 1988 DOI regulations, "marketable condition" is defined to mean "lease products which are sufficiently free from impurities and otherwise in a condition that they will be accepted by a purchaser under a sales contract typical for the field or area." 30 C.F.R. § 206.151. The marketable condition rule requires lessees to put gas into marketable condition at no cost to the United States. At issue here is DOI's interpretation of the rule to include the costs of compression and dehydration incurred after the gas leaves the CDPs to allow it to move through the pipelines that serve the market in which the gas is typically sold. Devon argues that this interpretation is inconsistent with the plain language of the regulations, because it improperly focuses the inquiry on the market where the gas is actually sold, as opposed to the requirements of a sales contract typical for the field or area.

In its Valuation Determination and Final Order, DOI held that costs associated with compression and dehydration are not deductible if their primary function is to prepare the gas to move through the pipelines to the point where gas is purchased. However, the parties disagree as to what "sales contract typical for the field or area" requires. DOI found that "typical" sales contracts require that gas be delivered to the purchaser at the terminus of a specified pipeline. Under this view, a producer must provide the compression and dehydration necessary to allow the gas to be delivered through the pipeline. Therefore, the agency reasonably found that Devon "could not meet the requirements of any of its sales contracts without compressing the gas to the pressure necessary to get it into" the pipelines, J.A. 88, and that Devon had "not shown that the dehydration performed. [was] for anything other than what is required to put the production into marketable condition to meet pipeline and purchaser requirements." J.A. 91.

It is true that the DOI marketable condition rule is ambiguous, and Devon's preferred interpretation of the rule is not unreasonable. In other words, we assume that the costs of dehydration and compression can reasonably be interpreted to fall within the compass of "transportation costs." However, we are obliged to afford "substantial deference to an agency's interpretation of its own regulations." Thomas Jefferson Univ., 512 U.S. at 512, 114 S.Ct. 2381 (citations omitted). On this record, we find that DOI's contested construction of the marketable condition rule is reasonable. Indeed, DOI's interpretation of the marketable condition rule is consistent with an interpretation that this court approved in Amoco, 410 F.3d 722.

In Amoco, we addressed DOI's interpretation of the marketable condition rule as it related to the cost of transporting excess carbon dioxide to the treatment plant. The court held that the marketable condition rule did not require DOI to "understand typical sales contracts and thus marketable condition-as relating to transactions at the leasehold or immediately nearby." Id. at 729. "The regulation stipulating that producers are to place gas in marketable condition at no cost to the government does not contain a geographic limit." Id. Therefore, DOI's interpretation of the marketable condition rule to require lessees to compress and dehydrate gas to meet the requirements of the pipelines that serve its typical purchasers is not "plainly erroneous or inconsistent with the regulation." Thomas Jefferson Univ., 512 U.S. at 512, 114 S.Ct. 2381. And as the court noted in Amoco, the deference that we owe to an agency's interpretation of its own regulations "is particularly appropriate in the context of a complex and highly technical regulatory program, in which the identification and classification of relevant criteria necessarily require significant expertise and entail the exercise of judgment grounded in policy concerns." 410 F.3d at 729 (citations and quotations omitted).

C. The Requirements of a Typical Sales Contract

Devon argues that there is no record support for the agency's conclusion that the typical sales contract for the field or area required Devon to compress its gas to 1,100 psi and dehydrate it in order to put the gas in marketable condition. However, although DOI provided Devon an opportunity to supplement the record after the first valuation determination, Devon merely asserted that it "believes that its working interest partner, Redstone Resources, Inc., sells gas to unrelated third parties in the field at pressures less than 1200 psi [sic] under contracts typical for the field or area." Request for Reconsideration and/or Clarification, reprinted in J.A. 194, 196. This cursory assertion is not sufficient to render DOI's interpretation unreasonable.

D. Prior Inconsistent Interpretation

Finally, Devon argues that the agency's interpretation of the marketable condition rule (embodied in the DOI Valuation Determination and Final Order) must be vacated because it was issued without notice-and-comment rulemaking required by § 553 of the APA. At bottom, Devon's central claim is that it acted in reliance on the guidance documents and this "reliance interest is protected by the APA." Appellant's Br. at 16. Devon's argument runs as follows:

> The marketable condition rule does not prohibit the deduction of transportation costs, and it does not attempt to differentiate between deductible transportation costs and nondeductible marketable condition costs. Because the regulations do not expressly address the issue, the Royalty Policy Board was called upon to interpret the regulations. [Id.]
>
> [The Board's] decision gave rise to [the guidance documents] which were consistently followed by Interior from 1995 until 2003. [Id.]
>
> Devon followed Interior's publicly-announced guidelines and instructions when it deducted its post-CDP dehydration and compression costs. [Id.]

Interior's decision in this case wrongly assumes that Interior was not bound by its 1995 guidelines and instructions because they were not embodied in a formal regulation. This Court has long recognized that an agency interpretation can be authoritatively adopted even if it was not embodied in a rule that was adopted through a notice and comment rulemaking. [Id. at 17.]

An agency's consistent advice-and here it was instruction-to the regulated community can evidence the agency's authoritative adoption of a regulatory interpretation. Such an interpretation can be changed only through a notice and comment rulemaking. [Id.]

DOI's description of the situation is quite different. According to the agency, there was no official or binding Royalty Policy Board action taken to address the issues now before the court. Rather, DOI contends that [n]otice and comment rulemaking was not required for Interior to change its interpretation of its regulation from how it had been applied as a result of ambiguous guidance documents. This Court has held that the very same guidance documents were not binding on the agency. [See Amoco, 410 F.3d at 732.] If they were not binding, then they are not evidence of a definitive agency interpretation and Interior can change its interpretation without going through notice and comment rulemaking? Absent a definitive interpretation, the APA does not require notice and comment rulemaking to effect a change in that interpretation.

Appellee's Br. at 15–16. For the reasons stated below, we agree with DOI.

First, it is telling that the agency's disputed Valuation Determination and Final Order came only after Devon sought confirmation from the agency that it was properly deducting the dehydration and compression costs (as part of its transportation allowance) incurred after the gas leaves the CDPs. This request for confirmation was made in 2002, long after the issuance of the guidance documents upon which Devon now relies. It is perplexing, to say the least, that Devon was seemingly confused over the propriety of its royalty accounting if, in its view, the matters at issue had been authoritatively resolved over five years earlier. In other words, there is much force to DOI's argument that, in fact, the guidance documents were far from conclusive in what they said.

Second, implicit in Devon's prior-inconsistent-interpretation argument is a claim that the judgments reached in DOI's Valuation Determination and Final Order do not reflect a supportable interpretation of the marketable condition rule. As we have already explained in part II.B, supra, we find no merit in this claim. Although the marketable condition rule is ambiguous and Devon's preferred construction of the rule is not unreasonable, we are obliged to defer to the agency's reasonable construction of the rule. Thomas Jefferson Univ., 512 U.S. at 512, 114 S.Ct. 2381 (holding that an agency's interpretation of its own regulation is entitled to "substantial deference," unless "plainly erroneous or inconsistent with the regulation").

Third, and most important, Devon is mistaken in its argument that the guidance documents constituted authoritative and binding interpretations of the marketable condition rule. In rejecting Devon's argument, we start with the principle that agency actions do not have the force of law unless they "mark the consummation of the agency's decision making process" and either determine "rights or obligations" or result in discernible "legal consequences" for regulated parties. Bennett v. Spear, 520 U.S. 154, 177–78, 117 S.Ct. 1154, 137 L.Ed.2d 281 (1997). The "Dear Operator" letter certainly does not satisfy this standard. Indeed, this court has previously considered a different aspect of the very same "Dear Operator" letter that is at issue in this case. See Amoco, 410 F.3d at 732.

In Amoco, coalbed methane producers challenged an Assistant Secretary's decision that cited the April 22, 1996 letter, arguing that it constituted a new rule that the agency could promulgate only through notice-and-comment rulemaking. Citing Independent Petroleum Ass'n of America v. Babbitt, 92 F.3d 1248, 1256–57 (D.C.Cir.1996), the court rejected Amoco's argument because the letter was not binding on the agency:

> As in Babbitt, the Payor Letter here is not an agency statement with future effect because nothing under DOI regulations vests the Letter's author-in Babbitt and this case MMS's Associate Director for Royalty Management-with the authority to announce rules binding on DOI. Id. at 1256. "The letter is not an agency rule at all, legislative or otherwise, because it does not purport to, nor is it capable of, binding the agency." Id. at 1257.

> The sort of "workaday advice letter[s] that agencies prepare countless times per year in dealing with the regulated community," Indep. Equip. Dealers Ass'n v. EPA, 372 F.3d 420, 427 (D.C.Cir.2004) (internal quotation marks omitted), do not retroactively become agency rules whenever they are referenced in an agency decision.

Amoco, 410 F.3d at 732.

In response to the Amoco holding, Devon says that it "does not contend that the 1996 Dear Operator letter in and of itself was a binding rule. Rather, Devon contends that the regulatory interpretation it relied on was authoritatively adopted by the agency through the cumulative effect of a number of agency actions, including but not limited to, the issuance of the 1996 Dear Operator letter." Devon Reply Br. at 14. There are two problems with this argument. First, it assumes that the two internal memoranda written by the Deputy Director of the Minerals Management Service in 1995 to the Associate Director for Royalty Management and the Associate Director for Policy and Management Improvement were final and binding agency interpretations of the marketable condition rule. Second, it assumes that the guidance documents have the force of law because Devon followed the advice contained in the documents. There is no merit to these contentions.

Devon argues that these 1995 documents were conclusive because they reflected the actions of the Royalty Policy Board, as if to suggest that the Board had authority to adopt regulations or guidelines that bind the agency. But when questioned about this at oral argument, Devon's counsel readily conceded that the Royalty Policy Board had no authority to issue authoritative guidelines, and that the guideline documents did not have the force of law. This concession is unsurprising, because there is nothing in the record here to indicate that the guidance documents purported to have the force of law.

At the very least, a definitive and binding statement on behalf of the agency must come from a source with the authority to bind the agency. See Ctr. for Auto Safety v. Nat'l Highway Traffic Safety Admin., 452 F.3d 798, 810 (D.C.Cir.2006) (holding that Associate Administrator for Safety Assurance had no authority to issue guidelines with binding effect on agency); Ass'n of Am. R.Rs. v. DOT, 198 F.3d 944, 948 (D.C.Cir.1999) (holding a letter and two emails from lower level officials did not amount to an authoritative agency interpretation); Paralyzed Veterans of Am. v. D.C. Arena L.P., 117 F.3d 579, 587 (D.C.Cir.1997) (stating that a speech of a mid-level official of an agency "is not the sort of 'fair and considered judgment' that can be thought of as an authoritative departmental position") (citing Auer v. Robbins, 519 U.S. 452, 462, 117 S.Ct. 905, 137 L.Ed.2d 79 (1997)); Amoco, 410 F.3d at 732 (noting "Dear Operator" letter not binding on agency because not authored by official with authority to announce binding rules). The guidance documents at issue here do not satisfy this standard.

Fourth, resting on its "reliance" theory, Devon suggests that the agency is bound by the guidance documents because, for a number of years, regulated parties followed the advice contained in the documents. This argument fails. In Center for Auto Safety, 452 F.3d 798, a case very much on point, the court held that policy guidelines issued by the Associate Administrator of the National Highway Traffic Safety Administration did not amount to a binding rule. The contested guidelines, which related to automakers' voluntary regional recalls, were found not binding because the Associate Administrator had no authority to issue binding regulations or make a final determination on the issue. Importantly, the court also rejected the petitioner's argument that, merely because the agency and automakers had followed the guidelines for seven years, the guidelines had binding "legal consequences." In addressing this point, the court said:

> The flaw in appellants' argument is that the "consequences" to which they allude are practical, not legal. It may be that, to the extent that they actually prescribe anything, the agency's guidelines have been voluntarily followed by automakers and have become a de facto industry standard for how to conduct regional recalls. But this does not demonstrate that the guidelines have had legal consequences. The Supreme Court's decision in Bennett makes it quite clear that agency action is only final if it determines "rights or obligations" or occasions

"legal consequences 520 U.S. at 178, 117 S.Ct. 1154. (citation and internal quotation marks omitted). Circuit case law cannot obviate the holding of Bennett.

Ctr. for Auto Safety, 452 F.3d at 811. See also Nat'l Ass'n of Home Builders v. Norton, 415 F.3d 8, 15 (D.C.Cir.2005) ("[I]f the practical effect of the agency action is not a certain change in the legal obligations of a party, the action is non-final for the purpose of judicial review.").

Devon argues that our decisions in Alaska Professional Hunters Ass'n v. FAA, 177 F.3d 1030 (D.C.Cir.1999), and Paralyzed Veterans of America, 117 F.3d 579, should control the disposition of this case. We disagree. In Alaska Professional, the court found that thirty years of uniform advice by the Alaskan regional office of the FAA "became an authoritative departmental interpretation" binding on the agency. The case is plainly distinguishable, however, because the disputed agency advice in that case had been upheld in a formal adjudication by the Civil Aeronautics Board, FAA's predecessor agency. See Alaska Prof'l, 177 F.3d at 1034 (discussing Administrator v. Marshall, 39 C.A.B. 948 (1963)). Indeed, the decision in Alaska Professional acknowledges that an interpretation or advice by an official without authority to bind the agency alone would not amount to an authoritative interpretation. Alaska Prof'l, 177 F.3d at 1035; see also Hudson v. FAA, 192 F.3d 1031, 1036 (D.C.Cir.1999) (distinguishing Alaska Professional as concerning a binding interpretation on the basis of the formal adjudication upon which the longstanding practice was based); Ass'n of Am. R.Rs., 198 F.3d at 949 (same). In this case, by contrast, the guidance documents have never been upheld in an agency adjudication, nor have they ever been endorsed in any other agency action having the force of law.

Paralyzed Veterans also lends no support to Devon's position. In that case, we held that Advisory Board guidelines that were not clearly adopted by the Department of Justice and a speech by a mid-level official did not amount to a binding interpretation of its regulation implementing the Americans with Disabilities Act. 117 F.3d at 588. The court noted that if the Department itself had adopted the Board's interpretation of the regulation the outcome might have been different. Id. The case surely does not stand for the proposition that guidance documents written by persons without authority to bind an agency and released with no indication that the documents purported to have the force of law may be taken as binding interpretations of an agency regulation.

In sum, we find no merit in Devon's claim that it acted in reliance on the 1995 and 1996 guidance documents and that this "reliance interest is protected by the APA." As noted above, the guidance documents were far from conclusive in what they said. In any event, on the record here, it is plain that the contested guidance documents did not come from sources who had the authority to bind the agency. Therefore, it does not matter whether the appellant, or others, followed the advice that was offered in these documents. These documents did not amount to a binding interpretation of the marketable condition rule, so the Agency was free to adopt the interpretation at issue in this case without providing an opportunity for notice and comment.

III. Conclusion

For the reasons indicated above, we deny Devon's challenge to DOI's Final Order and affirm the District Court's judgment in favor of the agency.

NOTES

1. A 2011 decision by the Director of the Office of Hearings and Appeals affirmed that lower level agency decisions are not binding on the Department. Statoil Gulf of Mexico LLC; ExxonMobil Corporation, 42 OHA 261 (May 31, 2011). When is it reasonable for industry to rely upon agency advice?

(c) Duty to Market at No Cost to the Lessor

Other litigation raised a distinct but related issue, namely, whether lessees may deduct costs incurred to market their production (as opposed to costs incurred to put the production into marketable condition). Amendments to the ONRR gas valuation rules effective in 1998 (see 30 C.F.R. §§ 1206.152(i) and 1206.153(i) (1998–2001)) (federal unprocessed and processed gas) and 1206.106 (2001) (federal crude oil) (effective June 1, 2000) provide that lessees must market production for the mutual benefit of the lessee and the lessor at no cost to the federal government. ONRR's position was that these provisions codified a longstanding implied covenant. The producing industry challenged both rules. The "duty to market" provisions in the gas valuation rule were held unlawful in Independent Petroleum Association of America v. Armstrong, 91 F. Supp. 2d 117 (D.D.C.2000) (Lamberth, J.). The D.C. Circuit reversed that ruling in February 2002.

INDEPENDENT PETROLEUM ASSOCIATION OF AMERICA v. DeWITT

279 F.3d 1036 (D.C. Cir. 2002).

WILLIAMS, SENIOR CIRCUIT JUDGE.

Producers of natural gas typically lease the mineral rights and compensate the owner by means of a royalty calculated as some fraction (such as 1/8 or 1/6) of the value of the gas produced. In exchange, lessees agree to bear the costs and risks of exploration and production. Federal and Indian gas leases are no exception.

But the federal government is not your standard oil-and-gas lessor. For the detailed ascertainment of the parties' rights, its leases give controlling effect not merely to extant Department of the Interior regulations but also to ones "hereafter promulgated." See, e.g., Department of Interior, Form 3100–11, at p. 1 (1992) [i.e., the lease form]. The regulations have historically called for calculation of royalty on the basis of "gross proceeds." See, e.g., 30 C.F.R. §§ 206.152(h) (federal unprocessed gas), 206.153(h) (federal processed gas). But to abide by the statutory mandate to base royalty on the "value of the production removed or sold from the lease," 30 U.S.C. § 226(b)(1)(A), Interior has allowed two deductions from gross proceeds when calculating value for royalty purposes. One deduction relates to certain processing costs and is irrelevant here; the other is for transportation costs when production is sold at a market away from the lease. 30 C.F.R. §§ 206.157, 206.177; see also, Final rule, Revision of Oil Product Valuation Regulations and Related Topics, 53 Fed. Reg. 1184, 1186 (1988). These are evidently the only deductions from gross proceeds. Walter Oil and Gas Corp., 111 IBLA 260, 265 (1989). Marketing costs have therefore not been deductible. See, e.g., Arco Oil & Gas Co., 112 IBLA 8, 10–11 (1989).

In the mid–1980s, a series of rulemakings by the Federal Energy Regulatory Commission somewhat changed the circumstances to which these principles applied. Previously, producers most commonly sold gas at the wellhead to natural gas pipeline companies, which then transported it and sold it to local distribution companies; less commonly, they made direct sales from producer to an end user or distributor, with the pipeline providing only transportation. [Citation omitted.] But FERC, starting with Order No. 436 and culminating in Order No. 636, in effect transformed the pipelines into "open access" transporters and required them to separate sales from transportation services [citation omitted], to charge unbundled rates for services such as transmission and storage [citation omitted], and to assign their merchant services to functionally independent market affiliates [citations omitted]. In effect, the pipelines as such became almost exclusively transporters of gas, and direct sales by producers to end users, distributors, or merchants became the norm.

In response to these changes, the Department of Interior in 1997 amended its gas royalty regulations "to clarify its existing policies" and to prevent lessees from claiming "improper deductions on their royalty reports and payments." Final Rule, Amendments to Transportation Allowance Regulations for Federal and Indian Leases to Specify Allowable Costs and Related Amendments to Gas Valuation Regulations, 62 Fed. Reg. 65,753/3–65,754/1 (1997) ("Final Rule"). Two trade associations representing the gas producers * * * brought suit challenging these regulations as arbitrary and capricious. Their primary contention was that Interior had impermissibly refused to permit deductions for costs incurred in marketing gas to markets "downstream" of the wellhead. Dispute focused especially on Interior's denial of deductions for (1) fees incurred in aggregating and marketing gas with respect to downstream sales; (2) "intra-hub transfer fees" charged by pipelines for assuring correct attribution of quantities to particular transactions (not for the physical transfers themselves); and (3) any "unused" pipeline demand charge (i.e., the portion of a demand charge paid to secure firm service but relating to quantities in excess of a producer's actual shipments).

* * *

* * * On the deductibility of marketing costs we find no legal error in Interior's rule and therefore reverse the district court; on the "unused" demand charge issue, we affirm the district court.

* * *

* * * [P]roducers urge that deference to Interior's interpretation of the statute under Chevron USA, Inc. v. Natural Resources Defense Council, Inc., 467 U.S. 837 (1984), is inappropriate for regulations that affect contracts in which Interior has financial interests.

But in the mineral leasing statutes Congress has granted rather sweeping authority "to prescribe necessary and proper rules and regulations and to do any and all things necessary to carry out and accomplish the purposes of [the leasing statutes]." 30 U.S.C. § 189 (federal lands); see also, 25 U.S.C. §§ 396, 396d (tribal lands); 43 U.S.C. § 1334(a) (outer Continental Shelf). These "purposes," of course, include the administration of federal leases, which involves collecting royalties and determining the methods by which they are calculated. See California Co. v. Udall, 296 F.2d 384, 387–88 (D.C.Cir.1961) * * *.

It is thus not surprising that the cases do not support producers' theory. Though no circuit appears ever to have ruled specifically on the issue of deference to financially self-interested agencies, courts have regularly applied Chevron in royalty cases [citing, inter alia, Mesa Operating Limited Partnership v. Dep't. of the Interior, Enron Oil & Gas Co. v. Lujan, and Marathon Oil Co. v. United States, all discussed above]. * * *

* * *

"Downstream" marketing costs and intra-hub transfer fees. We find nothing unreasonable in Interior's refusal to allow deductions for so-called "downstream" marketing costs. *See* Final Rule, 62 Fed. Reg. at 65,756. Both the producer groups acknowledge that marketing costs for sales at the lease have historically been nondeductible. API Br. at 30; IPAA Br. at 22. Yet at no point do they offer a persuasive distinction between marketing for leasehold sales and for "downstream" sales. Indeed, marketing does not even appear to be readily divisible between the two, as it would be if lessees stood on their lease boundaries and operated the equivalent of a lemonade stand for leasehold sales, but traveled to distant cities for "downstream ones." Rather, so far as it appears, marketing proceeds by means of the standard modern devices—face-to-face meeting, phone call, internet posting. See, e.g., Order 636, 57 Fed. Reg. at 13,282/2 (describing electronic bulletin boards, then precursors to the Internet, as having become "standard industry-wide practice"). Unlike the sale itself, which will presumably involve shifts of title and possession at specified points,

marketing has no locus—certainly none that ineluctably tracks the point where title shifts.

To be sure, transaction costs may be higher for sales in the current market; sales to a single (perhaps monopsonistic) pipeline may have been painfully simple. But a change in the dimension of a cost is hardly an argument for its reclassification, as the Interior Board of Land Appeals has observed. *Arco*, 112 IBLA at 11. * * *

Producers further argue that downstream marketing adds to the value of the gas at the leasehold, and thus that the royalty owner should share the costs. In support, they propose what amounts to an elegant theory suggesting that the sale of "marketable condition" gas at the leasehold represents a baseline, and that the costs of all further value-adding activities should be deductible. Under this view, producers explicitly condemn any distinction between marketing and transportation. But the argument in the end seems almost metaphysical; it is a claim that when the maximum value of gas can be realized by a downstream sale, then not only transportation costs but also the costs of efforts undertaken to identify and realize that value must somehow be more like transportation itself than they are like on-lease marketing.

Assuming *arguendo* that producer's metaphysical point is correct, we think it falls far short of compelling the Department to give up its usual distinction between marketing and transporting costs. Not only is the distinction traditional, Walter Oil, 111 IBLA at 265, but Interior has historically applied it to downstream sales, denying deductibility for a lessee's costs in hiring a marketing agent to arrange transportation downstream, to aggregate customers, and to deal with a local distribution company. Arco, 112 IBLA at 9–12. Given the difficulty of slicing up marketing costs on the basis of the point of sale, and given that Interior must take administrability into account, compare Owen L. Anderson, Royalty Valuation: Should Royalty Obligations Be Determined Intrinsically, Theoretically, or Realistically? (part 2), 37 Nat. Resources J. 611, 678 (1997) (discussing monitoring problems), we find nothing unreasonable in its hewing to the old line between marketing and transportation.

* * *

[The court then upheld the nondeductibility of aggregator/marketer fees and intra-hub transfer fees (reversing the district court), but affirmed that part of the district court's ruling that "unused" firm demand charges (the portion of firm pipeline capacity paid for beyond the actual volume transported) was deductible as a transportation cost. The court also affirmed the district court's holding that if a lessee sold unused firm capacity, it must correspondingly reduce a transportation allowance previously taken on the basis of the entire firm capacity payment.]

The judgment of the district court is reversed on all issues except for its ruling on unused firm demand charges, which we affirm.

NOTE

Do you see any relationship between the decision in this case and the Ninth Circuit's decision in *Marathon*, discussed in Subsection A.4.(a)(i), above?

(d) Allowable Deductions in Determining Royalty Value (Allowances)

Under ONRR rules, two types of deductions are allowed when lessees determine royalty value, transportation allowances (applicable to oil and gas) and processing allowances (applicable only to "wet" gas—see the discussion of "wet" gas below).

As mentioned above in the *IPAA v. DeWitt* and *Amoco Production Co. v. Watson* cases, and in the notes following the *Marathon Oil Co. v. United States* case, ONRR rules provide for the deduction of reasonable actual costs incurred to transport production to a point of sale not at or near the lease or unit where the oil or gas is produced. 30 C.F.R. §§ 1206.156–1206.157 (federal gas) and 1206.109–1206.111 (federal crude oil). The deduction recognizes that lessees are not obligated to transport production to distant markets at their own expense, and adjusts the value derived at a distant point of sale back to the lease.

In some circumstances, the distinction between transportation and "gathering" may be disputed between lessees and ONRR. As explained above, ONRR does not permit any allowance for gathering because gathering is part of putting production into marketable condition. (The term "gathering" may have different meanings in different contexts or jurisdictions). For federal royalty purposes, the ONRR regulations define "gathering" as "the movement of lease production to a central accumulation and/or treatment point on the lease, unit, or communitized area, or to a central accumulation or treatment point off the lease, unit, or communitized area as approved by BLM or Bureau of Safety and Environmental Enforcement OCS operations personnel for onshore and OCS leases, respectively." 30 C.F.R. § 1206.151 (gas); *see also* the functionally identical definition for crude oil at 30 C.F.R. § 1206.101. Both the IBLA and federal courts have addressed the difference between gathering and transportation under ONRR rules. See Amerada Hess Corp. v. Department of Interior, 170 F.3d 1032 (10th Cir. Okla. 1999); Kerr–McGee Corp., 147 IBLA 277 (1999).

Under the cited provisions, if transportation arrangements are at arm's length, the lessee may deduct the costs paid to the transporter. If transportation arrangements are not at arm's length (*e.g.*, the lessee also owns the pipeline), the lessee must calculate actual costs of constructing and operating the transportation system, and then allocate those costs to the production transported, according to requirements prescribed in the regulation.[420] The regulations in 30 C.F.R. §§ 1206.111 (crude oil) and 1206.157(b) (gas) provide details on what elements are includible in the calculation of actual costs. Those include costs such as operations, labor, maintenance, and directly related overhead, and either depreciation or a return on undepreciated capital investment. Though the rules are detailed, disputes still arise as to particular costs. For example, in Shell Offshore, Inc., 142 IBLA 71 (1997), the lessee prevailed in an argument that the costs to enlarge an offshore platform to accommodate transportation-related facilities was allowable as a transportation cost because it was an integral part of a transportation system.

The other allowance mentioned above is a "processing" allowance. A substantial portion of the natural gas produced is so-called "wet" gas— i.e., gas that has heavier entrained liquid hydrocarbons such as ethane (C_2H_6), propane (C_3H_8), butane (C_4H_{10}), etc., as part of the gas stream flowing from the well. ("Dry" gas is pure methane (CH_4).) "Wet" gas usually has an energy content (measured in British thermal units (Btu)) too high for the gas to be useable without separating out the heavier hydrocarbons, which themselves are valuable products. Removal of the heavier hydrocarbons is called "processing" or "manufacturing" and is done at a gas processing plant. When gas is processed, the lessee must use the processed gas royalty valuation rules at 30 C.F.R. § 1206.153.

The processing allowance recognizes that the lessee incurs cost to derive different and distinct products from the original gas stream. Removal of impurities to put gas into marketable condition, which the lessee must do at its own expense under the "marketable condition" rule discussed above, is not "processing."

Under ONRR rules (30 C.F.R. §§ 1206.158–1206.159), the lessee may deduct reasonable, actual costs of processing. The processing costs must be allocated among the gas plant products (i.e., the extracted liquid hydrocarbons). Unless ONRR approves an extraordinary processing cost allowance under § 206.158(d)(2), no processing allowance may be taken against the value of the "residue gas" (i.e., the dry methane remaining after the liquids are extracted).

Under paragraph (d)(2), an "extraordinary" processing allowance is permitted only when the lessee can show that the costs are "extraordinary, unusual, or unconventional" by reference to standard industry conditions and practice.[421]

Under § 1206.159, if the processing arrangements are at arm's length, the lessee may deduct the amount it pays to have the gas processed. If the processing arrangements are not at arm's length, (e.g., the lessee also owns the processing plant), the lessee must calculate the

---

420. In the natural gas context, the regulations provide for an exception to the requirement to calculate actual costs of constructing and operating a transportation system if the lessee has a tariff approved by the Federal Energy Regulatory Commission. 30 C.F.R. § 1206.157(b)(5). (An analogous exception for crude oil was removed when the June 2000 rule was promulgated.)

421. The scenario described in Exxon Corp., 118 IBLA 221 (1991) is just such an unusual situation that led to the extraordinary processing cost allowance exception being applied.

actual costs of construction and operation of the processing plant, and
then allocate those costs to the production processed under requirements
prescribed in the regulation. The provisions defining the allowable costs
for constructing and operating a processing plant at § 1206.159(b) are
analogous to the transportation cost rules described above.

(e) Affiliated Transactions

While gross proceeds objectively measure the value of production
when production is sold at arm's length, the premises underlying acceptance of the total consideration paid in the marketplace as the measure of
value break down when the transacting parties are not dealing at arm's
length. Transactions between related or affiliated entities have given rise
to disputes between ONRR and lessees. Lessees often argue that ONRR
should accept the price in the sale to the affiliate in various circumstances.
ONRR frequently wants to look behind the inter-affiliate transaction.

Initial transfers between affiliates may occur for a number of reasons.
For example, a producer may have both production and marketing operations that are separate subsidiaries (or one may be the subsidiary of the
other). An integrated crude oil producer may transfer production from the
producing corporate subsidiary to the refining subsidiary. A producer,
together with others, also may own part of a marketing entity.

The valuation regulations effectively are bifurcated between arm's-
length and non-arm's-length dispositions. In 30 C.F.R. §§ 1206.152 and
1206.153 (federal unprocessed and processed gas), paragraph (b) of each
section addresses arm's-length sales, while paragraph (c) addresses non-
arm's-length dispositions. Under paragraph (b), the gross proceeds derived
from an arm's-length sale generally are the value of the production, and
not just the minimum value. For non-arm's-length dispositions, paragraph
(c) establishes a hierarchical series of "benchmarks" intended to look at
more objective market indicia. (Under those benchmarks, the non-arm's-
length price may be the royalty value if it meets certain criteria of
comparability with arm's-length prices.) However, the "benchmark" price
must still be compared to the lessee's gross proceeds—the minimum
value—under paragraph (h).

Until June 1, 2000, the federal crude oil royalty valuation rule
contained analogous provisions. (Former 30 C.F.R. § 206.102(b) and (c)
(1999).) In the rule effective on that date, the value of oil sold at arm's
length is the lessee's gross proceeds. However, even under certain arm's-
length conditions, the lessee may exercise a conditional option to use a
spot market index-based value. 30 C.F.R. § 1206.102(a) and (d) (2001).

If production is not sold at arm's length before the oil is refined, the
measure of value a lessee must use under the rule (as amended in 2004)
depends on the area of the country in which the lease is located. 30 C.F.R.
§§ 1206.102(a)(1) and (2) and 1206.103. Specifically, if the oil is produced
from a federal lease in California or Alaska, value is based on the spot
market index price for Alaska North Slope oil in California, adjusted for

location and quality. 30 C.F.R. § 1206.103(a). If the oil is produced in the Rocky Mountain Region (as defined in section 1206.101), value is one of three measures, depending on the lessee's particular circumstances. 30 C.F.R. § 1206.103(b). If the oil is produced from a federal lease that is not located in California or Alaska or the Rocky Mountain Region, value is the average of the daily New York Mercantile Exchange ("NYMEX") price for the nearest month of delivery, plus the "roll" (which takes rising or falling market trends into account), and further adjusted for location and quality. 30 C.F.R. § 1206.103(c). The NYMEX provisions of paragraph (c) apply to oil produced from offshore leases in the Gulf of Mexico and from federal leases in the Permian Basin not sold at arm's length before refining.

One of the principal disputes between ONRR and industry that has arisen in the context of affiliate transactions is the proper measure of value when the lessee transfers to a wholly-owned affiliate (or to another affiliate that also is wholly owned by the same parent corporation), and the affiliate then resells at arm's length. (The 2000 crude oil rule resolves this question for oil by using the affiliate's arm's-length resale proceeds to establish value, 30 C.F.R. § 1206.102(a), but the issue remains for gas.) The question first arose when lessees challenged ONRR orders to produce documents regarding the affiliate's arm's-length resale. In Shell Oil Co. v. Babbitt, 125 F.3d 172 (3d Cir. 1997), and Santa Fe Energy Products Co. v. McCutcheon, 90 F.3d 409 (10th Cir. 1996), the courts upheld administrative decisions requiring lessees to produce documents regarding their affiliates' arm's-length resales.

Subsequently, in Texaco Exploration & Production, Inc., Docket No. MMS–92–0306–O & G (May 18, 1999), the Interior Department addressed the issue of whether a wholly-owned or wholly-commonly-owned affiliate's arm's-length resale proceeds are a proper measure of the lessee's gross proceeds. There, the Secretary held that the wholly-commonly-owned affiliate's resale proceeds were a proper measure of the lessee's gross proceeds. One of the principal grounds for the decision was the Secretary's view that a lessee should not be able to escape the gross proceeds requirement through internal corporate structuring arrangements that are within the lessee's unilateral control. The Secretary also took the view that the term "lessee" in the phrase "gross proceeds accruing to the lessee" in the regulation may be read to include wholly-owned or wholly-commonly-owned affiliates. While pending in the district court, Texaco's suit for judicial review of the Secretary's decision was settled.

Four years later, the D.C. Circuit rejected the Secretary's reasoning and holding in Texaco, holding that the wording of the regulation did not permit the result the Secretary reached in Texaco.

FINA OIL & CHEMICAL CO. v. NORTON

332 F.3d 672 (D.C. Cir. 2003).

TATEL, CIRCUIT JUDGE.

* * * This case involves a valuation dispute concerning gas that is sold twice: first by the producer to a gas marketing firm it controls, and then by the controlled marketing firm to end-users. The Secretary of the Interior valued the gas production based on the contract price of the resale. Challenging that decision, the producer argues that the Secretary should have valued the production based on the lower contract price of the initial sale. Because the applicable regulation unambiguously requires valuation based on the initial sale, we reject the Secretary's contrary interpretation. Though we express no opinion on whether the Secretary might have statutory authority to value production based on the resale price, the Secretary may not do so by interpreting a regulation to mean the opposite of its plain language.

* * *

* * * The regulation establishes three different valuation methodologies, depending on the particular entity to whom producers first sell the gas. Gas sold directly to non-affiliated purchasers under ordinary "arm's-length contracts" is valued on the basis of "gross proceeds accruing to the lessee"—a defined term meaning total direct and indirect consideration under the contract. 30 C.F.R. §§ 206.152(b)(1)(i) (unprocessed gas), 206.153(b)(1)(i) (processed gas), 206.151 (defining "arm's length contract" and "gross proceeds"). Gas sold to so-called marketing affiliates—entities that purchase gas exclusively from producers that own or control them—and subsequently resold by the marketing affiliates pursuant to arm's-length contracts is valued on the basis of downstream resales. 30 C.F.R. §§ 206.152(b)(1)(i) (unprocessed gas), 206.153(b)(1)(i) (processed gas), 206.151 (defining "marketing affiliate"). Gas sold to owned or controlled affiliated entities that, because they purchase at least some gas from sources other than their owning or controlling producer, are not "marketing affiliates" is valued on the basis of the first applicable of three benchmarks. 30 C.F.R. § 206.152(c) (unprocessed gas), 206.153(c) (processed gas). The first benchmark values gas based on "gross proceeds accruing to the lessee pursuant to a sale under its non-arm's-length contract, ... provided that those gross proceeds are equivalent to the gross proceeds derived from [comparable sales in the same field or area]." 30 C.F.R. § 206.152(c)(1) (unprocessed gas), 206.153(c)(1) (processed gas). The second benchmark values gas based on "information relevant in valuing like-quality gas," including "other reliable public sources of price or market information." 30 C.F.R. §§ 206.152(c)(2) (unprocessed gas), 206.153(c)(2) (processed gas). * * * Finally, and central to this case, the regulation contains a catch-all: "Notwithstanding any other provision of this section, under no circumstances shall the value of production for

royalty purposes be less than the gross proceeds accruing to the lessee for lease production." 30 C.F.R. §§ 206.152(h) (unprocessed gas), 206.153(h) (processed gas).

Appellants Fina Oil and Chemical Company and Petrofina Delaware, Inc. are natural gas producers holding onshore and offshore federal leases. (Like the parties, we shall call appellants "Fina.") Fina Natural Gas Company (FNGC) is a natural gas marketer that purchases gas from producers for resale to downstream end-users. Though controlled by Fina, FNGC is not a "marketing affiliate" because it purchases gas from both Fina and other gas producers. Fina therefore paid royalties based on its contract price with FNGC—a price which, according to Fina, complies with the first benchmark or, if the first benchmark is inapplicable, with the second.

* * *

Beginning with the gross proceeds provision, we of course agree with the Secretary that because the provision applies "notwithstanding any other provision of this section," it trumps any methodology, including the benchmarks, that yields valuations "less than the gross proceeds accruing to the lessee for lease production." 30 C.F.R. §§ 206.152(h) (unprocessed gas), 206.153(h) (processed gas), 206.102(h) (1999) (oil). At this point, however, our agreement with the Secretary ends. As we shall show, the underlying statute's definition of "lessee," the regulation's language and structure, and the agency's own pronouncements at the time of the regulation's promulgation all demonstrate that "gross proceeds accruing to the lessee" refers only to proceeds accruing to Fina, not to the entire corporate family of which Fina is a member.

* * * FOGRMA section 3(7) defines "lessee" as "any person to whom the United States, an Indian tribe, or an Indian allottee, issues a lease, or any person who has been assigned an obligation to make royalty or other payments required by the lease." Pub. L. No. 97–451 § 3(7), 96 Stat. 2447, 2449 (amended in 1996, after the events at issue in this case, to read "any person to whom the United States issues an oil and gas lease or any person to whom operating rights in a lease have been assigned" and codified at 30 U.S.C. § 1702(7)). The MMS incorporated this definition word for word in both its oil and gas valuation regulations. 30 C.F.R. §§ 206.101 (1988) (oil), 206.151 (1988) (gas). The definition could hardly be clearer. It defines "lessees" not as "persons ... issued ... leases *and their affiliates*," but rather restricts the definition to "persons ... issued ... leases." Although the administrative record in this case does not include the actual leases, the "person to whom the United States ... issued a lease" is clearly Fina. Not only does the Secretary allege no formal relationship between the United States and FNGC, but in its very first paragraph, the Board's decision identifies Fina as the "lessee[]/appellant[]" and FNGC simply as Fina's "affiliate." *Fina*, 149 I.B.L.A. at 169.

The regulation's overall structure and statements of agency intent at the time of promulgation provide additional reasons why the Secretary's interpretation of the gross proceeds provision is quite wrong. The marketing affiliate provision, which states that "gas which is sold or otherwise transferred to the lessee's marketing affiliate and then sold by the marketing affiliate pursuant to an arm's-length contract shall be valued ... based upon the sale by the marketing affiliate," 30 C.F.R. §§ 206.152(b)(1)(i) (unprocessed gas), 206.153(b)(1)(i) (processed gas), shows that the regulation's authors knew just how to require valuations based on downstream resales when they intended such methodology. Moreover, not only did they limit this methodology to marketing affiliates—which FNGC is not—but the regulation contains provisions that expressly deal with valuation of production sold to non-marketing affiliates, *i.e.*, the benchmarks, which provide for valuation based on non-arm's-length transactions, such as intra-corporate transfers.

Removing any doubt about the treatment of sales to nonmarketing affiliates, the regulation's preamble makes plain that the decision to restrict valuation based on downstream sales to marketing affiliates was intentional. In response to commenters who proposed expanding the marketing affiliate rule to encompass affiliates who acquire *any* gas from their owners or controllers, rather than affiliates who acquire gas *only* from their owners or controllers, the agency stated that: "The MMS is retaining the term 'only.' If the affiliate of the lessee also purchases gas from other sources, then that affiliate presumably will have comparable arm's-length contracts with the other parties which should demonstrate the acceptability of the gross proceeds accruing to the lessee from its affiliate." Revision of Gas Royalty Valuation Regulations, 53 Fed. Reg. 1230, 1243.

In sum, the overall import of the regulation's tripartite structure and "other indications of the [agency's] intent at the time of the regulation's promulgation," Gardebring v. Jenkins, 485 U.S. 415, 430, 99 L. Ed. 2d 515, 108 S. Ct. 1306 (1988), is crystal clear. Gas sold directly to unaffiliated entities is valued at the contract price, since that price reliably indicates objective value. In contrast, gas sold to marketing affiliates is valued not on the basis of the initial sale—obviously an unreliable indicator of objective value—but rather on the basis of the price at which it ultimately leaves the corporate family. But the agency expressly restricted non-recognition of intra-corporate sales to situations where no directly comparable arm's-length sales exist. Accordingly, gas sold to non-marketing affiliates-where objective value can be reliably approximated through comparable arm's-length sales—is valued through the benchmarks at the initial sales price and not the subsequent resale price.

As against this clear policy choice enshrined in the regulation, the Secretary takes the exact opposite position. Declining to recognize intra-corporate transfers of gas from Fina to FNGC, even though benchmark comparisons exist, the Secretary argues that Fina should calculate value as if FNGC were a marketing affiliate, *i.e.*, on the basis of downstream resales. At oral argument, we asked counsel for the Secretary to explain why this interpretation did not read the benchmarks out of the statute—

that is, if non-marketing affiliates are treated just like marketing affiliates, what purpose do the benchmarks serve? Although it is true, as counsel responded, that the benchmarks would still apply to non-marketing affiliates selling gas downstream for less than the price at which they bought it, Oral Arg. Tr. 15:6–16, nothing in either the regulation or its preamble suggests that the benchmarks cover only the limited subset of non-marketing affiliates who fail to turn a profit.

* * *

In *Texaco*, the Secretary warned that valuing production based on intra-corporate sales "allows any lessee to avoid the gross proceeds requirement by the simple and facile device of creating a wholly-owned subsidiary and then first transferring the production to the affiliate, for a price the lessee determines unilaterally, before selling the production at arm's length at a higher price." *Texaco* at 7. We disagree. Even Fina's position would not allow it to set prices "unilaterally," for the benchmarks require Fina to base value on the prices that its affiliate, FNGC, pays *other* producers. In other words, Fina must pay royalties based on the actual market value of the gas at the time Fina transfers the gas to its affiliate.

Although the Secretary does not expressly say so, her primary concern seems to be that valuing the gas based on the initial sale would allow Fina and other lessees to pay royalties on gas before its value increases through the transportation and marketing services provided by affiliates like FNGC. But this is precisely what the regulation permits. If the Secretary now believes—as *Texaco* and her position here indicate—that recognizing intra-corporate transfers is too favorable to producers, she should amend the regulations through notice-and-comment rulemaking, not under the guise of interpretation.

The Secretary's second ground for rejecting application of the benchmarks requires little discussion. The regulation states that "lessees [are] required to place gas in marketable condition at no cost to the federal Government ... unless otherwise provided in the lease agreement," 30 C.F.R. §§ 206.152(i) (1996) (unprocessed gas), 206.153(i) (1996) (processed gas), with "marketable condition" meaning fit for "acceptance by a purchaser under a sales contract typical for the field or area," id. § 206.151. Acknowledging that we have previously interpreted this provision to mean that only producers who market gas downstream, not producers who "opt to sell at the leasehold," must pay royalties based on the increase in gas value associated with marketing expenditures, Indep. Petroleum Ass'n v. DeWitt, 350 U.S. App. D.C. 53, 279 F.3d 1036, 1041 (D.C. Cir. 2002), the Secretary argues that "Fina did market its production downstream, through its affiliate FNGC," Appellee's Br. at 46. This argument, however, differs not at all from the Secretary's basic position against recognizing intracorporate sales for valuation purposes—a position that, as we have just explained, conflicts with the regulation's plain language.

The judgment of the district court is reversed.

NOTES

1. What practical effect, if any, do you think the Fina decision might have on the lessee's duty to market at no cost to the lessor, upheld in Independent Petroleum Association of America v. DeWitt, covered in Subsection A.4.(c), above?

2. To what extent should a producer's extended corporate structure control application of the royalty valuation rules?

3. Note that the federal crude oil royalty valuation rule amendments promulgated in 2004 addressed the issue involved in Fina and required that oil first sold to an affiliate and then re-sold at arm's length be valued based on the arm's-length resale price (unless the lessee opts to use a spot market index-based value). See 30 C.F.R. § 1206.102(a) (2007).

4. Both the federal gas and federal oil royalty valuation rules contain definitions of "arm's-length contract" and "affiliate." 30 C.F.R. §§ 1206.101 and 1206.151. An arm's-length contract is a contract between independent persons who are not affiliates and who have opposing economic interests regarding the contract. (A "person" includes a corporation, partnership, etc.) An affiliate is a person controlled by or under common control with another person. Control is established in the case of ownership or common ownership of more than 50 percent of the voting securities or other forms of ownership. In the case of ownership or common ownership of 10 through 50 percent of the voting securities or other instruments of ownership, ONRR will consider a number of specified factors in determining whether control exists in a particular case. Assume that each of three lessees owned a 1/3 interest in the purchaser who resells at arm's-length. In examining the factors listed in the regulation, could there be circumstances in which more than one of the three controlled the purchaser? Could there be circumstances in which none of the three controls the purchaser?

(f) Royalty in Kind

When the federal government leases oil and gas, the mineral leasing statutes provide for the payment of a royalty of a specified percentage of "the amount or value" of production removed or sold from the lease. 43 U.S.C. § 1337(a)(1) (OCSLA); 30 U.S.C. § 226(b) (Mineral Leasing Act). The reference to "amount" refers to the Secretary's authority to elect to take royalty in kind instead of in a cash payment. The Mineral Leasing Act's authority to take royalty in kind is found in 30 U.S.C. § 192, and the OCSLA authority is 43 U.S.C. § 1353(a)(1). Authority to take in kind is also expressly reserved to the Secretary in all leases issued under those statutes. Therefore, if a lessee were to produce 100 barrels of oil worth $1000 under a lease with a 12.5 percent royalty rate, the lessee would be obligated to pay $125 in royalties. However, if the Secretary chooses, the lessee must instead deliver 12.5 barrels of oil.

In a general sense, both statutes provide for three principal types of disposition for royalty taken in kind. First, the Secretary may sell the product through a competitive sale process. Second, the product may be reserved for use by, or sold to, government agencies, including the Defense Department or the Department of Energy for storage in the Strategic Petroleum Reserve. Third, under circumstances specified in both statutes, crude oil may be made available at market price on a preference basis to small refiners who do not have access to adequate supplies of crude oil.[422]

In section 342 of the Energy Policy Act of 2005, 42 U.S.C. § 15902, Congress added further provisions regarding royalty taken in kind from both offshore and onshore leases. Among other things, Congress specified:

1. Delivery of the royalty amount and quality due under the lease satisfies the lessee's royalty obligations. (Section 342(b)(1).)

2. The lessee must place production taken as royalty in kind ("RIK") in marketable condition at no cost to the United States. (Section 342(b)(2).)

3. The Secretary is given permanent authority to retain and use a portion of the revenues derived from the sale of RIK oil or gas that otherwise would be deposited to miscellaneous receipts to pay costs of transporting RIK production, processing RIK gas, and disposing of RIK production, or to reimburse lessees for such costs. (Section 342(b)(4)and (c).) The Secretary must deduct those amounts before making payments under existing statutory revenue disbursement provisions at 30 U.S.C. § 191 and 43 U.S.C. § 1337(g)(2) (discussed below). (Section 342(f)(1).)

(g) Enforcement Statutes—FOGRMA and RSFA

In 1982, Congress enacted the Federal Oil and Gas Royalty Management Act of 1982 ("FOGRMA"), 30 U.S.C. §§ 1701 et seq. FOGRMA does not address how much royalty a lessee is required to pay. Rather, Congress' principal purpose was to give the Secretary new and expanded authority to audit and enforce royalty payment obligations on federal and Indian oil and gas leases. Congress also imposed new fiscal accountability requirements on the Secretary regarding timely distribution of royalty revenues to designated recipients. Some of the major issues FOGRMA addressed include:

1. Record keeping. Lessees, operators, and others involved in producing, transporting or purchasing oil or gas are required to maintain records and make them available for inspection. Under FOGRMA as enacted (§ 103, 30 U.S.C. § 1713), records are required to be maintained for six years after they are generated, unless the Secretary has notified the record holder to keep them longer for purposes of an audit or investigation involving those records.

---

422. The ONRR royalty-in-kind regulations at 30 CFR Part 1208 address only sales of royalty oil to small refiners.

That requirement still applies to Indian leases. For federal leases, the Federal Oil and Gas Royalty Simplification and Fairness Act ("RSFA"), Pub. L. No. 104–185, 110 Stat. 1700, enacted in August 1996, changed the document retention period to seven years, with the period being extended only for administrative appeals and judicial proceedings that are timely commenced. RSFA section 4, enacting a new FOGRMA section 115(f), 30 U.S.C. § 1724(f).

2. Civil and criminal penalties. FOGRMA section 109, 30 U.S.C. § 1719, established a civil penalty regime for any person who did not pay royalties properly, did not allow inspections, submitted false reports, stole oil or gas, or committed other specified violations. The statute provides for civil penalties after notice and a failure to correct, and higher civil penalties for certain categories of knowing or willful violations where notice and an opportunity to correct are not required. (See Marathon Oil Co. v. Minerals Management Service, 106 IBLA 104 (1988), discussed above.) For the most serious knowing or willful violations, such as filing false reports or stealing oil or gas, the statute also provides for criminal penalties. FOGRMA section 110, 30 U.S.C. § 1720.

3. Interest. If a lessee pays its royalties late, FOGRMA section 111(a), 30 U.S.C. § 1721(a), requires payment of interest at the penalty rate established in section 6621 of the Internal Revenue Code, 26 U.S.C. § 6621. See 30 C.F.R. § 1218.54. FOGRMA sections 111(b) and (d), respectively, also require ONRR to pay interest if it is late in distributing to states their share of royalty payments received, or in distributing royalties derived from Indian leases to Indian tribes and allottees (see 30 C.F.R. § 1218.55).

4. Cooperative agreements/delegations of audit authority. FOGRMA authorizes the Secretary to enter into cooperative agreements with Indian Tribes (section 202, 30 U.S.C. § 1732) and to delegate to states (section 205, 30 U.S.C. § 1735) to undertake several of the Secretary's responsibilities under the Act, including audits, inspections and certain enforcement activities.[423]

When Congress enacted RSFA in 1996, it amended certain of FOGRMA provisions and added new provisions related to royalty management on federal oil and gas leases. (The RSFA amendments do not apply to Indian leases (RSFA section 9, 30 U.S.C. § 1701 note); FOGRMA provi-

---

423. The reason for giving the Secretary authority to delegate audit functions to states stems from how federal mineral lease revenues are distributed under applicable statutes. Revenues derived from leases of public domain lands under the Mineral Leasing Act are paid 50 percent to the state in which the lease is located (except for Alaska, which receives 90 percent), 40 percent to the Reclamation Fund (except for Alaska) and 10 percent to miscellaneous receipts in the Federal Treasury. 30 U.S.C. § 191(a). (Congress enacted a different scheme for Alaska when it became a state because Alaska is not a state that benefits from the Reclamation Fund.) Under the OCSLA, royalties and other revenues derived from leases or portions of leases within the first three miles of the Outer Continental Shelf are paid 27 percent to the State and 73 percent to miscellaneous receipts. 43 U.S.C. § 1337(g)(2). (Revenues derived from all other leases on the Outer Continental Shelf are deposited 100 percent to miscellaneous receipts in the Treasury. 43 U.S.C. § 1338.) The reasons for giving the Secretary authority to enter into cooperative agreements with Indian tribes are similar. Indian lessors receive 100 percent of revenues derived from leases on their lands.

sions as written and amended before August 1996 still apply to Indian leases.) Some of RSFA's significant provisions include:

1. Delegations of audit authority. RSFA section 3, amending 30 U.S.C. § 1735, expanded the functions that states may perform through delegation from the Secretary. The new authorities include issuing demands for royalty payments and subpoenas for documents.

2. Time limitations on royalty collection. RSFA section 4, enacting a new FOGRMA section 115(b), 30 U.S.C. 1324(b), established a seven-year statute of repose, with only limited tolling provisions—*i.e.*, ONRR can no longer pursue an underpayment through any means (including judicial lawsuit, administrative demand, or offset) after seven years from when a royalty payment is due. RSFA section 5 enacted a new FOGRMA section 111A, 30 U.S.C. § 1721a, that bars lessees from seeking a refund or credit for overpayments after six years.

3. Time limitations on administrative adjudications. See the discussion in the following subsection regarding administrative appeals.

4. Overpayment interest. RSFA section 6(a), enacting a new FOGRMA section 111(h), 30 U.S.C. § 1721(h), requires interest to be paid or credited on overpayments made by lessees (at the Internal Revenue Code overpayment rate, 26 U.S.C. § 6621(a)(1)(A) and (B)), and provides a source of funds for such payments.

(h) Administrative Appeals and Judicial Review

A lessee or a designee (a person designated by the lessee to make royalty or other payments on behalf of the lessee (30 C.F.R. §§ 1218.52 and 1290.102)) who receives an order from ONRR or a delegated State directing the payment of royalties, interest or other monies, or directing the lessee or designee to provide information, may appeal that order administratively to the ONRR Director. The appeal procedures are set out in ONRR regulations at 30 CFR part 1290, (§§ 1290.100–1290.110). The appellant has the opportunity to submit legal and factual arguments in support of its appeal. The Director will review the record and issue a written decision. The same procedures apply for appeals involving federal onshore, Outer Continental Shelf, and Indian leases, except that for Indian leases the decision on appeal is issued by the Director, Bureau of Indian Affairs (§ 1290.105(g)).

Any party to a case adversely affected by a decision of either the ONRR Director or the Director, Bureau of Indian Affairs, has the right to appeal that decision to the IBLA in the OHA (§ 1290.108). The ONRR regulations also provide that the IBLA use the procedures in 43 CFR Part 4, Subpart E, applicable to appeals from Bureau of Land Management land decisions, to process royalty appeals. See discussion above at the end of Subsection A.2., which describes the Department's administrative review process.

Before 1996, there was no time limit on the administrative appeals process in the Department. It sometimes took several years for an administrative appeal to move through both the ONRR Director and the IBLA for decision. Congress addressed this issue in RSFA. RSFA section 4 enacted a new FOGRMA section 115(h), 30 U.S.C. § 1724(h), requiring the Department to issue a final decision in any royalty-related administrative proceeding within 33 months from when the administrative proceeding is commenced, unless the appellant agrees in writing to an extension. The Department issued regulations addressing, inter alia (1) when an administrative proceeding commences (generally, when the ONRR Director receives the notice of appeal, due no later than 30 days after the appellant receives the appealed-from order) (30 C.F.R. § 1290.105(a)[424]); (2) when the 33–month period ends, and (3) procedures for requesting extensions (43 CFR Part 4), subpart J (§§ 4.901–4.909). The requirements of RSFA, including the appeal deadline, do not apply to appeals involving oil and gas royalties for Indian leases.

Section 1724(h)(2) addresses the consequences if the Department fails to issue a final decision within the prescribed 33–month period. In that event, if the appeal involves a non-monetary obligation (*e.g.*, an order to deliver royalty in kind) or if the monetary obligation in dispute is less than $10,000, the appeal is deemed decided in favor of the appellant and the dispute ends. However, if the appeal involves a monetary obligation of $10,000 or more, the Department will be deemed to have issued a decision affirming the decision that was appealed. That decision is judicially reviewable. For example, if the ONRR Director were to issue an appeal decision stating the appellant owed $10 million in additional royalty which was then further appealed to the IBLA, and if the IBLA did not issue a decision by the 33–month deadline, then the ONRR Director's decision becomes the final decision for the Department and is subject to review in the U.S. district courts.

Under the Administrative Procedure Act, judicial review of final royalty decisions is based on the administrative record, and generally is resolved through motions for summary judgment in the district courts. If an appellant paid the disputed royalties pending appeal, it would have the option of pursuing judicial review in a refund action in the U.S. Court of Federal Claims under the Tucker Act, 28 U.S.C. § 1491.

5. EXPRESS "IMPLIED" COVENANTS

The law of implied covenants is applied to federal leases largely as a result of express regulations that are incorporated into the terms of a federal or Indian lease. The following opinion illustrates some of the lessee's obligations to operate and develop reasonably and prudently.

---

424. In Murphy Exploration & Production Co. v. U.S. Dep't. of the Interior, 252 F.3d 473 (D.C.Cir.2001), the D.C. Circuit held that a lessee's request for a refund began the 33–month period, without action by ONRR denying the request or an administrative appeal from denial of the request.

NGC ENERGY CO. v. MONO POWER CO.

114 IBLA 141 (1990).

Appeal from a decision of the Colorado State Office, Bureau of Land Management, upholding a prior decision finding that drainage had occurred from lands within oil and gas lease C–17540, and providing for the assessment of compensatory royalties.

Vacated in part, reversed in part.

Opinion by ADMINISTRATIVE JUDGE MULLEN.

NGC Energy Company (NGC) and Mono Power Company (Mono) have appealed from a May 5, 1988, decision of the Colorado State Office, Bureau of Land Management (BLM), upholding a prior decision that drainage had occurred from land within federal oil and gas lease C–17540, and providing for the assessment of compensatory royalties.[1]

A brief history of lease C–17540 provides the necessary background for this appeal. Effective July 1, 1969, BLM issued lease C–8929 encompassing the SW 1/4, sec. 15, the N 1/2 NW 1/4, sec. 28, and the N 1/2 N 1/2, sec. 29, T. 1 N., R. 103 W., sixth principal meridian, Rio Blanco County, Colorado, for a term of 10 years. Effective January 3, 1973, a portion of the land subject to lease C–8929 (i.e., the N 1/2 NW 1/4, sec. 28) was committed to the Bantu Ridge Unit, and the uncommitted remainder was segregated and assigned serial number C–17540. A portion of the land subject to lease C–17540 was then committed to the Taiga Mountain Unit effective November 7, 1978, the uncommitted acreage was again segregated, and the new lease was assigned a new serial number. Following this second unitization and segregation, lease C–17540 embraced 160 acres in the N1/2 N1/2, sec. 29, T. 1 N., R. 103 W., sixth principal meridian. Production under the unit extended the term of lease C–17540 beyond the end of its original term.

As a result of development drilling in sec. 20, T. 1 N., R. 103 W. (which was not within the Taiga Mountain Unit), BLM placed the acreage subject to lease C–17540 in an undefined addition to an undefined known geologic structure (KGS), effective December 29, 1982. Effective June 23, 1984, when the Taiga Mountain Unit automatically contracted, lease C–17540 was eliminated from that unit. The term of lease C–17540 was extended for 2 years from the date of elimination pursuant to 43 C.F.R. 3107.4, and expired on June 23, 1986.

At all relevant times Coseka Resources (USA) Limited (Coseka) owned an undivided 50–percent interest, Mono owned an undivided 25–percent interest, and NGC owned the remaining undivided 25–percent interest in lease C–17540. Coseka was the operator of the lease. Coseka and Mono also held interests in a lease of adjacent fee lands in sec. 20, T. 1 N., R.

---

1. In its answer to NGC's statement of reasons, BLM admits error in its decision holding NGC liable for drainage. NGC was not a common lessee and did not have notice of the alleged drainage until 2 months prior to lease expiration. See Consolidation Coal Co., 87 IBLA 296, 301 (1985), finding that, when two or more lessees have an undivided interest in a lease, they hold the lease as tenants in common and there is no agency relationship between them. Therefore, notice to one lessee does not bind another lessee unless the notified lessee has the authority to act for the other. We therefore vacate BLM's liability determination as to NGC and will not specifically address the issues NGC raised on appeal.

103 W., sixth principal meridian. On December 29, 1982, Coseka completed the Coseka 3–20–1N–103 Coors (3–20 Coors) well as a producing gas
well in the SE1/4 SW1/4 of sec. 20, within its fee lease.

By letter dated April 25, 1986, BLM notified lessees that it was
conducting a statewide review of areas in which federal leases might be
drained by offset producing wells, including possible drainage of lease C–
17540 by the 3–20 Coors well. After noting that the lease and regulations
required lessees to protect the lease from drainage, BLM stated that, if
lessees believed that drainage was not occurring or that an economic well
could not be drilled, they should submit data supporting their position.
Coseka responded by letter dated June 4, 1986, stating that, because most
of lease C–17540 was in a separate fault block from the 3–20 Coors well, it
was not being drained by that well. Coseka did admit that a portion of the
lease, located in the NW1/4 NW1/4, sec. 29, fell within the same fault
block and could be drained by the well, but stated that well spacing closer
than 160 acres could not be justified, given the then current gas prices.

By letter dated July 31, 1987, BLM informed lessees that, based on
preliminary geologic and engineering reviews, it had determined that the
lease was subject to possible drainage by the 3–20 Coors well. While
recognizing that the lease had expired, BLM reminded lessees that, during
the term of the lease, they had a duty to protect the lease land from
drainage. BLM indicated that, if the lessees could not demonstrate that
drainage had not occurred, using detailed engineering or geologic data,
they would be assessed compensatory royalties from the date of first
production from the 3–20 Coors well until the date of expiration of lease
C–17540.

In a response dated September 21, 1987, Coseka submitted additional
engineering and geologic data in support of its position that, at the most,
minimal drainage had occurred, and that it would have been uneconomic
to drill a protective well. Coseka explained its rationale for defining the
extent of the reservoir and indicated that two wells, the 3–20 Coors and
the Coseka 9–20–1N–103 federal (located in the SE 1/4 NE 1/4, sec. 20, T.
1 N., R. 103 W.), were producing from the reservoir. Coseka concluded
that the majority of lease C–17540 was nonproductive, and that the small
quantity of hydrocarbons contained in the portion of the lease subject to
possible drainage was insufficient to warrant an offset well.

By decision dated March 18, 1988, BLM determined that drainage had
occurred from lease C–17540 and assessed compensatory royalty based
upon 18.8 percent of production from the 3–20 Coors well between
December 1982 and June 23, 1986. BLM did not specifically state the basis
for its decision. However, a final geologic report dated March 3, 1988, and
a final engineering report dated March 9, 1988, appear to be the foundation for its determination.

The final geologic report dated March 3, 1988, was prepared by BLM
based on Coseka's data. The drafters of this report agreed with the Coseka
findings that: (1) only the NW 1/4 NW 1/4 of sec. 29 was capable of

containing producible hydrocarbons; and (2) it was not economically feasible to drill a well on the lease. Having reached these conclusions, the author of the final geologic report concluded that compensatory royalties should be assessed.

The final engineering report dated March 9, 1988, also relied on data supplied by Coseka. In computing the drainage factor, the author of that report determined that the 3–20 Coors well would drain 53.1 acres of the reservoir, and that 10 of those acres were within lease C–17540. Based upon these findings, the drainage factor was determined to be 18.8 percent of the 3–20 Coors production.

Coseka, Mono, and NGC all sought state director review (SDR) of the BLM decision. Mono and NGC argued that the duty to protect against drainage did not arise until a reasonable time after BLM notification that drainage was occurring, and that BLM first notified them of the drainage in April 1986, less than 2 months prior to lease expiration. They contended that they had no obligation to drill a protective well or pay compensatory royalty because the lease expired before the passage of a reasonable time after BLM's notice. They further asserted that no compensatory royalty was due because a protective well would not have been economically justified, citing Board decisions holding that the prudent operator rule applies to federal drainage cases. The prudent operator rule provides that a lessee is not required to drill a protective well or pay compensatory royalty if the protective well is not economically justified. NGC submitted an additional analysis demonstrating that the drilling of a protective well on the lease at any time after December 1982 would not have been profitable.

Coseka's SDR submission included the arguments raised by Mono and NGC. In addition it argued that BLM's drainage determination was improper because BLM provided no geologic or engineering data to contradict Coseka's evidence that only a small amount of drainage was occurring from the federal lease, and no evidence that the drainage was sufficient to justify the assessment of compensatory royalties. Coseka further stated that it was operating under the protection of the U.S. Bankruptcy Code, and any assessment for compensatory royalty against it had been discharged because BLM had received notification and failed to file a claim.

In the May 5, 1988, decision, the State Director upheld the prior decision as to Mono and NGC, but found that Coseka's bankruptcy and subsequent reorganization precluded assessment of compensatory royalties against it. He identified two issues (in addition to the bankruptcy issue) raised in the SDR requests: (1) the notice requirement; and (2) the economic viability of a protective well. He found that the Board decisions cited by Mono and NGC were not controlling because they did not involve common ownership of the offending well and the drained federal lease, and concluded that "IBLA never intended to require an economic test in cases involving common ownership." The State Director also determined that, in the common lessee context, "since the operator of the offending well is also a lessee of the offset tract, notification of the drainage situation is not necessary. The lessee has obviously been aware of the offset from the beginning, therefore notification is irrelevant in the case of common ownership."

The State Director agreed with the allegation that BLM had offered no contradictory evidence to refute lessees' data, stating that BLM had "no contention with Coseka's interpretation of the reservoir limits or with well performance," and acknowledged that the 18.8–percent drainage factor "was calculated using the drainage area as determined by volumetric analysis of the 3–20 Coors well and the bounded reservoir area under lease [C–17540]. The parameters utilized in this analysis were those which Coseka supplied."[2] He further found that payment of compensatory royalties beyond the expiration date of the lease could extend the lease for as long as the offending well continued to produce and lessees tendered the compensatory royalties.

In its statement of reasons for appeal, Mono again asserts that, even though it is a common lessee, it is entitled to notification by BLM that drainage is occurring before incurring a duty to protect the lease against that drainage, and that the assessment of compensatory royalties can commence only after the expiration of a reasonable time following such notification. It alleges that the applicable regulations mandate that it be afforded the opportunity to drill a protective well to prevent drainage, and that BLM must provide notice of drainage and allow a lessee a reasonable amount of time in which to drill a protective well before it can assess compensatory royalties. Mono argues that compensatory royalties cannot be assessed because BLM advised it that drainage might be occurring less than 2 months prior to lease expiration thereby depriving it of its option to drill.

Mono further argues that the prudent operator rule should apply in the common lessee context,[3] and that BLM has failed to find that drilling a protective well would have been economic or in accordance with good oil field practices. Mono asserts that this conclusion is supported by the evidence submitted to BLM, which clearly demonstrates that drilling on lease C–17540 would not have been economically justified. Mono concludes that no compensatory royalty should be assessed in this case, or, alternatively, that the Board should refer the case for a hearing to determine the existence of drainage and, if drainage occurred, the date from which compensatory royalty should be assessed.

---

2. In the Final Engineering Report prepared for the SDR, BLM found that, in determining the volume per acre-foot of both the 3–20 Coors well and the Coseka 9–20–1N–103 federal well, Coseka had incorrectly applied the recovery factor twice, and, therefore, Coseka's calculations were invalid. The State Director's decision does not mention Coseka's error on this point.

3. Mono notes the following additional facts. In this case the owners of the offending well and the federal lease are not all the same. Mono owns a smaller interest in the 3–20 Coors well (20 percent before payout and 12.5 percent after payout) than it does in the federal lease (25 percent). It argues that it would defy common sense to assume that it would deliberately drain production from under the federal lease by producing from a well in which it owns a smaller interest.

In its response, BLM concedes that it was never economically feasible to drill a protective well on lease C–17540, but argues that this fact does not preclude BLM from assessing compensatory royalties in the common lessee context. BLM contends that a common lessee has a duty to unitize a lease being drained with other leases, including the offending well, even if a prudent operator would not drill a protective well, citing Williams v. Humble Oil & Refining Co., 432 F.2d 165 (5th Cir.1970), a case decided under Louisiana law, in support of this contention.[4] It asserts that, in common lessee drainage cases, the question is not whether the lessee could have drilled a profitable offset well, but whether the lessee has taken all reasonable steps to prevent drainage. BLM argues that these steps include unitization, forced pooling, or obtaining administrative relief from spacing orders. According to BLM, the imposition of this duty to unitize is necessary to prevent fraudulent drainage by circumventing the prudent operator rule.

The applicable regulations governing drainage and compensatory royalty, 43 CFR 3100.2–2 and 43 CFR 3162.2(a), provide in part, respectively:

> Where lands in any leases are being drained of their oil or gas content by wells either on a federal lease issued at a lower rate of royalty or on non-federal lands, the lessee shall both drill and produce all wells necessary to protect the leased lands from drainage. In lieu of drilling necessary wells, the lessee may, with the consent of the authorized officer, pay compensatory royalty in the amount determined in accordance with 30 CFR 221.21.

> (a) The lessee shall drill diligently and produce continuously from such wells as are necessary to protect the lessor from loss of royalty by reason of drainage. The authorized officer may assess compensatory royalty under which the lessee will pay a sum determined as adequate to compensate the lessor for the lessee's failure to drill and produce wells required to protect the lessor from loss through drainage by wells on adjacent lands.

In Atlantic Richfield Co., 105 IBLA 218, 95 I.D. 235 (1988), and Atlantic Richfield Co. (On Reconsideration), 110 IBLA 200, 96 I.D. 363 (1989), this Board considered the drainage issue in the context of a common lessee. In our initial decision we discussed the principle that compensatory royalties commence upon the passage of a reasonable time following notice to the lessee that drainage is occurring. We held:

> In a common lessee context, the lessee who drills the offending well is in the best position to know that drainage is occurring. In such context, we find no reason for requiring BLM to assume the initial burden of going forward with evidence that the common lessee knew or that a reasonably prudent operator should have known that drainage was occurring. See Elliott v. Pure Oil Co., [139 N.E.2d 295 (Ill.1956)]. The common lessee shall be presumed to have knowledge of the drainage upon first production from its offending well. Howev-

---

4. This argument was raised for the first time in the BLM answer.

er, this presumption is rebuttable by the common lessee, who bears the ultimate burden of persuasion as to notice of drainage.

Id. at 226, 95 I.D. at 240. See also Cordillera Corp., 111 IBLA 61, 65–66 (1989). Thus, contrary to Mono's assertion, BLM is not barred from assessing compensatory royalties by its failure to notify it of the possible drainage before April 1986.

Under the usual statement of the prudent operator rule, even if drainage is occurring, the lessee is not required to drill an offset well unless there is a sufficient quantity of oil or gas to pay a reasonable profit to the lessee over and above the cost of drilling the well. Nola Grace Ptasynski, 63 IBLA 240, 247, 89 I.D. 208, 212 (1982).

In Atlantic Richfield Co., supra at 224–25, 226, 95 I.D. at 239, 240, we determined that the prudent operator standard applies when a leased federal tract is being drained by a well operated by a common lessee. In that case we also refined our determination regarding the proper burdens of proof in the common lessee context. In such situations, BLM has the burden of establishing that the leased federal tract is being drained by the common lessee's non-federal well. However, it need not show, as a part of its cause of action, that a protective well would be economic. In the case of a common lessee, the burden of producing evidence and the ultimate burden of persuasion on this issue rest with the common lessee. Id. at 225, 95 I.D. at 239. See also Cordillera Corp., supra at 66.

In Atlantic Richfield Co., supra, we also discussed the appropriate test of prudent operation to be applied in common lessee cases. We noted that, because the loss to the lessor is an economic loss, economics should govern the duty to drill. We held that if the cost of drilling and operating an offset well is greater than the value of the recovered oil and/or gas, there would be no breach of a lessee's duty to prevent drainage. However, if a lessee can make a reasonable profit by drilling the well, the well should be drilled. We held that one must look to the reasonably anticipated recovery from the offset well, rather than the oil and/or gas that would be lost if the well were not drilled when applying the prudent operator test. Atlantic Richfield Co., supra at 226–27, 95 I.D. at 240–41.

In Atlantic Richfield Company (On Reconsideration), supra, we also considered the extent to which the prudent operator rule is applicable to drainage by a common lessee. In that decision we held that the prudent operator rule limits the duty of a common lessee to protect federal lands from drainage, i.e., a common lessee must pay compensatory royalty on oil and gas that it drained from a federal lease only if the reserves recoverable by a protective well on the federal lease are sufficient to pay a reasonable profit over and above the cost of drilling and operating the well.

BLM concedes that it would not have been economically feasible to drill a protective well on lease C–17540, because a protective well would not have produced sufficient oil or gas to recover the costs of drilling. That question is no longer in issue. Nevertheless, BLM now asserts that Mono must pay compensatory royalty because Mono had a duty to unitize the federal lease with the offending lease, even though it had no duty to drill an offset well. On appeal BLM argues that appellant's obligation to seek unitization arises from operation of the prudent operator rule. In other words, since lessees are generally required to take such actions as would be prudent to protect a lessor from unnecessary losses due to drainage, the scope of the lessee's responsibility cannot be limited to drilling an offset well, but must embrace all other actions which a prudent operator might consider.

As a general proposition, we do not find this formulation objectionable. Certainly, if a lessee unitized a lease rather than drilling an offset well, one could hardly say that the lessee did not fulfill the lease obligations merely because the regulations do not expressly state that unitization is an option. See, e.g., Cordillera Corp., supra at 65–66. By the same token, the failure to expressly delineate a unitization option in the regulations should not preclude a finding that a prudent operator would have unitized the lease. It follows that, if a prudent operator would unitize, a failure to do so would constitute a breach of the duty to protect the lease against drainage. As previously noted, in Nola Grace Ptasynski, supra, this Board found the prudent operator rule applicable to federal leases.

Notwithstanding the fact that a failure to unitize would constitute a breach of the lessee's duty to protect the lease against drainage if a prudent operator would unitize, BLM's assertion of a duty to unitize in the face of a clear showing that an offset well could not be economically drilled is fraught with both legal and practical difficulties. This is particularly true in the instant appeal. In the first place, none of the court decisions BLM cites to this Board imposes a duty to unitize. The decision of the Fifth Circuit Court of Appeals in Williams v. Humble Oil & Refining Co., supra, on which counsel seems to rely for the broad assertion that it is not "unreasonable to require a common lessee to unitize a lease being drained with others [Reply at 7]," establishes no such absolute duty. Rather, this decision[5] recognizes that the viability of unitization is a factor to be considered when determining whether a lessee has discharged his prudent operator duty to protect against drainage. Thus, the court noted:

> To require the lessee in certain circumstances to seek unitization will not place an unfair burden upon him. Indeed, the concept of a duty to unitize is thoroughly compatible with the "prudent administrator" standard governing his conduct with respect to other implied covenants. The lessee may always defend a suit based upon his failure to

---

5. The decision in Cook v. El Paso Natural Gas Co., 560 F.2d 978 (10th Cir.1977), cited by BLM, is essentially premised on the conclusion that the prudent operator rule does not apply at all in the common lessee situation. Indeed, on this point, rather than following the rationale of the Fifth Circuit, as suggested by BLM counsel, it is directly contrary to Williams v. Humble Oil & Refining Co., supra. In the Williams case, the requirement that a lessee consider unitization was directly derived from the prudent operator rule. The question of the applicability of the prudent operator rule in the common lessee situation was examined in Atlantic Richfield (On Reconsideration), supra. While *Cook* was not cited, the Board expressly rejected the theory that the prudent operator rule was inapplicable.

unitize by showing that a prudent operator would not have formed a unit or that he had attempted without success all reasonable means to establish a unit or that the costs of unitization would not leave him a profit. [Emphasis supplied.]

Id. at 174.

Thus, the Fifth Circuit expressly recognized that there was no absolute obligation to unitize, but that a lessee had the obligation to factor-in the possibility of unitization when carrying out its duties as a prudent operator. When an offsetting well is shown to be profitable, it makes eminent good sense that prudent lessees would consider unitization as a viable and practical alternative to drilling the offset well.[6] However, when an offset well would not now be, and never would have been, profitable, we find no legally defensible basis for requiring unitization. Such an approach ignores economics and simple practicalities.

In Nola Grace Ptasynski, supra at 251, 89 I.D. at 214–15, we addressed the economic basis of the prudent operator rule in the context of the obligation to drill an offset well to prevent drainage of leased lands:

> If the recoverable oil underlying the land where drainage is occurring is insufficient to support the cost of recovery, no intelligent landowner would make out-of-pocket expenditures to drill a well. The oil lost through drainage is not an economic loss to the landowner, because its attempted recovery would actually cost the landowner money. Thus, while in some conceptual sense the landowner has lost the oil drained, there has been no economic loss occasioned by the drainage. The landowner is no worse off than he was before the offending well commenced to drain his meager reserves, and considerably better off then he would be if he tried to recover them by drilling an offset well. A lessee should not be obligated to pursue a course of economic folly which a prudent owner would forego. [Emphasis in original, footnote omitted.]

These same considerations apply to an analysis of unitization in lieu of drilling an uneconomic offset well. When the owner of the property being drained seeks to compel unitization in such a situation, that party seeks compensation for oil or gas which could not be profitably produced. In short, it would be an attempt to share in proceeds properly appertaining to its neighbor's property, at its neighbor's expense, and with none of the risk its neighbor assumed when drilling the well.

As a practical matter, it is difficult to see how unitization could be accomplished in the situation now before us.[7] The operator of a producing well would not normally be disposed to unitize with an adjacent property

---

6. This prudent operator requirement should not be limited to a common lessee. It would apply to all drainage situations.

7. Forced pooling would not be an available option where, as in the instant case, the offending well was in one drilling unit and the land being drained in another.

merely to permit the adjacent property owner an opportunity to share in the proceeds from the producing well.[8] Thus, the unitization addressed in Williams v. Humble Oil & Refining Co., supra, was forced, and not consensual.[9] This fact was expressly recognized by the court at page 174 of that decision.

Nor would the protection of correlative rights apply if, as in this case, the drained mineral owner's ability to drill a protection well is constrained only by economic realities and not by legal impediments. Cf. Sinclair Oil & Gas Co. v. Bishop, 441 P.2d 436, 446–47 (Okl.1967) (implying obligation to seek unitization where production from an existing well would result in waste in violation of state conservation statutes).[10] Nor is the prevention of the drilling of unnecessary wells implicated. Assuming rationality on the part of the drained mineral lessee, no additional wells would be drilled in any event.

The relationship of a lessee to the adjacent property owners will normally be of no consequence when considering the economics of unitization. The presence of a common lessee is relevant only because of the need to gain the consent of a specified percentage of the interest owners (operating and nonoperating) in the area to be unitized.[11] This is the case for both voluntary and forced unitization. See generally Williams & Meyers, Oil & Gas Law § 913.5. Thus, quite apart from any theoretical difficulties in justifying unitization, it is virtually impossible to unitize a producing property with a property that could not be produced profitably under applicable spacing and drilling units. The operating and nonoperating interest owners of the producing property would have no practical or economic reason for consenting to such unitization.

---

8. While it is true that the adjacent mineral owner would be required to pay its aliquot share of production costs, it is also true that the owner of the drained mineral estate would not seek unitization if the owner expects that the allocated costs of production would be greater than the allocated share of the profits. If an absolute duty to unitize were applicable to both common and noncommon lessees, a situation could arise where an adjacent lessee would be required to unitize with land containing a nonprofitable well for the sole purpose of allowing his lessor to share in the royalty payments. See, e.g., Hardy, Drainage of Oil and Gas from Adjoining Tracts–A Further Development, 6 Nat.Res.J. 45, 57–58 (1966) (where an argument is made for precisely this result in the common lessee situation). Paradoxically, in this situation, the draining working interest owner would be happy to share his loss with the drained working interest owner. Such a result would, of course, be totally inconsistent with the entire prudent operator rule. That rule is clearly premised on the concept that the lessee should not be *required* to lose money solely for the purpose of permitting the lessor to obtain royalties.

9. To the extent that the leases involved may contain pooling clauses, it is possible that imposition of an obligation to unitize on a common lessee would give rise to an obligation to pool the royalty interest of the draining lease and thus the consent of the nonparticipating owners (generally required under both voluntary and forced unitization) would be obtained. Although such unitization might technically be deemed voluntary, it would occur only when a common lessee is forced to take action it would otherwise avoid. Moreover, it forces the common lessee to take actions with respect to the drained royalty owner's interests which might be deemed violative of its duty of fair dealing. *See* discussion in text *infra*.

10. Moreover, if legal impediments did exist, it seems difficult to justify forced unitization to protect correlative rights when the adjacent mineral owner would not drill a protective well if afforded the opportunity.

11. Colorado requires approval of 80 percent of both the operating and nonoperating interests. *See* Colo.Rev.Stat. § 34–60–118(5) (1973).

In the "uncomplicated" common lessee situation,[12] unitization would normally have no economic effect on the interests of the common lessee. The common lessee would still receive all net income less royalty payments.[13] Indeed, the essential neutrality of unitization to the lessee's economic interests in such cases has been expressly recognized and cited as supporting the imposition of the duty to seek unitization upon a common lessee. See Williams v. Humble Oil & Refining Co., supra at 174. However, this analysis conveniently overlooks the obvious fact that the benefits gained by the drained lessor are at the direct expense of the draining lessor. It could not be expected that a lessor of the draining parcel would favor unitization when faced with these economic realities.

It should be noted, however, that many oil and gas leases contain pooling clauses permitting the lessee to pool all mineral interests without the lessor's consent.[14] It might be argued, therefore, that in such situations, the common lessee would be obligated to utilize this provision to pool the nonworking interest of his lessor (unitize) to protect the adjacent land from drainage. See, e.g., Hardy, Drainage of Oil and Gas from Adjoining Tracts—A Further Development, 6 Nat.Res.J. 45, 55–56 (1966). However, to accept this premise one must ignore the lessee's affirmative "fair dealing" obligation to the lessor of the draining land. See generally, Williams & Meyers, Oil & Gas Law § 420.2.

It does not take much imagination to envision a legal basis for a suit to enjoin a lessee from unitizing a producing lease with land which is not and was never capable of economic production, when a common lessee is seeking unitization for the sole purpose of avoiding a possible conflict with the lessor of the drained land. It is questionable whether this action represents a reasonable discharge of the common lessee's obligation of "fair dealing" with the lessor of the productive tract. The lessor of the draining land obtains absolutely no benefit when a common lessee's actions are based on the desire to avoid the possibility of liability to the lessor of the drained land rather than rational economic considerations. This issue would arise only when two parcels of land happened to have a common lessee. Therefore, until policy considerations, not now apparent, are shown to militate against having a lessee control adjoining parcels, there appears to be absolutely no theoretical justification for imposing a general obligation on a common lessee which would not be imposed if the parcels had been leased by separate entities.[15]

---

12. By using this phrase we expressly refer to a common lessee owning 100 percent of the operating interests in both tracts of land.

13. The one obvious exception would be when the drained parcel has a nonoperating interests burden which is greater than that existing on the draining parcel. Another exception would be when the common lessee owns the entire mineral estate in the draining parcel.

14. Admittedly, most pooling clauses expressly limit the amount of acreage with which the leased land may be pooled or unitized. See generally Williams & Meyers § 669.10. Thus, the discussion in the text assumes that this limitation would not be exceeded. If it is, the royalty interest owner's consent would be needed—an unlikely event, as noted earlier in the text.

15. This is not to say that there may not be a specific fact situation under which a common lessee should be held to a higher standard. Such special circumstance should be addressed if and

All of the difficulties we have discussed are compounded when there are multiple lessees rather than a single common lessee holding the entire operating interests in both tracts. In this case, one party owned interests only in the drained tract, several entities held interests only in the draining tract, two parties owned interests in both tracts, and one of the two (Coseka, the operator under both leases) has since been discharged in bankruptcy of all further liability. Given the undisputed fact that an offsetting well would not be profitable, it is difficult to believe that there was even a remote possibility that unitization could have been effected by Mono.[16]

It may well be that the land which the United States leased has been, in some conceptual sense, drained of oil, but the United States has suffered no real economic loss as a result of that drainage. Such loss as might have occurred is simply damnum absque injuria. See generally Phillips Petroleum Co. v. Millette, 72 So.2d 176, 189 (Miss.1954) (Ethridge, J., dissenting) ("Since appellees could not have gained by the production of oil from their lands, they could not lose by its subterranean drainage"). Counsel for BLM seeks to have us award the Government what is essentially a windfall, merely because its lessee had also leased the adjacent tract. Such action is not justified.

Accordingly, pursuant to the authority delegated to the Board of Land Appeals by the Secretary of the Interior, 43 CFR 4.1, the decision appealed from is vacated in part and reversed in part.

NOTES

1. Is it reasonable to conclude that the duty to pool or to unitize can exist only if the drilling of an offset well is economically feasible? Does the IBLA's comments about the unfairness of pooling to the draining lessor suggest that the lessor is entitled to protection under the rule of capture at the expense of protecting the correlative rights of others who own interests in the common pool? Compare the reasoning of the IBLA in the principal case with the reasoning of the Texas Supreme Court in Amoco v. Alexander, in Chapter 2.

2. Lessees are required to protect the leasehold from drainage by drilling offset wells, or with permission of the Secretary, by paying compensatory royalty. 43 C.F.R. §§ 3100.2–2, 3162.2(a). Consistent with the general implied covenant to protect against drainage, the federal government, as lessor, must ordinarily prove that the drilling of an offset well would be profitable to the lessee. Nola Grace Ptasynski, 63 IBLA 240 (1982). However, the burden shifts to the lessee to show that an offset well would not be profitable where the lessee is the draining party. Atlantic Richfield Co., 105 IBLA 218 (1988).

when it arises. Clearly, no *general* rationale exists to justify such treatment in other than an exceptional case.

16. Coors Energy Company owned an after-payout working interest of 33.5–percent in the producing fee lease. There would be no earthly reason for Coors to agree to unitization with the federal tract and, therefore, no possible method to unitize the two leases under the Colorado statutes.

3. Lessees are also obligated to develop a productive lease. After the federal government notifies the lessee in writing, the lessee must "promptly drill and produce * * * other wells * * * in order that the lease may be properly and timely developed in accordance with good economic operating practices." 43 C.F.R. § 3162.2(c).

4. The lessee must also conduct all operations in compliance with applicable laws, regulations, lease terms, and other orders from the authorized officers. All operations must be conducted

> in a manner which ensures the proper handling, measurement, disposition, and site security of leasehold production; which protects other natural resources and environmental quality; which protects life and property; and which results in maximum ultimate economic recovery of oil and gas with minimum waste and with minimum adverse effect on ultimate recovery of other mineral resources.

Id. § 3162.1(a).

6. EXPLORATORY UNITS, "COMMUNITIZATION" AND UNITIZATION[425]

While federal leases do not contain pooling or unitization clauses, lessees may "communitize" their leases with the consent of the Secretary of the Interior.[426] Communitization is the federal term for pooling. Without Secretarial consent, federal lands are not affected by state compulsory pooling or unitization laws.[427] Nevertheless, the Department of the Interior has long advocated unit operations as a conservation tool and, compared to private lessors, is usually more sympathetic to unit operations. The Secretary may even require federal lessees to engage in unit operations when these operations are found to be in the public interest.[428] Accordingly, the Secretary will often consent to the pooling or unitization of federal acreage with private or state lands, and, on occasion, has used state compulsory pooling acts to force the pooling of federal acreage with private lands.[429]

---

425. For a thorough discussion of this complex topic, see, Kramer & Martin, Ch. 16 and 2 Rocky Mtn. Min.L.Found., Law of Federal Oil and Gas Leases, Ch. 18 (1997).

426. 30 U.S.C. § 226(m). Lessees may also engage in unit operations on offshore and Indian lands with approval of the Secretary. 43 U.S.C. § 1334(a)(4) (offshore) and 25 U.S.C. § 396d (tribal lands under the Indian Mineral Leasing Act). With respect to most leases covering Indian tribal lands, both the Secretary and the tribe must consent to unit operations. Leases for allotted lands may provide that the Secretary alone may approve unit operations on allotted lands. Unit regulations for Indian tribal lands under the Indian Mineral Leasing Act and for allotted lands under the Act of March 3, 1909, are found at 25 C.F.R. §§ 211.21(b) and 212.24(c), respectively. Regulations issued pursuant to the Indian Mineral Development Act of 1982 provide for the possible inclusion of unitization and communitization provisions in mineral agreements governed by the Act. 25 C.F.R. § 225.21(b)(19). For a discussion of Indian oil and gas leasing and agreements, see subsection 3, above.

427. Kirkpatrick Oil & Gas Co. v. United States, 675 F.2d 1122 (10th Cir.Okla.1982).

428. 30 U.S.C.A. § 226(m). The offshore regulations specifically provide for both voluntary and compulsory unit operations. 30 C.F.R. §§ 250.190–250.194. In Clark Oil Producing Co. v. Hodel, 667 F.Supp. 281 (E.D.La.1987), the court found that the Secretary could compel unitization of offshore leases to protect correlative rights and to avoid the drilling of unnecessary wells.

429. See, e.g., Ohmart v. Dennis, 196 N.W.2d 181 (Neb. 1972).

Communitization serves the same purpose as the pooling of interests to conform to well spacing, drilling unit, or proration unit requirements.[430] Like pooling, communitization may be voluntary or compulsory and it serves to perpetuate two or more leases by production from a single well. In general, however, only the communitized portions of federal leases will be held indefinitely by production from a unit well.[431]

Generally, unitization conjures up thoughts of secondary or enhanced recovery operations in a proven, developed field. Subject to Secretarial approval, federal land may be unitized for enhanced recovery or for pressure maintenance in much the same manner as private lands; federal units may also be created to further exploration and primary development.[432] Indeed, a unique feature of federal unitization policy is the "federal exploratory unit," whereby federal lessees, with the consent of the Secretary, may combine multiple federal leases,[433] sometimes including private fee leases, to conduct exploration and development drilling.

The objective of the federal exploratory unit is orderly exploration and development of the unit area, which is believed to be underlain by a common reservoir, without regard to the interior boundaries of the unit leases. Accordingly, the timely drilling of wells will hold all leases within the unit area for the duration of the unit. The lands are approved for inclusion in an exploratory unit on the basis of geological or geophysical inferences that the lands may overlie a common reservoir. Nevertheless, an exploratory unit can be created so as to encompass all formations within the unit area. The unit area may be as large as 25,000 acres (slightly larger than a township), and larger in Alaska, Nevada, and where more than an initial exploratory well is proposed. However, all proposed exploratory wells must be drilled regardless of the results of earlier wells.[434]

An onshore federal exploratory unit is governed by a model onshore unit agreement for unproven areas. 43 C.F.R. § 3186.1.[435] Unwilling federal lessees can be forced to join; Gordon H. Barrows, 36 IBLA 160

---

430. Communitization regulations are found at 43 C.F.R. § 3105.2. Secretarial consent to communitization is generally given after all lessees have consented to the creation of such a unit by entering into a communitization agreement on an approved form.

431. 30 U.S.C.A. § 226(m) contains language similar to the Pugh clause discussed in Chapter 6. At the time of communitization, the non-unit portion of the lease will continue for the balance of its primary term or two years, whichever is longer, subject to continued payment of rentals. Id. During the balance of that period, the lessee could perpetuate the non-unit portion of the lease by obtaining production from that portion.

432. Federal gas storage units may also be created. 43 C.F.R. § 3105.5.

433. Generally, units are limited to 25,000 acres for each exploratory well committed in the unit plan of operations; however, in New Mexico, a carbon dioxide exploratory unit comprises over 1,000,000 acres of federal, state, and private land. For a discussion of the implications for private landowners, see Chapter 2.

434. For more detailed information, see BLM Handbook 3180–1, Unitization (Exploratory) (Rel. 3–102, October 28, 1984).

435. The Rocky Mountain Mineral Law Foundation has promulgated a standard unit operating agreement for federal exploratory units. See Rocky Mountain Unit Operating Agreement, Form 2 (divided interest) (1994). Offshore unitization is addressed at 30 C.F.R. §§ 250.190–250.194 (1997).

(1978); however, a substantial majority of the lessees holding most of the leased acreage within the proposed unit area must approve of the basic unit plan of operations before the Secretary will give approval. With their consent, fee owners can also be included in the unit; and, where a fee lease includes a unitization clause, the lessee may consent on behalf of the fee owner.[436] Once participants are included in a unit, they can also be forced to accept changes in the unit. Chevron U.S.A., Inc., 111 IBLA 96 (1989), overruled in part on other grounds, Orvin Froholm, 132 IBLA 301 (1995). The Secretary may expand and contract existing units as reasonably necessary to achieve the conservation objectives of the unit.

Generally an initial exploratory well must be drilled within six months of approval. 43 C.F.R. § 3186.1, Model Agreement Section 9. In the event more than 25,000 acres are included in a unit, multiple exploratory wells drilled at six-month intervals may be required. If oil or gas is not discovered in paying quantities within five years from the date of approval, the unit ordinarily terminates. If oil or gas is discovered in paying quantities, additional development drilling is required. Id. Section 10. Generally, a unit must be fully explored within five years after the discovery of oil or gas in paying quantities. Thus, an operator may hold all unit acreage for up to ten years by complying with the exploration obligations. An operator may also qualify for up to a two-year extension. The unit agreement contains a liberal force majeure provision that may operate to suspend drilling obligations without loss of unit acreage. Id. Section 25. The unit agreement also allows the government to alter or modify the drilling and production obligations when "such alteration or modification is in the interest of attaining the conservation objectives stated in this agreement * * *." Id. Section 21.

In Koch Exploration Co., 100 IBLA 352 (1988), Koch, contending that there was an inadequate market for gas, requested that its exploratory-unit drilling obligations be suspended indefinitely until market conditions improved, and that the term of the unit be extended for the full period of the suspension. Koch had contracted to sell gas from the unit to Northwest Central Pipeline Corporation; however, Northwest exercised its right under a "market out" clause, which allowed Northwest to avoid its purchase obligations if the contract price of gas was deemed uneconomic. In response, Koch agreed to reduce the purchase price from $7.54/MMBtu to $3.00/MMBtu and reduce Northwest's take-or-pay obligation from 90 percent to 22 percent. Koch contended that it could no longer justify drilling additional wells until market conditions improved. Thus, Koch argued for relief under Section 25 (the force majeure provision) of the unit agreement. The force majeure provision allowed for the suspension of drilling obligations if the unit operator "despite the exercise of due care and diligence, is prevented from complying with such obligations, in whole

---

436. See, e.g., Froholm v. Cox, 934 F.2d 959 (8th Cir.N.D.1991); Amoco Prod. Co. v. Heimann, 904 F.2d 1405 (10th Cir.N.M.1990); and Amoco Prod. Co. v. Jacobs, 746 F.2d 1394 (10th Cir.N.M.1984). The consent of overriding royalty owners is not necessary. BLM Handbook 3180–1, Unitization (Exploratory) 7 (Rel. 3–102, October 28, 1984).

or in part, by * * * matters beyond the [operator's] reasonable control." While the IBLA agreed that the worldwide fluctuations in natural gas prices were beyond Koch's control, the IBLA refused to find that such fluctuations prevented Koch from complying with its drilling obligations. The IBLA concluded that the contract doctrines of commercial impracticability and impossibility of performance were not applicable, because Koch failed to prove that the decline in gas prices was reasonably unforeseeable and because Koch failed to prove that further drilling by Koch or by another operator would be unprofitable. Should these contract doctrines provide relief from express or implied development obligations under federal oil and gas leases or unit agreements?[437]

Koch also argued that suspension of its drilling obligations would be "in the interest of conservation."[438] Although the BLM may suspend drilling obligations if it determines that the sales price available to the operator for unit production "is so significantly less than that received for other comparable gas in the area as to adversely affect the federal royalty revenues," (BLM Instruction Memorandum No. 85–537 (July 9, 1985)), the BLM concluded that Koch was receiving a price that was comparable to prices received by other producers in the area on a Btu basis. The BLM rejected Koch's argument that "comparable gas" must take into account the cost of drilling and producing wells—Koch had contended that unit wells were more costly to drill and produce than other wells in the general area, because the unit wells were deeper and were produced from tight sands. What factors should be considered in determining comparability?

Although the unit agreement uses the familiar "paying quantities" language encountered in most oil and gas leases, in an exploratory unit agreement the term means that the well will recover all costs of drilling, completing, and producing operations plus a reasonable profit. 43 C.F.R. 3186.1, Section 9 and BLM Handbook 3180–1, Unitization (Exploratory) 10 (Rel. 3–102, October 28, 1984). See also, Koch, supra note 2; Amoco Production Co., 41 IBLA 348 (1979); and Yates Petroleum Corp., 67 IBLA 246 (1982). Thus, production sufficient to cover operating and marketing costs—the traditional paying-quantities measure—will hold the federal lease on which the well is located but, absent profitable production, will not qualify as a unit well that will hold other federal leases within an exploratory unit.

If a qualifying unit well is drilled, then the operator must submit a plan of development that includes the number of wells to be drilled, their locations, and the sequence of drilling. This plan must be updated yearly. Only approved development wells may be drilled except as may be necessary to prevent drainage. 43 C.F.R. 3186.1, Section 10.

---

437. For further discussion, see generally Marla E. Mansfield, Relief From Express Drilling Obligations in an Uneconomic Market: The Federal Response and the Doctrines of Force Majeure, Impracticability, and the Prudent Operator, 22 Tulsa L.J. 483 (1987).

438. The BLM may grant relief from express *lease* obligations where the lessee is denied the beneficial enjoyment of its *lease*. 30 U.S.C. § 209. This provision has no application to unit operations.

Unlike conventional unit agreements, only those portions of the unit that are "reasonably proven to be productive of unitized substances" share in production from a unit well. Id., Section 11. Generally, separate participating areas are established for each productive reservoir. The participating area is supposed to reflect the area that the well would reasonably and effectively drain. Radial drainage is presumed for vertical wells. The size of drilling units established by the state conservation agency is often accepted as appropriate for determining the size of the initial participating area, but the participating area for a vertical well is determined by drawing a circle around the well and encompassing the number of acres that would comprise a drilling unit. All 40–acre subdivisions that are cut by the circle with more than half the acreage included within the circle are included within the participating area.

As more unit wells are drilled the participating area is expanded. Productive unit (profitable) wells drilled within 10,000 feet of a producing unit well may be included in an expanded participating area by the "circle-tangent" method. A corresponding drainage circle is drawn around the new well and then straight tangent lines are drawn to create a corridor connecting with the circle of the prior well, and creating a participating area resembling the presumed drainage area for horizontal wells. Once again all 40–acre subdivisions intersected by these lines are included in the participating area if more than half of the subdivision acreage lie inside the lines. While the primary allocation basis for sharing production is surface acreage, (Id. § 3186.1 Section 12), working interest owners are free to negotiate their own allocation formula for costs and working-interest production. The fundamental point is that a lease included in an exploratory unit will not share in production except to the extent that it is part of the "participating area."

Respecting communitization and unitization, the federal government is required to act in the public interest to promote conservation and orderly development; however, in the case of Indian lands, the federal government is also obliged to act as a fiduciary in the best interest of the tribe or allottee. Accordingly, communitization and unitization of Indian lands present special problems. For example, if the unit well is being drilled, but is not producing, at the end of the Indian lease primary term, the unit agreement cannot be relied upon to extend the lease beyond its primary term. The model unit agreement provides, in essence, that the agreement will remain in effect for five years and as long thereafter as unitized substances are produced in paying (profitable) quantities from unitized lands. 43 C.F.R. § 3186.1, Section 20. However, this provision cannot be construed as extending the primary term of a Indian oil and gas lease with less than five years remaining[439] because the governing statute does not, either expressly or impliedly, provide for the extension of lease terms by any event other than actual production.

The most common conflict experienced in Indian law is the division of loyalties within administrative agencies charged with acting in the best interests of the public and in the best interests of Indians. Resolution of this

---

439. 25 U.S.C. § 396d.

conflict has resulted in many different approaches, running the gamut between complete deference to Indian interests to complete disregard. In arguing on behalf of Indians, in conjunction with a congressional investigation into this conflict-of-interest problem, Reid Chambers has testified:

> This "conflict" * * * is not one which properly can be resolved through the process of balancing conflicting interests. Such a balancing procedure within the executive department is desirable where competing public policies are being balanced; this, of course, is the method by which public policy is formulated. But private rights, which the United States is obligated as a fiduciary to defend, cannot be so balanced against conflicting public purposes. The government's relationship to the Indians is, in this respect, unique in character.

Comm. on the Judiciary, 91st Cong., 2d Sess., A Study of Administrative conflicts of Interest in the Protection of Indian Natural Resources 3 (Comm. Print 1971).[440]

When acting on a request to approve a unit operation, the Secretary must act in the best interests of the tribe in accord with the Indian trust doctrine. See, 25 U.S.C. § 396d (1983) and 25 C.F.R. § 211.28(a) (tribal land) and 25 U.S.C. § 396 and 25 C.F.R. § 212.28(a) (allotted land). When reviewing the Secretary's decision, the scope of review is whether the Secretary has considered all relevant factors and whether the action taken is arbitrary or capricious, an abuse of discretion, or contrary to law. In applying this scope of review, the Tenth Circuit has revealed a willingness, through a series of decisions, to second guess Secretarial discretion. Cf., Woods Petroleum Corp. v. Department of Interior, 47 F.3d 1032 (10th Cir.Okla.1995, en banc); Cheyenne–Arapaho Tribes of Oklahoma v. United States, 966 F.2d 583 (10th Cir.Okla.1992); Cotton Petroleum Corp. v. U.S. Dept. of Interior, 870 F.2d 1515 (10th Cir.Okla.1989); and Kenai Oil and Gas, Inc. v. Department of Interior, 671 F.2d 383 (10th Cir.Utah 1982).

In *Kenai*, the lessee sought to communitize an unproductive Indian lease with producing fee land just prior to the expiration of the primary term of the Indian lease. The Secretary's agent did not approve the communitization agreement, believing it not to be in the best economic interests of the Indians. In upholding this disapproval, the Tenth Circuit recognized that approval of communitization agreements is within the discretion of the Secretary, but "limited by the fiduciary responsibilities vested in the United States as trustee of Indian lands." 671 F.2d at 386. The court then defined this fiduciary responsibility as "a duty to maximize lease revenues." Id. at 386. The lessees unsuccessfully argued that the applicable statutes and regulations required the Secretary to approve a communitization agreement that was consistent with sound oil and gas conservation practices. The Tenth Circuit rejected this argument, finding that, in determining the best interests of the

---

440. See also Judith V. Royster, Equivocal Obligations: The Federal–Tribal Trust Relationship and Conflicts of Interest in the Development of Mineral Resources, 71 N.D. L. Rev. 327, 329, 358–59, 360 (1995) ("Balancing the tribal interest against public considerations, and in particular subordinating the tribal interest to public interests represented by agencies such as the BLM, violates the Secretary's trust obligations to the Indian tribes.... The Secretary is obligated under the mineral development scheme not to weigh tribal interests against public values, but to act in the best interests of the mineral owning tribes....").

tribe, all factors, including economic considerations, may be considered. After *Kenai*, the Secretary established guidelines so that superintendents and area directors of the BIA could evaluate proposed communitization agreements in accord with an "all relevant factors" test.

Cotton involved multiple Indian tracts within a 640–acre drilling and spacing unit. The communitization agreement was submitted just prior to the expiration of the Indian leases. After consultation with the MMS as required by the new guidelines, the Secretary's agents approved the agreement over the objections of one Indian owner, Rose. On administrative appeal, the Assistant Secretary for Indian Affairs reversed the approval respecting the Rose tract, causing the lease to expire, but then re-approved it as the communitization of an unleased tract. Under the terms of the communitization agreement, the unleased tract received a production allocation of 8/8 of the production attributed to that 80–acre tract. Cotton, the affected lessee, filed suit, and the Tenth Circuit found an abuse of discretion. The court stressed that no explanation was given for the inconsistent treatment of the various Indian lessors within the unit and that the disapproval appeared to be for the sole purpose of causing the underlying lease to expire. In its review of the proposed agreement, the Tenth Circuit observed that the Secretary must consider the economic effect of the agreement, as well as the possible long-term conservation benefits resulting from orderly development. The Court concluded that the Secretary had not followed his own guidelines, nor documented his departure from the guidelines. Thus, the Secretary abused his discretion because he did not consider "all relevant factors."

In *Cheyenne–Arapaho*, Indian lessors appealed the approval of a communitization agreement, and the Tenth Circuit found that the Secretary had abused his discretion. The court held that Secretarial discretion must be exercised in light of the government's fiduciary duties—a principal duty being to maximize lease revenues. Because the area in question was experiencing an oil and gas boom, the court found that the Secretary should have considered the marketability of a new lease. The court viewed its decision as consistent with *Cotton*, which overturned the disapproval of the unit based solely on economic factors, and consistent with *Kenai*, where the Secretary failed to consider all relevant factors. But is *Cheyenne–Arapaho* really consistent with *Cotton*? An important theme in *Cotton* (and *Woods*, below) is the impropriety of canceling a lease based solely upon the best economic interests of Indians. Yet, in *Cheyenne–Arapaho*, the Secretary was overturned for not considering economic factors, seemingly to the exclusion of other factors that would have supported communitization.

In *Woods*, the most recent of these four cases, the Secretary disapproved a communitization agreement so that the Indian lessors could enter into more profitable leases—a $400,000 bonus had already been offered for a new lease. After a new lease was issued, a new communitization agreement, essentially identical in substance to the agreement that had been disapproved, was approved, retroactive to date of first production. In overturning the Secretary's decision as an arbitrary and capricious abuse of discretion, the Tenth Circuit panel found that the sole reason for the Secretary's rejection was to further "the ulterior motive of enabling the Indian lessors to acquire an additional bonus payment." The Tenth Circuit en banc affirmed the panel decision by holding that the Secretary may not reject a proposed communitization for the sole purpose of allowing an existing Indian lease to lapse so that a new lease could be issued and then followed by the approval of a similar communitization agreement retroactive to the date of first production.

Despite the seeming inconsistencies in this line of case law since *Woods*, no reported decisions address Indian communitization. What are all the relevant factors that the Secretary should consider? How would a private lessor react to a communitization request? Suppose that a lease contained a pooling clause requiring the lessor's approval, at his sole discretion, of any pooling during the last year of the lease primary term. In contrast to the narrow self-interest of private parties, should the Secretary, acting as a fiduciary, consider a bigger picture than just the particular communitization request? Should the expectations of lessees be relevant? Should the Secretary look long term or short term when acting as a fiduciary? For further discussion see Owen L. Anderson, State Conservation Regulation—Single Well Spacing and Pooling—Vis–À–Vis Federal and Indian Lands, Special Institute on Federal Onshore Oil and Gas Pooling and Unitization (Rocky Mtn. Min. L. Foundation 2006).

B. DEVELOPMENT OF STATE LANDS

1. GRANT LANDS

Other than the original 13 colonies, Maine, Texas, West Virginia, and parts of Tennessee, most states were created from federal territories. Hence, the lands not already in private ownership were either federal public domain or Indian lands. After the admission of the State of Ohio in 1802, states were customarily given grants of land at statehood to use as a source of income to defray the costs of establishing and funding public schools, colleges, universities, and institutions, and for the costs of constructing various internal improvements.[441] Many states have also received land grants apart from those lands received at the time of their admission into the Union.[442] In many states, particularly in the West,

---

441. The practice of setting aside lands for the support of schools and other institutions can be found in post-Renaissance England. After Henry VIII confiscated church property, grammar schools that depended on the income from the property were forced to close. Supporters of education petitioned Henry's successors to reopen the schools, which were then endowed with the income from some of the confiscated lands. M. Orfield, Federal Land Grants to the States with Special Reference to Minnesota, Studies in Social Sciences No. 2, 7 (1915) (on file at the University of Minnesota Library). In Colonial America in 1639, the town of Dorchester in the Massachusetts Bay Colony set aside land for the support of a school. Id. at 8. There are many other examples, particularly in the Northern colonies. Id. at 8–13. Other colonial lands were set aside for the support of colleges, seminaries, militia, and industry. Id. at Chapters 2–5.

442. In a series of Acts, Congress authorized grants of swamp lands to states that agreed to reclaim these lands by draining them for cultivation or other uses. See, e.g., 9 Stat. 352 (1824); 10 Stat. 634 (1855); 11 Stat. 3; 12 Stat. 3 (1860); and 13 Stat. 3 (1860). Under the Carey Act of 1894, the Congress authorized grants of desert lands to states that would reclaim them for irrigation. 38 Stat. 422. In 1862, the Morrill Act made land grants in support of agricultural colleges. 16 Stat. 116 (1862).

state grant lands have been developed for oil, gas, coal, and other minerals.[443]

Unlike the federal government, which can give valuable resources to developers,[444] an interest in state grant lands (especially those west of the Mississippi River)[445] must generally be leased for fair market value, either pursuant to a given state's constitution, enabling act, or both.[446] Typically, the agency or board in charge of managing state grant lands is charged with a fiduciary duty to manage the lands for the benefit of the intended beneficiary (i.e., schools, colleges, universities, or institutions). As the following case illustrates, breach of this duty can cause problems for those who deal with the agency.

ASARCO INCORPORATED v. KADISH
490 U.S. 605 (1989).

JUSTICE KENNEDY delivered the opinion of the Court, except as to Part II—B1.

The ultimate question for our decision is whether Arizona's statute governing mineral leases on state lands is void because it does not conform with the federal laws that originally granted those lands from the United States to Arizona. First, however, there is a difficult question about our own jurisdiction, a matter which touches on essential aspects of the proper relation between state and federal courts.

I.

Various individual taxpayers and the Arizona Education Association, which represents approximately 20,000 public school teachers throughout the State, brought suit in Arizona state court, seeking a declaration that the state statute governing mineral leases on state lands, Ariz.Rev.Stat. Ann. § 27–234(B) (Supp.1988), is void, and also seeking appropriate injunctive relief. The state statute was challenged on the ground that it does not comply with the methods Congress required the State to follow before it could lease or sell the lands granted from the United States in the New Mexico–Arizona Enabling Act of 1910, 36 Stat. 557, and which are repeated in the Arizona Constitution. The suit was brought against the Arizona Land Department and others. ASARCO and other current mineral lessees of state school lands were permitted to intervene as defendants. Eventually the trial court certified the case as a defendant

---

443. In addition to grant lands, states own other lands managed for largely non-proprietary purposes, including parks, historic sites, rest areas, office sites, agricultural experiment stations, and wildlife preserves. Depending on the state or on the particular tract, these lands may or may not be open to oil, gas, and mineral development. Discussion of these lands is beyond the scope of this casebook.

444. Historically, oil and gas were locatable minerals that persons could acquire on the public domain without compensating the federal government. Even today, many minerals, including gold, silver, and copper, are still classified as locatable minerals. See discussion in Subsection A.1(a) above.

445. Kansas and Nevada received land grants, but promptly disposed of nearly all of their lands. The remainder of the states have retained much of their acreage. In some cases, such as North Dakota, many of the grant lands have been sold with a reservation of all or a fractional interest in the minerals to the State.

446. See, e.g., N.D. Const. art. IX, § 6 and Enabling Act of Feb. 22, 1889, ch. 180, § 11, 25 Stat. 676.

class action under Arizona Rule of Civil Procedure 23. The defendant class consisted of all present and future mineral lessees of state lands.

The trial court upheld the statute on cross-motions for summary judgment, and respondents (the original plaintiffs) appealed. The Arizona Supreme Court reversed over the dissent of one justice, ruling that the statute is "unconstitutional and invalid as it pertains to nonhydrocarbon mineral leases." Kadish v. Arizona State Land Dept., 155 Ariz. 484, 498, 747 P.2d 1183, 1197 (1987). It remanded the case to the trial court with instructions to enter summary judgment for respondents, to enter a judgment declaring § 27–234(B) invalid, and to consider what further relief, if any, might be appropriate.

Various of the mineral lessees filed a petition for certiorari, and we granted review.

II.

Before we may undertake to consider whether the state legislation authorizing the leases is valid under federal law, we must rule on whether we have jurisdiction in the case. [The court concluded that it had jurisdiction.]

III.

The issue on the merits is whether Arizona may lease mineral lands granted from the United States without meeting the specific requirements imposed by federal statute. We begin with a more detailed review of the statutes in question.

In 1910, Congress passed the New Mexico–Arizona Enabling Act, 36 Stat. 557, which authorized the people of those territories to form state governments. Among its other provisions, the Enabling Act granted Arizona certain lands within every township for the support of public schools. Congress provided, however, that the new State would hold those granted lands in trust and subject to the specific conditions set out in § 28 of the Act, 36 Stat. 574–575. Under the conditions, the granted lands could not be sold or leased except to the highest bidder at a public auction following notice by advertisements in two newspapers weekly for 10 weeks. Leases for a term of five years or less were exempt from the advertising requirement. Lands could not be sold or leased for less than the values set by an appraisal required by the statute. All proceeds derived from the lands would go to a permanent segregated fund, and interest, but not principal, was to be spent for support of public schools. Arizona incorporated those restrictions in its proposed constitution, Ariz. Const., Art. 10, and was admitted to the Union in 1912.

The grant of lands in the Enabling Act specifically excluded mineral lands, §§ 6, 24, 36 Stat. 561–562, 572, but this gave rise to uncertainty about what are known as "unknown" mineral lands, those lands on which minerals were not discovered until after the grant. In two subsequent decisions, this Court held that the exclusion applied only to lands known to be mineral at the time of the grant, and that unknown mineral lands were granted under the Act. Wyoming v. United States, 255 U.S. 489, 500–501 (1921); United States v. Sweet, 245 U.S. 563, 572–573 (1918). These holdings in turn spawned numerous disputes over whether lands were known to be mineral at the time they were granted from the Federal Government. See, e.g., Work v. Braffet, 276 U.S. 560, 561–563 (1928). Title to lands in many western States was in doubt, and the issue became more difficult to prove as the years passed. Accordingly, in 1927 Congress passed the Jones Act, 44 Stat. 1026, a brief statute that extended the terms of the original grant of lands in the western States to encompass mineral lands as well. Congress also has amended the Enabling Act twice, each time to clarify the procedures for leasing granted lands for specific purposes. See Act of June 5, 1936, ch. 517, 49 Stat. 1477; Act of June 2, 1951, 65 Stat. 51.

Arizona's own law governing the leasing of state mineral lands, enacted in 1941, requires every such lease to "provide for payment to the state by the lessee of a royalty of five percent of the net value of the minerals produced from the claim." Ariz.Rev.Stat.Ann. § 27–234(B) (Supp.1988). But it does not require those lands to be advertised or appraised before they are leased, and does not require the lands to be leased at their full appraised value. The lands in question here were granted to Arizona either in 1910, by the terms of the Enabling Act itself, or in 1927, under the Jones Act.

The grant of all lands under the Enabling Act is conditioned, by the statute's clear language, upon the specified requirements for leasing or selling those lands. The Act declares that "all lands hereby granted * * * shall be by the said State held in trust, to be disposed of in whole or in part only in the manner as herein provided, * * * and that the natural products and money proceeds of any of said lands shall be subject to the same trusts as the lands producing the same." § 28, 36 Stat. 574, 575 (emphasis added). "Disposition of any of said lands, or of any money or thing of value directly or indirectly derived therefrom, * * * in any manner contrary to the provisions of this Act, shall be deemed a breach of trust." Any such disposition is expressly stated to be "null and void" unless "made in substantial conformity with the provisions of this Act." Ibid. And, again, the requirements set forth in the Act apply to "[a]ll lands, leaseholds, timber, and other products of land." Ibid.

Petitioner cites Neel v. Barker, 27 N.M. 605, 204 P. 205 (1922), as standing for the proposition that because mineral lands originally were exempted by Congress from the grant made in the Enabling Act, its provisions for the sale or lease of granted lands did not apply to those lands later determined to be mineral in nature. That proposition, never tested in a federal court, is flawed in two respects. First, in Wyoming v. United States, supra, decided the year before but not mentioned or discussed in Neel, this Court held that unknown mineral lands were within the grant made by Congress. Second, since those lands were granted to the States under the authority of the Enabling Act itself, they could not be regarded as unburdened by its mandatory conditions. In consequence, the New Mexico Supreme Court erred in concluding that because "Congress did not intend to grant to the state any mineral lands * * * it follows that the state is not controlled nor restricted by said act in regard to leasing said lands for mineral purposes." 27 N.M., at 611, 204 P., at 207. All the lands granted under the Act are granted subject to its conditions.[1]

The lands granted under the Jones Act are subject to the same conditions. This very brief enactment was passed to address the continuing problems associated with the dual regime, under which the adjudication of title to lands would depend on whether they were known to be mineral at the time the Federal Government granted them. H.R.Rep. No. 1761, 69th Cong., 2d Sess., 2–3 (1927); S.Rep. No. 603, 69th Cong., 1st Sess., 1–6 (1926). Indeed, its formal title was: "An Act Confirming in States and Territories title to lands granted by the United States in the aid of common or public schools." 44 Stat. 1026. The Jones Act resolved the problem of the dual regime by simply "extend[ing]" the prior grants of lands "to embrace numbered school sections mineral in character." § 1, 44 Stat. 1026. The statute explicitly stated that "the grant of numbered mineral sections under this Act shall be of the same effect as prior grants for the numbered non-mineral sections." § 1(a), 44 Stat. 1026 (emphasis added).

Petitioners make two points about the proper reading of this statute. First, they argue that the "same effect" language was intended only to assure that the title to these lands passed and vested in the same manner and with the same validity as did the title to lands granted under the Enabling Act, but said nothing about the conditions upon which those lands were granted. Second, they argue that the language of § 1(b) of the Jones Act granted the States a broad authority to lease the mineral deposits in the newly granted lands "by the State as the State legislature may direct," with "the proceeds of rentals and royalties therefrom to be utilized for the support or in aid of the common or public schools." 44 Stat. 1026–1027. According to petitioners, therefore, the Jones Act did not impose the same restrictions on mineral lands as did the Enabling Act; on the contrary, it explicitly repudiated any such restrictions on the newly granted lands.

We do not agree with this reading of the Jones Act. First, the suggested interpretation of the "same effect" language would render that language redundant: the statute continues immediately with an additional clause that directly addresses the "vest[ing]" of "titles to such numbered mineral sections." § 1(a), 44 Stat. 1026. Instead, we believe that the

---

1. One possible distinction between mineral leases and the lease of lands for other purposes is that mineral rights can be difficult to appraise, which might make the Enabling Act's provisions less helpful in this setting. But this Court recognized long ago that such rights are subject to valuation in condemnation proceedings, and that whatever the difficulties may be in making such appraisals with complete accuracy, it does not defeat the existence of a "market value" in mineral rights, and it does not suffice as a reason to depart from the ordinary requirements that the law imposes on such transactions. Montana R. Co. v. Warren, 137 U.S. 348, 352–353 (1890).

"same effect" language has independent meaning, and that it achieved Congress' stated objective of "extend[ing]" the 1910 grants to encompass all mineral lands and of "[c]onfirming" title to such lands in the States. 44 Stat. 1026.

Second, the language of § 1(b) does not undermine the conclusion that § 1(a) of the Jones Act extended the coverage of the Enabling Act's express restrictions as well as of its grant of lands. Section 1(b) says that though the mineral lands may be sold, the rights to mine and remove the minerals themselves are reserved to the State and may only be leased. Such leases may be undertaken "as the State legislature may direct." Petitioners would read § 1(b) as containing the sole dispositional restrictions on the newly granted lands, and would read the latter passage as a blanket authority for the States to lease minerals on whatever terms they wish to set, as long as the proceeds of those leases go to the schools.

This interpretation suffers from several defects. To begin with, it does not offer a comprehensive understanding of the statutory regime. Section 1(b) contains no dispositional restrictions on the sale or lease of the newly granted lands except for the provision that the mineral rights on those lands are reserved to the State. If the "same effect" language in § 1(a) does not extend the dispositional restrictions in the Enabling Act to the lands granted in the Jones Act, then those lands are subject to no dispositional restrictions at all, though their mineral rights would be reserved. This is inconsistent with the view that the lands granted under the Jones Act are part of the school trust. Similarly, if the "as the State legislature may direct" language is the blanket authority for which petitioners contend, it would allow minerals to be leased for little or no royalty, and thus would leave room for all the abuses that the establishment of a school trust was designed to prevent.

Perhaps the most fundamental defect of the interpretation urged by petitioners is that it would largely perpetuate the dual regime that Congress sought to eliminate by enacting the Jones Act. Under that interpretation, the restrictions in the Enabling Act would continue to apply to unknown mineral lands, but would not apply to known mineral lands. As a result, for example, some of the leases involved in this case might be proper, under the Jones Act, while others would be improper, under the Enabling Act, and the critical difference would rest on a determination, to be made at some future point, whether those lands were known to be mineral in 1910. This is surely not the resolution Congress intended when it passed this statute, and it is neither a sensible nor an appealing one.[2]

---

2. Under the reading of the Jones Act we adopt, there may still be traces of the dual regime, though they are minimized. For example, it might be argued that "the right to prospect for, mine, and remove" minerals on unknown mineral lands can be sold, whereas those same rights on known mineral lands cannot, since the Jones Act's prohibition in this regard is limited to those lands in "the additional grant made by this Act." § 1(b), 44 Stat. 1026. We need not decide in this case, however, whether that reading of the statute is fair or necessary.

In addition, the "as the State legislature may direct" language is not inconsistent with the express restrictions set forth in the Enabling Act. Given the preceding restrictions on the sale of minerals in § 1(b), Congress may have thought it necessary to emphasize that leases were subject to no such novel limitations; instead, the States retained all the authority given under the conditional grants made in the Enabling Act. We thus agree with the court below that this language is properly viewed as authorizing the States to regulate the methods by which mineral leases are made and to specify any additional terms in those leases that are thought necessary or desirable, as long as the leases comply with the dispositional requirements set forth in the Enabling Act. See 155 Ariz., at 491, 747 P.2d, at 1190. But this language, in and of itself, does not dispense with those restrictions.[3]

Both sides place a great deal of emphasis on the later amendments to the Enabling Act, which occurred in 1936 and 1951. We think that the language of the original grants of these lands to Arizona is the decisive basis for decision here, and that subsequent amendments are at best only illustrative of how a later Congress read the original terms of the statute. Congress could not, for instance, grant lands to a State on certain specific conditions and then later, after the conditions had been met and the lands vested, succeed in upsetting settled expectations through a belated effort to render those conditions more onerous. Congress could relax the conditions upon which lands had been granted previously, of course, but we see nothing in the later amendments here to suggest that it has done so. Instead, the later amendments are wholly consistent with the view that Congress granted these lands in 1910 and 1927 subject to the conditions discussed previously, and has never removed those conditions.

IV.

"The Court's concern for the integrity of the conditions imposed by the [Enabling Act] has long been evident." Alamo Land & Cattle Co. v. Arizona, 424 U.S. 295, 302 (1976). We conclude that the sale or lease of mineral lands granted to the State of Arizona under these federal statutes must substantially conform to the mandatory requirements set out in the Enabling Act. The court below was correct in declaring Ariz.Rev.Stat.Ann. § 27–234(B) (Supp.1988) invalid as to nonhydrocarbon mineral leases. The judgment of the Arizona Supreme Court is

Affirmed.

JUSTICE O'CONNOR took no part in the consideration or decision of this case.

---

3. In the wake of the enactment of the Jones Act in 1927, the experience of New Mexico is instructive as a contemporaneous reading of the statute. Concerned that the Act had undermined whatever basis there might have been for the decision in *Neel v. Barker,* 27 N.M. 605, 204 P. 205 (1922), the New Mexico government immediately petitioned Congress to authorize a state plebiscite to codify its holding as law. In response, Congress passed a joint resolution to that effect. Joint Resolution No. 7, ch. 28, 45 Stat. 58. The language of the resolution explicitly permitted New Mexico to waive the advertising, appraisal, and bidding requirements on all mineral leases. This explicit language was conspicuously absent from the Jones Act itself.

JUSTICE BRENNAN, with whom JUSTICE WHITE, JUSTICE MARSHALL, and JUSTICE BLACKMUN join, concurring in part and concurring in the judgment. [omitted]

CHIEF JUSTICE REHNQUIST, with whom JUSTICE SCALIA joins, concurring in part and dissenting in part. [omitted]

NOTES

1. Congressional restrictions placed on the management of land grants must be determined on a state-by-state or act-by-act basis. Beginning with the admission of Colorado (18 Stat. 476 (1875)), Congress began restricting the manner in which a state managed and disposed of its public lands. These restrictions ordinarily address the manner of sale, minimum sale or lease prices, lease terms, and the management of revenues. The Enabling Acts of Arizona and New Mexico are the most restrictive. Even in the absence of an express enabling act or constitutional provision, the state likely owes a fiduciary obligation to manage trust lands for the benefit of the intended beneficiaries. State constitutions may contain restrictions beyond those required by the Enabling Act. For example, the North Dakota Constitution prohibits the sale of any grant land for less than fair market value. N.D. Const. art. IX, § 6. Another section prohibits the acquisition of any interest in grant lands by adverse possession. Id. § 9. Yet another general section prohibits the state from making donations of property or assets. Id. art. X, § 18. In 1951, the North Dakota legislature passed legislation purporting to divest the state of title to mineral interests initially acquired through foreclosure. In some instances, the state had sold the foreclosed land to the former owner-mortgagor, but had reserved mineral rights. This legislation, which attempted to transfer retained mineral rights to former owner-mortgagors who had repurchased the surface, was declared unconstitutional on the ground that the state was making an impermissible donation of state property to private parties. Solberg v. State Treasurer, 53 N.W.2d 49 (N.D. 1952).

2. Grants for the support of the common schools generally involved specific lands. Alabama, Arkansas, Florida, Illinois, Indiana, Iowa, Louisiana, Michigan, Mississippi, Missouri, Ohio, and Wisconsin each received Section 16 in every township. California, Colorado, Idaho, Kansas, Minnesota, Montana, Nebraska, North Dakota, Oklahoma, Oregon, South Dakota, Washington, and Wyoming received Sections 16 and 36 of every township. Arizona, New Mexico, and Utah received Sections 2, 16, 32, and 36 of every township.[447] If the designated sections had already been disposed of or were otherwise not available, the states were given indemnity or "in-lieu" lands in their place. Regarding in-lieu lands and other land grants, the states were ordinarily allowed to select lands from the available public domain. Several states have not yet made all of their selections. See Andrus v. Utah, 446 U.S. 500 (1980).

3. Because Texas entered the Union as an independent country in 1845, it held title to the public lands within the boundaries of the Republic of Texas.

---

447. Nevada disclaimed its initial grant of over 3.9 million acres in return for the right to make specific selections of public lands totaling 2 million acres. Alaska received grants in excess of 100 million acres.

Texas offered to cede 175 million acres of land to the United States in exchange for debt relief, but Congress refused the offer. Ultimately, however, as part of the Compromise of 1850, Texas ceded 67 million acres of land in return for $10 million dollars in debt relief. The ceded lands now form parts of New Mexico, Oklahoma, Colorado, and Wyoming. Thus, while the State of Texas did not receive federal land grants, it retained title to public lands within its borders. Although Texas patented much of this land into private ownership, the retained acreage and mineral rights, along with the state's offshore holdings, have been extensively developed for oil and gas resources, providing the state with an important source of income.

4. States have authorized oil and gas development of grant lands in a variety of ways. While leasing is clearly the most common arrangement, states have experimented with exploration licenses, as well as net profits contracts somewhat similar to farmout agreements. Most leases are issued competitively, either on a sealed bid or public auction basis. Royalty and rental rates are usually fixed, bonus bidding is the norm. A few states, including Texas and California, have experimented with royalty bidding. For many years, the State of Wyoming offered its lands for lease by lottery, but this practice was abandoned in the early 1980s. The State of Louisiana negotiates lease arrangements with developers. Which method is best? In the case of competitive bonus bidding, is a sealed bid or public auction preferable?

Lease primary terms are typically three, five, or ten years; annual rentals are usually nominal. Royalty rates generally range from one-eighth to one-fourth. A few states have reserved sliding scale royalties that begin at one-eighth and increase with the rate of production. States generally use their own lease forms, which are more lessor oriented than the forms prepared by lessees for use on privately owned land.

2. SUBMERGED AND OFFSHORE LANDS

After independence from England, the original 13 colonies succeeded to the rights of the English Crown, including what was believed to be the Crown's sovereign title to the beds of navigable lakes and streams that ebbed and flowed with the tide. These sovereign rights were ultimately extended to include title to all beds of navigable lakes and streams whether or not affected by the tide. Because new states were admitted to the Union on an "equal footing" with the original thirteen colonies, these states also hold title to the beds of navigable lakes and streams within their boundaries in trust for the public to use for navigation subject to the federal navigational servitude.[448] This sovereign title extends to ordinary high watermark; however, some states have enacted statutes that could be construed as limiting state title to low watermark, thereby implying that riparian owners own riparian lands bordering navigable waters to low watermark.

---

448. See, Montana v. United States, 450 U.S. 544 (1981) and Pollard v. Hagan, 44 U.S. (3 How.) 212 (1845). A state's title to such lands was not given by grant from the federal government to the states. Prior to statehood, the federal government held title to such lands for the benefit of future states. At statehood, title automatically vested in the state pursuant to the equal footing doctrine.

Historically, the coastal states generally believed that they held sovereign title to the beds of tidelands. But in 1947, the United States Supreme Court held that the federal government held paramount title to these lands.[449] The coastal states petitioned Congress for relief, and in 1953, Congress enacted the Submerged Lands Act,[450] which confirmed state title seaward a distance of three miles, as well as to the beds of inland navigable waters. Gulf coastal states were given an opportunity to claim additional acreage based upon historic claims. Texas and Florida have proven historic claims in the Gulf of Mexico, a distance of three marine leagues (nine nautical miles) from the coast.[451] Complex litigation is often necessary to determine the precise location of a state's coastal boundaries—a necessary step in measuring a state's tideland claims.[452]

Litigation also occurs over the title to the beds of lakes and streams. Among the issues commonly litigated are: whether a particular river or lake or portion thereof is navigable for purposes of determining a state's claim of ownership; whether the bed of a particular navigable lake or river or portion thereof is owned by an Indian Tribe or has been reserved by the federal government for a special federal purpose; whether the state has divested itself of title to any portion of the bed of a navigable lake or stream and whether such disposition is lawful; whether the state's title to the bed of a lake has been diminished by reliction (a permanent receding of the waters of a lake or river); whether the bed of a river has shifted by erosion and accretion (a slow, imperceptible shift in a river's course) or by avulsion (a sudden and perceptible shift—often as a result of flooding). Often the litigation arises over the ownership of resources lying beneath the bed, such as oil and gas reserves. The following case illustrates the nature of this type of litigation, provides an excellent summary of relevant legal principles, and is a classic example of the important role that legal history may play in resolving such a dispute.[453]

J.P. FURLONG ENTERPRISES, INC. v. SUN EXPLORATION AND PRODUCTION COMPANY

423 N.W.2d 130 (N.D.1988).

MESCHKE, JUSTICE.

---

449. United States v. California, 332 U.S. 19 (1947).

450. 43 U.S.C. §§ 1301–1315.

451. United States v. States of La., Tex., Miss., Ala., and Fla., 363 U.S. 121 (1960).

452. See, e.g., United States v. Alaska, 422 U.S. 184 (1975); United States v. Louisiana, 422 U.S. 13 (1975); United States v. Maine, 420 U.S. 515 (1975); United States v. Louisiana, 420 U.S. 529 (1975); United States v. Florida, 420 U.S. 531 (1975); United States v. Louisiana, 409 U.S. 909 (1972); United States v. Louisiana, 404 U.S. 388 (1971); United States v. Louisiana, 394 U.S. 836 (1969); United States v. Louisiana, 394 U.S. 11 (1969); United States v. Louisiana, 389 U.S. 155 (1967); United States v. California, 381 U.S. 139 (1965); United States v. States of La., Tex., Miss., Ala., and Fla., 363 U.S. 121 (1960).

453. For a companion case concerning title to the portion of the bed of a navigable lake that had been barred by reliction, see Matter of Ownership of Bed of Devils Lake, 423 N.W.2d 141 (N.D.1988).

We consider whether a man-made change in the course of the navigable Missouri River affects ownership of oil and gas underlying the former riverbed. Applying a statute derived from Napoleonic and Roman law through the Field Code, we hold that it does. Therefore, we reverse a summary judgment declining to apply the statute.

Facts

In 1957, the United States of America acquired land by eminent domain in section 15, Township 152, Range 103, McKenzie County, from Emery Papineau. The condemnation decree stipulated that Papineau retained "all oil and gas rights."

After acquiring the land, the U.S. Corps of Engineers dug a large trench through section 15. The navigable Missouri River formed a new channel through the trench, leaving a long oxbow of former riverbed north of the new channel. Part of that oxbow is located in the NE 1/4 of section 9 of the same township.

Ladd Petroleum Corporation obtained an oil and gas lease, dated August 9, 1983, from the State of North Dakota for the oxbow riverbed in section 9. Sun Exploration and Production Company obtained an oil and gas lease, dated October 5, 1982, from Grace M. Oyloe on related lands adjoining the oxbow in section 9.

The oxbow riverbed in section 9 was also leased by Marc A. Chorney on September 16, 1983 from David A. Papineau as successor in interest of Emery Papineau. Chorney assigned this lease to J.P. Furlong Enterprises, Inc. and Nantasket Petroleum Corporation.

In November 1985, Sun drilled a producing oil and gas well in the NE 1/4 of section 9.

This Litigation

Following completion of the oil well, Furlong, Nantasket, and Papineau ("Furlong plaintiffs") began this quiet title action against Sun, Ladd, Oyloes, State of North Dakota and several other associated mineral and royalty owners ("Sun defendants"). The Furlong plaintiffs claimed ownership of the oil and gas under the oxbow riverbed in section 9 and contended that the state owned the oil and gas beneath the new channel in section 15 on the basis of NDCC 47–06–07, which says:

> Ancient stream bed taken by owners of new course as indemnity.—If a stream, navigable or not navigable, forms a new course abandoning its ancient bed, the owners of the land newly occupied take by way of indemnity the ancient bed abandoned, each in proportion to the land of which he has been deprived.

The Sun defendants took the position that NDCC 47–06–07 did not apply to artificial changes in the course of a navigable river and did not apply to the oxbow riverbed which still contained water. After preliminary discovery and motions, the trial court apparently declined to apply the statute, dismissed the Furlong complaint, and granted summary judgment to the Sun defendants.

The Furlong plaintiffs appealed, arguing that the plain meaning of NDCC 47–06–07, as well as historical objectives of it and connected sections, call for application of that statute to both natural and artificial changes in the course of a navigable river and to an abandoned riverbed that still contains some water.

The Sun defendants do not dispute either the history or the policy of NDCC 47–06–07, but urge that it should be applied only to natural changes, not to man-made changes, and that the oxbow is not an abandoned riverbed. They argue that Papineau does not need "indemnity" and therefore still owns the minerals under section 15. They further argue that laches and limitations support the summary judgment below and that the United States is a necessary party if the statute is applied.

The State of North Dakota argues that we should strictly construe NDCC 47–06–07 to protect the state's "sovereign lands" from "intrusion." Since Papineau was compensated by the United States for taking of his land in section 15, while being allowed to retain the underlying oil and gas, the State submits that he has not been deprived of anything by the river change, so indemnification under NDCC 47–06–07 is unnecessary. If the statute applies, the State further argues that the oxbow riverbed has not been "abandoned," leaving factual issues to be addressed upon remand.

Background

When North Dakota became a state, the beds of navigable waters, including that of the Missouri River, became state property by virtue of the equal footing doctrine. The purpose of state title was to protect the public right of navigation. See Montana v. United States, 450 U.S. 544, 551 (1981) and Pollard's Lessee v. Hagan, 44 U.S. (3 How.) 212, 225 (1845) (at 229: " * * * to Alabama belong the navigable waters, and soils under them, * * * subject to the rights surrendered by the constitution to the United States.") Thus, the State of North Dakota holds title to the bed of the Missouri River.[1] See NDCC 47–01–14[2] and 47–01–15.[3] This title

---

1. Under the equal footing doctrine, a state's title to the beds of navigable waters can extend up to the ordinary high watermark, but is "governed by the local laws of the several States, * * * "Shively v. Bowlby, 152 U.S. 1, 26, 40 (1894). Several states have limited their ownership of the beds of navigable waters to the area below the low watermark. See 1 Patton on Land Titles, §§ 138 and 297 (2d ed. 1957 and Supp.). Whether North Dakota has limited its title to the area below the low watermark has not been decided. See NDCC 47–01–15 and Note, 59 N.Dak.L.Rev. 211 (1983). As in our contemporary decision, In the Matter of the Ownership of the Bed of Devils Lake, 423 N.W.2d 141 (Civil No. 870144), the trial court did not address that issue and we are not called upon to do so.

2. NDCC 47–01–14 says:

"Land below high watermark-Regulated by federal or state law.-The ownership of land below ordinary high watermark and of land below the water of a navigable lake or stream is regulated by the laws of the United States or by such laws as under authority thereof, the legislative assembly may enact."

3. NDCC 47–01–15 says:

includes underlying oil and gas. The Submerged Lands Act, § 3, 43 U.S.C. § 1311 (1976), reaffirmed the title of the states to lands beneath navigable waters at statehood, including "the natural resources within such lands and waters."

The Missouri River and the land adjoining it (i.e., riparian land) are subject to the processes of accretion, erosion, avulsion, and reliction.[4] The consequences of these processes are addressed in NDCC Ch. 47–06.

In the event of accretion and reliction, any accreted or bared land "belongs to the owner of the bank, * * * "NDCC 47–06–05.[5] This statute "is essentially a restatement of the well-established common law rule governing riparian rights;" Hogue v. Bourgois, 71 N.W.2d 47, 53 (N.D. 1955). It generally follows the common-law rule that a riparian owner gains land by accretion and reliction and loses it by erosion. See United States v. 11,993.32 Acres of Land, 116 F.Supp. 671 (D.N.D.1953) (at 678: "[T]he general rule rests upon the equitable idea that a riparian owner should have the opportunity to gain by accretion since he is subject to the hazard of loss by erosion.") In two situations, however, this statute, which originates in the Field Code, does not follow common law.

The first situation is where land, originally surveyed as riparian, is submerged by encroaching river erosion causing land, originally surveyed as nonriparian, to become riparian. When the river shifts back, causing the land originally surveyed as riparian to reemerge, this court, in construing NDCC 47–06–05, has held that title to the reemerging land rests with the owner of the original riparian land and not with the owner of the original non-riparian land.[6] Perry v. Erling, 132 N.W.2d 889, 897 (N.D. 1965).

"Banks and beds of streams—Boundary of ownership.—Except when the grant under which the land is held indicates a different intent, the owner of the upland, when it borders on a navigable lake or stream, takes to the edge of the lake or stream at low watermark. All navigable rivers shall remain and be deemed public highways. In all cases when the opposite banks of any stream not navigable belong to different persons, the stream and the bed thereof shall become common to both."

4. "Accretion" refers to the gradual deposit and addition of soil along the bank of a waterbody caused by the gradual shift of the waterbody away from the accreting bank.

"Erosion" refers to the gradual loss of soil along the bank of a waterbody caused by the gradual encroachment of water into the eroding bank.

"Avulsion" refers to the sudden inundation or sweeping away of land resulting from a sudden change in the course of a waterbody.

Technically, "reliction" refers to the sudden baring of land resulting from a sudden change in the course of a waterbody. However, the word "reliction" is also commonly used to describe the gradual receding of water resulting in the gradual baring of previously submerged land. See n. 1, In the Matter of the Ownership of the Bed of Devils Lake, supra.

See generally Robert E. Beck, The Wandering Missouri River: A Study in Accretion Law, 43 N.Dak.L.Rev. 429, 431 (1967) (hereafter cited as Beck II).

5. NDCC 47–06–05 says:

"Riparian accretions.—Where from natural causes land forms by imperceptible degrees upon the bank of a river or stream, navigable or not navigable, either by accumulation of material or by the recession of the stream, such land belongs to the owner of the bank, subject to any existing right of way over the bank."

6. So has South Dakota, with an identical Field Code provision. See Erickson v. Horlyk, 48 S.D. 544, 205 N.W. 613, 614 (1925) and Allard v. Curran, 41 S.D. 73, 168 N.W. 761 (1918). Under

The second situation, where NDCC 47–06–05 apparently does not square with common law, concerns accretion, erosion, and reliction caused by the nonnatural shifting of a river. NDCC 47–06–05 begins with the phrase "[w]here from natural causes...." (Emphasis added). The word "natural" tends to indicate that this provision excludes from the general rule accretion and reliction resulting from artificial or man-made efforts. Thus, if a river shifts due to artificial or man-made efforts, the accreted or bared land may not belong "to the owner of the bank...." See Beck II at p. 449–50. At common law, the benefit of nonnatural accretion and nonnatural reliction went to the owner of the accreting bank, provided that the benefitted owner was not the primary contributor to the artificial or man-made effort that caused the accretion or reliction.[7]

These general observations lead to consideration of two additional statutes, both on avulsion, NDCC 47–06–06[8] and, the subject of this decision, NDCC 47–06–07, which says:

> If a stream, navigable or not navigable, forms a new course abandoning its ancient bed, the owners of the land newly occupied take by way of indemnity the ancient bed abandoned, each in proportion to the land of which he has been deprived.

While this court has not construed either NDCC 47–06–06 or 47–06–07, it is evident that these sections also significantly modify common-law avulsion rules.[9]

At common law, avulsion did not result in a change of title; boundaries remained as before the avulsive change.[10] This basic common-law rule was applied whether the avulsive change resulted from natural or artificial causes.[11] Apparently, no court has refused to apply the common-

---

the prevailing view, however, title to the reemerging land would rest with the owner of the land originally surveyed as nonriparian, in accordance with the common-law accretion rule. See Wilcox v. Pinney, 250 Iowa 1378, 98 N.W.2d 720 (1959). See also 2 Patton on Land Titles, § 303, p. 65 (cases cited at n. 89) (2d ed. 1957); Robert E. Beck, Boundary Litigation and Legislation in North Dakota, 41 N.Dak.L.Rev. 424, 447 (1965) (hereafter cited as Beck I); and Beck II at 429–431 (cases cited at nn. 10, 11 & 12, p. 430).

7. See Annotation, Riparian Owner's Right to New Land Created By Reliction Or By Accretion Influenced By Artificial Condition Not Produced By Such Owner, 63 A.L.R.3d 249, 254–60 and 2 Patton on Land Titles, § 300, pp. 58–59, nn. 60 and 61 (2d ed. 1957). The Montana Supreme Court has followed this view even though Montana has a statute identical to NDCC 47–06–05. See City of Missoula v. Bakke, 121 Mont. 534, 198 P.2d 769, 772 (1948), construing Rev.Code of Mont. § 6820 (1935) (currently Mont.Code Ann. § 70–18–201). Compare City of Newport Beach v. Fager, 39 Cal.App.2d 23, 102 P.2d 438, 442 (1940) and City of Los Angeles v. Anderson, 206 Cal. 662, 275 P. 789, 791 (1929), construing an identical California statute, § 1014 of the California Civil Code, as applying only to natural accretion.

8. NDCC 47–06–06 says:

> If a river or stream, navigable or not navigable, carries away by sudden violence a considerable and distinguishable part of a bank and bears it to the opposite bank or to another part of the same bank, the owner of the part carried away may reclaim it within a year after the owner of the land to which it has been united takes possession thereof.

9. NDCC 47–06–07 does not refer to a river "suddenly" abandoning its former bed.

10. See Nebraska v. Iowa, 143 U.S. 359, 361 (1892). See also 2 R. Patton and C. Patton Land Titles § 303, p. 66 (cases cited at n. 90) (2d ed. 1957) and J. Grimes, Law of Surveying and Boundaries § 572 (4th ed. 1976) (formerly F. Clark, Clark on Surveying and Boundaries).

11. See Puyallup Tribe of Indians v. Port of Tacoma, 525 F.Supp. 65, 77 (W.D.Wash.1981), aff'd, 717 F.2d 1251, 1263 (9th Cir.1983) (1984) (Corps of Engineers dredged new channel);

law avulsion rule to artificial or man-made avulsion.[12] Consistent with the common-law rule, NDCC 47–06–07 appears to treat natural and artificial (man-made) avulsion alike.[13]

But, in another respect, NDCC 47–06–07 greatly modifies common law by providing that a particular kind of avulsion results in a change of title when a stream "forms a new course abandoning its ancient bed." In this situation, "the owners of the land newly occupied take by way of indemnity the ancient bed abandoned, each in proportion to the land of which he has been deprived." This transfer of title did not happen at common law.

Statutory History

Using the well-developed presentation of the Furlong plaintiffs about the derivation of NDCC 47–06–07, which is not contested by the Sun defendants or the State, we survey that statute's history.

NDCC 47–06–07 did not codify common-law principles. It came to us, through the Field Code, from the Code Napoleon and the Digest of Justinian (Roman law).

The Field Code, enacted in Dakota Territory in 1865, was the immediate source of NDCC 47–06–07, although the Century Code cites the Territorial Civil Code of 1877 as the earliest source. In 1877, the Dakota Territory Legislative Assembly did make some revisions in its Field Code, apparently based on the California Revised Field Code of 1872. No change, however, was made in what is now NDCC 47–06–07.

Both the 1865 Field Code and 1862 Draft Field Code annotate what is now NDCC 47–06–07. The relevant Field Code annotation says: "This and the four sections following are similar to those of the Code Napoleon, Art. 559–563." Field Code, p. 135, annotation to § 444 (1865). The fourth section following is § 448 which is identical to NDCC 47–06–07.[14]

Art. 563 of the Code Napoleon, referred to in the Field Code annotation, states:

Peterson v. Morton, 465 F.Supp. 986, 1003 (D.C.Nev.1979) rev'd on other grounds, 666 F.2d 361 (9th Cir.1982) (rechannelization); Witter v. County of St. Charles, 528 S.W.2d 160, 162 (Mo.App. 1975) (Corps of Engineers diked and diverted main channel); Gill v. Porter, 248 Ark. 140, 450 S.W.2d 306, 308 (1970) (Corps of Engineers dredged new channel); Parker v. Farrell, 74 Wash.2d 553, 445 P.2d 620, 622–23 (1968) (avulsion caused by a logjam); Whiteside v. Norton, 205 F. 5 (8th Cir.1913) (dredging changed channel); and State v. Bowen, 149 Wis. 203, 135 N.W. 494 (1912) (bridge construction changed channel).

12.   "[W]hen the bed and channel are changed by the natural and gradual processes known as erosion and accretion, the boundary follows the varying course of the stream; *while if the stream from any cause, natural or artificial,* suddenly leaves its old bed and forms a new one, by the process known as an avulsion, the resulting change of channel works no change of boundary, * * * " Arkansas v. Tennessee, 246 U.S. 158, 173 (1918) (Emphasis added).

13.   Like NDCC 47–06–05 (concerning accretion), NDCC 47–06–07 originates in the Field Code. But, unlike 47–06–05, which by its language applies only to "natural" accretion, 47–06–07 contains no such express limitation.

14.   * * *

1865 Field Code § 443 is identical to North Dakota's accretion statute, NDCC 47–06–05. The annotation to § 443 cites two common-law cases and Code Napoleon art. 556–557 as sources.

"If a river or creek, whether navigable or floatable or not, opens itself a new bed by leaving its former channel, the owners of the soil newly occupied take, by way of indemnification, the former bed of the river, everyone in proportion to the quantity of land he has lost." Annotation to 16 La.Civ.Code, Compiled Ed., art. 518 (1972) (translating Code Napoleon art. 563 (1804)).

Code Napoleon art. 563 was evolved from Roman law—specifically the Digest of Justinian.[15] The relevant part of the Digest, a statement of the whole of Roman law, says:

"(7) In like manner, if a river leaves its bed and begins to flow elsewhere, anything which was built in the old bed will not come under the terms of this interdict, for what belongs to the neighbors on both sides is not constructed in a public stream; or, if the land has boundaries, the bed of the river will belong to the first occupant, and it certainly ceases to be public property.

"Moreover, although the new bed which the river has made for itself was previously private property, it at once becomes public; because it is impossible for the bed of a public stream not to be public.

"(8) A canal, made by human hands, through which a public river flows is, nevertheless, public property to such an extent that if anything is built there, it is considered to have been built in a public stream." 9 Scott, The Civil Law 302 (1932), translating Dig.Just. 43.12.1 §§ (7)–(8) (Ulpianus, On the Edict, Book 68).

Thus, NDCC 47–06–07 did not come from common law, but from French and Roman civil law. It is clear that Field intended to depart from and to modify common law.[16]

This historical review also shows the public policy underlying NDCC 47–06–07, as well as related sections. The excerpt from the Digest of Justinian expresses the Roman policy of protecting the public right of navigation. This policy is also apparent in the Code Napoleon.

In the United States, the policy of protecting the public right of navigation has been continued in the federal navigational servitude which applies to any navigable stream.[17] Paralleling Roman and Napoleonic civil law, this servitude follows the movement of a river, even where there has been an avulsive change. Manifestations of this policy have also survived

---

15. See discussion in Dickson v. Sandefur, 259 La. 473, 250 So.2d 708, 716–17 (1971) and see 2 Civil Law Translations of Aubry and Rau, The Civil Law of France, "Property" § 203, Paragraph 208, Avulsion, n. 28 (Translation by Louisiana State Law Inst. 1966).

16. Field adopted civil-law provisions throughout the Field Code. This is reported in a study by Professor Rodolfo Batiza at Tulane University School of Law. See Rodolfo Batiza, Sources of the Field Civil Code: The Civil Law Influences on a Common Law Code, 60 Tul.L.Rev. 799 (1986).

17. United States v. Cherokee Nation of Oklahoma, 480 U.S. 700 (1987) held that the Cherokee Nation was not entitled to just compensation for damage to sand and gravel deposits in the riverbed it owned under the navigable Arkansas River, which had been disturbed by construction of a navigational channel. The Court declared that the tribal ownership under the river did "not include the right to be free from the navigational servitude, for exercise of the servitude is 'not an invasion of any private property rights in the stream [or] the lands underlying it * * *.' " 107 S.Ct. at 1492.

in the common law by which a state's title shifts with the process of accretion and reliction and in the equal footing and public trust doctrines by which states hold title to the beds of navigable waters. NDCC 47–01–14 and 47–01–15 recognize this policy. NDCC 47–01–15 says: "All navigable rivers shall remain and be deemed public highways." In cases of avulsion, however, the common law did not fully carry out this policy, since avulsion did not result in a change of title. In common law, a state's title to a riverbed did not follow an avulsive shifting of the course of a river.

On the other hand, at Roman law, the ownership of the bed of a river remained public with an avulsive change. Scott, supra, at § (7). This was so even if the avulsive change was man-made. Id. at § (8). The same result followed from the language of the Code Napoleon, which had evolved from the Digest of Justinian. See discussion in Dickson v. Sandefur, 259 La. 473, 250 So.2d 708, 716–17 (1971). The only difference between the Code Napoleon and Roman law was that, under Roman law, the owner of land riparian to the old bed took the old bed,[18] but under the Code Napoleon art. 563, the old bed was taken by the owner of land lost to the new channel. NDCC 47–06–07 also provides that the owner of land lost to a new channel becomes, proportionately, the owner of the old bed.

Precedent

Counterparts to NDCC 47–06–07 are found in Louisiana, Oklahoma and South Dakota. See La.Civ.Code Ann. art. 504 (West 1980) (formerly codified as art. 518 (West 1952)); Okla.Stat. tit. 60, § 340 (West 1971); and S.D.Codified Laws Ann. § 43–17–11 (1983). The South Dakota and Oklahoma Supreme Courts have not construed their statutes.[19]

Like the Field Code, the Louisiana statute came from Code Napoleon art. 563 (1804). The current Louisiana statute provides:

"When a navigable river or stream abandons its bed and opens a new one, the owners of the land on which the new bed is located shall take by way of indemnification the abandoned bed, each in proportion to

---

18. The Roman law scheme is also followed in Texas. In other words, the state's title to riverbeds always follows the movement of the river, whether the movement is gradual or avulsive. But, the owners of land riparian to the old bed take the old bed. Texas law is derived from Spanish civil law. For a thorough discussion, see Manry v. Robison, 122 Tex. 213, 56 S.W.2d 438, 442–449 (1932). See also Maufrais v. State, 142 Tex. 559, 180 S.W.2d 144, 148–49 (1944). The reason that the drafters of the Code Napoleon modified Roman law by giving the old bed to the owner of the land lost to the new bed is explained in Dickson v. Sandefur, 259 La. 473, 250 So.2d 708, 716, n. 2 (1971). [Editors' addition: In Brainard v. State, 12 S.W.3d 6 (Tex.1999), the Texas Supreme Court held that riparian owners gained title to the historical bed of the Canadian River when an upstream dam reduced the flow of the river and hence the width of the actual bed. Since Texas entered the Union as an independent nation, title to the beds of lakes and streams within Texas is a matter of state law. As a result, the boundary line between state and riparian ownership is not the ordinary high watermark, but the "gradient boundary" of a navigable stream—a line located halfway between the lowest level where the flowing water first touches the bank and the highest point at which the water reaches the top of the bank without overflowing it. Id.]

19. The Oklahoma statute and related statutes on accretion, avulsion and islands are identical to the Field Code. While Oklahoma is not regarded as a "Field Code state," it did derive many of its statutes from the Laws of Dakota Territory. See, e.g., source notes, Okla.Stat. tit. 60, §§ 335–340 (West 1971).

the quantity of land that he lost. If the river returns to the old bed, each shall take his former land."

La.Civ.Code Ann. art. 504 (West 1980) (formerly codified as art. 518 (West 1952)). Since originally enacted, this statute has been amended, but none of the amendments is relevant to this case (e.g., prior versions did refer to both navigable and nonnavigable rivers.) For history, including reference to the Code Napoleon, see Annotation to 16 La.Civ.Code, Compiled Ed., art. 518 (1972).

Louisiana courts have construed this statute several times. Since all cases refer to it by its former codification number of art. 518, rather than its current designation, we also refer to this statute as art. 518.

This statute was first applied in State v. Richardson, 140 La. 329, 72 So. 984 (1916), a case about title to producing oil wells as affected by accretion and the boundary of the state's title to the bed of the Red River. In a petition for rehearing the State contended that it owned the bed of a slough which formerly had been part of the riverbed. Noting that this argument had not been presented in the pleadings, the court said: "But where a river or stream changes[ ] its course, and opens a new bed, the owners of the soil newly occupied take the former bed of the river. Civil Code, art. 518." Id. 72 So. at 993.

This statute was applied in Fitzsimmons v. Cassity, 172 So. 824 (La.App.1937), where the Red River was eroding banks leading into and out of an oxbow. The Levee Board dug a cutoff which became the new channel of the river. The old channel became an oxbow lake. Defendant, who had built a duck blind in the old channel, contended that the oxbow lake belonged to the state since it was part of the original bed of the Red River. The court applied art. 518, held that the plaintiff, not the state, held title to the old bed, and declared that the state held title to the new bed.

> "The underlying philosophy, as well as the equitable effect of appropriate application of this article, is obvious. The state has no right to acquire private property and not compensate the owner therefor. The beds of rivers, it is conceded, belong to the state in its sovereign right. Therefore, when a river changes its course and for this purpose appropriates private property for its new bed, the lawmaker, out of a spirit of justice and fairness, has wisely ordained, in effect, that the owner of the appropriated land shall be compensated for his loss by becoming the owner of the abandoned bed. All persons who acquire property adjacent to navigable streams are impressed with knowledge of the existence of this law and, of course, the sovereign, the source of the law, is bound by it." Id. at 828–29.

In dealing with the claim that the abandoned oxbow still held water, the court went on to say:

> "It is contended that the abandoned part of the river is susceptible to navigation in fact and that for this reason its bed still belongs to the

state. The water therein is deep enough for light craft to ply, but we do not think this fact alters the situation. The depth of the 'Old River' has been reduced materially by silt from the Red [R]iver and partakes more of the character of a shallow lake than it does a navigable stream. Being disconnected from any navigable stream, and surrounded by plantation lands, it can serve no useful purpose commercially. Anyway, article 518 of the Civil Code makes no exceptions in conferring ownership of abandoned rivers on those whose land has been taken by the new channel." Id. at 829.

In addressing the man-made nature of the change, the court stated:

"It is also argued that article 518 of the Civil Code does not apply as the adoption of the new channel across the 286–foot neck was encouraged by the act of man. We do not think this tenable. It was certain the river was destined very soon to connect at this point and the cutting of the canal only accelerated this event a brief time. It remains that plaintiff's author's land was 'taken' by the river without any act of his." Id.

In Dickson v. Sandefur, 235 So.2d 579 (La.App.1970), a circuit Court of Appeal held that art. 518 applied only to very sudden avulsive changes. Accordingly, the court refused to apply art. 518 to a cutoff by the Red River that had gradually formed over several years and was finally completed by a five-month flood. In a vigorous dissent, Judge Dixon argued that the statute did apply, citing other cases that had applied art. 518, including Russ v. Stephens, 90 So.2d 501 (La.App.1956) and Stephens v. Drake, 134 So.2d 674 (La.App.1961).

On appeal, the Louisiana Supreme Court reversed, holding that art. 518 applied in any situation where a river forms a new channel and abandons the former channel "in such a manner as to be readily perceived in a departure not requiring the passage of much time." Dickson v. Sandefur, 259 La. 473, 250 So.2d 708, 719 (1971). A five-month flood caused the Red River to overflow its banks and to complete the formation of a new channel. Water flowed for a while in both the old and new channels, but when the floodwaters subsided siltation caused the flow in the old bed to cease, leaving an oxbow lake. Id. at 714–15. The supreme court discussed art. 518 in depth, comparing it with common-law decisions that more narrowly define avulsion.

"We recognize that the courts of other states and the federal courts have applied the terms 'avulsions' and 'cutoffs' in cases not too dissimilar to the present case. Of course we are not bound by these decisions. We do not find that they are clarifying of our specific Civil Code article or that they [sic] are illuminating for our determination here. Although the legal principle set forth in our Civil Code Article 518 may be contrary to some of the legal principles enunciated in the cited common law cases, the proposition stated in the Code article is very clear and concise, and we are bound by it." Id. at 718.

Moreover, the court stated that the Court of Appeal in Fitzsimmons, supra, (the case where the Levee Board cut an artificial channel) "correctly applied Civil Code Article 518 to situations where a river had abandoned its old channel and occupied the land of another." 250 So.2d at 719. The court concluded that the former owner of the new bed "owns all the land where the old bed flowed—whether covered with water or dry—by indemnification under Civil Code Article 518." Id. at 720.[20]

Article 518 was recently considered in Verzwyvelt v. Armstrong–Ratterree, Inc., 463 So.2d 979 (La.App.1985). An abandoned oxbow lake was occasionally inundated by overflow from the Red River. "The flow of water in the channel depends almost totally upon the level of the Red River." Id. at 985. Nonetheless, this oxbow was regarded as abandoned riverbed.

Decision

Construing our statute in light of its legal history and related public policy objectives, as well as the ample Louisiana precedents, we conclude that NDCC 47–06–07 applies in this case. Unless the Sun defendants or the State prevail on a remaining issue of fact or a separate defense, the Furlong plaintiffs have title to the oil and gas rights underlying the former riverbed.[21]

Given the development of the Field Code in North Dakota, this conclusion follows logically. The Territorial Legislative Assembly recognized that our state would receive title to the beds of navigable waters at statehood. Accordingly, by 1877, it had enacted a code that would secure title of the state to such lands and modify common law so that the state's title would follow the movement of the bed of the river. This accords with the underlying public policy, since the purpose of a state holding title to a navigable riverbed is to foster the public's right of navigation, traditionally the most important feature of the public trust doctrine. Moreover, it seems to us that other important aspects of the state's public trust interest, such as bathing, swimming, recreation and fishing, as well as irrigation, industrial and other water supplies, are most closely associated with where the water is in the new riverbed, not the old.[22]

---

20. The court stated that the boundary of ownership to the bed was to ordinary low watermark. 250 So.2d at 720. The court gave no citation for this reference, but Louisiana has a statute similar to NDCC 47–01–15. See La.Civ.Code Ann. art. 456 (West 1980) (formerly codified as arts. 455 and 457 (West 1952)). See also Pizanie v. Gauthreaux, 173 La. 737, 138 So. 650, 652 (1931).

21. We cannot, and do not, decide title to the bed of the new channel. That issue is not essential to our decision about title to the oil and gas under the old riverbed and the United States is not a party to this action. But, absent countervailing considerations, NDCC 47–06–07 and its ancestors, as well as the gist of the Louisiana precedents, imply the reciprocal of our holding today: The State of North Dakota ordinarily would have title to the oil and gas rights beneath the bed of the new channel. Compare Beck II at 445–446, speculating that the owner of the land under the new bed would continue to own it, along with that under the abandoned riverbed.

22. [Editors' Note (courts' footnote omitted)] Since most states do not have statutory law addressing the legal effect of a change in the course of a river, courts would resolve this matter in accordance with common law. In State By and Through State Land Bd. v. Corvallis Sand &

The statute makes no exceptions in transferring ownership of abandoned riverbeds. Therefore, we hold that it applies with equal force to oil and gas rights.

Our decision reverses a summary judgment and does not foreclose issues which have not yet been decided by the trial court. Whether the old riverbed has been abandoned or continues as a twin flowing channel of the Missouri River is a question of fact to be decided by the trial court on remand. Similarly, application of statutes of limitation and of the doctrine of laches turn on factual references which the trial court has not yet addressed.

Accordingly, we reverse the summary judgment and remand for further proceedings consistent with this opinion.

NOTES

1. Although it has been occasionally argued that the doctrines of accretion, erosion, avulsion, and reliction should not be applied to mineral rights, courts, either explicitly or implicitly, have consistently applied these doctrines to mineral rights. See, e.g., Ely v. Briley, 959 S.W.2d 723 (Tex. App.–Austin 1998, no writ) (applying the doctrine of accretion to severed mineral rights); Jackson v. Burlington Northern, Inc., 205 Mont. 200, 667 P.2d 406 (1983); (holding that severed mineral rights are subject to the doctrines of accretion and erosion); Nilsen v. Tenneco Oil Co., 614 P.2d 36 (Okla.1980) (holding that severed mineral rights are subject to the doctrines of accretion and erosion); Briggs v. Sarkeys, Inc., 418 P.2d 620 (Okla.1966) (holding that accretions added to riparian land inure to the benefit of an oil and gas lessee of such land); Esso Standard Oil Company v. Jones, 98 So.2d 236 (La. 1957) (applying doctrines of accretion, erosion and reliction to determine rights to oil royalties). But see, Eliason v. Northern Alberta Land Registration District, 115 D.L.R.3d 360, 6 W.W.R. 361 (Alberta Ct. of Queen's Bench 1980) (suggesting in dicta the possibility that severed mineral rights would not be subject to the doctrines of accretion, erosion, and reliction). What problems might arise if minerals rights in general were not subject to these doctrines? What problems might arise if only severed mineral rights were not subject to these doctrines?

2. Though purporting to follow surveying instructions issued by the Department of the Interior, surveyors often surveyed meander lines along lakes and streams. Meander lines are short straight lines that roughly parallel the bank of a stream or the shore of a lake. When a water body was "meandered," its bed was not included in the surveyed acreage for calculating the acreage subject to homesteading, mining claim, sale, or other disposition. The presence or absence of meander lines is not relevant to the issue of navigability, and these lines do not delineate the boundaries of state title.

3. States hold sovereign title to the beds of navigable waters. Thus, the threshold question to state ownership is whether the relevant portion of the water body is navigable. PPL Montana, LLC v. Montana, ___ U.S. ___, 132

Gravel Co., 582 P.2d 1352 (Ore.1978), the Supreme Court of Oregon felt compelled to follow the common law rule of avulsion, even though the court would have preferred the civil law rule. This decision has been harshly criticized in a case comment, 60 Or.L.Rev. 273 (1981).

S.Ct. 1215 (2012). To determine a state's claim, navigability is a federal question.[454] United States v. Oregon, 295 U.S. 1 (1935). The state carries the burden of proof to show navigability, at least against the federal government. Iowa–Wisconsin Bridge Co. v. United States, 84 F.Supp. 852 (Ct.Cl.1949). The federal test is whether, at the time a state entered the union, the water body was navigable in fact in its natural and ordinary condition. A river was navigable in fact if it was used for commercial navigation (or susceptible to such use) by customary modes of transportation for the area at the time the state entered the Union. The Daniel Ball, 77 U.S. (10 Wall) 557 (1870).

A river need not be navigable throughout its course. Occasional portages will not defeat navigability, provided that the river affords a means for useful commerce. United States v. Utah, 283 U.S. 64 (1931) and United States v. Holt State Bank, 270 U.S. 49 (1926). On the other hand, the "mere fact that logs, poles, and rafts are floated down a stream occasionally and in time of high water does not make it a navigable river." United States v. Rio Grande Dam & Irrigation Co., 174 U.S. 690, 698 (1899). Modern-day recreational use and other post-statehood use may be relevant in showing that the river was navigable at statehood. PPL Montana LLC v. Montana, ___ U.S. ___, 132 S.Ct. 1215 (2012).

Application of these tests to specific situations is not easy, and courts are not consistent in their rulings. For example, the State of North Dakota and the United States have had ongoing litigation over title to the bed of the Little Missouri River and to the oil and gas reserves beneath the bed. The United States, as the largest riparian landowner along the river, contended that the river is not navigable, in which case the riparian owners along the river own the bed.[455] The State of North Dakota argued that the river is navigable, in which case the state owns the bed. The United States District Court for North Dakota handed down two opinions on the navigability question. Following the first trial, the court concluded that the river is navigable. North Dakota ex rel. Board of University & School Lands v. Andrus, 506 F.Supp. 619 (D.N.D.1981), affirmed 671 F.2d 271 (8th Cir.N.D.1982), reversed on other grounds. Block v. North Dakota ex rel. Board of University & School Lands, 461 U.S. 273 (1983), judgment vacated North Dakota ex rel. Board of University & School Lands v. Block, 789 F.2d 1308 (8th Cir.N.D.1986). Following a second trial, the court (a different judge presiding) concluded that the river is not navigable, even though none other than Theodore Roosevelt navigated the river in the 1880s, just a few years prior to statehood, to pursue bandits who had stolen a boat! North Dakota ex rel. Board of University & School Lands v. United States, 770 F.Supp. 506 (D.N.D.1991), affirmed 972 F.2d 235 (8th Cir.1992). For other illustrative cases addressing navigability in the context of a dispute over mineral rights, see State ex rel. Indiana Department of Conservation v. Kivett, 95 N.E.2d 145 (Ind. 1950) (finding a river to be navigable) and Ozark–Mahoning Co. v. State, 37 N.W.2d 488 (N.D.1949) (finding a lake to be nonnavigable).

---

454. An exception is Texas, which entered the Union as an independent nation. Thus, that state's title to the beds of lakes and rivers is a question of state law.

455. If there are different riparian owners on opposite sides of a nonnavigable river, ownership of the bed is divided at the "thread" or center of the stream. Amoco Oil Co. v. State Highway Dept., 262 N.W.2d 726 (N.D.1978).

Unless the state has lawfully disposed of all or a portion of such acreage, a state normally holds title to the lands lying within the actual ordinary high watermark of a navigable water body. Thus, although state title depends upon navigability, which is a federal question, state law controls the subsequent disposition of such acreage. Oregon ex rel. State Land Bd. v. Corvallis Sand & Gravel Co., 429 U.S. 363 (1977). Several states appear to have purported to dispose of at least a portion of such lands to riparian owners. See, e.g., N.D. Cent. Code § 47–01–15. Query whether such disposition is valid in light of state constitutional provisions prohibiting the donation of state property or in light of the "public trust" doctrine. See, e.g., N.D. Const. art. IX, § 9 and art. X, § 18; Coastal Petroleum Company v. American Cyanamid Company, 492 So.2d 339 (Fla.1986); and Illinois Central R. Co. v. Illinois, 146 U.S. 387 (1892).

4. Where the bed of a navigable river forms a state boundary, the actual state boundary is located at the center of the "thalweg" (or "talweg") of the stream, the middle of the deepest or most navigable channel, as distinguished from the "thread," the midway line between the banks, the usually boundary line for tracts are separated by a non-navigable stream. United States v. Louisiana, 470 U.S. 93 (1985); Louisiana v. Mississippi, 202 U.S. 1 (1906). An important exception to this general rule is the Red River, which separates Texas and Oklahoma. The northern boundary of Texas was set by the 1819 Adams–Onis Treaty, 8 Stat. 252 (1819), as the southern bank of the Red River. Oklahoma v. Texas, 260 U.S. 606 (1923) and Oklahoma v. Texas, 256 U.S. 70 (1921).

5. Most states lease their sovereign lands in much the same manner and are subject to the same general terms and conditions as state grant lands. The lease itself, however, may not necessarily grant a right of surface occupancy. In other words, the lessee may not be allowed to locate a well on the water, although the lessee would ordinarily be permitted to drill a directional well beneath the bed from an upland location. Often, the drilling of a directional well is unnecessary, because the state's submerged acreage may be pooled with adjacent uplands with the well being vertically drilled from an upland location. If a well is located on the water, any operations from "vessels" would be governed by federal maritime law (see discussion, Subsection B.2.(f)) and would be subject to full compliance with a host of federal and state environmental laws and regulations.

3. TEXAS RELINQUISHMENT ACT LANDS

Texas has disposed of most of its public lands along with the mineral rights;[456] however, between 1895 and 1931, over six million acres of "mineral classified lands" were sold, subject to a reservation of mineral rights in the state. With the advent of oil and gas development, parties who owned the surface rights to these lands complained that they were

---

456. Under Spanish and Mexican law, the sovereign held title to all minerals. The Republic and State of Texas succeeded to this view; however, in a series of constitutional amendments and statutory enactments, the state retroactively relinquished its claim to mineral rights regarding lands that had already been patented into private ownership. The Relinquishment Act applies to approximately 7,400,000 acres of land patented into private ownership after September 1, 1895.

suffering surface damage without compensation or benefit. In response, in 1919 the Texas legislature enacted the Texas Relinquishment Act.[457] This Act gave these surface owners a share of oil and gas lease benefits. Although the provisions of the Act appear to grant the surface owner all oil and gas rights except a 1/16 royalty and 10 cents per acre delay rental,[458] the Act has been construed as merely giving the surface owner, as an agent of the state, the right to execute oil and gas leases on the state's behalf in return for a share of the lease benefits.[459] As construed, the surface owner retains one-half of all lease benefits as compensation for surface damages and for negotiating the lease. The State of Texas receives the other one-half, subject to statutory minimums.[460]

LEWIS v. OATES

195 S.W.2d 123 (Tex.1946).

TAYLOR, JUSTICE.

The * * * sole question presented for decision * * * is whether John S. Oates and Tryon Lewis, on September 25, 1929, had a right under the facts to effectuate by contract the transaction they undertook to enter into on that date. Oates was then, as at all times mentioned herein, the surface owner and original awardee of 640 acres of Pecos County school land. About three years prior to the above date (January 28, 1926), Oates, as surface owner of the land and as agent of the state, leased the land for oil and gas to Pure Oil Company for a term of ten years. Thereby the company, as lessee, became the owner of the lease interests for the duration of that lease and Oates became the owner of the agency compensation payable to him by the lessee for the same duration. The lease was still in force with about seven years of its term unexpired, the state was still the owner of the entire oil and gas mineral estate in the land, and Oates was still the owner of the surface estate. No oil or gas had been produced or discovered on the land and no oil or gas operations for the production of either had been begun. Oates owned the entire surface estate, having made no sale of any part thereof; and, so far as the record discloses, the territory was unproven as to oil or gas production prospects. Tryon Lewis was desirous of buying a permanent oil and gas royalty interest in the land and Oates was desirous of selling such permanent interest. Accordingly, they undertook, by contract, to enter into a transaction to effectuate their respective desires. The means whereby they undertook to enter into the transaction, was the execution and delivery

457. 1919 Tex.Gen.Laws ch. 81 (codified as amended at Tex.Nat.Res.Code Ann. §§ 52.171–52.189. For a thorough discussion of the Act, see A.W. Walker, Jr., The Texas Relinquishment Act, 1 Inst. on Oil & Gas L. & Tax'n 245 (1949).

458. 1919 Tex.Gen.Laws ch. 81 § 1.

459. Greene v. Robison, 8 S.W.2d 655 (Tex.1928) (upholding the constitutionality of the Act as construed).

460. Beginning in 1931, some state lands were sold subject to the reservation of a "free royalty." For a case discussing these lands, see Wintermann v. McDonald, 102 S.W.2d 167 (Tex.1937).

contemporaneously of two instruments bearing date, September 25, 1929, both signed by Oates, the promisor, and delivered to Lewis, the promisee. The instruments will be labeled as First Part of Proposed Mineral Conveyance, and Second Part of Proposed Mineral Conveyance, respectively. The first part, in so far as pertinent here, is as follows:

First Part of Proposed Mineral Conveyance.

"And the said above described land being now under an oil and gas lease * * *, it is * * * agreed that this sale is made subject to the said lease, but covers and includes 1/8th of all the oil royalty and gas rental or royalty due and to be paid under the terms of said lease, * * * whether covered by said original lease or not. * * * It is agreed * * * that one-eighth of the money rentals which may be paid to extend the term within which a well may be begun under the terms of said lease is to be paid to the said Tryon Lewis and that in the event said above described lease for any reason becomes cancelled or forfeited, then, and in that event, the lease interests and all future rentals, * * * for oil, gas and mineral privileges shall be owned jointly by the respective owners of record, * * * Lewis owning an undivided one-eighth interest therein being in and to all oil, gas and other minerals in and upon said land, together with a like interest in all future rents. * * * This sale is made for and in consideration of Ten Dollars ($10.00) and other valuable considerations, * * *.

"To Have and to Hold the above described property * * * (etc.), unto the said Tryon Lewis, * * * (etc.), forever, and we do hereby bind ourselves, * * * (etc.), to warrant and forever defend * * * (etc.)."

The second part of the proposed conveyance, in so far as pertinent here, is as follows:

* * *

"That whereas, on the 25th day of September, 1929, John S. Oates * * * did convey * * * a 1/8th undivided interest in and to all of the minerals in and under (said land, mineral classified) * * * to Tryon Lewis, * * *; (and) the above described * * * land, * * * is involved in the present litigation of the Relinquishment Act, which gives to the landowner fifteen-sixteenths of the interest in and to the minerals in and under all school lands bearing such classification; (and) * * * in the future the question might arise as to whether the landowner owning lands with such classification, owns any of the minerals after a specified lease has expired, and whether or not any mineral interest which he had sold during the time such land is under lease, will revert to the State at the expiration of such lease.

"Now, therefore, know all men by these presents: That I, John S. Oates, having sold * * * perpetual royalty or perpetual mineral interest as shown by the above mineral deed, do hereby agree and bind myself, my heirs * * * (etc.) to protect Tryon Lewis in the interest so conveyed as above described, in the following manner:

"If the Supreme Court rules that all minerals under the above described section of land, shall revert to the State of Texas, at the expiration of the present lease, now in good standing, then I hereby agree and bind myself, * * * (etc.) to carry the said Tryon Lewis, * * * (etc.), to the extent of the interest outlined in the above * * * mineral deed, in the sale of any future leases on the above described land and upon the execution of such lease or leases, the interest so conveyed in the * * * mineral deed, will again be in force and effect in * * * Tryon Lewis, * * * (etc.)." (Italics ours)

During the seven years that then remained of the term of the lease (executed in 1926), the only income from the State's mineral estate in the land was a leasing income. This was paid to Oates by the lessee company and Oates in turn paid to Lewis his pro rata part of the income. No question ever arose between them concerning the income from that lease. Such income was property which Oates, by leasing the land could lawfully acquire, and was assignable. On January 28, 1936, upon expiration of the first lease, Oates executed a second lease of the land to the same lessee for a ten-year term. While this was the second lease, it was, in relation to the purported conveyance the parties were undertaking to make, the first lease made after the purported sale of the permanent royalty interest. Oates did not pay over to Lewis any part of the income received by him under the first future lease. After it had run for about eight years Lewis, on September 11, 1944, filed suit in trespass to try title against Oates to establish, under the above transaction, a perpetual royalty interest in future leases, and to recover moneys paid over to Oates by the lessee under the first future lease. * * *

The trial court * * * rendered judgment that Lewis take nothing by his suit (filed some fifteen years after the undertaking referred to); and recited as a part of the judgment that the "purported mineral conveyance * * * is hereby declared to be, and it always has been absolutely void and of no force and effect whatever * * *." Lewis appealed direct to the Court of Civil Appeals. He was again denied the relief sued for. 188 S.W.2d 895. Writ of error was applied for by Lewis, and was granted, on the ground that the Court of Civil Appeals erred in its holding in effect, substantially, that Oates and Lewis had no right on September 25, 1929, to make the contract they undertook to enter into in that Oates at that time owned no permanent oil and gas royalty interest and could not lawfully acquire and therefore could not lawfully assign to Lewis, such interest. Upon further consideration we have concluded that the Court of Civil Appeals was not in error in so holding. Greene v. Robison, 117 Tex. 516, 8 S.W.2d 655; Empire Gas & Fuel Co. v. State, 126 Tex. 138, 47 S.W.2d 267; Lemar v. Garner, 121 Tex. 502, 50 S.W.2d 773.

As our conclusion as to the correctness of the holding of the Court of Civil Appeals is predicated upon the Greene and Empire cases they will be analyzed with respect to their holdings in regard to the legislative plan or policy of selling and developing the state's mineral estate, before stating the reasons for the conclusion reached.

The Court in the Greene case [117 Tex. 516, 8 S.W.2d 662] * * * after setting out the Relinquishment Act * * * said:

Therefore the very first words of this Mineral Act of 1919 disclosed that one of the purposes of the act was 'to promote the active co-operation of the owner of the soil.' This calls attention to the conditions that made it desirable to secure the co-operation of the owner of the soil. The state had sold the land, the soil with all that goes with it, to the purchaser thereof, and was under obligation to protect him in the use and enjoyment of what it had sold him; and this the state had failed to do. There was a dual or double ownership of the land, the surface estate and the mineral estate, each antagonistic to and conflicting with the other. There was no provision of law for the protection of the owner of the soil in his peaceable enjoyment and possession of his property. The development of an oil field on it would be disastrous to him and utterly destructive of his property. * * * The conditions were inimical to any effort at development, and the state was not realizing on its mineral estate in these lands. The purpose of the act was to meet this practical situation. Indeed, the rights of possession and user of the land as a whole by both the owner of the soil and the owner of the minerals, they being joint owners of the land, are mutual and blended. As in other joint ownerships, necessarily there must be co-operation. If the joint owners do not co-operate, confusion is bound to arise, the purposes and efforts of each are jeopardized and destroyed, and the state suffers loss, not only to its mineral estate, but likewise as a sovereign in the administration of justice. The legislature has brought about this desired result in a lawful manner by requiring the purchaser of the oil and gas to compensate the owner of the soil for the use he makes of the surface, independent of the price he pays for the minerals. He compensates said owner for the inevitable damages of oil exploration and operation. The landowner acquires no estate in the oil and gas. He simply has a right to receive the compensation from the lessee out of the lessee's production as the statute provides.

* * * The Court held in this connection that under the plan there was "no vesting of title or interest in the oil and gas" in the surface owner; and further held that there was not only "no vesting of title or interest in the oil and gas" in the surface owner under the provisions of the Relinquishment Act, but that no right thereunder passed to anyone "until a sale or lease" had been effected, "according to the terms of the Act."

* * *

It is clear, as applied to the present case and facts, that Oates, as the agent or intermediary through whom the state, which was "continuously" offering for sale its mineral estate in the land, was required, in making future leases (of which the 1936 lease was one) to sell same for a leasing income in the manner provided. Assume the contract undertaken was good. It follows that Oates, having sold to Lewis a part of the permanent royalty income, could not make the future lease as provided by the legislative plan. He could not, with Lewis owning a mineral estate or interest, deal on the basis of sixteen-sixteenths of the oil. He would not receive a "like amount" with the state. In event Oates sold his surface estate, the state's agent in selling a future lease could not receive as large pro rata of leasing income as Oates received. Lewis would be entitled to receive it. In other words, under the plan of Oates and Lewis, when Oates conveyed to Lewis the interest described in the purported mineral convey-ance, he thereby not only rendered both himself and the successor agent incapable of dealing with the principal's sixteen-sixteenths of the oil and gas mineral estate, but also varied the legislative plan or policy so as to make a future lease less attractive than the former, and less likely to keep the land under lease until oil is discovered—all detrimental to the state's organic plan to procure income in the interest of its permanent school fund. In other words, the Oates and Lewis plan tended to take away in part the inducement provided by the state's plan of keeping the land leased until the discovery of oil or gas. After discovery the sale and development of the mineral estate proceeds under rules of law and regulations with which we are not here concerned. Their plan of sale tends to make less likely the leasing of the land by the state's agent (whether Oates or another) and is obviously detrimental to the state's interest. It reduces or tends to reduce, leasing income in that it takes away a part of the incentive fixed to encourage leasing of the land. It sets at naught the legislative plan formulated for the purposes above indicated. According to the law as stated in the Greene case, it ignores the basis fixed to accomplish those purposes.

[T]he State of Texas was Oates' principal and that as an agent of the state the method of his procedure in selling the mineral estate in the land was fixed by the legislature as provided in the Relinquishment Act. He became such an agent by the provisions of that act and not on the basis or consideration of whether he would be derelict in leasing the land or would not be. He was no more selected on that basis as an agent than he was selected on that basis by the state as an awardee of the land in question. It would have been awarded to him whether saint or sinner in his method of dealing. Likewise Oates became the surface owner and agent of the state without regard to whether he would be derelict in his duty or whether he would not be derelict. The land was awarded to him pursuant to the state's homesteading policy and the state, in selling through him its mineral estate, protected him in the enjoyment of his surface estate and compensated him on the basis fixed by the legislature in the Relinquish-ment Act. He and Lewis could not, by contract, fix another basis of sale. The attempt to do so was void.

It is stated in the Lemar case that there is nothing in the Relinquish-ment Act that expressly prohibits the severance and separate assignment by the surface owner of the payments to him and that the mineral leases there in controversy were for a certain period of time and were executed by the owner of the soil. In holding the severed mineral interest to be assignable the Court pointed out that "the rule is well established that it is not the policy of the law of this state to favor restraints upon alienation of property." [121 Tex. 502, 50 S.W.2d 773.] In other words, as stated by Court, the share of the royalties and bonuses derived from the leases executed by the surface owner, had become property rights "during the period of time for which the lease runs." There is no inconsistency between the foregoing statement in regard to the assignability of the property right in question and the subsequent statement which the Court was careful to make that "prior to the making of the mineral lease, the owner of the land has no right to assign or convey any mineral rights in the property."

The trial court denied Lewis the relief sought by him and correctly stated in his judgment that the "purported mineral conveyance * * * is hereby declared to be and it always has been absolutely void and of no force and effect whatever * * *." We agree with the judgment of the trial court. The purported contract was, for reasons pointed out above, contrary to public policy.

* * *

It is therefore ordered that the judgment of the Court of Civil Appeals, affirming that of the trial court, be, and it is, hereby affirmed.

* * *

NOTES

1. Upon sale of Relinquishment Act land under a purchase contract, the purchaser is regarded as the "owner of the soil" having the right to execute a new lease. Although the seller may not reserve the right to execute future leases or to retain any interest in future leases, the seller may retain lease benefits that may accrue out of any lease subsisting at the time of sale. While surface owners may not reserve or convey a nonparticipating royalty, they may transfer their share of the landowner's royalty reserved in the lease.

2. Under the Relinquishment Act, the owner of the soil is required to share all leasing benefits proportionately with the state. He may not receive any income other than one-half of the bonuses, delay rentals and royalties, and may not acquire a working interest. In State v. Durham, 860 S.W.2d 63 (Tex.1993), the State sought damages in excess of $162 million against the descendants of a surface owner who had allegedly breached his fiduciary duty as the state's agent by participating in certain transactions subsequent to executing an oil and gas lease. The effect of the transactions was to allow the owner of the soil to acquire additional interests in the minerals without having to share the proceeds with the State. Reversing the lower courts, the Texas Supreme Court held that a fact issue existed as to whether the landowner had breached his fiduciary duties to the state and remanded to the trial court. The case then settled.

Under the Relinquishment Act, as amended, the surface owner is specifically charged with a fiduciary obligation and

> may not lease, either directly or indirectly, to himself or to a nominee, to any corporation or subsidiary in which he is a principal stockholder, or to

an employee of such a corporation or subsidiary, or to a partnership in which he is a partner, or to an employee of such a partnership. If the owner of the soil is a corporation or a partnership, then the owner of the soil may not lease, either directly or indirectly, to a principal stockholder of the corporation or to a partner of the partnership, or any employee of the corporation or partnership. The owner of the soil may not lease, either directly or indirectly, to his fiduciary, including but not limited to a guardian, trustee, executor, administrator, receiver, or conservator.

Tex.Nat.Res.Code Ann. § 52.189 (West 1998). Because of the interest and controversy generated by *Durham*, the Texas legislature further amended the Relinquishment Act to provide that the landowner may not lease to a person related to him within the second degree of affinity or consanguinity or to a corporation or partnership of which that person is the principal stockholder, partner or employee unless he obtains prior approval from the State. Id. As one of the prerequisites for seeking such approval, the applicant must file a sworn affidavit that he will not receive any benefit under the lease that will not be shared proportionately with the State. Tex. Nat. Res. Code Ann. § 52.190 (West 1998).

An additional but older limitation on the owner of the soil is the owner's inability to represent the state in any dispute with the lessee. And generally, the owner of the soil may not share in other income derived from a lessee apart from one-half of the bonuses, rents, and royalties.

3. Texas is a community property state. If a married woman owned a Relinquishment Act tract as her separate property, would her share of lease benefits be separate or community property?

4. Historically, the surface owner could execute a lease on any form that complied with the Act. Today, the General Land Office for the State of Texas has promulgated an official Relinquishment Act lease form that is lessor-oriented and that specifies the royalty and delay rental. Nonetheless, many old leases are still being held by production.

5. The State of Texas holds title to about 13 million acres dedicated to the support of the common schools. In addition to the Relinquishment Act lands, these lands include offshore holdings extending three marine leagues, and the beds of bays, inlets, and navigable lakes and streams. Texas also holds title to over two million acres of land, mostly in West Texas, dedicated to the support of the University of Texas and Texas A & M University. Leases for these lands are issued directly by the State of Texas.

6. Unlike state-owned lands in other jurisdictions, oil and gas interests owned by the State of Texas, including Relinquishment Act interests, are not subject to compulsory pooling without the express consent of the General Land Office.

7. For a more detailed discussion of Texas Public Lands and the Relinquishment Act, see E. Smith and J. Weaver, Texas Law of Oil and Gas §§ 2.3, 3.6(D), 4.6, 4.10, 11.5(D), 12.2(c).

INDEX

References are to Pages

References are to Pages

†